About the authors

Margo Daly is also the author of the *Rough Guide to Sydney*, and co-author of t[...] *Rough Guide to Tasmania*. She lives in the Blue Mountains, near Sydney.

Anne Dehne has lived in Melbourne since 1989. Apart from researching and writing part of this book, she has written titles for other travel publishers, mai[...] on Australia.

David Leffman is an established Rough Guide author and inveterate traveller. A[...] well as Australia, he writes the *Rough Guide to Hong Kong*, *China* and *Iceland*.

Chris Scott covers NT and WA. His other books include *Sahara Overland*, the *Adventure Motorcycling Handbook* and the *Overlanders' Handbook*.

[...] used the Rough [...] lishments [...] – a perfectly sited [...] restaurant. The [...] k recommendations [...] us your own [...] be happy to check

Accommodation price codes

All the accommodation listed in this book has been categorized according to the following price codes. For full details, see p.45.

❶ $50 and under   ❹ $76–100   ❼ $161–200
❷ $51–60   ❺ $101–130   ❽ $201–250
❸ $61–75   ❻ $131–160   ❾ $251 and over

The **Rough Guide** to

Australia

written and researched by

Margo Daly, Anne Dehne, David Leffman and Chris Scott

with additional research by

Terry Carter, Ben Connor, Lara Dunston, Helen Marsden, Catherine Le Nevez, Ian Osborn, James Stewart, Karoline Thomas and Paul Whitfield

www.roughguides.com

Contents

Watersports colour
section following p.408

Landscapes colour
section following p.600

Australian wildlife
colour section
following p.920

◄◄ New South Wales stockmen ◄ Outback Western Australia

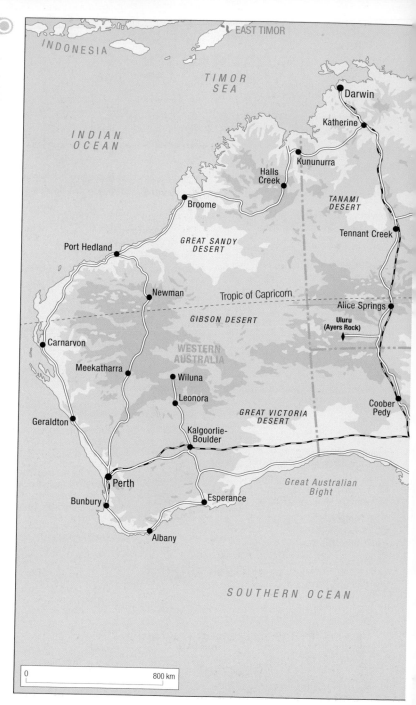

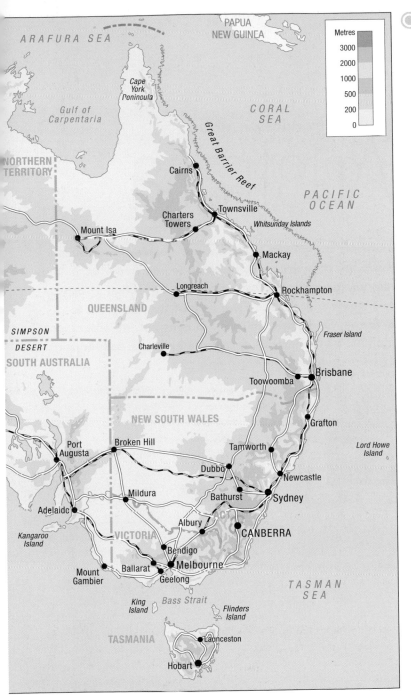

Metres
3000
2000
1000
500
200
0

ARAFURA SEA

PAPUA NEW GUINEA

Cape York Peninsula

Gulf of Carpentaria

CORAL SEA

NORTHERN TERRITORY

Cairns

Great Barrier Reef

PACIFIC OCEAN

Charters Towers

Townsville

Whitsunday Islands

Mount Isa

Mackay

Longreach

Rockhampton

QUEENSLAND

SIMPSON DESERT

Fraser Island

SOUTH AUSTRALIA

Charleville

Brisbane

Toowoomba

NEW SOUTH WALES

Grafton

Port Augusta

Broken Hill

Tamworth

Lord Howe Island

Dubbo

Mildura

Bathurst

Newcastle

Adelaide

Sydney

Kangaroo Island

Albury

CANBERRA

VICTORIA

ACT

Mount Gambier

Ballarat

Bendigo

Melbourne

Geelong

King Island

Bass Strait

Flinders Island

TASMAN SEA

TASMANIA

Launceston

Hobart

Introduction to
Australia

Australia is massive, and sparsely peopled: in size, it rivals the USA, yet its population is just under 22 million. It is an ancient land, and often looks it: much of central and western Australia – the bulk of the country – is overwhelmingly arid and flat. In contrast, its cities, most founded as recently as the mid-nineteenth century, express a vibrant, youthful energy.

The most memorable scenery is in the Outback, the vast desert in the interior of the country west of the Great Dividing Range. Here, vivid blue skies, cinnamon-red earth, deserted gorges and other striking geological features – as well as bizarre wildlife – comprise a unique ecology, one that has played host to the oldest surviving human culture for up to 70,000 years (just 10,000 years after *Homo sapiens* is thought to have emerged from Africa).

This harsh interior has forced modern Australia to become a **coastal country**. Most of the population lives within 20km of the ocean, occupying a suburban, southeastern arc extending from southern Queensland to Adelaide. These urban Australians celebrate the typical New World values of material self-improvement through hard work and hard play, with an easy-going vitality that visitors, especially Europeans, often find refreshingly hedonistic. A sunny climate also contributes to this exuberance, with an outdoor life in which a thriving beach culture and the congenial backyard "barbie" are central.

Although visitors might eventually find this *Home and Away* lifestyle rather prosaic, there are opportunities – particularly in the Northern Territory

– to experience **Australia's indigenous peoples** and their culture through visiting ancient art sites, taking tours and, less easily, making personal contact. Many Aboriginal people – especially in central Australia – have managed to maintain a traditional lifestyle (albeit with modern accoutrements), speaking their own languages and living according to their law. Conversely, most Aboriginal people you'll come across in country towns and cities are victims of what is scathingly referred to as "welfare colonialism" – a disempowering consequence of dole cheques and other subsidies combined with little chance of meaningful employment, often resulting in a destructive cycle of poverty, ill health and substance abuse. There's still a long way to go before black and white people in Australia can exist on genuinely equal terms.

◀ Melbourne

Fact file

- With an area of just over 7.5 million square kilometres, Australia is the sixth-largest country in the world.

- The population is estimated at just under 22 million, of whom some 85 percent live in urban areas, mainly along the coast. About 92 percent are of European origin, 2 percent Aboriginal, and around 6 percent Asian and Middle Eastern.

- Much of Australia is arid and flat. One third is desert and another third steppe or semi-desert. Only six percent of the country rises above 600m in elevation, and its tallest peak, Mount Kosciuszko, is just 2228m high.

- Australia's main exports are fossil fuels, minerals, metals, cotton, wool, wine and beef, and its most important trading partners are Japan, China and the USA.

- Australia is a federal parliamentary state (formally a constitutional monarchy) with two legislative houses, the Senate and the House of Representatives. The chief of state is the British Monarch, represented by the Governor-General, while the head of government is the Prime Minister.

Where to go

For visitors, deciding where to go can mean juggling distance, money and time. You could spend months driving around the Outback, exploring the national parks, or hanging out at beaches; or you could take an all-in, two-week "Reef 'n' Rock" package, encompassing Australia's outstanding trinity of must-sees.

Both options provide thoroughly Australian experiences, but neither will leave you with a feeling of having more than scraped the surface of this vast country. The two big natural attractions are the two-thousand-kilometre-long **Great Barrier Reef** off the Queensland coast, with its complex of islands and underwater splendour, and the brooding monolith of **Uluru** (Ayers Rock), in the Northern Territory's Red Centre. You should certainly try to see them, although exploration of other parts of the country will bring you into contact with more subtle, but equally rewarding, sights and opportunities.

The **cities** are surprisingly cosmopolitan: waves of postwar immigrants from southern Europe and, more recently, Southeast Asia have done much to erode Australia's Anglocentrism. Each Australian state has a capital stamped with its own personality, and nowhere is this more apparent than in New South Wales, where glamorous Sydney has the iconic landmarks of the Opera House and Harbour Bridge. Elsewhere,

◀ The Whitsundays, Coastal Queensland

Outdoor activities

Though there's fun to be had in the cities, it's really the **great outdoors** that makes Australia such a special place. Its multitude of national parks – around a thousand in total – embrace everything from isolated beaches and tropical rainforest to the vast wildernesses of the bush and the Outback. Visitors are spoilt for choice when it comes to getting out and about, with a huge range of outdoor pursuits on offer – everything from diving off the Great Barrier Reef or white-water rafting Tasmania's Franklin River to hot-air ballooning over Alice Springs or even skiing in the Australian Alps. Perhaps the best way to see something of the great outdoors, and certainly the cheapest and the most

▲ Hot-air ballooning over the Outback

popular, is bushwalking – you'll find trails marked in every national park. For more on outdoor activities, see p.60.

the sophisticated café society of Melbourne (Victoria) contrasts with the lively social scene in Brisbane (Queensland). Adelaide, in South Australia, has a human scale and old-fashioned charm, while Perth, in Western Australia, camouflages its isolation with a leisure-oriented urbanity. In Hobart, the capital of Tasmania, you'll encounter fine heritage architecture and a distinct maritime feel. The purpose-built administrative centre of Canberra, in the Australian Capital Territory, often fails to grip visitors, but Darwin's continuing regeneration enlivens an exploration of the distinctive "Territory".

Away from the suburbs, with their vast shopping malls and quarter-acre residential blocks, is the transitional "bush", and beyond that the wilderness of the **Outback** – the quintessential Australian environment. Protected from the arid interior, the **east coast** has the pick of the country's greenery and scenery, from the north's tropical rainforests and the Great Barrier Reef to the surf-lined beaches further south. The east coast is backed by the Great Dividing Range, which steadily decreases in elevation as it extends from Mount Kosciuszko (2228m) in New South Wales north into tropical Queensland. If you have time to spare, a trip to often-overlooked **Tasmania**, across the Bass Strait, is worthwhile: you'll be rewarded with vast tracts of temperate wilderness, as well as landscapes almost English in their bucolic appeal.

9

▼ Boab tree in the Kimberley, Western Australia

When to go

ustralia's **climate** has become less predictable in recent times, with phenomena such as an extended drought in the eastern Outback, the cyclic El Niño effect, and even the hole in the ozone layer – which is disturbingly close to the country – probably part of a long-term pattern. Climatic shift seemed confirmed by a spate of natural disasters in recent years. In 2008–09 alone, there were severe floods in the NT, droughts in New South Wales, hurricane-like storms in Western Australia, a record- and mercury-busting heat wave in South Australia and devastating bushfires in Victoria. With freak weather increasingly becoming a misnomer, some scientists suggest that storm clouds are gathering over the Lucky Country due to global warming.

Visitors from the northern hemisphere should remember that, as early colonials observed, in Australia "nature is horribly reversed": when it's winter or summer in the northern hemisphere, the opposite season prevails down under, a principle that becomes harder to apply to the transitional seasons of spring and autumn. To confuse things further, the four seasons only really exist in the **southern half of the country** outside of the tropics. Here, you'll find reliably warm summers at the coast with regular, but thankfully brief, heat waves in excess of 40°C. Head inland, and the temperatures rise further. Winters, on the other hand, can be miserable, particularly in Victoria, where the short days add to the gloom. Tasmania's highlands are unpredictable weather-wise year-round, although summer is a reliable time to explore the island's outdoor attractions.

In the **coastal tropics**, weather basically falls into two seasons. The best time to visit is during the hot and cloudless Dry (from April to Nov), with moderate coastal humidity maintaining a pleasant temperature day and night and cooler nights inland. In contrast, the Wet – particularly the "Build Up" in November or December before the rains commence – can be very uncomfortable, with stifling, near-total humidity. As storm clouds gather, rising temperatures, humidity and tension can provoke irrational behaviour in the psychologically unacclimatized – something known as "going troppo". Nevertheless, the mid-Wet's daily downpours and enervating mugginess can be quite intoxicating, compelling a hyper-relaxed inactivity for which these regions are known; furthermore, the countryside – if you can reach it – looks its best at this time.

Australia's interior is an arid semi-desert with very little rain, high summer temperatures and occasionally freezing winter nights. Unless you're properly equipped to cope with these extremes, you'd be better off coming here during the transitional seasons between April and June, or October and November.

In general, the **best time to visit** the south is during the Australian summer, from December to March, though long summer holidays from Christmas through January mean that prices are higher and beaches more crowded at this time. In the tropical north, the best months are from May to October, while in the Centre they are from October to November and from March to May. If you want to tour extensively, keep to the southern coasts in summer and head north for the winter.

Aboriginal art

Aboriginal art has grown into a million-dollar industry since the first canvas **dot paintings** of the central deserts emerged in the 1970s. Though seemingly abstract, early canvases are said to replicate ceremonial sand paintings – temporary "maps" fleetingly revealed to depict sacred knowledge. In the tropics, figurative **bark** and **cave paintings** are less enigmatic but much older, though until recently they were ceremonially repainted. The unusual **x-ray style** found in the Top End details the internal structure of animals. The Northern Territory – and Alice Springs, in particular – are the best places to look; for tips on buying Aboriginal art as well as didgeridoos, see pp.614–618.

▲ Aboriginal rock art, Keep River National Park, NT

▼ Sydney's skyline

Average temperatures (˚C) and rainfall (mm)

	Jan	Feb	Mar	Apr	May	Jun	Jul	Aug	Sep	Oct	Nov	Dec
Adelaide												
Av. temp. (°C)	28	27	25	22	18	16	14	15	17	21	22	25
Av. rainfall (mm)	20	20	25	45	65	70	65	60	55	40	25	20
Alice Springs												
Av. temp. (°C)	36	35	32	27	22	21	19	21	25	30	32	35
Av. rainfall (mm)	35	40	25	20	25	25	20	20	10	25	30	35
Brisbane												
Av. temp. (°C)	27	27	26	25	23	21	23	22	24	25	26	27
Av. rainfall (mm)	160	160	150	80	70	60	55	50	50	75	100	140
Cairns												
Av. temp. (°C)	31	31	30	29	28	25	25	27	27	28	30	31
Av. rainfall (mm)	400	440	450	180	100	50	30	25	35	35	90	160
Canberra												
Av. temp. (°C)	27	25	23	20	15	13	12	13	15	18	22	25
Av. rainfall (mm)	55	50	50	45	50	30	30	50	50	70	65	65
Darwin												
Av. temp. (°C)	31	30	31	32	31	30	30	31	32	32	33	32
Av. rainfall (mm)	400	430	435	75	50	10	5	10	15	70	110	310
Hobart												
Av. temp. (°C)	21	21	20	17	14	12	11	12	15	18	19	20
Av. rainfall (mm)	50	45	50	55	50	45	50	50	55	55	50	50
Melbourne												
Av. temp. (°C)	26	26	24	21	16	15	14	15	17	19	21	20
Av. rainfall (mm)	45	50	55	60	55	50	50	50	55	65	55	55
Perth												
Av. temp. (°C)	30	30	28	25	22	20	19	19	20	22	25	28
Av. rainfall (mm)	10	15	25	50	125	185	175	145	80	75	25	20
Sydney												
Av. temp. (°C)	25	25	24	23	20	17	16	17	19	22	23	24
Av. rainfall (mm)	100	105	125	130	125	130	110	75	60	75	70	75

All temperatures are in Centigrade: to convert to Fahrenheit multiply by 9, divide by 5 and add 32.

36

things not to miss

It's not possible to see everything that Australia has to offer in one trip – and we don't suggest you try. What follows, in no particular order, is a selective taste of the country's highlights: beautiful beaches, outstanding national parks, spectacular wildlife and lively festivals. They're arranged in five colour-coded categories, which you can browse through to find the very best things to see and experience. All highlights have a page reference to take you straight into the Guide, where you can find out more.

01 **Fraser Island (Qld)** Page **421** • The giant dunes, freshwater lakes and sculpted, coloured sands of the world's largest sand island form the backdrop to exciting 4WD safaris.

02 **Beer Can Regatta, Darwin (NT)** Page 575 • These wacky boat races in sea craft made entirely from beer cans are held every July.

04 **South Australia's wineries (SA)** Pages **776, 787** & **805** • Australia's premier wine-producing regions – the Barossa Valley, Adelaide Hills, McLaren Vale, Clare Valley and Coonawarra – are all easily accessible from Adelaide, and are wonderful places to unwind.

03 **The Franklin River (Tas)** Page **1106** • White-water rafting is the only way to explore the wild Franklin River, one of the great rivers of Australia.

05 Sailing in the Whitsundays (Qld) Page 450

• There's fantastic sailing and diving – and whale watching in season – in the idyllic white sand Whitsunday Islands.

07 Humpback whales (Qld) Page 419

• Australia's waters are the breeding ground for some sixty percent of the world's whales. Saved from extinction by a ban on whaling, humpback whales migrate up the Queensland coast between June and October, and can also be spotted along the western and southern coasts.

06 Athorton Tablelands (Qld) Page 486

• With its majestic rainforest, crater lakes and abundant wildlife, you could spend days exploring the Atherton Tablelands.

08 The Great Ocean Road (Vic) Page 932

• On two wheels or four, the 280-kilometre route along the rugged, surf-battered cliffs bordering the Great Ocean Road is perfect road-trip material, and can also be followed as a rewarding hike.

09 Aboriginal Dance Festival at Laura (Qld) Page **502** • This electrifying celebration of Aboriginal culture is held in June in odd-numbered years.

10 Bushtucker Page **53** • Wattle seeds, possum-tail soup, witchetty grubs and rooburgers – a few restaurants around the country are now experimenting with bushtucker.

11 Crocodiles (NT) Page **579** • Head up north to see the Territory's growing population of fearsome crocs.

12 Wilpena Pound (SA) Page **838** • There are some fantastic hikes amid spectacular scenery at the elevated basin of Wilpena Pound in the Flinders Ranges National Park.

13 Blue Mountains (NSW)
Page **200** • World Heritage-listed, the Blue Mountains, just west of Sydney, get their name from the blue mist of fragrant eucalyptus oil hanging in the air all year round.

14 Climbing Sydney Harbour Bridge (NSW)
Page **107** • Scale the bridge for adrenaline thrills and great views – or walk or cycle across it for free.

15 Birdsville Races (Qld) Page **527** • Birdsville Hotel is the focus for the annual Birdsville Races, when five thousand people descend on the tiny desert township in Queensland's Outback for a weekend of drinking, horse racing and mayhem.

16 **Canoeing up the Katherine Gorge (NT)** Page **594** ● Hop on a cruise or paddle a canoe through the dramatic orange cliffs of the Katherine Gorge – you won't have it to yourself, but it's still hugely enjoyable.

19 **Mutawintji National Park (NSW)** Page **361** ● Red, barren earth laced with ancient galleries of Aboriginal rock art, secluded gorges and quiet waterholes.

18 **Mardi Gras (NSW)** Page **168** ● The irreverent Oxford Street parade, from "dykes on bikes" to the "Melbourne marching boys", ends the summer season.

20 **Bondi Beach (NSW)** Page **143** • Beach, surf and café culture: Sydney's famous beach has something for everyone.

21 **Overland Track in Cradle Mountain-Lake St Clair National Park (Tas)** Page **1103** • The eighty-kilometre Overland Track is Australia's greatest extended bushwalk, spread over five or more mud- and leech-filled days of physical, exhilarating exhaustion.

22 Watching a match at the MCG (Vic) Page 871 •

Taking in a game of cricket or, even better, Aussie Rules football at the venerable Melbourne Cricket Ground (MCG) is a must for sports fans.

24 Giant termite mounds (NT) Page 589 •

These impressively huge towers – up to 4m tall – are a regular feature of the Top End.

23 Tall Timber Country (WA) Page 672 •

The primeval karri forests of the so-called Tall Timber Country are one of WA's greatest natural sights. Get a bird's-eye view from the Tree Top Walk.

25 Sydney Opera House (NSW) Page 105 •

Take in a performance at one of the world's busiest performing-arts centres – interval drinks certainly don't have such spectacular harbour views anywhere else in the world.

26 **Kakadu National Park (NT)** Page **579** • Australia's largest national park is a spectacular World Heritage-listed wilderness with abundant wildlife and some fascinating Aboriginal rock art to explore.

27 **Broken Hill (NSW)** Page **352** • Pay a visit to the Royal Flying Doctor Service and the School of the Air headquarters at NSW's historic Outback mining town and thriving arts centre.

28 **Melbourne Cup (Vic)** Page **59** • Melbourne's venerable horse race brings the entire country to a standstill around the radio or TV.

29 **Diving at the Great Barrier Reef (Qld)** Page **482** ● Come face to face with stunning coral and shoals of curious fish.

30 **Rent a 4WD** Page **40** ● Adventure off-road from Queensland's Cape York (p.477) to the Territory's Central Deserts (p.624) or WA's Kimberley (p.744).

31 Kangaroo Island (SA)

Page **793** • Unspoilt Kangaroo Island boasts fantastic coastal scenery and a huge variety of wildlife, from seals and sea lions to kangaroos, wallabies and koalas.

32 Hiking through Carnarvon Gorge (Qld)

Page **522** • With its Aboriginal art sites and magical scenery, a day-hike into the Carnarvon Gorge takes some beating.

33 Uluru (NT)

Page **632** • Uluru, otherwise known as Ayers Rock, is a sacred site for Aboriginal people, and a magnet for tourists the world over.

34 Manly Ferry (NSW)

Page **89** • The short ferry trip from Circular Quay to the excellent surfing beaches at Manly takes in picture-postcard views of Sydney Harbour.

23

35 **The Kimberley (WA)** Page **721** • Regarded as Australia's last frontier, the Kimberley is a sparsely populated, untamed wilderness that contains some stunning landscapes.

36 **Karijini National Park (WA)** Page **715** • The water-carved gorges of the Karijini National Park make a dramatic backdrop for challenging canyoneering adventures.

Basics

Basics

Getting there

You can fly pretty much every day to the main east-coast cities from Europe, North America and Southeast Asia. Airfares always depend on the season, with the highest fares being the two weeks either side of Christmas, when the weather is best in the main tourist areas. Fares drop during the "shoulder" seasons – mid-January to March and mid-August to November – and you'll get the best prices during the low season, mid-April to June. Because of the distance from most popular departure points, flying on weekends does not alter the price.

To cut costs, use a **specialist flight agent** or a discount agent, who may also offer special student and youth fares as well as travel insurance, rail passes, car rental, tours and the like. If Australia is only one stop on a longer journey, you might want to consider buying a Round-the-World (RTW) ticket (see p.28). Some travel agents sell pre-packaged RTW tickets that will have you touching down in about half a dozen cities, and Australia is frequently part of the regular eastbound RTW loop from Europe.

Flights from the UK and Ireland

The north Australian coast is just fifteen hours' **flying** time **from London**, though in practice the journey to Sydney or the other eastern cities takes a minimum of 21 hours including stopovers. If you break the trip in Southeast Asia or North America, getting to Australia need not be the tedious, seat-bound slog you may have imagined. Note there are no direct flights **from Ireland**.

Sydney and Melbourne are served by the greatest number of airlines, and carriers such as Qantas charge the same price to fly to any east-coast city between Cairns and Adelaide; flights to Darwin and Perth are around £100 cheaper, but you'll spend at least that much on the overland journey to the east coast. An **open-jaw ticket** (flying into one city and out from another) usually costs no more than an ordinary return.

Direct scheduled flights depart from London's Heathrow airport, although Singapore Airlines has flights from Manchester to Singapore that connect with onward flights to Sydney and Melbourne.

With Qantas you can fly from regional airports at Aberdeen, Edinburgh, Glasgow, Manchester or Newcastle to connect with your international flight at Heathrow.

Tourists and those on one-year working visas are generally required by Australian Immigration to arrive with a return ticket, so **one-way tickets** are really only viable for Australian and New Zealand residents.

The cheapest **fare** you're likely to find is around £650 return, available during the low-season months of April to June, though special offers can go as low as £550; if you insist on flying with Qantas, BA or Singapore Airlines, expect to pay from around £800 for a flight in this off-peak period, with special offers sometimes taking prices down to £700. The **most expensive time** to fly is in the two weeks either side of Christmas, when you'd be lucky to find anything for less than £1000 return: to stand a chance of getting one of the cheaper tickets, book at least six months in advance. Prices also go up from mid-June or the beginning of July to mid-August coinciding with the peak European holiday period. In between times (the shoulder seasons of mid-Aug to Nov and mid-Jan to March) you should expect to pay around £700 (or up to £950 with one of the prestige airlines).

An excellent alternative to a long direct flight is a **multi-stopover ticket**, which can cost the same or just a little more than the price of an ordinary return; check airlines for routings. Unusual routes are inevitably more expensive, but it's possible to fly via South America with Aerolineas Argentinas, which offers stops in Buenos Aires and Auckland return.

If you're considering booking a return ticket with Qantas or British Airways and are thinking of heading over to New Zealand or the South Pacific in between, you might want to consider buying a **Boomerang Pass**; see p.35 for details.

Most of the routings **from Ireland** involve a stopover in London and transfer to one of the airlines listed on p.27. Fares in low-season are usually around the €1000 mark, €1900 in high season. Singapore Airlines has flights ticketed through from Dublin or Cork via London to Singapore and Sydney, Adelaide, Brisbane, Melbourne and Perth, while Malaysian Airlines also goes from Dublin via London to Kuala Lumpur, from where you can fly to all major Australian cities. Dublin, Cork and Shannon are also served by the affiliated British Airways and Qantas: all their flights to Australia have a Dublin–London add-on included in the price. For youth and student discount fares, the best first stop is Usit.

Round-the-World (RTW) tickets provide a chance to see the world on your way to and from Australia; RTW flights come in a tantalizing variety of permutations, with stopovers chiefly in Asia, the Pacific and North America, but you can pretty much devise your fantasy itinerary and get it priced. A good agent should be able to piece together sector fares from various airlines: providing you keep your itinerary down to three continents, prices range from around £750 for a simple London–Bangkok–Sydney–LA–London deal to well over £1000 for more complicated routings.

Flights from the US and Canada

From Los Angeles it's possible to **fly nonstop** to Sydney in fourteen and a half hours.

Six steps to a better kind of travel

At Rough Guides we are passionately committed to travel. We feel strongly that only through travelling do we truly come to understand the world we live in and the people we share it with – plus tourism has brought a great deal of **benefit** to developing economies around the world over the last few decades. But the extraordinary growth in tourism has also damaged some places irreparably, and of course **climate change** is exacerbated by most forms of transport, especially flying. This means that now more than ever it's important to **travel thoughtfully** and **responsibly**, with respect for the cultures you're visiting – not only to derive the most benefit from your trip but also to preserve the best bits of the planet for everyone to enjoy. At Rough Guides we feel there are six main areas in which you can make a difference:

* Consider what you're contributing to the **local economy**, and how much the services you use do the same, whether it's through employing local workers and guides or sourcing locally grown produce and local services.
* Consider the **environment** on holiday as well as at home. Water is scarce in many developing destinations, and the biodiversity of local flora and fauna can be adversely affected by tourism. Try to patronize businesses that take account of this.
* Travel with a purpose, not just to tick off experiences. Consider **spending longer** in a place, and getting to know it and its people.
* Give thought to how often you **fly**. Try to avoid short hops by air and more harmful night flights.
* Consider **alternatives to flying**, travelling instead by bus, train, boat and even by bike or on foot where possible.
* Make your trips **"climate neutral"** via a reputable carbon offset scheme. All Rough Guide flights are offset, and every year we donate money to a variety of charities devoted to combating the effects of climate change.

Qantas, United and Air Canada all operate direct to the east coast of Australia. Flying on a national Asian airline will most likely involve a stop in their capital city (Singapore, Tokyo, Hong Kong, etc), and if you're travelling from the west coast of North America to the east coast of Australia you'll probably find fares on the Pacific route somewhat higher than their American and Australian competitors. However, if you're flying from the east coast of North America to, say, Perth, a carrier such as Singapore Airlines or Malaysia Airlines with a transatlantic routing may offer the best value.

Many of the major airlines offer deals whereby you can make stopovers either at **Pacific Rim destinations** such as Tokyo, Honolulu or Kuala Lumpur or at a number of exotic South Pacific locations. Either there will be a flat surcharge on your ticket or they may offer you a higher-priced ticket allowing you to make as many stops as you like, within certain parameters, over a fixed period of time.

Sample lowest standard scheduled **fares** for low/high seasons are approximately as follows: to Sydney or Melbourne from Chicago or New York (US$1600/2200); Los Angeles or San Francisco (US$1400/2100); Montréal or Toronto (CDN$1900/2700); Vancouver (CDN$1800/2200); to Perth from New York, Los Angeles or San Francisco (US$1950/2400); Vancouver, Toronto or Montréal (CDN$2300/2900). The price of an **open-jaw ticket** (flying into one city and returning from another) should be approximately the average of the return fares to the two cities. If you plan on flying around Australia, it may be more cost-effective to buy a Qantas AirPass (see p.35).

RTW or Circle Pacific tickets

The best deal, if you don't mind planning your itinerary in advance, will most likely be a Round-the-World (RTW) ticket or a Circle Pacific, which has stop-offs in Australia and New Zealand from North America.

A sample **RTW itinerary** would be: Los Angeles–Sydney–Singapore–Bangkok–Delhi–London–Los Angeles (US$4220), while a sample **Circle Pacific route** from Los Angeles via Hong Kong, Bangkok, Singapore, Cairns and Melbourne costs about US$1600.

Flights from New Zealand and South Africa

New Zealand–Australia routes are busy and competition is fierce, resulting in an ever-changing range of deals and special offers; your best bet is to check the latest with a specialist travel agent (see p.32) or the relevant airlines' websites. The recent influx of low cost, **no-frills airlines** has meant a further price drop, with the likes of Virgin Blue, Virgin's low-cost Pacific subsidiary, offering special "Happy Hour" fares daily, from NZ$1 plus tax. It's a relatively short hop across the Tasman Sea: **flying time** from Auckland to Sydney is around three and a half hours.

All **fares** quoted below are for travel during low or shoulder seasons; flying at peak times (primarily Dec to mid-Jan) can add substantially to these prices. Ultimately, the price you pay for your flight will depend on how much flexibility you want; many of the cheapest deals are hedged with restrictions – typically, a maximum stay of thirty days and a fourteen-day advance-purchase requirement. Air New Zealand offers return

FROM DEEP SEA TO SKY HIGH - THE ONLY PLACE TO SEE AUSTRALIA I A DAY IS ON THE DISCOVERY TRAIL.

Do the total Aussie experience right in the heart of Sydney on The Discovery Trail! Start at Sydney Aquarium where you'll see the amazing dugongs, walk underwater among sharks and experience Australia's largest Great Barrier Reef exhibit. Head to Sydney Wildlife World, Australia's number one family attraction, where you can have breakfast with the koalas*, feed the kangaroos and walk

through nine different Aussie wildlife ha And at Sydney Tower you'll enjoy 360 d views of Sydney, take an amazing virtua reality ride across Australia and venture breathtaking glass overhangs on Skywa

For tickets, come to Sydney Aquari Sydney Wildlife World or Sydney Tov or visit: 🏕 myfun.com.au

flights from Auckland, Christchurch, Dunedin, Palmerston North and Wellington starting from around NZ$490, while Pacific Blue flies from Christchurch and Wellington from around NZ$300–500 return. The cheapest regular return fare from Auckland to Sydney is usually with Aerolineas Argentinas (also to Melbourne) for around NZ$250, but flights tend to be heavily booked.

Flying **from South Africa**, the journey time is around twelve hours, travelling from Johannesburg to Sydney. The main carriers are Qantas and South African Airways, which both offer flights from around ZAR7800 in low season and ZAR11,800 in high season.

Getting there from Southeast Asia

This is a very popular route for travellers en route to Australia from Europe, or vice versa, especially Australian backpackers heading in the other direction at the start of their trip. Travelling **overland through Southeast Asia** is a bit more demanding than Australia, but it's a fascinating region and is unlikely to make a big dent in your budget. It also shouldn't make too much of a difference to the price of your plane ticket, since many Asian airlines stop in Bangkok, Singapore, Jakarta, Denpasar or Kuala Lumpur on the way to Australia, and breaking your journey is either free or possible for a small extra charge. If you want to go overland on the route detailed below between Bangkok and Bali, rather than just stop over, you could buy a Round-the-World ticket with an overland component. If you do buy a one-way ticket from Bali, you will still need to be in possession of a return ticket out of Australia to get through immigration, probably best routed via Bangkok.

Overland from Bangkok to Bali

Bangkok is a popular starting point for an overland route, with return flights available from around £380–450 in the UK and US$800 in the US. From Bangkok an inexpensive bus service leaves twice daily for the 2000-kilometre ride to Singapore, though it's a gruelling 48-hour trip unless you make a stop or two along the way; a more comfortable option is the International

Express train from Bangkok to Butterworth, in Malaysia (21hr), then an overnight train to Kuala Lumpur (9hr), and another train to Singapore (8hr); you will usually need to stay overnight in Butterworth or Penang to connect with the train to Kuala Lumpur, but at least a few days is recommended. Book both journeys a day or two in advance to be sure of a seat; the combined price for first class is £33/US$50, but considerably cheaper second- and third-class fares are available. Alternatively, you could plump for luxury on the *Eastern and Oriental Express* (@www.orient-express.com), modelled on the original *Orient Express*; the 41-hour journey via Kuala Lumpur costs from £1160/US$2210.

From Singapore, you can cross to the **Indonesian islands** of Sumatra or Kalimantan (Indonesian Borneo) and from there island-hop via local buses and ferries southeast through to Java and Bali, from where you can take a short flight to Darwin in Australia's Northern Territory.

Allow at least a month travelling overland from Bangkok to Bali, but be aware that there is still **political and social unrest** right through Indonesia, including Bali, and travel through some of these regions may not be wise or even possible. Check your country's Department of Foreign Affairs website (see p.75) for the latest information.

Airlines, agents and tour operators

If your time is short and you're reasonably sure of what you want to do, it may not be a bad idea to pre-book some of your accommodation and tours; see p.32 for a list of operators and Australian tour specialists.

Airlines

Aerolineas Argentinas @www.aerolineas.com.
Air Canada @www.aircanada.com.
Air China @www.airchina.com.cn.
Air New Zealand @www.airnz.co.nz.
Air Pacific @www.airpacific.com.
American Airlines @www.aa.com.
Austrian Airlines @www.aua.com.
British Airways @www.ba.com.
Cathay Pacific @www.cathaypacific.com.
China Airlines @www.china-airlines.com.
Emirates @www.emirates.com.

Garuda Indonesia @ www.garuda-indonesia.com.
JAL (Japan Air Lines) @ www.jal.com or
@ www.japanair.com.
KLM (Royal Dutch Airlines) @ www.klm.com.
Korean Air @ www.koreanair.com.
Malaysia Airlines @ www.malaysiaairlines.com.
Pacific Blue @ www.flypacificblue.com.
Qantas Airways @ www.qantas.com.
Royal Brunei @ www.bruneiair.com.
Singapore Airlines @ www.singaporeair.com.
South African Airways @ www.flysaa.com.
Thai Airways @ www.thaiair.com.
Tiger Airways @ www.tigerairways.com.
United Airlines @ www.united.com.
Virgin Atlantic @ www.virgin-atlantic.com.

Agents and tour operators

AAT Kings Australia ☏ 1300 556 100, NZ ☏ 0800
500 146, @ www.aatkings.com. Long-established
Australian coach-tour operator that offers escorted
and independent one-day tours from Melbourne.
Abercrombie and Kent US ☏ 1-800/554-7016,
@ www.abercrombiekent.com. 8- to 21-day
high-end tours, ranging from basic trips (including
Sydney, Melbourne and the Great Barrier Reef)
to more extensive ones (including Tasmania and
the Outback). Also family tours and customized
itineraries.

Air Brokers International US ☏ 1-800/883-3273,
@ www.airbrokers.com. Specialist in Round-the-
World and Circle Pacific tickets.
Airtreks.com US & Canada ☏ 1-877/AIRTREKS
or 415/977-7100, @ www.airtreks.com. RTW and
Circle Pacific tickets for North Americans. The website
features an interactive database that lets you build
and price your own itinerary.
Asia Transpacific Journeys US ☏ 1-800/642-
2742, @ www.asiatranspacific.com.
Long-established outfit with a wide range of
customized itineraries and group tours including
nature, adventure and Aboriginal rock art.
ATS Tours US ☏ 1-888/781 5170, @ www
.atstours.com. Huge Australian and New Zealand
specialist; dive deals, fly-drives, city stopovers,
rail/bus passes, motel vouchers and more.
Australia Travel Centre Republic of Ireland
☏ 01/804 7100, @ www.australia.ie. Specialists in
long-haul flights.
Australian Pacific Touring UK ☏ 020/8879 7444,
US & Canada ☏ 1-800/290-8687, Australia ☏ 1300
655 965, NZ ☏ 0800-APTOURS; @ www.aptours
.com. Comprehensive range of Australia-wide coach
tours including a 27-day "Rock, Kakadu, Reef" tour for
£4940 per person, twin share, including meals and
accommodation, plus escorted trips from North America.
Austravel UK ☏ 0844/873 0977, Republic of
Ireland ☏ 01/642 7009, @ www.austravel
.com. Specialists for flights and tours to Australia.
Issues ETAs (**see opposite**) and traditional visas for an
administration fee of £20.
Contiki Australia ☏ 1300/CONTIKI, @ www.contiki
.com. Big-group, countrywide bus and 4WD tours
for fun-loving 18- to 35-year-olds. All transport and
most meals covered; additional excursions (climbing,
diving, etc) extra.
ebookers UK ☏ 0871/223 5000, Republic of
Ireland ☏ 01/431 1311; @ www.ebookers.com.
Low fares on an extensive selection of scheduled
flights and package deals.
Explore UK ☏ 0845/013 1537, Republic of
Ireland ☏ 01/677 9479; @ www.explore.co.uk.
Bus and 4WD tours ranging from a 17-day "Outback
Adventure" (£2545) to a 30-day "Australia Adventure"
for £3625 – all with flights from the UK.
Flightcentre UK ☏ 0870/499 0040, US
☏ 1-866/967-5351, Canada ☏ 1-877/967-5302,
Australia ☏ 13 31 33, NZ ☏ 0800/243 544;
@ www.flightcentre.com. Rock-bottom fares.
Holiday Shoppe NZ ☏ 0800/866 654, @ www
.holidayshoppe.co.nz. Great deals on flights, hotels
and holidays.
Lee's Travel UK ☏ 0871/855 3338, @ www
.leestravel.com. Good deals from the UK, especially
on Southeast Asian airlines.

North South Travel UK ☎01245/608 291, Ⓦwww.northsouthtravel.co.uk. Friendly travel agency, offering discounted fares worldwide. Profits are used to support projects in the developing world, especially the promotion of sustainable tourism.

Quest Travel UK ☎0845/263 6963, Ⓦwww.questtravel.com. Specialists in RTW and Australian discount fares.

STA Travel UK ☎0871/2300 040, US ☎1-800/781-4040, Australia ☎134 782, NZ ☎0800/474 400, SA ☎0861/781 781; Ⓦwww.statravel.com. Specialists in independent travel; also student IDs, travel insurance, car rental, rail passes and more. Good discounts for students and under-26s.

Student Universe US & Canada ☎1-800/272-9676, Ⓦwww.studentuniverse.com. Competitive student-travel specialists for North Americans; no card or membership required.

Swain Australia Tours US ☎1-800/227-9246, Ⓦwww.swainaustralia.com. Excellent range of customized tours, including around Victoria, the Great Ocean Road and Phillip Island.

Trailfinders UK ☎0845/058 5858, Republic of Ireland ☎01/677 7888; Ⓦwww.trailfinders.com. One of the best-informed and most efficient agents for independent travellers.

Travel Bag UK ☎0800/804 8911, Ⓦwww.travelbag.co.uk. Specialists in RTW tickets and long-haul flights, with good deals to be had on leading airlines.

Travel Cuts US ☎1-800/592-CUTS, Canada ☎1-866/246-9762; Ⓦwww.travelcuts.com. Popular, long-established student-travel organization, with worldwide offers.

Usit Republic of Ireland ☎01/602 1906, Ⓦwww.usit.ie. Student and youth specialists for flights, accommodation and transport.

World Expeditions UK ☎020/8545 9030, US & Canada ☎1-800/567-2216, Australia ☎1300 720 000, NZ ☎09/ 368 4161; Ⓦwww.worldexpeditions.co.uk. Australian-owned adventure company; small-group active wilderness holidays; cycling, canoeing, rafting, 4WD excursions, walking and camping.

Entry requirements

All visitors to Australia, except New Zealanders, require a visa or Electronic Travel Authority (ETA) to enter the country; if you're heading overland, you'll obviously also need to check visa requirements for the countries en route. You can get visa application forms from the Australian high commissions, embassies or consulates listed below.

The easiest option for nationals of the UK, Ireland, the US, Canada, Malaysia, Singapore, Japan, Hong Kong, South Korea and most European countries who intend to stay for less than three months is to get an **ETA**, valid for multiple entry over one year. Applied for online at Ⓦwww.eta.immi.gov.au for AUS$20, or through travel agents and airlines for a small fee at the same time you book your flight, it replaces the visa stamp in your passport (ETAs are computerized) and saves the hassle of queuing or sending off your passport.

Citizens of other countries and visitors who intend to stay for longer than three months should apply for a **tourist visa**, valid for three to six months, which costs AUS$100, and can be lodged in person or by post to the embassy or consulate, or online at Ⓦwww.immi.gov.au; you'll need to complete an application form and deliver it either in person or by post to the embassy or consulate. If you think you might stay more than three months, it's best to get the longer visa before departure, because once you get to Australia extensions cost AUS$215. Once issued, a visa usually allows multiple entries, so long as your passport is valid.

An important condition for all holiday visa applications is that you have **adequate**

funds both to support yourself during your stay – at least AUS$1000 a month – and eventually to get yourself home again.

Twelve-month **working holiday visas** are available to citizens aged 18–30 of Britain, Ireland, Belgium, Denmark, Finland, Italy, Estonia, France, Taiwan, Malta, Sweden, Norway, Canada, the Netherlands, Germany, Hong Kong, Japan and Korea. The stress is on casual employment: you are meant to work for no more than six months at any one job. You must arrange the visa several months in advance of you arriving in Australia. Working visas cost AUS$195; some travel agents such as STA Travel (see p.33) can arrange them for you.

Young American citizens wishing to work in Australia might consider the **Special Youth Program**, designed to allow people aged 18–30 to holiday while working in short-term employment over a four-month period. See BUNAC (ⓦwww.bunac.com), Camp Counselors (ⓦwww.ccusa.com) or Council/CIEE (ⓦwww.ciee.org) for more information.

Australia has strict **quarantine laws** that apply to bringing fruit, vegetables, fresh and packaged food, seed and some animal products into the country, and when travelling interstate (see p.39); there are also strict laws prohibiting drugs, steroids, firearms, protected wildlife and associated products. If you've been snacking on the flight, throw any leftovers in the amnesty quarantine bins available in the arrival area or on the way to the luggage collection bay. You are allowed AUS$900 worth of goods, including gifts and souvenirs, while those over 18 can take advantage of a **duty-free allowance** on entry of 2.25 litres of alcohol and 250 cigarettes or 250g of tobacco. To find out more about specific goods that are prohibited in Australia before you travel, visit the Australian Customs Service website ⓦwww.customs.gov.au.

Australian embassies and consulates abroad

Bali Australian Consulate, Australian Consulate-General, Jalan Tantular, No 32, Renon, Denpasar, Bali 80234 ☏0361/241 118, ⓦwww.bali .indonesia.embassy.gov.au.

Canada Australian High Commission, Suite 710, 50 O'Connor St, Ottawa, ON K1P 6L2 ☏613/236-0841, ⓦwww.ahc-ottawa.org.

Jakarta Australian Embassy, Jalan HR Rasuna Said Kav C15–16, Jakarta Selatan 12940 ☏021/2550 5555, ⓦwww.austembjak.or.id.

Kuala Lumpur Australian High Commission, 6 Jalan Yap Kwan Seng, Kuala Lumpur ☏2146 5555, ⓦwww.australia.org.my.

Netherlands Australian Embassy, Carnegielaan 4, 2517 KH, The Hague ☏070/310 8200, ⓦwww .australian-embassy.nl.

New Zealand Australian Consulate, 72–76 Hobson St, Thorndon, Wellington ☏04/473 6411, ⓦwww .australia.org.nz.

Republic of Ireland Australian Embassy, 7th Floor, Fitzwilton House, Wilton Terrace, Dublin 2 ☏01/ 664 5300, ⓦwww.ireland.embassy.gov.au.

Singapore Australian High Commission, 25 Napier Rd, Singapore ☏065/6836 4100, ⓦwww .singapore.embassy.gov.au.

South Africa Australian High Commission, 292 Orient St, Arcadia, Pretoria ☏12/423 6000, ⓦwww.australia.co.za.

Thailand Australian Embassy, 37 South Sathorn Rd, Bangkok ☏02/344 6300, ⓦwww .austembassy.or.th.

UK Australian High Commission, Australia House, Strand, London WC2B 4LA ☏020/7379 4334, ⓦwww.australia.org.uk.

US Australian Embassy, 1601 Massachusetts Ave NW, Washington, DC 20036-2273 ☏202/797-3000, ⓦwww.usa.embassy.gov.au.

Getting around

Australia's vastness makes the distances, and how you cover them, a major feature of any stay in the country. In general, public transport will take you only along the major highways to capital cities, the bigger towns between them, and popular tourist destinations; to get off the beaten track you'll have to consider driving, either by buying or renting your own vehicle. Frequencies and journey times of long-distance bus, train and plane services can be found under "Travel details" at the end of each chapter, with local buses and trains covered in the main text.

If you're travelling by road, check out the route on a map first, as it's very easy to underestimate **distances and conditions** – you may well be letting yourself in for a three-day bus journey, or planning to drive 500km on bad roads. Bear in mind what the **weather** will be doing, too; you don't necessarily want to head into central Australia in a battered old car during the summer, or into the northern tropics in the wet season.

By plane

Flying between major destinations, your main choice of airlines is between Qantas, Jetstar and Virgin Blue; a typical one-way flight from Sydney to Adelaide with Jetstar costs from around AUS$119, from Perth to Darwin with Virgin Blue AUS$290, and from Cairns to Melbourne with Qantas AUS$189. Elsewhere, **regional routes** are served by smaller airlines such as Regional Express (Rex), which covers New South Wales, Victoria and South Australia; and state-based companies such as Skywest in Western Australia and Regional Link in the Northern Territory. It's worth checking websites for their latest deals, which are often very good, especially when you consider the time and money you'd otherwise spend on a long bus or train journey.

If you're flying from Britain or Ireland and want to include a trip to New Zealand or the South Pacific on your itinerary you could save money by booking a **Qantas Boomerang Pass**, which must be purchased before arrival. The pass divides these areas into three zones based on distance and you are required to book at least two flights costing from £65 for single-zone, £120 for two-zone, or £146 for three-zone flights. You pay according to how many zones your flight crosses. Note, though, that the Boomerang Pass is not always as good value as it sounds: check Qantas' internet rates first, as well as current deals with other domestic airlines. For those travelling from North America, the **Qantas Aussie AirPass** offers similar internal-flight discounts if purchased with the return airfare, starting from US$1199/CDN$1199 for three domestic flights.

Another type of flight offered all over Australia is brief **sightseeing** or joyrides. Everything is covered, from biplane spins above cities to excursions to the Great Barrier Reef and flights over well-known landscapes. A good example is a flight from Alice Springs to Uluru in a small plane, which enables you to visit the Rock in a day, but also observe the impressive central Australian landforms from the air. Bill Peach Journeys (℡02/9693 2233, ⊛www.aircruising.com.au) offers a twelve-day Outback tour by air that flies from Sydney and takes in the main sights and cities, including Darwin, Broome, Kakadu, Alice Springs and Uluru, from AUS$13,295, all-inclusive.

Domestic airlines

Jetstar ℡13 15 38, ⊛www.jetstar.com.au.
Qantas Airways ℡13 13 13, ⊛www.qantas.com.au.
Regional Express ℡13 17 13, ⊛www.rex.com.au.

Shortest driving distances in kilometres

	Adelaide	Alice Springs	Brisbane	Broken Hill	Broome	Cairns
Adelaide	x	1533	1959	508	3274	2854
Alice Springs	1533	x	2700	1638	1745	2163
Brisbane	1959	2700	x	1458	4250	1700
Broken Hill	508	1638	1458	x	3383	2344
Broome	3274	1745	4250	3383	x	3411
Cairns	2854	2163	1700	2344	3411	x
Canberra	1164	2561	1212	929	4305	2545
Darwin	3025	1489	3426	3135	1868	2596
Melbourne	731	2255	1690	835	3999	2812
Perth	2690	2475	4260	2802	2176	4638
Sydney	1371	2768	929	1160	4741	2414
Townsville	2532	1773	1361	2022	3319	348
Uluru	1582	440	3149	1690	2185	2603

Regional Link ☏1800 627 474, ⓦwww
.regionallink.com.au.
Skywest ☏1300/660 088, ⓦwww.skywest.com.au.
Virgin Blue ☏13 67 89, ⓦwww.virginblue.com.au.

By train

The populous southeast has a reasonably comprehensive service: interstate railways link the entire east coast from Cairns to Sydney, and on to Melbourne and Adelaide. Each state operates its own rail network. The two great (or perhaps just long) journeys are the twice-weekly **Indian Pacific** (Perth–Sydney; 66hr; one-way, seat only AUS$690; sleeper AUS$1350; luxury sleeper with meals AUS$1950), across the Nullarbor Plain; and the seasonally twice-weekly **Ghan** (Adelaide–Darwin; 47hr; one-way, seat only AUS$710; sleeper AUS$1440; luxury sleeper with meals AUS$1980). Services are operated by Great Southern Railway (☏13 21 47, ⓦwww.gsr .com.au), who offer good concessionary fares for students and YHA/Backpacker cardholders (see p.47) for the sleeper and seat only, which work out only around fifteen percent more than a bus. Remember though, this is not a European-style high-speed network; journey times are similar to those of buses.

On the overnight Ghan and Indian Pacific, a twin-share Red sleeper service provides washing facilities and converts from a day lounge into a sleeper, while the Gold service lays on a luxury en-suite cabin and all meals, for the full "Orient Express" treatment. Either of these options is well worth considering for the three-day trawl from Sydney to Perth if you don't want to fly. The seat-only option is a reclining chair with generous legroom and a reading light, with access to a lounge and buffet, DVDs and showers. With a pair of Gold tickets between capitals and/or Alice, you get the offer of motorail car transportation for just AUS$99 – something that's really caught on with southerners wanting to tour the Centre or Top End with their own vehicles, with the fun of the train ride there. Great Southern Railway also runs an overland interstate service between Melbourne and Adelaide (11hr; AUS$94–151.50).

Other than these, there are a couple of inland tracks in Queensland – to Mount Isa, Longreach and Charleville, plus the rustic Cairns–Forsayth run and isolated Croydon–Normanton stretch – and suburban networks around some of the major cities. Only around Sydney does this amount to much, with decent services to most of New

Canberra	Darwin	Melbourne	Perth	Sydney	Townsville	Uluru
1164	3025	731	2690	1371	2532	1582
2561	1489	2255	2475	2768	1773	110
1212	3426	1690	4260	929	1361	3149
929	3135	835	2802	1160	2022	1690
4305	1868	3999	2176	4741	3319	2185
2545	2596	2812	4638	2414	348	2603
x	3947	666	3724	286	2161	2612
3947	x	3752	3983	3926	2509	1937
666	3752	x	3419	875	2480	2310
3724	3983	3419	x	3932	4823	2035
286	3026	875	3032	x	2070	2820
2161	2509	2480	4823	2070	x	2219
2612	1937	2310	2035	2820	2219	x

South Wales. There are no passenger trains in Tasmania.

The advantages of travelling by train rather than bus are comfort and (usually) a bar; disadvantages are the slower pace, higher price and potential booking problems – Queensland trains, for example, travel at about 60kph and require a month's advance booking during the holiday season.

Rail Australia (ⓦwww.railaustralia.com.au) offers a range of **rail passes**, including the Rail Explorer Pass (AUS$690, AUS$590 concessions), which must be bought before you arrive in Australia and lets you loose without limit on the routes described above for a six-month period. To be sure that you can make full use of your pass, it's advisable to book your route when you buy it. Western Australia, Victoria, New South Wales and Queensland also have their own passes available through main stations, but check any travel restrictions before buying – interstate routes do not overlap as far as passes are concerned.

By bus

Bus travel is almost certainly the cheapest way to get around, but it's also the most tiresome. Even though the bus network reaches much further than the train network, routes follow the main highways between cities, and may mean arriving or departing at smaller places in the middle of the night. And services are not daily as you might think, especially in Western Australia, where there's only one bus a week to Adelaide. The buses are about as comfortable as they can be, with reclining seats, air conditioning, toilets and DVDs. If possible, try and plan for a stopover every twenty hours – If you try stoically to sit out a sixty-hour marathon trip, you'll need a day or more to get over it and the roadhouse food you'll have survived on. **Discounts** (ten percent, or fifteen percent if you buy your ticket before entering Australia) are available on many fares if you have a YHA, ISIC or recognized backpacker card such as VIP (see p.47), or if you are a pensioner.

The major **interstate bus company** on the mainland is Greyhound Australia (☏1300 473 946, ⓦwww.greyhound.com.au), which covers the entire country. Along the east coast, there's also Premier Motor Service (☏13 34 10, ⓦwww.premierms.com.au), calling in everywhere along the highway between Melbourne and Cairns, plus Countrylink (☏13 22 32, ⓦwww.countrylink .info), which runs between Brisbane and Melbourne and inland New South Wales,

RAIL AUSTRALIA
GREAT SOUTHERN RAIL
CountryLink
TRAVELTRAIN
Holidays

DISCOVER AUSTRALIA BY RAIL

Make new friends, meet fellow travellers including the locals, view the vast beauty of Australia's landscape or just sit back and relax. You can visit some spectacular cities from Sydney, Melbourne and Brisbane to Perth, Darwin and Adelaide as well as natural attractions such as The Whitsundays, Great Barrier Reef, Kangaroo Island and Uluru - whatever your interest is, let the train take you there.

CHOOSE FROM FOUR RAIL PASSES FROM AS LITTLE AS AUD$117

Austrail Pass - Discover all of Australia on one pass for up to 6 months unlimited travel!

Rail Explorer Pass - Travel the great trains - The Ghan, Indian Pacific and The Overland for up to 6 months!

Backtracker Pass - Explore Sydney and New South Wales with over 350 destinations to visit via CountryLink rail and coach services from 14 days to 6 months

East Coast Discovery Pass - Choose your destinations on the east coast from Melbourne to Cairns and enjoy up to 6 months travel in one direction - 6 different options!

Save 10% when you prepurchase your pass outside of Australia
www.railaustralia.com.au/railPasses.php

while in WA Integrity Coach lines (☎1800 226 339, ⓦwww.integritycoachlines.com.au) goes from Perth as far as Port Hedland. Firefly Express (☎1300 730 740, ⓦwww.fireflyexpress.com.au) runs to Sydney, Melbourne and Adelaide and usually has the cheapest fares for these routes. Tasmania is thoroughly covered by Tasmanian Redline Coaches (☎1300 360 000, ⓦwww.tasredline.com.au) and Tassielink (☎1300 300 520, ⓦwww.tassielink.com.au).

Sample direct **one-way fares** from Sydney are: Adelaide AUS$150 (23hr), Alice Springs AUS$440 (45hr), Brisbane AUS$100 (16hr), Cairns AUS$407 (45hr), Darwin AUS$790 (64hr) and Melbourne AUS$68 (13hr). Return fares are, at best, only marginally cheaper than two singles.

A good-value option for bus travellers is to buy a **pass**, though bear in mind that you won't save money over shorter routes and that passes are non-refundable. Greyhound offers a range of over twenty passes lasting between one and twelve months and covering preset routes, on which you can break your journey as often as you like and travel in any direction, but are not allowed to backtrack. Sample fares include the

six-month Perth–Darwin "Western Explorer" pass (AUS$819, AUS$737 concessions); a one-year "Best of the East", which goes everywhere between Adelaide, Uluru, Alice Springs, Mount Isa, Cairns, Sydney and Melbourne (AUS$1421, AUS$1279 concessions); and the "All Australian" pass (AUS$2968, AUS$2672 concessions). Year-long **kilometre passes** are more flexible, giving you unlimited travel up to 20,000 kilometres in any direction until you have used up the distance paid for – these work out around 9¢ per kilometre. Tasmania has its own passes, starting from AUS$135 for seven days' travel within a ten-day period.

By car

To explore Australia fully you'll **need your own vehicle**. This will enable you to get to the national parks, isolated beaches and ghost towns that aren't serviced by public transport and make the country such a special place. If your trip is a long one – three months or more – then **buying a vehicle** may well be the cheapest way of seeing Australia. On shorter trips you should consider **renting** – if not for the whole time then at least for short periods between bus rides, thereby allowing you to explore an area in depth.

Most foreign licences are valid for a year in Australia. An International Driving Permit (available from national motoring organizations) may be useful if you come from a non-English-speaking country. **Fuel** prices start at around $1.45 per litre for unleaded, with diesel about five percent more: prices increase by ten to fifteen percent along the Outback highways and can double at remote stations. The **rules of the road** are similar to those in the UK and US. Most importantly, drive on the left (as in the UK), remember that seat belts are compulsory for all, and that the speed limit in all built-up areas is 50kph or less. Outside built-up areas, maximums are around 110kph on long, isolated stretches – except in the Northern Territory, where common sense is your only limit between towns. Whatever else you do in a vehicle, avoid driving when you are tired – get out of the car every two hours – and don't drink alcohol; random breath tests are common even in rural areas, especially during the Christmas season and on Friday and Saturday nights. One rule that might catch you out in town is that **roadside parking** must be in the same direction as the traffic; in other words, don't cross oncoming traffic to park on the right.

Main **hazards** are boredom and fatigue, and animal collisions – a serious problem everywhere (not just in the Outback) at dawn, dusk and night-time. Driving in the Outback is by far the most dangerous tourist pursuit in Australia and every year several people get killed in single-vehicle rollovers or head-on collisions, particularly Europeans on short see-it-all holidays in cumbersome 4WDs or motor homes. Beware of fifty-metre-long **road trains**: these colossal trucks can't stop quickly or pull off the road safely, so if there's the slightest doubt, get out of their way; only

overtake a road train if you can see well ahead and are certain that your vehicle can manage it. On dirt roads be doubly cautious, or just pull over and let the road train pass.

Roads, Outback driving and breakdowns

Around the cities the only problem you'll face is inept signposting, but the quality of inter-state main roads – even Highway 1, which circles the country – isn't always great, and some of the minor routes are awful. **Conditions**, especially on unsealed roads, are unpredictable, and some roads will be impassable after a storm, so always seek reliable advice (from local police or a roadhouse) before starting out. Make it clear what sort of vehicle you're driving and remember that their idea of a "good" or "bad" road may be radically different from yours. Some so-called "4WD only" tracks are easily navigable in ordinary cars as long as you take it easy – high ground clearance, rather than four-driven wheels, is often the crucial factor.

Rain and flooding – particularly in the tropics and central Australia – can close roads to all vehicles within minutes, so driving through remote regions or even along the coastal highway in the wet season can be prone to delays. The stretches of highway between Broome and Kununurra and Cairns to Townsville are notorious for being cut by floods during the summer cyclone season. Several remote and unsealed roads through central Australia (the Sandover and Plenty highways, the Oodnadatta, Birdsville and Tanami tracks, and others) are theoretically open to all vehicles in dry winter weather, but unless you're well equipped with a tough car, don't attempt a crossing during the summer, when extreme temperatures place extra strain on both driver and vehicle.

Driving interstate

When driving across state borders bear in mind that your car may be subject to a customs search by officers on the lookout for fruit and fresh produce, which often cannot be carried from one state to another, to minimize the spread of plant pests and viruses. You'll see large bins at the side of the road as you approach a state border line for this purpose: dump any perishables here before crossing; otherwise, you risk receiving a large fine if pulled over and caught with them.

On **poor roads and dirt tracks**, the guidelines are to keep your speed down to 80kph, stick to the best section and never assume that the road is free from potholes and rocks. Long corrugated stretches can literally shake the vehicle apart – check radiators, fuel tanks and battery connections after rough stretches; reducing tyre pressures slightly softens the ride but can cause the tyres to overheat, making them more prone to punctures. Windscreens are often shattered by flying stones from passing traffic, so slow down and pull over to the left.

At all times carry plenty of **drinking water** and **fuel**, and if you're heading to the Outback let someone know your timetable, route and destination so that a rescue can be organized if you don't report in. Carry a detailed map, and don't count on finding regular signposts. In the event of a breakdown in the Outback, **always stay with your vehicle**: it's more visible to potential rescuers and you can use it for shade. If you're off a main track, as a last resort, burn a tyre or anything plastic – the black smoke will be distinctive from the average bushfire.

Car, 4WD and campervan rental

To **rent** a car you need a full, clean driver's licence and to be at least 21 years old, rising to 25 for 4WDs and motorcycles (see p.43). Check on any mileage limits or other restrictions, extras, and what you're covered for in an accident, before signing. The multinational operators Hertz, Budget, Avis and Thrifty have offices in the major cities, but outside of these, lack of competition makes their standard **rates** expensive at AUS$70–90 a day for a small car. Local firms – of which there are many in the cities – are almost always better value. A city-based non-multinational rental agency will supply new cars for around AUS$50 a day with unlimited kilometres. One-way rental might appear handy, but is usually very expensive: at least AUS$200 extra for the drop-off fee.

Four-wheel drives are best used for specific areas rather than long term, as rental and fuel costs are steep, starting at around AUS$120 a day. Some 4WD agents actually don't allow their vehicles to be driven off sealed roads, so check the fine print first.

Campervans and **motor homes** cost from AUS$90 a day for a two-berth campervan in low season (up to AUS$160 in high season) with unlimited kilometres – amazing value when you consider the independence, comfort and the saving on accommodation costs – plus one-way rental is possible. Like cars, campervans can be limited to sealed roads, but they give you the chance to create your own tour across Australia. Remember, though, that the sleeping capacity stated is an absolute maximum, which you wouldn't want to endure for too long. Furthermore, in the tropics the interior will never really cool enough overnight unless you leave the doors open – which brings the bugs in. Consider sleeping outside under a mozzie dome or inner tent.

For **4WD campervans**, the high-roofed Toyota Troop Carriers used by Britz, Apollo and Kea, to name a few, are tough, all-terrain vehicles fitted with 180-litre fuel tanks that will only be limited off-road by your 4WD experience or the height of the roof. With these models it's important to understand the operation of the free-wheeling hubs on the front axle to engage 4WD – many a campervan has become bogged by tourists who didn't engage 4WD correctly. The only drawback with this popular model is the high fuel consumption of around 7kpl. Lighter 4WD utes fitted with a cabin and a pop-up roof can't really take the same hammering but will be more economical, while the large Isuzu-based six-berthers look chunky but would really be a handful off-road and use even more fuel. With all these 4WD campers it's vital to appreciate the altered driving dynamics of an already high vehicle fitted with a heavy body. In the hands of overseas renters they regularly topple when an inexperienced driver drifts off the road, overcompensates and rolls over.

Prices for 4WD campers start around AUS$100 a day in the low season, up to AUS$250 in the high season. In addition to the big companies listed below, several smaller or local outfits buy in high-mileage, ex-rental vehicles to rent out at low prices. Branches of the big rental chains and local firms for all types of vehicles are detailed in "Listings" sections throughout the Guide.

Car rental agencies

Avis ⓦ www.avis.com.
Budget ⓦ www.budget.com.
Europcar ⓦ www.europcar.com.
Hertz ⓦ www.hertz.com.
Holiday Autos ⓦ www.holidayautos.co.uk.
National ⓦ www.nationalcar.com.
Rent-A-Bomb ⓦ www.rentabomb.com.au.
Thrifty ⓦ www.thrifty.com.

Campervan and motor-home rental agencies

Apollo Motorhome Holidays ☎ 1800 777 779, ⓦ www.apollocamper.com.au.
Backpacker Campervans ☎ 1800 670 232, ⓦ www.backpackercampervans.com.
Britz Australia ☎ 03/8379 8890, ⓦ www.britz.com.au.
Kea Campers ☎ 1800 252 555, ⓦ www.keacampers.com.
Maui ☎ 1300 363 800, ⓦ www.maui-rentals.com.

Buying a car

Buying a used vehicle needn't be an expensive business, and a well-kept car should resell at about two-thirds of the purchase price at the end of your trip. If you're lucky, or a skilful negotiator, you might even make a profit. A good place to evaluate vehicle prices and availability online is at ⓦ www.tradingpost.com.au.

If you don't know your axle from your elbow but are not too gullible, **car yards** can provide some advice: in Sydney, they're the most common place to buy a used vehicle, and some even cater specifically to travellers (see p.176) – but don't forget you're dealing with used-car salesmen whose worldwide reputation precedes them; a buy-back guarantee offered by some new car yards and dealers is usually a guarantee to pay you a fraction of the car's potential value. Assuming you have a little time and some mechanical knowledge, you'll save money by buying privately, **Backpackers' notice boards** in main exit points from Australia are the best places to look. One of the great advantages of buying from a fellow traveller is that you may get all sorts of stuff thrown in – camping gear, eskies and many of the spares listed below. The disadvantage is that the car may have been maintained on a backpacker's budget.

Four-wheel driving: some hints

The Outback is not the place to learn how to handle a 4WD and yet this is exactly where many tourists attracted by driving a tough off-road vehicle do so. Take all the spares listed on p.43, plus a shovel, hi-lift jack and gloves. In addition to the many "how to" manuals easily found in bookshops, if you're planning a long off-road tour, *Explore Australia by Four-Wheel Drive* (Viking) will suit recreational drivers. The following basic hints should help; see also the advice on creek crossings on p.505.

- Be aware of your limitations, and those of your vehicle.
- Know how to operate everything – including free-wheeling hubs (where present) and how to change a wheel – before you need it.
- Always cross deep water and very muddy sections on foot first.
- Don't persevere if you're stuck – avoid wheel spin (which will only dig you further in) and reverse out. Momentum is key on slippery surfaces such as mud, sand and snow – as long as you're moving forward, however slowly, resist the temptation to change gear, and so lose traction.
- Reducing tyre pressures down to 1 bar (15lb psi) dramatically increases traction in mud and sand, but causes tyre overheating, so keep speeds down. Carry a compressor or reinflate as soon as possible.
- If stuck, clear all the wheels with your hands or a shovel, create a shallow ramp (again, for all wheels), engage four-wheel drive, lower pressures if necessary, and drive or reverse out in low-range second.
- Keep to tracks – avoid unnecessary damage to the environment.
- Driving on beaches can be great fun, but is treacherous – observe other vehicles' tracks and be aware of tidal patterns.
- Consider a rented satellite phone for remote travel (see "Phones", p.73).

A **thorough inspection** is essential. Rust is one thing to watch for, especially in the tropics where humidity and salt air will turn scratches to holes within weeks – look out for poorly patched bodywork. Take cars for a spin and check the engine, gearbox, clutch and brakes for operation, unusual noises, vibration and leaks; repairs on some of these parts can be costly. Don't expect perfection, though: worn brake-pads and tyres, grating wheel-bearings and defective batteries can be fixed inexpensively, and if repairs are needed, it gives you a good excuse to haggle over the price. All tyres should be the same type and size. If you lack faith in your own abilities, the various state automobile associations offer rigorous pre-purchase inspections for about AUS$200, which isn't much to pay if it saves you from buying a wreck – and plenty of people do.

If you're **buying privately** (or from a dealer), you should also check the requirements of the state transport department: in most states you'll need a roadworthiness certificate to have the vehicle transferred from its previous owner's name to yours. This means having a garage check it over;

legally, the previous owner should do this, and theoretically it guarantees that the car is mechanically sound – but don't rely on it. You then proceed to the local Department of Transport with the certificate, a receipt of purchase, your driver's licence and passport; they charge a percentage of the price as stated on the receipt to register the vehicle in your name. WA-registered cars are a special case because a new roadworthy certificate is not necessary when the car is sold. This means that cars with WA plates are much easier to sell on wherever you are (as long as you keep the WA registration). You get some really clapped-out bangers still on the road in WA until the police slap an "unroadworthy" ticket on them.

If the annual **vehicle registration** is due, or you bought an interstate or deregistered vehicle ("as is", without number plates), you'll have to pay extra for registration, which is dependent on the engine size and runs into hundreds of dollars. Note that cars with interstate registration can be difficult to sell: if possible, go for a car with the registration of the state where you anticipate selling.

Best secondhand buys

Big-engined, mid-1980s **Holden Kingswood** or **Ford Falcon** station wagons are popular travellers' cars: cheap, roomy, reliable, mechanically simple and durable, with spares available in just about any city supermarket, roadhouse or wrecker's yard. At the bottom end, AUS$2000 plus a bit of luck should find you some kind of old car that runs reliably. Chances are, if a vehicle has survived this long, there's nothing seriously wrong with it and you should be able to nurse it through a bit further. Real bargains can also be secured from travellers desperate to get rid of their vehicle before flying out. Ideally, though, you should plan to pay at least AUS$4000 in total for a sound, well-equipped vehicle. Manual transmission models are more economical than old automatics, with the four-speed versions superior to the awkward, three-speed, steering-column-mounted models. Smaller and less robust, but much more economical to run, are old Japanese station wagons or vans such as **Mazda L300s** (also in 4WD version), suitable for one or two people. Any city backpackers' notice board will be covered in adverts of vehicles for sale.

Four-wheel drives are expensive and, with poor fuel economy and higher running costs, worth it only if you have some actual off-highway driving planned; to do that you can't buy an old wreck. **Toyota FJ** or **HJ Land Cruisers** are Outback legends, especially the long-wheelbase (LWB) models: tough, reliable and with plenty of new and used spares all over the country. If nothing goes wrong, a diesel (HJ) is preferable to a petrol (FJ) engine, being sturdier and more economical – although all Toyota engines, particularly the six-cylinder FJs, seem to keep on running, even if totally clapped out. The trouble with diesels is that problems, when they occur, tend to be serious, and repairs expensive. Generally, you're looking at AUS$8000 for a 20-year-old model.

Registration includes the legal minimum third-party personal **insurance**, but you might want to increase this cover to protect you against theft of the vehicle, or if you've bought something more flash go the whole way with comprehensive motor insurance. Joining one of the **automobile clubs** for another AUS$90 or so is well worth considering, as you'll get free roadside assistance (within certain limits), and discounts on road maps and other products. Each state has its own, but membership is reciprocal with overseas equivalents.

Equipping your car

Even if you expect to stick mostly to the main highways, you'll need to carry a fair number of **spares**: there are plenty of very isolated spots, even between Sydney and Melbourne. For ordinary cars, the cheapest place to buy spares is at a supermarket – head for the racks of any branch of K-Mart or Coles. A **towrope** is a good start; passing motorists are far cheaper than tow trucks. In addition – and especially if your vehicle is past its prime – you should have a set of spark plugs, points, fuses, fuel filters (for diesels), fan belt and radiator hoses – you need to check and maybe replace all these anyway. A selection of hose clamps, radiator sealant, water-dispersing spray, jump leads, tyre pump/compressor and a board to support the jack on soft ground will also come in handy. Again, if the car is old, establish its engine oil consumption early on; a car can carry on for thousands of kilometres guzzling oil at an alarming rate, but if the level drops too much the engine will cook itself. If you're confident, you might want to get hold of a Gregory's workshop manual for your vehicle; even if you're not, carry a copy and the above spares anyway – someone might help who knows how to use them. A ten-litre or bigger fuel container is also useful in case you run out.

Before you set off, check **battery** terminals for corrosion, and the battery for charge; buy a new one if necessary – don't risk money on a secondhand item. Carry two spare tyres. In fact, one of the best things you can do is start a long road trip with six new tyres, oil, filters, and radiator coolant, as well as points (if present) and plugs on a petrol

engine. **Off-road** drivers in remote regions should add to the list a puncture repair kit, bead breaker and tubes – and know how to use them. Keeping tyres at the correct pressure and having a wheel balance/alignment will reduce wear.

By motorcycle

Motorcycles, especially large-capacity trail bikes, are ideal for the Australian climate, although long distances place a premium on their comfort and fuel range. Japanese trail bikes, such as Yamaha's XT600, sell for around AUS$4000 and allow 100kph on-road cruising, are manageable on dirt roads and have readily available spares. A bike like the Honda XL650V Transalp is heavier but has a much smoother engine and fairing, which add up to better long-range comfort and reasonable gravel manners.

If it's likely that you'll return to your starting point, look out for dealers offering buy-back options that guarantee a resale at the end of your trip; bikes can be more difficult to sell privately than cars. Whether you're planning to ride off or on the bitumen, plenty of water-carrying capacity is essential in the Outback. **Outback night-riding** carries risks from collisions with wildlife from which a rider always comes off badly; all you can do is make sure your lights and brakes are up to it and keep your speed down to under 100kph.

Motorcycle **rental** has become widely available from the main southern cities. All types of models are available, but for extended touring you can't beat something like a BMW GS1150: comfortable, economical and a pleasure to ride loaded, two-up, day in, day out (although tyre choice will be critical for unsealed roads and it weighs a ton). Among other outlets, 1150s are available from ⓦ www.carconnection.com.au from around AUS$130 a day, or at a flat rate of AUS$6050 for three months (plus various deposits and bonds). *The Adventure Motorcycling Handbook* (Trailblazer) is a definitive manual for preparation and riding off the beaten track and includes a regional rundown of Australia's Outback tracks.

Hitching

The official advice for hitching in Australia is don't: with so many affordable forms of transport available, there's no real need to take the risk of jumping into a stranger's vehicle.

If you must do it, **never hitch alone**, and always avoid being dropped in the middle of nowhere between settlements. Remember that you don't have to get into a vehicle just because it stops: choose who to get in with and don't be afraid to ask questions before you do get in, making the arrangement clear from the start. Ask the driver where he or she is going rather than saying where you want to go. Try to keep your pack with you; having it locked in the boot makes a quick escape more difficult.

A much better method is lining up lifts through backpackers' notice boards (though this means sharing fuel costs). This option gives you the chance to meet the driver in advance, and – as a fellow traveller – they will most likely be stopping to see many of the same sights along the way. In out-of-the-way locations, roadhouses are a good place to head, as the owners often know of people who'll be heading in the same direction as you.

The best way to ensure your safety, apart from exercising your judgement and common sense, is to make concrete arrangements before your departure and stick to them.

Accommodation

Finding somewhere to bed down is rarely a problem, even in the smallest of places. However, on the east coast it's a good idea to book ahead for Christmas, January and the Easter holidays, as well as for long weekends, especially when big sporting events are held (see "Festivals", p.57).

The term "**hotel**" in Australia means a pub or bar. Although they were once legally required to provide somewhere for customers to sleep off a skinful – and many still do provide accommodation – the facilities are by no means luxurious. Those highlighted in the Guide do offer decent rooms, though the majority of them are still primarily places to drink, can be loud, and are not usually enticing places to stay.

The flip side of this is that many places that would call themselves hotels anywhere else prefer to use another name – hence the reason for so many motels and resorts, and, in the cities, "private hotels" or (especially in Sydney and Melbourne) boutique hotels that tend to be smaller and run along guesthouse lines. There are also a growing number of B&Bs and farmstays.

Australia caters extremely well for travellers, with a huge array of excellent hostels and "backpackers'", and caravan parks that offer accommodation in the form of permanent on-site vans and cabins or chalets, as well as campervan facilities and tent spaces, and sometimes self-catering apartments.

Hotels and motels

Cheaper Australian **hotels** tend to be basic – no TV, and shared bathrooms and plain furnishings – and aren't always the best choice for peace and quiet. In country areas hotels are often the social centre of town, especially on Friday and Saturday nights. But with double rooms at around AUS\$80–100 and singles from AUS\$60 (often with breakfast included), they can be better value – and more private – than hostel accommodation. **Motels** are typically a comfortable, bland choice, often found en masse at the edge of town to catch weary drivers, and priced on average upwards of AUS\$110 for a double room with TV and bath, not including breakfast. They rarely have single rooms, but they may have larger units for families, often with basic cooking facilities.

Accommodation price codes

All the accommodation listed in this book has been categorized into one of nine **price codes**, as set out below. These represent the cost of the **cheapest** available **double** or twin room in **high season**; single rooms are generally about two-thirds the price of doubles. Hostels and backpackers' accommodation mainly have beds in dorms. Where this is the case the price stated is in Australian dollars per dorm bed per night in high season. Where private rooms are also available, we have provided the price code. For units, cabins and caravans, the code covers the cost of the entire unit, which may sleep as many as six people.

In the lower categories, most rooms will be without private bath, though there's usually a washbasin in the room. From code ❹ upwards you'll most likely have private facilities. Remember that many of the cheaper places may also have more expensive rooms with en-suite facilities.

❶ $50 and under	❹ $76–100	❼ $161–200
❷ $51–60	❺ $101–130	❽ $201–250
❸ $61–75	❻ $131–160	❾ $251 and over

In cities, you're far more likely to come across a hotel in the conventional sense. The cheaper of these may well describe themselves as **"private hotels"** to distinguish themselves from pubs. Some of these, especially in inner cities, can be rather sleazy, but others are very pleasant, family-run guesthouses. Double rooms might cost anything from AUS$100 and up; more expensive hotels in the cities are standard places, aimed at the business community; in resorts and tourist areas they're more like upmarket motels. Prices can vary from around AUS$130 to well over AUS$350 In five-star establishments: a typical city three-star will probably cost you above AUS$160. Similar places in a resort or country area charge AUS$100 or more.

There are numerous nationwide hotel and **motel chains** that give certain guarantees of standards, among them familiar names such as Best Western and Travelodge, as well as Australian ones such as Budget, Golden Chain and Flag. While you might find it rather restrictive to use them for your whole stay, they offer dependable facilities and can be used to ensure that you have a reservation on arrival, or at anywhere else you know you'll be spending some time.

Resorts and self-catering apartments

You'll find establishments calling themselves **resorts** all over Australia, but the term is not a very clearly defined one. At the bottom

end, price, appearance and facilities may be little different to those of a motel, while top-flight places can be exclusive hideaways costing hundreds of dollars a night. Originally, the name implied that the price was all-inclusive of accommodation, drinks, meals, sports and anything else on offer, but this isn't always the case. These places tend to be set in picturesque locations – the Barrier Reef islands swarm with them – and are often brilliant value if you can wangle a stand-by or off-season price.

Self-catering apartments or country cabins can be a very good deal for families and larger groups. The places themselves range from larger units at a motel to purpose-built apartment hotels, but are usually excellent value. Cooking facilities are variable, but there'll always be a TV and fridge; linen (generally not included) can sometimes be rented for a small extra charge.

Farmstays and B&Bs

Another option in rural areas is **farmstays** on working farms, and **B&Bs** or guesthouses; the last two are predominantly in the south and east and can be anything from someone's large home to your own colonial cottage – ask what the "breakfast" actually includes. Farmstays are even more variable, with some offering very upmarket comforts, while at others you make do with the basic facilities in vacant shearers' quarters; their attraction is that they are always in out-of-the-way

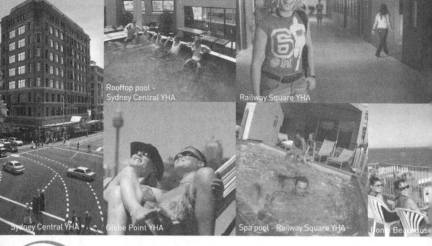

locations, and you'll often get a chance to participate in the working of the farm, or take advantage of guided tours around the property on horseback or by 4WD.

Hostels

There's a huge amount of budget accommodation in Australia, and though the more shambolic operations don't survive for long, standards are variable. Official **YHA youth hostels** (see opposite for a list of associations) are pretty dependable – if often relatively expensive – and in most places their regimented rules and regulations have been dropped in the face of competition, especially from the firmly established **VIP Backpacker Card** network, whose membership card is as useful and widely known as the YHA. Another well-known network of backpacker hostels is **Nomads**, which also issues a membership card entitling holders to plenty of discounts.

At their best, hostels and backpackers' accommodation are excellent value and are good places to meet other travellers and get on the grapevine. There's often a choice of dormitories, double or family rooms, plus bike rental, kitchen, games room, TV, internet access, a pool and help with finding work or planning trips. Many have useful notice boards, organized activities and tours. At their worst, their double rooms are poorer value than local hotel accommodation, and some are simply grubby, rapid-turnover dives – affiliation to an organization does not ensure quality. Hostels charge AUS$22–26 or more for a dormitory bed, with doubles – if available – from around AUS$60.

Most establishments prohibit the use of personal sleeping bags and instead provide all bedding, but it might be a good idea to carry at least a sheet sleeping bag for the few hostels that don't provide linen.

Youth hostel associations

The **International YHA card** is available through your national youth hostel association before you leave home, or you can purchase a one-year Hostelling International card in Australia for AUS$42, or AUS$32 for under-26s. YHA Membership and Travel Centres can be found in Sydney, Darwin, Brisbane, Cairns, Adelaide, Hobart, Melbourne and Perth, and at many YHA hostels. Australian YHA hostels number around 150, with thousands more worldwide.

UK and Republic of Ireland

Hostelling International Northern Ireland ☎028/9032 4733, ⓦwww.hini.org.uk.
Irish Youth Hostel Association Republic of Ireland ☎01/830 4555, ⓦwww.anoige.ie.
Scottish Youth Hostel Association ☎01786/891 400, ⓦwww.syha.org.uk.
Youth Hostel Association (YHA) England and Wales ☎01629/592 700, ⓦwww.yha.org.uk.

Hostel passes

If you're travelling on a budget, it's well worth laying your hands on at least one of the following **hostel passes**, which give you cheaper rates – around ten percent off on accommodation at member hostels, and also entitle you to a wide range of other discounts on everything from bus tickets and tours to phone calls, museum entry fees and meals.

Probably of most use in Australia is a **VIP Backpacker Card** (ⓦwww .vipbackpackers.com), which doubles as a rechargeable eKit phone card with a few dollars' worth of phone calls factored into the price of the card (AUS$43 for one year, AUS$57 for two years). At present, there are around 125 member hostels around the country, and your card will also be valid at one hundred more in New Zealand.

Nomads (ⓦwww.nomadsworld.com) works along similar lines; their card, which also doubles as a rechargeable phone card, costs AUS$35 a year. Their network comprises about 30 hostels in Australia, many of them in old pubs, a few of them "working hostels" in country areas specializing in harvest work, and there are also affiliated hostels in other countries, including New Zealand and Fiji.

US and Canada

Hostelling International-American Youth Hostels US ☎1-301/495-1240, ⓦwww.hiayh.org.
Hostelling International Canada ☎1-800/663-5777, ⓦwww.hihostels.ca.

Australia, New Zealand and South Africa

Australia Youth Hostels Association Australia ☎02/9281 9444, ⓦwww.yha.com.au.
Hostelling International South Africa Cape Town ☎021/424 2511, ⓔinfo@hisa.org.za.
Youth Hostelling Association NZ ☎0800/278 299 or 03/379 9970, ⓦwww.yha.co.nz.

Camping, caravan parks and roadhouses

Perhaps because Australian hostels are so widespread and inexpensive, simple tent **camping** is an option little used by foreign travellers. But don't let this put you off: national parks and nature reserves offer a host of camping grounds, which, depending on the location, will have an amenities block with flushing toilets, hot and cold showers, drinking water, plus a barbecue and picnic tables. Others, however, provide nothing at all, so come prepared, especially in national parks where **bushcamping** is often the only option for staying overnight. Vital equipment includes ground mats and a range of pegs – some wide (for sand), others narrow (for soil). A hatchet for splitting firewood is light to carry and doubles as a hammer. Fuel stoves are recommended, but if you do build a fire, make sure it doesn't get out of control – and always observe any fire bans. Prices depend on state policy and site facilities, and you'll usually need a permit from the local NPWS (National Parks and Wildlife Service) office, details of which are given throughout the Guide. Payment will be either by self-registration (fill in a form, put it into an envelope together with the required money, and drop it off in a box on the camp ground), or a park ranger will do the rounds and collect the money.

Camping rough by the road is not a good idea, even if you take the usual precautions of setting up away from the roadside and avoiding dry riverbeds. If you have to do it, try and ensure you're not too visible: having a group of drunks pitch into your camp at midnight is not an enjoyable experience. Animals are unlikely to pose a threat, except to your food – keep it in your tent or a secure container, or be prepared to be woken by their nocturnal shenanigans.

All over Australia, **caravan parks** (sometimes called holiday parks) are usually extraordinarily well equipped: in addition to an amenities block and a coin-operated laundry, very often you'll get an ironing board, a camp kitchen, a coin-operated barbecue, a kiosk and a swimming pool, maybe even a children's playground and a tennis court. If you are travelling without a tent, renting an on-site van (with cooking facilities but shared amenities) is a cheap, if somewhat basic, accommodation option, whereas cabins usually come with cooking facilities and an en-suite bathroom. In some upmarket caravan parks, cabins can even be slightly more expensive than a motel room, but as they are larger and better equipped, they are a good choice for families or groups travelling together.

Expect to pay AUS$10–18 per tent for an unpowered site, or AUS$36–90 for a van or cabin, depending on its location, age, size and equipment. Highway **roadhouses** are similar, combining a range of accommodation with fuel and restaurants for long-distance travellers.

Health

Australia has high standards of hygiene, and there are few exceptional health hazards – at least in terms of disease. No vaccination certificates are required unless you've come from a yellow-fever zone within the past week. Standards in Australia's hospitals are also very high, and medical costs are reasonable in comparison to Europe and the US.

The national healthcare scheme, **Medicare**, offers a reciprocal arrangement – free essential healthcare – for citizens of the UK, Ireland, New Zealand, Italy, Malta, Finland, the Netherlands, Norway and Sweden. This free treatment is limited to public hospitals and casualty departments (though the ambulance ride to get you there isn't covered); at GPs, you pay upfront (about AUS\$40 minimum), with two-thirds of your fee reimbursed by Medicare (does not apply to citizens of New Zealand and Ireland), or fill in a bulk bill form and the doctor bills Medicare directly (you don't pay anything).

Collect the reimbursement from a Medicare Centre (there are many branches) by presenting your doctor's bill together with a **Medicare Card**, available from any Medicare Centre. Anyone eligible who's staying in Australia for a while – particularly those on extended working holidays – is advised to obtain one. Applicants need to bring their passport and the National Health documents of their country. Dental treatment is not included: if you find yourself in need of dental treatment in one of the larger cities, try the dental hospital, where dental students may treat you cheaply or for free.

The sun

Australia's biggest health problem is also one of its chief attractions: **sunshine**. A sunny day in London, Toronto or even Miami is not the same as a cloudless day in Cairns, and the intensity of the Australian sun's damaging ultraviolet rays is far greater. Whether this is because of Australia's proximity to the ozone hole is a matter of debate, but there's absolutely no doubt that the southern sun burns more fiercely than anything in the northern hemisphere, so extra care is needed.

Australians of European origin, especially those of Anglo-Saxon or Celtic descent, could not be less suited to Australia's outdoor lifestyle, which is why two out of three Australians are statistically likely to develop **skin cancer** in their lifetime, the world's worst record. About five percent of these will develop potentially fatal melanomas, and about a thousand die each year. Looking at the ravaged complexions of some older Australians (who had prolonged exposure to the sun in the days before there was an awareness of the dangers of skin cancer) should be enough to make you want to cover yourself with lashings of the highest-factor **sun block** (SPF 35+), sold just about everywhere. Sunscreen should not be used on babies less than six months old: instead, keep them out of direct sunlight. What looks like war paint on the noses of surfers and small children is actually zinc cream; the thick, sticky waterproof cream, which comes in fun colours, provides a total blockout and is particularly useful when applied to protruding parts of the body, such as noses and shoulders.

These days, Australians are fully aware of the sun's dangers, and you're constantly reminded to "**Slip, Slop, Slap**", the government-approved catchphrase reminding you to slip on a T-shirt, slop on some sun block and slap on a hat – sound advice. Pay attention to any moles on your body: if you notice any changes, either during or after your trip, see a doctor; cancerous melanomas are generally easily removed if caught early. To prevent headaches and – in the long term – cataracts, it's a good idea to wear sunglasses; look for "UV block" ratings when you buy a pair.

The sun can also cause **heat exhaustion** and **sunstroke**, so in addition to keeping well covered up, stay in the shade if you can. Drink plenty of liquids: on hot days when walking, experts advise drinking a litre of water an hour – which is a lot to carry. Alcohol and sun don't mix well; when you're feeling particularly hot and thirsty, remember that a cold beer will actually dehydrate you.

Wildlife dangers

Although **mosquitoes** are found across the whole of the country, malaria is not endemic; however, in the tropical north there are regular outbreaks of similarly transmitted Ross River fever and dengue fever, chronically debilitating viruses that are potentially fatal to children and the elderly. Outbreaks of Ross River fever occur as far south as Tasmania, which is reason enough not to be too blasé about mozzie bites.

The danger from other **wildlife** is much overrated: snake and spider bites are an essential part of the perilous Outback myth, and crocodile and shark attacks are widely publicized – nonetheless, all are extremely rare.

The way to minimize danger from **saltwater crocodiles** (which actually range far inland; see p.579) is to keep your distance. If you're camping in the bush within 100km of the northern coast between Broome (WA) and Rockhampton (QLD), make sure your tent is at least 50m from waterholes or creeks, don't collect water at the same spot every day or leave any rubbish out, and always seek local advice before pitching up camp. Four-wheel drivers should take extra care when walking creeks prior to driving across.

Snakes almost always do their best to avoid people and you'll probably never see one. They're more likely to be active in hot weather, when you should be more careful. Treat them with respect, and it's unlikely you'll be bitten: most bites occur when people try to catch or kill snakes. Wear boots and long trousers when hiking through undergrowth, collect firewood carefully, and, in the event of a confrontation, back off. **Sea snakes** sometimes find divers intriguing, wrapping themselves around limbs or staring into masks, but they're seldom aggressive. If **bitten** by a snake, use a crepe bandage to bind the entire limb firmly and splint it, as if

for a sprain; this slows the distribution of venom into the lymphatic system. Don't clean the bite area (venom around the bite can identify the species, making treatment easier), and don't slash the bite or apply a tourniquet. Treat all bites as serious and always seek immediate medical attention, but remember: not all snakes are venomous, not all venomous snakes inject a lethal dose of venom every time they bite, and death from snakebite is rare.

Two **spiders** whose bites can be fatal are the funnel-web, a black, stocky creature found in the Sydney area, and the small redback, a relative of the notorious black widow of the Americas, usually found in dark, dry locations all over Australia (ie outdoor toilets, among shrubs, under rocks and timber logs), although they are less common in colder regions like Tasmania. Both are prolific in January and February, when there is the greatest danger of bites. Treat funnel-web bites as for snakebites, and apply ice to redback wounds to relieve pain; if bitten by either, get to a hospital – antivenins are available. Other spiders, centipedes and scorpions can deliver painful wounds but generally only cause serious problems if you have allergies.

Ticks, **mites** and **leeches** are the bane of bushwalkers, though spraying repellent over shoes and leggings will help keep these pests away in the first instance. **Ticks** are venomous – spring is the time when they produce the most toxins during feeding – and attach themselves to long grass and bushes, often latching on to passing animals that brush against them. Ticks can cause paralysis and death in humans, but the most common complaint is discomfort and allergic reactions. However, the paralysis tick, a native of Australia, can be found from Cairns to Lakes Entrance and is a life-threatening parasite of both man and animals. This tick is very common and regularly causes paralysis in dogs and cats.

Check yourself over after a hike: look for local stinging and swelling (usually just inside the hairline) and you'll find either a tiny black dot, or a pea-sized animal attached, depending on which species has bitten you. Use fine-pointed tweezers and grasp it as close to the skin as possible, and gently pull the tick out, trying to avoid squeezing the animal's body, which will inject more venom. Seek medical attention if you are not successful. A lot of bushwalkers advocate dabbing kerosene, alcohol or insect repellent on the ticks before pulling them out, but the official medical advice is not to – this will cause the ticks to inject more toxins into the host's body. **Mites** cause an infuriating rash known as "scrub itch", which characteristically appears wherever your clothes are tightest, such as around the hips and ankles. Unfortunately, there's not much you can do except take antihistamines and wait a day or two for the itching to stop. **Leeches** are gruesome but harmless: insect repellent, fire or salt gets them off the skin, though bites will bleed heavily for some time.

More serious is the threat from various types of **jellyfish** (also known as stingers or sea wasps), which occur in coastal tropical waters through the summer months. Two to watch out for are the tiny irukandji and the saucer-sized box jellyfish, though both are virtually invisible in water. **Irukandji** have initially painless stings, but their venom causes "irukandji syndrome", which can be fatal. Its symptoms are somewhat similar to those of decompression illness: elevated heart rate and increased blood pressure; and in addition, excruciating pain, anxiety and an overwhelming sense of doom and dread. **Box jellyfish** stings leave permanent red weals, and the venom can cause rapid unconsciousness and even kill, by paralyzing the heart muscles, if the weals cover more than half a limb. Treat stinger victims by dousing the sting area (front and back) with liberal amounts of vinegar – which you may find in small stands on affected beaches, such as North Queensland. Never rub with sand or towels, or attempt to remove tentacles from the skin – both could trigger the release of more venom; apply mouth-to-mouth resuscitation if needed, and get the victim to hospital for treatment. Whatever the locals are doing, don't risk swimming anywhere on tropical beaches during the stinger season (roughly Oct–May) – stinger nets don't offer any protection against the tiny irukandji that pass through the mesh designed to stop

the box jellyfish. For specific **reef hazards**, see the box on p.431.

For more background on Australian fauna, see p.1138.

Other health hazards

One thing to watch out for in the hot and humid north is **tropical ear**, a very painful fungal infection of the ear canal. Treatment is with ear drops, and if you think you might be susceptible, use them anyway after getting wet.

Although you're unlikely to find yourself in the path of a raging **bushfire**, it helps to know how to survive one. If you're in a car, don't attempt to drive through smoke but park at the side of the road in the clearest spot, put on your headlights, wind up the windows and close the air vents. Although it seems to go against common sense – and your natural instincts – it's safer to stay inside the car. Lie on the floor and cover all exposed skin with a blanket or any covering at hand. The car won't explode or catch on fire, and a fast-moving wildfire will pass quickly overhead. If you smell or see smoke and fire while walking, find a cleared rocky outcrop or an open space: if you're trapped in the path of the fire and the terrain and time permits, dig a shallow trench – in any event, lie face down and cover all exposed skin.

Medical resources for travellers

UK and Republic of Ireland

Hospital for Tropical Diseases Travel Clinic ☎0845/155 5000 or 020/7387 4411, ⦿www.thehtd.org.
MASTA (Medical Advisory Service for Travellers Abroad) ☎0870/606 2782 or ⦿www.masta-travel-health.com for the nearest clinic.
Tropical Medical Bureau Republic of Ireland ☎1850/487 674, ⦿www.tmb.ie.

US and Canada

CDC ☎1-800/311-3435, ⦿wwwn.cdc.gov/travel. Official US government travel health site.
International Society for Travel Medicine ☎1-770/736-7060, ⦿www.istm.org. Has a full list of travel health clinics.
Canadian Society for International Health ☎613/241-5785, ⦿www.csih.org. Extensive list of travel health centres.

Australia, New Zealand and South Africa

Travellers' Medical and Vaccination Centre
℡ 1300/658 844, 🖰 www.tmvc.com.au. Travel clinics in Australia.

The Travel Doctor NZ 🖰 www.traveldoctor.co.nz; SA ℡ 0861 300 911, 🖰 www.traveldoctor.co.za. Travel clinics in New Zealand and South Africa.

Food and drink

Australia is almost two separate nations when it comes to food. In the cities of the southeast – especially Melbourne – there's a range of cosmopolitan and inexpensive restaurants and cafés featuring almost every imaginable cuisine. Here, there's an exceptionally high ratio of eating places to people, and they survive because people eat out so much – three times a week is not unusual. Remote country areas are the complete antithesis of this, where the only thing better than meat pies and microwaveable fast-food is the plain, straightforward counter food served at the local hotel, or a slightly more upmarket bistro or basic Chinese restaurant.

Traditionally, Australian food found its roots in the English overcooked-meat-and-three-veg "common-sense cookery" mould. Two things have rescued the country from culinary destitution: **immigration** and an extraordinary range of superb, locally produced fresh ingredients. In addition to introducing their own cuisine, immigrants have had at least as profound an effect on mainstream Australian food. "Modern Australian" cuisine (or **Mod Oz**) is an exciting blend of tastes and influences from around the world – particularly Asia and the Mediterranean – and many not specifically "ethnic" restaurants will have a menu that includes properly prepared curry, dolmades and fettuccine alongside steak and prawns. This healthy, eclectic – and above all, fresh – cuisine has a lot in common with Californian cooking styles, and both go under the banner of "East meets West" or fusion cuisine.

Food

Meat is plentiful, cheap and excellent: steak forms the mainstay of the pub-counter meal and of the ubiquitous **barbie** – as Australian an institution as you could hope to find: free or coin-operated barbecues can be found in car parks, campsites and beauty spots all over the country. As well as beef and lamb, emu, buffalo, camel and witchetty grubs may be served, especially in more upmarket restaurants, but the two most common are kangaroo – a rich, tender and virtually fat-free meat – and crocodile, which tastes like a mix of chicken and pork and is at its best when simply grilled. At the coast, and elsewhere in specialist restaurants, there's tremendous **seafood**: prawns and oysters, mud crabs, Moreton Bay bugs (small crusta- ceans) and yabbies (sea- and freshwater crayfish), lobsters, and a wide variety of fresh- and seawater fish – barramundi has a reputation as one of the finest, but is easily beaten by sweetlips or coral trout.

Fruit is good, too, from Tasmanian apples and pears to tropical bananas, pawpaw (papaya), mangoes, avocados, citrus fruits, custard apples, lychees, pineapples, passion fruit, star fruit and coconuts – few of them native, but delicious nonetheless. **Vegetables** are also fresh, cheap and good, and include everything from pumpkin, European cauliflowers and potatoes to Chinese bok choy and Indian bitter gourds.

Note that aubergine is known as eggplant, courgettes as zucchini and red or green peppers as capsicums.

Vegetarians might assume that they'll face a narrow choice of food in "meato-centric" Australia, and in the country areas that's probably true. But elsewhere, most restaurants will have one vegetarian option at least, and in the cities veggie cafés have cultivated a wholesome, trendy image that suits Australians' active, health-conscious nature.

Finally, a word on **eskies** – insulated food containers varying from handy "six-pack" sizes to cavernous sixty-litre trunks capable of refrigerating a weekend's worth of food or beer. No barbie or camping trip is complete without a couple of eskies. The brand name "Esky" has been adopted to describe all similar products.

Ethnic food

Since World War II, wave after wave of immigrants have brought a huge variety of ethnic cuisines to Australia: first North European, then Mediterranean and most recently Asian.

An array of Asian cuisines – especially Chinese, Vietnamese, Malaysian, Thai, Japanese and Mongolian – can be found throughout Australia. European cuisines have also made their mark, with Italian food an enormous influence, and Greek, Turkish and Lebanese also popular.

Eating out

Restaurants are astonishingly good value compared with Britain and North America, particularly as many restaurants are BYO (see box, p.55). You should have no problem finding an excellent two-course meal in a BYO restaurant for AUS$25 or less, though a main course at a moderate restaurant is around AUS$17–26.

There are also lots of excellent **cafés** and **coffee shops**. In the cities and resorts, modern cafés are often the best places to go for a decent meal, and will be open from early in the morning until late at night, serving food all day; in the country, they may stick more or less to shop hours.

The **hotel** counter meal is another mainstay, and at times may be all that's available: if it is, make sure you get there in time – meals in pubs are generally served only from noon to 2.30pm and again from 6 to 9pm, and sometimes not at all on Sunday evening. The food – served at the bar – will be simple but substantial and inexpensive (usually around AUS$14 or less): steak, salad and chips, and variations on this theme. In more upmarket areas and cities such as Melbourne and Sydney you'll find the food is more in line with gastropub fare, with dishes such as pan-fried salmon and mash, porter-house steak and lamb and rosemary sausages featuring alongside club sandwiches and burgers. Many hotels and motels also have a restaurant where you sit

Bushtucker

Before the first European colonists settled on the continent, **Aborigines** followed a nomadic lifestyle within extensive tribal boundaries, following seasonal game and plants and promoting both by annually burning off grassland.

Along the coast, indigenous people speared turtles and dugong from outrigger canoes, and even cooperated with dolphins to herd fish into shallows. On land, animals caught were possums, snakes, goannas, emus and kangaroos, while more meagre pickings were provided by honey and green ants, water-holding frogs, moths and various grubs – the witchetty (or *witjuti*) being the best known. Plants were used extensively and formed the bulk of the diet. This food became known as **bushtucker**.

Until about twenty years ago, it was illegal to sell or serve kangaroo or emu anywhere outside of South Australia, but following legislation that allowed their consumption in other states, dishes featuring emu, kangaroo or crocodile are now readily available on most **restaurant** menus.

There are also several bushtucker tours and safaris available (particularly in the Northern Territory), which give an introduction to living off the land.

Infamous Australian foods

Chicko Roll Imagine a wrapper of stodgy dough covered in breadcrumbs, filled with a neutered mess of chicken, cabbage, thickeners and flavourings, and then deep-fried. You could only get away with it in Australia.

Damper Sounding positively wholesome in this company, "damper" is the swagman's staple – soda bread baked in a pot buried in the ashes of a fire. It's not hard to make after a few attempts – the secret is in the heat of the coals and a splash of beer.

Lamington A chocolate-coated sponge cube rolled in shredded coconut.

Pavlova ("pav"). A dessert concoction of meringue with layers of cream and fruit; named after the eminent Russian ballerina. Made properly with fresh fruit and minimum quantities of cream and sugar, it's not bad at all.

Pie floater The apotheosis of the meat pie; a "pie floater" is an inverted meat pie swamped in mashed green peas and tomato sauce; found especially in South Australia. Floaters can be surprisingly good, or horrible enough to put you off both pies and peas for life.

Vegemite Regarded by the English as an inferior form of Marmite and by almost every other nationality with total disgust, Vegemite is an Australian institution – a strong, dark, yeast spread.

Witchetty grubs (*witjuti*). About the size of your little finger, witchetty grubs are dug from the roots of mulga trees and are a well-known Australian bushtucker delicacy. Eating the plump, fawn-coloured caterpillars live (as is traditional) takes some nerve, so try giving them a brief roasting in embers. They're very tasty either way – reminiscent of peanut butter.

down to be served; these places often have a help-yourself salad bar, too. Usually the most expensive thing on the menu is a huge steak for AUS$15–20.

In cities and bigger resorts, you'll find fantastic fast-food in **food courts**, often in the basements of office buildings or in shopping malls, where dozens of small stalls compete to offer Thai, Chinese, Japanese or Italian food as well as burgers, steaks and sandwiches. On the road, you may be limited to what's available at the roadhouse, usually the lowest common denominator of reheated meat pies and microwaved ready-meals.

Drink

Australians have a reputation for enjoying a drink, and **hotels** (also sometimes called taverns, inns, pubs and bars) are where the drinking mostly takes place. Traditionally, public bars are male enclaves, the place where mates meet after work on their way home, with the emphasis more on the beer and banter than the surroundings. While changing attitudes have converted many city hotels into comfortable, relaxed bars, a lot of

Outback pubs are still pretty spartan and daunting for strangers of either sex, but you'll find barriers will come down if you're prepared to join in the conversation.

Friday and Saturday are the serious party nights, when there's likely to be a band and – in the case of some Outback establishments – literally everybody for a hundred kilometres around jammed into the building. **Opening hours** vary from state to state; they're usually 11am to 11pm, but are often much later, with early closing on Sunday. Some places are also "early openers", with hours from 6am to 6pm.

Off-licences or liquor stores are known as **bottle shops.** These are usually in a separate section attached to a pub or super-market – in some states, you can't buy alcohol from supermarkets or grocery stores. There are also **drive-in** bottle shops, sometimes attached to pubs, where you can load bulk purchases directly into the boot of your car. If you plan to visit **Aboriginal communities** in the Outback, bear in mind that some of them are "dry". Respect their regulations and don't take any alcohol with

BYO

In a restaurant, **BYO**, or **Bring Your Own**, means diners may bring their own wine to enjoy with their meal. Some establishments add "wine only" after BYO, but the understanding is generally that you may not bring spirits or beer. A small corkage fee – around AUS$3–7 – is usually charged, either per bottle or per head. Some licensed restaurants also allow BYO wine, but if you add their steeper corkage fee to the price of your bottle, you might as well stick to their wine list.

you, even if members of the communities ask you for "grog".

Beer

As anyone will tell you, the proper way to drink **beer** in a hot country such as Australia is ice-cold (the English can expect to be constantly berated for their warm beer preferences) and fast, from a small container so it doesn't heat up before you can down the contents. Tubular foam or polystyrene coolers are often supplied for **tinnies** (cans) or **stubbies** (short-necked bottles) to make sure they stay icy. Glasses are always on the small side, and are given confusingly different names state by state. The standard ten-ounce (half-pint) serving is known as a **pot** in Victoria and Queensland, and a **middie** in New South Wales and Western Australia, where the situation is further complicated by the presence of fifteen-ounce **schooners**. A **carton** or **slab** is a box of 24–30 tinnies or stubbies, bought in bulk from a bottle shop and always cheaper when not chilled (a "Darwin stubby", with typically Territorian eccentricity, is two litres of beer in an oversized bottle).

Australian beers are lager- or pilsner-style, and even the big mass-produced ones are pretty good – at least once you've worked up a thirst. They're considerably stronger than their US equivalents, and marginally stronger than the average British lager at just under five percent alcohol. Each state has its own **label** and there are fierce local loyalties, even though most are sold nationwide: Fourex (XXXX; see p.384) and Powers in Queensland; Swan in Western Australia; Coopers in South Australia; VB in Victoria; Tooheys in New South Wales; and Boags in Tasmania. Almost all of these companies produce more than one beer – usually a light low-alcohol version and a premium "gold" or

bitter brew. There are also a number of smaller "boutique" breweries and specialist beermakers: Tasmania's Cascade, WA's Redback or Matilda Bay, Queensland's Cairns' Draught and Eumundi are more distinctive but harder to find. Fosters is treated as a joke in Australia, something that's fit only for export. Larger bottle shops might have imported beers, but outside cities (where Irish pubs serve surprisingly authentic-tasting Guinness) it's rare that you'll find anything foreign on tap.

Wines and spirits

Australian **wines** have long been appreciated at home, and it's not hard to see why; even an inexpensive bottle (around AUS$12) will be better than just drinkable, while pricier varieties compare favourably with fine French wines – though some critics complain that Australian reds have become a bit too "woody" in recent years. If you're new to Australian wines, you'll always find Yalumba, Lindemans and Wolf Blass will give satisfaction, but the secret is to be adventurous: you're unlikely to be disappointed. Even the "chateau cardboard" four-litre bladders or wine casks that prevail at parties and barbecues are perfectly palatable. Whatever the colour, a mid-range bottle of wine will set you back about AUS$16.

The biggest wine-producing **regions** are the Hunter Valley in New South Wales and the Barossa Valley in South Australia, but you'll find smaller commercial vineyards from Kingaroy in Queensland to Margaret River in southwest Western Australia; all are detailed in the Guide. If you buy at these places, you'll be able to sample in advance (see box, p.781). Most bottle shops will, in any case, have a good range of very reasonably priced options. For more on Australian wines, check out Ⓦ www.wineaustralia.com

or www.australianwines.com.au, for maps and a description of the most important wine regions, as well as information on how to best serve and drink local wines.

The Australian wine industry also makes port and brandy as a sideline, though these are not up to international standards. Two excellent dark **rums** from Queensland's sugar belt are well worth tasting, however: the sweet, deliciously smoky Bundaberg (see p.428) and the more conventionally flavoured Beenleigh. They're of average strength, normally 33 percent alcohol, but beware of "overproof" variations, which will have you flat on your back if you try to drink them like ordinary spirits.

Coffee

Australia can thank its Italian immigrants for elevating **coffee** to a pastime rather than just a hot drink. Nowadays, every suburban café has an espresso machine, and it's not just used to make cappuccino. Other styles of coffee have adopted uniquely Australian names: a "flat white" is a plain white coffee, a "long black" is a regular cup of black coffee, and a "short black" is an espresso – transformed by a splash of milk into a macchiato. ("Espresso" is also a brand of instant coffee, so ask for a short black if you're after the genuine article.)

The media

Local papers are always a good source of listings, if not news. You should be able to track down some international papers, or their overseas editions – British, American, Asian and European – in the state capitals. Australian television isn't particularly exciting unless you're into sport, of which there's plenty.

Newspapers and magazines

The Murdoch-owned *Australian* (Ⓦwww .theaustralian.news.com.au) is the country's only national daily (that is, Mon–Sat) newspaper; aimed mainly at the business community, it has good overseas coverage but local news is often built around statistics. Each state (or more properly, each state capital) has its own daily paper, the best of which are two Fairfax-owned papers, the *Sydney Morning Herald* (Ⓦwww.smh.com.au) and Melbourne's venerable *The Age* (Ⓦwww .theage.com.au) – both available across the southeast (the two papers share similar content in their weekend-edition magazines). If you're interested in wildlife, pick up a copy of the quarterly *Australian Geographic* (related only in name to the US magazine) for some superb photography and in-depth coverage of Australia's remoter corners, or the quarterly *Australian Wildlife* magazine published by the

Wildlife Preservation Society of Australia. There are some excellent glossy Australian-focused adventure-travel magazines, too, such as the quarterly *Wild*, while the beautifully produced and written quarterly *40° South* concentrates on all things Tasmanian (it's hard to track down; see Ⓦwww.fortysouth.com.au for details). You'll find Australian versions of all the fashion mags, from *Vogue* to *Marie Claire*, plus enduring publications such as *Australian Women's Weekly*. The excellent *Australian Gourmet Traveller* celebrates both fine food and travel. Gossip magazines such as *Who Weekly* feature the lowdown on the antics of international and Australian celebs.

Television

Australia's first **television** station opened in 1956 and the country didn't get colour television until 1974 – both much later than other westernized countries. It is governed by Australian content rulings, which means that there a good amount of Australian dramas, series and soap operas, many of which go on to make it big overseas (from *Neighbours* and *Home and Away* to *The Secret Life of Us*). However, there's a predominance of American programmes and lots of repeats. Australian TV is also fairly permissive in terms of sexual content compared to the programming of Britain or North America. There are three predictable commercial stations: Channel Seven; Channel Nine, which aims for an older market with more conservative programming; and Channel Ten, which tries to grab the younger market with some good comedy. In addition, there is also the more serious ABC – a national, advertisement-free station still with a British bias, showing all the best British sitcoms and mini-series – and the livelier SBS, a government-sponsored, multicultural station, which has the best coverage of world news, as well

as interesting current-affairs programmes and plenty of foreign-language films. In more remote areas you won't be able to access all five channels, and often only ABC and one commercial offering are receivable. Foxtel is one of the main providers of cable TV.

Radio

The best **radio** is on the various ABC stations, both local and national. ABC Radio National – broadcast all over Australia – offers a popular mix of arty intellectual topics, and another ABC station, 2JJJ ("Triple J"), a former Sydney-based alternative-rock station, is aimed at the nation's youth and is available across the country in watered-down form. To find the frequency for ABC radio stations in your area visit ⓦwww.abc.net.au. You can listen to various ABC radio stations on the internet with live or on-demand audio (ⓦwww.abc.net.au/streaming).

Festivals and sporting events

The nationwide selection of festivals listed below all include, necessitate and are, in some cases, the imaginative product of prolonged beer-swilling. Why else would you drive to the edge of the Simpson Desert to watch a horse race? More seriously, each mainland capital tries to elevate its sophistication quotient with a regular celebration and showcase of art and culture, of which the biennial Adelaide Arts Festival is the best known.

Besides the major events listed below, there's a host of smaller, local events, many of which are detailed throughout the Guide. All cities and towns also have their own agricultural "shows", which are high points of the local calendar. The Christmas and Easter holiday periods, especially, are marked by celebrations at every turn, all over the country.

January

Sydney Festival Sydney, NSW. Starts the first week. Three weeks of festivities take place all over the city – in parks, theatres and cinemas – with

something for absolutely everyone, from new film and outdoor jazz to contemporary art and current-events lectures. ⓦwww.sydneyfestival.com.au.
Australian Open Tennis Championship Melbourne, VIC. Mid- to end Jan. The year's first Grand Slam attracts hordes of zinc-creamed tennis fans to see the best players in international tennis compete for two weeks at Melbourne Park. ⓦwww.australianopen.com.
Tamworth Country Music Festival NSW. Mid-Jan. Ten days of Slim Dusty and his ilk, attracting over 50,000 people and culminating in the Australian Country Music Awards. ⓦwww.tcmf.com.au.
Big Day Out Various locations. Late Jan to early Feb. This event has got bigger and bigger since the

first Big Day Out in Sydney over fifteen years ago and today is Australia and New Zealand's largest outdoor music festival, with over 250,000 people gathering at six different locations over successive weekends to see bands such as the Arctic Monkeys, Jet and Kasabian. Kicks off in Auckland, then moves on to the Gold Coast, Sydney, Melbourne, Adelaide and finally Perth. ⓦ www.bigdayout.com.

February

Sydney Gay and Lesbian Mardi Gras, NSW. Early Feb to early March. Sydney's proud gay community's festival runs throughout Feb and culminates at the beginning of March with an extravagant parade and an all-night dance party. ⓦ www.mardigras.org.au.

Perth International Arts Festival Perth, WA. Mid-Feb to early March. Australia's oldest and largest arts festival, attracting renowned international artists, performers and attendees to indoor and outdoor events all over the city for three weeks. ⓦ www.perthfestival.com.au.

Adelaide Arts Festival SA. Late Feb to early March. Held in even-numbered years. The country's best-known and most innovative biennial arts festival, featuring opera, theatre, music and dance, and including the largest literary festivals in the world; not to be missed. ⓦ www.adelaidefestival.org.au.

March

Australian Grand Prix Melbourne, VIC. Formula 1 mania takes over Melbourne for four days, with action centred on the purpose-built Albert Park race track. As well as the high-adrenalin 58-lap race, which takes place on Sunday, off-track entertainment includes air displays, rides, go-karting and glamour in the form of the pit girls. ⓦ www.grandprix.com.au.

Womadelaide Adelaide, SA. First or second weekend. Part of the Womad festival circuit; three-day party featuring world music, folk, blues and jazz. ⓦ www.womadelaide.com.au.

Moomba Waterfest VIC. Second weekend. A long weekend of partying in Melbourne, beginning and ending with fireworks, with lots of water-based fun on the Yarra River in between. Don't miss the "Birdman Rally" in which various flying contraptions assemble at Princes Bridge and attempt to defy gravity. ⓦ www.melbournemoombafestival.com.au.

April

Melbourne International Comedy Festival Melbourne, VIC. Leading laughathon that attracts more than a thousand home-grown and international comics throughout April. Based around the Melbourne Town Hall, but with programmes in over fifty other city venues, spanning stand-up comedy, plays, film, TV and street theatre. ⓦ www.comedyfestival.com.au.

June

Sydney International Film Festival Sydney, NSW. Early June. Important film festival, running for over two weeks and based at four CBD venues including the glorious State Theatre. ⓦ www.sydneyfilmfestival.org.

Barunga Cultural and Sports Festival NT. Queen's Birthday weekend. This three-day festival, held on Aboriginal land near Katherine, offers a rare and enjoyable opportunity to encounter Aboriginal culture in the NT. No alcohol. ⓦ www.barungafestival.com.au.

Laura Dance and Cultural Festival Cape York, QLD. Third weekend; held in odd-numbered years. Three-day, alcohol-free celebration of authentic Aboriginal culture. ⓦ www.laurafestival.tv.

July

Imparja Camel Cup Alice Springs, NT. Second Sat. This event originated with camels charging down the dry Todd River; the camel-racing now takes place at Blatherskite Park, with free buses to the site. Entry fee. ⓦ www.camelcup.com.au.

Brisbane Festival Brisbane, QLD. Mid-July; held in even years. Huge, biennial, seventeen-day festival featuring performing arts, food and drink, music, writing and children's events topped off with fireworks. ⓦ www.brisbanefestival.com.au.

Darwin Beer Can Regatta NT. Third Sun. Mindil Beach is the venue for the recycling of copious empties into a variety of "canstructed" seacraft. Also a thong-throwing contest; Territorian eccentricity personified. ⓦ www.beercanregatta.org.au.

Melbourne International Film Festival VIC. End July to mid-Aug. The country's largest and most prestigious film festival, lasting for nineteen days with a focus on Australian, cult and arty films, plus a multimedia component highlighting the latest in film technology. ⓦ www.melbournefilmfestival.com.au.

August

Isa Rodeo Mount Isa, QLD. Second or third weekend. Australia's largest rodeo – a gritty, down-to-earth encounter with bulls, horses and their riders. ⓦ www.isarodeo.com.au.

Henley-on-Todd Regatta Alice Springs, NT. Third Sat. Wacky races in bottomless boats running down the dry Todd River; the event is heavily insured against the river actually flowing. ⓦ www.henleyontodd.com.au.

Shinju Matsuri Festival Broome, WA. End Aug. Probably the most remote of the big festivals, but this doesn't stop the town packing out for WA's ten-day Oriental-themed pearl festival. ⊛ www .shinjumatsuri.com.

September

Birdsville Races QLD. First weekend. Once a year, the remote Outback town of Birdsville (population approx 120) comes alive for a weekend (Fri and Sat) of drinking and horse racing – a well-known and definitive Australian oddity. ⊛ www.birdsvilleraces.com.

Royal Melbourne Show VIC. Mid-Sept. Eleven-day agricultural bonanza, featuring sheep-shearing, dog and horse shows and performing pigs. Rides, baked potatoes and candyfloss stalls compete with contests featuring everything from Jersey-Holstein cows to wood-choppers. ⊛ www.royalshow.com.au.

AFL Grand Final Melbourne, VIC. Last Sat. I luge, testosterone-charged sporting event. The Australian Football League final is held at Melbourne's MCG and is accompanied by lots of beer drinking and celebrating, depending on which team wins. ⊛ www.afl.com.au.

October

Australian Motorcycle Grand Prix VIC. Held over one weekend on Phillip Island, this is one of the last races of the World Championship and a popular pilgrimage for all motorbike enthusiasts. ⊛ http://bikes.grandprix.com.au.

Manly Jazz Festival Sydney, NSW. First weekend. Long-established, free three-day jazz festival featuring artists from all over the world. ⊛ www.manly.nsw.gov .au/manlyjazz.

Melbourne International Arts Festival VIC. Mid-Oct. One of Australia's pre-eminent annual arts events, this seventeen-day festival has a cast of thousands drawn from the fields of music, multimedia, opera, dance and theatre. Ticketed and free performances are held both indoors at various venues and on Melbourne's streets. ⊛ www.melbournefestival.com.au.

November

Melbourne Cup Flemington Racecourse, VIC. First Tues. Australia's Ascot, a 148-year-old horse race that brings the entire country to a standstill around the radio or TV. ⊛ www.melbournecup.com.

December

Christmas Day Sydney, NSW. For travellers from the northern hemisphere, turkey on the beach is an awesome concept – on Sydney's Bondi Beach, it's coupled with a lot of alcohol, making this public holiday a raucous riot. Sadly, though, the days of free partying are long gone and the organized festivities are a ticket affair only.

New Year's Eve Sydney, NSW. The fireworks display from Sydney Harbour Bridge is a grand show, and a fine example to the rest of the world of how to welcome in the New Year. To get the best views along the water's edge, you'll need to get there while it's still light.

Sydney–Hobart Yacht Race Sydney, NSW. Crowds flock to the harbour to witness the start of this classic regatta, which departs Sydney at 1pm on Boxing Day and arrives in Hobart three days later. ⊛ www.rolexsydneyhobart.com.

Sports and outdoor activities

Australians are sports-mad, especially for the ostensibly passive spectator sports of cricket, Aussie Rules football, rugby (league or union), tennis or any type of racing, from cockroach to camel. No matter what it is, it'll draw a crowd – with thousands more watching on TV – and a crowd means a party. Even unpromising-sounding activities such as surf lifesaving and yacht racing (the start of the Sydney to Hobart race just after Christmas is a massive social event; see p.1034) are tremendously popular.

Football

The wintertime football (**footy**) season in Australia lasts from March to September, and comes in several varieties. Before World War II, soccer was played by British immigrants, but with postwar immigration it was branded as "ethnic", as new clubs became based on the country of origin of the players: Australian Rules (see below) was considered the game "real Australians" played. Before the National Soccer League's (NSL) competition was disbanded in 2004, more than fifty percent of the former NSL's twelve clubs had evolved from communities of postwar immigrants – mainly Italians, Greeks and Yugoslavs. The former chairman of Soccer Australia (now rebranded Football Federation Australia), David Hill, believed that their fervent nationalism marginalized the game; his mid-1990s ban on clubs that included national flags in their logos won support as well as accusations of the pursuance of a policy of "ethnic cleansing". The new A-League competition, with eight teams from Australia and New Zealand, is the latest attempt to promote national rather than localized, politicized interest in the sport. The best players invariably head off to play overseas but can usually be seen in Australia's national team, the **Socceroos**, interest in which has increased significantly since their appearance at the 2006 World Cup – their first for thirty years – where they (controversially) lost to eventual champions Italy in the second round.

Australian Rules ("**Aussie Rules**") football dominates Victoria, Tasmania, South Australia and Western Australia. It's an extraordinary, anarchic, no-holds-barred, eighteen-a-side brawl, most closely related to Gaelic football and known dismissively north of the Victorian border as "aerial ping pong". The ball can be propelled by any means necessary, and the fact that players aren't sent off for misconduct ensures a lively, skilful and, above all, gladiatorial confrontation. The game is mostly played on cricket grounds, with a ball similar to that used in rugby or American football. The aim is to get the ball through the central uprights for a goal (six points). There are four 20-minute quarters, though the clock is stopped each time the ball is out of play so quarters can go on for longer. Despite the violence on the pitch (or perhaps because of it), Aussie Rules fans tend to be loyal and well behaved, with a high proportion of fans being women and children. It's also worth noting that fans aren't segregated at matches. Victoria has traditionally been the home of the game with ten out of the sixteen AFL clubs, and an all-Victorian Grand Final (held in September; see p.59) usually warrants a sell-out crowd at the MCG.

Rugby

In New South Wales and Queensland, **Rugby League** attracts the fanatics, especially for the hard-fought State of Origin matches. The thirteen-a-side game is one at which the Australians – known as the **Kangaroos** – seem permanent world champions, despite having a relatively small professional league. Formerly run by the Australian Rugby League (ARL), the game was split down the middle in 1996, when Rupert Murdoch launched Super League in an attempt to gain ratings for his Foxtel TV

Gambling

Australians are obsessive about gambling, though legalities vary from state to state. Even small towns have their own racetracks, and there are government TAB betting agencies everywhere; you can often bet in pubs, too. Many states have huge casinos and clubs, open to anyone, with wall-to-wall one-armed bandits (poker machines or "pokies"); there are also big state lotteries.

station. It quickly became obvious that the game could not support two separate competitions, and in 1997 they united to form the National Rugby League (NRL).

Rugby League huge in Sydney, and the majority of the sixteen NRL teams are based there. One of the sadder consequences of this media-inspired revolution has been the loss of some of the traditional inner-city clubs through mergers. Many people also resent the way in which this one-time bastion of working-class culture has been coopted by pay TV.

Rugby Union is very much a minority interest domestically. However, the introduction of a Super 12 competition, involving teams from Australia, New Zealand and South Africa, has generated a much greater interest in what was formerly an elitist sport, and the national team, the **Wallabies**, are hugely popular. The league and union rugby season runs from April to September.

Cricket

In summer, **cricket** is played from October to March, and is a great spectator sport – for the crowd, the sunshine and the beer as much as the play. Every state is involved, and the three- or four-day Sheffield Shield matches of the interstate series are interspersed with one-day games and internationals, as well as full five-day international test matches.

The international competition that still arouses greatest interest is that of the biennial series (the next competition is in 2009) between Australia and England – **The Ashes**. Having been around for over 120 years, this is perhaps the oldest rivalry between nations in international sport. The "trophy" competed for has an interesting provenance: in 1882, an Australian touring side defeated England at the Oval in South London by seven runs, and the *Sporting Times* was moved to report, in a mock

obituary, that English cricket had "died at the Oval... deeply lamented by a large circle of sorrowing friends". The funeral ceremony involved the cremation of a set of bails, which were then preserved in a funerary urn. Each time the two countries compete, this is the trophy that is up for grabs, though the urn itself never actually leaves Lord's cricket ground in London, and a new crystal trophy goes to the winners. In 2006, Australia took the Ashes back down under after demolishing England in the first series whitewash since 1920.

Outdoor pursuits

Though the cities are fun, what really makes Australia special is the great outdoors: the vast and remote wilderness of the bush, legendary Outback, and the thousands of kilometres of unspoilt coastline. There's tremendous potential here to indulge in a huge range of **outdoor pursuits** – hiking, fishing, surfing, diving, even skiing – especially in the multitude of national parks that cover the country. Further information on all of these is available from local tourist visitor centres, which publicize what's available in their area: from **Parks Australia**, which has detailed maps of parks with walking trails, climbs, swimming holes and other activities, to specialist books. In addition, virtually any activity can be done as part of an organized excursion, often with all the gear supplied. If you want to go it alone, you'll find plenty of places ready to rent or sell you the necessary equipment. Before indulging in adventure activities, check your insurance cover (see p.70).

As with any wilderness area, the Australian interior does not suffer fools, and the coast conceals **dangers**, too: sunstroke and dehydration are risks everywhere, with riptides, currents and unexpectedly large waves to be wary of on exposed coasts. In the more remote regions, isolation and lack of surface water compromise energetic outdoor activities such as bushwalking or mountain biking, which are probably better practised in the cooler climes and more populated locations of the south.

For **watersports**, see the *Watersport* colour section.

Bushwalking

Bushwalking in Australia doesn't mean just a stroll in the bush, but refers to self-sufficient hikes, from a day to a week or longer. It's an increasingly popular activity nationwide, and you'll find trails marked in almost every national park, as well as local

National parks

The Australian Government federal **Department of the Environment, Water, Heritage and the Arts** (DEWHA) is tasked with protecting and conserving the nation's natural environment (and aspects of its cultural heritage). Its mandate includes dealing with international problems such as whaling, and making decisions about the Australian Antarctic Division. Under the DEWHA, Parks Australia (itself under the Director of National Parks) manages Commonwealth reserves including six **Commonwealth national parks**, three of which are jointly managed by traditional Aboriginal owners – Booderee in Jervis Bay Territory, and in the Northern Territory, Uluru-Kata Tjuta and Kakadu – while the remaining three protect unique island ecosystems, including Norfolk Island National Park. The DEWHA also manages the Australian National Botanic Garden in Canberra and botanic gardens at Booderee and Norfolk Island, as well as a number of marine protected areas.

Each state and territory has its own protected area management authority; departmental names vary from state to state, but Australians tend to generically dub them as the **National Parks and Wildlife Service (NPWS)**, which is how we refer to them in the Guide.

The thousand-odd **national parks** range from suburban commons to the Great Barrier Reef, and from popular hiking areas within striking distance of the big cities to wilderness regions that require days in a 4WD simply to reach. They protect everything within their boundaries: flora, fauna and landforms as well as Aboriginal art and sacred sites, although not always to the exclusion of mineral exploitation, as in Karijini in WA or Kakadu in the Northern Territory.

Entry and camping **fees** are variable. Some parks or states have no fees at all, some charge entry fees but often don't police the system, some charge for use of camping facilities, while others require permits – free or for a small fee – obtained in advance; each state or territory usually offers a pass – which makes it cheaper if you want to visit many national parks and for longer periods – but unfortunately no national pass is available. If you're camping you can usually pay on site, but booking ahead might be a good idea during the Christmas, Easter and school holidays.

Some parks have cabin accommodation, either self-catering or bunk-style with a camp kitchen, but nearby resorts or alternative accommodation are always independently run. For details on the names and vagaries of each state or territory's system, consult the websites listed below.

Australian Capital Territory ⓦ www.tams.act.gov.au/live/environment
Commonwealth ⓦ www.environment.gov.au
New South Wales ⓦ www.environment.nsw.gov.au/nationalparks
Northern Territory ⓦ www.nt.gov.au/ipe/pwcnt
Queensland ⓦ www.epa.qld.gov.au
South Australia ⓦ www.environment.sa.gov.au/parks
Tasmania ⓦ www.parks.tas.gov.au
Victoria ⓦ www.parkweb.vic.gov.au
Western Australia ⓦ www.dec.wa.gov.au

bushwalking clubs whose trips you may be able to join.

It's essential to be **properly equipped** for the conditions you'll encounter – and to know what those conditions are likely to be. Carry a map (often on hand at the ranger station or visitor centre in popular national parks), know how the trail is marked, and stay on the route. If your trip is a long one, let someone know where you're going, and confirm to them that you've arrived back safely – park rangers are useful contacts for this, and some will insist on it for overnight walks, which may require registration. One point worth noting is that in national park areas the estimated duration of a given walk is often exaggerated – certainly in the Territory and WA: you can comfortably divide the indicated time by half or more. On formed tracks a walking speed of 3 to 4kph

is average. The essentials, even for a short walk, are adequate clothing, including a wide-brimmed hat, enough food and, above all, water – and plenty of it (see below). Other useful items include a torch, matches or lighter, penknife, sun block, insect repellent, toilet paper, first-aid kit, and a whistle or mirror to attract attention if you get lost. A lot of this gear can be rented, or bought cheaply at disposal stores, which can often also put you in touch with local clubs or specialists.

Long-distance tracks exist mostly in the south of the country, with Tasmania's wilderness areas being perhaps the most rewarding bushwalking location; the eighty-kilometre Overland Track from Cradle Mountain to Lake St Clair is one of the country's best-known trails. On the mainland, the Blue Mountains, a two-hour train ride from Sydney, the Snowy Mountains

Bush essentials

Four things above all:

Fire The driest continent on Earth is covered by vegetation that has evolved with regular conflagrations, and is always at risk from bushfires. In February 2009 wildfires across Victoria destroyed over a million acres of bushland and killed 210 people, many of whom had little time to escape the flames, in the country's worst bushfire disaster in history. High winds, record temperatures and over a month without rain left conditions worse than those during the terrible bushfire season of 2002/2003, when a large part of the Alpine region in Australia's southeast was ablaze for almost two months. Even in wet years, there's a constant red alert during summer months. Always use an established fireplace where available, or dig a shallow pit and ring it with stones. Keep fires small and make absolutely sure embers are smothered before going to sleep or moving on. Never discard burning cigarette butts from cars. Periodic total fire bans – announced in the local media when in effect – prohibit any fire in the open, including wood, gas or electric barbecues, with heavy fines for offenders.

Check on the local fire danger before you go bushwalking – some walking trails are closed in the riskiest periods (summer – Dec, Jan & Feb – in the south; the end of the dry season – Sept/Oct – in the north). If driving, carry blankets and a filled water container, listen to your car radio and watch out for roadside fire-danger indicators. See "Health", p.50, for potential bushwalking hazards and advice on how to deal with them – including ways to survive if caught in a bushfire.

Water Carry plenty with you and do not contaminate local water resources. In particular, soaps and detergents can render water undrinkable and kill livestock and wild animals. Avoid washing in standing water, especially tanks and small lakes or reservoirs.

Waste Take only photographs, leave only footprints. That means carrying all your rubbish out with you – never burn or bury it – and making sure you urinate (and bury your excrement) at least 50m from a campsite or water source.

Hypothermia In Tasmania, where the weather is notoriously changeable, even in summer, prepare as you would for a walk in Scotland.

further south, and Victoria's spectacular Grampians are all popular regions for longer, marked walks.

South Australia's **Flinders Ranges**, 300km north of Adelaide, are accessible along the Heysen Trail from the Fleurieu Peninsula, the walk into the thousand-metre-high natural basin of Wilpena Pound being the highlight. In temperate southwestern WA, the 960-kilometre **Bibbulmun Track**, an old Aboriginal trail passing through the region's giant eucalypt forests, was completed in 2002 from Albany to Kalamunda near Perth. In the same year the 220-kilometre Larapinta Trail, along the McDonnell Ranges west of Alice Springs, was also completed: an initially strenuous hike out of Alice Springs that should only be attempted in winter. Queensland's rainforested coastal strip offers plenty more opportunities for walks, including the Lamington area in the south, and around northern Atherton Tablelands and Hinchinbrook Island.

Throughout the text of the Guide, we mention specialist bushwalking **guides and maps** that are relevant. Two of Australia's best-regarded bushwalkers are John Chapman and Tyrone T. Thomas, and both publish a range of walking guides. Try to get hold of the latest edition of Chapman's rigorously updated *Bushwalking in Australia*, which details the country's best bushwalks.

Other pursuits

Alice Springs' wide-open spaces make it the country's **hot-air-ballooning** capital and also the main base for **camel treks** into the surrounding desert.

More regular **riding**, on horseback, is offered all over the country – anything from a gentle hour at walking pace to a serious cattle roundup. **Cycling** and mountain biking

are tremendously popular, too, as well as being a good way of getting around resorts; just about all hostels rent out bikes, and we've listed other outlets throughout the Guide.

Australia's wilderness is an ideal venue for extended **off-road driving** and **motor-biking**, although permission may be needed to cross station- and Aboriginal-owned lands, and the fragile desert ecology should be respected at all times. Northern Queensland's Cape York and WA's Kimberley are the most adventurous destinations, 4WD-accessible in the dry season only. The great **Outback tracks** pushed out by explorers or drovers, such as the Warburton Road and Sandover Highway and the Tanami, Birdsville and Oodnadatta tracks, are actually two-wheel driveable in dry conditions, but can be hard on poorly prepared vehicles. Getting right to the tip of Queensland's eight-hundred-kilometre-long Cape York Peninsula will definitely require a 4WD or trail bike, while the Kimberley's notoriously corrugated Gibb River Road in WA is also popular in the Dry.

Finally, you may not associate Australia with **skiing**, but there's plenty of it in the 1500-metre-high Australian Alps on the border of Victoria and New South Wales, based around the winter resorts of Thredbo, Perisher, Falls Creek and Mount Hotham. Europeans tend to be sniffy about Australian skiing, and certainly it's limited, with a season that lasts barely two to three months – from the end of June until the end of September, if you're lucky – and very few challenging runs. The one area where it does match up to Europe is in the prices. On the other hand, it's fun if you're here, and the relatively gentle slopes of the mountains are ideal for cross-country skiing, which is increasingly being developed alongside downhill.

Travelling with children

Australians have an easy-going attitude to children and in most places they are made welcome. With plenty of beautiful beaches, parks and playgrounds, travelling Australia with children in tow can be great fun.

There are a few helpful publications available: in Sydney, look out for *Sydney's Child* (Ⓦwww.sydneyschild.com.au), a free monthly magazine listing kids' activities in and around the city and advertising a range of services including baby-sitting. Spin-offs *Canberra's Child* (Ⓦwww .canberraschild.com.au), *Melbourne's Child* (Ⓦ www.melbournechild.com.au), *Brisbane's Child* (Ⓦwww.brisbaneschild .com.au) and *Adelaide's Child* (Ⓦwww .adelaideschild.com.au) can be picked up at libraries and major museums.

Getting around

Most forms of **transport** within Australia offer child concessions. Throughout the country, metropolitan buses and trains give discounts of around fifty percent for children and many allow children under 4 or 5 to travel free. Most interstate buses offer around twenty percent off for under-14s.

Long-distance train travel is limited in Australia. It's also a slower and more expensive option, but if you're travelling with small children it does have the advantage of sleepers and a bit more freedom of movement. Domestic airlines offer discounts of around fifty percent of the full adult fare for children between 2 and 11 years. However, it's worth checking for adult discount deals, which are likely to be even cheaper. Infants usually travel free. Otherwise, there's always the option of **self-drive**. Car rental is reasonably priced, and motor homes and campervans are also available for rental (see p.40); don't forget to take more activities for the trip than usual – music, books, magnetic games, cards – to last the long distances.

Accommodation

Many **motels** give discounts for children and some offer a baby-sitting service – it's worth checking when you book. If you like the idea of a whinge-free bushwalk or cocktails by the pool, most resorts have kids' clubs, organized children's activities and baby-sitting services.

Although initially more expensive, **self-contained accommodation** can prove cheaper in the long run as it's possible to cook your own meals. These days, youth hostels are not exclusively for young backpackers and most provide affordable family rooms – some en suite. A few of the more modern hostels are positively luxurious, most are in fabulous locations, and in cities they're usually conveniently close to the city centre. They all have communal kitchens, lounge areas and television, and there are usually plenty of books and games.

Aside from camping, the most economical way to see the country is to stay in some of the thousands of **caravan parks**. Most have on-site vans or self-contained cabins at reasonable family rates. Check with visitor centres for details.

Eating out

In the cities especially, many of the more atmospheric upmarket **restaurants** are welcoming to children, often providing highchairs, toys, blackboards, drawing materials and a reasonable children's menu. Otherwise, there are still plenty of standard fast-food outlets, which often have enclosed play areas, and children are allowed in the dining section of pubs for counter meals. Most country towns have pubs and some have RSL clubs (Returned Servicemen's League), which are a cheap way to feed the family on basic pub food and make a welcome change from fast food.

Kids' gear

Car and van rental companies provide **child safety seats**. Taxis will also provide child seats if you request them when making a booking, although there may be a longer wait. Airlines will allow you to carry a pram or travel cot for free, and it's possible to rent baby equipment from some shops – check the local *Yellow Pages* for listings. When planning a sightseeing day that involves a lot of walking, check with the tourist attraction to see if they rent out pushchairs, as this can make the difference between a pleasant and an awful day out.

Activities

Most tours and entry fees for tourist destinations offer **concession rates** for children and many also offer family tickets. If you have two or more children these will usually work out substantially cheaper. Museums often have children's areas, and during **school holidays** many run supervised activities, along with programmes that include storytelling and performances (check "Opening hours and public holidays", p.72, for dates).

In most states, the National Parks and Wildlife Service (NPWS) runs entertaining and educational ranger-led walks and activities during the school holidays. The walks are free, but there's usually a park entrance fee. Check at visitor centres or with NPWS in each state for timetables and fees.

Sun care

The Australian **sun** is ferocious, making it essential to combine outdoor activities with sensible skin care; see "Health", p.49, for more on sunscreens. There's a "no hat, no play" policy in school playgrounds and most kids wear legionnaire-style caps, or broad-brimmed sun hats – easy to find in surf shops and department stores. Most kids wear UV-resistant Lycra swim tops or wetsuit-style all-in-ones to the beach. The Cancer Council Australia (🌐www.cancer.org.au) has shops in most Australian cities selling all these items.

Working in Australia

Most visitors' visas clearly state that no employment of any kind is to be undertaken during a visit to Australia. However, if you're in possession of a Working Holiday Visa (see "Entry requirements", p.33) and are prepared to try anything – officially for no more than six months at a time – there are plenty of possibilities for finding work. Organized work programmes, both paid and voluntary, are also a possibility.

In practice, this means that the only jobs officially open to you are unskilled, temporary ones. The **National Harvest Hotline** (☎1800 062 332, 🌐www.jobsearch.gov.au/harvesttrail) has information about harvesting or farm-labouring jobs and will put you in touch with potential employers. Just remember that crop-picking is hard work for low wages (usually paid on a commission basis). It's also worth noting that harvest work is often on farms or plantations that are quite some distance away from a town. In some cases,

employers or a workers' hostel in a nearby town will provide transport to and from work – sometimes, but not always, free of charge. In other cases, you will be given basic accommodation on the farm; or you may be required to pitch your own tent. There is no centralized agency for casual work, such as bar or restaurant, construction and factory work. A good place to start searching, however, is **Travellers' Contact Point** (☎1800 647 640, 🌐www.travellers.com.au), which has a branch in most of the major cities. Services include a job notice board, skills testing, CV updating and help with the required paperwork. You can view the jobs posted online by their recruitment agency, **Travellers At Work** (ⓦwww.taw.com.au), which has consultants in Sydney, Cairns and Brisbane. The travel centre **Backpackers World** (☎1800 676 763, ⓦwww.backpackersworld.com.au), with branches all over Australia except South Australia and Tasmania, also runs an employment agency (ⓦwww.worktravelcompany .com), based in Sydney. Quite a few hostels run their own employment agency or have a permanently staffed **employment desk**. Some charge a membership fee – about AUS$40 a year. All of these places will help with all aspects of working, from organizing tax file numbers to actually getting you jobs. In addition, more specialized **employment agencies** are worth a try in the cities if you have a marketable skill (computer training, accountancy, nursing, cooking and the like). They might have better, higher-paid jobs on their books, though they may be looking for full-time or at least longer-term commitment. **Newspaper job ads** are also worth checking out, especially in smaller local papers. One useful **website** is ⓦwww.mycareer.com.au, which is Australia's largest online job-search engine, and has links to the *Sydney Morning Herald* and Melbourne's *The Age* classified sections. Finally, fellow travellers, hostel staff in smaller hostels, and **notice boards** may be the best source of all, especially in remote areas: this is where you'll find out about local opportunities. The hostels themselves may occasionally offer free nights in lieu of cleaning work – or even pay you for jobs that involve a bit more skill.

Some of the hostels in the big cities or in country towns where there is a lot of harvesting work also arrange employment.

Australia is becoming increasingly tough on people working either on tourist visas or on expired working visas. If you're caught **working illegally**, you will have any visa cancelled and will be asked to leave the country immediately; you may be taken into detention if immediate arrangements cannot be made. Furthermore, you will be forbidden to reapply for a working visa for three years, but even after this time it is extremely unlikely that you would be granted another visa under normal circumstances. Employers can be fined up to AUS$10,000 for employing illegal workers, and are liable for prosecution.

Study and work programmes

AFS Intercultural Programs US ☎1-800/876-2376, Canada ☎514/288-3282, Australia ☎02/9215 0077, NZ ☎04/494 6020, SA ☎11/447 2673, international enquiries ☎1-212/807-8686; ⓦwww.afs.org. Intercultural exchange organization with programmes in over 50 countries.
American Institute for Foreign Study ☎1-866/906-2437, ⓦwww.aifs.com. Language study and cultural immersion, as well as au pair and Camp America programs.
ATCV (Australian Trust for Conservation Volunteers) Australia ☎1800 032 501, ⓦwww.atcv.com.au. Volunteer work (unpaid) on conservation projects across Australia; about AUS$40 a day charged for food and accommodation. The projects run from one day to four weeks.
BUNAC UK ☎020/7251 3472, US ☎1-800/GO-BUNAC; ⓦwww.bunac.org. Working holidays in a range of destinations for students.

Tax

In recent years, employers have been threatened with huge fines for offering cash-in-hand labour and, as a result, it's difficult to avoid paying income **tax**, which is levied at 29 percent for earnings under about $34,000 per annum and deducted at source. To become part of the system you'll need a **tax file number** (form available at post offices or taxation offices), which is pretty easy to obtain on presentation of a passport with relevant visa. Your employer will give you a couple of weeks' grace, but not much more – if you don't have a number, after that you'll be taxed at 46.5 percent. Nowadays, it's hard to claim a tax rebate, no matter how little you earn; however, it's worth a try, and possibly a trip to a tax advisor. Alternatively, go to ⓦwww.taxback.com, which offers a hassle-free service to reclaim tax and superannuation refunds.

B

Council on International Educational Exchange (CIEE) US ☎1-800/40-STUDY or 1-207/533-4000, ⓦwww.ciee.org. Leading NGO offering study programmes and volunteer projects around the world.

Earthwatch Institute UK ☎01865/318 838, US ☎1-800/776-0188 or 978/461-0081, Australia ☎03/9682 6828; ⓦwww.earthwatch.org. Scientific expedition project that spans over 50 countries with environmental and archeological ventures worldwide.

Visitoz UK ☎01865/861 516, Australia ☎07/4168 6185, ⓦwww.visitoz.org. Provides work on farms and stations and rural hospitality for those who would like to work in the bush. Previous experience not required. Participants must attend a four-day preparation and orientation course; during this period a suitable job is found. Driving licence necessary for most jobs.

Work Oz UK ☎01934/413 795, ⓦwww.workoz.com. An organization owned and run by ex-Australian high-commission staff, designed to assist working-holiday-visa applicants with help in finding employment in Australia, pre-book hostel accommodation prior to arrival, and arrange pick-ups from the airport and travel insurance.

WWOOF (Willing Workers on Organic Farms) Australia ☎03/5155 0218, ⓦwww.wwoof.com.au. Woofing is a great way to experience a side of Australia that you'd never see if you just worked in an office and then beach-bummed your way up the east coast. As you're not paid cash, a work visa is not required: you put in about half a day's work at your host's place in exchange for full board and lodging, and the rest of the time is yours to go exploring. You are expected to stay at least two nights; everything else is negotiable. The Australian WWOOF Book lists 1200 organic farms and 100 non-farm hosts (such as organic nurseries and greengrocers, and alternative schools). The book gives you membership (AUS$55 single, AUS$65 for two people travelling together), including basic work insurance for a year.

Gay and lesbian Australia

Australia is now well and truly planted on the Queer map as year after year the beautiful people flock down under, lured by the great climate and laid-back lifestyle, and eager to hang out with the homeboys on balmy beaches and sun-kissed city streets. Sydney is Australia's gay-friendly capital, especially in March when hundreds of thousands of people flock to Oxford Street and Moore Park for the Sydney Gay & Lesbian Mardi Gras. Despite its reputation as a macho culture, the country revels in a large and active scene: you'll find an air of confidence and a sense of community that is often missing in other parts of the world.

Australia is testimony to the power of the **pink dollar**, and there's an abundance of gay venues, services, businesses, travel clubs, country retreats and the like. Given the climate, the scene obviously makes use of sun and sport, and while it's far from limited to the tanned-and-toned muscle crowd, if you want to make the most of a thriving community, it's a good idea to pack your swimming, snorkelling and clubbing gear.

Australian dykes are refreshingly open and self-possessed – a relief after the more closed and cliquey scene in Europe. The flip side of their fearlessness is the predominance of S&M on the scene. Dyke and gay scenes are nothing if not mercurial, and Australia is no exception. We've done our best to list bars, clubs and meeting places, but be warned that venues open, change their names, shut for refurbishment, get relaunched and finally go out of business with frightening rapidity.

The **age of consent** varies: in Western Australia, it's still 21, whereas the ages of consent in ACT and Victoria (both 16), SA and Tasmania (both 17), are the same as the heterosexual age. In the Northern Territory and NSW, the homosexual age of consent is 18. In Queensland, the age of consent for homosexuals depends on the sexual act practised, with anal sex outlawed until 18, but otherwise 16. Sex between women is either not mentioned in state laws or is covered by the heterosexual age.

The foreign partner in a **de facto** gay relationship can apply to reside permanently in Australia, a much better situation than in many countries, but the current battle being waged by the gay and lesbian lobby groups is to make Australian federal law recognize same-sex marriages. A significant step forward was made in 2008 when Australian Parliament passed laws which made same-sex de facto couples completely equal in the eyes of the law to heterosexual ones, in terms of parenting, next-of-kin rights, taxation, superannuation and healthcare.

Where to go

Sydney is the jewel in Australia's luscious navel. Firmly established as one of the world's great gay cities – only San Francisco can really rival it – it attracts lesbian and gay visitors from around the world. Melbourne closely follows the scene in Sydney, but for a change of pace, take a trip to Brisbane and the Gold Coast. Perth, Adelaide and Darwin all have smaller, quieter scenes.

Away from the cities, things get more discreet, but a lot of **country areas** do have very friendly local scenes – impossible to pinpoint, but easy to stumble across. Australians on the city scene are a friendly bunch, but in a small country town they get really friendly, so if there's anything going on you'll probably get invited along.

The **Outback** covers the vast majority of the Australian continent and is, in European terms, sparsely populated. Mining and cattle ranching are the primary employers and they help to create a culture not famed for its tolerance of homosexuality. Tread carefully: bear in mind that Uluru may be 2000km from Sydney as the crow flies, but in many ways it's a million miles away in terms of attitudes.

Each chapter of the Guide has gay and lesbian listings, with a wealth of information

– see in particular the box on pp.168–169, which has all you need to know to join in Sydney's Mardi Gras celebrations.

Gay and lesbian contacts

Personal contacts

Pinkboard ⓦ www.pinkboard.com.au. Popular, long-running website featuring personal ads and classifieds sections with everything from houseshares, party tickets for sale, employment and a help and advice section. Posting ads is free.

Press and multimedia

Each major capital has excellent free gay newspapers, such as the *Sydney Star Observer* (ⓦ www.ssonet.com.au) and the *Melbourne Community Voice* (ⓦ http://mcv.e-p.net.au), which give the local lowdown. Otherwise, check out:
ALSO Foundation ⓦ www.also.org.au. Based in Victoria, they have a good website with an excellent nationwide business and community directory.
DNA ⓦ www.dnamagazine.com.au. National glossy – an upmarket lifestyle magazine for gay men.
LOTL (Lesbians on the Loose) ⓦ www.lotl.com. A monthly publication available at lesbian and gay venues.
The Pink Directory ⓦ www.thepinkdirectory.com .au. Online directory of gay and lesbian business and community information.

Tourist services and travel agents

GALTA (Gay and Lesbian Tourism Australia) ⓦ www.galta.com.au. An online resource and nonprofit organization set up to promote the gay and lesbian tourism industry. Website has links to accommodation, travel agents and tour operators, and gay and lesbian printed and online guides.
Gay Travel ⓦ www.gaytravel.com. Online travel agent, concentrating mostly on accommodation.
International Gay and Lesbian Travel Association ⓦ www.iglta.org. Trade group with lists of gay-owned or gay-friendly travel agents, accommodation and other travel businesses.
Q Beds ⓦ www.qbeds.com. An online accommodation directory and booking service for gay- and lesbian-owned, -operated or -friendly businesses.

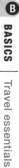

Travel essentials

Costs

If you've travelled down from Southeast Asia, you'll find Australia expensive on a day-to-day basis, but fresh from Europe or the US you'll find prices comparable or cheaper; note, though, that in Sydney the cost of living has crept up over the years, and any prolonged length of time spent in the city will quickly drain any savings you might have unless you have a contingency plan in place, such as finding work.

If you're prepared to camp, the absolute minimum **daily budget** is AUS$50 (£25/US$50/€30), but you should count on around AUS$75 (£40/US$70/€45) a day for food, board and transport if you stay in hostels, travel on buses and eat and drink fairly frugally. Stay in motels and B&Bs (assuming you're sharing costs) and eat out regularly, and you'll need to budget AUS$115 (£45/US$80/€70) or more: extras such as scuba-diving courses, clubbing, car rental, petrol and tours will all add to your costs. Under the Tourist Refund Scheme (TRS), visitors can claim **Goods and Services Tax** (GST) refunds for goods purchased in Australia as they clear customs (goods need to be worn or taken within hand luggage), providing individual receipts exceed AUS$300, and the claim is made within thirty days of purchase.

For **tipping**, see p.74.

Crime, personal safety and the law

Australia can pride itself on being a relatively safe country, although increasingly it is following the American trend in gun-related incidents. This is not to say there's no petty crime, but you're more likely to fall victim to a fellow traveller or an opportunist: theft is not unusual in hostels and many therefore provide lockable boxes. But if you leave valuables lying around, or on view in cars, you can expect them to be stolen.

One place where violence is common is at the ritual pub or bar fight – nearly always alcohol-fuelled and usually on a Friday or Saturday night in smaller, untouristed towns, or among groups of drunk males in the major cities. Strangers are seldom involved without at least some provocation. Be aware of drug-related crime, especially in hotspots such as Kings Cross in Sydney.

It's worth knowing about certain points of Australian **law**: Marijuana use is widespread, but you'd be foolish to carry it when you travel, and crazy to carry any other illegal narcotic. Each state has its own penalties, and though a small amount of grass may mean no more than confiscation and an on-the-spot fine, they're generally pretty tough – especially in Queensland. Driving in general makes you more likely to have a confrontation of some kind, if only for a minor traffic infringement. **Drink driving** is taken extremely seriously, so don't risk it – random breath tests are common around all cities and larger towns.

Lesser potential problems are **alcohol** – there are all sorts of controls on where and when you can drink, and taking alcohol onto Aboriginal lands can be a serious offence – and nude or topless sunbathing, which is quite acceptable in many places, but absolutely not in others; follow the locals' lead. Since 2007, **smoking** has been banned in all public places, including bars, pubs, restaurants and train stations.

Electricity

Australia's electrical current is 240v, 50Hz AC. British appliances will work with an adaptor for the Australian three-pin plug. American and Canadian 110v appliances will also need a transformer.

Insurance

Even if you're entitled to free emergency healthcare from Medicare (see "Health", p.49), some form of travel insurance is essential to help plug the gaps and cover you in the event of losing your baggage, missing a plane and the like. A typical travel insurance policy usually provides cover for the loss of baggage, tickets and – up to a certain limit – cash and cheques, as well as cancellation or curtailment of your journey. If you're thinking of doing any "high-risk" activities such as scuba diving, skiing or even just hiking, you may need to pay an extra premium; check carefully what you're covered for before you take out any policy. If you do take medical coverage, ascertain whether benefits will be paid as treatment proceeds or only after your return home, and whether there is a 24-hour medical emergency number. When securing baggage cover, make sure that the per-article limit – typically under £500/US$1000 – will cover your most valuable possession. If you need to make a claim, you should keep receipts for medicines and medical treatment, and in the event you have anything stolen, you must obtain an official written statement from the police.

Internet

Internet access is widespread, easy and cheap across Australia. In the cities, internet cafés are everywhere, typically charging AUS$3–6 an hour, with concessions as well as "happy hours". Many places to stay – especially hostels – also provide terminals for their guests at similar rates (hotels will charge more), although some places still opt for the user-reviled coin-operated booths, while at some places you buy a card that works like a phonecard.

Out in the country, even the smallest one-horse town will have a Telecentre – a council- or privately-run outlet, although opening times can be pretty provincial, too. Internet cafés are listed throughout the Guide, where available.

Laundry

Known as laundromats, these are rare outside urban centres. Hostels always have a laundry with at least one coin-operated washing machine and a dryer, as do most caravan parks, holiday units and a lot of motels. Five-star hotels, of course, will do your laundry for you at a cost.

Mail

Every town of any size will have a **post office**, or at least an Australia Post agency,

usually at the general store. Post offices and agencies are officially open Monday to Friday 9am to 5pm; big-city GPOs sometimes open late or on Saturday morning as well. Out in the country, it's rare to see post boxes.

Domestically, the **mail service** has a poor reputation, at least for long distances: it will take a week for a letter to get from Wittenoom (WA) to Wagga Wagga (NSW), though major cities have a guaranteed express-delivery service to other major cities – worth the expense for important packages. On the other hand, international mail is extremely efficient, taking four to five working days to the UK, four to six to the US and five to seven to Canada. **Stamps** are sold at post offices and agencies; most newsagents sell them for standard local letters only. A standard letter or postcard within Australia costs 55¢; postcards or cards to the US, Canada, South Africa and Europe cost AUS$1.35, and regular letters start at AUS$2.05. Large **parcels** are reasonably cheap to send home by surface mail – but it will take up to three months for them to get there. Economy Air is a good compromise for packages that you want to see again soon (up to 20kg) – expect a fortnight to Europe. For more information on letter and parcel postage rates, and delivery times, go to ⓦwww.austpost.com.au and click on "calculate postage rates".

Maps

The Rough Guide **map of Australia** (1:4,500,000) is printed on rip- and water-proof paper. Also finely produced are GeoCenter (including NZ) and Nelles, both 1:4,000,000, with good topographical detail: the Nelles (printed in northern and southern halves on both sides of the sheet) includes additional detail of major city environs. The Bartholomew and the new Globetrotter (both 1:5,000,000) are the best of the rest.

In Australia, UBD (ⓦwww.ubd.com.au), Gregory's (ⓦwww.gregorys-online.com), HEMA (ⓦwww.hemamaps.com.au), Westprint (ⓦwww.westprint.com.au) and the state-produced AusMap publish national, regional and city maps of varying sizes and quality. HEMA produces scores of regional and themed maps and atlases covering the entire country many times over; cities, states, national parks, fishing, hiking, 4WD and wine are some of the many themes covered. BP and the state motoring organizations have regularly updated touring guides, with regional maps, listings and details of things to see and do – something for the back shelf of the car rather than a backpack.

Money

Australia's **currency** is the Australian dollar, or "buck", written as $ or AUS$ and divided into 100 cents. The colourful plastic notes with forgery-proof clear windows come in AUS$100, AUS$50, AUS$20, AUS$10 and AUS$5 denominations, along with AUS$2, AUS$1, 50¢, 20¢, 10¢ and 5¢ coins. There are no longer 1¢ or 2¢ coins so an irregular bill, such as $1.98 etc, will be rounded up or down to the closest denomination, which can be confusing at first. To check the latest exchange rate, check ⓦwww.xe.com.

The unfortunate closure of local **banks** throughout much of Australia means you will no longer necessarily find a branch of one of the main banks in every town, though there will be a local agency that handles bank business – usually based at the general store, post office or roadhouse – though not necessarily a 24-hour **ATM**. The best policy is always to make sure you have some cash on you before leaving the bigger towns, especially at weekends. The major four banks, with branches countrywide, are Westpac (ⓦwww.westpac.com.au), ANZ (ⓦwww.anz .com.au), the Commonwealth (ⓦwww .commbank.com.au) and the National Australia Bank (ⓦwww.national.com.au); you can search their websites for branch locations. For banking hours, see "Opening hours and public holidays", opposite.

All **post offices** act as Commonwealth or National Australia Bank agents, which means there's a fair chance of changing money even in the smallest Outback settlements – withdrawals at these places are often limited by a lack of ready cash, however, though less remote post offices may have EFTPOS facilities (see below).

If you're spending some time in Australia, and plan to work or move around, it makes life a great deal easier if you **open a bank account**. To do this you'll need to take along every piece of ID documentation you own –

a passport may not be enough, though a letter from your bank manager at home may help – but it's otherwise a fairly straightforward process. The Commonwealth Bank and Westpac are the most widespread options, and their keycards give you access not only to ATMs but also anywhere that offers **EFTPOS** facilities (Electronic Funds Transfer at Point of Sale). This includes many Outback service stations and supermarkets, where you can use your card to pay directly for goods and to withdraw cash as well. Bear in mind that **bank fees** and charges are exorbitant in Australia; most banks allow only a few free withdrawal transactions per month (depending on whom you bank with – it's well worth shopping around before you open an account), and there are even charges for using a competitor's ATM, as well as monthly fees.

Discount cards soon pay for themselves in savings. If you're a full-time student, it's worth applying for an **International Student ID Card** (ISIC; ⓦwww.isic.org), which entitles the bearer to air, rail and bus fares and discounts at museums, theatres and other attractions. The card costs £9; US$22; CDN$16; NZ$20; and AUS$18 in Australia itself. If you're no longer a student, but are 26 or younger, you still qualify for the **International Youth Travel Card**, which costs the same price and carries the same benefits, while teachers qualify for the **International Teacher Card** (same price and some of the benefits). All these cards are available from the website above or branches of STA Travel or Travel Cuts.

Opening hours and public holidays

Shops and services are generally open Monday to Friday 9am to 5pm and until lunchtime or 5.30pm on Saturday. In cities and larger towns, many shops stay open late on Thursday or Friday evening – usually until 9pm – and all day on Saturday, and shopping malls and department stores in major cities are often open on Sunday as well.

In remote country areas, **roadhouses** provide all the essential services for the traveller and, on the major highways, are generally open 24 hours a day. **Visitor**

Holidays

National holidays are New Year's Day, Australia Day (Jan 26), Good Friday, Easter Monday, ANZAC Day (April 25), Queen's Birthday (second Mon in June; Sept/Oct in WA), Christmas Day and Boxing Day (except SA). Note that when a public holiday falls on a weekend, Australians take the following Monday off. State holidays are listed in the capital city accounts of each state or territory. **School holidays** transform beaches into bucket-and-spade war zones, national park campsites are full to overflowing, and the roads are jammed. Dates vary from year to year and state to state but all schools (except Tasmania) have four terms. Generally, things start to get busy mid-December to the end of January or beginning of February (January is the worst, as many people stay home until after Christmas), two weeks around Easter, another couple of weeks in late June to early July, and another two weeks in late September to early October. January and Easter are the **busiest periods**, when you are likely to find accommodation booked out.

centres – even ones well off the beaten track – are often open every day from 9am–5pm or at least through the week plus weekend mornings; urban visitor centres are more likely to conform to normal shopping hours.

Tourist attractions such as museums, galleries and attended historic monuments are often open daily, though those in rural communities may have erratic opening hours. Almost without exception, all are closed on Good Friday and Christmas Day, but most are open during school and other public holidays. Specific opening hours are given throughout the Guide.

Banking hours are generally Monday to Thursday 9.30am to 4pm, Friday 9.30am to 5pm. A change in the law has made Saturday bank opening legal, though it's not yet fully in practice. In country areas, some banks may have more limited hours, such as lunchtime closures, or some agencies may be open later, and some big-city branches might also have extended hours. ATMs are generally open 24 hours. See "Mail", p.71, for post office opening hours.

For **public holidays**, see box above.

Phones

Public telephones take coins or phone cards, which are sold through newsagents and other stores. Many bars, shops and restaurants have orange or blue payphones; watch out for these as they cost more than a regular call box. Whatever their type, payphones do not accept incoming calls.

Local calls are **untimed**, allowing you to talk for as long as you like; this costs around 17¢ on a domestic phone, though public phones charge a flat rate of 50¢. Many businesses and services operate freephone numbers, prefixed ℡1800, while others have six-digit numbers beginning ℡13 or 1300 that are charged at the local-call rate – all can only be dialled from within Australia. Numbers starting ℡1900 are premium-rate private information services.

Phone cards are a cheap way to call cross-country or abroad. Various brands are available, but all require a minimum of 50¢ to call the local centre, after which you key in your scratch number and telephone number. Rates are incredible, from as low as 5¢ a minute.

It's also possible to buy a **pre-paid mobile phone** for as little as AUS$99 with a pay-as-you-go SIM card. Alternatively, you can just buy the pre-paid SIM cards alone in various denominations for your own handset – CDMA and GSM are compatible. Telstra is the main provider and with the widest coverage, but does not include unpopulated areas in the north and west of the country. Vodafone is a long way behind on cross coverage but may work out cheaper solely for urban use.

As anywhere in the world, mobile phone reception will drop off in remote areas. A solution offering guaranteed reception (but at call rates several times higher) is a **satellite phone**. Little bigger than a conventional GSM, they can be rented from ⓦwww.rentasatphone.com.au from around

Making international calls

Calling Australia from home

Dial the relevant international access code + 61 + area code, omitting the initial zero.

The **international access code** for the UK, the Republic of Ireland, New Zealand and South Africa is ℡00; for the US and Canada ℡011.

Calling home from Australia

The **international access code** for Australia is ℡0011. Note that the initial zero is omitted from the area code when dialling the UK, the Republic of Ireland and New Zealand from abroad.

To New Zealand international access code + 64 + area code.
To the Republic of Ireland international access code + 353 + area code.
To South Africa international access code + 27 + area code.
To the UK international access code + 44 + area code.
To the US and Canada international access code + 1 + area code

---

AUS$21 per day and can run both GSM as well as the special satellite SIM cards.

Shopping

Australians love to shop, and you'll find plenty of outlets to tempt you to part with your cash, from designer boutiques to large department stores. Australians also do vintage very well, and there are some excellent thrift shops to be found, especially around Chapel Street in Melbourne and Paddington in Sydney.

Weekly **markets** take place in most cities and resort towns, selling everything from secondhand clothes and new-age remedies to fresh seafood and mouthwatering delicacies; the most popular ones are Mindil Beach in Darwin (see p.575), Queen Victoria Market in Melbourne (see p.870) and, in Tasmania, Hobart's Salamanca Market (see p.1027). In Sydney, Paddington Market is a great place to pick up one-off new designer clothes, while Glebe's Saturday market is good for crystals, tie-dye and lava lamps.

For **souvenirs**, there's no shortage of shops selling Australiana: mass-produced tat such as stuffed koalas, painted boomerangs and the like. If you're looking for something more authentic, there are a number of good art and craft stores around The Rocks in Sydney, selling genuine opals and handcrafted didgeridoos. The best place to shop for Aboriginal art, however, is Alice Springs, where many galleries sell on behalf of the artist and the money goes back to the Aboriginal communities. **Gemstones** such as

the Australian opal are a popular purchase, though the quality and price varies from place to place so be sure to shop around before you buy; of course, you could always try fossicking for your own at one of the mining towns such as Coober Pedy in South Australia (see p.830). Broome in Western Australia has long been the "pearl capital" of Australia, and is a good place to pick up your very own cultured pearl, plus all manner of mother-of-pearl trinkets. Note that if you buy goods worth more than AUS$300 in a single transaction, you can claim the tax back under the **Tourist Refund Scheme** (see p.67).

Time

Australia has three time zones: Eastern Standard Time (QLD, NSW, VIC, TAS, VIC), Central Standard Time (NT, SA) and Western Standard Time (WA). Eastern Standard Time is ten hours ahead of Greenwich Mean Time (GMT) and fifteen hours ahead of US Eastern Time. When it's 10pm in Sydney, it's noon in London, 7am in New York and 4am in Los Angeles – but don't forget daylight saving, which can affect this by one hour either way. Central Standard Time is thirty minutes behind Eastern Standard, and Western Standard two hours behind Eastern. Daylight saving (October–March) is adopted everywhere except QLD, NT and WA; clocks are put forward one hour.

Tipping

Tipping is not as widespread in Australia as it is in Europe and the US. In cafés and restaurants you might leave the change or round up the bill, while cab drivers will usually expect you to round up to the nearest dollar. Only in more upmarket restaurants is a service charge of ten percent the norm; note that on public holidays cafés and restaurants in cities may add a surcharge of ten percent to your bill.

Tourist information

Australian tourism abroad is represented by the Australian Tourist Commission, whose website Ⓦwww.australia.com has plenty of useful links.

More detailed information is available by the sackful once you're in the country. Each state or territory has its own **tourist authority**, which operates information offices throughout its own area and in major cities in other parts of Australia – some are even represented abroad (those with London offices are detailed below). A level below this is a host of regional and community-run visitor centres and information kiosks. Even the smallest Outback town has one – or at the very least an information board located at a rest spot at the side of the road.

Hostels are excellent places to pick up information, with notice boards where you'll often find offers of cheap excursions or ride shares, and comments and advice from people who've already passed that way.

Finally, most tourist hotspots will have a travellers' centre, such as Backpackers World Travel (Ⓦwww.backpackersworld.com.au) and Travellers Contact Point (Ⓦwww.travellers.com.au). Once you've signed up with them, they can help you find work and pre-book travel and accommodation as you move around; you also get discounted phone and internet rates, cheap drinks at selected pubs and use of notice boards.

Tourist offices and government sites

Australian Department of Foreign Affairs Ⓦwww.dfat.gov.au, Ⓦwww.smartraveller.gov.au.
British Foreign & Commonwealth Office Ⓦwww.fco.gov.uk.
Canadian Department of Foreign Affairs Ⓦwww.dfait-maeci.gc.ca.
Irish Department of Foreign Affairs Ⓦwww.foreignaffairs.gov.ie.
New Zealand Ministry of Foreign Affairs Ⓦwww.mft.govt.nz.
US State Department Ⓦwww.travel.state.gov.

Travellers with disabilities

The vast distances between Australia's cities and popular tourist resorts present visitors with mobility difficulties with a unique challenge but, overall, travel in Australia for people with disabilities is rather easier than it would be in, say, the UK and Europe.

The federal government provides information and various nationwide services through the National Information Communication Awareness Network (NICAN) and the National Disability Service (NDS) – see p.76 for contact details.

Much of Australia's tourist **accommodation** is well set up for people with disabilities, because buildings tend to be built outwards rather than upwards; all new buildings in Australia must comply with a legal minimum accessibility standard.

Disability needn't interfere with your **sightseeing**: Australia's major tourist attractions will provide assistance where they can. For example, you'll find you can view rock art at Kakadu National Park, do a tour around the base of Uluru, snorkel unhindered on the Great Barrier Reef, go on a cruise around Sydney Harbour, and see the penguins at Phillip Island.

Seasons

In the southern hemisphere, the seasons are reversed: summer lasts from December to February, winter from June to September. But, of course, it's not that simple: in the tropical north, the important seasonal distinction is between the Wet (effectively summer) and the Dry (winter) – for more on their significance to travellers, see p.570.

Clothing and shoe sizes

Clothing and shoe sizes

Women's clothing

American	4	6	8	10	12	14	16	18
Aus/British	6	8	10	12	14	16	18	20
Continental	34	36	38	40	42	44	46	48

Women's shoes

Aus/American	5	6	7	8	9	10	11	
British	3	4	5	6	7	8	9	
Continental	36	37	38	39	40	41	42	

Men's shirts

American	14	15	15.5	16	16.5	17	17.5	18
British	14	15	15.5	16	16.5	17	17.5	18
Aus/Continental	36	38	39	41	42	43	44	45

Men's shoes

American	7	7.5	8	8.5	9.5	10	10.5	11	11.5
Aus/British	6	7	7.5	8	9	9.5	10	11	12
Continental	39	40	41	42	43	44	44	45	46

Men's suits

American	34	36	38	40	42	44	46	48
Aus/British	34	36	38	40	42	44	46	48
Continental	44	46	48	50	52	54	56	58

For a good overview of accessible travel in Australia, *Easy Access Australia* (AUS$27.45; ⓦwww.easyaccessaustralia.com.au) is a comprehensive guide written by wheelchair-user Bruce Cameron for anyone with mobility difficulties, and has information on all the states, with maps, and a separate section with floor plans of hotel rooms.

Useful contacts

NDS (National Disability Service) ☏02/6283 3200, ⓦwww.nds.org.au. Regional offices provide lists of state-based help organizations, accommodation, travel agencies and tour operators.
NICAN (National Information Communication Awareness Network) ☏02/6241 1220 or 1800

806 769, ⓦwww.nican.com.au. A national, nonprofit, free information service on recreation, sport, tourism, the arts, and much more, for people with disabilities. Has a database of over 4500 organizations – such as wheelchair-accessible accommodation, sports organizations, and companies renting out accessible buses and vans.
Paraplegic and Quadriplegic Association of NSW ☏02/8741 5600 or 1300 886 601, ⓦwww.paraquad.org.au. Serves the interests of the spinally injured for NSW, with independent offices in each state capital.
ⓦwww.accessibility.com.au Lists of accessible accommodation and transport, as well as access maps of major Australian cities.

Guide

Guide

Sydney and around

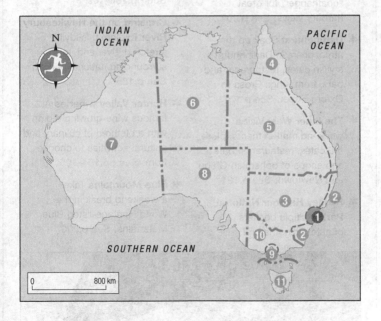

CHAPTER 1 # Highlights

✱ **Cruise the harbour** Sydney is at its best from the harbour; take it in cheaply on the popular Manly Ferry. See p.103

✱ **The Opera House** Catch a show or relax with a drink at the *Opera Bar*. See p.105

✱ **Climbing Sydney Harbour Bridge** Scale the famous "coathanger" for great harbour views. See p.107

✱ **Darlinghurst** Soak up the atmosphere in Darlinghurst's stylish cafés, restaurants and bars, from Kings Cross to Oxford Street. See p.127

✱ **The Inner West** Visit a weekend market then explore the cafés, restaurants, bars and shops of bohemian Glebe and Newtown. See p.131

✱ **Sydney Harbour National Park** Multiple pockets of astounding natural beauty with great views of the harbour and city. See p.136

✱ **Bondi Beach** Bold, brash Bondi is synonymous with Australian beach culture. See p.143

✱ **Mardi Gras** The world's biggest celebration of gay and lesbian culture. See pp.168–169

✱ **Cruising on the Hawkesbury River** Explore this idyllic stretch of river and its surrounding national parks. See p.185

✱ **Hunter Valley wineries** A famous wine-growing region with a plethora of culinary and cultural activities to choose from. See pp.194–195

✱ **Blue Mountains** Take a weekend break in the World Heritage-listed Blue Mountains. See p.200

▲ Sydney Harbour Bridge

Sydney and around

Flying into **Sydney** provides the first snapshot of Australia for most overseas visitors: toy-sized images of the Harbour Bridge and the Opera House, tilting in a glittering expanse of blue water. The Aussie city par excellence, Sydney stands head and shoulders above any other in Australia. Taken together with its surrounds, it's in many ways a microcosm of the country as a whole – if only in its ability to defy your expectations and prejudices as often as it confirms them. A thrusting, high-rise business centre, a high-profile gay community, and inner-city deprivation of unexpected harshness are as much part of the scene as the beaches, the bodies and the sparkling harbour. Its sophistication, cosmopolitan population and exuberant nightlife are a long way from the Outback, and yet Sydney has the highest Aboriginal population of any Australian city, and bushfires are a constant threat.

The area around – everything in this chapter is within day-trip distance – offers a taste of virtually everything you'll find in the rest of the country, with the exception of desert. There are magnificent **national parks** – Ku-ring-gai Chase and Royal being the best known – and native wildlife, each a mere hour's drive from the centre of town; while further north stretch endless ocean **beaches**, great for surfers, and more enclosed waters for safer swimming and sailing. Inland, the Blue Mountains, with three more national parks, offer isolated bushwalking and scenic viewpoints. On the way are historic colonial towns that were among the earliest foundations in the country – Sydney itself, of course, was the very first. The commercial and industrial heart of the state of New South Wales, especially the central coastal region, is bordered by **Wollongong** in the south and **Newcastle** in the north. Both were synonymous with coal and steel, but the smokestack industries that supported them for decades are now in severe decline. This is far from an industrial wasteland, though: the heart of the coal-mining country is the **Hunter Valley**, northwest of Newcastle, but to visit it you'd never guess, because this is also Australia's oldest, and arguably its best known, wine-growing region.

Sydney

The 2000 Olympics were a coming-of-age ceremony for **SYDNEY**, with fifty years' worth of development compressed into four years under the pressure of intense international scrutiny. The benefits are still being felt: Sydney has all the vigour of a world-class city, with the reputation of its restaurants in particular turning the lingering cultural sneers to swoons. It seems to have the best of both worlds: twenty minutes from Circular Quay by bus, the high-rise office buildings and skyscrapers give way to colourful inner-city suburbs where you can get an eyeful of sky and watch the lemons ripening above the pavemet, while to the centre's north and south are corridors of largely intact bushland where many have built their dream homes. During every heatwave, however, bushfires threaten the city, and sophisticated Sydney becomes closer to its roots than it sometimes feels. In the summer, the city's hot offices are abandoned for the remarkably unspoilt beaches strung along the eastern and northern suburbs.

It's also as beautiful a city as any in the world, with a **setting** that perhaps only Rio de Janeiro can rival: the water is what makes it so special, and no introduction to Sydney would be complete without paying tribute to one of the world's

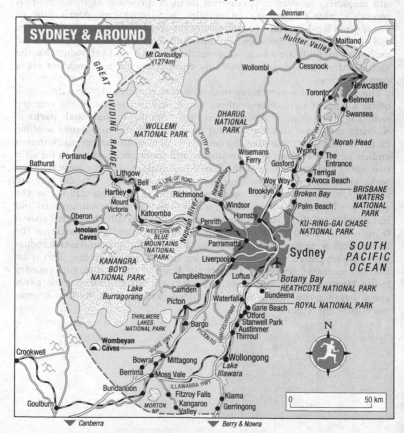

great **harbours**. Port Jackson is a sunken valley that twists inland to meet the fresh water of the Parramatta River; in the process it washes into a hundred coves and bays, winds around rocky points, flows past small harbour islands, slips under bridges and laps at the foot of the Opera House. Sydney is seen at its gleaming best from the deck of a harbour ferry, especially at weekends when the harbour's jagged jaws fill with a flotilla of small vessels, racing yachts and cabin cruisers; getting away from the city centre and exploring them is an essential part of Sydney's pleasures.

It might seem surprising that Sydney is not Australia's capital: the creation of Canberra in 1927 – intended to stem the intense rivalry between Sydney and Melbourne – has not affected the view of many Sydneysiders that their city remains the true capital of Australia, and certainly in many ways it feels like it. The city has a tangible sense of history: the old stone walls and well-worn steps in the backstreets around The Rocks are an evocative reminder that Sydney has more than two hundred years of white history behind it.

Some history

The city of Sydney was founded as a penal colony, amid brutality, deprivation and despair. In January 1788, the **First Fleet**, carrying over a thousand people, 736 of them convicts, arrived at **Botany Bay** expecting the "fine meadows" that Captain James Cook had described eight years earlier. In fact, what greeted them was mostly swamp, scrub and sand dunes: a desolate sight even for sea-weary eyes. An unsuccessful scouting expedition prompted Commander Arthur Phillip to move the fleet a few kilometres north, to the well-wooded Port Jackson, where a stream of fresh water was found. Based around the less than satisfactory Tank Stream, the settlement was named **Sydney Cove** after Viscount Sydney, then Secretary of State in Great Britain. In the first three years of settlement, the new colony nearly starved to death several times; the land around Sydney Cove proved to be barren. When supply ships did arrive, they inevitably came with hundreds more convicts to further burden the colony. It was not until 1790, when land was successfully farmed further west at **Parramatta**, that the hunger began to abate. Measure this suffering, however, with that of the original occupants, the **Eora Aborigines**: their land had been invaded, their people virtually wiped out by smallpox, and now they were stricken by hunger as the settlers shot at their game – and even, as they moved further inland, at the Eora themselves.

Under the leadership of **Pemulwuy**, a skilled Aboriginal warrior, the Eora commenced a guerilla war against the colony for much of the 1790s. Homesteads were attacked, crops burnt and livestock killed and maimed. In 1794 an attack on the western outskirts of the budding Sydney settlement, at Brickfield Lane (near the end of today's George Street), resulted in the death of thirty-six British and fourteen Eora. Other major attacks occurred at Prospect, Parramatta, Toongabbie and the Hawkesbury River. The numbers and firepower of the settlers proved too great for the Eora, however, and in 1802 Pemulwuy was captured and killed, his severed head sent back to England. With their numbers depleted and Pemulwuy gone, the Eora's resistance soon ended.

By the early 1800s, Sydney had become a stable colony and busy trading post. Army officers in charge of the colony, exploiting their access to free land and cheap labour, became rich farm-owners and virtually established a currency based on rum. The **military**, known as the New South Wales Corps (or more familiarly as "the rum corps"), became the supreme political force in the colony in 1809, even overthrowing the governor (mutiny-plagued Captain Bligh himself). This was the last straw for the government back home, and the rebellious officers were finally brought to heel when the reformist Governor **Lachlan Macquarie** arrived from England with forces of his own. He liberalized conditions, supported the prisoners' right to become citizens after they had served their time, and appointed several to public offices.

By the 1840s, the transportation of convicts to New South Wales had ended, the explorers Lawson and Blaxland had found a way through the Blue Mountains to the Western Plains, and **gold** had been struck in Bathurst. The population soared as free settlers arrived in ever-increasing numbers. In the Victorian era, Sydney's population became even more starkly divided into the **haves** and the **have-nots**: while the poor lived in slums where disease, crime, prostitution and alcoholism were rife, the genteel classes – self-consciously replicating life in the mother country – took tea on their verandas and erected grandiloquent monuments such as the Town Hall, the Strand Arcade and the Queen Victoria Building in homage to English architecture of the time. An outbreak of the plague in The Rocks at the beginning of the twentieth century made wholesale slum clearances inevitable, and with the demolitions came a change in attitudes. Strict new vice laws meant the end of the bad old days of backstreet knifings, drunk-filled taverns and makeshift brothels.

Over the next few decades, Sydney settled into comfortable **suburban living**. The metropolis sprawled westwards, creating a flat, unremarkable city with no real centre, an appropriate symbol for the era of shorts and knee socks and the stereotypical, barbecue-loving Bruce and Sheila – an international image that still plagues Australians. Sydney has come a long way since the parochialism of the 1950s, however: skyscrapers at the city's centre have rocketed heavenward and constructions such as the **Opera House** began to reflect the city's dynamism. The cultural clichés of cold tinnies of beer and meat pies with sauce have long been discarded, giving way to a city confident in itself and in its culinary attractions, too. Today, Sydney's citizens don't look inwards – and they certainly don't look towards England. Thousands of immigrants from around the globe have given Sydney a truly cosmopolitan air and it's a city as thrilling and alive as any.

Arrival

The dream way to **arrive** in Sydney is, of course, by ship, cruising in below the great coathanger of the Harbour Bridge to tie up at the Overseas Passenger Terminal alongside Circular Quay. The reality of the functional airport, bus and train stations is a good deal less romantic.

By air

Sydney's **Kingsford Smith Airport**, referred to as "Mascot" after the suburb where it's located, is 8km south of the city, near Botany Bay (international flight times ☎ 13 12 23, ⊛ www.sydneyairport.com.au). Passengers needing to transfer between domestic and international terminals may be eligible for a free shuttle service if travelling with Qantas (☎ 13 13 13) or Virgin Blue (☎ 13 67 89), or you can get a T-Bus (every 30min; $5.50), a taxi ($8–12) or the **Airport Link** underground railway ($5.60), which also connects the airport to the City Circle train line in the heart of Sydney in around fifteen minutes (every 10–15min;

Airport buses

State Transit Authority (STA)
STA's daily east–west commuter route #400 stops frequently at the international and domestic terminals bound for Bondi Junction via Maroubra and Randwick in one direction, and to Burwood in the other (tickets to Bondi Junction $4.80).

Shuttle service – Sydney area
KST Sydney Transporter ☎ 02/9666 9988, ⓦ www.kst.com.au. Private bus service dropping off at hotels or hostels in the area bounded by Kings Cross and Darling Harbour. Service leaves when the bus is full ($13 one-way, $22 return). Bookings three hours in advance for accommodation pick-up to the airport.

Coach and shuttle services – central coast and south coast
Aussie Shuttles ☎ 1300 130 557, ⓦ www.ben-air.com.au. Pre-booked door-to-door service to accommodation anywhere on the central coast ($60–75).
Premier Motor Service ☎ 13 34 10, outside Australia ☎ 02/4423 5233, ⓦ www .premierms.com.au. Departs daily at 9.30am and 3.35pm from the domestic terminal, ten minutes later from the international terminal, to south-coast towns as far as Eden ($68) with the 3.35pm service continuing to Melbourne ($83). Booking necessary.

$14.40 one-way; ⓦ www.airportlink.com.au). A return Airport Link transfer is included in the excellent-value Sydney Pass tourist transport package (see p.88), which you can buy at the airport train station, Circular Quay and Manly Ferry wharfs, CityRail stations, visitor centres and on Explorer Buses. Buses run regularly into the city (see box above), while a **taxi** to the city centre or Kings Cross costs $34–38.

Bureau de change offices at both terminals are open daily from 5am until last arrival with rates comparable to major banks. On the ground floor (Arrivals) of the international terminal, the **Sydney Visitor Centre** (daily 5am until last arrival; ☎ 02/9667 9386) can arrange car rental and city-bound shuttle bus tickets, and can **book hotels** anywhere in Sydney and New South Wales free of charge and at stand-by rates. Most hostels advertise on an adjacent notice board; there's a freephone line for reservations, and many of them will refund your bus fare; a few also offer free airport pick-ups.

By train and bus

All local and interstate **trains** arrive at **Central Station** on Eddy Avenue, just south of the city centre. There are no lockers at the station, but you can store **luggage** at Wanderers' Travel, 810 George St, a three-minute walk around the block (daily 8am–8pm; $7 per bag, per day, or $30 per week). From outside Central Station, and neighbouring **Railway Square**, you can hop onto nearly every major bus route, and from within Central Station you can take a CityRail train to any city or suburban station (see "City transport", p.86).

All **buses** to Sydney arrive and depart from Eddy Avenue and Pitt Street, bordering Central Station. The area is well set up, with decent cafés, a 24-hour police station and a huge YHA hostel, as well as the **Sydney Coach Terminal** (Mon–Fri 6am–6pm, Sat & Sun 8am–6pm; ☎ 02/9281 9366), which has a left-luggage room ($5–10 per bag per 24hr) and an internet kiosk, and can **book accommodation**, tours and coach tickets and passes.

Information

There are two **Sydney Visitor Centres** offering comprehensive information, free accommodation and tour-booking facilities, and selling transport tickets and sight-seeing passes. Both are centrally located at The Rocks, on the corner of Argyle and Playfair streets, and at Darling Harbour, beside the IMAX cinema (both daily 9.30am–5.30pm; ☎02/9240 8788 or 1800 067 676, ⑩www.sydneyvisitorcentre .com). Free **maps** and brochures can be picked up at both, including the very useful *Sydney: The Official Guide*. Tourism New South Wales (☎13 20 77, ⑩www .visitnsw.com) runs the **City Host information kiosks** (daily 9am–5pm) at Circular Quay (on the corner of Pitt and Alfred sts), Martin Place and Town Hall, providing brochures, maps and information.

Several free **magazines** are worth picking up at tourist offices: the quarterly *This Week in Sydney* is best for general information, while *TNT Magazine* is aimed at **backpackers**, giving the lowdown on Sydney on the cheap.

City transport

Sydney's **public transport network** is wide-reaching and relatively comprehensive, but not always punctual, and since the system relies heavily on buses, traffic jams can be a problem. **State Transit Authority (STA)** operate buses, trains and ferries – see the box on pp.88–89 for information on the great-value Sydney Pass, which enables travel on all three – and there's also a privately run light rail and monorail system whizzing about the city centre, as well as plenty of taxis. Trains stop around midnight, as do most regular buses, though several services towards the eastern and northern beaches, such as the #380 to Bondi Beach, the #372 and #373 to Coogee and the #151 to Manly, run through the night. Otherwise, a pretty good network of **Nightride buses** shadows the train routes to the suburbs, departing from Town Hall Station (in front of the Energy Australia Building on George St) and stopping at train stations – where taxis wait at designated ranks. For all public transport information, routes and timetables, call ☎13 15 00 (24hr) or check ⑩www.131500.info.

Buses

Within the central area, **buses** – hailed from yellow-signed bus stops – are the most convenient, widespread mode of transport, and cover more of the city than the trains. With few exceptions, buses radiate from the centre, with major interchanges at Railway Square near Central Station (especially southwest

Smartvisit Card

Both Sydney Visitor Centres sell the **See Sydney & Beyond Smartvisit Card** (☎1300 661 711, ⑩www.seesydneycard.com), which comes in two-, three- and seven-day versions (to be used over consecutive days), with or without a free transport (train, bus, ferry) option, and includes admission to forty attractions in Sydney and the Blue Mountains, as well as a range of discounts. The two-day pass costs $175, or $135 without transport, the three-day pass $225/$165, and the seven-day option $299/$225. If an action-packed, fast-paced itinerary is your thing, the card can be good value, and it's certainly a convenient way to bypass the queues.

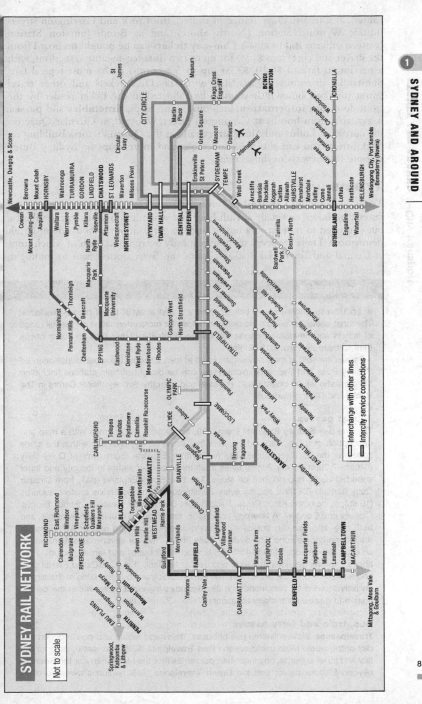

SYDNEY RAIL NETWORK

Not to scale

Interchange with other lines
Intercity service connections

routes), at Circular Quay (range of routes), from York and Carrington streets outside Wynyard Station (North Shore), and at Bondi Junction Station (eastern suburbs and beaches). One-way **tickets** can be bought on board from the driver and cost from $1.90 for up to two distance-measured sections, with a maximum fare of $6.10; $3.20 (up to 5 sections) is the most typical fare. Substantial discounts are available with TravelTen tickets and other travel passes (see box below); these must be validated in the ticket reader by the front door. Bus **information**, including route maps, **timetables** and **passes**, is available from booths at Carrington Street, Wynyard; at Circular Quay on the corner of Loftus and Alfred streets; and at the Queen Victoria Building on York Street. You can also view timetables and route maps on Sydney Buses' website (Ⓦ www.sydneybuses.info).

Trains

Trains, operated by **CityRail** (see map, p.87), will get you where you're going faster than buses, especially at rush hour and when heading out to the suburbs, but you need to transfer to a bus or ferry to get to most harbourside or beach destinations. There are seven train lines, mostly overground, each of which stops at Central and Town Hall stations. Trains run from around 5am to midnight,

---

Travel passes

In addition to single-journey tickets, there's a vast array of travel passes available. The most useful for visitors are outlined below; for more information on the full range of tickets and timetables, phone the Transport Infoline (24hr; ☏ 13 15 00) or check their website (Ⓦ www.131500.info).

Passes are sold at most newsagents and at train stations; the more tourist-oriented Sydney Pass and Sydney Explorer Pass can be bought at train stations (including airport stations), on board Explorer buses and from the Sydney Visitor Centre in The Rocks and Darling Harbour.

Tourist passes

The one-day **Sydney Explorer Pass** ($39, family pass $97) comes with a map and description of the sights, and includes free travel on any STA bus within the same zones as the Explorer routes. The red Sydney Explorer (from Circular Quay daily 8.40am–7.20pm; every 20min) takes in all the important sights in the city and inner suburbs, via 27 hop-on, hop-off stops. The blue Bondi Explorer (daily from Circular Quay 8.30am–6.11pm; approx every 30min) covers the waterside eastern suburbs (19 stops, including Kings Cross, Paddington, Double Bay, Vaucluse, Bondi, Bronte, Clovelly and Coogee). A **two-day** ticket ($68, family pass $170) is also available, and both one- and two-day tickets allow use of bus services and regular STA Buses in the inner-city blue zone. The **Sydney Pass** (three-, five- or seven-day options within an eight-day period; $110/$145/$165) is valid for all buses and ferries, including the above Explorer services, the ferry and JetCat to Manly, the RiverCat to Parramatta, and a return trip to the airport with the Airport Link train (buy the pass at the airport on arrival), valid for two months. It also includes travel on trains within the central area, and discounts at many attractions.

Bus, train and ferry passes

Travelpasses allow unlimited use of buses, trains and ferries and can begin on any day of the week. Most useful are the **Red Travelpass** ($38 for a week), valid for the city and inner suburbs, and inner-harbour ferries (not the Manly Ferry or the RiverCat beyond Meadowbank); and the **Green Travelpass** ($46), which allows use of all

with **tickets** starting at $3.20 for a single on the City Loop and for short hops; buying off-peak returns (after 9am and all weekend) means you can save up to thirty percent.

Automatic ticket machines (which give change) and barriers (insert magnetic tickets; otherwise, show ticket at the gate) have been introduced just about everywhere. On-the-spot fines for fare evasion start from $200, and transit officers patrol frequently. All platforms are painted with designated "nightsafe" waiting areas and all but two or three train carriages are closed after about 8pm, enforcing a cattle-like safety in numbers. Security guards also patrol trains at night; at other times, if the train is deserted, sit in the carriage nearest the guard – marked by a blue light.

Ferries

Sydney's distinctive green-and-yellow **ferries** are the fastest means of transport from Circular Quay to the North Shore, and to most places around the harbour. Even if you don't want to go anywhere, a ferry ride is a must, a chance to get out on the water and see the city from the harbour.

Ferries chug off in various directions from the wharves at Circular Quay (see map, p.90); cruises depart from Wharf 6. The Manly Ferry (30min) operates

ferries. Passes covering a wider area cost between $50 and $60 a week, and monthly passes are also available.

DayTripper tickets ($17) are also available for unlimited travel on all suburban network services offered by CityRail, Sydney Buses and Sydney Ferries, and they can even be purchased on board buses and ferries.

Bus and ferry

The **Blue Travelpass** ($34 for a week) gives unlimited travel on buses in the inner-city area and on inner-harbour ferries but cannot be used for Manly or beyond Meadowbank; the **Orange Travelpass** ($43 for a week) gets you further on the buses and is valid on all ferries; and the **Pittwater Travelpass** ($58 for a week) gives unlimited travel on all buses and ferries. These Travelpasses start with first use rather than on the day of purchase.

Bus

TravelTen tickets represent a twenty-percent saving over single fares by buying ten trips at once; they can be used over a space of time and for more than one person. The tickets are colour-coded according to how many sections they cover: the Brown TravelTen ($25.60), for example, is the choice for trips from Newtown or Glebe to the city and Circular Quay, while the Red TravelTen ($33.60) is the one to buy if you're staying at Bondi.

Ferry

FerryTen tickets, valid for ten single trips, start at $33.50 for Inner Harbour Services, going up to $48.10 for the Manly Ferry.

Train

Seven Day RailPass tickets allow unlimited travel between any two nominated stations and those in between, with savings of about twenty percent on the price of five return trips. For example, a pass between Bondi Junction and Town Hall would cost $27. A FlexiPass will give you the same journey for longer periods – 30 to 365 days (for the journey above: 30 days $105, 90 days $300).

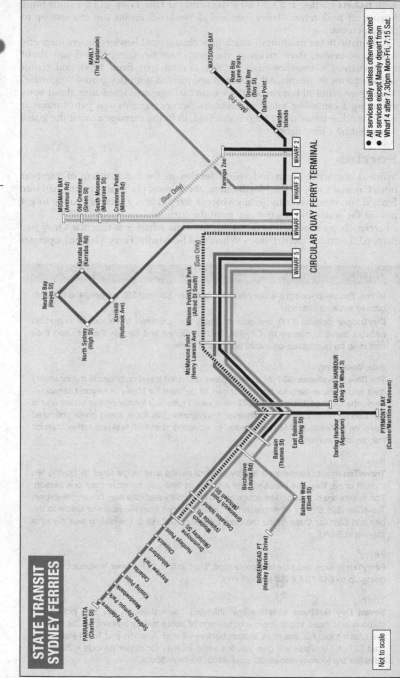

STATE TRANSIT SYDNEY FERRIES

Not to scale

until 11.45pm, 11pm on Sundays. Other ferry routes, such as those to Parramatta and Pyrmont Bay, run only until 10.50pm, while ferries to closer locations, including Neutral Bay and Balmain, continue to around 11.40pm. Except for the Manly Ferry, services on Sunday are greatly reduced and often finish earlier. **Timetables** for each route are available at Circular Quay and on the Sydney Ferries website ⓦ www.sydneyferries.info.

One-way **fares** are $5.20 ($6.40 for the Manly Ferry; $7.70 for the RiverCat to Parramatta); return fares are doubled. Travelpasses and FerryTen tickets can offer substantial savings (see box, pp.88–89).

Monorail and Light Rail

The city's monorail and light rail systems are run by **Metro Transport Sydney** (ⓣ 02/8584 5288 ⓦ www.metromonorail.com.au; see map p.87 for routes).

The **Monorail** is essentially a tourist shuttle designed to loop around Darling Harbour every three to five minutes, connecting it with the city centre. Thundering along tracks set above the older city streets, it doesn't exactly blend in with its surroundings. Still, the elevated view of the city, particularly from Pyrmont Bridge, makes it worth investing $4.80 (day-pass $9.50) and ten minutes to do the whole eight-stop circuit (Mon–Thurs 7am–10pm, Fri & Sat 7am–midnight, Sun 8am–10pm).

Light Rail (MLR) runs from Central Station to the Pyrmont Peninsula and on to Lilyfield in the inner west. There are fourteen stops on the route, which links Central Station with Chinatown, Darling Harbour, the fish markets at Pyrmont, Star City Casino, Wentworth Park's greyhound racecourse, Glebe (with stops near Pyrmont Bridge Road, Jubilee Park, and Rozelle Bay by Bicentennial Park) and Lilyfield, not far from Darling Street, Rozelle. The service operates 24 hours a day, every ten to fifteen minutes to the casino (every 30min midnight–6am), with reduced hours for stops beyond to Lilyfield (Mon–Thurs & Sun 6am–11pm, Fri & Sat 6am–midnight). There are two zones: Zone 1 is from Central to Convention Centre in Darling Harbour, and Zone 2 from Pyrmont Bay to Lilyfield.

▲ Sydney's Monorail

Tickets, purchased at machines by the stops, cost $3.20/$4.20 one-way (Zone 1/Zone 2), and $4.60/$5.70 return; a day-pass costs $9 and a weekly pass $22. A TramLink ticket, available from any CityRail station, combines a rail ticket to Central Station with an MLR ticket. If you plan on using the Monorail and Light Rail a lot, it might be worth buying a **METROcard** ($30), which gives seven days of unlimited travel on both lines.

Taxis

Taxis are vacant if the rooftop light is on, though they are notoriously difficult to find at 3pm, when the shifts change over. The four major city **cab ranks** are outside the *Four Seasons Hotel* at the start of George Street, The Rocks; on Park Street outside Woolworths, opposite the Town Hall; outside David Jones department store on Market Street; and at the Pitt Street ("CountryLink") entrance to Central Station. Drivers don't expect a tip but often need directions – try to have some idea of where you're going. Check the correct tariff rate is displayed: tariff 2 (10pm–6am) is twenty percent more than tariff 1 (6am–10pm). See "Listings", p.179, for phone numbers.

Accommodation

There are a tremendous number of places to stay in Sydney, and fierce competition helps keep prices down. Finding somewhere is usually only a problem around Christmas, throughout January, in late February/early March during the Gay Mardi Gras, and at Easter: at these times, **book ahead**. All types of accommodation offer a (sometimes substantial) discount for **weekly bookings**, and may also cut prices considerably during the **low season** (from May–Sept, school holidays excepted).

The larger **chain hotels** in The Rocks and the city centre generally charge upwards of $200 for a double room, although rates vary with demand: book early and you can often get a bargain. At such hotels, weekend rates are usually twenty

---

Flat-shares

If you're staying longer than a month, consider a **flat-share** as an alternative to hotels or hostels. You'll feel more at home and it will probably cost less. The average shared-house room price is around $160 a week (usually two weeks in advance, plus a bond/deposit of four weeks' rent; you'll usually need your own bed linen and towels). Furnished Property Group (☏ 02 8669 3678, ⒲ www.furnishedproperty.com .au) have a of wide range of places, both leased rooms in guesthouses in all the best areas, and furnished apartments (stays of 3–12 months). Sleeping With The Enemy, 617 Harris St, Ultimo (☏ 1300 309 468, ⒲ www.sleepingwiththeenemy.com), organizes house-shares for travellers (aimed at under-28s) in fully equipped inner-city houses with up to eight others. Rooms are mostly singles and twins and go for $180 a week for a minimum one-month stay. There's a $300 bond and the rate includes all bills including free internet and wi-fi. Other good bets include Wednesday and Saturday's real-estate section of the *Sydney Morning Herald*, and café notice boards, especially in King Street in Newtown, Glebe Point Road in Glebe, or Hall Street in Bondi Beach.

If you feel unsure about renting in a strange city, contact the New South Wales Tenants Union (☏ 02/9251 6590, ⒲ www.tenants.org.au) for information on lease agreements and **tenants' rights**.

percent higher than weekday rates, a pattern also found at **boutique hotels**, which get booked out in advance for Friday and Saturday nights. Rates in Kings Cross are much cheaper, with rooms in **hotels** available for $70 (sharing a bathroom) and around $90 en suite, and around $130–180 in three- or four-star hotels.

An increasing number of mid-range boutique hotels and **guesthouses** are smaller, more characterful places to stay, charging upwards of $150. **Serviced holiday apartments** can be very good value for a group, but are heavily booked.

Despite the number of **hostels** all over Sydney and the rivalry between them, standards are variable. Generally you get what you pay for: a couple of extra dollars may get you a less cramped dorm or airier room. Almost everywhere includes sheets and blankets in the price, which starts around $24, though you'll pay over $30 at the best places. Rates increase by around 10–20 percent from mid-December through to early February (especially at beachside hostels), but drop considerably in winter when three-for-two-nights deals and free breakfasts are common. All hostels have a laundry, kitchen and common room with TV unless stated otherwise. Office hours are restricted, so it's best to arrange an arrival time.

Big cities usually offer few options for **camping** (see box, p.94), but Sydney is an exception, with walk-in camping right in the middle of Sydney Harbour at Cockatoo Island, and several more distant drive-in sites.

Where to stay

The listings below are arranged by area. For short visits, you'll want to stay in the **city centre** or the immediate vicinity: **The Rocks**, the **CBD** and **Darling Harbour** have the greatest concentration of expensive hotels, while **Haymarket** is well endowed with backpackers' hostels, a couple of fine YHAs and a few mid-range hotels.

Kings Cross makes an excellent base, as it's only a ten-minute walk from the city, has its own train station and is always lively. In recent years, it has shaken the worst of its renowned red-light and drug-abuse sleaze and is once again popular with backpackers who frequent the dense cluster of hostels and cheap hotels in The Cross and along leafy Victoria Street.

Fashionable new restaurants and bars are opening up all the time in adjacent **Potts Point**, **Woolloomooloo** and **Darlinghurst**, and the buzz has attracted a cluster of chic boutique hotels and refined B&Bs to the area.

There's far less choice in southern Darlinghurst, Paddington and Surry Hills, though the vibrant gay scene along Oxford Street ensures there are **gay-friendly** places to stay. Few are exclusively gay, though *Governors on Fitzroy* (see p.100) comes close, and there are several welcoming places in the area that we've included in our general listings: try *BIG* (p.98), the *Kirketon* (p.99) and *Sullivans* (p.100).

To the west, verdant and peaceful **Glebe** is another slice of prime travellers' territory, featuring several backpackers' and a number of small, luxurious guesthouses.

For longer stays, consider somewhere further out, on the **North Shore**, where you'll get more of a feel for Sydney as a city. **Kirribilli**, **Neutral Bay** or **Cremorne Point**, only a short ferry ride from Circular Quay, offer serenity and affordable water views. Large old private hotels out this way are increasingly being converted into hostels, particularly on Carabella Street in Kirribilli.

This being Sydney, the beaches are a huge draw, and thanks to the good ferry and train system it's quite possible to stay at the beach and still sightsee quite comfortably. The closest ocean beach to the city is **Bondi**, which weighs in with a couple of great hostels and a boutique hotel. There's a more casual feel

Campsites around Sydney

The four campsites and caravan parks listed below are the closest sites to the centre. Camping rates rise in the listed peak season; expect to pay $10 less in low season.

Cockatoo Island Camping Cockatoo Island, Sydney Harbour [T]02/8898 9774, [W]www.cockatooisland.gov.au. Arguably one of the world's most uniquely sited campsites, affording magnificent views of the city across the water. Includes a campsite kitchen, BBQs, a fridge, hot showers and access to the island's café. Access is via ferry on the Parramatta River Service or Woolwich service ([W]www.sydneyferries.info; cars need to be parked near one of the wharfs). Unpowered sites $45; package including tent, mattresses, chairs and lantern $75.

Lakeside Caravan Park Lake Park Road, Narrabeen, 26km north of the city [T]1800 008 845, [W]www.sydneylakeside.com.au. Spacious campground in a great spot by Narrabeen Lakes on Sydney's northern beaches, with camp kitchens and coin-operated gas barbecues, and it's only a 10-minute walk to the supermarket. Powered sites $45, campervan sites with private bathroom $55, two-bedroom villas [8]. Bus #L90 from Railway Square by Central Station. Prices increase by 20 percent on peak holiday weekends.

Lane Cove River Tourist Park Plassey Rd, North Ryde, 14km northwest of the city [T]02/9888 9133, [W]www.lanecoverivertouristpark.com.au. Wonderful bush location beside Lane Cove National Park, right on the river, in Sydney's northern suburbs. Great facilities include a bush kitchen (with fridge), TV room, wi-fi and swimming pool. Train to Chatswood then bus #545. Camping $34–36; en-suite cabins [5]

Sheralee Tourist Caravan Park 88 Bryant St, Rockdale, 13km south of the city [T]02/9567 7161. Small, basic park, six blocks from Botany Bay, with good, clean facilities and friendly staff. Train to Rockdale station, then a 10-minute walk. Campsites $30–35, Caravans $45, Cabins $60.

to **Coogee**, a couple of headlands to the south, which is also popular with backpackers and has a chic hotel. A frequent and fast ferry service makes **Manly**, the first of the northern beaches, a good base. This seaside suburb with ocean and harbour beaches, just thirty minutes from Circular Quay, has a concentration of hostels and a limited supply of more upmarket accommodation. Lastly, the beaches to the north of Manly offer a couple of hostels and B&Bs that are inconvenient for visiting the city but make good spots for a short break.

The Rocks

The listings below are marked on the **map** on p.108.

Hotels and B&Bs

Lord Nelson Brewery Hotel Corner of Argyle and Kent sts [T]02/9251 4044, [W]www.lordnelson.com.au. This colonial-style B&B in a historic pub has ten cosy rooms. Price varies according to size and position: best is the corner room with views of Argyle St. Serves beer brewed on the premises, plus bar food daily and upmarket meals from its first-floor brasserie (lunch Wed–Fri, dinner Tues–Sat). [6]–[7] includes continental breakfast.

Mercantile 25 George St [T]02/9247 3570, [E]merc@tpg.com.au. This high-spirited Irish pub has a stash of great rooms upstairs, which are always booked out, so get in early. Original features include huge fireplaces in several rooms, all furnished in colonial style. Some have bathrooms complete with spa baths. In the pub itself, bistro meals are served at outdoor tables – a fine spot to watch the weekend market crowds. [5]–[6] includes cooked breakfast.

Old Sydney Holiday Inn 55 George St [T]02/9252 0524, [W]www.holidayinn.com. In a great location right in the heart of The Rocks, this hotel is impressively designed: eight levels of rooms around a central atrium create a remarkable feeling of space. The best rooms have harbour views, but the rooftop swimming pool (plus spa and sauna) also offers fantastic vistas. Variable rates start from $342. [9]

The Russell 143A George St ☎ 02/9241 3543, [W] www.therussell.com.au. A small hotel with popular shared-bathroom rooms, as well as en-suite options; the priciest of these have views of Circular Quay. There's a rooftop garden with a small restaurant serving continental breakfast. [6]–[8]

Hostel

Sydney Harbour YHA 106–128 Cumberland St ☎ 02/9261 1111, [W] www.sydneyharbouryha.com.au. This new, 106-room YHA, due to be completed by late 2009, will double as an innovative Archaeology Education Centre (the "Big Dig") – with the YHA's structure suspended over early nineteenth-century remains uncovered in the 1990s. The only budget accommodation in The Rocks.

Central Business District (CBD)

The listings below are marked on the **map** on p.96.

Hotels and B&Bs

Blacket 70 King St ☎ 02/9279 3030, [W] www.blackethotel.com.au. Stylish 42-room hotel in a converted former bank, with original features such as the 1850s staircase contrasting with the minimalist modern interiors. Suites come with designer kitchenettes, and there are also loft suites, as well as two-bedroom apartments and a suite with its own terrace. The basement bar, *Privilege*, is very trendy, and there's a smart on-site restaurant where a buffet breakfast ($9) is served. [8]

Central Park 185 Castlereagh St ☎ 02/9283 5000, [W] www.centralpark.com.au. A small, chic hotel in a central position, though rooms are quiet. There's a sofa, desk and kitchenette in the a/c rooms, and some come with a bathtub. The lobby café is open daytime only, but there's a 24hr reception. [7]

Grand 30 Hunter St ☎ 02/9232 3755, [W] www.merivale.com.au. Very well located budget accommodation occupying several floors above one of Sydney's oldest pubs. Rooms (all sharing bathrooms) are brightly painted, and come with fridge, kettle, TV, heating and ceiling fans. [5]

Intercontinental 117 Macquarie St ☎ 02/9253 9000, [W] www.intercontinental.com. The sandstone facade of the 1851 former Treasury building forms the lower floors of this 31-storey, five-star hotel, with stunning views of the Botanic Gardens, Opera House and harbour. Pool and gym on the top floor. Summer rates from around $350, more for city and harbour views. [9]

Travelodge Wynyard 7–9 York St ☎ 02/9274 1222 or 1300 886 886, [W] www.travelodge.com.au. This 22-storey hotel close to The Rocks has the usual motel-style rooms but excels with its spacious studios, which come with kitchen area and CD player. There's also a small gym and a pleasant café-brasserie. Cheaper weekend packages available. [6]–[7]

Y Hyde Park 5–11 Wentworth Ave ☎ 1800 994 994, [W] www.yhotel.com.au. Surprisingly stylish and very comfortable YWCA (both sexes welcome) near Hyde Park. Caters to all levels of traveller with four-bed dorm rooms (no bunks), standard hotel rooms and deluxe rooms. There's no common kitchen, but facilities include a café, laundry and pay wi-fi throughout. Dorms $35, rooms [5]–[6], including a light breakfast.

Hostel

BASE Backpackers 477 Kent St ☎ 1800 24 BASE, [W] www.basebackpackers.com. This huge, modern, 360-bed hostel is well set up with two TV rooms, laundry and internet facilities and a newly renovated kitchen. Well-furnished rooms and dorms (four-, six-, eight- and ten-bed), all have a/c with shared bathrooms. Globetrotting single gals can enjoy their women-only "Sanctuary", with hairdryers in the bathrooms, Aveda haircare products and feather pillows. Dorms $26–34, rooms [4]

Haymarket and around Central Station

The listings below are marked on the **map** on p.114.

Hotels and B&Bs

Citigate Central Sydney 169–179 Thomas St, Haymarket ☎ 1800 252 588, [W] www.mirvachotels.com. This modern eighteen-storey tower with plain decor in a quiet street near Central Station and Chinatown is fronted by the charming nineteenth-century facade of the site's former hospital. A heated outdoor swimming pool and spa and terrace garden with BBQ area are further pluses. [7]

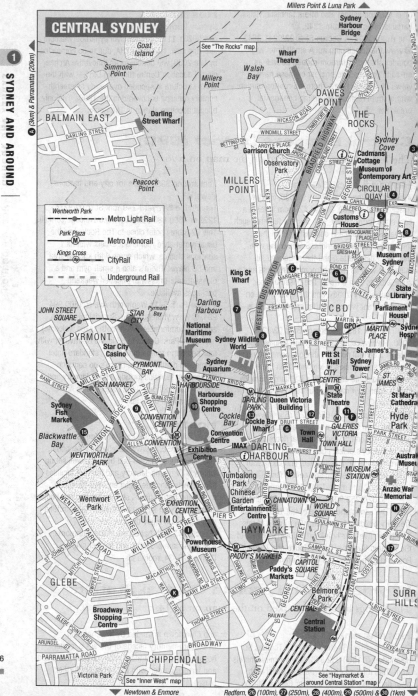

Millers Point & Luna Park ▲

SYDNEY AND AROUND

Goat Island

Simmons Point

(3km) & Parramatta (20km)

See "The Rocks" map

Wharf Theatre

Walsh Bay

Sydney Harbour Bridge

Millers Point

DAWES POINT

THE ROCKS

BALMAIN EAST

DARLING STREET

Darling Street Wharf

HICKSON ROAD

WINDMILL STREET

BETTINGTON

ARGYLE PLACE

Garrison Church

Observatory Park

MILLERS POINT

ARGYLE STREET

CUMBERLAND STREET

BRADFIELD HIGHWAY

LOWER FORT ST

GEORGE STREET

HICKSON ROAD

Sydney Cove

Cadmans Cottage

Museum of Contemporary Art

CIRCULAR QUAY

Peacock Point

HARRINGTON ST

KENT STREET

HICKSON ROAD

CAHILL

ALFRED STREET

Customs House

EXP

Wentworth Park

Metro Light Rail

Park Plaza

Metro Monorail

Kings Cross

CityRail

Underground Rail

Museum of Sydney

MACQUARIE PLACE

BRIDGE STREET

GRESHAM

BOND ST

SPRING

State Library

King St Wharf

MARGARET STREET

WYNYARD

ERSKINE ST

WESTERN DISTRIBUTOR

HUNTER ST

CBD

Parliament House

MARTIN PL

GPO

MARTIN PLACE

Sydney Hospi

JOHN STREET SQUARE

STAR CITY

Pyrmont Bay

Darling Harbour

PYRMONT

Star City Casino

PYRMONT BAY

National Maritime Museum

Sydney Wildlife World

Sydney Aquarium

CLARENCE STREET

KING STREET

SUSSEX STREET

YORK STREET

GEORGE STREET

Pitt St Mall

CITY CENTRE

St James's

Sydney Tower

ST JAMES RD

ST JAMES

BANK STREET

MILLER STREET

FISH MARKET

PYRMONT BRIDGE

HARBOURSIDE

Harbourside Shopping Centre

DARLING PARK

Queen Victoria Building

MARKET STREET

State Theatre

GALERIES VICTORIA

St Mary's Cathedra

Hyde Park

Sydney Fish Market

BUNN ST

MURRAY ST

CONVENTION CENTRE

Cockle Bay

Cockle Bay Wharf

Town Hall

DRUITT STREET

TOWN HALL

Blackwattle Bay

HARRIS ST

ALLEN ST

CONVENTION

Convention Centre

Exhibition Centre

IMAX

DARLING HARBOUR

BATHURST ST

Austra Muse

WENTWORTH PARK

WATTLE STREET

JONES STREET

BULWARA ROAD

DARLING DRIVE

Tumbalong Park

Chinese Garden

Entertainment Centre

MUSEUM STATION

LIVERPOOL ST

WILMOT ST

PITT STREET

Anzac War Memorial

Wentwort Park

WILLIAM HENRY STREET

EXHIBITION CENTRE

PIER ST

HAYMARKET

CHINATOWN

WORLD SQUARE

GOULBURN

ULTIMO

HARRIS STREET

Powerhouse Museum

PADDY'S MARKETS

CAPITOL SQUARE

Paddy's Markets

CAMPBELL ST

GOULBURN STREET

CASTLEREAGH STREET

SURR HILLS

GLEBE

ST JOHNS ROAD

MITCHELL STREET

COWPER STREET

MACARTHUR ST

JONES ST

ULTIMO ROAD

MARY ANN STREET

GEORGE STREET

PITT STREET

HAY ST

Belmore Park

ALBION STREET

Broadway Shopping Centre

GLEBE POINT ROAD

BAY STREET

WATTLE STREET

THOMAS STREET

RAILWAY SQ

Central Station

FOVEAUX STR

ARUNDEL ST

CENTRAL

LEE ST

REGENT ST

BROADWAY

CHIPPENDALE

PARRAMATTA ROAD

Victoria Park

CITY ROAD

See "Inner West" map

See "Haymarket & around Central Station" map

▼ Newtown & Enmore

Redfern, 26 (100m), 27 (250m), 28 (400m), 29 (500m) & 30 (1km) ▼

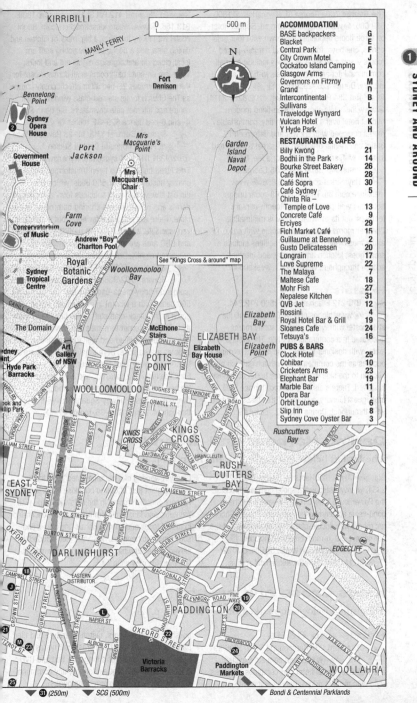

KIRRIBILLI

MANLY FERRY

0   500 m

N

Fort Denison

Bennelong Point

Sydney Opera House

Government House

Port Jackson

Mrs Macquarie's Point

Garden Island Naval Depot

Mrs Macquarie's Chair

Farm Cove

Conservatorium of Music

Andrew "Boy" Charlton Pool

Royal Botanic Gardens

Woolloomooloo Bay

See "Kings Cross & around" map

Sydney Tropical Centre

CAHILL EXP

The Domain

McElhone Stairs

Elizabeth Bay House

ELIZABETH BAY

Elizabeth Bay

Elizabeth Point

Sydney Art Gallery of NSW

POTTS POINT

Hyde Park Barracks

WOOLLOOMOOLOO

ook and illip Park

KINGS CROSS

KINGS CROSS

RUSH-CUTTERS BAY

Rushcutters Bay

EAST SYDNEY

CRAIGEND STREET

ILLIAM STREET

LIVERPOOL STREET

BURTON STREET

OXFORD STREET

DARLINGHURST

TAYLOR SQ

EASTERN DISTRIBUTOR

CAMPBELL STREET

NAPIER ST

PADDINGTON

OXFORD STREET

ALBION ST

Victoria Barracks

Paddington Markets

WOOLLAHRA

EDGECLIFF

❸ (250m)   SCG (500m)   Bondi & Centennial Parklands

ACCOMMODATION	
BASE backpackers	G
Blacket	E
Central Park	F
City Crown Motel	J
Cockatoo Island Camping	A
Glasgow Arms	I
Governors on Fitzroy	M
Grand	N
Intercontinental	D
Sullivans	B
Travelodge Wynyard	L
Vulcan Hotel	C
Y Hyde Park	K
Y Hyde Park	H

RESTAURANTS & CAFÉS	
Billy Kwong	21
Bodhi in the Park	14
Bourke Street Bakery	26
Café Mint	28
Café Sopra	30
Café Sydney	5
Chinta Ria – Temple of Love	13
Concrete Café	9
Erciyes	29
Fich Market Café	15
Guillaume at Bennelong	2
Gusto Delicatessen	20
Longrain	17
Love Supreme	22
The Malaya	7
Maltese Cafe	18
Mohr Fish	27
Nepalese Kitchen	31
QVB Jet	12
Rossini	4
Royal Hotel Bar & Grill	19
Sloanes Cafe	24
Tetsuya's	16

PUBS & BARS	
Clock Hotel	25
Cohibar	10
Cricketers Arms	23
Elephant Bar	19
Marble Bar	11
Opera Bar	1
Orbit Lounge	6
Slip Inn	8
Sydney Cove Oyster Bar	3

The George 700a George St, Haymarket ☏1800 679 606, ⓦwww.thegeorge.com.au. Budget hotel on three floors opposite Chinatown with four girls' dorms, one boys' four-share and bargain-priced rooms – some en suite. Facilities include a small communal kitchen/TV room, free wi-fi and a laundry. Dorms $26–29, rooms ❹–❺

Ibis Hotel 384 Pitt St, Haymarket ☏02/8267 3111, ⓦwww.ibishotels.com.au. Clean-lined modern budget hotel over 17 floors with tiny, comfortable rooms equipped with shower and flatscreen TV. Buffet continental breakfast, off-street parking and in-room wi-fi are all available for a fee. ❺–❻

Pensione Hotel 631–635 George St, Haymarket ☏1800 885 886, ⓦwww.pensione.com.au. This stylish 68-room budget hotel has well-preserved nineteenth-century features, but its overriding style is minimalist. Cheaper rooms are small, but come with cable TV and a mosaic-tiled bathroom. Facilities include a small guest kitchen and laundry, and internet access throughout. Weekday ❺, weekend ❻

Hostels

BIG 212 Elizabeth St ☏1800 212 244, ⓦwww.bighostel.com. Central, boutique-style hostel with well-equipped, sunny rooms decorated in a contemporary style. The ground-floor lobby, with designer lounges and internet terminals, doubles as the common area with a high-tech guest kitchen to the side where the free buffet breakfast is served. There's also a great roof-terrace BBQ area, guest laundry, a couple of free bikes and free wi-fi throughout. Dorms $28–32, rooms ❹

Nomads Westend 412 Pitt St, Haymarket ☏1800 013 186, ⓦwww.westendbackpackers.com. Bright hostel with funky furniture, a big, modern kitchen and dining area, and a pool table. The young staff are local, clued-up and organize nights out and tours. There are en-suite bathrooms in all dorms except for the one enormous 28-bed affair affectionately known as The Church for its stained-glass window. Travel centre and internet café downstairs. Big dorm $24, 4- and 6-bed dorms $29–31, rooms ❹

Sydney Central YHA 11–23 Rawson Place at Pitt St, opposite Central Station ☏02/9281 9111, Ⓔsydcentral@yhansw.org.au. This listed building has been transformed into a snazzy hostel with over 550 beds, which are almost always full, with spacious four- and six-bed dorms and private rooms sharing bathrooms or en suite. There are hotel-like facilities, but it still feels very sociable: a travel agency, rooftop pool, sauna and BBQ area are all on site, and movies are organized nightly. Dorms $35–40, rooms ❺

wake up! 509 Pitt St, opposite Railway Square ☏02/9288 7888, ⓦwww.wakeup.com.au. Trendy mega-backpackers' complex (over 500 beds) with a vibrant interior. Highly styled, right down to the black-clad staff in the huge foyer with its banks of internet terminals and travel/jobs desk. Rooms are light-filled and well furnished; only nine doubles are en suite. Dorms have lockers, there's a laundry on every floor and security is very good. Facilities include a café, bar and a huge modern kitchen, on a corner with gigantic windows overlooking busy Railway Square. Pay wi-fi throughout. Dorms $28–36, rooms ❹–❺

Darling Harbour and around

The listings below are marked on the **map** on p.96.

Glasgow Arms 527 Harris St, Ultimo ☏02/9211 2354, ⓦwww.glasgowarmshotel.com.au. Opposite the Powerhouse Museum, this pleasant pub has good-value accommodation upstairs. Polished-floor, a/c rooms with double-glazed windows keep out the bar noise. Light in-room breakfast included. ❻

Vulcan Hotel 500 Wattle St, Ultimo ☏02/9211 3283, ⓦwww.vulcanhotel.com.au.

Classy reworking of a heritage-listed 1894 former pub in a quiet part of Ultimo but close to Darling Harbour. Smallish rooms in the old wing (some with bathtubs) and larger modern rooms are all decorated in muted tones and come with a/c and fridge, and some have kitchenettes. Breakfast (not included) is served in the *Hummingbird* restaurant downstairs. Old wing ❻, new wing ❼

Kings Cross and around

The listings below are marked on the **map** on p.126.

Hotels and B&Bs

Altamont 207 Darlinghurst Rd ☏1800 991 110, ⓦwww.altamont.com.au. Excellent and well-sited small hotel that combines effortless style with modest prices. Rooms come with

polished concrete floors, tasteful furniture and tiled bathrooms, and some have small courtyards. Spacious loft rooms get a king-size bed and DVD player, plus there's a guest lounge, tiny communal kitchen, bar and spacious rooftop garden overlooking Kings Cross. Wi-fi throughout ($20 for your whole stay). [6]

Blue Sydney 6 Cowper Wharf Rd, Woolloomooloo [T] 02/9331 9000, [W] www.tajhotels.com/sydney. This luxury establishment has bags of smooth contemporary style and is located on the water's edge in a redeveloped wharf lined with fashionable cafés and restaurants. Rooms are of eclectic design and retain much of the building's original characteristics, with loft rooms boasting city views. There's also a day spa, indoor heated pool and gym. Rooms from around $300. [9]

Challis Lodge 21–23 Challis Ave, Potts Point [T] 02/9358 5422, [W] www.budgethotelssydney.com. A wonderful old mansion with polished timber floors throughout set on a quiet, tree-filled street a short walk from Woolloomooloo and Kings Cross. All rooms have TV, fridge and sink; there's a laundry but no kitchen. Rooms [3]–[5]

The Chelsea 49 Womerah Ave, Darlinghurst [T] 02/9380 5994, [W] www.chelsea.citysearch.com.au. Tasteful B&B with contemporary and French Provincial-style rooms in a leafy residential backstreet. Rooms come with fridge, kettle and TV and the price includes a light breakfast, served in the courtyard. [6]

🏃 **Highfield Private Hotel** 166 Victoria St, Kings Cross [T] 1800 285 534, [W] www.highfieldhotel.com. Very clean and secure 32-room budget hotel. The small, darkish rooms are well equipped and have access to a tiny kitchen/common room with TV, microwave, kettle and toaster. Three-bed dorms are also available. Dorms $25, rooms [3]

🏃 **Hotel 59** 59 Bayswater Rd, Kings Cross [T] 02/9360 5900, [W] www.hotel59.com.au. Small hotel (just nine rooms), reminiscent of a pleasant European pension, with a friendly owner and small and very clean, if slightly dated, a/c rooms. A cooked breakfast (included) is served in the downstairs café. One family room (sleeps four) has a small kitchenette and bathtub. Very popular, so book in advance. [5]–[6]

Kirketon 229 Darlinghurst Rd, Darlinghurst [T] 1800 332 920, [W] www.kirketon.com.au. Kings Cross CityRail. An excellent location, and high in the fashion stakes too, thanks to swish, meticulously designed yet understated interiors. Corridor flatscreen TVs showing Buster Keaton and Charlie Chaplin movies beckon you beyond the chic bar to the luxury beyond. Beautiful staff, slick service and a stack of great restaurants and cafés on the doorstep. [7]

Hostels

🏃 **Blue Parrot Backpackers** 87 Macleay St, Potts Point [T] 02/9356 4888, [W] www.blueparrot.com.au. A family-run hostel in a great position in the trendy (and quieter) part of Potts Point, this converted mansion is sunny, airy and brightly painted. Rooms consist of mostly six- and eight-bed dorms and a few shared-bath doubles. There's a common room with cable TV, gas fire and free internet and wi-fi, and the huge courtyard garden has wooden furniture and shady trees. Dorms $28–32, rooms [4]

🏃 **Eva's Backpackers** 6–8 Orwell St, Potts Point [T] 1800 802 517, [W] www.evasbackpackers.com.au. It's worth the extra couple of dollars to stay at this excellent, family-run hostel away from Darlinghurst Rd's clamour. Rooms and common areas are colourful and clean and there's a peaceful rooftop garden with table umbrellas, greenery, BBQ area and fantastic views over The Domain. The guest kitchen/dining room, positioned at street level, feels like a café and has a sociable feel, though this isn't a "party" hostel. Free internet and wi-fi throughout. Dorms $30–36, shared-bath rooms [4]

The Original Backpackers Lodge 160–162 Victoria St, Kings Cross [T] 1800 807 130, [W] www.originalbackpackers.com.au. In a spacious Victorian mansion with ornate ceilings, this upscale hostel tends to have a quieter clientele. All rooms have a TV and fridge and there are security lockers and a laundry available at the 24hr reception. A new wing has small but stylish en-suite doubles with TV/DVD (library of free DVDs available). Dorms $28, rooms [4]

🏃 **The Wood Duck Inn** 49 William St, East Sydney [T] 1800 110 025, [W] www.woodduckinn.com.au. Fun hostel run by two switched-on brothers. Don't be put off by the dingy concrete steps: they emerge onto a sunny rooftop, the nerve centre of the hostel, with fantastic park and city views. Spacious, clean dorms (mostly four- and six-bed) have polished floors, fans, good mattresses and lockers under the bunks. Lots of activities, including free lifts to the beach. Dorms $24.

Paddington and Surry Hills

The listings below are marked on the **map** on p.96.

City Crown Motel 289 Crown St, Surry Hills [T] 1800 358 666, [W] www.citycrownmotel.com.au. Standard motel in a great location. The smart a/c units come with free in-house movies and the added bonus of a large balcony looking onto Crown St. Limited parking. [5]

Governors on Fitzroy 64 Fitzroy St, Surry Hills [T] 02/9331 4652, [W] www.governors.com.au. Long-established gay B&B in a restored Victorian terrace just a few blocks from Oxford St. The five rooms share two bathrooms but have their own sinks. A full cooked breakfast (included) is served in the dining room or the garden courtyard. Guests – mostly men – can also meet and mingle in the spa. [6]

Sullivans 21 Oxford St, Paddington [T] 02/9361 0211, [W] www.sullivans.com.au. Medium-sized hotel in a trendy location, run by staff tuned into the local scene (free guided walking tour of Paddington included). Comfortable, modern en-suite rooms with TV and telephones. There's free (but limited) parking, as well as a garden courtyard and swimming pool, in-house movies, free internet, free guest bicycles, fitness room and laundry. The on-site café is open for a huge and yummy breakfast. [7]

Inner west: Glebe and Newtown

The listings below are marked on the **map** on p.132.

Hotels and B&Bs

Australian Sunrise Lodge 485 King St, Newtown [T] 02/9550 4999, [W] www.australiansunriselodge.com. Inexpensive and well-managed small private hotel well positioned for King St action but with good security. Rooms, some en suite, come with TV and fridge. Ground-floor rooms are darker, smaller and cheaper – better options are the sunny rooms on the top two floors, all with cute balconies. En-suite family rooms also available. [4]–[5]

Rooftop Travellers Lodge 146 Glebe Point Rd, Glebe [T] 02/9660 7711, [W] http://users.tpg.com.au/glebe146. This excellent-value budget retreat for short and long stays is right in the heart of Glebe and has a large kitchen and fabulous city views from the rooftop. Most rooms have a double and a single bed, a/c, PC and free broadband. Parking included. [5]

Tricketts Bed and Breakfast 270 Glebe Point Rd, Glebe [T] 02/9552 1141, [W] www.tricketts.com.au. Luxury B&B in an 1880s mansion. Rooms – en suite – are furnished with antiques and Persian rugs, and the lounge, complete with a billiard table and leather armchairs, was originally a small ballroom. Delicious, generous and sociable breakfast. [7]–[8]

Hostels

Billabong Gardens 5–22 Egan St, off King St, Newtown [T] 02/9550 3236, [W] www.billabonggardens.com.au. In a quiet street but close to the action, this long-running hostel is arranged around a peaceful inner courtyard with swimming pool, and has excellent communal facilities. Clean dorms (four- to six-bed; mostly en suite), as well as private rooms and motel-style en suites. Daily charge for the undercover car park. Dorms $25–27, rooms [3]–[4]

Glebe Village Backpackers 256 Glebe Point Rd, Glebe [T] 02/9660 8133 or 1800 801 983, [W] www.glebevillage.com. Three large old houses with a mellow, sociable atmosphere – the laid-back guests socialize in the streetside fairy-lit garden. Staffed by young locals who know what's going on around town. Private rooms plus four-, six-, ten- or twelve-bed dorms. Dorms $28–30, rooms [4]

North Shore

Cremorne Point Manor 6 Cremorne Rd, Cremorne Point [T] 02/9953 7899, [W] www.cremornepointmanor.com.au. Huge, restored Federation-style villa. Nearly all rooms are en suite, except for a few small singles (from $87), which have their own toilet and sink, and all have TV and fridge; some pricier rooms have harbour views. Communal kitchen and laundry. Ferry to Cremorne Point Wharf. Light breakfast included. [7]–[9]

Elite Private Hotel 133 Carabella St, Kirribilli [T] 02/9929 6365, [W] www.elitehotel.com.au. Great-value, bright place offering good rooms, most with shared bathrooms, with sink, TV, fridge and kettle; some more expensive ones have a harbour view. Small, communal cooking facility and garden courtyard. Only minutes by ferry from the city (to Kirribilli Wharf) and near Milsons Point train station. Cheaper weekly rates. [3]–[4]

Glenferrie Lodge 12A Carabella St, Kirribilli [T] 02/9955 1685, [W] www.glenferrielodge.com. Another made-over Kirribilli mansion: clean, light and secure with 24hr reception. Three-bed dorms and single, double or family rooms (all with shared bathroom). Some pricier rooms have their own balcony and harbour glimpses but guests can also hang out in the garden and on the guest

verandas. Ferry to Kirribilli Wharf or train to Milsons Point. Dorms $45, rooms ❺–❻ including breakfast.

Bondi Beach

Bondi Beachouse YHA 63 Fletcher St ☎02/9365 2088, ✉bondi@bondibeachouse.com.au. Actually nearer to peaceful Tamarama Beach than lively Bondi but still close enough to the action, this well-run and fully equipped hostel has a sunny internal courtyard with BBQ, and a rooftop deck with fabulous ocean views. Spacious, high-ceilinged dorms (four-, six- and eight-bed, with lockers) and rooms – some en suite, with fridges and kettles – all have ceiling fans. Free surfboards and body-boards. Book well ahead to get a beach-view room. Dorms $32, rooms ❹

Bondi Serviced Apartments 212 Bondi Rd ☎1300 364 200, ⓦwww.bondi-serviced -apartments.com.au. Good-value serviced motel studio apartments halfway between Bondi Junction and Bondi Beach and on bus routes. A/c units all have clean, modern furniture, TV, telephone, kitchen

and a balcony with sea view. The rooftop pool has far-off ocean views. Parking is included and there are discounts for weekly stays. ❺

Noah's Backpackers 2 Campbell Parade ☎1800 226 662, ⓦwww.noahsbondibeach.com. Huge hostel right opposite the beach with fantastic ocean views from the rooftop deck and BBQ area. Clean and well run with beach-view rooms, dorms (four-, six- and eight-bed), but with cramped bathrooms. On-site bar with bargain meals, TV room and pool table. Excellent security. Dorms $24–27, rooms ❸

Ravesi's Corner of Campbell Parade and Hall St ☎02/9365 4422, ⓦwww.ravooio.com.au. The first-floor restaurant and most of the 12 rooms at this boutique hotel have glorious ocean views. Interiors are totally modern with minimalist decor and some have French windows opening onto small balconies. ❼, beachside ❾

Coogee

Coogee Bay Boutique Hotel 9 Vicar St ☎02/9665 0000, ⓦwww.coogeebayhotel.com.au. New hotel attached to the rear of the older, sprawling Coogee Bay Hotel. Rooms – all with balconies, half with ocean views – look like something out of *Vogue Interiors*, with luxurious touches such as marble floors in the bathrooms. Cheaper "heritage wing" rooms are noisy at weekends but just as stylish. Heritage ❻, ocean view ❾

Dive 234 Arden St ☎02/9665 5538, ⓦwww.thedivehotel.com. A wonderful 16-room hotel opposite the beach with interiors that combine clean, modern lines with original Art Nouveau tiling and high, decorative-plaster ceilings. Two larger rooms at the front have splendid ocean views; one at the back has its own balcony and all

have funky little bathrooms, CD players, cable TV, queen-size beds and a handy kitchenette and breakfast included. Free internet access and wi-fi. Standard ❼, ocean view ❾

Wizard of Oz Backpackers 172 Coogee Bay Rd ☎02/9315 7876, ⓦwww.wizardofoz.com.au. Top-class hostel run by a friendly local couple in a big and beautiful Californian-style house with a huge veranda and polished wooden floors. Spacious, vibrantly painted dorms with ceiling fans, and some well-set-up doubles. TV/video room, dining area, modern kitchen, good showers and pleasant backyard with BBQ. Bus #372 from Central City-Rail & #373 & #374 from Circular Quay CityRail. Dorms $30.

Manly and the northern beaches

Avalon Beach Backpackers 59 Avalon Parade, Avalon ☎02/9918 9709, ⓦwww.avalonbeach .com.au. This hostel, at one of Sydney's best – and most beautiful – surf beaches, has seen better days, but its location and atmosphere still make it worth considering, especially if you're here to surf, as many of the longer-stay guests are. Dorms (four- and six-bed) and rooms have storage area and fans. Boat trips and surfboard rental can be

organized. Excellent local work contacts and weekly rates available. Dorms $25, rooms ❸

Manly Backpackers Beachside 28 Raglan St, Manly ☎02/9977 3411, ⓦwww .manlybackpackers.com.au. This fun and lively hostel in a purpose-built building one block from the surf attracts long-staying surfers. This place has free internet access, a spacious, well-equipped kitchen and outside terrace with BBQ and organizes nightly events. Four- and six-bed dorms, and doubles all share bathroom; the best dorm is at the front with a balcony. Dorms $35, rooms [5]

Manly Pacific Sydney 55 North Steyne, Manly ☎02/9977 7666, [W]www.accorhotels.com. Beach-front, multistorey, four-star hotel with 24hr reception, room service, spa, sauna, gym and heated rooftop pool. You pay for it all, and more for an ocean view, which is spectacular. [8], sea view [9]

Palm Beach Bed and Breakfast 122 Pacific Palm Rd, Palm Beach ☎02/9974 1608, [W]www.palmbeachbandb.com.au. Incredibly friendly and slightly quirky B&B (antique cars are scattered about the front lawn), perched on a hilltop on one of Sydney's most sought-after streets. All rooms have balconies and views of either Pittwater or the Pacific Ocean, and the emphasis is on relaxing and unwinding. The four simply furnished rooms have either en suite or shared bathroom. [7]

Periwinkle Guesthouse 18–19 East Esplanade ☎02/9977 4668, [W]www.periwinkle.citysearch.com.au. Pleasant 18-room B&B in a charming, restored 1895 villa on Manly Cove. Close to the ferry, shops and harbour and a perfect base for swimming, sailing or just watching the lorikeets. Rooms have fridges and fans; several larger and family rooms are available. There's also a communal kitchen, laundry, courtyard with BBQ and car park. Breakfast included. [6]–[7]

Sydney Beachouse YHA 4 Collaroy St, Collaroy Beach ☎02/9981 1177, [W]www.sydneybeachouse.com.au. Relaxed, purpose-built YHA across the road from the beach, with heated outdoor pool, sun deck, BBQs, open fireplaces, video lounge and games and pool rooms. Too far out for your entire Sydney stay (it's a 45min bus ride from the city), it's a good base for kicking back on the sand or exploring the northern beaches; bikes are free for guests, and kayaking and sailing can be organized. Bus #L90 from Railway Square by Central Station. Dorms $30, rooms [4]–[5]

Q Station Retreat North Head, Manly ☎02/9976 6220, [W]www.qstation.com.au. The stylishly modernized rooms in this former quarantine station enjoy a wonderfully peaceful setting, with harbour views from most rooms, best seen from wicker chairs stationed on the broad verandas. Rates from $290. [9]

Cronulla Beach

Cronulla Beach YHA 40 Kingsway, Cronulla ☎02/9527 7772, [W]www.cronullabeachyha.com. No-fuss hostel in this unpretentious, surf-oriented suburb, two minutes from the sand and even less to the shops and restaurants of Cronulla Mall. Also well situated for day-trips to the Royal National Park. Dorms $30–32, rooms [4]

The City

Port Jackson carves Sydney in two halves, linked by the Harbour Bridge and Harbour Tunnel. The **South Shore** is the hub of activity, and it's here that you'll find the **city centre** and most of the things to see and do. Many of the classic images of Sydney are within sight of **Circular Quay**, making this busy waterfront area on Sydney Cove a logical – and pleasurable – point to start discovering the city, with the **Sydney Opera House** and the expanse of the Royal Botanic Gardens to the east of Sydney Cove and the historic area of **The Rocks** to the west. By contrast, gleaming, slightly tawdry **Darling Harbour**, at the centre's western edge, is a shiny redeveloped tourist and entertainment area.

Circular Quay

At the southern end of Sydney Cove, **Circular Quay** is the launching pad for harbour and river ferries and sightseeing boats, the terminal for buses from the eastern and southern suburbs, and a major suburban train station to boot (some of the most fantastic views of the harbour can be seen from the above-ground station platforms). Circular Quay itself is always bustling with commuters during the week, and with people simply out to enjoy themselves at the weekend. Restaurants, cafés and fast-food outlets line the Quay, buskers entertain the crowds, and vendors of newspapers and trinkets add to the general

Harbour cruises

Sydney offers a wide choice of harbour cruises, almost all of them leaving from Wharf 6, Circular Quay, and the rest from Darling Harbour. While many offer a good insight into the harbour and an intimate experience of its bays and coves, the altogether much cheaper ordinary ferry rides, enjoyable cruises in themselves, are worth experiencing first. The best of these is the thirty-minute ride to Manly, but there's a ferry going somewhere worth checking out at almost any time of the day.

If you want to splash out, take a **water-taxi ride** – Circular Quay to Watsons Bay, for example, costs $110 for up to four passengers (max 20; extra $11 per person after the first four). Pick-ups are available from any wharf if booked in advance (try Water Taxis Combined on ☎02/9555 8888, ⓦwww.watertaxis.com.au). Water Taxis Combined also offers half-hour ($250) and hour-long tours ($360) in a sleek white water taxi (holds up to 20, but 15 is more comfortable) – the route is negotiable.

The Australian Travel Specialists (ATS) at Jetty 6, Circular Quay and the Harbour-side Shopping Centre at Darling Harbour (☎02/9211 3192, ⓦwww.atstravel.com.au) book all **cruises**; the majority are offered by Captain Cook Cruises (☎02/9206 1122, ⓦwww.captaincook.com.au) and Matilda (☎02/9264 7377, ⓦwww.matilda.com.au), which have now combined forces (while retaining separate titles), although those offered by the State Transit Authority (STA) – Heritage Cruises (☎02/9246 8363, ⓦwww.sydneyferries.nsw.gov.au) – are a little cheaper. The Captain Cook "Middle Harbour Coffee Cruise" (10am and 2.15pm; 2hr; $49) is probably the most popular and affordable of the private cruises, allowing you to venture into quaint little bays and coves (with commentary on local history and ecology). If you're willing to splurge, an even more pleasurable introduction to the Harbour is provided by the Captain Cook "2 Night Weekend Escape Cruise" ($423). Captain Cook Cruises also offer cheaper, shorter "highlight" tours on smaller sailing vessels, as well as breakfast, lunch, dinner and cocktail cruises.

There are also a number of more romantic sailing options. Sydney Harbour Tall Ships (☎1300 664 410, ⓦwww.sydneytallships.com.au) operate the *Svanen*, a beautiful, three-masted Danish ship, built in 1922, which moors at Campbells Cove. Two hour "Lunch" and "Twilight" cruises (both $79) sail past iconic harbour sights while guests devour gourmet seafood BBQ offerings. Sydney's oldest sailing ship, the *James Craig*, an 1874 three-masted iron barque, is part of the Sydney Heritage Fleet based at Wharf 7, Pirrama Rd, Pyrmont, near Star City Casino, and does six-hour cruises on Saturdays and Sundays (9.30am–4pm; ☎02/9298 3888, ⓦwww.shf.org.au; $205; over-12s only; refreshments and lunch provided). Sydney by Sail (☎02/9280 1110, ⓦwww.sydneybysail.com) offers the popular small-group, three-hour Port Jackson Explorer cruise (daily at 1pm; $150) on board a luxury Beneteau yacht, departing from the National Maritime Museum at Darling Harbour (free entry to the museum included). There are also a number of private **boats to hire** for various purposes (visit ⓦwww.sydneyharbourescapes .com.au).

Some **alternatives** offer more thrills (but noise pollution for the locals): Ocean Extreme (☎1300 887 373, ⓦwww.oceanextreme.com.au) offers a hair-raising, small-group (maximum ten) "Extreme Blast" on an RIB (Rigid Inflatable Boat). There's "Rush Hour" ($80; 1hr), a trip out to the heads and back; the "Bondi Bash" ($95; 1hr 30min), a trip beyond the heads to Bondi Beach; and "Palm Beach Pursuit" ($125; 2hr), to Palm Beach and back (times based on demand). At speeds of more than 100kph you will regularly find yourself airborne. Harbour Jet (☎1300 887 373, ⓦwww.harbourjet.com) runs the "Jet Blast" ($65; 35min); the "Sydney Harbour Adventure" ($80; 50min); and the "Middle Harbour Adventure" ($95; 2hr) on a boat that roars along at 75kph, executing spins, power breaks and fishtails.

hubbub. The sun reflecting on the water and its heave and splash as the ferries come and go make for a dreamy setting – best appreciated over an expensive beer at a waterfront bar. The inscribed bronze pavement-plaques of **Writers' Walk** beneath your feet as you stroll around the Circular Quay waterfront provide an introduction to the Australian literary canon. There are short biographies of writers ranging from Miles Franklin, author of *My Brilliant Career*, through Booker Prize-winner Peter Carey and Nobel Prize-awardee Patrick White, to the feminist Germaine Greer, and quotable quotes on what it means to be Australian. Notable literati who've visited Australia – including Joseph Conrad, Charles Darwin and Mark Twain – also feature.

Having dallied, read, and taken in the views, you could then embark on a sightseeing **cruise** or enjoy a ferry ride on the harbour (see box, p.103). Staying on dry land, you're only a short walk from most of the city-centre sights, along part of a continuous foreshore walkway beginning under the Harbour Bridge and passing through the historic area of Sydney's first settlement The Rocks, then extending beyond the Opera House to the Royal Botanic Gardens.

Besides ferries, Circular Quay still acts as a passenger terminal for ocean liners; head north past the Museum of Contemporary Art to Circular Quay West. It's a long time since the crowds waved their hankies regularly from the **Overseas Passenger Terminal**, looking for all the world like the deck of a ship itself, but you may still see an ocean liner docked here; even if there's no ship, take the escalator and the flight of stairs up for excellent views of the harbour. The rest of the recently redeveloped terminal is now given over to trendy and expensive restaurants and bars.

Leading up to the Opera House is the once-controversial **Opera Quays** development, which runs the length of **East Circular Quay**. Since its opening, locals and tourists alike have flocked to promenade along the pleasant colonnaded lower level with its outdoor cafés, bars and bistros, upmarket shops and Dendy Cinema, all looking out to sublime harbour views. The distasteful apartment building above, dubbed "The Toaster" by locals and described by Robert Hughes, the famous expat Australian art critic and historian, as "that dull, brash, intrusive apartment block which now obscures the Opera House from three directions", caused massive protests, but went up anyway, opening in 1999.

Customs House

The railway and the ugly Cahill Expressway block views to the city from Circular Quay, cutting it off from Alfred Street immediately opposite, with its architectural gem, the sandstone and granite **Customs House**. First constructed in 1845, it was redesigned in 1885 by the colonial architect James Barnet to give it its current Classical Revival-style facade; its interior was revamped in 2005. On the ground floor a **City Exhibition Space** keeps pace with the development of Sydney with a detailed 1:500 scale model of the city set into the floor under glass and accompanied by a multimedia presentation. Sydney's premier **public library** (Mon–Fri 10am–7pm, Sat 11am–4pm, closed public holidays) is housed on the first three floors, whilst the top floor is the only reminder of the building's previous incarnation, a pricey contemporary brasserie, *Cafe Sydney* (see p.151), with postcard harbour views. In front of the building a newly designed forecourt space incorporates seating for cafés and bars that, on weekday evenings, buzz with a twilight post-work euphoria.

Museum of Contemporary Art (MCA)

The **Museum of Contemporary Art** (**MCA**; daily 10am–5pm; free; free tours Mon–Fri 11am & 1pm, Sat & Sun noon & 1.30pm; ☎02/9252 2400 for details of special exhibitions and events; ⓦ www.mca.com.au), on the western side of Circular Quay with another entrance at 140 George Street, was developed out of a bequest by the art collector John Power in the 1940s to Sydney University to purchase international contemporary art. The growing collection finally found a permanent home in 1991 in the former Maritime Services Building, provided for peppercorn rent by the State Government. The striking Deco-style 1950s building is now dedicated to international twentieth-century art, with an eclectic approach encompassing lithographs, sculpture, film, video, drawings, paintings and Aboriginal art, shown in themed temporary exhibitions. The museum's superbly sited, if expensive, café has outdoor tables overlooking the waterfront and Opera House.

The Sydney Opera House

The **Sydney Opera House**, such an icon of Australiana that it almost seems kitsch, is just a short stroll from Circular Quay, by the water's edge on **Bennelong Point**. It's best seen in profile, when its high white roofs, at the same time evocative of full sails and white shells, give the building an almost ethereal quality. Some say the inspiration for the distinctive design came from the simple peeling of an orange into segments, though perhaps Danish architect **Jørn Utzon**'s childhood as the son of a yacht designer had something to do with their sail-like shape – he certainly envisaged a building that would appear to "float" on water. Despite its familiarity, or perhaps precisely because you already feel you know it so well, it's quite breathtaking at first sight. Close up, you can see that the shimmering effect is created by thousands of white tiles.

The feat of structural engineering required to bring to life Utzon's "sculpture", which he compared to a Gothic church and a Mayan temple, made the final price tag $102 million, ten times the original estimate. Now almost universally loved and admired, it's hard to believe quite how controversial a project this was during its long haul from plan – as a result of an international competition in the late 1950s – to completion in 1973. For sixteen years construction was plagued by quarrels and scandal, so much so that Utzon, who won the competition in 1957, was forced to resign in 1966. Some put it less kindly and say he was hounded out of the country by politicians – the newly elected Askin government disagreeing over his plans for the completion of the interior – and xenophobic local architects. Seven years and three Australian architects later the interior, which at completion never matched Utzon's vision, was finished: the focal Concert Hall, for instance, was designed by **Peter Hall** and his team.

Utzon did have a final say, however: in 1999, he was appointed as a design consultant to prepare a Statement of Design Principles for the building, which has become a permanent reference for its conservation and development. The Reception Hall has been refurbished to Utzon's specifications and was renamed the **Utzon Room** in 2004. He also remodelled the western side of the structure, with a colonnade and nine new glass openings, giving previously cement-walled theatre foyers a view of the harbour. Utzon died in November 2008. He had been working, at this time, with his business-partner and son, Jan, and Sydney-based architect Richard Johnson, on plans to renovate the much-maligned Opera Theatre.

"Opera House" is actually a misnomer: it's really a performing-arts centre, one of the busiest in the world, with five performance venues inside its shells, plus restaurants, cafés and bars, and a stash of upmarket souvenir shops on the lower concourse. The building's initial impetus, in fact, was as a home for the Sydney Symphony Orchestra, and it was designed with the huge **Concert Hall**, seating

2690, as the focal point; the smaller **Opera Theatre** (1547 seats) is used as the Sydney performance base for Opera Australia (seasons June–Nov & Feb–March) and the Australian Ballet (mid-March to May & Nov–Dec). There are three theatrical venues: the **Drama Theatre**, used primarily by the Sydney Theatre Company; The Playhouse, used by travelling performers; and the more intimate **The Studio**. There's plenty of action outside the Opera House, too, with the use of the Mayan temple-inspired **Forecourt** and Monumental Steps as an amphitheatre for free and ticketed concerts – rock, jazz and classical, with a capacity for around five thousand people. Sunday is also a lively day on the forecourt, when the **Tarpeian Markets** (10am–4pm), with an emphasis on Australian crafts, are held.

If you're not content with gazing at the outside and can't attend a performance, **guided tours** are available (book on ☏02/9250 7250 or via the website, Ⓦwww.sydneyoperahouse.com). "Essential" tours give an overview of the site, looking at the public areas, discussing the unique architecture and visiting one of the venues (daily 9am–5pm; 1hr; $35); "Backstage" tours include access to the scenery and docks, rehearsal rooms, technical areas, and breakfast in the Greenroom (daily 7am; 2hr; $150). These tours also visit the foyer of The Playhouse where two original Utzon models of the Opera House are displayed, alongside a series of small oil paintings depicting the life of **Bennelong**, the Iora tribesman who was initially kidnapped as little more than an Aboriginal "specimen" but later became a much-loved friend of Governor Arthur Phillip; Phillip later built a hut for him on what is now the site of the Opera House.

The best way to appreciate the Opera House, of course, is to attend an evening **performance**: the building is particularly stunning when floodlit and, once you're inside, the huge windows come into their own as the dark harbour waters reflect a shimmering night-time city – interval drinks certainly aren't like this anywhere else in the world. You could choose to **eat** at what is considered to be one of Sydney's best restaurants, *Guillaume at Bennelong* (see p.152) overlooking the city skyline, or take a **drink** at the spectacularly sited *Opera Bar* on the lower

▲ The Opera Bar, outside Sydney Opera House

concourse with outside tables overlooking the Harbour Bridge and an affordable all-day menu (see p.161), plus there's a sidewalk café, a bistro and several theatre bars. Good-value **packages**, which include tours, meals, dinner cruises, drinks and performances, can be purchased at the Opera House or via the website.

The Harbour Bridge

The charismatic **Harbour Bridge**, northeast of Circular Quay, has straddled the channel dividing North and South Sydney since 1932; today, it makes the view from Circular Quay complete. The largest arch bridge in the world when it was built, its construction costs weren't paid off until 1988. There's still a toll ($3) to drive across, payable only when heading south; you can walk or cycle it for free. Pedestrians should head up the steps to the bridge from Cumberland Street, opposite the *Glenmore Hotel* in The Rocks, and walk along the eastern side for fabulous views of the harbour and Opera House (cyclists keep to the western side).

The bridge demands full-time maintenance, and is protected from rust by continuous painting in trademark steel-grey. Comedian Paul Hogan, of *Crocodile Dundee* fame, worked as a rigger on "the coathanger" before being rescued by a *New Faces* talent quest in the 1970s. To check out Hogan's vista, you can follow a rigger's route and climb the bridge with **Bridge Climb**, who take specially equipped groups (maximum 12) to the top of the bridge from sunrise until after dark (twilight climbs $249; Mon–Fri day climbs $189; Mon–Sun night climbs $179; Sat & Sun day climbs $199; prices rise steeply in the two weeks following Christmas; children must be aged 10 or over; booking advised, particularly for weekends, on ℡02/8274 7777, ⓦwww.bridgeclimb.com). There are now two bridge climbs available: the original "Bridge Climb" over the arch of the bridge to its summit, and the newer "Discovery Climb", a journey through the interior of the arch, offering greater insight into the nuts and bolts of the bridge's engineering, views of Sydney through the bridge's functional though decorative framework, and the same impressive views at the summit. Though both take three and a half hours, only two hours is spent on the bridge, gradually ascending and pausing while the guide points out landmarks and offers interesting background snippets. The hour spent checking in and getting kitted up at the "Base" at 5 Cumberland St, The Rocks, and the grey *Star Trek*-style suits designed to blend in with the bridge, make you feel as if you're preparing to go into outer space. It's not as scary as it looks – harnessed into a cable system, there's no way you can fall off. So that nothing can be dropped onto cars or people below, cameras cannot be taken on the walk (only your glasses are allowed, attached by special cords), limiting scope for one of the world's greatest photo opportunities. Though one group photo on top of the bridge is included in the climb price, the jolly strangers, arms akimbo, crowd out the background. To get a good shot showing yourself with the splendours of the harbour behind, taken by the guide, you'll need to fork out another $20 ($10 for each additional shot after that).

If you can't stomach (or afford) the climb, there's a **lookout point** (daily 10am–5pm; $9.50; ⓦwww.pylonlookout.com.au; 5min walk from Cumberland St, then 200 steps) actually inside the bridge's southeastern pylon where, as well as gazing out across the harbour, you can study a photo exhibition on the bridge's history.

The Rocks

The Rocks, immediately beneath the bridge, is the heart of historic Sydney. On this rocky outcrop between Sydney Cove and Walsh Bay, Captain Arthur

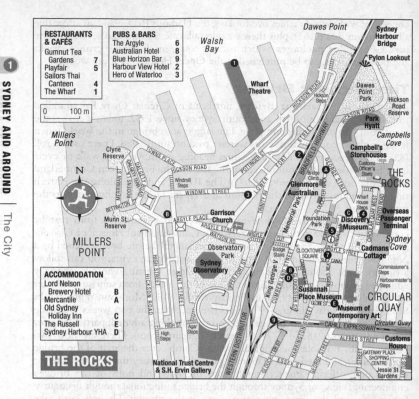

RESTAURANTS & CAFÉS
Gumnut Tea
Gardens 7
Playfair 5
Sailors Thai
Canteen 4
The Wharf 1

PUBS & BARS
The Argyle 6
Australian Hotel 8
Blue Horizon Bar 9
Harbour View Hotel 2
Hero of Waterloo 3

0   100 m

N

MILLERS POINT

ACCOMMODATION
Lord Nelson
Brewery Hotel   B
Mercantile   A
Old Sydney
Holiday Inn   C
The Russell   E
Sydney Harbour YHA   D

THE ROCKS

Phillip proclaimed the establishment of Sydney Town in 1788, the first permanent European settlement in Australia. Within decades, the area had degenerated into little more than a slum of dingy dwellings, narrow alleys and dubious taverns and brothels. In the 1830s and 1840s, merchants began building fine stone warehouses here, but as the focus for Sydney's shipping industry moved from Circular Quay, the area fell into decline. By the 1870s and 1880s, the notorious Rocks "pushes", gangs of "larrikins" (louts), mugged passers-by and brawled with each other: the narrow street named **Suez Canal** was a favourite place to hide in wait. Some say the name is a shortening of Sewers' Canal, and indeed the area was so filthy that whole streetfronts had to be torn down in 1900 to contain an outbreak of the bubonic plague. It remained a run-down, depressed and depressing quarter until the 1970s, when there were plans to raze the historic cottages, terraces and warehouses to make way for office towers. However, due to the foresight of a radical building-workers' union which opposed the demolition, the restored and renovated **historic quarter** is now one of Sydney's major tourist attractions and, despite a passing resemblance to a historic theme park, it's worth exploring. It's also the best place for souvenir shopping, especially at weekends when The Rocks Market (10am–5pm) takes over the northern end of George and Playfair streets.

There are times, though, when the old atmosphere still seems to prevail: Friday and Saturday nights in The Rocks can be thoroughly drunken, and New Year's Eve is also riotously celebrated here, to the backdrop of fireworks over the harbour. The best time to come for a drink is Sunday afternoon, when many of the pubs here offer live jazz or folk music.

Information, tours and transport
The Rocks Discovery Museum (daily 10am–5pm; free) is a good starting point and offers background information and displays on its rich history, from the lives of the original Cadigal inhabitants to the 1970s protests that helped preserve the area from major redevelopment. The small museum is tucked away down Kendall Lane in a restored 1850s sandstone warehouse facing the Rocks Centre, a busy arcade of boutiques and cafés. Above the arcade, on the corner of Argyle and Playfair streets, is the **Sydney Visitor Centre**, which supplies tourist information about The Rocks, Sydney and New South Wales (daily 9.30am–5.30pm; ☎1800 067 676). Further down Playfair Street, at number 23, **The Rocks Walking Tours** provide excellent guided tours of the area (Mon–Fri 10.30am, 12.30pm & 2.30pm; Jan 10.30am & 2.30pm only; Sat & Sun 11.30am & 2pm; $30; bookings ☎02/9247 6678, ⓦwww.rockswalkingtours.com.au).

The corner of Argyle and Kent streets, Millers Point, is a terminus for several useful **bus routes**; buses #431–434 go along George Street to Railway Square and from there to various locations including Glebe and Balmain, while #339 goes to the eastern beaches suburb of Clovelly via George Street in the city and Surry Hills.

Argyle Street and around
Exploring the narrow alleys and streets hewn out of the original rocky spur, which involves climbing and descending several stairs and cuts to different levels, is the area's chief delight. From Argyle Street, wander north up (and in between) Playfair Street, Kendall Lane, and George Street, then nip down cobbled pedestrian back alleys to the south towards the once sordid Suez Canal and Nurses Walk or take coffee or lunch in the charming old-world courtyards of *La Renaissance* or *Gumnut Tea Gardens* (see p.152). Leafy Argyle Street hosts **The Rocks Farmers Market** on Fridays (10am–3pm) and Saturdays (9am–3pm), where you can taste and buy delectable local produce, including bread, meat, cheeses, chutneys and other such tasty morsels.

From Cadmans Cottage to Dawes Point Park
Across George Street, next to the impressive Art Deco–style Museum of Contemporary Art in a small tree-filled reserve, is **Cadmans Cottage** (Mon–Fri 9.30am–4.30pm, Sat & Sun 10am–4.30pm; free), the oldest private house still standing in Sydney, built in 1816 for John Cadman, ex-convict and Government coxswain. You can poke around a few rooms to see how the original settlers lived, and browse in the **National Parks and Wildlife Service** bookshop and information centre (same hours; ☎02/9247 5033, ⓦwww.environment.nsw.gov.au/nationalparks), providing information about the Sydney Harbour National Park and taking bookings for trips to Fort Denison and other harbour islands that are part of the park.

From the cottage, head north along the waterfront walkway past the Overseas Passenger Terminal to **Campbells Cove**, where the beautifully restored 1830s **Campbells Storehouses**, once part of the private wharf of the merchant Robert Campbell, now house a shopping and eating complex. A replica of Captain Bligh's ship, the *Bounty*, is moored here between cruises, while a luxury hotel, the *Park Hyatt*, overlooks the whole area. The walkway continues adjacent to Hickson Road to **Dawes Point Park**, which sits beneath the Harbour

Bridge offering fantastic views, particularly at sunset. Looking out past the Opera House, you can see **Fort Denison** on a small island in the harbour: "Pinchgut", as the island is still known, was originally used as a special prison for the tough nuts the penal colony couldn't crack. During the Crimean Wars in the mid-nineteenth century, however, old fears of a Russian invasion were rekindled and the fort was built as part of a defence ring around the harbour.

Tours from Circular Quay are booked through, and leave from, Cadmans Cottage (daily 11.45am; 3hr 30min; $22; brunch tours with a cooked meal in the fort's café included, Sat & Sun 9am; 3hr; $47; ☎02/9247 5033).

Walsh Bay, Millers Point and Observatory Park

On the west side of Dawes Point Park, Hickson Road passes several luxurious old wharves, now renovated as luxury housing, and the **Wharf Theatre** (Pier 4/5), home to the Sydney Theatre Company and the Sydney Dance Company. From the restaurant and its bar (see p.168) you can revel in the sublime view across Walsh Bay to Balmain, Goat Island and the North Shore. Guided tours, including the costume department and a peek at set construction, run on the first and third Thursday of the month (10.30am; 1hr; $8; booking essential; ☎02/9250 1795, ⓦ www.sydneytheatre.com.au).

Surrounding the wharves, on the western side of the Bradfield Highway (Sydney Harbour Bridge), **Millers Point** is a reminder of how The Rocks used to be – with a surprisingly genuine community feel so close to the tourist hype of The Rocks, as much of the housing is government- or housing association-owned. The area has its upmarket pockets, but for the moment the traditional street-corner pubs and shabby terraced houses on the hill are reminiscent of the raffish atmosphere once typical of the whole area, and the mostly peaceful residential streets are a delight to wander through.

You can reach the area through the Argyle Cut (see p.111) or from the end of George Street, heading onto Lower Fort Street, where you could stop for a drink at the **Hero of Waterloo** at no. 81 (see p.162), built from sandstone excavated from the Argyle Cut in 1844, before peeking in at the **Garrison Church** (daily 9am–5pm) on the corner of Argyle Street, the place of worship for the military stationed at Dawes Point fort (the fort was demolished in the 1920s to make way for the Harbour Bridge) from the 1840s. Beside the church, **Argyle Place** has some of the area's prettiest old terraced houses.

From here, walk up the steps on Argyle Street opposite the church to **Observatory Park** with its shady Moreton Bay figs, benches and lawns, for a marvellous hilltop view over the whole harbour. It's also easy to reach the park from the **Bridge Stairs** off Cumberland Street by the Argyle Cut.

The Italianate-style **Sydney Observatory** from which the park takes its name marked the beginning of an accurate time standard for the city when it opened in 1858, calculating the correct time from the stars and signalling it to Martin Place's GPO and the ships in the harbour by the dropping of a time ball in its tower at 1pm every day – a custom that still continues. Set amongst some very pretty gardens, the Observatory is now a **museum of astronomy** (daily 10am–5pm; free; ⓦ www.sydneyobservatory.com.au). A large section is devoted to the Transit of Venus, a rare astronomical event occurring about twice every century; it was the observation of this that prompted Captain Cook's 1769 voyage. The extensive exhibition of astronomical equipment, both obsolete and high-tech, includes the (still-working) telescope installed under the copper dome to observe the 1874 Transit of Venus. Another highlight, in the "Stars of the Southern Sky" section, are three animated videos of Aboriginal creation stories, retellings of how the stars came to be, from the Milky Way to Orion.

Every evening, you can view the sky through telescopes and learn about the Southern Cross and other southern constellations (times vary with season; 2hr tours include a lecture, film, exhibition, guided view of the telescopes and a look at the sky, weather permitting; $15; booking essential on ☎02/9241 3767, usually up to a week in advance); the small planetarium is used during night visits when the sky is not clear enough for observation.

Argyle Cut and Gloucester Street

From the Observatory, head back to Argyle Street and walk under Bradfield Highway to the **Argyle Cut**, which slices through solid stone connecting Millers Point and Circular Quay. The cut took sixteen years to complete, carved first with chisel and hammer by convict chain gangs who began the work in 1843; when transportation ended ten years later the tunnel was still unfinished, and it took explosives and hired hands to complete it in 1859.

Once you've passed through the cut, look out for the **Argyle Steps**, which lead back up to Cumberland Street. The Harbour Bridge is accessible by foot from here via the pylon staircase or you can sit back and enjoy the splendid views from a couple of fine old boozers, the *Glenmore* and the *Australian*. From the latter, head down **Gloucester Street**; at nos. 58–64 is the **Susannah Place Museum** (Jan daily 10am–5pm; Feb–Dec Sat & Sun only 10am–5pm; $8; visit by guided tour only; book on ☎02/9241 1893; ⓦwww.hht.nct.au), a row of four brick terraces built in 1844 and occupied until 1990. It's now a "house museum" (including a re-created 1915 corner store), which conserves the domestic history of Sydney's working class.

City Centre

From Circular Quay south as far as King Street is Sydney's **Central Business District**, often referred to as the **CBD**, with **Martin Place** as its commercial nerve centre. A pedestrian mall stretching from George Street to Macquarie Street, lined with imposing banks and investment companies, Martin Place has its less serious moments at summer lunchtimes, when street performances are held at the little amphitheatre, and all year round, fruit and flower stalls add some colour. The vast **General Post Office (GPO)**, built between 1865 and 1887 with its landmark clock-tower added in 1900, broods over the George Street end in all its Victorian-era pomp. The upper floors have been incorporated into part of a five-star luxury hotel, the *Westin Sydney*; the rest of the hotel resides in the 31-storey tower behind. The old building and the new tower meet in the grand Atrium Courtyard, on the lower ground floor, with its restaurants, bars and classy designer stores. The eastern end of Martin Place emerges opposite the old civic buildings on lower Macquarie Street.

Museum of Sydney

North of Martin Place, on the corner of Bridge and Phillip streets, stands the **Museum of Sydney** (daily 9.30am–5pm; $10; ☎02/9251 5988, ⓦwww.hht .net.au). The site itself is the reason for the museum's existence: a ten-year archeological dig starting here in 1983 unearthed the foundations of the first Government House built by Governor Phillip in 1788, which was home to eight subsequent governors of New South Wales before being demolished in 1846. The museum, built next to the site, is totally original in its approach, presenting history in an interactive manner, through exhibitions, film, photography and multimedia. Around half the exhibition space is taken up with special exhibitions which have recently included Captain Bligh's Sydney mutiny of 1808 and the 1960s glamour photos of local snapper, David Mist.

Sydney Architecture Walks

If you're interested in the city's modern architecture, Sydney Architecture Walks (Sept–May; $25; ☎02/8239 2211, Ⓦwww.sydneyarchitecture.org) offer informal two-hour walking tours led by young architects, all starting from the Museum of Sydney entrance. "Sydney" (Wed 10.30am) looks at the forces shaping the cityscape with particular reference to a couple of modern masterpiece skyscrapers, while "Utzon" (Sat 10.30am) looks at the design and construction of the Sydney Opera House. A third tour, "Harbourings", only takes place once a month (call for details) and investigates the industrial heritage of The Rocks and the finger wharves of nearby Walsh Bay. Walk fees include free entrance to the Museum of Sydney.

First Government Place, a public square in front of the museum, preserves the site of the original Government House: its foundations are marked out in different-coloured sandstone on the pavement. It's easy to miss, as your eye is naturally drawn to the forest of vertical poles at the western end. This is **Edge of the Trees**, an emotive sculptural installation that was a collaboration between a European and an Aboriginal artist, and attempts to convey the complexity of a shared history that began in 1788. Each pole represents one of the original 29 clans that lived in the greater Sydney area, and you can't help but notice the symbolism of the poles, standing quietly to one side, overlooking the comings and goings of Government House.

Entering the museum, you hear a dramatized dialogue between the Eora woman Patyegarang and the First Fleeter Lieutenant Dawes, giving a strong impression of the meeting and misunderstanding between the two cultures. Straight ahead is a video screen which projects images of the bush, sea and Sydney sandstone across all three levels, stylistically linking together what is really quite a small museum. Head up to the Level 2 auditorium for short movies of mid-twentieth-century Sydney life and the construction of the Harbour Bridge, then work your way down past wonderful **panoramas** of Sydney Harbour, the **Bond Store Tales** section, in which holographic "ghosts" relate tales of old Sydney as an ocean port, and the **Trade Wall**, full of anecdotes and facts about goods Sydney imported in its early days – rice from Batavia, cheroots from India, ginger wine from the West Indies and tar from Sweden.

There's also an excellent **gift shop** with a wide range of photos, artworks and books on Sydney, as well as the expensive *MOS* **café** on First Government Place.

King Street to Liverpool Street

South of Martin Place, the streets get a little more interesting. The rectangle between Elizabeth, King, George and Park streets is Sydney's prime shopping area, with a number of beautifully restored **Victorian arcades** (the Imperial Arcade, Strand Arcade and Queen Victoria Building are all worth a look) and Sydney's two **department stores**, the very upmarket David Jones on the corner of Market and Elizabeth streets, established in 1838, and Myers on Pitt Street Mall.

The landmark **Sydney Tower** (daily 9am–10.30pm, Sat 9am–11.30pm; adults $25, seniors & students $19.50, children $15; Ⓦwww.sydneytower.com.au), on the corner of Market and Castlereagh streets, is the tallest poppy in the Sydney skyline – a giant golden gearstick thrusting up 305m. The 360-degree view from the top is especially fine at sunset, and on clear days you can even see the

Blue Mountains, 100km away. Once up at the observation level you can opt for the **Skywalk** (daily 9am–8pm every 30–60min; additional $40, children $30), a harnessed-up, 45-minute walking tour of the exterior of the tower complete with vertiginous, glass-floored viewing platforms, one of which extends out over the abyss. It obviously imitates the popular Harbour Bridge climb, the original and still the best thrill for your money. The ticket also includes **Oztrek** at the base of the tower, a tacky "virtual ride" introduction to a clichéd Australia that lasts forty long minutes.

To enjoy the Sydney Tower view without the crowds, put the cash towards a meal at one of the **revolving restaurants** at the top of the tower; the revolution takes about one hour ten minutes and nearly all the tables are by the windows (bookings ☎02/8223 3800, ⊛www.sydney-tower-restaurant.com). For à la carte dining visit *360 Bar and Dining*, which serves lunch (Wed–Fri noon–2pm; two courses $68, three courses $75) and dinner (daily; two courses $75, three $95, 15-percent surcharge on Sun). *Sydney Tower Restaurant* puts on buffet lunches (Mon–Sat $49.50, Sun $59.50) and dinners (Mon–Thurs $64.50, Fri–Sun $85).

Nearby, several fine old buildings – the State Theatre, the Queen Victoria Building and the Town Hall – provide a pointed contrast. If heaven has a hallway, it surely must resemble that of the restored **State Theatre**, just across from the Pitt Street Mall at 49 Market St. Step inside and take a look at the glorious interior of this picture palace opened in 1929, whose lavishly painted, gilded and sculpted corridor leads to the lush, red and wood-panelled foyer. To see more of the interior, you'll need to attend the Sydney Film Festival (see p.171) or other events held here, such as concerts and plays, or you can take a guided tour (monthly 10.30am; 1hr 30 min; $15; ☎02/9373 6655). Otherwise, pop into the beautiful little *Retro Café* next door for a coffee.

The stately **Queen Victoria Building** (QVB; shops Mon–Sat 9am–6pm, Thurs 9am–9pm, Sun 11am–5pm; cafés and restaurants open later; building open 24hr; ⊛www.qvb.com.au), taking up the block bounded by Market, Druitt, George and York streets, is another of Sydney's finest. Stern and matronly, a huge statue of Queen Victoria herself sits outside the magnificent building. Built as a market hall in 1898, two years before Victoria's death, the long-neglected building was beautifully restored and reborn in 1986 as an upmarket shopping mall with a focus on fashion: from the basement up, the four levels become progressively exclusive. The interior is magnificent, with its beautiful woodwork, gallery levels and antique lifts; Charles I is beheaded on the hour, every hour, by figurines on the mechanical **Royal Automata Clock** on Level 2. From Town Hall station you can walk right through the basement level (mainly bustling food stalls) and continue via Sydney Central Plaza to Myers department store, emerging on Pitt Street without having to go outside.

In the realm of architectural excess, however, the **Town Hall** is king – you'll find it across from the QVB on the corner of George and Druitt streets. It was built during the boom years of the 1870s and 1880s as a homage to Victorian England; the huge organ inside its Centennial Hall gives it the air of a secular cathedral. Throughout the interior, different styles of ornamentation compete in a riot of colour and detail; the splendidly dignified toilets are a must-see, though the place is closed for refurbishment until late 2009.

South to Haymarket and Chinatown

The section of the city centre south from Liverpool Street down to Central Station is known as **Haymarket**, a lively area that's effectively a downmarket

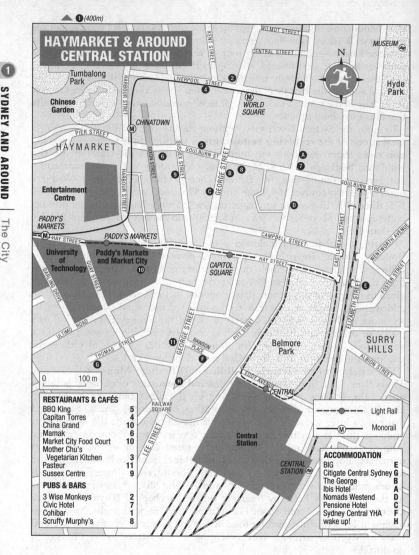

▲ ① (400m)

HAYMARKET & AROUND CENTRAL STATION

Tumbalong Park

Chinese Garden

CHINATOWN

HAYMARKET

Entertainment Centre

PADDY'S MARKETS

University of Technology

Paddy's Markets and Market City

CAPITOL SQUARE

Belmore Park

SURRY HILLS

RAILWAY SQUARE

Central Station

CENTRAL STATION

N

MUSEUM

Hyde Park

WORLD SQUARE

0   100 m

RESTAURANTS & CAFÉS	
BBQ King	5
Capitan Torres	4
China Grand	10
Mamak	6
Market City Food Court	10
Mother Chu's Vegetarian Kitchen	3
Pasteur	11
Sussex Centre	9

PUBS & BARS	
3 Wise Monkeys	2
Civic Hotel	7
Cohibar	1
Scruffy Murphy's	8

-----●----- Light Rail

Ⓜ Monorail

ACCOMMODATION	
BIG	E
Citigate Central Sydney	G
The George	B
Ibis Hotel	A
Nomads Westend	D
Pensione Hotel	C
Sydney Central YHA	F
wake up!	H

southern extension of the CBD. Between Town Hall and Central Station, **George Street** shifts gear as businesspeople and shoppers give way to backpackers, who jam the area's abundant hostels, and students from the University of Technology. It's also a markedly East Asian area with its own distinct **Chinatown**, a growing **Koreantown** and plenty of food courts with restaurants spanning the continent.

The short stretch between the Town Hall and Liverpool Street is for the most part teenage territory, a frenetic zone of **multiscreen cinemas**, pinball halls and fast-food joints, though the **Metro Theatre** is one of Sydney's best live-music venues (see p.164). The stretch is trouble-prone on Friday and Saturday nights when there are pleasanter places to catch a film (see p.170). Things change pace at Liverpool Street, where Sydney's **Spanish Corner** is gradually being taken over by Korean restaurants.

Sydney's **Chinatown** is a more full-blooded affair than Spanish Corner and probably the most active of the ethnic enclaves in the city. Through the ornate Chinese gates, **Dixon Street** is the main drag, buzzing day and night as people crowd into numerous restaurants, pubs, cafés, cinemas, food stalls and Asian grocery stores. Towards the end of January or in the first weeks of February, Chinese New Year is celebrated here with gusto: traditional dragon and lion dances, food festivals and musical entertainment compete with the noise and smoke from strings of Chinese crackers. For a calmer retreat, on the edge of Chinatown, at the southern fringes of Darling Harbour, is the serene **Chinese Garden** (see p.121).

The area immediately south of Chinatown is enlivened by Sydney's oldest market, bustling **Paddy's Market** (Thurs–Sun 10am–5pm), in its undercover home in between Thomas and Quay streets: a good place to buy cheap vegetables, seafood, clothes, souvenirs and bric-a-brac. Above Paddy's, the multilevel **Market City Shopping Centre** has a modern Asian feel as well as some excellent outlet stores for discounted fashion. There's also a first-rate Asian food court, on the top floor next to the multiscreen cinema.

The historic precinct: Hyde Park, College Street and Macquarie Street

Lachlan Macquarie, reformist governor of New South Wales between 1809 and 1821, gave the early settlement its first imposing public buildings, clustered on the southern half of his namesake Macquarie Street. He had a vision of an elegant, prosperous city – although the Imperial Office in London didn't share his enthusiasm for expensive civic projects. Refused both money and expertise, Macquarie was forced to be resourceful: many of the city's finest buildings were designed by the ex-convict architect **Francis Greenway** and paid for with rum money, the proceeds of a monopoly on liquor sales. Hyde Park was fenced off by Governor Macquarie in 1810 to mark the outskirts of his township, and with its war memorials and church, and peripheral museum and Catholic cathedral, is still very much a formal city park.

Hyde Park

From the Town Hall, it's a short walk east to **Hyde Park** along Park Street, which divides the park into two sections linked by a main north–south axis. The southern focus of this axis is the **ANZAC Memorial** (daily 9am–5pm but closed for renovations until late 2009; free), Sydney's most potent monument to those fallen in wartime. Fronted by the tree-lined Pool of Remembrance, the thirty-metre-high cenotaph, unveiled in 1934, is classic Art Deco right down to the detail of Rayner Hoff's stylized soldier figures which solemnly decorate the exterior. Downstairs, a mainly photographic exhibition looks at Australian wartime experiences.

In the northern half, the 1932 **Archibald Fountain** commemorates the alliance of Australia and France during World War I and is dripping in Greek and Roman iconography – all gods and minotaurs in a large hexagonal pool.

On the west side of the park the 1878 **Great Synagogue**, 187 Elizabeth St (tours Tues & Thurs at noon; $5; Ⓦ www.greatsynagogue.org.au), was inspired by English synagogues of the time in London and Liverpool and is the most beautiful in Australia, with domed towers flanking the wrought-iron gates and a big rose window facing Hyde Park.

College Street: the Australian Museum and St Mary's Cathedral

Facing Hyde Park across College Street, the **Australian Museum** (daily 9.30am–5pm; $12; free 40min tours daily 11am & 2pm; ⓦ www.australianmuseum.net.au) is primarily a museum of natural history, with an interest in human evolution and Aboriginal culture and history. The collection was founded in 1827, but the actual building, a grand sandstone affair with a facade of Corinthian pillars, wasn't fully finished until the 1860s and has been extended several times since. As well as the permanent exhibitions below, there are also **special exhibitions** throughout the year, for which there is usually an additional charge.

The core of the old museum is the three levels of the **Long Gallery**, Australia's first exhibition gallery, opened in 1855 to a Victorian public keen to gawk at the colony's curiosities. Many of the classic displays of the following hundred years remain here, Heritage-listed, contrasting with a very modern approach in the rest of the museum.

On the **ground floor**, the impressive **Australia's First Peoples** exhibition looks at the history of Australia's Aboriginal people from the Dreamtime to the more contemporary issues of the Stolen Generation and freedom rides. The ground-floor level of the Long Gallery houses the **Skeletons** exhibit, where you can see a skeletal human going through the motions of riding a bicycle, for example, and the elegantly complex bone structure of a python.

Level 1 is devoted to **minerals**, but far more exciting are the disparate collections on **level 2** – especially the Long Gallery's **Birds & Insects** exhibit, which includes chilling contextual displays of dangerous spiders such as redbacks and funnelwebs. On the same floor, adaptation is the key to **Surviving Australia**, which explores how monotremes, marsupials and humans have coped with the extremes of the Australian climate, or ultimately failed to in the case of the ancient marsupial lion or the Tasmanian tiger. Ancient beasts also form the bulk of **Dinosaurs** where the fun design-o-saurus programme allows you to create your own dinosaur on screen amid displays of dinosaur eggs and explanations of how the dinosaur world all came to an end 65 million years ago.

Kids, of course, will love the dinosaurs, and can pass an hour in **Kids' Space**, a fun play-space for under-5, while adults and older children will appreciate **Search and Discover**, a flora and fauna identification centre with internet access and books to consult.

The northern stretch of College Street flanks the large **Cook and Phillip Park** with its **recreation centre** (Mon–Fri 6am–10pm, Sat & Sun 7am–8pm; pool $6.20), which includes a fifty-metre swimming pool and gym. This is overlooked by the Catholic **St Mary's Cathedral** (Mon–Fri & Sun 6.30am–6.30pm, Sat 8am–6.30pm), a huge Gothic-style church opened in 1882, though the foundation stone was laid in 1821. In 1999, the cathedral at last gained the twin stone spires originally planned for the two southern towers by architect William Wardell in 1865.

Macquarie Street

Macquarie Street neatly divides business from pleasure, separating the office towers and cramped streets of the CBD from the open spaces of The Domain. The southern end of Governor Macquarie's namesake street is lined with the grand edifices that were the result of his dreams for a stately city: Hyde Park Barracks, Parliament House, the State Library, and the hospital he and his wife designed. The new Sydney – wealthy and international – shows itself on the corner of Bent and Macquarie streets in the curved glass sails of ABN AMRO's

41-floor **Aurora Place** tower, completed in 2000 to a design by Italian architect Renzo Piano, co-creator of the Georges Pompidou Centre in Paris.

St James's Church and Hyde Park Barracks

Immediately north of Hyde Park, the Anglican **St James's Church** (daily 9am–5pm) is Sydney's oldest existing place of worship, completed in 1824. It was one of Macquarie's schemes built to ex-convict Greenway's design, and the architect originally planned it as a courthouse – you can see how the simple design was converted into a graceful church. It's worth popping into the crypt (separate entrance on Phillip St) to see the richly coloured **Children's Chapel** mural painted in the 1930s.

Opposite, bordering Hyde Park, the **Hyde Park Barracks** (daily 9.30am–5pm; $10; ⓦwww.hht.net.au) were designed to house six hundred male convicts by convict-architect Francis Greenway and built in 1819, again without permission from London. It is the oldest institutional building in Australia and one of the most complete convict barracks in the former British Empire. Now a museum of the social and architectural history of Sydney, it's a great place to visit for a taste of prison life during the early years of the colony. Start on the top floor, where you can swing in re-creations of the prisoners' rough hammocks suspended from exposed beams. Computer terminals allow you to search for information on a selection of convicts' histories and backgrounds – several of those logged were American sailors nabbed for misdeeds while in Dublin or English ports (look up poor William Pink). Later the Barracks took in single immigrant women, many of them Irish, escaping the potato famine; an exhibition on the middle level looks specifically at the lives of Irish orphan girls, over 4000 of whom passed through the barracks between 1848 and 1850. Next door, you can see how buildings here were adapted to cope with the changing needs in a series of detailed scale models.

Ground-floor exhibits explore why the Australian colonies were set up in the first place, the reconstruction of one of the prison hulks that used to line the Thames in London giving a clear indication of how bad the situation had become once Britain could no longer transport its criminals to America after independence. Look out too for the excellent temporary historical exhibitions, as well as the room stripped back to reveal the building's original construction.

Sydney Hospital and the State Library

Next door to the barracks, sandstone **Sydney Hospital**, the so-called "Rum Hospital", funded by liquor-trade profits, was Macquarie's first enterprise, commissioned in 1814 and therefore one of the oldest buildings in Australia. From here it's a short walk through the grounds to The Domain and across to the Art Gallery of New South Wales. One of the original wings of the hospital was long ago converted into **Sydney Mint** (Mon–Fri 9am–5pm; free), originally a branch of the Royal Mint, opened in response to the first Australian gold rush. It closed in 1927 and after several incarnations received an award-winning $14 million redevelopment, which combined historic restoration with contemporary architecture. It now houses the head office of the Historic Houses Trust which maintains a small display on how the building was restored. On site is also the *Mint Café*, which extends onto the veranda looking over Macquarie Street.

The other, northernmost, hospital wing is now the **New South Wales Parliament House** (Mon–Fri 9.30am–4pm; free tours first Thurs of month at 1pm; call ⓣ02/9230 2047 or check ⓦwww.parliament.nsw.gov.au for parliamentary recesses), where as early as 1829 local councils called by the governor started to meet, making it by some way the oldest parliament building in Australia. However, it wasn't until the May 2003 state elections that an Aboriginal Australian was elected to the New South Wales Parliament – Linda Burney, former head of the New South Wales Department of Aboriginal Affairs and now Labor member for multicultural Canterbury as well as minister for Fair Trading, Youth and Volunteering. You can listen in on the politicians during question time, when Parliament is sitting. Look out for the varied exhibitions in the foyer which change every fortnight or so; all represent community or public-sector interests and range from painting, craft and sculpture to excellent photographic displays that often have an overt political content.

The row of public architecture along Macquarie Street ends with the **State Library of New South Wales** (Mon–Thurs 9am–8pm, Fri 9am–5pm, Sat & Sun 10am–5pm; Mitchell Library closed Sun; free tours Tues 11am & Thurs 2pm; ⓦ www.sl.nsw.gov.au). The complex of old and new buildings includes the 1906 sandstone **Mitchell Library**, its imposing Neoclassical facade gazing across to the Botanic Gardens. Inside the foyer the **Tasman Map** floor mosaic replicates an original drawn by the Dutch explorer Abel Tasman in the 1640s and now held in the library's collection. It depicts the Australian continent, still without an east coast, and its northern extremity joined to Papua New Guinea.

A walkway links the Mitchell Library with the modern building housing the **General Reference Library**. Free exhibitions relating to Australian history, art, photography and literature are a regular feature of the Reference Library vestibules, while lectures, films and video shows often take place in the **Metcalfe Auditorium** (☎02/9273 1414). The library's **bookshop** on the ground floor has one of the best collections of Australia-related books in Sydney, and every week the Metcalfe Auditorium hosts **free movies** (Thurs 12.10pm) from the extensive film and documentary archive.

The Domain and the Royal Botanic Gardens

Cook and Phillip Park fills in the green gap between Hyde Park and **The Domain**, a much larger, plainer open space that stretches from behind the historic precinct on Macquarie Street to the waterfront, divided from the Botanic Gardens by the ugly Cahill Expressway and Mrs Macquarie's Road. In the early days of the settlement, The Domain was the governor's private park; now it's a popular place for a stroll or a picnic, with the Art Gallery of New South Wales, an outdoor swimming pool and Mrs Macquarie's Chair to provide distraction. On Sundays, assorted cranks and revolutionaries assemble here for Speakers' Corner, and every January thousands of people gather on the lawns to enjoy the free open-air concerts of the Sydney Festival (see p.172).

Art Gallery of New South Wales

Beyond St Mary's Cathedral, Art Gallery Road runs through The Domain to the **Art Gallery of New South Wales** (Thurs–Tues 10am–5pm, Wed 10am–9pm; free; tours Mon 1pm & 2pm, Tues–Sat 11am, 1pm & 2pm, Sun 11am; free except for special exhibitions; excellent audio tour $5; ⓦ www.artgallery.nsw .gov.au). The collection was begun in 1874, moved into this building in 1897 and has been expanding ever since, most recently in 2003 when a gigantic cube of white glass, dubbed the "lightbox", was grafted onto the eastern Woolloomooloo facade to contain the gallery's Asian collection. As well as a wonderful permanent collection spanning European, Colonial, Aboriginal and Contemporary art, there's a strong programme of temporary exhibits.

You enter the gallery at Ground Level from where stairs lead down to three lower levels. Ground Level principally contains a large collection of European art dating from the eleventh to the twenty-first centuries and includes a vast, gilt-framed canvas by Edward John Poynter depicting *The Queen of Sheba before Solomon* in luminous detail. You should also be able to spot Cézanne's *Bords de la Marne*: the painting was bought for over $16 million in 2008, making it the most expensive work ever purchased by an Australian public gallery.

Classic **Australian paintings** to look out for are Frederick McCubbin's *On the Wallaby Track* from 1855, Tom Roberts' romanticized shearing-shed scene *The Golden Fleece* (1894) and an altogether less idyllic look at rural Australia in Russell Drysdale's *Sofala* (1947), a depressing vision of a drought-stricken town. Other luminaries such as Sidney Nolan and Brett Whitely are usually well represented, though works on show rotate from the greater collection. The **photographic collection** includes Max Dupain's iconic *Sunbaker* (1937), an early study of Australian hedonism that looks as if it could have been taken yesterday.

On Lower Level 3, the **Yiribana** gallery is devoted to the art and cultural artefacts of Aboriginal and Torres Strait Islanders – painting, sculpture, photography and multimedia installations. By joining one of the free hour-long tours of the indigenous collection (Thurs–Tues 11am, Wed 11am & 7.15pm) it's easier to gain an insight into works by artists such as Rusty Peters, Freddie Timms and Lin Onus, who created the lovely *Fruit Bats*, with almost a hundred cross-hatched bats hanging from a rotary clothesline.

Try to visit during "**Art After Hours**" (Wed 5–9pm) for the free talks and films (usually arthouse, often rare), along with live performances in the *ArtBar*. There's also an excellent bookshop, a café (Lower Level 1), and a well-regarded restaurant (Ground Level).

Mrs Macquarie's Chair and "The Boy"

Beyond the Art Gallery is the beginning of one of Sydney's most popular jogging routes – Mrs Macquarie's Road, built in 1816 at the urging of the governor's wife, Elizabeth. The road curves down from Art Gallery Road to Mrs Macquarie's Point, which separates idyllic Farm Cove from the grittier Woolloomooloo Bay. At the end is the celebrated lookout point known as **Mrs Macquarie's Chair**, a bench seat fashioned out of the rock. From here, Elizabeth could admire her favourite view of the harbour on her daily walk in what was then the governor's private park. On the route down to the point, the **Andrew "Boy" Charlton Pool** is an open-air, chlorinated saltwater swimming pool safely isolated from the harbour waters (daily Sept–April 6am–8pm; $5.70) on the Woolloomooloo side of the promontory, with views across to the engrossingly functional Garden Island Naval Depot. "The Boy", as the locals fondly call it, was named after the gold-medal-winning Manly swimmer, who turned 17 during the 1924 Paris Olympics. It's a popular hangout for trendy Darlinghurst types and gay sun-worshippers.

The Royal Botanic Gardens

The **Royal Botanic Gardens** (daily 7am–sunset; free; Ⓦ www.rbgsyd.nsw.gov .au), established in 1816, occupy the area between this strip of The Domain and the Sydney Opera House, around the headland on Farm Cove where the first white settlers struggled to grow vegetables for the hungry colony. While duck ponds, a romantic rose garden and fragrant herb garden strike a very English air, look out for native birds and, at dusk, the fruit bats flying overhead (hundreds of the giant bats hang by day in the Palm Grove area near the restaurant) as the nocturnal possums begin to stir. There are examples of trees and plants from all over the world, although it's the huge, gnarled, native Moreton Bay figs that stand out. The gardens provide some of the most stunning **views** of Sydney Harbour, particularly the section between Mrs Macquarie's Point and Main Pond, and are always crowded with workers at lunchtime, picnickers on fine weekends, and lovers entwined beneath the trees.

The southern area of the gardens has a herb garden, a cooling palm grove established in the 1860s, a café-restaurant by the duck ponds, and the **Sydney Tropical Centre** (daily 10am–4pm; $5.50) – a striking glass pyramid and adjacent glass arc respectively housing native tropical plants and exotics. Nearby, the **Rare and Threatened Plants** garden has the first example of a cultivated Wollemi Pine, planted in 1998. The "dinosaur" tree, thought long-extinct, was discovered by a national park ranger in 1994; there are only 38 naturally propagated examples of these trees in the world, growing in the Blue Mountains (see p.200).

Free **tours** of the gardens commence from the **visitor centre** (daily 9.30am–4.30pm; tours daily 10.30am; 1hr 30min; March–Nov Mon–Fri also 1pm; 1hr) at Palm Grove in the centre of the Gardens. The **Trackless Train**, which runs through the gardens about every twenty minutes, picks up from here; the main pick-up point is the entrance near the Opera House and there are also stops along the way (daily 9.30am–5pm; all-day hop-on-hop-off service $10, child $5).

Many **paths** run through the gardens. A popular and speedy route (roughly 15min) is to start at the northern gates near the Opera House and stroll along the waterfront path. Once you've passed through a second set of gates, walk up the **Fleet Steps** to Mrs Macquarie's Chair (see p.119) with fantastic views of the city skyline through trees. Within the northern boundaries of the park, the sandstone mansion glimpsed through a garden and enclosure is **Government House** (grounds daily 10am–4pm; entry to house by free guided tour only Fri–Sun 10.30am–3pm; tours half-hourly; 45min; Ⓦwww.hht.net.au), built between 1837 and 1845 as the seat of the governor of New South Wales. It is still used for vice-regal receptions and official engagements by the governor, who now lives in a private residence. The building was designed by Buckingham Palace architect, Edward Blore, and is furnished with an impressive array of Australian art and furniture from the past 150 years, including modern works introduced in the major 2007 refurbishment.

Further south, at the end of Bridge Street, the **Conservatorium of Music** is housed in what was intended to be the servants' quarters and stables of Government House. Public opinion in 1821, however, deemed the imposing castellated building far too grand for such a purpose and a complete conversion gave it a loftier aim of training the colony's future musicians. A major renovation project in the late 1990s uncovered an earlier convict-era site which led to an archeological dig being incorporated into the final redesign. Duck inside the modern entrance to see the preserved remains of an old drainage system and water cistern, or come for the free lunchtime recitals (Wed 1.10pm during term time) given by Conservatorium students. Tours of the building (Wed 12.30pm; $10) include the lunchtime concert; and there's a full programme of evening performances too (see Ⓦwww.music.uysd.edu.au).

Darling Harbour and around

Immediately east of the city centre lies **Darling Harbour**, once a grimy industrial docks area which lay moribund until the 1980s when the State

Government chose to pump millions of dollars into the regeneration of this prime city real estate as part of the 1988 Bicentenary Project. The huge redevelopment scheme around Cockle Bay, which opened in 1988, included the building of the above-ground monorail – one of only a few in the world – as well as a massive new shopping and entertainment precinct. In many ways it's a thoroughly stylish redevelopment of the old wharves, and Darling Harbour has plenty of attractions on offer: an aquarium, entertainment areas, a shopping mall, an IMAX cinema, a children's playground, gardens and a convention and exhibition centre. However, it's only recently that Sydneysiders themselves have embraced it. Sneered at for years by locals as tacky and touristy, it took the Cockle Bay and King Street wharf developments on the eastern side of the waterfront – with upmarket cafés, bars and restaurants – to finally lure the locals.

The eastern side of Darling Harbour blends straight into the CBD with office and apartment blocks overlooking the yacht-filled water. Across the old **Pyrmont Bridge**, the western side is a different matter. Push beyond the western wharfside developments and you're onto the Pyrmont–Ultimo Peninsula, an altogether older industrial quarter comprising the suburbs of **Pyrmont** and **Ultimo** that have only started to smarten up since the turn of the millennium. It still has a good way to go and there's pleasure in just wandering around marking the changes in between visits to the **Star City Casino**, the **Sydney Fish Market** and the superb **Powerhouse Museum**.

It's only a ten-minute walk from the Town Hall **to get to Darling Harbour**; from the QVB, walk down Market Street and along the overhead walkway. Further south, there's a pedestrian bridge from Bathurst Street, or cut through on Liverpool Street to Tumbalong Park. Alternatively, the **monorail** (see p.91) runs from the city centre to one of three stops around Darling Harbour. Getting to the wharf outside the Sydney Aquarium by **ferry** from Circular Quay gives you a chance to see a bit of the harbour – STA ferries stop at McMahons Point on the North Shore and Balmain en route. The *Matilda Ferry* runs from the Harbourmaster's Steps, outside the MCA, and goes via Luna Park. By **bus**, the #443 goes from Circular Quay via the QVB, Pyrmont and the casino, and the #449 runs between the casino, the Powerhouse Museum, Broadway Shopping Centre and Glebe. The large site can be navigated on the dinky **People Mover train** (daily 10am–5pm; full circuit 20min; $4.50).

There are always festivals and events here, particularly during school holidays; to find out what's on, visit the **Darling Harbour Visitor Centre** (daily 9.30am–5.30pm; ☎02/9240 8788, ⓦwww.darlingharbour.com.au), next door to the IMAX Theatre.

Tumbalong Park and Cockle Bay

The southern half of Darling Harbour, around **Cockle Bay**, is focused on **Tumbalong Park**, reached from the city via Liverpool Street. Backed by the Exhibition Centre, this is the "village green" of Darling Harbour – complete with water features and some interesting sculptures and public artworks – and serves as a venue for open-air concerts and free public entertainment. The area surrounding it can be Darling Harbour's most frenetic – at least on weekends and during school holidays – as most of the attractions, including a free playground and a stage for holiday concerts, are aimed at children.

For some peace and quiet head for the adjacent **Chinese Garden** (daily 9.30am–5pm; $6), completed for the Bicentenary in 1988 as a gift from Sydney's sister city Guangdong; the "Garden of Friendship" is designed in the traditional southern Chinese style. Although not large, it feels remarkably calm and spacious – a great place to retreat from the commercial hubbub. Stroll past the Water Pavilion of Lotus Fragrance to admire the vista across the Lake of Brightness to the pagoda on its hillock backed by city high-rises, then continue to the traditional tearoom, with views of the polychrome Dragon Wall, to enjoy a refreshing green tea as carp swim in the surrounding waters.

The Southern Promenade of Darling Harbour is dominated by the **IMAX Theatre** (films hourly from 10am; $19.50, children $14.50; ℡02/9281 3300, Ⓦ www.imax.com.au). Its eight-storey-high cinema screen (claimed as the world's biggest) shows a constantly changing programme of films, with an emphasis on scenic wonders, the animal kingdom and adventure sports.

Sydney Aquarium and Sydney WildlifeWorld

A little way north, at the eastern end of **Pyrmont Bridge**, is the impressive **Sydney Aquarium** (daily 9am–10pm; $30; Ⓦ www.sydneyaquarium.com.au), which, if you're not going to get the chance to explore the Great Barrier Reef, makes a good substitute. The highlights are the three vast ocean tanks. The first two cover the Southern Oceans, with underwater walkways allowing you to wander along as sharks, seals and gigantic stingrays swim overhead. There's a similarly grand approach to the Northern Oceans exhibit, where exotic species from the Great Barrier Reef drift past behind huge sheets of glass. Try to come at a quiet time (early or late in the day) when it can be breathtakingly beautiful: black-and-yellow-spotted butterfly fish drift by, undulating moon jellyfish loom into view, iridescent blue starfish glow and a spotted leopard shark seems disinterested in it all. The Great Barrier Reef Oceanarium finishes with a huge floor-to-ceiling tank where you can sit and watch the underwater world while classical music plays. Another section displays dangerous creatures like the moray eel and poisonous sea urchins, and Little penguins try to keep cool.

Next door is the equally impressive **Sydney WildlifeWorld** (daily 9am–6pm; $30; Ⓦ www.sydneywildlifeworld.com.au), a mesh-domed centre with free-flying birds and a compact collection of over 130 species of animals found throughout Australia. The elegant glass displays are carefully thought out, giving a good impression of the natural environment the animals live in. Koalas and kangaroos are the inevitable highlights, but snakes, spiders and other creepy-crawlies make interesting viewing, and you might even get the chance to handle some non-venomous species. Come early, or book in for the **Koala Breakfast** (Mon–Fri 7.30am; $55), a chance to photograph koalas up close, and enjoy a buffet breakfast as they dine on gum leaves nearby.

The National Maritime Museum and around

On the western side of Pyrmont Bridge, the **National Maritime Museum** (daily 9.30am–5pm, Jan until 6pm; free; Ⓦ www.anmm.gov.au), with its distinctive modern architecture topped by a wave-shaped roof, highlights the history of Australia as a seafaring nation, but goes beyond maritime interests to look at how the sea has shaped Australian life. It covers everything from immigration to beach culture and Aboriginal fishing methods in seven core themed exhibitions. Highlights include the "Merana Eora Nora – First People" exhibition, delving into indigenous culture, and "Navigators – Defining Australia", which focuses on the seventeenth-century Dutch explorers; major exhibits are continually being introduced. Look out for such delights as the replica of the winner of Darwin's Beer Can Regatta, a kind of raft built from hundreds of beer cans.

Outside you can wander along the shore, where there's a pleasant **café**, and stroll north past the Cape Bowling Green Lighthouse to the bronze **Welcome Wall**, which pays honour to Australia's six million immigrants. But the real highlights are several **moored vessels**, which you'll need to pay to board. The Navy ticket ($18) gives access to the 1950s destroyer HMAS *Vampire*, which on retirement operated as a naval training ship, and the submarine HMAS *Onslow*, which was decommissioned in 1999. In addition you can board the barque *James Craig* ($10) for a tour of this 1874 square-rigger, and get a sense of what Captain Cook's onboard life was like on the replica HM *Bark Endeavour* ($15). A Big ticket ($30, children $16) gives access to all the above. Moored around the wharves nearby is the Sydney Heritage Fleet's collection of smaller restored boats and ships, the oldest of which was built in 1888.

To the south, the two-level **Harbourside Shopping Centre** provides opportunities for souvenir hunting: don't miss the ground-floor **Gavala: Aboriginal Art & Cultural Education Centre** (daily 10am–9pm), the only fully Aboriginal-owned and -run store in Sydney (all profits go back to the artists), selling Aboriginal art, clothing, accessories and music.

Ultimo: the Powerhouse Museum

From Tumbalong Park, a signposted walkway leads to **Ultimo** and the **Power-house Museum** at 500 Harris St (daily 10am–5pm; $10, children $5, extra for special exhibitions; ⓦ www.phm.gov.au), located, as the name suggests, in a former power station. Arguably the best museum in Sydney, it's a huge, fresh and exciting place dedicated to science and design. Set aside at least a couple of hours to investigate the four-level museum properly, more if you visit one of the temporary exhibitions which are as varied as "The Lord of the Rings" and "The Untold Story of Modernism in Australia". You enter on Level 3, which is dominated by the huge **Boulton and Watt Steam Engine**, the oldest rotative steam engine in the world, first put to use in 1785 in a British brewery and used for over a hundred years. Still operational, the engine is often loudly demonstrated.

Downstairs, the old destination board from Sydney's Central Station is set to look as it would have on a Sunday in 1937, although the board was in use until 1982. It overlooks the transport section, including the venerable red-and-cream Rose Bay tram and one of the solar racers that competed in transcontinental races – effectively a streamlined solar panel on wheels.

Elsewhere you'll find *¡Inspired!*, an excellent design exhibit usually featuring pieces of furniture by top Australian industrial designer Marc Newsom, including his classic Lockheed Lounge Chair (1986), with aluminium panels riveted into a deliciously organic form.

The **Kings Cinema** on level 2, with its original Art Deco fittings, aptly shows the sorts of newsreels and films a Sydneysider would have watched in the 1930s. Judging by the tears at closing time, the **special children's areas** are proving a great success.

Pyrmont: Star City Casino and the Sydney Fish Market

Long an integral part of Sydney's industrial waterfront, with shipbuilding yards, a sugar refinery and wool stores, **Pyrmont**, which juts out into the water between Darling Harbour and Blackwattle Bay, was also Sydney's answer to Ellis Island. In the 1950s, thousands of immigrants disembarked here at the city's main overseas passenger terminal, Pier 13. Today the former industrial suburb, which had a population of only nine hundred in 1988, is being transformed into a residential suburb of some twenty thousand, with $2 billion worth of investment, and slick modern blocks and warehouse renovations to show for it. The area has certainly become glitzier, with Sydney's **casino** and the Channel

Ten TV company based here. Harris Street has filled up with new shops and cafés, and the area's old pubs have been given a new lease of life, attracting the young and upwardly mobile alongside the wharfies.

West of the Maritime Museum, on Pyrmont Bay, the palm-fronted **Star City** (Ⓦwww.starcity.com.au) is Sydney's spectacularly tasteless 24-hour casino. As well as the two hundred gaming tables (from Blackjack to Pai Gow – there are lots of Asian games, and gamblers), a big betting lounge and sports bar, and 1500 noisy poker machines, the building houses over a dozen restaurants, cafés (good for late-night eats) and theme bars, two theatres (see p.167) and a nightclub. The interior of the casino itself is a riot of giant palm sculptures, prize cars spinning on rotating bases, Aboriginal painting motifs on the ceiling, Australian critters scurrying across a red desert-coloured carpet and an endless array of flashing poker machines. Dress code is smart casual; you can just wander in and have a look around or a drink, without betting.

The best reason to visit this area, though, is the **Sydney Fish Market**, on the corner of Pyrmont Bridge Road and Bank Street (daily 7am–4pm; Ⓦwww .sydneyfishmarket.com.au), only a ten-minute walk via Pyrmont Bridge Road from Darling Harbour: the second-largest seafood market in the world for variety of fish, after the Tsukiji market in Tokyo. You need to visit early to see the **auctions** (Mon–Fri, with the biggest auction floor on Friday): buyers begin viewing the fish at 4.30am, auctions begin at 5.30am and the public viewing platform opens at 7am. Buyers log into computer terminals to register their bids in a Dutch-style auction: the price drops steadily until a bid is made and the first bid gets the fish. You don't get much of a view from the public platform, so consider joining one of the market tours (see below).

You can take away oysters, prawns and cooked seafood and (if you don't mind being pestered by seagulls) eat picnic-style on waterfront tables watching the boats come in. Everything is set up for throwing together an impromptu meal – there's a bakery, the Blackwattle Deli, with an extensive cheese selection, a bottle shop and a grocer. At lunchtime, you can eat in at *Doyles,* the casual and slightly more affordable version of the famous fish restaurant of the same name at Watsons Bay, or at the excellent sushi bar. Alternatively, plump for dirt-cheap fish and chips or a crack-of-dawn espresso at the *Fish Market Cafe*. Retail shops open at 7am.

To get a taste of the action on the auction floor and stand among buyers bidding for sashimi-grade yellowfin tuna, join one of the informative **fish market tours** (Mon & Thurs 7am; 90min; $20, coffee included; enclosed shoes required; ℡02/9004 1143). The tours also visit the rooms used by the **Sydney Seafood School** (℡02/9004 1111) which offers cookery lessons starting from $80 for a two-hour course, from Thai-style to Provençale, under the expert tuition of resident home economists as well as guest chefs drawn from the city's top restaurants. The most popular course, for which you need to book at least three months in advance, is the "Seafood Barbecue" (weekends; 4hr; $145).

The inner east

To the east of the city centre the adjacent districts of **Kings Cross** and **Potts Point** comprise one of the city's major entertainment districts and a popular spot for tourists (particularly backpackers). To the north you can descend a series of steps to **Woolloomooloo** with its busy naval dockyards and stylish Finger Wharf. South of Kings Cross, **Darlinghurst** and **Paddington** were once rather scruffy working-class suburbs, but were gradually taken over and revamped by the young, arty and upwardly mobile.

Oxford Street runs from the city southeast through **Taylor Square**, the heart of gay Sydney and on through the designer shopping and art gallery areas of Darlinghurst and Paddington to old-money **Woolahra** and the open grasslands of **Centennial Park**.

Oxford Street marks the northern boundary of rapidly gentrifying **Surry Hills**. While cutting-edge galleries and bars are still filling the area's backstreets, others are looking south to go-ahead **Waterloo** and even edgier **Redfern**

Kings Cross and Potts Point

The preserve of Sydney's bohemians in the 1950s, **Kings Cross** became an R&R spot for American soldiers during the Vietnam War and has long been considered Sydney's seedy red-light district. In recent years, however, the brothels have moved out to the suburbs and a facility for drug users has taken the drug abuse off the streets. What remains of the sex industry is a 700-metre-long strip of Darlinghurst Road where a handful of strip shows hang on – though even their time is limited as no new places are allowed to open up.

But Kings Cross certainly hasn't become lifeless. It still has a slight edginess from the interplay between disparate groups all staking their claim on the place – ageing bohemians, strung-out junkies, abstemious backpackers, a few confused and derelict souls, and the upwardly mobile who are increasingly moving into swanky apartments here. Somehow "The Cross" manages to cater to them all.

Kings Cross is always lively, with places to eat and drink that stay open all hours. Friday and Saturday nights can be rumbustious, but the constant flow of people (and police officers) makes it relatively safe. Generally, the area is much more subdued during the day, with a slightly hungover feel to it; local residents emerge and it's a good time to hang out in the cafés.

Eastbound from the city centre, **William Street** heads straight for the giant neon Coca-Cola sign that heralds Kings Cross. The street is an uneasy blend of cheap car and van rental places and dealerships for Ferrari, Lamborghini and Maserati. By the Coca-Cola sign, head left along Darlinghurst Road to the partly paved **Fitzroy Gardens** with its distinctive El Alamein fountain: the centre of the action. At weekends, people from the suburbs arrive in droves, emerging from the underground Kings Cross Station, near the beginning of the Darlinghurst Road "sin" strip, to wander the streets licking ice creams as touts try their best to haul them into the remaining tacky stripjoints and sleazy clubs. This same strip is increasingly being populated with hostels, budget travel agencies and internet cafés catering to the travellers staying in the area.

From Fitzroy Gardens, **Macleay Street** runs north through quieter **Potts Point**, an upmarket area of tree-lined streets, apartment blocks, classy boutique hotels, stylish restaurants, buzzy cafés and occasional harbour glimpses over wealthier Elizabeth Bay, just to the east; this is as close to European living as Sydney gets. The grand villas of colonial bureaucrats that distinguished Sydney's first suburb gave way in the 1920s and 1930s to Art Deco residential apartments, and in the 1950s big, splendid hotels were added to the scene, though many of these have been converted to luxury apartments. Beyond Macleay Street, Wylde Street heads downhill to Woolloomooloo.

You can get to Kings Cross by **train** (Eastern Suburbs line) or **bus** (#311, #324 or #325 from Circular Quay; many others from the city to Darlinghurst Rd), or it's not too far to walk: straight up William Street from Hyde Park. For a quieter route than William Street, you could head up from The Domain via Cowper Wharf Road in Woolloomooloo, and then up the McElhone Stairs to Victoria Street.

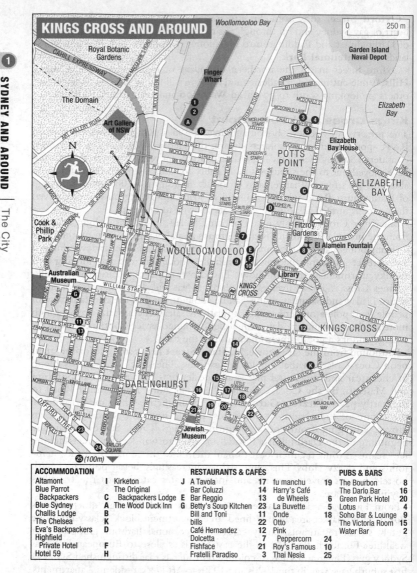

KINGS CROSS AND AROUND

ACCOMMODATION				RESTAURANTS & CAFÉS				PUBS & BARS	
Altamont		Kirketon	**J**	A Tavola	**17**	fu manchu	**19**	The Bourbon	**8**
Blue Parrot		The Original		Bar Coluzzi	**14**	Harry's Café		The Darlo Bar	**16**
Backpackers	**C**	Backpackers Lodge	**E**	Bar Reggio	**13**	de Wheels	**6**	Green Park Hotel	**20**
Blue Sydney	**A**	The Wood Duck Inn	**G**	Betty's Soup Kitchen	**23**	La Buvette	**5**	Lotus	**4**
Challis Lodge	**B**			Bill and Toni	**11**	Onde	**18**	Soho Bar & Lounge	
The Chelsea	**K**			bills	**22**	Otto	**1**	The Victoria Room	**15**
Eva's Backpackers	**D**			Café Hernandez	**12**	Pink		Water Bar	**2**
Highfield				Dolcetta	**7**	Peppercorn	**24**		
Private Hotel	**F**			Fishface	**21**	Roy's Famous	**10**		
Hotel 59	**H**			Fratelli Paradiso	**3**	Thai Nesia	**25**		

Woolloomooloo

North of William Street just below Kings Cross, **Woolloomooloo** occupies the old harbourside quarter between The Domain and the grey-painted fleet of the **Garden Island Naval Depot**. Once a narrow-streeted slum, Woolloomooloo is quickly being transformed, though its upmarket apartment developments sit uneasily side by side with problematic community housing, and you should still be careful in the backstreets at night. There are some lively pubs and some quieter, more old-fashioned drinking holes, as well as the legendary **Harry's**

Café de Wheels on Cowper Wharf Road, a late-closing pie-cart operating since 1945 and popular nowadays with Sydney cabbies and hungry clubbers (see p.154).

Next door, the 400-metre-long **Woolloomooloo Finger Wharf** was built in 1915 and for decades was where the bulk of New South Wales' wool left for markets overseas, and many new immigrants arrived. As containerization shifted the docks' trade elsewhere, the buildings became picturesquely dilapidated until the late 1980s when they were saved from demolition and converted into luxury residential apartments with some A-list tenants, a number of slick restaurants with alfresco dining and the cool *Blue Hotel* with its funky *Water Bar*. You can wander along the wharf and even go inside: there's a free exhibition space with a changing theme in the centre.

Woolloomooloo is best reached **on foot** from Kings Cross by taking the **McElhone Stairs** or the **Butlers Stairs** from Victoria Street; or from the Royal Botanic Gardens by walking south around the foreshore from Mrs Macquarie's Chair; alternatively, take **bus** #311 from Kings Cross, Circular Quay or Central Station.

Darlinghurst, Paddington and Woollahra

Hip and bohemian **Darlinghurst** mingles seediness with hedonism: some art students and clubbers never leave the district, save for a coffee at The Cross or a swim at "The Boy" in The Domain. South of Kings Cross and strung out along Oxford Street between Hyde Park and Paddington, it falls into distinct halves. In the north, the restaurants, bars and a couple of chic hotels along the diverging Darlinghurst Road and **Victoria Street** seem like a southern continuation of Kings Cross. It's a classic haunt of posers, boasting the legendary, street-smart *Bar Coluzzi* (see p.154), the elegantly worn-in, lounge-style *Darlo Bar* (see p.163) and up and-coming dining spots such as *A Tavola* (see p.154).

The southern strip along **Oxford Street**, and especially around **Taylor Square**, is very much the focus of Sydney's active **gay and lesbian** community. Some bars and clubs leave you in no doubt about the punters' sexual orientation, but Oxford Street also has plenty of restaurants and bars with a mixed clientele.

Oxford Street's shopping strip – many would argue Sydney's best for labels and stylish clothes shops – starts at the corner of Victoria Street in Darlinghurst and doesn't stop until the corner of Jersey Road in **Woollahra**. Two arthouse cinemas – the Academy Twin and the Verona (see p.171) – always have the latest local and international alternative flicks, and late-night bookshops Berkelouws (with its fabulous coffee shop upstairs) and Ariel across the street pack in students and the smart set alike till late.

From the intersection with South Dowling Street in Darlinghurst, Oxford Street strikes southeast through trendy, upmarket **Paddington** and wealthy, staid **Woollahra** to the verdant expanse of Centennial Park. **Buses** heading in this direction include #380 and #389 from Circular Quay; the #378, from Central Station, also heads along Oxford Street.

Paddington, a slum at the turn of the twentieth century, became a popular hangout for hipsters during the late 1960s and 1970s. Yuppies took over in the 1980s and turned Paddington into the smart and fashionable suburb it is today: the Victorian-era terraced houses, with their iron-lace verandas reminiscent of New Orleans, have been beautifully restored. Many of the terraces were originally built in the 1840s to house the artisans who worked on the graceful, sandstone **Victoria Barracks** on the southern side of Oxford Street, its walls stretching seven blocks, from Greens Road to just before the Paddington Town

Hall on Oatley Road. The barracks are still used by the army, though you can visit a small **museum** (Sun 10am–3pm; $2 donation) of uniforms, medals and firearms. Free **tours** (Thurs 10am) include an army band recital.

Shadforth Street, opposite the entrance gates, has many examples of the original artisans' homes. Follow this street north then turn right onto Glenmore Road to reach **Five Ways**, the focus of an area of pleasant, winding, tree-lined streets that make a great place for a stroll, and offer a chance to wander into speciality stores, cafés and numerous small art galleries.

The area's swankiest clothes **shopping** is around the junction of Glenmore Road and Oxford Street, and there are more classy shops further east on Elizabeth Street, which runs off Oxford Street almost 1km further southeast. Always bustling, the area comes alive on Saturday from 10am to around 4pm, when everyone descends on **Paddington Markets** in the church grounds at no. 395. The markets just keep getting bigger, selling everything from handmade jewellery to local artwork, cheap but fresh flowers and vintage clothes; you can even get a massage or a tarot reading between a cup of coffee and an organic sandwich. Nearby, photo fans shouldn't miss the **Australian Centre for Photography**, 257 Oxford St (Tues–Fri noon–7pm, Sat & Sun 10am–6pm; free; Ⓦ www.acp.au.com) with exhibitions of photo-based art from established and new international and Australian artists.

Woollahra, along Oxford Street from Paddington, is even more moneyed and correspondingly sober, with expensive **antiques shops** and **art galleries** along **Queen Street** replacing the fashion and lifestyle stores of Paddington. Leafy Moncur Street hides the gourmet *jones the grocer* at no. 68, where locals gather for coffee at the long central table.

Centennial Parklands

South of Paddington and Woollahra lies the great green expanse of **Centennial Parklands** (daily sunrise to sunset; Ⓦ www.cp.nsw.gov.au), opened to the citizens of Sydney at the Centennial Festival in 1888. With its vast lawns, rose

▲ Centennial Parklands

gardens and extensive network of ponds complete with ducks it resembles an English country park, but is reclaimed at dawn and dusk by distinctly antipodean residents, including possums and flying foxes. The park is crisscrossed by walking paths and tracks for cycling, rollerblading, jogging and horseriding: you can rent a bike or rollerblades nearby (see p.178) or hire a horse from the adjacent equestrian centre and then recover from your exertions in the café with its popular outside tables or, in the finer months, stay on until dark and catch an outdoor film at the Moonlight Cinema (see p.170). Adjoining **Moore Park** has facilities for tennis, golf, bowling, cricket and hockey; it's also home to the Sydney Cricket Ground and the Entertainment Quarter (for both, see p.129).

The Parklands also contain the Murdoch-owned **Fox Studios Australia** (no public access), opened in 1998 on the old Showgrounds site, where the Royal Agricultural Society held its annual Royal Easter Show from 1882 until 1997. The eight high-tech film and television sound stages have been put to good use making movies including *The Matrix*, *Mission Impossible II*, Baz Luhrmann's *Moulin Rouge* and *Episode I* and *II* of the *Star Wars* saga.

To get to Paddington Gates, take a **bus** along Oxford Street: either the #378 from Railway Square and Central Station or the #380 from Circular Quay. Alternatively, head straight into the heart of the park from Central Station (#372, #393 or #395). There is plenty of free **parking** for cars.

The Sydney Cricket Ground (SCG)

The venerated institution of the **Sydney Cricket Ground (SCG**; ☎02/9360 6601, ⓦ www.scgt.nsw.gov.au) earned its place in cricketing history for Don Bradman's score of 452 not out in 1929, and for the controversy over England's bodyline bowling techniques in 1932. Ideally, proceedings are observed from the lovely 1886 Members Stand, while sipping an ice-cold gin and tonic – but unless you're invited by a member, you'll end up elsewhere, probably drinking beer from a plastic cup. Cricket spectators aren't a sedate lot in Sydney, and the noisiest barrackers will probably come from the newly redeveloped Victor Trumper Stand. The Bill O'Reilly Stand gives comfortable viewing until the afternoon, when you'll be blinded by the sun, whereas the Brewongle Stand provides consistently good viewing. Best of all is the Bradman Stand, with a view directly behind the bowler's arm, and adjacent to the exclusive stand occupied by members, commentators and ex-players. The Test to see here is, of course, **The Ashes**; the Sydney leg of the five tests, each for five days, begins on New Year's Day. You can buy **tickets** for all matches at the gates on the day subject to availability, or purchase them in advance from Ticketek (☎13 28 49, ⓦ www.ticketek.com.au). Die-hard cricket fans can go on a **tour** of the SCG on non-match days (Mon–Fri 10am, noon & 2pm, Sat 10am; 1hr 30min; $25; ☎1300 724 737), which also covers the **Aussie Stadium** next door, where the focus is on international and national rugby league and rugby union, and Aussie Rules football matches, when Sydneysiders come out to support their local team, The Swans.

The Entertainment Quarter

The southern section of the old Showgrounds is now the **Entertainment Quarter** (ⓦ www.entertainmentquarter.com.au), a modern and rather characterless area of shops, cinemas, a dozen restaurants and a couple of events centres. There's little reason to spend time here unless you are coming for a show or a movie, or just need some sustenance when visiting Centennial Park.

The EQ is focused around the old **Showring**, once the preserve of woodchopping competitions and rodeo events, and now used for everything from open-air cinema and circuses to the food-oriented **Village Market** (Wed, Sat & Sun 10am–3.30pm). Arcing around the south side of the Showring is **Bent Street**, an anodyne pedestrian promenade partly shaded by palms and lined with middling restaurants and high-street fashion chains, most of which are open daily until 10pm.

Here you'll also find the twelve-screen Hoyts Entertainment Quarter **cinema complex**, the more arty Cinema Paris (for both see p.170) and the indoor **Lollipops Playground** (daily 9.30am–6pm; adults $5; under-1s free; children aged 1–2 midweek $10, weekends $14; aged 2 and over $14; ℡02/9331 0811). Just outside are two free playgrounds. On the way to a gig or movie, people often stop off at the *Fox and Lion* pub, just off Bent Street.

To get here, catch **buses** #339, #392, #394 or #396 from Central, Wynyard, or Town Hall.

Surry Hills

South of Darlinghurst's Oxford Street and due east of Central Station, **Surry Hills** was traditionally the centre of the rag trade. Rows of tiny terraces once housed its poor, working-class population, many of them of Irish origin. Considered a slum by the rest of Sydney, the dire and overcrowded conditions were given fictional life in Ruth Park's *The Harp in the South* trilogy (see p.1169), set in the Surry Hills of the 1940s. The area became something of a cultural melting pot with European postwar immigration, and doubled as a grungy, student heartland in the 1980s.

By the mid-1990s, the slickly fashionable scene of neighbouring Darlinghurst and Paddington had finally taken over Surry Hills' twin focal points of **Crown Street**, filled with cafés, swanky restaurants, funky clothes shops and designer galleries, and parallel **Bourke Street**, where a couple of Sydney's best cafés lurk among the trees. As rents have gone up, only **Cleveland Street**, running west to Redfern and east towards Moore Park and the Sydney Cricket Ground (see p.129), traffic-snarled and lined with cheap Indian, Lebanese and Turkish restaurants, retains its ethnically varied population.

Surry Hills is always a good area for a coffee, a meal, a few drinks or just a general mooch around the shops, but the only real sight is the **Brett Whiteley Gallery** (Sat & Sun 10am–4pm; free; ℡02/9225 1881, ⓦwww.brettwhiteley .org), at 2 Raper St, off Davies Street. Whiteley was one of Australia's best-known contemporary painters with an international reputation by the time he died, in 1992 at the age of 53, of a heroin overdose; wild self-portraits and expressive female nudes were some of his subjects, but it is his sensual paintings of Sydney Harbour for which he is best known, painted from his home in Lavender Bay. In 1986 Whitely converted this former T-shirt factory into a studio and living space, and since his death it has become a museum and gallery showing his paintings and memorabilia. The only painting permanently on display is 1973's *Alchemy*, a series of multimedia panels taking up most of two walls, which apparently gives a kind of snapshot of his state of mind at the time – working out just what that was could take you some time. Upstairs you can lounge around watching videos of his life and works, and peruse all manner of memorabilia from photos and furniture to the artist's vinyl – the music playing is from his collection. Through the wall is his studio, left chaotically scattered with works in progress.

Surry Hills is a short **walk** uphill from Central Station (Devonshire St or Elizabeth Street exit): take Foveaux or Devonshire streets and you'll soon hit Crown St, or it's an even quicker stroll from Oxford Street, Darlinghurst, heading south along Crown or Bourke streets. Several **buses** also run here from Circular Quay, including the #301 and #303, both to Crown Street.

Waterloo and Redfern

As Surry Hills becomes ever more gentrified, galleries in search of cheaper rent and restaurants out to create a buzz have gone in search of a new playground. They've found it on **Danks Street**, around its junction with Young Street on the northern fringes of **Waterloo**, about half a kilometre south of Cleveland Street. Although surrounded by uninspiring residential housing, Danks Street is a world apart, and it's worth making the effort to visit 2 Danks Street Galleries (Ⓦ www.2danksstreet.com.au) and highly regarded cafés such as *Café Sopra* (see p.156).

There's an equally resurgent feel to **Redfern**, northwest of Waterloo and less than 2km south of Central Station. Long considered Sydney's underbelly, you'll now find new cafés opening amid the more mundane shops and pubs: this is an area to catch at the beginning of its upward trajectory. Redfern is perhaps best known, at least among Sydneysiders, for **Eveleigh Street**, where Australia's biggest urban **Aboriginal community** lives in "the Block", a squalid street-scape of derelict terraced houses and rubbish-strewn streets not far from Redfern train station; this is the closest Sydney has to a no-go zone. The Aboriginal Housing Company, set up as a cooperative in 1973, has been unable to pay for repairs and renovation work, and Eveleigh Street appears in shocking contrast to Paddington's cutesy restored terraces. Derelict houses have been knocked down in recent years and residents relocated, which has upset many who want to keep the community together. A full-blown street riot in 2004 shows how close to the surface tensions are, and these may be further fuelled by current plans for indigenous developers to build a 62-house development on The Block.

The inner west

West of the centre, immediately beyond Darling Harbour, the inner-city areas of **Glebe** and **Newtown** surround Sydney University, their vibrant artistic communities and cultural mix enlivened by large student populations. On a peninsula north of Glebe and west of The Rocks, **Balmain** is a gentrified former working-class dock area popular for its village atmosphere, while west of Glebe **Leichhardt** is a focus for Sydney's Italian community.

Glebe

Right by Australia's oldest university, **Glebe** is simultaneously a café-oriented student quarter, a haven for artists, writers and musicians, an area of poor housing and a territory for upmarket thirtysomethings with New Age inclinations. Very much the centre of alternative culture in Sydney, Glebe's organic food stores, yoga schools and healing centres – offering every kind of therapy from Chinese massage to homeopathy and floatation tanks – are plentiful. **Glebe Point Road**, lined with a mix of cafés with leafy courtyards, restaurants, bookshops and secondhand shops, runs uphill from **Broadway**, becoming quietly residential as it slopes down towards the water of Rozelle Bay. The side streets here are fringed with renovated two-storey terraced houses with white-iron lacework verandas; not surprisingly, Glebe is popular with backpackers and offers several hostels (see p.100). The **Broadway Shopping Centre** on nearby Broadway, but linked to Glebe by an overhead walkway from Glebe Point Road opposite one of the street's most popular cafés, *Badde Manors*, is handy if you're

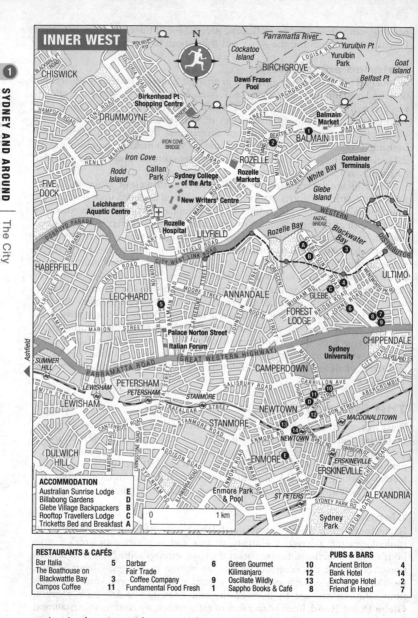

INNER WEST

WOLSELEY RD

Parramatta River

Yurulbin Pt

Cockatoo Island

BIRCHGROVE

LOUISA RD

Yurulbin Park

Goat Island

Belfast Pt

CHISWICK

Dawn Fraser Pool

BIRCHGROVE RD

WHARF RD

Birkenhead Pt Shopping Centre

Balmain Market

BALMAIN

DRUMMOYNE

Container Terminals

IRON COVE BRIDGE

ROZELLE

White Bay

Iron Cove

Rodd Island

Callan Park

Sydney College of the Arts

Rozelle Markets

Glebe Island

WESTERN

FIVE DOCK

Leichhardt Aquatic Centre

New Writers' Centre

ANZAC BRIDGE

Blackwater Bay

DISTRIBUTOR

HENLEY MARINE DRIVE

Rozelle Hospital

LILYFIELD

Rozelle Bay

ULTIMO

HABERFIELD

LILYFIELD ROAD

CITY WEST LINK ROAD

THE CRESCENT

GLEBE

FOREST LODGE

LEICHHARDT

ANNANDALE

CHIPPENDALE

Palace Norton Street Italian Forum

Sydney University

Ashfield

PARRAMATTA ROAD (GREAT WESTERN HIGHWAY)

CAMPERDOWN

SUMMER HILL

LEWISHAM

PETERSHAM

STANMORE

NEWTOWN

MACDONALDTOWN

DULWICH HILL

STANMORE

NEWTOWN

ENMORE

ERSKINEVILLE

ACCOMMODATION
Australian Sunrise Lodge	E
Billabong Gardens	D
Glebe Village Backpackers	B
Rooftop Travellers Lodge	C
Tricketts Bed and Breakfast	A

Enmore Park & Pool

ST PETERS

ALEXANDRIA

Sydney Park

0   1 km

RESTAURANTS & CAFÉS
Bar Italia	5	Darbar	6	Green Gourmet	10
The Boathouse on		Fair Trade		Kilimanjaro	12
Blackwattle Bay	3	Coffee Company	9	Oscillate Wildly	13
Campos Coffee	11	Fundamental Food Fresh	1	Sappho Books & Café	8

PUBS & BARS
Ancient Briton	4
Bank Hotel	14
Exchange Hotel	2
Friend in Hand	7

staying in the area, with supermarkets, speciality food shops, huge food court, record, book and clothes shops and twelve-screen cinema.

Just before the beginning of Glebe Point Road, on Broadway, **Victoria Park** has a pleasant, heated outdoor swimming pool (Mon–Fri 5.45am–7.45pm, Sat & Sun 7am–5.45pm; $4.80) with attached gym and a sophisticated café. From the park, a path and steps lead up into **Sydney University**, inaugurated in 1850; your gaze is led from the walkway up to the Main Quadrangle and its very Oxford-reminiscent clock tower and Great Hall. You can wander freely around the university grounds, and there are several free museums and galleries to visit.

Glebe itself is at its best on Saturday, when **Glebe Market** (10am–4pm), which takes place on the shady primary-school playground on Glebe Point Road, is in full swing. On sale are mainly secondhand clothes and accessories, CDs, the inevitable crystals and a bit of bric-a-brac. At 49 Glebe Point Rd, you'll find the excellent **Gleebooks** – one of Sydney's best-loved bookshops. The original, now selling secondhand and children's books, is worth the trek further up to no. 191, past St Johns Road and Glebe's pretty park. A few blocks on from here, Glebe Point Road trails off into a more residential area, petering out at **Jubilee Park**. The pleasantly landscaped waterfront park, complete with huge, shady Moreton Bay fig trees, children's playground and picturesque Harbour Foreshore Walk around Blackwattle Bay, offers an unusual view of far-off Sydney Harbour Bridge framed within the cabled ANZAC Bridge.

Buses #431, #433 and #434 run to Glebe from Millers Point, George Street and Central Station; #431 and #434 run right down the length of Glebe Point Road to Jubilee Park, with the #434 continuing on to Balmain, while the #433 runs halfway, turning at Wigram Road and heading on to Balmain. From Coogee beach, the #370 runs to Glebe via the University of New South Wales and Newtown. The Monorail runs between Central Station and Rozelle, stopping at the Glebe stop, just off Pyrmont Bridge Road, and the Jubilee stop at Jubilee Park. Otherwise, it's a fifteen-minute **walk** from Central Station up Broadway to the beginning of Glebe Point Road.

Newtown and around

Newtown, separated from Glebe by Sydney University and easily reached by train (to Newtown Station), is a hip inner-city neighbourhood. What was once a working-class district – a hotchpotch of derelict factories, junkyards and cheap accommodation – has transformed into a trendy, offbeat area where body piercing, shaved heads and weird fashions rule. Newtown is characterized by a large population of artists, devotees of numerous alternative cultures, a strong gay and lesbian community, a rich ethnic mix, and a healthy dose of students and lecturers from the nearby university. It also has an enviable number of cafés and diverse restaurants, especially Thai, making it an agreeable location for an evening meal, late-night drink or midday fortifying breakfast.

The main drag, gritty, traffic-fumed and invariably pedestrian-laden **King Street**, is filled with secondhand, funky fashion and homeware shops and a slew of bookshops, old and new. For two weeks in September and October, various shop windows are taken over by young, irreverent and in-your-face art in the "Walking the Street" exhibition, but the highlight of the year is the second Sunday in November, when the huge **Newtown Festival** takes over nearby Camperdown Memorial Park, with an eclectic mix of over 200 stalls and live music on three stages, with very fun, and very Newtown, punk rockabilly bands, and blues, funk, hip-hop and indie-electronica representatives. On the last Saturday of each month the small, but impressive, **Newtown Markets** are held in front of The Hub, opposite Newtown Station, where quirky toys, books, alternative fashion and works by talented local artists are perused by locals.

King Street becomes less crowded south of Newtown Station as it heads for 1km towards St Peters train station, but it's well worth strolling down to look at the more unusual speciality shops (such as vintage record stores and button shops), as well as some small art galleries and yet more retro and new clothes shops. The street is also well served with restaurants, ranging from Mexican to African.

Enmore Road, stretching west from King Street, opposite Newtown Station, offers a similar mix of shops and evidence of a migrant population – such as the African International Market at no. 2 and Amera's Palace Bellydancing Boutique at no. 83. It's generally much quieter than King Street, except when a big-name band or comedian is playing at the Art Deco **Enmore Theatre** at no. 130. Beyond here, the multicultural, lively but down-at-heel **Marrickville** stretches out, known for its Vietnamese and Greek restaurants.

Erskineville Road, extending from the eastern side of King Street, marks the beginning of the adjoining suburb of **Erskineville**, a favourite gay hangout; the *Imperial Hotel*, at 35 Erskineville Rd (see p.166), has long hosted popular drag shows, and is famous as the starting point for the gang in the 1994 hit film *The Adventures of Priscilla, Queen of the Desert*.

Buses #422, #423, #426 and #428 run to Newtown from Circular Quay via Castlereagh Street, Railway Square and City Road. They go down King Street as far as Newtown station, where the #422 continues to St Peters while the others turn off to Enmore and Marrickville. From Coogee beach, take the #370 bus to Glebe, which goes via Newtown. Alternatively, catch a **train** to Newtown, St Peters or Erskineville stations.

Leichhardt, Rozelle and Balmain

Bus #440 takes half an hour to get from The Rocks to **Leichhardt**, Sydney's "Little Italy", where the famous **Norton Street** strip of cafés and restaurants runs off unattractive, traffic-jammed **Parramatta Road** (buses #436, #437 and #438 from George St in the city centre will also take you here). Leichhardt is very much up and coming – shiny, trendy Italian cafés keep popping up all along the strip. Close to Parramatta Road is the **Italian Forum**, an upmarket shopping and dining centre and showcase for all things Italian. However, the lively, much-loved *Bar Italia*, a ten-minute walk further down Norton, is arguably still the best Italian café in Leichhardt (see p.158 for more). In between, the upmarket cinema complex, The Palace, hosts a two-week Italian film festival in late October.

From Leichhardt, the #445 bus runs along Rozelle High Street and down the hill to Balmain's waterfront. **Rozelle**, once very much the down-at-heel, poorer sister to Balmain, has emerged as a sophisticated and stylish area, with the Sydney College of the Arts and the Sydney Writers' Centre now based here, in

---

Goat Island

Just across the water from Balmain East, Goat Island is the site of a well-preserved gunpowder-magazine complex. The sandstone buildings, including a barracks, were built by two hundred convicts between 1833 and 1839. Treatment of the convicts was harsh: 18-year-old Charles Anderson, a mentally impaired convict with a wild, seemingly untameable temper who made several escape attempts, received over twelve hundred lashes in 1835 and was sentenced to be chained to a rock for two years, a cruel punishment even by the standards of the day. Tethered to the rock, which you can still see, his unhealed back crawling with maggots, he slept in a cavity hewn into the sandstone "couch". Eventually, Anderson ended up on Norfolk Island (see p.298), where under the humane prisoner-reform experiments of Alexander Maconochie, the feral 24-year-old made a startling transformation.

At the time of writing, the island was closed undergoing a major face-lift to make the buildings more accessible to the public.

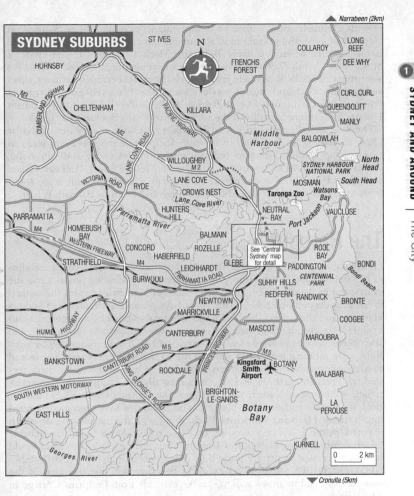

SYDNEY SUBURBS

Narrabeen (2km)

ST IVES

N

HURNSBY

FRENCHS
FOREST

COLLAROY

LONG
REEF

DEE WHY

CHELTENHAM

KILLARA

CURL CURL

QUEENSCLIFF

MANLY

Middle
Harbour

BALGOWLAH

WILLOUGHBY
M2

SYDNEY HARBOUR
NATIONAL PARK

North
Head

RYDE

LANE COVE

CROWS NEST

Lane Cove River

MOSMAN

Taronga Zoo

South Head

PARRAMATTA

HUNTERS
HILL

NEUTRAL
BAY

Port Jackson

Watsons
Bay

VAUCLUSE

HOMEBUSH
BAY

Parramatta River

BALMAIN

CONCORD

HABERFIELD

ROZELLE

GLEBE

See 'Central
Sydney' map
for detail

PADDINGTON

ROSE
BAY

BONDI

STRATHFIELD

LEICHHARDT

SURRY HILLS

CENTENNIAL
PARK

Bondi Beach

BURWOOD

PARRAMATTA ROAD

NEWTOWN

REDFERN

RANDWICK

BRONTE

MARRICKVILLE

MASCOT

COOGEE

CANTERBURY

MAROUBRA

BANKSTOWN

CANTERBURY ROAD

M5

Kingsford
Smith
Airport

BOTANY

MALABAR

ROCKDALE

BRIGHTON-
LE-SANDS

Botany
Bay

LA
PEROUSE

EAST HILLS

Georges River

KURNELL

0   2 km

Cronulla (5km)

the grounds of the 150-acre waterfront **Callan Park** on Balmain Road. Darling Street has a string of cafés, bookshops, speciality shops, gourmet grocers, restaurants, made-over pubs, and designer homeware stores, and is at its liveliest at the weekend, when a huge **flea market** (Sat & Sun 9am–4pm) takes over the grounds of Rozelle Primary School, near the Victoria Road end.

   Balmain, directly north of Glebe, is less than 2km from the Opera House, by ferry from Circular Quay to Darling Street Wharf, but stuck out on a spur in the harbour and kept apart from the centre by Darling Harbour and Johnston's Bay, it has a degree of separation that has helped it retain its village-like atmosphere and made it the favoured abode of many writers and filmmakers. Like better-known Paddington, Balmain was once a working-class quarter of terraced houses that has gradually been gentrified. Although the docks at White Bay no longer operate, the pubs that used to fuel the dockworkers still abound, and **Darling Street** and the surrounding backstreets are blessed with enough watering holes to warrant a pub crawl – two classics are the *London Hotel* on Darling Street and the *Exchange Hotel* on Beattie Street. Darling Street also rewards a leisurely stroll, with a bit of browsing in its quirky shops (focused on clothes and gifts), and grazing in its restaurants and cafés. The best time to come is on Saturday, when the lively **Balmain Market** occupies the grounds of St Andrews Church (7.30am–4pm), on the corner opposite the *London Hotel*. An assortment of books, handmade jewellery, clothing and ceramics, antiques, cakes and gourmet foods and organic produce are on sale. For a **self-guided tour** of Balmain and Birchgrove, buy a *Balmain Walks* leaflet ($2.20) from Balmain Library, 370 Darling St, or from the well-stocked Bray's Bookshop, at no. 268.

The most appealing way **to get to Balmain** is to catch a **ferry** from Circular Quay to Darling Street Wharf in Balmain East, where the #442 bus waits to take you up Darling Street to Balmain proper (or it's about a 10min walk). **Buses** #432 and #433 run out to Balmain via George Street, Railway Square and Glebe Point Road and down Darling Street; a quicker option is the #442 from the QVB, which crosses ANZAC Bridge and heads to Balmain Wharf.

The Harbour

Loftily flanking the mouth of Sydney Harbour are the rugged sandstone cliffs of North Head and South Head, providing spectacular viewing points across the calm water to the city 11km away, where the Harbour Bridge spans the sunken valley at its deepest point. The many coves, bays, points and headlands of Sydney Harbour, and their parks, bushland and swimmable beaches, are rewarding to explore. However, harbour beaches are not always as clean as ocean ones, and after storms are often closed to swimmers (see p.141). Finding your way by ferry is the most pleasurable method: services run to much of the **North Shore** and to harbourfront areas of the **eastern suburbs**. The eastern shores are characterized by a certain glitziness and are, fundamentally, the haunt of the nouveaux riches, while the leafy North Shore is largely the domain of Sydney's old money. Both sides of the harbour have pockets of bushland that have been incorporated into **Sydney Harbour National Park**, along with five islands, one of which – Fort Denison – can be visited by tour (see p.110); Shark Island is reachable by ferry from Darling Harbour or Circular Quay; while Clark Island and Rodd Island are accessed by private vessel only (bookings through NPWS; ☎02/9247 5033). The NPWS publishes an excellent free map detailing the areas of the national park and its many walking tracks, available from Cadmans Cottage in The Rocks.

Elizabeth Bay to South Head

The suburbs on the hilly southeast shores of the harbour are rich and exclusive. The area around **Darling Point**, the enviable postcode 2027, is the wealthiest in Australia, supporting the lifestyle of waterfront mansions and yacht-club memberships enjoyed by one-time residents Nicole Kidman and Lachlan Murdoch. A couple of early nineteenth-century mansions, Elizabeth Bay House and Vaucluse House, are open to visitors, providing an insight into the life of the pioneering upper crust, while the ferry to **Rose Bay** gives a good view of the pricey contemporary real estate; the bay is close to beautiful **Nielson Park** and the surrounding chunk of Sydney Harbour National Park. At South Head, **Watsons Bay** was once a fishing village, and there are spectacular views from **The Gap** in another section of the national park. Woollahra Council (ⓦ www.woollahra.nsw.gov.au) has brochures detailing three **waterside walks**: the 5.5-kilometre (3hr) **Rushcutters Bay** to Rose Bay harbour walk, which can then be continued with the eight-kilometre (4hr 30min) walk to Watsons Bay, and the fascinating five-kilometre cliffside walk from Christison Park in **Vaucluse** (off Old South Head Road) to Watsons Bay and **South Head**, with shipwreck sites, old lighthouses and military fortifications along the way.

Buses #324 and #325 from Circular Quay via Pitt Street, Kings Cross and Edgecliff cover the places listed below, heading to Watsons Bay via New South Head Road; #325 detours at Vaucluse for Nielson Park. Bus #327 runs between Martin Place and Bondi Junction stations via Edgecliff Station and Darling Point.

Elizabeth Bay and Rushcutters Bay

Barely five minutes' walk northeast of Kings Cross, **Elizabeth Bay** is a well-heeled residential area, centred on **Elizabeth Bay House**, at 7 Onslow Avenue (Fri–Sun 9.30am–4pm; open daily in Jan; $8; bus #311 from either Railway Square or Circular Quay, or walk from Kings Cross Station), a grand Regency residence with fine harbour views, built in 1835. Heading southeast, you're only a few minutes' walk from **Rushcutters Bay Park**, wonderfully set against a backdrop of the yacht- and cruiser-packed marina in the bay; the marina was revamped for the 2000 Olympics sailing competition. You can take it all in from the tables outside the very popular *Rushcutters Bay Kiosk*.

Double Bay and Rose Bay

Continuing northeast to **Darling Point**, McKell Park provides a wonderful view across to **Clarke Island** and **Bradleys Head**, both part of Sydney Harbour National Park; follow Darling Point Road (bus #327 from Edgecliff Station). Next port of call is **Double Bay**, dubbed "Double Pay" for obvious reasons. The noise and traffic of New South Head Road are redeemed by several excellent antiquarian and secondhand bookshops, while in the quieter "village", some of the most exclusive shops in Sydney are full of imported designer labels and expensive jewellery. Eastern-suburbs socialites meet on **Cross Street**, **Knox Street** and the small pedestrian lanes feeding them, where the swanky pavement cafés are filled with well-groomed women in Armani outfits. Double Bay's hidden gem is **Redleaf Pool** (Sept–May daily dawn–dusk; free), a peaceful, shady harbour beach enclosed by a wooden pier you can dive off or just laze on; there's also an excellent café here. A ferry stops at both Darling Point and Double Bay; otherwise, catch buses #323, #324, #325 or #327.

A ferry to **Rose Bay** from Circular Quay gives you a chance to check out the waterfront mansions of **Point Piper** as you skim past. Rose Bay itself is a haven of exclusivity, with the verdant expanse of the members-only Royal Sydney Golf Course. Directly across New South Head Road from the course, waterfront **Lyne Park's seaplane** service has been operating since the 1930s (℡02/9388 1978; ⓦwww.seaplanes.com.au). Rose Bay is also a popular **windsurfing** spot; you can rent equipment from Rose Bay Aquatic Hire (see p.179).

Nielson Park and Vaucluse

Sydney Harbour National Park emerges onto the waterfront at Bay View Hill, where the delightful 1.5-kilometre **Hermitage walking track** to Nielson Park begins; the starting point, Bay View Hill Road, is off South Head Road between the Kambala School and Rose Bay Convent (bus #324 or #325). The walk takes about an hour, with great views of the Opera House and Harbour

Bridge, some lovely little coves to swim in, and a picnic ground and sandy beach at yacht-filled **Hermit Point**. Extensive, tree-filled **Nielson Park**, on Shark Bay, is one of Sydney's delights, a great place for a swim, a picnic, or refreshment at the popular café. The decorative Victorian-era mansion, **Greycliffe House**, built for William Wentworth's daughter in 1852 (see below), is now the headquarters of Sydney Harbour National Park (Mon–Fri 10am–4pm; Ⓦwww .npws.nsw.gov.au) and provides excellent information and maps on all waterfront walks. With views across the harbour to the city skyline, the park is a prime spot to watch both the New Year's Eve fireworks and the Sydney-to-Hobart yachts racing out through the heads on Boxing Day.

Beyond Shark Bay, Vaucluse Bay shelters the magnificent Gothic-style 1803 **Vaucluse House** and its large estate on Wentworth Road (grounds daily 10am–5pm; house Fri–Sun 10am–4pm; $8), with tearooms in the grounds for refreshment. The house's original owner, explorer and reformer William Wentworth, was a member of the first party to cross the Blue Mountains. To get here, walk from Nielson Park along Coolong Road (or take bus #325). Beyond Vaucluse Bay, narrow **Parsley Bay**'s shady park is a popular picnic and swimming spot, crossed by a picturesque pedestrian suspension bridge.

Watsons Bay and South Head

On the finger of land culminating in South Head, with an expansive sheltered harbour bay on its west side, and the treacherous cliffs of The Gap on its ocean side, **Watsons Bay** was one of the earliest settlements outside of Sydney Cove. In 1790, Robert Watson was one of the first signalmen to man the clifftop flagstaffs nearby, and by 1792 the bay was the focus of a successful fishing village; the quaint old wooden fishermen's cottages are still found on the narrow streets around Camp Cove. It's an appropriate location for one of Sydney's longest-running fish restaurants, *Doyles* (see p.158), by the old Fishermans Wharf, now the ferry terminal (accessible by ferry from Circular Quay, or Rocket Harbour Explorer from Darling Harbour; see box, p.103). In fact, *Doyles* has taken over the waterfront here, with two restaurants, a takeaway, and a seafood bistro in the bayfront beer-garden of *Doyles Palace Hotel*.

Spectacular ocean views are just a two-minute walk away through grassy Robertson Park, across Gap Road to **The Gap** (buses terminate just opposite – the #324, #325, and faster #L24 from Circular Quay, and the #380 from Circular Quay via Bondi Beach), whose high cliffs are notorious as a place to commit suicide. You can follow a walking **track** north from here to South Head through another chunk of Sydney Harbour National Park, past the HMAS *Watson* Military Reserve. The track heads back to the bay side, and onto Cliff Street, which leads to pretty **Camp Cove**, a tiny, palm-fronted, unnetted harbour beach from which vantage point all harbour shores are lush national park.

Alternatively, reach Camp Cove by walking along the Watsons Bay beach and then along Pacific Street and through Green Point Reserve. From the northern end of Camp Cove, steps lead up to a boardwalk, which will take you to **South Head** (470m circuit), the lower jaw of the harbour mouth affording fantastic views of Port Jackson and the city, via Sydney's best-known **nudist beach**, "Lady Jane" (officially Lady Bay), a favourite gay haunt. It's not very private, however: a lookout point on the track provides full views, and ogling tour boats cruise past all weekend. From Lady Bay, it's a further fifteen minutes' walk along a boardwalked path to South Head itself, past nineteenth-century fortifications, lighthouse cottages, and the picturesquely red-and-white-striped Hornby Lighthouse.

The North Shore

The **North Shore** is generally more affluent than the South. **Cremorne Point**, **Clifton Gardens** and **Balmoral** in particular have some stunning waterfront real estate, priced to match. It's surprising just how much harbourside bushland remains intact here – "leafy" just doesn't do it justice – and superbly sited amongst it all is **Taronga Zoo**. A ride on any ferry lets you gaze at beaches, bush, yachts and swish harbourfront houses, and is one of the chief joys of this area.

North Sydney and around

Beside the Harbour Bridge on Lavender Bay at **Milsons Point**, you can't miss the huge laughing clown's face that belongs to **Luna Park**. Generations of Sydneysiders have walked through the grinning mouth, and the park's old rides and conserved 1930s fun hall, complete with period wall murals, slot machines, silly mirrors and giant slippery dips, have great nostalgia value for locals. Luna Park has had its ups and downs over the years, but in 2004 it was restored to its former glory and reopened to the public (opening times are variable – see ⓦ www.lunaparksydney.com; individual rides $10, unlimited-ride day pass $48). The ferry to Milsons Point Wharf from Circular Quay or Darling Harbour pulls up right outside (or train to Milsons Point Station). Beyond the park, a boardwalk goes right around Lavender Bay offering spectacular views of the Harbour Bridge and Opera House, most notably from McMahons Point Wharf and the adjacent park at Blues Point – which is a photographer's delight.

Right next door to Luna Park is Sydney's most picturesquely sited public swimming pool, with terrific vistas of the Harbour Bridge – the heated **North Sydney Olympic Pool**, Alfred South Street (Mon–Fri 5.30am–9pm, Sat & Sun 7am–7pm; $5.80). There's an indoor 25-metre pool as well as a 50-metre outdoor pool, a gym, sauna, spa, café, and an expensive restaurant, *Aqua*, overlooking the pool.

Just east of the Harbour Bridge and immediately opposite the Opera House, **Kirribilli** and adjacent Neutral Bay are mainly residential areas, although Kirribilli hosts a great general **market** on the fourth Saturday of the month in Bradfield Park (7am–3pm), the best and biggest of several rotating markets on the North Shore (see p.139). On Kirribilli Point, **Kirribilli House** is the Prime Minister's official Sydney residence, while next door, Admiralty House is the Sydney home of the Governor General, where the British royal family stay when they're in town.

Following the harbour round you'll come to upmarket **Neutral Bay**. A five-minute walk from Neutral Bay ferry wharf via Hayes Street and Lower Wycombe Road is **Nutcote**, at 5 Wallaringa Ave (Wed–Sun 11am–3pm; $8), the former home for 45 years of May Gibbs, the author and illustrator of the famous Australian children's book, *Snugglepot and Cuddlepie*, about two little gumnuts who come to life; published in 1918, it's an enduring classic. Bush-covered **Cremorne Point**, which juts into the harbour here, is also worth a jaunt. Catching the ferry from Circular Quay brings you in a short stroll from a quaint open-access sea pool; from here, you can walk right around the point to Mosman Bay (just under 2km), or in the other direction, past the pool, there's a very pretty walk into **Shell Cove** (1km).

Taronga Zoo

Taronga Zoo on Bradleys Head Road, Mosman, has a superb hilltop position overlooking the city (daily 9am–5pm; adult $39, child $19, family $98.50, under-4s free; Zoo Pass including return ferry and entry $44; child $21.50

Ⓦ www.taronga.org.au). The wonderful views and the natural bush surrounds are as much an attraction as the chance to get up close to the animals. The zoo houses bounding Australian marsupials, native birds (including kookaburras, galahs and cockatoos), reptiles, and sea lions and seals from the sub-Antarctic region. You'll also find exotic beasts from around the world, including giraffes, gorillas and many a playful chimpanzee. The **Wild Asia** exhibit includes a long-awaited new home for Taronga's five Asian elephants.

You can get close to kangaroos and wallabies in the **Australian Walkabout** area, and the **koala house** gives you eye-level views; to get closer, arrange to have your photo taken next to a koala (daily 11am–2.45pm; $19.95). For a more **hands-on experience**, a VIP Aussie Gold Tour (daily 9.15am & 1.15pm; 1hr 30min–2hr; $80; child $41; includes zoo entry; book 24hr in advance on ⓣ 02/9978 4782) will give you and a small group a session with a zookeeper, guiding you through the Australian animals, some of which can be handled. Keeper talks and feeding sessions – including a free-flight bird show and a seal show – run through the day; details are on the map handed out on arrival.

The zoo can be reached by **ferry** from Circular Quay to Taronga Zoo Wharf (every 30min). Although there's a lower entrance near the wharf on Athol Road, it's best to start your visit from the upper entrance and spend several leisurely hours winding downhill to exit for the ferry. State Transit buses meet the ferries for the trip uphill, but a better option is to take the **Sky Safari** cable car included in the entry price. **Bus** #247 from Wynyard or the QVB also goes to the zoo.

Bradleys Head

Beyond the zoo, at the termination of **Bradleys Head Road**, Bradleys Head is marked by an enormous mast that once belonged to HMAS *Sydney* (1912), a victorious World War I Royal Australian Navy battleship (not to be confused with the recently recovered ship of the same title, built in 1934). The rocky point is a peaceful spot with a dinky lighthouse and, of course, a fabulous view back over the south shore. A colony of ringtailed possums nests here, and boisterous flocks of rainbow lorikeets visit. The headland comprises another large chunk of Sydney Harbour National Park: you can walk to Bradleys Head via the six-kilometre **Ashton Park walking track**, which starts near Taronga Zoo Wharf, and continues beyond the headland to Taylors Bay and Chowder Head, finishing at **Clifton Gardens**, where there's a jetty and sea baths on **Chowder Bay**. It is worth wandering the streets of Clifton Gardens: the lofty hillside mansions here are arguably the most beautiful and superbly sited on the harbour, surrounded as they are by Sydney Harbour National Park – most significantly, picturesque Taylors Bay, with its lush, unadulterated wilderness shoreline. The now defunct military reserve that separates Chowder Bay from another chunk of Sydney Harbour National Park on Middle Head is open to the public (see p.141), reached by a boardwalk from the northern end of Clifton Gardens.

Middle Harbour

Middle Harbour is the largest inlet of Port Jackson, its two sides joined across the narrowest point at **The Spit**. The Spit Bridge opens regularly to let tall-masted yachts through – much the best way to explore its pretty, quiet coves and bays (see box, p.103). Crossing the Spit Bridge, you can walk all the way to Manly Beach along the ten-kilometre Manly Scenic Walkway (see p.147). The area also hides some architectural gems: the mock-Gothic 1889 bridge leading to **Northbridge**, and the idyllic enclave of **Castlecrag**, which was designed in 1924 by **Walter Burley Griffin**, fresh from planning Canberra and intent on building an environmentally friendly suburb – free of the fences and the red-tiled roofs he hated – that would be "for ever part of the bush". Bus #144 runs to Spit Road from Manly Wharf, taking a scenic route uphill overlooking the Spit marina. To get to Castlecrag, take bus #203 from Wynyard.

Between Clifton Gardens and Balmoral Beach, a military reserve and naval depot at **Chowder Bay** blocked coastal access to both **Georges Head** and the more spectacular **Middle Head** by foot for over a century. Since the military's 1997 withdrawal from the site, walkers can now trek all the way between Bradleys Head and Middle Head. The 1890s military settlement of Middle Head is open to visitors as a reserve, and the NPWS offers tours exploring the underground fortifications (fourth Sun of the month at 10.30am; 2hr; $13.20). You can reach the military reserve entrance from the northern end of Clifton Gardens (see p.140) or walk from Balmoral Beach. On the Hunters Bay (Balmoral) side of Middle Head, tiny **Cobblers Beach** is officially **nudist**, and is a much more peaceful, secluded option than the more famous Lady Bay at South Head.

The bush of Middle Head provides a gorgeous backdrop to the shady, tree-lined **Balmoral Beach** on Hunters Bay, which is very popular with families. Fronting the beach, there's something very Edwardian and genteel about palm-filled, grassy Hunters Park and its bandstand, which is still used for Sunday jazz concerts and Shakespeare performances in summer. The antiquated air is enhanced by the pretty, white-painted **Bathers Pavilion** at the northern end, now converted into a restaurant and café (see p.158). There are two sections of beach at Balmoral, separated by **Rocky Point**, a picturesque promontory and noted picnicking spot. South of Rocky Point, the "baths" – actually a netted bit of beach with a boardwalk and lanes for swimming laps – have been here in one form or another since 1899; you can rent sailboards, catamarans, kayaks and canoes; lessons are available from Balmoral Sailing Club (see p.179).

To get to Balmoral, catch a **ferry** from Circular Quay to Taronga Zoo Wharf and then bus #238 via Bradleys Head Road, or, after 7pm from Monday to Saturday, the ferry to South Mosman (Musgrave St) Wharf, at nearby Mosman, then bus #233.

Ocean beaches

Sydney's **beaches** are among its great natural joys. The water and sand seem remarkably clean – people actually eat fish caught in the harbour – and at Long Reef, just north of Manly, you can find rock pools teeming with starfish, anemones, sea-snails and crabs, and even a few shy moray eels. In recent years, whale populations have recovered to such an extent that humpback and southern right whales have been regularly sighted from the Sydney headlands in June and July on their migratory path from the Antarctic to the tropical waters of Queensland, and southern right whales even occasionally make an appearance in Sydney Harbour itself – the three whales frolicking under the Harbour Bridge in July 2002 caused a sensation. Don't be lulled into a false sense of security, however: the beaches do have **perils** as well as pleasures. Some are protected by special shark nets, but they don't keep out stingers such as bluebottles, which can suddenly swamp an entire beach; listen for loudspeaker announcements that will summon you from the water in the event of shark sightings or other dangers. Pacific **currents** can be very strong indeed – inexperienced swimmers and those with small children would do better sticking to the sheltered **harbour beaches** or **sea pools** at the ocean beaches. Ocean beaches are generally patrolled by **surf lifesavers** during the day between October and April (all year at Bondi): red and yellow flags (generally up from 6am until 6 or 7pm) indicate the safe areas to swim, avoiding dangerous rips and undertows. It's hard not to be impressed as **surfers** paddle out on a seething ocean, but don't follow them unless you're confident you know what you're doing. Surf schools can teach the basic skills, surfing etiquette and lingo (see "Listings", p.179). You can check daily **surf reports** on ⓦwww.realsurf.com.

The final hazard, despite the apparent cleanliness, is **pollution**. Monitoring shows that it is nearly always safe to swim at all of Sydney's beaches – except after storms, when storm water, currents and onshore breezes wash up sewage and other rubbish onto harbour beaches making them (as signs will indicate) unsuitable for swimming and surfing. To check pollution levels, consult the Beachwatch Bulletin (☏1800 036 677, ⓦwww.environment .nsw.gov.au).

Topless bathing for women, while legal, is accepted on many beaches but frowned on at others, so if in doubt, do as the locals do. There are two official **nudist** beaches around the harbour (see p.138 & p.141).

Bondi and the eastern beaches

Sydney's eastern beaches stretch from Bondi down to Maroubra. Heading south from Bondi, you can walk right along the coast to its smaller, less brazen but very lively cousin **Coogee**, passing through gay-favourite **Tamarama**, family focused, café-cultured **Bronte**, narrow **Clovelly** and **Gordons Bay**, the latter with an underwater nature trail. Randwick Council has designed the "Coastal Walkway" from Clovelly to Coogee and beyond to more downmarket **Maroubra**, with stretches of boardwalk and interpretive boards detailing environmental features. A free guide can be picked up at visitor centres and downloaded at ⓦwww.randwickcitytourism.com.au. It's also possible to walk north all the way from Bondi to South Head along the cliffs, now that missing links in the pathway have been connected with bridges and boardwalk.

Christmas Day on Bondi

For years, backpackers and Bondi Beach on **Christmas Day** were synonymous. The beach was transformed into a drunken party scene, as those from colder climes lived out their fantasy of spending Christmas on the beach under a scorching sun. The behaviour and litter began getting out of control, and after riots in 1995, and a rubbish-strewn beach, the local council began strictly controlling the whole performance, with the idea of trying to keep a spirit of goodwill towards the travellers while also tempting local families back to the beach on what is regarded as a family day. Nowadays, alcohol is banned from the beach and surrounding area on Christmas Day, and police enforce the rule with on-the-spot confiscations. However, a **party** is organized in the Pavilion, with a bar, DJs, food and entertainment running from noon to 10pm. Up to 3000 revellers cram into the Pavilion, while thousands of others – including a greater proportion of the desired family groups – enjoy the alcohol-free beach outside. In 2008, **tickets** for the Pavilion bash were $65 in advance from backpacker hostels, Moshtix (☏1300 438 849, ⓦwww.moshtix.com.au) or Ticketek (☏13 28 49, ⓦwww.Ticketek.com.au).

Bondi Beach

Bondi Beach is synonymous with Australian beach culture, and indeed the 1.5km-long curve of golden sand must be one of the best-known beaches in the world. It's also the closest ocean beach to the city centre; you can take a train to Bondi Junction and then a ten-minute bus ride, or drive there in twenty minutes. Big, brash and action-packed, it's probably not the best place for a quiet sunbathe and swim, but the sprawling sandy crescent really is spectacular. Red-tiled houses and apartment buildings crowd in to catch the view, many of them erected in the 1920s when Bondi was a working-class suburb. Although still residential, it's long since become a popular gathering place for backpackers from around the world (see box, p.142).

The beachfront **Campbell Parade** is both cosmopolitan and highly commercialized, lined with cafés and shops. For a gentler experience, explore some of the side streets, such as **Hall Street**, where an assortment of kosher bakeries and delis serve the area's Jewish community, and some of Bondi's best cafés are hidden. On Sunday, the **Bondi Beach Markets** (10am–5pm), in the grounds of the primary school on the corner of Campbell Parade and Warners Avenue facing the northern end of the beach, are good for fashion and jewellery. Between Campbell Parade and the beach, **Bondi Park** slopes down to the promenade, and is always full of sprawling bodies. The focus of the promenade is the arcaded, Spanish-style **Bondi Pavilion**, built in 1928 as a deluxe changing-room complex and converted into a community centre hosting an array of workshops, classes and events, from drama and comedy in the theatre and the Seagull Room (the former ballroom) to the outdoor Bondi Short Film Festival in the courtyard (Ⓦwww.bondishortfilmfestival.com), which takes place in late November. A community-access **art gallery** on the ground floor (daily 10am–5pm; free) features changing exhibitions by local artists. In September, the day-long Festival of the Winds, Australia's largest **kite festival**, takes over the beach.

Surfing is part of the Bondi legend, the big waves ensuring that there's always a pack of damp young things hanging around, bristling with surfboards. However, the beach is carefully delineated, with surfers using the southern end. There are two sets of flags for swimmers and boogie-boarders, with families congregating at the northern end near the sheltered saltwater pool (free), and everybody else using the middle flags. The beach is netted and there hasn't been a shark attack since 1929. If the sea is too rough, or if you want to swim laps, head for the sea-water swimming pool at the southern end of the beach under the **Bondi Icebergs Club** on Notts Avenue, with a fifty-metre lap pool, kids' pool, gym, sauna, massage service and poolside café (pool Mon–Wed & Fri 6am–6.30pm, Sat & Sun 6.30am–6.30pm; $4.50). The Icebergs Club has been part of the Bondi legend since 1929 – members must swim throughout the winter, and media coverage of their plunge, made truly wintry with the addition of huge chunks of ice, heralds the first day of winter. The very dilapidated club building was knocked down and rebuilt in 2002; the top floor houses the posh *Icebergs Dining Room and Bar*, while the floor below has the club's less salubrious *Icebergs Bistro* (for both, see p.159), which shares the fabulous view over pool and beach.

Topless bathing is condoned at Bondi – a far cry from conditions up to the late 1960s when stern beach inspectors were constantly on the lookout for indecent exposure. If you want to join in the sun and splash but don't have the gear, Beached at Bondi, below the lifeguard lookout tower, rents out everything from umbrellas, wet suits, cozzies and towels to surfboards and body-boards. It also sells hats and sun block and has lockers for valuables.

Bondi's surf lifesavers

Surf lifesavers are what made Bondi famous, so naturally a bronze sculpture of one is given pride of place outside the Bondi Pavilion. The surf lifesaving movement began in 1906 with the founding of the Bondi Surf Life Bathers' Lifesaving Club in response to the drownings that accompanied the increasing popularity of swimming. From the beginning of the colony, swimming was harshly discouraged as an unsuitable bare-fleshed activity. However, by the 1890s swimming in the ocean had become the latest fad, and a Pacific Islander introduced the concept of catching waves – or bodysurfing – that was to become an enduring national craze. Although "wowsers" (teetotal puritanical types) attempted to put a stop to it, by 1903 all-day swimming was every Sydneysider's right.

The bronzed and muscled surf lifesavers in their distinctive red-and-yellow caps are a highly photographed, world-famous Australian image. Surf lifesavers (members of what are now called Surf Life Saving Clubs, abbreviated to SLSC) are volunteers who work the beach at weekends, so come then to watch their exploits – or look out for a surf carnival. Lifeguards, on the other hand, are employed by the council and work all week during swimming season (year-round at Bondi).

Reach Bondi Beach on **bus** #333, #380 or #389 from Circular Quay via Oxford Street and Bondi Junction, or take the train to Bondi Junction Station, then transfer to these buses or to the #361, #381 and #382.

Tamarama to Gordons Bay

Many people find the smaller, quieter beaches to the south of Bondi more enticing, and the oceanfront and clifftop **walking track** to Clovelly (about 2hr) is popular – the track also includes a fitness circuit, so you'll see plenty of joggers en route. Walk past the Bondi Icebergs Club on Notts Avenue (see p.143), round Mackenzies Point and through Marks Park to the modest and secluded **Mackenzies Bay**. Next is **Tamarama Bay** ("Glamarama" to the locals), a deep, narrow beach favoured by the smart set and a hedonistic gay crowd, as well as surfers. The walk from Bondi takes about fifteen minutes, or if you want to come here directly, hop on bus #360 or #361 from Bondi Junction.

Walking through Tamarama's small park and following the oceanfront road for five minutes will bring you to the next beach along, **Bronte Beach** on Nelson Bay, easily reached on bus #378 from Central Station via Oxford Street and Bondi Junction. More of a family affair, with a large green park, a popular café strip and sea baths, the **northern end** as you arrive from Tamarama has inviting flat-rock platforms, popular as fishing and relaxation spots, and the beach here is cliff-backed, providing some shade. The **park** beyond is extensive with Norfolk Island Pines for shade; a **mini-train ride** for small children (Sat & Sun 11am–4pm) has been operating here since 1947, while further back there's a children's playground. At the **southern end** of the beach, palm trees lend a holiday feel as you relax at one of the outside tables of Bronte Road's cafés – there are several to choose from, plus a fish-and-chip shop. Back on the water at this end a natural rock enclosure, the "Bogey Hole", makes a calm area for snorkelling and kids to swim in, and there are rock ledges to lie on around the enclosed sea swimming pool known as **Bronte Baths** (open access; free), often a better option than the surf here, which can be very rough.

It's a pleasant five-minute walk past the Bronte Baths to **Waverley Cemetery**, a fantastic spot to spend eternity. Established in 1877, it contains the graves of many famous Australians, with the bush poet contingent well represented.

Henry Lawson, described on his headstone as poet, journalist and patriot, languishes in section 3G 516, while **Dorothea Mackeller**, who penned the famous poem "I love a sunburnt country", is in section 6 832–833.

Beyond here – another five-minute walk – on the other side of Shark Point, is the channel-like **Clovelly Bay**, with concrete platforms on either side and several sets of steps leading into the very deep water. Rocks at the far end keep out the waves, and the sheltered bay is popular with lap-swimmers and snorkellers; you're almost certain to see one of the bay's famous blue groupers. There's also a free swimming pool. A grassy park with several terraces extends back from the beach and is a great place for a picnic. The divinely sited café is packed at weekends, and on Sunday afternoons and evenings the nearby *Clovelly Hotel* is a popular hangout, with free live music and a great bistro, or get rock-bottom-priced drinks and lovely views at the beachside *Clovelly Bowling Club*. To get to Clovelly, take **bus** #339 from Millers Point via Central Station and Albion Street, Surry Hills; #360 from Bondi Junction; or the weekday peak-hour #X39 from Wynyard.

From Clovelly, it's best to stick to the road route along Cliffbrook Parade rather than rockhop around to equally narrow **Gordons Bay**. Unsupervised, undeveloped Gordons Bay itself is not a pretty beach, but another world exists beneath the sheltered water: the protected **underwater nature trail**, marked out for divers, is home to a range of sea creatures. From here, a walkway leads around the waterfront to Major Street and then onto **Dunningham Reserve** overlooking the northern end of Coogee Beach; the walk to Coogee proper takes about fifteen minutes in all.

Coogee

Laid-back, community-oriented **Coogee** is another long-popular seaside resort, almost on a par with Manly and Bondi, and teeming with young travellers who flock to the stack of backpackers' hostels here. With its hilly streets of Californian-style apartment blocks looking onto a compact, pretty beach enclosed by two cliffy, green-covered headlands, Coogee has a snugness that Bondi just can't match. Everything is close to hand: beachside **Arden Street** is dominated by the extensive *Coogee Bay Hotel*, one of Sydney's best-known music venues, while the main shopping street, **Coogee Bay Road**, runs uphill from the beach and has a choice selection of coffee spots and restaurants, plus a big supermarket.

The imaginatively modernized promenade is a great place to stroll and hang out; between it and the beach a grassy park has free electric barbecues, picnic tables and shelters. The beach is popular with families (there's an excellent children's playground above the southern end, while at the northern end you'll find the *Beach Palace Hotel*, a 1980s restoration of the 1887 Coogee Palace Aquarium. In its heyday it had a gigantic dancefloor that could accommodate three thousand pleasure-seekers; today the hotel is a popular drinking spot for backpackers, who crowd out its oceanfront balcony.

One of Coogee's chief pleasures is its baths, beyond the southern end of the beach. The first, the secluded, volunteer-run McIvers Baths, traditionally for women only (and boys up to age 3), is known by locals as **Coogee Women's Pool** (noon–5pm; 20¢). Just south of the women's pool is the 1917 **Wylies Baths**, a unisex saltwater pool on the edge of the sea (daily: Oct–April 7am–7pm, May–Sept 7am–5pm; $3), with big decks to lie on and solar-heated showers; its kiosk serves excellent coffee.

You can reach Coogee on **bus** #373 or #374 from Circular Quay via Randwick, or #372 from Eddy Avenue, outside Central Station; the journey time from Central is about 25 minutes. Alternatively, take bus #313 or #314 from Bondi Junction via Randwick.

Immediately south of Wylies, **Trenerry Reserve** is a huge green park jutting out into the ocean; its spread of big, flat rocks offers tremendous views and makes a great place to chill out. Probably the most impressive section of Randwick Council's **Eastern Beaches Coast Walk** commences here. You initially follow a boardwalk where interpretive panels detail the ongoing regeneration work on native flora and highlight the returning bird and animal life. Steps lead down to a rock platform full of small pools – you can wander down and look at the creatures there, and there's a large tear-shaped pool you can swim in, quite thrilling with the waves crashing over – but be careful of the waves and the blue-ringed octopus found here. At low tide you can continue walking along the rocks around Lurline Bay – otherwise you must follow the streets inland for a bit, rejoining the waterfront from Mermaid Avenue. Jack Vanny Memorial Park is fronted by the large rocks of Mistral Point, a great spot to sit and look at the water, and down by the sea there's the **Mahon Pool** (free; open access), a small, pleasant pool surrounded by great boulders, with an unspoilt, secluded feel. The isolated *Pool Caffe* across the road on Marine Parade makes a wonderful lunch or coffee spot.

Manly and the northern beaches

Manly, just above the North Head of Sydney Harbour, is doubly blessed, with both ocean and harbour beaches. It is this combination, and its easy accessibility from central Sydney, that give it the feeling of a holiday village still within the city limits. When Captain Arthur Phillip, the commander of the First Fleet, was exploring Sydney Harbour in 1788, he saw a group of well-built Aboriginal men onshore, proclaimed them to be "manly" and named the cove in the process. During the Edwardian era it became fashionable as a recreational retreat from the city, with the promotional slogan "Manly – seven miles from Sydney, but a thousand miles from care". An excellent time to visit is over the Labour Day long weekend in early October, for the **Jazz Festival**.

Beyond Manly, the **northern beaches** continue for 30km up to the Barrenjoey Peninsula and **Palm Beach**. Pick up the excellent, free *Sydney's Northern Beaches Map* from the Manly visitor centre (see below). The northern beaches can be reached by regular **bus** from various city bus terminals or from Manly Wharf; routes are detailed throughout the text below.

Manly

The ferry trip out to Manly has always been half the fun: the legendary **Manly Ferry** (Mon–Fri 6am–11.45pm, Sat 8am–11.45pm, Sun 8am–11pm; every 30–40min; $6.40 one-way) has run from Circular Quay since 1854. After the ferry finishes, the #151 **night bus** runs from Wynyard Station. Ferries terminate at **Manly Wharf** with its cafés, shops and **visitor centre** (Mon–Fri 9am–5pm, Sat & Sun 10am–4pm; ☏02/9976 1430, ⊛www .manlytourism.com.au). The wharf is now a hub for **adventure activities**: three watersports companies based here offer parasailing, kayaking and rigid-inflatable-boat tours through crashing surf to North Head; ask at the visitor centre for details.

From the wharf, walk north along West Esplanade to **Oceanworld** (daily 10am–5.30pm; $18.50; ☏02/8251 7877, ⊛www.oceanworld.com.au), where clear acrylic walls hold back the water so you can saunter along the harbour floor, gazing at sharks and stingrays. It's not a patch on the Sydney Aquarium at Darling Harbour, but is considerably cheaper, and kids love it. Divers hand-feed sharks three times weekly (Mon, Wed & Fri at 11am) and you can also organize dives among the big grey nurse sharks with Shark Dive Extreme (qualified diver $185, refresher diver course $220, unqualified diver $250; bookings ☎02/8251 7878).

Opposite Oceanworld, the screams come from the three giant waterslides at **Manly Waterworks** (Oct–Easter Sat, Sun, school & public holidays 10am–5pm, plus Dec–Feb Sat 10am–9pm; 1hr $14.50, all day $19.50; must be over 120cm tall to enter). Between the slides and Oceanworld, the **Manly Art Gallery and Museum** (Tues–Sun 10am–5pm, closed public holidays; free) has a collection started in the 1920s of Australian paintings, drawings, prints and etchings, and a stash of fun beach memorabilia including huge old wooden surfboards and old-fashioned swimming costumes.

Northeast of Manly Wharf, **The Corso** cuts directly across the isthmus 500m to South Steyne beach. The Corso is lined with surf shops, cafés, bakeries, restaurants and pubs, while **South Steyne** beach is characterized by the stands of Norfolk pine that line the shore. Every summer, Manly Beach Hire rents out just about anything to make the beach more fun, from surfboards to snorkel sets, and they also have lockers for your valuables. A six-kilometre-long shared pedestrian and **cycle path** begins at South Steyne and runs north to Seaforth, past North Steyne Beach and Queenscliff. You can join a two-hour **guided bike tour** around interesting corners of Manly with Manly Bike Tours, 2 West Promenade (daily 10.30am; $55; ☎02/8005 7368, ⓦwww.manlybiketours .com.au), who also offer bike hire.

For a more idyllic beach, follow the footpath from the southern end of South Steyne around the headland to Cabbage Tree Bay, with two very pretty – and protected – green-backed beaches at either end: **Fairy Bower** to the west (where you'll find *The Bower Café*) and **Shelley Beach** to the east (home to the swanky *Le Kiosk*).

Belgrave Street, running north from Manly Wharf, is Manly's alternative strip, with good cafés, interesting shops, yoga schools and the Manly Environment Centre at no. 41, whose aim is to educate the community about the local biodiversity and the issues affecting it.

North Head

More of the Sydney Harbour National Park can be explored at **North Head**, the harbour mouth's upper jaw, where you can follow the short, circuitous Fairfax Walking Track to three lookout points, including the **Fairfax Lookout**, for splendid views. A regular #135 **bus** leaves from Manly Wharf for North Head, or you can simply drive up there. Right in the middle of this national

The Manly Scenic Walkway

One of the finest harbourside walks anywhere in Sydney is the **Manly Scenic Walkway** (10km one-way; 3–4hr; mostly flat) which follows the harbour shore inland from Manly Cove all the way west to Spit Bridge on Middle Harbour, where you can catch a bus (#180 and many others) back to Wynyard Station in the city centre (20min). This wonderful walk takes you through some of the area's more expensive neighbourhoods before heading into a section of Sydney Harbour National Park (free entry) past a number of small beaches and coves – perfect for stopping off for a dip – Aboriginal middens and some subtropical rainforest. The walk can easily be broken up into six sections with obvious exit/entry points; pick up a map from the Manly visitor centre (see opposite) or NPWS offices.

park is a military reserve centred on the **North Fort – National Artillery Museum** (Wed–Sun 10am–4pm; $11; ⓦwww.northfort.org.au), sited in the historic North Fort, a curious system of tunnels built into the headland here during the Crimean Wars in the nineteenth century, as a reaction to fears of a Russian invasion. It takes around an hour and a half to wander through the tunnels with the obligatory guide.

There's a modern twist to historic Sydney at **Q Station** (ⓣ02/9977 5145, ⓦwww.qstation.com.au), a reworking of the old Quarantine Station, on the harbour side of North Head. From 1832 until 1984, arriving passengers and crew who had a contagious disease were set down here to serve forty days of isolation. Sydney residents, too, were forced here, most memorably during the plague which broke out in The Rocks in 1900, when 1828 people were quarantined (104 plague victims are buried in the grounds). The old quarantine accommodation has now been turned into a kind of historic luxury resort.

Although you can't just wander around the site, you can join a tour, attend a performance or dine at the *Boilerhouse Restaurant* – no bad thing in itself. To get a general feel for the old Quarantine Station join one of the two-hour **tours**, which mostly take place at weekends: the "Day Tour" ($35) is a fairly straight-forward walking visit, while "40 Days" ($35) takes a more interactive approach, with clues guiding you around the quarantine station as you get a sense of what it was like here during the 1918 flu epidemic. **Ghost tours** come in three guises: the child-friendly "Family Ghosty" (adults $34; children $22); the more nerve-wracking "Adult Ghost Tour" ($44); and the "Spirit Investigator" ($44), during which a medium takes you ghost-hunting.

There's a more traditional appeal to *Defiance* (early bookings $35, otherwise $50–65), a genuinely entertaining "immersion" play in which you'll find yourself sucked into the experience of life at the quarantine station during the 1881 smallpox epidemic, the 1901 bubonic plague, the 1918 Spanish influenza pandemic and a projected Avian flu epidemic in 2020. The two acts are performed in buildings where some of the events depicted took place.

You can get a water shuttle direct to Q Station ($26 return) from King Street Wharf, but it is often better value going for a tour **package**; see the website for details.

Freshwater to Palm Beach

Freshwater, just beyond Manly, sits snugly between two rocky headlands on Queenscliff Bay, and is one of the most picturesque of the northern beaches. There's plenty of surf culture around the headland at Curl Curl, and a walking track at its northern end, commencing from Huston Parade, will take you above the rocky coastline to the curve of **Dee Why Beach** (bus #136 or #156 from Manly Wharf; or bus #151, #169 or #178 from outside the QVB).

Several other picturesque beaches lie up the coast. The long, beautiful sweep of **Collaroy Beach** with its YHA (see p.102) shades into **Narrabeen Beach**, an idyllic spot backed by the extensive, swimmable and fishable **Narrabeen Lakes**, popular with anglers, kayakers and families. Beyond Narrabeen, **Mona Vale** is a long, straight stretch of beach with a large park behind and a sea pool dividing it from sheltered **Bongin Bay**.

After Bongin Bay the Barrenjoey Peninsula begins, with calm **Pittwater** (see p.183) on its western side and ocean beaches running up its eastern side. **Newport** is best known for the gargantuan beer-garden deck of *The Newport Arms* overlooking Heron Cove at Pittwater. Unassuming **Bilgola Beach**, next door to Newport and nestled at the base of a steep cliff, is one of the prettiest of the northern beaches, with its distinctive orange sand. From Bilgola Beach, a trio of Sydney's best beaches, for both surf and scenery, runs up the eastern fringe of the hammerhead peninsula. One of the most convenient is **Avalon Beach**, popular surfie territory backed by a set of shops and the *Avalon Beach Backpackers* (see p.101).

At the northern point of the peninsula is **Palm Beach**, a hangout for the rich and famous and a popular city escape. It's also the location of "Summer Bay" in the long-running Aussie soap *Home and Away*, with the picturesque bush-covered Barrenjoey Head – part of **Ku-ring-gai Chase National Park** – regularly in shot. The headland is topped by the 1881 **Barrenjoey Lighthouse** (Sun 11am–3pm with 30min tours every 30min; $3; ☎02/9472 9300), which can be reached by a steep walking path (2km return; 40–60min; 110m ascent) from the car park at the base; your reward is a stunning panorama of Palm Beach, Pittwater and the Hawkesbury River.

You can **stay** at the quirky *Palm Beach Bed and Breakfast* at 122 Pacific Rd (see p.102) with lovely views of the ocean. **Buses** #190 and #L90 run up the peninsula from Railway Square at Central via Wynyard to Avalon, continuing to Palm Beach via the Pittwater side; change at Avalon for bus #193 to Whale Beach. Bus #L88 goes from Central and Wynyard to Avalon, and the #187 from Milsons Point in The Rocks to Newport.

Botany Bay

The southern suburbs of Sydney, arranged around huge **Botany Bay**, are seen as the heartland of red-tiled-roof suburbia, a terracotta sea spied from above as the planes land at **Mascot**. Clive James, the area's most famous son, hails from Kogarah – described as a 1950s suburban wasteland in his tongue-in-cheek *Unreliable Memoirs*. The popular perception of Botany Bay is coloured by its proximity to an airport, a high-security prison (Long Bay), an oil refinery, a container terminal and a sewerage outlet. Yet the surprisingly clean-looking water is fringed by quiet, sandy beaches and the marshlands shelter a profusion of birdlife. Whole areas of the waterfront, at **La Perouse**, with its associations with eighteenth-century French exploration, and on the **Kurnell Peninsula** where Captain Cook first set anchor, are designated as part of **Botany Bay National Park**, and large stretches on either side of the Georges River form a State Recreation Area. **Brighton-Le-Sands**, the busy suburban strip on the west of the bay, is a hive of bars and restaurants and is something of a focus for Sydney's Greek community. Its long beach is also a popular spot for windsurfers and kite-surfers.

La Perouse

At least, is there any news of Monsieur de Laperouse?

Louis XVI, about to be guillotined, 1793

La Perouse, tucked into the northern shore of Botany Bay where it meets the Pacific Ocean, contains Sydney's oldest Aboriginal settlement, the legacy of a mission. The suburb took its name from the eighteenth-century French explorer, **Laperouse**, who set up camp here for six weeks, briefly and cordially meeting Captain Arthur Phillip, who was making his historic decision to forgo swampy Botany Bay and move on to Port Jackson. After leaving Botany Bay, the Laperouse expedition was never seen again. A monument erected in 1825 and the excellent NPWS-run **La Perouse Museum** (Wed–Sun 10am–4pm; $5.50), which sits on a grassy headland between the pretty beaches of

Congwong Bay and Frenchmans Bay, tell the whole fascinating story. There is also an exhibition that looks at the Aboriginal history and culture of the area.

The surrounding headlands and foreshore have been incorporated into the northern half of **Botany Bay National Park** (free; the other half is across Botany Bay on the Kurnell Peninsula). An **NPWS visitor centre** (℡02/9311 3379) in the museum building provides details of walks, including a fine one past Congwong Bay Beach to Henry Head and its lighthouse (5km round trip). The idyllic veranda of the *Boatshed Cafe*, on the small headland between Congwong and Frenchmans bays, sits right over the water with a white sand beach arcing from below and cranes puncturing the distant shoreline. La Perouse is at its most lively on **Sunday** (and public holidays) when, following a tradition established at the start of the twentieth century, Aboriginal people come down to sell boomerangs and other crafts, and demonstrate snake-handling skills (from 1.30pm) and boomerang throwing. There are also tours of the nineteenth-century fortifications on **Bare Island** (Sun 1.30pm, 2.30pm & 3.30pm; 45min; $5; no booking required, wait at the gate to the island), joined to La Perouse by a thin walkway; the island was originally built amid fears of a Russian invasion, and featured in *Mission Impossible II*.

To **get to La Perouse**, catch **bus** #394 or #399 from Circular Quay via Darlinghurst and Moore Park, or #393 from Railway Square via Surry Hills and Moore Park, or the #L94 express from Circular Quay.

The Kurnell Peninsula and Cronulla

From La Perouse, you can see across Botany Bay to Kurnell and the red buoy marking the spot where Captain James Cook and the crew of the *Endeavour* anchored on April 29, 1770, for an eight-day exploration. Back in England, many refused to believe that the uniquely Australian plants and animals they had recorded actually existed – the kangaroo and platypus in particular were thought to be a hoax. **Captain Cook's Landing Place** is now the south head of **Botany Bay National Park**, where the informative **NPWS Discovery Centre** (Mon–Fri 11am–3pm, Sat & Sun 10am–4.30pm; car $7; ℡02/9668 2000) looks at the wetlands ecology of the park and tells the story of Cook's visit and its implications for Aboriginal people. Indeed, the political sensitivity of the spot that effectively marks the beginning of the decline of an ancient culture has led to the planned renaming of the park to Kamay-Botany Bay National Park, "Kamay" being the original Dharawal people's name for the bay. Set aside as a public recreation area in 1899, the heath and woodland is unspoilt and there are some secluded beaches for swimming; you may even spot parrots and honeyeaters. To get here, take the train to Cronulla and then Kurnell Bus Services route #987.

On the ocean side of the **Kurnell Peninsula** sits Sydney's southernmost beach suburb and its longest stretch of beach – just under 5km; the sandy stretch of Bate Bay begins at **Cronulla** and continues as deserted, dune-backed **Wanda Beach**. This is prime **surfing** territory – and the only Sydney beach accessible by train (40min from Central Station on the Sutherland line; surfboards carried free). Steeped in surf culture, everything about Cronulla centres on watersports and a laid-back beach lifestyle, from the multitude of surf shops on Cronulla Street (which becomes a pedestrianized mall between Kingsway and Purley Place), to the outdoor cafés on the beachfront and the surfrider clubs and boating facilities on the bay. Even the *Cronulla Beach YHA* (see p.102) is aimed primarily at surfers, with excursions to Garie and free use of boogie-boards. Unfortunately, the ethnically-charged **riots** in December 2005 did much to damage Cronulla's reputation as a chilled beach-resort destination, and tensions between local surfers and Middle Eastern youths from the western suburbs still exist.

Eating and drinking

If the way its chefs are regularly poached by restaurants overseas is any indication, Sydney has blossomed into one of the great culinary capitals of the world, offering a fantastic range of cosmopolitan **restaurants**, covering every imaginable cuisine. Quality is uniformly high, with the freshest produce, meat and seafood always on hand, and a culture of discerning, well-informed diners. It's also a highly fashionable scene, with businesses rising in favour, falling in popularity and closing down or changing name and style at an astonishing rate. For a comprehensive guide, consider investing in *Cheap Eats in Sydney* or the *Sydney Morning Herald Good Food Guide* and check out ⓦ http://grabyourfork .blogspot.com, a good foodie blog with lots of restaurant reviews. All of New South Wales' restaurants are **nonsmoking**, except for reception areas and outside tables.

Sydney's well-developed **café culture** can be found most notably in Potts Point, Darlinghurst, Surry Hills, Glebe, Newtown, Leichhardt and the eastern beaches of Bondi, Bronte and Coogee. The many fascinating **ethnic** enclaves, representing the city's diverse communities, serve up authentic cuisines, including Jewish on Hall Street, Bondi Beach; Chinese in Haymarket; Turkish and Indian on Cleveland Street, Surry Hills; Italian in East Sydney, Leichhardt and Haberfield; Portuguese on New Canterbury Road, Petersham; Greek in Marrickville and Brighton-Le-Sands; and Indonesian on ANZAC Parade, in Kingsford and Kensington. Much further out, reached by train, Cabramatta is very much a Little Vietnam.

All restaurants in the following listings are **open** daily for lunch and dinner, unless otherwise stated, and the more specific café times are given (many are open early for breakfast, one of Sydney's most popular meals). A ten-percent surcharge is almost always applied on Sundays.

The CBD and Circular Quay

The cafés and food stalls in the business and shopping districts of the CBD cater mainly for lunchtime crowds, and there are lots of **food courts** serving fast food and snacks. Check out the selection in the basements of the **QVB**, **Quayside Shopping Centre** on Alfred Street, Circular Quay, **Myers** department store on Pitt Street Mall, and the **MLC Centre** near Martin Place, but the classiest is the foodie's paradise in the basement of the **David Jones** department store on Market Street. There are lots of great Italian espresso bars for quick coffee hits throughout the CBD, and many museums and tourist attractions also have surprisingly good **cafés** – notably the MCA, the Australian Museum, Hyde Park Barracks and the Art Gallery of New South Wales.

The listings below are marked on the **map** on p.96.

Bodhi in the Park Cook and Phillip Park, College St ☎ 02/9281 6162. Top-notch Chinese vegetarian and vegan *yum cha* (dishes $9–18) using predominantly organic and biodynamic produce. A good option near the Australian Museum, particularly on a sunny day when the outside seating is a treat. Licensed. Daily 10am–10pm.

Cafe Sydney Level 5, Customs House, 31 Alfred St, Circular Quay ☎ 02/9251 8683. The views of the Harbour Bridge and Opera House from the balcony are jaw-dropping, and the contemporary Australian cuisine with a seafood focus comes highly rated. Service is great and the atmosphere is fun (the Sunday lunch jazz, acoustic and percussion session is popular). Mains from $30. Licensed. Closed Sun dinner.

Guillaume at Bennelong Sydney Opera House, Bennelong Point ☎02/9241 1999. French chef Guillaume Brahimi has fused his name with the Opera House's top-notch restaurant, housed in one of the iconic building's smaller shells; the huge windows provide stunning harbour views. If you're going to have one splash-out, romantic meal in Sydney, come here. With mains at around $50 (elegant modern French fare), it's not the most expensive place in town and if you can't afford it you can always opt for a drink at the bar. Lunch Thurs & Fri, dinner Mon–Sat.

QVB Jet Corner of York and Druitt sts, City. Very lively Italian café-bar, on the corner of the QVB looking across to Town Hall, with big glass windows and outdoor seating providing people-watching opportunities. Coffee is predictably excellent, and the menu is big on breakfast. The rest of the day, choose from pasta, risotto, soups, salads and sandwiches. Licensed. Mon–Fri 7.30am–11pm, Sat 9am–midnight, Sun 10am–7pm.

Rossini Wharf 5, Circular Quay. Quality alfresco Italian fast food while you're waiting for a ferry or just watching the quay. *Panzerotto* – big, cinnamon-flavoured and ricotta-filled doughnuts ($7) – are a speciality. Pricey but excellent coffee. Licensed. Daily 7am–11pm.

Sydney Cove Oyster Bar Circular Quay East. En route to the Opera House, the quaint little building housing the bar and kitchen was once a public toilet, but don't let that put you off. The outdoor tables right on the water's edge provide a magical location to sample Sydney Rock Pacific oysters (around $22 for half a dozen), or just come for coffee, cake and the view. Licensed. Daily 8am till late.

Tetsuya's 529 Kent St ☎02/9267 2900, @www .tetsuyas.com. Stylish premises – a Japanese timber interior and a beautiful Japanese garden outside – and exquisite Japanese/French-style fare created by the internationally renowned chef Tetsuya Wakuda. As Sydneysiders will attest, an evening here is a once-in-a-lifetime experience and the month-long waiting list is worth it to sample the ten-course tasting menu ($195); wine teamed with each course starts from $70. Licensed & BYO. Lunch Sat, dinner Tues–Sat.

The Rocks

There are several good **pubs** in The Rocks (see p.107), many of which serve food, and some reasonably priced cafés with calm courtyards or street seating, as well as a choice of expensive restaurants, popular for business lunches, and trading on fantastic views.

The listings below are marked on the **map** on p.108.

Gumnut Tea Gardens 28 Harrington St. Popular lunchtime venue in historic Reynolds Cottage. Munch on delicious gourmet meat pies and plough-man's lunches in the serene courtyard, or sip tea in the antiquated lounge. Live jazz Fri night and Sun lunch. BYO. Daily 8am–5pm, dinner Wed–Fri. For an expensive but delectable pastry head to the equally salubrious adjoining café-courtyard of *La Renais-sance Patisserie*.

Playfair Shop 21, Playfair St. In a quaint old-meets-new pedestrian street this small, stylish hole-in-the-wall with mod plastic outdoor seating beneath a perspex awning serves the best coffee in The Rocks. Also deals in tasty frittatas, sandwiches, wraps and burgers. Daily 8am–5pm.

Sailors Thai Canteen 106 George St. Cheaper version of the much-praised, pricey downstairs restaurant (☎02/9251 2466), housed in the restored Sailors' Home. The ground-level canteen with a long stainless-steel communal table looks onto an open kitchen, where the chefs chop away to produce simple, delectable meals. Licensed. Mon–Sat noon–10pm.

The Wharf Pier 4, Hickson Rd, next to the Wharf Theatre ☎02/9250 1761. Innovative, expensive modern food (lots of seafood), served up in an old dock building with heaps of raw charm and a harbour vista; bag the outside tables for the best views. Cocktail bar open from noon until end of evening performance. Closed Sun.

Haymarket, Chinatown and around Central Station

The southern end of George Street and its backstreets have plenty of cheap restaurants of variable quality. Chinatown around the corner is a better bet: many places here specialize in *yum cha* (or *dim sum* as it's also known), and there are several late-night eating options. Inexpensive Asian **food courts** are also common, and a couple of blocks northeast of Chinatown there's an array of Spanish places on Liverpool Street, almost all of them boisterous and lively.

The listings below are marked on the **map** on p.114.

BBQ King 18 Goulburn St, Haymarket ☎02/9267 2433. Late-night hangout of chefs, rock stars and students alike, this unprepossessing but always packed Chinese restaurant does a mean meat dish, as suggested by its name and the duck roasting in the window, but there's a big vegetarian menu, too. Communal tables. Inexpensive to moderate. Licensed. Daily 11.30am–2am (last orders 1.30am).

Capitan Torres 73 Liverpool St, Haymarket ☎02/9264 5574. Atmospheric and enduring Spanish place specializing in seafood. Freshly displayed catch of the day and an authentic tapas menu (most dishes $12–16), plus great paella. Sit downstairs at the bar or upstairs in the restaurant. Inexpensive to moderate. Licensed. Daily noon–3pm & 6–11pm.

China Grand Level 3, Market City Shopping Centre, Hay St, Haymarket ☎02/9211 8988. Sitting proudly aside from the food court, this 800-seater Cantonese establishment is officially Australia's largest restaurant. You can eat some of the best *yum cha* in Sydney here, and you'll still have to queue for it at the weekend if you haven't booked. Moderate to expensive. Licensed. Daily 10am–3pm.

Mamak 15 Goulburn St, Haymarket ☎02/9211 1668. There's often a queue at this budget Malaysian place, but you're kept entertained while you wait, as you watch the chefs whip up super-flaky *roti canai*. Share dishes such as

tangy fish curry, stir-fried beans in shrimp paste or *nasi goreng* ($10–16) and leave space for the impressively conical sweet *roti* with ice cream. Delicious. BYO ($2 a bottle). Tues–Sun noon–3pm & 6–10.30pm.

Market City Food Court Level 3, Market City Shopping Centre, above Paddy's Markets. Almost entirely Asian – Japanese, Chinese, Malaysian, Indian, Cambodian, Thai and Singaporean. The best stall is McLuksa – the spicy coconut noodle soups which give it its name are delicious. Daily 10am–10pm.

Mother Chu's Vegetarian Kitchen 367 Pitt St. Taiwanese Buddhist cuisine in suitably plain surrounds and, true to its name, family run. Though onion and garlic aren't used, the eats here aren't bland. Inexpensive. No alcohol allowed. Closed Sun.

Pasteur 709 George St, Haymarket. Popular Vietnamese cheapie specializing in *pho*, a rice-noodle soup, served with fresh herbs, lemon and bean sprouts. Most noodles (mainly pork, chicken and beef) are $10, and there's nothing over $12. Refreshing pot of jasmine tea included. BYO. Daily 10.30am–9.30pm.

Sussex Centre 401 Sussex St, Haymarket. Good food court on first floor. Vietnamese, Korean BBQ, Thai, Japanese, Chinese and a juice bar. Daily 10am–9.30pm.

Darling Harbour and around

The Cockle Bay Wharf restaurant precinct harbours some excellent quality food. Beyond Darling Harbour, you can eat well at the Sydney Fish Market (see also p.124).

The listings below are marked on the **map** on p.96.

Chinta Ria – Temple of Love Roof Terrace, 201 Sussex St, Cockle Bay Wharf, Darling Harbour ☎02/9264 3211. People still queue to get in here (bookings lunch only) years after opening, as much for the fun atmosphere – a blues and jazz soundtrack, and decor that mixes a giant Buddha, a lotus pond and 50s-style furniture – as for the yummy Malaysian food. Dishes mostly $22–25. Licensed & BYO. Daily noon–2.30pm & 6–11pm.

Concrete Café 224 Harris St, Pyrmont ☎02/9518 9523. This minimalist café with outside tables that catch the morning sun is handy for both the Fish Market and the western shores of Darling Harbour. Tuck into the likes of baked eggs with chorizo and red capsicum and chutney on sourdough ($11) or

roast pumpkin and halloumi salad ($14). Mon–Fri 7am–4pm, Sat & Sun 8am–4pm.

Fish Market Cafe Sydney Fish Market, Pyrmont ☎02/9660 4280. Located on the left-hand side after the entrance of the undercover market, this is the pick of the hawkers for its excellent-value seafood platter with Kilpatrick oysters, lobster tails and steamed catch of the day. Mon–Fri 4am–4pm, Sat & Sun 5am–5pm.

The Malaya 39 Lime St, King St Wharf, Darling Harbour ☎02/9279 1170. Popular, veteran Chinese–Malaysian place in swish water surrounds, serving some of the best and spiciest *laksa* ($20–24) in town. Licensed. Mon noon–3pm & 6–9pm, Tues–Sat noon–3pm & 6–10pm, Sun 6–9pm.

Kings Cross, Potts Point and Woolloomooloo

Many of the coffee shops and restaurants in "The Cross" cater for the tastes (and wallets) of the area's backpackers, though there are also increasing numbers of stylish restaurants, particularly in Potts Point. Several of the places in the Darlinghurst listings (see below) are only a few steps away.

The listings below are marked on the **map** on p.126.

Cafe Hernandez 60 Kings Cross Rd, Kings Cross. Veteran Argentinian-run 24hr coffee shop. Relaxed and friendly with an old-time feel. You can linger here for ages and no one will make you feel unwelcome. Spanish food is served – *churros*, *tortilla*, *empanadas* and good pastries – but the coffee is the focus. Open daily.

Dolcetta 165 Victoria St, Potts Point ☏ 02/9331 5899. Tiny, down-to-earth Italian restaurant with a couple of tables on the street overlooking the fashionable *Dov* restaurant. All dishes under $15. BYO. Mon–Sat 6am–10pm, Sun 7am–4pm.

Fratelli Paradiso 12–16 Challis Ave, Potts Point ☏ 02/9357 1744. This place has everything, from gorgeous wallpaper and a dark furniture fit-out to flirty waiting staff and a diverse wine list. There's even an adjoining bakery, which runs out of stock before lunchtime most days. And the food's amazing, too – calamari, veal, pizzas and pastries – with a blackboard menu that changes daily. Moderate. Licensed. Mon–Fri 7am–11pm, Sat & Sun 7am–6pm.

Harry's Café de Wheels Cowper Wharf Rd, Woolloomooloo. Sometimes, there's nothing like a good old-fashioned pie, and this little cart has been serving them up for over sixty years. Some gourmet and vegetarian options have made it onto the menu but the standard meat pie with mashed peas and gravy is still the favourite. Open daily to 2am or later.

La Buvette 35 Challis Ave, Potts Point. Hole-in-the-wall coffee shop with streetside seating usually packed with mid-morning caffeine-seekers. The blackboard menu features some yummy delicacies such as baked egg with spinach, sun-dried tomatoes, goat's cheese and caramelized onion ($15) or vanilla French toast brioche ($12.50). Daily 6am–5.30pm.

Otto The Wharf, 6 Cowper Wharf Rd, Woolloomooloo ☏ 02/9368 7488. *Otto* is the sort of restaurant agents choose to take actors and models out to lunch, or a well-known politician could be dining at the next table. Trendy and glamorous, with a location not just by the water but *on* the water. The exquisite Italian cuisine – very fresh seafood – coupled with friendly service and a lively atmosphere, is what keeps them coming back. Mains $35–45. Licensed. Lunch and dinner daily.

Roy's Famous 176 Victoria St, Potts Point. It's all about the meal deal at this backstreet backpacker hangout, with Sunday roast for two people with a bottle of wine at $39 (from 6pm) and the Wednesday pasta night, with garlic bread and glass of wine for $19.50 (from 6pm). Two-for-one drinks (daily 5.30–6.30pm) and a friendly atmosphere. Daily 7am–10pm.

Darlinghurst and East Sydney

South of Kings Cross, Darlinghurst's **Victoria Street** has a thriving café and restaurant scene which spills west down the hill to **East Sydney**, focused on the intersection of **Stanley Street** and Crown Street. Traditionally an Italian stronghold, it is now branching out. Further south you hit **Oxford Street**, lined with restaurants and cafés from one end to the other. **Taylor Square** and its surroundings (the heart of the city's gay community) is a particularly busy area, with lots of ethnic restaurants and several pubs.

The listings below are marked on the **map** on p.96.

A Tavola 348 Victoria St, Darlinghurst ☏ 02/9331 7871. Stylish Italian pasta restaurant with a modern approach to traditional dishes selected from the daily blackboard menu. Mains (mostly $25–38) such as rabbit and home-made ravioli are supplemented by superb salads and desserts. Licensed. Lunch Fri, dinner Mon–Sat.

Bar Coluzzi 322 Victoria St, Darlinghurst. Veteran Italian café that's almost a Sydney legend: tiny and always packed with a diverse crew of regulars spilling out onto wooden stools on the pavement and partaking in the standard menu of focaccias, muffins, bagels and, of course, coffee. Daily 5am–7pm.

Bar Reggio 135 Crown St, East Sydney ☎02/9332 1129. Hugely popular neighbourhood Italian joint serving good food (including crisp-based pizzas from $13) in sizeable portions to an eager clientele. Not the place for a romantic dinner. BYO ($1 a head). Open daily.

Betty's Soup Kitchen 84 Oxford St, Darlinghurst. Soup is obviously the thing here, with continually changing specials that make for a cheap but filling meal, served with damper, but you can also order the simple things your ideal granny might serve: stews, sausages or fish fingers with mash, pasta, salads and desserts. Delicious home-made ginger beer and lemonade. All dishes under $15. BYO. Sun–Thurs noon–10.30pm, Fri & Sat noon–11.30pm.

Bill and Toni 74 Stanley St, East Sydney. Cheap-and-cheerful Italian, where it's worth the queue up the stairs for the huge servings of simple home-made pasta and sauces. The café downstairs serves tasty Italian sandwiches (daily 7am–10pm). Inexpensive. BYO. Daily noon–2.30pm & 6–10.30pm.

🏃 **bills** 433 Liverpool St, Darlinghurst. Owned by celebrity chef Bill Granger, this sunny corner café-restaurant in the quieter Darlinghurst backstreets is one of Sydney's favourite breakfast spots. Linger over ricotta hotcakes with honeycomb butter and banana ($17), muffins and newspapers. It's definitely worth a visit for breakfast; the modern Australian lunches start at about $17. Licensed. BYO. Mon–Sat 7.30am–3pm, Sun 8.30am–3pm.

Fishface 132 Darlinghurst Rd, Darlinghurst ☎02/9332 4803. Tiny restaurant where the excellent range of seafood and sushi speaks for itself. Everything is fresh: the fish and chips served in a paper cone, the pea soup with yabby tails or the sushi prepared before your eyes. Moderate–expensive. Licensed. BYO. Dinner Mon–Sat.

fu manchu 249 Victoria St, Darlinghurst ☎02/9360 9424. Perch on red stools at steel counters and enjoy stylish but inexpensive Chinese and Malaysian noodles and soups in this small, popular diner. Seasonal specials add variety to a standard but tasty menu, with organic chicken and many vegetarian options. BYO. Lunch Mon–Fri noon–3pm, dinner daily 5.30–10.30pm.

Onde 346 Liverpool St, Darlinghurst ☎02/9331 8749. People keep returning to this French-owned restaurant, situated in a Darlinghurst side-street, which serves outstanding and very authentic bistro-style food: soups and pâtés to start, mains (mostly $25–28) such as steak-*frites* or confit of duck, plus a fish dish. Portions are generous, service excellent and desserts decadent. Moderate. Licensed, with many wines available by the glass. Daily 5–11pm/midnight.

🏃 **Pink Peppercorn** 122 Oxford St, Darling-hurst ☎02/9360 9922. A place that keeps springing up on critics' favourites lists, lured by the unusual Laotian-inspired cooking – including the signature dish: stir-fried king prawns and pink peppercorns. Mains $21–25. Licensed. BYO. Daily 6pm–midnight.

🏃 **Thai Nesia** 243 Oxford St, Darlinghurst ☎02/9361 4817. Ever-popular, low-key place serving delectable Thai dishes. Get the juices flowing with the betel leaf with prawn ($3.50) then choose from the likes of pumpkin chicken curry ($16) and roast duck salad ($18). It's great value and attracts a strong gay following. BYO ($2 a head). Daily 5.30–10.30pm.

Paddington

Oxford Street becomes gradually more upmarket as it heads east from the city through Paddington; the majority of restaurants here are attached to gracious old pubs and most have had a complete culinary overhaul and now offer far more than the steak-and-three-veg option of times past.

The listings below are marked on the **map** on p.96.

Gusto Delicatessen 2a Heeley St, Five Ways. Sit at the breakfast bar at this relaxed local café to tuck into mushrooms on sourdough, a croissant and coffee or one of the salads, quiches and cold meats from the counter. Mon–Sat 7am–5pm.

Love Supreme 180 Oxford St ☎02/9331 1779. Delicious, thin-based pizzas (three sizes: $14, $19 & $25) served up in a sometimes frenetic atmos-phere. Try Ya Basta! (ham, pumpkin, chilli and pecorino) with a rocket salad and one of their delicious desserts. Always popular and can get pretty stifling on a hot day, when you may prefer to take away. Brunch Sat & Sun, dinner daily.

Royal Hotel Bar & Grill *Royal Hotel*, 237 Glenmore Rd, Five Ways. Grand old triple-storey pub-restaurant serving some of the most mouth-watering steaks in Sydney. Eating on the veranda is a real treat, with views over the art gallery and Five Ways action below. Tables fill fast – no bookings. There's also the *Elephant Bar* upstairs

(see p.163). Moderate. Mon–Fri noon–3pm & 6–10pm, Sat noon–10pm, Sun noon–9pm.
Sloanes Cafe 312 Oxford St. The emphasis in this veteran café is on good, unusual vegetarian food, moderately priced, but some meatier dishes have slipped onto the menu, including a BLT with

guacamole to die for; the fresh juice bar has always been superb. The stone-floored dining room opens onto the street with a view of all the Saturday market action, or eat out back under vines in the delightful courtyard. Breakfast and lunch served all day. BYO. Daily 6am–5pm.

Surry Hills and Redfern

Surry Hills' **Crown Street**, and the streets running off either side, are home to numerous funky cafés and some upmarket restaurants. At its southern end, **Cleveland Street**, running west towards Central Station, is lined with cheap Turkish, Lebanese and Indian restaurants, which are among the cheapest and most atmospheric in Sydney. And half a kilometre further south, cool **Danks Street** is the focus of Waterloo's resurgence.

The listings below are marked on the **map** on p.96.

Billy Kwong 355 Crown St, Surry Hills. Traditional Chinese cooking gets a stylish slant at this restaurant owned by celebrity chef Kylie Kwong. The space itself – all dark polished wood and Chinese antiques but brightly lit and with contemporary fittings – complements the often adventurous combination of dishes and flavours. Mains from $26, but mostly $37–49. No bookings. Licensed. BYO ($10 per bottle). Daily 6–11pm.

Bourke Street Bakery 633 Bourke St ☎02/9699 1011. Superb bakery-café with just three mini-tables inside plus seats outside which catch the afternoon sun. Great for tucking into a flaky pain au chocolat or a pear and rhubarb tart. Mon–Fri 7am–6pm, Sat & Sun 8am–5pm.

Café Mint 579 Crown St. Wonderful smart-casual café that gives a Mediterranean–Middle Eastern twist to the usual urban breakfasting scene. Try the beautifully presented Turkish breakfast of roast tomato, spinach, boiled egg, olives, grilled halloumi and *za'atar* toast ($14.50). At dinner you might tuck into beef cheek with merguez sausage, white beans, preserved lime and figs ($23). Licensed. No bookings or credit cards. Mon 7am–5pm, Tues–Sat 7am–9.30pm.

Café Sopra 7 Danks St, Waterloo. Wonderful modern Italian café serving dishes such as butternut, pumpkin, roast garlic and mozzarella risotto, and braised squid with peas and potatoes. Popular and they don't take bookings, so aim for a less busy time. Most mains $15–22. Licensed. Tues–Fri 10am–3pm, Sat 8am–3pm.

Erciyes 409 Cleveland St, Surry Hills ☎02/9319 1309. Among the offerings of this busy family-run Turkish restaurant is delicious $10 *pide* – a bit

like pizza – available with 30 different toppings, many vegetarian; there's a takeout section, too. Belly-dancing Fri & Sat nights when bookings are essential. Inexpensive. BYO. Daily 11am–midnight.

Longrain 85 Commonwealth St, Surry Hills ☎02/9280 2888. Hip restaurant and bar housed in a converted warehouse on a quiet edge of Surry Hills. The contemporary Thai flavours are much raved-about, and dining is on three long community-style wooden tables. Most mains $23–38. Licensed. Lunch Mon–Fri noon–2.30pm, dinner daily 6–11pm. Bookings for lunch only.

Maltese Cafe 310 Crown St, Surry Hills. Established in the early 1940s, this café is known for its delicious (and ridiculously cheap at $1.50) Maltese *pastizzi* – flaky pastry pockets of ricotta cheese, plain or with meat, spinach or peas – to eat in or take away. Tues–Sat 9am–8pm, Sun & Mon 9am–6pm.

Mohr Fish 202 Devonshire St, Surry Hills. This tiny but stylish and convivial fish-and-chip bar, with stools and tiled walls, packs in the customers and provides fresh, well-priced, well-prepared and sometimes distinctive seafood options. Pop into the pub next door and they'll come and fetch you when a table is free – you can even bring your drink in with you. BYO. Daily 10am–10pm.

Nepalese Kitchen 481 Crown St, Surry Hills ☎02/9319 4264. Peaceful establishment with cozy wooden furniture, religious wall hangings and traditional music. The speciality here is goat curry, served with freshly cooked relishes that traditionally accompany the mild Nepalese dishes, and simple but delicious *momos* (stuffed handmade dumplings). Vegetarian options, too. Lovely courtyard for warmer nights. Mains $12–16. BYO. Daily 6–10.30pm.

Glebe

Glebe has a bit of everything: both cheap and upmarket restaurants, ethnic takeaways and delis. **Glebe Point Road** is dominated by cafés – with a cluster of particularly good places at the Broadway end. See also p.163 for reasonably priced Italian food at the characterful *Friend in Hand*.

The listings below are marked on the **map** on p.132.

The Boathouse on Blackwattle Bay End of Ferry Rd ☎02/9518 9011. Atmospheric restaurant located above Sydney Women's Rowing Club, with fantastic views across the bay to ANZAC Bridge and the fishmarkets opposite. Unsurprisingly, seafood is the thing here (and this is one of the best places to sample some), from the six different kinds of oysters to the raved-about snapper pie. Expensive at around $42 for mains, but worth it. Licensed. Closed Mon.

Darbar 134 Glebe Point Rd ☎02/9660 5666. A cavernous old sandstone building with stone pillars and arched doors and windows provides a gorgeous setting for a surprisingly inexpensive – but superb – Indian meal. Mains around $18–20. Licensed and BYO. Closed Mon lunch.

🏃 **Fair Trade Coffee Company** 33 Glebe Point Rd. Warm, earthy tones and a delightful ambience, with great music and dishes from around the world – Colombia, Morocco, Indonesia and the Middle East are all featured, with nothing over $17. Plenty of vegetarian options, and the all-day cooked breakfast is fantastic. Daily 7am–9pm.

Sappho Books & Café 51 Glebe Point Rd. Colourful graffiti and murals (remnants of a grittier past) combine beautifully with rainforest plants, timber lattice sidewalls, parasols and a sail shelter in this quintessential Glebe courtyard café, joined to a secondhand bookstore. Great coffee is the focus here, but the paninis ($7–10) and salads ($11–13) satisfy – and who could resist hot toasted banana bread with ricotta ($5)? Mon–Sat 8am–7pm, Sun 9am–7pm.

Newtown

On the other side of Sydney University from Glebe, **King Street** in Newtown is lined with cafés, takeaways and restaurants of every ethnic persuasion, particularly Thai. For gorgeous courtyard Thai dining, see also *Sumalee* at the *Bank Hotel* (p.163).

The listings below are marked on the **map** on p.132.

🏃 **Campos Coffee** 193 Missenden Rd, just off King St. Superb coffee (among the best in Sydney) is what this pocket-sized timber café does best – roasted, blended and ground in-house and served up to perfection by trained baristas. The only nibbles on offer are a few delicious biscuits and pastries. Mon–Fri 7am–4pm, Sat 8am–5pm.

Green Gourmet 115 King St. Loud and busy Chinese vegan eatery, which always has plenty of Asian customers, including the odd Buddhist monk. The devout Buddhist owner's creativity is reflected in the divine tofu variations on offer. Order off-menu (mains around $15) or to get a taste of everything, there's a nightly buffet, or *yum cha* at weekend lunch. The same owners run the excellent Vegan's Choice Grocery next door. Daily lunch and dinner.

Kilimanjaro 280 King St. Long-running Senegalese-owned place serving authentic and simple dishes that span Africa – from West African marinated chicken to North African couscous. Casual and friendly atmosphere, with African art and craft adorning the walls. Inexpensive. BYO.

Oscillate Wildly 275 Australia St, Newtown ☎02/9517 4700. Newtown has plenty of fine places to eat but if you're looking to treat yourself with some tasty contemporary cuisine, the eight-course tasting menu here ($95) is exceptional. Vegetarian tasting menu also available. Dinner Tues–Sat.

Vegetarian eating

Vegetarians are well catered for on just about every café menu, and most contemporary restaurant menus, too. The following are specifically vegetarian: *Fair Trade Coffee Company* (see p.157), *Bodhi in the Park* (see p.151), *Green Gourmet* (see p.157) and *Mother Chu's Vegetarian Kitchen* (see p.153).

Balmain and Leichhardt

Further west is **Leichhardt**, Sydney's "Little Italy", which has a concentration of cafés and restaurants on **Norton Street**, while the **Darling Street** strip of restaurants runs from Rozelle to upmarket **Balmain**.

The listings below are marked on the **map** on p.132.

Bar Italia 169 Norton St, Leichhardt. There's a community-centre feel to this place, with the day-long comings and goings of Leichhardt locals, and it's positively packed at night. The focaccia, served during the day, comes big and tasty, the coffee is spot-on and it serves some of the best *gelato* in Sydney. There's pasta from $13, plus some more substantial meat dishes ($16.50–20). Shady courtyard out back. BYO. Open daily till midnight or 1am.

Fundamental Food Fresh 266 Darling St, Balmain. A funky, modern space with two long rows of tables – both with comfortable cushioned wall seating. Serves great breakfasts till 4pm, and the massive seafood Sizzling Platter ($26, and worth sharing) comes highly recommended. Mon 7.30am–5pm, Tues–Sun 7.30am till late.

The Harbour

Military Road, running from Neutral Bay to Mosman, has a string of good restaurants, mainly on the expensive side, but there are a number of tempting pastry shops and well-stocked delis. The intersection of **Willoughby Road** and the Pacific Highway in Crows Nest, north of North Sydney, also has a great range of options. At South Head, **Watsons Bay** is known for its famous seafood restaurant, *Doyles*.

The Bathers Pavilion 4 The Esplanade, Balmoral Beach ☏02/9969 5050. Indulgent beach-house-style dining in the former (1930s) changing rooms on Balmoral Beach. The very pricey restaurant and café double-act is presided over by one of Sydney's top chefs, Serge Dansereau. Fixed-price dinner menu in the restaurant is $125 for three courses (from $110 at lunch). Weekend breakfast in the café is a North Shore ritual – expect to queue to get in – while the wood-fired pizzas are popular later in the day. Licensed. Café daily 7am–midnight, restaurant lunch and dinner daily.

Bottom of the Harbour Seafoods 21 The Esplanade, Balmoral Beach ☏02/9969 7911. An exceptionally good takeaway. Regress into a childlike state with lightly battered fish and chips, yummy prawn cutlets, creative salads or something from the grill. A licensed sit-down breakfast/lunch bistro attached offers something for those with more adventurous palates: try the truffle toast or zucchini fritters. Eat inside or dine on the grass overlooking one of the most picturesque of Sydney's harbour beaches. Mon–Thurs 9am–8.30pm, Fri–Sun 9am–9pm.

Doyles on the Beach 11 Marine Parade, Watsons Bay ☏02/9337 2007; also *Doyles Wharf Restaurant* ☏02/9337 1572. The former is the original of the long-running Sydney fish-restaurant institution, but both serve great if overpriced seafood and have wonderful views of the city across the water. The

adjacent boozer serves pub versions in its beer garden, with slightly more affordable takeaway options. A ferry or water taxi can transport you from Circular Quay to Watsons Bay. Daily lunch and dinner.

Maisy's Cafe 164 Military Rd, Neutral Bay. Cool hangout on a hot day or night (open 24hr), with lively interior and music and great coffee. Good for breakfast – from mixed berry yoghurt ($7.90) to eggs Benedict ($13). The quesadillas are also a treat, as is the vegetarian frittata. BYO; ten-percent surcharge for early hours at weekends.

Radio Cairo Cafe 83 Spofforth St, Cremorne ☏02/9908 2649. Oozing African exotica – with African art, crafts, artefacts and ornate brass-framed flatscreen monitors showing *Tarzan*, *Tin Tin* and *Casabalanca* – this funky café, directly opposite the fabulous Orpheum cinema, features a creative and varied menu with a strong emphasis on African flavours – complemented by a suburb selection of wines and cocktails (try the "Cosmic Cairo"). Mains $16.75–23.75. Licensed & BYO. Dinner daily.

Tea Garden Cafe 8 Marine Parade, Watsons Bay. Picturesque, parasol-protected alfresco courtyard, backed by bright green lawns and vibrant gardens, with a cute play area (with toys) for the kids and a killer view across the harbour. Affordable too: big breakfast ($16), asparagus bruschetta ($13.50), nutella crepes ($12), focaccias ($10). Daily breakfast and lunch.

Ocean beaches

Bondi is a cosmopolitan centre with the area's many Eastern European and Jewish residents giving its cafés a continental flair; there are also some fantastic kosher restaurants, delis and cake shops. The Bondi Beach area is full of cheap takeaways, fish-and-chip shops and beer gardens, as well as some seriously trendy cafés and restaurants. South of Bondi, **Bronte**'s beachfront café strip is wonderfully laid-back, and **Coogee** has a thriving café scene too. At the northern mouth of the harbour, **Manly** offers something for every taste and budget.

Bacino Bar 1a The Corso, Manly. All-day café with a wide range of mainly Italian food, including lasagne, pasta and risotto (all $9), though there are some Australian favourites too. Upstairs is a lounge area and communal tables, which add to the beachside vibe. Licensed & BYO. Mon–Sat 6am–5pm, Sun 7am–5pm.

Barzura 62 Carr St, Coogee ☎02/9665 5546. Fantastic spot providing up-close ocean views. Both a café and a fully fledged restaurant, with wholesome breakfast until 1pm, snacks until 7pm, and restaurant meals – such as seafood spaghetti or grilled kangaroo rump – served at lunch and dinner. Unpretentious, though stylish service encourages a large local crowd. Mains $14–30; pasta deals 5–7pm. Licensed & BYO. Daily 7am–11pm.

Bondi Social First Floor, 38 Campbell Parade, Bondi Beach ☎02/9365 1788. You could easily miss the sandwich-board sign pointing you to this hidden gem, but once found a million-dollar balcony view of the beach awaits those wanting to escape the melee of the Campbell Parade pavement. The wood interior is rich and dim-lit at night; the mood promises romance and an interesting dining experience with a worldwide influence. Tapas-style dishes $11–15. Licensed. Mon–Fri noon–late, Sat & Sun 8am–late.

Gertrude & Alice Cafe Bookstore 46 Hall St, Bondi Beach. It's hard to decide if *Gertrude & Alice* is a café or a secondhand literary bookshop. With small tables crammed into every available space, a big communal table and a comfy couch to lounge on, it can be tough going for browsers to get to the books at busy café times. A homely hangout with generous, affordable servings of Greek and Mediterranean food, great cakes, even greater coffee and lots of conversation. Daily 7.30am–9.30pm.

Icebergs Bistro 1 Notts Ave, Bondi Beach ☎02/9130 3120. Effectively the clubrooms of the Icebergs swimming club, this straightforward bistro shares the fabulous view of the far flashier *Icebergs Dining Room* (see p.159) on the floor above. Just show a photo ID, sign in and settle down for a beer and everything from a fry-up breakfast to half a dozen oysters ($15) or a rump steak and chips ($22). There are often cover bands playing at weekends. Mon–Fri 11am till late, Sat & Sun 9am till late.

Jack & Jill's Fish Café 98 Beach St, Coogee ☎02/9665 8429. This down-to-earth fish restaurant on the north side of the beach is a local legend. Come here to enjoy wonderfully cooked fish, from the basic battered variety to tasty tandoori perch. Mains $14–23. Daily from 5pm, Sun from noon.

Melonhead 256 Coogee Bay Rd, Coogee. The smell of fresh fruit wafts down the street from this fantastic juice bar. Apart from custom-made smoothies, crushes and milkshakes, there are enticing salads and Turkish rolls to choose from. Daily 6am–8pm.

North Bondi Italian Food 118 Ramsgate Ave, North Bondi ☎02/9300 4400. This trattoria offers the best combination of gorgeous beach views and wonderful food at reasonable prices. Try the warm beef, salsa and chilli panini ($17) or the rigatoni with pork sausage, sage and garlic sauce ($27). For quiet dining eat early, or come late when it's buzzing with the fashionable set. Licensed. Lunch Fri–Sun noon–4pm, dinner daily from 6pm.

Out of Africa 43–45 East Esplanade, Manly, opposite Manly Wharf ☎02/9977 0055. The zebra-skin seat covers and tribal spears, masks and colourful photos on the walls set the tone for this modern-Moroccan-cum-traditional-African place serving the likes of "Couscous Royale" ($45 for two), and fish tagine ($26). Licensed. Lunch Thurs–Sun, dinner daily.

Pacific Thai Cuisine 2nd floor, 48 Victoria Parade, corner of South Steyne, Manly ☎02/9977 7220. With crisp decor and fantastic views of the beach from its upstairs location, this low-key Thai restaurant offers a variety of fresh favourites as well as chef's specials such as *chu chi* curry (red curry with kaffir lime leaves). Vegetarian options too. Inexpensive to moderate. Licensed & BYO. Lunch Tues–Sun, dinner daily 5.30–10pm.

Sabbaba 82 Hall St, Bondi ☎ 02/9365 7500. Excellent-value non-kosher Israeli-run café (Sabbaba is Hebrew for "great" or "cool") in the heart of Bondi's small Jewish quarter. Great felafel (around $9), grilled chicken, salads, tabouleh and a selection of gooey baklava made from all sorts of different nuts. Daily 11am–8pm or later.

Speedo's 126 Ramsgate Ave, North Bondi. Totally casual café bang opposite the north end of the beach, where the locals and their kids and dogs hang out, with no busy road to obscure the view.

The inexpensive breakfast specials are very popular; expect long waits for your order. Daily 5.30am–6pm.

Swell Restaurant 465 Bronte Rd, Bronte ☎ 02/9386 5001. One of the few Bronte café-restaurants to open in the evening down at the beach. Sit inside for the sharp interior, or out on the pavement for a delightful Bronte Beach view. There's plenty of competition alongside, so prices are reasonable for what you're getting. Dinner mains $28–32. Daily 7am–10pm.

Entertainment, nightlife and culture

To find out exactly **what's on** in Sydney, Friday's *Sydney Morning Herald* offers *Metro*, a weekly entertainment supplement. In addition to this and the rather bland tourist monthlies (see p.86), there is a plethora of **free listings magazines** for more alternative goings-on – clubbing, bands, fashion, music and the like – which can be found in the cafés, record shops and boutiques of Bondi, Paddington, Darlinghurst, Glebe, Newtown and Kings Cross: these include *The Brag* and *Drum Media*, with their weekly band listings and reviews, and *3D World* covering the club scene. *City Hub*, a politically aware, free weekly newspaper, also has excellent events listings, and *Time Out Sydney* is a weekly magazine with listings and plenty of ideas as to how to spend your time. The Sydney Citysearch **website** (ⓦ www.sydney.citysearch.com.au) has details of film, theatre and music events.

The main **booking agencies** are Ticketek (outlets at Hum, 55 Oxford St, Ticketek@Park, 50 Park St, and the Theatre Royal; ☎ 132 849; ⓦ www.ticketek .com.au), Ticketmaster7 (outlets include the State Theatre, Market St, CBD, and Sydney Entertainment Centre at Darling Harbour ☎ 13 61 00,

▲ Vertiginous views from the Orbit Lounge

Legendary beer gardens

Many Sydney pubs have an outdoor drinking area, perfect for enjoying the sunny weather – the four listed below, however, are outright legends.

The Coogee Bay Hotel Arden Street, Coogee. Loud, rowdy and crammed with backpackers, this enormous beer garden across from the beach is renowned in the eastern suburbs. The hotel has six bars in all, including a big screen sports bar for all international sporting events. Revellers can buy jugs of beer and cook their own meat from 9.30am till late.

Newport Arms Hotel Beaconsfield Street, Newport. Famous beer-garden pub established in 1880 with a huge deck looking out over Heron Cove at Pittwater. Good for families, with a children's play area. The bistro's range of pasta, pizza, grills and salads complements a large wine list.

The Oaks Hotel 118 Military Rd, Neutral Bay. The North Shore's most popular pub takes its name from the huge oak tree that shades the entire beer garden. Cook your own (expensive) steak, or order a gourmet pizza from the restaurant inside.

Watsons Bay Hotel 10 Marine Parade, Watsons Bay. The beer garden here gives uninterrupted views across the harbour, which you can enjoy with fresh fish and chips from the renowned *Doyles* kitchen (see p.158) or a steak from the outdoor BBQ.

Ⓦwww.ticketmaster7.com) and Moshtix (outlets at Utopia Records, 233 Broadway, and The Music Shop, Shop 5050, Level 5, Westfield, 500 Oxford St, Bondi Junction; Ⓣ1300 438 849, Ⓦwww.moshtix.com.au).

Bars and pubs

The differences between a restaurant, bar, pub and nightclub are often blurred in Sydney, and one establishment may be a combination of all these under one roof. Sydney's bland, pub-dominated wilderness has all but disappeared and you'll find a fashionable **bar** on almost every corner, offering everything from poetry readings and art classes to groovy Sunday-afternoon jazz or DJ sessions. Not to be outdone, the traditional hotels are getting in renowned chefs and putting on food far beyond the old pub-grub fare. Sydney has many **Art Deco pubs**, a style notably seen in the tilework; we've included some of the best below. Opening hours vary considerably: traditional pubs and beer gardens will be open 11am–11pm or later, while more fashionable cocktail bars may not open until the evening but won't close until 2am (perhaps 4am or later at weekends).

The CBD and Circular Quay

The listings below are marked on the **map** on p.96.

Marble Bar 259 Pitt St. A sightseeing stop as well as a great place for a drink: this was the original 1893 basement bar of the *Tattersalls Hotel*, and the stunningly ornate *fin de siècle* interior is now encased within the 1973 *Hilton Hotel*. Drinks are modestly priced and there is free comedy or music most nights. Also check out the glamorous *Zeta Bar* on Level 4 of the same building.

Orbit Lounge Level 47, Australia Square, 264 George St. The views from this stylish revolving bar are best when darkness falls and the city is dramatically lit up, all seen from the 47th floor of Australia's first Manhattan-style skyscraper. The drinks list is very James Bond (try the delicious Maserati cocktail, $18), and there's bar food if you're peckish. Open all night when custom justifies it.

Opera Bar Lower Concourse Level, Sydney Opera House. Stunningly located – a tiered deck beneath the Opera House sails – with alfresco bar, tables and stylish parasols overlooking the Quay, the Bridge and the harbour, and a sleek glass-walled interior – the Opera Bar is almost perfect. All the more so for the entertainment, with some of Sydney's best DJs and live music nightly from 8.30pm (2pm at weekends), and a delectable menu of bar snacks.

Slip Inn 111 Sussex St. Now famous as the place where Mary Donaldson met her Prince Frederick of Denmark, this huge three-level place has several bars, a bistro and *The Chinese Laundry* nightclub, overlooking Darling Harbour. The front bars have a pool room, while downstairs a boisterous beer garden fills up on balmy nights, with the quieter, more sophisticated *Sand Bar* beside it. Excellent wine list, with lots available by the glass; bar food includes Thai.

The Rocks and CBD

The listings below are marked on the **map** on p.108.

The Argyle 18 Argyle St. A seamless and cinematic blend of the best of the past and the future in a vast, multi-zoned glass, stone and timber playground. Early nineteenth-century wool stores have been transformed with chic cubic furniture, sleek bars, impressive use of recycled timber and a suspended glass DJ booth. The numerous Bavarian beers are definitely worth sampling, and the diverse food and cocktail menus certainly deliver.

Australian Hotel 100 Cumberland St. This corner hotel is seemingly always full of Brits. Inside, original fittings give a lovely old-pub feel while outside tables on the footpath provide a convivial atmosphere to take in the neighbourhood's historic charm. Known and loved for its Bavarian-style draught beer brewed in Picton, plus delicious gourmet pizzas with extravagant toppings that extend to native animals – emu, kangaroo and crocodile.

Blue Horizon Bar *Shangri-La Hotel*, 176 Cumberland St. The top-floor bar of the five-star *Shangri-La Hotel* has a stunning 270-degree view – the Opera House, Darling Harbour, Middle Harbour and Homebush Bay to the Blue Mountains. The mega-expensive lounge is worth it for the view alone – dress smart to get in.

Harbour View Hotel 18 Lower Fort St. Sibling to the stately *Exchange Hotel* in Balmain, this three-storey renovated gem puts you right under the bridge – and close enough from the top balcony cocktail bar to raise a glass to the grey-overall-clad bridge climbers making their way back from the summit. The crowd is mixed, and better for it, although drinks are a little pricey. Fine-dining restaurant upstairs.

Hero of Waterloo 81 Lower Fort St, Millers Point. One of Sydney's oldest pubs, built in 1843 from sandstone dug out from the Argyle Cut (see p.111), this place is redolent with history, the atmosphere enhanced by a complete absence of TV monitors, and with blazing fireplaces in winter, simple meals

and music almost every night of the week, from folk through to dirty blues, trad Irish and jazz. Check out the classic ageing jazz quartet on weekend afternoons.

Darling Harbour, Haymarket and around

The listings below are marked on the **maps** on p.96 and p.114.

3 Wise Monkeys 555 George St, corner of Liverpool St, Haymarket. Good mix of Sydneysiders and travellers who come for the relaxed pub atmosphere, beers on tap, pool tables, live music and DJs to 3am.

Civic Hotel 388 Pitt St, corner of Goulburn St, Haymarket ☎02/8267 3186. Beautiful 1940s Art Deco–style pub, its original features in great condition. Upstairs, there's a glamorous dining room and cocktail bar. Handy meeting point for Chinatown and George St cinema trips.

Cohibar Harbourside Shopping Centre, Darling Harbour ☎02/9281 4440. Classy cocktail bar across the water from the main Darling Harbour strip topped by a "cigar loft" that's perfect for a leisurely cohiba (they're available in six grades) with great city views. Limited bar food, and DJs at weekends.

Scruffy Murphy's 43 Goulburn St. Rowdy Irish pub with Guinness on tap, of course; phenomenally popular with travellers and expats, who come for some hearty home cooking, including $6 meal deals. Open till 4am most nights.

Kings Cross, Potts Point and Woolloomooloo

The listings below are marked on the **map** on p.126.

The Bourbon 24 Darlinghurst Rd, Kings Cross. Established in 1968 when it was frequented by US soldiers on R&R, this infamous 24hr Kings Cross restaurant and drinking hole has been given a swish new look, which hasn't done much to deter some of its more colourful regulars. There's a new terrace upstairs, a lounge bar out back, the lure of happy hour (daily 6–9pm) and all-day $10 steaks. Cover bands and DJs at weekends.

Lotus 22 Challis Ave, Potts Point. Kings Cross CityRail ☎02/9326 9000. Style and substance combine in the back room of the *Lotus Bistro*, and the padded snakeskin walls and retro wallpaper provide the perfect setting in which to sip the famous Lotus Martini. Cocktails are a speciality, and there's an extensive list – enough to keep you happy all night, if you can afford it. Closed Mon.

Soho Bar & Lounge *Piccadilly Hotel*, 171 Victoria St, Kings Cross. Trendy, Art Deco pub on leafy

Victoria St. The ground-floor *Piccadilly* bar is the most Deco, but locals head for the upstairs *Leopard Room* bar (Fri & Sat nights) to hang out on the back balcony and sample the seasonally updated cocktail menu. The attached club, *Yu*, runs on Fri, Sat & Sun nights from 10pm to sunrise.

Water Bar Que Sydney, Cowper Wharf Rd, Woolloomooloo. Kings Cross CityRail. The bar of Sydney's hippest hotel (see p.99), this place is fabulously located in a dramatically renovated old iron and timber finger wharf. The sense of space is sensational, the lighting atmospheric, and the sofas gorgeously designed – all of which make it a favourite with local celebrities. The pricey drinks (cocktails from $17) are worth it for the architecture and ambience.

Darlinghurst, Paddington and Surry Hills

The listings below are marked on the maps on p.96 and p.126.

Clock Hotel 470 Crown St, Surry Hills. Classy former pub with fashionable clientele draped around the chocolate-coloured lounge bar and filling the booths and tables downstairs. It's popular for after-work drinks, and the restaurant really excels, with prime position seating on the veranda and a satisfying menu of burgers, pasta and risotto dishes (mains $15–25) and plenty of creative touches; tapas is available too.

Cricketers Arms 106 Fitzroy St, Surry Hills. Just down the road from the live-music scene at the *Hopetoun* (see p.165), the *Cricketers* has an equally dedicated clientele. A young, offbeat crowd – plenty of piercings and shaved heads – cram in and fall about the bar, pool room and tiny beer garden, and yell at each other over a funky soundtrack. Hearty bar snacks and a bistro.

Darlo Bar Corner of Darlinghurst Rd and Liverpool St, Darlinghurst. Popular meeting place, with a lounge-room atmosphere. Comfy colourful chairs and sofas have a 1950s feel but there aren't enough to accommodate the mixed and unpretentious crowd who are there to play pool or just curl up under the lamps and chat. Drinks, including the house wines, aren't expensive. At night you can order from the menus of local restaurants (Thai, pizza, etc) and they'll fetch the food for you.

Elephant Bar *Royal Hotel*, 237 Glenmore Rd, Paddington. The top-floor bar of this beautifully renovated, Victorian-era hotel has knockout views of the city, best appreciated at sunset (happy hour 5.30–6.30pm). The small interior is great, too, with its fireplaces, paintings and elephant prints. As it gets crowded later on, people pack onto the stairwell, creating a party atmosphere.

Green Park Hotel 360 Victoria St, Darlinghurst. A Darlinghurst stalwart, partly because of the stash of pool tables in the back room, but mainly thanks to the unpretentious vibe. The bar couldn't be more unassuming; there's nothing decorating the walls, and humble bar tables with stools and a few lounges out back accommodate the regular arty crowd. Very popular with gay men on Sunday evening.

The Victoria Room Level 1, 235 Victoria St, Darlinghurst. Atmospheric drawing room from the Colonial era with elegant sofas, a grand piano and chandeliers, yet a positively trendy atmosphere makes it popular with the chill-out crowd. Tapas are served at the cocktail bar, and there's high tea on Sat and Sun afternoons.

Inner west: Glebe, Newtown and Balmain

The listings below are marked on the map on p.132.

Ancient Briton 225 Glebe Point Rd. This lively pub, popular with the area's travellers, has been recently refurbished into a stylish boozer, with a sleek upstairs "Pacific Penthouse" area sporting the world's largest fish-tank bar, professional poker tournaments (2pm and 7.30pm) DJs on weekend nights, live jazz, soul and blues on Thurs night and world music on Sun afternoon. The food is Asian and modern Australian (check out the $10 deals) and goes down well in the Spanish-style courtyard.

Bank Hotel 324 King St, next to Newtown Station. Smart-looking pub open late and always packed with local arty residents and visiting musos. Upstairs, the stylish Velvet Room, with a side deck for smokers, is usually good for a dance, while downstairs, the cocktail bar leads out on to fantastic timber decking (lovely in summer), with a great Thai restaurant, *Sumalee*, in the leafy beer garden below.

Exchange Hotel Corner of Beattie & Mullens sts, Balmain. This classic Balmain backstreet corner pub, built in 1885, popular with the locals, has a stylish and comfortably furnished wrought-iron balcony upstairs. Relax with a beer or combine a hearty breakfast with a Bloody Mary on the balcony at the "*Bloody Mary Breakfast Club*" on Sat and Sun mornings (10am–3pm). The gourmet pizzas are also popular.

Friend in Hand 58 Cowper St, corner of Queen St, Glebe ☎02/9660 2326. Character-filled pub in the leafy backstreets of Glebe, with all manner of curious objects dangling from the walls and ceilings of the public bar; a popular haunt for backpackers. Diverse entertainment in the upstairs bar (where you can also play pool), poetry, stand-up comedy and crab-racing nights – call to check what's on when. There's also a good Italian restaurant serving pasta dishes from $10 (closed Sun lunch).

Ocean beaches

4 Pines Brewing Company 43 The Esplanade, Manly ☏02/9976 2300. Slick yet casual bar with polished concrete floors, recycled timber tables and a harbourview deck. Its own microbrewery produces toothsome handcrafted beers, typically including a pale ale, a bitter, a hefeweizen and a kolsch (light ale from Cologne), plus seasonal brews. Good, modern bar meals for around $20.

Beach Palace Hotel 169 Dolphin St, Coogee. Home to a young and drunken crowd, made up of locals, beach babes and backpackers. Features five bars, two restaurants and a great view of the beach from the balcony under the distinctive dome.

Beach Road Hotel 71 Beach Rd, Bondi Beach ⓦwww.beachrdhotel.com.au. Huge, stylishly decorated pub with a bewildering range of bars on two levels, and a beer garden. Popular with both travellers and locals for its atmosphere. Entertainment, mostly free, comes from rock bands and DJs

(see website for details). The cheap Italian bistro, *No Names*, takes over the beer garden; there's an upmarket modern Australian restaurant upstairs.

Bondi Hotel 178 Campbell Parade, Bondi Beach. Huge pub dating from the 1920s, with many of its original features intact, outside seating and an open bar area where locals hang out with sand still on their feet. Sedate during the day but at night an over-the-top, late-night backpackers' hangout.

Bondi Icebergs Club 1 Notts Ave, Bondi Beach. Famous for its winter swimming club (see p.143), *Icebergs* is a fantastic place to sip a beer on the balcony and soak up the views and atmosphere of Bondi Beach. The *bistro* within the club serves oysters ($15 for half a dozen), rump steak and chips ($22), burgers and more. Cover bands often play at weekends.

Manly Wharf Hotel Manly Wharf, Manly ☏02/9977 1266. Modern, light and airy pub that makes a great spot to catch the afternoon sun and sunset over the city. With four bars, there's something to suit everyone, including the *Harbour Bar* restaurant serving great seafood, grills ($18–30) and pizza ($20).

Live music: jazz, blues and rock

The live-music scene in Sydney has passed its boom time, and pub venues keep closing down to make way for the dreaded poker machines. However, there are still enough venues to just barely nourish a steady stream of local, interstate and overseas acts passing through each month, peaking in summer with a well-established open-air festival circuit. Bands in pubs and clubs are often free, especially if you arrive early; door charge is usually from $5, with $30 the top price for smaller international acts or the latest interstate sensation. Sunday afternoon and early evening is a mellow time to catch some music, particularly jazz, around town.

The **venues for major events**, with bookings direct or through Ticketek, Ticketmaster or Moshtix (see p.142), are the Sydney Entertainment Centre at Haymarket near Darling Harbour (☏02/9320 4200); The Hordern Pavilion at Driver Avenue, Entertainment Quarter, Moore Park (☏02/9921 5333); the Capitol Theatre, 13 Campbell St, Haymarket (☏02/9320 5000); the Enmore Theatre, 130 Enmore Rd, just up from Newtown (☏02/9550 3666); the centrally located Metro Theatre, 624 George St (also ☏02/9550 3666); and the State Theatre, on Market Street in the city (☏13 61 00).

There are now several big outdoor rock concerts throughout spring and summer, but Homebake and the Big Day Out are still the best. **Homebake** (around $95; ⓦwww.homebake.com.au) is a huge annual open-air festival in The Domain in early December with food and market stalls, rides, roving performers and a line-up of up to forty famous and underground Australian bands, from Spiderbait to Jet. The **Big Day Out**, on the Australia Day weekend (around $140; ⓦwww.bigdayout.com), at the Showground at Sydney Olympic Park, features big international names like Neil Young, Arctic Monkeys and The Prodigy as well as local talent like Something for Kate and The Drones. See also "Festivals", p.172, for the Manly Jazz Festival.

The Basement 29 Reiby Place, Circular Quay ⊕ 02/9251 2797, ⓦ www .thebasement.com.au. This dark and moody venue attracts the great and rising names in jazz, funk, acoustic and world music, as well as a roster of the world's most renowned blues performers. To take in a show, book a table and dine in front of the low stage; otherwise, you'll have to stand all night at the bar at the back.

Bridge Hotel 135 Victoria Rd, Rozelle ⊕ 02/9810 1260. Legendary inner-west venue specializing in blues, jazz and pub rock, with the occasional big international act (B.B. King and Jon Cleary have played here), but mostly hosting local performers. Laid-back, no-frills atmosphere.

Hopetoun Hotel 416 Bourke St, corner of Fitzroy St, Surry Hills ⊕ 02/9361 5257. One of Sydney's best venues for the indie band scene, "The Hoey" focuses on new young bands: local, interstate and international acts all play in the small and inevitably packed front bar (Mon–Sat from 7.30pm; cover charge depends on the act, though sometimes free), and on Sun there are DJs (5–10pm; $6). Pool room, drinking pit in the basement, and inexpensive restaurant upstairs (meals $9–16). Closes midnight.

Oxford Art Factory 38–46 Oxford St, Darlinghurst ⊕ 02/9332 3711, ⓦ www.oxfordartfactory.com.

Andy Warhol-inspired cultural hub and arts space with an industrial feel. As well as running a bar and cutting-edge art gallery, they put on an enormously wide range of shows from album launches and avant-garde plays to gigs — anything from relatively well-established rock, funk and punk to DJ nights.

Rose of Australia Hotel 1 Swanson St, Erskineville ⊕ 02/9565 1441. Trendy inner-city types mix with goths, locals and gays to sample some favourites of the pub circuit. Line-up changes regularly, and there are no set days for performances (check the free magazine *Drum Media*). Catch anything from an original rock act through to a country-and-western cover band; music is from 9pm and is usually free.

Sandringham Hotel 387 King St, Newtown ⊕ 02/9557 1254. "The Sando" features local and interstate indie bands, who play on the stage upstairs (daily 8–11pm, $5–15; big shows $20) or on the small corner stage downstairs (Wed, Thurs & Sat 7.30–9pm; free)

The Vanguard 42 King St, Newtown ⊕ 02/9557 7992. Billed as bringing jazz, blues and roots to Newtown, this 1920s-style venue – resplendent in racy crimson – with restaurant and cocktail bar, attracts some important international acts, plus some excellent raw local talent. Most acts play from 7pm till 11.45pm.

Clubs

From dark den to opulent fantasy, Sydney's thriving club scene, attracting international DJ celebrities and impressive local talent, is likely to satisfy. A long strip of clubs stretches from Kings Cross to Oxford Street and down towards Hyde Park. The scene can be pretty snobby, with door gorillas frequently vetting your style, so don your finest threads and be sure to spruce up. Along with the places listed below, most of the clubs in our "Gay and lesbian" listings (see p.166) have a fairly mixed clientele.

Admission ranges from $10 to $30; many clubs stay open until 5am or 6am on Saturday and Sunday mornings. There are also good clubs attached to several of the drinking spots listed on pp.161–164. Below are the bigger venues or places with something unusual to offer.

Candy's Apartment 22 Bayswater Rd, Kings Cross. The most happening place in town, this music portal transforms itself every night with the coolest DJs playing gigs early and then churning out fresh dance mixes as the night progresses. Wed–Sun 10pm–6am. $10–20.

Club 77 77 William St, East Sydney. The DJ nights are Fri and Sat (Thurs gets some great live acts) at this intimate and relaxed club. Drinks are cheap and a lot of regulars come for the progressive and rare funk, experimental and house music. Wed–Sat 9pm–3am. $10.

Havana Club 169 Oxford St, Darlinghurst. Alternating resident DJs and live musicians/ percussionists ensures that there's always something new happening. The younger crowd comes on Fri for the high-octane beats, while the clientele on Sat are predominantly 25- to 30-year-olds. Fri & Sat 10pm–6am. $15–25.

Home Cockle Bay Wharf, Darling Harbour. The first really big club venture in Sydney, lavish *Home* can cram 2000 punters into its cool, cavernous interior. There's also a mezzanine, a chill-out room, and outdoor balconies. Decks are often manned by big-name DJs, drinks are expensive, and staff beautiful. Packed with a younger crowd on Fri for its flagship night "Sublime", with four musical genres across four levels. On Sat, "Together at Home" plays progressive and funky house. Fri & Sat 11pm till late. $20–25.

Le Panic 20 Bayswater Rd, Kings Cross. This one-stop-shop for late-night partying has a sizeable dance floor surrounded by a dimly lit bar and comfy booths. A private and exclusive lounge off to the side acts as a chill-out room. Thurs & Sun 9pm–1pm, Fri & Sat 9pm–6am. $20.

Tank 3 Bridge Lane, off George St, City. This is for the glamorous industry crowd – fashion, music and film aficionados. If you don't belong, the style

police will spot you a mile away. All very funky – from the house music played by regular or guest DJs on Sat to the bathroom fittings. Try Fri if R 'n' B is your thing. Attire is smart casual to cool streetwear, but attitude and good looks override the dress code. Fri & Sat 10pm–6am. $20–25.

The World Bar 24 Bayswater Rd, Kings Cross. With a relatively relaxed door policy, *The World* is popular with a fun, party-loving crowd of travellers, who jive to a pleasing mix of funk and house grooves in a pleasant Victorian-era building with a big front balcony. Mon–Thurs & Sun noon–4am, Fri & Sat noon–6am. $15, free before midnight.

Gay and lesbian bars and clubs

The last few years have seen a quiet diminishing of specifically gay and lesbian bars, and due to Sydney's highly restrictive licensing laws, the smaller venues vanish and the large ones just get bigger. The city's gay and lesbian scene is concentrated in two areas, so it's easy to bar hop: in the inner east around Oxford Street, Darlinghurst, including Surry Hills and Kings Cross, and in the inner west in adjoining Newtown and Erskineville. Those wanting a comfortable place to drink with a mixed clientele should also check out pubs such as the *Green Park Hotel* (p.163). Entry is free unless otherwise indicated.

Arq 16 Flinders St, corner of Taylor Square, Darlinghurst ⓦwww.arqsydney.com.au. Huge, state-of-the-art mainstream club with everything from DJs and drag shows to pool competitions. Two levels, each with a very different scene: the "Arena", on the top floor, is mostly gay, while the ground-floor "Vortex" is a quieter, less crowded mix of gay and straight, with pool tables. Chill-out booths, laser lighting, viewing decks and fishtanks add to the fun, friendly atmosphere. Sun is the big night. Check website for events. Thurs–Sun from 9pm. Fri $10, Sat $15 before 11pm, $25 after, Sun $5.

Colombian Hotel 117 Oxford St, corner of Crown St, Darlinghurst. Mixed-clientele bar where people come to get revved up in the evenings and renew their energy the day after. The downstairs bar offers an airy, comfortable space to drink, bop and chat, with open windows onto the street. Upstairs there's a more intimate cocktail bar – which includes a giant red tribal mask. There are different DJs and musical styles (Wed–Sun), from R 'n' B to funky house and drag-cum-variety nights Wed & Thurs. Thurs is glamour night in the cocktail lounge. Hip but not pretentious. Mon & Tues 10am–4pm, Wed–Sun 9am–5am.

Imperial Hotel 35 Erskineville Rd, Erskineville ⓣ02/9519 9899. This gay icon, brought to the world's attention in the hit film *The Adventures of Priscilla, Queen of the Desert*, which both started and ended here, was closed for renovations at the

time of research. When operational, drag queen shows never fail to delight all manner of patrons, while, down the stairs, the basement jumps, jiggies and jives on full-throttle club nights.

Midnight Shift 85 Oxford St, Darlinghurst. "The Shift", running for over 25 years, is a veteran of the Oxford St scene. The *Shift Video Bar* is a large drinking and cruising space to a music-video backdrop, with pool tables out back. Upstairs, the weekend-only club is a massive space with drag shows, DJs and events; cover charge $5–20. Mainly men. Downstairs bar daily noon–6am, club Fri & Sat 11pm–7am.

Stonewall Hotel 175 Oxford St at Taylor Square, Darlinghurst ⓣ02/9360 1963, ⓦwww .stonewallhotel.com. Extending over three action-packed levels, this pub is a big hit with both young gays and lesbians and their straight friends. The airy downstairs bar (with a few outside tables) plays commercial dance, the cocktail bar on the next level accelerates on uplifting house, while the top-floor, weekend-only VIP Bar gets off on campy, "handbag" sounds (Fri & Sat 11pm–6am). You can expect theme nights like karaoke, celebrity drag, or Mailbox (a dating game), and there are DJs Wed–Sat. Daily 11am–6am.

Taxi Club 40 Flinders St, Darlinghurst. A Sydney legend famous (or notorious) for being the only place you can buy a drink after 10pm on Good Friday or Christmas Day, but don't bother before

2/3am, and you'll need to be suitably intoxicated to appreciate it fully. There's a strange blend of drag queens, taxi drivers, lesbians and boys (straight and gay) to observe, and the cheapest drinks in gay Sydney. An upstairs dance club (free) operates Fri and Sat from 1am. Supposedly a members' club but bring ID to show you're from out of town. Mon–Thurs 4pm–midnight, Fri & Sat 2pm–6am, Sun 2pm–4am.

Classical music, theatre and dance

Sydney's **arts scene** is vibrant and extensive. The Sydney Symphony Orchestra plays at the Opera House, and sometimes at the City Recital Hall, while the Australian Ballet performs at the Opera House and the Capitol Theatre. The free outdoor performances in The Domain, under the auspices of the Sydney Festival, are one of the year's highlights, with crowds gathering to enjoy the music with a picnic.

Concert halls

City Recital Hall Angel Place, between George and Pitt sts, City ☏ 02/8256 2222. Opened in 1999, this classical music venue right next to Martin Place was specifically designed for chamber music. Seats 1200, but on three levels, giving it an intimate atmosphere.

Conservatorium of Music Royal Botanic Gardens, off Macquarie St, City ☏ 02/9351 1438, ⓦwww.usyd .edu.au/su/conmusic. Students of the "Con" give lunchtime recitals every Wed at 1.10pm during term time in Verbrugghen Hall (donation expected). Other concerts, both free and ticketed ($10–35) are given by students and staff both here and at venues around town; check website for details and see also p.120.

St James' Church King St, beside Hyde Park, City ☏ 02/9232 3022. St James' highly acclaimed chamber choir, whose repertoire extends from Gregorian chants to more contemporary pieces, can be heard on Sun at 11am (plus 4pm last Sun of the month). St James' music programme also includes a series of lunchtime concerts (Wed 1.15pm; 30min; $5 donation).

Sydney Opera House Bennelong Point ☏ 02/9250 7777. The Opera House is, of course, the place for the most prestigious performances in Sydney, hosting not just opera and classical music but also theatre and ballet in its many auditoriums. Forget quibbles about ticket prices (classical concerts from $50, ballet from $65, opera from $100) – it's worth going just to say you've been. See pp.105–107 for more.

Town Hall Corner of Druitt and George sts, City ☏ 02/9265 9189. Centrally located concert hall (seats 2000) with a splendid high-Victorian interior – hosts everything from chamber orchestras to bush dances and public lectures, but closed for major refurbishment until late 2009.

Theatre and dance

Bangarra Dance Theatre Pier 4, Hickson Rd, Millers Point, The Rocks ☏ 02/9251 533,

ⓦwww.bangarra.com.au. Formed in 1989, Bangarra's innovative style fuses contemporary movement with the traditional dances and culture of the Yirrkala Community in the Northern Territory's Arnhem Land. Although based at the same pier as the Wharf Theatre, the company performs at other venues in Sydney and tours nationally and internationally.

Belvoir St Theatre 25 Belvoir St, Surry Hills ☏ 02/9699 3444. Highly regarded two-stage venue for a wide range of contemporary Australian and international theatre.

Ensemble Theatre 78 McDougall St, Milsons Point ☏ 02/9929 0644. Hosts Australian contemporary and classic plays.

Lyric Theatre Star City Casino, Pirrama Rd, Pyrmont ☏ 02/9777 9000. The place to see big musical extravaganzas imported from the West End and Broadway. The casino's smaller theatre, the Star City Showroom, puts on more offbeat musicals – such as the *Rocky Horror Picture Show* – and comedy.

The Playhouse, Drama Theatre and The Studio Sydney Opera House, Bennelong Point ☏ 02/9250 7777. The Playhouse and Drama Theatre show modern and traditional Australian and international plays mostly put on by the Sydney Theatre Company, while the Studio, the Opera House's smallest venue (with the most affordable ticket prices), has a theatre-in-the-round format, and offers an innovative and wide-ranging programme of contemporary performance: theatre, cabaret, dance, comedy and hybrid works.

Sydney Dance Company Pier 4, Hickson Rd, Millers Point ☏ 02/9221 4811, ⓦwww .sydneydance.com.au. Graeme Murphy, Australia's doyen of dance, was at the helm here from 1976 to 2007, and his successors continue to raise the bar with ambitious sets and beautifully designed costumes. The company is based at the Wharf Theatre but tours nationally and internationally.

Sydney is indisputably one of the world's great gay cities – indeed, many people think it capable of snatching San Francisco's crown as the queen of them all. There's something for everyone – whether you want to lie on a beach during the warmer months (Oct–April) or party hard all year round. Gays and lesbians are pretty much accepted, particularly in the inner-city and eastern areas. They have to be – there's too many of them for anyone to argue.

Even if you can't be here for Mardi Gras or the Sleaze Ball (see both below), you'll still find the city has much to offer. **Oxford Street (mostly around Taylor Square)** is Sydney's official "pink strip" of gay-frequented restaurants, coffee shops, bookshops and bars, and here you'll find countless pairs of tight-T-shirted guys strolling hand-in-hand, or checking out the passing talent in hip, streetside cafés. However, the gay–straight divide in Sydney has less relevance for a new generation, perhaps as a result of Mardi Gras' mainstream success. Several of the long-running gay venues on and around Oxford Street have closed down and many of those remaining attract older customers, as younger gays and lesbians embrace inclusiveness and party with their straight friends and peers or choose to meet new friends on the internet instead of in bars. **King Street**, Newtown, and nearby **Erskineville** are centres of gay culture, while lesbian communities have carved out territory of their own in **Leichhardt** (known affectionately as "Dykehart") and **Marrackville**.

Little of the **accommodation** in Sydney is gay-exclusive, but anywhere within a stone's throw of Taylor Square will be very gay-friendly. Best bets in our accommodation listings are *City Crown Motel* (see p.99), *Governors on Fitzroy* (see p.100), *Kirketon* (see p.99) and *Sullivans* (see p.100). Most of the cafés and **restaurants** in the same area have a strong gay following; for a lowdown on the gay and lesbian **club scene** see p.166. Weekly event listings are included in the free magazines (see p.86).

If you've come for the sun, popular **gay beaches** are Tamarama (see p.144), Bondi (see p.143) and "clothing-optional" Lady Jane, while pools of choice are Redleaf harbour pool at Double Bay (see p.137) and the appropriately named Andrew "Boy" Charlton pool in The Domain (see p.118). The Coogee Women's Baths, at the southern end of Coogee Beach (see p.145), are popular with lesbians.

Mardi Gras and the Sleaze Ball

The year's highlight is the **Sydney Gay & Lesbian Mardi Gras** (℡02/9568 8600, ⓦwww.mardigras.org.au): three weeks of exhibitions, performances and other events, including the **Mardi Gras Film Festival** (ⓦwww.queerscreen.com.au), showcasing the latest in queer cinema. Mardi Gras starts the second week of **February**, kicking off with a free Fair Day in Victoria Park, Camperdown, and culminating with a massive parade and party, usually on the first weekend of March. The first parade was held in 1978 as a gay-rights protest and today it's the biggest celebration of gay and lesbian culture in the world. In 1992, an unprecedented crowd of 400,000, including a broad spectrum of straight society, turned up to watch the parade, and two years later it began to be broadcast nationally on television. By 1999, the combined festival, parade and party was making the local economy $100 million richer each year, and the increasing commercialization of Mardi Gras was drawing criticism from the gay and lesbian community. Its bubble burst in 2002, after financial mismanagement saw the Mardi Gras organization in the red to the tune of $500,000. Instead of throwing in the towel, the fundraising

---

Wharf Theatre Pier 4/5, Hickson Rd, Millers Point, The Rocks ℡02/9250 1777. Home to the Sydney Dance Company and the highly regarded Sydney Theatre Company (currently with Cate Blanchett and her husband, Andrew Upton, at the helm), producing Shakespeare and modern pieces. Atmospheric waterfront location, two performance spaces and a good restaurant (see p.152), bar and café.

organization was rebuilt as the "New Mardi Gras", drawing on the resources and creativity of its talented community, along with the desire to keep the festival going, and continuing to build. The thirtieth anniversary Mardi Gras in 2008 was a triumph, and one of the biggest yet.

The main event is the exuberant night-time **parade** down Oxford Street, when up to half-a-million gays and straights jostle for the best viewing positions, before the Dykes on Bikes – traditional leaders of the parade since 1988 – roar into view. Participants devote months to the preparation of outlandish floats and outrageous costumes at Mardi Gras workshops, and even more time is devoted to the preparation of beautiful bodies in Sydney's packed gyms. The **parade** begins at 7.45pm (finishing around 10.30pm), but people line the barricades along Oxford Street from mid-morning (brandishing stolen milk crates to stand on for a better view). If you can't get to Oxford Street until late afternoon, your best chance of finding a spot is along Flinders Street near Moore Park Road, where the parade ends. Otherwise, AIDS charity The Bobby Goldsmith Foundation (Wwww.bgf.org.au) has around 7000 grandstand ("Glamstand") seats on Flinders Street, at $120 each.

The all-night **dance party** that follows the parade attracts up to 25,000 people and is held in several differently themed dance spaces at The Entertainment Quarter in Moore Park (with Paul Oakenfold headlining in 2009). You may have to plan ahead if you want to get a **ticket**: party tickets ($135 from Ticketek on T 13 28 49, Wwww .ticketek.com.au) sometimes sell out by the end of January. The **Sydney Gay & Lesbian Mardi Gras Guide**, available from mid-December, can be picked up from bookshops, cafés and restaurants around Oxford Street or viewed online on the Mardi Gras website.

Sydney just can't wait all year for Mardi Gras, so the **Sleaze Ball** (tickets $120 through Ticketek, see above) is a very welcome stopgap in early October, and acts as a fundraiser for the Mardi Gras organizers. Similar to the Mardi Gras party, it's held at The Entertainment Quarter, and goes on through the night. For those who miss the main event, the **recovery parties** the next day are nearly as good; virtually all the bars and clubs host all-day sessions after the parties, especially the lanes behind the *Flinders Bar*, which are packed with exhausted but deliriously happy party-people.

Groups and information

First stop for information on gay Sydney is The Bookshop, 207 Oxford St, Darlinghurst (T 02/9331 1103, Wwww.thebookshop.com.au), a friendly place with a complete stock of gay- and lesbian-related books, cards and magazines. You can pick up the free gay and lesbian weeklies *Sydney Star Observer* (Wwww.starobserver.com.au), *SX* (Wwww.eevolution.com.au) and the lesbian-specific monthly *LOTL* (*Lesbians on the Loose*; Wwww.lotl.com) here and in other gay-friendly businesses in the eastern suburbs and inner west. The websites are good for trip planning and the mags will tell you where and when the weekly dance parties are being held, and where you can buy tickets.

Support networks include: the Gay & Lesbian Counselling Service (daily 5.30–10.30pm; T 02/8594 9596, Wwww.glcsnsw.org.au); the AIDS Council of New South Wales (ACON), 9 Commonwealth St, Surry Hills (T 1800 063 060, Wwww.acon.com .au); Albion Street Centre, 150–154 Albion St, Surry Hills (T 02/9332 1090), which offers counselling, a testing clinic, information and a library; and the Anti-Discrimination Board (T 02/9268 5544).

Fringe theatre, comedy and cabaret

As well as the venues listed below, also see the *Friend In Hand* pub (p.163), which has Thursday comedy nights, and *The Imperial* (see p.166) for brilliant, free drag shows.

New Theatre 542 King St, Newtown ☎02/9519 3403. Professional and amateur actors (all unpaid) perform contemporary dramas with socially relevant themes. Tickets $28.

NIDA 215 ANZAC Parade, Kensington ☎02/9697 7613. Australia's premier dramatic training ground – the National Institute of Dramatic Art – where the likes of Mel Gibson, Judy Davis and Colin Friels started out, also offers student productions for talent-spotting.

Stables Theatre 10 Nimrod St, Darlinghurst ☎02/9361 3817. Home theatre for the Griffin

Theatre Company, whose mission is to develop and foster new Australian playwrights.

Sydney Comedy Store Entertainment Quarter, Driver Ave, Moore Park ☎02/9357 1419, ⓦwww .comedystore.com.au. International (often American) and Australian stand-up comics Tues to Sat; door open 8.15pm; shows start 8.30pm. Meals aren't available, but nearby restaurants offer meal discounts for *Comedy Store* ticket-holders. Bookings recommended. Tues & Wed $15, Thurs $20, Fri $27.50, Sat $29.50.

Cinemas

Sydney's commercial movie hub is on George Street, two blocks south of the Town Hall, where you'll find the Greater Union (see below). This is mainstream, fast-food, teenager territory, and there are much nicer places to watch a film, particularly at the Entertainment Quarter and around the groovier inner-city suburbs. Standard tickets cost around $16, but reduced-price tickets (around $10) are available on Tuesday at all of these cinemas and their suburban outlets, and on Monday or Tuesday at most of the art-house and local cinemas listed below.

In the summer, there are two **open-air cinemas**: from November to the end of March, the **Moonlight Cinema**, in the Centennial Park Amphitheatre (Oxford St, Woollahra entrance; Tues–Sun, films start 8.45pm, tickets available when gates open from 7pm, or book online at ⓦwww.moonlight .com.au; $17), shows classic, art-house and cult films; and throughout January and February, the **Open Air Cinema** (tickets from 6.30pm; ☎1300 366 649; $28) is put up over the water at Mrs Macquarie's Point, the Royal Botanic Gardens, for a picturesque harbour screening, backed by the Opera House and Harbour Bridge (mainly mainstream recent releases and some classics). See box, opposite for film festivals.

Chauvel Cinema Paddington Town Hall, corner of Oatley Rd and Oxford St, Paddington ☎02/9361 5398. Varied programme of Australian and foreign films, plus classics, at this cinephile's cinema. Discount Tues.

Cinema Paris Entertainment Quarter ☎02/9332 1633. Hoyts' four-screen art-house option also has mini-festivals and events throughout the year.

Cremorne Orpheum 380 Military Rd, Cremorne ☎02/9908 4344. Charming heritage-listed, six-screen cinema built in 1935, with a splendid Art Deco interior and old-fashioned, friendly service. The main cinema has never dispensed with its Wurlitzer organ recitals before Sat night and Sun afternoon films. Mainstream and foreign new releases. Discount Tues.

Dendy 261 King St, Newtown ☎02/9550 5699. Trendy four-screen cinema complex with attached café, bar and bookshop, showing new-release films. The newer, three-screen Dendy Opera Quays, 2 East Circular Quay (☎02/9247 3800), is superbly sited. Discount Tues.

Govinda's Movie Room 112 Darlinghurst Rd, Darlinghurst ☎02/9380 5155. Run by the Hare Krishnas, Govinda's shows two films every night from a range of classics and recent releases in a pleasantly unorthodox screening room with cushions. The movie-and-dinner deal (all-you-can-eat vegetarian buffet) is popular – $19.80 for the meal with an extra $8.80 to see a movie. Buy your film ticket when you order your meal, or you may miss out on busy nights. Film only is $12.80 but diners are given preference.

Greater Union 505–525 George St, CBD ☎02/9267 8666. Seventeen screens of the latest releases right in the heart of town.

Hoyts Broadway Broadway Shopping Centre, near Glebe ☎02/9211 1911. This multiplex offers a more pleasant experience than heading into George St.

Hoyts Entertainment Quarter Entertainment Quarter ☎02/9332 1300. Twelve-screener with six sporting a special deluxe section, La Premiere,

Film festivals

The **Sydney Film Festival**, held two weeks in early June, has an exciting programme of features, shorts, documentaries and retrospective screenings from Australia and around the world. Founded in 1954 by a group of film enthusiasts at Sydney University, the festival struggled with prudish censors and parochial attitudes until freedom from censorship for festival films was introduced in 1971. From the early, relaxed atmosphere of picnics on the lawns between screenings and hardy film-lovers crouching under blankets in freezing prefabricated sheds, it has gradually moved off-campus, to find a home from 1974 in the magnificent State Theatre (see p.113). Films are now also shown at the wonderfully sited three-screen Dendy Quays in Circular Quay, Greater Union on George Street, the Metro Theatre (opposite Greater Union), The Studio at the Opera House, and more. For information on tickets contact the festival office (Mon–Fri 9am–5pm; ℡02/9318 0999; ⓦwww.sydneyfilmfestival.org).

There are also two short film festivals in the summer with the sort of irreverent approach that once fuelled the Sydney Film Festival. Starry skies and the lapping of Bondi's waves accompany the week-long **Flickerfest International Short Film Festival** (tickets $15, season pass $130; ℡02/9365 6888, ⓦwww.flickerfest.com .au), held in the amphitheatre of the Bondi Pavilion in early January, showcasing foreign and Australian productions, including documentaries. The **Tropfest** (℡02/9368 0434, ⓦwww.tropfest.com) is a competition festival for short films held annually around the end of February; its name comes from the *Tropicana Cafe* on Victoria Street, Darlinghurst, where the festival began almost by chance in 1993 when a young actor, John Polsen, forced his local coffee spot to show the short film he had made. He pushed other filmmakers to follow suit, and the following year a huge crowd of punters packed themselves into the café to watch around twenty films. These days, the entire street is closed to traffic to enable an outdoor screening, while cafés along the strip also screen films inside. The focus of the event in Sydney has moved to The Domain, with huge crowds turning up to picnic and watch the free 8pm screening (plus live entertainment from 3pm), while outdoor screenings are held simultaneously in capital cities Australia-wide. The judges are often famous international actors, and Polsen himself, still the festival's director, has made it as a Hollywood director with his films *Swimfan* (2002) and *Hide and Seek* (2005). Films must be specifically produced for the festival and be up-to-the-minute – a theme is announced a few months in advance of the entry date that must feature in the shorts. In 2009, it was "spring" – however filmmakers chose to interpret it.

Other film festivals include the **World of Women's Cinema** (WOW) Festival held over five days in early October at the Chauvel Cinema, Paddington and surrounding venues (ⓦwww.wift.org/wow); and a **gay and lesbian film festival** in late February as part of the Gay and Lesbian Mardi Gras.

---

aimed at couples, where custom-made sofa seats for two have wine holders and tables for food – you can buy bottles of wine and cheese plates; soft drinks and popcorn are all included in the ticket price ($33, Tues $23). Standard tickets $16 (Tues $10).

IMAX Theatre Southern Promenade, Darling Harbour ℡02/9281 3300. State-of-the-art giant cinema screen showing a choice of six films (many of them in 3D) designed to thrill your senses. Films under 1hr cost $19.50, those over 1hr $25. Films hourly 10am–10pm.

Palace Cinemas Chain of inner-city cinemas showing foreign-language, art-house and new releases: Academy Twin, 3A Oxford St, corner of South Dowling St, Paddington (℡02/9361 4453); Verona, 17 Oxford St, corner of Verona St, Paddington (℡02/9360 6099), which has a bar; Norton, 99 Norton St, Leichhardt (℡02/9550 0122), the newest, with a bookshop and café. Discount Mon.

Art galleries and exhibitions

The Citysearch Sydney website (Ⓦ www.sydney.citysearch.com.au) has comprehensive listings of art galleries and current exhibitions, while Friday's *Metro* section of the *Sydney Morning Herald* offers reviews of recently opened shows, or check out the useful *Artfind Guide* online (Ⓦ www.artfind.com.au). Galleries tend to be concentrated in Paddington and Surry Hills, with a few smaller ones on King Street, Newtown.

Artspace The Gunnery Arts Centre, 43–51 Cowper Wharf Rd, Woolloomooloo ☎ 02/9356 0555. In a wonderful location, showing provocative young artists with a focus on installations and new media. Tues–Sat 11am–5pm.

Australian Centre for Photography 257 Oxford St, Paddington ☎ 02/9332 1455. Exhibitions of photo-based art from established and new international and Australian artists in four galleries. Emerging photographers are showcased on the Project Wall. There's an extensive specialist library, photography courses, and a darkroom, studio and digital media suite hire, Tues–Fri noon–7pm, Sat & Sun 10am–6pm.

Australian Galleries: Painting & Sculpture 15 Roylston St, Paddington ☎ 02/9360 5177. A serene gallery selling and exhibiting contemporary Australian art, including works by Gary Shead, Jeffrey Smart and John Coburn. Mon–Sat 10am–6pm.

Australian Galleries: Works on Paper 24 Glenmore Rd, Paddington ☎ 02/9380 8744. Includes works by William Robinson, Lloyd Rees and Arthur Boyd, as well as prints and sketches by young Australian artists. Mon–Sat 10am–6pm, Sun noon–5pm.

Hogarth Galleries Aboriginal Art Centre 7 Walker Lane, Paddington ☎ 02/9360 6839. Extensive collection of work by contemporary Aboriginal artists, both tribal and urban, and special exhibitions. Tues–Sat 10am–5pm.

Ivan Dougherty Gallery Corner of Albion Ave and Selwyn St, Paddington ☎ 02/9385 0726. This is the exhibition space for the College of Fine Arts (COFA), University of New South Wales. The ten shows per year focus on Australian and international contemporary art with accompanying forums, lectures and performances. Mon–Sat 10am–5pm.

Josef Lebovic Gallery 34 Paddington St, Paddington ☎ 02/9332 1840. Renowned print and graphic gallery specializing in Australian and international prints from the nineteenth, twentieth and twenty-first centuries, as well as vintage photography. Wed–Fri 1–6pm, Sat 11am–5pm.

Ray Hughes Gallery 270 Devonshire St, Surry Hills ☎ 02/9698 3200. Influential dealer with a stable of high-profile, contemporary Australian, New Zealand and Chinese artists. Openings monthly, with two artists per show. Tues–Sat 10am–6pm.

Festivals and events

The Sydney year is interspersed with festivals and events of various sorts that reach their peak in the summer. Check the City of Sydney Council's online "What's On" section (Ⓦ www.cityofsydney.nsw.gov.au) for details of events year-round.

The **New Year** begins with a spectacular **fireworks** display from the Harbour Bridge and Darling Harbour. There's a brief hiatus of a week or so until the annual **Sydney Festival** (☎ 02/8248 6500, Ⓦ www.sydneyfestival.org.au), an exhaustive and exhausting arts event that lasts for most of **January** and ranges from concerts, plays and outdoor art installations to circus performances. Numerous free events are based around urban public spaces, focusing on Circular Quay, The Domain, Darling Harbour and Sydney Olympic Park; the remainder – mostly international performances – can cost a packet. The **Big Day Out** (see p.164) is usually held at the end of January at Sydney Olympic Park, featuring around sixty local and international bands and DJs.

Later in the month, on January 26, **Australia Day** (Ⓦ www.australiaday.com .au) is a huge celebration in Sydney, with activities focused on the water. Sydney's passenger ferries race from Fort Denison to the Harbour Bridge, via Shark Island, and there's a Tall Ships Race from Bradleys Head to the Harbour

Horse racing in Sydney

There are horse-racing meetings on Wednesday, Saturday and most public holidays throughout the year, but the best times to hit the track are during the **Spring and Autumn Carnivals** (Aug–Sept and March–April), when prize money rockets, and the quality of racing rivals the best in the world. The venues are well maintained, and peopled with colourful characters, and often massive crowds. Principal racecourses are: Royal Randwick (Alison Rd, Randwick), which featured in *Mission: Impossible II*; Rosehill Gardens (James Ruse Drive, Rosehill); and Canterbury Park (King St, Canterbury), which has midweek racing, plus floodlit Thursday-night racing from September to March. Entry is around $12, or $20–25 on carnival days. Contact the Australian Jockey Club (℡02/9663 8400, ⓦwww.ajc.org.au) for details of many other picturesque country venues. Every Friday, the *Sydney Morning Herald* publishes its racing guide, "The Form". Bets are placed at TAB shops; these are scattered throughout the city, and most pubs also have TAB access.

Bridge, as well as an aerial display of military planes. The **Australia Day Regatta** takes place in the afternoon, with hundreds of yachts racing all over the harbour, from Botany Bay to the Parramatta River. There are also free events at The Rocks, Hyde Park, and at Darling Harbour, where the day culminates with the Australia Day Spectacular at around 9pm with a "multimedia symphony of light, sound and music" concluding with a massive fireworks display. In addition, many museums let visitors in for free or half price.

Besides all this, there are at least two outdoor festivals to choose from: **Yabun**, which celebrates Aboriginal culture and acts as an antidote to the mainstream, white Australia Day festivities, is held at Victoria Park, Broadway (free; contact Koori Radio on ℡02/9384 4000 or check ⓦwww.gadigal.org .au); and **Rocksong at The Rocks**, an all-day festival (at The Rocks) featuring high-calibre singers and songwriters of a variety of genres from all over Australia.

An entirely different side of Sydney life is on view at the impressive summer **surf carnivals**, staged regularly by local surf lifesaving clubs (contact Surf Life Saving NSW for details on ℡02/9984 7188, ⓦwww.surflifesaving.com.au), while at the end of **February** the city is engulfed by the **Sydney Gay and Lesbian Mardi Gras** (see p.168).

Another big event is the **Sydney Royal Easter Show** (ⓦwww.eastershow .com.au), an agricultural and garden show based at the Showground at Sydney Olympic Park. For twelve consecutive days (with the second weekend always the Easter weekend) the country comes to the city for a frantic array of amusement-park rides, fireworks, parades of prize animals, a rodeo and wood-chopping displays.

A clutch of cultural events takes place around May and June: in **May**, the week-long **Sydney Writers Festival** (mostly free; ⓦwww.swf.org.au) takes place in the very scenically located Wharf Theatre complex, while the **Sydney International Film Festival** takes over many of the city's screens in **June** (see box, p.171). Every even-numbered year, the **Biennale of Sydney** takes place over six weeks from early June until mid-August, with provocative contemporary art exhibitions at various venues and public spaces around town. The **City to Surf Race**, a fourteen-kilometre fun-run from the city to Bondi, happens every **August**. Labour Day weekend in early **October** is marked by the **Manly International Jazz Festival**, with several free outdoor, waterfront events and a few indoor concerts charging entry.

▲ A Sculpture By The Sea exhibit

In late **October**, the coast between Bondi and Tamarama is transformed for two weeks by the magical **Sculpture By The Sea** exhibition (ⓦwww.sculpturebythesea.com). The year is brought to a close by the **Sydney to Hobart Yacht Race**, when it seems that half of the city turns up at the harbour on December 26 to cheer the start of this classic regatta and watch the colourful spectacle of two hundred or so yachts setting sail for a 630-nautical-mile slog.

Shopping

Sydney's main shopping focus is the city centre, in the stretch between Martin Place and the QVB. Apart from its charming old nineteenth-century arcades and two **department stores**, David Jones and Myers, the city centre also has several modern **shopping complexes** where you can hunt down clothes and accessories without raising a sweat, among them Skygarden (between Pitt and Castlereagh streets) and Centrepoint on Pitt Street Mall, on the corner of Market Street. Much of the area from the QVB to the mall is linked by underground arcades, which will also keep you cool.

Most stores are **open** Monday to Saturday 9am to 6pm, with Thursday late-night shopping until 9pm. Many of the larger shops and department stores in the city are also open on Sunday 10am to 5pm, as are shopping centres in tourist areas such as Darling Harbour. If you've run out of time to buy presents and souvenirs, don't worry: the revamped **Sydney Airport** is attached to one of the biggest shopping malls in Sydney, with outlets for everything from surfwear to R.M. Williams bush outfitters, at the same prices as the downtown stores. The Rocks is the best place for souvenir and duty- and GST-free (VAT-free) shopping.

Fashion

Oxford Street in Paddington is the place to go for interesting fashion, with outlets of most Australian designers along the strip. You'll find more expensive designer gear in the city, at the Strand Arcade, 412 George St, and David Jones department store (see p.174). For striking street fashion, check out Crown Street in Surry Hills, with places such as Wheels & Doll Baby at no. 259, and King Street in Newtown running up to St Peters, where you'll also find cheaper styles, retro clothes and other interesting junk. To go with the outfits, funky Australian **jewellery** can be found in the Strand Arcade at Dinosaur Designs (also at 339 Oxford St, Paddington), and at Love and Hatred, both on Level 1.

The quality Australian **bush outfitters** R.M. Williams, with branches at no. 71 and no. 389 George St, is great for moleskin trousers, Drizabone coats and Akubra hats. However, for an even wider range of Akubra **hats**, check out Strand Hatters at shop 8, Strand Arcade. If it's interesting **surfwear** you're after, head for Mambo at 80 The Corso, Manly (or samples of Mambo at Beach Culture, 105 George St), and an array of surf shops at Manly and Bondi Beach.

Arts and crafts

The Rocks is heaving with **Australiana** and **arts and crafts** souvenirs, from opals to sheepskin – weekends are particularly busy when the open-air market takes over George Street. Tourists flock to Ken Done's emporium here at 123 George St and 1 Hickson Rd (in the restored Australian Steam and Navigation Building) to buy his colourful designs, which feature Sydney's harbour, boats and flowers; there's also a Done Art & Design store at Opera Quays and Darling Harbour. The best place to buy **Aboriginal** art and crafts is the Aboriginal-owned and -run Gavala, in the Harbourside shopping centre in Darling Harbour.

Music and books

For a take-home sample of the **Australian music** scene in all its variety visit Red Eye Records at 66 King St in the CBD, which has a large section on Australian pop and indie, and the Australian Music Centre shop, Level 4, The Arts Exchange, 10 Hickson Rd, The Rocks, which stocks music by Australian composers working within a variety of genres including electroacoustic, contemporary jazz, electronica and sound art.

One of the biggest **bookshops** in the city is the long-running, Australian-owned Dymocks, 424 George St (also in Broadway Shopping Centre near Glebe), open daily, on several floors with an impressive Australian selection and a café. Gleebooks, 49 Glebe Point Rd, Glebe, is one of Australia's best bookshops, specializing in academic and alternative books, contemporary Australian and international literature, and is open daily until 9pm; book launches and other literary events are regularly held. **Secondhand books** can be found at Glebe and Paddington markets, at characterful Sappho Books and Café, 51 Glebe Point Rd (daily until 7pm), Gleebooks (see above); and in the secondhand bookshops on King Street, Newtown – in particular, check out the amazingly chaotic piles of books at Gould's Book Arcade, nos. 32–38 (daily 9am–midnight).

Food and drink

There are several handy **supermarkets** in the city centre with extended opening hours: one is in the basement of Woolworths on the corner of Park and George streets, above Town Hall Station (Mon–Fri 6am–midnight, Sat & Sun 8am–midnight); and there are two small Coles supermarkets in the city – Shop A40, 289–307 George St, Wynyard; and 580 George St in The Pavilion – while the larger Coles in Kings Cross, at 88 Darlinghurst Rd, and on the ground floor of Broadway Shopping Centre near Glebe, are both also handy for travellers (all daily 6am–midnight). In the suburbs, large supermarkets stay open daily until about 10pm or midnight, and there are plenty of (albeit overpriced) 24-hour convenience stores in the inner city and suburbs. For **delicatessen** items, look no further than the splendid food hall at David Jones (see p.174). The **Australian Wine Centre**, corner of George and Alfred streets, Circular Quay (Mon, Tues, Wed & Sat 9.30am–7pm, Thurs–Fri 9.30am–8pm, Sun 10am–6pm), sells more than a thousand **wines** from around Australia and even has an in-house wine bar.

Markets

The two best **markets** are the Paddington Market (10am–4pm) and Balmain Market (8.30am–4pm), both on Saturday, while the relaxed Glebe Markets (Sat 10am–4pm), the flea market at Rozelle (Sat & Sun 9am–4pm) and Bondi Markets (Sun 10am–4pm) are also worth a look, if only for the atmosphere. The

Cars: buying and selling

Sydney is the most popular place to buy a car or campervan in which to travel around Australia. The information below is specific to buying a car in New South Wales – for general background on buying and selling a car, see pp.41–43. Before you start looking, it's a good idea to join the NRMA motoring association, 74 King St, City (☎13 21 32, international ☎612/9848 5201; ⓦwww.mynrma.com.au; $55 joining fee plus $90.70 annual charge per vehicle, or $162.50 for extra benefits); overseas motoring association members may have reciprocal membership. Membership entitles you to roadside assistance and a reduced rate for a vehicle inspection of a potential purchase (members $149, non-members $199; ☎13 11 22). The NRMA's website has an excellent "Motoring" section and The Red Book (ⓦwww.redbook.com.au) provides detailed, up-to-date information on the value of all makes of new and used cars. The Office of Fair Trading's useful *The Car Buyers Handbook: Buying and Maintaining a Car in NSW* can be viewed online (☎13 32 20, ⓦwww.fairtrading.nsw.gov.au).

Thursday's *Weekly Trading Post* (ⓦwww.tradingpost.com.au) has a big second-hand-car section, while the *Sydney Morning Herald*'s Friday "Drive" supplement has ads for secondhand dealers (most on Parramatta Rd from Annandale onwards) and private used cars for sale at the pricier end of the market. Demand to see a "pink slip" (certificate of roadworthiness) that is less than 28 days old. You can contact REVS (☎13 32 20, ⓦwww.revs.nsw.gov.au) to check if there are any payments owing and call the Roads and Traffic Authority (RTA; ☎13 22 13, ⓦwww.rta.nsw.gov.au) to check registration is still current.

Sydney is well equipped with dealerships who will arrange to buy back the vehicle they've sold you at the end of your trip – expect to get thirty to fifty percent back. The longest running is Travellers Auto Barn, 177 William St, Kings Cross (☎1800 674 374; ⓦwww.travellers-autobarn.com.au), with offices in Melbourne, Brisbane, Cairns, Perth and Darwin, or the more down-to-earth Traveller's Mate (☎02/9556 2113, ⓦwww.travellersmate.com.au), in Arncliffe near Mascot airport. The Car Market, 110 Bourke St, Woolloomooloo (9am–5pm; ☎02/9358 5000 or 1800 808 188, ⓦwww.carmarket.com.au), is specifically aimed at travellers, with help with paperwork and contract exchange provided. It's also one of the few places where you will be able to sell a car registered in another state. Dealers are barred, and fees for sellers are $60–85 per week. Many of the vehicles come equipped with camping gear and other extras. Third-party property insurance ($210 for 3 months, $375 for 12 months) can be arranged – the NRMA often refuses to cover overseas travellers. It's worth checking The Car Market's website, where sellers can advertise for $50.

Rocks Market on George Street (Sat & Sun 10am–5pm) is more touristy but good for a browse, while Paddy's Market, in Haymarket near Chinatown (Thurs–Sun 9am–5pm), is Sydney's oldest, selling fresh produce and deli items, plus large quantities of bargain-basement clothes and toys. There's also a series of alternating Saturday markets on the North Shore; the scenically sited Kirribilli Market (fourth Sat of month; 7am–3.30pm) is the best known. Foodies should check the **produce markets**: The Rocks Farmers Market on Argyle Street, The Rocks (Fri 10am–3pm, Sat 9am–3pm); Pymont Growers Market at Pyrmont Bay Park in front of the Star City Casino (first Sat of month 7–11am); EQ Village Markets at the Showring in The Entertainment Quarter (Wed & Sat 10am–4pm); and Northside Produce Market on Miller Street, North Sydney, between Ridge and McClaren streets (third Sat of month 8am–noon).

Listings

Airlines (domestic) Aeropelican (☎ 02/4928 9600) to Inverell and Newcastle; Qantas, see address below (☎ 13 13 13), Australia-wide including Albury, Armidale, Ballina, Coffs Harbour, Dubbo, Lord Howe Island, Moree, Narrabri, Newcastle, Norfolk Island, Port Macquarie, Tamworth and Wagga Wagga; Regional Express (REX; ☎ 13 17 13) to Albury, Ballina, Bathurst, Bourke, Broken Hill, Dubbo, Griffith, Lismore, Melbourne, Merimbula, Mildura, Moruya, Narrandera, Orange, Parkes, Taree and Wagga Wagga; Air Link (☎ 1300 662 823) to Bathurst, Bourke, Cobar, Coonamble, Dubbo, Lightning Ridge, Mudgee and Walgett; Jetstar (☎ 13 15 38) to Adelaide, Brisbane, Ballina/Byron-Cairns, Gold Coast, Hamilton Island, Hobart, Launceston, Melbourne, Mackay, Rockhampton, Sunshine Coast, Townsville and Whitsunday Coast; Virgin Blue (☎ 13 67 89), Australia-wide to all state capitals as well as much of coastal Queensland, and Coffs Harbour.

Airlines (international) Aeroflot, Level 24, 44 Market St ☎ 02/9262 2233; Air Canada, Level 12, 92 Pitt St ☎ 02/9232 5222; Air New Zealand, Level 18, 264 George St ☎ 13 24 76; Air Pacific, Level 10, 403 George St ☎ 1800 230 150; Alitalia, 64 York St ☎ 02/9244 2400; British Airways, Level 19, AAP Centre, 259 George St ☎ 1300 767 177; Cathay Pacific, Third Floor, Sydney Airport ☎ 13 17 47; Continental, 64 York St ☎ 02/9244 2242; Delta Air Lines, Level 4/9, 13 Young St ☎ 1300 302 849; Finnair, 64 York St ☎ 02/9244 2271 or 1300 798 188; Garuda, 55 Hunter St ☎ 1300 365 330; Gulf Air, 64 York St ☎ 1300 366 337; Japan Airlines, Level 14, 201 Sussex St ☎ 02/9272 1111; KLM, 13th floor, 115 Pitt St ☎ 1300 303 747; Korean Air, Level 4, 333 George St ☎ 02/9262 6000; Lufthansa, 143 Macquarie St ☎ 1300 655 727; Malaysia Airlines, 16 Spring St ☎ 02/9364 3500;

Olympic, Third Floor, 37–49 Pitt St ☎ 02/9251 1048; Qantas, 10 Bridge St ☎ 13 13 13, Scandinavian Airlines, Level 15, 31 Market St ☎ 1300 727 707; Singapore Airlines, 31 Market St ☎ 13 10 11; Thai Airways, 75 Pitt St ☎ 1300 651 960; Virgin Atlantic, Level 8, 403 George St ☎ 02/9244 2747.

Banks and exchange Head offices of banks are mostly in the CBD, around Martin Place; hours are Mon–Thurs 9.30am–4pm, Fri 9.30am–5pm, with some suburban branches open later and on Sat. American Express outlets include Ground Floor 50 Pitt St (inside Westpac; Mon–Fri 9am–5pm; ☎ 1300 139 060); 296 George St (daily 8.30am–5.30pm). Money can also be exchanged at Travelex bureaux de change at the airport, 570 George St and 28 Bridge St (Mon–Fri 9.30am–4pm; for more locations visit ⊕ www.travelex.com.au/StoreLocator).

Camping equipment and rental Kent St in the city behind the Town Hall (and near YHA headquarters) is nicknamed "Adventure Alley" for its preponderance of outdoor equipment stores; the best known is the high-quality Paddy Pallin at no. 507. Cheaper options include army surplus stores at the downtown ends of George and Pitt sts near Central Station, and suburban K-Mart stores (closest to the city are at Spring St, Bondi Junction, and at the Broadway Shopping Centre, Bay St) or hostel notice boards. Only a few places rent gear, mostly based in the suburbs: try Alpsport, 1045 Victoria Rd, West Ryde (☎ 02/9858 5844), with weekend rental of a backpack for around $50, sleeping bag from $40 and tent from $80.

Car rental see "Moving on from Sydney" box, p.180

Consulates Embassies are all in Canberra (see p.240), and it's usually easier to call them when in difficulty than to go to the consulates in Sydney: Canadian, Level 5, 111 Harrington St ☎ 02/9364 3000; New Zealand, Level 10, 55 Hunter St ☎ 02/8256 2000; UK, Level 16, Gateway Building, 1 Macquarie Place ☎ 02/9247 7521; US, Level 59, MLC Centre, 19–29 Martin Place ☎ 02/9373 9200. For visas for onward travel, consult "Consulates and Legations" in the *Yellow Pages*.

Cycling Bicycles are carried free on trains outside of peak hours (Mon–Fri 6–9am & 3.30–7.30pm) and on ferries at all times. The Roads and Traffic Authority (RTA; ☎ 1800 060 607, ⓦ www.rta.nsw .gov.au) produces a fold-out map, *Sydney Cycleways*, showing off-road paths and bicycle routes, which they will post out. The best source of information, however, is the organization Bicycle NSW, Level 5, 822 George St (Mon–Fri 9am–5.30pm; ☎ 02/9218 5400, ⓦ www .bicyclensw.org.au). Two useful publications are *Bike It Sydney* ($24.95), which has backstreet inner-city bike routes, and *Cycling Around Sydney* ($25), which details 25 of the best rides; they also have free council and RTA bike-route maps. Popular cycling spots are Centennial Park and the bike path that runs from Manly (see p.147). The international cycling activist group Critical Mass has a Sydney movement; on the last Fri of the month meet at the Archibald Fountain in Hyde Park for an hour-long mass ride through the city at 6pm.

Recommended central bike shops include Clarence Street Cyclery, 104 Clarence St (☎ 02/9299 4962); Woolys Wheels, 82 Oxford St, Paddington (☎ 02/9331 2671); and Inner City Cycles, 151 Glebe Point Rd, Glebe (☎ 02/9660 6605). Clarence Street Cyclery also rents mountain bikes ($50 per day), as does Inner City Cycles ($33 for 24hr, $55 per weekend). For a leisurely ride in the park, Centennial Park Cycles, 50 Clovelly Rd, Randwick (☎ 02/9398 5027), rents various types of bike (mountain bikes $12 per hr, $40 per day), as well as rollerblades ($18 per hr) and pedal cars ($25–35 per hr).

Diving One of the best places to dive is at Gordon Bay in Clovelly, and off North and South heads. Nearby Pro Dive Coogee, 27 Alfreda St, Coogee (☎ 02/9665 6333), offers boat and shore dives anywhere between Camp Cove (Watsons Bay) and La Perouse, plus dives all over Sydney. Aquatic Explorers, 40 Kingsway, Cronulla (☎ 02/9523 1518), does local weekend coordinated shore dives and also organizes boat dives, night dives and weekends away up and down the NSW coast. Dive Centre Manly, 10 Belgrave St, Manly (☎ 02/9977 4355), offers shore dives to Shelley Beach, Fairlight and Little Manly, plus Harbord if conditions are good, and boat dives off North and South heads and

Long Reef (boat dives, double $175; shore dives twice daily; single shore dive $75, double $95; "Discover Scuba" $155; rates include equipment).

Hospitals (with emergency departments) St Vincent's, corner of Victoria & Burton sts, Darlinghurst ☎ 02/8382 1111; Royal Prince Alfred, Missenden Rd, Camperdown ☎ 02/9515 6111; Prince of Wales, Barker St, Randwick ☎ 02/9382 2222.

Immigration Department of Immigration, 26 Lee St, near Central Station, City ☎ 13 18 81.

Internet There's free internet access at the State Library, Macquarie St, for up to an hour a day, but you can't send emails. Global Gossip ($4 per 30min–1hr) has several offices, including 790 George St, near Central Station; 415 Pitt St, near Chinatown (both daily 9am–11pm); 14 Wentworth Ave, next to Hyde Park (Mon–Fri 9am–6pm); 63 Darlinghurst Rd, Kings Cross (daily 8am–1am); 37 Hall St, Bondi (Mon–Thurs 9am–midnight, Fri–Sun 9am–11pm); they also offer cut-rate international calls and parcel post. Phone Net Cafe, 73–75 Hall St, Bondi (Mon–Fri 8am–10pm, Sat & Sun 8am–9pm; $3.30 for 1hr), is a lively haunt in its own right.

Left luggage There are lockers at Wanderers' Travel, 810 George St, near Central Station (daily 7am–8pm; $7 per day). Also lockers at the airport.

Libraries See the State Library, p.118, and City of Sydney Library, p.104.

Maps Map World, 280 Pitt St (☎ 02/9261 3601, ⓦ www.mapworld.net.au), has Sydney's biggest selection of maps and travel guides; see also "Parks and wildlife", below.

Medical centres Broadway Medical Centre, 185–211 Broadway, near Glebe (Mon–Fri 9am–7pm, Sat & Sun 11am–5pm; no appointment necessary ☎ 02/9281 5085); Sydney Sexual Health Centre, Sydney Hospital, Macquarie St (☎ 02/9382 7440 or 1800 451 624); The Travel Doctor, 7th Floor, 428 George St (☎ 02/9221 7133, ⓦ www.traveldoctor .com.au).

Parks and wildlife information The NPWS, Cadmans Cottage, 110 George St, The Rocks (☎ 02/9247 5033, ⓦ www.npws.nsw.gov.au), is the information centre for Sydney Harbour National Park and books tours to its islands. The Sydney Map Shop, part of the Surveyor-General's Depart-ment, 22 Bridge St (☎ 02/9228 6111), sells detailed National Park, State Forest and bushwalking maps of New South Wales.

Pharmacy (late-night) Crest Hotel Pharmacy, 91–93 Darlinghurst Rd, Kings Cross (daily 8.30am–midnight; ☎ 02/9358 1822).

Police Headquarters at 14 College St (☎ 02/9339 0277 or 13 14 44); emergency ☎ 000.

Post office The General Post Office (GPO) is in Martin Place (Mon–Fri 8.15am–5.30pm, Sat 10am–2pm). Poste restante (addressed to Poste Restante, Sydney GPO, Sydney, NSW 2000) is located at the post office in the Hunter Connection shopping mall at 310 George St (Mon–Fri 8.15am–5.30pm), opposite Wynyard Station. Log your name into the computer to see if you have any post before queuing.

Public holidays In addition to the Australia-wide public holidays (see p.73), the following are celebrated only in New South Wales: Bank Holiday – first Mon in Aug; Labour Day – first Mon in Oct; Queen's Birthday – first Mon in June.

Scenic flights Sydney Harbour Seaplanes, Rose Bay (⊕02/9388 1978), can take you on a 15min scenic flight over Sydney Harbour and Bondi Beach ($160 per person, minimum 2 people, max 8), or the harbour and the Northern beaches ($225), or drop you off for lunch at Palm Beach or one of the Hawkesbury River restaurants ($465, including lunch). Wine or gold tours to the Hunter Valley ($715–735) are also offered.

Surfing Surf schools can teach you the basic skills, and enlighten you on surfing etiquette and lingo. In the Eastern beaches, the best is Lets Go Surfing, 128 Ramsgate Ave, North Bondi (daily 9am–6pm; ⊕02/9365 1800, ⊛www.letsgosurfing.com.au), which sells surfing gear, rents boards ($25 for 2hr, $40 per day, plus $5–10 for a wet suit) and offers lessons: a group lesson (2hr; $79–89) includes board and wet suit, or go for a private lesson (1hr; $130, $70 each extra person). Manly Surf School (⊕02/9977 6977, ⊛www.manlysurfschool.com) run $55 group lessons and offer private lessons for $80 per hr per person. Nearby, Dripping Wet, 93 North Steyne, Manly (⊕02/9977 3549, ⊛www.drippingwetsurf.com), rent Malibu boards ($35 for 4hr) and bodyboards and wet suits ($15 for 4hr).

Swimming pools Most pools are outdoors and unheated, and open from the long weekend in Oct until Easter. Those detailed in the text, with times and prices given, are: Cook and Phillip Park Aquatic and Leisure Centre, near Hyde Park (p.115); Andrew "Boy" Charlton in The Domain (p.118); North Sydney Olympic Pool, North Sydney (p.139); Victoria Park, City Rd, next to Sydney University (p.132); and the pool of champions, the Sydney International Aquatic Centre at Homebush Bay (p.199).

Taxis Legion ⊕13 14 51; Premier ⊕13 10 17; St George ⊕13 21 66; Taxis Combined ⊕13 33 00. For harbour water-taxis, call Water Taxis Combined ⊕02/9555 8888.

Telephones The unattended Telstra Pay Phone Centre, 231 Elizabeth St, City (Mon–Fri 7am–11pm, Sat & Sun 7am–5pm), has private booths; bring change or a phonecard. Global Gossip (see "Internet" above) offers discount-rate international calls, and Backpackers World Travel (see "Travel agents" below) sells their own rechargeable discount phonecard.

Tennis Rushcutters Bay Tennis Centre, 7 Waratah St, Rushcutters Bay (daily 8am–11pm, courts $20 per hr; $24 after 4pm and on Sat & Sun; racket rental $3; ⊕02/9357 1675). If you don't have anyone to play, the managers will try to provide a partner for you.

Travel agents Backpackers World Travel, 234 Sussex St (⊕02/8268 6001, ⊛www.backpackersworld.com.au), does everything from international flights to bus passes; offices also at 91 York St (⊕02/8268 5000); at 488 Pitt St, near Central Station (⊕02/9282 9711); 212 Victoria St, Kings Cross (⊕02/9380 2700); and 2B Grosvenor St, Bondi Junction (⊕02/9369 2011). Flight Centre, 52 Martin Place (⊕13 18 66), also at several other locations, offers cheap domestic and international air tickets. STA Travel has many branches, including Town Hall Square, 464 Kent St (⊕02/9262 9763), or try Student Flights (⊕1300 762 410), with several offices including 140 King St, Newtown; 50 Spring St, Bondi Junction; and 87 Glebe Point Rd, Glebe. Trailfinders is at 8 Spring St (⊕1300 780 285). YHA Travel, 422 Kent St (⊕02/9261 1111), is a full travel agent and also has a branch at *Sydney Central YHA*, 11 Rawson Place off Eddy Ave (⊕02/9281 9444), and offers an excellent range of Sydney tours.

Travellers with disablities See also "Travellers with Disabilities", p.75. Disability Australia, 52 Pitt St, Redfern, NSW 2016 (⊕02/9319 6622) can provide advice. Spinal Cord Injuries Australia, PO Box 397, Matraville, NSW 2036 (⊕02/9661 8855, ⊛www.spinalcordinjuries.com.au), publishes the very useful *Access Sydney* ($10 plus postage). Most national parks have wheelchair-accessible walks; check ⊛www.nationalparks.nsw.gov.au. Post-Olympic improvements include many wheelchair-accessible train stations; check ⊛www.cityrail.nsw.gov.au. All taxi companies take wheelchair bookings.

Watersports Rose Bay Aquatic Hire, near the waterfront at 1 Vickery Ave, Rose Bay (⊕02/9371 7036), rents out kayaks (Wed–Sun; $20 per hr single kayak, $30 double) and motorboats (Sat & Sun; $80for the first two hours, $15 for each subsequent hour). Balmoral Windsurfing, Sailing and Kayaking School, at the Balmoral Sailing Club, southern end of the Esplanade (Oct–April; ⊕02/9960 5344), rents out kayaks ($15 per hr) and windsurf kits ($50 for the first hour, then $20

By bus

Most **bus** services from Sydney depart from **Eddy Avenue**, alongside Central Station; buy tickets from the Sydney Coach Terminal, corner of Eddy Ave and Pitt St (daily 6am–10pm; ☏02/9281 9366) or direct from bus companies. There are four **interstate services**: Greyhound Australia has Australia-wide services (☏1300 473 946, ⓦwww.greyhound.com.au); Firefly Express (☏1300 730 740, ⓦwww.fireflyexpress.com.au), twice daily to Melbourne and connecting to Adelaide; Murray's (☏13 22 51, ⓦwww.murrays.com.au; also from Strathfield Station), to Canberra many times daily – with onward services to the Southeast Coast (Batemans Bay, Moruya and Narooma) or The Snowy Mountains; while Premier Motor Service departs just around the corner at 490 Pitt St (☏13 34 10, ⓦwww.premierms.com.au), heading to Cairns via the north coast, and to Melbourne via the south coast. Most bus services to **destinations within New South Wales** also depart from Eddy Avenue: Rover Coaches (☏02/4990 1699, ⓦwww.rovercoaches.com.au; also from the *Four Seasons Hotel*, The Rocks), daily to Cessnock and Hunter Valley resorts; Port Stephens Coaches (☏02/4982 2940 or 1800 045 949, ⓦwww.pscoaches.com.au), daily to Port Stephens via Newcastle outskirts; Selwoods (☏02/6362 7963, ⓦwww.selwoods.com.au), daily to Orange via the Blue Mountains, Lithgow and Bathurst; Prior's Scenic Express departs from Parramatta, Liverpool and Campbelltown train stations (☏02/4472 4040 or 1800 816 234), daily except Saturday to the Southern Highlands and Kangaroo Valley, and from there to Moruya or Narooma via the south coast including Batemans Bay and Ulladulla.

By train

All out-of-town trains depart from the **country trains terminal** of Central Station (information and booking at the CountryLink Travel Centre 6.30am–10pm; ☏13 22 32, ⓦwww.countrylink.info). The *Indian Pacific*, the *Ghan* and the *Overland* are managed by Great Southern Railway (☏13 21 47, ⓦwww.gsr.com.au). Interstate trains should be booked as early as possible, especially the *Indian Pacific* and Brisbane–Cairns trains.

per hr thereafter), and offers sailboarding and Hobie Cat dinghy sailing courses (both 4hr; $270), as well as one- to five-day courses for kids ($145–370). Northside Sailing School, Spit Bridge, Mosman (☏02/9969 3972), specializes in weekend dinghy sailing courses on Middle Harbour during the sailing season (Sept–April); tuition is one-on-one ($110 for 2hr). Sydney by Sail, Darling Harbour (☏02/9280 1110), has "Learn To Sail" programmes for yacht sailing throughout the year, from a Level 1 "Introductory Course" (12 per hr, 2-day course; $425) to a Level 4 "Inshore Skipper Course" (3-day, 2-night live-aboard; $695). Experienced sailors can charter the yachts from $495 per half-day. For other sailing courses and yacht rental, contact the NSW Yachting Association (☏02/9660 1266, ⓦwww.nsw.yachting.org.au). Natural Wanders Sea Kayak Adventures (☏02/9899 1001) arrange sea-kayaking in the harbour: their most popular trip is the Balmain Island Paddle (3hr 30min; $90), or for experienced kayakers there's the Bridge Paddle (3hr 30min; $90), from Lavender Bay near Luna Park, under the Harbour Bridge and exploring the North Shore; picnic brunch included.

Work If you have a working holiday visa, you shouldn't have too much trouble finding some sort of work, particularly in hospitality or retail. Offices of the government-run Centrelink (☏13 28 50) have a database of jobs. Centrelink also refers jobseekers to several private "Job Network" agencies, including Employment National (☏13 34 44). The private agency Troys, at Level 11, 89 York St (☏02/9290 2955), specializes in the hospitality industry. If you have some office or professional skills, there are plenty of temp agencies that are more than keen to take on travellers: flick through "Employment Services" in the *Yellow Pages*. For a range of work, from unskilled to professional, the multinational Manpower is a good bet (ⓦwww.manpower.com.au). Otherwise, scour hostel notice boards and the *Sydney Morning Herald*'s employment pages – Saturday's bumper edition is best.

By car and motorbike

The big four **car-rental companies**, with expensive new-model cars, charge from $50 per day for a small manual, with much cheaper rates for five- to seven-day and longer rentals: Avis, airport (℡02/8374 2847) and 200 William St, Kings Cross (℡02/9357 2000); Budget, airport (℡02/9207 9165) and 93 William St, Kings Cross (℡02/8255 9600); Hertz (bookings ℡13 30 39, international ℡613/9698 2555), airport (℡02/8337 7500) and corner of William and Riley sts, Kings Cross (℡02/9360 6621); Thrifty, airport (℡1300 367 227 or 612/8337 2700) and 75 William St, Kings Cross (℡02/8374 6177). There are cheaper deals with the popular Bayswater, 180 William St, Kings Cross (℡02/9360 3622), which has low rates often linked, however, with limited kilometres; Travellers Auto Barn, 177 William St, Kings Cross (℡02/9360 1500 or 1800 674 374), does cheap one-way rentals to Melbourne, Brisbane or Cairns, but with a minimum ten-day hire.

For **motorbike** rental, there's Bikescape, 183 Parramatta Rd, Annandale (℡1300 736 869, ⓦwww.bikescape.com.au), with scooters from $70 per day and motorbikes from $120 (cheaper weekend and longer-term rates available).

By campervan and 4WD

All Seasons Campervans, 178 Railway Parade, Kogarah (℡02/9553 4666 or 1800 226 737), is 15 minutes from the airport and offers a wide range of campervans and motorhomes with linen, sleeping bags and free delivery within the CBD. Britz Campervan Rentals, 653 Gardeners Rd, Mascot (domestic and international ℡00 800 200 80 801), has campervans, 4WD campers and camping gear, available one-way to Adelaide, Alice Springs, Brisbane, Cairns, Darwin, Melbourne and Perth. Travel Car Centre, 26 Orchard Rd, Brookvale (℡02/9905 6928), has been established for over twenty years and has hatchbacks, station wagons, campervans and 4WDs available for long- or short-term rental. Travellers Auto Barn (see above) also offers budget campervan and 4WD bushcamper rentals.

Around Sydney

If life in the fast lane is taking its toll, Sydney's residents can easily get away from it all. Right on their doorstep, golden beaches and magnificent national parks beckon, interwoven with intricate waterways. Everything in this part of the chapter can be done as a day-trip from the city, although some require an overnight stay to explore more fully. See the box on p.182 for some of the huge variety of tours on offer.

North of Sydney, the Hawkesbury River flows into the jagged jaws of the aptly named **Broken Bay**. The entire area is surrounded by bush, with the huge spaces of the **Ku-ring-gai Chase National Park** in the south and the **Brisbane Waters National Park** in the north. Beyond Broken Bay, the **Central Coast** between Gosford and Newcastle is an ideal spot for a bit of fishing, sailing and lazing around. **Newcastle** is escaping its industrial-city tag: an up-and-coming, attractive beach metropolis, with a surfing, student, café and music culture all part of the mix. Immediately beyond are the wineries of the **Hunter Valley**.

To the **west**, you escape suburbia to emerge at the foot of the beautiful World Heritage-listed **Blue Mountains**, while the scenic Hawkesbury–Nepean river valley is home to historic rural towns such as **Windsor**.

Tours from Sydney

Day-tours from Sydney range from a sedentary bus trip to a wildlife park to a day of canyoning in the Blue Mountains, and there are many overnight trips, too. You'll almost certainly have a better time with one of the outfits specializing in small-group tours, quite often with an emphasis on physical activities such as bushwalking, horseriding, whitewater rafting or abseiling, as opposed to taking one of the commercial bus-tour operators such as AAT Kings. One-way tours can be the next best thing to going by car: small groups in minibuses travel from Sydney to Melbourne (for example), taking detours to attractions along the way that you'd never be able to reach on public transport. As well as booking direct, you can book most of the tours below through YHA Travel (☏ 02/9261 1111, ⓦ www.yha.com.au).

Day and overnight trips around Sydney

Oz Trek ☏ 02/9666 4262 or 1300 66 1234, ⓦ www.oztrek.com.au. Recommended active full-day tours to the Blue Mountains ($55), with a choice of bushwalks. Small groups (max 20). The trip can be extended to overnight packages with either abseiling ($255) or a Jenolan Caves visit ($210–230). City, Glebe, Kings Cross, Bondi and Coogee pick-ups.

Waves Surf School ☏ 02/9369 3010 or 1800 851 101, ⓦ www.wavessurfschool.com .au. "Learn To Surf" trips to the Royal National Park, Seal Rocks or up the north coast to Byron Bay, learning surfing technique and etiquette and beach safety, with a chance to spot wildlife. Prices start from $79 (one day, with lunch) and go up to $699 for seven days, meals included. Two- to seven-day trips include bushwalking and cabins; $30–60 surcharge on four- to seven-day trips Jan–April. City, Bondi and Coogee pick-ups.

Wildframe Ecotours ☏ 02/9440 9915, ⓦ www.wildframe.com. Two full-day tours to the Blue Mountains ($85) and overnight tours starting at $136. The "Grand Canyon Ecotour" is for fit walkers as it includes a small-group bushwalk (max 21) through the Grand Canyon (5km; 3hr), with BYO lunch in Katoomba. The "Blue Mountains Bush Tour" is more relaxed, with several short bushwalks and BYO lunch in Blackheath. Kangaroo-spotting promised on both trips.

Extended and one-way tours

Ando's Outback Tours ☏ 02/6842 8286 or 1800 228 828, ⓦ www.outbacktours.com .au. Popular five-day tour from Sydney to Byron Bay but getting well off the beaten track inland via the Blue Mountains, the Warrumbungles, Coonabarabran and Lightning Ridge ($485 all-inclusive; departs Sydney every Sun); includes a stay on the rural property of the true-blue family who run the tours. Finding farm work is a common bonus.

Autopia Tours ☏ 03/9419 8878 or 1800 000 507, ⓦ www.autopiatours.com.au. This excellent, long-established Melbourne-based tour company has a three-day Sydney-to-Melbourne tour via Canberra, the Snowy Mountains and Wilsons Promontory National Park ($395; includes meals and dorm accommodation). Small-seater buses with the driver acting as guide.

Oz Experience ☏ 02/9213 1766 or 1300 300 028, ⓦ www.ozexperience.com. A cross between transport and tours that go a little off the beaten track, with a hop-on, hop-off component lasting six months; accommodation and meals not included. Among the many scheduled routes are Sydney to Cairns in nine days ($595); Sydney to Brisbane via the Warrumbungles and Byron Bay in four days ($280); and Sydney to Melbourne in three days via the south coast, Canberra and the Snowy Mountains ($280).

Heading **south**, the **Royal National Park** is an hour's drive away, while on the coast beyond is a string of small, laid-back towns – Waterfall, Stanwell Park, Wombarra – with beautiful, unspoilt **beaches**. The industrial city of **Wollongong** and neighbouring Port Kembla are impressively located between the Illawarra Escarpment and the sea, but of paltry interest to visitors, although more interesting spots cluster around. Inland, the **Southern Highlands** are covered with yet more national parks, punctuated by pleasing little towns such as **Bundanoon** and **Berrima**.

North

The **Hawkesbury River** widens and slows as it approaches the South Pacific, joining Berowra Creek, Cowan Creek, Pittwater and Brisbane Water in the system of flooded valleys that form **Broken Bay**. The bay and its inlets are a haven for anglers, sailors and windsurfers, while the adjoining bushland is virtually untouched. Two major **national parks** surround the Hawkesbury River: **Ku-ring-gai Chase** in the south and **Dharug**, inland to the west.

The **Pacific Highway**, partly supplanted by the **Sydney–Newcastle Freeway**, is fast and efficient, though not particularly attractive until you're approaching Ku-ring-gai Chase; if you want to detour into the national parks or towards Brooklyn, don't take the freeway. The **rail** lines follow the road almost as far as Broken Bay, before they take a scenic diversion through the **Central Coast**, passing Brooklyn, Brisbane Waters, Woy Woy and Gosford en route to **Newcastle**.

Ku-ring-gai Chase National Park

Only 24km north of the centre of Sydney, **Ku-ring-gai Chase** (sunrise–sunset; $11 per vehicle per day) is much the best known of New South Wales' national parks and, with the Pacific Highway running all the way up one side, is also the easiest to get to. The bushland scenery is crisscrossed by walking tracks, which you can explore to seek out Aboriginal rock carvings, or just to get away from it all and see the forest and its wildlife. The park's most popular picnic spot is at **Bobbin Head**, 6km east of the Sydney–Newcastle Freeway, essentially just a colourful marina with a café, a picnic area and NPWS **Bobbin Head Information Centre** (daily 10am–4pm; ☎02/9472 8949), located inside the Art Deco *Bobbin Inn*, which is neither a pub nor a hotel. From here, the **Mangrove Boardwalk** (10min return) pleasantly traces the water's edge past thousands of bright red crabs and continues as the **Gibberagong Track** (additional 20min return) through a small sandstone canyon to some aboriginal rock art featuring figures and axe-grinding grooves.

To the northeast, West Head Road leads to West Head, which juts into Broken Bay marking the entrance to **Pittwater**, a deep ten-kilometre-long sheltered waterway. There are superb views from here across to Barrenjoey Head and Barrenjoey Lighthouse at Palm Beach on the eastern shore of Pittwater. From West Head, the **Garigal Aboriginal Heritage Walk** (3.5km loop; 2–3hr) leads past the Aboriginal rock-engraving site, the most accessible Aboriginal art in the park.

Without your own transport, it's more rewarding to explore the Pittwater and eastern Ku-Ring-Gai by ferry, which provides access to a couple of great places

Koala patting and other wildlife experiences

It is no longer legal to pick up and hold a koala in New South Wales' wildlife parks, but photo-opportunity "patting" sessions are still on offer. Below are several hands-on wildlife experiences around Sydney.

Australian Reptile Park (daily 9am–5pm; $22; Ⓦwww.reptilepark.com.au). 65km north of Sydney, just off the Pacific Highway before the Gosford turn-off, this park offers photographic opportunities with koalas, and has roaming kangaroos that you can tickle and hand-feed, though its real stars are the reptiles, with native Australian species well represented and visible all year round thanks to heat lamps in the enclosures. The highlights are Elvis, New South Wales' largest saltwater crocodile, and the sizeable perentie lizard of central Australia. There are reptile shows and talks throughout the day, including giant Galapagos tortoise-feeding (daily 10.45am), alligator feeding (Sat & Sun at noon) and a crocodile show (Sat & Sun 1.30pm), featuring Elvis.

Featherdale Wildlife Park (daily 9am–5pm; $20; Ⓦwww.featherdale.com.au). Located at 217 Kildare Rd, Doonside, 30km west of Sydney off the M4 motorway between Parramatta and Penrith. Patting koalas is the special all-day attraction here. Train to Blacktown Station, then bus #725.

Koala Park Sanctuary (daily 9am–5pm; $19; Ⓦwww.koalapark.com.au) was established as a safe haven for koalas in 1935 and has since opened its gates to wombats, possums, kangaroos and native birds of all kinds. Koala-feeding sessions (daily 10.20am, 11.45am, 2pm & 3pm) are the patting and photo-opportunity times. Around 25km north of Sydney, not far from the Pacific Highway on Castle Hill Road, West Pennant Hills; train to Pennant Hills then bus #651 or #655 towards Glenorie (Mon–Sat).

to stay. The only place to **camp** is *The Basin* (Ⓣ02/9974 1011 for bookings; Ⓦwww.basincampground.com.au; $14 per person) on Pittwater, reached via the Palm Beach Ferry Service. Facilities at the site are minimal, so bring everything with you. If you want to stay in the park in rather more comfort, there's the very popular *Pittwater YHA* (Ⓣ02/9999 5748, Ⓔpittwater@yhansw.org.au; dorms $28, rooms ❸; bookings essential and well in advance for weekends). The hostel is accessed by regular **ferry** from Church Point Wharf (15min; $12.50 return; last departure Mon–Fri 7pm, Sat & Sun 6.30pm; Ⓣ02/9999 3492, Ⓦwww.churchpointferryservice.com) or water taxi (freephone at the wharf), alighting at Halls Wharf and walking 15 minutes up the hill. It's one of New South Wales' most scenically sited hostels – a rambling old house overlooking the water (kayaks available) and surrounded by spectacular bushwalks. Bring supplies with you – the last food (and bottle) shop is at Church Point. Two direct **buses** run to Church Point: #E86 from Central Station (Mon–Fri) or #156 from Manly Wharf.

The Hawkesbury River

One of New South Wales' prettiest rivers, lined with sandstone cliffs and bush-covered banks for much of its course and with some interesting old settlements alongside, the **Hawkesbury River** has its source in the Great Dividing Range and flows out to sea at Broken Bay. For information about the many national parks along the river, contact the NPWS (Sydney Ⓣ02/9995 5000; Richmond Ⓣ02/4588 5247; Ⓦwww.environment.nsw.gov.au). Short of chartering your own boat (see box opposite), the best way to explore the river system is to take a cruise with the Riverboat Postman.

Brooklyn and the Riverboat Postman

For a brief taste of the bucolic pleasures of the Hawkesbury River, turn east off the Sydney–Newcastle Freeway to **Brooklyn**, 40km north of Sydney, a small riverside community with a train station that featured prominently in the movie *The Oyster Farmer*. A few steps away, the **Riverboat Postman** (Mon–Fri 9.30am excluding public holidays; $50; booking essential on ☎02/9985 7566, ⓦ www.hawkesburyriverferries.com.au) leaves to deliver letters, as well as tourists, up and down the river on a four-hour cruise, including morning tea. A connecting CountryLink train leaves Sydney's Central Station at 8.15am.

Brooklyn also offers modestly priced seafood and water views at *Leah's Alfresco*, on the wharf, who do half a dozen oysters for $12 and a plate of fish, chips and salad for $15.

Upstream: Wisemans Ferry

WISEMANS FERRY is a popular recreational spot for day-trippers from Sydney – just a little over an hour from the city centre by car, and with access to the **Dharug National Park** over the river by a free 24-hour car ferry. Dharug's rugged sandstone cliffs and gullies shelter Aboriginal rock engravings, which can be visited only on ranger-led trips during school holidays; there's a camping area at Mill Creek, 8km east of Wisemans Ferry ($10; book on ☎02/4320 4203 for summer weekends and holidays).

The village of Wisemans Ferry was based around ex-convict Solomon Wiseman's home, Cobham Hall, built in 1827. Much of the original building still exists as *Wisemans Ferry Inn* on the Old Great North Road (☎02/4566 4301, ⓦ www.wisemansinnhotel.com.au; ❹), with characterful shared-bath **rooms** upstairs, and poky en-suite motel rooms out back. *Del Rio Riverside Resort*, Webbs Creek, across the Webbs Creek car ferry, 3km south of Wisemans Ferry (☎02/4566 4330, ⓦ www.delrioresort.com.au; camping $25–35 per site, studio cabins ❹, waterview villas ❼), offers a campsite, bistro, swimming pool, tennis court and golf course.

Taking the ferry across the river from Wisemans Ferry, it's then a scenic nineteen-kilometre river drive north along the convict-built Settlers Road to **St Albans**, where you can partake of a cooling brew (or stay awhile) at a pub built in 1836, the hewn sandstone *Settlers Arms Inn* (☎02/4568 2111, ⓦ www .settlersarms.com.au; en-suite rooms ❻). The pub is set on two and a half acres, and much of the vegetables and herbs for the delicious home-cooked food are grown on site (lunch daily, dinner Fri–Sun).

Exploring the Hawkesbury River system

If a cruise with Brooklyn's Riverboat Postman (see above) doesn't suit, consider these alternatives. Barrenjoey Boating Services at Governor Phillip Park, Palm Beach (☎02/9974 4229, ⓦ www.barrenjoeyboathire.com), hires out **boats** that seat up to six people (2hr $60, 4hr $80, 8hr $130) and are perfect for fishing expeditions around the mouth of the Hawkesbury. The centre has a fishing shop and sells bait supplies and hires out rods. Otherwise, if you're keen to fish and can get four people together, you can charter a boat, including all the gear and bait, plus a skipper who knows exactly where to go, with Fishabout Tours (☎02/9451 5420; $175 per person; 7hr), who have a great reputation on the Hawkesbury. **Houseboats** can be good value if you can get a group together, with prices starting from $700 for a weekend and $1200 for a week for four people. Try Able Hawkesbury River Houseboats, on River Road in Wisemans Ferry (☎1800 024 979, ⓦ www.hawkesburyhouseboats.com.au), or Ripples Houseboats, 87 Brooklyn Rd, Brooklyn (☎02/9985 5534, ⓦ www.ripples.com.au).

The Upper Hawkesbury: Windsor

About 50km inland from Sydney and reached easily by train from Central Station via Blacktown, **WINDSOR** is probably the best preserved of all the historic Hawkesbury towns, with a lively centre of narrow streets, spacious old pubs and numerous historic colonial buildings. It's terrifically popular on Sundays, when a **market** takes over the shady, tree-lined mall end of the main drag, George Street, and the *Macquarie Arms Hotel*, which claims to be the oldest pub in Australia, sponsors live rock'n'roll on the adjacent grassy village green. Around the corner from the pub, the **Hawkesbury Regional Museum and Tourist Information Centre** (Mon–Fri 10am–4pm, Sat & Sun 10am–3pm; ☎02/4560 4655) doles out local information, and can point you towards the *Hawkesbury Paddlewheeler* (☎02/4575 1171, ⓦwww.paddlewheeler.com.au), which has a good-value Sunday-afternoon Jazz Cruise: live jazz and a BBQ lunch for $35 (12.30–2.30pm; advance bookings essential).

From Windsor, Putty Road (Route 69) heads north through beautiful forest country, along the eastern edge of the Wollemi National Park, to Singleton in the Hunter Valley. From Richmond, just 7km northwest of Windsor, the **Bells Line of Road** (Route 40) goes to Lithgow via Kurrajong and is a great scenic drive; along the way are fruit stalls stacked with produce from the valley, and there's a wonderful view of the Upper Hawkesbury Valley from the lookout point at **Kurrajong Heights**, on the edge of the Blue Mountains. Another appealing drive from Richmond to the Blue Mountains, emerging near Springwood (see p.201), is south along the Hawkesbury Road, with the **Hawkesbury Heights Lookout** halfway along providing panoramic views. Not far from the lookout, the modern, solar-powered *Hawkesbury Heights YHA* (☎02/4754 5621; dorm beds $24–27) also has lovely views from its secluded bush setting.

The Central Coast

The shoreline between Broken Bay and Newcastle, known as the **Central Coast**, is characterized by large **coastal lakes** – saltwater lagoons almost entirely enclosed, but connected to the ocean by small waterways. The northernmost, **Lake Macquarie**, is the biggest saltwater lake in New South Wales. Most travellers bypass the Central Coast altogether on the Sydney–Newcastle Freeway, which runs some way inland, but to see a bit more of the coastal scenery and the lakes, stay on the older Pacific Highway, which heads to Newcastle via **Gosford**, home of the Australian Reptile Park (see box, p.184).

North of Gosford, Tuggerah and Munmorah lakes meet the sea at **The Entrance**, a favourite fishing spot with anglers – and with swarms of pelicans, which descend upon Memorial Park for the afternoon fish-feeds (3.30pm). The beaches and lakes along the coast from here to Newcastle are crowded with caravan parks, motels and outfits offering the opportunity to fish, windsurf, sail or water-ski; although less attractive than places further north, they make a great day-trip or weekend escape from Sydney. The **Entrance Visitor Centre**, Marine Parade (daily 9am–5pm; ☎1300 132 975, ⓦwww.cctourism.com.au), has a free accommodation booking service.

Newcastle

NEWCASTLE was founded in 1804 for convicts too hard even for Sydney to cope with, but the river is the real reason for the city's existence: coal, which lies in great abundance beneath the Hunter Valley, was and still is ferried from the countryside to be exported around the country and the world. The proximity of the mines encouraged the establishment of other **heavy industries**, though the production of steel here ceased in late 2000 and most of the slag heaps have been worked over, but the docks are still functional, particularly with the through traffic of coal from the Hunter Valley. Today, Newcastle remains the world's largest coal-exporting port, and there may be a couple of dozen bulk carriers queued off the beaches at any one time; ironically, the city also has a reputation as one of the most environmentally progressive places on Earth.

New South Wales' second city, with a population of over a quarter of a million, Newcastle has long suffered from comparison with nearby Sydney. However, for a former major industrial city, it's surprisingly attractive in parts, a fact now being more widely recognized. The city has been experiencing a **real-estate boom**: hundreds of apartments and hotels have gone up, and old icons have been redeveloped, such as the once grand *Great Northern Hotel* at 89 Scott St, first built in 1938 and now benefiting from a $3 million face-lift (check out the fabulous old map of the world on the ceiling).

Years of accumulated soot has been scraped off the city's stately buildings, riverside gardens have been created in front of the city centre, and a former goods yard has been converted into a waterside entertainment venue. The once blue-collar town is taking to tourism in a big way, trading particularly on its **waterside location** – the surf beaches are wonderful, and there are some more sheltered sandy beaches around the rocky promontory at the mouth of the Hunter River; the extraordinary dunes of Stockton Beach are just a ferry ride

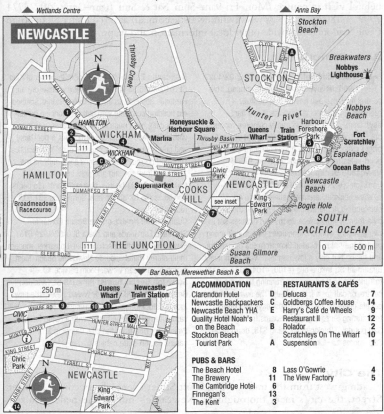

away. The large and lively student community keeps the atmosphere vibrant, and there's a serious **surf culture** too – many surfwear- and surfboard-makers operate here, several champion surfers hail from the city, and there's a big contest, Surfest, in March. You might not choose to spend your entire holiday here, but it can be a good base for excursions, particularly to the wineries of the nearby Hunter Valley.

Arrival, public transport and information

If you're not driving, you'll arrive by **train or bus** at Newcastle train station and coach terminal, right in the heart of the city on the corner of Scott and Watt streets. It's easy to get around using Newcastle's **public transport** system, Newcastle Bus and Ferry Services (☎13 15 00; ⓦwww.newcastlebuses.info). Bus fares are time-based, allowing changes (1hr $3; 4hr $5.90; all-day bus and ferry $9); tickets can be bought on board. The one ferry operating goes to Stockton, departing from Queens Wharf (Mon–Thurs 5.15am–11pm, Fri & Sat 5.15am–midnight, Sun 8.30am–10pm; $2.10 one-way). Two passenger-train lines have several suburban stops, the most useful heading towards Sydney, with handy stops at Civic for Darby Street and Hamilton for Beaumont Street (fares from $3.20 one-way). You can familiarize yourself with the city sights on **Newcastle's Famous Tram** (Mon–Fri and school holidays 11am & 1pm; 1hr; $15; ☎02/4977 2270), the usual twee coach-done-out-as-a-tram deal, departing from Newcastle Station. The very helpful **visitor centre** (Mon–Fri 9am–5pm, Sat & Sun 10am–3pm; ☎02/4974 2999 or 1800 654 558, ⓦwww.visitnewcastle.com.au) at 361 Hunter St, opposite Civic Station, can provide other local information and maps.

Accommodation

Clarendon Hotel 347 Hunter St ☎02/4927 0966, ⓦwww.clarendonhotel.com.au. This central Art Deco pub has been beautifully renovated, with original features in the bar downstairs. The stylish, vibrantly coloured rooms are totally contemporary and offer great value. A bright café-bistro with a huge courtyard does good-value meals from breakfast on. ❻–❼

Newcastle Backpackers 42 & 44 Denison St, Hamilton ☎02/4969 3436 or 1800 333 436, ⓦwww.backpackersnewcastle.com.au. An outstanding home-style hostel and guesthouse run by a friendly family with dorms and doubles set in two adjacent wooden bungalows with a swimming pool at the back. Located 3km from the city centre and beach but only a few minutes' walk from lively Beaumont St; take a bus (#100, #104, #111, #118) to Tudor St, in the free zone, running from the city centre, or call for a free pick-up. The owner runs people down to the beach most days and offers free surfing lessons (boogie-boards free, surfboards $20 per day). Backyard camping $15; dorm beds $26, rooms ❷–❸

Newcastle Beach YHA 30 Pacific St, corner of King St ☎02/4925 3544, ⓔnewcastle@yhansw.org.au. Fantastic hostel in an impressively restored, spacious old building complete with ballroom (once a gentle-men's club), with huge timber staircases, a lounge with a fireplace and leather armchairs, a pool table and courtyard with BBQ, plus the usual YHA facilities. Four-bed dorms, doubles, twins and family rooms. Just 50m from the surf and right in the centre of town; free boogie-boards, plus surfboards ($5 per hr) and bikes ($5 for 3hr) to hire. Dorm beds $31.50, rooms ❸

Quality Hotel Noah's on the Beach Corner of Shortland Esplanade and Zaara St ☎02/4929 5181, ⓦwww.noahsonthebeach.com.au. Upmarket, modern multi-storey motel opposite Newcastle Beach. Most rooms have ocean views. Room service. ❽–❾

Stockton Beach Tourist Park Pitt St, Stockton Beach ☎02/4928 1393, ⓦwww1.newcastle.nsw .gov.au/stocktonbeach. Picturesquely sited campsite right on the beach with a camp kitchen. 2min ferry ride from the city. Camping $31–40, cabins ❹, en-suite cabins ❻

The City

Heading west from the train station, Scott Street eventually becomes **Hunter Street**, the city's main thoroughfare. Newcastle's hub is the pedestrianized, tree-lined Hunter Street Mall, with its department store, shops, fruit stalls and buskers, linked by a footbridge across to the harbour foreshore. From the mall, continuing west along Hunter Street, Civic train station marks the city's cultural and administrative district centred on City Hall and Civic Park. A short walk south of here, **Cooks Hill** is focused on café- and restaurant-lined Darby Street. Newcastle has whole streetscapes of beautiful **Victorian terraces** that put Sydney's to shame – pick up a free *Newcastle Visitor Guide* from the tourist office, to steer you around some of the old buildings. A couple of buildings in **Newcastle Harbour Foreshore Park** show the trend for the city's wealth of disused public architecture: on one corner of the park stands the beautiful Italianate brick **Customs House**, now a popular pub. Nearby is the wooden two-storey **Paymasters House**, where you can sit with a coffee in its fine veranda café and contemplate the water. The restored **Queens Wharf**, a landmark with its distinctive observation tower, is located on the south bank of the Hunter River. It's linked to the city centre by an elevated walkway from Hunter Street Mall and boasts *The Brewery*, a popular and stylish waterfront drinking spot (see p.192).

Further along the foreshore is the new **Honeysuckle** development, an assortment of renovated rail sheds, wharves, pristine walkways and smart new apartments centring on Harbour Square. You'll find a string of stylish cafés, restaurants and bars here, definitely worthy of a twilight drink or mid-morning slap-up breakfast.

Besides Newcastle's waterside attractions, the **Newcastle Region Art Gallery**, 1 Laman St (Tues–Sun 10am–5pm; free), might be of interest. Considered one of the best in Australia, the gallery holds an impressive collection of works by esteemed Australian artists such as Brett Whitely, Arthur Boyd and Russell Drysdale, as well as regularly hosting touring exhibitions of significant local, national and international artists.

Beaches and wildlife reserves

The city centre, positioned on a narrow length of land between the Hunter River to the west and the Pacific Ocean to the east, has several popular and pleasantly low-key beaches close by. **Newcastle Beach**, only a few hundred metres from the city on Shortland Esplanade, has patrolled swimming between flags, a sandy saltwater pool perfect for children, shaded picnic tables and good surfing at its southern end. At the northern end, the beautifully painted, Art Deco-style, free **Ocean Baths** houses the changing pavilions for the huge saltwater pool, which has its own diving board. North of Newcastle Beach, beyond Fort Scratchley, is the long, uncrowded stretch of **Nobbys Beach**, with a lovely old beach pavilion. A walkway leads to Nobbys Head and its nineteenth-century lighthouse.

If you follow Shortland Esplanade south from Newcastle Beach, you'll come to the huge, undulating expanse of **King Edward Park**, with good walking paths and cliff views over this rocky stretch of waterfront. One section of the rock ledge holds Australia's first man-made ocean pool, the **Bogie Hole**, chiselled out of the rock by convicts in the early nineteenth century for the Military Commandant's personal bathing pleasure. The cliffs are momentarily interrupted by **Susan Gilmore Beach**, arguably Newcastle's most beautiful beach and definitely its most visually unadulterated – cliff-rimmed and secluded enough to indulge in some nude bathing, this is a great place for a swim. Further around the rocks is **Bar Beach**, a popular surfing spot with a good beachfront café and ugly surrounding development. The longer **Merewether Beach** next door has a fabulous ocean bath at its southern end and a separate children's pool; overlooking the beach is *The Beach Hotel*, a fine place for a drink.

Just two minutes by ferry from Queens Wharf across the Hunter River, the beachside suburb of **Stockton** is the starting point for the vast, extraordinary **Stockton Beach**, which extends 32km north to **Anna Bay**. Two kilometres wide at some points and covered in moving sand dunes, some of which are up to 30m high, Stockton Bight, as it's officially known, looks strikingly like a mini-desert and has been the location for a Bollywood film. It's become something of an adventure playground in recent years, with thrilling quad-bike tours offered by Quad Bike King ($110 for 1hr 30min; $130 for 2hr 30min; ☎02/4919 0088, ⓦwww.quadbikeking.com.au), which also take in the 1974 shipwreck, the *Sygna Bergen*. You can sandboard down the dunes on the 4WD beach tours offered by Dawsons Scenic Tours (from $20 per hr; pick-ups from Anna Bay; ☎02/4982 0602, ⓦwww.portstephensadventure.com.au), or explore them on horseback with Horse Paradise Tours, based at Williamtown (beginners $40 per hr; ☎02/4965 1877, ⓦwww.users.bigpond.com/horseparadise).

Inland, **Blackbutt Reserve** is a large slab of beautiful bushland in the middle of Newcastle suburbia in New Lambton Heights, about 10km southwest of the city with a number of multi-award-winning wildlife exhibits (daily 9am–5pm; free; koala encounters daily at 2pm; $3). Consisting of four valleys, it includes a remnant of rainforest, creeks, lakes and ponds and 20km of walking tracks to explore them. En route you'll see kangaroos, koalas, wombats, emus and other native animals in the reserve's wildlife enclosures. To get here from the city, take bus #222 or #224 to the main Carnley Avenue entrance (for the best enclosures – including koalas); for the entrances on Lookout Road, you can take bus #363; the tourist office produces a free map.

Northwest of the city, the **Hunter Wetlands Centre**, Sandgate Road, Shortland (Mon–Fri 10am–5pm; Sat & Sun 9am–5pm; $8.50; ☎02/4951 6466, ⓦwww.wetlands.org.au), is situated on Hexham Swamp by Ironbark Creek, and is home to a plethora of birdlife. There are walking and cycling trails here, and you can rent canoes or participate in canoe tours, ecotours or bird and reptile feeding talks (11am). Reach the Wetlands Centre by train from Newcastle to Sandgate, from where it's a ten-minute walk.

Eating

The two streets to head for are **Darby Street**, close to the city centre, which has a multicultural mix of restaurants and some very hip cafés, as well as some second-hand bookshops and retro clothes stores to browse in between coffees; and **Beaumont Street** in Hamilton, 3km northwest of the city centre (train to Hamilton Station or bus #235 from Scott Street or Hunter Street, west of Hunter Mall), which also has great cafés and a concentration of Italian places, as well as Turkish, Lebanese, Indonesian, Thai and Indian; it's jam-packed Friday and Saturday nights. Newcastle has the only franchise of the Sydney legend, *Harry's Café de Wheels*, an all-day, **late-night** pie-cart (Mon & Tues 8.30am–10pm, Wed 8.30am–2.30am, Thurs 8.30am–midnight, Fri 8.30am–3.30am, Sat 10.30am–4.30am, Sun 10.30am–11pm) stationed on Wharf Road near *The Brewery* (see p.192).

Delucas 159 Darby St. This dimly lit, groovy little place, populated by hip locals, dishes out delicious Italian cuisine. There are fabulous pizzas and pastas, the risottos are lovely ($18–24) and the tiramisu is out of this world ($11). Tues–Sat 5.30pm till late, Sun 5.30–10pm.

Goldbergs Coffee House 137 Darby St. This perennially popular Darby St institution is big, buzzy and airy with modish green walls and polished wooden floors. The emphasis is on the excellent coffee, plus very reasonably priced, eclectic modern meals. Has a great outside courtyard. Licensed. Daily 7am–midnight.

Restaurant II 8 Bolton St ☎02/4929 1233. Newcastle's best fine dining restaurant serves contemporary cuisine with Asian and Mediterranean influences in a relaxed atmosphere. The seared duck breast is popular (mains $34–37). Tues–Sat 6–9pm.

Rolador 1 Beaumont St, Hamilton. Fabulous music and coffee, and divine, cheap meals in this artfully assembled establishment straight out of Melbourne's hip café scene. Owner Fiona Smart is a bona fide Melbourne café queen. The menu is diverse and interesting – try the pumpkin, spinach and polenta loaf served with avocado and fresh tomato ($7.50). Daily 6am–5.30pm.

Scratchleys On The Wharf 200 Wharf Rd. Opposite *Harry's Café de Wheels* on the waterfront,

this is a great seafood restaurant. Dine in the beautiful, airy glass-walled interior or get takeaway and devour it happily on the grass overlooking the water. Restaurant Mon–Sat 11.30am–3pm & 5.30–9pm; Sun 11.30am–9pm, takeaway daily 10.30am–9pm.

Suspension 3–5 Beaumont St, Islington. Like coffee? With a pleasingly slapdash aesthetic that only struggling artists can properly pull off, this coffee-only café is just crazy about coffee beans. Owner Mishka Golski acquires the finest beans from across the globe and combines them into five regularly changing blends. Local artists exhibit inside. Mon–Fri 7am–6pm, Sat 8am–5pm, Sun 9am–5am.

Arts and festivals

The area known as "the cultural precinct", near Civic Park on King, Hunter and Auckland streets, is the location for three venues (☎02/4929 1977), Civic Theatre, City Hall and the Playhouse; pick up a monthly calendar from the visitor centre for details of what's on. The grand, Art Deco **Civic Theatre**, with its opulent 1920s interior, and the more intimate **Playhouse**, have a diverse programme, featuring dance, theatre, comedy, film and shows for children, while the **City Hall**, 290 King St, primarily reserved for functions and conferences, hosts occasional music events by the likes of the Australian Chamber Orchestra. Wheeler Place, flanking Civic Theatre and the mushroom-like Newcastle City Council building, is a palm tree-fringed, attractive space, which hosts occasional outdoor community events (and the *Juicy Beans Café*, with its alfresco seating, which is well worth a visit). Between July and October at the **University Conservatorium of Music** on Auckland Street (☎02/4921 8900) there are free lunchtime concerts (1pm) on Thursdays, as well as Friday-evening performances (7.30pm; $20). Mainstream **cinema** is on offer at the three-screen Greater Union at 183 King St (☎02/4926 2233).

Try to time your visit to Newcastle with the *This Is Not Art* **festival** (☎02/4927 0470; ⊛http://octapod.org), a dynamic, multi-disciplinary experimental arts festival with free performances, exhibitions and talks all over the city over the October long weekend; the Mattara Festival (Festival of Newcastle) is held at the same time. It's also worth investigating the Street Performers Festival and Surfest in March, Cultural Stomp in June and the Newcastle Jazz Festival in August.

Nightlife

During term time, the students of Newcastle University bring a buzz to the city, but there's a thriving **live-music scene** year-round. Good venues in town are *The View Factory* at 66 Scott St (☎02/4929 4580), the *Lass O'Gowrie* (see p.192), the university's *Bar on the Hill* at Callaghan, 12km west of the city (☎02/49683717; bus #100, #225, #226, or train to Warabrook Station), and the *Cambridge Hotel* at 789 Hunter St, West Newcastle (☎02/4962 2459), which attracts touring interstate and international bands.

On Friday and Saturday nights, the city pubs on Hunter Street and parallel King Street are lively and there are a few **clubs** too – *King Street Hotel* on the corner of King and Steel streets is very popular, while near the harbour, *Fanny's*, 311 Wharf Rd, has a wild reputation. Due to recent antisocial behaviour, clubs are required to close at 3.30am, with no entry beyond 1.30am.

For **nightlife listings**, check out the supplement "TE" in Wednesday's *Post*, or the fortnightly free music mag, *U Turn*.

Pubs and bars

The Beach Hotel Opposite Merewether Beach ☏02/4963 1574. With a huge, beachfront beer garden, this is popular all weekend and there are free live bands Thurs–Sun.

The Brewery Queens Wharf, 150 Wharf Rd ☏02/4929 6333. Popular waterfront drinking hole with three bars – grab tables right on the wharf or on the upstairs balcony. Food from the busy bistro can be eaten outside (weekend breakfasts too). Free live music or DJs Thurs–Sun.

Finnegan's Corner of Darby and King sts. Newcastle's obligatory Irish theme pub is inevitably lively and popular, especially with travellers.

The Kent 59 Beaumont St, corner of Cleary St, Hamilton ☏02/4961 3303. This beautifully renovated old pub and music venue is busy most nights with pool competitions, quizzes, karaoke, and bands Fri– Sun, but there are refuges, including a plant-filled beer garden, big upstairs balcony and a great bistro.

Lass O'Gowrie 14 Railway St, Wickham ☏02/4962 1248. This down-to-earth Aussie pub attracts a hip, alternative crowd. Its beer garden has a backyard feel, and local bands bash out original tunes from Wed–Sun (from 9pm). Good, cheap pub grub is served. The Moulin Rouge-esque ladies' toilets are a sight to behold. To get there, take bus #100, #104, #111 or #118 (free).

Listings

Banks and exchange American Express, 49 Hunter St ☏1300 139 060; Commonwealth Bank, 136 Hunter St Mall ☏02/4927 2777.
Car rental A.R.A, 86 Belford St, Broadmeadow ☏02/4962 2488 or 1800 243 122; Thrifty, 272 Pacific Highway, Charlestown ☏02/4942 2266.
Left luggage At the train station (daily 8am–5pm; $1.50 per article for one day; $4.50 each day after).

Post office Newcastle GPO, 1 Market St (Mon–Fri 8.45am–5pm). Also American Express traveller's cheques, foreign currency and Travelex cash passport services.
Supermarket Coles, corner of King and National Park sts; open 24hr.
Taxi Newcastle Taxis ☏13 33 00

The Hunter Valley

New South Wales' best-known wine region and Australia's oldest, the **Hunter Valley** is an area long synonymous with fine **wine** – in particular, its golden, citrusy **Sémillon** and soft and earthy **Shiraz**. In recent years the region has become equally prized for its restaurant and cultural scene: visitors are treated to some of the best the country has to offer in the way of fine dining, gourmet delis, arts and crafts and outdoor events and festivals.

Wine, however, is still the main attraction. The first vines were planted in 1828, and some still-existing wine-maker families, such as the Draytons, date back to the 1850s. In what seems a bizarre juxtaposition, this is also a very important **coal-mining region**, in the **Upper Hunter Valley** especially. By far the best-known wine area is the **Lower Hunter Valley**, nestled under the picturesque **Brokenback Range**, fanning north from the main town of **Cessnock** to the main wine-tasting area of **Pokolbin**. Cessnock, unfortunately, is a depressingly unattractive introduction to the salubrious wine culture surrounding it. Its big old country pubs are probably its best feature, and for a taste of Australian rural life, past and present, you might even consider staying in one. The wine-tasting area of Pokolbin is twelve to fifteen kilometres northwest, offering much in the way of luxurious accommodation and fine dining. The area can, however, seem a little like an exhausting winery theme park; to experience the real appeal of the Hunter Valley wine country – stone and timber cottages surrounded by vast vineyards somehow lost among forested ridges, red-soiled dirt tracks and paddocks with grazing cattle – explore the region's periphery. Take the scenic, winding Wollombi Road to the charming

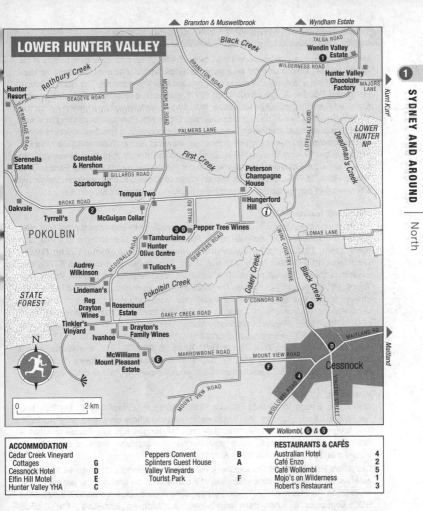

LOWER HUNTER VALLEY

Branxton & Muswellbrook   Wyndham Estate

TALGA ROAD
Wandin Valley Estate
WILDERNESS ROAD
Black Creek
BRANXTON ROAD
Rothbury Creek
Hunter Resort
DEASEYS ROAD
MCDONALDS ROAD
PALMERS LANE
Hunter Valley Chocolate Factory
MAJORS LANE
Kurri Kurri
LOVEDALE ROAD
LOWER HUNTER NP
Deadman's Creek
First Creek
Serenella Estate
GILLARDS ROAD
Constable & Hershon
Scarborough
Peterson Champagne House
Tempus Two
HALLS RD
Hungerford Hill
Oakvale
BROKE ROAD
Tyrrell's
McGuigan Cellar
Pepper Tree Wines
LOMAS LANE
POKOLBIN
DEGSTERS ROAD
Tamburlaine
Hunter Olive Centre
Audrey Wilkinson
Tulloch's
WINE COUNTRY DRIVE
Black Creek
Lindeman's
Pokolbin Creek
Oakey Creek
Reg Drayton Wines
Rosemount Estate
O'CONNORS RD
Tinkler's Vinyard
OAKEY CREEK ROAD
Drayton's Family Wines
Ivanhoe
MAITLAND ROAD
Maitland
McWilliams Mount Pleasant Estate
MARROWBONE ROAD
MOUNT VIEW ROAD
Cessnock
STATE FOREST
N
MOUNT VIEW ROAD
WOLLOMBI ROAD
VINCENT STREET
0   2 km

Wollombi

ACCOMMODATION			RESTAURANTS & CAFÉS	
Cedar Creek Vineyard Cottages	G	Peppers Convent	B	Australian Hotel	4
Cessnock Hotel	D	Splinters Guest House	A	Café Enzo	2
Elfin Hill Motel	E	Valley Vineyards Tourist Park	F	Café Wollombi	5
Hunter Valley YHA	C			Mojo's on Wilderness	1
				Robert's Restaurant	3

historic town of **Wollombi**, 28km southwest of Cessnock; or try the Lovedale/ Wilderness Road area, to the northeast, and the still unspoilt **Upper Hunter**, west of Muswellbrook, with its marvellous ridges and rocky outcrops.

Getting there and around

By car, the Lower Hunter Valley is two hours north of Sydney along National Highway 1 (F3 Freeway). For a more scenic route, and an eminently more pleasurable start to your stay, turn off the F3 to join Peats Ridge Road and continue to the pretty village of Wollombi on the outskirts of the region. A meandering route from the Blue Mountains via **Putty Road** is also popular with motorcyclists. Rover Coaches (☎02/4990 1699, ⒲www.rovercoaches .com.au) run daily services from Sydney Central Station, The Rocks and Chatswood to Cessnock, and on to Pokolbin resorts. If you're feeling flush, you might consider arriving in style on a scenic amphibious seaplane flight from Sydney Harbour with Sydney Seaplanes (see p.179).

Wine-tasting in the Hunter Valley

Nearly 150 wineries cluster around the Lower Hunter Valley and fewer than twenty in the Upper Hunter; almost all offer **free wine tastings**. Virtually all are open daily, at least between 10am and 4pm, and many offer **guided tours** (see below). The Hunter Resort, Hermitage Road, Pokolbin (℡02/4998 7777), also runs a recommended **wine course** (daily 9–11am; $50; bookings essential), including a tour followed by a tasting instruction tutorial. The "Old Shop" museum at Oakvale, Broke Rd, Pokolbin, consisting of a slab cottage replicating a nineteenth-century general store, sells a great selection of **wine-related books**. You can enjoy fine panoramic **views** at Audrey Wilkinson (Debeyers Rd, Pokolbin) and Tinklers Vineyard (Pokolbin Mountains Rd, Pokolbin), from where you can continue to the Pokolbin Mountains Lookout, while the award-winning Pepper Tree Wines, Halls Rd, Pokolbin, with its French-rustic feel, has beautiful **gardens**. Below are a few more of our favourites, but you'll inevitably discover your own gems.

Vineyard tours

A huge range of **vineyard tours** is on offer, and many of the wineries themselves offer guided tours, including: McWilliams Mt Pleasant Estate, Marrowbone Rd, Pokolbin (daily 11am; $3.30; no booking required); Hermitage Road Cellars, Hunter Resort, Hermitage Rd, Pokolbin (daily 11am & 2pm; $10; bookings ℡02/4998 7777); and several of those detailed below. The excellent, long-established **Hunter Valley Day Tours** (℡02/4951 4574, ⓦwww.huntervalleydaytours.com.au) offers a wine-and-cheese tasting tour ($95 for Hunter Valley pick-ups; restaurant lunch included), with very informative commentary. The long-established, family-run **Hunter Vineyard Tours** (℡02/4991 1659, ⓦwww.huntervineyardtours.com.au) visits five wineries (Hunter Valley pick-up $60, Newcastle, Maitland or Wollombi $65; restaurant lunch $30 extra). Also recommended are **Trek About 4WD Tours** (℡02/4990 8277, ⓦwww.hunterweb.com.au/trekabout; half-day $45; full day $55) and **Aussie Wine Tours** (℡0412 735 809, ⓦwww.aussiewinetours.com.au; $50), both supportive of small local wineries.

Wineries

Constable Estate Vineyards Gillards Road, Pokolbin. Established in 1981 by two best friends from England, this small establishment offers unhurried wine-tastings. The thirty-acre vineyard under the Brokenback Ranges has five formal gardens – Sculpture, Camellia, Rose, Herb and Secret; the gardener leads a tour Mon & Wed–Fri at 10.30am. Mon & Wed–Sun 10am–5pm.

Drayton's Family Wines Oakey Creek Rd, Pokolbin. Friendly, down-to-earth winery, established in 1853. All processes are still carried out on site and the excellent free tours (Mon–Fri 11am; 40min) guide you through. A pretty picnic area with wood-fired BBQ overlooks a small dam and vineyards. Mon–Fri 8am–5pm, Sat & Sun 10am–5pm.

Hungerford Hill Broke Rd, Pokolbin. This space-station-like winery has a fine-dining restaurant, *Terroir* (mains $39–59; tasting menu $110), as well as the chic *Terroir Bar & Dining* (bar open evenings only Wed–Sat) with its light day menu (daily 10am–5pm; $12–20).

To get around the area, you can **rent bikes** from Grapemobile, on the corner of McDonalds Road and Palmers Lane, Pokolbin (℡02/404 039; ⓦwww.grapemobile.com.au; $25 per day; booking required), or hire a **taxi** from Cessnock RadioCabs (℡02/4990 1111). The more extravagant can get around in horse coaches (℡0408 161 133, ⓦwww.pokolbinhorsecoaches.com.au), limousine (℡02/4984 7766, ⓦwww.huntervalleylimos.com.au) or even convertible Cadillac (℡02/4996 4959, ⓦwww.cadillactours.com.au).

Peterson House Corner of Broke and Wine Country Drive, Pokolbin. The only Hunter Valley winery to specialize in sparkling wines, also using their *methode champenoise* expertise to produce for other wineries. The pretty stone building with duck pond makes a pleasant tasting spot, and a good place to sample the *Restaurant Cuvée's* fantastic, well-priced cooked breakfast. For more indulgence, the Hunter Valley Chocolate Factory is right next door. Daily 9am–5pm.

Rosemount Estate McDonalds Road, Pokolbin. Occupying a converted blue church built in 1909, next to a delightful café and art gallery, this intimate cellar-only location offers some of Australia's best-known award-winning wines grown at its famous vineyards in the Upper Hunter. Daily 10am–5pm.

Scarborough Gilliards Rd, Pokolbin. Small, friendly winery with a reputation for outstanding wines; specializes in Chardonnay and Pinot Noir. Pleasantly relaxed sit-down tastings are held in a small cottage on Hungerford Hill with wonderful valley views. Daily 9am–5pm.

Tamburlaine Mcdonalds Road, Pokolbin. The jasmine-scented garden outside provides a hint of the flowery, elegant wines within. Tastings are well orchestrated and delivered with a heap of experience. Daily 9am–5pm.

Tempus Two Broke Road, Pokolbin. This huge, contemporary winery – all steel, glass and stone – has a high-tech, urban-chic exterior. Owned by Lisa McGuigan, of the well-known wine-making family, whose unique-tasting wines are the result of using lesser-known varieties such as Pinot Gris, Viognier and Marsanne. The attached Japanese–Thai *Oishi* (11.30am–9.30pm; ☎02/4999 7051) has surprisingly moderate prices, and there's a lounge area where you can relax over an espresso. Daily 9am–5pm.

Tyrrell's Broke Road, Pokolbin. The oldest independent family vineyards, producing consistently fine wines. The tiny ironbark slab hut, where Edward Tyrrell lived when he began the winery in 1858, is still in the grounds, and the old winery with its cool earth floor is much as it was. Beautiful setting against the Brokenback Range. Mon–Sat 8.30am–5pm, with free tour at 1.30pm.

Wandin Valley Estate Corner of Wilderness and Lovedale roads. Picturesquely sited on a hundred acres of vineyards, producing a variety of wines but best known for its hot-selling rosé. There are magnificent views across the Wategos and the Brokenback Ranges, especially from the balcony of the European-style *Bel Posto* café-restaurant (☎02/4930 9199; mains $30; cellar-door priced wine). Daily 10am–5pm.

Wyndham Estate Dalwood Road, Dalwood. A scenic drive through the Dalwood Hills leads to the Lower Hunter's northern extent, where Englishman George Wyndham first planted Shiraz in 1828. Now owned by multinational Pernod Ricard, there's an excellent, free guided tour (daily 11am), which covers the vines and wine-making techniques and equipment, including the original basket press. The idyllic riverside setting – grassy lawns, free BBQs – makes a great spot for picnics and the annual opera concert (see p.197). Restaurant open for lunch Thurs–Sun. Daily 9.30am–4.30pm.

Accommodation in the Hunter Valley

Since the Hunter Valley is a popular weekend trip for Sydneysiders, accommodation **prices** rise on Friday and Saturday nights when most places only offer two-night deals; the price ranges below indicate the substantial midweek to weekend variable. Advance **booking** is essential for weekends, and during the October-to-November events season.

Cedar Creek Vineyard Cottages Wollombi Rd, Cedar Creek, 10km northwest of Wollombi ☏02/4998 1576, ⓦwww.cedarcreekcottages.com.au. An idyllic choice on a 550-acre deer- and cattle-stocked farm. Run by the delightful Stonehurst Wines, whose tiny chapel-like tasting room, with wine from insecticide-free, handpicked, estate-grown grapes, illustrates the owner's philosophy. Delightful self-catering cottages, for couples or big groups, are made from recycled timber with views over vineyards and bush-clad mountainsides. Expect queen-sized beds, wood combustion stoves, ceiling fans and a/c, CD players, stylish decor, breakfast hampers and a BBQ. ❻–❼

Cessnock Hotel 234 Wollombi Rd, Cessnock ☏02/4990 1002, ⓦwww.huntervalleyhotels.com.au. Renovated pub with a great restaurant, *The Wright Taste Cafe*. Rooms share bathrooms but they're huge with high ceilings, fans and really comfortable beds, with a big veranda to hang out on and cooked breakfasts (included) served in the café. ❹

Elfin Hill Motel Marrowbone Rd, Pokolbin ☏02/4998 7543, ⓔelfinhill@hunterlink.com.au. Friendly, family-run hilltop motel with comfortable timber cabin-style a/c units and extensive views – particularly good value midweek. Facilities include a pool, BBQ area and spacious, glass-walled common room with table-tennis table and guest kitchen, though a hearty breakfast is included. ❺–❻

Hunter Valley YHA 100 Wine Country Drive, Nulkaba ☏02/4991 3278, ⓦwww.yha.com.au.

A single-storey long timber building with wrap-around balcony offering everything one would expect from a YHA: there's a communal kitchen, fridge, laundry and TV lounge, plus a sauna and swimming pool. Bicycles are available for hire, as are cheap tours to local vineyards and, for nightlife, *Potters Hotel and Brewery* is only 400m away. Dorms beds $26–32, rooms ❸, en suite ❹

Peppers Convent Halls Rd, Pokolbin ☏02/4993 8999. The swankiest place to stay in the Hunter Valley, with a price to match (midweek $396 per night, weekend $849 for 2 nights minimum). The guesthouse, converted from an old nunnery, is decidedly regal, with fireplaces, low beams and luxurious rooms, and is part of the Pepper Tree Winery (see box, pp.194–195), with fine-dining at *Robert's* restaurant (see p.198) just a stroll away. ❾

Splinters Guest House 617 Hermitage Rd, Pokolbin ☏02/6574 7118, ⓦwww.splinters.com.au. The mezzanine-bedroomed cottages on this 10-acre property come with slate floors, wood-combustion stoves, leather armchairs and kitchens with coffee machines (cook-your-own breakfast supplied). En-suite rooms have mini espresso machines (light breakfast included). Guests are served with cheese and wine on arrival. There's a covered BBQ area, a putting green, swimming pool and walking tracks. Cottages for two couples $180–425; en-suite rooms ❻–❼

▲ Hunter Valley vineyards

Valley Vineyards Tourist Park Mount View Rd, 2km northwest of Cessnock ☎02/4990 2573, ⓦwww.valleyvineyard.com.au. High-standard campsite with kitchen, BBQ area, pool and on-site Thai restaurant. Cabins (BYO linen) have external bathrooms; cottages (linen included) have en-suite facilities. Cabins ❸–❹, cottages ❹–❺

Information and activities

You can pick up the excellent, free *Hunter Valley Wine Country* guide with a pull-out map from the **visitor centre** at Wine Country Drive, Pokolbin (Mon–Sat 9am–5pm, Sun 9am–4pm; ☎02/4990 0900, ⓦwww.winecountry .com.au), scenically sited among vineyards with the pleasant *Wine Country Café*. If it's closed, you can still pick up the free guide from a rack under the shelter outside. Try to tour the wineries during the week; at weekends both the number of visitors and accommodation prices go up, and the area can get booked out completely when there's a concert on in the valley.

Events take place throughout the year. From early October to mid-January the Wollombi region hosts **Sculpture in the Vineyards**, in which surreal and innovative site-specific sculptures dazzle among the vineyards, valleys, dirt roads and bushy ridges of picturesque Wollombi's wineries. In late October Wyndham Estate (see box, pp.194–195) hosts the night-time **Opera in the Vineyards** (☎1800 675 875; ⓦwww.4di.com.au), followed a week later by a day of fine food, wine and music at **Jazz in the Vines** (☎02/4930 9190, ⓦwww.jazzinthevines .com.au; tickets $55–70) based at Tyrrell's vineyard (see box, pp.194–195). On multiple dates from November to February, Bimbadgen Estate holds **A Day on the Green**, featuring local and international performers (tickets through ⓦwww .ticketek.com.au; $105–129; ⓦwww.adayonthegreen.com.au). For information on numerous other events visit ⓦwww.winecountry.com.au/events.

If you've had your fill of wine, there are plenty of other **activities** to keep you busy. Sunrise hot-air balloon rides (ⓦwww.balloonaloft.com), horse rides (ⓦwww.huntervalleyhorseriding.com.au), helicopter flights (ⓦwww .hunterwinehelicopters.com.au), aerobatic warbird, sport and vintage aircraft flights (ⓦwww.airaction.com.au) and golf (ⓦwww.thevintage.com.au) are just some of the options available, and those looking to get up close and personal with Australian wildlife can visit the **Hunter Valley Zoo** (ⓦwww .huntervalleyzoo.com.au; $8–14), where, in interactive yards, you can happily picnic with baby kangaroos and emus.

Eating and drinking

Many of the Hunter's excellent (and pricey) restaurants are attached to wineries or are among vineyards rather than in the towns (see box, pp.194–195), while the large old pubs dish out less fancy but more affordable grub – see "Accommodation" above for bistro options. Every year over a mid-May weekend around eight wineries along and around the scenic Lovedale and Wilderness roads team up with local restaurants to host the **Lovedale Long Lunch** (☎02/4990 4526, ⓦwww.lovedalelonglunch.com.au). The Hunter olive-growing industry has also taken off: check out the Hunter Olive Centre (Pokolbin Estate Vineyard, McDonalds Rd, Pokolbin; ☎02/4998 7524; ⓦwww.hunterolivecentre.com.au), which puts on the weekend-long **Feast of the Olive Festival** (ⓦwww .hunterolives.asn.au/feast) in late September. Other places where you can taste the local wares include The Hunter Valley Cheese Company at the McGuigans Complex, McDonalds Road (ⓦwww.huntervalleycheese.com.au); the newer Binnorie Dairy, just across the road from the Hunter Resort (p.194), which specializes in soft fresh cheeses; and farm produce at Tinkler's Vineyard, Pokolbin Mountain Road. You can also try local-brewed beer at *Potters Hotel & Brewery* on

Wine Country Drive or the Blue Tongue Brewery, Hunter Resort. Just about every winery and accommodation place in the valley has a BBQ or cooking facilities – for picnic or self-catering supplies (a budgeter's necessity in this area) there's the large Coles **supermarket** in Cessnock, at 1 North Ave (Mon–Sat 6am–midnight, Sun 8am–8pm), or the small supermarket in the Hunter Valley Gardens Village. You can also pick up delectable deli supplies at the Australian Regional Food Store at the Small Winemakers Centre on McDonalds Rd, from Stone Pantry @ Peppers Creek on Broke Road or, for a real treat, *Mojo's on Wilderness* (see below).

Australian Hotel 136 Wollombi Rd, Cessnock. The excellent bistro here is popular with the locals, and the pub showcases the Hunter's coal-mining roots with mining paraphernalia and related art. Though steaks hit the $28 mark, mains average $15–25, and the menu encompasses stir-fries, gourmet salads and vegetarian dishes. Daily noon–3pm 6–10pm.

Café Enzo Peppers Creek Antiques, Broke Rd, Pokolbin. Charming café of stone and timber with an old-world, earthy interior and elegant garden seating; feels like it's been lifted from the south of France; light Mediterranean menu ($19–32) and excellent coffee, or start the day here with a cooked breakfast ($16–22). Daily 9am–5pm.

Café Wollombi Wollombi Rd, Wollombi ☏02/4998 3220. In a beautiful old timber building on a hill, with delightful views of the leafy and historic surrounds of Wollombi from the seating on its wrap-around balcony. Serves cheap and delicious eats (with good vegetarian options) including Turkish toasties ($13), salads ($14.50–16.50), pizza ($16.50), laksa ($17.50) and burgers, with tasty home-made patties ($12.50–13.50). Daily breakfast & lunch. Dinner Thurs–Sun.

Mojo's on Wilderness Wilderness Rd, Lovedale ☏02/4930 7244. A British Michelin-rated chef and his Australian chef wife create the divine modern British-Australian food at this bush-set restaurant with a warm, arty interior, flowery courtyard with hillside views, cheerful staff and a laid-back vibe. The set dinner menu (2 courses $56, 3 courses $70) has suggested wines for each course, available by the glass. Open daily from 6.30pm. The attached deli (Mon–Fri 10am–5pm; Sat & Sun 9am–4pm) serves scrumptious gourmet pizzas ($9), paninis ($8) and desserts ($2–12), as well as coffee; consume it all on brightly coloured bean bags on a lush green lawn beneath stylish parasols – or take away.

Robert's Restaurant Peppertree Winery, Halls Rd, Pokolbin ☏02/4998 7330. This restaurant in a fairytale wooden farmhouse (built 1876) is as romantic a dining experience as one could possibly wish for. Oodles of dark polished timber contrast with cream walls and gleaming white tablecloths while gothic antiques, candles and flowers do the rest. The modern European cuisine is outstanding – but pricey. Mains $38–56; tasting menu (highly recommended) $150. Booking essential. Daily noon–3pm, 6.30–9pm.

West

For over sixty years, Sydney has slid ever westwards in a monotonous sprawl of shopping centres, brick-veneer homes and fast-food chains, along the way swallowing up towns and villages, some dating back to colonial times. The first settlers to explore inland found well-watered, fertile river flats, and quickly established agricultural outposts to support the fledgling colony. **Parramatta**, **Liverpool**, **Penrith** and **Campbelltown**, once separate communities, are now satellite towns inside Sydney's commuter belt. Yet, despite Sydney's advance, bushwalkers will find there's still plenty of wild west to explore in the beauty of the **Blue Mountains**. A trip west, however, now starts for many travellers with a visit to the Olympic site at **Homebush Bay**.

Parramatta and Penrith

Situated on the Parramatta River, a little over 20km upstream from the harbour mouth, **PARRAMATTA** was the first of Sydney's rural satellites – the first

Sydney Olympic Park at Homebush Bay

The main focus of the 2000 Olympic events was **Sydney Olympic Park** at Homebush Bay. Virtually the geographical heart of the westward-sprawling city, Homebush Bay already had some heavy-duty sporting facilities – the State Sports Centre and the Aquatic Centre – in place. The Sydney Olympic Park Authority (SOPA) has turned Sydney Olympic Park into an entertainment and sporting complex with family-oriented recreation in mind, with events such as free outdoor movies, multicultural festivals and children's holiday activities. For details, check Ⓦwww.sydneyolympicpark.nsw.gov.au.

The $470-million Olympic site was centred on the 110,000-seat Telstra Stadium, the venue for the opening and closing ceremonies, track and field events, and marathon and soccer finals. And despite a $68-million overhaul to reduce the number of seats to 83,500, it's still Sydney's largest stadium, though with a more realistic number for its use as an Australian Rules football, cricket, rugby league, rugby union, soccer and concert venue. Tours of the stadium, with commentary, are available daily (hourly 10.30am–3.30pm; $28.50; child $18.50; turn up at Gate C but check it's a non-event day first by contacting ⓣ02/8765 2300 or checking Ⓦwww.anzstadium.com.au).

Opposite the Olympic site is the huge **Bicentennial Park**, opened in 1988; more than half of the expanse is conservation wetlands – a delightful, zigzagging boardwalk explores thick subtropical mangroves, and there's a bird hide from which you can observe a profusion of native birds. Around 8km of cycling and walking tracks facilitate proper appreciation, and the odd dramatic steel sculpture is a nice touch. Further north, the green-friendly Athletes' Village is now a solar-powered suburb, Newington. To get an overview of the site, there's an **observation centre** on the seventeenth floor of the *Novotel Hotel* (daily 10am–4pm; $5; contact ⓣ02/8762 1111), on Olympic Boulevard between ANZ Stadium and the Aquatic Centre. A number of cafés, restaurants and stores, on Dawn Fraser Avenue by the station, offer refreshments.

Visiting the venues

The best way to get out to Olympic Park is to take a **ferry** up the Parramatta River: the RiverCat from Circular Quay ($7.50 one-way to Homebush Bay) stops off frequently en route to Parramatta. Otherwise, a direct **train** from Central to Olympic Park Station runs four times daily on weekdays (at weekends change at Lidcombe station, from where trains depart every 10min). You can get to some venues directly by **bus** from Strathfield train station: #401–404 run regularly to the Homebush Bay Olympic Centre, the State Sports Centre and the Athletic Centre via the Olympic Park ferry wharf. **Car parks** at Sydney Olympic Park charge $4 per hour with a maximum daily charge of $20. To get around the extensive site there are 35km of **cycleways**, including those in Bicentennial Park. **Bike hire** is available (contact the visitor centre – see p.200; from $12 per hr, $22 per half-day) and bikes are permitted on trains and ferries (charges apply during peak hours). A self-guided audio tour, "Listen Live", is available from the visitor centre with interesting information on the Olympic Games and Olympic Park site, venues and attractions (9am–4pm; $20) – worth doing in conjunction with bike hire. Guided **Segway tours** are also available on weekends (11am & 2pm; $55 per hr; $99 for 2hr).

farm settlement in Australia, in fact. The fertile soil of "Rosehill", as it was originally called, saved the fledgling colony from starvation with its first wheat crop of 1789. It's hard to believe today, but dotted here and there among the malls and busy roads are a few remnants from that time – eighteenth-century public buildings and original settlers' dwellings that warrant a visit if you're interested in Australian history.

It's a thirty-minute train ride from Central Station to Parramatta, but the most enjoyable way to get here is on the sleek RiverCat ferry from Circular Quay up the Parramatta River (1hr; $7.70 one-way). The wharf is on Phillip Street, a couple of blocks away from the helpful visitor centre within the **Parramatta Heritage Centre**, corner of Church and Market streets (daily 9am–5pm; ☎02/8839 3311, ⓦwww.visitsydney.org/parramatta), by the convict-built Lennox Bridge. The centre hands out free walking-route maps detailing its many historical attractions. Parramatta's most important historic feature is the National Trust-owned **Old Government House** (Mon–Fri 10am–4pm, Sat & Sun 10.30am–4pm; $8) in **Parramatta Park** by the river. Entered through the 1885 gatehouse on O'Connell Street, the park – filled with native trees – rises up to the gracious old Georgian-style building, the oldest remaining public edifice in Australia. It was built between 1799 and 1816 and used as the Viceregal residence until 1855; one wing has been converted into a pleasant teahouse. History aside, Parramatta today is a modern multicultural suburban town with a wealth of international restaurants around Church and Phillip streets, and bargain shops and factory outlets on its outskirts.

The Western Highway and the rail lines head on to **PENRITH**, the western-most of Sydney's satellite towns, in a curve of the Nepean River at the foot of the Blue Mountains (on the way out here you pass **Featherdale Wildlife Park**; see box, p.184). Penrith has an old-fashioned Aussie feel to it – a tight community that is immensely proud of the Panthers, its boisterous rugby-league team. The area is also the home of the extensive International Regatta Centre on Penrith Lakes, spreading between Castlereagh and Cranebrook roads north of the town centre, and used in the Olympics; at **Penrith Whitewater Stadium** you can go white-water rafting ($85; 1hr 30min; ☎02/4730 4333, ⓦwww.penrithwhitewater.com.au).

The Blue Mountains region

The section of the Great Dividing Range nearest Sydney gets its name from the blue mist that rises from millions of eucalyptus trees and hangs in the mountain air, tinting the sky and the range alike. In the colony's early days, the **Blue Mountains** were believed to be an insurmountable barrier to the west. The first expeditions followed the streams in the valleys until they were defeated by cliff faces rising vertically above them. Only in 1813, when the explorers Wentworth, Blaxland and Lawson followed the ridges instead of the valleys, were the "mountains" (actually a series of canyons) finally conquered, allowing the western plains to be opened up for settlement. The range is surmounted by a plateau at an altitude of more than 1000m where, over millions of years, rivers have carved deep valleys into the sandstone, and winds and driving rain have helped to deepen the ravines, creating a spectacular scenery of sheer precipices and walled canyons. Before white settlement, the Daruk Aborigines lived here, dressed in animal-skin cloaks to ward off the cold. An early coal-mining industry, based in Katoomba, was followed by tourism, which snowballed after the arrival of the railway in 1868; by 1900, the first three mountain stations of Wentworth Falls, Katoomba and Mount Victoria had been established as fashionable resorts, extolling the health-giving benefits of eucalyptus-tinged mountain air. In 2000, the Blue Mountains became a **UNESCO World Heritage Site**, joining the Great Barrier Reef; the listing came after abseiling was finally banned on the mountains' most famous scenic wonder, the **Three Sisters**, after forty years of clambering had caused significant erosion. The Blue Mountains stand out from other Australian forests in particular for the **Wollemi**

Pine, discovered in 1994 (see p.120), a "living fossil" that dates back to the dinosaur era.

All the villages and towns of the romantically dubbed "**City of the Blue Mountains**" – principally Glenbrook, Springwood, Wentworth Falls, Leura, Katoomba and Blackheath – lie on a ridge, connected by the Great Western Highway. Around them is the **Blue Mountains National Park**, the state's fourth-largest national park and to many minds the best. The region makes a great weekend break from the city, with stunning views and clean air complemented by a wide range of accommodation, cafés and restaurants. But be warned: at weekends, and during the summer holidays, Katoomba is thronged with escapees from the city, and prices escalate accordingly. Even at their most crowded, though, the Blue Mountains offer somewhere where you can find peace and quiet, and even solitude – the deep gorges and high rocks make much of the terrain inaccessible except to bushwalkers and mountaineers. Climbing schools offer courses in rock-climbing, abseiling and canyoning for both beginners and experienced climbers, while Glenbrook is a popular mountain-biking spot.

Transport, tours and information

Public transport to the mountains is quite good but your own vehicle will give you much greater flexibility, allowing you to take detours to old mansions, cottage gardens and the lookout points scattered along the ridge. **Trains** leave from Central Station for Mount Victoria and/or Lithgow and follow the highway, stopping at all the major towns en route (frequent departures until about midnight; 2hr; $12.30 one-way to Katoomba, $16.80 off-peak day return). If you're dependent on public transport, Katoomba makes the best base: facilities and services are concentrated here, and the Blue Mountains Bus Company (℡02/4751 1077, Ⓦwww.bmbc.com.au) has half-hourly **bus** services to Blackheath, Mount Victoria (no service at weekends), Echo Point and the Scenic World complex, Leura, Wentworth Falls and North Katoomba. Buses leave from Katoomba Street outside the *Carrington Hotel*, and opposite the *Savoy*.

The two Katoomba-based, hop-on-hop-off tour buses have offices by the train station exit on Main Street; passes include discounts to some of the attractions en route. **Trolley Tours** (℡1800 801 577, Ⓦwww.trolleytours .com.au) is a minibus decked out like a tram, which does a scenic circuit with commentary from Katoomba to Leura around Cliff Drive to the Three Sisters and back, taking in 29 attractions along the way (departs Katoomba hourly Mon–Fri 9.15am–4.15pm, Sat & Sun 9.45am–3.45pm; $20 all-day pass also valid on all ordinary bus routes). The slightly more extensive **Blue Mountains Explorer Bus** (℡02/4782 1866 or 1300 300 915, Ⓦwww.explorerbus.com .au) also links Katoomba and Leura but in a red double-decker bus (departs Katoomba roughly hourly 9.45am–4.15pm, last return 5.15pm; 30 stops; $33 all day pass). There's no commentary with the Explorer Bus, but you do get a guide with maps detailing bushwalk and sightseeing options. Blue Mountains Explorer Link tickets (available from train stations) combine a return rail ticket from Sydney to Katoomba with all-day or 3-day access to the Explorer Bus (both $51).

The **Blue Mountains Information Centre** (9am–4.30pm; ℡1300 653 408, Ⓦwww.bluemts.com.au) is on the Great Western Highway at Glenbrook (see p.204), the gateway to the Blue Mountains. The centre has a huge amount of information on the area, including two free publications: the *Blue Mountains Wonderland Visitors Guide* (Ⓦwww.bluemountainswonderland.com), which has

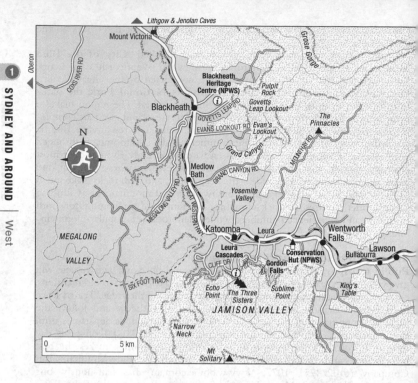

several detailed colour maps and bushwalking notes, and an events guide. The other official tourist information centre is at **Echo Point**, near Katoomba (see p.206); both offices offer a **free accommodation booking** service.

The **Blue Mountains National Park** has its main ranger station at Blackheath (see p.208), where you can get comprehensive walking and camping information – there are car-accessible NPWS camping and picnic sites near Glenbrook, Woodford, Wentworth Falls, Blackheath and Oberon, and bush camping is allowed in most areas. The only point where you must pay vehicle entry into the park is at Glenbrook ($7).

Accommodation in the Blue Mountains

Accommodation rates rise on Friday and Saturday nights – aim to visit on weekdays when it's quieter and cheaper. The tourist offices at Glenbrook and Echo Point have a booking service. **Katoomba** is the obvious choice if arriving by train, particularly for those on a budget, since it has several **hostels** to choose from, but if you have your own transport you can indulge in some of the more unusual and characterful **guesthouses** in **Blackheath** and **Mount Victoria**.

There are also many charming **holiday homes**; contact Soper Bros, 173 The Mall, Leura (℡02/4784 1633, ⓦwww.soperbros.com.au) and check out homes like the idyllic *Brookside Cottage*, overlooking the Charles Darwin Walk, in Wentworth Falls (4 people; 3-night weekend $475), or the less exotic bargain of *Geebung Cottage*, Katoomba (8 people; 3-night weekend $480). There are two council-run **caravan parks**: *Katoomba Falls*, at Katoomba Falls Road (℡02/4782 1835; en-suite cabins ➍–➎), and *Blackheath*, at Prince Edward Street (℡02/4787 8101; cabins ➋). You can **camp** at both of these, as

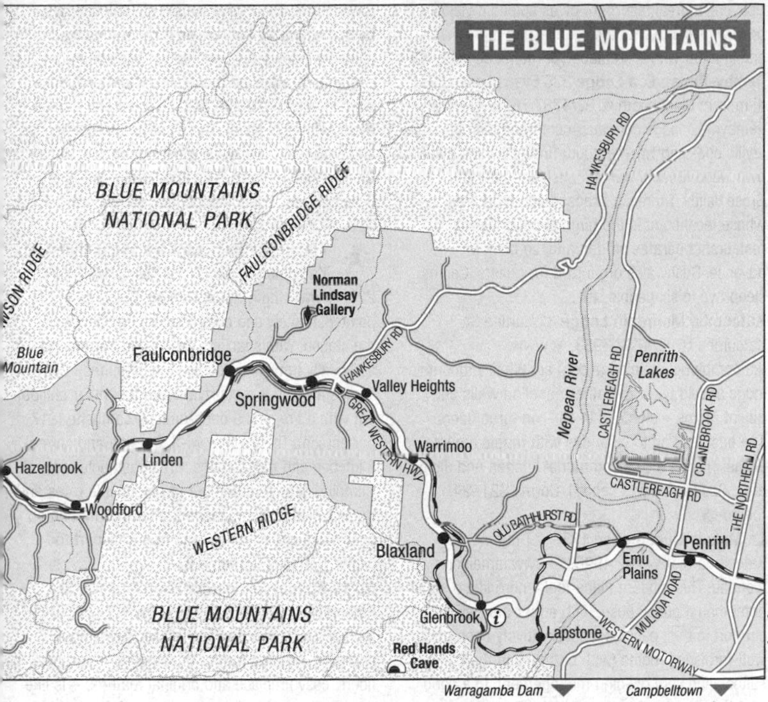
THE BLUE MOUNTAINS
BLUE MOUNTAINS
NATIONAL PARK
FAULCONBRIDGE RIDGE
Norman
Lindsay
Gallery
Blue
Mountain
Faulconbridge
Springwood
HAWKESBURY RD
Valley Heights
GREAT WESTERN HWY
Warrimoo
Linden
Hazelbrook
Woodford
WESTERN RIDGE
Blaxland
OLD BATHURST RD
BLUE MOUNTAINS
NATIONAL PARK
Glenbrook
Red Hands
Cave
Lapstone
WESTERN MOTORWAY
MULGOA ROAD
Emu
Plains
Penrith
CASTLEREAGH RD
THE NORTHERN RD
CRANEBROOK RD
Penrith
Lakes
Nepean River
HAWKESBURY RD
Richmond
Windsor
Sydney
Warragamba Dam
Campbelltown

well as in the grounds of *Flying Fox Backpackers* (see p.204), and in the bush at several NPWS sites (see p.206).

Hotels, motels and guest-houses

Carrington Hotel 15–47 Katoomba St, Katoomba ☎ 02/4782 1111, Ⓦ www.thecarrington.com.au. When it opened in 1882, the *Carrington* was the region's finest hotel. Now fully restored, original features include stained-glass windows, open fireplaces, a splendid dining room and ballroom, cocktail bar, snooker and games room, library and guest lounges. The spacious en-suite rooms are beautifully decorated in rich heritage colours. Rooms [6], en suite [8]

Cecil Guesthouse 108 Katoomba St, Katoomba ☎ 02/4782 1411, Ⓦ www.ourguest.com.au. Old-world, very central choice, set back from the main street. There are great views over the town and Jamison Valley from the common areas and some bedrooms. A little dilapidated but charming, with original 1904 wallpaper, dark-polished timber, log fires, games room and an abandoned, overgrown tennis court all providing an old-fashioned atmosphere with a pleasing sense of regal decay. [4]

Glenella 56 Govett's Leap Rd, Blackheath ☎ 02/4787 8352, Ⓦ www.glenellabluemountainshotel.com.au. Guesthouse in a charming 1905 homestead with antiques-furnished rooms, mostly en suite, but there are slightly cheaper shared-bathroom options. [5]–[6]

Imperial 1 Station St, Mount Victoria ☎ 02/4787 1233, Ⓦ www.hotelimperial.com.au. Beautifully restored nineteenth century resort that once hosted croquet-playing ministers and royalty. Its old-world charms are still in evidence: there are beautifully appointed en-suite rooms and spacious, pleasantly decorated guesthouse-style shared-bathroom options, as well as more basic pub-style rooms. Breakfast included. [4]–[7]

Jamison House 48 Merriwa St, corner of Cliff Drive, Katoomba ☎ 02/4782 1206, Ⓦ www.jamisonhouse.com. Built as a guesthouse in 1903, this seriously charming place has amazing, unimpeded views across the Jamison Valley. The feel is of a small European hotel, enhanced by the French restaurant downstairs, *The Rooster*, with its gorgeous dining room full of original fixtures.

Upstairs, a breakfast room gives splendid views – provisions come with the room – and there's a sitting room with a fireplace. All rooms en suite. **7**

Jemby-Rinjah Eco Lodge 336 Evans Lookout Rd, 4km from Blackheath ☎02/4787 7622, ⓦwww .jembyrinjahlodge.com.au. Accommodation in idyllic one- and two-bedroom timber cabins (with own wood fires) in tranquil bushland near the Grose Valley. There's a licensed common area whose focal point is the huge circular "fire pit"; a restaurant operates on demand, so book in advance. Bushwalks organized for guests. Cabins sleep two to six people. **8**

Katoomba Mountain Lodge 31 Lurline St, Katoomba ☎02/4782 3933, ⓦwww .katoombamountainlodge.com.au. What a mountain lodge should be, with timber-panelled walls and quaint rooms – eighteen in all – on three floors. The best lead on to verandas with magic mountain vistas. There's also a communal kitchen and dining area. Good value and central. Dorms $21–24, rooms **4**

La Maison Guesthouse 175–177 Lurline St, Katoomba ☎02/4782 4996, ⓦwww.lamaison .com.au. This modern place feels more like a small hotel than a guesthouse, with a four-star level of comfort in the spacious, conservatively decorated, well-furnished rooms (with bathtubs in the en suites), and very obliging management. In a good spot between the town centre and Echo Point. There's also a garden, deck, spa and sauna. **6**

Hostels

Blue Mountains YHA 207 Katoomba St, Katoomba ☎02/4782 1416, ⓔbluemountains @yhansw.org.au. Huge 200-bed YHA right in the town centre. The former 1930s guesthouse has been modernized but retains its charming lead-lighted windows, Art Deco decor, huge ballroom and an old-fashioned mountain-retreat ambience, with an open fire in the reading room and games room (with pool table). There's also internet access and a pleasant courtyard. Most rooms and some of the four-bed dorms are en suite (there are also 8-bed dorms). Friendly reception staff. Dorms $27–30, rooms **4**

Flying Fox Backpackers 190 Bathurst Rd, Katoomba ☎02/4782 4226 or 1800 624 226, ⓦwww.theflyingfox.com.au. Colourfully painted, homely and comfortable bungalow near the station, with spacious seven-bed dorms and artistically furnished doubles (no en suites). Cosy lounge area, plus a courtyard and a popular chillout hut with a fire, and a bush-outlook campsite ($17 per person). There's free wi-fi, free tea and coffee, a kitchen and fridge space. Breakfast included. Camping gear is rented out at reasonable rates and the knowledgeable managers offer information on bushwalks and camping, and free transport to walks. Dorms $29, rooms **3**

No 14 Budget Accommodation 14 Lovel St, Katoomba ☎02/4782 7104, ⓦwww .numberfourteen.com. This relaxed hostel in a charming restored former guesthouse – polished floors, cosy fireplace and original features – is like a home away from home, run by an informative, friendly young couple. Mostly twin and double rooms, some en suite, plus four-share dorms with comfy beds instead of bunks; all centrally heated. Peaceful veranda surrounded by pretty plants and valley views. Dorms $25, rooms **3**

Glenbrook to Wentworth Falls

The first stop off the busy highway from Sydney is **GLENBROOK**, a pleasant village arranged around the train station, with an adventure shop and a strip of cafés on Ross Street. The section of the **Blue Mountains National Park** here is popular for **mountain biking** along the **Oaks Fire Trail** (it's best to start the thirty-kilometre trail higher up the mountain in **WOODFORD** and head downhill, ending up in Glenbrook; bike rental is available at Katoomba, see p.210). Several bushwalks commence from the part-time NPWS office at the outside end of Bruce Road (hours variable; ☎02/4739 2950). In summer, head for the swimmable **Blue Pool** and **Jellybean Pool**, an easy, one-kilometre walk away. One of the best hikes from here is to see the Aboriginal hand stencils on the walls of Red Hands Cave (6km; 3hr return; medium difficulty). With a car or bike you can get there via road and continue to the grassy creekside Eoroka picnic ground (also camping) where there are lots of eastern grey kangaroos.

The small town of **WENTWORTH FALLS**, 32km further west, was named after William Wentworth, one of the famous trio who conquered the mountains in 1813. A signposted road leads from the Great Western Highway to the **Wentworth Falls Reserve**, with superb views of the waterfall tumbling down into the Jamison Valley. You can reach this picnic area from Wentworth train station by following the easy creekside 2.5-kilometre **Darwin's Walk** – the route followed by the famous naturalist in 1836 to the cliff edge, where he described the view from the great precipice as one of the most stupendous he'd ever seen. Most of the other bushwalks in the area start from the national park's **Conservation Hut** (Mon–Fri 9am–4pm, Sat & Sun 9am–5pm; ☎02/4757 3827), about 3km from the railway station at the end of Fletcher Street.

Leura

Just 2km west of Wentworth Falls, well-heeled **LEURA**, packed with cafés and antiques stores, is a scenic spot with views across the Jamison Valley to the imposing plateau that is **Mount Solitary**. The main shopping strip, **Leura Mall**, has a wide grassy area lined with cherry trees and makes a popular picnicking spot. In fact, Leura is renowned for its beautiful gardens, and nine are open to the public during the **Leura Gardens Festival** (early to mid-Oct; $5 per garden, or $18 all gardens; ⓦ www.leuragardensfestival.com.au). Open all year round, though, is the beautiful National Trust-listed **Everglades Gardens** (daily 10am–5pm; $7) at 37 Everglades Ave, 2km southeast of the Mall. There

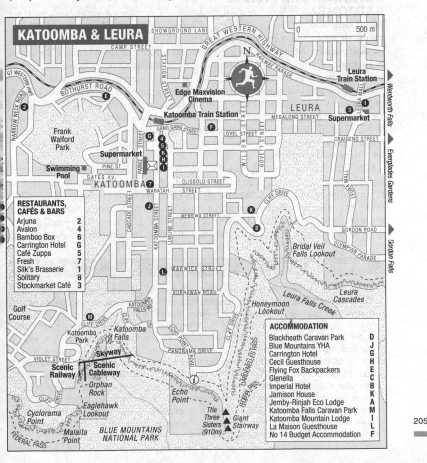

KATOOMBA & LEURA

RESTAURANTS, CAFÉS & BARS
Arjuna 2
Avalon 4
Bamboo Box 6
Carrington Hotel G
Café Zuppa 5
Fresh 7
Silk's Brasserie 1
Solitary 8
Stockmarket Café 3

ACCOMMODATION
Blackheath Caravan Park D
Blue Mountains YHA J
Carrington Hotel G
Cecil Guesthouse H
Flying Fox Backpackers E
Glenella C
Imperial Hotel B
Jamison House K
Jemby-Rinjah Eco Lodge A
Katoomba Falls Caravan Park M
Katoomba Mountain Lodge I
La Maison Guesthouse L
No 14 Budget Accommodation F

are wonderful Jamison Valley views from its formal terraces, a colourful display of azaleas and rhododendrons, an arboretum, and a simple tearoom. Just over 1km south of the Mall is the Gordon Falls picnic area on Lone Pine Avenue, where Leura's mansions and gardens give way to the bush of the **Blue Mountains National Park**; it's an easy ten-minute return walk to the lookout over the falls, or there's a canyon walk (2hr return; medium difficulty) via Lyre Bird Dell and the Pool of Siloam, which takes in some of the Blue Mountains' distinctive hanging swamps, an Aboriginal rock shelter and cooling rainforest. From Gordon Falls, a 45-minute bushwalk part-way along the Prince Henry Cliff Walk (see p.208) heads to **Leura Cascades** picnic area off **Cliff Drive** (the scenic route around the cliffs that extends from Leura to beyond Katoomba) where there are several bushwalks, including a two- to three-hour circuit walk to the base of the cascading **Bridal Veil Falls** (not to be confused with Bridal Veil Falls on the north side of Leura at Grose Valley, see p.208). To the east of Gordon Falls, Sublime Point Road leads to the aptly named **Sublime Point** lookout, with panoramic views of the Jamison Valley.

Katoomba and around

KATOOMBA, 103km west of Sydney, is the biggest town in the Blue Mountains and the area's commercial heart; it's also the best located for the major sights of Echo Point and The Three Sisters. There's a lively café scene on **Katoomba Street**, which runs downhill from the train station; the street is also full of vintage clothes shops, secondhand bookstores, antiques dealers and gift shops. When the town was first discovered by fashionable city-dwellers in the late nineteenth century, the grandiose **Carrington Hotel**, prominently located at the top of Katoomba Street, was the height of elegance (a historian gives 1hr–1hr 30min tours of the hotel; bookings ℡02/4754 5726). It's recently been restored to its former glory, with elegant sloping lawns running down to the street, half of which has been taken over by a new **town square**.

Across the railway line (use the foot-tunnel under the station and follow the signs), a stunning introduction to the ecology of the Blue Mountains can be had at the **Edge Maxvision Cinema**, at 225 Great Western Highway (℡02/4782 8900, ⊛www.edgecinema.com.au), a huge six-storey cinema screen created as a venue to show *The Edge Movie* (daily 10.20am, 11.05am, 12.10pm, 1.30pm, 2.15pm & 5.30pm; $15). The highlight of the forty-minute film is the segment

---

The Six Foot Track

Along the Great Western Highway, about 2.5km west of Katoomba train station, is the **Explorers Tree**, inscribed with the initials of Blaxland, Lawson and Wentworth during their famous 1813 expedition. From Nellies Glen Road here is the start of the 42-kilometre **Six Foot Track** to the Jenolan Caves (2–3 days; carry plenty of water) and shorter walks to Pulpit Rock and Bonnie Doon Falls. There are four basic campsites along the way, plus well-equipped cabins at Binda Flats (see p.212). Blackheath NPWS can provide more bushwalking and camping information. Blue Mountains Guides (℡02/4782 6109, ⊛www.bluemountainsguides.com .au) offer a guided walk along the track (3-day; $750). Otherwise, Fantastic Aussie Tours (see p.211) provide a return service from Jenolan Caves for those who have completed the walk (1hr 30min; $35). A more unusual way to do the track is to enter Australia's largest annual off-road marathon, the Six Foot Track Marathon held in March (⊛www.coolrunning.com.au).

▲ The Scenic Skyway

about the "dinosaur trees", a stand of thirty-metre-high **Wollemi pine**, previously known only from fossil material over sixty million years old. The trees – miraculously still existing – survive deep within a sheltered rainforest gully in the **Wollemi National Park**, north of Katoomba, and they made headlines when they were first discovered in 1994 by a group of canyoners. Since the discovery, the first cultivated Wollemi pine was planted in 1998 at Sydney's Royal Botanic Gardens.

A 25-minute walk south from the train station down Katoomba Street and along Lurline Street and Echo Point Road (or by tour or regular bus from outside the Savoy Theatre; see p.209) will bring you to **Echo Point**. From the projecting lookout platform between the **visitor centre** (daily 9am–5pm, ☎ 1300 653 408) and souvenir shops and eateries at the Three Sisters Heritage Plaza, breathtaking vistas take in the Kedumba and Jamison valleys, Mount Solitary, the Ruined Castle, Kings Tableland and the Blue Mountains' most famous landmark, the **Three Sisters** (910m). These three gnarled rocky points take their name from an Aboriginal Dreamtime story that relates how the Kedumba people were losing a battle against the rival Nepean people: the Kedumba leader, fearing that his three beautiful daughters would be carried off by the enemy, turned them to stone, but was tragically killed before he could reverse his spell. The Three Sisters are at the top of the **Giant Stairway** (1hr 45min one-way), the beginning of the very steep 800 steps into the 300-metre-deep **Jamison Valley** below, passing **Katoomba Falls** en route. There's a popular walking route, taking about two hours and graded medium, down the stairway and part-way along the **Federal Pass** to the **Landslide**, and then on to the Scenic Railway or Cableway (see p.208), either of which you can take back up to the ridge.

To spare yourself the trek down into the Jamison Valley or the walk back up, head for the very touristy **Scenic World complex** at the end of Violet Street off Cliff Drive. Apart from housing a small cinema showing a documentary of the area (free with purchase of any ticket), you can take a short and pricey glass-bottomed cable-car ride over the valley in the **Scenic Skyway** ($10 one-way, $16 return) or choose between two modes of transport to get to the valley floor: the original **Scenic Railway** or the modern **Scenic Cableway** (daily 9am–4.50pm; every 10min; $10 one-way; $19 return; ⓦwww.scenicworld.com.au). The Railway and Cableway offer steep descents to the valley floor with fantastic views of the Three Sisters along the way, and end up about 100m away from each other, making it easy to go down by one and up by the other. Once at the bottom, a scenic two-kilometre, wheelchair-accessible boardwalk meanders through the rainforest, with boards detailing natural features and history along the way. For the more energetic, there's a tranquil but moderately difficult twelve-kilometre return bushwalk to the Ruined Castle.

A short walk from the Scenic World complex along Cliff Drive is the **Katoomba Falls picnic area** in Katoomba Park, where there's a kiosk and several bushwalking options. The **Prince Henry Cliff Walk** (9km one-way; 9hr; easy) is a long, pleasant stroll along the plateau clifftop via Echo Point all the way to **Gordon Falls** (see p.206) with glorious lookouts along the way. A scenic drive following Cliff Drive southwest of Katoomba Falls leads to several other spectacular lookouts: Eaglehawk, the Landslide and Narrow Neck – a great sunset spot, with views into both the Jamison and Megalong valleys.

Blackheath

Two train stops beyond Katoomba, and 11km further northwest along the Great Western Highway, there are more lookout points at **BLACKHEATH** – just as impressive as Echo Point and much less busy. One of the best is **Govetts Leap**, at the end of Govetts Leap Road (just over 2km east of the highway through the village centre), near the **Blue Mountains Heritage Centre** at Black-heath (daily 9am–4.30pm; ⓣ02/4787 8877), which acts as the **Blue Mountains National Park headquarters**. The two-kilometre **Fairfax Heritage Track** from the NPWS centre is wheelchair- and pram-accessible and takes in the Govetts Leap Lookout with its marvellous panorama of the **Grose Valley** and the much-photographed Bridal Veil Falls. Many walks start from the centre, but one of the most popular, **The Grand Canyon** (5km; 3hr 30min; medium difficulty), begins from **Evans Lookout Road** at the south end of town, west of the Great Western Highway.

Govetts Leap Road and its shady cross-street, Wentworth Street, have lots of antiques and craft shops, an antiquarian bookshop, and great cafés and restaurants. Some 10km southwest of Blackheath, across the railway line, the beautiful, unspoilt **Megalong Valley** is reached via winding Megalong Road; it's popular for **horseriding** (see "Listings" p.211), and there are creeks with swimmable waterholes.

Mount Victoria and around

At the top of the Blue Mountains, secluded and leafy **MOUNT VICTORIA**, 6km northwest of Blackheath along the Great Western Highway and the last mountain-settlement proper, is the only one with an authentic village feel. The great old pub, the *Imperial* (see p.203), is good for a drink or meal, and there are old-fashioned scones at the *Bay Tree Tea Shop* opposite. Several antiques shops and secondhand bookstores are worth a browse. Some short **walks** start from the Fairy Bower picnic area, a ten-minute walk from the Great Western Highway via Mount Piddington Road.

Beyond Mount Victoria, drivers can circle back towards Sydney via the scenic **Bells Line of Road**, which heads east through the fruit- and vegetable-growing areas of Bilpin and Kurrajong to Richmond, with growers selling their produce at roadside stalls. On the way, **Mount Tomah Botanic Garden** (daily: April–Sept 10am–4pm; Oct–March 10am–5pm; $5.50; ⊛www.rbgsyd.nsw.gov .au; no public transport) has been the cool-climate outpost of Sydney's Royal Botanic Gardens since 1987. The popular *Restaurant Tomah* (lunch daily; licensed; mains $22–28.50; ☏02/4567 2060, ⊛www.restauranttomah.com.au), with a contemporary Australian menu, has fantastic north-facing views over the gardens, Wollemi National Park and Bilbin orchards. Cheaper light lunches are also available and there's a kiosk, plus free electric barbecues and picnic tables. By car, you can continue west along the Bells Line of Road to the Zig Zag Railway at Clarence, just over 35km away (see p.211).

Eating, drinking and entertainment

Cuisine in the Blue Mountains has gone way beyond the ubiquitous "Devonshire teas", with many well-regarded restaurants, and a real **café culture** in Katoomba and Leura. There are some great bakeries, too: top of the list is *Hominy*, 185 Katoomba St (daily 6am–5.30pm), with no eating area of its own, but the street's public picnic tables just outside. See also the *Conservation Hut Café* (p.205) and accommodation listings (p.203) for other eating options.

There are a number of **nightlife** options in Katoomba. The salubrious cocktail bar and cabaret room at *The Carrington* (see below) hosts eclectic folk, blues, jazz and world music (Fri–Sun from $12; dinner plus show $35). On the other side of the tracks, opposite the station, the huge and now rather hip *Gearin Hotel* (☏02/4782 4395) is a hive of activity, with several bars where you can play pool, see touring bands (Fri & Sat nights) or boogie at the club nights. There's more action at the many bars of the *Carrington*, below.

Arjuna 16 Valley Rd, just off the Great Western Highway, Katoomba ☏02/4782 4662. Excellent, authentic Indian restaurant. A bit out of the way but well positioned for spectacular sunset views, so get there early. Good veggie choices, too. BYO. Mon & Thurs–Sun from 6pm.

Avalon 18 Katoomba St ☏02/4782 5532. Stylish place with the ambience of a quirky café, in the dress circle of the old Savoy Theatre, with many Art Deco features. Beautiful views down the valley, too – turn up for lunch or early dinner to see them. Moderately expensive menu, but generous servings and to-die-for desserts, or just drop by for a drink. BYO & licensed. Lunch & dinner Wed–Sun.

Bamboo Box 50 Katoomba St, Katoomba ☏02/4782 6998. Very friendly, simple white space, with ergonomic seating and appealing tropical plant art along the wall. A favourite with locals for its many cheap and tasty Asian eats (the laksas are

particularly delicious, $11.80–14.80). Eat in or take away (sushi packs are a good option for bushwalk picnics), and be sure to check out the cheap lunch specials. Tues–Sat 10am–9pm.

Café Zuppa 36 Katoomba St, Katoomba, ☏02/4782 9247. Wall-to-wall waist-high mirrors, crystal ball lightshades and a glass and timber facade are just some of the attributes of this charming Art Deco place. The coffee's tasty, while the food – burgers, salads, pastas and pizzas (like the delicious roasted vegetable and feta "Zuppa Pizza"; $12.95) – could feasibly inspire a sonnet. Daily 7.30am–late.

Carrington Hotel 15–47 Katoomba St, Katoomba ☏02/4782 1111. The *Carrington* has a host of bars in and around its grand old building: *Champagne Charlie's Cocktail Bar* has a decorative glass ceiling dome and chandeliers. You can order tasty poly-syllabic cocktails and down them in one of the classic Kentia-palm-filled lounges or out on the front veranda overlooking the lawns. Cheaper drinks and a livelier atmosphere are to be found at the bottom of the *Carrington*'s driveway at stately *Old City Bank Bar* (live music most Fri & Sat evenings) with its award-winning upstairs brasserie serving great pizzas, pastas and gourmet burgers. The *Carrington Public Bar*, with a separate entrance around the corner, on Bathurst St opposite the train station, is more down-to-earth, and upstairs is the *Baroque Bar & Nightclub*, a dimly illuminated Art Deco retreat hosting a mix of DJs and live music (Fri & Sat 10pm till late).

Fresh 181 Katoomba St, Katoomba. The spacious goldfish bowl at the bottom end of the main street is the most popular café with locals, from the local police to arty types. It has an open kitchen, wooden interior, good music and sunny tables outside, and serves great breakfasts, from build-your-own eggs and bacon bonanzas to ricotta hotcakes with home-made butterscotch sauce ($12.90), while the slightly more health-conscious might go for the organic muesli with rhubarb compote and greek yoghurt ($10.90). Also serves raved-about burgers, risotto and wraps ($12.50–15.50), and the coffee is the best in town. Daily 8am–5pm.

Il Postino 13 Station St, opposite the train station, Wentworth Falls. Great, relaxed café in the old post office – the cracked walls have become part of an artfully distressed, light and airy interior; there are tables on a street-facing courtyard. The menu is Mediterranean- and Thai-slanted, with plenty for vegetarians (nothing over $16). Excellent all-day breakfast. BYO. Daily 8.30am–6pm.

Silk's Brasserie 128 The Mall, Leura ☎02/4784 2534. Parisian-style bar with excellent service and great food. For dinner, the sophisticated European-style dishes, from confit of duck to Tasmanian salmon, range from $29–34. Both fine dining and cheaper, more relaxed fare ($17–28) at lunch. Licensed, with many wines available by the glass. Daily noon–3pm & 6–10pm.

Solitary 90 Cliff Drive, Leura Falls ☎02/4782 1164. Perched on a hairpin bend on the mountains' scenic cliff-hugging road, the views of the Jamison Valley and Mount Solitary from this modern Australian restaurant are sublime. Expect beautifully laid tables, eager service, a reasonably priced wine list and superb food. There's a fireplace in the back room and rattan tables and chairs beneath parasols on the lawn outside overlooking the valley. You can enjoy it all more cheaply when it morphs into the laid-back *Solitary Kiosk* (little above $16.50). Kiosk: daily 10am–4pm. Restaurant: lunch Sat & Sun, dinner Wed–Sun.

Stockmarket Cafe 179 The Mall. A rustic narrow place serving consistently good coffee, delicious breakfasts, gourmet pies, great salads and paninis and mood-altering desserts. Mon–Fri 7.30am–3.30pm, Sat & Sun 8am–3.30pm.

Victory Café 17 Govetts Leap Rd, Blackheath ☎02/4787 6777. A very pleasant space in the front of an old Art Deco theatre now converted into an antiques centre. Gourmet sandwiches and café favourites with an interesting spin, with special mains such as Szechuan chicken, and an all-day breakfast. There's plenty for vegetarians too. Daily 8.30am–5pm.

Listings

Adventure activities Australian School of Mountaineering, at Paddy Pallin, 166 Katoomba St, Katoomba (☎02/4782 2014, ⊛www.asmguides.com) offers daily day-long abseiling courses ($145), plus canyoning to Grand, Empress or Fortress canyons (Oct–May daily 9am; $165; also less frequent trips to other canyons), rock-climbing and bush-survival courses. Another long-established operator, High 'n' Wild Mountain Adventures, 3–5 Katoomba St, Katoomba (☎02/4782 6224, ⊛www.high-n-wild.com.au), has great beginners' courses in abseiling (half-day $90, full day $145), canyoning (from $179), rock-climbing (half-day $159, full day $179), plus guided bushwalking and bushcraft courses. Both include lunch on full-day courses.

Bike rental Vélo Nova, 182 Katoomba St, Katoomba (☎02/4782 2800), has mountain bikes from $40 half-day, $50 full day.

Camping equipment Paddy Pallin, 166 Katoomba St, Katoomba (☎02/4782 4466), sells camping gear and a good range of topographic maps and bushwalking guides and supplies. For cheap gear, go to K-Mart (next door to Coles supermarket, Katoomba St).

Car rental Redicar, 121 The Mall, Leura (50m from Leura Station; ☎02/4784 3443, ⊛www.redicar.com.au).

Festivals The Blue Mountains Music Festival is a three-day, mid-March festival of folk, roots and blues featuring Australian and international musicians on several indoor and outdoor stages

($165 weekend, $95 one day, $65–70 night ticket; ⓦ www.bmff.org.au). Celebrating the winter solstice in late June, the Winter Magic Festival (ⓦ www.wintermagic.com.au) consists of a number of events over several weeks culminating on Sat, when Katoomba St is closed off to traffic and taken over by performers and a parade of locals in colourful pagan garments.

Horseriding Blue Mountains Horse Riding Adventures (☎ 02/4787 8188, ⓦ www.megalong.cc; pick-ups from Blackheath) offer escorted trail rides in the Megalong Valley and along the Coxs River, with the beginners' one-hour "Wilderness Ride" ($45), plus experienced riders' all-day adventures along the river (from $165). Werriberri Trail Rides offer horseriding and overnight stays for all abilities in the Megalong Valley ($90 for 2hr; $190 per day; pony rides from $5.50 for 5min; ☎ 02/4787 9171; ⓦ http://australianbluehoroorides.com.au)

Hospital Blue Mountains District ANZAC Memorial, Katoomba ☎ 02/4784 6500.

Internet Katoomba Book Exchange, 34 Katoomba St, Katoomba ☎ 2/4782 9997 (17 cents per min, 15min free with a cup of coffee, 10am–6pm).

Laundry The Washing Well, K-Mart car park, Katoomba (daily 7am–6pm; ☎ 02/4782 2377).

Pharmacies Blooms Springwood Pharmacy, 161 Macquarie Rd, Springwood (Mon–Fri 8.30am–9pm, Sat & Sun 9am–7pm); Greenwell & Thomas, 145 Katoomba St, Katoomba (Mon–Fri 8.30am–7pm, Sat & Sun 9am–6pm).

Post office Katoomba Post Office, Pioneer Place, off Katoomba St, Katoomba. Mon–Fri 9am–5pm.

Supermarket Coles, Pioneer Place off Katoomba St, Katoomba (daily 6am–midnight).

Swimming pool Katoomba Aquatic Centre, Gates Ave, Katoomba (Mon–Fri 6am–8pm, Sat & Sun 8am–8pm, winter weekends closes 6.30pm; ☎ 02/4782 5156; $10), has outdoor and indoor complexes with a toddlers' pool, sauna, spa and gym.

Taxis Taxis wait outside the main train stations to meet arrivals; otherwise, for the upper mountains call Katoomba Radio Cabs (☎ 02/4782 1311), or for the middle mountains call Blue Mountains Taxi Cabs (☎ 02/4759 3000).

Tours Most tours of the Blue Mountains start from Sydney; see box, p.182. For hop-on hop-off tour services from Katoomba, see p.201. Fantastic Aussie Tours (283 Main St, Katoomba; ☎ 02/4782 1866, ⓦ www.fantastic-aussie-tours.com.au) also do large-group coach tours to the Jenolan Caves: a day-tour (daily; $70–78 with one cave entry), or adventure caving ($105). The excellent Blue Mountains Walkabout (☎ 0408 443 822, ⓦ www .bluemountainswalkabout.com) offers half-day ($75) and all-day ($95), off-the-beaten-track bush roams (around 10km) between Faulconbridge and Springwood, led by an Aboriginal guide. Tread Lightly Eco Tours (☎ 02/4788 1229, ⓦ www .treadlightly.com.au) offer small-group, expert-guided 2hr, half-day and full-day bushwalk and 4WD tours from Katoomba.

Trains Katoomba station general enquiries ☎ 02/4782 1902.

Lithgow and the Zig Zag Railway

En route to Bathurst and the Central West on the Great Western Highway, **Lithgow**, 21km northwest of Mount Victoria, is a coal-mining town nestled under bush-clad hills, with wide, leafy streets, quaint mining cottages and some imposing old buildings. About 13km east of the town on the Bells Line of Road, by the small settlement of **Clarence**, is the **Zig Zag Railway**. In the 1860s, engineers were faced with the problem of how to get the main western railway line from the top of the Blue Mountains down the steep drop to the Lithgow Valley, so they came up with a series of zigzag ramps. These fell into disuse in the early twentieth century, but tracks were relaid by rail enthusiasts in the 1970s. Served by old steam trains, the picturesque line passes through two tunnels and over three viaducts, and you can stop at points along the way and rejoin a later train. The Zig Zag Railway can be reached by ordinary State Rail train on the regular service between Sydney and Lithgow, by asking the guard in advance to stop at the Zig Zag platform; you then walk across the line to Bottom Point platform at the base of the Lithgow Valley. To catch the Zig Zag Railway from Clarence, at the top of the valley, you'll need to have your own transport. Zig Zag trains depart from Clarence daily (11am, 1pm & 3pm; from the Zig Zag platform add 50min to these times; $19 one-way, $25 return;

☎02/635 2955, ⓦwww.zigzagrailway.com.au). There are plenty of **motels** in and around Lithgow, especially on the Great Western Highway – and the **Lithgow Visitor Centre**, 1 Cooerwull Rd (daily 9am–5pm; ☎1300 760 276 or 02/6350 3230, ⓦwww.tourism.lithgow.com), can advise on them.

Kanangra Boyd National Park and the Jenolan Caves

Kanangra Boyd National Park shares a boundary with the Blue Mountains National Park. Further south than the latter, much of it is inaccessible, but you can explore the rugged beauty of **Kanangra Walls**, where the Boyd Plateau falls away to reveal a wilderness area of creeks, deep gorges and rivers below. Reached via Jenolan Caves, three **walks** leave from the car park at Kanangra Walls: a short lookout walk, a waterfall stroll and a longer plateau walk – contact the NPWS in **Oberon** for details (38 Ross St; ☎02/6336 1972). Vehicle entry to the park is $7. *Boyd River* and *Dingo Dell* campsites, both off Kanangra Walls Road, have **free bush camping** (pit toilets; limited drinking water at *Dingo Dell*).

The **Jenolan Caves** lie 30km southwest across the mountains from Katoomba on the far edge of the Kanangra Boyd National Park – over 80km by road – and contain New South Wales' most spectacular limestone formations. There are ten "show" caves, with daily guided tours at various times throughout the day (9.30am–5.30pm; 2hr adult-oriented ghost tours depart 8pm Sat only). If you're coming for just a day, plan to see one or two caves: the best general one is the Lucas Cave ($25; 1hr 30min), though a more spectacular cave is the Temple of Baal ($33; 1hr 30min), while the extensive River Cave, with its tranquil Pool of Reflection, is the longest and priciest ($38; 2hr). The system of caves is surrounded by the **Jenolan Karst Conservation Reserve**, a fauna and flora sanctuary with picnic facilities and walking trails to small waterfalls and lookout points. It and the caves are administered by the Jenolan Caves Trust (☎02/6359 3911 and 1300 763 311, ⓦwww.jenolancaves.org.au), which also offers **adventure caving** in various other caves ("Plughole" tour $60 for 2hr; "Central River Adventure Cave" tour $187.50 for 7hr).

The Jenolan Caves Trust also looks after several **places to stay** in the vicinity. The most central is *Jenolan Caves House* (en suite ❼, shared facilities ❺), a charming old hotel that was a popular honeymoon destination in the 1920s. In the old hotel section, there's a good restaurant, a bar and a more casual bistro. About ten minutes by car from the caves in a secluded woodland setting are the *Jenolan Caves Cottages* at Binda Flats (sleeps 6; BYO linen; ❻). Other places to stay in the area include ☀*Jenolan Cabins*, 42 Edith Rd, 4km west on Porcupine Hill (☎02/6335 6239, ⓦwww.jenolancabins.com.au; ❺), whose reasonably priced, well-equipped two-bedroom timber cabins with wood fires accommodate six (BYO linen) – all with magnificent views over the Blue Mountains and Kanangra Boyd national parks and the Jenolan Karst Conservation Reserve; 4WD tours of the area are also offered (from $80 per half-day, including lunch).

There's **transport** to Jenolan Caves with Fantastic Aussie Tours (see p.211; 1hr 30min; $35; departs Katoomba 11.15am; departs Jenolan Caves 3.45pm), designed as an overnight rather than a day-return service; otherwise, the same company offers day-tours from Katoomba, as do several other operators (see "Listings", p.210), and there are also many tours from Sydney (see box, p.182).

South

Once you escape Sydney's uninspiring outer suburbs, the journey south is very enjoyable, offering two main choices. Staying **inland**, you're soon into the softly rolling hills of the **Southern Highlands**, dotted with old country towns such as **Berrima**, **Bowral** and **Bundanoon**, with access to a cluster of waterfall-strung national parks, notably the wild and windswept crags of **Morton National Park**. Taking the **coastal route** south out of Sydney, beyond Botany Bay and Port Hacking, the Princes Highway and the Illawarra railway hug the edge of the **Royal National Park** for more than 20km. The railway and the scenic Grand Pacific Drive (Route 68) then follow the coast to **Wollongong**. Between here and Nowra, the ocean beaches of the Leisure Coast are popular with local holidaymakers, while fishermen, windsurfers and yachtsmen gather at **Lake Illawarra**, a huge coastal lake near Port Kembla. A few kilometres further down the coast is the famous, and occasionally lethal, blowhole at **Kiama**.

Transport down south is good. The Southern Highlands are well served by a frequent train service between Sydney and Canberra stopping at Picton, Mittagong, Bowral, Moss Vale, Bundanoon and Goulburn. Priors (☏1800 816 234) run a once-daily (not Sat) bus service through the region from Campbelltown train station with stops at Mittagong, Bowral, Fitzroy Falls and Kangaroo Valley before continuing to the coast. Berrima Buslines provides a local bus service (☏02/4871 3211, ⓦwww.berrimabuslines.com.au). Down the coast, there's a frequent train service operating between Sydney and Nowra, stopping at most of the coastal locations detailed below. The main bus service is Premier Motor Service (☏13 34 10, ⓦwww.premierms.com.au), which stops at Wollongong and Kiama en route to Bega and Eden.

The Southern Highlands and the road to Canberra

Heading southwest out of Sydney out through Campbelltown along the speedy South Western Motorway (M5), you'll eventually find yourself on the Hume Highway bound for Goulburn and Canberra. It's a straightforward drive, but best broken by detours into the picturesque **Southern Highlands**, a favourite weekend retreat for Sydneysiders since the 1920s. The pretty Highlands towns are full of cafés, restaurants, antiques shops and secondhand bookstores, and there's an emerging wine industry too. The cooler-climate wines produced here are building a good reputation, and visiting the wineries – an excellent alternative to the better-known Hunter Valley – is a great way to enjoy the beautiful countryside of the area.

Southwest of Campbelltown, **Mount Annan Botanical Garden** and **Wirrimbirra Sanctuary** make appealing short stops. To get into the Highlands proper you'll need to continue to Mittagong, a base for accessing the limestone underworld of **Wombeyan Caves**. All true Australians know that the world's best ever batsman, Donald Bradman, grew up in **Bowral**, a short drive from historic **Berrima** with its ancient inn. **Bundanoon** sits on the edge of the wild Morton National Park, where **Fitzroy Falls** are a justified highlight. Further south, fabulous views are the main reward for visiting the Illawarra Fly **treetops walkway**, while the boardwalk at **Minnamurra** highlights the charms down at floor level. The last stop before the coast is **Kangaroo Valley**, another quaint and ancient little village, with some lovely kayaking through Shoalhaven Gorge.

Mount Annan Botanical Garden and Wirrimbirra Sanctuary

About 40km south of Parramatta, the Camden Valley Way heads west from the motorway to **CAMDEN** on the Nepean River, where John Macarthur pioneered the breeding of merino sheep in 1805. The town still has a rural feel and several well-preserved nineteenth-century buildings, the oldest of which dates from 1816. En route, you'll pass **Mount Annan Botanical Garden** (daily 10am–5pm; $9 per car; ⓦ www.rbgsyd.nsw.gov.au). The native-plant section of the Royal Botanic Gardens in Sydney, this outstanding collection of flora is the largest of its kind in Australia. Within the grounds, you can eat well at the idyllically sited *Gardens Restaurant* at outside tables surrounded by trees. A major attraction, it makes sense to book if you intend to dine (ⓣ 02/4647 1363); there's also a café in the park.

From Camden, Remembrance Drive passes through **Picton** and on to the **Wirrimbirra Sanctuary** at **Bargo**, 30km south of Camden (Tues–Sun 9.30am–4.30pm; free; ⓣ 02/4684 1112, ⓦ www.wirrimbirra.com.au), a peaceful bushland spot owned by the National Trust, with a field studies centre, a native-plant nursery, bushwalking trails and a visitor centre. You can stay over in the bunk-style cabins ($15 per person) with the opportunity of spotting wallabies, kangaroos, wombats, brush-tailed possums and goannas, along with 150 different species of birds in the wild. Without your own **transport**, you can get here by train from Sydney to Bargo and then walk a couple of kilometres.

Mittagong and Wombeyan Caves

Just over 100km south of Sydney, the small agricultural and tourist town of **MITTAGONG** is mostly visited on the way to the limestone, NPWS-run **Wombeyan Caves** (daily 9am–5.30pm), 65km west on a tortuously winding road. Take as long as you like in the self-guided Figtree Cave ($13), with its wild formations inventively lit; other caves are visited on tours ($16 each; 1hr–1hr 30min each), either individually or with the Explorer Pass ($28) which includes two tours and the Figtree Cave. There's a well-run **campsite** near the caves (ⓣ 02/4843 5976, ⓦ www.nationalparks.nsw.gov. au; camping $10 per person, cabins and cottages ⓢ).

Bowral and Berrima

Neighbouring **BOWRAL**, 6km southwest of Mittagong, is a busy, well-to-do town; its main strip, Bong Bong Street, is full of upmarket clothes and homeware shops and it has a good bookstore and a cinema. It was also the birthplace of cricket legend Don Bradman; cricket fans should check out the **Bradman Museum** (daily 10am–5pm; $12) on Jude Street, in an idyllic spot between a park and the well-used cricket oval and club. Inside, a history of the game's development in Australia is accompanied by great 1930s and 1940s films of "The Don", and a chance to try your hand at Bradman's childhood game using a golf ball and a stump as a bat, playing knock back against the brick base of a water tank. He claimed this as the foundation of his skills.

The picturesque village of **BERRIMA**, 7km west of Bowral, boasts a complement of well-preserved and restored old buildings, including the *Surveyor General Inn*, which has been serving beer since 1835. The **visitor centre** (daily 10am–4pm; ⓣ 02/4877 1505) is inside the 1838 sandstone **Courthouse Museum** (same hours; $7; ⓦ www.berrimacourthouse.org.au), on the corner of Argyle and Wiltshire streets, while across the road is the still-operational

Berrima Gaol, which once held the infamous bushranger Thunderbolt, and acted as an internment camp for POWs and immigrants in wartime; it also has the dubious distinction of being the first place in Australia to execute a woman, in 1841.

Bundanoon

Some 5km south of **Moss Vale** on the Old Hume Highway is the turn-off south to **BUNDANOON**, famous for its April celebration of its Scottish heritage with the annual Highland Games – Aussie-style. Bundanoon is in an attractive spot, set in hilly countryside scarred by deep gullies and with splendid views over the gorges and mountains of the huge **Morton National Park** (car fee $7), which extends east from Bundanoon to near Kangaroo Valley (see p.217).

You can start your explorations by setting off at sunset armed with a torch on an evening stroll to **Glow Worm Glen**; after dark the small sandstone grotto is transformed by the naturally flickering lights of these insects, and you may be lucky enough to see wombats along the way. It's a 25-minute walk from Bundanoon via the end of William Street, or an easy forty-minute signposted trek from Riverview Road in the national park. The national park, and Bundanoon, are great for **cycling**, with the long-established Ye Olde Bicycle Shoppe, 9 Church Street, near the railway station in Bundanoon, renting out bikes (Mon–Fri 9am–4.30pm, Sat & Sun 9am–5pm; $18.50 per hour, $28 half-day, $45 full day; T02/4883 6043).

Opposite the station, the cosy *Bundanoon Hotel* (W www.bundanoonhotel .com.au) is a good place to recover with a pint of stout and a filling meal after a cycling adventure, with plain, affordable **food** on offer in its *Thistle* carvery (lunch Wed–Sun, dinner Wed–Sat); you'll need to book ahead at weekends. **Accommodation** options in Bundanoon include the *Bundanoon Country Inn Motel*, ANZAC Parade (T02/4883 6068, W www.bundanoonmotel.com.au; ❹–❺), with great facilities. About 1km northeast is the ⚑ *Bundanoon YHA* on Railway Avenue (T02/4883 6010; camping $15.50, dorms $25, rooms ❸; book ahead), a spacious Edwardian-era guesthouse complete with open fireplaces, set in extensive grounds where you can also camp. A few metres away is the antiques-furnished *Tree Tops Country Guesthouse*, 101 Railway Ave (T02/4883 6372, W www.treetopsguesthouse.com.au; ❼–❽ including breakfast), which occupies a 1910 house; dinner is available.

Buderoo National Park and Minnamura Rainforest Centre

Leaving the Southern Highlands via Moss Vale, one route to the coast (see p.218) heads southwest past Fitzroy Falls to Kangaroo Valley and Berry, while a second initially follows the Illawarra Highway due east then cuts southeast at **Robertson**, 25km east of Moss Vale. This runs through **BUDDEROO NATIONAL PARK** past the impressive, fifty-metre **Carrington Falls**, 8km southeast of Robertson off Jamberoo Mountain Road, which can be accessed by a short bushwalk leading to lookout points over the waterfalls.

Some 6km further southwest, **Illawarra Fly**, 182 Knights Hill Rd (daily 9am–5pm; $19; W www.illawarrafly.com.au), gives you the chance to walk out on a massive 500m-long treetop walkway cantilevered out over the edge of the Illawarra Escarpment. On a fine day the views can seem never-ending, north and south along the coast, and down into the gumtrees below.

Continuing southwest, Jamberoo Mountain Road heads down the escarpment, twisting and turning until, when you feel you've reached the foothills, a turn-off leads to the **Minnamurra Rainforest Centre** (daily 9am–5pm; $11 per car; ☎02/4236 0469), which hugs the base of the escarpment. From the centre you can wander along a wheelchair-accessible elevated boardwalk (1.6km return; 30min–1hr; last entry 4pm) which winds through cabbage tree palms, staghorn ferns and impressive Illawarra fig trees with the distinctive call of whip birds and the undergrowth rustle of lyre birds for company. Midway along the boardwalk, a path (2.6km return; last entry 3pm) spurs off steeply uphill (quickly gaining 100m) to a platform with views to the delicate 25-metre **Upper Minnamurra Fall**. A second platform allows you to peer down the 50-metre lower fall as it cascades into a dark slot canyon.

From Minnamurra it is a further 17km west to coastal Kiama.

Fitzroy Falls and Kangaroo Valley

Nowra Road heads directly southeast from Moss Vale and after 15km reaches **Fitzroy Falls** (daily: Oct–April 9am–5.30pm, May–Sept 9am–5pm; parking $3), on the fringes of Morton National Park. A short boardwalk from the car park takes you to the falls, which plunge 80m into the valley below, with glorious views of the Yarrunga Valley beyond. The **NPWS visitor centre** (☎02/4887 7270) at the falls has a buffet-style café with a very pleasant outside deck, and can provide detailed information about the many walking tracks and scenic drives in the park.

From Fitzroy Falls, Kangaroo Valley Road winds steeply down 20km to **KANGAROO VALLEY**. Hidden between the lush dairy country of Nowra and the Highlands, the town is a popular base for walkers and canoeists, and is brimming with cafés, craft and gift shops, plus an imposing old character pub, *The Friendly Inn*.

Just over 1km west of the township, the road from Fitzroy Falls crosses the Kangaroo River on the picturesque 1898 **Hampden Suspension Bridge**, with its castellated turrets made from local sandstone. Lying to one side of the bridge, the **Pioneer Museum Park** (Fri–Mon: Nov–April 10am–4pm, May–Oct 11am–3pm; $4; ⓦwww.kangaroovalleymuseum.com) provides an insight into the origins of the area, in and around an 1850 homestead. The shop next door is the base for Kangaroo Valley Safaris (☎02/4465 1502, ⓦwww.kangaroovalleycanoes.com.au) who offer leisurely **self-guided kayak trips** along the placid Kangaroo River and between the escarpments of the Shoalhaven Gorge. Rates include basic instruction, maps, waterproof containers and a return bus trip so you only need to paddle downstream. Opt for a day-trip ($35–65 per person depending on kayak type) or an overnight trip ($85–130), camping beside the river. They also offer rental of tents ($40) and cooking stoves ($30).

Some of the same waters are also accessible on kayaks and canoes rented from the very pleasant *Kangaroo Valley Tourist Park* **campsite**, on Moss Vale Road (☎1300 559 977, ⓦwww.kvtouristpark.com.au), with camping ($11–13 per person), a bunkhouse ($20–25 per person) and en-suite timber cabins equipped with DVD and air-conditioning, sleeping from two to seven people (midweek ❸–❻, weekend ❺–❼). A kilometre east of Kangaroo Village, *Tall Trees B&B*, 8 Nugents Creek Rd (☎02/4465 1208, ⓦwww.talltreesbandb .com.au; midweek ❻, weekend ❼), is a home from home, with great views across the valley and hearty breakfasts. Self-contained accommodation in a studio or treehouse is also available (studio midweek $180, weekend $435 for two nights).

Of the many **cafés** in Kangaroo Valley, *Café Bella*, 151 Main Rd (Thurs–Sun; ☎02/4465 1660; BYO), stands out from the crowd with its relaxed, friendly feel, good-value breakfasts and delicious lunches. It also opens on Friday and Saturday evenings with a small but well chosen menu (mains $20–30). Alternatively, you can sit beneath a shady veranda and enjoy a cup of tea at *Jing Jo Café* **restaurant** by the Hampden Suspension Bridge, with a modern Australian daytime menu and Thai in the evening (Thurs–Mon; ☏02/4465 1314). A service station near the bridge sells **groceries**.

Bus access to Kangaroo Valley is with Priors (☏1800 816 234; not Sat) on their run from Campbelltown train station on the outskirts of Sydney through Bowral to Narooma on the coast. They stop at 5.25pm southbound and 10.45am northbound.

The Royal and Heathcote national parks

The **Royal National Park** (always open; $11 per car per 24hr) is a huge nature reserve right on Sydney's doorstep, only 36km south of the city. Established in 1879, it was the second national park in the world (after Yellowstone in the USA). The railway between Sydney and Wollongong marks its western border, and from the train the scenery is fantastic – streams, waterfalls, rock formations and rainforest flora fly past the window. If you want to explore more closely, get off at one of the stations along the way – Loftus, Engadine, Heathcote, Waterfall or Otford – all starting points for walking trails into the park. On the eastern side, from Jibbon Head to Garie Beach, the park falls away abruptly to the ocean, creating a spectacular coastline of steep cliffs broken here and there by creeks cascading into the sea and little coves with fine sandy beaches; the remains of **Aboriginal rock carvings** are the only traces of the original Dharawal people.

You can also drive in at various points: so long as you don't stop, cars are allowed right through the park without paying, exiting at **Waterfall** on the Princes Highway or **Stanwell Park** at the start of Grand Pacific Drive. Approaching the park from the north, stop 3km south of Loftus at the easy, concrete Bungoona Lookout **nature trail** (1km return; 20min; flat) with its panoramic views, or continue 1km to the **NPWS Visitor Centre** (daily 8.30am–4.30pm; ☏02/9542 0648, ⊛www.environment.nsw.gov.au), at tiny **Audley**. Here, beside the Hacking River you can rent a bike or canoe or just laze around with a picnic. Deeper into the park, on the ocean shore, **Wattamolla** and **Garie beaches** have good surfing waves; the two beaches are connected by a walking track. There are kiosks at Audley, Wattamolla and Garie Beach.

There's a small, very basic but secluded **YHA hostel** inside the park, 1km from Garie Beach (book in advance; key must be collected in advance; dorms $14), with solar lights and access to cold showers at Garie Beach. The **bushcamp** at North Era ($5 per person) requires a permit from the visitor centre; you'll often need to book full weeks in advance at weekends, and the permit can be posted out to you (which can take up to five days), or you can buy it before leaving Sydney at the NPWS centre at 110 George St (see p.178).

Heathcote National Park, across the Princes Highway from the Royal National Park, is much smaller and quieter. This is a serious bushwalkers' park with no roads and a ban on trail bikes. The best **train** station for the park is Waterfall, from where you can follow the fairly hilly **Bullawarring Track** (12km one-way; 5hr; moderate difficulty) north and join a later train from Heathcote. The track weaves through a variety of vegetation, including scribbly gums with their intriguing bark patterns, and spectacular gymea lilies with bright red flowers atop tall flowering spears in the spring. Along the path are several swimmable pools fed by Heathcote Creek – the carved sandstone of the **Kingfisher Pool** is the largest and most picturesque. The *Royal National Park Tourist Map* ($6.50 from NPWS) is invaluable for route finding.

There's a small, very basic 18-person **campsite** here (no drinking water; $5 per person), and another one at Mirang Pool (space for 12 people; $5 per person). Water is not guaranteed, and you'll need to book through the NPWS (Mon–Fri 10.30am–1.30pm; ☎02/9542 0683).

By car, you can reach the **picnic area** at **Woronora Dam** on the western edge of the park: turn east off the Princes Highway onto Woronora Road (free entry); parking available.

South down the coast

For a **scenic drive from Sydney** – bush, coast and cliff views and beautiful beaches – follow the Princes Highway south, exiting into the Royal National Park after Loftus onto Farnell Drive; the entry fee at the gate is waived if you are just driving through without stopping. The road through the national park emerges above the cliffs at **Otford**, beyond which runs **Lawrence Hargrave Drive** (Route 68), part of the newly dubbed **Grand Pacific Drive**, which ends south of Wollongong.

A couple of kilometres south of Otford is Bald Hill, a great viewpoint looking down the coast past the 665-metre-long Sea Cliff Bridge, which curls around the seacliffs. It's above **Stanwell Park** where you're likely to see the breath-taking sight of **hang-gliders** taking off. The Sydney Hang Gliding Centre (☎02/4294 4294, ⓦwww.hanggliding.com.au) offers tandem flights with an instructor ($195 during the week, $220 at weekends) and runs courses (from $275 per day).

By the time you get to **AUSTINMER**, 10km south of Bald Hill, you're at a break in the stunning cliffs and into some heavy surf territory. The down-to-earth town has a popular, very clean, patrolled surf beach that gets packed out on summer weekends.

THIRROUL, 2km south of Austinmer, is the spot where English novelist D.H. Lawrence wrote *Kangaroo* during his short Australian interlude in 1922 (the bungalow he stayed in is at 3 Craig St). The town and surrounding area are described in some depth in the novel, though he renamed the then-sleepy village Mullumbimby. Today, Thirroul is gradually being swallowed up by the suburban sprawl of Wollongong but makes a lively spot to stop for a coffee at the *Tin Shed*, 364 Lawrence Hargrave Drive, or a sophisticated but moderately priced dinner at *Samuels*, 382 Lawrence Hargrave Drive (☎02/4268 2244; closed Mon), which opens for lunch at weekends. At the southern end of Thirroul's beach, **Sandford Point** (labelled Bulli Point on maps) is a famous surfing break. A sixty-kilometre cycle track runs from Thirroul south along the coast through Wollongong to Lake Illawarra.

After Thirroul, Lawrence Hargrave Drive joins up with the Princes Highway going south into Wollongong (Route 60) or heading northwest, uphill to a section of the forested **Illawarra Escarpment** and the **Bulli Pass**. There are fantastic views from the Bulli Lookout, which has its own café, and further towards Sydney at the appropriately named **Sublime Point Lookout**. You can explore the escarpment using the **walking tracks** that start from the lookouts, and there's an extensive part of the **Illawarra Escarpment State Recreation Area**, about 10km west of Wollongong's city centre on Mount Kembla and Mount Keira.

Wollongong

Although it's New South Wales' third-largest city, **WOLLONGONG** has more of a country-town feel; the students of Wollongong University give it extra life in term time and it also enjoys a big dose of surf culture as the city centre is set right on the ocean. Some 80km south of Sydney, it's essentially a working-class industrial centre – Australia's largest steelworks at nearby Port Kembla looms unattractively over Wollongong City Beach – but the **Illawarra Escarpment** (see p.218), rising dramatically beyond the city, provides a lush backdrop.

There's not much to see in the **city centre** itself (concentrated between Wollongong train station and the beach), which has been swallowed up by a giant shopping mall on **Crown Street**, but the regional art centre, the **Wollongong City Gallery**, on the corner of Kembla and Burelli streets (Tues–Fri 10am–5pm, Sat & Sun noon–4pm; free), shows changing exhibitions and has a permanent collection with an emphasis on contemporary Aboriginal and colonial Illawarra artists. If you continue east down Crown Street and cross Marine Drive, you'll hit **Wollongong City Beach**, a surf beach that stretches over 2km to the south. One of the most pleasant activities is simply wandering along the coastal **City Walk** which starts at the eastern end of Crown Street and runs 2km north to **North Wollongong Beach**. The walk passes Flagstaff Point, a grassy headland overlooking the lovely **Wollongong Harbour**, with its fishing fleet, fish market, seafood restaurants, and a picturesque nineteenth-century lighthouse on the breakwater. Around the middle of October, the **Viva la Gong festival** (Ⓦ www.vivalagongfestival.org) livens up the city with a sculpture exhibition along the seafront, and events every night, including circus acts, dance and live music.

Away from the centre, science and religion provide the most interest. Just over 2km north of the city centre, off Grand Pacific Drive, is the $6-million **Science Centre**, Squires Way (daily 10am–4pm; $10; Ⓦ http://sciencecentre.uow.edu .au); attractions include the state's best **planetarium** (shows daily at noon & 3pm; 30min; laser concert Sat, Sun & school holidays at 1pm) and over a hundred themed kid-friendly, hands-on exhibits.

Some 8km south of the centre, the vast **Nan Tien Buddhist Temple**, Berkeley Road, Berkeley (Tues–Sun & public holidays 9am–4pm; free; Ⓦ www .nantien.org.au), is the largest in Australia. The Fo Guang Shan Buddhists welcome visitors to the temple (Tues–Sun 9am–5pm) and offer a good-value $9 vegetarian lunch, weekend meditation and Buddhist activity retreats in peaceful and surprisingly upmarket guesthouse accommodation (Ⓣ 02/4272 0500; ❺). The temple is well signposted off the Princes Highway, and is a twenty-minute walk from the Unanderra CityRail train station, two stops south of Wollongong.

Practicalities

The best and cheapest way to get to Wollongong from Sydney by public transport is the frequent **train** from Central Station, which hugs the coast and stops at most of the small towns en route; Wollongong station is right in the centre just off Crown Street. Premier Motor Service (see p.85) has two **bus** services a day in each direction on its Sydney–Melbourne run, stopping at the junction of Keira and Campbell streets. **Wollongong Tourist Information Centre**, near the mall at 93 Crown St (Mon–Fri 9am–5pm, Sat 9am–4pm, Sun 10am–4pm; Ⓣ 02/4227 5545, Ⓦ www.tourismwollongong.com), can advise on **accommodation**; there's nowhere central to camp but there are **caravan parks**.

Wollongong isn't renowned for its **food**, through there are a couple of highlights, and a few cafés on Crown Street near the tourist information centre.

Accommodation

Boat Harbour Motel Corner of Campbell St and Wilson St ℗02/4228 9166, ⓦwww.boatharbour -motel.com.au. Large, central motel with comfortable and spacious rooms with balconies, some with sea views. Restaurant on site. ❺, seaview ❻

Corrimal Beach Tourist Park Lake Parade, Corrimal, 6km north ℗02/4285 5688, ⓦhttp://touristparks.wollongong.nsw.gov.au. Just back from the beach at the mouth of Towradgi Lagoon, with good facilities. Sites $20–25, en-suite cabins ❹, beachside ❺

Ibis 72 Market St ℗02/4223 6000, ⓦwww .accorhotels.com.au. Simple, modern three-star hotel in the centre of town with phone, cable TV and in-room internet access. ❺

Novotel Northbeach 2–14 Cliff Rd, North Wollongong ℗02/4224 3111, ⓦwww.novotelnorthbeach .com.au. Upmarket four-and-a-half-star hotel with water views, pool, gym, restaurant and bars. Wollongong's finest. ❽

YHA Wollongong 75–79 Keira St, near the intersection with Smith St ℗02/4229 1132, ⓔwollongong@yhansw.org.au. This modern hostel with central alfresco courtyard shares a building with a student halls of residence. Rooms have en-suite facilities and shared balconies. Dorms $30, rooms ❹

Eating and drinking

Caveau 122 Keira St ℗02/4226 4855. Wollongong's finest dining is French, immaculately presented and eased down with superb old-world wines. Lunch: two courses plus coffee for $45. Dinner: two courses for $58, 3 for $72 and a 7-course tasting for $90. Licensed. Lunch Thurs & Fri, dinner Tues–Sat.

Diggies 1 Clift Rd, North Beach ℗02/4226 2688. A beachside location, top coffee and excellent café fare at moderate prices make this a very popular place, especially for weekend brunch. There's food cooked in the same kitchen, similar views from the

outdoor tables and much lower prices from the kiosk next door. Breakfast and lunch daily, plus dinner Fri & Sat in summer.

Five Islands Brewing Company Crown St, by the beachside Entertainment Centre ℗02/ 4220 2854. Popular waterfront bar where you can try at least ten delicious and varied ales with an imaginative bar menu.

Mylan 193 Keira St ℗02/4228 1588. Fresh ingredients, modest prices and a lively atmosphere make this Vietnamese place a great spot for lunch or dinner. BYO. Closed Sun.

Kiama and around

Of the coastal resorts south of Sydney, **KIAMA**, 35km south of Wollongong, is probably the most attractive. A large resort and fishing town, Kiama is famous for its star attraction, the **Blowhole**, a five-minute walk from the **train station** on Blowhole Point. Stemming from a natural fault in the cliffs, the Blowhole explodes into a waterspout when a wave hits with sufficient force. It's impressive, but also potentially dangerous: freak waves can be thrown over 60m into the air and have swept several over-curious bystanders into the raging sea – so stand well back. The **visitor centre**, nearby on Blowhole Point Road (daily 9am–5pm; ℗02/4232 3322, ⓦwww.kiama.com.au), books accommodation and supplies details of other local attractions such as **Cathedral Rocks**, a few kilometres to the north, whose rocky outcrops drop abruptly to the ocean.

There's an abundance of **accommodation** (mostly motels) along the Princes Highway, and a few places downtown. Budget alternatives include the rather basic

Coverage of towns along the coast further south continues on p.225.

Kiama Backpackers, 31 Bong Bong St (☎02/4233 1881, ⓔkiamabackpackers @hotmail.com; dorms $20, rooms ❷), which is next to the train station and right near the beach, though it sometimes closes down in winter. Next door, the *Grand Hotel*, on the corner of Manning and Bong Bong streets (☎02/4232 1037; ❸), is one of Kiama's oldest hotels, with shared-bath rooms; the pub restaurant serves decent filling meals at lunch and dinner daily. There's convenient **camping** right in town at *Surf Beach Holiday Park*, Bourrool St (☎02/4232 1791, ⓦwww.kiama .net/holiday; camping $26, on-site vans $90, cabins ❻); and swankier accommodation at *Kiama Harbour Cabins*, Blowhole Point Road (☎1800 823 824, ⓦwww .kiama.net/holiday/blowhole; en-suite cabins ❼), with great views of the harbour and coast, but a two-night minimum at weekends.

There are plenty of **places to eat** in Kiama – Thai, Chinese and Italian restaurants and lots of cafés – with a concentration on Manning and Terralong streets. The best is *55 on Collins*, 55 Collins St (☎02/4232 2811; breakfast and lunch daily; dinner Thurs–Sat), which is casual enough for coffee and cake in the daytime and serves very good contemporary cuisine in the evening (mains around $30).

Gerringong, 15km south of Kiama, is wonderfully scenic, set against green hills with glorious sweeping views. There's little to do, but you can eat well at *Gerringong Deli & Café* on Fern Street, the best café in town, with divine fish and chips and gourmet burgers, or try *Perfect Break Vegetarian Café*, just along the street, for outstanding veggie food such as nachos and lentil burgers, washed down with freshly squeezed fruit juice.

Seven Mile Beach, 4km south of Gerringong, is beautiful: you can camp beside the beach at *Seven Mile Beach Holiday Park* (☎02/4234 1340, ⓦwww .kiamacoast.com.au; camping $29–35, cabins ❹, safari tents ❺, en-suite cabins ❻), located beside Crooked River almost 4km south of Gerringong, but with cafés and a restaurant close by.

Travel details

Sydney is very much the centre of the Australian transport network, and you can get to virtually anywhere in the country from here on a variety of competing services. The following list represents a minimum; as well as the dedicated services listed below, many places will also be served by long-distance services stopping en route.

Trains

Sydney to: Adelaide (Indian Pacific; Sat & Wed 2.55pm; 24hr 10min); Brisbane (2 daily; 14hr 10min); Broken Hill (1 daily; 15hr); Canberra (2 daily; 4hr 15min); Dubbo (2 daily; 6hr 30min); Goulburn (4 daily; 2hr 45min); Katoomba (29 daily; 2hr 10min); Maitland (6 daily; 2hr 45min); Melbourne (2 daily; 11hr; plus daily bus/train Speedlink via Albury; 12–13hr); Murwillumbah (3 daily; 13hr 45min); Newcastle (28 daily; 2hr 45min); Perth (Indian Pacific; Sat & Wed 2.55pm; 67hr 45min); Richmond (14 daily; 2hr); Windsor (14 daily; 1hr 45min); Wollongong (32 daily; 1hr 30min).

Buses

Sydney to: Adelaide (3 daily; 22hr); Albury (4 daily; 8hr 30min); Armidale (2 daily; 8hr 30min); Batemans Bay (2 daily; 5hr 20min); Bathurst (1 daily; 3hr 15min); Bega (2 daily; 8hr); Brisbane (9 daily; 15–17hr, with connections to Cairns and Darwin); Broken Hill (1 daily; 15hr 40min); Byron Bay (7 daily; 13hr 15min); Canberra (11–14 daily; 4hr); Cessnock (1 daily; 2hr 30min); Coffs Harbour (7 daily; 9hr); Eden (2 daily; 8hr 30min–9hr 30min); Forster (1 daily; 6hr); Glen Innes (2 daily; 10hr); Grafton (3 daily; 10hr); Melbourne (6 daily; 12–18hr); Mildura (3 daily; 16hr); Mittagong (4 daily; 2hr 20min); Moss Vale (1 daily; 2hr

45min); Muswellbrook (1 daily; 3hr 30min); Narooma (2 daily; 8hr); Newcastle (8 daily; 3hr); Nowra (2 daily; 3hr–4hr 20min); Orange (1 daily; 4hr 15min); Perth (2–3 daily; 52–56hr); Port Macquarie (6 daily; 7hr); Port Stephens (1 daily; 3hr); Scone (1 daily; 6hr); Tamworth (1 daily; 7hr); Taree (2 daily; 6hr 30min); Tenterfield (1 daily; 12hr).

Flights

Sydney to: Adelaide (16 daily; 2hr 10min); Albury (8 daily; 1hr 20min); Alice Springs (1 daily; 3hr 15min); Armidale (4 daily; 1hr 10min); Ballina (4–7 daily; 1hr 40min); Bathurst (3 daily Mon–Fri; 40min); Bourke (1 daily except Sat; 3hr 10min); Brisbane (42 daily; 1hr 30min); Broken Hill (1 daily; 1hr 50min); Cairns (8 daily; 3hr 10min); Canberra (20–25 daily; 45min); Cobar (2 daily except Sat; 2hr 25min); Coffs Harbour (7 daily; 1hr 15min); Cooma (1–2 daily; 1hr); Darwin (1 daily; 4hr 25min); Dubbo (5–7 daily Mon–Fri; 1hr); Fraser Coast (1–2 daily; 1hr 40min); Gold Coast (17 daily; 1hr 20min); Grafton (1 daily; 2hr); Griffith (3–4 daily; 1hr 25min); Hamilton Island (2 daily; 2hr 25min); Hobart (8 daily; 1hr 50min); Inverell (1–2 daily; 1hr 55min); Launceston (2 daily; 1hr 40min); Lismore (3–4 daily; 1hr 35min); Lord Howe Island (1 daily; 1hr 50min); Melbourne (58 daily; 1hr 20min); Merimbula (3 daily; 1hr 35min); Mildura (1 daily; 2hr 40min); Moruya (2 daily; 50min); Mudgee (2 daily Mon–Fri, 1 daily Sat & Sun; 1hr); Narrandera (2 daily; 1hr 30min); Newcastle (1 daily except Sun; 40min); Norfolk Island (4 weekly; 2hr 20min); Orange (3–4 daily; 45min); Parkes (2–3 daily; 1hr); Perth (8 daily; 4hr 50min); Port Macquarie (6 daily; 1hr); Port Stephens (Mon–Fri 1 daily; 1hr); Prosperine (1 daily; 2hr 30min); Rockhampton (1 daily; 2hr); Sunshine Coast (4 daily; 1hr 30min); Tamworth (4 daily; 1hr); Taree (2–3 daily; 50min); Townsville (1 daily; 2hr 40min); Uluru (2 daily; 3hr 30min); Wagga Wagga (3–6 daily; 1hr 10min).

2

Coastal New South Wales and the ACT

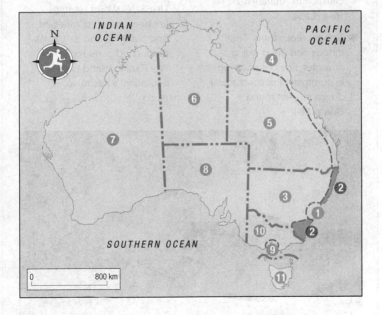

Highlights

✳ **New Parliament House, Canberra** The stunning angular design of the New Parliament House is matched by its interior, which shows contemporary Australian design at its best. See p.234

✳ **Australian War Memorial** Located near the heart of Canberra, this moving memorial commemorates Australia's war dead from Gallipoli to Afghanistan. See p.236

✳ **Snowy Mountains** Cosy lodges and good skiing in winter, fine bushwalking in summer, plus spectacular drives all year round. See p.254

✳ **Bellingen** Arty little town in the beautiful Bellinger Valley where everyone has a smile on their face – take a lazy canoe trip, drink great coffee at the enticing cafés and soak up the good vibes. See p.269

✳ **Byron Bay** Hippie-Chic Mecca with 30km of sandy beaches. See p.280

✳ **Lord Howe Island** On the UNESCO World Heritage list because of its rare bird and plant life and its virtually untouched coral reef, this tiny Pacific island is an ecotourist's paradise. See p.291

▲ Lagoon Beach, Lord Howe Island

Coastal New South Wales and the ACT

New South Wales is Australia's premier state in more ways than one. The oldest of the six states, and also the most densely populated, its 6.7 million residents make up a third of the country's population. The vast majority occupy the urban and suburban sprawl which straggles along the state's thousand-plus kilometres of **Pacific coastline**, and the consistently mild climate and many beaches draw a fairly constant stream of visitors, especially during the summer holiday season, when thousands of Australians descend on the coast to enjoy the extensive surf beaches and other oceanside attractions.

South of Sydney, there's a string of low-key family resorts and fishing ports, good for watersports and idle pottering. To the **north** the climate gradually

National parks in New South Wales

The **National Parks and Wildlife Service (NPWS)** charges **entrance fees** at many of its most popular parks – usually $7–11 a day per vehicle (often on an honour system; bring plenty of coins). If you intend to "go bush" a lot in New South Wales you can buy an **annual pass** for $65, which includes all parks except Kosciuszko. Remember that the pass is vehicle specific and can't be transferred.

Because of its popularity as a skiing destination, entrance to Kosciuszko is a steep $27 per car per day in winter and $16 per car per day in summer – if you plan on spending any length of time here, or are going to visit other parks as well, consider the $190 annual pass which covers entry to all parks, including Kosciuszko. Passes can be bought at NPWS offices and some park entry-stations, over the phone using a credit card (☎02/9585 6068 or 1300 361 967) or online (⊛www.environment.nsw .gov.au/nationalparks; expect 5–10 working days for delivery).

You can **camp** in most national parks. Bushcamping is generally free, but where there is a ranger station and a designated campsite with facilities, fees are charged, usually $10–14 per day. If the amenities are of a high standard, including hot showers and the like, or if the spot is just plain popular, fees can be as high as $25 per tent. There are often electric or gas barbecues on campsites, but you'll need a fuel stove for hard-core bushcamping. Open **fires** are banned in most parks and forbidden everywhere on days when there is high danger of fire – it's worth checking the NPWS for details of any current bushfires and park closures before you visit.

QUEENSLAND

Coolangatta
Tweed Heads
Woodenbong
Murwillumbah
Kyogle
Nimbin
Byron Bay
Bald Rock
Lismore
Lennox Head
Casino
Ballina
Dumaresq
Tenterfield
Evans Head
Mungindi
Moree
Yamba
Warialda
Emmaville
GWYDIR HWY
Glen Innes
Grafton
Bingara
Inverell
Tingha
Ben Lomond
Guyra
NEW ENGLAND NP
Woolgoolga
Wee Waa
Narrabri
Dorrigo
Coffs Harbour
Mylestom
Walgett
Manilla
Uralla
Armidale
Bellingen
Bowraville
Nambucca Heads
Maclean
WARRUMBUNGLES
Gunnedah
Walcha
Coonabarabran
Tamworth
Kempsey
Crescent Head
Nundle
Wauchope
Port Macquarie
Quirindi
Crowdy Head
Gilgandra
Coolah
Murrurundi
BARRINGTON TOPS NP
Wingham
Merriwa
Scone
Gloucester
Taree
Dubbo
Gulgong
Muswellbrook
Forster-Tuncurry
Wallis Lake
Bulahdelah
Seal Rocks
Mudgee
Singleton
Myall Lake
Hunter
Port Stephens
Maitland
Nelson Bay
Cessnock
Parkes
Newcastle
Forbes
Orange
Bathurst
Lithgow
0   3 km
Cowra
Katoomba
Lord Howe Island
Camden
Picton
Sydney
Young
Bargo
SOUTH PACIFIC OCEAN
Boorowa
Crookwell
Bowral
Wollongong
Moss Vale
Robertson
Bundanoon
Kiama
Cootamundra
Berry
Gundagai
Yass
Goulburn
0   3 km
Tumut
MORTON NP
Jervis Bay
BOODEREE NP
Yarrangobilly Caves
CANBERRA
Queanbeyan
Ulladulla
ACT
Braidwood
Tharwa
Norfolk Island
Tumbarumba
NAMADGI NP
Batemans Bay
DEUA NP
KOSCIUSZKO NP
Cooma
Narooma
Thredbo
WADBILLIGA NP
Tilba Tilba
Jindabyne
Bermagui
Mt Kosciuszko (2228m)
Bega
Tathra
Candelo
Merimbula
Bombala
Eden
N
BEN BOYD NP
VICTORIA
0   100 km

COASTAL NEW SOUTH WALES

becomes warmer, and the coastline more popular – the series of big resorts up here includes **Port Macquarie** and **Coffs Harbour** – but there are plenty of tiny national parks and inland towns where you can escape it all. One of the most enjoyable beach resorts in Australia is **Byron Bay**, chic these days, but still retaining something of its slightly offbeat, alternative appeal, radiating from the thriving hippie communes of the lush, hilly **North Coast Hinterland**.

Just over 280km southwest of Sydney is the **Australian Capital Territory (ACT)**, which was carved out of New South Wales at the beginning of the twentieth century as an independent base for the new national capital. While **Canberra** struggles to shed its dull image, it is the principal gateway to the **Snowy Mountains**, where the Great Dividing Range builds to a crescendo at **Mount Kosciuszko** (Australia's highest at 2228m), which offer skiing in winter and glorious hiking in summer.

Also included in this chapter are the Pacific islands far off the north coast of New South Wales: subtropical **Lord Howe Island**, 700km northeast of Sydney, and **Norfolk Island**, 900km further northeast and actually closer to New Zealand, inhabited by the descendants of the *Bounty* mutineers.

Australian Capital Territory

The first European squatters settled in the valleys and plains north of the Snowy Mountains in the 1820s, though until 1900 this remained a remote rural area. When the Australian colonies united in the **Commonwealth of Australia** in 1901, a capital city had to be chosen, with Melbourne and Sydney the two obvious and eager rivals. After much wrangling, and partly in order to avoid having to decide on one of the two, it was agreed to establish a brand-new capital instead. In 1909, Limestone Plains, south of Yass, was chosen out of several possible sites as the future seat of the Australian government. An area of 2368 square kilometres was excised from the state of New South Wales and named the **Australian Capital Territory**, or **ACT**. The name for the future capital was supposedly taken from the language of local Aborigines: **Canberra** – the meeting place.

Canberra is situated on a high plain (600m above sea level) giving it a predominantly dry, sunny climate but with often chilly winters.

Canberra

In 1912 **Walter Burley Griffin**, an American landscape architect from Chicago, won the international competition for the design of the future Australian capital, **CANBERRA**. His plan envisaged a garden city for about 25,000 people based in five main centres, each with separate city functions, located on three axes: land, water and municipal. Roads were to be in concentric circles, with arcs linking the radiating design. Construction started in 1913, but political squabbling and the effects of World War I, the Depression and World War II prevented any real progress being made until 1958, when growth began in earnest. In 1963 the Molonglo River was dammed to form long, artificial **Lake Burley Griffin**; the city centre, **Civic**, coalesced along the north shore to face **parliamentary buildings** to the south; while a host of outlying **satellite suburbs**, each connected to Civic by a main road cutting through the intervening bushland, took shape. The population grew rapidly, from fifteen thousand in 1947 to over three hundred thousand today, completely outstripping Burley Griffin's original estimates – though Canberra's decentralized design means that the city never feels crowded.

Being such an overtly planned place populated by civil servants and politicians, Canberra is in many ways a city in search of a soul: while there are all the galleries, museums and attractions that there should be, many seem to exist simply because it would be ridiculous to have omitted them from a

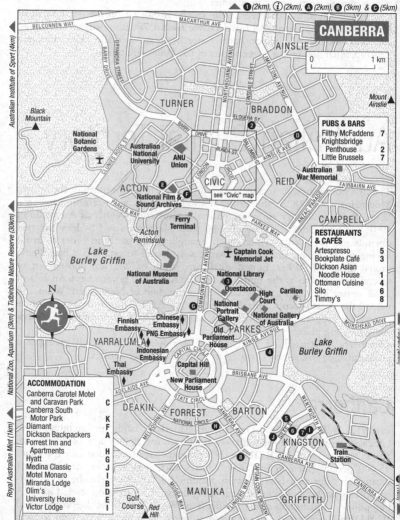

▲ **①** (2km), **ⓘ** (2km), **Ⓐ** (2km), **Ⓑ** (3km) & **Ⓒ** (5km)

CANBERRA

0 _____ 1 km

PUBS & BARS
Filthy McFaddens 7
Knightsbridge
  Penthouse 2
Little Brussels 7

RESTAURANTS & CAFÉS
Artespresso 5
Bookplate Café 3
Dickson Asian
  Noodle House 1
Ottoman Cuisine 4
Silo 6
Timmy's 8

ACCOMMODATION
Canberra Carotel Motel
  and Caravan Park C
Canberra South
  Motor Park K
Diamant F
Dickson Backpackers A
Forrest Inn and
  Apartments H
Hyatt G
Medina Classic J
Motel Monaro I
Miranda Lodge B
Olim's D
University House E
Victor Lodge I

national capital. Still, several key sights definitely justify staying a couple of nights, particularly the **War Memorial**, the extraordinary, partly subterranean **Parliament House**, the **National Gallery** and the **National Botanic Gardens**. With so much of the city being dotted with trees, visiting the bush might seem a bit pointless, but the **Brindabella Ranges** and the **Namadgi National Park** on the outskirts definitely warrant a short visit.

Canberra's **nightlife** – in term time at least – is alive and kicking. The two universities here (and the Duntroon Military Academy) mean there's a large and lively **student population** (good news for those who have student cards, as most attractions offer hefty discounts), and the city is also said to have more **restaurants** per capita than any other in Australia, which is saying something. Canberra also holds the dubious title of Australia's **porn capital**, due to its liberal licensing laws, which legalize and regulate the sex industry.

Arrival and information

Canberra's **airport**, 7km east of the city, handles domestic flights only. The Airliner Shuttle bus ($9 one-way, $15 return; ☎02/6299 3722, ⓦwww.airliner .com.au) runs from the airport to Civic every thirty minutes from about 6.30am to 7pm Monday to Friday, and 10am to 6pm at weekends. The **train station** is located 2km southeast of the centre, on Wentworth Avenue in Kingston. The one-way fare from Sydney is around $40. Bus #8 (#980 at weekends) can get you to Civic; Kingston accommodation is a short walk (or taxi ride) away. The **long-distance bus terminal** is in Civic at the **Jolimont Centre**, 65–67 Northbourne Ave; the centre has **tourist information** (with free direct telephone line to the main visitor centre), **ticket booking desks** for tours, trains and buses, and an internet kiosk.

The main **visitor centre** is inconveniently located 3km north of the centre at 330 Northbourne Ave (Mon–Fri 9am–5pm, Sat & Sun 9am–4pm; ☎1300/733 228, ⓦwww.visitcanberra.com.au) – it's on the #4 and #5 bus routes (weekends #932 and others).

City transport

With Canberra's sights so spread out, you'd have to be very enthusiastic to consider walking everywhere. A good option is to rent a **bike** and take advantage of the city's excellent network of cycle paths (see "Listings", p.240); city buses have bike-racks on the front for when you get tired.

If you're driving, make sure you carry a good-quality **map** – Canberra's baffling concentric street plan can turn navigating the city's roads into a Kafka-esque nightmare. You typically pay $1.20 an hour for **parking** in Civic, or head for the Canberra Centre parking building, accessed off Ballumbir Street.

City buses run by Action (☎13 17 10, ⓦwww.action.act.gov.au) operate daily from around 6.30am to 8pm or later, though weekend services are greatly reduced. Almost all services pass through the **City Bus Interchange** in Civic, a set of open-air bays around the eastern end of Alinga Street. **Tickets** are available from drivers, and cost $3 for a single journey (with transfers available), $4.10 for an off-peak pass (valid Mon–Fri 9am–4.30pm and after 6pm, and all weekend) and $6.60 for an all-day pass. These two passes, plus bulk tickets (ten rides for $22) and weekly passes are also available from most newsagents. A more expensive option is the **Explorer Bus** (☎0418/455 099, ⓦwww.canberradaytours.com .au), which circuits the major sights around five times a day, with a pick-up from central accommodation. Go for a stay-on-the-bus sightseeing tour (1hr; $15) or a hop-on-hop-off day pass ($35).

Activities around Canberra

Driving around Canberra gives a pretty skewed impression of its layout, and it is a whole lot more pleasant seeing it from the waters of Lake Burley Griffin on a **lake cruise** (daily 10.30am, 1.30pm & 2.30pm, plus Sat & Sun 11.30am & 3.30pm; $13; ☎0419 418 846, ⊛www.lakecruises.com.au) from the Ferry Terminal less than 1km southwest of Civic.

Even better is the aerial view from the ever-popular sunrise **hot-air ballooning** trips with Dawn Drifters (☎02/6285 4450, ⊛www.dawndrifters.com.au). An hour-long flight costs $250 (weekends $300) and you can add in a champagne breakfast for $22.

Accommodation

Most of Canberra's **accommodation** is located either in Civic or south of the lake at Kingston, both on bus routes and within striking distance of sights and places to eat. **Rates** fall at weekends, when the city empties, but hotel rooms can become scarce during big **conferences**, which can happen at any time through the year.

If you have a vehicle it's better to stay outside Civic where **parking** is easier and cheaper.

Hotels, motels and guesthouses

Diamant 15 Edinburgh Ave, Civic ☎02/6175 2222, ⊛www.diamant.com.au. Bright sofas around an exposed fire in the lobby set the tone for this classy 80-room boutique hotel fashioned from former public servants' accommodation. The designer landscape gardens, very good coffee bar and excellent restaurant make this a haven in the heart of the city, but the standard rooms are small, so upgrade if possible. Standard and deluxe ❼, premiere ❽

Forrest Inn and Apartments 30 National Circuit, Forrest ☎02/6295 3433, ⊛www.forrestinn.com .au. Next to the pretty Serbian church, this modern, clean and clinical motel is lacking in atmosphere, but is professionally run. Restaurant and bar on site. Bus #3 & #6 (#935 at weekends). ❻

Hyatt Commonwealth Ave, Yarralumla ☎02/6270 1234, ⊛www.canberra.park.hyatt.com. One of the most stylish (and expensive) hotels in Canberra, set amongst lawn and gardens in a complex of low-set 1930s buildings. Rates from $280 at weekends, more midweek. ❾

Medina Classic 11 Giles St, Kingston ☎02/6239 8100, ⊛www.medina.com.au. Tasteful, upmarket one-, two- and three-bedroom, self-catering serviced apartments with fully equipped kitchens (except for a couple of smaller apartments). Facilities include laundry, swimming pool, spa and undercover parking; bike rental available. Popular with families, and staff are friendly. Bus #4 or #5 (weekends #938). Internet deals. ❼

Miranda Lodge 524 Northbourne Ave, Downer, 4km north ☎02/6249 8038, ⊛www .mirandalodge.com.au. Good, non-smoking B&B with off-street parking and en-suite rooms with TV and fridge (some also have spa baths). Bus #39 (#939 at weekends). ❺

Motel Monaro 27 Dawes St, Kingston ☎02/6295 2111, ⊛www.motelmonaro.bestwestern.com.au. Next door to Victor Lodge (see opposite) and run by the same management, this 1970s motel has clean and tidy, smallish rooms equipped with microwave, kettle, hairdryer and TV. ❻

Olim's Corner of Ainslie Ave and Limestone Ave, Braddon ☎02/6248 5511, ⊛www.olimshotel.com. Close to the War Memorial, this is one of Canberra's cheaper "real" hotels, with a range of rooms in the older, National Trust-listed main building, and modern, self-contained apartments in a newer wing. Definitely needs to be booked ahead. Bus #2 or #3 (weekends #931). Heritage rooms ❺, newer rooms ❻

Quest Canberra 28 West Row, Civic ☎02/6243 2222, ⊛www.questapartments.com.au. Smart, self-contained apartments in the city centre, though kitchens in the cheaper Studio rooms are fairly basic. ❼

University House 1 Balmain Crescent, Acton, 1km southeast of Civic ☎1800/814 864, ⊛www.anu.edu.au/unihouse. Excellent-value 100-room hotel run by the Australian National University on the edge of their huge, semi-rural campus, just a short way from the National Film Archive. Very popular with conference delegates and visiting lecturers – book ahead. Bus #3. ❻

Hostels

Canberra City YHA 7 Akuna St, Civic ☏ 02/6248 9155, ✉ canberracity@yhansw.org.au. This cavernous, organized hostel is located right in the heart of Civic and comes with basement pool, spa and sauna, rooftop BBQ deck, laundry, internet café, TV, lockers in every room and 24hr check-in Dorms $30, rooms ❹–❻

Dickson Backpackers 4/14 Woolley St, Dickson, 4km north of Civic ☏ 02/6262 9922 or 1300 734 911, ⓦ www.dicksonbackpackers.com.au. Clean, comfortable and modern, if a little clinical, hostel inconveniently sited away from Civic and the main sights but on a high-frequency bus route (#2, #39 and others). Facilities include a/c, broadband internet, bike hire and games area. Dorms $35, rooms ❹

Victor Lodge 29 Dawes St, Kingston, 4km southwest of Civic ☏ 02/6295 7777, ⓦ www.victorlodge.com.au. Small, friendly and very popular family-run hostel-cum-guesthouse, situated close to lots of good restaurants. The four-bunk dorms are clean and bright, while the shared-bath rooms are small and neat. A buffet continental breakfast is included, and facilities extend to a well-equipped kitchen and BBQ area, laundry, TV room, internet access and wi-fi and bike rental ($20 per day). Bus #4, #5 or #8 (weekends #938). Dorms $33, rooms ❻

Camping and caravan parks

Canberra Carotel Motel and Caravan Park Federal Highway, Watson, 7km north of Civic ☏ 02/6241 1377, ⓦ www.carotel.com.au. Caravan park with a swimming pool and café, plus camping space and assorted cabins and motel rooms. Bus #36. Camping $23 per site, cabins and rooms ❹–❻

Canberra South Motor Park Canberra Ave, Symonstone, 4km southeast of Parliament ☏ 02/6280 6176, ⓦ www.csmp.net.au. Well-equipped park on a little creek with a/c options and en-suite cabins. Camping $28 per site, cabins and motel rooms ❹

The City

North of Lake Burley Griffin, Civic's shops, restaurants, cafés and pubs sit immediately west of the **Australian National University (ANU)**, whose grounds house the National Film and Sound Archive. This in turn borders the lakeside **National Museum of Australia**, the **National Botanic Gardens** and the flanks of 806-metre-high **Black Mountain**, topped by its distinctive tower. East of Civic is one of Canberra's key sights, the **Australian War Memorial**.

South of the lake, the main landmark is **Parliament House**, dug into the top of Capital Hill. This looks lakewards over the **old Parliament House**, and a clutch of cultural institutions, housed in architecturally distinctive buildings: the **National Library**, **Questacon** (the National Science and Technology Centre), the **National Gallery**, the **National Portrait Gallery** and the **High Court**. Most of the city's foreign **embassies** – intended to resemble the vernacular architecture of their home countries – cluster around Yarralumla and Forrest, on the far side of Capital Hill.

Civic and around

The commercial heart of Canberra is known as **Civic**, occupying a series of concentric streets between London Circuit and the huge **Canberra Centre** shopping mall. Though you may stay in Civic, and will almost certainly visit the cafés, restaurants and bars, it is not a place to come for the sights. One exception is the **Canberra Museum and Gallery**, Civic Square (Tues–Fri 10am–5pm, Sat & Sun noon–5pm; free; ⓦ www.museumsandgalleries.act.gov.au), which contains good material on social history, and the **Nolan Collection**, where you'll find paintings by renowned Australian artist Sidney Nolan.

The area immediately west of Civic is filled by the green and spacious **ANU (Australian National University)** campus. Here, on McCoy Circuit, the **National Film and Sound Archive** (Mon–Fri 9am–5pm, Sat & Sun

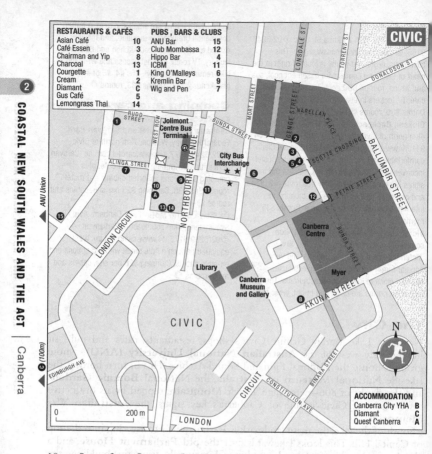

RESTAURANTS & CAFÉS
Asian Café   10
Café Essen   3
Chairman and Yip   8
Charcoal   13
Courgette   1
Cream   2
Diamant   C
Gus Café   5
Lemongrass Thai   14

PUBS , BARS & CLUBS
ANU Bar   15
Club Mombassa   12
Hippo Bar   4
ICBM   11
King O'Malleys   6
Kremlin Bar   9
Wig and Pen   7

CIVIC

ACCOMMODATION
Canberra City YHA   B
Diamant   C
Quest Canberra   A

10am–5pm; free; Ⓦwww.nfsa.gov.au) houses a comprehensive collection of Australian sound and screen recordings dating back to the 1890s. One of the Archive's gems is their reconstruction of the fifteen surviving minutes of *The History of the Kelly Gang*, made in 1906 and quite possibly the world's first feature film. There's coverage of this in their displays on film-making and restoration, and longer segments are shown during free **screenings** (usually Sat & Sun 11am & 3pm).

Moving south, the **National Museum of Australia** (daily 9am–5pm; free; Ⓦwww.nma.gov.au) occupies the little Acton Peninsula on the shores of Lake Burley Griffin. The unmistakable piecemeal building, topped by a giant black and orange loop, is considerably more interesting than the contents, which come across as self-consciously postmodern. Traditional gallery and museum displays are largely shunned in favour of experience spaces, but style doesn't completely overshadow content, which might cover anything from the First Australians to the country's early Greek cafés and the sad decline of Tasmania's **thylacine**, or marsupial wolf, which became extinct in the 1930s. Buildings are ranged around the **Garden of Australian Dreams**, a challenging and initially baffling "map" of the continent which attempts to marry colonial and Aboriginal geopolitical perspectives.

Questacon and the National Library

Crossing the lake south from Civic over Commonwealth Avenue Bridge, you turn left onto King Edward Terrace. The odd-shaped truncated tower before you contains **Questacon** (daily 9am–5pm; $16, children $11.50; ⊛www .questacon.edu.au), the hands-on National Science and Technology Centre. This is great fun, especially for children, with heaps of interactive exhibits explaining sound, light, geology and other bits of physics; favourites include a simulated earthquake and lightning storm, a roller-coaster simulator and the Mini Q section for under-6s. You'll easily kill a couple of hours here, though it does get very busy during school holidays and on rainy days.

Looming behind Questacon is the **National Library** (Mon–Thurs 9am–9pm, Fri & Sat 9am–5pm, Sun 1.30–5pm; free; ⊛www.nla.gov.au), whose reading room has a comprehensive selection of overseas newspapers and magazines (Mon–Sat 9am–5pm). The archives are mostly hidden away, but can be seen if you're particularly interested in something. A facsimile of Captain Cook's journal from the *Endeavour* is on display on Level 2. More accessible are the top-quality temporary exhibitions, often on maps, documents or photography. There's also an interesting behind-the-scenes tour (Thurs 12.30pm; 1hr; free) and the *Bookplate Café* (see p.238).

The High Court and National Portrait Gallery

East of Questacon lies the **High Court of Australia** (Mon–Fri 9.45am–4.30pm; free), set in an appropriately grandiose, glass-fronted concrete-block edifice with a stylized waterfall running alongside the walkway up to the entrance. Visitors can watch a short video which explains the court's function and examines two of its landmark cases: the 1983 ruling that saved Tasmania's wild Franklin River from damming, and its finding on the 1992 land-rights case of Mabo versus Queensland (see p.1131) – a momentous decision that overturned the British legal concept of *terra nullius* whereby Australia was considered uninhabited prior to white settlement in 1788. You can watch judgements while the court is in session.

The High Court is approached past the brand-new **National Portrait Gallery of Australia**, King Edward Terrace (daily 10am–5pm; free; ⊛www .portrait.gov.au), which contains portraits – oils, photos, drawings, sculptures, etc – of over four hundred people who have helped shape the nation. Often the most interesting sections are the temporary exhibits (fee sometimes applies), which change every few weeks.

The National Gallery of Australia

The **National Gallery of Australia** (daily 10am–5pm; free; tours daily at 11am & 2pm; ⊛www.nga.gov.au) is immediately east of the High Court, to which it is linked by a footbridge. The whole place is impressive, though by far the best display is the upper-level **Australian Art gallery**. Starting right back at the time of settlement, paintings here include some of the earliest recorded impressions of landscape, wildlife and Aborigines, and proceed through European-inspired art movements to the emphatically Australian *Ned Kelly* series by Sidney Nolan; there are also some Brett Whiteleys, samples of the nightmarish work of Albert Tucker, and fine pieces by Arthur Boyd, Ian Fairweather and the Aboriginal-influenced John Olson. Other works on permanent display include Russell Drysdale's *The Drover's Wife* (1945), probably his best-known painting.

Move downstairs for work by **Aboriginal and Torres Strait Islands artists**, ranging from traditional bark paintings from the Northern Territory to politically aware contemporary work in different media. Far more of such work will be on display with the opening of a new extension (expected in early 2010).

Perhaps unsurprisingly, the collection of work from outside Australia seems dutiful and somewhat eclectic. Displays of European art touch on everything from pre-Renaissance onwards, though the strength is in nineteenth- and twentieth-century works: one of Monet's waterlily canvases, a couple of good Warhols, a scintillating Hockney of the Grand Canyon, and Jackson Pollock's vibrant *Blue Poles*, which caused a national outcry when the government bought it for $5 million in 1974.

There's also a fine display of **Indian and Southeast Asian antiquities**, including some wonderful textiles, a lovely gilt Buddha and a twelfth-century Shiva, all strikingly displayed amid the concrete brutalism of the gallery.

Outside, the **Sculpture Garden** overlooking Lake Burley Griffin includes a dispersed version of Rodin's freestanding bronze statues *The Burghers of Calais*. Also visible and audible across the water from here is the **National Carillon** stranded on Aspen Island, whose three elegant bell-towers and 55 bronze bells – ranging from tiny to huge – were a gift from the British government to mark Canberra's fiftieth birthday. It's pleasant to sit on the lawns under a shady tree by the lake and listen to the Carillon recitals (Wed & Sun 12.30–1.20pm).

The Old and New Parliament houses

Away from the lake and at the foot of Capital Hill, the **Old Parliament House** (daily 9am–5pm; $2; Ⓦwww.oph.gov.au) is a grand, white Neoclassical wedding cake of a building, in use between 1927 and 1988. Hourly **tours** show just how crowded and inconvenient the building actually was, all imposingly gloomy, Victorian-style wood panelling and moulded plaster, though the leather seats in the old senate are pretty comfortable. There are always interesting temporary exhibits, and a new **democracy section** showcasing the history of democracy in Australia.

Outside, you can wander in the adjacent **Senate Rose Garden**, or take a look at the so-called **Aboriginal Tent Embassy** on the lawn in front, which has been here, on and off, since 1972 and serves as a focus for the million-odd representatives of Australia's oldest culture – you'll be welcomed for a cup of tea and a (political) chat.

Behind Old Parliament House, (New) **Parliament House** (daily 9am–5pm; free; Ⓦwww.aph.gov.au) is an extraordinary construction which appears to be built into Capital Hill. All you see from a distance are grassy slopes leading up to the landmark, four-legged **flagpole**, though closer inspection reveals a modern white colonnaded entry. Designed by the American-Italian architect (and now Canberra resident) Romaldo Giurgola, it opened in May 1988 to much derision. Former Prime Minister Malcolm Fraser, who commissioned the building, described it later as "an unmitigated disaster" and "my one very serious political mistake". Twenty years on, it is ageing well and most now concede that, while not an iconic building, it is still a good one – impressive in scale and concept, with over 4500 rooms tucked away from prying eyes.

Outside the ground-floor entrance level is a **mosaic** by the Aboriginal artist Michael Nelson Jagamara – a piece that conveys the idea of a sacred meeting place. It is all explained next to the original painting on which it is based, which can be found inside the cool and serene **foyer**. The foyer is dominated by marble staircases and over forty columns clad in grey-green and rose-pink marble, representing a eucalypt forest. Around the walls, native wood panels feature delightful marquetry designs of native flora designed by Michael Retter.

Simply wandering around the remaining public areas isn't very instructive, so make sure you catch one of the 45-minute **guided tours** (daily 9am–4pm, roughly every 30min; free) which visit both chambers of parliament when they're not sitting.

Beyond the foyer, the **Great Hall** sports a 20-metre-high **tapestry** based on a painting of blackened trees by Arthur Boyd: guides will point out the cockatoo and Haley's comet which was in the sky when the weavers were at work. Portraits of former Prime Ministers and Governors General surround the adjacent **Members' Hall**, where you can admire Queen Victoria's writing desk and one of only four extant original copies of the **Magna Carta**, this one bought for the National Archive in 1952.

Lifts from the Members' Hall rise to the grassy roof, where Walter Burley Griffin's masterplan becomes evident. Here you stand at the apex of the city's triangular core with Kings Road leading across the lake to the War Memorial and Commonwealth Avenue heading past the National Library to Civic.

When Parliament is in session – usually from sixty to eighty days a year – you can sit in the **public galleries** and watch the proceedings in the House of Representatives (the lower chamber of Parliament) or the Senate (the upper chamber of the legislature); Question Time in both chambers starts at 2pm, with the House of Representatives making for better viewing. To guarantee a seat at busy times (like budget day), book in advance on ☎02/6277 4889.

The diplomatic quarters and the mint

A trip among the upmarket suburban homes in Canberra's diplomatic quarters – **Yarralumla** and **Forrest** – completes the political sightseeing tour. The consulates and high commissions were asked to construct buildings that exemplified the typical architecture of the countries they represent – look out for the eye-catching embassies of Thailand, Indonesia, China, Papua New Guinea and Finland.

Australia's coins are produced at the **Royal Australian Mint**, Denison Street, Deakin (Mon–Fri 9am–4pm, Sat & Sun 10am–4pm; free; ⓦwww.ramint.gov .au), 4km southwest of Parliament. Once the renovations are complete (in mid-2009) you will again be able to see stamping presses in action (Mon–Fri only), and they promise improvements to the existing small display of historic Australian currency, including gold bars and "holey" dollars. The kids are most likely to be impressed by being able to stamp out their own dollar coin from a polished blank ($2.60 per coin).

Lake Burley Griffin and around

Canberra is oriented around **Lake Burley Griffin**, which stretches for 11km from west to east. A **cycle track** circuits the entire lake; **buses** from Civic link (or come very close to) almost all of the following sights – there's no regular weekday service, but #981 runs at weekends and #81 on weekdays during school holidays.

Commonwealth Avenue Bridge links Civic with Parliament passing the **Captain Cook Memorial Jet**, which spurts a column of water 140m into the air (daily 11am–4pm). It was built in 1970 to mark the bicentenary of Captain Cook's "discovery" of Australia. The park immediately behind it is the venue for all sorts of outdoor shows, from the springtime **Floriade** flower festival (ⓦwww.floriadeaustralia.com), to New Year's Eve firework displays.

Black Mountain rises just north of the lake's mid-point, with **Black Mountain Tower** (daily 9am–10pm; $7.50) poking upwards from the summit like a two-hundred-metre-high homing beacon for the city, visible from many kilometres away. Bus #81 goes up to the tower's base, and there are magnificent panoramic views of Canberra from the 66-metre-high viewing platform or the revolving restaurant just below. There's also a walking track up here from the **National Botanic Gardens** below on Clunies Ross Street (daily 8.30am–5pm; free; tours daily at 11am & 2pm), which has done an amazing job recreating a wide swathe of native habitats in what was a dairy farm until the 1950s. Strolling through the lush rainforest section, it is astonishing to consider that this was a dry valley until 1968.

You can spend a couple of tranquil hours here walking through the undergrowth and spotting reptiles and birds, including rare **gang-gang cockatoos**. The visitor centre (daily 9am–4.30pm) has a leaflet on the Aboriginal walk, highlighting significant plants and how they were used. The outdoor **café** (same hours) is beautifully set amongst shaded fern-gardens and lawns.

The **National Zoo and Aquarium**, Lady Denman Drive (daily 10am–5pm; $26.50, children $14.50; ℡02/6287 8400, Ⓦwww.nationalzoo.com.au) sits on the lake's far western shore, 6km west of Civic. All the usual native suspects are here, but the zoo's best feature is its **big cats**, which include tigers, lions, cheetahs and snow leopards. The two-hour Zoo Venture **tour** (daily at 3.30pm; Mon–Fri $95, Sat & Sun $125) lets you hand-feed most of these, along with some of the native animals; $150 gets you in to pet a cheetah for fifteen minutes – you need to book both in advance.

The Australian War Memorial

Due east of Civic on Limestone Avenue, the **Australian War Memorial** (daily 10am–5pm; free; Ⓦwww.awm.gov.au) does an admirable job of positively commemorating Australia's war dead whilst avoiding any glorification of war itself – a notable achievement for a country that sees participation in world wars as the core of its identity. Free **tours** take place at 10am, 10.30am, 11am, 1pm, 1.30pm & 2pm.

▲ The Australian War Memorial

The ANZACs

Travelling around Australia you'll notice that almost every town, large or small, has a war memorial dedicated to the memory of the ANZACs, the **Australia and New Zealand Army Corps**. When war erupted in Europe in 1914, Australia was overwhelmed by a wave of pro-British sentiment. On August 5, 1914, one day after Great Britain had declared war against Germany, the Australian prime minister summed up the feelings of his compatriots: "When the Empire is at war so Australia is at war." On November 1, 1914, a contingent of twenty thousand enthusiastic volunteers – the **ANZACs** – left from the port of Albany in Western Australia to assist the mother country in her struggle.

In Europe, Turkey had entered the war on the German side in October 1914. At the beginning of 1915, military planners in London (Winston Churchill prominent among them) came up with a plan to capture the strategically important Turkish peninsula of the Dardanelles with a surprise attack near **Gallipoli**, thus opening the way to the Black Sea. On April 25, 1915, sixteen thousand Australian soldiers landed at dawn in a small bay flanked by steep cliffs: by nightfall, two thousand men had died in a hail of Turkish bullets from above. The plan, whose one chance of success was surprise, had been signalled by troop and ship movements long in advance; by the time it was carried out, it was already doomed to failure. Nonetheless, Allied soldiers continued to lose their lives for another eight months without ever gaining more than a foothold. In December, London finally issued the order to withdraw. Eleven thousand Australians and New Zealanders had been killed, along with as many French and three times as many British troops. The Turks lost 86,000 men.

Official Australian historiography continues to mythologize the battle for Gallipoli, elevating it to the level of a national legend on which Australian identity is founded. From this point of view, in the war's baptism of fire, the ANZAC soldiers proved themselves heroes who did the new nation proud, their loyalty and bravery evidence of how far Australia had developed. It was "the birth of a nation", and at the same time a loss of innocence, a national rite of passage – never again would Australians so unquestioningly involve themselves in foreign ventures. Today the legend is as fiercely defended as ever, the focal point of Australian national pride, commemorated each year on April 25, **ANZAC Day**.

The centrepiece is the Byzantine-style, domed **Hall of Memory**, approached past an eternal flame which rises from a rectangular pond. Look up at the ceiling to see mosaics depicting veterans of World War II, while the lovely blue stained-glass windows commemorate those who fought in World War I. In the centre is the tomb of the Unknown Australian Soldier, while over 102,000 names of the fallen are etched onto the walls outside. This is where you should be just before closing time when a bugler or piper plays the **Last Post** in moving testament to the war dead.

Wings either side house paintings by war artists, battle dioramas, military relics and films to illustrate Australia's involvement in both world wars, as well as Vietnam and more recent conflicts. Fighter aircraft and huge naval guns compete for your attention with the ANZAC Hall with its giant Lancaster bomber, Messerschmidt fighters and coverage of the Japanese submarine attack on Sydney.

The Australian Institute of Sport

Some 7km northwest of Civic is the ultramodern **Australian Institute of Sport (AIS)**, on Leverrier Street in Bruce (Mon–Fri 9am–5pm, Sat & Sun 10am–4pm; ⓦ www.ausport.gov.au; bus #80). Founded to improve the national sports profile after Australia's dismal showing in the 1976 Olympics (when they won just three medals), AIS has since churned out world-beating athletes with such regularity that other countries now copy their training techniques. **Tours** (10am, 11.30am, 1pm & 2.30pm; 1hr 30min; $16, children $9) are guided by athletes and introduce you to their intensive schedules, while the **Sportex** interactive exhibition gives you the chance to test your prowess at virtual football, cycling, rowing, wheelchair basketball and rock climbing.

Eating

There are so many **cafés and restaurants** around Civic and Kingston (and nearby **Manuka**) that finding somewhere to eat is never a problem. The cafés all serve light meals, while the restaurants feature a definite bias towards Southeast Asian food. Almost all the sights, museums and galleries have a café of some sort, but we've only listed the best below.

North of the lake: Civic and Dickson

Asian Café 32 West Row ☏02/6262 6233. Extremely popular, inexpensive restaurant serving tasty versions of Malay and Chinese staples – fried noodles, sweet-and-sour and the rest. Mains around $16.

Café Essen Garema Arcade. Much-loved coffee house with enormous, cheap and unusual brunches, all-day breakfasts and a great range of teas. Daily from 7.30am.

Chairman and Yip 108 Bunda St ☏02/6248 7109. This stylish and eccentric restaurant offers Eastern Chinese classics such as meltingly tender, aromatic Shandong Lamb. Not cheap at around $30 for a main, though they also offer early-evening two-course set meals for $29. Lunch Tues–Fri, dinner Mon–Sat.

Charcoal 61 London Circuit ☏02/6248 8015. Grilled steak, in shamelessly large servings, is the mainstay here, though they also offer grilled reef fish. Steaks $30–40.

Courgette 54 Marcus Clarke St ☏02/6247 4042. Probably Canberra's finest cooking is served up at this smart yet intimate restaurant. Modern European leanings inform a menu which might include John Dory with Balmain bugs, black olive mash and red pepper foam ($36). Top-notch wine list too. Lunch Mon–Fri, dinner Mon–Sat.

Cream Bunda St ☏02/6162 1448. Good food served with panache at moderate prices is the key to the success of this always-buzzing downtown café-bar and restaurant. The menu is contemporary with Asian and Mediterranean influences (mains mostly $20–25). On a warm evening head for the marble cocktail bar or shun the echoey interior for the streetside seating. Closed Sun eve.

Dickson Asian Noodle House 29 Woolley St, Dickson, 4km north of Civic ☏02/6247 6380. Predominantly Thai and Lao cheapie that's always packed, thanks to its superb laksas and tangy noodle dishes. Daily 11am–10pm.

Gus Café Bunda St. This long-standing café serves inexpensive light meals, good pasta and fresh soups, with lots of choice for vegetarians. It's popular with students and an arty crowd, and has outside tables under vines. Daily 7.30am–10pm, later at weekends.

Lemongrass Thai 65 London Circuit ☏02/6247 2779. There are posher Thai restaurants than this one, but none match the fast service and tasty, good-value menu. Mains around $15. Licensed & BYO. Closed Sat lunch & Sun.

South of the lake: Parkes, Kingston and Manuka

Artespresso 31 Giles St, Kingston ☏02/6295 8055. Executives plot global domination over barra-mundi and duck in this classy bar-restaurant, which also has fine artworks on the walls. Lunches $15–20, dinner mains around $35. Tues–Sat noon till late.

Bookplate Café National Library, Parkes ☏02/6262 1154. The best café in the Parliamentary district. Sit inside surrounded by modern stained glass, or out on the sunny terrace overlooking Lake Burley Griffin and tuck into superb pastries and coffee or lunch, which might include sourdough and focaccia sandwiches or pancetta, feta and roasted pumpkin salad ($15). Daily 11am–3pm.

Ottoman Cuisine Corner of Broughton St and Blackall St, Barton ☏02/6273 6111. There's a suitably Arabian Nights feel to the entrance to this swanky restaurant, but inside it's all white linen and crystal – a delightfully surreal setting for top-end Turkish dishes such as slow-braised lamb filo rolls ($21), perhaps followed by sliced veal seasoned with mild Aleppo chilli ($33) and rose-petal Turkish delight ($6). Closed Sat lunch, Sun & Mon.

Silo 36 Giles St, Kingston ☎02/6260 6060. Narrow and cramped yet always packed with Canberra's smart set, this suburban café and specialist cheese shop serves excellent coffee, and its pastries and breads have made it an institution

Be prepared to wait for a table for their imaginative and delicious breakfasts, but you can book for their equally scrumptious lunches. Closed Sun.

Timmy's Corner of Furneaux St and Bougainville St, Manuka ☎02/6295 6537. This friendly and very popular Malay restaurant is particularly good for seafood. Mains $15–22. Licensed & BYO. Closed Mon.

Drinking, nightlife and entertainment

Canberra has a lively entertainment scene, though it's nothing you'd make a special journey for. Most of the **drinking** action is in Civic, but Braddon (immediately north) and Dickson (4km north) also have small scenes. South of the lake there are a couple of worthwhile bars among the restaurants of Kingston. Canberra's **clubs** are mostly in Civic, and open Thursday to Saturday or Sunday from about 8pm. The best **live music** is usually at the university's *ANU Bar*.

For **information** about upcoming events, the daily *Canberra Times* is your best bet; the most extensive listings are published every Thursday in the "Good Times" supplement. For details of gigs and club nights, check out the free monthly music magazines *BMA* (ⓦwww.bmamag.com) or *3D World* (ⓦwww.threedworld.com.au), available from record shops, hostels and bars.

Pubs and bars

Filthy McFaddens Green Square, Kingston. The pick of the suburban pubs; Irish-styled and surprisingly cosy in this suburban shopping centre.

King O'Malleys 131 City Walk, Civic. This vibrant Irish-style pub in the heart of town becomes the place to get the party started at weekends. At quieter times it's a good spot for meals – pizza, pasta and beef and Guinness pie ($12–16).

Knightsbridge Penthouse 34 Mort St, Braddon. Sleek cocktail bar a short walk north of Civic that has a good party vibe at weekends, with DJs on duty. Like being in someone's (large) lounge.

Kremlin Bar 65 Northbourne Ave, Civic. The curtains are more red velvet than iron in this cruisey Soviet-themed bar that's a world away from the frenetic weekend scene elsewhere in Civic.

Little Brussels 29 Jardine St, Kingston. All the Belgian beers (on tap and in bottles) and pots of mussels you'd expect, in friendly, wood-panelled surroundings. It is fairly pricey but weekend lunch specials (mussels and Stella for $15) and a weekday wine and spirits happy hour (6–8pm) help.

Wig and Pen on Alinga St, Civic. English-style pub serving the best beer in town in convivial surroundings with bar meals (mostly $12) available. They brew their own excellent lager, ale and bitter on site, including a delicious Pale Ale, the American hops giving an almost fruity flavour. A four-beer tasting tray is just $7.

Clubs and live music

ANU Bar University Ave, Civic ☎02/6125 3660, ⓦwww.anuunion.com.au. Also known as the Uni Bar and not to be confused with the Uni Pub, this venue hosts most small to mid-range touring bands. The Fratellis and Sydneyside favourites, Cassette Kids, played recently. Also hosts club nights till dawn.

Club Mombassa 128 Bunda St, Civic. Plays laid-back African, Latin and Pacific sounds to an older crowd. Wed–Sun.

Hippo Bar 17 Garema Place, Civic. Stylish, hard-to-spot bar that's all ottomans and low lighting. Smart people sip sumptuous cocktails as DJs ramp up the music, from loungy electronica to soulful funk fusion. Wed–Sat.

ICBM 50 Northbourne Ave. Hugely popular club with no cover charge and a mix of students and civil servants letting their hair down. Wed–Sat.

Theatre and cinema

ANU Arts Centre Union Court, ANU ☎02/6215 2419, ⓦhttp://cass.anu.edu.au/artscentre. Inexpensive student theatre, putting on anything from Shakespeare to Shepherd.

ARC National Film and Sound Archive, McCoy Circuit ☎02/6248 2000, ⓦwww.nfsa.gov.au. Excellent art-house movies from around the world, many of them historic, though with occasional new releases. Mostly Thurs and Sat.

Canberra Theatre Centre London Circuit ☎02/6243 5711, ⓦwww.canberratheatre.org.au.

Moving on from Canberra

Long-distance **bus services** use the Jolimont Centre terminal (see p.229); tickets are available here for direct services with Greyhound (℡13 14 99, ⓦwww .greyhound.com.au) to Sydney, Brisbane, Melbourne and Adelaide; and Murrays Coaches (℡13 22 51, ⓦwww.murrays.com.au) to Sydney, Bateman's Bay, Wollongong and, during winter, a Snow Express to Thredbo. There are also daily **trains** to Sydney from the train station in Kingston (℡13 22 32, ⓦwww.countrylink.info).

Canberra's main drama space, with several theatres hosting plays, concerts, dance performances and travelling shows.
The Dendy Upstairs in the Canberra Centre, Civic ℡02/6221 8900, ⓦwww.dendy.com.au. Mainstream multiplex with a smattering of international and art-house films.
Greater Union 6 Mort St at Bunda St, Civic ℡02/6247 5522, ⓦwww.greaterunion.com.au.

Downtown multiplex with a smaller sibling on the corner of Furneaux St and Canberra Ave in Manuka (℡02/6295 9042).
The Street Theatre Corner of Childers St and University Ave ℡02/6247 1519, ⓦwww.thestreet .org.au. The one to try for something away from the mainstream.

Listings

Banks ANZ, Commonwealth, National Australia Bank and Westpac all have branches in Civic.
Bike rental To make the most of Canberra's cycle tracks, Mr Spokes Bike Hire (℡02/6257 1188) is located next to the ferry dock on the north side of the lake, and hires out bikes ($12 per hr, or $38 per day), tandems ($24/$75) and pedal "cars" ($30 an hour).
Books Smiths Alternative Bookshop, 76 Alinga St, opposite the post office is a small but interesting independent book store.
Car rental Canberra is an expensive place to rent a car, but relatively good deals are available with Rumbles, 11 Paragon Mall, Gladstone St, Fyshwick (℡02/6280 7444). Others, with desks at the airport, include: Avis ℡02/6249 6088; Budget ℡02/6257 2200; Hertz ℡02/6257 4877; and Thrifty ℡1300 367 227.
Embassies and high commissions There are over seventy in Canberra (all the following are in Yarralumla, unless otherwise stated): Britain, Commonwealth Ave ℡02/6270 6666; Canada, Commonwealth Ave ℡02/6270 4000; China, 15 Coronation Drive ℡02/6273 4780; Ireland, 20 Arkana St ℡02/6273 3022; Malaysia, 7 Perth Ave ℡02/6273 1543; New Zealand, Commonwealth Ave ℡02/6270 4211; Singapore, 17 Forster Crescent ℡02/6271 2000; Thailand, 111 Empire Circuit ℡02/6273 1149; USA, 21 Moonah Place ℡02/6214 5600.
Festivals The big event of the year is the Canberra Festival – the anniversary of the city's

foundation – celebrated with concerts, theatre, exhibitions, street parades and fireworks for nine days from the beginning of March. The Royal Canberra Show is an agricultural fair lasting three days over the last weekend in February, while Floriade (ⓦwww.floriadeaustralia.com) is a spring festival marked by floral displays, theatre and music, from mid-Sept to mid-Oct. The Canberra International Film Festival (early Nov) is held at Dendy Cinemas in Civic with new and retrospective international and Australian films.
Gay and lesbian Canberra Gay Information and Support Service ℡02/6247 2726; daily 6–10pm.
Hospitals John James Memorial Hospital, Strickland Crescent, Deakin ℡02/6281 8100 (private); The Canberra Hospital, Yamba Drive, Garran ℡02/6244 2222.
Internet access If your accommodation can't help out, there are some terminals at the bus station in Jolimont Centre, several internet cafés around Civic and free wi-fi at the National Library of Australia.
Post office Alinga St, Canberra, ACT 2600 (Mon–Fri 8.30am–5.30pm; ℡02/6209 1680).
Skiing Canberra has good connections to the winter snowfields at Thredbo and Perisher; contact Murrays Coaches (℡13 22 51, ⓦwww.murrays .com.au) or Transborder (℡02/6241 0033, ⓦwww .transborder.com.au).
Taxis Canberra Cabs (℡13 22 27); there's also a taxi rank on Bunda St, Civic, outside the cinema.

Around Canberra: Namadgi National Park

Canberra's reputation for being surrounded by attractively rugged country-side took a sad beating from the awful 2003 **bushfires** which burned out two thirds of the ACT and gutted over five hundred homes. Australian native vegetation is generally fire-tolerant, with some species even needing occasional conflagrations to pop open seed pods or encourage new growth, but these fires were so intense that huge areas of forest were totally incinerated, and will take decades to fully recover. Still, many of the visible scars are already largely healed and a visit to the **Namadgi National Park**, occupying almost half of the ACT, in the west and southwest, is well worth considering. Its mountain ranges and high plains rise to 1900m, have a far more severe climate than low-lying Canberra and give rise to the Cotter River and many smaller streams.

You really need a **vehicle** to go exploring, best done on an eighty-kilometre loop from Canberra which initially heads west along Cotter Road to **Cotter Dam**, 15km from Civic, a popular swimming spot with simple **camping** ($7.50 per person) and hot showers. From here, continue south past the extra-terrestrial exhibits at the **Canberra Deep Space Communication Centre** and the wonderful **Tidbinbilla Nature Reserve**, then loop back north along the valley of the Murrumbidgee River past the historic **Lanyon Homestead**.

The **Namadgi Visitors Information Centre** at Naas Road, 7km south of Lanyon Homestead (Mon–Fri 9am–4pm, Sat, Sun & public holidays 9am–4.30pm; ℡02/6207 2900, ⓦwww.environment.act.gov.au), has displays and videos about the park, and provides tours on request. This is also the place to make bookings for **camping** at simple drive-in sites *Honeysuckle*, Orroral (which has flush toilets), or Mt Clear (all $5 per person).

Canberra Deep Space Communication Centre

Amid the foothills of the Tidbinbilla Range 30km southwest of Canberra you'll glimpse the big white satellite dishes of the **Canberra Deep Space Communication Centre**, Discovery Drive (daily 9am–5pm, till 8pm in summer; free; ⓦwww.cdscc.nasa.gov). They're the largest in Australia and are operated in conjunction with NASA for communicating with spacecraft exploring the solar system; there are only two others in the world – one near Madrid, the other in Goldstone, California. In their shadow, a small visitor centre gives fairly pedestrian but interesting coverage of their activities, in particular the work of the Mars Exploration Rover. It is all slotted into displays on understanding the universe, space exploration and general rocketry, including a 1970s-vintage minicomputer (all big brown switches and hubcap-sized hard disk) once used for mission control. There's enough interactive stuff to keep kids happy for a while.

Tidbinbilla Nature Reserve

The small **Tidbinbilla Nature Reserve**, 3km south of the satellite dishes, (daily: Oct–March 9am–8pm, April–Sept 9am–6pm), is an enjoyable place of rocks and gum trees with relatively easy walks, picnic grounds, a good chance of seeing emus and even the possibility of spotting platypus. Consequently, it's a popular place on long weekends and during the school holidays, especially with families.

The area around the park entrance and **visitor centre** (Mon–Fri 9am–4.30pm, Sat & Sun 9am–5pm; ☎02/6205 1233, ⓦwww.tams.act.gov.au) is home to kangaroos and wallabies in spacious bush enclosures, and you can also see koalas, birds and **corroboree frogs**, an extremely rare alpine amphibian. From here, a sixteen-kilometre sealed loop road runs through the reserve with short trails off to panoramic viewpoints and historic sites – a once heavily used Aboriginal shelter rock and the spire-like Church Rock, where services were held in pioneering times. The reserve's highlight is the new **Sanctuary**, a few hectares fenced off from predators where a two-kilometre wheelchair-accessible boardwalk path winds though some wetlands. Landscaping allows you to get a duck's-eye view of one lake, the signage is entertaining and informative and at the Vet Centre you can get up close and personal with the reptiles.

Lanyon Homestead

Some 4km north of the little hamlet of Tharwa, and 30km south of Canberra, the convict-built **Lanyon Homestead** (Tues–Sun 10am–4pm; $8, admission to grounds free) dates back to the earliest European settlement of the region. The house itself has been thoroughly restored to its original mid-Victorian style and is a prime example of how life in colonial Australia was lived, at least for wealthy landowners. It also houses a small display outlining the history of the area before Canberra existed.

The south coast and Snowy Mountains

The **south coast**, with its green dairylands and small fishing villages, is delightful in a quiet sort of way – an area for casting a rod, surfing or relaxing on the many stunning beaches – with no huge resorts or commercial developments. Inland are the **Snowy Mountains**, the Great Dividing Range's highest peaks, which have Australia's best skiing and, in summer, some fine bushwalking.

The direct route from Sydney to Melbourne via the inland **Hume Highway** (covered in Chapter 3) passes close to Canberra and the Snowy Mountains; the coastal route, the **Princes Highway**, is slightly longer but much more scenic. Give yourself four or more days if you want to appreciate the national parks, sandy beaches, mountains, valleys and forests that comprise this beautiful stretch of the coast.

The south coast

The **south coast** of New South Wales is all rather low-key and family-oriented, with a few wildlife and amusement parks to keep the children happy, and plenty of opportunities for traditional outdoor pursuits. Exposed parts on this stretch of the coast are perfect for **surfing**, while the numerous coastal lakes, bays and inlets are suited for **swimming**, windsurfing, sailing or canoeing. Away from the ocean there's some superb rugged scenery, with some great **bushwalking** and **horseriding** in the forest-clad, mountainous hinterland. The stretch between **Jervis Bay** and **Batemans Bay** in particular can get busy during the summer months, especially from Christmas to the end of January.

Berry

On the Princes Highway some 25km south of Kiama and 65km south of Wollongong, **BERRY** is a pretty, historic town with many listed buildings, surrounded by dairy country and green hills. The main reason to stop is to eat well, do a little craft and homeware shopping then eat some more. The main drag, **Queen Street**, is packed with upmarket shops, little art galleries, cafés and restaurants, and is home to two country pubs. Understandably enough, Berry is a favourite with weekending Sydneysiders, and the place can get unbearably crowded. The town's popularity is further enhanced by the proximity of **Kangaroo Valley** (16km west), the beach at **Gerringong** (18km east) and a monthly market (first Sun of the month).

 Wineries are another draw: Coolangatta Estate (daily 10am–5pm; ☎02/4448 7131, ⓦwww.coolangattaestate.com.au), just 5km southeast of Berry on Bolong Road, and Silos Estate, 8km southwest at Jasper's Brush (Wed–Sun 10am–5pm; ☎02/4448 6082, ⓦwww.thesilos.com), are among the best.

Practicalities

Berry is easily reached by **train** on CityRail's South Coast Line from Sydney. The Shoalhaven **visitor centre** (daily 9am–5pm; ☎1300 662 808, ⓦwww.shoalhavenholidays.com.au) can help you out with any queries and accommodation bookings – it's located on the Princes Highway, 18km south of Berry just after the road bridge between Nowra and Bomaderry.

Accommodation

As well as the places listed below, there are dozens of rural **B&Bs** in the hills around town (check out ⓦwww.shoalhavenholidays.com.au for listings).

The Berry Hotel 120 Queen St ☎02/4464 1011, ⓦwww.berryhotel.com.au. A lovely old coach house offering pretty, old-fashioned rooms, including a huge family flat sleeping eight. A full country breakfast is included in the price at weekends. Weekdays ❸, weekends ❺
Berry Orchard 17a George St ☎02/4464 2583, ⓦwww.berryorchard.com.au. Lovely, central B&B with a delightful, sunny self-contained cottage for two, and a smaller studio, both coming with fresh flowers, cheese and wine on arrival. Two-night minimum. ❼
The Bunyip Inn 122 Queen St ☎02/4464 2064. Thirteen-room B&B mostly in an imposing National Trust-classified former bank, with a lovely leafy garden and swimming pool. Every room is different

(nearly all are en suite) and the modern stables accommodation includes one wheelchair-accessible unit and one with a kitchen. Good value. ❹
Great Southern Hotel 95 Queen St, Berry ☎02/4464 1009. These wackily decorated and hand-painted rooms attached to the hotel are fun and cheap, and you don't have to stumble back

far after a night at the pub. Weekday ❸, weekend ❺
Silo Estates Jaspers Bush, 8km south ☎02/4448 6082, ⓦwww.thesilos.com. Boutique accommodation on a vineyard with four delightfully appointed suites, some with spa. Two-night minimum at weekends. Suite ❻, spa suite ❼

Eating

The Berry Hotel 120 Queen St. This much-loved place boasts the best-value food in town, served in either the pub itself, the large courtyard at the back, or a cosy-cottage dining room with open fire. Food consists of posh pub tucker at lunch (around $15) and affordable Mod Oz offerings in the evening, including the likes of cumin-spiced lamb rump with puy lentils, aubergine and yoghurt ($26). Entertainment Sat eve.

Berry Woodfired Sourdough Bakery 23 Prince Alfred St ☎02/4464 1617. Virtually everything is made on the premises at this wonderful bakery/café just off the main street. A coffee and one of their delectable tarts is a treat, but aim to come for breakfast or lunch, which might be toasted brioche with lemon curd ($8) or corn fritters with caramelized prosciutto and tomato relish ($14). Outdoor seating. Wed–Sun 8am–3pm.
Cuttlefish 98 Queen St ☎02/4464 3065. Stylish pizza-bar located above the *Hedgehog Café*, overlooking a beautiful nursery. Also serves Italian

mains and desserts. Lunch Sat & Sun, dinner Thurs–Sun.
Emporium Food Co. 127 Queen St. This deli serves posh sandwiches, savoury pies, beautiful little cakes and excellent coffee – try and grab one of the little tables at the front of the shop. Mon–Sat 9am–5pm, Sun 10am–4.30pm.
The Posthouse 137 Queen St ☎02/4464 2444. Quality, contemporary Oz dining at moderate prices is the motif at this lively restaurant with seating either in the former post office or on the leafy patio. Lunch mains $15–18; dinner mains $19–28. Closed Wed.
Silos Winery Princes Highway, Jaspers Bush, 8km southwest ☎02/4448 6160, ⓦwww.thesilos.com .au. The finest dining in the area, with an eclectic, Asian-inspired Mod Oz menu, beautifully crafted desserts and idyllic views over the vineyard. Expect five-spice duck with scallops ($36) and their own variation on moussaka ($27). Lunch Wed–Sun, dinner Wed–Sat.

Jervis Bay

Around 40km south of Berry, the sheltered waters of **Jervis Bay** (often mispronounced Jarvis Bay), now a marine reserve, are surrounded by small towns. On the southern hook of the bay is the town of the same name which, by a political quirk, is technically part of the ACT, in order to provide Canberra with theoretical access to the sea.

The area attracts a lot of visitors due to its proximity to Sydney, and the delights of the nearby Booderee National Park. The best place to base yourself if you don't fancy bushcamping is the small, slightly lacklustre town of **HUSKISSON**, at the midpoint of the bay, which isn't much more than a few streets centred on the small marina backed by a handful of cafés and takeaways, and a street of shops. **Sealife-watching tours** are available with eco-certified Dolphin Watch Cruises, 50 Owen St (2hr; $25; ☎1800 246 010, ⓦwww .dolphinwatch.com.au), who run year-round; from September to November there are opportunities for spotting **whales**. **Snorkelling** trips (2hr; $60) generally run early morning and late afternoon.

If you'd prefer to be underwater, visit Dive Jervis Bay, 64 Owen St (☎02/4441 5255, ⓦwww.divejervisbay.com), who offer **diving** in pristine waters – surprisingly enough, it's the second most popular dive spot in Australia after the Great Barrier Reef, with an extremely diverse range of marine life. Four-hour, two-dive trips go for $110 ($170 including all gear), and you can tag along to snorkel for $75. They also have backpacker-style budget accommodation ($35 per person), mainly aimed at divers. Topside, Jervis Bay Kayak Co, 13 Hawke St (℡02/4441 7157, ⓦwww.jervisbaykayaks.com), run a wide range of trips.

The beautiful coast of **Booderee National Park** ("bay of plenty", or "plenty of fish"), at the southern end of the bay, is very popular: rugged cliffs face the pounding ocean along its eastern boundary, while the park's northern side, within the confines of the bay, is marked by tranquil beaches of dazzling white sand and clear water. Inland, heaths, wetlands and forests offer strolls and bushwalks; there's also great snorkelling from the park and around nearby Bowen Island, with a chance of spotting a range of marine life including dolphins, stingrays and – around the island – a penguin colony. The park is jointly run by Wreck Bay Aboriginal Community and Environment Australia, and NPWS passes are not valid. For an aboriginal perspective on the place, contact Barry Moore of Barry's Bushtucker Tours (℡02/4442 1168). Booderee National Park's visitor centre (daily 9am–4pm; ℡02/4443 0977, ⓦwww.booderee.np.gov.au) is at the entrance to the park on Jervis Bay Road; detailed walking maps are available, and you also pay the entry fee here ($10 per vehicle for 48 hours). They handle all bookings for the three insanely popular unpowered **campsites** in the park – a ballot is held in August for spots over the Christmas holiday period. The *Cave Beach* site ($7–11 per site, plus $5–7 per person) is the most sought-after, despite its cold showers and 300-metre walk-in, but *Bristol Point* and *Green Patch* (both $10–20 per site, plus $5–10 per person) also get plenty of guests; the latter is the only one of the three suitable for campervans.

Booderee Botanic Gardens (May–Sept daily 9am–4pm, Oct–April Mon–Fri 9am–5pm, Sat & Sun 8am–6pm; free), on Cave Beach Road, focuses on regional coastal flora and has a number of pleasant walks with interpretative boards.

Practicalities

Ideally you'll want your own transport to get to Jervis Bay. The Shoalhaven **visitor centre** on Princes Highway in Nowra (daily 9am–5pm; ℡1300/662 808, ⓦwww.shoalhavenholidays.com.au) has the broadest information on the area, though there's a volunteer-run **information desk** (daily 9am–5pm; ℡02/4441 5241) in Huskisson at 1 Tomerong St. They offer electric mopeds ($29 for 2hr), and Dive Jervis Bay (see opposite) have mountain **bike rental** ($13 per hr, $45 per day).

Accommodation

Huskisson B&B 12 Tomerong St, Huskisson ℡02/4441 7551, ⓦwww.huskissonbnb.com.au. Lovely, beachy B&B in a 1913 weatherboard cottage with well-decorated "shabby chic" rooms, nourishing breakfasts and a multitude of home comforts. Two-night minimum at weekends and in Jan. ❽

Jervis Bay Backpackers ℡02/4441 6880, ⓦwww.jervisbaybackpackers.com.au. This very homely and welcoming place offers the most convenient budget accommodation in the area, with a self-contained flat or two in Huskisson and a house with dorm beds and a double room 2km south of Huskisson. Call for directions and details of buses. Dorms $30, doubles ❸

Jervis Bay Caravan Park 785 Woollamia Rd, 2km northwest of town ℡02/4441 5046,

ⓦwww.jervisbaycaravanpark.com.au. Waterside campsite with cabins, solar-heated pool and kayak rental. Sites $25, cabins ❸, luxury cabins ❺–❼

Paper Bark Camp 571 Woollamia Rd, 4km northwest of Huskisson ℡02/4441 6066, ⓦwww.paperbarkcamp.com.au. Unusual luxury eco-resort set in the middle of the bush, with accommodation in romantic en-suite safari tents on stilts, huge beds, private verandas, solar-powered lighting and a superb restaurant (see below). Rates from $320, but deluxe tents ($450) are larger and have a freestanding bath. Breakfast, bikes and canoe all included. ❾

Eating and drinking

The Gunyah Paper Bark Camp (see above) ℡02/4441 7299. Fabulously sited in the treetops, this airy restaurant allows you to view the resident possums and sugar gliders through the windows. Very good contemporary cuisine with mains at $30–35. Good value. Booking essential.

Husky Pub Owen St. Beachfront boozer with a good bistro and plenty of pool tables – very much the focus of the town.

Supply Café 54 Owen St. Daytime café which does the best all-day breakfasts and excellent espresso.

Ulladulla, Milton and around

ULLADULLA, 60km south of Jervis Bay, is a pleasant but uninspiring fishing port arranged along the Princes Highway, whose saving grace is its small, pretty harbour. The best local beach is **Mollymook**, 2km north, which has a few shops, motels and cafés. In terms of **activities**, there's swimming at Ulladulla's free seawater pool by the wharf (Nov–March 7–11am & 2–6pm; closed Tues), and scuba diving run by Ulladulla Dive & Adventure (℡02/4455 3029, ⓦwww.ulladulladive.com.au), 211 Princes Highway. The local Budamurra Aboriginal community (℡02/4455 5883, ⓦwww.budamurra.asn.au) has constructed an interesting cultural trail, "One track for all", at Ulladulla Head; turn off the highway at North Street and keep going.

It's also worth taking a detour 7km north along the Princes Highway to the village of **Milton**, a vaguely alternative place that's home to several craft shops, cafés and the **Milton Theatre** (ⓦwww.miltontheatre.com.au), which attracts predominantly acoustic acts – anything from classical to world music.

Ulladulla and Milton are set within a beautiful area, dominated by the sandstone plateau of the **Morton National Park** to the west, one of the biggest and wildest national parks in New South Wales. Towards the south of the park in the Budawang Ranges there's a good bushwalk to the top of the 720-metre **Pigeon House Mountain** (4.6km return; 3–4hr; 500m ascent), a fairly steep affair with some ladders for the final ascent. To get there, turn west off the Princes Highway 8km south of town along Wheelbarrow Road then follow signs 26km inland.

There are attractive river mouths, beaches and lakes along the coast in both directions. Pretty **Lake Conjola** (10km north), **Lake Burrill** (5km south) and **Lake Tabourie** (13km south) are popular with fishermen, canoeists and campers.

Practicalities

Premier Motor Service (℡13 34 10, ⓦwww.premierms.com.au) and Transborder (℡02/6241 0033, ⓦwww.transborder.com.au) buses call at Ulladulla, connecting the town with the coastal towns and Canberra respectively; Priors (℡1800 816 234) run through the Southern Highlands to Parramatta. There's a **visitor centre** (Mon–Fri 10am–6pm, Sat & Sun 9am–5pm; ℡02/4455 1269, ⓦwww.shoalhavenholidays.com.au) on the Princes Highway as it runs through Ulladulla, which has an activities and accommodation booking service and **internet** access.

Accommodation

Bannister's 191 Mitchell Parade, Mollymook, 2km north ℡02/4455 3044, ⓦwww.bannisters .com.au. Just south of Milton, the 31 rooms in this designer place are all decorated to the highest specifications: all have balconies with sea views, huge rainforest showers, and some have outdoor plunge pools. A spectacular cliff-top infinity pool adjoins a Moroccan-style bar with Campari-bottle lamp shades; a pricey, award-winning restaurant and indulgent day-spa are also on site. Summer off-peak rates from $260. ❾

Harbour Royal 29 Burrill St ℡02/4455 5444, ⓦwww.harbourroyal.com.au. Modest town-centre motel on a quiet street with all the usual facilities. ❹

Marlin Hotel 191 Mitchell Parade ℡02/4455 1999. Old-style shared-bath rooms with TV above one of the town's busiest pubs. At $30 per person, it's a bargain for singles. ❸

Seaspray Motel 70 Ocean St, Mollymook
☎02/4455 5311, ⓦwww.mollymookseaspray.com
.au. Pleasant, mainstream motel just across from
Mollymook beach, with welcoming owners. ➍

Southcoast Backpackers 63 Princes Highway,
500m north of town ☎02/4454 0500, ⓦwww
.southcoastbackpackers.com. Small and reasonable backpackers with cosy lounge and kitchen,
BBQ area, double rooms and 4- to 6-bed dorms.
Dorms $25, doubles ➋

Ulladulla Headland Tourist Park South St
☎1300 733 021, ⓦwww.holidayhaven.com.au.
Superb cliff-top location overlooking the harbour,
plus excellent amenities, including a swimming
pool, tennis court, children's playground and
cabins. Camping $10–15 per person, cabins ➋–➏

Eating

Bannister's Point Lodge 191 Mitchell Parade,
Ulladulla ☎02/4455 3044, ⓦwww.bannisters.com
.au. The restaurant at *Bannister's* (see opposite) is
one of the best on the south coast, with award-
winning food and a particularly good wine cellar.
Mains $30–40. Dinner Tues–Sun.

Edge Café Corner of Boree and Green sts,
Ulladulla. The best lunch option in town, this
spacious hideaway offers gourmet pizza, pasta,
salads and lots of veggie plates, plus great
brunches. Licensed & BYO. Open Mon–Sat daytime,
and dinner in summer.

Millard's Cottage 81 Princes Hwy, Ulladulla
☎02/4455 3287. This striking pink building, just
before you cross Millard's Creek, is one of Ulladulla's oldest. The interior is fairly traditional too, while
the menu offers very fine dining with lots of wines
by the glass and some pricey, unusual seafood and
meat mains such as pork with strawberry-and-
balsamic-vinegar sauce. Licensed & BYO. Mon–Sat
from 6pm.

Pilgrims Princes Hwy, Milton. Excellent vegetarian
wholefood place with courtyard seating. Their
buttermilk pancakes make a great breakfast, and
the "Millennium burger", made with curried lentil
patty, goes nicely with a mango lassi. Daily
9am–3pm.

Yes, I Am 22 Wason St, Ulladulla. Good town-
centre Thai restaurant with all the usual favourites
and harbour views. BYO.

Batemans Bay and around

At the mouth of the Clyde River and the end of the highway from Canberra,
BATEMANS BAY is a favourite escape for the landlocked residents of the
capital, just 152km away. It's not the most exciting place on the coast, but it's
a fair-sized resort with plenty to do. The town itself is focused around Clyde
and Orient streets, which run into one another. Beach Road runs alongside
the river to the pleasant marina, then southeast past a string of good beaches
– the further you go, the nicer they get. You can take a **cruise** on the Clyde
River with Merinda Cruises (3hr; $27; ☎02/4472 4052) whose trips include
a stop at the pretty village of **Nelligen**, 6km upstream (which is also accessible
off the road to Canberra). Alternatively, Straight Up Kayaks (☎0418 970 751,
ⓦwww.straightupkayaks.com.au) offer dusk paddles ($85) and full-day tours
to Nelligen ($115).

A number of small zoos and theme parks are dotted around town, including
Birdland Animal Park, 55 Beach Rd, Bateman, 2km southeast (daily
9.30am–4pm; $16; ⓦwww.birdlandanimalpark.com.au), where you can feed
the wallabies, watch koalas being fed, cuddle wombats and get draped in snakes.
In **MOGO**, 10km to the south, you can step back in time at the open-air **Old
Mogo Town Goldrush Theme Park** (daily 10am–4pm; $15; ⓦwww
.oldmogotown.com.au), a reconstruction of a mid-nineteenth-century goldrush
town. Nearby, the privately owned **Mogo Zoo** (daily 9am–5pm; feeding at
10.30am & 1.30pm; $20; ⓦwww.mogozoo.com.au) began life as a small
sanctuary, and has grown to something more akin to the Serengeti, housing
snow leopards, giraffe, monkeys and Australia's only pride of white lions. Just
north of town, the **Murramarang National Park** ($7 per vehicle per 24hr)
offers good bushcamping, and is popular not only with campers but also with
kangaroos, which come here at dawn and dusk to frolic on the beach –
especially Pebbly Beach (see p.248).

Practicalities

Transborder and Premier Motor Service buses call at Batemans Bay, stopping where Orient Street becomes Clyde Street. The **visitor centre** (daily 9am–5pm; [T]02/4472 6900 or 1800 802 528, [W]www.eurobodalla.com.au) is on Princes Highway, at the corner of Beach Road.

Accommodation

Accommodation consists mainly of motels and a wide range of holiday units; most of the latter require a minimum booking during school and public holidays.

Araluen Motor Lodge 226 Beach Rd, Batehaven [T]02/4472 6266, [W]www.araluenmotorlodge.com.au. Well-appointed motel with its own pool and restaurant across from Corrigans Beach. Units [4], kitchen units [5]

Batemans Bay Beach Resort 51 Beach Rd [T]02/4472 4541 or 1800 217 533, [W]www.beachresort.com.au. Smart, spacious resort with very plush beachfront cabins, some prime camping spots overlooking the water, and some reasonably priced backpacker rooms with TV and access to communal kitchen and bathrooms. Sites $31–34, backpacker rooms [3], cabins [8]

Batemans Bay YHA & Shady Willows Holiday Park Old Princes Hwy, 800m south of the town centre [T]02/4472 4972, [W]www.shadywillows.com.au. Slightly cramped holiday park with pool and menagerie located close to town, though it's quite a walk to the beaches. They've wedged in a small YHA section too, offering a rare chance to break out of the backpacker posse and mix with some "outsiders". Sites $22, dorms $25, doubles [2], cabins [3]

Old Post Office Nelligen Guesthouse 7 Braidwood St, Nelligen, 9km inland [T]02/4478 1079, [E]alison.peter1@bigpond.com.au. Recently renovated 1900 house with wooden floors, period decor and three en-suite rooms. [5]

Pebbly Beach 21km north [T]02/4478 6023. Drive-in bushcamping with showers, water, BBQs and lots of kangaroos. Also electricity-free cabins sleeping 4–6 with gas stove, fridge and bush shower. There's a two-night minimum and you'll need to bring bedding. Camping $10 per person, cabins [5]

Eating

There are several decent **places to eat** in Batemans Bay, especially down Clyde and Orient streets and on the esplanade.

Barkala 3 Orient St [T]02/4472 1888. Chic tapas bar with sea views, elegant decor, a great list of wines, sherries and cocktails plus large plates of, say, serrano ham ($12), manchego cheese ($8) and mushrooms with garlic and sherry vinegar.

The Boatshed Clyde St. Long-standing waterfront chippy that's excellent for fresh local seafood.

North St Café and Bar 5 North St [T]02/4472 5710. Stylish modern café that's fine for home-made cakes and coffee but also serves great food, most of it organic, with gluten-free dishes and even healthy options for kids. Expect the likes of wholemeal spelt pappardelle with roast pumpkin, pine nuts and pecorino ($18), or chicken breast with asparagus, olives and kipfler potatoes ($25). Daytime daily, plus dinner Fri & Sat.

On the Pier 2 Old Punt Rd, just over the bridge to the north [T]02/4472 6405, [W]www.onthepier.com.au. The nicest restaurant in town by a stretch. It's a bright, breezy place with good lounging possibilities, a great Aussie wine list, and imaginative seafood mains. As promised, you can actually eat on the pier. Daily noon–2.30pm & 6–8.30pm.

Sam's 3 Orient St [T]02/4472 6687. Long-standing family pizza and pasta restaurant with great views over the water. Large pizzas for $20. Licensed & BYO.

Narooma

Surrounded on three sides by beautiful beaches, inlets and coastal lakes, **NAROOMA**, 70km south of Batemans Bay, is perfect for watery pursuits, and lies at the heart of an area famous for its succulent **freshwater oysters**. The town is rather spread out along the Princes Highway – first Wagonga then

Campbell Street as it runs through the centre – with a marina down to the west and beaches to the east. First impressions are best from the pretty, 350m-long **Mill Bay Boardwalk**, which skirts the northern shore of Wagonga Inlet. Southern right and humpback whales migrate past the bay from September to early November; there's also a decent chance of seeing seals from the lookout at the end of Bar Rocks Road, particularly in spring.

You can canoe on the **Wagonga Inlet** and sail to the town's star attraction, **Montague Island**, an offshore sanctuary for sea birds, seals and Little penguins 9km offshore; Pelicans, at the marina on Riverside Drive (ⓣ02/4476 2403), rents out kayaks and boats. If you want to actually disembark at the island, you'll have to go on a tour with Narooma Charters (3–4hr; $130; ⓣ0407 909 111, ⓦwww.naroomacharters.com.au), since it's a protected wildlife reserve. Morning tours include a nature walk on the island with an NPWS guide, whilst evening tours have time set aside to see the penguins come ashore. Narooma Charters also offer **diving** and snorkelling, often combining time underwater with a trip to Montague Island for a small additional cost. Stand-alone dives go for around $75; if you don't have your own gear, rent it from Ocean Hut, on the corner of Field and Graham streets.

Scenic inlet **cruises** through the mangroves are available aboard the *Wagonga Princess* (Wed, Fri & Sun; 3hr; $33; ⓣ02/4476 2665, ⓦwww.wagongainletcruises .com), a charming little pine ferry very different from the usual glass bottomed tourist hulks. If catching marine life is more your thing, try Island Charters (6hr for $130; ⓣ02/4476 1047, ⓦwww.islandchartersnarooma.com) for reef and game fishing.

If you're in town over the long weekend at the start of October, don't miss the annual **Great Southern Blues and Rockabilly Festival** (ⓦwww .bluesfestival.tv).

Practicalities

Murray's Coaches run buses to Narooma from Canberra and Batemans Bay, while Premier Motor Service buses stop here on their Sydney–Melbourne route and Prior's end their run from Parramatta and the Southern Highlands here. The **visitor centre** (daily 9am–5pm; ⓣ02/4476 2881, ⓦwww.eurobodalla.com.au) is on the Princes Highway.

Accommodation

Ecotel 44 Princes Highway, on the northern side of the inlet ⓣ02/4476 2217, ⓦwww.ecotel.com.au. Good-value, simple motel rooms on a former dairy farm with views towards the coast. Everything is done with the environment in mind, so you can holiday and salve your conscience at the same time. ❹

Lyrebird Lodge 99 Armitage Rd, 13km southwest of Narooma ⓣ02/4476 3370, ⓦwww.tilba.com .au/lyrebirdlodge.htm. Fully self-contained mudbrick-and-boards, three-bedroom cottage among the gum trees, roughly equidistant from Narooma and Central Tilba, and worth the drive. ❼

Narooma Surfbeach Resort Ballingalla St ⓣ02/4476 2275, ⓦwww.naroomagolf.com.au. Adjoins the much-celebrated Narooma Golf Club, the beach and a creek. It's spacious, well situated, and far nicer than the caravan parks in town. Sites $22, cabins ❸–❺

Pub Hill Farm Tourist Drive 4, just south of Narooma, then 6km inland ⓣ02/4476 3177, ⓦwww.pubhillfarm.com. Great country-style B&B with four well-decorated en-suite rooms. It's extremely scenically situated, right on Punkallah Creek and overlooking Wagonga Inlet and Mount Dromedary. They also have a self-contained cottage with mezzanine bedroom, CDs and DVDs. B&B ❺, cottage ❻

Eating

Casey's Café Corner of Canty and Wagonga sts. A bright, cheery establishment, serving healthy, hearty food with many veggie options, giant smoothies and the best coffee in town. Daily 8am–4.30pm.

Lynch's Restaurant On the Princes Highway ⓣ02/4476 3002. Posh pub serving excellent contemporary Australian cuisine and local oysters. Mains $25–30. Daily from 6pm.

Pelicans Riverside Drive, by the marina ☎02/4476
2403. An upmarket, nautical-style option offering
fancy breakfasts and lunches, plus excellent
seafood in the evening, including beer-battered
flathead ($20) and bouillabaisse ($27). Tues–Thurs
& Sun 8am–5pm, Fri & Sat 8am–late.
Quarterdeck Marina Riverside Drive, by the
marina ☎02/4476 2723. An eclectic and colourful
restaurant with a great deck, good breakfast

pancakes, and Oz-style tapas. Mon & Thurs–Sun
8am–4pm.
The Whale Restaurant *Whale Motor Inn*, 104
Wagonga St ☎02/4476 2411. White tablecloths
and river views set the tone for this slow-food
restaurant serving the likes of lamb rump with
lemon myrtle jus ($30) and kelp-crusted salmon
with lime leaf and lemongrass beurre blanc ($29).
Licensed & BYO. Dinner Mon–Sat.

Central Tilba and Tilba Tilba

Some 15km south of Narooma, stop for a little wine-tasting at **Tilba Valley Wines**, 947 Old Highway (May–Sept Wed–Sun 11am–4pm; Oct–April daily 10am–5pm, ⓦwww.tilbavalleywines.com). Situated beside Corunna Lake, the winery provides an idyllic spot for a home-made lunch on the terrace or a game of croquet with the English owner. There's live music every first and third Sunday of the month.

A couple of kilometres south, signs direct you on a loop road off the highway inland through picturesque hill country to a couple of tiny villages. A few hundred metres off the highway, **CENTRAL TILBA** is by far the quaintest village on the south coast. Beautifully set against the forested slopes of Mount Dromedary, with many an old timber shop selling art, fudge, jewellery and gourmet foodstuffs, it invariably gets packed at weekends. The area is also famous for its cheeses, and Central Tilba's 1891 **ABC Cheese Factory**, 37 Bate St (daily 9am–5pm), on the main street, is open for visits and free tastings.

Almost everything happens on Bate Street where the *Rose & Sparrow Café* and *Tilba Teapot* offer decent cream teas and light **meals**. You'll probably appreciate the village better if you stay over, perhaps at *Two Story Bed and Breakfast*, Bate Street (☎1800 355 850, ⓦwww.tilbatwostory.com; ❺), a delightful place with chintzy decor and very friendly owners. A kilometre down Bate Street on the Tilba–Punkalla Road is *The Bryn* (☎02/4473 7385, ⓦwww.thebrynattilba .com.au; ❻–❼), a great B&B boasting bucolic views and a huge lounge with a wood-burning stove.

Some 2km south along the loop road, pretty **TILBA TILBA** is a tiny community with a pleasant walking trail up to the 797-metre summit of **Mount Dromedary** (11km return; 5–6hr; 600m ascent), which starts from Pam's Store. Nearby, the *Green Gables B&B* (☎02/4473 7435, ⓦwww.greengables.com.au; ❻–❼) is stylish, comfortable, and has gourmet breakfasts.

Wallaga Lake and around

South of Tilba Tilba the Princes Highway cuts inland for the next 85km down to Merimbula. On the whole, it's better to stick to the slower coast road which turns off at Tilba Tilba heading for Tathra, 60km south – as pleasant a drive as you'll find in this area, crossing wooden bridges over pristine lagoons, traversing bush and beach.

Some 7km south of the highway junction, *Wallaga Lake Park* (☎02/6493 4655; sites $25, cabins ❷, en suites ❹) is in a terrific location backing onto the lake and 400m from the wild Camel Rock Beach. The road continues 8km to **Bermagui**, 15km southeast from the highway, a pleasant fishing village with a limited range of places to stay and eat, and a **visitor centre** (daily 10am–4pm; ☎1800 645 808) on Lamont Street. One essential stop is *Saltwater*, 75 Lamont St, serving great **fish and chips** and local **oysters** beside the marina.

Burnum Burnum: Aboriginal activist

Wallaga Lake is the birthplace of one of Australia's most important Aboriginal figures, the elder named **Burnum Burnum**, an ancestral name meaning "great warrior". He was best known for his flamboyant political stunts, which included planting the Aboriginal flag at Dover to claim England as Aboriginal territory in Australia's bicentennial year, in order to highlight the dispossession of his native country. He was born under a sacred tree by Wallaga Lake in January 1936. His mother died soon afterwards and he was taken by the Aborigines Protection Board and placed in a mission at Bomaderry, constituting one of the "stolen generation" of indigenous children removed from their families in this period. After graduating in law and playing professional rugby union for New South Wales, he became a prominent political activist in the 1970s. He was involved in various environmental and indigenous protests, including erecting the "tent embassy" outside the Federal Parliament in Canberra (see p.234), and standing twice, unsuccessfully, for the senate. Burnum Burnum died in August 1997 and his ashes were scattered near the tree where he was born.

South of Bermagui, the terrain gets wilder for the remaining 45km to Tathra. Unsealed tracks branch off the coast road to **Mimosa Rocks National Park**, where there are opportunities for bushwalking, camping and swimming – check the National Parks website (W www.environment.nsw.gov.au) for details.

At **Thatra**, a pleasant fishing village, either cut inland to pick up the Princes Highway, or stick to the quieter coast route to Merimbula passing the coastal **Bournda National Park**, and many little art galleries and wineries en route.

Merimbula

The pretty town of **MERIMBULA** is surrounded by lagoons, lakes, rivers and ocean, making it ideal for watersports or an evening stroll along the shore. By day, you can explore Merimbula Lake (actually the wide mouth of the Merimbula River) and Pambula Lake with Merimbula Marina (T 02/6495 3611 or 1800 651 861, W www.merimbulamarina.com). They offer dolphin tours, boat rental, fishing charters and whale-watching tours (Sept–Nov; $69). So confident are they of seeing whales they offer a money-back guarantee.

There are some good **dive** sites around town. Merimbula Diver's Lodge (T 02/6495 3611, W www.merimbuladiverslodge.com.au) offer single and double boat dives ($66/$99), and also run a comfortable lodge at 15 Park St (from $29 per person).

You've a chance in a million of seeing a whale while you're underwater, but it has happened. To see sharks and tropical fish that are firmly under control, check out the **Merimbula Aquarium** (daily 10am–5pm; $11.50; T 02/6495 4446, W www.merimbulawharf.com.au) at the Wharf Restaurant at the end of Lake Street. Fish feeding (Mon, Wed & Fri 11.30am) is always popular.

For a chance to get up close and personal with wombats and koalas, stroke a python and learn something about Australia's diverse environments, visit **Potoroo Palace**, 2372 Princes Hwy, 9km north of town (Mon & Thurs–Sun and daily during school holidays 10am–4pm; $15; T 02/6494 9225, W www .potoroopalace.com.au), a not-for-profit wildlife sanctuary that also has kangaroos, crocodiles, a toy train and a good café.

Practicalities

Merimbula is well served with **buses**: Premier Motor Service down the coast from Sydney; CountryLink from Canberra, Cooma and on to Eden; and V/Line from Melbourne and Eden, and on to Batemans Bay. The **visitor centre**, 2 Beach St (Mon–Fri 9am–5pm, Sat 9am–4pm, Sun 10am–4pm; [T]02/6495 1129, [W]www.sapphirecoast.com.au) can advise on accommodation and has **internet** access. For national park information visit the **NPWS office** (Mon–Fri 8.30am–4.30pm; [T]02/6495 5000) on the corner of Sapphire Coast Drive and Merimbula Drive. Cycle 'N' Surf, Marine Parade ([T]02/6495 2171), **rent bikes and body boards**.

Accommodation

There are dozens of **motels** ([4]) and **holiday apartments** in Merimbula, all of which get booked up during the summer holidays, when many places hike their rates considerably and accept only weekly bookings.

Bella Vista 16 Main St [T]02/6495 1373, [W]www.merimbulabellavista.com.au. Mediterranean-style B&B a 5min walk from town, with a deck right on the waterfront where a lovely breakfast is served. [7]

Mandeni Resort Sapphire Coast Drive, 7km north from Merimbula on the road to Tathra [T]02/6495 9644 or 1800 358 354, [W]www.mandeni.com.au. Fully equipped timber cottages in a bushland setting, sleeping up to six. Facilities include tennis courts, swimming pools, a golf course, walking and mountain biking trails and, bizarrely, a needlecraft centre. Two-night minimum stay. [7]

Merimbula Beach Cabins 47–65 Short Point Rd [T]02/6495 1216 or 1800 825 555, [W]www.beachcabins.com.au. Spacious studios plus one- or two-bed cabins with inspiring ocean views, in a pleasant bushland setting overlooking Short Beach and Back Lake. Also has a pool and BBQ area. [4]–[5]

Merimbula Beach Holiday Park 2 Short Point Rd [T]02/6499 8988 or 1300 787 837, [W]www.merimbulabeachholidaypark.com.au. The nicest of several caravan parks in town, this one is scenically located in a breezy spot above the lovely Short Point Beach, and has a great pool. Good for families. Sites $28–32, cabins and villas [3]–[8]

Wandarrah Lodge YHA 8 Marine Parade [T]02/6495 3503, [E]meribula@yhansw.org.au. Modern, purpose-built youth hostel close to both the beach and lake, with good communal areas, games room, BBQ and bright, clean dorms. The very friendly owners take groups out to Ben Boyd National Park, or to see the 'roos at Pambula Beach on request, though the place is for sale. Phone to check it's still open. Dorms $28, doubles [3]

Eating

The Cantina 56 Market St. Great little tapas and wine bar also open during the day for breakfast and coffee.

Merimbula RSL Main St. A cut above the usual Returned and Services League club, with pokies well away from the dining area, which has big windows with distant harbour views. Huge range of menu options at reasonable prices. Free wi-fi too.

Sante Fe 23 Beach St. The chilli-fanatics here do a range of Mexican dishes ($18–25) and even habanero-flavoured wood-fired pizzas ($22). Licensed and BYO. Open daily for lunch & dinner.

Waterfront Café On the promenade by the visitor centre. Smart, with good breakfasts and lunches, including a delicious coconut, lime and prawn salad.

Zanzibar Café Corner of of Market and Main sts [T]02/6495 3636. The best restaurant in town, poorly located on a busy corner but with superb Mod Oz cuisine including the renowned Eden mussel chowder. Their 4-course tasting menu ($50) is good value. Tues–Sat 6–9pm.

Eden and around

EDEN, on pretty Twofold Bay, is just about the last seaside stop before the Princes Highway heads south towards Victoria, and by far the nicest coastal village in the south. In 1818 the first **whaling station** on the Australian mainland was established here, and **whaling** remained a major industry until the 1920s. Today Eden is touristy in a quiet sort of way, with good fishing and plenty of reminders of the old days, including the excellent **Killer Whale Museum** (Mon–Sat 9.15am–3.45pm, Sun 11.15am–3.45pm; $7.50;

@www.killerwhalemuseum.com.au) on the main drag, Imlay Street. The star attraction is the huge skeleton of "Old Tom", an orca who used to herd baleen whales into the bay then lead whaling boats towards the pods, in order to get his chops around the discarded bits of carcass. There's also plenty of old whale bones, boats, some interesting Aboriginal history, and a (literally) incredible account of a man being swallowed by a sperm whale and coming out alive fifteen hours later.

The busy main **wharf** in Snug Cove, at the bottom of Imlay Street, is a good place for a stroll, as are the two pretty **beaches**, Aslings and Cocora. Cat Balou Cruises (☏0427 962 027, @www.catbalou.com.au), based at the main wharf, offer two-hour dolphin-spotting tours ($30) and **whale-watching cruises** (late Sept–late Nov; 3hr 30min; $65). Ocean Wilderness (☏02/6495 3669, @www.oceanwilderness.com.au) run half-day **kayaking** adventures ($80), while Freedom Charters (☏02/6496 1209, @www.freedomcharters.com.au) are the town's **fishing** specialists.

Practicalities

Premier's Sydney–Eden buses stop here, while CountryLink buses link the town with Canberra, Cooma and Merimbula, and V/Line from Victoria continue up the coast to Batemans Bay. The **visitor centre** (daily 9am–5pm; ☏02/6496 1953, @www.edentourism.com.au), at the corner of Mitchell Sreet and Princes Highway, can advise on accommodation and book activities. The best area for **eating** is down at the main wharf, where bright and breezy *Taste of Eden* (BYO) is the pick of the daytime cafés, serving breakfast and lunch at long wooden tables – seafood and mussels are a mainstay of the changing menu. The excellent and airy *Wheelhouse* (daily from 6pm; ☏02/6496 3392) has strong surf and turf leanings, with dishes such as kangaroo fillet in oyster sauce ($32) and steamed local mussels ($29).

Accommodation

Cocora Cottage 2 Cocora St ☏02/6496 1241, @www.cocoracottage.com. Pretty, heritage-listed B&B with fine rooms, a cute garden bedecked with flowers, and a stunning sun deck with views over the bay at the rear. ❻

🏃 **Crown & Anchor Inn** 239 Imlay St ☏02/6496 1017, @www.crownandanchoreden.com.au. This little gem is the best B&B on the south coast, set in a beautiful historic building packed with antique furniture. Most of the exceedingly comfy rooms have super-lative ocean views, while breakfast is served on the back deck, overlooking the water. Complimentary champagne on arrival. ❼

Eden Tourist Park Aslings Beach Rd ☏02/6496 1139, @www.edentouristpark.com.au. Peaceful, leafy park with Lake Curalo on one side, and Aslings Beach on the other. Sites $20–23, cabins ❸–❹

Heritage House Motel & Units 178 Imlay St ☏02/6496 1657, @www.heritagehouseunits.com. Pleasant motel rooms and one- or two-bed units right in the centre of Eden; it's all a cut above the usual motel fare, with some rooms boasting striking views over Twofold Bay. Motel ❹, units ❺–❻

South of Eden

Heading south from Eden, you become increasingly surrounded by the vast temperate rainforests that characterize southeastern Australia. Roads lead off the highway to the east into the magnificent **Ben Boyd National Park** which hugs the coast to the north and south of Eden. As well as lovely beaches you can seek out the nineteenth-century folly of Boyd's Tower, and the Cape Green lightstation. The tower and lightstation can be linked by walking the **Light to Light Walk** (31km one-way; 2 days), which is predominantly coastal but also traverses heathland areas. There's no public transport, so the easiest way to tackle it is to base yourself midway at *Saltwater Creek* campsite ($10 per adult) and explore north and south on successive days. You can also stay in the self-contained former assistant lightkeeper's cottage at Cape Green ($200–300; book through Merimbula NPWS, see p.252), which sleeps six.

Inland, the summit of **Mount Imlay** can be reached via a walking track (6km return; 3–4hr; 600m ascent) that starts at the picnic grounds on Burrawang Forest Road, 14km south of Eden. The steep, strenuous ascent is rewarded by a panoramic view over the coast and across the dense forests of the hinterland onto the Monaro Plain.

The Snowy Mountains

Australia's highest terrain is in the **Snowy Mountains**, which peak at the 2228-metre **Mount Kosciuszko**, named in 1840 by the Polish-born explorer Paul Strzelecki, after the Polish freedom fighter General Tadeusz Kosciuszko. The Snowies are just one section of the Australian Alps which sprawl from northeast Victoria into New South Wales via the Crackenback Range, with much of the New South Wales section falling within the **Kosciuszko National Park** (Ⓦwww.nationalparks.nsw.gov.au/kosciuszko). This is the state's largest national park, extending 200km north to south and encompassing ten peaks above 2100m, forested valleys and a beautiful plateau with glacial lakes and rivers. Compared to the high mountain ranges of other continents, the "roof of Australia" is relatively low and the rounded and granite-strewn mountaintops lie below the line of permanent snow. Nonetheless, in **winter** (roughly late June–early Oct), skiers and boarders flock to Australia's most concentrated cluster of **ski resorts**, almost all in the Mount Kosciuszko area.

The downhilling isn't world-class and the snow is rarely dry, but it's better than you might think, and if you're into back-country skiing, the Snowy Mountains offer a paradise of huge, empty valleys, snowgum forests and wildlife. In summer, some of the resorts close completely but the towns are less crowded and work as bases for excellent hiking along with mountain biking, horse trekking, fishing and white-water rafting in crystal-clear mountain rivers.

The main resort town is **Thredbo** which operates ski-lifts throughout the year up to a high plateau, from where you can bushwalk across the wildflower-covered high country and reach Australia's highest summit. The other main ski town is lakeside **Jindabyne**, 35km further west along the scenic Alpine Way and just outside the eastern boundary of the park. It doesn't have its own ski-field but provides access along Kosciuszko Road to a string of resorts which virtually close down in summer. Smiggin Holes, Blue Cow, Guthega and Perisher Valley are jointly managed as **Perisher**, while **Charlotte Pass** is further uphill at the road end.

Eastern access to the region is through the small town of **Cooma**, where the hour-long drive to the snow guarantees lower accommodation prices. From here you can head for the northern reaches of the park and **Yarrangobilly Caves**, which are well worth the long drive.

Kosciuszko National Park practicalities

Visitors to Cooma and Jindabyne (both outside the park) and those driving through without stopping do not have to pay, but visitors to Thredbo, all the ski resorts and Yarrangobilly Caves must pay the **vehicle entry fee** (June–early Oct $27, early Oct–May $16) which is charged per 24-hour period. Pay

▲ The Snowy Mountains, Kosciuszko National Park

at the entrance station between Jindabyne and Thredbo, the NPWS visitor centre in Jindabyne or the newsagent in Thredbo and attach the sticker to your windscreen. Arriving by **bus**, you'll still have to make a one-off payment of $11.45 ($6.60 in summer). The New South Wales annual park pass ($190) is only a wise investment if you intend to spend a good chunk of time here in the snow season.

When you pay you'll be supplied with *Kosciuszko Today*, a seasonal newspaper with stacks of **information** on the national park and surrounds. Also look out for the free *Snowy Times*, which has resort information, maps, and listings of skiing prices and packages.

Getting there and around

In summer there is no useful public transport into or around the park so a car is pretty much essential. The **Snowy Mountains Highway** leads straight through the mountain ranges across the northern section of the Kosciuzko National Park. If you want to see more of the alpine scenery, head along the spectacular **Alpine Way**, turning off the highway at Kiandra in the heart of the park and heading south via Khancoban to Thredbo. In **winter**, check road conditions before driving anywhere; **snow chains** must be carried by two-wheel drives between June and early October, and are recommended for 4WD: some roads might be closed altogether. Numerous winter **bus** services operate around the area. The most useful is Transborder Alpinexpress (℡02/6241 0033, ⓦwww.transborder.com.au), which links Canberra, Cooma, Jindabyne and Thredbo daily. Cooma is also accessible from Canberra and Melbourne with V/Line (℡13 61 96, ⓦwww.vline.com.au). A number of small bus companies link Jindabyne and all the ski-fields in the winter – contact the visitor centre in Jindabyne (see p.257) for details.

Autopia Tours (℡03/9419 8878, ⓦwww.autopiatours.com.au) operate a Melbourne–Sydney three-day tour via the region for $395. Winter road access to the resorts of Perisher Valley and Mount Blue Cow is quite hairy and usually requires chains, but there's an intriguing alternative in the form of the **Skitube**

Skiing and snowboarding in the Snowy Mountains

The easiest option for **skiing in the Snowy Mountains** is to arrange a **ski package** departing from Sydney or Canberra – always check exactly what's included in the price. Be aware that snow conditions can let you down and that the resorts' interpretation of "good" conditions may not match yours, so check an independent source like the excellent ⓦ www.ski.com.au (which also has links for accommodation) before you go. Sydney-based Ski Kaos (ⓣ 02/9976 5555, ⓦ www.skikaos.com.au) offer weekend deals from $250 – you'll have to add food, lift pass and equipment to this.

The longest **downhill runs** are at Thredbo (ⓦ www.thredbo.com.au), while the Perisher Valley/Mount Blue Cow/Smiggin Holes/Guthega complex (known as Perisher; all one lift pass; ⓦ www.perisher.com.au) is the largest and most varied; other resorts include family-oriented Selwyn Snowfields, in the far north of the park (ⓦ www.selwynsnow.com.au), and Charlotte Pass (ⓦ www.charlottepass.com.au) which has more advanced runs. If you have your own equipment and vehicle, and don't need a package, check out the resort websites for details of lift pass prices and lift-and-lesson deals. Resorts are generally **child-friendly**, particularly Thredbo's Friday Flats area and Perisher's Smiggin Holes.

Paddy Pallin (ⓣ 1800 623 459, ⓦ www.mountainadventurecentre.com.au), in Jindabyne, run all manner of cross-country ski trips, plus mountain biking in summer.

(late June to mid-Sept daily every 20–60min; ⓦ www.perisher.com.au/winter/skitube). This rack railway ascends 8.5km (6.3km in tunnels) under the mountains from Bullocks Flat, roughly midway between Jindabyne and Thredbo, up to the resorts.

Cooma and around

The small town of **COOMA** is outside the national park and at least an hour from the nearest resort, but it successfully functions as a service centre for skiers. It's a fairly attractive place in its own right, with a number of fine old buildings on Lambie and Vale streets in particular; the visitor centre (see below) has a map of the five-kilometre "Lambie Town Walk".

If you're interested in the history and technical details of the Snowy hydro-electric project, which utilizes the water of the area's rivers to provide electricity to the ACT, New South Wales and Victoria, check out the **Snowy Mountains Hydro Information Centre** (Mon–Fri 8am–5pm, Sat & Sun 9am–2pm; ⓦ www.snowyhydro.com.au), on the Monaro Highway, 2km north of Cooma. The long-established Yarramba Trail Rides (1hr; $50; ⓣ 02/6453 7204, ⓦ www.yarramba.com.au) is located 25km northwest of town on Dry Plains Road, on the way to Adaminaby.

Cooma is also a base for **rafting**. Upper Murray Whitewater Rafting (ⓣ 1800 677 179, ⓔ rafting@snowy.net.au) offer a springtime half-day trip ($85) and a popular overnight trip ($310), camping beside the river.

Practicalities

The staff at the **visitor centre** (daily 9am–5pm; ⓣ 1800 636 525, ⓦ www.visitcooma.com.au) on the main road, Sharp Street, will just about vault over the counter in their eagerness to give you information about Kosciuszko National Park; they also offer internet access, an accommodation booking service and details of local farmstays. For **eating**, call at *The Lott*, 178 Sharp St, a smart organic foodstore and café turning out good breakfasts and lunches, or *Thai Continental*, 76 Sharp St (closed Mon) which serves plenty of spicy Thai favourites.

Accommodation

In summer you're better off **staying** in Jindabyne or Thredbo, but in winter prices are lower here and availability a little easier: most motels charge around $95 year-round.

Bunkhouse Motel 28–30 Soho St ☎02/6452 2983, [W] www.bunkhousemotel.com.au. Set around a pleasant central courtyard, this long-established, homely hostel and motel has a slightly Wild West feel to it. The wooden-walled dorms are chalet-cosy and the doubles adequate. Dorms $30, doubles [3]

Royal Hotel Corner of Lambie and Sharp sts ☎02/6552 2132. Fairly average rooms with shared bathrooms, most with French windows opening onto the pretty wrought-iron balcony. A bistro serving pub food is attached. [2]

Snowtels Caravan Park 286 Sharp St ☎02/6452 1828, [W] www.snowtels.com.au. Probably the best of the town's campsites, though not particularly salubrious. Sites $19–23, cabins [1]–[3]

White Manor Motel 252 Sharp St ☎02/6452 1152, [W] www.whitemanor.com. Far pleasanter than the majority of motels, with large, bright rooms, an abundance of potted plants and a good helping of chintz. [4]–[5]

Yarrangobilly Caves

In the northern reaches of Kosciuszko National Park, the **Yarrangobilly Caves** ([W] www.environment.nsw.gov.au), a vast system of about sixty limestone caves at the edge of a rocky plateau surrounded by unspoiled bushland, are one of the few specific sights in the park. They're located 6.5km off the Snowy Mountains Highway near Kiandra, 110km northwest of Cooma and 70km southwest of Canberra. There are guided tours daily to the **Jersey** (1pm; $13) and **Jillabenan** (11am & 3pm; $13) **caves**. A third cave, the **South Glory Cave** (daily 9am–4pm; $10.50), can be explored on a self-guided tour. From walking trails along the edge of the rock plateau there are panoramic views of the Yarrangobilly Gorge, and a steep trail leads from the Glory Hole car park to a **thermal pool** at the bottom of the gorge near the Yarrangobilly River. The spring-fed pool, which you can swim in (free), has a year-round temperature of 27°C.

Jindabyne and around

A scenic settlement beside the man-made lake of the same name, **JINDABYNE**, 63km west of Cooma, is the jumping-off point for most of the national park's ski resorts. From here Kosciuszko Road heads north then west, passing Smiggin Holes on the way and finishing up at Charlotte Pass.

The town itself sits just outside the national park and was created in the 1960s after the Snowy Mountains Scheme dammed the Snowy River and drowned the original settlement. There's good fishing on the lake and in summer you can also swim and sail – equipment is available to rent in town. The **Snowy Region Visitor Centre** (daily 8.30am–5pm; ☎02/6450 5600) in Jindabyne is the park's main visitor centre, and has details of walking trails, ranger-guided tours and campsites, as well as a free map and a café. There are also small NPWS **visitor centres** at Perisher Valley (☎02/6457 5214), Khancoban (☎02/6076 9373), Yarrangobilly (☎02/6454 9597) and Tumut (☎02/6947 7025).

Accommodation

Accommodation prices and availability follow the same seasonal pattern as Thredbo: moderately priced in summer but expensive and hard to get during the ski season, especially during school holidays and at weekends, so book ahead. You can expect the high-season winter prices below to drop by two price codes in summer.

Bimble Gumbie Alpine Way, Crackenback, 10km west of Jindabyne ☏ 02/6456 2185, ⊛ www.bimblegumbie.com.au. The most characterful place in the mountains by a long way: a tranquil cluster of eclectically decorated farmhouses set in sculpture-filled bushland, overflowing with art from every continent and century. The shelves are full of books, breakfast is included and dinner can be arranged. Excellent value, and not to be missed. **❼**–**❽**

Crackenback Farm Alpine Way, Crackenback, 10km west of Jindabyne ☏ 02/6456 2601, ⊛ www .crackenback.com.au. Plush loft rooms in a very cosy farmhouse with tiny indoor pool, sauna, day-spa, billiard table and the obligatory roaring fires. **❻**

Discovery Holiday Park Junction of Alpine Way and Kosciuszko Rd, 3km west of Jindabyne

☏ 02/6456 2099, ⊛ www.discoveryholidayparks .com.au. Right on the lakeshore, this excellent campsite has dorms, as well as a spa, sauna, Thai café-restaurant, tennis courts, and motor boat and canoe rental. Dorms $45, sites $40–45, cabins **❻**–**❾**

Kosciuszko Mountain Retreat Sawpit Creek, 12km north of Jindabyne ☏ 02/6456 2224, ⊛ www .kositreat.com.au. Beautiful, tranquil campsite set amongst a snowgum forest; kangaroos are regular visitors. Sites $25–35, cabins **❺**–**❽**

Snowy Mountains Backpackers 7–8 Gippsland St, Jindabyne ☏ 1800 333 468, ⊛ www .snowybackpackers.com.au. Pleasant hostel with clean, light dorms, BBQ area, comfy kitchen and common area and disabled access. There's also an internet café downstairs. Dorms $42, rooms **❺**

Eating

Crackenback Cottage Restaurant Alpine Way, 10km west of Jindabyne ☏ 02/6456 2198. Probably the best food in the Snowy Mountains, served with relaxed panache in a chalet with French country decor. Everything is freshly prepared, from home-made scones and jam to the modern cuisine (mains $25–35), and there's plenty of wines by the glass, some local. Closed Mon, and Tues outside of ski season.

Sublime NPWS visitor centre, Jindabyne (see p.254). Good café with big windows and decent

coffee and a range of muffins and cakes, plus the likes of prawn and noodle soup ($16) and quiche with salad ($14).

Wild Brumby Wollondibby Rd, Crackenback, 11km west. Modern schnapps distillery making all manner of fruit spirits (including one using their own raspberries) in a glass-walled room where you can also dine on great food such as Monaro lamb ragout slow-cooked with vegetables ($15).

Thredbo

From Jindabyne, the Alpine Way continues 35km west into the national park to **THREDBO**, an attractive, bustling little village at 1380m, entirely devoted to the needs of hikers, bikers and winter sports enthusiasts. The array of pitched-roof houses and condos huddles against the mountainside in a narrow valley between the road and the infant Thredbo River.

Unlike the other resorts, Thredbo is reasonably lively in summer, with activity focused on the Village Square where the bulk of the restaurants, bars and shops stay open year-round. There's a chairlift ticket and ski/board rental shop at the Valley Terminal, 100m away across the river. From here, the Kosciuszko Express **chairlift** (daily 8.30am–4pm; $28 return, $34 for a 2-day pass) carries you 560m up to the *Eagles Nest* **restaurant** (open all year) giving easy access to the hiking in the high country (see box opposite).

Once the snows have melted, some of the valley trails are open for **mountain biking**. **Bikes** can be rented from Southeast MTB Co, in the service station by the Village Square (☏ 02/6457 6234, ⊛ www.mountainbikingco.com.au; half-day $45–80). To get onto the fantastically steep runs down the ski slopes, go for the full-day package ($199) which includes fully sprung bike, lift ticket, full-face helmet with body armour and a compulsory first run down with an instructor. Nearby, the **Thredbo Bobsled** offers luge-style rides (1 ride $6, 10 rides $44) throughout the summer – take it easy on your first run. When the weather turns foul, head for the Thredbo Leisure Centre (⊛ www.thredbo.com.au), which has a fifty-metre **heated pool** with waterslide, plus gym and squash courts.

Hiking around Thredbo

Once the snows have melted, hikers take over the hills, with the main **hiking season** running from December through to April or May. Some of Australia's most interesting and beautiful bushwalking tracks pass through the area. Initially you might find yourself between beautiful snow gums with multicoloured bark in greens and yellows, before climbing up to the barren tops. Thredbo's Kosciuszko Express **chairlift** gives easy access to the high country and you can book guided **walks** through ⓦwww .thredbo.com.au.

Kosciuszko Summit (13km return; 4–6hr; 300m ascent). This relatively gentle hike starts with a ride on the Kosciuszko Express chairlift to the *Eagles Nest* restaurant on the edge of a high plateau. The altitude at the top of the chairlift will have you struggling to catch your breath, and it can be -5°C up here even in summer, so check conditions at the bottom. Views are particularly panoramic from Kosciuszko Lookout (after 2km), from where Australia's highest peak seems barely higher than the surrounding country. Can be hiked from Thredbo village using Merritts Nature Track (see below).

Main Range Walk (32km loop; 8–10hr; 600m ascent). Perhaps the best hike in the park, this starts from the top of the Kosciuszko Express chairlift and follows the Kosciuszko Summit track, then skirts a beautiful glacial lake before dropping down to Charlotte Pass ski resort and looping back via the stone Seaman's Hut. Can be done in one very long day, as an overnight hike with camping gear, or as a half-length guided hike ($60; ⓦwww.thredbo.com.au) with a bus pick-up from Charlotte Pass.

Merritts Nature Track (4km one-way; 2–3hr; 560m ascent). A picturesque alternative to riding the Kosciuszko Express chairlift to the *Eagles Nest* restaurant. Best done downhill, unless you relish the slog.

Practicalities

The **visitor centre** (daily 10am–4pm or later; ☎02/6459 4100, ⓦwww .thredbo.com.au), in the Village Square, has details of annual events such as the **Thredbo Blues Festival** (ⓦwww.thredboblues.com.au) in mid-January, the **Rocks the Snowys** roots and country music festival in March (ⓦwww .countrymusicchannel.com.au) and the **Thredbo Jazz Festival** (ⓦwww .thredbojazz.net.au) in early May.

Accommodation

In winter, **rooms** are almost impossible to come by without a reservation; minimum stays are enforced and **prices** are high. In summer the situation is far better – you should have little difficulty finding somewhere, and you can expect the rates below to drop by two price codes. There are a couple of campsites (see below), and walk-in **camping** is permitted (free) in most of the national park, except day areas and within 200m of any road.

The Denman Diggings Terrace ☎02/6457 6222, ⓦwww.thedenman.com.au. Smart boutique hotel in the heart of the village with upmarket, minimalist (and minimal-sized) rooms, a swanky cocktail bar, day-spa and *The Terrace*, an award-winning restaurant. Breakfast is included, and dinner packages are available. ⑨

Kasees Lodge 4 Banjo Drive ☎02/6457 6370, ⓦwww.kasees.com.au. An excellent guesthouse centred around a European-style guest lounge, which has a piano for après-ski singalongs. The eight large rooms have the best mountain views in town. 2-night deals from $390.

Ngarigo Alpine Way, 10km east of Thredbo. Basic but very pleasant streamside camping with longdrops and river water. Free.

Thredbo Diggins Alpine Way, 14km east of Thredbo. More streamside camping with longdrops and river water. Free.

Thredbo YHA 8 Jack Adams Path ☎02/6457 6376, ⓔthredbo@yhansw.org .au. Central and spacious, purpose-built hostel with cosy fires and communal areas and great views across the mountains. Also some en-suite dorms. Unfortunately for backpackers, in peak season this must be the most expensive hostel in Australia, and in July & Aug they have special 2- and 3-night packages. Access off Buckwing Place. Dorms $52 (peak season weekends $81), doubles [5]

Eating and drinking

Some of Thredbo's **restaurants** close down in summer, but there are always a few places open around the Village Square.

Altitude 1380 Village Square, Thredbo. Handy spot for coffee, hearty breakfasts and the likes of burgers and wedges for lunch (around $11), plus fancier stuff like hearty broths ($12), Caesar salad ($14) and pasta dishes ($18–22).

🏃 **Apres Bar** *The Denman*, Diggings Terrace. With its glowing yellow bar, admirable cocktail list and prices no more expensive than the rest of town, the *Apres Bar* has long been a Thredbo favourite.

Bernti's 4 Mowomba Place ☎02/6457 6332. Cheerful tapas bar with offerings from around the world, such as Tandoori lamb cutlets with lime and coriander salsa ($14) and smoked trout bruschetta ($12).

🏃 **T-Bar** Village Square ☎02 6457 6355. Year-round chargrilled steak ($35) and gourmet pizza ($25) restaurant with a relaxed vibe and snug interior.

The north coast

The coast from Sydney **north to Queensland** is more densely populated and much more touristy than its southern counterpart, with popular holiday destinations such as **Port Stephens**, **Port Macquarie** and **Coffs Harbour** strung along the coast north of Newcastle. Since the 1970s, the area around **Byron Bay** has been a favoured destination for people seeking an alternative lifestyle; this movement has left in its wake not only disillusioned hippie farmers (as well as a few who've survived with their illusions intact), but also a firmly established artistic and alternative scene.

As in the south, the **coastline** consists of myriad inlets, bays and coastal lakes, interspersed with white, sandy beaches and rocky promontories. Parallel to the coast are the rocky plateaus of the **Great Dividing Range**, whose national parks provide bushwalkers with remote, rugged terrain to explore. Numerous streams tumble down from the escarpment in mighty waterfalls, creating fertile river valleys where the predominant agricultural activity is cattle breeding; in the north, subtropical and tropical agriculture takes over, especially the cultivation of bananas. In essence, the further you go, the better this coast gets.

Getting up the north coast is easy, with frequent **train** and **bus** services between Sydney and Brisbane, as well as a number of local bus services (detailed within individual town accounts and on p.303).

Port Stephens

Just north of Newcastle, the wide bay of **Port Stephens**, which extends inland for some 25km, offers calm waters and numerous coves ideal for swimming, watersports and fishing, while the ocean side has good surf and wide, sandy beaches. In January, thousands of families arrive to take their annual holiday in the area dubbed "Blue Water Paradise". The main township of **NELSON BAY** is perched at the tip of the bay's southern arm, together with the quieter settlements of Shoal Bay, Soldiers Point, Fingal Bay and Anna Bay. Stockton Beach, to the south, has some of the largest sand dunes in the eastern Australian mainland. Port Stephens 4WD Tours ([T]02/4984 4760, [W]www.portstephens4wd.com.au), 35 Stockton St, Nelson Bay, run trips to the giant slopes – try sandboarding or driving down the slopes in a 4WD; the black, metallic pyramids rising out of the sand (World War II anti-tank defences) give the experience a sci-fi twist.

From May to November you might see **whales** as they migrate first north then south, while **dolphin cruises** are available all year round, most leaving from d'Albora Marina in Nelson Bay. Try Moonshadow Cruises (1hr 30min; $26; [T]02/4984 9388, [W]www.moonshadow.com.au;) or Simba II Cruises (3hr; $27; [T]02/4984 3843, [W]www.psboats.nelsonbay.com), which departs from Nelson Bay and Tea Gardens; they also run a ferry service between the two places ($22 return). Much more satisfying than a motor cruise, though, are the eco-friendly trips aboard a fifteen-metre catamaran run by Imagine Cruises (dolphin cruise around 1hr 30min, $30; whale-and-dolphin cruise from May to November, 3hr, $60; [T]02/4984 9000, [W]www.imaginecruises.com.au) out of Nelson Bay. To swim among the dolphins and other marine life contact Pro Dive ([T]02/4981 4331, [W]www.prodivenelsonbay.com; from $120). You can go **surfing**, **horse-trekking**, **parasailing**, **sea-kayaking** and rent jet skis all around the bay; see the visitor centre or check their excellent website (see below) for details.

Practicalities

Getting around the bay is easiest if you have your own vehicle, though Busways call at Tea Gardens en route between Sydney and Taree, and Greyhound and Premier Motor Service stop at Karuah, midway around the bay. Port Stephens Coaches ([W]www.pscoaches.com.au) links all the smaller beach settlements with Nelson Bay, and runs an express service from Sydney and Newcastle. The **visitor centre** (daily 9am–5pm; [T]02/4980 6900, [W]www.portstephens.org.au) is at Victoria Parade in Nelson Bay, and offers an accommodation, tour and cruise booking service.

Accommodation-wise, there are scores of motels ([4]–[5]) and even more holiday apartments to choose from in the area, though many insist on weekly bookings during the holiday season – the visitor centre will be able to help you out if you find yourself homeless.

Accommodation

Halifax Holiday Park Beach Rd, Shoal Bay Beach, 2km east of Nelson Bay [T]02/4981 1522 or 1800 600 201, [W]www.beachsideholidays.com.au. A well-equipped beachside caravan park resort with campsite with camp kitchen, BBQ area and kids' activities. Sites $55, cabins and villas [7]–[9]

Melaleuca Surfside Backpackers 2 Koala Place, One Mile Beach [T]02/4981 9422, [W]www.melaleucabackpackers.com.au. Red cedar timber bungalows, camping and dorms set in tranquil bushland roamed by koalas and possums. A great option, especially as it's only minutes from an excellent surf beach. Sites $15–20pp, dorms $28–32, doubles [4]

Nelson Bay B&B 81 Stockton St, Nelson Bay [T]02/4984 3655, [W]www.nelsonbaybandb.com.au. Light and bright 4-star B&B with three airy rooms, 10min walk from town. [4]–[7]

Samurai Beach Bungalows YHA Corner of Frost Rd and Robert Connell Close, Anna Bay [T]02/4982 1921, [W]www.yha.com.au. Set in lush gardens, this is the best budget option in the area: four smart bungalows, with polished floorboards – and resident possums – arranged around an undercover "bush" kitchen. There are free boards and bikes, a small pool and a BBQ area. Port Stephens Buses from Sydney stop outside. Dorms $26–29, doubles [3]–[4]

Myall Lakes National Park and around

From Port Stephens the Pacific Highway continues north past the beautiful **Myall Lakes National Park**, which well rewards a day or so of exploration. About 20km before the small town of **Bulahdelah**, turn right onto Tea Gardens Road for a heavenly drive to **Mungo Brush**, along the shores of Myall Lake. There are plenty of gentle walking tracks around here, while a more challenging 21-kilometre hike leads back to **Hawks Nest**, on Port Stephens Bay. Just after Mungo Brush, the charming Bombah Point Ferry takes you and your car over Myall Lake (daily 8am–6pm; every 30min; $5; ℡02/6591 0300) and back to Bulahdelah and the highway via the unsealed Bombah Point Road; the service is occasionally suspended when water is low or due to mechanical problems, so always call ahead.

Heading north again towards Forster–Tuncurry, you can turn east just after Bulahdelah onto the extremely scenic **Lakes Way** (tourist drive 6). A short distance away, at Bungwahl, a turn-off leads down mostly unsealed roads to **SEAL ROCKS**, a remote, unspoilt fishing village and the only settlement in the **national park**. The first beach you come to, the inspirationally named Number One Beach, is truly beautiful, with crystal-clear waters marooned between two headlands. Two minutes to the south, there are great waves for surfing. **Sugar Loaf Point Lighthouse** is around ten minutes' walk up a steep path; the grounds offer fantastic 360-degree views, and the lookout below leads down to a deserted, rocky beach. Seal Rocks' seasonal agglomerations of nurse sharks make it one of the best **dive sites** in New South Wales; contact Forster Dive Centre (see p.262) to arrange a trip.

North of Seal Rocks, the exhilarating drive through the tiny **Booti Booti National Park** takes you through endless forests, over a narrow spit of land between Wallis Lake and Elizabeth Bay where it's hard to keep your eyes on the road, especially at sunset. Ten kilometres further north, a bridge connects the twin holiday towns of **FORSTER–TUNCURRY**, the former set on the strip of land separating **Wallis Lake** from the ocean. The lake is very pretty, but Forster itself decidedly isn't, being somewhat blighted by high-rise development. It's a good base for all manner of cruises and watersports though, and famous for its **oysters** and playful resident **dolphins** – Amaroo Cruises (10am most days; 2hr; $45; ℡0419 333 445, ⊛www.amaroocruises.com.au), at the end of Memorial Drive, run dolphin-watching trips. Forster Dive Centre (℡02/6555 4477, ⊛www.forsterdivecentre.com.au), at 11–13 Little St, offers diving at Seal Rocks, fishing trips, and swimming with dolphins, while the nearby Boatshed Number One (℡02/6554 7733) at 1 Little St, rents out luxury houseboats, canoes and wave skis. For non water-babies, Tobwabba Art Gallery (Mon–Fri 9am–5pm; free; ℡02/6554 5755; ⊛www.tobwabba.com.au) at 10 Breckenbridge St has some wonderful indigenous art by the Worimi people.

Practicalities

To explore the Myall Lakes National Park in your own time you really need a vehicle, although Busways runs along the Lake Way to Bungwahl. Greyhound and Premier Motor Service **buses** both serve Forster, with Greyhound also stopping at Bulahdelah. The well-organized **visitor centre** (daily 9am–5pm; ℡02/6554 8799 or 1800 802 692, ⊛www.greatlakes.org.au), on Little Street in Forster, is responsible for the Myall Lakes area and offers an accommodation booking service.

Wharf Street, the main strip in Forster, has numerous cafés, restaurants and takeaways; the buzzy *Reef Bar Grill* (☎02/6555 7092) has the rarity of an all-day menu, one of the best waterfront locations, and dishes up deliciously fresh seafood, including local Wallis Lake Oysters. Nearby on Memorial Drive, *Bella Bellissimo* (☎02/6555 6411) has long been a local favourite, offering gourmet pizza, pasta and risotto. If you want to **stay** in the area overnight, bushcamping in the Myall Lakes is an appealing option; check the national parks website ([W] www.nationalparks.nsw.gov.au) for listings. There are scores of holiday apartments and motels (❺–❾) in Forster.

Accommodation

BreakFree Mobys Boomerang Beach, Pacific Palms ☎1800 655 322, [W] www.breakfreemobys.com.au These stylish beach houses come with all mod cons, including CD/DVD players, and are minutes from the beach. There's a chic restaurant serving up creative cuisine and a bar on site. Beach houses ❼–❾

EcoPoint Myall Shores Resort Right by the Bombah Point Ferry on the northern side of the lake (see p.262), 16km southeast of Bulahdelah ☎02/4997 4495, [W] www.myallshores.com.au. Beautifully located, tranquil resort, boasting rather stylish waterfront villas, cabins, bunks, camping and a smart café-restaurant, plus loads of activities including canoe, boat and bike rental. The best option in the national park by far if you don't like to stay under canvas. All sites $25, cabins and villas ❹–❽

Forster Caravan Park Reserve Rd, Forster ☎1800 240 632 [W] www.forsterbeachcaravan.com.au Centrally located caravan park overlooking the marina and a minute's walk to the beach. Spotless amenities, playground and beach frontage. All sites $33, cabins ❺–❼

Seal Rocks Camping Reserve Seal Rocks ☎02/4997 6164 or 1800 112 234, [W] www.sealrockscampingreserve.com.au. Glorious, unspoilt site right on beautiful Number One Beach, with great-value facilities. Although there's a small general store in the settlement, you should bring supplies in with you. If it's full, *Treachery Camp* (☎02/4997 6138, basic camping only $13pp, cabins ❹–❼) is at 166 Thomas Rd, a couple of minutes' drive around the headland. Un/powered sites $24/28–25, 5/6-berth cabins ❸–❺

Sundowner Tiona Tourist Park The Lakes Way, 19km south of Forster ☎02 6554 0291, [W] www.sundownerholidays.com. Beautiful location right on Seven Mile Beach, in the Booti Booti National Park, with good facilities, and a wide array of accommodation options, from a backpackers lodge to beachside, lakeside and sand dune cabins. Un/powered sites $28–35, dorms $22.50, cabins ❺–❾

Barrington Tops and Ellenborough Falls

Heading from Forster–Tuncurry via Nabiac and Gloucester, you arrive at the World Heritage–listed **Barrington Tops National Park** ([W] www.barringtons.com.au). It's gentle, hilly farming country up to the country town of **Gloucester**; about 40km beyond here, unsealed roads lead through the park. The closest you'll get to the park with public transport is on the train from Sydney or Newcastle to Gloucester or Dungog; *The Barringtons Country Retreat* (see p.264) offers free pick-ups from the latter.

The Barrington Tops themselves are two high, cliff-ringed plateaus, **Barrington** and **Gloucester**, which rise steeply from the surrounding valleys. The changes in altitude within the park are so great – the highest point is 1586m – that within a few minutes you can pass from areas of subtropical rainforest to high, windswept plateaus covered with snow gums, meadows and subalpine bog. Up on the plateau, snow is common from the end of April to early October.

The **Great Lakes Visitors Centre** in Forster (see opposite) can help with specific routes or organized 4WD tours into the national park. There are plenty of picnic grounds, walking trails and scenic **lookouts** in the park. A 4WD is often required to access the many **campsites** ($14 per person, vehicle entry fee $7 per day): check out the New South Wales National Parks and Wildlife website (Ⓦwww.environment.nsw.gov.au) or contact the NPWS in Gloucester (Ⓣ02/6538 5300) or Scone (Ⓣ02/6540 2300) for locations and advice. The other **accommodation** in the area is relatively pricey, but there are lots of options. One of the closest places to the park is *Salisbury Lodges* (Ⓣ02/4995 3285, Ⓦwww.salisburylodges.com.au; ❾), at 2930 Salisbury Rd in Salisbury, 40km northwest of Dungog. This wilderness retreat is perfect for a cozy country weekend, with timber lodges, with fireplaces and spas, a good restaurant and a gorgeous rainforest setting. You'll find a range of cheaper alternatives, from snug cottages to timber lodges on Ⓦwww.thebarringtons.com.au (❹–❽), including *Wangat Lodge and Melia & Overflow Cottages* (Ⓣ02/4995 9265) on 1938 Chichester Dam Rd, 23km north of Dungog, whose cabins and lodges boast log fires and corner spa baths.

Heading north to Port Macquarie via Gloucester and Wingham, you can call at the two-hundred-metre-high **Ellenborough Falls**, one of the most spectacular waterfalls on the whole coast; the falls are located near Elands on Bulga Forest Drive – unsealed for much of the way.

Port Macquarie and around

The fast-growing town of **PORT MACQUARIE**, at the mouth of the Hastings River, has a beautiful natural setting. Long, sandy **beaches** extend far along the coast, while the hinterland is dotted with forests, mountains and pretty towns. The town was established in 1821 as a place of secondary punishment for convicts who continued their criminal ways after arrival in New South Wales, though by the late 1820s the **penal settlement** was closed and the area opened up to free settlers. An increasing number of independent travellers call into "Port", but it remains primarily a family-focused resort. The **activities** on offer are really the thing here, with mini-zoos, nature parks, cruises on the Hastings River, horseriding and, above all, watersports and fishing outlets all vying for your attention.

Arrival and information

Greyhound and Premier Motor Service stop at Port Macquarie on their runs between Sydney and Brisbane, while Kean's run to Tamworth, Nambucca Heads and Coffs Harbour. **Buses** drop you in the centre of town on Hayward Street, although not all make the detour from the Pacific Highway, so check carefully. Countrylink **trains** stop in Wauchope, 22km to the west, from where there's a connecting bus service. You can **fly** to Port Macquarie from Sydney with Qantas; the airport is about 6km west of town.

Horton Street is the main downtown street, running north to the Hastings River. The helpful **visitor centre** (Mon–Fri 8.30am–5pm, Sat & Sun 9am–4pm; Ⓣ02/6581 8000 or 1300 303 155, Ⓦwww.portmacquarieinfo.com.au), just out of the CBD on the corner of Gore and Gordon streets, can book rooms and activities. The town's attractions and beaches are far-flung, and local transport isn't the best. You can **get around** much of town on Busways (Ⓣ02/6583 2499, Ⓦwww.busways.com.au), but the best option is **cycling** (see p.267).

Accommodation

Despite the huge number of motels and apartments in town, Port Macquarie still gets booked out over summer and during school holidays, so make reservations

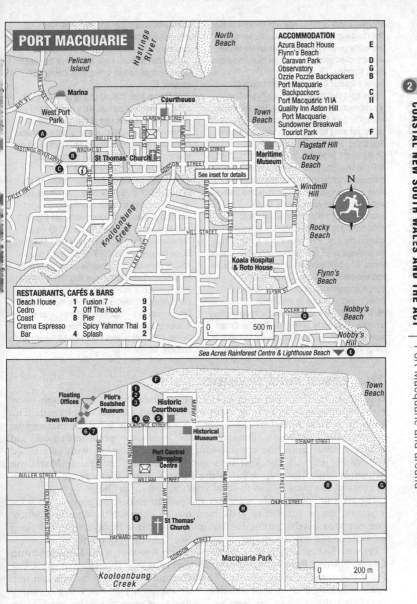

PORT MACQUARIE

See inset for details

ACCOMMODATION

Azura Beach House	E
Flynn's Beach Caravan Park	D
Observatory	G
Ozzie Pozzie Backpackers	B
Port Macquarie Backpackers	C
Port Macquarie YHA	H
Quality Inn Aston Hill Port Macquarie	A
Sundowner Breakwall Tourist Park	F

RESTAURANTS, CAFÉS & BARS

Beach House	1	Fusion 7	9
Cedro	7	Off The Hook	3
Coast	8	Pier	6
Crema Espresso Bar	4	Spicy Yahmor Thai	5
		Splash	2

Sea Acres Rainforest Centre & Lighthouse Beach ▼ **E**

in advance – out of season, prices drop dramatically. The visitor centre can book you an apartment, but the motels are all pretty similar, so off-season just cruise around town to see which takes your fancy. The backpackers' do free pick-ups from the coach stop.

Azura Beach House B&B 109 Pacific Drive ☏ 02/6582 2700, ⍟ www.azura.com.au. A rather

smart B&B close to Shelly Beach with modern, comfortable rooms with balconies, a small pool,

BBQ and comfy guest-lounge with books and films. The considerate hosts provide picnics on request and rustle up very nice breakfasts on the wooden veranda, overlooking lush gardens. Complimentary travel transfers. [5]–[9]

Flynn's Beach Caravan Park 22 Ocean St, 2.5km from the centre ☎02/6583 5754, [W]www.flynnsbeachcaravanpark.com.au. This leafy park just 200m from Flynn's Beach has a range of cabins set amid ferns and gum trees, a pool and BBQ areas. Sites $32–38, cabins [5]–[6]

Observatory 40 William St, Town Beach ☎02/6586 8000, [W]www.observatory.net.au. These stylish contemporary apartments and hotel rooms are sleek and spacious with all mod cons and balconies with stunning sea views. Rooms [4]–[9]

Ozzie Pozzie Backpackers 36 Waugh St ☎02/6583 8133 or 1800 620 020, [W]www.ozziepozzie.com. Friendly, vibrantly painted place set around a small central courtyard, with standard dorms, free boogie-boards, bikes for $5, BBQ area and free breakfast. Dorm $26, doubles [3]

Port Macquarie Backpackers 2 Hastings River Drive, corner of Gordon St ☎02/6583 1791 or 1800 688 882, [W]www.portmacquariebackpackers.com.au. Great hostel in an 1888 Victorian Gothic weatherboarded building, instantly recognizable by the globe outside. Colourful, comfy dorms, fine communal areas, pool and BBQ area, plus a fun atmosphere. The enthusiastic ex-backpacker owner runs kangaroo camping trips to the beautiful Crowdy Bay National Park, and there's free use of bikes, surfboards and fishing gear. Dorms $27, doubles [3]

Port Macquarie YHA 40 Church St ☎02/6583 5512, [W]www.yha.com.au. Very compact and very yellow YHA in a quiet part of town, with laid-back atmosphere to match. Nice dorms and reasonable communal areas are supplemented by free boogie-boards, bikes ($5), and a small outdoor area. Dorms $27–30, double rooms [4]

Quality Inn Aston Hill Port Macquarie 15 Mort St ☎02/6583 3266, [W]www.qualityportmac.com.au. This modern motel and contemporary apartments in a separate building nearby are a good option for overnight stays. Rooms [4]–[9]

Sundowner Breakwall Tourist Park 1 Munster St, on the riverfront ☎02/6583 2755 or 1800 636 452, [W]www.sundownerholidays.com. Right in the heart of town next to the river, this family-oriented park is superbly located and feels roomy despite the number of cottages and cabins packed into it. Lots of activities – including surf trips – are offered in case the pool and kids' club lose their appeal. Dorms $25, un/powered sites $47–59, cabins and cottages [6]–[9]

The town and around

Port Macquarie has a tendency to destroy reminders of its past, though a few early buildings survive; pick up a historic walk leaflet at the visitor centre. The 1835 **Historical Museum** (Mon–Sat 9.30am–4.30pm; $6) at 22 Clarence St, opposite the courthouse, illuminates early life in the penal settlement, and houses a rather gruesome convict-whipping stool complete with fake blood that should frighten the kids into good behaviour. The quaint **Maritime Museum** (daily 10am–4pm; $5) in the **Pilot Station Cottages** at 6 William St contains the usual mix of nautical artefacts and model boats.

The river foreshore, with its anglers and pelican colony, is a pleasant place for a peaceful sunset stroll or to grab some fish and chips. Floating offices where you can book anything from dolphin tours to seaplane flights are located along its western end, towards the town wharf (see "Listings", opposite).

Perhaps the best attraction in the town centre, however, is the **Kooloonbung Creek Nature Park**, a large bushland reserve remarkably close to the CBD. From the entrance at the corner of Horton and Gordon streets, you can step onto trails among casuarinas, eucalypts and swampy mangroves, visit a cemetery containing the graves of eminent early settlers, or sweat through a small patch of rainforest – were it not for the boardwalks and faint hum of traffic, it'd be amazingly easy to believe that you were lost in the bush.

A string of fine beaches runs down the ocean-facing side of town (Town, Flynn's and Lighthouse are patrolled); perhaps the best way to spend a day in Port Macquarie is to rent a bike and explore the cliff-top paths and roads that link them all. You can call in at the **Sea Acres Rainforest Centre** (daily 9am–4.30pm; free guided walks at regular intervals, including bushtucker walks with indigenous guides; $6), 4km south of town on Pacific Drive at Shelly Beach – the impressive centre features a 1.5-kilometre boardwalk through rare types of sub-tropical rainforest, which can be enjoyed at close quarters.

Back towards the town centre on Lord Street, in the grounds of **Roto House**, is Australia's oldest **koala hospital** (daily 8am–4.30pm; free; "Feed, Walk & Talk" guided tour 3pm, additional feeding 8am; W www.koalahospital.org.au)   you can even adopt one of the "patients" if you get particularly attached. For more cuddly creatures, the **Billabong Koala & Wildlife Park** (daily 9am–5pm; koala petting at 10.30am, 1.30pm & 3.30pm; $18; W www.billabongkoala.com.au) at 61 Billabong Drive, off the Oxley Highway west of the town centre, has koalas as well as emu chicks, kangaroos, monkeys and reptiles.

You'll find the **wines** produced at Cassegrain Winery (daily 9am–5pm; W www.cassegrainwines.com.au), at 764 Fernbank Creek Rd, off the Pacific Highway, 10 minutes west of town, on many a wine list in the area; the award-winning restaurant here, Ça Marche (daily 10am–4pm snacks, noon–3pm & Fri 6–9pm meals; T 02/6582 8320, W www.camarche.com.au), is a great spot for a long lunch overlooking the vineyards.

Eating and drinking

There are a growing number of good, innovative places to **eat** in town. You can buy fresh fish and seafood for the BBQ from the **Fishermen's Co-op**, by the town wharf. Where a phone number is listed, it's best to book.

Beach House 1 Horton St. The waterside bar with wraparound wooden veranda overlooking the river is a great spot for a morning coffee or sunset drinks.
Cedro 70 Clarence St T 02/6583 5529. Breakfast and lunch are so good at this casual café with sunny tables in a garden setting that locals wish it was open for dinner. The enticing breakfast menu includes delights such as Turkish bread with eggs, chorizo and bacon, and scrambled eggs with freshly caught crab and preserved lemon, while lunch is Mediterranean meets Middle East. Daily 7.30am–2.30pm.
Coast 40 William St, Port Macquarie T 02/6583 9300. Expect bistro standards based on fresh regional produce and prepared with panache by Marco Pierre White-protégé Charlie Rushton at this relaxed place, run by him and his wife Lucia. Don't miss the salmon fishcakes with Asian greens or salt-and-pepper squid salad.
Crema Espresso Bar 2/17–19 Horton St T 02/6589 2837. This is where you'll find the best coffee in town, along with quiches, sandwiches and soups, and "babycinos" for the little ones. Daily from breakfast until late afternoon.
Fusion 7 6/124 Horton St T 02 6584 1171. Aussie chef Lindsey Schwab perfected the art of fusion

cuisine, specifically Pacific Rim, while working in London under Paul Gordon, and has brought his skills back to his "hometown" bistro, where he artfully applies his talents to dishes such as scallop, shiso and white pepper gyoza with ponzu dressing and flying fish roe.
Off The Hook 5/2 Horton St. Catchily named takeaway serving the best fish and chips in town, handily located thirty seconds from the river.
Pier 2/72 Clarence St. The impressive range of Belgian and European designer beers on tap attracts a young crowd to this large, airy bar; snacks available at the adjoining café.
Spicy Yahmor Thai Corner of Clarence and Hay sts T 02/6583 9043. Busy local Thai serving good-value favourites including tangy Thai salads, stir-fries, and rich red and green curries. Daily from 5.30pm.
Splash 3/2 Horton St T 02/6584 4027, W www .restaurantsplash.com. Seafood is the speciality at this award-winning restaurant, with wonderful alfresco seating overlooking the river. Their Hastings River oysters with condiments are some of the tastiest around (and priciest at $34 a dozen); try the chilli lime salsa, Bloody Mary and champagne oysters! Mon–Fri lunch & Mon–Sat dinner.

Listings

Bike rental Graham Seers Cyclery, Shop 2 Port Marina, Bay St T 02/6583 2333. $30 for half-day or $40 for full day.

Boat rental The Settlement Point Boatshed (T 02/6583 6300), 2km north of the CBD next to the Settlement Point Ferry (follow Park St north over the road bridges), rents out canoes (singles $6 per hr, doubles $10 per hr) and a range of boats ($10 for 1hr up to $85 for full day).

Camel safaris Port Macquarie Camel Safaris ☎ 0437 672 080. Half-hour ($25) from Lighthouse Beach (daily except Sat).

Car rental Hertz, 102 Gordon St ☎ 02/6583 6599; Thrifty, corner of Horton and Hayward sts ☎ 02/6584 2122.

Cruises Boats leave from the cruise terminal: Port Macquarie Cruise Adventures ☎ 1300 555 890, [W] www.cruiseadventures.com.au; prices range from $15 for a short sunset cruise (1hr 30min) to $69 for a trip to the Everglades rainforest (5hr 30min); Port Venture (☎ 02/6583 3058 or 1300 795 577, [W] www.portventure.com.au; $12.50–40; 2–4 hr) offers sunset cruises and whale-watching. They also offer watersports.

Diving Rick's Dive School ☎ 02/6584 7759.

Fishing Ocean Star, Town Wharf ☎ 02/6584 6965 or 0416 240 877, [W] www.oceanstarfishing.com.

Horseriding Bellrowan Valley Horse Riding ☎ 02/6587 5227, [W] www.bellrowanvalley.com.au. 30min drive from Port Macquarie in beautiful bushland. Rides range from a one-hour trip ($55) to a two-day tour with overnight pub-stay ($319).

Hospital Port Macquarie Hospital, Wright's Rd ☎ 02/6581 2000.

Internet access Port Surf Hub, 57 Clarence St.

Police ☎ 02/6583 0199.

Post office Shop 2 Palm Court Centre 14–16 Short St.

Seaplane flights Akuna Seaplanes ☎ 1300 369 216, [W] www.akunaseaplanes.com.au. Flights range from $50 for 12min up to $185 for longer jaunts. Minimum two people.

Surfing Port Macquarie Surf School ☎ 02/6585 5453, [W] www.portmacquariesurfschool.com.au.

Taxi Port Macquarie Taxicabs ☎ 02/6581 0081.

The coast north to Nambucca Heads

The coastline between Port Macquarie and Nambucca Heads, 115km to the north, has some magical spots. **KEMPSEY**, though not one of them, is a large service-town 49km from Port Macquarie, and home to a prominent Aboriginal population, the **Dunghutti** people. The Dunghutti's ability to demonstrate continuous links with their territory led in 1996 to a successful native title claim for a portion of land at **CRESCENT HEAD**, 21km southeast of Kempsey. The agreement was both the first recognition of native title by an Australian government on the mainland, and the first time that an Australian government negotiated an agreement with indigenous people to acquire their land.

There are some wonderful waterfront **campsites** around Crescent Head, including the amusingly named *Delicate Nobby Camping Ground* (☎ 02/6566 0144, [W] www.delicatenobby.com.au; un/powered sites $20/25 per person) on Point Plomer Road, set in secluded bushland ten minutes' drive from the township.

Slightly further up the coast is **Hat Head National Park** and the small town of **SOUTH WEST ROCKS**, perched on a picturesque headland. The excellent *Hat Head Holiday Park* (☎ 02/6567 7501, [W] www.4shoreholidayparks .com.au; un/powered sites $31/35, bungalows, units & cabins 5–8) is the best place to stay. Further north, back on the Pacific Highway, you'll pick up signs for **TAYLORS ARM** and its famous pub, **The Pub with No Beer**, which claims to have provided the inspiration for the popular Australian folk song of the same name, penned by Slim Dusty and Gordon Parsons.

Further north again is the laid-back holiday town of **NAMBUCCA HEADS**. There's some excellent **surf** on Main, Beilby's and Shelly beaches, and great **swimming** in the crystal-clear water at the extremely scenic rivermouth. Whales can be sighted from Scotts Head, a popular surfing spot to the south, during their southern migration (July–Oct). The town is on the main Sydney–Brisbane **bus** and **train** routes, with Greyhound, Premier Motor Service and Countrylink calling in. Busways also operate a daily service to Urunga, Coffs Harbour and Bellingen.

Good places to **stay** include *Marcel Towers Beach House* (T02/6568 7041, Wwww.marceltowers.com.au; ❸–❹) at 12 Wellington Drive, which is not really a beach house at all; the modern apartments won't win any interior design awards but they're seconds from the water with wonderful sea views. The cabins at the exceptionally well-located *White Albatross Holiday Resort* (T02/6568 6468 or 1800 152 505, Wwww.whitealbatross.com.au; powered sites $45, cabins and vans ❻ ❼) are within splashing distance of the sea; the adjoining *V-Wall Tavern* (T02/6568 6344) serves good pub grub on a veranda overlooking the lagoon. Upriver, ⚓ *Matilda's* (Mon–Sat lunch & dinner; T02/6568 6024), on Wellington Drive, is a long-standing favourite with locals. Chef Kel and wife Cissy serve up delicious Mod Oz food in a cute turquoise building.

The Bellinger Region

The **Bellinger Region** is a beautiful area just south of Coffs Harbour, which truly has something for everyone. It comprises the country village of Dorrigo and its spectacular plateau, the charming town of **Bellingen** and the Bellinger Valley, and the pristine seaboard around **Urunga** and **Mylestom**.

Urunga and Mylestom

URUNGA, 20km north of Nambucca Heads, is a small beachside town where the Bellinger and Kalang rivers meet the sea. Nearby, **MYLESTOM**, 7km further down the highway, is an undeveloped backwater which occupies a stunningly beautiful spot on the wide Bellinger River. You can take advantage of its riverside setting at the **Alma Doepel Reserve**'s sheltered, sandy river beach. Two minutes' walk to the east is a gorgeous sweep of surf beach – often gloriously deserted. If you want to **stay** overnight, the *North Beach Caravan Park* is on Beach Parade in Mylestom (T02/6655 4250, Wwww.nbcp.net; un/ powered sites $32/38, cabins ❹–❺), along with a couple of eateries, but you're better off having a quick swim, then heading inland up into the valley.

Bellingen

Just after Urunga, a turn-off heads 12km west to the bewitching town of **BELLINGEN**, one of the prettiest and most characterful spots in New South Wales. The colourful Tibetan prayer flags fluttering throughout the town hint at Bellingen's alternative bent, confirmed once you stick your head inside one of the many esoteric bookshops, kooky cafés, or arts and crafts galleries. Most people come to "Bello" for a day-trip and end up staying a week.

Arrival and information

Busways (Wwww.busways.com.au) operates a **bus** service from Coffs Harbour, Urunga, Mylestom and Nambucca Heads, while Kean's (Wwww.keans.com.au) runs from Coffs, Armidale and Dorrigo three times a week – the bus stop is at the corner of Hyde and Church streets, by the mural. The Waterfall Way **visitor centre** (daily 9am–5pm; T02/6655 1522, Wwww.bellingermagic.com) is at 29–31 Hyde St, and can book accommodation, activities and festival tickets.

Accommodation

Bellingen has a few great places to rest your head. The creekfront ⚓ *Bellingen YHA* (T02/6655 1116, Wwww.bellingenyha.com.au; dorms $25, doubles ❸), at

2 Short St, is one of the best hostels in Australia. Located in a beautiful two-storey timber house with wide verandas facing Bellingen Island, it boasts a lovely garden of jacaranda trees that come alive with flying foxes at dusk. If you don't want to sleep in one of the comfortable dorms you can join the queue for the hammock or outdoor gazebo. The hostel can arrange excursions to Dorrigo National Park ($25) and has bikes for rent ($5), pick-ups from Urunga, honesty-box cookies and a wall of nudey pics – join it if you dare. A charming option is the renovated 1930s Federation-style *Rivendell Guesthouse* (☏02/6655 0060, Ⓦwww.rivendellguesthouse.com.au; Ⓖ), centrally located at 10–12 Hyde St with four comfy rooms with private verandas, and a small pool; a cooked breakfast plus after-dinner port and choccies are included. The *Koompartoo Retreat* (☏02/6655 2326, Ⓦwww.koompartoo.com.au; Ⓖ), five minutes' walk from town on the corner of Rawson and Dudley streets, has four hardwood chalets with stained-glass windows and cosy rooms inside and big verandas out, tucked away amongst five acres of rainforest rich in birdlife.

The Town

Just before town, the 100-year-old **Old Butter Factory**, a renovated dairy, contains a complex of art galleries and craft shops; massages are on offer at **Serenity Relaxation** (book ahead: ☏0413 104 800; 2hr; $85) and there's a lovely café (9am–5pm). The enjoyable **Bellingen Community Markets** (third Saturday of the month; 8am–2pm), in Bellingen Park, is one of Australia's largest local markets, with plenty of buskers and over 250 stalls selling arts, crafts, clothes and organic food; the predominantly foodie **Growers' Market** is held on the second and fourth Saturday (8am–1pm) at Bellingen Showground. There's more eclectic shopping at the **Emporium Bellingen** in the 1902 **Hammond and Wheatley building** on Hyde Street, a glorious restored department store. At **Heartland Didgeridoos**, opposite the Shell garage, you can buy a didj from the craftsmen themselves. For a cooling break from crafts and culture, walk for five minutes down Waterfall Way before hopping over a white gate and heading down to the river; the **rope swings** here are popular, and you can **swim** back into town.

Just east of town in Fernmount is the much-loved ✡ **Bellingen Canoe Adventures** (☏02/6655 9955, Ⓦwww.canoeadventures.com.au), whose daily meanders down the tranquil Bellinger River bring sightings of koalas, eagles and the odd dolphin. Half-day tours cost $48, full-day rapids tours are $90, while sunset and full-moon trips with champagne are also available ($25; 1hr). One of the town's most popular activities are rides in the charming **horse-drawn carriage** – the thirty-minute Town Explorer rides cost $15, the one-hour Heritage Tour costs $30, while a full-day Picnic Tour is $60 per person (☏02/6655 0270, Ⓦwww.fairytaletours.com.au).

Each year Bellingen hosts a lively **jazz festival** (Ⓦwww.bellingenjazzfestival.com.au) in August, followed by the **Global Carnival** (Ⓦwww.globalcarnival.com) of world music in October. David Helfgott (whose life was dramatized in the 1996 film, *Shine*) lives nearby; if you're very lucky, you might catch one of his rare piano performances somewhere in town.

Eating and drinking

The town is full of great **cafés and restaurants**, making eating out here a delight.

Bellingen Gelato Bar 101 Hyde St. Stylish *gelateria* with fifties-style decor, a cool old jukebox, funky lighting, delicious home-made cakes and mouthwatering ice cream – try the pistachio. Daily 10am–5pm.

Boiling Billy 7F Church St. An old-fashioned place serving excellent coffee, hearty breakfasts and gourmet sandwiches. Mon–Fri 8am–4pm, Sat & Sun 8am–2pm.

Federal Hotel Hyde St ☎02/6655 1003, ⓦwww .federalhotel.com.au. This renovated heritage-listed pub is the only one in town, and Bello's social hub. There's live music (check the board outside); *Relish*, a lively brasserie (try the $10 weekday lunch or the $12.50 Schnitzel and Schooner combo); comfortable, great-value rooms (④) and backpacker bunks ($40); and a breezy, lace-work veranda with battered brown-leather sofas and funky lighting.

🏃 Lodge 241 117–212 Hyde St ☎02/6655 2470. Standing at the end of town as you head up to Dorrigo, this imposing three-storey Federation-style building with big verandas houses

a bustling, award-winning café and gallery, and has bucolic views over hills and creeks. The big blackboard menus feature the likes of wild game pâté and lemon tart – you can have a game of chess or peruse a newspaper while you wait. BYO. Wed–Sun 8.30am–5pm.

No. 2 Oak St ☎02/6655 9000. This multiple award-winning restaurant is everyone's favourite, rustling up some truly stunning contemporary Australian food in a cute candelit heritage cottage. Try the sweet pork belly with braised bok choy and five-spice reduction. Book ahead. Tues–Sat from 6.30pm.

Sis de Lane Church St. Funky café with communal tables, fresh juices, ricotta pancakes for breakfast, delicious antipasto for lunch, and scrumptious carrot cake for afternoon tea.

Inland to Dorrigo

The Waterfall Way winds steeply from Bellingen up to **DORRIGO**, past some spectacular lookouts. **Dorrigo** is a quiet country town with sleepy, wide streets lined with plenty of little shops, art galleries and cafés, which, in combination with the natural attractions nearby, make it well worth a day or so of exploration. **Dorrigo National Park** should be first on your list of things to do: the protected area contains a startlingly beautiful remnant of World Heritage–listed rainforest in a region that was once heavily forested, due to the lure of the valuable Australian cedar or "red gold". The **Rainforest Centre** (daily 9am–5pm; free; ☎02/6657 2309), 2km east of town on Dome Road, is a wonderful facility with interpretative displays on flora and fauna, a café and walking-trail maps. Several walks start right behind the centre: the boarded **Skywalk** is the most spectacular and also the least strenuous, extending high over the rainforest canopy for 200m. Other **trails** here range from the eight-hundred-metre Lyrebird Walk up to the Wonga Walk (6.6km return), which winds through the rainforest and underneath the Crystal Shower and Tristania falls. It's cool, misty and slightly eerie down on the forest floor, and easy to believe you're kilometres from anywhere as huge trees and vines soar overhead. All the walks starting behind the centre are open from 5am to 10pm daily, so visitors can observe the forest's nocturnal creatures. Wilder trails, with more majestic waterfalls and great escarpment views, begin from the Never Never Picnic Area, a further 10km down Dome Road. Aside from visiting the magnificent Dangar Falls, 2km north along Hickory Street, the main strip, there isn't much to do in town, although it's a pleasant little place. The **Dorrigo Folk and Bluegrass Festival** (ⓦwww.dorrigofolkbluegrass.com.au) is held in October each year.

Practicalities

The only way to get to Dorrigo on **public transport** is with Kean's, which runs to the town from Coffs Harbour via Bellingen, and on up to Armidale three times a week – buses stop at the corner of Hickory and Cudgery streets. The **visitor centre** (daily 10am–4pm; ☎02/6657 2486) at 36 Hickory St can advise you on the many **farmstays** in the area, but there's plenty of **accommodation** in town: budget travellers can try the friendly *Beds on a Budget* (☎02/6657 2431; beds $20 per person ❶) at 14 Bielsdown St; it's like staying in someone's house, but a chilled-out one at that, as is *Gracemere Grange B&B* (☎02/6657 2630, ⓦ www.gracemeregrange.com.au; ask about backpackers' rates; doubles ④), nearer the park at 325 Dome Rd. This cosy guesthouse is stuffed with trinkets from the owner's travels around the world – try to book the attic room.

For **eating**, *Misty's* (Wed–Sun from 6pm & Sun lunch from noon; ☎02/6657 2855) at 33 Hickory St, is a local favourite, housed in a charming 1920s weatherboard cottage with stained-glass windows, and serving gorgeous contemporary regional cuisine – cosy rooms are also available (④). The *Waterfall Winery* and attached *Lick the Spoon Café*, at 51–53 Hickory St, has a gourmet deli and lunches, home-made gluten-free cakes, and wines fermenting in vast steel drums out the back – persimmon and other fruity flavours are the house specialities (available for tasting Mon–Fri 10am–4pm & Sat 10am–noon).

Coffs Harbour

Back on the Pacific Highway, **COFFS HARBOUR** – or "Coffs" – is beautifully set at a point where the mountains of the Great Dividing Range fall into the South Pacific Ocean, and boasts glorious expanses of white sand to the north. The town is a lot of fun, with more activities than you can shake a stick at – in particular, the **Solitary Islands**, just offshore, are notable for diving, with fringing coral reefs, a plethora of fish, and migrating whales between late May and late November.

Arrival and information

All long-distance **buses** stop at the **bus station** on the corner of McLean Street and the Pacific Highway; the **train station** is by the harbour. Greyhound and Premier Motor Service stop here on their east-coast runs; Kean's link the town with Bellingen, Dorrigo, Armidale and Tamworth; Busways run to

▲ The marina at Coffs Harbour

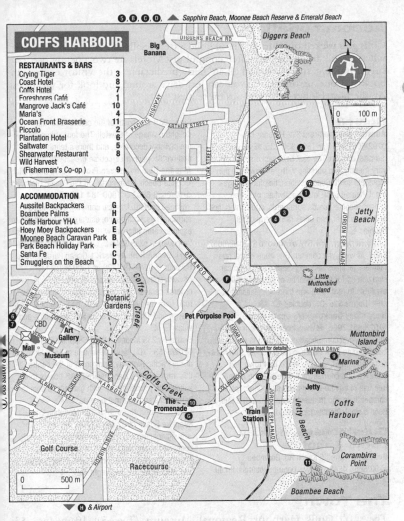

❺, ❻, ❼, ❽, ▲ Sapphire Beach, Moonee Beach Reserve & Emerald Beach

COFFS HARBOUR

Diggers Beach

RESTAURANTS & BARS

Crying Tiger	3
Coast Hotel	8
Coffs Hotel	7
Foreshores Café	1
Mangrove Jack's Café	10
Maria's	4
Ocean Front Brasserie	11
Piccolo	2
Plantation Hotel	6
Saltwater	5
Shearwater Restaurant	8
Wild Harvest	
(Fisherman's Co-op)	9

ACCOMMODATION

Aussitel Backpackers	G
Boambee Palms	H
Coffs Harbour YHA	A
Hoey Moey Backpackers	E
Moonee Beach Caravan Park	B
Park Beach Holiday Park	F
Santa Fe	C
Smugglers on the Beach	D

Bellingen, Urunga and Nambucca Heads; and Ryan's to Grafton. You can **fly** to Coffs with Qantas, Virgin Blue or Brindabella; the **airport** is about 5km south of town. Coffs is rather spread out, and if you haven't rented a bike or car (see p.276) you'll have to use either taxis or the half-hourly **bus** (Busways ☎02/6583 2499, ⓦwww.busways.com.au) which runs between the town centre, Coffs Jetty and Park Beach.

The town is split into three distinct sections: the CBD and mall; the jetty, around 2km to the east; and Sapphire, Moonee and Emerald **beaches** to the north – Ryan's run buses to all three from Monday to Saturday. The helpful **visitor centre** (daily 9am–5pm; ☎02/6652 1522 or 1300 369 070, ⓦwww .coffscoast.com.au), next to the bus station, can book accommodation for you. The **NPWS** (☎02/6652 0900 or 6657 2309) has an office down at the marina and offers a variety of guided walks, talks and activities.

Accommodation

Coffs gets packed out during school holidays, especially at Christmas and Easter when weekly **bookings** are often compulsory. Motels are two a penny, particularly down Ocean Parade, and all are fairly predictable – the visitor centre can book you one, or, off-season, you can just drive around and look for vacancies. All the hostels offer free pick-ups on request.

Hostels

Aussitel Backpackers 312 Harbour Drive ☏02/6651 1871 or 1800 330 335, ⓦwww .aussitel.com.au. The best backpackers' in Coffs – very friendly and bursting with "all down the pub together" spirit. Good facilities, helpful management, heated pool, lots of activities, plus free canoes, boogie-boards/surfboards, and fishing, golf and tennis gear, and bikes ($5). Dorms $28, doubles ❸

Coffs Harbour YHA 51 Collingwood St ☏02/6652 6462, ⓦwww.yha.com.au. This huge hostel has faultless facilities and very helpful staff who can sign you up for an avalanche of activities. Bikes are available to rent ($10) and there's a pleasant pool area. Dorms $25–31, doubles ❸–❹

Hoey Moey Backpackers Ocean Parade ☏02/6651 7966, ⓦwww.hoeymoey.com.au. This motel-style accommodation attached to a pub and backing onto Park Beach is party central. The facilities aren't great, and it's way out of town, but there's a free courtesy bus, free beer on arrival, free use of boogie-boards and surfboards, pool competitions and frequent live music at the pub. Rooms single/double/triple/quads ❶–❹

Guesthouses, holiday parks & motels

Boambee Palms 5 Kasch Rd, Boambee ☏02/6658 4545, ⓦwww.boambeepalms.com.au.

Smart B&B just south of the centre, near the delightful village of Sawtell. The four suites here are stylishly decorated, and there's tennis, a pool and barbie, plus three-course breakfasts. ❼–❽

Moonee Beach Caravan Park Moonee Beach Rd, Moonee Beach,12km north, off the Pacific Highway ☏02/6653 6803 or 1800 184 120, ⓦwww .moonee.com.au. Magical camping spot in bush surroundings, with beach, estuary and headlands to explore, camp kitchen, wi-fi and loads of activities. Un/powered sites $34/42, vans ❸, cabins ❻–❾

Park Beach Holiday Park 1 Ocean Parade, Coffs Harbour ☏02/6648 4888 or 1800 200 111, ⓦwww.coffscoastholidayparks.com.au. Huge, well-ordered caravan and camping ground across the road from the beach, with BBQ, pool and children's playground. Un/powered sites $37/46, cabins and villas ❺–❾

Santa Fe 235 Mountain Way, Sapphire Beach ☏02/6653 7700, ⓦwww.santefe.net.au. Just west of the Pacific Highway, 9km north of the centre, this attractive Mexican-inspired B&B boasts three suites with private decks, lush gardens, a pool, hammocks and gourmet breakfasts. ❼–❾

Smugglers on the Beach 235 Mountain Way, Sapphire Beach ☏02/6653 7700, ⓦwww .smugglers.com.au. These comfortable, fully self-contained apartments are right on the beach. There's a pool, tennis, cricket gear, body boards, and BBQ. Minimum two-night stay. ❻–❾

The Town

The small **Coffs Harbour Regional Museum** (Tues–Sat 10am–4pm; $3; ☏02/6652 5794), at 191A Harbour Drive, has an interesting collection of early pioneering relics and artefacts belonging to the **Gumbaingirr** people. The star exhibit is the original, Doctor Who–esque Solitary Islands lighthouse – ask for a demo.

The **CBD** and shopping mall, clustered around the western end of Harbour Drive and Grafton Street, is where the major shops and services are located. A charming **creek walk** and **cycle trail** begins on nearby Coffs Street and winds its way down the creek's southern bank to the sea; halfway along, on Hardacre Street, are the magnificent **Botanic Gardens** (daily 9am–5pm; donation). These delightfully tranquil subtropical gardens feature a mangrove boardwalk, sensory herb garden and a slice of rainforest; guided walks are available. A little further on is **The Promenade**, a breezy boutique shopping centre on Harbour Drive. Promenade Canoes (☏02/6651 1032, ⓦwww.promenadecanoes.com.au), on the ground floor, rents out single canoes ($12 per hr), doubles ($17 per hr) and pedal boats ($15 per hr).

The boat-filled **marina**, with its adjacent Jetty Beach and historic pier, is unquestionably the nicest part of town, and perfect for a pre-dinner sunset stroll. A fifteen-minute walk from here takes you to **Muttonbird Island Nature Reserve**, offering fantastic views back over Coffs Harbour, its beaches and the Great Dividing Ranges beyond. Thousands of wedge-tailed shearwaters, or muttonbirds, travel to the island from Southeast Asia each year to breed (Aug–April). Partially visible to the north are the five islands and several islets making up the **Solitary Islands Marine Reserve**, the largest such preserved area in New South Wales; the mingling of tropical and temperate waters means that there's a huge variety of sealife – see p.276 for dive operators. Over Coffs Creek from the marina, Park Beach is a decent stretch of sand, as is Boambee Beach to the south and Digger's Beach around the headland to the north. Little Digger's Beach, to the north again, is the spot to get rid of your white bits.

Aside from the beaches, there are a couple of must-see family attractions in Coffs: the **Pet Porpoise Pool** (daily 9am–4pm; performances at 9.30am & 12.30pm; adults $27, kids $14; Ⓦ www.petporpoisepool.com), on Orlando Street, is home to rescued dolphins (which used to be known as porpoises, hence the misleading moniker), fairy penguins, seals, emu, kangaroo and sea lions.

A highlight for lovers of kitsch is the iconic **Big Banana** (daily 9am–4.30pm; free entry, but passes for rides and shows, adults $16–33, kids $14–27; Ⓦ www.bigbanana.com), a "horticultural theme park" 3km north of Coffs on the Pacific Highway, dominated by a big yellow concrete banana. There's a show shedding light on the town's $70-million-a-year banana industry, but after you've seen it you can get down to the more serious business of tobogganing, taking a monorail tour, buying banana-related merchandise and eating chocolate-covered bananas – it's good for kids, but best avoided by theme-park phobics.

Eating, drinking and nightlife

The mall has a wealth of cafés which are fine for lunch and a coffee, albeit in less-than-scenic surrounds. Much more relaxing is the marina end of Harbour Drive, crammed with restaurants of all persuasions; it's hardly worth looking beyond this buzzy little stretch – where a telephone number is listed, you need to book, especially on weekends and during holidays. Nightlife is covered by the *Coast*, *Coffs* and *Plantation* hotels on Grafton Street, which cater for locals and travellers – all are lively in summer, and between them you'll find live music on most nights.

Crying Tiger Harbour Drive ☏ 02/6650 0195. Expect quality Thai food at this excellent Thai restaurant with an Asian-inspired interior. The curries are deliciously fragrant and a notch above your average small-town Thai. Daily from 5.30pm.
Foreshores Café 394 Harbour Drive. Large, airy place with takeaway standards served up in generous proportions. The burgers with the lot are especially enormous. Daily 7.30am–3pm & Wed–Sun dinner in high season.
Mangrove Jack's Café The Promenade ☏ 02/6652 5517. Honest food served up in simple

surrounds with fine creek views. Daily from 7am for breakfast & lunch, Tues–Sat for dinner.
Maria's 368 Harbour Drive ☏ 02/6651 3000. Traditional, bustling Italian place with lively atmosphere, huge pepper-grinders, and lots of seafood, pasta ($13–17) and pizza ($13–15). Licensed. Takeaway available. Wed–Mon from 5.45pm.
Ocean Front Brasserie Coffs Harbour Deep Sea Fishing Club, Jordan Esplanade ☏ 02/6651 2819. The bistro standards won't win any awards; however, most people come for the stunning beach and sea views. Mains $15–29. Daily, breakfast, lunch and dinner.

Piccolo Jetty Strip, 390 Harbour Drive ☏ 02/6651 9599. This intimate, award-winning Italian eatery is super-stylish with moody lighting and a comfy cushioned window seat at the front, a lovely courtyard at the back, and a sophisticated menu to match. Mains $24–29. Tues–Sat from 6pm.

Saltwater 104 Fiddaman Rd, Emerald Beach ☏ 02/6656 1888. This sophisticated eatery is one of the north coast's few truly beachside restaurants. Opt for eggs with truffled mushrooms for breakfast, or Asian and Middle East-inspired mains for lunch and dinner. Mains $24–29. Breakfast, lunch and dinner.

Shearwater Restaurant 321 Harbour Drive ☏ 02/6651 6053. Grab a veranda table overlooking Coffs Creek and feast on anything from French toast for breakfast to Asian-inspired seafood for lunch or dinner. Wine available by glass only, so you may want to BYO. Mains $22–29. Daily 8am–9pm.

Wild Harvest The Marina ☏ 02/6651 6888. This fine eatery owned by the local Fisherman's Co-op serves the freshest seafood straight from their trawlers (which you can see from your table), prepared in countless ways. There's also a takeaway. Entrees $7–15, mains $14–24. Lunch 11.30am–3pm, Tue–Sat 6–10pm.

Listings

Bike rental Bob Wallis Cycles, Shop 30 Homebase, 252 Pacific Hwy ☏ 02/6652 5102. $18 for half-day, $25 for full day, or $40 for two days.

Car rental Europcar ☏ 02/6651 8558; Hertz ☏ 02/6651 1899; Thrifty ☏ 02/6652 8622.

Cruises Spirit of Coffs Harbour Cruises, Marina Drive ☏ 02/6650 0155. Whale-watching trips (late May–late Nov; $39), dolphin cruises ($25) and lunch tours ($45). Pacific Explorer, in the yellow floating shed at the marina ☏ 02/6652 8988. Whale-watching trips only in season ($30).

Diving Jetty Dive Centre, 398 Harbour Drive ☏ 02/6651 1611, ⓦ www.jettydive.com.au. $55 for a pool session, $195 for a one-day Discover Scuba course (minimum two people). Snorkelling and whale-watching trips also available.

Horseriding Valery Trails, Valery Rd, 20km southwest of Coffs off the Pacific Highway at Bonville ☏ 02/6653 4301, ⓦ www.valerytrails.com .au. Twice-daily, two-hour excursions ($50), breakfast or BBQ rides ($60) and two-day trips overnighting at the pub in Bellingen ($300).

Hospital 345 Pacific Highway ☏ 02/6656 7000.

Internet access Jetty Dive Centre, Harbour Drive.

Police 22 Moonee St ☏ 02/6652 0299.

Post office In the Palms Centre at the CBD end of Harbour Drive; there's a smaller branch at the marina end of the road, on the corner with Camperdown St.

Skydiving Coffs City Skydivers ☏ 02/6651 1167, ⓦ www.coffsskydivers.com.au. Tandem dives from 3000m for $325.

Surfing East Coast Surf School, Digger's Beach ☏ 02/6651 5515, ⓦ www.eastcoastsurfschool .com.au. Introductory lessons ($55, 2hr 30min), five-lesson courses ($200).

Taxi ☏ 13 10 08.

Watersports Liquid Assets Adventure Tours, 38 Marina Drive ☏ 02/6658 0850, ⓦ www.surfrafting .com. Sea- and river-kayaking, surf rafting (all $50 for half-day) and white-water rafting on the Goolang ($80 for half-day) or Nymboida ($160 for full day) rivers. Coffs Ocean Jet Ski Hire (☏ 02/6651 3177 or 0418 665 656, ⓦ www.coffsjetskihire.com.au) rent out single ($100 for half-hour) or double machines ($120 for half-hour) from Park Beach.

Grafton and around

GRAFTON, 83km along the Pacific Highway, north of Coffs Harbour, is a pleasant country town on a bend of the wide **Clarence River**, which almost encircles the city. It's a genteel, old-fashioned place with wide, tree-lined avenues; Victoria and Fitzroy streets are lined with pretty, Federation-style houses, while the main commercial strip is Prince Street. The week-long **Jacaranda Festival** (late Oct–early Nov; ⓦ www.jacarandafestival.org.au) celebrates the town's jacaranda and flame trees, which come ablaze with mauve, maroon and white blossoms in the spring. Out of festival time this is a tranquil place, where the main attraction is visiting some of the historic buildings preserved by the National Trust. **Schaeffer House** (Tues–Thurs & Sun 1–4pm; $3), at 190 Fitzroy St, dating to 1900, has a collection of beautiful china, glassware and period furniture; on the same street at no. 158 is the **Grafton Regional Gallery** (Tues–Sun 10am–4pm), which has some fine temporary exhibitions and local artwork.

Practicalities

The staff at the **visitor centre** (daily 9am–5pm; ℡02/6642 4677, ⓦwww .clarencetourism.com), on the Pacific Highway at the corner of Spring Street in South Grafton, can give you information on scenic drives, national parks and other activities. Countrylink **train** services along the north coast stop at Grafton Station, close to the river crossing in South Grafton, while **long-distance buses** stop near the visitor centre. Either way, it's a half-hour walk into the town proper, across a fine, split-level road-and-rail bridge. Grafton is on the main Sydney–Brisbane Greyhound and Premier Motor Service routes; Ryan's also run to Coffs Harbour, while Busways operate regular buses between the town and South Grafton.

There's some decent **accommodation** in Grafton, notably in the two old pubs: the *Roches Family Hotel* (℡02/6642 2866, ⓦwww.roches.com.au; rooms with shared bathrooms ❶–❷) at 85 Victoria St, and the *Crown Hotel-Motel* (℡02/6642 4000, ⓦwww.crownhotelmotel.com; pub rooms ❶–❸, motel rooms ❹) at 1 Prince St. Both offer great-value rooms and even better-value pub grub (including $5.90 lunch specials at *Roches*). The location, overlooking the river, is more appealing at the latter, but the food is pretty good at both. More in keeping with the town's style, *Arcola B&B* (℡02/6643 1760, ⓦwww .arcola.com.au; ❻–❼), at 150 Victoria St, is a gracious heritage house on the banks of the river, furnished with antiques, and serving scrumptious breakfasts.

A lovely place to **eat** is the award-winning *Georgie's Café* (Tues–Sun 9am–4pm, dinner from 6pm to late Wed–Sat; book for dinner ℡02/6642 6996), at the Regional Art Gallery, which serves delicious light meals for lunch and slightly more sophisticated dishes for dinner, in a leafy courtyard or inside amongst the art.

Around Grafton

From Grafton it's 47km northeast to **Maclean**, a small delta town which proclaims its Scottish heritage with tartan lampposts and street signs in Gaelic – turn off the Pacific Highway at Cowper for a more scenic run into town along the Clarence River. Continuing east along the same road, you reach the twin settlements of **YAMBA** and **ILUKA** – two pretty holiday villages facing each other across the mouth of the river. Yamba, long a popular family holiday resort, was voted Australia's number one town by *Australian Traveller* magazine in 2009, for its postcard-perfect scenery, superlative surfing and laid-back vibe. Clarence River Ferries shuttle between the two communities (foot passengers only; 4 daily; $5.70; ℡02/6646 6423) and also cruise along the river. Busways run daily services to both settlements from Grafton.

While there are many motels (❹–❺) in sun-drenched Yamba, holiday-makers like the low-key, riverfront *Calypso Holiday Park* (℡02/6646 8847, ⓦwww .calypsoyamba.com.au; un/powered sites $30/35, units, cabins & villas ❹–❻) on Harbour Street. The *Pacific Hotel* (℡02/6646 2466, ⓦwww.pacifichotelyamba .com.au; 4-bed bunk rooms $60, doubles ❷, motel rooms ❺) commands a terrific location overlooking the picturesque Main Beach at 18 Pilot St, and has decent pub rooms and good live music (Thurs–Sat). Its restaurant, the *Pacific Hotel Bistro*, boasts a globally inspired menu (entrees $12–20, mains $22–30). Also try the funky *Caperberry Café* on the corner of Coldstream and Yamba streets for lunch, and, at 16 Clarence St, *Sea Spray Fine Food Café* (☎02/6646 8336) for casual bistro fare made from fresh local produce.

A few kilometres south of Yamba is **Yuraygir National Park**, with plenty of basic but attractive **bushcamping** (book via Grafton NPWS; ☎02/6441 1500; $10 per adult per night, vehicles $7 per day) and a spectacular strip of sand at Angourie Point, which became New South Wales' first **surfing reserve** in 2007.

Eighty kilometres west of Grafton, the **Gwydir Highway** runs through the rugged and densely forested **Gibraltar Range** and **Washpool** national parks, both with walking tracks, bushcamping, lookout points and waterfalls galore.

Ballina and around

North of Grafton are **Ballina** and **Lennox Head**, the latter in particular worth a stop before the madness of Byron Bay. The old port of **BALLINA**, at the mouth of the Richmond River, is a tranquil holiday town that hasn't escaped the clutches of the "big things", with the **Big Prawn** marking the entrance to town on the highway from Grafton.

Arrival, information and accommodation

You can **fly** to Ballina from Sydney with Virgin Blue, Regional Express or Jetstar, who also have flights from Melbourne. Greyhound and Premier Motor Service connect the town by **bus** to all stops between Sydney and Brisbane; Kirklands run to Byron Bay, Brisbane, Lismore and Lennox Head; while Blanch's operate services to and from the airport, and to Lennox Head and Byron Bay. To get around town, you can rent **bikes** from Jack Ransom Cycles (☎02/6685 3485) at 16 Cherry St. The **visitor centre** (Mon–Fri 9am–5pm; ☎02/6686 3484, Ⓦwww.discoverballina.com) is in Las Balsas Plaza, and can book accommodation, river cruises and other tours.

Accommodation

Ballina Lakeside Holiday Park North of the river on Fenwick Drive ☎02/6686 3953 or 1800 888 268, Ⓦwww.ballinalakeside.com.au. Good holiday park, right next to the lagoon, with plenty of good facilities. Powered sites $26–68, studios, cabins and villas ❻–❾

Ballina Manor 25 Norton St ☎02/6681 5888, Ⓦwww.ballinamanor.com.au. This elegant boutique hotel in a grand Victorian house is Ballina's most atmospheric option: expect brass beds, four-posters, ceiling fans and lace curtains. ❽–❾

Ballina YHA Travellers Lodge 36 Tamar St ☎02/6686 6737, Ⓦwww.yha.com.au. Clean, motel-style place with a swimming pool, bikes for rent ($5) and free fishing rods, boogie-boards and snorkel gear. Dorms $28, doubles ❸

Brundah B&B 37 Norton St ☎02/6686 8166, Ⓦwww.babs.com.au/brundah. This beautiful boutique B&B is set in a splendid heritage-listed 1908 Federation house amidst lovely gardens. ❼

Flat Rock Tent Park Just off Coast Rd, 5km northeast of town, at 38 Flat Rock Rd ☎02/6686 4848. Set right on Angels Beach, this unspoilt campsite with unpowered sites is for tents only. Sites $30.

The Town

On Regatta Avenue by Las Balsas Plaza is the **Maritime Museum** (daily 9am–4pm; donation; Ⓦwww.ballinamaritimemuseum.org.au). Its star exhibit is a raft from the 1973 Las Balsas expedition, in which three vessels set sail from Ecuador with the aim of proving that ancient South American civilizations could have traversed the Pacific. A mere 179 days and 14,400km later the twelve-strong crew arrived in Ballina, sporting some choice facial hair. A few doors down is **Richmond River Cruises** (2hr; $26; ℡02/6687 5688, ⓦwww .rrcruises.com.au), who run morning tea and afternoon tea cruises downriver. To go it alone, visit **Ballina Boat Hire** (℡403 810 277), at 268 River St, to rent out a tinnie ($45 for 2hr).

Eating and drinking

For tasty **food**, *Shelly's on the Beach* has hearty breakfasts and lunches, enticing cakes, and alfresco seating with unbeatable views over Shelly's Beach – follow the bridge and sea wall 2km north of town. In the historic Riversleigh house at 5 River St, *River Thai* (Tues–Sat from 6pm; ℡02/6686 9774; bookings required; BYO) serves excellent traditional Thai cuisine; book a veranda table on a balmy night. For very civilized fine dining in an elegant wood-panelled room, try *Ballina Manor Restaurant*. For a special experience, try the super-stylish *Sandbar and Restaurant* (Wed–Sat lunch & dinner; Sun lunch; ℡02/6686 6602; bookings essential; licensed and BYO), at 23 Compton Drive, with spectacular river views from the bar and restaurant; you'll want to dine early to enjoy the sunset over the river.

Lennox Head

LENNOX HEAD, 11km north of Ballina, is a small, relaxed town with a surfie feel. At the southern end of the fabulous Seven-Mile Beach, The Point rates among the best **surfing** spots in the world, and professionals congregate here for the big waves in May, June and July. Adding to Lennox Head's appeal is the calm, fresh water of **Lake Ainsworth**; stained dark by the tea trees around its banks, it's a popular swimming spot for families seeking refuge from the crashing surf in the soft medicinal water (it's effectively diluted tea-tree oil).

There are a few good places **to stay** in town. *Lennox Head Beach House YHA* (℡02/6687 7636, ⓦwww.yha.com.au; dorms $29, rooms ❸), at 3 Ross St, is a great little hostel ideally situated between the lake and the beach. Reiki massage, reflexology and Bowen therapy are available in-house (free 10min sessions on Thurs). For $5 you have unlimited use of fishing gear, bikes, windsurfers (free lessons) and paddle-skis (all $5), surfboards extra. *Lake Ainsworth Caravan Park* (℡02/6687 7249, ⓦwww.bscp.com.au/lakeainsworth; un/powered sites $30/37, cabins ❹–❺), on Pacific Parade, is a fairly standard holiday park superbly located right by the water. *Randall's on Ross* (℡02/6687 7922, ⓦwww .tropicalnsw.com.au/randalls; ❻–❽) is a homely B&B option at 9 Ross St, with excellent breakfasts and comfy queen-sized beds.

Eating out is a very casual affair. Before you hit the waves, stop by cute *Café de Mer* for a full Aussie breakfast on Turkish bread or scrumptious home-made cakes. *Lennox Head Pizza & Pasta* on Ballina Street is good for takeaway pizza and calzone, while a few doors down at 2/76 you'll find terrific Thai (the Choo Chee Prawns are divine) at *Mi Thai* (Wed–Sun from 6pm; ℡02/6687 5820). *Seven Mile Café* (Wed–Sun from 6pm & Fri–Sun from noon; ℡02/6687 6210) on Pacific Parade has fine sea views, bright decor and bold Mod Oz food to match. There's more Mod Oz in the bistro, *Ruby's by the Sea* at the *Lennox Point Hotel*. The pub itself is a convivial sort of place, with live music from Thursday to Sunday.

Since Lennox Head is off the Pacific Highway, no long-distance **bus** services call here; jump on a local service to/from Byron Bay, Ballina, Lismore or Evans Head (Kirklands or Blanch's), or catch the Greyhound and Premier Motor Service buses at Ballina.

Byron Bay and around

Situated at the end of a long sweeping bay, the vibrant township of **BYRON BAY** boasts 30km of almost unbroken sandy beaches and is high on most travellers' lists. Once a favourite with barefoot hippies, Byron's small-community feel and bohemian atmosphere has been disappearing over the past years, and it now has stylish hotels, restaurants and bars, lively pubs and chic boutiques.

Arrival and information

Trains no longer call into Byron, although Countrylink still operate a bus service to a large number of east-coast destinations. Greyhound and Premier Motor Service stop in town on their east-coast runs, and drop you at the bus stop on Jonson Street. Local bus services include Kirklands, which run to Brisbane, Surfers, Tweed Heads, Murwillumbah, Brunswick Heads, Lennox Head and Ballina; and Blanch's, which call at Ballina, Lennox Head and Mullumbimby. The closest **airport** is Ballina, 39km south, served by Jetstar, Virgin and Regional Express; Blanch's run a connecting bus service (3–7 daily). Brisbane 2 Byron (☎07/5429 8759 or 1800 626 222, ⊛www.brisbane2byron .com) serve Brisbane airport daily ($46), and Kirklands run to the Gold Coast airport at Coolangatta (2–3 daily).

The helpful **visitor centre** (daily 9am–5pm; ☎02/6680 8558, ⊛www.visit byronbay.com), in the old Stationmaster's Cottage at 80 Jonson St near the bus stop, has a huge range of printed information and activities on offer. Byron Bus & Backpacker Travel (daily 7.30am–7pm; ☎02/6685 5517), a few doors down at no. 84, can book all manner of tours, activities, travel tickets and cheap car rental, and has internet access. There is a plethora of other "information centres" along Jonson Street that are really private travel agencies selling adventure tours.

▲ Byron Bay

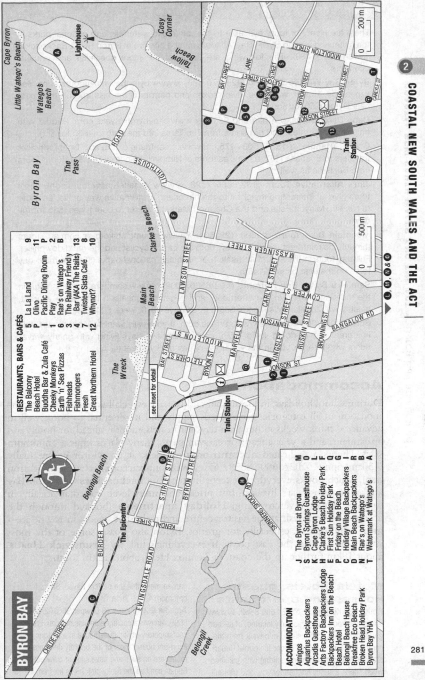

BYRON BAY

Arts and Industry Estate & Pacific Highway ▼

RESTAURANTS, BARS & CAFÉS

The Balcony	5	La La Land	9
Beach Hotel	P	Olivo	11
Buddha Bar & Zula Café	1	Pacific Dining Room	2
Cheeky Monkeys	6	Play	B
Earth 'n' Sea Pizzas	3	Rae's on Watego's	
Fishheads	4	The Railway Friendly Bar (AKA The Rails)	13
Fishmongers	7	Twisted Sista Café	8
Fresh	12	Whynot?	10
Great Northern Hotel	10		

ACCOMMODATION

Amigos	M	The Byron at Byron	J
Aquarius Backpackers	O	Byron Springs Guesthouse	S
Arcadia Guesthouse	L	Cape Byron Lodge	K
Arts Factory Backpackers Lodge	F	Clarke's Beach Holiday Park	H
Backpackers Inn on the Beach	E	First Sun Holiday Park	P
Beach Hotel	Q	Friday on the Beach	G
Belongil Beach House	G	Holiday Village Backpackers	I
Breakfree Eco Beach	D	Main Beach Backpackers	R
Broken Head Holiday Park	B	Rae's on Watego's	N
Byron Bay YHA	A	Watermark at Watego's	T

0   500 m

0   200 m

► O, M, N & O

Tours from Byron Bay

There are plenty of tours available to the rainforest, waterfalls and national parks in the hinterland around Byron Bay. All tours can be booked at Byron Bus & Backpacker Travel (see p.280). The following are some of the more specialist and unusual operators.

Byron Bay Wildlife Tours ☏0429 770 686, ⓦwww.byronbaywildlifetours.com. See kangaroos, koalas, wallabies, flying foxes and parrots in the hills and on the coast near Byron ($50 for 5hr).

Cape Byron Kayaks ☏02/6680 9555, ⓦwww.capebyronkayaks.com. Paddle with dolphins and turtles, and get some free Tim Tams into the bargain ($60 for 3hr).

Green Triangle ☏1800 503 475, ⓦwww.greentriangle.com.au. Does efficient transfers to Brisbane ($32) as well as tours of Nimbin ($13 one-way, $24 return). Tours from Brisbane as well.

Jim's Alternative Tours ☏02/6685 7720, ⓦwww.jimsalternativetours.com. Jim's tours give an interesting insight into the hinterland's alternative way of life, en route to Nimbin, Minyon Falls and the Channon Markets, all set to cool tunes ($35 for full day).

Mountain Bike Tours ☏1800 122 504, ⓦwww.mountainbiketours.com.au. Tours through the rainforest that will satisfy both the casual cyclist and the rabid downhiller. Full-day tours in the Mount Jerusalem or Nightcap national parks ($99), or multi-day tours on the east coast ($1450).

Samudra Byron Bay Retreats ☏02/6566 0009, ⓦwww.samudra.com.au. Yoga in the morning, surfing in the afternoon, and vegetarian meals in between – a great, healthy way to relax. Weekends $630, three days $910, week $2450.

Surfari ☏02/6684 8111, ⓦwww.surfaris.com. If you really want to learn to surf, this is a great way of doing it. For $599 you'll spend five days living with gnarly wave-riders who'll chuck you in the water every day until you get it.

Accommodation

During school holidays, in December and January especially, demand for accommodation in all categories far exceeds supply, and it's essential to book well in advance – think weeks rather than days for hostels, months ahead for hotels and apartments, and a year ahead for caravan parks; many places impose minimum stays. There's a dedicated **accommodation** desk at the visitor centre (daily 9.30am–5pm; ☏02/6680 8558, ⓦwww.byronbayaccom.net/accommodation.asp), which books everything except hostels. The **backpackers'** in Byron Bay are among Australia's liveliest, but prices and stress levels rise dramatically in summer due to overcrowding. **Holiday apartments** (booked through the accommodation desk at the visitor centre and real-estate agents in town) are a great-value option, especially for groups. Byron also boasts some of the most stylish options on the east coast. If everything's full, try **Brunswick Heads**, about 18km further up the coast, or Lennox Head, about 12km south.

Motels, hotels, guest-houses and apartments

Amigos 32 Kingsley St ☏02/6680 8662, ⓦwww.amigosbb.com. This peacefully located, blue- and green-painted guesthouse is 5min walk from the centre. The Latin-inspired decor (colourful Cuban artwork, Mexican hammocks) along with polished wood floors, a sunny kitchen/lounge, and tranquil garden make this the perfect haven. Shared bathroom ⑤, en suite ⑥

Arcadia Guesthouse 48 Cowper St ☏02/6680 8699, ⓦwww.arcadiaguesthouse.com.au. Fresh, contemporary-styled guesthouse in a historic Federation-era house; most of the brightly decorated rooms are en suite and have spa- or clawfoot baths. Guests can use the funky pink bikes for free. ⑥–⑦

Beach Hotel Bay St ℡ 02/6685 6402, ⓦ www
.beachotel.com.au. Byron's famous hotel, located
directly opposite the beach, has comfortable,
spacious rooms and suites set around a lush
garden and swimming pool. Rooms ❼–❾
Belongil Beach House 25 Childe St ℡ 02/6685
7868, ⓦ www.belongilbeachouse.com. This
Balinese-style complex has spacious timber
cottages set around a landscaped garden.
Accommodation ranges from en-suite dorms to
self-contained apartments with stained-glass
windows and mosaic floors. There's a café,
Cicada, on site with a short breakfast and lunch
menu. Dorms $36, doubles, studios and apart-
ments ❹–❼
Breakfree Eco Beach 35–37 Shirley St ℡ 02/6639
5700, ⓦ www.ecobeachbyron.com.au. Clean, stylish
contemporary motel free of the dreadful interior
design tendencies that usual bedevil this type of
place. Pristine pool, lush gardens and a good BBQ
area; all motels should be like this. ❻–❽
The Byron at Byron 77–97 Brokenhead Rd,
℡ 1300 554 362, ⓦ www.thebyronatbyron.com.au.
Stunningly set amid 45 acres of rainforest and
waterways, this stylish resort is Byron's most
luxurious, with complimentary yoga each day,
sublime spa treatments on offer, and a superb
restaurant and bar. ❾
Byron Springs Guesthouse 2 Oodgeroo Gardens,
corner of Mahogany Drive ℡ 02/6685 5836,
ⓦ www.byronspringsguesthouse.com. This lovely,
light, airy guesthouse, set amid topical gardens, is
ideal for budget travellers who are over the
backpacker scene. Rate includes a generous
breakfast; pick-up by arrangement. ❷–❺
Friday on the Beach 45 Lawson St ℡ 02/6685
6373, ⓦ www.fridayonthebeach.com.au. This chic
contemporary motel in the centre of town has a
bright and breezy feel to it and boasts absolute
beach frontage. ❻–❾
Rae's on Watego's Watego's Beach ℡ 02/6685
5366, ⓦ www.raes.com.au. This idiosyncratic
boutique hotel has long had a cult following, its
unique sense of style, intimacy (just seven rooms),
personal service, superb restaurant, and unbeatable location on gorgeous Watego's beach
attracting jetsetters, celebrities and travellers in
need of pampering – and romance (double beds
only). ❾
Watermark at Watego's 29 Marine Parade,
Watego's ℡ 02/6685 8999, ⓦ www
.wategoswatermark.com.au. These stunning suites
and apartments may be luxurious (think Italian
marble bathrooms, Egyptian cotton sheets, Bose
sound system) but the place still has that laid-back
sense of beach style synonymous with Byron. ❾

Hostels

Aquarius Backpackers Motel 16 Lawson St
℡ 02/6685 7663 or 1800 029 909, ⓦ www
.aquarius-backpackers.com.au. Excellent hostel
boasting characterful, split-level en-suite dorms
with fridge, motel rooms and some cute apartments. There's also a small "beach", BBQ, tour
desk, excellent communal areas, pool, and a bar
with a daily happy hour. Dorms $30, doubles ❸,
motel rooms ❹–❺, apartments ❻
Arts Factory Backpackers Lodge Skinners
Shoot Rd ℡ 02/6685 7709, ⓦ www.artsfactory
.com.au. In a bushland setting with a hippie atmosphere, this is a love-it-or-hate-it kind of place, and
the sheer number of backpackers wanting to stay
here means it can be a bit of a scrum. Facilities
include an arts studio, café, cinema, spa, pool,
beach volleyball, ping pong, boards, bikes ($7), as
well as poi twirling classes. There's a huge array of
"funky abodes", including tents, dorms, tepees,
cottages, wagons, cubes, surfshacks and
loveshacks, and prices vary: ❷–❼
Backpackers Inn on the Beach 29 Shirley St
℡ 02/6685 8231, ⓦ www.backpackersinnbyronbay
.com.au. Sociable hostel with direct access to
Belongil Beach, a cozy cushion-strewn lounge, large
clean dorms, and pool. Dorms $26–42, doubles ❹
Byron Bay YHA 7 Carlyle St ℡ 02/6685 8853,
ⓦ www.yha.com.au. Bright, peaceful option with a
BBQ area and pool, comfy dorms, plus free boogie-
boards and bikes. An excellent choice if you're not
that into Byron's party-hostel scene. Dorms $33,
doubles ❹
Cape Byron Lodge 78 Bangalow Rd ℡ 02/6685
6445 or 1800 111 030, ⓦ www.capebyronlodge
.com. Simple, friendly place with popular learn-to-
surf packages, good-value dorms, plus the usual
bikes, boards and activities, though it's a bit out of
town. Dorms $27, rooms ❸–❹
Holiday Village Backpackers 116 Jonson St
℡ 02/6685 8888 or 1800 350 388, ⓦ www
.byronbaybackpackers.com.au. Well-equipped,
motel-style hostel with standard dorms, a pool, BBQ
and free boards and bikes. Dorms $32, doubles ❹
Main Beach Backpackers Corner of Lawson
and Fletcher sts ℡ 02/6685 8695, ⓦ www
.mainbeachbackpackers.com. Safe, pleasant
hostel with standard dorms, a great sundeck,
pool, free bikes and boogie-boards, a great BBQ
two nights a week, and it's the best-located
hostel in town to boot, just 100m from Main
Beach. Dorms $30, doubles ❸–❹

Campsites

Broken Head Holiday Park Beach Rd, Broken
Head, 6km south ℡ 02/6685 3245 or 1800 450 036,

ⓦwww.brokenhd.com.au. The best of the bay's holiday parks, this site has good facilities and gentle, wooded inclines that afford great sea views over the southern end of Tallow Beach and the aptly named Broken Head Rocks. Un/powered sites $45/50, cabins ⑤–⑨

Clarke's Beach Holiday Park Off Lighthouse Rd ⓣ02/6685 6496, ⓦwww.clarkesbeach.com.au. Pleasant wooded site with standard amenities but

a fantastic setting right on the fabulous Clarke's Beach. Un/powered sites $45–49, cabins ⑥–⑧

First Sun Holiday Park Lawson St ⓣ02/6685 6544, ⓦwww.bshp.com.au/first-sun. Excellent central location on Main Beach with superb facilities, including camp kitchens you'd be happy to have at home, and free wireless internet. Un/powered sites ①, cabins ⑦–⑨

The town and around

There's plenty of opportunity to soak up the local atmosphere – and the fascinating mix of subcultures as surfie meets soap starlet meets hippie – simply by wandering the streets. If you want to explore, one of the first places to visit is the **lighthouse** on the rocky promontory of **Cape Byron**. The cape is the easternmost point of the Australian mainland and is a popular spot to greet the dawn (see p.282 for tours); with a bit of luck you'll see **dolphins**, who like to sport in the surf off the headland, or **humpback whales**, which pass this way heading north in June or July and again on their return south in September or October.

Alternative and artistic Byron Bay

Byron Bay offers a huge variety of alternative therapies, New Age bookshops, crystals, palmists and tarot readers – all with a good dose of capitalism, as prices are hiked up during the lucrative summer months. The alternative culture attracts artists and artisans in droves, and galleries and artists' studios abound.

Alternative therapies

Notice boards around town advertise hundreds of conventional and slightly wackier therapies. Get a copy of *Body & Soul* from the visitor centre for the full gamut of good vibes. **Quintessence** (ⓣ02/6685 5533, ⓦwww.quintessencebyron.com.au), 6/11 Fletcher St, is more for good old-fashioned pampering, with aromatherapy, massage and a range of indulgent packages ($60–145). Heading off the deep end of the purple spectrum, the Ambaji House of Wellbeing (ⓣ02/6685 6620/8538, ⓦwww .ambajihouseofwellbeing.com) at 1 Marvel St is very New Age, and offers a wide range of treatments from massage and reflexology to tarot readings, crystal healing and chakra clearing.

Arts and crafts

Local arts and crafts are on display at the **Byron Bay market**, held on the first Sunday of each month on Butler Street, behind the train station. There is also a farmers' market there every Thursday (8–11am). There are others at The Channon and Alstonville on the second Sunday, Mullumbimby on the third Saturday, Uki (north of Nimbin) and Ballina on the third Sunday, and at the showground at Bangalow, 13km southwest, on the fourth Sunday of each month. The **Arts Factory**, on Skinners Shoot Road, has an artists' workshop that you can visit (Mon–Sat 9am–2pm; ⓣ0438 949 398, ⓦwww.byrontik.com), and 3km west of town off Ewingsdale Road (the road to the Pacific Highway), the **Arts and Industry Estate** is a browser's dream, with over three hundred studios run by local artisans selling furniture, jewellery, art and glassware. Back in town, Jonson Street is lined with shops selling clothes and locally made crafts, particularly jewellery.

The **Byron Bay Writers' Festival** (ⓣ02/6685 5115, ⓦwww.byronbaywritersfestival .com.au) is held annually around the beginning of August; check the website for exact dates and details of readings, workshops and film screenings.

Main Beach in town is as good as any to swim from, and usually has relatively gentle surf. One reason why Byron Bay is so popular with surfers is because its beaches face in all directions, so there's almost always one with a good swell; conversely, you can usually find somewhere for a calmer swim. West of Main Beach, you can always find a spot to yourself on **Belongil Beach**, from where there's sand virtually all the way to **Brunswick Heads**.

To the east, Main Beach curves round towards Cape Byron to become **Clarke's Beach**; The Pass, a famous surfing spot, is at its eastern end. This and neighbouring **Watego's Beach** – beautifully framed between two rocky spurs – face north, and usually have the best surfing. On the far side of the cape, **Tallow Beach** extends towards the **Broken Head Nature Reserve**, 6km south of the town centre at Suffolk Park; there's good surf at Tallow just around the cape at Cosy Corner, and also at Broken Head. From the car park here, a short stroll through rainforest leads to the secluded, nudist **Kings Beach**.

The diversity of marine life in the waters of Byron Bay makes it a prime place to **dive**, though these are rock – rather than coral – reefs. Tropical marine life and creatures from warm temperate seas mingle at the granite outcrop of **Julian Rocks Aquatic Reserve**, 3km offshore; by far the most popular spot here is **Cod Hole**, an extensive underwater cave inhabited by large moray eels and other fish. Between April and June is the best time to dive, before the plankton bloom (see p.284 for dive operators).

Eating

Byron Bay is a great place to eat, with street food stalls, cafés and restaurants galore sprinkled down Jonson Street and the roads leading off it, although the alternative, vegetarian joints that once prevailed are being hustled out of town by upmarket delis and lunch spots.

Cafés and takeaways

Fishmongers Bay Lane, behind the *Beach Hotel*. Locals love this excellent little fish-and-chip place for its battered fish with hand-cut chips, and kumara crisps. Daily noon–9.30pm.

Twisted Sista Café Lawson St. Banana smoothies and big slices of cakes, plus the usual sandwiches, wraps and burgers. Daily 7am–4.30pm.

Restaurants

The Balcony Lawson St ☏02/6680 9666. An early-evening cocktail on the balcony of this eclectically decorated bar-restaurant is a relaxing way to kick off a night in Byron. Delicious food is served at breakfast, lunch and dinner, when the style turns to Mod Oz with a Spanish twist. Booking essential, sometimes even for drinks. Daily 8am–12.30am.

Buddha Bar & Zula Café At the Arts Factory, Skinners Shoot Rd ☏02/6685 5833. Definitely not everyone's cup of herb tea, but this kooky bar and café, with their booths and sofas, frequent live music and fire-twirling galore, are popular with hippies and backpackers. BYO. Mon–Sat 4pm–midnight, Sun 4–10pm.

Earth 'n' Sea Pizzas 11 Lawson St ☏02/6685 6029. The long pizza menu at this popular place includes all the classics, along with more off-the-wall combos such as the Beethoven, an alarming medley of prawn, banana and pineapple. BYO and licensed. Daily from 5.30pm.

Fishheads Right at the beach end of Jonson St ☏02/6680 7632, ⊛www.fishheadsbyron.com.au. Seafood restaurant opposite the sea that would be entirely perfect were it not for its car-park views. Still, you can hear the waves crashing on the shore from the wooden deck, and the seafood is delicious. BYO. Daily 7.30am–late.

Fresh 7 Jonson St ☏02/6685 7810. This funky casual eatery specializes in globally-inspired cuisine focused on the freshest produce with an emphasis on locally caught seafood, organic vegetables and free-range poultry. Daily 7.30am–10pm.

Olivo 34 Jonson St ☏02/6685 7950. Food and service can be hit and miss here, but the cozy atmosphere is appealing and the duck confit heavenly. BYO and licensed. Daily from 6.30pm.

Pacific Dining Room Beach Hotel, Bay St ☏02/6685 6402, ⊛www.beachotel.com.au. Long considered Byron's best restaurant, Chef David Moyle (formerly of Melbourne's *Circa*) dishes up light, refined cuisine to match the breezy, laid-back beach-shack-inspired decor. Small plates $10–18, larger plates $25–32. Breakfast 7–10am & cocktails and dinner 6pm to late.

Rae's on Watego's Watego's Beach ⓉT 02/6685 5366, Ⓦwww.raes.com.au. The romantic atmosphere is reason enough to book a table at this superb restaurant, but Chef Andrew Gimber's superb cuisine is another – Gimber worked under

some of Australia's best chefs, including Neil Perry, Christine Mansfield and David Thompson.

Whynot? 18 Jonson St ⓉT 02/6680 7994. This popular café-restaurant is an all-day kind of affair with Aussie-style tapas, cocktails (happy hour 5–7pm) and delicious Mod Oz cuisine served in the arty interior or at outdoor tables. Daily 6am–midnight.

Entertainment and nightlife

The weekly free community newspaper, *The Byron Shire Echo*, has a comprehensive gig guide. Many of the festivals and events are held in venues in the hinterland. There's plenty of activity in summer: **New Year's Eve** is such a big event that the council has taken to closing the town off, so come early. The huge **Blues and Roots Festival** (Ⓦwww.bluesfest.com.au) takes over Red Devil Park every Easter; check the website for dates and to book tickets. Similarly, the **Splendour in the Grass** music festival (Ⓦwww.splendourinthegrass.com), usually held in June/July, brings in huge crowds. In the Arts Factory complex, **The Lounge Cinema** (ⓉT 02/6685 5828) has pigskin-covered seats, a large disco ball, and several art-house or mainstream films screened daily at reasonable prices.

Beach Hotel Corner of Jonson and Bay sts ⓉT 02/6685 6402. Byron's beloved *Beach Hotel*, opposite Main Beach, has a large sunny terrace that attracts a mix of locals and visitors, and there's live music from Thurs–Sun year-round, and every night in high season, including jazz sessions on Sun afternoon.

Cheeky Monkeys 115 Jonson St ⓉT 02/6685 5886. Renowned backpacker party zone, with loud music, lots of frolicking, and junk food from 7pm to see you through to closing time eight hours later. Closed Sun.

Great Northern Hotel Corner of Jonson and Byron sts ⓉT 02/6685 6454. Huge and occasionally raucous Aussie pub with nightly live music in high season. Closes anywhere between 1am and 3am, depending on the crowd.

La La Land Lawson St. The little sister of the Melbourne institution, this is one of the hippest

nightspots in town, and a stop on the international DJ circuit. The cavernous, chandelier-bedecked interior is fairly chilled until 10.30pm, after which it gets reliably rammed with locals and well-heeled backpackers. $10–25 cover, depending on the DJ. Mon–Sat 8pm–3am, Sun 8pm–midnight.

Play Plaza car park ⓉT 02/6685 8989. This funky club attracts big-name DJs, with music ranging from electro house to drum 'n' bass. Cover charge; varies enormously depending on how big the DJ is. Daily 10pm–3am.

The Railway Friendly Bar (AKA The Rails) at the old train station. Good local bands rock the mike at this busy backpacker place a few times a week, and with its covered outdoor area it's a better bet than the pub.

Listings

Bike rental Most hostels have bikes which can either be used free or rented by guests; otherwise try Byron Bay Bicycles (ⓉT 02/6685 6067, Ⓦwww.byronbaybicycles.com.au), Shop 8 The Plaza, behind Woolworth's ($15 per 4hr or $22 per 8hr).

Car rental Jetset, Shop 6, Old Bakery Complex, Corner of Marvel & Jonson sts ⓉT 02/6685 6554; Hertz, 5 Marvel St ⓉT 02/6621 8855; Thrifty, corner of Butler & Lawson sts ⓉT 02/6685 6345.

Circus School Circus Arts (ⓉT 02/6685 6566, Ⓦwww.circusarts.com.au) will have you swinging

from the chandeliers and generally clowning about in no time. 1hr 30min trapeze workshops ($45), and circus-skills taster courses from $25.

Diving Sundive, next door to *Cape Byron YHA* on Middleton St ⓉT 02/6685 7755, Ⓦwww.sundive.com.au. Byron's only five-star PADI centre offers Open Water courses ($450), an introductory half-day dive course ($150, including ocean dive), dives at Julian Rocks ($90 first dive, $80 for subsequent dives) for qualified divers, plus snorkelling and whale-watching trips.

Hang-gliding Byron Airwaves Hang Gliding School ☏02/6629 0354, ⊛www.byronair.cjb.net. 30min tandem flights cost $145.

Horseriding Pegasus Park ☏02/6687 1446, ⊛www.pegasuspark.com.au. Trot through the hinterland ($50 per hr or $70 for 1hr 30min) or fulfil that galloping-down-a-deserted-beach fantasy ($70 per hr or $110 for 2hr).

Hospital Byron District Hospital, Wordsworth St, off Shirley St ☏02/6685 6200.

Internet access It won't move on Jonson St for internet cafés; just shop around for the cheapest prices, as it's very competitive.

Left luggage Byron Bus & Backpacker Travel (see p.280) have storage lockers ($4 for 5hr/$8 per 24hr).

Police 2 Shirley St ☏02/6685 9499.

Post office 61 Jonson St.

Skydiving Skydive Byron Bay (☏02/6684 1323, ⊛www.skydivebyronbay.com) offer Australia's highest jump (14,000ft), with spectacular views over Cape Byron for $299.

Surfing Black Dog Surfing, Shop 8, The Plaza ☏02/6680 9828, ⊛www.blackdogsurfing.com. The best of many outlets offering gear hire and lessons; they guarantee you'll stand up on your first lesson, a bold claim worth testing out. One- to five-day courses range from $60 to $150.

Taxi Byron Bay Transport Services ☏02/6685 5008. There's a taxi rank on Jonson St, opposite the Great Northern Hotel.

Far north coast hinterland

The beautiful **far north coast hinterland** lies between the major service town of **Lismore**, in the fertile Richmond River valley to the south, and **Murwillumbah**, in the even lusher valley of the Tweed River near the Queensland border. Much of the area dances to a different tune, with hippies, communes and Kombi vans very much the norm in this "Rainbow Region". The hinterland's three rainforest national parks and several reserves are World Heritage–listed: **Mount Warning National Park** rises in the middle of a massive caldera, on whose northwest and southern rims lie the **Border Ranges** and **Nightcap national parks**, the latter near countercultural **Nimbin** and **The Channon**, home to the largest and most colourful market in the area.

You need your own **vehicle** to get the best out of the area, particularly to complete one of the most **scenic drives** in New South Wales, the short round-trip over the mountainous, winding country roads north and northeast of Lismore to Nimbin, The Channon and Clunes, and then via Eltham and Bexhill, with superb views from the ridges and hilltops.

Nimbin and around

Some 50km inland from Byron via Lismore is **NIMBIN**, site of the famed Aquarius Festival that launched Australian hippie culture in 1973; it's a friendly little place and synonymous with the country's alternative life.

Arrival, information and accommodation

Nimbin has its own **visitor centre** (daily 9am–5pm; ☏02/6689 1764) at 8 Cullen St. There's no regular public transport to the town: the **Nimbin Shuttle Bus** runs up from Byron (Mon–Sat; $28 return; ☏02/6680 9189, ⊛www .nimbintours.com) but is really as much a day-tour as the other options running out of the bay (p.282).

During Mardi Grass, Nimbin is booked up well in advance, so be prepared to **camp**; all the hostels have pitches available.

Granny's Farm Backpackers & Camping 112 Cullen St ☏02/6689 1333. On the edge of town, you can sleep in a converted old train carriage by the creek, camp out on the grass, or bunk down in a dorm. There are two pools, but you can also swim in the creek. Dorms $22, doubles ❷–❸

Grey Gum Lodge 2 High St ☎02/6689 1713. Right in town, this comfortable guesthouse in an old "Queenslander" (picture a house on stilts with verandas) is about as smart as they get here, with a saltwater swimming pool but not much Nimbin vibe – a plus for some people. ❸–❹

Nimbin Rox 74 Thorburn St ☎02/6689 0022, ⓦwww.nimbinrox.com.au. The pick of the hostels, this friendly, well-managed place has a range of accommodation, from tepees to bush camps plus a pool, flotation tank and massage room in its fruit garden. It's set in a superb hilltop location just outside town and named after the huge sacred rocks it overlooks. Camping $14, dorms $26, canvas lodges, doubles and tepees ❶–❷

Rainbow Retreat 75 Thorburn St ☎02/6689 1262, ⓦwww.rainbowretreat.net. The hippiest place in town, with accommodation in a dorm, an old VW Kombi, gypsy wagon, bungalows or budget rooms. You can also camp. The property shares a stretch of Goolmanger Creek with the resident platypus, while horses munch between the tent spaces. Camping $13, dorms $20, doubles ❶–❷

The Town

The surrounding rainforest is dotted with as many as fifty communes, while the town itself is famous for live music, crafts and New Age therapies, but mainly **marijuana**. Visitors are invariably offered dope as soon as they set foot in town and you'll see it smoked openly on the streets; however, that doesn't mean to say you can wave joints around and expect not to get arrested should the police make one of their infrequent visits. Try to time your visit to coincide with the annual **Mardi Grass and Cannabis Law Reform Rally** (ⓦwww.nimbinmardigrass.com), held on the first weekend in May, when the town becomes a tent city and a high proportion of the temporary population have dreadlocks – bong throwing, joint rolling and campaigning rallies are amongst the activities on offer. Alternatively, aim to make it here on a **market** day (third and fifth Sunday of the month), where you'll catch some music, crafts and great organic food.

The tiny centre of Nimbin is aglow with buildings painted in bright, psychedelic designs, while small stores sell health food and incense sticks; everything of interest is on the main strip, Cullen Street. The **Nimbin Museum** (daily 9am–5pm; gold-coin donation, ⓦwww.nimbinaustralia.com/museum) at 61 Cullen St is a weird and wonderful living museum run by hippies, with a Kombi van left where it was driven through the front wall, lots of way-out graffiti and a ceiling mobile made from hand whisks – it nevertheless manages to impart a message of sorts about the value of Bundjalung Aboriginal culture and the benefits of cannabis use. If you have Green leanings, the **Nimbin Environmental Centre** might be of interest – they campaign on environmental issues, and can arrange visits to the **Djanbung Gardens Permaculture Centre** (ⓦwww.permaculture.com.au), a showcase for a system of sustainable agriculture that has gained ground worldwide. The **Hemp Embassy** (daily 10am–5pm; ⓦwww.hempembassy.net) too is worth a look; learn why the Hemp Party believe the herb should be legalized, and browse through some of their previous campaigns and press releases.

Eating, drinking and nightlife

Cullen Street is full of **places to eat**, including the legendary *Rainbow Café*, which has a garden out the back and serves good coffee, all-day breakfasts, burgers and salads. The *Nimbin Retro Café* specializes in veggie fare and cakes, while *Nimbin Pizza & Pasta* is a long-established favourite offering gargantuan pizzas topped with local organic produce. For **nightlife and entertainment** there's the *Nimbin Hotel*, which sees plenty of live music and some interesting local characters; the *Rainbow Retreat* (see above), with more live bands; and the *Hemp Bar*, next to the Hemp Embassy, a cozy, Amsterdam-esque drinking hole.

The Nimbin Bush Theatre (☎02/6689 1111), located in an old butter factory over the bridge opposite *Granny's Farm Backpackers*, serves tasty food and is home to a charming little cinema – call or check the notice boards in town for screenings.

The Channon and the Nightcap National Park

THE CHANNON, a 26-kilometre drive south of Nimbin, is a pretty village on the banks of **Terania Creek**. It's home to the **Channon Craft Market** (second Sunday of the month), the best – and the first – of its type in the Rainbow Region. Begun in 1976 to provide the rapidly starving hippies with some cash, the rule that you have to "make it or bake it" still holds fast – it's a colourful spectacle and well worth a trip. The funky, heritage-listed *Channon Tavern* is located within an old butter factory, and serves up hearty dinners and local gossip.

A fourteen-kilometre drive into the **Nightcap National Park**, along the unsealed Terania Creek Road, brings you to **Protestors Falls** and a rainforest valley filled with ancient brush box trees, saved by the 1979 protest which was the first successful anti-logging campaign in Australia. You can walk down to the bottom of the falls, named after the dispute, to the Terania Creek Picnic Area. Also within the park are the one-hundred-metre cascades of **Minyon Falls**, often more of a trickle in summer; a steep walk (2hr return) leads down to the base. You're allowed to **camp** at the *Rummery Park Camping Ground* ($5 per adult) in nearby **Whian Whian State Conservation Area**, 2km from Minyon Falls along Peates Mountain Road; for something more comfortable try the arty *Havan's Ecotourist Retreat* (☎02/6688 6108, ⓦwww.rainbowregion .com/havan; ❹–❺), just off Terania Creek Road on Lawler Road, overlooking the creek and rainforest.

Murwillumbah and around

MURWILLUMBAH is a quiet, inland town on a bend of the Tweed River, a little over 30km northwest of Byron Bay. It's a good base for exploring the beautiful Tweed Valley and the mountains that extend to the Queensland border. It's well worth dropping by the superb **Tweed River Regional Art Gallery** (Wed–Sun 10am–5pm; free), at the corner of Tweed Valley Way and Minstral Road, which displays the work of Australian artists and features travelling exhibitions. The gallery's Australian Portrait Collection is engaging.

At the Murwillumbah exit on the Pacific Highway, the **Big Avocado** lures the visitor towards **Tropical Fruit World** (daily 10am–4.30pm; $35; ⓦwww .tropicalfruitworld.com.au), slightly to the south on Duranbah Road. A plantation which has been turned into a miniature theme park, it grows avocados, macadamia nuts and many kinds of tropical fruit; you can ride around in open-air buses and miniature trains, or cruise around on man-made "tropical canals". There are canoes and aqua-bikes for rent, and a fruit market sells plantation produce.

The **Tweed Valley** and the surrounding land close to the Queensland border are among the most beautiful areas of New South Wales, ringed by mountain ranges that are actually the remains of an extinct volcano. Some twenty million years ago a huge shield **volcano** spewed lava through a central vent onto the surrounding plain. Erosion carved out a vast bowl around the centre of the resultant mass of lava, while the more resistant rocks around the edges stood firm. Right at the bowl's heart is **Mount Warning** (1157m), or Wollumbin ("cloud catcher") to the local **Bundjalung** Aborigines, the original vent of the volcano, whose unmistakable, twisted profile rises like a sentinel from the Tweed Valley. The mountain is a place of great cultural significance to the Bundjalung, who believe that only expressly chosen people may attempt the steep three-hour path to the summit; however, as at Uluru, many visitors can't resist the dazzling views on offer.

North of Murwillumbah is Tourist Drive 40, a 57-kilometre **scenic drive** through the **Tweed Valley**, which takes in some of its best features en route from Murwillumbah up to Tweed Heads and the state border.

Practicalities

Greyhound and Premier Motor Service long-distance **buses** stop in town. The **visitor centre** (Mon–Sat 9am–4.30pm, Sun 9.30am–4pm; ☎1800 674 414, ⓦwww.tweedtourism.com.au) is located in the Rainforest Heritage Centre on Alma Street, and has an accommodation booking service.

Places to stay in Murwillumbah include the Art Deco *Imperial Hotel* (☎02/6672 1036; rooms ❷–❸) at 115 Main St, a grand old building right in the centre of town, with good-value singles and doubles, a decent bistro and local bands at weekends. *Mount Warning Riverside YHA Backpackers* (☎02/6672 3763, ⓦwww.yha.com.au; dorms $26–30, doubles ❷), at 1 Tumbulgum Rd, is a truly wonderful find; a cozy hostel in an atmospheric old Sea Captain's house overlooking the picturesque Tweed River, with swimming, bikes for rent, free canoes and rowing boat, plus free ice cream every evening at 9pm – stay for two nights and you'll get a free trip to Mount Warning. Alternatively, make the most of the countryside by staying in rural accommodation: *Mount Warning Forest Hideaway* (☎02/6679 7277, ⓦwww.foresthideaway.com.au; ❹–❽), on Byrill Creek Road near the village of Uki, southwest of town, occupies a hundred acres of lush forest and offers motel-style units with cooking facilities, plus a swimming pool.

Places to eat include the *Blue Frog*, on Wharf Street, for breakfast and lunch, and the *Imperial Hotel*, where you'll find the best bistro food in town.

Lord Howe and Norfolk islands

Lord Howe Island, 700km northeast of Sydney, and on the same latitude as Port Macquarie, is technically a part of New South Wales, despite its distance from the mainland. Its nearest neighbour is **Norfolk Island**, 900km further northeast, an external independent territory of Australia, though geographically it's closer to New Zealand. The approach to tourism of the two subtropical islands couldn't be more different: Lord Howe is the perfect eco-destination, attracting outdoor types with its rugged beauty, while Norfolk Island concentrates primarily on its status as a tax haven. Neither island caters to budget travellers.

Getting there

You can **fly to Lord Howe Island** with Qantas from Sydney (daily) from around $800–1000 return in summer and $700 in winter, with advance booking a definite advantage. Qantas charge similar prices for their summer flights from Lord Howe to Brisbane and Port Macquarie (both 1–2 weekly), though most flights route through Sydney. Overseas visitors can fly to Lord Howe as an add on fare on an air pass (see p.35).

Norfolk Air (T1800 612 960, Wwww.norfolkair.com) operate **flights to Norfolk Island** from Sydney (three per week), Brisbane (three per week), Newcastle (one per week) and Melbourne (one per week), while Air New Zealand fly to the island twice a week from Auckland – flights from Australia cost around $800–1000 return, and those from New Zealand around $600. There are no scheduled flights between the two islands.

On both islands, **accommodation** has to be arranged before you book your air travel, to limit the number of tourists staying each night. It's often much easier – and better value – to buy an accommodation and flights **package deal**. Prices for seven nights on either island range from around $900 in winter and from $1400 in summer: try Oxley Travel (T1800 671 546, Wwww.oxleytravel .com.au) or Talpacific Holidays (T1300 665 737, Wwww.talpacific.com).

One way to combine visits to Lord Howe and Norfolk islands is with Heron Airlines (T02/9792 4544, Wwww.heronairlines.com.au) who offer an all-inclusive ten-day trip from Sydney to Lord Howe, on to Norfolk and New Caledonia, then finally back to Sydney, for $6000.

Lord Howe Island

I would strongly urge preserving this beautiful island from further intrusions of any kind...

Government Expedition, 1882

World Heritage-listed **LORD HOWE ISLAND** is a kind of Australian Galapagos, and a favourite destination for ecotourists. Just 11km long and 2.8km across at its widest point, the crescent-shaped island's only industry other than tourism is its plantations of **kentia palms** (see p.293), and two-thirds of the island is designated as Permanent Park Reserve. As you fly in, you'll get a stunning view of the whole of the volcanic island: the towering summits of rainforest-clad **Mount Gower** (875m) and **Mount Lidgbird** (777m) at the southern end; the narrow centre with its idyllic lagoon and a **coral reef** extending about 6km along the west coast; and a group of tiny islets off the lower northern end of the island providing sanctuary for the prolific **birdlife**. Much of the surrounding waters and islands fall within Lord Howe's protective **marine park**.

The emphasis here is on tranquillity: there are only 350 islanders; no rowdy nightclubs spoiling the peace; no mobile-phone coverage; and most of the 400 visitors allowed at any one time are couples and families. Even disregarding the island's ecological attractions, it's a fascinating place to stay: most visitors are intrigued by the small details of island life, such as how children are schooled and how food is brought from the mainland, and are generally eager to sample life in this egalitarian paradise where no one locks their car (or even takes the key out of the ignition), bike or house. Though it's expensive to get to the island, once here you'll find that cruises, activities and bike rental are all relatively affordable. The island's **climate** is subtropical, with temperatures rising from a

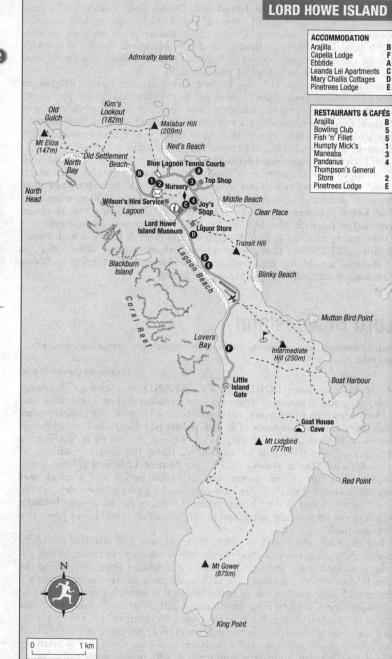

LORD HOWE ISLAND

ACCOMMODATION
Arajilla	B
Capella Lodge	F
Ebbtide	A
Leanda Lei Apartments	C
Mary Challis Cottages	D
Pinetrees Lodge	E

RESTAURANTS & CAFÉS
Arajilla	B
Bowling Club	5
Fish 'n' Fillet	5
Humpty Mick's	1
Maneaba	3
Pandanus	4
Thompson's General Store	2
Pinetrees Lodge	E

Admiralty Islets

Old Gulch

Kim's Lookout (182m)

Mt Eliza (147m)

▲ Malabar Hill (209m)

Ned's Beach

Old Settlement Beach

North Bay

North Head

Blue Lagoon Tennis Courts

B

1 2

A

3 Top Shop

Wilson's Hire Service

Lagoon

i

4 Joy's Shop

Middle Beach

Clear Place

Lord Howe Island Museum

Liquor Store

D

Transit Hill ▲

Blackburn Island

Lagoon Beach

5 E

Blinky Beach

Coral Reef

Mutton Bird Point

Lovers Bay

F

Intermediate Hill (250m)

Boat Harbour

Little Island Gate

Goat House Cave

▲ Mt Lidgbird (777m)

Red Point

N

▲ Mt Gower (875m)

King Point

0 —————— 1 km

▼ Ball's Pyramid (23km)

mild 19°C in winter to 26°C in the summer, and an annual rainfall of 1650mm. It's cheaper to visit in the winter, though some places are closed.

Some history

Lord Howe Island was discovered in 1788 by Lieutenant Henry Lidgbird Ball (who named the island after the British admiral Richard Howe), commander of the First Fleet ship *Supply*, during a journey from Sydney to found a penal colony on Norfolk Island. The island wasn't inhabited for another 55 years, however; the first **settlers** came in 1833, and others followed in the 1840s. In 1853 two white men arrived with three women from the Gilbert Islands in the central Pacific, and it is from this small group that many of Lord Howe's present population are descended. In the 1840s and 1850s the island served as a stopover for **whaling ships** from the US and Britain, with as many as fifty ships a year passing through. In 1882, a government expedition from the mainland recommended that in order to preserve the island, no one other than the present "happy, industrious" leaseholders and their families be allowed to make permanent settlement.

With the decline of whaling, economic salvation came in the form of the "thatch" palm, one of the four endemic species of the **kentia palm**. Previously used as roofing for the islanders' homes, it began to be exported as a decorative interior plant, boosting the island's economy. The profits from the kentia trade were shared out equally amongst the Lord Howe residents, each of whom was in turn expected to take on an equal share of the (not overly hard) work on the kentia plantations. In 1918, however, the kentia industry was damaged by the appearance of **rats**, which escaped onto the island from a ship. **Tourism** was eventually to become the mainstay of the island – Lord Howe became a popular stopover on the cruise-ship circuit before World War II, and after the war it began to be visited by holidaymakers from Sydney, who came by seaplane.

Today, rats still pose a hazard to the palms, but the **kentia industry** is nonetheless in resurgence, with profits going towards the preservation of the island's unique ecosystem. Seeds are no longer exported but instead are cultivated in the Lord Howe Island Board's own **nursery** (tours Fri at 10.30am; book at the visitor centre; $15), which sells two and a half million plants annually and grows seedlings for regeneration around the island.

Arrival, orientation and information

On arrival at the **airport**, located in the narrow central part of the island, you'll be met by hotel staff who will take you to your lodging. These are dotted around the populated northern end of the island, often tucked away behind rows of palms. There's no town as such, though people jokingly refer to the **CBD**, where Ned's Beach Road meets Lagoon Road. Here you'll find the **post office** (Mon–Fri 10am–1pm & 2–4pm), a community hall-cum-summer cinema and Thompson's General Store (daily 8am–6pm; ☎02/6563 2155), where you can book most activities, order roast chickens, and rent fishing or snorkelling gear. About 500m south along Lagoon Road you'll find the **visitor centre** (Mon–Fri 9.30am–3pm, Sun 9.30am–2.30pm; ☎02/6563 2114 or 1800 240 937, ⓦwww.lordhoweisland.info), inside the Lord Howe Island Museum. They book all tours and activities, hand out good island maps and sell the *Ramblers Guide to Lord Howe Island* ($10), which covers all the walks on the island in detail.

There are no ATMs on the island, but the two **banks** and many shops will give cash out on EFTPOS or credit cards to customers. Credit cards are fairly

Lord Howe ecology

Seven million years ago, a volcanic eruption on the sea floor created Lord Howe Island and its 27 surrounding islets and outcrops – the island's boomerang shape is a mere remnant (around two percent) of its original form, mostly eroded by the sea. While much of the **flora** on the island is similar to that of Australia, New Zealand, New Caledonia and Norfolk Island, the island's relative isolation has led to the evolution of many **new species** – of the 241 native plants found here, 113 are endemic, including the important indigenous **kentia palm** (see p.293).

Similarly, until the arrival of settlers, fifteen species of flightless **land birds** (nine of which are now extinct) lived on the island, undisturbed by predators and coexisting with migrating sea birds, skinks, geckos, spiders, snails and the now-extinct giant horned turtle. However, in the nineteenth century Lord Howe became a port of call for ships en route to Norfolk Island, whose hungry crews eradicated the island's stocks of **white gallinule** and **white-throated pigeon**. The small, plump and flightless **woodhen** managed to survive, protected on Mount Gower, and an intensive captive breeding programme in the early 1980s (aided by eradication of feral goats and pigs) saved the species. There are now about 350 woodhens on the island, and you'll often spot them pecking around your lodging. About one million **sea birds** – fourteen species – nest on Lord Howe annually: it is one of the few known breeding grounds of the providence petrel; has the world's largest colony of red-tailed tropic birds; and is the most southerly breeding location of the sooty tern, the noddy tern and the masked booby. Cats have now been eradicated from the island, as a result of which bird numbers have soared, and a plan to exterminate rats and mice is being examined. Nervous travellers can rest in peace on Lord Howe, safe in the knowledge that there are none of the poisonous spiders and snakes that blight the mainland.

The cold waters of the **Tasman Sea**, which surround Lord Howe, host the world's southernmost **coral reef**, a tropical oddity which is sustained by the warm summer current sweeping in from the Great Barrier Reef. There are about sixty varieties of brilliantly coloured and fantastically shaped coral, and the meeting of warm and cold currents means that a huge variety of both **tropical and temperate fish** can be spotted in the crystal-clear waters. Some of the most colourful species include the yellow moon wrasse, parrotfish and the yellow-and-black banner fish. Unique to Lord Howe is the doubleheader, with its bizarre, bulbous forehead and fat lips. Beyond the lagoon, the water becomes very deep, with particularly good diving in the seas around the **Admiralty Islets**, which have sheer underwater precipices and chasms.

widely accepted, but it's a good idea to bring all the **cash** you'll need with you. Many hotels now offer **internet access**, and it's also available at the visitor centre (daily 10am–2pm; coin-op $2 for 20min; network cable $3 for 20min).

Transport

The island has few **roads** and only a small number of cars: the speed limit is just 25km per hr. The majority of places you want to go are within 3km of each other so most people get around on foot or by **bicycle**. Lodges generally offer **bikes** to guests (free or for a small daily charge), or you can rent from Wilson's Hire Service (see box, p.297). If you really want to **rent a car**, be sure to reserve one before you arrive, either from Wilson's or *Leanda Lei Apartments* (see opposite). There are sporadic streetlights down Lagoon Road, but if you are walking or cycling after dark you'll need to bring a torch with you, or buy one from one of the stores – in wet conditions, you might see some glow-in-the-dark fungi. For island **tours**, see box, p.297.

Accommodation

Most of the accommodation on the island is **self-catering** and of a good standard. Room rates drop as low as $150 in winter, but $200 is the cheapest you'll find in summer. All the lodges are centrally located, with the exception of *Capella Lodge*, where the privacy, views and air of luxury more than compensate.

Arajilla Lagoon Rd ☎1800 063 928, ⓦwww .arajilla.com.au. The one- and two-bedroom suites at this luxury lodge nestle among the kentia palms and banyan trees, with buildings linked by sinuous boardwalks. With private decks, a day-spa and a lovely restaurant there's all the pampering and seclusion you could want, and the beach is just a few steps away. Full board only, from $520 per person ⓥ

Capella Lodge Lagoon Rd ☎02/9918 4355, ⓦwww.lordhowe.com. Nestling under Mount Gower and Mount Lidgbird, this is the most luxurious place to stay on the island. The stunning bar, restaurant and infinity pool overlook the mountains, and the suites and loft apartments are all interior-designed to within an inch of their lives. Breakfast, sunset drinks and canapés, and fusion-style dinner are included in the price. There's also a hot tub and a spa. The one niggle is that the restaurant isn't open to non-residents – it seems a shame not to share those views. Full board only, $550–790 per person ⓥ

Ebbtide Muttonbird Drive ☎02/6563 2023, ⓦwww.ebbtide-lhi.com.au. Nestling up on the cliff by Searles Point, this very friendly place has simple, stylish apartments and cottages set in a tropical garden of pawpaw and banana (guests can

help themselves). A private bush-track leads down to Ned's Beach. ⓧ

Leanda Lei Apartments Middle Beach Rd ☎02/6563 2195, ⓦwww.leandalei.com.au. Smart, clean and run with friendly efficiency by the Riddle family. The studios and one- and two-bedroom apartments here are set in lush manicured grounds with BBQs, close to Lagoon Beach. They also have a couple of cars for rent at $88 per day. Summer rates from $270. ⓥ

Mary Challis Cottages Lagoon Rd ☎02/6563 2076, ⓔgretmock@clearmail.com.au. Situated right by Lagoon Beach, these two cute cottages have everything you'll need, plus some home-baked goodies on arrival, and a couple of docile cows. ⓧ

Pinetrees Lodge Lagoon Rd ☎02/9262 6585, ⓦwww.pinetrees.com.au. The island's original guesthouse is a family-friendly place, set in extensive, forested grounds. Accommodation is in motel-style units or newer "garden cottages" around the original lodge, where everyone takes full advantage of the delicious meals included in the price. There's also a tennis court, and a boatshed over the road on Lagoon Beach, a delightful place for a sundowner from the honesty bar. Full board only, $250–400. ⓥ

The island

A good way to kick off your island idyll is with a trip to the **Lord Howe Island Museum** (Mon–Fri 9am–3pm, Sat & Sun 10am–2pm; free), on the corner of Middle Beach and Lagoon roads, which goes a long way to answering all those "so who's related to whom?" questions you inevitably bore your lodge-owner with. The museum hosts very good slide-shows on island history and ecology a few evenings a week, narrated by the island naturalist, Ian Hutton (check times at the visitor centre; $6), as well as occasional cultural nights. A couple of hundred metres north along Lagoon Road you'll come across a series of beach huts from where most of the water-related businesses operate – glass-bottom boats, round-island cruises, diving, snorkelling and kayak rental (see box, p.297 for operators).

North Bay and around

At the island's **northern end**, Lagoon Road ends at Old Settlement Beach where a 300-metre walk northeast across a cow paddock takes you to the wreckage of a **Catalina** flying boat which ditched here in 1948. Old Settlement Beach is a good starting point for lovely, easy to moderate **hikes** around the top of the island. Memorial Track is a steep two-kilometre hike over a hill to **North Bay**, where there's a picnic area, toilets and free gas barbecue. It's a good place to hang out for the day, perhaps swimming, snorkelling or taking in a couple more short hikes. There's a twenty-minute trek to the summit of **Mount Eliza** (147m), the most accessible place to see **sooty terns** in their southernmost breeding grounds. When the colony visits the island between September and March each female lays a single speckled egg on the bare ground, which means that the summit has to be closed for the birds' protection. Also from **North Bay**, a five-minute walk through forest leads to **Old Gulch**, a beach of boulders, where at low tide you can rock-hop to the **Herring Pools** at the base of the cliff front and examine the colourful marine life before returning to the picnic area. It's worth taking a boat to **North Bay** with Islander Cruises (see box opposite, $10 each way) and beginning the walk from there, as the initial hike from Old Settlement Beach takes a lot out of you without giving a lot back.

Keen hikers should consider continuing northeast from North Bay to Ned's Beach (3km one-way; 1–2hr) along the spectacular clifftop path past **Kim's Lookout** (182m) to the top of **Malabar Hill** (209m) then down to the beach. The route provides a good view of the settlement and the lagoon beaches and islets, and Malabar Hill gives access to one of the world's largest nesting concentrations of **red-tailed tropic birds**, which between September and May make their homes in the crannies of the cliff face below, laying only one egg and looking after the chick for twelve weeks until it can fly. From the summit, you can just see Ball's Pyramid way down to the south around the corner of Mount Lidgbird.

Ned's Beach

Some 500m northwest of the CBD, **Ned's Beach** is the most accessible ocean beach and is always popular for its **fish-feeding** frenzy. Pretty much any time of the day you'll find people throwing stale bread or fish food pellets into the water, attracting a throng of big trevally, whiting and kingfish. Stand knee-deep in the water and you'll have metre-long kingfish brushing past your calves in the melee. If you want to get amongst them, rent **snorkelling gear** and wet suits from the hut at the back of Ned's Beach (snorkel set $3.50 per hr or $10 a day; wet suit $6/20); put your money in the honesty box. Snorkelling is probably best around low tide, when most of the fish life is concentrated in a narrow channel that cuts between banks of coral and the sea. Harmless but menacing-looking, metre-long Galapagos sharks are usually around.

Consider returning at dusk for the clumsy arrival of the **muttonbirds** (sooty shearwaters; here Sept–May) which return from their day's fishing to burrows in among the palms at the back of the beach. You'll see them circling, then they'll start landing all around you and waddling to their burrows, seemingly unconcerned by your presence.

Mount Gower

The ultimate view on the island is at its **southern end**, where the lofty summit of **Mount Gower** (875m) gives vistas over the whole island and out to sea towards the world's tallest sea stack, **Balls Pyramid** (548m), a spike of volcanic rock which breaks dramatically up out of the ocean 23km southeast of Lord Howe. Mount Gower is high enough to have a true **mist forest** on its summit, with a profusion of ferns, tree trunks and rocks covered in mosses. This extremely strenuous walk can be undertaken only with a licensed **guide** (best with Sea to Summit Expeditions – see box opposite) and is definitely not for the faint-hearted – one section of the walk runs precariously along a narrow cliff-face above the sea, and in parts the track is so steep that you have to pull yourself up the guide ropes. The path to the top was blazed by botanists in 1869, who took two days to get there, but they were rewarded with the discovery of a plant seen nowhere else on earth – the **pumpkin tree**, bearing fleshy orange flowers. You can see other rare endemic plants here, including the island apple and the blue plum, as well as birds such as the providence petrel and the woodhen.

The Lagoon and ocean

The island has some sensational swimming, snorkelling and diving sites, as well as a large number of boat trips (see box, p.297). The beaches here are lovely, though the white sand comprises rather rough little bits of broken-up coral. There's stunning snorkelling and diving at **Sylphs Hole**, off Old Settlement

---

Tours and activities

Tours

All of the following can be booked at Thompson's Store (⏽02/6563 2155) or direct with the operator.

Ron's Rambles ⏽02/6563 2010. Ron will have you sniffing herbs, feeling rocks and believing some tall stories about the early islanders' bushcraft on his three-hour ambles. Mon, Wed & Fri at 2pm; $20.

Pro Dive Lagoon Road ⏽02/6563 2253, Ⓦwww.prodivelordhowelsland.com.au. Professional diving (Sept–May) with single dives ($90 including gear), doubles ($165), and three-day PADI courses for $500, with all your training in the lagoon.

Marine Adventures Lagoon Rd ⏽02/6563 2448. A wide array of marine-oriented trips including: turtle-spotting in a glass-bottomed boat with snorkelling (2hr; $40); turtle-spotting with a nature tour of North Bay (3hr 30min; $45); a round-island cruise ($50); and boat trips out to Ball's Pyramid ($100).

Lord Howe Nature Tours ⏽02/6563 2447. Walking tours with the island's fabulously knowledgeable naturalist, Ian Hutton, from $55 for half a day.

Islander Cruises ⏽02/6563 2021, Ⓔislcru@etelecom.com.au. Diving, snorkelling, and turtle- and coral-viewing can be combined on assorted tours from $40.

Sea to Summit Expeditions ⏽02/6563 2218. Excellent and informative guided hikes up Mount Gower (Mon & Thurs; 8hr; $40) with fifth-generation islander, Jack Shick, whose grandfather started treks up the peak. Booking is essential and you'll need lunch and water. To join the walk, you have to be at the Little Island Gate on the south of the island by 7.30am: you can get a lift there with **Whitfield's Island Tours** (see below; $10 return), or it's about a half-hour cycle ride from the north of the island. Also runs fishing trips when the weather behaves.

Whitfield's Island Tours ⏽02/6563 2115. Informative 3hr minibus tours of the island (daily 9.30am; $30) comprise a visit to the palm nursery and school, and morning tea at the family home, where Greg scales a palm tree to get at the seeds.

Activities and rentals

A good place for rental of all types of gear is Wilson's Hire Service at Lagoon Road (⏽02/6563 2045; closed Sat), including cars ($60 per day), bikes ($7 per day), snorkel set ($6 per day) and wet suits (additional $2 per day).

Golf There's a nine-hole golf course near *Capella Lodge* ($20 with your own clubs, $35 with theirs). It is done on an honesty system, and you'll need $1 coins to buy balls. During competitions (Fri from 3pm and Sun from 1.30pm) the bar is open.

Spa Both *Capella* and *Arajilla* have day spas open to non-guests. Full-body massages start around $100 per hr.

Tennis There's a court across the road from Thompson's General Store where you can book ($10 per hr), rent rackets ($2 per hr) and buy balls.

Beach, and on the east side of the island at Ned's Beach (see p.296), where corals lie only 10m from the shore. The combination of temperate and tropical waters makes double-headed wrasse, lobsters and angelfish a common sight. Rent snorkelling gear from Ned's Beach, or more cheaply from Wilson's Hire Service (see box, p.297).

If you'd rather not get wet, join one of the glass-bottom boat cruises over the reef, all run from a string of boatsheds on Lagoon Road. In the same area you'll find companies offering fishing trips, kayak rental and just about any kind of **boat trip**.

Eating and drinking

Bookings are necessary for evening meals; not much vegetarian food is available, so state your preferences beforehand. Most restaurants will drop you back home after dinner. There are four places to buy **groceries** and sundries on the island, including Thompson's General Store (see below). Inevitably, transport costs make things more **expensive** than on the mainland. There's no pub on Lord Howe; the closest thing to a **bar** is the *Bowling Club* ("The Bowlo"; daily 4.30–9.30pm), which stays open late on Friday when people bring down their iPods and play a few tunes (generally 9.30pm–1am).

Arajilla Lagoon Rd ☎02/6563 2002. This luxury resort has a restaurant serving delicious Australian cuisine in the evenings, although due to full board being offered to guests it rarely has space for non-residents. Mains around $40.

Fish 'n' Fillet ☎02/6563 2208. *Fish 'n' Fillet* hold fish-fry nights at the bowling club on Tues, Thurs and Sat from 5.30pm with a basket of fish, calamari and chips going for $22. They also sell super-fresh fish from their shop (Mon, Wed & Fri 4–6pm) at Earl's Anchorage on Anderson Rd.

Humpty Mick's Ned's Beach Rd. Recently revamped café that's an essential lunch or snack stop offering affordable salads, speciality burgers, focaccias and daily fish specials. Daily 9am–7.30pm.

Pandanus Anderson Rd ☎02/6563 2400. This pleasant, minimalist restaurant has wooden floors,

starchy white table linen and beachy artwork, and serves pizza, pasta and mains (mostly around $30) with an Italian flavour. Lunch Thurs–Sat, dinner daily from 6pm.

Pinetrees Lodge Lagoon Rd ☎02/6563 2177. The Monday-night fish fry here is the best of several on the island; it's well worth booking for this quintessential Lord Howe experience, including as it does vast plates of sushi, fried kingfish, chips, salads and groaning tables of desserts. Three-course dinner $40; fish fry $50. Go early and have a glass of wine over at the lodge's boatshed on the lagoon, where you can watch the often spectacular sunset.

Thompson's General Store Ned's Beach Rd. Inexpensive takeaway sandwiches, fish and beef burgers at lunchtime only, plus pastries and ice cream cones.

Norfolk Island

Just 8km long and 5km wide, tiny, isolated **NORFOLK ISLAND** is an External Territory of Australia, located 1450km east of Brisbane. The island has had an eventful history, being linked with early convict settlements and later with the descendants of Fletcher Christian and other "mutiny-on-the-*Bounty*" rebels. It's a unique place, forested with grand indigenous pine trees, and with a mild subtropical **climate** ranging between 12°C and 19°C in the winter and from 19°C to 28°C in the summer; Norfolk is also said to have some of the world's **cleanest air** after Antarctica. The island's **tax-haven** status makes it a refuge for millionaires, though its **duty-free stores** are less popular than they once were.

Norfolk mainly attracts honeymooners or retired Australians and New Zealanders (known as the "newly weds and nearly deads"). Australian and New

Zealand **passport** holders need no further documentation, but all others will need a multi-entry Australian visa to get onto the island. Everyone needs a return air ticket and accommodation booked before arrival. The island has no income tax, finances being raised from sources such as departure tax ($30) and a road levy included in the price of petrol.

Most of the 1800 local people remain unaffected by tourism, maintaining their friendly attitude, amusing nicknames (confusingly used in the island's telephone directory) and the remnants of their dialect, **Norfolk**, a mixture of old West Country English and Tahitian (see p.300).

Much of the land is cleared for cultivation, as islanders have to grow all their own fresh food; cattle roam freely on the green island and are given right of way, creating a positively bucolic atmosphere. At the centre of the island is its only significant settlement, **Burnt Pine** – on the south coast, picturesque **Kingston** is the sightseeing focus. Scenic winding roads provide access to the **Norfolk Island National Park** and the **Botanic Garden** in the northern half of the island, which together cover twenty percent of Norfolk's area with subtropical rainforest. Norfolk Island is also an ornithologist's paradise, with nine endemic **land-bird** species, including the endangered **Norfolk Island green parrot**, with its distinctive chuckling call. The two small, uninhabited islands immediately south of Norfolk, **Nepean** and **Phillip** islands, are important **sea bird** nesting sites.

Some history

A violent **volcanic eruption** three million years ago produced the Norfolk Ridge, extending from New Zealand to New Caledonia (Norfolk Island's closest neighbour, 700km north), with only Norfolk, Phillip and Nepean islands remaining above sea level. **Captain Cook** "discovered" the then-uninhabited islands in 1774, but it's now known that migrating Polynesian people lived here as far back as the tenth century – their main settlement at Emily Bay has been excavated and stone tools found. Cook thought the tall **Norfolk pines** would make fine ships' masts, with accompanying sails woven

▲ Norfolk Island

from the native flax. Norfolk Island was settled in 1788, only six weeks after Sydney. However, plans to use the fertile island as a base to grow food for the starving young colony of Australia floundered when, in 1790, a First Fleet ship, the *Sirius*, was wrecked on a reef off the island, highlighting its lack of a navigable harbour. This **first settlement** was proved unviable when the pines were found not to be strong enough for masts, and it was finally abandoned in 1814. Most of the buildings were destroyed to discourage settlement by other powers.

Norfolk's isolation was one of the major reasons for its **second settlement** as a **prison** (1825–55), described officially as "a place of the extremest punishment short of death"; up to two thousand convicts were held on Norfolk, overseen by sadistic commandants who had virtually unlimited power to run the settlement and inflict punishments as they saw fit. Some of the imposing stone buildings designed by Royal Engineers still stand in **Kingston** on the southern coast.

Norfolk Island was again abandoned in 1855, but this time the buildings remained and were used a year later during the **third settlement**, which consisted of 194 Pitcairn Islanders (the entire population of the island), who left behind their overcrowded conditions over 6000km east across the Pacific to establish a new life here. The new settlers had only eight family surnames among them – five of which (Christian, Quintal, Adams, McCoy and Young) were the names of the original mutineers of the *Bounty*. These names – especially Christian – are still common on the island, and today about one in three can claim descent from the mutineers. These descendants still speak some of their original language to each other: listen for expressions such as "Watawieh Yorlye?" (how are you?) and "Si Yorlye Morla" (see you tomorrow). **Bounty Day**, the day the Pitcairners arrived, is celebrated in Kingston on June 8.

Information and transport

The **airport** is on the western side of the island, just outside **Burnt Pine**, the main service centre; here you'll find the **visitor centre** (Mon, Tues, Thurs & Fri 8.30am–5pm, Wed 8.30am–4pm, Sat & Sun 8.30am–3pm; ℡6723/22147, Ⓦwww.norfolkisland.com), which books tours and activities; the liquor bond store, which sells discounted alcohol on production of your airline ticket; the **post office**; the Communications Centre, where you can make international **phone calls**; and two **banks**, Westpac and Commonwealth (the latter has the island's only ATM).

There's no public transport on Norfolk Island and it's rather hilly, so getting around by **car** is much the best option. Many accommodation places offer a car as part of the package or give you a big discount on **car rental**. It's very cheap anyway, with rates around $30 per day – Aloha Rent A Car (℡6723/22510, Ⓦwww.aloha.nlk.nf) is based opposite the airport. No one bothers with seat belts or even driving mirrors, and the maximum speed limit is only 50kph (40kph in town). There are also a limited number of **bikes** for rent, which can be arranged through the visitor centre or your accommodation.

Tours

Pinetree Tours (℡6723/22424, Ⓦwww.pinetreetours.com), on the main street next to the Commonwealth Bank, offer a slew of **tours**, including a half-day bus trip around the island ($34), a convict settlement tour ($34) and meals in islanders' homes ($68). Baunti Escapes (℡6723/23693, Ⓔbounty@ninet.nf) also runs a range of cultural and historic trips, while Culla & Co (book through Pinetree Tours, above) offers shire-horse-drawn carriage rides of the island on weekdays.

The island is surrounded by a coral reef and pristine waters, so at least one waterborne tour is a must; the volcanic sea floor is full of caves and swim-throughs and the whole area is a marine reserve – commercial fishing is banned. Bounty Divers (℡6723/24375, Ⓦwww.bountydivers.com) runs PADI courses (from $450), discovery dives ($120) and has **dive** charters (from $135 per dive, including gear), **snorkelling** and **diving** gear for rent, as well as scenic boat tours. Tropical Sea Kayaks (℡6723/23208, Ⓦwww.seakayaking.nf) runs an easy tour (1hr 30min; $25) and a beautiful, longer paddle taking in tall cliffs, tiny islands, sea stacks and arches before culminating in a swim in the tranquil lagoon (4hr; $45). For **fishing** trips, call Advance Fishing (℡6723/23363, Ⓦwww.nf/advancefishing).

Accommodation

With no camping and no hostel, the cheapest **accommodation** is in one of several comfortable 1970s-style motels which dot the island. In recent years a clutch of newer "romantic hideaway"-style places has sprung up, many of them self-contained. All places below include a small car in the rates unless specified.

Christian's of Bucks Point ℡6723/23833, Ⓦwww.christians.nf. Frilly, historic, 3-bedroom property on the southeast coast, where much of the timber used is from original convict buildings. Perfect for groups of up to six, with airport pick-up, a bottle of bubbly on arrival and you can pick what's in season from the orchard. $365 for two, then $65 each extra. ⑨

Forrester Court Clifftop Cottages ℡6723/22838, Ⓦwww.forrestercourt.com. Lovely boutique cottages with great views over Cascade Bay and a tennis court. A breakfast basket is included in the price. From $360. ⑨

Hillcrest Gardens Hotel Taylor's Rd ℡6723/22255, Ⓦwww.hillcrest.nf. Welcoming hotel with pool, restaurant and courtesy car service, but no free rental. Rooms (some with views over Kingston towards Phillip Island) range from motel style (including buffet breakfast) to

2-bedroom self-contained cottages. Rooms ④, cottages ⑦

Shearwater Scenic Villas ℡6723/22539, Ⓦwww.shearwater.nf. Self-contained accommodation in 1- and 2-bedroom villas in extensive grounds, with terrific water views over Bumbora Reserve. Rates from $260. ⑨

Tintoela of Norfolk ℡6723/22946, Ⓦwww.tintoela.nf. Luxury 1- and 2-bedroom cottages equipped with everything you need, plus a large wooden house, sleeping up to ten, with panoramic views of Cockpit Valley and Cascade Bay. From $315. ⑨

Whispering Pines Mount Pitt Rd ℡6723/22114, Ⓦwww.norfolk-pines-group.nf. Charming, hexagonal timber 2-bedroom, self-contained cottages hidden in thickly wooded gardens on the edge of the national park. ⑥

The island

The island's main settlement, **BURNT PINE**, is a fairly modern affair crammed with shops selling everything from cosmetics to stereos, all at almost duty-free prices; most shops are closed on Wednesday and Saturday afternoons and all day Sunday. The island's ecotourism attraction, **A Walk in the Wild** (daily 2–5pm; free), is based here at Taylor's Road, educating visitors about the fragile, disappearing rainforest and its bird life.

KINGSTON is the place to come for a taste of Norfolk Island history. This is the site of the second settlement penal colony and is now Norfolk's administrative centre, with the Legislative Assembly meeting in the military barracks, and the old colonial Government House now home to the island's Administrator. There's an excellent view from the **Queen Elizabeth Lookout** over the **Kingston and Arthur's Vale Historic Area** and the poignant seafront

cemetery, containing a number of graves from the brutal second settlement and detailed interpretative boards.

A string of lovely houses known as **Quality Row** bears some of the world's most impressive examples of Georgian **military architecture**; looking at the buildings now, it's difficult to imagine the suffering that took place behind their walls. Enter **No. 10 Quality Row** (daily 11am–3pm; $10) to see the interior, including examples of Norfolk pine furniture made by convicts. Further west, the basement of the 1835 former **Commissariat Store** (Mon–Sat 11am–3pm; $10) contains an archeological museum and an extensive collection of colonial-era china. Over by the wharf, the **Pier Store** (Mon–Sat 11am–3pm; $10) contains various artefacts recovered from the 1790 wreck of the *Sirius*, including its huge anchor, but more compelling is the *Bounty*-related paraphernalia brought here by Pitcairners, including the ship's cannon and even the kettle that was used on Pitcairn Island for everything from fermenting liquor to boiling sea water for salt.

The Kingston area is also the site of the island's main swimming **beaches**, protected by a small reef. Immediately in front of the walls of the ruined barracks is **Slaughter Bay**, which has a sandy beach dotted with interestingly gnarled and eroded basalt rock formations; the small hard-coral reef is excellent for **snorkelling**. At low tide you can take a **glass-bottomed boat cruise** ($30) from nearby Emily Bay, which is also a beautiful, safe swimming area backed by a large pine forest.

In **Bumbora Reserve**, just west of Kingston, reached by car via Bumbora Road, you can see the natural regrowth of Norfolk pines; from the reserve you can walk down to Bumbora Beach, a shady little strip of sand where you'll find some safe pools for children to swim in at low tide. There's another track down to **Crystal Pool**, which has more swimming and snorkelling.

The west coast

West of Burnt Pine, along Douglas Drive, you'll find the exquisite **St Barnabas Chapel**, once the property of the Melanesian Mission (Anglican), which relocated gradually here from New Zealand between 1866 and 1921. The chapel's rose window was designed by William Morris and some of the others by Sir Edward Burne-Jones; the altar was carved by Solomon Islanders – ancestral masters of the craft.

Further north along the **west coast** there's a scenic picnic area with tables and barbecues high over **Anson Bay**, from where it's a satisfying walk down to the beach. Immediately north of here, the **national park** has 8km of walking trails, many of them old logging tracks. Many walks start from **Mount Pitt** (316m), a pleasing drive up a fairly narrow and winding sealed road surrounded by palms and trees – worth it for the panoramic views. The most enjoyable walk from here is the three-kilometre route to the **Captain Cook Memorial** (1hr 45min), which starts as a beautiful grassy path but soon becomes a downward-sloping dirt track with some steps. Just south of the national park, on Pitt Road, the tranquil rainforest of the **Botanic Gardens** (unrestricted access) is worth a stroll. Here you can observe the forty endemic plant species, including the pretty native hibiscus, the native palm, and the island's best-known symbol, the **Norfolk pine**, which can grow as high as 57m with a circumference of up to 11m.

No. 10 Quality Row, the Commissariat Store and the Pier Store are all part of the **Norfolk Island Museum**) ⓦ www.museums.gov.nf), which offers a joint ticket for $25 allowing multiple access over several days.

Eating, drinking and entertainment

Norfolk Island **food** is plain and fresh, with an emphasis on locally caught fish and home-grown seasonal produce. Tahitian influence remains in the tradition of big fish-fries, and in some novel ways of preparing bananas. As most accommodation is self-catering, you'll need to head to the Foodland Supermarket in Burnt Pine (daily to 6pm). On Sunday afternoon fresh fish is sold at the Kingston pier.

The **clubs** on the island are good places to eat, drink and mingle with the locals.

The Brewery opposite the airport. The island's only pub, with pool tables, serving local ales such as "Bee Sting" and "Bligh's Revenge". A rough, late-night crowd that can be a bit intimidating for single women.

Dino's Bumboras Rd ☎6723/24225. A quality licensed Italian place with dining inside and on the veranda of a late 1800s house. Closed Mon & Tues.

Golden Orb Café Taylor's Rd, Burnt Pine ☎6723/24295. Peaceful subtropical sanctuary just off the main street with wholesome café meals and snacks, good coffee and juices served inside on the deck, plus a decent range of books, many of local interest.

Golf Club Kingston. This wonderfully scenic 9-holer (with 18 tees) has a popular bar that also serves meals.

Homestead Restaurant New Farm Rd ☎6723/22068. Great lunch spot when you're exploring the west coast. Dine on the veranda shaded by a huge Morton Bay fig, tucking into king prawn salad ($19), savoury crepes or chicken, lime and coconut curry (mostly around $20).

The Olive off Taylor's Rd, Burnt Pine ☎6723/24406. New daytime café with great coffee, fresh salads and a funky vibe.

Sports & Workers Club Taylor's Rd, Burnt Pine. A great opportunity to eat, drink and mingle with the locals.

Travel details

Most public transport in New South Wales originates in Sydney, and the main services are outlined in the "Travel details" section on p.221; check individual town accounts in this chapter to see which operator you need to contact.

Trains

Local train services around Sydney and its suburbs are run by CityRail (☎13 15 00, ⓦwww.cityrail.info), which extends out as far north as Newcastle, west to the Blue Mountains and Lithgow, and south to Wollongong and Kiama. Trains to the rest of the region are operated by CountryLink (☎13 22 32, ⓦwww.countrylink.info), which also operates a bus network to small places.

Canberra–Sydney (2 daily; 4hr 20min).
Sydney to: Bowral (2–3 daily; 1hr 50min); Bundanoon (2 daily; 2hr); Canberra (2 daily; 4hr 20min); Gosford (every 30min; 1hr 30min); Goulburn (4 daily; 2hr 40min); Hawkesbury River (every 30min; 1hr); Kiama (1 daily; 1hr); Mittagong (2 daily; 1hr 40min); Waterfall (every 20–40min; 1hr); Wollongong (hourly; 1hr 30min).

Buses

The most extensive bus networks along the coast of New South Wales are CountryLink (☎13 22 32, ⓦwww.countrylink.info), who run many services integrated with their train network; and Greyhound (☎1300 473 946, ⓦwww.greyhound.com.au). Both operate frequent services along the east coast from Melbourne via Sydney to Brisbane, stopping at many places en route. Other major players are Premier Motor Service (☎13 34 10, ⓦwww.premierms.com.au) and Transborder (☎02/6241 0033, ⓦwww.transborderexpress.com.au), supplemented by several regional companies with limited range.

Batemans Bay to: Bowral (1–2 daily; 3hr 30min); Canberra (2–3 daily; 2hr 30min); Eden (2 daily; 3hr); Melbourne (1 daily; 11hr); Merimbula (2 daily; 2hr 45min); Narooma (3–4 daily; 1–2hr); Nowra (3–4 daily; 1hr–1hr 30min); Sydney (2 daily; 4hr); Ulladulla (4–5 daily; 1hr); Wollongong (2 daily; 2hr).

Bowral to: Batemans Bay (1–2 daily; 3hr 30min); Wollongong (1 daily; 1hr 30min).

Byron Bay to: Ballina (13–22 daily; 40min); Brisbane (9 daily; 2hr 30min); Buladelah (6 daily; 9hr 20min); Brunswick Heads (10–13 daily; 15min); Coffs Harbour (8 daily; 4hr); Forster (1 daily; 8hr 45min); Grafton (8 daily; 3hr); Karuah (7 daily; 9hr 45min); Lennox Head (8–12 daily; 25min); Lismore (6–10 daily; 2hr 5min); Maclean (5 daily; 2hr 15min); Murwillumbah (5 daily; 55min); Nambucca Heads (6 daily; 3hr 30min); Port Macquarie (5 daily; 8hr); Surfers Paradise (9 daily; 1hr 20min); Sydney (4 daily; 14hr 15min); Tweed Heads (4–5 daily; 1hr 20min); Urunga (6 daily; 3hr 20min).

Canberra to: Batemans Bay (2–3 daily; 2hr 30min); Cooma (1–4 daily; 1hr 20min); Eden (1 daily; 4hr 30min); Goulburn (1 daily; 1hr 10min); Moss Vale (1 daily; 2hr); Narooma (1–2 daily; 4hr 30min); Sydney (9–11 daily; 3hr 30min); Thredbo (winter 2 daily; 3hr); Wollongong (1 daily; 3hr 20min).

Coffs Harbour to: Bellingen (Mon–Fri 4–5 daily, Sun 1 daily; 1hr); Byron Bay (8 daily; 3hr 50min); Dorrigo (Tues, Thurs & Sun 1 daily; 1hr 10min); Grafton (8–12 daily; 1hr 10min); Nambucca Heads (6–11 daily; 1hr); Port Macquarie (6–7 daily; 2hr 40min); Urunga (6–11 daily; 40min).

Merimbula to: Batemans Bay (2 daily; 2hr 45min); Melbourne (2 daily; 9hr).

Port Macquarie to: Ballina (5 daily; 6hr); Bellingen (Tues, Thurs & Sun; 3hr 15min); Byron Bay (6 daily; 7hr); Coffs Harbour (6 daily; 2hr 40min); Dorrigo (Tues, Thurs & Sun; 3hr 50min); Grafton (5 daily; 4hr 10min); Nambucca Heads; Wauchope (2–6 daily; 1hr).

Sydney to: Batemans Bay (2 daily; 4hr); Canberra (9–11 daily; 3hr 30min); Goulburn (1 daily; 3hr 30min); Gosford (1 daily; 1hr 30min); Kiama (0–1 daily; 2hr); Mittagong (1 daily; 2hr 30min); Wollongong (2–3 daily; 2hr).

Wollongong to: Batemans Bay (2 daily; 2hr); Bowral (1 daily; 1hr 30min); Canberra (1 daily; 3hr 20min); Sydney (2–3 daily; 2hr).

Flights

The main airlines operating in New South Wales are Qantas (☎ 13 13 13, ⊛ www.qantas.com.au), its budget subsidiary Jetstar (☎ 13 15 38, ⊛ www.jetstar.com), Virgin Blue (☎ 13 67 89, ⊛ www.virginblue.com.au), Regional Express (☎ 13 17 13, ⊛ www.regionalexpress.com.au) and Brindabella (☎ 1300 668 824, ⊛ www.brindabellaairlines.com.au).

Ballina to: Melbourne (2–6 weekly; 2hr 5min); Sydney (5 daily; 1hr 50min).

Canberra to: Adelaide (1–4 daily; 1hr 45min); Albury (Mon–Fri 2 daily; 45min); Brisbane (9–11 daily; 1h 40min); Melbourne (10–15 daily; 1hr); Newcastle (1–3 daily; 1hr 10min); Sydney (20–30 daily; 50min).

Coffs Harbour to: Brisbane (1–2 daily; 1hr); Port Macquarie (1–2 daily; 1hr 30min); Sydney (6–7 daily; 1hr 25min).

Lismore to: Sydney (3–4 daily; 1hr 50min).

Lord Howe Island to: Brisbane (Sat & Sun 1 daily; 1hr 35min); Port Macquarie (summer only; 1 weekly; 1hr 30min); Sydney (1–3 daily; 2hr).

Merimbula to: Sydney (2–3 daily; 1hr 10min).

Norfolk Island to: Brisbane (3 weekly; 2hr 25min); Newcastle (1 per week; 2hr 30min); Sydney (4 weekly; 2hr 30min).

Port Macquarie to: Coffs Harbour (1–2 daily; 30min); Lord Howe Island (summer only; 1 weekly; 1hr 30min); Sydney (3–8 daily; 1hr).

3

Inland New South Wales

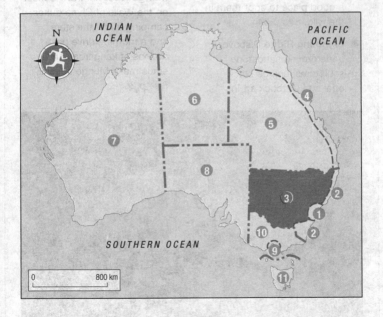

CHAPTER 3 # Highlights

* **Tamworth** Boot-scoot with country music fans from all over the world during Tamworth's famous annual festival. See p.334

* **Coonabarabran** Gaze at a multitude of stars in Australia's "astronomy capital". See p.342

* **Gunnedah** Home to one of the healthiest koala populations in the state, and a good place to spot them in the wild. See p.344

* **Lightning Ridge** Discover underground sandstone sculptures, unique black opal and Outback art in this off-beat mining outpost. See p.346

* **Broken Hill** Take a mine tour, visit the Royal Flying Doctor Service or browse the art galleries of this gracious Outback town. See p.352

* **Mutawintji National Park** Aboriginal rock art is the main draw of the remote Mutawintji National Park. See p.361

* **Mungo National Park** Sunset on the Walls of China dunes, camping under the stars and a morning drive past dozens of kangaroos and emus make Mungo special. See p.363

▲ Sculptures near Broken Hill

Inland New South Wales

nland New South Wales is a very different proposition from the populous coast, and although it's not a stand-alone holiday destination and it might strike you as boring at times, travelling here gives you a real insight into the Australian way of life. The region stretches inland for around a thousand kilometres, covering a strikingly wide range of landscapes, from the rugged slopes of the **Great Dividing Range** to the red-earth desert of the Outback, dotted with relatively small agricultural and mining communities. The Great Dividing Range itself runs parallel to the coast, splitting the state in two.

West of the range, towns such as **Bathurst** and **Dubbo** date back to the early days of Australian exploration, when the discovery of a passage through the Blue Mountains opened up the rolling plains of the west. Free (non-convict) settlers appropriated vast areas of rich pastureland here and made immense fortunes off the back of sheep farming, establishing the agricultural prosperity that continues to this day. When gold was discovered near Bathurst in 1851, and the first **goldrush** began, New South Wales' fortunes were assured. Although penal transportations ceased the following year, the population continued to increase rapidly and the economy boomed as fortune-seekers arrived in droves. At much

Getting around inland New South Wales

Inland New South Wales still has a fairly extensive **rail** network, although the operator, Countrylink (☏13 22 32, ⓦwww.countrylink.info), has replaced many train services with buses. The train journey from Sydney to Broken Hill ($120 each way; 13hr) is a great way to see the vast desert in air-conditioned comfort – if you're lucky the train will pass through one of the huge sandstorms that ravage the region from time to time. A one-month Backtracker pass ($275) with Countrylink will get you just about anywhere in the state. Greyhound **buses** (ⓦwww.greyhound.com.au) run through Scone, Tamworth, Armidale and Glen Innes en route between Sydney and Brisbane via the New England Highway, and Kean's Travel services Armidale, Uralla, Walcha and Tamworth once a week in each direction on its way between Port Macquarie and Scone. For details of the **National Parks and Wildlife Service (NPWS)** in New South Wales, including park entry fees, see p.225.

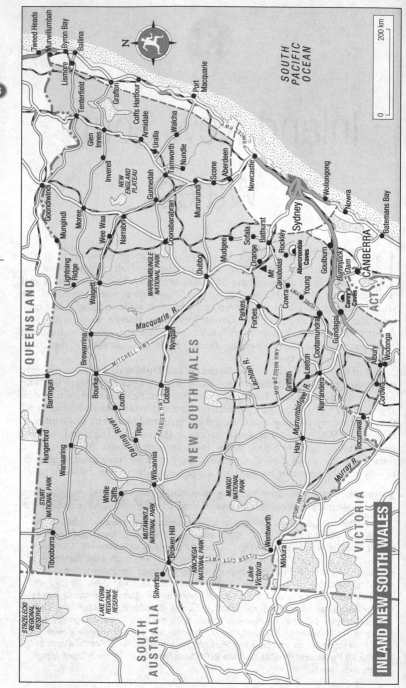

INLAND NEW SOUTH WALES

the same time, Victoria broke off to form a separate colony, followed by Queensland in 1859.

Agriculture also dominates the southern section of the state, where the fertile **Riverina** occupies the area between the Murrumbidgee, Darling and Murray rivers (the last dividing New South Wales from Victoria). In the north, falling away from the Great Dividing Range, the gentle sheep- and cattle-farming tablelands of the **New England Plateau** extend from the northern end of the Hunter Valley to the border with Queensland.

Moving west away from the coast the land becomes increasingly desolate and arid as you head into the state's harsh **Outback** regions, where the mercury can climb well above the 40°C mark in summer and even places which look large on the map turn out to be tiny, isolated communities. The small town of **Bourke** is traditionally regarded as the beginning of the real Outback ("Back O'Bourke" is Australian slang for a remote place in the Outback); other destinations in the area include the opal-mining town of **Lightning Ridge** and, in the far west of the state almost at the South Australian border, the mining settlement of **Broken Hill**, a surprisingly gracious city surrounded by the desert landscape of *Mad Max*.

Out beyond the Blue Mountains, the **Great Western Highway** takes you as far as Bathurst; from there the **Mid-Western Highway** goes on to join the **Sturt Highway**, which heads, via Mildura on the Victorian border, to Adelaide. Any route west is eventually obliged to cross the **Newell Highway**, the direct route between Melbourne and Brisbane that cuts straight across the heart of central New South Wales.

The central west

The **central west** of New South Wales is rich farmland, and the undulating green hills provide both seasonal work and easy hiking tracks. Although **Dubbo** is the region's major hub, and home to a famous zoo, **Bathurst** is the most sophisticated town, attracting the Sydney crowds on weekends with fine architecture and numerous museums. **Cowra**'s fame derives from the breakout of Japanese prisoners here during World War II, while **Young** was the site of the Lambing Flat Riots against Chinese miners in 1861, both significant events in Australian history. Both towns lack major draws though, and could easily be overlooked. **Parkes'** only attraction is its nearby observatory. While not tremendously cosmopolitan, the central west is picking up its culinary act and **Orange** has developed a bit of a café society. Alternatively, you could lunch at one of the wineries around **Mudgee** and **Young**, which are gaining popularity and make a pleasant break from the road.

Bathurst and around

The pleasant city of **BATHURST**, elegantly situated on the western slopes of the Great Dividing Range 210km west of Sydney, is Australia's oldest inland settlement. Its beautifully preserved nineteenth-century architecture, antique shops, lively arts scene and good cafés make it a pleasant overnight stop. The settlement was founded by Governor Macquarie in 1815, but Bathurst remained nothing more than a small convict and military settlement for years, only slowly developing into the main supply centre for the rich surrounding pastoral area. It was the discovery of **gold** nearby at Lewis Ponds Creek at Ophir in 1851 (see p.315), and on the Turon River later the same year, which changed the life of the town and the colony forever. Soon rich fields of alluvial gold were discovered in every direction and, being the first town over the mountains for those on the way to the goldfields, Bathurst prospered and grew. The population increased dramatically: in 1885 Bathurst was proclaimed a city, and by the late 1890s it was even proposing itself as the site for the capital of the new Commonwealth of Australia.

Although there's still the odd speck of gold and a few gemstones (especially sapphires) to be found in the surrounding area, modern Bathurst has reverted to its role as capital of one of the richest fruit- and grain-growing districts in Australia. The presence of the **Charles Sturt University**, one of Australia's leading institutes, gives the city an academic feel and adds to its liveliness. Over the second weekend in October, rev-heads turn up for the big annual motor-racing meetings – centred on the famous **Bathurst 1000** endurance race – at the Mount Panorama Racing Circuit. If V8 supercars do it for you, this is the place to be.

Arrival, information and accommodation

Daily Countrylink **trains** and long-distance **buses** run to Bathurst from Sydney, with onward services to Broken Hill. The **tourist office**, 1 Kendall Ave (daily 9am–5pm; ☏02/6332 1444 or 1800 681 000, ⓦ www.visitbathurst.com .au), is on the eastern edge of town on the Sydney road.

Accommodation is abundant in Bathurst, with a dozen motels along the highway. Rates are relatively high, and if you visit during the two weeks leading up to race day prices rise by at least fifty percent and everywhere gets booked solid.

Accommodation

Accommodation in an Historic Warehouse 121A Keppel St ☏02/6332 2801, ⓦ www .accomwarehouse.com.au. Self-contained, bright modern rooms in a converted warehouse make this a little different to most places. Continental breakfast provided. ⑤

Bathurst Heritage Apartments 108 William St ☏02/6332 4920, ⓦ www.bathurstheritage.com.au. A selection of fully self-contained apartments around town, best at the *Royal Hotel*, the town's jewel-in-the-crown heritage building where two antique-filled serviced apartments take up the top floor (one with one bedroom, one with three), complete with access to the wide veranda with views over the King's Parade Park. Also excellent modern apartments just behind. ⑥

Big 4 Bathurst Panorama Holiday Park Sydney Rd, Kelso, 5km east of town ☏1800/669 911,

ⓦ www.bathurstholidaypark.com.au. A spacious, well-kept park, with a large swimming pool with waterslides and nightly movies on a big screen. Camping $25, powered site $29, cabins ③, cottages ⑥

Commercial Hotel 135 George St ☏02/6331 2712, ⓦ http://commercialhotel.6te.net. Functional place with the cheapest rooms in town. Dorms $25, doubles ②

Dinta Glen B&B 3 Strathmore Drive, Forest Grove ☏02/6332 6662, ⓦ www.ix.net.au/~dinta. Tranquil and rustic B&B in the bush around 12km northeast of the centre. Very relaxing. ④

The Russells 286 William St ☏02/6332 4686, ⓦ www.therussells.com.au. Small family home offering four-star B&B rooms with log fires and generous cooked breakfasts. ⑤

The City

Because of its cool climate – proximity to the mountains means it can be cold at night – and a smattering of grand nineteenth-century buildings, the city has a very different feel to anywhere on the baking plains further west. Large city blocks form a gridplan around a striking brick **carillon** in King's Parade Park. Russell Street, on its western side, is home to the 1880 **Courthouse**, which contains a little **museum** tucked away in the east wing (Tues, Wed & Sat 10am–4pm, Sun 11am–2pm; $3), displaying relics and archives of regional pioneer history along with some interesting Aboriginal artefacts. Behind the Courthouse, **Machattie Park** is a great place to relax in the landscaped Victorian-era gardens with duck ponds and spreading shady trees.

On the western side of Machattie Park, Keppel Street runs south to the train station past the **Regional Art Gallery**, at nos. 70–78 (Tues–Sat 10am–5pm, Sun 11am–2pm; free; Ⓦ www.bathurstart.com.au), which houses a fine provincial art collection strong on ceramics and paintings by Lloyd Rees (though not often on display), as well as regular special and travelling exhibitions. Also in the centre, a block east of the carillon, is the **Australian Fossil and Mineral Museum** at 224 Howick St (Mon–Sat 10am–4pm, Sun 10am–2pm; $8), which does a great job of displaying a fairly small but broad-ranging collection including Australia's only complete *tyrannosaurus rex* skeleton – a fearsome sight. There's a world class array of trilobites along with superb amber (including one piece with an entire preserved gecko) and some absolutely beautiful minerals, all well lit.

About six blocks southwest of the centre the well-preserved **Chifley Home**, 10 Busby St (Sat, Sun & Mon 10am–2pm; $6.50; Ⓦ www.chifleyhome.org.au), was once the residence of Ben Chifley, Bathurst's most famous son, who was born to a blacksmith here in 1885 and served as prime minister of Australia between 1945 and 1949.

Driving 3km west from the centre along William Street leads you to **Mount Panorama** and its famous six-kilometre-long racing circuit, providing panoramic views of the city. The circuit is accessible by car, making every boy's dream of racing on an official circuit come true (albeit at 60kph). The **National Motor Racing Museum** (daily 9am–4.30pm; $8; Ⓦ www .nmrm.com.au), at Murray's Corner at the beginning of the circuit, features a few dozen famous racing cars and bikes, plus photographs and memorabilia from races since the 1960s. One wing is devoted to Australian supercar legend Peter Brock, who won "The Great Race" nine times before his untimely death in 2006.

The **Bathurst Sheep and Cattle Drome** on Limekilns Road, 8km northeast of the city, has an entertaining and educational show (call ☏ 02/6337 3634 for times; $14, children $8.80; Ⓦ www.bathurstsheepandcattledrome.com.au) covering everything you always wanted to know about sheepshearing and milking cows.

Eating and drinking

There's a variety of **restaurants** in the city centre, offering Thai, Indian and modern Australian cuisine. Most of the town's **pubs** also serve counter meals or have bistros at the back. Due to the presence of so many students, Bathurst has a reasonable **nightlife**, centred mainly on pubs close to the university.

Church Bar 1 Ribbon Gang Lane ☏ 02/6334 2300, Ⓦ www.churchbar.com.au. Drinks and tasty wood-fired pizzas (both traditional and fancy gourmet) in the impressive surrounds of the neo-Gothic Old School House; you can eat inside, or out in the leafy courtyard. Closed Sun evening.

Cobblestone Lane 173 George St at Keppel St ☏ 02/6331 2202. Bathurst's best restaurant. A casual affair located in the historic Webb building, and serving modern Australian cuisine with Mediterranean influences. Mains around $35. Closed Sun & Mon.

Legall 56 Keppel St ☎02/6331 5800. Great French-run, sit-in and takeaway patisserie doing wonderful bread and croissants, delicious lemon tarts, plus quiches, soups and espresso. Closed Sun & Mon.

Maalouf's 159 George St at Russell St ☎02/6331 1477. Basic eat-in and takeaway Lebanese place serving authentic versions of Middle Eastern favourites – fattouch salad ($9), chawarma plate ($22) and a mixed vegetarian plate ($21). BYO. Closed Sun.

Oxford Corner of William and Piper sts ⓦwww.theoxfordbathurst.com.au. Particularly popular amongst students, with a regular club night on Friday, a huge alfresco bar and good-value meals from its Piper Bistro.

Tully's 72 William St. Good daytime café with breakfast to 11am, build-your-own sandwiches, wraps and wel-prepared lunches such as salt-and-pepper squid and chips ($14). Closed Sun.

Around Bathurst: Abercrombie Caves

An enjoyable excursion from Bathurst takes in the former gold-mining towns of **Rockley**, 35km to the south, and **Trunkey Creek**, before continuing to the spectacular **Abercrombie Caves**, 72km south of town in the middle of a large nature reserve. The principal and most impressive cavern, the **Grand Arch** (daily 9am–4pm, longer in school holidays; $13; ☎02/6368 8603, ⓦwww.jenolancaves.org.au), is 221m long, about 39m wide at the north and south entrances, and in some places over 30m high – it's said to be the largest natural limestone arch in the southern hemisphere. More than eighty other caves are dotted around the reserve; more than a century ago, miners constructed a dancefloor in one of them, and concerts and church services are still held here occasionally.

Also within the reserve are old gold mines, and swimming holes in **Grove Creek**, which runs through the reserve, plunging 70m over the **Grove Creek Falls** at the southern edge. There's unpowered **camping** at Abercrombie Caves ($10 per person) and a selection of cabins and cottages (from $50 for 4).

North of Bathurst: Sofala, Hill End and the Mudgee wine country

The area north of Bathurst, heading towards the **Mudgee wine country**, is dotted with semi-derelict villages and ghost towns dating back to the goldrushes of the nineteenth century. A scenic drive 45km north from Bathurst leads to the picturesque hamlet of **SOFALA**, on the Turon River. Gold was found in the river here in 1851, just three weeks after the first gold strikes in Australia, and today the narrow, winding main street still follows the course of the water. You can **stay** at the *Old Gaol* on Barkly Street (☎02/6337 7064, ⓦwww.oldsofalagaol.com.au; rooms ❸, self-contained cottage ❹), a rustic B&B in the former police station with a warm welcome and comfy beds. A good spot for a drink is the *Sofala Royal Hotel* on Denison Street, a very atmospheric, classic wooden pub with a big balcony; it also offers meals with a seasonal flavour.

Hill End

From Sofala, a partly unsealed road follows the Turon River west 38km to **HILL END**, an even more important goldrush town located on a plateau above the Turon Valley. In 1870, Hill End was the largest inland centre in New South Wales, a booming gold-mining town with a population of about twenty thousand, with 53 hotels and all the accoutrements of a wealthy settlement. Within ten years, however, gold production had faltered and Hill End became a virtual ghost town. It stayed that way until 1967, when the area was proclaimed a historic site and huge efforts were made to restore and preserve the town. Now it is a strange place with under a hundred residents living in the remaining buildings, all widely scattered across the grassy reserve. Church, courthouse, chapel, hotel, post office, general store and half a dozen other brick buildings lend grace to the broken streetscapes. You can pick up a leaflet at the **NPWS visitor centre** in the old hospital (daily 9.30am–12.30pm & 1.30–4.30pm; ℡02/6337 8206), where there's also a small **museum** ($2.20), and take a self-guided walk around the village. Ask, too, about trying your hand at gold panning and taking a mine tour into the old underground workings (generally daily 1.30pm; $37.50, bookings on ℡02/6337 8224 or through the general store).

You can **stay** in basic shared-bath rooms at the last of Hill End's pubs, the *Royal Hotel* (℡02/6337 8261, ✉hotel@hillendnsw.co.au; ❸) or the *Hill End Lodge*, 1km toward Sofala (℡02/637 8200, ⓦwww.hillendlodge.com.au; ❺), with comfortable but slightly soulless motel-style rooms. There's also the four-star *Cooke's Cottage B&B* (℡02/6332 5832, ⓦwww.stayz.com.au/8505; ❻), and camping at the grassy NPWS *Village Camping* (camping $7 per person, powered site $10 per person), right in the centre.

There are reasonable **restaurants** at both the pub and *Hill End Lodge*, and excellent Devonshire teas at *Rose Cottage*, on Germantown Lane in the centre of town. Continuing north it is 75km to Mudgee, about 10km of which is unsealed.

Mudgee

About 120km north of Bathurst on good roads, the large, old country town of **MUDGEE** (meaning "the nest in the hills" in the Wiradjuri language) is the

Mudgee wineries: five of the best

The majority of the 40-odd cellar doors are immediately north of Mudgee and offer free **tastings**. Consider cycling around the vineyards with a bike rented from Countryfit, 32 Short St ($25 for 4hr; ℡02/6372 3955, ⓦwww.countryfitbicyclehire .com.au), which also offers guided half-day bike tours ($90) including a café lunch.

Botobolar Botobolar Lane, 16km northeast of town ℡02/6373 3840, ⓦwww .botobolar.com. Australia's first organic winery is known for its Marsanne, with tastings on a shady terrace. There's also a picnic area and BBQs. Mon–Sat 10am–5pm, Sun 10am–3pm.

Huntington Estate Wines Cassilis Rd, 6km northeast of town ℡02/6373 3825, ⓦwww.huntingtonestate.com.au. Delicious wines, notably the young Semillons and the intense, heady Cabernet Sauvignon. An excellent annual chamber-music festival takes place here in November. Daily 10am–4pm.

Miramar Wines Henry Lawson Drive, 3km north of town ℡02/6373 3874, ⓦwww .miramarwines.com.au. Established by respected wine-maker Ian MacRae in 1977, this winery specializes in delicious whites, with atmospheric tastings among old cobwebbed casks. Daily 9am–5pm.

Pieter Van Gent 141 Black Springs Rd, 6km northwest of town ℡02/6373 3030, ⓦwww.pvgwinery.com.au. Tastings in a delightful setting: beautiful nineteenth-century choir stalls on cool earth floors, overshadowed by huge old barrels salvaged from Penfolds Winery. Try the Pipeclay Port, a tawny specimen aged in wood. The wine-maker is Dutch, and the herbs he uses in his traditional vermouth are specially imported from the Netherlands. Mon–Sat 9am–5pm, Sun 10.30am–4pm.

Logan Castlereagh Hwy, 16km southeast of town ℡02/6373 1333, ⓦwww.loganwines .com.au. Modern winery with free tasting plus coffee and cake in a striking concrete and glass room overlooking the vines. Great wines too. Daily 10am–5pm.

centre of an increasingly important wine region that's the original home of Aussie Chardonnay. The town is set along the lush banks of the Cudgegong River, and the countryside appears to have more grazing cows and sheep than vineyards. Once known for Mudgee Mud, a particularly dire local beer, it is now famous for its wines and is popular with the Sydney crowd, not least because of the many art galleries and local produce shops that dot the town.

Arrival, information and accommodation

Countrylink **trains** run from Sydney to Lithgow, just east of Bathurst, where you connect with a bus on to Mudgee. The useful **visitor centre**, 84 Market St (daily 9am–5pm; ☎02/6372 1020, ⓦwww.visitmudgeeregion.com.au), has detailed winery information and maps. Mudgee's popularity and proximity to Sydney means that **accommodation** is booked out at weekends, when it's best to call in advance.

Accommodation

Bleak House 7 Lawson St ☎02/6372 4888, ⓦwww.bleakhouse.com.au. Delightful B&B in as 1860s heritage house with pool. All four en-suite rooms have broad, lace-ironwork verandas perfect for a sundowner, and two have deep, clawfoot baths. ❼

Central Motel 120 Church St ☎1800 457 222, ⓔcentral@hwy.com.au. Basic but well-equipped motel with small rooms and a great barbecue-equipped deck overlooking the street. ❸

Mudgee Riverside Caravan & Tourist Park 22 Short St ☎02/6372 2531, ⓦwww.mudgeeriverside.com.au. Shady caravan park with a children's playground and barbecue area. Camping $20, powered site $23, cabins ❸

The Tannery 48 Lawson St ☎02/6373 3701, ⓦwww.wildwoodmudgee.com.au. Chic and stylish renovation of a central 1850s cottage into a two-bedroom self-catering suite with all the luxuries you need and a small garden. ❽

Wanderlight Motor Inn 107 Market St ☎1800 813 468, ⓦwww.wanderlight.bestwestern .com.au. Welcoming and central three-star motel with a good restaurant a pool and spa. ❺

Eating and drinking

In town, *Butcher Shop Café*, 49 Church St, is the place to go for great coffee, all-day **breakfasts** and tasty lunches (around $15). The *Lawson Park Hotel*, a fine old country pub at 1 Church St, is also good value, or consider heading out to the **wineries**. *Wild Oats Café* at Oatley Wines, Craigmore Road, 3km north (☎02/6372 2208), is ideal for a relaxed lunch, but for something more formal head to the *Blue Wren Winery*, 433 Cassilis Rd, 3km northeast (☎02/6372 6205, ⓦwww.bluewrenwines.com.au), which uses mainly local produce and has lovely outdoor dining.

Orange and around

ORANGE, 55km west of Bathurst on the Mitchell Highway en route to Dubbo, is a pretty town of around 40,000 set amid rolling countryside. There's not an orange tree to be seen – the Surveyor General apparently named it after William, Prince of Orange under whom he fought Napoleon – but the hills hereabouts are draped in **fruit**, principally apples, cherries and grapes. You can find apple-picking **work** here from late February through into April, while cherry picking takes place from late November to early January – contact employment agency Ready Workforce (☎02/6360 3044, ⓦwww .readyworkforce.com.au). Many growers have rough accommodation on their properties but demand often outstrips supply, so bring a tent. If you want to

sample the local produce rather than pick it, turn up for **Food Week** (Ⓦwww
.orangefoodweek.com.au) in April or Wine Week (Ⓦwww.winesoforange
.com.au) in October.

Just out of town, take the drive 15km southwest to the 1395-metre summit
of **Mount Canobolas**, with great views all around.

Practicalities

Countrylink has daily **train** services from Sydney and Dubbo and you can **fly**
here with Regional Express (Ⓣ13 17 13, Ⓦwww.rex.com.au). The **visitor
centre**, on Byng Street in Civic Square (daily 9am–5pm; Ⓣ1800 069 466,
Ⓦwww.visitorange.com.au), has information on local attractions including
fossicking for gold in the **Ophir Reserve**. Just behind the tourist office the
library has **internet** access.

There's a pretty good range of **accommodation** in and around Orange
(though no hostel). The cheapest place is *Colour City Caravan Park*, 203 Margaret
St, 1.5km north (Ⓣ02/6362 7254, Ⓔkpratt@orange.nsw.gov.au; camping $14,
powered site $17, cabins ❸, cottages ❻), the best of the local caravan parks with a
good range of cabins and cottages sleeping six. *Oriana Motor Inn*, Woodward St,
1km west of the centre (Ⓣ02/6362 3066, Ⓦwww.orianamotorinn.com.au; ❹),
offers clean and comfortable motel-style accommodation with air conditioning
and fridge in rooms and pool and restaurant on site, while ⚔ *Cotehele*, 177 Anson
St, two blocks south of the centre (Ⓣ02/6361 2520, Ⓦwww.cotehele.com.au; ❻),
occupies an 1878 magistrate's home with high ceilings. The five en-suite rooms
are all distinctly decorated and breakfast can be served in the shady yard. For equally
luxurious B&B with views, head 5km southwest of town to *Arancia*, 69 Wrights
Lane (Ⓣ02/6365 3305, Ⓦwww.arancia.com.au; ❼), where rooms are stylish and
well appointed, each with its own entrance.

Orange's **eating** scene is fairly cosmopolitan with gourmet sandwiches at
modest prices available from *Scottys on Summer*, 202 Summer St. Nearby, *DNA
Coffee*, 190 Anson St, offers internet access and wi-fi (both $5 per hr) in a
Starbucksy café. For evening dining, head straight for ⚔ *Union Bank*, 84 Byng St
(closed Sun evening), a classy but not too expensive wine cellar and bar which
serves great meze platters ($10), wine-matched bistro meals ($17–27) and a select
cheeseboard ($18) in its compact courtyard. Fine dining is the name of the game
at *Selkirks*, 179 Anson St (Ⓣ02/6361 1179; Tues–Sat dinner plus Fri lunch),
where a Federation-era house provides the setting for lunch (when it is a
bargain) or dinner (2 courses $55, 3 $68) when it is still good value. Contemporary Australian dishes come matched with local wines. Heading 15km southwest
of town to the lower slopes of Mount Canobolas you'll find *The Mountain
Teahouse*, 42 Mount Canobolas Rd (Ⓣ02/6365 3227), a very pleasant spot for
brunch, lunch and Devonshire teas with a shady veranda, and a fire in winter.

Forbes and Parkes

West of Orange are the important regional towns of Forbes and Parkes.
FORBES, on the Lachlan River 110km west of Orange, is a graceful old place
famous as the stomping ground of the nineteenth-century bushranger Ben
Hall, who is buried in the town's cemetery. It is serviced from Sydney by
Countrylink, with a changeover at Lithgow, while Greyhound has direct
services from Melbourne and Brisbane. Several motels offer **accommodation**
or there's the *Big 4 Forbes Lachlan View HolidayPark*, 141 Flint St (Ⓣ1800 641
207, Ⓦwww.big4forbeslachlanview.com.au; camping $19, powered site $25,
en-suite cabin ❸, villa ❺).

Countrylink and Greyhound buses link Forbes with the small town of **PARKES**, 30km northeast, which puts on an **Elvis Festival** (Ⓦwww.parkeselvisfestival.com .au) each January. For the rest of the year the only point of interest is the **Parkes Observatory**, a further 25km north along the Newell Highway. It is famous for its 64-metre radio telescope which was used for tracking the Apollo 11 mission to the moon, as well as featuring in the 2000 film *The Dish*. The observatory's visitor centre (daily 8.30am–4.15pm; free; Ⓣ02/6861 1777, Ⓦwww.parkes.atnf.csiro.au) has displays on space and the observatory's work, and continuously screens the 22-minute **Invisible Universe** ($6.50) and a changing roster of short 3D films ($6.50). The *Dish Café* provides refreshment.

Dubbo

DUBBO, named after an Aboriginal word meaning "red earth", lies on the banks of the Macquarie River, 420km northwest of Sydney and about 200km from Bathurst. The regional capital for the west of the state (with around 40,000 people), it supports many agricultural industries and is located at a vital crossroads where the Melbourne–Brisbane Newell Highway meets the Mitchell Highway and routes west to Bourke or Broken Hill. As such, it's well used to people passing through, but not staying long. If you do stop, the only real attraction is the Taronga Western Plains Zoo, which can easily fill a day or more.

Arrival, information and accommodation

The **visitor centre** (daily 9am–5pm; Ⓣ02/6801 4450, Ⓦwww.dubbotourism .com.au) is set in a riverside park at the corner of Erskine and Macquarie streets, just off the Newell Highway. Two long blocks east, the **train station** has services from Bathurst, Orange and Sydney: Countrylink buses arrive just outside from Broken Hill, Bourke and Lightning Ridge. Greyhound buses (direct from Brisbane, Melbourne and Narrandera) stop on the western side of town at the junction of the Mitchell and Newell highways.

Dubbo's airport, 5km northwest of town, receives daily flights from Sydney and Broken Hill: a taxi (Ⓣ13 10 08) into the centre will set you back around $10. Thrifty, 142 Talbragar St near the train station, **rents cars** from $60 a day. The **library**, at the corner of Macquarie and Talbragar sreets, has **internet** access.

Accommodation

As you'd expect, there are plenty of **motels**, with the majority on the Mitchell Highway (Cobra Street as it passes through town). Unfortunately there is no backpackers' hostel, and Dubbo has problems with theft, even from caravan parks, so keep an eye on your belongings at all times. Also consider a couple of accommodation options out at the zoo (see p.317).

Amaroo Hotel 83 Macquarie St Ⓣ02/6882 3533, Ⓔamaroohotel@bigpond.com. The most salubrious pub-hotel in town, with comfortable rooms, some with views over town. Breakfast is included. ❹
Castlereagh Hotel Corner of Brisbane and Talbragar sts Ⓣ02/6882 4877. This old hotel has the cheapest singles in town ($40, $45 en suite). The en-suite doubles aren't quite as good as you'd get in a motel, though they've got a lot more charm. ❹

De Russi Hotel 95 Cobra St Ⓣ02/6882 7888, Ⓦwww.derussihotels.com.au. The trendiest option of the lot, with stylish motel-style rooms, king-size beds, a pool, wi-fi throughout (with 1hr free), and a restaurant (closed Sun) serving modern Australian cuisine. ❺
Dubbo City Caravan Park Whylandra St Ⓣ1800 824 820, Ⓦwww.dubbocaravanpark.com.au. Central caravan park with good security and

facilities including pool and games room. Camping $20, powered site $28, cabins ❷, en-suite cabins ❸

Dubbo Parklands 154 Whylandra St ☎1800 033 0722, ⓦwww.dubboparkland.com.au. Typically anodyne but well-appointed Big 4 caravan park, occupying a green spot right on the river, though the luxurious cabins (some even have spas) are expensive. Located 2km south of Dubbo off the Newell Hwy near the Western Plains Zoo. Camping $25, powered site $28, cabins ❺

Mayfair Cottage 10 Baird St ☎02/6882 5226, ⓔ donjstephens@bigpond.com. Centrally located B&B with very comfortable and well-decorated rooms in a separate guest wing, plus a pool. ❺

The Town

Easily the biggest attraction in these parts is the open-range 🦒 **Taronga Western Plains Zoo** on Obley Road, 5km south of Dubbo off the Newell Highway (daily 9am–5pm; $39 ticket valid for 2 consecutive days; ☎02/6881 1488, ⓦwww.taronga.org.au). The vast zoo-cum-safari park is mostly populated with Australian and African animals used to a hot, dry climate similar to Dubbo's. Beasts – white rhinos, giraffes, Sumatran tigers and so on – roam in expansive landscaped habitats separated by moats, giving a good approximation of being on safari. Close encounters include face-to-face photo ops with giraffes (March–Nov daily 2.30pm; $5), and the chance to hand-feed lions and tigers from behind a strong mesh fence (daily except Wed 11.30am; $59).

The zoo is threaded by a six-kilometre road you can drive at your own pace. Of course, you can also walk the many paths, cycle around (rentals from $15 for 4hr), or rent an electric cart ($69 for 3hr). It's best to start exploring early, as temperatures can become unbearable by noon and the animals sometimes slink off out of sight into the shade.

Early birds can opt for the Morning Walk, which is a good opportunity to get close to the animals without the crowds (every Sat & Sun, plus Wed & Fri during school holidays, 6.40am; $10). Even better is waking up with the sound of roaring lions, possible in a couple of ways: the family-oriented Roar and Snore package ($145, kids $95, must be 5 or older) includes an Outback dinner, guided evening safari, a night under canvas, the Morning Walk and general zoo access; the luxurious *Zoofari Lodge* ($269 per person twin-share midweek, $298 at weekends and school holidays) gets you two days' general zoo admission, bike rental, three behind-the-scenes tours, à la carte dinner, breakfast and a night in a deluxe tent with double bed and bathroom. Giraffes, eland and oryx graze nearby.

There's no public transport to the zoo, so **cycling** there (and around) is a good option; Wheeler Cycles, 25 Bultje St (☎02/6882 9899), rents out basic bikes for $15 per day.

A couple of kilometres south of the zoo along Obley Road the National Trust property **Dundullimal Homestead** (Tues–Thurs 10am–4pm; $8) deserves a quick look. This 1840s timber slab house is one of the oldest in the district and comes with sandstone stables, and Devonshire teas served in a 1920s shed.

In the centre of town, **Old Dubbo Gaol**, 90 Macquarie St (daily 9am–5pm; $15; ⓦwww.olddubbogaol.com.au), is worth an hour or so. Back in the 1880s, this fortress-style building housed some of the west's most notorious criminals, and today it glories in the details of nineteenth-century prison life, giving loving attention to the macabre – the gallows, the hangman's kit and the criminal careers of some of those who were executed here.

Nearby, the revamped **Western Plains Cultural Centre** at 76 Wingewarra St (daily except Tues 10am–4pm; free; ⓦwww.wpccdubbo.org.au) houses both the **Art Gallery**, which has regularly changing exhibitions, and the **Dubbo Regional Museum**, showing pastoral scenes of early settlers.

The state's largest **Livestock Market**, 3km north of town on the Newell Highway, auctions sheep (Mon noon) and cattle (Thurs & Fri 8.30am). It's worth a visit just to see the local farmers decked out in their Akubra hats and Drizabone coats, and to inhale the authentic smell of country life.

Eating and drinking

Given its remoteness, Dubbo's **café society** is well developed, with restaurants just as creative as the ones you'd find on the coast. For the less adventurous, there are decent pub meals in the many hotels.

Amaroo Hotel 83 Macquarie St. Your best bet if you crave the usual steak and veggies at rock-bottom prices.

Grapevine Café 144 Brisbane St. A low-key and relaxing daytime café with a lovely shady courtyard and delicious meals in generous portions (around $15). Free wi-fi.

Rose Garden 208 Brisbane St ☎02/6882 8322. Superb Thai restaurant that's a cut above the average (but no more expensive), set in a wood-panelled heritage home decorated with classy pewter.

Sticks and Stones 215 Macquarie St ☎02/6885 4852. Gourmet pizzas in a former doctor's house, four long blocks south of the visitor centre. Daily from 6pm.

Two Doors Tapas and Wine Bar 215B Macquarie St ☎02/6885 2333, ☉www .twodoors.com.au. Occupying a lovely stone cellar below *Sticks and Stones*, and with a leafy courtyard, this place is perfect for a few glasses of wine and something from the well-thought-out, Spanish-influenced menu (dishes $16–20), all also sold as half-portion tapas. Expect the likes of asparagus-filled tortilla and fish skewers on an orange salad. Closed Sun.

Village Hot Bake 113A Darling St, by the train station. The best place for fresh bread, cakes, sandwiches and fries. The pies have won numerous awards. Daily 6am–5.30pm.

Cowra

Nestled on the banks of the Lachlan River, 107km southwest of Bathurst along the Mid-Western Highway, **COWRA** is a green little town, though it doesn't invite you to stay longer than necessary. Its only claim to fame is the **Cowra Breakout** of World War II. August 5, 1944, saw the escape of 378 Japanese prisoners of war armed with baseball bats, staves, home-made clubs and sharpened kitchen knives – those who were sick and remained behind hung or disembowelled themselves, unable to endure the disgrace of capture. It took nine days to recapture all the prisoners, during which four Australian soldiers and 231 Japanese died. The breakout was little known until the publication of Harry Gordon's excellent 1970s account *Die Like the Carp* (republished as *Voyage of Shame*).

You can see the site of the **POW camp**, now just ruins and fields, on Sakura Avenue on the northeast edge of town. The graves of the escapees, who were buried in Cowra, were well cared for by members of the local Returned Servicemen's League, a humanitarian gesture that touched Japanese embassy officials who then broached the idea of an official **Japanese War Cemetery**. Designed by Shigeru Yura, the tranquil burial ground lies north of the camp, on Doncaster Drive. The theme of Japanese–Australian friendship and recon-ciliation continued in Cowra with the establishment of the **Japanese Garden** (daily 8.30am–5pm; $9.50) in 1979, with funding from Japanese and Australian governments and companies. The large garden, designed to represent the landscape of Japan, is set on a hill overlooking the town, on a scenic drive running north off Kendal Street, the main thoroughfare. There's another antiwar symbol in the shape of the **World Peace Bell** on Civic Square, while an avenue of cherry trees connects the war cemeteries, the POW camp and the Japanese Garden.

A holographic explanation of the breakout can be seen at the **visitor centre** at the junction of the Olympic Highway, Lachlan Valley Way and Mid-Western Highway (daily 9am–5pm; ℡02/6342 4333, ⊛www.cowratourism.com.au), although its emphasis is more on the few Australian casualties than the Japanese prisoners who died. The only public transport here is Countrylink **buses** from Bathurst.

If you want to taste the local **wine** (the region is best known for its Chardonnays), head for the *Quarry Cellar Restaurant & Cellar Door* on Boorowa Road, 4km south of Cowra (cellar Tues–Sun 10am–4pm, lunch Thurs–Sun, dinner Fri & Sat; ℡02/6342 3650). If you're interested in some **grape-picking** work, contact Oz Jobs (⊛www.ozjobsonline.com).

Young

Seventy kilometres southwest of Cowra along the Olympic Highway and serviced daily by Countrylink, the hilly town of **YOUNG** is a good spot to pick up some **cherry-picking** work during the season (approximately six weeks from the first week of Nov); being monotonous rather than strenuous, the work is popular with retired Queenslanders. To just pick your own and have a look at some orchards and packing sheds, head to any one of a number of places on the way into town from Cowra; you could also contact Ready Workforce on Boorowa Street (℡02/6382 4728). The long weekend in October generally coincides with the **cherry blossoms** being in full bloom – a glorious sight – and there's even an annual Cherry Festival (early Dec) celebrating the harvest with games and competitions. There are also several vineyards on the slopes of the undulating area, which is becoming known as the **Hilltops wine region**. Two worth visiting are the small, family-run Lindsays Woodonga Hill Winery, 10km north of Young on Olympic Highway (daily 9am–5pm), and Chalkers Crossing winery on Grenfell Road (daily except Sat 9am–5pm; ⊛www.chalkerscrossing.com.au).

A former gold-mining centre previously known as Lambing Flat, the town was the scene of racist violence – the notorious **Lambing Flat Riots** – against Chinese miners in June 1861. As the gold ran out, European miners resented what they saw as the greater success of the more industrious Chinese, and troops had to be called in when the Chinese were chased violently from the diggings and their property destroyed. Carried at the head of the mob was a flag made from a tent flysheet, with the Southern Cross in the centre and the slogan "Roll Up, Roll Up, No Chinese" painted on. Following the riots, the Chinese Immigration Restriction Act was passed, one of the first steps on the slippery slope towards the White Australia Policy of 1901. You can see the original flag, and other exhibits relating to the riots, in the **Lambing Flat Folk Museum** (daily 10am–4pm; $4) in the Community Arts Centre, Campbell Street. Apart from the museum and seasonal work, there's no real reason to make the detour to Young.

For more information, contact the **visitor centre**, 2 Short St (Mon–Fri 9am–5pm, Sat & Sun 9.30am–4pm; ℡02/6382 3394, ⊛www.visityoung.com .au). A recommended **farmstay** outside town on the Olympic Highway is

Old Nubba School House (☎02/6943 2513, ✉nubba@dragnet.com.au; ❺), offering peaceful self-contained accommodation in the grounds of a friendly family farm. By far the most enjoyable spot for **lunch** is *Café Lunch A lot*, 67 Lynch St, with a tiny French terrace, creative salads and a vast selection of teas.

The Hume Highway and the Riverina

The rolling plains of southwestern New South Wales, spreading west from the Great Dividing Range, are bounded by two great rivers: the **Murrumbidgee** to the north and the **Murray** to the south, the latter forming the border with the state of Victoria. This area is now known as the **Riverina**. The land the explorer John Oxley described as "uninhabitable and useless to civilized man" began its transformation to fertile fruit-bowl when the ambitious **Murrumbidgee Irrigation Scheme** was launched in 1907. Though times are tough in the current drought, the area around **Griffith** normally produces ninety percent of Australia's rice, most of its citrus fruits and twenty percent of its wine grapes, so if you're looking for work on the land, you've a reasonable chance of finding it here.

The eastern limit of the region is defined by the **Hume Highway**, the rather tedious route between Sydney and Melbourne. It is often choked with trucks, particularly at night, and still occasionally narrows to one lane either way, so you'll want to keep your wits about you. Better still, stop off at towns along the way, many of them truly and typically Australian – rich in food, wine, flora and fauna, and friendly locals. Tick off the big sheep at **Goulburn**, but don't miss the town's old brewery. **Yass** has associations with Hamilton Hume – after whom the highway is named – while **Gundagai** is more famous for a fictional dog's behaviour. You'll have to detour 50km off route to visit likeable **Wagga Wagga**, the capital of the central Riverina and the largest inland town in New South Wales, while the last stop in the state is **Albury**, twinned with Wodonga on the Victorian shore of the Murray River.

Heading west **Narrandera** really only justifies a meal stop, while **Griffith** is good for wine tasting and fruit picking. There are several interesting **festivals** in the region, including the Wagga Wagga Jazz Festival in September (🖥www .waggajazz.org.au) and Griffith's La Festa (🖥www.lafesta.org.au), an orgy of Aussie wine, food and culture held on Easter Saturday.

Goulburn and beyond

GOULBURN, just off the Hume Highway, is a large regional centre and home to a quality **wool industry**, established in the 1820s. The town, with its wide streets, has a conservative country feel, but boasts some large and impressive public buildings. Goulburn's wool traditions have been immortalized by the

Big Merino (daily 8.30am–5.30pm; free), a fifteen-metre-high sheep which stands proudly next to the Mobil service station on the Old Hume Highway 2km southwest of the town centre; the first floor has a display on the industry. To get closer to the real thing and enjoy a glimpse into Australian country life, head for the long-established **Pelican Sheep Station** on Braidwood Road, 10km south of town (☎02/4821 4668, ⓦwww.pelicansheepstation.com.au; bunkhouses ❷, cabins ❺, cottage ❹, plus camping at $11 per person), where 75-minute tours ($6.50; by appointment only) include a shearing demonstration and the chance to see sheepdogs being put through their paces – kids can cuddle newborn lambs in April. It is a working farm so call in advance.

There are several historic places to visit in Goulburn, including the National Trust property **Riversdale**, an 1840 coaching inn on Maud Street (Sept–May Mon & Tues 9am–1pm, Sun 10am–3pm; ⓦwww.nsw.nationaltrust.org.au; $5), and the **Old Goulburn Brewery** on Bungonia Road (daily 11am–5pm; $5.50 including a generous tasting), which has been brewing traditional ales and stouts since 1836. As well as seeing the buildings, you can enjoy a snack in the sunny courtyard and explore some curious displays on the philosophy of numbers in relation to architecture, particularly that of early nineteenth century convict Francis Howard Greenway, designer of Sydney's Hyde Park Barracks and this brewery building.

The **Cathedral of Saint Saviour** on Church Street (daily 10am–4pm), completed in 1884, is one of the most attractive old churches in Australia, with some beautiful stained glass and a fine organ.

Practicalities

Now bypassed by the Hume Highway, Goulburn is still the traditional stop-off point en route to Canberra from Sydney, with regular Countrylink **trains** and Greyhound **buses** passing by. The **visitor centre** opposite the shady, flower-filled Belmore Park at 201 Sloane St (daily 9am–5pm; ☎1800 353 646, ⓦwww.igoulburn.com) stocks the local brochure detailing walks and heritage buildings.

The most intriguing place to **stay** in the area is at the *Gunningbar Yurtfarm*, 20km northwest of town on Grabben Gullen Road (☎02/4829 2114, ⓦwww .yurtworks.com.au/yurtfarm; free as a helper with four hours' work per day – all meals included as part of a WWOOF placement, see p.68). Essentially a sheep property, the several yurts here provide an educational centre for groups of children to help them become more self-sufficient and environmentally aware. If you want to stay in the back-to-basics yurts ($12 per person with own bedding), you must call in advance; someone can pick you up if you don't have your own transport.

In town, *Tattersalls Hotel*, 74 Auburn St (☎02/4821 3088; dorms $30, rooms ❶), is a hostel offering good and clean, if basic, dorm accommodation and shared-bath rooms. There are also cheapish rooms and swankier heritage rooms at *Alpine Heritage Motel*, 248 Sloane St (☎02/4821 2930, ⓦwww .alpineheritagemotel.com.au; double ❸, heritage queen ❹), in a listed building opposite the train station. Nearby, *Mandelson's*, 160 Sloane St (☎02/4821 0707, ⓦwww.mandelsons.com.au; ❻), offers luxurious rooms in another heritage building. There's **camping** at *Governors Hill Carapark*, 77 Sydney Rd, 3km northeast of town (☎1800 227 373, ⓔgovernorshillcp @bigpond.com.au; $28, powered site $32).

The essential Goulburn **eating** experience is the licensed *Paragon Café* at 174 Auburn St, which dates back to the 1940s and serves up inexpensive breakfasts, hamburgers, steaks, fish and Italian fare. A host of other good, multi-ethnic eateries can be found close by on the same street, and in the evening there's great wood-fired pizza at *Sasso*, 173 Bourke St (licensed & BYO; closed Mon & Tues).

The Bungonia State Conservation Area and the Wombeyan Caves

The **Bungonia State Conservation Area**, 35km east of Goulburn, covers a rugged strip of the Southern Tablelands containing some of the deepest **caves** in Australia, the spectacular limestone Bungonia Gorge and the Shoalhaven River. There are also plenty of bushwalking tracks with good river and canyon views, and a well-equipped **campsite** near the entrance of the park (T 02/4844 4277; Oct–April $10 per person, May–Sept $5).

Some 70km north of Goulburn via Taralga are the huge and more accessible **Wombeyan Caves** (daily 9am–5.30pm; W www.nationalparks.nsw.gov.au), with a self-guided tour of Figtree Cave ($13) and assorted guided tours of four other caves (from $16).

Yass and the Burrinjuck Waters State Park

YASS, 87km west of Goulburn just off the Hume Highway, is an appealing little place with a rural feel, kept green by the Yass River. Both Countrylink and Greyhound pass through the town which, before European settlement, had a high Aboriginal population, who gave the town its name, "yharr", meaning running water. The famous explorer **Hamilton Hume** chose to retire here, the town's main claim to fame. The National Trust-owned **Cooma Cottage** (mid-Aug to mid-June Thurs–Sun 10am–4pm; $5), a well-preserved nineteenth-century homestead 4km south on the Canberra road, was his former home and is now a museum, set in a hundred acres of rolling country-side and containing excellent material on Hume and his expeditions. Hume was different from many of his contemporaries in that he was born in Australia – in Parramatta, to free settlers in 1797 – and his explorations relied on his first-hand knowledge of the bush and of Aboriginal skills and languages. Hume's best-known exploration was in 1828 when he paired with **Hovell**, an English sea captain, to head for Port Phillip Bay; you can follow in their footsteps on the **Hume & Hovell Walking Track** (W www.lands.nsw.gov.au) which starts at Yass, and runs over 440km southwest to Albury (the visitor centre has a free brochure and a more detailed guide pack for $20). He also assisted Sturt in tracing the Murray and Darling rivers.

The **Yass and District Museum** on Comur Street (Oct–April Sat & Sun 10am–4pm, weekdays when volunteers available; $2) contains displays on what the town looked like back in the 1890s. About 20km along the road west towards Gundagai at Gap Range amid landscaped gardens is the **gallery** of the internationally renowned glass sculptor Peter Crisp (daily 10am–5pm; free; T 02/6227 6073, W www.petercrisp.com.au), whose exquisite work is available for sale – little bowls from $50 up to commemorative pieces for thousands.

The **visitor centre**, 259 Comur St (Mon–Fri 9am–4.30pm, Sat & Sun 9am–4pm; T 02/6226 2557, W www.yass.nsw.gov.au), has maps outlining an informative, two-kilometre walk through town and will point you to good wineries in this up-and-coming cool-climate wine region.

There are some lovely **bed and breakfasts** in Yass. One of the best is *Kerrow-gair*, an elegant historical residence at 24 Grampian St (T 02/6226 4932,

ⓦwww.kerrowgair.com.au; ⓖ). The *Thunderbird Motel*, 264 Comur St (☎02/6226 1158, ⓦwww.thunderbirdmotelyass.com.au; ⓖ), offers comfortable units and a nice pool, while the *Australian Motel*, at 180 Comur St (☎02/6226 1744; ❸), is decent value and has singles for as little as $25. *Yass Caravan Park* (☎02/6226 1173; camping $16, powered site $20, cabins ❶, en suite ❸) is central though lacks character, and there are lots of places to **eat** on Comur Street.

Some 20km west of Yass, a worthwhile detour off the Hume Highway leads 15km north to the peaceful village of **BINALONG**. Australia's best-known poet, Banjo Patterson, spent much of his childhood here, attending the local school. Binalong railway station was used to transport gold from nearby Lambing Flat (Young), which made it a lucrative area for bushrangers; the grave of one of the most daring, "Flash" Johnny Gilbert, lies alongside the road to Harden. A Countrylink **coach** passes through Binalong on its way to Harden from Yass.

Continuing for 27km along the Hume Highway from the Binalong junction towards Gundagai, you'll reach a turn-off for the Burrinjuck Waters State Park. From here it's a 25-kilometre drive south to the park, set around the gigantic (at 2.5 times the size of Sydney Harbour) **Burrinjuck Dam** ($7 per car per day), with camping (☎02/6227 8114, ⓦwww.stateparks.nsw.gov.au; camping $15, powered site $18, cabins ❶–❷, cottages ❸–❹) and picnic areas filled with kangaroos and chirping rosellas.

For some downtime away from the Hume Highway, head south from Yass along Tourist Route 7 which rejoins the Hume south of Gundagai. Around 50km southwest of Yass you reach the picturesque tiny village of **WEE JASPER**, comprising little more than a general store and a pub beside the headwaters of the Burrinjuck Waters. There are basic campsites ($7.50 per person; ☎02/6227 9626, ⓦwww.weejasperreserves.com.au).

From here you can take an hour-long tour of **Carey's Caves**, 6km northwest of Wee Jasper (Fri–Mon noon & 1.30pm, Sat & Sun also at 3pm; $11; ⓦwww .weejaspercaves.com), for a look at some of Australia's most spectacular limestone rock formations.

Gundagai

Some 100km west of Yass, **GUNDAGAI** sits on the banks of the Murrumbidgee, at the foot of the rounded bump of Mount Parnassus. The town was once situated on the alluvial flats north of the river, despite warnings from local Aborigines that the area was prone to major flooding. Proving them correct, old Gundagai was the scene of Australia's worst flood disaster in 1852, when 89 people drowned. Gold was eventually discovered here in 1858, and by 1864 Gundagai had become a boom town, preyed upon by the romantically dubbed bushranger Captain Moonlight. The relocated town, on the main route between Sydney and Melbourne until bypassed by the Hume Highway, became a favoured overnight stopping-point amongst pioneers heading into the interior by bullock cart. A large punt was the only means of crossing the Murrumbidgee until the **Prince Alfred Bridge** was erected in 1867, a pretty wooden structure which can still be used by pedestrians.

Gundagai found immortality through a **Jack Moses** poem, in which "the dog sat on the tuckerbox, nine miles from Gundagai" and stubbornly refused to help its master pull the bogged bullock team from the creek. Somehow the image became elevated from that of a disobedient dog and a cursing teamster to a symbol of the pioneer with his faithful hound at his side. As a consequence, a statue of the dog was erected 8km north of town at **Five Mile Creek**, where pioneers used to camp overnight – it's still a very pleasant spot to take a break.

The tiny town itself lacks much character, but the **visitor centre**, 249 Sherridan St (Mon–Fri 8am–5pm, Sat & Sun 9am–noon & 1–5pm; ☎02/6944 0250, ⓦwww.gundagai.nsw.gov.au), can help with accommodation should you wish to stay. Countrylink and Greyhound **buses** both service the town on a regular basis. The most luxurious **accommodation** option is the old convent at ⌖ *Lanigan Abbey* (☎02/6944 2852, ⓦwww.laniganabbey.com.au; ⓞ), complete with intact chapel behind St Patrick's church and an art gallery next door. Otherwise there are plenty of hotels along the main road.

Stop for great home-made daytime **meals**, and cakes at *Bullocky Bills* on Dog on the Tuckerbox Road, 8km north of town beside the Hume Highway.

Wagga Wagga

WAGGA WAGGA, known simply as "Wagga" (and pronounced "Wogga"), is capital of the Riverina region and by far its largest town, with around 60,000 inhabitants, though despite its size it remains a green and pleasant place. Its curious name is thought to come from the Widadjuri, the largest of the New South Wales Aboriginal peoples: "wagga" means crow, and its repetition signifies the plural (though some claim it means "dancing men").

Arrival, information and accommodation

Roughly halfway between Sydney (470km) and Melbourne (435km), Wagga is just off the Sturt Highway, the main route between Adelaide and Sydney. Baylis Street, the main strip (and Fitzmaurice St, its continuation), extends from the bridge spanning the Murrumbidgee River 1km south through town to the train station which receives daily Countrylink **trains** from Sydney and Melbourne. The station is also the stop for interstate Greyhound **buses** between Brisbane, Sydney, Adelaide, Melbourne and Canberra, and Fearnes Coaches (☎02/6921 2316, ⓦwww.fearnes.com.au) services to Canberra and Sydney

Timetables for the seven **local bus routes** can be picked up at the **visitor centre**, 183 Tarcutta St, close to the river (daily 9am–5pm; ☎1300 100 122, ⓦwww.visitwaggawagga.com), which has an **accommodation** booking service.

There's **internet access** at the library in the Civic Centre (Mon 11am–7pm, Tues–Fri 10am–7pm, Sat 10am–5pm) and at Wagga Systems, 114 Fitzmaurice St, which has wi-fi.

Accommodation

Lawson Motor Inn 117–121 Tarcutta St ☎02/6921 2200, ⓦwww.thelawson.com.au. Well-run four-star motel with spacious, well-furnished rooms with satellite TV, free broadband and kitchenettes. ⓖ

The Manor 38 Morrow St ☎02/6921 2958, ⓦwww.themanor.com.au. Historic B&B next to the beautiful lagoon-front park, with heavy wooden furniture, old gramophones and pleasant communal areas. ⓖ–ⓞ

Romano's Hotel Corner of Sturt and Fitzmaurice sts ☎02/6921 2013, ⓦwww.romanoshotel.com.au.

Old hotel with a nineteenth-century feel and rather old-fashioned rooms including singles (around $40). Rooms ❷, en suites ❹

Victoria Hotel 55 Baylis St ☎02/6921 5233, ⓦwww.vichotel.net. "The Vic" has good doubles with shared bathrooms – but none of the character of *Romano's*. Singles $25, doubles ❶

Wagga Beach Caravan Park 2 Johnston St ☎02/6931 0603, ⓦwww.wwbcp.com.au. The town's best-situated caravan park, this shady and tranquil place has a free gas barbecue right on the town beach, 5min walk north of the main shops. Camping $20, powered site $22, en-suite cabins ❷

The Town

Wagga's main attractions are on the edge of the city. A half-hour walk to the south at the base of Willans Hill are the huge and impressive **Botanic Gardens**, whose attractions include a walk-through bird aviary, a mini zoo (daily 8am–4pm or 5pm in summer; free), bush trails and picnic areas. The **Museum of the Riverina** has two sites: one near the Botanic Gardens on Lord Baden Powell Drive (Tues–Sat 10am–5pm, Sun noon–4pm; free), which hosts a hotch-potch collection of old farm machinery, printing presses and a display of over two hundred door-knockers; and the other back in town at the **Civic Centre** (same hours), at the corner of Baylis and Morrow streets, which often hosts travelling exhibitions.

Also in the Civic Centre, the **Wagga Wagga Art Gallery** (Tues–Sat 10am–5pm, Sun noon–4pm; free; ⓦ www.waggaartgallery.org) is home to a collection of over 1200 original Australian prints (some of which are usually on display) and the **National Art Glass Collection**, comprising around four hundred pieces, mostly non-representational studio glass made since the 1970s.

On Sunday mornings a bit of life is sparked by the **market** (7.30am–noon) at the Myer car park on O'Reilly Street, which has secondhand clothes and books, crafts, local produce and cakes. The city's **Charles Sturt University** boasts a well-regarded wine course and has its own on-campus **winery** (and cheesery) on Coolamon Road, both of which are open for tastings and sales (Mon–Fri 11am–5pm, Sat & Sun 11am–4pm; ⓣ 02/6933 2435) – try the unusual lemon Myrtle cheese. Sweet teeth can tour the heavenly Green Grove Organics **liquorice and chocolate factory** at 8 Lord St in **Junee**, 37km to the north (daily tours 10am–4pm; $4; ⓦ www.greengroveorganics.com).

Eating and drinking

In the town centre, the Baylis/Fitzmaurice strip and its side streets provide fertile **eating** ground, though there's little that's really special. For **drinking** and **dancing**, the town's most popular spots are the lively *Victoria Hotel* ("The Vic") and the *Black Swan Hotel*.

Black Swan Hotel 37 Gardiner St, North Wagga, 1.5km north. Known as "The Muddy Duck", this friendly booze barn is eternally popular with the student population.

Eat@Romano's At *Romano's Hotel*. This hotel has a good modern restaurant with lots of seafood and other dishes (mostly under $20), plus decent espresso and all-day breakfasts. Great terrace for summer eating. Closed Sun.

Indian Tavern Tandoori Restaurant 81 Peter St ⓣ 02/6921 3121. A popular spot with authentic tandoori dishes, though can be a bit liberal with the chilli sauce.

Montezuma's 85 Baylis St. Cosy wooden cantina where you can enjoy the best Mexican food in town, surrounded by kitschy relics. The friendly and exuberant owners add to the atmosphere. Wed–Sat lunch, Tues–Sun dinner.

Premium Coffee Roasters 34 Trail St. They don't do much, but they do it well. Top espresso and a few snacks, inside or out. Closed Sun.

Three Chefs In the *Townhouse International Motel*, 70 Morgan St. One of the classiest restaurants in Wagga with white linen tablecloths, and a Mod Oz menu using lots of local produce. Expect the likes of boneless rack of lamb with roasted truss tomatoes ($32). Closed Sun.

Victoria Hotel 55 Baylis St. Extensive bistro menu with everything from avocado salad to rump steak; the upstairs balcony is open Fri and Sat nights.

Wagga Wagga Winery Oura Rd, a 15-min drive northeast of town ⓣ 02/6922 1221, ⓦ www .waggawaggawinery.com.au. One of the best local places to eat. The wines themselves are nothing special, but the excellent local food (from $20 a head) and the setting, in an old pine-log building with a large veranda and a garden area, is very pleasant. Wed–Sun for lunch and dinner.

Albury/Wodonga and around

The small city of **ALBURY** and its smaller twin **Wodonga**, across the Murray River in Victoria, are traditionally regarded as a stopping point en route between Sydney and Melbourne. The Hume Highway now cuts through the twin cities on a new freeway, but drivers tempted to shoot straight through miss out on a bustling district with a pleasant atmosphere and a few key sights.

Arrival, information and accommodation

Trains (from Sydney, Melbourne and Wagga Wagga) and Countrylink, Greyhound and V/Line long-distance **buses** (from lots of places) all stop at the magnificent train station, 100m east of the shops and cafés of Dean Street and only ten minutes' walk from the Cultural Precinct and Botanic Gardens.

There's a small and only occasionally staffed **information booth** at the train station, but the principal **visitor centre** is on the Wodonga side of the river on The Causeway (daily 9am–5pm; ☏1300 796 222, ⓦwww .destinationalburywodonga.com.au). The LibraryMuseum (see p.326) has free **internet** and **wi-fi**.

Being a major stopover has contributed to the ridiculous number of **motels** in a city that can be explored within a day. The cheapest ones are along the highway, the truck noise being the only difference from the ones in the centre.

Accommodation

Albury Motor Village 372 Wagga Rd, 4.5km north ☏02/6040 2999, ⓦwww .alburymotorvillage.com.au. Holiday park and associate YHA with pool, free wi-fi, van hookups and cabins but no tent sites. Bus #907 from Dean St. Dorms $29, powered sites $32, rooms ❸, cabins ❹–❺

All Season Tourist Park 481 Wagga Rd, 7km north ☏02/6025 1619, ⓦwww.alburyallseasons .com.au. Well-kept campsite with pool. Bus #907 from Dean St. Camping $26, en-suite cabins ❹

Chifley Albury Corner of Dean and Elizabeth sts ☏02/6021 5366, ⓦwww.chifleyhotels.com/albury. Plush eight-storey, four-and-a-half-star hotel in the heart of town. ❻

Fraunfelder Cottage 791 David St, 1km north ☏02/6023 5948. Cute B&B cottage sleeping four in Albury's oldest dwelling. ❹

New Albury Hotel 491 Kiewa St just off Dean St ☏02/6021 3599, ⓦwww.newalburyhotel.com.au. Smart, modern en-suite rooms with fridge and TV on three floors above a popular Irish bar. ❸

The Town

Albury is where you'll spend most of your time, most likely around the so-called Cultural Precinct in the block northeast of the junction of Dean and Kiewa streets. Here, the excellent, modern **LibraryMuseum**, at the corner of Kiewa and Swift streets (Mon, Wed & Thurs 10am–7pm, Tues & Fri 10am–5pm, Sat 10am–4pm, Sun noon–4pm, free; ⓦwww.alburycity.nsw.gov.au/library museum), has a small but well-presented display on the city's history and culture including material on Bonegilla (see p.327) and a great poster showing *Spirit of Progress*, one of the sleek trains which once called at the train station here. Victoria and New South Wales run on different track gauges and until 1962 when a standard-gauge track to Melbourne was completed, everyone had to change trains at Albury. Always on display are three oils by Australian artist Russell Drysdale (1912–81), who lived in the area in the 1920s and married into a local family. If this has sparked your interest in his work, nip around the corner to the equally superb **Albury Art Gallery**, 546 Dean St (Mon–Fri 10am–5pm, Sat 10am–4pm, Sun noon–4pm; free; ⓦwww.alburycity.nsw.gov .au/gallery), in the decorative old town hall. It has a large collection of his work (not always on display) and a great collection of Australian photography, including works by Max Dupain, Tracey Moffat, Bill Henson and Anne Zahalka; it also sponsors a biennial national photography prize.

When you get cultured out, head west along Dean Street to the **Albury Botanical Gardens**. Established in 1877, the gardens house some impressive old trees, including a huge, 41-metre Queensland kauri pine. At their southern end the Gardens abut **Noreuil Park**, a peaceful place looking across to a bush-covered riverbank in Victoria. People swim in the river and picnic under the large gum trees here – one of which was marked by the explorer Hovell at the point where he and Hume crossed the Murray.

To get out on the water, rent a **canoe** from Murray River Canoe Hire (☎02/6041 1822, ✉thecanoeguy@hotmail.com; $25 half-day, $35 full day, $70 2-day camping trip). They generally drop you upstream and let you paddle back into town where they pick you up.

Eating, drinking and nightlife

Most of the **eating** action happens along or just off the main shopping drag, Dean Street. There are bars in the same area and a little bit of **nightlife**.

Bended Elbow 480 Dean St. A lively English-style pub, with good meal deals ($12 steaks on Tues), karaoke, trivia nights, and club nights at weekends.

Commercial Club 620 Dean St. If you are ravenous and broke, head here for a cheap deal with all the pasta, steak, seafood and salad you can eat for $16 and pizzas starting at $12.

Electra Café 441 Dean St at Macauley St. Popular with locals for great breakfasts and lunches in a retro setting. Also open for modern Australian dinners ($25 mains). Closed Sun evening and all day Mon and Tues.

Roi Bar 491 Dean St ⊛www.roibar.com.au. Albury's main nightclub open Wed (university night), and Fri & Sat for DJs and live music. Biggish bands and club nights often stop in on their way between Sydney and Melbourne.

Sourcedining 664 Dean St ☎02/6041 1288, ⊛www.sourcedining.com. Probably the finest restaurant in the district with elegant presentation and delectable modern dishes such as nectarine and gorgonzola tart with blue cheese barvois ($17) followed by slow-braised lamb neck ($33). Lunch Thurs & Fri, dinner Tues–Sat.

Around Albury: Bonegilla and Corowa

Thousands of older Australians have strong memories (fond or otherwise) of the **Bonegilla**, the Migrant Reception and Training Centre located 15km east of Wodonga. It was set up after World War II to cope with immigrants from over thirty countries wanting a new life in "the lucky country". Between 1947 and 1971 over 300,000 people were processed here, most staying just a couple of months before being shipped off to where labour was in short supply, many to the Snowy Mountains hydroelectric scheme nearby. When it closed, most of the 26 self-contained living areas were flattened, but Block 19 has been restored and contains an interpretive centre (daily 9am–5pm; free; ⊛www.parklands-alburywodonga.org.au), the starting point for a self-guided tour around the rest of the site.

It's 56km northwest from Albury to the pleasant town of **COROWA**, across the Murray from Victoria's Rutherglen wine region (see p.1000). This is the birthplace of **Federation**, since the Federation Conference of 1893 was held at Corowa's courthouse on Queen Street in the centre. If you're here at the weekend, call in at the **Corowa Federation Museum**, a few steps along Queens Street (Sat & Sun 1–4pm; $2 donation), which contains documents and photos of the Federation Conference along with displays on local artists including Aboriginal artist Tommy McRae, who painted around here.

You can reach Corowa from Albury using Countrylink and local buses (2 daily on average). The **visitor centre** is at 88 Sanger St (Mon–Fri 10am–5pm, Sat 10am–3pm, Sun 10am–1pm; ☎1800 814 054, Ⓦwww.visitcorowashire.com .au). There are stacks of motels in town offering very reasonable **accommodation**, such as the three-star, riverside *Corowa Golf Club Motel*, on Hume Street, 4km south of town (☎1800 334 288, Ⓦwww.corowagolfclubmotel.com.au; ❹), or *Murray Bank Holiday Units*, 76 Federation Ave, 1km southwest of town (☎02/6033 2922, Ⓦwww.murraybank.com.au; ❹), with one- and two-bedroom units on a yabby farm where you can barbecue your own yabby.

Campers should try *Bindaree Motel & Holiday Park*, 454 Honour Ave, 3km north of town (☎02/6033 2500, Ⓦwww.bindaree.net; camping $15–60, self-contained cabins ❹, motel rooms ❺), which has riverside views. There are several places on the main street where you can get a **meal**, including the *Royal Hotel*, which serves up decent counter food, *D'Amico's* Italian restaurant (closed Wed), and the *Corowa Bakery*, a popular café-bakery that opens early.

The Murrumbidgee Irrigation Area

Irrigation has transformed the area northwest of Wagga Wagga, between the Lachlan and the Murrumbidgee rivers, into a fertile valley full of orchards, vineyards and rice paddies, cut through with irrigation canals. The **Murrumbidgee Irrigation Area** (or **MIA**) extends over two thousand square kilometres, a mostly flat and – from ground level at least – featureless landscape that is nonetheless responsible for producing enormous amounts of rice, wine grapes and citrus fruits. Sadly, the years of **drought** have left the place largely parched and rice production has dropped to less than two percent of what it was in the years of plenty.

Probably the main reason you'll visit this off-the-beaten-track area is to find **work**, particularly around Griffith, with abundant fruit picking available roughly between August and March. Save yourself a potentially wasted trip by checking for a late harvest or poor crop with Skilled (☎02/6964 2547, Ⓦwww.skilled.com.au) or Summit Personnel (☎02/6964 2718, Ⓦwww .summitpersonnel.com.au).

You'll also pass through if you're driving along the **Sturt Highway** between Sydney and Adelaide. Laid-back **Narrandera** is just off the highway but you'll have to stray a little further to visit **Griffith**, with its Italian community and their wines, notably "stickies". Lastly, if you're passing through **Hay**, be sure to call in at the Australian Shearers' Hall of Fame.

Narrandera

Almost 100km northwest of Wagga Wagga, at the junction of the Sturt and Newell highways, leafy **NARRANDERA** is a popular overnight stop en route from Adelaide to Sydney, or from Melbourne to Brisbane. It's a pleasant place to take a break, set on the **Murrumbidgee River** with streets lined with tall native trees; its white cedars, which blossom in November, are particularly beautiful. In mid-March the town hosts the **John O'Brien Festival** (Ⓦwww .johnobrien.com.au), a commemoration of the famous poet-priest who lived here in the early 1900s, with bush poetry and Irish music.

A good place to cool down is **Lake Talbot**, a willow-fringed expanse of water flowing from the Murrumbidgee River. Right next to the lake are the Lake Talbot pools (Nov–March daily 10am–dusk; adults $3; Ⓦwww.laketalbot.com.au), a family-friendly complex with picnic areas, barbecues, water slides and an Olympic-sized swimming pool. Nearby, the riverside **Koala Regeneration Reserve** has been set aside for a disease-free colony of koalas; to get there, follow the Bundidgerry Walking Track (map from visitor centre) around Lake Talbot and the Murrumbidgee River.

Fishing fans could try out the lake or river for some Murray cod, yellowbelly and redfin.

Practicalities

Countrylink **buses** between Griffith and Wagga Wagga stop outside the **train station**, from where a train service runs to Sydney once a week. Greyhound stops at Narrandera South en route to Adelaide, Brisbane, Melbourne or Sydney. The friendly **visitor centre** is in Narrandera Park on the Newell Highway (Mon–Sat 9am–5pm, Sun variable hours; ☎1800 672 392, ⓦwww .narrandera.nsw.gov.au).

There's **accommodation** in various classic country hotels, the most appealing and best value being the *Murrumbidgee Hotel*, 159 East St (☎02/6959 2011; ➊), complete with iron-lace balconies lining East Street. Another good bet is the nearby *Midtown Motor Inn*, on the corner of East and Larmer streets (☎02/6959 2122, ✉budleaf@itginternet.net.au; ➍), a clean motel with pool and a Mediterranean feel in its modern rooms; but Narrandera's best place to stay is the ⚜ *Historic Star Lodge*, 64 Whitton St (☎02/6959 1768, ⓦwww .historicstarlodge.com.au; ➍–➎), a fine B&B with many original 1916 features, a huge balcony and friendly owners. On the southeastern edge of town *Lake Talbot Caravan Park*, Gordon Street (☎02/6959 1302, ⓦwww.laketalbot.com; camping $18, powered site $21, cabins ➊, en-suite cabin ➌–➎), offers quiet and shady camping that's well positioned above the lake and pool.

Daytime **eating** is good at *Café G*, 124A East St, with tasty sandwiches, wraps and smoothies served either inside or out on the back deck. For a reliable evening meal try the *Ex-Servicemen's Club*, opposite the visitor centre on Bolton Street – but don't expect a cosy atmosphere.

Griffith

Citrus orchards line the way into **GRIFFITH**, 70km northwest of Narrandera, with a range of low hills in the background. The major centre of the MIA, it's known for its large **Italian population**, the descendants of immigrants who came in the 1920s, having already tried mining in Broken Hill, and again after World War II. Needless to say, excellent Italian cafés and restaurants line the tree-filled main street of Banna Avenue, and many **wineries** are run by Italian families. The city was laid out by **Walter Burley Griffin**, the landscape architect from Chicago who was also responsible for Canberra's confusing layout; although Griffith suffers from a similar charm deficit, it does have a rather spacious feel.

Arrival, information and accommodation

Only one **train** a week (on Sat) reaches Griffith, but Countrylink and Greyhound **buses** pull up outside the combined Griffith Travel and Transit Centre (☎02/6962 7199) and **visitor centre**, on the corner of Jondaryan and Banna avenues (daily 9am–5pm; ☎02/6962 4145, ⓦwww.griffith.com.au). For details of camping and bushwalking ask at the **NPWS office**, 200 Yambil St (Mon–Fri 8.30am–4.30pm; ☎02/6966 8100).

With virtually no public transport out to the wineries, if you arrive by bus you'll need to **rent a bike**, best done from Abest Bikes, 475 Banna Ave (☎02/6962 1234, ⓦhttp://abestbikes.com; $36 a day, $70 a week).

Accommodation

There's a reasonable range of places to stay both in town and scattered around about, much of the cheaper stuff geared towards temporary workers.

The Clarendon 22 Palla St ☎02/6962 5284. This central, classically decorated self-contained bedroom apartment comes with breakfast hamper, private gazebo and a pool. [6]

Globe Backpackers 26 Wayeela St ☎02/6962 3619, 🌐www.theglobebackpackersgriffith.com.au. Very central and reasonably well-equipped hostel in a brick house with weekly rates from $110. Four-bed dorms and good work connections. Dorms $25

Griffith Tourist Caravan Park 919 Willandra Ave, 2km south of the centre ☎02/6964 2144. Popular with fruit-pickers and other labourers, with a large tennis court and well-kept amenities. Camping $20, powered site $22, cabins [2]

Lake Wayngan 12km north of town. Free lakeside camping for up to three nights with toilets, water and cold showers.

Myalbangera Outstation Rankin Springs Rd, 12km northeast of town ☎0428 130 093, 🌐http://myalbangera.com. Great hostel set amid farmland with comfy four-bed dorms and doubles, large modern kitchen and well set up for organizing work. $130 a week in a dorm, $250 for a double room. Dorms $25, rooms [1]

Victoria Hotel 384 Banna Ave ☎02/6962 1299, 🌐www.hotelvictoria.com.au. The best option in the centre of town, with basic rooms, a covered courtyard, and quality bistro meals downstairs. [5]

Wilga Park Cottage Coghlan Rd ☎02/6963 6527, 🌐www.ingleden.com.au. One two-bedroom and one three-bedroom cottage, both fully self-contained, prettily set on a working farm 15km southeast of town. [5]

The town and wineries

The best way to get an overview of the area is to head for **Scenic Hill**, the escarpment that forms the northern boundary of the city, where the **Sir Dudley de Chair's Lookout** gives a panoramic view of the horticultural enterprises below. Immediately beneath this rocky outcrop is the **Hermit's Cave**, where Valerio Recetti, an Italian immigrant, lived alone and undetected for ten years, working only at night and early in the morning with Stone-Age tools to create a home in the caves. **Pioneer Park** (daily 9.30am–4pm; $9), in an extensive bushland setting 2km north from the city centre, has 36 buildings recreating the era of the early MIA, and also houses the **Italian Museum** (same hours and entrance fee), which gives an overview of early immigrants and their traditions.

There are eighteen **wineries** in the area surrounding Griffith, thirteen of which are open to the public (some by appointment only). The oldest winery, McWilliam's Hanwood Estate (Mon–Fri 10am–4pm, Sat 10am–5pm; 🌐www.mcwilliams.com.au), was established in 1913 and holds tastings in a building resembling a wine barrel; while one of the more celebrated vineyards is De Bortoli Wines (Mon–Sat 9am–5pm, Sun 9am–4pm; 🌐www.debortoli.com.au) at De Bortoli Road, Bilbul, the birthplace of the sensational Noble One Botrytis Semillon dessert wine, which has raked in over three hundred gold medals across the world. For a complete overview of the wineries, head for the visitor centre.

Eating and drinking

There's no shortage of good Italian places to **eat** and **drink** on Banna Avenue. For gourmet picnic supplies, Riverina Grove on Whybrow Street is a fantastic deli stocking a wide range of regional produce like plums in port, local salami and cheeses.

Bertoldo's Pasticceria 324 Banna Ave. Cheap, bakery-style place with inexpensive and filling pasta dishes and wraps for lunch. Also has a superb selection of mouthwatering *gelati*.

Clock 239 Banna Ave ☎02/6962 7111, 🌐www.theclockgriffith.com.au. Right by the town clocktower, this classy, contemporary Italian restaurant dishes up great pizza ($15–25) and pasta ($19)

along with the likes of chicken supreme with a salad of Cannellini beans, grilled aubergine, yogurt and dukkah ($28). Lunch and dinner Tues–Sat.
Coro Club 20–26 Harward Rd. Large, cheap portions of Chinese food if you've had enough of Italian. Lunch and dinner Wed–Sun.
Gemini Hotel 201 Banna Ave. The town convenes here to down a schooner or sip a cocktail while listening to live music most weekends.

Il Corso Café & Pizza 232 Banna Ave. Popular mainstream Italian serving good trad pizza (plus a few gourmet concoctions), pasta and reliable *secondi piatti* for $22–25. Licensed. Takeaway available.
Vita's 252–254 Banna Ave. One of the more upmarket Italian places, serving risotto, pasta and seafood – no pizza though. The covered terrace is a good place for people-watching. Closed Sun.

Around Griffith

The **Cocoparra National Park**, 25km northeast of Griffith (always open; free), is draped across the wooded Cocoparra Range, the blue-green cypresses contrasting with the classic red Aussie rocks. The park has several walking tracks, most taking less than an hour, though **Mount Brogden** (4km; 3hr) is moderately difficult and turns back at a trig point with long views to Murrumbidgee River. NPWS in Griffith has info on walks and drive-in **camping**, principally at Woolshed Flat (free), on a forest road off Whitton Stock Route.

Much further away, on the flat plains 185km northwest of town, is **Willandra National Park** (always open; $7 per vehicle for 24hr), reached via **Hillston** (64km from Griffith) on the unsealed Hillston–Mossgiel road. The park was created in 1971 from a section of the vast Big Willandra pastoral station, a famous stud-merino property founded in the 1860s. As well as allowing you to experience the semi-arid riverine plains country at close quarters, a visit to the 1918 **homestead** gives an insight into station life and the wool industry. Wet weather makes all the roads to Willandra impassable, so check before you head out with the **NPWS** in Griffith or at Ⓦ www.carrathool.nsw.gov.au/roads/roads.htm. The NPWS also handles **accommodation** bookings for shared rooms in a fully self-contained cottage ($50 for up to 4 people) and the former Men's Quarters ($25 per room for up to 4) with shared kitchen and shower block. There's also drive-in camping ($3 per person) near the homestead.

You'll need your own transport to get to both parks: take extra supplies in case you get rained in.

Hay

Heading west from the MIA it is a lengthy run along the Sturt Highway to Mildura and Wentworth. Break the journey at the modest town of **Hay**, 120km west of Griffith, by spending an hour at **Shear Outback: The Australian Shearers' Hall of Fame**, at the junction of Sturt and Cobb highways (daily 9am–5pm; $15; Ⓦ www.shearoutback.com.au). With its clear and vibrant descriptions of Outback station life and the history of Australian pastoralism, this striking, interpretive centre-cum-museum perfectly complements a visit to the great former sheep stations at Willandra or Kinchega national parks. Along with exhibits on sheepshearing technology there's wool art, a woolshed relocated from Murray Downs (120km to the southwest), and, of course, shearing demos (daily 10.30am, 1pm & 3.30pm).

The New England Plateau

The **New England Plateau** rises parallel to the coast, extending from the northern end of the Hunter Valley, some 200km north of Sydney, all the way to the Queensland border. At the top it's between 1000m and 1400m above sea level, and on the eastern edge an escarpment falls away steeply towards the coast. This eastern rim consists of precipitous cliff-faces, deep gorges, thickly forested valleys, streams and mighty waterfalls, and because of its inaccessibility remains a largely undisturbed wilderness. On the plateau itself the scene is far more pastoral, as sheep and cattle graze on the undulating highland. Because of the altitude, the **climate** up here is fundamentally different from the subtropical coast, a mere 150km or so away: winters are cold and frosty, with occasional snowfalls, while in summer the fresh, dry air can offer welcome relief after the coastal heat and humidity. Even during a heatwave the nights will be pleasantly cool – perhaps attracting the mainly Scottish immigrants who, despite the name, transformed the New England highlands into pastures in the nineteenth century.

The **New England Highway**, one of the main links between Brisbane and Sydney, passes all the major towns – **Tamworth**, **Armidale**, **Glen Innes** and **Tenterfield** – from where scenic side-roads branch off towards the coast. Farms and stations all over the highlands provide farmstay accommodation, offering horseriding and other activities. The area is well served by **bus**: Greyhound Australia (T13 20 30) has daily services between Sydney or Canberra and Brisbane, and between Brisbane and Melbourne, both via New England. Keans Travel (T02/6543 1322) runs once a week between Port Macquarie and Scone via Nambucca Heads, Coffs Harbour, Bellingen, Dorrigo, Armidale, Uralla, Walcha and Tamworth. **Trains** also serve the region: Sydney's Cityrail trains go as far north as Scone, while Countrylink has services to Tamworth where the line forks, continuing to Moree to the west, and, to the east, Tenterfield and points north.

The Upper Hunter Valley

The upper end of the **Hunter Valley** is Australia's main horse-breeding area – indeed it claims to deal in as much horseflesh as anywhere in the world – with at least thirty stud farms; sires are flown in from all over the world to breed with the local mares. There are cattle- and sheep-breeding stations up here too, while the fertile soils of the Upper Hunter also yield a harvest of cereals and fruits including, of course, grapes – see box, pp.194–195 for a sampling of Hunter Valley wineries.

The pretty township of **SCONE** is at the centre of the Hunter Valley horse trade; you can get further details of the business from the **visitor centre** on the corner of Susan and Kelly streets (daily 9am–5pm; T02/6545 1526, Wwww.upperhuntertourism.com.au), which also has an excellent internet café. The best time to visit is during the **Scone Horse Festival** – ten days in the middle of May – which features local prize specimens in horse shows, rodeos and races including the Scone Cup; book your accommodation well in advance. Any time of year, ask at the tourist information centre about regular races held in the area, and visits to the studs (particularly during breeding season, September to Christmas).

Lake Glenbawn, 15km east of Scone, makes for a pleasant excursion. The dam holds back the waters of the Upper Hunter, storing up to 750 billion litres for irrigation purposes. Recreation facilities at the reserve here include a caravan park and boat rental: the lake is great for water-skiing, canoeing, sailing and fishing. You can continue past the dam and climb to the plateau of the Barrington Tops (see p.333) to the national park of the same name.

Northeast of Scone is polo country, the haunt of mega-rich Australians. If you fancy seeing the elitist sport in action, there are polo grounds at **Gundy** and at **Ellerston**. Heading on towards the heart of the New England Plateau you'll pass **Burning Mountain**, about 20km north of Scone, near the village of Wingen. The smoking vents don't indicate volcanic activity but rather a seam of coal burning 30m under the surface: the fire was ignited naturally, perhaps by a lightning strike or spontaneous combustion, over a thousand years ago. The area, protected as a nature reserve, can be reached via a signposted **walking trail** that starts at the picnic grounds at the foot of the hill, just off the New England Highway; pick up the informative NPWS guide to the area's walking tracks from any NPWS office; the nearest is in Scone. You might also see aquatic fossils on your walk – this area was once under the ocean. Fourteen kilometres north of Wingen, **MURRU-RUNDI** marks the end of the Upper Hunter Valley. It's a scenic spot, enclosed by the Liverpool Ranges; the landmark *Café Telegraph* here makes a cheerful refreshment stop, and has seats outside in the garden with the creek flowing past.

Practicalities

Countrylink **trains** run daily from Sydney to Scone, while Cityrail has three services per day (change in Hamilton for Sydney); the trip is around four hours. Greyhound **buses** stop at Murrurundi and Scone en route between Sydney and Brisbane.

Places to **stay** in the area are widely scattered. By far the most atmospheric, located between Gundy and Ellerston, is 🏚 *Belltrees* (☎02/6546 1123, ⓦwww .belltrees.com), the family estate of the White family, who gave the world the Nobel Prize-winning novelist Patrick White. The station's collection of buildings includes the 1832 Semphill Cottage, set among pepper trees; there's even a small school, established in 1879. You can stay at the country house next door to the Whites' residence (❽) or in self-contained **cottages** sleeping four (❾). Polo tuition can be arranged and dinner is available for $45, but it's unlicensed so you'll need to BYO.

Right in Scone, the *Royal Hotel-Motel* on St Aubins Street (☎02/6545 1722; ❷–❸) offers simple pub accommodation and fancier motel units – it also serves good counter meals.

In nearby Aberdeen, 10km south on the New England Highway, is *Segenhoe B&B*, at 55 Main Rd (☎02/6543 7382, ⓦwww.segenhoeinn.com; ❸), a charming sandstone residence from the early 1800s with large, period-style rooms, a white-linen, silver-service restaurant, and coffee shop serving high tea; the staff can arrange a host of activities. Also highly recommended is the forested mountain-retreat *Craigmhor* (☎02/6543 6394, ⓦwww.craigmhor.com .au; ❸), on Upper Rouchel Road in the foothills of the Barrington Tops, 48km east of Aberdeen, which, in addition to its tranquil surrounds, only accommodates one booking at a time. Meals are available on request.

If you're hungry for scones in Scone, try the old-fashioned *Asser House Café* at 202 Kelly St. Otherwise, smart new daytime spots in town include *The Larda* (closed Sun), a stylish chocolate-toned gourmet deli/café two blocks north at 122 Kelly St, or, around the corner at 108 Liverpool St, *Kerv* (closed Sun). Scone's finest **food** is at 🏚 *Canter*, 109 Susan St (Wed–Sat 8am–4pm & from 6pm, Sun 9am–3pm, closed Mon & Tues; ☎02/6545 2286,

@www.canterrestaurant.com.au), next door to the visitor centre, whose Mod Oz cuisine ranges from the likes of tempura-battered zucchini flowers filled with white beans and gorgonzola to crispy-skin barramundi with pickled green pawpaw, and sticky date pudding with butterscotch sauce for dessert. Be sure to peek at its onsite boutique, *William's Workshop* (Thurs–Sun 10am–4pm), in an original worker's cottage in the back garden, selling retro tin toys and contemporary arts and crafts.

Tamworth and around

TAMWORTH – on the New England Highway, 130km north of Scone – is also known as the "City of Lights" because it was the first in Australia to be fitted with electric street lighting, in 1888. To most Australians, however, Tamworth means **country music** – it's a sort of antipodean Nashville.

Arrival and information

Countrylink **train** services run daily between Sydney and Armidale via Tamworth, and both Greyhound and Kean's Travel **buses** pass through on a daily basis, the former en route between Sydney and Brisbane. At the intersection of Peel Street, the town's main drag, with Murray Street, Tamworth's guitar-shaped **visitor centre** (daily 9am–5pm; ☎02/6767 5300, @www .visittamworth.com) can give you information on local bus services to Nundle. At the time of writing, a new visitor centre was about to open in Nundle – check with the Tamworth centre for updates.

Accommodation

There's a fair spread of **accommodation** in Tamworth, including a string of **motels** on the New England Highway outside town, though you might have trouble finding a room during the festival if you haven't booked ahead.

Tamworth

Paradise Caravan Park Peel St ☎&℉02/6766 3120, @www.paradisetouristpark.com.au. The closest place to town for campers and caravanners, on the river about 5min walk from the centre. Camping $21–30, powered sites $21–36, cabins ❹–❺
Quality Hotel Powerhouse Corner of East St and Armidale Rd ☎02/6766 7000, @www .qualityhotelpowerhouse.com.au. This smart motel has a corporate feel and five-star facilities, including room service, gym, swimming pool and sauna. ❻
Tamworth YHA 169 Marius St ☎02/6761 2600, @www.yha.com.au. Bang opposite the train station with well-maintained, if old, facilities. Dorms $23–28, rooms ❷

Around Tamworth

Austin Caravan Park 4km north of town off the New England Hwy ☎02/6762 2380, @www .austintouristpark.com.au. Occupies a riverside spot with a postage-stamp of a pool and a

children's playground. Camping $23, powered site $28.50, cabins ❷–❹
Jenkins St Guest House 85 Jenkins St, Nundle ☎02/6769 3239, @www.jenkinsstguesthouse .com.au. Beautiful place with polished-wood floors, open fires in winter, fresh flowers in the rooms, trout fishing and croquet. Three of its six rooms have en suites; all rates include a country breakfast. ❻–❼
Leconfield 50km east of Tamworth ☎02/6769 4328, @www.leconfield.com. If you want a taste of Australian country living, this place offers a five-day residential Jackeroo and Jilleroo school ($550) where you learn to ride and groom horses, shear and throw fleeces, lasso, whip crack and muster. It can arrange pick-ups from *Tamworth YHA*.
Peel Inn Jenkins St, Nundle ☎02/6769 3377, @www.peelinn.com.au. Historic 1860-built pub flanked by a six-metre-deep wraparound veranda, run by the fourth and fifth generations of the Schofield family, with antique-filled rooms (some en suite) and hearty meals. ❸–❹

The town and around

The twelve-metre-high golden guitar in front of the **Golden Guitar Complex** (daily 9am–5pm; $8; ⓦ www.biggoldenguitar.com.au), on the southern edge of town, sums up the town's role as the country-and-western capital of Australasia. Inside the complex you'll find waxwork figures of the great Australian country stars such as Chad Morgan, Buddy Williams, Smoky Dawson and his horse Flash, Slim Dusty, Reg Lindsay and Tex Morton. In the second half of January each year, fans from all over Australia and beyond descend on the town for the ten-day **Tamworth Country Music Festival**. Every pub, club and hall in town hosts gigs, record launches and bush poetry, culminating in the presentation of "Golden Guitars", the Australian Country Music Awards – for info and bookings, contact the visitor centre (see opposite). Inside the visitor centre itself, you can "Walk a Country Mile" at the exhibition of the same name, with interactive displays, film and music clips and old albums (same hours as visitor centre; $5). There's yet more musical memorabilia at the corner of Brisbane Street and Kable Avenue, where the **Hands of Fame** cornerstone bears the palm-prints of various country greats.

Don't give up on Tamworth if country music isn't your thing. The **Powerstation Museum** at 216 Peel St (Wed–Sat 9am–1pm; $3.50) celebrates those pioneering street lights, and there are numerous **art galleries** and crafts studios around town – the **Tamworth Regional Gallery**, above the library at 466 Peel St (Tues–Fri 10am–5pm, Sat 10am–4pm; free; ⓦ www.tamworthregionalgallery .com.au), has frequently changing exhibitions, with good contemporary and Aboriginal art. Natural attractions include the **Oxley Lookout and Nature Reserve** at the end of White Street, with panoramic views of the city and the Peel River Valley; and Lake Keepit, 56km northwest of the city, where you can rent boats to mess about on the water.

Nundle

The former gold-mining township of **NUNDLE** lies some 60km southeast of town via a sealed loop road off the highway in the "hills of gold" – people still visit with picks, shovels and sieves in the hope of striking it lucky. If you want to join them, drop by the General Store on Jenkins Street; they'll point you in the right direction to start digging.

Eating, drinking and entertainment

Tamworth isn't a gourmand's paradise but you'll find decent pubs, restaurants and cafés scattered around. Despite the town's affinity with country music, surprisingly it's rarely performed in the **clubs and pubs** outside festival time. Various other genres are performed by bands and DJs from Thursday to Saturday at the town's major venue, the *Imperial Hotel*, on the corner of Brisbane and Marius streets. The *Central Hotel*, on the corner of Peel and Brisbane streets, has bands from Wednesday to Saturday. Live acts also occasionally hit the stage of *West's Diggers*.

Inland Café 407 Peel St. A busy lunch spot with cakes, focaccia and pasta, plus good coffee.

Jack Style 15 Fitzroy St. Large and inexpensive Thai restaurant with Buddhas hanging on the wall.

Joe Maguires 148 Peel St. Old-fashioned watering hole at the northern end of Peel St with top-notch pub grub including chargrills.

Quality Hotel Powerhouse Corner of East St and Armidale Rd. Good-quality modern Australian mains ($30) in a very genteel setting.

West's Diggers Club Corner of Bourke St and Kable Ave. This local landmark houses three separate, inexpensive and filling eateries: a steakhouse upstairs, and a Mexican restaurant and a café downstairs.

Armidale and around

Australia's highest city, at 980m, **ARMIDALE** is home to the **University of New England**, which, together with a couple of famous boarding schools, gives an unexpectedly academic feel to a place so far up-country. Significantly cooler than the surrounding plains, Armidale is also a place of considerable natural beauty, especially in autumn, when its many parks are transformed into a sea of red and golden leaves.

Arrival, information and accommodation

Armidale has a helpful **visitor centre** at 82 Marsh St (daily 9am–5pm; ☏02/6772 4655, ⊛www.armidaletourism.com.au), which adjoins the **bus** terminal, from where Countrylink, Greyhound and Kean's Travel services arrive and depart. There's also a daily **train** to/from Sydney. Plenty of places offer car rental, among them Budget, at the airport (☏02/6772 5872), and Realistic Car Rentals, at Armidale Exhaust Centre on the corner of Rusden and Dangar streets (☏02/6772 8078). Bikes can be rented from Armidale Bicycle Centre, 244 Beardy St (☏02/6772 3718). For taxis, call Armidale Radio Taxis (☏13 10 08).

Accommodation

Due to its size and central location on the New England Highway, Armidale has plenty of accommodation to choose from. Standards are high, and competition keeps prices reasonable.

Glenhope Homestead Red Gum Lane ☏02/6772 1940, ⊛www.glenhopealpacas.com. For a real country feel, head 4km northwest of the city to this working alpaca farm. The self-contained doubles with kitchenette are modern, and boast a scenic location overlooking the farm. ❺–❻

Hideaway Motor Inn 70 Glen Innes Rd ☏02/6772 5177. Right in the centre of town, this clean motel is the cheapest of its kind, with small but well-furnished rooms. ❹

Lindsay House 128 Faulkner St ☏02/6771 4554, ⊛www.lindsayhouse.com.au. This nineteenth-century Tudor-style residence is the nicest place to stay in Armidale, with large, antique-filled en-suite rooms, a bar and a garden. ❺–❼

Pembroke Tourist and Leisure Park 39 Waterfall Way, 2km east of town ☏02/6772 6470, ⊛www .pembroke.com.au. This leisure-park complex has good facilities including a swimming pool and tennis court, and is also home to a small YHA dormitory. Dorms $29.50, camping $22, powered site $27, en-suite site $33, on-site vans ❶–❷, cabins ❸–❺

Poppy's Cottage Dangarsleigh Rd ☏02/6775 1277, ⊛www.poppyscottage.com.au. B&B set in a farm cottage 5min drive from town and close to a local vineyard. ❻

Tattersalls Hotel 147 Beardy St ☏02/6772 2247. Inexpensive and good-value singles and doubles in a central yet quiet location. ❷–❸

The Town

The central pedestrian mall, **Beardy Street**, is flanked by quaint Australian country pubs with wide, iron-lace verandas – on the last Sunday of the month the street comes alive with an extensive morning **market** complete with buskers. The excellent **New England Regional Art Museum** on Kentucky Street (Tues–Fri 10am–5pm, Sat & Sun 9am–4pm; free; ⊛www.neram.com .au) includes fine surrealist work by Clifford Bayliss among others, displays by Arthur Streeton and Tom Roberts, plus big-name temporary exhibits from Sydney (most $5–10). Next door, the arresting modern building with the distinctive ochre-coloured tin roof is the indigenous-run **Aboriginal Centre and Keeping Place** (Mon–Fri 9am–4pm, Sat & Sun 10am–2pm; ☏02/6771

1242; free), an educational, visual and performing-arts centre which has displays of artefacts and interpretive material, plus special exhibitions. You might also want to visit the **Folk Museum**, at the corner of Rusden and Faulkner streets (daily 1–4pm; donation), which has a collection of artefacts from the New England region and displays on local history. There's more history at the **Saumarez Homestead** (entry to homestead by guided tour only at 10.30am & 2pm Sat, Sun & public holidays, closed mid-June to Sept; $8) behind the airport, a perfectly preserved dwelling dating from the 1800s. A two-hour **free bus tour** of the city with Heritage Tours departs from the visitor centre daily at 10am (bookings essential), or you can pick up the self-drive leaflet from the centre.

One of the best ways to get around town is by **bike**: there's a signposted city tour, as well as a bike path to the **university campus**, 5km northwest of the city. On the campus are two small specialized museums (Antiquity and Zoology; Mon–Fri 9am–4.30pm; both free), a kangaroo and deer park, and the historic Booloominbah homestead, built in the 1880s as a fashionable gentlemen's residence and now housing the university's principal administration office.

Eating, drinking and nightlife

Many of Armidale's appealing range of **restaurants** are found around Beardy and Marsh streets, such as the venerable *Jean Pierre's* on Marsh Street, serving Chateaubriand and filet mignon (closed Sun & Mon). Sophisticated **cafés** along the Beardy Street Mall include *Rumours*, with strong coffee and a range of healthy meals; there's also superb daytime fare at the Art Museum (see opposite; café closed Mon & Tues). Inexpensive **counter meals** are served at many of the grand old pubs on Beardy Street, including the *New England Hotel* and the *Imperial*. The visitor centre's dining guide leaflet contains a complete list. For term-time **entertainment** (March–Nov) head to the *St Kilda*, *Tattersalls*, *New England* or *Wicklows* hotels in the centre for live music on Friday and Saturday nights.

Around Armidale

Armidale makes a good staging post north through the **New England Plains** or east to the coast through some of Australia's most beautiful national parks. The main access road, the sealed World Heritage drive **Waterfall Way** (Ⓦwww.visitwaterfallway.com.au), travels to Coffs Harbour via hundreds of kilometres of rainforest roads, waterfalls and lookouts. The exceptional **New England National Park**, 85km east on the Waterfall Way, and the several patchwork sections of the **Oxley Wild Rivers**, **Guy Fawkes River**, and **Cathedral Rock** national parks around it are full of ancient ferns, towering canopy trees, gorges and spectacular **waterfalls** (although the falls can diminish to a trickle during prolonged dry spells). The most impressive are the **Wollomombi Falls**, among the highest in Australia, plunging 225m into a gorge just over 40km east of Armidale, off the road to Dorrigo. Nearby are the **Chandler Falls**, while **Ebor Falls**, a stunning double drop of the Guy Fawkes River, can be viewed from platforms just off Waterfall Way, another 40km beyond Wollomombi. Between Wollomombi and Ebor, **Point Lookout** in the New England National Park offers a truly wonderful panoramic view across the forested ranges – you'd be forgiven for thinking you were in the middle of the Amazon. The road to the lookout is unsealed gravel, but is usually in reasonable condition, and there are simple **cabins** (from $35 per person, per night; minimum stay 2 nights) and bush **campsites** ($5 per person per night): book

▲ Ebor Falls

through the NPWS in Armidale (☎02/6776 0000). The rest of the park is virtually inaccessible wilderness.

URALLA, 23km south of Armidale, is another old gold-town, with a small but thriving population of around two-and-a-half thousand. The Historic Building Walk takes you past the town's highlights, including **McCrossin's Mill Museum** (Mon–Fri noon–5pm, Sat & Sun 10am–5pm; $4), a historic red-brick, three-storey flour mill on Salisbury Street. Fossicking is possible at the old Rocky River diggings: the **visitor centre** on the New England Highway (daily 9.30am–4.30pm; ☎02/6778 4496, ⓦwww.uralla.com) rents equipment for $10 per day and can advise on accommodation in town.

Uralla's other claim to fame is the ongoing mystery surrounding **Captain Thunderbolt**, a bushranger who terrorized the gold-rich New England region in the nineteenth century when the town was on the major Sydney–Brisbane route. A charismatic fellow, he promised his Aboriginal wife never to shoot anyone, and he never did. The police, however, had made no such promises, and Thunderbolt was apparently killed here in 1870 – although evidence suggests the corpse was actually his brother and that Thunderbolt escaped to North America. There's a bronze statue of the bushranger and his horse at the corner of Bridge and Salisbury streets.

About 20km south of Armidale towards Walcha is **Dangars Lagoon**, a wetland region visited by more than a hundred different kinds of bird; a hide is provided for spotters. **Dangars Falls** and a network of twenty walking tracks and lookouts around **Dangars Gorge** are only 22km from Armidale on a partially sealed road. Beyond these, about 20km east of Walcha, a turn-off from the Oxley Highway leads to Apsley Gorge and two more waterfalls in another section of the Oxley Wild Rivers National Park. The town of **WALCHA** (pronounced *Wol*-ka), 65km southwest of Armidale, is surrounded by national parks, making it a great base for nature freaks and trout anglers. For more information on the area, head for the **visitor centre** on Fitzroy St (Mon–Fri 9am–4.30pm, Sat & Sun 9am–4pm; ☎02/6774 2460, ⓦwww.walchansw.com.au). West of Armidale, 27km along the Bundarra Road, is the **Mount Yarrowyck**

Nature Reserve, where an Aboriginal cave-painting site can be accessed via a three-kilometre circuit walk.

Glen Innes and around

GLEN INNES, the next major stop north on the New England Highway, about 100km north of Armidale, is a decent-sized town in a beautiful setting. Although agriculture is still important up here, you begin to see more and more evidence of the gemfields – sapphires are big business (the visitor centre, below, can advise on fossicking opportunities), as, to a lesser extent, is tin mining. In the centre, on **Grey Street** especially, numerous century-old public buildings and parks have been renovated and spruced up, and there's some fine country architecture, including a couple of large corner pubs with iron-lace verandas.

The **Land of the Beardies History House** (Mon–Fri 10am–noon & 1–4pm, Sat & Sun 1–4pm; $6; @www.beardieshistoryhouse.info), in the town's first hospital on the corner of Ferguson Street and West Avenue, displays pioneer relics, period room settings and a reconstructed slab hut. The name alludes to the two hairy stockmen who settled the area in the nineteenth century, and the title is one of which the town is proud; the **Land of the Beardies Festival** is held in early November, with everything from a beard-growing contest to dances, parades and arts-and-crafts exhibits. The **Scottish legacy** of the original settlers is reflected in the name of the town itself and in many of its streets, which are rendered in both English and Gaelic. The local granite **Australian Standing Stones** at Martins Lookout, Watsons Drive, are based on the Ring of Brodgar in Scotland and honour the "contribution of the Celtic races to Australia's development". The stones are the site of the **Australian Celtic Festival** (@www.australiancelticfestival.com) during the first weekend of May, when locals dust off their bagpipes, brave haggis, stage highland games and see the Celtic slaves take on the Roman legions.

While you're in the area, you might also consider a horseback pub-crawl with **Pub Crawls on Horseback** (T02/6732 1599, @www.pubcrawlsonhorseback.com.au), who run half-hour to four-day horse-riding adventures through the bush with overnight stops at traditional Aussie pubs – a weekend trip costs $395, all-inclusive.

Practicalities

Greyhound **buses** and Countrylink services stop in town en route between Sydney and Melbourne. The **visitor centre** is at 152 Church St (Mon–Fri 9am–5pm, Sat & Sun 9am–3pm; T02/6732 2400, @www.gleninnestourism.com), as the New England Highway is called as it passes through town; it has a sapphire shop attached and can help book **accommodation**. Numerous motels line Church Street, of which the best value is *Alpha Motel* at no. 60 (T02/6732 2688; ❸–❹) – don't be fooled by the dated exterior; inside rooms are spacious and stylishly renovated, with a large pool, free broadband internet and free breakfast. Wildlife spotters should head to *Craigieburn Tourist Park*, 2km south of town off the New England Highway (T02/6732 1283; camping $20, powered site $25, cabins ❹), set in lush forest.

For **food**, head to Grey Street, where you can choose between the *Tea and Coffee Shop*, a cosy tearoom with loads of pancakes, an array of interesting sandwiches, savoury croissants and hot breakfasts; modern Australian cuisine at

The Myall Creek massacre

In the first decades of the nineteenth century, when European settlers started to move up to the highlands and to use Aboriginal-occupied land on the plateau as sheep and cattle pasture, many of the local Aborigines fought back. Time and again bloody skirmishes flared up, though most were never mentioned in pioneer circles and have subsequently been erased from public memory. The **Myall Creek massacre** is one of the few that has found a place in the history of white Australia.

For Aboriginal people, expulsion from the lands of their ancestors amounted to spiritual as well as physical dispossession, and they resisted as best they could: white stockmen staying in huts far away from pioneer townships or homesteads feared for their lives. In 1837 and 1838, Aborigines repeatedly ambushed and killed stockmen near the Gwydir and Namoi rivers. Then, during the absence of the overseer at Myall Creek Station, near present-day Inverell, twelve farm hands organized a raid in retribution, killing 28 Aborigines. In court, the farm hands were acquitted – public opinion saw nothing wrong with their deed, and neither did the jury. The case was later taken up again, however, and seven of the participants in the massacre were sentenced to death on the gallows.

the *Tasting Room* (closed Mon & Sun); or a hefty, bargain-priced feed at the *Imperial Hotel*.

Inverell

The area between Glen Innes and **INVERELL**, 67km to the west and serviced daily from Tamworth by Countrylink, is one huge gemfield. Industrial diamonds, garnets, topaz, zircons and over half the world's sapphires are mined in the area – Inverell is in fact known as "Sapphire City", and at the **Dejon Sapphire Centre**, on the Gwydir Highway 18km east of town, you can watch gems being washed, sorted and cut (daily 9am–5pm; free). The showroom has a display of sapphires in 155 colours, from pale blue and green to gold, lemon and pink.

If you want to try your own luck, you'll need to contact the **visitor centre** on Campbell Street (Mon–Fri 9am–5pm, Sat & Sun 9am–2pm; ☎02/6728 8161, ⓦwww.inverell-online.com.au), which can direct you to the designated areas. If you decide to **stay**, try the *Royal Hotel* on Byron Street (☎02/6722 2811; ❸), which has clean rooms with shared facilities, open fires, air conditioning and a restaurant; or the leafy *Sapphire City Caravan Park* on Moore Street (☎02/6722 1830; camping $14, powered site $18, cabins ❷–❹).

Tenterfield and around

Less than 20km from the Queensland border, the buzzing little town of **TENTERFIELD** marks the northern end of the New England Plateau. From here you can go straight to Ballina on the coast or continue north on the New England Highway. Settled by 61 German families, today Tenterfield honours its Germanic origins with a week-long **beer festival** in the March of odd-numbered years. Tenterfield has a confirmed place in Australian history, being the birthplace of the **Australian Federation**. Its title was earned when the Prime Minister of New South Wales, Sir Henry Parkes, made his famous Federation speech here in 1889, advocating the union of the Australian colonies; twelve years later the **Commonwealth of Australia** was inaugurated.

The **Sir Henry Parkes museum** (daily 10am–4pm; $5) recalls the occasion, and you'll still see the federation flag flown around town. Tenterfield's other claim to fame is as the birthplace of **Peter Allen**, the flamboyant singer who penned the popular *Tenterfield Saddler* – the saddlery itself (Tues–Sun 10am–4pm; free) is on High Street with memorabilia on display and knowledgeable staff – and *I still call Australia home* (he moved to the USA).

Tenterfield's real attractions lie outside town. Just 30km to the northeast is **Bald Rock**, in the national park of the same name, which claims to be Australia's second-largest monolith after Uluru, but a grey-granite version, 213m high. You can walk up the northeast side to the summit, from where there are breathtaking panoramic views well into Queensland.

The excursion to Bald Rock combines nicely with a visit to the nearby 210-metre-high **Boonoo Boonoo Falls**, also set in a national park of the same name, which is home to endangered brush-tailed rock wallabies. The road is sealed as far as Bald Rock, but there's an unsealed road (usually passable in a 2WD) branching off before you reach the rock and running for around 12km to the falls. En route to Bald Rock on the left you'll pass **Thunderbolt's Hideout**, the rock shelter and stable of the bushranger Captain Thunderbolt (see p.338). Details are available from the **visitor centre**, 157 Rouse St (Mon–Fri 9.30am–5pm, Sat 9.30am–4.30pm, Sun 9.30am–4pm; ℡02/6736 1082, ⓦwww.tenterfield.com), which has some Peter Allen memorabilia of its own including a glittering pair of his maracas. To get to Tenterfield, use Greyhound from Brisbane or Sydney, or Countrylink from Armidale.

Accommodation in Tenterfield includes a wide range of motels, pubs and B&Bs as well as a handful of places to camp, including the showground (℡02/6736 3666; camping $10–14, powered site $16). The *Telegraph Hotel/Motel* on Manners Street (℡02/6736 2888; ❷–❸) is central, clean and has good counter meals, while the old, renovated *Tenterfield Tavern* on Rouse Street (℡02/6736 2888; ❹) has comfortable motel rooms behind the pub.

The northwest

From Dubbo, the **Newell Highway**, the main route from Melbourne to Brisbane, continues through the wheat plains of the northwest, their relentless flatness relieved by the ancient eroded mountain ranges of the **Warrumbungles**, near Coonabarabran, and **Mount Kaputar**, near Narrabri, with the Pillaga Scrub between the two towns. Clear skies and the lack of large towns make this an ideal area for stargazing, and large telescopes stare into space at both **Coonabarabran** and **Narrabri**. The thinly populated northwest is home to a relatively large number of Aboriginal people, particularly in the town of Moree, the area's largest. In 1971 Charles Perkins, an Aboriginal activist, led the **Freedom Ride**, a group of thirty people – mostly university students – who bussed through New South Wales on a mission to root out racism in the state. The biggest victory was in Moree itself when the riders, facing hostile townsfolk, broke the race bar by escorting Aboriginal children into the public swimming pool.

The **Namoi Valley** – extending from **Gunnedah**, just west of Tamworth, to Walgett – with its rich black soil is **cotton country**. Beyond Walgett, just off the Castlereagh Highway that runs from Dubbo, is **Lightning Ridge**, a scorching-hot opal-mining town relieved by hot artesian bore baths.

Coonabarabran and the Warrumbungles

People come to **COONABARABRAN** on the Castlereagh River, 160km north of Dubbo via the Newell Highway, to **gaze at stars** in the clear skies, or for bushwalking and climbing in the spectacular **Warrumbungles** mountain range 35km to the west.

By virtue of its proximity to the **Siding Spring Observatory Complex** (Mon–Fri 9.30am–4pm, Sat & Sun 10am–2pm; $5.50; Ⓦwww.siding springexploratory.com.au), perched high above the township on the edge of Warrumbungle National Park, Coonabarabran considers itself the astronomy capital of Australia. The skies are exceptionally clear out here, due to the dry climate and a lack of pollution and population. The giant 3.9-metre optical telescope (one of the largest in the world) can be viewed close up from an observation gallery, and there's an astronomy exhibition, complemented by hands-on exhibits and a film.

You can't actually view the stars at Siding Spring because, as a working observatory, it's closed at night. However, the aptly named Peter Starr, a retired Siding Spring astronomer, offers **star-gazing tours** by request (Ⓣ0488 425 112) utilizing his five telescopes. The one night of the year Siding Spring does open to the public is during October's ten-day **Festival of the Stars**, when you can also catch pub talks by astronomers, as well as markets and Coonabarabran's annual racing carnival.

Cultural tours focusing on the Gamilaroi Aboriginal history of the region are run by Ukerbarley Tours (Ⓣ02/6843 4446). Some 4km north of town on Dandry Road, boutique local winery **Coonandry Wines** (Ⓣ 02/6842 1649) specializes in Chardonnay and Cabernet Sauvignon and offers free tastings on Saturday and Sunday from 10am to 5pm.

In addition to the National Park Visitors Centre (see p.343), Coonabarabran has its own **visitor centre** on the Newell Highway, or John Street as it's called as it passes through town (daily 9am–5pm; Ⓣ02/6849 2144 or 1800 242 881, Ⓦwww.warrumbungleregion.com.au). Inside there's a display of ancient megafauna – the large animals that used to roam the continent before human habitation – including a diprotodon, a wombat the size of a hippo. Greyhound **buses** pass through town four times per week from Melbourne to Brisbane, while CountryLink has six services a week via Mudgee to/from Sydney (none on Sat).

Warrumbungle National Park

The rugged **Warrumbungles** are ancient mountains of volcanic origin with jagged cliffs, rocky pinnacles and crags jutting from the western horizon. The dry western plains and the moister environment of the east coast meet at these ranges, with plant and animal species from both habitats coexisting in the park. Resident fauna include four species of kangaroo, plus koalas and a variety of birds including wedgetail eagles, superb blue wrens, eastern spinebills and mountain galaxies.

Arrival, information and accommodation

There's **no public transport** to the Warrumbungles, so you'll need your own. The **National Park Visitor Centre** is in the park near the campsite (daily 9am–4pm; [T] 02/6825 4364, [W] www.nationalparks.nsw.gov.au). **Accommodation** in the national park itself is limited to **campsites** ($5 per person, powered site $10 per person plus $7 per vehicle), some of which have hot showers, electric barbecues and fireplaces (note that wood is not supplied, and while plenty of places sell it, there's a fine for collecting it in the park); and *Balor Hut*, an eight-bunk hut adjacent to the Breadknife ($5; mattresses aren't provided). Bookings aren't necessary for any of the sites, but you may need to book the hut; reservations can be made at the National Park Visitors Centre. Anyone planning to stay in the park will need to bring provisions. There are plenty of alternative **accommodation** options in town.

Accommodation in the park

Tibuc Farm Timor Rd, 16km from town [T] 02/6842 1740, [W] www.coonabarabran.com/tibuc. Nestled under Bulleamble Mountain, with three rustic, self-contained cabins varying from the decently equipped to the extremely basic (cold water only and no power). If you're not bringing your own linen, mention it when booking. Sleeps four. [4]–[5]

Warrumbungles Mountain Motel Timor Rd, 9km from town en route to the park [T] 02/6842 1832, [W] www.warrumbungle.com. Set in bushland on the Castlereagh River. Rooms (BYO linen) have extra bunks and kitchens; there's also a small saltwater pool and facilities for tennis and basketball. Dorms $19 (groups), cabins & motel [3]

Accommodation in town

Acacia Motor Lodge John St [T] 02/6842 1922, [W] www.acaciamotorlodge.com.au. The flashest place in town, with plush furnishings, broadband internet, and spas in some rooms. [5]–[6]

All Travellers Motor Inn John St [T] 02/6842 1133, [W] www.alltravellers.com.au. Modern brick-and-timber motel with spacious rooms (one wheelchair-accessible) and a cooling swimming pool. [4]–[5]

El Paso Motel Newell Highway, 1km from the centre [T] 02/6842 1722. One of the cheaper places to stay, but with good facilities including a large pool and licensed restaurant. [4]

Imperial Hotel John St [T] 02/6842 1023, [E] imphotel@tpg.com.au. Excellent hotel which has a guest lounge, kitchenette, very reasonable singles and doubles (some en suite), a huge veranda with tables and armchairs and cooked breakfasts on weekdays. [1]–[2]

John Oxley Caravan Park 1.5km along the Oxley Hwy [T] 02/6842 1635. Shady and relaxing caravan park, one of two in town. $17–20, powered site $21–26, cabins [2]–[4]

The park

The **Warrumbungle National Park** ("crooked mountains") was once bordered by three different language groups – the Kamilaroi, the Weilwan and the Kawambarai – and evidence of past Aboriginal habitation here is common, with stone flakes used to make tools indicating old campsites. The park is particularly spectacular in spring when wild flowers in the sandstone areas bloom. Remember to bring plenty of water when walking in summer and warm clothing in winter as nights can be chilly and snow is not uncommon.

The **National Park Visitors Centre** (see above) has hands-on displays and detailed maps of walking tracks. The wheelchair-accessible bitumen **Gurianawa Track** makes a short circuit around the centre and overlooks the flats where eastern grey kangaroos gather at dusk. Another good introduction to the park is the short **White Gum Lookout Walk** (1km), with panoramic views over the ranges that are especially dramatic at sunset. However, the ultimate – for the reasonably fit only – is the 14.5-kilometre (roughly 5hr) **Grand High Tops Trail** along the main ridge and back. The walk begins at the kangaroo-filled Camp Pincham and follows the flat floor of Spirey Creek through open forests full of colourful rosellas and lorikeets, and lizards basking on rocks. As the trail climbs, there are views of the three-hundred-metre-high Belougery Spire, and more scrambling gets you to the foot of the **Breadknife**, the park's most famous feature, a 2.5-metre-wide rock flake thrusting 90m up into the sky. From here the main track heads on to the rocky slabs of the Grand High Tops, with tremendous views of most of the surrounding peaks. Experienced walkers could carry on to climb Bluff Mountain and then head west for Mount Exmouth (1205m), the park's highest peak; both are great spots from which to watch the sunrise. During school holidays, the visitor centre runs a range of activities including bird- and flower-identification, caving and events for kids, mostly costing around $5. **Rock climbers** are allowed to climb anywhere except the Breadknife; permits are required.

Eating

Most places to **eat** are on John Street in town: the bright and airy *Jolly Cauli* offers a wide choice of dishes, delicious coffee and home-made cakes, and also serves as the town's internet café, although more terminals can be found at the community centre just across the road next to the post office, and at the town library. The *Imperial Hotel* has the best counter meals, while the lime-green-painted daytime café *Eat It* has better than average fare to take away or eat on site, including tasty fish burgers.

The Namoi Valley: Gunnedah and around

On the Oxley Highway, 76km west of Tamworth, **GUNNEDAH** is one of the largest towns in the northwest and the inspiration for the Australian poet **Dorothea MacKellar** (1885–1968) and her ode to this drought-stricken land, *My Country*, penned while staying on her family's property here. The opening stanza is familiar to most Australians, who learn it by rote at school:

I love a sunburnt country
A land of sweeping plains
Of ragged mountain ranges
Of drought and flooding rains...

Today, Dorothea MacKeller lends her name to Gunnedah's nationally recognized poetry award (Ⓦwww.dorothea.com).

Gunnedah is often referred to as Australia's **koala capital**, and the **visitor centre** (Mon–Fri 9am–5pm, Sat & Sun 10am–3pm; ☎02/6740 2230 or 1800 562 527, Ⓦwww.infogunnedah.com.au) in ANZAC Park on South Street has updated information from local spotters on the whereabouts of the town's bears (it even sells "koala kitsch" – ie koala droppings – for $1). Otherwise, you have a good chance of seeing the bears on the **Bindea Walking Track**, a 7.4-kilometre walk from the visitor centre, or a 4.5-kilometre trek through the bush from the car park at Porcupine's Lookout in the porcupine reserve, just southeast of the centre. Directly behind the visitor centre in ANZAC Park, the **Old Water Tower** (Sat & Mon 10am–4pm, other days by appointment; $4) has exhibits on the town's indigenous and European settlement history including some of Dorothea MacKeller's childhood dolls, as well as a panoramic viewing deck.

Gunnedah is a major **beef cattle-selling** centre, with auctions on Tuesdays; there are also **markets** on the third Saturday of the month, at Wolseley Park in Conadilly Street. The **Waterways Wildlife Park** (daily 10am–4pm; $5), 7km west of Gunnedah on Mullaley Road (the Oxley Highway), is a green lakeside spot which makes an inviting break from the highway and is home to emus, kangaroos, wombats, lizards and possums.

A daily Countrylink **train** stops in Gunnedah on its way from Sydney to Moree. Should you want to **stay**, try the friendly *Regal Hotel* at 298 Conadilly St (☎02/6742 2355; ❶), which has a guest lounge with an open fire and good bistro meals and comfortable rooms (all a/c; some en suite), or *Roseneath Manor* at 91 Maitland St (☎02/6742 1906; ❹), a historic nineteenth-century B&B with three cosy rooms and cooked breakfasts. The nearest **caravan park** is 1km east of town on Henry Street (☎02/6742 1372; camping $20, powered site $22, cabins ❷–❸). **Eating** out of an evening is confined to pub and club meals; otherwise, head for Conadilly Street for a couple of decent daytime cafés including the *Redgum Outdoor*, *The Verdict*, on the corner of Chandos Street, and the excellent, Aboriginal café *Footprints*, which serves tasty fare such as cheese melts and burgers in airy, art-filled surrounds.

Narrabri, Mount Kaputar National Park and Wee Waa

NARRABRI, 97km northwest via the communities of Boggabri and Baan Baa, is recognized as the commercial centre of cotton growing. The **visitor centre** is on the Newell Highway (Mon–Fri 9am–5pm, Sat & Sun 9am–2pm; ☎02/6799 6760, ⓦwww.narrabri.nsw.gov.au). Next door to the visitor centre, the gleaming **Australian Cotton Centre** (daily 8.30am–4.30pm; $8) has some fun interactive exhibits covering cotton production. The **Australia Telescope** complex lies 20km west on the Yarrie Lake road and consists of six antennae, five of which move along a three-kilometre railtrack. Opening times vary (ask at the visitor centre), entry is free and there are lots of computer models to play with.

The other draw around Narrabri is **Mount Kaputar National Park**. The fifty-kilometre drive into the park to the 1524-metre-high **lookout** – with views over the vast Pillaga Scrub – is steep, narrow and partly unsealed. There are nine marked bushwalking trails in the park, with brochures available from the **NPWS office** at 100 Maitland St in Narrabri (Mon–Fri 8.30am–4.30pm; ☎02/6792 7300). The most striking geological feature of the park is **Sawn Rocks**, a basalt formation that looks like a series of organ pipes; it's reached via the northern end of the park on the unsealed road heading to Bingara. There are **camping** facilities at **Dawsons Spring** ($5, no vans) with hot showers, and a couple of cabins sleeping a maximum of six, with bathroom, kitchen and wood stove (reservations via NPWS, minimum stay 2 nights; cabins ❹). If you want to **stay** in Narrabri itself, try the good-value *Tourist Hotel* at 142 Maitland St (☎02/6792 2312; ❶–❷), which offers homely, clean rooms, some en suite. To grab something to **eat**, the adjacent daytime spot *The Café* is a good bet, while the large *Bowling Club* at 176 Maitland St does hearty lunches and dinners.

The town of **WEE WAA**, roughly 40km west, was where the Namoi cotton industry began in the 1960s, and the large cotton "gins" or processing plants are located here. If you can stand the rather raw, dispirited town and the blazing summer heat, you could earn some cash from the abundant **cotton-chipping** work available here in December and January; ask at one of the two pubs on Rose Street, the main drag, and someone will send you in the right direction. From Wee Waa you can head west to Walgett and on to Lightning Ridge.

Lightning Ridge

The population of **LIGHTNING RIDGE**, 74km north of Walgett on the Castlereagh Highway, is a transient one, where people in their hordes pitch up, lured by the promise of **opal**. Amid this harsh landscape scarred by holes and slag heaps, Lightning Ridge's opal fields are the only place in the world where black opal is found. Against their dark background, these "black" stones display a vivid spectrum of colours, and command top dollar. Opal galleries and mines proliferate in town, among them the **Walk-in Mine**, 1 Bald Hill Rd (Mon–Sat 9am–5pm; tours $8), which has tours to an underground mine and the opportunity to go fossicking; and the **Chambers of the Black Hand**, a hundred-year-old mine on Three Mile Road, 5km south of town (4 tours daily winter, 2 tours daily summer; ☎02/6829 0221, ⓦwww.blackopalsaustralia.com; carvings only $25, carvings and mine tour $35), where owner/miner Ron Canlin has hand-chiselled surreal life-size carvings – everything from Egyptian tombs to superheroes – in the mine's soft sandstone walls and installed an underground opal shop.

Lightning Ridge's rugged scenery and colourful local characters have long inspired **artists**: in addition to Ron Canlin, local notables include John Murray, whose intricately detailed images of the town and its residents are on show at the *John Murray Gallery* at 8 Opal St (Mon–Fri 9am–5pm, Sat 9am–2pm, Sun 9am–1pm; ⓦwww.johnmurrayart.com.au), and Aboriginal artist Johanna Parker, whose work can be viewed and bought at the visitor centre. The *Garrawal Aboriginal Artefacts Shop*, at 29 Nobby Rd (hours vary; ☎02/6829 0357), is also well worth a visit.

In late July, the **opal and gem festival** sees the population shoot up by a few thousand, as does the **Great Goat Race**, held down the main street over the Easter weekend. The effects of the opal obsession can also be seen in the gloriously crazy constructions of the few who have struck it lucky, such as the **Bottle House**, 60 Opal St (daily 9am–5pm; $5), a bizarrely beautiful cottage and dog kennel built entirely from wine bottles set in stone.

For a good overview of the town's attractions, you can take one of the three-hour **bus tours** ($25) that set off three to six times daily from the visitor centre (see opposite). To explore by yourself, pick up a leaflet at the visitor centre ($1) to follow one of four colour-coded **car door trails** covering various points of interest, each marked with an original old car door resting in the scrub.

You can try your luck at finding opals in clearly demarcated **fossicking** areas (in 2007, a tourist unearthed a $20,000 black opal), but don't do it anywhere else, or you may stray onto others' claims and infringements are taken *very* seriously. Recover afterwards in the 42°C water of the hot **artesian bore baths** on Pandora Street (open 24hr; free), which tap into the great Artesian Basin, an underground lake of fresh water about the size of Queensland. More cooling is the **Olympic Pool & Theme Park** on Gem Street (late Sept to Easter daily 11am–6pm, to 7pm early Oct to early April; $5.50), with waterslides, a wave pool and beach volleyball, plus an indoor Olympic diving pool.

Practicalities

Countrylink runs **buses** to Lightning Ridge from Sydney via Dubbo daily. The **visitor centre** is in the Lions Park, on the Bill O'Brian Way (daily 9am–5pm; ☎02/6829 1670, ⓦwww.lightningridge.net.au); ask for the useful *Lightning Ridge Walgett and District* brochure, which contains a handy guide to buying the stones.

The centre can also fill you in on **accommodation** possibilities (all have rooms with a/c; book ahead for the winter high season). Among the cheapest are the central *Black Opal Motel* on the corner of Opal and Morilla streets (☎02/6829 0518; ❸), but there's a knack to opening the doors – ask the staff to show you before you go out at night or risk being locked out; and *Lightning Ridge Hotel Motel & Caravan Park*, a friendly pub on Onyx Street (☎02/6829 0304; ❹) which also has cabins (❸) and camping ($12, powered site $15). Other good places to camp are *Crocodile Caravan and Camping Park* on Morilla Street (☎02/6829 0437; powered site $17, on-site vans ❶, cabins ❷), which has a pool, spa and air-cooled cabins; and *Chasin' Opal Holiday Park*, just up from the visitor centre (☎02/ 6829 0448, ⓦwww.chasinopal.com.au), with brand-new cabins (❹).

Meals catering to miners' appetites are served at the legendary *Wong's Chinese Restaurant* on Opal Street, and at the *Bowling Club* on Morilla Street (lunch daily, dinner Tues–Sat). Also on Morilla Street, the daytime *Morilla's Café* (also open Fri and Sat nights from 5pm from Easter–Oct) cooks up crispy wood-fired pizzas.

Back O'Bourke: the Outback

Travelling beyond Dubbo into the northwest corner of New South Wales, the landscape transforms into an endless expanse of largely uninhabited red plain – the quintessential **Australian Outback**. The searing summer heat makes touring uncomfortable from December to February. Bourke, about 370km along the Mitchell Highway, is generally considered the turning point; venture further and you're into the land known as **"Back O'Bourke"** – the back of beyond.

En route to Bourke, the Mitchell passes through **Nyngan**, the geographical centre of New South Wales, where the Barrier Highway heads west for 584 sweltering kilometres, through **Cobar** and **Wilcannia**, to **Broken Hill**.

Bourke and around

BOURKE is mainly known for its remoteness, and this alone is enough to attract tourists; once you've crossed the North Bourke Bridge that spans the Darling River, you're officially "out back".

Bourke was a **bustling river port** from the 1860s to the 1930s, and there remain some fine examples of riverboat-era architecture, including the huge reconstructed wharf, from where a track winds along the magnificent, tree-lined river. The Darling River water has seen crops as diverse as cotton, lucerne, citrus, grapes and sorghum successfully grown here despite the 40°C-plus summer heat, while Bourke is also the commercial centre for a vast sheep- and cattle-breeding area. River **cruises** are available aboard the old paddleboat *Jandra*, which operates between Easter and October (daily; 1hr; $14 – call the visitor centre for bookings).

However, Bourke is suffering. Since the **onset of drought** in 2002, the town has lost one third of its population (some 1000 people), who have had to move out of the region to find employment. Many services, such as large supermarkets, have simply shut up shop, pubs have closed and passenger air services have ceased. It's hoped that **tourism** will help Bourke back on its feet, and the new **Back O' Bourke Centre** (℡02/6872 1321; $17.50), in a vast new sail-covered building on the Mitchell Highway, a couple of kilometres north of town on the road towards Cunnamulla, is a brand-new draw for the town with multimedia displays on Outback life.

Practicalities

The helpful **visitor centre**, inside the former train station on Anson Street (Easter–Oct daily 9am–5pm; Nov–Easter Mon–Sat 9am–5pm; ℡02/6872 1222, ⓦwww.visitbourke.com), can provide hand-drawn "mud maps" marking places of interest off the beaten track in the surrounding area, though bear in mind that these destinations can be as far as 200km away and lesser-travelled roads little more than dirt tracks. Staff at the centre can arrange **tours** (Mon–Fri 2–5.30pm, Sat 9.30am–1pm; $27.50) covering orchards and vineyards in summer, and historical buildings and cotton farms in winter.

Countrylink **buses** arrive here from Dubbo four times weekly. **Accommodation** in town includes the pleasant *Port of Bourke Hotel* on Mitchell Street (℡02/6872 2544; ❸), which has a restaurant and air-conditioned rooms, some en suite and all opening out onto a sociable veranda. An ideal way to see how life is lived out here is to stay on an **Outback station**; the visitor centre has details of those that welcome guests, among them *Comeroo Camel Station* (℡02/6874 7735, ⓦwww.comeroo.com; $88 per person dinner and bed & breakfast and $110 full-board in the homestead, camping $10, powered site $12), a unique experience with artesian hot bores, river waterholes with yabbying and fishing opportunities, and resident buffalo and ostriches. For those interested in **seasonal work** in Bourke – harvesting tomatoes, onions and grapes between November and February and cotton chipping between December and February – *Kidman's Camp Tourist Park* (℡02/6872 1612), 8km north of town on the Darling River, may be able to point you in the right direction.

The *Port of Bourke Hotel* is the best place in town for **food** and **drink**, with fresh and healthy bistro fare, or counter meals out in the shady beer garden. The *Bowling Club Restaurant*, on the corner of Richard and Mitchell streets, serves counter lunches and dinners as well as Chinese food, while the *Oxford Hotel* at 71 Anson St in town also cooks up filling meals.

West and north of Bourke

West of Bourke, it's 193km to the small settlement of **WANAARING**, past a reconstruction of Fort Bourke, built by Major Mitchell in 1835 as a secure depot to protect his stocks from Aboriginal people while he explored the Darling River.

Northwest, the road runs 215km to **HUNGERFORD**, on the Queensland border, and the **Dingo Fence** (see p.1139). The state border bisects Hungerford, which consists of little more than a couple of houses, a post office and a pub but was made famous (amongst Australians) by poet Henry Lawson's short story, *Hungerford*. Make sure you shut the steel dingo-proof fence behind you when you drive through – there's a heavy fine if you don't.

Heading directly north from Bourke, the sealed Mitchell Highway goes right up to just past Charleville in Queensland (see p.524). If you're passing this way, the four-person hamlet of **BARRINGUN**, on the border 135km from Bourke, is worth a stopoff just to have a drink at the remarkably genteel *Tattersalls Hotel*, set amid a flower-scented garden. Across the road and closer to the border is the painted tin shed that comprises the *Bush Tucker Inn* (℡02/6874 7584; ❶), which has hot, home-cooked meals, rooms and camping space, but no fuel – fill up in Bourke as the next opportunity is 250km north in Cunnamulla.

South and east of Bourke

Amidst the empty, featureless plains, the elongated **Mount Gunderbooka** (498m), about 70km south of Bourke en route to Cobar, appears all the more striking. Likened to a mini-Uluru, the mountain was of similar cultural significance to the Aboriginal people of the area, with semi-permanent waterholes

> ### Southwest of Bourke: The Darling River Run
>
> Adventurous travellers wanting to see a remoter tranche of Outback should consider heading southwest from Bourke on the **Darling River Run** (🌐www.darlingriverrun .com.au) – one of Australia's last great adventures taking in 829km of Outback history, heritage and landscape running from Brewarrina near Bourke southwest to Wentworth. The whole area is in the midst of a long drought, not helped by the amount of water that has been sucked out of the watershed for irrigation – for more on the issue consult Don't Kill our Darling (🌐www.d-r-a-g.org).
>
> The route is unsealed and closely follows the east and west banks of the Darling River. When dry it is passable in ordinary vehicles but it always pays to ask local advice about the roads and take spare fuel, water and food. There's a good map of the region downloadable from 🌐www.outbackbeds.com.au which has excellent links to **accommodation** in the area. You can also just **camp** beside the river pretty much wherever you want.
>
> First stop, 100km southwest of Bourke, is tiny **Louth**, where there's a river crossing and *Shindy's Inn* (℡02/6874 7422; cabins $30, cottage ❹) sells diesel and petrol, and has basic **accommodation**. In early August the population of thirty briefly balloons to around 4000 for the **Louth Races**, along the lines of its more famous Birdsville cousin.
>
> You can get a real Outback experience by staying either *Trilby Station*, 25km downstream (℡02/6874 7420, 🌐www.trilbystation.com.au; camping $18, powered site $20, bunks $30, a/c rooms ❹), or *Kallara Station*, a further 50km southwest (℡02/6837 3963, 🌐www.kallarastation.com.au; camping from $5 per person, bunkhouse $25, a/c rooms ❹). Both offer meals by arrangement.
>
> At Tilpa, 15km on, there's a bridge over the river and the classic Outback pub, the 1890s *Tilpa Hotel* (℡02/6837 3928; ❸), with shared-bath rooms, meals (the steak sandwiches are huge) and fuel; for a $2 donation towards the Royal Flying Doctor Service, you can immortalize your name on the pub's tin wall.
>
> The 130-kilometre run down to Wilcannia passes **Mount Murchinson Station**, on the west side of the river, allegedly once managed by the son of Charles Dickens. From Wilcannia you can follow the river downstream to Menindee (see p.361) and explore the Kinchega National Park before the final 250-kilometre run down to Wentworth on the Victorian border.

and caves with rock art – contact the **NPWS** on Oxley Street in Bourke for details ([T]02/6872 2744).

Twenty-eight kilometres east of Bourke, en route to Brewarrina, is a turn-off south to **Mount Oxley**, climbed by the explorers Sturt and Hume in 1829 to herald white settlement in the area. It's on private property, so you must first pick up a key from the visitor centre in Bourke, which also organizes three-and-a-half-hour tours here ($27.50). The town of **BREWARRINA** (locals call it "Bre") lies 100km east of Bourke on the Barwon River. Abundant fish stocks made the area a natural fishery for the original Aboriginal population; their stone fish-traps – a labyrinth of large, partly submerged boulders – can still be seen in the river, where as many as five thousand Aborigines used to gather to catch fish. However, like Bourke, Brewarrina has also been hard-hit by the drought and many shops and services have closed.

Cobar

Since copper was discovered here in 1870, **COBAR**, just under 160km south of Bourke and the first real stop on the Barrier Highway between Nyngan and Broken Hill, has experienced three mining booms. Today, this town of around 7000 people is home to the vast **CSA Copper Mine**, which extracts well over half a million tonnes of copper ore every year, and smaller gold and silver mines. Earlier booms resulted in a number of impressive public buildings, among them the 1882 courthouse and the police station, as well as the *Great Western Hotel* on Marshall Street, whose iron-lace verandas are among the longest in the state. Most people only stop here to refuel before the monotonous 260-kilometre stretch to Wilcannia; there is, however, a lovely picnic spot in Drummond Park, just off the highway on Linsley Street.

For more about the town, head for the excellent **visitor centre** (Mon–Fri 8.30am–5pm, Sat & Sun 9am–5pm; [T]02/6836 2448, [W]www.cobar.nsw.gov.au) on Marshall Street. The attached **Great Cobar Heritage Centre** (Mon–Fri 8.30am–4.30pm, Sat & Sun 9am–5pm; $9) has some great exhibits on mining, local Aborigines and the colonial social history. Outside, the 1907 train carriage fitted out as a travelling clinic was used until the 1960s by the Far West Children's Health Scheme which still brings medical assistance to remote communities. Staff at the visitor centre can provide a mud map showing places of interest around Cobar, including the platform giving views down into the open-cast gold mine. They can also advise on **Outback bush-stays**. If you're headed out to the Mount Grenfell Historic Site (see p.351), pick up a leaflet from the **NPWS**, 19 Barton St (Mon–Fri 8.30am–4.30pm; [T]02/6836 2692).

There are lots of **motels** along the highway in Cobar, all with air conditioning and pool: you should book ahead in the peak season of June to September. The nicest place is the *Town & Country Motor Inn*, 52 Marshall St ([T]02/6836 1244, [E]townandctry@gmail.com; [5]), with all mod cons and its own restaurant. The *Cross Roads Motel*, at the corner of Bourke and Louth roads ([T]&[F]02/6836 2711; [4]), is also good, while the *Cobar Caravan Park*, 101 Marshall St ([T]02/6836 2425, [E]cobvanpk@bigpond.net.au; camping $20, powered site $22, cabins [3]), has smart cabins and shady trees. There are several basic cafés and pub **restaurants**, but for something a little more sophisticated visit *Gecko Espresso*, 35 Marshall St (closed Sun), or *Twisted Sisters*, 32 Linsley St, half a block off the Barrier Highway.

Mount Grenfell Historic Site

Arguably one of the most significant Aboriginal rock-art locations in New South Wales, the **Mount Grenfell Historic Site** (sunrise to sunset; free; Ⓦwww.environment.nsw.gov.au) lies 40km west of Cobar along the Barrier Highway then 32km north along a gravel road.

The rocky ridge contains three art sites with over 1300 motifs – human and animal figures, including the emus that you're still likely to see around the site, plus abstract designs and hand stencils. Older layers are visible beneath the more recent pigments, but there's no way to tell exactly how old the art is. The adjacent semi-permanent waterhole explains the significance of the site for the Ngiyampaa people. The signposted **Ngiyampaa Walkabout** (5km return) goes to the top of the ridge with wide views.

Wilcannia and around

The next major town on the Barrier Highway is **WILCANNIA**, 260km west of Cobar. The former "Queen City of the West" was founded in 1864 and until the early 1900s was a major port on the Darling River, from where produce was transported by paddle-steamers and barges down the Darling–Murray river system to Adelaide. Droughts, the advent of the railways and road transport put an end to the river trade, and today, after a decade of hard drought, it is difficult to imagine a steamer getting anywhere near the place. The only reminders of that prosperous era are the ruins of the docks and the old lift-up bridge, along with a few impressive public buildings such as the post office, police station, courthouse, Catholic convent and the Council Chambers on Reid Street. Nowadays Wilcannia is a cheerless, boarded-up place, with high unemployment and alcoholism affecting the significant Aboriginal population.

There's a bank, shop, motel, post office and service station in town, but the fortified pub is only open a couple of hours a day. **Meals and drinks** are best sought at the golf club on Ross Street.

The only fuel stop between Wilcannia and Broken Hill is at the *Little Topar Hotel*, roughly halfway along the 195-kilometre stretch of the Barrier Highway.

White Cliffs

From Wilcannia, you can head north off the Barrier Highway to the opal fields at **WHITE CLIFFS**, 98km away. Four kangaroo shooters found opals here in 1889 and four thousand miners followed. Besides opals, White Cliffs is famous for its extraordinary summer heat, and many of the two hundred residents **live underground** in "dug-outs". For a few dollars, several people will show you their one-man mining operations, dug-out homes and opal collections, and you can inspect the solar power station that looks like something out of a space odyssey. PJ's (see below) runs twenty-minute tours of its B&B (daily 10am, 1pm & 5pm; $8).

For the authentic underground experience, there are two places to **stay**. The original and very friendly *White Cliffs Underground Motel* (☎08/8091 6647, Ⓦwww.undergroundmotel.com.au; ❹) comes with a warren of thirty white-painted rooms (almost all shared-bath) dug into the hillside, underground bar, and topside licensed restaurant and outdoor swimming pool. The only subterranean B&B in town is ⚑ *PJ's* (☎08/8091 6626, Ⓦwww.babs.com.au/pj; ❺–❻), with its underground spa-bath and 64-million-year-old rock roof. Cheaper above-ground options include the *White Cliffs Hotel/Motel* (℡08/8091 6606, Ⓦwww.whitecliffshotelmotel.com.au; ➍) or, if you can bear the heat, **camping** (with hot showers) at *Opal Pioneer*, right in town (℡08/8091 6688; camping $10, powered site $15). **Tourist information** is available on Keraro Road at the White Cliffs General Store and Café (daily 7.30am–7.30pm; ℡08/8091 6611) and at the **NPWS Paroo-Darling Visitor Centre** (generally open daily) in the middle of town, which has info on local national parks.

There are several **tours** to White Cliffs from Broken Hill, including a day-trip with Tri State Safaris ($168; ℡08/8088 2389, Ⓦwww.tristate.com.au) or as part of a longer trip with Broken Hill's Outback Tours (from $1170 for 3 days; ℡08/8087 7800, Ⓦwww.outbacktours.net).

Broken Hill and around

The ghosts of mining towns that died when the precious minerals ran out are scattered all over Australia. **BROKEN HILL**, on the other hand, has been riding the minerals market roller-coaster continuously since 1888. Its famous "Line of Lode", one of the world's major lead-silver-zinc ore bodies and the city's *raison d'être*, still has a little life left in it yet.

Almost 1200km west of Sydney and about 500km east of Adelaide, this surprisingly gracious Outback mining-town – with a population of around 21,000 and a feel and architecture reminiscent of the South Australian capital – manages to create a welcome splash of green in the harsh desert landscape that surrounds it. Extensive re-vegetation schemes around Broken Hill have created grasslands that, apart from being visually pleasing, help contain the dust that used to make the residents' lives a misery. It's aided by a reliable water supply – secured for the first time only in 1953 – via a one-hundred-kilometre pipeline from the Darling River at Menindee.

Inevitably, Broken Hill revolves around the **mines**, but since the 1970s it has also evolved into a thriving **arts centre**, thanks to the initiative of the **Brushmen of the Bush**, a painting school comprising local artists Hugh Schulz, Jack Absalom, John Pickup, Eric Minchin and Pro Hart. Diverse talents have been attracted to Broken Hill, and their works are displayed in galleries scattered all over town. Some may be a bit on the tacky side, but others are excellent, and it's well worth devoting some time to gallery browsing.

The city is also a convenient base for touring far-northwest New South Wales and nearby areas in South Australia.

Arrival and information

Indian Pacific trains from Sydney and Adelaide, and one weekly Countrylink train from Sydney, arrive at the **train station** on Crystal Street at the foot of the slag heap. From here it's 200m to the main Argent Street and 500m to the combined **bus station** and **visitor centre**, at the corner of Bromide and

Check your watch

Remember to adjust your watch here: Broken Hill operates on **South Australian Central Standard Time**, half an hour behind the rest of New South Wales. All local transport schedules are in CST, but you should always check.

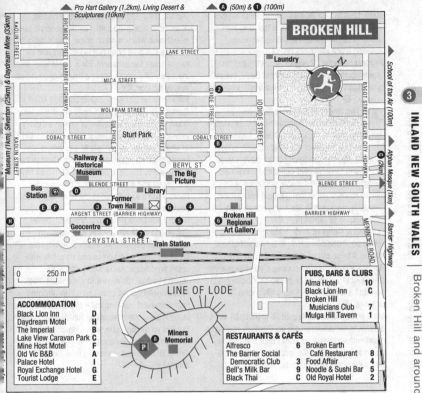

Photographic Recollections (2km), ⑨ (2km) & ⑩ (2km) ▼

Blende streets (daily 8.30am–5pm; ☎08/8080 3560, Ⓦwww.visitbrokenhill .com.au), where you can buy a map ($2.20) for a self-guided heritage walk along Argent and Blende streets, or information on tours (see p.359). Countrylink **buses** arrive here from Dubbo, and Buses R Us (☎08/8285 6900, Ⓦwww.busesrus.com.au) runs services from Adelaide and Mildura.

The **airport** is 5km south of town but there's no shuttle bus – either catch a taxi (around $15) or arrange to have a rental car waiting (see p.359). Murton's **City Bus** (☎08/8087 3311) runs hourly or half-hourly along four routes through Broken Hill – the visitor centre can provide a combined timetable and route map.

For information on the surrounding national parks, visit the nearby **NPWS** at 183 Argent St (Mon–Fri 8.30am–4.30pm; ☎08/8080 3200).

Accommodation

Broken Hill has the best range of **accommodation** for several hundred kilometres with everything from campsites and a hostel to mainstream hotels, pubs and a few nice B&Bs in grand old buildings. **Booking** ahead is sensible in the popular cooler months from May to October but rarely absolutely necessary.

Black Lion Inn 34 Bromide St, opposite the bus station [T] 08/8087 4801. This is the town's cheapest but simplest pub, with quiet rooms including some singles ($33). [1]

Daydream Motel 77 Argent St [T] 08/8088 3033, [W] www.budgetmotelchain.com.au. Basic, central motel that's clean and well looked after. Breakfast included. [4]

The Imperial 88 Oxide St [T] 08/8087 7444, [W] www.imperialfineaccommodation.com. The pick of the crop: a classy, four-and-a-half-star in a beautiful old building with huge veranda. The five spacious rooms (plus a large apartment) have all mod cons, and there's also a kitchenette, free self-serve breakfast, a billiard room, a guest lounge, pool and garden. Complimentary port in the lounge area. Free wi-fi. Rooms [7], apartment [9]

Lake View Caravan Park 1 Mann St, 3km northeast [T] 08/8088 2250, [E] bhlvevp@bigpond.net.au. A large site on the edge of town with Outback views, disabled access, a good swimming pool, a kiosk and an array of cabins. Camping $22, powered site $26, on-site vans [1], cabins [2], cottages [4]

Mine Host Motel 120 Argent St [T] 08/8088 4044, [W] www.minehostmotel.com.au. Recently revamped motel with stylish rooms with fridge and minibar, plus a small pool. Central location right near the bus station, and close to clubs and pubs. [5]

Old Vic B&B 230 Oxide St [T] 08/8087 1169, [E] theoldvic@bigpond.com. Farmhouse-style family guesthouse which is much cosier than it looks from the street. A good breakfast is included and all rooms share the bathroom. It's a 15min walk from the centre, though there are a couple of good pubs nearby for food. [3]

Palace Hotel 227 Argent St [T] 08/8088 1699. Corner pub with the largest hotel balcony in New South Wales and a profusion of murals on every available surface, including a Botticelli-style *Birth of Venus* (painted by the late Mario, former landlord) which featured to hilarious effect in the film *Priscilla, Queen of the Desert*. All rooms have a/c, phone and a sink, and some are en suite. Room #102 also featured in the film. Singles $37, doubles [3]–[4]

Royal Exchange Hotel 320 Argent St, corner of Chloride St [T] 08/8087 2308, [W] www.royalexchangehotel.com. Plush 24-room hotel with lovely Art Deco public areas and en suites with smart furnishings, some with bathtub. [8]

Tourist Lodge 100 Argent St [T] 08/8088 2086, [E] bhlodge@bigpond.com. Large YHA-affiliated hostel near the bus terminal – the only backpacker place in town. After becoming run-down it looks like it is on the up again, with fridges and TVs in many rooms, a well-equipped, shared kitchen/dining/TV room and swimming pool. Dorms $25, doubles [3]–[4]

The City

Broken Hill grew up around the **Line of Lode**, a strip of mines that runs from northeast to southwest through town, most obviously marked by a fifty-metre high **slag heap**, a hill of mine waste topped by the Miners Memorial steel sculpture. The CBD and the bulk of town lies to the northwest while the mostly residential South Broken Hill lies southeast and feels quite separate.

The slag heap towering over the city centre leaves you in no doubt that, above all, this is still a mining town. Take care shaking hands with anyone you suspect might have gripped a drill and shovel for forty years; the old-timers can put a serious squeeze on you without noticing. The streets – laid out in a grid – are mostly named after chemicals; **Argent Street** (Latin for silver) is the main thoroughfare, with the highest concentration of historic buildings and a really good art gallery. Art and mining also form the foundation for sights elsewhere around the centre, particularly the slightly oddball **White's Mineral Art and Mining Museum** and the **Pro Hart Gallery**. Aussie icons the **Royal Flying Doctor Service** and the **School of the Air** show off their talents on the outskirts, and just beyond there's a great **wildlife sanctuary**-cum-**sculpture park**.

Argent Street and around

You'll get a pretty good feel for Broken Hill just strolling along broad Argent Street with its grand edifices, century-old pubs with ornate iron verandas and commemorative plaques. The two finest buildings, both from the early

1890s, are near the junction with Chloride Street. The brick **Post Office**, with its large square tower and double-height veranda, still fulfils its original function, while the former **Town Hall** is possibly the finest building on the street, done in South Australian Italianate style with its distinctive, almost minaret-like tower.

Two blocks northeast, the **Broken Hill Regional Art Gallery**, 404 Argent St (daily 10am–5pm; donation), has an excellent representative collection of artists from Broken Hill as well as Australian art in general. Established in 1904, it's the second-oldest gallery in the state – after Sydney's Art Gallery of New South Wales – with a small collection of nineteenth- and early twentieth-century paintings including works by Sidney Nolan, John Olsen and the "Brushmen of the Bush" (see p.352), though these last are sometimes moved to make way for special exhibitions.

Art of a different kind is on show at **The Big Picture**, 66 Chloride St (daily 10am–4pm; $4.95), tucked in the back room of an art gallery. Here, renowned photorealist bird painter Peter Anderson spent two solid years working on what is said to be the largest acrylic-on-canvas painting in the world. The vast hundred-metre long tableau of local desert and scenes features the Sculpture Park, Silverton and the distant Flinders Range.

The **Railway & Historical Museum**, opposite the visitor centre on Blende Street (daily 10am–3pm; $2.50), occupies the former station of a rail service which ran from here to the mines at Silverton. A highlight among the old railway carriages and machinery is the sleek, diesel Silver City Comet, the first air-conditioned train in the southern hemisphere, which ran from here to Parkes from 1937–89. There's also a small hospital museum, a good section on immigrants to the region, and an extensive mineral collection.

Finally, the **Geocentre**, in a nineteenth-century bond store on the corner of Bromide and Crystal streets (Mon–Fri 10am–4.45pm, Sat & Sun 1–4.45pm; $3.50), looks at Broken Hill's geology, mineralogy and metallurgy. Highlights include a 42-kilogram silver ingot and the spectacular *Silver Tree*, a 68-centimetre figurine wrought of pure silver from the Broken Hill Mines, depicting five Aborigines, a drover on horseback, kangaroos, emus and sheep gathered under a tree.

The rest of the city

Other sights are scattered a little further out, and if you don't have your own vehicle, a **tour** (see "Listings", p.359) is really the only solution.

Start by getting a fix on your bearings by driving up to the top of the slag heap either for a coffee at *Broken Earth* (see p.358) or to visit the **Miners Memorial** (daily 10am–5pm; $5), a modern rusted-steel sculpture commemorating the lives of lost miners.

A visit to the bizarre but wonderful **White's Mineral Art and Mining Museum**, 1 Allendale St, 2km west of the centre off Silverton Road (daily 9am–5pm; $5), is the next best thing to going underground, though it occupies part of a suburban house. The art section is pretty extraordinary, consisting mainly of collages of crushed minerals depicting Broken Hill scenes, and at the back there's a convincingly recreated walk-in underground mine. Inside, ex-miner Kevin White gives an entertaining talk, with videos and models, on the history of Broken Hill and its mines, while a shop at the front of the museum sells minerals, opals, jewellery and pottery.

If you only go to one gallery in Broken Hill, make it the **Pro Hart Gallery** at 108 Wyman St (Mon–Sat 9am–5pm, Sun 1.30–5pm; $4; ⓦwww.prohart .com.au). The gallery showcases the work of Broken Hill miner-turned-artist,

Pro Hart, who died in 2006. Sculptures, etchings and prints typically depict Outback events and people such as race meetings, backyard barbecues and union leaders – look out for the fantastic ten-metre-long *History of Australia* showing scenes of Aboriginal life before the arrival of Captain Cook, the early pioneers, bush rangers and the founding of Broken Hill. Hart's delightfully chaotic studio has now been moved in its entirety into the museum with one of his final iconic dragonfly paintings on the easel. To celebrate the millennium Hart also took his paintbrush to one of his Rolls-Royces, now garaged outside.

There's also a collection of Hart's sculptures in a lot across the road which you can check out for free. If you're buying, you can get a framed print for $30; a small painting will set you back about $3500.

Following the bush-art theme, call in at **D'Art De Main Gallery**, 233 Rowe St (Wed–Sun 10am–5pm; free), where there's a good collection of sculptures, portraits and landscapes by Geoff De Main, who also painted many of the wall murals you'll see around town.

Almost 2km north of the centre it is easy to miss the corrugated-iron, minaret-less **Afghan Mosque**, on the corner of William and Buck streets (Sun 2–4pm; free), on the site of the former **camel camp** where Afghan and Indian camel-drivers loaded and unloaded the camel teams which used to accompany explorers on their harsh route through the desert.

You'll need to head south around the slag heap to reach **Photographic Recollections**, on Eyre Street in South Broken Hill (Mon–Fri 10am–4.30pm, Sat 1–4.30pm; $5), which provides a pictorial history of Broken Hill, with over six hundred photographs accompanied by well-researched text that delves into mining, union and social history. The location itself, in the former **Central Power Station**, tells a story of the city's very Outback past; Broken Hill produced all its power here from the 1930s until as late as 1986, when it finally went onto the national grid.

The Royal Flying Doctor Service and the School of the Air

Broken Hill offers an excellent opportunity to visit two Australian Outback institutions: the Royal Flying Doctor Service (RFDS) and the School of the Air. The **Royal Flying Doctor Service**, at Broken Hill Airport, 5km south of town (Mon–Fri 9am–5pm, Sat & Sun 11am–4pm; $5.50; ✆08/8080 3714, Ⓦwww.rfds.org.au), offers guided tours with an accompanying video and talk – phone in advance as places are limited. In the headquarters you'll see the radio room where calls from remote places in New South Wales, South Australia and Queensland are handled, before going out to the hangar to see the aircraft. The popularity of the tours is due to the Australian television series *The Flying Doctors*, which is shown worldwide, and since a third of the service's annual budget of $30 million has to come through fundraising – the rest of the money is from the State and Federal governments – whatever you spend on the tour and at the souvenir shop here is going to a good cause.

In many ways the **School of the Air** on Lane Street, 2km north of the centre, is indebted to the RFDS: lessons for children in the Outback, in a transmission area of 1.8 million square kilometres, were formerly conducted via RFDS two-way radio (these days it's all by webcam). The radio service was established in 1956 to improve education for children in the isolated Outback, and you can still listen to the transmission in a schoolroom surrounded by children's artwork (Mon–Fri term time only 8.20am; book the day before at the visitor centre; $4.40). It's frighteningly like being back

Mining and unionism in Broken Hill

The story of Broken Hill began in 1883 when a German-born boundary rider from Mount Gipps Station, Charles Rasp, pegged out a forty-acre lease of a "broken hill" that he believed was tin. A syndicate of seven was formed, founding the **Broken Hill Proprietary (BHP)** to work what turned out to be rich silver, lead and zinc deposits. Broken Hill's mines, dominated by BHP until they withdrew operations in 1939, have contributed greatly to the wealth of Australia: the deposit, more than 7km long and up to 250m wide, is thought originally to have contained more than three hundred million tonnes of silver, zinc and lead ores. Even now there's said to be ten years left in the "Line of Lode" currently being worked by the Perilya and CBH companies.

In the early years, living and working **conditions** for the miners were atrocious. The climate was harsh, housing was poor and diseases such as typhoid, scarlet fever and dysentery – to say nothing of work-related illnesses such as lead poisoning and mining accidents – contributed to a death rate almost twice the New South Wales average; there have been around eight hundred deaths in mining accidents since operations began. The mine and the growing town rapidly stripped the landscape of timber, leaving the settlement surrounded by a vast, bleak plain and beleaguered by dust storms. Not surprisingly, perhaps, Broken Hill was at the forefront of **trade union** development in Australia, as the miners, many of them recent immigrants, fought to improve their living and working conditions. It was their ability to unite that ultimately won them their battles, above all in the Big Strike of 1919–20, when, after eighteen months of holding out against the police and strikebreakers, major concessions were won from BHP.

The unions typified the precious Australian concept of **mateship** – some miners literally died for each other, or worked for fifteen years side by side with the same partner. Not that the trade union movement at Broken Hill should be viewed through too-rosy glasses: the union, which effectively ran the town in conjunction with the mine companies, was also a bastion of racism and male supremacy – non-whites were not tolerated in town, nor were working women who happened to be married – and local attitudes remain strongly conservative.

Despite the life left in Broken Hill's mineral deposits, the **future** is none too certain. With modern mining technology the ore is removed faster, and the numbers employed are lower. Between 1970 and 1975, about four thousand people were employed in the mines. By the early 1980s this number had been reduced to 2500, and less than six hundred work there now. The population continues to decrease gradually and every few years another of the city's many pubs closes down.

at school, with jolly primary-school teachers hosting singalongs, but the children in the far-flung areas seem to enjoy it.

The Living Desert and the Sculpture Park

Ten kilometres northwest of town, 24 square kilometres of the eroded Barrier Ranges desert region has been sectioned off as the **Living Desert Flora & Fauna Sanctuary** (dawn–dusk; $10 per vehicle), a beautiful area, especially at either end of the day when the wildlife is more active. The **Cultural Walk Trail** (2km loop; 1hr 30min) takes in an Aboriginal quartz quarry, mining claim markers and lots of desert flora (possibly including the lovely red Sturt's desert pea). At the beginning of the walk, an electrified predator-proof fence keeps introduced pests (mainly cats and foxes) out of a large compound now re-populated with threatened species such as yellow-footed rock wallabies, brush-tailed bettongs and bilbies.

The highest hill within the Living Desert is crowned by the **Broken Hill Sculpture Park** (included in entry to Living Desert), easily the most dramatic of Broken Hill's art exhibits. Carved from Wilcannia sandstone boulders, the sculptures are the work of twelve artists who took part in a sculpture symposium in 1993. They were drawn from diverse cultures – two apiece from Mexico and Syria, three from Georgia (in the Caucasus), and five Australians, including two Bathurst Islanders – as reflected in the variety of their works. Antonio Nava Tirado's Aztec-influenced *Bajo El Sol Jaguar* (Under the Jaguar Sun) is particularly fine: the image is re-created everywhere and has become a kind of de facto symbol of Broken Hill.

Everyone comes up to visit the sculptures at sunset, no surprise since on a clear evening the light can be magical and the rocks glow crimson. It's a pleasant fifteen-minute walk up the hill from the Sanctuary car park, or you can drive right up to the car park beside the sculptures using a **key** available (at no extra charge) from the visitor centre in Broken Hill, where you can also pick up an **information brochure**.

Eating, drinking and nightlife

Restaurants aren't really Broken Hill's style – the town is famous for its bad **food** and, while things are slowly improving, if your meal looks like it was trucked a thousand kilometres through a sandstorm to get here, that's because it probably was. Broken Hill still has the proverbial pub on every corner, and most of them serve **counter meals** where quantity usually prevails over quality. For **grocery** supplies, visit the central IGA on Blende Street at Oxide Street (daily 9am–9pm), or Woolworths in Centro Westside, 1km southwest of the centre (Mon–Sat 7am–10pm, Sun 8am–8pm).

The city has always been a legendary **drinking hole**, and once had over seventy hotels. Many pubs have been converted for other uses, but there are still more than twenty licensed establishments and a pub crawl is highly recommended. Another option is to sample the local culture at one of the numerous clubs which often host live entertainment on Friday and Saturday nights: just sign yourself in.

Eating

Alfresco 397 Argent St. Reliable if hardly outstanding pavement dining with a large selection of gourmet salads, pastas and pizza at modest prices. Licensed.

The Barrier Social Democratic Club 218 Argent St. Passable salad bar plus good, inexpensive breakfasts from 7–9am.

Bell's Milk Bar 160 Patton St, South Broken Hill ⓦ www.bellsmilkbar.com.au. A great spot – a bit like a 1950s diner with a rock 'n' roll jukebox and vinyl booths. They specialize in spiders (soda ice-cream floats), milkshakes and smoothies, with hot waffles the only food option. The back room takes a nostalgic look at the 1950s and 1960s heyday of Aussie milk bars. Mon–Sat 10.30am–6pm, 9pm in summer.

Black Thai Inside the Black Lion Inn, 34 Bromide St. The city's only southeast Asian place is surprisingly good, with a limited range of tasty mains (around $14) such as Malaysian laksa and Thai green curry. Thurs–Sat 6–9pm only.

Broken Earth Café Restaurant Federation Way, on top of the slag heap. The place for smart dining, with a funky winged roof which is visible all over town. Some of the best dining around, augmented by fabulous views. Fine for a coffee or semi-formal lunch, but perfect for dining around sunset on modern Australian food and wine. Mains around $30.

Food Affair 362 Argent St. Unassuming café serving tasty made-to-order sandwiches and the town's best coffee, either inside or at a couple of pavement tables. Closed Sat afternoon and Sun.

Noodle & Sushi Bar 351 Argent St. Something completely different, with everything from Nasi goreng to Singapore noodles as well as Japanese sushi. Mains around $10. Daily 11.30am–8.30pm.

Old Royal Hotel 146 Oxide St. Some of the best straightforward pub meals in town, in large portions. You won't go hungry.

Drinking and nightlife

Alma Hotel Corner of Hebbard and South sts, South Broken Hill. Substantially revamped local that's good for a drink any time and is the only place with live music on Sun night.

Black Lion Inn 34 Bromide St. Always good but especially during the happy hours – 5–7pm for beer, 5pm–midnight for fairly weak but decent cocktails.

Broken Hill Musicians Club 276 Crystal St. This club has covers bands towards the weekend and was immortalized by Kenneth Cook's 1961 novel (and later film), *Wake in Fright*. Try to make it here on Fri and Sat (10.30pm–1.30am) when it operates Broken Hill's famous *Two Up School*, once an illegal back-lane gambling operation. The boys from the bush turn up to bet as much as $200 on one flip of a coin, though $10 or $20 is more common.

Mulga Hill Tavern Corner of Oxide and Williams sts. Recently revamped pub with a wide variety of clientele, cold beer and good bar food.

Listings

Airline Regional Express ☎ 13 17 13.

Bookshop Browzers Bookshop at 345 Argent St stocks new and secondhand books.

Car rental Avis, 195 Argent St ☎ 08/8087 7532; Hertz, at the visitor centre ☎ 08/8087 2719; Thrifty, 190 Argent St ☎ 08/8088 1928. All have desks at the airport too. You'll pay around $75/125 a day for a saloon car/4WD; small cars are nonexistent here – utes with giant roo-bars are the vehicle of choice.

Cinema Village Silver City Cinema, 41 Oxide St (☎ 08/8087 4569), has mostly mainstream and some festival showings. Tickets just $10.

Hospital Broken Hill Base Hospital and Health Services, 176 Thomas St ☎ 08/8080 1333.

Internet Free access at the library, on the corner of Blende and Chloride sts, but you have to book (Mon–Wed 10am–8pm, Thurs & Fri 10am–6pm, Sat 10am–1pm, Sun 1–5pm; ⊛www .bhlibrary.org.au). Also at Café Rendezvous in the visitor centre building ($8 per hr).

Laundry Wilsons Dry Cleaners, 457 Lane St at Oxide St (☎ 08/8087 3379), is open daily 8am–9pm as a coin-op laundry and for dry-cleaning.

Pharmacies Handiest is Outback Pharmacies, 323 Argent St, but Nettings, 274 McCulloch St, 2km north of the centre, is open daily 9am–9pm.

Post office Corner of Argent and Chloride sts (daily 9am–5pm).

Swimming pool Broken Hill Aquatic Centre, 2km north of the oentre on McCulloch St (daily April–Oct 6am–6pm; Nov–March 5.30–9pm; $3), is heated in winter.

Taxi Yellow Taxis ☎ 13 10 08.

Tours Contact the visitor centre for a guided **walking tour** delving into Broken Hill's history (March–Nov Mon, Wed, Fri 10am; 1hr 30min–2hr; donation). The **Bush Mail Run** (Wed & Sat 7am–4pm; $120) takes you through a great slice of the surrounding countryside as it delivers mail to distant homesteads. Lunch (bring your own) is eaten beside the Darling River. For local **minibus tours**, contact Broken Hill Sightseeing Co (☎ 08/8088 6900) whose assorted half- ($50) and full-day ($80) trips generally include the city sights, Silverton and the sculpture park.

Around Broken Hill

A good deal of the pleasure in visiting Broken Hill involves discovering what lies within 100km or so in all directions. Day-trippers visit the nearby mining semi-ghost town of **Silverton**, while you might consider going overnight to visit the excellent national parks of **Mutawintji**, with its gorge hiking and Aboriginal rock art, and **Kinchega**, a former sheep run with camping beside the Darling River.

Silverton and around

The only opportunity to experience something of what it was like to mine underground is to visit **Day Dream Mine** (Easter–Dec daily 10am–3.30pm with hour-long tours on demand; Jan–Easter open for tours at 10am & 11.30am; 1hr; $20), 20km northeast of Broken Hill on Silverton Road then 13km north along a dirt road. Predating the discovery at Broken Hill, the Day Dream operated between 1882 and 1889, and you can see the old workings where children as young as 8 laboured.

Back on Silverton Road it is just 5km further, on a good road, to the semi-ghost town of **SILVERTON**, which makes a great day out. If the scene looks vaguely familiar, you've probably seen it before: parts of *Mad Max II* were shot around here, and the *Silverton Hotel* has appeared as the "Gamulla Hotel" in *Razorback*, "Hotel Australia" in *A Town Like Alice*, and in Aussie gangster movie *Dirty Deeds* with Toni Colette. It also seems to star in just about every commercial – usually beer-related – that features an Outback scene. In the tradition of all Outback pubs, it has its own in-jokes; you'll find out what all the laughter is about if you ask to "take the test" (gold coin donation to charity).

Taking the **Silverton Heritage Trail**, a two-hour stroll around town marked by white arrows, is a good way to work up a thirst, though it's far too hot to attempt in the summer. Along the way you'll pass the 1889 vintage **Silverton Gaol Museum** (daily 9.30am–4.30pm; $3), with a bit of just about everything you could imagine there ever was in Silverton – washboards, typewriters, masonic garb, assay scales and so on. There's also material on Dame Mary Gilmore (that's her on the $10 note), who was assistant teacher here from 1887 to 1889 and later became a noted socialist journalist and poet.

There's a burgeoning **art scene** here too, with several galleries to browse through, including **Horizon Gallery** (daily 10am–5pm; Ⓦ www.horizongalleries .com.au) run by fine local artists Albert Woodroffe and Bronwen Standley-Woodroffe, and also stocking work by some of their peers.

One of the most enjoyable things to do in Silverton is to go on a camel tour. The Cannard family, who run **Silverton Camels** (Ⓣ08/8088 5316, Ⓔ silvertoncamels@bigpond.com), come from a long line of camel trainers and have forty working animals. You can't miss their farm on the way into Silverton, with the shapes of camels looming like desert mirages. You can hop on for half an hour ($25), or trot for an hour along the nearby creek ($35). Better still is the great sunset trek (2hr; $65) out into the desert with a return trip in the twilight. Dawn and moonlight rides are occasionally available, and they'll organize multiday trips on demand.

Beyond Silverton, the sealed road continues 5km north to the **Mundi Mundi Plains Lookout**, where the undulating plateau you have been driving across descends gradually to a vast plain. On clear days you can see the blurred outline of the northern Flinders Ranges in South Australia in the distance (the lookout is the spot where, at the end of *Mad Max II*, Mel Gibson tipped the semi-trailer). A further 5km on there's a picnic area overlooking the **Umberumberka reservoir**, Broken Hill's only source of water until the Menindee Lakes Scheme was set up.

Practicalities

Most people visit Silverton for half a day or so from Broken Hill, but it is possible to **stay**. Camping is best at *Penrose Park* (Ⓣ08/8088 5307; camping $9 per person, room ❷), a particularly well-kept place with its own mini-zoo and rooms sleeping four, with kitchen. The *Silverton Hotel* (Ⓣ08/8088 5313; ❶) has a handful of en-suite cabins with access to a barbecue but no kitchen. Bring your own bedding or rent here. There's also the self-contained *Blue Bush Country Cottage* (Ⓣ08/8088 5506; ❹), sleeping four.

The *Silverton Hotel* is the place to drink, but for **meals** visit the excellent ※ *Silverton Café*, right in the centre (closed Mon), which does a great line in home-made country food including stews, damper and pies made from quandong, a native Australian fruit with a taste somewhere between plum and rhubarb.

Note that there's no **fuel** available at Silverton.

Mutawintji National Park

Mutawintji National Park, 130km northeast of Broken Hill in the Byngnano Ranges, has magnificent scenery to offer, with secluded gorges and quiet waterholes attracting a profusion of wildlife. The main highlights of the park are the ancient galleries of **Aboriginal rock art** in the caves and overhangs. The best can only be visited accompanied by an Aboriginal tour guide (April–Oct Wed & Sat at 11am Eastern Standard Time; 3hr; $20; no bookings but contact the Broken Hill NPWS office to confirm times) – there are no tours in the hot summer months. While on the tour you get to visit the **Mutawintji Cultural Centre**, an amazing multimedia collaboration between indigenous Australians and the NPWS which tells of tribal history and myth in sound and pictures.

More Aboriginal rock art can be seen on a series of walks from the Homestead Creek day area, ranging from the wheelchair-accessible **Thaaklatjika Mingkana Walk** (500m return; 20min; flat) to the excellent **Byngnano Range Walk** (7.5km loop; 4–5hr; moderate to hard). About 10km southeast, the **Mutawintji Gorge Walk** (6km return; 3hr; easy) is equally good, heading into one of the park's most picturesque gorges, ending at a peaceful rock pool enclosed by towering rusty red cliffs.

There's a **camping** area at Homestead Creek ($5 per person) among river red gums with barbecues, hot showers and flush toilets.

Access to the park is largely on unsealed dirt roads and there's no fuel so fill up before leaving Broken Hill. The road is normally fine for 2WD vehicles, but check locally as the roads can quickly become impassable after even a light rain; bring extra food and water just in case. The NPWS office in Broken Hill can provide other information. You can also get here from Broken Hill on a one-day **tour** with Tri-State Safari ($160; ☎08/8088 2389, ⓦwww.tristate.com.au).

Kinchega National Park and the Menindee Lakes

From Broken Hill it is a predominantly flat 110-kilometre tar-sealed run southeast to the township of Menindee, amid the **Menindee Lakes**, actually a series of flood plains fed by the Darling River. The upper lakes have been harnessed and channelled to provide water for Broken Hill and generally have water in; those downstream within the **Kinchega National Park** have been dry for several years. Together they are a major habitat for **water birds**; there are over 210 species here in total, including numerous little black cormorants (shags), pelicans, ibis, white egrets and whistling kites.

Menindee itself, on the Darling River Run (see p.349), isn't much to look at but provides limited services including fuel and a small **visitor centre** (daily 10am–2pm, longer during high season; ☎08/8091 4274), where you can get a free, detailed, hand-drawn "mud map" of the lakes area. If you need to **stay**, visit *Maidens Hotel*, Yartla Street (☎08/8091 4208; ❷), where Burke and Wills stayed on their ill-fated trip north in 1860 (see box, p.526). Unfortunately the room in which they stayed burned down a few years back. Still, the green courtyard is a good place for a drink or a counter meal. Otherwise, you can stay at the *Burke & Wills Motel* (☎08/8091 4313, ⒻＰ08/8091 4406; ❸) across the street. There's also free **camping** (with septic toilets), 20km north of town beside Wetherell Lake which Burke and Wills used as a base camp from October 1860 until January 1861 – a tree marks the spot.

Most of the promo photos you'll see of **Kinchega National Park** ($7 per vehicle per 24hr) show skeletal trees emerging from placid waters silhouetted against a late dusk sky. It's a beguiling image, but sadly there hasn't been any significant water in these lakes for the best part of a decade. All is not lost, though. There's still good camping amid large red river gums along the Darling River and fascinating history in the form of a massive shearing shed in great condition.

Before heading out to Kinchega, check road conditions with Broken Hill NPWS: road are all dirt and fine in a 2WD car in the dry seasson but impassable after rain. If you don't have transport, you can take a **day-trip** out here from Broken Hill with Tri-State Safari (℡08/8088 2389, ⓦwww.tristate.com.au) and Silvercity Tours (℡08/8087 6956, ⓦwww.silvercitytours.com.au).

Heading 5km west of Menindee into the park there's an **information shelter** where you pay your park fees. From here a good dirt road heads 10km to a sporadically staffed visitor centre beside the historic and exceptionally well preserved **Kinchega Woolshed**, on the vast Kinchega Station. This was one of the first pastoral settlements in the area when it was established in 1850, and it continued to operate until 1967; you can explore it by following the signposted **woolshed walk**.

Accommodation is available in shearers' quarters next to the old woolshed ($16.50 per adult; book at Broken Hill NPWS), and there's a shared kitchen, coin-op showers and even a payphone nearby.

You can take a slightly longer loop back to Menindee along the Darling River where you'll find numerous **campsites** ($5 per person) scattered in the gum trees.

▲ Fishermen on the Murray River

Wentworth and Mungo National Park

Tucked into the far southwestern corner of the state, **Wentworth**, 260km south of Broken Hill, is an interesting old port town with a storehouse of ancient Aboriginal history around **Lake Victoria** and in the remote **Mungo National Park**.

Wentworth and Lake Victoria

Once a thriving river port, **WENTWORTH** was founded in 1859 at the confluence of the Murray and Darling rivers. For over fifty years it was the hub of paddle-steamer traffic between New South Wales, Victoria and South Australia, but in 1903 the railway reached Mildura, 30km southeast in Victoria. Mildura burgeoned at Wentworth's expense and the "two rivers" town is now a sleepy place of around 1500 people. It makes a good base for exploring Mungo National Park, and with a handful of attractive buildings, the river confluence and some sand dunes it's a pleasant spot to overnight.

Buses run by Broken Hill-based operator Buses-R-Us (T08/8285 6900, Wwww.busesrus.com.au) call at Wentworth on their thrice-weekly Mildura–Broken Hill route, and there's a weekday local service linking Mildura with Wentworth (stopping outside the post office). The **visitor centre** (Mon–Fri 9am–5pm, Sat & Sun 10am–2pm; T03/5027 3624, Wwww.wentworth.nsw .gov.au) is nearby at 66 Darling St.

The National Trust's striking **Old Wentworth Gaol** on Beverly Street (daily 10am–5pm; $6) ranks as the first Australian-designed jail, the work of colonial architect James Barnett who also designed the Sydney Post Office. It was built of handmade bricks in 1879, and ghosts of former prisoners are believed to make the occasional appearance, leaving shadows on pictures taken. Opposite, **Pioneer World** (daily 10am–4pm; $5) is a folk museum exhibiting items related to Aboriginal and European history of the area, and models of extinct megafauna once found hereabouts.

A small park on Cadell Street has a viewing tower from where you can see the **confluence of the two rivers**, and there's a reminder of headier days with the *Ruby*, a restored **paddle steamer**, tied up near where the main road crosses the Darling. Perhaps the most interesting thing to do, however, is simply to drive 6km north of town along Old Renmark Road and have a look at the amazing, Sahara-like dunes of the **Perry Sandhills**.

Wentworth-based Harry Nanya Tours (T03/5027 2076, Wwww.harrynanya tours.com.au) organize excellent daily trips into Mungo National Park (see p.364) and less frequent trips to significant **Aboriginal sites** around **Lake Victoria**, accompanied by accredited Barkindji guides. In 1994, ancient Aboriginal graves were discovered at Lake Victoria, 65km west of Wentworth, when the partial draining of the eleven-square-kilometre lake revealed skeletons buried side by side and in deep layers. Some of the estimated ten thousand graves (well-known to the Barkindji people) date back six thousand years, in what is believed to be Australia's largest pre-industrial burial site, surpassing any such finds in Europe, Asia or North and South America. The site also challenges the premise that Aboriginal lifestyles were solely nomadic, suggesting that here at least they lived in semi-permanent dwellings around the lake.

Among the various places to **stay** in Wentworth, the best waterfront choice is the shady *Willow Bend Caravan Park* on Darling Street (T03/5027 3213, Wwww .willowbendcaravanpark.com; camping $20, powered site $25, cabins ❸), right near the shops but also at the confluence of the Darling and Murray rivers. Otherwise try the *Wentworth Grande Resort*, 61 Darling St (℡03/5027 2225, Ⓦhttp://wentworthgranderesort.com.au; ❹), for more luxury with a pool and river views.

Mungo National Park

Mungo National Park, 135km northeast of Wentworth (always open; $7 per vehicle per 24hr), is most easily reached from the river townships of Wentworth, and Mildura (over the Victorian border about 110km away). Organized tours run to the park from both towns (see p.363), but as long as the roads are dry it is easy enough to drive yourself in an ordinary vehicle. The last 90km to the park are dirt, as are all the roads in the park.

The park is part of the dried-up **Willandra Lakes System** which contains the longest continuous record of Aboriginal life in Australia, dating back more than forty thousand years. During the last Ice Age the system formed a vast chain of freshwater lakes, teeming with fish and attracting waterbirds and mammals. Aborigines camped at the shores of the lake to fish and hunt, and buried their dead in the sand dunes. When the lakes started drying out fifteen thousand years ago, Aborigines continued to live near soaks along the old river channel. The park covers most of one of these dry lake beds, and its dominant feature is a long, crescent-shaped dune, at the eastern edge of the lake, commonly referred to as the **Walls of China**.

There's a NPWS office (daily 8.30am–4.30pm; ℡03/5021 8900) on the corner of the Sturt Highway at Buronga, 3km northeast of Mildura in Victoria, where you can book accommodation in the park. The park's **visitor centre** (daily 8.30am–4.30pm) is near the southwest entrance, and has a very informative display on its geological and Aboriginal history. Nearby, the impressive old **Mungo Woolshed** is open for inspection at any time. From here a fifty-kilometre loop road heads out across the dry lake bed to the dunes then around behind them and back through malee scrub to the visitor centre. Many people just drive the first 10km to a car park from where a short boardwalk takes you onto the **Walls of China** dunes. This low dune system barely rises 30m from the level of the lake bed, but it is a dramatic spot especially around dawn and sunset when the otherworldly shapes and ripple patterns glow golden and kangaroos and goats make their way onto the dunes for meagre pickings. It is a 500-metre walk to the top of the dunes and views over the other side.

Practicalities

There's basic **camping** in the park at the Main Camp, 2km southwest of the visitor centre ($5 per person) and the small, peaceful Belah Campground, 25km east of the visitor centre ($5 per person) in an area rich in wildlife. Roofed **accommodation** is available beside the visitor centre in the *Shearers Quarters* ($20 per person), with a fully equipped communal kitchen and dining area: bring your own sheets. For something a little special there's also *Mungo Lodge*, on the Mildura Road, 3km southwest of the visitor centre (℡03/5029 7297, Ⓦwww.mungolodge.com.au; ❽), comprising sophisticated, modern cabins (and one self-contained apartment sleeping 6; ❾) with lovely decks, and a central lodge with quality restaurant and bar (both open to non-residents).

Probably the best of the companies running **tours** to the park is the Aboriginal-owned Harry Nanya Tours (℡03/5027 2076, ⓦwww.harrynanyatours .com.au) who pick up in Wentworth and Mildura. In summer they do a Sunset Tour (Nov–March daily from 2.30pm; 8hr; $155) that visits the Walls of China and includes afternoon tea and dinner; the winter trips (April–Oct daily from 8.30am; 8hr; $155) include lunch. Both can be joined in the park ($115) and you can tag along in your own vehicle ($80). Cheaper, but still very good, trips are run by Mildura-based Sunraysia Discovery Tours ($115; ℡03/5023 5937, ⓦwww.sunraysiadiscoverytours.com.au).

Travel details

Most public transport in New South Wales originates in Sydney, and the main services are outlined at the end of Chapter 1 on pp.221–222.

Trains

Almost all trains are run by Countrylink (℡13 22 32, ⓦwww.countrylink.info), which extends its network considerably with additional integrated bus services. The New South Wales leg of the Indian Pacific (ⓦwww.trainways.com.au) linking Sydney and Perth takes in Broken Hill and Adelaide. Services listed below are train only.

Broken Hill to: Adelaide (2 per week; 6hr 45min); Menindee (3 weekly; 50min); Sydney (3 per week; 16hr).

Dubbo to: Bathurst (1–2 daily; 3hr); Orange (1–2 daily; 1hr 45in); Sydney (1–2 daily; 6hr).

Sydney to: Adelaide (2 per week; 24hr); Albury (2 daily; 7hr 30min); Armidale (1 daily; 8hr 10min), via Tamworth (6hr 15min); Bathurst (1–2 daily; 3hr 30min); Cootamundra (2–3 daily; 5hr 15min); Dubbo (daily; 6hr 30min); Goulburn (2 daily; 2hr 30min); Griffith (Sat only; 8hr 40min); Menindee (3 per week; 12hr); Moree (1 daily; 9hr) via Gunnedah (6hr 20min) and Narrabri (7hr 45min); Narrandera (Sat only; 7hr 30min); Orange (1–2 daily; 5hr 45min); Parkes (3 per week; 6hr 30min); Scone (4 daily; 4hr 20min); Wagga Wagga (2 daily; 6hr 15min).

Buses

Bus services are mostly run by Countrylink in conjunction with their trains (see above) and by Greyhound (℡1300 473 946, ⓦwww.greyhound .com.au).

Albury to: Corowa (3 per week; 1hr).

Armidale to: Brisbane (1–2 daily; 7hr 30min); Melbourne (1 daily; 18hr 45min); Port Macquarie (2–3 per week; 6hr 15min); Sydney (1 daily; 9hr);

Tamworth (1 daily; 2hr 10min); Tenterfield (2–3 daily; 3hr).

Bathurst to: Cootamundra (3 per week; 4hr); Cowra (0–3 daily; 2hr); Dubbo (0–3 daily; 2hr 45min); Lithgow (1–6 daily; 1hr); Orange (1–6 daily; 40min–1hr).

Bourke to: Dubbo (4 per week; 4hr 10min).

Broken Hill to: Adelaide (3 per week; 7hr); Cobar (1 daily; 4hr 30min); Dubbo (1 daily; 9hr 30min); Mildura (3 per week; 4hr).

Coonabarabran to: Lithgow (1 daily; 5hr); Melbourne (1 daily; 7hr 30min); Sydney (6 per week; 8hr 15min).

Dubbo to: Bathurst (6 per week; 1hr); Bourke (4 per week; 4hr 10min); Broken Hill (1 daily; 8hr 30min); Cobar (1 daily; 3hr 30min); Cootamundra (3 per week; 4hr); Forbes (4 per week; 2hr 20min); Lightning Ridge (1 daily; 4hr 20min); Melbourne (4 per week; 12hr); Orange (1 daily; 2hr); Parkes (4 per week; 1hr 15min).

Griffith to: Canberra (1 daily; 6hr); Hay (1 daily; 1hr 45min); Narrandera (1 daily; 1hr 15min); Sydney (1 daily; 10hr 30min); Wagga Wagga (1 daily; 3hr).

Lithgow to: Bathurst (1–6 daily; 1hr); Coonabarabran (1 daily; 5hr); Cowra (6 per week; 2hr 40min); Dubbo (daily; 3hr 30min); Mudgee (2 daily; 2hr); Orange (1–6 daily; 1hr 45min–2hr).

Orange to: Bathurst (1–6 daily; 40min–1hr); Cootamundra (3 per week; 3hr); Dubbo (1 daily; 2hr); Lithgow (1–6 daily; 1hr 45min–2hr); Parkes (1 daily; 1hr 15min–2hr).

Tamworth to: Armidale (1 daily; 2hr 10min); Dorrigo (1 daily; 4hr 10min); Port Macquarie (3 per week; 8hr 30min); Scone (1 per week; 2hr 15min); Tenterfield (1 daily; 4hr 30min).

Wagga Wagga to: Griffith (1 daily; 3hr).

Flights

The main airlines operating in inland New South Wales are Qantas (☎ 13 13 13, ⊛ www.qantas .com.au), its budget subsidiary Jetstar (☎ 13 15 38, ⊛ www.jetstar.com), Virgin Blue (☎ 13 67 89, ⊛ www.virginblue.com.au), Regional Express (☎ 13 17 13, ⊛ www.regionalexpress.com.au), Airlink (☎ 1300 662 823, ⊛ www.airlinkairlines.com.au) and Brindabella (☎ 1300 668 824, ⊛ www .brindabellaairlines.com.au).

Albury to: Sydney (9 daily; 1hr 15min).

Armidale to: Sydney (4 daily; 1hr 15min).
Bathurst to: Sydney (2 daily; 45min).
Broken Hill to: Adelaide (1–3 daily; 1hr 10min); Dubbo (Mon–Fri 1 daily; 1hr 30min); Sydney (1–2 daily; 2hr 20min).
Dubbo to: Broken Hill (1–2 daily; 2hr); Sydney (8–13 daily; 1hr 10min).
Griffith to: Sydney (1–2 daily; 1hr 20min).
Narrandera to: Sydney (1 daily; 1hr 15min).
Orange to: Sydney (1–4 daily; 45min).
Parkes to: Sydney (1–3 daily; 1hr).
Wagga Wagga to: Sydney (5–7 daily; 1hr 10min).

Coastal Queensland

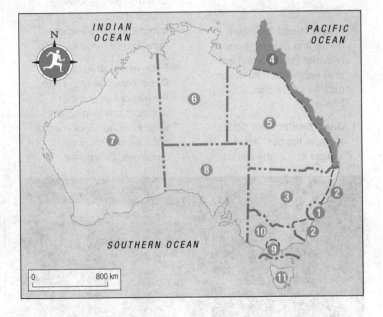

CHAPTER 4

Highlights

✳ **Gold Coast** The beaches, bars and theme parks of Australia's prime domestic holiday destination provide raucous thrills around the clock. See p.394

✳ **Glass House Mountains National Park** One of the few really special places on the Sunshine Coast; it's worth climbing at least one of the dramatic pinnacles for the fantastic views. See p.408

✳ **Fraser Island** The giant dunes and pristine lakes of beautiful Fraser Island are best explored on an action-packed 4WD safari. See p.421

✳ **Great Barrier Reef** Scuba diving is the best way to explore one of the world's most beautiful coral complexes. See p.430

✳ **The Whitsundays** Lying inside the Great Barrier Reef, the rainforested peaks and long white beaches of the Whitsunday Islands offer some of Australia's most picturesque cruising. See p.445

✳ **The Sanctuary at Mission Beach** Rare cassowaries inhabit the rainforest at this outstanding eco-friendly retreat. See p.469

✳ **Four-wheel driving on Cape York** The Cape York Peninsula has some of the most challenging 4WD territory in Australia – watch out for crocs on river crossings. See p.498

▲ Four-wheel driving on Cape York

Coastal Queensland

R unning for over 2500km from the New South Wales border to Australia's northernmost tip at Cape York, **Coastal Queensland** contains almost everything that lures visitors to Australia. Set down in the more developed southeastern corner, the state capital **Brisbane** is a relaxed city with a lively social scene and good work possibilities. South between here and the border, the **Gold Coast** is Australia's prime holiday destination, with a reputation founded on some of the country's best surf – though this now takes second place to a belt of beachfront high-rises, theme parks, and the host of lively bars and nightclubs surrounding **Surfers Paradise**. An hour inland, the **Gold Coast Hinterland**'s green heights offer a chain of national parks packed with wildlife and stunning views. Heading north of Brisbane, fruit and vegetable plantations behind the gentle **Sunshine Coast** benefit from rich volcanic soils and a subtropical climate, overlooked by the spiky, isolated peaks of the **Glass House Mountains**. Down on the coast, **Noosa** is a fashionable resort town with more famous surf. Beyond looms **Fraser Island**, whose surrounding waters host an annual **whale migration** and where huge wooded dunes, freshwater lakes and sculpted coloured sands form the backdrop for exciting safaris.

North of Fraser the humidity and temperature begin to rise as you head **into the tropics**. Though there's still an ever-narrowing farming strip hugging the coast, the Great Dividing Range edges coastwards as it progresses north, dry at first, but gradually acquiring a green sward which culminates in the steamy, rainforest-draped scenery around **Cairns**. Along the way are scores of beaches, archipelagos of islands and a further wealth of national parks, some – such as **Hinchinbrook Island** – with superb walking trails. Those with work visas can also recharge their bank balances along the way by **fruit and vegetable picking** around the towns of **Bundaberg**, **Bowen**, **Ayr** and **Innisfail**. Moving north of Cairns, rainforested ranges ultimately give way to the savannah of the huge, triangular **Cape York Peninsula**, a sparsely populated setting for what is widely regarded as the most rugged 4WD adventure in the country.

Offshore, the tropical coast is marked by the appearance of the **Great Barrier Reef**, among the most extensive coral complexes in the world. The southern reaches out from Bundaberg and **1770** are peppered with sand islands or **cays**, while further north there's a wealth of beautiful granite islands between the coast and reef, covered in thick pine forests and fringed with white sand – the pick of which are the **Whitsundays** near **Airlie Beach** and **Magnetic Island** off Townsville. Many of these islands are accessible on day-trips, though some offer everything from campsites to luxury resorts if you fancy a change of pace from tearing up and down the coast. The reef itself can be explored from **boat**

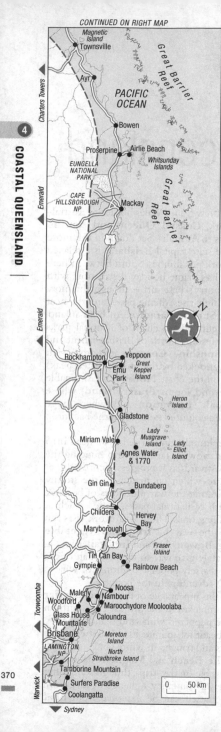

Magnetic Island
Townsville

Great Barrier Reef

PACIFIC OCEAN

Ayr

◄ Charters Towers

Bowen

Proserpine Airlie Beach

EUNGELLA NATIONAL PARK

Whitsunday Islands

CAPE HILLSBOROUGH NP

Mackay

Great Barrier Reef

◄ Emerald

◄ Emerald

Rockhampton Yeppoon
Great Keppel Island
Emu Park

Heron Island

Gladstone

Miriam Vale

Lady Musgrave Island

Lady Elliot Island

Agnes Water & 1770

Gin Gin Bundaberg

Childers Hervey Bay

Maryborough

Fraser Island

Tin Can Bay

Gympie Rainbow Beach

Maleny Noosa
Woodford Nambour
Maroochydore Mooloolaba
Glass House Mountains Caloundra

◄ Toowoomba

Brisbane

Moreton Island

LAMINGTON NP

North Stradbroke Island

Tamborine Mountain

◄ Warwick

Surfers Paradise

Coolangatta

▼ Sydney

0   50 km

4

COASTAL QUEENSLAND

370

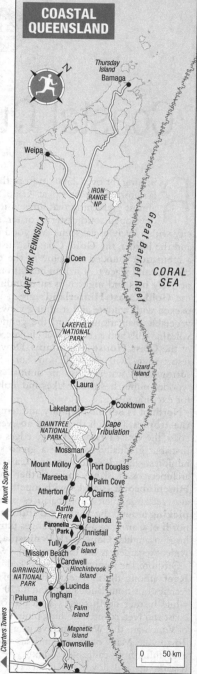

COASTAL QUEENSLAND

N

Thursday Island
Bamaga

Weipa

IRON RANGE NP

CAPE YORK PENINSULA

Coen

CORAL SEA

LAKEFIELD NATIONAL PARK

Great Barrier Reef

Lizard Island

Laura

Lakeland Cooktown

DAINTREE NATIONAL PARK

Cape Tribulation

Mossman

Mount Molloy Port Douglas
Mareeba Palm Cove
Atherton Cairns

◄ Mount Surprise

Bartle Frere
Paronella Park Babinda
Tully Innisfail
Mission Beach Dunk Island
GIRRINGUN NATIONAL PARK Cardwell Hinchinbrook Island
Lucinda
Paluma Ingham

Palm Island

◄ Charters Towers

Magnetic Island
Townsville

1

Ayr

0   50 km

excursions of between a few hours and several days' duration; **scuba divers** are well catered for, though the best of the coral is within easy snorkelling range of the surface.

As a prime tourist destination, Queensland's coast seldom presents **accommodation** problems, with a good range of everything from budget to upmarket options in just about every location. Just be aware that the Easter and Christmas holidays – or even just weekends – can see **room shortages** and price hikes at popular locations, including some national parks: booking in advance is wise, and may even get you discounted rates.

The **rail line** runs north from Brisbane to Cairns and south from Brisbane to Surfers Paradise; incredibly, there's no train between Surfers Paradise and Byron Bay in New South Wales, just a connecting bus. Travelling by **road**, the more-or-less coastal Highway 1 connects Brisbane to Cairns, with frequent long-distance **buses** serving all towns along the route. A few out-of-the-way spots are covered on local transport, but it's worth renting a car from time to time to reach some of the less accessible parks or beaches. **Driving**, Queensland's road signs are infuriatingly confusing and contradictory, and tailgating seems to be mandatory – have a good look at a detailed road **map** (those put out by the state automobile association, the RACQ, are the best) before setting out anywhere. From the Bundaberg area north, you also need to watch out for **cane trains** that cross roads during the sugar-crushing season (roughly June–Dec); crossings are usually marked by flashing red lights.

As for **weather**, winters are dry and pleasant throughout the region, but the summer climate (Dec–April) becomes more oppressive the further north you travel, with the possibility of cyclones bringing torrential rain and devastating storms to the entire tropical coast.

Some history

In a way, Queensland's popularity as a holiday hot spot is surprising, as this is perhaps Australia's most **conservative** state, often lampooned as being slow and regressive. There are, however, very physical and **social divisions** between the densely settled, city-oriented southeastern corner and the large rural remainder, which is mostly given over to mining and farming. These divisions date back to when Brisbane was chosen as capital on Queensland's **separation** from New South Wales in 1859; the city proved an unpopular choice with the northern pioneers, who felt that the government was too far away to understand, or even care about, their needs. These needs centred around the north's **sugar plantations** and the use of Solomon Islanders for labour, a practice the government equated with **slavery** and finally banned in 1872. Ensuing demands for further separation, this time between tropical Queensland and the southeast, never bore fruit, but the remoteness of northern settlements from the capital led to local self-sufficiency, making Queensland far less homogeneous than the other eastern states.

The darker side of this conservatism has seen Queensland endure more than its fair share of extreme or simply **dirty politics**. During the 1970s and early 1980s, the repressive stranglehold of a strongly conservative National Party government, led by the charismatic and slippery Sir Johannes Bjelke-Petersen (better known as "**Joh**"), did nothing to enhance the state's image. Despite a long-term Labor government since his time, state politics remain predominantly right-wing, as was seen in the late 1990s by the emergence from southeast Queensland of Pauline Hanson and her One Nation Party, whose shallow, racist outbursts won favour with a fair number of Australians who felt ignored by the main parties. Labor Premier **Peter Beattie** served for three successive terms between 2001 and 2007 and was the first state premier to act on the Australia-wide **water shortage** caused by a decade of poor rainfall, by implementing water-recycling measures for domestic, industrial and agricultural use in 2007. He resigned from politics shortly afterwards, and was succeeded by his deputy, Anna Bligh, who became the State's first female premier.

Brisbane and around

By far the largest city in Queensland, **BRISBANE** is not quite what you'd expect from a state capital with over one and a half million residents. Although there is urban sprawl, high-rise buildings, slow-moving traffic, crowded streets and the other trappings of a business and trade centre, there's little of the pushiness that usually accompanies them. To urbanites used to a more aggressive approach, the atmosphere is slow, even backward (a reputation the city would be pleased to lose), but to others the languid pace is a welcome change and reflects relaxed rather than regressive attitudes.

Brisbane is an attractive enough place, with the typical features of any Australian city of a comparable age and size – a historic precinct, museums and botanic gardens – though there are neither outstanding sights nor funky beach settlements. It's a fairly easy place to find casual, short-term **employment** however, and there's a healthy, unpredictable social scene, tempting many travellers to spend longer here than they had planned. As for exploring further afield, you'll find empty beaches and surf on **North Stradbroke Island** and dolphins around **Moreton Island** – both easy to reach from the city.

Some history

In 1823, responding to political pressure to shift the "worst type of felons" away from Sydney, the New South Wales government sent Surveyor General **John Oxley** north to find a suitable site for a new prison colony. Sailing into **Moreton Bay**, he was shown a previously unknown river by three shipwrecked convicts who had been living with Aborigines. He explored it briefly, named it "Brisbane" after the governor, and the next year established a convict settlement at **Redcliffe** on the coast. This was immediately abandoned in favour of better anchorage further upstream, and by the end of 1824 today's city centre had become the site of Brisbane Town.

Twenty years on, a land shortage down south persuaded the government to move out the convicts and free up the Moreton Bay area to settlers. Immigrants on government-assisted passages poured in and Brisbane began to shape up as a busy **port** – an unattractive, awkward town of rutted streets and wooden shacks. As the largest regional settlement of the times, Brisbane was the obvious choice as capital of the new state of Queensland on its formation in 1859, though the city's first substantial buildings were constructed only in the late 1860s, after fire had destroyed the original centre and state bankruptcy was averted by Queensland's first gold strikes at Gympie. Even so, development was slow and uneven: new townships were

Aboriginal Brisbane

John Oxley recorded that the **Brisbane Aborigines** were friendly; in the early days, they even rounded up and returned runaways from the settlement. In his orders to Oxley on how to deal with the indigenous peoples, Governor Brisbane admitted, though in a roundabout way, that the land belonged to them: "All uncivilized people have wants ... when treated justly they acquire many comforts by their union with the more civilized. This justifies our occupation of their lands."

But future governors were not so liberal, and things had soured long before the first squatters moved into the Brisbane area and began leaving out "gifts" of poisoned flour and calling in the Native Mounted Police to disperse local Aborigines – a euphemism for exterminating them. In the later part of the nineteenth century, survivors from these early days were dispossessed by the **Protection Act** (in force until the 1970s) which saw them rounded up and relocated onto special reserves away from traditional lands.

A trace of Brisbane's Aboriginal past is found at the Nudgee Bora Ring about 12km north of the centre at Nudgee Waterhole Reserve, at the junction of Nudgee and Childs roads. Last used in 1860, two low mounds where boys were initiated form little more than an icon today, and you'll probably feel that it's not worth the trip. More rewarding are the several Aboriginal walking trails at Mount Coot-tha; the City Hall information desk has leaflets on these which explain traditional uses of the area (see p.379).

founded around the centre at Fortitude Valley, Kangaroo Point and Breakfast Creek, gradually merging into a city.

After World War II, when General Douglas MacArthur used Brisbane as his headquarters to coordinate attacks on Japanese forces based throughout the Pacific, Brisbane stagnated, earning a reputation as a dull, underdeveloped backwater – not least thanks to the Bjelke-Petersen regime. Since his time, escalating development has impressed upon the city's skyline and for the past decade Brisbane has boasted the country's highest internal migration figures and a quarter of the national **population growth**, resulting in booming house prices and the redevelopment of the dilapidated Brisbane River foreshore into upmarket apartments.

Arrival, information and city transport

Brisbane Airport is located 9km northeast of the city centre, at the end of Kingsford Smith Drive. Inconveniently, the domestic and international terminals are sited 2km apart, and are not connected by complimentary shuttle bus, so unless you're prepared to walk you'll have to catch a taxi ($9) or the half-hourly Airtrain (see below; $4). You'll find banks and ATMs at both terminals, but no luggage storage, although a company called Store-a-Bag (⊤07/3503 8538; $13 per suitcase per day plus $10 pick-up/drop-off charge) will pick up items on request. To get to the city from either terminal, there's the speedy **Airtrain** ($14 one-way, $26 return; ⊛www.airtrain.com.au), which takes just twenty minutes to reach Brisbane's Transit Centre; or the **Coachtrans bus** ($12 one-way, $22 return; ⊛www.coachtrans.com.au), which takes up to forty minutes but delivers direct to central accommodation as well as the Transit Centre. A **taxi** into the city costs around $40 for the half-hour trip. For the Gold Coast, Coachtrans delivers direct to accommodation for $39 one-way

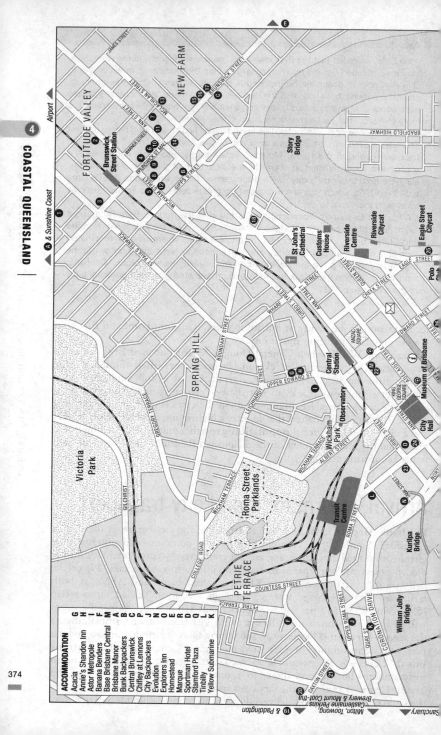

COASTAL QUEENSLAND

4

NEW FARM

FORTITUDE VALLEY

Brunswick Street Station

SPRING HILL

Victoria Park

Roma Street Parklands

PETRIE TERRACE

Transit Centre

Wickham Park Observatory

Central Station

St John's Cathedral

Customs House

Riverside Centre

Story Bridge

Riverside Citycat

Eagle Street Citycat

Museum of Brisbane

City Hall

Kurilpa Bridge

William Jolly Bridge

Airport

A & Sunshine Coast

BRADFIELD HIGHWAY

JAMES STREET

ANN STREET

BRUNSWICK STREET

McLACHLAN STREET

WARNER STREET

BRUNSWICK ST MALL

WICKHAM STREET

GIPPS STREET

ST PAULS TERRACE

BOUNDARY STREET

WHARF STREET

TURBOT STREET

ANN STREET

EAGLE STREET

QUEEN STREET

CREEK STREET

EDWARD STREET

LEICHHARDT STREET

UPPER EDWARD ST

WICKHAM TERRACE

GREGORY TERRACE

GILCHRIST

COLLEGE ROAD

ALBERT STREET

GEORGE STREET

ROMA STREET

COUNTESS STREET

PETRIE TERRACE

UPPER ROMA STREET

QUAY STREET

CORONATION DRIVE

CLAYTON STREET

ANZAC SQUARE

KING GEORGE SQUARE

Polo Club

Milton, Toowong, Brewery & Mount Coot-tha

Castlemaine Perkins

Sanctuary

ACCOMMODATION

Acacia	G
Annie's Shandon Inn	H
Astor Metropole	I
Banana Benders	F
Base Brisbane Central	M
Brisbane Manor	A
Bunk Backpackers	B
Central Brunswick	C
Chifley at Lennons	P
City Backpackers	J
Evolution	N
Explorers Inn	O
Homestead	E
Marque	R
Sportman Hotel	D
Stamford Plaza	Q
Timbilly	L
Yellow Submarine	K

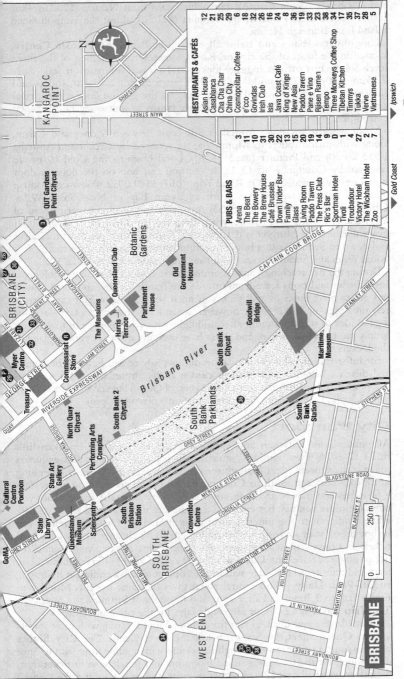

BRISBANE

Ipswich, St Lucia & Lone Pine

▶ Ipswich

▶ Gold Coast

PUBS & BARS

Arena	3
The Beat	11
The Bowery	10
The Brew House	31
Café Brussels	30
Down Under Bar	22
Family	13
Glass	15
Living Room	20
Paddo Tavern	19
The Press Club	14
Ric's Bar	9
Sportman Hotel	D
Tivoli	1
Troubadour	4
Victory Hotel	27
The Wickham Hotel	2
Zoo	7

RESTAURANTS & CAFES

Asian House	12
Casablanca	21
Cha Cha Char	25
China City	29
Cosmopolitan Coffee	6
e'cco	18
Govindas	32
Irish Club	26
Isis	16
Java Coast Café	24
King of Kings	8
New Asia	36
Paddo Tavern	19
Pane e Vino	33
Rijsen Ramen	23
Tempo	38
Three Monkeys Coffee Shop	34
Tibetan Kitchen	17
Timmys	35
Tukka	37
Verve	28
Vietnamese	5

and is a better option than Airtrain which calls in at Nerang ($26.10) 4km inland from Surfers Paradise, and Robina ($27.30), about the same distance inland from Burleigh Heads.

Long-distance buses and trains all end up at Brisbane's **Transit Centre**, located in the heart of the city on Roma Street. On the highest of the three levels are the **bus offices**, luggage lockers and a hostel information desk (daily 7.30am–5.30pm). The middle floor has fast-food joints, a bar, toilets and showers, a medical centre and ATMs, while on the ground floor is the arrival and departure point for local and interstate **trains** as well as several car-rental companies.

Major destinations along Australia's east coast between Sydney and Cairns, along with inland routes to Mount Isa, are serviced by Greyhound Australia (☎13 20 30) and Premier (☎13 34 10). Local buses to the Gold Coast are operated by Coachtrans (☎13 12 30) or you can hop on the door-to-door hostel service provided by Oz Road Trip (☎07/3349 0052, ⓦwww.ozroadtrip .com.au) which travels as far south as Byron Bay in New South Wales. Otherwise, Crisp's (☎07/4661 8333) runs daily to the southeastern towns of Warwick, Tenterfield and Moree, while Brisbane Bus Lines (☎07/3355 0034) heads northeast to Murgon and Toowooba. Trains run up the coast to Cairns and down to Sydney, with a bus connection between Casino in northern New South Wales and Surfers Paradise – for rail information call ☎13 12 30.

During the day, reaching your accommodation seldom poses any problems as **local buses** and **taxis** leave from outside the Transit Centre, and most hostel-iers either meet buses or will pick you up if you call them. You can't always rely on a pick-up late at night, however, when it's best to take a taxi – it's not a good idea to wander around after midnight with your luggage in tow. If you simply must get somewhere and don't have the cab fare, leave your luggage in the lockers.

For **information**, all accommodation can give advice and heaps of brochures, and there's a helpful official **visitor centre** at the airport (Mon–Fri 8.30am–4.30pm, Sat 10am–1pm) and at the eastern end of Queen Street Mall (Mon–Thurs 9am–5.30pm, Fri 9am–7pm, Sat 9am–5pm, Sun 9.30am–4.30pm).

City transport

All public buses, Citytrain and Council ferries are operated by **Translink** (☎13 12 30, ⓦwww.transinfo.com.au), which has a bookings and enquiries office at the Queen Street Mall visitor centre and services 23 zones extending north to Noosa and south to Coolangatta. All tickets are valid on all services – boat, bus and train – and fares are calculated by zone: the more zones you cross, the more you pay. For example, a single fare in the central zone is $2.40, while a ride out to the inner suburbs costs around $4. One-way **tickets** can be bought on your journey, but for multiple trips it's cheaper to buy a book of tickets or a **pass** – most newsagents sell them. Some passes give discounts for day or off-peak travel: the **Day Pass** ($4.80 central zone) offers unlimited bus, ferry and train travel for a day within the zone purchased, ending at midnight; an **Off-Peak Daily** ($3.60 central zone) gives the same benefits Monday to Friday 9am to 3.30pm and after 7pm, and throughout Saturday and Sunday. A **Ten-Trip Saver** is a book of ten single fares for the price of eight.

Buses (drivers give change) run from about 5am to 11pm, with most travel-ling via Queen Street Bus Station below the Myer Centre. The **City Sights** blue bus tours a preset route through the centre with a guide from 9am to 5pm daily – look for the specially marked blue stops and purchase your ticket from the driver (valid all day; $20). Another popular way to get around the Central

Business District is on the **free City Loop** (Mon–Fri 7am–5.50pm). The distinctive red buses circle every ten minutes both clockwise and anticlockwise between Central Station and Botanic Gardens with ten red-bus stops en route in each direction.

The electric **Citytrain** network provides a faster service than the buses, but it's not as frequent or comprehensive. Trains through central Brisbane run every few minutes, but for the more distant suburbs you may have to wait an hour. The last trains leave Central Station on Ann Street at about 11.45pm – timetables are available from ticket offices. You can buy tickets and passes at most stations.

Brisbane's **ferries** are a quick way of getting across the city. Running every ten to thirty minutes between 5.30am and 11.30pm, there are a couple of easy cross-river connections, but the **Inner City** and **City Cat** services are the most useful, the latter running at a bracing 27 knots between the University of Queensland campus in the southwest to Bretts Wharf, up towards the airport on Kingsford Smith Drive. The central departure points for Inner City and City Cat are from South Bank Parklands, Eagle Street Pier and North Quay, next to Victoria Bridge.

After dark, **taxis** (☎13 10 08) tend to cruise round the clubs and hotels; during the day Roma Street is a good place to find one. **Cyclists** have a good number of bike routes from which to choose, with maps available from the visitor centres and libraries. A few hostels **loan** bikes, or they can be easily rented elsewhere (see p.389).

Accommodation

Being Australia's fastest growing city, Brisbane has a dire shortage of inner-city accommodation, with hostels bursting with travelling casual workers, and the luxury boutique apartments often rented long-term by the expanding business and law fraternity. Although there's good diversity in accommodation styles, you should book at least a week ahead to guarantee a room to your liking; during major sports events such as the annual Brisbane Cup horse race in June, and the Royal Queensland Show (the "Ekka") in August, and also the week-long Brisbane Festival in July, it's wise to enquire a month before your arrival. Prices at more upmarket places may drop at weekends and during December and January, due to the scarcity of business customers and competition from the Gold Coast.

City centre

All the following are within a short walk of Central Station, on the Citytrain line.

Acacia 413 Upper Edward St ☎07/3832 1663, ⓦwww.acaciainn.com. This austere brick exterior building with a similarly low-key atmosphere offers very affordable but tiny shared and en-suite rooms with complimentary breakfast. ❸

Annie's Shandon Inn 405 Upper Edward St ☎07/3831 8684, ⓔanniesshandoninn @hotmail.com. A cosy, family-run B&B with single, double and en-suite rooms just 5min walk from the city centre. ❸

Astor Metropole 193 Wickham Terrace ☎1800 046 835 4000, ⓦwww.astorhotel.com.au. Boutique hotel in a smart, renovated nineteenth-century colonial building, with a range of en-suite rooms and fully serviced apartments. Rooms ❹, two-bedroom apartments ❻

Base Brisbane Central Corner of Ann and Edward sts ☎1800 242 273, ⓦwww.stayatbase .com. Formerly *Palace Backpackers*, this huge downtown hostel, purpose-built in 1911, has been completely revamped (except for the ancient lift). The noise from the attached *Down Under Bar* prompts some travellers to move elsewhere for some sleep. Poky singles, high-ceilinged and spacious doubles, and three- to nine-bed dorms. Dorms $26–33, rooms ❸

Chifley at Lennons 66 Queen St Mall ☎07/3222 3222, ⓦwww.chifleyhotels.com. Bang in the city centre, this new place offers tidy, ordinary hotel rooms at a good price. ❻

Evolution 18 Tank St ☎07/3034 3700, ⓦwww.evolutionapartments.com.au. Fully equipped one- and two-bedroom modern apartments, most with outstanding views overlooking the river, though the city-view rooms are not as good. ❼

Explorers Inn 63 Turbot St (corner of George St) ☎07/3211 3488, ⓦwww.explorers.com.au. Popular with rural Queenslanders visiting the city, this centrally positioned and friendly budget hotel has simply furnished standard rooms and amply spacious superior rooms – ask for one of the newly renovated rooms. ❺

Marque 103 George St ☎07/3221 6044, ⓦwww.marquehotels.com. Stylish hotel

rooms, some with partial views over the river, make this one of the best boutique options in town, often with substantial weekend or special package deals. ❼

Sportsman Hotel 130 Leichhardt St, Spring Hill ☎07/3831 2892, ⓦwww.sportsmanhotel.com.au. Gay-friendly pub with rooms; predominantly male clientele but both sexes welcome. ❷

Stamford Plaza Edward St ☎07/3221 1999, ⓦwww.stamford.com. Top-notch hotel with a grand mix of colonial and modern buildings overlooking the river and Botanic Gardens. ❾

Tinbilly Corner of George and Herschel sts ☎1800 446 646, ⓦwww.tinbilly.com. Lively hostel almost directly opposite the Transit Centre; facilities are good though doubles are expensive and the noise level from the on-site bar can build through the evening. Dorms $28–32, rooms ❺

Petrie Terrace

The following cluster of hostels are a ten-minute walk west of Roma Street Station, or take bus #144 from opposite the Transit Centre.

Banana Benders 118 Petrie Terrace ☎07/3367 1157, ⓦwww.bananabenders.com.au. A small, friendly hostel with a homely, easy-going feel. There's a small kitchen and BBQ/dining area, a casual TV-and-video lounge and an on-site job centre. Dorms $26–28, rooms ❸

City Backpackers 380 Upper Roma St ☎07/3211 3221, ⓦwww.citybackpackers.com. One of Brisbane's biggest hostels, this busy, well-run place has clean facilities, fair-sized rooms, its own bar

with budget meal deals, swimming pool, free under-cover parking and good work connections attracting long-term stays. Dorms $21–30, rooms ❹

Yellow Submarine 66 Quay St ☎07/3211 3424, ⓦwww.yellowsubmarinebackpackers.com. Small, comfortable hostel in a refurbished 1860s building with landscaped courtyard. Full kitchen facilities, laundry, BBQ and pool. The staff can help out with work connections. Dorms $25, rooms ❸

Fortitude Valley and New Farm

The Valley's accommodation is well placed for clubs but the area can be seedy late at night. Most buses travelling up Adelaide Street pass through here, or you can take the Citytrain to Brunswick Street Station. For New Farm, take a bus (#177, #178, #167 or #168) from Adelaide St.

Brisbane Manor 555 Gregory Terrace, Fortitude Valley ☎1800 800 589, ⓦwww.brisbanemanor.com. A clean, quiet, heritage lodge with beautiful landscaping, some parking space, laundry and kitchen. ❸

Bunk Backpackers Corner of Ann and Gipp sts ☎1800 682 865, ⓦwww.bunkbrisbane.com.au. From the outside, this place looks like a stark fortress badly located between two busy roads, but good-quality facilities including a pool and spa make this warehouse-sized backpackers' bearable. The attached nightclub-bar adds to the noise though. Dorms $28, doubles ❹, apartments ❻

Central Brunswick 455 Brunswick St, Fortitude Valley ☎07/3852 1411, ⓦwww.centralbrunswickhotel.com.au. Sparkling modern red-brick building with comfortable hotel rooms, all with own bath and TV, some apartment-style with kitchen facilities. Shared amenities include spa and gym. ❻

Homestead 57 Annie St, New Farm ☎07/3358 3538 or 1800 658 344. A large house converted to a hostel, with quiet atmosphere and plenty of outdoor space. There are free bikes, and the hostel arranges trips to Mount Coot-tha. Dorms $23, rooms ❸

The City

The city is focused around the meandering loops of the **Brisbane River**, with the triangular wedge of the business centre on the north bank surrounded by community-oriented suburbs. At the city's heart are the busy, upmarket commercial and administrative precincts around Queen Street and George Street, an area of glass towers, cafés and century old sandstone façades that extends southeast to the Botanic Gardens on the river. Radiating north, the polish gives way to less conservative shops, accommodation and eateries around Spring Hill, Fortitude Valley and New Farm, and the aspiring suburbs of Petrie Terrace and Paddington. To the west is a blaze of riverside homes at Milton and Toowong and the fringes of Mount Coot-tha. Across the river, the major landmarks are the South Bank Cultural Centre and South Bank Parklands, which stretch to Kangaroo Point. Beyond are the open, bustling streets of South Brisbane and the West End, more relaxed than their northern counterparts.

Downtown

Queen Street is Brisbane's oldest thoroughfare, the stretch between George and Edward streets a **pedestrian mall** flanked by multistorey shopping centres. The area is always busy with people running errands, eating at the many cafés, window-shopping or just socializing, and there's usually some kind of entertainment too: either informal efforts – acrobats, buskers and the occasional soap-box orator – or more organized events such as dancing or jazz sessions on the small stage about halfway down the street.

City Hall, Museum of Brisbane and Central Business District

North from the mall along Albert Street, you arrive at the open space of **King George Square**, a popular gathering place for the city's business workers. Facing the square to the west is **City Hall**, an ornate stately 1920s building with

▲ The Brisbane River

a strikingly bland 92-metre clock tower. Inside, the **Museum of Brisbane** (daily 10am–5pm; free) has five rotating exhibition spaces usually with a Queensland theme, with one gallery reserved for emerging Brisbane artists. Whilst you're there, pick up a free historical **self-guided walking pamphlet**, which highlights the city's architecture and history in great detail. The **clock tower** is open, too, if you want a view of the city centre (daily 10am–3pm; free); access is through the City Hall foyer.

Flanked by roads further up Albert Street, tiny **Wickham Park** is overlooked by the grey cone of Brisbane's oldest building, a windmill known locally as the **Observatory**, built by convicts in 1829 to grind corn for the early settlement. The original wooden sails were too heavy to turn but found use as a gallows until being pulled off in 1850, and all grinding was done by a treadmill – severe punishment for the convicts who had to work it. After the convict era the building became a signal station and now stands locked up and empty, held together with a cement glaze.

East between here and the river lies Brisbane's **Central Business District**, which was heavily developed in the 1990s and left with a legacy of glassy high-rises sprouting alongside the restaurants and shops of the Riverside Centre; the few surviving old buildings are hidden among the modern ones. The copper-domed **Customs House** (daily 9am–4pm; guided tour 10am Sun; free) at the upper end of Queen Street, built in 1889, harbours a small collection of Chinese antiques and hosts free concerts given by the Queensland University Orchestra, usually on the last Sunday of the month, while the neo-Gothic **St John's Cathedral** (daily 9.30am–4.30pm; donation) on Ann Street has some elegant stained-glass windows and the only fully stone-vaulted ceiling in Australia. Sunday morning is made lively by the Eagle Street Markets between the river and the road – too trendy for bargains, but not bad for jewellery and leatherwork, clothing and $25 massages.

The historic precinct

The area south between Queen Street and the Botanic Gardens contains some of Brisbane's finest architecture, dating from the earliest days of settlement until the late nineteenth century. Between Elizabeth and Queen streets, occupying an entire block, is the former **Treasury** with its classical facade. Built in the 1890s, its grandeur reflects the wealth of Queensland's gold mines (though by this point most were on the decline) and was a slap in the face to New South Wales, which had spitefully withdrawn all financial support from the fledgling state on separation some forty years previously, leaving it bankrupt. With irony typical of a state torn between conservatism and tourism, the building is now Brisbane's 24-hour **casino**.

South along William Street, the **Commissariat Store** is contemporary with the Observatory, though in considerably better shape. Originally a granary, it's now a museum (Tues–Fri 10am–4pm; $5) and headquarters of the Royal Historical Society of Queensland; the knowledgeable staff pep up an otherwise dusty collection of relics dating back to convict times. Further south along George Street you pass **Harris Terrace** and **The Mansions**, two of the city centre's last surviving rows of Victorian-era terraced houses, the latter guarded by stone cats on the parapet corners. Nearby, on the corner of George and Alice streets, the **Queensland Club** was founded in 1859, just four days before the separation of Queensland from New South Wales. Heavy walls, columns and spacious balconies evoke a tropical version of a traditional London club; entrance and membership – women are still not allowed to join – are by invitation only. Diagonally opposite, **Parliament House** (Mon–Fri 9am–4.15pm,

Sat & Sun 10am–2pm; free guided tours when Parliament not in session) was built to a design by Charles Tiffin in 1868, in an appealingly compromised French Renaissance style which incorporates shuttered north windows, shaded colonnades and a high, arched roof to allow for the tropical climate. You can see the grand interior on an hour-long guided tour, and there's access to the chambers when there's no debate in progress.

South of Parliament House, George Street becomes a pedestrian lane along the western side of the Botanic Gardens and home to the Queensland University of Technology. Here you'll find the **Old Government House** (Mon–Fri 10am–4pm, open some weekends – ⓣ07/3864 8005; free), the official residence of Queensland's governors and premiers between 1862 and 1910. Another of Tiffin's designs, the building has been comprehensively restored to its stately, early twentieth-century condition, and is well worth a look for its furnishings.

The Botanic Gardens

Bordered by Alice Street, George Street and the river, Brisbane's **Botanic Gardens** overlook the cliffs of Kangaroo Point and, while more of a park than a botanic garden, provide a generous arrangement of flowers, shrubs, bamboo thickets and green grass for sprawling on, all offering an easy escape from city claustrophobia. Free **guided tours** (Mon–Sat 11am & 1pm except mid-Dec to Jan) leave from the rotunda, 100m inside the gardens' main entrance, halfway along Alice Street.

Once a vegetable patch cultivated by convicts, formal gardens were laid out in 1855 by Walter Hill, who experimented with local and imported plants to see which would grow well in Queensland's then untried climate. Some of his more successful efforts are the oversized **bunya pines** around the Edward Street entrance at the east end of Alice Street, planted in 1860, and a residual patch of the **rainforest** that once blanketed the area, at the southern end of the park. **Mangroves** along the river, accessible by a **boardwalk**, are another native species more recently protected. During the day, cyclists flock to the park, as it's at one end of a popular cycling and jogging track that follows the north bank of the river south to St Lucia and the University of Queensland. At the southern end of the gardens, classical music recitals are held on an open-air stage in the summer, beyond which the pedestrian **Goodwill Bridge** crosses over the river to South Bank Parklands.

The northern neighbourhoods

North of the river, just beyond Brisbane's central business district, are several former suburbs which have been absorbed by the city sprawl: **Paddington** and **Petrie Terrace** to the west, **Spring Hill** and **Fortitude Valley** to the north, and **New Farm** to the east. Houses in these areas are popular with Brisbane's aspiring professional class, and while office buildings and one-way streets are beginning to encroach, there's also an older character reflected in the many high-set, wooden-balconied and tin-roofed Queenslander houses still standing – some lovingly restored to original condition.

Fortitude Valley

While the other northern neighbourhoods are mainly residential, **Fortitude Valley** – better known as just "**the Valley**" – is a tangled mix of shops, restaurants, bars and clubs, comprising Brisbane's unofficial centre of artistic, gastronomic and alcoholic pursuits. An eclectic mix of the gay, the groovy and the grubby, the Valley is mostly focused along partially pedestrianized

Brunswick Street, which sports a kilometre-long melange of nightclubs, an Irish pub, a compact Chinatown complete with the usual busy restaurants and stores, and a burgeoning European street-café scene. The area is in a state of inner-city gentrification, when the urban poor make way for hipsters, artists and students, though Brunswick Street itself has so far avoided the yuppies and smarmy wine-bars which have descended on parallel **James Street**, and remains a good spot to enjoy an evening out among Brisbane's young, fun and adventurous. It's best at weekends when cafés buzz and live musicians compete for your attention; on Saturday there's a secondhand market in the mall. After dark the Valley's streets can be somewhat sleazy, with an element of drug-related petty crime – if you've any distance to go on your own after the pubs close, take a taxi.

South Brisbane

Across the river from the city centre, best reached using the pedestrian-only Kurilpa Bridge or Goodwill Bridge, the main points of interest are the **South Bank Cultural Centre** and the nearby **South Bank Parklands**. Both are also accessible by Citytrain to South Brisbane Station, while plenty of buses from all parts of the city stop outside the station on Melbourne Street.

Beyond here, the **West End** is South Brisbane's answer to Fortitude Valley, with no sights as such but popular for the escalating number of **restaurants and cafés** strung out along Boundary Street.

The Brisbane River

The sluggish, meandering **Brisbane River** is, at four hundred million years old, one of the world's most ancient waterways. It flows from above Lake Wivenhoe – 55km inland – past farmland, into quiet suburbs and through the city before emptying 150km downstream into Moreton Bay. Once an essential trade and transport link with the rest of Australia and the world, it now seems to do little but separate the main part of the city from South Brisbane; though it's superficially active around the city centre, with ferries and dredgers keeping it navigable, most of the old wharves and shipyards now lie derelict or buried under parkland.

If the locals seem to have forgotten the river, it has a habit of reasserting its presence through **flooding**. In February 1893 cyclonic rains swelled the flow through downtown Brisbane, carrying off Victoria Bridge and scores of buildings: eyewitness accounts stated that "debris of all descriptions – whole houses, trees, cattle and homes – went floating past". This has since been repeated many times, notably in January 1974 when rains from **Cyclone Wanda** completely swamped the centre, swelling the river to a width of 3km at one stage. Despite reminders of this in brass plaques marking the depths of the worst floods at **Naldham House Polo Club** (at 1 Eagle St), some of Brisbane's poshest real estate flanks the river, with waterfront mansions at Yeerongpilly, Graceville and Chelmer, southwest of the centre. They're all banking on protection from the Lake Wivenhoe dam, completed in 1984, which should act as a buffer against future floods.

The most enjoyable and cheapest way to explore the downtown reaches of the river is simply to take a return ride on the **City Cat** (see p.377 for details); this popular, if unofficial, sightseeing trip means that the service can be severely overcrowded during holidays. You can also take **sightseeing cruises** with River City Cruises (daily 10.30am & 12.30pm; $25; ☎0428 278 473 for bookings) from the South Bank Cruise Terminal at South Bank Parklands; or aboard the quaint paddlewheeler *Kookaburra River Queen* (daily 12.15pm & 2pm; $20 cruise only; seafood buffet dinner cruise 7.30pm & 9.30pm, $75; ☎07/3221 1300, ⓦwww.kookaburrariverqueens.com).

The South Bank Cultural Centre

The **South Bank Cultural Centre** comprises separate adjacent buildings between Grey Street and the river housing the Queensland Museum, Sciencentre, the Queensland Art Gallery, State Library and Gallery of Modern Art (better known as GoMA). The buildings themselves are a mass of dull, 1980s-style concrete facades, but they hide some of Australia's better museum collections and are well worth a visit.

The **Queensland Museum** (daily 9.30am–5pm; free, except for special exhibitions) is essentially a natural history museum. It kicks off with full-scale models of a humpback-whale family suspended from the lobby ceiling, then takes you past displays of finds from the state's fossil sites, including a reconstruction of Queensland's own *Muttaburrasaurus*. There's also a little bit on the marine environment, particularly turtles, and the **Museum Zoo**, where hundreds of models, skeletons and remains of wildlife are arranged in a long conga line in order of size. The topmost floor has an exhibition on **Aboriginal Queensland**, with the usual cases of stone tools and boomerangs enlivened by photos, accounts by early settlers and Aboriginal elders, interactive videos and Dreamtime stories.

In the same building but with a separate entrance, the **Sciencentre** (daily 9.30am–5pm; $11) is good for those who prefer to prod and dismantle exhibits rather than peer at them through a protective glass case. It's great for children, with favourites including the "perception tunnel", which gives the impression of rotating although you remain stock still, and the "Thongophone", a set of giant pan pipes played by whacking the top with a flip-flop – all good rainy-day material.

The adjoining **Queensland Art Gallery** (Mon–Fri 10am–5pm, Sat & Sun 9am–5pm; free, except for special exhibitions) houses a collection of Australian painting from the early days of local settlement up to the present, with most important artists represented. Top of the bill are astounding works by Sidney Nolan from his series on **Mrs Fraser** (of Fraser Island fame), watercolours by iconic Aboriginal artist Albert Namatjira, Ian Fairweather's abstract canvases, and a nineteenth-century **stained-glass window** of a kangaroo hunt. The selection is broad enough to trace how Australian art began by aping European tastes and then, during the twentieth century, found its own style in the alienated works of Nolan, Boyd and Whiteley, who were all inspired by Australian landscape and legends.

To browse newspapers and access the internet for free, stop in at the Interzone on the ground floor of the adjoining **State Library** (Mon–Thurs 10am–8pm, Fri–Sat 10am–5pm). Across Stanley Place, GoMA, the **Gallery of Modern Art** (Mon–Fri 10am–5pm, Sat & Sun 9am–5pm; free, except for special exhibitions), opened in 2006 and announced Brisbane's emergence as a thriving arts centre. The museum really came of age in 2008 with two massive coups: it was chosen as the sole Australian host to Picasso's collection on its world tour, and it staged an exciting Andy Warhol exhibition. The gallery is a huge, airy space ideally suited to contemporary displays, with constantly changing exhibitions including Queensland's most impressive collection of indigenous art. The largest space though is an unobstructed wall-to-ceiling view through huge glass windows revealing the architecturally zany Kurilpa Bridge and beyond the river to the evolving urban skyline.

The South Bank Parklands

The **South Bank Parklands** date back to just 1988 but despite this are one of the nicest parts of the city – you can promenade under shady fig trees along the riverfront; **picnic** under rainforest plants and bamboo on lawns lining the banks of shallow, stone-lined "streams" (which are convincing enough to attract large, sunbathing water dragons and birds); or make use of the **artificial beach** and accompanying saltwater pool. **Bands** play most Saturday nights, either on the outdoor stage or at the *Plough Inn*, a restored, century-old pub on the cobbled high street; other attractions include the exhibits at the **Maritime Museum** (daily 9.30am–4.30pm; $7), where there's a 90-year-old Torres Strait pearling lugger and a World War II frigate, *Diamantina*, on show in the dry dock.

You can reach South Bank Parklands on Citytrain to **South Bank Station**; by ferry or City Cat; or by taking the pedestrian Goodwill Bridge from the city Botanic Gardens to the Maritime Museum.

Southwest of the centre

A few worthwhile sights lie southwest of the city centre, some of which – such as Lone Pine Sanctuary – you can reach **by boat** along the Brisbane River, though all are also accessible by other forms of public transport.

The Castlemaine Perkins Brewery: XXXX

Just west from Petrie Terrace on Milton Road (take the Citytrain to Milton and it's just across the street), the **Castlemaine Perkins Brewery** (☎07/3361 7597, ⓦwww.xxxx.com.au) has been making Queensland's own beer since 1878. Its famous yellow-and-red **XXXX** emblem is part of the Queensland landscape – it's splashed across T-shirts, the roofs of Outback hotels, and the labels of countless discarded bottles and cans littering everything from roadsides to the Great Barrier Reef. For enthusiasts, the adjacent **XXXX Ale House** runs tours (Mon–Fri 10am–4pm on the hour, Sat 10.30am, 11am & noon, plus Wed evening at 6pm; $20; bookings essential and you must wear fully enclosed shoes) which incorporate a one-hour overview of the brewing process and four free beers in the Ale House.

Mount Coot-tha

The lower slopes of **Mount Coot-tha**, about 5km from the city centre away from the river along Sir Samuel Griffith Drive (bus #471 from Adelaide St runs hourly 7.50am–6.15pm weekdays, 10.20am–4.35pm weekends), are the setting for Brisbane's second **botanic gardens** (daily 8am–5pm; free). Sunday picnickers are a common sight in this leafy haven, where careful landscaping and the use of enclosures have created a variety of climates – dry pine and eucalypt groves, a cool subtropical rainforest complete with waterfalls and streams, and the elegant Japanese Gardens with bonsai and fern houses. The steamy **tropical plant dome** contains a pond stocked with lotus lilies and fish, overhung by lush

---

Drinks for women: the Regatta Hotel

Though Australian **pubs** still tend towards being all-male enclaves, women were once legally barred to "protect" them from the corrupting influence of foul language. On April 11, 1965, Merle Thornton (mother of the actress Sigrid Thornton) and her friend Rosalie Bogner chained themselves to the footrail of the **Regatta Hotel** bar at Toowong in protest; the movement they inspired led to the granting of "the right to drink alongside men" in the mid-1970s. The grand, pink-and-white colonial hotel, now a trendy place for a drink after work on Fridays, is on the west bank of the river along Coronation Drive, about 2km from the city centre towards St Lucia – catch the City Cat ferry to Regatta.

greenery dripping with moisture. Informative **free guided walks** depart from the information kiosk at 11am and 1pm daily except Sunday.

The other dome in the gardens does duty as a **planetarium** (Tues–Sun 10am 4.30pm with a daily public show at 3pm, and additional shows Sat & Sun at 11.30am, 12.30pm & 2pm, and evening shows Sat only 6pm & 7.30pm; $12.70; ℡07/3403 2578). While the foyer display is dated, the show itself, which you view lying back under the dome's ceiling, gives a unique perspective of the key features of Brisbane's night sky.

After visiting the botanic gardens most people head up the road to Mount Coot-tha's **summit** for panoramas of the city and, on a good day, the Moreton Bay islands. Walking tracks from here make for moderate hikes of an hour or two through dry gum woodland, and include several **Aboriginal trails** – the best of these branches off the Slaughter Falls track with informative signs pointing out plants and their uses. Pamphlets on the tracks are available from the botanical gardens or the information desk in the foyer of Brisbane's City Hall.

Lone Pine Sanctuary

Lone Pine Sanctuary, on Jesmond Road in Fig Tree Pocket (daily 8.30am–5pm; $22), has been a popular day-trip upstream since first opening its gates in 1927. Here you can see native Australian fauna in its natural state which, in the case of the sanctuary's hundred-odd koalas, means being asleep for eighteen hours a day. In nearby cages you'll find other slumbering animals, including Tasmanian devils, fruit bats, blue-tongued lizards and dingoes. Indeed, about the only lively creatures you'll see are birds and a colony of hyperactive sugar gliders in the nocturnal house. Alternatively, head for the outdoor paddock where tolerant wallabies and kangaroos allow themselves to be petted and fed by visitors.

You can catch **bus** #430 or #431 from outside the Myer Centre on Elizabeth Street to Lone Pine, but the best way of getting there is to take a ninety-minute **river cruise** past Brisbane's waterfront suburbs with Mirimar Cruises (daily 10am, returns to city 2.45pm; $50, including entry to Lone Pine; ℡1300 729 742), whose boats depart from the Cultural Centre Pontoon beside the State Library. Free pick-up from central accommodation is usually possible if you call ahead. Note that the City Cat and other public ferries do not go as far upstream as Lone Pine.

Eating

Brisbane has no gastronomic tradition to exploit, but there's a good variety of **cafés and restaurants** all over the city, with a trend towards "modern Australian" cuisine (creative use of local produce, with Asian and Mediterranean influences). Fortitude Valley has a dense grouping of Asian restaurants (and a fashionable café society), while South Brisbane's Boundary Street has more of a European flavour.

The **counter meals** offered by many downtown hotels (especially during the week) are the cheapest route to a full stomach – aim for lunch at around noon and dinner between 5 and 6pm – or try one of the scores of cafés and **food courts** in the centre catering to office workers. Restaurants **open** from around 11am to 2pm for lunch, and from 6 to 10pm or later for evening meals; many are closed for one day a week (often Monday).

City centre

Cha Cha Char Pier 9, Eagle St ☎ 07/3211 9944. With an owner who is well connected to the beef industry, steak is the thing to go for here, and around $40 will buy you one of the best you will ever eat. Also recommended for its wine selection and riverside location.

China City 76 Queen St Mall. Probably the most authentic Cantonese food in Brisbane – though also relatively expensive – especially good for its seafood and *yum cha* (dim sum) selection. Seafood mains from $25.

e'cco 100 Boundary St ☎ 07/3831 8344, ⓦ www .eccobistro.com. Obscure location but boasts an impressive awards list, not to mention its own cookbook – you'll have to book here, and sometimes days ahead. Not cheap but good value, with all mains at $40. Open for lunch Tues–Fri, dinner Tues–Sat.

Govindas First floor, 99 Elizabeth St. Hare Krishna-run vegetarian food bar, with a $10 all-you-can-eat menu. Mon–Thurs 11am–7.30pm, Fri 11am–8.30pm, Sat 11am–2.30pm.

Irish Club 171 Elizabeth St. Not a theme-bar clone but the genuine deal, with set pub lunches and dinners from $13 and nightly live entertainment.

🏃 **Java Coast Café** 340 George St. This delightful café is tucked down an alley with a brick-laid courtyard doused in tropical vegetation. It's a serene place to escape the city and enjoy coffee and carrot cake or an all-day brekkie. Lunch specials include spinach and feta quiche or Vietnamese noodle salad, all for under $15. Mon–Fri 7.30am–4pm.

Pane e Vino Corner of Charlotte and Albert sts. Likeable Italian café-restaurant with pavement tables, catering mainly to nearby office executives. Light meals from $13, otherwise main courses are around $25.

Rjisen Ramen 414 George St. Popular with a Japanese clientele, this unassuming place specializes in healthy Japanese noodle soups (around $15) including the sumptuous ramen spicy dumplings. You can also order a multitude of side dishes for under $10 from tofu salad to teriyaki beef.

Verve 109 Edward St. Modern Italian in an ambient basement cellar with funky music and art. Pastas and risottos $11–16, mains under $20 and enticing blackboard specials such as goat's-cheese gnocchi. Closed Sun.

Petrie Terrace

Casablanca 52 Petrie Terrace. Inexpensive brasserie and café on the corner of fashionable Caxton St serving the young and pretentious. Tapas

are served at the bar for around $15, and the food is excellent and mouthwateringly spicy, with leanings towards North African cuisine. R&B, hip-hop or live music provides atmosphere at weekends and there are Latin dance classes in the cellar Tues–Thurs.

Paddo Tavern 186 Given Terrace (corner of Caxton St). Huge Irish pub with a dozen pool tables plus beer and steak for $12. Live comedy acts downstairs.

Fortitude Valley

Asian House 165 Wickham St. Good, filling Chinese food at very reasonable prices – most mains, such as roast pork or greens in oyster sauce, are under $15.

Cosmopolitan Coffee 322 Brunswick St Mall. This relaxed place is something of an institution with Brisbane's café society; it opens early for breakfast and is less pretentious than the surrounding competition.

Isis Corner of Brunswick and Robertson sts ☎ 07/3852 1155. Smart, popular, long-running brasserie with a predominantly French-influenced menu and mains at around $39.

King of Kings 169 Wickham St. Two restaurants with separate entrances, in the same building: upstairs it's huge and tacky, but popular with the local Chinese community thanks to its fine late-morning *yum cha* tea selections – be prepared to queue at weekend lunchtimes. Open daily for lunch and dinner.

🏃 **Tibetan Kitchen** 454 Brunswick St ☎ 07/3358 5906. It's hard to resist any place that advertises "traditional Tibetan, Sherpa, Nepalese foods", and luckily the stuff on offer here, including the Valley's best samosas and curries, is tasty, cheap, and served in a very attractive setting. Mains $15–18. Open daily for dinner only; booking advisable at weekends. Also at 216 Petrie Terrace ☎ 07/3367 0955.

The Vietnamese 194 Wickham St ☎ 07/3252 4112. With an interior as plain and unassuming as the name over the door, this is no-frills, genuine Vietnamese food – the crispy duck in plum sauce is excellent, as are the Vietnamese spring rolls (self-assembled using a boiled rice-noodle wrapper). Most mains cost around $15, but if you finish dining by 7pm you'll get 15 percent off the bill. Bookings recommended for later tables.

South Brisbane

New Asia 153 Boundary St, West End. Forget the flashier Vietnamese restaurants in the neighbour-hood, this is the best – prawns grilled on sugar cane, deep-fried quail, rice-noodle dishes – most for less than $12 a dish.

Tempo 181 Boundary St, West End. Great Italian-style home cooking, with fresh salads and fine seafood pasta – even humble sandwiches come with a salad big enough to be a meal in itself. The most expensive dish costs around $12. Tues–Sun 9am–late.

Three Monkeys Coffee Shop 58 Mollison St, West End. Decorated with a funky assortment of African oddments; serves average coffee, awesome cakes, and effortlessly achieves the sort of bohemian atmosphere most cafés merely aspire to. Greek-influenced menu with plenty of vegetarian options, and nothing over $15. Daily 9am–late.

🏃 Timmy's Galleria Complex, corner of Grey and Tribune sts, Southbank. Tucked away in a corner, you could easily mistake this discreet but fashionable restaurant overlooking the parklands as another cheap café. The food though is exceptional, with masterly Asian and Australian fusion dishes including lamb shanks in yellow curry or spicy quail. Mains around $35. Tues–Sat 11am–late, Sun 8am–3pm.

🏃 Tukka 145 Boundary St, West End ☎07/3846 6333. Combines native fruits, seeds, herbs and meats with European-style cooking techniques for a genuinely Australian meal, loosely inspired by Aboriginal bushtucker. Mains around $30, with a $69 five-course set meal available. Booking essential.

Nightlife

The days when Brisbane nights were a byword for boredom have long gone, with the city enjoying an explosion of home-grown musical talent: **bands** such as Savage Garden and Powderfinger have put Brisbane firmly on the Australian pop-culture map whilst up-and-coming bands include The Grates and Yves Klein Blue. While there are plenty of central places to fire up with a few drinks on Friday and Saturday nights, the big push is out to Fortitude Valley's **bars and clubs**. Live-music venues are very fluid and tend to open and close in the blink of an eye; places listed below should be here to stay, but check with **music stores** such as Rocking Horse, just off Queen Street Mall in Albert Street, or weekly **free magazines** for up-to-the-minute reviews and listings – *Rave* for general information, *Time Off* for rock and live bands, and *Scene* for dance. The city's two main music festivals are the

Gay and lesbian Brisbane

Brisbane's gays and lesbians revel in a loud and energetic scene which gets better every year. In June the Pride Collective hosts the annual **Pride Festival** (@www.pride brisbane.org.au), a diverse three-week event with a street march, fair, art exhibitions, a film festival, sports events and general exhibitionism, culminating with a dance party – the Queen's Birthday Ball. Other events to look out for include the **Northern Exposure** in October organized by Brisbears (@www.brisbears.org.au) at various locations around the city.

The **gay scene** is largely clustered around the suburbs of Spring Hill, Fortitude Valley, New Valley, New Farm and Paddington. For up-to-the-moment information, listen to Queer Radio, Station ZZZ 102.1FM (Wed 9–11pm) or pick up a copy of the fortnightly *Qnews* (@www.qnews.com.au) or *Queensland Pride* from gay nightclubs, street distributors and some coffee shops.

For **gay-friendly accommodation**, try *Central Brunswick Apartment Hotel*, or the *Sportsman Hotel* (see p.378); nightlife focuses on *Cockatoo Club* above *The Beat*, *The Wickham Hotel* and *Sportsman Hotel* – all listed under "Nightlife" on p.388. Bent Books, on the corner of Vulture and Boundary streets in the West End, is the longest-established gay **bookshop** in Brisbane, and **medical advice** is available at the Central Brunswick Medical Centre, 421 Brunswick St, Fortitude Valley (☎07/3852 2733; Mon–Sat from 8am).

world-music celebration of Fete de la Musique at King George Square in June and the outdoor Sunset Sounds rock concert at the Botanical Gardens in January – see ⊛www.brispop.com for updated news and weekly gig listings. There's no standard charge for club entry, and many places offer free nights and special deals.

City centre

The Brew House 142 Albert St ☎07/3003 0098. Microbrewery producing British-style ale, bitter and stout as well as lager, plus a sports bar with live bands or DJ Fri and Sat nights. Call first to arrange a brewery tour.

Café Brussels Corner of Mary and Edward sts. Ice-cold European beers served amongst century-old wooden panelling, tiles and light fittings.

Down Under Bar At *Palace Backpackers* (corner of Ann and Edward sts). Hugely popular and often overtly get-drunk-throw-up-and-fall-down venue for travellers.

Victory Hotel 127 Edward St. Nice beer garden with braziers taking the chill off in winter and live bands Wed–Sun.

Petrie Terrace and Spring Hill

The Living Room 2 Caxton St. The latest place to be seen, this is a modern hip-hop club with live bands and guest DJs on weekends, jazz every Wed and mellow acoustic shows on Sun.

Paddo Tavern 186 Given Terrace. Band and disco on Fri night and a sit-down comedy club most days of the week.

Sportsman Hotel 130 Leichhardt St. Gay, lesbian and straight crowds fill the two floors, which have pool tables, pinball, bands, bottle shop and bistro. Fantastic drag nights Thurs–Sun.

Fortitude Valley and New Farm

Arena 201 Brunswick St ☎07/3252 5690. Long-established venue hosting popular DJs and dance parties as well as local and international touring bands. Call for listings.

The Beat 677 Ann St. Small, crowded and sweaty pub with a beer garden outside where you can recharge your batteries on bar food. The $10 cover charge is a bit off-putting, but it's one of the best techno/dance venues in town, and open until 5am.

Upstairs is the *Cockatoo Club*, a stridently gay venue with both indoor and outdoor bars, and a penchant for commercial dance music. Open Wed–Sun.

The Bowery 676 Ann St. Award-winning bar in the heart of Fortitude Valley makes a good place to meet for an early cocktail or an ambient retreat in the middle of the night.

Family 8 McLachlan St. Serious dance venue with three huge floors, where established DJs play everything from house to 1970s funk.

Glass 420 Brunswick St. Funky wine bar serving wicked tapas, this is a popular spot to start the evening, with live jazz Wed–Fri from 8pm and DJs on Sat. Open Tues–Sat.

The Press Club In the *Empire Hotel* (corner of Brunswick and Ann sts). Club with door gorillas, leather lounges, big cushions to rest your feet on and a huge glam/industrial fan as the centrepiece, all of it enveloped in a relaxed and funky dance beat. Rather a "fabulous" crowd, out to see and be seen, with drinks prices to match. Closed Mon.

Ric's Bar 321 Brunswick St. Narrow, crowded place and overtly pretentious – getting to the bar takes some effort. Nightly mix of live Aussie bands downstairs and DJ-driven techno upstairs at the *Upbar*.

Tivoli 52 Costin St. Originally an Art-Deco theatre, now one of Brisbane's most popular live venues for big-name domestic touring bands.

Troubadour 322 Brunswick St. Nightly live music, usually pub-style acoustic or rock – it's a bit of a low-key option, but you can at least have a conversation with your mates here.

The Wickham Hotel Corner of Wickham and Alden sts. Queensland's most popular gay pub. Drag show on Thurs and DJs every night.

Zoo 711 Ann St. Best of the long-standing clubs in the valley, offering a hectic night out featuring dub or local bands, and jazz every last Sun of the month. Wed–Sun 5pm–late.

Listings

Airlines Air New Zealand, 243 Edward St ☎13 24 76; Air Niugini, Level 4, 99 Creek St ☎07/3229 5844; Air Pacific ☎1800 230 150; Air Vanuatu,

Brisbane International Airport ☎1300 780 737; British Airways ☎1300 767 1770; Cathay Pacific ☎13 17 47; China Airlines ☎1300 668 052;

Emirates ☏ 1300 303 777; Japan Airlines, Level 14, 1 Waterfront Place, Eagle St ☏ 07/3221 2200; Jetstar ☏ 13 15 38; Korean Air, Level 6, 320 Adelaide St ☏ 07/3226 6000; Malaysia Airlines, 17th Floor, 80 Albert St ☏ 13 26 27; Pacific Blue ☏ 13 16 45; Qantas, 247 Adelaide St ☏ 13 13 13; Royal Brunei, 60 Edward St ☏ 07/3017 5000; Singapore Airlines, 344 Queen St ☏ 13 10 11; Thai International ☏ 1300 651 960; Virgin Blue ☏ 13 67 89.

Banks Queensland banking hours are Mon–Fri 9.30am–4pm; major branches in the centre are around Queen and Edward sts.

Bike rental Valet Cycle Hire (☏ 0408 003 198, ⓦ www.cyclebrisbane.com) delivers bikes direct to your accommodation ($60 for one full day and $80 for two full days); their van is usually parked inside the Botanic Gardens off Alice St.

Car rental You'll pay around $35 for a single-day's car rental; longer terms work out from $29 a day, while campervans start at $59 a day for long-term rental. Shop around and read rental conditions before signing; most places will deliver and the minimum age is 21. Alpha (☏ 1300 227 473, ⓦ www.alphacarhire.com.au); East Coast (☏ 1800 028 881, ⓦ www.eastcoastcarrentals.com.au); Ezy (☏ 1300 661 938, ⓦ www.ezycarhire.com.au); Travellers Auto Barn (☏ 1800 674 374, ⓦ www .travellers-autobarn.com.au) have campers for $70 a day and station wagons for $47 a day but with a minimum two-week rental period; Wicked (☏ 1800 246 869, ⓦ www.wickedcampers.com.au) specializes in discount long-term campervan rentals.

Cinemas Greater Union, inside the Myer Centre, Queen St Mall (ⓦ www.greaterunion.com.au); Moonlight (ⓦ www.moonlight.com.au) shows outdoor screenings of current and classic films through the summer in public parks; Palace Centro Cinema, The Barracks, 61 Petrie Terrace (ⓦ www .palacecinemas.com.au).

Consulates Britain, Level 26, 1 Eagle St ☏ 07/3223 3200; Japan, 12 Creek St ☏ 07/3221 5188; Malaysia, 239 George St ☏ 07/3210 2833; Papua New Guinea, 320 Adelaide St ☏ 07/3221 7915; Philippines, 126 Wickham St, Fortitude Valley ☏ 07/3252 8215; Thailand, 87 Annerley Rd ☏ 07/3846 7771.

Environmental Protection Agency 160 Ann St (Mon–Fri 8.30am–5pm; ☏ 1300 130 372, ⓦ www .epa.qld.gov.au). Head office for Queensland Parks and Wildlife Service with a massive array of pamphlets, maps and books embracing Queensland's parks, marine protected areas and cultural heritage.

Hospitals/medical centres Royal Brisbane, Herston Rd, Herston (☏ 07/3636 8111; buses #126, #144 or #172 from outside City Hall); Travellers' Medical Service, Level 1, 245 Albert St (Mon–Fri 7.30am–7pm, Sat 8.30am–5pm, Sun 9.30am–5pm; ☏ 07/3211 3611, ⓦ www .cbdmedical.com.au), for general services, vaccinations and women's health.

Internet Most hostels have terminals where you can log on from around $4 an hour; the Infozone at the State Library on South Bank offers free, limited-use internet and plenty of terminals.

Left luggage None at the airport, but available at the Transit Centre for $6 per day per locker.

Markets Eagle St (Sun until 3pm) and Brunswick St Mall (Sat until 4pm) for bits and pieces; South Bank Parklands (Fri night, Sat & Sun until 5pm) for clothing, arts and crafts and a family atmosphere; King George Square Market in front of City Hall

Tours from Brisbane

Most **tours** from Brisbane are pretty straightforward day-trips by bus to take in the highlights of Lamington, Tamborine Mountain, the Sunshine Coast or Gold Coast. Australian Day Tours (☏ 07/3236 4155, ⓦ www.daytours.com.au) has a dozen or so day-tours to the Sunshine Coast, Gold Coast theme parks, or Lamington and Tamborine Mountain costing between $80 and $120.

If you want a bit more depth to your trips, or to visit more distant regions, try the highly recommended Bushwacker (☏ 1300 559 355, ⓦ www.bushwacker-ecotours .com.au) for day-trips to various parts of the Gold Coast Hinterland and Moreton Island, featuring plenty of wildlife, rainforests, bushtucker and swimming holes ($95) as well as overnight camping trips, or you can try your hand at adrenalin sports from abseiling to kayaking with Riverlife (☏ 07 3891 5766, ⓦ www.riverlife.com.au; $39 for 2hr sessions). Sunrover Expeditions (☏ 1800 353 717, ⓦ www.sunrover.com.au) and Moreton Bay Escapes (☏ 1300 559 355, ⓦ www.moretonbayescapes.com.au) offer one- to three-day 4WD safaris to Moreton, North Stradbroke and Fraser islands from $70–170 and also get great reviews. Cat-o'-Nine-Tails (see p.391) run trips to St Helena Island. MiCat (see p.392) organize tours to Moreton Island.

(Sun 8am–4pm) is small but has nice contemporary crafts; while the Riverside Centre (Sun) is more "arty" than the rest.

Pharmacies Transit Centre Pharmacy (Mon–Fri 7am–6pm, Sat 7.30am–1.30pm); Day & Night Pharmacy, Queen St Mall (Mon–Sat 7am–9pm, Sun 8.30am–6pm).

Police Queensland Police Headquarters is opposite the Transit Centre on Roma St ☏ 07/3364 6464 or in an emergency call 000.

Post office 261 Queen St (Mon–Fri 9am–5pm; ☏ 13 13 18 for poste restante; bring photo ID to collect).

Sport Queensland's sport is rugby league, and the Broncos' stomping ground is the Suncorp Stadium on Castlemain St, 5min walk west of the city with matches played between March and Sept and the all-Important State of Origin series in May or June. The Queensland Reds rugby union team also play all home Super 14 games at Suncorp stadium

between Feb and May. Tickets for most sports events cost $25–45 and are available from Ticketek outlets or ⓦ www.ticketek.com.au. Cricket matches are played at "The Gabba" on Vulture St, 3km southeast of the City (tickets cost $25–55 available from Ticketmaster outlets or ⓦ www.ticketmaster.com.au).

Travel agents Backpackers World Travel, 131 Elizabeth St ☏ 1800 676 763; Flight Centre, 181 George St ☏ 07/3229 0150; STA, 243 Edward St ☏ 07/3221 3722; Student Flights, Mayfair Arcade, 126 Adelaide St ☏ 07/3229 8449; Trailfinders, 101 Adelaide St ☏ 07/3331 8700; YHA, 450 George St, opposite the Transit Centre ☏ 07/3236 1680.

Work Brisbane offers fairly good employment prospects if you're not too choosy. Many hostels run effective ad hoc agencies for their guests, or for out-of-town work, try Brisbane's WWOOF office at *Banana Benders* backpackers', 118 Petrie Terrace (☏ 07/3367 1157).

The Moreton Bay Islands

Offshore from Brisbane are the shallow waters of **Moreton Bay**, famous throughout Australia as the home of the unfortunately named Moreton Bay Bug, which is actually a small, delicious lobster-like crustacean. The largest of the bay's islands, **Moreton** and **North Stradbroke**, are generously endowed with sand dunes and beaches, and are just the right distance from the city to make their beaches accessible but seldom crowded. The island of **St Helena** is not somewhere you'd visit for sun and surf, but its prison ruins recall the convict era and make for an interesting day-trip. In the bay itself, look for dolphins, dugong (sea cows) and **humpback whales**, which pass by in winter en route to their calving grounds up north.

St Helena Island

Small, low and triangular, **St Helena Island** sits 8km from the mouth of the Brisbane River, and from the 1850s until the early twentieth century served as a **prison**. The government found it particularly useful for political troublemakers, such as the leaders of the 1891 shearers' strike and, with more justice, a couple of slave-trading "Blackbirder" captains.

A tour of the penal settlement, tagged the "Hell Hole of the South Pacific" during its working life, leaves you thankful you missed out on the "good old days". Escape attempts (there were only ever three) were deterred by sharks, whose presence was actively encouraged around the island. Evidence of the prisoners' industry and self-sufficiency is still to be seen in the stone houses, as well as in the remains of a sugar mill, paddocks, wells, and an ingenious lime kiln built into the shoreline. The Deputy Superintendent's house has been turned into a bare **museum** (reached from the jetty on a mini-tramway), displaying a ball and chain lying in a corner and photographs from the prison era. Outside, the two cemeteries have been desecrated: many headstones were carried off as souvenir coffee-tables, and the corpses dug up and sold as medical specimens. The remaining stones comprise simple concrete crosses stamped with a number for the prisoners, or inscribed marble tablets for the warders and their children.

Cat-o'-Nine-Tails offers day-trips (Wed departing 9.15am and returning 2.15pm, Sun departing 10am and returning at 3pm; $69 including lunch; ☎07/3893 1240, ⓦwww.sthelenaisland.com.au) and **Saturday-night tours** ($90 includes three-course meal), the latter including a theatrical sound-and-light show on the island. Advance bookings are essential. Boats leave around 15km east of the city from the public jetty in the suburb of **Manly**, a ten-minute walk from Manly train station – from Brisbane, you can reach Manly direct from Roma Street, Central and South Brisbane train stations.

Moreton Island

A 38-kilometre-long, narrow band of stabilized, partly wooded sand dunes, **Moreton Island**'s faultless beaches are distinctly underpopulated for much of the year, and perfect for lounging, surfing or fishing. Many people just come over for the day, but it's also possible to camp or stay in a resort, and even bring your own vehicle across – driving though is on soft sand tracks only so 4WD is essential, and stock up on fuel as it's hard to find on the island (permits $37 available via Environmental Protection Agency, ⓦwww.epa.qld.gov.au).

The main arrival point on the island is **TANGALOOMA** along Moreton's west coast. Offshore here is a set of wrecks, deliberately sunk to create an artificial reef, providing fine **snorkelling** at high tide and the beach resort setting of *Tangalooma Wild Dolphin Resort* (☎07/3268 6333, ⓦwww.tangalooma.com; ⑨). The resort is a casual, family-oriented affair with a range of rooms, apartments and holiday villas built around a former **whaling station**; it organizes daily **dolphin feeding** for wild dolphins who rock up every evening for a handout, a sand-tobogganing trip ($25), whale watching cruises ($58) and full- and half-day tours of the island ($75). The resort is also the only place on the island that has a restaurant and serves cold drinks – tidy dress is required. There's a National Parks **campsite** nearby (with water, showers and toilets), which gets as crowded as anywhere on the island – permits are available from the ranger based at *Tangalooma Resort* (☎07/3408 2710). A three-kilometre track heads south from Tangalooma to the **desert**, where the dunes are a great place to try **sand-tobogganing**.

With your own vehicle, or on foot if you don't mind hiking, you can take the ten-kilometre track from Tangalooma across to Moreton's more attractive eastern side, where the beach has good **surf** and it's less crowded. Before reaching the eastern coast at **Eagers Creek**, a sandy track branches off, winding its way to **Mount Tempest**'s 280-metre peak – it's an exhausting 2.5-kilometre climb but the view from the top is outstanding. Back at Eagers Creek, head 10km north up the beach and you'll find Blue Lagoon, the largest of the island's freshwater lakes, only 500m from the beach campsite and adjacent to the smaller, picturesque **Honeyeater Lake**. Blessed with shady trees, the dunes behind the beach make an ideal place to camp, and the site is supplied with water, showers and toilets. Dolphins come in close to shore – a practice that Moreton's Aborigines turned to their advantage by using them to chase fish into the shallows. Writing in the 1870s about his life in Brisbane, Tom Petrie reported that the Ngugi men would beat the surf with their spears, and:

By and by, as in response, porpoises would be seen as they rose to the surface making for the shore and in front of them schools of tailor fish. It may seem wonderful, but they were apparently driving the fish towards the land. When they came near, [the Ngugi] would run out into the surf, and with their spears would jab down here and there at the fish, at times even getting two on one spear, so plentiful were they.

The north and south ends of the island are only accessible from the Tangalooma area by 4WD, often driving on the beach, though there are tiny settlements at both. **BULWER**, on the island's northwest coast, comprises a cluster of weatherboard "weekenders" and a general store stocking beer. You can stay in basic six-person units (☎07/3203 6399; ❺) or at the island's largest National Park campsite with cold-water showers and toilets. From Bulwer there's road access to Cape Moreton Lighthouse on the northern tip of the island – from the cliffs you should easily spot migrating humpback whales between May and October as well as sea turtles bobbing in the ocean. At Moreton's southern tip, tiny **KOORINGAL** has a store offering supplies and drinks from its bar (daily 8am–midnight), as well as **holiday units** that sleep up to ten (☎07/3217 9965; ❺).

Getting to Moreton

Tangalooma Wild Dolphin Resort operates **fast ferries** direct to the resort from its wharf, 8km out of the city at the end of Holt Street, off Kingsford Smith Drive at Pinkenba (daily at 7.30am, 10am and 5pm; $70 open return). For an extra $14 you can book a pick-up from Brisbane hotels to the wharf when you make your booking.

The other main option is MiCat (☎07/3909 3333, ⓦwww.micat.com.au; 4WD $205 return includes 2 adults, foot passengers $45 return, day cruise and adventure tour $90), a huge modern catamaran crossing daily at 8.30am to the wrecks just north of *Tangalooma Wild Dolphin Resort* from its wharf at 14 Howard Smith Drive, Lytton – you can get here from Brisbane in an hour by catching the train to Wynnum Central from the Transit Centre, then a bus from outside the station on Andrew Street to the wharf.

Aside from **tours** listed in the box on p.389, MiCat also offers a range of day and overnight trips, including sandboarding and four-wheel-driving, and can also organize National Park **camping permits** at $4.85 a night. If you're planning to stay a while, note that there are **no banks** on the island (although there is an ATM at *Tangalooma Resort*), and that supplies are expensive – it's best to be self-sufficient and have enough water if you are camping. Before you go in the sea, remember that the beaches aren't patrolled and there are no shark nets. The worst times to visit are at Christmas and Easter, when up to a thousand vehicles crowd onto the island all at once.

North Stradbroke Island

North Stradbroke Island is, at 40km long, the largest and most established of the bay's islands, with sealed roads and the fully serviced townships of Dunwich, Amity and Point Lookout. Ninety percent of "**Straddie**" is given over to mining the island's titanium-rich sands, and the majority of the 3200 residents are employees of Consolidated Rutile Ltd. The mine sites south of Amity, and in the central west and south, are far from exhausted but their future is precarious, thanks to an oversupply on the world market. Other industries focus on timber, a by-product of preparing land for mining, and, increasingly, tourism.

Stradbroke's **diving** is renowned for congregations of the increasingly rare grey nurse shark, along with moray eels, dopey leopard sharks, and summertime manta rays. Courses, dives and accommodation can be arranged through *Manta Lodge* (see opposite).

Unless you need to fuel up or visit the bank, there's little to keep you at **Dunwich**, Straddie's ferry port. Two sealed roads head out of town, east through the island's centre towards Main Beach, or north to Amity and Point

Lookout. The road through the centre passes two lakes – the second and smaller of these, **Blue Lake**, is a national park and source of fresh water for the island's wildlife, which is most visible early in the morning. Beyond Blue Lake you have to cross the **Eighteen Mile Swamp** to reach **Main Beach** and, though there's a causeway, the rest of the route is for 4WDs only. You can **camp** behind the beach anywhere south of the causeway (north of it is mining company land), but be prepared for the mosquitoes that swarm around the mangroves; the southernmost point is an angling and wildlife mecca, with birdlife and kangaroos lounging around on the beaches.

Heading north from Dunwich, it's 11km to where the road forks left for a further 6km to **AMITY**, a sleepy place built around a jetty at the northwestern point of the island; there's a store, **campsite** and *Sea Shanties* at 9A Cook St (℡07/3409 7161, ⓦwww.seashanties.com.au; ❹), which offers low-key beachfront **accommodation** in self-contained cabins sleeping four (bring your own sleeping bag or bedding).

Point Lookout

Stay on the road from Dunwich past the Amity turn-off, and it's another 10km to **POINT LOOKOUT**, at Straddie's northeastern tip. The township spreads out around the island's single-rock headland, overlooking a string of beaches, a sports pub, a takeaway pizza place, a store, some cafés and various **places to stay**. Top of the range are *Straddie Views B&B* at 26 Cumming Parade (℡07/3409 8875, ⓔstraddiebedandbrekky@bigpond.com; ❻), with a nice veranda offering ocean views; and *Samarinda* (℡07/3409 8785, ⓦwww.samarinda.com.au; ❺), with motel rooms and two-bedroom units. At the other end of the scale, *Manta Lodge*, at 1 Eastcoast Rd (℡07/3409 8888, ⓦwww.stradbrokeislandscuba.com.au; dorms $28, rooms ❸), offers budget rooms and has surfboards, bikes and fishing gear for rent; it also organizes scuba diving, and 4WD, walking and trail-riding trips. *Amity Point Holiday Park* (℡1300 551 253; camping $32, four- to six-person cabins ❺) is the best of the local caravan parks.

Point Lookout's **beaches** are picturesque, with shallow, protected swimming along the shore. Home and Cylinder beaches are both patrolled and, therefore, crowded during holiday weekends; if you don't mind swimming in unwatched waters, head for the more easterly Deadman's Beach or Frenchman's Bay. On the headland above the township, there are fine views and the chance to see loggerhead turtles and dolphins; from the walking track around North Gorge down to Main Beach you might see whales, if you have binoculars.

Getting to the island, and getting around

Island ferries leave from Toondah Harbour at **Cleveland** – take the train to Cleveland from Brisbane's Transit Centre, then catch the special red-and-yellow National Bus to the harbour. Stradbroke Ferries (℡07/3488 5300, ⓦwww.stradbrokeferries.com.au) and Sea Stradbroke (℡07/3488 9777, ⓦwww.seastradbroke.com) cross to Dunwich around twenty times daily between them, commencing at 5.30am, both charging $11 return for walk-on passengers and $135 for vehicles and two passengers.

To **get around** the island, the Dunwich–Point Lookout **bus** ($9 return) connects with all water taxis, and various operators offer **4WD safaris**: Sunrover Expeditions (℡07/3880 0719, ⓦwww.sunrover.com.au) and Straddie Kingfisher Tours (℡07/3409 9502, ⓦwww.straddiekingfishertours.com.au) both come recommended. Some roads on Stradbroke are open to mining vehicles only, so drivers should look out for the signs. **Off-roading** through the centre on non-designated roads is not advised: quite apart from the damage caused to the dune systems, the sand is very soft and having your vehicle pulled out will be very expensive. Driving on the beach requires a 4WD and a **permit** ($44.50), which can be obtained from either ferry operator. Beach camping is available at either Main Beach or Flinders Beach and must be booked in advance through Straddie Holiday Parks (℡ 1300 551 253).

The Gold Coast

Beneath a jagged skyline shaped by countless high-rise beachfront apartments, the **Gold Coast** is Australia's Miami Beach or Costa del Sol, a striking contrast to Brisbane, only an hour away to the north. Aggressively superficial, it's not the place to go if you're seeking peace and quiet, but its sheer brashness can be fun for a couple of days – perhaps as a weekend break from Brisbane. There's little variation on the beach and nightclub scene, however, and if you're concerned this will leave you jaded, bored or broke, you'd be better off avoiding this corner of the state altogether.

The coast forms a virtually unbroken beach 40km long, from **South Strad-broke Island** past **Surfers Paradise** and **Burleigh Heads** to the New South Wales border at **Coolangatta**. The **beaches**, nominally why everyone comes to the Gold Coast, swarm with bathers and board-riders all year round: **surfing** first blossomed here in the 1930s and the key surf beaches at Coolangatta, Burleigh Heads and South Stradbroke still pull daily crowds of veterans and novices. In the meantime, other attractions have sprung up, notably the **club and party scene** centred on Surfers Paradise, and several action-packed **theme parks**, domestic holiday blackspots mostly based about 15km northwest of the town.

With around three hundred days of sunshine each year there's little "off-season" as such. **Rain** can, however, fall at any time during the year, including midwinter – when it's usually dry in the rest of the state – but even if the crowds do thin out a little, they reappear in time for the **Gold Coast Indy** car race in October and then continue to swell, peaking over Christmas and New Year. The end of the school year in mid-November also heralds the phenomenon that is **Schoolies Week**, when thousands of high-school leavers from across the country ditch exam rooms and flock to Surfers for a few days of hard partying, a rite of passage which causes an annual budget-accommodation crisis.

Getting there and around

From Brisbane, the only local bus operator offering regular transfers to the Gold Coast is Coachtrans (℡ 13 12 30), which runs three services daily from Roma Street Transit Centre to Southport, Surfers, Burleigh Heads and Coolangatta, and can also organize transfers direct **from Brisbane airport** to Gold Coast accommodation or theme parks. You can also get to the Gold Coast from Brisbane airport and the city by taking the **Citytrain** to Nerang Station, where you pick up Surfside Bus connections on to Surfers Paradise – a total cost of around $35.

From **New South Wales**, the coastal highway enters Queensland at Coolangatta, where you'll also find the **Gold Coast airport**. The Gold Coast Tourist Shuttle (℡07/5574 5111, ⓦwww.gcshuttle.com.au) runs buses to all points between the airport and Surfers Paradise for $18 one-way, while Con-X-ion (℡07/5556 9888, ⓦwww.con-x-ion.com) offers theme-park transfers.

Getting around, Surfside Buses run a 24-hour bus service (up to six times hourly; timetables available from bus drivers, on ℡13 12 30 or at ⓦwww.surfside.com.au) along the Gold Coast Highway from Tweed Heads and Coolangatta to Surfers Paradise and out to all the theme parks. Their various **passes** give unlimited travel for between three and fourteen days ($26–63). Otherwise, you'll need to take a **taxi** or rent a vehicle; there are more details in accounts of the individual resorts.

Surfers Paradise

Spiritually, if not geographically, **SURFERS PARADISE** is the heart of the Gold Coast, the place where its aims and aspirations are most evident. For the residents, this involves making money by providing services and entertainment for tourists; visitors reciprocate by parting with their cash. All around and irrespective of what you're doing – sitting on the beach, **partying** in one of the frenetic nightclubs along Orchid or Cavill avenues, shopping for clothes or even finding a bed – the pace is brash and glib. Don't come here expecting to be allowed to relax; subtlety is nonexistent and you'll find that enjoying Surfers depends largely on how much it bothers you having the party mood rammed down your throat.

Surfers' **beaches** have been attracting tourists for over a century, though the town only started developing along commercial lines during the 1950s when the first multistorey beachfront apartments were built. The demand for views over the ocean led to ever-higher towers which began to encroach on the dunes; together with the sheer volume of people attracted here, this has caused **erosion** problems along the entire coast. But none of this really matters. Though Surfers Paradise is a firm tribute to the successful marketing of the ideal Aussie lifestyle as an eternal beach party, most people no longer come here for the sun and sand but simply because everyone else does.

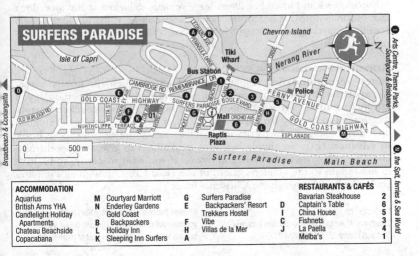

ACCOMMODATION					RESTAURANTS & CAFÉS	
Aquarius		Courtyard Marriott	M		Bavarian Steakhouse	2
British Arms YHA		Enderley Gardens	N	Surfers Paradise	Captain's Table	6
Candlelight Holiday		Gold Coast		Backpackers' Resort D	China House	5
Apartments	B	Backpackers		Trekkers Hostel I	Fishnets	3
Chateau Beachside	L	Holiday Inn	G	Vibe C	La Paella	4
Copacabana	K	Sleeping Inn Surfers	E	Villas de la Mer J	Melba's	1
			F			
			H			
			A			

▲ Surfers Paradise

Arrival and information

Surfers' **bus station** (daily 6am–10pm) is on Beach Road on the corner of the highway, one street down from Cavill Avenue. Coachtrans run to Brisbane (☎13 12 30); Kirkland's to Brisbane, Byron Bay and Lismore (☎1300 367 077); and Greyhound Australia (☎13 20 30) and Premier (☎13 34 10) right down the east coast. At the bus station you'll find luggage lockers, bus-company desks and an accommodation-information counter. The **visitor centre** is in a booth on Cavill Avenue (Mon–Fri 8.30am–5.30pm, Sat 8.30am–5pm, Sun 9am–4pm; ☎1300 309 440, ⓦwww.verygc.com), but the accommodation desk is usually just as well informed.

Security is worth bearing in mind: many people come here simply to prey on tourists, especially around Christmas and Easter, or on teenagers during Schoolies Week in November. Don't leave vehicles unlocked at any time, don't take valuables onto the beach, and don't wander alone at night; muggings are common, especially around nightclubs, so take advantage of the courtesy buses run by hostels.

Accommodation

Surfers' **accommodation** is split between high-end, high-rise **hotels**; lower-rise **apartment blocks** that can be an excellent deal for a group, though you usually have to stay for a minimum of three nights; and **backpacker hostels**, which tend to be very hard-sell – don't expect any peace until you've signed up for trips to nightclubs, parties and beach events. Whatever you choose, **book in advance**. There are simply too many possibilities to give a comprehensive list; those below are central and good value. If you want to **camp**, you'll have to head south to the quieter sections of the Gold Coast, though all campsites get booked solid through the Christmas break.

Hotels

Courtyard Marriott Corner of Surfers Paradise Blvd and Hanlan St ☎1800 074 317, ⓦwww.marriott.com.au/oolcy. Very flash, very central international chain offering a good deal if you're looking for something in this sort of market. ❻

396

Holiday Inn 22 View Ave ℡07/5579 1000, Ⓦwww.holidayinnsurfersparadise.com.au. Another reliable big chain set just a short walk back from the beach, and offering online booking discounts. ❼

Vibe 42 Ferny Ave ℡07/5539 0444, Ⓦwww.vibehotels.com.au. Uninspiring from the outside but with a slickly designed interior, a nice swimming pool and spa, and great service, this medium-sized central hotel is excellent value for money. The Aqua Rooms are worth the extra dollars for their fabulous river views. ❻

Motels and apartments

Candlelight Holiday Apartments 22–24 Leonard Ave ℡07/5538 1277, Ⓦwww.candlelightholiday apartments.com.au. Very pleasant, self-contained one-bedroom units in a quiet street close to the bus station with very helpful and friendly owners. Minimum three-night stay. ❺

Chateau Beachside Corner of Esplanade and Elkhorn Ave ℡07/5538 1022, Ⓦwww .chateaubeachside.com.au. In the heart of Surfers and overlooking the beach, this modern tower block is a great mid-range deal, with good-sized hotel rooms and studio apartments with cooking facilities. ❺

Copacabana 24 Hamilton Ave ℡07/5592 1866, Ⓦwww.copa.com.au. Rooms on three levels arranged around an ornamental garden laden with palms; rooms are clean, if simple, and there's a small indoor pool. ❻

Enderley Gardens 38 Enderley Ave ℡07/5570 1511, Ⓦwww.enderleygardens.com.au. Self-contained units, one block away from the beach and 10min from the heart of Surfers. Facilities include pool, spa and tennis court. ❺

Villas de la Mer Corner of Markwell Ave and Northcliffe Terrace ℡07/5592 6644, Ⓦwww .villasdelamer.com.au. Attractive two- and three-bedroom apartments in a three-storey security complex. Simple but modern and well furnished. ❻

Hostels

Aquarius 44 Queen St, Southport ℡1800 229 955, Ⓦwww.aquariusbackpackers.com.au. Offers a tiny TV lounge on each floor, pool and communal kitchen, plus a courtesy bus to and from Surfers. Small four- and six-bed dorms. Dorms $32, rooms ❹

British Arms YHA 70 Sea World Drive ℡07/5571 1776 or 1800 680 269, Ⓦwww.yha.com.au. Well placed for Sea World, about 5km north of the centre. Good facilities, plus a lively English bar and grill serving up pub fare, occasional entertainment and a range of beers till late. Dorms $28, rooms ❹

Gold Coast Backpackers 28 Hamilton Ave ℡1800 801 230, Ⓦwww.goldcoastbackpackers .com.au. Secure, purpose-built hostel, with safe car park. Facilities include a small kitchen and a bar, but there's no pool and the place feels a bit sterile. Four-bed dorms $25, tiny doubles ❸

Sleeping Inn Surfers 26 Peninsula Drive ℡1800 817 832, Ⓦwww.sleepinginn.com.au. Close to the bus station, these nicely furnished, self-contained units, all with TV, provide quality budget accommodation. There are also simply furnished three-bedroom apartments for $295 per night closer to the beach on Surfers Paradise Blbd. Dorms $26, rooms ❸

Surfers Paradise Backpackers' Resort 2837 Gold Coast Highway ℡1800 282 800, Ⓦwww .surfersparadisebackpackers.com.au. Purpose-built, sparklingly clean and efficient, with spacious rooms; the price per bed covers everything, including use of washing machines. Dorms $27, rooms ❸

Trekkers Hostel 22 White St, Southport ℡1800 100 004, Ⓦwww.trekkersbackpackers.com.au. Restored old house 3km from the centre, with heaps of deals and trips. Price includes a basic breakfast. There's a courtesy bus, or you can catch local transport to the hostel. Dorms $32, rooms ❸

The City

Downtown Surfers Paradise is a thin ribbon of partially reclaimed land between the ocean and the **Nerang River** which – as the Broadwater – flows north, parallel with the beach, past **the Spit** and South Stradbroke Island into the choked channels at the bottom end of Moreton Bay. Reclaimed land in the river forms islands whose names reflect the fantasies of their founders – Isle of Capri, Sorrento, Miami Keys – and which have become much-sought-after real estate.

From its dingiest club to its best restaurant, Surfers exudes entertainment, and at times – most notoriously at New Year and Christmas – you can spend 24 hours a day out on the town. Another thing you'll spend is money: the only free venue is the beach and with such a variety of distractions it can be financial suicide venturing out too early in the day – the city is full of tourists staggering around

Surfing the Gold Coast

As locals will tell you, the Gold Coast has some of the best **surfing beaches** in the world. In terms of consistency this might be true – on any given day there will be good surf somewhere along the coast – with 200-metre-long sand-bottom point breaks and rideable waves peaking at about 4m in prime conditions.

The coast is known for its **barrels**, particularly during the summer storm season when the winds shift around to the north; in winter the swell is smaller but more reliable, making it easier to learn to surf. A rule of thumb for finding the best surf is to **follow the wind**: head to the north end of the coast when the wind blows from the north and the south when it comes from the south. Generally, you'll find the **best swell** along the southern beaches, and on South Stradbroke Island. Sea temperatures range between 26°C in December and 17°C in June, so a 2–3mm wet suit is adequate. Hard-core surfies come for Christmas and the cyclone season, though spring is usually the busiest time. On the subject of **general safety**, all beaches as far north as Surfers are patrolled – look for the signs – and while sharks might worry you, more commonplace hostility is likely to come from the local surfies, who form tight-knit cliques with very protective attitudes towards their patches.

For expert **tuition**, **tours**, or **advice** anywhere on the Gold Coast, contact Go Ride a Wave (℡1300 132 441, ⊛www.gorideawave.com.au); beginners pay around $70 for a two-hour session, or you can simply rent a surfboard for the day for $45). **Competitions** or events are held somewhere along the coast on most weekends, advertised through local surf shops. To try your hand at **kitesurfing**, another popular Gold Coast pastime, contact Pureaqua (℡04/1626 7654, ⊛www.pureaqua.com.au) on the Broadwater at Southport – beginners pay $185 for a three-hour intro package.

at noon with terrible hangovers and empty wallets, complaining how expensive their holiday has become. The area around **Orchid Avenue** and partially pedestrianized **Cavill Avenue** is a bustle of activity from early morning – when the first surfers head down to the beach and the shops open – to after midnight, when there's a constant exchange of bodies between the bars and nightclubs. If you spend any length of time in town, you'll get to know the district intimately.

Surfers' tower-block cityscape makes an immediate impression, but the stakes in who can build highest and so block their neighbours' view of the beach have recently been upped considerably: occupying an entire block on the highway between Clifford Street and Hamilton Avenue, **Q1** is – at 80 storeys and 322.5m high – the world's tallest residential building. You can ride the lift up 78 storeys in 42.7 seconds to the **observation deck** (Fri & Sat 8am–midnight, Sun–Thurs 9am–9pm; $28) for a drink at the bar and stupendous views down on the puny high-rises below, the endless strip of golden sand fringing the sea, and inland as far south as Mount Warning in New South Wales.

Across the Esplanade, the **beach** is all you could want as a place to recover from your night out; it runs 5km or more north from here via **Main Beach** to **the Spit**, so finding empty sand shouldn't be too difficult. If you're feeling energetic, seek out a game of volleyball or head for the surf: the swell here is good in a northerly wind, but most of the time it's better for boogie-boards.

The theme parks

All the theme parks are a bundle of fun, especially for children, and are easy to spend a full day at – Wet 'n' Wild takes some beating on a hot day, though. All are located to the north of town on Surfside and Gold Coast Shuttle bus routes. Check out the park websites for the latest discounted deals on entry and **combination passes** to more than one park.

Around 5km north of Surfers at the Spit, **Sea World** (daily 10am–5pm; $69; access on the Surfside Bus from the highway; Ⓦwww.seaworld.com.au) is the longest running of the Gold Coast's theme parks. Besides various stomach-churning rides, the park features immaculately trained dolphins and killer whales, and helps rehabilitate stranded wild dolphins for later release.

Movie World (daily 10am–5pm; $69; Ⓦwww.movieworld.com.au), on the Pacific Highway 14km north of Surfers, is a slice of Hollywood featuring studio tours, Western shows and stunt demonstrations. Adjacent to Movie World, **Wet 'n' Wild** (daily 10am–5pm or later; $49; Ⓦwww.wetnwild.com .au) is an adrenaline-inspired water park – the back-breaking "kamikaze" and the vicious 25-metre-tall, high-speed water slide alone are worth the entrance fee. **Dreamworld** (daily 10am–5pm; $69; Ⓦwww.dreamworld.com.au), also on the Pacific Highway at Coomera, 17km north of Surfers Paradise, has a violent double-loop roller-coaster and a fairground atmosphere, as well as a collection of hand-reared tigers in a large enclosure.

Although not strictly speaking a theme park, a themed show which gets great reviews is the **Australian Outback Spectacular**, located on the Pacific Highway between Wet 'n' Wild and Movie World (Tues–Sun 6.15–9pm, entertainment commences 7.30pm; $99; bookings essential; ☎13 33 86, Ⓦwww.outbackspectacular.com.au). This two-hour evening show features stunning demonstrations of horsemanship, camel races and a cattle roundup, plus a huge meal.

Eating

Surfers has somewhere to eat wherever you look, though most places are forget-table **snack bars and cafés**. In fact, there are surprisingly few **restaurants**, which have mostly migrated south to Broadbeach Mall or north to Broadwater and Southport, where there's usually a Porsche or two parked along Tedder Avenue's trendy café strip. For **supplies**, there's a supermarket downstairs in the Centro Centre (on Cavill Ave) and a 24-hour Night Owl store on the highway near Trickett Street. If a phone number is listed, it's best to book.

Bavarian Steakhouse 41 Cavill Ave ☎07/5531 7150. Wood-panelled theme restaurant on several floors, where you can wolf down steins of beer and plates of beef while staff dressed in leather and lace pump away on Bavarian brass instruments. Good fun if you're in the mood and fair value – about $34 for steak, salad and fries.
Captain's Table 17 Orchid Ave ☎07/5531 5766. Award-winning restaurant with excellent Aussie game and seafood variations – the $28 plate of delicious barbecued Moreton Bay Bugs should not be missed.
China House 3286 Surfers Paradise Blvd. Centrally located, with a daily three-course lunch special ($9.80; noon–3pm) that's the best value in town – try the tasty Mongolian lamb, satay chicken or Sichuan noodles. Otherwise, mains are around $13.

Fishnets Circle on Cavill, 3184 Surfers Paradise Blvd. Smartly presented fish and chips with on-site fishmonger serving fresh oysters. The fish cakes at $1.80 a pop are delicious, while the seafood bucket at $17.50 will keep you going for the day. Daily 11am–7pm.
La Paella 3114 Surfers Paradise Blvd. Tiny yet lively Spanish restaurant with excellent tapas for $17, sangria by the bucket and sumptuous veal casserole for $27. Dinner only.
Melba's 46 Cavill Ave ☎07/5592 6922. Ambitious café-restaurant attached to the nightclub of the same name, with a mix of Mediterranean-style light meals and snacks served – unusually for Surfers – at pavement tables. Tassie salmon and Mediterranean salads are the chef's specialities, with mains between $25 and $35. Daily 7am–5am.

Nightlife and entertainment

Next to the beach, Surfers' **nightclubs** and **bars** – mostly located in Orchid Avenue – are its reason to be. Initially, particularly if you're staying at a hostel or have picked up a free pass somewhere, your choice will most likely be influenced by the various **deals** on entry and drinks. In addition, there are booze-cruise nightclub **tours** offered by various places for around $60, which includes transport and often a club pass valid for the rest of your stay. Opening times are from around 6pm to 3am or later; bars are open daily and clubs from Thursday to Sunday.

In addition to the nightspots below, the Gold Coast often hosts big **dance parties** and live **music festivals** (Good Vibrations, in February, is one of the biggest), usually held at outdoor venues such as Doug Jennings Park at the Spit. You can find out the latest in the free Brisbane **magazines** *Scene*, *Rave* and *Time Off* (see p.387), and also in the more locally oriented *Tsunami*.

Bedroom 26 Orchid Ave. The best place for house and dance on the coast, with an ever-changing array of local and international DJs.

Cocktails and Dreams Orchid Ave. Nightly dance crowd in the late teen bracket who party against a background of neon and disco lighting.

Gilhooley's Raptis Plaza, 39 Cavill Ave. Rowdy Irish pub serving Guinness and other draught beers, and usually overflowing with travellers. Live bands throughout the week.

Howl at the Moon Upstairs at Centro Centre on Cavill Ave ⊕07/5527 5522. Hugely popular restaurant, bar and nightclub with two live pianists performing their own sing-along renditions of popular hits. Daily 8pm–2am, bookings advisable.

Melba's 46 Cavill Ave. Big and relatively upmarket nightclub with a monstrous, atmospherically lit bar and powerful sound system – plus a noticeably older crowd than the rest of Surfers' clubs.

The Party At *The Mark*, Orchid Ave. Live rock bands on Friday and Sunday (with a variable cover charge); DJs for the rest of the week.

Platinum 19 Victoria Ave, Broadbeach. Chill-out dance club and lounge bar with international DJs. Open Fri & Sat only.

Shooters Orchid Ave, next to *Cocktails and Dreams*. Crowds heading for more serious dance spots start out here for a game of pool and a few drinks; a definite stop on the backpacker bar-crawl trail.

Sin City Orchid Ave. DJ sessions and regular drinks specials make this the liveliest club outside of weekends.

Surfers Beergarden Cavill Ave, opposite Orchid Ave. Good for live music, with local and interstate band talent on Thurs and Sat nights.

Listings

Car rental CY Rent a Car, 9 Trickett St ⓦwww .cyrentacar.com.au; East Coast Car Rentals, 25 Elkhorn Ave ⓦwww.eastcoastcarrentals.com.au; Surfers Paradise Car Hire, inside the Transit Centre ⓦwww.surfersparadisecarhire.com; Red Back

Rentals, inside the Transit Centre, Beach Rd ⓦwww.redbackrentals.com.au; Red Rocket, Centre Arcade, 16 Orchid Ave ⓦwww.redrocketrentals .com.au.

Gold Coast tours and cruises

Land-based **day-trips** from the Gold Coast concentrate on various Hinterland national parks (see p.404). Bushwacker Ecotours (⊕07/3871 0057, ⓦwww .bushwacker-ecotours.com.au), Mountain Trek Adventures (⊕07/5578 3157) and Southern Cross (⊕07/5574 5041, ⓦwww.sc4wd.com.au) are all in the adventurous bracket, with 4WD day-tours and night-time wildlife-spotting ventures ($115–230). Mountain Coach Company (⊕07/5524 4249) runs up daily to O'Reilly's at Lamington ($55 return), and Scenic Hinterland Tours (⊕07/5531 5536, ⓦwww.hinterlandtours .com.au) do comfortable trips to almost all the Hinterland national parks (from $65).

The following explore the Nerang River and seafront on one-hour to half-day **cruises**: Adventure Duck (⊕07/5528 4544), an amphibious bus, departs nine times daily from Orchid Avenue for an hour-long trip ($35); or Wyndham Cruises (⊕07/5539 9299) spend a couple of hours on the water for $45. See p.401 for trips to South Stradbroke Island.

Hospitals and medical centres Gold Coast Hospital, Nerang St, Southport ☎07/5519 8211; Paradise Medical Centre, Centro Centre, on Cavill Ave ☎07/5538 8099.
Pharmacy Piazza Shopping Plaza, corner of Elkhorn Ave and Gold Coast Highway (daily 7am–midnight).
Post office The main post office is in the Centro Centre on Cavill Ave.

Surf rental Go Ride A Wave, in an orange kiosk beside the Paradise Centre on Cavill Ave ☎1300 132 441. Typical prices are $25 a day for board rental, plus credit-card deposit. For tuition, see the box on p.398.
Taxis ☎13 10 08.

South Stradbroke Island

South Stradbroke Island is a twenty-kilometre-long, narrow strip of sand, separated from North Stradbroke Island by the 1896 cyclone and, as apartment buildings edge closer, doomed to become an extension of the Gold Coast. For now, though, South Stradbroke's relatively isolated and quiet beaches offer something of an escape from the mainland, though most day-trippers come over simply to get plastered in the bar at *South Stradbroke Island Resort* (☎07/5577 3311, ⊛www.ssir.com.au; rooms ❻; four-bed cabins ❸). Alternative accommodation is available at the new *Couran Cove Resort* (☎1800 268 726, ⊛www.couran.com; cabins and rooms ❼), which offers a much more exclusive atmosphere, and doesn't welcome day-guests. There's also some of the coast's finest **surf** to ride along the southeast shore, though local surfies are notoriously protective.

Day-trippers can get to South Stradbroke on the *South Stradbroke Island Resort* fast **ferry** (daily 10.30am, return between 2.30pm and 5pm depending on the day; $49 includes BBQ lunch) from Runaway Bay Marina, 5km north of Surfers on Bayview Street – bookings (through the *Resort*) are essential.

Surfers Paradise to Currumbin

The central section of the Gold Coast lacks any real focus. Haphazardly developed and visually unattractive, it exists very much in the shadow of Surfers Paradise, but can't match its intensity. The highway is just a continuous maze of crowded, multi-lane traffic systems and drab buildings which lose momentum the further south you drive, but once you leave the road there are fine **beaches**, two **wildlife sanctuaries** and – unbelievably amidst all the commotion and noise – a tiny **national park**, which preserves the coast's original environment.

Burleigh Heads National Park and around

Around 7km south of Surfers, **Burleigh Heads** consists of a traffic bottleneck where the highway dodges between the beach and a rounded headland; there can be very good surf here but the rocks make it rough for novices. Sixty years ago, before the bitumen and paving took over, this was all dense eucalypt and vine forest, the last fragment of which survives as **Burleigh Head National Park**. Entrance is on foot from the car park on the Esplanade, or turn sharply at the lights below the hill just south of the headland for the **visitor centre** (Mon–Fri 10am–3pm, Sat & Sun 10am–4pm).

Geologically, Burleigh Heads stems from the prehistoric eruptions of the Mount Warning volcano (p.289), 30km to the southwest. Lava surfaced through vents, cooling to tall hexagonal basalt columns, now mostly tumbled and covered in vines. Rainforest colonized the richer volcanic soils, while stands of red gum grew in weaker sandy loam; along the eastern seafront there's a patch of exposed heathland bordered by groups of pandanus, and a beach along the mouth of Tallebudgera Creek. This diversity is amazing considering the minimal space, but urban encroachment has seriously affected the **wildlife** – you can still see butterflies, scrub turkeys and sunbathing dragons though.

Less than 2km inland on West Burleigh Road, the **David Fleay Wildlife Park** (daily 9am–5pm; $16.60; take the Surfside Bus; ⊕07/5576 2411) is an informal park with boardwalks through forest pens and plenty of rangers at hand to answer your questions. The late David Fleay was the first person to persuade platypus to breed in captivity and the park has a special section devoted to this curious animal, along with crocodiles, koalas, glider possums and plenty of birds. There are various guided tours through the day, including through the **nocturnal house** – a chance to see normally somnambulant Australian wildlife in action.

Currumbin Beach and Sanctuary

A further 6km past Burleigh Heads, **Currumbin Beach** is a good, relatively undeveloped stretch of coast between Elephant Rock and Currumbin Point, and given a breeze there are usually some decent rollers to ride. Just to the north, **Palm Beach** is more sheltered. *Vikings*, in the surf-club building below Elephant Rock, serves Chinese **food**, or you can fill up on regular pub fare at the *Palm Beach Surf Club* along the beachfront.

CURRUMBIN is a leftover from the days before high-density development, just a few streets of houses off the highway down a bumpy lane – though a major housing estate is on the drawing board. The focus is **Currumbin Sanctuary**, on Tomewin Street (daily 8am–5pm; $39; ⊛www.currumbin-sanctuary.org.au), which was started in 1946 by Alex Griffiths, who developed this seventy-acre reserve of forest and water as a native wildlife refuge. There are the usual feeding times (throughout the day), shows and tame kangaroos, but the park's strongest point is its beautiful natural surroundings, best experienced from the **elevated walkways** through the forest, where you'll see koalas, tree kangaroos and birds at eye level. The park reopens every night at 7pm for a two-hour guided nocturnal walk followed by a traditional Aboriginal dance performance ($52). A Saturday morning **farmers' market** sets up opposite the sanctuary once or twice a month.

Coolangatta

On the Queensland–New South Wales border 10km south of Currumbin, **COOLANGATTA** merges seamlessly with Tweed Heads (in New South Wales) along Boundary Street. With only a giant concrete plinth just off the main road marking the border, you'll probably make the crossing between states without realizing it. Unless it's New Year, when everyone takes advantage of the one-hour time difference between the states to celebrate twice, most travellers bypass Coolangatta completely; in doing so, they miss some of the best surf, least crowded beaches and the only place along the Gold Coast which can boast a real "local" community. Even the motel towers on Point Danger are well spaced, and the general ambience is that of a small seaside town.

Arrival and information

The **Gold Coast airport** is 3km west of Coolangatta – see p.395 for local buses and transfers. There are two **long-distance bus stops**: Premier set down in Wharf Street, just over the border in Tweed Heads (and inside the New South Wales time zone); while Greyhound use a bus shelter at the corner of Warner and Chalk streets, in Coolangatta and Queensland. Coolangatta's helpful **visitor** centre is about halfway down Griffith Street (Mon–Fri 8.30am–5.30pm, Sat 9am–3pm; ☎07/5569 3380, ⊛www.goldcoasttourism.com.au). **Taxis** can be booked on ☎13 10 08, while **car rental** is available through Alpha Car Hire, 41 Mclean St (☎07/5599 2301); prices start at around $30 a day.

Accommodation

Accommodation is concentrated down towards the border, where apartment buildings overlook the sea on Marine Parade and Point Danger.

Calypso Plaza 99 Griffith St ☎07/5599 0000. Modern and expensive resort hotel, with suites and two-bedroom penthouse apartments, right across from Greenmount Beach. **❼**

Kirra Beach Hotel Marine Parade, across from the beach at Kirra Point ☎07/5599 3400, ⊛www .kirrabeachhotel.com.au. Ideal location for board-riders. Some rooms are quite spacious, and all have bath, TV and fridge. **❹**

Kirra Tourist Park 1km west on Charlotte St, Kirra ☎07/5581 7744. Probably the cheapest bet in the area, with four- and two-person cabins and tent sites. Rates drop for longer stays. Camping $29, powered sites $33, cabins **❹–❼**

Sunset Strip Budget Resort 199 Boundary St ☎07/5599 5517, ⊛www.sunsetstrip.com.au. Offers family rooms, singles and good facilities – there's a huge kitchen, living area (with three TVs), 20-metre pool and sun deck. Backpacker rooms **❷**, self-contained flats **❹**

YHA 3km up the coast at 230 Coolangatta Rd/Gold Coast Highway, Bilinga, near the airport ☎07/5536 7644, ⊛www.coolangattayha.com. Helpful management and nicely located for the quieter beaches, though a bit far from Coolangatta itself. Dorms $29, rooms **❸**

The Town

Coolangatta is set out one block back from **Greenmount Beach** along **Griffith Street**, where you'll find banks, shops and little in the way of high-density development. Running parallel, and connected by a handful of short streets, **Marine Parade** fronts the shore, the view north over sand and sea ending with the jagged teeth of the skyscrapers on the horizon at Surfers Paradise. The state border runs along Griffith Street and uphill to the east along its continuation, Boundary Street, up to Point Danger at the end of the small peninsula.

At **Point Danger**, the Captain Cook Memorial Lighthouse forms a shrine where pillars enclose a large bronze globe detailing Cook's peregrinations around the southern hemisphere (see also p.1121). Twenty-five metres below, surfers in their colourful wet suits make the most of **Flagstaff Beach**'s swell – at weekends this area is very crowded.

Other good spots to **surf** include the area between Point Danger and Kirra Point, to the west (the latter was nominated by world surfing champion Kelly Slater as his favourite break); Greenmount, which is fairly reliable and a good beach for beginners; and Snapper Rocks and Point Danger, at the end of the peninsula, for the more dedicated – exactly where depends on the wind. For sun worshippers, Coolangatta Beach, just west of Greenmount, is right in town, but the six-kilometre stretch of sand further west, beyond Kirra Point, is wider and less crowded. **Surfing gear and information** are available from Pipedream Surf Shop, Showcase Centre, Griffith Street (☎07/5599 1129), and Mount Woodgee, 122 Griffith St (☎07/5536 5937); surfboard and ski rental is around $30 a day plus credit-card deposit. All shops have decent secondhand boards for sale, though local boards tend to be too thin and lightweight to use elsewhere. For **tuition**, see the box on p.398.

Eating, drinking and nightlife

There are plenty of **snack bars** along Griffith Street, while the best deals on **restaurant meals** are at the *Surf Club* on the corner of Marine Parade and

Dutton Street, where you can get huge counter lunches with sea views from $16. At *Little Malaya*, at the western end of Marine Parade, you can get large noodle soups with chicken or seafood for $10, along with satays and curries for $15 or so. *L9One*, at *Calypso Hotel* down near the border on Griffith Street, is a large bar-bistro complex with an expensive surf-and-turf menu and **live bands** most weekends – you can also catch bands at the *Coolangatta Hotel*'s **nightclub**, on the corner of Marine Parade and Warner Street. If you're doing your own cooking, there's a 24-hour Night Owl convenience store at the Showcase Shopping Centre beside the *Coolangatta Hotel*, and bigger **supermarkets** across the border at the main shopping centre on Wharf Street, in Tweed Heads.

The Gold Coast Hinterland

Beginning around 30km inland from the coast's jangling excesses, the **Gold Coast Hinterland** is a mountainous, rainforested plateau encompassing a series of beautifully wild **national parks**, all packed with scenery, animals and birds. The pick of the bunch is **Green Mountain** at **Lamington National Park**, with atmospheric **hiking trails** through beech forest and a stunning density of birdlife. **Tamborine Mountain**'s less rugged walking tracks and country "villages" also provide a relaxing weekend escape, while waterfalls in **Springbrook National Park** make for an easy day-trip. **Access** is by **tour bus** from Brisbane and the Gold Coast – see the boxes on p.389 and p.400 – but to explore to any degree you'll need your own vehicle, which will also work out the cheapest option for a group. If you're **driving**, carry a good road map, as **signposts** are few and far between – all places are reached off the Pacific Highway between Brisbane and the Gold Coast.

Weather ranges from very wet in summer (when there are leeches in abundance and some hiking trails are closed) to fairly cool and dry in winter, though **rain** is a year-round possibility. If you're planning to **hike**, you'll need good footwear for the slippery paths, although trails are well marked. **Accommodation** is in resorts, motels and campsites, so if you're on a tight budget bring a **tent** – make sure you book all accommodation in advance. You'll need a **fuel stove** if you're camping, as collecting firewood in national parks is forbidden; barbecues and wood are often supplied on sites, however.

Tamborine Mountain

Tamborine Mountain is a volcanic plateau about 40km inland as the crow flies from the Gold Coast, whose remaining pockets of rainforest are interspersed with the little satellite suburbs of northerly **Eagle Heights**, adjoining **North Tamborine** and **Mount Tamborine**, about 5km south. Once the haunt of the Wangeriburra Aborigines, Tamborine Mountain's forests were targeted by the timber industry in the late nineteenth century until locals succeeded in getting the area declared Queensland's **first national park** in 1908. A trip here provides a pleasant escape from the city, with a surplus of tearooms, country accommodation and easy walking tracks through accessibly small, jungly stands of timber.

EAGLE HEIGHTS is the largest settlement, though it's not much more than a five-hundred-metre-long strip, **Gallery Road**, lined with cafés and craft showrooms. The **botanic gardens** (free), off Long Road, are very pretty, with small picnic lawns surrounding a pond overlooked by tall trees; for something a little more energetic, head to **Palm Grove Circuit** at the end of Palm Grove Avenue, a 2.5-kilometre-long mix of dry forest, a few small creeks, and a limpid, eerie gloom created by an extensive stand of elegant piccabean palms. Hidden 20m up in the canopy are elusive wompoo pigeons, often heard but seldom seen, despite their vivid purple-and-green plumage and onomatopoeic call.

A few kilometres west, **NORTH TAMBORINE** sports a **visitor centre** at the junction of Western Road and Geissmann Drive (Sat 9.30am–3.30pm, Sun–Fri 10am–3.30pm; ℡07/5545 3200), a post office, ATMs, fuel stations and even more cafés. The best walk here is about 1km south down Western Road, where a three-kilometre track slaloms downhill through open scrub and rainforest to **Witches Falls**. The easy walk is more rewarding for the views off the plateau than for the falls themselves, which are only a trickle that disappears over a narrow ledge below the lookout. Far more impressive is **Cedar Creek Falls**, a good swimming spot a couple of kilometres north of North Tamborine along Geissmann Drive (the road to Brisbane). Finally, down near **Mount Tamborine** – which is otherwise purely residential – there's a stand of primitive, slow-growing cycads (see box, p.495) and a relatively dry climate at **Lepidozamia National Park** on Main Western Road.

Practicalities

Driving from the coast, turn off the Pacific Highway north of the theme parks at Oxenford and follow Route 95 up to Eagle Heights; from Brisbane, turn off the highway at Beenleigh and take Route 92 to North Tamborine.

The mountain's abundant **accommodation** is generally of a romantic-getaway nature, including cozy rooms at *The Polish Place*, 333 Main Western Rd, North Tamborine (℡07/5545 1603, ⓦwww.polishplace.com.au; self-contained chalet ❽); or suites with four-poster beds, plus a pool and surrounding forest at *Maz's Ambience Retreat*, 25 Eagle Heights Rd, North Tamborine (℡07/5545 1766, ⓦwww.mazsretreat.com; ❻). Alternatively, there's *The Cottages*, 23 Kootenai Drive, North Tamborine (℡07/5545 2574, ⓦwww.thecottages.com .au; ❼), or the very stylish, wooden pole-frame buildings at *Pethers Rainforest Retreat* (℡07/5545 4577, ⓦwww.pethers.com.au; ❾). The sole budget option is *Tamborine Mountain Caravan and Campsite* at Thunderbird Park, near Cedar Creek on Tamborine Mountain Road (℡07/5545 0034, ⓦwww.tamborine .info; camping $9 per person, powered sites $22).

Springbrook National Park

At the edge of a plateau along the New South Wales border, **Springbrook National Park** comprises several separate fragments – the best of which are **Purling Brook Falls** and **Natural Bridge** – featuring abundant forest, waterfalls and swimming holes. To get there, turn off the Pacific Highway inland from Burleigh Heads at **Mudgeeraba** and then follow the twisty road 20km southwest to a junction, where Route 99 heads left to Purlingbrook, and Route 97 heads right to Natural Bridge.

Purling Brook Falls is about 8km south of the junction. The 109-metre falls are very impressive after rain has swollen the flow; a four-kilometre track zigzags down the escarpment and into the rainforest at the base of the falls before curving underneath the waterfall (expect a soaking from the spray) and going back up the other side. In the plunge pool at the foot of the falls, the force of the water is enough to push you under; swimming is more relaxed in a couple of pools downstream, picturesquely encircled by lianas and red cedar. There's a **campsite** outside the forest, near the top of the falls, with a **store** about 4km back along the main road.

A ten-kilometre drive beyond the falls brings you to a handy information centre (℡07/5533 5147), with maps of the region, and another 1km along is the aptly named **Best of All Lookout** which affords a panoramic vista south to Mount Warning.

Natural Bridge is about 24km from the Purling Brook Falls junction. It's a dark, damp and hauntingly eerie place, where a collapsed cave ceiling beneath the riverbed has created a subterranean waterfall. You can walk in through the original cave-mouth some 50m downstream; from the back of the cave the forest outside frames the waterfall and blue plunge pool, surreally lit from above; **glow-worms** illuminate the ceiling at night.

Lamington National Park

Lamington National Park occupies the northeastern rim of a vast 1156-metre-high caldera centred on Mount Warning, 15km away in New South Wales. An enthralling world of rainforest-flanked rivers, open heathland and ancient eucalypt woods, Lamington's position on a crossover zone between subtropical and temperate climes has made it home to a staggering variety of plants, animals and birds, with isolated populations of species found nowhere else in the world. There are two possible bases for exploring the park: **Binna Burra** on the drier northern edge, and **Green Mountain** (better known for the well-publicized **O'Reilly's Guesthouse**) in the thick of the forest, with a twenty-kilometre-long hiking track linking the two.

By road from Brisbane or the coast, it's simplest to first aim for **Nerang**, inland from Surfers Paradise on the Pacific Highway. From here, Binna Burra is 36km southwest via tiny **Beechmont**, while Green Mountain/O'Reilly's is about 65km away via **Canungra township**. If you don't have a car, accommodation might provide a **pick-up** from the coast, and some tour operators may be willing to take you up one day and pick you up on another if asked in advance.

Beechmont or Canungra are the last proper sources of **supplies**, fuel and cash, though there's resort and campsite **accommodation** at both Green Mountain and Binna Burra, which must be booked in advance. Once here, Lamington has to be explored on foot: most of the tracks described below are clearly signposted and **free maps** are available from local National Parks ranger stations.

Binna Burra

Binna Burra is a massive tract of highland forest where, overlooking the Numinbah Valley from woodland on the crown of Mount Roberts, you'll find **accommodation** at the upmarket *Binna Burra Mountain Lodge* (℡1300 246 622, @www.binnaburralodge.com.au; camping $24, powered sites $30, on-site tents ❷, cabins ❼). They offer wooden twin-share cabins with log fires, along with on-site tents and a campsite with hot showers; phone in advance to arrange a **pick-up** from the Gold Coast airport and Nerang Station (to connect with the train from Brisbane airport). The *Lodge* also has an expensive **restaurant** and less formal café if you're not self-catering. Hikers can also **bushcamp** inside the national park between February and November; for details contact the ranger in Beechmont (daily 8am–4pm; ℡07/5533 3584).

Of the **walks**, try the easy five-kilometre **Caves Circuit**, which follows the edge of the Coomera Valley past the white, wind-sculpted Talangai Caves to remains of Aboriginal camps, strands of *psilotum nudum* (a rootless ancestor of the ferns), and a hillside of strangler figs and red cedar. The **Ballunji Falls Track** is a little more demanding, with some vertical drops off the path; key features along the way include views of Egg Rock from **Bellbird Lookout**, at its most mysterious when shrouded in dawn mists, and a stand of majestic forty-metre-tall box brush trees. The trail can be extended out to **Ships Stern**, a tiring and dry 21-kilometre hike (8hr return), with some wonderful views off the escarpment. **Dave's Creek Circuit** is similar but about half as long, crossing bands of rainforest and sclerophyll before emerging onto heathland. Look for tiny clumps of red **sundew** plants along the track, which supplement their nitrogen intake by trapping insects in sticky globules of nectar.

By far the best of the longer tracks is the **Border Track**; a relatively easy 21-kilometre, 7-hour path (one-way) through rainforest and beech groves linking Binna Burra with Green Mountain. If you need road transport between the two, the *Lodge* usually runs a free weekly service to *O'Reilly's* for its guests, and will often take others for a fee if there's room – departures depend on demand, so all arrangements have to be made on site.

Green Mountain

Green Mountain is Lamington at its best, a huge spread of cloud forest filled with ancient, moss-covered trees and a mass of wildlife including so many birds that you hardly know where to start looking. The road up from Canungra ends at ⚜ *O'Reilly's Guesthouse* (℡07/5544 0644, ⓦwww.oreillys.com.au; ⑨), a splendid and comfortable place opened in 1926; there's a limited **store** (with EFTPOS facilities) and a moderately priced **restaurant** here for meals and snacks throughout the day. An exposed **National Parks campsite** with showers (℡07/5544 0634 or ⓦwww.epa.qld.gov.au for essential advance booking) is nearby. If you can't get in here, head back 7km towards Canungra and *Cainbable Mountain Lodge* (℡07/5544 9207, ⓦwww.cainbable.com; ⑦), whose modern, self-contained chalets sleep from four to eight people and have splendid views.

The **birdlife** around *O'Reilly's* is prolific and distracting: you can't miss the chattering swarms of crimson rosellas mingling with visitors on the lawn, and determined twitchers can clock up over fifty species without even reaching the forest – most spectacular is the black-and-gold regent bowerbird. But it's worth pushing on to the **treetop walk** just beyond the clearing, where a suspended walkway swings 15m above ground level. At the halfway anchor point you scale a narrow ladder to vertigo-inducing mesh platforms 30m up the trunk of a strangler fig to see the canopy at eye level. Soaking up the increased sunlight at this height above the forest floor, tree branches become miniature gardens of mosses, ferns and orchids. By night the walkway is the preserve of possums, leaf-tailed geckoes and weird stalking insects.

If you manage only one day-walk at Lamington, make it the exceptional fifteen-kilometre **Blue Pool–Canungra Creek** track (5hr return), which features all the jungle trimmings: fantastic trees, river crossings and countless opportunities to fall off slippery rocks and get soaked. The first hour is dry enough as you tramp downhill past some huge red cedars to Blue Pool, a deep, placid waterhole where platypuses are sometimes seen on winter mornings; this makes a good walk in itself. After a dip, head upstream along Canungra Creek; the path traverses the river a few times (there are no bridges, but occasionally a fallen tree conveniently spans the water) – look for yellow or red arrows painted on rocks that indicate where to cross. Seasonally, the creek can be almost dried up; if the water is more than knee-deep, you shouldn't attempt a crossing and will need to retrace your steps. Follow the creek as far as Elabana Falls and another swimming hole, or bypass the falls; either way, the path climbs back to the guesthouse.

Another excellent trail (17.5km return) takes six hours via **Box Creek Falls** to the eastern escarpment at **Toolona Lookout**, on the Border Track to Binna Burra; rewards are a half-dozen waterfalls, dramatic views into New South Wales, and encounters with clumps of moss-covered **Antarctic beech trees**, a Gondwanan relic also found in South America.

The Sunshine Coast

The **Sunshine Coast**, stretching north of Brisbane to Noosa, is a more pedestrian version of the Gold Coast, where largely domestic tourist development is tempered by, and sometimes combined with, agriculture. Much of the local character is due to the lack of death taxes in Queensland, something which, together with the mild climate, attracts retirees from all over Australia. The towns tend to be bland places, though there's striking scenery at the **Glass House Mountains**, good beaches and surf at **Maloolaba** and **Maroochydore**, and upmarket beach life at **Noosa**. Though you'll find the **hinterland** far tamer than that behind the Gold Coast, it still has some pleasant landscapes and scattered hamlets rife with Devonshire cream teas and weekend markets.

Without your own transport, the easiest way through the area is by **bus**, either with local transport or tour companies, or the national long-distance carriers. Brisbane's **Citytrain** network can also take you into the region, with stops at the Glass House Mountains, Woombye, Nambour and Eumundi, from where there's a connecting local bus to Noosa. There's also the **Sunshine Coast airport** just north of Maroochydore, serving Brisbane, Sydney and Melbourne.

Woodford, the Glass House Mountains and Australia Zoo

The unremarkable town of **Caboolture** marks the start of the Sunshine Coast, 40km north of Brisbane, though the first place of interest lies 20km northwest, where the two-street town of **WOODFORD** draws thousands for the annual folk festival in December (W www.woodfordfolkfestival.com).

Route 60 runs 30km north from Caboolture to **Beerwah**, providing access to **Glass House Mountains National Park**: nine dramatic, isolated pinnacles

Watersports

While most visitors mythologize Australia as a rust-red never-never, baking beneath epic blue skies, it's the beach that is hardwired into the Aussie mentality – even in dusty Outback towns, an incongruous surf shop will peddle the beach lifestyle. No surprise, then, that around ninety percent of the population live within a couple of hours of the coast, nor that Australians have found countless ways of getting in, on or under the water.

Surfing

In the century since Hawaiian legend Duke Kahanamoku paddled out at North Sydney's Freshwater Beach to demonstrate the wave-riding of his homeland, Australians have made **surfing** their own, thanks to world-class waves on all coastlines except the north. Forget any impressions of surfing as the counter-culture activity of beach bums, however – in Australia it is a mainstream sport where the standard is high and the mentality is territorial; cliquey at best, aggressive at worst. Learners, therefore, should familiarize themselves with a lesson or two at resorts such as Byron Bay first, and keep clear of the pack.

The **surfari road-trip** is not just one of the great joys of Aussie travel – it's a rite of passage for all surfers, where new breaks and dazzling scenery await around every bend in the road. Hot spots in New South Wales are Newcastle and the strip from Lennox Head to Byron Bay – still

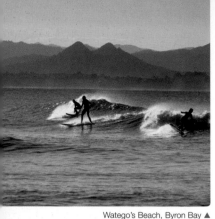

Watego's Beach, Byron Bay ▲

Lifeguard, Manly Beach, Sydney ▼

Lifesavers' watchtower, Surfers Paradise, Queensland ▼

Surf lifesaving

Pioneered off Sydney beaches in 1906, **surf lifesaving** is now as much a visual shorthand for Australia as Uluru. When they're not patrolling beaches, volunteer lifeguards of the 305 lifesaving clubs, each with its own club colours emblazoned on cossies and caps, take part in inter-club competitions. Events at these colourful beach extravaganzas range from first-aid contests and running races via surf-ski paddles to the long-boat rescue; these five-crew, 200–250kg row-boats now buck through breaking surf only for competitions. Equally worthy of respect is the **Ironman** event, a gruelling nonstop discipline whose entrants paddle, swim and run up to 50km. Small wonder it is often seen as the pinnacle of Aussie athleticism.

a surfing hub, even if it's moved on since its days as an icon of Sixties soul-surfing. Queensland boasts regional classics like the perfect right-hand point of Snapper Rocks near Coolangatta and the mellow longboarders' wave at Noosa. South Australia and Victoria are characterized by cold Southern Ocean seas – the latter is home to Bells Beach, venue for the world's oldest surf competition, the Rip Curl Pro Surf at Easter – while powerful reef breaks make Margaret River the undisputed surf capital of Western Australia.

▲ Sailing in Sydney Harbour

▼ Sea-kayaking in Coles Bay, Tasmania

Kayaking

You can dip a paddle all over Australia, from sit-on floats off Queensland resorts to sea kayaks in Sydney Harbour. For true adventure, however, go to Tasmania, whose UNESCO-listed Southwest National Park provides two of the greatest eco-trips on Earth. Book a canoe-and-camp expedition to explore Port Davey's remote natural harbour (see p.1108), or sign up for a trip on the Franklin River, the wildest whitewater roller-coaster in Australia, and you'll tumble over rapids up to Grade IV in an otherwise inaccessible canyon (see p.1106).

▼ Kayaking in Lawn Hill National Park, Queensland

Sailing

The top **sailing** destination is Queensland's Whitsunday Islands, a concentrated Caribbean of azure sea and powder beaches. You can either join an organized trip or charter a yacht to snorkel with dolphins and turtles, or simply gawp at postcard-perfect wonders like Whitehaven Beach. Other premier sailing destinations include Western Australia's west coast – try the marina at Fremantle or take a cruise from Coral Bay – and Sydney Harbour, which hosts weekend racers and cruises alike.

Potato grouper fish ▲

Green turtle ▼

School of tropical fish ▼

Diving

For many, the Great Barrier Reef is reason alone to visit Australia. A huge draw for **divers**, the world's largest living organism is a kaleidoscope of coral and tropical fish – the dilemma is which bit of its 2000km to visit, and whether to go with a live-aboard dive school or day-trip; either takes the hassle out of hiring gear and organizing transport. **Snorkelling** is a low-tech alternative that still gets you up close to the life around a reef.

Top dive sites

Bougainville Reef Coral Sea, Great Barrier Reef, QLD. Coral walls, clear water and reef life in abundance. Trips from Cairns and Port Douglas. See p.484.

Cod Hole Far North Reef, Great Barrier Reef, QLD. Where giant potato cod and divers meet. Trips from Cairns. See p.484.

Geographe Bay WA. The HMS *Swan* was scuppered off Cape Naturaliste. Trips from Dunsborough. See p.667.

Lord Howe Island NSW. The world's southernmost reef surrounds one of its most beautiful islands. See p.297.

Ningaloo Reef WA. Whale sharks from April to June. Tours from Exmouth or Coral Bay. See p.709.

Port Lincoln SA. These waters are a last bastion for the unfairly maligned great white shark. Shark-cage diving trips from Port Lincoln. See p.824.

SS Yongala QLD. Huge fish and the wreck of an early twentieth-century passenger liner sunk by a cyclone. Trips from Townsville and Cairns. See p.453.

Tasman Peninsula TAS. Caves and kelp forests in the world's most accessible underwater wilderness. Trips from Eaglehawk Neck. See p.1048.

jutting out of a flat plain, visible from as far away as Brisbane. To the Kabi Aborigines, the mountains are the petrified forms of a family fleeing the incoming tide, though their current name was bestowed by Captain Cook because of their "shape and elevation" – a resemblance that's obscure today. The peaks themselves vary enormously: some are rounded and fairly easy to scale, while a couple have vertical faces and sharp spires requiring competent climbing skills. It's worth conquering at least one of the easier peaks, as the views are superb: **Beerburrum**, overlooking the township of the same name, and **Ngungun**, near the Glass House Mountains township, are two of the easiest to climb, with well-used tracks which shouldn't take more than two hours return; the latter's views and scenery outclass some of the tougher peaks, though the lower parts of the track are steep and slippery. **Tibberoowuccum**, a small peak at 220m just outside the national-park boundary, must be climbed from the northwest, with access from the car park off Marsh's Road. The taller mountains – **Tibrogargan** and **Beerwah** (the highest at 556m) – are at best tricky, and **Coonowrin** should be attempted only by experienced climbers after contacting the National Parks office in Beerwah (℡07/5494 0150).

For maps of the region and local climbing conditions, ask the experienced volunteers at the **visitor centre** at the Matthew Flinders Park Rest Area, 2km north of **Beerburrum town** and about 20km north of Caboolture. The most convenient **accommodation** in the area is at *Glasshouse Mountains Holiday Village* (℡07/5496 9338; camping $23, powered sites $25, cabins ❸), south of the Glass House Mountains township, 25km north of Caboolture at the foot of Mount Tibrogargan.

Australia Zoo

Australia Zoo (daily 9am–4.30pm; $52; ℡07/5494 1134, ⓦwww .crocodilehunter.com), just north of Beerwah, became famous through the antics of the late zoo director **Steve Irwin**, otherwise known for his "Crocodile Hunter" screen persona. Despite his tragic death in 2006, the staff here continue Irwin's tradition of exuberant exhibitionism, and it remains one of the largest and most enjoyable commercial zoos in Australia, with plenty of hands-on experience with both foreign and native animals. The best way into the area is up along Route 60 via Beerwah, or south along Route 6 from Landsborough; contact the zoo in advance for a **free pick-up** from Beerwah Station (on the Citytrain network from Brisbane) and most places along the coast between Caloundra and Noosa. Otherwise, numerous **tours** run here from Brisbane or you can catch the Greyhound bus from Brisbane or Noosa.

Caloundra

On the coast 20km east of Landsborough – there's a local bus from Landsborough train station – **CALOUNDRA** just manages to hold on to its small seaside-town atmosphere, and as such is unique along the Sunshine Coast, where busy highways and beachfront overdevelopment have long since put paid to this elsewhere. Even so, there are plenty of towering apartment blocks, though central **Bulcock Street** has only low-rise buildings and is lined with trees. Caloundra's **beaches** are very pleasant: the closest is at Deepwater Point, just two streets south of Bulcock Street – Shelley Beach and Moffat Beach, about 1km distant, are much quieter. The **bus terminal** is on Cooma Terrace, one street south of Bulcock, where there's also a **visitor centre** (Mon–Fri 8am–5pm; ℡07/5491 2555). For **accommodation** try *Caloundra City Backpackers*, 84 Omrah Ave (℡07/5499 7655; dorms $25, rooms ❸), which is clean, well run, and just two minutes from Deepwater Point. *Estoril*, at 38 McIlwraith St (℡07/5491 5988, Ⓦwww.estoril.com.au; ❼), offers self-catering apartments sleeping four in a high-rise block right next to Moffat Beach, and has a huge pool.

Mooloolaba

The coast north of Caloundra kicks off with **MOOLOOLABA**, a mess of high-rise units, boutiques and flashy, forgettable dining experiences – though the beaches are long, sandy and excellent for surfing. The town's sole land-based attraction is **Underwater World** on Parkyn Parade (daily 9am–5pm, last entry at 4pm; $28.50), with superb views of sharks, turtles and nonchalant freshwater crocodiles staring blankly at you through observation windows. For the real thing, Sunreef at 110 Brisbane Rd (℡07/5444 5656, Ⓦwww .sunreef.com.au) can take qualified **scuba divers** fifteen minutes offshore to where the HMAS *Brisbane* lies in 8–28m of water; the 133m-long destroyer was deliberately sunk as a dive site in 2005 and has already become home to a large array of marine life. A two-tank dive costs $145 plus gear rental, but it's an unpleasant experience in heavy swell; if you're heading north, save your dollars for the *Yongala* (see p.453).

Buses set down on Smith Street, a short way back from shops and restaurants lining the hundred-metre-long, seafront Esplanade. The Esplanade has plenty of modern high-rise **holiday apartments** all charging around $300 and up for a two bedroom, self-contained unit: options include *Sirocco* (℡07/5444 1400, Ⓦwww.siroccoapartments.com.au) and *Peninsular* (℡07/5444 4477, Ⓦwww .peninsular.com.au). Alternatively, *Sandcastles*, on the corner of Esplanade and Parkyn Parade (℡07/5478 0666, Ⓦwww.sandcastlesonthebeach.com.au; ❼), offers older rooms right next to the Surf Club, while *Mooloolaba Beach Backpackers* at 75 Brisbane Rd (℡07/5444 3399, Ⓦwww.mooloolababackpackers.com; dorms $26, rooms ❸) is a clean and friendly budget option where the price includes a free breakfast, bike, kayak and boogie-board loans, and barbecue nights. **Eating** options are everywhere, though the best deals and sea views are at *Mooloolaba Surf Club*'s smart café, bar and restaurant on the Esplanade (daily noon–2pm & 6pm–late, plus Sun from 8am). *Mooloolaba Hotel*, on the Esplanade, hosts rock bands every Friday and Saturday, and opens its doors as a **nightclub** on Sundays.

Maroochydore

Most of the other accommodation options for independent travellers are 3km north of Mooloolaba at **MAROOCHYDORE**. With a multi-lane highway tearing through the middle of the town, this isn't an immediately attractive place, but away from the centre the beaches and surrounding streets are quiet, and the surf – as usual – is great. **Buses** set down beside the visitor centre on Sixth Avenue, just a short walk from **accommodation** at *Sea Breeze Caravan Park* (℡1800 461 167, Ⓦwww.maroochypark.qld.gov.au; camping $33, powered sites $37, 1- and 2-bedroom cabins ❻–❼), on Cotton Tree Parade right at the northern end of the beach. Just around the corner, *Cotton Tree Backpackers*, 15 Esplanade (℡07/5443 1755, Ⓦwww.cottontreebackpackers.com; dorms $29, rooms ❻), is a bright, airy place in an old beach house and hands out surfboards and kayaks. A final option is the hidden *Maroochydore Backpackers*, 1km from the bus and beach at 24 Schirrmann Drive (℡07/5443 3151, Ⓦwww.yhabackpackers.com.au; dorms $22–29, rooms ❷); facilities include a pool, free use of bikes and surfboards and a courtesy bus into the town centre. **Moving on**, Noosa is an easy 30km north of

Maroochydore along the coastal David Low Way, or a little more along Route 70 to Tewantin.

Nambour, the hinterland, and on to Noosa

Bisected by tramways from surrounding sugar plantations, the functional town of **Nambour** sits 15km inland from Maroochydore on Highway 1 in the centre of the Sunshine Coast's farming region. There's not much in town to detain you, though 5km south between the highway and **Woombye** you'll find it hard not to at least pause and gawk at the renowned and ridiculous **Big Pineapple** which overshadows the eponymous plantation (daily 9am–5pm; free except tours and rides; ☎07/5442 1333). Activities include trips around the plantation on a cane train and, of course, climbing the fibreglass fruit. Woombye is a stop on Brisbane's **Citytrain** network, or Sunshine Coast Coaches run here from Nambour.

A two-hour (90km) circuit drive from Nambour along the Blackall Range takes you into the **Sunshine Coast hinterland**, a rural English-style idyll with fields dotted by herds of pied dairy cattle, and occasional long views out to the coast. Several settlements – such as **Montville** and **Mapleton** – have dolled themselves up as "villages" and suffer from an overdose of potteries and twee tearooms, though it's worth stretching your legs to reach a couple of respectably sized **waterfalls** up here: Kondalilla, 3km north from Montville towards Nambour, with swimming holes along Obi Obi Creek; and Mapleton Falls, just west of Mapleton, where the river plunges over basalt cliffs.

A much more genuine place is **MALENY**, whose ageing hippy population, single street of cafés (the *Upfront Club* on Maple Street has good food with a healthy inclination and live bands at weekends), co-operative supermarket, and short river walk all create a pleasantly alternative atmosphere. About 5km south out of town, **Mary Cairncross Reserve** (winter 9am–4pm; summer 9am–5pm; donation) is a small patch of rainforest inhabited by snakes, wallabies and plenty of birds; there's a fantastic view south over the Glass House Mountains from the entrance. Maleny's handful of cottage-industry **accommodation** options include the friendly *Maleny Hills Motel* (☎07/5494 2551, ⊛www.malenyhills.com.au; ❺), about 5km east of town on the Montville road; and ⊁ *Lyndon Lodge B&B* (☎07/5494 3307, ⊛www.lyndonlodge.com.au; ❹–❺), also on the Maleny–Montville road, and with superb views and very helpful owners.

Back down near Nambour and heading north on Highway 1, you can reach Noosa by turning coastwards at **EUMUNDI**, a tiny town also on the Citytrain line and known for its Wednesday and Saturday **markets**, reputed to be the biggest and best in Australia. An appealing place to **stay overnight** here is *Hidden Valley B&B and Cookery School* (☎07/5442 8685, ⊛www.eumundibed .com; ❼), an old Queenslander home with great decor set on four acres of land – one separate guest room is a beautifully renovated railway caboose.

Noosa

The exclusive end of the Sunshine Coast and an established celebrity "des-res" area, **NOOSA** is dominated by an enviably beautiful headland, defined by the mouth of the placid **Noosa River** and a strip of beach to the southeast. Popular since **surfers** first came in the 1960s to ride the fierce waves around the headland, the setting compensates for the density of cloned apartment boxes in "Mediterranean" colours around town. Beach and river aside, there's also a tiny national park with beautiful coastal walks where you'll almost certainly see **koalas**, and a couple of shallow **lakes** just north with good paddling potential.

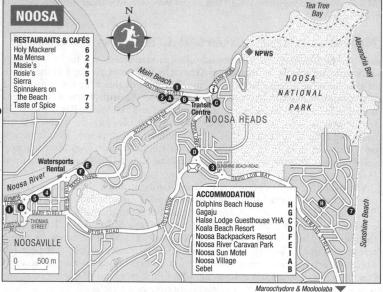

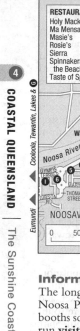
NOOSA

RESTAURANTS & CAFÉS	
Holy Mackerel	6
Ma Mensa	2
Masie's	4
Rosie's	5
Sierra	1
Spinnakers on the Beach	7
Taste of Spice	3

ACCOMMODATION	
Dolphins Beach House	H
Gagaju	G
Halse Lodge Guesthouse YHA	C
Koala Beach Resort	D
Noosa Backpackers Resort	F
Noosa River Caravan Park	E
Noosa Sun Motel	I
Noosa Village	A
Sebel	B

Maroochydore & Mooloolaba ▼

Information and accommodation

The long-distance "**Transit Centre**" – just a bus shelter – is at the junction of Noosa Parade and Noosa Drive. Avoid the commercially driven information booths scattered all over Noosa and head to the government-backed, volunteer-run **visitor centre** alongside the Surf Club on Hastings Street (daily 9am–5pm; ☏07/5447 4988).

All **accommodation** will help organize activities and tours, from surfing lessons to Fraser Island safaris. Van parks and a couple of hostels are the budget options but are often booked up in advance so plan ahead; most places here are motels, apartments or expensive chain hotels. **Prices** double everywhere apart from the hostels during school holidays.

Dolphins Beach House 14 Duke St, Sunshine Beach ☏1800 454 456, ⓦwww.dolphinsbeach house.com. Budget rooms and self-contained units with a distinctly mellow, New Age feel and surfboards to rent, about 5min walk from the sea. Dorms $27, rooms ❸, units. ❻

Gagaju Call ahead for directions or pick-up ☏07/5474 3522. An eco-friendly bush camp near the lakes north of Noosa, with very basic timber bunkhouses and space for campers. Canoes and camping equipment, advice on hikes and canoe trips, and fireside bush-poetry readings are among the attractions. Their three-day independent canoe trip ($90 excluding food which you buy and cook yourself) is highly recommended. Dorms $15, camping $10.

Halse Lodge Guesthouse YHA 17 Noosa Drive, Noosa Heads ☏1800 242 567, ⓦwww.halselodge .com.au. Immaculate 1888 Queenslander building

in leafy grounds with shared rooms and dorms close to Noosa Beach; there's a large kitchen, comfy lounge and good-value dinner deals, although it's not a place for partying. Often full so book in advance. Dorms $29–35, rooms ❹

Koala Beach Resort 44 Noosa Drive, Noosa Heads ☏1800 357 457, ⓦwww.koalaresort.com .au. Central budget accommodation in dorms and motel units. Nowhere near the beach, and not especially clean, but the party atmosphere and live music might compensate. Dorms $28, rooms ❸

Noosa Backpackers Resort 9 William St, Noosaville ☏1800 626 673, ⓦwww.noosaback packers.com.au. Converted motel units with small dorms and basic rooms but close to the activities centre on Gympie Terrace and free use of boogie-boards and surfboards. Dorms $25, rooms ❸

Noosa River Caravan Park Russell St, Noosaville ☎07/5449 7050. Large campsite and van park with splendid river views, but with no cabins or on-site vans. Sites $33.

Noosa Village 10 Hastings St ☎07/5447 5800, [W]www.noosavillage.com.au. Unpretentious, tidy motel that's an extraordinarily good deal given its location on Noosa's most glitzy, upmarket street. Rooms are not huge, though some have balconies. [5]

Noosa Sun Motel 131 Gympie Terrace, Noosaville ☎07/5474 0477, [W]www.noosasunmotel.com. Clean, spacious and affordable self-contained apartment accommodation – one of the best deals in town although it's set slightly away from the main tourist hubs. [5]

Sebel Hasting St [W]www.sebelnoosa.com. Stylish comforts around a pool and other water features in this low-set international chain; apartments have well-equipped kitchens and spa baths. [9]

The town and around

"Noosa" is a loose term covering a seven-kilometre-long sprawl of merging settlements stretched along the south side of the Noosa River, culminating at **Noosa Heads**. This forms the core of the town, with a chic and brash shopping-and-dining enclave along beachside **Hastings Street**, and a far more down-to-earth area of shops, banks and cafés 1km inland along **Sunshine Beach Road**. East of this is the headland itself and **Noosa National Park**, worth a look for its mix of mature rainforest, coastal heath and fine **beaches** – Tea Tree Bay and Alexandria Bay ("swimwear optional") have good sand pounded by unpatrolled surf – all reached along graded paths with gorgeous views. These start from the picnic area at the end of Park Road (a continuation of Hastings Street), where you'll probably see **koalas** in gum trees above the car park. South of the headland and national park is the discreet suburb of **Sunshine Beach**, which features Noosa's longest and least crowded stretch of

Noosa water activities

Noosa's original reason to be was the **surf**, and if you know what you're doing you'll find all the necessary gear at Go Ride A Wave, 77 Noosa Drive, Noosa Junction (☎1300 132 441). The best surf is found around Noosa Heads; if you're a novice and put off by the crowds, try a lesson with Learn to Surf (☎0418 787 577, [W]www.learntosurf.com.au) or Wavesense (☎0414 369 076, [W]www.wavesense.com.au); costs are around $55 for a two-hour introduction, and from $220–550 for a five-day course depending on group size and intensity.

Most other water activities, including the popular **river cruises**, are based to the west around Noosaville and Tewantin. Noosa River Cruises, on Gympie Terrace in Noosaville (☎07/5449 7362), and Everglade Cruises, Harbour Town Complex, Tewantin (☎07/5449 0393, [W]www.noosaevergladescruises.com), have day-tours on the river and lakes for around $80. To get as far as Lake Cootharaba, Beyond (☎1800 657 666, [W]www.beyondnoosa.com.au) has three-hour cruises upriver for $89 and full-day tours for $149, which includes a cruise and a 4WD run up the sands to Rainbow Beach.

For **watersports**, Pro Ski, on the river bank at Gympie Terrace in Noosaville (☎07/5449 7740), has **water-skiing** ($140 for 45min up to 4 people), **jet skis** ($80 for 30min) and canoes ($20 per hour); next door, Pelican Boat Hire (☎07/5449 7239, [W]www.pelicanboathire.com.au) has small **outboard** boats for rent ($34 for the first hour and $14 for additional hours). Kingfisher Boat Hire (☎07/5449 9353), at the Harbour Town Complex in Tewantin, rents out **fishing boats** with fuel, rods, bait pumps, crab pots, ice boxes and the rest, for around $35 an hour. Adventure Sports, at the Noosa River Shopping Centre on Gympie Terrace (☎07/5455 6677, [W]www.kite-surf.com.au), has two-hour **kite surfing courses** ($150), and also rents out kayaks and mountain bikes.

sand. All three suburbs are connected by a **bus service** (Sunbus), which goes by every thirty minutes or so between 5.50am and 7.50pm, with an hourly service thereafter to midnight.

West from Noosa Heads, **Noosaville** is a mainly residential district along the riverfront. In the late afternoon, half of Noosa promenades along **Gympie Terrace** as the sinking sun colours a gentle tableau: mangroves on the opposite shore, pelicans eyeing anglers for scraps and landing clumsily midstream, and everything from cruise boats to windsurfers and kayaks out on the water. If you just want to take a quick ride along the river, hop on the **Noosa ferry** (Sun–Thurs 9.05am–5.50pm, 10 daily; Fri & Sat 9.05am–9.50pm, 13 daily) from the Sheraton Noosa Jetty off Hastings Street upstream to the suburb of **Tewantin**; it costs $13.50 one-way for the forty-minute journey to Tewantin, or $19.50 for an all-day pass.

Eating

Noosa's **nightlife** is pretty tame, and eating out is the main pastime. Hastings Street has long been the place to dine and be seen in Noosa, but it's dominated by pretentious Italian restaurants clogging up the pavements with tables – soaring rents have seen the best eateries relocate to Noosaville, where you'll now find lots of casual diners checking out the places clustered along Gympie Terrace and Thomas Street.

Holy Mackerel 187 Gympie Terrace, Noosaville. Unquestionably the place for fish and chips – try the sensational coconut prawns and handmade ice creams. Daily 10.30am–7.30pm.

Ma Mensa Hastings St, Noosa Heads. Best of the Italian bistros with obligatory outdoor tables with home-made pizza and pasta dishes for $25, with more flamboyant mains starting from $32.

Masie's 247 Gympie Terrace, Noosaville. Excellent steak and seafood dishes served in a rather formal and airy setting with some outside tables. Try the seafood pie or pan-fried veal – mains cost around $29. Closed Mon.

Rosie's Gympie Terrace, near the corner of Albert St, Noosaville ☏07/5449 7888. Tiny and intimate BYO place, with a new menu every week. It's popular with locals, with mains from around $24.

Sierra 10 Hastings St, Noosa Heads. Cheapest of Hastings' restaurants with a broad menu including the obligatory Italian pastas for $20 and a more enticing Thai fish laksa for $27. Live music most evenings makes this a more casual affair than its neighbours. Daily 7.30am to late.

Spinnakers on the Beach Sunshine Beach Surf Club. Spacious bar and restaurant with unbeatable views. Big servings of seafood, steaks, pasta and salad, all in the $15–25 range. Courtesy bus from Noosa on Wed and Fri nights.

Taste of Spice 36 Sunshine Beach Rd, Noosa Heads. Inconspicuous noodle bar serving tasty Malaysian curries and Vietnamese wraps for under $15. BYO.

Around Noosa: lakes Cooroibah and Cootharaba

North of Noosa, a winding six-kilometre stretch of the Noosa River pools into lakes **Cooroibah** and **Cootharaba** as it nears Tewantin. Placid, and fringed with paperbarks and reedbeds, the lakes look their best at dawn before there's any traffic; they're saltwater and average just 1m in depth, subject to tides.

You can **cruise** the lakes from Noosa (see p.411), or drive up from Tewantin; turn off the main road onto Werin Street at the school – there is a sign, but it's easy to miss – then turn left again and follow the signposts. About 6km along is **Cooroibah township** on Cooroibah's western shore, where there's a boat ramp. It's 10km by water from here to Lake Cootharaba, or 17km by road to lakeshore **BOREEN POINT**, a small place with fuel, a general store and the low-slung, colonial-era wooden *Apollonian Hotel* (☏07/5485 3100; ❷), which oozes character and serves cold drinks and pub lunches; there's also a council-run **campsite** here. Another 4km and the road runs out at **Elanda Point** (where there's another small store) from where there's a footpath to Cootharaba's northernmost edge at **Kinaba**, basically a visitor centre set where Kin Kin Creek and the Noosa River spill lazily into the lake through thickets of mangroves, hibiscus and tea trees – the so-called **Everglades**. A boardwalk from Kinaba leads to a hide where you can spy on birdlife, and the picnic area here is a former **corroboree ground**, which featured in the saga of Eliza Fraser (see p.422). **Canoes** and kayaks can be rented at all the townships from around $40 a day.

The Fraser Coast

The **Fraser Coast** covers over 190km of the coastline north from Noosa, forming a world of giant dunes, forests, coloured sands and freshwater lakes where fishing and four-wheel driving are the activities of preference. But it doesn't have to be a macho tangle with the elements: for once it's relatively easy and inexpensive to rent tents and a 4WD and set off to explore in some comfort. The main destination for all of this is **Fraser Island**, an enormous, elongated and largely forested sand island, which has just about enough room for the crowds of tourists who visit each year. On the way there, the small townships of **Rainbow Beach** and **Tin Can Bay**, on the mainland off Fraser's southernmost tip, offer a more laid-back view of the region, with another long strip of beach and the chance to come into contact with wild **dolphins**. You can catch a ferry to Fraser Island from the Rainbow Beach area, though the main access point is **Hervey Bay**, a tourist hub which also offers seasonal **whale watching cruises**.

The Fraser Coast's abundant fresh water, seafood and plants must have supported a very healthy Aboriginal population; campfires along the beach allowed Matthew Flinders to navigate Fraser Island at night in 1802. The area was declared an Aboriginal reserve in the early 1860s but, with the discovery of **gold** at Gympie in 1867, Europeans flocked in thousands into the region. The subsequent economic boom sparked by the goldrush saved the fledgling Queensland from bankruptcy, but the growth in white settlement saw the Aboriginal population cleared out so that the area could be opened up for recreation. More recently, the big issues here have been caused by the local logging, tourism and conservationist camps all struggling for control of resources: the balance between protection and "development" – a word with almost religious connotations in Queensland – is far from being established.

The main route into the area is off Highway 1, 60km north of Noosa at **Gympie** for Tin Can Bay and Rainbow Beach, or a further 85km north up the highway at **Maryborough** for Hervey Bay; **long-distance buses** serve all three towns daily. **Tours** around the region run from Noosa, Rainbow Beach and Hervey Bay (the best place to arrange self-drive 4WD expeditions); those from Noosa often zip straight up **Cooloola Beach** in a 4WD from Tewantin to Rainbow Beach, a forty-kilometre run of uninterrupted sand.

Tin Can Bay and Rainbow Beach

Tin Can Bay and **Rainbow Beach** are small, slowly developing coastal townships reached off Route 15 northeast of Gympie. Some 55km along, **TIN CAN BAY** occupies a long wooded spit jutting north into a convoluted inlet; the main drag, **Tin Can Bay Road**, runs for a couple of kilometres past a small shopping centre, post office and a few places to stay and eat before petering out at the Yacht Club. The reason to come here is to see – and even feed – the wild **Indo-Pacific dolphins** who pull in around 8am most mornings at **Norman Point** boat ramp next to Barnacles kiosk, but it's also just a nice place to kick back and do nothing for a day, though there's no beach.

Greyhound **buses** set down just off the main road in Bream Street at the *Sleepy Lagoon Motel* (℡07/5486 4124, ⓦwww.tincanbaybackpackers.com.au; dorms $25, motel rooms ❷), which is attached to the pub. A more upmarket alternative is *Seychelle Luxury Units* at 23 Bream St (℡07/5486 2056; ❺), while *Kingfisher Caravan Park*, a little further up off Tin Can Bay Road (℡07/5486 4198; ❶), is well equipped and has camping and shared-facility cabins. For **eating**, there are a couple of cafés and a pub, though *Barnacles*, at the dolphin feeding station at Barnacle Point, does great, inexpensive lunches.

Rainbow Beach

RAINBOW BEACH, 80km from Gympie and 48km from Tin Can Bay, is a very casual knot of streets set back from a fantastic **beach** facing into **Wide Bay**. The main recreations here are fishing, surfing and kite-boarding – there's almost always a moderate southeasterly blowing – but you can also take a 4WD (when the tide is right) or walk 10km south along the beach to the coloured sand cliffs at **Double Island Point**, whose streaks of red, orange and white are caused by minerals leaching down from the cliff-top. On the far side of the point lies the rusty frame of the *Cherry Venture* **shipwreck**, beached during a storm in 1973, then – for 4WDs only – it's a clear forty-kilometre run down the beach to Tewantin.

The township lies either side of **Rainbow Beach Road**, which ends above the surf at a small **shopping complex** housing a post office, service station and store – **buses** pull in nearby on Spectrum Street. **Accommodation** includes *Rainbow Beach Holiday Village*, at 13 Rainbow Beach Rd (℡07/5486 3222, ⓦwww.beach-village.com.au; camping $31, powered sites $38, self-contained units ❺), and *Fraser's Backpackers*, 18 Spectrum St (℡07/5486 8885, ⓦwwwfraseronrainbow.com; dorms $24, rooms ❸). There's a lively **pub** on the main road serving huge steaks at around $20, while *Coloured Sands Café* in the shopping complex does good coffee and cooked breakfasts.

Heading to Fraser, the island is only accessible to 4WD vehicles (see pp.423 for full information). *Fraser's Backpackers* arrange an all-inclusive three-day, two-night **four-wheel-drive tour** for $225; you can also **rent** a vehicle with Safari (℡1800 689 819, ⓦwww.safari4wdhire.com.au), which offers five-seater off-roaders from about $150 per day for a three-day rental, and can sort out **packages** including vehicle permits and National Park camping fees (the latter can also be booked at ⓦwww.epa.gov.qld.au).

Barges to Fraser leave from **Inskip Point**, 10km north of Rainbow Beach, for the fifteen-minute crossing to Hook Point on the island's south coast – be aware that this is a difficult landing, not for novice drivers. There are two **barge services**, both charging the same rates (4WDs $65 one-way, pedestrians free; bookings on ℡07/5486 8888, ⓦwww.fraserislandbarge.com.au); the first barge leaves Inskip Point at 6.30am, while the last departs Fraser at 5.30pm. If you're driving your own vehicle over, you need to buy a **vehicle permit** and pay **camping fees** for the island – these can both be arranged through the backpackers or Safari.

Hervey Bay

Around 35km northeast of Maryborough along Route 57, **HERVEY BAY** is a rapidly expanding sprawl of coastal suburbs known locally as "God's Waiting Room" due to the large number of retirees living here. Though very spread out, it's in fact a straightforward enough place, somewhere to pull up for only as long as it takes to join the throng crossing to **Fraser Island**, or to venture into the bay to spot **whales** in the spring.

Pialba is Hervey Bay's commercial centre, an ugly blob of car parks, shopping malls and industrial estates where the road from Maryborough enters town. It's about 1km from here to the **Esplanade**, which forms a pleasant seven-kilometre string of motels and shops facing a wooded foreshore as it runs east through the conjoined beachfront suburbs of **Scarness** and **Torquay**, and on to beach-less **Urangan** with its protruding pier and boat harbour for whale watching and Fraser Island trips.

Arrival and information

Buses wind up in Pialba at the Centro Shopping Complex, where there's a helpful **visitor centre** (Mon–Fri 6am–5.30pm, Sat 6am–1pm; ℡07/4124 4000); your accommodation won't be short on advice either. The **airport** is about 5km south of Urangan off Booral Road. Hervey Bay has a decent **local bus** service, travelling from Centro Shopping Centre in Pialba and along the Esplanade every hour or so between 7am and 6pm, though you'll need a taxi for the airport ($15–20; ℡13 10 08). Otherwise, bicycles can be rented from Bay Bicycle Hire (℡ 04/1764 4814; $20 per day) which operates from a mobile van and delivers to your doorstep.

Accommodation

Accommodation is packed during the whale watching season and at Christmas and Easter, when motel prices can double. Most places will pick you up from the bus station, and all can organize tours to Fraser, with the hostels specializing in putting together budget self-drive packages. If you're **camping**, the best van parks are those fronting the beach on the Esplanade at Scarness (℡07/4128 1274) and Torquay (℡07/4125 1278).

Arlia Sands 13 Ann St, Torquay ℡07/4125 4360, ⓦwww.arliasands.com.au. Extremely comfortable, well-equipped apartments sleeping from two to four people in a quiet street off the Esplanade – an ideal family option. One- or two-bedroom apartments ❺

Beaches 195 Torquay Rd, Torquay ℡1800 655 501, ⓦwww.beaches.com.au. Busy party hostel with lively bar/bistro and cheerful staff, one street back from the Esplanade. Dorms $27, rooms ❹

Coconut Palms 335 Esplanade, Scarness ℡07/4124 0200, ⓦwww.coconutpalmsonthebay .com.au. Balinese-inspired decor with friendly hosts

and small but well-presented one- and two-bedroom apartments. A tropical landscaped swimming pool adds to the calming atmosphere. ❹

Fraser Roving 412 Esplanade, Torquay ℡07/4125 6386, ⓦwww.fraserroving.com. Barracks-like but clean and efficient backpackers' with its own bar and pool, and specializing in Fraser trips. Dorms $23, rooms ❸

Friendly Hostel 182 Torquay Rd, Scarness ℡1800 244 107, ⓦwww.thefriendlyhostel.com.au. Relaxed, intimate guesthouse, with comfy three-bed self-contained dorms and a nice, family

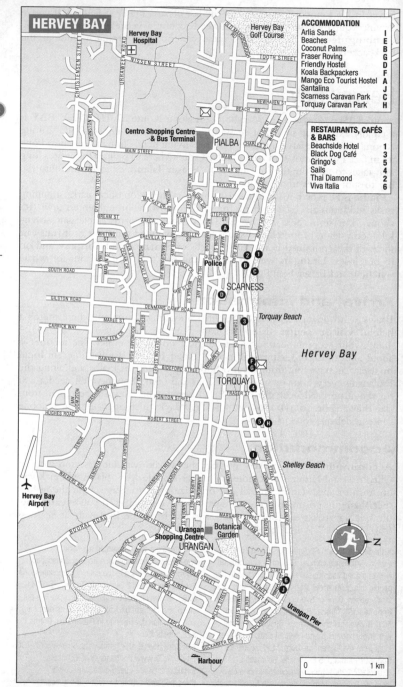

HERVEY BAY

Hervey Bay Hospital

Hervey Bay Golf Course

ACCOMMODATION

Arlia Sands	I
Beaches	E
Coconut Palms	B
Fraser Roving	G
Friendly Hostel	D
Koala Backpackers	F
Mango Eco Tourist Hostel	A
Santalina	J
Scarness Caravan Park	C
Torquay Caravan Park	H

RESTAURANTS, CAFÉS & BARS

Beachside Hotel	1
Black Dog Café	3
Gringo's	5
Sails	4
Thai Diamond	2
Viva Italia	6

Centro Shopping Centre & Bus Terminal

PIALBA

SCARNESS

Police

Torquay Beach

Hervey Bay

TORQUAY

Shelley Beach

Hervey Bay Airport

Urangan Shopping Centre

Botanical Garden

URANGAN

Urangan Pier

Harbour

N

0   1 km

atmosphere. Dorms $22, rooms ❶, self-contained apartments sleeping six ❻

Koala Backpackers 408 Esplanade, Torquay ☎1800 354 535, ⓦwww.koalaresort.com.au. Large hostel with party atmosphere in a handy location close to shops, with its own fleet of 4WDs. Dorms $28, rooms ❸

Mango Eco Tourist Hostel 110 Torquay Rd, Torquay ☎07/4124 2832, ⓦwww.mangohostel .com. Delightful old Queenslander with polished

floors and just three rooms. The hosts are extremely knowledgeable on Fraser Island and can organize alternative nature-based walking tours, ecotours or sailing trips. Dorms $22, rooms ❶

Santalina 566 Esplanade, Urangan ☎07/4125 4500, ⓦwww.santalina.com.au. Comfortable and spacious apartments surrounded by palms and ferns, and one of the few places in Hervey Bay with ocean views, although you'll pay a premium for the best outlooks. ❻

Whale watching from Hervey Bay

Humpback whales are among the most exciting marine creatures you can encounter: growing to 16m long and weighing up to 36 tonnes, they make their presence known from a distance by their habit of "breaching" – making spectacular, crashing leaps out of the water – and expelling jets of spray as they exhale. Prior to 1952 an estimated ten thousand whales made the annual journey between the Antarctic and tropics to breed and give birth in shallow coastal waters; a decade later whaling had reduced the population to just two hundred. Now protected, their numbers have increased to over five thousand, many of which pass along the eastern coast of Australia on their annual migration. An estimated two-thirds enter Hervey Bay, making it the best place to spot humpbacks in the country. The **whale watching season** here lasts from August to November, a little later than northern waters because Fraser Island leans outwards, deflecting the creatures away from the bay as they migrate north, but funnelling them in to the constricted waters when returning south.

In the early months you're more likely to see mature **bulls** which, being inquisitive, swim directly under the boat and raise their heads out of the water, close enough to touch. You may even see them fighting over mating rights and hear their enchanting mating songs; of course you may also see and hear nothing at all. The later part of the season sees **mothers and playful calves** coming into the bay to rest before their great migration south, a good time to watch the humpbacks breaching. Whether all this voyeurism disturbs the animals is unclear, but they seem at least tolerant of the attention paid to them.

The town makes the most of their visit with an August **Whale Festival**, and operators are always searching for new gimmicks to promote day-cruises and flights. For **flights**, try Air Fraser Island (☎07/4125 3600, ⓦwww.airfraserisland .com.au), costing from $85 per person (depending on the number of passengers) for a thirty-minute buzz. **Cruises** last for a morning or a full day and cost around $100 per person; some boats can take up to 150 passengers but this doesn't necessarily mean they feel overcrowded – check the boat size, viewing space, speed of vessel and how many will be going before committing yourself. The fastest vessel in the water is the zippy *Awesome* (☎1800 653 775), which offers dawn and dusk tours with a maximum of 35 passengers and is owned by long-time operator Quick Cat (☎07/4128 9611). The campan also has a much larger and taller boat that works with a spotter plane to almost guarantee sightings; *Spirit of Hervey Bay* (☎1800 642 544) has underwater portals to view the whales if they come close; while Whalesong (☎1800 689 610, ⓦwww .whalesong.com.au), Tasman Venture (☎07/4124 3222, ⓦwww.tasmanventure .com.au) and the full-day sailing catamaran *Blue Dolphin* (☎07/4124 9600, ⓦwww.bluedolphintours.com.au) also come recommended.

▲ Taylor Bay, Fraser Island

Trips to Fraser Island

Before crossing **to Fraser Island**, remember that the island's roads are 4WD only – see pp.421–426 for the full island account. For a quick trip without a vehicle, there's a **passenger-only ferry** from Urangan harbour to the west-coast *Kingfisher Bay Resort* six times a day (℡1800 072 555; $55 return). **Vehicle barges to Fraser** – which also allow foot-passengers – cross to the island's west coast from Urangan harbour and River Heads, 17km south. Those **from Urangan** make for a very difficult landing at Moon Point, departing daily at 8.30am and 3.30pm, returning at 9.30am and 4.30pm. The **River Heads** barge crosses to Wangoolba Creek daily at 8.30am, 10.15am and 3.30pm, returning at 9.30am, 2.30pm and 4pm; this is the easiest place to land a vehicle on Fraser and is recommended if you haven't had much 4WD experience.

Unless on an organized tour, you need a **barge ticket** (returns are $140 for vehicle including driver and three passengers, $24 for pedestrians), **vehicle permit** for the island if driving ($37.10; book at ⓦwww.epa.qld.gov.au), plus you'll have to pay **camping fees** in advance for national-park sites if you're planning to camp ($4.85 per person per night; book at ⓦwww.epa.qld.gov.au). All these can also be arranged where you rent your vehicle – and are usually covered in package deals – or from barge offices at Urangan and River Heads. It's essential to **pre-book barge services** (℡07/4194 9222). Note that you can use return tickets only on the same barge; if you're planning a different exit from the island, you'll have to buy two one-way tickets. For **tours of Fraser**, see the box on p.422.

Eating and drinking

Apart from snack bars and fast-food joints in Pialba, most of the places to eat and spend the evening are along the Esplanade at Torquay.

Beachside Hotel Corner of Esplanade and Queens St, Scarness. Lively bar with retro furnishings and an open front for sea views. DJ Wed–Sat nights.
Black Dog Café Corner of Esplanade and Denman Camp Rd, Scarness. An odd name for what is actually a small, smart restaurant with heavy Asian leanings – mostly Japanese. Udon soup, sushi and beef teriyaki sit strangely alongside Cajun fish and Caesar salad. Good value, with mains around $18.
Gringo's 449 Esplanade, Torquay. Good Mexican menu with enchiladas, chilli con carne and nachos, spiced to individual tolerances and with bean fillings as an alternative to meat. Main courses cost around $19. Daily from 5.30pm.
Sails Corner of Fraser St and Esplanade, Torquay ☎07/4125 5170. Moderately upmarket

Mediterranean/Asian brasserie, and a good place to splash out a little. Good choices are the Shanghai noodles and seafood risotto, and there are some decent vegetarian options too, along with good old Aussie steaks. Alternatively, just plump for the tapas platter and a cocktail. Daily 10am–midnight.
Thai Diamond 353 Esplanade, Scarness. Inexpensive yet filling dishes with cheerful service in an unassuming cafeteria-style setting. Licensed and BYO. Daily 11.30am–midnight. Also at Shelley Bay Resort at 466 Esplanade, Torquay.
Viva Italia 564 Esplanade, Urangan. Lively all-day Italian café with savoury pizza, pasta and focaccias, and delicious home-made chocolate mousse. Daily 11am–late.

Listings

Airlines Air Fraser Island (☎07/4125 3600, ⓦwww.airfraserisland.com.au) for whale spotting and flights to Fraser; Jetstar (ⓦwww.jetstar.com.au) and Virgin Blue (ⓦwww.virginblue.com.au) for intercity flights. For Lady Elliot Island, contact the resort direct (see p.429).
Banks Most banks are in Pialba, with a few scattered along the Esplanade at Torquay.
Camping equipment Some 4WD operators also rent camping equipment.
Car rental Nifty, 463 Esplanade (☎1800 627 583), has decent runarounds from $29 a day. For 4WD, Fraser Magic in Urangan (☎07/4125 6612, ⓦwww.fraser-magic-4wdhire.com.au) has the lowest rates and has been going forever; Bay 4WD

Centre, 54 Boat Harbour Drive, Pialba (☎1800 687 178, ⓦwww.bay4wd.com.au), offers much the same deal. For more information about 4WD rental for Fraser Island, see the box on p.423.
Internet access Several hostels can oblige, as can the visitor centre at 401 Esplanade in Torquay ($4 an hour).
Pharmacy Day and Night Pharmacy, 419 Esplanade, Torquay (daily 8am–8pm).
Post office On the Esplanade, Torquay.
Taxi ☎13 10 08.
Watersports Torquay Beach Hire, 415 Esplanade at Torquay (☎07/4125 5528), offers sailing catamarans ($50 per hr) and outboard-driven tinnies ($80 for 2hr) for fishing.

Fraser Island

With a length of 123km, **Fraser Island** is the world's largest sand island, but this dry fact does little to prepare you for the experience. Accumulated from sediments swept north from New South Wales over the last two million years, the scenery ranges from silent forests and beaches sculpted by wind and surf to crystal-clear streams and dark, tannin-stained lakes. The east coast forms a ninety-kilometre razor-edge from which Fraser's tremendous scale can be absorbed as you travel its length; with the sea as a constant, the dunes along the edge seem to evolve before your eyes – in places low and soft, elsewhere hard and worn into intriguing canyons. By contrast, slower progress through the forests of the island's interior creates more subtle impressions of its age and permanence – a primal world predating European settlement – brought into question only when the view opens suddenly onto a lake or a bald blow. In 1992, the entire island was recognized as a UNESCO **World Heritage Site**, with all but a few pockets of freehold land and the tiny township of Eurong being national park.

Tours and cruises from Hervey Bay

Not surprisingly, all **tours from Hervey Bay** involve Fraser Island: day-trips start at around $110, overnight camping trips from $275 – all include guides. For **day-trips**, Fraser Island Co (℡1800 063 933, ⓦwww.fraserislandco.com.au) is a little pricey at $155, but has an excellent BBQ lunch, great vehicles and first-rate guides – it also seems to work out of sync with rival tours' schedules, so you don't keep bumping into busloads of other visitors. Alternatively, Fraser Venture Tours (℡1800 249 122, ⓦwww.fraser-is.com) does recommended **overnight trips** with accommodation at Eurong ($322). For **three-day all-inclusive packages** covering just about the whole island, the best is again offered by Fraser Island Co (see above; $461), along with the more adventurous Cool Dingo ($409; ℡1800 072 555, ⓦwww.coolingotour.com) or the rowdy Trailblazer Tours ($334; ℡1800 639 518, ⓦwww.trailblazertours.com.au).

Cruises are offered by most of the boat operators outside the whale watching season (see p.419) and spend about four hours searching for dolphins, turtles and – with real luck – dugongs (sea cows) at $95 per person. Alternatively, Krystal Klear (℡07/4124 0066) and Blue Horizon (℡1800 247 992) allow four to five hours for snorkelling, coral viewing, and a BBQ lunch for $85–90.

Some history

To the Kabi Aborigines, Fraser Island is **K'gari**, a beautiful woman so taken with the Earth that she stayed behind after creation, her eyes becoming lakes that mirrored the sky and teemed with wildlife so that she wouldn't be lonely. The story behind the European name is far less enchanting. In 1836, survivors of the wreck of the *Stirling Castle*, including the captain's wife **Eliza Fraser**, landed at Waddy Point. Though runaway convicts had already been welcomed into Kabi life, the castaways suffered "dreadful slavery, cruel toil and excruciating tortures", and two months after the captain's death Eliza was presented as a prize during a corroboree at Lake Cootharaba. She was rescued at this dramatic point by former convict John Graham, who had lived with the Kabi and was part of a search party alerted by three other survivors from the *Stirling Castle*. The exact details of Eliza's captivity remain obscure as she produced several conflicting accounts, but her role as an "anti-Crusoe" inspired the work of novelist Patrick White and artist Sidney Nolan.

Arrival and information

The easiest way to reach Fraser – albeit a very small fragment – is to take the daily fast **passenger ferry** from Hervey Bay to *Kingfisher Bay Resort* (p.424). Alternatively, guided **day-tours** from Hervey Bay whip around the main sights – usually some of the forest, a couple of lakes, and the beach as far as Indian Head – but the wildlife and overall feel of the area are elusive unless you get away from the more popular places, camp for the night and explore early on in the day. Again, you can take an overnight tour, but it's far cheaper to assemble a group and **rent a 4WD**, either independently or through accommodation, and then catch a **vehicle barge** from Rainbow Beach or Hervey Bay.

Once on the island, there are a couple of **safety points** to bear in mind. As there have never been domestic dogs on the island, Fraser's **dingoes** are considered to be Australia's purest strain, and they used to be a common sight. After one killed a child in 2000, however, dingoes which frequented public areas were culled and you'll probably not see many. If you do encounter some, keep your distance, back off rather than run if approached, and – despite their misleadingly scrawny appearance – **don't feed them**, as it's the expectation of hand-outs which makes them aggressive. You should also be aware that **sharks** and severe currents make Fraser a dangerous place to get in the sea; if you want to swim, stick to the freshwater lakes. Lastly, pack some powerful **insect repellent**.

For **supplies**, the east coast settlements of Happy Valley and Eurong have stores, telephones, bars and fuel; there's another store at *Cathedral Beach Resort* but no shops or restaurant at Dilli. You'll save money by bringing whatever you need with you; and make sure you **take all garbage home** or place it in the large, wildlife-proof metal skips you'll find along the way.

Getting around

Driving on the island requires a **4WD vehicle**. The east beach serves as the main highway, with roads running inland to popular spots; make sure you pick up a **tide timetable** from barge operators, as parts of the beach are only reliably negotiable at low tide. Other tracks, always slower than the beach, crisscross the interior; the main tracks are often rough from heavy use, and minor roads tend to be in better shape. **General 4WD advice** is to lower your tyre pressure to around 12psi to increase traction on the sand, but this isn't generally necessary (if you get bogged, however, try it first before panicking). Rain and high tides harden sand surfaces, making driving easier. **Road rules** are the same as those on the mainland. Most **accidents** involve collisions on blind corners, rolling in soft sand (avoid hard braking or making sudden turns – you don't have to be going very fast for your front wheels to dig in, turning you over), and trying to cross apparently insignificant creeks on the beach at 60kph – 4WDs are not invincible. Don't drive your vehicle into the surf; you'll probably get stuck and even if you don't, this much saltwater exposure will rust out the bodywork within days (something the rental company will notice and charge you for). Noise from the surf means that pedestrians can't hear vehicles on the beach and

---

Renting a 4WD for Fraser Island

Fraser Island is simply too large and varied to appreciate fully on a day-trip, and with competition in Hervey Bay keeping prices to a minimum it's a great opportunity to learn how to handle a 4WD. See p.421 for some recommended outfits; a stipulation of the Fraser Coast 4 Hire Association is that the company should take time to protect both itself and you with a full briefing on the island and driving practicalities. Renting a 4WD over three days, expect to pay around $115 per day for two-seaters such as a Suzuki, up to $200 per day for an eight-seater Land-Rover Defender or Toyota Landcruiser, including insurance. Note that older ex-army Land-Rovers, while mechanically sound, are uncomfortable and best avoided unless you're trying to save money.

Conditions include a minimum driver age of 21 and a $500 deposit, payable in plastic or cash – note that advertised prices are normally for renting the vehicle only, so tents, food, fuel, and ferry and vehicle permit for the island are extra, available separately or as part of a package. To help cut costs, you'll want to form a group of five or six which should make a three-day, two-night trip work out to about $195 a person.

Almost every backpackers' hostel organizes its own much-touted three-day self-guided camping trip to the island for around $150 per person but you usually have to wait a few days until the vehicle is packed full of paying passengers before departing. Fuel surcharge is also a point of contention – most hostels currently charge $40 extra per person, expensive considering a three-day trip would commonly use less than $100 of fuel. If you're not happy with what's being offered, or don't want to wait around, consider one of the independent tour companies on p.422.

won't be aware of your presence until you barrel through from behind, so give them a wide berth.

Walking is an excellent way to see the island. There's only one established circuit, and even that is very under-used, running from Central Station south past lakes Birrabeen and Boomanjin, then up the coast and back to Central Station via lakes Wabby and McKenzie; highlights are circumnavigating the lakes, chance encounters with goannas and dingoes, and the energetic burst up Wongi Blow for sweeping views out to sea. A good three-day hike that by each sundown renders you all but unconscious after all that walking across sand, it requires no special skills beyond endurance and the ability to set up camp before you pass out. If this is your thing, head to *Mango Tourist Hostel* (℡07/4124 2832) in Torquay for more details.

Accommodation

All **accommodation** needs to be booked in advance. Top of the range are the plush hotel rooms and self-contained villas at *Kingfisher Bay Resort* (℡07/4125 5511 or 1800 072 555, ⓦwww.kingfisherbay.com; ⓞ) on the west coast; it's close to forest but 15km across the island to the beach. Most of the other options are along **Seventy-Five Mile Beach** on the east coast: the southernmost (and first if you're coming up from Rainbow Beach) is friendly and low-key *Dilli Village* (℡07/4127 9130, ⓦwww.dillivillage.com; camping $10 per person, powered sites $25, bunkhouse ❶, cabins ❷), not far from Lake Boomanjin. Moving north up the beach, *Eurong Beach Resort* (℡07/4127 9122, ⓦwww.eurongbeach.com; ⓞ) has motel-style rooms near the road exit from Central Station but a minimum three-night stay. From here, it's a good way up to *Yidney Rocks Beachfront Units* (℡07/4127 9167, ⓦwww.yidneyrocks.com.au; ⓞ), whose motel-like self-contained units are a little overpriced, and *Fraser Island Backpackers YHA* at Happy Valley (℡07/4127 9144, ⓦwww.fraserislandco.com.au/backpackers; dorm $29–49, doubles ❺), which provides timber-lodge dorms, a pool, good kitchen and a decent bistro.

With a National Parks **camping permit** (bookings ℡13 13 04 or ⓦwww.epa.qld.gov.au), you can **camp** anywhere along the eastern foreshore except where signs forbid, or if you need tank water, showers, toilets and barbecue areas, use the **National Park campsites** at Central Station, Lake Boomanjin or Lake Allom, Dundubara and Waddy Point on the east coast. There are also **privately run campsites** at *Cathedral Beach Resort* (℡07/4127 9177, camping $27, cabins ⓞ) and the nicer *Dilli Village* (see above).

Around Central Station

Most people get their bearings by making their first stop at **Central Station**, an old logging depot with campsite, telephone and information hut under some monstrous bunya pines in the middle of the island, halfway between the landing at Wanggoolba Creek and Eurong on the east coast. From the station, take a stroll along **Wanggoolba Creek**'s upper reaches, a magical, sandy-bottomed stream so clear that it's hard at first to see the water as it runs across the forest floor. It's a largely botanic walk from here to **Pile Valley**, where satinay trees humble you to insignificance as they reach 60m to the sky. The trees produce a very dense timber, durable enough to be used as sidings on the Suez Canal, and are consequently in such demand that the trees on Fraser have almost been logged out.

There are several **lakes** around Central Station, all close enough to walk to and all along main roads. A nine-kilometre track leads north to **Lake McKenzie**, the most popular on the island, often very crowded and sometimes tarnished by discarded plastic rubbish: despite this, it's a wonderful place to spend the day, ringed by white sand, with clear, tea-coloured water reflecting a blue sky. Eight kilometres to the south, **Birrabeen** is mostly hemmed in by trees, while **Boomanjin**, 8km further, is open and perched in a basin above the island's water table – there's a National Parks campsite here, or it's not too far to the coast at *Dilli Village* if you want to spend the night in the area.

Seventy-Five Mile Beach

East-coast **Seventy-Five Mile Beach** is Fraser's main road and camping ground, and one of the busiest places on the island. Vehicles hurtle along, pedestrians and anglers hug the surf, and tents dot the foredunes; this is what beckons the crowds over from the mainland. Coming from Central Station, you exit onto the beach at **Eurong**, a complex of motel accommodation and shops; 6km north, **Hammerstone Blow** is slowly engulfing **Lake Wabby**, a small but deep patch of blue below the dunes with excellent swimming potential – another century and it will be gone. Another 10km along at **Rainbow Gorge**, a short trail runs between two blows, through a hot, silent desert landscape where sandblasted trees emerge denuded by their ordeal. Incredibly, a dismal spring seeps water into the valley where the sand swallows it up; "upstream" are the gorge's stubby, eroded red fingers.

Another 5km brings you to **Happy Valley**, another source of supplies and beds, and then after the same distance again you cross picturesque **Eli Creek**, where water splashes briskly between briefly verdant banks before spilling into the sea. Sand-filtered, it's the nicest swimming spot on the island, though icy-cold. Back on the beach, another 4km brings you to the *Maheno* **shipwreck**, beached in 1935 and now a skeleton almost consumed by the elements, and the start of a line of multicoloured sand cliffs known as the **Cathedrals**. About 5km up the beach from here is the **Dundubara campsite**, behind which is the tiring, hot four-kilometre walk up Wungul Sandblow through what may as well be the Sahara; turn around at the top, though, and the glaring grey dune-scape is set off by distant views of a rich blue sea.

Approximately 20km north from Dundubara, **Indian Head** is a rare – and pretty tall – rocky outcrop, the anchor around which the island probably formed originally. It's not a hard walk to the top, and on a sunny day the rewards are likely to include views down into the surf full of dolphins, sharks and other large fish chasing each other; in season you'll certainly see pods of whales too, breaching, blowing jets of spray, and just lying on their backs, slapping the water with outstretched fins. From here there's a tricky bit of soft sand to negotiate for a final nine-kilometre run around to **Champagne Pools**, a cluster of shallow, safe swimming pools right above the surf line, which mark as far north as vehicles are allowed to travel.

The interior, west coast and far north

Fraser's wooded **interior**, a real contrast to the busy coast and popular southern lakes, gets relatively few visitors. It encloses **Yidney Scrub**, the only major stand of rainforest left on the island, and although the name doesn't conjure up a very appealing image, the trees are majestic and include towering kauri pines. There's a circuit through Yidney from Happy Valley, taking in Boomerang and Allom **lakes** on the long way back to the beach near the *Maheno*. You can camp at Allom, a small lake surrounded by pines and cycads, and completely different in character from its flashy southern cousins. Further north, another road heads in from Dundubara township to **Lake Bowarrady**, a not particularly exciting body of water famed for turtles which pester you for bread – if you can't imagine being pestered by a turtle, try refusing to hand it over.

The island's **west coast** is a mix of mangrove swamp and treacherously soft beaches, both largely inaccessible to vehicles. Access is via rough tracks which cross the island via Lake Bowarrady and Happy Valley to where the Urangan barge lands at Moon Point, though there's a better road to *Kingfisher Bay Resort* from the Central Station area.

The Southern Reef

Sand carried north up the coast by ocean currents is swept out to sea by Fraser Island's massive outwards-leaning edge, eventually being deposited 80km offshore as a cluster of tiny, coral-fringed sand islands – **cays** – which mark the southernmost tip of Queensland's mighty **Great Barrier Reef**. The coastal settlements of **Bundaberg**, **1770** and **Gladstone** each offer access to a cay, either on day-trips or for an overnight stay in a resort; either way, there's the chance to do some excellent **scuba diving**. Bundaberg – along with the nearby hamlet of **Childers** – also lies at the heart of a rich sugar-cane, fruit and vegetable farming area, and both are popular places to find short-term crop-picking **work**.

All the towns are either on, or accessed from, Highway 1 and are served by **long-distance buses**; Bundaberg and Gladstone are also on the **train line**.

Childers

About 60km up the highway from Hervey Bay, **CHILDERS** is a pretty, one-horse highway town, sadly known for the terrible **fire** which burned down the old *Palace Backpackers* in 2000, killing fifteen people. The town has moved on, however, and the site has been rebuilt as a tasteful, low-key memorial and **visitor centre** (Mon–Fri 8.30am–4pm, Sat & Sun 9am–3pm; ☎07/4126 3886). Childers' core of old buildings offers an excuse to pull up and stretch your legs; these include the photogenic *Federal Hotel*, a wooden pub built in 1907, and the musty, bottle-filled and slightly dull **Childers Pharmaceutical Museum** (Mon–Fri 9am–4pm, Sat 8.30am–noon; $3). Just west of Childers, **Flying High** (daily 10am–3pm, closed on rainy days; $18) is a huge aviary with just about every type of Australian parrot and finch zipping around, squawking, or chewing the furnishings.

For farm work, the *Childers Tourist Park* (☎07/4126 1371; camping $12.40, powered sites $30.80, cabins ❸) has good contacts with surrounding farmers but it's a six-kilometre ride out of town on the back road to Bundaberg. Otherwise, the nicest place to stay in town is the *Childers Hotel* on Churchill Street (☎07/4126 1719; ❸), with very cute "country-style" rooms, a spacious beer garden and the best **meals** in Childers – the *Laurel Tree Cottage*, on the main street at the Bundaberg end of town, comes a close second with traditional fare including delightful pies.

Bundaberg and around

Fifty kilometres off the highway from Childers, surrounded by canefields and fruit farms, **BUNDABERG** is famous for its **rum**, though the town is otherwise a humdrum place whose attractions are scarcely advertised. The adjacent coast is, however, an important place for **marine turtles**, who mass in huge numbers every summer to lay their eggs on the beaches surrounding Mon Repos, and those wanting **work** are virtually guaranteed seasonal employment (mostly Feb–Nov) picking avocados, tomatoes, snow peas and courgettes on farms in the area. You can also fly from town to the local Barrier Reef cay, **Lady Elliot Island**, which offers a basic resort and good scuba diving.

Arrival and information

Bundaberg lies along the south bank of the **Burnett River**, about 15km from the coast. **Bourbong Street**, the main thoroughfare, runs parallel to the river and is where you'll find banks, the post office and internet cafés. The **bus terminal** is on Targo Street, and the **train station** is 500m west on McLean Street. The **airport**, for departures to Lady Elliot Island amongst other places, is 4km from the centre on the Childers Road. The **visitor centre** (daily 9am–5pm; ☎07/4153 8888, ⓦ www.bundabergregion.info) is at 271 Bourbong St. **Moving on**, trains and long-distance buses – Greyhound (☎13 20 30) and Premier (☎13 34 10) – head up the coast to Gladstone and down to Childers and beyond; Greyhound also runs to Agnes Water daily (for 1770).

Accommodation and eating

The first two backpackers' listed can find you work. Most motels are west of the centre, and camping is also available at Mon Repos Beach – see p.428. For **eating**, *Indulge*, 80 Bourbong St, offers all-day breakfasts, while the nearby *Club Hotel* serves filling counter meals for lunch and dinner, and sports a beer garden. For modern Italian, try *Statics*, on Targo Street.

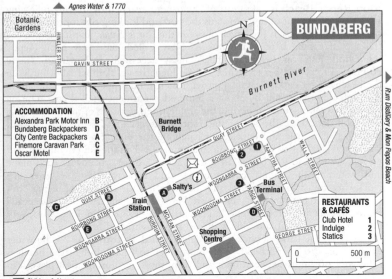

Agnes Water & 1770

Botanic Gardens

BUNDABERG

N

HINKLER STREET
GAVIN STREET
Burnett River

ACCOMMODATION
Alexandra Park Motor Inn   **B**
Bundaberg Backpackers   **D**
City Centre Backpackers   **A**
Finemore Caravan Park   **C**
Oscar Motel   **E**

Burnett Bridge
QUAY STREET
BOURBONG STREET
WOONGARRA
TANTITHA STREET
WALLA STREET

Salty's
Bus Terminal
TARGO STREET

QUAY STREET
Train Station
BURRUM STREET
MCLEAN STREET
WOONDOOMA STREET
Shopping Centre
GEORGE STREET

BOURBONG STREET
WOONGARRA STREET
WOONDOOMA STREET

RESTAURANTS & CAFÉS
Club Hotel   **1**
Indulge   **2**
Statics   **3**

0   500 m

Rum Distillery & Mon Repos Beach

Childers & Airport

427

Alexandra Park Motor Inn 66 Quay St ☏07/4152 7255, ⓦwww.alexandras.com.au. A modern Queenslander-style place with huge rooms. ❹

Bundaberg Backpackers Opposite the bus terminal on Targo St ☏07/4152 2080. Central workers' hostel. Dorms $25 or $170 per week.

City Centre Backpackers 216 Bourbong St, near the train station ☏07/4151 3501. Similar to

Bundaberg Backpackers, and just as full of workers. Dorms $25 or $170 per week.

Finemore Caravan Park Quay St ☏07/4151 3663. Pleasant location overlooking the river. Cabins ❷

Oscar Motel 252 Bourbong St ☏07/4152 3666, ⓦwww.oscarmotel.com.au. Motel just west of the centre, with a pool and barbecue area. Rooms and units ❸–❹

The Town

"**Bundie**", as it's affectionately known, is synonymous with rum throughout Australia and, if you believe its advertising pitch, the town's **rum distillery** on Whittered Street, about 2km east of the town centre along Bourbong Street (tours Mon–Fri 10am–3pm, Sat & Sun 10am–2pm; $9.90), accounts for half the rum consumed in the country each year. A distillery tour allows fans to wallow in the overpowering pungency of raw molasses and ends, of course, with a free sample – though you probably won't need to drink much after inhaling the fumes in the vat sheds, where electronic devices are prohibited in case a spark ignites the vapour.

Flying 1270km from Sydney to Bundaberg in 1921, **Bert Hinkler** set a world record for continuous flight in his flimsy wire-and-canvas Baby Avro, demonstrating its potential as transport for remote areas and so encouraging the formation of Qantas the following year (see p.534). In 1983, the house where Hinkler lived at the time of his death in England was transported to Bundaberg and rebuilt in the Botanic Gardens, 4km from the centre over the Burnett Bridge towards Gin Gin, sharing its desirable surroundings with a Sugar Museum and Historical Museum (daily 10am–4pm; $5 each). Outside the house, landscaped gardens flank ponds where Hinkler was supposedly inspired to design aircraft by watching ibises in flight.

Mon Repos Beach and the turtle rookery

Mon Repos Beach is 15km east of Bundaberg, reached by initially following Bourbong Street out of town towards the port and looking out for small brown signposts for the beach (or larger ones for the *Turtle Sands Tourist Park*). Once the site of a French telegraph link to New Caledonia, today Mon Repos' reputation rests on being Australia's most accessible **loggerhead turtle rookery**. From October to March, female loggerheads clamber laboriously up the beaches after dark, excavate a pit with their hind flippers in the sand above the high-tide mark, and lay about a hundred parchment-shelled eggs. During the eight-week incubation period, the ambient temperature of the surrounding sand will determine the sex of the entire clutch; 28.5°C is the change-over point between male and female. On hatching, the endearing, rubbery-brown youngsters stay buried in the nest until after dark, when they dig themselves out en masse and head for the sea. In season, about a dozen turtles lay each night, and watching the young leave the nest and race towards the water like clockwork toys is both comical and touching – your chances of seeing both laying and hatching in one evening are best during January. The loggerhead's future doesn't look too bright at present: since 1980 Mon Repos' rookery population has halved, most likely due to net-trawling offshore.

The National Parks service runs nightly **guided tours** ($9.35; bookings essential on ☏07/4153 8888) from November to March, when the beach is otherwise off limits between 6pm and 6am; most accommodation places can book you on a tour and transport package ($70). For **accommodation** at Mon Repos Beach, the first-rate 🏕 *Turtle Sands Tourist Park* (☎07/4159 2340, ⓦwww.turtlesands.com.au; camping $23, powered sites $25, cabins ❹) is right next to the turtle rookery and a kilometre of beach.

Lady Elliot Island

The Great Barrier Reef's southernmost outpost, **Lady Elliot Island**, is a two-kilometre-square patch of casuarina and pandanus trees stabilizing a bed of coral rubble, sand and – in common with all the southern cays – a thick layer of **guano**, courtesy of the generations of birds to have roosted here. The elegant **lighthouse** on Lady Elliot's west side was built in 1866 after an extraordinary number of wrecks on the reef; on average, one vessel a year still manages to come to grief here. Wailing shearwaters and the occasional suicide of lighthouse staff didn't endear Lady Elliot to early visitors, but a low-key **resort** and excellent reef have now turned the island into a popular escape.

Shearwaters aside, there's a good deal of **birdlife** on the island; residents include thousands of black noddies and bridled terns, along with much larger frigate birds and a few rare **red-tailed tropicbirds** – a white, gull-like bird with a red beak and wire-like tail – which nest under bushes on the foreshore. Both loggerhead and green **turtles** nest on the beaches too, and in a good summer there are scores laying their eggs here each night. The main reason to come to Lady Elliot, however, is to go **scuba diving**: the best spots for diving are out from the lighthouse, but check on daily currents with the dive staff at the resort before getting wet. The Blowhole is a favourite with divers, with a descent into a cavern (keep an eye out for the "gnomefish" here), and there's also the 1999 wreck of the yacht *Severence* to explore. You've a good chance of encountering harmless leopard sharks, sea snakes, barracuda, turtles and gigantic manta rays wherever you go. Shore dives cost $35 per person, while boat dives are $50 ($70 for night dives), plus gear rental.

Lady Elliot can only be reached **by air** on daily flights from Hervey Bay or Bundaberg (overnight return $231; book through the resort). **Accommodation** on the island is with the comfortable *Lady Elliot Island Resort* (☎1800 072 200, ⓦwww.ladyelliot.com.au; ❾), which has basic four-person tented cabins as well as motel-like suites with private bathrooms and ocean views. Breakfast and dinner (but not lunch or flights) are included in the rates, and it's worth enquiring about discounts for longer-term packages – if you're not interested in underwater activities, a day or two is ample time to see everything and unwind, though.

Agnes Water, 1770 and around

On the coast 100km north of Bundaberg along the Rosedale road, the tiny settlements of **Agnes Water** and nearby **1770** mark the spot where Captain Cook first set foot in Queensland on May 24, 1770. It's a pretty area whose attractions include pockets of mangrove, fan palm and paperbark wetlands, and Queensland's northernmost **surf beach** at Agnes Water, while 1770 is the closest point on the mainland with boats out to **Lady Musgrave Island** and nearby reefs. Greyhound Australia operates a **daily bus** in both directions between Bundaberg and Agnes Water, stopping opposite *Cool Bananas Hostel* on Spring Road.

AGNES WATER consists of a service station, two shopping complexes, several large resort villages and the *Agnes Water Tavern* – which does excellent meals. The town is fronted by a stunning, sweeping **beach** backed by sand dunes,

The Great Barrier Reef

The **Great Barrier Reef** is to Australia what rolling savannahs and game parks are to Africa, and is equally subject to the corniest of representations. "Another world" is the commonest cliché, which, while being completely true, doesn't begin to describe the feeling of donning mask and fins and coming face to face with extraordinary animals, shapes and colours. There's so little relationship to life above the surface that distinctions normally taken for granted – such as that between animal, plant and plain rock – seem blurred, while the respective roles of observer and observed are constantly challenged by shoals of curious fish following you about.

Beginning with Lady Elliot Island, out from Bundaberg, and extending 2300km north to New Guinea, the Barrier Reef follows the outer edge of Australia's continental plate, running closer to land as it moves north: while it's 300km to the main body from Gladstone, Cairns is barely 50km distant from the reef. Far from being a continuous, unified structure, the nature of the reef varies along its length: the majority is made up by an intricate maze of individual, disconnected patch reefs, which – especially in the southern sections – sometimes act as anchors for the formation of low sand islands known as **cays**; continental islands everywhere become ringed by **fringing reefs**; and northern sections form long **ribbons**. All of it, however, was built by one animal: the tiny **coral polyp**. Simple organisms, related to sea anemones, polyps grow together like building blocks to create modular colonies – **corals** – which form the framework of the reef's ecology by providing food, shelter and hunting grounds for larger, more mobile species. Around their walls and canyons flows a bewildering assortment of creatures: large rays and turtles "fly" effortlessly by, fish dodge between caves and coral branches, snails sift the sand for edibles, and brightly coloured nudibranchs dance above rocks.

The reef is administered by the **Marine Parks Authority**, which battles against – or at least attempts to gauge – the effects of overfishing, pollution, agricultural runoff, environmental fluctuations and tourism. All these things are beginning to have a serious effect on the Reef, with many formerly colourful coral gardens reduced to weed-strewn rubble. Don't let this put you off going – the Reef is still unquestionably worth seeing, and if the government realizes how much tourism will be lost if the Reef dies, they may get more involved in protecting it. In order to **minimize damage**, visitors should never stand on or hold onto reefs when snorkelling or diving; even if you don't break off branches, you'll certainly crush the delicate polyps.

Diving and other ways of seeing the Reef

Scuba diving is the best way to get to grips with the Reef, and **dive courses** are on offer right along the coast. Five days is the minimum needed to safely cover the course work – three days pool and theory, two days at sea – and secure you the all-important C-card. The quality of training and the price you pay vary; before signing up, ask others who have taken courses about specific businesses' general attitude and whether they just seem concerned about processing as many students in as short a time as possible – you need to know that any problems you may encounter while training will be taken seriously. Another consideration is whether you ever plan to dive again: if this seems unlikely, **resort dives** (a single dive with an instructor) will set you

and there are some delightful coastal walks in the area, including the three-kilometre trail from Agnes Headland along the wooded ridge to Springs Beach, which is best reached from the Museum on Springs Road. **Accommodation** includes *1770 Getaway* (☎07/4974 9323, [W]www.1770getaway.com.au; [5]) on Springs Road, featuring nicely designed apartments with balconies overlooking

back only $70 or so, and they're usually available on day-trips to the Reef and island resorts. **Qualified divers** can save on rental costs by bringing some gear along; tanks and weightbelts are covered in dive packages but anything else is extra. You need an alternative air source, timer, C-card and log book to dive in Queensland (the last is often ignored, but some places insist, especially for deep or night-time dives).

Snorkelling is a good alternative to diving: you can pick up the basics in five minutes and with a little practice the only thing you sacrifice is the extended dive time that a tank allows. If you think you'll do a fair amount, buy your own mask and snorkel – they're not dramatically expensive – as rental gear nearly always leaks. Look for a silicone rubber and toughened glass mask and ask the shop staff to show you how to find a good fit. If getting wet just isn't for you, try **glass-bottomed boats** or "subs", which can still turn up everything from sharks to oysters.

Reef hazards

Stories of shark attacks, savage octopuses and giant clams all make good press, but are mostly the stuff of fiction. However, there are a few things at the Reef capable of putting a dampener on your holiday, and it makes sense to be careful. The best protection is simply to **look and not touch**, as nothing is actively out to harm you.

Seasickness and **sunburn** are the two most common problems to afflict visitors to the Reef, so take precautions. Coral and shell **cuts** become badly infected if not treated immediately by removing any fragments and dousing with antiseptic. Some corals can also give you a nasty **sting**, but this is more a warning to keep away in future than something to worry about seriously. Animals to avoid tend to be small. Some dangerous **jellyfish** (see p.51) are found at the Reef during summer – wear a protective Lycra "stinger suit" or full wet suit with hood. Conical **cone shells** are home to a fish-eating snail armed with a poisonous barb which has caused fatalities. Don't pick them up: there is no "safe" end to hold them. Similarly, the shy, small, **blue-ringed octopus** has a fatal bite and should never be handled. **Stonefish** are camouflaged so that they're almost impossible to distinguish from a rock or lump of coral. They spend their days immobile, protected from attack by a series of poisonous spines along their back. If you tread on one, you'll end up in hospital – an excellent argument against reef-walking. Of the larger animals, **rays** are flattened fish with a sharp tail-spine capable of causing deep wounds – don't swim close over sandy floors where they hide. At the Reef, the most commonly encountered **sharks** are the black-tip and white-tip varieties, and the bottom-dwelling, aptly named carpet shark, or wobbegong – all of these are inoffensive unless hassled.

Reef tax

The Marine Park Authority levies an Environmental Management Charge (EMC), sometimes referred to as **reef tax** (currently $5 per person per day, though some tour operators add $5 extra for administration) to help fund monitoring and management of human impact on the Reef. On most tours and boat trips, you will be required to pay the EMC in addition to the cost of the tour. You may feel a little annoyed at having to fork out the extra money, especially if you've already paid quite a lot for your trip, but this is simply a "user-pays" system to help ensure that the Reef is maintained for everyone to experience and enjoy.

four acres of landscaped gardens; spacious motel rooms at *Sandcastles* (☎07/4974 7200, ⓦwww.sandcastles1770.com.au; ❹), off Captain Cook Drive heading towards 1770 and fronted by tropical bush just 200m from the beach; and *Cool Bananas Backpackers Lodge* (☎07/4974 7660, ⓦwww.coolbananas.net.au; dorms $25) on Springs Road. Street Beat (☎07/4974 7697), 1km before town on

Round Hill Road, rents out scooters ($90 per day), cars ($65 per day) and 4WD vehicles ($120 per day).

1770 is even smaller, occupying the foreshore of a narrow promontory some 6km to the north. At the end of the road is windswept Round Hill, with exposed walking trails and coastal views, though the main reason to come here is to take a **day-trip to the reef**. Boats leave from the marina: *SeaQuest* ($170; ☎1800 177 011, 🖰www1770seaquest.com.au) runs day-trips to **Fitzroy Reef** lagoon, while *Spirit of 1770* ($160; ☎1800 631 770, 🖰www.spiritof1770.com.au) visits **Lady Musgrave Island**. Snorkelling gear is included in the price, but **scuba diving** at either is an extra $65. At 1770, **places to stay** include *The Beach Shacks* (☎07/4974 9463, 🖰www.1770beachshacks.com; **❼**), which has four beautifully furnished tropical pole homes facing the ocean sleeping four to six people; a budget alternative is the cabins and tent sites at *Captain Cook Holiday Village* (☎07/4974 9219, 🖰www.1770holidayvillage.com; camping $24, powered sites $27, cabins **❹**), which has a store, bar and bistro. For **eating**, *Saltwater Café* overlooks the ocean on Captain Cook Drive and does an excellent fish and chips – other mains cost around $20, and there's a lively **bar** next door.

Eurimbula National Park, on the west side of 1770 across Round Hill Creek, abounds with birdlife. You can **tour** the region aboard *The Larc* **amphibious bus** (☎07/4974 9422; Mon, Wed & Fri, full day $132, 1hr evening cruise $33), which explores the remote coastline. For 4WD road access to the park, head 10.5km back towards Miriam Vale from Agnes Water, where you'll see the track and national-park sign to the north of the road. You can **bushcamp** about 15km inside the park in the dunes behind Bustard Beach, but beware of the prolific sand flies.

Lady Musgrave Island

Lady Musgrave Island, the southernmost island of the eight tiny coral cays constituting Capricornia Cays National Park, is covered in soft-leaved **pisonia trees** which host the usual throng of roosting birdlife, ringed by a coral wall which forms a large turquoise **lagoon**. Diving inside the lagoon here is safe but pretty tame (though snorkelling is good); outside the wall is more exciting. Relatively easy, inexpensive access means that Lady Musgrave is the best of the southern cays on which to **camp** (April–Jan; $4.85 per person; 🖰www.epa.qld .gov.au). There are **no facilities** at all on the island, so make sure you bring absolutely everything you need with you, including all camping and cooking gear, a fuel stove, food and more water than you need (which is at least five litres a day). If you're planning on a long stay, make prior arrangements with the *Spirit of 1770*, which runs out here daily for snorkelling tours (see p.431), to bring supplementary provisions across for you.

Gladstone and Heron Island

Around 90km up Highway 1 from the Miriam Vale turn-off, **GLADSTONE** is a busy port, and also the site of the Boyne Island processing plant, which refines aluminium from ore mined at Weipa on the remote Cape York Peninsula. Glaringly hot, there's no reason to visit unless you're trying to reach **Heron Island**. If you've time to spare, the **Tondoon Botanic Gardens**, about 7km south of town, comprise a partly wild spread of wetlands, woodlands, forests and native shrubs, all expertly laid out – you'll probably clock up wallabies and birdlife here too.

The main strip is **Goondoon Street**, where there's a "mall" – just the usual high-street shops, post office and banks – plus a couple of hotels and motels. You'll find the regions' **visitor centre** (Mon–Fri 8.30am–5pm, Sat & Sun 9am–5pm) inside the ferry terminal at the marina, about 2km north of the centre on Bryan Jordan Drive. *Gladstone Reef Motel*, 38 Goondoon St (℗07/4972 1000; ❹), has ordinary motel rooms and good views from a rooftop pool. Places to eat include *The Yacht Club*, 1 Goondoon St, with reasonably priced bistro meals and outdoor dining overlooking the water, or the more fashionable *Scotties*, 46 Goondoon St, open for dinner only, with contemporary cuisine at gourmet prices.

Heron Island

Famous for its diving, **Heron Island** is small enough to walk around in an hour, with half the cay occupied by a comfortable **resort** and **research station**, and the rest covered in groves of pandanus, coconuts and shady pisonias. You can literally walk off the beach and into the reef's maze of coral, or swim along the shallow walls looking for action. The eastern edges of the lagoon are good for snorkelling at any time although some of the best coral is on the outer reefs, accessible only by boat for $130 per person on a half-day cruise; **scuba diving** costs $55 for a standard dive and $80 to venture out at night. A drift along the wall facing Wistari reef to Heron Bommie covers about everything you're likely to encounter. The coral isn't that good but the amount of life is astonishing: tiny boxfish hide under ledges; turtles, cowries, wobbegong, reef sharks, moray eels, butterfly cod and octopuses secrete themselves among the coral; manta rays soar majestically; and larger reef fish gape vacantly as you drift past. The bommie itself makes first-rate **snorkelling**, with an interesting swim-through if your lungs are up to it, while the Tenements along the reef's northern edge are good for bigger game – including sharks.

There's a price to pay for all this natural wonder, namely no day-trips and no camping. ⚓ *Heron Island Resort* (reservations ℗13 24 69, island reception ℗07/4972 9055, ⓦwww.heronisland.com; ❾) is excellent, but its rates, coupled with that of the two-hour ferry transfer to the island from Gladstone Marina ($230 return), are steep, even after taking advantage of the regular **web specials** and packages.

The tropics: Rockhampton to Cape York

The tropics kick in at **Rockhampton**, 100km north of Gladstone, but with the exception of the **Mackay region** – a splash of green with a couple of good national parks – it's not until you're well past the tropic line and north of **Townsville** that the tropical greenery associated with north Queensland finally appears. Then it comes in a rush, and by the time you've reached the tourist haven of **Cairns** there's no doubt that the area deserves its reputation: coastal ranges covered in rainforest and cloud descend right to the sea. **Islands** along the way lure you with good beaches, hiking tracks and opportunities for snorkelling and diving: Great Keppel near Rockhampton, the Whitsundays off **Airlie Beach**, Magnetic Island opposite Townsville, and Hinchinbrook and Dunk further north are all must-sees. **Cairns** itself serves as a base for exploring highland rainforest on the **Atherton Tablelands**, coastal jungles in the **Daintree** and, of course, for trips out to the most accessible sections of the Great Barrier Reef.

Until recently, the region's **weather** involved dry, relatively cool winters (June–Aug) and extremely humid summers (Dec–Feb) with torrential rainfall and devastating cyclones. As with everywhere else, the climate is less predictable these days, though the pattern still holds to some degree. All the main towns between Rockhampton and Cairns are on Highway 1, served by Greyhound and Premier long-distance **buses** and also the **train**.

Rockhampton

Straddling the Tropic of Capricorn, **ROCKHAMPTON** was founded after a false goldrush in 1858 left hundreds of miners stranded at a depot 40km inland on the banks of the sluggish **Fitzroy River**, and their rough camp was adopted by local stockmen as a convenient port. The iron trelliswork and sandstone buildings fronting the river recall the balmy 1890s, when money was pouring into the city from a prosperous cattle industry and nearby gold and copper mines; today Rockhampton feels a bit despondent – the mines have closed (though before they did, they managed to fund the fledgling BP company), the beef industry is down in the dumps and the summers, unrelieved by coastal breezes, are appallingly humid. Bearing this in mind, the city is best seen as a springboard for the adjacent Capricorn Coast.

Arrival and information

Rockhampton is divided by the Fitzroy River, with all services clustered directly south of the **Fitzroy Bridge** along Quay and East streets; the Bruce Highway runs right through town past two pairs of fibreglass bulls (repeatedly "de-balled" by pranksters). Greyhound and Premier **buses** stop at the Mobil service station just north of the bridge on the highway; **local buses** to or from Yeppoon and the coast set down, amongst other places, along Bolsover Street. The **train station** is 1km south of the centre on Murray Street, and the **airport** is 4km to the west at the end of Hunter Street – Virgin and Qantas fly daily from Brisbane. **Banks**, the post office and other services are mostly along East Street, and there's an internet bar at *Jungle* (see p.436). The **visitor centre** is in the old riverside customs house on Quay Street (Mon–Fri 8.30am–4.30pm, Sat & Sun 9am–4pm; ☏07/4922 5339). Recent reports of nasty incidents involving gangs of Aboriginal teenagers are unfortunately too numerous to ignore; there's no need for paranoia, but do follow local advice and don't walk alone at night.

Accommodation

If your only reason for being in Rockhampton is to get to Great Keppel, there's little reason to stay over – catch a local bus to Rosslyn Bay or Yeppoon (see p.436).

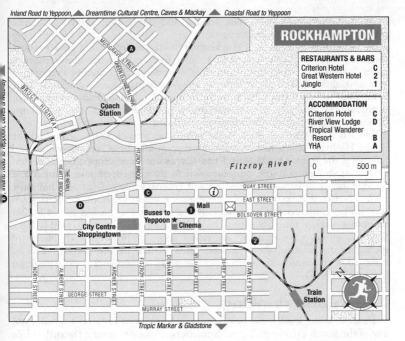

ROCKHAMPTON

RESTAURANTS & BARS
Criterion Hotel	C
Great Western Hotel	2
Jungle	1

ACCOMMODATION
Criterion Hotel	C
River View Lodge	D
Tropical Wanderer Resort	B
YHA	A

Fitzroy River

0   500 m

QUAY STREET
EAST STREET
BOLSOVER STREET

Mall

Buses to Yeppoon
Cinema

City Centre Shoppingtown

MUSGRAVE STREET
QUEEN ELIZABETH DRIVE
BRUCE HIGHWAY
Coach Station
FITZROY BRIDGE
THE NERIUL
HEWITT BRIDGE
NORTH STREET
ALBERT STREET
ARCHER STREET
FITZROY STREET
DENHAM STREET
WILLIAM STREET
DERBY STREET
STANLEY STREET
GEORGE STREET
MURRAY STREET

Train Station

Tropic Marker & Gladstone

The pick of the city's **accommodation** choices is the reasonably priced though often noisy suites above the pub at the historic *Criterion Hotel* on Quay Street (℡07/4922 1225, Ⓦwww.thecriterion.com.au; ❸), which overlooks the river. Budget options include *River View Lodge* at 48 Victoria Parade (℡07/4922 2077; ❷), with shared facilities but in a pleasant and central location; the YHA's well-appointed compound north of the river at 60 MacFarlane St, close to the long-distance bus stop (℡07/4927 5288, Ⓦwww.yha.com.au; dorms $22, rooms ❷); or the *Tropical Wanderer Resort*, on the highway 3km north of the river (℡1800 815 563, Ⓦwww.tropicalwanderer.com.au; cabins ❸, units ❺), with a restaurant, pool and attractive gardens.

The City and around

It doesn't take long to look around the city. The **Tropic Marker**, 3km from the river at Rockhampton's southern entrance, is just a spire informing you of your position at 23° 26' 30" S. Apart from a riverside stroll to take in the early twentieth-century architecture or the brown-stained boulders midstream that gave the city its name, there's very little else to detain you.

About 6km north of town on the Bruce Highway, the **Dreamtime Cultural Centre** (Mon–Fri 10am–3.30pm; tours with an Aboriginal guide from 10.30am; $13.50; Ⓦwww.dreamtimecentre.com.au) offers a good introduction to central Queensland's Aboriginal heritage. Inside, chronological and Dreamtime histories are intermingled, with a broad dissection of the archeology and mythology of Carnarvon Gorge (see p.522). Outside, surrounded by woodland, gunyahs (shelters of bark and branches) and stencil art, you'll find an unlikely walk-through dugong (sea cow), and the original stone rings of a **bora ground** which marked the main camp of the Darumbal, whose territory reached from the Keppel Bay coastline inland to Mount Morgan. The tour also discusses plant usage and introduces boomerang, dance and didgeridoo skills – audience participation is definitely encouraged.

The limestone hills north of Rockhampton are riddled with a **cave system**, thick with tree roots encased in stone after forcing their way down through rocks, "cave corals" and "frozen waterfalls" – minerals deposited by evaporation after annual floods. The **ghost bat** (Australia's only carnivorous species) and the **little bent-winged bat** – both now endangered – seasonally use the caves for roosts, and you might catch the odd group huddled together on the ceilings, eyes peering down at you over leaf-shaped noses.

Two sets of caverns are open to the public, both reached by turning off the Bruce Highway 25km north of Rockhampton at **The Caves** township and following the signs. The **Mount Etna Caves** are undeveloped but none too extensive; you can explore on your own (daily 6am–8pm; take a torch and durable shoes); or between December and February you can go on a **bat tour** with a National Parks ranger (four evenings a week; $8; book on ☎07/4936 0511). The **Capricorn Caverns** (daily 9am–4pm; 1hr guided tour $20, 2hr adventure caving tour $60, must be booked in advance; ☎07/4934 2883, ⓦwww.capricorncaves.com.au) are rather more impressive, with plenty of spotlights illuminating their interiors. **Bus tours** to the Caverns can be arranged with Johnny ($55 from Rockhampton, minimum 2 people; book on ☎04/1479 3637).

Eating and drinking

A **steak** of some kind is the obvious choice in Australia's "Beef Capital", and any of the hotels can oblige. There's a smattering of cafés around the mall, while the *Great Western Hotel* over on Stanley Street (☎07/4922 3888) serves quality steak, and has a weekly rodeo "out back", sometimes with **live country music** – call ahead for times as they change frequently. A perch at the *Criterion*'s bar on Quay Street, overlooking the Fitzroy River, is recommended for less flamboyant steak and beer, along with elbow-to-elbow closeness with a few locals. *Jungle*, on the corner of East and William streets, is a popular café-restaurant-bar which stays open late, and serves sandwiches and light meals for under $10 – the *Strutters* **nightclub** is upstairs.

The Capricorn Coast

Views from the volcanic outcrops overlooking the **Capricorn Coast**, some 40km east of Rockhampton, stretch across graziers' estates and pineapple planta-tions to exposed headlands, estuarine mudflats and the Keppel Islands. The coastal townships of **Yeppoon** and **Emu Park**, 20km apart and settled by cattle barons in the 1860s, were soon adopted by Rockhampton's elite as places to beat the summer temperatures, and retain a pleasantly dated holiday atmosphere – besides being much nicer places to stay than Rockhampton. **Great Keppel Island** is the coast's main draw, however, accessed from **Rosslyn Bay**, just south of Yeppoon.

There are **two roads** to the coast from Rockhampton: on the north side of the river, turn east and it's 50km to Emu Park; or drive 5km further up Highway 1 and then turn coastwards for the forty-kilometre run to Yeppoon. Young's **buses** run from Rockhampton to Yeppoon, Emu Park and Rosslyn Bay (6–10 services daily from the stop beside the car park in Bolsover Street, near the junction with William; ☎07/4922 3813).

Emu Park and Yeppoon

EMU PARK comprises a pleasant sandy beach and breezy hillside covered by scattered Queenslander houses, where the wind howls mournful tunes through the wires of the **Singing Ship**, a peculiar monument to Captain Cook. A five-minute stroll north of the memorial is *Emu's Beach Resort* (☎1800 333 349, ⊛www.emusbeachresort.com; dorm $22, rooms ❹), a modern backpacker retreat on Pattison Street, or closer to the town centre is the motel-like *Endeavour Inn* on Hill Street (☎1800 252 112, ⊛www.endeavourinn.com.au; ❹).

Heading north up the coast from here, it's 18km via **Rosslyn Bay** to **YEPPOON**'s quiet handful of streets, which face the Keppel Islands over a blustery expanse of sand and sea. All services are on **Normanby Street**, at right angles to the seafront ANZAC Parade. **Buses** pull into the depot on Hill Street, which also runs off ANZAC Parade parallel with Normanby. For **accommodation**, *Driftwood Motel*, about 2km north of town at 7 Todd Ave (☎07/4939 2446, ⊛www.driftwoodunits.com.au; ❺), has straightforward but smartly equipped self-contained rooms overlooking the beach, while the *Strand Hotel* (☎07/4939 1301; ❸), on the corner of ANZAC Parade and James Street, offers basic, four-bed units. Just south of town off the Emu Park road, the *Poinciana Tourist Park* (☎07/4939 1601, ⊛www.poincianatouristpark.com; camping $25.50, powered sites $29.50, cabins ❷) is the cheapest place to stay, with inexpensive, self-contained cabins and shady tent sites.

Yeppoon prides itself on its fresh **fish**, and there are plenty of **restaurants** where you can sample it. The pick of the lot is *Seagulls Seafood* on ANZAC Parade, which specializes in local Spanish mackerel dishes, and its bucket of seafood is excellent value at $16.50. *Spinnaker Restaurant* at the nearby *Keppel Bay Sailing Club* has an all-you-can-eat menu of breakfasts ($15), lunches ($13) and dinners ($16), or you can sip a beer admiring the long views of the islands from the clubhouse. For weekend **entertainment**, try *Bonkers Nightclub*, one road back from ANZAC Parade on Hill Street.

Rosslyn Bay and Great Keppel Island

Great Keppel is the largest of the eighteen Keppel islands, a windswept hillock covered in casuarinas and ringed by white sand so fine that it squeaks when you walk through it, all surrounded by an invitingly clear blue sea – just the place for a few days of indolence. **Ferries** leave from **ROSSLYN BAY**, 5km south of Yeppoon: the *Freedom Fast Cat* departs from the marina at 9.15am daily except Monday, with an additional trip to the island on Friday at 3pm (☎07/4933 6888; $45 return). There's exposed **free parking** at the harbour, though for protection from salt spray, leave your car undercover at Great Keppel Island Security Car Park ($10 a day; ☎07/4933 6670), opposite the Rosslyn Bay junction on the main road.

Great Keppel Island

Arriving at Great Keppel, the ferry leaves you on a spit near several **accommodation** choices including the friendly *Great Keppel Island Holiday Village* (☎1800 180 235, ⊛www.gkiholidayvillage.com.au; tent cabins ❹, cabins ❺). Along the beach, *Keppel Lodge* (☎07/4939 4251, ⊛www.keppellodge.com.au; ❹) is a pleasant, motel-like affair, or you can rent one of the island's many beachfront holiday houses by contacting the local store and post office, Rainbow Hut (☎07/4939 5596, ⊜rainbowhut@bigpond.com), which can work out economical for small groups. For **food**, there's a tearoom at the Shell House boutique on Fisherman's Beach, and a late-opening pizza shack.

Once a popular retreat for Australian holiday-makers, the island's only large resort, the *Great Keppel Island Resort* (℡07/4939 2050), is under long-term redevelopment and is scheduled to reopen in late 2010. For those looking for seclusion, the beautiful and once bustling main beaches of Putney and Fisherman's are temporarily empty and doubly breathtaking. Long Beach, half an hour's walk along a woodland path beyond the resort, is an even more secluded spot for sun-lovers, while snorkellers can make the short haul over sand dunes at the western end to shallow coral on Monkey Beach. **Middens** (shell mounds) on Monkey Beach were left by Woppaburra Aborigines, who were enslaved and forcibly removed to Fraser Island by early settlers.

Mackay and around

Some 360km north of Rockhampton along a famously unexciting stretch of Highway 1, the fertile Pioneer Valley makes the **MACKAY** area a welcome break from the otherwise dry country between Bundaberg and Townsville. Despite encounters with aggressive Juipera Aborigines, John Mackay was impressed enough to settle the valley in 1861, and within four years the city was founded and the first **sugar cane** plantations were established. Sugar remains the main industry today, though the **coal mines** out west in the Bowen Basin have forced Mackay to become a service centre and its dreary parade of motel accommodation is usually full with casual workers and travelling business people. Though the city itself has no specific sights and is barely geared up to tourism, Mackay's proximity to two stunning and seldom-visited national parks at seafront **Cape Hillsborough** and rainforested **Eungella** –

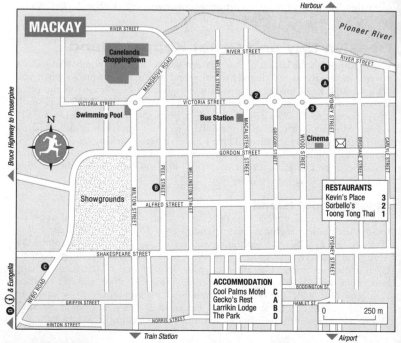

Sugar cane on the Tropical Coast

Sugar cane, grown in an almost continuous belt between Bundaberg and Mossman, north of Cairns, is the Tropical Coast's economic pillar of strength. Introduced in the 1860s, the crop subtly undermined the racial ideals of British colonialists when farmers, planning a system along the lines of the southern United States, employed **Kanakas** – Solomon Islanders– to work the plantations. Though only indentured for a few years, and theoretically given wages and passage home when their term expired, Kanakas on plantations suffered greatly from unfamiliar diseases, while the recruiting methods used by **"Blackbirder"** traders were at best dubious and often slipped into wholesale kidnapping. Growing white unemployment and nationalism through the 1880s eventually forced the government to ban blackbirding and repatriate the islanders. Those allowed to stay were joined over the next fifty years by immigrants from Italy and Malta, who mostly settled in the far north and today form large communities scattered between Mackay and Cairns.

After cane has been planted in November, the land is quickly covered by a blanket of dusky green. Before cutting, seven months later, the fields are traditionally fired to burn off leaves and maximize sugar content – though the practice is dying out. Cane fires often take place at dusk and are as photogenic as they are brief; the best way to be at the right place at the right time is to ask at a mill. Cut cane is then transported to the mills along a rambling rail network. The mills themselves are incredible buildings, with machinery looming out of makeshift walls and giant pipes which belch out steam around the clock when the mill is in operation. Cane is juiced for raw sugar or molasses, as the market dictates; crushed fibre becomes fuel for the boilers that sustain the process; and ash is returned to the fields as fertilizer. **Farleigh Mill** (℡07/4959 8360), north of Mackay, is open for **tours** (daily 9am & 1pm; $22) during the crushing season (June–Nov); sturdy shoes, a long-sleeve shirt and long trousers are essential.

where you are almost certain to see platypus – makes the region well worth a visit.

Practicalities

Mackay's centre straddles the crossroads of **Victoria** and **Sydney** streets, with the **bus station** – just a set-down point outside Mackay Travelworld – off Victoria on Macalister Street. Both **trains** (the station is on Connors Rd, 3km south off Milton St along Boundary Rd or Paradise St) and **planes** arrive south of town; a taxi into town from either terminal will set you back around $15. Virgin and Qantas have direct flights from Mackay to all the major cities between Cairns and Brisbane. Mackay Travelworld (Mon–Fri 7am–6pm, Sat 7am–2pm; ℡07/4944 2144) is the **ticket agent** for bus, train and air travel, and free maps are available from the **visitor centre** (℡07/4951 4803) in the town hall on Sydney Street.

It's sometimes hard to find a bed in Mackay, as many motels and van parks can be almost permanently full of mine workers – book well ahead or try the accommodation near the national parks which tend to be quieter – see pp.440–441. There are plenty of small ordinary roadside motels along the Nebo Road heading into Mackay, the closest to the centre being Cool Palms Motel (℡07/4957 5477; ❹) at no. 4, which offers clean and quiet rooms. Another good option on the Nebo Road is 2km south from the centre at *The Park* (℡07/4952 1211; ❸), a tidy caravan park with self-contained cabins in a pleasant garden setting. Budget options include *Gecko's Rest* at 34 Sydney St (℡07/4944 1230, ⓦwww.geckosrest.com.au; dorms $24, rooms ❷), a slightly sterile modern hostel set in a converted shopping arcade but with spacious rooms and a large, well-equipped kitchen; or *Larrikin Lodge* at 32 Peel St (℗07/4951 3728, Ⓦwww .larrikinlodge.com.au; dorms $24, rooms ❷; office hours 7am–2pm & 5–8.30pm, phone ahead to arrange check-in at other times), a low-set, comfortable Queenslander house with a laid-back feel, two minutes' walk from the bus station. The staff at *Larrikin* are extremely knowledgeable about the region, and the lodge runs its own bus to Eungella National Park.

There is no shortage of places to eat, with several downtown pubs and restaurants offering filling week-time lunch specials for around $10. For a good Singaporean–Chinese restaurant with fixed-price lunches (try the *laksa* – a colossal bowl of noodles, seafood and spicy coconut soup) and dinners from around $22 (featuring five-spice squid and whole fried fish) head to *Kevin's Place* on the corner of Wood and Victoria streets. Another long-established Asian restaurant is the cheap and cheerful *Toong Tong Thai* at 10 Sydney St with authentically hot and spicy takeaway or eat-in food. Upmarket *Sorbello's* at 166 Victoria St is the best choice for pastas and other Italian dishes and one of the few places open for a late-night tipple.

Cape Hillsborough National Park

Cape Hillsborough, about an hour's drive north of Mackay, is the site of a pretty beachfront national park; Reeforest Tours in Mackay (℗07/4959 8360, Ⓦwww.reeforest.com) sometimes run here, but you'll probably need your own vehicle to reach it. First head north up Highway 1 for about 20km and then take the signposted **Seaforth road**, past the inevitable canefields and the imposing bulk of Mount Jukes, for a further 30km to Cape Hillsborough.

The main area of the national park is set around a broad two-kilometre **beach**, backed by a good picnic area and framed by the beautifully wooded cliffs of Cape Hillsborough to the north and Andrews Point to the south; the shallow bay is good for swimming outside the stinger season. Hidden in bushland at the end of the road, the *Cape Hillsborough Resort* (℗07/4959 0152, Ⓦwww.capehillsboroughresort.com.au; camping $23, powered sites $28, hut ❷, cabins ❺) has a pool, basic store (which closes at 6pm) and restaurant. A good **walk** heads out 2km past here to **Hidden Valley**, a patch of cool, shady forest on a rocky beach where you'll find the outline of an Aboriginal fish trap; keep your eyes peeled for dolphins, turtles and pelicans out in the bay.

Five hundred metres back up the road towards Mackay, an excellent two-kilometre trail follows a **boardwalk** through coastal mangroves (bring insect repellent) and then snakes up to a ridge for views out over the area from open gum woodland peppered with grevillias, cycads (see box, p.495) and grasstrees – the latter identified by their tall, spear-like flower spike. There's also a huge **midden** up here, the remains of Aboriginal shellfish feasts, and plenty of reptiles sunning themselves around the edges of the path.

Eungella National Park

Some 80km west of Mackay, magical rainforest and rivers would make **Eungella National Park** (pronounced "young-g'lla") worth the journey even if you weren't almost guaranteed to see **platypuses**. There are two separate sections: lowland swimming holes and tropical rainforest at **Finch Hatton Gorge**, and highland rainforest at **Broken River**. The park's isolation has produced several unique species, including the Mackay tulip oak, the Eungella honeyeater and the much-discussed but probably extinct **gastric brooding frog**, known for incubating its young in its stomach.

Day-trips taking in both sections of the park can be arranged from Mackay with Reeforest Tours ($115; ℡1800 500 353, ⓦwww.reeforest.com) or the *Larrikin Lodge* (see opposite; $90). Both run only if they have sufficient numbers – otherwise, you'll need your own vehicle. **From Mackay**, head south down the Nebo Road (Highway 1) to the city limits and follow signs initially west along the Peak Downs Highway; if you're coming south down the highway **from Proserpine**, follow the signs just south of tiny Kuttabul, around 30km north of Mackay.

Finch Hatton Gorge

The Eungella road cuts through prime cane country and past several **sugar mills** as it runs the length of the Pioneer Valley, past the townships of **Marian** and **Mirani**. Some 60km from Mackay, signposts just before Finch Hatton township mark the turn-off to **Finch Hatton Gorge**, 12km from the main road across several fords – access depends on the season, though generally it's negotiable by all vehicles, and although there's no public transport into the park, both accommodations listed below will pick up from Mackay for $30 per person. Immediately across the first creek, *Platypus Bush Camp* (℡07/4958 3204, ⓦwww.bushcamp.net; camping $7.50 per person, dorms $25, cabins ❸) provides camping and basic cabin accommodation: mattress, pillow, amenities and kitchen are supplied; the rest (including food) is up to you. This is the most authentic rainforest experience you can have anywhere in Queensland: you'll see an astonishing array of bird- and animal-life (including the elusive platypus), sit by a fire under the stars, shower in the rainforest amidst fairy-like fireflies, and be lulled to sleep by a gurgling creek. About 1km and three creeks further on you'll find comfortable units at *Finch Hatton Gorge Cabins* (℡07/4958 3281, ⓦwww.finchhattongorgecabins.com.au; dorms $22, cabins ❹) and a small **tearoom**. This is also the pick-up point for **Forest Flying** ($45; advance booking essential on ℡07/4958 3359), which can take you for a ride 25m up through the tree tops (and a flying-fox colony) on a wire-and-sling affair – much more secure than it sounds, and offering as close a view of the forest canopy as you'll ever get.

Another kilometre past the tearoom, the road ends at a picnic area, from where graded **walking tracks** ascend through a hot jungle of palms, vines and creepers to where the gorge winds down the side of Mount Dalrymple as a rocky creek pocked with swimming holes. **Araluen Falls** (1.5km from the picnic area), a beautiful – if icy – pool and cascade, is the perfect place to spend a summer's day; further up (3km from the picnic area) is an even more attractive cascade at the **Wheel of Fire Falls**, where you can sit up to your neck in the water.

Eungella township and Broken River

About 15km past Finch Hatton township, the main road makes an unforgettably steep and twisting ascent up the range to **EUNGELLA**. This spread-out hamlet comprises a general store, fish-and-chip shop, a couple of cafés and the *Eungella Chalet* **hotel**, whose back-lawn beer garden and swimming pool sit just metres away from a seven-hundred-metre drop into the forest, with a fantastic panorama down the valley. The best **place to stay** here is the friendly *Eungella Holiday Park* (℡07/4958 4590; camping $20, cabins ❹) – take the first right at the top of the range – which has log cabins, units and campsites, more great views, plus its own store and an ATM.

A final 5km further from Eungella through patches of forest and dairy pasture and beside a tiny bridge is **Broken River** where you can pick up free **maps** from the unmanned National Parks **interpretation centre**, usually unlocked by 8am by the park ranger. There's also a bush **campsite** (book on ☎ 13 13 04 or ⓦ www.epa.qld.gov.au) with cold showers, a picnic area and the excellent *Broken River Mountain Resort* (☎ 07/4958 4528, ⓦ www.brokenrivermr.com.au; doubles ❺, four-person self-contained cabins with fireplaces ❻). Be prepared for **rain**: Eungella translates as "Land of Cloud".

The best vantage point for **platypus watching** is the purpose-built **platform** by the picnic area; normally fairly timid creatures, here they've become quite tolerant of people, and you can often see them right through the day. The real star of Broken River, though, is the **forest** itself, whose ancient trees with buttressed roots and immensely high canopies conceal a floor of rich rotting timber, ferns, palms and vines. Local cabbage palms, with their straight trunks and crown of large, fringed leaves; huge, scaly-barked Mackay cedar; and tulip oaks are all endemic – many others shrubs and trees here are otherwise only found further south, indicating that Eungella may have once been part of far more extensive forests. It can be difficult to see **animals** in the undergrowth, but the sun-splashed paths along riverbanks attract goannas and snakes, and you'll certainly hear plenty of birds. The best two **walking tracks** are either following the river upstream to Crediton and then returning along the road (16km return), or heading through the forest and down to *Eungella Chalet* (13km return). If you're not that dedicated, there's also an easy **forty-minute circuit** from the picnic grounds upstream to Crystal Cascades.

On to Whitsunday

PROSERPINE, 123km north of Mackay, is a small workaday sugar town on the turn-off from Highway 1 to Whitsunday, and site of the regional **train station** and **airport**, though there's another major airport on Hamilton Island. Arriving by **long-distance bus**, there's no need to get out here as all services continue to Airlie Beach. If you do wind up in town, Whitsunday Transit (☎ 07/4946 1800) runs a **local bus** seven times daily between Proserpine and Whitsunday; contact them in advance to arrange train station and airport **pick-ups** (the airport is 10km south of town). Late arrivals can stay at the functional *Proserpine Motor Lodge*, 184 Main St (☎ 07/4945 1788; ❸), or the van park on Jupp Street.

Twenty kilometres east off the highway, **WHITSUNDAY** is the cover-all name for the sprawling communities of Cannonvale, Airlie Beach and Shutehaven (aka Shute Harbour), access points for the **Whitsunday Islands** (see p.445). Despite an attractive setting, nobody comes to Whitsunday to spend time in town – it's just a place to be while deciding which island to visit. **Cannonvale** and **Airlie Beach** are the service centres, while island ferries generally leave from **Shutehaven**, 10km on from Airlie past Cape Conway National Park. Other cruises leave from **Abel Point Marina**, just on the Cannonvale side of Airlie.

Cannonvale, Airlie Beach and Shutehaven

Coming from Proserpine, Whitsunday's first community is **CANNONVALE**, a scattering of modern buildings fringing the highway for about 1km or so, overlooked by luxury homes set higher up on the wooded slopes of the

Conway Range. Just around the headland past Abel Point Marina, **AIRLIE BEACH** is nestled between the sea and a hillside covered in apartment blocks, with all services crammed into one short stretch of **Shute Harbour Road** and the hundred-metre-long **Esplanade**. Despite the name, Airlie Beach has only a couple of gritty stretches of sand, which get covered at high tide – though the view of the deep turquoise bay, dotted with yachts and cruisers, is gorgeous. To make up the shortfall, there's a free, open-air **landscaped pool** between Shute Harbour Road and the sea, complete with showers, changing rooms, picnic hotplates, benches and a little sand.

A final 3km on, **SHUTEHAVEN** (Shute Harbour) consists of a cluster of houses with stunning views overlooking the islands from wooded hills above **Coral Point**; it's one of Australia's busiest harbours, and most of the island ferries and bareboat charters depart from here.

Arrival and information

Airlie's **long-distance bus terminal** is at the eastern end of town, off the Esplanade past the *Airlie Beach Hotel*. By **air**, island transfers are available with Air Whitsunday (℡07/4946 9111, ⊛www.airwhitsunday.com.au), and intercity flights with Virgin Blue (⊛www.virginblue.com.au) and Jetstar (⊛www.jetstar.com.au); long-distance flights use Proserpine or Hamilton Island, while local flights to or around the islands depart from Whitsunday Airport, about halfway between Airlie and Shutehaven. The Whitsunday Transit **bus** runs between Cannonvale, Airlie and Shutehaven roughly twice an hour from around 6am to 6pm, and around once an hour between Cannonvale and Airlie from 6pm until 10.30pm. Staff at the town's hotels, hostels and other places offer limitless **information**, though don't expect it to be unbiased; the information office, Whitsunday.com, up at the Cannonvale end of Airlie (℡07/4946 5299, ⊛www.airliebeach.com) is probably the most objective source, but it's a good idea to ask other visitors about which cruises they recommend before making a decision.

Accommodation

Unless you're in town during the September Whitsunday Fun Race, Christmas or New Year, you'll have little trouble finding **accommodation**, which is concentrated in Airlie Beach itself. **Hostels** are all cramped, but a pool and kitchen are standard amenities; **motels** and **resorts** often insist on minimum stays of three nights during Christmas and Easter, though might offer discounted rates at other times. All places act as booking agents for tours and transport.

Airlie Beach Hotel On the Esplanade near the bus station, Airlie ℡07/4964 1999, ⊛www .airliebeachhotel.com.au. This formerly seedy motel is now one of the smartest places to stay in Airlie. Refurbished older motel rooms ❻, new beachfront hotel rooms ❼

Airlie Beach YHA 394 Shute Harbour Rd, Airlie ℡07/4946 6312, ⊛www.yha.com.au. Generally busy and somewhat crowded, with tidy dorms and doubles. Dorms $28, rooms ❸

Airlie Cove Van Park Three kilometre towards Shutehaven on Shute Harbour Rd ℡07/4946 6727, ⊛www.airliecove.com.au. Try this place for camping and upmarket cabins. Camping $32, powered sites $39, cabins ❹

Airlie Waterfront Backpackers Near the *Airlie Beach Hotel*, Airlie ℡1800 089 000, ⊛www .airliewaterfront.com. Six-person apartments above a boutique food plaza with private bedrooms, shared bathrooms and kitchens; also has dorms and is close to the bus stop. Dorms $25, rooms ❷–❹

Airlie Waterfront Bed and Breakfast Corner of Broadwater and Mazlin sts, Airlie ℡07/4946 7631, ⊛www.airliewaterfrontbnb.com.au. One- or two-bedroom serviced apartments in a modern timber house with fantastic bay views; rooms are comfortably furnished, and some have outdoor spa baths. ❾

Beaches 362 Shute Harbour Rd, Airlie ℡1800 636 630, ⊛www.beaches.com.au. Brash backpackers' hostel, with plenty of bunks and double rooms available. Dorms $27, rooms ❹

Coral Point Lodge 54 Harbour Ave, Shute Harbour ☎07/4946 9500, ⓦwww .coralpointlodge.com.au. Delightful, excellent-value rooms and apartments with the best views in the Whitsundays. It's a bit hard to find – turn up the hill immediately after the Shell garage and keep going to the end. The attached café-restaurant is well worth a stop even if you're not staying here. ❻

Coral Sea Resort 25 Oceanview Ave, at the Cannonvale end of Airlie ☎07/4946 1300, ⓦwww .coralsearesort.com. Airlie Beach's only real full-blown resort; rooms (some with ocean views) are all very smart, and there's a private jetty, popular bar and pool area too. ❽

Koalas Shute Harbour Rd, at the Cannonvale end of Airlie ☎1800 466 444, ⓦwww.koalaadventures .com. Basic six-bed dorms, each with bathroom

and TV. Facilities include a communal kitchen, volleyball court and large pool in pleasant landscaped grounds; you can also camp here. Dorms $28, rooms ❸

Magnum's By the bridge on Shute Harbour Rd, Airlie ☎1800 624 634, ⓦwww.magnums.com.au. Tidy cabins with en-suite bathrooms, pleasantly sheltered tropical lawns, and a loud bar and nightclub next door. Dorms $17, rooms ❷

On the Beach 269 Shute Harbour Rd, Cannonvale end of Airlie ☎07/4946 6359, ⓦwww .whitsundayonthebeach.com. Unpretentious central motel with self-contained serviced units overlooking Airlie's artificial pool and the bay. ❹

Whitehaven Holiday Units 285 Shute Harbour Rd, Airlie. Extraordinarily quiet, given its central location, with friendly staff. Rooms are simply furnished and face the sea. ❺

Airlie activities

Airlie's main preoccupation is with **organizing cruises** (see box, p.450), but you can also rent **watersports gear** from the kiosk on the beach, or organize half-day to six-day **sea-kayaking** expeditions with Salty Dog (☎07/4946 1388, ⓦwww.saltydog.com.au). A **flea market** is held near the long-distance bus stop on Saturday mornings, for local produce and souvenirs (8am–noon). Otherwise, **Conway National Park** comprises a mostly inaccessible stretch of forested mountains and mangroves facing the islands, but there's a small picnic area on the roadside about 7km from Airlie on Shute Harbour Road, from where an easy walking track climbs Mount Rooper to an observation platform giving views of the islands' white peaks jutting out of the unbelievably blue sea.

Eating and entertainment

As with the accommodation, the majority of **restaurants**, as well as the liveliest **nightclubs**, are in Airlie – there are also busy clubs at *Beaches* and *Magnum's* backpackers'.

Café Mykonos 287 Shute Harbour Rd, Airlie. Cheap and cheerful kebabs, souvlakia, dolmades and salads, with nothing over $13. Basically a takeaway, but there are a few tables and chairs if the nearby beach doesn't appeal.

Capers Airlie Beach Hotel, Esplanade, Airlie. Australian contemporary menu, a little pricey but worth it for the alfresco atmosphere and stunning ocean views. Mains from $35.

Evolution Lounge Bar Cannonvale end of Shute Harbour Rd. Nightly grind to loud music. Daily 10pm–late.

Fish D'vine Beach Plaza Food Court, Esplanade, Airlie. Pick of a fantastic assortment of eateries, this award-winning fish and rum bar serves exceptionally well-cooked fish and chips and delicious seafood baskets for around $18.

Golden Temple 252 Shute Harbour Rd, Cannon-vale. Popular and friendly Chinese restaurant with spacious dining and the usual takeaway menu – all mains are under $20.

KC's 50 Shute Harbour Rd, Airlie. Popular with backpackers for its $10 steak-and-chips dinner specials before 7pm, or you can blow out on kangaroo, croc and seafood in noisy comfort; this place stays open until 3am and often has live bands. Mains from $30.

Morocco's Shute Harbour Rd, at the Cannonvale end of Airlie. Lively bar with a huge video screen, party atmosphere, and cheap Mexican and Cajun dishes. Daily 3pm–2am.

Paddy Shenanigan's A popular place to down endless pints, listen to live music or watch sports on the huge TV screen.

Sailing Club Up past the bus stop off the Esplanade. Bar and decent pub food from 10am until late, with views out over the bay.

Listings

Banks NAB and Commonwealth in Airlie, plus ANZ and Westpac in Cannonvale.

Boat charters Unless you know exactly what you want, bookings are best made through an agent. Bareboat charters should be undertaken by experienced sailors only: the average wind speed in the Whitsundays is 15–25 knots, which means serious sailing. Five-person yachts start at around $550 a day; add another $75 during holiday seasons. Whitsunday Rent-a-Yacht (☏07/4946 9232, ⓦwww.rentayacht.com.au) and Queensland Yacht Charters (☏07/4946 7400, ⓦwww.yachtcharters .com.au) have been going for years and are thoroughly reliable.

Car, scooter and bicycle rental Cars cost around $50 a day, scooters from $35 and bicycles at $25. Airlie Beach Budget Autos, 285 Shute Harbour Rd, Airlie ☏07/4948 0300; Fun Rentals, next to the Caltex fuel station at the Cannonvale end of Airlie, has bicycles as well as cars and scooters ☏07/4948 0489; Tropic Car Hire, 15 Commerce Close, Cannonvale ☏07/4948 3415; We Do Scooters ☏07/4946 5425.

Car lockup There's limited parking space at Shutehaven; undercover facilities are available behind the Shell garage ($8 a day, or $14 for 24hr); there's an open-air grid at the harbour itself ($8 a day), and a free but unguarded area at the Lions Lookout up the hill from the Shell garage. Otherwise, contact Shute Harbour Secured Parking (☏07/4946 9666) or Whitsunday Airport Secured Parking, midway between Airlie and Shutehaven (☏04/1979 0995).

Diving The best of Airlie's limited scuba-diving options is aboard *Fantasea* (☏07/4946 5111, ⓦwww.fantasea.com.au), which makes daily trips to the company's "Reef World" pontoon at Hardy Reef; from here, you take a smaller launch to various dive sites. Two dives cost $359. Scuba is also often available on island cruises – see box, p.450. You might be asked to provide a dive medical certificate, especially if you are over 45 years old.

Doctor Opposite *McDonald's*, Shute Harbour Rd, Airlie (Mon–Fri 8am–7pm, Sat & Sun 8am–5pm; 24hr phoneline ☏07/4948 0900).

Internet If your accommodation can't help out, airliebeach.com, up near the *Hog's Breath Café* at the Cannonvale end of town, has a stack of terminals.

Joy flights Whitsunday Tigermoth Adventures (☏07/4946 9911, ⓦwww.tigermothadventures .com.au) take you on rides over the Whitsundays in a vintage biplane (10min–1hr; $99–360); Air Whitsunday (☏07/4946 9911, ⓦwww .airwhitsunday.com.au) offers flights out to the islands and Great Barrier Reef in a seaplane ($220–390); and Flying Tours (☏07/4946 9102, ⓦwww.avta.com.au) run sea planes and helicopter tours of the reef and islands ($144–284).

Left luggage There's a set of lockers with 24hr access on the corner of Shute Harbour Rd and the Esplanade ($4–6 per day).

National Parks office Shute Harbour Rd, 3km out towards Shutehaven on the left of the road (Mon–Fri 9am–4.30pm; ☏07/4946 7022, ⓦwww .epa.qld.gov.au). Island camping permits and a small environmental display.

Pharmacy Airlie Day and Night Pharmacy, Shute Harbour Rd (daily 8am–8pm).

Police 8 Altmann Ave, off Shute Harbour Rd, Cannonvale ☏07/4948 8888.

Post office In the centre of town, right behind *McDonald's*.

Supermarket The biggest is in Cannonvale, though Airlie has a well-stocked local food store about halfway through the town on Shute Harbour Rd.

Taxi ☏13 10 08.

The Whitsundays

The **Whitsunday Islands** look just like the granite mountain peaks they once were before rising sea levels cut them off from the mainland six thousand years ago. They were seasonally inhabited by the Ngaro Aborigines when Captain Cook sailed through in 1770; he proceeded to name the area after the day he arrived, and various locations after his expedition's sponsors. Today, dense green pine forests, vivid blue water and roughly contoured coastlines give the 74 islands

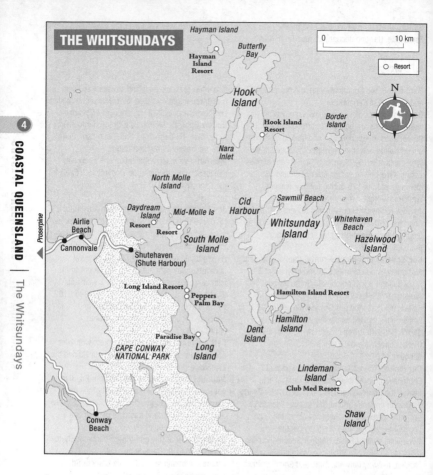

instant appeal, and the surrounding seas bustle with yachts and cruisers. Resorts first opened here in the 1930s and now number eight, but the majority of islands are still undeveloped national parks, with campsites on seventeen of them. Resorts aside, the few islands left in private hands are mainly uninhabited and largely the domain of local yachties. Those covered below all have regular connections to the mainland.

There are two ways to explore the Whitsundays: staying on the islands or cruising around them. **Staying** allows you to choose between camping and resort facilities, with snorkelling, bushwalks and beach sports to pass the time. **Cruises** spend one or more days around the islands, perhaps putting ashore at times (check this, if it's the islands themselves you want to see) or diving and snorkelling. Don't miss the chance to do some **whale watching** if you're here between June and September, when humpbacks (see p.419) arrive from their Antarctic wintering grounds to give birth and raise their calves before heading south again.

If you're planning to make use of the 32 island **campsites**, you'll first need to arrange transport, then obtain **permits** from the local National Parks office (see

"Listings", p.445). At most, campsite facilities comprise a pit toilet, picnic tables and rainwater tanks, so take everything you'll need with you, especially insect repellent, a fuel stove (wood fires are prohibited) and **drinking water** – if you're planning a long stay, you can arrange for cruise boats to ferry in supplies. **Resorts** sometimes have a higher profile than the islands they're built on, though staying at them is often beyond most budget travellers' means; stand by deals can slash prices, though, and polite bargaining is always worth a try. Most, in any case, allow day-trippers to use their facilities, an economical way to explore the islands whilst staying at the cheaper accommodation available around Airlie Beach.

The resort islands all offer relatively expensive return **ferry transfers** to and from the mainland. If you'd like to see more than one island, or plan to camp away from a resort, it's cheaper to choose some sort of a **cruise** or **camping transfer** – for details, see the box on pp.450–451. Once you've arranged everything else, check your **departure points**; most cruises leave from Abel Point Marina, while resort ferries and island transfers tend to use Shutehaven – both stops on the Whitsunday Transit bus.

Whitsunday Island

The largest island in the group, National Parks-run **Whitsunday Island**, is also one of the most enjoyable. Its east coast is home to the five-kilometre-long **Whitehaven Beach**, easily the finest in all the islands, and on the agenda of just about every cruise boat in the region. Blindingly white, and still clean despite the numbers of day-trippers and campers, it's a beautiful spot so long as you can handle the lack of distractions. The **campsite** on the southern end of the beach facing Haslewood Island is above the tide line, with minimal shelter provided by whispering casuarinas, and the headland here is the best place for snorkelling. On the northern end of the beach is a short track leading up to popular Hill Inlet Lookout with its keenly photographed views of the sand-ridden bay.

Over on Whitsunday's west side, **Cid Harbour** is a quieter hideaway which lacks a great beach but instead enjoys a backdrop of giant granite boulders and tropical forests, with several more campsites above coral and pebble shingle. **Dugong Beach** is the nicest, sheltered under the protective arms and buttressed roots of giant trees; it's a twenty-minute walk along narrow hill paths from Sawmill Beach, where you're likely to be dropped off.

There's no resort on Whitsunday; aside from day-trips to Whitehaven (see box, p.450), Camping Whitsunday and Island Camping Connections offer campsite transfers for $60–160 (see p.450 for contact details).

Hook Island

Directly north of Whitsunday, and pretty similar in appearance, **Hook Island** is the second largest in the group. The easiest passage to the island is on a transfer with *Voyager* from Shute Harbour ($40) to the low-key and fairly basic **resort** (☎07/4946 9380, [W]www.hookislandresort.com; dorms $45, rooms [5]) at the island's southeastern end, which has fine views over the channel to Whitsunday, as well as a bar, a small store and a cafeteria serving meals and snacks. There are also several National Parks **campsites** around the island, the pick of which is at southern **Curlew Beach** – sheltered, pretty and accessible only with your own vessel or by prior arrangement with a tour operator.

Cruises often pull into southern **Nara Inlet** for a look at the **Aboriginal paintings** on the roof of a small cave above a tiny shingle beach. Though not dramatic in scale or design, the art is significant for its net patterns, which are otherwise found only at central highland sites such as Carnarvon Gorge (see p.522). On the rocks below the cave is more recent graffiti, left by boat crews over the last thirty years.

Snorkelling on the reef directly in front of the resort is a must; snorkelling gear and surf skis are free (with deposit) to guests. The water is cloudy on large tides, but the coral outcrops are all in fairly good condition and there's plenty of life around, from flatworms to morays and parrotfish. Day-cruises run from Airlie to the snorkelling spots and visit the top-rate fringing coral at **Manta Ray Bay**, **Langford Reef** and **Butterfly Bay**, on the northern and north-eastern tips of the island – visibility can be poor here, but on a good day these sites offer some of the best diving in the Whitsundays.

Hayman Island

The extremely high price of accommodation at the *Hayman Island Resort* (℡07/4940 1244, ⓦwww.hayman.com.au; ⑨) pales into insignificance when compared with the resort's building costs, which topped $300 million. Guests indulge in lush rooms with extravagant and genuine Baroque and Renaissance furnishings, and staff move about through underground tunnels so that they don't get in the way. Not surprisingly, day-trippers aren't allowed anywhere near the place, although cruises and some dive-trips stop off for a look at the coral off **Blue Pearl Bay** – which isn't actually that exciting – on the island's west coast.

The Molles and nearby islands

South Molle Island was a source of fine-grained stone for Ngaro Aborigines, a unique material for the tools that have been found on other islands and may help in mapping trade routes. The slightly dated **resort** (℡07/4946 9433, ⓦwww.southmolleisland.com.au; ⑧) in the north of the island offers heaps of extras – such as guided walks, and all sports and facilities – along with stand-by rates. A series of fabulous coastal **walking tracks** from behind the golf course leads through gum trees and light forest, encompassing vistas of the islands

▲ South Molle Island

from the top of Spion Kop and Mount Jeffreys, and on to some quiet beaches at the south end.

South Molle's resort can sometimes organize a lift to the **campsite** on uninhabited **North Molle Island**, only 2km away (or contact Camping Whitsunday; see box, p.450); the beach here is made up of rough coral fragments, but the snorkelling is fairly good. There are another couple of campsites on **Mid-Molle Island**, joined to South Molle by a low-tide causeway about half a kilometre from the resort.

Daydream Island is little more than a tiny wooded rise between South Molle and the mainland, with a narrow coarse-sand beach running the length of the east side, and coral to snorkel over at the north end. The **resort** (⊙07/4948 8488, ⓦwww.daydreamisland.com; ❾) with its regimental lines of hotel rooms has three meandering swimming pools and a large open-air aquarium stocked with reef sharks and manta rays, making it a haven for kids. Cruise Whitsunday (see p.450 for details) offers day-trips for $75 including lunch at the resort.

Tiny **Planton**, **Tancred** and **Denman** islands are just offshore from South Molle – with no facilities and limited camping at the National Parks sites here, they're about as isolated as you'll get in the Whitsundays. All three are surrounded by reef, but be careful of strong currents. Again, Camping Whitsunday and Island Camping Connections offer drop-offs for $45 one-way (see p.450).

Long Island

Long Island is exactly that, being not much more than a narrow, ten-kilometre ribbon almost within reach of the mainland forests. There are a few looping hikes through the rainforest to **Sandy Bay** (where there's a National Parks campsite) or up **Humpy Point**, as well as **three resorts**. *Long Island Resort* at Happy Bay (⊙07/4946 9400, ⓦwww.oceanhotels.com.au; dorm $25, lodge rooms ❹, hotel rooms including meals and transfers ❻) has the only budget accommodation in the Whitsundays, although it's primarily a beach resort popular with couples and families with all sorts of entertainment on hand; Cruise Whitsunday (see p.450) runs a day-trip here for $85. *Peppers Palm Bay* (⊙07/4946 9233, ⓦwww.peppers.com.au; cabins and bungalows ❾), half a kilometre south at the island's waist, is a more exclusive upmarket retreat, but for a real tropical escape, head to ⌘ *Paradise Bay* (⊙07/4946 9777, ⓦwww.paradisebay.com.au; ❾), whose self-contained waterfront cabins, superb food and attentive service are only accessible by helicopter.

Hamilton and Lindeman Islands

With a large marina, an airstrip, tons of motorized sports and several high-rise apartment towers, **Hamilton Island** is the only brazenly commercial spot on the islands. Privately owned, its businesses operate under a lease: development includes a quaint **colonial waterfront** with bank, post office, bakery, nightclub, a handful of overpriced restaurants (the most affordable being *Popeye*, for fish and chips), and six hotels that fall under the umbrella of *Hamilton Island Resort* (⊙13 73 33, ⓦwww.hamiltonisland.com.au; ❾). The twin towers of *Reef View Hotel* loom over the east beach complex, and the best view of the whole area is from one of its **external glass lifts**, which run up to penthouse level. To explore the island, you can rent a motorized dinghy from the marina ($90 per half-day) or a golf buggy from opposite the ferry terminal ($55 for 2 hr) to ride around the residential roads twisting along the northern peninsula. The best option, though, is the well-used walking track to the 239-metre-high Passage

Island resort transfers to Hamilton, Daydream, *Long Island Resort* and South Molle are offered by Fantasea (℡07/4946 5111, ⓦwww.fantasea.com.au) and Cruise Whitsundays (℡07/4946 4662, ⓦwww.cruisewhitsundays.com.au); other resorts run their own transfers for guests only. Both companies also offer good-value **island-hopping day-cruises** where you get to do your own thing: Fantasea calls in at Daydream, Hamilton and Whitehaven Beach on Whitsunday ($134 includes buffet lunch on board), and Cruise Whitsundays visits Daydream, South Molle and Long Island ($79 boat only); alternatively, Voyager (℡1800 642 717; $130 including lunch, glass-bottom boat tour and snorkelling gear) offers a three-island cruise to Hook, Daydream and Whitehaven Beach. For **camping transfers** to National Parks campsites, contact Island Camping Connections (℡07/4946 9330) or Camping Whitsundays (℡07/4946 9330).

Day-cruises usually take in two or more islands, and offer the chance to experience the thrills of boom-netting – sitting in a large rope hammock stretched above the water at the front of the boat so that you can catch the full soaking force of the waves – and do some snorkelling; others may concentrate on a single theme, such as whale watching, fishing or lazing on Whitehaven Beach. **Multi-day cruises** cover much the same territory but at a slower pace, and may give sailing lessons. **Scuba diving** is also often available to certified divers on cruises, at wildly variable rates upwards of $60 a dive. Groups with yachting experience might consider a **bareboat charter** (see "Listings" on p.445 for operators).

The list below is not exhaustive; word of mouth is the best method of finding out about who is still in business, what the current deals are and if operators live up to their advertisements. Check the **length** of trips carefully – "three days" might mean one full day and two half-days – along with how much time is actually spent cruising and at the destination, how many other people will be on the cruise, and the size of the vessel. There are scores of beautiful boats, so you'll be swayed by your preference for a performance racing yacht or a fun trip with lots of deck space on which to lounge. Bear in mind that a cheerful (or jaded) crew can make all the difference, and that **weather conditions** can affect destinations offered. Many yachts also have poor environmental practices and pump waste directly into the sea, so it's wise to ask probing questions. Finally, if you want to save money, shop around as close to departure times as possible, when advertised prices tend to drop.

Day-trips

Sailing

The following cost $105–140.

Illusions ℡07/4946 5255, ⓦwww.illusions.net.au. Catamaran trip to Hayman's Blue Pearl Bay includes snorkelling, boom-netting and lunch.

Maxi Ragamuffin ℡1800 454 777, ⓦwww.maxiaction.com.au. This 24-metre-long racer runs to Blue Pearl Bay (Mon, Wed, Fri & Sat) and Whitehaven Beach (Thurs & Sun), with snorkelling and diving available. Lunch included.

Powered vessels

With the exception of *Ocean Rafting*, the following cost around $140, and include lunch unless otherwise stated.

Peak which offers the finest 360-degree panorama in the Whitsundays. Fantasea (see above) runs a day-trip here for $129 with lunch.

Lindeman Island suffered as a victim of feral goats, though their eradication has seen native plants making a comeback in a small melaleuca swamp and on the wooded northeast side. **Mount Oldfield** offers panoramic views, while other walking tracks lead to swimming beaches on the north shore. The family-oriented *Club Med* **resort** (℡1300 855 052, ⓦwww.clubmed.com.au; ⑨),

Mantaray ⊤07/4948 3711, ⓦwww.mantaraycharters.com. Fast and relatively roomy boat out to Whitehaven, where you spend around three hours at leisure before heading north to Mantaray Bay and some good snorkelling.

Ocean Rafting ⊤07/4946 6848, ⓦwww.oceanrafting.com. Great-value, action-packed cruise on a zippy inflatable to Whitehaven Beach, with options to visit either Hill Inlet or the Aboriginal caves at Nara Inlet ($109). Maximum 25 passengers.

Reefjet ⊤07/4946 5366, ⓦwww.reefjet.com.au. Fast run out to Whitehaven Beach and Hook Island for snorkelling or diving.

Whitehaven Express ⊤07/4946 7172, ⓦwww.whitehavenxpress.com.au. Trips to Whitsunday Island, stopping for scenery at Hill Inlet before a snorkel and beach BBQ at Whitehaven.

Longer trips

The following cost $360–500 for two-night, three-day outings; trips depart at around 9am from Abel Point Marina, returning on day three about 4pm. The basic itinerary is to visit Hook Island via Nara Inlet, then move round to Whitehaven Beach on Whitsunday. There are two major sailboat companies in town, fronting for the majority of vessels: **Oz Adventure Sailing** (⊤1300 653 100, ⓦwww.ozsailing.com.au) specializes in classic tall and vintage-style ships, while **Southern Cross** (⊤07/4946 4999, ⓦwww.soxsail.com.au) puts the emphasis on maxi-yacht racers.

Anaconda III ⊤1800 677 119, ⓦwww.airliebeach.com. The largest party yacht in the Whitsundays, taking up to fifty passengers, and fantastically comfortable. Relatively expensive, but you do get three full days and three nights aboard.

Avatar ⊤1800 607 050, ⓦwww.ozsail.com.au. Slick trimaran with majestic speed and spacious lounging. Maximum of 22 passengers.

Derwent Hunter (Oz Adventure Sailing). Ninety-foot schooner built in 1945 and totally refitted with timber decking and fittings after years spent as a research vessel and a film set, and yet more time engaged in dubious activities in the South China Seas.

Pacific Sunrise (Oz Adventure Sailing). Beautiful, classic 33-metre wooden ketch with eight rather plush a/c cabins.

Pegasus ⊤07/4946 4777, ⓦwww.tallarookdive.com.au. Leisurely lugger with a lively reputation, spacious sun decks with some of the cheapest prices plus diving.

Siska (Southern Cross). A 25-metre ocean maxi-yacht with room for twenty passengers, and winner of races between the UK and Australia.

Southern Cross (Southern Cross). The company's flagship: a high-speed, 21-metre-long America's Cup challenger accommodating fourteen passengers, aimed at couples.

Waltzing Matilda (Oz Adventure Sailing). A more modern design than most of Oz Adventure Sailing's fleet, this eighteen-metre ketch is not that roomy, but has a great atmosphere.

Australia's first, has all the services you'd expect including a golf course. You can visit on a day-trip (⊤07 4946 9333; $95 includes lunch but not transfers) with access to all resort activities, catching the first Fantasea ferry from Shute Harbour via Hamilton Island, arriving at Club Med around 9.45am. The ferry returns to Shute Harbour at 12.15pm, so to take full advantage of the day-trip price and buffet lunch you'll need to arrange a helicopter or water taxi to pick you up from the resort later in the afternoon.

Bowen and the route to Townsville

BOWEN, a quiet seafront settlement 60km northwest of Proserpine, was once under consideration as the site of the state capital, but it floundered after Townsville's foundation. Overlooked and undeveloped, the wide sleepy streets and historic clapboard buildings made Bowen's town centre the perfect film-set location for the 2008 Baz Luhrmann epic, *Australia*, standing in as 1930s Darwin. Nothing remains from the mass Hollywood intrusion except for the many tales of almost every resident whose world was briefly turned upside down. Stark first impressions created by the sterile bulk of the saltworks on the highway are offset by a certain small-town charm and some pretty beaches just off to the north. The main attraction for travellers, though, is the prospect of seasonal **farm work**: Bowen's mangoes and tomatoes are famous throughout Queensland, and there's a large floating population of itinerant pickers in town between April and January. The backpackers' hostels (see below) can help with finding work, though nothing is guaranteed.

Bowen's attractive **beaches** lie a couple of kilometres north of the town centre. **Queens Beach**, which faces north, is sheltered, long and has a stinger net for the jellyfish season, but the best is **Horseshoe Bay**, small, and hemmed in by some sizeable boulders, with good waters for a swim or snorkel – though the construction of an oversized resort nearby threatens to ruin the atmosphere.

If you're looking for work, try the ranch-style *Bogie River Bush House* (℡07/4785 3407, ⑩www.bogiebushhouse.com.au; dorms $17.50, rooms ❹), about 60km inland from town towards Collinsville. This splendid retreat has a pool and offers the chance to go horseriding, fishing, or to play with tame wildlife in your spare time.

Bowen practicalities

Bowen's centre overlooks **Edgecumbe Bay**, with all the shops and services spaced out along broad but empty **Herbert Street**. The **train station** is a few kilometres west of town near the highway, while **buses** stop outside Bowen Travel (℡07/4786 2835), just off Herbert on Williams Street, which can organize tickets for both.

Budget **accommodation** – which should be booked in advance and is usually offered at weekly rates to potential farm workers – consists of *Bowen Backpackers*, at the beach end of Herbert Street (℡07/4786 3433, ⓔbowenbackpackers @bigpond.com; sometimes closes Feb–March; dorms $23.50, rooms ❷), with a huge pool out the back; and *Reefers by the Beach* at 93 Horseshoe Bay Rd (℡07/4786 4199, ⑩www.reefers.com.au; dorms $30, rooms ❶), a spacious place with a pool located 3km from town near the beaches. **Mid-range** choices include *Castle Motor Lodge*, 6 Don St (℡07/4786 1322, ⑩www.castlemotor-lodge.com.au; ❺), about the closest option to the centre of town, or *Queens Beach Motor Hotel* (℡07/4785 1555, ⑩www.queensbeachmotorhotel.com.au; ❸), north of town and overlooking Queens Beach. You can **eat** at the *Grand View Hotel*, down near the Harbour Office on Herbert, or *Moody Blues*, on the corner of Herbert and George streets; alternatively, stock up at Magee's **supermarket** on Williams Street and at the town's numerous fruit and vegetable stalls.

The Burdekin River, Ayr and the Yongala

Further on up the highway, 115km past Bowen, are the towns of **Home Hill** and **Ayr**, separated by a mill, a few kilometres of canefields and the iron framework of the **Burdekin River Bridge**. The river, one of the north's most famous landmarks, is still liable to flood during severe wet seasons, despite having to fight its way across three weirs and a dam. On the northern side, **AYR** is a compact farming town fast becoming another popular stop on the **farm work** trail. The highway – which runs through town as Queen Street – is where you'll find the **bus stop** and all essential services, as well as two workers' hostels which can find you employment picking and packing capsicums, amongst other things – *Ayr Backpackers*, on Willmington Street (☎07/4783 5837; phone in advance for pick-up; dorms $110 per week; single nights only available outside of the fruit-picking season and on special request), is definitely the better option.

Ayr's other attraction is easy access to the wreck of the **Yongala**, a 109-metre-long passenger ship which sank with all hands during a cyclone in 1911. It now lies intact and encrusted in coral in 18–30m of water, and is home to turtles, rays, moray eels and huge schools of barracuda, mackerel and trevally, making for a staggeringly good **wreck dive**. *Yongala Dive*, out from Ayr at 56 Narrah St, Alva Beach (☎07/4783 1519, ⓦwww.yongaladive .com.au; dorms $27, rooms ❷), runs trips for **certified divers only** from $220, including all gear rental, pick-up from town, and two dives. It also has very comfortable **accommodation** if you plan to stay overnight. Be aware that the wreck is in an exposed location, and it's not much fun diving here if the weather is rough; this is also a demanding site – deep, with strong currents and startlingly big fish – and it's best not to go unless you've logged twenty dives or more.

Townsville

Hot and stuffy **TOWNSVILLE** sprawls around a broad spit of land between the isolated hump of Castle Hill and swampy Ross Creek. Industrial in make-up, the town has a rough edge and an air of racial tension, a hangover of the riots that broke out on Palm Island in 2004 after an Aboriginal man died in police custody; reports of stabbings, predominantly by belligerent out-of-towners hanging around Flinders Mall after dark, now appear in the news on an almost weekly basis. Whilst most travellers skip town altogether and head straight out to the beaches of laid-back **Magnetic Island**, just offshore, the city does have its moments: there's a visible maritime history; long sea views from the Strand promenade; and the muggy, salty evening air and old pile houses on the surrounding hills which mark out Townsville as the coast's first really tropical city.

Townsville was founded in 1864 by John Melton Black and Robert Towns, entrepreneurs who felt that a settlement was needed for northern stockmen who couldn't reach Bowen when the Burdekin River was in flood. Despite an inferior harbour, the town soon outstripped Bowen in terms of both size and prosperity, its growth accelerated by **gold** finds inland at Ravenswood and Charters Towers (see p.540). Today, it's the gateway to the far north and transit point for routes west to Mount Isa and the Northern Territory; it's also an important military centre, seat of a university and home to substantial Torres Strait Islander and Aboriginal communities.

Arrival and information

Townsville's roughly triangular city centre is hemmed in by Cleveland Bay to the north, Ross Creek to the south and Castle Hill to the west. Following the north

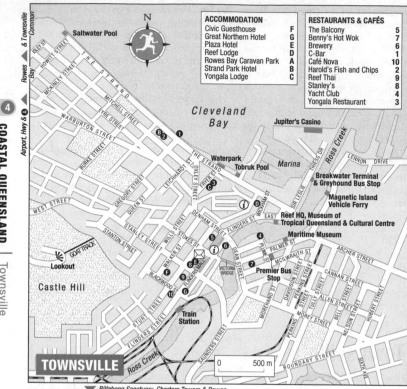

ACCOMMODATION
Civic Guesthouse   F
Great Northern Hotel   G
Plaza Hotel   E
Reef Lodge   D
Rowes Bay Caravan Park   A
Strand Park Hotel   B
Yongala Lodge   C

RESTAURANTS & CAFÉS
The Balcony   5
Benny's Hot Wok   7
Brewery   6
C-Bar   1
Café Nova   10
Harold's Fish and Chips   2
Reef Thai   9
Stanley's   8
Yacht Club   4
Yongala Restaurant   3

Billabong Sanctuary, Charters Towers & Bowen

bank of Ross Creek, **Flinders Street** is the main drag, sectioned into a downtown pedestrian mall before running its last five hundred metres as **Flinders Street East**. The **train station** is central, just southwest of the centre along Flinders Street; the **airport** is 5km northwest of town, served by a shuttle bus ($10 single, $18 return; book in advance on ☎07/4775 5544). Virgin Blue flies to town from Brisbane, and Jetstar and Qantas from everywhere else. At the moment there are **two long-distance bus stops**: Premier (☎13 34 10) pull in on the south side of Ross Creek on Palmer Street, with a short walk across a bridge to the city centre; Greyhound (☎13 14 19) stop north of the centre outside the Magnetic Island Breakwater ferry terminal on Sir Leslie Theiss Drive.

Public transport serves the suburbs rather than the sights, though much of what there is to see is central; some hostels have **bikes** available. A very helpful **information booth**, with a separate counter handling and booking diving, cruises and tours, is located in Flinders Street Mall (daily 9am–5pm).

Accommodation

Lodgings are concentrated around the city centre and might collect you from transit points if you call ahead.

Civic Guesthouse 262 Walker St ☎1800 646 619, ⓦwww.civicguesthouse.com. Clean and helpful backpackers' with a well-equipped kitchen, spa pool and free Friday-night BBQs. Deals on dive courses with Ocean Dive next door. Dorms $24, rooms ➋

Great Northern Hotel Corner of Flinders and Blackwood sts ☎07/4771 6191. The downstairs bar in this old Queenslander pub has lots of character, and serves huge meals from $10. Rooms are rather tired in appearance, though, and have shared facilities. ❸
Plaza Hotel Corner of Flinders and Stanley sts ☎07/4772 1888, ⓦwww.leisureinnhotels.com.au. Downtown, motel-like apartments; modern, friendly and with a bit more panache than the average hotel. ❺
Reef Lodge 4–6 Wickham St ☎07/4721 1112, ⓦwww.reeflodge.com.au. The cheapest place in town, and friendly enough with all facilities including a women-only dorm, though a bit cramped. Dorms $21, rooms ❷
Rowes Bay Caravan Park Heatley Parade ☎07/4771 3576, ⓦwww.rowesbaycp.com.au. Off

The Strand, 3km north of the centre towards Pallarenda, overlooking Magnetic Island across the bay; take bus #7 from the mall. Very popular cabins and campsites, so worth booking in advance. Camping $23, powered sites $29, cabins (with or without en suite) ❸–❹
Strand Park Hotel 59–60 The Strand ☎07/4750 7888, ⓦwww.strandparkhotel.com.au. Small boutique motel in Townsville's prettiest area, offering self-contained double rooms and suites with either garden or sea views. Rooms ❺–❼
Yongala Lodge 11 Fryer St ☎07/4772 4633, ⓦwww.historicyongala.com.au. A welcoming place, named after the city's most famous shipwreck, with spacious if slightly shabby motel rooms joined to a historic old Queenslander with original furnishings. ❺

The City and around

Funded by inland gold mines during the late nineteenth century, some of Townsville's solid stone colonial buildings are quite imposing, especially along Flinders Street East. On the corner of the Mall and Denham Street, the **Perc Tucker Art Gallery** (Mon–Fri 10am–5pm, Sat & Sun 10am–2pm; free) is another grand old building, featuring travelling exhibitions of mainly antique art. On Sunday (8.30am–1pm), the Mall itself hosts **Cotters Market**, which has good local produce and crafts.

Castle Hill looms over the city centre, an obvious target if you're after clear views of the region. There's a road to the top from Stanley Street; on foot, head along Gregory Street to Stanton Terrace and join a walking path of sorts that climbs to the lookout, for vistas over the city to the distant Hervey Range and Magnetic Island.

The Strand runs northwest along Cleveland Bay, lined with more old houses and fig trees looking out to Magnetic Island. The busy waterfront strip here is a beautiful stretch of palms, beach, shady lawns and free hotplates for picnics, plus cafés, a swimming pool and excellent **children's waterpark**, plus a specially built jetty for fishing. Off the eastern end of the road along Sir Leslie Theiss Drive, you'll find the Magnetic Island Breakwater ferry terminal, a **marina** (where most dive-trips depart) and the adjacent **Jupiter's Casino** – once the only legal gaming venue in Queensland.

The Reef HQ, Museum of Tropical Queensland and Cultural Centre

The **Reef HQ**, on Flinders Street East (daily 9.30am–5pm; aquarium $24.75, IMAX theatre $14), houses a terrific aquarium and **IMAX theatre** (hourly shows), which projects films with a popular science theme onto a domed ceiling to create an overwhelming, wraparound image. The huge live tanks in the **aquarium** contain recreations of the reef, where you can watch schools of fish drifting over coral, clown fish hiding inside anemones' tentacles and myopic turtles cruising past. Between the main tanks are smaller ones for oddities – sea snakes, deep-sea nautiluses, baby turtles and lobsters. Upstairs, videos about the reef are shown, and you can handle some inoffensive invertebrates including tiny clams, sea slugs and starfish. In the same building, the **Cultural Centre**

The Bounty and the Pandora

In 1788, the British Admiralty vessel **Bounty** sailed from England to Tahiti, with a mission to collect **breadfruit** seedlings, intended to provide a cheap source of food for Britain's plantation slaves in the West Indies. But the stay in Tahiti's mellow climate proved so much better than life on board the *Bounty* that on the return journey in April 1789 the crew **mutinied**, led by the officer **Fletcher Christian**. Along with eighteen crew who refused to join in the mutiny, **Captain William Bligh** was set adrift in a longboat far out in the Pacific, while the mutineers returned to Tahiti, intending to settle there.

Things didn't go as planned, however. After an incredible feat of navigation over 3600 nautical miles of open sea, Bligh and all but one of his companions reached the Portuguese colony of Timor in June, emaciated but still alive, from where Bligh lost no time in catching a vessel back to England, arriving there in March 1790. His report on the mutiny immediately saw the Admiralty dispatch the frigate **Pandora** off to Tahiti under the cold-hearted **Captain Edwards**, with instructions to bring back the mutineers to stand trial in London.

Meanwhile in Tahiti, Christian and seven of the mutiny's ringleaders – knowing that sooner or later the Admiralty would try to find them – had, along with a group of Tahitians, taken the *Bounty* and sailed off into the Pacific. Fourteen of the *Bounty*'s crew stayed behind on Tahiti, however, and when the *Pandora* arrived there in March 1791, they were rounded up, clapped in chains and incarcerated in the ship's brig, a three-metre-long wooden cell known as **"Pandora's Box"**.

Having spent a fruitless few months island-hopping in search of the *Bounty*, Captain Edwards headed up the east coast of Australia where, on the night of August 29, the *Pandora* hit a northern section of the Great Barrier Reef. As waves began to break up the vessel on the following day, Edwards ordered the longboats to be loaded with supplies and abandoned the ship, leaving his prisoners still locked up on board; it was only thanks to one of the crew that ten of them managed to scramble out as the *Pandora* slid beneath the waves.

In a minor replay of Bligh's voyage, the *Pandora*'s survivors took three weeks to make it to Timor in their longboats, and arrived back in England the following year. Edwards was castigated for the heartless treatment of his prisoners, but otherwise held blameless for the wreck. The ten surviving mutineers were court-martialled: four were acquitted, three hanged, and three had their death sentences commuted. Captain Bligh was later made Governor of New South Wales, where he suffered another mutiny known as the **"Rum Rebellion"** (see "History", p.1122). To add insult to injury, the *Bounty*'s whole project proved a failure; when breadfruit trees were eventually introduced to the West Indies, the slaves refused to eat them.

Seventeen years later, the American vessel *Topaz* stopped mid-Pacific at the isolated rocky fastness of **Pitcairn Island** and, to the amazement of its crew, found it settled by a small colony of English-speaking people. These turned out to be the descendants of the *Bounty* mutineers, along with the last survivor, the elderly **John Adams** (also known as Alexander Smith). Adams told the *Topaz*'s crew that, having settled Pitcairn and burned the *Bounty*, the mutineers had fought with the Tahitian men over the women, and that Christian and all the men – except Adams and three other mutineers – had been killed. The other three had since died, leaving only Adams, the women, and their children on the island. After Adams' death, Pitcairn's population was briefly moved to Norfolk Island in the 1850s (see p.300), where some settled, though many of their descendants returned and still live on Pitcairn.

helps promote indigenous artwork, particularly from the Torres Islands, and its walls act as a gallery for paintings and craft for sale.

Next door, an innovative building houses the **Museum of Tropical Queensland** (daily 9.30am–5pm; $12), which showcases the Queensland Museum's marine archeology collection. The centrepiece is a full-sized, cut-away replica – figurehead and all – of the front third of the **Pandora**, a British frigate tied up in the tale of the **Bounty mutiny**, which sank on the outer reef in 1791 (see box, p.456 for the full tale). Accompanying artefacts salvaged off the wreck since its discovery in 1977 include water jars and bottles, tankards owned by the crew, and the surgeon's pocket watch, with glass face and finely chased gold and silver mountings. Dioramas recreate life on board, with views into the captain's cramped cabin and a dramatic reconstruction of the sinking, while a life-sized blueprint of the *Pandora*'s upper deck is mapped out on the carpet. You can also join in the twice-daily "Running Out the Gun", the loading and mock firing of a replica cannon from the *Pandora*. Other sections of the museum cover Outback Queensland's extensive **fossil finds** (including several life-sized dinosaur models).

Townsville Common and Billabong Sanctuary

The **Townsville Common Conservation Park** (daily 6.30am–6.30pm; free) is 6.5km north of the centre, on the coast at **Pallarenda**. The Bohle River pools into wetlands below the Many Peaks Range, a habitat perfect for wildfowl including the brolga, the stately symbol of the northern marshes. Less popular – with rice farmers anyway – are the huge flocks of magpie geese that visit after rains and are a familiar sight over the city. You need a vehicle to reach the park, but once there you can get about on foot, although a car or bike makes short work of the less interesting tracks between lagoons. Camouflaged **hides** at Long Swamp and Pink Lily Lagoon let you clock up a few of the hundred or more bird species in the park: egrets stalk frogs around waterlilies, ibises and spoonbills strain the water for edibles and geese honk at each other, undisturbed by the low-flying airport traffic – bring binoculars.

Seventeen kilometres south of Townsville on the highway, **Billabong Sanctuary** (daily 8am–5pm; $28; Ⓦ www.billabongsanctuary.com.au) is a well-kept collection of penned and wild Australian fauna laid out around a large waterhole. Amongst the free-ranging wildlife you'll find wallabies and flocks of demanding whistling ducks on the prowl for handouts; animals you'll probably be happier to see are caged include saltwater crocs, cassowaries (bred for release into the wild), dingoes, wedge-tailed eagles and snakes. A swimming pool and accompanying snack-bar make the sanctuary a fine place to spend a few hours, and you can also tour the grounds with an Aboriginal guide and get an introduction to bush foods.

Eating, drinking and entertainment

There are plenty of good **eating** options in Townsville, with restaurants grouped in three main areas: in the centre on Flinders Street; south on Palmer Street; and out along The Strand. For evening **entertainment**, many of the town's hotels cater to the sizeable military and student presence and have regular live music, for which you might have to pay a cover charge.

Cafés and restaurants

The Balcony 287 Flinders St Mall. Mediterranean-style salads and grills, good coffee and cakes, and a great view over the mall from upper-storey balcony tables. Mains around $18.

Benny's Hot Wok Palmer St, South Townsville. Stylish and popular Singaporean and Asian café-restaurant, with tasty bowls of noodle soup for around $20, and Indonesian or Thai curries for about $23.

Brewery Corner of Denham and Flinders sts. Café, bar and boutique brewery housed in the old post-office building. You can sample each of the six in-house beers for $7. The ambience is good, although the outdoor tables are a bit noisy thanks to the adjacent main road.

C-Bar The Strand. One of several café-restaurants in the area, right on the seafront with outside tables and a bar overlooking Magnetic Island. Good for anything from a coffee or beer to succulent char-grilled steak or lamb kebabs and salad. Mains around $25.

Café Nova Corner of Blackwood and Flinders sts, near the station. Long-running student venue, with generous helpings and meals, including tasty salads, for under $12. Tues–Thurs 10.30am–10.30pm, Fri & Sat 10.30am–11.30pm.

Harold's Fish and Chips The Strand, opposite *C-Bar*. If you can't catch your own from the nearby fishing jetty, console yourself with a takeaway from this excellent establishment.

Reef Thai 455 Flinders St. Seafood green curry, satays and a chilli-packed beef dish known as "crying tiger". Mains under $20. Daily 5.30–10pm.

Stanley's Corner of Flinders and Stanley sts. Airy café and bistro serving early breakfasts, pasta, ornate sandwiches and grills.

Yacht Club Plume St, South Townsville. Hearty, bistro-style meals including chicken and wild mushroom or roast of the day for $15, but the main reason to come here is to enjoy the views from the waterfront deck. Closed Mon & Tues.

Yongala Restaurant 11 Fryer St, in front of the *Yongala Lodge*. Historic, authentically furnished surroundings where you can enjoy live music and good, Greek-influenced food. Appropriately, the building's architect was on board the *Yongala* when it sank.

Pubs, bars and clubs

Bully's Flinders St East. Tamest of the town's rowdy clubs, with DJs playing dance music at weekends and theme nights Tues to Thurs.

Exchange Hotel Flinders St East. This pub is a real locals' watering hole, with occasional live bands.

Heritage Bar Flinders St East. Fashionable wine bar playing frisky music till 2am and serving delicious oyster snacks.

Molly Malones Flinders St East. Standard Irish bar with stout on tap, some pavement tables and live bands Wed–Sat. Closed Sun.

Listings

Banks All located on Flinders St Mall, and there are ATMs in most pubs.

Bookshops Mary Who?, at 414 Flinders St, has a fine range of just about everything.

Car rental Independent (☏07/4725 2771, ⓦwww.independentrentals.com.au) has basic models from $35 a day.

Hospital Townsville General Hospital, Angus Smith Drive, 15min southwest of city centre beside James Cook University ☏07/4796 1111.

Internet At Internet Den, 265 Flinders St Mall ($3–4 per hr).

Police 30 Stanley St ☏07/4760 7777.

Post office Behind Flinders St Mall on Sturt St, near the junction with Stanley St.

Taxi There's a stand at Flinders St Mall ☏13 10 08.

Tours Detours (☏07/4728 5311, ⓦwww .detourcoaches.com) run day-tours to the old gold-mining town of Charters Towers ($115) and rainforest at Paluma ($98); Kookaburra (☏0448 794 798, ⓦwww.kookaburratours.com.au) provides city tours ($40) most days and visits Wallaman Falls ($125) on Thurs; whilst Hidden Valley (☏1800 466 509, ⓦwww.hiddenvalleytours.com.au) has two- and three-day overnight tours visiting Paluma, Mt Fox Crater and Wallaman Falls (from $279).

Diving and reef trips from Townsville

The main diving attraction out from Townsville is the *Yongala* shipwreck (see p.456), though there's also access to the local stretch of the Barrier Reef. For **reef day-trips**, the best option is *Sunsea* (☏07/4726 0800, ⓦwww.sunferries.com.au; $260 including 2 dives), a big tourist catamaran which runs to John Brewer Reef. For the **Yongala**, Adrenaline (☏07/4724 0600, ⓦwww.adrenalinedive.com.au) runs day-trips ($240 including 2 dives), while Prodive (☏07/4721 1760, ⓦwww.prodivetownsville.com.au; $210 including 2 dives) also offers three-day live-aboard trips including both the *Yongala* and Barrier Reef ($720).

Magnetic Island

Another island named by Captain Cook in 1770 – after his compass played up as he sailed past – **Magnetic Island** is a beautiful triangular granite core 12km from Townsville. There's a lot to be said for a trip here: lounging on a beach, swimming over coral, bouncing around in a moke from one roadside lookout to another, and enjoying the sea breeze and the island's vivid colours. Small enough to drive around in half a day, but large enough to harbour several small settlements, Magnetic Island's accommodation and transfer costs are considerably lower than on many of Queensland's other islands, and if you've ever wanted to spot a **koala** in the wild, this could be your chance – they're often seen wedged into gum trees up in the northeast corner of the island.

Seen from the sea, the island's apex, **Mount Cook**, hovers above eucalypt woods variegated with patches of darker green vine forest. The north and east coasts are pinched into shallow **sandy bays** punctuated by granite headlands and coral reefs, while the western part of the island is flatter and edged with mangroves. A little less than half the island is designated as national park, with the settlements of **Picnic Bay**, **Nelly Bay**, **Arcadia** and **Horseshoe Bay** dotted along the east coast. Shops and supplies are available on the island, so there's no need to bring anything with you.

Arrival and island transport

Two ferries operate between Townsville and Magnetic Island. **Sunferries** leaves from the Breakwater terminal on Sir Leslie Theiss Drive for the twenty-minute ride across to the marina at Nelly Bay, midway along the east coast, at least sixteen times daily ($29 return; ☎07/4726 0800); pick up a **timetable** from any information booth. There's no need to book, just buy a ticket at the jetty and hop on board. The **car ferry** is operated by Fantasea ($156 return for a car and up to three passengers, pedestrians $24 return; ☎07/4772 5422, ⓦwww.fantaseacruisingmagnetic.com.au), also heading to Nelly Bay at least seven times daily from Ross Street, at the end of Palmer Street on the south bank of the creek in Townsville.

Magnetic Island has 35km of road, including a dirt track to West Point and a sealed stretch between Picnic and Horseshoe bays. **Magnetic Island Bus Service** (☎07/4778 5130) meets all Sunferries and runs between Picnic Bay and Horseshoe Bay more or less hourly between 6.35am and 9.10pm with late services to 12.40am on weekends; its day-pass ($6.20) allows unlimited travel and can be purchased from the bus driver or at the visitor centre in the Nelly Bay Ferry Terminal. For your **own transport**, Moke Magnetic at Nelly Bay (☎07/4778 5377, ⓦwww.mokemagnetic.com) rents out fun mini-mokes for a flat $73 a day including 60km of fuel plus $200 deposit, while Tropical Topless (☎07/4758 1111), across the car park from the same ferry terminal, charges $78 a day including 40km of fuel; both require a minimum driver age of 21, and ask that you stick to sealed roads. Some accommodation options rent out **bicycles** for about $15 a day, as does Island Bike (☎0425 244 193), which delivers anywhere on the island.

Accommodation

Magnetic Island's **accommodation** is ubiquitous, with options for all budgets. Most lodgings have internet access, rent out snorkelling gear, bikes, beach gear and watersports equipment, can make tour bookings and might pick you up if you call in advance. If you're looking for something more intimate, try one of the many holiday homes around the island promoted by Best of Magnetic (☎07/4778 5955, [W]www.bestofmagnetic.com; [5]–[9]).

Picnic Bay and Nelly Bay

Base Backpackers 1 Nelly Bay Rd ☎1800 242 273, [W]www.basebackpackers.com. Large, modern backpackers' with a lively atmosphere, large pool, bar and DJ, situated at the secluded southern end of Nelly Beach. It has excellent facilities, and there's a restaurant serving cheap meals. Dorms $26, female-only dorm $30, doubles [5]

Beachside Palms 7 Esplanade, Nelly Bay ☎04/1966 0078, [W]www.magnetic-island-qld.com. Four clean and spacious one- and two-bed apartments facing the beach, with pool and laundry facilities. [5]

Segara Villas 20 Mango Parkway, Nelly Bay ☎07/4778 5151, [W]www.segara.com.au. Three beautiful Balinese-style villas with polished wooden floors, set around a pool amidst tropical gardens. [7]

Travellers Backpackers 32 Picnic St, Picnic Bay ☎1800 000 290, [W]www.travellersbackpackers.com. Low-key budget accommodation boasting converted motel units with a/c, one street back from the beach at Picnic Bay. Dorms $24, doubles [3]

Arcadia

Arcadia Beach Guest House 27 Marine Parade ☎07/4778 5668, [W]www.arcadiabeachguesthouse.com.au. Nautically themed modern units with a slightly quirky touch; the pricier units are aimed at the "romantic-getaway" market. [3]–[6]

Foresthaven 11–13 Cook Rd ☎07/4778 5153. Self-contained apartments with pool and tropical garden backing onto national park; it also offers dorms, though it's not primarily a backpackers'. Dorms $20, doubles [2]–[4]

Horseshoe Bay

Bungalow Bay YHA 40 Horseshoe Bay Rd ☎07/4778 5577, [W]www.bungalowbay.com.au. Quiet retreat with cabin accommodation in a large wooded setting with pool, restaurant, large kitchen and a campsite about ten minutes' walk to the beach. The owner feeds hundreds of wild lorikeets every afternoon. Camping $12.50 per person, dorms $28, rooms [3]

Sails 13 Pacific Drive ☎07/4778 5117, [W]www.sailsonhorseshoe.com.au. Self-contained apartments with a full range of modern amenities, including pool and outdoor BBQ area, at the quiet end of Horseshoe Bay. One-bedroom apartments [8], villas [9]

The island

Set on the southernmost tip of the island at the end of the sealed road, **PICNIC BAY** is a languid spot, well shaded by surrounding gum woodland and beach-front fig trees. The tiny settlement faces a nice beach with views back towards Townsville and a wooden pier protruding over the ocean which once served as

Magnetic Island tours and excursions

For a **tour** of the island, plump for a day out in a 4WD with Tropicana (☎07/4758 1800, [W]www.tropicanatours.com.au; $198); the cost seems steep, but you'll be very well fed and looked after, plus you'll see just about all the island's beaches and bays. You could also spend a day **sailing** to hard-to-reach beaches and bays with Jazza (☎04/0487 5530, [W]www.jazza.com.au; $95), including snorkelling, lunch and afternoon tea; or try your hand at **sea-kayaking** with Magnetic Island Sea Kayaks (☎07/4778 5424, [W]www.seakayak.com.au; $69 guided tour or $55 per day for single kayak rental).

Relatively murky waters don't make Magnetic Island the most dramatic place to learn to **scuba dive**, but with easy shore access it's very cheap – certification courses start at $299 – and on a good day there's some fair coral, a couple of small shipwrecks and decent fish-life. Pleasure Divers (☎1800 797 797, [W]www.pleasuredivers.com.au) run dive courses, snorkelling tours and can also arrange dives to the *Yongala* for experienced divers (see p.453).

the island's ferry terminal before it was relocated to Nelly Bay, but there's little to do here.

Moving up the east coast, **NELLY BAY** is thriving thanks to the modern marina complex and ferry terminal, and comprises a sprawl of houses fronted by a good beach, with a little reef some way out. Two streets back is a shopping complex with a supermarket and a couple of places to eat, while a rather poky **aquarium** (daily 9.30am–4.30pm; $3), just around the corner on Elena Street, has tank-loads of giant clams, some weighing up to 85kg, as well as coral and reef fish displays. Alternatively, there's a **walking track to Arcadia** from here, though it can be hot work – start early and take plenty of water. A little further along the coast, **ARCADIA** surrounds Geoffrey Bay and counts the good-value *Banister's Seafood Restaurant* at 22 McCabe Crescent among its attractions. At Arcadia's northern end is the perfect swimming beach of **Alma Bay**, hemmed in by cliffs and boulders, and with good snorkelling over the coral just offshore. A **walking track** from the end of Cook Road leads towards Mount Cook and the track to Nelly Bay, or up to Sphinx Lookout for sea views. At dawn or dusk you might see the diminutive island **rock wallaby** on an outcrop or boulder near Arcadia's jetty.

North of Arcadia the road forks, with the right branch (prohibited to rental vehicles) leading via tiny **Florence Bay** – one of the prettiest on the island – to Radical Bay, and the main road carrying on to Horseshoe. Leave your car at the junction here and continue uphill on foot to **the Forts**, built during World War II to protect Townsville from attack by the Japanese. The walking track climbs gently for about 1.5km through gum-tree scenery to gun emplacements (now just deserted blockhouses) set one above the other among granite boulders and pine trees. The best views are from the slit windows at the command centre, right at the pinnacle of the hill. The woods below the Forts are the best place to see **koalas**, introduced to the island in 1930. They sleep during the day, so tracking them down involves plenty of wandering around – although if you hear ferocious pig-like grunts and squeals, then some lively koalas are not far away.

Horseshoe Bay and around

The road ends in the north at **HORSESHOE BAY** on the island's longest and busiest beach, half of which is developed and half of which remains blissfully secluded, with views north beyond the bobbing yachts to distant Palm Island. The cluster of shops at the road's eastern end features a general store and bakery, and there's a decent craft market on the last Sunday of every month. Places **to eat** include the quaint *Ferrari's Restaurant*, which serves excellent seafood, and the more flamboyant *Marlin Bar and Grill* with cheap steaks, several beers on tap and cocktails by the jug. The beach, which is good for swimming most of the year, is also a great place for activities – several beachfront operators **rent** out jet skis, kayaks, surf skis and boats, and provide joyrides on inflated tubes and water-skis. Other diversions include **horse rides** with the experienced Bluey's Horseshoe Ranch ($90 for the popular 2hr beach ride, $120 for a half-day ride; both depart 9am or 3pm, advance bookings necessary on ☏07/4778 5109). **Walking tracks** lead over the headland to Radical Bay by way of tiny **Balding Bay**, arguably the nicest on the island; you can spend a perfect day here snorkelling around the coral gardens just offshore and cooking on the hotplate provided. **Radical Bay** itself is another pretty spot, half a kilometre of sandy beach sandwiched between two huge, pine-covered granite fists.

Townsville to Cairns

Just an hour to the north of Townsville the arid landscape that has predominated since Bundaberg transforms into dark green plateaus shrouded in cloud. There's superlative scenery at **Wallaman Falls**, inland from **Ingham**, and also near Cairns as the slopes of the coastal mountains rise up to front the **Bellenden Ker Range**. Forests here once formed a continuous belt but, though logging has thinned them to a disjointed necklace of national parks, it still seems that almost every side-track off the highway leads to a waterhole or falls surrounded by jungle – this is where it really pays to have your own vehicle. There's also a handful of **islands** to explore, including the wilds of **Hinchinbrook**, as well as the **Mission Beach** area between **Tully** and **Innisfail**, where you might find regular work on fruit plantations or further opportunities to slump on the sand.

Paluma and Jourama Falls

The change in climate starts some 60km north of Townsville, where the Mount Spec road turns west off the highway and climbs a crooked 21km into the hills to **Paluma** township. Halfway there, a solid stone bridge, built by relief labour during the Great Depression of the 1930s, spans **Little Crystal Creek**, with some picnic tables and barbecue hotplates by the road, and deep swimming holes overshadowed by rainforest just up from the bridge – beware of slippery rocks and potentially strong currents. Look out too for large, metallic-blue **Ulysses butterflies** bobbing around the canopy.

PALUMA itself consists of a handful of weatherboard cottages in the rainforest at the top of the range. A couple of **walking tracks** from the town (from 500m to 2km in length) take you into the gloom, including a ridgetop track to Witt's Lookout. Keep your eyes open for **chowchillas**, plump little birds with a dark body and white front which forage by kicking the leaf litter sideways; you'll also hear whipbirds and the snarls of the black-and-blue **Victoria riflebird**, a bird of paradise – they're fairly common in highland rainforest between here and the Atherton Tablelands, but elusive. You can stay at the *Rainforest Inn* (☎07/4770 8688; ❻), which is primarily a restaurant (closed Tues) but has comfy motel rooms at the back; or self-contained cabins at *Paluma Rainforest Cottages* (☎07/4770 8520, ⓦwww.palumarainforest.com.au; ❻).

Past Paluma the range descends west, leaving the dark, wet coastal forest for open gum woodland. *Hidden Valley Cabins* (☎07/4770 8088, ⓦwww.hidden valleycabins.com.au; ❹–❻), 24km beyond Paluma on a dirt road near Running River, provides a spa, pool, beer, meals and packed lunches. Nearby is **the Gorge**, a lively section of river with falls, rapids and pools – drive down in a 4WD or walk the last kilometre.

Back on the coastal highway heading north, you pass the **Frosty Mango roadhouse** (daily 8am–6pm), whose exotic fresh cakes and ice creams are made from locally grown fruit, before encountering more aquatic fun at **Jourama Falls**, accessed west off the highway down a six-kilometre part-asphalt road. This ends at a low-key **National Parks campsite** (book on ☎13 13 04 or at ⓦwww.epa.qld.gov.au) set amongst gum and wattle bushland peppered with huge **cycads** (see box, p.495). From here an hour-long walking track follows chains across the rocky riverbed to more swimming holes surrounded by gigantic granite boulders and cliffs, finally winding up at the falls themselves – which are impressive in full flood but fairly insignificant by the end of the dry season.

Ingham and around

Home to Australia's largest Italian community, the small town of **INGHAM**, 110km north of Townsville, is well placed for trips inland to **Girringun National Park** – home to Australia's highest waterfall – and also gives access to the tiny port of **Lucinda**, the southern terminus for ferries to Hinchinbrook Island (p.464). Pasta and wine are to be had in abundance during the May **Italian Festival**, but the town is better known for events surrounding the former *Day Dawn Hotel* (now *Lee's Hotel*) on Lannercost Street, the legendary "**Pub with No Beer**". During World War II, Ingham was the first stop for servicemen heading north from Townsville, and in 1941 they drank the bar dry, a momentous occasion recorded by local poet Dan Sheahan and later turned into a popular ballad – it's not the only pub in Australia which claims to be the inspiration for this ditty, however. If you've an hour or so to kill in town, there's a nice easy **walk** around the well-signposted **Tyto Wetlands** on the southern outskirts; call in at the Tyto Wetlands Centre (Mon–Fri 8.45am–5pm, Sat & Sun 9am–4pm; free) on Cooper Street for interactive bird displays and maps.

The highway curves through town as Herbert Street, though most services are located slightly to the west along **Lannercost Street**. Long-distance **buses** stop ten times daily just where the southern highway meets Lannercost Street; **trains** stop 1km east on Lynch Street – you can buy **tickets** from Ingham Travel at 28 Lannercost St. Information is available at the well-informed **Hinchinbrook Visitor Centre** (Mon–Fri 8.45am–5pm, Sat & Sun 9am–2pm; Ⓦwww.hinchinbrooknq.com.au), on the corner where the highway from Townsville meets Lannercost Street; they also stock brochures on local national parks.

Accommodation options include *Palm Tree Caravan Park* (℡07/4776 2403; cabins ❸), on the southern outskirts of town, clean rooms at *Motel Ingham* (℡07/4776 2355, Ⓦwww.motelingham.com.au; ❺) opposite the Tyto Wetlands Centre on Townsville Street, or basic dorm beds at the *Royal Hotel* (℡07/4776 2024; $18), on Lannercost Street. *Lee's* does filling budget **meals** and the bar hasn't run out of beer since the 1940s. The *Olive Tree Coffee Lounge*, just a few doors along from the Visitor Centre, is a great Italian lunchtime venue, with home-made pizza and pasta.

Leaving, Highway 1 is well marked, but for the various sections of Girringun National Park, turn west down Lannercost Street and follow the **Trebonne** road (lucidly signposted, "This road is not Route 1"); for Lucinda, follow the signs for Forest Beach and Halifax from the town centre.

Girringun National Park

Several disconnected areas of wilds west of Ingham together form **Girringun National Park**, named after a mythical storyteller from the local Aboriginal tribe. The road from Ingham divides 20km along at Trebonne, with separate routes from here to either Mount Fox or Wallaman Falls. For **Mount Fox**, stay on the road for 55km as it crosses cattle country to the base of this extinct volcanic cone; the last 2km are dirt and can be unstable. A rocky, unmarked path climbs to the crater rim through scanty forest; it's hot work, so start early. The crater itself is only about 10m deep, tangled in vine forest and open woodland. With prior permission, you might be able to camp at the nearby township's cricket grounds – either ask at the school, or call ℡07/4777 5104.

The signposted forty-kilometre route to **Wallaman Falls** runs along a mostly sealed road up the tight and twisting range. Tunnelling through thick rainforest along the ridge (where cassowaries are commonly sighted), the road emerges at a bettong-infested National Parks **campsite** (bookings on ☏13 13 04 or Ⓦ www.epa.qld.gov.au) before reaching a picnic area at the falls **lookout**. The falls – at 268m, Australia's highest – are spectacular, leaping in a thin ribbon over the sheer cliffs of the plateau opposite and appearing to vaporize by the time they reach the gorge floor. A walk down a narrow and slippery path from the lookout to the base dispels this impression, as the mist turns out to be from the force of water hitting the plunge pool. If you're staying the night, walk from the campsite along the adjacent quiet stretch of **Stoney Creek** at dawn or late afternoon to see platypuses.

Cardwell

Some 50km north from Ingham lies the modest little town of **CARDWELL** – just a quiet string of shops on one side of the highway, with the sea on the other. It's made attractive by the outline of **Hinchinbrook Island**, which hovers just offshore, so close that it almost seems to be part of the mainland. Access to the island is the main reason to stop here, though you can also buy very cheap **lychees** from roadside stalls in December.

Cardwell spreads for about 2km along the highway, with banks, the post office, supermarket and hotel all near or south of the **old jetty**, itself about halfway along the road. Just north of the jetty, the National Parks-run **Rainforest and Reef Centre** (daily 8am–4.30pm; free) has a walk-through rainforest and mangrove display, plus a ranger on hand to answer any questions. For island permits, see opposite.

If you'd like to spend a few days **cruising** around Hinchinbrook's crocodile- and dugong-infested coastline instead of hiking its trails, Hinchinbrook Rent a Yacht, based south of town at the Port Hinchinbrook Marina (☏07/4066 8007, Ⓦ www.hinchinbrookrentayacht.com.au), rents out bareboat **yachts** and **houseboats** sleeping from six to twelve people; prices work out at around $90 per person per day in a group of six for a minimum four-day charter.

Buses pull up beside the BP service station and *Seaview Café* at the "Transit Centre" – actually just an open-sided bus shelter; the **train station** is about 200m further back. You can buy **tickets** at *Seaview Café* (daily 8am until late).

Accommodation options include nice gardens and cute rooms at *Cardwell Bed & Breakfast*, two streets behind the bus stop at 18 Gregory St (☏07/4066 8330, Ⓦ www.cardwellhomestay.com.au; ❹); self-contained, simple units at *Cardwell Beachfront Motel*, 1 Scott St (☏07/4066 8776; ❸); or *Kookaburra Holiday Park*, 175 Bruce Highway (☏07/4066 8648, Ⓦ www.kookaburraholidaypark.com.au; camping $15 per person, powered sites $26, dorms $20, cabins ❷, motel rooms ❹). For **food**, *Holy Dooly*, across from the bus stop on the corner of Brasenose and Victoria streets, is the best of the town's numerous cafés; fish and chips can be had from *Seafood Fish & Chips* opposite the Rainforest and Reef Centre. If you're self-catering, head for the small supermarket on the north side of town.

Hinchinbrook Island

Across the channel from Cardwell, **Hinchinbrook Island** looms huge and green, with mangroves rising to forest along the mountain range that forms the island's spine, peaking at **Mount Bowen**. The island's drier east side, hidden behind the mountains, has long beaches separated by headlands and the occasional sluggish creek. This is Bandjin Aboriginal land, and though early Europeans reported the people as friendly, attitudes later changed and nineteenth-century "dispersals" had the same effect here as elsewhere. The island was never subsequently occupied, and apart from a single resort, Hinchinbrook remains much as it was two hundred years ago. Today, the island's main attraction is the superb **Thorsborne Trail**, a moderately demanding hiking track along the east coast, taking in forests, mangroves, waterfalls and beaches.

Practicalities

If you're not interested in a serious hike then Hinchinbrook Ferries (☎1800 777 021, ⓦwww.hinchinbrookferries.com.au) offers an excellent **day-trip** ($125), departing daily at 9am from the marina at Cardwell, cruising after **dugong** and stopping for a three-kilometre beach and rainforest walk before winding up with a dip in the pool at the island's sole proper **accommodation**, *Hinchinbrook Island Wilderness Lodge* (☎1800 777 021, ⓦwww.hinchinbrook resort.com.au; six-person cabins ❽, luxury treehouse doubles with all meals ❾). The lodge is set on Cape Richards at Hinchinbrook's northernmost tip and makes a comfortable retreat.

The Thorsborne Trail needs some **advance planning**. The National Parks **campsites** charge $4.85 per person per night, and are best booked online at ⓦwww.epa.qld.gov.au (where you can also read current warnings and download a **trail map**). Do this as far ahead as possible – visitor numbers on the island are restricted and the trail is usually booked solid. Next you need to book **ferry transfers**, though note there are **only three ferries a week** from January to March, and different operators service the north and south ends of the island. For ferries to Ramsay Bay at Hinchinbrook's **north end**, contact Hinchinbrook Island Ferries at Cardwell's marina ($85 one-way, $125 return; ☎1800 777 021, ⓦwww.hinchinbrookferries.com.au); for George Point at the **south end**, contact Hinchinbrook Wilderness Safaris in Lucinda ($66 one-way, $77 return; ☎07/4777 8307, ⓦwww.hinchinbrookwildernesssafaris.com.au), who also offer transfers to Bluff Creek and Zoe Bay. You can book **buses** from Lucinda to Ingham or Cardwell for $30 per person with Ingham Travel (☎07/4776 5666).

The drier winter months (June–Oct) provide optimum **hiking conditions**, though it can rain throughout the year. **Hiking essentials** include water-resistant footgear, pack and tent, a lightweight raincoat and insect repellent. Wood fires are prohibited, so bring a **fuel stove**. *Kookaburra Holiday Park* in Cardwell (see opposite) rents out camping gear. Although streams with **drinking water** are fairly evenly distributed, they might be dry by the end of winter, or only flowing upstream from the beach – collect from flowing sources only. As for **wildlife**, you need to beware of crocodiles in lowland creek systems. Less worrying are the white-tailed rats and marsupial mice that will gnaw through tents to reach food; there are metal food-stores at campsites, though hanging anything edible from a branch may foil their attempts.

The Thorsborne Trail

The 32-kilometre **Thorsborne Trail** is manageable in two days, though at that pace you won't see much. **Trailheads** are at Ramsay Bay in the north and George Point in the south, and the route is marked with orange triangles (north to south), or yellow triangles (south to north). The north to south route is considered slightly more forgiving as it eases into ascents, although the advantage of ending up in the north is that the pick-up with Hinchinbrook Ferries includes a welcome few hours unwinding at the *Hinchinbrook Island Wilderness Lodge*'s bar and pool.

Boats **from Cardwell** take you through the mangroves of Missionary Bay in the north to a boardwalk that crosses to the eastern side of the island at **Ramsay Bay**. The walk from here to **Nina Bay**, which takes a couple of hours, is along a fantastic stretch of coast with rainforest sweeping right down to the sand and Mount Bowen and Nina Peak as a backdrop. If long bushwalks don't appeal, you could spend a few days camped at the forest edge at Nina instead; a creek at the southern end provides drinking water and Nina Peak can be climbed in an hour or so. Otherwise, continue beyond a small cliff at the southern end of Nina, and walk for another two hours or so through a pine forest to **Little Ramsay Bay** (drinking water from Warrawilla Creek), which is about as far as you're likely to get on the first day.

Moving on, you scramble over boulders at the far end of the beach before crossing another creek (at low tide, as it gets fairly deep) and entering the forest beyond. From here to the next camp at **Zoe Bay** takes about five hours, following creek beds through lowland casuarina woods and rainforest, before exiting onto the beach near Cypress Pine waterhole. A clearing and pit toilets at the southern end of Zoe Bay mark the **campsite** – though you'll need to check with the National Parks service about the safest areas to camp, as **crocodiles** have recently been seen here. This is one of those places where you'll be very glad you brought insect repellent.

Next day, take the path to the base of **Zoe Falls** – the waterhole here is fabulous but not safe for swimming – then struggle straight up beside them to the cliff top, from where there are great vistas. Across the river, forest and heathland alternate: the hardest part is crossing **Diamantina Creek** – a fast-flowing river with huge, slippery granite boulders. **Mulligan Falls**, not much further on, is the last source of fresh water, with several rock ledges for sunbathing around a pool full of curious fish – stay off the dangerously slippery rocks above the falls. Zoe to Mulligan takes around four hours, and from here to George Point is only a couple more if you push it, but the falls are a better place to camp and give you the chance to backtrack a little to take a look at the beachside lagoon at **Sunken Reef Bay**.

The last leg to **George Point** is the least interesting: rainforest replaces the highland trees around the falls as the path crosses a final creek before arriving at unattractive Mulligan Bay. The campsite at George Point has a table and toilet in the shelter of a coconut grove, but there's no fresh water, nothing to see except Lucinda's sugar terminal, and little to do except wait for your ferry.

Murray Falls and Tully

North of Cardwell up Highway 1, it's 20km to where a side road heads another 20km inland past banana plantations to attractive **Murray Falls**, right at the edge of the Cardwell Range. It's really just worth a look to break your journey, but there's a large **camping area** here (book online at Ⓦwww.epa.qld.gov.au) and tracks through the forest to permanent swimming holes and lookouts across the bowl of the valley. There's a basic store on the approach road, some distance from the falls, but it's best to stock up in Cardwell beforehand.

Some 45km north of Cardwell, **TULLY** lies to the left of the highway on the slopes of **Mount Tyson**, whose 450-centimetre annual rainfall is the highest in Australia. Chinese settlers pioneered banana plantations here at the beginning of the twentieth century, and it's now a stopover for **white-water rafting** day-trips out of Cairns and Mission Beach on the fierce and reliable Tully River, 45km inland. Otherwise the town is nothing special, a triangle of narrow streets with cultivated lawns and flowerbeds backing onto roaring jungle at the end of Brannigan Street, a constant reminder of the colonists' struggle to keep chaos at bay. Though most people drive the extra thirty minutes to Mission Beach, there's **accommodation** here at *Green Way Caravan Park* (Ⓣ07/4068 2055;

▲ White-water rafting on the Tully River

cabins ❸), although it's often fully booked, or the well-managed *Banana Barracks* hostel at 50 Butler St (℡07/4068 0455, Ⓦwww.bananabarracks.com; dorms $24), which has excellent **farm work** connections for travellers, plus free weekend beach-trips and barbecues.

Mission Beach and around

After branching east off the Bruce Highway a couple of kilometres past Tully, a loop road runs 18km through canefields and patches of rainforest to **Mission Beach**, the collective name for four peaceful hamlets strung out along a fourteen-kilometre stretch of sand. The coastal forest is home to the largest surviving **cassowary** population in Australia, while not far offshore lies little **Dunk Island**, whose idyllic beaches and rainforest track make it a pleasant day-trip.

The area owes its name to the former Hull River Mission, destroyed by a savage **cyclone** in 1918. In 2006, **Cyclone Larry** stripped the rainforest canopy and flattened farms between here and Cairns, wiping out the entire year's banana crop – though the effects will be visible for years, the forest is already well on the way to recovery.

Arrival and information

From south to north, Mission Beach comprises the communities of **South Mission**, **Wongaling Beach**, **Mission Beach** and **Bingil Bay**, each around four or five kilometres from its neighbours. **Long-distance buses** set down outside the shopping-centre office at Wongaling Beach, from where your accommodation might collect you if forewarned. Alternatively, a **local bus** plies the route between South Mission and Bingil Bay (roughly eight per day Mon–Sat 8.30am–6pm; ℡07/4068 7400, Ⓦwww.transnorthbus.com); for a taxi call ℡07/4068 8155. The **visitor centre** (daily 9am–5pm) is just north of Mission Beach township along Porter Promenade; right behind it, the **Environmental Information Centre** (Mon–Fri 10am–4.30pm; free) has a display on local habitat, along with a nursery

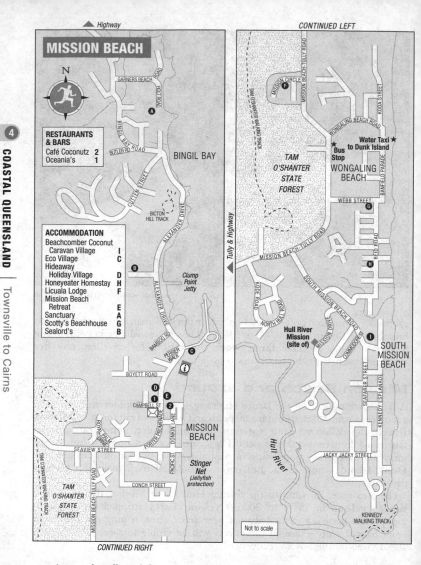

MISSION BEACH

N

▲ Highway

CONTINUED LEFT

CONTINUED RIGHT

RESTAURANTS & BARS

Café Coconutz	2
Oceania's	1

ACCOMMODATION

Beachcomber Coconut Caravan Village	I
Eco Village	C
Hideaway Holiday Village	D
Honeyeater Homestay	H
Licuala Lodge	F
Mission Beach Retreat	E
Sanctuary	A
Scotty's Beachhouse	G
Sealord's	B

GARNERS BEACH

BINGIL BAY

Clump Point Jetty

MISSION BEACH

Stinger Net (Jellyfish protection)

TAM O'SHANTER STATE FOREST

Tully & Highway ▲

TAM O'SHANTER STATE FOREST

Water Taxi ★ to Dunk Island

WONGALING BEACH

Hull River Mission (site of)

SOUTH MISSION BEACH

KENNEDY WALKING TRACK

Not to scale

growing seeds collected from cassowary droppings, with the aim of safeguarding the food supply for future generations of this giant bird.

Accommodation

Accommodation is fairly evenly distributed along the coast and covers everything from camping to resorts. All can provide information and book you on white-water rafting trips and other tours in the area. **Campsites** include the tidy *Beachcomber Coconut Caravan Village* at South Mission (☎07/4068 8129, ⓦwww .beachcombercoconut.com.au; camping $30, powered sites $38, units ❸), and the *Hideaway Holiday Village* at Mission Beach (☎07/4068 7104, ⓦwww.mission beachhideaway.com.au; camping $33, powered sites $39, cabins ❹, villas ❼).

Eco Village Clump Point, Mission Beach ☎07/4068 7534, ⓦwww.ecovillage.com.au. Smart motel accommodation set just back from the beach amongst pandanus, native nutmeg trees and tropical gardens with a natural rock pool. The luxury rooms all have a jacuzzi. **❼**

Honeyeater Homestay 53 Reid Rd, Wongaling ☎07/4068 8741, ⓦwww.honeyeater.com.au. Balinese-inspired house, whose lush tropical gardens surrounding the pool make the place look far larger and more secluded than it actually is. Takes a maximum of six people. **❺**

Licuala Lodge 11 Mission Circle, Mission Beach ☎07/4068 8194, ⓦwww.licualalodge.com.au. Delightful tropical-style B&B with airy wooden verandas and traditional, high-ceilinged interior; the landscaped garden and pool are worth a stay in themselves, and the huge breakfast will keep you going all day. **❺**

Mission Beach Retreat 49 Porters Promenade, Mission Beach ☎07/4088 6229, ⓦwww .missionbeachretreat.com.au. Conveniently located next to the shops in Mission Beach, close to the beach and with a small pool and laundry. Dorms $21, rooms **❶**

Sanctuary 72 Holt Rd, Bingil Bay ☎07/4088 6064, ⓦwww.sanctuaryretreat .com.au. An outstanding operation set in fifty acres of thick rainforest. There's abundant wildlife – including cassowary – and a 700-metre forest track down to a beach. Huts are on stilts (and walled with fine-meshed netting, so you wake up surrounded by greenery), while cabins have verandas; there's also a bar, pool, yoga lessons and an excellent-value restaurant. Note that hut-access paths follow steep slopes, and some find the wildlife's proximity unsettling. Advance booking essential. Huts **❸**, cabins **❼**

Scotty's Beachhouse 167 Reid Rd, Wongaling ☎1800 665 567, ⓦwww.scottysbeachhouse.com .au. A popular party backpackers' near the bus stop and right across from the beach at Wongaling, with bunkhouses, a pool and a fine restaurant offering cheap meals. Dorms $21, rooms **❷**

Sealord's 4 James Rd, Clump Point, Mission Beach ☎07/4088 6444, ⓦwww.sealords.com.au. Smart B&B just up the road from the Dunk Island jetty, with polished wooden floors and themed bedrooms. **❺**

Mission Beach

Right down at the bottom end of the beach, **SOUTH MISSION** is a quiet, mostly residential spot, with a long, clean beach. Signposted off the main road on Mission Drive is a monument to the original site of the **Hull River Mission**; after the 1918 cyclone, the mission was relocated to safer surroundings on Palm Island. At the end of beachfront Kennedy Esplanade, the **Kennedy Walking Track** weaves through coastal swamp and forest for a couple of hours to the spot where Edmund Kennedy originally landed near the mouth of the Hull River – a good place to spot coastal birdlife and, quite likely, crocodiles.

Heading 4km north of South Mission takes you to **WONGALING BEACH**, a slowly expanding settlement based around a shopping centre and Mission's only **pub**. A further 4km lands you at **MISSION BEACH** itself, a cluster of shops, boutiques, restaurants, banks and a post office one block back from the beach on Porter Promenade. Inland between the two, a six-kilometre walking track weaves through **Tam O'Shanter State Forest**, a dense maze

---

Cassowaries

Aside from the lure of the beach, Mission's forests are a reliable place to spot **cassowaries**, a blue-headed and bone-crested rainforest version of the emu, whose survival is being threatened as their habitat is carved up – estimates suggest that there are only a couple of thousand birds left in tropical Queensland (though they are also found in New Guinea and parts of Indonesia). Many larger trees rely on the cassowary to eat their fruit and distribute their seeds, meaning that the very make-up of the forest hinges on the bird's presence. Unlike the emu, cassowaries are not at all timid and may attack if they feel threatened: if you see one, remain quiet and keep a safe distance.

Tours from Mission Beach

Among the local tours worth seeking out, Raging Thunder (☏1800 337 116, ⊛www
.ragingthunder.com.au) offers the best-value **river rafting** down the Tully River in
small groups – a full day costs $145 plus a $30 levy but it's worth forking out an
extra $40 for the "Xtreme" package which guarantees that you're first on the river
and not caught up in a conveyor belt of rafts. Skydive Mission (☏1800 444 568,
⊛www.jumpthebeach.com.au) can take you to 3000m for **freefall** fun ($220), and
also offers skydiving over Dunk Island ($449). If it's riverine wildlife you're after,
River Rat Cruise (☏07/4068 8018) runs four-hour croc-spotting trips departing 4pm
($40), or you can go paddling around Dunk Island for the day with Coral Sea
Kayaking ($126; ☏07/4068 9154, ⊛www.coralseakayaking.com). For **reef trips**,
Quick Cat (☏07/4068 7289, ⊛www.quickcatcruises.com.au) run a passenger ferry
daily to Beaver Cay on the Barrier Reef for coral viewing and snorkelling ($160),
while Calypso II (☏07/4068 8432, ⊛www.calypsodive.com) caters more specifically to **scuba divers**, but is pretty pricey at $215 for a reef trip with two dives –
you'll get a better deal out of Cairns.

of muddy creeks, vine thickets and stands of licuala palms (identified by their
frilly, saucer-shaped leaves). If you don't see **cassowaries** here – sometimes
leading their knee-high, striped chicks through the undergrowth – you'd be
very unlucky. Continuing 6km north of Mission township past **Clump Point**
– a black basalt outcrop with views south down the beach sitting above
Clump Point Jetty – the road winds along the coast to sleepy **BINGIL
BAY**. Just before, there's a parking bay on the roadside for the excellent
Bicton Hill track, a four-kilometre hilly walk through wet tropics forest
where encounters with cassowaries are again likely. From here, the road
continues inland alongside the **Clump Mountain National Park** and back
to the main highway.

There are stores and **places to eat** at all four hamlets, though only Mission
Beach has a comprehensive range – the best of the restaurants here are *Oceania's*,
with an eclectic "Asian" menu, and *Café Coconutz*, which serves light meals and
fresh juices, and also has a **bar**.

Dunk Island

In 1898 Edmund Banfield, a Townsville journalist who had been given only
weeks to live, waded ashore on **Dunk Island**. He spent his remaining years – 25
of them – as Dunk's first European resident, crediting his unanticipated
longevity to the relaxed island life. A tiny version of Hinchinbrook, Dunk
attracts far more visitors to its resort and camping grounds. While there's a satisfying track over and around the island, it's more the kind of place where you
make the most of the beach – as Banfield discovered.

Vessels from the Mission Beach area put ashore on or near the jetty, next to
Jetty Café, which sells fish and chips and sandwiches, and there's a small store
adjacent to it for basic provisions. On the far side is the shady National Parks
campsite (book online at ⊛www.epa.qld.gov.au), with toilets, showers and
drinking water. Five minutes along the track is the **resort** (☏07/4068 8199,
⊛www.dunk-island.com; ➐), a low-key affair well hidden by vegetation; day-
guests have to pay $40 to use the resort facilities, which includes lunch. The best
places to relax are either on **Brammo Bay**, in front of the resort, or **Pallon
Beach**, behind the campsite. Note that the beaches are narrow at high tide and
the island is close enough to the coast to attract box jellyfish in season, but you
can always retreat to the resort pool.

Before falling victim to incipient lethargy, head into the interior past the resort and **Banfield's grave** for a circuit of the island's west. The full nine-kilometre **trail** up Mount Cootaloo, down to Palm Valley and back along the coast is a three-hour rainforest trek, best tackled clockwise from the resort. You'll see green pigeons and yellow-footed scrubfowl foraging in leaf litter, vines, trunkless palms and, from the peak, a vivid blue sea dotted with hunch-backed islands.

Two **ferry** operators run to Dunk daily: Quick Cat (20min; Ⓣ07/4068 7289, Ⓦwww.quickcatcruises.com.au, $28 one-way or $52 return) departs from the Clump Point Jetty at 8.30am, 10am, 2pm and 4pm; the last ferry leaves Dunk at 4.30pm; Water Taxis (10min; Ⓣ07/4068 8310, $20 one-way, bookings recommended) leave from Wongaling Beach at 8.30am, 9.30am, 11am, 12.30pm, 2.30pm and 4pm. Phone operators to see if they offer bus transfers from your accommodation. The island is 5km and barely fifteen minutes offshore, but even so the tiny **water taxis** are not really suitable if you have much luggage. **Camping gear** can be rented from the complex next to the post office in Mission Beach; you can also leave surplus equipment with them.

Paronella Park, Innisfail and the Bellenden Ker Range

Back on the highway around 25km north of Tully, tiny **Silkwood** marks the turn inland for the 23-kilometre run through canefields to **Paronella Park** (daily 9.30am–5pm; $30; Ⓣ07/4065 3225, Ⓦwww.paronellapark.com.au). This extraordinary estate was laid out by **José Paronella**, a Spanish immigrant who settled here in 1929 and constructed a **castle** complete with florid staircases, water features and avenues of exotic kauri pines amongst the tropical forests. Left to moulder for twenty years, the park was reclaimed from the jungle and restored during the 1990s, and now forms a splendidly romantic theme park, with half-ruined buildings artfully part-covered in undergrowth, lush gardens and arrays of tinkling fountains – all gravity-fed from the adjacent Mena Creek. A former walk-through aquarium has become the roost of endangered little bent-winged bats, and native vegetation includes a bamboo forest and dozens of *angiopteris* ferns, rare elsewhere. Fifteen-minute indigenous cultural performances held four times a day and educational bushtucker walking tours add to the park's appeal, so you'll need a good couple of hours to do the place justice; it's possible to **camp** here and explore after dark – phone ahead for details. There's a **restaurant** on site, or you can eat across Mena Creek at the old pub.

The Paronella Park road and highway converge again 25km on at **INNISFAIL**, a small but busy town on the Johnstone River and a good spot to find work **picking bananas**: the specialists here are *Innisfail Budget Backpackers*, on the highway just on the northern side of town (Ⓣ07/4061 7833, Ⓦwww .jobsforbackpackers.com.au; dorms $140 per week); and the much smarter *Codge Lodge*, near the pale-pink Catholic church on Rankin Street (Ⓣ07/4061 8055, Ⓦwww.codgelodge.com; ❶), with single rooms available for $150 per week. Innisfail is worth a quick stop anyway as a reminder that modern Australia was in no way built by the British alone: there's a sizeable **Italian community** here, represented by the handful of delicatessens displaying herb sausages and fresh pasta along central Edith Street. The tiny red **Lit Sin Gong temple** on Owen Street (and the huge longan tree next to it) was first established in the 1880s by migrant workers from southern China, who cleared scrub and created market gardens here; many of Innisfail's banana plantations have been bought up recently by **Hmong** immigrants from Vietnam.

The Bellenden Ker Range

Just north of Innisfail, the Palmerston Highway turns off Highway 1 for its ascent to the bottom end of the Atherton Tablelands (see p.486), and at about the same point you begin to see the **Bellenden Ker Range**, which dominates the remaining 80km to Cairns and includes Queensland's highest mountain, **Bartle Frere**. While the fifteen-kilometre, two-day return climb through **Wooroonooran National Park** to the 1600-metre summit is within the reach of any fit, well-prepared bushwalker, you should check the National Parks website first (ⓦwww.epa.qld.gov.au) or contact the park ranger (☎07/4067 6304) for accurate information about the route. Peak climb or not, it's worth visiting **Josephine Falls**, at the start of the summit track, which forms wonderfully enclosed jungle waterslides: leave the highway 19km north of Ingham at one-house **Pawngilly** and continue for 8km via Bartle Frere township. The **summit track** itself – closed at the time of writing due to damage from the 2006 cyclone – is marked from here with orange triangles and passes through rainforest, over large granite boulders and out onto moorland with wind-stunted vegetation. Much of the summit is blinded by scrub and usually cloaked in rain, but there are great views of the tablelands and coast during the ascent.

Further along the highway, there's a detour at **BABINDA** township – dwarfed by a huge sugar mill – to another waterhole 7km inland at **the Boulders**, where an arm of Babinda Creek forms a wide pool before spilling down a collection of house-sized granite slabs. Cool and relatively shallow, the pale blue waterhole is an excellent place to swim, though several deaths have been caused by subtle undertows dragging people over the falls – be very careful and stay well clear of the falls side of the waterhole. You can also **camp** here for free.

Nearing the end of the range is **Gordonvale**, the place where the notorious **cane toad** was first introduced to Australia (see box, p.486), from where the tortuous Gillies Highway climbs from the coast to lakes Barrine and Eacham on the Atherton Tablelands. Marking the turn-off is **Walsh's Pyramid**, a natural formation which really does look like an overgrown version of its Egyptian counterpart. From here, the last section of Highway 1

Cane toads

Native to South America, the huge, charismatically ugly **cane toad** was recruited in 1935 to combat a plague of greyback beetles, whose larvae were wreaking havoc on Queensland's sugar cane. The industry was desperate – beetles had cut production by ninety percent in plague years – and resorted to seeding tadpoles in waterholes around Gordonvale. They thrived, but it soon became clear that toads couldn't reach the adult insects (who never landed on the ground), and they didn't burrow after the grubs. Instead they bred whenever possible, ate anything they could swallow, and killed potential predators with poisonous secretions from their neck glands. Native wildlife suffered: birds learned to eat nontoxic parts, but snake populations have been seriously affected. Judging from the quantity of flattened carcasses on summer roads (running them over is an unofficial sport), there must be millions lurking in the canefields, and they're gradually spreading into New South Wales and the Northern Territory – they arrived in Darwin, via Kakadu, in 2006. Given enough time, they seem certain to infiltrate most of the northern half of the country.

The toad's outlaw character has generated a cult following, with its warty features and nature the subject of songs, toad races, T-shirt designs, a brand of beer and the award-winning **film** Cane Toads: An Unnatural History – worth seeing if you come across it on video. The record for the largest specimen goes to a 1.8-kilogram monster found in Mackay in 1988.

carries you – in thirty minutes – through the suburbs of Edmonton and White Rock to Cairns.

Cairns and around

CAIRNS was pegged out over the site of a sea-slug fishing camp when gold was found to the north in 1876, though it was the Atherton Tablelands' tin and timber resources that established the town and kept it ahead of its nearby rival, Port Douglas (see p.493). The harbour is the focus of the north's fish and prawn concerns, and tourism began modestly when marlin fishing became popular after World War II. But with the "discovery" of the reef in the 1970s and the appeal of the local climate, tourism snowballed, and high-profile development has now replaced the unspoiled, lazy tropical atmosphere that everyone originally came to Cairns to enjoy.

For many visitors primed by hype, the city falls far short of expectations. However, if you can accept the tourist industry's shocking intrusiveness and the fact that you're unlikely to escape the crowds, you'll find Cairns a convenient base with a great deal on offer, and easy access to the surrounding area – especially the Atherton Tablelands and, naturally, the **Great Barrier Reef** and islands.

Arrival and getting around

Downtown Cairns is the grid of streets behind the Esplanade, overlooking the harbour and Trinity Bay. **Long-distance buses** are operated by Greyhound Australia (℡13 20 30), which sets down and has an office at the Reef Fleet Terminal (office open Mon–Fri 8.30am–5.30pm, Sat & Sun 8.30am–3pm) and Premier (℡13 34 10), which sets down at the south end of Lake Street. Trans North (℡07/4061 7944) runs daily to several Atherton Tablelands towns from their depot at 46 Spence St or the Cairns Central Shopping Centre; Country Road Coachlines (℡07/4045 2794) run to Cooktown via Port Douglas and Cape Tribulation, or Mareeba and Lakeland Downs; Coral Reef Coaches (℡07/4098 2800) and Sun Palm Coaches (℡07/4084 2626) both operate a daily service to Cape Tribulation via Port Douglas. The **train station** is 750m from the main drag, under the Cairns Central development between Bunda and McLeod streets. Queensland Rail (℡13 22 32, ⓦwww.qr.com.au) trains head south down the coast to Brisbane and up to Kuranda on the Atherton Tablelands, while the Savannahlander (℡07/4053 6848, ⓦwww.savannahlander.com.au) runs west to Forsayth in the Gulf region (p.493). The **airport** is about 7km north along the Cook Highway; a taxi into Cairns costs around $20, or a **shuttle bus** ($10) connects with most flights and delivers to all central accommodation. Some accommodation also collects from arrival points if contacted in advance.

For **getting around**, Sunbus, the **local bus** service, is based at the Transit Mall on City Place (Lake St), and serves the city and Northern Beaches as far as Palm Cove; daily, weekly and monthly passes are available, and you can get **free timetables** from the driver. You may also be able to **rent bikes** at your accommodation, or check out the rental outfits on p.479. If you want to buy a **secondhand car**, try Travellers' Auto Barn at 123–125 Bunda St (℡07/4041 3722, ⓦwww.travellers-autobarn.com), or check the classified ads in the Wednesday and Saturday editions of the local paper, the *Cairns Post*. Cars for sale are also advertised on a notice board in an arcade beside the museum at City Place or at Global Gossip, 125 Abbott St.

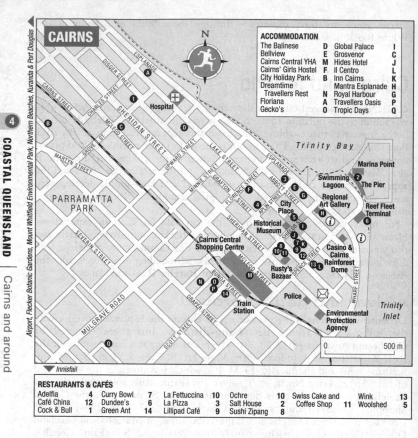

CAIRNS

Trinity Bay

Marina Point

Swimming Lagoon

The Pier

Regional Art Gallery

Reef Fleet Terminal

City Place

Historical Museum

Cairns Central Shopping Centre

Casino & Cairns Rainforest Dome

Rusty's Bazaar

Police

Train Station

Environmental Protection Agency

Trinity Inlet

Hospital

PARRAMATTA PARK

0   500 m

Innisfail

RESTAURANTS & CAFÉS

Adelfia	**4**	Curry Bowl	**7**	La Fettuccina	**10**	Ochre	**10**	Swiss Cake and		Wink	**13**
Café China	**12**	Dundee's	**6**	La Pizza	**3**	Salt House	**2**	Coffee Shop	**11**	Woolshed	**5**
Cock & Bull	**1**	Green Ant	**14**	Lillipad Café	**9**	Sushi Zipang	**8**				

Information

Cairns' official **visitor centre** is the Gateway Discovery Centre, housed in the old Shire Offices at 51 Esplanade (☎07/4041 3588, ⊕www.tropicalaustralia.com.au); though this promotes only those operators that pay to be featured, the staff are friendly and they have a wealth of brochures and flyers. Other places around town with prominent blue "i" signs, along with the backpacker agents on Shields Street, tend to focus on selling the tours that they'll make the most commission on – don't expect them to provide unbiased, informed opinions. One exception – though based out of town – is **Cairns Discount Tours** (☎07/4055 7158, ⓔtours@iig .com.au) which specializes in last-minute deals and comes recommended for its honest approach and comprehensive knowledge of the local tour options.

Accommodation

Cairns has a prolific number of **places to stay** in every price bracket, and the following is just a selection. Most are pretty central, though there's a knot of backpacker hostels west of the train station, of which *Dreamtime* and *Tropic Days* are the pick. The nearest official **campsite** is the recently refurbished *City Holiday Park* at 12–30 Little St (☎07/4051 1467, ⊕www.cairnscamping .com.au; camping $23, powered sites $29, cabins ❸), with good amenities and a pool. If Cairns itself doesn't appeal but you want access to all its attractions, consider staying 15km north beyond the airport at the city's Northern Beaches (see p.480).

Expect seasonal **price fluctuations** at all accommodation, with Christmas and Easter being the busiest times, and February to March the quietest; **book ahead** but beware of committing yourself to a long-term deal until you've seen the room – you won't be able to get a refund. All hostels have kitchens, and most have a courtesy bus service, laundry and a pool. Hostels make as much profit through commissions as they do beds, so don't admit to making tour bookings elsewhere if you want your room to remain available.

For something a little different, try the farmstay accommodation at enterprising *Mount N Ride* (℡07/4056 5406, Ⓦwww.mountnride.com.au; $150 per person includes meals and free pick-up from Cairns) on the Gilles Highway between Gordonvale and Little Mulgrave, where you can take in mountain biking, horseriding and fishing.

Hotels, motels and guesthouses

The Balinese 215 Lake St ℡1800 023 331, Ⓦwww.balinese.com.au. Slightly sterile but comfy motel with carved wooden doors, bamboo blinds and lots of tiling. There's a small pool, satellite TV, inclusive breakfast and airport courtesy bus. ❹

Floriana 183 Esplanade ℡07/4051 7886, Ⓦwww.florianaguesthouse.com. Amiable old guesthouse with sea views and Art Deco decor in the reception. Rooms overlooking the Esplanade have polished timber floors and are nice and airy, as are the self-contained flats; the cheaper downstairs rooms have no windows and get pretty stuffy. ❹

Grosvenor 188 McLeod St ℡1800 629 179, Ⓦwww.grosvenorcairns.com.au. Bright and cheerful motel offering self-contained apartments and deluxe units; not very central but close to the highway. Apartments ❻, units ❼

Hides Hotel Corner of Lake and Shields sts ℡07/4051 1266, Ⓦwww.hideshotel.com.au. Very central, convenient and affordable, with long corridors of comfortable motel rooms and unadorned high-ceilinged box rooms with shared bathrooms on the third floor. ❹–❺

Il Centro 26–30 Sheridan St ℡07/4031 6699, Ⓦwww.ilcentro.com.au. Modern and fairly spacious self-contained apartments with either pool or street views. ❼

Inn Cairns 71 Lake St ℡07/4041 2350, Ⓦwww.inncairns.com.au. Smart boutique apartments slap in the centre of town, with pool and BBQ area, plus rooftop views out to sea. ❼

Mantra Esplanade 53–57 Esplanade ℡07/4046 4141, Ⓦwww.mantraesplanadecairns.com.au. Plush high-rise hotel in a prime location close to the casino, restaurants, shops and the "beach". ❼

Royal Harbour 73–75 Esplanade ℡07/5665 4450, Ⓦwww.stellaresorts.com.au. Self-contained hotel apartments with sea views – it feels surprisingly secluded given the location. ❼

Hostels

Bellview 85 Esplanade ℡07/4031 4377, Ⓦwww.bellviewcairns.com.au. Family-run hostel that has been around forever, though the site is being eyed by property speculators. Motel-like facilities and a range of rooms. Dorms $22, rooms ❷

Cairns Central YHA 20–26 McLeod St ℡07/4041 0722, Ⓦwww.yha.com.au. Large hostel facing Central Shopping Plaza, a little barracks-like with motel-style rooms surrounding the swimming pool, but with good security, lots of doubles and some family rooms. Dorms $23–33, rooms ❸–❹

Cairns' Girls Hostel 147 Lake St ℡07/4051 2016, Ⓦwww.cairnsgirlshostel.com.au. Renovated 1930s Queenslander, with tidy rooms and secure feel. Can be hard to locate; look for the adjacent laundry. Dorms $20, rooms ❶

🏃 **Dreamtime Travellers Rest** 4 Terminus St, behind the train station ℡1800 058 440, Ⓦwww.dreamtimetravel.com.au. Small, friendly hostel with a keen owner and very relaxed tropical atmosphere about ten minutes' walk from the centre. There's also a great café run by the same family next door. Dorms $22, rooms ❷

Gecko's 187 Bunda St ℡1800 011 344, Ⓦwww.geckosbackpackers.com.au. Overcrowded hostel in an old Queenslander, with wooden floors and period furnishings; staff are good but rooms are

pretty airless and hot in the summer. Dorms $22, rooms ❶
Global Palace 86–88 Lake St ☎1800 819 024, ⓦwww.globalpalace.com.au. This large, modern backpackers' right in the centre of town has an industrial feel but is well organized and offers good facilities. Dorms $26, rooms ❷
Travellers Oasis 8 Scott St ☎1800 621 353, ⓦwww.travoasis.com.au. Very friendly old Queenslander with comfortable double rooms boasting

balconies but slightly stuffy four-bed dorms. Dorms $25, rooms ❷
Tropic Days 28 Bunting St ☎1800 421 521, ⓦwww.tropicdays.com.au. Though a little bit out of town, this friendly hostel has a big pool, nice gardens, colourful rooms and a highly sociable atmosphere. There's a small campsite too, and a courtesy bus through the day. Camping $11 per person, dorms $25, rooms ❷

The City

Cairns' strength is in doing, not seeing: there are few monuments, natural or otherwise. This is partly because the Cape York goldfields were too far away and profits were channelled through Cooktown, and partly because Cairns was remote, lacking a rail link with Townsville until 1924; people came here to exploit resources, not to settle. Your best introduction to the region's heritage is at the **Cairns Historical Museum**, at the junction of Shields and Lake streets (Mon–Sat 10am–4pm; $5), which uses photos and trinkets to explore maritime history, the Tjapukai and Bama Aborigines of the tablelands, and Chinese involvement in the city and Palmer goldfields.

At **City Place**, the open-air pedestrian mall outside the museum, you'll find Cairns' souvenir-shopping centre, with a rash of cafés, and shops selling didgeridoos, T-shirts, paintings and cuddly toy koalas. Local performers do their best at the small **sound shell** here from time to time, and there are often more professional offerings in the evenings. Between Grafton and Sheridan streets, towards Spence Street, **Rusty's Bazaar markets** (Fri, Sat & Sun morning) sell a fantastic range of local produce from crafts to herbs, tropical fruit and veg, coffee and fish, with excellent deals on surplus produce around noon on Sunday.

Moving east, the seafront **Esplanade** is packed through the day and into the night with people cruising between accommodation, shops and restaurants. Grabbing an early-morning coffee here, you'll witness a quintessentially Cairns scene: fig trees framing the waterfront, with a couple of trawlers, cruise boats and seaplanes bobbing at anchor in the harbour. A three-kilometre pedestrian walkway hugs the tidal coastline from where you can watch pelicans lazing in the sun and other smaller birds feeding in the shallows – identification charts along the route help you pick out a tern from a shearwater – while an excellent **skateboard park** is thoughtfully located up towards the hospital. In the opposite direction, Cairns' well-planned **artificial beach** actually sits way above the tide-line, but encloses five landscaped swimming lagoons which are packed at weekends. Facing the lagoon on the far end of the Esplanade is the glass-domed **casino** and Cairns Rainforest Dome (daily 9am–7pm; $22), an equally artificial replica, this time of the rainforest with caged birds and several depressed-looking crocodiles. Opposite, the **Reef Fleet Terminal** is where most day-cruises to the reef depart from, while **The Pier**, facing Cairns' expanding marina, is lined with cliquey, overpriced restaurants.

The Esplanade's **night market** (daily 5pm until late) runs through to Abbott Street and has a mix of fast-food courts, $10 massage stalls, trendy tack and good-quality souvenirs, plus a great location near plenty of bars. Just around the corner from the Esplanade on Shields Street, **Cairns Regional Art Gallery** (Mon–Sat 10am–5pm, Sun 1–5pm; $5) is worth a look if Cairns' crasser commercial side is beginning to grate; exhibitions include both local artists' work and travelling shows.

Heading out of the centre, the city's natural attractions include the wonderful **Flecker Botanic Gardens** (Mon–Fri 7.30am–5.30pm, Sat & Sun 8.30am–5.30pm; free guided walks Tues & Thurs 10am & 1pm, private guided walks Mon–Fri 10am $11.50, minimum 2 people) and adjacent **Mount Whitfield Environmental Park**, whose cool, tranquil rainforest is dense enough for wallabies. Both are accessed off Collins Avenue, west off the northern end of Sheridan Street; several buses run up here from the City Place Transit Mall, or it's a forty-minute walk. Also worth a look are the **mangrove walks** on the airport approach road nearby, whose boardwalks and hides give you a chance to see different varieties of mangrove trees, mudskippers and red-clawed, asymmetric fiddler crabs. Take some insect repellent or you'll end up giving the flies a free lunch. Alternatively, Habitat Cruises ($59; ℡07/4041 3851, ⓦwww.cairnshabitatcruises.com.au) explore the local mangrove creeks for birds and also work in a visit to a crocodile farm.

Activities

In addition to the tours covered in the box below, several operators offer more activity-led excursions. For **bushwalking**, Wooroonooran Safaris (℡1300 661 113, ⓦwww.wooroonooran-safaris.com.au) spends a moderately strenuous day hiking through thick rainforest just north of Bartle Frere, where you're guaranteed to see wildlife and get wet crossing creeks ($169 all-inclusive). **Wildlife-spotting tours** focus on the Atherton Tablelands' platypus, tree kangaroos and rare possums, and are run by Wildscapes Safaris (℡07/4057 6272), Wait-a-While Tours (℡07/4098 2422, ⓦwww.waitawhile.com.au) and Wild Watch (℡07/4097 7408, ⓦwww.wildwatch.com.au); expect to pay in the region of $195 for an afternoon-to-night excursion. Wild Watch also offers specialized **birding** trips, as does Cassowary Tours (℡07/4043 1202, ⓦwww.cassowarytours.com.au) – both can put together week-long packages to the Tablelands and Cape York.

Bicycle tours around the Atherton Tablelands are on offer four times a week with Bandicoot ($99; ℡0418 967 201, ⓦwww.bandicootbicycles.com), or you can get stuck into some moderate to extreme off-road biking around Cairns

---

Tours from Cairns

Before exploring locally or around the Atherton Tablelands, Port Douglas and Cape Tribulation, bear in mind that the cheapest day-tours will set you back $110 per person, while it costs as little as $55 per day to rent a four-seat car, plus perhaps a bit less for fuel – though of course you'll miss out on a tour guide's local knowledge.

For day-trips to the **Atherton Tablelands**, **the Daintree** and **Cape Tribulation**, both Uncle Brian (℡07/4050 0615, ⓦwww.unclebrian.com.au) and Cape Trib Connections (℡07/4053 3833, ⓦwww.capetribconnections.com) come highly recommended in the $110 bracket. Ranging further afield, Trek North Safaris (℡07/4033 2600, ⓦwww.treknorth.com.au) has day-trips to the Daintree ($128) and Cape Tribulation ($148), whilst Wilderness Challenge (℡07/4035 4488, ⓦwww.wilderness-challenge.com.au) offers an excellent three-night trip to Cooktown and the Aboriginal rock-art sites around **Laura** ($845 for 2 people). For **Cape York**, the following organize trips to the tip by 4WD, boat and plane, and enjoy reliable reputations; you're looking at $2000–3000 for an all-inclusive, week-long trip, depending on the level of comfort offered: Heritage Tours (℡07/4038 2628, ⓦwww.heritagetours.com.au); Billy Tea Bush Safaris (℡07/4032 0077, ⓦwww.billytea.com.au); and Oz Tours (℡1800 079 006; ⓦwww.oztours.com.au).

and Cape Tribulation with Dan's Mountain Biking ($85–165; ☎07/4032 0066, ⓦwww.dansmountainbiking.com.au); both come highly recommended. Cairns' **bungee-jumping** venue is a purpose-built platform surrounded by rainforest, in the hills off the coastal highway 8km north of Cairns; contact A.J. Hackett ($125; ☎07/4057 7188), which offers heaps of combined package deals with other extreme-sport operators.

White-water rafting is organized on the reliable Tully River near Tully or the slightly less turbulent Barron River behind Cairns, and is wild fun despite being a conveyor-belt business: as you pick yourself out of the river, the raft is dragged back for the next busload. A "day" means around five hours' rafting; a "half-day" about two. Agents include RnR (☎07/4041 9444, ⓦwww.raft.com.au) and Raging Thunder (☎07/4030 7990, ⓦwww.ragingthunder.com.au); day-trips with either company cost from $98–$155 plus a compulsory rafting levy of $30 per day. RnR also offers an all-inclusive, four-day camping adventure further inland along the North Johnstone River for $1500 per person, also departing Cairns.

Finally, if you want to arrange a spot of small-scale **fishing** for barramundi and other estuary fish, contact Paradise Sportfishing (☎07/4055 6088) which charges $160 per person for a full day fishing from a boat.

For **trips to the Great Barrier Reef**, see the box on pp.482–483.

Eating and nightlife

Cairns has no shortage of places to **eat**. Least expensive are the Esplanade takeaways serving Chinese food, falafel, kebabs and pasta. Some, like *La Pizza* on the corner of Aplin Street, open early and close very late, switching from coffee and croissants at dawn to fast food during the day and evening. The night market also houses a fast-food plaza, with a choice ranging from fish and chips to pizza or sushi; alternatively, you can stock up at the **supermarkets** on Abbott Street or in Cairns Central.

Openly drinking on the streets is illegal in Cairns, but the **pub and club** culture thrives undaunted. Clubs open around 6pm, most charging $5 entry for the bar and disco, or more if there's a band playing. Many pubs also feature live music once a week – reviews and details are given in Cairns' free weekly **listings magazine**, *Time Out*; for some indigenous sounds, try to catch one of the up-and-coming local **Torres Strait Islander** performers, such as the Brisco Sisters. Try not to make yourself an obvious target for the **pickpockets** and bag-snatchers who work the nightclubs, though the steady reports of drink-spikings, rapes and muggings are more worrying – don't hang around outside venues, and get a taxi home.

Cafés and restaurants

Adelfia Corner of Grafton and Aplin sts. Lively Greek taverna with particularly tasty seafood and grills. Most main dishes around $28.

Café China Corner of Spence and Grafton sts. Two sections here cater to an increasing number of Chinese visitors to Cairns: there's an inexpensive noodle house on Spence St where most dishes are under $14, and a more sophisticated Cantonese restaurant on Grafton, with great roast meat or seafood dishes from $25, and daily *yum cha* sessions from 11am (best selection at weekends).

Cock & Bull 6 Grove St, corner of Grafton St. Keg Guinness, hearty counter meals (from around $15) and a pleasant garden atmosphere.

Curry Bowl In Mainstreet Arcade between Grafton and Lake sts, just south of Shields St. Very ordinary-looking fast-food counter, but the portions of (mostly vegetarian) Sri Lankan dhals and curries are large, cheap and pretty authentic.

Dundee's Waterfront, 1 Marlin Parade. One of a dozen restaurants gracing the waterfront, this popular upmarket bistro has leanings towards native fauna – choose from kangaroo, emu or crocodile – and seafood. The best dishes are the kangaroo satay and seafood platter (includes crays and mud crab). Mains around $35.

Green Ant 83 Bunda St. Cheap, cheerful and tasty evening meals with unbeatable $5 meal deals every day from 5–7pm. Mains – such as spicy chicken salsa or meat grills served with rice or chips – go for around $12, while the burgers taste like burgers used to before fast-food versions appeared. Live bands at weekends. Daily 4pm–midnight.

La Fettuccina 41 Shields St ☎07/4031 5959. Superb home-made pasta and sauces for around $18, though it's very popular, so get in early or book – the "small" servings will be enough for most people.

Lillipad Café 72 Grafton St. Well-presented chill-out café adorned with interesting artwork, serving decent coffee and with a simple but hearty snack menu ranging from vegan burgers to all-day breakfasts. Live jazz most evenings from 7.30pm. Daily 7am–late.

Ochre 43 Shields St. Long-running restaurant with Outback decor and a menu revolving around truly Australian ingredients such as kangaroo and crocodile – although emu meat seems to have been replaced by ostrich. Tasty, but some dishes are a bit overworked. Mains $23 and up.

Salt House Marina Point ☎07/4041 7733. Cairns' most prestigious waterfront location, overlooking the marina, with alfresco fine dining (mains from $35) and a more casual wet bar serving draught beer and snacks for around $15.

Sushi Zipang 39 Shields St. The best place in town for sushi, which parades across a conveyor belt in colour-coded bowls, noodle soups or other Japanese light meals – popular with Japanese tourists. Most meals around $18.

Swiss Cake and Coffee Shop 93 Grafton St. Top-notch patisserie with crisp strudels, rich cakes and fine coffee.

Wink Corner of Grafton and Spence sts. Modern Australian with a diverse menu (mains around $35) and blackboard specials around $25 with several inspiring vegetarian dishes including tarragon gnocchi and curry goat's cheese. Closed Tues.

Woolshed 22 Shields St. Budget backpackers' diner, with huge and inexpensive meals, beer by the jug and party fever. Hostels give out vouchers for various discount meal deals here; it's worth "upgrading" these for a couple more dollars and getting a full-blown feed.

Nightlife

Bā8 1 Marlin Parade. Fashionable wine bar facing Reef Fleet Terminal. Good spot for a sunset cocktail with large comfy loungers overlooking the marina and daily happy-hour prices from 5–7pm.

Buddha Bar Corner of Shields St and the Esplanade. Ambient lounge bar, a decent place to chat with your mates, and with live chill-out music at weekends.

Casa De Meze Corner of Aplin St and the Esplanade. Week-time karaoke venue but perks up on Fri, with live bands, and Sat, with free salsa dance classes.

Gilligans 89 Grafton St. Attached to the massive backpackers', this is the liveliest nightspot in Cairns, popular with both travellers and locals. Nightly DJs with live bands on Tues, Sat & Sun.

Heritage Corner of Spence and Lake sts. Large pub with balcony tables and daily theme nights which get the crowds pumping after 10pm.

The Lounge Ground floor of the *Woolshed*, 22 Shields St. Fri- and Sat-night house and trance, with guest DJs from 11pm–5am.

P.J. O'Brien's City Place, next to *Hides Hotel*, Shields St. This Irish bar attracts a mix of locals and tourists, and hosts some big-name Queensland indie band nights. Best on Fri, Sat & Sun nights.

Listings

Airlines All of the following fly to Cairns: Airlines PNG ☎1300 764 696, ⊛www.apng.com; Air New Zealand ☎13 24 76, ⊛www.airnz.com .au; Air Niugini ☎1300 361 380, ⊛www.airniugini .com.pg; Cathay Pacific ☎13 17 47, ⊛www .cathaypacific.com; Continental ☎1300 737 640, ⊛www.continental.com; JAL ☎07/4031 1912, ⊛www.jal.com; Jetstar ☎13 15 38, ⊛www .jetstar.com; Skytrans ☎07 4040 6700, ⊛www .skytrans.com.au; Qantas ☎13 13 13, ⊛www .qantas.com.au; Virgin Blue ☎13 67 89, ⊛www .virginblue.com.

Banks and exchange Banks are scattered throughout the city centre, mostly around the inter-section of Shields and Abbott sts and in Cairns Central. Some booths around the Esplanade also offer bureau de change facilities, though rates are lower than at the banks.

Bike rentals Cairns Scooter & Bicycle Hire, 47 Shields St ☎07/4031 3444; bike rental from $20 a day.

Books Exchange Book Shop, 78 Grafton St, has an excellent range of secondhand books to buy or exchange.

Camping equipment Adventure Equipment, 133 Grafton St (℡07/4031 2669), stocks and rents out all types of outdoor gear and even kayaks; City Place Disposals, on the corner of Shields and Grafton sts, has more down-to-earth, non-brand-name equipment.

Car rental On a day-by-day basis you're looking at around $55 for a four-person runaround, though longer rentals might come in at only $45 a day. Four-wheel-drive vehicles are around $165 per day. A1 Car Rental, 141 Lake St ℡07/4031 1326, Ⓦwww.a1carrentalscairns.com.au; All Day, 1/62 Abbott St ℡07/4031 3348, Ⓦwww.cairns-car-rentals.com; Billabong, 134 Sheridan St ℡1800 354 299, Ⓦwww.billabongrentals com.au; Integra Car, 131 Lake St ℡1800 069 263, Ⓦwww.abcintegra.com.au; Minicar Rentals, 150 Sheridan St ℡1300 735 577, Ⓦwww.minicarrentals.com.au.

Cinemas There are multi-screens at BC City Cinemas, at 108 Grafton St and in Cairns Central.

Environmental Protection Agency At the southern end of Sheridan St, just past the police station – look for the building with green and yellow trim (Mon–Fri 8.30am–5pm; ℡07/4046 6600). Staff are very helpful, and have plenty of free brochures on regional National Parks, plus books for sale on wildlife and hiking.

Hospital and medical centres Cairns Medical Centre, on the corner of Florence and Grafton sts (℡07/4052 1119) is open 24hr for vaccinations and GP consultations (free if you have reciprocal national health cover).

Hospitals include Base Hospital, at the northern end of the Esplanade (℡07/4050 6333), or Cairns Private Hospital (℡07/4052 5200) on the corner of Upward and Lake sts, if you have insurance.

Internet access If your accommodation isn't connected, try the backpacker places around the intersection of Shields and Abbott sts ($1 for 15min).

Pharmacy VP Pharmacy 86 Lake St (Mon–Sat 8.30am–7pm, Sun 10am–7pm).

Police 5 Sheridan St ℡07/4030 7000.

Post office 13 Grafton St and upstairs in Orchid Plaza off the Transit Mall, Lake St.

Scenic flights Daintree Air Services (℡07/4034 9300, Ⓦwww.daintreeair.com.au) charge $199 for an hour's flight over the reef; they also buzz up to Lizard Island (see p.502; $590) or Cape York ($1089) for the day.

Taxis The main cab rank is on Lake St, west of City Place, or call ℡13 10 08.

Travel agents Flight Centre, 24 Spence St ℡07/4052 1077; Trailfinders, next to *Hides Hotel*, Shields St ℡07/4050 9600.

Work The backpacker contact points along Shields St or your accommodation may be able to help out with WWOOF placements on the Atherton Tablelands.

Yacht Club Marina Point ℡07/4031 2750. Worth contacting for hitching/crewing north to Cape York and the Torres Strait, south to the Whitsundays and beyond, and even to New Guinea and the Pacific.

Around Cairns

There's a fair amount to see and do **around Cairns** (unless otherwise stated, the areas below can be reached on Sunbus services from City Place; see p.473). About 12km northwest near Redlynch, **Crystal Cascades** (Wongalee Falls) is a narrow forest gorge gushing with rapids, small waterfalls and swimming opportunities – somewhere to picnic rather than explore. Don't leave valuables in your car, and heed warnings about the large, serrated, heart-shaped leaves of the stinging tree (also known locally as "Dead man's itch") found beside the paths here; the stories about this plant's sting may seem exaggerated, but if stung you'll believe them all. Backtracking through **Kamerunga** township – as far as you'll get on the bus – there's a marked, fairly steep track through the **Barron Gorge National Park** up through forests to Kuranda (see p.487).

Cairns' variously developed **Northern Beaches** all lie off the highway past the airport. They offer a slower pace than the city, while still being close enough for easy access – all but distant Ellis are on bus routes. Around 8km north, **HOLLOWAYS BEACH** is a string of suburban streets fronting a long strip of sand, quiet except for the airport to the south; *Strait on the Beach* **café** has ordinary takeaway food but great views from its shaded terrace, while *Billabong B&B* on Caribbean Street (℡07/4037 0162, Ⓦwww.cairns-bed-breakfast.com; ◉) is a delightful and secluded spot set on a man-made island, surrounded by water and full of birdlife – the tariff includes a sumptuous gourmet breakfast but the proximity to Cairns Airport can make it a noisy place to stay. **YORKEYS KNOB**, 2km further up the highway and away from the airport noise, is one of the best **kite-surfing** beaches in Australia – Kiterite at 471 Varley St (T04/0928 3322) offers introductory lessons for $79 an hour or two-day certified courses for $199. ⚑ *Villa Marine*, 8 Rutherford St (T07/4055 7158, Wwww.villamarine.com.au; ❺), has self-contained, spacious units, most clad in funky artefacts from the Torres Islands, and set 50m back from the beach beside a cool patch of rainforest; the manager here is a mine of useful information about the Cairns region. You can **eat** at the popular and picturesque **marina**.

About 12km north of Cairns on the highway, the township of **Smithfield** marks the starting point for the Kennedy Highway's ascent to Kuranda, in the Atherton Tablelands. Shortly before, a large complex on the roadside houses both the **Kuranda Skyrail** cable-car terminus (see p.487) and the **Tjapukai Aboriginal Park** (daily 9am–5pm; $31 plus transfers, 7.30pm night tour $90 plus transfers). The park's hefty admission price isn't bad value, as it includes entry to boomerang and didgeridoo displays, a fine museum, and three separate theatre shows featuring Dreamtime tales and dancing; it's not eye-opening stuff, but does offer a light-hearted and entertaining introduction to Aboriginal culture.

Up the highway beyond Smithfield are the more developed and upmarket tourist areas of **TRINITY BEACH** and **PALM COVE**, both with spotlessly clean, palm-fringed beaches and lots of luxury holiday apartments, beach resorts, cafés, boutique shops, restaurants and watersports. You can expect to pay from $150 per night at the resorts here, with minimum stays enforced during the high seasons. The *Sebel Reef House & Spa* at Palm Cove (T07/4055 3633, Wwww.reefhouse.com.au; ❾) is the grandest of all the resorts along the coast, whilst the most exclusive is *Kewarra Beach Resort*, also at Palm Cove (T07/4057 6666, Wwww.kewarrabeachresort.com.au; ❾), tucked away in a secluded patch of rainforest on the quietest stretch of beach. **Cairns Tropical Zoo** (daily 8.30am–5pm; $31), nearby on the main highway, offers close-up views of Australia's often-elusive fauna – their night tour (Mon–Thurs & Sat 7–10pm; $85 plus transfers) is particularly recommended.

If you want to really escape for a few days, however, you couldn't ask for a finer place to unwind than **ELLIS BEACH**, thirty minutes north of Cairns on the way to Port Douglas (and unfortunately beyond the reach of bus services) and nothing more than an endless strip of sand and coastal belt of trees beside ⚑ *Ellis Beach Bungalows* (T07/4055 3538, Wwww.ellisbeach.com; camping $26, powered sites $30, cabins ❹, bungalows ❻).

The Reef and diving

One of Cairns' major draws is the **Great Barrier Reef**, and there are so many cruise or dive options that making a choice can be very daunting. A lot of fuss is made about the differences between the **inner reef** (closer to the coast, and visited by slower boats), the **outer reef** (closest to the open sea and the target of most speedy operators) and **fringing reef** (surrounding Fitzroy and Green islands), but the coral and fishlife at any of them can be either excellent or tragic. The state of Cairns' **coral** is the subject of much debate: years of agricultural runoff and recent **coral-bleaching** events – not to

The **reef cruises** and **diving** listings given below are not mutually exclusive – most outfits offer diving (typically $45 per dive including gear), snorkelling (usually free) or just plain old sailing. **Prices** can come down by as much as thirty percent during the low seasons (Feb–April & Nov). All dive schools run trips in their own boats, primarily to take students on their certification dives – **experienced divers** may want to avoid these, and should always make their qualifications known to onboard dive staff, who might then be able to arrange something a bit more adventurous than simply joining the heavily shepherded groups. Beware of "**expenses only**" boat trips offered to backpackers, which usually end up in sexual harassment once out at sea. If in doubt, find out from any booking office in town if you're dealing with an authorized, registered operator.

Reef cruises
SAILBOATS
Day-trips $120–190; three days (two nights) $420–580.

Ocean Free ☏07/4041 1118, ⊛www.oceanfree.com.au. Day-trips to Green Island, aboard a nineteen-metre rigged schooner.

Ocean Spirit Cruises ☏07/4031 2920, ⊛www.oceanspirit.com.au. Large vessel that holds up to a hundred passengers – it sails out to Michaelmas Cay, reputed for its clams, and motors back, ensuring adequate time on the reef. Great presentation but one of the more expensive sailing trips.

Passions of Paradise ☏1800 111 346, ⊛www.passions.com.au. Popular with backpackers, this roomy and very stable sail-catamaran cruises out to Paradise Reef.

Santa Maria ☏07/4055 6130, ⊛www.reefcharter.com. Twenty-metre, replica nineteenth-century rigged schooner with maximum of ten passengers for overnight trips to Thetford and Moore reefs.

POWERBOATS
$100–200 (day-trips only).

Great Adventures ☏1800 079 080, ⊛www.greatadventures.com.au. Trips on a large, fast catamaran to a private reef pontoon via Green Island.

Osprey V ☏1800 079 099, ⊛www.downunderdive.com.au. Speedy vessel which runs out to the outer Norman and Hastings reefs; comfortable boat, great crew and the best meals of any day-trip.

Quicksilver ☏07/4087 2100, ⊛www.quicksilver-cruises.com. Probably the highest priced in this bracket, but also one of the largest, comfiest vessels, docking at its own stable pontoon mooring at Agincourt reef.

Reef Magic ☏07/4031 1588, ⊛www.reefmagiccruises.com. High-speed catamaran which spends five hours at the Marine World pontoon, on the outer reef, for snorkelling and glass-bottom-boat trips.

Sunlover Cruises ☏1800 810 512, ⊛www.sunlover.com.au. Fast catamaran to a private pontoon where you spend four hours exploring the outer reef.

Diving
DAY-TRIPS
$95–155; diving upwards of $90 for two dives, including gear rental.

Reef Experience ☏07/4051 5777, ⊛www.reefexperience.com.au. Diving at two different reef locations with the thrill of boom-netting on the way back.

Reef Quest ☏1800 612 223, ⊛www.diversden.com.au. Stable, well-equipped catamaran and the cheapest of the outer reef tours visiting various sites depending on conditions.

Seastar II ☏07/4041 6218, ⊛www.seastarcruises.com.au. Long-established family-run business with permits for some of the best sections of Hastings Reef and Michaelmas Cay – slow boat leaves at 8am to ensure adequate time on the reefs.

COASTAL QUEENSLAND

Silverswift ☎07/4044 9944, ⓦwww.silverseries.com.au. Large 24-metre catamaran whose speed means that you get longer at the reef – there's just enough time to get in three dives if you want.

Sun-Kist ☎07/4051 0294, ⓦwww.cairnsdive.com.au. Budget dive and snorkel operator visiting Moore and Thetford reefs. Twenty-eight passengers are sometimes squashed onto the 18-metre monohull, but the diving is excellent.

Super Cat ☎1800 079 099, ⓦwww.downunderdive.com.au. Another well-organized budget option, though a faster, newer vessel than most in the price range.

Tusa ☎07/4047 9100, ⓦwww.tusadive.com. Purpose-built vessel holding a maximum of 60 passengers, visiting any one of fifteen separate reefs depending on conditions and offering excellent-value multi-trip packages.

LIVE-ABOARDS

Live-aboard trips cater to more serious divers, last from three days upwards and cover the best of the reefs. **Prices** vary seasonally, with cheaper rates from February to June. All costs below include berth, meals and dives, but not gear rental. Remember that weather conditions can affect the destinations offered. For further information and **comparisons** of various operations, check out Diversion Travel (☎07/4039 0200, ⓦwww.diversionoz.com).

Mike Ball ☎07/4053 0500, ⓦwww.mikeball.com. Luxury diving with one of Queensland's best-equipped and longest-running operations; venues include the Cod Hole and Coral Sea sites, with most trips including dives with minke whales. Four- to eight-day trips from $1430–2840.

Nimrod Explorer ☎07/4031 5566, ⓦwww.explorerventures.com. Motorized catamaran with basic or plush cabins; four- to eight-day Cod Hole and Coral Sea trips cost $1095–2195 for quad-share cabins.

Spirit of Freedom ☎07/4047 9150, ⓦwww.spiritoffreedom.com.au. Huge 33-metre vessel with superlative facilities, sailing to Cod Hole, the Ribbons and Coral Sea. Three days from $1300, four days from $1625, seven days from $2675.

Taka ☎07/4046 7333, ⓦwww.takadive.com.au. Fast, thirty-metre chunky vessel with four levels and onboard facilities including digital-photography equipment rental and computers. Four days at the Cod Hole and Ribbon reefs $1180; five days (including Coral Sea sites) $1380.

Undersea Explorer ☎07/4099 5911, ⓦwww.undersea.com.au. Scientific research vessel where guests are allowed to participate in ongoing projects; destinations include Osprey Reef, Cod Hole and the Ribbons, and occasional trips to the historic *Pandora* wreck (see p.456). Four days $1365, seven days $2215.

Vagabond ☎07/4059 0477, ⓦwww.vagabond-dive.com. Twenty-metre yacht with maximum of eleven passengers and a roving permit to suit weather conditions. Two days from $290, dives $30 each.

DIVE SCHOOLS

Ask around about what each **dive school** offers, though training standards in Cairns are uniformly sound. You'll pay around $400 for a budget Open-Water Certification course, diving lesser reefs whilst training and returning to Cairns each night; and $600–725 for a four- or five-day course using better sites and staying on a live-aboard at the reef for a couple of days doing your certification. The following schools are long-established and have a solid reputation; certification dives are either made north at Norman, Hastings and Saxon reefs, or south at Flynn, Moore and Tetford.

CDC 121 Abbott St ☎1800 642 591, ⓦwww.cairnsdive.com.au.

Deep Sea Divers Den 319 Draper St ☎1800 612 2233, ⓦwww.diversden.com.au.

Down Under Dive 287 Draper St ☎07/4052 8307, ⓦwww.downunderdive.com.au.

Pro-Dive Corner of Grafton and Shields sts ☎07/4031 5255, ⓦwww.prodivecairns.com.

mention the sheer number of visitors – have had a visibly detrimental effect in the most visited areas, though remoter sections tend to be in better condition. Having said that, almost everywhere is still packed with marine life, ranging from tiny gobies to squid, turtles and big pelagic fish – only seasoned divers might come away disappointed.

Vessels to take you there range from old trawlers to racing yachts and high-speed cruisers; **cruises** and **dive trips** last from a day to over a week. All day-trip operators have **ticket desks** at, and depart from, the **Reef Fleet Terminal** at the end of Spence Street; you can also **book** through an agent, but either way you need to do so at least a day in advance. One way to choose the right boat is simply to check out the **price**: small, cramped, slow tubs are the cheapest while roomy, faster catamarans are more expensive; to narrow things down further, find out which serves the best **food**. Before going to the reef (or even if you're not), take in the superb two-hour **Reef Teach** multimedia and interactive show in Cairns at the Mainstreet Arcade, 85 Lake St (Mon–Sat 6.30pm, 2hr; $15; ⓦ www .reefteach.com.au), at which eccentric marine biologist Paddy Colwell gives more essential background than the dive schools and tour operators have time to impart – this is the most worthwhile thing you can do in Cairns.

Dive sites

The dozen or more **inner reef** sites are much of a muchness. Concentrated day-tripping means that you'll probably be sharing the experience with several other boatloads of people, with scores of divers in the water at once. On a good day, snorkelling over shallow outcrops is enjoyable; going deeper, the coral shows more damage, but there's plenty of patchily distributed marine life. **Michaelmas Cay**, a small, vegetated crescent of sand, is worth a visit: over thirty thousand sooty, common and crested terns roost on the island, while giant clams, sweetlips and reef sharks can be found in the surrounding waters. Nearby **Hastings Reef** has better coral, resident moray eel and bulky Maori wrasse, as well as plenty of sea stars and snails in the sand beneath. The two are often included in dive- or reef-trip packages, providing shallow, easy and fun diving. Another favourite, **Norman Reef**, tends to have very clear water, and some sites preserve decent coral gardens with abundant marine life.

One of the cheaper options for diving the **outer reef** is to take an overnight trip (sleep on board) to nearby sections such as **Moore** or **Arlington** reefs, which take between ninety minutes and two hours to reach – it's rather gener-alized terrain, but the advantages over a simple day-excursion are that you get longer in the water plus the opportunity for night dives. **Longer trips** of three days or more venture further from Cairns into two areas: a circuit north to the Cod Hole and Ribbon reefs, or straight out into the Coral Sea. **The Cod Hole**, near Lizard Island (see p.502), has no coral but is justifiably famous for the mobs of hulking potato cod which rise from the depths to receive hand-outs; currents here are strong, but having these monsters come close enough to cuddle is awesome. **The Ribbons** are a two-hundred-kilometre string boasting relatively pristine locations and good visibility, as do the **Coral Sea** sites; these are isolated, vertically walled reefs some distance out from the main structure and surrounded by open water teeming with seasonal bundles of pelagic species including mantas, turtles and seasonal minke whales. The most-visited Coral Sea sites are **Osprey** and **Holmes** reefs, but try to get out to **Bougainville Reef**, home to everything from brightly coloured anthias fish to fast and powerful silvertip sharks.

Green Island and Fitzroy Island

Heart-shaped, tiny and sandy, **Green Island** is the easiest of any of the Barrier Reef's coral cays to reach, making it an accessible, if expensive, day-trip from Cairns. This, combined with the island's size, means that it can be difficult to escape other visitors, but you only need to put on some fins, visit the **underwater observatory** ($10) or go for a cruise in a glass-bottomed boat to see plentiful coral, fish and turtles. The five-star rooms at the *Green Island Resort* (℡07/4031 3300, ⓦwww.greenislandresort.com.au; ⑨) attract long-term guests, and there's a restaurant and pool open to day-trippers, plus plenty of sand to laze on. **Daily ferries** from the Reef Fleet Terminal in Cairns include Big Cat ($69; ℡07/4051 0444, ⓦwww.bigcat-cruises.com.au), which departs at 9am, 11am and 1pm, and Great Adventures ($69; ℡07/4044 9944, ⓦwww.greatadventures .com.au), departing at 8.30am, 10.30am and 1pm. Both run buses which will collect you from your accommodation for $12 return. Day-trippers on a budget should bring their own lunches, as the resort's restaurant is very expensive. Alternatively, Ocean Free ($119; ℡07/4050 0550, ⓦwww.oceanfree.com.au) offers **sailing tours** to Green Island with offshore snorkelling at Pinnacle Reef, departing from the Marlin Marina at 7.30am.

Fitzroy Island is a small rugged continental island covered in tropical forest just 35km southeast of Cairns but just 4km off the Yarrabah Peninsula, and sports the upmarket *Fitzroy Island Resort* (℡1300 308 303, ⓦwww.huntgroup .com.au; ⑨). You can visit as a day-tripper, and away from the manicured beach fronting the resort there are some worthwhile walks through highland greenery, notably the two-hour trek to the Lighthouse for excellent views. A daily **ferry** departs from Reef Fleet Terminal at 8.30am (45min each way; $63 return; ℡07/4030 7907).

▲ A sea turtle in the Great Barrier Reef

The Atherton Tablelands

The **Atherton Tablelands**, the highlands behind Cairns, are named after **John Atherton**, who made the tin deposits at Herberton accessible by opening a route to the coast in 1877. Dense forest covered these highlands before the majority was felled for timber and given over to dairy cattle, tobacco and grain. The remaining pockets of forest are magnificent, but it's the area's understated beauty that draws most visitors today, and though **Kuranda** and its markets pull in busloads from the coast, there are several quieter national parks brimming

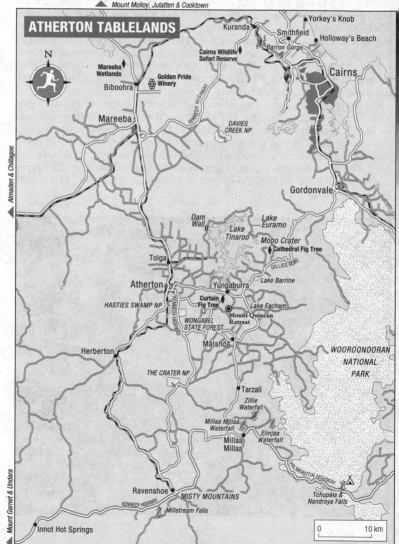

ATHERTON TABLELANDS

Mount Molloy, Julatten & Cooktown

Almaden & Chillagoe

Mount Garnet & Undara

N

Kuranda
Yorkey's Knob
Smithfield
Holloway's Beach
Barron Gorge
Cairns Wildlife Safari Reserve
Mareeba Wetlands
Golden Pride Winery
Biboohra
KENNEDY HIGHWAY
Cairns
DAVIES CREEK NP
Mareeba
Gordonvale
Dam Wall
Lake Euramo
Lake Tinaroo
Mobo Crater
Cathedral Fig Tree
Tolga
GILLIES ROAD
Atherton
Yungaburra
Lake Barrine
Curtain Fig Tree
Lake Eacham
HASTIES SWAMP NP
Mount Quincan Retreat
KENNEDY HIGHWAY
WONGABEL STATE FOREST
Malanda
Herberton
WOOROONOORAN NATIONAL PARK
THE CRATER NP
Tarzali
Zillie Waterfall
Millaa Millaa Waterfall
Elinjaa Waterfall
Millaa Millaa
PALMERSTON HIGHWAY
Ravenshoe
MISTY MOUNTAINS
Tchupala & Nandroya Falls
KENNEDY HIGHWAY
Millstream Falls
Innot Hot Springs

0   10 km

Queensland's **wet tropics** – the coastal belt from the Paluma Range, near Townsville, to the Daintree north of Cairns – are **UNESCO World Heritage** listed, as they contain one of the oldest surviving tracts of rainforest anywhere on Earth. Whether this listing has benefited the region is questionable, however; logging has slowed, but the tourist industry has vigorously exploited the area's status as an untouched wilderness, constantly pushing for more development so that a greater number of visitors can be accommodated. The clearing of mangroves for a marina and resort at Cardwell is a worst-case example; Kuranda's **Skyrail** was one of the few projects designed to lessen the ultimate impact (another highway – with more buses – was the alternative). Given the profits to be made, development is inevitable, but it's sad that a scheme designed to promote the region's unique beauty may accelerate its destruction.

with rare species. You could spend days here, driving or hiking through rainforest to crater lakes and endless small waterfalls, or simply camp out for a night and search for wildlife with a torch. For a contrast, consider a trip west to the mining town of **Chillagoe**, whose dust, limestone caves and Aboriginal art place it firmly in the Outback.

Numerous **tours** run here from Cairns (see box, p.477), and there's a regular **bus service** with Trans North (℡07/4776 5124), which runs from Cairns Central to Kuranda, Marreba and Atherton three times daily on weekdays, twice on a Saturday and once on a Sunday. To explore properly you really need your own car: **drivers** can reach the tablelands on the Palmerston Highway from Innisfail; the twisty Gillies Highway from Gordonvale; the Kennedy Highway from Smithfield to Kuranda; or Route 81 from Mossman to Mareeba. Two unforgettable alternatives are to ride up to the tablelands **by train** from Cairns to Kuranda, which winds through gorges and rainforest; or in the green gondolas of the **Kuranda Skyrail cable car**, with fantastic aerial views of the forest canopy en route between Smithfield and Kuranda – either method costs $40 one-way or $58 return.

Kuranda and the Barron Gorge

A constant stream of visitors arriving from the coast has turned the formerly atavistic community of **KURANDA** into a stereotypical resort village, though it's still a pretty spot and good for a half-day excursion. Most people come for the much-hyped daily **markets**, best from 8.30am to 3pm on Wednesday, Friday and Sunday, though these are shrinking as less-regulated events at Yungaburra and Port Douglas gain momentum. There are also a number of good wildlife enclosures, notably the **Butterfly Sanctuary** (daily 9.45am–4pm; $16), a mix of streams and "feed trees" where giant Ulysses and birdwing butterflies' numbers are being pumped up by a breeding programme; and **Birdworld** (daily 9am–4pm; $15), a superb aviary with realistically arranged vegetation and nothing between you and a host of native and exotic rarities. At the **Koala Gardens** (daily 9am–4pm; $15) next door you can cuddle koalas and see wallabies, wombats, snakes and crocodiles in a rather bland environment. Look out for discounted combined deals to all three attractions.

Kuranda sits at the top of the **Barron Gorge**, spectacular in the wet season when the river rages down the falls, which are otherwise tamed by a hydroelectric dam upstream. Cross the rail bridge next to the station and take a path leading down to the river to hop on the Kuranda Riverboat (5 daily; $14;

⊕07/4093 7476) for a 45-minute informative **cruise**. On foot, a **walking track** descends to cold swimming spots along the railway and river from the lookout at the end of Barron Falls Road, 2km from town. Other trails follow the road beyond the falls through the Barron Gorge National Park and down to Kamerunga, near Cairns – see p.480 for details.

Just 9km from Kuranda down the Mareeba road, **Cairns Wildlife Safari Reserve** (daily 9am–4.30pm; $28; ⊕07/4093 7777, ⊛www .cairnswildlifesafarireserve.com.au) has a few native species but draws the crowds with Sumatran tigers, pigmy hippos, white rhinos and ring-tailed lemurs in pretty authentic, savannah surroundings – there are guided tours and feeding sessions throughout the day.

Practicalities

The road from Cairns comes in at the top of town, while trains and the Skyrail cable car arrive 500m downhill; **essential services** – post office, store (EFTPOS), bank, cafés – are laid out between them along Coondoo Street.

Given its accessibility from Cairns, Kuranda doesn't tempt many people to stay overnight; it's virtually a ghost town after the markets close, and there's little **accommodation**. Just up from the Skyrail terminus and orchid-shrouded train station, you'll find the quiet *Kuranda Backpackers' Hostel* at 6 Arara St (⊕07/4093 7355, ⊛www.kurandabackpackershostel.com; dorms $19, rooms ❷), with a plentiful supply of bunks, large grounds, kitchen and laundry. Around the corner is *Kuranda Hotel* (⊕07/4093 7206, ⊛www.kurandahotel.com.au; ❸), with motel rooms out the back of an incongruous Irish theme pub. The nearest **campsite** is just out of town across the Mareeba road at the pleasantly shaded *Kuranda Rainforest Accommodation Park* (⊕07/4093 7316, ⊛www.kurandarainforestpark .com.au; camping $24, powered sites $28, rooms ❷, units ❹), which also has a decent restaurant overlooking the forest.

Cafés are legion, though pricey: *Annabel's Pastry*, across from the main markets, has excellent croissants and pies, while *Billy's* at the *Middle Pub* (halfway down Coondoo St) does tasty charcoal grills and salads.

Mareeba and around

West of Kuranda, rainforest quickly gives way to dry woodland and tobacco plantations, quite a change from the coast's greenery. **MAREEBA**, 35km along,

---

Birding on the tablelands

The northern end of the Atherton Tablelands, as it slopes downhill between Mareeba and Mossman, encompasses a broad range of habitats, from dry gum woodland to highland rainforest, open farmland, lowland wetlands and the coast, and as such is one of the richest areas for **birding** in Australia, with over 350 species recorded, including thirteen endemics. Several places along the Mareeba–Mossman road have now set themselves up as **birdwatchers' retreats**, and can fill you in on places to improve your tallies: near the tiny hamlet of **Julatten**, about 50km north of Mareeba via Mount Molloy, ❧ *Kingfisher Park* (⊕07/4094 1263, ⊛www.birdwatchers.com.au; rooms ❷, units ❺) has clued-up owners, a choice of bunkhouse rooms with shared bathrooms or self-contained units, and guided walks. The retreat is within striking distance of fabled (in birding circles at least) **Mount Lewis**, and features in Sean Dooley's book *The Big Twitch*, a humorous insight into the obsessive world of serious birdwatching.

is a quiet place and the tablelands' oldest town, founded in the 1900s after the area was opened up for **tobacco** farming. **Coffee** has largely replaced this now – Coffee Works, on Mason Street at the southern end of town (daily 9am–4pm; $19), offers tours of its facilities with tastings of 21 varieties of coffee and twelve chocolates, an impressive coffee museum and a courtyard café with free coffee refills. Fruit plantations have also become a profitable business, with several farms recently branching out into **tropical fruit wine** production and opening cellar doors to promote their mango wines, coffee liqueurs and banana brandy – try Golden Pride Winery (daily 8am–6.30pm), 10km north of Mareeba off the highway at Biboohra.

Just beyond Biboohra, the **Mareeba Wetlands** (daily 9am–4.30pm, closed Jan–March; $10; ℗07/4093 2514, ⓦwww.mareebawetlands.com) is a stunning five-thousand-acre reserve of tropical savannah woodlands with grass-fringed lagoons that attract seasonal flocks of brolgas, jabiru storks and black cockatoos, along with resident wallabies and goannas. The wetlands are also part of a breeding programme for rainbow-coloured **Gouldian finches**, a formerly common bird now virtually extinct in the wild, but which you can see in the aviary here. You can rent canoes or join a boat, book twilight ranger-led walks, or **stay** in tented cabins (◐) at the **safari camp** here when it's not being used by researchers – all of these need to be booked in advance.

Back in Mareeba, all the shops and banks can be found on Byrnes Street, with the **visitor centre** (daily 8am–4pm) about 1km south of town along the Atherton road, marked by a memorial to James Venture Mulligan, the veteran prospector who discovered the Palmer River Goldfields. Just opposite, the *Jackaroo Motel* (℗07/4092 2677, ⓦwww.jackaroomotel.com; ◑) is one of Mareeba's better **places to stay**, or try the *Mareeba Country Caravan Park* (℗07/4092 3281; cabins ❷) in a rural setting tucked along the Emerald End Road off the Kennedy Highway. The town itself is pretty seedy **after dark**, with plenty of drunks staggering around even early on. **Moving on**, Atherton is 30km south, while roads north head via the township of Mount Molloy to Cooktown or the coast at Mossman. For Chillagoe, follow signs from the northern end of town for Dimbulah, just beyond which you can stay at a working farm at the quaint *Emu Creek Station* (℗07/4094 8313; camping $14, rooms ◑), which serves hearty home-cooked meals.

West to Chillagoe

The 150-kilometre road to **Chillagoe** mysteriously alternates between corrugated gravel and isolated sections of bitumen, but poses no real problem during the dry season. Thirty kilometres before town, the *Almaden Hotel*'s cool, mirrored, well-supplied bar and beer garden are an incredible oasis in ramshackle, dilapidated **Almaden**.

CHILLAGOE dates from 1887, when enough copper ore was found to keep a smelter running until the 1950s; nowadays a gold mine 16km west at Mungana seems to keep the place ticking over. Red dust, hillocks, a service station, a general store and a single, short street of oversized hotels complete the picture. The main point of coming here is to see Chillagoe's **caves**, ancient limestone hillocks hollowed out by rain and half-buried in the scrub, explored on tours from the Hub (see p.490). The most interesting caves are **Royal Arch**, **Donna** and **Trezkinn**, full of natural sculptures including a few large **stalagmites**. Wildlife here includes grey swiftlets and agile pythons, which somehow manage to catch bats on the wing. A footpath leads through grassland between the caves, where you'll find echidnas, kangaroos, black cockatoos and frogmouths, the last being odd birds whose name fits them perfectly. **Balancing Rock** offers panoramic views, with Chillagoe hidden by low trees, while obscure Aboriginal paintings and engravings have been found near **the Arches**, west at Mungana.

The **Hub visitor centre** (℡07/4094 7111) is on Queen Street, Chillagoe's main drag, and can arrange **tours** of three of the town's caves (daily 9am, 11am & 1.30pm; $15; 1hr); check well in advance as the tours may not run during the wet season and numbers are limited. **Accommodation** is available at the *Chillagoe Cabins* on Queen Street (℡07/4094 7206, ⓦwww.chillagoe .com; ❻), which has a pool and serves meals, or at *Chillagoe Observatory & Eco Lodge* on Hospital Avenue (℡07/4094 7155, ⓦwww.coel.com.au; ❹), with shared rooms, family units and a mini observatory for star-gazing. **Heading west** from Chillagoe, the road continues 500km to Karumba and the Gulf of Carpentaria (see p.550), but it doesn't improve, and there's little fuel or help along the way.

Atherton and around

Thirty kilometres south of Mareeba and centrally placed for forays to most of the area's attractions, the bland setting of **ATHERTON** is the largest town in the tablelands. It was founded in part by Chinese miners who settled here in the 1880s after being chased off the goldfields: 2km south of the centre, the corrugated-iron **Hou Wang Temple** (daily 10am–4pm; $7.50) is the last surviving building of Atherton's old **Chinatown**, a once-busy enclave of market gardens and homes which was abandoned after the government gave the land to returning World War I servicemen. The temple was restored in 2000, with an accompanying museum containing photographs and artefacts found on site – the excellent **birds of prey show** is also held here (Wed–Sun 11am & 2pm; closed Feb, March & Nov; $13).

You can clock up more local **birdlife** at **Hasties Swamp**, a big waterhole and two-storey observation hide about 5km south of town. While nothing astounding, it's a peaceful place populated by magpie geese, pink-eared ducks, swamp hens and assorted marsh tiggets.

Atherton's banks, shops and early-opening **cafés** – *Chatterbox* is the most lively – can be found along Main Street, with a supermarket right at the south end past the post office. There's a friendly **visitor centre** (daily 9am–5pm; ℡07/4091 4222) just south of the centre. **Accommodation** includes green and spacious campsites at the *Woodlands Tourist Park*, just at the edge of town on Herberton Road (℡07/4091 1407, ⓦwww.woodlandscp.com.au; cabins ❹); the heavily tiled and hospitable *Atherton Travellers Lodge*, 37 Alice St, off Vernon Street (℡07/4091 3552, ⓦwww.athertontravellerslodge.com.au; dorms $25, rooms ❶), which specializes in finding farm work; and the very pleasant *Atherton Blue Gum* at 36 Twelfth Ave (℡07/4091 5149, ⓦwww.athertonbluegum.com; ❺–❼), a modern, timber B&B which also runs regional tours.

Lake Tinaroo

At the village of **Tolga**, 5km north of Atherton, a turn-off leads to **Lake Tinaroo**, a convoluted reservoir formed by pooling the Barron River's headwaters. At the end of the fifteen-kilometre sealed road is the dam wall and nearby *Lake Tinaroo Holiday Park* (℡07/4095 8232, ⓦwww.ltholidaypark.com .au; cabins ❸), which also rents out canoes for $50 a day. Past here, a gravel road runs 25km around the lake to the Gillies Highway, 15km east of Yungaburra, passing five very cheap **campsites** on the north shore before cutting deep into native forests. It's worth stopping along the way for the short walks to bright-green **Mobo Crater**, spooky **Lake Euramo**, and the **Cathedral Fig**, a giant tree some 50m tall and 43m around the base; the thick mass of tendrils supporting the crown has fused together like molten wax.

Yungaburra and around

Just 13km east of Atherton at the start of the Gillies Highway to Gordon-vale, the self-consciously pretty village of **YUNGABURRA**, consisting of the old wooden *Lake Eacham Hotel*, a store, a handful of houses and some quaint restaurants, makes an excellent base to explore the tablelands. The village is also the venue for a huge **market** held on the last Saturday of each month. Good places for wildlife spotting include a **platypus-viewing platform** on the river where the road from Atherton comes into town, and the **Curtain Fig Tree** (again signposted off the Atherton road), another extraordinarily big parasitic strangler fig whose base is entirely overhung by a stringy mass of aerial roots drooping off the higher branches. Informative **wildlife guides** can help you spot some of the rarer nocturnal marsupials around town; contact Alan's Wildlife Tours ($60; ☏07/4095 3784, ⓦwww.alanswildlifetours.com.au).

Considering its diminutive size, Yungaburra has plenty of **places to stay**. The pine-and-slate ⚘ *On the Wallaby Hostel*, 37 Eacham Rd (☏07/4095 2031, ⓦwww.onthewallaby.com; dorms $22, rooms ❷), is an excellent budget option which organizes canoe and wildlife-spotting trips. Also on Eacham Road are the value-for-money motel rooms of *Kookaburra Lodge* (☏07/4095 3222, ⓦwww.kookaburra-lodge.com; ❹) or the rather more pricey but stylish *Eden House* (☏07/4095 3355, ⓦwww.edenhouse.com.au; ❻) on Gillies Highway. For a **romantic weekend**, though, the secluded, self-contained wooden-pole houses which overlook an extinct volcano crater at ⚘ *Mt Quincan Crater Retreat*, on the Peeramon road about 8km southeast of Yungaburra (☏07/4095 2255, ⓦwww.mtquincan.com.au; ❾), are absolutely unbeatable – and it's also infested with tree kangaroos. For **eating**, *Flynn's Café* does an excellent breakfast, *Eden House* has an "Australian contemporary" menu and inexpensive set dinners, or try the bratwurst and rosti at *Nick's Swiss Italian Restaurant* (closed Mon).

Lakes Eacham and Barrine

A few kilometres east of Yungaburra at the start of the Gillies Highway down to Gordonvale are the **crater lakes**, or "maars", of Barrine and Eacham – blue, still discs surrounded by thick rainforest (though parts of this were badly battered by **Cyclone Larry** in 2006). **Lake Eacham** has a picnic area and an easy four-kilometre trail around its shores, taking you past birds and insects foraging on the forest floor, and inoffensive **amethystine pythons** – Australia's largest snake – sunning themselves down by the water. There's **accommodation** near the lake at the cozy *Crater Lake Rainforest Cottages* (☏07/4095 2322, ⓦwww.craterlakes.com.au; ❻), with four self-contained themed cottages set in a forest clearing; and *Chambers Wildlife Lodges* (☏07/4095 3754, ⓦwww.rainforest-australia.com; minimum three-night stay ❽), something of a magnet for local birdlife and mammals.

For its part, **Lake Barrine** has a tearoom overlooking the water serving good cream teas and canteen-style meals, and a **cruise boat** (daily 9.30am,

11.30am, 1.30pm, 2.30pm & 3.15pm; $14.50) which spends an hour circuiting the lake. To get away from the crowds, head for the two enormous kauri pines which mark the start of an underused six-kilometre **walking track** around the lake; keep your eyes peeled for spiky-headed water dragons, more pythons and hordes of musky rat-kangaroos, which look exactly as you'd expect them to.

The Southern Tablelands

The Kennedy Highway continues 80km down from Atherton to Ravenshoe, the highlands' southernmost town, past easy walking tracks at first **Wongabel State Forest** and then **the Crater** at Mount Hypipamee, a 56-metre vertical rift formed by volcanic gases blowing through fractured granite that's now filled with deep, weed-covered water. There are picnic tables here but camping is prohibited. An alternative road south from Atherton – and the train (see p.487) – circles west via **HERBERTON**, a quaint, one-time timber town without a modern building in sight. During the 1880s there were thirty thousand people here (a century before Cairns' population numbered so many), and the railway from Atherton was built to service the town. If you happen to be in Herberton at lunchtime on Sunday, there are huge outdoor **barbecues** at the *Royal Hotel*'s beer garden.

RAVENSHOE is notable for the *Tully Falls Hotel*, Queensland's highest pub, and **Millstream Falls**, Australia's broadest waterfall, 5km southwest. There's a **steam railway** here, with a train departing Sunday at 1.30pm ($18) to the tiny siding of Tumoulin, Queensland's highest train station – call Ravenshoe's **visitor centre** (daily 9am–4pm; ☏07/4097 7700) for information. Southeast of town, a series of marked **hiking trails** through the **Misty Mountains**' forests and streams offers walks of between a day and a week in length, with campsites laid out at regular intervals – for practical information check out Ⓦwww.mistymountains.com.au, or call the National Parks Service on ☏07/4046 6600.

For **accommodation** in Ravenshoe, try the *Old Convent B&B* (☏07/4097 6454, Ⓦwww.theoldconvent.com.au; ❹) or *Tall Timbers Caravan Park* (☏07/4097 6325; units ❷). Southwest, the road drops off the tablelands past **Innot Hot Springs** – with its huge ant hills and steamy upwellings behind the *Hot Springs Hotel* – and the township of **Mount Garnet**, to the start of the Gulf Developmental Road.

Malanda, Millaa Millaa and the Palmerston Highway

About 25km southeast of Atherton, the **dairy** at **MALANDA** provides milk and cheese for the whole of Queensland's far north, plus most of the Northern Territory and even New Guinea. In the centre of town, the *Malanda Hotel* (☏07/4096 5488; ❷) was built in 1911 to sleep three hundred people and claims to be the **largest wooden building** in the southern hemisphere; its old furnishings and excellent restaurant are worth a look even if you're not staying here, though the bar is so cavernous it always feels empty. Back less than 1km towards Atherton, there's a roadside swimming hole and short rainforest walk at **Malanda Falls Environmental Park**; the display at the **visitor centre** here (daily 9.30am–4.30pm; donation) gives a rundown of the tablelands' geology and its Aboriginal and settler history. For **somewhere to stay**, *Canopy Treehouses*, about 7km south via Tarzali (☏07/4096 5364, Ⓦwww.canopytreehouses.com .au; ❽), is another of the tablelands' superlative accommodation options, with wooden pole-frame treehouses set amongst a hundred acres of thick, wildlife-packed rainforest.

From Malanda it's about 20km south to **MILLAA MILLAA**, a quiet, five-hundred-metre street with the usual hotel and general store. A waterfall circuit starts 2km east of the town, where a fifteen-kilometre road passes three small cascades. There's a National Parks **campsite** about 27km southeast of Millaa Millaa, from where walking tracks lead to mossy **Tchupala Falls** and the impressive **Nandroya Falls**, before the Palmerston highway descends 40km to Innisfail and the coast.

Cairns to Cape Tribulation

Just a couple of hours' drive **north of Cairns** on the Cook Highway are the Daintree and Cape Tribulation, the tamed fringes of the Cape York Peninsula. The highway initially runs to **Port Douglas** and **Mossman**, a beautiful drive past isolated beaches where hang-gliders patrol the headlands. North of Mossman is **the Daintree**, Australia's largest and the world's oldest surviving stretch of tropical rainforest. World Heritage listing hasn't saved it from development: roads are being surfaced, land has been subdivided, and there's an ever-increasing number of services in place, undermining the wild and remote brochure image. While this disappoints some visitors, the majestic forest still descends thick and dark right to the sea around **Cape Tribulation**, and you can explore paths through the jungle, watch for wildlife, or just rest on the beach.

Tours from Cairns will show you the sights, but you really need longer to take in the rich scenery and atmosphere – without your own transport, Sun Palm Coaches (℡07/4087 2900, Ⓦwww.sunpalmtransport.com) runs a twice-daily shuttle bus from Cairns to Cape Tribulation ($75 one-way) via Port Douglas and Mossman, whilst Coral Reef Coaches (℡07/4098 2800, Ⓦwww.coralreefcoaches.com.au) offers a slightly cheaper and more frequent service but only as far as Mossman ($35 one-way).

Port Douglas and around

Massive development in recent years has seen the once pretty fishing village of **PORT DOUGLAS**, an hour north of Cairns, turned into an upmarket tourist hub, with a main street full of boutiques, shopping malls and holidaying hordes. However, the town does have a huge **beach**, along with plenty of distractions to keep you busy for a day or two, and it's getting to be as good a place as Cairns to pick up a regional tour or dive trip to the reef.

The town comprises a small grid of leafy streets centred around Macrossan Street – which runs between Four Mile Beach and ANZAC Park – with the **marina** a couple of blocks back. Between the end of Macrossan Street and the sea, **ANZAC Park** is the scene of an increasingly busy Sunday-morning **market**, good for fruit, vegetables and souvenirs. Near the park's **jetty** you'll find the whitewashed timber church of **St Mary's by the Sea**, built after the 1911 cyclone carried off the previous structure.

Out to sea, the vegetated sand cays known as **the Low Isles** make a good day-trip, with fine snorkelling, a lighthouse and an interpretive centre; you can get there with *Wavedancer* ($132; ℡07/4087 2100, Ⓦwww.quicksilver-cruises.com), *Sailaway* ($165; ℡07/4099 4772, Ⓦwww.sailawayportdouglas.com) and

Shaolin ($160; ☎07/4099 4772, ⓦwww.shaolinportdouglas.com), a romantic Chinese junk. **Reef trips** mostly head to Agincourt; Quicksilver's fast catamaran ($195; ☎07/4087 2100, ⓦwww.quicksilver-cruises.com) is best for a day-trip cruise, while **divers** should contact Poseidon, 34 Macrossan St ($225 for three dives; ☎07/4099 4772, ⓦwww.poseidon-cruises.com.au).

Practicalities

As in Cairns, a prolific number of businesses offer tourist information – the Port Douglas **visitor centre** at 23 Macrossan St (daily 8.30am–6.30pm; ☎07/4099 5599) can sort out everything from Aboriginal-guided tours of Mossman Gorge to sailing trips and buses to the Daintree.

The most intimate of the town's **accommodation** options is the adults-only *Pink Flamingo* (☎07/4099 6622, ⓦwww.pinkflamingo.com.au; ⑤–⑦), off Davidson Street on the way into town. There is a pack of more conventional apartments along Macrossan Street, all offering comfortable rooms and a pool, including *Macrossan House* at no. 19 (☎07/4099 4366, ⓦwww.macrossanhouse-port-douglas.com.au; ⑦) and *New Port* at no. 16 (☎07/4099 5700, ⓦwww.thenewport.com.au; ⑥). Budget options include the centrally located backpackers' hostel *Parrotfish Lodge* on Warner Street (☎07/4099 5011, ⓦwww.parrotfishlodge.com; dorms $25–38, rooms ④), while the pleasant *Port O'Call Lodge*, about 1km from town on Port Street (☎07/4099 5422, ⓦwww.portocall.com.au; dorms $26.50, rooms ④), has an altogether more sedate atmosphere.

Places to eat abound along Macrossan Street. Near the visitor centre, *EJ Seamarket* is a licensed fish-and-chip shop, so you can grab a cold beer while waiting for your meal to crisp. The *Iron Bar* has rough-cut timber furniture and a mid-range surf 'n' turf menu; *Mango Jam Café* across the road opens late over wood-fired pizza; but the cheapest decent meal is from the *Combined Club*, a locals' haunt in a large tin shed overlooking Dickson Inlet. *The Living Room*, around the corner on Wharf Street (Tues–Sun 6.30pm–late; ☎07/4099 4011), sports a huge outdoor deck leading into the cool interior of a renovated wooden Queenslander house; its Asian-fusion menu is thick with seafood specialities such as blue swimmer crab and tiger prawns (mains around $30). If it's just a cooling **drink** you're after, both the *Court House Hotel* and *Central Hotel* are old-style wooden pubs with plenty of local atmosphere.

Mossman

MOSSMAN, 14km past Port Douglas, is a quiet town which has hardly changed since the 1950s; rail lines between the canefields and mill still run along the main street. Ten minutes inland, **Mossman Gorge** looks like all rainforest rivers should; the boulder-strewn flow is good for messing around in on a quiet day, but attracts streams of tour buses and car break-ins in peak season. There are also plenty of **walking trails** taking in the gorge and rainforest, lasting from a few minutes to a couple of hours. **Kuku Yalanji**, the local Aboriginal community, also conduct **tours** of the gorge explaining its history and local plant usage (Mon–Sat 9am, 11am, 1pm & 3pm; $32; bookings on ☎07/4098 2595, ⓦwww.yalanji.com.au). If you want to stay somewhere plush in the area, book in at the exclusive *Silky Oaks Lodge* (☎1300 134 044, ⓦwww.silkyoakslodge.com.au; ⑨), 12km from town through the canefields; there's not much rainforest here, but you get very well looked after.

Continuing north, the road splits left to Daintree township or right for the Daintree Ferry to Cape Tribulation. Backtracking southeast, you leave the highway and climb to **Mount Molloy** and either Mareeba or the Peninsula Developmental Road – the easier, inland route to Cooktown.

The Daintree

Set off the Mossman to Cape Tribulation road, riverside **DAINTREE** township – a former timber camp – is now more or less just one big pub, a general store and a campsite. For exceptional two-hour dawn **birding tours** contact Chris Dahlberg (℡07/4098 7997, ⓦwwwdaintreerivertours .com.au; $55), though most people bypass Daintree completely and instead follow the road to the **Daintree River Ferry** (6am–midnight; vehicles $20 return) and the start of the Cape Tribulation road. The river crossing can be very busy, with the 25-vehicle-capacity cable ferry taking around fifteen minutes for the return trip.

The Cape Tribulation road

Across the river is the start of the **Daintree National Park** and the 35-kilometre scenic drive to the tiny settlement of Cape Tribulation, beyond which the sealed road ends and becomes a 4WD-only route to Cooktown. From the ferry crossing at Daintree River, it's 8km through rainforest over the convoluted Alexandra Range to the **Daintree Discovery Centre** (daily 8.30am–5pm; $33), which features a five-level, 27-metre-high tower with identification charts for the plants and birds you're likely to see at each stage – the top also provides a fabulous view over the canopy. Just up the road, **Floraville** has the regional pub and a café; past here, a six-kilometre side road from the airstrip heads straight to the coast and **Cow Bay**'s excellent **beach**. **Accommodation** along the Cow Bay road includes the open-plan, laid-back *Epiphyte Bed and Breakfast*, off a short track about 4km along (℡07/4098 9039, ⓦwww.rainforestbb.com; ❹), and the jungle-clad cabins of *Crocodylus Village*, about 3km along (℡07/4098 9166, ⓦwww.crocodyluscapetrib.com; dorms $23, rooms ❸). Meals at the latter are healthy and inexpensive, and they arrange night walks, kayak trips to Snapper Island, and diving at the local reef.

Back on the Cape Tribulation road, another few kilometres lands you at *Fanpalm Café*, which marks the start of a **boardwalk** through a forest of fan palms, and the cabins, self-contained units and camping at *Lync-Haven Retreat* (℡07/4098 9155, ⓦwww.lynchaven.com.au; ❻). Moving on past a tea plantation and tiny **ALEXANDRA BAY** township, there's further **accommodation** up against the forest fence at *Deep Forest Lodge* (℡07/4098 9102, ⓦwww.daintreedeepforestlodge.com.au; ❺), which has well-furnished, self-contained cabins, and *Heritage Lodge*, inland off the main road (℡07/4098 9138, ⓦwww.heritagelodge.net.au; ❻), which has boutique cabins, a fancy

---

Cycads

Cycads are extremely slow-growing, fire-resistant plants found throughout the tropics, with tough, palm-like fronds – relics of the age of dinosaurs. Female plants produce large cones which break up into bright orange segments, each containing a seed; these are eaten (and so distributed) by emus, amongst other creatures. Despite being highly toxic to humans – almost every early Australian explorer made himself violently ill trying them – these seeds were a staple of Aborigines, who detoxified flour made from the nuts by prolonged washing. They also applied "fire-stick farming" techniques, encouraging groves to grow and seed by annual burning.

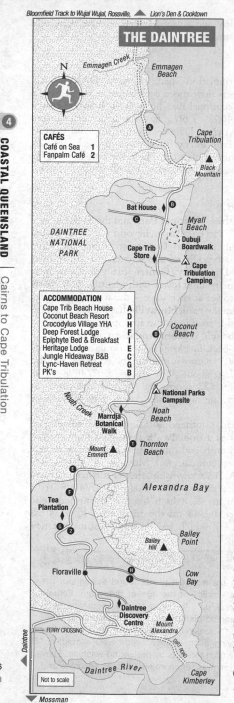

THE DAINTREE

N

Emmagen Creek

Emmagen Beach

Cape Tribulation

CAFÉS
Café on Sea   1
Fanpalm Café   2

Black Mountain

Bat House

Myall Beach

DAINTREE NATIONAL PARK

Dubuji Boardwalk

Cape Trib Store

▲ **Cape Tribulation Camping**

ACCOMMODATION
Cape Trib Beach House   A
Coconut Beach Resort   D
Crocodylus Village YHA   H
Deep Forest Lodge   F
Epiphyte Bed & Breakfast   I
Heritage Lodge   E
Jungle Hideaway B&B   C
Lync-Haven Retreat   G
PK's   B

Coconut Beach

▲ **National Parks Campsite**

Noah Creek

Marrdja Botanical Walk

Noah Beach

Mount Emmett ▲

❶ **Thornton Beach**

Alexandra Bay

Tea Plantation

❷

Bailey Hill ▲

Bailey Point

Floraville

❽

Cow Bay

Daintree Discovery Centre

Mount Alexandra

DIRT ROAD

FERRY CROSSING

Daintree

496

Not to scale

Daintree River

Cape Kimberley

▼ Mossman

restaurant and walking trails along **Cooper Creek**. Based on the river here are *Cape Tribulation Wilderness Cruises* (☎07/4033 2052; 1hr cruise $25, 6hr cruise $120) which meander along the mangrove estuaries spotting wildlife including huge crocodiles. The next stop is 4km on at sandy Thornton Beach, where you'll find a **licensed kiosk** at *Café on Sea*; from here it's another few kilometres to the **Marrdja Botanical Walk**, where concrete paths and boardwalks follow the creek through a mixture of forest to mangroves at the river mouth on **Noah Beach**. Look for spiky lawyer cane, lianas twisted into corkscrew shapes where they once surrounded a tree, and the spherical pods of the cannonball mangrove – dried and dismembered, they were used as puzzles by Aboriginal peoples, the object being to fit the irregular segments back together. There's a National Parks **campsite** (pre-book via ⓦwww.epa.qld.gov.au) in woodland behind the beach; it's big but prone to be muddy and is closed during the wet season.

Just up the road is the exclusive beachfront *Coconut Beach Resort* (☎1300 144 044, ⓦwww.coconut beach.com.au; ❾), with an extensive array of facilities including a huge A-frame restaurant where "smart tropical dress" is required. North of here, the **Cape Trib Store** has a café and supplies, with a natural swimming hole in the forest close by. The store is also the base for **Mason's Tours** (☎07/4098 0070, ⓦ www.masonstours.com.au), which organizes 4WD safaris and local day and night walks – they also publish a very detailed map ($5) of the Bloomfield Track to Cooktown if you're heading that way. Opposite the store, a short road heads through thick forest to **Myall Beach** and *Cape Tribulation Camping* (☎07/4098 0077, ⓦwww.capetribcamping.com.au; camping $30, powered sites $36, safari tents ❸). Plants close in again a couple of kilometres up the main road at **Dubuji Boardwalk**, a 1.2-kilometre-long replay of Marrdja, though with a greater variety of forests.

Cape Tribulation

Cape Tribulation – a forty-minute drive from the ferry crossing – was named when Captain Cook's vessel hit a reef offshore in June 1770. The cleared area below the steep, forested slopes of **Mount Sorrow** has a café, store, ATM, pharmacy and a **Bat House** (Tues–Sun 10.30am–3.30pm; $4), worth a visit to handle tame, orphaned flying foxes. The beach here is attractive and accessed along a boardwalk from the township. Beds and camping are available at the often noisy and overcrowded *PK's* hostel (T 1800 232 333, W www.pksjunglevillage.com; camping $10 per person, dorms $23–28, rooms ❺). Alternatively, there are comfy but rustic wooden cabins hidden in the forest at *Jungle Hideaway B&B* (T 07/4098 0108, W www.rainforesthideaway .com; ❹), set 200m up in the hills, as well as the supremely idyllic jungle-beachfront *Cape Trib Beach House*, 2.5km north (T 1800 111 124, W www .capetribbeach.com.au, dorms $25, rooms ❻, cabins ❾). All can organize horseriding, sea-kayaking, guided forest walks and the exhilarating experience of abseiling through the canopy with Jungle Surfing Tours ($85; T 07/4098 0043, W www.junglesurfingcanopytours.com).

The area is best explored on foot, for the simple pleasure of walking through the forest with the sea breaking on a beach not five minutes distant. A **path** runs out to the cape, where you may see brilliantly coloured pittas (small, tailless birds with a buff chest, green back and black-and-rust heads) bouncing around in the leaf litter, or even a crocodile sunning itself on the beach. One way to penetrate the undergrowth away from the paths is to follow small creeks: **Emmagen**, about 6km north, runs halfway up Mount Sorrow and is recommended for its safe swimming holes, but get advice on the route first from your accommodation.

The Bloomfield Track

Spanning 80km from Cape Tribulation to where it joins the Cooktown Road at Black Mountain, the **Bloomfield Track** is completely impassable after rain and otherwise requires a 4WD. If you don't have your own, the Country Road Coachlines **bus** (T 07/4045 2794; Cow Bay to Cooktown $47 one-way) runs up it three times per week on its Cairns–Cooktown run, weather permitting – contact them in advance for a pick-up anywhere along the Cape Tribulation road.

The Bloomfield Track's exciting section with virgin rainforest and drastic gradients lies below the halfway mark of the tidal **Bloomfield River**, which has to be crossed at low water. Beyond the **Wujal Wujal Aboriginal community** on the north side, the road flattens out to run past *Haley's Cabins and Camping* (T 07/4060 8207, W www.bloomfieldcabins.com; camping $10 per person, ❸), where there's plentiful camping space and three basic cabins with shared bathrooms. *Home Rule Rainforest Lodge*, at **ROSSVILLE** (T 07/4060 3925; W www.home-rule.com; ❶), offers kitchen facilities and inexpensive meals; alternatively, you could fork out for the exclusive *Peppers Bloomfield Lodge* (T 07/4035 9166, W www.bloomfieldlodge.com.au; ❾), but you'll need to stay at least four nights. Moving on, it's not far now to the more down-to-earth *Lions Den* **pub** at Helenvale near **Black Mountain** (see p.499), about thirty minutes from Cooktown.

The Cape York Peninsula and Torres Strait Islands

The **Cape York Peninsula** points north towards the Torres Strait and New Guinea, and tackling the rugged tracks and hectic river crossings on the "Trip To The Tip" is an adventure in itself – besides being a means to reach **Australia's northernmost point** and the communities at **Bamaga** and **Thursday Island**, so different from anywhere else in Australia that they could easily be in another country. But it's not all four-wheel driving across the savannah: during the dry season the historic settlement of **Cooktown**, the wetlands at **Lakefield National Park** and **Laura**'s Aboriginal heritage are only a day's journey from Cairns in any decent vehicle. Given longer, you might get as far as the mining company town of **Weipa**, but don't go further than this without off-road transport; while some have managed to reach the Tip in family sedans, most who try fail miserably.

With thousands making the overland journey between May and October, a **breakdown** won't necessarily leave you stranded, but the cost of repairs will make you regret it. **Bikers** should travel in groups and have off-roading experience. Those without their own vehicle can take **overland tours** right to the Tip (see box, p.477), or get as far as Cooktown with the Country Road Coachlines **bus**. It's also possible to **cruise** from Cairns up to Bamaga, Horn Island and Thursday Island (see p.507). **Airlines** servicing the Cape from Cairns include Qantas (T 13 13 13, W www.qantas.com.au), Skytrans (T 1300 759 872, W www.skytrans.com.au) and Regional Pacific Airlines (T 1300 797 667, W www.regionalpacific.com.au).

You'll find a few roadhouses and motels along the way, but north of Weipa **accommodation** on the Cape is mostly limited to camping, and it's inevitable if you head right to the Tip that one night at least will be spent in the bush. Settlements also supply meals and provisions, but there won't be much on offer, so take all you can carry. Don't turn bush campsites into rubbish dumps: take a pack of bin liners and remove all your garbage. **Estuarine crocodiles** are present throughout the Cape: read the warning under "Wildlife dangers" in Basics (p.50) and see also p.579. There are few **banks**, so take enough cash to carry you between points – some roadhouses accept plastic. In Cairns, the National Parks office stocks **maps** and brochures on the Cape's national parks, whilst the RACQ (W www.racq.com) has up-to-date information regarding current road conditions. **Essential items** for any vehicles heading to the Tip include a first-aid kit, a comprehensive tool kit and spares, extra fuel cans and a tarpaulin for creek crossings. A winch, and equipment for removing, patching and inflating tyres may also come in handy.

Mossman to Cape York

Not as pretty as the coastal Bloomfield Track but considerably easier, the 260-kilometre inland road to Cooktown and points north leaves the Cook Highway just before Mossman and climbs to the drier scrub at **MOUNT CARBINE**, a former tungsten mine whose roadhouse and *Mt Carbine Hotel* (T 07/4094 3108; ❸), with simple but clean rooms, fulfil all functions. Next stop is **LAKELAND**, whose café, hotel and fuel stop marks the junction for routes north along the Peninsula Developmental Road to Laura. The road to Cooktown lies east, past cataracts at the **Annan River Gorge**, and the mysterious **Black Mountain**, two huge dark piles of lichen-covered granite boulders near the road. Aborigines reckon the formation to be the result of a building competition between two rivals fighting over a girl, and tell stories of people wandering into the eerie, whistling caverns, never to return.

At this point it's worth making the four-kilometre detour south along the Bloomfield Track to the *Lions Den* at **HELENVALE** (☏07/4060 3911, ⓦwww.lionsdenhotel.com.au; safari tents ❸). The *Den* is an old-style pub playing up for tourists during the day, but one hundred percent authentic at

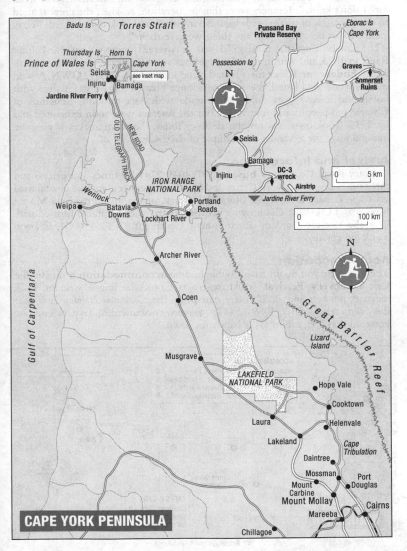

CAPE YORK PENINSULA

night, from the iron sheeting and beam decor to the nasty exhibits in glass bottles on the piano. Those with 4WD vehicles can follow the track south from Helenvale to Cape Tribulation (see p.497), while back on the main road it's another twenty minutes to Cooktown past the birdlife-filled waterholes of **Keatings Lagoon Conservation Park**, just 5km short of town.

Cooktown

After the *Endeavour* nearly sank at Cape Tribulation in 1770, Captain Cook landed at a natural harbour to the north, where he spent two months repairing the vessel, observing the "Genius, Temper, Disposition and Number of the Natives" and – legend has it – naming the kangaroo after an Aboriginal word for "I don't know". Tempers wore thin on occasion, as when the crew refused to share a catch of turtles with local Aborigines and Cook commented: "They seem'd to set no value upon any thing we gave them."

The site lay dormant until **gold** was discovered southwest on the Palmer River in 1873, and within months a harbour was being surveyed at the mouth of the **Endeavour River** for a tented camp known as **COOKTOWN**. A wild success while gold lasted, the settlement once boasted a main street alive with hotels and a busy port doing brisk trade with Asia through thousands of Chinese prospectors and merchants. But the reserves were soon exhausted and by 1910 Cooktown was on the decline. Today, the town makes a pleasant, tranquil place for a wander or a couple of days' stay.

Arrival and information

Country Road Coachlines **buses** (☎07/4045 2794 for times and prices) run three times a week between Cairns and Cooktown, either along the coastal road via Cape Tribulation and the Bloomfield Track, or the inland road via Mount Molloy and Lakeland. Cooktown's **visitor centre**, with helpful, informed staff, is at the Botanic Gardens' Environment Centre (☎07/4069 6004, ⓦwww .cook.qld.gov.au).

Accommodation

The only time you might have trouble finding **accommodation** is during the June **Discovery Festival**, which re-enacts Cook's landing – wooden boat, redcoats, muskets and all. If you're **camping**, the *Cooktown Holiday Park* near the cemetery (☎07/4069 5417, ⓦwww.cooktownholidaypark.com.au; powered sites $35, cabins ❹) is handy for town.

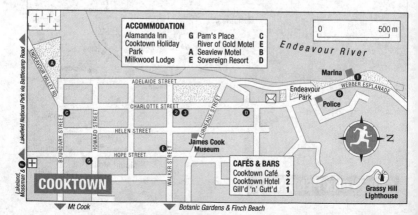

Alamanda Inn Hope St ℡ 07/4069 5203. More upmarket than Cooktown's budget options, *Alamanda Inn* offers quiet motel rooms and a big pool. ❸

Milkwood Lodge Annan Rd ℡ 07/4069 5007, ⊛ www.milkwoodlodge.com. Two kilometres out of town on a secluded hillside, *Milkwood Lodge* offers self-contained cabins with veranda views out over the valley. ❺

Pam's Place Charlotte St ℡ 07/4069 5166, ⊛ www.cooktownhostel.com. A good bet for budget beds, with bright rooms in shared dorms and self-contained units. Good hostel facilities, such as kitchen, laundry, pool room and bar. Dorms \$25, rooms ❷, motel units ❹

River of Gold Motel ℡ 07/4069 5222, ⊛ www .riverofgoldmotel.com. Clean, comfortable self-contained units with a good pool and BBQ area. ❻

Seaview Motel Webber Esplanade ℡ 07/4069 5377, ⓔ seaviewmotel@bigpond.com. The two-storey *Seaview Motel* is central and tidy, with balconies overlooking the bay. ❹

Sovereign Resort ℡ 07/4043 0500, ⊛ www .sovereign-resort.com.au. This lavish resort-style hotel has a pool set in award-winning tropical gardens and a café-bar-restaurant. The rooms are airy and tastefully furnished. ❼

The Town

Today, the town's main drag, Charlotte Street, is neat but quiet, good for random wandering past the old wharves and **Endeavour Park**, the site of Cook's landing, now graced by a statue of the great navigator. Among monuments on the lawn are the remains of defences sent from Brisbane in the nineteenth century to ward off a threatened Russian invasion: one cannon, three cannonballs and two rifles. Just outside town, 500m along Endeavour Valley Road, Cooktown's half-wild **cemetery**, divided into Jewish, Chinese, Protestant and Catholic sections, suggests how cosmopolitan the town once was. The cemetery's most famous resident is **Mary Watson** of Lizard Island (see p.502), whose grave near the entrance is decorated with seashells and a painting of a pietà.

The best **views** of the town and river are from the top floor of the old Sisters of Mercy Convent, now the **James Cook Museum** (daily 9.30am–4pm; \$9) containing a bit of everything: artefacts jettisoned from the *Endeavour*; a reconstructed joss house; a display on pearling around Thursday Island; and an account of the "hopelessly insolvent" Cooktown–Laura railway. There are more views of the district from the red-and-white, corrugated-iron cone of **Grassy Hill Lighthouse**, reached on a concrete track from the end of Hope Street. **Mount Cook** is a rather tougher proposition, a two-hour return hike through thick forest on meagre paths – follow the orange triangles from the nondescript starting point beyond Ida Street (you can pick up free maps of the route from the Council Offices next to the post office, open Mon–Fri 9am–4.30pm). At the end of Walker Street, the **Botanic Gardens** date back to the 1870s and house galleries of plant illustrations inside **Nature's Power House Environment Centre** (\$3). The road past the gardens runs down to sandy **Finch Beach** on Cherry Tree Bay; although it's reputedly a safe swimming beach, you should heed the home-made warning signs saying "Dispela Stap Hia", with a picture of a croc underneath.

Eating and drinking

For **eating**, other than motel restaurants, there are riverside views from *Gill'd 'n' Gutt'd*, a chip shop at Fisherman's Wharf, or hearty pies at the *Cooktown Café* at 99 Charlotte St. The *Cooktown Hotel* (also known as the *Top Pub*) on the corner of Charlotte and Walker streets is the best spot for drink and bar meals. The **supermarket** is the last reliable source of fresh provisions before Weipa.

Moving on

To **get out and about around Cooktown** without your own transport, contact Guurrbi Tours (℡ 07/4069 6043; \$90), an Aborigine-led half-day adventure exploring ancient rock-art sites along the Endeavour Valley. **Moving on**, Country

Road Coachlines (☎07/4045 2794) head back to Cairns three times a week, either via inland or coastal routes – this is a genuine bus service rather than a tour, so you can get off along the way. Those continuing **up Cape York** have two options: vehicles other than 4WDs have to head southwest to Lakeland for Laura and points north; stronger sets of wheels can reach Lakefield National Park more directly by heading towards the Hope Vale community and then taking the Battle Camp road. The **last fuel** this way until Musgrave is about 33km from Cooktown at the *Endeavour Falls Tourist Park* (☎07/4069 5431; self-contained units ❹), a nice spot in itself with a neighbouring waterfall, forest and an apparently croc-free swimming hole – though don't swim here without advice from the tourist park.

Lizard Island

Lizard Island is one of the most isolated resorts in Australia, a granite rise covered in stunted trees and heath, 90km north of Cooktown and 30km offshore within sight of the outer reef – **divers** rave about the fringing coral here. Shell middens show that Lizard was regularly visited by Aboriginal peoples, but the island was uninhabited when **Robert Watson** built a cottage and started a sea-slug processing operation here in the 1870s, accompanied by his wife **Mary** and two Chinese servants. Aborigines attacked the house while Robert was at sea in October 1881, killing one of the Chinese and forcing Mary, her baby and Ah Sam to flee in a water tank; they paddled west for five days before dying of thirst. Despite this sad story, there are far worse places to spend a few days than in the exclusive lodge here or even simply camped in a tent.

The only regular access is on **flights from Cairns** with either Hinterland Aviation ($490 return; ☎07/4035 9323), which provides transfers for those staying on the island, or on a day tour with Daintree Air Services (☎07/4034 9300, ⓦwww.daintreeair.com.au; $590) with snorkelling, guided walks and lunch. Those unable to afford the swish but exorbitantly priced *Voyages Lizard Island* **lodge** (☎1300 134 044, ⓦwww.lizardisland.com.au; ❾) – which has a bar and restaurant – can use the **National Parks campsite** (permits from Cairns' National Parks office or book online at ⓦwww.epa.qld.gov.au) down on Watson Beach. Campers should be self-sufficient in food and bring charcoal beads for cooking (gas cylinders and fuel are not allowed on the plane); the lodge is off-limits apart from in serious emergencies. The lodge can arrange diving for its guests.

Quinkan Country: Laura

Back on the now-unsealed Peninsula Road, 60km north of Lakeland, **LAURA**'s store-cum-post office and roadhouse (☎07/4060 3440) support the two-day **Aboriginal Dance Festival** (ⓦwww.laurafestival.tv), an electrifying assertion of Aboriginal identity held in June of odd-numbered years. At any time you can visit the sandstone caves and ridges covered in **Aboriginal art** at **Split Rock**, 13km south of town, where a steep track leads to a two-hour gallery circuit. Paintings depict animals, humans and startling spirit figures associated with sorcery: spidery, frightening **Quinkan** with pendulous earlobes, and dumpy **Anurra**, often with their legs twisted upwards. Other sites show scenes from post-Contact life, depicting horses, rifles and clothed figures; some caves here were probably in use until the 1930s. The **Quinkan and Regional Cultural Centre** (open daily, but irregular hours; ☎07/4060 3457, ⓦwww.quinkancc.com.au) organizes guided rock-art **tours** and has current information on upcoming dance festivals.

Moving on, it's a straight 170km run up the Cape York road to **Musgrave** (not suitable for 2WD after rain), or – in the right vehicle – you can detour north to Musgrave via Lakefield National Park.

Lakefield National Park

Ideally you'd take at least a week to absorb **Lakefield National Park**'s fifty thousand square kilometres of savannah and riverine floodplain, but even a single night spent here will give you a feel for the Cape's most accessible wilderness area. Apart from the **Old Laura Homestead** – built between 1892 and 1940 and standing abandoned in the scrub on the **Laura River** – the park's pleasures revolve around outdoor pursuits, fishing and exploring lagoons for wildlife. Lakefield's **crocodile-conservation** programme means you might see both fresh- and saltwater types; birdlife is plentiful and plenty of kangaroos put in an appearance. **Magnetic ant hills** are a common landmark: the ants build flattened towers aligned north to south to prevent overheating in the midday sun.

Four-wheel-drive vehicles are strongly recommended for all routes, though lesser vehicles can usually manage the rough **170-kilometre track** through the park between Laura and Musgrave Roadhouse if there hasn't been any rain for a good while. **Ranger stations**, where you pick up **camping permits**, are located at New Laura (☎07/4060 3260), 50km from Laura at the southern end of the park, and at Lakefield (☎07/4060 3271), 30km further on at the centre of the park. Pick of the many **campsites** are *Kalpowar Crossing* (near Lakefield, with showers and toilets); *Seven Mile Waterhole*, 13km west of Lakefield ranger station; and *Hann Crossing*, in the north of the park.

Laura to Iron Range and Weipa

Following the main road, the 300km that stretches between Laura and Archer River passes in a haze of dust, jolts and **roadhouses** supplying fuel, food, beds and drink. First on the list is **MUSGRAVE** (135km from Laura), a converted homestead where the track from Lakefield National Park joins the Cape York road; there's **accommodation** about 28km east towards the park at *Lotus Bird Lodge* (☎07/4060 3400, ⓦwww.lotusbird.com.au; ❾), whose spacious wooden cottages are surrounded by much the same scenery as you'll find in the national park. Back on the road north, the next two hours are a wild roller-coaster ride – look out for "Dip" signs warning of monster gullies – down to **COEN**, 107km from Musgrave. Coen's **Ambrust Store** handles camping, provisions, fuel, post-office business and has an ATM; the *Exchange Hotel* is the place to find bar **meals** and a cooling drink. The *Homestead Guest House*, on Regent Street, has **beds** (☎07/4060 1157; ❹).

Back on the main road north, it's 70km to the friendly **Archer River Roadhouse** (☎07/4060 3266, ❹), which has a campsite and accommodation in units, an EFTPOS for emergency cash, and the last reliable **fuel** on the main Cape York road before Bamaga, 400km away. Beyond are routes east to Iron Range (155km) and west to Weipa (190km).

Iron Range

There's nothing else in Australia quite like the magnificent jungle at **Iron Range National Park**, a leftover from the Ice Age link to New Guinea, which hides fauna found nowhere else on the continent – the nocturnal **green python** and brilliant blue-and-red **eclectus parrot** are the best-known species. Three hours bouncing along a 110-kilometre 4WD track from the main road should bring you to a clearing where the army simulated a nuclear strike in the 1960s – fortunately using tons of conventional explosives instead of the real thing. Turning right at the junction here takes you past the **ranger station** (☎07/4060 7170 – contact them about campsites and walking tracks in the park) to **LOCKHART RIVER**, an Aboriginal mission and fishing beach; supplies and fuel are sold here during weekday trading hours. The road left passes two bush campsites near the Claudie River and Gordon's Creek crossings, before winding up at **PORTLAND ROADS** and the remains of a harbour used by US forces in World War II – there are a few houses and beach **accommodation** here (☎07/4060 7193, Ⓦwww .portlandhouse.com.au; ❻), though no stores or any public services. There's further **bush camping** a few kilometres back towards the junction at **Chili Beach**, a perpetually blustery, tropical setting backed by forest and coconut palms.

Next day, you have the chance to experience something unique on the mainland – seeing sunrise and sunset over different seas – by taking **Frenchman's Road** to Weipa. This runs northwest 30km back from the Lockhart/Portland junction, crosses the difficult Pascoe and Wenlock rivers, and emerges on the Peninsula Developmental Road, 2km north of **Batavia Downs**. Head through Batavia and cross more creeks – which look worse than they are – to the main Weipa road; the trip from coast to coast takes between six and eight hours.

Weipa

West-coast **WEIPA** is a company town of red clay and yellow mining trucks dealing in kaolin and bauxite. The area was one of the first in Australia to be described by Europeans: Willem Janz encountered "savage, cruel blacks" here in 1606, a report whose findings were subsequently reiterated by Jan Carstensz, who found nothing of interest and sailed off to chart the Gulf of Carpentaria instead. Apart from a mission built at **Mappoon** in the nineteenth century, little changed until aluminium ore was first mined here in the 1950s, and Comalco built the town and began mining.

All traffic in Weipa gives way to the gargantuan mine vehicles and stays out of the restricted areas. The town comprises mostly company housing, but does offer long-forgotten luxuries: you can pick up **vehicle spares** at the auto wreckers and service station on the way into town, and there's a **supermarket** and post office just in front of *Weipa Camping Ground* (☎07/4069 7871, Ⓦwww .campweipa.com; camping $24, powered sites $28, units ❸–❺), a large campsite featuring hot showers and a laundry, where you can unwind and swap tales about the rigours of the trip. The *Albatross Hotel* (☎07/4090 6666, Ⓔalbatrosshotel @bigpond.com; ❻) up the road has rooms and bungalows, and its beer deck looks out over the western sea.

Around town, the **library**'s Cape York Collection contains a unique collection of books and documents relating to the area, while the **Uningan Nature Reserve**, situated on the Mission River, preserves sixteen-metre-high middens composed entirely of shells left over from Aboriginal meals – some over 1600 years old. Driving is the only way to get here, and guidebooks are available from the campsite. Keep an eye out for crocs while walking around the reserve. **Moving on**, there is no reliable source of fuel between Weipa and Bamaga (340km).

North of the Wenlock River

The bridge over the seasonally deep, fast-flowing **Wenlock River**, an hour north of the Weipa junction on the main road up the Cape, marks the start of the most challenging part of the journey north, with road conditions changing every wet season. The road divides 42km further on, where die-hards follow the **Old Telegraph Track**, which has all the interesting scenery and creek crossings, though the telegraph lines have been dismantled, and many of the poles have been robbed of their ceramic caps by souvenir hunters. The first travellers of the year build simple rafts and log bridges to cross the creeks; as tracks dry and traffic increases, jarring corrugations and potholes are more likely to pose a problem, constituting a serious test of vehicle strength. There are some fine **creek**

Crossing creeks by 4WD

While Cape York's **crocodiles** make the standard 4WD procedure of walking creek crossings before driving them potentially dangerous, wherever possible you should make some effort to gauge the water's depth and find the best route. *Never* blindly follow others across. Make sure all **rescue equipment** – shovel, winch, rope, etc – is easy to reach, outside the vehicle. **Electrics** on petrol engines need to be water-proofed. On deep crossings, block off air inlets to prevent water entering the engine, slacken off the fan belt and cover the radiator grille with a tarpaulin; this diverts water around the engine as long as the vehicle is moving. Select an appropriate **gear** (changing it in midstream will let water into the clutch) and drive through at walking speed; clear the opposite embankment before stopping again. In deep water, there's a chance the vehicle might float slightly, and so get pushed off-track by the current – though there's not much you can do about this. If you **stall**, switch off the ignition immediately, exit through windows, disconnect the battery (a short might restart the engine) and winch out. Don't restart the vehicle until you've made sure that water hasn't been sucked in through the air filter – which will destroy the engine. If you have severe problems, recovery will be very expensive; see Basics, p.41.

crossings on this route: **Bertie**'s potholes are large enough to submerge an entire vehicle; **Gunshot**'s three-metre vertical clay banks are a real test of skill (use low range first, and keep your foot off the brake); and the north exit at **Cockatoo** is deceptively sandy. Dozens wipe out on Gunshot every season; for the cautious there's a 24-kilometre detour via open scrub at Heathlands to the north side.

Those less certain of their abilities avoid the Old Telegraph Track and take the longer **New Road** to the east, consisting of 200km of loose gravel, bulldust and shocking **corrugations**. The two routes rejoin one another briefly after 75km, after which the New Road diverges left for 54km to the **Jardine River Ferry** crossing ($90 return, including use of the Injinu campsite at Bamaga), while the Old Telegraph Track ploughs on past beautiful clear green water and basalt formations at **Twin Falls**' safe swimming holes, through the deep **Nolans Brook**, before reaching the hundred-metre-wide **Jardine River** – the likeli-hood of crocodiles here only adds to the risks. However, it's worth the trip to camp (assuming you have enough fuel) before heading back via the ferry. From here, the last hour to Bamaga passes the remains of a **DC-3** that crashed just short of the airstrip in 1945.

Bamaga and around

BAMAGA, a community of stilt houses and banana palms founded by Saibai islanders in 1946, owes nothing to the rest of Australia's suburban values. Around the intersection you'll find a workshop and **service station** selling fuel (Mon–Fri 9am–5pm, Sat 9am–12.30pm, Sun 1.30–3pm), airline offices, a hotel and a **shopping centre** containing fresh veggies, a National Australia Bank agent, telephones, a café and post office. For **accommodation**, there's the central *Resort Bamaga* (℡07/4069 3050, 🌐www.resortbamaga.com.au; ❻), which has motel rooms, or turn left at the junction to **Injinu campsite** (Cowall Creek). Turning right past the shopping centre, you come to the coast at **SEISIA** (Red Island Point). There's another fuel station and well-stocked store here, and you can stay at the *Seisia Holiday Park* (℡07/4069 3243, 🌐www.seisiaholidaypark .com; camping $8 per person, powered sites $20, cabins ❺), under palms near the jetty, and take advantage of showers, laundry facilities, a canteen and **fishing safaris**. Peddell's **ferry** departs from Seisia to Thursday Island (see p.506).

Cape York and Somerset

To make local contacts, hang around Bamaga. To stay with the overland crowd, head 16km north to a road junction, then bear left for 11km to the idyllic beach at **Punsand Bay Camping Resort** (℡07/4069 1722, ⓦ www.punsand.com.au; camping $10 per person, powered sites $22, cabins/prefab tents including three meals ⑨), a just reward for the trials of the journey, with a licensed restaurant and basic provisions. Around here you might spot the rare **palm cockatoo**, a huge, crested black parrot with a curved bill. You could spend a day recuperating on the beach, or return to the junction and take the seventeen-kilometre road to the very **tip of Cape York**, past the Somerset fork, to its end at another campsite (shower, water and kiosk). Follow the footpath through vine forest onto a rocky, barren headland and down to a turbulent sea opposite the lighthouse on Eborac Island, where a sign concreted into an oil drum marks the tip of mainland Australia and the end of the journey.

Somerset

Established on government orders in 1864 to balance the French naval station in New Caledonia, **Somerset** is known for one of its first settlers, **Frank Jardine**, whose legendary exploits assume larger-than-life proportions (fearless pioneer to some, brutal colonial to others). Though envisaged as a second Singapore, Somerset never amounted to more than a military outpost, and in 1877, after the pearling trade in the Torres Strait erupted into lawlessness, the settlement was abandoned in favour of a seat of government closer to the problem at Thursday Island.

Today, only a few cannons, machine parts and mango trees testify to Somerset's former inhabitants; the buildings succumbed to white ants or were moved long ago. Frank and his wife Sana are buried on the beach directly below (standing up, say locals), next to a **Chinese cemetery** and traces of a jetty into the Adolphus Channel. Dogged exploration of the dense undergrowth above the beach to the left will uncover remains of a **sentry post** and a cave with stick-figure paintings, presumably Aboriginal.

Thursday Island and the Torres Strait

Just a short boat ride beyond Cape York, little **Thursday Island** is the administrative centre for the dozens of other populated specks of land which lie scattered across the two-hundred-kilometre-wide **Torres Strait**, which separates Australia from New Guinea. Thursday Island is easily reached from Cape York by ferry and from Cairns by air, and offers a fascinating glimpse into an all-but-forgotten corner of Australia, and one whose inhabitants, the **Torres Strait Islanders**, have a very different world view from the country's white population.

The strait is named after **Luís Vaez de Torres**, who navigated its waters in 1606; at this time, the different Torres Strait Islands existed in a complicated state of trade and warfare, which was brought to an end when the islanders enthusiastically embraced the arrival of Christianity – known here as the "**Coming of the Light**" – in 1871. **Pearling** (for mother of pearl) was the main source of employment here from this point until after World War II, when the advent of plastics saw the industry collapse and a mass migration of islanders to the Australian mainland. Those who chose to stay formed a movement to establish an Islander Nation, which bore its first fruit on June 3, 1992, when the **Mabo Decision** acknowledged the Merriam as traditional owners of easterly Murray Island, thereby setting a precedent for mainland Aboriginal claims and sending shock waves through the establishment.

Coming over by ferry from the mainland, you pass **Possession Island** and come within sight of a plaque commemorating James Cook's landing here on August 22, 1770, when he planted the flag for George III and Great Britain. Then it's into the shallow channel between Horn Island and **Prince of Wales Island**, the strait's largest, stocked with deer and settled by an overflow population unable to afford Thursday's exorbitant land premiums.

Thursday Island and around

A three-square-kilometre dot within sight of the mainland, **Thursday Island** wears a few aliases: known simply as "T. I." in day-to-day use, it was coined "Sink of the Pacific" for the variety of peoples who passed through in pearling days, and the local tag is Waiben or (very loosely) "Thirsty Island" – once a reference to the availability of drinking water and now a laconic aside on the quantity of beer consumed. The hotel clock with no hands hints at the pace of life and it's only for events like Christmas, when wall-to-wall aluminium punts from neighbouring islands make the harbour look like a maritime supermarket car park, that things liven up. Other chances to catch Thursday in carnival spirit are during the annual **Coming of the Light festivities** on July 1, and the full-bore **Island of Origin** rugby-league matches later in the same month – in one year 25 players were hospitalized, and another killed.

In town there are traces of the **old Chinatown** district around Milman Street, and a reminder of Queensland's worst shipping disaster in the **Quetta Memorial Church**, way down Douglas Street, built after the ship hit an uncharted rock in the straits in 1890 and went down with virtually all the Europeans on board. The Aplin Road **cemetery**, where two of the victims are buried, has tiled Islander tombs and depressing numbers of **Japanese graves**, all victims of pearl diving during the early twentieth century. As a by-product of the industry, Japanese crews had accurately mapped the strait before World War II and it's no coincidence that the airstrip was **bombed** when hostilities were declared in 1942; fortifications are still in place on Thursday's east coast. Bunkers and naval cannon at the **Old Fort** on the opposite side date from the 1890s.

The **Gab Titui Cultural Centre** across from the ferry terminal provides an interesting insight into island affairs and has a daily dance performance (Mon–Sat 9am–5pm, reduced opening times Jan–Feb; $6; ☎07/4090 2130); the town's only **café** is inside.

Just fifteen minutes from Thursday's wharf on the Horn Island Ferry ($15, departs hourly 6am–5pm), **Horn Island** is another small chunk of land surrounded by mangroves and coral, the site of an open-cut gold mine and the **regional airport** (with regular flights to and from Cairns). The main reason to take a trip across is to visit the **pearling museum**, run by an ex-diver and stocked with his memorabilia – including an old-fashioned bronze dive helmet. He also owns Horn's sole **place to stay** and eat, the *Gateway Torres Strait Resort* (☎07/4069 2222, [W]www.torresstrait.com.au; [5]).

Practicalities

Ferries run to Thursday Island from Seisia with Peddell's (June–Sept Mon–Sat; Oct–May Mon, Wed & Fri; $48 one-way; ☎07/4069 1551, [W]www.peddellsferry.com.au). Between June and October, Peddell's Buses (☎07/4069 1551) meet incoming ferries for a ninety-minute **island tour** ($29). It's also possible to **cruise** up to Thursday Island aboard the Trinity Bay passenger and car ferry (☎07/4035 1234, [W]www.seaswift.com.au). The ferry departs Cairns at 2pm every Friday, arriving in Thursday Island approximately 6pm on Sunday. Accommodation is in air-conditioned four-bed cabins which cost $753 for one-person private use, or $451 per person if three or four people travel together; taking along a 4WD vehicle costs an additional $724.

Flying, Qantas (℡13 13 13, ⓦwww.qantas.com.au) heads twice daily from Cairns direct to Horn Island, whilst local operator Aero-Tropics (℡07/4040 1222, ⓦwww.aero-tropics.com.au) has in the past flown daily from Horn Island to a dozen outer Torres Islands including Yorke and Badu but at the time of writing had been closed down by aviation authorities. Regional Pacific Airlines (℡07/4040 1400, ⓦwww.regionalpacific.com.au) flies daily from Cairns to Bamaga, with water-taxi connections over to nearby Thursday Island.

Thursday's **wharf** sits below the colonial-style Customs House, a minute from the **town centre** on Douglas Street. Here you'll find a post office with payphones, a **bank** and two of the island's **hotels**: the *Torres* just beats the neighbouring *Royal* as Australia's northernmost bar. Facing the water on Victoria Parade, there are clean **lodgings** at the *Federal Hotel* (℡07/4069 1569, ⓦwww.federalhotelti.com.au; ⑥), while on the corner with Normanby Street, *Jardine Motel* (℡07/4069 1555, ⓔjardinemotel@bigpond.com; ⑥) is a slightly cheaper option.

Travel details

Trains

Two trains, the Tilt and Sunlander, trundle along the 1680-kilometre track from Brisbane to Cairns and back again, each making the journey three times a week. Contact Rail Australia (℡07/4069 1569, ⓦwww.railaustralia.com.au) for more information.

Brisbane to: Ayr (6 per week; 17hr); Bowen (6 per week; 15hr); Bundaberg (6 per week; 5hr); Caboolture (6 per week; 1hr); Cairns (6 per week; 24hr); Cardwell (6 per week; 20hr); Gladstone (6 per week; 7hr); Ingham (6 per week; 20hr); Innisfail (6 per week; 22hr); Mackay (6 per week; 12hr); Proserpine (6 per week; 14hr 30min); Rockhampton (6 per week; 7hr 30min); Townsville (6 per week; 17hr 30min); Tully (6 per week; 21hr).

Bundaberg to: Ayr (6 per week; 11hr 30min); Bowen (6 per week; 10hr); Brisbane (6 per week; 5hr); Caboolture (6 per week; 4hr); Cairns (5 per week; 19hr); Cardwell (6 per week; 15hr 30min); Gladstone (6 per week; 1hr 45min); Ingham (6 per week; 14hr 30min); Innisfail (5 per week; 17hr); Mackay (6 per week; 7hr 15min); Proserpine (6 per week; 9hr 15min); Rockhampton (6 per week; 2hr 45min); Townsville (6 per week; 12hr 30min); Tully (6 per week; 16hr 15min).

Cairns to: Ayr (6 per week; 7hr 30min); Bowen (6 per week; 9hr); Brisbane (6 per week; 24hr); Bundaberg (6 per week; 19hr); Caboolture (6 per week; 23hr); Cardwell (6 per week; 3hr 30min); Gladstone (6 per week; 17hr 30min); Ingham (6 per week; 4hr 30min); Innisfail (6 per week; 2hr); Kuranda (2 daily; 1hr 45min); Mackay (6 per week; 11hr 15min); Proserpine (6 per week; 9hr 30min); Rockhampton (6 per

week; 16hr); Townsville (6 per week; 6hr); Tully (6 per week; 3hr).

Ingham to: Ayr (6 per week; 3hr); Bowen (6 per week; 4hr 30min); Brisbane (6 per week; 20hr); Bundaberg (6 per week; 15hr); Caboolture (6 per week; 19hr); Cairns (6 per week; 4hr 30min); Cardwell (6 per week; 1hr); Gladstone (6 per week; 13hr); Innisfail (6 per week; 3hr); Mackay (6 per week; 7hr); Proserpine (6 per week; 5hr); Rockhampton (6 per week; 11hr 30min); Townsville (6 per week; 1hr 30min); Tully (6 per week; 1hr 45min).

Mackay to: Ayr (6 per week; 4hr); Bowen (6 per week; 2hr 30min); Brisbane (6 per week; 12hr 30min); Bundaberg (6 per week; 7hr 45min); Caboolture (6 per week; 12hr); Cairns (6 per week; 12hr); Cardwell (6 per week; 8hr); Gladstone (6 per week; 6hr); Ingham (6 per week; 7hr); Innisfail (6 per week; 10hr); Proserpine (6 per week; 1hr 30min); Rockhampton (6 per week; 4hr 15min); Townsville (6 per week; 5hr); Tully (6 per week; 9hr).

Proserpine to: Ayr (6 per week; 2hr 15min); Bowen (6 per week; 45min); Brisbane (6 per week; 14hr 30min); Bundaberg (6 per week; 9hr 30min); Caboolture (6 per week; 13hr 30min); Cairns (6 per week; 9hr 30min); Cardwell (6 per week; 6hr); Gladstone (6 per week; 8hr); Ingham (6 per week; 5hr); Innisfail (6 per week; 8hr); Mackay (6 per week; 1hr 30min); Rockhampton (6 per week; 6hr 30min); Townsville (6 per week; 3hr 30min); Tully (6 per week; 7hr).

Rockhampton to: Ayr (6 per week; 8hr 30min); Bowen (6 per week; 7hr); Brisbane (6 per week; 7hr 30min); Bundaberg (6 per week; 3hr); Caboolture (6 per week; 7hr); Cairns (6 per week; 16hr);

Cardwell (6 per week; 12hr 30min); Gladstone (6 per week; 1hr 15min); Ingham (6 per week; 11hr 30min); Innisfail (6 per week; 14hr 15min); Mackay (6 per week; 4hr 15min); Proserpine (6 per week; 6hr 30min); Townsville (6 per week; 9hr 30min); Tully (6 per week; 13hr 30min).

Townsville to: Ayr (6 per week; 1hr 15min); Bowen (6 per week; 2hr 30min); Brisbane (6 per week; 17hr 30min); Bundaberg (6 per week; 12hr 30min); Caboolture (6 per week; 17hr); Cairns (6 per week; 6hr); Cardwell (6 per week; 2hr 30min); Gladstone (6 per week; 11hr 15min); Ingham (6 per week; 1hr 30min); Innisfail (6 per week; 4hr 30min); Mackay (6 per week; 5hr); Proserpine (6 per week; 3hr 30min); Rockhampton (6 per week; 9hr 30min); Tully (6 per week; 3hr 30min).

Buses

Greyhound Australia (☎13 20 30, ⊛www.greyhound .com.au) is the main bus company with five daily buses running between Brisbane and Cairns and between Cairns and Sydney via Brisbane, stopping at all major towns and tourist hotspots. Premier (☎13 34 10, ⊛www.premierms.com.au) operates a similar service once daily.

Airlie Beach to: Ayr (6 daily; 3hr 15min); Brisbane (5 daily; 19hr); Bundaberg (4 daily; 12hr 30min); Cairns (6 daily; 10hr); Cardwell (6 daily; 6hr 45min); Childers (5 daily; 13hr 15min); Hervey Bay (5 daily; 14hr); Ingham (6 daily; 6hr); Innisfail (6 daily; 9hr); Mackay (6 daily; 2hr 15min); Mission Beach (6 daily; 8hr); Mooloolaba (1 daily; 17hr 30min); Noosa (1 daily; 16hr 45min); Rockhampton (5 daily; 7hr 30min); Townsville (6 daily; 4hr); Tully (6 daily; 7hr 35min).

Brisbane to: Airlie Beach (5 daily; 19hr); Ayr (5 daily; 22hr 30min); Agnes Water (1 daily, 11hr); Bowen (5 daily; 20hr 30min); Bundaberg (5 daily; 9hr); Burleigh Heads (6 daily; 1hr 30min); Byron Bay (10 daily; 4hr); Cairns (5 daily; 28hr 30min); Cardwell (6 daily; 26hr); Childers (5 daily; 0hr); Coolangatta (8 daily; 2hr 30min); Gladstone (4 daily; 11hr); Hervey Bay (7 daily; 5hr); Ingham (5 daily; 24hr); Innisfail (7 daily; 27hr); Mackay (8 daily; 15hr 30min); Mission Beach (5 daily; 26hr 25min); Mooloolaba (6 daily; 2hr 30min); Noosa (9 daily; 2hr 50min); Rockhampton (5 daily; 11hr 30min); Surfers Paradise (every 30min; 1hr 30min); Sydney (7 daily; 17hr 30min); Townsville (5 daily; 24hr); Tully (5 daily; 27hr).

Bundaberg to: Airlie Beach (5 daily; 10hr 30min); Agnes Water (1 daily; 1hr 30min); Ayr (5 daily; 14hr); Brisbane (5 daily; 6hr 30min); Cairns (6 daily; 20hr 30min); Cardwell (6 daily; 17hr); Childers (5 daily; 50min); Hervey Bay (5 daily; 1hr 45min); Ingham (5 daily; 19hr); Innisfail (5 daily; 3hr); Mackay (5 daily;

9hr); Mission Beach (5 daily; 20hr); Noosa (2 daily; 7hr); Rainbow Beach (1 daily; 4hr 30min); Rockhampton (5 daily; 3hr 30min); Townsville (5 daily; 15hr 30min); Tully (5 daily; 19hr 30min).

Cairns to: Airlie Beach (5 daily; 11hr); Atherton Tablelands (2 per day Mon–Fri); Ayr (5 daily; 7hr 30min); Brisbane (5 daily; 28hr 30min); Bundaberg (6 daily; 20hr 30min); Cape Tribulation (2 daily; 5hr); Cardwell (6 daily; 3hr); Childers (5 daily; 23hr); Cooktown (up to 6 per week; 12hr); Hervey Bay (5 daily; 24hr); Ingham (6 daily; 3hr 30min); Innisfail (6 daily; 1hr 15min); Mackay (5 daily; 13hr); Mission Beach (4 daily; 2hr 30min); Noosa (2 daily; 27hr 30min); Port Douglas (2 daily; 2hr); Rockhampton (5 daily; 17hr 30min); Townsville (6 daily; 6hr); Tully (6 daily; 2hr 45min).

Hervey Bay to: Airlie Beach (5 daily; 14hr); Agnes Water (1 daily; 4hr); Ayr (5 daily; 15hr 30min); Brisbane (7 daily; 5hr); Bundaberg (5 daily; 1hr 45min); Cairns (6 daily; 20hr 30min); Cardwell (5 daily; 20hr); Childers (5 daily; 50min); Ingham (5 daily; 19hr); Innisfail (5 daily; 22hr); Mackay (5 daily; 10hr 30min); Mission Beach (5 daily; 21hr); Noosa (4 daily; 4hr); Rainbow Beach (1 daily; 2hr); Rockhampton (5 daily; 6hr); Townsville (5 daily; 19hr); Tully (5 daily; 20hr 30min).

Mackay to: Airlie Beach (6 daily; 2hr 15min); Ayr (6 daily; 5hr); Brisbane (8 daily; 15hr 30min); Bundaberg (5 daily; 9hr); Cairns (5 daily; 13hr); Cardwell (6 daily; 9hr); Childers (5 daily; 11hr); Hervey Bay (5 daily; 10hr 30min); Ingham (6 daily; 9hr); Innisfail (6 daily; 12hr); Mission Beach (6 daily; 10hr 30min); Noosa (2 daily; 14hr); Rockhampton (5 daily; 5hr); Townsville (6 daily; 6hr 30min); Tully (6 daily; 10hr).

Mission Beach to: Airlie Beach (6 daily; 8hr); Ayr (5 daily; 5hr 30min); Brisbane (5 daily; 26hr 25min); Bundaberg (5 daily; 20hr); Cairns (4 daily; 2hr 30min); Cardwell (5 daily; 1hr); Childers (4 daily; 21hr); Hervey Bay (5 daily; 21hr); Ingham (5 daily; 2hr); Innisfail (5 daily; 1hr); Mackay (6 daily; 10hr 30min); Noosa (2 daily; 25hr); Rockhampton (4 daily; 16hr); Townsville (5 daily; 3hr 30min); Tully (5 daily; 30min).

Noosa to: Airlie Beach (1 daily; 16hr 45min); Agnes Water (1 daily; 9hr); Ayr (1 daily; 20hr); Brisbane (9 daily; 2hr 50min); Bundaberg (2 daily; 7hr); Cairns (2 daily; 27hr 30min); Cardwell (2 daily; 24hr); Childers (2 daily; 5hr 30min); Hervey Bay (4 daily; 4hr); Ingham (2 daily; 23hr); Innisfail (2 daily; 26hr); Mackay (2 daily; 14hr); Mission Beach (2 daily; 25hr); Rainbow Beach (2 daily; 3hr); Rockhampton (2 daily; 10hr); Tin Can Bay (1 daily; 2hr 30min); Townsville (2 daily; 21hr); Tully (2 daily; 25hr).

Rockhampton to: Airlie Beach (5 daily; 7hr 30min); Ayr (5 daily; 10hr); Brisbane (5 daily; 11hr 30min);

Bundaberg (5 daily; 3hr 30min); Cairns (5 daily; 17hr 30min); Cardwell (5 daily; 14hr); Childers (5 daily; 5hr); Hervey Bay (5 daily; 6hr); Ingham (5 daily; 11hr 30min); Innisfail (5 daily; 16hr); Mackay (5 daily; 5hr); Mission Beach (4 daily; 16hr); Noosa (2 daily; 10hr); Townsville (2 daily; 11hr); Tully (5 daily; 14hr).

Surfers Paradise to: Brisbane (every 30min; 1hr 30min); Burleigh Heads (every 10min; 30min); Byron Bay (10 daily; 3hr); Coolangatta (every 10min; 1hr); Sydney (7 daily; 15hr 30min).

Townsville to: Airlie Beach (6 daily; 4hr); Ayr (5 daily; 1hr); Brisbane (5 daily; 24hr); Bundaberg (5 daily; 15hr 30min); Cairns (6 daily; 6hr); Cardwell (5 daily; 2hr); Childers (5 daily; 18hr); Hervey Bay (5 daily; 19hr); Ingham (5 daily; 1hr 30min); Innisfail (5 daily; 4hr 30min); Mackay (6 daily; 6hr 30min); Mission Beach (5 daily; 3hr 30min); Noosa (2 daily; 17hr); Rockhampton (2 daily; 11hr); Tully (5 daily; 3hr).

Ferries

Airlie Beach/Shute Harbour to: Daydream Island (14 daily; 30min); Hamilton Island (12 daily; 30min); Hook Island (1–2 daily; 1hr 30min); Lindeman Island (1 daily; 1hr 30min); Long Island (4 daily; 20min); South Molle Island (5 daily; 45min); Whitsunday Island (2 daily; 2hr).

Brisbane to: Moreton Island (4 daily; 2hr); North Stradbroke Island (20 daily; 30min); St Helena (2 per week; 2hr).

Cairns to: Thursday Island (1 per week; 36hr).

Cape York to: Thursday Island (Mon–Fri 2 daily; 1hr 15min–2hr).

Cardwell to: Hinchinbrook Island (2 daily; 1–2hr).

Hervey Bay to: Fraser Island (9 daily; 30min–1hr).

Mission Beach to: Dunk Island (10 daily; 15min).

Rosslyn Bay to: Great Keppel Island (1 daily; 1hr).

Surfers Paradise to: South Stradbroke Island (3 or more daily; 30min).

Townsville to: Magnetic Island (20 or more daily; 45min).

Weipa to: Normanton (1 per week; 24hr).

Flights

Virgin Blue (☎13 67 89, ⊕www.virginblue.com.au), with its headquarters based at Brisbane, together with Qantas (☎13 13 13, ⊕www.qantas.com.au) and its budget side-kick, Jetstar (☎13 15 38, ⊕www.jetstar.com), account for the vast majority of commercial domestic flights in Queensland. Brisbane Domestic Airport is the state's hub, handling almost all flights to regional towns, although both Cairns and

Gold Coast-Coolangatta are international airports and have flights to Australia's main cities. The following represent direct flights only:

Brisbane to: Adelaide (8 daily; 3hr 30min); Alice Springs (2 per week; 4hr 30min); Biloela (1 daily; 1hr 15min); Blackall (3 per week; 2hr); Bundaberg (3 daily; 1hr); Cairns (10 daily; 2hr 10min); Canberra (9 daily; 2hr); Charleville (2 per week; 2hr); Coffs Harbour (2 daily; 1hr); Darwin (4 daily; 3hr 40min); Emerald (3 daily; 1hr 40min); Gladstone (5 daily; 1hr); Hamilton Island (2 daily; 1hr 30min); Hervey Bay (3 daily; 50min); Hobart (1 daily; 3hr 50min); Launceston (1 daily; 3hr 30min); Longreach (2 daily; 2hr); Lord Howe Island (2 per week; 1hr 30min); Mackay (10 daily; 3hr); Melbourne (many daily; 2hr 25min); Mount Isa (2 daily; 4hr); Newcastle (6 daily; 2hr 20min); Norfolk Island (3 per week; 3hr 45min); Perth (6 daily; 5hr); Proserpine (2 daily; 1hr 50min); Rockhampton (11 daily; 1hr 5min); Roma (1 daily; 1hr 10min); Sydney (many daily; 1hr 35min); Townsville (11 daily; 1hr 50min).

Bundaberg to: Brisbane (3 daily; 1hr); Lady Elliot (1 daily; 45min).

Cairns to: Adelaide (4 per week; 3hr 45min); Alice Springs (1 daily; 2hr); Bamaga (1 daily; 1hr 45min); Brisbane (10 daily; 2hr); Cooktown (2 daily; 45min); Darwin (2 daily; 1hr); Dunk Island (3 daily; 45min); Lizard Island (2 daily; 1hr); Melbourne (4 daily; 3hr 20min); Palm Island (2 per week; 1hr); Perth (2 per week; 5hr); Sydney (8 daily; 3hr); Thursday Island/Horn Island (1–2 daily; 2hr); Townsville (4 daily; 1hr); Uluru (2 daily; 2 hr); Weipa (1 daily; 1hr 15min).

Gladstone to: Brisbane (5 daily; 1hr); Rockhampton (5 per week; 25min).

Gold Coast–Coolangatta to: Adelaide (2 daily; 2hr 40min); Melbourne (10 daily; 2hr 15min); Newcastle (1 daily; 1hr 10min); Sydney (many daily; 1hr 15min).

Mackay to: Brisbane (10 daily; 2hr 45min); Rockhampton (2 daily; 45min); Sydney (2 daily; 2hr 45min); Townsville (2 daily; 1hr).

Rockhampton to: Brisbane (10 daily; 1hr); Gladstone (5 per week; 25min); Great Keppel Island (2 daily; 25min); Mackay (2 daily; 50min); Sydney (1 daily; 2hr).

Sunshine Coast–Maroochydore to: Melbourne (4 daily; 2hr 30min); Sydney (5 daily; 1hr 45min).

Townsville to: Brisbane (11 daily; 1hr 45min); Cairns (4 daily; 50min); Mackay (2 daily; 50min); Melbourne (3 per week; 3hr); Palm Island (4 daily; 20min); Sydney (2 daily; 2hr 30min).

Outback Queensland

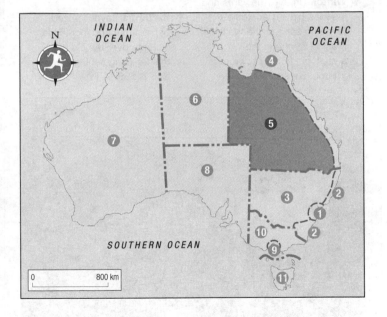

CHAPTER 5 # Highlights

✳ **Carnarvon Gorge** Hike through the verdant Carnarvon Gorge to reach ancient Aboriginal art sites. See p.522

✳ **Longreach** Walk on the wing of a 747 in Qantas' thriving home town and visit a School of the Air class in progress. See p.534

✳ **Winton** Unravel the yarns and legends behind Australia's favourite song at the Waltzing Matilda Centre in the archetypal frontier town of Winton. See p.536

✳ **Boulia** Spot the mysterious Min Min lights in the Channel Country around Boulia or at this rustic town's automated sound-and-light show. See p.538

✳ **Undara** Explore Undara's massive, contorted lava tubes, formed by a 190,000-year-old volcanic eruption. See p.552

✳ **Karumba** Savour prized barramundi and incredible sunsets over the Gulf at this far-flung fishing town. See p.555

▲ Carnarvon Gorge

Outback Queensland

O utback Queensland, the vast area west of the state's heavily touristed coast, is sparsely populated by tenacious farming communities swinging precariously between famine and survival, and a dramatic change from Queensland's lush, wet tropics. The population is concentrated in the relatively fertile highlands along the Great Dividing Range, which run low behind the coast; on the far side, expansive, empty plains slide over a hot horizon into the fringes of South Australia and the Northern Territory. The only places attracting Australian or international visitors in any numbers are Longreach, with its mega-museum the Stockman's Hall of Fame, and the Central Highlands oasis of Carnarvon Gorge. But opportunities for exploration are immense, with precious stones, fossils, waterholes and Aboriginal art in abundance. The region has also produced two of Australia's best-known icons: Banjo Paterson first performed *Waltzing Matilda* in a Winton hotel, and the same town was the birthplace of Qantas airlines before its launch at nearby Longreach.

Choosing where to go is usually determined by the most convenient starting point. **Main roads** and **trains** head west from the coast at Brisbane, Rockhampton, Townsville and Cairns; **buses** from Brisbane, Cairns and Townsville cross Outback Queensland as they head interstate, but otherwise there's little in the way of public transport. If you're **driving**, your vehicle must be well maintained and you should carry essential spares, as even main centres often lack replacement parts. A number of sealed minor roads are single-vehicle width – pull over to let traffic pass or overtake, and pull off and stop completely to give way to road trains.

Western summers frequently hamper or prohibit travel, as searing temperatures and violent flash floods regularly isolate areas (especially in the Channel Country on the far side of the Great Dividing Range) for days or weeks on end. Consequently, many tour companies, visitor centres and motels close completely between November and March, or at least during January and February. On the other hand, water revives dormant seeds and fast-growing desert flowers. At other times, expect hot days, cool, star-filled nights and plenty of red dust.

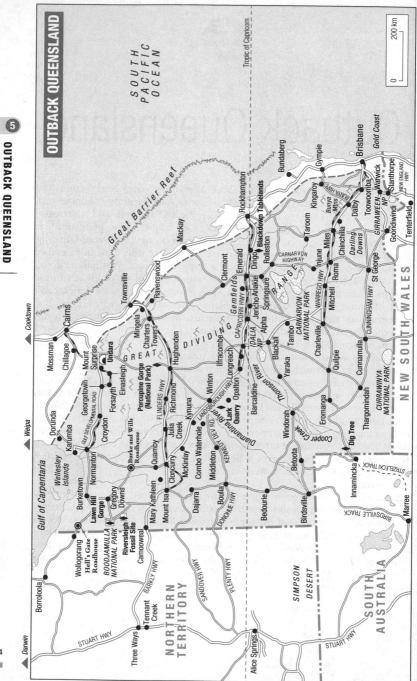

OUTBACK QUEENSLAND

Brisbane to Cooper Creek and Birdsville

The thousand–plus–kilometre haul from the coast to Queensland's remote southwestern corner dumps you tired and dusty on the South Australian border, with some exciting routes down the Birdsville and Strzelecki tracks or through the hostile red barrier of the Simpson Desert yet to come. There are two ultimate targets: the outpost of **Birdsville**, with its annual horse races, and the **Dig Tree** at Nappa Merrie on **Cooper Creek**, monument to the Burke and Wills tragedy (see box, p.526). After crossing the fertile disc of the **Darling Downs**, the country withers and dries, marooning communities in isolation and hardship. Detour north through Queensland's **Central Highlands** however, and you'll find forested sandstone gorges and the Aboriginal sites at **Carnarvon National Park** – worth the journey even if you don't go any further.

   From Brisbane, the most practical route is the **Warrego Highway**, through Toowoomba, Roma and Charleville towards Quilpie. Roma is the jumping-off point for the highlands and from Quilpie there are primarily unsurfaced roads to Birdsville and the Dig Tree. The twice-weekly Westlander **train** runs in this direction from Brisbane to Charleville, as do daily **buses** en route from Brisbane to Mount Isa. Alternatively, the southern **Cunningham Highway** runs via Warwick and Goondiwindi (the limit of bus services in this direction) to Cunnamulla, beyond which unsealed roads requiring a 4WD forge across oil, gas and opal fields towards the Dig Tree.

The Darling Downs

The **Darling Downs**, a broad spread of prime agricultural land first explored by **Ludwig Leichhardt** in the 1840s, sprawl westwards from the back of the Great Dividing Range behind Brisbane. Settlements strung out along the main roads here are for the most part unadorned farming centres, though solid stone architecture lends some sense of style to the gateway towns of **Toowoomba** and **Warwick**. A far bigger draw is the scenery along the downs' fringes, particularly the **Bunya Mountains** between Toowoomba and Kingaroy in the north and around the southeasterly **Granite Belt** – where there are also some superb traditional and innovative new wineries and possibilities for **farm work**. The flat grasslands provide clear evidence of Aboriginal custodial practices – created by controlled burning designed to clear woodland and increase grazing land for game, they perfectly suited European pastoral needs. The downs are relatively fertile and stud farms, dairy, cotton, wool and cereal farming have all flourished at one time or another. Even unwanted plants thrive – during the 1920s millions of acres of land were infested by South American **prickly pear** cacti that was finally brought to heel by the tiny parasitic *cactoblastis* moth in 1930 – a success story of biological control on a scale to match the later failure of the introduction of the cane toad (see *Australian Wildlife* colour section).

From Brisbane, the Warrego Highway climbs a steep escarpment to Toowoomba and the central downs (as do long-distance **buses**), while the Cunningham Highway cuts through Cunningham's Gap to Warwick and the south.

Toowoomba

TOOWOOMBA, 160km west of Brisbane, is a stately university city perched on the edge of a six-hundred-metre escarpment, with stylish houses and a blaze of late nineteenth-century sandstone architecture along its central Main and Ruthven streets. A prolonged drought has seen the development of water-conserving horticulture methods here, and the city still lives up to its moniker of "the Garden City", with several free gardens around town including the State Rose Garden in Newtown Park; Queens Park Gardens, at the end of Godsall Street; Laurel Bank Park Gardens, on the corner of West and Hill streets; and most peaceful of all, Ju Raku En, twelve acres of Japanese gardens adjoining the University of Southern Queensland's northern car park. The gardens are at their finest during September's **flower festival**, displaying prize blooms. Toowoomba's other notable attraction is the **Cobb & Co. Museum**, 27 Lindsay St (daily 10am–4pm; $9.50), 500m northeast of the centre across spacious Queens Park, which recalls the period from the 1860s to 1924 when intrepid coaches bounced across the Outback delivering mail and passengers. Aside from an impressive collection of these vehicles, the museum also houses interactive exhibitions on local history and flora and fauna, along with a working smithy at the back. Splendid views from the escarpment unfold from the café, bar and restaurant and picnic area at **Picnic Point** at the top of Tourist Road, 2.5km east of the centre, as do several bushwalking tracks ranging from 850m to 5.3km.

Downtown Toowoomba is a compact area based around the intersection of **Ruthven Street**, which runs north to south, and **Margaret Street** (here also known by locals as "Eat Street" for its plethora of cafés and restaurants), which runs east to west. The **bus station** is one block east along Neil Street; **trains** pull up 500m northwest on Railway Street. The **visitor centre** is in James Street, south off Ruthven (daily 9am–5pm; ☏1800 331 1155, ⓦwww .toowoombarc.qld.gov.au). **Accommodation** prospects include the well laid-out *Jolly Swagman Caravan Park*, at 47 Kitchener Rd (☏07/4632 8735; camping $22, cabins ❸–❹), about 1km southeast of the centre (there's also a parkland walking track into town); the spotless and friendly Garden City Motor Inn, near the visitor centre at 718 Ruthven St; and the central *James Street Motor Inn* on the corner of James and Kitchener streets (☏07/4639 0200, ⓦwww.jamesstmotorinn.com.au; ❹), with barbecue facilities and a licensed restaurant and bar. *Jilly's Café* on Ruthven Street has a varied menu which includes some vegetarian options – check for daily specials such as pumpkin and pine-nut risotto, or five-spice chicken. Otherwise take your pick from the places on Margaret Street.

Moving on from Toowoomba, Greyhound Australia buses (☏13 14 99, ⓦwww.greyhound.com.au) continue northwest on their Charleville to Mount Isa run, while Crisps (☏07/3236 5266, ⓦwww.crisps.com.au) run south to Warwick, where you can connect with services to Stanthorpe and Goondiwindi.

Kingaroy and around: the Northern Downs

KINGAROY is a thriving town in the heart of peanut country on the fringes of the downs, 120km north of Toowoomba. A cluster of castle-like peanut silos in the middle of town aptly symbolize the fame Kingaroy owes to the late **Johannes Bjelke-Petersen** – better known simply as "Joh" – who farmed nuts here before becoming Queensland Premier in 1968, an office he held for nineteen years. His equally charismatic wife, Flo, also attained fame with her iconic pumpkin scone recipe. Joh passed away in April 2005, but remains in no danger of obscurity, with a dam, bridge, road and sportsground named after him, and his ominous catchphrase "Don't you worry about that" still in use. You can tour the family property, Bethany, just south of town at Peterson Drive (tours Wed & Sat 2pm; $10; ☎07/4162 7046, ⓦwww.bethany.net.au). Tours include Sir Joh's gravesite, memorabilia and afternoon tea of pumpkin scones; cottage accommodation is available by request. Otherwise, get in touch with what Kingaroy is all about by stopping at the **Peanut Van** outside Lions Park, between the factory and town, which sells over twenty varieties of boiled and roasted nuts – from chilli-and-lime to butterscotch-and-caramel or ginger-and-honey. The last few years have also seen dozens of **wineries** springing up around Kingaroy, most open daily for tasting – and, of course, buying. The **visitor centre** (Mon–Fri 9am–5pm, Sat & Sun 10am–4pm; ☎07/4162 6272), facing the peanut silos along Haly Street, has a food and wine trail map listing their locations as well as details of cheese and biscuit factories that can be toured by reservation, and also screens a short film on how peanuts are grown and harvested.

For **somewhere to stay**, *Kingaroy Holiday Park* (☎07/4162 1808, ⓦwww.kingaroycaravanpark.com.au; camping $21, powered sites $24, cabins & villas ❸–❼), 1km south near the peanut factory on Walter Road, has a variety of accommodation options in leafy surroundings. Alternatively, *Kingaroy Hotel-Motel* (☎07/4162 1677; ❸) on the corner of Youngman and Haly streets, and the central *Club Hotel* (☎07/4162 2204; ❸) on Kingaroy Street have good-value rooms; the latter also offers occasional **live music**. Kingaroy's only bus services run to and from Brisbane (1–2 daily).

The Bunya Mountains

Southwest of Kingaroy, a sixty-kilometre section of road twists through the **Bunya Mountains** before reaching Dalby, back on the Warrego Highway. Among the mountains' greenery and clusters of unlikely flowers are enormous **bunya pines**, whose seeds were a valuable seasonal food source for local Aborigines. On his trip across the downs in 1844, the indefatigable Ludwig Leichhardt witnessed the collection and roasting of nuts at such a feast and persuaded the government to make the area an Aboriginal reserve, free from logging or settlement. The decree was revoked in 1860, but today the Bunya Mountains still retain a significant stand of pines, along with orange-flowering silky oaks and ancient **grass trees**, with their three-metre-high, spear-like flower heads.

Two national parks along the road at Burton's Well and Westcott make for good **bushcamping**, with another wallaby-overrun site at the hamlet of Dandabah; the **ranger's office** here deals with enquiries on all three (daily 2–4pm; ☎07/4668 3127, ⓦwww.epa.qld.gov.au; advance booking essential during holiday periods; camping $4.85 per person). Less frugal accommodation is on hand about 500m north along the main road at the cosy and fun *Rice's Log Cabins* (☎07/4668 3133, ⓦwww.riceslogcabins.com.au; minimum 2-night stay; ❹), or you can find a **chalet rental** through ⓦwww.bunyamountains.com.au (minimum stays required during busy periods; ❹–❽). Note that the mountains are cooler than the plains below and seriously cold in winter. Walking tracks between the three campsites lead through the forest to orchid-covered lookouts and waterfalls –

satin **bowerbirds** and **paradise riflebirds**, with their deep blue-black plumage and long curved beaks, are both fairly common here.

The Granite Belt

The southeastern edge of the Darling Downs along the New South Wales border, known as Queensland's **Granite Belt**, is a major wine- and fruit-producing area, which regularly records the state's **coldest temperatures** that drop well below freezing on winter nights. Heading south from Toowoomba, you'll pass through the one-horse town of **NOBBY**, whose former resident **Steele Rudd** created archetypal Australian country characters in his "Dad and Dave" tales – commemorated at the *Nobby Hotel* in paintings and farming bric-a-brac.

Around 85km south of Toowoomba, the 11,000-strong town of **WARWICK** makes a fine base for exploring the region, and is widely known for its cheese. Services centre on Grafton and Palmerin streets, where sandstone buildings date back to the time when Warwick graziers competed fiercely with Toowoomba's merchants to establish the downs' premier settlement. Warwick itself sits beside the **Condamine River**, which later joins the Murray/Darling river system, Australia's longest. At **Queen Mary Falls**, 43km east from Warwick beyond Killarney, a tributary exits the forest in a plunge off the top of the plateau. A two-kilometre-long track climbs to the escarpment at the head of the falls from the road, with a kiosk, accommodation and lunches provided by *Queen Mary Falls Tourist Park* (☎07/4664 7151, ⓦwww.queenmaryfallscaravanpark.com.au; camping $22, powered sites $24, cabins ❸); you need your own transport to get here.

Warwick's **visitor centre** is on Albion Street (daily 8.30am–5pm; ☎07/4661 3122, ⓦwww.southerndownsholidays.com.au), while **buses** pull up on central Grafton Street, adjacent to the library with internet access, and the town's small but impressive art gallery (Tues–Fri 10am–4pm, Sat & Sun 10am–1pm; admission by donation). During the **October rodeo** particularly, **accommodation** can be tight – try *Warwick Tourist Caravan Park*, 18 Palmer Ave (☎07/4661 8335; camping $18, powered sites $24, cabins ❸), 1.2km north of town on the highway, *Warwick Motor Inn*, 17 Albion St (☎07/4661 1533; ❸), or *Country Rose Motel* (☎07/4661 7700; ❹). **Heading on**, both Crisps Coaches (☎07/4661 8333, ⓦwww.crisps.com.au) and Greyhound Australia (☎13 14 99, ⓦwww.greyhound .com.au) run south to Stanthorpe along the New England Highway and southwest to Goondiwindi along the Cunningham Highway.

Stanthorpe

Sixty kilometres south of Warwick along the New England Highway, **STANTHORPE** was founded in the 1880s around a tin-mining operation on Quart Pot Creek, but really took off in the 1940s after Italian migrants started up the fruit farms, and some 62 wineries now throng the region – in season there are plenty of opportunities for **fruit-picking work**. A number of wineries are represented at the Market in the Mountains (ⓦwww.marketinthemountains .org), where local producers also sell preserves, jams, crafts and more every second Sunday at the Civic Centre on the corner of Victoria and Lock streets. Several companies run half- and full-day vineyard tours including Maxi Tours (☎07/4681 3969, ⓦwww.maxitours.com.au) and Filippo's (☎07/4681 3130, ⓦwww.filippostours.com.au); half-day tours around $60/65 (midweek/ weekend), full-day tours around $70/75 – prices include pick-up and lunch. If you'd rather drive yourself, a full list of traditional and emerging "alternative" wineries – and advice on the best – is available at Stanthorpe's **visitor centre** (daily 8.30am–5pm; ☎07/4681 2057), overlooking the river just south of the centre on Leslie Parade. Staff can also organize permits ($6.15 per month) to fossick for semi-precious **topaz** (found near tin deposits), 13km northwest of Stanthorpe at Swiper's Gully.

Stanthorpe's **accommodation** includes a growing number of luxurious B&Bs, but cheaper accommodation is also plentiful. For camping your best bet is the spacious *Top of Town* (☎07/4681 4888, ⓦwww.topoftown.com.au; camping $22, powered sites $24, cabins ❺), on the main street 2km north of Stanthorpe's main shopping precinct. Hostel beds are available on a weekly basis only at the excellent *Backpackers of Queensland*, 80 High St (☎0429 810 998, ⓦwww.backpackersofqueensland.com.au; dorms $170 per week), which also arranges **farm work** including free transportation to and from the farms, while the central *Stannum Lodge Motor Inn* (☎07/4681 2000, ⓦwww.stannumlodge .com.au; ❺) on Wallangarra Road has good facilities including the town's only motel swimming pool. Unsurprisingly, the abundance of fresh produce means the region boasts some outstanding restaurants such as the long-established and surprisingly affordable Anna's Restaurant, on the corner of Wallengarra Road and O'Mara Terrace, set in a romantic Queenslander timber house with log fires and alfresco tables (open dinner Mon–Sat; ☎07/4681 1265). On the highway 10km north of town, Vincenzo's makes a mouthwatering stop for breakfast, lunch or gourmet picnic items from the deli including antipasto, cheeses and aromatic coffee.

Girraween National Park

The granite hills around Stanthorpe are exposed as fantastic monoliths at **Girraween National Park**, accessed by a turn-off 26km south down the New England Highway. From here it's another eleven sealed kilometres to the National Parks **campsite and ranger's office** (☎07/4684 5157, ⓦwww.epa .qld.gov.au; camping $4.85) with showers, toilets and the chance of seeing small, shy, active **sugar gliders** just after dark. Listen for claws clattering over bark and then shine your torch overhead to catch a set of glowing eyes in the spotlight.

With more energy than skill, you can climb several of the giant hills with little risk, as long as rain hasn't made them dangerously slippery – trails are well marked and **free maps** are available from the ranger's office. The **Castle Rock** track (2hr return) initially follows a gentle incline past lichen-covered boulders in the forest, then a dotted white line into a fissure – look up and you'll see loose rocks balanced above you – before emerging onto a thin ledge above the campsite. Follow this around to the north side and clamber to the very top for superb views of the Pyramids, the Sphinx and Mount Norman, the park's 1267-metre apex, poking rudely out of the woods. It's a further forty minutes' walk from the Castle Rock campsite to the Sphinx and Turtle Rock: **Sphinx** is a broad pillar topped by a boulder, while **Turtle Rock**'s more conventional shape means a scramble, with no handholds on the final stretch to the top of the completely bald **South Pyramid** (2hr return from Castle Rock). At the top is Balancing Rock, a precariously teetering oval boulder. From here you can take a well-earned rest and look across to the unscaleable North Pyramid.

The Central Downs and around

To break the unexciting journey northwest across the downs from Toowoomba to Dalby, turn off the highway about 45km from Toowoomba at tiny Jondaryan township and head 3km south to the **Jondaryan Woolshed** (daily 10am–4pm;

$9, or $13 including tour; ☎07/4692 2229, ⓦwww.jondaryanwoolshed.com). This collection of mostly resited old buildings gives a glimpse of old-time life on the downs: exhibits include a document dating from 1880 itemizing the schoolmistress's tasks – including splinting broken legs, wallpapering buildings to keep out snakes and fighting off swagmen hoping to sleep in the school-house. Make sure you catch one of the **tours** (Sat, Sun & holidays 10.30am & 1.30pm) when the smithy is working and you can watch sheep shearers at work in the vast woolshed, lit by a bare bulb – a very surreal tableau. There are also various **accommodation** options including shearers' quarters or a self-contained cottage ($50–75; meals by arrangement), as well as safari tents ($29–36) and campsites (camping $11, powered sites $14).

Stops over the next 200km include **Dalby**, **Chinchilla** and **Miles**, rural centres largely devoid of attractions but with services and places to stay. One worthwhile stop, however, is ⚘ *Possum Park* (☎07/4627 1651, ⓦwww.possumpark.com.au; camping $18, powered sites $22, bunkers and carriages ❹), some 20km north of Miles. Sited in World War II ammunition bunkers in prime bushland, accommodation here is in restored train carriages, the bunkers or campsites – you'll need your own vehicle to get here, and to bring your own food.

Roma and Mitchell

ROMA, 140km west of Miles, thrives on farming, supplemented by the **oil and gas** fields. Not long after it was settled in 1862, Roma was the venue for the 1871 trial of the audacious **Captain Starlight** (also known as Harry Redford), who stole a thousand head of cattle from a nearby property and drove them down through the South Australian deserts to Adelaide for sale. An unusual white bull in the herd was recognized and Redford arrested, but his pioneering of a new stock route won such popular approval that the judge refused to convict him.

Roma's wide streets are lined with **bottle trees** (not only bottle-shaped but also full of moisture for emergency stock-watering), and are lent a slightly dated air by the iron decorations and wraparound balconies of its hotels. About 1km north of town **Romavilla Winery** (Mon–Fri 8am–5pm, Sat 9am–noon & 2–4pm; ☎07/4622 1822, ⓦwww.romavilla.com), on the Carnarvon road, at Quintin Street, has been producing prize-winning wine since 1863.

The Warrego Highway runs through Roma as Bowen Street and it's here, on the eastern side of town, that you're greeted by the **Big Rig** (daily 9am–5pm; $10 or $15.50 with night show, $8 night show only; ☎07/4622 4355, ⓦwww.thebigrig.com.au), originally a drilling tower left as a monument to the oil boom of the 1920s and now a multimillion-dollar complex exploring the history of Australia's oil and gas industry, which doubles as the town's **visitor centre**. Most of the shops, banks and businesses are one block north of Bowen Street, on parallel McDowall Street. Roma's broad range of **accommodation** includes the *Starlight Motor Inn* (☎07/4622 2666; ❺), with standard motel beds, the slightly less pricey *Bottle Tree Gardens* (☎07/4622 6111; ❹), on the corner of Bowen and Charles streets, and the *Big Rig Tourist Park*, 4 McDowall St (☎07/4622 2538; camping $20, powered sites $26, cabins ❹–❺), near the Big Rig, which has bright modern cabins and hot showers, welcome during the sub-zero winter nights. Book well ahead during the town's biggest annual shindig, Easter in the Country (ⓦwww.wheninroma.com.au): six days of enter-tainment including goat races, a bush poets breakfast and a Sunday-night rodeo. **Restaurants** in Roma are fairly basic, though many of the motels have decent bars and grills, and the *Golden Dragon* at 60–62 McDowall St serves reasonable Chinese food.

Roma's **train station** is one block south of the highway at the corner of Station and Charles streets, and **buses** pull up along the highway at the more central of the two BP roadhouses. **Tickets** for both can be obtained from Maranoa Travel Centre, 71 Arthur St (☎07/4622 1416). **Heading on**, the Carnarvon Highway (take Quintin St from the town centre) heads north for access to Carnarvon National Park; otherwise, the next stops west along the highway are Mitchell and Charleville.

Mitchell

MITCHELL is a delightful, single-street highway town 88km west of Roma beside the Maranoa River. Like Roma, Mitchell has its local outlaw legend; the protagonists this time were the two **Kenniff Brothers**, who raided the district for cattle and horses in the early 1900s. After killing a policeman during one arrest attempt, they were finally ambushed south of town.

There are two reasons to pass through Mitchell – either to follow the two-hundred-kilometre track north to **Mount Moffat** in Carnarvon National Park, or to take a dip in the town's **hot artesian springs**, which have been channelled into an open-air swimming pool and spa (daily 8am–6pm; $6.60) in the grounds of the old **Kenniff Courthouse** on the main street (here called Cambridge St) – good, steamy fun on a cold winter's morning. The courthouse itself now houses a **visitor centre** (daily 8am–6pm; ☎07/4624 6923), and also incorporates the *Healthy Byte* internet café serving tasty snacks. For **somewhere to stay**, try the campsite back across the Maranoa River (camping $16, powered sites $17–19, en-suite sites $25; ☎07/4623 6600); the *Mitchell Motel* (☎07/4623 1355; ❹), on Caroline Street on the western side of town; or the spacious and well-equipped Berkeley Lodge Motor Inn (☎07/4623 1666, ⓦwww.berkeleylodge.net; ❺) just near the visitor centre on Cambridge Street with a pool and a licensed restaurant; otherwise the town's pubs serve inexpensive counter meals.

Moving on, all transport and the Warrego Highway continue a further 180km west to Charleville. The **train station** is 500m from the courthouse at the western side of town, and the newsagent on the main street doubles as the bus agent.

Carnarvon National Park

North of Roma and Mitchell, Queensland's Central Highlands consist of a broad band of weathered sandstone plateaus, thickly wooded and spectacularly sculpted into sheer cliffs and pinnacles. It's an extraordinarily primeval landscape, and one still visibly central to Aboriginal culture, as poor pasture left the highlands relatively unscathed by European colonization. Covering a huge slice of the region, the fragmented sections of **Carnarvon National Park** include **Carnarvon Gorge** and **Mount Moffatt**: Carnarvon Gorge has the highest concentration of Aboriginal art and arguably the best scenery, while Mount Moffatt is harder to reach but wilder – it isn't possible to drive directly between the two sections, though you can usually hike with the rangers' permission.

As there's **no public transport** to any section of the park (and no organized tours), you'll need your own vehicle: **access** to the gorge is from Roma to the south, or Emerald to the north, and to Mount Moffatt from Roma or Mitchell.

All these roads involve some stretches of dirt, making them impassable even in a 4WD after heavy rain (most likely Nov–May). Always carry extra rations in case you get stranded and – unless you're desperately short of supplies – stay put in wet weather so you don't churn the road up and make it harder to use. Summer **temperatures** often reach 40°C, while winter nights can be below freezing. Gathering firewood is prohibited inside the park, so stop on the way in or bring a gas stove. For **information** and **campsite bookings** visit [W]www.epa.qld.gov.au.

5 Carnarvon Gorge

The Carnarvon Gorge **access road** (sealed except for the final 20km) is reached off the Carnarvon Highway between Roma (200km) and Emerald (250km), from where it runs 45km west, past views of the Consuelo Tableland standing out magnificently above dark forests, to the park's edge at the mouth of the gorge. The **ranger station** here (daily 8am–5pm; ☎07/4984 4505) has an orientation model of the gorge, free maps and a library, and also runs night-time wildlife-spotting tours (Fri–Tues 5pm; $25).

Accommodation is best booked well in advance: nearby options are *Carnarvon Gorge Wilderness Lodge* (☎1800 644 150, [W]www.carnarvon-gorge.com; from $155 per person, per night), 2km before the ranger station, where comfortable rooms are surrounded by a neat lawn and cycad palms, and which also has a bar and a store selling basics, fuel and LP gas refills; or a further 2km away at the creekside *Takarakka Bush Resort* (☎07/4984 4535, [W]www.takarakka.com.au; camping $28, powered sites $34, safari-style canvas "cabins" [4]).

Along the gorge

Carnarvon Creek's journey between the vertical faces of the gorge has created some magical scenery, where low cloud often blends with the cliffs, making them appear infinitely tall. Before setting off between them, scale **Boolimba Bluff** from the *Takarakka* campsite for a rare chance to see the gorge system from above; the views from the "Roof of Queensland" make the tiring three-kilometre track worth the effort.

Boomerangs

Curved **throwing sticks** were once found throughout the world. Several were discovered in Tutankhamun's tomb, Hopi Indians once used them and a 23,000-year-old example made from mammoth ivory was recently found in Poland. Since that time the invention of the bow and arrow superseded what Aborigines call a **boomerang** or *karli*, but their innovation of a stick that returns has kept the boomerang alive, not least in people's imaginations – they were originally used as children's toys but were then modified into decoys for hunting wildfowl. The non-returning types depicted in Carnarvon Gorge show how sophisticated they became as **hunting weapons**. Usually made from tough acacia wood, some are hooked like a pick, while others are designed to cartwheel along the ground to break the legs of game. Thus immobilized, one animal would be killed while another could be easily tracked to meet the same fate. Besides hunting, the boomerang was also used for digging, levering or cutting, as well as for musical or ceremonial accompaniment, when pairs would be banged together. At Carnarvon Gorge, the long, gently curved boomerangs stencilled on the walls in pairs are not repetitions but portraits of two weapons with identical flight paths; if the first missed through a gust of wind, for instance, the user could immediately throw the second, correcting his aim for the conditions.

The superb **day-walk** (19km return from the ranger station) into the gorge features several intriguing side-gorges. The best of these contain the **Moss Garden** (3.5km), a vibrant green carpet of liverworts and ferns lapping up a spring as it seeps through the rockface, and **Alijon Falls** (5km), which conceal the enchanting Wards Canyon, where a remnant group of *angiopteris* ferns hang close to extinction in front of a second waterfall and gorge, complete with bats and blood-red river stones.

Carnarvon's two major **Aboriginal art sites** are the Gallery (5.6km) and Cathedral Cave (at the end of the trail, 9.3km from the *Takarakka* campsite), both on the gorge track, though if you keep your eyes open you'll spot plenty more. These are Queensland's most documented Aboriginal art sites, though the paintings themselves remain enigmatic. A rockface covered with engravings of vulvas lends a pornographic air to **the Gallery**, and other symbols include kangaroo, emu and human tracks. A long, wavy line here might represent the rainbow serpent, shaper of many Aboriginal landscapes. Overlaying the engravings are hundreds of coloured stencils, made by placing an object against the wall and spraying it with a mixture of ochre and water held in the mouth. In addition to adults' and children's hands there are also artefacts, boomerangs and complex crosses formed by four arms, while goannas and mysterious net patterns at the near end of the wall have been painted with a stick. **Cathedral Cave** is larger, with an even greater range of designs, including seashell pendant stencils – proof that trade networks reached from here to the sea – and engravings of animal tracks and emu eggs.

Mount Moffatt

Mount Moffatt is part of an open landscape of ridges and lightly wooded grassland, at the top of a plateau to the west of Carnarvon Gorge. It was here that the Kenniff Brothers murdered a policeman and station manager in 1902, events which were to lead to their being run to ground by a group of vigilantes. Years later in 1960, archeological excavations at their hideout, **Kenniff Cave** (closed due to instability), were the first to establish that Aboriginal occupation of Australia predated the last Ice Age.

Access to this area of the park is direct from Mitchell (220km), or from Roma (250km) via the small town of **INJUNE** (150km), which has a visitor centre (daily 9am–5pm; ☎07/4626 1053, ⓦ www.discoverinjune.com.au) on the highway (here called Hutton St), as well as a caravan park (camping $12; ☎07/4626 1053) on Third Avenue, and a free town swimming pool. Although the park perimeter can be reached in 2WD vehicles in dry conditions, you'll need a 4WD to get around once inside. As there is **no fuel or supplies** of any kind available in the park, make sure you have enough – last sources for either are at Injune or Mitchell. There are four **bush campgrounds** ($4.85 per person) in the park, two of which have drinking water; check out ⓦ www.epa.qld.gov.au as you'll need to book in advance.

Mount Moffatt's attractions spread out over an extensive area. At the park's southern entrance, the **Chimneys** area has some interesting sandstone pinnacles and alcoves that once housed bark burial-cylinders. Around 6km on from here the road forks, and the right track continues 10km to the **ranger station** (☎07/4626 3581), where you can collect your map of the area and plan bushwalking. The left track, meanwhile, runs 6km past *Dargonelly* campsite to **Marlong Arch**, a sandstone formation decorated with handprints and engravings. Five kilometres northeast from here, a trail leads to **Kookaburra Cave**, named after a weathered, bird-shaped hand stencil. A further 5km beyond the cave is **Marlong Plain**, a pretty expanse of blue grass surrounded by peaks, and another sandstone tower known as **Lot's Wife**. Ten kilometres north of Marlong Plain, a lesser track leads to several sites associated with the Kenniff legend, including the murder scene, and the rock where they are believed to have burned the evidence. Finally, for pure scenery, head 15km due east of Marlong Plain to the **Mahogany Forest**, a stand of giant stringybark trees.

Charleville to Cooper Creek and Birdsville

The last place of any size on the journey west from Roma is **CHARLEVILLE**, a busy country town whose broad streets and shaded pavements are flanked by some solid buildings constructed when the town was a droving centre and staging post for Cobb & Co. It's well known as a victim of **contradictory weather** – in November 1947 a hot summer afternoon was interrupted for twenty minutes as a blast of massive hailstones stripped trees, smashed windows and roofs and killed poultry. In 1990 the town centre was struck by five-metre-deep floodwaters from the Warrego River, requiring mass evacuation – a dramatic end to years of drought.

The weather doesn't deter the area's wildlife: the **National Parks Centre**, right on the Warrego Highway as you come in from Mitchell on the eastern side of town (Mon–Fri 9am–4pm; free), is dedicated to studying and breeding populations of regional rarities such as the absurdly cute **bilby** (for more on which see p.525) and the graceful **yellow-footed rock wallaby**, both of which are on show. The lack of industrial light and pollution, combined with a low horizon, also makes Charleville's location ideal for star-gazing. Three kilometres south of town, on Qantas Drive (off the Matilda Highway), the **Cosmos Centre and Observatory** (April to mid-Oct daily 10am–6pm, with night shows at 7.30pm; Nov–March Mon–Sat 10am–5pm, with night shows Mon, Wed, Fri & Sat at 8pm; day/night/combined shows $10/20/26, closed mid- to late Oct; ☎07/4654 7771, ⓦwww.cosmoscentre.com) provides visitors with the opportunity to observe the night sky through powerful **Meade telescopes**. During daylight hours, the centre has interactive displays and films explaining the history of astronomy and the formation of the universe. **Bookings** are essential.

Charleville practicalities

The town's small hub centres on the intersection of Wills and Galatea streets. Most services – banks, shops and post office – are along Wills, and trains and (in this direction) buses also terminate here. The **visitor centre** is situated within the Cosmos Centre (see above). Comfortable **rooms** can be found at the peaceful and modern *Charleville Motel* (☎07/4654 1566; ❹), near the train station on King Street, or the town's historic *Corones Hotel* on Wills Street (☎07/4654 1022, ⓦwww.hotelcorones.com.au; ❶–❹), whose accommodation options span basic pub-style to heritage rooms and adjoining motel units. To **camp**, head for *Bailey Bar Caravan Park*, on King Street (☎07/4654 1744, ⓦwww.charlevillebaileybar.com.au; camping $21, powered sites $24, cabins ❹). The best **meals** in town are at the *Corones Hotel*, whose timber-and-stained-glass dining rooms have been refurbished to original 1925 condition.

Moving on from Charleville, sealed roads head north to Blackall and Longreach (covered by Brisbane–Mount Isa buses), south via Cunnamulla to New South Wales, and further west to Quilpie. **Flights** to eastern destinations as far as Brisbane, and western destinations as far as Birdsville, leave from the tiny strip outside town.

Cunnamulla and Currawinya National Park

A trucking stop 200km south of Charleville on the long run down the Mitchell Highway to Bourke in New South Wales, the isolated town of **CUNNAMULLA** comprises a handful of service stations and motels, as well as a couple of diversions. The helpful **visitor centre** (Mon–Fri 9am–4.30pm, April–Oct also Sat & Sun 10am–2pm; ℡07/4655 8470, ⓦwww.paroo.info), in the old schoolhouse on central Jane Street, is part of the Cunnamulla Fella Centre (admission free), incorporating the town's museum of local history, an Artesian Time Tunnel, showing how the Artesian Basin shaped the current landscape and its opal formations, and the superb Outback Dreaming Art Gallery, where you can buy or simply admire local indigenous art. The "Cunnamulla Fella" himself comes from country singer Slim Dusty's song; a bronze statue of the young stockman sits on Stockyard Street in town. The stockman is also celebrated during the Cunnamulla Fella Festival each November – a weekend of rodeo bull riding, bush poetry and live music.

Accommodation is surprisingly tight, not only during the festival but throughout the year due to the high volume of workers and travellers passing through, and should be booked in advance. Options include the family-run *Cunnamulla Hotel* (℡07/4655 1102; ❷–❸) on the corner of Jane and Stockyard streets, which has both shared facilities and en-suite rooms; a couple of friendly motels on Louise Street; and *Jack Tonkin Caravan Park* (℡07/4655 1421; camping $16, powered sites $19, cabins ❸). Otherwise, you can experience life on a working sheep and cattle station, Nardoo (℡07/4655 4833, ⓔdcmeurant @bigpond.com.au), 38km north of town on the Matilda Highway, which has a variety of rooms (some en suite) and camping, a camp kitchen and free artesian spas, and can provide meals – call directly for prices.

Cunnamulla's Council Offices (℡07/4655 8400), on the corner of Stockyard and Louise streets, can arrange a **fossicking licence** ($8, valid for a month) if you're planning to head 160km northwest to the **Yowah Opal Fields**, where shallow deposits yield much-sought-after Yowah Nuts. At the fields, beware of vertical shafts – always look where you're going and never step backwards. Yowah has bore water, fuel and the Artesian Waters Caravan Park (℡07/4655 4953; camping from $16, cabins ❶).

If you have a 4WD, venturing 200km southwest of Cunnamulla brings you to **Currawinya National Park** (ⓦwww.epa.qld.gov.au), featuring mallee scrub, wetlands and associated wildlife, in contrast to the semi-arid land more typical of the region. One animal to benefit is the highly endangered **bilby**, which, with its long ears and nose, looks like a cross between a rabbit and a bandicoot. Feral cats, rabbits and grazing cattle have brought the bilby close to extinction, but a **fence** at Currawinya keeps these pests out, allowing the new bilby population – reintroduced from Charleville's National Parks Centre – to prosper. You can camp at Currawinya, but check on road conditions and practicalities with the National Parks ranger first (℡07/4655 4001). Past Currawinya is the tiny border town of **Hungerford**, where you can stock-up on fuel and groceries at the *Royal Mail Hotel*. From here it's a 200-kilometre run southeast on a mainly unsealed road to Bourke.

Quilpie and the road to the Dig Tree

A sealed 200km west of Charleville, **QUILPIE** is a compact, dusty farming community with a handful of amenities including a supermarket and fuel depot. The **visitor centre** (Mon–Fri 8am–5pm, April–Sept also Sat & Sun 10am–4.30pm; ☎07/4656 2166), on Brolga Street, can help if you'd like to stay; options include the *Channel Country* **caravan park** at 21 Chipu St (☎07/4656 2087; camping $18, powered sites $22, twin-bed cabins ❶, en-suite cabins ❹) and the *Quilpie Motor Inn* (☎07/4656 1277; ❹). There's a bakery and a daytime café in town, while the *Imperial Hotel* serves evening meals.

As there are few signposts, a **map** is essential if you plan to follow the 490-kilometre, largely unsealed route from Quilpie to the Dig Tree at Nappa Merrie, just 30km from the South Australian border. The **last fuel** along the way lies an hour west of Quilpie at **EROMANGA**, which is famed for being the furthest town from the ocean in Australia – no small claim on this vast continent. Eromanga's 1885-built *Royal Hotel* (☎07/4656 4837; ❸) provides beer, food, information and comfortable rooms. From here you head across the stony plains above the huge gas and oil reserves of the **Cooper Basin**, past the cattle stations of Durham Downs and Karmona, lonely "nodding donkeys" and unaccountably healthy-looking droughtmaster cattle, to the **Dig Tree on Cooper Creek**. The creek itself also achieved fame through references in the works of poet AB "Banjo" Paterson.

The Burke and Wills saga

In 1860 the government of Victoria, then Australia's richest state, decided to sponsor a lavish expedition to make the first south to north **crossing** of the continent to the Gulf of Carpentaria. Eighteen men, twenty camels (shipped, along with their handlers, from Asia) and over twenty tons of provisions started out from Melbourne in August, led by **Robert O'Hara Burke** and **William John Wills**. It didn't take long for the leaders' personalities to cause problems, and by December, Burke had impatiently left the bulk of the expedition and supplies racing behind and raced ahead with a handful of men to establish a base camp on **Cooper Creek**. Having built a stockade, Burke and Wills started north, along with two other members of their team (Gray and King), six camels, a couple of horses and food for three months. Four men remained at camp, led by William Brahe, waiting for the rest of the expedition to catch up. In fact, most of the supplies and camels were dithering halfway between Melbourne and Cooper Creek, unsure of what to do next.

As Burke and Wills failed to keep a regular diary, few details of the **"rush to the Gulf"** are known. They were seen by Kalkadoon Aborigines following the Corella River into the Gulf, where they found that vast salt marshes lay between them and the sea. Disappointed, they left the banks of the Bynoe (near present-day Normanton) on February 11, 1861, and headed back south. Their progress slowed by the wet season, they killed and ate the camels and horses as their food ran out. Gray died after being beaten by Burke for stealing flour; remorse was heightened when they staggered into the Cooper Creek stockade on April 21 to find that, having already waited an extra month for them to return, Brahe had decamped that morning. Too weak to follow him, they found supplies buried under a tree marked "**Dig**", but failed to change the sign when they moved on, which meant that when the first rescue teams arrived on the scene, they assumed the explorers had never returned from the Gulf. Trying to walk south, the three reached the Innamincka area, where Aborigines fed them fish and nardoo (water fern) seeds, but by the time a rescue party tracked them down in September, only King was still alive. The full, sad tale of their trek is expertly told by Alan Moorehead in his classic account *Cooper's Creek*, which is well worth tracking down (see "Books", p.1164).

The site of Burke and Wills' **stockade** (see box opposite), Depot Camp 65, is a beautiful shaded river bank alive with pelicans and parrots – it's hard to believe that anyone could have starved to death nearby. The **Dig Tree** is still standing and protected by a walkway, but the three original blaze marks reading "BLXV, DIG 3FT NW, DEC 6 60-APR 21 61" have been cemented over to keep the tree alive. Burke's face was carved into the tree on the right by John Dickins in 1898, and is still clearly visible.

Pressing on, you'll be relieved to know that it's only 50km to **Innamincka's** pub, at the top of the Strzelecki Track in South Australia.

Quilpie to Birdsville

Depth markers en route from Quilpie to Birdsville give an idea of how saturated this **Channel Country** becomes after rainfall – always check forecasts before setting out. First stop is **WINDORAH**, with a clutch of buildings offering fuel, a post office and a general store, as well as a visitor centre on Maryborough Street (March–Oct daily 8.30am–5pm; Nov–Feb Mon–Fri 8.30am–5pm; ☏07/4656 3063), which has leaflets on nature trails in the area. The *Western Star Hotel* (☏07/4656 3166; hotel room ❷, motel room ❹) is hard to resist for a cold drink, a meal and a look at its collection of old photos; its air-conditioned motel **rooms** book up quickly. In the same street is the tidy, council-run Windorah Caravan Park (☏07/4656 3063; camping $10). Around 10km west of town along a sealed road, Windorah's rippled red sand hills change colour throughout the day, turning an astonishingly vivid shade of red at sunset. Windorah is the last place with **fuel** before Birdsville, 385km west along a mostly unsealed road (generally manageable in good conditions without a 4WD). Heading northeast via Jundah it's sealed all the way to Longreach.

The ruins of the John Costello hotel lie 80km further west, opposite a windmill. Tired of riding 30km every morning to round up his stockmen from the bar, the manager of a nearby station had the local liquor licence transferred from the JC to his homestead in the 1950s; there's now little left beyond the foundations and some posts. Another 140km brings you to more remains at **Betoota**, whose only building, the 1880s-built Betoota Hotel, was in business until 1997, when this was Australia's smallest town (population 1). Beyond here the country turns into a rocky, silent plain, with circling crows and wedge-tailed eagles the only signs of life. Driving can be hazardous here – you'll pass plenty of wrecks and shredded tyres – but with care (and good luck), the Diamantina River and Birdsville are just three hours away.

Birdsville and beyond

Legendary for its **horse races** on the first weekend in September, when several thousand beer-swilling spectators pack out the dusty little settlement, **BIRDSVILLE** is at other times merely a far-flung handful of buildings where only the hotel and roadhouses seem to be doing business. But unless you've flown in (there are currently two runs each way per week to and from Brisbane, stopping at towns en route), you'll probably be glad simply to have arrived intact. The **caravan park** (☏07/4656 3214; camping $20, powered sites $25, en-suite cabins ❺, rooms ❸) is situated by the creek, or you can **camp for free** outside the town limits along the Diamantina River, where huge flocks of raucous corellas seem to justify the township's name – though it's actually a corruption of "Burt's Ville", after the first storekeeper. Given the lack of alternatives, be sure to book ahead for the comfy accommodation at the iconic ⚑ *Birdsville Hotel* (☏07/4656 3244, ⓦwww.theoutback.com.au; ❺).

For more on the **race weekend** – alcohol and horses, in that order; the hotel trades over 50,000 cans of beer in just two nights – check out ⓦwww .birdsvilleraces.com. **Provisions** and snacks can be bought from the general store. You owe yourself at least one drink in the hotel's mighty bar; order early if you want a full evening meal, such as kangaroo fillet with parmesan puree and rocket pesto beetroot relish – the "seven-course takeaway" is a pie and a six-pack.

The town's visitor centre, the **Wirrarri Information Centre** (March–Oct 9am–noon & 1–5pm; Oct to mid-Dec & mid-Jan to Feb Mon–Fri 8.30am–noon & 1–4.30pm; ⓣ07/4656 3300) on Billabong Boulevard will give you the lowdown on the state of the various Outback tracks, or ask at the fuel station (ⓣ07/4656 3236) across from the hotel. The visitor centre can also direct you to another **tree** blazed by Burke and Wills across the Diamantina, otherwise hard to locate among the scrub, or to attractions in town such as the stone shell of the original 1923 **Australian Inland Mission**. The **Birdsville Working Museum** (March–Oct daily 8am–6pm; $10; ⓣ07/4656 3259), as its name suggests, is more than just a collection of old stuff: all the exhibits, from petrol pumps and farm machinery to a complete blacksmith's shop, are fully restored and regularly operated.

Outside Birdsville, 12km north on the Bedourie road, some slow-growing, old and very rare **Waddi trees** stand about 5m tall and resemble sparse conifers wrapped in prickly feather boas with warped, circular seed-pods; the wind blowing through the needles makes an eerie noise like the roar of a distant fire. For something more dramatic, head out west 38km to **Big Red**, the desert's largest dune, at the start of the Simpson Desert crossing. If you're having a hard time getting up the long western face, there's a less steep track immediately on the right, which has a couple of quick turns near the summit. Two-wheel-drive vehicles can often reach the base (check with the fuel station before setting off) and it's worth it to see the dunes, flood plains and stony gibber country (red desert, covered with loose stone) on the way.

North of Birdsville, the next substantial settlement, Mount Isa, is a lonely 700km further on, with fuel available about every 200km. Those heading **west across the Simpson Desert** to Dalhousie Springs in South Australia need a Desert Parks Pass ($105), available online at ⓦwww.parks.sa.gov.au, or from the Birdsville National Parks office on the corner of Jardine Street and Billabong Boulevard (Mon–Fri 8am–5pm; ⓣ07/4656 3272); it may not be open if the ranger's out of town, in which case drop into the visitor centre. Feasible in any sound vehicle during a dry winter, the 520-kilometre **Birdsville Track** heads from the racecourse down to Marree in South Australia (see p.842).

Rockhampton to Winton

Heading west from Rockhampton, the Capricorn and Landsborough highways run through the heart of **central Queensland** to Winton and ultimately Mount Isa. There's a lot to see here – just a couple of hours from the coast you'll find magical scenery atop the forested, sandstone plateau of the **Blackdown**

Tablelands, while the town of **Emerald** offers the chance of seasonal farm work, and is also a gateway to the **Gemfields'** sapphire mines. Continuing inland, both **Barcaldine** and **Longreach** are historically significant towns, while further west, **Winton** sits surrounded by a timeless, harsh orange landscape, with access to remote bush imprinted with a dramatic set of dinosaur footprints at **Lark Quarry**.

Buses run by both Greyhound and Paradise Coaches (℡07/4933 1127, ⓦwww.paradisecoaches.com.au) connect Rockhampton, via all stops along the Capricorn Highway, with Barcaldine and Longreach, from either of which you can pick up a Greyhound service to Winton on its Brisbane–Mount Isa run. Both also operate buses between Emerald and Mackay. Alternatively, you can catch the twice-weekly *Spirit of the Outback* **train** (with economy seats and sleeper cars) from Rockhampton as far as Longreach.

Into the Northern Highlands

As you move inland, the coastal humidity is left behind and the gently undulating landscape becomes baked instead of steamed. The highway loops over low hills, running straight for many kilometres followed by an unexpected bend. Gradually, the deep-blue platform of the **Blackdown Tablelands** emerges from the horizon and, by the time you reach tiny Dingo, 150km from Rockhampton, dominates the landscape. Buses drop off in **DINGO** which has a hotel, van park, fuel station and store, and a bronze monument to the town's namesake.

The Blackdown Tablelands

Floating 600m above the heat haze, the **Blackdown Tablelands'** gum forests, waterfalls and escarpments are a delight, and a scenic refuge from the dry, flat lands below. A twenty-kilometre **access road** is signposted on the highway 11km west of Dingo, and runs flat through open scrub to the base of the range; it's sealed up to the top, but there's no public transport into the park. Views over a haze of eucalyptus woodland are generally blocked by the thicker forest at the top of the plateau, but at **Horseshoe Lookout** there's a fabulous view north and, after rain, **Two Mile Falls** rockets over the edge of the cliffs. From here the road runs past **Mimosa Creek campground** (bookings through the National Parks office in Emerald on ℡07/4982 4555 or with the special booking service on ℡13 13 04; $4.85 per person), an excellent spot shaded by massive stringybark trees, with tank water, tables, toilets, fire pits and a creek to bathe in. At night the air fills with the sharp scent of woodsmoke, and the occasional dingo howls in the distance – with a torch, you might see **greater gliders** or the more active brushtail possum. Watch out for **currawongs** (crows) that raid unattended tables, tents and cars for anything, edible or not. Temperatures can reach 40°C on summer days, and drop below zero on winter nights.

Walks in the park include short marked trails from the campsite to **Officers Pocket**, a moist amphitheatre of ferns and palms with the facing cliffs picked out yellow and white in the late afternoon; and a circuit track along **Mimosa Creek**, past remains of cattle pens and stock huts to some beautifully clear ochre stencils of hands and weapons made by the Gungaloo people over a century ago. Blackdown's finest scenery, however, is at **Rainbow Falls**, at the end of the vehicle track 6km past the campsite. At their glorious best around dawn, the falls are surrounded by eerie gum forest; from the lookout above you can spy on birds in the rainforest below and hear the explosive thumps of rock wallabies tearing across ledges hardly big enough for a mouse. A long staircase descends into a cool world of spring-fed gardens, ending on a large shelf where the falls spray from above into a wide pool of beautifully clear but paralyzingly cold water.

Emerald and around

The highway west of Dingo crosses the lower reaches of the **Bowen Basin coalfields** into cotton country, signalled by fluffy white tailings along the roadside. Despite its proximity to the Gemfield towns of Sapphire and Rubyvale, **EMERALD**, 125km along, was named by a surveyor who passed through after heavy rains had greened the landscape. A dormitory town for nearby coal mines, at the junction of routes north to Mackay and south to Carnarvon Gorge, Emerald's rich soil supports sunflowers, citrus trees, grapevines, lychees and rock melons, all of which attract swarms of seasonal **fruit-pickers**. Despite being over a hundred years old, the town appears quite modern due to rebuilding after a series of disastrous fires in the 1930s and 40s.

Most essential services are on the Capricorn Highway, here called **Clermont Street**. Its main feature is the pristine **train station**, built at the turn of the twentieth century and restored in the late 1980s, where **buses** also pull up. At the west end of Clermont Street, the **visitor centre** (Mon–Sat 9am–5pm, Sun 10am–2pm; ☎07/4982 4142, ⦿www.centralhighlandstourism.org.au) sits in a shady park in front of the world's largest Van Gogh sunflower print, mounted on a giant easel.

Due to a steady influx of workers, **accommodation** is tight all year round (particularly midweek) and especially during the April harvest or November cotton-chipping season – book ahead. The *Central Inn* (☎07/4982 0800; ❸), near the station on Clermont Street, has a big kitchen, simply furnished rooms, and offers good advice for either farm work or visiting the Gemfields; the friendly, family-run *Motel 707* (☎07/4982 1707; ❹) on the corner of the Capricorn and Gregory highways, just around the corner from the visitor centre, has clean, comfortable rooms and a good steak restaurant; and the *Explorers Inn Motel* (☎07/4987 6222, ⦿www.emeraldexplorersinn.com.au; ❻) is in a quiet spot at the edge of town, with comfortable, well-appointed rooms (some with spas) and a saltwater pool as well as a licensed restaurant and cocktail bar.

South to Springsure and Carnarvon Gorge

Carnarvon Gorge (p.522) lies 200km or so south of Emerald via the town of **SPRINGSURE**, which is set below the weathered orange cliffs of Mount Zamia, also known as Virgin Rock – though today you can barely see the likeness of the Madonna and Child. If you wind up here for the night, the *Zamia Motel* (☎07/4984 1455; ❹) has comfortable rooms and a café. It's worth pausing in the area to detour 10km southwest to **Rainworth Fort** (daily except Thurs 9am–2pm, closed Dec–Feb; $7), to see how Aborigines put up a strong resistance to their land being invaded. The fort is a squat stockade of basalt blocks and corrugated iron built by settlers for protection after "**the Wills Massacre**", when on October 17, 1861, Kari Aboriginal forces stormed Cullin-la-ringo station and killed nineteen people in apparent retaliation for the slaughter of a dozen Aborigines by a local squatter. White response was savage, spurred on by vigilantes – newspapers reported that "a great massacre has been made among the blacks of the Nogoa [river district]". The fort, and newer structures of Cairdbeign School and Homestead at the same site, house a few relics of the period. Back on the Carnarvon road, it's 70km from Springsure to **Rolleston**, the last source of fuel, supplies and accommodation in this direction before Carnarvon Gorge.

The Gemfields

The hot, sparse, rubble-covered country an hour west of Emerald masks one of the world's richest **sapphire fields** and, with hard work, the chances of finding some are good – though you're unlikely to get rich. The closest fields to

Gem mining

Gems were first discovered in 1870 near Anakie, but until Thai buyers came onto the scene a century later operations were low-key; even today there are still solo fossickers making a living from their claims. Formed by prehistoric volcanic actions and later dispersed along waterways and covered by sediment, the **zircons**, **rubies** and especially **sapphires** found here lie in a layer of gravel above the clay base of ancient riverbeds. This layer can be up to 15m down, so gullies and dry rivers, where nature has already done some of the excavation for you, are good places to start digging.

Looking for surface gems, or **specking**, is best after rain, when a trained eye can see the stones sparkle in the mud. It's erratic but certainly easier than the alternative – **fossicking** – which requires a pick, shovel, sieve, washtub full of water and a canvas sack before even starting (this gear can be rented at all of the fields). Cut and polished, local zircons are pale yellow, sapphires pale green or yellow to deep blue, and rubies are light pink, but when they're covered in mud it's hard to tell them from gravel, which is where the washing comes in: the wet gems glitter like fragments of coloured glass.

You have to be extremely enthusiastic to spend a summer on the fields, as the mercury soars, topsoil erodes and everything becomes coated in dust. The first rains bring floods as the sunbaked ground sheds water, and if you're here at this time you'll be treated to the sight of locals specking in the rain, dressed in Akubra hats and long Drizabone raincoats and shuffling around like mobile mushrooms. Conditions are best (and hence the fields busiest) as soon after the wet season as possible (around May), when the ground is soft and fresh pickings have been uncovered.

If this all seems like too much hard work, try a **gem park** such as Pat's Gem Tourist Fossicking Park (p.532), where they've done the digging for you and supply a bucket of wash along with all the necessary gear ($8). All you have to do is sieve the wash, flip it onto the canvas and check it for stones. There's an art to sieving and flipping, but visitors frequently find stones. Alternatively, Pat's sells bags for $15 that include among the wash a sapphire ready for faceting (cutting). Gem parks can also value and cut stones for you. Another break from the business end of a pick is to take a **mine tour** (p.532) and see if the professionals fare any better. In some ways they do – the chilled air 5m down is wonderful – but the main difference is one of scale rather than method or intent.

If you're still keen you'll need a **fossicker's licence**, available from shops and gem parks, which allows digging in areas set aside for the purpose or on no-man's-land. The $6.15 licence is valid for one month and gives you no rights at all other than to keep what you find and to camp at fossick grounds. To "stake a claim" – which gives you temporary ownership of the land to keep others away – you need a **Miner's Right** from the field officer in Emerald (Department of Mines and Energy, Hospital Rd; ☎07/4987 9373). This also carries obligations to restore the land to its original state and maintain it for two years after quitting the site.

Emerald (and the best-geared for beginners) are Sapphire and Rubyvale, reached by sealed roads: the turn-off to both is off the Capricorn Highway about 43km west; from here Sapphire is 11km north and Rubyvale a further 7km north. There's **no transport**, but Emerald's visitor centre (p.530) can advise on car rental.

The well-worked country around **SAPPHIRE** looks like a war zone, with mine remnants scarring the countryside. You'll find a post office and houses scattered along the road and a section of Retreat Creek, where the first gems were found. The *New Sapphire Caravan Park* (℡07/4985 4281; powered sites $25, cabins ❷) has cabins and tent sites across the road from the medical centre, in sight of the creek. *Blue Gem Caravan Park* (℡07/4985 4162; camping $18, powered sites $20, cabins ❹) has a store, fuel and fast food. Towards Rubyvale is Pat's Gem Tourist Fossicking Park (daily 8.30am–5pm; ℡07/4985 4544) with a café and licensed restaurant, jewellery, craft displays and **fossicking lessons** – for more see p.531.

RUBYVALE itself has several shops, service stations and a few **exhibition mines**. Tour groups tend to visit Miner's Heritage (mid-March to mid-Oct daily 9am–5pm, mid-Oct to mid-March daily 9am–3pm; 30min tours $12), but equally interesting is Bobby Dazzler (daily 8am–3.30pm; 20min tours $8), on the hill as you approach town. Rubyvale's facilities include fuel, a general store, a couple of caravan parks including the *Rubyvale Caravan Park* with campsites and cabins (℡07/4985 4118; camping $16, powered sites $20, cabins ❸), and *Rubyvale Holiday Units* (℡07/4985 4518; ❹–❺), which has very comfortable motel-style rooms, a sparkling, shaded pool and a couple of luxurious, brand-new spa units with private outdoor areas. For **eating**, the best place around is the *New Royal Hotel*, a smart stone-and-timber building with a mighty fireplace and tasty pub food.

The ground beneath each new development in the area has to be mined first; the surfaced road was built only after years of wrangling over whether the ground had given up all its treasures. You'll hear plenty of tall stories during the annual **August Gemfest** (ⓦwww.gemfest.com.au), held at the Allen King Memorial Park in Anakie, just opposite the turn-off from the Capricorn Highway to Sapphire and Rubyvale. Some 27km west of this turn-off, the **Willows Gemfield**, part mining camp, part township, is the most recent designated fossicking area and some fair-sized gems have been found. The immaculate, well-shaded *Willows Caravan Park* (℡07/4985 5128; camping $15, powered sites $18, cabins ❶) has wangled a liquor licence and acts as a post office as well as supplying fuel. The gemfields are just down the track from the park; through-buses heading west from Emerald can drop you off.

Over the Range to Winton

Vistas from the rounded sandstone boulders at the top of the Great Dividing Range reveal a dead-flat country beyond. Rivers flow to the Gulf of Carpentaria or towards the great dry lakes of South Australia, while unsealed roads run north to Clermont and south to Charleville. You'll notice an increase in temperature as flies appear from nowhere, tumbleweeds pile up against fences and trees never seem closer than the horizon. In terms of numbers, **sheep** dominate these parts, though there are some cattle and even a few people out here. The next stops on the road or rail line before Barcaldine are the townships of **Alpha** (ⓦwww.alphaqueensland.com.au), where you can find fuel and a café or two, and **Jericho** (ⓦ www.jericho.qld.gov.au), one of the last places in Queensland with a drive-in movie theatre, which shows films usually on the third Saturday night of each month, year-round.

Barcaldine, Blackall and Ilfracombe

It was near **BARCALDINE**, 300km west of Emerald, during the 1885 drought that geologists first tapped Queensland's **artesian water**, revolutionizing Outback development. The town further secured its place in history during the 1891 **shearers' strike** which – though a failure itself – ultimately led to the formation of the **Australian Labor Party**. On the highway, outside the station which became the focus of the dispute, is a granite monument – sculpted to resemble the tips of a pair of shears – to shearers arrested during the strike. Right next to it, the **Tree of Knowledge** was a rallying point for shearers. The tree itself was poisoned in 2006 in mysterious circumstances and has now died, but its stump and root-ball have been preserved as part of a multimillion-dollar monument, encased in a walk-in Perspex box topped by windchime-like green poles representing leaves.

The town's only other sight as such is the **Australian Workers' Heritage Centre** (Mon–Sat 9am–5pm, Sun 10am–5pm; $13), unmissable underneath a yellow-and-blue marquee on Ash Street. Its expanding collection of displays concentrates on the history of the workers' movement after the shearers' strike, as well as film footage, artefacts and plenty of sepia-tinted photos covering themes including Outback women and Aboriginal stockmen. On the highway, the **visitor centre** (Mon–Fri 8.30am–4.30pm; ⓣ07/4651 1724, ⓦwww .barcaldine.qld.gov.au) rents bikes for a gold coin donation. For a closer look at Outback caves, waterholes and **Aboriginal art** – much of it on private property – with a tall tale or two thrown in, contact Artesian Country Tours (ⓣ07/4651 2211, ⓦwww.artesiancountrytours.com.au); their day-long "Aramac & Graceville" tour (Wed & Sat; $145 including all transport, lunch and tea) is highly recommended.

Both Paradise Coaches and Greyhound **buses** stop in Barcaldine; the bank, ATM and other **services** are mostly on Box Street, which runs south off the highway. **Accommodation** options include the corrugated-roofed *Ironbark Inn* (ⓣ07/4651 2311; ❸–❹), an "Outback-style" motel with attached steakhouse, *Barcaldine Motel* (ⓣ07/4651 1244; ❸–❹) and *Barcaldine Tourist Park* (ⓣ07/4651 6066; camping $18, powered sites $20, cabins ❸), all on Box Street. Barcaldine has a disproportionate number of **bars** (six) in iconic veranda-shaded buildings, including the *Artesian*, *Commercial* and *Union* hotels, all offering cold drinks and counter meals.

Blackall and Idalia National Park

One hour south of Barcaldine on the Landsborough Highway, it was here in the Merino Country surrounding **BLACKALL** in 1892 that **Jackie Howe** fleeced 321 sheep in under eight hours using hand shears, a still-unbroken record. You can learn more at the steam-driven **woolscour** (where the freshly sheared fleeces are vigorously washed and cleaned), 1.4km north of town, which was built in 1908 and in operation for seventy years; guides are on hand to show you around the restored plant (daily 9am–5pm; $12). Back in town, a sign points to the famous **black stump**, a surveying point used in pinpointing Queensland's borders in the nineteenth century. The original stump has been replaced by a more interesting (if less blackened) fossilized one. In Aussie parlance, anything east of here is "this side of the black stump", while anything west is "beyond the black stump", another term for Outback remoteness. Before heading in either direction, be sure to cool off at the **artesian spa** (summer Mon–Fri 6–10am & 2.30–6pm, Sat & Sun 11am–6pm; winter daily 10am–6pm; $1.65), a large pool at the town's Aquatic Centre on Salvia Street.

The town sits on the banks of the often dry (but occasionally five-metre-deep) Barcoo River. **Shamrock Street**, shaded by palms and bottle trees, is the main road on which you'll find banks, supplies, the friendly visitor centre (daily 9am–noon & 1–5pm; ☎07/4657 4637), and a few places **to eat** – if you're neatly dressed you can savour good food at the *Blackall Club*. The most central **places to stay** are the smart *Acacia Motor Inn* (☎07/4657 6022; ❹), on Shamrock Street, or at *Blackall Caravan Park* (☎07/4657 4816; camping $17, powered sites $20, cabins ❸) on Hart Lane, where you can yarn with other travellers around a huge campfire and, between April and September, enjoy a communal pot roast with billy tea and damper. Greyhound **buses** heading to Brisbane stop in town; tickets are available from Blackall's BP Roadhouse (☎07/4657 4453) on Shamrock Street.

Around 155km southwest of Blackall, **Idalia National Park** preserves one of Queensland's last wild groups of **yellow-footed rock wallabies**, fantastically pretty animals with long, ringed tails (though these can be seen more easily at Charleville, if you're heading that way). You can generally (but not always) get into the park in a 2WD; for current **access details** contact the ranger on ☎07/4657 5033, or check out ⓦwww.epa.qld.gov.au.

Ilfracombe

Back on the Landsborough Highway between Barcaldine and Longreach, 80km west of the former and just 27km east of the latter, the entire one-street bush township of **ILFRACOMBE** (ⓦwww.ilfracombe.qld.gov.au) essentially forms a living museum. The main drag comprises the "Machinery Mile" with pastoral machinery, vehicles and farming equipment lined up next to the highway. Also here are an artesian spa in the town's Memorial Park, Australia's biggest bottle collection at Hilton's Bottles, a folk museum, and a hundred-year-old homestead – all of which have free admission. The town's centrepiece, however, is the iconic Queenslander pub, the *Wellshot Hotel* (☎07/4658 2106; ❶), boasting local memorabilia, ice-cold beer and seven colourful, clean budget rooms. Alternatively, the caravan park (☎07/4658 1510; camping $12, powered sites $17.50, cabins ❸) has a free barbecue area and a nightly happy hour.

Longreach

Unlike many other western towns, **LONGREACH**, 110km west of Barcaldine and right on the Tropic of Capricorn, is more than surviving. The lynchpin for

Qantas

Though **Qantas** (the Queensland and Northern Territories Aerial Service) officially formed at Winton, the first joy-flights and taxi service actually flew from Longreach in 1921, pioneered by Hudson Fysh and Paul McGinness. Their idea – that an airline could play an important role by carrying mail and passengers, dropping supplies to remote districts and providing an emergency link into the Outback – inspired other projects such as the Flying Doctor Service. Though the company's headquarters moved to Brisbane in 1930, Qantas maintained its offices at Longreach until after World War II – during the war US Flying Fortresses were stationed here – by which time both the company and its planes had outgrown the town.

▲ Historic Douglas DC3 aircraft at the Qantas Founders Outback Museum

this is the ambitious Stockman's Hall of Fame museum, but the town was also one of the first to realize the potential of tapping Queensland's artesian water reserves for stock farming, and was the original headquarters of **Qantas** (see box opposite).

On the highway 2km north of the town centre, the **Stockman's Hall of Fame** (daily 9am–5pm; $22.50; ⓦ www.outbackheritage.com.au) is a master-piece not just in architectural design – it's a blend of aircraft hangar and cathedral – but in being an encyclopedia of the Outback in its heart. The displays unashamedly romance the Outback through film footage, multimedia presentations, photographs and exhibits. History starts in the Dreamtime and moves on to early European explorers and pioneers (including a large section on women in the Outback), before ending with personal accounts of life in the bush. Among more day-to-day features are some offbeat selections: over a hundred types of barbed wire, from the old hook design to modern razor wire, boxing kangaroos, rodeos, bark huts and tall stories. Onsite there's also an art gallery, a daytime café and an excellent restaurant (p.536); allow half a day to take it all in.

Opposite the Hall of Fame is the **Qantas Founders Outback Museum** (daily 9am–5pm; museum $19, 747 tours from $19, 707 tours from $16; ⓦ www.qfom.com.au), whose prized possessions are a decommissioned Qantas jumbo jet and a restored 1950s Boeing 707, Australia's (and Qantas') inaugural registered passenger jet. Each can be viewed on various guided tours (booking advisable), including a 747 "wing walk" tour ($85). An original 1922 hangar forms part of the exhibition, which also includes classic advertising posters and cabin staff uniforms from days gone by.

Next door to the Hall of Fame towards Barcaldine along the Landsborough Highway, the School of the Air offers guided tours (Mon–Fri 9am & 10.30am excluding public and Christmas school holidays; ☏07/4658 4222; $5), where you can see a school lesson for kids in isolated locations in progress.

Back in town, the farmer-run Station Store, at 126 Eagle St (☏07/4658 2006), is a drought-inspired enterprise comprising a former pub-turned-shop (Mon–Fri

9am–5pm, Sat 9am–noon) selling quality Outback crafts and clothing; a bark-strewn cinema, with canvas sling chairs, screening classic Australian films (Mon–Fri 3 shows daily; tickets $7.50); a café (Easter–Oct Mon–Fri 9am–5pm) with an original Cobb & Co. coach parked in the corner; and a reproduction horse-drawn coach that can take you on a galloping tour through the scrub (Easter–Oct Mon–Fri; $44) or, twice-weekly during the same period, on an overnight campout including a three-course dinner ($165). Also in town, the Powerhouse Museum, on the corner of Swan and Ibis streets (Mon–Fri 2–5pm; $8), gathers together an interesting collection of rural generating machinery alongside exhibits on the town's history.

Practicalities

Longreach's main drag is south off the highway along **Eagle Street**, where you'll find hotels, cafés, banks, a cinema screening first-release films (upstairs from the Hideaway Café), and a supermarket. The **airport** is off the highway directly behind the Qantas museum, while **trains** terminate at the station at the junction of Galah Street and the highway. Greyhound and Paradise Coaches **buses** set down on Eagle Street at Longreach Outback Travel Centre (℡07/4658 1776, ⓦwww.lotc.com.au), which can arrange tickets for onward travel, as well as cruises on a paddle-boat ($50) or dinner or bush-tucker cruises ($59/46) on a modern vessel along the Thomson River, also known as Longreach Waterhole, one of the major streams of the Lake Eyre Basin that joins Cooper Creek. Cruises run daily during winter; less frequently during summer.

The **visitor centre** (April–Oct Mon–Fri 9am–5pm, Sat & Sun 9am–noon; Nov–March Mon–Fri 9am–4.30pm; ℡07/4658 4150), in a replica of Qantas's original office, on the corner of Eagle and Duck streets opposite the post office, has a leaflet about exploring the river yourself, including free camping available at the riverside park, which has toilets but no showers, or try *The Discovery Van Park* (℡07/4658 1781; camping $26, powered sites $28, cabins ❺), on Thrush Road looking across to the Hall of Fame. Rooms are comfortable and well equipped at the motel-style *Albert Park Motor Inn* on Hudson Fysh Drive (℡07/4658 2411; ❺), and at the retro-contemporary *Longreach Motor Inn* on Galah Street (℡07/4658 2322; ❹–❺), with a palm-shaded pool, free broadband internet and the town's best restaurant. Other good options for meals include the *Longreach RSL Club* on Duck Street; Longreach's main nightlife spot, *Starlight's Hideout Tavern*, on Eagle Street; and the open-sided, shed-like *Cattlemen's Bar & Grill* (closed Mon & Tues), adjacent to the Stockman's Hall of Fame, cooled by an enormous ceiling fan, serving gourmet Aussie tucker like beer-battered barra and chips, damper, deep-dish pies such as lamb, rosemary and mustard or red wine and beef, and hearty burgers (including vege burgers).y

Winton and around

A 173-kilometre-long run northwest from Longreach across the barren Mitchell Plains, **WINTON** is a real frontier town where dust devils blow tumbleweeds down the streets – a fitting backdrop for the 1800s-set film *The Proposition* (2004), written by Nick Cave, which was filmed in and around town. As Queensland's largest cattle-trucking depot, Winton has a constant stream of road trains rumbling through, and a fair swag of history: **Waltzing Matilda** premiered

Waltzing Matilda

The first public performance of "Banjo" Paterson's ballad **Waltzing Matilda** was held in April 1895 at Winton's *North Gregory Hotel*, and has stirred up gossip and speculation ever since. Legend has it that Christina MacPherson told Paterson the tale of a swagman's brush with the law at the Combo Waterhole, near Kynuna, while the poet was staying with her family at nearby Dagwood Station. Christina wrote the music to the ballad, a collaboration which so incensed Paterson's fiancée, Sarah Riley, that she broke off their engagement. (Neither woman ever married.) While a straightforward "translation" of the poem is easy enough – "Waltzing Matilda" was contemporary slang for tramping (carrying a bedroll or swag from place to place), "jumbuck" for a sheep, and "squatters" refers to landowners – there is some contention as to what the poem actually describes. The most obvious interpretation is of a poor tramp, hounded to death by the law, but first drafts of the poem suggest that Paterson – generally known as a romantic rather than a social commentator – originally wrote the piece about the arrest of a union leader during the shearers' strike. Either version would account for its popularity – it was one of four songs Australians voted for to become the national anthem in 1977, coming in second, and Aussies readily identify with an underdog who dares to confront the system.

at the *North Gregory Hotel*, and Qantas was founded here in 1920. The surrounding country is an eerie world of windswept plains and eroded **jump-ups** (flat-topped hills layered in orange, grey and red dust), **opal deposits** and **dinosaur footprints**.

Winton's central drag is **Elderslie Street**, where you'll find banks, a post office and service stations. From April to September, if there's a film on, treat yourself to a session in the **open-air cinema**, complete with canvas seats and original projector, at the corner of Elderslie and Cobb streets – enquire next door at the general goods shop Wookatook. A few doors down, next to the *North Gregory Hotel*, the immense wooden **Corfield & Fitzmaurice building** (Mon–Fri 9am–5pm, Sat 9am–12.30pm, Sun 11am–3pm; $5) opened as a store in 1916 and now houses a vast collection of rocks and fossils from around the world, along with a life-size diorama of the Lark Quarry dinosaurs – garbage bins around town are also shaped as dinosaur feet.

Further down Elderslie Street, opposite a bronze statue of the jolly swagman, the **Waltzing Matilda Centre** (daily 9am–5pm; $19; ☎07/4657 1466, Ⓦ www.matildacentre.com.au), a major highlight of this corner of the Outback, has a fantastic multimedia show presented by the "ghost" of the swaggie himself in an indoor billabong and a host of unusual items, including a fine display of Aboriginal artefacts, reconstructed historic buildings and vehicle sheds, and a research library. The centre also doubles as a **visitor centre**, which books **tours** to local sights. For some really ludicrous fun, the **Australian Crayfish Derby**, part of the Outback Festival held in September in odd-numbered years, sees the owner of the winning crustacean net around $1500, while the runner-up gets to eat all the competitors. Every April the **Waltzing Matilda Festival** incorporates a rodeo and bush poetry.

Winton's **accommodation** prospects include the *Matilda Country Tourist Park* (☎07/4657 1607; camping $21, powered sites $26, cabins ❸–❹) on Chirnside Street, about 700km from Elderslie Street where the Landsborough Highway kinks into town; the neat and trim *Banjo Holiday Units* (☎07/4657 1213; ❸) on nearby Manuka Street; and the *North Gregory Hotel* (☎07/4657 1375; shared-facility hotel rooms ❸, en-suite motel rooms ❸), situated opposite the early-opening *Twilight Café* (last orders 7.30pm). Alternatively, **Carisbrooke Station**,

85km southwest of Winton amid rugged scenery (☎07/4657 3885, ⓦwww
.carisbrooketours.com.au; camping $5, powered sites $17, units ❸–❹), a
working sheep and cattle station where Lyndon B. Johnson made an emergency
landing after Pearl Harbor, offers units with shared facilities and space for tents
and vans as well as meals on request and **tours** from the property by arrangement, including one to Lark Quarry.

Moving on, Greyhound **buses** depart from the Matilda Centre once daily in
each direction towards Mount Isa and Brisbane. Check with the visitor centre
about road conditions before driving out to Opalton or Lark Quarry

Opalton

South of Winton, a 120-kilometre-long unsealed road runs south through the
beautifully stark jump-ups and spinifex scrub to **OPALTON**, a multicultural
shantytown where Yugoslav, Czech and Australian miners are reworking
century-old **opal diggings** with Chinese and Korean finance. You need to be
entirely self-sufficient here (including bringing your own drinking water); the
only modern feature is a solar-powered telephone. Fossicking zones have been
established where you can pick over old tailings for scraps. There's a **camping**
and van park (sites from $10, units ❸), washing water, and a small **store** that's
usually open from 10am to 2pm, though it doesn't sell fuel.

Lark Quarry

It takes about two hours to drive the 120-kilometre unsealed road southwest
from Winton to **Lark Quarry**, dodging kamikaze kangaroos and patches of
bulldust. It's not surprising to find **dinosaur** remains here: the place looks
prehistoric, swarming with flies and surrounded by stubby hills where stunted
trees and tufts of grass tussle with rocks for space. A hundred million years ago
a carnivorous dinosaur chased a group of various turkey-sized herbivores
through the mud to a rockface where it caught and killed one as the others fled.
Over **three thousand footprints** have been found recording these few
seconds of action, excavated in the 1970s and now protected by an awning and
walkway around them maintained by the National Parks and Wildlife Service.
Indentations left by small, amazingly sharp, three-clawed feet – some very light
as the prey panicked and ran on tiptoe – stream in all directions, while those
left by the larger predator go only one way. Paths lead around to other, buried
tracks where the chase ended.

Beyond Winton

From Winton, it's 340km northwest to Cloncurry (covered by the Greyhound
bus). Some 165km along, the **Combo Waterhole** is a shaded, muddy soak just
off the road which provided the inspiration for Banjo Paterson's classic ballad
Waltzing Matilda. A shade further on, **KYNUNA's** low-slung *Blue Heeler Hotel*
(☎07/4746 8650; camping $5, powered sites $12.50, cabins ❸, motel rooms ❹),
another of the first places the song was performed, has ice-cold beer – as does
the single-storey, clay-coloured *Walkabout Creek Hotel* (☎07/4746 8424;
camping $19.80, powered sites $23.80, motel rooms with shared amenities ❷)
at **McKINLAY**, 75km past Kynuna, which you might recognize as the rowdy
Outback pub in the film *Crocodile Dundee*.

West of Winton – there's no bus – it's 366 sealed kilometres to **BOULIA**
along one of the most beautiful and surprisingly varied stretches of scenery in

Queensland's Outback, alternating between endless plains, lush creeks and blood-red hills. Fuel is available 163km west of Winton at Middleton's combined pub/general store; drop in for a drink with its owner Stoney and his family and assorted local characters and wayfarers. Boulia is best known for its enigmatic **Min Min Light**, an eerie, unexplained car-headlamp-like light reputedly seen in the bush at night. If you miss the real thing (locals maintain "you don't go looking for it, it comes looking for you"), drop in to the **Min Min Encounter Centre** (Mon–Fri 8.30am–5pm, Sat & Sun 9am–2pm, to 5pm summer; $13), a 45-minute sound-and-light show where you're directed through a series of rooms to meet automated characters depicting real-life locals and hear about their close personal encounters with the lights. Boulia's **visitor centre** (same hours; ☎07/4746 3386, ⓦwww.boulia.qld.gov.au) is here too, along with *Encounters Café*. The Old Stone House Museum (check with the visitor centre for times; $2.20), on the corner of Pituri and Hamilton streets, was built in 1884 out of local stone bonded with limestone, gidyea ash and sand and has some rare Aboriginal artefacts and lots of fossils. Services in town include a van park (☎07/4746 3122), well-kept motel rooms at the *Desert Sands Motel* (☎07/4746 3000; ●), and hotel and motel **rooms** at the *Australian Hotel* (☎07/4746 3144; ●), which also has good counter meals, a store and roadhouse. Families flock to Boulia for the **July camel races**; camping at the rodeo grounds is free up to one week beforehand and during the three-day event, which also features live bands.

Moving on from Boulia, Mount Isa is 303km north on bitumen, and Birdsville is 400km south on a mostly reasonable unsealed road. If you're really enjoying the ride, Alice Springs is 814km west on the Donohue and Plenty "highways" – a long stretch of dust and gravel. Be sure to fuel up in Boulia if you're heading that way, as the next chance is 467km west in Jervois in the NT.

Townsville to the Territory

All the major settlements along the thousand-kilometre stretch between Townsville and the Northern Territory border are **mining** towns, spaced so far apart that precise names are redundant: **Mount Isa** becomes "the Isa", **Cloncurry** "the Curry", and **Charters Towers** "the Towers". It's a shame that most people see this vast area as something to be crossed as quickly as possible – even if time is limited, Charters Towers' century-old feel and Mount Isa's strange setting are worth a stopover. With the freedom of your own vehicle, there's untramped bush at **Porcupine Gorge**, north of Hughenden in the heart of **dinosaur country**, and the spectacular oasis of **Lawn Hill Gorge**. The main route through into the Territory is along the Flinders and Barkly highways – covered daily by Greyhound **buses** – and there's also the twice-weekly Inlander **train** between Townsville and Mount Isa.

Gold country

Two hours west of the coast, the dry scrub at the heights of the inland range at the community of **Mingela** once covered seams of ore which had the streets of both **Charters Towers** and **Ravenswood** bustling with lucky-strike miners. Those times are long gone – though gold is still extracted from old tailings or sporadically panned from the creek beds – and the towns have survived at opposite extremes: connected by road and rail to Townsville, Charters Towers became a busy rural centre, while Ravenswood, half an hour south of Mingela, was just too far off the track and is a shadow of its former self. Between April and October, Detour Coaches (☏07/4728 5311, ⓦwww.detourcoaches.com) run **day-trips** from Townsville to the Gold country for about $115.

Ravenswood

As the wind blows dust and dried grass around the streets between mine shafts and lonely old buildings, **RAVENSWOOD**, reached by a sealed road detouring some 50km south off the main highway, fulfils ideas of what a ghost town should look like. Gold was discovered here in 1868 and within two years there were seven hundred miners on Elphinstone Creek. As one historian put it, "Every building on the main street was either a public house and dance house or a public house and general store."

The main attraction is to wander among the restored buildings. The curator of the **Court House Museum** (April–Sept daily 10am–1.30pm; Oct–March Mon–Fri 11am–1pm Sat & Sun 10.30am–1pm; $2; ☏07/4770 2047 to book) gives – with sufficient notice – entertaining tours of the museum, town and current mining efforts. Built in 1879, the **post office** doubles as the town's store and fuel supply. The two most complete survivals are **hotels** – the solid, dark-brick *Railway* (☏07/4770 2144; ❹), and the gracious, recently restored *Imperial* (☏07/4770 2131; ❷), with original wood panelling. You'll probably end up in one of them as the day heats up, for a drink or a **meal**; both also offer atmospheric, antique-furnished pub rooms with shared bathrooms.

Charters Towers and around

Once Queensland's second-largest city, and often referred to in its heyday simply as "the World", **CHARTERS TOWERS** is a showcase of colonial-era architecture. An Aboriginal boy named **Jupiter Mosman** found gold here in 1871 and within twelve months three thousand prospectors had stripped the landscape of trees and covered it with shafts, chimneys and crushing mills. At first, little money was reinvested – the **cemetery** is a sad record of cholera and typhoid outbreaks from poor sanitation – but by 1900, despite diminishing returns, Charters Towers had become a prosperous centre. There's been minimal change since, and the population, now mainly sustained by cattle farming, has shrunk to about a third of its prime. Good times to visit are for the May Day weekend **Country Music Festival**, and the Easter **Rodeo**. Films are screened on Fridays, Saturdays, Sundays and public holidays at the drive-in cinema 5km north of town.

Arrival and information

Charters Towers and its surrounds have several highly worthwhile attractions to justify a couple of days in the area, all of them bookable at the visitor centre at Mosman St (daily 9am–5pm; ☏07/4752 0314). The most entertaining by day, the **Venus Gold Battery** (April–Sept guided tours every half-hour

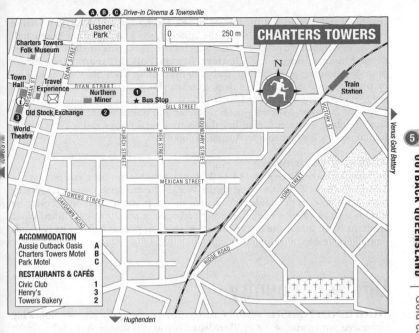

Lissner Park

0   250 m

CHARTERS TOWERS

Charters Towers
Folk Museum

DEANE STREET

MARY STREET

Town Hall

MOSMAN ST

Travel Experience

RYAN STREET

Northern Miner

❶ ★ Bus Stop

GILL STREET

Old Stock Exchange   **❷**

World Theatre   **❸**

N

Train Station

VICTORY ST

CHURCH STREET

HIGH STREET

BOUNDARY STREET

MEXICAN STREET

TOWERS STREET

DAYDAWN ROAD

YORK STREET

RIDGE ROAD

Venus Gold Battery

ACCOMMODATION
Aussie Outback Oasis   A
Charters Towers Motel   B
Park Motel   C

RESTAURANTS & CAFÉS
Civic Club   1
Henry's   3
Towers Bakery   2

▼ *Hughenden*

9.30am–3.30pm; Oct–March guided tours 9am & 10am; $12), 4km out of town down Gill Street, is a fascinating illustration of the monumental efforts needed to separate gold from rock. Abandoned in 1972 after a century of operations, the battery is a huge, gloomy temple to the past, its machinery belying the fact that this was once a sweatbox filled with noxious mercury fumes and the noise of huge hammers smashing ore into manageable pieces. Heading 2km west of town brings you to Towers Hill Lookout, offering a sweeping panorama of the city. Of an evening, an atmospheric 45-minute outdoor film (nightly; $7) evokes the former mining town's ghosts.

Accommodation

For **accommodation**, the *Charters Towers Motel* (☎07/4787 1366; **❹**), at 95 Hackett Terrace, is a simple but very well-kept family-run motel with one highly worthwhile luxury: magnetic mattress and pillow underlays that are incredibly restful before or after a long day's drive. The *Park Motel* (☎07/4787 1022; **❹**), on the corner of Mosman and Deane streets, is also central and comfortable. If you're **camping**, the Aussie Outback Oasis van park (☎1800 812 417, ⓦhttp://aussie-outback-oasis.qld.big4.com.au; camping $20, powered sites $30, cabins **❹–❺**), 3km northeast of the city centre on Dr George Ellis Drive, has well-spaced, shady sites and amenities including a landscaped saltwater pool set amongst rocks and waterfalls, and wireless internet.

The City

The city centre has plenty of spruce old buildings along Gill and Mosman streets, including the 1871-established headquarters of the twice-weekly *Northern Miner*, one of Queensland's oldest surviving newspapers, the classical elegance of the post office and the **World Theatre** (guided tours $2; book at the visitor centre), and the shaded country arcades outside the stores. The

courtyard and glass roof at the former **Stock Exchange** and **Assayer's Office**
now front some quiet shops, while the adjacent, solid facade of the **town hall**
betrays its original purpose as a bank, which stored gold bars smelted locally. Just
down Mosman Street is the **Charters Towers Folk Museum** (daily 10am–
3pm; $5), housing an absorbing jumble of everything from old wagons to a set
of silver tongs for eating frogs' legs. Further along the road there's plenty of
shade under giant fig trees at **Lissner Park**, whose Boer War memorial recalls
stories of **Breaker Morant** – a local soldier and poet executed by the British
after shooting a prisoner, who has, thanks to several books and a 1980 feature
film about his life, become an Australian folk hero.

Eating and drinking

For **food**, *Towers Bakery* at 114 Gill St has award-winning meat pies, while
Henry's Café and Restaurant, next to the World Theatre on Mosman, is a pricey
place with an eclectic, modern Australian menu. If you're here on a Friday, be
sure to stop by for the weekly evening barbecue at the 1900-established Civic
Club on Ryan Street; the rest of the week, you can pocket balls on its two full-
size billiards tables.

Dinosaur country

HUGHENDEN, 245km west of Charters Towers along the highway, looks big
compared with some of the small settlements you pass on the way, with a dozen
wide streets, a supermarket, a couple of hotels and banks. Its main draw for
visitors, the **Dinosaur Museum and information centre** (daily 9am–5pm;
$3; ☎07/4741 1021) on Gray Street, focuses on the swamp-dwelling
Muttaburrasaurus, bones of which were found south of town in 1963 and
assembled into a ten-metre-long skeleton. For **accommodation**, *Wrights Motel*
(☎07/4741 1677; ❹) opposite the museum has reasonably priced rooms and a
restaurant, and the *Rest Easi Motel* (☎07/4741 1633; camping $16, rooms ❹),
on the Flinders Highway to the west of the town centre, also has camping facilities. *Pete's Country Café*, before the tracks on the other side of town, has good
burgers, while *FJ Holden's Café* at 55 Brodie St is a 1950s-style diner complete
with gingham tablecloths and Elvis memorabilia.

Ten kilometres south of town, Mount Walker rises 152m above the pancake-
flat plains, offering a 360-degree panorama of the district that's especially
photogenic at sunset. The road is sealed as far as the turn-off, then again to the
summit's six lookout points.

Porcupine Gorge is 70km north of Hughenden along the partially
surfaced Kennedy Developmental Road, accessible only if you have your
own vehicle (you can usually get by without a 4WD). It's best seen at the
start of the dry season (May–July) before the **Flinders River** stops flowing,
when good swimming holes, richly coloured cliffs, flowering bottlebrush and
banksia trees reward the effort of getting here. A National Parks **campsite**
(book on ☎13 13 04 or ⊛www.epa.qld.gov.au; $4.85) at the top of the
gorge has limited cold water and toilets; you can self-register on arrival. Look
for wallabies on the walk into the gorge, which leads down steps from the
campsite and becomes an increasingly steep, rough path carpeted in loose
stones. The white riverbed, sculpted by water, curves into a pool below the
orange, yellow and white bands of **Pyramid Rock**. This is the bush at its
best – sandstone glowing in the afternoon sun against a deep-blue sky, with

wildlife calls echoing along the gorge as the shadow of the gorge wall creeps over distant woods.

Richmond

More of the regional fossil record is on show 115km west of Hughenden along the highway at the small town of **RICHMOND**, whose **Marine Fossil Museum** and **information centre** (daily 8.30am–4.45pm; $12; ☏07/4741 3429) displays the petrified remains of hundred-million-year-old fish, long-necked elasmosaurs, and models of a "**kronosaurus Queenslandius**" excavated in the 1920s by a team from Harvard University and now on show in the USA. Pride of the collection is a complete skeleton of a seal-like **pliosaur** – the most intact vertebrate fossil ever found in Australia – and the **minmi ankylosaur**, with its armour-plated hide.

The roadside park makes a good spot to stretch your legs, with an original Cobb & Co. coach and views out across the Flinders River. The best-sited **accommodation** is the *Richmond Lake View Caravan Park* (☏07/4741 3772; camping $17/22, bunkhouse ❶, cabins ❹). The museum's **café** is the only one in town – otherwise head to the old wooden *Federal Palace Hotel* or one of the service stations for a feed.

Julia Creek

Along the main highway, 149km west of Richmond, **JULIA CREEK** is best known in Australia as the home of April's Dirt & Dust Festival, which combines serious sporting competition with more offbeat events such as bog snorkelling (a bog is artificially dug out of the dry soil for the occasion). Year-round, it's the home of the endangered dunnart, a nocturnal, insect-eating, mouse-like marsupial measuring just 10cm to 12cm in length.

Julia Creek's visitor centre (☏07/4746 7690) was planning its relocation from the town's library at the time of writing – call for updates. There are several hotels and motels in town, all of a good standard and all charging around $85 per double; otherwise you can camp at the Julia Creek *Caravan Park* (☏07/4746 7108; camping $15, powered sites $16.50, cabins ❶–❷). For a hearty meal, drop into the Julia Creek Hotel (☏07/4746 7727; ❹), also known as the "Top Pub", on the corner of Goldring and Julia streets.

Cloncurry and around

CLONCURRY, 137km west of Julia Creek, is caught between two landscapes, where the flat eastern plains rise to a rough and rocky plateau. Signs at either end of the town wish you "a warm welcome indeed", given that Australia's **highest temperature** (53.1°C) was recorded here. Cloncurry offers glimpses into the **mining history** that permeates the whole stretch west to larger Mount Isa. Copper was discovered here in 1867 but as the town lacked a rail link to the coast until 1908, profits were eroded by the necessity of transporting the ore by camel to Normanton. These days miners are flown in from the coast to the mines, work their two-week shifts at their self-contained mine sites, then head home again.

Buildings at the **Mary Kathleen Memorial Park Museum and Visitor Centre** (March–April Mon–Fri 8am–4.30pm; May–Oct same hours plus Sat & Sun 9am–3pm; $8.50; ☏07/4742 1361, ⓦwww.cloncurry.qld.gov.au) were salvaged from the short-lived town of Mary Kathleen (p.545). The museum is primarily of geological interest, a comprehensive catalogue of local ores, fossils and gemstones arranged in long cases, though Aboriginal tools and Burke's water bottle add some historical depth. The centre also has good tips on where to go bush-bashing for gemstones in the area.

Cloncurry's isolation inspired the formation of the **Royal Flying Doctor Service**. Over on the corner of King and Daintree streets, **John Flynn Place** (March–April Mon–Fri 8am–4.30pm; May–Oct same hours plus Sat & Sun 9am–3pm; $9.70) is a monument to the man who pioneered the use of radio and plane to provide a "mantle of safety over the Outback". The exhibition explains how ideas progressed with technology, from pedal-powered radios to assistance from the young Qantas, resulting in the opening of the first Flying Doctor base in Cloncurry in 1928. A very different aspect of Cloncurry's past is evident in the two foreign **cemeteries** on the outskirts of town. To the south of the highway, before you cross the creek on the way to Mount Isa, a hundred plots recall a brief nineteenth-century goldrush when the harsh conditions took a terrible toll on **Chinese** prospectors, while at the north end of Henry Street the unnamed graves of **Afghanis** are all aligned with Mecca. Afghanis were vital to Cloncurry's survival before the coming of the railway, organizing camel trains which carried the ore to Normanton whence it was shipped to Europe.

Practicalities

The highway runs through town as **McIlwraith Street** in the east, and **Ramsay Street** in the west. Most services – banks, supermarket, half-dozen bars and a post office – are along Ramsay or the grid of streets immediately north. Cloncurry's **train station** is a couple of kilometres southeast of the centre, while **buses** drop off along Ramsay (and at the Roadrunner Roadhouse east of town on the highway) – you can buy **tickets** for either at Cloncurry Agencies, 45 Ramsay St (Mon–Fri 8am–6pm, Sat 8am–noon; ℡07/4742 1107). The best **campsite**, *Cloncurry Caravan Park Oasis* (℡07/4742 1313; camping $20, powered sites $26, cabins ❹–❺), is on McIlwraith Street, with cooling pool and comfy cabins. Otherwise, you'll find **accommodation** right in town at the welcoming *Wagon Wheel Motel* (℡07/4742 1866; ❷–❹) on Ramsay Street, founded in 1867 with both older pub rooms and newer motel rooms, or at the eco-conscious *Gidgee Inn* (℡07/4742 1599, ⓦwww.gidgeeinn.com.au; ❺–❻) on McIlwraith Street, built from recycled timber and rammed earth and named for the surrounding gidyea trees. Both also have good **restaurants**, the latter specializing in char-grills. During the day, *Cuppa's*, a café on Ramsay Street, is cool, spacious, and serves up strong coffee and good-value food, while the *Bio Café*, one block north of Ramsay on Scarr Street, has healthy, freshly prepared light meals and adjoins Cloncurry's 1913-established open-air cinema, which screens films once or twice a week.

Moving on, the highway, buses and trains continue west for 118km to Mount Isa, while the (sealed) Burke Developmental Road heads 380km north past forests of anthills and kapok trees to Normanton, via the one-pub settlement of **Quamby**, and the **Burke and Wills Roadhouse**. Aside from being a welcome break in the journey, with fuel pumps, a bar and canteen, the roadhouse also marks the turning west on a sealed road to Gregory Downs, gateway to the oasis of Lawn Hill Gorge.

Onwards to Mount Isa: Mary Kathleen

The rough country between Cloncurry and Mount Isa is evidence of ancient upheavals which shattered the landscape and created the region's extensive mineral deposits. While the highway continues safely to Mount Isa past the **Burke and Wills monument** and the Kalkadoon/Mitakoodi **tribal boundary** at Corella Creek, forays into the bush will uncover remains of less fortunate mining settlements. About halfway to Mount Isa, **uranium** was found at **MARY KATHLEEN** by accident when a car broke down; while waiting for help, the driver and his friends tried fossicking. About 3km off the highway (on an unsealed road normally reachable in a 2WD in dry conditions), the two-street town was built in 1956 and completely dismantled in 1982 when export restrictions halted mining; only the floors of the houses have been preserved. Another kilometre or so past the old town the dirt road splits; the right fork leads to a bumpy uphill track (4WD only) and the terraces of the open-cast mine, now reminiscent of a flooded Greek amphitheatre, about 7km from the abandoned township. On a cloudy day you can be sure that the alarming blue-green colour of the water is not simply a reflection of the sky. Locals maintain it's safe to swim here though, and some even claim health benefits.

Mount Isa and around

As the only place of consequence for 700km in any direction, the industrial smokestacks, concrete paving and sterile hills at **MOUNT ISA** assume oasis-like qualities on arrival. Though the novelty might have worn off by the time you've had a cold drink in an air-conditioned bar (and absorbed the faint scent – and taste – of sulphur that lingers in the air), the city has a few points to savour before heading on: the area's **Aboriginal heritage**, a couple of unusual **museums**, tours of the local mines, Australia's **largest rodeo** every August and simply the fascinating situation and the community it has fostered.

The world's largest city in terms of surface area – its administrative boundaries stretch halfway to Cloncurry and all the way to Camooweal – Mount Isa sits astride a wealth of zinc, silver, lead and copper. The city's founding father was **John Miles**, who discovered ore in 1923, established **Mount Isa Mines** (MIM) the next year and began commercial mining in 1925 – see also box, p.547.

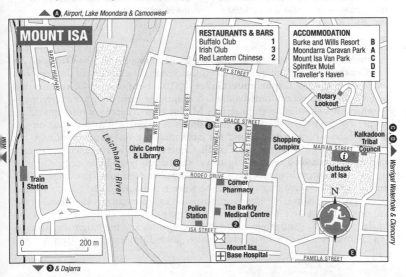

Arrival and information

West of the often-dry **Leichhardt River**, **MIM** – with its two huge chimneys illuminated at night – is the city's major landmark; the Rotary lookout on Hilary Street gives a good view. The Barkly Highway runs through town as Marian and Grace streets, with the city centre immediately south of the latter between Simpson and West streets; the highway then crosses the river and joins the road to Camooweal in front of MIM. **Buses** pull in at the **Outback At Isa Centre** on Marian Street; **trains** terminate at the station in front of MIM; and the **airport** is 7km to the north, where taxis meet arrivals. The excellent **visitor centre** is located in the Outback At Isa Centre (daily 8.30am–5pm; ☏07/4749 1555, ⓦwww.outbackatisa.com.au) and can make all tour bookings and find accommodation.

Accommodation

The mining boom has seen rents skyrocket, and this, combined with the town's role as a staging post for interstate travellers, means accommodation is surprisingly expensive and in short supply. You'll find motels clustered on and around Marian Street.

Burke and Wills Resort ☏07/4743 8000. Smart and central low-rise motel on the corner of Grace and Camooweal sts, close to everything but traffic noise can be a problem. ❺

Moondarra Caravan Park ☏07/4743 9780. Four kilometres north of the city off Camooweal Rd, and close to a creek that draws plenty of local birdlife. The cabins are nothing special, but the shady, picturesque location compensates. Camping $20, powered sites $25, cabins ❸–❹

Mount Isa Van Park ☏07/4743 3252, ⓦwww .mtisacaravanpark.com.au. Situated on the eastern side of town just off Marian St, this is a well-kept campsite with attractive white-and-red cabins and en-suite villas and a children's

play area. Camping $20, powered sites $25, cabins ❸, villas ❹

Spinifex Motel ☏07/4749 2944, ⓦwww .spinifexmotel.com.au. Stylish new family-owned motel a 600-metre stroll from the Outback At Isa Centre on Marian St with cool, clean, uncluttered rooms in neutral tones, with kitchenettes and broadband internet. ❻–❼

Traveller's Haven ☏07/4743 0313, ⓦwww .users.bigpond.net.au/travellershaven. Suburban-style hostel on the corner of Spence and Pamela sts, with a pool and limited off-street parking. Staff can pick you up from the train and bus stations if you arrange it in advance. Dorms $25, doubles (shared facilities) ❷

The City

All the city's main attractions are handily grouped together in the **Outback At Isa Centre** (same opening hours as visitor centre). The history of the region is explored in the **Isa Experience Gallery** ($10): the ground floor consists of a series of informative multimedia displays examining early prehistoric life, indigenous culture and the development of Mount Isa as a centre of mining activity, while the theatre on the upper level shows a poignant film focusing on the personalities who helped to build the city's multinational community over the years. The adjacent **Riversleigh Fossils Centre** ($10) gives an excellent insight into how paleontologists working at the Riversleigh Fossil Site (see p.546) have discovered an incredible record of the marsupial and mammalian evolution and environmental change that occurred between ten thousand and twenty million years ago. Imaginative, life-sized dioramas and an informative video recreate the region at a time when it was a lush wetland, populated by ancestral platypus and koalas, giant snakes and emus, carnivorous kangaroos and the enigmatic "thinga-donta". You can also visit the **laboratory** (guided tours daily at 10am & 1pm;

The **Mount Isa Mines** complex is a land of trundling yellow mine-trucks, mountains of slag, intense activity and kilometres of noisy vibrating pipelines. Copper, silver, lead and zinc deposits are mined almost 2km down by a workforce of 1200; the rock is roughly crushed and hoisted to the surface before undergoing a second crushing, grinding and washing in flotation tanks, to separate ore from waste. Zinc is sold as it is, copper is smelted into ingots and transported to Townsville for refining, while four-ton ingots of lead and silver mix are sent to England for the few grams of silver to be separated. **Power** for the mines and the entire region comes from MIM's own plant, and any surplus is sold to the state grid.

included in admission) out the back, where fossils are prepared by soaking boulders collected at Riversleigh in weak acid, dissolving the rock but leaving bones, beaks and teeth intact.

Mount Isa's working mines are not accessible to the general public. However, you can get a fairly vivid taste by taking the miner-led **Hard Times Underground Mine Tour** ($45; not suitable for children under 7). Visitors are equipped with full protective gear, including hard-helmet and torch, before descending into the 1.2km of tunnels that make up the specially constructed mine.

Eating and drinking

Mount Isa boasts inhabitants of over fifty nationalities, many of whom have their own **clubs** with **restaurants** and **bars**. The best is probably the central and flashy *Buffalo Club*, on the corner of Grace and Simpson streets. Known to one and all as "The Buffs", it hosts an **Oktoberfest** and has a comfy, heavily air-conditioned bar, and a bistro serving the best steaks in town. The other mainstay, the *Irish Club* on Buckley Avenue, 2km south of the centre, has weekend-night bands and inexpensive food; both places offer **courtesy buses** to and from accommodation. Hotels are the alternatives, or try the *Red Lantern Chinese*, on the corner of Simpson and Isa streets.

Listings

Airline Qantas (☏13 13 13) flies daily to Brisbane.
Bus Greyhound Australia (☏13 14 99, ⊛www .greyhound.com.au) covers routes to Townsville and Brisbane daily, and Tennant Creek three times per week; its booking office is in the Outback At Isa Centre.
Car rental Avis, Marian St (and at the airport) ☏07/4743 3733; Sargent, Simpson St (☏07/4743 3962, ⊛www.sargent.com.au), rent 4WDs. Also at the airport are Budget (☏07/4743 3733) and Hertz (☏07/4743 4142).
Hospitals 30 Camooweal St ☏07/4744 4444; The Barkly Medical Centre, 71 Camooweal St ☏07/4749 5300.
Internet Back of Mount Isa newsagent at 25 Miles St; $5.50 per hr; Outback At Isa Centre $2/20min.

Pharmacy Corner Pharmacy, corner of Marian and Miles sts.
Police 7 Isa St ☏07/4744 1111.
Post office For poste restante, use the Isa St branch (☏07/4743 4805); there's another office on Simpson St opposite the shopping complex.
Taxi ☏13 10 08 .
Tours Campbell's, located at the Outback At Isa Centre (☏07/4743 2006, ⊛www.campbellstravel .com.au), runs day-tours to local mines ($27.50).
Trains Queensland Rail operates a twice-weekly service to/from Townsville. For information and bookings call ☏13 16 17, or check ⊛www.qr .com.au.

Kalkadoon country

The scrub around Mount Isa is thick with abandoned mines, waterholes and Aboriginal sites; to explore the area you need your own vehicle – check at the visitor centre for the latest road conditions. The city marks the centre of territory belonging to the **Kalkadoons**, a tribe who strongly resisted white invasion in the nineteenth century. After ten years of guerrilla tactics, they were decimated in a pitched battle with an army of local settlers and Native Mounted Police near **Kajabbi** in 1884 – Kalkadoon bones littered the battle-ground for years.

Numerous sites around Mount Isa attest to the Kalkadoons' abilities in toolmaking and painting, and it's worth checking out their Tribal Council office (hours vary; no phone), next to the Outback At Isa Centre on Marian Street. Bear in mind that many local sites have been vandalized so information may be difficult to obtain.

Lake Moondarra

Lake Moondarra, 20km along on a good unsealed road (follow the signs from the highway heading towards Camooweal), is packed with windsurfers and boats at weekends. During the week it's nearly deserted and other animals are attracted to the water – goannas, wallabies and flocks of pelicans. Beyond the dam wall at the north end of the lake, the unexpectedly green and shady **Warrina Park** is the unlikely home of peacocks and apostle birds.

Camooweal and Boodjamulla National Park

West of Mount Isa, the **Barkly Highway** (and buses) continues to Camooweal and the NT, passing routes to **Boodjamulla National Park**. The park has two sections: **Riversleigh** – a huge fossil site – and the oasis of **Lawn Hill Gorge**; if you're making for either, ensure you have a campsite booked (see p.550) and check the latest road conditions (☎1300 130 595, ⊛www.racq.com.au). The unsealed route via Riversleigh is sometimes 4WD-only or closed altogether, but the Lawn Hill road via the **Gregory Downs** roadhouse, while also unsealed, is fine for most cars if it's dry (you can get as far as Gregory Downs on bitumen from Cloncurry by taking the Burke Development Road to the *Burke and Wills Roadhouse*, then turning northwest on the Wills Development Rd). Wherever you're driving, **fuel up**; from Mount Isa it's two hundred monotonous kilometres to Camooweal and the fringes of the black-soil Barkly Tablelands, and over twice that to Boodjamulla.

Camooweal

Just 13km east of the NT's border (and different time zone) is the small highway town of **CAMOOWEAL**. In fact, the highway from Mount Isa, 188km to the east, forms the main street and was built in 1944 by American servicemen whose names are painted on a rock at the edge of town, and the town has something of a "wild west" feel of eras past. In addition to a roadhouse, mechanic and post office, you'll find a couple of hotels serving cold beer and a general store. The store's old decor is worth a peek, and murals at the *Camooweal Roadhouse* (☎07/4748 2155, ⊛kikai@bigpond.com; camping $5.50 per person, cabins with shared facilities ❶) should raise a chuckle. There's also camping (bookings on ⓣ13 13 04 or ⓦwww.epa.qld.gov.au; $4.85 per person) beside Nowranie Waterhole at the Camooweal Caves National Park, 14km from the park entrance, which has pit toilets but no drinking water (bring your own). The park sprawls 24km south of town off an unsealed road – 2WDs can usually gain access in fine weather, but it's often closed completely after rain. Take care around the edges of these dolomite sinkholes, whose labyrinths, up to 75m deep, are generally not accessible for visitors – the Outback At Isa Centre in Mount Isa (p.546) can provide advice. Camooweal's biggest annual event is the Drovers Festival, a weekend-long, Outback-style celebration held between the end of August and early October.

Heading on from Camooweal there's an unsealed track north to Lawn Hill via Riversleigh (see p.549), while 200km south (4WD-only) is **Urandangie** from where it's a 650-kilometre "short cut", across to Alice Springs. On the Barkly Highway to the west, the next fuel is at the Barkly Homestead in the NT, 275km away.

Gregory Downs and Boodjamulla National Park

Hidden from the rest of the world by the Constance Range and bleached grass are the red sandstone walls and splash of tropical greenery at **Boodjamulla National Park**. There's little warning of this change in scenery; within moments, a land which barely supports scattered herds of cattle is exchanged for palm forests and creeks teeming with wildlife. There are two sections to the park, **Riversleigh Fossil Site** and **Lawn Hill Gorge**, connected by a seventy-kilometre track (sometimes closed or 4WD-only), both highly worthwhile.

The gateway to the area, **GREGORY DOWNS**, is a tiny community of just nine inhabitants, whose roadhouse acts as a pub and general store, and undertakes mechanical repairs; each May Day weekend, there's a wild **canoe race** down the Gregory River. From here, the gorge is 76km west along a decent gravel road, via the controversial **zinc mine** (the world's second-largest), where work was halted by a sit-in of the local Waayni, Mingginda, Gkuthaarn and Kukatji Aboriginal peoples. After several years, amicable negotiations on all sides over the use of the land resulted in the reopening of the mine.

Riversleigh Fossil Site

Around 110km north of Camooweal, **Riversleigh Fossil Site** was once cloaked in rainforest supporting many ancestral forms of Australian fauna. The road from Camooweal to Riversleigh crosses the Gregory River three times around **Riversleigh Fossil Site** (hence the need for a 4WD), offering sudden patches of shady green and cool air in an otherwise hostile landscape.

Riversleigh's **fossil finds** cover a period from twenty million to just ten thousand years ago, a staggering range for a single site, and one which details the transitional period from Australia's climatic heyday to its current parched state. Riversleigh may ultimately produce a fossil record of evolutionary change for an entire ecosystem, but don't expect to see much *in situ* as the fossils are trapped in limestone boulders which have to be carefully blasted out and treated with acid to release their contents. A roadside shelter houses a map of the landscape with fossil sites indicated on a rock outcrop nearby where, with some diligence, you can find bones and teeth protruding from the stones.

Camping is not allowed at Riversleigh; the nearest place is at Lawn Hill Gorge (p.550).

Lawn Hill Gorge

When **Lawn Hill Creek** started carving its forty-metre-deep gorge the region was still a tropical wetland, but as the climate began to dry out, vegetation retreated to a handful of moist, isolated pockets. Animals were drawn to creeks and waterholes and people followed the game – middens and art detail an **Aboriginal culture** at least seventeen thousand years old. The National Parks **campsite** (tank water, showers, toilets) occupies a tamed edge of the creek at the mouth of the gorge (bookings essential; ☎ 13 13 04 or ⓦ www.epa.qld.gov .au; $4.85 per person). You'll also need to book ahead for accommodation at *Adel's Grove* (☎ 07/4748 5502, ⓦ www.adelsgrove.com.au; camping $12 per person, safari tent cabins ❷, rooms ❹), a Savannah Guides (see opposite) post 5km from the gorge, which does meals by prior arrangement (dinner, bed and breakfast from $88 per person), and also rents **canoes** ($20 per hour). An easy hour's paddle over calm green water takes you from the National Parks campsite between the stark, vertical cliffs of the **Middle Gorge** to **Indari Falls**, a wonderfully refreshing swimming spot with a ramp so you can carry your gear down. Beyond here the creek alternates between calm ponds and slack channels choked with vegetation before slowing to a trickle under the rock faces of the **Upper Gorge**. You'll see plenty of birds – egrets, bitterns and kites – though **freshwater crocodiles** are harder to spot. Since visitor numbers have increased, this timid reptile has retreated to the **Lower Gorge**, a sluggish tract edged in water lilies and forest where goannas lounge during the day and rare purple-crowned fairy wrens forage in pandanus leaves. The rocks along the banks of the Lower Gorge – reached on a short walking track from the campsite – are daubed with designs relating to the **Dingo Dreaming**, a reminder of the sanctity of the gorge to the Waanyi people.

In the creek itself are turtles, shockingly large catfish, and sharp-eyed **archer fish** that spit jets of water at insects above the surface. Just how isolated all this is becomes clear from the flat top of the **Island Stack**, a twenty-minute walk from the camp. A pre-dawn hike up the steep sides gives you a commanding view of the sun creeping into the gorge, highlighting orange walls against green palm-tops, which hug the river through a flat, undernourished country.

The Gulf of Carpentaria

The great savannahs of the **Gulf of Carpentaria** were described in 1623 by the Dutch explorer Jan Carstensz as being full of hostile tribes – not surprising, since he'd spent his time here kidnapping and shooting any Aborigines he saw. The Gulf was ignored for centuries thereafter, except by Indonesians gathering sea slugs to sell to the Chinese. Interest in its potential, however, was stirred in 1841 by **John Lort Stokes**, a lieutenant on the *Beagle* (which had been graced by a young Charles Darwin on an earlier voyage), who absurdly described the coast as "Plains of Promise":

A vast boundless plain lay before us, here and there dotted with woodland isles...
I could discover the rudiments of future prosperity and ample justification of the
name which I had bestowed upon them.

Gulf trains

Two unconnected, anachronistic and highly atmospheric **railways** still operate in the Gulf region, mostly as tourist attractions.

The **Savannahlander** (T 07/4053 6848, W www.savannahlander.com.au) runs every Wednesday morning from Cairns to Almaden on the Chillagoe road, where it overnights before continuing via Mount Surprise and Einasleigh to Forsayth, arriving Thursday afternoon. Friday morning it leaves Forsayth for Mount Surprise, arriving back in Cairns on Saturday evening. You spend the snail's-pace journey being hauled over rickety bridges in carriages with corrugated-iron ceilings and wooden dunnies – a pastiche of Outback iconography. The cheapest one-way trip costs from $159.50 including one night's accommodation (a host of more expensive **packages** and various add-on excursions can also be booked online), and you'll need to bring extra for additional accommodation and meals.

The **Gulflander**, run by Queensland Rail (T 07/4745 1391, W www.traveltrain.com .au), runs once a week each way along an isolated stretch of line between Croydon and Normanton, a journey that takes a mere four hours. The train departs Croydon at 8.30am on Thursday and Normanton 8.30am on Wednesday ($59 each way), but you can also return the same day by bus ($08 each way).

It took Burke and Wills' awful 1861 trek to discover that the "woodland isles" were deficient in nutrients and that the black soil became a quagmire during the wet season. Too awkward to develop, the Gulf hung in limbo as settlements sprang up, staggered on for a while, then disappeared – even today few places could be described as thriving communities. Not that this should put you off visiting – with few real destinations but plenty to see, the Gulf is a perfect destination for those who just like to travel. On the way, and only half a day's drive from Cairns, the awesome lava tubes at **Undara** shouldn't be missed, while further afield there are **gemstones** to be fossicked, the coast's birdlife and exciting **barramundi fishing** to enjoy, and the Gulf's extraordinary sunsets and sheer remoteness to savour.

The main route through the region is along the sealed, 580-kilometre-long **Gulf Developmental Road** west off the Atherton Tablelands, covered three times weekly from Cairns by Trans North **buses** (a subsidiary of Greyhound) which continue north of Normanton to Karumba. If you want to travel further afield you'll need either your own vehicle, to take a **safari** from Cairns (see box, p..477), or make use of one of the region's two rustic **railways** (see box above). Be warned that wet-season **flooding** (possible from Dec–April) can cut main roads and isolate areas of the Gulf for weeks at a time, and that you shouldn't venture far off-road without a 4WD at any time.

Visitors to the Gulf need to be reasonably **self-sufficient**, as there are few banks and accommodation is limited for the most part to campsites or pricey motels. For **information** before you go, contact *Gulf Savannah Development* at 212 McLeod St, Cairns (T 07/4031 1631, W www.gulf-savannah.com.au), which offers brochures and advice, but doesn't make bookings. Many of the regional reserves are managed by the **Savannah Guides** (T 08/8985 3890, W www.savannah-guides.com.au), a private ranger organization voted the best of its type in the world, which runs campsites with guides to show you around. On a more alarming note, you might also come face to face with the Gulf's two **crocodile** species – locals stress that the only place you're safe in the water is the shower and even habitually check swimming pools before plunging in, as these amphibians often wander in – stay away from the edges of waterways at all times. Also be sure to bring plenty of insect repellent.

Undara Lava Tubes

The **Undara Lava Tubes** are astounding, massive subterranean tunnels running in broken chambers for up to 160km beneath the scrub – most weren't even uncovered until the 1980s, although tool sites around the cave mouths show that local Aboriginal groups knew of their existence. The tubes were created 190,000 years ago after lava flowing from the now-extinct **Undara volcano** followed rivers and gullies as it snaked northwest towards the Gulf. Away from the cone, the surface of these lava rivers hardened, forming insulating tubes which kept the lava inside in a liquid state and allowed it to run until the tubes were drained. Today, thick vegetation and soil have completely covered the tubes, and they'd still be hidden if some of their ceilings hadn't collapsed, creating a way in. These **entrance caves** are decked in rubble and remnant pockets of thick prehistoric vegetation quite out of place among the dry scrub on the surface.

Once **inside**, the scale of the 52 tubes is overpowering. Up to 19m high, their glazed walls bear evidence of the terrible forces that created them – coil patterns and ledges formed by cooling lava, whirlpools where lava forged its way through rock from other flows, and "stalactites" made when solidifying lava dribbled from the ceiling. Some end in lakes, while others are blocked by lava plugs. Animal tracks in the dust indicate the regular passage of kangaroos, snakes and invertebrates, but the overall scale of the tubes tends to deaden any sounds or signs of life. Four species of microbats use some of the tubes as a maternity chamber, emerging at night en masse to feed – up to 150,000 at a time. Lying in wait (though harmless to humans) are brown tree snakes, commonly known as night tigers, which dangle from the treetops.

Practicalities

Run by Savannah Guides, Undara is 130km from the Atherton Tablelands next to **Yarramulla Station**, which lies 16km south of the Gulf Developmental Road – buses drop off at the junction and the *Lodge* can pick you up if forewarned. A bar, and an excellent restaurant at the 🍴 *Lava Lodge* (☎07/4097 1411,

▲ Undara Lava Tubes

W www.undara.com.au; camping $10–18 per person, safari tents $25–30 per person, dorms $35, railway carriages ⑥–⑦) plus some accommodation options are housed in eleven restored early 1900s railway carriages brought over from Mareeba and set up amongst a eucalypt forest, with beautiful original features like leather seats, pull-down stainless-steel handbasins and polished timber fittings intact.

Access to the lava tunnels themselves is only allowed on a Savannah Guides-led **tour** booked at the *Lodge* ($45 for a 2hr introduction, $80 half-day, $125 full day), which takes you through some of the tubes and delivers an intimate rundown on local geology, flora, fauna and history. In addition to the grounds' refreshing swimming pool, you'll find plenty of other activities to occupy a few days here, such as sunset wildlife-spotting tours ($45), campfire stories and a "bush breakfast" where you can make your own toast and billy tea over the fire – enquire when you book about package prices. There are also plenty of good self-guided walks to make through woodland and up to lookout points in the low hills above the *Lava Lodge*.

Mount Surprise, Georgetown and around

Aside from being a stop for the *Savannahlander* **train** on its weekly return leg to Cairns, there's little more to **MOUNT SURPRISE**, 40km north of Undara, than a service station, *Mount Surprise Hotel* (☎07/4062 3118; ②) and a couple of van parks: *Mount Surprise Tourist Park and Motel* (☎07/4062 3153; camping $16, powered sites $22, cabins ②–③, motel rooms ④), which has a **gem shop** and plenty of **information**; and Bedrock Village (☎07/4062 3193; camping $16, powered sites $24, cabins ③–④), which runs tours to Undara (p.552). The area's main attraction lies a bumpy 40km north at **O'Briens Creek Topaz Field** (check on road conditions at W www.racq.com.au or call ☎1300 130 595), and its waterhole known as **the Oasis**, where you might find a handful of topaz while fossicking, although you will need a fossicker's licence first (available from *Mount Surprise Tourist Park*). **Moving on** from Mount Surprise, buses continue west to Georgetown, while the train heads south to Einasleigh and then Forsayth.

Beyond Mount Surprise, the Gulf Developmental Road – sealed, but among the worst in Queensland for stray cattle – crosses **the Wall**, where expanding gases in a blocked subterranean lava tube forced the ground above it up 20m into a long ridge. After 25km, there's a turning south for a forty-kilometre unsealed detour to **EINASLEIGH**, a handful of weatherboard and iron houses made memorable by the huge, delicious evening meals served at the *Central Hotel* (☎07/4062 5222, ✉einasleighpub@bigpond.com; ③), and summer dips in Einasleigh Creek's deep **basalt gorge**. Campers can stay at the Copperfield Lodge Camping & Caravan Park (☎07/4062 5102; camping from $12). If you don't have your own vehicle (and you might need 4WD after rain), the *Savannahlander* **train** also passes this way.

Back on the Gulf Developmental Road about 90km west of Mount Surprise, **GEORGETOWN** is a diminutive but nonetheless lively little place, home to several accommodation options including the *Midway Caravan Park* (☎07/4062 1219; camping $11, powered sites $13, cabins ①–②), with a saltwater swimming pool and spa, and the rather plusher *La Tara Resort Motel* (☎07/4062 1190; ④), along with shops and a supermarket along the main street, and **hotels** (*Wenaru* has the best meals). The area around Georgetown has a reputation as somewhere to fossick for **gold nuggets** such as Flat Creek Station (mid-March–Aug; ☎07/4062 5304, ✉enquiries@flatcreekstation; camping or day visitors $7, station stay including meals ❻), a private cattle-grazing property 45km southeast of town along an unsealed road. For more information on the region and its fossicking possibilities, head for **TerrEstrial** on Low Street (daily: April–Sept 8am–5pm; Oct–March 8.30am–4.30pm; exhibition $10; ☎07/4062 1485), which acts as both **visitor centre** and home to the Ted Elliott Mineral Collection, an impressive display of precious stones. **Buses** stop on the highway at the BP fuel station, and then continue west to Croydon.

Forty kilometres south of Georgetown down a decent gravel road is **FORSAYTH**, terminus for the *Savannahlander* **train** and home to the *Goldfields Hotel* (☎07/4062 5374; ❺ including dinner), and the Forsayth Tourist Park & Store (☎07/4062 5324; camping $12.50, powered sites $14.50). It's also the last place to stock up before heading into the bush to two unusual locations. Two hours south in a 4WD through the scrub, at **Agate Creek** fossickers scour the creek banks after each wet season for these semiprecious stones; the colours, ranging from honey through to delicate blue, justify the time spent grubbing around with a pick looking for them. Ask the visitor centre in Georgetown about camping possibilities here during the dry season. Some 50km south of Forsayth on a passable dirt road, **Cobbold Gorge** is a starkly attractive oasis inhabited by freshwater crocodiles and crayfish and surrounded by baking-hot sandstone country. From Easter to October *Cobbold Camping Village* (☎07/4062 5470, ⓦwww.cobboldgorge.com.au; camping $14, powered sites $25, rooms ❹) organizes two excellent **tours** (each $65) to experience this very remote corner of the Outback: either a 4WD trip around the station, or a scout up the kilometre-long gorge in a motorized punt.

Croydon

CROYDON, 150km west of Georgetown along the Gulf Developmental Road, was the site of Queensland's **last major goldrush** after two station hands found nuggets in a fence-post hole in 1885. Within five years the **railway** was built, carrying up to two hundred passengers a week, and lucky miners whooped it up at Croydon's 36 hotels, before chaotic management brought operations to a close in 1900. Today, despite rumours of a new gold strike near town, the place has the air of being frozen in time, with most of its elegant buildings predating 1920. Several of these now form the core of the heritage precinct, including the general store and the restored old courthouse which have their original fittings; it's free to wander inside. Pick up a self-guided walking tour leaflet from the friendly visitor centre on Samwell Street (May–Sept daily 8am–5pm; Oct–March Mon–Fri 8am–5pm; ☎07/4745 6125, ⓦwww.croydon.qld.gov.au), which can also provide directions to other scattered relics, as well as the area's jewel, Lake Belmore, 4km along a sealed road north of town, with free electric BBQs and fishing for barramundi (camping's not allowed). Locals regularly swim here, though there are some freshwater crocs about. Otherwise, leave a key deposit to use the town's Olympic-size swimming pool for free. If you're tempted to stay, the *Club Hotel* (☎07/4745 6184; ❷), the last of the 36 to survive, has **rooms**, or you can pitch a tent at the well-shaded *Croydon Gold Van Park* (☎07/4745 6238; camping $11, powered sites $15) on the Georgetown side of town.

Moving on, buses and the main road plough on to Normanton, 154km west, as does the **Gulflander train**, which departs from the station on Helen Street (see box, p.551).

Normanton

Founded on the flat, gritty banks of the Norman River in 1868, **NORMANTON** was once the Gulf's main port, connected to the Croydon goldfield by rail and Cloncurry's copper mines by camel train. Normanton's fortunes declined along with regional mineral deposits and today there's only a sparse collection of stores and service stations, a bank and post office, with shop awnings and a handful of trees providing scant shade. A worthy survivor of former times is the beautiful timber **Burns Philp Store**, built in the 1880s, which covers almost an acre and remains upright despite the attentions of over a century's worth of termites. It now houses the library, along with the visitor centre (winter Mon–Fri 9am–5pm, Sat 9am–1pm; summer Mon, Wed, Fri & Sat 9am–1pm, Tues 10am–5pm, Thurs noon–4pm; ☏07/4745 1065). Pick up a self-guided walking trail leaflet taking in the town's historical points of interest including Normanton's toy-town-like railway station, from where Gulflander trains (p.551) arrive and depart, which incorporates a small, free museum. To see the area from the water, you can take various wildlife-spotting tours with Ferryman River Cruises (☏07/4745 9155, ⊛www.ferryman.net.au; tours from $30).

Normanton's **accommodation** prospects include the *Gulfland Motel* (☏07/4745 1290, ⊛www.gulflandmotel.com.au; camping $18, powered sites $22, rooms ❺) at the south entrance to the town, with a large pool and an artesian spa; or the liveliest of Normanton's three pubs, the aubergine-coloured *Purple Pub* (☏07/4745 1324; ❹). This is also a good place to **eat**, with a beer garden and tasty char-grilled steaks and fish.

Moving on, Karumba lies north, covered by the **bus**; Cloncurry is 400km south via the Burke and Wills Roadhouse; Burketown is a dusty, unsealed trip west; and **trains** run once a week east to Croydon.

Karumba

Reached from Normanton along a seventy-kilometre sealed stretch of cracked, burning saltpan, patrolled by saurus cranes and jabiru storks, **KARUMBA** sits near the mouth of the Norman River. Once an airforce base for **Catalina flying boats** moving between Brisbane and Singapore, today the town mostly survives on prawn trawling and fishing, though a major landmark is the huge **sheds** storing slurry from the zinc mine near Lawn Hill Gorge; the slurry is fed through pipes to Karumba, then dried and shipped overseas for refining. The tides here are so immense that there's usually only one per day. Declining stocks of barramundi in the Gulf have inspired the opening of the **Barramundi Discovery Centre** (shop Mon–Fri 10am–3pm, tours by appointment; $12.50), 2km from town along the river, which raises fish for release into the wild; during a one-hour tour you have the chance to hand-feed them and learn about their regeneration. One thing that you'll notice is that there are few Aboriginal people – they shun the area, as many died in a tribal battle nearby. There's no visitor centre but all accommodation options have plenty of information on the region.

Karumba comprises **two areas** – central Karumba itself, and Karumba Point, 10km downstream by the estuary. **Central Karumba** is along Yappar Street on the Norman River's south bank, with a supermarket, the *Karumba Café* (serving good barraburgers), a post office, and a smattering of **accommodation** including the *Karumba Lodge* (☏07/4745 9121; ❹), which started life as the airforce mess – the ramp that runs alongside the lodge down to the river was where the Catalina aircraft berthed. The *Lodge* has two **bars**: the lounge-style *Suave Bar* and the infamous **Animal Bar** – once known for its heavy drinking and hand-to-hand combat, but now a lot tamer. However, the nicer of the two areas to stay is **Karumba Point**, overlooking mudflats and mangroves along the river mouth where it meets the Gulf's open seas, which has many more accommodation options. Of these, *Karumba Point Tourist Park* (☎07/4745 9306; camping $20, unpowered sites $25, on-site vans ❶) is a good bet for campers and hosts occasional free fish barbecues, while anyone in need of some luxury will find it at the new ⚓ *End of the Road Motel* (☎07/4745 9599, ⓦwww.endoftheroadmotel.com.au; ❹–❺) on Palmer Street, with the pick of its self-contained apartments decked out in cool tropical colours opening directly onto the waterfront. For incredible sunsets, good meals and ice-cold beer, head next door to the riverside *Sunset Tavern*. Across the road on Palmer Street, the bright-yellow *Ash's Holiday Units & Café* (daily 7.30am–7.30pm; ☎07/4745 9132, ⓦwww.ashsholidayunits.com.au; cabins or units ❹) cooks delicious, ocean-fresh barra and sells groceries, and can also advise about boat rental. Alternatively, consider a fishing charter with Kerry D (☎07/4745 9275) or Kathryn M (☎07/4745 9449), or book in for a Croc & Crab Sunset Tour (☎0428 496 026; $50).

Buses terminate outside *Ash's* at Karumba Point, and head back to Cairns three times a week.

Burketown and on to the Territory

Set on the Albert River some 230km west of Normanton, via the site of Burke and Wills' northernmost camp near the Bynoe River, **BURKETOWN** balances on the dusty frontier between grassland and the Gulf's thirty-kilometre-deep coastal flats. Another Gulf fishing hotspot, it achieved local fame for providing background to Nevil Shute's *A Town Like Alice*. The lack of sealed roads into town makes Burketown something of an outpost (the closest bitumen extends as far as Gregory Downs, p.549, 117km to the south), but you'll find a good range of facilities including the welcoming and historic *Burketown Pub* (☎07/4745 5104; en-suite rooms ❹–❺), the equally welcoming *Burketown Caravan Park* (☎07/4745 5118, ⓦwww.burketowncaravanpark.com.au; powered sites $25, cabins ❹, en-suite villas ❺), a **hot artesian spring**, a store, fuel and a post office; accommodation spots can organize barra fishing.

The Hell's Gate Track

If you have a 4WD, head 170km west from Burketown via the Aboriginal community at **Doomadgee**, to the **Hell's Gate Roadhouse**, 50km from the NT (☎07/4745 8258, ⓦwww.hellsgateroadhouse.com.au; camping $12, powered sites $22, safari tents ❹, cabins ❶, rooms ❹). Giant anthills, pandanus-frilled waterholes and irregular tides are the rewards – and the area is stacked with wildlife, including saltwater crocodiles. Besides supplying fresh provisions, fuel and accommodation, the roadhouse is a Savannah Guide station, and organizes **tours** of the area (2hr/4hr/full-day $30/50/100), taking in Aboriginal painting sites and extraordinary rock formations more than 500 million years old.

The road on from Hell's Gate improves inside the Territory and once there you shouldn't have any trouble reaching **Borroloola**, 266km up the track.

Travel details

Trains and buses serve Outback Queensland's major towns (if infrequently), along with a surprising number of flights operated by QantasLink (Ⓦwww .qantas.com.au).

Trains

Barcaldine to: Emerald (2 per week; 6hr); Longreach (2 per week; 2hr); Rockhampton (2 per week; 10hr).

Charleville to: Brisbane (2 per week; 17hr); Mitchell (2 per week; 3hr 30min); Roma (2 per week; 5hr); Toowoomba (2 per week; 11hr 30min).

Charters Towers to: Cloncurry (2 per week; 13hr 30min); Hughenden (2 per week; 4hr 30min); Mount Isa (2 per week; 18hr); Richmond (2 per week; 7hr); Townsville (2 per week; 3hr).

Cloncurry to: Charters Towers (2 per week; 13hr); Hughenden (2 per week; 8hr 30min); Mount Isa (2 per week; 4hr 30min); Richmond (2 per week; 6hr); Townsville (2 per week; 16hr).

Croydon to: Normanton (weekly; 4hr).

Emerald to: Barcaldine (2 per week; 6hr 45min); Longreach (2 per week; 9hr); Rockhampton (2 per week; 4hr).

Forsayth to: Cairns (weekly; 2 days); Mount Surprise (weekly; 5hr 15min).

Hughenden to: Charters Towers (2 per week; 5hr); Cloncurry (2 per week; 9hr); Mount Isa (2 per week; 13hr); Richmond (2 per week; 2hr 15min); Townsville (2 per week; 8hr).

Longreach to: Barcaldine (2 per week; 2hr); Emerald (2 per week; 8hr 30min); Rockhampton (2 per week; 12hr 30min).

Mitchell to: Brisbane (2 per week; 13hr 30min); Charleville (2 per week; 4hr); Roma (2 per week; 2hr); Toowoomba (2 per week; 10hr).

Mount Isa to: Charters Towers (2 per week; 17hr 30min); Cloncurry (2 per week; 4hr); Hughenden (2 per week; 13hr); Richmond (2 per week; 10hr 30min); Townsville (2 per week; 22hr).

Mount Surprise to: Cairns (weekly; 11hr).

Normanton to: Croydon (weekly; 4hr).

Richmond to: Charters Towers (2 per week; 7hr); Cloncurry (2 per week; 6hr 15min); Hughenden (2 per week; 2hr 20min); Mount Isa (2 per week; 13hr); Townsville (2 per week; 8hr 30min).

Roma to: Brisbane (2 per week; 12hr); Charleville (2 per week; 5hr 30min); Mitchell (2 per week; 2hr); Toowoomba (2 per week; 7hr 30min).

Toowoomba to: Brisbane (2 per week; 4hr); Charleville (2 per week; 12hr 30min); Mitchell (2 per week; 9hr); Roma (2 per week; 7hr).

Buses

Barcaldine to: Blackall (1 daily; 2hr); Brisbane (1 daily; 16hr 30min); Charleville (1 daily; 5hr 30min); Cloncurry (1 daily; 8hr); Longreach (1 daily; 1hr 15min); Mitchell (1 daily; 7hr 30min); Mount Isa (1 daily; 10hr 30min); Rockhampton (2 per week; 7hr 30min); Roma (1 daily; 8hr 30min); Toowoomba (1 daily; 14hr 30min); Winton (1 daily; 3hr).

Charleville to: Barcaldine (1 daily; 5hr 30min); Blackall (1 daily; 4hr 10min); Brisbane (2 daily; 11hr); Cloncurry (1 daily; 13hr); Longreach (1 daily; 6hr 30min); Mount Isa (2 daily; 15hr); Roma (2 daily; 3hr 15min); Toowoomba (2 daily; 8hr); Winton (1 daily; 8hr 30min).

Charters Towers to: Camooweal (5 weekly; 13hr); Cloncurry (1 daily; 8hr); Hughenden (1 daily; 3hr); Mount Isa (1 daily; 10hr); Richmond (1 daily; 5hr); Townsville (1 daily; 1hr 40min).

Cloncurry to: Barcaldine (1 daily; 7hr); Camooweal (5 weekly; 5hr); Hughenden (1 daily; 5hr 30min); Mount Isa (1 daily; 1hr 30min); Richmond (1 daily; 3hr 30min); Townsville (1 daily; 10hr).

Emerald to: Barcaldine (2 per week; 4hr); Dingo (2 daily; 1hr 30min); Longreach (2 per week; 5hr); Mackay (2 daily; 5hr 30min); Rockhampton (2 daily; 3hr 30min).

Longreach to: Barcaldine (1 daily; 1hr 15min); Blackall (1 daily; 3hr 15min); Brisbane (1 daily; 17hr 30min); Charleville (1 daily; 6hr 30min); Cloncurry (1 daily; 6hr 30min); Dingo (2 per week; 7hr); Emerald (2 per week; 5hr); Mitchell (1 daily; 9hr); Mount Isa (1 daily; 8hr 30min); Rockhampton (2 per week; 9hr); Roma (1 daily; 10hr); Toowoomba (1 daily; 15hr); Winton (1 daily; 2hr).

Mitchell to: Barcaldine (1 daily; 8hr); Blackall (1 daily; 6hr); Brisbane (2 daily; 7hr 45min); Charleville (2 daily; 2hr 15min); Cloncurry (1 daily; 15hr); Longreach (1 daily; 9hr); Mount Isa (1 daily; 17hr); Roma (2 daily; 1hr); Toowoomba (2 daily; 6hr); Winton (1 daily; 9hr).

Mount Isa to: Barcaldine (1 daily; 10hr); Blackall (1 daily; 11hr); Brisbane (1 daily; 26hr); Charleville (1 daily; 15hr); Charters Towers (1 daily; 10hr 30min); Cloncurry (2 daily; 1hr 30min); Hughenden (1 daily; 7hr 30min); Longreach (1 daily; 8hr 30min); Mitchell (1 daily; 17hr); Richmond (1 daily; 5hr 30min); Roma (1 daily; 18hr);

Toowoomba (1 daily; 24hr); Townsville (1 daily; 12hr); Winton (1 daily; 6hr).

Richmond to: Charters Towers (1 daily; 5hr); Cloncurry (1 daily; 3hr); Hughenden (1 daily; 1hr 20min); Mount Isa (1 daily; 5hr 30min); Townsville (1 daily; 6hr 30min).

Roma to: Barcaldine (1 daily; 8hr 30min); Blackall (1 daily; 7hr); Brisbane (2 daily; 8hr); Charleville (1 daily; 3hr 15min); Cloncurry (1 daily; 16hr); Longreach (1 daily; 10hr); Mitchell (2 daily; 1hr); Mount Isa (1 daily; 18hr 30min); Toowoomba (2 daily; 5hr); Winton (1 daily; 12hr).

Stanthorpe to: Brisbane (1 daily; 5hr); Toowoomba (2 daily; 2hr 30min); Warwick (2 daily; 40min).

Toowoomba to: Barcaldine (2–3 daily; 13hr 30min); Blackall (2–3 daily; 12hr); Brisbane (15–20 daily; 1hr 50min); Charleville (2–3 daily; 8hr); Cloncurry (2–3 daily; 21hr); Longreach (2–3 daily; 15hr); Mitchell (2–3 daily; 6hr); Mount Isa (2–3 daily; 23hr); Roma (2–3 daily; 5hr); Stanthorpe (4–5 weekly; 2hr 30min); Warwick (4–5 weekly; 3hr); Winton (1 daily; 18hr 30min).

Warwick to: Brisbane (2 daily; 3hr); Stanthorpe (4–5 weekly; 40min); Toowoomba (4–5 weekly; 3hr).

Winton to: Barcaldine (1 daily; 3hr); Blackall (1 daily; 5hr 10min); Brisbane (1 daily; 19hr 30min); Charleville (1 daily; 9hr 30min); Cloncurry (1 daily; 3hr 30min); Longreach (1 daily; 2hr); Mitchell (1 daily; 11hr); Mount Isa (1 daily; 6hr); Roma (1 daily; 12hr); Toowoomba (1 daily; 17hr).

Flights

Barcaldine to: Brisbane (3 weekly; 2hr).
Emerald to: Brisbane (2 daily; 2hr).
Longreach to: Brisbane (1 daily; 2hr 25min); Townsville (5 weekly; 2hr).
Mount Isa to: Brisbane (1–2 daily; 2hr 15min); Burketown (weekly; 1hr 35min); Cairns (1–2 daily; 5hr 20min); Mackay (1 daily except Sun; 8hr); Mornington Island (5 weekly; 1hr 50min); Rockhampton (1–2 daily; 4hr); Townsville (1–3 daily; 2hr).
Roma to: Brisbane (1–2 daily; 1hr 10min)
Winton to: Townsville (2 weekly; 1hr 25min).

Northern Territory

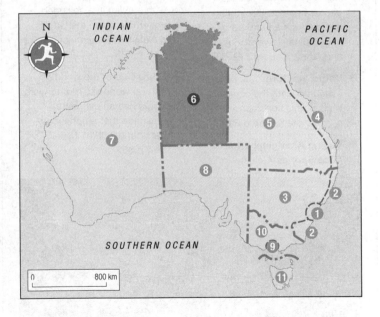

CHAPTER 6 Highlights

* **Aboriginal culture** Get a taste of 40,000 years of indigenous Australian culture. See p.568

* **Top End crocs** The Mary River Wetlands have the highest concentration of crocodiles in Australia. See p.579

* **Kakadu National Park** Australia's largest national park is home to fascinating ancient rock art and an extraordinary diversity of flora and fauna. See pp.579–587

* **Katherine Gorge** Cruise or canoe beneath the ochre walls of this spectacular gorge system. See p.595

* **Buying Aboriginal art in Alice Springs** A cluster of galleries in and around Todd Mall makes finding a special souvenir easy. See p.614

* **Four-wheel driving in the Red Centre** Hop into a 4WD to explore the network of dirt tracks that radiate outwards from Alice Springs. See p.624–625

* **Kings Canyon** The three-hour walk around Kings Canyon, with a swim in a secluded waterhole along the way, is a classic NT experience. See p.628

* **Uluru** One of the world's natural wonders, Uluru (Ayers Rock) has an elemental presence that emphatically transcends all the hype. See p.632

▲ Katherine Gorge

Northern Territory

For most Australians the **Northern Territory** – known simply as "the Territory" or "NT" – embodies the antithesis of the country's cushy suburban seaboard. The name conjures up a distant frontier province, and to some extent that's still the case. Within the Territory's boundaries are some of Australia's oldest sites of Aboriginal occupation and some of the last regions to be colonized by Europeans – even today, a little over one percent of Australians inhabit an area covering a fifth of the continent, which partly explains why the Territory has never achieved full statehood. Territorians love to play up the extremes of climate, distance and isolation that mould their temperaments and accentuate their tough, maverick image as outsiders in a land of "southerners", and the Territory attracts those wanting to escape their past. It's a place where people ask few questions: most people were born elsewhere, and that Aussie institution, the "character", is in his element here, propping up the bars and bolstering the more palatable myths of the Territory's frontier history. The real "Crocodile Dundee" (see p.598) met his end here, and regular croc attacks and the occasional highway psycho killer help augment the Territory's untamed Outback mystique.

Travellers from around the world flock to the prosperous and sultry city of **Darwin**, the Territory's capital, making it their base for explorations around the **Top End**, as tropical NT is known. Most make a beeline for World Heritage-listed, Aboriginal-managed **Kakadu National Park** to take in its astonishing array of wildlife, waterways and wonderful Aboriginal art sites. Adjacent **Arnhem Land**, to the east, is Aboriginal land, requiring a permit to enter – Darwinites think nothing of getting a permit every weekend to go fishing – while if you don't want to go it alone, certain tours are authorized to visit the spectacular wilderness of scattered indigenous communities.

Around 100km south of Kakadu, the main attraction near the town of **Katherine** is the magnificent gorge complex within **Nitmiluk National Park**. By the time you reach **Tennant Creek**, 650km south of Katherine, you've left the Top End's savannah woodland, wetlands and stone country to pass through pastoral tablelands on your way to the central deserts surrounding **Alice Springs**. By no means the dusty Outback town many expect, Alice Springs makes an excellent base to explore the region's natural wonders, of which the famous monolith, **Uluru** – formerly known as **Ayers Rock** – 450km to the southwest, is one of many. This is one of the best areas to learn about the Aborigines of the Western Desert, among the last to come into contact with European settlers and consequently the most studied by anthropologists.

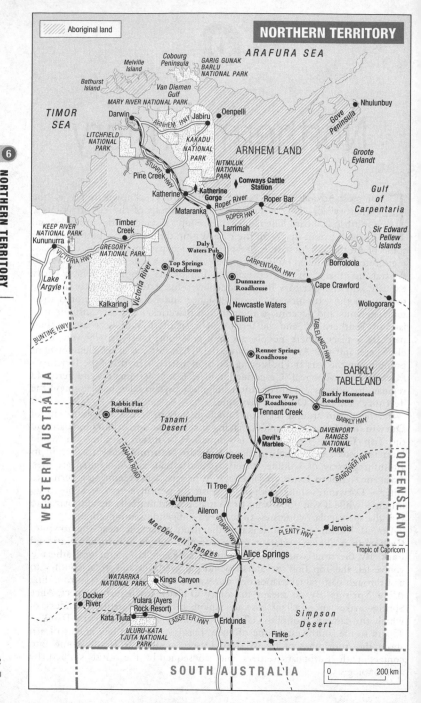

Darwin and the Top End

Darwin, the Territory's capital, lies midway along Australia's convoluted northern coast. Most tourists come here to visit nearby **Kakadu** and **Litchfield National Parks**, or fly to Asia or Europe, but the little city has enough to detain visitors for a few days, and there are plenty more within half a day's drive. The **proposed Mary River National Park** is a croc-infested wetland environment, while further east, pristine Aboriginal-owned **Arnhem Land** is slowly opening up to tourism. In the southwest, the little-visited **Daly River** region comprises small Aboriginal communities and riverside fishing haunts.

Darwin and around

In spite of its history and languid tropical torpor, Darwin manages to feel young, vibrant and cosmopolitan, a mood that's illustrated as much by an evening on buzzing Mitchell Street as it is joining the fitness fanatics cycling, hiking and jogging through the lush parks and waterfront suburbs. The fact that Darwin is an ocean city isn't always fully appreciated – to make sure you do, visit Stokes Hill Wharf, Cullen and Fannie Bays, East Point, and do a sunset cruise.

Some history

Setting up a colonial settlement on Australia's remote northern shores was never going to be easy, and it took four abortive attempts in various locations over 45 years before **DARWIN** (originally called Palmerston) was established in 1869 by the new South Australian state keen to exploit its recently acquired "northern territory". The early colonists' aim was to pre-empt foreign occupation and create a trading post – a "new Singapore" for the British Empire.

Things got off to a promising start with the 1872 arrival of the **Overland Telegraph Line (OTL)**, following the route pioneered by explorer **John McDouall Stuart** in 1862 that finally linked Australia with the rest of the world. **Gold** was discovered at Pine Creek while pylons were being erected for the OTL, prompting a goldrush and construction of a southbound railway. After the goldrush ran its course, a cyclone flattened the depressed town in 1897, but by 1911, when Darwin adopted its present name, the rough-and-ready frontier outpost had grown into a small government centre, servicing the mines and properties of the Top End. Yet even by 1937, after being razed by a second cyclone, the town had a population of just 1500.

During World War II, **Japanese air raids** destroyed Darwin, killing hundreds, information that was suppressed at the time. The fear of invasion and an urgent need to get troops to the war zone led to the swift construction of the **Stuart Highway**, the first reliable land link between Darwin and the rest of Australia.

Three decades of guarded postwar prosperity followed until Christmas Day 1974, when **Cyclone Tracy** devastated Darwin. Fortunately a low tide limited storm surges and no more than 66 people lost their lives, but Tracy marked the end of old Darwin, psychologically as well as architecturally. The city was hastily rebuilt, but for many residents this was the last straw, and, having been evacuated, they never returned.

Kakadu's starring role in the film *Crocodile Dundee* put Darwin on the tourist map, while strong links with Asia, and an influx of Aussies seeking warmer weather and a slower pace of life, have transformed the city into a vibrant multi-cultural destination worth visiting in its own right. Mining and tourism were boosted by the completion in 2004 of the **Darwin rail link** with Alice Springs (and Adelaide).

Day-trips from Darwin include the popular Litchfield National Park (see p.589) as well as the Aboriginal-owned Tiwi islands, a thirty-minute flight from town. Crocodylus Park, on the city's edge, and the Darwin Crocodile Farm, south of town, make for a great day out when combined with the excellent Territory Wildlife Park (see p.589). To really appreciate Kakadu, you'll need more than a day; for tours there, see p.573.

Arrival and information

Darwin airport (Ⓦwww.darwin-airport.com.au) is 12km northeast of the CBD; a **shuttle bus** service (℗08/8981 5066 or 1800 358 945; $10, $18 return) meets international flights and drops passengers at major hotels and the **Transit Centre** behind 69 Mitchell St; a **taxi** (℗13 10 08) to town from the airport costs about $30.

Given the proximity of Indonesia, Darwin is the cheapest place from which to leave Australia (see "Listings", p.576, for details). On the other hand, it's a long way from anywhere in Australia – the bus journey from Townsville, in Queensland, takes a gruelling two-and-a-half days, including a twenty-hour layover in Tennant Creek; from Sydney, Melbourne or Perth, you're better off flying. **Interstate buses** arrive at the Transit Centre, where you can make reservations for onward journeys. Trains arrive at the forlorn **Darwin Passenger Rail Terminal** 20km from town, south of Berrimah, on Tuesday afternoons, heading back on the two-day journey to Adelaide via Alice Springs on Wednesday and

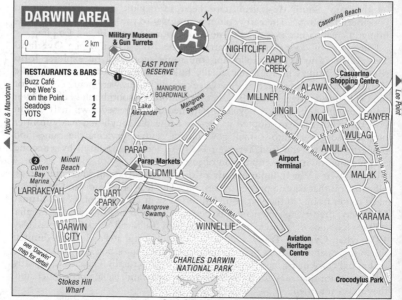

Saturday mornings. A shuttle bus ($9) ferries passengers between the Transit Centre and rail terminal.

Five minutes' walk from the Mitchell Street Transit Centre, on the corner of Bennett and Smith streets, the helpful **visitor centre** (Mon–Fri 9am–5pm, Sat 9am–3pm, Sun 10am–3pm; Ⓣ1300 138 886, Ⓦwww.tourismtopend.com.au) has plenty of brochures. Note that local rental cars booked through here can come with unlimited kilometres (albeit at a higher rate), a deal not always available if you approach rental agencies yourself. The free glossies, *This Week in Darwin* and *Destination Darwin and the Top End*, can be picked up around town and are handy for their **maps**, bus routes and tour times.

City transport

The city's inexpensive **bus service** can deliver you to most corners of Darwin. Services operate daily from around 7am to 8pm, with some routes running until 11pm on Friday and Saturday. The **bus terminal** (Ⓣ08/8924 7666) is on Harry Chan Avenue, at the bottom of Cavenagh Street, with a major **interchange** at Casuarina shopping centre in the suburbs. A "Show&Go" ticket, offering unlimited travel (1–7 days; $5–15), is available at both places. Buses leaving the city for the suburbs head along Cavenagh Street, running as far as Palmerston, and return via Mitchell and Smith streets.

Most hostels and some hotels rent **bicycles** for around $20 a day. Although Darwin is fairly flat, it's perennially hot and humid, so East Point Reserve, 7km from the centre, is about as far as you'd want to ride for fun. A "twist and go" **scooter** is much more entertaining; you can rent them from E-Summer, corner of Mitchell & Peel streets (Ⓣ08/8941 2434, Ⓦwww.esummer.com. au), as well as 50cc mopeds ($50 per day; car driver's licence) and 150cc bikes (from $80 per day; motorbike driver's licence). Several local **car rental** outfits do battle along Mitchell and Smith streets, with prices starting from as little as $35 a day for an economy car, plus mileage (see "Listings" on p.576, for more). **Taxis** work out at about $1.50 per km but there are few cruising around: book one on Ⓣ13 10 08.

Accommodation

Darwin has plentiful **accommodation** ranging from backpackers' to hotels, most of it conveniently central. Rates in the town's apartments and more expensive hotels can drop by half during the Wet from **October through to April**, and even hostels drop a few dollars from their rates, especially for longer stays. Ring around and check websites before making reservations during this period – but also keep an eye on the weather reports.

Hotels, motels and apartments

Most **accommodation** is in the city centre, with properties along the Esplanade offering bay views. If you're looking for self-catering accommodation, there are excellent **apartments** around.

Atrium Novotel 100 Esplanade Ⓣ08/8941 0755, Ⓦwww.noveldarwin.com.au. An upmarket hotel with a foliage-draped atrium, gym, pool, sea views, bar and restaurant. ❽

City Gardens Apartments 93 Woods St Ⓣ1800 891 138, Ⓦwww.citygardensapts.com.au. Modern, spacious and centrally located family units with a small pool, a 2min walk from Frogshollow Park. ❼

Darwin Central Hotel 21 Knuckey St Ⓣ08/8944 9000, Ⓦwww.darwincentral.com.au. The exterior of this high-rise hotel is more modern than the dowdy rooms, but the location is unbeatable, as are the off-season/internet rates. ❾

Escape for a Break Apartments in CBD & villas at 6 Gardens Hill Crescent, The Gardens ℡ 08/08/8981 8850, ⓦ www.escapeforabreak.com. Choose from chic apartments in several CBD locations or contemporary tropical-style two-storey villas with fashionable corrugated-iron walls, louvred windows and polished floorboards within lush gardens with plunge pool; super-luxurious accommodation with every amenity imaginable and a fridge stocked with champagne and goodies. Apartments ⓼, villas ⓽

Mirambeena Travelodge Resort 64 Cavenagh St ℡ 08/8946 0111, ⓦ www.travelodge.com.au. This busy central high-rise hotel boasts spacious modern rooms and a pool surrounded by tropical gardens, and offers an enormous breakfast buffet in its popular restaurant. ⓻

Palms City Resort 64 The Esplanade, corner of Knuckey St ℡ 08/8982 9200, ⓦ www.citypalms.com. These motel rooms (standard/superior) and villas (duplex/freestanding) with decks and BBQs are set in tropical gardens in the CBD. There's a pool, parking and breakfast for $20. Motel rooms ⓻, villas ⓼

SkyCity Gilruth Ave, The Gardens St ℡ 08/8943 8888 or 1800 891 118, ⓦ www.skycitydarwin.com.au. Darwin's best hotel, attached to Darwin's famous casino, boasts gorgeous beachfront gardens, a swimming pool, the city's finest restaurant, *Evoo*, and an excellent location adjoining Mindil Beach Markets. ⓽

Value Inn 50 Mitchell St ℡ 08/8981 4733, ⓦ www.valueinn.com.au. No-frills motel with small en-suite rooms (TV, a/c and fridge) that sleep up to three at a squeeze; central location and there's a plunge pool. ⓺

Backpackers' and budget accommodation

Some hostels pay for the airport shuttle if you stay three nights or more. Ask about air conditioning, as some only turn it on at night; without it a fan is essential. All have internet facilities, and most include basic breakfasts.

Banyan View Lodge 119 Mitchell St ℡ 08/8981 8644, ⓦ www.banyanviewlodge.com.au. This spotlessly clean YWCA (accepts males too) has dorms, doubles and twin rooms, TV lounges, tropical garden, BBQ, pool and free internet. Parking available. Four-bed dorms from $19–25, doubles ⓸

Chilli's Backpackers & Youth Shack 69 & 69A Mitchell St ℡ 08/8923 9790, 08/8980 5800 or 1800 351 313, ⓦ www.youthshack.com.au, ⓦ www.chillis.com.au. These similar adjoining sister-properties near the Transit Centre are bookable via the same website and share facilities. The Youth Shack has a spacious dining area overlooking the pool, while Chilli's has airy decks ideal for socializing. There's also a tour desk. Four-bed dorms from $29.

Darwin YHA 97 Mitchell St ℡ 08/8981 5385, ⓦ www.yha.com.au. This YHA may lack personality but it's clean and has a pool, bar and tour office. Dorms (4/6-bed) $20–28, rooms ⓶

Elke's 112 Mitchell St ℡ 08/8981 8399 or 1800 808 365, ⓦ www.elkesbackpackers.com.au. Set in a renovated old tropical house, *Elke's* has snug twins, doubles and four-bed dorms, friendly staff, pool, leafy garden, and parking. Dorms $33, rooms ⓸

Frogshollow Backpackers 27 Lindsay St ℡ 08/8941 2600 or 1800 068 686, ⓦ www.frogs-hollow.com.au. This popular party hostel on the edge of the CBD is set in tropical gardens with a pool and big breezy veranda off the snug rooms. Huge range of dorms from $20, doubles ⓷

Melaleuca on Mitchell 52 Mitchell St ℡ 08/8941 7800 or 1300 723 437, ⓦ www.momdarwin.com. This enormous, award-winning backpackers' has accommodation ranging from twins to 6-bed dorms, good security, off-street parking, women-only floor, and array of facilities including a huge sundeck, two pools and a bar. Dorms $31, rooms ⓹–⓺

Camping and caravan parks

The following places are near the airport, 7–10km from the centre. Buses #5 and #8 run here from the central bus terminal.

Hidden Valley Caravan Park 25 Hidden Valley Rd, Berrimah ℡ 08/8947 1422, ⓦ www.hiddenvalleytouristpark.com.au. Set in lush tropical gardens, this neat and tidy caravan park has a pool, kiosk and Internet access, and offers family villas ($380), units ($195) and un/powered sites $30/39.

Shady Glen Caravan Park Corner of Farrell Crescent and Stuart Highway, Winnellie ℡ 08/ 8984 3330 or 1800 662 253, ⓦ www.shadyglen.com.au. This leafy park with grassy lawns, a decent pool and picnic tables, boasts spotless facilities and transport to the markets. Family villas (from $130), cabins ($89–120) and powered sites $29.

The City

The modern city spreads north from the end of a stubby peninsula where a settlement was originally established on the lands of the Larrakeyah Aborigines. Over the years, leafy suburbs have sprung up across the fairly flat, mangrove-fringed headland, but for the visitor most of the action lies between the Wharf Precinct and East Point, 9km to the north. Cyclones, air raids and termites have destroyed much of Darwin's old buildings, although a few architectural gems

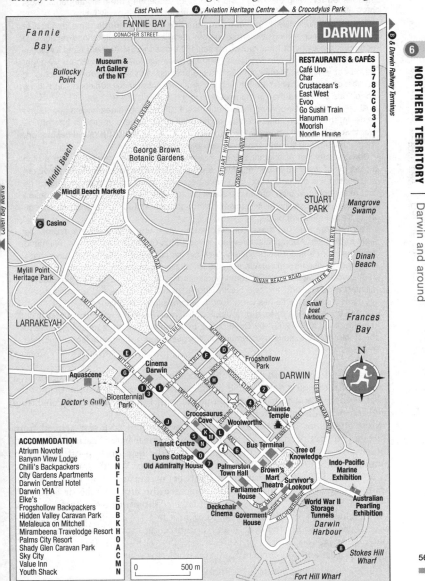

East Point ▲ **Ⓐ**, Aviation Heritage Centre ▲ & Crocodylus Park

DARWIN

Ⓑ & Darwin Railway Terminus

RESTAURANTS & CAFÉS

Café Uno	5
Char	7
Crustacean's	8
East West	2
Evoo	C
Go Sushi Train	6
Hanuman	3
Moorish	4
Noodle House	1

Fannie Bay

CONACHER STREET

FANNIE BAY

Bullocky Point

Museum & Art Gallery of the NT

Mindil Beach

George Brown Botanic Gardens

STUART PARK

Mangrove Swamp

■ **Mindil Beach Markets**

Ⓒ Casino

Cullen Bay Marina

Dinah Beach

DINAH BEACH ROAD

Mylill Point Heritage Park

Small boat harbour

Frances Bay

LARRAKEYAH

N

Ⓔ

Cinema Darwin

Frogshollow Park

DARWIN

Ⓖ

Aquascene

Ⓕ

Ⓗ

Bicentennial Park

Doctor's Gully

Ⓙ

Crocosaurus Cove

Chinese Temple

Woolworths

Transit Centre

Ⓚ Ⓛ Ⓜ

Ⓝ

ⓘ

Ⓞ

Bus Terminal

Tree of Knowledge

Lyons Cottage

Old Admiralty House

Ⓟ

Palmerston Town Hall

Brown's Mart Theatre

Survivor's Lookout

Indo-Pacific Marine Exhibition

Parliament House

Deckchair Cinema

Government House

World War II Storage Tunnels

Australian Pearling Exhibition

Darwin Harbour

Ⓡ Stokes Hill Wharf

Fort Hill Wharf

ACCOMMODATION

Atrium Novotel	J
Banyan View Lodge	G
Chilli's Backpackers	N
City Gardens Apartments	F
Darwin Central Hotel	L
Darwin YHA	I
Elke's	E
Frogshollow Backpackers	D
Hidden Valley Caravan Park	B
Melaleuca on Mitchell	K
Mirambeena Travelodge Resort	H
Palms City Resort	O
Shady Glen Caravan Park	A
Sky City	C
Value Inn	M
Youth Shack	N

0 — 500 m

Aborigines in the Northern Territory

Over a quarter of the Territory's population are Aborigines, a far higher proportion than anywhere else in Australia. Maps show that half of the Territory is once again **Aboriginal-owned land**, returned to Aboriginal control following protracted land claims. This uniquely Territorian demography is the result of a sympathetic federal government's cooperation with the politically powerful Land Councils within the NT, established following the 1976 Land Rights Act. Excepting the national parks, most Aboriginal land is out of bounds to visitors without a permit or invitation.

Most Aborigines live in remote **communities** or **outstations**, smaller satellite communities supporting a clan or several families. While outstations replicate a nomadic, pre-Contact tribal group, particularly those in East Arnhem Land's Aboriginal homelands, communities have been less successful, mixing clans who might have been enemies. Many communities are plagued with social problems, including domestic violence, child abuse, alcoholism and substance addiction, and living conditions are worse than in many developing nations.

Aboriginal society appears divided at present. Some Aborigines have a new-found pride in their culture and identity demonstrated in superb museum interpretive displays, successful Aboriginal tourism projects, and a flowering of indigenous art, media, music, and writing, especially autobiography and poetry.

Some sectors of Aboriginal society, however, seem to be imploding, with a high incidence of violence in communities, led by men whose roles as family providers and custodians of the law and land have been eliminated, eroding self-esteem. The fact that Aboriginal men make up a disproportionately high percentage of the prison population is not solely due to racism – although such attitudes may well have driven them there in the first place.

You'll be reminded of these complex issues when you encounter the depressing sight of drunken Aboriginals sprawled on footpaths or parks in NT towns. Alienated from the more affluent white society, they are casualties of a clash of cultures that's greater than visitors realize. Although the failed assimilation policies of the 1950s and 1960s were followed by self-determination, land rights reform, a long-awaited reconciliation process, and in 2008 Kevin Rudd's highly symbolic and enthusiastically welcomed apology, little has been done to improve living conditions.

In March 2009, the release of a much-anticipated Federal Government report on the outcomes of the 2007–08 Government Intervention – an emergency response to the deplorable situation in communities – argued that indigenous Territorians had

have survived. Away from Mitchell Street's shops, restaurants and bars there is a handful of interesting sights, while beaches and parks offer a healthy slice of the great outdoors, and lush gardens abundant with bougainvillea and palm trees give Darwin a distinctly tropical feel.

Most attractions are accessible on foot, though if you've just arrived from Europe you may need time to acclimatize to the heat before haring off around the city. An easy way to see the city is to take the hop-on hop-off **Tour Tub** minibus (daily 9am–4pm; $30, includes entry to World War II Tunnels; ☏08/8985 6322), which visits most sights below, departing on the hour from Smith Street Mall. Alternatively, you could see the city on bike or foot with **Darwin Walking & Bicycle Tours** (daily 2/3hr tours; $25–40; ☏08/8942 1022), which also rents bikes, delivered to your hotel ($25–35 a day), or experience Darwin through the eyes of an Aboriginal guide with indigenous-owned **Batji Tours** (Mon, Wed & Fri, 2hr tours; $45; ☏1300 881 186). If you don't like tours, cars and scooters are readily available for rent.

benefited from the Intervention, citing the creation of 1700 jobs in communities, including police, night patrols and rangers, and a subsequent reduction of violence and disadvantage. The Opposition points out that there are still serious social and health problems, and that 15,000 people receive their welfare payments in the form of food, not cash.

Despite the bleak realities, for those interested in getting to the heart of the enigmatic Australian Outback and meeting indigenous Australians, the Territory offers enriching and memorable experiences, providing an introduction to a land that's sustained a fascinating and complex culture for at least sixty thousand years.

Indigenous tours

The term **"Indigenous tour"**, while seeming to offer the promise of a privileged insight into indigenous culture, can be misleading. Some tours are offered by white-managed agencies, while others are run by Aboriginal-owned tourism organizations. Always choose the latter but keep in mind that while these might appear to offer an opportunity to learn about Aboriginal customs and laws, secrecy is one of the pillars that supports traditional society, so what you'll probably learn is a watered-down version from people reluctant to give away closely guarded "business".

Some communities invite responsible tour operators to visit, or have set up their own operations, and these allow you to experience something of their way of life. Keep in mind, however, that even in the Territory, Aborigines no longer live solely off the land, although hunting and gathering is still a beloved pastime to supplement conventional food sources.

As a tourist, meeting Aboriginal people by chance and getting to know them can be difficult or take some nerve, especially as Aboriginal land is, for the most part, out of bounds. Many Territorian Aborigines are shy and can get weary of endless questions, well-meaning though they are, rendering exchanges awkward and super-ficial. The most meaningful contact for the short-term visitor will therefore be from an indigenous tour guide or a knowledgeable non-Aboriginal guide.

The message here is that you should not expect the earth by doing an Aboriginal tour – in most cases it will only scrape the surface of a complex way of life – but if you're content to learn about the meaning of the country for Aborigines, about languages, bushtucker, bush medicine, and Dreamtime stories, doing one of these tours can be an enriching experience.

The City Centre

The city's shopping centre is **Smith Street Mall**. Kids love the walk-through fountain near the century-old **Hotel Victoria**, once Darwin's answer to a Wild West saloon, now a stinky, dimly lit, beer-soaked place, subsumed by modern development. On and around the Mall, several galleries and gift shops sell pearls, croc-skin products, Aboriginal art and crafts, and kitschy Australiana.

Historic buildings found further along Smith Street as you cross Bennett Street include the ruins of **Palmerston Town Hall**, built in 1883, demolished by Cyclone Tracy, and occasionally used as a location for outdoor performances by the Darwin Theatre Company based in the atmospheric 1885 **Brown's Mart Theatre** opposite. In the park adjoining Brown's Mart is a huge banyan tree known as the **Tree of Knowledge**, marking the location of the former Chinatown, destroyed during World War II air raids. At the beginning of the twentieth century the industrious Chinese outnumbered Europeans three-to-one in the Top End, and were involved in everything from building the Pine Creek

Top End weather

There is a certain amount of misunderstanding about the Top End's **tropical climate**, usually summed up as the hot and humid "Dry" and the hotter and very humid "Wet". Give or take a couple of weeks either way, this is the pattern: the **Dry** begins in April when rains stop and humidity decreases – although this always remains high, whatever the season. The bush is at its greenest, and engorged waterfalls pound the base of the escarpments, although it may take a couple of months for vehicle access to be restored to all far-flung tracks. From April until October skies are generally cloud-free, with daily temperatures reliably peaking in the low thirties centigrade, though June and July nights might cool down to 10°C – sheer agony for seasoned Top Enders, but bliss for unacclimatized tourists.

From October until December temperatures and humidity begin to rise during the dreaded **Build Up**. Clouds accumulate to discharge brief showers, and it's a time of year when the weak-willed or insufficiently drunk can flip out and "go troppo" as the unbearable tensions of heat, humidity and dysfunctional air conditioning push people over the edge. Around November storms can still be frustratingly dry but often give rise to spectacular lightning shows; Darwin is the world's most lightning-prone city. While rain showers become longer and more frequent towards Christmas – the onset of the **Wet** – access on sealed roads is rarely a problem.

Only when the actual **monsoon** commences at the turn of the year do the daily afternoon storms rejuvenate and saturate the land. This daily cycle lasts for two months or so and is much more tolerable than you might expect, with a daily thunderous downpour cooling things down from the mid- to low-thirties. Along with Queensland's Cape York and Western Australia's northern Kimberley, Darwin's proximity to the equator gives it a true monsoon. Several hundred kilometres south the rains are lighter, though a Wet Season is experienced along the coast as far southwest as Exmouth in Western Australia and Rockhampton in central Queensland.

Coming in from the west, **cyclones**, sometimes just a week apart, occur most commonly at either end of the Wet and can dump 30cm of rain in as many hours, with winds of 100kph and gusts twice that speed. Frequent updates on the erratic path and intensity of these tropical depressions are given on the radio, so most people are prepared when a storm hits. Some fizzle out or head back out to sea; others can intensify and zigzag across the land, as nearly every community between Exmouth, Western Australia (1999) and Darwin (1974) has found to its cost.

railroad to running market gardens. Backtracking up Bennett Street to Woods Street you'll find the working **Chinese Temple** (daily 8am–4pm; free), another post-Tracy restoration, employing the altar and statues from the 1887 original.

Turn left on Knuckey Street and head toward the Esplanade for the former **Old Admiralty House**, a tropical 1920s stilted house that survived cyclones and air raids. Recently renovated, it now houses a restaurant. Opposite, the 1925 stone **Lyons Cottage** (daily 10am–4.30pm; free) was built to house the Darwin Cable Company staff, but now holds a museum to Darwin's early history. Back on Mitchell Street near the Transit Centre, the **Mitchell Street Precinct** is home to a welcome cluster of lively bars and cafés with alfresco terraces and entertainment, as well as Crocosaurus Cove (daily 8am–6pm; free ⊤08/8981 7522, ⓦwww.crocosauruscove.com.au; $28). Boasting the largest display of reptiles in Australia and a two-storey aquarium, you can swim with crocs (actually, you swim in an adjoining pool) and, if you so choose, hop into the "Cage of Death", to be lowered into the croc enclosure.

The leafy Bicentennial Park lawns along the **Esplanade** make for a pleasant stroll, looking over the aquamarine sea. Walking north along the Esplanade you'll arrive at Daly Street, which leads to the Stuart Highway; from here it's a straight 2722-kilometre run to Port Augusta in South Australia. Otherwise, a left turn down the dog-legged Doctor's Gully Road takes you to **Aquascene** (ⓣ08/8981 7837, ⓦwww.aquascene.com.au, tide-dependent feeding hours; $8), where at high tide scores of catfish, mullet and milkfish swim in to be hand-fed on stale bread. Heading south along the Esplanade, you'll come to the striking modern white **Parliament House** (daily 8am–6pm; free; free 90min tours available Sat 9am & 11am all year, Wed 10.30am May–Sept).

Across the road, the restored **Government House** was built in 1883 after the original residence was devoured by white ants, and is a fine example of an elegant, tropical building. It's periodically open to the public; check dates with the visitor centre. Further along, at Survivor's Lookout, paths lead down to World War II Oil Storage Tunnels (included on the Tour Tub itinerary, otherwise $5 including guided tour; daily May–Sept 9am–4pm, Oct–Apr 9am–1pm), which run beneath the city, then down to the Wharf Precinct.

The Wharf Precinct

At the southern end of town, lively **Stokes Hill Wharf** is home to a couple of seafood restaurants and a handful of fish-and-chip places with quayside seating, and is at its buzziest around sunset and on weekend evenings. **Sunset boat tours** set sail from here on the historic pearl luggers *Streeter* (ⓣ0423 522 423/4; $65 including champagne at sunset and a "Taste of the Territory", i.e. kangaroo, buffalo and crocodile hors d'oeuvres) and *Cape Adieu* (ⓣ08/8942 2011; $85 including seafood dinner; BYO & licensed), which depart for approximately three-hour cruises daily around 5pm April to December.

Also worth a look while you are here is the live coral display at **Indo-Pacific Marine Exhibition** (Apr–Oct daily 10am–5pm, Nov–Mar Mon–Fri 9am–1pm & Sat & Sun 10am–5pm; $18; ⓣ08/8981 1294, ⓦwww .indopacificmarine.com.au), where informative talks will set you straight about corals – the Timor Sea north of Darwin is one of the world's richest and most diverse coral environments, though they're obscured from view by the tidal silt which feeds them. Night shows (Wed, Fri & Sun 7pm; $104)

▲ Outdoor dining at Stokes Hill Wharf, Darwin

focus on nocturnal coral life followed by a seafood dinner and time to observe fluorescing species. Next door, the sleek **Australian Pearling Exhibition** (daily 10am–5pm; $6.60; ℡08/8999 6573) describes Darwin's role in north-western Australia's pearling boom.

Cullen Bay Marina and the Fannie Bay museums

If you walk north about 4km along the full length of Smith Street (best not attempted on a hot day) you'll arrive at a small roundabout where a sign points down to Cullen Bay Marina. At the roundabout is **Mylill Point Heritage Park**, home to four historic pre-Tracy buildings, including Burnett House, Mines House, Audit House and Magistrates House. Considered fine examples of 1930s tropical architecture, the houses are set on stilts with the slatted, breeze-inducing, louvered windows typical of Top End architecture.

From here the road winds down 1km to **Cullen Bay Marina** where there are some good cafés and restaurants (see p.574) with an attractive waterside setting, lovely on a balmy evening if there's a breeze blowing. You can also take **boat trips** from Cullen Bay; the *Spirit of Darwin* (℡08/8981 3781; $40) is the more affordable option, but for something a little more memorable, try the pearl lugger *Anniki* (℡0428 414 000; $60 including antipasto and champagne at sunset) – both have licensed bars.

From the marina roundabout it's a one-kilometre walk downhill along Gilruth Avenue to the lush **George Brown Botanic Gardens** (daily 7am–7pm; free), and from there another 2km north to Conacher Street and the excellent **Museum and Art Gallery of the NT** (Mon–Fri 9am–5pm, Sat & Sun 10am–5pm; free; ℡08/8999 8264; ⓦwww.magnt.nt.gov.au) overlooking the waters of Fannie Bay. The museum features an absorbing Gallery of Indigenous Art, with displays by the Tiwi people of Bathurst and Melville islands, along with Arnhem Land bark paintings, and pointillist work by the Central Desert peoples. Other highlights include the brilliant Cyclone Tracy exhibition commemorating Darwin's tragic destruction on Christmas Eve 1974 when 48,000 people were made homeless (don't miss the chilling footage of the aftermath), and the excellent Maritime Gallery located in a massive boat-shed housing various historic craft including pearl luggers, Indonesian *praus*, Polynesian outriggers and bark canoes. Elsewhere there are stuffed examples of everything that flies, swims, hops, skips or jumps in the Territory, including everyone's favourite, Sweetheart, a colossal stuffed 5.1-metre crocodile that was 50 years old and weighed 780kg when caught in 1979.

On to East Point

Back on the main drag, Gilruth Road (served by buses #4 and #6) leads to East Point Road and, 5km away, **East Point Reserve**, an area of bushland that's home to around two thousand wallabies. On the way you'll pass **Lake Alexander**, a recreational saltwater lake that's the only place in Darwin suitable for year-round swimming.

The road ends at the engaging **East Point Military Museum** (daily 9.30am–5pm; $10; ℡08/8981 9702), the World War II command post during the relentless bombing of Darwin by the Japanese between 1942 and 1944. At the time, news of both the air raids and the thirty thousand enemy troops massed on Timor was suppressed. The museum describes these events with fascinating archival footage and displays of uniforms, medals and wartime memorabilia, while in the grounds a collection of aircraft engines, military vehicles and guns quietly rusts away. **East Point** itself is also a splendid spot to observe the breathtaking hues of Darwin's sunsets; if driving, watch out for the wallabies on the way back.

Aviation Heritage Centre and Crocodylus Park

Set in a hangar on the Stuart Highway, 10km from the city centre at Winnellie, on the southeastern edge of the airport, the fascinating **Aviation Heritage Centre** (daily 9am–5pm; $12; ☏08/8947 2145, ⓦwww.darwinsairwar.com.au; bus #5 or #8) is dominated by the huge bulk of a B-52 bomber on loan from the US Air Force, along with numerous other planes, which together describe the engaging story of civil and military aviation in the region.

Further down the Stuart Highway, a left at the Berrimah traffic lights leads you to the crocodile research facility and farm of **Crocodylus Park** (daily 9am–5pm; tours & croc feeding at 10am, noon, 2pm & 3.30pm; $27.50; ☏08/8922 4500, ⓦwww.crocodyluspark.com; bus #5) on McMillans Road. You can get within kissing distance of a three-metre man-eater; the indolent reptiles are coaxed into action for feeding sessions during guided tours. There's also an absorbing museum giving you the lowdown on crocs, a must

---

Tours from Darwin around the Top End

For many visitors, Darwin is simply a convenient base for trips into the surrounding area. **Kakadu** is the must-do, but if you only have a day, **Litchfield Park** is nearer and has several easily accessible swimming holes. Litchfield is a popular day-trip, while most Kakadu tour operators offer two- to five-day tours, including possible excursions into **Arnhem Land** or a return via Litchfield.

Like anywhere, tour experiences vary wildly in quality and group dynamics and the tour guides' sensitivity to this is an important part of enjoying your trip. If you're interested more in Aboriginal art than the art of boozing, opt for one of the smaller group tours, which tend to attract more mature travellers, couples and people interested in taking in the landscape rather than a member of the opposite sex. "Pitching in" and helping your guide is expected on many tours.

Connections ☏1300 886 332, ⓦwww.connections.travel. Very professional outfit operating tours all over Australia. A wide range of camping and hotel-based tours is on offer, with their Top End tours ranging from two-day large group tours to Kakadu ($520) to a three-day "Dreamtime Safari" ($1095) with six people and accommodation in permanent tents at a wonderful private camp next to a billabong.

Kakadu Dreams 50 Mitchell St ☏08/8981 3266, ⓦwww.kakadudreams.com.au. Low-cost full-on fun and games in packed 4WDs, aimed at a young, fit crowd. Two-day tours from $340.

Lords Safaris ☏08/8948 2200, ⓦwww.lordsafaris.com. Award-winning Arnhem Land operator, Sab Lord, grew up with the traditional owners, as is evident from his intimate knowledge of the land, people and culture, his use of indigenous guides and his phenomenal access to places: he can essentially go anywhere. Small-group 4WD tours range from one-day trips, picking up from Darwin/Jabiru, to customized charters. One-day trip from $195.

Odyssey Tours and Safaris 50 Mitchell St ☏1800 891 190, ⓦwww.odysaf.com.au. Safari-tented or motel-based tours across the Top End and Kimberley for those who don't want to rough it. Three-day "Top End Splendour" tours ($1828 in air-conditioned lodges) as well as five-day and one-week see-it-all trips.

Top End Escapes ☏1300 736 892, ⓦwww.topendescapes.com.au. Offers a mix of tours ranging from Darwin day-trips ($49) to longer trips that can be broken up to allow hop-on hop-off access to Top End sights (weekly passes from $399).

Wilderness 4WD Adventures ☏08/8941 2161, ⓦwww.wildernessadventures.com.au. Competitively priced tours (2–5 days; $465–765) through Kakadu and Litchfield, with plenty of fun and action. The longer tours are a better deal.

if you're heading to Kakadu, Mary River, or anywhere else where you could come across them.

Eating

There are plenty of great eating options for every budget, but local favourites fill up most nights, so book ahead. Like anywhere in Australia, the climate makes it likely that even "fresh" locally caught **seafood** will have been snap-frozen. Look out for **barramundi**, a sweet-tasting fighting fish which draws anglers from far and wide, and the flavoursome **snapper** or red emperor. Mindil Beach and Parap markets boast a plethora of Asian food stalls (see opposite), while there are inexpensive seafood takeaways on Stokes Hill Wharf – a good option for a casual sunset drink and dinner.

City centre and the wharf area

Café Uno 4/69 Mitchell St. Casual Italian café serving coffee and food all day; dishes average $25. Daily 7.30am–late.

Char Admiralty House, The Esplanade ☏ 08/8981 4544. This chic bar and restaurant has alfresco seating out front and Mod-Oz cuisine on the menu. The prawn cocktail shots ($18) are fun, while the crispy pork belly, seared scallops, apple peanut salad and chilli caramel sauce are scrumptious. Starters average $18, mains $30. Mon–Fri noon–late, Sat & Sun 5pm–late.

Crustacean's Stokes Hill Wharf ☏ 08/8981 8658. Enjoy fresh seafood, including fantastic oysters and mud crab, at this restaurant at the end of the pier, with seating in the high-ceilinged interior or on the boardwalk in the Dry. Thurs–Sun 11.30am–2pm, daily from 6pm.

EastWest Mantra Pandanas, 43 Knuckey St ☏ 08/8901 2900. This stylish eatery serves up delicious contemporary Asian-Australian cuisine, from barramundi spring rolls to crocodile wrapped in bacon and pandanus leaves. Mains from $24–45. Daily 8.30am–late.

🏃 **Evoo** SkyCity Casino, Gilruth Ave, The Gardens ☏ 08/8943 8888. Darwin's best restaurant serves adventurous, inventive cuisine by Chef Rebecca Bridges; try the Chef's Tasting Plate (changes daily) and the tortellini of red emperor, pearl meat and sweet potato served with caper salsa, and a bouillabaise and mascarpone foam. If it's not on the menu, ask for it. Starters av. $17, mains $30.

Go Sushi Train Mitchell St. A great place for a quick lunch; sushi, bento boxes, *udon* soup and tempura. Mon–Sat 11am–3pm & 5.30–8.30pm.

🏃 **Hanuman** 93 Mitchell St ☏ 08/8941 3500. Book a table in the buzzy front room for delicious Indian, Nonya and Thai dishes. The famous poached Hanuman oysters with coriander, lemongrass, sweet basil, galangal and chilli are a must, as are the wild barramundi fillets with turmeric, fresh curry leaf and coconut. Mon–Fri noon–2pm & daily from 6.30pm.

Moorish 37 Knuckey St. Locals love this atmospheric place which fills most nights, but. The Spanish and North African-inspired tapas (for around $7.50) can be hit-and-miss and scant, but when they're good, they're delish! The house-made merguez sausages and berber-spiced kangaroo with tomato jam are scrummy. Mon–Sat 10am–late.

Noodle House 89 Mitchell St ☏ 08/8942 1888. Snag a table on the terrace overlooking lively Mitchell St to tuck into big plates of spicy salted chilli squid and bigger bowls of curry laksa soup. The tangy steamed oysters with ginger and shallots are delicious. Mon–Sat 10am–10.30pm, Sun 6–10.30pm. Starters $4–24, mains $19–30.

Cullen Bay, Fannie Bay and East Point

Buzz Café Marina Blvd, Cullen Bay ☏ 08/8941 1141. A popular waterfront bar and restaurant dishing up upmarket Aussie pub grub; expect anything from salt-and-pepper squid ($18) to beer-battered barramundi ($29). Mon–Fri 11am–late, Sat & Sun 9am–late.

🏃 **Pee Wee's on the Point** East Point Road ☏ 08/8981 6868. Darwin's most romantic restaurant, set on an alfresco terrace overlooking the beach and Fannie Bay, serves up contemporary Aussie fusion cuisine. Starters include a tasting plate of four entrées, while mains include dishes such as grilled Charles Point black jewfish fillet with a seafood and pumpkin bisque, and flying fish caviar.

Seadogs Marina Blvd, Cullen Bay ☏ 08/8941 2877. Book a table on the terrace of this local favourite (always busy in the Dry), for delicious pizzas ($14–24; try the Seadogs Special topped with fresh seafood), pastas ($15), risottos ($19). Tues–Sun 5.30pm–late.

YOTS Marina Blvd, Cullen Bay ☏08/8981 4433. This chic restaurant overlooking the marina does great home-style Greek food. The freshly shucked oysters are a must. Nov–May Tues–Sun 6pm–late; June–Oct Tues–Sun 7.30am–late.

Drinking and nightlife

Darwin's alcohol consumption is notorious, well above the national average. If you're not a big drinker, go for a movie under the stars.

Pubs and bars

Mitchell Street is the venue for most of Darwin's drinking and live-music scene. Unless otherwise mentioned, all of the places listed below are open from 11am until around 2am most nights.

The Cavenagh Cavenagh St. Affectionately known as the "Cav", this place attracts the young, backpacking crowd and hosts live music.

Ducks Nuts 76 Mitchell St. This casual place has blaring music videos inside and a big breezy terrace that gets busy with drinkers in the evenings.

The Fox Mitchell St. Opposite the *Ducks Nuts*, this is a popular British-style pub where it's standing room only come weekend evenings.

Lizards Bar and Grill Corner of Mitchell and Daly sts. There are four drinking venues to choose from in the *Top End Hotel*, and *Lizards* is the most salubrious; DJs from 10pm.

Shenannigans 69 Mitchell St. Popular with backpackers, this Irish pub has live music, sports on the TV, and Guinness on tap.

The Tap Mitchell St. Opposite the Transit Centre, *The Tap* is a good place for a drink, with plenty of outdoor seating, well-priced snacks and wireless internet connection.

Throb 64 Smith St. Darwin's best-known gay club, *Throb* has nightly DJs and regular themed nights. Open Thurs–Sun from 10pm.

Wisdom Mitchell St. This upscale bar has over 50 beers on offer and challenges you to try them all (hopefully not in one night) to get your name inscribed on the "Wall of Wisdom".

Entertainment

For something a little more cultured, the Darwin Entertainment Centre at 93 Mitchell St (☏08/8980 3333, ⓦwww.darwinentertainment.com.au) has a full programme, from symphony orchestras and string quartets to theatre, comedy, musicals, jazz and blues. Opposite, the five-screen **Cinema Darwin** has cheap tickets on Tuesdays, while the open-air **Deckchair Cinema**, on the Esplanade below Parliament House (☏08/8981 0700, ⓦwww.deckchaircinema.com; $13 or $20 for a double session; closed Nov–March), shows a mix of homegrown, art-house and cult classic movies; snacks and drinks, including wine and beer, are all available.

Festivals and events

The onset of the Dry season sees an upsurge in activity as the city shakes off the languor of the Wet. As well as agricultural shows, rodeos, gymkhanas, campdrafts and racing, Darwin plays host to theatre, cabaret, music, movies and workshops around the city for June's Fringe Festival and August's **Festival of Darwin**. In July, the famous and eccentric **Beer Can Regatta** – wacky boat races in sea craft made from beer cans – takes place on Mindil Beach in Fannie Bay.

Markets

Every Thursday (5–10pm) and Sunday (4–9pm) during the Dry (May–Oct) **Mindil Beach Markets** attracts locals who unpack their eskies and fold-up furniture and settle in on the sand for the sunset. There's a mouthwatering array of sizzling food stalls from all corners of the Earth (mostly Asia); stalls sell Aboriginal art, handicrafts and New Age stuff, while performers add to the bustling atmosphere. It's a three-kilometre walk from town or a short bus journey (#4 or #6) from the centre; alternatively, a minibus service runs to and from most accommodation ($2.50 each way).

Parap's Saturday market (8am–2pm, year-round) in the streets around the stylish Parap Shopping Village on Parap Road (bus #6) has Asian food stalls, crafts, jewellery, vintage and handmade clothes and knick-knacks.

Listings

Airlines The Flight Centre (☎1300 727 706) in the Mitchell Centre can organize overseas flights and visits to Bali and the Palau Islands.

Banks All major banks are located in or near Smith St Mall.

Bookshop Readback Book Exchange has a branch on the Mall near Star Arcade.

Buses Greyhound Australia, Transit Centre, behind 69 Mitchell St ☎08/8981 8700.

Camping equipment The NT General Store, 42 Cavenagh St, has everything you need for going out into the bush, from a new pair of Blunnies to mozzie nets, eskies, potties and billies.

Car and campervan rental Britz 4WDs and campervans, 17 Bombing Rd ☎1800 331 454, ⓦwww.britz.com; Europcar, 77 Cavenagh St ☎08/9841 0300; Thrifty Rental Cars, 64 Stuart Highway ☎1800 891 125 (they also have an office at the *Value Inn* in Mitchell St); Traveller's Auto Barn, 13 Daly St ☎1800 674 374, ⓦwww.travellers-autobarn.com.au.

Consulate Indonesia, 20 Harry Chan Ave (Mon–Fri 9am–1pm & 2–4.30pm; ☎08/8941 0048).

Hospital Royal Darwin Hospital, Rocklands Drive, Casuarina ☎08/8922 8888.

Internet access Most of the hostels have internet access, or there's Global Gossip on the corner of Mitchell and Knuckey sts ($4 per hr). Wireless internet is accessible along Mitchell St as far as *Shenannigans*.

Permits for Aboriginal Land Northern Land Council, PO Box 42921, Casuarina 0811 ☎08/8920 5100, ⓦwww.nlc.org.au.

Pharmacy Amcal, next to the Woolworths between Smith and Cavenagh sts (☎08/8981 8522) is open until 8pm on weekdays.

Police Mitchell Centre, end of Knuckey St ☎08/8901 0200.

Post office 48 Cavenagh St, corner of Edmunds St.

Supermarket Coles, in the Mitchell Precinct, is open 24hr; Woolworths on Cavenagh St is open till midnight.

Swimming The nearest decent-sized pool is at Ross Smith Ave, Parap (☎08/8981 2662); take bus #4 or #10 from the city centre. Or try Lake Alexander at East Point.

Vaccinations If you're travelling on to Southeast Asia and need vaccinations, call in advance to book appointments at all of the following: Carpentaria Medical Centre, 13 Cavenagh St (☎08/8981 4233); Cavenagh Medical Centre, 50 Woods St (☎08/8981 8566); International Immunisation Clinic, 43 Cavenagh St (☎08/8981 7492).

Bathurst and Melville islands

Around six thousand years ago, rising sea levels created **Bathurst and Melville islands**, 80km north of Darwin. Also known as the **Tiwi Islands**, they're home to the **Tiwi** Aborigines, who had only limited contact with Aboriginal mainland tribes until the nineteenth century. Tiwi hostility towards intruders doubtless hastened the failure of **Fort Dundas** on Melville Island, Britain's first north Australian outpost, which survived for just five years until 1829. The Tiwi word for white men, *murantani* or "hot, red face", probably originates from this time.

In 1912 a Belgian missionary cautiously established the present-day town of **NGUIU** on Bathurst, and in a few generations the Tiwi have moved from a hunter-gatherer lifestyle to a commodity-based economy. Though they seem to have adapted more easily than some mainland Aborigines, alcoholism, drug addiction and suicide are all problems. **Tours** are the only way to see the islands: Aussie Adventures (☎1300 721 365, ⓦwww.aussieadventure.com.au) offers one-day Tiwi Island Cultural Tours (Mon–Fri, Mar–Nov), flying you over in thirty minutes for a day-trip ($449, including return flight and permit, but not airport transfers), while Sea-Cat Ferries (☎08/8941 1991; from $259 plus $16.50 Land Use permit) departs from Cullen Bay, taking you across the Van Diemen Gulf to Nguiu Beach in two hours. Both tours take you around the Nguiu community, to visit the Mission, an old church and museum, and to shop for Tiwi arts and crafts. The flight, however, gives you time to see a lot more, including a smoking ceremony, traditional totem dances, and artisans at work, as well as a drive around the island.

East along the Arnhem Highway

The **Arnhem Highway**, which runs east to Kakadu, parts company with the main southbound Stuart Highway 10km beyond Howard Springs. Soon after passing Humpty Doo's farms you'll spot the turn-off to the lush **Fogg Dam Conservation Reserve**, 65km east of Darwin. The dam was originally established in the mid-1950s to irrigate Humpty Doo's experimental rice project that was to transform the Territory's economy. It failed for various "operational" reasons, not least the migrating birds, which munched their way through the crops. Since then, the dam has naturally experienced greater success as a bird sanctuary, and driving across the barrage you'll quickly spot jacanas, egrets and geese, as well as one or two of the countless pythons which feed on the water rats, goannas and wallabies. It is the first bit of wetland on the arid drive out of Darwin, and all the more pleasant if you do the 2.2-kilometre return Woodlands to Waterlily Walk along a boardwalk through the mangrove forests fringing the lagoon onto the dam, and the 2.7-kilometre return Monsoon Forest Walk which takes you through several habitats including paperbark forests and flood plains. Across the dam wall there are wonderful views from the Pandanus Lookout (2.5km return). Don't leave the boardwalks and stay clear of the water's edge as there are saltwater crocs here.

Back on the highway you'll spot the distinctive observation platform of the **Windows on the Wetlands Visitors Centre** (daily 8am–7.30pm), which overlooks the Adelaide River flood plain from the top of Beatrice Hill. Known as Ludawei by the indigenous Limilngan-Wulna people, the hill represents "lulak" or "turtle dreaming". On the top floor you can play with interactive displays describing the surrounding ecology, seasons, and problems with feral animals and weeds.

Adelaide River jumping crocs

Seeing crocodiles in their natural habitat is one of the Top End's undoubted highlights, but at the nearby **Adelaide River Crossing**, 1km down the road, you can join a **jumping crocodile cruise**. You'll see signs for several croc-jumping outfits en route, but the Original Jumping Crocodile Cruise on the *Adelaide River Queen* ($34 for 1hr cruise; 4 times daily at 9am, 11am, 1pm & 3pm; ☎08/8988 8144, ⓦwww.jumpingcrocodilecruises.com.au) is indeed the original. The spectacle involves enticing the river's wild saltwater crocodiles to surge 2m out of the water to snap at bony offal on a string. While the cruises make it safe and easy to snap great photos, the crocodiles are actually being trained in potentially dangerous behaviour. Sea eagles swooping in to snatch the meat from the crocs' jaws add to the drama and – ethics aside – it's an astonishing spectacle.

The Mary River

Continuing along the Arnhem Highway, you'll pass some enormous cathedral **termite mounds** on the south side of the road, a popular photo stop. Seventeen kilometres past the *Bark Hut Inn* roadhouse, the unsealed **Jim Jim Road** (formerly the Old Darwin Road) on the right leads southeast to Cooinda in Kakadu, while the Point Stuart Road turns left (north) to the proposed **Mary River National Park** on Chambers Bay where the explorer Stuart was carried lame and blind to reach the sea in 1862. It was here that legendary bushman Tom Cole made his living for a while, shooting crocs and buffalo, a tough life described with wry stoicism in his book, *Riding the Wildman Plains* – and where the original Crocodile Dundee, Rod Ansell (see p.598), briefly ran Melaleuca station.

The Mary River's attractions won't be giving Kakadu too much to worry about, but it offers a chance to explore a wetland environment recreationally (it's a popular fishing spot with Darwinites) and get as close as you dare to huge crocs. Before leaving Darwin, pick up a copy of the *Northern Territory Discovery Trails: Mary River Wetlands* map from the visitor centre.

After turning off the highway onto Point Stuart Road, there is 8km of sealed section before the route turns into a sandy road, best negotiated in a 4WD or AWD vehicle; during the Wet season (Oct–April) this area is subject to flooding. Another 8km takes you to the turn-off to Rockhole Road on the left for the Wildman Ranger Station (℡08/8978 8986), and **Couzens Lookout**, where there is a basic campsite near a lookout over the river. Nearby **Rockhole** is a popular place to put a boat in for some barra fishing, despite the river teeming with crocs; take care. Experienced off-road drivers with a 4WD could try the **Wildman 4WD Track**, a bumpy drive along a little-used trail amidst hopping marsupials, flocks of birds, huge termite mounds and crocs cruising among the lilies at Connellan Lagoon. If you're in a high 4WD, beware of scratching the vehicle on overhanging trees. From Connellan Lagoon the Wildman Track gets sandier before it meets Wildman Road.

Back on Point Stuart Road, it's another 17km to the turn-off (left again) for *Point Stuart Wilderness Lodge* (℡08/8978 8914, ⊛www.pointstuart.com.au), which boasts a pool, bar and restaurant, plus a range of rooms and powered/unpowered sites ($30/15). They offer fishing and boar-hunting, run wildlife cruises from Rockhole (8am, 10am, 2pm & 4pm) and rent four-person boats from **Shady Camp** ($120/90 per half-day for large/small boat). To reach Shady Camp, drive another 8km along Point Stuart Road, turn left onto Harold Knowles Road then left again after 2.6km. Here, a barrage separates the Mary River's fresh water from the tidal reach of the open sea. Both habitats are home to countless birds, including beautiful jabirus (black-necked storks), and a whole lot of crocs – hire a boat and you'll see dozens of them lolling on the banks either side of the barrage. While you'll see local fishermen knee-deep in water when launching their boats, it's advisable not to follow suit; even locals admit they become blasé.

Harold Knowles Road takes you to the very special Bamurru Plains (℡1300 790 561, ⊛www.bamurruplains.com; rooms including all meals, beverages and activities $930 per person per day), accessible only to guests who arrange in advance to be met at Swim Creek Station gate. Accommodation is in luxurious African safari-style tents with floor-to-ceiling mesh "windows" that look onto the lush flood plains where buffalo roam and kangaroos and wallabies graze. An array of activities includes wildlife-spotting safaris, birdwatching and exhilarating air-boat rides across the mangroves.

Kakadu National Park

Some 150km east of Darwin lies the World Heritage Site, **KAKADU NATIONAL PARK**. The park derives its name from the Bininj/Mungguy people, the area's traditional owners who jointly manage the park with the Department of Environment and Heritage. Their website (Ⓦ www.environment .gov.au/parks/kakadu) is excellent.

Crocodiles and swimming in the Top End

Two distinct types of crocodile inhabit the Top End. Bashful **Johnston** or **freshwater** crocodiles ("freshies") grow up to 3m in length, and are almost exclusively fish-eaters, living in freshwater rivers and billabongs. Unique to Australia, and distinguishable by their narrow snouts and neat rows of spiky teeth, they look relatively benign and are considered harmless to man.

Estuarine, or **saltwater**, crocodiles ("salties") can live in both salt and fresh water and are the world's biggest reptiles. Once fully mature (they can grow up to 6m long and weigh up to 1000kg), they have no natural predators other than each other and have been known to take buffaloes trapped in the mud. Their broad, powerful snouts and gnarled jaw lines have changed little since the time of the dinosaurs – only then salties were four times bigger. Apart from the jumping croc spectacle at Adelaide River, you'll see crocs basking on mudbanks, cruising menacingly through the water, and snapping at a bird or two throughout the Top End. They are opportunistic hunters, catching their prey in sudden, short bursts of speed, then resuming their customary inactivity for days if not weeks at a time.

Aborigines have lived alongside crocodiles, and eaten them and their eggs, for thousands of years; however, in the early twentieth century crocodiles were hunted close to extinction – for sport, as vermin, or for their skin. Legislation in the 1960s reversed the trend, leading to a return of the big crocs; their current population is estimated at around 80,000 in the Top End. While there were only 11 fatalities in northern Australia from 2003 to 2009, there was a flurry of croc attacks and incidents in March and April 2009, including two deaths in the Top End alone, that of an 11-year-old girl taken while splashing about with friends at Black Jungle Swamp in the Litchfield area, and a man attacked while swimming across Daly River. Darwin residents were banned from swimming in the harbour after crocs were spotted near East Point and Rapid Creek, a dog was stalked by a croc on Casuarina Beach, and Nitmiluk Gorge rangers warned against swimming in Katherine River after catching two monster salties. The NT was not alone, with a saltwater croc shot around the same time at Coral Bay in Western Australia after harassing beach-goers. In mid-April 2009 the NT Government released a revised crocodile management plan proposing a reintroduction of culling and safari-hunting to be managed by Aboriginal rangers, and the removal of crocodiles from a fifty-kilometre zone around Darwin. Conservationists opposed the plan, arguing for greater education for new arrivals and visitors to the area.

However, most of the Top End's crocodile-infested waters are already well signposted, with two types of warning signs essentially saying "don't swim here" or "swim at your own risk". Unfortunately, many visitors ignore this advice, running the risk of becoming a statistic. Sadly, one such statistic was 23-year-old German backpacker Isabel von Jordan, who was killed by a 4.5-metre, 500-kilogram saltie in October 2002 at Kakadu, after her tour guide, ignoring the warning signs, took his group for a midnight swim in Sandy Billabong, near Nourlangie Rock – a spot well known for its resident salties. The timing could not have been worse: crocs are most active at night, and it was the breeding season when males are particularly aggressive. The story provides a persuasive argument for following the signs – no matter what your guide says.

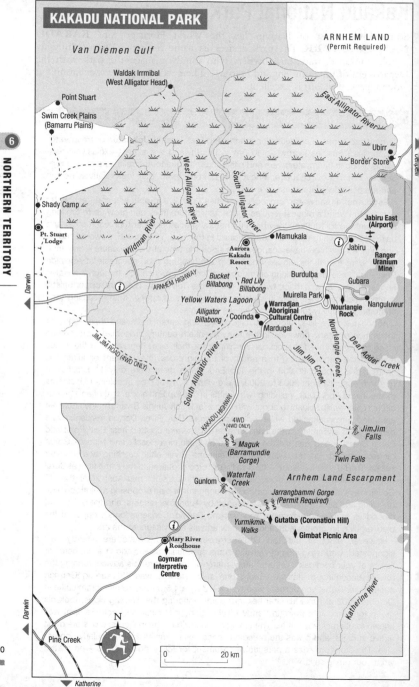

KAKADU NATIONAL PARK

ARNHEM LAND
(Permit Required)

Van Diemen Gulf

Waldak Irrmibal
(West Alligator Head)

Point Stuart

Swim Creek Plains
(Bamarru Plains)

East Alligator River

Ubirr
Border Store

West Alligator River

South Alligator River

Shady Camp

Wildman River

Pt. Stuart
Lodge

Mamukala

Jabiru East
(Airport)

Jabiru

Ranger
Uranium
Mine

Aurora
Kakadu
Resort

Burdulba

ARNHEM HIGHWAY

Bucket
Billabong

Red Lily
Billabong

Gubara

Muirella Park

Nanguluwur

Yellow Waters Lagoon

Warradjan
Aboriginal
Cultural Centre

Nourlangie
Rock

Alligator
Billabong

Cooinda

Mardugal

Deaf Adder Creek

JIM JIM ROAD (4WD ONLY)

South Alligator River

Jim Jim Creek

Nourlangie Creek

KAKADU HIGHWAY

4WD
(4WD ONLY)

Jim Jim
Falls

Maguk
(Barramundie
Gorge)

Twin Falls

Arnhem Land Escarpment

Gunlom

Waterfall
Creek

Jarrangbammi Gorge
(Permit Required)

Yurmikmik
Walks

Gutatba (Coronation Hill)

Gimbat Picnic Area

Mary River
Roadhouse

Goymarr
Interpretive
Centre

Katherine River

N

Darwin

Pine Creek

0   20 km

Katherine

Kakadu was originally brought to worldwide attention in the mid-1980s when it was used as a location in the film *Crocodile Dundee* – though previously it was the environmental debate in the late 1970s over the rather less appealing subject of **uranium mining** that was instrumental in establishing the park. Areas on the border with Arnhem Land contain fifteen percent of the world's known reserves, and together with the Ranger Uranium Mine (see p.585) near Jabiru, have yielded some $145 million dollars in royalties for the traditional owners since 1978. In 1998 the proposed mining of a second site at Jabiluka, located close to Ubirr, one of the park's most beautiful spots, created widespread controversy. Protestors occupied the site, and in the end the proposal was abandoned. In spite of this, mining continues in Kakadu, and not without controversy – in 2004 a number of miners were poisoned by contaminated water, and there have been over 150 leaks and spills at the Ranger Uranium mine since it opened in 1981. In April 2009 a Senate Committee was informed that over the past month around 100,000 litres of contaminated water had been leaking into Kakadu National Park every day from a dam at the Ranger mine.

The park's 20,000 square kilometres encompass the entire catchment area of the **South Alligator River**, misnamed by an early British explorer after the river's prolific crocodile population. In its short run to the sea, the river passes through – and creates – a number of varied topographical features: ravines run through the southern sandstone **escarpment**, itself topped with plateau **heathlands**, while, downstream, **savannah woodlands** merge into the paperbark **swamps**, tidal **wetlands** and **mangroves** of the coastal fringe. There are also scattered pockets of monsoonal **rainforest**. Within these varied habitats an extraordinary diversity of flora and fauna thrives, including 2000 different **plants**, over 10,000 species of **insect**, half the Territory's species of **frog**, a quarter of Australia's **freshwater fish**, five out of the world's seven types of **turtle**, 68 mammals, and 120 different **reptiles** – more than you'll find in the whole of Europe. There are even animals, such as the freshwater – or Johnston – crocodile, that are unique to Kakadu. A third of Australia's **bird** species can also be spotted in Kakadu, including the elegant jabiru (black-necked stork), the similarly large brolga, with its curious courting dance, lily-hopping jacanas, white-breasted sea eagles, as well as galahs and magpie geese by the thousand. **Mammals** include kangaroos, wallabies, wallaroos, 26 species of bats, and dingoes.

With so many interdependent ecosystems, maintaining the park's natural balance is a full-time job. The **water buffalo**, brought in from Timor early in the nineteenth century (one of a handful of **feral species** found in the park), proliferated so successfully that their wallowing behaviour soon turned the fragile wetlands into saltwater mudbaths. Reducing buffalo numbers, however, allowed their main food source, the *salvinia molesta* weed, to choke all other life out of the billabongs until a weevil was introduced to limit it. The long-feared arrival of the **cane toad** in 2002 has been a cause for concern; scientists are working on a genetically engineered control. Exotic **grasses** blown in from the east also pose an ecological threat to the park, due to the higher temperature at which they burn and so the greater damage they cause. **Burning off** has long been recognized as a technique of land management by Aborigines who have a safe, effective process that involves lighting small, controllable fires in a patchwork quilt-like pattern to stimulate new plant growth and as an aid to hunting. Today, rangers imitate these age-old practices, burning off the drying speargrass during Yegge, the indigenous 'cool weather time' season from May to June, to preclude catastrophic fires at the end of the Dry, when the desiccated countryside could be devastated by a wildfire.

Visiting the park

It must be stressed that Australia's largest national park is a challenging place to appreciate in a short visit; allow a minimum of three days, either hire a 4WD or join a 4WD tour, and if you really want to access the park's diverse features and experience the bush humming with wildlife, especially birdlife you should be prepared to do short boat tours such as those on Yellow Waters,. Also keep in mind that the most popular times of year for visitors are when Kakadu is **drier** than might be imagined, and most of the wildlife is active only around sunrise and sunset, when they're feeding, or in the evening for nocturnal creatures. Early-morning drives or walks along dirt tracks will certainly increase wildlife-spotting opportunities. The danger from crocodiles and the need to keep certain important Aboriginal sites secret – not to mention the harsh terrain and climate – mean that the wetlands and, especially, the most interesting escarpment country, can be difficult to fully appreciate, though it is something that is becoming easier to do on tours in adjacent Arnhem Land (see p.587).

Kakadu's Aborigines distinguish six **seasons** throughout the year: Yegge (cool weather time, May to June); Banggerreng (harvest time, April); Gudjewg (monsoon, Dec–March); Wurrgeng (early dry season, June–Aug); Gurrung (hot dry season, Aug–Oct); and Gunumeleng (pre-monsoon, Oct–Dec). To almost everybody else, it's either the Wet or the Dry, although in reality there are three seasons: the Dry (April–Sept), the Build-up (Oct–Nov) and the Wet (Dec–March). The **dry-season months** are the most popular times to visit the park – this is the busy tourist season across northern Australia – with little or no rain, acceptable humidity and temperatures, and fairly conspicuous wildlife. Towards the end of the Dry, birdlife congregates around the shrinking waterholes, while November's rising temperatures and epic electrical storms herald the onset of the Wet. To see Kakadu during the Wet, which sees up to 1600mm of torrential rainfall between December and March, or the early Dry is, many argue, to see it at its best. Water is everywhere, and while many sights are inaccessible and the wildlife dispersed, the land possesses a verdant splendour that can be quite breathtaking.

Ancient rock art

Over five thousand known **Aboriginal art sites** cover the walls of Kakadu's caves and sheltered outcrops, ranging in age from just thirty years old to over twenty thousand. Most of the art sites are of spiritual significance to the three hundred or so Gagudju and other language groups who live in the park, and most of them are consequently inaccessible to visitors. There are also estimated to be several thousand more sites still to be discovered. The paintings include a variety of styles, from handprints to detailed cross-hatched depictions of animals and fish from the rich **Estuarine period** of six thousand years ago. At this time, rising sea levels are thought to have submerged the land bridge by which Aborigines crossed into Australia. It's not unusual to see paintings from successive eras on one wall. **Contact period** images of seventeenth-century Macassar fishing *praus* and larger European schooners might be superimposed (a common feature of petroglyphs worldwide) over depictions of ancient Mimi spirits or creation ancestors. Kakadu's rock art may provide a fascinating record of a culture that has been present in the Top End for over sixty thousand years, but for the indigenous people, the art sites are djang (dreaming places), depicting Dreamtime stories, and the images serve as prompts to communicate valuable lessons that are still passed down from generation to generation.

Getting there and information

The **Arnhem Highway** leaves the Stuart Highway 43km south of Darwin, after which it's a 215-kilometre drive to the **Park Headquarters and Bowali Visitors Centre** (daily 8am–5pm; ☎08/8938 1120) at the eastern edge of the park near Jabiru, at the junction of the Arnhem and Kakadu highways. There you can pick up the excellent Kakadu Visitor Guide (also available online: ⓦwww.kakadu.com.au) with helpful maps and itineraries and Park Notes on various walks, wildlife and flora and find out about **Dry-season ranger-led walks** and many other activities. An innovative walk-through **exhibition** takes you through a condensed Kakadu habitat, passing by stuffed snakes and under a stuffed croc's belly. A café, gift shop and art gallery round off the facilities.

From Jabiru the sealed **Kakadu Highway** heads southwest through to Pine Creek on the Stuart Highway (an alternative entry point into the park if approaching from the south), passing Cooinda, pretty much the heart of the park. The unsealed 4WD-only **Old Jim Jim Road** (formerly known as the **Old Darwin Road**) starts 12km east of the *Bark Hut Inn* on the Arnhem Highway. It offers an alternative route back to Darwin and en route you can take a turn-off along a rough track to see wildlife at Alligator Billabong and Red Lily Lagoon.

Greyhound Australia operates a bus service between Darwin, Jabiru and Cooinda on Monday, Wednesday and Friday. With careful planning, you could see the park in day-tours from Jabiru and Cooinda, but you are better off taking a tour from Darwin or Katherine (see p.573 & p.594), or **renting** a car from Darwin (see p.576) or Jabiru. Try the Thrifty office at the *Gagudju Crocodile Holiday Inn* hotel in Jabiru (☎08/8979 2552) or look for cheaper deals online at ⓦwww.thrifty.com.au. Although the **maps** in the Visitor Guide are helpful, the HEMA 1:400,000 *Kakadu National Park* map is more detailed.

Accommodation

Within Kakadu, most accommodation is at **Cooinda** or **Jabiru**. The park also offers 24 campsites: category one ($10 per person, paid at campsite) boasts good facilities, including **Merl** at Ubirr, **Mardugal** near Cooinda, **Muirella Park** near Nourlangie Rock, **Garnamarr** near Jim Jim Falls, and **Gunlom**; category two ($5 per person; paid into collection box) offers basic facilities at Waldak Irrmbal (West Alligator Head), Malabanjbanjdju, Burdulba, Sandy Billabong, Jim Jim Billabong, Maguk, Kambolgie, Gungurul and Jarrang-barnmi (Koolpin Gorge); while category three (free) covers no-frills sites at 2 Mile Hole, 4 Mile Hole, Bucket Billabong, Red Lily and Alligator Billabongs, Giyamungkurr (Black Jungle Springs), Bilkbilkmi (Graveside Gorge), Ikoymarrwa (Moline Rockhole, top and bottom) and Ferny Gully. Bookings are not possible – it's first-come-first-served – and many are only accessible and open during the Dry. Check accessibility and opening times online at ⓦwww.kakadu.com.au/access.

Aurora Kakadu Arnhem Hwy, 2.5km west of South Alligator Bridge ☎08/8979 0166, ⓦwww.auroraresorts.com.au. Attractively landscaped resort with a restaurant, bar, and central pool area visited by birds and wallabies. There are spacious standard and superior motel rooms with terraces overlooking the lawns. **❼**

Gagudju Crocodile Holiday Inn Jabiru ☎08/8979 9000, ⓦwww.gagudju-dreaming.com. Managed by the Holiday Inn but partly owned by the traditional custodians, this crocodile-shaped hotel is Kakadu's most luxurious accommodation with plush modern rooms with satellite TV and Aboriginal art on the walls, a good restaurant, and an ATM. **❾**

Gagudju Lodge Cooinda ☎08/8979 0145, ⓦwww.gagudjulodgecooinda.com.au. Handy to Yellow Waters and Warradjan Cultural Centre, and also owned by the traditional custodians, these attractive leafy grounds boast modern bungalows, "Outback double dorms", and a camping and caravan park ($20–35). There are enticing swimming pools, a restaurant and bar, tour desk, gift shop and general store, and lots of activities from April–Oct including an open-air cinema and live music. Bungalows [8]–[9], dorms [4]–[5]

Lake View Park Lakeside Drive, Jabiru ☎08/8979 3144, [W]www.lakeviewkakadu.com.au. The best-value place in the park is traditionally owned, with a range of options including contemporary corrugated-iron cabins with bathrooms and kitchens, en-suite double/twin rooms, and safari-style "bush bungalows" with external bathrooms. The en-suite camping/van sites ($30) have access to shared BBQ area. [4]–[7]

Around the park

Seeing the **rock art** at Ubirr or Nourlangie Rock, taking a **cruise** at Guluyambi or Yellow Waters and checking out the Bowali Visitors Centre or Warradjan Cultural Centre will give you a taste of the park, and can just about be fitted into a day. However, you can easily spend a week visiting all the spots detailed below, ideally followed by a return visit six months later to observe the seasonal changes. All the places below are reached off either the Arnhem or **Kakadu highways**. Most roads are accessible to 2WDs, except where indicated; 4WD tracks are closed during the Wet when even the highways can be underwater at times. Check [W]www.kakadu.com.au/access for updates as to accessibility.

East along the Arnhem Highway

Just 2km after entering the national park, fishing fanatics and wildlife spotters will want to take the turn-off heading north 81km to **Waldak Irrmbal**. This rough-as-guts 4WD-only track, impassable during the Wet and for months afterwards, should be attempted only by experienced off-road drivers from August to October; allow two to three hours. A fishing and birdwatching paradise, it's the only place in Kakadu where you can get to the sea. However, as both ocean and river are croc-infested, swimming is impossible. You need to be completely self-sufficient as there are no facilities at the free camping areas, no toilets, no drinking water, and little shade. The main attraction of the drive is the chance to see abundant wildlife, especially early in the morning. On the way up you pass turn-offs to two **basic campsites** on the Wildman River at **Two Mile Hole** (12km from the highway and the slightly nicer of the two) and **Four Mile Hole** (38km from the highway). After Four Mile the narrow corrugated track wends through savannah woodlands, before emerging onto a grassy flood plain, which retains water for months after the Wet ends, so check conditions ([W]www.kakadu.com.au/access) before attempting the drive. On the last stretch, you drive on the edge of the sand dunes before reaching the beach and the camping areas at West Alligator Head (very basic facilities) and **Pocock's Beach** (none). Beachcombing is fun, with jumping fish fluttering across the water, but stay well away from the ocean and mangroves. You'll find shade (but not much else) 4km further on at **Middle Beach**, a kilometre-wide bay, nice enough to walk around, but just as unsafe to swim without sniper support. There's room for a couple of tents but no facilities.

Jabiru and the Ranger Uranium Mine

JABIRU, a couple of kilometres east of the Park HQ, was originally built to serve Kakadu's uranium-mining leases before the park was established. There are three mine leases in the park (and another in Arnhem Land) and at the time of writing the Ranger mine was seeking to expand, much to the anger of environmentalists. Jabiru is now populated by mine workers, park employees, Aboriginal corporations and tour operators, and boasts a **tour booking centre** (☎08/8979 2548), a small **supermarket**, café, excellent bakery, post office and bank, all located in the **shopping plaza**. You'll also find police (℡08/8979 2122), **health clinic** (℡08/8979 2018) and swimming pool (daily 9am–7pm; $3), the only year-round safe public swimming spot in Kakadu!

Kakadu Air (℡1800 089 113, ✆www.kakaduair.com.au) operates out of the airport (6km east of Jabiru), offering thirty-minute **scenic flights** along the escarpment and wetlands (from $120; 20min helicopter rides from $195). From Jabiru Air Terminal you can also take a one-hour tour ($25; ℡1800 089 113) of **Ranger Uranium Mine**. However, as the mine consists of nothing more than a pit, pipelines and mysterious-looking buildings where the ore is processed, the tour itself is largely a public-relations exercise.

Ubirr and the Guluyambi Cruise

A one-kilometre circular walking track takes you by five impressive rock galleries at **Ubirr** (Dry season 8.30am–sunset; Wet season 2pm–sunset), 43km north of the Park HQ, which illustrate the rich food resources of the wetlands. Fish, mussels, lizards, marsupials and the now-extinct Tasmanian tiger (or thylacine) are depicted, as well as stick-like Mimi spirits, the first Creation Ancestors to be painted on the rocks. A moderate 250-metre clamber up the rocky escarpment brings you to a **lookout** offering one of the park's most beautiful views (especially at sunset) across the Nardab flood plain and the East Alligator River to the rocky outcrops of Arnhem Land. There are several walks in the area including the 6.5-kilometre return **sandstone and river bushwalk** along the East Alligator River, one of the few longish walks in the park.

Not far from the Sandstone and River Walk you can take the 🕊 **Guluyambi Cruise** ($70/50; 2hr/1hr 30min; 3–4 times daily; ℡1800 089 113) along the East Alligator River. A local Aboriginal guide takes you upstream to view the rocky escarpment while pointing out crocs and birdlife on the water. Once there, you get the chance to set foot, briefly, on Arnhem Land and enjoy a demonstration of some canny bush trickery. The combination of Aboriginal insight and lush scenery makes it a special experience. If you like this, you'll love the Yellow Waters cruise from Cooinda (see p.582).

Nourlangie Rock Area

Nourlangie Rock, one of Kakadu's most accessible and most visited sites, is 31km south of the Park HQ. Here, the protected **Anbangbang Shelter** has preserved evidence of occupation stretching back twenty thousand years; dimples on boulders show where ochre was ground and then mixed with blood for painting. Nearby, the paintings at the **Anbangbang Gallery** depict the dramatic figures of Nabulwinjbulwinj, Namarrgon (the Lightning Man) and his wife Barrginj. Unusually vivid, they were in fact repainted (a traditional and sometimes ritual practice) in the 1960s over similar faded designs. The **lookout** over the Arnhem Land escarpment, traditionally recognized as the home of Namarrgon, marks the beginning of the twelve-kilometre **Barrk Sandstone Walk** (see box, p.586). Other signposted walks include **Nanguluwur**, a 3.4-kilometre return walk from Nourlangie car park to a fascinating art site featuring images from the contact period when Aborigines first encountered explorers and settlers. **Nawulandja Lookout** has views onto the imposing hulk of Nourlangie Rock itself, which looms over **Anbangbang Billabong**, a *Crocodile Dundee* location. During the Dry, a 2.5-kilometre/one hour return track circles the billabong. Almost halfway along Nourlangie road toward the Arnhem Highway, a nine-kilometre 4WD track to the right leads to the starting point of the Dry season-only six-kilometre/four-hour return **Gubara Pools**

Bushwalking in Kakadu

For bushwalking enthusiasts, the lack of long-distance trails in Kakadu is disappointing. A leaflet at the Park HQ lists around twenty marked trails in the park, with only a handful of half-to full-day walks; most are short **nature trails**. The twelve-kilometre return **Barrk Sandstone Bushwalk**, named after the black wallaroo that inhabits the area – a rugged six- to eight-hour trek through Nourlangie Rock's backcountry – offers a challenge and should not be attempted in the hot months. The trail is marked, should not be undertaken lightly, and is best started in the cool of daybreak. For the very fit, there is a steep hike up to the top of **Jim Jim Falls** with fine views across the escarpment; allow six hours return and take at least 4 litres of water.

In the often-overlooked southwest of the park near Gunlom, the **Yurmikmik** area on the edge of the escarpment offers a similar challenge in the unmarked **Motor Car Creek Walk** (11km return; 7hr) and **Motor Car and Kurrundie Creek Circle Walk** (14km return; 10hr overnight walk). Before attempting these walks, ask for the **Park Notes** at Park HQ at Bowali Visitor Centre. If walking and camping overnight, you need to get your walking plans approved and obtain camping permits from the Permits Officer at Park HQ (℡08/8938 1140; kakadu.permits@environment.gov.au). You'll need good topographic maps, a compass, plenty of water (at least one litre per hour of walking) and wear appropriate footwear and clothing. Many also recommend hiring a satellite phone. No matter how hot you get, don't even think about a dip in the river or billabongs!

Walk, which takes you to a string of small pools along a palm-shaded creek. Check on accessibility and crocs before heading out (swimming at your own risk; see box, p.579).

Jim Jim Falls and Twin Falls

Allow a full day to visit these two dramatic waterfalls 100km south of Park HQ, including a bumpy four-hour return drive from the Kakadu Highway along a 60-kilometre 4WD-only track, open 6.30am to 8.30pm Dry season only. Alternatively, visit with an operator from Darwin or Kakadu: *Gagudju Lodge's* (℡08/8979 0145) full-day Kakadu Gorge and Waterfall Tour costs $195, departing from Jabiru (6.45am) and Cooinda (7.30am), from May/June to October.

Jim Jim Falls plunge 150m off the escarpment and are best viewed from a plane in the Wet or from the ground when they're reopened around June; the falls stop flowing around August. The rocky trail to the base may only be 1km long, but you need to be in good shape as the rocks are hard going, and although the track runs beside a pool, it's like an oven within the canyon walls from September to November. Swim at your own risk (see box, p.579). Another track leads to the top of the cliffs, but again, it's quite a slog and should only be attempted by the fit; check conditions first at Park HQ (see p.583).

Twin Falls is a sandy ten-kilometre drive from Jim Jim, involving a creek crossing, which, even in a high-clearance 4WD (ensure it comes with a snorkel), you'll need to take cautiously. From the car park, the Twin Falls Gorge Boat Shuttle ($12.50 per person) ferries you up the gorge where a stroll along a boardwalk takes you to the waterhole (no swimming). There's a three-kilometre hike up to the top: once there you can look over the falls and, providing they have been cleared of crocs, swim in natural pools (see box, p.579).

Yellow Waters and the Warradjan Aboriginal Cultural Centre

As Jim Jim Creek meanders into the flood plains close to Cooinda, 50km southwest of Jabiru, it forms the inland lagoon of **Yellow Waters**. From the car park, a short walk leads along the edge of the billabong from where 🚢 **cruises** ($70/50; 2hr/1hr 30min; 6 daily; book in advance on ☏08/8979 0145) weave through the lushly vegetated waterways, stopping periodically to view abundant birdlife and crocs. The early-morning cruises (6.45am & 9am, 2hr) catch the lagoon and wildlife at their best, although the heat-of-the-day tours are still worthwhile if a little warm.

The turtle-shaped **Warradjan Aboriginal Cultural Centre** (daily 9am–5pm), on the Cooinda access road, offers a compelling, cutting-edge interpretive display on the culture and lore of the local Aborigines that warrants an hour or two of your time. There is also a good gift shop here.

Maguk, Gunlom and other beauty spots

The twelve-kilometre corrugated 4WD track to **Maguk** (also known as Barramundi Gorge) leaves Kakadu Highway 53km southwest of Cooinda. A path from the car park runs alongside the creek to a lovely tranquil waterhole. The top of the waterfall and more rock pools can be reached by clambering up the tree roots to the right of the falls. Saltwater crocs have been found here so ensure you check the status of croc surveys before swimming (see box, p.579).

Gunlom (also known as Waterfall Creek) is another *Crocodile Dundee* location accessed by an unsealed road 37km off the Kakadu Highway close to the park's southwestern exit; at the junction at 26km, turn left. Although the falls don't flow all year, it's a lovely paperbark-shaded place (swim at own risk; see box, p.579), and as you can camp here it's worth the diversion if travelling via Pine Creek (if your car can take it). The steep two-kilometre climb to the top of the falls reveals still more pools (again, swim at own risk).

A right turn at the 26km junction leads to the shady Gimbat Picnic Area near Gutatba or Coronation Hill, the site of a former uranium mine: to local Jawoyn Aborigines this area is traditionally "Sickness Country", suggesting that even in its natural state, uranium, along with other toxic minerals found in the area, has proved harmful to humans. About 7km before Gimbat, a turn-off to the left takes you along a 4WD-only track (inaccessible during the Wet) to **Jarrangbarnmi** or **Koolpin Gorge**. As the number of daily visitors is limited, you need to obtain a permit through the Permits Officer at Park HQ (☏08/8938 1140).

Arnhem Land

Pristine **ARNHEM LAND** is geographically the continuation of Kakadu eastwards to the Gulf of Carpentaria, but without the infrastructure and picnic areas. Never colonized and too rough to graze, the 91,000 square kilometre wilderness was designated an Aboriginal reserve in 1931 and has remained in Aboriginal hands since that time. In 1963 the Yirrkala of northwestern Arnhem Land appealed against the proposed mining of bauxite on their land. It was the first protest of its kind and included the presentation of sacred artefacts and a petition in the form of a bark painting to the government in Canberra. Their actions brought the issue of Aboriginal land rights to the public eye, paving the way for subsequent successful land claims in the Territory.

Independent tourists are not allowed to visit Arnhem Land without a permit, and the twelve thousand Aborigines who live here prefer it that way. Little disturbed for over forty thousand years, Arnhem Land, like Kakadu, holds thousands of rock-art sites and burial grounds, wild coastline, rivers teeming

▲ Aboriginal women and girls gather pandanus for weaving, Central Arnhem Land

with fish, stunning stone escarpments, monsoon forests, savannah woodlands and abundant wildlife.

In recent years, the mystique of this "forbidden land" has proved a profitable source of income for Arnhem Land's more accessible communities, and **tours** (see box, p.573), particularly to the areas adjacent to Kakadu, are now offered in partnership with a select few operators who have earned the trust of the Aboriginal custodians. The award-winning ⚓ Lords Safaris (☎08/8948 2200, Ⓦwww.lords-safaris.com, see p.573) is the longest-running operator into Arnhem Land; Sab Lord grew up with the traditional owners and employs indigenous guides on his small-group 4WD day-trips ($195), which include a climb up Injalak Hill (Long Tom Dreaming) to see impressive rock art, and the chance to meet artists, watch painting and basket weaving, and purchase art at Injalak Arts and Crafts Centre. Davidson's Arnhem Land Safaris (☎08/8927 5240, Ⓦwww.arnhemland-safaris.com) offers 3-4 and 5-day tours in the Mount Borradaile area from around $500 per person per day including flights from Darwin. A visit here, even for a day, is a special experience: with its intangible allure, amazing rock galleries and unique sites, you'll capture the sense of an ancient, untamed land that a national park can never imitate.

The major settlement is **NHULUNBUY** on the **Gove Peninsula**, in the northeast corner, which boasts sublime white sand beaches and aquamarine water. On the northwest corner, the Coburg Peninsula is one of Australia's finest fishing spots (best appreciated by boat), and home to the Garig Gunak Barlu National Park, a paradise for birdwatchers. Many travellers are happy simply to visit Injalak Arts and Crafts Centre (Mon–Fri 8am–5pm, also June–Sept Sat 8am–noon; ☎08/8979 0190, Ⓦwww.injalak.com) in **GUNBALANYA** (also known as **OENPELLI**), 15km from the East Alligator River crossing at Ubirr's Border Store, where they can talk to artists and buy beautiful art. Permits ($13.20 per person) to visit any of these places must be applied for at least ten days in advance from the Northern Land Council (NLC; Darwin ☎08/8931 1910; Ⓦwww.nlc.org.au); permits are for specific places and purposes, detours are not permitted, and liquor cannot be taken in.

Along the Stuart Highway

From Darwin, the **Stuart Highway** passes old mining outposts and overgrown, but still commemorated, World War II airstrips. Along its length are a number of attractions that can be visited either as excursions from Darwin or as diversions on the journey to Katherine, 320km to the south. Don't expect to get to any of the places off the highway without organizing local transport.

Territory Wildlife Park and termite mounds

South along the Stuart Highway, 50km from Darwin, the Cox Peninsula Road turn-off west to Berry Springs leads to the superb **Territory Wildlife Park** (℡08/8988 7200, daily 8.30am–6pm, last admission 4pm; $20), where you can easily spend half a day wandering through a variety of Territorian habitats, including walk-in aviaries, nocturnal houses and walk-through aquariums. The entry fee – worth every cent – includes free rides on the circulating train to different habitats, saving trudging along the four-kilometre roadway in the sticky heat.

Twenty kilometres west before the Cox Peninsula road veers north to Mandorah there's a turn-off onto the northern approach track to Litchfield National Park (see below). Crossing through the usually dry Finniss River, this road passes fields of **termite mounds**, a combination of fluted "cathedral" mounds, up to 4m high, and so-called "magnetic" or "meridian" mounds. Not often seen in the same vicinity, both designs are made of digested grass and are designed to create a regulated internal temperature.

Litchfield National Park

"Kaka-don't, Litchfield-do" is an oversimplified quip expressing many Darwin residents' preference for **LITCHFIELD NATIONAL PARK** over its neighbour; however, its vicinity to Darwin means it can get uncomfortably crowded on weekends. Situated 100km south of Darwin, and roughly 16km west of the Stuart Highway, the park encompasses the Tabletop Range, a spring-fringed plateau from which gush several easily accessible **waterfalls**. The whole park is a popular and enjoyable destination, free of restrictions, long drives, the need for 4WDs and intangible expectations. Crocodiles are also found here, so you still need to pay attention to warning signs.

If you're coming from Darwin you can enter the park from the north, passing the Territory Wildlife Park (40km of gravel road), and exit via Batchelor to the east or, with a 4WD, leave to the south via the Reynolds River Track passing some of the park's less visited waterfalls. For details of **organized tours**, which are the only way to see the park without your own transport, see box, p.573.

Batchelor

Lush, leafy **BATCHELOR** – 8km west of the Stuart Highway – was originally built to serve the postwar rush to mine uranium at nearby Rum Jungle. In the early 1970s, when large-scale mining ceased, the establishment of Litchfield gave the town a new lease of life. Pick up **information** on sights, bushwalks and a map for Litchfield from the unmanned visitor centre on the main road. **Coomalie Cultural Centre** (℡08/8939 7404, Mon–Fri 10am–4pm & Sat 8am–2pm, free) on the corner of Awillia Street and Nurndina Road has beautiful Aboriginal arts and crafts on display and for sale. There are several **caravan parks** in and around the Batchelor area, but choose your time and place carefully, especially at weekends, when Litchfield is popular. The *Batchelor*

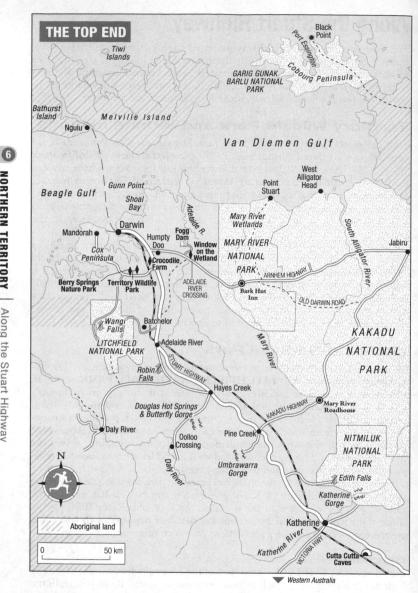

THE TOP END

Tiwi
Islands

Black
Point

Port Essington

GARIG GUNAK
BARLU NATIONAL
PARK

Cobourg Peninsula

Bathurst
Island

Melville Island

Van Diemen Gulf

Nguiu

West
Alligator
Head

Point
Stuart

Beagle Gulf

Gunn Point

Shoal
Bay

Mary River
Wetlands

South Alligator River

Jabiru

Mandorah

Darwin

Humpty
Doo

Fogg
Dam

Adelaide R.

Window
on the Wetland

MARY RIVER
NATIONAL
PARK

Cox
Peninsula

Crocodile
Farm

Berry Springs
Nature Park

Territory Wildlife
Park

ADELAIDE
RIVER
CROSSING

Bark Hut
Inn

ARNHEM HIGHWAY

OLD DARWIN ROAD

Mary River

KAKADU

NATIONAL

PARK

Wangi
Falls

Batchelor

LITCHFIELD
NATIONAL PARK

Adelaide River

STUART HIGHWAY

Robin
Falls

Hayes Creek

KAKADU HIGHWAY

Mary River
Roadhouse

Douglas Hot Springs
& Butterfly Gorge

Daly River

Oolloo
Crossing

Pine Creek

NITMILUK
NATIONAL
PARK

Umbrawarra
Gorge

Daly River

Edith Falls

Katherine
Gorge

N

Katherine

Aboriginal land

Katherine River

VICTORIA HWY

Cutta Cutta
Caves

0   50 km

Western Australia

Resort (☎08/8976 0123, 37–49 Rum Jungle Rd) has basic rooms (❼) around a palm-fringed swimming pool and un/powered sites $12/30, but the best accommodation in town is at the Asian-chic B&B ⚹ *Rum Jungle Bungalows* (☎08/8976 0555, ⓦ www.rumjunglebungalows.com.au, bungalows ❼, breakfast $15 per person), which has a reputation for serving up one of the most lavish breakfast buffets in the NT. For dinner you can cook up your own BBQ in the leafy garden near the swimming pool.

Along Litchfield Park Road

Heading into the park from Batchelor you'll pass red-dirt plains dotted with grey, tombstone-like termite mounds. The first chance for a splash is at the **Buley Rock Holes**, a string of easily accessible rock pools with basic camping nearby. Both the road and a three-kilometre trail follow the Buley Creek to **Florence Falls**. A lookout surveys the twin twenty-metre falls from above, where a convoluted stairway drops right down to the shady plunge pool where it's possible to swim.

Back on the Litchfield Park Road (the main sealed road in the park linking all the most visited spots), a turn-off south leads to the rough-as-guts, Dry season-only, 4WD track (most car rental companies will not allow you to take a vehicle here) to the **Lost City**, a jumble of unusually weathered sandstone columns. Back on the main park road the uninteresting Tabletop Swamp is followed soon after by **Tolmer Falls**, 450m from the road, probably the park's most photogenic waterfall, though you can only view it from the cliffs opposite due to the resident rare orange horseshoe bats. Look carefully above the chute and you'll notice a natural rock arch bridging the falls. From the clifftop lookout, a half-hour walk goes via pools at the top of the falls, passing examples of ancient cycads (see p.495) on the way, before returning to the car park, but as the track is dangerous – it's easy to slip off and go over the edge – it can only be done with a professional guide. From **Green Ant Creek** a one-hour return walk leads through pockets of rainforest to the top of the **Tjaetaba Falls**, with a pool to cool off in right on the lip of the cascade.

Packed out at weekends and during school holidays, **Wangi Falls**, 1.6km from the main road, on the west side of the park, has easy access past tree-shaded lawns, low-rise picnic tables (whatever you do, do not sit on the ground, because you'll more than likely catch scrub typhus from the microscopic bush mites) and a café to an enormous natural swimming hole. Near the base of the main cascade is a sun-warmed natural spa, but note the multilingual signs warning of the risk of drowning (the pool closes in the Wet when undertows develop and crocs lurk). A trail leads through a rainforest boardwalk up over the falls and down the other side via a **lookout** – a good way to work off lunch.

The road leads north from Wangi out of the park to the rather grandly named **Litchfield Tourist Precinct**; basically a pair of "safari" parks. *Latitude 1308* (℡08/8978 2077; safari tents $95 per person) has a café serving home-style meals. Twice-daily **billabong cruises** on the Reynolds River also leave from here (℡08/8978 2330). A kilometre along a dirt road, *Litchfield Safari Camp* (℡08/8978 2185, ⓦwww.litchfieldsafaricamp.com.au; un/powered $10/15 per person) is a cheap, basic option, with safari cabins with en suites ($130) and backpacker tents ($25).

Southern Litchfield: the Reynolds River Track

Near Green Ant Creek, the high-clearance 4WD-only **Reynolds River Track** leads 44km south out of the park to the sealed Daly River Road. The half-metre-deep creek crossing near the start of the track is a sign of things to come, with a particularly sandy section before Surprise Creek Falls, and some steep drops into deep creek crossings. The track (closed during the Wet and after any rain) passes huge termite mounds and verdant woodland.

A few kilometres after the start of the track is a turn-off left (sometimes closed) to the spooky, abandoned **Blyth Homestead**, established by grazier Harry Sargent and his family in 1928 and testament to the guts and determination of the early pioneering families. Back on the main track, you soon reach a turn-off leading in a couple of kilometres to **Tjaynera Falls** campsite (also known as Sandy Creek). From the campsite car park it's a 1.7-kilometre walk to the falls above a large plunge pool. At the Tjaynera turn-off, on the main track, take note of the sign warning that 4WDs should have a raised air-intake to cross the Reynolds River, 6km further on. **Surprise Creek Falls** (with camping), about 20km further on, are the highlight along the track. A short walk from the campsite car park leads to a sunny plunge pool and, tucked away on the rocks above, two perfectly positioned ten-metre-wide natural water-holes overlooking the whole scene. From this point it's about a twenty-minute drive over a few more humps to the junction with the Daly River Road.

Adelaide River and around

Established during the construction of the Overland Telegraph Line, the town of **ADELAIDE RIVER** was the supply head for Darwin's defence during World War II and consequently suffered sporadic Japanese bombing. Today the town, 110km south of Darwin, provides little more than a lunch-stop along the Stuart Highway, unless you want to visit the town's **war cemetery**, where many of the victims of the air raids are buried. Officially, 243 people died as a result of the eighteen months of Japanese bombing, which began in February 1942, but the cemetery has twice as many graves. There are lovely picnic grounds here and friendly peacocks. The *Mobil Roadhouse* has **camping**, but there's no reason to stay.

Just south of town, the old highway forks west along a rolling 75-kilometre scenic drive before rejoining the main road at *Hayes Creek* roadhouse. After the first 17km on this route you'll come to the turn-off for **Robin Falls**, a pretty little cascade reached after a ten-minute scramble up the creek bed from the car park. Seventeen kilometres south of the Robin Falls turn-off, a road leads to **Daly River** community (passing a southern entrance into Litchfield Park; 4WD only), a dead end favoured by barra fishermen; beyond is Aboriginal land.

Pine Creek and around

Site of the Territory's first goldrush, **PINE CREEK**, 230km from Darwin, is one of the Territory's oldest towns and has managed to hang onto an unreconstructed charm despite (or perhaps because of) its low tourist status. Gold was discovered here while digging holes for the Overland Telegraph Line pylons in 1871, and fools rushed in, hoping to pan their way to fortune. Unfortunately the gold was in the rock, not the riverbeds, requiring laborious crushing with heavy stamp batteries, which, for most prospectors, was too much like hard work for unpredictable returns. The subsequent labour shortage was solved by importing Chinese workers who kept the progressively poorer-quality ore coming for a few more years until fears of Asian dominance led to their being banned from the Territory in 1888. Ah Toys general store on Main Terrace is still run by the descendants of its original Chinese owner.

Around the town, the various time-worn buildings, such as the 1889 **Old Playford Hotel** and **Old Bakery**, may lead you to contemplate the crucial role of corrugated iron (now fashionable again) in the colonial pioneering process. The **Miners Park**, at the northern end of town, displays crude mining hardware from over a century ago, and there's a small **museum** (Mon–Fri 1–5pm; $2.50) on Railway Terrace, near the police station, and an old locomotive at the old train station itself. The *Pine Creek Hotel* (☎08/8976 1288; $115) was the only accommodation open at the time of research but there's little reason to spend longer here than it takes to fill up on petrol and grab a pie at *Mayse's Café*.

From Pine Creek it's 200km along the sealed **Kakadu Highway** to Jabiru, in the heart of Kakadu National Park, passing the majority of the park's highlights on the way. Down the Stuart Highway, 91km south of Pine Creek, a turn-off leads 20km east to **Edith Falls** (Leliyn). Like Wangi in Litchfield, Edith Falls is popular on weekends, with a refreshment kiosk and small waterfall at the back of a large pool. To get away from the crowds you can walk round to the secluded upper pools, on to Sweetwater Pool (9km return) or indeed all the way to Katherine Gorge along a 66-kilometre trail (see p.596).

Katherine to Alice Springs

An obligatory stopover for visitors to the Top End, **Katherine** is a small regional centre on the southern banks of the Katherine River, just 30km from **Nitmiluk Gorge** (formerly Katherine Gorge), part of the region's primary attraction, **Nitmiluk National Park**.

From Katherine, the **Victoria Highway** leads for 500km west to the Wetern Australia also border, passing Timber Creek and **Gregory National Park**. South of town is a vast touristic no-man's-land all the way to Alice Springs. A dip in **Mataranka**'s thermal pools and a few "bush pubs" are the highlights of the 670km to **Tennant Creek**. South of Tennant Creek, only the rotund boulders of the **Devil's Marbles** brighten the string of roadhouses along the Stuart Highway, which rolls on for just over 500km to Alice Springs. If you are aiming to drive straight through, allow a good ten hours: and whatever you do, don't drive in the dark, as there is a strong likelihood of hitting a kangaroo.

Katherine

Traditionally home of the Jawoyn and Dagoman people, the **Katherine River** area must have been a sight for explorer John McDouall Stuart's sore eyes as he struggled north in 1862. Having got this far, he named the river after a benefactor's daughter, and within ten years the completion of the Overland Telegraph Line (OTL) encouraged European settlement, as drovers and prospectors converged on the first reliable water north of the Davenport Ranges. In 1926 a railway from Darwin finally spanned the river and **KATHERINE** was established on its present site. It's essentially a "one-street" town, though in January 1998 when the river rose to 22m and broke its banks that street found itself under 2m of water when two cyclones dumped a Wet-season's worth of rain over southern Arnhem Land – a crocodile was even spotted cruising lazily past the semi-submerged Woolworths. April 2006 saw the river rise again to 19m but fortunately it subsided as quickly as it rose with nowhere near the devastation and loss of 1998.

The town and around

The Stuart Highway becomes **Katherine Terrace**, the main street, as it passes through town. Along it lie most of the shops and services, as well as several excellent Aboriginal art and craft galleries, giving Katherine a compact and unexpectedly busy feel. If you want to base yourself here for a while, the town is also a good place to pick up **casual work** at the surrounding stations and market gardens.

If you want the full story on the town head 3km up Giles Street to the **Katherine Outback Heritage Museum** (Mon–Fri 9am–4pm; $5), on Gorge Road, in the old aerodrome building, just before the original town site at Knotts Crossing, where a few original OTL pylons still remain upright. Inside are displays on Katherine's pioneering history, from the 1870s through to the mid-twentieth century, including early medical instruments and a 1930s Gypsy Moth plane from the time when the building did duty as a Flying Doctor base. On Tuesday, Thursday and Sunday nights the museum grounds play host to Stockman's Dinners (7pm Apr–Oct; $45 food & entertainment only, BYO alcohol; ℡0427 112 806) where you can try the tucker typical of a stockman's camp including roasts, roo fillets, coal-fired veggies, damper, scones and billy tea, and be entertained by Aussie yarns around a campfire.

The crystal-clear waters of Katherine Hot Springs, a five-minute drive from the centre, accessed by the Victoria Highway or Riverbank Drive, are worth a look – and swim – if you're not visiting Mataranka. The grassy banks are a great place for a picnic.

Cutta Cutta Caves, 27km south of town, can only be visited on guided tours (hourly 9–11am & 1–3pm; $13.50; ℡08/8972 1940). The two caves display subterranean karst features as diverse as they are delicate, and are home to the rare orange horseshoe bat, as well as rather alarming stalactite-climbing brown snakes.

Practicalities

The **train station** is a few kilometres west off the Victoria Highway, from where a **taxi** (℡08/8972 1777) to Katherine costs about $20. All buses arrive at the **Transit Centre**, at the south end of Katherine Terrace, next to the 24-hour *BP Roadhouse*. Katherine is a busy interchange for buses, with at least one daily arrival or departure for Darwin, Kununurra (WA) and Alice Springs.

Tours from Katherine

Conway's Cattle Station, Central Arnhem Road, ℡08/8974 4252. Travel by helicopter or 4WD to this working cattle station a few hours east of Katherine for station tours, fishing, swimming, birdwatching, wildlife spotting, and if your timing is right, aerial mustering or horse-breaking. Stay in a guesthouse adjoining the jackaroo bunkroom and share yarns as you dine under the stars. Room, meals and all activities from $320 per person.

Gecko Canoe Tours ℡08/8972 2224 or 1800 634 319, ℡www.geckocanoeing.com .au. One- to six-day relaxed and peaceful canoeing trips on the Katherine River system downstream of town for around $200 per day.

Katherine Aviation ℡08/8971 1277. This professional outfit offers scenic flights in 5-seater single-engine Cessna 210s and twin-engine Beechcraft Baron planes over the 13 gorges of Nitmiluk, Edith Falls and Kakadu starting at $160 per person from 40 minutes to $435 per person for 5 hours including stops for sightseeing, cruises and swimming.

Manyallaluk ℡1800 644 727. Long-established Aboriginal culture tours now operated by Gecko (see above); a fun day out with didgeridoo-playing, painting, spear-throwing, fire-lighting and bushtucker, all for $165 (or $125 self-drive).

Travelnorth ℡08/8971 9999 or 1800 089 103, ℡www.travelnorth.com.au. Offers plenty of Katherine-based tours such as the evening wildlife-spotting tour ($59), which includes a BBQ dinner and some croc spotting.

Opposite you'll find the **visitor centre** (March–Oct daily 8.30am–5pm; Nov–Feb Mon–Fri 8.30am–5pm, Sat & Sun 9am–2pm; ℡1800 653 142, ⊛www.visitkatherine.com.au), with shelves weighed down with leaflets. For more detailed information on Nitmiluk, Gregory and Keep River national parks visit the **Parks and Wildlife Commission** (℡08/8973 8888) on Giles Street, 1km Art Gallery opposite Woolworths at 12 Katherine Terrace and in the library, also on the main street. To **rent a car** phone Thrifty (℡08/8972 3183 or 13 61 39, ⊛www.rentacar.com.au) or Hertz Rent-A-Car (℡08/8971 1111, ⊛www.hertz.com.au). Taxis can be called on ℡08/8972 1777. **Bikes** can be rented from the backpackers' or the bike shop on the main street in town.

Accommodation and eating

The visitor centre maintains an accommodation list with current prices; the best options are detailed below. There are four caravan parks around town (although none very central) offering camping (un/powered sites from $24/27) and en-suite cabins (from $130 per night). **Eating out** in Katherine is nothing to get excited about. The *Terrace Café* in the Woolworths Shopping Centre is a popular spot for a daytime snack and there are several fast-food places; in the evening your best bet is the Stockman's Dinner (see opposite) or a meal at one of the motel restaurants.

Backpackers

Kookaburra Palm Court Backpackers Corner of Giles and Third sts ℡08/8972 2722 or 1800 626 722, ⊛www.travelnorth.com.au. This friendly hostel in an old motel has a communal kitchen and laundry, small pool, BBQ facilities, car parking, and offers free transfers, luggage storage, bike hire and tour bookings. Dorms have en-suite bathrooms. Dorms ❶, rooms ❷–❸

Motels

All Seasons Katherine Stuart Highway ℡08/8972 1744, ⊛www.allseasons.com.au. Katherine's best motel, located 4km south of town and set back from the road (so you're guaranteed a good night's sleep), also has a pool, bar and bistro. ❼
Best Western Pine Tree Motel Third St ℡08/8972 2533, ⊛www.pinetree.bestwestern.com.au. This decent motel in the centre of town has spacious rooms and a palm-lined swimming pool, and offers laundry access and free bus pick-ups. ❻

Maud Creek Country Lodge Lot 4179 Gorge Road, Katherine ℡08/8971 1814, ⊛www.maudcreeklodge.com.au. This lovely lodge 6km from the gorge is a great option if you have your own car, offering a rather special experience including hot breakfast, Stockman's dinner with campfire yarns, sunset drinks and appetizers, use of boat, fishing gear and bicycles, and transfers for Ghan arrivals. Set within lush tropical gardens, there's a self-contained cottage plus comfortable rooms opening onto a big wooden veranda, with a guest lounge/kitchen, library and swimming pool. Between the property and river are trees teeming with birdlife. ❾
Paraway Motel Corner of O'Shea and First sts ℡08/8972 2644, ⊛www.parawaymotel.com.au. A comfortable motel in the town centre with spacious rooms (all with queens and single beds), microwaves, and an on-site restaurant, *The Carriage* (Wed–Mon) offering a buffet, stonegrill dishes, and the popular *Junction Bar*. ❺

Nitmiluk National Park

The central attraction of **Nitmiluk National Park** – jointly managed by the traditional indigenous owners, the Jawoyn, and the Parks and Wildlife Commission – is the magnificent twelve-kilometre **Nitmiluk Gorge** (formerly Katherine Gorge), carved by the Katherine River through the Arnhem Land plateau. Described as thirteen gorges, it is in fact one continuous cleft, turning left and right along fault lines and separated during the Dry season by rock bars. The spectacle of the river, hemmed in by sheer ochre cliffs, makes for a spectacular **cruise**. Nitmiluk also welcomes bushwalkers along its eight marked walking **trails**. There is **accommodation** at the shady ⚘ campsites (un/powered site $14/32 per person, chalets $165), a popular spot with wallabies, near Nitmiluk visitor centre, at Leliyn (Edith Falls), and at the Nitmiluk-managed Maud Creek Country Lodge (see p.595), 6km from the gorge.

The Jawoyn-owned Nitmiluk Tours (☎1300 146 743; ⓦwww.nitmiluktours .com.au) operates **shuttle buses** from April to September between Katherine and the gorge for $24 return. The **visitor centre** (March–Nov daily 8am–7pm) has a fascinating interpretive display on the Jawoyn and the park's geology, flora and fauna, and a tour desk with information and maps detailing walking trails, including the *Guide to Nitmiluk National Park* ($6.55) with topographical maps. There's also a café and mini-mart/gift shop. As you sit on the terrace overlooking the river, consider that in January 1998 you would have been under 1m of water.

The Southern Walks information sheet details seven marked **trails** (from 1.8km/1hr to 39km/2–3 days), while **Jatbula Trail** has basic information on the 66-kilometre walk to Edith Falls, open June to September, which takes four to five days. You need to register with the rangers for any overnight walks as well as book the ferry crossing and return bus service. A minimum of two people is required, along with a $50 refundable deposit. Rangers also offer guided two- to four-hour walks, from $45–65.

Exploring Nitmiluk Gorge

Buses from Katherine terminate at the canoe ramp and jetty. Tickets for cruises are sold at the visitor centre. There is relatively safe swimming in the Dry season, although the gorges are closed to swimmers and canoeists from December (when high water levels enable saltwater crocs to swim between the gorges) until April or May (when the water has subsided low enough for rangers to trap the crocs). In February and March 2009 two monster salties were captured in the first and second gorges. While waiting for a cruise, you can take the steep, nine-hundred-metre walk leading from the jetty to the Baruwei clifftop **lookout** for superb river views.

A variety of Nitmiluk Tours **boat cruises** (☎1300 146 743) ply the gorge throughout the day. The best are the two-hour Dawn Break Breakfast Cruises for $63 when the light has a gorgeous clarity and the three-and-a-half-hour Nabilil Dreaming Sunset Cruises for $123 (including a three-course meal and drinks), when the setting sun gives the rocks a golden hue. Nitmiluk Tours also operate exhilarating **helicopter flights** up the gorge from as little as $75 per person for eight minutes – it's a magnificent sight from the air.

Canoeing up the gorge is an option for the energetic, but don't expect to paddle up to the "thirteenth" in a day; canoeing is hard work, especially against the breeze which blows down the gorge. Nitmiluk Tours rent single and double canoes (available at 8am and 1pm) for $54 a day, $42 per half-day, and $104 overnight for a single – add about fifty percent for two-person canoes (easier to control and a shared load for beginners). A deposit of $60 and a permit ($3.30) is required for overnight trips, payable on site. You need to provide your own camping equipment. Expect long sections of canoe-carrying over boulders and successively shorter sections of water as you progress up the gorges. Those determined to reach the thirteenth gorge (which, scenically speaking, is not really worthwhile) will find it easier to leave their canoe at the fifth and swim/walk the last couple of kilometres.

The first permissible overnight **campsite** is 9km from the visitor centre in the fifth gorge (or anywhere upstream from there) – this is regarded as a fair day's paddling and portaging. Canoeing is best done early in the Dry season, when small waterfalls run off cliff walls and the water level is still high enough to reduce the length of the walking sections.

The Victoria Highway to Western Australia

The **Victoria Highway** stretches for 510km southwest of Katherine to Kununurra in Western Australia. South of the highway, between Gregory and Keep River national parks, is the legendary Victoria River Downs (VRD) station, once the country's biggest cattle station and the base of Australia's biggest heli-mustering outfit, pursuing the daredevil practice of mustering widely dispersed stock with helicopters.

The two pit stops on the long journey west along the Victoria Highway are the Victoria River Roadhouse, 194km west of Katherine, access point for the eastern sector of the remote and wild **Gregory National Park**; and **Timber Creek**, another 92km along the highway, near the entrance to the park's western sector. With a 4WD and the right gear, you can explore the Park's Outback tracks, walk along spectacular escarpments and dramatic gorges, and do a spot of bush camping. More accessible and also worth a diversion is the **Keep River National Park**, just before the Western Australia border.

Timber Creek

Although little more than a pair of roadhouse-cum-bars with adjacent campsites, **TIMBER CREEK**, almost 300km west of Katherine, makes a welcome break on the long run to Kununurra. In 1856, the explorer Augustus Gregory's ship ran aground on the Victoria River and, forced to make repairs, Timber Creek was born, an inland port to serve the vast pastoral properties then being established throughout the region. This remote outpost was soon the scene of bitter disputes between Aborigines and the settlers, and in 1898 a **police station** was set up in a hut at Timber Creek, staffed by two policemen and an Aboriginal tracker whose task was to patrol an area the size of Tasmania. Upgraded to corrugated iron and steel in 1908, the old police station is now a **museum** (Mon–Fri 10am–noon, April–Aug; $3), a rare survivor of early NT architecture and construction, featuring a display of pioneering relics dragged out of the surrounding undergrowth or abandoned homesteads and used to illustrate a pithy historical commentary about the region. The town also boasts the easternmost examples of the bottle-trunked **boab trees**; according to Aboriginal mythology, the boab was a once-arrogant tree which was turned upside down to teach it a lesson in humility.

Practicalities

Tourist information is dispensed from the Victoria River Cruise office's Crock Stock Shop (Mon–Sat 8am–4pm; ☎08/8975 0850, ⓦwww .victoriarivercruise.com). Inside you'll find one of the finest selections of "croco-bilia" north of the 26th parallel. An afternoon **boat tour** (Mon–Sat 4–7.30pm; $80; BYO) runs 40km down the Victoria River, on which you'll see some real crocs, as well as roos and birds, arriving back for sunset on the crags.

Life and death of the real Crocodile Dundee

The survival story of **Rod Ansell** and his subsequent media exposure are generally agreed to be the inspiration for the character of Mick "Croc" Dundee in the popular 1980s films that portrayed a tough bushman as a "fish out of water" in the big city. In 1977, Ansell, then 27 years old, claimed he became marooned when his boat was overturned while fishing at the mouth of the Victoria River, northwest of Timber Creek. With just one oar he paddled a dinghy up the Fitzmaurice River to fresh water and survived for seven weeks using the bush skills he'd been brought up with. Living on a diet of feral cattle, berries and sharks, Ansell and his two bull terriers were found, emaciated but coherent, seven weeks later by stockmen. He played down his ordeal but the tale grew legs and, as in the film, journalist Rachel Percy tracked him down and publicized his story in a TV documentary and later in a slim book, *To Fight the Wild*. Sensing an opportunity, Ansell hit the TV chat-show circuit, where his story allegedly inspired the comedian Paul Hogan to co-write *Crocodile Dundee*. The film came out in 1985 and was a worldwide hit, helping to put Australia's Outback on the map.

Following the film's success, Ansell took on a station near Shady Camp on the Mary River, but his tourist plans were foiled when he was barred from using the "Crocodile Dundee" epithet and his entire stock was subsequently shot as part of a bovine disease-eradication programme for which he felt he was not adequately compensated. Under financial pressure, he lost his station and was later charged with assault and cattle stealing in Arnhem Land. Embittered by his own failure compared with the success of the film, Ansell left his family and became a speed-addled recluse living near Roper Bar. In August 1999, weighing less than 45kg and in the grip of drug-induced paranoia, he shot at strangers near Berry Springs who he thought had kidnapped his sons, before shooting dead a policeman on the Stuart Highway. A shoot-out ensued, and when reinforcements arrived Ansell came out of hiding, firing, and was himself shot dead. Kate Finlayson's 2003 book *A Lot of Croc* describes a semi-fictionalized search to unravel the Rod Ansell story and, on the way, describes many definitively Territorian and politically incorrect characters, encounters and situations.

Accommodation, **fuel** and **food** can be found at indigenous-owned *Gunamu Tourist Park and Timber Creek Hotel* (☎08/8975 0772), which has camping (un/powered sites $8/20), cabins (④) and motel rooms (⑥). The hotel does a daily croc-feeding session during the Dry at 5pm from the bridge at the back of the place. You can also buy food at the roadhouses and store.

Gregory National Park

Gregory National Park, the Territory's second-largest park, is divided into two sectors, the eastern Victoria River sector, accessible from the Victoria Highway around the Victoria River Roadhouse, and the western Gregory sector, best reached from an unsealed road 14km east of Timber Creek. The park is accessible during the Dry season, from May to November. At other times, roads may be closed due to flooding – even the sealed Victoria Highway becomes impassable during the Wet. Created from unviable pastoral leases, the park exhibits striking sandstone escarpments, deep dramatic gorges, and limestone hills covered in light woodland. Because of its remoteness and rough terrain, the park should only be explored in a high-clearance **4WD vehicle** with snorkel, spare tyres, and lots of fuel, food and water; you need to be completely self-sufficient. Stop at the **Parks & Wildlife** office at Timber Creek (turn right just before Watch Creek, west of town; ☎08/8975 0888) to get a map and information about 4WD tracks, walks and camping, check road conditions, and to register your trip plans. Look out for crocodile warning signs as the park's rivers are home to saltwater crocs; as ever, you should only swim where recommended.

Accessible from the Victoria Highway, 2km west of Victoria River Roadhouse in the eastern sector, the steep three-kilometre return Escarpment Walk boasts breathtaking vistas of the surrounding red escarpments and picturesque valley, as does the 1.7-kilometre Nawulbinbin Walk, another 7km down the road, which takes in Aboriginal paintings on the rocky walls.

In the western sector, **Limestone Gorge** can only be reached by high-clearance 4WD on a corrugated track 48km south of the highway. The 1.8- kilometre Limestone Ridge Loop Walk winds through a stunning karst landscape that affords magnificent views of the valley and East Baines River. There's a campsite, and while you can swim in the billabong, you can only fish the river. The historic Bullita Homestead and stockyards are 9km south of the Limestone Gorge turn-off. From here, the one-way seventy-kilometre **Bullita Stockroute** loops in a northern and easterly direction, following the old stock route to Wyndham. The eight-hour drive involves a couple of challenging river crossings and crawling over extremely rocky terrain. For avid off-roaders, this is 4WD paradise; **camping** is permitted at designated spots along the way.

The rocky **Humbert River Track** follows another stock route south between Bullita and Humbert River station (allow at least six hours for the challenging 62.5-kilometre route), from where you can head east to Victoria River Downs Station then north to the Victoria Highway. Alternatively, from Bullita you can continue south to the **Buntine Highway** along the Wickham Track and then either the Gibbie Track via Kalkaringi (allow a day) or the **Broadarrow Track** via Depot Creek (allow two full days and take two spare tyres and a puncture repair kit). Keep in mind these routes are closed from December to April and can still be boggy in May. It's vital to check conditions before attempting these routes (℡ 1800 246 199; ⓦ www.ntlis.nt.gov.au/roadreport/).

Keep River National Park and the Western Australia border

West of Timber Creek, the land flattens out into the evocatively named **Whirlwind Plains**, where the East and West Baines rivers frequently flood the Victoria Highway in the Wet. **Keep River National Park** lies just before the Western Australia border, 185km from Timber Creek. The corrugated gravel roads are accessible to high 2WDs, although are often closed due to flooding from November to April. It's an easily explored park, teaming with wallabies and birds, and boasting colossal domed rocks (similar to the formations at Purnululu and Mirima National Parks in Western Australia), dissected sandstone ridges, dramatic gorges and Aboriginal art sites, the best of which is **Nganalam**, 24km from the park entrance. Marked walking trails start from the two **campsites**, Gurrandalng, 18km from the park entrance, and Jarnem, 31km. Call into the Cockatoo Lagoon Information Centre (℡ 08/9167 8827), 3km from the highway, but note that it's necessary to get a permit one week in advance for longer walks.

Eat or discard any fresh produce or honey before you get to the border as there are restrictions on what you can take into Western Australia. Kununurra's intensively irrigated agricultural area is hoping to remain free from pests found elsewhere in Australia. If you're not sure what to discard, checkpoint staff will set you right. Note that **Western Australia time** is an hour and thirty minutes behind the Territory. Kununurra (see p.738) is 40km from the border.

South to Alice Springs

The 1100km south from Katherine down "**the track**", as the Stuart Highway is known, to Alice Springs, are something of a **no-man's-land** for travellers – taken up by a sparsely populated, flat, arid plain rolling all the way from the Top End's big rivers to the waterholes of the Red Centre.

West of the Track, the vast Aboriginal lands of the Warlpiri and neighbouring groups occupy just about the entire **Tanami Desert**, while to the east are the grasslands of the **Barkly Tableland**, a dramatic drought-affected pastoral region extending north to the seldom-visited coast of the **Gulf of Carpentaria**. The town of **Tennant Creek**, just over halfway, is an anticlimactic break to a journey. The bleak landscape along the Stuart Highway tends to provoke either an agoraphobic urgency or such imponderables as "Just how many anthills *are* there in the Northern Territory?"

Mataranka and the Roper River region

The tiny town of **MATARANKA** – just over 100km from Katherine – is the capital of "Never Never" country. Named after Jeannie Gunn's 1908 novel of a pioneering woman's life set in the area, *We of the Never Never*, which in turn evokes Henry Lawson's poem The Never Never Land about a place of rainless skies and hopeless deserts, Mataranka was the site of reviled Administrator John Gilruth's planned Northern Territory capital. Nearby, the hot springs of **Elsey National Park**, **Mataranka Homestead** and the freshwater wetlands of the **Roper River** lure passing travellers from May to September.

You'll find **accommodation**, roadhouses, a supermarket and museum on **Roper Terrace** (Stuart Highway). *Territory Manor* (☎08/8975 4516; [W]www.matarankamotel.com.au) has rooms ([5]) and caravan/camping sites (un/powered $21/25) set in leafy grounds with a swimming pool and daily barramundi feeding show, while *Mataranka Cabins* (☎08/8975 4838, [W]www.matarankacabins.com.au) has attractive cabins ([5]) and camping (un/powered/en suite $10/24/28) by the river, close to Bitter Springs.

Elsey National Park, the Roper River and Mataranka Homestead

The main attractions in the 4,000-acre **Elsey National Park** are the natural springs that feed the Roper River. Set amid tropical woodlands off Martin Road, 2km northeast of Mataranka, the swampy pools of **Bitter Springs** have lukewarm minty-blue mineral waters, which you can swim in. You'll need a mask though – as they stink! The rotten-egg gas or hydrogen sulphide is a by-product of bacteria that break down the floating mats of green algae growing in the nutrient-rich waters; they, in turn, provide food for the insects, lizards and birds.

The clear 34°C waters of Rainbow Springs and Mataranka Thermal Pool, adjoining Mataranka Homestead Tourist Resort, 6km east of town off Homestead Road, may be less smelly, but the surrounding palm forest reeks of excrement produced by the colossal colony of nomadic little red flying foxes. What started as a small colony of 5000, which roosted here from October to May each year, grew to an unmanageable 250,000 in 1995 when they stayed

Landscapes

The popular image of Australia as a brown desert surrounded by picture-postcard beaches has some truth to it, but gives only a very partial description of this vast island continent. Snow-covered mountains, inland lakes, wild rivers, deep gorges, lush pastures, magnificent forests – both temperate and tropical – and immense underground caves add variety, and the Australian love of the outdoor life ensures a host of different ways to enjoy them.

Great Ocean Road ▲
Wineglass Bay ▼

The coast

Most Australians live within a couple of hours of the ocean, and beach culture is central to the Australian way of life. The 35,000km of coast (nearer 60,000km if you include all the islands) have an abundance of beaches that can seem impossibly perfect, with vast stretches of brilliant white sands caressed by deep blue seas under cloudless skies. From the geometric curve of temperate **Wineglass Bay** (Tas) to the cosmopolitan bustle of **Byron Bay** (NSW), the choice seems endless – and the country's disproportionately small population means you're likely to be alone on beaches that would be crowded anywhere else in the world.

Other areas of the coast have a more active appeal. Victoria's **Great Ocean Road** is an inspiring drive (or a wonderful walk) past spectacular columns of rock, sculpted by the ocean and standing offshore like sentinels against the waves. Whether snorkelling with whale sharks at **Ningaloo Reef** (WA), diving in the **Great Barrier Reef** (Qld), surfing at **Bells Beach** (Vic), sailing at the **Whitsunday Islands** or fishing (pretty much anywhere), a lot of Australian life is lived in, on or near the ocean – see the *Watersports* colour section for how to join in.

Forest and mountains

Despite the fact that most of Australia is flat, the **Great Dividing Range**, which runs roughly parallel to the eastern coast, is the fourth-longest mountain range in the world. The area around the country's highest peak, **Mount Kosciuszko** (2228m) in the **Snowy Mountains** (NSW), offers the full gamut of winter alpine activities, from skiing to snow-tubing, but elsewhere much of the Range is covered with lush forests that provide spectacular bushwalking country. In the popular **Blue Mountains** (NSW), also renowned for its rock-climbing and caving, the roads and towns are on top of the escarpment, so you look down into immense canyons of dense forest. It's a genuine "land that time forgot" – near here, the dinosaur-contemporary **Wollemi pine** was discovered just fifteen years ago, a tree previously believed to be extinct for more than two million years.

Equally ancient are the magnificent trees of Tasmania's **Tarkine** forests, the second-largest temperate rainforest in the world and host to no fewer than 56 threatened and endangered species. At the other end of the country, the **Daintree** rainforest (Qld) is Australia's largest, and the world's oldest, surviving stretch of tropical rainforest, sheltering the largest range of plants and animals on Earth.

▲ Blue Mountains
▼ Driving Outback Australia

The Outback

The **Outback** – everything west of the Great Dividing Range – is the essence of Australia, where the myths, facts and uncertainties of Australian identity interweave with the uncompromising harshness, scale and beauty of this ancient land. Covering an area almost as big as Europe, there is a lot of Outback to enjoy. The ever-popular **Uluru (Ayers Rock)** is Australia's most-visited single site – one of the world's great natural wonders; getting up close to its vast bulk is nothing short of awe-inspiring. But you may find that your lasting memories are more elusive: countless scrubby

Daintree rainforest ▲

The Tasmanian wilderness ▼

bushes, termite mounds and eucalypts, epic horizons and an empty, endless road that threads across a vast, flat nothingness to the shimmering haze where intense red yields to saturated blue.

Either in your own vehicle or as part of a tour, **driving** is the best way to experience the Outback. You can also travel by **train** from Adelaide to Darwin on the Ghan Railway, but some places, such as the beehive-shaped Bungle Bungles (WA), are best seen from the **air**, while others, particularly the Red Centre, are appreciated more **on foot**.

National parks

Nearly ten percent of Australia's great outdoors is protected within national parks, many of them – such as **Kakadu** (NT), a vast area of natural beauty and Aboriginal rock art dating back tens of thousands of years – significant enough to be listed as World Heritage Sites. The **Tasmanian wilderness** is one of the largest conservation reserves in Australia, and the 80-kilometre **Overland Track** from **Cradle Mountain** to **Lake St Clair** one of the world's great walks – a challenging five days of mud and leeches, but worth it for the spectacular scenery every step of the way. Other equally spectacular parks include **Karajini** (WA), astonishing for its wild flowers, gorges and red dust, and the **Flinders Ranges** (SA), 300km north of Adelaide, renowned for the great kilometre-high natural bowl of **Wilpena Pound** and as the start of the **Heysen Trail**, a punishing twelve-hundred-kilometre walk. There are less visited, but equally rewarding national parks too, such as **Mutawintji**, 130km northeast of Broken Hill in New South Wales, with secluded gorges, quiet waterholes and ancient galleries of Aboriginal rock art to be discovered in the caves and overhangs.

until July, wreaking havoc: their faecal output was so great, a boardwalk was constructed and canopies erected to protect visitors. Rangers have struggled ever since to manage the flying foxes, facing dwindling tourist numbers and a conservation dilemma. On the one hand, the flying foxes destroy branches and natural ground covering, on the other, they act as pollinators, dispersing seeds of native plants over great distances. While management techniques (sprinklers and sound guns) and a mystery virus have reduced numbers, the stench remains strong. If you can handle the pong, stroll to the springs for a dip and to watch the flying foxes in action.

Mataranka Homestead was established by Gilruth in 1916 as an experimental sheep and cattle station and is a fine example of tropical Top End architecture, begging to be restored and turned into a museum. On the other side of the car park is the fascinating Elsey Homestead replica built for the 1982 film *We of the Never Never*, which is screened daily at Maluka's Bar/Jeannie's Kitchen at the Mataranka Homestead Tourist Resort (☎08/8975 4544 or 1800 754 544, ⓔmatarankahomestead@bigpond.com.au), where you'll find food and free nightly entertainment (April–Sept only). **Accommodation** includes basic motel rooms (❹), self-catering cabins (❺), dorms ($17–36) and a campsite (un/powered sites $14/27).

There is another basic **campsite** ($7.70) offering canoe rental and swimming in some areas (observe croc warning signs) at 12 Mile Yards and Jalmurark Campgrounds on the upper Roper River, accessed from John Hauser Drive; you'll find the turn-off as you head back toward Mataranka, halfway along Homestead Road. There are no powered sites and generators are not permitted.

During the Dry, experienced off-roaders with a 4WD (and spare tyres) can take the **Roper Highway**, south of Mataranka, east for 185km (the single-lane bitumen ends at around 130km) to the remote **ROPER BAR** community where the Roper Bar Store (☎08/8975 4636; Mon–Sat 9am–6pm, essential to call ahead) has food, fuel and some accommodation. Take care crossing the causeway. If you've got this far, you're probably taking the track to **Borroloola**, 380km away (see p.602), for some fishing; stock up on food, water and fuel as there's nothing on the way.

Down the Track to Three Ways

LARRIMAH, 72km south of Mataranka, was where the old Darwin railway terminated until 1976 when it closed for good following Cyclone Tracy. Up until then, it had been a busy road–rail terminus, receiving goods brought up from Alice Springs. Now it's just a fuel stop on the highway with a bit more history than most. The *Larrimah Hotel* is a typical **bush pub**, full of eccentricity and historic memorabilia (for more of the same check out the free museum across the way and Fran's pies and Devonshire Teas); you can **camp** here (un/powered sites $7/12) or take one of the pub's basic rooms (❹).

Another 89km south brings you to **DALY WATERS**, 3km off the highway. The Daly Waters Pub has held a "gallon licence" since 1893, and it's laden with memorabilia, including money and IDs stuck to the bar and underwear hanging from the ceilings: you're welcome to contribute. During the 1930s, when Qantas's Singapore flights refuelled here, world-class aviators would pop in for a pint. These days tourists come to marvel at the nutty quaintness of it all over a cold beer and barra burger. If you fancy a break there's camping (un/powered sites $5/9) and a range of **rooms** (❶–❸) **en suites** (❸) and cabins (❹).

Just beyond, at the *Hi Way Inn Roadhouse* (open 24hr) the turn-off to the **Carpentaria Highway** heads east to Cape Crawford, 270km away, and

Borroloola, 414km (see below); Further down the Track, just before *Dunmarra Roadhouse*, there's a turn-off west to the **Buchanan Highway** to *Top Springs Roadhouse* (185km) and ultimately, if you turn off south, Halls Creek in Western Australia (see p.736) along almost 800km of mostly unsealed road (Dry season only, 4WD recommended).

Further down the Track, there's a turn-off west, 4km, to **NEWCASTLE WATERS**, a semi-abandoned, historic droving township that's worth a look; the ramshackle buildings are beautiful at sunset.

Further south, **ELLIOTT** has a couple of roadhouses and a few shops serving the Jingili Aboriginal community, but there's little reason to linger other than to refuel. If you have to stop, *Midland Caravan Park* (☎08/8969 2037; powered sites $21.50, cabins ❸), attached to the BP roadhouse, post office and super-market, locks its gates at 9pm, opening again at 6am.

Heading south, the trees that dotted the landscape start to recede into low-lying mallee scrubland as you approach Central Australia. Worth a quick look if you're ticking off bush pubs, **Renner Springs** is plastered with eccentric knick-knacks.

On the way to **THREE WAYS** (roadhouse open 24hr) watch out for the turn-off to **Attack Creek Memorial** where explorer Stuart was repelled by Aborigines on one of his expeditions. From Three Ways, the **Barkly Highway** heads east to Camooweal, Mount Isa and Townsville in Queensland; at 210km you'll hit *Barkly Homestead* (☎08/8964 4549; 6am–1am), with the usual services. From here, the single-lane **Tablelands Highway** offers a narrow bitumen alternative to the Carpentaria Highway (above). From Three Ways, Tennant Creek (see p.603) is just 26km south.

Cape Crawford, Borroloola and the Tablelands Highway

From *Barkly Homestead*, the **Tablelands Highway** takes you north to **remote Cape Crawford** (bizarrely sited 113km away from the sea), the gateway to the spectacular towering sandstone rock formations of the Lost City. It's best viewed from the air on a helicopter tour (☎08/8975 9611, 2hr, $300 per person) operated by Cape Crawford Tourism on behalf of the Gudanji people, which includes a swim at beautiful Poppy's Pool and waterfall. Their office is opposite the *Heartbreak Hotel* roadhouse (☎08/8975 9928), which has camping (un/powered $6/24 per person), backpacker rooms (❶) and cabins (❹).

Borroloola

Situated on the croc-infested **McArthur River**, **BORROLOOLA** is a rough and depressing Aboriginal welfare town of interest only if you need fuel and a feed. It does, however, have a colourful history. Explorers Leichhardt and Gregory passed through in the mid-nineteenth century, reporting good pasture, and cattle drovers followed. By the early 1880s, when Tennant Creek and Katherine were still shacks on the Overland Telegraph Line, Borroloola was a wild outpost that even missionaries avoided. Ships that had supplied the OTL brought in provisions for the hard-living drovers, who were stocking the pastoral leases across northern Australia. Borroloola's was proclaimed, or gazetted, in 1886 and a police station was established in an attempt to stop the lawlessness. Shortly afterwards, the Barkly Highway was established, and soon became the favoured stock route, taking traffic away from Borroloola. By 1900 only a handful of settlers remained and the local Aboriginal groups reclaimed the area.

The bookworms and recluses of Borroloola

Perhaps the most bizarre feature of Borroloola is that its facilities include a library of classic literature. One theory for the impressive library is that a bored policeman requested reading matter from New York's Carnegie Foundation. In truth, it was a gradual acquisition of well over two thousand literary classics by the town's McArthur Institute at the beginning of the twentieth century. Termites tucked into the library, a cyclone destroyed the remains and only a handful of books survived, many of which found their way to the town's jail – creating a very well read criminal class.

In 1963 a boyish David Attenborough made a TV documentary about three **hermits** who had chosen to retreat to the 'Loo. Jack Mulholland came across as a slightly jaded recluse when pressed about "loneliness and…women", and the reputedly aristocratic "Mad Fiddler" was too deranged to face the camera, but **Roger Jose** was, and looked like, the real thing. Having devoured the library ahead of the ants, he lived in a water tank with his Aboriginal wife and was a humane if eccentric "bush philosopher" who once observed that "a man's riches are the fewness of his needs". He is buried at the end of the airstrip in Borroloola.

The only original building to have survived punch-ups, white ants and floods is the **Old Police Station**, now a fascinating museum (Mar–Oct Mon–Fri 10am–4pm; free) documenting Borroloola's wild history (see box above). If you want to know more, get hold of a copy of E.Gaunt's hair-raising *The Birth of Borroloola*, recalling the early days and the toxic home-brew known as "Come Hither", whose label showed a red-eyed Lucifer beckoning malevolently. By contrast, coverage of local Aboriginal history is lightweight. Despite all this history, don't be misled. Borroloola is now a popular base for fishermen here for the famed barramundi.

The attractive *Borroloola Guesthouse* (☎08/8975 8883) offers a range of accommodation (❺) in lush tropical gardens. Borroloola is accessible from the west via the **Carpentaria Highway** and Cape Crawford, and from the east from **Hell's Gate** roadhouse in Queensland (see p.556) via the unsealed Savannah Way, a route that can be challenging, and impassable during the Wet, and is best attempted by high-clearance 4WD.

Tennant Creek

Visitors expect to be disappointed by **TENNANT CREEK**, 26km south of Three Ways, and often are. The town has long been plagued by alcohol-fuelled social problems and violence, which escalated to disturbing proportions in 2008 – a local doctor described the night shift at the hospital as a "bloodbath" and hoteliers warned guests not to venture out at night. At the time of writing, it remained to be seen whether alcohol restrictions were having an effect. Regardless, with its handful of shops, restaurants and sights, including an excellent Aboriginal cultural centre, Tennant Creek remains the best stopover on the long haul between Katherine and Alice.

At the heart of the Barkly region, Tennant is a key hub for the rich mining and beef industries, and is home to the NT's oldest, and some of the world's biggest, cattle stations (the largest is over 12,000 square kilometres and runs around 65,000 head of cattle). If you're in town for one of the many campdrafts and rodeos that dominate the social calendar (March–Oct), you might just have one of the best experiences of your trip.

John McDouall Stuart came through Tennant Creek in the early 1860s, followed by the Overland Telegraph Line ten years later. Pastoralists and prospectors arrived from the south and east, and in 1933 it was the site of Australia's last major **goldrush**. This was the time of gritty "gougers", such as Jack Noble and partner Bill Weaber (with one eye between them), who defied the Depression by pegging some of the most productive claims. Mining corporations continue to exploit the rich deposits here, with mineral exploration the most important industry alongside beef.

Arrival and information

Tennant Creek is 507km from Alice Springs and 669km from Katherine. The **train station** is off the highway 5km south of town and The Ghan (Wwww .gsr.com.au) stops here twice a week. On the main road of Paterson Street (Stuart Highway), diagonally opposite El Dorado Motor Inn, you'll find the 24-hour *BP Roadhouse* (with takeaway and mini-market) where interstate **buses** stop. As both north- and southbound buses come through around 2am, when reception offices are shut, you'll need to arrange accommodation well in advance. On Paterson Street, there's **internet** access at *Switch* next to the *Top of the Town* **café**. The helpful **visitor centre** is at Battery Hill (daily 9am–5.30pm; T08/8962 1281 or 1800 500 879, Wwww.barklytourism.com.au), 1.5km east along Peko Road.

Accommodation

There are motels at each end of town and one in the middle, but book ahead as they fill up with tour buses, contractors and government workers.

El Dorado Motor Inn Paterson St T08/8962 2402 or 1800 888 010, Wwww.eldoradomotorinn .com.au. Comfortable motel at the north end of town with a decent licensed restaurant and small pool. ❹

Safari Lodge Motel 12 Davidson St T08/8962 2207 Wwww.safari.budgetmotelchain.com.au. Basic motel in the town centre, with functional rooms. ❹

Tennant Creek Caravan Park Next to the Shell service station, 208 Paterson St T08/8962 2325, Wwww.users.bigpond.com/tennantcreek. One of

three caravan parks in town, this one has good deals for camping (un/powered site $20/25), backpackers' bunkhouse doubles (❸) and simple cabins (❹).

Tennant Creek Tourist's Rest Leichhardt St T08/8962 2719, Wwww.touristrest.com.au. The three- and four-bed dorms and two-, three-bed and family rooms at this hostel have a lived-in feel. There's an above-ground pool, kitchen, tour desk, 24-hour check-in, and free pick-ups off the bus. Dorms $22pp, rooms ❸.

The town and around

The scale of the 1930s goldrush was significant; for a year the equivalent of around a million dollars of gold was extracted from Tennant each day. To find out more, head to the visitor centre, and take the entertaining ninety-minute guided tour of the adjoining underground **Battery Hill Mining Centre** (T088/962 1281; daily 9am–5pm; 4 tours daily in peak season, fewer in quiet periods; $20 day tour, $25 night tour; free bus pick-up). On site there is also a **museum** ($5) which houses an impressive minerals collection and traces the region's social history in the fascinating Freedom, Fortitude and Flies exhibition. Outside you can check out the old stamp battery (crushing machinery) for free.

At the southern end of Paterson Street, the superb Nyinkka Nyunyu **Cultural Centre** (T08/8962 2699; May–Sept Mon–Sat 8am–6pm, Sun 10am–2pm; Oct–Apr Mon–Fri 9am–5pm, Sat & Sun 10am–2pm; Wwww .nyinkkanyunyu.com.au; $15 per person including guided tour) provides a wonderful insight into the local indigenous Warumungu people from their perspectives, with innovative displays on their involvement in the cattle and mining histories, land claims, skin groups and bushtucker, among other topics, including films of Warumungu talking about their experiences. An on-site shop sells art, crafts, CDs and souvenirs.

For those with their own vehicle, the beautiful old **Telegraph Station**, 11km north of town, is worth a look; get the keys from the visitor centre.

Eating and drinking

Your options are café fare at the *Top of the Town* (daytime only); fast food from one of the takeaways on Paterson Street; Chinese at *Woks Up* (Mon–Sat from 6pm) at the Sporties Club on Ambrose Street; a buffet meal at the motels; or you can sign in as a guest at the *Memorial Club* on Schmidt Street for gigantic steaks and a drink. Bars are few and far between: try the motel bistros, clubs or the two pubs on Paterson Street.

Towards Alice Springs and the Centre

If you're feeling a bit "Top Ended" then the 505km from Tennant to Alice Springs offers some respite as the land opens out into the subtle hues of the central deserts. Unless you have a 4WD, only the surreal boulder-like rock formations known as the Devil's Marbles are worth breaking the journey for. If you've not got your own transport, they can be visited on a day-tour from Tennant Creek with Devil's Marbles Tours (℡0418 891 711; $80 per person, 2 people minimum).

Eighty-seven kilometres south of town, a sign points east towards the **Davenport Ranges National Park**. Here a 4WD track runs east along the north side of the ranges and then south some 160km to Old Police Station Waterhole before looping back west along the rougher but scenically more interesting southern side, passing a couple of waterholes, station homesteads and outstations. While you could do the loop with a stop for swimming and lunch in a day, an overnight camp at the Waterhole is more fun. The only problem is that you'll emerge 63km further down the Stuart Highway and will have to backtrack 46km to see the Devil's Marbles; alternatively, see them in the morning (when the light is better anyway) before heading to the Davenports. Get a leaflet and map from Tennant Creek's visitor centre and ensure you have sufficient fuel and provisions.

South to Ti Tree

Just off the highway about 130km south of Tennant Creek, the marvellous **DEVIL'S MARBLES** (basic camping) are worth an hour or two of your time. Aim to arrive soon after sunrise when the light is at its best. A genuine geological oddity, the local Warumungu people believe these huge round boulders are the eggs of the Rainbow Serpent. A short drive south of the Marbles, the 1930s pub and roadhouse at **WAUCHOPE** (pronounced "Walkup"; ℡08/8964 1963) has rooms (❸–❹), caravan/camping sites (un/powered sites $7/18) and a basic restaurant. **WYCLIFFE WELL Holiday Park** (℡08/8964 1966), a little further south, is proud of its extensive range of beer and reputation as a hotspot for UFO sightings (see box, p.606). There's camping (un/powered sites $14–20/18–25) and a wide range of cabins (❷–❺), internet access, and a sorry collection of wildlife in the so-called animal sanctuary.

Once an Overland Telegraph Line outpost, the 1926 pub at **BARROW CREEK**, 90km further on, is one of the oldest around and as quirky as they come, its walls daubed in coarse humour and foreign banknotes (a "bush bank"). Barrow Creek was the site of the 1874 massacre of around 90 Kaytetye people in reprisal for the killing of the two men whose graves are in the forecourt, while 54 years later, the last of the Territory's massacres occurred at

6

For decades there have been apparent sightings of UFOs in the skies over Wycliffe Well and the roadhouse here has well and truly capitalized on this. There is kitsch "alien-obilia", a space ship on the forecourt and scores of newspaper articles inside attesting to the regular sightings of UFOs, if not necessarily bug-eyed ETs. The location has certain parallels with Nevada's Area 51, a sparsely populated semi-desert, and the shady goings-on at the Pine Gap US military base near Alice Springs are just 400km to the south, fuelling the fantasies of conspiracy theorists. Rationalizations of the sightings include that they are merely "glowing birds" or the "Min Min Light" (see p.539). Whatever the truth is, though it might be unfair to suggest that Wycliffe Well's global selection of beers has any connection with the phenomenon, it does at least give you something to do while you watch the skies and wait.

Coniston, 100km southwest, when around 70 Aboriginal men, women and children were killed by a police-led posse following a dingo trapper's death. In 2001, a few kilometres down the highway from Barrow Creek, British tourist Peter Falconio was murdered (although his body was never found) and his girlfriend Joanna Lees abducted by drug-runner Bradley John Murdoch. If you're still up for staying, the pub (☏08/8956 9753) has basic rooms (❶) and unpowered sites ($7).

At **TI TREE**, an Aboriginal community close to the middle of the continent, you can buy artefacts and paintings by the local indigenous communities, and delicious mango ice cream, jam, chutney and wine from the store at Red Centre Farm (ⓦwww.redcentrefarm.com; 9am–7pm daily). Another 58km away, **AILERON** roadhouse (☏08/8956 9703) is the last fuel stop before Alice Springs, 132km away. It's also home to a 17-metre statue of the Anmatjere Man, a memorial to Charlie Quartpot, a rainmaker from the area. There's good pub grub at Glen Maggie Bar, camping (unpowered $8.50), backpacker dorms ($30) and rooms (❹), and Aboriginal art for sale in the gallery.

The Plenty Highway and Tanami Road

Heading towards Alice Springs, the land begins to crumble as you near the MacDonnell Ranges. The **Plenty** and **Sandover highways**, which run off the Stuart Highway 66km south of Aileron, head northeast to Queensland through the scenic Harts and Jervois ranges. After the first sealed 145km, the Plenty becomes a dirt track, deteriorating after Jervois homestead into large ruts and bull dust and becoming a goat track at the NT-Queensland border, where it's called the Donohue Highway. After the first 30km of sealed road, the Sandover is a dirt track for the remaining 520km with only one fuel supply en route at Ammaroo. These routes are susceptible to flooding, impassable after rain, and prone to washouts, remaining shut for months at a time until repaired and graded. They should only be attempted by experienced off-road drivers in a high-clearance 4WD with plenty of spare fuel, food, water and tyres. The Donohue Highway down to Boulia and on to Birdsville is not much better. Unbelievably, road trains use these tracks, so take care.

Twenty kilometres north of Alice Springs, the legendary **Tanami Road** leads 1055km northwest to Halls Creek in Western Australia. The 4WD-recommended road is sealed for the first 188km to Tilmouth Roadhouse, after which it's a corrugated dirt road to the Granites mines just before the Western Australia border, from where things get rougher and sandier. If you're heading from Alice Springs to Purnululu (see p.737), the Tanami is quicker than the bitumen via Katherine. You need to plan your trip well: the only place to get fuel is 322km from Yuendumu at **Rabbit Flat** roadhouse (☎08/8956 8744; closed Tues–Thurs, camping not allowed when closed). While there's little to see on the way, you can drop into the art centre at the Aboriginal community of **Balgo Hills** (☎08/9168 8900), but it's essential to call first.

Before embarking on any of these tracks, it's essential to check the latest conditions online at the official NT Government Road Report website (ⓦwww.ntlis.nt.gov.au/roadreport/) or phone Emergency Services in Alice Springs (☎08/8951 6686) or the Main Roads Dept, Halls Creek (☎08/9168 6007). The Australian government was commencing substantial upgrading work on both the Tanami Road and Plenty Highway in 2009, due to be completed in 2011.

Alice Springs and the Red Centre

Stunningly set at the geographical centre of Australia, **Alice Springs** may have a population of just 26,000, yet it's still the largest settlement in the interior. A modern, compact town in the midst of the MacDonnell Ranges, it makes an excellent base from which to explore Australia's "Red Centre".

The **Red Centre** is the name given to the area around Alice Springs, a historically rich and scenically spectacular region. It includes the lands inhabited by the "Anangu", which means simply "Aboriginal people" in the languages of the Western Desert. Tribes include the Arrernte from the Alice Springs area, Luritja from the Papunya area, the Pitjantjatjara from the region stretching from Uluru/Yulara to Docker River, and the Yankuntjatjara and Antakarinja, from the areas in between. Notwithstanding massacres as late as 1928, the **Aborigines of the central deserts** were fortunate in being among the last to come into contact with white settlers, by which time the exterminations of the nineteenth century had passed and anthropologists like Ted Strehlow were busy recording the "dying race". However, their isolation is thought to have made adjustment to modern life more challenging for them than for Aborigines of the northern coast, whose contact with foreigners stretches back to before European colonization.

Uluru – formerly known as **Ayers Rock** – is Australia's most famous and most visited natural sight, and the primary reason most people head to the Centre. At first sight, even jaded "seen-it-all" cynics will find it hard to take their eyes off its stupendous beauty, but despite its allure, there's much more to the Centre than "the Rock". The **West MacDonnell** ranges, a series of rugged ridges cut at intervals by slender chasms and huge gorges, start on Alice Springs's western doorstep. On the other side of town, the **Eastern MacDonnells** are less visited but no less appealing, while the remote tracks of the **Simpson Desert** to the south attract intrepid off-roaders. To the west, lush **Palm Valley** is accessible via a rough 4WD route (mostly along a riverbed) and linked to **Kings Canyon** via a dirt track, the Mereenie Loop (closed after rain). These sights combined make for a memorable tour of the Outback. Hiring a 4WD is recommended to get the most out of the trip; off-road tracks are detailed in the box, p.624.

When to go and what to take

The aridity of the Centre results in seasonal extremes of temperature. In the midwinter months of July and August the weather is lovely and the light clear, although **freezing nights**, especially around Uluru, are not uncommon. In December and January the temperature can reach 40°C by 10am and not drop below 30°C all night. The transitional seasons of autumn (April–June) and spring (Sept & Oct) are the best times to explore the region in comfort, although in spring there's the chance of rain. Although you may encounter floods and road closures, rain can magically transform the desert into a green garden with wild flowers sprouting everywhere, though generally it's the **midsummer storms** that bring the most rain.

Out here a **wide-brimmed hat** is not so much a fashion accessory as a lifesaver, keeping your head and face in permanent shadow. All walks require a **water bottle**, loose long-sleeved clothing, plus lashings of **sun block**. Australia's venomous (but rarely seen) snakes, rocky paths and the prickly spinifex grass that covers a fifth of the continent, make a pair of **covered shoes or boots** the final precaution to safe, comfortable tramping around the Centre.

Alice Springs and around

The bright, clear desert air of **ALICE SPRINGS** gives the Outback town and its people a charge that you don't get in the languid, tropical north. In Alice Springs, the shopping centre is in the middle of town, not in some distant suburb, so allusions to Nevil Shute's flyblown *A Town Like Alice* or Robyn Davidson's *Tracks* have long been obsolete.

The area has been inhabited for at least forty thousand years by the Arrernte (also known as Aranda), who moved between reliable water sources along the MacDonnell Ranges. But, as elsewhere in the Territory, it was only the arrival of the Overland Telegraph Line in the 1870s that led to a permanent settlement here. Following **John McDouall Stuart**'s exploratory journeys through the area in the early 1860s, it was the visionary **Charles Todd**, then South Australia's Superintendent of Telegraphs, who saw the need to link Australia with the rest of the empire. The town's river and its tributary carry his name, while the "spring" (actually a billabong) and town are named for his wife, Alice.

With repeater stations needed every 250km from Adelaide to Darwin to boost the OTL signal, the billabong north of today's town was chosen as the spot at which to establish the telegraph station. When a spurious ruby rush led to the discovery of gold at Arltunga in the Eastern MacDonnells, **Stuart Town** (the town's official name in its early years) became a departure point for the long slog to the riches east. Arltunga's goldrush fizzled out, but the township of Stuart remained, a collection of shanty dwellings serving a stream of pastoralists, prospectors and missionaries.

In 1929 the **railway line** from Adelaide finally reached Stuart Town. Journeys that had once taken weeks by camel from the Oodnadatta railhead could now be undertaken in just a few days, so by 1933, when the town officially became Alice Springs, the population had mushroomed to nearly five hundred white Australians. The 1942 bombing and evacuation of Darwin saw Alice Springs

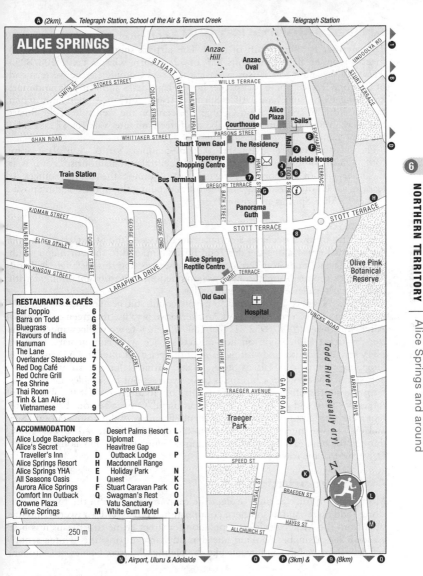

become the Territory's administrative capital and a busy military base, supplying the northern war zone.

After hostilities ceased, some of the wartime population stayed on and Alice Springs's fortunes continued to rise, boosted in the mid-1960s by the establishment of **Pine Gap**, a US base southwest of town, and in the mid-1980s by the reconstruction of the poorly built rail link from Adelaide and the sealing of the Stuart Highway. A tourist boom, spurred by the massive publicity surrounding Azaria Chamberlain's abduction by a dingo at Ayers Rock in 1980, took a knock when direct flights to Uluru were established, but Alice Springs and the surrounding area remain a worthwhile destination in their own right.

Arrival, information and transport

The **airport** is 14km south of town. The airport shuttle (☎08/8953 0310) meets incoming flights and costs $15, or $28 return, while a taxi (☎08/8953 0979) will be about $30. **Buses** arrive at the Coles Complex at the western end of Gregory Terrace. Some backpacker hostels have desks at the airport, and meet incoming flights and buses. Alice Springs's **train station** – open only when trains are due to arrive – is on George Crescent on the west side of the Stuart Highway, just off Larapinta Drive, about a fifteen-minute walk (or $7 taxi ride) from the centre.

The **visitor centre** (Mon–Fri 8.30am–5.30pm, Sat & Sun 9am–4pm; ☎08/8952 5800 or 1800 645 199, ⓦwww.centralaustraliantourism.com) is at the river end of Gregory Terrace (no. 60) adjoining the council offices. It features a well-organized range of brochures detailing the mind-boggling possibilities in Alice Springs and around.

Transport

The centre of town occupies a compact area between the Stuart Highway and Leichhardt Terrace, along the dry Todd River, bordered to the north and south by Wills Terrace and Stott Terrace respectively. Bisecting this rectangle is **Todd Mall**, once the main street, now a relaxing pedestrian thoroughfare lined with alfresco cafés, galleries and souvenir outlets.

The town's sights are scattered, but you could still get around them easily enough on foot in a couple of days. An alternative is to use the green-and-yellow **Alice Wanderer** (☎08/8952 2111 or 1800 722 111, ⓦwww.alicewanderer.com .au; day-ticket $40), a hop-on hop-off bus service with commentary, running every seventy minutes and visiting most of the places of interest. The Yepereneye Shopping Centre, on Hartley Street, is the terminus for the **suburban bus** network; it's best to check bus times before you set out (timetables are available from the tourist office or the Civic Centre on Todd Street). Of the four main routes, #1 West and #4 South are the most useful. Otherwise your best bet is to rent a **car** (see "Listings", p.617) or a **bicycle** from any of the hostels (around $25 a day). There's an enjoyable seventeen-kilometre partly **paved cycle track** through the bush to Simpson's Gap, starting at Flynn's Grave, 7km along Larapinta Drive, west of the town centre.

Accommodation

Most places in Alice Springs (except the caravan parks) are in the town centre along Todd Street and its southern continuation, **Gap Road** – a twenty-minute walk from the Mall, but with a reputation for street crime that means it is best avoided late at night. Booking ahead is advisable during the winter school holidays (June & July) and events like the biennial Masters Games in October.

Motels and hotels

Alice Springs Resort 34 Stott Terrace ☎08/8951 4545 or 1300 134 044, ⓦwww .voyages.com.au. Just over the river, this plush four-star has stylish, spacious rooms (book one overlooking the river) and the fine *Barra-on-Todd* restaurant and Barra Bar overlooking the pool. ❼

All Seasons Oasis 10 Gap Rd ☎08/8952 1444, ⓦwww.accorhotels.com.au. Good motel with landscaped pool area, comfortable rooms and a decent bar-restaurant; breakfast included. ❺

Aurora Alice Springs 11 Leichhardt Terrace ☎08/8950 6666, ⓦwww.auroraresorts.com.au. Slap-bang in the centre, with covered parking, and stylish contemporary executive rooms with balconies. Also home to the excellent *Red Ochre Grill*. ❺–❼

Comfort Inn Outback 46 Stephens Rd ☎08/8952 6100, ⓦwww.comfortinn.com. Tucked under the MacDonnell Ranges on the edge of town, this well-equipped modern four-star hotel has spacious rooms, gym, pool and the *Cat's Tango* restaurant. ❼

Crowne Plaza Alice Springs 82 Barrett Drive ☏ 1800 899 960, ⊛ www.crowneplaza.com. This five-star hotel may be a little dated but it's extremely comfortable with a pleasant pool area and the superb *Hanuman* restaurant. ❻–❾

Desert Palms Resort 74 Barrett Drive ☏ 08/8952 5077 or 1800 678 037, ⊛ www.desertpalms.com .au. Rows of semi-detached villas in lush tropical gardens just over the river, with well-equipped kitchens and pool. ❺

Diplomat 15 Gregory Terrace, corner of Hartley St ☏ 08/8952 8977, ⊛ www.diplomatmotel.com.au. Right in town, a decent four-star motel popular with coach groups and the *Red Sea* restaurant on site. ❺

Heavitree Gap Outback Lodge Palm Circuit ☏ 08/8950 4444, ⊛ www.auroraresorts.com.au. This good three-star at The Gap best suits those with their own transport, although there are shuttle buses into town. There's a nice pool, BBQs, tavern, wallaby-feeding at dusk and indigenous Red Centre Dreaming performances every night. Good discounts off-season. ❺

Quest 9–10 South Terrace ☏ 08/8959 0000, ⊛ www.questalicesprings.com.au. Sleek, contemporary apartments well equipped with great kitchens and laundries. ❼

Swagman's Rest 67–69 Gap Rd ☏ 08/8953 1333 or 1800 089 612, ⊛ www.theswagmansrest.com .au. Basic but fully self-contained rooms sleeping up to three or six people. Double rooms, ❺ $15 per extra person.

🏃 **Vatu Sanctuary** Corner of Knuckey & Babbage sts ☏ 0417 274 431, ⊛ www .vatusanctuary.com.au. Run by the owners of Gondwana Gallery and stylishly decorated with Aboriginal art and Asian furniture, these super-comfortable, self-contained apartments have more character than any in Alice. There's a pool, BBQ area, spa tub, and lots of outdoor chill-out areas. ❼–❾

White Gum Motel 17 Gap Rd ☏ 08/8952 5144, ⊛ www.whitegum.com.au. A notch below the

Swagman's, this place has seen better days, but its self-contained motel units are the closest to the town centre. ❺

Backpackers

Alice Lodge Backpackers 4 Mueller St ☏ 08/8953 1975 or 1800 351 925, ⊛ www .alicelodge.com.au. This converted house in a quiet residential street on the east side of the river is Alice's most popular hostel. Nearer to the centre than it feels, there's a shady garden area and pool. Breakfast, internet and pick-ups included. 6-/3-4-bed dorms $22/25, double ❸

Alice's Secret Traveller's Inn 6 Khalick St ☏ 08/8952 8686, ⊛ www.asecret.com.au. With its family atmosphere, this homey hostel in a converted house near Alice Lodge is one of those love-it-or-hate-it places. Facilities include a big kitchen and off otroot parking; free internet access and breakfast are included. Six-/four-/three-share dorms $22/25/26, double rooms ❷

Alice Springs YHA Corner of Leichhardt Terrace and Parsons St ☏ 08/8952 8855, ⊛ www.yha.com .au. In a historic Art Deco cinema building, this popular hostel is the most central in town, one block from the main drag, with a pool and good-sized kitchen. Only downside is a lack of parking, but don't leave your car by the river as vandalism and theft are commonplace. Four-bed dorms $25.50–30.50, "multi-share" dorms $22.50–27.50.

Caravan parks

Macdonnell Range Holiday Park Palm Place ☏ 08/8952 6111. Camping (powered sites $33, unpowered $29) and cabins with all mod cons in a leafy setting on the south edge of town. Cabins ❺

Stuart Caravan Park Opposite Araluen Centre, Larapinta Drive ☏ 08/8952 2547, ⊛ www .stuartcaravanpark.com.au. The most central caravan park, about 2km west of town, with regular camping and powered sites ($27). Cabins ❺

The Town

Start your tour of town by nipping up to **ANZAC Hill** (off Wills Terrace) for views over Alice Springs to Heavitree Gap, the break in the MacDonnell Ranges that serves as the town's southern entrance. In town, on Parsons Street, is the Old Courthouse and, across the street, **The Residency** (Mon–Fri 9am–4pm, Sat 10am–4pm; free), a neat 1928 dwelling and a tangible symbol of the brief independence Central Australia once had from the Northern Territory. Further along Parsons Street is the **Stuart Town Gaol** (Tues–Thurs 10.30am–noon; free), Alice Springs's oldest building, dating from 1907.

From the shade sails at the centre of Todd Street Mall, a short stroll brings you to the 1926 **Adelaide House Museum** (March–Nov Mon–Fri 10am–4pm; $5), an ingenious convection-cooled building designed by the Reverend John

Flynn, founder of the Royal Flying Doctor Service (RFDS). Once the Bush Nursing Hostel, it was also the place where Flynn and Alf Treager conducted innovative radio experiments using portable, pedal-generated electricity. Early medical and RFDS memorabilia is on display inside. Next door to Adelaide House is the **John Flynn Memorial Church**.

Half a kilometre southwest is the diminutive **Alice Springs Reptile Centre** (daily 9.30am–5pm; $12; ☎08/8952 8900, ⓦwww.reptilecentre.com.au) at 9 Stuart Terrace. Worth an hour of your time, it highlights the countless reptiles that inhabit this region, along with species from elsewhere in Australia. Deadly creatures such as the Inland Taipan, Australia's most venomous snake, vie for attention alongside less fearsome but equally fascinating reptiles such as the comedic thorny devils. The enclosures are informatively captioned and there are feeding displays and playful shows where you'll have the opportunity to handle lizards and a giant olive python.

Opposite the Reptile Centre at 2 Stuart Terrace, the National Pioneer Women's Hall of Fame (March–Nov daily 10am–5pm; $6.50; ☎08/8952 9006, ⓦwww.pioneerwomen.com.au), within the walls of the **Old Alice Springs Gaol**, has a stirring exhibition detailing the achievements of admirable women such as Olive Pink. A passionate defender of Aboriginal rights long before the issue gained importance, Olive Pink, like T.G.H. Strehlow, with whom she briefly worked, dedicated herself to the welfare and preservation of full-blood tribal Aborigines and their lore. When you've had enough of artefacts and memorabilia, visit the **Olive Pink Botanical Garden** (daily 8am–6pm; by donation; ☎08/8952 9006; guided walks April–Oct only; ⓦwww.opbg.com .au), just across the causeway on Tuncks Road. Pink also found time to collect native flora from the surrounding area, which is identified here along pathways winding through the reserve. You can also enjoy the company of local birdlife at "Breakfast with the birds" at 8.30am weekends at the on-site *Bean Tree Café* (Tues–Fri 10am–4pm & Sat–Sun 8.30am–4pm).

The Telegraph Station and School of the Air

The atmospheric buildings of the restored old **Telegraph Station** (daily 8am–5pm, picnic grounds until 9pm; $7.80; ☎08/8952 3993) are tucked in the hills 4km north of the centre on Heritage Drive, accessible by car from the Stuart Highway or by foot along a three-kilometre riverside walk from Wills Terrace. Tranquilly set within a striking landscape by the natural waterhole (take your swimmers) from which the town derives its name, the historic reserve faithfully re-creates the settlement's earliest years. Use the free map for a self-guided **tour** or call ahead to book a guided tour. The leafy grounds, grassy banks of the waterhole, and surrounding picnic area make for a pleasant place to while away an afternoon. The station is also the starting point of the **Larapinta Trail** bushwalk to Standley Chasm in the Western MacDonnells (see p.617).

Across the Stuart Highway at 80 Head St, the **School of the Air** (Mon–Sat 8.30am–4.30pm, Sun 1.30–4.30pm; $6.50; ☎08/8951 6834) offers regular explanatory sessions on this famous Outback institution ("the largest classroom in the world") through which children living on remote stations (in areas still not serviced by telephone or broadband) are taught over the radio. From town, take bus #3 and alight at stop 5 or 11.

Along Larapinta Drive to the Alice Springs Desert Park

Larapinta Drive heads out through the western suburbs to the **Alice Springs Cultural Precinct** (Mon–Fri 10am–4pm, Sat–Sun 11am–4pm; $10;

⊤08/8951 1120), some 2km from the town. While it's not far to walk, take a bus during the warmer months or hottest part of the day. The precinct takes in the **Araluen Arts Centre**, the focal point for the visual and performing arts scene with a 500-seat theatre-cum-art-house cinema and superb art galleries showing paintings from the wonderful Albert Namatjira Collection, the Hermannsburg School and early Papunya art, as well as temporary exhibitions. The **Museum of Central Australia** contains local fauna, and an impressive display of locally found meteorites. In the same building the **Strehlow Research Centre** commemorates the life and work of T.G.H. Strehlow. Around the corner on Memorial Drive is the **Alice Springs Memorial Cemetery**, which includes the graves of pioneer aviator Eddie Connellan, artist Albert Namatjira and legendary, luckless prospector Harold Lasseter (see p.637), after whom, with some irony, the town's casino is named. The **Central Australian Aviation Museum**, located in the Old Connellan Hangar, houses many of the aircraft in which Outback plane travel was pioneered, along with a memorial to the 1929 "Coffee Royale Incident", in which rescuers searching for missing aviator Charles Kingsford-Smith perished in the northern Tanami Desert. Kingsford Smith was accused of staging the crash for publicity purposes, though this was never proved; the memorial poignantly displays the wreckage of the long-lost *Kookaburra* used in the search.

A little further along on Larapinta Drive you will come to Alice Springs's premier attraction, **Alice Springs Desert Park** (daily 7.30am–6pm, last admission 4.30pm; $20; ⊤08/8951 8788, Ⓦwww.alicespringsdesertpark.com .au). Set beneath Mount Gillen, this brilliant park boasts a thoughtful and imaginative design featuring several of the Territory's natural environments. Allow a minimum of two hours for the self-guided walk through the park's creek, sand-dune and woodland habitats, more if you're planning on enjoying the informative presentations, such as the Birds of Prey show. The real highlights are the various aviaries and the large **nocturnal house** where the Territory's myriad, but rarely seen, fauna can be seen scurrying around in artificial moonlight. The park succeeds in blurring the boundary between the surrounding bush and the fenced interior – there's as much birdlife darting about outside the aviaries as in!

Eating, drinking and nightlife

There are plenty of good places to **eat** in Alice Springs. Todd Mall boasts a handful of **cafés and restaurants** with outdoor seating.

Cafés and restaurants

Barra on Todd Alice Springs Resort, 34 Stott Tce ⊤08/8951 4545. The speciality of the Mod-Oz menu at this smart hotel bistro is seafood, with scrumptious dishes like Thai-style barramundi spring rolls and crispy soft-shell crab with lime and mango. Two- to three-course dinner $40/50. Lunch and dinner.

Bar Doppio Fan Arcade, Todd St Mall. With its mismatched furniture, leaflets plastered over the glass, vegetarian options, good coffee and student vibe, this casual café would be equally at home in inner-city Sydney or Melbourne. Mon–Sat 7.30am–5.30pm, Fri & Sat 6–9pm, Sun 10am–4.20pm.

Bluegrass Corner of Stott Terrace and Todd St, ⊤08/8955 5188. This heritage building sees locals cramming the terrace tables for lunch and on Sundays for live jazz. The seafood comes direct from Adelaide's markets, and the laksa is especially good, as are local specialities such as camel and kangaroo. Licensed. Wed–Mon lunch & dinner.

Flavours of India 20 Undoolya Rd ⊤08/8952 3721. Expect classic Indian dishes like chicken tikka and beef vindaloo ($14–17) along with a decent selection of vegetarian mains from $13. Licensed, BYO & takeaway. Daily from 5.30pm.

Hanuman Crowne Plaza Hotel, 82 Barrett Drive, ⊤08/8953 7188. This stylish Asian restaurant, specialising in Thai, Nonya and Indian, serves up a combination of spicy classics (from roast red duck to lamb rogan josh; from $22–35) alongside contemporary dishes such as tangy hanuman oysters ($18) with lemongrass and basil. Daily from 6pm.

Overlander Steakhouse 72 Hartley St ☎08/8952 2159, ⓦwww.overlanders.com.au. This long-established rustic steakhouse is a favourite with tourists who come to order the Drovers Blowout ($60), a huge Territorian meat plate, featuring barramundi, crocodile, camel, emu, kangaroo and beef, served with soup, damper and pavlova. Entrees $16–22 & mains $29–42. Licensed. Daily 6pm till late.

Red Dog Café Todd Mall, southern end. A good spot for breakfast, snacks and coffee in the sunshine from one of the tables on the mall.

Red Ochre Grill Todd Mall ☎08/8952 9614. This stylish bistro has an air-conditioned interior and pleasant patio from which to watch the world wander by whilst enjoying bushtucker-inspired Mod-Oz dishes, such as the meze-style Bushman's Plate ($16.50) and kangaroo soft taco ($16.50) with a glass of Australian wine. A rarity, it's open and serves food from 6.30am until late.

Tea Shrine Yeperenye Shopping Centre, Hartley St. This simple little eatery has a short Asian menu, daily lunch specials ($6.50–8; Friday laksa is a favourite) and, of course, a long list of teas. Mon–Sat 9.30am–5pm.

Thai Room Fan Arcade, Todd St Mall ☎08/8952 0191. Book a table at this casual but hugely popular eatery, for its traditional Thai food – everything from tangy paw paw salad ($9.50) to Masaman curries ($14.50). BYO and takeaway. Mon–Fri 11am–2pm & 6–8.30pm & Sat 5–8.30pm. BYO and takeaway.

The Lane 58 Todd St Mall ☎08/8952 5522. Chic place with a nice vibe, cool music, friendly service, good Mod-Oz cuisine and delicious woodfire pizzas. Tues–Sun 10am–late.

Tinh & Lan Alice Vietnamese Lot 1900 Heffernan Rd, near the airport ☎08/8952 8396. You'll need your own car or a taxi to reach this local favourite out near the airport. Run by a Vietnamese husband and wife team who have their own market garden, the Vietnamese food is delicious, fresh and authentic. Bookings essential. Tues–Sun 11am–2pm & 5–10pm.

Drinking, nightlife and entertainment

Alice Springs' nightlife is low-key. Locals prefer to entertain at home or go camping and enjoy beer around a campfire with friends. However, there's something on somewhere most nights, particularly at weekends. The daily *Centralian Advocate* carries details.

The *Todd Tavern*, at the top of Todd Mall, is the town's landmark **drinking** spot, while weekend nights get busy at the popular *Bojangles Saloon*. *Lasseters Hotel Casino* on Barrett Drive along the river's east bank has the best bars in town, which is handy if you're feeling lucky.

If nothing else appeals, there's a mainstream **cinema** at the top of Todd Mall, and an art-house cinema, along with a programme of theatre, music and dance, at **Araluen Arts Centre** (☎08/8951 1120) on Larapinta Drive.

Events

More energetic activities naturally occur in the cooler months, starting with the **Bangtail Muster** on the first Monday in May, followed by May's **Heritage Week** celebrating Alice Springs's history, a colourful and irreverent parade of silliness. The **Camel Cup races** (ⓦwww.camelcup.com.au) in mid-July are Australia's biggest camel race meeting, ending in a huge fireworks display. The string of **rodeos** along the Track hits Alice Springs in late August, while the town's most famous event, the wacky **Henley-on-Todd Regatta**, kicks off at the end of August (ⓦwww.henleyontodd.com.au) when bottomless boats and other contraptions are run down the dry riverbed. **Todd Mall Markets** are held every second Sunday from 9am–1pm.

Shopping for Aboriginal art

Alice Springs has become the country's foremost centre for **Aboriginal art and crafts** and Todd Mall is full of galleries. Most distinctive are the **dot paintings**, which derive from the temporary sand paintings once used to pass on sacred knowledge during ceremonies. The first dot paintings on canvas

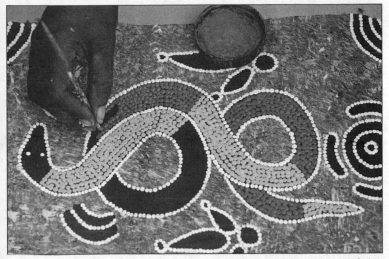

▲ Aboriginal art, Alice Springs

were produced in the early 1970s at Papunya, northwest of Alice Springs, under the encouragement of local teacher Geoffrey Bardon. Bardon encouraged the elders to paint in their own style, not in Western styles. In Aboriginal art, elements such as a footprint, a man, a woman and a star, for example, had a way of being represented in a graphic form. This became the genesis of the Central and Western Desert art movement. What was intended as a kind of constructive graffiti for youngsters was taken up by the elders and has since blossomed into one of the more positive aspects of Aboriginal self-determination, as well as a highly rewarding industry. What's more astonishing is that in the early 1970s, art galleries around Australia rejected much of what is now considered significant work.

Clifford Possum and Billy Stockman were among the earliest of the Papunya artists to find fame, but they've since been superseded by astute, more commercially minded painters from communities throughout the Central Desert, the most successful of whom have experimented with innovative abstract and minimalist styles. Art dealers and gallery owners in Alice have fanned the market, supplying artists with materials and studio space and even subbing them thousands of dollars when funds run low. However, while many artists won't work if they don't feel inspired, others are pressured by their families and communities to keep bringing in the cash from churning out countless variations of their most marketable designs.

Some of the most sought-after **modernists** working in the Alice Springs area include sisters Gloria and Kathleen Petyarre, and Barbara Weir (daughter of the late Minnie Pwerle, see p.616), who all come from the famously productive Utopia community 270km northeast of town; Papunya artist George Tjungurrayi; the Pintupi Walala Tjapaltjarri, who only encountered white people for the first time in 1984 when he and his family emerged from the Gibson Desert; Kathleen Wallace of Santa Teresa's Keringke Arts Centre; and Alice Springs–based Margaret Turner, daughter of Clifford Possum.

Most of these artists are represented by more than one of Alice Springs's top galleries, and it only takes a few hours' browsing to become familiar with their

Buying and playing a didgeridoo

Didgeridoos, the simple wooden instruments whose eerie drone instantly evokes the mysteries of Aboriginal Australia, have become phenomenally popular souvenirs, and even a New Age musical cult. Authentic didges are created from termite-hollowed branches of stringybark, woollybark and bloodwood trees that are indigenous from the Gulf to the Kimberley. Most commonly they are associated with Arnhem Land, where they were introduced around 2000 years ago and are properly called *yidaka* or *molo* by the Yolngu people of that region. "Didgeridoo" is an Anglicized name relating to the sound produced.

Minuscule, bamboo and even painted pocket didges have found their way onto the market, but a real didge is a natural tube of wood with a rough interior. Painted versions haven't necessarily got any symbolic meaning; plain ones can look less tacky and are less expensive. Branches being what they are, every didge is different, but if you're considering playing it rather than hanging it over the fireplace, aim for one around 1.3m in length with a 30–40mm diameter mouthpiece. The bend doesn't affect the sound, but the length, tapering and wall thickness (ideally around 10mm) do. Avoid cumbersome, thick-walled items that get in the way of your face and sound flat.

The key to making the right sound is to hum while letting your pressed lips flap, or vibrate, with the right pressure behind them – it's easier using the side of your mouth. The tricky bit – beyond the ability of most beginners – is to master circular breathing; this entails refilling your lungs through your nose while maintaining the sound from your lips with air squeezed from your cheeks. A good way to get your head round this concept is to blow or "squirt" bubbles into a glass of water with a straw, while simultaneously inhaling through the nose. Unless you get the hang of circular breathing you'll be limited to making the same lung's worth of droning again and again.

Most shops that sell didges also sell tapes and CDs and inexpensive "how to" booklets which offer hints on the mysteries of circular breathing and how to emit advanced sounds using your vocal chords.

The Sounds of Starlight show in Todd Mall (April–Nov Tues, Fri & Sat 8pm; $30; ⊤08/8953 0826, Ⓦwww.soundsofstarlight.com) features Alice Springs didge impresario Andrew Langford and friends and is an entertaining night out – but a "traditional" experience it's not. You'll also be given a free lesson afterwards, if you choose. Women should keep in mind, though, that many Aboriginal communities forbid women to play the didge – as actress Nicole Kidman found out after she played one on German television to promote the film Australia. Besides being heavily criticized for cultural insensitivity, Nicole was later informed that many Aboriginal groups believe that playing it makes women infertile.

idiosyncratic styles; their best works can sell for hundreds of thousands of dollars. Don't fall into the trap that many people do, which is to buy a piece because of the name of the artist rather than because you like it, and always buy from reputable dealers who have relationships directly with the artist.

Of Alice Springs's dozen or so **Aboriginal art galleries**, the most serious include that of the founders of the Central and Western Desert Art Movement, the Aboriginal-owned Papunya Tula Artists, at 63 Todd Mall (Ⓦwww.papunyatula .com.au), which formed in 1971 at the encouragement of school teacher Geoffrey Bardon. Mbantua Gallery, at 71 Gregory Terrace (Ⓦwww.mbantua.com.au), has a cultural museum upstairs with displays on bushtucker, weapons, traditional handicrafts and paintings (Mon–Fri 9am–6pm, Sat 9.30am–5pm, Sun noon–4pm; $6.60), housing works by Albert Namatjira and Minnie Pwerle; and Gallery Gondwana, 43 Todd Mall (Ⓦwww.gallerygondwana.com.au), which specializes in Warlpiri and Pintupi arts. All of these are enjoyable to browse even if you can't afford to buy. Souvenir shops on Todd Mall also sell paintings starting from around

$25, including Red Sand, Desert Art Gallery and Australian Aboriginal Dreamtime Gallery: however, this pieces are purely decorative. The more you spend, the more chance there is of getting a discount, shipping and insurance included. Reputable galleries provide certificates or labels of **authenticity** with each artwork to assure buyers they're getting a genuine article.

To see Arrernte artists at work, visit the Many Hands Art Centre (Mon–Fri 10am–4pm; free) at 29 Wilkinson St, where you can buy reasonably priced paintings, then drop into the nearby Tjanpi Desert Weavers (ⓦ www.tjanpi.com .au; Mon–Fri 10am–4pm) at 3 Wilkinson St, where you can admire and buy beautiful indigenous-made baskets and other woven products.

Listings

Camping supplies Barbeques Galore on the corner of Whittaker and Colsen sts, or Lone Dingo on Todd Mall.

Car rental Thrifty (☎08/8952 9999), on the corner of Hartley St and Stott Terrace, has the usual range of vehicles, but it pays to book ahead. For 4WDs, Britz/Maui (☎1800 331 454) is on the Stuart Highway north of Alice Springs and has fully equipped Toyota Bushcampers sleeping two inside, or Adventurers sleeping four in two roof tents, as well as regular campervans.

Hospital Gap Rd ☎08/8951 7777.

Internet access Try the library on Gregory Terrace (one hour per day limit when busy); Adventchanet on Todd Mall; Outback Internet on the opposite corner (very cheap and open on Sun); or the JPC computer shop in the Coles complex off Bath St.

Maps The Map Shop, Alice Springs Plaza, first floor (☎08/8951 5393), for detailed maps of the Centre.

Permits for Aboriginal Land Central Land Council, 33 North Stuart Highway, PO Box 3321, Alice Springs 0871 ☎08/8951 6320, ⓦ www.clc .org.au. Blank forms and subsequent permits can be faxed. For the WA section of the Great Central Rd (see p.688) get your permit from the Ngaanyatjarra Council, 58 Head St, next to *Sammy's Pizza* ☎08/8950 1711, ⓦ www.ngaanyatjarra.org.au. You can also get permits from the visitor centre.

Police Parsons St ☎08/8951 8888.

Post office Hartley St ☎08/8952 1020.

South of Alice Springs

Several sites of interest are located beyond **Heavitree Gap**, a couple of kilometres south of the centre. The museum and camel farm are reachable by #4 bus, which terminates just off the Stuart Highway. The rest are easily reached by bike, or on the Alice Springs Wanderer bus route.

A few kilometres down the Ross Highway you'll find the **Frontier Homestead** (daily 9am–4pm; free), which offers short rides on camels ($5), plus a camel museum. Back down the Stuart Highway just before the airport, about 10km south of town, the Alice Springs Transport Heritage Centre (daily 8am–5pm; $12) at MacDonnell Siding is home to the **Old Ghan Train Museum** and original Ghan carriages; the **Kenworth Hall of Fame**, which has the first Kenworth truck ever built in Australia; and the **National Transport Hall of Fame**, featuring a collection of old vehicles, including the first road trains used to slog up to Darwin during the 1930s at 30kph.

The MacDonnell Ranges

The **MacDonnell Ranges** are among the longest of the parallel ridge systems that corrugate the Centre's landscape. Their east–west axis, passing through Alice Springs, is broken by myriad gaps carved through the ranges during better-watered epochs. It is these striking ruptures, along with the grandeur and colours of the rugged landscape – particularly west of Alice Springs – which make a few days spent in the MacDonnells so worthwhile. The

A large number of **tour operators** offer adventure, cultural or historic tours throughout the area, best booked directly with the operator, or at one of the travel shops around the corners of Todd Street and Gregory Terrace. Though Uluru could be visited from Alice in a long day, to fully appreciate the Rock, a two- to three-day tour is best, combined with a visit to Kings Canyon. Costs start at $300; the $25 Uluru park entry fee may or may not be included.

Aboriginal Sacred Sites & Culture Tours ☏1800 089 644, ⓦwww .aboriginalculturaltours.com.au. Indigenous guide Patricia Dodds shows visitors local historical and cultural sights through the eyes of the Arrernte people (Mon–Wed & Fri–Sat 10am; from $99).

Austour ☏1800 335 009, ⓦwww.austour.com.au. Daily one-day bus trips to Uluru (from $210) and two-day visits including Kings Canyon (from $405 in a tent or from $475 accommodated).

Australasian Jet ☏08/8953 1444, ⓦwww.ausjet.com.au. Scenic flights around Alice Springs and the MacDonnells (from $95 for 30min) or to Uluru and Kata Tjuta (from $595).

Ballooning Downunder ☏1800 801 601, ⓦwww.ballooningdownunder.com.au; **Outback Ballooning** ☏08/8952 8273 or 1800 809 790, ⓦwww.outbackballooning .com.au; Alice Springs is Australia's ballooning capital and these excellent operators will take you up, up and away – and back down for a traditional chicken and champagne breakfast (from $230 for a 30min flight). Don't wear your best clothes, as the landings are less than smooth.

Beanies, Baskets and Bushtucker ☏1300 369 699. Pitjantjatjara women share their beanie crocheting and basket-weaving skills while sharing stories about bushtucker and culture in the grounds of Alice Springs Desert Park (Tues–Fri 9am–noon; from $77).

Connections ☏1800 077 251, ⓦwww.connections.travel. Professional operation offering two- to five-day camping and accommodated tours through the West MacDonnells, to Kings Canyon and Uluru using comfortable minibuses. As is often the case, the longer tours are the best value.

Dot Painted Mountain Bike Tours ☏0415 815 033. Indigenous-operated half-day mountain bike tours to cultural sites (Wed–Sun only; from $110 per person).

Frontier Camel Tours ☏08/8950 3030, ⓦwww.ananguwaai.com.au. One-hour camel rides down the Todd River plus breakfast or dinner ($110–165), or short rides (from $10).

Mulga Tours ☏08/8952 1545 or 1800 359 089, ⓦwww.mulgas.com.au. Cheap ($250 plus entry fees) and cheerful three-day Rock tours sleeping in swags.

Outback Experience ☏08/8953 2666, ⓦwww.outbackexperience.com.au. Four-wheel-drive day-trips to Chambers Pillar, Rainbow Valley and other spots in the northern Simpson for around $150.

Outback Quad Adventures ☏08/8953 0697, ⓦwww.oqa.com.au. Fun quad-bike rides on a cattle station close to town using automatic machines: all you have to do is turn the throttle and steer (from $109 for an hour's ride). Dress for extreme dust. There's another quad operation at Kings Creek Station (p.628).

Wayoutback ☏08/8952 4324 or 1300 551 510, ⓦwww.wayoutback.com.au. Popular three- to five-day Rock and Canyon tours packed into a Troopcarrier (around $150 a day).

expansive **West MacDonnell Ranges National Park** is best appreciated with at least one overnight stay at any of the campsites mentioned below, while the often-overlooked **East MacDonnells** are a better bet if your time is limited. Both can be visited as part of a tour (see box, p.618) or with your own vehicle – a 4WD is recommended to get the most out of a visit as some of the best spots are along corrugated dirt tracks. For **off-road driving advice** see Basics (p.11) and the box on pp.624–625.

A wonderful way to experience the West MacDonnells is to trek the long-distance **Larapinta Trail**, which follows the ranges, beginning at the Telegraph Station north of Alice Springs and ending 223km to the west on the 1347-metre Mount Sonder summit. The walk is divided into around a dozen sections, but these don't necessarily delineate a day's walk. Trailside water tanks are situated no more than two days' walk or 30km apart. The more impressive and more arduous sections are near town. Section 2 from Simpson's Gap to Jay Creek is 25km long – an overnight stop is advised, while the next section is a short but hard 14km to Standley Chasm with 350m of climbing. Visit Alice Springs's visitor centre for the latest details on conditions and weather. You can also print the trail guide and maps from the NT government website (ⓦ www.nt.gov.au/ nreta/parks/walks/larapinta/; look under "Walks, Talks and Trails").

The West MacDonnell Ranges and Finke Gorge national parks

The **route** described below follows an anticlockwise loop out along Larapinta Drive, then north along Namatjira Drive to *Glen Helen Resort*, from where a 110-kilometre dirt road takes you south past Gosses Bluff to the Mereenie Loop and turn-off (east) for Palm Valley and Hermannsburg, and back to Alice Springs. A total distance of 370km, it can be slow-going depending on the condition of the road after Glen Helen and the Mereenie Loop, which is prone to flash flooding in rain and can be closed for weeks after. The Mereenie Loop passes through **Aboriginal land**; get a permit from the Alice Springs visitor centre and check road conditions; regardless of any advice to the contrary, do not attempt the route if rain is forecast.

About 18km west of town, **Simpsons Gap** (gates open daily 5am–8pm) is the nearest and most popular of the West MacDonnells' gaps, where a sandy riverbed lined with red and ghost gums leads up to a small pool. Black-footed rock wallabies live on the cliffs and there's a **visitor centre** and barbecues. You can cycle here along a seventeen-kilometre bike track. The first stage of the **Larapinta Trail** ends here – a 24-kilometre walk from the Telegraph Station in Alice Springs.

Further along Larapinta Drive are the **Twin Ghost Gums**, immortalized in Albert Namatjira's definitive painting of the Centralian landscape; just beyond is a turn-off north to **Standley Chasm** (daily 8am–5pm; $6), 50km from Alice Springs. Situated on Iwupataka Aboriginal land, this is another very popular spot, where a walk along the cycad palm-lined riverbed leads to a narrow chasm formed by the erosion of softer rock that once lay between the red-quartzite walls. Between 11am and 1pm the eighty-metre-high walls blaze golden red from the overhead sun. There is a café with a terrace and a souvenir shop; black-footed rock wallabies are fed here daily at 9.30am.

Along Namatjira Drive

Another 6km along Larapinta Drive, **Namatjira Drive** turns north amid the West MacDonnell Ranges. Continuing on Larapinta brings you to Hermannsburg and Palm Valley (see p.623). Along Namatjira Drive, a scenic 42km ahead is **Ellery Creek Big Hole** (barbecues, toilets and camping), the biggest waterhole in the area, which floods a large gap in the ranges. Nevertheless,

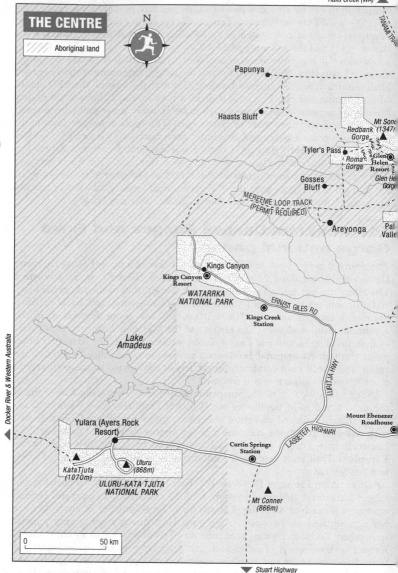

THE CENTRE

Aboriginal land

N

Halls Creek (WA)

TANAMI TRACK

Papunya

Haasts Bluff

Mt Sond
Redbank (1347r
Gorge

Tyler's Pass

Glen
Helen
Resort

Glen He
Gorge

Roma
Gorge

Gosses
Bluff

MEREENIE LOOP TRACK
(PERMIT REQUIRED)

Areyonga

Pal
Valle

Kings Canyon

Kings Canyon
Resort

WATARRKA
NATIONAL PARK

ERNEST GILES RD

Kings Creek
Station

Lake
Amadeus

LURITJA HWY

Yulara (Ayers Rock
Resort)

Mount Ebenezer
Roadhouse

LASSETER HIGHWAY

Curtin Springs
Station

Kata Tjuta
(1070m)

Uluru
(868m)

ULURU–KATA TJUTA
NATIONAL PARK

Mt Conner
(866m)

0   50 km

Stuart Highway

caught between the brief ebb and flow of visiting bus tours, it's a great spot to splash about with the ducks if you can stand the cold water (swimmers are advised not to enter the water without a floatation device). Eleven kilometres to the west is **Serpentine Gorge** (toilets but no camping), where you can do a half-hour walk into the gorge or climb up the ridge to a lookout with sweeping views. As with many concealed perennial pools in Central Australia, the Arrernte believe the pool is the home of a serpent, and even today they visit

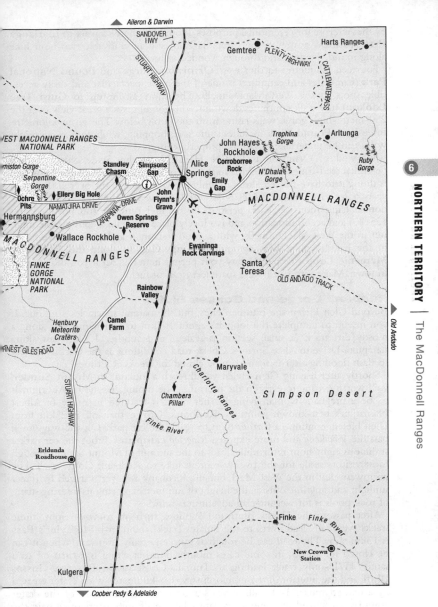

the place reluctantly and never enter the water. In this way, the story acted as a device to ensure the pool – a drought-proof source of water – was never polluted or carelessly used. Just down the road, the **Serpentine Chalet** bush camping area has pitches among the rather arid bushland and a twenty-minute walk to a silted-up dam.

The stunning **Ochre Pits**, signposted off Namatjira Drive, make an interesting diversion. Ochre was a highly valued trading commodity and is still used by the Arrernte for ceremonial purposes. From here there's a walk to **Inarlanga Pass** (a narrow gorge on the Larapinta Trail) and an enjoyable two-hour hike along rounded ridges and through wooded valleys.

Fourteen kilometres further west, **Ormiston Gorge** and **Pound National Park** (barbecues and camping) is one of the most spectacular and easily accessible spots in the West MacDonnells. The short ascent up to **Gum Tree Lookout** (the walk continues down into the gorge) gives a great view over the 250-metre-high gorge walls rising from the pools below. The seven-kilometre, three-hour **Pound Walk** includes some rock hopping, while longer overnight walks can be undertaken by those properly equipped.

Just west of Ormiston is **GLEN HELEN**, another wide chasm with a perennial reed-fringed waterhole in the bed of the ancient **Finke River**, which is thought to have flowed along roughly the same course for over 100 million years. *Glen Helen Resort* (☎08/8956 7489, ⓦwww.glenhelen.com.au; single/double/triple rooms ❻, extra person $25) has fuel, camping (un/powered sites $25/30) and accommodation and is a lovely place to spend a comfortable night out in the West MacDonnells, with a good restaurant and frequent live music in the bar. If you're heading towards Kings Canyon along the 4WD-only **Mereenie Loop** (see p.624), buy your permit here ($2.20) if you didn't get it in town. Make sure you have a spare jerry can of fuel.

Redbank Gorge and Gosses Bluff

Beyond Glen Helen the bitumen ends, but the natural spectacles continue. If you intend to complete the loop, it's about 107km to Hermannsburg along a mostly dirt track (a small section is sealed), and another 126km east along Larapinta Drive to Alice Springs. Check road conditions as the track is subject to flash flooding after rain and can be closed for weeks at a time.

Shortly after leaving Glen Helen you'll reach a lookout to **Mount Sonder**, well worth getting to early in the morning. The mountain, said by Aboriginals to be a pregnant woman lying on her back, is featured in many of Albert Namatjira's best-known paintings. **Redbank Gorge** turn-off is 25km from Glen Helen; continue a further 8km to reach the car park. On the way you'll pass the *Woodland* and more exposed *Ridgetop* **campsites**. From the car park a strenuous eight-hour return hike leads to the summit of Mount Sonder, though most visitors settle for the twenty-minute hike to Redbank Gorge itself. The narrowest cleft in the West MacDonnells, Redbank is never warmed by direct sunlight and, anytime outside the height of summer, exploring its freezing string of rock pools is for wetsuit-clad adventurers only.

After passing the Haasts Bluff and Papunya turn-off to your right (these tracks eventually lead north to the Tanami Track), the turn-off to **Tyler's Pass** is 13km away. The road can be rough as guts, especially after rain, when it can be closed for weeks, in some cases months. Further along is a turn-off to a sandy 4WD-only track leading to Tnorala Conservation Reserve, **Gosses Bluff**, and the interior of the extraordinary two-kilometre-wide crater created by a comet impact 140 million years ago. Inside, the majority of the crater comprises a fenced-off ceremonial site where male miscreants once paid the penalty for sexual indiscretions. A good way to appreciate the wonder of it all is to scramble up to the rim; there's no path, though it's less steep on the outside slope.

South of the bluff, you reach the Hermannsburg–Mereenie Loop junction. Left leads to Palm Valley, Hermannsburg and Alice Springs; right to Kings Canyon and close encounters of the incredibly corrugated kind (see p.628).

Finke Gorge National Park and the road back to Alice Springs

The popularity of **FINKE GORGE NATIONAL PARK** is founded on its prehistoric cycads and the unique red cabbage palms that have survived in the park's sheltered **Palm Valley** for over ten thousand years. Despite the challenging 4WD track leading to the lush valley, the gorge is on every tour itinerary – unsurprisingly, as the forty-minute Arankaia Walk and longer two-hour Mpulungkinya Walk through the palm-filled valley and back across the plateau above are both magical. Visiting the park requires a high-clearance 4WD vehicle, as most of the sixteen-kilometre track follows the sandy and rocky bed of the Finke River, impassable after rain. On the way in or out of the valley, you can climb up to the once-sacred **Kalarranga Lookout** (1.5km, 45min return), giving a fine view over the amphitheatre, a cirque of sandstone cliffs. The park has barbecues, toilets, solar-heated showers and camping.

Now a Western Arrernte community, **HERMANNSBURG**, to the north of the park, was the first Aboriginal mission in the Northern Territory, established by the Lutherans in 1877. You can visit the original 18 mission buildings at the **Historic Precinct** (daily 9am–4pm; $10), one of which has been converted into tearooms and an art gallery. Albert Namatjira and Theodore Strehlow were both born here (see box below). There is a supermarket and fuel (cash only) in town, but no accommodation; if driving the Mereenic Loop, check road conditions at the police station here first.

On the way back to Alice Springs, you'll pass the **Albert Namatjira Memorial** before reaching the Aboriginal community of **Wallace Rockhole**, (☎08/8956 7415) where you can do a self-guided ($6) or an escorted one-hour tour ($14) to see Aboriginal petroglyphs. There is an art centre, fuel and camping here as well.

Albert Namatjira

Born on the Hermannsburg Lutheran mission in 1902, Albert Namatjira, a member of the Arrernte tribe, was the first of the Hermannsburg mission's much-copied school of **landscape watercolourists**. Although lacking much painting experience, Namatjira assisted white artist Rex Battarbee on his painting expeditions through the Central Australian deserts in the 1930s during which his talent soon became obvious to Battarbee, who later became Namatjira's agent. Like all NT Aborigines at that time, Namatjira was forbidden to buy alcohol, stay overnight in Alice Springs or leave the Territory without permission, but at the insistence of southern do-gooders – and against his wishes – he was the first Aborigine to be awarded **Australian citizenship**, in 1956. This meant he could travel without limitations, but needed a permit to visit his own family on Aboriginal reserves, while the house in Alice Springs he longed for was denied him for fear of the entourage he might have attracted. Following the success of his first exhibition in the south, which sold out in three days, he became a reluctant celebrity, compelled to pay taxes on his relatively huge earnings. A shy and modest man, much respected for his earnestness and generosity, he died in 1959 following a sordid conviction and short imprisonment for supplying alcohol to fellow Aborigines.

Critics could never make up their minds about his work, but his popular appeal was undoubted: exhibitions in the southern cities, which he rarely attended, persistently sold out within hours of opening, and today his paintings remain among the most valuable examples of Australia's artistic preoccupation with its landscape.

Renting a 4WD for a few days of off-road driving is great fun and can get you to some beautiful corners of the central deserts. Below are some **4WD-only** routes close to Alice Springs, which could all be linked into a memorable week in the dirt. Pick up information and maps and check road conditions from the Alice Springs Visitor Centre before setting out and ensure you are completely self-sufficient, with plenty of food, water and spare fuel. Remember that 4WD vehicles are not invincible and inexperienced drivers can easily get bogged, lose control or damage the vehicle. The vehicles can also make a mess of the terrain if driven off main tracks, so try to avoid wheel spins and tearing up vegetated ground, which takes years to recover. Make sure the rental company you're using understands and approves your proposed 4WD itinerary and read the advice and carry the gear recommended in Basics, p.43. Ask at Alice Springs's tourist office for the *4×4 Guide* booklet, which details 4WD routes in the area. It's a good idea to hire a recovery kit (rarely included with vehicles), and satellite phone. Although most rental 4WDs are in good shape, closely inspect the vehicle. Also make sure you are appropriately equipped for travelling in remote areas with tow ropes, a second spare tyre, and spare jerry cans. For recommended 4WD rental agents, see the "Listings" for Alice Springs on p.617.

Mereenie Loop Track

The main appeal of the 195-kilometre Mereenie Loop, linking the West MacDonnells with Kings Canyon (allow 3–4hr), is that it avoids backtracking on the usual "Canyon and Rock" tour. However, it is a stunning drive with plenty of desert oaks, river crossings, wild horses, donkeys and dingoes. The corrugations can be fearsome; don't even think about the trip if rain is forecast as it's prone to flash flooding and inaccessible after rain. Obtain a permit at Alice Springs Visitor Centre, Glen Helen or Kings Canyon. Note that you're not allowed to stop or camp.

Finke River Route

With a day to spare and experience with a 4WD, following the Finke Riverbed from **Hermannsburg** down to the **Ernest Giles Road** offers an adventurous alternative to the highway and saves some backtracking. Rewards include stark gorge scenery, a reliable waterhole and the likelihood that you'll have it all to yourself. Before you set off, check the road conditions (℡1800 246 199). On the route follow the small signs for "Kings Canyon".

The hundred-kilometre track starts immediately south of Hermannsburg. After 10km of corrugated road you descend into the riverbed. From here on driving is slow, along a pair of sandy or pebbly ruts – you should deflate your tyres to at least 25psi/1.7bar and keep in the ruts to minimize the risk of getting stuck. The sole designated campsite is at **Boggy Hole**, much nicer than it sounds and almost two hours (28.5km) from Hermannsburg. The campsite looks out from beneath river red gums to permanent reed-fringed waterholes, best seen at dawn as the sunlight creeps across the gorge and the ponds are alive with birdlife.

Beyond Boggy Hole, the track crisscrosses rather than follows the riverbed before taking a roller-coaster ride to the Giles Road across some low dunes thinly wooded with desert oaks – beware of oncoming traffic on blind crests. Boggy Hole to the Giles Road is 65km, so allow at least three hours. If you fancy risking the direct route

The East MacDonnells and the northern Simpson Desert

Heading out of Alice Springs through **Heavitree Gap** and along the Ross Highway you soon reach tranquil **Emily Gap**, Alice Springs's nearest waterhole, 10km from town. This is one of the most significant Arrernte sacred sites, the

to the Ernest Giles Road from the Tempe Downs station track, keep straight over the dunes just after a saltpan instead of turning sharply east; subsequent dunes can be avoided but the Palmer River crossing can be very sandy and may require further tyre deflation. Back on the road, keep speeds down until you can reflate your tyres.

Arltunga to Ruby Gap

Call the ranger at the **Arltunga Visitors Centre** (℡08/8951 8211), 101km east of Alice Springs, for the latest track conditions for this scenic, if bumpy, 47-kilometre drive (allow 2hr) through the ranges. It includes some steep creek crossings until you reach the sandy riverbed of the Hale and the **Ruby Gap Nature Park**. From here, keep to the sandy ruts and inch carefully over the rocks for 5km, at which point you'll need to stop and walk the last 2km to **Glen Annie Gorge**, a dead-end with maroon cliffs, bright green reeds and creamy sand.

Binns Track

Another challenging track (impassable after the rain) heads north from Arltunga past Claraville station and up over the Hails Ranges through **Cattlewater Pass** to the Plenty Highway, 67km or three hours from Arltunga. It's a scenic way of returning to Alice Springs from Arltunga and you're bound to see some hopping marsupials along the way, but ensure you allow plenty of time as it's slow-going in places. Once you reach the Plenty Highway it's a fairly easy dirt road (in dry weather) via Gemtree to the Stuart Highway and Alice Springs, 150km away.

The Finke and Old Andado tracks

More ambitious is the 550-kilometre loop into the fringes of the Simpson Desert along the **Finke** and **Old Andado tracks**, which diverge at Alice Springs's airport and meet at the community of Finke. At the airport, the Finke Track is also known as the **Old Ghan Heritage Trail**, as it follows the route of the old railway all the way past Oodnadatta to Port Augusta in South Australia. On the way, you'll pass stands of desert oak and may see camels, descendants of the original beasts led by Afghan cameleers before the Ghan train reached Alice Springs in 1928. It passes Ewaninga Rock Carvings but detours east before Maryvale to the ruins of Rodinga sidings. The section from Rodinga to Finke is the best part of this route, either on the embankments of the actual railway or on the rougher track alongside it, passing other sidings with interpretive boards on the history of this pioneering overland route. As you near Finke, the red sand ridges create some sandy passages, after which you cross the sandy Finke River itself and enter the community.

After Finke, the nature of the route changes as you traverse overgrazed plains to New Crown station; you may prefer to call it a day here and turn west from Finke to Kulgera on the Stuart Highway. To complete the loop via Andado, head east, recrossing the broad Finke, and follow the denuded pasturelands past Andado homestead and on to the ramshackle but still occupied *Old Andado* homestead. North of here the track remains easy but gets bleaker still as the sand ridges thin out. After a while, the ranges of the East MacDonnells rise from the horizon and bring you back into vegetated and then wooded country for the rough, final 150km past Santa Teresa community and the airport close to town.

start of Caterpillar Dreaming (see Contexts, p.1119.) The Arrernte believe they are Caterpillar people, direct descendants of the Caterpillar ancestors, and they consider this the place of their birth. There are some interesting stylized depictions of the caterpillars on the far side of a natural pool; and again at the equally peaceful **Jessie Gap**, a little further east. **Corroboree Rock**, 47km east of Alice Springs, is an unusual, fin-like outcrop of limestone with an altar-like platform and two crevices piercing the fin. The rock was once a repository for sacred objects and a site of initiation ceremonies, or *corroborees*.

Trephina Gorge Nature Park

Trephina Gorge Nature Park, just 85km from Alice Springs, is one of the most satisfying destinations in the East MacDonnell Ranges, offering superb scenery and a selection of enjoyable walks. **Trephina Gorge**, perhaps the most impressive spot in the eastern part of the range, is a beautiful, sheer-sided sandy gorge whose golden-red walls support slender, white-barked ghost gums and a small natural pool, while huge river red gums grow in the bed providing welcome shade. There's a pleasant **campsite** and two enjoyable walks, the Gorge and Panorama, both taking about 30 minutes. **John Hayes Rockhole** (limited camping space) is actually a series of pools linked by waterfalls through a canyon. The rockhole can be reached either along a rocky four-kilometre track requiring a high-clearance 4WD vehicle or by a four-hour hike from Trephina Gorge. Once there, the ninety-minute Chain of Pools walk runs above the pools before meandering down to the waterhole. Alternatively, the lower pools are accessible on a ten-minute walk from the car park.

Arltunga and N'Dhala Gorge

Five kilometres beyond Trephina Gorge is the turn-off northeast to a corrugated track leading the 33km to **ARLTUNGA**, the site of Central Australia's first goldrush. Allow plenty of time to get here as driving conditions vary depending on whether the road has been graded or not. There's a fascinating exhibit at the unmanned **visitors centre** (daily 8am–5pm; ☎08/8951 8211), where you can pick up walking itineraries.

Arltunga's story began in the 1890s, when, in the midst of the country's first economic depression, gold was discovered by miners originally drawn to the garnets at Ruby Gap (see p.627). Over the next fifteen years, they regularly pushed barrows the 600km from Oodnadatta railhead, groping in desperate conditions for pitiful returns. Arltunga was never a particularly rich field and remains yet another abandoned testament to pioneer optimism. With a high-clearance 4WD it's possible to continue on to Ruby Gap or north over the ranges along the rough-as-guts Binns Track to the Plenty Highway (see 4WD box, p.625).

Further along the Ross Highway is the Ross River Resort (☎08/8956 9711, cabins ❼, bunkhouse $20, camping $15), located at the historic 1890s Loves Creek Homestead, where there's fuel, a bar and restaurant (dinner only); for lunch bring your own food to throw on the barbie. Just before the resort a right turn leads along an eleven-kilometre track to **N'Dhala Gorge**. A high-clearance 4WD is required to negotiate the rough track and wide sandy riverbeds. On the way in you have a chance to appreciate the immense geological forces that have shaped the MacDonnell Ranges, warping formerly horizontal beds by ninety degrees or more. The gorge itself is home to various **Aboriginal rock engravings** representing aspects of Caterpillar Dreaming, with which other sites in the East MacDonnells are also associated; the tall feather-like symbol (also found at Ruby Gorge) is said to represent the stages of a newly hatched moth taking flight.

About 4km before you arrive at N'Dhala, a track to the left (signposted with the "Explorer Territory" logo) leads for a pleasant 13km south through a valley and over a couple of sandy river crossings to a station access track, which joins the Ross Highway just before Jessie Gap.

Ruby Gap and Glen Annie Gorge

From Arltunga, there's a rough 47-kilometre high-clearance 4WD-only track (impassable after rain) along the sandy bed of the Hale River to Ruby Gap and Glen Annie Gorge (see box, p.624–625). Both are beautiful and wild places. Back in 1885, the explorer Lindsay discovered "rubies" while in the process of digging for water, thereby initiating the customary rush for what turned out to be garnets. Once at **Ruby Gap** (no facilities except camping), the drive gets even more challenging, and after 5km you need to leave your vehicle for the final 2-kilometre walk to **Glen Annie Gorge**. At the end of the day, even with the flies handing over to the mozzies, it's one of the most tranquil places you'll find in Central Australia.

The Old South Road and the northern Simpson Desert

Just 14km out of Alice Springs, shortly after the airport turn-off, a sign indicates "Chambers Pillar (4WD)". This is the **Old South Road**, which follows the abandoned course of the Ghan and original Overland Telegraph Line to Adelaide, 1550km away; these days, the sandy route has become part of the Old Ghan Heritage Trail, which takes adventurous off-roaders all the way to South Australia (see box, pp.624–625).

Ordinary cars can easily cover the 35km to **Ewaninga Rock Carvings**, a jumble of rocks by a small claypan that is a sacred Aboriginal Rain Dreaming site, but after the store at **MARYVALE** (shop and fuel) you'll need a 4WD vehicle and to be in the mood for a thorough shaking until Charlotte Ranges. After the ranges there are sand ridges all the way to **Chambers Pillar** (camping), a historic dead-end, 165km from Alice Springs. Named by Stuart after one of his benefactors (who had natural features named after him and his family all the way to the Arafura Sea), the eighty-metre-high sandstone pillar was used as a landmark by early overlanders heading up from the railhead at Oodnadatta, in South Australia. The plinth is carved with their names as well as those of many others, and can be seen from the platform at the pillar's base. If you're not an experienced off-road driver, Outback Experience in Alice Springs (see box, p.618) has full-day tours that include Chambers Pillar.

South to Kings Canyon

Kings Canyon in Watarrka National Park, southwest of Alice Springs, is accessible by three different routes. Most travel the bitumen four-hour 453-kilometre journey south from Alice Springs on the Stuart Highway, then west on the Lasseter Highway, then north on the Luritja Road. More intrepid travellers with a 4WD generally prefer to take either the Mereenie Loop (see p.624) if it's open, or the Stuart Highway, and then head west on the Ernest Giles Road. If you're heading straight down the track from Alice Springs be prepared for an increasingly barren run of nearly 700km to Coober Pedy (itself no oasis; see p.830) in South Australia.

Alternatively, most **tours** of two days or more departing from Alice Springs include Kings Canyon on their itineraries, the easiest and cheapest way to enjoy the canyon. There are also daily **bus services** from Alice Springs to Kings Canyon with Greyhound Australia, or from Ayers Rock Resort with AAT Kings.

The Stuart Highway to Kings Canyon

Around 76km along the Stuart Highway from Alice Springs, the turn-off east to **Rainbow Valley** (basic camping) follows a twenty-kilometre dirt track (some of which is very sandy) to the "valley", a much-photographed outcrop set behind claypans said to produce rainbows following rain. What you are more likely to see is the spectacular way the sunset catches the red-stained walls. This is a wild place to spend the night, best followed in the morning by a climb up the crag.

From the Stuart Highway, the next turn-off west is the Ernest Giles Road for Kings Canyon, a strictly 4WD-only road, inaccessible after rain and closed for long periods. Not far along this track is the turn-off to **Henbury Meteorite Craters**. The extraterrestrial shower that caused these twelve depressions, from 2m to 180m in diameter, may have occurred in the last twenty thousand years, given that one of the Arrernte's names for the place translates as "sun walk fire devil rock". A walk with interpretive signs winds among the craters, long since picked clean of any unearthly fragments. There is camping, barbecues and toilets.

The bone-shaking Ernest Giles Road continues west, joining the sealed Luritja Highway linking Ayers Rock Resort to Kings Canyon. The bitumen road continues west, past **Kings Creek station** (☎08/8956 7474, ⓦwww .kingscreekstation.com.au), 35km from the canyon. Kings Creek has taken to rounding up and raising the wild camels that other station owners regard as vermin. There are camel rides at sunrise or sunset ($7.50), quad tours (from $67) and helicopter flights (from $45). You'll also find a well-equipped campsite (powered sites $33, unpowered $14 per person), safari-style tented accommodation ($65 per person), fuel and a shop/café.

Kings Canyon (Watarrka National Park)

As you cross the boundary of the **Watarrka National Park**, you'll see the turn-off to **Kathleen Springs**, where a walk (90min return) takes you to a sacred Aboriginal waterhole. Once used to corral livestock, it's now a good place to catch sight of colourful birdlife.

Another twenty minutes' drive down the road is **KINGS CANYON** itself. The big attraction here is the three- to four-hour, six-kilometre **Rim Walk** up and around the canyon, one of the Centre's best hikes. **Early morning** is the most popular time, and for a couple of hours from sunrise, visitors swarm out from the car park along the track – if you don't mind missing the sunrise, you might have the place to yourself in the late afternoon when the light is better, but avoid the middle of the day, especially during the warmer months (Sept–April). Undertaken in a now mandatory clockwise direction, the walk starts with a well-constructed stepped ascent (the toughest part of the walk), after which the trail leads through a maze of sandstone domes, known as the **Lost City**, where interpretive boards fill you in on the geology and botany. About halfway along, you clamber down into a palm-filled chasm known as the **Garden of Eden**, bridged by an impressive array of staircases. Coming up the far side, there's an easily missed detour downstream to a shady **pool** where you can swim. The highlight of the walk, looking out from the throat of the canyon above a (usually) dry waterfall, is just a minute beyond, accessible either by wading knee-deep for a few steps round the right bank of the pool, or simply swimming across. Peering from the brink you get a perfectly framed **view** of the sunlit south wall and the canyon below. Returning to the staircase, the walk comes to the very edge of the south wall and then descends gently to the car park. For a different perspective, the easy two-kilometre return walk along the canyon bottom is also worthwhile.

There is no camping at Kings Canyon or in the national park. The nearest accommodation is 10km away at *Kings Canyon Resort* (☎08/8956 7442,

@ www.voyages.com.au) which has luxurious deluxe rooms (●) with decks overlooking bushland, lodge rooms with TV and fridge (sleeping up to six; $39 per person), and grassy **camping** (powered sites $29, unpowered $13 per person). There are two swimming pools, two good restaurants with bars, including *Carmichaels Restaurant* (5.30–10am & 6–9pm) and the *Outback BBQ & Grill* (6–9pm), a café (10am–5pm), service station/mini-mart (7am–7pm), and plenty of cooking and washing facilities at the caravan park. The Sounds of Firelight offers a romantic four-course dinner with wines ($129 per person) served around a fire, under the stars.

Uluru–Kata Tjuta National Park and Ayers Rock Resort

Uluru–Kata Tjuta National Park encompasses **Uluru** (formerly known as **Ayers Rock**) and **Kata Tjuta** (once known as the **Olgas**) and is the most visited single site in Australia. If you're wondering whether all the hype is worth it, the answer is, emphatically, yes. The Rock, its textures, colours and not least its elemental presence, is without question one of the world's natural wonders. While overt commercialization has been controlled within the park, designated a World Heritage Site by UNESCO in 1987, it's impossible to avoid other tourists, but this shouldn't affect your experience.

Kata Tjuta (meaning "Many Heads") lies 45km west from the park entry station. A cluster of rounded domes divided by narrow chasms and valleys, it is geologically quite distinct from Uluru. Public access is limited to the Walpa Gorge (formerly Olga Gorge) and Valley of the Winds walks; none of the domes, including Mount Olga, 200m higher than Uluru, can be climbed.

As the park is on Aboriginal land, you can't go anywhere other than Uluru, Kata Tjuta, the Cultural Centre and the few roads and paths linking them, which explains why these spots get so crowded. All accommodation, camping, fuel, shops and restaurants are at the **Ayers Rock Resort**, part of the settlement of Yulara, just outside the park.

Getting there

It's 200km from Alice Springs to **ERLDUNDA**, a busy roadhouse on the Stuart Highway, from where the **Lasseter Highway** heads to Ayers Rock Resort, 249km to the west. After 56km is *Mount Ebenezer Roadhouse* and later the turning for the **Luritja Highway**, which leads 168km up to Kings Canyon.

The next thing to catch your eye will be the flat-topped mesa of **Mount Conner**, sometimes mistaken for Uluru. *Curtin Springs Station* (☎08/8956 2906; @ www.curtinsprings.com), 11km west of Mount Conner, offers good-value accommodation, including free camping ($2 charge for showers), snug budget rooms (●) and more comfortable en-suite rooms (●). There's a reasonably priced restaurant (daily 7am–2pm and 6.30–8.30pm), as well as a bar, shop, fuel, and station tours. A variety of 4WD excursions to Mount Conner, including climbs, is operated by Uncle's Tours (☎08/8956 2906, @ www .unclestours.com.au; $65–185). You-know-what is now only 106km away.

Ayers Rock Resort and Yulara

The purpose-built **AYERS ROCK RESORT** at the township of Yulara is far from the eyesore it could have been. Low-impact, and environmentally aware,

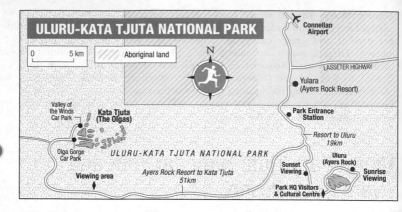

the resort was ahead of its time when it was built between 1983 and 1990, keeping building heights below the adjacent landscape, desalinating bore water (and recycling some of it to keep the gardens fresh), and using solar-powered electricity. Over the years, it has aged well, helped along by occasional refurbishments and carefully considered extensions.

Practicalities

All the town's facilities branch off a central ring road called Yulara Drive, around which a **free bus** circulates (10.30am–6pm & 6.30pm–midnight; every 20min). Within this ring the natural bushland is crisscrossed with walking tracks and a couple of **lookouts** to the Rock and Kata Tjuta on the horizon. In the **Shopping Square**, the hub of the resort, off the north side of Yulara Drive, you'll find a post office, supermarket (daily 8am–9pm), newsagent, cafés, restaurants and an ANZ **bank** (Mon–Thurs 9.30am–4pm, Fri 9.30am–5pm) with an ATM. Apart from hotel bars, the sole liquor store is the **bottle shop** at the *Outback Pioneer Lodge*, where you'll also find the only **laundry**. There's also the all-important **Tours and Information Centre** (daily 8am–8.30pm; ☎08/8957 7524) where you can rent a car and book everything that's going – see the box, p.633, for some ideas. You'll also find coin-operated **internet access** here for $18 per hour. In case of emergencies, there's a Flying Doctor **Medical Centre** (Mon–Fri 9am–noon & 2–5pm; ☎08/8956 2286), as well as fire and police stations near the campsite on Yulara Drive.

All incoming **flights** to Ayers Rock Airport (formerly known as Connellan Airport), 6km from town, are met by a free shuttle bus. If you miss one, there are private shuttles (☎08/8956 2152) for $10 per person. **Buses** will drop you at your chosen accommodation, where you'll be given a town map, or at the Shopping Square. The main Uluru–Kata Tjuta Cultural Centre (see p.632) is located within the park. There is also a **visitor centre** (daily 9am–5pm; ☎08/8957 7377), tucked out of the way between the Shopping Square and the *Desert Gardens Hotel*. Worth an hour's browse, there are absorbing visual displays on the geology, ecology and Anangu connections with Uluru. If you want more detailed information, there are audioguides available in four languages for $2.

Accommodation

The cost of accommodation at Ayers Rock Resort may come as a shock to some, as it's on a par with Sydney and Melbourne rather than Alice Springs, although prices drop a little in summer. No matter what the season, **book ahead**, because the constant flow of tour groups from all over the world fills the hotels quickly, while the campsite overflows during winter and school holidays. All accommodation is operated by the Sydney-based Voyages group who manage Ayers Rock Resort (℡1300 134 044, ℮reservations@voyages .com.au). To ring the actual hotels, call ℡08/8957 7888. To book a site at the campsite, call ℡08/8957 7001 or email ℮campground.reception@ayers .voyages.com.au.

All the places below are situated off Yulara Drive, and none is more than fifteen minutes' walk from the Shopping Square.

Ayers Rock Campground Offers electric BBQs, a small shop and swimming pool and does its best to keep the sites grassy for tents, with camping at $16.50 per person unpowered and powered sites at $19 per person. The campsite also has permanent tents ($95) and air-con cabins that sleep six, with fully equipped kitchens and TV ($150) – if you don't mind sharing bathroom facilities, these are almost a good deal.

Desert Gardens Hotel Excellent four-star property with a native flora theme and spacious, well-appointed studio rooms with all mod cons and stunning views of Uluru from the big balconies. ❾

Emu Walk Apartments Apartments with fully equipped kitchens, a lounge and a balcony, close to the Shopping Square and with either one bedroom ($490) or two bedrooms and a balcony ($570).

Longitude 131° A two-night minimum package ($4200 based on two people sharing) at this unique eco-friendly property includes all meals, alcohol and other beverages, a full schedule of brilliant tours and activities with knowledgeable guides, park entrance tickets, and transfers. A stay here is memorable, from the dramatic arrival (the property is hidden among the dunes) to your first glimpse of the Rock (this is as close as any accommodation gets). The stilted safari-style tent-roofed cabins are super-luxurious and each is individually themed after a Centralian pioneer. Meals in the *Dune House* are a delight (the chef is a Gordon Ramsay-protégé), with a new menu each day based on fine Australian products. ❾

The Lost Camel Hotel Right behind the Shopping Square and set around two courtyards, one with a grassy lawn, the other with an attractive swimming pool, this chic boutique hotel has snug, stylish rooms with CD players but no TV. There's a casual lounge and bar with big-screen TV in the funky foyer. ❾

Outback Pioneer Lodge It's a 15min walk from the Shopping Square, but there's a casual eatery, BBQ areas, camp kitchen, bar and bottle shop on-site. Beds in the twenty-bed single-sex dorms go for $36 while the mixed four-bed dorms go for $44. There are also en-suite motel rooms with a/c, TV and fridge. ❻

Sails in the Desert Hotel Until *Longitude* opened, this smart 5-star was the resort's flagship, and is still the favoured choice of affluent travellers. The spacious rooms come with all mod cons and have a balcony or enormous sun terrace with jacuzzi. There's a superb fine dining restaurant, casual eatery, gallery-cum-gift shop, spa, and a leafy swimming pool area. ❾

Eating and drinking

There are restaurants and eateries at the resort to suit all budgets and you can handily eat at any and bill it to your room even if you're staying at a different property. Like anywhere, prices tend to reflect the level of quality, service and surroundings. There is also a casual licensed eatery, café, takeaway and supermarket at the Shopping Square.

Arnguli Grill Desert Gardens Hotel. This relaxed restaurant dishes up Australian bistro standards that draw upon quality regional produce – appetizers such as Coffin Bay Oysters and beef carpaccio from grain-fed Black Angus, and mains such as Wagyu Beef and the Arnguli Grill Tasting Plate featuring barramundi, smoked kangaroo and slow-cooked crocodile served with bush plum chutney and wild lime pickle. The sticky date pudding is scrumptious.

Bough House Restaurant Outback Pioneer Lodge. This casual place offers a buffet laden with traditional Aussie favourites including countless meats, salads and desserts. A wheelbarrow ride back to your room is extra. Nearby, you'll find the Pioneer BBQ where you can cook-your-own steak

(6–9.30pm) for around $20 including unlimited salad, and an all-day kiosk selling takeaway fish and chips or burgers.

Gecko's Café Shopping Square. A laid-back bistro and bar serving up Mediterranean-style dishes, including pasta and wood-fired pizza, along with steaks, burgers and sandwiches, from around $18–30. Mid-morning to late.

Kuniya Restaurant Sails in the Desert. The resort's finest restaurant after *Longitude*'s Dune House serves up elegant and innovative contemporary Australian cuisine with European and Asian accents. Expect to see dishes such as spiced kangaroo carpaccio with truffled parmesan

shavings, sourdough grissini, rocket and baby capers ($23) and marron with grilled asparagus risotto, pancetta with crispy soft-shell crab and crab bisque ($55). Dinner only.

Sounds of Silence Desert location. If you fancy the idea of cocktails overlooking Uluru while the sun goes down to a live didge soundtrack, followed by dinner under the stars, then sign up for the popular Sounds of Silence, booked at the hotel tour desks. The food can be hit and miss but the talks by both the didgeridoo player and astronomer are brilliant, and it's a great way to meet fellow travellers. Buses pick up from the hotels one hour before sunset. A pricey $149 per person.

Uluru–Kata Tjuta National Park

And the dead tree gives no shelter, the cricket no relief,
And the dry stone no sound of water. Only
There is shadow under this red rock
(Come in under the shadow of this red rock)

T.S. Eliot, *The Wasteland*

The entry fee for **ULURU–KATA TJUTA NATIONAL PARK** (daily from one hour before dawn to one hour after dusk; $25, under-16s free) allows unlimited access for up to three days, though it's easily extendable. Besides the two major sites of Uluru and Kata Tjuta the park incorporates the closed Aboriginal community of Mutujulu, near the base of the Rock, the site of the original caravan park before the resort was built.

The strikingly designed **Uluru–Kata Tjuta Cultural Centre** (daily 7am–6pm, last entry 5.30pm; ☏08/8956 1128; free), situated 1km before the Rock, opened in 1995, on the tenth anniversary of the handback of Uluru to its traditional owners. The compelling exhibition covers aspects of traditional

▲ Uluru

Uluru National Park: tours from Ayers Rock Resort

All tours can be booked at your hotel desk or at the **Tours and Information Centre** in the Shopping Square, but note that some do not include the $25 park entry fee, so you need to have your permit with you. **Car rentals** can also be booked at the Tours and Information Centre or directly from Hertz (☏08/8956 2244), Avis (☏08/8956 2266) and Thrifty (☏08/8956 2030) for around $60 a day for a medium-sized vehicle, including 100km free mileage.

Anangu Tours ☏08/8950 3030, ⓦwww.ananguwaai.com.au. Indigenous cultural tours focused on Dreamtime myths, traditional customs and bushtucker along the Liru, Kuniya and Mala walks at Uluru, led by a local Aboriginal guide and an interpreter from around $87 (self-drive $69) for a 3hr 30min tour with pick-ups. Unfortunately, the advertised "small groups" can consist of up to 35 people.

Discovery Ecotours ☏08/8956 2563, ⓦwww.ecotours.com.au. Small group tours around Uluru and Kata Tjuta with local experts from $84. For $115 the morning Uluru Walk circling the Rock is particularly informative, covering both scientific and cultural aspects – perhaps the best tour in the park. The Spirit of Uluru (same price) covers a similar area but is vehicle-based. Both tours include breakfast. Also has afternoon tours (3–4hr, including walks) to Kata Tjuta and Mount Conner from around $80 to $233 with dinner.

Professional Helicopter Services ☏08/8956 2003. Fifteen-minute helicopter rides over the Rock from $115, with longer options such as one covering Uluru (Ayers Rock) and Kata Tjuta (the Olgas) in half an hour ($220).

Scenic Flights ☏08/8956 2345, ⓦwww.ayersrockflights.com.au. Scenic flights (40min; $165) over Uluru and Kata Tjuta, or add Kings Canyon and Lake Amadeus for $410 (2hr). The half-day Ultimate Outback ($665) gives you enough time to do a walk at Kings Canyon, while an Aboriginal Art Tour ($445) stops at engravings and community art centres.

Uluru Camel Tours ☏08/8950 3030, ⓦwww.ananguwaai.com.au. Operated by Anangu Tours (see above), sunrise and sunset camel rides are on offer from $99.

Uluru Express ☏08/8956 2152, ⓦwww.uluruexpress.com.au. Not really a tour but a small minibus that shuttles you from your accommodation to the Rock or the Olgas (from $60/$65 for a sunrise/sunset trip to $160 for a three-day pass, including park entry fee). Excellent if you don't have your own transport.

Uluru Motorcycle Tours ☏08/8956 2019. Pillion rides round the Rock on the back of a Harley-Davidson. Sunrise tours lasting an hour and a half $160, two-hour rental from $275.

life and customs of the indigenous peoples of the area, Dreaming stories related to Uluru, land care and bushtucker know-how. The centre also houses a café, souvenir shop and two galleries: allow at least an hour to look around.

While you're here drop by the National Parks **information desk** to check the schedule for the free ninety-minute ranger-guided walks (usually 8am Oct–April, 10am May–Sept). You could also take a look at the exhibition on the park's geology, flora and fauna, and pick up the informative *Park Notes* on various topics. The park is home to over 400 species of plants, 25 native mammals, 178 different birds and no less than 72 species of reptiles, and features subtly diverse habitats ranging from spinifex-covered sand hills to desert oak woodlands.

Maruku Arts specializes in rustic handicrafts from the Central and Western Desert, such as boomerangs, spears and music sticks, while Walkatjara Arts sells fine paintings from the talented local artisans, some of whom have exhibited at Australia's best museums and galleries. You can walk the 4km from the Cultural Centre to the base of the climb along the **Liru Walk**.

Uluru

It is thought that Aboriginal people arrived at the Rock over 20,000 years ago, having occupied the Centre more than 10,000 years earlier. These days **Uluru** straddles the ancestral lands of the people who still speak the Yankunytjatjara and Pitjantjatjara dialects of what is called the Western Desert Language (the most used and, area-wise, most extensive of Aboriginal languages). They survived in this semi-arid environment in small mobile groups, moving from one waterhole to another. Water was their most valued resource, and so any site like Uluru or Kata Tjuta which had permanent waterholes and attracted game was of vital practical – and therefore religious – significance.

The first European to set eyes on Uluru was the explorer Ernest Giles, in 1872, but it was a year later that William Gosse followed his Afghan guide up the Rock and thereby made the first ascent by a European, naming it **Ayers Rock** after a South Australian politician. With white settlement of the Centre came the relocation of its occupants from their traditional lands, to enable pastoralists' stock to deplete the fragile desert environment.

The first tourists visited the Rock in 1936, and in 1958 the national park was excised from what was then an Aboriginal reserve. Sadly, it wasn't long before tour operators succeeded in having most of the people who lived in the park relocated to a new community at Docker River (Kaltukatjarra), 300km to the west, close to the Western Australia border. By the early 1970s the tourist facilities in the park were failing to cope and the purpose-built township and resort of Yulara was conceived and completed within a decade. At the same time the traditional custodians of Uluru began to protest about the desecration of their sacred sites by tourists, who at that time could roam anywhere. After a long land-claim the park was subsequently returned with much flourish to the Yankunytjatjara and Pitjantjatjara peoples in 1985. Reclaimed, the site was initially unchanged under Aboriginal ownership, since it was a condition of handback that the park was leased straight back to the Department of Environment and Heritage, which now jointly manages the park with the Anangu.

These days over 400,000 tourists visit the park every year and, as many come in bus tour groups, the place can sometimes feel crowded.

Anangu culture

Uluru, Kata Tjuta and the surrounding desert are integral to a culture whose holistic cosmology sees the Anangu – here, the Pitjantjatjara and Yankunytjatjara Aboriginal peoples of the Western Desert – as having their land, laws and moral systems, or *Tjukurpa/Wapar*, as central to their belief system. *Tjukurpa* (in Pitjantjatjara)/ *Wapar* (in Yankunytjatjara) is a complex concept that encompasses the past, present and future; the creation period when the ancestral beings created the world; the relationship between people, plants, animals and the land; and the knowledge of how these relationships formed, what their meaning was, and how they should be maintained through daily life and ceremony. *Tjukurpa/ Wapar* provides the Anangu with a connection with the past and a moral code. In Aboriginal society their stories (which can sound simplistic when related to tourists) acquire more complex meanings as an individual's level of knowledge increases with successive initiations. (The Pitjantjatjara translation, *Tjukurpa*, is mainly used by guides at Uluru.)

Uluru is actually the name of one of the many temporary waterholes near the summit. While Uluru has been considered to be a key intersection along many "Dreamtime" or "Dreaming" trails (Bruce Chatwin's book described them as "Songlines"), these concepts were created by non-Aboriginal people; to the Anangu the stories are not "dreams", but are real. Nor is Uluru, as one often reads, the pre-eminent shrine to which Aborigines flocked like pilgrims from around the country, although Uluru was important to the Anangu as a reliable source of water and food and is still an important site for ceremony. Sites where significant events in stories took place were linked by iwara (tracks), sometimes stretching hundreds of kilometres. The **Mala** (rufous hare wallaby) *Tjukurpa* involves three groups of Mala people who travel from the north to Uluru. When you visit the Cultural Centre, join an Anangu tour, and read the interpretive signs at the base of Uluru you will also learn about other *Tjukurpa*, such as the **Liru** (poisonous snake), **Kuniya** (python) and **Kurpany** (monster dog).

Geology

The reason Uluru rises so dramatically from the surrounding plain is because it is a **monolith** – that is, a single piece of rock. With few cracks to be exploited by weathering, and the layers of very hard, coarse-grained **sandstone** (or arkose) tilted to a near-vertical plane, the Rock successfully resists the denudation of the landscape surrounding it. If one can visualize the tilted layers of rock, then Uluru is like a cut loaf, its strata pushed up to near-vertical slices so that from one side you look at the flat ends (the classic, steep-sided sunset profile). Elsewhere the separate vertical layers or slices are clearly evident as eroded grooves – the pronounced fluting and chasms along the Rock's southeast and northwest flanks. Brief, but spectacular, waterfalls stream down these channels following storms. In places, the surface of the monolith has peeled or worn away, producing bizarre features and many caves, mostly out-of-bounds but some accessible on the Kantju Gorge walk left of the car park by the start of the climb. The striking orangey-red hue, enhanced by the rising and setting sun, is merely superficial, the result of oxidation ("rusting") of the normally grey sandstone which can be seen in these caves.

Up and around Uluru

You can appreciate Uluru in any number of ways on various tours, but to climb or not to climb…that is the question. "Anangu don't climb" is the oft-repeated message found at the base of the climb, along with the plea that "Anangu feel sad" when someone hurts themselves or dies on the Rock.

Many visitors to the Rock do attempt the hour-long **climb** to the summit, regardless of Anangu sentiment, but make no mistake, if you do decide to climb, it will probably be the greatest exertion you will undertake during your visit to Australia. Around a third who try give up and, on average, one tourist a year dies, usually from a heart attack, with scores more needing rescuing – action that puts rescuers in danger. If you slip or collapse you'll roll straight back to the car park. But with a firmly attached hat, plenty of water, secure footwear and frequent rests, you can safely attain the end of the chain from where the gradient eases off considerably and continues up and down gullies to the **summit**, often a windy spot, especially in the morning. Most people hang around only long enough for their legs to de-jellify and then climb back down; the daunting view into the car park can cause some freak-outs. But the summit plateau is quite an interesting place with gnarled trees surviving in wind-scooped gullies. Take great care, especially near the edges. And in case you're wondering, mobile phones do work on the summit.

If you're at all unfit or are nervous about heights and exposed places, do not attempt the climb. These days, it is regularly closed during high winds or by 8am if the temperature that day is expected to exceed 36°C. During August/September and April/May it gets windy; November to January is the hottest period when temperatures can hover around or above 40°C; and January to March is wet when the annual average of 300mm of rain can fall in the park (though this figure is extremely variable); it can also rain during the build-up and lightning season from late November through December. Daily weather forecasts are posted in the resort's accommodation and information centres.

Far less strenuous, no less satisfying and certainly more in keeping with the spirit of the place are the **walks** one can take along the base of the rock. At the very least, the one-kilometre Kuniya Walk from the Kuniya car park to **Mutitjulu Waterhole**, a perennial pool, rock art site and scene of epic ancestral clashes, is recommended. In the other direction from the base of the climb at the Mala car park, the two-kilometre Mala Walk to **Kantju Gorge** is even better, passing unusually eroded caves, more rock art, as well as pools shaded by groves of desert oaks, ending at the huge cliff above Kantju Gorge itself. Best of all is combining this with the 9.8-kilometre Base Walk **around the Rock**, which takes three to four hours, including time for nosing about. It offers a closer look at some Anangu sites (though most are closed – heed any warning notices), as well as a chance to appreciate the extraordinary textural variations and surface features you'll have noticed if driving round the rock. Remember, though, to take plenty of water, hat and appropriate footwear.

Kata Tjuta

The "Many Heads", as **Kata Tjuta** – formerly the **Olgas** – translates from the local Aboriginal languages, are situated 53km from the resort or Uluru. This remarkable formation may have once been a monolith ten times the size of Uluru, but has since been carved by eons of weathering into 36 "monstrous domes", to use explorer Ernest Giles' words, each smooth, rounded mass divided by slender chasms or broader valleys. The composition of Kata Tjuta – markedly different from Uluru's fine-grained rock – can be clearly seen in the massive, sometimes sheared, boulders set in a **conglomerate** of sandstone cement. Access to this fascinating maze is unfortunately limited to just two walks, in part because of earlier problems with overambitious tourists, but also because the east of Kata Tjuta is a site sacred to Anangu men so is not accessible to the public.

The first of the permitted walks, the 2.6-kilometre **Walpa Gorge Walk**, involves an easy stroll into the dead-end chasm flanking Mount Olga (which, at 1070m, is the highest point in the massif), with dramatic views on the return leg. Better by far is the **Valley of the Winds Walk**, a 7.5-kilometre loop which takes about three hours, or the two-kilometre walk to **Karu Lookout**. This is as much as you can see of Kata Tjuta's interior. The longer stretch from Karu Lookout onwards is closed at 11am if temperatures are forecast at 36 degrees or higher.

The Great Central Road

From Kata Tjuta the **Great Central Road** leads west over 1100km to Laverton, 350km northeast of Kalgoorlie. The track is also known as the "Warburton Road" or, to tourism-marketing types, the "Outback Highway". Work on the road has recently been completed, and, while it's still unsealed, the road has been raised, gravel has been laid, and drainage improved, so the duration of road closures following rain is reduced. It's still important to check conditions well ahead of travel so you can plan around any closures.

A **permit** (free) is needed to travel the Great Central Road and can easily be obtained in Alice Springs or in Perth, either in person at the Central Land Council (CLC) in Alice Springs (it can take up to three days to get the pass, which then lasts for the duration of the drive) over the counter at the Ngaany-atjarra Council, which covers most of the Western Australia section (for addresses see "Listings", p.617 – or, if coming from Perth, p.654); or (by far the easiest option) online at ⓦ www.dia.wa.gov.au/Land/Entry-Permits/. Showing the CLC permit at the entrance to Uluru national park allows nonstop transit through the park without paying the entry fee. Even once you're out of the park, both permits are for a **direct transit only**. You're not allowed to stop anywhere along the way and only camp at the designated campsites next to roadhouses.

As long as you don't get caught in a storm (check weather forecasts and do not attempt the route if rain is predicted), a 4WD isn't necessary on the Great Central Road but the usual precautions for driving on remote dirt roads should be taken: take more than enough fuel (note unleaded petrol restrictions below), satellite phone, spare tyres and water, especially in summer. Filling up at Yulara, the greatest diesel range needed is around 350km, while for modern vehicles specifically requiring unleaded petrol, it's a rather daunting 816km to **Tjukayirla roadhouse**. The restricted availability of petrol exists to curb the epidemic of petrol-sniffing which has claimed many lives in remote Aboriginal communities. Opal is a non-stupefying unleaded petrol substitute available at the Warakunna and Warburton roadhouses which works fine in most vehicles designed to use unleaded. Fuel prices are around 25 percent higher than in Alice Springs.

Along the road

Scenically the first half of the route is more interesting, passing **Lasseters Cave** in the Petermann Ranges where the prospector **Harold Lasseter** sheltered with an Aboriginal family in 1931 after his camels bolted. He died trying to get to the Olgas, and the location of the now legendary gold claim he had pegged went with him. Soon after, a dense woodland of desert oaks spreads across the valley leading to the Aboriginal community of **DOCKER RIVER** (or **Kaltu-katjara**; store), 240km from Yulara (basic camping 2km down the road). Ten kilometres later you reach the Western Australia border with the Rawlinson Ranges to the north and, soon after, more desert oaks.

Next up is **WARAKURNA** (**Giles**) community, where there's camping ($13–15 per person) plus budget and self-contained motel rooms (☎08/8956 7344; ❹–❻), as well as a store, Opal and diesel. West from here the land flattens all the way to **WARBURTON**, more or less halfway between Yulara and Laverton, where there's a roadhouse (☎08/8956 7344), Opal and diesel, a store and a campsite round the back with budget and motel rooms (❹–❺). Just past the roadhouse is the Ngaanyatjarra shire office with a café and **gallery** which is well worth a look (some local paintings are also on show at the Kalgoorlie's Mining Hall of Fame, see p.687). From Warburton the 255km to **Tjukayirla roadhouse** (unleaded petrol and diesel, plus camping $34 per person and rooms ❸) and the following 320km to **LAVERTON** look very much like each other, especially if you're concentrating mainly on not joining the countless roadside wrecks. Laverton itself is not an overly noteworthy spot to rejoin civilization – if you have it in you, **LEONORA** is just another 134km down the road.

Travel details

Trains

The 'Ghan' train service between Alice Springs and Darwin runs twice-weekly in both directions.
Alice Springs to: Adelaide (Thurs & Sun; 24hr); Darwin (Mon & Thurs; 24hr).
Darwin to: Alice Springs (Wed & Sat; 23hr) and on to Adelaide (51hr).

Buses

Alice Springs to: Adelaide (1 daily; 20hr); Darwin (1 daily; 22hr); Katherine (1 daily; 17hr; change here for WA); Tennant Creek/Three Ways Roadhouse (1 daily; 7hr; change at Tennant Creek for Queensland destinations); Yulara (1 daily; 5hr).
Darwin to: Alice Springs (1 daily; 22hr); Katherine (1 daily; 4hr; change for WA); Tennant Creek/Three Ways Roadhouse (1 daily; 14hr).
Katherine to: Alice Springs (1 daily; 17hr); Darwin (1 daily; 4hr); Kununurra (1 daily; 6hr 30min); Tennant Creek/Three Ways Roadhouse (1 daily; 10hr).
Tennant Creek to: Alice Springs (1 daily; 7hr); Darwin (1 daily; 14hr); Katherine (1 daily; 10hr); Townsville (1 daily; 20hr).

Domestic flights

Alice Springs to: Adelaide (1–2 daily; 2hr); Brisbane (1–2 daily; 2hr 35min); Darwin (1–2 daily; 2hr); Melbourne (1–2 daily; 2hr 35min); Sydney (1–2 daily; 3hr); Yulara (1–2 daily; 50min).
Darwin to: Adelaide (5 weekly, more via Alice Springs; 3hr 35min); Alice Springs (1–2 daily; 2hr); Brisbane (2–3 daily; 4hr); Broome (1 daily; 2hr); Cairns (1 daily; 2hr 25min); Perth (1 daily; 3hr 45min).
Yulara (Ayers Rock) to: Alice Springs (1–2 daily; 45min); Brisbane (1 daily; 5hr 30min); Melbourne (1 daily; 6hr 25min); Perth (3–5 weekly; 4hr 30min); Sydney (1–2 daily; 4hr 30min).

International flights

Darwin to: Denpasar, Bali (3 weekly direct); Kuala Lumpur, Malaysia (1 direct weekly, or change at Singapore); Kupang and Dili, East Timor (4 weekly); Singapore (2 daily).

7

Western Australia

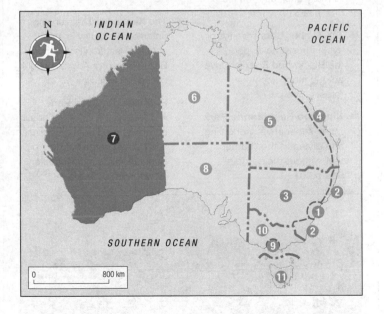

CHAPTER 7

Highlights

＊ **South Coast** Between Walpole and Cape Le Grand you'll find sublime sandy beaches and crescent bays squeezed between granite headlands pounded by the Southern Ocean. See p.652

＊ **Fremantle** Eclectic, authentic and alive – base yourself here instead of Perth's CBD to really soak up Freo life. See p.655

＊ **Tall Timber Country** Hike or cycle forest tracks, paddle the Blackwood River or drive among magnificent karri forests. See p.672

＊ **Ningaloo Reef Marine Park** Enjoy superlative snorkelling and diving at the "barrier reef without the barriers". See p.701

＊ **Shark Bay** The friendly Monkey Mia dolphins are still No.1 on everyone's to-do list, but there's much more to this incredibly biodiverse region. See p.701

＊ **Karijini National Park** Take a detour inland to experience exhilarating camping and canyoning in gorgeously gorge-ridden Karijini. See p.715

＊ **The Kimberley** The stunning, untamed Kimberley is the country's last frontier, although Baz Luhrmann's *Australia* might change all that. See p.721

＊ **Purnululu National Park** Accessible only by 4WD or air, but the striped beehive domes and narrow gorges of the Bungle Bungle massif make it all worthwhile. See p.737

▲ The Bungle Bungles

Western Australia

W estern Australia (WA) covers a third of the Australian continent, yet has a population of just 1.9 million. Conscious of its isolation from the more populous eastern states or indeed anywhere else, WA is ironically the most suburban of Australian states: almost all of its inhabitants live within 200km of Perth and most of the rest live in communities strung along the coastline. The state offers an enticing mix of Outback grandeur and laid-back living, albeit more dispersed than elsewhere, and is attracting increasing numbers of tourists keen to break away from "the East", as the rest of Australia is known in these parts.

Perth retains the leisure-oriented vitality of a young city, while the atmospheric port of **Fremantle**, really just a suburb of the city, resonates with a largely European charm. South of Perth, the wooded hills and trickling streams of the **southwest** support the state's celebrated wine-growing region and a popular holiday-making area, and the giant **eucalyptus forests** around **Pemberton** further ripen a land fed by generous winter rains. East of the forests is the state's intensively farmed **wheat belt**, an interminable man-made prairie struggling against the saline soils it has created. Along the Southern Ocean's stunning storm-washed coastline, **Albany** is the primary settlement, part summer holiday, part retirement resort; the dramatic granite peaks of the **Stirling Ranges** just visible from its hilltops are among the most botanically diverse habitats on the planet. Further east, past **Esperance** on the edge of the Great Australian Bight, is the **Nullarbor Plain**, while inland are the Eastern Goldfields around **Kalgoorlie**, the largest inland town in this region and a survivor of the century-old mineral boom on which WA's prosperity is still firmly based.

While the temperate southwest of WA has been tamed by colonization, the north of the state is where you'll discover the raw appeal of the **Outback**. The virtually unpopulated inland deserts are blanketed with spinifex and support remote Aboriginal and mining communities, while the west coast's winds abate once you venture into the tropics north of **Shark Bay**, home of the friendly dolphins at **Monkey Mia**. From here, the mineral-rich **Pilbara** region fills the state's northwest shoulder, with the dramatic gorges of the **Karijini National Park** at its core. Visitors also home in on the submarine spectacle of the easily accessible **Ningaloo Reef**, which surrounds the beaches of the **Cape Range National Park** – those in the know rate it more than Queensland's attention-grabbing Barrier Reef.

Northeast of the Pilbara, the **Kimberley** is regarded as Australia's last frontier. **Broome**, once the world's pearling capital, is a beacon of civilization in this

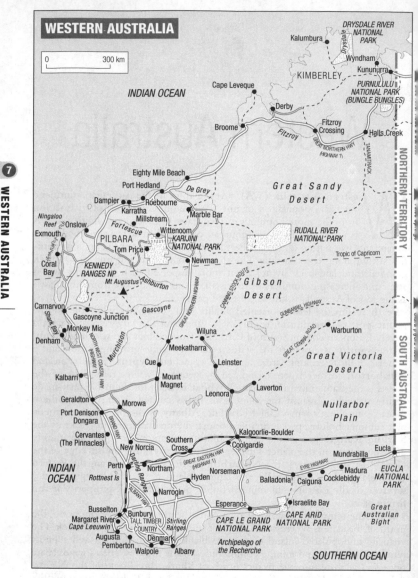

WESTERN AUSTRALIA

DRYSDALE RIVER NATIONAL PARK
Kalumbura
Wyndham
Kununurra
KIMBERLEY
PURNULULU NATIONAL PARK (BUNGLE BUNGLES)
Cape Leveque
INDIAN OCEAN
Derby
Fitzroy Crossing
Halls Creek
Broome
Fitzroy
GREAT NORTHERN HWY (HIGHWAY 1)
TANAMI TRACK
Eighty Mile Beach
Port Hedland
De Grey
Great Sandy Desert
Dampier
Roebourne
Karratha
Millstream
Marble Bar
Fortescue
RUDALL RIVER NATIONAL PARK
Ningaloo Reef
Onslow
Exmouth
PILBARA
Wittenoom
KARIJINI NATIONAL PARK
Tom Price
Coral Bay
KENNEDY RANGES NP
Newman
Tropic of Capricorn
Mt Augustus
Ashburton
Gibson Desert
Carnarvon
Gascoyne Junction
Gascoyne
CANNING STOCK ROUTE
GUNBARREL HIGHWAY
Shark Bay
Monkey Mia
Denham
Murchison
Wiluna
Warburton
GREAT CENTRAL ROAD
Meekatharra
Great Victoria Desert
Kalbarri
Cue
Leinster
NORTH WEST COASTAL HWY (HIGHWAY 1)
Mount Magnet
Geraldton
Morowa
Leonora
Laverton
Port Denison
Dongara
BRAND HWY
Nullarbor Plain
Cervantes (The Pinnacles)
New Norcia
Southern Cross
Kalgoorlie-Boulder
Coolgardie
Mundrabilla
Eucla
Perth
Northam
GREAT EASTERN HWY (HIGHWAY 1)
Madura
EUCLA NATIONAL PARK
INDIAN OCEAN
Rottnest Is
Darling Ranges
Hyden
Norseman
EYRE HIGHWAY
Caiguna
Cocklebiddy
Balladonia
Madura
Narrogin
Esperance
Israelite Bay
Great Australian Bight
Busselton
Bunbury
TALL TIMBER COUNTRY
Stirling Ranges
CAPE LE GRAND NATIONAL PARK
CAPE ARID NATIONAL PARK
Margaret River
Cape Leeuwin
ALBANY HWY
Augusta
Pemberton
Denmark
Walpole
Albany
Archipelago of the Recherche
SOUTHERN OCEAN
NORTHERN TERRITORY
SOUTH AUSTRALIA
0   300 km

hard-won cattle country, while adventurous travellers fall in love with the stirring, dusty scenery around **Cape Leveque** and the **Gibb River Road**. The region's convoluted, barely accessible coasts are washed by huge tides and occupied only by secluded pearling operations, a handful of Aboriginal communities, a couple of luxury retreats, and crocodiles. On the way to the Northern Territory border is **Purnululu National Park**, home to the surreal **Bungle Bungle** massif – one of Australia's greatest natural wonders.

Travellers never fail to underestimate the **massive distances** in WA. If you hope to explore any significant part of the state's 2.5 million square kilometres, and in particular the remote northwest, your own **vehicle** (preferably a 4WD) is essential, although you can still get to many interesting places by combining local tours with buses.

WA's **climate** is a seasonal mix of temperate, arid and tropical. **Winters** are cool in the south and wet in the southwest corner, while at this time the far north basks in daily temperatures of around 30°C, with no rain and tolerable humidity: this is the tropical dry season. Come the **summer**, the wet season or "Wet" (Dec–April) renders the Kimberley lush but inaccessible, while the rest of the state, particularly inland areas, crackles in the mid-40s°C heat. The southern coast is the only retreat for the heat-struck; the southwest coast is cooled by dependable afternoon sea breezes, known in Perth as the "Fremantle Doctor".

WA is eight hours ahead of GMT, one and a half hours behind the Northern Territory and South Australia and two hours behind the other eastern states. **Daylight saving** between late October and late March was introduced in WA in December 2006 – a referendum is due to be held in mid-2009 to see whether the three-year experiment will continue, but it seems unlikely

Some history

Aborigines had lived in WA for at least forty thousand years by the time the seventeenth-century traders of the **Dutch East India Company** began wrecking themselves on the west coast mid-journey to the Dutch East Indies (modern-day Indonesia), where they sought valuable spices. While some dispute remains about the first foreigner to see Australia, with French, Portuguese and Chinese explorers all laying a claim, it can safely be said that Dutch mariner **Dirk Hartog** was the first European to set foot on Western Australian soil, leaving an inscribed pewter plate on the island off Shark Bay that now bears his name, in 1616. For the next two hundred years, however, WA's barren lands remained – commercially at least – uninspiring to European colonists.

France's interest in Australia's southwest corner at the beginning of the nineteenth century led the **British** to hastily claim the unknown western part of the continent in 1826, establishing **Fredrickstown** (Albany) on the south coast; the **Swan River Colony**, today's Perth, followed three years later. The **new colony** initially rejected convict labour and as a result struggled desperately in its early years, but it had the familiar effect on an Aboriginal population that was at best misunderstood and at worst annihilated. Aborigines and their lands were cleared for agriculture – these days indigenous faces are rarely seen south of Perth.

Economic problems continued for the settlers until stalwart explorers in the mid-nineteenth century opened up the country's interior, leading to the goldrushes of the 1890s which propelled the colony into autonomous statehood by the time of Australian federation in 1901. This **autonomy**, and growing antipathy towards the eastern states, led to a move to secede in the depressed 1930s, when WA felt the rest of the country was dragging it down – an attitude that persists today. However, following World War II the whole of white Australia – and especially WA – began to thrive, making money first from wool and later from huge iron ore and offshore gas discoveries that continue to form the basis of the state's wealth and now account for a quarter of the nation's entire economy. Meanwhile, most of WA's forty thousand Aborigines – predominantly in the Kimberley – continue to live in desperately poor and remote communities, as if in another country.

DEC (the state government Department of Environment and Conservation) maintains WA's parks; to enter the most-visited parks, you need to pay an entry fee or buy a pass – the prices of the various passes are listed below. Throughout this chapter parks that require an entry fee have the phrase "DEC fee" placed in brackets after their names. The DEC website (⊕ www.dec.wa.gov.au) contains details of all passes, which you can buy online, as well as useful information about all of WA's national parks. You can also obtain a pass from the entry station (often unattended), local DEC offices and some visitor centres.

Day Pass $10 per car, $5 per motorbike. For any number of WA parks visited on that day; useful in the Southwest.

Annual Local Park Pass $20 per vehicle; gives unlimited access to parks in a given area for a year.

Holiday Pass $35 per vehicle; allows entry into all WA parks for four weeks.

Annual All Parks Pass $75 per vehicle; allows entry into all WA parks for a year.

Walking

In some national parks in WA, despite the many outstanding examples of natural beauty, you can feel as though you're just driving from lookout to lookout, with a few unsatisfactorily short, carefully prescribed walking trails thrown in. If you want to really experience a park, longer overnight trails are often possible – you need to discuss your intended route with the appropriate park ranger though, and be reasonably competent in the outdoors (including advanced map-reading skills and the ability to use a compass), not to mention being able to carry a tent, food and water if necessary.

Right across the state (if not the entire country) signs for short walking trails consistently exaggerate a suggested duration time to the point where it dissuades many from even trying. Experience has shown that you can comfortably halve the indicated times and still factor in a picnic and a siesta. Where shown, the chapter gives actual walking times: the minimum time it takes to complete the walk at a normal pace without stops.

School holiday dates in southern WA

Summer: mid-December to the end of January
Easter: middle two weeks of April
Winter: middle two weeks of July
Spring: first two weeks in October

Perth and the South

South of the **Great Eastern Highway**, which joins **Perth** to **Kalgoorlie**, is the most climatically benign portion of WA, something you can only appreciate if you've spent much time up north. It supports intensive agriculture and coastal resorts, with all points eventually connected to Perth, the modern expression of the state's wealth. East of the state capital, the **Darling Ranges** offer a number of appealing day-trip destinations, while south of Perth, the **Margaret River Region**'s verdant landscape is especially attractive, supporting orchards, wineries and numerous holiday hideaways in the giant karri forests around **Pemberton**. Both **Albany** and **Esperance** are engaging resort towns on the Southern

Ocean's rugged coastline, where sea breezes take the edge off the summertime heat. They make ideal bases for exploration of their adjacent national parks, while the dreary **Wheatlands**, north of the coast, is a region to pass through rather than head for. **Kalgoorlie**, at the still-thriving heart of the **Eastern Goldfields**, is a colourful caricature of an Outback mining town and certainly deserves a stop if you're travelling east.

Perth

Western Australia's modern hub of **PERTH** is home to just over 1.5 million people and has a reputation for endless sunshine and an easy-going lifestyle. After work, it's typical for people to go surfing, sailing, swimming or fire up a barbie somewhere on the shores of the Swan River, which forms a broad lagoon ideal for recreation and sport. This enviable social life partly explains Perthites' contented detachment from the rest of the country. Another factor is simply the physical distance: Perth is Australia's most isolated city, almost 4000km from Sydney by road, and in a different time zone (Western Standard Time, two hours behind the east coast).

The state's wave of mineral prosperity saw the city grow quickly in the 1980s, and, considering its modest population, development continues today. The city's Central Business District (CBD) is essentially an open-air shopping mall with two pedestrian-only retail precincts, museums, galleries, and some beautiful historic buildings. Strangely, the city fails to take advantage of its stunning riverside frontage, which is left to the joggers, cyclists and gulls. Just north of the CBD, **Northbridge** is the restaurant and club district, as well as being the centre for Perth's Asian community with a buzzy eat street, while the inner western suburbs of Leederville and Subiaco boast boutiques, cafés, restaurants and pubs galore. On weekends, city dwellers head for the hills (York and Toodyay are favourites) or wineries (Swan Valley and Margaret River are closest), or stay closer to home and hit the beaches (Cottesloe is the spot) and markets (Fremantle's are an institution, followed by fish and chips).

Arrival and information

Perth's **international airport** (☎13 12 23, ⓦwww.perthairport.com) is 16km east of the city centre and the busier **domestic** terminal a few kilometres closer. **Shuttle buses** (international $20, domestic $15; ☎08/9277 7958) meet arrivals at both airports and take you to your accommodation. Poorly signposted, but directly opposite the Qantas domestic terminal, you can also catch a green Transperth bus (ⓦwww.transperth.wa.gov.au); #36 runs to the Esplanade Busport, Perth City, #37 runs to Perth City and Kings Park, #40 goes to Esplanade Busport, Perth City. All run seven days a week, straight to the city ($3.50), at least every twenty minutes during the day, but slowing at night. Otherwise, a trip by **taxi** to or from the international airport will take thirty minutes and cost around $30, less from the domestic terminal. An airport shuttle runs to **Fremantle** (from $35 one-way; ☎08/9335 1614, ⓦwww .fremantleairportshuttle.com.au) once an hour in peak times.

Interstate **trains** and **buses** as well as Transwa (formerly Transco) buses serving rural WA use the **East Perth Rail and Bus Terminal**, three train stops east of the city central Transperth **Perth train station** on Wellington Street. Near the latter you will find the **Wellington Street Bus Station** for suburban

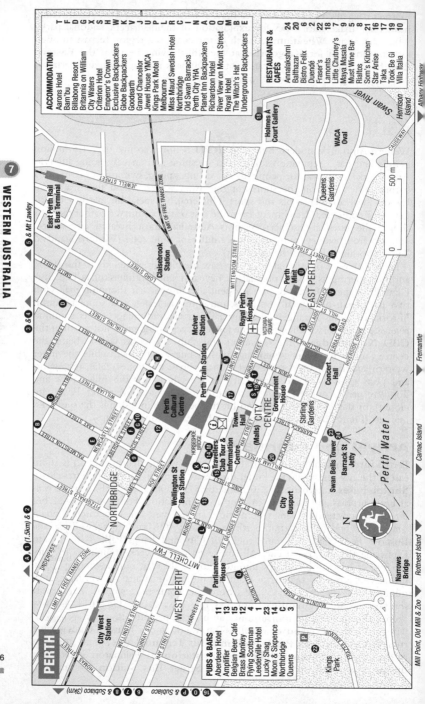

PERTH

WESTERN AUSTRALIA | 7

ACCOMMODATION

Aarons Hotel	T
Bam'bu	F
Billabong Resort	D
Britannia on William	G
City Waters	X
Criterion Hotel	S
Emperor's Crown	H
Exclusive Backpackers	W
Globe Backpackers	K
Goodearth	Y
Grand Chancellor	J
Jewel House YMCA	U
Kings Park Motel	P
Melbourne	L
Miss Maud Swedish Hotel	R
Northbridge	C
Old Swan Barracks	I
Perth City YHA	N
Planet Inn Backpackers	A
Richardson Hotel	O
River View on Mount Street	Q
Royal Hotel	M
The Witch's Hat	B
Underground Backpackers	E

RESTAURANTS & CAFÉS

Annalakshmi	24
Balthazar	20
Bistro Felix	6
Duendé	2
Fraser's	22
Lamonts	18
Little Chutney's	7
Maya Masala	9
Must Wine Bar	5
Rialtos	8
Som's Kitchen	21
Star Anise	16
Taka	17
Took Be Gi	19
Villa Italia	10

PUBS & BARS

Aberdeen Hotel	11
Amplifier	13
Belgian Beer Café	15
Brass Monkey	4
Flying Scotsman	1
Leederville Hotel	12
Lucky Shag	23
Moon & Sixpence	14
Northbridge	C
Queens	3

services, and to confuse matters further there is also the **Esplanade Bus Station** on Mill Street by the Perth Conference Centre.

The main **visitor information centre** (Mon–Thurs 8am–6pm, Fri 8am–7pm, Sat 9.30am–4.30pm, Sun noon–4.30pm; ☏1300 361 351, ⓦwww.westernaustralia.com), just across the road from the Transperth station in Forrest Chase precinct, has numerous free city guides and maps, tour information and statewide promotional videos. An alternative is the **Travellers' Club Tour and Information Centre** (Mon–Fri 9am–5.30pm, Sat 10am–4pm; ☏08/9226 0660, ⓦwww.travellersclub.com.au), at 92–94 Barrack St, with an information service for backpackers and budget travellers as well as inexpensive **internet** access and notice boards for work and car sales.

City transport

Transperth, Perth's efficient and inexpensive **suburban transport** network, has frequent **trains** to Fremantle and the northern, eastern and southern suburbs of Joondalup, Midland, Armadale and Mandurah, plus a fleet of **buses** filling in the gaps. The city centre has two suburban **bus stations**, one on Wellington Street (information office Mon–Fri 7.30am–5.30pm, Sat 8am–1pm; ☏13 62 13), next to the central train station, and the Esplanade Bus Station (information office Mon–Fri 7.30am–6.30pm, Sat 10am–2pm, Sun noon–4pm; ☏13 62 13) ten minutes' walk south at the bottom of Mill Street which caters mostly for services south of the river. Any southbound bus crossing the railway line at Horseshoe Bridge near the Wellington Street bus station goes to the Esplanade Bus Station.

Outside the **Free Transit Zone** (see box below), Perth is divided into eight concentric zones – zones 1 and 2 (tickets $3.50) are the most useful to visitors, incorporating Fremantle, the northern beaches and Midland. **Tickets** are available from bus conductors or vending machines at all (mostly unstaffed) stations; they are valid for up to two hours' (some for 1hr 30min) unlimited travel within the specified zones on Transperth buses, trains and the ferry to South Perth from Barrack Street Jetty. All-zone day-passes ($8.40) are also available from certain newsagents.

Perth has a far-reaching network of **cycle lanes**, which spread out to the suburbs and can make cycling a pleasant and viable option; the government agency Bikewest (☏08/9216 8000) or the Bicycle Transportation Alliance (☏08/9420 7210, ⓦwww.btawa.org.au) can provide more information.

Free transport in central Perth: the FTZ

Both of Perth's central bus stations, as well as the local train stations' stop on either side of the main Wellington Street train station, are within the **Free Transit Zone**, or **FTZ**. Most buses passing through the FTZ offer free travel within it, as do the snazzy "CAT" (Central Area Transit) buses serving the city centre. You can board the buses at special CAT stops to take you along two circular CAT routes, with a third route, the Yellow CAT, running up and down Wellington Street to East Perth. Press a button at the bus stops and a voice tells you when the next bus is due. The Blue CAT runs from Barrack Street Jetty along the Foreshore and up Mounts Bay Road to Barrack Street and Aberdeen Street and then down William Street and over Horseshoe Bridge back to the river, while the Red CAT runs east to west along St Georges Terrace, the non-pedestrianized part of Hay Street, and Wellington Street. All routes run Mon–Thurs 7am–6pm, Fri 7am–1am, Sat 8.30am–1am, and Sun 10am–5pm, with intervals of fifteen minutes at the most.

Accommodation

There's a full range of **accommodation** around the centre of Perth – from backpackers' hostels to hotels and apartments – conveniently close to, or even right in, the city centre. Self-contained apartments can be great value for groups of four or more. The nearest campsites are 7km from the city. Booking ahead for hotels and apartments is advisable if you want to stay at the first place on your list.

Hotels and self-contained apartments

Aarons Hotel 70 Pier St ☎08/9325 2133, Ⓦwww.aaronsperth.com.au. Standard mid-range hotel in a great location in the CBD, close to bars and restaurants. ❺

City Waters 118 Terrace Rd ☎08/9325 1556, Ⓦwww.citywaters.com.au. Snug one- and two-bedroom three-star units with kitchens in a motel-style block. Close to the river, a 10min walk from the shopping centre. Doubles ❺, 2-bed units ❼

Criterion Hotel 560 Hay St ☎08/9325 5155, Ⓦwww.criterion-hotel-perth.com.au. The rooms at this central heritage hotel might not live up to the beautiful renovated Art Deco exterior, but they're clean, comfortable and spacious. English pub, free wi-fi and some secure parking. ❺

Goodearth 195 Adelaide Terrace ☎08/9492 7777, Ⓦwww.goodearthhotel.com.au. Large modern hotel, with a range of rooms, including two-bedroom apartments with kitchenettes. Views to the river. ❼

Grand Chancellor 707 Wellington St ☎08/9327 7000 or 1800 753 379, Ⓦwww.ghihotels.com. Central four-star providing spacious rooms with mini-bar and internet access, as well as a gym, sauna and rooftop pool. ❼

Jewel House YMCA 180 Goderich St ☎08/9325 8488, Ⓦwww.ymcajewellhouse.com.au. Simple, clean and cheap in a pleasant part of the city. Rooms have shared facilities with fan and heater – some have TV and fridge. Popular with students and families. Singles ❶, doubles ❷

Kings Park Motel 255 Thomas St, Subiaco ☎08/9381 0000 or 1800 655 362, Ⓦwww.kingsparkmotel.com.au. Some rooms at this rather old-fashioned motel come with spa baths and kitchens, although the highlight is the swimming pool. A 10min drive from the city centre at Shenton Park, not far from Subiaco shops and Kings Park. ❻

Melbourne 942 Hay St at Milligan St ☎08/9320 3333 or 1800 685 671, Ⓦwww.melbournehotel.com.au. The rooms at this heritage-listed Federation-era boutique hotel on Hay St aren't as lovely as the beautiful exterior would suggest, but they're comfortable and well equipped with mini-bar and internet access, and a buzzy bar downstairs. Breakfast included. Windowless rooms ❻, with balcony ❽

Miss Maud Swedish Hotel 97 Murray St ☎08/9325 3900, Ⓦwww.missmaud.com.au. These comfortable, well-equipped rooms include a good smorgasbord breakfast with Miss Maud's famous Swedish pastries. Handy central location. ❼

Northbridge 210 Lake St, Northbridge ☎08/9328 5254, Ⓦwww.hotelnorthbridge.com.au. The rooms, which come with spa baths, are rather frumpy (expect lots of floral) for such a stylish local pub, but the Northbridge location is unbeatable. Off-street parking and pub bars downstairs. ❼

🏃 **Richardson Hotel** 32 Richardson St ☎08/9217 8888, Ⓦwww.therichardson.com.au. Perth's best and rather plush five-star boutique hotel has all the amenities you'd expect, including an award-winning spa and a well-regarded mod-Oz restaurant. Rooms start at $415. ❾

River View on Mount Street 42 Mount St ☎08/9321 8963, Ⓕ9322 5956. Nestled at the foot of Kings Park on the edge of the city, a 5min bus ride to the centre, these surprisingly chic rooms are well equipped, and some have kitchens. ❽

Royal Hotel 531 Wellington St at William St ☎08/9338 5100, Ⓦwww.royalhotelperth.com.au. These clean simple rooms and apartments (some en suite) in this historic hotel come with fridge and TV. Reception open Mon–Fri 8am–5pm. ❸

Backpackers'

The majority of Perth's backpackers' are located in Northbridge, where a variety of converted hotels and houses have been turned into sociable dens for working holiday-makers and travellers. Northbridge has few free on-street daytime parking spots, but off-street parking is available at some accommodation as indicated in the reviews. The keener establishments meet incoming trains and buses at East Perth Rail and Bus Station and will also collect you from the airports, though a two-night minimum stay might be required.

City Centre

Exclusive Backpackers 158 Adelaide Terrace ☎08/9221 9991, ⓦwww.exclusivebackpackers .com. At the East Perth end of Adelaide St, minutes from the Swan River and WACA, this is an excellent location for those here for the summer cricket. Loyal return travellers like the spacious rooms, polished floorboards, retro atmosphere and big balcony. A good café next door supplements the kitchen. Off-street parking. Five- to three-bed dorms $26–32, rooms ❸

Globe Backpackers 561 Wellington St at Queen St, ☎08/9321 4080, ⓦwww .globebackpackers.com.au. About as central as you can get, with a small kitchen, sociable outdoor eating area, TV rooms and internet access. Four- to sixteen-bed dorms $25–32, en suites $2 extra, rooms ❹

Perth City YHA 300 Wellington St ☎08/9287 3333, ⓦwww.yha.com.au. Located in a splendid renovated 1940s building close to everything, a stylish flashpacker YHA with polished wooden floorboards, spacious lounge areas, and a first-rate kitchen. The train line opposite means earplugs are needed. Booking essential. Secure parking available for $10 a night. Four-bed dorms $29–36, rooms ❹

Northbridge: central

Bam'bu 75 Aberdeen St ☎08/9328 1211, ⓦwww.bambu.net.au. This renovated former warehouse and self-styled "boutique" hostel is decked out with Asian arts and crafts collected by owner-adventurer Dave. With its weekend club nights and mood lighting, it's one for travellers who like to party. Complimentary breakfast, wi-fi and rice. Limited parking. Eight- to four-bed dorms $25–31, rooms ❸

Britannia on William 253 William St ☎08/9227 6000, ⓦwww.perthbritannia.com.au. This huge, three-storey warren in the heart of Northbridge is a stone's throw from clubs and cafés, so affected by the noise of late-night revels and early-morning garbage collection. There's 24hr reception but no parking. Four-, six- or eight-bed dorms $24–26, rooms ❶

Emperor's Crown 85 Stirling St ☎08/9227 1400 or 1800 991 553, ⓦwww.emperorscrown.com.au. Outstanding flashpacker hostel, with a clean, modern interior, plasma-screen TV/DVD, internet, a fully equipped kitchen, and a café. Standard six- or four-bed dorms and several double or triple configurations, some with en suite, TV/DVD and fridges. Limited parking. Dorms $32, rooms ❹

Old Swan Barracks 2–8 Francis St ☎08/9428 0000, ⓦwww.theoldswanbarracks.com. Renovated in 2008, this unique hostel in a grand, historic stone building (built in 1896) boasts the clubby *Barracks Bar* with illuminated whiskey barrels and pool tables. Rooms are simple and clean, and there's parking available. Twelve- to four-bed dorms $21–26, rooms ❸

Underground Backpackers 268 Newcastle St ☎08/9228 3755 or 1800 033 089, ⓦwww .undergroundbackpackers.com.au. Friendly backpackers', formerly a pub, boasting a pool, free breakfast, bar with nightly specials, cheap internet access, a/c in all rooms, a video lounge and 24hr reception. Ten- to four-bed dorms $27–31, rooms ❸

Northbridge: north of Newcastle Street

Billabong Resort 381 Beaufort St ☎08/9328 7720, ⓦwww.billabongresort.com.au. Not as central as others (1km north of CBD) but a long-standing favourite. There's a palm-shaded pool area, beach volleyball court, murals on the walls, parking, free breakfast, and just about every possible service on offer, short of tucking you in at night. Close to Mt Lawley shops and bars. Eight- to four-bed dorms ($25–27) with en-suites, rooms ❹

Planet Inn Backpackers 496 Newcastle St ☎08/9227 9969, ⓦwww.planetinn.com.au. It's hardly central, but this party hostel is popular with "fun-loving guys and girls" keen to "share in an unrestricted spirit of self-discovery", according to the website. There's a bar, mini-shop, and plenty of freebies including breakfast and 24hr pick-up. Twelve- to four-bed dorms $24–27, rooms ❸

The Witch's Hat 148 Palmerston St ☎08/9228 4228 or 1800 818 358, ⓦwww.witchs-hat.com. Exceptionally well-managed hostel located in a beautiful heritage building in a residential area northeast of Northbridge with a real home-from-home feel. There are comfy communal areas and BBQ, excellent computer facilities and internet access, along with parking, job and tour service, and friendly staff. Dorms $32, rooms ❹

Caravan park

Central 34 Central Ave, 7km east of Perth ☎08/9277 1704, [W]www.perthcentral.com.au. Located in Ascot, by the domestic airport, a 15min drive to the city. Camping $33, cabins [5]–[6]

The City

The most engaging area within Perth's compact **CBD** is a walkable, easy-to-negotiate grid extending from Wellington Street down to St Georges Terrace, and from Hill Street to the east and Milligan Street to the west. Much of your time will be spent exploring the area in and around the pedestrianized shopping precincts of **Hay Street** and **Murray Street**, particularly between William and Barrack streets, which are connected by several shopping arcades. William Street runs north over the railway at **Horseshoe Bridge** and on into the pubs, clubs and Asian eateries of Northbridge, while Barrack Street runs south to the **Barrack Street Jetty** on the Swan River and **Swan Bells Tower** (daily 10am–3.45pm; $11; [W]www.swanbells.com.au). The distinctive tower houses the 280-year-old bells of London's St-Martin-in-the-Fields Church, presented to WA on the 1988 bicentenary.

In front of the tower, the **Swan River**, between **Narrows Bridge** to the west and the Causeway over **Heirisson Island** to the east, is popular with windsurfers, sailors and jet-skiers. From the jetty, a Transperth ferry (Sept–April 6.50am–9.15pm; May–Aug 6.50am–7.24pm) regularly sails to Mends Street Jetty on the south shore, while tourist boats ply the river upstream to the Swan Valley wineries and downstream to **Fremantle** and **Rottnest Island** (see box, p.656).

Museums and old buildings

Situated just over the railway tracks in Northbridge, on James Street Mall, the **Perth Cultural Centre** comprises the impressive **Art Gallery of Western Australia** (daily 10am–5pm; donation; [W]www.artgallery.wa.gov.au), the engaging **Western Australian Museum** (daily 9.30am–5pm; donation; [W]www.museum.wa.gov.au) and the state library. The Gallery's permanent collection includes one of the country's most highly regarded collections of Aboriginal art, along with other contemporary and classic work by Western Australian artists, as well as constantly changing temporary exhibitions. There's always something worth seeing, the air conditioning is blissful in summer, and the free guided tours are informative. On the other side of the square, the Western Australian Museum includes a floor devoted to Aboriginal culture, plus exhibitions of vintage cars, stuffed marsupials, meteorites, a diorama of a swamp and a reconstruction of an old jail, among other interesting exhibits.

In a striking building on the banks of the Swan River in East Perth, the **Holmes À Court Gallery** at Level 1, 11 Brown St (Wed–Sun noon–5pm; donation; ☎08/9218 4540, [W]www.holmesacourtgallery.com.au), boasts one of the most outstanding private collections of Australian and indigenous art (4000 works in total), and hosts engaging guided art walks.

Perth has some wonderful examples of colonial and Federation-era architecture dotted around the city centre. One fine building is the splendid **Perth Mint** (Mon–Fri 9am–5pm, Sat & Sun 9am–1pm; $15; [W]www.perthmint.com.au) on Hill Street, between Hay and Goderich streets. Operating from its original 1899 base, Perth's mint was responsible for producing and distributing gold sovereigns for Britain's colonies, and was owned by the British until as late as 1970. It still trades in precious metals in bar and coin form, as well as minting for international clients. Its fascinating exhibition includes the world's largest gold bars and largest gold nugget collection, historic coins, the chance to

▲ Perth at night

observe hourly gold-pouring and minting operations in the refurbished foundry, and hourly (on the half-hour) guided tours.

Kings Park and Botanic Garden

The five-square-kilometre expanse of **Kings Park**, two-thirds of which is native bushland, is situated 2km west of the centre up on Mount Street (bus #37 from St Georges Terrace). Created with great foresight in 1872, the park is Perth's most popular attraction and its sweeping parklands are flooded with locals on weekends, celebrating weddings and birthdays, enjoying picnics and barbecues, and jogging and playing sports. The **Botanic Garden** is a showcase for Western Australia's unique flora – incredibly, the state has half of Australia's 25,000 species, most of which aren't found anywhere else on Earth. There are walking trails, bike tracks, playgrounds, picnic/BBQ areas, an elevated walkway through the trees, and free guided tours and maps at the **visitor centre** (daily 9.30am–4pm; ☎08/9480 3634, ⓦwww.bgpa.wa.gov.au) next to the car park. The adjoining shop, Aspects of Kings Park (daily 9am–5pm), stocks art, crafts and design products by local artists including textiles, ceramics, jewellery and prints, as well as eco-friendly and educational gifts.

Eating and drinking

Perth is blessed with a great food scene. You'll find plenty of cafés and restaurants in the **CBD**, **Northbridge** (especially on James and Lake streets, and Beaufort, an Asian eat street), nearby at **Mount Lawley**, at **Leederville** in the inner-west, at **Subiaco**, close to Kings Park, and of course at **Fremantle** (see p.655). All areas get busy from Friday through to Sunday nights, especially during the warmer months.

If you're on a tight budget, try the food courts in the city and Northbridge, including the predominantly Asian *Shang Hai* on James Street, while in the city you'll find *Metro* and the *Carillon* off Hay Street Mall, where you can get a bowl of noodles for around $15 or pile your plate high at an all-you-can-eat for around $17. If you're more interested in quality than quantity, at the other end of the scale eating at some of Perth's finest restaurants may cost you around $50 per head for two courses without drinks. A good local **website** with restaurant reviews is Ⓦ www.eatingwa.com.au.

Annalakshmi Jetty no. 4, Barrack St ☎ 08/9221 3003, Ⓦ www.annalakshmi.com.au. Brainchild of a Hindu monk and named after the Hindu goddess of food, this vegetarian place is staffed by volunteer chefs (mostly Asian grandmas) who dish up delicious Indian, Malaysian and Sri Lankan food. Fabulous waterfront location. No prices – you pay what you want. Profits go to the poor in India. Tues–Fri & Sun noon–2pm & Tues–Sun 6.30–9pm.

Balthazar 6 The Esplanade ☎ 08/9421 1206. In a stunning Art Deco building, this is one of Perth's best restaurants, with a gentlemen's-club vibe by day but a more romantic atmosphere after dark. Dress up to enjoy the elegant cuisine and superb local wines. Mon–Fri noon–10.30pm & Sat 6–10.30pm.

Bistro Felix 118 Rockeby Rd, Subiaco ☎ 08/9388 3077, Ⓦ www.bistrofelix.com.au. A chic spot with a buzzy atmosphere that's renowned for exquisite mod-Oz cuisine and warm service. Mon–Sat noon–3pm & 6–10.30pm.

Duendé 662 Newcastle St, Leederville ☎ 08/9228 0123, Ⓦ www.duendetapasbar.com.au. At Perth's best Spanish joint, you can expect traditional tapas alongside more creative contemporary versions of classics. Great wines by the glass too. Mon–Thurs 6–11pm, Fri noon–midnight, Sat 6pm–midnight.

Fraser's Fraser Ave, Kings Park ☎ 08/9481 7100, Ⓦ www.frasersrestaurant.com.au. With its elegant decor, stunning Kings Park location, panoramic views and refined cuisine, this is the sort of restaurant locals book for romantic dinners, proposals and anniversaries, so it makes for a memorable first/last night in Perth/Australia. Daily noon–3pm & 6–10.30pm.

Lamonts 11 Brown St, East Perth ☎ 08/9202 1566, Ⓦ www.lamonts.com.au. Fresh regional products cooked exceptionally well and great WA wines are the reasons to hit Kate Lamont's restaurant. Wed–Sun noon–9.30pm.

Little Chutney's 71–75 Rockeby Rd, Subiaco ☎ 08/9381 7755, Ⓦ www.littlechutneys.com.au. This funky Indian place serves up fiery Indian cuisine (trad and fusion) to a loyal local crowd. If you can't score a table, try its adjoining sister-establishment

Chutney Mary's. Tues–Sun noon–2.30pm & daily 5.30–10.30pm.

Maya Masala 49–51 Lake St, at Francis St, Northbridge ☎ 08/9328 5655. Branch of a family-owned chain of Indian restaurants, with *masala dosa* from $13, seafood *thali* for $17 and curries from $15–20. Tues–Sun 11.30am–2.30pm & 5.30pm–late.

Must Wine Bar 519 Beaufort St, Highgate ☎ 08/9328 8255, Ⓦ www.must.com.au. One of Perth's hippest spots is a fine-diner, casual eatery and bar all in one, so while you can stick to sipping the excellent Western Aussie wines, the bar snacks and the meals in the Parisian-style brasserie are both fabulous – French classics with a twist, using fantastic fresh local produce. Daily noon–midnight.

Rialtos 424 Hay St, Subiaco ☎ 08/9328 3292, Ⓦ www.rialtos.com.au. This local favourite is a traditional Italian-Australian *trattoria* dishing up rustic Italian cuisine to happy locals. Italian wines by the glass alongside WA wines. Tues–Sun 11.30am–2.30pm & 5.30pm–late.

Som's Kitchen 240 Adelaide Terrace, CBD. This tiny, great-value family-run Thai restaurant fills up with students feasting on the spicy curries. Mon–Fri 11am–2pm & 6–8pm.

Star Anise 225 Onslow Rd, Shenton Park ☎ 08/9381 9811, Ⓦ www .staraniserestaurant.com.au. Perth's finest restaurant, *Star Anise* specializes in adventurous, contemporary Asian-inspired cuisine – a must for foodies. Tues–Sat 6.30–10pm.

Taka Corner of Barrack and Wellington sts, CBD. It may not be the most authentic sushi around, but portions are huge and cheap, making it popular with students, backpackers and the lunchtime office crowd. Mon–Sat 11am–9pm, Sun 11am–5pm.

Took Be Gi Pier St, CBD. Good-value Korean food (soups and noodles are popular) keeps the Asian students and travellers happy. BYO. Wed–Mon 11am–11pm.

Villa Italia Corner of Aberdeen and William sts, Northbridge. Casual Italian café serving up hearty pastas, good pizzas and great coffee. Mon–Fri 7am–late, Sat 8am–late.

Entertainment and nightlife

Northbridge and **Fremantle** (see p.655) are the focal points for after-dark action, with plenty of **pubs**, **bars** and **dance clubs**, but there are also lively bars in the city and other suburbs. Late at night on weekends, however, North-bridge has an edge to it that many find intimidating, with a reputation for violence, and many locals avoid the place between Friday and Sunday these days. Perth's nightlife centres around drinking and live music, and although the city is attempting to promote responsible behaviour, it's not helped by the many pubs and bars offering **cheap beer** and happy hours.

The free weekly *X Press* newspaper (ⓦ www.xpressmag.com.au), available at boutiques, music stores, cafés, bars and pubs, has comprehensive movie, music and club **listings**. Also check the entertainment section of Thursday's *West Australian* newspaper. For the lowdown on the **gay and lesbian scene**, see "Listings".

Pubs and bars

7

Aberdeen Hotel 84 Aberdeen St, Northbridge. "The Deen" has six bars, live gigs, several DJs and themed nights: a backpacker/student night (Mon), salsa classes (Thurs), hip hop/R&B (Fri) and DJs and bizarro live band Booty Joooo (Sat).

Amplifier 383 Murray St, CBD (access via laneway). Excellent late-night bar-club, with live music midweek (mainly punk/hardcore) and DJs weekends (everything from alternative, new wave and art rock to electronica).

Belgian Beer Café 347 Murray St, CBD. This popular global franchise is a favourite with the after-work crowd for its fantastic Trappist beers and tasting trays.

Brass Monkey Corner of William and James sts, Northbridge. Enduringly popular pub with a buzzy atmosphere in the heart of Northbridge. Live gigs, themed nights, great range of local beers, and the stylish *Grapeskin* wine bar.

Flying Scotsman 639 Beaufort St, Mt Lawley. A popular student hangout, with cover bands, nightly drink specials and cheap meals.

Hotel Northbridge 198 Brisbane St, Northbridge.

Karaoke in the hotel's *210 Bar* on a Friday night can be interesting.

Leederville Hotel 742 Newcastle St at Oxford St, Leederville ⓦ www.theleederville.com. This popular local has five bars, a beer garden, pool tabloo, sports, bands and DJs, yet it has a strict dress code after 7pm – better check the website for what's acceptable if you didn't pack your going-out shirt.

Lucky Shag Barrack St Jetty, CBD. Perth's only city pub with a bar right on the Swan river – the tables on the wooden boardwalk are a wonderful place to be for sunset or on a sunny afternoon. Weekends typically see the Brit backpacker boys stripping to their underwear and jumping into the water.

Moon & Sixpence 300 Murray St, CBD. One for homesick UK travellers, this English pub serves up British pub grub and has UK beers on tap.

The Queens 520 Beaufort St, Mt Lawley. This fun bar, in an 1899 coach house, has a buzzy local vibe, good Aussie-brewed beers and a great Sunday brunch.

Cinemas and theatres

Most of Perth's mainstream **cinemas** are located in the arcades off Hay and Murray streets in the centre. Tuesday nights are cheap, with matinees also discounted at some places. Cinemas in the Luna Palace chain (ⓦ www.lunapalace .com.au) show art-house and independent films: the Paradiso in the Galleria complex on James Street, Northbridge; The Luna on Oxford Street, Leederville, a fifteen-minute walk west of Northbridge; and the Luna On SX at Fremantle. There's also the beautiful Art Deco-style Astor (ⓦ www.astorcinema.com.au), at Mount Lawley on the corner of Beaufort and Walcott streets, but this was closed for renovation at the time of writing.

Just over the Causeway, southeast of the centre, the vast *Burswood Entertainment Complex and Casino* (ⓣ 08/9362 7777, ⓦ www.burswood.com.au), within the five-star *InterContinental Hotel*, has a dozen restaurants and bars and hosts big touring shows and musicals such as *Phantom of the Opera* and *Stomp*. The acclaimed Western Australian Symphony Orchestra plays at the stunning Perth Concert Hall on St Georges Terrace (ⓣ 08/9231 9900, ⓦ www.perthconcerthall.com.au), while the West Australian Ballet, West Australia Opera and the Perth Theatre Company all perform at the splendidly restored Edwardian His Majesty's Theatre (℡08/9322 2929, ⓦwww.hismajestystheatre.com) on the corner of King and Hay streets.

Listings

Airline Skywest ℡1300 660 088, ⓦwww.skywest .com.au. Flights to Albany, Broome, Carnarvon, Esperance, Exmouth, Geraldton, Goldfields, Kalbarri, Karratha, Kununurra, Monkey Mia and Port Hedland.
Bike rental About Bike Hire, Point Fraser Reserve (Causeway Car Park), 1–7 Riverside Drive ℡08/9221 2665, ⓦwww.aboutbikehire.com.au (Daily 9am–5pm, until 6pm summer); or available from most backpackers' from $33 a day.
Buses Greyhound Australia (ⓦwww.greyhound .com.au) goes up along the coast to Darwin daily, less frequently to Port Hedland via Newman on the inland route; Integrity Coach Lines (℡08/9226 1399 or 1800 226 339, ⓦwww.integritycoachlines .com.au) heads north via the Great Northern Highway to Port Headland (Thurs); South West Coach Lines (℡08/9324 2333, ⓦwww .southwestcoachlines.com.au) has daily services to the Margaret River region as far as Augusta; and Transwa (℡1300 662 205, ⓦwww.transwa.wa .gov.au) operates daily bus services as far as Esperance and, less frequently, north to Kalbarri and Meekatharra via Mullewa. It also does a four-week Southern Discovery Pass for around $175.
Car purchase For used vehicles, backpackers' notice boards and the many internet cafés and travel shops like Travellers Club at 92–94 Barrack St are best for private sales. Try to avoid buying non-WA-registered vehicles in WA as the change of ownership requires an inspection in the state of origin, or a local inspection prior to registration on WA plates, which might entail expensive repairs. Buying and running WA-plated cars within the state is simple as there is no annual roadworthy or change-of-ownership inspection; all you do is renew the annual vehicle-registration document, aka "rego".
Car rental Travellers Auto Barn, 365 Newcastle St, Northbridge (℡08/9228 9500, ⓦwww.travellers -autobarn.com), is well respected and has offices throughout the country. Prices start around $35 a

day. For **scooter rental** go to Scootaround, 127 Hill St, East Perth (℡08/9201 2990, ⓦwww.scootarama .com.au), or Modomio, 14 (rear) Norfolk St, Fremantle (℡08/9433 2377, ⓦwww.modomio.com.au).
Gay and lesbian Perth The quickest way to plug into the scene is to pick up the weekly community paper *Out in Perth* (ⓦwww .outinperth.com), free from Cinema Paradiso on James St or the Arcane Bookshop, 212 William St, Northbridge (℡08/9328 5073).
Hospitals Royal Perth, Victoria Square ℡08/9224 2244; Fremantle, Alma St ℡08/9242 5544.
Maps Perth Map Centre, 900 Hay St (℡08/9322 5733), has a full range of topographic and touring maps.
Motoring associations RACWA, 228 Adelaide Terrace (℡08/9421 4444), offers a complete range of services, as well as maps.
Permits for Aboriginal Land Aboriginal Affairs Department, 197 St Georges Terrace ℡08/9235 8000, ⓦwww.dia.wa.gov.au/Land/Entry-Permits/.
Police 2 Adelaide Terrace ℡08/9222 111 or 13 14 44 for non-urgent calls.
Post office Forrest Chase, opposite the train station. Mail collection service.
Taxi Swan Taxis ℡13 13 30.
Trains The Indian-Pacific rail service, operated by Great Southern Railways (℡13 21 47, ⓦwww.gsr .com.au), leaves on Wed and Sun, getting to Sydney or Melbourne two days later, and there are great deals like half-price backpackers/overseas concessions and the six-month Great Southern Rail Pass ($690, conc. $590. Check the website for latest prices, but over very long distances a flight becomes better value with the savings in travel time. Transwa also has daily rail services south to Bunbury and twice on weekdays to Kalgoorlie. Both Transwa and Indian-Pacific have offices at the Wellington St Bus Station.

Around Perth

For excursions beyond central Perth, the port of **Fremantle**, at the mouth of the Swan River, should not be overlooked, nor should a trip over to **Rottnest Island**, an eighty-minute ferry ride from the city or half that from Fremantle. Perth's **beaches** form a near-unbroken line north of Fremantle, just a short train or bus ride from the centre, while with your own vehicle you can escape to the

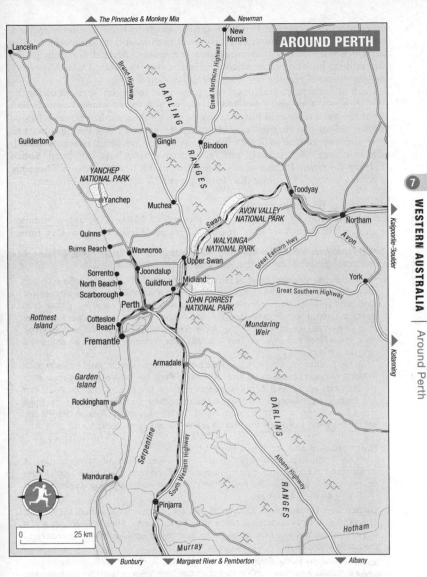

AROUND PERTH

Lancelin

New Norcia

Guilderton

DARLING

Great Northern Highway

Brand Highway

Gingin   Bindoon

RANGES

Toodyay

YANCHEP NATIONAL PARK

Yanchep

Muchea

AVON VALLEY NATIONAL PARK

Swan

Northam

Avon

Kalgoorlie-Boulder

Quinns

WALYUNGA NATIONAL PARK

Great Eastern Hwy

Burns Beach   Wanneroo

Sorrento   Joondalup

Upper Swan

York

North Beach   Guildford   Midland

Great Southern Highway

Scarborough

Perth

Rottnest Island

Cottesloe Beach

JOHN FORREST NATIONAL PARK

Fremantle

Mundaring Weir

Garden Island

Armadale

Katanning

Rockingham

DARLING

Serpentine

South Western Highway

RANGES

Albany Highway

N

Mandurah

Hotham

Pinjarra

0   25 km

Murray

Bunbury   Margaret River & Pemberton   Albany

Upper Swan Valley wineries and the **national parks** north of Perth, which run parallel to the coast and atop the **Darling Ranges**, where patchily forested hills, just half an hour's drive east of the city, offer a network of scenic drives and marked walking trails among the jarrah woodlands. Further afield, **York**, **Toodyay** and **New Norcia** can make a satisfying day-trip with a tour or in a rented car.

Fremantle

Although long since merged into the metropolitan area's suburban sprawl, Perth's port of **FREMANTLE** – "Freo" – retains a character altogether different to the centre of Perth. It's small enough to keep its energy focused, with a real working harbour and busy yacht marina, and it has an eclectic, arty ambience without too many upmarket pretensions. Myriad buildings in the atmospheric historic precinct have been taken over by Notre Dame University and the students give the town a youthful, vibrant feeling.

Much of the convict-built dock, dating from the 1890s, was spruced up for the 1987 Americas Cup yacht race and the eagerly anticipated tourist boom. Before the makeover Freo was as rough as any port – the historic hotels were "bloodhouses" full of brawling sailors – but today the town attracts Perthites from all over the city and all walks of life for its famed weekend **markets** (worth planning your visit around) and "Cappuccino Strip", as café-lined **South Terrace** is known. It's also worth noting that in the heat of summer Fremantle is often a breezy 5°C cooler than Perth, a mere 25 minutes away by train.

Arrival and information

Fremantle Station is located at the top end of Market Street, five minutes' walk north of the town centre; **trains** to Fremantle leave the city every fifteen

---

River cruises and tours from Perth

Commercial ferry operators are all based at Barrack St Jetty and offer cruises up and down the Swan River from as little as $20 to Fremantle or $70 for a full day upriver. Collecting you from your accommodation, bus and 4WD tours also leave daily in all directions from Perth. Popular day-tour destinations include the peculiar Pinnacles, near Cervantes, the wineries of the Upper Swan Valley, New Norcia and Toodyay, York, Wave Rock and even the Tree Top Walk near Walpole – the last two entailing a long day on a bus.

For the Southwest, overnight tours are better: a three-night trip will typically pack in all the highlights in a loop via Albany. North of Perth the west-coast hot spots after the Pinnacles are Kalbarri, Shark Bay and then Coral Bay on the Ningaloo Reef, with four days or more being a good relaxed pace for the trip up. From here some tours shoot back down to Perth or head inland to Karijini National Park in the Pilbara, something that's well worth the effort if you've come this far north.

River cruises and Rottnest Island ferries

Captain Cook Cruises ☎08/9325 3341, ⓦwww.captaincookcruises.com.au. A whole range of cruises including one upriver to some wineries ($139.50 with three-course lunch), one down to Fremantle ($21) and some evening dinner cruises ($95–109) on the Swan River.

Golden Sun Cruises ☎08/9325 9916, ⓦwww.goldensuncruises.com.au. Cruises upriver to visit the National Trust property at Tranby House, historic Guildford, and a day-cruise and bus tour around the Swan Valley wineries. Also downriver cruises to Fremantle from $28 return, $17 one-way.

Oceanic Cruises Perth ☎08/9325 1191, Fremantle ☎08/9430 2666, ⓦwww.oceanic cruises.com.au. Four daily Perth–Rottnest cruises from $68 and six daily from Fremantle to Rottnest from $54, as well as all-in Rottnest tours for $84 and overnight backpacker deals from $79. Also five daily Perth–Fremantle services for around $21 one-way.

Rottnest Express ☎08/9335 6406, ⓦwww.rottnestexpress.com.au. Up to ten Fremantle departures daily from $54, with overnight packages and bike rental.

Day-tours

Feature Tours 26 St Georges Terrace ☎1800 999 819, ⓦwww.ft.com.au. Daily coach tours from Perth along the Swan Valley up to New Norcia and Toodyay as well as Margaret River, the Tree Top Walk and Wave Rock from $180.

minutes. **Buses** (routes #102–106 and #151 from Perth's Esplanade Busport) also stop here; local **taxis** can be called on ☎13 13 30 or 13 10 08. **Ferries** to Rottnest and Perth leave from the wharfside B Shed (behind E Shed), which is five minutes' walk from the station along Phillimore Street (see box below for details and prices). The orange **Fremantle CAT** (Mon–Thurs 7.30am–6.30pm, Fri 7.30am–8pm, Sat & Sun 10am–6.30pm) is a free bus service which runs from Fremantle train station every ten minutes along a figure-of-eight route that covers all places covered here. You could also consider hopping aboard the **Fremantle Tram**, which offers informative commentaries on its various tours (daily 10am–4pm; hourly; from $22; ⓦwww.fremantletrams.com.au), and departs from outside the town hall on Kings Square. There's a busy **visitor centre** in the town hall on Kings Square (Mon–Fri 9am–5pm, Sat 10am–3pm, Sun 11.30am–2.30pm; ☎08/9431 7878, ⓦwww.fremantlewa.com.au).

Accommodation

Fremantle has no less than five backpackers' all within 1km of each other, as well as a caravan park. Grand-era hotels have been splendidly refurbished, their

Western Travel Bug ☎08/9204 4600 or 1800 627 488, ⓦwww.travelbug.com.au. Pinnacles, Wave Rock and Margaret River for around $150, all with plenty of activities.

Swan Valley wine tours

Various operators run **bus and boat tours** of the valley from Perth, among them Swan Valley Tours (☎08/9274 1199, ⓦwww.svtours.com.au; $90), Captain Cook Cruises (see opposite), who run a daily wine cruise from Barrack St Jetty in Perth for around $139 including three-course lunch, and Out and About Wine Tours (☎08/9377 3376, ⓦwww.outandabouttours.com.au), who have group day-tours every day except Mon including a three-course lunch, for $89.

Overnight tours

Easyrider Backpacker Tours 224 William St, Northbridge ☎08/9227 0824, ⓦwww .easyridertours.com.au. Hop on and off the yellow bus, with tickets valid from three days up to six months, as far as Darwin via Coral Bay, Karijini and Broome, or over to Kalgoorlie, Esperance and Albany. The seven-day Broometime tour is $799 with discounts available when booked online.

Planet Perth Tours ☎08/9225 6622, ⓦwww.planettours.com.au. Accommodated tours into the Southwest and five- to seven-day trips up to Exmouth and Broome from around $135 a day.

Red Earth Safaris ☎08/9279 9011 or 1800 501 968, ⓦwww.redearthsafaris.com.au. Mon departures for one-week coastal trips up to Exmouth and back ($795/655 with YHA VIP card).

Westernxposure 179 William St, Northbridge ☎08/9414 8423 or 1800 621 200, ⓦwww.westernxposure.com.au. Four-day Monkey Mia trips, three-day Southwest tours or ten-day jaunts via Exmouth and Karijini to Broome. Around $135 a day.

Surf tours

Lancelin Beach Surf School ☎08/9444 5399, ⓦwww.surfschool.com.au. Picks you up early from Perth for up to four days, at around $122 a day, with wet suits, accommodation and food included.

WA Surf ☎1800 927 873, ⓦwww.wasurf.com.au. Day-trips and two-day trips to Lancelin, including overnight camp for $240.

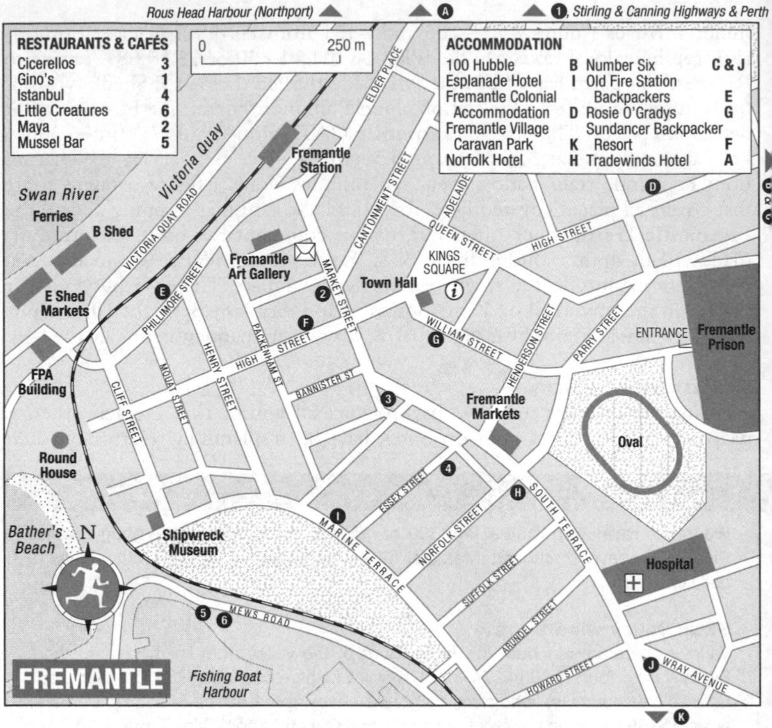
Rous Head Harbour (Northport)
A
1, Stirling & Canning Highways & Perth
RESTAURANTS & CAFÉS
Cicerellos 3
Gino's 1
Istanbul 4
Little Creatures 6
Maya 2
Mussel Bar 5
0 250 m
ACCOMMODATION
100 Hubble B
Esplanade Hotel I
Fremantle Colonial Accommodation D
Fremantle Village Caravan Park K
Norfolk Hotel H
Number Six C & J
Old Fire Station Backpackers E
Rosie O'Gradys G
Sundancer Backpacker Resort F
Tradewinds Hotel A
Swan River
Ferries
B Shed
E Shed Markets
Victoria Quay
VICTORIA QUAY ROAD
ELDER PLACE
Fremantle Station
CANTONMENT STREET
ADELAIDE
QUEEN STREET
HIGH STREET
KINGS SQUARE
Fremantle Art Gallery
MARKET STREET
Town Hall
PHILLIMORE STREET
PACKENHAM ST
HIGH STREET
WILLIAM STREET
HENDERSON STREET
PARRY STREET
ENTRANCE
Fremantle Prison
Western Australia Maritime Museum
FPA Building
CLIFF STREET
MOUAT STREET
HENRY STREET
BANNISTER ST
Fremantle Markets
Oval
Round House
ESSEX STREET
SOUTH TERRACE
Bather's Beach
N
Shipwreck Museum
MARINE TERRACE
NORFOLK STREET
SUFFOLK STREET
Hospital
ARUNDEL STREET
MEWS ROAD
WRAY AVENUE
HOWARD STREET
FREMANTLE
Fishing Boat Harbour
K

only drawback being shared bathrooms for most rooms. There are also plenty of historic B&Bs and apartments in and around the centre. Freo is busy with tourists year-round so always book in advance.

100 Hubble 100 Hubble St, East Fremantle [T] 08/9339 8080, [W] www.100hubble.com. You'll either love or hate this eccentric, eco-friendly hippy place where rooms (one an old train carriage) are decked out in a mishmash of bric-a-brac and plants. Rooms sleep one to six people. [4]–[9]

Esplanade Hotel Corner of Marina Terrace and Essex St [T] 08/9432 4000, [W] www.esplanadehotelfremantle.com.au. Fremantle's finest hotel boasts comfortable rooms with all amenities in a huge old heritage hotel opposite the park, not far from the fishing harbour. [8]

Fremantle Colonial Accommodation 215 High St, [T] 08/9430 6568, [W] www.fremantlecolonialaccommodation.com.au. Three former colonial prison cottages and terrace houses divided into self-contained apartments. All have lovely balconies and are charmingly decorated with old iron beds. B&B room [6], cottages [7]

Fremantle Village Caravan Park Corner of Cockburn and Rockingham rds, South Fremantle [T] 08/9430 4866, [W] www.fremantlevillage.com.au. The nearest campsite to the centre of town, with a range of on-site cabins and rooms. Camping $30, powered site $36, cabins and rooms [5]

Norfolk Hotel 47 South Terrace [T] 08/9335 5405, [W] www.norfolkhotel.com.au. Centrally located pub accommodation with mostly en-suite rooms plus a few budget options, all with kettle and fridge. Quiet despite bands playing most nights in the basement. Parking available. Doubles [4]–[5]

Number Six 47 South Terrace [T] 08/9252 1380, [W] www.numbersix.com.au. This family-owned operation has chic, fully-equipped studios, apartments and heritage houses scattered around Freo, available for short and long stays. [4]–[8]

Old Fire Station Backpackers 18 Phillimore St [T] 08/9430 5454, [W] www.old-firestation.net. Two minutes from the station, this sprawling hostel has a huge common room, outdoor cinema area, women-only lounge and dorms, and discount food from the Indian restaurant downstairs. And there's even an old fireman's pole. Four- to fifteen-bed dorms from $26, rooms [3]

Rosie O'Gradys 23 William St ☎08/9335 1645, ⓦwww.rosieogradys.com.au. Old pub in the centre of town with simple rooms (some en suite); noisy when bands play downstairs on weekends. Prices go up at the weekend. Standard rooms ❹–❺, en-suite rooms ❻

Sundancer Backpacker Resort 80 High St ☎08/9336 6080 or 1800 061 144, ⓦwww .sundancer-resort.com.au. Fremantle's designated party hostel. Huge, slightly impersonal, with an outdoor pool, beer garden and bar with various drink specials. Congested ten-bed dorms $24, four-bed dorms $26, rooms (some en suite) ❸

Tradewinds Hotel 59 Canning Hwy ☎08/9339 8188, ⓦwww.tradewindshotel.com.au. Good-looking, Federation-era hotel with well-equipped, self-catering apartments, close to the river and 2km from the centre. Apartments ❾

The Town

Exploring Fremantle on foot, with plenty of streetside café breaks, is the most agreeable way of visiting the town's compactly grouped sights. If you want to tick off all of them, start your appraisal on the east side before moving down to the ocean to end up at the Fishing Boat Harbour, ready for a sunset seafood dinner.

Kick off with a tour of the hillside **Fremantle Prison** (daily 10am–5pm; day tour $17.50, night tour $23, tunnel tour $59; ⓦwww.fremantleprison.com), whose entrance is on The Terrace, on the west side of the compound. Built by convicts in 1855, soon after the struggling colony found it couldn't do without their labour, the complex was only decommissioned in 1991. The excellent, informative tours are sometimes guided by ex-wardens.

Not far from the prison are the more cheerful **Fremantle Markets** (Fri 9am–8pm, Sat 9am–6pm, Sun & Mon 10am–6pm; ⓦwww.fremantlemarkets .com.au), on the corner of Henderson Street and South Terrace, with a locals' fruit and veg market, and a more tourist-focused section crammed with stalls selling souvenirs, arts and crafts and New Age paraphernalia. Moving down the main street, **South Terrace**, known locally as "Cappuccino Strip", Freo's Italian heritage is on full display. Take a seat at one of the many alfresco cafés and take in the buzzy atmosphere.

Suitably recaffeinated, browse the funky boutiques on South Terrace on your way towards the "**West End**", as the old shipping office and freight district of Freo is known. A left-turn on High Street will lead you past art galleries, bookshops and boutiques, before reaching the **Round House** (daily 10am–3pm; donation), the state's oldest building and original gaol, which boasts fine views of the headland, sea and town.

From here you'll see the striking **Western Australian Museum's Maritime Museum** on Victoria Quay (daily 9.30am–5pm; $10 or $15 including submarine *Ovens*, free every second Tues of the month; ⓦwww.museum .wa.gov.au/maritime), which covers just about every nautical aspect of WA with displays on fishing, whaling, pearling and trade across the Indian Ocean. Pride of place goes to the glossy-hulled *Australia II* yacht that won the America's Cup several times, while other highlights include the first Indonesian *prau* seized in WA for illegal fishing, and the weather-beaten *Parry Endeavour* belonging to world circumnavigator John Sanders. The **submarine** *Ovens* is round the back (free 1hr tours every half-hour 10am–3.30pm).

Outside the Fremantle Port Authority building at the end of Phillimore Street, there's a statue to C.Y. O'Connor, who masterminded the rebuilding of the docks in the 1890s, as well as the construction of the vital water pipeline to Kalgoorlie. Nearby, where the Rottnest ferries berth, the **E-Shed markets** (Fri 10am–9pm, Sat & Sun 10am–5pm) are worth a quick look, although they are nowhere near as good as the Fremantle Markets.

Wander back along Cliff Street to another branch of WA Museum, the **Shipwreck Galleries** (daily 9.30am–5pm; donation), near the Roundhouse, which tells the compelling stories of the myriad vessels lost on WA's treacherous coast. The centrepiece is the *Batavia,* the Dutch East Indiaman wrecked off present-day Geraldton in 1629. The exhibit includes the ship's reconstructed stern, a stone portico bound for the Dutch East India Company's unfinished fort at Batavia (modern-day Jakarta), numerous corroded artefacts, and a fascinating film about the extraordinary drama of the wrecking (and subsequent salvage) of the ship. If WA's past still intrigues you, the WA Museum has a third Freo branch, **Fremantle History** (daily 10.30am–4.30pm; donation) at 1 Finnerty St. Housed in a former convict-built 1860 asylum, it traces the development of the port from its colonial foundations through postwar immigration.

Coming out of the Shipwreck Galleries you find yourself on the grassy esplanade park with its towering Norfolk pines, busy on weekends with picnicking families and games of cricket. Cross the railway tracks and you're at Fremantle's busy **Fishing Boat Harbour** (see "Eating", below), with its numerous seafood restaurants.

Eating

Seafood restaurants line the perimeter of Freo's Fishing Boat Harbour off Mews Road, while in town, South Terrace and its surrounding streets are crammed with all kinds of eateries, from **Italian** to **Asian**. There's also a **food hall** (Thurs–Sun noon–9pm) on Henderson Street, next to the markets, where you'll find mostly Asian food stalls.

Cicerellos Fishermans Wharf, 44 Mews Rd. Hugely popular casual seafood joint right on the harbour, with tables on the wooden boardwalk. Seafood platters are a good deal if there are a few of you, while the "Catch of the Day" generally goes for around $25. Daily 8am–late.

Gino's 1 South Terrace. This enduringly popular and unpretentious sidewalk café serves great coffee and cakes, as well as a range of traditional pastas from around $17. Daily 8am–late.

Istanbul 19 Essex St. This casual, no-nonsense place is a long-standing favourite with locals and tourists alike, serving generous portions of traditional Turkish food, from meze to grills. Daily 11am–late.

Little Creatures 40 Mews Rd, Fishing Boat Harbour ☎08/9430 5555, ⓦwww.littlecreatures.com.au. Sit amidst towering vats of fermenting ale in this atmospheric old aircraft hangar, and enjoy wood-fired pizzas with toppings such as harissa lamb or Atlantic salmon that wash down nicely with one of *Little Creatures'* own delicious ales. Tables overlooking the water. Mon–Fri 10am–midnight, Sat & Sun 9am–midnight.

Maya 75 Market St ☎08/9335 2796. Expect fine Indian cuisine in a stylish contemporary setting, but while the standard of food is exemplary (the appetizer tasting plate is a must), service is slow and the wine list disappointing (you're better off taking your own and paying corkage). Bookings essential. Tues–Sun dinner from 6pm, plus Fri lunch from noon.

Mussel Bar 42 Mews Rd ☎08/9433 1800. Sublime seafood with an emphasis on mussel dishes (the Thai green curry is a favourite) at this stylish harbourside restaurant. Bookings essential. Tues–Sun 11am–3pm & 6pm–late.

Drinking and entertainment

Like the town itself, entertainment in Fremantle is generally a laid-back, easy-going affair. The *Norfolk Hotel,* diagonally opposite the markets on South Terrace, is the most popular watering hole for a drink in Freo, anytime of the day or night but especially on weekends when its beer garden gets crowded with locals. Nearby, the *Sail & Anchor* at 64 South Terrace is another local favourite, serving a variety of **boutique beers**, and its bars, downstairs and upstairs on the veranda, are *the* place for a late-afternoon weekend drink.

The *Left Bank Bar & Café* at 15 Riverside Rd on the Swan River in East Freo is a beautifully renovated nineteenth-century house that gets packed on sunny weekends.

Bars with **live music** include *Rosie O'Grady's* at 23 William St, the intimate basement at the *Norfolk Hotel* and the rowdy *Newport Hotel*, 2 South Terrace. Some of the country's eminent bands, such as the John Butler Trio, Eskimo Joe and Little Birdy, started out playing Freo's pubs and you can catch bands of this calibre at *Metropolis* on 52 South Terrace, a live-music venue and **nightclub**, offering a choice of bars and dancefloors. The *Market Bar* in the Fremantle Markets also has musicians (generally an acoustic guitarist) playing throughout the day. At the back of the markets, the *Fly By Night*, at the prison end of Queen Street, is a musicians' co-op and a great place to see local talent. Just over the river, *Mojos Bar* at 237 Queen Victoria St is good for original music, or try the *Swan Basement* at the *Swan* hotel down the road at no. 201.

Fremantle has no less than four **cinemas**, on Essex Street, William Street, Collie Street and Adelaide Street, all with cut-price tickets on Tuesdays and for some matinees.

Rottnest Island

Eighteen kilometres offshore, west of Fremantle, **Rottnest Island** was so-named by seventeenth-century Dutch mariners who mistook its unique, indigenous **quokkas**, beaver-like marsupials, for rats. Today, following an ignominious period as a brutal Aboriginal penal colony in the nineteenth century, Rottnest is a popular holiday destination, easily accessible from Perth or Fremantle by ferry and – at the very least – makes for a fun day out.

The island, inevitably abbreviated to "Rotto", is 11km long and less than half as wide, with a historic settlement of charming colonial houses stretching along the sheltered Thompson Bay on the east side. West of the settlement, a low heathland of salt lakes meets the coastline, which boasts twenty clear scalloped bays, 63 small beaches, and fascinating offshore reefs ending at the "West End", as the seaward "tail" of the island is known. Although well attuned to the demands of its daily stream of visitors (the island receives over 500,000 of them a year), Rotto gets packed out during school summer holidays (for dates see p.644), Schoolies Week, and around Christmas and New Year when accommodation is booked months ahead. Motorized traffic on the island is virtually nonexistent, a real treat that makes **cycling** from bay to sparkling bay the best way to appreciate Rotto. Besides riding around the island, you can take a **train ride** up to Oliver Hill (3 trips daily; 2hr; $23.50), or get in the water with the help of the Dive Shop (departs Perth daily 7.30am, returns 5.30pm; ☏08/9292 5111, ⓦ www.rottnestdiving.com.au), which runs snorkelling tours ($80) and diving tours ($165) including all gear and lunch. The diving and snorkelling off Rotto's beautiful coves are unlike anywhere on the adjacent mainland and a couple of days spent here, especially midweek when it's less busy, are well worth the excursion from Perth. On the Little Salmon Bay Snorkel Trail there are underwater plaques describing the surroundings. The *Underwater Explorer* (☏08/9325 1191, ⓦ www.underwaterexplorer.com.au) is a glass-bottomed boat that operates reef-and-wreck tours (Sept–May; $29; 45min) for those who don't want to get wet.

Practicalities

Ferry operators servicing Rotto depart from the B-Shed in Fremantle and Perth's Barrack Street Jetty from Pier 2. Prices are around $54 for same-day return from Freo and $69 from Perth (see box, p.656, for details). The trip from

Perth takes about eighty minutes and less than half that from Fremantle, so to make the most of your day aim to board at the latter. You can also **fly** to Rotto in twenty minutes from Jandakot airport, about 20km south of Perth, with the Rottnest Air Taxi (☏1800 500 006 within Perth/WA, or 08/9292 5027, ⓦwww.rottnest.de; from $80 return; 15min each way) among others. Rottnest Airport is 800m from the settlement and 600m from the bike-rental building, and there's a free courtesy bus.

Ferries arrive at the jetty in Thompson Bay right in front of the island's **visitor centre** (daily 7.30am–5pm; ☏08/9372 9732, ⓦwww.rottnestisland .com), which has maps and bus timetables and also serves as a **post office**. Daily two-hour **bus tours** depart from the bus stop behind the visitor centre at varying times throughout the day ($24.30). There is also the more-or-less half-hourly Bayseeker **bus service** (Oct–April daily 8.30am–5.15pm; $11 day-ticket) which takes you to the island's bays as far as the isthmus, Narrow Neck, 3km from the West End. Also behind the visitor centre is the Salt Store building, which is where the Rottnest Voluntary Guides begin free daily walking tours; see the visitor centre for details. The **bike-rental** building (daily, hours vary seasonally; from $20 per day; ☏08/9292 5105) is behind the *Hotel Rottnest* (the old *Quokka Arms Hotel*) a couple of minutes south of the visitor centre.

Accommodation is found along Thompson, Longreach and Geordie bays, all adjacent to each other at the developed northeast end of the island and linked by the Bayseeker bus service. Accommodation, ranging from backpackers' to self-contained cottages, can be booked online (ⓦwww.rottnestislandonline .com) or via the central reservations number (☏08/9432 9111); note that prices drop about twenty percent in winter. The *Rottnest Lodge Resort* (☏08/9292 5161, ⓦwww.rottnestlodge.com.au; ⑨) is a former prison converted into first-class motel units. The newly renovated, historic *Hotel Rottnest* (☏08/9292 5011, ⓦwww.rottnestisland.com; ❽, minium 2-night stay), a five-minute walk from the visitor centre, has rather chic contemporary rooms with sea views. **Allison Camping Area** (☏08/9432 9111; tent sites around $9) is available just behind the settlement; camping is not permitted anywhere else on the island. There are many **eating** options, including, for better or worse, *Red Rooster* and a *Subway* (thanks to the schoolies). *Hotel Rottnest* does good bistro and café-style fare, including tasty gourmet pizzas, and sipping a beer at one of its tables beside the sea is sublime.

Perth's beaches

Perth's closest beaches extend along the **Sunset Coast**, 30km of near-unbroken sand and coastal suburbs stretching north of the Swan River, bordered by the Indian Ocean and cooled by afternoon sea breezes. There are also tiny inshore beaches worth a look along the **Swan River** at Crawley, Nedlands, Peppermint Grove and Mosman Bay on the north shore, and Como, Canning Bridge and Applecross on the south shore, which are calm and safe for children, and make wonderful picnic spots.

Cottesloe Beach, 7km north of Fremantle, is the most popular city beach, with safe swimming. There are ice-cream vendors, cafés and watercraft-rental outlets aplenty, all just a ten-minute walk from Cottesloe train station. Two kilometres north of here, **Swanbourne Free Beach** – cut off by army land in both directions but accessible from the road – has nude bathing. North of **Scarborough Beach**, itself another favoured venue 6km north of Swanbourne, the surf and currents are more suited to wave-riding and experienced swimmers, though with fewer beachside facilities, crowds are reduced. Bus #400 leaves from Perth's Wellington Street Bus Station for the 35-minute journey.

Guildford and the Swan Valley

North of **GUILDFORD**, a twenty-minute drive from the city centre, is the **Upper Swan Valley** – WA's oldest wine-growing region. It makes for a pleasant day's **wine-tasting**, even if the wines here – though lovely – are no match for those of the Margaret River region, which are some of Australia's finest. **Guildford** itself is a historic town dating back to the earliest years of the colony, with several Federation-era grand hotels, a number of historic buildings, antique shops and cafés. The **visitor centre** (daily 9am–4pm; Ⓦwww .swanvalley.com.au) is on the corner of Swan and Meadow streets. If you're heading to the valley, pick up the *Swan Valley* booklet with maps and information on the wineries, cycle tracks and driving trails.

The Swan Valley Drive
Heading north from Guildford, a clearly marked thirty-kilometre drive follows the west side of the river. On Route 203, the **Little River Winery & Café** (daily 10am–5.30pm) is a small, independent winery with a pleasant café. The most notable winery of the region is **Houghton's** on Dale Road (daily 10am–5pm; Ⓦwww.houghton-wines.com.au), the area's biggest and most diverse producer of wines, with an art gallery, excellent café and tended lawns on which to contemplate your tastings. Other wineries of note include Moondah Brook, Faber, Garbin Estate, Heafod Glen, Jane Brook Estate and Lamonts, all marked on the tourist map. The route returns to Guildford via Midland and thence to the city. From Midland you can take Toodyay Road to the Darling Ranges. For Swan Valley tours, see p.656.

New Norcia and Toodyay

One of WA's most unusual architectural sights is **NEW NORCIA**, a monastic community dating from the nineteenth century, 130km northeast of Perth on the Great Northern Highway. This unexpected collection of Spanish-inspired buildings in the Australian bush is part of a community founded by Benedictine monks in 1846 with the aim of converting the local Aborigines to Christianity. Nowadays the community is a much-visited tourist attraction.

There is a roadhouse, **visitor centre** (daily 9am–4.30pm; Ⓣ08/9654 8056, Ⓦwww.newnorcia.wa.edu.au), and a **museum and art gallery** (daily 9am–4.30pm; $23) that explains the Benedictines' motivation in coming here and displays a fine collection of religious art. The museum entry ticket includes a two-hour guided walk of the town leaving at 11am and 1.30pm. The **rooms** in the *New Norcia Hotel* (Ⓣ08/9654 8034, Ⓦwww.newnorcia.wa.edu.au; ❹) don't quite live up to the grandeur of this colossal historic hotel (nor does the restaurant's food for that matter), although the experience of staying here is still an old-fashioned treat. The two-kilometre self-guided New Norcia **heritage trail** begins here and takes you on a circuit past the community's impressive buildings.

The two most ornate buildings, on either side of the cemetery, are **St Gertrude's Residence for Girls** and **St Ildephonsus's for Boys** (both open only for tours). Among other buildings, you can also visit the **Flour Mills** (arrange at visitor centre) and the Abbey Church (open daily; mass times Sun ·7.30am & 9am) – both relatively ordinary in comparison. You'll find the famous wood-fired **bread** made at the mills in Perth's best restaurants, and sold here in the **gift shop** (along with chocolate, preserves, wine, CDs, books and crafts) and at a retail outlet at 163 Scarborough Beach Rd, Mount Lawley.

Several bus-tour companies offer **day-trips** from Perth to New Norcia (see box, pp.656–657), which is otherwise served only three times a week by Transwa's rural bus service.

Toodyay

The historic town of **TOODYAY** (pronounced "2J"), set among the wooded hills of the Avon Valley, 85km northwest of Perth, makes an agreeable diversion on the way to – or from – New Norcia. The charming town was founded in 1836, making it one of the earliest inland settlements of the Swan River Colony, and a number of buildings survive from that era. The **visitor centre** (Mon–Sat 9am–5pm, Sun 10am–5pm; ☎08/9574 2435, ⓦwww.toodyay.com), situated on Piesse Street behind **Connor's Mill** on Stirling Terrace, the town's main road, has a booklet with a map and information on the historic sites. The mill is now a **museum** ($3.50), as is the **Old Newcastle Gaol** (Mon–Fri 10am–3pm, Sat & Sun 10am–4pm; $3.50), just over the rails on Clinton Street, which dates from the 1830s. Other historic buildings include the riverside **St Stephen's Church**, opposite the mill, as well as the former Mechanics' Institute – now the **library** – on Stirling Terrace.

York

Stranded in the Avon Valley, 97km from Perth via the Great Southern Highway, **YORK** looks like a film set for an Australian western. The town is the state's most complete pioneering settlement, filled with attractive and well-preserved early architecture. The commercial centre of the Avon Valley until the railway – and with it the Great Eastern Highway – bypassed it 30km to the north, York is now an agricultural centre but also plays a historic role as a venerable museum of ornate nineteenth-century public buildings, coaching inns and churches. On weekends its streets are busy with Perthites looking for a change of scenery. Be warned, though: this inland region regularly bakes at 40°C in midsummer.

The **Old Courthouse** (daily 10am–4pm; $5) on Avon Terrace harks back to the town's pioneer history, while the **York Motor Museum** (daily 9.30am–4pm, summer till 3pm; $8.50), in the centre of town, capitalizes on York's antiquarian charisma with a large collection of vintage and classic vehicles – from a hundred-year-old single-cylinder tricycle to Ossie Cranston's 1936 Ford V8 racer. At the north end of the terrace are the **Sandalwood Yards**, where the perfumed wood – once prolific in WA and highly prized in the Orient – was stored during York's heyday. Near here you can take a walk down to the wobbly **suspension bridge** spanning the peaceful Avon River and take a look at the 1854 **Holy Trinity Church**, with its modern stained-glass designs by Robert Juniper, one of WA's foremost artists.

Practicalities

York's **visitor centre** (daily 9am–5pm; ☎08/9641 1301, ⓦwww.yorkwa.org) is at 105 Avon Terrace, the main road on which most of York's fine old buildings are located. It has a **town map** and information sheet, which locates and describes the town's key structures as well as listing places to stay and eat. The restored *Imperial Hotel* (☎08/9641 1255, ⓦwww.imperialhotelyork.com .au; ➐) has stylish contemporary rooms, a lively bar, a brilliant alfresco terrace

Wave Rock

WA's best-known natural oddity is the striking **Wave Rock** (Ⓦwww.waverock.com
.au; $7 per car), four hours' drive through the Wheatlands from Perth via historic York,
and 3km from the tiny farming settlement of Hyden. At 15m high and 110m long, the
formation resembles a breaking wave, an impression enhanced by the vertical water
stains running down the overhanging face. From the base of the rock a marked
twenty-minute walking trail leads to another outcrop, Hippo's Yawn.

Accommodation includes *Wave Rock Caravan Park* (Ⓣ08/9880 5022; cabin/
cottages Ⓖ) at Wave Rock, and in town the *Hyden Wave Rock Hotel* on Lynch
Street (Ⓣ08/9880 5052; Ⓖ). The *Bush Shopping Village* has a few places to eat,
including the *Wave Rock Bush Bakehouse* (Mon–Fri 6.30am–3pm, Sat 6.30am–
noon), which does breakfast and lunches as well as freshly baked bread and
pastries.

If you can't face the drive, Western Travel Bug offers full-day tours three times a
week (Ⓦwww.travelbug.com.au; $150 including a couple of other sights, meals and
entrance fees).

that's popular on weekends and the town's best restaurant. There are
several B&Bs, guesthouses and motels in and around town; the visitor centre
has details.

The Southwest

The region south of Perth and west of the Albany Highway, known as **the
Southwest**, is the temperate corner of the continent, where the cool Southern
and warm Indian oceans meet to drop heavy winter rains. North of **Bunbury**,
180km from Perth, lies a knot of satellite and retirement towns, such as
Rockingham and Mandurah, which offer little of interest to the visitor
compared to what's ahead. South of Bunbury things improve greatly. The
Margaret River region, WA's most popular holiday destination, is justly
famous for its fabulous surf beaches, wineries and boutique accommodation.
Tall Timber Country, to the southeast, encompasses towns set amid the
remnants of the giant karri forests and offers a chance to experience one of the
world's last stands of temperate old-growth forest.

At its best in spring and outside school holidays (dates on p.644), the Southwest's lush bucolic scenery is all the more appealing in that it can be enjoyed
without donning a hat, water bottle and sunblock while swatting away flies and
avoiding the crowds, an experience augmented by **gourmet produce-makers**
and **art galleries** and **woodcraft studios** displaying the work of local artisans.
There is also better-quality, and more varied, **accommodation** in this region
and, backpackers' apart, the recommendations given here barely scratch the
surface. Make the most of the visitor centres, and their invaluable sources of
places to stay.

South West Coach Lines (Ⓦwww.southwestcoachlines.com.au) offers a Perth
to Bunbury route, and serves Augusta via Margaret River and Busselton, as well
as Collie, Donnybrook, Bridgetown and Manjimup. Transwa (Ⓦwww.transwa
.gov.au) has a train link, *The Australind*, to Bunbury and a similar provincial **bus**
service with a 28-day unlimited-travel Southern Discovery Pass for around
$175. The best way to get about, however, is with a car, making use of Perth's

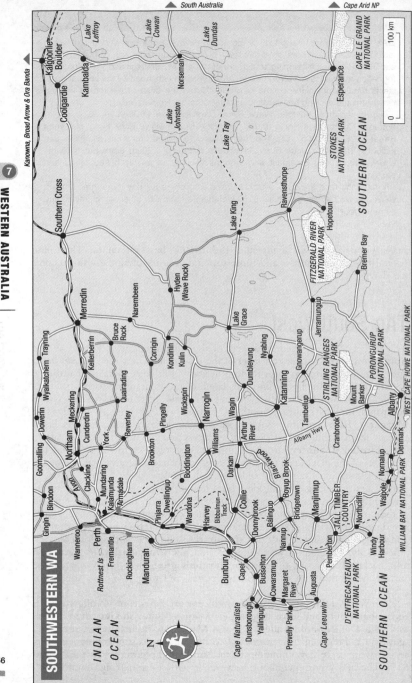

SOUTHWESTERN WA

Kanowna, Broad Arrow & Ora Banda

South Australia

Cape Arid NP

100 km

0

Kalgoorlie
Boulder

Kambalda

Coolgardie

Lake Leffroy

Lake Cowan

Lake Dundas

Norseman

Esperance

CAPE LE GRAND
NATIONAL PARK

CAPE GRAND
NATIONAL PARK

STOKES
NATIONAL PARK

SOUTHERN OCEAN

Lake Johnston

Lake Tay

Southern Cross

Ravensthorpe

Hopetoun

Lake King

FITZGERALD RIVER
NATIONAL PARK

Bremer Bay

Hyden
(Wave Rock)

Merredin

Narembeen

Lake Grace

Gnowangerup

Jerramungup

PORONGURUP
NATIONAL PARK

Trayning

Bruce Rock

Kellerberrin

Corrigin

Kondinin

Kulin

Dumbleyung

Katanning

Nyabing

STIRLING RANGES
NATIONAL PARK

Mount Barker

Albany

WEST CAPE HOWE NATIONAL PARK

Wyalkatchem

Dowerin

Meckering

Cunderdin

Quairading

Wickepin

Narrogin

Wagin

Arthur River

Tambellup

Cranbrook

Goomalling

Northam

York

Beverley

Pingelly

Williams

Denmark

Brookton

Boddington

Darkan

Blackwood

Boyup Brook

Manjimup

Normalup

Walpole

Gingin

Bindoon

Clackline

Mundaring

Kalamunda

Armadale

Pinjarra

Dwellingup

Wardona

Harvey

Bibbulmun
Track

Collie

Donnybrook

Balingup

Bridgetown

TALL TIMBER
COUNTRY

Northcliffe

Wanneroo

Perth

Fremantle

Rottnest Is

Rockingham

Mandurah

Bunbury

Capel

Busselton

Nannup

Pemberton

Windy
Harbour

WILLIAM BAY NATIONAL PARK

INDIAN
OCEAN

Cape Naturaliste

Dunsborough

Yallingup

Cowaramup

Margaret River

Augusta

Cape Leeuwin

Prevelly Park

D'ENTRECASTEAUX
NATIONAL PARK

SOUTHERN OCEAN

N

Avon

inexpensive rental agencies. Expect to cover at least 2000km in a typical week's tour as far as Albany but note that some attractions and scenic drives are on unsealed roads that may not be permitted in your rental agreement, so check with the company.

You might also wish to consider walking parts of the **Bibbulmun Track** (Ⓦwww.bibbulmuntrack.org.au), a 1000-kilomctre long-distance path that winds down from Kalamunda, east of Perth, to Albany on the south coast. The full trek takes six to eight weeks, but there are plenty of easy day-walks. There are huts on the way, but B&B owners do pick-ups and drop-offs. Some of the best sections of the track are found between the coastal inlets around Walpole and the forests and pastures south of Bunbury.

Designated the "Mountain Bikers' Bib", the **Munda Biddi Trail** (Ⓦwww .mundabiddi.org.au) follows a similar route to the Bibbulmun Track, starting from Mundaring, 40km east of Perth, and currently finishing at Nannup. The final stage to Albany should be completed in the next year or two. Both tracks are lined with camp huts and tent sites.

Bunbury

Described as the capital of the Southwest, **BUNBURY**, the state's second-largest population centre, is clearly prosperous and content, yet not the sort of place you'd cross oceans to see. A day's dallying here on the way south offers a chance to commune with **dolphins** (found around The Cut on Leschenault Inlet, and in the inlets around Mandurah and Rockingham), although the sightings are less predictable than at Monkey Mia (see p.705). Bunbury Dolphin Discovery Centre at the beach off Koombana Drive (daily 8am–4pm; $8; ℡08/9791 3088, Ⓦwww.dolphindiscovery.com.au) runs interactive dolphin tours from a boat ($47), as well as a swim-with-dolphins tour ($148) with a marine biologist as a guide.

Daily **bus services** from Perth (3hr) drop you at the well-stocked **visitor centre** (Mon–Sat 9am–5pm, Sun 9.30am–4.30pm; ℡08/9721 7922 or 1800 286 287, Ⓦwww.visitbunbury.com.au) in the old train station on Carmody Place. Shuttle buses to the town operate regularly from the **train station**, 3km from the centre, during the day and otherwise usually meet evening arrivals. The train from Perth takes two hours.

There is plenty of **accommodation** in and around town including the pleasant, laid-back *Wander Inn* at 16 Clifton St (℡1800 039 032, Ⓦwww .bunburybackpackers.com.au; dorms $27, rooms ❸), off Victoria Street (the main road), which has bikes, boogie-boards and local tours available. Likewise, the clean *Dolphin Retreat YHA* (℡08/9792 4690, Ⓦwww.dolphinretreatbunbury .com.au; dorms $26, rooms ❸) at 14 Wellington St is close to everything and has good facilities. The historic 1865 *Rose Hotel* (℡08/9721 4533, Ⓦwww.rosehotel .com.au; ❺) on Victoria Street has elegant heritage-style accommodation, a popular restaurant with meals for around $26, and two atmospheric bars. There are plenty of good sidewalk **cafés** and **restaurants** along Victoria Street.

Geographe Bay to Cape Naturaliste

South of Bunbury, the Bussell Highway curves west around **Geographe Bay** to **BUSSELTON**, named after a prominent pioneering family. The sheltered white-sand beaches of this sprawling holiday town make it a popular "bucket and spade" resort. On Peel Street, the **visitor centre** (Mon–Fri 9am–5pm, Sat 9am–4pm, Sun 10am–4pm; ℡08/9752 1288, Ⓦwww.geographebay.com) has lots of information on accommodation, restaurants, beaches, wineries and other nearby attractions. The town's foremost sight is its famously long (1842-metre), 142-year-old **jetty** (Ⓦ www.busseltonjetty.com.au; pedestrian access $2.50). Although the popular jetty train has been suspended until the pier is restored (the community raised $9 million to repair it), you can enjoy the aquatic activity 8m below the surface at the **underwater observatory** (daily 8am–5pm; $20; book ahead for tours on Ⓣ 08/9754 0900,), where well over a century of maritime growth and soft corals adorn the jetty's supports.

Out of town the highway turns south towards Margaret River, though continuing west brings you to the small resort town of **DUNSBOROUGH**, 21km from Busselton. The well-equipped **visitor centre** (daily 9am–5pm; Ⓣ 08/9752 1288, Ⓦ www.geographebay.com), at the Dunsborough Park Shopping Centre, offers accommodation- and tour-booking services. In town, just 100m from the water, the *Dunsborough Beach Lodge* (Ⓣ 08/9756 7144, Ⓦ www.dunsboroughbeachlodge.com.au; dorms $20, rooms ❷), at 13 Dunn Bay Rd, has clean rooms and a big balcony where people congregate at night. The *Dunsborough Motel* (Ⓣ 08/9756 7711, Ⓦ www.dunsboroughmotel.com.au; ❺), at no. 50, in the heart of town, has rather stylish "Superior" rooms and frumpy "Standard" ones, while *Newberry Manor* (Ⓣ 08/9756 7542, Ⓦ www.newberrymanor.com.au; ❽), 16 Newberry Rd, is an old-fashioned B&B with comfortable suites.

Two kilometres southeast of town, within splashing distance of the sea, the beachfront backpackers' *Dunsborough Beachouse* (Ⓣ 08/9755 3107, Ⓦ www.dunsboroughbeachouse.com.au; dorms $24, rooms ❷) has a relaxed surfer vibe (get off the bus at Quindalup), while 12km northwest on Cape Naturaliste, overlooking stunning Bunker's Bay, the sleek, chic *Quay West Resort* (Ⓣ 08/9756 9100, Ⓦ www.mirvac.com.au; ❾) has a colossal beachside swimming pool and a superb restaurant. Adjoining the resort, with possibly the most sublime seaside location of any eatery in Australia, the award-winning 🍴 *Bunker's Beach Café* (Ⓣ 08/9756 8284, Ⓦ www.bunkersbeachcafe.com.au; daily 9am–5pm, Thurs–Sun till 8pm for sundowners) does fantastic mod-Oz cuisine. In town, Dunsborough Bakery at Centrepoint Shopping Centre has been selling tasty pies since 1941, while the *Three Bears Bar*, at 536 Naturaliste Terrace (Ⓣ 08/9755 3657), serves decent pub grub and hosts impressive live bands.

With its sheltered position and minimal tides, Geographe Bay is ideal for **diving** – all the more so since the scuttling of the old *Swan* warship in 1997 in 30m of water (see the *Watersports* colour section). Cape Dive, 222 Naturaliste Terrace in Dunsborough (Ⓣ 08/9756 8778, Ⓦ www.capediveexperience.com), visits this and other sites in the bay (from $100). Surfboard rental is available at Yahoo Surfboards (Ⓣ 08/9756 8336), on the corner of Clark and Naturaliste Terrace, for $40 per day, or $20 per day for six days or more.

Cape Naturaliste itself, 14km northwest of the resort, is the less impressive of the two capes that define the Margaret River region. You can visit its truncated **lighthouse** (daily 9am–4.30pm; $6) and explore secluded beaches and coves on the way.

Along Caves Road to Margaret River

South of Dunsborough you head into the **Margaret River region** proper, characterized by brilliant beaches, ancient caves, superb wineries, choice restaurants and snug hideaways, all interspersed with art galleries, glass-blowing and woodcraft studios, and potteries. There's plenty to see, do, taste and spend your money on here.

Passing **Ngilgi Cave** you come to the turn-off for **YALLINGUP**, a small seaside settlement with a superb beach, populated by surfers waiting for the big one. **Caves Road** leads south from here, passing Gunyulgup Galleries (daily 10am–5pm; @www.gunyulgupgalleries.com.au), overlooking a lake, which has a fine selection of contemporary art, pottery, glass, ceramics and jewellery by local artisans. Adjoining it is the well-regarded restaurant *Lamont's* (Thurs–Mon 11.30am–5pm, Sat 6pm–late, ℡08/9755 2434, @www.lamonts.com.au).

You'll receive a warm welcome and be pampered silly at stylish family-owned boutique hotel ⚿ *Windmills Break* (℡08/9755 2341, @www.windmillsbreak .com.au; ❾), on the corner of Caves and Hemsley roads, which boasts a big swimming pool and gardens. If you're settling in for a while, consider self-contained homesteads nearby at *Yallingup Forest Resort* (℡08/9755 2550, @www.yallingupforestresort.com.au; ❽–❾, min 2-night-stay) on Hemsley Road with pool and tennis court. On Yallingup Beach Road, the heritage-listed 1938 *Caves House Hotel* (℡08/9755 2131, @www.caveshouse.com.au; ❼) has attractive rooms.

Back on Caves Road a right turn leads to **Canal Rocks**, where the waves relentlessly pound the pink-granite outcrops into curious, scalloped forms. Some 5km further south, turn left onto Injidup Springs Road for the **Wardan Aboriginal Cultural Centre** (℡08/9756 6566, @www.wardan.com.au) where you can do a bushtucker walk, learn to make traditional tools and buy indigenous art. Nearby, at luxurious ⚿ *Moondance Lodge* (℡08/9750 1777, @www.moondancelodge.com; ❾) in the heart of native bushland, the focus is on wellness and spiritual nourishment with indigenous experiences offered in partnership with local Aboriginal custodians; rooms are a whopping $475.

Further south, ⚿ *Cape Lodge* (℡08/9755 6311, @www.capelodge.com.au; ❾) is the quintessential Margaret River boutique place (rooms $375) and a popular foodie destination, with the region's finest restaurant on site. On Puzey Road, **Bootleg Brewery** (daily 10am–4.30pm; ℡08/9755 6300, @www.bootlegbrewery.com.au) cheekily claims to be "a beer oasis in a desert of wine". Those here to visit wineries (and breweries) in the region should pick up the *Margaret River Map and Guide* from the Margaret River visitor centre; see p.670.

Further down Caves Road you come to the crossroads leading 5km inland to Margaret River township. A right turn takes you to the oceanside resort of **PREVELLY PARK**, close to the estuary of the Margaret River. The Greek **Chapel of St John** will catch your eye: a memorial to the Preveli Monastery on Crete which sheltered Allied soldiers, Australians among them, in World War II. The turning opposite leads down to the blustery Prevelly beach where November's annual Margaret River Classic **surfing** championships are held.

Back at the chapel, the road continues on to the beachside community, where chic, architect-designed homes sit alongside holiday chalets and caravan parks. The spacious and well-equipped *Surfpoint Resort*, on Reidle Drive (℡08/9757 1777 or 1800 071 777, @www.surfpoint.com.au; dorms $29, rooms ❹), opposite Gnarabup beach, is one of the best backpackers' in the region, offering free pick-ups from Margaret River if you call ahead, as well as free shuttles for those here to work the vineyards (pruning June–Sept, grape-picking Feb–April).

Margaret River, Cape Leeuwin and around

The **wine-lovers'** town of **MARGARET RIVER** and the surrounding region is busy at weekends and holidays with surfers, tourists and gastronomes escaping from Perth and the East Coast cities, with many making it their base for wine tasting by day and fine dining by night. Though you may not want to stay here if it's beach or rural bliss you're seeking, you'll still find the town handy for shopping (supermarket open till 9pm), eating out and browsing for art, crafts and gourmet goodies. Also worth visiting are remote Cape Leeuwin and historic Augusta.

Arrival, information and accommodation

Transwa and South West **buses** visit daily from Perth. The **visitor centre** (daily 9am–5pm; ℡08/9757 2911, ⓦwww.margaretriver.com), on the main street, can book accommodation, transport and winery tours. Grab the essential *Margaret River Map and Guide* which pinpoints all wineries, and the *Map & Guide to Studios and Galleries of the South West Cape Region* (available on ⓦwww .margaretriverartisans.com.au). The range of **accommodation** is daunting, with scores of options in the immediate vicinity. While the visitor centre has loads of information, it's wise to book before you arrive in town.

Accommodation

Bridgefield 73 Bussell Hwy ℡08/9757 3007, ⓦwww.bridgefield.com.au. This historic guest-house on the edge of town has charming antique rooms, and plenty of character, and is minutes from restaurants and bars. Includes breakfast. ❺

Central Avenue Apartments 1 Charles West Ave, ℡08/9758 7025, ⓦwww.centralavenue.com.au. These light, airy, contemporary apartments have enormous balconies and are centrally located, ideal for wine tasting by day and dining in town by night. One-bedroom apartment ❼, two-bedroom ❾

Margaret River Backpackers & Lodge Backpackers' at 66 Townview Terrace ℡08/9757 9572; Lodge at 220 Railway Terrace ℡08/9757 9532, ⓦwww.margaretriverbackpackers.com.au. Two jointly managed backpackers' – the first a smart new "working" hostel slap-bang in the town centre, with wi-fi, jobs desk and free transport to vineyards (for work) and beaches, the second a huge YHA resort-style place in a bushland setting 1.5km southeast of town, with pool, volleyball court, and bike rental. Dorms from $25, en-suite rooms ❸

Margaret River Hotel 139 Bussell Hwy ℡08/9757 2655, ⓦwww.margaretriverhotel.com .au. Large country pub in the heart of town, with spacious heritage-style rooms and some smaller ones. ❺–❻

Redgate Beach Escape 14 Redgate Rd ℡08/9757 6677, ⓦwww.redgatebeachescape .com.au. A 10min drive southwest of town. Four contemporary two-bedroom chalets on a hill overlooking the coast with great views of the surrounding landscape. ❾

Riverview Tourist Park 8 Wilmott Ave ℡1300 666 105, ⓦwww.riverviewcabin.com. Camping sites and cabins set in a picturesque setting on the river, 800m from town. Camping $17, powered site $30, en-suite cabins ❷, riverfront cabins ❺

Tour operators

Wine-tasting **tours** (which also include breweries), with Margaret River Tours (℡0419 917 166, ⓦwww.cmargaretrivertours.com.au), Wine For Dudes (℡0427 774 994, ⓦwww.winefordudes.com), and Margaret River Discovery Tours (℡0439 910 064, ⓦwww.margaretriverdiscovery.com.au), cost around $65 to $165 including lunch. Bushtucker Tours (℡08/9757 1084, ⓦwww .bushtuckertours.com; $80) offer just that from a canoe at the river mouth on Prevelly Beach, and the Margaret River Surf School (℡08/9757 1111, ⓦwww .margaretriversurfschool.com) has daily two-hour lessons for $45 or a three-day course for around $110, while Escape Safaris (℡08/9755 2488, ⓦwww .escapesafaris.com.au) do women–only tours combining surfing lessons, yoga, horseriding and other fun stuff.

Eating and drinking

The countryside surrounding Margaret River is dotted with brilliant **restaurants** attached to wineries, such as the outstanding *Vasse Felix* (℡08/9756 5050, ⓦwww.vassefelix.com.au), on the corner of Caves and Harmans roads in Cowaramup, although most only open for lunch. For dinner, the restaurants in town are your best option; most are on the main road, the Bussell Highway. Try

A band of limestone passing through the cape has created some 350 caves around Margaret River, four of which are open to the public. Most involve guided tours to avoid damage and accidents, with relatively steep entrance fees ($19.50 per cave) and shuffling crowds detracting from the cavernous spectacle. All are fairly humid and include some long, stepped ascents, with temperatures around 17°C. Tours are less frequent from May to August. For more details about all except Ngilgi Cave, see the website or enquire at the visitor centre in Margaret River or Augusta. The Cave Works Interpretive Centre (dealing with all things speleological) at Lake Cave (daily 9am–5pm; free with cave ticket; ☎08/9757 7411) sells a Grand Tour pass for $45 (valid for 7 days), which includes entry to Lake, Jewel and Mammoth caves.

Jewel Cave (daily 9.30am–3.30pm; 7 tours per day, 1hr), the best cave, features extraordinary formations such as five-metre-high "helictites" (delicate, straw-like formations) protected by breeze-proof doors, while a collapsed cavern overgrown with huge karri trees marks the impressive entrance to **Lake Cave** (daily 9.30am–3.30pm; 7 tours per day, 45min), where a unique "suspended table" hangs over the subterranean lake. **Mammoth Cave** (daily 9am–4pm; self-guiding) is a large cavern with easy access but is the least impressive. Note that lighting is dim in all caves, doing nothing to enhance an experience that won't appeal to all. **Ngilgi Cave** (daily 9.30am–4pm; $19.50) near Yallingup is not included on the above cave ticket but has plenty of nooks to explore and delicate features to admire.

the rustic-chic *Wino's* (☎08/9758 7155; daily 6pm–late) at no. 85 for delicious tapas and mod-Oz dishes. *Rasas* (☎08/9758 8443; Thurs–Sun noon–2.30pm & Tues–Sun 5–10pm) at no. 113 serves up tasty Asian, from satays to laksa, while *Margaret River Hotel* has backpacker specials on Tuesdays. On Willmott Avenue, *Wild Thyme* (Mon–Fri 7.30am–5pm, Sat 8am–3.30pm), does hearty breakfasts and typical café fare. *VAT 107* has the hippest and buzziest bar in town, while *Settlers* puts on live music in summer.

Augusta and Cape Leeuwin

If you're not doing much driving in WA, where you'll see plenty of birds of prey in the wild, visit **Eagles Heritage** (daily 10am–4pm; $12; Ⓦwww .eaglesheritage.com.au), on Boodjidup Road 5km southwest of Margaret River, for wedge-tail eagles, white-breasted sea eagles, peregrine falcons and owls in aviaries.

Rejoining Caves Road, having passed the turn-off for **Leeuwin Estate Winery** (daily 10am–4.30pm; Ⓦwww.leeuwinestate.com.au) with its fine restaurant, head south into the magnificent silvery-barked **karri forest**, worth taking some time to appreciate if you're not planning to visit the Pemberton area. Down the road are Mammoth and Lake caves (see box above), while Boranup Drive provides a scenic off-road detour through the **Boranup Forest**, and Boranup Gallery (☎08/9757 7585, Ⓦwww.boranupgallery.com) sells local art and **furniture** made from local timbers.

South of the forest, the Brockman Highway leads 90km east to Nannup, while continuing 3km south down Caves Road brings you to the turn-off to the old timber port of **Hamelin Bay**, which has a sheltered beach and a couple of shipwrecks ideal for snorkellers and scuba divers. At beachside *Hamelin Bay Caravan Park* (☎08/9758 5540, Ⓦwww.mronline.com.au/accom/hamelin/), you can choose from small bush cabins (❺) to oceanview cottages (❾), as well as camping ($25, powered site $28).

Passing **Jewel Cave**, the Bussell Highway takes you 8km further to the popular holiday town of **AUGUSTA**, on the estuary of the Blackwood River – WA's oldest settlement after Albany and Perth. The town's **museum** (daily: May–Aug 10am–noon; Sept–April 10am–noon & 2–4pm; $4) on Blackwood Avenue, the main road, tells Augusta's story. The **visitor centre** (daily 9am–5pm; ☎08/9758 0166, ⓦwww.augusta-wa.com.au) is on Ellis Street. On Blackwood Avenue, the *Augusta Hotel Motel* (☎08/9758 1944, ⓦwww.augusta-resorts.com.au; ❺) has river views. On the same road, *Baywatch Manor YHA* (☎08/9758 1290, ⓦwww.baywatchmanor.com.au) offers backpacker accommodation from $21, and rents bikes. On the main road, *Augusta Bakery & Café* (open to 4pm daily) does delicious pies and pastries, while the *Augusta Hotel Motel* has counter meals and cold beer.

Cape Leeuwin, 9km south of town, is probably why you've come this far, and it's worth the journey, with its windswept "land's end" feel, especially on a moody day. A Dutch captain named the cape after his ship in 1622, and Matthew Flinders began the onerous task of mapping Australia's coast right here in 1851. From the top of mainland Australia's tallest **lighthouse** (daily 8.45am–5pm; tours every 40min; entrance fee $5, tour $14), built in 1895 and still operational, you can contemplate Australia's most treacherous reef and your own location – halfway between the equator and Antarctic coast. There's a busy café on site. Nearby, an **old water wheel**, originally constructed for the lighthouse builders, is petrified in salt.

Hikers may want to consider the 140-kilometre coastal walk from Cape Leeuwin to Cape Naturaliste, the **Cape to Cape Track**, which can be tackled in five separate stages. The DEC office in Busselton (☎08/9752 1677) can provide information, although the Cape Leeuwin lighthouse store has maps and advice.

Tall Timber Country

Sandwiched between the popular tourist areas of the Margaret River region and Albany's dramatic coast, the forests of the so-called **Tall Timber Country**

▲ The lighthouse at Cape Leeuwin

Logging in Tall Timber Country

After a century and a half, the controversial **logging** of the Southwest's irreplaceable old-growth forest officially came to an end in 2001. Public debate over logging, and the sell-off of old-growth forests by DEC (the government department which also looks after WA's parks) to logging mills had grown ever more intense throughout the 1990s. Campaigners criticized DEC's sell-off as a display of mind-boggling environmental shortsightedness, pointing out that the ancient trees of old-growth forest predate colonization, and support a complex ecological system. As you explore the area along scenic drives you may assume the forest looks healthy and dense, but at times you're travelling in a 200-metre tree-lined corridor, outside of which lies an area still devastated by old-growth clear-felling. Quick to capitalize on a vote-winning issue, Labor had won the 2001 state election by promising to outlaw the logging of old-growth forests. Some backtracking followed and loopholes remain, but since that time the recession predicted in the logging industry has not materialized, and fast-growing plantations of blue gum trees (aka Tasmanian oak) have been found to offer a viable future to sustainable plantation logging in WA. Today the Forest Product Commission – Western Australia's trading enterprise – is continuing to focus on plantations, working with local governments, private landholders and communities to try to augment the attractiveness of tree farming. Debate continues as to how best to address the effect of tree farming on the land: issues such as farming communities, blending monocultures with bushland areas, accessing water and changing weather patterns dominate.

are some of WA's greatest sights. Along with the sinuous **Blackwood River** (ideal for sedate canoeing, especially downstream of Nannup; see below), the highlight of the region is the brooding, primeval majesty of the **karri forests**, famed not as much for their arboreal gimmicks – of which the **Gloucester Tree** near Pemberton is the best known – as for the raw, elemental nature of the unique forest environment. Since the practice of tearing down or clear-felling the irreplaceable ancient forests was greatly reduced in 2001 (see box above), logging towns like Pemberton and Manjimup are adjusting to an economy based around sustainable tree plantations and tourism. Check out Ⓦwww.southernforests.com.au for further details on this area as far as Walpole.

The Blackwood River Valley and south

The northern part of the forest country is watered by the **Blackwood River** and divided by scenic roads that link the riverside mill towns. Once an insular loggers' town, in the late hippy era **NANNUP**, 60km southeast of Busselton, was compared to New South Wales' Nimbin. These days it's an idyllic settlement of wooden cabins nestling quietly among wooded hills. The **visitor centre** (daily 9am–5pm; ℡08/9756 1211, Ⓦwww.nannupwa.com.au), on Brockman Street, has a portfolio of local **accommodation**. Set in lovely gardens, the B&B *Holberry House* (℡08/9756 1276, Ⓦwww.holberryhouse .com; ❺) has heritage-style rooms. On Warren Road, the *Blackwood Café* opens all day for big breakfasts and burgers in a picturesque garden setting, or up the road, there's the popular *Mulberry Tree Restaurant* (Tues–Sun 10am–4pm & 6pm–late).

If not walking, then a great way to enjoy the region is by **canoe**. Blackwood Canoeing (℡08/9756 1209, Ⓦwww.blackwoodrivercanoeing.com) offers self-guided one- to five-day **trips** on the lower Blackwood River, starting 27km south of town, from $35 a day, and offers a pick-up service from Nannup, or you can just paddle around for an hour or two. River levels vary with the seasons, making the overnight trips easier in the summer months.

From Nannup, a **scenic drive** winds 41km along the river to unremarkable Balingup, while the tree-lined Brockman Highway heads east 46km to **BRIDGETOWN**, a historic mill town that's becoming known for its organic produce, marron and olive oil. The busy **visitor centre** (Mon–Fri 10am–5pm, Sat 10am–3pm, Sun 10am–1pm; [T]08/9761 1740, [W]www.bridgetown.com.au) is on the main Hampton Street, as is a good **accommodation** option: the restored 1920s *Bridgetown Hotel* ([T]08/9761 1034, [W]www.bridgetownhotel.com.au; [5]) at no. 157 has contemporary spa suites and does pastas and burgers, while at no. 88 *The Barking Cow* ([T]08/9761 4619; daily 8.30am–4.30pm) is a charming deli-style **café** with a full menu focused on local products. Next to the rail crossing, at no. 30, *Horti Towers* ([T]08/761 2216; daily 10am–5pm except Wed) serves light lunches, cakes and Devonshire teas in rooms crammed with bric-a-brac.

Thirty-seven kilometres south of Bridgetown, **MANJIMUP** is the region's commercial centre, known for its truffles which can be tasted and purchased at *The Wine & Truffle Co* (daily 10am–4.30pm; [T]08/9777 2474, [W]www.wineandtruffle.com.au) on Seven Day Road. **Timber Park** celebrates the local timber industry behind the **visitor centre** (daily 9am–5pm; [T]08/9771 1831) on Rose Street, which has loads of information and maps detailing local bush walks and attractions, including a 600-year-old **King Jarrah Tree** 3km from town. Some 10km south of town you can climb the **Diamond Tree Lookout** at the top of a 51-metre karri tree, while about 20km from Manjimup there's a **100 Year Old Forest**. **One Tree Bridge**, made from a single karri tree felled to cross the Donnelly River in 1904, and the magnificent **Four Aces**, a quartet of huge 350-year-old karri trees standing in a row, are accessible from Graphite Road on a picturesque forest drive heading west 22km. The most luxurious and atmospheric **accommodation** (and best food) in the area is twenty minutes south of Manjimup (and 20min east of Pemberton) at ★ *Stonebarn* ([T]08/9761 1034, [W]www.stonebarn.com.au; [9]), an intimate and luxurious boutique retreat in a converted stone barn, set in 160 acres of forest; the $275 per room includes breakfast.

Pemberton and around

The quaint town of **PEMBERTON** makes a central base for Tall Timber touring, with enough craft shops, galleries, wineries and gourmet destinations to keep you a while. Stop at the **visitor centre** (daily 9am–5pm; [T]08/9776 1133, [W]www.pembertontourist.com.au) halfway up the hill on Brockman Street, to pick up a map and information on **fly-fishing**, **horseriding**, **canoe** and **bike rental**, local **tours** and maps of **walking trails** in the area, including part of the Bibbulmun Track. Here you'll also find the Pioneer Museum and the interactive Karri Forest Discovery Centre (both daily 9am–5pm; donation) which replicates the forest environment, giving a detailed explanation of the area's fauna and wildlife.

On Dickinson Street, Fine Woodcraft ([W]www.finewoodcraft.com.au) is one of the best craft galleries in the Southwest with everything you see, including the building itself, made from old-growth timber, either reclaimed or rejected by the mills. A fun way of enjoying the surrounding forest is to take the **tram** ([T]08/9776 1322, [W]www.pemtram.com.au; from $18) from Pemberton to Warren Bridge (daily 10.45am & 2pm; 1hr 45min return). The diesel tram rattles noisily along the old logging railway, over timber bridges spanning tiny creeks, visiting the **Cascades**, a local beauty spot also accessible by road.

The most popular attraction is the **Gloucester Tree** (DEC fee; see box, p.644), 3km southeast of town. At 61m, it's the world's tallest fire-lookout tree and its platform is accessible by climbing a terrifying spiral of horizontal stakes. Only a small proportion of people actually climb to the platform – these being people with courage to spare and no fear of heights.

The surrounding countryside is crisscrossed with peaceful walking trails and enchanting forest drives venturing deep into the karri woodlands. From **Beedelup National Park**, on the Vasse Highway 20km west of town, there's a short walk to a wobbly suspension bridge over **Beedelup Falls**, while the drive through the native karri forests of the **Warren National Park**, 10km southwest of town, will leave you in awe of these colossal trees. The specially signed 86-kilometre **Karri Forest Explorer** is a scenic drive that winds past many of the above attractions on a mixture of dirt and sealed roads. Otherwise, Pemberton Hiking and Canoeing (T08/9776 1559, W www.hikingandcanoeing.com.au) or Pemberton Discovery Tours (T08/9776 0484, W www.pembertondiscoverytours.com.au) can take you on a day-trip to see the sights above, including the spectacular D'Entrecasteaux dunes (see below).

As for **accommodation**, the centrally located *Pemberton Backpackers* (T08/9776 1105, W www.pembertonbackpackers.com.au; dorms $26, rooms ❸) has comfy doubles and a self-contained cottage (❹). A quirky option is the restored *Old Picture Theatre* (T08/9776 0258, W www.oldpicturetheatre.com.au; ❻), built in 1929 to entertain the townspeople, which has, rather oddly, been converted into comfy apartments. The **caravan park** (T08/9776 1300, W www .pembertonpark.com.au) has camping ($28–32), cabins (❹), cottages (❺) and bungalows (❻). The surrounding countryside abounds with tranquil woodland retreats, like the rustic cottages on *Pump Hill* (T08/9776 1379, W www .pumphill.com.au; ❻), a working farm, or the colonial mud-brick *Treenbrook Cottages* (T08/9776 1638, W www.treenbrook.com.au; ❼), with open fireplaces, nestled amongst the trees, 5km west.

For a **meal**, *Millhouse Café* (daily 9am–5pm), on Brockman Street, does scrumptious soups, quiches and cakes, while the grand old *Pemberton Hotel* serves decent pub grub (daily lunch and dinner). You can try local delicacies such as trout and marron (like freshwater crayfish) everywhere in town, but at *King Trout Restaurant & Marron Farm* (T08/9776 1352; daily 9.30am–5pm, book ahead for dinner), on the corner of Northcliffe and Old Vasse roads, you can try to catch your own and have the chef prepare it for you. You can taste locally brewed beers with the usual café fare at *Jarrah Jacks Brewery* (T08/9776 1333, W www.jarrahjacks.com.au; Mon–Fri 9am–5pm, Sat & Sun 9am–6pm).

Northcliffe and D'Entrecasteaux National Park

Some 30km south of Pemberton, **NORTHCLIFFE**, a small logging town, is a good stop for those doing the Bibbulman Track. Note that after rain the road here is a muddy track suitable for 4WD only. On Karri Hill Road near the Bibbulman Track, the *Watermark Kilns Farmstay and Marron Farm* (T08/9776 7349, W www.watermarkkilns.com.au; shared ❶, own kiln ❼) consists of heritage-listed 1950s tobacco kiln buildings converted into simple, clean accommodation. Dinner is, naturally, fresh marron.

To the southwest a long spread of coastal heathland and inland dunes makes up the mostly inaccessible **D'Entrecasteaux National Park**. Driving south of Northcliffe you emerge from the forest and onto the heathland, passing a short, steep walk up the 187-metre Mount Chudalup for views of the Southern Ocean breaking against Sandy Island, 30km south of Northcliffe, just off **WINDY HARBOUR**. The tidy and seemingly deserted settlement has about fifteen permanent residents, one shop at the campsite and a few dozen weatherboard holiday homes. As long as you're suitably equipped, a grassy **campsite** (℡08/9776 8398; no dogs allowed) in the centre of the hamlet makes an inviting stopover. West of the main bay you can walk to a broader, slightly more sheltered beach, also accessible from a car park off Old Lighthouse Road, a dead end that leads west out of the settlement. From here it's possible to walk the 2km up the clifftop to **Point D'Entrecasteaux**, where a platform hangs out over the pounding surf below. You can also reach the Point in your car by following the Salmon Beach turn-off just before Windy Harbour. **Salmon Beach** itself is a wild, exposed strand below Point D'Entrecasteaux, facing the prevailing southwesterlies and therefore good for a hair-tussling stroll.

Albany and the southern coast

Alternating sheltered bays and rounded granite headlands make up the southern coast, or "Great Southern", around Albany. As elsewhere in the Southwest, the temperate climate and changeable weather create a rural antipodean–English idyll unknown in the rest of WA. Site of the region's original settlement, nowadays it's an appealing area of wineries, art and craft galleries and fine restaurants.

Albany, 410km from Perth, is an agricultural centre and holiday destination, while **Denmark**, 54km to the west, is a quaint, arty hamlet. **Walpole**'s bays and tingle forests mark the western limit of the southern coast. An hour's drive north of Albany lie the burgeoning wine-making region of Mount Barker and the mountainous **Porongurup** and **Stirling Ranges national parks**.

While Perth's radial **bus services** to the main centres run on a fairly frequent basis, moving around by bus requires considerable planning to avoid inconvenient delays, making the area best explored by car. Transwa buses depart from Perth for Albany at least daily, either directly down the Albany Highway (6hr) or via Bunbury and Walpole (8hr 30min). It's also possible to see some of the area on **tours** (see pp.656–657).

Albany and around

In 1826, two years before the establishment of the Swan River Colony, the British sent Major Lockyer and a team of hopeful colonists to settle Albany's strategic **harbour** where they built the Princess Royal Fortress. It was a hasty pre-emptive response to French exploration of Australia's Southwest, and the small colony, originally called Fredrickstown, was allowed to grow at a natural pace – thus avoiding the vicissitudes of "Swan River Mania" that plagued Perth in the 1880s, when thousands of starry-eyed settlers poured into the riverside shanty town. Prior to the establishment of Fremantle Harbour in the 1890s, **ALBANY**'s huge natural harbour was a key port on the route between England and Botany Bay: a coaling station in the age of steamers. It was also the last of Australia that many ANZACs saw on their way to Gallipoli in 1914.

Now serving the southern farming belt, Albany has also become one of the Southwest's main holiday areas. Factors such as proximity to Perth, moderate summer temperatures, a surfeit of natural splendour and historical kudos all combine to make an agreeable and genuine destination, largely bereft of bogus tourist traps.

Arrival, information and accommodation

Transwa **buses** arrive near the old train station on Lower Stirling Terrace, not far from the **visitor centre** on Proudlove Parade (daily 9am–5.30pm; ℡08/9841 9290, ⊛www.amazingalbany.com), which dispenses handy local and regional **maps** and brochures detailing walking itineraries and cycling routes. Loves Bus Service (timetables at the visitor centre) provides in-town **public transport**: the #301 route between York Street, the town's main road, and Middleton Beach/Emu Point is particularly useful (Mon–Fri 9am–3pm, Sat 9.15–11am). For **car rental** try Mike at King Sound Vehicle Hire at 6 Sanford Rd (℡08/9841 8466, 0427 418 150, ⊛www.kingsoundcars.com, from $40 per day). Note that Albany can only be reached by bus from Esperance (see p.682) on Tuesdays and Fridays and that buses leave from Albany to Esperance on Monday and Thursday (6hr 30min).

Several **guesthouses** and **B&Bs** are situated along Stirling Terrace, a block from the harbour; there are also motels, self-contained units, and caravan and camping grounds in the Middleton Bay area, 3km east of the centre. In the countryside, you can stay on working farms or in cosy cottages. The visitor centre has a detailed portfolio of accommodation options. Note that prices drop by up to fifty percent in winter, especially for apartments.

Motels, backpackers', B&Bs and guesthouses

Albany Backpackers Corner of Stirling Terrace and Spencer St ℡1800 260130, ⊛www .albanybackpackers.com.au. One of Albany's oldest buildings: a warren of corridors and rooms with murals at every turn, plenty of amenities, and a good atmosphere. Breakfast, internet access on arrival, one beer, and coffee and cake each day are included in price. Dorms $25, rooms ❷

Bayview Backpackers YHA 49 Duke St ℡08/9842 3388, ℮albanyyha@westnet.com.au. Old wooden building, 5min from the centre, with dorms, twins, BBQs and some parking. Dorms $22.50, rooms ❷

Discovery Inn 9 Middleton Rd ℡08/9842 5535, ⊛www.discoveryinn.com.au. One block from Middleton Beach, this 1920s guesthouse has a chilled-out beach-house vibe. Breakfast included. ❸

Dog Rock Motel 303 Middleton Rd ℡08/9841 4422, ⊛www.dogrockmotel.com.au. Stylish contemporary rooms, a 5min walk from the town-centre shops, and Albany's best restaurant, *Lime 303*, on the premises. ❺

My Place Colonial Accommodation 47–61 Grey St East ℡08/9842 3242, ⊛www.myplace.com.au. A variety of charming options: from renovated, fully self-contained historic cottages to modern units and apartments with wi-fi and DVD players. ❺

Vancouver House 86 Stirling Terrace ℡08/9842 1071, ⊛www.vancouverhousebnb.com.au. This historic nineteenth-century guesthouse, now an old-fashioned five-room B&B, is famous for its hot breakfast; three rooms are en suite, some boast harbour views. ❸

Caravan parks

Emu Beach Emu Point, 7km from the town centre ℡08/9844 1147, ⊛www.emubeach.com. As well as the beach on its doorstep, the plentiful amenities here include trampolines and mini-golf. Camping $32–43, on-site chalet ❼, cabin (BYO linen) ❺

Middleton Beach 28 Flinders Parade, Middleton Beach ℡08/9841 3593, ⊛http://middleton-beach -holiday-park.wa.big4.com.au. Right on the beach, this swish holiday park boasts a solar-heated swimming pool and spa, wi-fi, and Devonshire tea on Wednesdays. Camping $33–48, powered sites $34–50, chalets ❺, units ❹

The town and around

Albany's attractions are spread between the Foreshore – where the original settlers set up camp – the calm white-sand beaches around **Middleton Beach**, and Emu Point on the still waters of Oyster Harbour. Some 40km east round the harbour is the idyllic nature reserve at **Two Peoples Bay**, while the natural spectacles and attractions on the **Torndirrup Peninsula**, 20km southwest of town, along Frenchman's Bay Road, are also well worth a look.

On the **Foreshore**, there's a replica of the *Amity* (daily 9.30am–4pm; $5; ☎08/9841 6885), the brig that landed its sixty-odd settlers here on Boxing Day 1826, after six months at sea. Nearby, the **Old Gaol & Convict Museum** (daily 10am–4pm; $5; ☎08/9841 6174), built in 1852, is an early surviving relic of colonization in the area, and offers spooky night tours (Fri & Sat 7.30pm or by arrangement; $20; ☎08/9845 1020). **WA Museum's Residency Museum** (daily 9.30am–4.30pm; gold coin donation; ☎08/9841 4844) has meticulous displays on the town's maritime history and Aboriginal bush medicines, and an educational see-and-touch gallery for children upstairs.

Closer to Middleton Beach, the curious tower on top of **Mount Melville Lookout**, off Serpentine Road, is colloquially known as "the spark plug". One of two lookouts in Albany, this one offers good seaward vistas. From here, backtrack to York Street, turn left and head 2km down Middleton Road to the **Old Farm Strawberry Hill** (Sept–June daily 10am–4pm; $5; ☎08/9841 3735). Reminiscent of an English cottage, the farm (WA's first) provided settlers with locally grown produce, while the building (built in 1836) once housed the visiting Governor Stirling. Devonshire tea is available to take full advantage of the enchanting gardens and historic landscape.

Middleton Beach itself, Albany's centre beach, was undergoing redevelopment at the time of writing, with the upmarket *Esplanade Hotel* demolished. From Middleton Beach, head up Marine Drive and turn right for **Mount Clarence Lookout**, with its ANZAC memorial, where, on a clear day, you can see the Stirling Ranges, 80km to the north. On the way down you pass the **Princess Royal Fortress** (daily 9am–5pm; $6; ☎08/9841 9369, ⓦ www .forts.albany.wa.gov.au), an impressively restored naval installation dating from the end of the nineteenth century.

Eating

Albany shares the rest of the Southwest's laudable preoccupation with quality eating. Food markets are big here and great for picnic supplies. Try Albany Farmers Market on Collie Street (Sat 8am–noon) for fresh seasonal produce with that just-picked taste, and the Boat Shed Markets (Sun 10am–1pm).

Dylans on the Terrace 82 Stirling St ☎08/9841 8720. This popular place does breakfasts, burgers and pancakes. Tues–Sat 7am–late, Sun 8am–5pm.

Lime 303 *Dog Rock Motel*, 303 Middleton Rd ☎08/9841 4422. A local favourite, this chic restaurant serves creative, contemporary Asian- and Med-inspired cuisine, such as Shark Bay prawns with lemongrass on shaved Parma ham. Daily 6pm–late.

Nonna's 135 Lower York St ☎08/9841 4626. Decent pastas and brasserie food served in a big atmospheric building. The great-value "seafood Fridays" draw locals. Mon–Fri 11am–late, Sat & Sun 5pm–late.

Rookleys Corner of Peels Place and York St. Deli-style café with outdoor seating and good coffee. Mon–Sat 9am–5pm (summer), 9am–3pm (winter).

The Squid Shack Boat Ramp, Emu Point ☎08/9844 9771. This local institution with outdoor tables by the beach is the spot for the freshest takeaway seafood; squid and calamari are the speciality, but the oysters and chilli mussels (weekends only) are delish. BYO. Daily 10am–7pm.

Tangle Head Brewery 72 Stirling St ☎08/9841 1733. This stylish brewery-restaurant does delicious gourmet pizzas (around $20) and has a variety of boutique beers, including the popular "harbourside lager". Brewery tours also on offer (Wed & Sat 2pm). Daily 11am–late.

Listings

Bicycle rental Albany Bicycle Hire offers a free drop-off/pick-up service (☎08/9842 2468).

Bus Transwa (☎1300 662 205) or call in at the visitor centre.

DEC 120 Albany Hwy (Mon–Fri 9am–5pm; ☎08/9842 4500). Information on parks and birdwatching, and passes sold for WA national parks (see box, p.644).

Diving Dive Locker (☎08/9842 6886, ⓦwww .albanydive.com), on the corner of York St and Proudlove Parade, is a PADI 5-star centre offering courses and dives to local sites (year-round visibility apart from Jan) from $202 with full gear rental. Popular wrecks include HMAS *Perth* that was scuttled in 2001, and the older *Cheyne III* whaler on nearby Michaelmas Island.

Fishing Spinners Charters (☎08/9844 1906, ⓦwww.spinnerscharters.com.au) does full-day charters including all fishing gear, breakfast and BBQ, for $210 per person. Prices for its whale-watching tours (July–Nov) vary depending on numbers.

Post office 218 York St ☎13 13 18.

Taxi ☎08/9844 4444.

Tours and cruises Albany Whale Tours (☎0408 451 068, ⓦwww.albanywhaletours.com.au) offers three-hour whale-watching cruises on a catamaran to King George Sound (June–Oct; $60), along with twilight cruises, while Silver Star Cruises (☎0428 429 876, ⓦwww.whales.com.au) takes you whale-watching (June–Oct; twice daily) and to historic whaling sights for around $75 including morning tea. JJ Tours (☎08/9841 3180; Mon-Sat) offers fascinating two-hour history walking tours for $18. Grape Southern Wine Tours (☎0429 479 463, ⓦwww.grapesoutherntours .com.au) has half- and full-day minibus tours to wineries including lunch ($65/95) and scenic tours around Albany ($65).

Torndirrup National Park and Whaleworld

Frenchman's Bay Road leads onto a peninsula incorporating the **Torndirrup National Park** (DEC fees; see box, p.644), 20km southwest of town, where there are stunning beaches, lookouts and other natural attractions. Passing the turn-off to the **Wind Farm** with its ridge-top boardwalk, **the Gap** and **Natural Bridge** are the first attractions worth visiting. Take care: this area has claimed several lives. People die by slipping or getting blown into the sea by **king waves**, immense waves that are indistinguishable in the swell. From the car park, a path leads down to the sloping granite shoreline of **Cable Beach**.

Further along, the views from Stony Hill and Misery Beach are worth a look. Nearby, a track leads to the summit of **Isthmus Hill** (1km), in spring passing varieties of orchids on the way. A bracing **walk** (around 4km) leads from the summit, culminating at Bald Head on the tip of the Flinders Peninsula.

Frenchman's Bay Road arrives at pretty, sheltered **Frenchman's Bay** on Princess Royal Harbour, a sublime spot for a swim. Just before, you'll have passed the turn-off to **Whaleworld** (daily 9am–5pm; $20; free tours on the hour 10am–4pm; ☎08/9844 4021; ⓦwww.whaleworld.org), site of Australia's last whaling station, which closed in 1978. The facility is now an engaging museum dedicated to the world's biggest creatures, once hunted to near extinction. The informative half-hour **tours** explain Australia's role in ending the hunting, though not before describing the process of dismembering and boiling down the whale blubber and bones, and displaying the machinery that did the job. Don't miss seeing the towering *Cheyne IV* whale chaser beached in the middle of the complex.

Along the southern coast

An hour's drive west of Albany, **West Cape Howe National Park** is a coastal wilderness area that requires a 4WD to fully explore, while **William Bay National Park**, 15km west of Denmark, has many inviting coves accessible to regular vehicles. A few kilometres before Walpole, the **Valley of the Giants** is home to the breathtaking **Tree Top Walk** and marks the edge of the giant tingle tree country. Transwa buses run on Monday and Friday between Albany and Perth (6hr), but you won't see much this way – renting a car is a better bet.

Denmark and William Bay National Park

DENMARK, set on the river of the same name, is a quaint little country town and a pleasant spot to enjoy lunch or boat up the river. By the coast, the big lagoon of Wilson Inlet can turn an unappealing tannin colour if the moving sand bar happens to plug the lagoon's narrow mouth to the sea. Just outside the lagoon mouth is **Ocean Beach** (accessible via Ocean Beach Rd), with spectacular views across the broad Ratcliffe Bay, where the swells sweep in to create good **surfing** conditions for learners. Mike Neunuebel's well-regarded South Coast Surfing (℡08/9848 2057 or 0401 349 854) offers one-to-one lessons and group sessions (2hr per day; $60–90), and gear rental.

Denmark's **visitor centre** (daily 9am–5pm; ℡08/9848 2055, ⊛www .denmark.com.au), 73 South Coast Hwy, on the corner of Ocean Beach Road, can advise on the myriad **places to stay** in the vicinity and book on your behalf. Grab a copy of the *Wine Lovers' Guide to Denmark* brochure, which lists over twenty local wineries. In town, *Pensione Verde*, 31 Strickland St (℡08/98481700, ⊛www.denmarkaccommodation.com.au; ❺), has nine individually decorated rooms, a cooking school and offers walking packages, while the *Blue Wren Travellers' Rest YHA*, 17 Price St (℡08/9848 3300, ⊛www .denmarkbluewren.com.au; dorms $24, rooms ❸), has a laid-back atmosphere. *Denmark Waterfront*, 63 Inlet Drive (℡08/9848 1147, ⊛www.denmarkwater front.com.au; ❻), has timber units and cottages, some with water views, while in the mountains above town ⚇ *Denmark Observatory Resort*, Mount Shadforth Rd (℡08/9848 2233, ⊛www.denmarkobservatoryresort.com.au; ❼), offers the most stylish and luxurious accommodation with spacious bungalows and split-level studios boasting kitchenettes, mod cons, spa baths and spectacular views. It also has slick caravan and RV bays with en suites.

Denmark's **dining** options are limited: *McSweeney's*, 5B Strickland St (℡08/9848 2362; daily 7.30am–4.30pm), does delicious breakfasts and light lunches, while *Southern End* at 427 Mt Shadforth Rd (℡08/9848 2600; dinner 6–9pm) is by far the best option in the area, serving fine classic bistro dishes based on local produce.

From Denmark you can head west along hilly **Shadforth Scenic Drive**, dotted with wineries, cheese-makers and animal farms, to **William Bay National Park**, passing **wineries** such as West Cape Howe. At William Bay **Green Pool** cove is one of the prettiest spots along the coast, while Madfish Bay and Waterfall Bay further west are also worth a visit.

The Valley of the Giants' Tree Top Walk and Walpole

About 40km west of Denmark you can turn south to **Peaceful Bay**, a pleasant lunch stop with a caravan park and chalets. The forest of massive tingle and karri trees that make up the **Valley of the Giants** is known for its **Tree Top Walk** (daily 9am–4.15pm; $8; ℡08/9840 8263), an amazingly engineered 600-metre walkway (accessible to wheelchairs), which sways on half a dozen pylons among the tingle-tree crowns, 40m above the ground. To gain a better impression of the surrounding forest, take the **Ancient Empire Walkway** that winds through the forest floor (same hours as above).

On the coastal highway, **NORNALUP** has a roadside tea house and restaurant and, next door, red cedar chalets overlooking the tranquil Frankland River (℡08/9840 1107, ⊛www.walpole.org.au/NornalupRiversideChalets; studios ❹). Take the track 6km west of town to lovely **Conspicuous Beach**. **WALPOLE**, 10km from Nornalup, is the hub of many scenic drives to more towering forests, oceanic lookouts and sheltered inlets. The **Walpole–Nornalup visitor centre** is on the South Coast Highway (Mon–Fri 9am–5pm, Sat & Sun 9am–4pm;

ⓣ08/9840 1111, ⓦwww.walpole.com.au), as is the *Valley of the Giants Eco Park* (ⓣ08/9840 1313, ⓦwww.valleyofthegiantsecopark.biz), offering eco-activities in a natural bushland setting during school holidays. Backpackers head for the *Tingle All Over YHA* (ⓣ08/9840 1041, ⓔtingleallover2000@yahoo.com.au; 5-bed dorms $20, rooms ❷); situated at the west end of town, it has a wood fire in the lounge (a must in winter) and seems to own one of the biggest chess sets in the southern hemisphere (the pieces are around 60cm). On the corner of Pier Street and Park Avenue, *Walpole Lodge* (ⓣ08/9840 1244, ⓦwww.walpolelodge .com.au; dorms $25, rooms ❷) is popular with walkers, and has a relaxed atmosphere.

West of Walpole the **South Western Highway** starts its scenic run northwest – through more colossal forests – to Northcliffe (100km) and Pemberton (138km) at the heart of the Tall Timber Country.

The Porongurups and the Stirling Ranges

North of Albany lie the ancient granite highlands of the Porongurups and the impressive thousand-metre-high Stirling Ranges, 40km and 80km from Albany respectively. Both have been designated **national parks**; the DEC office in Albany provides further information and maps.

Porongurup National Park

The granite hills comprising the **Porongurup National Park** (DEC fees; see box, p.644) are often described as "among the oldest rocks on Earth" and encompass a dozen wooded peaks, whose protruding bald summits are over 600m high. The fifteen-kilometre-long ridge catches coastal moisture to support its isle of karri forests, thereby leaving the loftier Stirlings to the north dry and treeless.

Once at the park, most people are happy to do no more than take the five-minute stroll to **Tree in a Rock**, a natural oddity near the park's northern entrance. However, if you want to get your teeth into a good walk, head up the marked trail to **Devil's Slide** (671m) and return via Nancy and Hayward peaks; the full route warrants at least half a day. **Balancing Rock**, at the eastern end of the park, can be reached in 45 minutes from the car park, with a cage on the exposed outcrop of Castle Rock providing safe viewing.

The Stirling Range National Park

Taking the Chester Pass Road north towards the looming **Stirling Range National Park** (DEC fees; see box, p.644), the distinctive profile of Bluff Knoll will, if you're lucky, emerge from the cloudbanks often obscuring its summit. Avid hillwalkers could spend a few days "peakbagging" here and come away well satisfied; the Stirlings are WA's best – if not only – mountain-walking area, with as many as five peaks over 1000m. Be aware, however, that the area can experience blizzards as late as October. **Bluff Knoll** (1073m), the park's highest and most popular ascent, has a well-built path involving a three-hour-return slog. Like much of the area, the floral biodiversity in the Range is exceptional.

The unsealed 45-kilometre Stirling Range **scenic drive** winds amid the peaks to Red Gum Pass in the west, where you can turn around and go back the same way (with superior views). Halfway along the drive **Talyuberup** (800m) is a short, steep ascent, with great vistas at the top, while **Toolbrunup Peak** (1052m), accessed by a track next to the park campsite (see p.682), is a steep, four-kilometre, three-hour trip, with some exposed scrambling near the summit. Many other **trails** wander between the peaks and link up into overnight walks. Before heading off, check conditions and pick up a brochure from the DEC office at Albany and enter your name, details of your party, destination and route in the log books at *Bluff Knoll* picnic site and *Moingup Springs* **campsite** off Chester Pass Road. With a lack of showers, the campsite is basic; more comfortable option is the *Stirling Range Retreat* (☎08/9827 9229, ⓦwww .stirlingrange.com.au; dorms $30, cabins ❸, four-bed chalets ❺), just outside the park's northern boundary, opposite the Bluff Knoll turn-off. There's a café here, whose owners can fill you in on wild-flower locales; they also sell DEC park passes. *Mount Trio Bush Camping & Caravan Park* (☎08/9827 9270, ⓦwww .mounttrio.com.au; camping $12) is on the park's south side on Salt River Road, with tent sites, a campers' kitchen and showers. Ten kilometres north of the Bluff Knoll turn-off is *The Lily*, 9793 Chester Pass Rd (☎08/9827 9205, ⓦwww.thelily.com.au; ❺), which offers a charming touch of Holland in the middle of nowhere; look for the sixteenth-century replica windmill (that used to grind flour), and prepare yourself for incredibly good food, quaint Dutch cottages and Dutch bicycle-riding owners.

Esperance and the south coast

Esperance, 721km southeast of Perth, is at the western end of the **Archipelago of the Recherche**. Both town and archipelago were named after the French ships that visited the area in the late eighteenth century, and whose persistent interest in the region precipitated the hasty colonization of WA by the edgy British. The archipelago's string of haze-softened granite isles, bobbing in the inky blue Southern Ocean, presents an almost surreal seascape common to coasts washed by cold currents. The mild summer weather (rarely exceeding 30°C), abundant fishing opportunities and surrounding national parks ensure the town is a popular destination for heat-sensitive holiday-makers.

Around 50km southeast of Esperance is the **Cape Le Grand National Park**, and a further 70km the more remote **Cape Arid National Park**, on the edge of the Great Australian Bight. Care should be taken all along this coastline, as unpredictable **king waves** frequently sweep the unwary away from exposed, rocky shores.

You can get to Esperance from Kalgoorlie with Transwa's **bus service** (3 weekly; 5hr) or direct from Perth on the *Spirit of Esperance* bus service (6 weekly; 10hr). Buses leave from Albany to Esperance on Monday and Thursday.

Esperance and around

The town of **ESPERANCE** prospered briefly as a supply port during the heyday of the Eastern Goldfields, and was revived after World War II when its salty soils were made fertile with the simple addition of certain missing trace elements. Now an established farming and holiday centre, it makes an ideal base from which to explore the south coast's dazzling beaches and storm-washed headlands. The town boasts a certain laid-back charm that's appealing – most evident in the mornings when the Coffee Kat van (7am–2pm) pulls up in the jetty car park and the locals lounge around in the sun with their takeaway cappuccinos and socialize for a couple of hours.

Dempster Street is the town's main road, where you'll find the visitor centre (see opposite) and various tourist-oriented shops, cafés, art galleries and crafts shops in a dozen historic bungalows known as the **Museum Village**; the visitor centre's Heritage Walk booklet explains the history of the buildings. Nearby on James Street, the **Esperance Museum** (daily 1.30–4.30pm; $5) in the historic railway goods shed is a good repository of local memorabilia and is very proud of its Skylab satellite display: it disintegrated over Esperance in 1979 and NASA was reputedly fined $400 for littering.

After you've taken a stroll along the Norfolk pine-lined esplanade and visited Sammy the Seal under the jetty, you could rent a bike or car and do the forty-kilometre **Great Ocean Drive scenic loop** west of town. Travelling clockwise, stop first at the **Rotary Lookout** to survey the captivating seascape. You'll see the **wind farm** on the way to **Twilight Cove**, an idyllic and sheltered spot that's much prettier than the beaches in the centre of town. From here settle in for more windswept grandeur (and a nudist beach) at **Observation Point Lookout**, before the road turns inland towards **Pink Lake**. This is one of many lakes between here and Merredin, sometimes so-coloured by salt-tolerant algae, whose seafaring cousins give the coastline its enchanting turquoise hue.

The hundred or so islands of the romantically named Archipelago of the Recherche – known as the **Bay of Isles** – around Esperance are chiefly occupied by seals, feral goats and multitudes of seabirds. Dolphins may also be spotted offshore and southern right whales are commonly observed migrating to the Antarctic in spring. Mackenzies Island Cruises, 71 The Esplanade (℡08/9071 5757, ⊛www.woodyisland.com.au), offer daily trips with the possibility of overnight stays in comfortable eco-friendly huts on idyllic **Woody Island** (Sept–April only) where you can go bushwalking, fishing and snorkelling.

Practicalities

Transwa **buses** stop in the town centre, with **taxis** available on ℡08/9071 1782. The **visitor centre** (Mon, Tues, Thurs 9am–5pm, Wed & Fri 8am–5pm, Sat 9am–4pm, winter till 2pm, Sun 9am–2pm, winter till noon; ℡08/9083 1555, ⊛www.visitesperance.com) is in the Historic Museum Village on Dempster Street and can book Transwa buses and trains. The **shopping centre** is on Andrew Street. The DEC office, at 92 Dempster St (℡08/9071 3733), provides information and sells passes for WA national parks including those around Esperance. **Bicycles** can be rented from the visitor centre or along the Esplanade. For **car rental**, try Budget (℡08/9071 2775) or Avis (℡08/9071 3998). Esperance Diving and Fishing, 72 The Esplanade (℡08/9071 5111, ⊛www.esperancedivingandfishing.com.au), runs **dive** charters and courses, while Kepa Kurl (℡08/9072 1688, ⊛www.kepakurl.com.au; $105 per day tour) offers an excellent and engaging series of tours, including some exploring Cape Le Grand/Frenchmans Peak and Mount Ridley from the perspective of the indigenous Noongar people.

Most **accommodation** is reserved well ahead of time during school holidays (see p.644) so book in advance. Note that air conditioning is rarely necessary. One of the best options is *Esperance B&B By the Sea*, 34 Stewart St (℡08/9071 5640, ⊛www.esperancebb.com; ❺), with panoramic sea views and a comfy, homely feel. Two motels on the Esplanade offer sea views: the well-appointed, two-storey *Jetty Resort* at no. 1 (℡08/9071 3333, ⊛www.thejettyresort.com.au; ❺), which has a pool, and the frilly, floral *Captain Huon Motel* at no. 5 (℡08/9071 2383, ⊛www.captainhuonmotel.com.au; ❻), with self-catering units and breakfast included. For a chic antidote to motel sterility, *Esperance Clearwater Motel Apartments*, partly set in the historic old hospital at 1A William St (℡08/9071 3587, ⊛clearwatermotel.com.au; ❻), are stylish, contemporary apartments with all mod cons. Finally, the backpackers', *Blue Waters Lodge YHA*, 299 Goldfields Rd

(☎08/9071 1040, ✉yhaesperance@hotmail.com; dorms $23, rooms ❷), is just 20m from the seafront and offers pick-ups, bikes and a huge kitchen.

For a creative mod-Oz **meal** head to family-run local favourite 🏃 *Loose Goose* (☎08/9071 2320; open daily for dinner) at 9A Andrew St, which serves up surprisingly hearty and adventurous French-inspired food and sublime local seafood. A few metres away at no. 5, the *Kebab and Turkish Bakery* (☎08/9071 7704; daily 8am–8pm) does tasty kebabs, felafel, salads and dips, although service is slow for a fast-food place, while *Taylor Street Jetty Café-Restaurant* on the jetty (☎08/9071 4317; daily 7am–10pm, dinner until 9pm) serves everything from sandwiches and salads to pasta and seafood.

Cape Le Grand National Park

Once in Esperance, a visit to **Cape Le Grand National Park** (DEC fee; see box, p.644) is well worth the expense of renting a car or taking a tour; it's essentially a climb up a hill and a beach-hop – but on a good day they're the kind of beaches you want to roll up and take home with you. Once in the park, the first turn-off is to the picturesque **Le Grand Beach**, then (just before the Frenchman's Peak turn-off), a road leads to **Hellfire Bay** – sheltered coves don't come any more perfect than this. The climb to the summit of **Frenchman's Peak** (262m) is not as hard as it looks, and warrants the half-hour's exertion if you have a sturdy pair of shoes. The secret of its distinctive, hooked summit is an unexpected hole that frames an impressive view out to sea. From here you can also take a tough, three-hour walk to **Le Grand Beach** (limited camping), which is also accessible in a 4WD from Wylie Bay at the end of Bandy Creek Road if the tide is right. There is also a less demanding two-hour trek east to **Thistle Cove**, from where an easier trail leads to the broad arc of the most beautiful beach in the area, **Lucky Bay**. Here you'll find kangaroos on the sand, great camping facilities, sheltered swimming and wonderful hues of ocean colours. **Rossiter Bay**, another 6km east, is pleasant enough, while **Orleans Bay** is a further 42km from here.

The Eastern Goldfields

Six hundred kilometres east of Perth, at the end of the **Great Eastern Highway**, are the **Eastern Goldfields**. In the late nineteenth century, gold was found in what still remains one of the world's richest gold-producing regions. Lack of fresh water made life very hard for the early prospectors, driven by a national economic depression into miserable living conditions, disease and, in most cases, premature graves. Nevertheless, boom towns of thousands, boasting grand public buildings, several hotels and a vast periphery of hovels, would spring up and collapse in the time it took to extract any ore.

In 1892 the railway from Perth reached the town of **Southern Cross**, just as big finds turned the rush into a national stampede. This huge influx of people accentuated the water shortage, until the visionary engineer C.Y. O'Connor oversaw the construction of a 556-kilometre **pipeline** from Mundaring Weir, in the hills above Perth, to Kalgoorlie in 1903. Around this time many of the smaller gold towns were already in decline, but the Goldfields' wealth and boost in population finally gave WA the economic autonomy it sought in its claim for statehood in 1901.

In the years preceding the goldrush, the area was briefly one of the world's richest sources of **sandalwood**, an aromatic wood greatly prized throughout

Asia for joss sticks, and still a staple in modern perfumery. Supplies in the Pacific had become exhausted, so by 1880 the fragrant wood was WA's second-largest exportable commodity after wool. Exacerbating the inevitable over-cutting was the goldrush's demand for timber to prop up shafts, or to fire the pre-pipeline water desalinators. Today the region is a pit-scarred and prematurely desertified landscape, dotted with the scavenged vestiges of past settlements, while at its core the **Super Pit** gold mine in Kalgoorlie gets wider and deeper year by year.

Moribund **Coolgardie** may have been the original goldrush settlement, but the Goldfields are now centred around the twinned towns of **Kalgoorlie–Boulder**. A thriving, energetic hub, Kalgoorlie is one of Australia's richest towns. Even if you're not planning to pass through the Goldfields, there's enough to see in Kalgoorlie to make a couple of days' excursion from Perth worthwhile – if for nothing else than the novelty of riding on the new "high-speed" **Prospector**, the daily six-hour rail link between Perth and Kalgoorlie.

Coolgardie

Not quite dilapidated and abandoned enough to carry the name "ghost mining town", **COOLGARDIE** is more of a museum to itself, a town which – at its peak – had twenty-three hotels, three breweries and six newspapers serving a population ten times greater than its present twelve hundred. Arthur Bayley cranked the gold fever up when he arrived into Southern Cross – then the easternmost extent of the rush – in 1892 with nearly sixteen kilos of gold. The ensuing wave of prospectors started within hours – ten thousand men rushed out of Southern Cross, culminating in a fourfold increase in WA's population by the end of the century.

The grand **Mining Warden's Court Building** at 62 Bayley St is home to the town's **visitor centre** (Mon–Fri 8.30am–4.30pm; ☏08/9026 6090, ⓦwww.coolgardie.wa.gov.au) and, upstairs, the **Goldfields Exhibition Museum** (same hours; $4), which boasts one of WA's most comprehensive displays on the goldrush and its impact. Next door, a fascinating **Pharmacy Museum** (same hours; $4) displays a collection of eighteenth- and nineteenth-century medicines and cool retro posters.

Outside the museum is an index to the 155 **historic markers** around the town. Diagonally opposite, you can't miss the junk comprising **Ben Prior's Open-Air Museum** (free). Half a kilometre up Hunt Street, off McKenzie Street, is **Warden Finnerty's Residence** (daily except Wed 11am–4pm; $4), the finely restored 1895 stone home of the man whose unenviable job it was to set the ground rules for mining at the height of the rush.

The visitor centre can book accommodation ^ ..suggest places to eat in town, but there's a far better range at Kalgoorlie, 40km away.

Kalgoorlie-Boulder

Whichever way you approach **Kalgoorlie** – the bustling gold capital of Australia: officially twinned, municipally merged but still fervently distinct from **Boulder** (see p.687) – it comes as a surprise after hundreds of kilometres of desolation. The conurbation possesses the idiosyncratic quality of places like Coober Pedy (see p.830) or Las Vegas. All three blithely disregard their isolation and bleak surroundings, so devoted is their attention to the pursuit of earthly riches – which, in Kalgoorlie's case, is **gold**.

Arrival and information

Transwa's six-hour **Prospector** train travels between Perth and Kalgoorlie daily; buses no longer do the trek. **Taxis** (℡13 10 08) meet the trains and will be your best bet with heavy bags. In the central town hall at 316 Hannan St, Kalgoorlie's **visitor centre** (Mon–Fri 8.30am–5pm, Sat & Sun 9am–5pm; ℡08/9021 1966, Ⓦwww.kalgoorlie.com) has maps and lots of information on local attractions and activities, and can book tours. The post office is at 204 Hannan St and there's an internet café on St Barbara's Square.

A local **bus service** operates between Kalgoorlie and Boulder every 25 minutes (Mon–Sat 8am–6pm; $4), with timetables available from Kalgoorlie's visitor centre. Halfpenny Rentals at 544 Hannan St (℡08/9021 1804) tries to live up to the name by offering good car-rental rates.

Accommodation

The town's motels get busy with "fly-in fly-outs" and corporate travellers, and with holiday-makers during the winter school holidays, so check room availability in advance. The many splendidly fronted hotels along Hannan Street offer inexpensive rooms with either shared or en-suite facilities.

All Seasons Kalgoorlie 45 Egan St ℡1300 656 565, Ⓦwww.allseasons.com.au. This renovated motel is the best in town with comfortable rooms with all mod cons and balconies looking over the town, as well as a bar and restaurant. Ⓖ

Comfort Inn Midas Motel 409 Hannan St ℡08/9021 3088, Ⓦwww.midasmotel.com.au. Comfortable motel with restaurant and pool, within walking distance of the station and town centre. Ⓖ

Kalgoorlie Backpackers 166 Hay St ℡08/9091 1482, Ⓦwww.kalgoorliebackpackers.com.au. Former brothel in the centre with a big kitchen, dorms and twins, as well as a pool and train pick-up. Dorms $25, single room Ⓞ

Palace Hotel 137 Hannan St ℡08/9021 2788, Ⓦwww.palacehotel.com.au. Beautiful old building slap-bang in the centre with an assortment of rooms; those on the veranda are more expensive. Wi-fi in lounge downstairs. Backpacker doubles Ⓒ, doubles Ⓖ

YHA Gold Dust Backpackers 192 Hay St ℡08/9091 3737, Ⓦwww.yha.com.au. Purpose-built hostel with a/c, pool, free bikes, internet and pick-ups. Dorms $25, rooms Ⓑ

Kalgoorlie

In 1893 **Paddy Hannan** (then 53 years old) and his mates, Tom Flannigan and Dan O'Shea, brought renewed meaning to the expression "the luck of the Irish" when a lame horse forced them to camp by the tree which still stands at the top of Egan Street in **KALGOORLIE**. With their instincts highly attuned after eight months of prospecting around Coolgardie, they soon found gold all around them, and as the first on the scene enjoyed the unusually easy pickings of surface gold. Ten years later, when the desperately needed water pipeline finally gushed into the Mount Charlotte Reservoir, Kalgoorlie was already the established heart of WA's rapidly growing mineral-based prosperity. As sole survivor of the original rush, and revitalized by the 1960s nickel boom, Kalgoorlie has benefited from new technology that has largely dispensed with slow and dangerous underground mining. Instead, the fabulously rich "**Golden Mile**" reef east of town, near Boulder, is being excavated around the clock, creating a colossal hole, the open-cast "Super Pit", which is still going strong and being expanded every day.

Proud of its history and continued prosperity, Kalgoorlie is one of the most parochial towns in Australia, but first and foremost "Kal" is a "Working Man's Town" of twelve-hour, seven-day shifts, a testament to the ethos of hard work and hard play that flourished in Australia's Anglo-Celtic heyday. A pub without a half-dressed barmaid (known in WA as "skimpies") is the exception, and in the sniggeringly louche red-light district of Hay Street, three of the infamous "tin shack" brothels remain conspicuously in business.

Start your tour of the town by taking a walk to the top of Hannan Street to the red 33-metre-high headframe (with a viewing platform boasting 360-degree views of the city and mines) at the **Western Australian Museum** (daily 10am–4.30pm; donation; ☎08/9021 8533, ⓦ www.museum.wa.gov.au), right next to the spot where Paddy and his crew found their first, auspicious nuggets. Inside is a display of Goldfields artefacts and history, with the very stuff that keeps the town going viewable in the basement vault. Aboriginal history and the sandalwood industry are also covered in this excellent summary of the area, and there's a lookout over the town from the top of the red headframe.

Hannan Street itself is one of Kalgoorlie's finest sights, with its superbly restored **Federation-era architecture**, imposing public buildings and numerous flamboyant hotel facades. You're welcome to inspect the grandiose interior of the **town hall** (Mon–Fri 8.30am–5pm), with its splendid hall and decent art gallery. It's only when you stop to reflect that this is a remote, century-old town in the Western Australia desert that the stunning wealth of the still continuing boom years is brought home to you. Outside the hall, a replica of a bronze **statue** of Paddy himself invites you to drink from his chrome-nozzled waterbag – the much vandalized original is now safely in the Mining Hall of Fame.

If it's merely your curiosity that's drawn you to Hay Street then *Langtrees 181* at no. 181 and *Questa Casa* at no. 133 have found a novel and successful way of perking up business in the quiet daylight hours – by offering **brothel tours**, one of Kalgoorlie's most popular activities. While prostitution has long been legal in WA, living off the earnings of prostitution was not until brothels were legalized in 2008, giving prostitutes basic working rights, including superannuation and worker's compensation. Brothels like *Langtrees* (daily 1pm, 3pm & 6pm; 1hr 30min; $35; ☎08/9026 2181) and the tin *Questa Casa* (daily 2pm; $20; ☎08/9021 4897), Kalgoorlie's oldest brothel at over 100 years, operated for so long due to Kalgoorlie's perceived "special needs" and an unofficial "containment" policy which essentially meant police looked the other way. The guide at *Langtrees* leads you through themed rooms whilst relating fascinating anecdotes about the history of prostitution in WA, and answering all the questions you dare to ask.

Another unmissable attraction is the **Australian Prospectors and Mining Hall of Fame** on Goldfields Highway (daily 9am–4.30pm; $30; ☎08/9026 2700, ⓦ www.mininghall.com), a former mine site transformed into an engaging museum and mining theme-park. Here you can have a crack at gold panning, watch a gold-pouring demo (and handle a bar of gold), and take a guided underground tour led by former miners. This is probably as long as you'd want to spend down a mine – especially after the brief demonstration of the pneumatic "air leg" drill. Above ground, the Hall of Fame building has a comprehensive display of rocks and minerals, as well as Aboriginal and other contemporary art.

Boulder

BOULDER, 5km south of Kalgoorlie, is quieter and smaller than its twin – a place to visit rather than stay in. It was originally set up as a separate settlement to serve the Golden Mile, but Boulder's heyday passed as Kalgoorlie's suburbs slowly absorbed the quaint little town. Boulder has a similar collection of grand old buildings and pubs that – like Kal's – have received a face-lift. Most people do a lap of the main street on their way up the hill to the astonishing **Super Pit Lookout** (off Goldfields Hwy), an absolute must. Phone or drop into the **Super Pit Shop** at 2 Burt St (daily 9am–4pm; ℡08/9093 3488, Ⓦwww .superpit.com.au) when you get to town to find out when a blast is scheduled – an experience you won't forget easily. Or if you're around on Boulder Market Days on the third Sunday of the month, join a **tour** (departs from shop; 10am, 10.30am, 11am & 11.30am; 1hr; $5). Finders Keepers at 20 Burt St also runs daily **Super Pit Tours** (℡08/9093 2222, Ⓦwww.superpittour.com; 2hr; $50).

Eating and drinking

For the most atmospheric location, excellent service and best food in town, book a table on the veranda at 🔥 *Judd's Balcony Bar & Restaurant* at the *Palace Hotel* (see p.686; 6pm–late), which serves up superb modern-Australian cuisine with an Italian influence; the wood-fired pizzas ($22–24) are fantastic (try the Moroccan lamb with caramelized onions). The bright and breezy *Blue Monkey* at 418 Hannan St (℡08/9091 3833) offers all-day dining and dishes up hearty portions of mod-Oz. Also on Hannan Street, at no. 71, *Top End Thai* does decent Aussie-style Thai and is open from 6pm daily, while the *Star and Garter* pub at no. 197 does cheap **counter meals**. For the blokes in town, Kal's **nightlife** revolves around scantily clad pub barmaids laying on beer jugs all down Hannan Street, while the hippest and most happening bar in town is *Judd's Balcony Bar* which is surprisingly chic.

The Northern Goldfields

North of Kalgoorlie, there are a number of mining and Aboriginal communities along the 726-kilometre stretch up to Meekatharra, itself halfway up the Great Northern Highway. For those who like their road trips, this is the real Outback, with lots of wildlife to spot, including kangaroos, emus, wedge-tailed eagles, kites and thorny devils. It's a useful route if you're heading northeast to Alice via the Great Central Road (see p.636), or if you want to get from the Eyre Highway to northern WA in a hurry, avoiding Perth. The **ghost towns** close to Kalgoorlie consist of little more than ruins of long-gone buildings, best photographed at sunrise or sunset. The **Golden Quest Discovery Trail** self-guides tourists through the region to Leonora and Laverton – ask for the free map and guide at Kalgoorlie's visitor centre.

Though it once boasted twelve thousand residents, two breweries and an hourly train to Kalgoorlie, you might want to give the rubble remains of **Kanowna** a miss. The ghost towns of **BROAD ARROW** and **ORA BANDA** (respectively 38km and 66km from Kalgoorlie) consist of dilapidated bush shacks and a "bush pub" each. At **Kookynie**, a short distance off the highway, is another bush pub, the rather quaint *Grand Hotel* (℡08/903 1310; ❸), standing alone in the dust.

LEONORA, 237km north of Kalgoorlie, is a sprightly century-old mining town – a "one-horse" version of Kalgoorlie with a photogenic Federation-era main street and a few old pubs, including the 1902 *White House Hotel* (℡08/9037 6030). Just south of town is the reconstructed **Gwalia** ghost town – an evocative scattering of tin sheds, a general store and a mining **museum** (daily 10am–4pm; Ⓦwww.gwalia.org.au; $5) at the top of the hill.

A sealed road branches northeast to **Laverton**, from where the seemingly endless **Great Central Road** runs around 1100km to Yulara, NT (see p.636 for a full description). Back on the road to Meekatharra, **Leinster** is a company town servicing a local mine, with a supermarket, while **Wiluna**, 175km north of Leinster, is the polar opposite – a century-old settlement and Aboriginal community. At *Tjukurba Art Gallery* (Mon–Fri 9am 4pm; ℡08/9981 8000) you can buy Aboriginal art and chat with the artists, before bunking down at the *Gunbarrel Laager Travellers Rest* (℡08/9981 7161, ⓦwww.users.bigpond.com /gunbarrel.camp; camping $30, single room ❸, twin/family room ❹) which has motel units and caravan sites. From Wiluna the **Gunbarrel "Highway"** winds east towards the NT border, while the **Canning Stock Route** runs northeast across the Great Sandy Desert for 1900km to Halls Creek; both routes should only be attempted by well-prepared and experienced off-road drivers in 4WD convoys from April to September. The last 180km from Wiluna to Meekatharra is a gravel road.

The Eyre Highway to South Australia

South of Kalgoorlie the Great Eastern Highway runs 190km to Norseman, at the western end of the **Eyre Highway**. The highway is named after the explorer John Eyre, who crossed the southern edge of the continent in 1841, a gruelling five-month trek that would have cost him his life but for some Aborigines who helped him locate water. Eyre crawled into Albany on his last legs but set the route for future crossings, the telegraph lines and the highway.

NORSEMAN was named after a prospector's horse that kicked up a large nugget in 1894 – a genuine case of lucky horseshoes. A bronze effigy of the nag now stands proudly on the corner of Roberts and Ramsay streets. Arrivals from South Australia may be eager to pick up their "I've crossed the Nullarbor" certificate from the **visitor centre** (daily 9am–5pm; ℡08/9039 1071, ⓦwww .norseman.info) on Roberts Street. At no. 106 the renovated Art Deco *Railway Hotel/Motel* (℡08/9039 0003, ⓦwww.therailwayatnorseman.com.au; ❶–❸) has simple budget and en-suite rooms and serves up decent pub meals, although the best food in town and slightly better accommodation is on Prinsep Street at the *Norseman Great Western Travel Village* (℡08/9039 1633; ❺), which has motel rooms and an adjoining caravan park with on site vans (❹). If you've come from the east and are in a quandary about which route to take to Perth, consider nipping up to Kal then returning south and heading west along the coast.

If you're heading back east on the Eyre Highway, it's about 730km to the South Australian border and another 480km from there to Ceduna, where the legendary **Nullarbor** ends, though that still leaves 800km before you reach Adelaide – a drive of notorious monotony. Although the longest stretch without fuel is only 200km, do not underestimate the rigours of the journey on your vehicle. Carry reserves of fuel and water, take rests every few hours and don't drive at dawn or dusk when kangaroos are crossing the road to feed. There are no banks between Norseman and Ceduna, and there's a quarantine check-point at the border where a large range of prohibited animal and vegetable goods (mainly fruit and veg) must be discarded.

BALLADONIA, 193km east from Norseman, has the *Balladonia Hotel Motel* (℡08/9039 3453; camping $13, powered site $17, rooms ❺) with ATM, restau-rant and caravan/camping park. Some 270km of virtually dead-straight road further along, you reach **COCKLEBIDDY**, which has a motel (℡08/9039 3462; camping $13, powered site $17, rooms ❺), while **MADURA**, 92km east, is halfway between Perth and Adelaide if you're still counting, and has rooms and caravan sites at *Madura Pass Oasis Motel* (℡08/9039 3464; camping $12, powered site $20, rooms ❺). **MUNDRABILLA**, 116km further on, where you rise up into the actual Nullarbor plain, also has a motel and caravan/campsite, the *Mundrabilla Roadhouse* (℡08/9039 3465; camping $15, powered site $20, rooms ❺).

EUCLA, just 12km from the border, was re-established up on the escarpment after sand dunes engulfed the original settlement by the sea. Down near the sea, the old telegraph and weather station, 4km away, are still visible above the sands, an eerie sight well worth a look. South of town is the **Eucla National Park** (DEC fee; see box, p.644), where the coastal cliffs extend east for 290km along the coast of South Australia. There are motel units and caravan-camping sites at the *Eucla Motor Hotel* (℡08/9039 3468; camping $6, powered sites $18, rooms ❺), or right on the border, at the *Border Village* (℡08/9039 3474; camping $12, powered sites $18, rooms ❺). For the South Australian section of this route, see p.826.

From Perth to Kununurra

The 4400-kilometre drive up Highway 1 along Western Australia's arching coastline from Perth to Broome, across the Kimberley and on to Darwin in the Northern Territory is one of Australia's great road journeys. Even without detours, it's a huge, transcontinental trek between the country's two most isolated capitals, fringing the barely inhabited desert that separates them. Contrary perhaps to expectations, the **Batavia** and **Coral** coasts, **Central Midlands** region, the **Pilbara** and the **Kimberley** all have distinct personalities that become evident as you rack up the kilometres. On some days – particularly in the Pilbara and the Kimberley – it'll seem like all you've seen are road trains, road kill and roadhouses, but to compensate there are innumerable places en route whose beauty will take your breath away, and even more that give an insight into Australia that you rarely get on the East Coast.

For many, the confrontation with **Aboriginal Australia** will be just as intense here as in the Northern Territory. Just as in the NT though, the complex relationship between "indigenous" and "white" Australias is here for all to see; Aboriginal welfare towns in the Kimberley challenge perceptions and misconceptions, whilst some areas boast burgeoning indigenous tourism industries that are seen variously as signs of success or selling-out depending on whom you listen to. To read more about the history of Aboriginal groups in northern WA see p.723.

If any single trip across Australia benefits from independent **mobility** it's this one: a car will allow you to explore intimately and linger indefinitely. If you want to discover the wayside attractions, allow at least four to five weeks for the journey from Perth to Darwin. Three weeks will whizz you through the highlights; anything less and you may as well fly. Highway 1 is sealed all the way, but to really experience northern WA you'll need to get off the beaten track and explore its many national parks and unsealed tracks, as towns en route are almost without exception lacking in charm. This means that a 4WD is a good idea – we've indicated where a 4WD is generally required but this can vary seasonally.

A glance at a map shows the long distances between roadhouses, let alone settlements; plan your next petrol stop and make sure your vehicle is in sound condition, particularly the tyres and the cooling system, both of which will be working hard. For more tips on driving in the Outback see p.39. If you undertake a trip in the northwest during the Wet (Jan–March) expect very high temperatures, humidity and huge amounts of **rain**, with associated flooding and disruption. **Cyclones** are an annual threat to coastal communities between Exmouth and Broome from November to April – acquaint yourself with the safety advice in each town during this time. Following weather damage, roads and bridges on Highway 1 are repaired amazingly quickly, but back roads can be closed for weeks – keep up to date with road conditions and closures at ranger stations, visitor centres, roadhouses and ⓦwww.exploroz.com.

If you don't have a car, the rigid schedules and butt-numbing nature of long-distance **bus** travel require a certain equanimity. Greyhound Australia offers a range of **regional passes** up the coast, while Integrity Coachlines covers the inland route to Port Hedland.

North to Cervantes

There are few must-see attractions before you get to Cervantes, although Yanchep, Guilderton and Lancelin all receive their fair share of holiday-makers due to their proximity to Perth, and in Lancelin's case, big winds which attract the kite-surfers and windsurfers. The first obligatory detour from the Brand Highway (as Highway 1 is known in these parts) is to view the weird and wonderful Pinnacles in **Nambung National Park**, 245km from Perth and 70km west off the highway. Just 17km away, **CERVANTES** is the closest overnight stop. There's little to occupy you in this young, windswept crayfishing town save some white sands and good views over to the Cervantes Islands from Thirsty Point – plan on arriving at sunset to view the Pinnacles before heading north in the morning.

Practicalities

Greyhound **buses** from Perth stop at the BP Roadhouse here. The **post office** on Cadiz Street houses the small **visitor centre** (daily 7.30am–5.30pm; ⓣ08/9652 7700 or 1800 610 660, ⓦwww.turquoisecoast.org.au), which has internet access and a list of things to do in the area. There's a bottle shop and small **general store** on the same strip. If you're looking for **accommodation**, the *Pinnacles Caravan Park* at 35 Aragon St (ⓣ08/9652 7060, ⓦwww.pinnaclespark.com.au; camping $24, powered site $27, cabins ❹) is a fairly standard site right by the beach, with some excellent wooded pitches for campers and the usual rows of cabins further back. Between *Cervantes Lodge* and *Pinnacles Beach Backpackers* there's a room to suit everyone at 91 Seville St (ⓣ08/9652 7377 or 1800 245 232, ⓦwww.cervanteslodge .com.au; dorms $29, rooms ❸–❺). Whilst some of the rooms are a bit bland, the friendly owners, characterful lounge area and superbly stocked kitchen make this a real home from home. The *Edge* chain is due to open a swish resort here – go to ⓦwww.edgeresorts.wa.com to check on its progress.

For **meals**, the newly opened *Seashell's Café*, at the entrance to the caravan park, is a good spot for breakfast or lunch, while the *Ronsard Bay Tavern* on Cadiz Street has pub fare for lunch and dinner. Turquoise Coast Enviro Tours

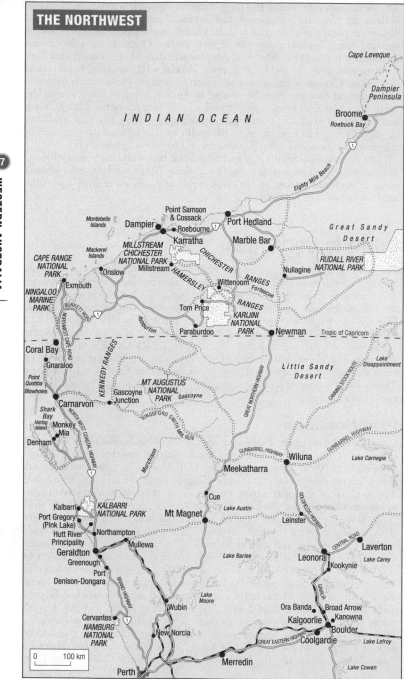

THE NORTHWEST

Cape Leveque

Dampier Peninsula

Broome
Roebuck Bay

INDIAN OCEAN

Eighty Mile Beach

Montebello Islands

Point Samson & Cossack
Dampier
Roebourne
Karratha
Port Hedland

Great Sandy Desert

Mackerel Islands

MILLSTREAM CHICHESTER NATIONAL PARK

CHICHESTER

Marble Bar

CAPE RANGE NATIONAL PARK

Onslow
Millstream

HAMERSLEY

Wittenoom
Fortescue

Nullagine

RUDALL RIVER NATIONAL PARK

NINGALOO MARINE PARK

Exmouth

BURKETT ROAD

NORTH WEST CAPE ROAD

RANGES

Tom Price

RANGES

KARIJINI NATIONAL PARK

Ashburton

Paraburdoo

Newman

Tropic of Capricorn

Coral Bay

Gnaraloo

KENNEDY RANGES

Little Sandy Desert

Lake Disappointment

Point Quobba Blowholes

Carnarvon

MT AUGUSTUS NATIONAL PARK

Gascoyne Junction
Gascoyne

CANNING STOCK ROUTE

Shark Bay

Hartog Island

Monkey Mia

NORTH WEST COASTAL HIGHWAY

KINGSFORD SMITH MAIL RUN

GREAT NORTHERN HIGHWAY

GUNBARREL HIGHWAY

GUNBARREL HIGHWAY

Denham

Murchison

GUNBARREL HIGHWAY

Wiluna

Lake Carnegie

Meekatharra

Cue
Lake Austin

Kalbarri

KALBARRI NATIONAL PARK

Mt Magnet

Leinster

GOLDFIELDS HIGHWAY

Port Gregory (Pink Lake)
Hutt River Principality

Northampton
Mullewa

Lake Barlee

CENTRAL ROAD

Laverton
Lake Carey

Geraldton
Greenough
Port Denison-Dongara

BRAND HIGHWAY

Leonora
Kookynie

GOLDFIELDS HIGHWAY

GWALIA

Wubin

Lake Moore

Cervantes

NAMBURG NATIONAL PARK

New Norcia

Ora Banda
Broad Arrow
Kanowna
Kalgoorlie
Boulder

Coolgardie

GREAT EASTERN HIGHWAY

Lake Lefroy

Perth

Merredin

Lake Cowan

0   100 km

(☎08/9652 7047, ⓦwww.thepinnacles.com.au) run three-hour walking trips through the Pinnacles at 8am and 2.5 hours before sunset ($55), or full-day excursions which take in other local attractions including Leseur National Park and Stockyard Tunnel Cave ($155); if you choose the full-day option a tour of the Pinnacles the evening before or morning after is included at no extra cost.

Nambung National Park

Right before Cervantes an entry road leads south into the **Nambung National Park** (DEC fee; see box, p.644); just off the road, beachside **Kangaroo Point** and **Hangover Bay** have picnic and barbecue facilities. Further on, the **Pinnacles** are the park's main attraction: this spread of three-metre-high limestone columns was originally formed underground and has since been exhumed from the sands, like a terracotta army, by the perennial southwesterlies. The brand-new **Pinnacles Desert Discovery Centre** (daily 9.30am–4.30pm; ☎08/9652 7043) at the Pinnacles car park explains the geology on show; just behind the centre a three-kilometre drive winds among the pillars. However lazy you're feeling though, you'll find it hard not to park up and wander around this eerie expanse, sometimes enhanced by a mist of fine, windblown sand. Most day-tours from Perth arrive around noon, missing the evening sun's long shadows, which add still further to the Pinnacles' photogenic qualities.

The Batavia Coast

The Batavia Coast's moniker comes from the Dutch East India Company's ship the *Batavia*, which was wrecked off the **Houtman Abrolhos** islands, 80km west of Geraldton, in 1629 – for more on ships and shipwrecks in the area see p.697. The region's administrative centre, **Geraldton**, has a bustling feel that's rare in these parts, while historic **Northampton** and **Greenhough** provide an alternative to the seaside resorts such as **Port Denison–Dongara** and **Kalbarri** that the region is known for.

Port Denison-Dongara

Continuing north from Cervantes a road runs down the coast past the fishing villages of Jurien Bay, Greenhead and Leeman – an alternative to the Brand Highway that saves you around 70km. While the three fishing villages all attract holiday-makers looking for some quiet time, there's really little of interest after the Pinnacles until you get to the twin towns of **Port Denison–Dongara**, 130km north of Cervantes via the coast road. Set slightly back from the coast, Dongara's pleasant main street is lined with Moreton Bay fig trees and fine old buildings; 1km or so further on, the beach and marina at Denison are both good for a stroll.

Practicalities

The **visitor centre** at 9 Waldeck St in Dongara (Mon–Fri 9am–5pm, Sat 9am–noon; ☎08/9927 1404) has a leaflet with some ideas on how to occupy yourself; Greyhound **buses** from Perth stop outside. There's some characterful **accommodation** here, which makes it a good option for an overnight stop. Try the great-value ♣ *Old Rectory B&B* at 19 Waldeck St in Dongara (☎08/9927 2252, ⓦwww.theoldrectorybandb.com; ❺), bursting with olde-worlde charm, iron bedsteads and beautiful linen, without descending into chintz. Also in Dongara at 11 St Dominic's Rd, the colonial-style *Priory Hotel* ([T]08/9927 1090, [W]www.prioryhotel.com.au; [4]–[6]) on the banks of the Irwin River offers a real all-round experience; the assortment of rooms here all have polished jarrah floorboards and lots of charm, while an evening can be whiled away with a drink in the characterful bar and a famous steak sandwich in the *1881* restaurant. The best caravan park is *Dongara Tourist Park* at 8 George St in Denison ([T]08/9927 1210 or 1800 052 077, [W]www.dongaratouristpark.com.au; camping $18, powered site $26, vans [2], one- to two-bed cabins [5]–[6]); this leafy campsite has some superb brightly coloured cabins overlooking South Beach.

For **eating**, the *Dongara Hotel* on Moreton Terrace in Dongara serves pub grub and Thai food that's recommended by locals, while great smoothies, cakes, breakfasts and lunches can be had on the buoy-strewn terrace at *Little Starfish* (Wed–Sun), next to South Beach in Denison.

Greenough

Forty kilometres north of Port Denison-Dongara is the tiny village of **GREENOUGH**, now in name at least part of the city of Geraldton-Greenough (see below) following their 2007 amalgamation. A thriving agricultural centre during the 1860s, it declined in the late nineteenth century after flooding, cyclones and the discovery of gold in the goldfields. The beautifully restored and curated 🏃 **Central Greenough Historical Settlement** remains, with eleven buildings including a courthouse, social hall, churches and various cottages still standing in golden fields by the incongruously close Brand Highway. Entry is through the visitor centre (daily 9am–5pm; $6; [T]08/9926 1084), which houses a surprisingly classy, airy café (same hours) serving delicious light lunches and possibly the best caramel slices in the world.

Another fine hour or so can be passed at the excellent *Hampton Arms* ([T]08/9926 1057, [W]www.hamptonarms.com.au; [4]), over the other side of the highway. This cute English-style pub has lots of nooks and crannies to explore, a secondhand bookshop containing over 17,000 titles, plus light lunches, rooms and dinner on request. The last stop before you leave the village is the **Pioneer Museum** (daily 10am–4pm; $4.50; [T]08/9926 1058), home to the Maley family from 1862 to 1932 and almost entirely unchanged. Around the village you'll notice Greenough's strange **leaning trees** – some bent almost flat against the ground by the prevailing salt-laden winds.

Geraldton and around

GERALDTON is situated in the middle of the **Batavia Coast**, 420km north of Perth and just 25km beyond Greenough. Now officially called Geraldton-Greenough after the 2007 amalgamation with its neighbour, it's the state's second-largest city and the traffic, bustling feel and busy shopping streets can feel a bit alien if you're coming from the north.

Culture vultures will find some relief in Geraldton; in a fairly barren region art-wise, the museum and art gallery here are both excellent.

Arrival and information

The helpful **visitor centre** (Mon–Fri 9am–5pm, Sat & Sun 10am–4pm; [T]08/9921 3999, [W]www.geraldtontourist.com.au), in the Bill Sewell Complex on Chapman Road 2km north of town, will happily sort out all accommodation and tour bookings. Greyhound services pull in here, while Transwa buses alight at the old train station just down the road. The **post office** is located on Durlacher Street, and there are pharmacies in the Northgate shopping complex on Chapman Street.

Accommodation

Motels are mostly located down Cathedral Avenue, with the Best Western, Comfort Inn and Mercure chains all represented. The *Edge* chain is due to open what will probably be a very smart resort here in late 2009 – go to ⓦwww .edgeresorts.wa.com to check on its progress.

Belair Gardens Tourist Park 463 Marine Terrace ☎08/9921 1997 or 1800 240 938, ⓦwww.belairbig4geraldton.com.au. Small, slightly cramped site but with good facilities including a campers' kitchen and pool, and well situated next to beautiful Point Moore beach and lighthouse. Camping $25, powered site $30, cabins ❸, 1–2 bed chalets ❹–❺, 1–2 bed deluxe units ❹–❽

Foreshore Backpackers 172 Marine Terrace ☎08/9921 3275, ⓦwww .foreshorebackpackers.bigpondhosting.com. Beautiful, rambling house right in the centre of town. The great rooms with polished floorboards, retro furniture and pot plants, funky lounge and relaxed spirit imbued by the friendly young owner make this a top pick. Dorms $24, singles ❶, twins/ doubles ❷

Geraldton Backpackers Behind the Bill Sewell Complex ☎08/9964 3001, ⓔgeraldtonback packers@hotmail.com. Housed in a beautiful heritage building, the austere feel, strong religious bent and total alcohol ban in this one-time hospital and jail mean party animals should steer well clear. Dorms $25, singles ❶, doubles ❷, family room ❸

Ocean Centre Hotel Corner of Foreshore Drive and Cathedral Ave ☎08/9921 7777, ⓦwww.ocean centrehotel.com.au. The motel-style rooms here are of a good size and standard; some have sea views, and the seaside theme is carried through to the blue-and-white decor. The *Sirocco* bar downstairs is a popular place to start the night. ❺–❽

The Town

Geraldton's main drag, Marine Terrace, is lined with shops and restaurants. The next block over is Foreshore Drive, with the family-friendly Town Beach at its centre, and a new **marina** complex full of swanky boats at its eastern end. West of town, beyond the harbour and **Fisherman's Wharf**, are good beaches and a striking red-and-white-striped lighthouse at **Point Moore**. Fresh seafood can be bought at the wharf, although for kite-surfers and adrenalin junkies the real attraction at this end of town is the blustery beach at the point.

On Cathedral Avenue, the striking **St Francis Xavier Cathedral** completed in 1938 (tours Mon, Wed & Fri 10am; free) is the crowning glory of Monsignor John Hawes' career – have a peek inside to see the bright stained-glass windows and very "now" orange-and-grey striped interior. Combining the unlikely professions of architect and priest, Hawes' distinctive hand can be seen in sixteen other churches and myriad religious buildings in the mid-West; you can buy a **Monsignor John Hawes Heritage Trail** leaflet at the visitor centre – the self-drive trail takes a good three days.

Looming over the city at the corner of George and Victoria streets is the **HMAS Sydney memorial**, a rather grandiose domed monument to the lost ship that's in urgent need of an information update since the wreck was discovered 207km off Shark Bay in 2008, solving a mystery that has taxed Australians and conspiracy theorists since World War II – for more on the HMAS *Sydney* see p.697. There are great views out to sea from here, and volunteers run tours around the memorial from the car park daily at 10.30am (30min; donation).

It's easy to get engrossed in the **Western Australian Museum Geraldton** at 1 Museum Place (daily 9.30am–4.30pm; donation; ☎08/9921 5080, ⓦwww .museum.wa.gov.au), down near the new marina. Covering regional flora and fauna, Dreamtime stories and Aboriginal history, it also has a room dedicated to the moving story of the HMAS *Sydney* and another on earlier wrecks around the Batavia Coast, including the Dutch East India Company ships the *Batavia* and the *Zuytdorp* – for more on ships and shipwrecks see opposite.

The **Geraldton Regional Art Gallery** at 24 Chapman St (Tues–Sat 10am–4pm, Sun 1–4pm; free; T08/9964 7171, Wwww.cgg.wa.gov.au/artgallery), a couple of blocks back from the front, hosts excellent local, national and international exhibitions.

Eating, drinking and nightlife

There are restaurants and cafés scattered all the way down Marine Terrace; for self-caterers, Coles and Woolworths are both located on Chapman Street. Good places for a **drink** include the *Freemason's Hotel* on the corner of Durlacher Street and Marine Terrace, which often hosts live music and serves huge portions of pubby food; *Breakers* and *Camel Bar* on Chapman Street are popular with a younger (and slightly trashier) crowd. Dance moves and chat-up lines can be practised at *Vibe* and *Nighty*, both on Fitzgerald Street.

Bellavista Café 205 Marine Terrace T08/9964 2681. Jazzy tunes, old bus seats, fabulous coffee, local art and modern, rustic Italian food including unctuous pastas, a daily risotto and interesting salads – this place is a real winner, and the most stylish thing in Geraldton by a country mile. Mon–Sat 7am–3pm, plus Fri & Sat dinner.

Boatshed 357 Marine Terrace T08/ 9921 5500. Right next door to the fish market, so you can guarantee the honey chilli prawns, seafood chowder and lobster served in this cute little restaurant are as fresh as you can get. BYO & licensed. Mon–Sat 6pm–late.

Conversations by Indigo Town Marina T08/9965 0800, Wwww.conversationsbyindigo.com.au.

Slightly pretentious name, slightly pretentious food, including "deconstruction of a lemon meringue pie". The pleasant terrace and interior overlooking the new marina complex are quite plain, with the well-made Mod-Oz food and excellent wine list the focus. During the day, there's a good brunch menu and dishes tailored to ladies who lunch. Daily 10am–late.

Skeetas Corner of Foreshore Drive and Cathedral Ave T08/ 9964 1619, Wwww.skeetas.com.au. Bag a table on the seafront terrace and opt for the tasty seafood rather than the slightly dated meat and pasta dishes. Breakfast and more lunchy fare also available. Daily 7am–9pm.

Around Geraldton

Fifty-two kilometres north of Geraldton, **Northampton** is a small historic town of the sort that's rare in northern WA, and makes an excellent tea-and-cake stop. The annual **Airing of the Quilts** in October is a real spectacle, with all the buildings on the main street hanging patchwork quilts off their verandas.

From Northampton it's worth taking a detour 42km west to Port Gregory, to get a better view of the Hutt Lagoon – better known as the **Pink Lake** due to the high levels of beta carotene in the water which produce its rosy hue. From here you can continue up the coast to Kalbarri, past the coastal bluffs of Kalbarri National Park.

From Geraldton, the self-drive **Wool Wagon Pathway** takes the inland route north 1300km to Exmouth, taking in plenty of wool country and the Kennedy Ranges along the way – the Gascoyne Murchison Outback Pathways brochure is available at local visitor centres or you can download it at Wwww.carnarvon.org.au.

Geraldton is also the departure point for flights to the **Houtman Abrolhos** islands, 80km offshore, and the cause of many a historic shipwreck. The 122 islands, spread over more than 100km, are renowned for their warm waters which allow both temperate and tropical marine life to thrive. There's no accommodation on the Abrolhos, but several companies offer scenic flights (from $175),

This stretch of coast is very much dominated by the sea and its maritime history, with the fate of the many ships wrecked off the coast continuing to consume professional and amateur historians alike. The seventeenth and eighteenth centuries were notable for the wrecking of numerous Dutch East India Company ships, including the *Batavia* in 1629, and the *Zuytdorp* in 1710. The **Batavia**'s story is especially compelling, if gory: the ship set sail from Amsterdam in 1628 for the Dutch East Indies, laden with silver and other goodies to trade for precious spices on arrival. During the journey, merchants Adriaene Jacobsz and Jeronimus Cornelisz hatched a plan to hijack the ship and effect a mutiny, allowing them to steal the booty on board and start a new life somewhere. After Jacobsz deliberately steered the ship off course, the *Batavia* struck a reef close to the Houtman Abrolhos Islands. Most passengers managed to get ashore, but on finding no fresh water Captain François Pelsaert, Jacobsz and other crew members set off to find help, eventually arriving at Batavia (modern-day Jakarta) 33 days later, an astonishing feat of nagivation given their lack of equipment. Pelsaert was given a new ship with which to rescue those left on the island, but on his return found that Cornelisz had unleashed a bloody mutiny to ensure he gained control of the riches aboard the wrecked *Batavia*, killing 125 survivors. Pelsaert set to trying the mutineers on his return, executing Cornelisz and his worst-offending cronies. Others were tried in Batavia, while two sailors found guilty of committing minor offences were abandoned on mainland Australia – reports of light-skinned Aborigines in the area have led to theories that the two men were adopted into a clan. The wreck of the Batavia was salvaged in the 1970s, with many of the items on board now displayed in museums in **Geraldton** and **Fremantle**.

In the 1920s the remains of a castaway's camp were discovered on the cliff tops between Kalbarri and Shark Bay, subsequently named the Zuytdorp Cliffs. The fate of the **Zuytdorp** survivors had been a three-hundred-year-old mystery until a rare disease endemic amongst seventeenth-century Afrikaaners (ships en route to the Dutch East Indies routinely stopped in South Africa to stock up on provisions) was discovered in local Aborigines, which again suggests that some of the castaways survived long enough to pass the gene on. Recent research seems to have discredited this idea, but controversy surrounding the wreck remains, with various locals claiming its discovery between the 1920s and 1960s, and accusations of looting rife.

In modern times, the ship that has most interested WA and indeed Australia is the **HMAS Sydney**, whose success in the early years of World War II was the source of much national pride. It was sunk in mysterious circumstances off the West Australian coast in 1941, after a confrontation with the *Kormoran*, a German merchant trader disguised as a Dutch ship. Conspiracy theories about the significantly more powerful HMAS *Sydney*'s fate ran out of control well into the twenty-first century, until the iconic ship was found 200km off Steep Point near Shark Bay, after a $3.5 million search effort. The ship's discovery on 16 March 2008, 22km away from the *Kormoran*, made front-page news in Australia and finally granted some peace to the families of the 645-strong crew who were lost.

and some land on the islands for lunch and snorkelling (from $240); try Geraldton Air Charters (☎08/9923 3434, ⓦwww.geraldtonaircharter.com.au) or Batavia Coast Air Charter (☎08/9921 5168, ⓦwww.abrolhosbat.com.au).

Kalbarri and around

About 70km north of Geraldton, your curiosity may be aroused by a sign for the **Hutt River Principality** (ⓦwww.principality-hutt-river.com), an old pastoral property which "seceded" from the Australian Commonwealth in 1970 on an arcane legal technicality, after a dispute over wheat quotas with the state government. While the principality rigorously defends its right to be known as a sovereign state, it has never been recognized by any international entity but nonetheless has thirteen thousand fans (or citizens) across the world. The principality issues its own postage and passport stamps, and welcomes visitors (daily 10am–4pm), who can be expected to be met and shown around by HRH Prince Leonard or one of the "royal family".

Idyllic **KALBARRI** is one of the best of the west coast's resorts. With the dramatic scenery of Kalbarri National Park on its doorstep, it's a refreshing place to spend a day or so, with good, inexpensive accommodation and a host of activities on offer. Situated on the mouth of the Murchison River nearly 600km north of Perth, the town can be accessed via the Port Gregory road, which leaves Highway 1 at Northampton (108km), or from Ajana–Kalbarri Road, which heads west off the highway just north of Binnu (66km).

Arrival and information

Greyhound Australia **buses** from Perth drop passengers at Binnu, to be met by a shuttle bus on Monday, Wednesday and Friday only; Transwa buses from Perth stop at the visitor centre or in the centre of town. The **visitor centre** (daily 9am–5pm; ☎08/9937 1104 or 1800 639 468, ⊛ www.kalbarriwa.info), in the Allen Centre on Grey Street, can book accommodation, tours and activities.

Accommodation

The accommodation in town is almost uniformly clean, spacious and good value, without being particularly stylish. School holidays can be busy, so book early; some places require a minimum stay at this time. For groups or longer stays, Ray White Holiday Homes in Kalbarri Arcade on Grey Street might be able to help (☎08/9937 1711, ⊛ www.kalbarriaccommodation.com.au).

Anchorage Holiday Village & Caravan Park Anchorage Lane ☎08/9937 1181. Ten minutes from the centre at the marina end of town, but for your efforts you get great pitches with tranquil river views, lots of shade, a good pool and a communal BBQ (Thurs). Camping $27, powered site $30, cabins ❸, en-suite cabins ❹

Blue Ocean Villas Auger St ☎08/9937 2442, ⊛ www.blueoceanvillas.com.au. Six light, spacious two-bed apartments that are the size of a standard suburban house; the pick of the many apartments in Kalbarri in this price bracket. There's a small pool too. ❻

Gecko Lodge 9 Glass St ☎08/9937 1900, ⊛ www.geckolodgekalbarri.com.au. This stylish, modern B&B stands out amidst the bland apartments and resorts in Kalbarri. A short walk from town, it has four supremely comfortable rooms and a nice pool; nothing is too much trouble for guests, and complimentary afternoon tea, choccies and port are included. ❼–❽

Kalbarri Backpackers Corner of Mortimer and Wood sts ☎08/9937 1430, ⊛ www.yha.com.au.

Clean and spacious if not overly atmospheric, with large, bright eaved dorms in one building and plenty of kitchen facilities. Hopefully guests get a warmer reception than travel writers. Free snorkel and boogie-board hire, plus bike hire – they'll drop you in the coastal section of the national park and you can cycle back. Dorms $27, doubles ❸

Kalbarri Edge Resort Porter St ☎1800 286 155, ⊛ www.kalbarriedge.com.au. Not quite finished at the time of writing, but this new resort should raise the bar for accommodation in Kalbarri – expect stylish, minimalist decor and high-spec fittings. Studios ❼, 2-bed apartments ❽, spa suites ❾

Pelican Shore Villas Corner of Grey and Kaiber sts ☎08/9937 1708 or 1800 671 708, ⊛ www .members.westnet.com.au/pelicanshores. The nicest of the many resort-style places in town – the spacious, well-kept apartments are centred around a pleasant pool, and the latticed verandas and many pot plants give it a cheery, welcoming air. Two-bed apartment ❻, 3-bed apartment ❼

The Town

Entering Kalbarri via Ajana–Kalbarri Road, you can see exactly why its setting is so unique; rugged gorge-scarred bush slides unexpectedly quickly into the mouth of the Murchison River, offering stunning views as you approach the town. Kalbarri is conveniently laid out along Grey Street, which runs from the **marina** alongside the river all the way to **Chinaman's Rock**, where big rollers break over the reef at the river mouth; just below the rock is the family-friendly **Chinaman's Beach**. Attractions around town include the **pelican feeding** in front of *The Grass Tree Café* (see p.700), popular with kids and big kids alike (daily 8.45am), and the **Kalbarri Wildflower Centre** at 882 Ajana–Kalbarri Road (July–Oct 9am–5pm except Tues; donation; T08/9937 1229), which is a good alternative if you can't get to see any of the state's wonderful wildflowers in situ.

Eating and drinking

Of the two so-so **pubs**, the *Kalbarri Hotel* on Grey Street is where the locals hang out, while the livelier *Gilgai Tavern* on Porter Street also serves decent meals. If none of the places below tempt you, there's an IGA supermarket midway down Grey Street.

Black Rock Café 80 Grey St T08/9937 1062, Wwww.blackrockcafe.com.au. Very similar menu and feel to *The Gorges Café*, with great crepe stacks for breakfast, salads and paninis for lunch and Mod-Oz mains in the evening. Licensed or BYO wine only. Tues–Sat 7am–8.30pm, Sun 7am–2pm.

Echo Beach Porter St T08/9937 1033. The smartest place in town, with a sleek industrial-style interior and sail-topped terrace on which to enjoy classy dishes like dhufish with scalloped potatoes, Thai beef salad and twice-cooked duck. Daily 5pm–late.

Tours and activities

There are enough tours and activities on offer here to keep you occupied for days.

Big River Ranch Ajana–Kalbarri Road T08/9937 1214, Wwww.bigriverranch.net. Horseriding for beginners and experts in beautiful bush just 2km east of town (20min $20, 1hr $50, 2hr $80).

Kalbarri Abseil T08/9937 1618, Wwww.abseilaustralia.com.au. Abseil into the gorges of Kalbarri National Park (half day $80, full day $125).

Kalbarri Boat Hire Grey St, opposite Murchison Caravan Park T08/9937 1245, Wwww.kalbarriboathire.com. Various vessels from paddle boats to power boats can be rented for trips upriver; prices start at $15. They also run half-day canoe safaris ($65, breakfast or lunch included).

Kalbarri Explorer T08/9937 2027, Wwww.kalbarriexplorer.com.au. Fishing charters ($210), sunset cruises ($45) and whale-watching (June–Dec; $65) aboard the *Explorer*. Reefwalker Adventure Tours (T08/9937 1356, Wwww.reefwalker.com.au) offer much the same.

Kalbarri Safari Tours T08/9937 1001, Wwww.kalbarrisafaritours.com.au. Kayaking and quad-biking trips in the national park ($59–139).

Kalbarri Sandboarding T08/9937 2377, Wwww.sandboardingaustralia.com.au. Like skate ramps but with sand dunes (full day $80).

Kalbarri Scenic Flights T08/9937 1130, Wwww.kalbarriaircharter.com.au. Offers six scenic flights out of Kalbarri, from $59 for the short but spectacular Coastal Cliffs run (20min) to $285 for a five-hour visit to Monkey Mia.

Kalbarri Sports and Dive Kalbarri Arcade, Grey St T08/9937 1126. Can organize dives and equipment rental.

Finlay's Fish BBQ Magee Crescent ☎08/9937 1260. Don't leave Kalbarri without checking out this unique place. Choose from the bewildering array of seafood chalked up on the huge blackboard, and munch on fresh damper (wrapped in newspaper and served with your very own tub of butter) until your perfectly cooked fish comes off the BBQ. The guiding principles in this unusual indoor/outdoor setting are BYO and DIY; songs around the campfire and a nightly charity raffle add to the warm vibes. Tues–Sun from 6pm, daily in school holidays.

The Grass Tree Café 94–96 Grey St ☎08/9937 2288. The menu at this casual waterfront place has all the usual suspects for breakfast and lunch, but is more popular for its Asian-influenced mod-Oz dishes in the evening, including excellent laksa and Goan prawns. Breakfast, lunch and dinner daily except Wed (closed) and Thurs (dinner only).

Listings

Bike rental Bikes can be hired at the Family Entertainment Centre, on Magee Crescent.
Internet Access is available at the Traveller's Book Exchange on Grey St.

Post office At the BP garage, opposite the marina.
Shopping There are several small shopping arcades along Grey St, housing pharmacies, bakeries, banks and the like.

Kalbarri National Park

Kalbarri National Park (DEC fee; see box, p.644) has two distinct sections: the **coastal gorges** just south of Kalbarri, and the serpentine **river gorges** of the upper Murchison River to the east. Kalbarri Coach Tours visit both areas several times a week ($45 half day; ☎08/9937 1161, ⓦwww.kalbarricoachtours.com.au), and also offer kayaking in the river gorges (from $60).

A fun day can be had cycling between the many beaches and **coastal gorges** south of Kalbarri along Red Bluff Road and George Grey Drive – around 40km return from town if you visit them all. The top picks from north to south are Red Bluff Beach, Mushroom Rock, Rainbow Valley, Pot Alley, Eagle Gorge and Natural Bridge. A gusty cliff-top trail links Eagle Gorge and Natural Bridge (8km; 3hr 30min one-way; easy), and there's also a track between Mushroom Rock and Rainbow Valley (3km; 1–2hr return; easy). There are great coastal views throughout this section of the park, especially as you come into Kalbarri.

Eleven kilometres east of Kalbarri on the Ajana–Kalbarri Road, a corrugated, wildflower-flanked track turns north for 20km to the **river gorges** along the Murchison River, before reaching a T-junction where you can go a further 6km north to **Nature's Window** and **The Loop**, or 5km south to **Z Bend**. From the right-hand northern car park, a short track leads to Nature's Window, for superlative 360-degree views and impressive photographs through the rock formation that forms the window. From here, you can continue on The Loop walk (8km; 3hr return; moderate) around a horseshoe bend in the Murchison River; if the heat or laziness prevails there's a lookout over The Loop at the left-hand car park. To the south, Z Bend lookout gives a real sense of how the river has shaped the land here, and the small birds zigzagging the gorge far below put its great size into perspective. From here, you can continue on a walk into the gorge itself (2.5km; 2hr return; moderate with some steep sections). Back on Ajana–Kalbarri Road heading east, you come to the turn-off for Hawks Head and Ross Graham lookouts, both a few kilometres off the road, with river access at the latter; the views here are less impressive but worth a quick look. It's typically ten degrees hotter in the river gorges than in Kalbarri, so take the necessary precautions.

It's possible to **walk** from Ross Graham Lookout to Z Bend (2 days) or the Loop (4 days), or from Z Bend to The Loop (2 days), but these are all demanding treks so consult the **park ranger** (☎08/9937 1140) first – apart from in these circumstances, there's no camping in the park.

The Coral Coast

The beautiful Coral Coast stretches from **Shark Bay**, an ecological and evolutionary hot spot of the highest order, up to the arid spike of land on which **Exmouth** and **Coral Bay** rest. People head here to see the stunning 250-kilometre **Ningaloo Reef** which fringes the western edge of the peninsula, never more than 7km offshore and in places accessible right from the beach. Increasing numbers head to the tiny, laid-back resort of Coral Bay at the southern end of the reef, rather than basing themselves in sterile Exmouth, near the tip of the peninsula.

Aside from viewing the reef, people flock here for the rare opportunity to swim with the world's largest fish, the **whale shark**, which feeds in the area between April and July each year. In between Shark Bay and Exmouth is **Carnarvon**, a good base for exploring the exhilarating 4WD track north to Gnaraloo Station, past wild beaches and tumultuous seas.

Shark Bay

Shark Bay is the name given to the two prongs of land and their corresponding lagoons situated west of Overlander Roadhouse on Highway 1. **Denham**, the only settlement, is on the western side of the northern Peron Peninsula, while at **Monkey Mia** on the sheltered eastern side, bottlenose dolphins have been coming in to the beach to meet people almost daily since the 1960s. The **southern peninsula**, accessed by Useless Loop Road 43km west of the Overlander, ends at Steep Point, mainland Australia's westernmost spot. There's much to see along the road to **Steep Point**, including blowholes, sheltered white beaches and the endless Zuytdorp Cliffs – a 4WD is required, and you'll need to be able to deflate and re-inflate your tyres to make it over some soft dunes. There are no facilities at all down this peninsula, so come prepared – call the ranger ahead of arrival for instructions (☎08/9948 3993, ⓦwww.steeppoint.com.au).

South Passage separates Steep Point from **Dirk Hartog Island** (March–Oct; ☎08/9948 1211 ⓦwww.dirkhartogisland.com.au), which offers good snorkelling, scuba-diving, fishing and walking opportunities, as well as the very unique experience that is setting foot on Cape Inscription, as Dirk Hartog did in 1616. If you want to explore the island fully, you'll need to bring your own 4WD; for more information and details about staying at the homestead (❾) or the island's campsites ($18 per person) check out the website. If you'd prefer to do a day tour, the website also has details of fly-in-fly-out trips, or see the box on p.704 for day tours by boat.

Shark Bay was **World Heritage** listed in 1991, and if you weren't aware of this fact before you arrived, tourism efforts have ensured that you certainly will be by the time you leave; the upside of this marketing drive is that the dolphins are quite rightly no longer the be-all and end-all in this remarkable place, which qualifies for listing under no less than four of UNESCO's "natural" criteria for World Heritage status.

Greyhound Australia **buses** from Perth and Broome stop at *Overlander Roadhouse*, where they are met by shuttle services (open to the public) on to Denham and Monkey Mia on Monday, Wednesday and Friday.

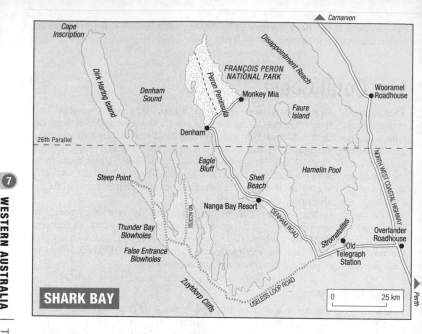

FRANÇOIS PERON
NATIONAL PARK

Cape
Inscription

Dirk Hartog Island

Denham
Sound

Peron Peninsula

Monkey Mia

Faure
Island

Wooramel
Roadhouse

26th Parallel

Denham

Disappointment Reach

Eagle
Bluff

Shell
Beach

Hamelin Pool

NORTH WEST COASTAL HIGHWAY

Steep Point

NO ACCESS

Nanga Bay Resort

DENHAM ROAD

Thunder Bay
Blowholes

False Entrance
Blowholes

Stromatolites

Old
Telegraph
Station

Overlander
Roadhouse

Zuytdorp Cliffs

USELESS LOOP ROAD

SHARK BAY

0   25 km

▶ Perth

The road to Denham and Monkey Mia

It's 125km to Denham and a further 25km to Monkey Mia from *Overlander Roadhouse* down the newly named World Heritage Drive. Twenty-nine kilometres west of the *Overlander*, a road leads 5km north to the **Old Telegraph Station** and **Old Postmaster's Residence**, the basic *Hamelin Pool Caravan Park* (☎08/9942 5905; camping $18, powered site $20) and **Hamelin Pool** itself. The pool is home to a community of **stromatolites**, colonies of sediment-trapping algae which are direct descendants of the Earth's earliest life forms, dating back over three billion years – you'll only find similar examples in the Bahamas and the Persian Gulf. It is their ancestors we can thank for diligently oxygenating the Earth's atmosphere, which eventually led to more complex life forms. Viewed from a boardwalk behind the Old Postmaster's Residence, the examples in Hamelin Pool flourish because no predators can handle the pool's hyper-saline water; the Faure Sill, a natural seagrass and sediment barrier on the ocean floor, creates both the "pool" and the salinity, as it allows water to flow in but not out, which after evaporation leaves very salty water. Inside the Old Postmaster's Residence there's now a café; they also deal with camping enquiries. Enquire here too about tours through the Old Telegraph Station opposite (daily on demand; $5); it gives useful information about stromatolites that might prevent you from thinking they're just big lumps of rock, and also gives a rundown of the telegraph station's interesting history.

Continuing on the main road towards Denham, on the left you'll pass *Nanga Bay Resort* (☎08/9948 3992, ⓦwww.nangabayresort.com.au; camping $25, powered site $30, dorms $40, cabins and villas ❹–❽), a laid-back park with good facilities and a cute restaurant on wide Nanga Bay. Across the isthmus is stunning **Shell Beach**, composed entirely of millions of tiny bivalve Cardiid Cockle shells – one of only two such beaches in the world. Lying up to 10m deep, where they've consolidated under their own weight they're cut into blocks to restore local buildings – you can see the only shell brick quarry in Shark Bay at Hamelin Pool.

The isthmus is now spanned by an electric fence which emits a recording of barking dogs, part of **Project Eden**, which is trying to re-establish native species such as the mallee fowl and the echidna on the Peron Peninsula by eradicating feral animals; the herbal "1080" poison you see signed all over WA – to which native fauna is immune – is also part of the project. Twenty kilometres before Denham, **Eagle Bluff** is an impressive cliff-top lookout with views of Dirk Hartog Island. The shallow green waters of Denham Sound and Henri Freycinet Harbour, below the bluff, are perfect for spotting dolphins, manta rays and even dugongs – almost ten thousand, or around ten percent of the world's dugong population, live in Shark Bay, attracted here by the plentiful supply of their favourite snack, seagrass.

Denham and beyond

A small prawning port and holiday resort, **DENHAM** thrives in the lee of Monkey Mia's unflagging popularity. Arranged down the breezy seafront Knight Terrace, and with more amenities than the resort at Monkey Mia, it can be a better place to base yourself. Four kilometres out of Denham along Monkey Mia Road is **Little Lagoon**, filled with clear turquoise waters and fringed by a narrow strip of white sand; when the wind gets up here it's ideal for windsurfing (bring your own).

Practicalities

The brand-new **Shark Bay Discovery Centre and Visitors Centre** at 33 Knight Terrace (daily 9am–6pm; $10 for discovery centre; ℡08/9948 1550, Ⓦ www.sharkbayworldheritagedrive.com.au) is well worth an hour of your time. This innovative facility about all things Shark Bay has displays arranged geographically on the floor, creating a 3D multimedia "map" of the area. Denham's main strip also has a **post office** and a couple of small **supermarkets**.

There's some good low-key **accommodation** in Denham. *Bay Lodge* at 113 Knight Terrace (℡08/9948 1278, Ⓦ www.baylodge.info; dorms $25, rooms ❷–❻) is a fairly ramshackle but homely backpackers', with a scatter of random furniture, a football-shirt-festooned kitchen, sun-baked pool area and an aviary. Nearby *Oceanside Village* at 117 Knight Terrace (℡08/9948 3003 or 1800 680 600, Ⓦ www.oceanside.com.au; ❺–❻) has cute blue-and-white one- and two-bed cottages with matching interiors that are functional rather than stylish. Some are right on the seafront though, and others perched on stilts up a hill at the rear have terrific views. *Seaside Tourist Village* at 1 Stella Rowley Drive (℡08/9948 1242 or 1300 133 733, Ⓦ www.sharkbayfun.com; camping $22, powered site $26.50, en-suite site $32, cabins ❸–❺) is the best of the three caravan parks in town, opening onto a small beach and with an excellent camp kitchen and wooded pitches. The pick of the apartments in town is at *Tradewinds Holiday Village* on Knight Terrace (℡08/9948 1222 or 1800 816 160, Ⓦ www .tradewindsdenham.com.au; ❺–❻); run by the lovely Fay and Trevor, these self-contained one- and two-bed apartments are great value and have more kitchen equipment than most homes. Proving that some things in life do come for free after all, you can camp for no charge for one night only at Eagle Bluff, Whalebone and Fowler's camps (℡08/9948 1550), all beautiful spots on the way into Denham. None has any facilities whatsoever.

The only notable **restaurant** is the *Old Pearler* on Knight Terrace (daily from 5pm; BYO and licensed; ℡08/9948 1373), an adorable little place made

Shark Bay is hub for tours and activities. Most of the excursions listed here, except for fishing charters, are based in or depart from Monkey Mia; check when you book – pick-ups are often available. With luck, on most water-based tours you'll see plenty of marine life, including dolphins, rays and dugongs.

Aquarush ☎08/9948 1446, ⓦwww.sharkbaysnorkel.com.au. Extreme boat tours that cover a lot of ground, very quickly. Prices range from $125–160, and they offer "Ocean and Earth" 4WD combos with Shark Bay Safaris.

Blue Lagoon Pearls ☎08/9948 1325, ⓦwww.bluelagoonpearls.com.au. See how black and cultured pearls are grown, eight minutes by ferry from Monkey Mia (daily; 1hr 10min; $15).

Jetwave Boat Charters ☎08/0423 954 679, ⓦwww.jetwaveboatcharters.com.au. Day-trips from Denham to Dirk Hartog Island (early April to mid-Oct Tues & Fri; $199).

Mac Attack ☎08/9948 3776, ⓦwww.sportfish.com.au. Full ($190) and half-day ($145) fishing trips out of Denham. **Unreel Fishing Charters** offer much the same service (☎08/9948 1185, ⓦwww.sharkbayfishing.com.au).

Monkey Mia Wildsights ☎08/9948 1481 or 1800 241 481, ⓦwww.monkeymiawild sights.com.au. 4WD tours to south Peron (5hr; $99) and François Peron National Park (8hr; $169). They also operate the popular *Shotover* cruises from Monkey Mia; with the promise of $100 cash if you get seasick, and free cruises if you don't spot as much marine life as you'd like. **Shark Bay Majestic Tours** (☎08/ 9948 1627, ⓦwww .sharkbayholiday.com.au) and **Shark Bay Safaris** (☎08/9948 3136 or 1800 441 828, ⓦwww.sharkbaysafaris.com) also offer 4WD tours to similar areas at similar prices, although the less in-your-face Majestic runs the only scheduled tour to Steep Point and the Zuytdorp Cliffs (full day; $169).

Monkey Mia Yacht Charters ☎08/9948 1446 or 1800 030 427, ⓦwww.monkey-mia .net. Gentle cruises aboard *Aristocat II*. Similar tours to those on *Shotover*, with the added thrill of boom-netting – both companies run a huge range of cruises so check websites to find one that suits.

PowerDive Shark Bay Monkey Mia Dolphin Resort ☎08/1300 553 031, ⓦwww .divefun.com.au. Dive and snorkelling safaris in François Peron National Park ($69–119), power-dive courses plus equipment rental.

Shark Bay Camel Safaris ☎08/9948 3136, ⓦwww.myweb.westnet.com.au /sharkbaycamels. Short rides between 9am and 11am ($20–35), with a 2-hour safari at 11am ($60). Doesn't operate Mon.

Shark Bay Coaches Tours and **Shark Bay Scenic Quad Bike Tours** ☎08/9948 1081, ⓦwww.sbcoaches.com. Coach trips around Shark Bay (Tues, Thurs & Sun; 4hr; $70) and quad bike tours around the Little Lagoon and south Peron areas by day and dusk (2/3hr; $70/$90). They also offer a combo for $130.

Shark Bay Scenic Flights ☎0417 919 059, ⓦwww.sharkbayair.com.au. Scenic flights over the area ranging from $55 for a 15-min flight over Monkey Mia and the Peron Homestead, to $400-plus for full-day trips up to Coral Bay and inland to Mount Augustus.

Wula Guda Nyinda ☎0429 708 847, ⓦwww.wulaguda.com.au. Aside from the obvious, one of the most worthwhile things you can do at Monkey Mia is take a tour with award-winning guide Darren "Capes" Capewell, who runs three very well-received Aboriginal cultural tours daily: Banu Dreaming by day (8.30am; 1hr 30min; $30); Maru Maru Dreaming at dusk (4.30pm; 2hr; $35); and Didgeridoo Dreaming later on still (8.30pm; 1hr; $30). The company name means "you come this way"; all tours can also be booked at the Monkey Mia Dolphin Resort (see opposite).

from local shell block, with an interior straight out of rural France. Food is hearty and retro – think steaks with sauce and catch of the day. Other than that, there are a couple of cafés and bakeries along the same road. Note that fresh **water** is very precious in the Shark Bay area: salty bore water is used as much as possible.

François Peron National Park

Four kilometres east of Denham on Monkey Mia Road is the access road for **François Peron National Park** (DEC fee; see box, p.644) at the northern tip of the peninsula, named after the naturalist on the *Geographe*, which sailed past in 1801. The park gets rave reviews from travellers entranced by its turquoise waters, fishing opportunities, red dunes and white sandy beaches, and by the wildlife that can be spotted from **Cape Peron**. **Big Lagoon** offers superb swimming and kayaking (BYO); fans of remote camping will love the sites here and at Bottle Bay, Gregories, South Gregories and Herald Bight. **Peron Homestead**, a former sheep station, is just 8km off the Denham–Monkey Mia road and usually accessible by 2WD – the hot tub of artesian water here is great for any aches and pains acquired on your travels. The park is paradise for four-wheel-drivers – a sturdy high-clearance vehicle is needed to go beyond the homestead, and tyre pressure should be reduced to 20psi on many tracks. For **tours** to the park see opposite. There's no drinking water or fuel here; make sure you have enough of both for the 130-kilometre return trip to Denham.

Monkey Mia

After all the hype, you might be surprised to find that **Monkey Mia** (DEC day fee $6 per person, two days or more $9; park passes don't apply) is just a resort and a jetty by a pretty beach. It's to this beach that scores of people flock to see the almost daily visits by between five and ten adult female **dolphins** and their attendant calves, all known by name. Get here at 7.30am for almost guaranteed dolphin time, and to watch the first feeding at around 8am. There are usually another two feeds per day, always before noon, to encourage the dolphins to spend the afternoon foraging for food in the bay as nature intended – these two later feeds can be a better option if you don't want to fight your way through the excitable crowds standing in the shallows. Displays in the **information centre** focus on dolphin behaviour and explain how the entirely unprompted interaction began in the 1960s – much of what has been learned about dolphins has been gleaned from studies of Monkey Mia's regular troupe of visitors.

If you want to get more involved, you can **volunteer** at Monkey Mia for periods from four days to up to two weeks; contact DEC for more information (℡08/6467 5000, ⓦwww.dec.wa.gov.au).

The middle-of-the-road *Monkey Mia Dolphin Resort* (℡08/9948 1320 or 1800 653 611, ⓦwww.monkeymia.com.au), arranged along the beautiful beach to the left of the dolphin interaction zone, is the only place to stay – the resort is currently undergoing a multi-million-dollar redevelopment. The sometimes confusing scatter of **accommodation** here is all clean and spacious without winning any style awards, and includes beachfront (❾) and garden villas (❽), budget rooms (❹), *Dolphin Lodge Backpackers* (dorms $27–32) and camping facilities ($14, powered site $33). There's also a pool, spa, tennis court, bar, restaurant, internet access and a small shop with basic groceries.

The booking office by the beach can organize all tours and activities (see opposite), and also rents out glass-bottom boats ($35 per hr), single ($10 per hr) or double kayaks ($17.50 per hr), pedal boats $30 per hr) and sun loungers.

Carnarvon and around

CARNARVON is a service town for prawning fleets and the sheep stations of the Upper Gascoyne region, located 900km from Perth and 200km north of *Overlander Roadhouse*. The town also supports a large agricultural zone, thanks to the superficially dry Gascoyne River's retrievable subterranean water, and is increasingly popular with fruit pickers. The town has had a bad reputation in the past due to its proclivity for drunken violence, but it's actually a pretty easy-going place to stock up and spend a night, and those expecting a brawl will most likely be disappointed. A good half day can be spent moseying around Carnarvon's **Heritage Precinct** on Babbage Island (March–Oct daily 9am–5pm; Nov–Feb Mon–Fri 10am–2pm, Sat & Sun 9am–5pm; $3 for train plus gold coin donations; ☏08/9941 3423), accessed from the end of Robinson Street, the main strip, via a footbridge and old railway track which make for an excellent 2.5-kilometre walk or cycle. The precinct contains a number of gentle attractions, including a trip along One Mile Jetty (currently being restored after an arson attack) on a tiny train.

Practicalities

Carnarvon's helpful **visitor centre** (Mon–Fri 9am–5pm, Sat 9am–noon, Sun 10am–1pm; ☏08/9941 1146, ⓦwww.carnarvon.org.au) is in the Civic Centre on the corner of Robinson Street and Camel Lane. Greyhound **buses** also arrive here, and the **post office** is just opposite. In the shopping centre close by you'll find a Woolworths and all the services you could need. Stockman Safaris (☏08/9941 2687, ⓦwww.stockmansafaris.com.au) and Outback Coast Safaris (☏08/9941 3448, ⓦwww.outbackcoastsafaris.com.au) run Aboriginal cultural tours and trips to the Kennedy Range and Mount Augustus national parks, and Lake Macleod.

The best **accommodation** in Carnarvon is at the *Fish and Whistle Backpackers/Port Hotel* at 35 Robinson St (☏08/9941 1704, ⓦwww.fishandwhistle.com.au; singles and twins with fridge $40 per person, twins, doubles and quads $25 per person, motel rooms ❹), a sprawling pub being slowly renovated by its lovely owners. So far they're doing admirably, with most rooms boasting light-wood floorboards and nice bed linen. A large, bright kitchen and a multitude of communal spaces are now in place, with a café, a pub renovation and a beer garden to follow. There are standard motel rooms, a bistro and pool at *Best Western Hospitality Inn*, 6 West St (☏08/9941 1600, ⓦwww.carnarvon.wa.hospitalityinns.com.au; ❻), or you can choose from the seven caravan parks that line the road into town. *Coral Coast Tourist Park* on Robinson Street ☏08/9941 1438, ⓦwww.coralcoasttouristpark.com.au; camping $25, powered site $27, en-suite site $37, cabins and chalets ❸–❻) is the best of the bunch, and also the closest to the centre.

There are a couple of good **eating** options too. *Avocadeau Tree* at 12–14 Robinson St (closed Sun) comes up trumps for breakfast and lunch with good focaccias, burgers and cakes in a modern space. *The Crab Shack* (daily 9am–5pm) at the Small Boat Harbour just south of town offers pure seafood fixes to take away, including steamed crab, prawns and fish. If you want to eat in, there's the nearby *Harbourside Café* (☏08/9941 4111; daily 10am–late), a sunny, casual joint with a good selection of breakfasts and lunches. People mainly come in the evenings though, to sit on the waterfront terrace and feast on specials such as Moroccan-spiced snapper and "Carnarvon bouillabaisse". In the centre of town your best bet is the *Old Post Office* at 10 Robinson St (☏08/9941 1800; daily from 5pm), with cute French-style red-and-white-checked tablecloths and a funky, corrugated-iron bar inside, and a large veranda. Locals rate the pizzas but there's a wide-ranging menu. For **drinks**, locals head to the *Gascoyne Hotel* on waterfront Olivia Terrace, at least until the *Port* is renovated.

Around Carnarvon

There are a couple of top-quality **4WD routes** close to town. The eight-hundred-kilometre **Kingsford Smith Mail Run** snakes inland from Carnarvon to Meekatharra, and gives intrepid travellers a real taste of the Outback. Named after Charles Kingsford Smith – who set a number of aviation "firsts" in the early twentieth century before setting up a mail delivery service to isolated pastoral stations – the route runs by the **Kennedy Range** and **Mount Augustus national parks**. The Gascoyne Murchison Outback Pathways brochure, available at local visitor centres or to download at ⓦ www.carnarvon .org.au, outlines the route and all necessary precautions.

Coast crawlers might prefer the awe-inspiring 154-kilometre run up to Gnaraloo Station, best done as an overnighter: 24km north of town, the sealed Blowholes Road heads 41km west to a T-junction with a sign bearing the legend "King Waves Kill"; take note before viewing the **Blowholes** at Point Quobba, just to the left. On all but the calmest days, incoming waves compress air through vents in the craggy coastline and erupt noisily up to 20m into the air. The road north from here is unsealed and a 4WD is required. You can camp cheaply ($8, powered site $10) at two spots on *Quobba Station* (ⓣ08/9948 5098, ⓦ www.quobba.com.au; ❶–❹), either just south of the blowholes (no water) or at the homestead 8km to the north, which also has a range of rustic accommodation. Continuing over a couple of private roads belonging to the Dampier Saltworks (watch out for road trains), you'll come to a signed turn-off which heads down a rocky track to spectacular **Red Bluff** (ⓣ08/9948 5001, ⓦ www .quobba.com.au), a broad sweep of white sand with some of the craziest surf you'll ever see. There's basic camping here ($20; no water), plus beach shacks ($15 per person), bungalows (❻) and luxurious eco-tents (❾). Departing Red Bluff, you move onto windy, sun-bleached 🏕 *Gnaraloo Station* (ⓣ08/9315 4809, ⓦ www.gnaraloo.com.au; dorms $25, accommodation ❷–❺). You'll pass another stunning lagoon-side camping spot at **Three Mile Camp** ($18 per person) before you reach the homestead, which boasts enticing, ramshackle accommodation, world-class wave-sailing and mesmerizing views. Seven kilometres beyond the homestead are the turquoise waters of deserted, tranquil **Gnaraloo Bay**, perfect for snorkelling and a spot of skinny dipping.

Coral Bay and on to Exmouth

Back on Highway 1, 140km north of Carnarvon, the Northwest Cape Road turning 6km past *Minilya Roadhouse* leads to beautiful **CORAL BAY**, an idyllic spot from which to enjoy Ningaloo Reef. The tiny, laid-back community stretches for little more than 150m down one side of the road, with a stunning

Ningaloo marine-spotters' calendar

Manta rays – all year in Coral Bay, between May and November in Exmouth
Turtle hatching – January to March
Coral spawning – March and April
Whale sharks – April to July
Whale watching – July to October
Turtle nesting – November to February
Reef Sharks – September to February in Coral Bay

▲ Whale shark, Ningaloo Reef

beach almost taking the place of a pavement on the other. At the northern end of the beach, reef sharks gather in season at Point Maud, while just south of the beach past the lookout there's good snorkelling at Purdy Point and beach-lounging spots on Paradise Beach. Hot salty bore water and a lack of available land have kept tourism fairly low-key, and the resort remains little more than a couple of caravan parks which between them own all the associated shops, services and cafés. At the time of writing, a marina development was under consideration.

You can have fun in Coral Bay just hanging out, strolling down the white sand and having an occasional dip. There are enough **tours** and **activities** to keep more active sorts occupied for weeks, though (see box opposite)

Practicalities

Shuttle **buses** to Coral Bay drop you at *Ningaloo Club*, and connect with Greyhound buses stopping at *Minilya Roadhouse* from Friday to Sunday only; the return service runs from Thursday to Saturday. In terms of facilities, **internet** access, **ATM**s and **fuel** are all available, and the small **supermarkets** should satisfy self-caterers for a couple of days. There's no official **visitor centre** here; the many booking offices displaying the familiar blue-and-white "i" logo are all run by Coral Bay's three resorts.

All **accommodation** is on the same (and only) strip, Robinson Street. A new motel should be up and running behind *Ningaloo Club* by mid-2009. *Bayview Coral Bay* (advance bookings ☎08/9385 6655, otherwise ☎08/9942 5932, [W]www.coralbaywa.com; camping $30, powered site $33, apartments [4]–[9]) is the first place on your left as you come into town, with pleasant sandy pitches, a good camp kitchen (you pay for the BBQ though), a pool and tennis courts. The various self-contained apartments range from average one-bed units with shared facilities through to the White House, a four-bed veritable palace. Not all units have drinking water. *Ningaloo Club* (advance bookings ☎08/9385 6655, otherwise ☎08/9948 5100, [W]www.ningalooclub.com; dorms $25–27, doubles and twins [4]–[5]), just opposite, is a cheery, purpose-built hostel with the same owners; highlights are a sparkling pool and great bar/veranda area with pool and ping pong. The dorms are serviceable although a little worn, but all in all a great choice.

Continuing down the main strip, the next place on your left is *Peoples Park Caravan Village* (℡08/9942 5933, ⓦwww.peoplesparkcoralbay.com; camping $27–28, powered site $34–46, 1-bed cabins ❼, 2-bed ❽), a bit more upmarket than *Bayview* and popular with an older crowd; it has more private pitches, nicer cabins and is generally greener and better laid out. Situated at the end of Robinson Street is *Ningaloo Reef Resort* (℡08/9942 5934, ⓦwww.ningalooreefresort.com.au; ❻–❾); the motel units and two- to four-bed apartments in this lively resort are of a good standard, and a nice pool overlooks the beach. The apartments fronting the pool and the *Coral Bay Hotel* can be noisy at night.

For **eating**, the *Coral Resort Bakery*, in the shopping centre opposite *Bayview*, is good for lunch, with excellent pies, pastries, cakes, sandwiches and coffee. *Fin's Café* (daily breakfast, lunch and dinner), in the shopping village adjacent to *Peoples Park*, is always busy in the evening; food is served on a busy terrace strewn with fairy lights, and the tiger prawns, surf and turf, burgers, focaccias, shakes and ice cream all deserve attention. Slightly less attractive are *Ningaloo Reef Café* (daily 6pm–late) at *Bayview*, and *Shades Restaurant* (Mon–Sat 8am–9pm, Sun 8am–2pm) at *Ningaloo Reef Resort*. For **drinking** there's the *Coral Bay Hotel* at *Ningaloo Reef Resort*, a lively pub with frequent live music in the courtyard; happy hours (Tues & Fri 5.30–6.30pm) only add to the holiday atmosphere.

Towards Exmouth

Continuing for 53km on the Northwest Cape Road to Exmouth you pass Burkett Road, which cuts 150km from the journey if you're coming from the north – enjoyable station stays are possible along this route at stylish *Bullara*

Tours and activities in Coral Bay

There is a bewildering array of tour companies in Coral Bay, offering catamaran cruises, fishing charters, resort dives or full PADI courses, scenic flights, sea-kayaking or glass-bottom boat trips, nature tours, whale-watching, 4WD safaris, tours around the cape, snorkelling, and quad-bike tours. Check out the websites below or call in once you get there to find one that suits you – unless otherwise noted, the companies mentioned run the whole gamut of tours and activities at similar prices, with trips lasting anything from an hour to a couple of days. With water-based trips, longer is generally better, as snorkelling on the more impressive outer reef is often included.

There's a booking office incorporating Coral Bay Charter at *Bayview Coral Bay* (℡08/9942 5932), with Coral Bay Adventures/The Boat Shed (℡08/9942 5955, ⓦwww.coralbayadventures.com.au) in the small shopping centre opposite, alongside Coral Bay Discoveries/Coral Coast Tours (fishing and 4WD trips only; ℡08/9948 5052, ⓦwww.coralcoasttours.com), Coastal Adventure Tours (℡08/9948 5190 ⓦwww.coralbaytours.com.au) and Ningaloo Reef Dive (diving and boat trips only; ℡08/9942 5824, ⓦwww.ningalooreefdive.com). Ningaloo Experience (℡08/9942 5877, ⓦwww.ningalooexperience.com) and Coral Bay Ecotours (℡08/9942 5885, ⓦwww.coralbayecotours.com.au) are based in the small "shopping village" next door to *Peoples Park*. A caravan towards the southern end of the beach rents glass-bottom kayaks, snorkelling gear, sun loungers and umbrellas; they also run sea-kayaking tours (℡08/9948 5034, ⓦwww.ningalookayakadventures.com).

([T]08/9942 5938, [W]www.bullara-station.com.au; camping $11, rooms [5]) and more basic *Giralia* ([T]08/9942 5937; [4]). Beyond the Burkett Road turn-off, two roads lead up onto the rugged eastern Cape Range: **Charles Knife Road**, which climbs precipitously to the top of the range 311m above sea level; and **Shothole Canyon Road** (closed indefinitely at the time of writing due to a washaway) 5km further down the main road. Short trails and lookouts down both roads offer fine views of the area; a longer walk which traverses the top of the range is possible from Thomas Carter Lookout, at the end of Charles Knife Road (8km; 3hr return; moderate).

Exmouth and around

EXMOUTH was built in 1967 to serve a former US Navy Communications Station. Nowadays the town has little to recommend it aside from a bed for the night and a plethora of tours – canny travellers will just stock up and head along the beautiful western side of the cape to Cape Range National Park and Ningaloo Marine Park. Exmouth is situated a couple of kilometres from the ocean (a necessary cyclone precaution), although the long-promised marina complex just south of town will enjoy sea frontage when it's finally completed. The **Muiron Islands**, just offshore, are popular with snorkellers, divers and fisherpeople; you can camp there outside of turtle-nesting season – apply to DEC in Exmouth for permits (camping 1 April–31 Oct only; [T]08/9947 8000).

Arrival and information

Shuttle **buses** connect Exmouth with Greyhound buses pulling in at *Minilya Roadhouse* from Friday to Sunday; the return trip runs Thursday to Saturday. The shuttle buses stop outside the **visitor centre** (April–Oct daily 9am–5pm; Nov–March Mon–Fri 9am–5pm, Sat & Sun 9am–1pm; [T]08/9949 1176, [W]www.exmouthwa.com.au) on the main Murat road opposite *Ningaloo Caravan Holiday Resort*; the centre can book accommodation and tours. To find the main **shopping centre**, turn left onto Maidstone Crescent at the Caltex fuel station on Murat Road; banks, the post office and other services are located around the crescent.

Accommodation

Accommodation in Exmouth is comfortable without being spectacular, with the notable exception of the *Novotel*.

Exmouth Cape Holiday Park and **Blue Reef Backpackers** Corner of Murat Rd and Truscott Crescent [T]08/9949 1101 or 1800 621 101, [W]www.aspenparks.com.au. This site, 2km south of town, has benefited from the input of new owners Aspen, and now boasts a great campers' kitchen, spotless amenities, an OK pool and large shady pitches, though unpowered sites are stuffed into an unshaded corner. Backpacker accommodation is brand-new, clean and functional but lacks a good communal area; motel rooms in the same block are of a good standard. Dorms $27, camping $34, powered site $40, motel rooms [5], cabins [4]–[7]

Ningaloo Caravan Holiday Resort and **Winston's Backpackers** Murat Rd [T]08/9949 2377, [W]www.exmouthresort.com. A similar standard to *Exmouth Cape* but with a better pool, nicer unpowered sites and more of a backpacker communal area. Backpacker rooms are good and chalets pleasant and very clean, with wicker furniture and bed linen. A large site, it can feel empty in low season. Dorms $28, doubles [4], camping $30, powered site $35, cabins [6]–[7]

Ningaloo Lodge Lefroy St, off Maidstone Crescent [T]08/9949 4949 or 1800 880 949, [W]www.ningaloolodge.com.au. Great-value motel accommodation with a small pool, and indoor and outdoor communal areas. Bed linen is chintzy but adds to the homely feel, with breakfast mugs stacked up in the kitchen and lots of garden ornaments. [4]

Novotel Ningaloo Resort Madaffari Drive, Marina [T]08/9949 0000, [W]www.novotelningaloo.com. The upmarket *Novotel* is simply but elegantly decked out in earthy tones and boasts the only ocean views in town. The resort focuses on the stylish central pool and also has a first-rate restaurant, *Mantaray's* (see below). All the studios and apartments have large balconies, supremely comfortable beds and sleek bathrooms. The only downsides are the distance from town (5km to the south) and – until the rest of the marina is developed – the construction-site appearance of the area, although you won't notice this once inside. ➒

Potshot Hotel Resort and **Excape Backpackers YHA** Murat Rd ☎08/9949 1200, ⓦwww .potshotresort.com and www.yha.com.au.

Sprawling resort at the top end of town with standard en-suite dorms, a scruffy lounge and good outdoor communal area in the backpackers' section, plus three pools, a bottleshop, bistro and *Brad's Bar* (see below). Aside from the backpacker rooms, there's a wide variety of decent accommodation here and at the fancier *Osprey Apartments* over the road, ranging from budget motel rooms to deluxe three-bed apartments. Dorms $25, singles, twins, doubles ➋, rooms ➍–➑

Tours and activities

There are plenty of trips you can take from Exmouth, notably swimming with whale sharks (see p.707 for wildlife seasons). Expect to pay at least $350 to get up close to these gentle giants, and make sure you have enough time to wait around for sightings. Tours can be booked direct, through the visitor centre, and at most accommodation.

Capricorn Sea Kayaking ⓣ08/6267 8059, ⓦwww.capricornseakayaking.com.au. Ride the waves from April–Oct from $149 for a full day.
Ningaloo Ecology Cruises ☎08/9949 2255, ⓦwww.ecology.com.au. See the reef without getting wet on the glass-bottom *Reefwalker* (from $120); they also offer snorkelling to all sites down the western cape.
Ningaloo Reef Dreaming ☎08/9949 4777, ⓦwww.ningaloodreaming.com. Ningaloo Reef is a diver's paradise, with world-class dive sites at the Muiron Islands and Exmouth's Navy Pier. Options include snorkelling ($140), dives (from $120 per dive), dive courses ($205–1300) and whale shark tours ($350). **Exmouth Dive Centre** (ⓣ08/9949

1201 or 1800 811 338, ⓦwww.exmouthdiving .com.au) and **Ningaloo Whaleshark-n-Dive** (ⓣ08/9949 1116 or 1800 224 060, ⓦwww .ningaloowhalesharkndive.com.au) run similar tours at similar prices.
Ningaloo Safari Tours ⓣ08/9949 1550, ⓦwww .ningaloosafari.com. See the cape at ground level from a 4WD with Ningaloo Safari Tours or **WestTreks Safaris** (ⓣ08/9949 2659); both outfits run full-day tours of the cape from $175.
Norwest Airwork ⓣ08/9949 2888, ⓦwww .norwestairwork.com. If you fancy viewing the region from the air these guys offer scenic plane trips ($250 for 3 people).

Eating and drinking

There are the usual takeaways, cafés and a Chinese restaurant in the shopping centre near Maidstone Crescent, which also has a decent-sized IGA supermarket. Self-caterers wanting to create the ultimate fish barbecue in Exmouth should take the time to visit Kailis Seafoods, at the Charles Knife turn-off before town.

Brad's Bar *Potshot Hotel Resort*. Offers a less fear-filled night out than the other pubs in town, with a smart purple interior, courtyard and attached sports bar.
Grace's Tavern Murat Rd, opposite Exmouth Cape. Not a fine example of a pub, with a rough-and-ready feel and an outdoor area that doubles as a car park. Inside there's a bistro and a fancier section with tablecloths and candles; the menu's the same, though – pizza, steak, burgers, seafood 'n' chips and curry. Lunch Wed–Sun 11am–2pm, dinner daily 6.30–9.30pm.
Mantaray's Novotel Ningaloo Resort ⓣ08/9949 0000. The town's top pick by a long stretch; mains

are in the $40 bracket but for that you can expect the likes of fresh crab in chilli-and-coconut broth, in classy surrounds. Daily 8am–late.
Ningaloo Health Foods Kennedy St, near the shopping centre. Good little joint doing gourmet brekkies, unctuous smoothies, focaccias and health-foodie lunches such as tuna-and-lentil patties. Good coffee. Daily 8am–4.30pm.
Whalers Kennedy St, near the shopping centre. Fairy lights surround the slightly retro veranda and the tasty food has a similar 1970s vibe, with garlic-and-chilli prawns, steak and chips, ice-cream sundaes and boozy desserts all popular. Daily breakfast, lunch and dinner.

To explore the area beyond Exmouth, you really need your own vehicle. Heading north out of town past Yardie Creek Road (the turn-off for Cape Range and Ningaloo) and the navy base you come to **Bundegi Beach**, set right below some ugly navy antennae – it's still nicer than the town beaches though, and there's a dark platform of **coral** a couple of hundred metres offshore so bring a snorkel. A new whale-shark interpretative centre, spotting tower and café should open here sometime in 2009 (March–Dec; ☎08/9949 4499), all of which will doubtless change the character of the beach. Glass-bottom boat tours on the *Ningaloo Coral Explorer II* are also available here, along with snorkelling equipment and beach gear.

After backtracking and heading down Yardie Creek Road another turn-off leads to unsignposted **Surfers Beach** and the wreck of the *Mildura*, which clipped the reef in 1907 during a cyclone. Continuing down Yardie Creek Road you'll reach the very tip of the cape and **Vlaming Head Lighthouse**; the lookout here offers fine views of the surrounding area and of the Muiron Islands to the northeast, especially at sunset. At the base of the lookout is the peaceful *Lighthouse Caravan Park* (☎08/9949 1478, ⓦwww.ningaloolighthouse .com; camping $24, powered site $26, chalets ❹–❽). It has good shaded pitches, fuel, a pool, café (May–Sept), camp kitchen, snorkelling equipment to rent (24hr; $15) and seven hilltop chalets.

Beyond Vlaming Head before the park entrance you'll pass the **Jurabi Turtle Centre**, an unmanned pagoda with interesting information on the green, hawksbill and loggerhead turtles which nest on the beach, and some alarming stuffed animals.

Cape Range National Park and Ningaloo Marine Park

Beyond the turtle centre is the entrance station for **Cape Range National Park** (DEC fee; see box, p.644) and the adjoining **Ningaloo Marine Park**. The proximity of the continental shelf is what gives this marine park such a stunning variety of marine life: over 500 species of fish and 250 species of coral have been recorded here, attracting migrating whales and whale sharks.

Moving south from the park entrance a sublime day can be had beach-hopping between deserted beaches and swimming in pristine lagoons. There's superb snorkelling at sheltered **Lakeside** and in **Turquoise Bay**, where the famous drift snorkel floats you across 200m of colourful coral: drop your clothes by the sandbar, enter the water at the southern end of the beach and hop out in time to pick up your clothes – the drift snorkel should only be completed at low- to mid-tide due to the strong currents. The pick of the snorkelling sites though is at **Oyster Stacks** just to the south, where legions of colourful fish huddle under the archways created by the four shelly protrusions – the coral is so close to the surface here that you can only snorkel at high tide.

The **Milyering Visitor Centre** (daily 9am–3.45pm; ☎08/9949 2808), just after the T-Bone Bay turn-off, has displays on the parks and tide times. Twelve idyllic **camping** spots ($6.50) line the coast: the best are at Osprey Bay, with swimming in the milky waters of adjacent Sandy Bay and good vantage points for sunsets or whale-watching; and Ned's Camp. You can't book ahead for any of the campsites, which have toilets but no other facilities: check availability at the park entrance or the DEC in Exmouth (Mon–Fri only; ☎08/9947 8000) and pay the fee ($6.50 per person) at the park entrance or to the campsite host where available.

For an altogether more pampering overnight experience, flush travellers might like to try *Sal Salis Ningaloo Resort* (℡1300 790 561 or 02/9571 6399, ⓦwww .salsalis.com.au; ⓔ), an exclusive safari camp with just five luxury tents ($685 per person per night) hidden in the white dunes near Mandu Mandu Gorge. An eco-friendly philosophy, lush sunsets, contemporary Australian cuisine and roaming wildlife are among the attractions. Close by, a walking trail from Mandu Mandu Gorge car park takes you along a creek bed before returning along the gorge rim (3km return; 2hr; moderate).

The final stop in the park for most will be **Yardie Creek**, 82km in total from Exmouth without detours. Those with 4WDs can cross the creek at low tide with reduced tyre pressure and fingers crossed, before continuing south past *Ningaloo Homestead*, enjoying beach camping and picnics all the way to Coral Bay, a drive that takes about a day. Walks from Yardie Creek include a gentle nature trail along the edge of the creek, which leads into the surprisingly steep gorge trail (2km return total; 2hr; easy–moderate). A boat cruise heads into the gorge from here daily at 11am and 12.30pm – book at the Milyering Visitor Centre (1hr; $25).

The Central Midlands – inland to the Pilbara

About 1000km north of Perth are the ancient, mineral-rich highlands of the **Pilbara**, an area which includes Mount Meharry, at 1249m the highest point in WA. The world's richest surface deposits of **iron ore** were developed here in the 1950s and rich discoveries of ore, crude oil, natural gas and salt continue to be made as private railroads cart the booty to the coast for export to Japan's and China's hungry markets. As a result, company towns such as **Tom Price** and **Newman** abound, offering little to travellers except mine tours and overpriced accommodation. While the Pilbara is unquestionably the economic powerhouse of the state and indeed the nation, the unquenchable growth of the mining industries has had knock-on effects throughout the region. Chronic housing shortages plague many towns, **Karratha** and **Port Hedland** in particular, and hotels and hostels are increasingly bought up by companies desperate to house their staff. Surrounding the huge open-cast mine sites are vast, arid pastoral stations, recovering from or surrendering to early overgrazing. In the middle of all this environmental chaos **Karijini National Park** serenely remains, safeguarding along with the gentler **Millstream–Chichester National Park** some of Australia's most spectacular and timeless natural scenery. Up the coast towards Broome, **Cossack** and **Port Samson** offer respite from the relentless heat and mining mentality.

The Great Northern Highway

Apart from the passage through the Hamersley Ranges north of Newman, scenically there's little to commend the **Great Northern Highway**'s 1600-kilometre inland section from Perth to Port Hedland – most people shoot through in two long days. But like the famed Nullarbor, the monotony can have its own fascination as you pass from the wooded farmlands northward into ever more marginal sheep country, until the only viable commodity is the mineral riches below ground. Soon after New Norcia on the still narrow Great Northern Highway you'll encounter **road trains**, the iconic Outback transporters. North of Wubin they're made up into full-length trains up to 55m long, and run around the clock serving the Pilbara and the northwest coastal ports. Unless you fancy overnighting in often-unhygienic and noisy roadside parking areas (ear-plugs may help), note that **motels** and **hotels** can be up to 260km apart and tend not to be the pick of the crop. Integrity **buses** (℡08/9226 1339, Ⓦwww.integritycoachlines.com.au) make the 22-hour journey between Perth and Port Hedland once a week.

Among the half-dozen surviving towns along this inland route, semi-abandoned **CUE**, 650km north of Perth, retains some character from the goldrush era and is a good place to stretch your legs. The **visitor centre** on the main strip, Austin Street (Mon–Fri 9am–4pm; ℡08/9963 1041, Ⓦwww.cue .wa.gov.au), has information on the Cue Heritage Trail and sights around town, including the Aboriginal rock paintings at **Walga Rock**, a few kilometres to the west. A night in the spacious jarrah interior of the *Queen of the Murchison Guest House* at 10 Austin St (℡08/9963 1625; ❺) beats any anodyne motel.

Beyond Cue the landscape outruns the south's rain-bearing fronts, scrub replace the trees and games of "count the roadkill" reach high double figures. **MEEKATHARRA**, 115km to the north, is a mining and pastoral centre with some century-old **hotels** such as the *Royal Mail Hotel* (℡08/9981 1148, Ⓦwww.royalmail.com.au; ❹) on Main Street offering good accommodation and food. From "Meeka", as it's known, it's 180km of dirt east to forlorn Wiluna, then another 600km of dull bitumen south to Kalgoorlie–Boulder, while to the west Carnarvon lies at the end of the Kingsford Smith Mail Run (see p.707), a good 800-kilometre dirt road. Continuing north from Meekatharra on the Great Northern Highway, you'll see a road sign marking the **26th parallel**, welcoming you to the fabled "Nor'west", and clumps of the spiky spinifex grass which carpets Australia's interior deserts begin to appear.

NEWMAN, 350km north of Meeka, is a company town built to serve BHP Billiton's **Mount Whaleback Mine**, the world's largest open-cut iron-ore mine. Besides stocking up at the Woolworths supermarket, the **mine tours** (Mon–Fri 9.30am plus Sat 9.30am May–Sept; 1hr 30min; long-sleeved shirt, trousers and enclosed shoes required; $20), which can booked through, and depart, from the excellent **visitor centre** (Feb–Dec daily 8am–5pm; Jan Mon–Sat 8am–5pm; ℡08/9175 2888, Ⓦwww.newman-wa.org) on the corner of Fortescue Avenue and Newman Drive, are the only reason you'd want to stop here. The tours clearly demonstrate the scale and astonishing simplicity of the operation, as **Mount Whaleback** is gradually turned inside out and shipped to Asia. For **accommodation**, try the fairly upmarket *Seasons Hotel* (℡08/9177 8666, Ⓦwww.seasonshotel.com.au; ❺–❼); the restaurant here is one of a few so-so **food** options, including the *Red Sands Tavern* and various Chinese, Thai and takeaway places.

Marble Bar

From Newman, a dirt road leads north for 300km through the scenic east Pilbara to **Nullagine** and **MARBLE BAR**. The latter, linked to Port Hedland by a sealed road, became known as Australia's hottest town after clocking up 160 consecutive days over 37.8°C in 1923 and 1924. This is the sole reason many visitors come to "the Bar", misnamed after a colourful bar of jasper in a rock face by the Coongan River 5km south of town. You can **stay** at the *Marble Bar Travellers Rest Stop* motel on Halse Street (℡08/9176 1066; ❺), *Marble Bar Holiday Park* (℡08/9176 1569; camping $20, powered site $24, cabins ❸–❺) on Contest Road, or at the town's famed *Ironclad Hotel* on Francis Street

(☎08/9176 1066; ❺) – a good place to get some drinking done or, if you're a "sheila", be stared at. The motel and hotel both serve **food**.

Karijini National Park

Karijini National Park (DEC fee; see box, p.644) is WA's second-largest protected area, with spectacular, accessible gorges in the north and a vast unvisited section to the south, separated roughly by Karijini Drive, the southernmost of the two roads running through the park. Travellers rave about the nerve-jangling walks, timeless scenery and sparkling waterholes here, and are often taken aback at the lush, spinifex-covered hills and proliferation of white-trunked snappy gums that sprout from the blood-red rock, distinguishing the Pilbara from the better-known but drier Kimberley, especially in July and August (the busiest months). Karijini Drive is sealed, but the northern Banjima Drive, which runs between the gorges, is predominantly corrugated dirt – barring adverse weather however, the park remains accessible for all vehicles throughout the year, although 2WD may find things a little bumpy. Gorges may flood and get extremely hot between November and April, so this is worth bearing in mind.

The **gorges** themselves cut through the north-facing escarpment of the Hamersley Ranges and all offer spectacular views as well as a range of **graded walks** through their interiors. Classes 1–3 can be completed comfortably by most, Class 4 requires a reasonable level of fitness, while Class 5 weeks tend to be exhilarating semi-Indiana Jones-style adventures. Class 6 requires you to either be a qualified rock climber and abseiler with all the necessary equipment, or on a guided tour. While lesser trails are not uniformly well marked, the "**Trail Risk**" signs certainly are, and will warn you if you're about to venture into a Class 6 area. Injuries are common in the park, and fatalities do occur, so think carefully about which trail your level of fitness will allow you to complete comfortably, and wear solid walking sandals – on many walks a small slip could see you plunge a fair distance down a gorge face. There are scores of superlative **swimming holes** in the park, but they tend to be situated deep in the gorges, and are rarely less than absolutely freezing, even on the hottest days. You should always keep a keen eye on the **weather forecast** and your watch within the park – gorges can flood very quickly if it rains, while ascending out of the gorges in anything less than full daylight is a definite no-no.

Tours of Karijini are run by Lestok Tours (☎08/9189 2032, ⓦwww.lestoktours .com.au), Pilbara Gorge Tours (☎08/9188 1534, ⓦwww.pilbaragorgetours .au) and West Oz Active (☎08/9189 8013, ⓦwww.westozactive.com.au). The first two pretty much run coach tours around the park ($130–140), including guided walks on Class 1–5 trails – tours depart from the visitor centre, *Karijini Eco Retreat* or Tom Price. If you prefer something a little more heart-pumping, West Oz Active climb and abseil deep into the gorges ($140–215). To see the gorges from the air, contact Karijini Heli Tours (☎08/9176 6942, ⓦwww.heliwest.com .au; $60–490).

The park has a western entrance, accessed from Highway 1 (303km) via Tom Price (50km), and an eastern entrance, accessed via the Great Northern Highway from Newman in the south (160km) or Port Hedland via the *Auski Roadhouse* to the north (296km). Whichever way you enter, make sure you fill up at the last available fuel station as **driving distances** in the park tend to be underestimated; count on doing around 250km. There's limited **food** and **drinking water** in the park, so it's best to bring your own just in case. Unless you fly into Parabardoo and take a local tour (see p.715) or you're on a tour from Perth, you'll need your own **vehicle** to visit Karijini.

The visitor centre and eastern gorges

Around 30km from the Karijini Drive turn-off on the Great Northern Highway is the park's eastern entrance; a further 10km down Banjima Drive brings you to the **visitor centre** (April–Oct daily 9am–4pm; Nov–March 10am–noon; ☏08/9189 8121). The design of the building represents a goanna moving through the country; inside are some great displays on Karijini's plants, animals and people and some better-than-nothing maps.

Backtracking slightly from the visitor centre, a road leads 10km east to the **Dales Gorge** area, first passing the basic **Dales Campground** (toilets and gas barbecues only). Slightly further on are the Fortescue Falls and Dales Day Use Area car parks, linked by an easy pathway along the gorge rim and a more scrambly one over boulders and through water along the gorge floor. Together, the pathways create a memorable walk (3km return to either car park; 3–4hr; Class 2–4) with various lookouts and idyllic swimming spots at the stepped **Fortescue Falls** and tranquil **Circular and Fern pools**, where the rusty gorge walls soar overhead. Alternatively, you can drive your vehicle to both car parks and just complete shorter sections.

The central gorges

Continuing west of the visitor centre, Banjima Drive turns to dirt and you soon reach a turn-off leading north to **Kalamina Gorge**, with a stream-side walk (3km; 3hr return; Class 3) and swimming at Rock Arch Pool. Though pretty enough, Kalamina can be given a miss if you don't have much time. Back on Banjima Drive, the next turn-off leads to two impressive lookouts: the first onto the tiered amphitheatre of **Joffre Falls** (usually just a trickle) and **Joffre Gorge**, and the second over **Knox Gorge**; there are walks into both gorges from the corresponding lookout (2–3km; 2–3hr return; Class 4).

Returning to Banjima Drive, the next turning north brings you to ⚐ **Karijini Eco Retreat/Savannah Campground** (☏08/9425 5591, ⓦ www.karijiniecoretreat.com.au; camping $25, standard eco-tent ❼, deluxe en-suite eco-tent ❾), owned by the Gumala Aboriginal Corporation which represents the collective interests of the Pilbara's Niapiali, Banyjima and Innawonga people – "gumala" means "all together" in Banyjima. On one side of the camp are smart safari-style eco-tents, an outdoor restaurant, kiosk and bar, and on the other old-school pitches, camp kitchens and hot showers. Various guided walks and tag-a-long tours run from the retreat, which scales down operations between December and March – the bar and restaurant close completely.

Continuing down the same turn-off, the road ends at Weano Day Use Area car park. A short stroll away, Red, Hancock, Joffre and Weano gorges come together spectacularly at **Oxer Lookout**, the park's big draw-card, with the only slightly less striking **Junction Pool Lookout** right next door. A number of exhilarating walking trails depart from the car park: a steep descent into **Weano Gorge**, large boulders, river-wading and narrow ledges all have to be negotiated before a slightly nerve-wracking entry into magical **Handrail Pool**, with the assistance of a metal railing and a length of knotted rope. You can swim across the pool and scramble a short distance further before you reach the Class 6 warning sign – inching carefully past the sign, stopping at the top of a steep waterfall you can get a good look into the next pool, which leads into Red Gorge (1km; 1hr 30min return to car park; Class 2–5). Only venture into Handrail Pool if you're confident that you can winch yourself back out using the rope. To add another kilometre or so onto this walk, you can head west rather than east at the end of the descent into Weano, and follow the river bed for around 500m before returning to the car park along the gorge rim (1km; 45min; Class 3).

The park's second Class 5 trail descends from the car park into **Hancock Gorge** via a metal stepladder before more boulders, thigh-deep pools and narrow ledges lie between you and a small amphitheatre. To exit the amphitheatre and have a rewarding dip in icy **Kermit's Pool** just beyond, you'll need to navigate narrow **Spider Walk**: as the name suggests, the least dangerous way to do this is to bridge the chasm with a hand and leg on each wall, avoiding the slippery rocks below. Beyond Kermit's Pool, where most will need to turn back, is a Class 6 trail into Regan's Pool and Junction Pool.

Mount Bruce, the western gorges and Tom Price

Continuing west along Banjima Drive, the road snakes across the roof of the Pilbara to the park's western entrance, rejoining Karijini Drive which links Tom Price in the west and the Great Northern Highway in the east. Overlooking the junction is **Mount Bruce**, at 1235m WA's second-highest peak and climbable along a nine-kilometre path. Shorter trails from the same car park climb to Marandoo View, a lookout surveying Rio Tinto's iron-ore-producing Marandoo Mine.

From the junction, if you skirt the park's northwestern boundary for 44km you'll come to **Hamersley Gorge**, quite a detour if you're heading back out to Highway 1. Should you make the effort you'll find the spa-like Grotto and unique, acutely folded beds of blue-grey and orange rock: walks here include an easy stroll to Hamersley Waterfall (400m) and a longer walk into the gorge itself (1km; 3hr return; Class 3). Continuing around Nanutarra-Wittenoom Road you'll find the little-visited Range, Bee and Wittenoom gorges.

Given the pariah status of Wittenoom (see box below), geographically the closest town to the park, **TOM PRICE**, 51km west of the park entrance, is the government-approved base for exploring Karijini. The neat company town is named after Thomas Moore Price, an employee of the American company Kaiser Steel, who convinced mining companies that having a dig around the area might be worth their while. The **visitor centre** (May–Oct Mon–Fri 8.30am–5pm, Sat & Sun 8.30am–12.30pm; Nov–April Mon–Fri 9.30am–3.30pm, Sat 9am–noon; ℡08/9188 1112, ⑩www.tompricewa.com.au) on

---

Wittenoom: to visit or not to visit...

At each end of **Wittenoom** signs warn of the possible health hazards associated with visiting the town. It's estimated that over a thousand ex-miners and former inhabitants have died as a result of the asbestos mining carried out here until 1966.

In its natural state **blue asbestos** (or crocidolite) is a harmless mineral, readily found in upper Wittenoom Gorge and once valued by manufacturers for its strength and resistance to heat, but the dust produced during milling operations can cause mesothelioma and lung cancer. Despite many arguing that setting foot in the town presents only a minute risk, the WA government is nonetheless committed to shutting down Wittenoom, removing it from maps, withdrawing services and shutting off power – much to the anger of the town's six or so remaining residents.

Partly because of its tragic history and partly due to its spectacular setting, the town possesses an intangible, eerie ambience, with a guesthouse and campsite the only services for visitors. Once a week Integrity **buses** stop at the Wittenoom visitor centre – after that, the decision whether to visit or not is entirely up to you.

Central Road can book accommodation and **tours** of Pilbara Iron's open-cut iron-ore mine (daily subject to minimum numbers; enclosed shoes required; 1hr 30min; $21). Accommodation is limited to the *Tom Price Hotel Motel* (℡08/9189 1101; ❹–❼) on Central Road, whose bistro is better than in most WA pubs, with several retro favourites on the menu, or the *Tom Price Tourist Park* (℡08/9189 1515; camping $25, powered site $27, dorms $29, cabins ❺–❼), nestled below Mount Nameless on Nameless Valley Road just out of town. The town has all the services you'd expect, including a good supermarket, bakery and pharmacy in the shopping mall.

Millstream–Chichester National Park

Often overshadowed by its showier neighbour, **Millstream–Chichester National Park** (DEC fee; see box, p.644) nonetheless draws increasing numbers of visitors for walks, bushcamping and scenic drives through the ancient and stirring Pilbara landscape. Almost 200km northwest of Karijini as the crow flies, the park can be accessed via the new Millstream Link road, which runs from Karratha to Barowanna Hill, or the Roebourne-Wittenoom road, which links northern Karijini with Highway 1 28km northeast of Roebourne. Heading south on the 61-kilometre stretch from Highway 1 you'll pass *Pyramid Homestead*: looking northwards from the many lookouts in the park, atop the **Chichester Ranges**, you'll see why the homestead is so-named.

Just inside the park, **Python Pool** is a striking waterhole backed with black-and-orange cliffs, where the silence is cut by the shriek of birds. From this photoworthy point it's a sixty-kilometre run south to **Millstream**, where an old homestead has been converted into an unusually good **visitor centre** (daily 8am–5pm; ℡08/9184 5144). **Chinderwarriner Pool**, a short walk from the homestead, is a lily-dappled pool surrounded by palm trees. Walking trails in the park range from 100m to 8km and include the palm- and paperbark-lined trails along the Fortescue River to Crossing and Deep Reach pools, where there are basic **campsites** (toilets and gas BBQs; fees apply).

Up the coast to Broome

Back on Highway 1, it's around 380km from the Burkett Road turn-off (for Exmouth) to the industrial twin towns of **Dampier** and **Karratha**, with just sleepy **Onslow** – jumping-off point for the **Mackerel Islands** – and some roadhouses to break the journey. Further up the coast there's only **Port Hedland** to look forward to, although wily travellers will bypass this less-than-charming town, and break the drive to Broome at **Eighty Mile Beach** instead.

The Mackerel Islands

Cyclone-battered Onslow, 81km northwest off Highway 1, is the departure point for trips to the **Mackerel Islands** (℡08/9184 6444, ⊕www.mackerelislands .com.au), 22km offshore: Thevenard Island is a small coral atoll fringed by good beaches and has accommodation in beach bungalows sleeping up to ten (❾) or at *Club Thevenard*, a converted mining camp (full board ❻–❼). Nearby Direction Island, fringed by its own coral reef, offers real solitude as there's only one deluxe eco-villa sleeping up to four ($1200), and no staff. A **dive school** offering the full range of courses, dives and equipment runs from Thevenard Island (℡08/9184 6046, ⊕www.scubaroodive.com); fishing, swimming and general relaxation are key activities for non-divers. You can arrange return **transport to the islands** by boat from Onslow (25–45min) on Wednesdays and Sundays for $80, or fly to Thevenard Island from Karratha, Onslow and Exmouth with Norwest Airwork (☎08/9949 2888, ⓦwww.norwestairwork.com.au) or Karratha Flying Services (☎08/9144 2444).

Dampier and Karratha

Further up Highway 1, the two young towns of **DAMPIER** and **KARRATHA** make up the northwest's biggest industrial centre – Dampier houses the huge export facilities for Pilbara Iron and Dampier Salt amongst others. Rapidly growing Karratha, 20km to the east, was established in 1968 when space ran out around Dampier, and grew dramatically when the **North West Shelf Natural Gas Project** got under way in the early 1980s. The project collects gas from offshore platforms 135km northwest of Dampier, from where it's piped to Perth (the project contributes sixty percent of WA's domestic gas) or liquefied locally for export to Japan and China.

After travelling in rural WA, arriving in Karratha is like entering another world, with lines of white industry utes, teeming throngs of mine workers and a range of shops not seen since Perth in the Centro complex. It's useful for stocking up, but has precious little to detain the passing traveller – Dampier has even less to offer. If you have your own vehicle you can visit the **Burrup Peninsula**, which lies between the two towns; here, Aboriginal rock paintings at Deep Gorge and swimming at high tide in Hearson's Cove provide low-key respite from the industrial mania.

Practicalities

Greyhound **buses** stop at the coach bay on Welcome Street in the town centre; local buses also run between Dampier and Port Samson four times a week, calling at Karratha and Roebourne along the way. Karratha's **visitor centre** is on Karratha Road (late Oct to mid-April Mon–Fri 8.30am–4pm, Sat 8.30am–noon; mid-April to late Oct Mon–Fri 8.30am–5pm, Sat 8.30am–4pm, Sun 8.30am–3pm; ☎08/9144 4600), the main access road off Highway 1, and can book various **industrial tours**.

There are huge **accommodation** shortages in Karratha as a result of the mining boom – don't show up without an advance booking. There are a couple of smart, pricey hotels in town; *Karratha International* (☎08/9187 3333, ⓦwww .karrathainternational.com.au; ⓽), on the corner of Hillview and Millstream roads, is the flashiest, followed by *All Seasons Karratha* on Searipple Road (☎08/9159 1000, ⓦwww.accorhotels.com.au; ⓽). For those on a budget there's the spick-and-span *Pilbara Holiday Park*, 2.5km down Rosemary Road on the way to Dampier (☎08/9185 1855, ⓦwww.aspenparks.com.au; camping $36, powered site $40, units ⓻–⓼), or the very "lived-in" *Karratha Backpackers* at 10 Wellard Way (☎08/9144 4904), another victim of the accommodation crisis – an engineering firm now commandeers a number of the double rooms here for its employees, although dorm beds are usually still available ($25).

For **food**, *Hearson's Bistro* at the *All Seasons* could do with a charm injection, but *Gecko's* and *Montebello* bars and *Etcetera* restaurant at the *International* are actually quite nice for the Pilbara. Other options include the many restaurants around the Centro and Karratha Village complexes.

Roebourne

Established in 1864 and once the capital of the northwest, **ROEBOURNE**, 33km east of Karratha, is the oldest surviving settlement between Port Gregory and Darwin. Now home to local Aboriginal people displaced by pastoral settlement, Roebourne feels just as much a ghost town as formally abandoned Cossack (see below) down the road. The **visitor centre** and **museum** (May–Oct Mon–Fri 9am–5pm, Sat & Sun 9am–3pm; Nov–April Mon–Fri 9am–3pm; $2 donation for museum; ☎08/9182 1060) are housed in the **Old Gaol** on Queen Street, a fine example of nineteenth-century English penal architecture – the octagonal central courtyard allowed jailers to keep an eye on all cells at once. The majority of prisoners here were indigenous folk who had offended against their sheep station "owners" – for more on Aboriginal history in northern WA see p.723. The prison was closed in 1924 but astonishingly (given the conditions) was reopened in 1975 and pressed into active service once more until 1984. Other nineteenth-century institutional buildings are dotted around the town, along with a couple of indigenous art galleries, the best of which is **Yinjaa Barni Arts Centre** (irregular hours; ☎08/9182 1959), located in Old Dalgety House at 3 Roe St. The *Harding River Caravan Park* (☎08/9182 1063; camping $18, powered site $24, cabins ❹), on De Grey Street at the eastern end of town, has plenty of shady pitches and a pool. Greyhound **buses** stop in the middle of town on the highway.

Cossack and Point Samson

From Roebourne, Roebourne–Port Samson Road leads north a few kilometres to Wickham and Point Samson (see below), after passing a turn-off right to **COSSACK**, originally Roebourne's port and well worth a visit. Cossack used to be quite the little town, with stores, boarding houses and Japanese brothels lining the streets to cater for the Asian pearlers, prospectors and pastoralists who all passed through in the late nineteenth century. But by the end of the century the port began silting up: by the 1950s, Cossack was abandoned and to this day can feel quite eerie if you're the only one prowling the streets.

What's left of this historic ghost town has been finely restored, with interpretive signs filling you in on its origins and history – five buildings remain (open in daylight hours; honesty box), along with a number of ruins and **cemeteries**. At the end of the town, **Readers Head Lookout** offers fine 360-degree views over **Settlers Beach** just below, Point Samson and Jarman Island and Lighthouse – both the island and lighthouse are accessible with Cossack Cruises (☎08/9187 0296, ⓦwww.cossackcruise.com.au). *Cossack Budget Accommodation* (☎08/9182 1190), in the centre of the village, used to be a fun, well-run facility with a lively café and art gallery next door but the town's new caretakers don't seem keen to continue in the same vein – plain rooms (❷) and a kiosk remain.

Close to the end of the small peninsula is **POINT SAMSON**, a tranquil fishing port that's popular with retirees. East of town is pretty **Honeymoon Cove**, which has good swimming at high tide. **Places to stay** are on the main Samson Road unless noted and include *Point Samson Resort* (☎08/9187 1052, ⓦwww.pointsamson.com; ❽–❾), a smart little complex with large, comfortable rooms, or the brand-new *Cove Caravan Park* (☎08/9187 0199, ⓦwww.thecovecaravanpark.com.au; camping $28, powered site $33, cabins ❼–❽), which has excellent facilities but no shade. *Samson Beach Chalets* (☎08/9187 0202, ⓦwww.samsonbeach.com.au; ❼–❾) offers deluxe, architect-designed accommodation, while *Delilah's B&B* (☎08/9187 1471; ❽) on Meares Drive is a very homely, frangipani-themed treat. The lively *Samson Beach Tavern*, at the end of town, serves mainly grills and other **food** on its first-floor terrace (daily 11am–late), while the pricier *Moby's Kitchen* downstairs does a huge array of takeaway seafood (daily lunch and dinner). Minimalist *Ta Ta's*, at the *Point Samson Resort*, serves the most upmarket food in town – mains cost around $40.

Port Hedland

Approaching **PORT HEDLAND**, 190km east of Roebourne, you'll spot the dazzlingly white stockpile of industrial salt at the Dampier Salt Works, an only mildly interesting sight that is nonetheless about as good as "BHP Billiton-town" gets in the way of tourist attractions. The main strip is Wedge Street, but most of the useful **shops** including Woolworths are the Boulevard Shopping Centre on nearby Anderson Street. After stocking up, make a visit to the **Courthouse Gallery** (Mon–Sat 9am–4.30pm; ℡08/9173 1064, Ⓦwww.courthousegallery.com.au) on Edgar Street, an incongruously classy art space hosting good temporary exhibitions, with a similarly inviting gift shop attached.

Practicalities

The **visitor centre** (April–Sept Mon–Fri 8.30am–4.30pm, Sat & Sun 10am–2pm; Oct–Mar Mon–Fri 9am–4pm, Sat 10am–2pm; ℡08/9173 1711), where Greyhound and Integrity **buses** stop, is on Wedge Street, and can organize tours of the **BHP Billiton loading facility** (May–Sept daily on demand; 1hr30min; $26).

   Accommodation includes the *Best Western Hospitality Inn* (℡08/9173 1044, Ⓦwww.porthedland.wa.hospitalityinns.com.au; ❺) on Webster Street and the *All Seasons/Mercure Inn* (℡08/9173 1511, Ⓦwww.accorhotels.com.au; ❻–❾) on the corner of nearby Lukis and McGregor streets; both have decent motel rooms but are grossly overpriced and invariably booked out. The *Cooke Point Caravan Park* (℡08/9173 1271 or 1800 459 999, Ⓦwww.aspenparks.com.au; powered site $39, budget rooms ❹, chalets ❼), on Athol Street 8km from town, is also overpriced but better than the other grim campsites in town. Confine your **eating** to self-catering or a meal in one of the motel bistros, and steer clear of the pubs.

Port Hedland to Broome

The six-hundred-kilometre drive northeast from Port Hedland to Broome is one of world-class boredom, a dreary plain of spinifex and mulga marking the northern edge of the Great Sandy Desert, broken only by a couple of roadhouses and the pleasant **Eighty Mile Beach Caravan Park** (℡08/7176 5941, Ⓦwww.eightymilebeach.com.au; camping $28.50, powered site $32.50, cabins ❻–❼) around the halfway point. Despite Highway 1's proximity to the ocean, this is one of few points on the drive with beach access. There isn't much to do here, but a drive along the sand at low tide is always exhilarating and turtles can sometimes be seen laying their eggs on the beach by moonlight.

The Kimberley

A region of red dust, endless skies, stunning sunsets, big rivers and huge gorges, the **Kimberley** is often romantically described as Australia's last frontier. It's a wilderness dotted with barely viable cattle stations often turned to tourism, isolated Aboriginal communities and, increasingly, vast tracts of Aboriginal land, all edged with a ragged, tide-swept coastline inhabited chiefly by crocodiles, secluded pearling operations and a couple of exclusive, fly-in getaways. The land is king here, with devoted locals making annual pilgrimages to their favourite spots armed with only a swag and an esky in the Dry, before retreating in the Wet. When the dry season sets in around April, tourism in the

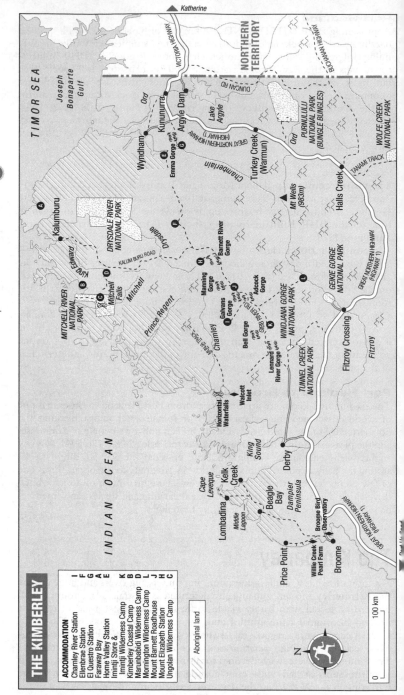

THE KIMBERLEY

ACCOMMODATION
Charnley River Station	I
Ellenbrae Station	F
El Questro Station	G
Faraway Bay	A
Home Valley Station	E
Imintji Store &	
Imintji Wilderness Camp	K
Kimberley Coastal Camp	B
Marunbabidi Wilderness Camp	D
Mornington Wilderness Camp	J
Mount Barnett Roadhouse	L
Mount Elizabeth Station	H
Ungolan Wilderness Camp	C

Aboriginal land

0   100 km

N

Katherine

NORTHERN TERRITORY

TIMOR SEA

Joseph Bonaparte Gulf

INDIAN OCEAN

Kimberley gradually comes back to life, with **tours** (see boxes on p.728 & p.740) running mainly between thriving **Broome** and **Kununurra** along the iconic **Gibb River Road**, or down to the mysterious **Bungle Bungles**, south of Highway 1 near Halls Creek. Adventurous travellers are increasingly heading for the stirring scenery around **Cape Leveque** and **Mitchell River National Park**: the many warnings that accompany journeys to these parts can be

Indigenous history in northern WA

The history of Aboriginal people in Australia's northwest differs greatly from those on the east coast or in southern WA due to a colonial quirk. The British Colonial Secretaries Office decreed in 1865 that no convict labour was to be used further north than the **26th parallel** due to the extreme heat that was considered too great for pallid northern hemisphere "criminals". So it came to be that rather than being slaughtered as on the East Coast, local indigenous people were pressed into service in the burgeoning pastoral and pearling industries of the northwest. Thus, their white "owners" were paradoxically depleting their workforces whenever they wanted to imprison local Aborigines for minor offences (an unsurprisingly regular occurrence). This is not to suggest that massacres did not occur; the **Flying Foam Massacre** of 1868, in which the Yaburura people of the Burrup Peninsula near Karratha were slaughtered in huge numbers, did as much to deplete the indigenous workforce as any number of prison stays.

The **prisons** scattered across the area (particularly at Derby, p.734 and Roebourne, p.719) highlight the appalling conditions in which Aboriginal "offenders" were kept – the neck chains and leg manacles which remain in many walls are a particularly stark reminder.

The story of **Jandamarra** or "Pigeon" gives an interesting perspective on relations between Aboriginals and white settlers. Jandamarra, a member of the Bunaba group whose land stretched from Fitzroy Crossing to the present-day Devonian Reef national parks, was made a "tracker" in the 1890s, and was expected to work with the white police force to weed out Aboriginal criminals. When rounding up a group of such "criminals" at Lillimooloora Police Station (see p.743) in 1894, Jandamarra's loyalties to his people returned to the fore, and he killed a policeman, Constable Richardson, instigating a three-year "war" between the now-iconic Jandamarra and his followers and the police force. His escapes from Windjana Gorge and Tunnel Creek entered folklore – in the latter case the police staked out one end of the tunnel for days, in the belief that it was a cave, while Jandamarra escaped from the other end. Ironically, it was another Aboriginal tracker who caught and shot Jandamarra back at Tunnel Creek in 1987.

By the 1880s, huge numbers of Aboriginal people were **"black-birded"**, or uprooted from their traditional communities in the Kimberley, and marched for hundreds of kilometres to pastoral or pearling stations; the Boab Prison Trees (see p.735) scattered across the region are the result of these exoduses, as temporary prisons were often needed en route. With pastoralism dominating the area's economy for the next hundred years, it took a shamefully long time for the mistreatment of indigenous workers to end, and it was only in 1966 that equal pay was granted to Aboriginal stockmen and farm workers. Unfortunately, this did not bring an end to Aboriginal suffering, as the increased mechanization of the farming industry resulted in the now-unwanted labourers being driven off the stations and into towns far away from their traditional land, with many developing into the deprived welfare towns you see across the Kimberley today.

On a more positive note, **Aboriginal art** is a growing force across the Kimberley, bringing funds into poor communities and in some cases alleviating the social problems that have befallen the region's original inhabitants. The **galleries** and workshops in Broome, Roebourne and Kununurra are well worth a visit on your trip.

daunting, but armed with a good 4WD and a dash of Outback knowledge you should be fine.

The harsh realities of indigenous history and life are displayed at every turn in the Kimberley, particularly in towns along the highway such as **Halls Creek** and **Fitzroy Crossing**. One of the less confronting manifestations of this is the region's array of **Aboriginal art**; Broome's narrow streets are crammed with gorgeous small galleries, while rural rocks hold many examples of enigmatic Wandjina paintings and the slender Bradshaw figures, some thought to be around 17,000 years old.

The **best time to visit** is from June to September, the coolest months; by late September the heat is already building up and even Highway 1 closes periodically from January to March following storms or cyclones. Night comes early and fast in the Kimberley – most visitors adapt to a routine of rising with the sun (often the best time to get some driving done) and retiring soon after sunset. Temperatures can stay stifling into the early hours, so a 4WD and a mozzie dome can be preferable to a campervan in these parts – make sure you erect tents and insect domes well away from waterholes in crocodile country. Greyhound **buses** ply the Great Northern Highway between Broome and Darwin, but to see this area you either need your own vehicle or to join a **tour** (see p.728 & 740).

Broome and around

"Slip into Broometime" is a well-worn local aphorism that still captures the tropical charm of **BROOME**, which clings to a peninsula overhanging Roebuck Bay. The accommodation market in Broome has expanded a great deal over the last few years, particularly at the pricey end, and to some extent the town is struggling to catch up, with a bit of a "wild west" air still pervading – this is not the west-coast Byron Bay many expect, with fancy restaurants and bars aplenty. Nonetheless, it's the classiest town in the northwest by quite a stretch; the nearby Kimberley's "frontier" appeal and the introduction of cheap flights from Sydney and Melbourne will only increase visitor numbers.

William Dampier, the English buccaneer-explorer, passed through in 1699 while on the run from an irate Spanish flotilla, and 160 years later the local Aboriginal people repelled an early fleet of prospective pastoralists. Easily collected pearl shell heaped along Eighty Mile Beach led to the northwestern "**pearl rush**" of the 1880s, initially enabled by the now enslaved Aborigines. Later, indentured workers from Asia sought the shell in ever-greater depths below the waves, boosted by the invention of hard-hat diving apparatus. Broome originated as a camp on sheltered Roebuck Bay where the pearl luggers laid up during the cyclone season. After the violent and raucous beginning common to many frontier towns of that era, the port finally achieved prosperity, which lasted until the outbreak of World War I.

It was actually the nacre-lined oyster shells, or **mother-of-pearl**, rather than extremely rare pearls themselves, which brought fortune to the town. By 1910, eighty percent of the world's pearl shell – used in the manufacture of buttons and cutlery handles amongst other things – came from Broome, by which time a rich ethnic mix and a rigidly racially stratified society had developed. Chinatown teemed with riotous Koepangers, Filipinos and Malays crewing for the predominantly Japanese divers – a boiling pot collectively termed "Saltwater Cowboys" in a well-known album by local musicians, the Pigram Brothers. Each season one in five divers died, several more became paralyzed and, as Broome's cemeteries steadily filled, only one shell in five thousand produced a

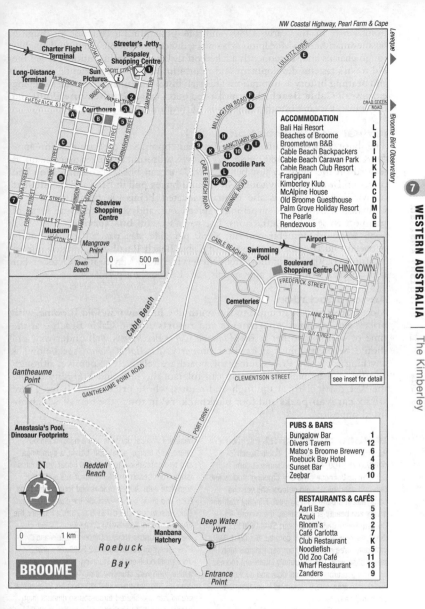

ACCOMMODATION

Bali Hai Resort	L
Beaches of Broome	J
Broometown B&B	B
Cable Beach Backpackers	I
Cable Beach Caravan Park	H
Cable Beach Club Resort	K
Frangipani	F
Kimberley Klub	A
McAlpine House	C
Old Broome Guesthouse	D
Palm Grove Holiday Resort	M
The Pearle	G
Rendezvous	E

PUBS & BARS

Bungalow Bar	1
Divers Tavern	12
Matso's Broome Brewery	6
Roebuck Bay Hotel	4
Sunset Bar	8
Zeebar	10

RESTAURANTS & CAFÉS

Aarli Bar	5
Azuki	3
Bloom's	2
Café Carlotta	7
Club Restaurant	K
Noodlefish	5
Old Zoo Café	11
Wharf Restaurant	13
Zanders	9

BROOME

7

WESTERN AUSTRALIA | The Kimberley

perfect example of the silvery pearls unique to this area – a fascinating story vividly told in John Bailey's book *The White Divers of Broome*, available in local bookshops.

Stagnation then rebuilding followed both world wars, after the second of which the Japanese – masters in the secret art of pearl culturing – warily returned and invested in the pearl-farming ventures around Broome's well-suited coastal habitat. Things improved with the sealing of the coastal highway

725

from Perth in the early 1980s and the philanthropic interest of English businessman Alistair McAlpine, who was seduced by Broome's diamond-in-the-rough charms and subsequently kicked off its latter-day reinvention. He led the old town's tasteful development and refurbishment, using its oriental mystique and pearling history as inspiration. This rich history is enhanced by the sweeping expanse of **Cable Beach**, the paprika-red outcrops at **Gantheaume Point** and the Indian Ocean's breathtaking shade of turquoise.

Arrival and information

The busy **visitor centre** (Mon–Fri 9am–5pm, Sat & Sun 8.30am–4pm; ☎08/9192 2222 or 1800 883 777, ⓦwww.broomevisitorcentre.com.au) is located on the highway just before town, and can book accommodation and places on Broome's many tours. Greyhound **buses** pull in here, and the **airport** on McPherson Street is also centrally located, being less than 1km west of Chinatown. Broome is surprisingly spread out, and you need some form of transport to see all its attractions. The town's useful **bus service** (☎08/9193 6585 ⓦwww.broomebus.com.au; $3.50 per ride, day pass $10) runs hourly between Old Broome and the end of Cable Beach Road via Chinatown from 7.10am to 6.30pm, with more frequent services from May to mid-October. For taxis and car, scooter and bike rentals, see "Listings" on p.732.

Accommodation

Most **hotels** are situated just to the south of Chinatown in Old Broome, with pricey self-contained **apartments** and **resorts** around Cable Beach – at the time of writing another resort, *Pinctada Cable Beach*, was well under way, and should be pretty plush if its sister property (*McAlpine House*, see below) is anything to go by. Prices across the board are relatively expensive, although bargains can be picked up if you can tolerate the heat and humidity during the Wet, particularly at the high-end resorts, whose prices often halve. There are six **caravan parks** and four **backpackers'** in town, the best of which are listed opposite.

Hotels, B&Bs and resorts

Bali Hai Resort 6 Murray Rd, Cable Beach ☎08/9191 3100, ⓦwww.balihairesort.com. Sumptuous Balinese-style self-catering studios and two-bed apartments with outdoor shower and patio, all set around a lovely pool. Friendly staff and a very zen beauty spa complete the picture. ❾

Broometown B&B 15 Stewart St ☎08/9192 2006, ⓦwww.broometown.com.au. Boutique B&B with only three rooms and correspondingly high levels of service. The beautifully kitted-out rooms are arranged around a small pool and decked communal area where awesome breakfasts are devoured daily. ❾

Cable Beach Club Resort Cable Beach Rd ☎08/9192 0400, ⓦwww.cablebeachclub.com. Established by Alistair McAlpine, who signed the lease to build the resort on the back of a beer mat in the "Roey" (see p.732), this is the resort that kicked off Broome's renaissance. It's still the best of its kind in town, with impeccable service,

beautiful tropical gardens and a relaxed atmosphere, and tennis, a day spa, bowls, a gym, yoga and two great pools to keep you occupied. Rooms range from beach shacks to luxurious suites complete with Sidney Nolans and four-poster beds. Food and drink options include the *Sunset Bar* and *Club Restaurant* (see p.731 & p.732), a carvery, the *Thai Pearl* and *Boardwalk Café*.

McAlpine House Corner of Louis and Herbert sts ☎08/9192 3886, ⓦwww.mcalpinehouse.com. A stunning, intimate guesthouse, with very attentive staff. The library, lush grounds, myriad cushioned lounging areas, gourmet breakfasts and shared three-course dinners (high season only; $70) cooked by the in-house chef encourage relaxation and socializing. Latticework verandas are filled with heavy, Oriental furniture, and rooms contain every creature comfort. ❾

Old Broome Guesthouse 64 Walcott St ☎08/9192 6106, ⓦwww.oldbroomeguesthouse.com.au. Charming guesthouse with four funky, individually decorated rooms, and great en-suite bathrooms with sunken tiled baths. Breakfast is served on the central deck amid much greenery. ❾

The Pearle 14 Millington Rd ☎08/9194 0900, ⓦwww.thepearle.com.au. Much-hyped new resort whose plush minimalist accommodation ranges from hotel rooms through to three-bed apartments. The poolside café-restaurant serves fancy-pants food at breakfast, lunch and dinner – non-guests are welcome – but all apartments have private plunge pools and kitchens so you don't have to socialize if you don't want to. ❾

The Frangipani (☎08/9195 5000, ⓦwww.thefrangipani.com.au), on the same road, and **Rendezvous** (☎08/9192 8088, ⓦwww.rendezvoushotels.com.au/broome) on Lullfitz Drive all offer near-identical levels of comfort and dining at the same inflated prices. ❾

Backpackers' and caravan parks

Beaches of Broome 4 Sanctuary Rd, Cable Beach ☎08/9192 6665, ⓦwww.beachesofbroome.com.au. "Flashpacker" accommodation with flawless, smart facilities that would put many hotels to shame, perhaps at the expense of the hostel spirit – the clientele are a slightly weird mix of students and retired couples. Dorms $30–45, rooms ❺–❼

Cable Beach Backpackers 12 Sanctuary Rd, Cable Beach ☎08/9193 5511 or 1800 655 011, ⓦwww.cablebeachbackpackers.com. Everything looks a little "pre-loved", but once you're ensconced in a hammock by the pool you won't care. Laid-back atmosphere with lots of activities and a free bus to town. Dorms $26–29, singles ❷, doubles ❸

Cable Beach Caravan Park 8 Millington Rd ☎08/9192 2066. Cable Beach's best campsite by a whisker, with large, shady pitches and a fabulous pool. No cabins. Camping $29, powered site $33.

🏃 **Kimberley Klub** 62 Frederick St ☎08/9192 3233 or 1800 004 345, ⓦwww.kimberleyklub.com. Five-star YHA-rated backpackers', run by friendly, enthusiastic staff. Good-quality rooms surround a breezy, slightly manic communal area with a good pool, bar, ping pong, "beach" volleyball and a novel round pool table – there's always something going on here. Doubles in particular are above the usual backpacker standard, not least because the hostel receives all of owner *Cable Beach Resort*'s cast-off furniture. Dorms $28–30, rooms ❺–❻

Palm Grove Holiday Resort Corner of Murray and Cable Beach rds ☎08/9192 3336 or 1800 803 336, ⓦwww.palmgrove.com.au. Excellent campsite with a good pool, campers' kitchen and decent cabins, although unpowered sites are a bit cramped. Camping $35–38.50, powered site $38–42.50, chalets ❼

The Town

Broome originally flourished around the old port area – centred on Carnarvon Street and bordered by Short Street, Napier Terrace and Dampier Terrace – known as **Chinatown**, somewhat of a misnomer given that people from many Asian cultures once lived here. This old quarter's original buildings have gradually been reconstructed along the same oriental lines, with corrugated iron, latticework and old verandas the prominent architectural features, but nowadays feel a little "Disneyfied". **Pearl showrooms**, cafés, **art galleries** and boutiques occupy most of the buildings; some of the best places to see art are classy Gecko Gallery and the attractively ramshackle Short Street Gallery, both on Short Street, with Paspaley Pearls, over the road, the showroom of one of Australia's most prestigious pearling families. Narrow alleys including **Sheba Lane** and **Johnny Chi Lane** run between Dampier and Carnarvon streets; like much of Chinatown, these days they're mostly full of boutiques, though historical plaques fill you in on the events which begat Broome right where you stand, over 120 years ago. **Sun Pictures** (see p.731) on Carnarvon Street opened in 1916, which makes it as old as Hollywood itself. During the day you can wander or take a tour (Mon–Fri 10.30am & 1pm; $5) around the virtually unchanged interior and see photographs showing the segregated seating order of the bad old days. At the end of the street, **Paspaley Shopping Centre** houses supermarkets, pharmacies and the **post office**.

Although just hanging out in Broome can be satisfying, the town's growing popularity means there's no shortage of things to do. There are too many activities and tours on offer to do justice to here: suffice to say they include helicopters, town tours by double-decker bus, trikes, fishing, whale-watching, hovercraft, hang-gliders, hot-air balloons, boat rental or sunset cruises, photography, sky-diving, scenic flights, indigenous cultural tours, sea-kayaking and star-gazing – ask at the visitor centre for operators and contact details. The classic Broome activity, the **sunset camel ride** down Cable Beach, is offered by four operators from around $40.

Kimberley coast

Luxury cruise boats glide along the convoluted inlets of the north **Kimberley coast**; with craft often featuring à la carte menus and helidecks for incoming guests, prices can be as spectacular as the coastline ($1000-plus per person per day). A cheaper way to see the coastline is to take a half-day tour.

Horizontal Falls Adventure Tours ☏08/9192 2885, ⊛www.horizontalfalls.com.au. Fly to the Horizontal Waterfalls before your seaplane lands on Talbot Bay, then transfer to a fast boat that takes you through the falls (half day; $595). Kimberley Extreme (☏08/9192 6208, ⊛www.kimberleyextreme.com.au) run a pretty much identical trip.

Matrix Ocean Safaris ☏08/9437 1777, ⊛www.matrixoceanadventures.com.au.

North Star Cruises ☏08/9192 1829, ⊛www.northstarcruises.com.au.

Dampier Peninsula, Cape Leveque and West Kimberley

The following companies run short (1–6-day) 4WD tours departing and returning to Broome, focusing on the Dampier Peninsula, Cape Leveque and West Kimberley (usually Derby, Windjana Gorge, Tunnel Creek and Geikie Gorge). Expect to pay from $230 per day, with gourmet meals around the campfire and a choice of accommodation in swags, tents or cabins often included. Some tours only run in the **Dry**.

Australian Pinnacle Tours ☏08/9192 8080, ⊛www.pinnacletours.com.au. They also run longer trips out of Broome to the Bungle Bungles, with scenic flights over most areas and cruises to the Horizontal Waterfalls available as add-ons.

Chomley's Tours ☏08/9191 6195, ⊛www.chomleystours.com.au. Operate to the Dampier Peninsula and Cape Leveque only; slightly cheaper than others, with flights over the peninsula, Horizontal Waterfalls and the Buccaneer Archipelago also

At the eastern end of Short Street is **Streeter's Jetty** and **Pearl Luggers** (daily 9am–5pm; ☏08/9192 0022, ⊛www.pearlluggers.com.au), a free exposition of Broome's pearling heritage, with a couple of dry-docked luggers and informative one-hour tours (3 daily; $18.50) which include a taste of pearl meat. At the corner of Frederick and Hamersley streets is the 1888 telegraph office and colonial-style **courthouse**; all of Broome turns out to the Saturday-morning **markets** here to exchange gossip, indulge in street food and browse the stalls full of local arts and crafts. Hamersley Street leads south to Old Broome: following the road round along the edge of Roebuck Bay, you'll come to the former Customs House, now home to **Broome Museum** (June–Oct Mon–Fri 10am–4pm, Sat & Sun 10am–1pm; Nov–May daily 10am–1pm; $5; ☏08/9192 2075, ⊛www.broomemuseum.org.au), an interesting little place that deserves a more prominent position in town. New displays outline Broome's pearling history, with evocative photographs and an old diving suit doing much to highlight the perils that faced divers.

possible. They also run return transfers from Broome to Cape Leveque, Beagle Bay and Lombadina (Sun, Tues, Wed, Fri & Sun outbound; Wed, Fri & Sun return; $180), should you want to explore on your own and not have a vehicle.

Kimberley Wild Expeditions ⊕08/9193 7778, ⊛www.kimberleywild.com. Extra tours and add-ons as per Australian Pinnacle Tours (see opposite).

Over The Top Adventure Tours ⊕08/9192 6225, ⊛www.4wdtours.wa.com. One-day tours to the southwest Dampier Peninsula, also known as the "northern beaches" (see p.733). **Aussie Off Road Tours** (⊕08/9192 3617, ⊛www.aussieoffroadtours.com.au) run to the same area.

Kimberley tours

Travelling from Broome to Kununurra or Darwin on an organized tour is a great way to see the remote Kimberley without the pressures associated with taking your own vehicle. The following outfits take in some or all of the Gibb River Road, Bungle Bungles, Drysdale National Park and Mitchell Falls – they're all fairly similar in terms of quality so shop around until you find one that matches your schedule and budget. Most companies offer return tours from Broome and Kununurra, along with one-way trips running both east and west. Expect to pay from $150–260 per day with meals and accommodation included as above, and add-on scenic flights and cruises costing extra; as above, bear in mind that many tours only run in the **Dry**.

Try one of Adventure Wild (⊕1800 359 008, ⊛www.adventurewild.com.au), Australian Adventure Travel (⊕08/9248 2355 or 1800 621 625, ⊛www.australianadventuretravel .com), Australian Pinnacle Tours (see opposite), Kimberley Wild Expeditions (see above), All Terrain Safaris (⊕1800 633 456, ⊛www.allterrainsafaris.com.au), Western Exposure (⊕08/9371 3695, ⊛www.westernxposure.com.au), Wilderness 4WD Adventures (⊕08/8941 2161, ⊛www.wildernessadventures.com.au) or Kimberley Wilderness Adventures/APT (⊕03/9277 8444 or 1800 889 389, ⊛www.kimberleywilderness .com).

In addition to the usual range of tours, Kimberley Wilderness Accommodation/APT also runs **four luxury camps** that are a great option for **self-drivers** who want to overnight in style: hot showers, three-course dinners around the campfire and plush safari tents are invariably on the menu at Bungle Bungle Wilderness Lodge, Imintji Wilderness Camp on the Gibb River Road, Ungolan Wilderness Camp at Drysdale River and Marunbabidi Wilderness Camp at Mitchell Falls ($170–210 per person per night).

Round the back of the museum, the old **Pioneer Cemetery** overlooks **Town Beach**, the nearest sand to the town centre but some way short of Cable Beach's glorious expanses. This is a good vantage point for observing the **"Staircase to the Moon"**, the reflections of the full moon rising over the mud flats, which occur at very low tides a few nights a month between March and October. You can observe the same phenomenon at many places along the northwest coast, but Broome capitalizes on it with nightly markets – dates and times can be obtained from the visitor centre.

The cemeteries and Gantheaume Point

An enjoyable day can be spent cycling, driving or scootering around Broome's outlying attractions. Heading down Frederick Street past the **Boulevard Shopping Centre** (daily 8am–8pm) and the Cable Beach turn-off, you'll get to Broome's old **cemeteries**. The rows of enigmatic headstones in the Japanese section (refurbished by a philanthropic countryman) testify to the hundreds of lives lost in the hazardous collection of mother-of-pearl; most deaths were due to "the bends", although the 1908 cyclone took its fair share – 150 men were killed, five percent of the workforce at the time. The Chinese cemetery next door is less well tended, and the Muslim and Aboriginal graveyards at the back are barely distinguishable, though the latter group's enslavement prior to the hard-hat era contributed greatly to Broome's early pearling boom.

Port Drive continues past the cemeteries to the deep-water port and **Reddell Beach**; tides permitting, you can walk right along the shore to **Gantheaume Point**, where the bright red sandstone formations contrast sharply with the pearly white expanse of Cable Beach and turquoise ocean stretching northwards. If tides don't conspire, a corrugated unsealed road follows the same route at the back of the beach. Flamboyant Irishman Patrick Percy, an ex-proprietor of the "Roey" (see p.732) who had a penchant for wearing large diamonds, bought the old **lighthouse** here in 1922, once a new automated warning light had been installed. He had a somewhat murky past, being variously accused of bigamy and murder, but it seems he was at least at times a loving husband; he built **Anastasia's Pool** amongst the tidal rocks here to soothe his wife's chronic arthritis. A cast of some 130-million-year-old **dinosaur footprints** is also set in the rocks – the originals are out to sea and visible at very low tides, one of nine different dinosaur classifications whose footprints have been fossilized on the stretch between Broome and Cape Leveque.

Cable Beach

Named after the nineteenth-century telegraph cable from Singapore which came ashore here, **Cable Beach** extends for an immaculate 22km north of Gantheaume Point to Willie Creek, providing the inspiring sea vistas which are strangely absent in town considering Broome's sea-bound position. The suburb of Cable Beach itself is where much of Broome's development is taking place, with new retail outlets down Millington Road on the way. Vehicle access to the beach is at Gantheaume Point or in front of *Cable Beach Club Resort* – to drive along the beach itself a 4WD is required. Patrolled swimming is available in front of the same resort in season (stingers are a danger Nov–March), with no cars, dogs or nudity allowed in this family section. The Beach Hut operates here between April and November (daily 8am–5pm), renting out surf- and boogie-boards, deckchairs and umbrellas. To get rid of the white bits, go instead to the nude-sunbathing area north of the rocks, from where 4WD can head all the way up to Willie Creek.

The **Broome Crocodile Park** (April–Nov Mon–Fri 10am–5pm, Sat & Sun 2–5pm, feeding tours daily 3pm plus 11am Mon–Fri; Dec–March 4.15–5.45pm, feeding tours daily 4.30pm; $25; ℡08/9192 1489, ⓦwww.malcolmdouglas .com.au/crocpark) on Cable Beach Road has scores of gruesome salties to wince over; the crocs here have all been relocated from the wild after terrorizing various Outback communities.

Eating

Despite the hype, no self-respecting Melburnian or Sydneysider would call Broome a foodie paradise. That said, the food here is quite literally the best for thousands of kilometres, so make the most of it.

Aarli Bar Corner of Hamersley and Frederick sts
☎08/9192 5529. The lovely tiled bar and glass
lanterns match the Middle-Eastern influenced food
well, with shared plates, wood-fired pizzas and
Moroccan lamb balls all popular. Tables are on a
stylish terrace under drooping frangipani trees,
although the car park views spoil the effect
somewhat. BYO. Daily 8am–late.

Azuki 15 Napier Terrace, Chinatown ☎08/9193
7211. Cute and modern Japanese fusion restaurant
serving excellent bento boxes at lunch and teriyaki,
sashimi, gyoza, katsu curry and all the rest in the
evening. BYO and licensed. Tues–Sat noon–3pm &
6pm–late.

Bloom's 12 Carnarvon St, Chinatown
☎08/9193 6366. Everyone's favourite café,
with a beautiful, fan-cooled jarrah interior and
colourful art lining the walls. Great smoothies,
ooffoo and oggy breakfasts start the day, before
sandwiches, salads and huge cakes take over at
lunch, and curries, burgers, pastas and cocktails
before bed. Daily 7.30am–late, live music Fri
6–9pm & Sun noon–3pm.

Café Carlotta Jones Place, off Dora St ☎08/9192
1706, ⓦwww.cafecarlotta.com.au. Authentic,
inventive wood-fired pizzas, risotto and fresh pasta,
and cute blue-and-orange decor. Make sure you
book ahead. Tues–Sat 5.30pm–late.

Club Restaurant *Cable Beach Resort* ☎08/9192
0400, ⓦwww.cablebeachclub.com. The original
and still the best restaurant in Broome. Hundreds
of bird cages hanging from the ceiling, molten
candelabra, antique furniture, lots of white linen,
shiny cutlery and a couple of Sidney Nolans make

up the decor side. On the food side, things are as
classy as you'd expect, with lamb rack, salmon and
steak to deliberate over, and fancy little desserts to
finish. Daily for dinner.

Noodlefish Corner of Hamersley and Frederick sts
☎08/9192 1697. In the same slightly odd space as
Aarli Bar, but only opens at night so you don't
really notice as steaming Asian fusion dishes like
prawn wontons with chilli and ginger arrive at your
outdoor table, followed by mango pudding and
coconut ice cream. BYO.

Old Zoo Café Challenor Drive, Cable Beach
☎08/9193 6200. Stylish yet chilled-out place
that's worthy of Broome's foodie reputation, serving
Mod-Oz fusion food – the Kimberley platter with
pearl meat, barra, crocodile and camel is more
than just a novelty – and with an excellent wine
list. Eat on the decking or in the red, beamed
interior. Daily breakfast, lunch and dinner.

Wharf Restaurant 401 Port Drive
☎08/9192 5800. Smart-casual restaurant
down by the deep-water port serving superb
fresh seafood – try the jumbo barbecue prawns
with aioli, with a glass of WA wine from the
excellent list. Try and grab the bench seats, the
only ones with a real water view. Daily
11am–late.

Zanders Cable Beach Rd, Cable Beach
☎08/9193 5090, ⓦwww.zanders.com.au. Airy
modern place with ocean views that's very much
an all-day job – punters pile in from morning until
night for food that pleases everyone without being
anything to write home about. Daily breakfast,
lunch and dinner.

Nightlife and entertainment

Sun Pictures **cinema** in Chinatown is a uniquely "Broometime" experience:
watch the latest movies from a deckchair while mosquitoes nibble your
ankles and the odd light aircraft comes in low across the screen. The huge
ten-day **Shinju Matsuri** festival in September celebrates Broome's ethnic
diversity, and the pearl that created it, finishing up with a huge fireworks
display. The town can get packed out for the Shinju, so book your accommodation in advance.

Bungalow Bar 18 Dampier Terrace, Chinatown
ⓦwww.bungalowbar.com.au. Nightclub owned by
the "Roey" (see p.732) so expect shenanigans,
albeit with a hint more class, DJs and a clubbier
feel. Check websites for nights – opening hours
vary with the season.

Divers Tavern 12 Cable Beach Rd, Cable Beach
ⓦwww.diverstavern.com.au. Large pub and bistro
with surrounding terrace that's actually quite

pleasant. Big-name bands sometimes play here –
check the website for listings. Daily 11am–late.

Matso's Broome Brewery Corner of
Hamersley and Carnarvon sts ☎08/9193
5811, ⓦwww.matsos.com.au. A bone-fide Broome
institution. The famous Monsoonal Blonde and
ginger beers can be (sensibly) gulped down on the
colonial-style veranda, or at a squashy couch in the
fanned interior. Great food served all day – from

breakfast through to beer-battered fish or authentic Indian curries in the evening. Daily 7am–late.

Roebuck Bay Hotel Carnarvon St. Incorporates *Pearlers Lounge* and *Cheffy's* restaurant, which has a decent beer garden and *Oasis* bar, a larger outdoor space with a stage for live music and plenty of room for happy-hour carousing. Depending on your views about an international panel of girls, white T-shirts and water you might want to attend/stay away on Thursday evenings as appropriate. Daily 11am–late.

Sunset Bar *Cable Beach Club Resort* ⓣ08/9192 0400, ⓦwww.cablebeachclub.com. A sundowner here is as much part of Broome as the camels – get there an hour before sunset to snag a table. It also does good bar food including pizzas, seafood platters and curries. Daily lunch–late.

Zeebar 4 Sanctuary Rd, Cable Beach ⓣ08/ 9193 6511, ⓦwww.zeebar.com.au. Bars without pokies, sports betting rooms and bikini shows are sorely needed in Broome, and *Zeebar* delivers on all counts. Things it does have are a huge well-stocked bar, minimalist decor, scatter cushions, friendly staff, wine-tasting (Fri eve) and excellent share plates. Daily 5pm.

Listings

Bicycle rental Broome Cycles, next to the Shell Garage in Chinatown (ⓣ08/9192 1871) and outside the Broome Crocodile Zoo on Cable Beach Rd (ⓣ0409 192 289), rent bikes from $24 per day.

Bookshop Kimberley Books on Napier Terrace has an excellent range of local titles, while Woody's Book Exchange in Johnny Chi Lane has second-hand stuff.

Car and 4WD rental Besides the big names with offices at the airport, there's Broome Broome Car

Rentals at 15 Napier Terrace (ⓣ08/9192 2210, ⓦwww.broomebroome.com.au) or Australian 4WD Hire (ⓣ1300 360 339, ⓦwww.australian4wdhire .com.au).

Hospital Robinson St ⓣ08/9194 2222.

Scooter rental Broome Scooter Hire, 52 Coughlin St (ⓣ08/9193 5626, ⓦwww.broomescooter.com .au), near the BP on Frederick St, rents scooters from $12 per day.

Taxi ⓣ08/9192 1133.

Around Broome: Broome Bird Observatory and Willie Creek Pearl Farm

Leaving Broome, Crab Creek Road branches off the highway around 10km north of town, leading 15km southeast down a corrugated dirt road to the tranquil **Broome Bird Observatory** (ⓣ08/9193 5600, ⓦwww .broomebirdobservatory.com), on the shores of Roebuck Bay. The rich mudflats around the observatory are one of the top five global spots for shorebirds, with over 150,000 visiting during the Wet after travelling from their annual breeding grounds in Asia and Siberia. The centre runs a variety of twitcher tours and courses ($60–820), with basic accommodation (camping $22, powered site $30, rooms ❶–❺) and pick-ups from Broome available for overnight guests or those booked on tours ($35 return).

Almost opposite the turn-off for the observatory, Broome–Cape Leveque Road leads north to the Aboriginal lands of the Dampier Peninsula, ending at Cape Leveque (see opposite). Shortly afterwards, the unsealed Manari Road turn-off heads west past **Willie Creek Pearl Farm** (ⓣ08/9192 0000, ⓦwww .williecreekpearls.com.au; daily 4hr tour with pick-up in town $80, 2hr self-drive tour $40, pre-booking essential), a popular day-tour 38km from Broome and the only Kimberley pearl farm easily accessible to the public – the pearls cultivated here are among the finest and biggest in the world. Although the main showroom is still based on the banks of beautiful Willie Creek, most of the operation, which involves regularly cleaning and turning a quarter of a million shells by hand, has now moved offshore for security reasons. The tour includes a talk on the pearl-farming process, and a boat trip in the creek to inspect the racks of seeded oysters, which build up layers of pearlescent nacre as they feed off the tidal nutrients – a process which takes half the normal time. A **4WD** is recommended for both attractions.

The Dampier Peninsula

Continuing along Manari Road past the pearl farm you'll find isolated **bushcamping** along the "northern beaches" on the southwest side of the Dampier Peninsula. Some tours come here from Broome (see p.728); anyone travelling the road on their own should be well prepared as there are no facilities whatsoever. The first of the beaches is **Barred Creek**, followed by **Quondong Point** and **Price Point**. The road can get pretty slippery after only a small amount of rain, and continuing beyond **Coulomb Point**, 78km from Broome, will be beyond most vehicles and drivers.

Fun though this detour is, it's just an hors d'oeuvre for the main course that is the Broome–Cape Leveque Road – for information on the area see ⓦwww .ardi.com.au. This beautiful area, with its pristine, deserted beaches, dusty red cliffs and mind-altering sunsets, is slowly opening up to low-key tourism, with indigenous cultural experiences now tending to be as much a highlight as the stunning scenery for many visitors – tours are offered at all of the Aboriginal communities listed on below.

The first stop on the road is the Aboriginal community of **Beagle Bay** (ⓣ08/9192 4913), 125km from Broome. The highlight here is the **Sacred Heart Church** built by German missionaries in 1918, a beautiful building with an unusual altar decorated with mother-of-pearl – pay the $5 entry fee when announcing your arrival at the community office. After Beagle Bay the track to Cape Leveque gets narrower and sandier and after a further 20km you'll reach the turn-off leading after 33km to Nature's Hideaway at **Middle Lagoon** (ⓣ08/9192 4002; entry $8), a lovely white-sand cove with camping ($32), good swimming and snorkelling, partially equipped four-bed cabins (❻) and a six-bed self-contained cabin (❼). Backtracking to the main road, a further 48km takes you to the community of **Lombadina/Djarindjin** (ⓣ08/9192 4936, ⓦwww .lombadina.com.au), another ex-mission settlement where you'll now find well-equipped backpacker accommodation ($44), two-bed self-contained units (❼), a range of water- and land-based tours ($5.50–220) and a beautiful wide bay. At pretty **Chile Creek** (ⓣ08/9192 4141, ⓦwww.chilecreek.com), just to the south, there's basic camping ($17) and bush shelters (❶). On the opposite side of the peninsula at Djugargagyn is **Kelk Creek** bush retreat (ⓣ08/9192 4377, ⓦwww.kelkcreek.com.au), which offers two- and three-night packages with all meals and tours included (two-night $350pp, three-night $500 per person); accommodation, tours and meals can also all be booked separately.

A stay at *Kooljaman Resort* at spectacular **Cape Leveque** (ⓣ08/9192 4970, ⓦwww.kooljaman.com; entry fees apply if not staying overnight), 220km from Broome at the very tip of the peninsula, is the reason why you've put your vehicle through such heartache. This is the original Dampier Peninsula resort, with accommodation ranging from camping ($33), powered site $38) and beach shelters (❸) to luxury stilted tents (❾) overlooking the ocean. *Dinkas* restaurant is open daily for lunch and dinner from April to October, or you can use the "Bush Butler" service if you can't drag yourself from your room. From *Kooljaman* guests and day visitors can occupy themselves with fishing, mud-crabbing, cultural tours, scenic flights and cruises to the old mission buildings on nearby Sunday Island – ask at the resort for information.

Practicalities

Unless you don't mind giving your car a hammering, it's best to arm yourself with a solidly built **4WD** rental, or to join a **tour** (see p.728) for the corrugated 220-kilometre track to Cape Leveque – note that access can be restricted in the Wet. Advance **permits** are required to visit or pass through Beagle Bay and Bardi (One Arm Point); apply online at Ⓦwww.dia.wa.gov.au or call ℡08/9235 8000. Even with a permit, phone ahead then announce your arrival at each community listed on p.733, and make sure you stick to public roads when driving on the peninsula – some communities here don't want to be disturbed. Limited supplies are available from the **stores** at Beagle Bay, Lombadina/ Djarindjin, Ardyaloon and Kooljaman, with **fuel** available weekdays and Saturday mornings at all but the last. There's no free camping along the road or in any communities, and all accommodation must be booked in advance; check with your host whether you can BYO alcohol.

Derby to Kununurra – the Great Northern Highway

There are two routes from Derby to Kununurra: the Gibb River Road (see p.742) and the Great Northern Highway, which passes through **Fitzroy Crossing** and **Halls Creek** before you come to the access road to **Purnululu National Park** (the Bungle Bungles). Most visitors will do one or the other, although the Bungle Bungles (the only real attraction down this wearying stretch of Highway 1) are close enough to Kununurra to be accessed on an overnight trip if you choose to do the "Gibb".

Derby

Situated 220km northeast of Broome, and 41km north of Highway 1 on a spur of land jutting into the mud flats of King Sound, **DERBY** (pronounced "dur-bee") is a neat, industrious little town and a centre for local Aboriginal communities, which make up sixty percent of the population. One of the few sights in town is the **old gaol** on the corner of Loch and Hensman streets, where rusting ruins and interpretative boards highlight the horrifying treatment of local indigenous people at the hands of pastoralists and the police; there's a similarly strong sense of history at the **Boab Prison Tree** (see opposite) 5km to the south.

A **scenic flight** or **cruise** to see the impressive West Kimberley coastline and Buccaneer Archipelago is a must, and cheaper than doing the same trips from Broome. Huge tides rage through a tiny gap in the cliffs at the **Horizontal Waterfalls** in Talbot Bay, one of many small inlets on this rugged shoreline; try Horizontal Falls Adventure Tours and Kimberley Extreme Adventures (6hr; $495; see p.728), or Buccaneer Sea Safaris (4–10 day; $2790–7690; ℡08/9191 1991, Ⓦwww.buccaneerseasafaris.com). **Derby Bus Service** runs an excellent-value day-trip ($121 including snacks and lunch; ℡08/9193 1550, Ⓦwww.derbybus.com.au) to Windjana Gorge and Tunnel Creek national parks, and Lillimooloora Police Station, scene of a local policeman's death at the hands of his now infamous Aboriginal tracker, Jandamarra or "Pigeon" (see p.723); they also run Gibb River Road tours (2–7 days; from $198 per day). Four kilometres down the Gibb River Road, whose western entrance is just south of town, is the brand-new and much-recommended **Mowanjum Art and Cultural Centre** (check opening times and prices at the visitor centre; ℡08/9191 1008, Ⓦwww.mowanjumarts.com).

The Boab – symbol of the Kimberley

East of Derby as you enter the Kimberley proper you'll start to notice the region's distinctive **boab** trees, their bulbous trunks and spindly branches creating startling silhouettes against the bowl-like sky. As much a symbol of the Kimberley as cattle stations and deep red sunsets, it's widely believed that seeds from the African **baobab** – the common name of the genus *Adansonia* and of which the Australian name is a contraction – arrived in the Kimberley by sea from Africa thousands of years ago, gradually evolving into this distinct species.

The trees' huge size has enabled their most dubious function as temporary prisons for local Aboriginal people. The most notorious example of a **prison tree**, located 5km south of Derby, held indigenous people kidnapped in the mid- to late nineteenth century from the Fitzroy Crossing and Halls Creek areas.

Today you'll see carved **boab nuts** sold as homewares across the Kimberley, the intricate patterns worked into the flesh by Aboriginal artists. At the beginning of the rainy season the tree produces flowers and fruit, foretelling the beginning of the Wet. Aboriginal people also chew the bark for water – the huge trunks can hold up to 120,000 litres.

The building's architecture celebrates the spirit of the Wandjina, the supreme spirit for the Worarra, Ngarinyin and Wunumbul peoples of the Mowanjum community just behind the centre. This Aboriginal-owned cultural haven houses a gallery, art studio, performance space and museum, as well as hosting an excellent annual festival in July.

Practicalities

The **visitor centre** (broadly Mon–Fri 8.30am–4.30pm, Sat & Sun 9am–noon; [T]08/9191 1426 or 1800 621 426, [W]www.derbytourism.com.au) is at the top end of town on the main strip, Clarendon Street, where Greyhound **buses** also arrive. Woolworths **supermarket** is on the highway just south of town.

Places to stay include the *Kimberley Entrance Caravan Park* at 2 Rowan St ([T]08/9193 1055, [W]www.kimberleyentrancecaravanpark.com; camping $26, powered site $30), the best of the two campsites in town, overlooking the mudflats and with lovely owners; *Jila Apartment* ([T]08/9193 2560; [7]) on the corner of Clarendon and Johnston streets, a pleasant two-bed apartment that's a cut above the rest of the rooms in Derby, with an adjacent **art gallery**; or *Derby Lodge and Backpackers* ([T]08/9191 2924, [W]www.derbylodge.com.au; dorms $30, rooms [4]–[5]), opposite the visitor centre, the pick of the motel-style rooms in town. For breakfast and lunch, *Diamonds and Pearls* at 56 Clarendon St is the best bet, serving smoothies, sandwiches and cakes. There's decent pub **food** at the *Boab Inn*, but watching the sun go down behind the jetty over seafood at *The Point* restaurant ([T]08/9191 1195; Tues–Sun 5pm–late), out by the wharf, is the best way to spend an evening in Derby. It also does takeaways.

Fitzroy Crossing and around

Since the pastoral expansion into the Kimberley in the late nineteenth century, **FITZROY CROSSING** has been a rest stop for travellers and a crucial crossing over the ever-flooding Fitzroy River. Today it's also a fairly desolate welfare town serving the Aboriginal communities strung out along the Fitzroy Valley – it's a better overnight option than Halls Creek (see p.736) however. The Fitzroy River's runoff is second only to the Amazon during flood peaks, at which time two cubic kilometres of water a minute surge under the road bridge, gushing out across a forty-kilometre-wide flood plain before disgorging into King Sound. The **visitor centre** (Mon–Fri 8.30am–noon & 1–4.30pm; ☏08/9191 5355) is on Flynn Drive by the roadhouse, and there's a **super-market** with limited stock and a **post office** on Forrest Road. **Tours** to Windjana Gorge and Tunnel Creek national parks (full day; $160) and Geikie Gorge (3hr; $60) are run from the *Fitzroy River Lodge* (see below) by Eco Adventure Day Tours (☏08/9191 5141).

For **accommodation**, don't look past *Fitzroy River Lodge* (☏08/9191 5141, ⓦwww.kimberleyhotels.com.au; camping $22, powered site $27, rooms ❻–❾), on the highway east of the bridge. This lush, sprawling oasis in dusty Fitzroy Crossing has lodges on stilts (to avoid flooding), smart motel-style rooms and less smart apartments, acres of camping space and excellent facilities including a pool, restaurants, a bar and internet access. The most memorable experience in town is a few **drinks** or some pub **food** at the atmospheric century-old *Crossing Inn* (☏08/9191 5080, ⓦwww.kimberleyhotels.com.au; camping $22, powered site $25, rooms ❺–❻), a true Outback pub on Skuthorpe Road with a small art gallery, rooms and camping in a natural bush setting. It can get fairly raucous on Thursdays – pay day.

Geikie Gorge National Park

The five-kilometre **Geikie Gorge**, one of the three Devonian Reef national parks (see p.743 for the others), is accessed from Fitzroy Crossing via Forrest Road, an eighteen-kilometre trip. This mighty gorge carved by the Fitzroy River is best seen by **boat** between May and October, either with DEC (2–3 daily; 1hr; $25 cash only; ☏08/9191 5121) or Darngku Heritage Cruises (1–4hr; $25–148; ☏08/9191 5552), who tag on some indigenous cultural experiences. For both, arrive at the pagoda near the car park fifteen minutes before the tour departs and take a hat, as boats are unshaded. Watermarks on the gorge walls clearly show how high the river can rise, while below the surface freshwater crocodiles jostle with freshwater-adapted stingrays and sawfish. **Walking trails** lead along the forested western banks, which are dotted with picnic sites and barbecues. The park is normally closed in the Wet, and camping is prohibited.

Halls Creek and around

Further down the Great Northern Highway is **HALLS CREEK**, 288km east of Fitzroy Crossing. The goldrush of 1885 took place in the hills 17km south of town; in less than four years thousands of prospectors exhausted the area's potential before stampeding off to Kalgoorlie. Nowadays new diamond mines are opening up, but Halls Creek itself remains a pretty desperate Aboriginal welfare town; wise travellers will fuel up and move on. Note also that this is not the place to break for a meal: with only weekly deliveries, fresh food can be scarce in the shops and the takeaway food on offer from the roadhouses is abysmal. If you have to stop, the **visitor centre** (Mon–Fri 9am–4pm; ☏08/9168 6262) is in the middle of town. For somewhere to **stay**, the grim, dusty *Halls Creek Caravan Park* (☏08/9168 6169; camping $22, powered site $26, cabins ❶–❸) on Roberta Avenue is the only option for campers; the *Kimberley Hotel* (☏08/9168 6101, ⓦwww.kimberleyaccommodation.com.au; ❹–❼) just opposite is far more comfortable, with a pool and the only **pub** in town.

There are a few attractions south of town down Duncan Road for those with their own transport, including the interesting ruins of **Old Halls Creek**;

China Wall, a block-like outcrop of quartzite rising from the hillside; swimming holes at Caroline and Palm springs; and finally Saw Tooth Gorge, 45km out of town, where you can also camp – all bar the final creek crossing just before the gorge are manageable in a 2WD during the Dry, although a 4WD makes life easier. Sixteen kilometres west of town, the **Tanami Track** heads south past **Wolfe Creek National Park** (where a 50,000-tonne meteorite crash-landed around 300,000 years ago, making an impressively large crater) on its way to Alice Springs, a remote road for hardened Outbackers only. The brutal Australian horror film *Wolf Creek* (1995) has led many travellers to approach the area with trepidation.

Purnululu National Park (Bungle Bungles)

The spectacular **Bungle Bungle** massif, seldom referred to by its official name, the **Purnululu National Park** (open April 1–Dec 20; DEC fee, see box, p.737), is one of Australia's greatest natural wonders and in 2003 earned prestigious UNESCO World Heritage listing. The nickname is believed to be a misspelling of the common Kimberley grass, Bundle Bundle, while "Purnululu" means "sandstone" in the local Kija tongue. A couple of days spent exploring the park's famous striped beehive domes, chasms and gorges is well worth the effort (or expense if you're taking a tour). Though visited by Europeans a century earlier, and long inhabited by Aboriginal people, the Bungles were brought to prominence in the early 1980s when a Dutch film crew flew over the area, and have quickly attracted a mystique matching that of Uluru.

Scenic flights are available over the Bungles if you don't want to drive into the park; choose between fixed-wing aircraft departing from Kununurra (see p.739) or an exhilarating helicopter flight from the park's Bellburn Airstrip just south of Walardi campsite (April–Nov; 18–48min; $205–495; ☎08/9168 7335, ⓦwww.slingair.com.au) or Warmun/Turkey Creek (April–Oct; 50min; $220; ☎08/9162 7337, ⓦwww.slingair.com.au). The helicopters are permitted to fly much lower – if you've ever wanted to fly in a chopper you won't be disappointed. The **tours** available from Broome and Kununurra (see p.728 & p.740), which often involve flying to the airstrip and then being driven around in a 4WD, offer the best of both worlds. You can sometimes "walk-in" to the luxury camps used by the tour groups – ask at the visitor centre for availability.

Because of the need to protect the fragile rock formations from mass tourism, and the very rough access road from the Great Northern Highway, 52km south of **Warmun/Turkey Creek**, entry is strictly limited to **4WD**s, with all tow vehicles prohibited. Accommodation and food are available at the *Warmun Roadhouse* (☎08/9168 7882, ⓦwww.warmunroadhouse.com.au; camping $20, powered site $28, rooms ❶–❻) here, ahead of a morning drive into the park. It gets stiflingly **hot** in the Bungles, with temperatures soaring well over 40°C from September onwards, so make sure you carry water, use sunblock and wear a hat on all walks.

From the highway it's a fun, if nerve-wracking, 53-kilometre drive through pastoral station land to the **visitor centre** and entry station (April to mid-Oct daily 8am–noon & 1–4.30pm; ☎08/9168 7300), where you should register your arrival – self-registration must be completed here from mid-October. The centre has cold drinks, park information and souvenirs only; bring all the food, fuel and water you need unless you're coming with a tour group – it's a good idea to freeze as much water as you can before entering the park if you don't have a fridge. Take it easy on the road in as the track is narrow and corrugated, with oncoming traffic in the morning – expect the journey to take from two to three hours. There are usually at least three creek crossings and frequent heavily rutted sections, meaning that low range and high clearance are a must.

In the park

From the entry station the roads are better and you can head to either of the two basic campsites (pay camping fees at visitor centre; toilets and bore water only) on the north or south side of the park. **Kurrajong Camp** is on the northern side, 7km from the entry station; 13km and 14km further on respectively are Echidna Chasm and Mini Palms car parks, with excellent short walks from both. The walk into **Echidna Chasm** (2km; 1hr return; easy) takes you deep into the soaring, maze-like incision, which opens into a small amphitheatre at the end – the perfect picnic spot. Do the walk at midday when the sun enters the chasm and you can see the colours in the rock to their best advantage. On the way out, make sure you check out the view over the Osmond Ranges and Osmond Creek from **Echidna Chasm Lookout**; the creek is the only permanent source of water in the park, and was historically used by Aboriginal groups as a travel pathway. Once overgrazed, sterling work by DEC to improve the soil and eradicate feral animals has gone some way to helping the land recover sufficiently for indigenous groups to live in the park once more. The **Mini Palms** walk (5km; 2–3hr return; moderate) runs along a creek bed then squeezes through tiny gaps between boulders, before ascending to a viewing platform and finally a palm-filled amphitheatre. Along the walk you can see tufts of palms clinging to the rock walls hundreds of metres above you; the scale of the clefts is emphasized when you realize the palms can be up to 20m high.

Walardi Camp, on the south side of the park 12km from the entry station, is the better laid-out campsite; 15km further on is Piccaninny Creek car park and classic Bungle vistas every way you look. From the car park, the short **Domes Walk** leads you among some bungles on the way to the walk into **Cathedral Gorge** (3km; 1–2hr return; moderate), an awe-inspiring overhanging amphitheatre with stunning acoustics and a seasonal pool whose rippled reflections flicker across the roof above. The nearby **Piccaninny Creek Lookout** provides more great views. **Piccaninny Gorge** is a tough, thirty-kilometre overnight walk for which you need to register at the visitor centre and carry vast quantities of water – between five and eight litres per person per day. Most people are understandably put off; if this is the case it's possible to do a shorter version to the gorge entry at the **Elbow** (14km; 8hr return; easy). Just north of the visitor centre, **Kungkalahayi Lookout** is a great place for sunset drinks, and sweeping views over this monumental land that you don't really get otherwise as a "ground visitor". The rest of the park is currently inaccessible, the northeast being the ancestral burial grounds of the Djaru and Gidja people. DEC is currently negotiating the opening of new, longer walking trails with the park's traditional owners.

Kununurra and around

From Turkey Creek/Warmun the road continues directly north, passing the Argyle Diamond Mine (tours from Kununurra; see box, p.740), which currently produces 25 percent of the world's diamonds. The scenery hereabouts takes a rugged turn as you pass the Ragged and Carr Boyd ranges en route to the junction with the Victoria Highway. At the junction, Kununurra is 45km to the east and Wyndham 56km northwest.

▲ Aboriginal rock art, Kununurra

Thriving **KUNUNURRA** is the Kimberley's youngest town, built in the early 1960s to serve the **Ord River Irrigation Project**, fed by Lake Kununurra. The Diversion Dam Wall to the west of town created this lake, essentially the bloated Ord River. Fifty kilometres upstream is the bigger Argyle Dam Wall, built in 1971 to ensure a year-round flow to the project, which in turn created **Lake Argyle**, the world's largest man-made body of water and home to an estimated twenty-five thousand crocodiles. Enhanced by the copious amounts of nearby fresh water which lends itself to recreational use, Kununurra escapes the listless feel of older Kimberley towns. Easy-to-produce sugar cane has become the most viable crop, along with more labour-intensive watermelons and other produce which offer steady opportunities for **farm work**; see the backpackers' notice boards for this or cattle-station work. There are some excellent **art galleries** in the centre of town, including the Lovell Gallery (March & April plus Sept–Dec Mon–Fri 9am–4pm, Sat 9am–noon; May–Aug daily 9am–5pm; ☎08/9168 1781, ⓦwww.lovellgallery.com.au) at 144 Konkerberry Drive, which sells Kimberley-focused works in a lovely, airy space, and Our Land Gallery (☎08/9168 1881) on Papuana Street, which sells paintings by local Aboriginal artists in traditional ochres and newer, brighter acrylics. **Kelly's Knob**, a small hill behind town, is a popular place to watch the sun go down.

A couple of kilometres east of town is Hidden Valley or **Mirima National Park** (DEC fee; see box, p.644), a narrow valley of "mini-bungles" with some fun short trails. Another popular spot is **Ivanhoe Crossing**, 13km north of town on the Ord River. The crossing is often closed, and you need a pretty hefty high-clearance 4WD to navigate the fast-flowing waters when it's open. Downstream you can continue along an unsealed road all the way to **Parry Lagoons Nature Reserve** (see p.742); this is saltwater crocodile country – don't copy the locals swimming in the pools here if you value life and limb. North of town on Weaber Plains Road is the **Hoochery**, which produces the

Tours in Kununurra and the East Kimberley

Triple J Tours (ⓣ08/9168 2682, ⓦwww.triplejtours.net.au) offer cruises ($145–250) up the Ord River to Lake Argyle in the Dry, as do the long-established Lake Argyle Cruises (ⓣ08/9168 7687, ⓦwww.lakeargylecruises.com), whose **boat trips** ($65–230) include sunset sails and birdwatching. The *BBQ Boat* (ⓣ08/9168 1718, ⓦwww.thebbqboat.com.au) does a three-hour sunset cruise (April–Oct daily 4pm; 2hr 30min; $67 including dinner) around **Lily Creek Lagoon**, just south of the highway in town, where you'll see crocodiles and trees full of bats, which all take to the air in a dramatic sky-darkening mass at dusk. Ask about **canoe rentals** for use on the lagoon at *Kimberleyland* (see opposite) or contact Go Wild Adventure Tours (ⓣ1300 663 369, ⓦwww.gowild.com.au), who run self-guided "eco-noeing" trips down the Ord River (1–3 day; $150–180) as well as climbing and abseiling ($50–180).

Regional tours

Kununurra is an excellent base from which to visit the Bungle Bungles and the East Kimberley. Many of the outfits operating out of Broome also run return or one-way tours from Kununurra – see p.728 for details.

Alligator Airways ⓣ08/9168 1333 or 1800 632 533, ⓦwww.alligatorairways.com.au. Plane flights only over Lake Argyle, Mitchell Plateau, Kimberley coast and fly-drive Bungles tours ($265–715). El Questro pick-ups and drop-offs and Aboriginal culture tours cost extra.

East Kimberley Tours ⓣ08/9168 2213 or 1800 682 213, ⓦwww.eastkimberleytours.com.au. Long-established operators offering Bungle tours which overnight in their comfortable Bungle Bungle Bushcamp. Tours depart from Kununurra or Warmun/Turkey Creek and include fly-drive options of varying length ($545–1255).

Slingair ⓣ08/9169 1300 or 1800 095 500, ⓦwww.slingair.com.au. Flights over the Argyle Diamond Mine (from $575) and fly-drive (from $640) or fly-drive-helicopter (from $935) trips into the Bungles. They also run flights from the park itself, scenic flights from *Drysdale River Homestead* and scenic flights and tours around the Mitchell Falls area (for all see p.744). Pick-ups and drop-offs at El Questro are available, along with combo packages (1–3 days).

infamous Ord River rum (May–Sept daily 9am–4pm, 30min tours 11am & 2pm; Oct–April Mon–Fri 9am–4pm, Sat 9am–noon, 30min tours 11am; tours $7.50 including rum cake and coffee; ⓣ08/9168 2467, ⓦwww.hoochery.com.au), the only rum produced in WA and probably none the better for the lack of competition.

The **Ord Valley Muster** (ⓦwww.ordvalleymuster.com) is the region's biggest event, an annual two-week extravaganza in May which has branched out from cows and cowboys to include concerts, arts and markets.

Practicalities

The **visitor centre** (Mon–Fri 8am–5pm, Sat & Sun 9am–4pm; ⓣ08/9168 1177, ⓦwww.kununurratourism.com) is on Coolibah Drive; they sell national park passes and have stacks of information on the Gibb River Road. You'll find a **telecentre** next door, along with a perennially warm **swimming pool**. The **post office** is also on Coolibah Drive, while Greyhound **buses** arrive outside the BP **roadhouse** on Messmate Way. There's a large Coles **supermarket** on Konkerberry Drive, where you should stock up if you're heading west.

Kununurra is well equipped with **accommodation**. In the centre of town, *Kimberley Croc* hostel at 120 Konkerberry Drive (℡08/9168 2702 or 1300 136 702, Ⓦwww.kimberleycroc.com.au; dorms $28, rooms ❶–❺) has a nice pool, standard dorms and a great kitchen, with lots of outdoor areas to lounge in and some long-term rooms for workers. It's also the booking agent for Go Wild Adventure Tours (see opposite). *Kununurra Backpackers* at 24 Nutwood Crescent (℡08/9169 1998 or 1800 641 998, Ⓦwww.adventure.kimberley.net.au; dorms $22–25, rooms ❶–❷) is similarly relaxing, although a little bit shabbier than *Croc* – Big Waters Tours are situated here. The hostel is in a quiet residential street a hot ten-minute walk from town, overlooked by the red craggy rocks of the Mirima National Park. In contrast, the *Kimberley Grande* at 20 Victoria Highway (℡08/ 9166 5600, Ⓦwww.kimberleygrande.com.au; ❼–❾) offers smart resort-style accommodation, with a pool and a couple of restaurants; the *Kununurra Country Club Resort* at 47 Coolibah Drive (℡08/9168 1024 or 1800 808 999, Ⓦwww.kununurracountryclub.com.au) is similar in style and price. The most central of Kununurra's six **caravan parks**, *The Town*, on the corner of Konkerberry and Bloodwood drives (℡08/9168 1763 or 1800 500 830, Ⓦwww.townpark.com.au; camping $26, powered site $28, cabins ❻), has helpful staff and a welcome pool. If you have your own vehicle though, *Kimberleyland* (℡08/9168 1280 or 1800 681 280, Ⓦwww.kimberleyland.com.au; camping $24, powered site $28, cabins ❻), on Lakeview Drive just south of town, is perched on the edge of Lake Kununurra overlooking a glowing red monolith, and is a lovely, peaceful spot to camp.

Places to eat include the *Boab Bookshop* (closed Sun; ℡08/9169 2574) on Papuana Street, which serves excellent breakfasts, lunches and local mango smoothies amidst the bookshelves. The stand-out, though, is the 🍴 *Pumphouse Restaurant* (daily 7.30am–late), on Lakeview Drive overlooking Lake Kununurra, where you can take in the gorgeous sunsets from the veranda over a glass of WA's finest, and indulge in gourmet pub food in the industrial interior. *Hotel Kununurra* on Messmate Way is buzzy with workers in the evening, and a good place for a cooling **drink**.

Lake Argyle

Thirty-five kilometres east of Kununurra on the Victoria Highway, a sealed road of the same distance leads to vast, scenic **Lake Argyle**. When the **Argyle Dam** was completed in 1972, the Ord River managed to fill the lake in just one wet season. Along with the neighbouring Victoria and the Fitzroy, these rivers account for a third of Australia's freshwater runoff and plans are often mooted to pipe it south where it's needed. Creating the lake was an engineer's dream: only a small defile needed damming to back up a shallow lake covering up to two thousand square kilometres. Since that time the fish population has grown over the years to support commercial fishing, as well as numerous birds and crocodiles, both estuarine and freshwater.

When the lake was proposed, the Durack family's **Argyle Homestead** was moved to its present site, 2km before the end of the road, and is now a **museum** (April–Oct daily 9am–3pm; $3; ℡08/9167 8088) of early pioneering life in the Kimberley, as described in Mary Durack's droving classic, *Kings in Grass Castles*. At the end of the road is *Lake Argyle Tourist Village*, with camping on the shores of the lake, a shop and a bistro (℡08/9168 7777, Ⓦwww.lakeargyle.com; camping $18, powered site $24, cabins ❺–❼). For **lake cruises**, see opposite.

Wyndham

Strung out in three built-up areas along the muddy banks of the Cambridge Gulf, **WYNDHAM** was the port established to serve the brief goldrush at Halls Creek; these days the East Kimberley's only port ticks over quietly serving local Aboriginal people. At the top of the town is **Wyndham Crocodile Farm** (Dry daily 8.30am–4pm; Wet daily 10.30am–12.30pm; feeding 11am; $16.50; ☎08/9161 1124), with plenty of big "salties" and pens packed with almost-cute crocodile hatchlings draped over each other. Nearby **Five Rivers Lookout** has good views over the gulf, where the Ord, King, Pentecost, Durack and Forrest rivers reach the end of their journeys. Sixteen kilometres south of town is the short unsealed road to **Parry Lagoons Nature Reserve** and Marlgu Billabong, internationally renowned birdwatching spots which are especially rewarding at sunrise or sunset.

The **visitor centre** (daily 6am–6pm; ☎08/9161 1281) is on the Great Northern Highway at Kimberley Motors, and you can **camp** at the *Wyndham Caravan Park* (☎08/9161 1064; camping $20, powered site $26, cabins ❶) on Baker Street. The *Wyndham Town Hotel* (☎08/9161 1003; ❹–❺) on O'Donnell Street has basic rooms and the town's only **restaurant**. You need a vehicle to visit Wyndham unless you can arrange a pick-up – Greyhound **buses** drop you at the junction of the Great Northern and Victoria highways 56km south of town.

The Gibb River Road

The alternative to the Great Northern Highway is the epic Gibb River Road (GRR). Originally built to transport beef out of the central Kimberley cattle stations to Wyndham and Derby, the "Gibb" cuts through the region's heart, offering a vivid slice of this vast and rugged expanse. It's 670km from its western end just south of Derby to its eastern end between Kununurra and Wyndham, 230km shorter than the Great Northern Highway. Although some people have mistaken it as such, the Gibb is no short cut, with corrugations and punctures guaranteed – heed the advice on off-highway driving on p.41. Accessed from the Gibb, the even more remote Kalumburu Road leads to the increasingly popular Mitchell River National Park.

As a scenic drive in itself the Gibb is very satisfying, but it's the wayside attractions that make this route what it is – the homesteads, gorges and pools here are almost uniformly spectacular, and offer a real glimpse of Outback Australia. A comprehensive and annually updated *Travellers Guide to the Inland Kimberley and Mitchell Plateau* ($5) is available at local visitor centres and and is worth picking up. Distances given in brackets below refer to an attraction's distance from the GRR proper; all other distances refer to the number of kilometres from Derby.

If you're traversing the GRR west to east and want to spare your car the full ordeal, turn back at Manning Gorge and head back down to the highway via Windjana Gorge, as the best and most accessible gorges are along the western half of the GRR. If you just want a taste of the Gibb, it's possible to visit **Windjana Gorge** and **Tunnel Creek** national parks in a day from Derby or Fitzroy Crossing; this snippet is just about doable in a solid 2WD in the Dry. Otherwise, a sturdy **4WD** that you know how to drive and maintain is a must – at the very least carry two spares and know how to change them.

Make sure you have enough **food and water** for five extra days, and around twenty litres of spare **fuel** – fuel stops along the road are noted below. **Camping** is only allowed where indicated below, and camping fees of around

$10 per person always apply: Bell Creek Gorge excepted, all campsites have toilets, drinking water and showers – some also have gas barbecues and other facilities. **Tours** are available from Broome and Kununurra (see p.128 & p.140). Most roads, gorges, services and accommodation are closed in the **Wet** from around November to March – always check conditions and opening dates before you set out. It's best to visit at the start of the Dry, when the land is lush from the rains and rivers are full. Where **phone numbers** are listed below, always call in advance to get the go-ahead from the station owner to enter their land, and similarly make sure you have all the necessary permits to enter Aboriginal land – it's noted below where these are necessary. Finally, take plenty of **cash**.

Tunnel Creek and Windjana Gorge national parks
During the Devonian era, 350 million years ago, a large barrier reef grew around the then-submerged Kimberley plateau. The limestone remnants of this reef are today exposed in the national parks of Geikie Gorge (see p.736), Tunnel Creek and Windjana Gorge, known collectively as the Devonian Reef national parks.

A turn-off south 124km from Derby leads to the most impressive remainders of the reef, the towering ramparts of **Windjana Gorge** (21km; camping), where the Lennard River cuts through the Napier Ranges. A walking trail leads into the spectacular gorge, where freshwater crocodiles sun themselves in the afternoon at a small permanent pool, and fruit-bat-filled paperbark and Leichhardt trees line the riverbanks. Look out also for the striped archer fish, which kills insects by spitting jets of water at them. Three kilometres east of the gorge are the ruins of **Lillimooloora Police Station**, where a Constable Richardson died after an altercation with his Aboriginal tracker Jandamarra or "Pigeon" – see p.723 for the full story.

It's a further 37km to fun **Tunnel Creek National Park**, where the creek has burrowed its way under the range, creating a 750-metre tunnel hung with fruit- and ghost-faced bats. Although the collapsed roof illuminates the cavern halfway, the wade through the progressively deeper and colder water to the other end still takes some nerve, especially with the golden eyes of freshwater crocs following your progress from the side of the pool – they shouldn't bother you, though. You'll need a torch and sturdy shoes that you don't mind getting soaked. Moving into the Wet, check **weather conditions** at Fitzroy Crossing, as the tunnel can fill quickly if the Fitzroy River receives a lot of water – hard-to-spot rock art on the walls of the tunnel reinforces this warning. The tunnel was another of Jandamarra's stomping grounds – for more see p.723.

The western Gibb River Road
Back on the GRR, you continue to wind your way through the impressive **King Leopold** and **Napier ranges** in the King Leopold Ranges Conservation Park (DEC fees apply; see p.644), passing a famous rock bearing more than a little resemblance to Queen Victoria at 133km. At 189km is the turning north for *Mt Hart Wilderness Lodge* (50km; ☎08/9191 4645, ⓦwww.mthart.com.au; camping $20pp, rooms $205 per person half-board plus lunch for any stays over one night; no day-visits). You can use the lodge's private radio at the GRR turn-off to book if you haven't already. The former homestead has been transformed into a cosy retreat by the welcoming owners, and has private gorges to explore a few kilometres away. Scenic flights and helicopters use the lodge's airstrip to stop for lunch, but at other times it could be all yours.

Though a common-enough destination in the Dry, the Northern Kimberley is a very **remote** region where a well-equipped 4WD and Outback skills are essential; trips here should only be undertaken by experienced four-wheel-drivers. The full exploitation of minerals known to exist on the region's Mitchell plateau is made uneconomical by the climate and location, which alone indicates the region's remoteness in a state where precious materials are normally scavenged eagerly from the ground.

Heading north at the Kalumburu Road junction, midway along the Gibb River Road, you'll come to *Drysdale River Homestead* (59km; daily 8am–5pm; ℡08/9161 4326, ⓦwww.drysdaleriver.com.au; rooms ❹), which also offers **fuel**, camping at two sites, an excellent bar, meals and scenic flights (from 2hr; $270) over Mitchell Falls and King Cascades. The beautiful, four-tiered **Mitchell Falls**, on the Mitchell Plateau, are the main attraction hereabouts, and the reason most people take on the Kalumburu Road – this once remote spot is getting less so by the year and is now a national park. Take the left turn-off from the Kalumburu Road, 160km north of the GRR, and head 80km west over **King Edward River** to the falls; the turn-off is extremely rough and takes up to four hours one-way. There's more basic **camping** at the Mitchell Falls car park, from where it's a tough three-kilometre walk (4–6hr return) northwest to the falls themselves (passing Little and Big Merten's Falls on the way). You can swim in the upper pools of the main falls, or arrange a scenic flight or a six-minute lift back to the car park via helicopter (℡08/9161 4512, ⓦwww.slingair.com.au; $100–660). Just before you arrive at Mitchell Falls there's an extremely rough turn-off north to **Surveyors Pool** and beyond to Port Warrender on the coast. Kimberley Wilderness Adventures/APT

At 196km is the access road for **Lennard River Gorge** (8km), a dramatic cleft carved through tiers of tilted rock, just south of the GRR in the middle of the King Leopold Ranges. You may find it quicker to walk the last two kilometres, which are very rough in parts unless they've recently been graded. At 219km is the access track north to popular **Bell Gorge** (29km; $10 per vehicle entrance fee; camping at Bell Creek and Silent Gorge). Well worth some extra corrugations, this is the loveliest gorge along the GRR, with a pretty swimming hole.

At 227km just after Saddlers Creek is *Imintji Wilderness Camp* (see p.729; half-board ❼); the **Imintji Store** (℡08/9191 7471) just down the road sells **diesel fuel** only, ice and a good supply of groceries, as well as carrying out basic vehicle repairs. Back on the GRR 253km from Derby, a long 82-kilometre detour south over some creeks brings you to enjoyable *Mornington Wilderness Camp* (℡08/9191 7406 or 1800 631 946, ⓦwww.australianwildlife.org; $20 per vehicle), a former station that has been bought out by a conservation organization aiming to preserve native fauna. The camp now boasts en-suite safari tents (full-board $235 per person) and creekside camping as well as a bar and restaurant. From here, you can access the impressive **Sir John Gorge**, which has broad pools ideal for swimming; exploring upstream leads you to even greater grandeur – for $200 the camp gives you a canoe, lunch and the exclusive use of the gorge for a day. To appreciate nearby **Dimond Gorge** you need to paddle downstream beyond the sheer walls ($60 per day).

Charnley River Station (℡08/9191 4646, ⓦwww.charnleyriverstation.com.au; en-suite rondaval bungalows $170 per person half-board) is 43km north of the GRR, 257km along the road from Derby; camping, gorge access, canoeing ($50 per day), swimming and homestead meals are all available. Continuing down the

(see p.729; half-board ②) run the luxury **Marunbabidi** and **Ungolan** wilderness camps at King Edward River and just before Mitchell Falls car park; both camps are used on their tours but also provide a welcome touch of comfort for self-drivers doing it the tough way.

Continuing along the Kalumburu Road from the Mitchell Falls turn-off, **Kalumburu** (267km from GRR; Mon–Fri 8.30am–4.30pm; $40 vehicle permit; ☎08/9161 4300) is an Aboriginal community with the languorous feel of an African village, where ancient cars lie rusting and palms flap and sway in the tropical breeze. Buy your one-week vehicle permit on arrival from the community office (if there's anyone there); you'll also need to get another (free) permit in advance from the Department of Indigenous Affairs (☎08/9235 8000, ⊛www.dia.wa.gov.au). As well as being able to get (expensive) **fuel** and basics from the store here (Mon–Fri 8am–12.30pm & 2–4pm, Sat 7.30–1am), you can visit a mission set up in the nineteenth century by Benedictine monks ($10). Kalumburu is a completely dry community, so don't even BYO alcohol. North of the community along sandy tracks, there are basic campsites run by Kalumburu families at pretty *McGowans Beach*, *Pago* (both 22km from town) and *Honeymoon Beach* (26km; ☎08/9161 4300); for the first two ask in town.

There are a couple of other accommodation options on the rugged, otherwise unpopulated Kimberley coast: the stunning **all-inclusive resorts** at *Kimberley Coastal Camp* (☎0417 902 006, ⊛www.kimberleycoastalcamp.com.au) close to Mitchell Falls, and *Faraway Bay* (☎08/9169 1214, ⊛www.farawaybay.com.au), northeast of Kalumburu, cost from $2400 per person for two nights and are once-in-a-lifetime experiences. Both can only be accessed by air or sea.

GRR for 16km you reach **Adcock Gorge** (5km) and a further 19km brings you to **Galvans Gorge** (700m), both scenic without being spectacular. At 306km is *Mount Barnett Roadhouse* (April–Sept daily 7am–5pm; Oct–March Mon–Sat 8am–noon & 2–4pm; ☎08/9191 7007), which has **fuel** and some supplies. Camping is permitted behind the roadhouse by Manning River ($12.50 per person), where a five-kilometre trail leads to **Manning Gorge**, with a large swimming hole and a pretty waterfall. Another 29km down the GRR is **Barnett River Gorge** (5km north of GRR), with swimming in a billabong.

Seventy kilometres short of the Kalumburu Road junction, and 345km along the GRR from Derby, is *Mount Elizabeth Station* (30km north of GRR; ☎08/9191 4644; half-board in homestead $160 per person), where you can visit private gorges before eating at the homestead and camping amidst shady gum trees. Beyond the station is the **Munja Track**, an exceedingly rough trail to the sea at **Walcott Inlet**, 226km to the east. Camping and cabins (③) are available mid-route at Bachsten Camp; call ☎08/9191 1547 to arrange permissions and bookings – vehicle fees are payable at Mount Elizabeth Station ($50) and at the camp ($50).

Travel details

Trains

Perth to: Adelaide/Sydney (2 weekly; Adelaide 50hr, Sydney 60hr); Bunbury (2–3 daily; 2hr); Kalgoorlie (1–2 daily; 6hr).

Buses

Many **tour buses** ply the entire length of the northern WA coast, the most popular of which are Easyrider (☎08/9227 0824, ⊛www.easyrider.com.au) and

WesternXposure (℡08/9414 8423 or 1800 621 200, ⓦwww.westernxposure.com.au). Greyhound buses run from Perth to Broome five times a week (Mon & Wed–Sat), stopping at Cervantes (4hr 50min); Dongara (5hr 30min); Geraldton (6hr 30min); Northampton (7hr 50min); Carnarvon (13hr 30min); Onslow (18hr 40min); Karratha (21hr 30min); Roebourne (23hr); Port Hedland (26hr); and Broome (33hr 30min), with connections to Kalbarri from Binnu (Mon, Wed & Fri; 9hr 20min); Denham (12hr) and Monkey Mia (12hr 30min) from Overlander Roadhouse (Mon, Wed & Fri); and Coral Bay (17hr 20min) and Exmouth (18hr 50min) from Minilya Roadhouse (Fri, Sat & Sun outbound; Thurs, Fri & Sat return). The reverse service from Broome to Perth runs five times a week (Tues & Thurs–Sun). Greyhound continues from Broome to Darwin once a day, stopping at Derby (2hr 30min); Fitzroy Crossing (6hr); Halls Creek (9hr 30min); Warnum/Turkey Creek (12hr); Wyndham (13hr 30min); and Kununurra (14hr), before continuing through the NT to Darwin (26hr). The reverse service also runs once a day.

Integrity Coachlines run from Perth to Port Hedland on Wednesday, calling at New Norcia (2hr); Cue (9hr); Meekatharra (11hr); Newman (16hr); Wittenoom (19hr); and Port Hedland (22hr).

Kalgoorlie to: Esperance (3 weekly; 5hr).

Perth to: Albany (3 daily; from 6hr); Augusta (6 weekly; 6hr); Broome (daily; 33hr); Bunbury (1–2 daily; 2hr); Carnarvon (daily; 13hr); Coral Bay (6 weekly; 16hr); Darwin (daily; 59hr – stopover Broome); Derby (daily; 36hr– stopover Broome); Esperance (4 weekly; 10hr); Exmouth (6 weekly; 18hr); Fitzroy Crossing (daily; 40hr); Geraldton (2 daily; 6hr–8hr 30min); Halls Creek (daily; 43hr); Hyden (for Wave Rock; 2 weekly; 5hr); Kalbarri (daily; 8hr 30min–9hr); Karratha (1 daily; 22hr); Kununurra (daily; 48hr); Margaret River (3 daily; 5hr); Meekatharra (1 weekly; 10hr); Monkey Mia (3 weekly; 13hr); Port Hedland (8 weekly; 22–26hr).

Flights

Flights are with Qantas (ⓦwww.qantas.com), Virgin Blue (ⓦwww.virginblue.com.au) and Skywest (ⓦwww.skywest.com.au). Skywest also connects some destinations in WA without routing through Perth.

Perth to: Adelaide (8 daily; 4hr 15min); Alice Springs (5 weekly; 2hr 40min); Ayers Rock Resort (3 weekly; 2hr 15min); Brisbane (5 daily; 4hr 30min); Broome (3–7 daily; 2hr 30min); Carnarvon (1 daily; 2hr); Darwin (2 daily; 4hr); Esperance (2 daily; 1hr 40min); Exmouth (1–2 daily; 1hr 45min–2hr 45min); Geraldton (2–6 daily; 1hr 20min); Kalbarri (3 weekly; 1hr 25min); Esperance (2 daily; 1hr 40min); Karratha (4–11 daily; 2hr); Kununurra (4 weekly; 4hr 20min); Meekatharra (4 weekly; 1hr 30min); Melbourne (14 daily; 3hr 30min); Newman (2–5 daily; 1hr 40min); Paraburdoo (1–3 daily; 1hr 40min); Port Hedland (2–5 weekly; 2hr–3hr 50min); Shark Bay (4 weekly; 2hr); Sydney (12 daily; 4hr 15min); Tom Price (daily; 2hr).

South Australia

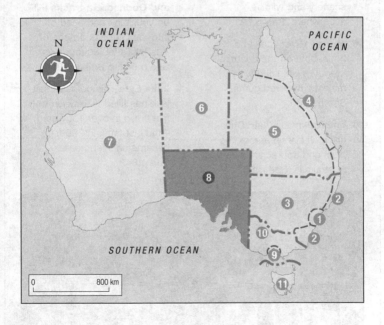

CHAPTER 8

Highlights

* **Adelaide Festival of Arts** The country's best-known and most innovative arts festival. See p.768

* **Barossa Valley** A day-trip from Adelaide, the Barossa Valley is home to some of Australia's finest wineries. See p.778

* **Kangaroo Island** Spectacular scenery and wildlife everywhere. See p.793

* **Murray River** Stay in a houseboat on the beautiful Murray River, lined with majestic river red gums. See p.810

* **The Nullarbor Plain** Drive or catch a train across the plain and appreciate how vast Australia is. See p.827

* **Coober Pedy** Gape at the cool underground homes of the residents of scorching Coober Pedy. See p.830

* **Wilpena Pound** The main attraction of the Flinders Ranges National Park is the enormous natural basin of Wilpena Pound. See p.836

* **The Strzelecki, Birdsville and Oodnadatta tracks** Fill up your tank and head off into the Outback on one of Australia's fabled journeys. See p.844, p.840 & p.844

* **Lake Eyre** This colossal salt lake has filled with water only five times in over 130 years – the last time, in 2009, it became an inland sea. See p.842

▲ Adelaide

South Australia

Outh Australia, the driest state of the driest continent, is split into two very distinct halves. The long-settled southern part, watered by the **Murray River**, with **Adelaide** as its cosmopolitan centre, has a Mediterranean climate, is tremendously fertile and has been thoroughly tamed. The northern half, however, is arid and depopulated, and as you head further north the temperature heats up to such an extreme that by **Coober Pedy** people are living underground to escape the searing summer temperatures.

Some of the highlights of southeastern South Australia lie within three hours' drive of Adelaide. Food and especially **wine** are among the area's chief pleasures: this is prime grape-growing and wine-making country. As well as wineries the **Fleurieu Peninsula**, just south of Adelaide, has a string of fine beaches, while nearby **Kangaroo Island** is a wonderful place to see Australian wildlife at its unfettered best. Facing Adelaide across the Investigator Strait, the **Yorke Peninsula** is primarily an agricultural area, preserving a copper-mining history and offering excellent fishing. The superb wineries of the **Barossa Valley**, originally settled by German immigrants in the nineteenth century, are only an hour from Adelaide on the **Sturt Highway**, the main road to Sydney. This crosses the Murray River at Blanchetown and follows the fertile Riverland region to the New South Wales border.

Following the southeast coast along the **Princes Highway**, you can head towards Melbourne via the extensive coastal Coorong lagoon system and enjoyable seaside towns such as Robe, before exiting the state at **Mount Gambier**, with its deep blue crater lakes. The inland trawl via the **Dukes Highway** is faster but less interesting. Heading north from Adelaide, there are old copper-mining towns to explore at **Kapunda** and **Burra**, the area known as the mid-north, which also encompasses the **Clare Valley**, another wonderful wine centre, famous for its Rieslings.

In contrast with the gentle and cultured southeast, the remainder of South Australia — with the exception of the relatively refined **Eyre Peninsula** and its strikingly scenic west coast — is unremittingly harsh **desert**, a naked country of vast horizons, salt lakes, glazed gibber plains and ancient mountain ranges. Although it's tempting to scud over the forbidding distances quickly, you'll miss the essence of this introspective and subtle landscape by hurrying. For every predictable, monotonous highway there's a dirt alternative, which may be physically draining but enables you to get closer to this precarious environment. The folded red rocks of the central **Flinders Ranges** and

Coober Pedy's post-apocalyptic scenery are on most agendas and could be worked into a sizeable circuit. Making the most of the journey is what counts here though – the fabled routes to **Oodnadatta**, **Birdsville** and **Innamincka** – are still real adventures.

Rail and **road** routes converge in Adelaide before the long cross-country hauls west to Perth via Port Augusta on the Indian Pacific train, or north to Alice Springs and Darwin on the Ghan – both ranking as two of Australia's great train journeys.

Some history

The coast of South Australia was first explored by the **Dutch** in 1627. In 1792 the French explorer Bruni d'Entrecasteaux sailed along the Great Australian Bight before heading to southern Tasmania, and in 1802 the Englishman Matthew Flinders thoroughly charted the coast. The most important expedition, though – and the one which led to the foundation of a colony here – was

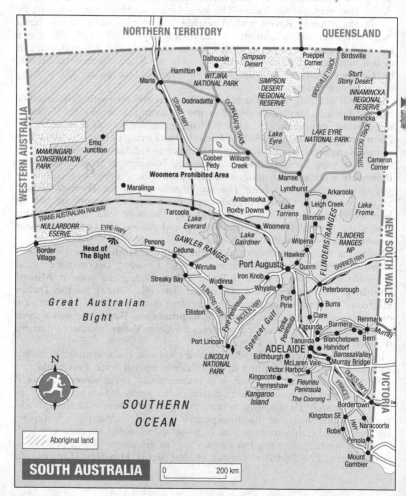

SOUTH AUSTRALIA   0   200 km

Captain Charles Sturt's 1830 navigation of the Murray River, from its source in New South Wales to its mouth in South Australia. In 1836, **Governor John Hindmarsh** landed at Holdfast Bay – now the Adelaide beachside suburb of Glenelg – with the first settlers, and the next year Colonel William Light planned the spacious, attractive city of Adelaide, with broad streets and plenty of parks and squares.

Early problems caused by the harsh, dry climate and financial incompetence (the colony went bankrupt in 1841) were eased by the discovery of substantial reserves of **copper**. The population of Adelaide boomed over the following decades, while the state's tradition of civil and religious **libertarianism** which was guaranteed to the early settlers continued; in 1894, South Australia's women were the first in the world to be permitted to stand for parliament and the second in the world to gain the vote (after New Zealand). The depressions and recessions of the interwar period hit South Australia hard, but the situation eased following World War II when new immigrants arrived, boosting industry and injecting fresh life into the state.

The 1970s were the decade of **Don Dunstan**: the flamboyant Labor Premier was an enlightened reformer who had a strong sense of social justice, abolishing capital punishment, outlawing racial discrimination and decriminalizing homosexuality. It appears that since his retirement in 1979, South Australia has gone back to being a sleepy state – after all, how can you follow up a premier who once wore tight pink hot pants to work?

Perhaps this is part of why South Australians themselves feel that their state's attractions have been unfairly eclipsed in the past by the lure of other Australian destinations. However, today South Australia has a renewed confidence buoyed in part by its strong art, culture, and food and wine scenes, as well as a renewed interest in its natural features and wildlife.

When South Australia was first settled by Europeans in 1836, it was home to as many as fifty distinct **Aboriginal groups**, with a population estimated at fifteen thousand. Three distinct cultural regions existed: the Western Desert, the Central Lakes, and the Murray and southeast region. It was the people of the comparatively well-watered southeast who felt the full impact of white settlement, and those who survived were shunted onto missions controlled by the government. Some Aboriginal people have clung tenaciously to their way of life in the Western Desert, where they have gained title to some of their land, but most now live south of Port Augusta, many in Adelaide.

Adelaide and around

ADELAIDE is a gracious city and an easy place to live, and despite its population of around one million, it never feels crowded. It's a pretty place, laid out on either side of the **Torrens River**, ringed with a green belt of parks and set against the rolling hills of the **Mount Lofty Ranges**. During the hot, dry summer the parklands are kept green by irrigation from the waters of the Murray River, upon which the city depends, though there's always a sense that the rawness of the Outback is waiting to take over.

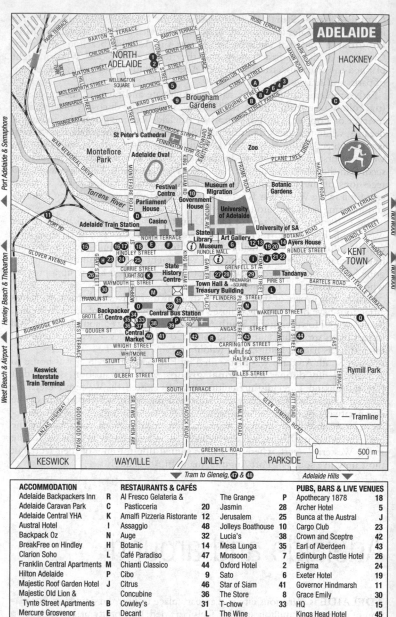

ADELAIDE

NORTH ADELAIDE

HACKNEY

PARK TERRACE

JEFFCOTT STREET
CHILDERS STREET
BARTON TERRACE
O'CONNELL STREET
GOVER STREET
LEFEVRE TERRACE
ROBE TERRACE

MILLS STREET
BUXTON STREET
WELLINGTON SQUARE
ARCHERS STREET
TYNTE STREET
KINGSTON TERRACE

MOLESWORTH STREET
WARD STREET
STANLEY STREET

BARNARDS STREET
BROUGHAM PL
Brougham Gardens
MELBOURNE STREET
FINNISS STREET PARADE

STRANGWAYS
KERMODE STREET
PENNINGTON TERR

St Peter's Cathedral
Zoo
Botanic Gardens

Montefiore Park
Adelaide Oval
PLANE TREE DRIVE
NORTH TERRACE

Torrens River
Festival Centre
Museum of Migration
Botanic Gardens

Adelaide Train Station
Parliament House
Government House
University of Adelaide
RUNDLE STREET

Casino
State Library
Art Gallery
University of SA
Ayers House
KENT TOWN

Museum
RUNDLE MALL
GRENFELL ST

HINDLEY STREET
State History Centre
Tandanya
PIRIE ST
BARTELS ROAD

CURRIE STREET
LIGHT SQ
WINDMARSH SQUARE
Town Hall & Treasury Building

WAYMOUTH STREET
FLINDERS STREET
WAKEFIELD STREET

FRANKLIN ST
Backpacker Centre
Central Bus Station
ANGAS STREET

GROTE ST
Central Market
VICTORIA SQ
CARRINGTON STREET

GOUGER ST
WRIGHT STREET
HURTLE SQ
HALIFAX STREET
Rymill Park

WHITMORE SQ
STURT STREET
GILLES STREET

GILBERT STREET

SOUTH TERRACE

KESWICK
WAYVILLE
UNLEY
PARKSIDE

Keswick Interstate Train Terminal

GREENHILL ROAD

Tram to Glenelg, 47 & 48
Adelaide Hills

0   500 m

--- Tramline

ACCOMMODATION	
Adelaide Backpackers Inn	R
Adelaide Caravan Park	C
Adelaide Central YHA	K
Austral Hotel	I
Backpack Oz	N
BreakFree on Hindley	H
Clarion Soho	L
Franklin Central Apartments	M
Hilton Adelaide	P
Majestic Roof Garden Hotel	J
Majestic Old Lion & Tynte Street Apartments	B
Mercure Grosvenor	E
Minima Hotel	A
Norwood Apartments	Q
Oaks Horizons	D
Richmond	
Stamford Plaza Adelaide	F
Sunny's	O

RESTAURANTS & CAFÉS	
Al Fresco Gelateria & Pasticceria	20
Amalfi Pizzeria Ristorante	48
Assaggio	
Auge	32
Botanic	14
Café Paradiso	47
Chianti Classico	44
Cibo	9
Citrus	46
Concubine	36
Cowley's	31
Decant	L
Elephant Walk	3
Eros Ouzeri	21
Farina Kitchen & Bar	29
Gaucho's	40

The Grange	P
Jasmin	28
Jerusalem	25
Jolleys Boathouse	10
Lucia's	
Mesa Lunga	35
Monsoon	7
Oxford Hotel	2
Sato	6
Star of Siam	41
The Store	8
T-chow	33
The Wine Underground	27
Wild Thyme	4
Ying Chow	37
Zuma	39

PUBS, BARS & LIVE VENUES	
Apothecary 1878	18
Archer Hotel	5
Bunca at the Austral	J
Cargo Club	23
Crown and Sceptre	42
Earl of Aberdeen	43
Edinburgh Castle Hotel	26
Enigma	24
Exeter Hotel	19
Governor Hindmarsh	11
Grace Emily	30
HQ	15
Kings Head Hotel	45
The Lion	B
Mars Bar	34
Rhino Room	13
Royal Oak Hotel	1
Supermild	17
Universal Wine Bar	22
Worldsend	16

Port Adelaide & Semaphore
Henley Beach & Thebarton
West Beach & Airport

The original occupants of the Adelaide plains were the **Kaurna people**, whose traditional way of life was destroyed within twenty years of European settlement. After a long struggle with Governor John Hindmarsh, who wanted to build the city around a harbour, the colony's surveyor-general, Colonel William Light, got his wish for an inland city with a strong connection to the river, formed around wide and spacious avenues and squares.

Postwar **immigration** provided the final element missing from Light's plan: the human one. **Italians** now make up the city's biggest non-Anglo cultural group, and in summer Mediterranean-style alfresco eating and drinking lend the city a vaguely European air. Not surprisingly, one of Adelaide's chief delights is its **food and wine**, with South Australian vintages in every cellar, and restaurants and cafés as varied as those in Sydney and Melbourne.

Adelaide may not be an obvious destination in itself, but its free-and-easy lifestyle and liberal traditions make it a fine place for a relaxed break on your way up to the Northern Territory or across to Western Australia.

Arrival

Buses from out of town, including the airport bus, will drop you off at the basic **Central Bus Station** on Franklin Street. The **airport**, 7km southwest from the centre, is modern and well equipped and has a currency exchange, car rental desks and information booth. It's serviced by the Skylink **airport bus** (daily 6.15am–9.45pm; 1–2 departures hourly; $8 coming from the airport; hotel pick-ups available, contact ℡08/8413 6196, ⓦwww.skylinkadelaide.com), which will drop you off at most city accommodation on request. The bus also stops at Victoria Square, North Terrace and Central Bus Station, as well as at the **Keswick Interstate Train Terminal**, about 1km southwest of the centre, from where it costs $5 to the city or airport.

You can also catch a train from the airport into **Adelaide Train Station**, situated on North Terrace in the city centre; walk across the terminal to the suburban platform. A **taxi** from the airport costs around $17 to either the city or the beachside suburb of Glenelg; taxis to the city from the interstate train terminal cost about $10.

Information

The first stop for information is the **South Australian Travel Centre**, at 18 King William St between Rundle Mall and North Terrace (Mon–Fri 8.30am–5pm, Sat & Sun 9am–2pm; ℡1300 655 276, ⓦwww.southaustralia.com). This large, modern office has helpful staff and masses of general information, including excellent free touring guides and maps of Adelaide and the state. You can also purchase a discount booklet if you plan to do a lot of sightseeing. Just around the corner on Rundle Mall itself is the **Rundle Mall Visitor Information Centre** (Mon–Thurs 10am–5pm, Fri 10am–8pm, Sat 10am–3pm, Sun 11am–4pm; ℡08/8203 7611, ⓦwww.southaustralia.com), a smaller version of the above.

Opposite the bus station at 110 Franklin St, the bright pink **Backpacker Transit and Travel Centre** (daily 9am–6pm; ℡08/8410 3000) can provide free maps and book all domestic tours; there's also a good notice board and internet access ($3 for 1hr).

City transport

The city centre is compact and flat, making walking an easy option, but if the heat becomes too much there are **free bus** and **tram** services. The **Terrace to Terrace** (Mon–Fri 8am–6pm, Sat–Sun 9am–6pm) tram service travels between South Terrace and North Terrace – essentially right through the heart of the city centre every 7 minutes 30 seconds Mon–Fri and every 15 minutes Sat–Sun. The **City Loop Bus** (#99C, Mon–Thurs 8am–6pm, Fri 8am–9.30pm, Sat 8.15am–5.45pm, Sun 10.15am–5.45pm) takes in all the city's major cultural and commercial centres, beginning at Adelaide Train Station. Buses run every 15 minutes during the week and every 30 minutes on weekends and Friday after 6.15pm.

To explore further out of the city centre, you'll need to use the integrated **Adelaide Metro system**, which comprises buses, suburban trains and one tramline from the city to Glenelg. Metro buses and trains run until about 11.30pm, with reduced services at night and on Sundays, while the **After Midnight** night-bus service operates Saturday nights (from around 12.30–5am). The **O-Bahn** is a fast-track bus that runs on concrete tracks through scenic Torrens Linear Park, between the city (Grenfell St) and Tea Tree Plaza in Modbury, 12km northeast. Four suburban train lines run from Adelaide Train Station, west to Grange and Outer Harbour and south to Noarlunga and Belair. The **tram** to seaside Glenelg (every 15–20min; 30min; $2.30–3.80, depending on the time of day) leaves from Victoria Square.

Information on all of the above services as well as free timetables can be found at **Adelaide Metro Info Centre**, on the corner of King William and Currie streets (Mon–Fri 8am–6pm, Sat 9am–5pm, Sun 11am–4pm; ⓦwww .adelaidemetro.com.au); staff also sell tickets and hand out copies of *The Metroguide*, a free information booklet including a handy map of the system. You can also get transport information on ⓣ08/8210 1000 (daily 7am–8pm).

Tickets for the Metro system come in single-trip, multi-trip and day-trip permutations, and can be used on buses, trains and the tram; if you need to use more than one form of transport for a single journey, one ticket will suffice. Single tickets range in price from $1.70 to $4.20, depending on the time of day, and are valid for two hours. You can buy single-journey tickets from machines on board trains, buses and trams, as well as from train-station ticket offices and the Adelaide Metro Info Centre. Other types of ticket, including the day-trip ticket ($8), can be bought from the Adelaide Metro Info Centre, train stations, post offices and some newsagents – look for the Metroticket sign.

Cycling is a popular and excellent alternative to public transport: the wide streets and level surfaces make riding a breeze, and there are several good cycling routes – including the Torrens Linear Park track, which weaves along the river from the sea at Westbeach to the hills at Athelston. Bike SA has an overview of all cycling routes and **maps**; they also rent out bikes (see "Listings", p.772).

Accommodation

Adelaide has a fantastic choice of accommodation, from contemporary boutique hotels to charming B&Bs, as well as loads of **hostels**. B&Bs (and farm stays) can be booked through ⓦwww.bandfsa.com.au which has over 150 places on their books. Hostels outside the centre will pick you up from the bus or train station if you phone ahead (several also send minibuses to scout for custom), and some offer airport pick-ups. There are lots of **hotel** rooms and serviced apartments on Hindley Street, Adelaide's nightclub area, while the swankiest accommodation is along **North Terrace**. The only time you may have difficulty finding accommodation is during March, when the annual **Womadelaide** festival and the **Arts Festival** (even-numbered years only) attract throngs of visitors. Rooms also fill up quickly at weekends, at both hotels and the more popular hostels around the Central Bus Station on Franklin Street and Waymouth Street.

The seaside suburb of **Glenelg** and the nearby beach resorts (see p.764), about half an hour away from Adelaide by public transport, are good alternatives to the city centre, with plenty of self-catering apartments and one of Adelaide's liveliest hostels.

City centre

Hotels, motels and pubs

Austral Hotel 205 Rundle St ☏ 08/8223 4660, ⓦwww.theaustral.com. Basic rooms in one of Adelaide's best pubs on this happening street. There are bands or DJs nearly every night, so it can be noisy. ❸–❹

Breakfree on Hindley 255 Hindley St ☏ 08/8217 2500, ⓦwww.savillehotelgroup.com. These great-value studio, one- and two-bedroom apartments have fully equipped kitchens and internet access. There's parking, a bistro, and it's handy to the club area. ❹–❺

🏃 **Clarion Soho** 264 Flinders St ☏ 08/8412 5600, ⓦwww.clarionhotelsoho.com.au. This intimate boutique hotel has stylish rooms, chic Italian designer furniture, art on the walls, broadband internet, LCD televisions and iPod docking stations, as well as one of Adelaide's best new restaurants, *Decant*. ❺–❼

Franklin Central Apartments 36 Franklin St, corner of Betham St ☏ 08/8221 7050, ⓦwww .franklinapartments.com.au. Fully serviced one-, two- and three-bedroom apartments in a good location, aimed at business travellers, but ideal for extended stays. ❺–❻

Hilton Adelaide 233 Victoria Square ☏ 08/8217 2000, ⓦwww.hilton.com. Centrally located, this luxury high-rise hotel boasts super-spacious, contemporary rooms with all mod cons and stunning city views, as well as one of the city's finest restaurants. Good online rates. ❼–❾

🏃 **Hotel Richmond** 128 Rundle Mall ☏ 08/8215 4444, ⓕ 8232 2290, ⓦwww .hotelrichmond.com.au. Ideally placed for shoppers, this idiosyncratically designed hotel has sleek contemporary rooms, a fabulous restaurant-bar-lounge, *First*, decorated with funky ottomans, Rajasthan furniture, billowing drapes and mirrors, and a terrace overlooking Rundle Mall. The suites on the top floors are truly special. There's a DJ some evenings. ❻–❼

Majestic Roof Garden Hotel 55 Frome St ☏ 08/8100 4499, ⓦwww.majestichotels.com.au. This smart property offers well-appointed contemporary rooms and suites with good amenities including internet access, at surprisingly affordable rates. Facilities include gym and a rooftop garden with wonderful city views. ❻–❽

Mercure Grosvenor 125 North Terrace ☏ 08/8407 8888 or 1800 888 222, ⓦwww .mercuregrosvenorhotel.com.au. Dating from 1918, this historic building houses a comfortable hotel with spacious, modern rooms with internet access. There's a gym and sauna, bar and bistro, and parking. ❻–❼

Oaks Horizons 104 North Terrace ☏ 08/8210 8000 or 1300 721 916, ⓦwww.theoaksgroup .com.au. These modern, self-catering apartments have balconies. Great city or river views from those on the top floor. Facilities include pool, spa and gym. ❻–❼

Stamford Plaza Adelaide 150 North Terrace ☏ 08/8461 1111, ⓦwww.stamford.com.au. This central hotel has comfortable rooms, swimming pool, sauna and restaurants, and views of the Festival Centre. Cheaper weekend rates available. ❼

Hostels

Adelaide Backpackers Inn 112 Carrington St ☏ 08/8223 6635 or 1800 247 725, ⓦwww .adelaidebackpackersinn.net.au. Shabby place in a converted pub, with a friendly ambience and helpful staff. Generous breakfast thrown in and internet access available. There's a travel service at reception selling bus and train tickets. Dorm accommodation only, $24.

Adelaide Central YHA 135 Waymouth St ☏ 08/8414 3010, ⓦwww.yha.com.au. Modern and efficient youth hostel with over two hundred beds in the city centre. There are well-equipped kitchens, a large laundry, lockers, a travel centre and internet access. Some off-street parking spaces can be reserved. Dorms $24–26, rooms ❸

Backpack Oz 144 Wakefield St, corner of Pulteney St ☏ & ℻ 8223 3551, ⓦwww .backpackoz.com.au. Converted from a nineteenth-century hotel, this low-key hostel has light, spacious rooms, dorms (four-, six- and ten-bed) and a guesthouse. There's a comfortable common room plus a laundry and small kitchen. Pick-ups

from bus, train and airport, and tour bookings available. Dorms $22–24, rooms ❸

Sunny's 139 Franklin St ☏ 08/8231 2430 or 1800 631 391, ⓦwww.sunnys.com.au. A friendly place in an old house next to the bus station. Facilities include a pool table, sound system, TV and video, and train, bus and plane tickets are sold and tours booked. There's cheap internet access, plus off-street parking. Rates include tea, coffee and breakfast. Dorms $24, rooms ❷

North Adelaide and Kent Town

Majestic Old Lion & Tynte Street Apartments 9 Jerningham St, North Adelaide ☏ 1800 779 919 ⓦwww.majestichotels.com.au. Set around a leafy landscaped courtyard, these spacious suites and apartments can accommodate up to seven people and have kitchens and laundry facilities, making them ideal for long stays. ❺–❻

Minima Hotel 146 Melbourne St ☏ 08/8334 7766, ⓦwww.majestichotels .com.au. This chic, contemporary self-check-in hotel (there are no staff on site) boasts snug, stylish rooms that are Adelaide's best-value ($99)

for such brilliant amenities: LCD television, broadband internet, kingsize bed, tea and coffee facilities, and mini-ironing board and iron. There's also a guest laundry, parking, vending machine in the foyer, and lovely rooftop area. ❹

Norwood Apartments 7 Wakefield St, Kent Town ☏ 08/8338 6555, ℻ 8336 4555, ⓦwww .norwoodapartments.com.au. Five self-contained two-person units, each containing kitchen facilities, washing machine, TV, video and CD player. Good value and convenient location. ❹

Beach suburbs

Glenelg Beach Hostel 1–7 Moseley St, Glenelg ☏ 08/8376 0007 or 1800 066 422, ⓦwww .glenelgbeachhostel.com.au. Award-winning hostel near the beach, located in a beautiful building with high ceilings and veranda. Lots of doubles as well as five- to six-bed dorms (no bunks). The lively common area downstairs has a popular bar open to the public, with occasional live music. Both the daily breakfast and weekend BBQ are included. Dorms $27, rooms ❸

Glenelg Jetty Hotel 28 Jetty Rd, Glenelg ☏ 08/8294 4377, ℻ 8295 4412. When all other options have failed, this friendly, homely pub accommodation – popular with country people visiting the city – has basic rooms. A warning: it gets noisy. ❹

Oaks Plaza Pier Hotel 16 Holdfast Promenade ☏ 08/8350 6688, ⓦwww.theoaksgroup.com.au. These sleek contemporary suites come with private balconies affording unspoilt ocean views and have

all the comforts you'd expect. Facilities include a pool, gym, spa and sauna. ❼–❾

Seawall Apartments 21–25 South Esplanade, Glenelg ☏ 08/8295 1197, ⓦwww .seawallapartments.com.au. Opposite the ocean and spread across several grand old buildings that are now chic self-contained apartments, this place oozes charm – the exterior's eccentric maritime decor (for one, there's an enormous old fishing boat dominating the courtyard) reflecting the tastes of the old sailor who owns the property, and the stylish interiors that of his daughter. ❺–❽

Taft Motor Inn 18 Moseley St, Glenelg ☏ 08/8376 1233, ⓦwww.taftmotorinn.com.au. Well-equipped if drab motel units and spacious one- and two-bedroom self-catering apartments near the beach; all have a/c, microwave and TV. The playground, garden, swimming pool (and toddler pool) and babysitting make it a good choice for families. ❺

Camping and caravan parks

All caravan parks need to be booked well ahead of time during school holidays, especially summer.

Adelaide Beachfront Tourist Park 349 Military Rd, Semaphore Park ☏ 08/8449 7726,

ⓦwww.adelaidebeachfront.com.au. A lovely seaside location with swimming pool, recreation room, playground and a free shuttle-bus service to West Lakes Mall and Ethelton train station. Un/powered sites $21/29, Cabins [4]–[7]

Adelaide Caravan Park 46 Richmond St, Hackney, on the Torrens River 2km northeast of the centre ☎08/8363 1566, 🌐www.adelaidecaravanpark.com.au. The most central option, right on the Torrens Linear Park cycling route, reachable by bus #281 or #282 from North Terrace, or on foot through parkland and along the river. Un/powered sites $22/28, cabins & units [4]–[6], villas [5]–[7]

Adelaide Shores Caravan Resort 1 Military Rd, West Beach ☎08/8355 7320, 🌐www.adelaideshores.com.au. Wonderful beach-front setting with lots of grass, heated pool, barbecues. Take bus #276 or #278 from Currie St. Un/powered sites $21/29, cabins [4]–[6]

The City

Adelaide's city centre is laid out on a strict grid plan surrounded by parkland: at the heart of the grid is **Victoria Square**, and each city quarter is centred on its own smaller square. **North Terrace** is the cultural precinct, home to the city's major museums, two universities and the state library. **Hindley Street** is the liveliest in town, and the focus of the city's nightlife, while **Rundle Mall**, its continuation, is the main shopping area; **Rundle Street**, further east, is home to the city's arty café strip, with hip boutiques, bars and pubs, and casual restaurants. West of Victoria Square between **Grote** and **Gouger** streets is the lively **Central Market** and the small **Chinatown**. The **Torrens River** flows to the north of North Terrace, with the Botanic Gardens and zoo set on its south bank. Three main roads cross the river to the distinctive colonial architecture and café culture of **North Adelaide**.

Adelaide suffered numerous economic setbacks and built up its wealth slowly, and its well-preserved **Victorian architecture** has a reassuring permanence quite unlike the over-the-top style of 1850s Melbourne, with its grandiose municipal buildings funded by easy goldrush money. The bourgeois solidity of Adelaide's streets is enhanced by the fact that virtually every building, public or domestic, is made of **stone**, whether sandstone, bluestone, South Australian freestone or slate.

The Botanic Gardens and Ayers House

There's really only one place to start your tour, and that's tree-lined **North Terrace**, a long heritage streetscape perfect for exploring on foot. At its eastern extremity is the main entrance to the impressive **Botanic Gardens** (Mon–Fri 8am–dusk, Sat & Sun 9am–dusk; free guided tours operate daily from the visitor centre at 10.30am; 🌐www.botanicgardens.sa.gov.au). Opened in 1857, the lovely gardens boast ponds, fountains, wisteria arbours, statues and heritage buildings just like a classic English-style garden, but with plenty of native trees too. The elegant glass-and-wrought-iron **Palm House**, completed in 1877, was based on a similar building in Germany and used to display tropical plant species, a role now taken over by the stunning **Bicentennial Conservatory** (daily 10am–4pm, summer until 5pm; $5). This, the largest glasshouse in Australia, houses a complete tropical rainforest environment with its own computer-controlled cloud-making system. Other attractions include a fragrant herb garden, a rose garden and **Simpson House**, a pleasantly cool thatched hut containing palms and ferns beside a stream. The **visitor centre** (daily 10am–4pm) is located in the centre of the park and has a shop selling books on botany and gardening, plus other souvenirs and a lovely café next door.

Heading away from the gardens at 288 North Terrace, the first notable building you come to is the National Trust–owned **Ayers House** (☎08/8223 1234,

Tues–Fri 10am–4pm, Sat & Sun 1–4pm; $8). Home to the politician **Henry Ayers**, who was premier of South Australia seven times between 1855 and 1897 and after whom the Rock was named, it began as a small brick dwelling in 1845 – the fine bluestone mansion you now see is the result of thirty years of extensions. Inside, it's elaborately decorated in late nineteenth-century style, with portraits of the Ayers family.

The university and the Art Gallery of South Australia

Between Frome Road and Kintore Avenue, a whole block of North Terrace is occupied by the **University of Adelaide**, and the art gallery, museum and state library. The University of Adelaide, the city's oldest, was established in 1874 and began to admit women right from its founding – another example of South Australia's advanced social thinking. The grounds are pleasant to stroll through: along North Terrace are **Bonython Hall**, built in 1936 in a vaguely medieval style, and **Elder Hall**, an early twentieth-century Gothic-Florentine design now occupied by the **Conservatorium of Music** (concerts Fri 1.10pm; $6.50; ℡ 08/8303 5925, ⓦ www.music.adelaide.edu.au).

Overbearing Victorian busts of the upright founders of Adelaide line the strip between Bonython Hall and Kintore Avenue until you reach the **Art Gallery of South Australia**, established in 1881 (daily 10am–5pm; free daily guided tours 11am & 2pm; free lunchtime talks on exhibits Tues 12.45pm; free; ℡ 08/8207 7000, ⓦ www.artgallery.sa.gov.au). The gallery has an impressive collection of **Aboriginal art**, including many non-traditional works with overtly political content; major works by the **Western Desert school** of Aboriginal artists are on permanent display in Gallery 7. There's a fine selection of colonial art, too, and it's interesting to trace the development of Australian art from its European-inspired beginnings up to the point where the influence of the local light, colours and landscape begin to take over. The collection of twentieth-century Australian art includes works by Sidney Nolan, Margaret Preston and Grace Cossington-Smith. There's also a large collection of twentieth-century **British art**, including paintings by Roger Fry and Vanessa Bell (Virginia Woolf's sister). The gallery has an excellent bookshop and coffee shop too.

The South Australian Museum, State Library and Migration Museum

Next to the art gallery, a huge whale skeleton guards the entrance to the **South Australian Museum** (daily 10am–5pm; tours Mon–Fri 11am, Sat & Sun 2pm & 3pm; free; ℡ 08/8207 7377, ⓦ www.samuseum.sa.gov.au). The museum's east wing houses the engrossing **Australian Aboriginal Cultures Gallery** (40min guided tours Wed–Sun; $10; book at the museum shop or on ℡ 08/8207 7370), home to the world's largest collection of Aboriginal artefacts. Amongst the exhibits are a 10,000-year-old boomerang and the *Yanardilyi (Cockatoo Creek) Jukurrpa*, a huge painting by a collection of artists from across the continent recalling four important Dreaming stories.

The west wing focuses on **natural history** and **geology**, including an extensive collection of minerals from around the world. There's also a permanent exhibition on local geologist **Sir Douglas Mawson** (1882–1958), who was commissioned by the museum to explore much of Australia in the early 1900s and who undertook the historic Australasian Antarctic Expedition in 1911. Some of the animals he brought back from this expedition are still on display, along with others from around Australia. The **fossil gallery** includes a skeleton of *Diprotodon*, the largest marsupial ever to walk the earth, plus the Normandy Nugget (at the east wing entrance on the ground floor), the second-largest gold nugget in the world, weighing 26kg. For those wishing to gain a more comprehensive understanding of the museum's treasures, the **Science Centre** (Mon–Fri 10am–4pm) holds the museum archives (booking essential: ☎08/8207 7500) as well as the entire Douglas Mawson Collection.

Next door to the museum, on the corner of Kintore Avenue, the 1884 **State Library** (Mon–Wed 10am–8pm, Thurs & Fri 10am–6pm, Sat & Sun 10am–5pm; ☎08/8207 7250, ⓦwww.slsa.sa.gov.au) has everything from archives to newspaper- and magazine-reading rooms and free internet access.

Around the corner at 82 Kintore Ave is the **Migration Museum** (Mon–Fri 10am–5pm, Sat & Sun 1–5pm; free; ☎08/8207 7570, ⓦwww.history.sa.gov .au), which takes you on a journey from port to settlement in the company of South Australia's settlers, through innovative, interactive displays and reconstructions – the "White Australia Walk" has a push-button questionnaire to allow you to see if you would have been allowed to immigrate under the guidelines of the **White Australia policy**, which was in force from 1901 to 1958.

The government buildings and arts spaces

Continue west along North Terrace, past the War Memorial, to reach **Government House**, Adelaide's oldest public building, completed in 1855: every governor except the first has lived here. Across King William Road, two parliament houses, the old and the new, compete for space. The current **Parliament House**, begun in 1889, wasn't finished until 1939 because of a dispute over a dome, and while there's still no dome (and only half a coat of arms), it's a stately building all the same, with a facade of marble columns. Alongside is the modest **Old Parliament House** (closed to the public), built between 1855 and 1876.

On the corner of North Terrace and Morphett Street, the **Lion Arts Centre** is home to theatres, bars, a cinema, galleries and the **Experimental Art Foundation**, which houses artists' studios upstairs and provocative exhibitions in the gallery downstairs (gallery Tues–Fri 11am–5pm, Sat 2–5pm). A short stroll south of here to 19 Morphett St, the **Jam Factory Craft and Design Centre** (Mon–Thurs 9.30am–5.30pm, Fri 9.30am–9.30pm, Sat 1–5pm, Sun 1–5pm; ⓦwww .jamfactory.com.au) displays beautiful objects made of ceramic, metal, leather, glass, wood and clay, with exhibition areas, retail galleries, a shop, and studios where you can view artisans at work. A block west of here is the latest addition to Adelaide's contemporary art scene, the **Light Square Gallery** (Mon–Fri 10am–5pm; free) in the basement of the Roma Mitchell Arts Education Centre on Light Square. The focus here is on contemporary art in the digital age.

Along the Torrens River

The **Torrens River** meanders between central Adelaide and North Adelaide, surrounded by parklands. Between Parliament House and the river is the **Festival Centre**, two geometric constructions of concrete, steel and smoked glass, in a concrete arena scattered with abstract 1970s civic sculpture. The main auditorium, the **Festival Theatre** (ⓦwww.adelaidefestivalcentre.com.au), has the largest stage in the southern hemisphere, hosting opera, ballet and various concerts; the foyer is often the venue for **free Sunday-afternoon concerts**. The smaller Playhouse Theatre is the drama theatre, while the Space Theatre is used for cabaret and stand-up comedy.

A short walk across **Elder Park** is the river, with its stunning fountain and black swans. **Popeye Cruises** leave from here for the zoo (Mon–Fri 1–3pm hourly, Sat & Sun 11am–5pm every 20min; more frequent during holidays; $6 one–way, $10 return), and you can rent paddleboats ($10 per 30min). Nearby, the green shed at **Jolleys Boathouse**, across King William Road, is an Adelaide institution, housing a popular restaurant (see p.766) and cheaper kiosk, both with river views.

The most pleasant way to get to **Adelaide Zoo**, whose main entrance is on Frome Road (daily 9.30am–5pm; free guided walks at 11am & 2pm; $20, children $12; call ☏08/8267 3255 for feeding times and keeper talks, ⊛www .adelaidezoo.com.au), is to follow the river, either by boat (see above) or on foot, a fifteen-minute stroll. Alternatively, walk from the **Botanic Gardens** through Botanic Park, entering through the children's zoo entrance on Plane Tree Drive, or take bus #271 or #273 from Grenfell or Currie streets. Opened in 1883, the country's second-oldest zoo (after Melbourne's) is full of century-old European and native trees, including a huge **Moreton Bay fig**, as well as being provided with picnic tables. The Victorian architecture here is well preserved, and a few classic examples of the old-fashioned animal houses have survived, such as the **Elephant House**, built in 1900 in the style of an Indian temple. The zoo is best known for its extensive collection of **native birds**, with two large walk-through aviaries, while the Southeast Asian Rainforest exhibit has naturalistic settings that are home to sixteen animal species, including the endangered Malaysian tapir.

King William Street and Victoria Square

The city's main thoroughfare, **King William Street**, is lined with imposing civic buildings and always crowded with traffic. Look out for the **Edmund Wright House** at no. 59, whose elaborate Renaissance-style facade is one of Adelaide's most flamboyant. Inside the building, the **State History Centre** (Mon–Fri 9am–4.30pm) sometimes hosts free travelling exhibitions. On the other side of the street a couple of blocks south, the **Town Hall** (1866) is another of Edmund Wright's Italianate designs. The **General Post Office**, on the corner of Franklin Street, is yet another portentous Victorian edifice, this time with a central clock-tower: look inside at the main hall with its decorative roof lantern framed by opaque skylights. Opposite, on the corner of Flinders Street, the **Old Treasury Building** retains its beautiful facade, although it now houses apartments.

Halfway down King William Street lies pleasant **Victoria Square**, a favourite Aboriginal meeting place and home to the **Catholic Cathedral of St Francis Xavier** (1856) and the imposing **Supreme Court**, on the corner of Gouger Street. Just to the west, the covered **Central Market** (Tues 7am–5.30pm, Thurs 11am–5.30pm, Fri 7am–9pm, Sat 7am–3pm) has been a well-loved feature of Adelaide for over a hundred years. Here you can find delectable fresh produce in a riot of stalls and lively banter, as well as heaps of shops and cafés, and, adjoining the market, a superb **Asian food hall** (see p.765) with sushi and noodle bars. Nearby Gouger and Grote streets also have a fantastic array of options for a meal, drink or coffee.

Rundle Mall and Rundle Street

The main shopping area in the central business district is the pedestrianized **Rundle Mall**, which manages to be bustling yet relaxed, enhanced by trees, benches, alfresco cafés, fruit and flower stalls, and usually a busker or two. The two main shopping centres are the **Myer Centre**, with over 120 speciality stores over five floors, and the **Adelaide Central Plaza**, dominated by the upmarket **David Jones** department store with a fantastic foodmart in the basement. Towards the east end of the mall is the decorative **Adelaide Arcade** and the **Regent Theatre**. By night, Rundle Mall is quiet, a strange contrast to Hindley and Rundle streets on either side, which really come to life after dark. On Sundays, from 9am to 4pm, however, the mall comes alive with the Rundle Street Market, when stalls take over the street at the East End, and the cafés, bars and pubs really buzz.

Rundle Street was once the home of Adelaide's wholesale fruit and vegetable market, but was later appropriated by the alternative and arty, and by university students from the nearby campuses on North Terrace. It's now home to dozens of **cafés** and **restaurants**, many of them with alfresco seating, several slick wine bars and two of the best pubs in town (*The Austral* and *The Exeter*, see p.769). The disused **Adelaide Fruit and Produce Exchange** (1903) is also worth a peek: it's a classically Edwardian building built of red brick, with curved archways decorated with yellow plaster friezes of fruit, vegetables and wheat. The facade has remained, but the interior has been transformed into apartments.

Tandanya: the National Aboriginal Cultural Institute

Tandanya: the National Aboriginal Cultural Institute is situated opposite the classic old market buildings at 253 Grenfell St (daily 10am–5pm; free; ☎08/8224 3200, ⓦwww.tandanya.com.au). The centre is managed by the Kaurna people, the traditional owners of the Adelaide plains area, and its main focus is the visual arts, with a permanent display and temporary exhibitions of significance. Displays cover everything including Dreamtime stories, history and contemporary Aboriginal writing, and political paintings confronting black deaths in custody and the Stolen Generation. There's also a 160-seat theatre for live performances, with daily **didgeridoo** or **dance performances** held Tuesday to Sunday at noon ($5), and a great gift shop.

North Adelaide

North Adelaide, a ten-minute walk from the city centre, makes for an enjoyable stroll past stately mansions and small, bluestone cottages, or a good pub crawl around the many old hotels. The best walking route to North Adelaide is up King William Road past the Festival Centre (if you are feeling lazy, nearly every bus from outside the Festival Centre also goes this way). From Elder Park you cross the pretty 1874 **Adelaide Bridge** over the river to Cresswell Gardens, home of the **Adelaide Oval** cricket ground (guided tour April–Sept Mon–Fri 10am; Oct–March Tues & Thurs 2pm except match days; 2hr; $10). Cricket fans shouldn't miss the sleek new **Bradman Collection Museum** (daily 9.30am–4.30pm; free; ⓦwww.cricketsa.com .au), at Adelaide Oval, War Memorial Drive, which follows the progress of Sir Donald Bradman, Australia's greatest cricketer and the world's greatest batsman, documenting his rise to hero status in the 1930s. The museum displays his personal collection of cricket memorabilia, including his own memoirs of the infamous Bodyline series with England, and films feature interviews and footage of his finest moments.

The oval affords superb views of **St Peter's Cathedral** (daily 9.15am–4pm; free guided tours Wed 11am & Sun 2.30pm) on Pennington Terrace. This Anglican cathedral was built in 1869 in the French Gothic-Revival style, with an entrance suggestive of Notre-Dame in Paris. The *Cathedral Hotel* opposite, built in 1850, is Adelaide's second-oldest hotel. At the top of King William Road, the peaceful and shady **Brougham Gardens** boast palm trees set against the backdrop of the Adelaide Hills. If you continue straight up, you'll come to North Adelaide's main commercial strip, **O'Connell Street**, whose restaurant scene rivals that of Rundle Street.

The district's best range of early **colonial architecture** lies a block west of here along **Jeffcott Street**. Just south of here in Montefiore Park is **Light's Vision**, a bronze statue of Colonel William Light pointing proudly to the city he designed. On Jeffcott Street itself is the neo-Gothic 1890 mansion **Carclew**, with its round turret, and the **Lutheran Theological College**, a fine bluestone and red-brick building with a clock tower and cast-iron decoration. Halfway up the street, on peaceful **Wellington Square**, lies the pretty 1851 *Wellington Hotel*, complete with its original wooden balcony. Turning into tree-lined **Gover Street** you'll find rows of simple bluestone cottages; in contrast, **Barton Terrace West**, two blocks north, has grand homes facing parklands.

East of O'Connell Street is **Melbourne Street** (buses #207, #208 or #209 from King William St, and #271 or #273 from Currie and Grenfell sts), an **upmarket strip** of cafés, antique stores, restaurants, designer clothing boutiques and speciality shops. The **Banana Room**, at no. 125, is probably the best retro-chic clothes store in Australia, with an immaculate range of designer dresses from the 1920s through to the 1950s. Don't expect bargains – most things are over $100 – but it's fascinating to browse.

The suburbs

Adelaide's **suburbs** spread a long way, and though they remain little visited, some of the inner suburbs – such as **Norwood** and **Thebarton** – have plenty of local character, inexpensive restaurants and out-of-the-ordinary shopping that's worth venturing out of the city centre for. West of the city lies a string of beaches, from **Henley** via **Glenelg** to **Brighton**, sheltered by the Gulf St Vincent. Further north, **Port Adelaide** has some excellent museums to set off its dockside atmosphere.

Norwood, Thebarton and Unley

Norwood, just east of the city, has two interesting streets: **Magill Road** (bus #106 from Grenfell or Currie sts), with a concentration of antique shops, and **The Parade** (bus #122–125 from Grenfell or Currie st), a lively shopping strip with some great cafés, pubs and bookshops. The small **Orange Lane Market** (Sat & Sun 10am–5pm), at the corner of Edward Street and The Parade, is a sedate place to browse among secondhand and new clothes, books and bric-a-brac, or eat at Asian food stalls.

In **Thebarton**, west of the city, the lively **Brickworks Market** (Fri–Sun 9am–5pm; bus #110–113 from Grenfell or Currie sts) spreads out from the 1912 Brickworks Kilns at 36 South Rd. There are plaza shops and indoor and outdoor stalls, mostly selling new clothes, and it's always busy with buskers and crowds of people.

Immediately south of the city, **Unley Road** (buses #190–199 from King William St) is known for its antique shops and expensive boutiques. The parallel King William Road at Hyde Park (bus #203 from King William St) is shaded by lots of trees, plants and vine-covered awnings, and has some good cafés to relax in.

Port Adelaide and Torrens Island

The unfortunate early settlers had to wade through swamps when they arrived at Port Misery, but thanks to William Light's visionary flair, **Port Adelaide** became the primary gateway to the state. Established not far from Port Misery in 1840, by 1870 it had become a substantial shipping area with solid stone warehouses, wharves and a host of pubs. The area bounded by Nelson, St Vincent and Todd streets and McLaren Parade is a well-preserved nineteenth-century streetscape; several ships' chandlers and shipping agents show that it's still a living port, a fact confirmed by the many corner pubs (with pretty decorative iron-lace balconies) still in business.

The **visitor centre**, near the waterfront at 66 Commercial Rd on the corner of St Vincent Street (daily 9am–5pm; ☎08/8405 6560), provides up-to-date details of attractions, cruises, themed guided walking tours and self-guided history-focused walks; the *Port Adelaide Enfield Museum Trail* is a must for museum fans, while the more "experiential" *Heritage Pub Trail* is loads of fun. To get here, take a **train** from Adelaide Train Station or bus #151 or #153 from North Terrace.

The best day to visit is Sunday or public-holiday Mondays, when the **Sunday Markets** (9am–5pm) take over a large waterfront warehouse near the Port Adelaide Lighthouse on Queens Wharf. Specializing in books and bric-a-brac, the market adds life to the waterfront. When you're hungry, try one of Adelaide's famous meat pies with peas from one of the many purveyors who set up. The quaint metal **lighthouse** (Mon–Fri 10am–2pm, Sun 10am–5pm), dating from 1869, can be seen as part of a visit to the South Australian Maritime Museum (see below), as can the museum's two floating vessels moored 300m away, the steam tug *Yelta* and the coastal trader *Nelcebee*.

The pick of Port Adelaide's several museums is the **South Australian Maritime Museum**, located in the old Bond Store at 126 Lipson St (daily 10am–5pm; $9; ⓦ www.history.sa.gov.au), with both temporary and permanent exhibitions tracing the connection South Australia has with the sea. Further along Lipson Street, the **National Railway Museum** (daily 10am–5pm; $12; ⓦ www.natrailmuseum.org.au) is a trainspotter's delight, with a collection of over twenty steam and diesel locomotives. The museum operates the historic Semaphore to Fort Glanville Tourist Railway on weekends and holidays, between noon and 4pm, frequencies on demand.

A few kilometres north of Port Adelaide is **Torrens Island**. Apart from a lively fresh seafood and produce market on Sunday (6am–1pm), its main attraction is its intricate **mangrove forests**. This tranquil habitat rich in marine life can be explored on foot on the **St Kilda Mangrove Trail** (Mon–Fri 10am–4pm, Sat & Sun 10am–5pm; $6.90; booking essential on ☎08/8280 8172), which has an interpretive centre and a 1.7-kilometre boardwalk for self-guided tours; or by **kayak** with Blue Water Sea Kayaking (self-guided tour $35 for 2hr; booking essential; ☎08/8295 8812, ⓦ www.adventurekayak.com.au), giving the chance to spot Port River dolphins along the way.

Semaphore to Henley Beach

On the coast just west of Port Adelaide, **Semaphore**, with its picturesque jetty and many grand heritage buildings, was important as the site of Adelaide's signal station from 1856, but it was George Coppin who named the place after establishing a fine old timber pub on the edge of the sand hills. With the establishment of the rail line here in 1878, boarding houses, carnivals, sideshows, tearooms and an open-air cinema were built, and Semaphore became Adelaide's most desirable holiday resort until the tram service ceased in 1935 and its popularity started to dwindle. Its current incarnation is as a popular **gay and lesbian area** (see box, p.770), with several gay- and lesbian-run cafés and a pub on **Semaphore Road**, a charming street running at right angles to the beach, with historic buildings with awnings and stained-glass windows, charming shops, good bookstores and a historic cinema. In the summer a steam train runs once a month from Semaphore Jetty to **Fort Glanville** at 359 Military Rd (Sept–May every third Sun 1–5pm; $6), the only complete example of the many forts built in Australia in the mid-nineteenth century, when fear of Russian invasion reached hysterical heights after the Crimean War. To get to Semaphore from the city centre by public transport, take a #151 or #153 from North Terrace to Port Adelaide, then catch bus #330 or #333; from Glenelg take the #340 (Mon–Fri only).

About 8km south of Semaphore, **Grange** is a charming beachside suburb, with a row of Victorian terraced houses facing the sands and a popular pier with an upmarket kiosk. Take bus #110 from Grenfell Street (30min) or a Grange line train (20min). The next beach along is atmospheric **Henley Beach**, where the focus is **Henley Square**, opposite the long wooden pier. The square is lined with classic Federation-style buildings housing several popular restaurants and cafés (Mon–Sat bus #137, Sun #130, both 20min from Currie St; #286 or #287 from North Terrace, 35min).

Glenelg and Brighton

The most popular and easily accessible of the city's beaches is **Glenelg**, 11km southwest of the city. Travel here by tram from Victoria Square (25min), or take bus #167 or #168 from Currie or Grenfell streets. Glenelg was the site of the landing of **Governor John Hindmarsh** and the first colonists on Holdfast Bay; the **Old Gum Tree** where he read the proclamation establishing the government of the colony still stands on McFarlane Street, and there's a re-enactment here every year on Proclamation Day (Dec 28).

Holidaymakers have been parading along Glenelg's seaside promenade for over 160 years and nowadays Glenelg still has the atmosphere of a busy holiday town, even in off-season. **Jetty Road**, the main drag, is crowded with casual places to eat (for the obligatory seaside fish and chips, try the *Bay Fish Shop* at no. 27 or the award-winning *The Oyster Shop* at no. 40, which is probably one of the few takeaways that serves beer and wine), while **Marina Pier** (Ⓦwww .marinapier.com.au) at the northern end of Holdfast Promenade is home to a dozen bars, cafés and seaside restaurants, such as *Sammy's* (see p.767). There's lots of **accommodation** (see p.756). The tram terminates at **Moseley Square**, dominated by the imposing **Glenelg Town Hall** and clock tower. At the opposite corner, the original *Victorian Pier Hotel*, now part of the imposing seafront *Stamford Grand Hotel*, is crowded with drinkers on Sunday, when Glenelg is at its most vibrant. From Moseley Square, the old jetty juts out into the bay, and in summer the beach is crowded with people swimming; it's a popular windsurfing spot year-round.

Glenelg Town Hall is home to the **Bay Discovery Centre** (daily 10am–3pm; by donation; Ⓣ08/8179 9508, Ⓦwww.baydiscovery.com.au), a wonderful social history museum documenting stories of life by the sea through the use of multimedia and archival images, and covering everything from old seaside amusements from the 1930s to changing beach fashions. Just around the corner and facing the shore, **Glenelg Visitor Centre** (Mon–Fri 9.30am–4.30pm, Sat 9.30am–3pm, Sun 10am–2pm; Ⓣ08/8294 5833, Ⓦwww.coastaladelaide.com .au) can book accommodation, tours and rental cars, and has some self-guided walking trail brochures; there's a 24-hour touch-screen information terminal outside. Beach volleyball, jogging and cycling are popular activities in Glenelg, with a **bike track** south of the square. Hostels rent or loan bikes.

South of Glenelg, **Brighton** has an old-fashioned, sleepy air, dominated by the stone **Arch of Remembrance**, flanked by palm trees, which stands in front of the long jetty. Running inland from the beach, **Jetty Road** has a string of appealing one- and two-storey buildings shaded with awnings that contain an assortment of art, craft and secondhand stores, and two popular alfresco cafés: *A Cafe Etc* and *Horta's*. Brighton can be reached by train from Adelaide (25min) or bus #265 from Grote Street. For beaches further south, see p.786.

Eating

Eating out is a local obsession in Adelaide, and one of the city's most popular places for a meal is **Gouger Street** – many of the restaurants have outdoor tables and are at their busiest on Friday night, when the nearby **Central Market** stays open until 9pm. **Moonta Street**, right next to Central Market, is the home of Adelaide's small **Chinatown**, and has several Chinese restaurants and supermarkets, while the excellent **food plaza** off Moonta Street (Mon 11am–2.30pm, Tues–Thurs 11am–4pm, Fri 11am–9pm, Sat 7am–3pm) serves Chinese, Vietnamese, Indian, Singaporean, Thai and Malaysian food. **Hutt Street**, on the eastern edge of the city, has a string of fine Italian eateries and is a good place to go for breakfast. Café society is based around **Rundle Street** in the centre, and **O'Connell Street** and **Melbourne Street** in North Adelaide. In Adelaide, eating in pubs doesn't just mean the usual steak and salad bar but covers the whole spectrum, from some fine contemporary Australian food in the commercial centre to bargain specials in several pubs along **King William Street**.

Thanks to the state's liberal licensing laws most cafés are **licensed**, with South Australian wine featuring heavily.

City centre

Cafés

Al Fresco Gelateria & Pasticceria 260 Rundle St. Packed every night, largely with Italian-Australians, this is the place to people-watch, while sipping superb coffee, biscotti, delicious home-made *gelati* and focaccia. Daily 6.30am until late.

Cowley's Franklin St. An Adelaide institution that's famous for its pie floaters, this mobile pie-cart takes its position each night. Sun–Thurs 6pm–1am, Fri & Sat 6pm–3.30am.

Zuma 56 Gouger St. Locals flock here for the huge breakfasts, big salads, and bruschetta, focaccia and quiche baked on the premises. Mon–Thurs 7am–6pm, Fri 7am–10pm, Sat 7am–4am.

Pubs and wine bars

Bunca at the Austral Hotel 205 Rundle St. The old beer garden here has been transformed into a funky venue with an industrial feel. Main dishes like butter chicken curry or

spinach lasagne go for around $18, and the wine list is largely sourced from SA wineries. Daily lunch & dinner.

Earl of Aberdeen 316 Pulteney St, Hindmarsh Square. Set in a gazebo dripping with greenery, this place serves huge portions of moderately priced, imaginatively cooked pasta, steak, fish and kangaroo. Attentive service too. Open daily from noon until late.

Kings Head Hotel 357 King William St. Wide selection of wines by the glass and inexpensive meals like Thai green curry or simple burgers or steaks. Tasteful interior with plush seats and a dark wooden floor. The rear of the pub doubles as a disco on Fri. Tues–Sun lunch & dinner.

Universal Wine Bar 258 Rundle St ☎08/8232 5000. Stylish casual place with alfresco seating and decent Mod Oz and Italian cooking, including good pizza. Tues–Sun lunch & dinner.

Restaurants

Amalfi Pizzeria Ristorante 29 Frome St ☎08/8223 1948. A local institution, this Italian trattoria and pizzeria offers up moderately priced pasta and pizza, including good vegetarian options. Crowded, and open very late. Closed Sat lunch & Sun.

Assaggio 92–94 King William Rd ☎08/8272 4748. This chic restaurant offers contemporary interpretations of classical Italian dishes, such as Saffron *chitarre* (guitar string pasta) with South Australian blue swimmer crab and roasted tomato and shellfish sauce, and a wine list of over 400 wines, 100 imported from Italy. Lunch Mon–Fri from noon, dinner daily from 6pm to late.

Auge 22 Grote St ☎08/8410 9332. Offering impeccable modern Italian cuisine in stylish surroundings, this award-winning restaurant is one of the city's best. Lunch Tues–Fri noon–3pm, dinner Tues–Sat 6pm–late.

Botanic 310 North Terrace ☎08/8227 0799. A funky Italian family-owned restaurant with mama in the kitchen making the pasta. Aside from the fantastic cuisine, the Botanic has a lovely vibe and some of the best service in town. Closed Sat lunch & Sun.

Chianti Classico 160 Hutt St ☎08/8232 7955. You're in for a special experience at this rustic-chic Italian restaurant, a local favourite with Adelaide's Italian-Australian community, run by a warm and welcoming Italian family. Let the staff guide you on your food and wine selection. Daily lunch and dinner.

Citrus 199 Hutt St ☎08/8224 0100. One of a handful of excellent restaurants on this leafy street, *Citrus* boasts a lovely outdoor eating area, a Mod Oz menu, and unusually for a restaurant of this quality, serves one of the best breakfasts in town, as well as lunch and dinner. Breakfast daily from 7am, lunch from noon, dinner Mon–Sat from 6pm.

Concubine 132 Gouger St ☎08/8212 8288. Gorgeously decorated in a retro Asian style, this fashionable restaurant does delicious contemporary Asian fusion cuisine, such as mussels in brown soybean and chilli sauce with Chivas Regal. Lunch Tues–Fri & Sun noon–2pm, dinner Tues–Sun 6–10pm.

🏃 **Decant** 264 Flinders St ☎08/8412 5600. This tiny restaurant serves some of Adelaide's finest contemporary cuisine with a focus on seasonal regional products, with creative dishes such as ginger beer battered zucchini flowers with Spencer Gulf prawn mousse on salsa verde ($18.50) and snapper carpaccio with cucumber sorbet, chilli, onion seeds, coriander, lime and extra virgin olive oil ($17). Breakfast 7–10am daily, lunch Mon–Fri noon–2.30pm & dinner Mon–Sat 6pm–late.

Eros Ouzeri 275–277 Rundle St ☎08/8223 4022. The speciality is delicious Greek *meze* and traditional dishes like *saganaki, souvlaki* and *moussaka*, dished up in a light and airy room in a renovated old building with high ceilings. The adjoining café serves Greek pastries and coffee. Daily noon until late.

Farina Kitchen & Bar 39 Hindmarsh Square ☎08/8227 1007. This funky restaurant serves up creative seasonal cuisine in contemporary Scandinavian-inspired surroundings. Licensed and BYO. Mon–Fri midday until late.

Gaucho's 91 Gouger St ☎08/8231 2299. Book ahead for this popular Argentinian place, serving some of the best steaks in town, ordered by weight. Licensed and BYO. Daily lunch and dinner.

The Grange *Hilton Adelaide*, 233 Victoria Square ☎08/8217 2000. This celebrated fine-dining restaurant, run by one of Australia's best chefs, Cheong Liew, delivers creative cuisine based on classical French technique. Expensive. Tues–Sat dinner; closed Dec & Jan.

Jasmin 31 Hindmarsh Square ☎08/8223 7837. The menu at this highly regarded North Indian restaurant may not be adventurous, but the food is delicious. Thurs & Fri lunch, Tues–Sat dinner.

Jerusalem Shishkebab House 131B Hindley St. This casual eatery is enormously popular for its excellent Middle East cuisine. BYO. Tues–Sat noon–2.30pm, Tues–Sun 5.30–10pm.

Jolleys Boathouse Jolleys Lane, off Victoria Drive next to City Bridge ☎08/8223 2891. Converted boathouse on the banks of the River Torrens, with wonderful water views, respectable Mod Oz cuisine and extensive wine list, is a popular lunch spot, especially on Sundays. Lunch daily, closed Sun night.

Lucia's Shop 1–2 Western Mall, Central Market ☎08/8231 2303. Lucia's has been keeping Adelaide's Italian-Australians sated with superb espresso and scrumptious Italian staples for over 50 years, and although Lucia herself passed away in 2002, her daughters still keep the locals coming back for more. Mon–Thurs 7am–5pm, Fri 7am–9pm & Sat 7am–3pm.

Mesa Lunga 140 Gouger St ☎08/8410 7617. This is the buzziest place in the city, serving delicious generously sized tapas at the bar and on the casual side of the eatery, and more refined Spanish offerings, such as Coorong Angus bistecca with panzanella salad, at the slightly more formal tables. Gets boisterous in the evenings, especially on weekends when there's a DJ. Lunch & dinner Tues–Sun, tapas until 11pm and pizza until midnight.

Star of Siam 67 Gouger St ⊕ 08/8231 3527. Popular Thai restaurant with an excellent, reasonably priced menu, including a good range of vegetarian dishes. Mon–Fri lunch, Mon–Sat dinner.

T-chow 68 Moonta St ⊕ 08/8410 1413. This enormously popular Chinese restaurant serves Teochew regional specialities such as tender duck and green-peppercorn chicken.

The Wine Underground 121 Pirie St ⊕ 08/8232 1222. Whether you choose from the (cheaper) casual bar-cum-bistro upstairs or the more formal restaurant downstairs, you're in for a treat – from the Wagyu rump steak and rochefort sandwiches to the buttered Kangaroo Island lobster with ponzu dressing. Lunch Mon–Fri noon–3pm, dinner Mon–Sat 6–10pm.

Ying Chow 114 Gouger St ⊕ 08/8211 7998. Unpretentious and always crowded place, serving inexpensive Northern Chinese cuisine including specialities such as aniseed-tea duck or scallops cooked with coriander and Chinese thyme. Vegetarians can enjoy delicious dishes such as bean curd with Chinese chutney. Licensed and BYO. Lunch Mon–Fri noon–3pm, dinner Mon–Sat 6–10pm.

North Adelaide, Norwood and Unley

Cafés

Café Paradiso 150 King William Rd, Hyde Park, near Unley. A long-established Italian favourite, with great coffee and biscotti plus alfresco dining out front. Daily 7.30am–10pm.

Elephant Walk 76 Melbourne St, North Adelaide. Lively but intimate coffee and late-night snack place, with small private lounge areas divided by carved wooden elephants and bamboo screens. Daily 8pm until late.

Oxford Hotel 101 O'Connell St, North Adelaide. Recently refurbished into a groovy pub with flaming red walls and a stainless-steel kitchen. The upgrade has also upgraded the price, with mains averaging between $10 and $22. Daily lunch, dinner Mon–Sat.

The Store Level 1, 157 Melbourne St, North Adelaide A gourmet delicatessen, corner store and café in one, with plenty of outdoor tables, and tasty breakfast and lunch menus. Daily 7am–7pm.

Wild Thyme 151 Melbourne St, North Adelaide. This big funky café-cum-organic food store does delicious light meals and snacks throughout the day. Daily 8am–late.

Restaurants

Cibo 10 O'Connell St, North Adelaide ⊕ 08/8267 2444. While most locals come for the excellent coffee (it's busy all day, especially at lunch time), they also do great wood-fired pizza, delicious pasta and Italian classics. Daily morning to late.

Monsoon 135 Melbourne St, North Adelaide ⊕ 08/8267 3822. Popular Indian place dishing up authentic cuisine at reasonable prices ($8–15 entrees, $14–18 mains), including a short menu of Southern Indian dishes (Masala Dosa is scrumptious; here the pancakes are filled with potatoes, cumin, onions, peas and coriander) and a long list of vegetarian dishes. Indian sweets are a speciality. Licensed and BYO. Daily lunch & dinner.

Sato 131 Melbourne St, North Adelaide ⊕ 08/8267 3381. Japanese restaurant with plenty of choice in sushi, sashimi and tempura dishes. BYO and licensed. Tues–Sun dinner.

Beach suburbs

Cafés & restaurants

Estias Henley Square, Henley Beach ⊕ 08/8353 2875. This award-winning modern Greek-Australian restaurant is within steps from the beach, but most patrons are too focused on the modern Greek-Australian fare, including delicious *meze*, to worry about the wonderful beach views nearby. Licensed and BYO. Book ahead; lunch & dinner Tues–Sun.

Europa 12–14 Jetty Rd, Glenelg. This popular espresso bar and casual eatery boasts a stylish contemporary interior and a menu dominated by pasta and risotto, but the main reason locals drop in here is for the authentic Italian coffee.

Salt Marina Pier, Glenelg. Contemporary bar and casual eatery, dishing up bistro standards, with DJs on weekend summer evenings. Open daily.

Sammy's Marina Pier, Glenelg ⊕ 08/8376 8211. Something of a local institution, *Sammy's* is considered to be one of Adelaide's best seafood restaurants on the water, serving up South Australia's freshest and finest. There's alfresco seating overlooking the marina and bay, and elegant

seating inside for windy days. Book for weekend lunch. Open daily noon–3pm & 6pm–late.
Sarah's 85 Dale St, Port Adelaide ☎08/8341 2103. Probably the best vegetarian eatery in Adelaide. Without any menus, diners are asked to place their trust in chef Stuart Gifford's capable hands – disappointment is unlikely. Tues–Sat lunch, Thurs–Sat dinner.

Stamford Grand Hotel The Foreshore, Glenelg ☎08/8376 1222..There are several good places to eat and drink here, including the excellent Asian eatery *Rickshaw's*, offering up Chinese, Thai and Indian dishes, with an open kitchen where you can see the chefs in action, and a modern café-cum-restaurant, *The Promenade*, with an international menu and sea views.

Nightlife and entertainment

Adelaide is a lively little city with something going on somewhere every night of the week from live bands and dance clubs to art-house film and avant-garde theatre. To find out **what's on** check out *The Guide* in Thursday's *Advertiser*, which has film and theatre listings and reviews. There's also a thriving free **press**: top of the culture stakes is *The Adelaide Review*, a monthly covering the visual and performing arts, dance, film, literature, history, wine and food, available from bookshops such as Imprints on Hindley Street, museums and galleries. *Rip It Up* is a gig listings magazine out every Thursday, with film, theatre, club and music reviews and interviews; *db Magazine*, in the same vein, is published every two weeks on Wednesdays – both can be picked up at record stores such as B# Records, 240 Rundle St, and Muses, 112–118 Rundle Mall. B# Records also sells tickets for underground events around town, but most big music events can be booked through Bass (☎13 12 46, ⊛www.bass.net.au).

The Adelaide Festival of Arts and Womadelaide

The huge Adelaide Festival of Arts (⊛www.adelaidefestival.org.au), which takes over the city for three weeks from late February to mid-March in even-numbered years, attracts an extraordinary range of international and Australian theatre companies, performers, musicians, writers and artists. An avant-garde Fringe has grown up around the main festival, which for many people is more exciting than the main event. The official festival began in 1960 and has been based at the purpose-built Festival Centre (see p.759) since 1973. In addition, free outdoor concerts, opera and films are held outside the Festival Centre and at various other locations during the period, while other venues around town host an Artists' Week, Writers' Week and a small film festival.

The Fringe Festival (⊛www.adelaidefringe.com.au) begins with a wild street parade on Rundle Street a week before the main festival, and events are held at venues all over town, with bands, cabaret and comedy at the *Fringe Club*, plus free outdoor shows and activities, while full use is made of the 24-hour licensing laws. Advance programmes for both the main and the fringe festival and further information are available from the offices of Tourism South Australia, or from all Bass outlets.

The Womadelaide (⊛www.womadelaide.com.au) world-music weekend began in 1992 as part of the Arts Festival but has now developed its own separate identity, attracting over thirty thousand people annually. Held in early March in the Botanic Park – with four stages, two workshop areas, multicultural food stalls and visual arts – it's a great place to hear some of Australia's local talent, with a broad selection of Aboriginal musicians, as well as internationally acclaimed world music artists from around the globe. The full weekend (Fri night–Sun night) costs $168, but day- and session-passes are also available. Tickets are available from Bass (☎13 12 46, ⊛www.bass.net.au).

At night, the two spots to head for are **Rundle Street**, which boasts popular pubs and bars, and the more edgy **Hindley Street**, where the young hipsters and arty university students hang out, where you'll find several funky clubs and live-music venues east of Morphett Street catering for the nearby university crowd. Near the train station, **Adelaide Casino** (open 24hr daily; neat dress required) has a stunning domed marble entrance, glitzy gaming rooms and jaw-dropping crystal chandeliers.

Pubs and bars

Apothecary 1878 118 Hindley St. One of the coolest venues in town, this atmospheric multi-level wine bar, housed in a nineteenth-century pharmacy, does decadent cocktails and delicious bar snacks. Tues–Thurs & Sat from 4pm until late, Fri noon until late.

Archer Hotel 60 O'Connell St, North Adelaide. This renovated pub has chic retro decor, with a good range of Aussie beers on the ground floor and a cocktail bar upstairs.

Austral Hotel 205 Rundle St ☎08/8223 4660. More arty and music-oriented than the *Exeter* (see below), the *Austral* is frequented by students who come for the local indie bands (Fri & Sat nights) and DJs (Tues–Thurs & Sun nights). DJs are free, as is most of the music – when there's

a cover charge, it's around $10. Fri & Sat open until 3am.

Exeter Hotel 246 Rundle St ☎08/8223 2623. This spacious old pub with an iron-lace balcony is a long-established hangout for Adelaide's artists, writers and students, yet remains totally unpretentious. Good lunches served, and music nightly.

Grace Emily 232 Waymouth St ☎08/8231 5500. Relaxed atmosphere, a young, alternative crowd and a range of local acts to suit everyone. Nightly until late.

Worldsend 208 Hindley St ☎08/8231 9137. Large, multifunctional pub popular with the nearby university crowd and boasting two bars, a restaurant, cocktail bar, lounge, beer garden, and live music at weekends. Licensed till 4am.

Clubs, comedy and live music

Cargo Club 213 Hindley St ☎08/8231 2327. Laid-back club featuring live jazz, spoken word, cabaret, soul, Latin, African and reggae acts plus local and international DJs. The decor is a mix of classic cool and trendy design, and there's something on most nights.

Crown and Sceptre 308 King William St ☎08/8212 4159, ⊛www.sceptre.com.au. One of Adelaide's best venues, this heritage-listed pub has sparkly bar stools, cozy couches in the intimate band area, and a busy espresso machine. Local bands and DJs Tues–Fri & Sun (usually free); Sat is club night (until 5am; around $10).

Enigma 173 Hindley St ☎08/8212 2313. Hip venue for the alternative university crowd. The small bar spills out into the street at weekends, and there's either a DJ or live music upstairs. Wed–Sat until late.

Governor Hindmarsh 59 Port Rd, Hindmarsh ☎08/8340 0744, ⊛www.thegov.com.au. The Gov, as this Adelaide institution is affectionately known, is one of Adelaide's leading live venues and hosts a

broad range of live music and cabaret, with gigs Tues–Sat at 8pm.

HQ 1 North Terrace ☎08/7221 1245, ⊛www .hqcomplex.com.au. By far the largest venue in Adelaide, with themed dance nights and well-known DJ's on Sat.

Rhino Room Upstairs at 13 Frome St ☎08/8227 1611. Underground club venue with an intimate lounge atmosphere: come casual or get glammed up, nobody minds. Comedy Wed & Fri and live music Fri & Sat. Wed 7.30–11pm, Fri 7.30pm–2am, Sat 9pm–3am. Standard charge $6.

Royal Oak Hotel 123 O'Connell St, North Adelaide ☎08/8267 2488, ⊛www.royaloakhotel.com.au. Popular North Adelaide bar and restaurant with arty decor and a young crowd. Live music (Tues & Sun), jazz (Wed) and DJs (Thurs and Fri).

Supermild 182 Hindley St West ☎08/8212 9000. One of the best clubs in town, with a laid-back atmosphere, chilled tunes and good cocktails. Wed 9pm–1am, Thurs 9pm–3am, Fri & Sat 9pm–5am, Sun 9pm–midnight.

Gay and lesbian nightspots

Edinburgh Castle Hotel 233 Currie St ☎08/8410 1211. Friendly gay- and lesbian-only venue with a dance floor from Thurs–Sun plus jukebox, bistro, beer garden and drag shows on Sun. Mon–Sat 11am–late, Sun 2pm–late.

Mars Bar 122 Gouger St ☎08/8231 9639. This Adelaide institution has been around for years and hosts drag acts for a big, friendly mixed crowd. Wed–Sat 9pm–late.

Film

Book ahead for the **Adelaide Film Festival** (☎08/8271 1029, ⓦwww .adelaidefilmfestival.org), held in odd-numbered years and running for two weeks from late February to early March. As well as several city and suburban mainstream film complexes, Adelaide now has a handful of art-house cinemas. The main **discount day** for mainstream cinemas is Tuesday. In the summer, you can watch films outdoors at the **Moonlight Cinema** in the Botanic Gardens (around $15; ☎1300 551 908, ⓦwww.moonlight.com.au); bookshops around town also have programmes.

Capri 141 Goodwood Rd, Goodwood ☎08/8272 1177. Alternative and arty films complete with pre-show Wurlitzer organ on Tues, Fri and Sat evenings. Take the tram to Glenelg to get here.

Chelsea 275 Kensington Rd, Kensington Park ☎08/8431 5080. The latest releases and a "crying room" for parents and babies.

Gay and lesbian Adelaide

South Australia was the first state to legalize gay sex and remains one of the most tolerant of lesbian and gay lifestyles, although Adelaide's gay scene remains more modest than Sydney's or Melbourne's. Apart from the city's more mainstream annual festivals, there are a few strictly gay and lesbian fiestas. The biggest and best is Feast (☎08/8231 2155, ⓦwww.feast.org.au), launched in 1997, which runs for two weeks in November. Events include theatre, music, visual art, literature, dance cabaret and historical walks, plus a Gay and Lesbian Film Festival at the Mercury Cinema (see opposite). The festival culminates in Picnic in the Park, an outdoor celebration in the parklands that surround central Adelaide that includes a very camp dog-show. Earlier in the year, June's Stonewall Celebrations are less flamboyant, featuring serious talks and exhibitions in a number of venues. A popular male gay hangout is Pulteney 431 Sauna, 431 Pulteney St (Mon & Tues 7pm–1am, Sun, Wed & Thurs noon–1am, Fri & Sat noon–3am; ☎08/8223 7506), with a spa, sauna, steam room, pool and snack bar.

To find out where the action is, pick up a copy of *Blaze* or check out "Listings" p.773.

Useful organizations and publications

Blaze 213 Franklin St ⓦwww.blazemedia.com .au. Fortnightly gay and lesbian newspaper with news, features and listings. Free from venues and bookshops. *Blaze* also publishes the handy free *Lesbian & Gay Adelaide Map*.
Darling House Gay and Lesbian Community Library 64 Fullarton Rd, Norwood. Fiction, non-fiction and newspapers. Mon–Fri 9am–5pm.

Liberation Monthly newsletter for lesbians – good for contacts and local events.
Murphy Sisters Bookshop 240 The Parade, Norwood. Gay/lesbian bookshop with a handy notice board. Wed–Sat only.
Parkside Travel 70 Glen Osmond Rd, Parkside ☎08/8274 1222 or 1800 888 501. Gay-owned and operated company offering hotel reservations, information and travel services.

Mercury Cinema Lion Arts Centre, 13 Morphett St ☎08/8410 1934, ⓦwww.mercurycinema.org.au. A wonderful art-house cinema showing shorts and foreign films.

Nova Cinema 251 Rundle St ☎08/8223 6333. Arts cinema complex with three screens; discounts available to students and backpackers with relevant identification.

Odeon Star Cinema 65 Semaphore Rd, Semaphore ☎08/8341 5988. Quaint local beachside cinema showing mainstream films.

Palace East End 274 Rundle St ☎08/8232 3434. Alternative venue showing foreign-language and art-house films plus other new releases. Discounts for backpackers.

Trak Cinemas 375 Greenhill Rd, Toorak Gardens ☎08/8332 8020. Good alternative cinema with two screens. Bus #145 from North Terrace to stop 10.

Theatre and the performing arts

Out of festival time, mainstream theatre, ballet, opera, contemporary dance, comedy and cabaret continue to thrive at the **Festival Centre** (see p.759). Classical concerts are held at the **Adelaide Town Hall** (usually performed by the Adelaide Symphony Orchestra) and at **Elder Hall** in the Conservatorium of Music on North Terrace. The **Lion Theatre**, on the corner of Morphett Street and North Terrace, is the main venue of the Lion Arts Centre with inter-state performers, jazz bands and comedy line-ups (☎08/8218 8400), while **Theatre 62**, 145 Burbridge Rd, offers two venues under one roof with pantomime, a theatre-restaurant and experimental productions (☎08/8234 0838). Almost anything that's on can be booked through Bass (☎13 12 46, ⓦwww.bass.net.au).

Shopping

You can find most things you'll need on the pedestrianized **Rundle Mall** (see p.760), which boasts several department stores, and a handy Woolworths at no. 86 with a small supermarket attached. There's also a Coles supermarket at 21 Grote St (open daily), next to the Central Market. For alternative fashion, **Rundle Street** and, particularly, Miss Gladys Sym Choon at no. 235 is the place to go. For **retro** clothing visit Naked at no. 238, Irving Baby, 33 Twin St, off Rundle Mall, or The Banana Room (see p.762). For **Aboriginal arts** and crafts try Tandanya (see p.761) or the Otherway Centre at 185 Pirie St. B# Records, at 240 Rundle St, and Krypton Discs, at 34 Jetty Rd, Glenelg, are both good for music.

There are several good **bookshops** around the city: the excellent Unibooks, at Adelaide University, provides an excuse to nose around the university; Angus & Robertsons, 138 Rundle Mall, is a large mainstream store, while the huge Borders, in Rundle Mall, has an excellent range of international newspapers and magazines plus an in-store café. All of the museums also have wonderful bookstores and gift shops. Adelaide Booksellers, at 6A Rundle Mall, sells good secondhand titles, as does O'Connell's Bookshop at 62 Hindley St – they also buy or exchange books.

Markets include Central Market (Tues 7am–5.30pm, Thurs 9am–5.30pm, Fri 7am–9pm, Sat 7am–3pm), Orange Lane Market, Brickworks Market, Port Adelaide Market and Torrens Island Fish and Produce Market. **Shopping hours** are generally Monday to Saturday 9am to 5pm or 6pm, with late-night shopping until 9pm on Friday in the city and Thursday in the suburbs, plus Sunday trading (11am–5pm) in the city only.

Adelaide Listings

Airlines Air New Zealand ⊤13 24 76; British Airways ⊤1300 767 177; Garuda ⊤1300 365 330; Japan Airlines ⊤1800 772 778; Lufthansa ⊤1300 655 727; Malaysia Airlines ⊤13 26 27; Qantas ⊤13 13 13; Singapore Airlines ⊤13 10 11.

American Express Shop 32, City Centre, Rundle Mall (Mon–Fri 9am–5pm, Sat 9am–noon; ⊤1300 139 060).

Banks and foreign exchange All the major banks are located on King William St. Exchange services are available at the international airport, at American Express (see above) and at Travelex, 45 Grenfell St (Mon–Fri 9am–5pm; ⊤1800 637 642). Outside these hours, the casino (see p.769) or international hotels on North Terrace can help, but obviously the exchange rates will be poor.

Bikes and bike rental Flinders Camping, 187 Rundle St (⊤08/8223 1913), rents bikes for $20 per day and offers weekly rates; Linear Park Mountain Bike Hire at Elder Park (⊤08/8223 6271), situated near a section of the River Torrens Linear Park bike track, rents bikes by the hour or day at competitive prices; Bike SA, 46 Hurtle Square (⊤08/8232 2644), is a nonprofit cycling organization providing information and cycling maps and organizing regular touring trips. They offer free bikes for the first two hours and charge $6 per hour thereafter; they also have a pick-up point at *Cannon Street Backpackers*.

Camping equipment and rental Rundle St is the place: for rental, try Flinders Camping at no. 187 (⊤08/8223 1913); they are also the only place in town that repairs backpacks. Paddy Pallin at no. 228 sells a range of high-quality gear, plus maps, or there's the Scout Outdoor Centre at no. 192.

Canoe rental and tours Adelaide Canoe Works, 74 Daws Rd, Edwardstown (⊤08/8277 8422), offer a range of courses and expeditions as well as very reasonably priced canoe and kayak hire.

Car rental Avis (⊤13 63 33), Hertz (⊤13 26 07) and Thrifty (⊤1300 367 227) have desks at the airport. Otherwise, small and friendly Access, 60 Frome St (⊤08/8359 3200 or 1800 812 580), does free airport deliveries; they also rent out sports cars. Other options include Action (⊤08/8352 7044 or 1800 888 282) or Excel (⊤08/8234 1666). Older, cheaper cars can be obtained from Cut Price Car Rentals (⊤08/8443 7788), which also does one-way rentals and buy-backs, or Rent-a-Bug (⊤08/8234 0911). Britz Campervan, Car and 4WD Rentals (⊤08/8234 4701 or 1800 331 454) have a full range of campervans for hire.

Environment and conservation The Conservation Council of South Australia, 120 Wakefield St

Tours from Adelaide

There are a huge number of tour companies operating out of Adelaide, offering everything from leisurely day-trips to hard-core camping excursions.

Adelaide Explorer City Sights Tour ⊤08/8293 2966. This hop-on hop-off tour covers the city, Glenelg and West Beach, with daily departures from the Travel Centre, 18 King William St, at 9.05am, 10.30am & 1.30pm (3hr; $30).

Gray Line (⊤1300 858 687, ⊛www.grayline.com) and **Adelaide Sightseeing** (⊤08/8413 6199, ⊛www.adelaidesightseeing.com.au) both head for the Barossa Valley (see p.778), Kangaroo Island (see p.793) and the Fleurieu Peninsula (see p.786), and can also arrange trips further afield to the Murray River, or the Coorong and Flinders ranges.

Groovy Grape Getaways ⊤1800 661 177, ⊛www.groovygrape.com.au. The Groovy Grape people offer several tours from Adelaide including two to Kangaroo Island (two days; $345, three days; $445 all-inclusive) and a tour to Alice Springs via the Flinders Ranges (seven days; $865 all-inclusive). Their Barossa day-trip visits four large wineries with a barbecue lunch ($79).

Heading Bush 4WD Adventures ⊤08/8356 5501, ⊛www.headingbush.com. Operates an epic ten-seater camping tour to Alice Springs, taking in Flinders Ranges, Coober Pedy, the Simpson Desert and Uluru (ten days; $1595).

Wayward Bus 115 Waymouth St ⊤08/8132 8230 or 1300 653 510, ⊛www.waywardbus.com.au. Adelaide is the home base for this excellent company, which does good one-way, small-group tours from Adelaide to Melbourne (or vice versa) via the scenic coastal route (three days; $395 including breakfast, lunch and hostel accommodation). They also run one-way tours to Alice Springs taking in the Clare Valley, Flinders Ranges, Oodnadatta Track, Lake Eyre, Coober Pedy, Uluru, Kata Tjuta and Kings Canyon (eight days; $895 all-inclusive).

(☎08/8223 5155), is a good place to find out what's going on. The Wilderness Society has its campaign office at 118 King William St (☎08/8231 6586) and a shop in Victoria Square Arcade, Victoria Square (☎08/8231 0625).

Hospital Royal Adelaide Hospital, North Terrace ☎08/8222 4000; Dental Hospital, Flinders St ☎08/8222 8222.

Internet access There's limited-time free access at the State Library (see p.759); book in advance), and cheap access at iNet Zone, 42 Grote St ($5 per hour). Most of the backpackers places have internet access for guests as well.

Laundries Adelaide Launderette, 152 Sturt St (daily 7am–9.30pm; service washes Mon–Fri 9am–5pm).

Left luggage Adelaide Train Station has 24-hour lockers. There are also facilities at the Central Bus Station with Premier Stateliner ($2 per 24hr) and Greyhound Australia (from $8 per 24hr).

Maps The Map Shop, 6–10 Peel St, between Hindley and Currie sts, has the largest range of local and state maps. If you're a member of an affiliated overseas automobile association, you can get free regional maps and advice on road conditions from the Royal Automobile Association, 55 Hindmarsh Square (☎08/8202 4600, ⓦwww.raa.net).

Motorbike rental Show & Go Motorcycles, 236 Brighton Rd, Somerton Park ☎08/8376 0333.

Newspapers The *Advertiser* is very provincial and doesn't have good coverage of national and international news, but is useful on Thurs for entertainment listings, and Wed and Sat for classifieds if you're looking for a car or other travel equipment. Alternatively, Melbourne's *The Age* is widely available. The best place to buy foreign and interstate newspapers is Rundle Arcade Newsagency, off Gawler Place, or Borders in Rundle Mall.

Pharmacy Midnight Pharmacy, 13 West Terrace (☎08/8231 6333, Mon–Sat 7am–midnight, Sun 9am–midnight). In Glenelg try Stephens Pharmacy, on the corner of Jetty Rd and Gordon St (daily 8.30am–10pm).

Police For emergencies call ☎000.

Post office GPO, 141 King William St, corner of Franklin St (Mon–Fri 8am–6pm, Sat 8.30am–noon); for poste restante use Adelaide GPO, SA 5000.

Swimming pool Adelaide City Swim, 235 Flinders St (Mon 6am–8.30pm, Sat 7.30am–2pm, Sun 8.30am–12.30pm; $10 per hour). Adelaide Aquatic Centre, corner of Jeffcott Rd and Fitzroy Terrace, North Adelaide (Mon–Sat 5am–10pm, Sun 7am–8pm; swimming $5.90), is an indoor centre with pool, gym, sauna and spa; take bus #231 from North Terrace.

Taxis There's a taxi rank on the corner of Pulteney and Rundle sts, otherwise call Adelaide Independent (☎13 22 11), Suburban Taxis (☎13 10 08) or Yellow Cabs (☎13 22 27).

Telephones Rundle Mall has lots of phones, including ones that take credit cards. For peace and quiet, try the Phone Room in the GPO.

Travel agents Adelaide YHA Travel, 135 Waymouth St ☎08/8414 3000; City Centre Travel, 75 King William St ☎08/8221 5044; Flight Centre, 186 Rundle St ☎08/8227 0404; Jetset, 23 Leigh St, off Hindley St ☎08/8231 2422; Peregrine Travel, upstairs at 192 Rundle St ☎08/8223 5905; STA Travel, 235 Rundle St ☎08/8223 2426; Thor Travel, 22–32 Frome St ☎08/8232 3071.

Travellers with disablties Disability Information and Resource Centre, 195 Gilles St ☎08/8236 0555.

Work Information on work rights is available from the Department of Immigration and Multicultural Affairs (☎13 18 81, ⓦwww.immi.gov.au /employers). Adelaide is a good place to find out about casual fruit-picking work in the Riverland. Hostels can help with finding work, and often provide a source of employment for young travellers.

Moving on from Adelaide

For **domestic flights** from Adelaide, Air South (☎08/8234 4988, ⓦwww.airsouth.com.au) flies to Kangaroo Island; Jetstar (☎13 15 38, ⓦwww.jetstar.com.au) flies to most capital cities as well as Cairns; Regional Express (☎13 17 13, ⓦwww.rex.com.au) serves a range of regional destinations including Broken Hill, Ceduna, Mount Gambier, Port Lincoln, Whyalla, Coober Pedy, Olympic Dam and Kangaroo Island; and Virgin Blue (☎13 67 89, ⓦwww.virginblue.com.au) flies to major cities countrywide.

The *State Guide*, available from the South Australian Travel Centre (see p.753), has route maps and timetables for all of South Australia's bus routes. Most **long-distance buses** leave from the Central Bus Station on Franklin Street. Greyhound Australia (☎1300 473 946863) has a nationwide service that includes Alice Springs in its destinations, while Firefly Express (☎1300 730 740, ⓦwww.fireflyexpress.com.au) runs to Melbourne and Sydney. V/Line (☎08/8231 7620 or 13 61 96, ⓦwww.vline.com.au) also runs to Melbourne from Adelaide and Mount Gambier.

State services are dominated by Premier Stateliner Coach Service (☎08/8415 5555, ⓦwww.premierstateliner.com.au), which goes to the Riverland, Whyalla, Port Lincoln, Ceduna, Woomera, Roxby Downs and Olympic Dam, the Yorke and Fleurieu peninsulas and to Mount Gambier either inland or along the coast. Other local operators include LinkSA Barossa Valley (☎08/8564 3022), which stops at the main towns in the Barossa Valley en route to Angaston; the Yorke Peninsula Passenger Service (☎08/8821 2755), which runs from Adelaide to Yorketown down the east coast via Ardrossan, Port Vincent and Edithburgh, and down the centre via Maitland and Minlaton; the Mid North Passenger Service (☎08/8823 2375) via the Clare Valley and/or Burra to Peterborough; and LinkSA Murray Bridge (☎08/8532 2633) to Pinnaroo via Murray Bridge and to Murray Bridge via Mannum and Meningie. Tickets can be purchased at the Central Bus Station. The **Bus & Train Booking Centre** at Station Arcade, 52 Hindley St (☎08/8212 5200), can arrange travel on any bus service.

There are three options for onward **train** travel – The *Overlander* to Melbourne, the *Ghan* to Darwin via Alice Springs, and the *Indian Pacific*, which runs east to Sydney and west to Perth. Tickets can be booked through the Great Southern Railway Travel Pty (☎13 21 47, ⓦwww.gsr.com.au), which produces a glossy brochure with current timetables.

Around Adelaide

Escaping Adelaide for a day or two is easy and enjoyable, with a tempting range of beaches, hills and wineries to choose from. Close at hand are the **Adelaide Hills**, southeast of the city, which are popular for weekend outings and have numerous small national and conservation parks that are great for walking. To the south, the **Fleurieu Peninsula** extends towards Cape Jervis and has plenty of fine beaches and around 50 wineries at McLaren Vale.

If wine is your priority, head for McLaren Vale first, then the **Barossa Valley**, Australia's premier wine-producing region, with another sixty or so excellent wineries within 50km of Adelaide. The valley is easily visited in a day from the city, but is also a great place to chill out for a few days. The **Yorke Peninsula**, across the gulf from Adelaide, is often ignored by foreigners, though many locals holiday here: as well as the wonderful beaches, it's home to the remains of an old copper-mining industry and an excellent national park.

The Adelaide Hills

The beautiful **Adelaide Hills** are the section of the **Mount Lofty Ranges** that run closest to the city, just thirty minutes' drive away, and largely accessible by train and the Transit Plus bus service (☎08/8339 7544); several tours heading for the Fleurieu Peninsula also take in the area. Many people have set up home in the hills to take advantage of the cooler air, and there are some grand old summer houses here as well as sleek contemporary weekenders. The **Heysen Trail**, a long-distance walk from Cape Jervis to Parachilna Gorge, cuts across the hills, with four quaint YHA hostels along it; most are run on a limited-access basis and you'll have to pick the key up first from the Adelaide

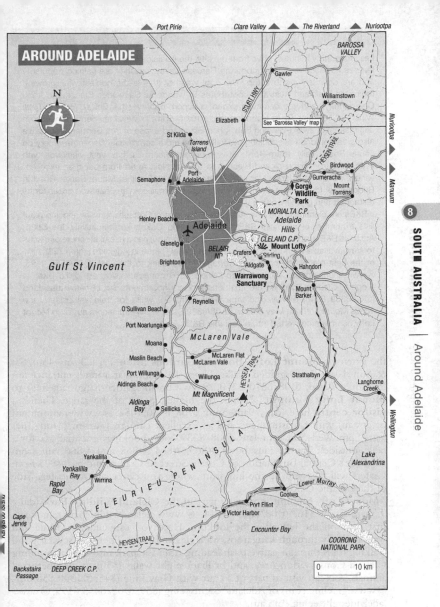

office at 135 Waymouth St (☎08/8414 3010). The **Adelaide Hills visitor centre** in Hahndorf (see p.777) is a good source of information about the area, and can book accommodation.

Leaving the city by Glen Osmond Road you join the **South Eastern Freeway**, the main road to Melbourne – there's an old tollhouse not far out of the city at Urrbrae and several fine old coaching hotels such as the *Crafers Inn*. At **CRAFERS** itself you can leave the freeway for the scenic Mount Lofty Summit Road, which runs along the top of the hills, past the western side of

Wineries and B&Bs in the hills

Less than thirty minutes' drive from the city, the Adelaide Hills' wineries may not be as famous as those in the neighbouring Barossa Valley, but they are gaining popularity and are definitely worth a trip. The cool weather (this is the coolest wine-growing region on mainland Australia) contributes to wonderful Sauvignon Blancs and fresh Chardonnays and you can even expect a superb cool-weather Shiraz. *Hahndorf Hill Winery* at 10 Pains Rd in Hahndorf (daily 10am–5pm; ⓦwww.hahndorfhillwinery.com .au) makes an award-winning Sauvignon Blanc and a rosé of rare German grapes; it's also great for lunch overlooking the valley. The more commercial *Nepenthe* winery on Jones Road (daily 10am–4pm, ⓦwww.nepenthe.com.au) has vast vineyards with everything from hand-picked Riesling to a Pinot Noir. Apart from being an excellent winery, *Petaluma Bridgewater Mill*, located in an 1860 mill at Mount Barker Road in Bridgewater (daily 10am–5pm; ⓦwww.bridgewatermill.com.au), has won prizes for its restaurant and is well worth a visit.

B&Bs are plentiful in the hills. Adelaide Hills Country Cottages (ⓦwww.ahcc.com.au) lists a number of excellent B&Bs in and around Oakbank; alternatively, the South Australia B&B and Farmstay (ⓦwww.bandbfsa.com.au) has a useful brochure of places to stay, available from the South Australian Travel Centre in Adelaide (see p.753). One of the best places is *Apple Tree Cottage*, in Oakbank to the east (☏08/8388 4193, ⓦwww.ahcc.com.au; ❼), a self-contained 1860 cottage beside an idyllic lake. In Aldgate, *Cladich Pavilions* are luxurious modern apartments set in native bushland (☏08/8339 8248, ⓦwww.cladichpavilions.com; ❻), while for train enthusiasts, the 1880s *Mount Lofty Railway Station* (☏08/8339 7400, ⓦwww.mlrs.com.au; ❹) in Mount Lofty has been converted into a sociable B&B.

the extensive **Mount Lofty Botanic Gardens** (Mon–Fri 8.30am–4pm, Sat & Sun 10am–5pm; guided walks Thurs 10.30am year round; entrance on Piccadilly Road; ☏08/8370 8370, ⓦwww.botanicgardens.sa.gov.au; free) to **Mount Lofty Summit** (710m), the highest point of the range. There's a **visitor centre** here (daily 9am–5pm; ☏08/8370 1054, ⓦwww.environment .sa.gov.au) with fantastic views and an excellent **café–restaurant** (Mon–Tues 9am–5pm, Wed–Sun 9am–late; ☏08/8339 2600; bookings essential; ask for a table outside). Transit Plus buses #863, #864, #865 and #866 run from Adelaide's Central Bus Station or Currie Street to Crafers, and bus #823 from Crafers will take you up the hill, from where you can access the eastern side of the Botanic Gardens.

Mount Lofty Summit is actually part of the **Cleland Wildlife Park** (daily 9.30am–5pm; $16; ☏08/8339 2444, ⓦwww.clelandwildlifepark.sa.gov.au), first turn on the left after the lookout. Here you can cuddle a koala and wander freely through kangaroos, wallabies and emus. There are several good walking trails through native bush leading from the park into the surrounding Cleland Conservation Area, and brilliant night walks ($30) to see nocturnal animals. You can visit as part of a tour with Gray Line ($45; ☏1300 858 687, ⓦwww.grayline.com) or Adelaide Sightseeing ($59; ☏08/8413 6199, ⓦwww .adelaidesightseeing.com.au).

The **Morialta Conservation Park**, to the north, is easily reached by taking the #105 bus (35min) from Grenfell Street in the city centre, which goes right into the park along the scenic Morialta Falls Road; from the entrance it's a 1.5-kilometre bushwalk to a lovely waterfall or a 7.3-kilometre hike to Three Falls Grand for stunning gorges and three falls. By car you can approach the park along the equally impressive Old Norton Summit Road; the *Scenic Hotel*, clinging to the side of the hill at Norton Summit, is a great place to stop for a drink.

South of Crafers, virtually in the southern suburbs of Adelaide, is **Belair National Park** (daily 8am till sunset; $3 (if arriving by train) or $8 per car; Ⓦ www.environment.sa.gov.au/parks/), South Australia's first national park, dedicated in 1891. Getting there is half the pleasure – you take a suburban train from Adelaide Train Station (35min), which winds upwards through tunnels and valleys with views of Adelaide and Gulf St Vincent. From Belair Station, steps lead to the valley and the grassy recreation grounds and kiosk. With its joggers, tennis courts, man-made lake, hedge maze and **Old Government House** (open to visitors Sun 12.30–4pm), a residence built in 1859 as a summer retreat for the governor, this seems more like a garden than a national park, though there are also some more secluded bush trails through gum forests.

The **Warrawong Sanctuary** (free), southeast of Belair National Park on Stock Road, reached by Sturt Valley Road, Heather Road and Longwood Road, was set up in the late 1960s as a sustainable conservation model to halt the loss of Australian wildlife. While you can do self-guided walks, there are also guided **bushwalks** at dawn, at one hour before sunset and at dusk ($25; bookings essential; ☎08/8370 9197, Ⓦ www.warrawong.com). These give the opportunity to spot the sanctuary's mostly nocturnal animals in their natural habitat, including several endangered species such as bettongs and potoroos (both from the marsupial family) as well as the elusive platypus. The sanctuary is home to the *Bilby Café and Restaurant* (licensed; $60 for two-course dinner and nocturnal walk) as well as **accommodation** in air-conditioned, en-suite tent-cabins ($125 per person including animal show, guided nocturnal walk, two-course dinner and breakfast). They have daily interactive animal shows (11am & 2pm; $5) where you get to meet the locals, from birds of prey to snakes and reptiles. There's no public transport or tours to Warrawong, but Transit Plus bus #866 goes to Stirling, where you can get a taxi for the remaining 5km.

Hahndorf

HAHNDORF, 28km southeast of the city, is the most touristy destination in the hills, and gets crowded at weekends. There are frequent Transit Plus bus services here from Adelaide Central Bus Station (40min). Founded in 1839, it's Australia's oldest **German settlement** and still has the look of a nineteenth-century village. The Bavarian-style restaurants and coffee houses, crafts, antique and gift shops are thoroughly commercial, but it's still enjoyable, especially in autumn when the chestnuts and elms lining the main street have turned golden.

The **Hahndorf Academy** (Mon–Sat 10am–5pm, 4pm in winter; free) is a working artist's studio with a small collection of photographs, prints, displays and well-written interpretive boards that shed light on the lives of early German settlers, plus a few sketches by the town's most famous resident and one of Australia's best-known artists, **Hans Heysen**, who settled here in 1908. There's a more comprehensive collection of Heysen's paintings on display at his old home, **The Cedars**, still maintained by the Heysen family, about 2.5km northwest of the village off Ambleside Road (Tues–Sun 10am–4pm; Sept–May guided tours 11am, 1pm & 3pm, June–Aug 11am & 2pm; $10 studio and house; shop and garden free).

The **Adelaide Hills visitor centre** at 41 Main St (June–Aug Mon–Fri 9.30am–4.30pm, Sat & Sun 10am–4pm; Sept–May Mon–Fri 9am–5pm, Sat & Sun 10am–4pm; ☎08/8388 1185 or 1800 353 323, Ⓦ www.visitadelaide hills.com.au or Ⓦ www.hahndorfsouthaustralia.com.au) has lots of information on **accommodation** (no charge for bookings) and can provide information about the area, though you won't need much help in the village itself – it's basically one street and all the buildings have blue plaques recounting their history. The best sleep in town is at *The Manna* at 25 Main St (☎08/8121 9755, Ⓦwww.themanna.com.au; ❻—❼), stylish, contemporary executive and spa rooms, slap-bang in the centre of town.

For lunch, the light seasonal dishes at *Udder Delights* (☎08/8388 1588, Ⓦwww .udderdelights.com.au), 91A Main St, are created from fresh regional products; the caramelized onion and goat cheese tart is sublime, especially accompanied by local wine. Buy some of their divine cheese (try the pungent goat camembert) handcrafted by cheesemaker Sheree Sullivan, who holds cheesemaking classes on site (book ahead). As the departure point for the *Adelaide Hills Cheese and Wine Trail* (Ⓦhttp://adelaidehillsfood.com.au; standard/silver $55/85 for two; $20 deposit on hamper, cutlery, cutting board and ice), a four-course progressive picnic following a wine route through the hills, this is where you pick up your hamper full of cheese and goodies. For a more serious lunch, you can't beat the stunning cuisine of Chef Le Tu Thai on the leafy terrace overlooking the atmospheric mill and creek at *Petaluma's Bridgewater Mill* (☎08/8339 9200; Ⓦwww.bridgewatermill.com.au) ten minutes' drive away on Mount Baker Road at Bridgewater. The **German Cake Shop** on Pine Avenue, near the visitor centre (daily 8.30am–5.30pm), is a busy bakery and coffee shop specializing in *bienenstich*, a yeast cake topped with honey and almonds and filled with cream, butter and custard. For a glass of authentic locally brewed pilsner with hearty German fare (be warned: it's hit and miss), head to popular *Hahndorf Inn Hotel* or *The German Arms*, which has a log fire and old photos. Hahndorf becomes a ghost town after 5.30pm, when you're better off heading to *The Stirling Hotel*'s stylish award-winning bistro (daily noon–9pm) or more elegant restaurant (lunch Fri & Sun; dinner Wed–Sun; bookings essential), 52 Mount Barker Rd, Stirling.

Torrens River Gorge

Further north in the upper valley, the 27-kilometre **Gorge Scenic Drive** beside the Torrens River Gorge is one of the loveliest areas in the Adelaide Hills, but you'll need your own car to get there: take the Gorge Road off the A11 from Adelaide, a few kilometres past the suburb of Campbelltown. Fourteen kilometres along this road is the **Gorge Wildlife Park** (daily 9am–5pm; koala cuddling 11.30am, 1.30pm & 3.30pm; $13; Ⓦwww.gorgewildlifepark.com.au), a 14-acre private park with native and exotic birds and animals housed in walk-through enclosures. A few kilometres past the park, at Cudlee Creek, the Gorge Scenic Drive turns southeast away from the river and passes through picturesque valleys and vineyards to Mount Torrens. If you want to stick with the river, turn north before Cudlee Creek towards the Chain of Ponds, where the road connects after a few kilometres to the equally stunning Torrens Valley Scenic Drive.

GUMERACHA, the first town east of here, is home to **The Toy Factory**, 389 Birdwood Rd (daily 9am–5pm; Ⓦwww.thetoyfactory.com.au), which sells wooden toys, games and puzzles and has a colossal eighteen-metre-high rocking horse which children (and adults) like to climb for views of the countryside. At the eastern end of the Torrens Valley Scenic Drive is **BIRDWOOD** and the impressive **National Motor Museum** on Shannon Street (daily 9am–5pm; $9; Ⓦwww.history.sa.gov.au), Australia's largest collection of veteran, vintage and classic cars, trucks and motorcycles. You can arrange for the Hills Explorer Bus (☎0411 725 603) to drop you here and pick you up.

The Barossa Valley

The **Barossa Valley**, only an hour's drive from Adelaide, produces internationally acclaimed wines and is the largest premium wine producer in Australia.

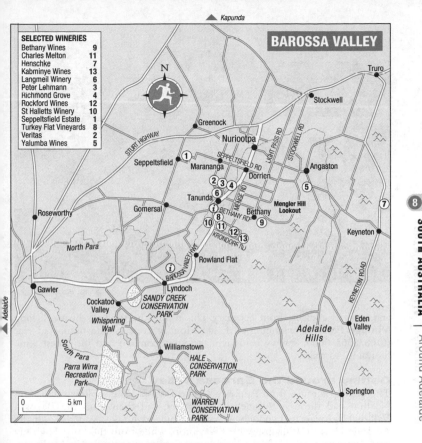

SELECTED WINERIES

Bethany Wines	9
Charles Melton	11
Henschke	7
Kabminye Wines	13
Langmeil Winery	6
Peter Lehmann	3
Richmond Grove	4
Rockford Wines	12
St Halletts Winery	10
Seppeltsfield Estate	1
Turkey Flat Vineyards	8
Veritas	2
Yalumba Wines	5

BAROSSA VALLEY

Small stone **Lutheran churches** dot the valley, which was settled in the 1840s by German Lutherans fleeing from religious persecution: by 1847 over 2500 German immigrants had arrived and after the 1848 revolution more poured in. German continued to be spoken in the area until World War I, when the language was frowned upon and German place names were changed by an act of parliament. The towns, however – most notably Tanunda – still remain German in character, and the valley is well worth visiting for the **vineyards**, wineries, bakeries and butcher's shops, where old German recipes have been handed down through generations. With up to eight hundred thousand visitors per annum, the valley can seem thoroughly touristy and traffic-laden if you whizz through it quickly, but the peaceful back roads are more interesting, with a number of small, family-owned wineries to explore.

The first vines were planted in 1847 at the Orlando vineyards, an estate which is still a big producer. There are now over sixty **wineries** with cellar doors, from multinationals to tiny specialists. Because of the variety of soil and climate, the Barossa seems able to produce a wide range of wine types of consistently high quality; the white Rieslings are among the best. The region has a typically Mediterranean climate, with dry summers and mild winters; the best time to visit is autumn (March–May), when the vines turn russet and golden and the harvest has begun in earnest. Much of the grape-picking is still done by hand

▲ Grape harvest, Barossa Wineries

and work is available from February. This is also the time of the week-long **Vintage Festival**, beginning on Easter Monday in every odd-numbered year (☎08/8563 0600, ⓦwww.barossavintagefestival.com.au) and the oldest wine festival in Australia.

Getting around the Barossa Valley

The principal route from Adelaide to the Barossa Valley follows the Main North Road through Elizabeth and Gawler, and then joins the **Barossa Valley Highway** to Lyndoch. A more scenic drive takes you through the Adelaide Hills to Williamstown or Angaston, while from the Sturt Highway you can turn into the valley at Nuriootpa. Getting to the valley by **bus** is also reasonably easy: LinkSA Barossa Valley (Mon–Sat 2 daily, Sun 1 daily; ☎08/8564 3022) stops at the main Barossa towns en route to Angaston from Adelaide, while the daily Premier Stateliner (☎08/8415 5555) service to Riverland from Adelaide can drop you at Nuriootpa on request. If you're cycling, you might want to consider taking your bike on the train to Gawler, 14km west of Lyndoch.

Driving obviously isn't the ideal way to explore the Barossa if you want to enjoy tasting wines – once here, you can always rent a bike or take a tour. If you decide you do need a **car** to get around, you can rent one from the Caltex service station, 212 Murray St, Tanunda ($65 per day; ☎08/8563 2677). A better way to experience the area is to **cycle**; there's a sealed bike track avoiding the busy highway between Tanunda and Nuriootpa and bike rental (around $30 a day) is available at *Novotel Barossa Valley Resort*, Rowland Flat, Tanunda (☎08/8524 0000), and *Barossa Secrets*, 91 Murray St, Tanunda (☎08/8563 0665), as well as at some other accommodation. Alternatively, you can take a two-day cycling tour with Ecotrek (☎08/8346 4155, ⓦwww.ecotrek.com.au), with an emphasis on wine tasting, gourmet food and heritage accommodation. There's also a range of **sightseeing tours** from Adelaide offered by all the big commercial tour operators (see "Listings", p.773).

Lyndoch and around

"A beautiful place, good land, plenty of grass and its general appearance open with some patches of wood and many kangaroos," reported Colonel William Light in 1837 on first sighting the **LYNDOCH** area. Settled in 1839, it's one of the oldest towns in South Australia, and although vineyards were established from the outset, the primary activity until 1896 was the growing of wheat, until someone had the bright idea of converting a flour mill into a winery. Today there are ten wineries in the immediate Lyndoch area, from some of the smallest to one of the largest in the Barossa, all still family-owned. **Kies Family Wineries** on Barossa Valley Way provides free informal tourist information (daily 9.30am–4.30pm; ☎08/8524 4110); their wine-tasting cellars (same hours) are in the same building.

Eight kilometres southwest of Lyndoch, off Yettie Road, is the Whispering Wall, a retaining wall for the Barossa Reservoir; it's shaped in such a way that words spoken on one side of the reservoir can be heard plainly on the opposite side 140m away. To the northeast, 4km along the Barossa Valley Highway, the village of **ROWLAND FLAT** is dominated by the **Orlando Winery** complex, the oldest winery in the valley and home of some of Australia's best-known wines, sold under the **Jacob's Creek** label. Johann Gramp planted the first commercial vines at nearby Jacob's Creek in 1847, and forty years later his son expanded the winery and moved it to Rowland Flat. The **Jacob's Creek Visitor's Centre**, located on the banks of Jacob's Creek itself, has a tasting centre, a good restaurant, and a gallery that includes information on production techniques and the history of the area (daily 10am–5pm).

Four kilometres north of Rowland Flat, the peaceful **Krondorf Road/ Hallet Valley** area runs east of the Barossa Valley Highway, with three charming wineries – Rockford, St Hallets and Charles Melton – each with its own philosophy of wine making and tasting (see box below). Next to St Hallets Winery you can watch skilled coopers at work at the **Keg Factory** on St Hallet Road (Mon–Sat 8am–4.30pm, Sun 10am–4.30pm); the huge stainless-steel

Wine-tasting tips

The smaller wineries tend to have more charm and intrinsic interest than the larger commercial operators and it's here you'll often get to talk personally to the winemaker or snare some wines that are not generally available in wine shops. Groups are welcomed by most wineries but are encouraged to book, although some wineries are too small to accommodate them. You're under no obligation to buy wine, but coming away with a few of your favourites of the day – often only available at the cellar door – and a few fruity adjectives to describe them is part of the fun.

For a novice, wine tasting can be an intimidating experience. On entering the tasting area (or cellar door) you'll be shown a list of wines that may be tasted, divided into whites through to reds, all of which are printed in the order that the winemaker considers best on the palate. This is fine, but if you are visiting several wineries and are only interested in reds, by all means concentrate on the reds. Always look at the colour and clarity of the wine first, then give it a swirl and a sniff. Then take a deeper sniff with your nose inside the rim of the glass to try to appreciate the aroma or bouquets you can pick up. Then take a sip, rolling it around on your tongue before swallowing; there's always a spittoon if you don't want to swallow. A great way to learn more is to think about what you can pick up on your palate and then check it against the winemaker's notes. Don't be shy about discussing the wines with the person serving – that's exactly what they're there for and even wine snobs are down-to-earth Australians at heart.

fermentation tanks you'll see around the valley aren't suitable for all wines, many of which still need to be aged in wood to impart flavour.

Parallel to Krondorf Road to the north, Bethany Road runs east off the Barossa Valley Highway to **BETHANY**, the first German settlement in the Barossa. The land is still laid out in the eighteenth-century Hufendorf style, with long, narrow farming strips stretching out behind the cottages, and the creek running through each property. Pretty gardens set off the old stone cottages, which remain well cared for. At dusk each Saturday the bell tolls at **Herberge Christi Church**, keeping up a tradition to mark the end of the working week, and Bethany – without even a pub or shop – retains its peaceful, rural village feel.

Tanunda and around

TANUNDA is the Barossa's most quintessentially German town. The tree-lined main drag, **Murray Street**, boasts several old and beautiful buildings and proclaims its pedigree with German music wafting out of small wooden kegs above the shops. There's a more authentic atmosphere in the narrow streets on the western side of town, towards the river. Here, **Goat Square** was the site of the first town market and is bordered by the original cottages; the early market is re-enacted during the Vintage Festival (see p.780). Many wineries dot the town, the largest concentration being along **Para Road**, beside the Para River, including Stanley Brothers, Peter Lehmann, Richmond Grove, Langmeil and Veritas, all of which can be visited in the course of a pleasant stroll along the road and river.

For a good introduction to the region, head to the **Barossa visitor centre**, 66–68 Murray St (Mon–Fri 9am–5pm, Sat & Sun 10am–4pm; wine centre daily 10am–4pm; $2; ☏08/8563 0600 or 1300 852 982, ⓦwww.barossa .com). The low-key **Historical Museum**, 47 Murray St (Mon–Fri 10am–5pm, Sat & Sun 10am–4pm; $3), crams local history into a small quaint building which it shares with an antiques shop.

Three kilometres out of town, **Norm's Coolies**, at "Breezy Gully" off Gomersal Road (Mon, Wed & Sat 2pm; $12, children $5; ☏08/8563 2198), could only be in Australia: 28 sheepdogs are put through their paces by Norm and a herd of sheep. Note that the dogs are not allowed to perform when the temperature exceeds thirty degrees. **Mengler's Hill Lookout**, east of Tanunda along Basedow Road and then the Mengler's Hill Road Scenic Drive, provides an unmatched view of the valley and its vineyards: there's a **sculpture garden** with white marble sculptures on the slopes below, and at night you can see the lights of Adelaide.

Seppeltsfield, off the highway 4km northwest of Tanunda, must be, visually at least, the most spectacular of the wineries. During the Great Depression the Seppelt family paid their workers in food to plant an avenue of date palms from Marananga to Seppeltsfield; on a hill halfway along the palm-lined avenue stands the Seppelt **family mausoleum**, resting place of the male members of the family. The estate itself was founded in 1851 when Joseph Seppelt, a wealthy merchant, arrived from Silesia with his workers: he turned to wine making when his tobacco crop failed, establishing the largest winery in the colony, with everything from a port-maturation cellar to a distillery, vinegar factory and brandy bond store. All have been preserved in their original condition, and can be seen on one of the many **tours** and **private tastings** offered (daily 11.30am, 1.30pm & 3.30pm; $10–79; ⓦwww.seppeltsfield.com.au; ☏08/8568 6217).

While there is a mind-boggling array of wineries here, this selection should start you off on a good footing.

Bethany Wines Bethany Rd, Bethany ⓦ www .bethany.com.au. A hillside winery set in an old quarry, with views over Bethany Village; the Schrapel family have grown grapes here for over 150 years and produce consistently good wines. Very good reds (the Shiraz is outstanding) and a decent Semillon. Mon–Sat 10am–5pm, Sun 1–5pm.

Charles Melton Krondorf Rd, Tanunda ⓦ www .charlesmeltonwines.com.au. Small, friendly winery concentrating on a limited range of handcrafted, full-bodied reds that sell out fast. Look for the Nine Popes, their Shiraz and Cabornot Sauvignon, as you sit at their informal tasting area.

Henschke Moculta Rd, Keyneton, 14km southeast of Angaston ⓦ www.henschke.com .au. Fifth-generation winemakers, the Henschke family's red wines are some of the best in Australia – their Hill of Grace red is second only to Penfold's Grange in terms of prestige, taste and price. It's located in a peaceful setting off the beaten track and you'll need to ring the bell to rouse the amiable staff and start tasting their outstanding range. Mon–Fri 9am–4.30pm, Sat 9am–noon.

Kabminye Wines Krondorf Rd, Tanunda ⓦ www.kabminye.com. Relatively new family-run winery with a modern restaurant serving authentic Barossa food in a loungey atmosphere, and an art gallery upstairs. Best known for their rare combination of Mataro, Carignan, Cinsaut and Black Frontignac grapes in their red Schliebs Block wine. Daily 11am–5pm.

Langmeil Winery Langmeil Rd, near Tanunda ⓦ www.langmeilwinery.com.au. This was the original Langmeil village, built in the 1840s; the little vineyard you can see from the tasting area was planted in 1846. Prints of nineteenth-century photos on the walls document the local wine industry. An outstanding winery with excellent reds, particularly the Shiraz – try their increasingly popular sparkling variety. Daily 10.30am–4.30pm.

Peter Lehmann Para Rd, near Tanunda ⓦ www.peterlehmannwines.com.au. A pleasant spot for a picnic as well as a tasting, the cellar door is housed in a homestead with vine-entwined verandas surrounded by flower-beds, gum trees and palms, overlooking a lawn leading down to the Para River. While the winery is now American-owned and the wines satisfy several price points, there are still some excellent wines produced here, such as their Reserve Riesling and their more expensive Shiraz wines. Mon–Fri 9.30am–5pm, Sat & Sun 10.30am–4.30pm.

Richmond Grove Para Rd, near Tanunda ⓦ www.richmondgrovewines.com. Large, historic winery with a lovely picnic area alongside the North Para River. The winery is a big producer, sourcing grapes widely to produce their wines. They do a decent Watervale Riesling. Daily 10.30am–4.30pm.

Rockford Wines Krondorf Rd, Tanunda. Excellent winery with outstanding wines by Robert O'Callahan, produced using old-fashioned techniques. The wines are hard to find, so snap up the Basket Press Shiraz, the amazing fizzy Black Shiraz or their Eden Valley Riesling. Mon–Sat 11am–5pm.

Seppeltsfield Estate Seppeltsfield Rd, Seppeltsfield via Nuriootpa ⓦ www.seppelt.com .au. This historic property (see opposite0) is known for its wonderful collection of fortified wines as well as its historic buildings. They also have guided tours of their fortification facilities – book in advance. Mon–Fri 10am–5pm, Sat & Sun 11am–5pm.

St Halletts Winery St Hallett's Rd, Tanunda ⓦ www.sthallet.com.au. Medium-size, quality producer whose star wine is Old Block Shiraz, sourced from vines eighty to a hundred years old, with an intense flavour and a velvety softness. Daily 10am–5pm.

Turkey Flat Vineyards Bethany Rd, Tanunda ⓦ www.turkeyflat.com.au. Named after the bush turkeys that used to wander here, this vineyard has the second-oldest Shiraz grapes of the valley, planted 158 years ago. Also famous for their rosé. Daily 11am–5pm.

Yalumba Wines Eden Valley Rd, Angaston ⓦ www.yalumba.com. Largest and oldest family-operated Barossa winery, established in 1849, set in a lovely building and gardens. Daily 10am–5pm.

Nuriootpa, Angaston and Springton

Just 7km from Tanunda, **NURIOOTPA** is the valley's commercial centre: as the place where local Aborigines gathered to barter, it takes its name from the word for "meeting place". The town is dominated by **Penfolds**, the Barossa's largest winery and famous for producing Australia's most collectable wine, Penfolds Grange. The finest building here is **Coulthard House**, a gracious, two-storey edifice commissioned by the area's first settler, William Coulthard. The town grew around his red-gum slab hotel, now the site of the *Vine Inn* hotel.

ANGASTON, southeast of Nuriootpa, is a pretty little town situated in the Barossa Ranges, an area of predominantly grazing land, red gums and rolling hills, although a few of the Barossa's oldest winemakers have been here for more than a century. This is the side of the Barossa that attracted the British pioneers, including George Fife Angas, the Scotsman after whom the town is named. The **Collingrove Homestead** (guided tours only Mon–Fri 1–4.30pm, Sat & Sun noon–4.30pm; $10; Ⓦ www.collingrovehomestead.com.au), 6km from town on Eden Valley Road, was one of his homes. Now the National Trust-protected home is a **B&B** (Ⓞ) surrounded by lush gardens. Angas also lived at nearby Lindsay Park, now the private **Lindsay Park Stud**, Australia's leading racehorse breeding and training complex.

The major attraction at **SPRINGTON**, 20km south of Angaston, is the **Herbig family tree**, a hollowed-out gum tree in which a pioneer German couple lived for five years from 1855; they began their married life in the tree and had two of their sixteen children in it. Inevitably, Springton's old buildings have undergone the "boutique-ing" process: the blacksmith's is now a winery, and the old post office has been transformed into an arts and crafts gallery.

Barossa accommodation

There's comfortable **accommodation** throughout the valley and you shouldn't have a problem finding somewhere to stay. If you need help, try Getaways Reservation Service (☎1300 136 970, Ⓦ www.grs.com.au), or for B&Bs, try Barossa B&B Booking Service (☎1800 227 677, Ⓦ www.bnbbookings.com.au).

Barossa Brauhaus Hotel 41 Murray St, Angaston ☎08/8564 2014. Basic rooms and cheap singles in a centrally located, historic pub, first licensed in 1849. Light breakfast included. No en suite. ❸

Barossa Doubles Dvine Barossa Valley Highway, 1.5km south of Nuriootpa ☎&Ⓕ08/8562 2260, Ⓦ www.doublesdvine.com.au. A simple, friendly, family-run plane set in vineyards, the self-contained accommodation is in a cottage or lodge. Bike rental $25 per day. Lodge ❸, cottage ❹

Blickinstal Vineyard Retreat Rifle Range Rd, Tanunda ☎08/8563 2716. Great views over the valley from this peacefully set six-suite B&B nestled into the foothills of the Barossa. All units are self-contained and a four-course breakfast and afternoon tea are included. ❻–❼

Caithness Manor 12 Hill St, Angaston ☎08/8564 2761, Ⓦ www.caithness.com.au. A former girls' grammar school whose lower storey has been transformed into a gracious guesthouse run by a friendly family. There's a sitting room with open fires, a swimming pool and spa. The spacious guest rooms are decorated with antique furnishings. Gourmet breakfast included. ❽

Langmeil Cottages Langmeil Rd, Tanunda ☎08/8563 2987, Ⓦ www.langmeilcottages.com. German-style stone cottage in a peaceful setting with kitchenette, spa and pool. Extras include champagne on arrival, breakfast provisions, free bicycles, and laundry facilities. ❺

Lawley Farm Krondorf Rd, south of Tanunda ☎08/8563 2141, Ⓦ www.lawleyfarm.com.au. Full of charm, these restored historic stone cottages, shaded by peppertrees, are within walking distance of wineries. Fresh flowers, fruit baskets and complimentary port, and breakfast provisions are provided. ❼–❽

The Louise Seppeltsfield Rd, Marananga ☎08/8562 2722, Ⓦ www.thelouise.com.au /thelouise. The luxurious rooms at this intimate boutique hotel have private terraces and all the mod cons you can imagine, from BOSE sound systems to espresso machines. The most expensive suites have outdoor showers. ❾

Novotel Barossa Valley Resort Golf Links
Rd, Rowland Flat, Tanunda ☏ 08/8524 0000,
ⓦ www.novotelbarossa.com.au. The best option for
those who want comfort, style and the convenience
of resort facilities – a superb restaurant *Harry's*, a
gourmet gift shop, good swimming pool, crèche for
the kids – without paying a fortune. Topping those
off: sweeping valley views. ❼–❾

Seppeltsfield Vineyard Cottage Gerald
Roberts Rd, Seppeltsfield ☏ 08/ 8563
4059, ⓦ www.seppeltsfieldvineyardcottage.com.
au. It doesn't get more exclusive than this, with
an entire elegant German settler's cottage all to
yourself. Enjoy wonderful views over the valley
from your bathtub. The award-winning B&B
requires a two-night minimum stay, though you'll
probably need little encouragement to stay
longer. ❾

Tanunda Caravan and Tourist Park Barossa
Valley Way, Tanunda ☏ 08/8563 2784,
ⓦ www.tanundacaravantouristpark.com.au. Set in
parkland among beautiful waratah trees, this park
caters well for families with heated swimming pool,
playground and a "jumping pillow". Powered sites
$25, cabins ❸, cottages ❺–❻

Tanunda Hotel 51 Murray St, Tanunda ☏ 08/8563
2030 or 8563 2165, ⓦ www.tanundapub.com. Built
from local stone and marble in 1845, with
Edwardian additions and decor inside. All rooms
have TV, a/c, fridge, tea and coffee; some are en
suite. ❸–❹

Vine Inn Hotel Motel 14 Murray St, Nuriootpa
☏ 08/8562 2133, ⓦ www.vineinn.com.au.
Spacious, modern motel-style units with a/c and
queen-size beds; continental breakfast included
and there's a spa and heated pool. ❺

Barossa eating and drinking

There are excellent **restaurants** throughout the valley, as well as plenty of picnic
spots and barbecue areas. Make the most of the restaurants at the wineries, as they
are usually blessed with a picturesque setting overlooking vineyards.

1918 Bistro and Grill 94 Murray St, Tanunda
☏ 08/8563 0405. The focus of this fine restaurant is
on Asian- and Middle Eastern-inspired modern
cuisine, which makes use of the freshest Australian
ingredients. Dine outside on the shady veranda, or
inside the atmospheric old house, built in 1918,
with its cosy fireplace. A blackboard features a well-
chosen list of local wines. Daily lunch & dinner.

Alfresco at Junipers 33 Murray St, Angaston
☏ 08/ 8564 3277. Open seven days a week for
breakfast, lunch and dinner. Australian cuisine with
Mediterranean influences in a lovely leafy garden.

Appellation Seppeltsfield Rd, Marananga
☏ 08/8562 4144. The food is chosen to match the
wine on the nine-course degustation menu ($195
per person) at boutique hotel *The Louise's* (see
opposite) elegant on-site restaurant. While it may
be expensive, unfortunately the food can be hit and
miss, although service is consistently excellent.

Barossa Wurst Haus and Bakery 86A Murray St,
Tanunda. Specializing in traditional Barossa
Mettwurst (German sausage) and other German
delights, this delicatessen offers tasty great-value
food. Daily 7.30am–5pm.

Harry's Golf Links Rd, Rowland Flat, Tanunda,
☏ 08/8524 0000. The impressive cuisine is
based on the freshest of regional produce,
from South Australian grain-fed beef to fish
straight from Adelaide's markets to local
Woodside cheeses. Dishes such as Westbridge
rabbit and wild mushroom terrine served with
red onion marmalade are divine. That it's such

great value (2 courses $46; 3 courses $58) is a
bonus. ❼–❾

Harvesters Café 29D Murray St, Nuriootpa
☏ 08/8562 1348. Spacious, contemporary café
with a pleasant courtyard serving cooked breakfasts, home-made soups and vegetarian dishes.
Tues–Sun 9am–5.30pm.

Lyndoch Bakery & Restaurant Barossa Valley
Highway, Lyndoch. The best German bakery in the
Barossa. The adjoining licensed restaurant serves
hearty, moderately priced traditional dishes. Daily
11am–2.30pm & 6pm until late.

Salters Saltram Winery, Nuriootpa Rd, Angaston
☏ 08/8561 0200. Elegant bistro serving delicious
modern Australian-Italian cuisine, all freshly
prepared and reasonably priced. The nineteenth-
century winery specializes in full-bodied reds – try
them at the cellar door before eating. Open daily
for lunch, dinner Fri & Sat. Book ahead in summer.

Vintners Bar and Grill Corner of Stockwell and
Nuriootpa rds, Angaston ☏ 08/8564 2488. A
winemakers' hangout with Mediterranean-inspired
regional produce on the menu and a suitably impressive wine list. The design seamlessly melds contemporary style with old stone walls, fireplaces and
wooden beams, and there's a vine-covered courtyard
for warm days. Open daily for lunch, dinner Mon–Sat.

Zinfandel Tea Rooms 58 Murray St, Tanunda.
Popular place for hot, cooked breakfasts, German
and Australian dishes for lunch and delicious
strudels and cakes. You can sit inside the cozy
cottage or out on the veranda. Daily 8.30am–5pm.

The Fleurieu Peninsula

The **Fleurieu Peninsula** (ⓦwww.fleurieupeninsula.com.au), thirty minutes south of Adelaide by car, is bounded by Gulf St Vincent to the west and the Southern Ocean to the south, the two connected by the Backstairs Passage at **Cape Jervis** (where ferries leave for Kangaroo Island, see p.793). There are fine beaches on both coasts and more wineries inland in the rolling **McLaren Vale** region. It's a picturesque area: many of the towns were settled from the 1830s, and there's a lot of colonial architecture, much of it now housing restaurants or B&Bs.

For a round trip, leave the city via the Adelaide Hills and cut down through Mount Barker to well-preserved Strathalbyn and then down to Goolwa on the south coast, before circling round through Victor Harbor, Yankalilla, Willunga and McLaren Vale. The peninsula is a good place to **cycle** – in addition to its roads it has two sealed bike paths: the 24-kilometre **Encounter Bikeway** (see box, p.789) follows the coast from Goolwa to just beyond Victor Harbor; and another shorter path runs between Willunga and McLaren Vale. For walkers, the **Heysen Trail** starts at the southern tip of the peninsula at Cape Jervis and winds its way across the hilly countryside north to the Adelaide Hills and beyond. Although the trail is meant for long-distance walking, there are a number of well-signposted short walks along the way, including the 3.5-kilometre **Deep Creek Waterfall Trail**, just east of Cape Jervis with its wild coastal scenery. The Heysen Trail also passes through the Mount Magnificent Conservation Park, which contains a number of shorter walks offering excellent panoramic views.

If you're relying on **public transport**, Premier Stateliner (ⓣ08/8415 5555) makes four trips daily from Adelaide to Goolwa via McLaren Vale, Willunga, Victor Harbor and Port Elliot. There's also a sporadic service provided by the *Southern Encounter* and *Highlander* **steam trains** (occasionally replaced by a diesel locomotive) which chug from Mount Barker to Victor Harbor and Strathalbyn respectively (first Sun of month June–Nov; ⓣ1300 655 991, ⓦwww.steamranger.org.au). Adelaide Sightseeing Tours run **tours** to the area (Wed & Sat; $79; ⓣ08/8413 6199, ⓦwww.adelaidesightseeing.com.au), visiting Goolwa, Victor Harbor and McLaren Vale and connecting with Coorong Pelican cruises from Goolwa, with optional overnight stays at Victor Harbor to see the penguins at Granite Island.

The McLaren Vales

The wineries of **McLaren Vale**, in the northwest of the peninsula, are virtually in Adelaide, as the suburban fringes of the city now push right up to **REYNELLA**, where the first vineyards were planted in 1838. Among the earliest was Hardy's Reynella Winery (daily 10am–4.30pm), on Reynella Road, where the tasting room occupies the original ironstone and brick building, set in botanical gardens. There are several other wineries in Reynella, but the largest concentration – often in bush settings only an hour's drive from Adelaide – is around the small town of **McLAREN VALE**, a "boutique" town, with many B&Bs and restaurants catering for the wine-buff weekend crowd, which has about fifty wineries, mostly small and family run. Since the 1960s there has been a trend for grape growers to switch from supplying winemakers to producing their own wine, and there's a swath of "boutique" wineries here as a result. More recently, the area has gained a reputation for its **olives**, and a number of shops have opened for tastings and sales. The Olive Grove (daily 9am–5pm), opposite the D'Arenberg winery, is the best, with excellent olives, oils, pesto and other sauces.

Listed below are seven favourites from a wide choice of excellent wineries.

Chapel Hill Chapel Hill Rd, McLaren Vale, adjacent to the Onkaparinga Gorge ⓦ www .chapelhillwine.com.au. A small but very civilized winery in an old stone chapel with nice views over the vineyards. Daily noon–5pm.

D'Arenberg Osborn Rd, McLaren Vale ⓦ www .darenberg.com.au. A family winery set up in 1928, well known for its prize-winning reds and excellent restaurant. Daily 10am–5pm.

Hoffmann's Ingoldby Rd, McLaren Flat ⓦ www.hoffmannwine.com.au. One of the smaller wineries with only a few wines to choose from, available exclusively through the cellar door or by mail order. A great place to sit in a peaceful setting and chat about wines with the friendly owners. Cellar door Thurs–Tues 11am–5pm, lunch Thurs–Tues.

Kay Brothers Amery Wines Kays Rd, McLaren Vale ⓦ www.kaybrothersamerywines.com. A wonderful family winery established in 1890; old photos of the family and the area cover the oak casks containing port. It's renowned for its Block 6 Shiraz from vines planted in 1892,

though it sells out quickly. Also has a picnic area set amid towering gum trees. Mon–Fri 9am–5pm, Sat & Sun noon–5pm.

Samuel's Gorge Corner of Chaffey and Chapel rds, McLaren Vale ⓦ www.gorge.com.au. The smallest winery, located in an 1853 homestead with a Jamaican-born winemaker who won't discuss wines with you without a glass himself. His Shiraz is one of the most outstanding in the region, and there's also a fine Tempranillo and Grenache. Fri–Mon 11am–5pm.

Scarpantoni Scarpantoni Drive, McLaren Flat ⓦ www.scarpantoniwines.com. Small, prize-winning winery run by an Italian family, with a contemporary cellar more akin to a city wine bar. Mon–Fri 9am–5pm, Sat & Sun 11am–5pm.

Wirra Wirra McMurtie Rd, McLaren Vale ⓦ www.wirrawirra.com. A large, classic ironstone building provides the setting for an impressive range of reds (especially Shiraz) and whites (try the Chardonnay). Mon–Sat 10am–5pm, Sun 11am–5pm.

Practicalities

Information on the area's wineries can be found at the **McLaren Vale and Fleurieu visitor centre** on Main Road, about 2km from the centre (daily 10am–5pm; ☏08/8323 9944, ⓦ www.mclarenvale.info), and the welcoming staff can also book **accommodation**. Among the town's B&Bs are the historic *Claddagh Cottages*, Lot 8, Caffrey St (☏08/8323 9806; ⓦ www.3divas .com.au ❼–❽), three comfortable cottages within walking distance of the town centre, and *Southern Vales*, 13 Chalk Hill Rd (☏08/8323 8144; ❻), a bit larger and with vineyard views. If you have a **tent**, the *Lakeside Caravan Park*, Field Street (☏08/8323 9255, ⓦ www.mclarenvale.net; un/powered sites $22/26, cabins ❹–❺), is your best bet, with a pool, tennis and volleyball in a scenic setting.

Most places to **eat** in town are fairly casual cafés although a few of the wineries have fine restaurants. For a relaxed lunch, try *Blessed Cheese* at 150 Main Rd, where, aside from the divine dairy products, you can sample locally grown olives and great coffee. This is also the pick-up point for your cheese hamper for the *Cheese and Wine Trail* (ⓦ www.cheeseandwinetrails.com.au; $50), taking you past several wineries where you can taste matching wines. The award-winning *Magnum Bistro* in the *Hotel McLaren*, 208 Main Rd (☏08/8323 8208), has delicious main courses, all reasonably priced. Across the road at no. 201, the stylish *Oscar's* serves Mediterranean salads, pizza and pasta. Good restaurants include *The Barn*, on the corner of Main and Chalk Hill roads (☏08/8323 8618), where you can dine on moderately priced contemporary cuisine accompanied by lovely local wines. On the corner of McMurtie Road, in the direction of Willunga, the award-winning *Salopian*

Inn (℡08/8323 8769; Fri & Sat lunch, dinner daily except Tues & Sun) is set in an atmospheric 1851 stone inn with a seasonally varying menu. The best restaurant, however, is *d'Arry's Verandah* at d'Arenberg Winery (℡08/8329 4848, ⓦwww.darenberg.com.au) which dishes up sublime plates of exquisitely prepared regional produce.

Gulf St Vincent beaches

A series of superb swimming beaches, often known as the **wine coast**, runs along the Gulf St Vincent shore roughly parallel to McLaren Vale, from **O'Sullivan Beach** down to **Sellicks Beach**. All are easily accessible from Adelaide on public transport: take the train from Adelaide to Noarlunga Centre and bus #750 or #751 to the various beaches.

   PORT NOARLUNGA is the main town, surrounded by steep cliffs and sand hills. Its jetty is popular with anglers and with wetsuit-clad teenagers who dive from it; at low tide a natural reef is exposed. Lifesavers patrol the beaches, and you can rent surf and snorkelling gear at Ocean Graffix Surf and Skate Centre, 21 Salt Fleet Point. **Moana**, two beaches south, has fairly tame surf that's perfect for novices. The southern end of **Maslins Beach**, south again, broke new ground by becoming Australia's first legal nude beach in 1975. The wide, isolated beach is reached by a long, steep walking track down the colourful cliffs from the Tait Road car park, deterring all but the committed naturist. **Port Willunga**, the next stop down, offers interesting diving around the wreck of the *Star of Greece*, while just further south is Aldinga Beach, reached by the daily Adelaide–Cape Jervis Public Coach Service. From here there's a connecting bus to Sellicks Beach where, if you have your own car, you can drive along 6km of firm sand.

   The coastal region south of here is more rugged, although there are some nice secluded beaches as well as the popular Heritage-listed sand dunes at **NORMANVILLE**. You can camp here at *Jetty Caravan Park Normanville* (℡08/8558 2038, ⓦwww.normanvillebeach.net.au; un/powered sites $20/25, en-suite cabins & villas ❺). A few kilometres inland, the **Yankalilla Bay and Beyond visitor centre**, 104 Main Rd (Mon–Fri 9am–5pm, Sat & Sun 10am–4pm; ℡08/8558 2999, ⓦwww.yankalilla.sa.gov.au), has a complete list of accommodation and information on diving, fishing and surfing. A bit further down the coast, the basic campsite (℡08/8598 4139; $5) at unspoilt **Rapid Bay** is a good base if you want to go underwater exploring and try to spot the rare **Leafy Sea Dragon**. Ferries for Kangaroo Island (see p.793) depart from Cape Jervis at the end of Main South Road.

Victor Harbor

The historic holiday town of **VICTOR HARBOR**, on Encounter Bay, is experiencing a renaissance, thanks principally to whales and penguins. In the 1830s there were three whaling stations here, hunting **southern right whales**, which came to Encounter Bay to mate and breed between June and September, heading close to shore, where they became easy targets. Not surprisingly, their numbers began to decline, and by 1930 they had been hunted almost to extinction. Half a century later there were signs of recovery: in 1991, forty were spotted in the bay and eighty thousand people flocked to see them, while in 1998, sixteen females stayed in the bay to calf, and a dozen humpback whales were also spotted. In recent years, there have been regular sightings of hundreds of calves each year enjoying the calm waters.

   A Heritage-listed former railway goods shed on Railway Terrace now houses the **South Australian Whale Centre** (daily 9.30am–5pm; $8; ℡08/8551

The Encounter Bikeway

The Encounter Bikeway follows a scenic 24-kilometre stretch of coast between Victor Harbor and Goolwa. Parts of the route are on-road and slightly inland, but mostly it follows the coastline and is for cyclists and walkers only. The return trip can be completed comfortably in a day; the most scenic – and hilliest – section is between Dump Beach in Victor Harbor and the town of Port Elliot. Mountain-bike rental is available at Victor Harbor Cycle & Skate, 73 Victoria St, Victor Harbor ($20 per day; ☏08/8552 1417), or at the *Whalers Inn*, 121 Franklin Parade, Victor Harbor (from $30 per day; ☏08/8552 4400). Unfortunately, there's no bike rental available in Goolwa and none offers a drop-off service for one-way journeys, but on Sundays you can take your bike on the *Cockle Train* (see below) between Victor Harbor and Goolwa and cycle back.

0750; ⓦwww.sawhalecentre.com.au), with excellent interpretive displays, exhibits and screenings on whaling and the natural history of whales, dolphins and the marine environment. The centre also acts as a monitoring station, locating and tracking whales, and confirming sightings, most likely between June and August. Call the **Whale Information Hotline** (☏1900 942 537) if you spot a whale, or for information on where you can see them. Two-hour **whale cruises** depart from Granite Island in season (daily June–Sept; $90; ☏08/8552 7000).

As well as whales, **Little penguins** come to nest, roost and moult on **Granite Island**, which is linked to the esplanade by a narrow causeway. At dusk they come back from feeding – this is the best time to see them, on one of the ranger-led **penguin walks** run by Granite Island Nature Park (daily at dusk; 1hr; $12.50; bookings essential on ☏08/8552 7555, ⓦwww.graniteisland.com .au). A warning: it's not possible to predict how many penguins will be around it differs each year, and could be just a dozen. Before exploring the island you can visit the **Penguin Centre**, to see rescued penguins being hand-fed (1pm & 2.30pm Wed–Fri; $6). There's also a display giving the lowdown on daily penguin life (daily 12.30–3.30pm plus an hour before the start of the walk). You can walk across the six-hundred-metre causeway to the island at any time, or take a traditional holiday ride with the **Victor Harbor Horse Tram** (daily 10am–4pm, longer in summer depending on demand; $8 return).

Other local attractions include the **Cockle Train**, a Wednesday and Sunday steam train (sometimes diesel-hauled) which runs on the otherwise disused line along the coast to Goolwa via Port Elliot and back (Sun & daily during school holidays; $26 return; ⓦwww.steamranger.org.au). If you're travelling with restless children, **Greenhills Adventure Park** on Waggon Road, alongside the Hindmarsh River (daily 10am–5pm, 6pm in summer; $22 adult, $17 child; ☏08/8552 5999, ⓦwww.greenhills.com.au), has activities from canoeing to waterslides, while the **Urimbirra Wildlife Experience** (daily 9am–6pm; $9, child $4.50), 5km north of Victor Harbor on Adelaide Road, is an open-range park with native animals from all over the continent.

Practicalities

For information on the area, head to **Victor Harbor visitor centre** next to the causeway (daily 9am–5pm; ☏08/8552 5738, ⓦwww.tourismvictorharbor .com.au); in the same building, **Top Choice Travel Booking Centre** (☏1800 088 552, ⓦwww.topchoicetravel.com.au) can book accommodation and tours. The best **place to stay** is the *Anchorage*, 21 Flinders Parade (☏08/8552 5970, ⓦwww.anchorageseafronthotel.com; ❸–❻), a lovingly restored beachfront pub dating to 1905 that was one of the earliest guesthouses in Victor Harbor, with en-suite and spa rooms with sea views and balconies.

Good places to **eat and drink** abound; those listed below are some of the best.

Café Bavaria 11 Albert Place. A popular local spot with delicious fresh-baked German cakes and light snacks at reasonable prices. Tues–Sun 8.30am–5pm.
Hotel Crown The Esplanade. A fun place to drink, with cheap counter meals, streetside tables, and bands and DJs on weekends.
Nino's 16 Albert Place. The place to be if you're after Italian food, where you can plough into some generous portions of pasta, authentic pizza, and home-made *gelati*. Daily lunch and dinner.

Ocean Grill 21 Flinders Parade at the *Anchorage* hotel. The best place to eat in town, with alfresco seats out front overlooking the sea (and lawns bowl club), generous portions of fresh seafood, and a cosy café out the back. Order at the counter. Open daily.
The Original Victor Harbor Fish Shop 20 Ocean St. This excellent, award-winning fish and chip shop has been grilling and deep-frying since 1927.

Port Elliot

PORT ELLIOT, just 5km east of Victor Harbor, is a pleasant little town with good coastal walks along the cliffs at Freeman Knob and an attractive sandy beach with safe swimming at **Horseshoe Bay**. Campers can enjoy the beachside setting at the award-winning *Port Elliot Holiday Park* (☎08/8554 2134, ⓦwww.portelliotholidaypark.com.au; un/powered sites $30/35, cabins ❹–❺, cottages ❻–❼). A more pleasant though pricier option is *Trafalgar House*, a lovely 1890 brick homestead and English-style cottage (☎08/8554 3888, ⓦwww.trafalgarhouse.com.au; ❻–❼).

Expect a queue for the mouthwatering pastries and pies of *Port Elliot Bakery* on 31 North Terrace, a great spot for **lunch**. For a superb (if expensive) meal overlooking the bay, head for the *Flying Fish Café* on The Foreshore. From here you can explore the coastal Encounter Bikeway (see box, p.789), or surf at nearby **MIDDLETON**, 4km from Goolwa, a top surfing spot with a number of well-regarded surf schools: Surf Culture (☎08/8327 2802, ⓦwww .surfcultureaustralia.com) has a brilliant reputation for success and a long list of programmes, from beginner lessons to surf camps and personal training; Surf and Sun (☎1800 786 386, ⓦwww.surfandsun.com.au) are also very good; and girls can try Learn to Surf Chicks (☎0414 341 545, ⓦwww.danosurf.com.au). Most include wet suits, boards and fins in the price, and rates range from $40 for a two-hour lesson to a three-lesson programme for $100. For experienced surfers, Waitpinga Parsons and Chiton offer more thrills, and gear can be rented from Southern Surf, 36 North Terrace (☎08/8554 2375).

Goolwa

GOOLWA lies 14km east of Port Elliot, and 12km upstream from the ever-shifting sand bar at the mouth of the Murray River. Boaties love its position adjacent to vast **Lake Alexandrina**, with easy access to the **Coorong** (see p.801) and ocean. Although it's so close to the coast, Goolwa feels like a real river town. It thrived in the days of the Murray paddle-steamer trade, when it was the steamers' final offloading port – a rip-roaring place with almost a hundred taverns and the biggest police station in South Australia. The railways brought the good times to an end, and today only a few reminders of the era remain along Railway Terrace, with its old buildings painted in Federation colours.

Steam trains make a comeback on Wednesdays and Sundays, however, when the **Cockle Train** heads along the coast to Victor Harbor and back (see p.789), and the **Southern Encounter** runs from Mount Barker in the Adelaide Hills to Goolwa via Strathalbyn and on to Port Elliot (see opposite) and Victor Harbor. There are also frequent **coaches** from Adelaide to Goolwa, run by Premier Stateliner (Mon–Fri 4 daily, Sat 2 daily, Sun 1 daily; ℡08/8414 5555).

Overlooking the wharf beside the Hindmarsh bridge is **Signal Point Interpretive Centre** (daily 10am–5pm; $5.50), housing an innovative exhibition telling the story of the Murray and its river trade, a small souvenir shop and café, as well as the helpful **Goolwa visitor centre** (daily 10am–5pm; ℡08/8555 3488, ⓦwww.alexandrina.sa.gov.au), which can book local river tours and accommodation.

For **B&Bs**, *Cottages of Goolwa* (℡0433 571 927, ⓦwww.cottagesofgoolwa .com) has a few self-catering cottages, including *Joseph's* (❼), a comfortable historic option near the centre of town. The *PS Federal* on Barrage Road (℡08/8362 6229; minimum two-night stay; ❼) started life as a working paddlesteamer in 1902 and now provides comfortable, self-contained accommodation. *Riverport Motel*, on Noble Avenue 3km northeast of Goolwa (℡08/8555 5033, ⓕ8555 5022; ❺), has motel units in a quiet setting beside the Lower Murray River, plus a pool, tennis court, bar and inexpensive dining room. Alternatively, try the *Corio Hotel* on Railway Terrace (℡08/8555 2011, ⓕ8555 1109; ❹), which has a popular bistro. The *Whistlestop Café* on Hays Street, and *Café Lime* just across the road, both do good coffee, cakes, snacks and light meals. Campers can head for *Goolwa Caravan Park*, Noble Avenue (℡08/8555 2737, ⓕ8555 1095, ⓦwww.goolwacaravanpark.com.au; un/powered sites $28/32, cabins ❸).

Strathalbyn

The pretty town of **STRATHALBYN** sits quietly among rolling hills about 25km north of Goolwa and an hour's drive southeast of Adelaide. Settled in 1839 by Scottish immigrants, the historic town is the market centre for the surrounding farming community, but is also renowned for its antique shops, Heritage-listed buildings and serene atmosphere. Strathalbyn comes alive during its irregular but well-publicized horse-racing meetings and for a few traditional **festivals**: an antiques fair held in the third week of August, and an agricultural show and duck race in October or November. For a self-guided walking tour of the town, pick up a brochure from the **Strathalbyn visitor centre**, at the Old Railway Station on South Terrace (daily 9am–5pm; ℡08/8536 3212).

The best of the town's many **B&Bs** is the *Watervilla*, 2 Mill St (℡08/8536 4099; ❼), a beautiful 1840s cottage overlooking landscaped gardens and the River Angas Park. Alternatively, the historic *Victoria Hotel* has decent motel rooms and a reasonable bistro (℡08/8536 2202, ⓕ8536 2469; ❺). For **eating**, *Café Ruffino*, on the High Street, serves excellent home-made pastries and cakes, while *Jack's Bakery*, on the other side of the street, has good coffee and an interesting gourmet menu. The only regular **public transport** is from Adelaide on

Transit bus #843 via Adelaide Hills (Mon–Fri only); alternatively, if your timing's right, the *Southern Encounter* and *Highlander* steam trains chug in from Mount Barker and Goolwa on selected Sundays (see p.786).

The Yorke Peninsula

The **Yorke Peninsula** was almost the last section of the Australian coastline to be mapped by Matthew Flinders in 1802. Flat plains stretch out to the sea, so extensively cleared for farming that only tiny areas of original vegetation remain – in the Innes National Park at the very tip of the peninsula and in a couple of conservation parks. While much is made of the northern peninsula's **Cornish heritage**, the miners from Cornwall who flocked to the area when **copper** was discovered in 1859 have left behind little but their names and the ubiquitous Cornish pasty. The three towns of the Copper Triangle or "**Little Cornwall**" – Kadina, Wallaroo and Moonta – celebrate their heritage at the Kernewek Lowender (Cornish Festival), held over the long weekend in May of odd-numbered years.

Just two hours' drive from Adelaide, the peninsula offers a peaceful weekend break as well as good **fishing**. The east-coast ports of Ardrossan, Port Vincent and Edithburgh on the Gulf St Vincent were visited first by ketches and schooners, and later by steamers transporting wheat and barley to England; now, the remaining jetties are used by anglers. They're all pleasant to visit, but **EDITHBURGH** offers the most facilities – once a substantial salt-production town and grain port, it still has a few fine old buildings and a long jetty. There's also a tidal swimming pool set in a rocky cove, and from Troubridge Hill you can see across to the Fleurieu Peninsula and the offshore **Troubridge Island Conservation Park**, with its 1850s iron lighthouse, migrating seabirds and **Little penguin population**: guided tours are available (on demand only; 2hr; $40; ☎08/8852 6290). **Accommodation** is available in the lighthouse-keeper's cottage, which sleeps up to ten and a minimum of four – if you stay here you'll have the whole island to yourself (arrange through the tour guide; minimum two-night stay; ❼–❽).

In Edithburgh itself, accommodation options include foreshore motel units and comfortable two-bedroom apartments at *The Anchorage Motel and Holiday Units*, 25 O'Halloran Parade (☎08/8852 6262, ℱ8852 6147; holiday units and rooms ❹–❺), and *Edithburgh Caravan Park* (☎08/8852 6056, ⓦwww .edithburghcaravanpark.com) further along the foreshore, which has un/powered sites $22/26 and en-suite cabins (❸–❺). There are also motel units at the back of the *Troubridge Hotel* on Main Street (☎08/8852 6013, ℱ8852 6323; ❹–❺). Across the road, the 1878 *Edithburgh Hotel* is the best place for **meals**; don't miss the sublime oysters.

At the tip of the peninsula lies the **Innes National Park**, with its contrasting coastline of rough cliffs, sweeps of beach and sand dunes, and its interior of mallee scrub. The park is untouched except for the ruins of the gypsum-mining town of **Inneston**, near **Stenhouse Bay**. The **visitor centre** (☎08/8854 3200) in the park sells entry permits ($8 per car) and **camping permits** ($4–16 per car depending on which campsite you choose) with facilities such as hot showers and barbecues. The main camping area is at **Pondalowie Bay**, which has some of the best **surf** in the state; there are several other good surfing spots around the park and north towards Corny Point. Other more sheltered coves and bays are good for **snorkelling**, with shallow reef areas of colourful marine life, while on land you might see emus, western grey kangaroos, pygmy possums and mallee fowl. The **Department of Environment and Heritage (DEH)** also operates five self-contained lodges around Inneston (☎08/8854 3200, ℱ8854 3299; ❸–❼).

Premier Stateliner (℡08/8415 5555) has a daily **bus service** from Adelaide to Moonta, via Kadina and Wallaroo. The Yorke Peninsula Passenger Service (℡08/8391 2977) runs from Adelaide to Yorketown, alternating daily between the east coast via Ardrossan, Port Vincent and Edithburgh and the centre via Maitland and Minlaton. There's no transport to Innes National Park. For more information, visit Ⓦwww.yorkepeninsula.com.au.

Kangaroo Island

As you head towards **Cape Jervis** along the west coast of the Fleurieu Peninsula, **KANGAROO ISLAND**, only 13km offshore, first appears behind a vale of rolling hills. Once you're on the island, its size and lack of development – there's only one person for every square kilometre – leave a strong impression. This is actually Australia's third-largest island (after Tasmania and Melville Island, north of Darwin), with 450km of spectacular, wild coastline, and so takes some time to explore. To see all the island's unusual geological features and **wildlife** habitats, you'll need at least three days, though most people only visit the major attractions on the south coast – Seal Bay, Little Sahara, Remarkable Rocks and Flinders Chase National Park.

Although the island is promoted as South Australia's premier destination for tourism, it's still very unspoilt; only in the peak holiday period (Christmas to the end of Jan, when most of the accommodation is booked up) does it feel busy. Once out of the island's few small towns, there's little sign of human presence to break the long, straight stretches of road which run through

▲ Kangaroo Island

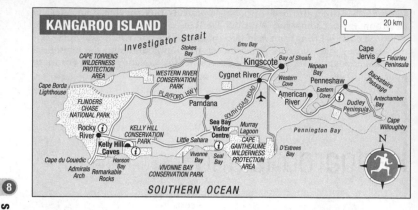

undulating fields, dense gum forests and mallee scrub. There's often a strong wind off the Southern Ocean, so bring something warm whatever the season, and take care when swimming – there are strong rips on many beaches. **Safe swimming spots** include Hog Bay and Antechamber Bay, both near Penneshaw; Emu Bay, northwest of Kingscote; Stokes Bay, further west; and Vivonne Bay, on the south side of the island.

A third of Kangaroo Island is protected in some form, and is consequently one of the best places in Australia for **wildlife spotting**; there's an astonishing range of animals here, largely untroubled by disease or natural predators. When Matthew Flinders first sighted the island in 1802, "black substances" seen on shore in the twilight turned out to be **kangaroos**, prolific and easily hunted; they still abound, as do wallabies. **Koalas** were introduced at Flinders Chase National Park in 1923 as a conservation measure. They have remained free of chlamydia, which is common in the mainland population, and have spread so widely that they are killing off many of the gum trees, and need to be culled in some parts. Other animals found here include echidnas, platypuses, Little penguins, fur seals, sea lions and, in passing, southern right whales. The island is also home to over two hundred other kinds of **birds**, as well as snakes, some of them venomous.

Wild pigs and feral goats, the descendants of those left here by early seafarers, can also be found, while a pure strain of **Ligurian bees** brought by early settlers now forms the basis of a local honey industry. There are also over a million **sheep** on the island, most of them merino, and a sheep dairy here makes delicious cheeses. The latest local craze is for **marron farming**, with about 140 licensed producers of the freshwater crustacean, a bit like a cross between a lobster and a yabbie. Other diverse new industries include abalone farming, oyster and mussel production, olive-oil pressing and the revival of eucalyptus-oil distilling.

Getting to the island

The expensive Kangaroo Island Sealink **ferries** ply across the Backstairs Passage from Cape Jervis to Penneshaw – often a rough journey, though mercifully short. Two large vehicle ferries make the journey at least three times daily, and up to seven times during peak holiday periods, taking about forty minutes to cross: buses connect the service with Adelaide twice daily ($86 ferry return, $44 extra for transfers to/from Adelaide, cars $168, motorbikes $54, bikes/

windsurfers/surfboards $20; ☎13 13 01, ⓦwww.sealink.com.au). At Penneshaw, connecting Sealink buses run to American River ($12 one-way) and Kingscote ($15), though they need to be booked in advance on the same number.

In addition, it's worth checking out various cheap **packages**, including accommodation and tours or car rental, often with special backpacker rates. At one end of the scale, Adelaide Sightseeing does a whirlwind $230 one-day coach tour leaving Adelaide at 6.45am and returning at 10.40pm – that's a long day. The Groovy Grape (☎08/8440 1640 or 1800 66 11 77, ⓦwww.groovygrape.com.au) people offer a couple of tours from Adelaide (two days; $345, three days; $445 all-inclusive). The Wayward Bus's two-day tour from Adelaide also takes advantage of an overnight stop near the Flinders Chase National Park, giving more time for viewing the spectacular sights there ($380 per person, or $417 to upgrade from dorm to twin or double room; ☎08/8410 8833, ⓦwww.waywardbus.com.au).

It takes thirty minutes to **fly** to Kingscote Airport (actually closer to Cygnet River) on Kangaroo Island from Adelaide – costs vary, starting from $120 for a return ticket. There's a bus to Kingscote for about $10 with Airport Shuttle Services (☎08/8553 2390).

Getting around, tours and activities

There's no public transport on the island apart from a coach service that runs between Kingscote, American River and Penneshaw connecting with SeaLink ferry services, so without a tour or your own vehicle, hiring a car is pretty much essential. There are two **car rental** firms; it's best to book ahead to be sure of getting a vehicle and ensure you'll be met with it off the ferry or plane. Budget Rent a Car has an office at Penneshaw Ferry Terminal (☎08/8553 3133), or you could try Kangaroo Island Rental/Hertz in Kingscote, on the corner of Franklin Street and Telegraph Road (☎08/8553 2390 or 1800 088 296, ⓦwww.hertz.com.au). Both have a desk at the airport and prices range from around $65 for a small car to 4WDs starting from around $120 a day. Always book ahead for Kangaroo Island rentals.

Roads to most major attractions are bitumen-sealed, including the scenic eighty-kilometre **South Coast Road** from Cygnet River to the Flinders Chase National Park, Remarkable Rocks and Admirals Arch. The main drag is the **Playford Highway**, running from Kingscote through Cygnet River and Parndana to the western tip of the island at Cape Borda; the last part of the highway along the northern edge of Flinders Chase National Park is not sealed and can be rough. At the eastern end of the highway, sealed roads feed off to the airport, Emu Bay, American River and Penneshaw. Most other roads are constructed of ironstone rubble on red dirt and can be very dangerous; the recommended maximum speed on these roads is 60kph. Driving at night on all roads is best avoided due to the high risk of collision with kangaroos and wallabies; you'll see animal remains alongside the road at depressingly short intervals – most are hit by speeding trucks. Cars have far less protection from impact and insurance excesses are often a mandatory $2000 for animal collision. The main roads are all good for **cycling** – you can rent bikes at most accommodation or at KI Cycling Adventures ($35 per day; ☎0412 860 034).

Most people opt to visit the island on a **tour**, which can be good value if bought as part of a package (see above). There are several small-group tour companies based on the island: Exceptional Kangaroo Island in Kingscote (☎08/8553 9119, ⓦwww.adventurecharters.com.au), led by an ex-park ranger, offers 4WD tours with an emphasis on fine food, wine and accommodation as well as nature. There are also a couple of dive-tour operators:

Kangaroo Island Diving Safaris (☎08/8559 3225, ⓦ www.kidivingsafaris.com), based at Telhawk Farm on the north coast, offers diving charters and residential dive courses with special backpacker rates; and K.I. Diving on Beach Crescent, American River (☎08/8553 1072, ⓦ www.kidiving.com), offers a three-day residential scuba course and certification ($425), as well as a half-day Discover Scuba course ($89).

Information and park entrance fees

Many of the national or conservation parks on the island charge entry fees and extras for guided tours. However, a one-year **Kangaroo Island Pass** ($46.50 per person) gives you unlimited access to all parks and most tours (except for camping, Seal Bay's pre-sunset tour, and adventure caving; see p.799), and is worth it if you're here for a while. The entry fees and tour prices quoted in the following accounts apply only if you don't have a pass – add up the cost of what you want to see and work out which is cheaper. Passes can be bought from the parks themselves or from the NPWS office at 37 Dauncey St, Kingscote (Mon–Fri 8.45am–5pm; ☎08/8553 2381, ⓦ www .environment.sa.gov/parks/kangaroo_is.html); this office can also arrange camping permits and heritage accommodation in the parks and conservation areas around the island. Passes can also be purchased from the **Kangaroo Island Gateway visitor centre**, at the edge of Penneshaw on the main road to Kingscote (Mon–Fri 9am–5pm, Sat & Sun 10am–4pm; ☎08/8553 1185, ⓦ www.tourkangarooisland.com.au), which also has an interpretive display on the island's history, geology and ecology, and dispenses free brochures and maps.

The island

Coming by boat, you'll arrive at Kangaroo Island's eastern end, either at the small settlement of **Penneshaw**, with its Little penguin colony, or **Kingscote**, a little further west, the island's administrative centre and South Australia's second-oldest colonial settlement, though little remains to show for it. Between Penneshaw and Kingscote, sheltered **American River** is another good base. The airport is situated near **Cygnet River**, a quiet spot inland from Kingscote. From here, the Playford Highway and South Coast Road branch out to traverse the island, entering **Flinders Chase National Park** from the north and south respectively. The national park and surrounding wilderness protection area cover the entire western end of the island.

The rugged **south coast** provides more wildlife spotting and fine scenery: running west to east you can visit the aptly named **Remarkable Rocks** and **Admirals Arch**, both within the national park; go bushwalking in Hanson Bay; tour the limestone caves of Kelly Hill; camp at Vivonne Bay Conservation Park; play Lawrence of Arabia among the impressive sand dunes of Little Sahara; or roam amongst sea lions at Seal Bay. The quieter **north coast** has a series of sheltered beaches, including Emu Bay and Stokes Bay, and wild coastal cliff walks around Scotts Cove.

Kingscote and the north coast

With banks, shops, internet access, a hospital, library and the only high school, **KINGSCOTE** is the island's main town. The coast here has been the scene of several shipwrecks – interpretive boards on the foreshore provide details. For more history, you can walk north along the Esplanade to the **Reeves Point Historic Site**, where boards commemorate the South Australia Company's first landing of settlers in July 1836, before they headed off to establish nearby Adelaide. The settlement never numbered more than three hundred people, and folded in 1839. Less than 1km up the hill above, on Centenary Street, is **Hope Cottage Folk Museum** (Sept–July daily 1–4pm, Jan 10am–4pm; $5; ☎08/8553 3017), the restored 1850's home of a pioneering family. There's also pelican feeding around the Fisherman's Jetty, with a small talk about their habits and habitat (daily 5pm; $2).

Upmarket motel **accommodation** with sea views is found at *Wisteria Lodge*, Cygnet Road (☎08/8553 2707, ⓦwww.wisterialodgeki.com; ➏). For the budget-conscious there's the *Kingscote Nepean Bay Tourist Park* (☎ & 🅕08/8553 2394, ⓦwww.kingscotetouristpark.com.au; un/powered sites $27/33, cabins ➌–➍) at Brownlow Beach, 3km away. Established in 1907, the waterfront *Ozone Hotel* (☎08/8553 2011 or 1800 083 133, ⓦwww.ozonehotel.com; ➏–➑) is a local institution with comfortable rooms and a lively dining area. The best **restaurant** in town is *Bella* at 54 Dauncey St (☎08/8553 0400), a cozy space where the specialities are pizza and pasta using local ingredients; licensed and delivery service available. Also on Dauncey Street is the *Queenscliffe Family Hotel* (☎08/8553 2254, ⓔqueenscliffehotel@bigpond.com; ➌–➍), an old pub offering simple rooms and meals.

The **beaches** on the north coast are more sheltered than those on the south. Emu Bay, 21km along a sealed road from Kingscote, is one of the most popular beaches on the island with a clean stretch of sand and a small penguin colony, lots of holiday homes and beach houses to rent, but no shops. Emu Bay Holidays (☎08/8553 5163, ⓦwww.emubayholidays.com.au) manages a variety of self-contained beach houses and cottages (➏–➒) along the bay and in the nearby hills. *Seascape Lodge* (☎08/8559 5033, ⓦwww.seascapelodge.com.au; ➐) on Bates Road is a boutique-style B&B overlooking the bay with friendly hosts, gourmet dinners on request, and informative tours of the island.

About 30km further west, secluded **Stokes Bay** is reached along a dirt road passing through a natural tunnel between overhanging boulders. There's a delightful, calm rock pool – a perfect semicircle of rounded black stones which conveniently provides protection from the dangerous rip in the bay. Outside the tunnel, the *Rockpool Café* (Sept–May daily 11am–6pm; ☎08/8559 2277; book a table for evening meals 24 hours in advance) offers alfresco dining with local wine, does takeaway, and has some basic provisions for sale.

Penneshaw and around

It's a 45-minute drive on a sealed road from Kingscote to **PENNESHAW**, set on low, penguin-inhabited cliffs. This is a popular base, with comfortable accommodation and plenty of places to eat. Penneshaw's crescent of sandy beach at Hog Bay curves from the rocks below the wharf, where the ferries come in, around to a wooded headland. The bay provides safe **swimming** and a shady shelter on the sand. Above, there's a grassy picnic reserve with barbecues and the **Penguin Interpretive Centre** (check opening hours with visitor centre). Penneshaw Penguin Tours (daily: winter 7.30pm & 8.30pm; summer 8.30pm & 9.30pm; $9; ☎08/8553 1103) provide an excellent informative commentary on the antics of the **Little penguins** from the centre at dusk. This is the time they return from feeding in the unpolluted sea and cross the beach at Hog Bay to their cliffside burrows – a specially lit boardwalk provides a rookery viewing area.

Antechamber Bay, 10km southeast of Penneshaw, also has good, safe swimming. If you drive or cycle a further 10km along the unsealed dusty road you'll come to **Cape Willoughby Lighthouse**, at the eastern end of the island. Guided tours are offered by the DEH (daily 11.30am, 12.30pm & 2pm; summer, spring and autumn also at 3.15pm & 4pm; $12.50: ⓦwww .environment.sa.gov.au), and you can stay in the sandstone cottages of the original keepers (see below). You'll find more safe swimming at **American Beach**, southwest of Penneshaw along the scenic road that hugs Eastern Cove.

The **Dudley Peninsula**, on which Penneshaw stands, is attached to the rest of the island by a narrow neck of sand; at the isthmus 511 steps lead up to **Mount Thisby** (Prospect Hill), a 99-metre hill of sand with views across to the mainland, to Hungry Beach, Pelican Lagoon and American River on the island's north coast, and in the opposite direction to Pennington Bay.

⑧ Penneshaw practicalities

Penneshaw's Sealink office is at 7 North Terrace (daily 8am–5.45pm; ⓣ08/8553 1122, ⓦwww.sealink.com.au). There's a bank, **post office**, many shops and pubs, and EFTPOS at Grimshaw's. Good **accommodation** options include the comfortable *Kangaroo Island YHA*, 33 Middle Terrace (ⓣ08/8553 1344, ⓦwww.yha.com.au; dorms $27, rooms ❸), for budget travellers, and the friendly *Kangaroo Island Seafront Hotel* (ⓣ08/8553 1028, ⓦwww.seafront.com .au; ❾), set in landscaped gardens with motel-style rooms and fully equipped cabins, plus a heated pool, spa, sauna and tennis court, bar and restaurant. You can also stay in the two lighthouse-keepers' cottages at **Cape Willoughby** (ⓣ08/8559 7235, ⓦwww.environment.sa.gov.au/; ❺).

Good **restaurants** in town include the local favourite *Fish* (Sept–June daily 4.30–8.30pm), a neat black-and-white-tiled place cooking up a wonderful array of locally caught produce such as lobster, marron, whiting and oysters. *Sorrento's* in the *Seafront Hotel* specializes in seafood, steaks and local wines, while the tin-roofed bungalow of the *Penneshaw Hotel* is a small and friendly place to drink, with a veranda overlooking the water.

American River

Facing Penneshaw across Eastern Cove, **AMERICAN RIVER** is actually a sheltered bay where many small fishing boats moor, aiming to catch some of its abundant whiting. It's a peaceful place to stay, with a concentration of accommodation along the hilly shoreline and a general store. Boats can be chartered for local **fishing and sailing** from the kiosk at American River Rendezvous (ⓣ08/8553 7150) or direct from Cooinda Charter Services (ⓣ&ⓕ08/8553 7063).

For **accommodation**, *Matthew Flinders Terraces* (ⓣ08/8553 7100, ⓦwww .kangaroo-island-au.com/matthewflinders/; ❺) is a beautifully located retreat with modern rooms, pool and spa, while *Wanderers Rest* (ⓣ08/8553 7140, ⓦwww.wanderersrest.com.au; ❽) is situated high on a hill and is an old-fashioned guesthouse with a quality seafood restaurant. Other options include the budget *Casuarina Coastal Units* (ⓣ08/8553 7020; ❹) and *Ulonga Lodge* (ⓣ 08/8553 7171, ⓦwww.ulonga.com.au; ❺), which has five two-bedroom cabins, and a café.

The south coast

There are several conservation parks strung out along the exposed south coast. The largest is **Cape Gantheaume**, an area of low mallee scrub supporting prolific birdlife around **Murray Lagoon**, the largest freshwater lagoon on the island. The adjacent **Seal Bay Conservation Park** is home to hundreds of sea lions, one of the largest breeding populations in Australia. They are fairly tolerant of humans and you can walk quietly among the colony on the beach at **Seal Bay** when accompanied by a national park guide (daily 9am–5.15pm in holidays, all other times until 4.15pm; $14, pre-sunset tour $32; T08/8559 4207), or take a stroll to the boardwalk and lookout entry ($10).

Vivonne Bay, with its long, sandy beach and bush setting, is a great place to camp. There's a **beachside campsite** ($10) with toilets, water and barbecues, and a well-stocked store and bottle shop 1km away on the main South Coast Road. It's safe to swim near the jetty or boat ramp or in the Harriet River, but the bay itself has a dangerous undertow. Between Seal Bay and Vivonne Bay, "**Little Sahara**" comprises 15km of perfect white-sand dunes rising out of mallee scrub.

The main features of the **Kelly Hill Conservation Park** are the **Kelly Hill Caves**, extensive limestone cave formations (DEH guided tours daily 10.30am–4.15pm, seven daily; $12). The tour explores the largest cave – not the usual damp, bat-filled cavern, but very dry, with a constant temperature of 16°C. The DEH runs **adventure caving tours** of three other caves at 2.15pm daily ($30; T08/8559 7231 for details and advance bookings). The eighteen-kilometre return **Hanson Bay Trail** runs from the caves to the sea, passing freshwater lagoons and dune systems: allow at least eight hours, or longer if you'll be tempted to stop for a swim. *Hanson Bay Sanctuary Homestead* (T08/8559 7344, Wwww.hansonbay.com.au; minimum three-night stay; ○), just west of the Kelly Hill Conservation Park, is situated in a lovely secluded spot surrounded by bushland with excellent walking trails.

Flinders Chase National Park

Flinders Chase National Park, Kangaroo Island's largest, occupies the entire western end of the island. It became a park as early as 1919, and in the 1920s and 1930s koalas, platypuses and Cape Barren geese from the Bass Strait islands were introduced. The land is mainly low-lying mallee forest, with occasional patches of taller sugar-gum trees. The **Flinders Chase Visitors Centre** (daily 9am–5pm; park entry fee $8 per person; T08/8559 7235, Eflinders.chase @saugov.sa.gov.au) is surrounded by open grasslands where large numbers of kangaroos and wallabies graze. Koala signs lead to a glade of trees where you can see the creatures swaying overhead, within binocular range. Follow the **Platypus Waterhole Walk** for 3km to a platypus-viewing area, but be warned that to get a glimpse of the creatures requires endless patience. The winding sealed road through the park will take you to its most spectacular features: the huge, weirdly shaped, rust-coloured **Remarkable Rocks** on Kirkpatrick Point, and the impressive natural formation of **Admirals Arch**, where hundreds of New Zealand fur seals bask around the rocks. At the northern corner of the park, you can go on a guided tour of the 1858 **Cape Borda Lighthouse** (daily 11am, 12.30pm & 2pm; summer, spring and autumn also at 3.15pm & 4pm; $12; T08/8559 3257).

The main **camping** area is at Rocky River, or there are various **cottages** (○) throughout the park – bookable through the Flinders Chase Visitors Centre – and several other good places to stay along the South Coast Road near the park. Spectacularly set in wilderness on a headland overlooking the sea, the eco-friendly *Southern Ocean Lodge* (T02/9918 4355, Wwww.southernoceanlodge; ○ includes all meals, beverages, tours and activities) is the island's most luxurious accommodation, with a spa and stylish, spacious contemporary suites, a light and airy lounge

8

SOUTH AUSTRALIA | The island

and bar, superb restaurant serving up refined cuisine based on fresh local produce, and loads of guided activities, including sunset canapés and cocktails amongst the kangaroos, bushwalks, and food- and art-themed island tours. Nearby, the *Western KI Caravan Park* (℡08/8559 7201, ⓦwww.westernki.com .au; powered/unpowered sites $25/$20 cabins ❺–❻) is set in an expansive wildlife reserve, where you can camp under the tall gum trees and try to spot koala bears. By staying at this end of the island you'll also see the spectacular coastal sights at their best – particularly Remarkable Rocks, which turn a deep orange with the setting and rising sun.

The southeast

Most travellers en route between Adelaide and Melbourne pass through southeast South Australia as quickly as possible, which is a shame, as the coastal route offers wild, pristine beaches and tranquil fishing villages, while inland there are a couple of brilliant wine regions. From Tailem Bend, just beyond Murray Bridge some 85km out of Adelaide, three highways branch out. The northernmost, the **Mallee Highway**, is the quintessential road to nowhere, leading through the sleepy settlements of Lameroo and Pinnaroo to the insignificant town of Ouyen in Victoria's mallee country (see p.975). The second, the **Dukes Highway**, offers a fast but boring route to Melbourne via the South Australian mallee scrub and farming towns of **Keith** and **Bordertown**, before continuing in Victoria as the Western Highway across the monotonous Wimmera (see p.975). It is, however, well worth breaking your journey to visit the **Coonawarra** and **Naracoorte**, in between the Dukes Highway and the coastal route: the former is a tiny wine-producing area that makes some of the country's finest **red wine**; the latter is a fair-sized town with a freshwater lagoon system that attracts prolific birdlife, and a conservation park with impressive World Heritage-listed caves.

The third option, the **Princes Highway** (Highway 1), is much less direct but far more interesting. It follows the extensive coastal lagoon system of the **Coorong** to **Kingston SE**, and then runs a short way inland to the lake craters of **Mount Gambier** before crossing into Victoria. There's another possible route on this last stretch, the **Southern Ports Highway**, which sticks closer to the coast, plus a potential detour along the Riddoch Highway into the scenic Coonawarra wine region.

Premier Stateliner (℡08/8415 5555) **buses** serve two routes between Adelaide and Mount Gambier, one inland via Keith, Bordertown, Naracoorte, Coonawarra and Penola; the other along the coast via Meningie, Kingston SE, Robe and Millicent. The DEH free newspaper, *The Tatler*, gives practical details relating to the southeastern coastal parks – pick up the latest copy from the Adelaide Travel Centre (see p.753), or regional offices en route. Further information can be found at the regional visitor information website (ⓦwww.thelimestonecoast.com).

Coorong National Park

From Tailem Bend, the Princes Highway skirts Lake Alexandrina and the freshwater Lake Albert before passing the edge of the **Coorong National Park**. The coastal saline lagoon system of the Coorong (from the Aboriginal "Karangk", meaning long neck) is separated from the sea for over 100km by the high sand dunes of the **Younghusband Peninsula**. This is the state's most prolific **pelican breeding ground**, and an excellent place to observe these awkward yet graceful birds – there's a shelter with seating and a telescope focused on the small islands where some birds breed at Jacks Point, 3km north of Policemans Point on the Princes Highway. If you don't have your own transport, you can get to the park on a **cruise** from Goolwa (see box, p.810).

There are several designated **camping areas** with shelters, barbecues, toilets, running water (but no showers) and marked **walking trails**. The Coorong is also good for beach camping: with a permit (see p.48) you can camp anywhere along the beach, but cars must be parked in designated places and you must bring your own drinking water, which can be collected outside the seldom-manned **Salt Creek DEH ranger station** on the edge of the park. Information, camping permits ($8 per car) and maps of the park and campsites can be obtained at the **ranger's office** at 32–34 Princes Highway, Meningie (Mon–Wed 9am–5pm; ℡08/8575 1200), the Coorong **visitor centre**, in the heart of the park at Tintinara (daily 9am–5pm; ℡08/8757 2220), and most petrol stations on the way to the park.

There are **caravan parks** at Long Point, Parnka Point, Gemini Downs and 42-Mile Crossing – the only land access to the Younghusband Peninsula. If you're passing by, park your car at the 42-Mile Crossing information area and walk 1km along a sandy 4WD track for **great views** of the sand dunes and the wild Southern Ocean. This track runs alongside the beach all the way up the peninsula to Barkers Knoll and down to Kingston SE, with camping along the way. If you want to stay in more comfort, there are plenty of motels at the popular, if dull, fishing centre of **Meningie**, by Lake Albert.

Camp Coorong, run by the Ngarrindjeri Lands and Progress Association, is 10km south of Meningie. This cultural centre attempts to explain the heritage and culture of the **Ngarrindjeri Aborigines**, once one of the largest groups in South Australia, occupying the land around the Coorong and the lower Murray River and lakes, through cultural programmes and a range of activities, from candle-lit bushwalks to basketweaving (prices based on group rate; see Ⓦwww.ngarrindjeri.com for details). There's a fascinating museum (Mon–Fri 10am–5pm; $5 per vehicle), and you can camp here or in the nearby bush reserve or stay in the well-fitted-out cabins (booking required on ℡08/8575 1557, Ⓦwww.ngarrindjeri.com; tents/bush camping $10/5pp, cabins ❸, all meals $60 a head). A few kilometres further south is the Ngarrindjeri-owned *Coorong Wilderness Lodge*, designed in the shape of a fish (℡08/8575 6001, Ⓦwww.cooronglodge.com; camping $10 per car, en-suite cabin ❸–❹). The **restaurant** serves indigenous meals (advance booking essential), and the traditional owners offer short tours, including kayaking and Dreamtime stories, along with a comprehensive three-day wilderness and cultural tour.

Southern Ports Highway: Kingston to Robe

KINGSTON South East (SE), on Lacepede Bay, is the first town past the Coorong: here the Princes Highway turns inland, while the Southern Ports Highway continues along the coast before rejoining the main road at Millicent. As the **Big Lobster** on the highway in Kingston attests, the town has an important lobster industry: you can buy them freshly cooked at Lacepede Seafood by the jetty (daily 9am–6pm Oct–May) for around $50 a kilo. The old *Crown Inn Hotel* at 31 Agnes St has a modern bistro (daily 12–2pm & 6–8pm) serving up scrumptious local seafood, succulent steaks and live music, albeit simple rooms (☎08/8767 2005, [W]www.crowninnkingston.com.au; rooms [6]). There's an attractive foreshore lined with pine trees, but apart from locals fishing off the jetty, there's little else happening.

Lobsters apart, you're better off continuing down the coast to the quaint seaside community of **ROBE**. On the south side of Guichen Bay, 44km from Kingston, Robe was one of South Australia's first settlements, established as a deep-water port in 1847. After 1857, over sixteen thousand Chinese landed here and walked to the goldfields, 400km away, to avoid the poll tax levied in Victoria. As trade declined and the highway bypassed the town, Robe managed to maintain both dignity and a low-key charm, and during the busy summer period the population of fewer than eight hundred expands to over eleven thousand. Summer is also the season for **crayfishing**, Robe's major industry.

Robe practicalities

Tourist information is available inside the library on the corner of Smiley and Victoria streets (Mon–Fri 9am–5pm, Sat & Sun 10am–4pm; ☎08/8768 2465, [W]www.robe.com.au); they also have walking and driving maps, and free, limited-time internet access. Premier Stateliner **buses** pass through on their way from Adelaide to Mount Gambier.

Accommodation

There are dozens of places to **stay**, most of which double up as places to eat. You can also book B&Bs, cottages and guesthouses through B&B Secrets (☎1800 227 677, [W]www.bnbsecrets.com.au; [4]).

Bushland Cabins & Caravan Park Nora Criena Rd ☎08/8768 2386, [W]www.robe.com.au/bushland/. Basic cabins and camping southeast of the centre, with walking trails into the surrounding bush, including a one-kilometre cliff-top track into Robe. Un/powered sites $20/23, dorms $18–30, cabins [4]

🏃 **Caledonian Inn** 1 Victoria St ☎08/8768 2029, [W]www.caledonian.net.au. The charming, ivy-covered building was first licensed in 1858 and wouldn't look out of place in an English village – it offers charming B&B rooms, bright and airy cottages with sea views, and a chic luxury retreat. They also serve scrumptious food at lunch and dinner. Rooms [4]–[5], cottages [8], retreat [9]

Guichen Bay Motel 42 Victoria St ☎08/8768 2001, [W]www.oceanroadaccommodation.com.au. While the simple, spacious rooms could do with a renovation, some come with kitchenette. The price includes a hearty hot breakfast, and the owners are friendly. Their licensed *Cottage Restaurant* dishes up crayfish in season. [4]–[5]

Lakeside Manor Backpackers 22 Main Rd ☎08/8768 1995 or 1800 155 350, [W]www.lakesidemanorbackpackers.com.au. Pick of the town for backpackers is this attractive lodge with spacious old-English-style dorms and an impressive library. Free internet access and bike hire is included. Dorms $26, double [3]

Robe Hotel Mundy Terrace ☎08/8768 2077, [W]www.robehotel.com.au. An old stone beachfront hotel, with backpacker rooms, en-suite motel-style rooms with views and spa suites; the downstairs bars serve good bistro meals. Bunks $25, rooms & suites ❸–❻

Sea Vu Caravan Park 1 Squire Drive ☎08/8768 2273, ⓦwww.robescavu.com. Family-run and one of the four caravan parks close to town, with a swimming beach right next door. Un/powered site $30/32, cabins ❻

Eating

For **meals**, *The Gallerie*, 2 Victoria St, serves good breakfasts, lunches and dinners and has a good selection of Limestone Coast wines in the adjacent wine bar. *Robe Seafood and Takeaway*, 21 Victoria St, provides the ubiquitous fish and chips, while *Sails* (☎08/8768 1954) next door is not only the most stylish place in town but serves up fabulous locally caught lobster and local seafood with an Asian accent such as seafood laksa; you'll need to book a table for dinner in summer. Adjoining it, *Vic Street Pizzeria* does delicious pizzas to go. For self-caterers, Foodland Supermarket, opposite the Ampol petrol station, is open daily 7.30am–7pm.

Beyond Robe

Between Robe and Beachport are four lakes: for part of the way you can take the Nora Criena Drive through **Little Dip Conservation Park**, 14km of coastal dune systems. The drive provides views of Lake Eliza and Lake St Clair before returning to Southern Ports Highway and the former whaling port of **BEACHPORT**, which boasts one of the longest jetties in Australia and many lobster-fishing boats at anchor on Rivoli Bay. Beachport has plenty of **accommodation**, but the pick of the town is the renovated historic pub, *Bompas*, overlooking the bay at 3 Railway Terrace (☎08/8735 8333, ⓦwww.bompas .com.au; dorms $35, en-suite rooms ❹–❻), with a buzzy bar and café and a lovely light restaurant serving modern Australian dishes. The helpful **visitor centre** on Millicent Road (Mon–Fri 9am–5pm, Sat & Sun 10am–1pm, summer Sat & Sun until 4pm; ☎08/8735 8029, ⓦwww.wattlerange.sa.gov.au) can provide information on the region.

Continuing south on Southern Ports Highway, there are several turn-offs to **Canunda National Park**, which has giant sand dunes, signposted coastal walking trails, an abundance of birdlife and camping facilities ($8 per vehicle). The best place to explore the park from is **SOUTHEND** but there's also access to the park near historic **MILLICENT**, 15km to the south, which has a **visitor centre**, 1 Mt Gambier Rd (Mon–Fri 9am–5pm, Sat & Sun 10am–4pm; ☎08/8733 0904), and information on local drives, walks and accommodation. The Southern Ports Highway rejoins the Princes Highway at Millicent.

Mount Gambier and around

Set close to the border with Victoria, **MOUNT GAMBIER** is the south-east's commercial centre. The small city sprawls up the slopes of an extinct volcano whose three craters – each with its own lake surrounded by heavily wooded slopes and filled from underground waterways – are perfect for subterranean diving.

The **Blue Lake** is the largest and most stunning of the three, up to 70m deep and 5km in circumference. From November to March it's a mesmerizing cobalt blue, reverting to a moody steel blue in the colder months. There are lookout spots and a **scenic drive** around the lake, and guided tours are offered by

Aquifer Tours (daily on the hour: Feb–May & Sept–Oct 9am–2pm; June–Aug 9am–noon; Nov–Jan 9am–5pm, 45min; $7; ℡08/8723 1199). The second-largest crater holds Valley Lake and a **Wildlife Park** (daily 7am–dusk; free), where indigenous animals range free amid native flora; there are also lookouts, walking trails and boardwalks.

West of the city centre, on Jubilee Highway West, is the extensive complex of underground caverns at **Engelbrecht Cave** (guided tours hourly 10am–3pm, check times in winter with visitor centre; 45min; $6). You can dive here in limestone waterways under the city, though you'll need a CDAA (Cave Divers Association of Australia) qualification to tackle these dark and dangerous waters. Contact the DEH at 11 Helen St (℡08/8735 1114, ⓦwww.environment.sa .gov.au/parks) for further information.

The centrepiece of Mount Gambier itself is **Cave Gardens**, a shady park surrounding a deep limestone cavern with steps leading some way down; the stream running into it eventually filters into the Blue Lake. Fronting the park is the former Town Hall and the **Riddoch Art Gallery** (Tues–Fri 10am–5pm, Sat 11am–3pm; free; ℡08/8723 9566, ⓦwww.riddochartgallery.org.au) whose focus is the impressive Rodney Gooch collection of Aboriginal art from the Utopia region of the Northern Territory.

The CDAA issues permits for snorkelling in the crystal-clear waters of **Picca-ninnie Ponds Conservation Park** and **Ewans Pond Conservation Park**, both south of Mount Gambier near Port Macdonnell. At Piccaninnie Ponds, a deep chasm with white limestone walls contains clear water that is filtered underground from the Blue Lake – apparently taking an astonishing five hundred years to get here. East of the city is Umpherston Sinkhole (open access), also known as the **Sunken Garden** for its Victorian-era terraced gardens – they are floodlit at night when possums come out to feed.

Practicalities

For more information on Mount Gambier's attractions, head for the excellent **Lady Nelson Victory and Discovery Centre**, on Jubilee Highway East (daily 9am–5pm; exhibition $10; ℡08/8724 9750, ⓦwww.mountgambiertourism .com.au), where the ecology, geology and history of Mount Gambier are explored from Aboriginal and European perspectives. They also have free limited-time internet access.

Mount Gambier has heaps of **places to stay**, with motels lining the highway either side of town – the pick of them, down the hill from the lakes on Nelson Road, is 🦌 *The Barn* (℡08/8726 8250, ⓦwww.barn.com.au; ❺–❻), with friendly owners, stylish well-equipped rooms and one of the finest restaurants in the region, the *Barn Steakhouse*, which does divine cuts of meat and boasts an impressive wine cellar. Budget travellers may care to experience *The Jail* on Margaret Street (℡08/8723 0032, ⓦwww.jailbackpackers.com; dorms $22, double ❶), built in 1866 and now a Heritage-listed building. The last inmates left in 1995 and you can stay in the original cells behind locked doors (the solitary loo in the corner is referred to as in-suite instead of en suite). There's also a bar, laundry facilities, internet access and lots of activities. Centrally located at 2 Commercial St West, *The G Hotel* (℡08/8725 0611, ⓦwww .mountgambierhotel.com.au; ❹) has rather old-fashioned albeit spacious rooms, a popular restaurant and bar downstairs with live music and DJs on weekends.

Dining options are plentiful – after *Barn Steakhouse*, the pick of the bunch in town is the award-winning but unassuming *Sage and Muntries* at 72 Commercial St West, serving up fine modern Australian cuisine (lunch and dinner; closed

Sun). Alternatively, try the *Anno Domani* at 17 Commercial St West, serving pasta and an excellent seafood risotto. Classic Italian pizza and more pasta can be found at *Caffè Belgiorno* on Percy Street, although the service can be hit and miss. The town's cinema is next door in the Oatmill Building.

Heading on to Melbourne from Mount Gambier, V/Line (☎13 61 96) has a daily **bus** service via Portland, Warrnambool, Geelong and Ballarat.

The Coonawarra wine region

Directly north of Mount Gambier, the Riddoch Highway heads through the lovely, low-key **Coonawarra wine region**, and past some World Heritage-listed caves at **Naracoorte**, eventually linking up with the Dukes Highway at Keith. Most wineries are located on a ninety-kilometre stretch of highway between **Penola** and Padthaway – the region is renowned for the quality of its reds, which have been compared to those of Bordeaux. The soil and drainage are ideal, classic Terra Rossa over limestone, and the climate is perfect – as the weather is not really variable from year to year, the wines are consistently good. Premier Stateliner (☎08/8415 5555) stops daily at Penola and Naracoorte on its Adelaide-to-Mount Gambier inland service, while Penola Coonawarra Tour Service (☎08/8733 2422) offers restaurant transfers and winery tours around the area.

Penola and around

Twenty-two kilometres north of Mount Gambier, **PENOLA**, gateway to the Coonawarra wine region, is a simple but dignified country town with well-preserved nineteenth-century architecture. For information, head to the excellent **visitor centre** (Ⓦwww.coonawarra.org) in the historic **John Riddoch Centre** (Mon–Fri 9am–5pm, Sat & Sun 10am–4pm; ☎08/8737 2855, Ⓦwww.wattlerange.sa.gov.au), at 27 Arthur St, which houses a display on this Coonawarra pioneer. Grab a copy of the *Coonawarra: Australia's Other Red Centre* map, which marks out the region's wineries, and the *Walk with History* map identifying Penola's rich historic architecture.

Coonawarra wineries

There are around twenty Coonawarra wineries that do tastings (most open Mon–Fri 9am–5pm, Sat & Sun 10am–4pm); for more information visit the Coonawarra Wine Association website (Ⓦwww.coonawarra.org). A few favourites (arranged in order if you are driving north along the Riddoch Highway from Penola towards Coonawarra Township) include Hollick Wines (Ⓦwww.hollick.com), once a tiny 1870s wood-and-stone slab cottage, now a modern winery with a superb stylish restaurant attached; Balnaves (Ⓦwww.balnaves.com.au), notable for its innovative architecture; Leconfield (Ⓦwww.leconfieldwines.com), with very well-regarded Cabernet Sauvignons; and Zema Estate (Ⓦwww.zema.com.au), a small family-run winery with Italian roots. Wynns Coonawarra Estate (Ⓦwww.wynns.com.au), west of the Riddoch Highway on Memorial Drive at Coonawarra Township, is Coonawarra's longest-established (1896) and best-known winery. Continuing back on the Riddoch Highway towards Padthaway, the down-to-earth Redman family winery (Ⓦwww.redman.com.au) has been making red wine for generations. Beyond Redman, the modern winery complex of Rymill (Ⓦwww.rymill.com.au), attractively located on Clayfield Road west of the Riddoch Highway, includes a glass-walled tasting area overlooking the vineyards, and platforms upstairs for viewing the testing lab.

Beside the 1857 Cobb & Co booking office on the corner of Portland Street and Petticoat Lane, the 1860s Woods-MacKillop Schoolhouse is a world away from the sleek, modern **Mary MacKillop Interpretative Centre** (daily 10am–4pm; $4; [T]08/8737 2092) next door. Sister Mary MacKillop (1842–1909) was Penola's most famous resident, and Australia's first would-be saint – in 1995 Pope John Paul II pronounced her "Blessed", though she still awaits full sanctification. MacKillop set up a school, established her own teaching method and, with Father Julian Tennyson Woods, co-founded the Sisters of St Joseph of the Sacred Heart, a charitable teaching order that spread throughout Australia and New Zealand. Episodes of alleged disobedience and excommunication give her story a certain drama – there's an informative display in the centre, with Barbie-doll lookalike "nuns on the run" and dressed-up dummies in the original schoolroom. Across the fields stand the National Trust-listed cottages of **Petticoat Lane**, where many of Mary's poverty-stricken students lived.

The focus of the town is the friendly, National Trust-listed *Heyward's Royal Oak Hotel*, 31 Church St ([T]08/8737 2322, [W]www.heywardshotel.com.au; [5]), with four-poster doubles and some twin rooms. *Penola Caravan Park* on South Terrace ([T]08/8737 2381) has good-value en-suite cabins ([4]). A welcoming sight is the striking contemporary architecture of ★ *Must* at 126 Church St ([T]08/8737 3444, [W]www.mustatcoonawarra.com.au; [8]), with its warm, welcoming owners and stylish, self-contained apartments, studios and B&B rooms with all mod cons, including free broadband internet and plasma TV screens.

There are a couple of great **eating** options in Penola including the superb *Pipers of Penola* ([T]08/8737 3999, [W]www.pipersofpenola.com.au; Fri–Sun lunch from noon, Wed–Sat dinner from 6pm) at 58 Riddoch St, which serves up creative contemporary cuisine in elegant surroundings, while for a more casual meal, *Heyward's Royal Oak Hotel* has a pleasant beer garden and good bistro.

Coonawarra Township

There isn't much to **COONAWARRA TOWNSHIP**, a settlement developed to service the adjacent Wynns Coonawarra Estate (see box, p.805), and with Penola so close by it's not really necessary to stay here to tour the local vineyards. If you like the idea of having them on your doorstep, **accommodation** here includes *Coonawarra Country Cottages* ([T]08/8737 2683, [W]www.coonawarracountrycottages.com.au; [4]–[5]), and just out of town on the Riddoch Highway, *Chardonnay Lodge* ([T]08/8736 3309, [W]www.chardonnaylodge.com.au; [6]), a motel set amongst rose gardens, with a swimming pool and café-restaurant. The best eating option here is *Upstairs at Hollick* ([T]08/8737 2752; [W]www.hollick.com; lunch Tues–Sun, dinner Fri & Sat from 6pm) overlooking the vineyards at Hollick Winery on Ravenswood Lane, which serves up exquisitely prepared dishes based on the freshest of regional produce.

Naracoorte Caves

Midway between Penola and Padthaway, the **Naracoorte Caves Conservation Park** protects a World Heritage-listed system of limestone caves. Your first point of call should be the **Wonambi Fossil Centre Wet Cave** (daily 9am–5pm; [T]08/8762 2340), where you can book tours to the caves below. The centre gives an insight into the area's archeological significance – important fossils of extinct Pleistocene megafauna, including giant kangaroos and wombats, were discovered here in the Victoria Fossil Cave in 1969. You can guide yourself through the **Wet Cave** (daily 9am–5pm; ☎08/8762 2340), named after the very wet chamber at its deepest part; an automatic lighting system switches on as you walk through. A walking trail from here leads to another notable feature, the **Bat Centre** (3.30pm; 1hr), where you can see bats inside a cave with the help of infrared remote-control cameras.

The other caves are spread out over the conservation park: **Alexandra Cave** has the prettiest limestone formations (tours daily 9.30am & 1.30pm; 30min), while **Victoria Fossil Cave**, not surprisingly, is popular for its fossils (daily 10.15am & 2.15pm; 1hr). **Admission fees** are $15 for one cave, $24 for two, $33 for three or $42 for all four of the show caves. There are also **adventure caving** tours in several other caves (2hr novice tours $32.50; 3hr advanced tours $60; overalls can be rented for $5, lights and helmets supplied; ☎08/8762 2340).

You can **camp** within the park ($21 per car), where facilities include powered sites, hot showers and a free laundry, or stay in dorms at *Wirreanda Bunkhouse* (☎08/8762 2340; $15). More appealing is the bush setting and rural tranquillity at *Cave Park Cabins* (☎08/8762 0696, ℱ8762 3180; ❷–❹), only 1.5km from the caves. For **meals**, the licensed *Bent Wing Cafe* by the Fossil Centre dishes up everything from Greek salads to chargrilled kangaroo fillets with native-plum chutney.

On the highway 12km west of the caves, the town of **NARACOORTE** is a small regional centre with a supermarket (open daily) and several places to **eat** and **stay**. *Naracoorte Hotel Motel*, 73 Ormerod St (☎08/8762 2400, ⓦwww .naracoortehotel.com.au; ❸), has cosy motel rooms and cheap meals, while the relaxed *Naracoorte Backpackers* (☎08/8762 3835, ⓦwww.naracoortebackpackers .com.au; dorms $22) at 4 Jones St can take you to the caves and find you seasonal work. A ten-minute walk north of town at 81 Park Terrace, *Naracoorte Holiday Park* (☎08/8762 2128, ⓦwww.naracoorteholidaypark.com.au; cabins ❸–❹) is set in a shady spot by a creek, close to a swimming lake.

The Riverland

The **Riverland** is the name given to the long irrigated strip on either side of the **Murray River** as it meanders for 300km from Blanchetown to Renmark near the Victorian border. The Riverland's deep red-orange alluvial soil – helped by extensive irrigation – is very fertile, making the area the state's major supplier of oranges, stone fruit and grapes. Fruit stalls along the roadsides add to the impression of a year-long harvest, and if you're after **fruit-picking** work it's an excellent place to start; contact the Harvest Labour Office on Riverview Drive in Berri (☎08/8582 9307). The area is also Australia's major **wine-producing** region, though the high-tech wineries here mainly make mass-produced wines for casks and export. Many are open to visitors, but their scale and commercialism make them less enjoyable than those in other wine regions.

The **Sturt Highway**, the major route between Adelaide and Sydney, passes straight through the Riverland. Premier Stateliner runs a twice-daily **bus** service along the highway from Adelaide to Renmark via Blanchetown, Waikerie, Barmera and Berri, and also goes daily (except Sat) to Loxton.

Between Waikerie and Renmark all the towns feel pretty much the same, with a raw edge, and little in the way of charm or sophistication.

Blanchetown to Waikerie

BLANCHETOWN, 130km east of Adelaide, is the first Riverland town and the starting point of the Murray's lock and weir system, which helps maintain the river at a constant height between the town and Wentworth in New South Wales. Eleven kilometres west of town, **Brookfield Conservation Park**, a gift to South Australia from the Chicago Zoological Society, is home to the endangered **southern hairy-nosed wombat**; the creatures also thrive at nearby *Portee Station* (℡08/8540 5211, ⓦwww.portee.com.au; ❻–❽), a picturesque, two-hundred-square-kilometre sheep-grazing property where you can stay in elegantly decorated rooms in the 1873 riverfront homestead. They run a range of tours, including river trips in a small boat to look at the prolific birdlife, and a 4WD station tour where you'll see wombats close up.

Following the river from Blanchetown, it's 36km directly north to **MORGAN**, one of the most attractive of the Riverland towns. At the height of the river trade between 1880 and 1915 Morgan was one of South Australia's busiest river ports, transferring wool from New South Wales and Victoria onto trains bound for Adelaide; parts of its mainly red-gum and jarrah river-wharf remain intact. You can wander through the riverfront park, past the old train station and the stationmaster's building, now a **museum** (tours by appointment; ℡08/8540 2130), and up onto the wharves overlooking moored houseboats on the river to bushland beyond. The well-preserved nineteenth-century streetscape of Railway Terrace, the main street, sits above the old railway line and wharf, dominated by the huge Landseer shipping warehouse. There's standard accommodation in two adjacent old pubs: the *Terminus Hotel* (℡08/8540 2006, ⓦwww.riverlandlocal.com.au/terminushotel; ❸) and the 1880 *Commercial* (℡08/8540 2107, ⓦwww.riverlandlocal.com.au /commercialhotel; ❷). A more comfortable option is the *Morgan Colonial Motel*, 1 Federal St (℡08/8540 2277, ⓦwww.murrayriver.com.au/morgan-colonial –motel-757; ❹). You can also stay at the *Morgan Riverside Caravan Park* (℡08/8540 2207, ⓔmorgancp@riverland.net.au; un/powered sites $20/25, cabins ❸), in a great spot right in town by the river.

From Morgan the river takes a sharp bend east, meandering south to **WAIKERIE**; it's 32km from Morgan to Waikerie on a riverside road, with a free ferry crossing at Cadell. A less attractive drive from Blanchetown bypasses the river loop, reaching Waikerie by heading 42km northeast along the Sturt Highway. Waikerie is at the heart of the largest citrus-growing area in Australia; the first thing you notice is a huge complex owned by **Nippy's** that takes up both sides of a street, allegedly the largest fruit-packing house in the southern hemisphere. A good base for fruit-picking work is *Nomads-on-Murray* (℡08/8583 0211 or 1800 665 166; dorms $22, rooms ❷–❸), on the Sturt Highway about 30km east of Waikerie.

Loxton and around

Some 35km east of Waikerie, the Murray makes another large loop away from the Sturt highway, bypassing **Barmera** and twisting instead through **LOXTON** and **Berri**. Leaving the highway at Kingston-on-Murray, you pass the **Moorook Game Reserve**, a large swamp fringed with river red gums and home to many waterbirds. In Loxton itself, the **Tourist & Art Centre**, at Bookpurnong Terrace (Mon–Fri 9am–5pm, Sat 9.30am–12.30pm, Sun 1–4pm; ☎08/8584 7919, ⓦwww.loxtontourism.com.au), is the local visitor centre, acting as an agent for Stateliner, and can brief you on local attractions such as the riverside **Loxton Historical Village** (Mon–Fri 10am–4pm, Sat & Sun 10am–5pm; $8; ⓦwww.loxtonhistoricalvillage.com.au), a charming (if slightly kitsch) replica of an early twentieth-century Riverland town.

Altogether more compelling is the **Katarapko Game Reserve**, opposite Loxton where Katarapko Creek and the Murray have cut deep channels and lagoons, creating an island. Access from Loxton is by water only – perfect for canoeing and observing birdlife; to camp, you need a permit from the DEH, 28 Vaughan Terrace, Berri (☎08/8595 2111). *Loxton Riverfront Caravan Park*, Packard Bend (☎08/8584 7862, ⓦwww.lrcp.com.au; un/powered sites $23/30, cabins ❸–❹), is a peaceful spot opposite the game reserve, with canoes for rent ($12 per hour, $60 per day).

The most comfortable place to **stay** in town is the *Loxton Hotel-Motel*, East Terrace (☎08/8584 7266, ⓦwww.loxtonhotel.com.au; ❹–❺), where you can also get good bistro **meals** (daily noon–2pm & 6–8pm). Primarily aimed at seasonal fruit pickers, the slightly shabby *Harvest Trail Lodge* (☎08/8584 5646, ⓦwww.harvesttrail.com; dorms $45, worker's rate $15) has small dorms and can help you find fruit-picking work.

Barmera and Herons Bend Reserve

If you haven't followed the river to Loxton, **BARMERA**, on the shores of Lake Bonney, is the next major stopping point along the highway. At **Pelican Point**, on the lake's western shore, there's an official **nudist beach** (and a nearby nudist resort on Morgan Road with camping and on-site vans ❷; ☎08/8588 7366, ⓦwww.riverland.net.au/pelicanpoint; bookings essential), while every June, the **South Australian Country Music Festival** and Awards are held in the lovely old Bonney Theatre. For information about the awards and local attractions stop by the **visitor centre** at the Council at 19 Wilson St (Mon–Fri 9am–5.15pm, Sat 9am–noon, Sun 10am–1pm; ☎08/8582 1922, ⓦwww.berribarmera.sa.gov.au).

The best bet for fully clothed **accommodation** is the *Barmera Lake Resort Motel*, Lakeside Drive (☎08/8588 2555, ⓦwww.barmeralakeresortmotel.com .au; ❹–❺), overlooking the lake with a pool, laundry, games room, barbecue and *Cafe Mudz*, a bright and attractive café/wine bar serving Australian country-style breakfasts, lunches and evening meals. The extensive *Lake Bonney Holiday Park* is close by on Lakeside Drive (☎08/8588 2234; cabins & cottages ❸), superbly located next to the lake and great for kids.

At the time of research, the government had closed off Lake Bonney's water supply from the Murray River, to help battle the drought in South Australia; while the closure was meant to be for 12 months only, it had gone on for some 13 months, angering the local community, and having a disastrous impact on the local economy of Barmera.

Just under 16km from Barmera towards Morgan, you pass a bend in the river dubbed **Overland Corner**, the former crossing point for the overland cattle trade heading to New South Wales. Built in 1859, the charming National Trust-protected *Overland Corner Hotel* (☎08/8588 7021, ⓔochotel@dodo.com.au; daily 11am–midnight (closes early if quiet); ❸–❹ including continental breakfast) serves food, has basic old-fashioned accommodation, and is a museum – note the marks indicating the level of the 1956 flood, practically up to the roof. You can camp and bushwalk in the adjacent **Herons Bend Reserve**, where an eight-kilometre trail (around 3hr) takes you past old Aboriginal campsites; a pamphlet detailing sites on the walk is available from the pub.

Berri

The Big Orange sets the scene in **BERRI**, announcing the fact that this is the town where the trademark orange juice comes from, and many travellers are drawn here between October and April by the prospect of fruit-picking work. The river is the main attraction, of course, with scenic river walks above coloured sandstone cliffs. You can also climb up the **Big Orange** for a good view of the Riverland, or watch the juice being produced in vast quantities at Berri Ltd on the Old Sturt Highway (℡08/8582 3321). For more information, head for the **visitor centre** on Riverview Drive (Mon–Fri 9am–5.30pm, Sat & Sun 10am–4pm; ℡08/8582 5511, ⓦwww.berribarmera.sa.gov.au).

In terms of places to **stay** in town, the *Berri Resort Hotel*, Riverview Drive (℡08/8582 1411 or ℡1800 088 226, ⓦwww.berriresorthotel.com; ⑥), is a huge riverfront hotel with a swimming pool, tennis courts, good food and a café with great river views. The quirky *Berri Backpackers* (℡08/8582 3144, ⓦwww .berribackpackers.com; dorms $26, rooms ②–③), 1km out of town towards Barmera on the Old Sturt Highway opposite the *Berri Club*, is the place to stay if you're fruit-picking, but is incredibly popular, so book ahead. Amenities include free bikes, internet access, a sauna, swimming pool, gym, tennis and

The Murray River

The Murray River is Australia's Mississippi – or so the American author Mark Twain declared when he saw it in the early 1900s. It's a fraction of the size of the American river, but in a country of seasonal, intermittent streams it counts as a major river and, like the Mississippi, the Murray helped open up a new continent. Fed by melting snow from the Snowy Mountains, as well as by the Murrumbidgee and Darling rivers, the Murray flows through the arid plains, reaching the Southern Ocean southwest of Adelaide near Goolwa. With the Darling and its tributaries, it makes up one of the biggest and longest watercourses in the world, giving life to Australia's most important agricultural region, the Murray–Darling basin. For much of its length it also forms the border between New South Wales and Victoria, slowing as it reaches South Australia, where it meanders through extensive alluvial plains and irrigation areas. Almost half of South Australia's water comes from the Murray; even far-off Woomera in the Outback relies on it.

Historically, the Riverland was densely populated by various Aboriginal peoples who navigated the river in bark canoes, the bark being cut from river red gums in a single perfect piece – many trees along the river still bear the scars. The Ngarrindjeri people's Dreamtime story of the river's creation explains how Ngurunderi travelled down the Murray, looking for his runaway wives. The Murray was then just a small stream, but, as Ngurunderi searched, a giant Murray cod surged ahead of him, widening the river with swipes of its tail. Ngurunderi tried to spear the fish, which he chased to the ocean, and the thrashing cod carved out the pattern of the Murray River during the chase.

The explorers Hume and Hovell came across the Murray at Albury in 1824. In 1830 Sturt and Mitchell navigated the Murray and Darling in a whale boat, Sturt naming it after the then Secretary of State for the Colonies (coincidentally, Murrundi was the Aboriginal name for part of the river). Their exploration opened up the interior, and from 1838 the Murray was followed as a stock route by "overlanders" taking sheep and cattle to newly established Adelaide. In 1853 the first paddle steamer, the *Mary*

volleyball courts, plus Balinese-style tree houses, tepees, and charming shacks. The well-equipped *Berri Riverside Caravan Park* (☎08/8582 3723, [W]www.berricaravanpark.com.au; un/powered sites $20/25, dorms $33, en-suite cabins 5) at the eastern end of Riverview Drive has a pool, barbecue area, cabins and snug bunkhouses.

For **food**, *Primo* at 1 Worman St is a rustic Aussie-style Italian restaurant open daily for lunch and dinner, while the *Mallee Fowl* restaurant, on the Sturt Highway 4km west of Berri (lunch & dinner Thurs–Sat), serves excellent barbecue-style meals in a busy and kitsch setting full of Australiana.

Renmark

RENMARK, on a bend of the Murray 254km from Adelaide, is the last major town before the New South Wales border. As with the other Riverland towns, the main attraction of Renmark is the river and its surrounding wetlands, and there's not a great deal to see in the town apart from **Olivewood Estate**, a fascinating National Trust property on the corner of Renmark Avenue and 21st Street (Thurs–Mon 10am–4pm, Tues 2–4pm; $5; ☎08 8586 6175). The former home of the Chaffey brothers, the Canadians who pioneered the irrigation and settlement of the Murray region, a palm-lined drive leads through a citrus orchard and olive trees to the house, which is a strange hybrid of Canadian log

Ann, was launched near Mannum. Goods were transported far inland, while wool was carried to market. River transport reached its peak in the 1870s, but by the mid-1930s it was virtually finished, thanks to the superior speed of the railways.

Seeing the river

The best way to appreciate the beauty of the Murray – lined with majestic river red gums and towering cliffs that reveal the area's colourful soils – is to get out on the water. Several old paddle steamers and a variety of other craft still cruise the Murray for pleasure – try the *Murray Princess* (three-night wetlands cruise from $775 per person, four-night Outback cruise $1033 per person, seven-night Murraylands and wildlife cruise $1596 per person; ☎08/9206 1122, [W]www.captaincook.com.au), based at Mannum, an hour's drive east of Adelaide (or take the Murray Bridge Passenger Service; Mon–Fri 1 daily; ☎08/8532 2633). Other cruises from Mannum include sporadic trips on the paddle steamer *Marion* (book at Mannum visitor centre, 67 Randell St; ☎08/8569 1303, [W]www.psmarion.com), and regular outings on the MV *Proud Mary* (morning tea cruises Mon 11am; 1hr 15min; two-, three- and five-night cruises also available; book at Mannum visitor centre or on ☎08/8231 9472, [W]www.proudmary.com.au).

Renting a houseboat is a relaxing and enjoyable way to see the river. All you need is a driving licence, and the cost isn't astronomical if you get a group of people together and avoid the peak holiday seasons. A week in an eight-berth houseboat out of season should cost around $1250, in a four-berth $950. The South Australian Tourism Commission (☎1300 655 276, [W]www.southaustralia.com) has pamphlets giving costs and facilities and can also book for you; alternatively, contact the Houseboat Hirers Association (☎08/8231 8466, [W]www.houseboat-centre.com.au).

A more hands-on way to explore the wetlands and creek systems is in a canoe, while the flat country, short distances between towns and dry climate are perfect for cycling – bikes can be rented at various hostels along the way.

cabin and Australian lean-to. The attached museum is the usual hotchpotch of local memorabilia, unrelated to the Chaffeys or their ambitious irrigation project. The **Chaffey Theatre** on 18th Street (℡08/8586 1800) has an impressive performing-arts centre hosting amateur and professional plays, films and concerts, anything from the Australian String Quintet to *Meet Me in St Louis*.

The riverfront **Renmark Paringa visitor centre** at 84 Murray Ave (Mon–Fri 9am–5pm, Sat 9am–4pm, Sun 10am–4pm; ℡08/8586 6704 or 1300 661 704, Ⓦwww.renmarkparinga.sa.gov.au) can book **river cruises**. The PS *Industry* – one of the few wood-fuelled paddle steamers left on the Murray – is moored outside and cruises on the first Sunday of the month (1hr 30min; $17; contact the visitor centre for times and bookings). Other cruises are run by Renmark River Cruises, which offers trips aboard the *Big River Rambler* (Tues, Thurs & Sat 2pm, Sun 11am; 2hr; $30; ℡08/8595 1862, Ⓦwww.renmarkrivercruises.com .au); the vessel leaves from Renmark wharf and heads upstream for 7km past colourful river cliffs. Riverland Leisure Canoe Tours (℡08/8588 2053, Ⓦwww .riverlandcanoes.com.au) rents out **kayaks** (single/double $30/40 per day) and **canoes** ($40 per day), and arranges day and overnight guided tours.

The obvious place to **stay** in Renmark is the landmark *Renmark Hotel/Motel* (℡08/8586 6755, Ⓦwww.renmarkhotel.com.au; ❸–❻), overlooking the river. Built in 1897 and given its current facade in the 1930s, the hotel has been thoroughly modernized and has a stylish bistro, outdoor swimming pool and spa. The *Renmark Riverfront Holiday Park*, on Patey Drive 2km east of town (℡08/8586 6315, Ⓦwww.big4renmark.com.au; un/powered sites $36/38, en-suite cabins & villas ❻–❾), has an idyllic setting along 1km of riverfront, with villas overlooking the river or the lagoon-style pool. *Café Sorelle* is a rustic Italian eatery at 179 Murray Ave with home-made lasagne and focaccias, while *The Golden Palace*, 114 Renmark Ave, does Aussie-Chinese; both are closed Mon.

The mid-north

Stretching north of Adelaide up to Port Augusta and the south Flinders Ranges is the fertile agricultural region known as the **mid-north**. The gateway to the region is the town of **Kapunda**, 16km northwest of Nuriootpa in the Barossa Valley (see p.778), which became Australia's first mining town when copper was discovered here in 1842. Kapunda can also be reached as a short detour from the **Barrier Highway** en route to Broken Hill in New South Wales, a route that continues through the larger mining town of **Burra**, and close to Peterborough, the self-proclaimed "frontier to the Outback". The centre of the mid-north's wine area, **Clare**, is 45km southwest of Burra on the Main North Road, the alternative route to Port Augusta. Heading north to Port Augusta on **Highway 1** for the Northern Territory or Western Australia, you'll pass through the ugly lead-smelting city of Port Pirie, and from there on to the south **Flinders Ranges**.

Getting around the area by **bus** is problematic – while most of the major towns have transport links to Adelaide, there are virtually no buses between towns, however close they might be. The Mid North Passenger Service (℡08/8823 2375, part of Yorke Peninsula Coaches) from Adelaide takes in Burra, Peterborough and the main Clare Valley settlements. In addition, LinkSA Barossa Valley (℡08/8564 3022) has a weekday service from Gawler – which can be reached by train – to Kapunda. All interstate buses to Darwin or Perth take Highway 1 through Port Pirie.

Kapunda and Burra

At the beginning of the 1840s South Australia was in serious economic trouble, until the discovery of **copper** at Kapunda in 1842 rescued the young colony and put it at the vanguard of Australia's mining boom. The early finds at **Kapunda** were, however, soon overshadowed by those at **Burra**, 65km north: the Burra "**Monster Mine**" was the largest in Australia until 1860, creating fabulous wealth and attracting huge numbers of Cornish miners. The boom ended as suddenly as it began, as resources were exhausted – mining finished at Burra in 1877 and Kapunda in 1878.

Heading to **KAPUNDA** from the Barossa, the landscape changes as vineyards are replaced by crops and grazing sheep. As you come into town, you're greeted by a colossal sculpture of a Cornish miner entitled *Map Kernow* – "Son of Cornwall". A place that once had its own daily newspaper, eleven hotels and a busy train station is now a rural service town, pleasantly undeveloped and with many old buildings decorated with locally designed and manufactured iron lacework.

If you have your own transport, you can follow a ten-kilometre **heritage trail** that takes in the ruins of the Kapunda mine, with panoramic views from the mine chimney lookout; details are available from the **Kapunda visitor centre** on the corner of Main and Hill streets (Mon–Fri 9am–5pm, Sat & Sun 10am–4pm; ℡08/8566 2902, ⓦ www.kapundatourism.com.au), where you can also book accommodation. At 11 Hill Street, the **Kapunda Museum** (daily 1–4pm; $5; ℡0402 247 419), occupying the massive Romanesque-style, 1866 former Baptist church, covers the history of the town. The best time to visit Kapunda is during the **Celtic festival**, held on the weekend before Easter, when Celtic music, bush and folk bands feature at the four pubs.

For **accommodation**, there's the lovely 1860s bluestone B&B *Ford House* at 80 Main St (℡08/8566 2280; ❺–❻). Backpackers could try the *Sir John Franklin Hotel* at 57 Main St (℡08/8566 3233; ❸), with simple rooms and inexpensive meals, or the *Kapunda Tourist and Leisure Park* on Montefiore Street (℡08/8556 2094, ⓦ www.kapundatouristpark.com; cabins ❸–❺) which has a range of cabins and cottages, and, impressively, wireless broadband.

Burra

In 1851 the mine at **BURRA** was producing five percent of the world's copper, but when the mines closed in 1877, it became a service centre for the surrounding farming community, and nowadays takes advantage of its mining heritage to attract visitors. Plenty of money has been spent restoring and beautifying the place, and the town's well-preserved stone architecture, shady tree-lined streets, lively country pubs and engaging art-and-craft and antiques shops make it a popular weekend escape between March and November, before it gets too hot. The creek divides the town in two: the mine is in the north, while the southern section has the shopping centre, based around

▲ The mine at Burra

Market Square, where you'll also find the **visitor centre** (daily 9am–5pm; ☎08/8892 2154, ⓦwww.visitburra.com). Its main function is to issue the Burra Heritage Passport to people driving the eleven-kilometre **heritage trail** ($50 for 2 people, including museum entry, and ($10 deposit) a key that gives you access to eight sites en route.

Heading north along Market Street you come to the **Burra Monster Mine** site, where there are extensive remains and interpretive walking trails, including the 1858 **Morphetts Enginehouse Museum** (daily 11am–1pm; 1hr; $5). Continuing north, the **Bon Accord Mine Complex** on Linkson Street (Thurs–Mon 2–4pm; 45min; $5) was a short-lived failure compared to its hugely successful neighbour; there's a scale model of the monster mine and a shaft and mining relics on view. Other key-pass places in the northern section of the town include the **old police lock-up and stables**, **Redruth Gaol**, and **Hampton**, a now-deserted private township in the style of an English village. Back in the main part of the town, the pass gets you entry to the **Unicorn Brewery Cellars** (1873) and the two fascinating remaining miners' dugouts: by 1851, because of a housing shortage nearly two thousand people were living in homes clawed out of the soft clay along Burra Creek. There are two further museums: the **Market Square Museum** (March–Jan daily 2–4pm; donation) was a general store, post office and home from 1880 to 1920, while the **Malowen Lowarth Museum cottages** on Kingston Street (daily tours at 9am & 10am, book at the visitor centre, also open for groups; $5) are decorated in 1860s style.

You can **stay** in one of a dozen or so self-contained miners' cottages (❹–❾) dotted around town, booked through the visitor centre. Book well ahead of time: on weekends from mid-March to October they fill with Adelaidians on short breaks. It can get very cold in the winter, but most cottages have fireplaces (free wood provided), plenty of blankets, and modern kitchens; breakfast is also available. Other accommodation in town includes the tree-surrounded *Burra*

Motor Inn, Market Street (☎08/8892 2777, ✉burramotel@bigpond.com.au; ❹), with modern rooms backing onto a creek, an indoor swimming pool and a well-priced restaurant. If you have a tent you could try the *Burra Caravan Park*, Bridge Terrace (☎08/8892 2442; un/powered sites $15/18, on-site vans ❶), in a pretty spot beside the creek, a couple of minutes' walk from the shops.

The *Burra Hotel*, 5 Market St, does typical bistro **meals**, but if you're in the mood for a real treat head for ☂ *White Cedars Café* (☎08/8892 2867) on Commercial Street. This Indonesian café offers authentic Balinese cuisine and the chef might even perform a traditional Balinese dance if asked nicely.

The Clare Valley

The wine industry in the **Clare Valley**, west of the Barrier Highway between Kapunda and Burra, was pioneered by Jesuit priests at **Sevenhill** in the 1850s. There's no tourist overkill here: bus trips are not encouraged, and because it's a small area with just over **forty cellar doors**, you can learn a lot about the local styles of wine (the valley is especially recognized for its fine Rieslings). You'll often get personal treatment too, with the winemaker presiding. In the cool uplands of the **North Mount Lofty Ranges**, Clare Valley is really a series of gum-fringed ridges and valleys running roughly 30km north from **Auburn** to the main township of **Clare**, on either side of Main North Road. Huge sheep runs were established here in the nineteenth century and the area, which is prime merino land, still has a pastoral feel; several stations can be visited. There are beautiful historic villages, well-preserved mansions, quaint old pubs, plenty of atmospheric accommodation, and superb restaurants attached to wineries. The region's calendar is crammed for most of the year but the biggest event is the **Clare Valley Gourmet Weekend**, held in May at local wineries.

Between Clare and Auburn, the old railway line has been transformed into the **Riesling Trail**, a 27-kilometre cycling path; to cycle one-way takes about two hours. Mountain bikes can be rented from Clare Valley Cycle Hire, 32 Victoria Rd, Clare ($30 per day; ☎08/8842 2782), which will deliver to anywhere in the valley.

Auburn to Watervale

Heading north through the valley the first settlement you come to is the small village of **AUBURN**, 120km from Adelaide, which began life as a halfway resting point for wagons carrying copper ore from Burra to Port Adelaide. On the Main North Road, the *Rising Sun Hotel* (☎08/8849 2015, ✉rising@capri .net.au; ❹–❺), first licensed in 1850, is one of many characterful pubs in the valley. It has snug bedrooms in mews-style accommodation in old stone stables, as well as a very affordable modern Australian menu and an appropriately local wine list. A more luxurious place to stay is the delightful *Dennis Cottage* (☎08/8277 8177, ⊛www.denniscottage.com.au; ❾), which has bags of charm, a spa, and paraphernalia associated with C.J. Dennis, the popular poet who was born here in 1876; the owners have added several other properties to their portfolio. *Cygnets*, on Main North Road (daily 9.30am–3.30pm and Fri & Sat 6.30pm–late; ☎08/8849 2030, ⊛www.cygnetsatauburn.com.au; ❻), is an atmospheric restaurant with rooms, delicious regional cuisine, and the departure point for the cheese and wine trail (⊛www.cheeseandwinetrail .com.au). They also host "la masseria" every Saturday night, a traditional Italian feast served on a long table. Two of the region's best small wineries are nearby:

Grosset (Wed–Sun 10am–5pm; although they close shop for the season when they run out; Ⓦwww.grosset.com.au) and **Mount Horrocks** (Sat & Sun 10am–5pm; Ⓦwww.mounthorrocks.com).

The next small village is **LEASINGHAM**, where you can camp or stay at *Leasingham Village Caravan & Cabins* (Ⓣ08/8843 0136, Ⓦwww.leasingham villagecabins.com.au; cabins ❸), a popular place for **grape-pickers** from March to May. You can taste **wines** nearby at **Tim Gramp Wines** (Sat & Sun 11am–4pm, Ⓦwww.timgrampwines.com.au). There are four small wineries at **WATERVALE**, 2km north: of them, **Crabtree of Watervale**, North Terrace (Mon–Sat 11am–5pm; Ⓦwww.crabtreewines.com.au), is one of the most enjoyable in the valley.

Mintaro

From Leasingham, you can turn off east to **MINTARO**, a village whose tree-lined streets and cottages are beautifully preserved from the 1850s, when it was a resting place for bullock teams travelling from the Burra copper mines. There's no general store or petrol supply here; the emphasis is on atmospheric cottage accommodation, popular with Adelaide weekenders. The focus of the village is the *Magpie and Stump Hotel*, which is particularly lively on Sunday afternoons. Opposite, at **Reilly's Wines** (daily 10am–4pm; Ⓦwww.reillyswines.com), housed in an 1856 Irish bootmaker's building, you can taste vintages produced since 1994 from Watervale grapes; the **restaurant** here serves hearty, globally inspired food for lunch (Ⓣ08/8843 9013) and has accommodation in cosy country cottages including the nearby *Mintaro Pay Office Cottages* (❺). *Mintaro Mews*, on Burra Street (Ⓣ08/8843 9001, Ⓕ8843 9002; ❺), has upmarket B&B accommodation with an indoor heated pool and spa; Saturday nights are package-only ($120 per person), including a four-course meal in the charming restaurant.

Southeast of the town lies the Georgian-style **Martindale Hall** (Mon–Fri 11am–4pm, Sat & Sun noon–4pm; $10; Ⓣ08/8843 9088, Ⓦwww.martindalehall .com; ❺–❼ including breakfast), the grand mansion featured in the 1975 film *Picnic at Hanging Rock*. You can visit during the day and do a tour, or for $210 per person you can stay overnight and enjoy a four-course meal and cooked breakfast, or for $235 per person you and your friends can have the full run of the place – it's freezing in winter though.

Heading northwest from Mintaro to Sevenhill (see below) takes you through the rolling hills of the Polish Hill River area. About 8km along, **Paulett Wines** (daily 10am–5pm; Ⓦwww.paulettwines.com.au) has fabulous views, its veranda overlooking the "river" – a dry creek for eleven months of the year.

Sevenhill and the Spring Gully Conservation Park

The village of **SEVENHILL** is home to the valley's oldest winery, **Sevenhill Cellars**, on College Road (Mon–Fri 9am–5pm, Sat & Sun 10am–5pm; Ⓦwww .sevenhillcellars.com.au). This is still run by a religious order that mainly makes sacramental wine, though the brothers have diversified into table wines, sweet sherry and port, doing everything from growing the grapes to bottling. The sandstone building has a tasting room with lots of character and history, and there's an old Catholic church in the grounds. Nearby, on College Road, *Thorn Park Country House* (Ⓣ08/8843 4304, Ⓦwww.thornpark.com.au; ❼–❽) occupies an 1850 stone-and-slate building in a gorgeous setting; it offers B&B and a superb dinner for an extra $110 per person. *Sevenhill Hotel*, on Main

North Road, is a classic country pub serving popular inexpensive **meals** (daily except Sun).

To the west of Main North Road, **Spring Gully Conservation Park** has the last remnant of red stringybark forest in South Australia. There are steep gullies, waterfalls, wildlife and, in spring, lovely wild flowers; free camping is allowed outside the fire ban season (usually early Dec–late April). Nearby, **Eldredge Wines**, Spring Gully Road (tastings daily 11am–5pm; Ⓦwww .eldredge.com.au), is located in a small farmhouse fronting a dam, while **Skillogalee Winery** (daily 10am–5pm; lunch bookings advised; Ⓣ08/8843 4311, Ⓦwww.skillogalee.com) boasts an excellent **restaurant** serving delicious meals made from fresh local produce, at moderate prices; they also do picnic baskets. It occupies a wonderful spot set against the backdrop of a clunking windmill, bush-clad hill and vineyards, with meals and tastings by the fire in the 1850s cottage or on the veranda.

Clare

CLARE itself is a surprisingly ordinary town, with few concessions to the weekend visitors who pour in from Adelaide: it consists primarily of Main North Road, and virtually everything is closed on Sunday. The **visitor centre**, right next to the caravan park at the corner of Main North and Spring Gully roads (Mon–Fri 9am–5pm, Sat 10am–4pm, Sun 11am–5pm; Ⓣ08/8842 2131, Ⓦwww.clarevalley.com.au), provides an excellent free visitors' guide and can book accommodation and restaurants. **Wineries** nearby include **Knappstein Wines**, 2 Pioneer Ave (Mon–Fri 9am–5pm, Sat 11am–5pm, Sun 11am–4pm; Ⓦwww.knappsteinwines.com.au), in an ivy-covered sandstone building with a veranda and an open log fire in winter; **Jim Barry**, a friendly, family-run place on Main North Road (Mon–Fri 9am–5pm, Sat & Sun 9am–4pm; Ⓦwww .jimbarry.com); and **Leasingham**, 7 Dominic St (Mon–Fri 8.30am–5pm, Sat & Sun 10am–4pm; Ⓦwww.leasingham-wines.com.au), a large commercial winery established in 1893.

Some local sheep stations are open for tours, and **farmstays** are also available: pick of the bunch is *Bungaree Station* (Ⓣ08/8842 2677, Ⓦwww.bungareestation .com.au; shearers' quarters $22, B&B cottages ❶–❷), a working merino station 12km north of Clare on Main North Road; one of the oldest and largest properties in the district, it has its own church as well as a swimming pool. Accommodation is spread across seven atmospheric cottages, houses and stables, while you can also bunk down in shearers' quarters (BYO swag). Activities include wildlife-spotting, horseriding and toasting marshmallows around a fire.

For **accommodation**, take advantage of the many charming B&Bs scattered around the valley; the visitor centre will make a booking for you. Otherwise head for one of the hotels along Main North Road. One of the handiest is the *Comfort Inn Clare Central* at the north end of town at no. 325 (Ⓣ08/8842 2277, Ⓦwww .clarecentral.com.au; ❺–❻) which has a pool. You can camp 4km south of town at *Clare Caravan Park* on Main North Road (Ⓣ08/8842 2724, Ⓦwww.clare-caravan -park.com.au; un/powered sites $20/27, en-suite cabins ❹–❺), which also has a swimming pool. For lunch, make the most of what the wineries have to offer as it's generally of higher standard than what the pubs in town will serve you.

Port Pirie

From Clare, the Main North Road heads to Jamestown, 65km north. To the west, a road branches off towards Crystal Brook, where there's a hikers' lodge at Bowman Park providing basic overnight shelter for hikers on the Heysen Trail.

From here it's not far up Highway 1 to **PORT PIRIE**, the fourth-largest urban centre in South Australia. While it appears to be an ugly industrial city on initial approach, its skyline dominated by smelters' chimneys, the centre boasts some impressive historic architecture from big old corner pubs to Art Deco shops. As the nearest seaport to Broken Hill, the lead and zinc smelting industry here dates back to the discovery of the rich vein of lead-silver-zinc found there in 1883. The **Port Pirie visitor centre and Arts Centre**, on Mary Elie Street (Mon–Fri 9am–5pm, Sat 9am–4pm, Sun 10am–4pm; ☎08/8633 8700 or 1800 000 424, ⓦwww.pirie.sa.gov.au), has interpretive brochures and self-guided walking tours of the town if you're interested in **historic buildings** and the smelting industry. If not, there's little else to keep you here. Beyond Port Pirie, Telowie Gorge and Mount Remarkable National Park, in the southern stretches of the Flinders Ranges (see p.834), are within easy reach.

Outback South Australia

...a country such as I firmly believe has no parallel on earth's surface.

The explorer Charles Sturt, 1844

Leaving behind the civilized south, the wild and vast expanses of South Australia's **Outback** can take some adjusting to. With little in the way of obvious destinations, the experience is the thing – few areas of the planet feel quite so isolated or hostile to human habitation. All routes radiate from **Port Augusta**, the commercial centre for the far north, and though buses cover the highways, elsewhere you'll need to have your own transport or take a tour. To the west, the Eyre Highway runs 950km to the border of Western Australia; the journey can be broken by taking a detour around the coast of the **Eyre Peninsula**, which has sandy white beaches, aquamarine sea, excellent fishing, and **Australia's finest seafood**, most of which sadly goes directly to Sydney's fish markets. Once past **Ceduna**, on the eastern edge of the **Nullarbor Plain**, there's little beyond you and the desert. The Indian Pacific **train** traverses the Nullarbor further inland, through even more extreme desolation. To the north, the Stuart Highway and the New Ghan rail line link Port Augusta with the Northern Territory through 890km of progressively drier scenery, where regular markers along the roadside record the distance covered, as well as how far there is to go. Prohibited zones surround much of the highway, though about the only places you'd want to leave it anyway are at **Woomera** and the opal-mining town of **Coober Pedy**, with its unusual underground dwellings; both lie outside the military areas and the boundaries of Aboriginal land.

All other roads north from Port Augusta follow the route taken by the legendary but now defunct Old Ghan to the country towns of **Quorn** and **Hawker**, where routes diverge. To the northeast lie the **Flinders Ranges**, a series of spectacularly beautiful gorges and geological curiosities, most famous of which is **Wilpena Pound**. Continuing northeast will take you along the **Strzelecki Track** to **Innamincka** and beyond to Queensland. Heading due north takes you to **Marree**, at the head of the **Birdsville** and **Oodnadatta** tracks. Travel beyond Marree is not for the faint-hearted, but worth the effort for those wishing to experience the eerie silence and emptiness of **Lake Eyre** and the sheer isolation of the Dalhousie Hot Springs and the Simpson Desert.

A **Desert Parks Pass** is required for legal entry into Innamincka Regional Reserve, Lake Eyre National Park, Witjira National Park and the Simpson Desert: $107 per vehicle allows unlimited access and use of campsites for twelve months, with copies of the detailed *DEH Desert Parks Handbook* and Westprint Heritage Maps' surveys thrown in. Passes are available from agencies throughout the north, can be purchased online (Ⓦ www.environment.sa.gov .au/parks/visitor/onlinepass; allow 7 days), or bought at the Port Augusta **Department of Environment and Heritage (DEH) office** at 9 Mackay St (Ⓣ 08/8648 5300).

To find out about **road conditions** in these regions, call Ⓣ 1300 361 033 or visit the SA Transport website (Ⓦ www.transport.sa.gov.au). Many roadhouses and fuel pumps have EFTPOS facilities. **Water** is vital: with few exceptions, lakes and waterways are dry or highly saline, and most Outback deaths are related to dehydration or heatstroke – bikers seem particularly prone. As always, stay with your vehicle if you break down. Summer temperatures can be lethally hot, and winters pleasant during the day and subzero at night; rain can fall at any time of year, but is most likely to do so between January and May.

RAA road **maps** are good but lack topographical information, so if you're spending any time in the north, pick up the excellent Westprint Heritage maps and the cluttered Landsmap *Outback: Central and South Australia*. The **South Australia Tourist Association** issues a road map of the Flinders Ranges, but it's inadequate for walking; hikers traversing the Flinders on the **Heysen Trail** need topographic maps of each section and advice from the nearest DEH office. Conditions of minor roads are so variable that maps seldom do more than indicate the surface type; local police and roadhouses will have current information.

Port Augusta and the west

How you see **Port Augusta** depends on where you've come from. Arriving from the Outback, the town's trees, shops and hotels can be a real thrill, but compared with the southeast of the state, there's little here. Its role as a transport hub has saved the town from destitution, while recent developments have made the foreshore area with its city beach more attractive. While you're deciding where to head next, there are a couple of brilliant sights to see in town and some good **bushwalking** country around Mount Remarkable, at the tail end of the Flinders Ranges.

The direct route west from Port Augusta, the Eyre Highway, begins its daunting journey towards Western Australia across the top of the Eyre Peninsula, but going this way you'll see virtually nothing. An alternative route detours around the peninsula's coastline (via the Lincoln and Flinders highways) before rejoining the highway at Ceduna on the brink of the Nullarbor Plain, while the **rail** line parallels the coast some 100km inland.

Port Augusta

PORT AUGUSTA sits at the tip of the Spencer Gulf with the Outback all around. Despite the name, the docks closed long ago, while the power station and railways were drastically scaled down during the 1980s – the former rail buildings have been converted to Employment Service offices.

During summer, you should make the most of the **swimming beach** at the end of Young Street or escape the dust and heat at the attractive foreshore – the old wooden pile crossing, now a footbridge, and a hundred-year-old jetty, all that remains of the port, make good perches for fishing and there are barbecue facilities and swimming pontoons in the water. The chief source of information is the very helpful **visitor centre** (Mon–Fri 9am–5.30pm, Sat & Sun 10am–4pm; ☎08/8641 9194) at 41 Flinders Terrace, where you can pick up a brochure detailing a self-guided heritage walk, book **tours** including scenic flights, fishing expeditions, whale and dolphin watching cruises, 4WD tours, camel rides, and sheep station experiences, and get your tickets for the Pitchi Richi Railway (see p.834). Internet access is also available ($5 for 30min). This is where you'll also find the superb **Wadlata Outback Centre** (same opening times; ☎08/8641 9193, [W]www.wadlata.sa.gov.au; $10.95). This compelling interpretative centre is dedicated to the Outback and its characters, covering everything from the indigenous people's deep relationship to the land to the explorers who opened up the unforgiving country. There's an impressive use of multimedia and audiovisual technology, lots of interactive elements to keep you amused (it's wonderful for families), and even a small cinema designed like an early "picture house". Allow a couple of hours to do the place justice; there's a café here too, and they'll give you a "pass out" if you want to return later.

The **Homestead Park Pioneer Museum** (daily 9am–4pm; $3), on Elsie Street behind McDonald's, is housed in a 140-year-old log homestead that was moved here from Yudnapinna, 100km away. It's crammed with 19th-century furnishings, and there's a buggy shed with two 1920s carriages and an original blacksmith's shop with machinery.

Flanking the north side of town on the Stuart Highway is the stunning **Australian Arid Lands Botanic Garden** (Mon–Fri 9am–5pm, Sat & Sun 10am–4pm; free entry, but it's worth taking the 1hr guided tour Monday to Friday at 10am for $6.95; [W]www.australian-aridlands-botanic-garden.org), a showcase and research centre for native Australian desert flora with 12km of self-guided walking trails and bird hides. The rain-gathering, solar-powered information centre, shop and café underline the ideals of the garden as an ongoing ecological project.

Practicalities

The centre of town overlooks the east side of the **Spencer Gulf**, more like a river where it divides the town. The **airport** (☎08/8642 3100) is down Caroona Road, 5km west of the centre – taxis travel into the centre (☎08/8642 4466). The **bus** terminal, serving Greyhound from Adelaide to Alice Springs and Stateliner from Adelaide to Whyalla and Ceduna, is at 21 Mackay St (all services ☎08/8642 5055), while **trains** from Sydney, Perth and Darwin pull in at Stirling Road (☎08/8642 6699). Shops, banks and the post office are clustered along narrow **Commercial Road**. If you need maps and information beyond what's available at the Outback Centre, visit the helpful **DEH** at 9 Mackay St (☎08/8648 5300) where you can pick up park info, maps and passes (if you're visiting four or more SA parks, get a Holiday Pass, $32; including camping $52); if you're a member, the RAA, at 7 Caroona Rd (☎08/8642 2576), provides very good road maps. **Cars** can be rented from Budget, at 14 Young St (☎08/8642 6040).

The best **accommodation** in town is the stylish *Majestic Oasis Apartments* (☎08/8648 9000 [W]www.majestichotels.com.au; [5]–[8]), within walking distance of pubs, eateries and shops; if all you need is a bed for the night, you'll be comfortable in any one of these smart self-contained units, but if you're staying a couple of nights, book one with balcony and water views. There are several motels, including the comfortable *Best Western Standpipe* (℡08/8642 4033, ⊛www.standpipe.com.au; ❺–❼), which is home to a popular Indian restaurant. The friendly *Flinders Hotel* at 39 Commercial Rd (℡08/8642 2544; dorms \$25, rooms ❸) is the best bet for budget travellers. The town's closest **campsites** include the *Shoreline Top Tourist Park* at the end of Gardiner Avenue (℡08/8642 2965; un/powered sites \$22/25, bunks \$36, cabins ❸) and the *Big 4 Holiday Park* at the junction of the Eyre and Stuart highways (℡08/8642 2974, ⊛www.aspenparks.com.au; un/powered sites \$27, cabins ❷–❹, units ❹–❺).

The best places to **eat** are *The Standpipe* (see above); dinner only) for hearty Indian, and the *Hannahville Hotel* (℡08/8642 2921; daily, lunch and dinner), on the corner of Gibson and Flinders streets, which dishes up decent Mod Oz bistro standards to its loyal locals. Out of the cafés dotted around town, *Ozzies Coffee Lounge* at 22 Commercial Rd (the northern end of the mall) is the best, with good coffee, croissants, quiches, scones and focaccia. There's no shortage of fast-food eateries on Victoria Parade, of which *Barnacle Bill's* (a South Australian chain) is the local favourite with great-value **seafood** (\$36 for a huge seafood platter for two). You can get counter meals at most pubs, including the central *Commonwealth Hotel* on Commercial Road and *Hotel Augusta* on the western foreshore, with fine views of the water, mangroves and distant Flinders Ranges from the tables out the front. The *Transcontinental*, Port Augusta's weekly rag, will have details of anything happening around town.

Mount Remarkable National Park

Mount Remarkable National Park (vehicle entry fee: \$8) lies in two sections, encircled by a ring road that starts 45km southeast of Port Augusta and runs via Wilmington, **Melrose** and Port Germein. The larger western slice contains **Mambray Creek** and **Mount Cavern**, and connecting tracks run from them to **Alligator Gorge**; **Mount Remarkable** and sections of the Heysen Trail rise to the east behind Melrose. If time is short, there are easy walks in Alligator Gorge, while the Mount Cavern circuit is considerably harder – both make good day-trips from Port Augusta. There are toilets, gas barbecues and picnic tables at the popular *Mambray Creek Campground* (book ahead at the DEH Mambray Creek office ℡08/8634 7068; \$15 per night;), which also has a cabin (\$50) and lodge (\$75), while bushcamping (\$5) is allowed at 11 designated sites from May to October. In hot weather, the park may be closed if there's a high risk of fire; check conditions with the CFS (℡1300 362 361). Stateliner **buses** go daily to Mambray Creek and Wilmington.

Alligator Gorge, Mount Remarkable and Melrose

The thirteen-kilometre dirt road (turn-off 1km south of Wilmington) to **Alligator Gorge** ends at a car park and picnic area perched on a spur above two bush campsites at Teal and Eaglehawk dams. Stairs descend into the gorge, with several **walking** options once you reach the gorge floor, including a two-kilometre 90-minute loop taking you along the rocky bed of Alligator Creek and through "the narrows" in spectacular Alligator Gorge, a tight red canyon alive with frog calls, moss gardens and echoes. Although it sometimes gets flooded, there are usually enough stepping stones to avoid wet feet. The path returns to the car park via Blue Gum Flat picnic area. A nine-kilometre, four-hour loop follows Alligator Creek upstream beyond the rippled Terraces (the remains of a fossilized lake shore), returning along a park management track and walking trail to the car park. For longer hikes down to Mambray Creek you'll need maps and approval from the DEH.

Nearby, the historic buildings of the tranquil former 1840s copper-mining town of **MELROSE** have been painstakingly restored. Melrose is home to Rock the Mount (ⓦwww.remarkablefestivals.com.au), a popular country music festival and ute muster held in April. There are a few hotels, including the hip *North Star Hotel* (ⓣ08/8666 2060, ⓦwww.northstarhotel.com.au; rooms ❹–❽) on Nott Street, with a funky restaurant serving fine regional cuisine, quality live entertainment, and a wide range of stylish rooms. There's a pleasant creekside **caravan park** (ⓣ08/8666 2060; dorms $15, cabins ❷) and a **B&B** in a barn behind *Bluey Blundstone's Blacksmith Shop* (ⓣ08/8666 2173; ❹), carefully restored to its original 1865 condition. When the proprietor isn't producing decorative wrought-ironwork he serves cakes in a coffee shop at the back of the forge. The summit of **Mount Remarkable**, with its panoramic views of Willochra Plain and the Spencer Gulf, can be reached on foot in a five-hour hike (12.5km) via the Heysen Trail, starting from the War Memorial Monument behind Melrose campsite.

Telowie Gorge, Mambray Creek and Mount Cavern

The small and appealing **Telowie Conservation Park** lies to the south off the Port Germein to Murray Town road. A very short path leads between the gorge walls, but unless you're properly equipped for a long hike over to Wirrabara Forest and the Heysen Trail, you'll get more of a flavour of the area by **camping** along the creek where you can enjoy spotting yellow-footed rock wallabies at dawn and dusk.

The access track to **Mambray Creek** is east off the highway, halfway between Port Germein and the Wilmington road. Here you'll find a **campsite** (with water and toilets) and the national park headquarters. Mambray Creek is the start of some serious hikes, either into the north part of the park along the **Battery Track** and **Alligator Creek**, or on the tough but shorter **Mount Cavern circuit**, which follows the path anticlockwise along the Black Range, giving spectacular views. The descent runs down a loose stone slope held together by grasstrees, before entering cool woodland at Mambray Creek Gorge, where you might be able to get close to large groups of emus.

The Eyre Peninsula

Long appreciated by Adelaidians as an antidote to city stress, the Eyre Peninsula's broad triangle is protected by the **Gawler Ranges** from the arid climate further north. The area began to be farmed in the 1880s, fishing communities sprang up at regular intervals and iron ore, discovered around 1900, is still mined around **Whyalla**. The drive around the coast passes stunning scenery and superlative **surfing** and **beach fishing**, especially where the Great Australian Bight's elemental weather hammers into the western shore – a chance to give your senses a workout before dealing with the Nullarbor's deadening horizons.

Stateliner **buses** from Port Augusta run either across the top of the peninsula to Ceduna, or via Whyalla down the east coast to Port Lincoln at the southern tip – you'll need your own transport to tackle the western side. Major **car** rental companies have outlets at both Whyalla and Port Lincoln which, if time is limited, are only fifty minutes by **air** from Adelaide.

Whyalla and the east coast

First visible, about an hour from Port Augusta, as a smudge of grey over Long Sleep Plain, **WHYALLA**, the state's second most important city and headquarters of its **heavy industry**, isn't the prettiest of places. **OneSteel** has its massive steelworks here (tours Mon, Wed & Fri 9.30am; 2hr; $18; book in advance through the visitor centre) and tankers queue offshore to fill up at Santos' oil and gas refinery. Until it closed in 1978, the shipyard produced a few famous **vessels**, including World War II warships, the first and most famous being the HMAS *Whyalla*, which now guards the northern entrance to town, as part of the **Whyalla Maritime Museum** (daily 10am–4pm; $8 including ship tour; 5 daily, times vary depending on season). Specializing in naval history, the museum features displays on the warships, the shipbuilding industry and the area's maritime heritage. Buy your tickets and enter the museum through the adjoining **visitor centre** (Mon–Fri 9am–5pm, Sat & Sun 9.30am–4pm; ℡08/8645 8900, 🌐www .whyalla.com). From the southwest, Whyalla presents a much greener aspect – at the junction of Broadbent Terrace and Playford Avenue an old aerodrome site has been landscaped into a series of ponds to recycle stormwater. Architecture buffs will also enjoy the many **Art Deco buildings** dotted around town, especially in the centre.

The highway curves through the old town under the name of Darling Terrace; you'll find a **post office**, **banks**, a **bus station**, hotels and shops around the junction with Forsyth and Patterson streets, all periodically covered in harmless red fallout from the steelworks' mysterious pellet plant.

Accommodation options include the *Foreshore Caravan Park* on Broadbent Terrace (℡08/8645 7474, 🌐www.bestonparks.com.au; cabins ❸) and *Whyalla Foreshore Motor Inn* on Watson Terrace (℡08/8645 8877, 🌐www .whyallaforeshore.com.au; ❻), both a ten-minute walk from the centre along a surprisingly attractive beach, with Hummock Hill mercifully obscuring the view of the steelworks; people and pelicans find good fishing off the jetty. Otherwise, try your luck at one of the **hotels**: *Spencer* on Forsyth Street (℡08/8645 8411; ❸) has rooms, good food and weekend music. For **food**, try *Watersedge* at the *Whyalla Foreshore Motor Inn* for bistro standards with water views, or sizzling seafood on a stone at *Broady's Stonegrill Café Lounge & Wine Bar* (11am till late; you need to book on Sundays, ℡08/8645 2666) at 84B Essington Lewis Ave. You can get counter meals at the *Spencer Hotel* and *New Whyalla Hotel* at City Plaza on Forsyth Street. After dinner, walk past the rows of fifty-year-old workers' homes to the top of Hummock Hill for a view over the brightly illuminated industrial complexes by night.

Beyond Whyalla, the **east coast** is an unassuming string of sheltered beaches and fishing villages, many with attractive historic architecture, nestled beneath towering grain silos – the sort of places you could drive through without a second glance or else get waylaid beachcombing for a week. **COWELL** is known for its whiting and as the world's largest source of black "nephrite" jade, though not much of it is in evidence, since it's largely exported rough. Arno Bay, Port Neill and the larger Tumby Bay all boast clean, quiet beaches, good fishing and decent accommodation.

Port Lincoln

Australia's seafood capital and largest fishing port, built on a hillside above Boston Bay, **PORT LINCOLN** has the liveliest atmosphere on the peninsula. The town's harbour bobs with trawlers, and the main seafront streets of Tasman Terrace and Liverpool Street are full of cafés, eateries and big old Aussie pubs. There's a **visitor centre** here too, between the post office and shopping mall (daily 9am–5pm; ☎08/8683 3544 or 1300 788 378, Ⓦwww.visitportlincoln.net), for accommodation, tours and national park passes,; Stateliner **buses** (☎08/8415 5555) terminate a couple of streets away on Darling Terrace.

The seafood farmed or caught wild in the oceans around here – southern bluefin tuna (April–Sept), yellow tail kingfish (year-round), southern rock lobster (Nov–May), wild king prawns (Nov–Dec, March–June), Boston Bay mussels (seasonal variations), Pacific oysters (Feb–Nov), and wild and farmed abalone (year-round) – is considered to be the country's finest, earning the town and state hundreds of millions of dollars a year. Tasting it involves some work, however, with the best stuff snap-frozen on deck and either trucked to Sydney's fish markets to be served in the country's finest restaurants or immediately exported overseas. If you're spending a few days on the Peninsula then buy the *Seafood and Aquaculture Trail* card from the visitor centre ($89) which gets you discounts and extras at restaurants all around the coast, and free guided tours (with tastings) of various seafood processing plants such as *The Fresh Fish Place* (Mon–Fri 8.30am–5.30pm, Sat 8.30am–12.30pm; guided tours 10.30am Mon, Wed & Fri; ☎08/8682 2166) at 20 Proper Bay Rd, where you can buy ready-to-eat oysters. Alternatively, head to one of the seafood restaurants or takeaways below or try your hand at catching your own. Get tackle and bait from *Spot On* at 39 Tasman Terrace where the friendly staff will draw you a mad map to their secret fishing and camping spots, or simply **fish** off the town jetty. The visitor centre can book boat charters, fishing trips, sailing, cruises to spot dolphins, seals, sea lions and birdlife, and shark cage-diving: the

▲ Cliffs near Port Lincoln

seas off Lincoln have been rated as the best place in the world to see the endangered **great white sharks** (footage for *Jaws* was filmed here). Boats leave from the **Marina**, Port Lincoln's commercial fishing headquarters, where the impressive trawlers are worth a look.

You can indulge in the sea's finest at local favourite *Sarins Restaurant and Bar* (daily, breakfast, lunch and dinner) at the Port Lincoln Hotel; the *Boardwalk Bistro Bar* (daily noon–2.30pm & 6–8.30pm) at the Marina Hotel at 13 Jubilee Drive, which boasts a deck overlooking the sea; the award-winning *Del Giorno's* (daily 9am–9pm), at 80 Tasman Terrace, where you can eat alfresco on the footpath; or *King Neptune's Takeaway* at 5 Light St. Make sure that, whatever you eat, you pair it with a bottle from the local *Boston Bay Wines*. While their wines are in local bottle shops and appear on all wine lists, you can buy direct from their cellar door, 6km north of Port Lincoln on the Lincoln Highway (Thurs–Mon noon–4pm; [W] www.bostonbaywines.com.au).

Entering Port Lincoln from the north, the Lincoln Highway (which later becomes Tasman Terrace and then London St) affords splendid views of Boston Bay and presents you with myriad **accommodation** options, such as the sleek *Port Lincoln Hotel* ([T] 1300 766 100; [W] www.portlincolnhotel.com.au; [5]–[9]), one of the best on the peninsula, with comfortable, contemporary rooms; book a room if you can with a balcony overlooking the sea. Also good, if a little frumpy, is the *Limani Motel* ([T] 08/8682 2200, [W] www.limanimotel.com.au; [5]–[7]), which has sea views. At the highway's far end lie the terraced tent sites of *Port Lincoln Tourist Park* ([T] 08/8621 4444, [W] www.portlincolnaccommodation.com; un/powered sites $23/26, cabins [3]–[5]). The visitor centre can also book stays on farms and stations ([1]–[2]).

Around Port Lincoln

Lincoln National Park, just south of Port Lincoln, covers a rough peninsula of sandy coves, steep cliffs and mallee scrub, which is home to the discreet rock parrot. The DEH at 75 Liverpool St in Port Lincoln ([T] 08/8688 3111) can supply maps and advice on road conditions. There's more stunning scenery 32km south at **Whalers Way**, a privately owned stretch of road to some of the coast's most ruggedly beautiful landscapes, including Cape Carnot and Cape Wiles. You'll need to collect a permit and key from the visitor centre or service stations in Port Lincoln, or from the Port Lincoln Caravan Park ($25, plus $10 key deposit); there's bush camping with toilets, picnic tables and gas barbecues at Redbanks. The name Whalers Way derives from the whaling station which once operated at Cape Wiles – its relics are stacked up around the gate – where you can spot fur seals, kangaroos and emus. The power of the Southern Ocean is memorably demonstrated at **Cape Carnot**, in the southern section, where giant waves and frosty blue surf force their way through blowholes which sigh as they erupt in sync with the swell.

The picturesque setting of the town of **COFFIN BAY**, home to Australia's finest oysters, is worth a look; book ahead during school holidays, when the caravan park ([T] 08/8685 4170; on-site vans [3], cabins [4]–[6]) and abundant holiday cottages are full to bursting. On the Esplanade, *The Oysterbeds* ([T] 08/8685 4000; Wed–Sat 10.30am–late, Sun–Mon 11am–4pm; closed in winter) serves up some of the most sublime seafood you'll taste between Adelaide and Perth. A stroll along the coastal "Oyster Walk" takes you past old fishermen's shacks, now mostly summer houses, and reveals a wealth of bird and plant life – a taste of the national park to the west.

Coffin Bay National Park (vehicle entry fee: $8), an hour's drive west from Port Lincoln, comprises a landscape of dunes and salt marsh, mostly accessible only by 4WD, though parts are open to other types of vehicle – consult the DEH office in Port Lincoln before visiting. You'll be rewarded by isolation, sand sculptures at Sensation and Mullalong beaches, and the quality of the fishing. Semicircular stone walls on the northern shore are **Aboriginal fish traps** – fish were chased in at high tide and then the gaps in the side blocked with nets as the water receded. If you don't have your own 4WD, Great Australian Bight Safaris (☏08/8682 2750, ⓦwww.greatsafaris .com.au) offers various day-trips ($100–180), as well as longer camping and fishing adventures.

The west coast

To catch the best of the west coast and the townships along the way, you'll need to detour off the main road between Coffin Bay and Ceduna. The region's coastal communities are a mix of fishermen, farmers and surfies who come to ride the endless succession of strong, hundred-metre-long crests rolling into Waterloo Bay at **ELLISTON**, one of the state's most highly regarded **surf beaches**. Bold murals at the Community Hall between the café and campsite address local themes – including a long-suppressed incident when Aboriginal people were driven over the cliffs.

North of Elliston just before Venus Bay, rocks have been hollowed by the sea to form the **Talia Caves**, but the lengthy beach is more compelling, though camping is prohibited. To the north again, if you turn to the coast about 20km north of Port Kenny, you pass the striking **Murphy's Haystacks**, a group of low granite monoliths that look like giant mushrooms. Pushing on to **Point Labatt** brings you to one of mainland Australia's only colony of fur seals – binoculars or a telephoto lens help to distinguish mother seals teaching pups to swim from the torpid, bulkier males basking on the rocks. Then it's back to the highway at **Streaky Bay** – the only place on the west coast that has a real centre – and then to drier country as you approach Ceduna and the Nullarbor.

The Eyre Highway and Gawler Ranges

Taking the **Eyre Highway** directly across the top of the peninsula from Port Augusta ensures an easy crossing to Ceduna, speeding past the mines at **Iron Knob** and dry scrub populated by green ring-necked parrots. Unusual geology appears around Wudinna in the form of isolated granite mounds (inselbergs) of various shapes and sizes. The largest, **Mount Wudinna**, 10km to the northeast of town, is the largest monolith in South Australia, while 30km southwest lies **Ucontichie Hill**, whose curved natural formations include a **wave rock** similar to Hyden's in Western Australia (see p.665).

Iron Knob is the start of forays along dirt tracks into the **Gawler Ranges**, before you rejoin the highway at Wirrulla. While you might not need a 4WD, it's a remote area that requires advance preparation and advice from the DEH. The ranges are low, rounded volcanic ridges coloured orange by dust, with occasional speckled boulders poking through a thin grass cover, and it's worth frightening the sheep and pink Major Mitchell cockatoos by walking up one of the peaks for a closer look. *Mount Ive Station* (☏08/8648 1817, ⓦwww .mtive.com.au; ❸–❹), 135km west of Iron Knob and right in the heart of the Ranges, has fuel, information and **accommodation** in basic rooms, plus camping space, but don't turn up unannounced. The track into the ranges passes **Lake Gairdner**, largest of the Gawler's **salt lakes**, with the ruins of Pondanna Homestead on a lonely plain at its southern end.

Ceduna and the Nullarbor Plain

You know where you are in **CEDUNA**: a large signpost in the centre gives distances to everywhere between Perth and Port Augusta. Despite being small enough to walk around in twenty minutes, there's no lack of **caravan parks**, **banks** or **service stations**. Depending on which direction you're travelling in, this is either the first or last bit of civilization you've seen or will see in a while after or before your crossing the Nullarbor. Statcliner **buses** pass through town on their way from Adelaide to Port Augusta. It's a punishing 1200km west from here to the next town of any note, so don't leave without a full tank of fuel.

The *Foreshore Van Park* on South Terrace (☎08/8625 2290 or 1300 666 290, [W]www.cedunaforeshorecaravanpark.com.au; cabins [4]–[5]) and the spiffy *Ceduna Foreshore Hotel-Motel* on O'Loughlin Terrace (☎08/8625 2008 or 1800 655 300, [W]www.ceduna.bestwestern.com.au; [5]), which has a good bistro, are right opposite the ocean – you can fish for whiting from the jetty on the turn of the high tide. Try Ceduna's famous oysters at *Ceduna Oyster Bar* (☎08/8626 9086) on the highway on the way out of town – if the place is closed phone them; they do 24-hour delivery. Seriously. Don't miss the wonderful Ceduna Aboriginal Arts and Culture Centre (☎08/8625 2487, [W]www.visitaboriginalart.com), on the corner of Eyre Highway and Kuhlmann Street, where you can buy vibrant artwork produced from indigenous people from the Far West region. Before your early-morning start, call in at the **visitor centre** on Poynton Street (Mon–Fri 9am–5.30pm, Sat & Sun 9.30am–5pm; ☎08/8625 2780 or 1800 639 413, [W]www.cedunatourism.com.au) and the DEH on McKenzie Street (☎08/8625 3144) for the latest on the Nullarbor's attractions. Incidentally, it almost never rains on the plain, and there's always a charge for **water**, which has to be distilled from underground reserves – so carry your own.

The Nullarbor Plain

Nullarbor, from the Latin "Nullus Arbor" or "treeless", is an apt description of the plain which stretches flat and infertile for over 1200km across the Great Australian Bight. Taking the **train** brings you closer to the dead heart than the **road** does, which allows some breaks in the monotony of the journey to scan the sea for southern right whales and visit at least one Aboriginal site. From Ceduna to the Western Australian border it's 480km, which you can easily cover in under five hours if you want; the Dalíesque fridges standing along the highway in the early stages of the drive are actually makeshift mailboxes for remote properties.

The last chance to catch some **waves** is at **Cactus Beach/Point Sinclair** south of **Penong**, and while its popularity took a dive after a fatal shark attack by a massive great white in 2000, the excellent waves still lure surfers from all over the world. Even for non-surfies it's worth the drive (closed after rain) through white dunes, green shrubbery and blue lagoons to watch the extraordinary wave formations; there's a **campsite** with firewood provided (but no drinking water). In Penong itself, **accommodation** is provided by the pretty basic *Penong Hotel* (☎08/8625 1050; [3]–[4]) on the highway, and *Penong Caravan Park* (☎08/8625 1111, [E]oatsfarm@bigpond.com; cabins [3]–[4]) on Stiggants

Road. There's also a general store and post office with EFTPOS (Mon–Fri 8am–5.30pm, Sat & Sun 9am–1pm).

Two hours beyond Penong you arrive at **Yalata Community**, settled by the Maralinga peoples cleared off their ancestral land by the British atomic bomb tests at Maralinga in the 1950s. The White Well ranger station (℡08/8625 2780) can issue permits ($7.50) to visit the community of some 400 people, and fish from the beaches and view whales from the platforms on Aboriginal land. Note that Yalata Roadhouse, which appears on maps, was closed at the time of research for renovation, all the more reason to fill up with fuel in Ceduna.

At the 290-kilometre point from Ceduna, you'll arrive at the turn-off to a 13-kilometre dirt road to the **Head of the Bight** and its sleek **Interpretive Centre** (daily 8am–5pm; permits required during the whale season only), on Yalata Aboriginal lands. This is the best place to see southern right whales as they migrate along the coast here between June and October. It's a stirring setting, with the dramatic cliffs plunging to the sea – you can't help feeling that this is how early cartographers must have envisaged the edge of the world. Twenty minutes away is the *Nullarbor Roadhouse* (℡08/8625 6271; open 7am–11pm; ❹–❻), which has budget **beds**, motel rooms and a campsite, and is the last place to get fuel before Border Village. One of the famous triple yellow signs warning of camels, wombats and kangaroos on the highway marks the beginning of the treeless run.

Curiously enough for a land with minimal rainfall, the Nullarbor is under-mined by partially flooded limestone **caverns**. From the outside, **Koonalda Cave** (just north of the *Nullarbor Roadhouse*) is a large hole with fruit trees growing in the mouth; inside, a tremendously deep network of tunnels leads to an underground lake, the shafts grooved by fingers being dragged over their soft walls. Although the patterns are clearly deliberate, their meaning is unknown. The cave is closed off to protect the engravings, but the Ceduna DEH (see p.827) might be able to arrange a visit.

Border Village (℡08/9039 3474; open 24 hours; ❺–❼) is the best roadhouse along the route, with good accommodation, bistro, takeaway, shop, BBQs, and even an EFTPOS machine – as well as a natty fibreglass kangaroo in the car park. **Eucla** (see p.690) and the rest of the Nullarbor lie 16km over the border in Western Australia on a noticeably worse road and in a considerably earlier time zone. You need to discard any fruit and vegetables and honey before you reach the quarantine checkpoint at the border.

The Stuart Highway: Woomera and beyond

Heading north of Port Augusta along the Stuart Highway, the first place of any consequence is **WOOMERA**, an uncharismatic but well-appointed barracks town two hours beyond Port Augusta. The town is synonymous with two things: the NASA deep tracking station that operated here in the 1960s, and its harsh **detention centre** which housed political asylum seekers before public pressure brought about its closure in 2003. The whole town was actually closed to the public until 1982, as it sits at the southeast corner of a five-hundred-kilometre corridor known locally as "the Range", ominously identified on maps as **Woomera Prohibited Area**, the largest land-based missile and rocket range in the world.

There is a **visitor centre** (daily March–Nov 9am–5pm; Dec–Feb 10am–2pm; ☎08/8673 7042) at the mostly military Heritage Centre (same hours; $5), at the crossroads of Dewrang and Banool avenues. Models, rocket-relics and plenty of pictures detail the European Launcher Development Organisation's efforts to launch the Europa rocket here in the 1960s, but there is no mention of the main reasons for the creation of the Prohibited Area – weapons-testing and the British-run 1950s **atomic bomb tests**, which contaminated dust that is still being scraped up and vitrified. For a first-hand account, read chief engineer Len Beadell's *Outback Highways*, cheerful tales of the bomb tests and the construction of "some sort of rocket range – or something".

There are two places to **stay**: the retro *Eldo Hotel* on Kotara Crescent (☎08/8673 7867, ⓦwww.eldohotel.com.au; ❻ ❼), with simple rooms that don't meet expectations formed by its rather stylish bistro; and the welcoming *Woomera Travellers Village* on Wirruna Avenue (☎08/8673 7800, ⓦwww.woomera.com; ❹–❺) which offers dirt-cheap accommodation including **camping** (un/powered $10/15), cabins and units (❶–❸). The "**shopping centre**" has banks and a small leisure centre with a café, bar and bowling alley. Greyhound Australia **buses** travelling on the Stuart Highway don't go into Woomera but will drop you off at the roadhouse at Pimba, 7km away; Stateliner services call into the town, however.

Roxby Downs, Andamooka and Lake Torrens

Instead of returning to the highway, you might want to carry on past Woomera to the strangest two companion towns in Australia. The first, **ROXBY DOWNS**, 80km away, is a modern service centre built in 1986 for miners working the copper, gold, silver and uranium deposits at the nearby **Olympic Dam Mine**. It's possible to do a surface **tour** of the mine (Mon, Thurs & Sat 9–10.30am), which should be booked well in advance through the friendly **visitor centre** (daily 9am–5pm; ☎08/8671 2001, ⓦwww.roxbydowns.com) at Richardson Place, where you'll also find a café. You can get as far as Olympic Dam and Port Augusta with Stateliner **buses**.

Another thirty minutes on an unsurfaced road lies **ANDAMOOKA**, an opal-mining shantytown of block and scrap-iron construction whose red-earth high street becomes a river after rain. The soil proved to be too loose for the underground homes which became *de rigueur* at Coober Pedy (see p.830), but mud lean-tos, built in the 1930s, are still standing opposite the post office. **Facilities** include fuel, a supermarket, the *Tuckerbox Restaurant* (☎08/8672 7137; daily 11am until late) on Main Road, two pubs, and the Andamooka Opal Showroom, which distributes maps and advice and runs *Duke's Bottlehouse Motel* (☎08/86727007; ⓦwww.andamookaopal.com.au) on Opal Creek Boulevard, and offers a package ($155 per person) including tours of mines and cottages, breakfast and use of their barbecue. If you're not staying overnight, at least do a tour ($10). If you fancy your luck "noodling", head to **German Gully**; opals here are more vivid than those at Coober Pedy.

Another thirty-minute 4WD ride away is **Lake Torrens**, a sickle-shaped salt lake related to the Acraman meteorite (see box, p.836) which gets popular with birdwatchers in wet years. The lake is also renowned in paleontological circles for traces of the 630-million-year-old **Ediacaran fauna**, the earliest-known evidence of animal life anywhere on the planet, first found in Australia and possibly wiped out by the meteorite. Delicate fossil impressions of jellyfish and obscure organisms are preserved in layered rock; the South Australian Museum in Adelaide (see p.758) has an extensive selection, but rarely issues directions to the site, which has been plundered by collectors since its discovery back in 1946 by the geologist Reg Sprigg.

Coober Pedy

COOBER PEDY is the most enduring symbol of the harshness of Australia's Outback and the determination of those who live there. It's a place where the terrain and temperatures are so extreme that homes – and even churches – have been built underground, yet it has managed to attract thousands of opal prospectors. In a virtually waterless desert 380km from Woomera, 845km from Adelaide, and considerably further from anywhere else, the most remarkable thing about the town – whose name stems from an Aboriginal phrase meaning "white man's burrow" – is that it exists at all. **Opal** was discovered by William Hutchison on a gold-prospecting expedition to the Stuart Range in February 1915, and the town itself dates from the end of World War I, when returning servicemen headed for the fields to try their luck, using their trench-digging skills to construct underground dwellings.

In summer Coober Pedy is seriously depopulated, but, if you can handle the intense heat, it's a good time to look for bargain opal purchases – though not to scratch around for them yourself: gem hunting is better reserved for the "cooler" winter months. At the start of the year, spectacular **dust storms** often enclose the town in an abrasive orange twilight for hours.

The local scenery might be familiar to you if you're a film fan, as it was used to great effect in *Mad Max III*, *Pitch Black* and Wim Wenders' epic *Until The End Of The World*. There's not much to it, just an arid plain disturbed by conical pink mullock (slag) heaps, and dotted with clusters of trucks and home-made contraptions, and **warning signs** alerting you to treacherously invisible, unfenced thirty-metre shafts. Be very careful where you tread: even if you have transport, the safest way to explore is to take a tour, follow a map, then return on your own. Past the diggings, the **Breakaway Range** consists of a brightly coloured plateau off the highway about 11km north of town, with good views, close-ups of the hostile terrain, and bushwalking through two-hundred-year-old stands of mulga.

Wandering around the dusty streets, it can be hard to tell whether some of the odd machinery lying about is bona-fide mining equipment or leftover film props. The **Big Winch Lookout** in the centre gives a grandstand view of the mix of low houses and hills pocked with ventilation shafts. The welded metal "tree" up here was assembled before any real ones grew in the area, though in the last few years there have been some attempts to encourage greenery with recycled waste water. There are two museums in former mines, including the **Old Timers Mine**, Crowders Gully Road (☏08/8672 5555, ⊛www.oldtimersmine.com;

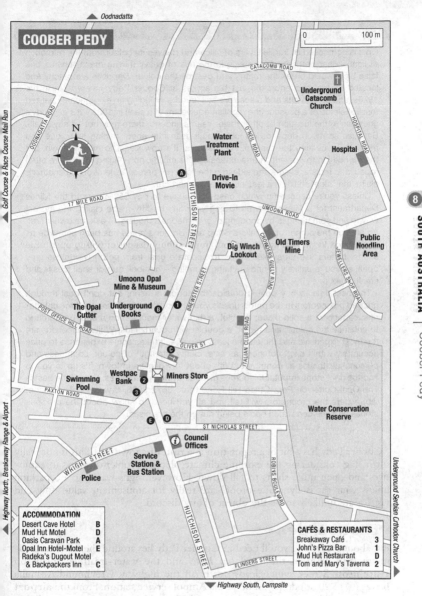

N

CATACOMB ROAD

Underground
Catacomb
Church

Water
Treatment
Plant

Hospital

O'NEIL ROAD

HOSPITAL ROAD

Drive-in
Movie

UMOONA ROAD

17 MILE ROAD

CRUNCHERS GULLY ROAD

Dig Winch
Lookout

Old Timers
Mine

Public
Noodling
Area

JEWELLERS SHOP ROAD

Umoona Opal
Mine & Museum

The Opal
Cutter

Underground
Books

BREWSTER STREET

HUTCHISON STREET

POST OFFICE HILL ROAD

OLIVER ST

ITALIAN CLUB ROAD

Swimming
Pool

Westpac
Bank

Miners Store

PAXTON ROAD

Water Conservation
Reserve

ST NICHOLAS STREET

Council
Offices

ROBIN'S BOULEVARD

Service
Station &
Bus Station

WRIGHT STREET

Police

HUTCHISON STREET

ACCOMMODATION
Desert Cave Hotel   B
Mud Hut Motel   D
Oasis Caravan Park   A
Opal Inn Hotel-Motel   E
Radeka's Dugout Motel   C
 & Backpackers Inn

CAFÉS & RESTAURANTS
Breakaway Café   3
John's Pizza Bar   1
Mud Hut Restaurant   D
Tom and Mary's Taverna   2

FLINDERS STREET

▼ Highway South, Campsite

Golf Course & Race Course Mail Run

Highway North, Breakaway Range & Airport

Underground Serbian Orthodox Church

\$10), and **Umoona Opal Mine and Museum** on Hutchison Street (☎08/8672 5288, ⓦwww.umoonaopalmine.com.au; entrance free, tours \$10). There are numerous **tours** on offer (all of which can be booked at the **visitor centre**), featuring a town drive, a spot of noodling and a visit to an underground home. One of the best is Radeka's four-hour Desert Breakaways Tour (\$50; ☎08/8672 5223; from 1pm) and one-hour Stargazing Tour (\$20) which includes a look at the Breakaway Range. Alternatively, book through your accommodation.

Finding and buying an opal

Opal is composed of fragile layers of silica and derives its colour from the refraction of light – characteristics that preclude the use of heavy mining machinery, as one false blow would break the matrix and destroy the colour. Deposits are patchy and located by trial and error: the last big strikes at Coober Pedy petered out in the 1970s, and though bits and pieces are still found – including an exceptional opalized fossil skeleton of a pliosaur (the reptilian equivalent of a seal) in 1983 – it's anybody's guess as to the location of other major seams (indeed, there may not be any at all). Because so much depends on luck, you'll hear little about mining technique and more about beating the system. For instance, it's now illegal to mine in town, but there's nothing to prevent "home extensions"; similarly, non-mining friends are often roped in to register claims and sidestep the "one per person" rule. Working another's claim (the "night shift") is a less honourable short cut.

Unless you're serious (in which case you'll have to pay $52 a year to the Mines Department for a Miner's Permit to peg your fifty-by-fifty-metre claim), the easiest way to find something is by noodling over someone's diggings – ask the owner first. An area on the corner of Jewellers Shop and Umoona roads has been set aside as a safe area for tourists to poke about freely without danger of finding open mine shafts. Miners use ultraviolet lamps to separate opal from potch (worthless grey opal), so you're unlikely to find anything stunning – but look out for shell fossils and small chips.

The best time to buy opal is outside the tourist season, but don't deal through grizzled prospectors in the hotels unless you're very clued in. There are three categories: cabochon, a solid piece; doublet, a thin wafer mounted on a dark background to enhance the colour; and triplet, a doublet with quartz lens. While cabochons are the most expensive and triplets the least valuable, it takes some experience to price accurately within each category, as size, clarity, strength of colour, brightness and personal aesthetics all contribute. With about fifty dealers in town, it's up to you to find the right stone; reputable sources give full written guarantees. One of the best is The Opal Cutter on Post Office Hill Road (℡08/8672 3086, ⓦwww.opalcutter.com .au), where the proprietors will tell you all you need to know about the precious stones and you can watch opals being cut on the premises.

Coober Pedy has a bit of a reputation as a **raucous** township. This is not really surprising considering the extreme climate, alcohol problems, access to explosives and open mine shafts to fall down. However, signs warning "no parking unless your car is dynamite-proof" are really for amusement value only, and visitors are unlikely to be the object of any discord.

Practicalities

Just about everything you'll need in Coober Pedy lies around the five-hundred-metre strip between the *Opal Inn Hotel* and the water-treatment plant on **Hutchison Street** which leads north off the highway. Greyhound Australia **buses** (℡13 20 30) drop you off at the Ampol service station. From the **airport** you may be able to get a lift with one of the hostel buses that meet most flights, or make an advance reservation to ensure that someone meets you.

The **visitor centre** on Hutchison Street (Mon–Fri 8.30am–5pm, Sat & Sun 10am–1pm; ℡1800 637 076, ⓦwww.opalcapitaloftheworld.com.au), in the District Council building, is a mine of local information. Underground Books (℡08/8672 5558), on Post Office Hill Road opposite the Mobil service station, is a good alternative source – it stocks packs of local mud maps which are a useful back-up to road maps. The Miners Store supermarket on Hutchison

Street (☎08/8672 5051) is also the **post office** and Commonwealth **bank** agent (there's a Westpac branch opposite). The **hospital** is on Hospital Road, at the north end of town (☎08/8672 5009), and there's a **pharmacy** at the Medical Centre in the middle of Hutchison Street. The **swimming pool** at the school on Paxton Road provides a welcome chance to cool down; check the opening hours at the visitor centre.

Accommodation

Coober Pedy relies heavily on tourist income, so finding **lodgings** can be challenging during the cooler months, although you shouldn't have problems during summer. To some people, the idea of sleeping underground is disturbing but, while not all accommodation is subterranean, it's worth spending at least one night in naturally cooled tunnels for the experience.

Desert Cave Hotel Hutchison St ☎08/8672 5688, ⓦwww.desertcave.com.au. The below- or above-ground four-star accommodation is expensive for what it is, but there's a swimming pool, restaurant, café and bar. Scenic flights, tours and car rental can be arranged. ❽–❾

Mud Hut Motel St Nicholas St ☎08/8672 3003, ⓦwww.mudhutmotel.com.au. The best-value accommodation in town. The bare, rammed-earth construction of this well-furnished motel gives a flavour of the subterranean without losing out on daylight. ❺–❾

Oasis Caravan Park Opposite the water-treatment plant, Hutchison St ☎08/8672 5169, ⓔbig4cooberpedy@bigpond.com. Spacious, a/c cabins (❸–❹) as well as camping facilities (un/powered sites $20/25).

Opal Inn Hotel-Motel Hutchison St ☎08/8672 5054 or 1800 088 523, ⓦwww.opalinn.com.au. A standard motel block behind a hotel with a bistro, bar, bottle shop and tour bookings. ❹–❻

Radeka's Dugout Motel and Backpackers Inn 1 Oliver St ☎08/8672 5223 or 1800 633 891, ⓦwww.radekadownunder.com.au. The best backpacker in town with snaking tunnels downstairs with alcoves holding from two to six beds – though it can be a long trek upstairs to the well-appointed kitchen and toilets – and a bar and pool table to provide evening entertainment. Dorms $22, motel rooms ❺

Underground Motel Catacomb Rd ☎08/8672 5324 or 1800 622 979, ⓦwww.theundergroundmotel.com.au. This tiny motel has clean, tiled rooms with views over the desert from the front porch. Breakfast included. ❹

Eating and drinking

Restaurants in town are scarce but good value and portions are huge – beware of over-ordering. Most are open for dinner only, from 6–8pm. The ♪ *Mud Hut Motel Restaurant* is the town's finest, serving up Mod Oz bistro standards with reasonably priced wines. *Tom and Mary's Taverna* on the main road is explained by Coober Pedy's large Greek-Australian population; it serves large portions of authentic, good-value Greek food as well as pizzas. Otherwise, head for the nearby *John's Pizza Bar*, a popular pizza and fast-food joint, or *Breakaway Café*, with a pleasant covered terrace; both on the main road.

The town lacks decent **watering holes** so make the best of the bar in your accommodation. The drive-in **cinema** on Hutchison Street shows a double bill most Saturday nights.

Beyond Coober Pedy

The Stuart Highway ploughs 350km north from Coober Pedy to the state border. From **Marla** township (where there's a shop, post office and Commonwealth Bank at the roadhouse) you could head east to Oodnadatta across the **Painted Desert** at Arkaringa Hills, a larger version of the Breakaway Range, or 35km west into Aboriginal land to the state's newest opal strike at Mintabie – seek permission from Marla's police (☎08/8670 7006). If you want to get to **Oodnadatta** and don't have your own vehicle, the direct two-hundred-kilometre dirt road from Coober Pedy across the pan of Giddi-Gidna (the **Moon Plain**) is covered by the **Mail Run Tour** (☎1800 069 911, Ⓦwww .desertdiversity.com; $185). The service departs from Underground Books in Coober Pedy on a roughly twelve-hour triangular route to William Creek and Oodnadatta every Monday at 9am (anticlockwise) and Thursday (clockwise); this is the only public transport in the area.

Australia's hottest 4WD journey has to be west from Coober Pedy to the **atomic bomb sites** at **Emu Junction**: concrete slabs cap pits where contaminated equipment lies buried, and sand fused into sheets of glass by the blasts covers the ground – the area is still highly radioactive and you'd be advised to pass through quickly. Beyond lies the virgin **Mamungari Conservation Park** (formerly the "Unnamed" Conservation Park) routes across the sand dunes and Aboriginal land to the **Great Central Road** in Western Australia (see p.688). The NPWS at 11 McKenzie St in Ceduna (☎08/8625 3144) supplies practical details and permits to 4WD convoys only.

The Flinders Ranges and northeast

If you're heading north from Port Augusta but want to avoid the Stuart Highway, an adventurous alternative route leads up to the spectacular **Flinders Ranges National Park** passing the quaint villages of **Quorn** and **Hawker** on the way. From the off-the-beaten-track settlement of **Blinman** in the **Northern Flinders**, the route continues down the isolated **Strzelecki Track** and beyond to the far-flung settlements of **Marree** and **Innamincka**.

Quorn and around

The first stop between Port Augusta and the Flinders Ranges National Park is 50km northeast at **QUORN**, whose wide streets, big old pubs, and historic stone buildings offer a last taste of the pastoral south before the austerities of the Outback set in. Best known for the **Pichi Richi railway**, the sole operational section of the old Ghan line, Quorn was a major rail centre until the line was re-routed through Port Augusta in the 1950s. Enthusiasts restored the service twenty years later and started taking passengers on a two-hour return haul to Woolshed Flats through the **Pichi Richi Pass** – whose name has been variously attributed to a medicinal herb or an Aboriginal word for "gorge".

Punctuated by a break at Woolshed Flats for a cream tea, it makes a relaxing and mildly scenic journey. Trains run only on a few weekends and holidays between April and October; call ahead to check and book (℡08/8658 6598 or 1800 440 101, ⓦwww.prr.org.au). More regular **public transport** includes Wayward Bus to Coober Pedy and Adelaide or Gulf Getaways (℡08/8642 6827) to Wilpena Pound and Port Augusta. First Street and the block between it and Railway Terrace contain a couple of antique and bric-a-brac shops and a good bookstore. A warning: avoid the town from January to February, the hottest part of the year, when the locals shut shop and head to the beach and the place is a ghost town.

The **visitor centre** at 3 Seventh St (daily 9am–5pm; ℡08/8648 6419, ⓦwww.flindersranges.com) can provide you with a self-guided walking tour of Old Quorn; book 4WD and camel tours; and supply you with heaps of information on the entire region. Established in 1878, *The Austral* at 16 Railway Terrace (℡08/8648 6017, ⓦwww.australinn.com.au; ❸–❺) is the most agreeable **hotel** in town, with a pleasant renovated bar and restaurant, smart rooms at the pub, and basic rooms in the motel section. They can also book scenic flights and camel rides. An even cheaper option, on the opposite side of the road, is the *Transcontinental Hotel* (℡08/8648 6076, ⓔtranshotel @bigpond.com.au; ❸), also dating to 1878, with an easy-going crowd of truckies and drovers for company. *Quorn Caravan Park* (℡08/8648 6206, ⓦwww.quorncaravanpark.com.au; un/powered sites $21/25, cabins ❸) may be pretty basic but it's eco-friendly. The main road through town is Railway Terrace, where you'll find the atmospheric old railway station, the town's post office and hotels, which all do good-value **meals** but are quite strict about serving times (usually 5.30–7.30pm/8pm for dinner). *The Austral*'s restaurant is the best, serving up great-value Mod Oz dishes such as duck sausages, potato mash with caramelized onion, roasted tomato and spinach, served with a port wine sauce ($14.50)

Around Quorn

There's great bushwalking off the back road to Hawker along a string of ridges and cliffs, outrunners from the main body of the central Flinders Ranges, 100km north. Ten kilometres northwest of Quorn is **The Dutchmans Stern**, a five-hour 10.5 kilometre hike for the reasonably fit from the car park to various lookouts. Less-dedicated walkers will find **Warren**, **Buckaringa** and **Middle gorges** an easier proposition. The 5.2-kilometre Warren Gorge Loop takes 2–3 hours to complete. Buckaringa's steep face is the most reliable place in the ranges to see the rare and ravishingly pretty **yellow-footed rock wallaby**, with its bushy, ringed tail and yellow paws – climb to the top at around 4pm and sit quietly until they appear. Closer to Hawker, it's also worth taking in the well-preserved remains of **Kanyaka Homestead**, abandoned after a drought in the 1880s, and **Yourambulla Cave**, which has some unusual charcoal symbols in a high overhang, reached by a ladder. Both are signposted from the road.

HAWKER itself, some 100km from Port Augusta, is somewhere to fuel up, make use of the last banks and shops, and have a hearty bushtucker-inspired meal at the *Old Ghan Restaurant* (℡08/8648 4176; Wed 10.30am–2.30pm, Thurs–Sat 10.30am–late; closed Jan–Feb) at Hawker Railway Station. If staying, try the *Hawker Holiday Park* at the Wilpena exit (℡08/8648 4006, ⓦwww .hawkerbig4holidaypark.com.au; ❸–❺) or Flinders Ranges Accommodation Booking Service (℡1800 777 880, ⓦwww.frabs.com.au) on the corner of

Cradock and Wilpena roads, which can arrange self-catering accommodation in and around Hawker, on Outback stations, and in shearers' quarters, cottages and huts (❶–❻). Note that, like Quorn, the town practically closes down from January to February, the hottest part of the year.

If you don't have your own wheels, the Port Augusta-based *Gulf Getaways* (☎08/8642 6827, ⓦwww.gulfgetaways.com.au) passes through Quorn and Hawker on its way to Wilpena Pound. Once in Hawker, you'll have to decide whether to press on into the Flinders Ranges and the northeast or continue following the former Ghan line north towards Marree; the bitumen on the latter route extends past the Leigh Creek coalfields to Lyndhurst, at the start of the Strzelecki Track.

⑧ Flinders Ranges National Park

The procession of glowing red mountains at **Flinders Ranges National Park** (vehicle entry fee $8), folded and crumpled with age, produces some of the Outback's most spectacular and timeless scenery, rising from flat scrub to form abrupt escarpments, gorges and the famous elevated basin of **Wilpena Pound**, a colossal crater rim rising from the plains. The contrast between sky and ranges is softened by native cypresses and river red gums, and in spring the land is burnished by **wild flowers** of all colours and there are more kangaroos than you can count. Bushwalkers, photographers and painters flock here in their hundreds, but with a system of graded **walking tracks** ranging in length from a few minutes to several days – not to mention roads of varying quality – the park is busy without being crowded. Most tracks lead into Wilpena Pound, though you can also pick up the Heysen Trail and follow it north from Wilpena for a couple of days around the ABC Range to **Aroona Ruins** on the northern edge of the park.

Nestling up against the edge of Wilpena Pound, **WILPENA** is a good place to orient yourself a range of accommodation, fuel and food.

Practicalities

The **visitor centre** (daily: 8.30am–5pm in summer; 8am–6pm in winter; ☎08/8648 0048) is at *Wilpena Pound Resort*, at the end of the sealed road to Wilpena Pound. Pick up the excellent *Flinders Ranges Holiday Map* here.

The Acraman meteorite

In the mid-1980s a band of red earth from 600-million-year-old deposits in the Flinders Ranges was bafflingly identified as coming from the Gawler Ranges, 400km away. Investigations and satellite mapping suggested that 35-kilometre-wide Lake Acraman in the Gawler Ranges was an eroded meteorite crater, while Lake Gairdner and fragmented saltpans (such as Lake Torrens, see p.830) further east were set in ripples caused by the force of the strike. Estimates suggest that to have created such a crater the meteorite must have been 4km across; the mystery band in the Flinders Ranges was dust settling after impact. Though there is fossil evidence of animal life prior to this event – notably the *Ediacaran fauna* – recent research indicates that the Acraman meteorite may well have killed it all. It's certainly true that the ancestors of almost all species living today evolved after this impact.

Flinders Dreaming and geology

The almost tangible spirit of the Flinders Ranges is reflected in the wealth of Adnyamathanha ("hill people") legends associated with them. Perhaps more obvious here than anywhere else in Australia is the connection between landscapes and Dreamtime stories, which recount how scenery was created by animal or human action – though, as Dreamtime spirits took several forms, this distinction is often blurred. A central character is Akurra, a gigantic maned serpent (or serpents) who guards waterholes and formed the Flinders' contours by wriggling north to drink dry the huge salt lakes of Frome and Callabonna. You may well prefer the Aboriginal legends to the complexities of geology illustrated on boards placed at intervals along the Brachina Gorge track, which explain how movements of the "Adelaide Geosyncline" brought about the changes in scenery over hundreds of millions of years.

Wayward Bus **coaches** will get you here from as far as Adelaide and Alice Springs; Gulf Getaways travel to and from Port Augusta twice a week.

In Wilpena, *Wilpena Pound Resort* (℡08/8648 0004 or 1800 805 802, Ⓦwww.wilpenapound.com.au; ❻–❾) was undergoing renovation at the time of writing, promising to provide more comfortable albeit expensive **accommodation**. Their pool wasn't going anywhere, though, and should still provide welcoming relief after a long sweaty hike. They can also arrange 4WD tours and scenic flights, a great idea to grasp the vastness of the pound. The adjacent *Wilpena Campsite* (℡08/8648 0004) is wooded and well equipped, and has permanent tent accommodation. Beautifully located below Rawnsley Bluff and overlooking the southern side of Wilpena Pound, you'll find a range of accommodation, from luxury self-contained eco-villas to more basic cabins at *Rawnsley Park Station* (℡08/8648 0030, Ⓦwww.rawnsleypark.com.au; eco-villas ❾, cabins ❹–❺, and un/powered sites $20/29). They also offer scenic flights, 4WD tours, horseriding and mountain-biking, and there's a licensed shop, ice, fuel and internet. Their stylish restaurant *The Woolshed* is excellent.

Wilder places further into the park to set up camp for a few days include the national park campsite at **Bunyeroo** and **Brachina Gorge** in the west, **Trezona** and **Oraparinna** in the centre, and **Wilkawillana Gorge** in the extreme northeast, all accessible on unsealed roads. For a longer stay consider renting a jackeroo's cottage or shearers' quarters from **Flinders Ranges Accommodation Booking Service** (see p.835). About 20km north of the pound, *Willow Springs* (℡08/8648 6282, Ⓦwww.frabs.com.au/willowsprings .htm; ❹) is a working sheep station with blockhouse dormitories and cottage.

The visitor centre offers booklets, maps and the latest information on routes; you're required to log out and back with them on any walk exceeding three hours. Hiking is restricted to the cooler winter months between May and October, as scant shade and reflective rocks raise summer temperatures above 40°C. Don't underestimate conditions for even short excursions: you'll need good footwear, a hat, sunscreen and **water** – at least a litre per hour is recommended. **Camping out**, a waterproof tent, ground mat and fuel stove are essential, and note that the **weather** is very changeable; wind-driven rain can be a menace along the ridges and heavy downpours cause roads to be closed (check conditions on ℡1300 361 033).

Wilpena Pound

Wilpena Pound's two main walks are the **Hills Homestead Walk** (6.6km, 2hr) from the visitor centre, and the **Yoluna Hike** (8km, 4hr), from the Aroona car park, 50km north of Wilpena Pound. Consult the visitor centre before attempting the less-publicised full-day hikes to **St Mary's Peak** on the rim, and **Edowie Gorge** inside the pound, or any **overnight** trips. The walk to **Hill's Homestead** across the pound's flat, grassy bowl takes you to the remains of evidence of the region's unsuitability for farming. From here you can follow the track northwest to **Cooinda Camp**, about three hours from Wilpena. Assuming you left early, there should be time to pitch a tent and spend the rest of the day following the creek upstream past **Malloga Falls** to **Glenora Falls** and views into Edowie Gorge before returning to Cooinda. Next morning, you could do the steep climb to **Tanderra Saddle** below the peak, followed by the last burst up to the summit of St Mary's Peak itself. The effort is rewarded by unequalled views west to Lake Torrens and north along the length of the ABC Ranges towards Parachilna; on exceptional mornings the peak stands proud of low cloud inside the pound. The direct descent from the saddle back to Wilpena is initially steep, but shouldn't take more than three hours. Shorter routes from Wilpena lead up **Mount Ohlssen Bagge** (a not-too-tiring four hours) and **Wangara Lookout** (2hr) for lower vistas of the pound floor, and southwest across the pound to **Bridle Gap** (6hr) following the Heysen Trail's red markers. Things to look out for are wallabies, emus and parrots inside the pound, and cauliflower-shaped fossil **stromatolites** – algal corals – on the Mount Ohlssen Bagge route, similar to those still living at Hamelin Pool in Western Australia (see p.702).

Arkaroo Rock, Sacred Canyon and nearby gorges

Two **Aboriginal galleries** worth seeing (although erosion and contact have damaged the paintings) are Arkaroo Rock, Sacred Canyon, and Perawurtinia cultural heritage sites, a short drive from Wilpena. **Arkaroo** is off the main road towards Rawnsley Park Station and involves an hour's walk up the outside of Wilpena Pound to see mesh-protected rockfaces covered in symbols relating to an initiation ceremony and the pound's formation, some dating back six thousand years. Snake patterns depict St Mary's Peak as the head of a male Akurra coiled round the pound. To reach **Sacred Canyon**, briefly take the road from Wilpena into the north of the park, past the **Cazneaux Tree** – a river red gum made famous by Harold Cazneaux's prize-winning 1930 photograph *Spirit of Endurance* – before turning right and following a bumpy track to its end. Rock-hop up the narrow, shattered gorge to clusters of painted swirls covered in a sooty patina and clearer engraved emu prints and geometric patterns; the best examples are around the second cascade.

The main road through the park heads straight out to Blinman, but another track detours to **Bunyeroo and Brachina gorges** on the western limits. The gorges make good campsites: you have to walk into Bunyeroo but the track passes through Brachina on its way to the surfaced Hawker-to-Marree road. If you're pressing directly on to the Northern Flinders, you can avoid Blinman by turning right off the main road about 20km from Wilpena, heading to **Wirrealpa Homestead**.

The Northern Flinders

The Wilpena–Blinman road passes through a low group of hills, thin in timber but still swarming with wallabies, emus and galahs. Set against a stunning hilly landscape, historic **BLINMAN**, established in 1859, comprises a handful of charming old houses with well-tended gardens, fuel, and the 1869 *Blinman Hotel* (℡08/8648 4867, ⓔblinman@senet.com.au; ❹–❻) with log fires, games room, pool and heritage-style accommodation. The *Wild Lime Café* (℡08/8648 4679, Mar–Nov Tues–Sun 9am–4pm) does delicious Devonshire teas and light meals. The main track winds west through beautiful Parachilna Gorge, where (as long as you're not too fussy) you could stay at *Angorichina Village* (℡08/8648 4842; ⓦwww.angorichinavillage.com.au; ❶–❷), which has a range of basic accommodation and a dirt campsite. The track meets the Hawker–Marree road at characterful **Parachilna**, where there's wonderful bushtucker-inspired cuisine and smart rooms at the atmospheric *Prairie Hotel* (℡08/8648 4844, ⓦwww.prairiehotel.com.au; ❻–❾). Four-wheel-drive tours and helicopter flights can also be arranged.

According to the Adnyamathanha people, **coal** was made by Yoolayoola the kingfisher man, who built fires at **Leigh Creek**, halfway between Hawker and Marree. Today, 2.6 million tonnes of it are scooped out of the ground annually to be sent by rail and burnt at the power station in Port Augusta. At a car park just off the road you can climb around an old dragline crane and look over the edge of an open-cast mine; there are **free tours** daily if you have a minimum of six people, booked through the visitor centre (℡08/8675 2056). Coal-workers live either in the well-planned modern township of **Leigh Creek South** or at more traditional **Copley**, where *Tulloch's Bush Bakery* does a decent cappuccino and quandong pie. Fuel, accommodation (❸–❺) and food are available at both towns. *Leigh Creek Tavern* (℡08/8675 2025 ⓔleighcreektavern@flinderspower.com.au) has motel rooms and cabins (❹–❺) and a bistro serving breakfast, lunch and dinner.

The route into the Northern Flinders lies east, joining up with the direct road from Wilpena and then running north to the **Gammon Ranges National Park** and Arkaroola. Arkaroola marks the limit of **public transport** in the area, running its own connection to meet the Stateliner bus at Hawker on Monday and Friday; you really need your own vehicle to explore properly though.

Chambers Gorge and Big Moro

On the road to the Gammon Ranges are the remote and little-visited sites of Chambers Gorge and Big Moro, worth every groan and twang of your vehicle springs for their stark beauty and Aboriginal significance. The ten-kilometre access track east into **Chambers Gorge** (28km after Wirrealpa) is decidedly dodgy after rain when you'll need a 4WD, but at other times 2WD vehicles should – with care – reach the natural campsite at the foot of **Mount Chambers**, within twenty minutes' walk of the gorge mouth.

In a Dreamtime story, Yuduyudulya, the Fairy Wren spirit, threw a boomerang which split Mount Chambers' eastern end and then circled back to form the crown. An indistinct left fork before the gorge leads to a dense gallery of **pecked engravings**; most are circles, though a goanna stands out clearly on the right, facing the main body of art. Chambers Gorge itself is huge and silent, the broad stony entrance guarded by high, perpendicular cliffs and brilliant green waterholes that would take days to explore properly.

Big Moro is sacred to the Adnyamathanha as the residence of an Akurra (the Dreamtime snake). The creek trickles through a crumbling gorge into two clear green pools, while limestone outcrops on the south side conceal miniature caves. The gorge lies west down an exceptionally tortuous fifteen-kilometre 4WD track opposite **Wertaloona Homestead**, 60km from the Mount Chambers junction. Pay attention to any signs and leave the three gates as you found them.

The Gammon Ranges

Arid and bald, the **Gammon Ranges** are the Flinders' last fling, a vicious flurry of compressed folds plunging abruptly onto the northern plains. Balcanoona is the DEH headquarters for the otherwise undeveloped **Gammon Ranges National Park**, a thick band of sandstone cliffs. There are two ways to experience the area: either carry on to Arkaroola (outside the park), or take the road west across the park through **Italowie Gorge** to Copley on the Hawker–Marree road. The steep red walls of the gorge are home to iga – native orange trees which symbolize the Adnyamathanha. There are **bush campsites** here and shearers' quarters at **Balcanoona** (book through the Wilpina DEH ℡08/8648 0049; ❸).

On the northern edge of the park, the award-winning, eco-friendly, **Arkaroola Wilderness Sanctuary** (℡08/8648 4848, ⓦwww.arkaroola.com .au; un/powered sites $15/20, cabins & cottages ❶–❼) has an atmospheric restaurant, bar, an array of accommodation choices, bush camping, swimming pool, shop and fuel, and offers a range of tours, from 4WD trips to scenic flights. Scene of Australia's most recent volcanic activity, the area is a geologist's dream: **Paralana Hot Springs** (two hours away by 4WD) bubble out radioactive radon gas, and walks into the shattered hills surrounding the resort turn up fossils and semiprecious minerals. According to Aboriginal legend, the springs mark the site where a Dreamtime warrior extinguished his firestick after using it to kill a rival. The area is so rugged that conventional mining isn't really a profitable venture – drilling rigs are airlifted in, then ferried around on the lower half of a Chieftain tank. The resort's **Ridgetop Tour** ($99 per person) brings you closest to the heart of the scenery: four hair-raising hours in an open 4WD (wear something warm) following precipitous contours to **Sillers Lookout** and views east to the shimmering salt lakes of **Frome** and **Callabonna**. Remains of the hippopotamus-sized marsupial *Diprotodon* have been found at Callabonna. It survived well into Aboriginal times, but died out as the climate changed after the last Ice Age.

High-clearance 4WD vehicles with experienced off-road drivers behind the wheel can continue directly north to join the **Strzelecki Track** at Mount Hopeless, a little under half the distance to Innamincka. If you're unsure, the track can also be reached via Lyndhurst on the Hawker–Marree road, but this involves a three-hundred-kilometre detour from Arkaroola.

The Strzelecki Track

The 460-kilometre **Strzelecki Track** between Lyndhurst and Innamincka was pioneered in 1870 by **Harry Redford** (see p.520), better known as Captain Starlight, who stole a thousand cattle from a property near Longreach in Queensland and drove them south across the Strzelecki Desert and down to Adelaide. Later used for more orthodox purposes, the track had a reputation as one of the roughest stock routes in the country, a serious obstacle for transport.

Much of its epic nature has since been flattened, along with the road surface, by companies draining the **Moomba gas and oil fields**, but it's still rough-as-guts in parts, heavily corrugated, single-lane mostly, and easily damaged after rain; it's restricted to 4WD vehicles only by the state's Road Transport Authority.

You need to be completely self-sufficient and carry plenty of water and food and extra fuel. Start at Lyndhurst by filling the tank – the next **fuel** is at the other end – and heading off at the northern tip of the Flinders Ranges; once past them, the journey becomes flat and pretty dull. Around the 105-kilometre mark you cross the 4850-kilometre-long **Dog Fence** (or Great Dingo Fence), designed to keep dingoes away from southern flocks, which stretches from the Nullarbor Plain east into New South Wales. Although its value is debatable, you do frequently see desiccated canine corpses poisoned by "1080" bait lying nearby. The road from Arkaroola connects within sight of **Mount Hopeless** (a pathetic hill, appropriately named); the next place to stop and perhaps camp is at the hot outflow from **Montecollina Bore**, 30km on. From here the scenery improves slightly as the road runs between dunes, and it's hard to resist leaving footprints along one of the pristine red crests.

At **Strzelecki Crossing** there's a choice of routes: you could abandon the track and head east to where Queensland, New South Wales and South Australia meet at **Cameron Corner**, where there's a store with fuel, a campsite (☎08/8091 3872; $5 per car, fee donated to the Royal Flying Doctors Service) and a small bar; alternatively, you could continue to Innamincka either via Moomba or by following the direct but less-frequented **Old Strzelecki Track**. Cameron Corner and the old track are 4WD only, and all of the routes are crossed by straight **seismic test lines** which run off to dead ends in the bush – you risk becoming permanently lost if you accidentally follow one, so take care. **Moomba**'s jumble of pipes and lick of flame are sometimes marked as a township on maps but, though visible from the road, the refinery is closed to the public. Within an hour you've crossed into the **Innamincka Regional Reserve** and are approaching Innamincka's charms.

Innamincka

Cooper Creek, which runs through Innamincka, is best known for the misadventures of explorers Burke and Wills, who ended their tragic 1861 expedition by dying here (see box, p.526). **INNAMINCKA** was later founded on much the same spot as a customs house to collect taxes on stock being moved between Queensland and South Australia. Never more than a handful of buildings, it found fame mainly because John Flynn's Flying Doctor Service ran a mission here and because the hotel piled up decades of empties into a legendary 180-metre-long bottle dump before the town was abandoned in 1952. Now the area falls within the 3-million-acre **Innamincka Regional Reserve and Coongie Lakes National Park** (apply for a Desert Parks Pass in advance ☎1800 816 078, [E]desertparks@saugov.sa.gov.au; [W]www.parkssa.gov.au; $68 per vehicle, valid for one year for entry to a range of parks) and the increase in popularity of recreational four-wheel driving has led to a renaissance. The new *Innimincka Hotel* (☎&[F]08/8675 9901; [5]) has weekend barbecues, a video jukebox and impromptu dancing on weekend nights, while the *Innamincka Trading Post* (☎08/8675 9900) has comfortable **cabins** ([4]), provisions and fuel. The mission was rebuilt in 1994 as a **museum** (for opening hours see the *Trading Post*), and there's a solar-powered telephone and spotless shower block opposite. Pelicans, parrots and inquisitive dingoes will be your companions if you camp out for free along the creek.

It only takes an hour to look around the museum and hunt for evidence of the bottle dump before you're ready for other distractions – you can take your pick from bushwalking, **fishing** for yellowbelly, bream and catfish, swimming in the creek, or renting a canoe from the hotel or the *Trading Post*. With a vehicle you could strike out 20km west to **Wills' grave** or 8km east to where **Burke** was buried (both bodies were removed to Adelaide in 1862). Another 8km beyond Burke's cairn is **Cullyamurra waterhole**, the largest permanent body of water in central Australia, and a footpath to rock engravings of crosses, rainbow patterns and bird tracks. With a 4WD you can also tackle the 110-kilometre track north to the shallow **Coongie Lakes**, where you can swim and watch the abundant birdlife. An hour's drive east of Innamincka along a rather poor track is Queensland, the Dig Tree and a fuelless route to Quilpie (see p.526).

The far north: Marree and beyond

MARREE consists of a collection of tattered houses which somehow outlived the old Ghan's demise in 1980, leaving carriages to rust on sidings and rails to be used for tethering posts outside the wonderful big old pub. Although it was first a camel depot, then a staging post for the overland telegraph line, and finally the point where the rail line skirted northwest around **Lake Eyre**, today all traffic comes by road and is bound for the **Birdsville Track** into Queensland or the **Oodnadatta Track**, which follows the former train route to Oodnadatta and beyond into the Northern Territory or **Simpson Desert**.

Accommodation is limited to the 100-year-old *Marree Hotel-Motel* on the main street (☎08/8675 8344, **ⓔ**marreepub@bigpond.com; ❹), which has an ATM, book exchange, swimming pool and serves generous meals for lunch or dinner. Or you could try the caravan park operated by *Oasis Café* (☎08/8675 8352; cabins ❸). If it's open, visit the **Arabunna Aboriginal Community Centre**, where you can buy art and artefacts and whose friendly staff will explain the uses of different types of boomerang.

Lake Eyre

Lake Eyre is a massive and eerily desolate salt lake caught between the Simpson and Strzelecki deserts in a region where the annual evaporation rate is thirty times greater than the rainfall. Most years a little water trickles into the lake from its million-square-kilometre catchment area, which extends well into central Queensland and the Northern Territory. However, in 2009 major

▲ Lake Eyre

floods in Queensland and New South Wales filled the basin, transforming it into a massive inland sea, for only the fifth time since white settlement of the region, and the most dramatic since 1974, when the lake expanded to a length of 140km. A hypnotic, glaring **salt crust** usually covers the southern bays, creating a mysterious landscape whose harsh surrounds are paved by shiny gibber stones and walled by red dunes – in 1964 the crust was thick enough to be used as a range for Donald Campbell's successful crack at the world land-speed record. Some **wildlife** also manages to get by in the incredible emptiness. The resident Lake Eyre dragon is a diminutive, spotted grey lizard often seen skimming over the crust, and the rare flooding attracts dense flocks of birds, wakes the plump water-holding frog from hibernation and causes plants to burst into colour. Designated a **national park**, you'll need a Desert Pass to visit (see p.841). It's an isolated area and only high-clearance 4WDs are permitted; you'll need to be self-sufficient with plenty of fuel, food and water, and a satellite phone is recommended. Check road conditions before departing (☏ 1300 361 033, Ⓦ www.transport.sa.gov.au/northern), as the roads are closed after flooding.

You can reach the shore 95km north of Marree to Level Post Bay via **Muloorina Station** (bush camping; donation). Timber at the lake is sparse and protected, which means that there's little shade and no firewood. There's no one to help you if something goes wrong, so don't drive on the lake's crust – should you fall through, it's impossible to extricate your vehicle from the grey slush below. This isn't a place to wander off to unprepared, but if you wish to grasp the vastness and emptiness of the state, don't miss it. Several companies offer **scenic flights** over the lake, from Coober Pedy, Marree and William Creek, booked at visitor centres, including Wrights Air (Ⓦ www.wrightsair.com.au; $210 per person) departing from William Creek.

The Birdsville Track

If there's been no rain, the 520-kilometre **Birdsville Track** is no obstacle to careful drivers during the winter: the biggest problem is getting caught in dried wheel ruts and being pulled off the road, and sections can be closed after rain. Check conditions before travelling (see p.845). Tearing north from Marree, the distant tips of the Flinders Ranges dip below the horizon behind, leaving you on a bare plain with the road as the only feature. Look for the **MV Tom Brennan**, a vessel donated to the area in 1949 to ferry stock around during floods, but now bearing an absurd resemblance to a large grey bathtub. Before the halfway house at Mungeranie Gap, a scenic variation is offered by the **Natterannie Sandhills** (150km), once a severe obstacle which has now been graded by digging out the soft sand and replacing it with clay. The *Mungerannie Hotel* (T08/8675 8317, Wwww .mungeranniehotel.com.au; ❸–❹) provides the only services on the track (fuel, beds and snacks). In a 4WD you can head west from the roadhouse to **Kalamurina campsite** near Cowarie Homestead (58km) for the thrill of desert fishing on Warburton Creek.

Back on the track, a windmill at **Mirra Mitta bore** (37km from the roadhouse) draws piping-hot water out of the ground beside long-abandoned buildings; the water smells of tar and drains into cooler pools, providing somewhere to camp. By now you're crossing the polished gibber lands of the **Sturt Stony Desert**, and it's worth going for a walk to feel the cold wind and watch the dunes dancing in the heat haze away to the west. The low edge of **Coonchera Dune** to the right of the track (190km from the roadhouse) marks the start of a run along the mudpans between the sandhills; look for desert plants and dingoes. In two more hours you should be pulling up outside the Birdsville pub (see p.527).

The Oodnadatta Track

The road from **Marree** to **Oodnadatta** is the most interesting of the three famous Outback tracks, mainly because abandoned sidings and fettlers' cottages from the old Ghan provide frequent excuses to get out of the car and explore. Disintegrating sleepers lie by the roadside along parts of the route, otherwise embankments and rickety bridges are all that remain of the line. As with the roads to Birdsville and Innamincka, with care, any sound vehicle can drive the route in dry winter weather.

About 100km into the journey, near **Curdimurka ruins**, the road runs within sight of **Lake Eyre South**, giving a flavour of its bigger sister if you can't get out there. Twenty-five kilometres later, a short track south ends below three conical hills – two of which have hot, bubbling **mound springs** at the top, created when water escaping from the artesian basin deposits heaps of mud and minerals. The perfectly symmetrical **Blanche Cup** looks out across a plain – stripped of every shred of greenery by rabbits and cattle – to **Hamilton Hill**, an extinct spring, while further south the **Bubbler** gurgles a verdant stream into the desert where it evaporates after a couple of hundred metres. Important to the Arabana, these springs were used by Sturt in the 1850s and later by the telegraph and rail depots, but tapping the artesian basin for bore water has greatly reduced their flow.

One of these bores is not far up the road at **Coward Springs** (open daily 9am–5pm; $1), where a corroded pipe spilling into ponds has created an artificial environment of grasses and palms behind a **campsite** (T08/8675 8336, Wwww.cowardsprings.com.au; unpowered only $8 per person), with toilet blocks and showers built from sleepers. One of the old railway buildings is now a display centre. **WILLIAM CREEK**, 75km further, has a resident population of just ten – and is a source of fuel, camping and relaxation in the **hotel** (T08/8670 7880, Wwww.williamcreekhotel.net.au; ❸–❹). Bar, walls and ceiling are heavily decorated with cards and photographs of 4WD disasters, and it also serves as a hangout for stockmen from **Anna Creek Station**, the world's largest cattle property, covering an area the size of Belgium. A solar-powered phone outside faces the battered remains of a Black Arrow **missile** dragged off the Woomera Range, just a few minutes' drive away. Off-road drivers can take a seventy-kilometre track from here to Lake Eyre's western shore; in the other direction is a more passable road to Coober Pedy, though there's almost nothing to see on the way except **Lake Cadibarrawirracanna**, a salt lake with permanent water and birdlife at the halfway mark.

After William Creek the track gets rougher, crossing sand dunes and then moving into stony country cut by frequent creeks – shallow for most of the year. Hardy mulgas line the banks, their soft yellow blooms giving off a distinctive acrid scent. On the last stretch to Oodnadatta, look out for a sight of the extraordinary red and black crescent petals of **Sturt's desert pea**, the state emblem, growing by the roadside.

Oodnadatta

Unless you stay long enough to meet some locals, you'll probably feel that, like Marree, **OODNADATTA** survived the Ghan's closure with little to show for it. Oodnadatta was founded as a railhead in 1890, and mail and baggage for further north had to make do with camel trains from here until the line to Alice Springs was completed in 1928. Now that has gone, the town has become a base for the Aranda community – utnadata ("mulga blossom") is the Aranda name for a local waterway – and 4WD crews heading into the Simpson Desert. After rain you'll even need a 4WD for the last slippery kilometre into town, past the racecourse. If your visit coincides with the **race weekend** in May, helicopters will be circling the track on the left, trying to dry it out, and the town will be deserted, so stop at the track, buy a pass and join in. With neat clothes and some sort of tie, you'll even get into the "formal" ball afterwards.

You can camp at the quirky **Pink Roadhouse** (T08/8670 7822, Wwww .pinkroadhouse.com.au), unless the relative luxury of a bed at the *Transcontinental Hotel* appeals (T08/8670 7804; ❹). The roadhouse acts as a store, bank and café (home of the famous Oodnaburger), and sells detailed sketch maps of the area. The hotel holds the key to the **Railway Museum** opposite, where you'll find a strangely timeless photographic record of the town – scenes are hard to date because so little seems to have changed. Stock up with provisions and then check the Transport SA hotline (T1300 361 033) for road conditions and fuel supplies if you plan to head north towards Dalhousie Springs and the Simpson Desert (4WD only), or west to the Stuart Highway at Coober Pedy or Marla.

The Simpson Desert and Dalhousie Hot Springs

Apart from the track out to the Stuart Highway, the area north of Oodnadatta is strictly for 4WDs, with **Dalhousie Hot Springs** in the Witjira National Park a worthwhile destination, or the **Simpson Desert** for the ultimate challenge. The route directly north, towards Finke and the Northern Territory, is relatively good as far as **Hamilton Homestead** (110km), though Fogarty's Claypan, around halfway, might present a sticky problem. From Hamilton the direct route east to Dalhousie Springs, shown on some maps, is now closed; take the longer route via **Eringa ruins** (160km) and **Bloods Creek bore** on the edge of **Witjira National Park**.

From Bloods Creek you can detour 30km northeast to **Mount Dare Hotel** (T 08/8670 7835, W www.mtdare.com.au; cabins; ❹) for fuel, accommodation, food (dinner $20) and provisions. In winter the homestead is busy with groups of 4WDs arriving from or departing for the desert crossing; it's at least 550km to the next fuel stop at Birdsville in Queensland.

Dalhousie Hot Springs

From the homestead it's a rough and bleak drive southeast to **Dalhousie Hot Springs**. The explorer Giles passed through this way in the 1870s, before the artesian basin had been extensively tapped by pastoralists, and described the scene:

The ground we had been traversing abruptly disappeared, and we found ourselves on the brink of limestone cliffs...From the foot of these stretched an almost illimitable expanse of – welcome sight – waving green reeds, with large pools of water at intervals, and dotted with island cones topped with reeds or acacia bushes.

Though reeds and water are less abundant today, Giles' account still rings true. The collection of over one hundred **mound springs** form Arabian-like oases, an impression enhanced by the green circle of date palms clustered around many of the pools. The largest spring, next to the **campsite** (which has showers and toilets), is cool enough to swim in and hot enough to unkink your back. What survives of the vegetation simmers with birdlife: budgerigars, galahs and the eye-catching purple, blue and red fairy wren. As nothing flows into the springs, the presence of **fish** – some, like the Dalhousie hardyhead, unique to the system – has prompted a variety of improbable explanations. One theory is that fish eggs were swept up in dust storms and later fell with rain at Dalhousie, but it's more likely that fish were brought in during an ancient deluge or that the population survives from when the area was an inland sea.

While the main springs area is flat and trampled by years of abuse from campers and cars – stay on the marked paths here to avoid causing further erosion – trudging out to other groups over the salt and samphire-bush flats armed with a packed lunch and camera gives you an idea of what Giles was describing, and a good overview of the region from the top of well-formed, overgrown mounds. More views can be had from the stony hills to the west, and from **Dalhousie Homestead**, 16km south of the springs along the Pedirka road. The homestead was abandoned after the Ghan line was laid down, and today the stone walls, undermined by rabbit burrows, are gradually falling apart in the extreme climate.

The Simpson Desert crossing

Crossing the approximately 550km of steep north–south dunes through the Simpson Desert between Dalhousie in South Australia and Birdsville in Queensland is the ultimate challenge for any off-roader. In late September, 4WD groups are joined by bikes attempting to complete the punishing Simpson Desert Cycling Classic (🌐www.sdcc.org.au). In winter, a steady stream of vehicles moves from west to east (the easier direction since the dunes' eastern slopes are steeper and harder to climb), but there's no help along the way, so don't underestimate the difficulties. Convoys need to include at least one skilled mechanic and, apart from the usual spares, a long-handled shovel and a strong tow-rope. While keeping weight to a minimum, you'll also need more than adequate food and water (six litres a day per person), and of course fuel – around a hundred litres of diesel, or two hundred litres of petrol, if you take the shortest route. Dune-ascent techniques start with reducing tyre pressures to around 15psi to increase traction; select the gear and build up revs before starting. Don't attempt a gear change on the way up, and beware of oncoming vehicles on blind dune crests. If you don't make it over, slide down and try again; lighter vehicles may end up towing overburdened trucks. If all else fails, detours bypass many dunes.

The most testing, direct route follows the French Line, with the Rig Road detouring around the worst section but adding substantial distance (and fuel requirements) to the crossing. The enjoyment is mostly in the driving, though there's more than sand to look at: trees and shrubs grow in stabilized areas and at dusk you'll find dune crests patrolled by reptiles, birds, small mammals and insects. Photographers can take advantage of clear skies at night to make timed exposures of the stars circling the heavens. Purni Bore, 70km from Dalhousie, is another uncapped spout (though this may change with growing concerns over diminished ground water), where birdlife and reeds fringe a 27°C pool; camping facilities here include a shower and toilet. A post battling to stay above shifting sand at Poeppel Corner (269km) marks the junction of Queensland, South Australia and the Northern Territory; salt lakes here vary in their water content and sometimes have to be skirted around. After the corner the dunes become higher but further apart, separated by claypans covered in mulga and grassland; you'll have to negotiate some of Eyre Creek's channels too, which can be very muddy. Big Red, the last dune, is also the tallest; once over this it's a clear 41-kilometre run to Birdsville.

A large area of the Simpson Desert outside the Witjira National Park and the Simpson Desert Conservation Park is now a Regional Reserve under the control of the NPWS, from whom you should seek advice and a Desert Parks Pass before setting out. Contact the NPWS at Port Augusta (☎1800 816 078).

Travel details

Trains

For all trains contact Great Southern Railway ☎13 21 47, 🌐www.gsr.com.au.
Adelaide to: Alice Springs (Ghan, 2 weekly; 20hr); Darwin (Ghan, 1 weekly; 47hr); Melbourne (Overlander, 4 weekly; 12hr 30min); Perth (Indian Pacific, 2 weekly; 38hr); Sydney (1 weekly, 23hr; Indian Pacific, 2 weekly; 26hr).

Buses

Further details of bus services can be found at 🌐www.bussa.com.au.
Adelaide to: Alice Springs (1 daily; 18hr 30min); Barossa Valley (1–2 daily; 1hr 30min); Broken Hill (3 weekly; 7hr); Ceduna (1 daily; 12hr); Clare (1 daily; 2hr 15min); Coober Pedy (1 daily; 10hr 30min); Goolwa (1–4 daily; 1hr 55min); Loxton

(1 daily except Sat; 3hr 30min); McLaren Vale
(1–3 daily; 50min); Melbourne (6 daily; 9hr 30min–
14hr); Mount Gambier (1–3 daily; 6hr); Port
Augusta (4–6 daily; 6hr); Port Lincoln (1–2 daily;
10hr); Renmark (2 daily; 4hr); Sydney (3 daily;
21–24hr); Victor Harbor (1–4 daily; 1hr 30min);
Whyalla (3–6 daily; 5hr); Woomera (1 daily; 6hr);
Yorke Peninsula (1–2 daily; 3–4hr).
Ceduna to: Adelaide (1 daily; 9hr 30min); Port
Augusta (1 daily; 5hr); Port Pirie (1 daily; 5hr 30min).
Coober Pedy to: Adelaide (1 daily; 11hr); Alice
Springs (1 daily; 7hr); Port Augusta (1 daily; 6hr
10min).
Port Augusta to: Adelaide (3–5 daily; 4hr 15min);
Alice Springs (1 daily; 14hr); Ceduna (1 daily; 5hr);
Coober Pedy (1 daily; 6hr 10min); Mambray Creek
(for Mount Remarkable; 3–5 daily; 1hr); Marla
(1 daily; 10hr); Port Lincoln (2 daily; 4hr 30min);
Quorn (3 weekly; 40min); Roxby Downs (1 daily
except Sat; 3hr); Whyalla (3–4 daily; 50min);

Woomera (1 daily except Sat; 2hr).
Port Lincoln to: Adelaide (1 daily; 10hr); Port
Augusta (1 daily; 4hr 30min); Whyalla (1 daily; 3hr
30min).

Flights

Adelaide to: Alice Springs (1 daily; 2hr); Brisbane
(6–8 daily; 4hr); Broken Hill (1–3 daily; 1hr 40min);
Cairns (1 daily; 4hr); Canberra (1–3 daily; 3hr
10min); Ceduna (1–2 daily; 1hr 30min); Coober
Pedy (1 daily except Sat; 1hr 30min); Darwin
(2 daily; 5hr); Kangaroo Island (4–5 daily; 30min);
Melbourne (11–12 daily; 1hr); Perth (4–6 daily;
5hr); Port Augusta (2 daily Mon–Fri; 1hr); Port
Lincoln (5–7 daily; 30min); Sydney (9 daily; 2hr
10min); Whyalla (2–4 daily; 45min).
Ceduna to: Adelaide (1–2 daily; 1hr 20min).
Coober Pedy to: Adelaide (1 daily except Sat; 2hr).
Port Lincoln to: Adelaide (6–7 daily; 45min).

9

Melbourne and around

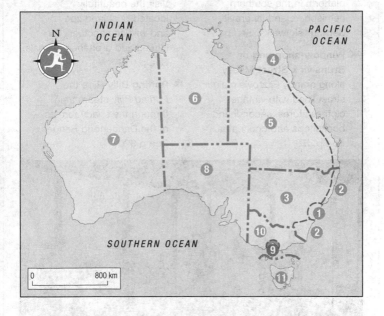

CHAPTER 9

Highlights

✳ **Chinatown** The low-rise, narrow streets of Melbourne's Chinatown have changed little since the nineteenth century. See p.868

✳ **Aussie Rules match at the MCG** Join the cheering Melbourne crowds for an action-packed footy game at the MCG. See p.871

✳ **Eureka Tower** See the city from the highest viewing platform in the southern hemisphere and its gravity-defying "skywalk". See p.873

✳ **Window-shopping on Brunswick Street** Mosey along grungy Fitzroy's main street lined with vintage clothes stores, secondhand bookshops and cool cafés. See p.879

✳ **Penguin Parade, Phillip Island** See thousands of Little penguins emerge from the sea and waddle up the sand to their burrows. See p.914

✳ **Yarra Valley** Victoria's answer to South Australia's Barossa Valley boasts pretty scenery and some great wineries. See pp.917–920

✳ **Healesville Sanctuary** Visit the beautifully located bushland zoo and wildlife sanctuary for injured and orphaned animals. See p.918

✳ **Puffing Billy** Ride the *Puffing Billy* steam train through the shady forests of the Dandenong Ranges. See p.920

▲ Views from the Eureka Tower

Melbourne and around

MELBOURNE is Australia's second-largest city, with a population of 3.8 million, around half a million less than Sydney. Rivalry between the two cities – in every sphere from cricket to business – is on an almost childish level. In purely monetary terms, Sydney is clearly in the ascendancy, having stolen a march on Melbourne as the nation's financial centre. However, as Melburnians never tire of pointing out, they have the incredible good fortune to inhabit what is often described as "one of the world's most liveable cities", and while Melbourne may lack a truly stunning natural setting or in-your-face sights, its subtle charms grow on all who spend time here, making it an undeniably pleasant place to live, and enjoyable to visit too.

In many ways, Melbourne is the most European of all Australian cities: magnificent landscaped gardens and parks provide green spaces near the centre, while beneath the skyscrapers of the Central Business District (CBD), an understorey of solid, Victorian-era facades ranged along tree-lined boulevards presents the city on a more human scale. The European influence is perhaps most obvious in winter, as trams rattle past warm cafés and bookshops, and promenaders dress stylishly against the chill. Not that Europe has supplied the city's only influences: large-scale immigration since World War II has shaken up the city's formerly self-absorbed, parochial WASP mind-set for good. Whole villages have come here from Vietnam, Lebanon, Turkey, Italy and all over Europe, most especially from Greece, furnishing the well-worn statistic that Melbourne is the third-largest Greek city after Athens and Thessaloniki. Not surprisingly, the immigrant blend has transformed the city into a **foodie mecca**, and tucking into a different cuisine each night – or new hybrids of East, West and South – is one of its great treats.

Melbourne's strong claim to being the nation's **cultural capital** is well founded: laced with a healthy dash of counterculture, the city's artistic life flourishes, culminating in the highbrow Melbourne International Arts Festival for two weeks in October, and its slightly more offbeat (and shoestring) cousin, the Fringe Festival. The city also takes pride in its leading role in Australian literary life, based around the Writers' Festival in August. Throughout the year, there are jam-packed seasons of classical music and theatre, a wacky array of exhibitions

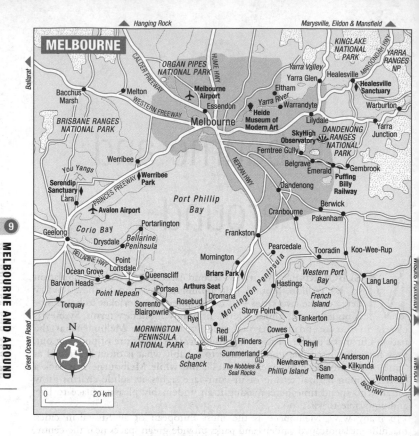

MELBOURNE

Ballarat ◄

KINGLAKE
NATIONAL
PARK

YARRA
RANGES
NP

ORGAN PIPES
NATIONAL PARK

Yarra Valley

Yarra Glen Healesville

Bacchus
Marsh

Melton

Melbourne
Airport

Eltham

Healesville
Sanctuary

Essendon

Yarra River Warrandyte

Warburton

BRISBANE RANGES
NATIONAL PARK

Melbourne

Heide
Museum of
Modern Art

Lilydale

Yarra
Junction

SkyHigh
Observatory

DANDENONG
RANGES
NATIONAL
PARK

You Yangs

Werribee

Ferntree Gully

Belgrave

Gembrook

Serendip
Sanctuary
Lara

Werribee
Park

Emerald

Puffing
Billy
Railway

Avalon Airport

Port Phillip
Bay

Dandenong

Berwick

Corio Bay

Portarlington

Cranbourne

Pakenham

Geelong

Drysdale

Frankston

Koo-Wee-Rup

Bellarine
Peninsula

Pearcedale

Tooradin

Point
Lonsdale

Ocean Grove

Queenscliff

Mornington

Western Port
Bay

Lang Lang

Barwon Heads

Point Nepean

Portsea

Briars Park

Hastings

Arthurs Seat

Dromana

French
Island

Torquay

Sorrento
Blairgowrie

Rosebud

Rye

Stony Point

Tankerton

N

Red
Hill

Cowes

MORNINGTON
PENINSULA
NATIONAL PARK

Flinders

Rhyll

Anderson

Cape
Schanck

Summerland

Newhaven

Kilkunda

The Nobbies &
Seal Rocks

Phillip Island

San
Remo

Wonthaggi

0   20 km

in small galleries, and enough art-house movies to last a lifetime. **Sport**, especially Australian Rules Football, is almost a religion here, while the Melbourne Cup in November is a public holiday, celebrated with gusto.

Melbourne is an excellent base for day-trips out into the surrounding countryside. Closest to Melbourne are the quaint villages of the eucalypt-covered **Dandenong Ranges**, while the scenic **Yarra Valley**, in the northeast, is Victoria's answer to South Australia's Barossa Valley, and one of many wine-producing areas around Melbourne. To the south, huge **Port Phillip Bay** is encircled by the arms of the Bellarine and Mornington peninsulas. **Mornington Peninsula** offers more opportunity for wine-tasting, and in addition to bucolic scenery there are beaches galore, the windswept coast facing the sea popular with surfers, while the placid waters of the bay are good for swimming and messing about in boats. **Geelong** and most of the **Bellarine Peninsula** are maybe not quite so captivating, but Queenscliff near the narrow entrance to Port Phillip Bay, with its beautiful, refurbished grand hotels, is a stylish (and expensive) weekend getaway.

Melbourne boasts a reasonably cool **climate**, although January and February are prone to barbaric hot spells when temperatures can climb into the forties with the threat of bushfires (see box, p.919) which may close off certain areas to the public.

Arrival and information

Melbourne's main airport is called Tullamarine (03/9297 1600, Ⓦwww
.melbourneairport.com.au), and is located 25km northwest of the city; the
Skybus Super Shuttle (every 15min 6am–9.30pm, every 30min–1hr outside
these times; $16 one-way, $26 return, valid one year; Ⓣ03/9335 2811) will take
you to Southern Cross Station on Spencer Street on the west side of the city. If
you book in advance, Skybus have a complimentary minibus service (Mon–Fri
6am–9.30pm, Sat & Sun 7.30am–5.30pm; Ⓣ03/9600 1711, Ⓦwww.skybus
.com.au) that picks up passengers from the coach terminal and drops them off
at most of the hotels in the city centre and the adjacent suburbs of Carlton, East
Melbourne and South Melbourne. Travelling time between Melbourne Airport
and the coach terminal is about thirty minutes. A taxi from Melbourne Airport
costs around $40–45 to the city centre, $60 to St Kilda.

Jetstar Airways, a budget subsidiary of Qantas, operates a limited number of
domestic flights from **Avalon Airport** (Ⓣ03/5227 9100, Ⓦwww.avalonairport
.com.au), located just off the Princes Freeway, 55km southwest of Melbourne.
Transport is provided by **Sunbus** (Ⓣ03/9689 6888; $22 one way), which meets
all arriving Jetstar flights and drops off passengers at Spencer Street, as well as
various suburbs and towns in the area if booked 48 hours in advance (one-way
$32), and takes about 45 minutes, depending on traffic.

Greyhound Australia, V/Line and Firefly buses all arrive at the **Southern
Cross Station Coach Terminal**. Some hostels pick up from Southern Cross
Station, as well as from the Tasmanian **ferry terminal** located about 4km
southwest of the city centre at Station Pier in Port Melbourne. The terminal is
served by the #109 **tram** to Collins Street in the CBD.

Information

The **Melbourne Visitor Centre**, housed in the northwest corner of Federation Square, directly opposite Flinders Street (daily 9am–6pm; Ⓣ03/9658
9658, Ⓦwww.thatsmelbourne.com.au/touristinformation), has brochures and
maps galore about Melbourne and the rest of the state. The pocket-sized
Melbourne Walks series is probably the most useful: each one describes a
themed, self-guided walk (1hr 30min–2hr 30min) around the city and has a
good reference map. There's also information on public transport and major
events, and a tour and accommodation booking service. Available at the centre
is the discount sightseeing card, *See Melbourne & Beyond Smartvisit Card* (also
sold online at Ⓦwww.seemelbournecard.com), which provides free admission
to more than sixty attractions in and around Melbourne and costs $69 for one
day, $105 for two days, $135 for three days and $205 for seven days. It's well
worth the expense if you intend doing some serious sightseeing. A free
Greeter Service matches up visitors with local volunteers for half a day
(starting at 10am), giving them an unparalleled insider's view of the city – book
at least a week in advance (Ⓣ0401 993 101, Ⓔgreeter@melbourne.vic.gov.au).
Tourism Victoria (daily 8am–6pm; Ⓣ13 28 42, Ⓦwww.visitvictoria.com) is
a phone and internet service providing information on attractions, accommodation and upcoming events.

Volunteers in red uniforms – so-called **City Ambassadors** – roam the CBD
between Elizabeth, Russell, La Trobe and Flinders streets (Mon–Sat 10am–4pm).
They'll try to assist with all kinds of tourist enquiries, and at the very least can
point you in the right direction. There's also a **Visitor Information Booth** in

the middle of Bourke Street Mall (Mon–Sat 9am–5pm, Sun 10am–4pm). For information on national parks and conservation areas in Victoria contact **Parks Victoria** (℡13 19 63, Ⓦwww.parkweb.vic.gov.au). Another good resource is the **National Trust** office, Tasma Terrace, 4 Parliament Place, East Melbourne (Mon–Fri 9am–5pm; ℡03/9656 9800, Ⓦwww.nattrust.com.au), which sells several historical walking-tour guides. *Melway*, available from all newsagents, is the city's best **street directory** and there are good maps online at Ⓦwww .zoomin.com.au.

City transport

Melbourne has an efficient public transport system of trams, trains and buses, run by **Metlink**. Unless you're going on a day-trip to the outer suburbs, you can get anywhere you need to, including St Kilda and Williamstown, on **a zone 1 ticket** ($3.70); this is valid for two hours (or all evening if bought after 7pm) and can be used for multiple trips on trams, buses and trains within zone 1. A **day-ticket** ($6.80 for zone 1; $10.60 for zones 1 & 2) is better value if you're making a few trips in zone 1, or if you are planning a trip to the outer suburbs. For longer stays, a **weekly ticket** ($29.40 for zone 1; $49.60 for zones 1 & 2) is an even better bargain. On Sundays, the **Sunday Saver Metcard** (just $3.10) entitles the bearer to travel within zones 1 and 2 for the entire day, but tickets must be purchased at ticket windows at Metlink stations and are not available through ticket machines. The **City Saver** ($2.80) is valid for a single trip on a tram or bus or between two stations in the City Saver area (the CBD and out to Richmond, Jolimont and North Melbourne). Transfers between bus, tram and train are not possible with this card.

You'll need to **validate** your ticket by machine every time you board a new vehicle; those bought on board a tram are automatically validated for that journey only. Two-hour and day-tickets are available from **vending machines** on board trams and at train stations. Machines on trams accept coins only, but change is given. You can't buy tickets from the tram driver. The reverse applies on buses: there are no vending machines, so buy your ticket from the driver (exact change preferred). Major train stations have staffed ticket offices; other stations are equipped with coin-only vending machines. You can also buy Metcards and get travel advice at the Melbourne Visitor Centre at Federation

---

Melbourne's vintage trams

Melbourne's tram system dates back to 1885, and some of the trams are vintage wooden vehicles dating back as far as the 1920s. The vintage **City Circle tram** is a **free service** that runs in a loop along Flinders, Spring, Nicholson, La Trobe and Spencer streets (daily except Christmas Day and Good Friday every 10min 10am–6pm, Nov–March Thurs–Sat until 9pm). The **Colonial Tramcar Restaurant** (℡03/9696 4000, Ⓦwww.tramrestaurant.com.au) is a converted 1927 tram offering a traditional silver- and white-linen restaurant service as you trundle around Melbourne. The service starts at Normanby Road near the Crown Casino, South Melbourne; the restaurant (no-smoking) offers a three-course early dinner (daily 5.45–7.15pm; $70) and a five-course dinner (8.35–11.30pm: Mon–Thurs & Sun $115; Fri & Sat $130), plus a four-course lunch (Sun 1–3pm; $75). All drinks are included. You'll need to reserve at least two to three weeks ahead, or up to three or four months in advance for Friday and Saturday evenings.

Driving in Melbourne requires some care, mainly because of the trams. You can overtake a tram only on the left and must stop and wait behind it while passengers get on and off, as they step directly into the road (though there's no need to stop if there's a central pedestrian island). A peculiar rule has developed to accommodate trams at major intersections in the city centre: when turning right, you pull over to the left-hand lane (leaving the tram tracks clear for trams) and wait for the lights to change to amber before turning – a so-called "hook turn". Signs overhead indicate when this rule applies.

Cyclists should also watch out for tram lines – tyres can easily get wedged in them. This apart, Melbourne is perfect for cycling and you'll be in good company as it's a popular way of getting around. The friendly staff at **Bicycle Victoria** on Level 10, 446 Collins St (Mon–Fri 9am–5pm; ☎03/8636 8888), can assist with practical information; their website ⓦwww.bv.com.au has a list of organized bike-rides in Victoria and interstate. Alternatively, the **Visitor Centre** at Federation Square has cycling **maps** and downloadable maps online at ⓦwww.vicroads.vic.gov.au. There are 24 urban routes in and around Melbourne, including the popular 35-kilometre Main Yarra Trail that follows the river out to the suburbs. See "Listings", p.000, for **bike rental**. A good way of getting a handle on Melbourne is to join one of the guided, 4-hour cycling tours run by **Real Melbourne Bike Tours** (☎0417 339 203, ⓦwww.byohouse .com.au/biketours; $89 everything included; bookings necessary). They operate daily on demand and include a refreshment stop for coffee and cake.

Square, the Metlink shop (Mon–Fri 9am–5.30pm, Sat 9am–1pm) at the Melbourne Town Hall near the corner of Swanston and Little Collins streets, and at other shops, including most newsagents, a few milk bars and pharmacies – look for the flag with the Metcard logo.

Train and tram services operate Monday to Thursday from 5am until midnight, until 1am on Friday and Saturday and Sunday from 7am until 11pm, supplemented in the early hours of Saturday and Sunday by **NightRider buses** (see p.858). For further information, call Metlink (☎13 16 38). For a range of public-transport information including timetables and disability services, visit ⓦwww.metlinkmelbourne.com.au.

Trams

Melbourne's **trams** give the city a distinctive character and provide a pleasant, environmentally friendly way of getting around: the **City Circle** (see box opposite) is particularly convenient, and free. Trams run down the centre of the road; passengers can board trams from stops at the side of the road, or, in the CBD only, from central islands. Stops are signposted (the "Central Melbourne" map on p.856 shows the main routes in the centre), and they often have a map with route numbers and times – the route number is displayed at the front of the tram. Although motorists are prohibited from passing trams that are stationary at stops, always look left as you disembark to make sure there are no vehicles approaching.

Trains

Trains are the fastest way to reach distant suburbs. An underground loop system feeding into sixteen suburban lines connects the city centre's five train stations: **Southern Cross**, which also serves as the station for interstate and country trains; **Flagstaff**, on the corner of La Trobe and William streets; **Melbourne**

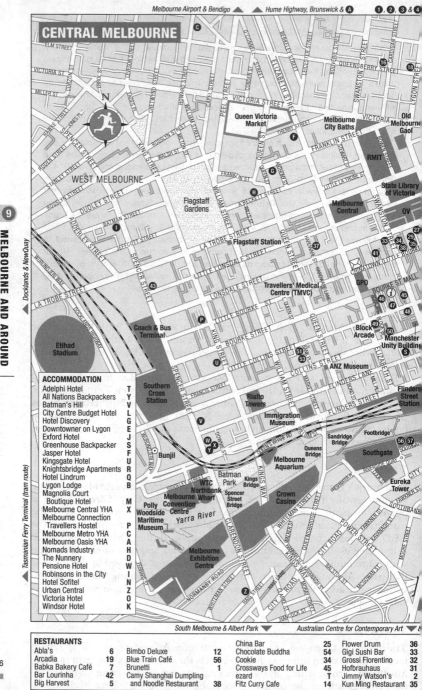

CENTRAL MELBOURNE

ELM STREET

VICTORIA ST

MILLER ST

Ⓒ

O'CONNELL STREET

BERKELEY STREET

QUEENSBERRY STREET

⑯

⑲

CARDIGAN STREET

VICTORIA STREET

Queen Victoria Market

Melbourne City Baths

Ⓕ

THERRY STREET

FRANKLIN STREET

Melbourne City Baths

VICTORIA

Old Melbourne Gaol

RMIT

HAWKE STREET
SPENCER STREET
JONES PL.
ERROL ST
CURZON ST
CHETWYND ST
ROSSLYN STREET
WALSH ST
HOWARD STREET
CAPEL STREET
PEEL STREET
QUEEN STREET
ELIZABETH STREET
SWANSTON STREET
BOUVERIE STREET

WEST MELBOURNE

Flagstaff Gardens

FRANKLIN ST

Ⓖ

FRANKLIN STREET

A'BECKETT STREET

State Library of Victoria

QV

DUDLEY STREET

BATMAN STREET

Ⓙ

LA TROBE STREET

LITTLE LA TROBE STREET

Melbourne Central

RODEN STREET
STANLEY STREET
ADDERLEY STREET
ROSSLYN STREET
SPENCER STREET
LEEFCOTT STREET
WILLIAM STREET
KING STREET
QUEEN STREET
HARDWARE ST
SWANSTON STREET

Flagstaff Station

Flagstaff Station

LA TROBE STREET

⑳

LITTLE LONSDALE STREET

㉗

㉙ ㉟
㉝ ㉞ ㉛
㉘

Docklands & NewQuay

WURUNDJERI WAY

LA TROBE STREET

DOCKLANDS HIGHWAY

LONSDALE STREET

Travellers' Medical Centre (TMVC)

CHINATOWN

LITTLE BOURKE

BOURKE ST MALL

⑪

⑤

㊳
㊵
GPO
ⓘ
㊺
㊻

Etihad Stadium

㊸

Ⓟ

LITTLE LONSDALE STREET

KING STREET

QUEEN STREET

WILLIAM STREET

LITTLE BOURKE STREET

Coach & Bus Terminal

BOURKE STREET

㊽

Block Arcade

㊾
㊿

Manchester Unity Building

Ⓢ

Southern Cross Station

LITTLE COLLINS STREET

Ⓤ

㊿
㊽

Tasmanian Ferry Terminal (tram route)

SPENCER STREET

FRANCIS STREET

COLLINS STREET

ANZ Museum

Rialto Towers

FLINDERS LANE

Flinders Street Station

ACCOMMODATION

Adelphi Hotel	T
All Nations Backpackers	Y
Batman's Hill	L
City Centre Budget Hotel	G
Hotel Discovery	E
Downtowner on Lygon	J
Exford Hotel	S
Greenhouse Backpacker	F
Jasper Hotel	U
Kingsgate Hotel	R
Knightsbridge Apartments	Q
Hotel Lindrum	B
Lygon Lodge	
Magnolia Court	M
Boutique Hotel	X
Melbourne Central YHA	
Melbourne Connection	P
Travellers Hostel	C
Melbourne Metro YHA	A
Melbourne Oasis YHA	H
Nomads Industry	D
The Nunnery	W
Pensione Hotel	I
Robinsons in the City	N
Hotel Sofitel	Z
Urban Central	O
Victoria Hotel	K
Windsor Hotel	

Rialto Towers

Immigration Museum

Ⓥ

Ⓦ Ⓧ
Ⓨ

Bunjil

Sandridge Bridge

Footbridge

Flinders Street Station

Queens Bridge

WTC Northbank Wharf

Batman Park

Kings Bridge

Spencer Street Bridge

Polly Woodside Maritime Museum

Melbourne Convention Centre

Yarra River

Melbourne Aquarium

Crown Casino

Southgate

㊶ ㊷

Eureka Tower

SOUTHBANK

RIVERSIDE QUAY

CITY RD

Melbourne Exhibition Centre

Ⓩ

NORMANBY ROAD

CLARENDON STREET

KINGS WAY

CITY ROAD

POWER STREET

STURT STREET

RESTAURANTS

Abla's	6	Bimbo Deluxe	12	China Bar	25	Flower Drum	36
Arcadia	19	Blue Train Café	56	Chocolate Buddha	54	Gigi Sushi Bar	33
Babka Bakery Café	7	Brunetti	1	Cookie	34	Grossi Florentino	32
Bar Lourinha	42	Camy Shanghai Dumpling		Crossways Food for Life	45	Hofbrauhaus	31
Big Harvest	5	and Noodle Restaurant	38	ezard	T	Jimmy Watson's	2
				Fitz Curry Cafe	14	Kun Ming Restaurant	35

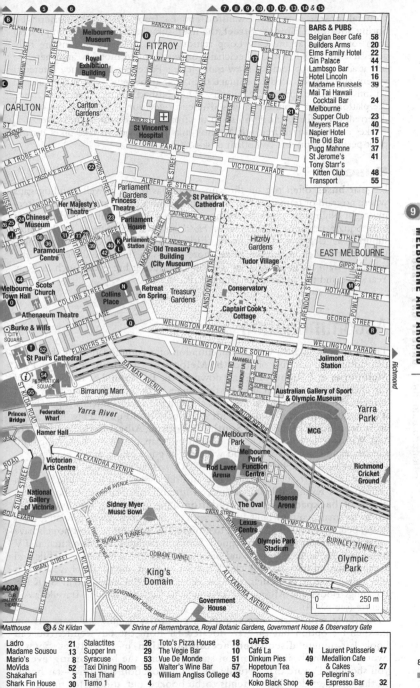

BARS & PUBS

Belgian Beer Café	58
Builders Arms	20
Elms Family Hotel	22
Gin Palace	44
Lambsgo Bar	11
Hotel Lincoln	16
Madame Brussels	39
Mai Tai Hawaii Cocktail Bar	24
Melbourne Supper Club	23
Meyers Place	40
Napier Hotel	17
The Old Bar	15
Pugg Mahone	37
St Jerome's	41
Tony Starr's Kitten Club	48
Transport	55

Richmond

Malthouse   58 & St Kildan ▼   ▼ Shrine of Remembrance, Royal Botanic Gardens, Government House & Observatory Gate

Ladro	21	Stalactites	26	Toto's Pizza House	18	**CAFÉS**
Madame Sousou	13	Supper Inn	29	The Vegie Bar	10	Café La	N
Mario's	8	Syracuse	53	Vue De Monde	51	Dinkum Pies	49
MoVida	52	Taxi Dining Room	55	Walter's Wine Bar	57	Hopetoun Tea Rooms	50
Shakahari	3	Thai Thani	9	William Angliss College	43	Koko Black Shop	46
Shark Fin House	30	Tiamo 1	4			

Laurent Patisserie	47
Medallion Cafe & Cakes	27
Pellegrini's Espresso Bar	32

Central, on the corner of Swanston and La Trobe streets; **Parliament**, on Spring Street; and **Flinders Street**, the main suburban station. You can pick up train route maps at any City Loop station. Trains and train stations are fully accessible for people using wheelchairs or with limited mobility, and there are lifts at all City Loop stations. New trains have a Passenger Emergency Intercom system that can be used to contact train staff (emergency use only), and all stations have a red emergency button – when pushed, a central operator can see the platform on a monitor via closed-circuit television (CCTV). If the train is deserted, you'll feel safest if you sit in the front carriage nearest the driver.

Bikes can be carried free, but Metlink asks people not to take bikes during peak periods (Mon–Fri 7–9.30am & 4–6.30pm).

Buses

Regular **buses** often run on the same routes as trams, as well as filling gaps where no train or tram lines run. Probably the most useful are the special after-midnight Nightrider buses (every hour 12.30–4.30am), which head from the City Square (in front of the *Westin Hotel* on Swanston Street) to the outer suburbs of Belgrave, Dandenong, Eltham, Frankston, Croydon, Epping, Craigieburn, Melton and Werribee, more or less in the same direction as the suburban train routes. The buses also operate during big events such as New Year's Eve and the Melbourne Grand Prix.

Accommodation

The most obvious areas with a concentration of accommodation are the CBD, the adjoining suburbs of **North Melbourne**, **Carlton**, **Fitzroy**, **East Melbourne** and **Richmond**, and down by the bay around St Kilda. Some of the cheap accommodation areas on the fringes of the city centre are fairly dead at night, though they're within easy reach of all the action. St Kilda is very lively, if a bit rough around the edges, with a few hostels and quite a few motels and apartments. South of the CBD, **South Melbourne**, **Albert Park**, **South Yarra** and **Windsor** (see the "Melbourne Suburbs" map, p.878) are handy for both the city centre and the beach, and with lots of good eating options.

The most exclusive **hotels** are in the CBD, particularly around Collins Street and the leisure precincts of Southgate and the Crown Casino, while there's a collection of revamped hotels around Southern Cross Station. Melbourne has plenty of **backpacker accommodation**, ranging from fairly basic, scruffy places to smart, custom-built hostels with all mod cons. During winter, most hostel beds cost around $23, rising to around $28 in summer. Most hostels have separate dorms for females on request. Standard facilities include a kitchen, TV room, laundry, luggage storage and internet access. If you're staying a while and are interested in **flat-sharing**, check the Saturday edition of *The Age*, as well as the notice boards of hostels, the *Galleon Café* at 9 Carlisle St in St Kilda, Readings Books and Music, 309 Lygon St in Carlton, and the Traveller's Aid Centre (see p.904).

For those with their own transport, **campsite** cabins and vans are an inexpensive option but they are located far from the city centre. You can book last-minute **discounted accommodation** in the city at ⓦwww .wotif.com. Finally, if you plan on staying during the big **sporting events** you should be aware that virtually all accommodation (from five-star hotels to the scruffiest doss-house) tends to be booked out, usually for months, if not a year, in advance. This applies particularly during the Australian Open Tennis in January and the Grand Prix (first or second weekend in March); other events and times to avoid or pre-book long in advance are the Melbourne Cup (first Tues in Nov and the preceding weekend) and the AFL Grand Final (last Sat in Sept).

City centre

The listings below are marked on the **map** on p.856.

Hotels and motels

Adelphi Hotel 187 Flinders Lane [T]03/8080 8888, [W]www.adelphi.com.au. Stylish hotel with a striking exterior and a sparse, ultramodern interior design, large guestrooms, contemporary art, a sauna and, most strikingly, a glass-bottomed pool that looks over the street. [9]

Batman's Hill 623 Collins St [T]03/9614 6344, [W]www.batmanshill.com. An elegant Edwardian exterior belies a functional and modern interior. The wide range of facilities includes bars, a restaurant and 24hr room service, and it's handy for Southern Cross Station, Telstra Dome, Docklands and the Casino Entertainment Complex just south of the river. [7]

🏃 **Jasper Hotel** 489 Elizabeth St [T]03/8327 2777 or 1800 468 359, [W]www.jasperhotel.com.au. A complete design makeover has raised this YWCA-owned hostel (formerly Hotel Y), just across the road from the Queen Victoria Market, to boutique hotel status and its rating to four stars. Cool and contemporary from the outside, spacious and bold inside, each hallway is painted a different colour. The 65 rooms are well appointed and stylishly furnished with queen-size beds, flat-screen TVs and sleek bathrooms. The hotel also offers in-room treatments and massage. Next door, Jasper Kitchen is open for breakfast ($20) and well-priced lunches. [6]

Kingsgate Hotel 131 King St [T]03/9629 4171, [W]www.kingsgatehotel.com.au. Huge, refurbished private hotel. The en-suite rooms with colour TV, heating and a/c are good value; and there are also inexpensive no-frills budget rooms with shared facilities, as well as a few rooms for small groups or families (up to four beds). Facilities include a laundry, internet access, a pleasant TV lounge and a bar and café (but no kitchen). Breakfast available. [4]–[8]

Hotel Lindrum 26 Flinders St [T]03/9668 1111, [W]www.hotellindrum.com.au. Named after Australia's most famous billiard-player Walter Lindrum (the billiard room has one of his original tables), this luxurious five-storey boutique hotel has a reading room with large comfy chairs, an open fireplace and books. Rather than a formal reception you register at the front bar. Each of the 59 rooms is designed with rich wood furnishings, huge bed, CD player and complimentary in-house movies. [9]

🏃 **Pensione Hotel** 16 Spencer St [T]03/9621 3333 or 1800 816 168, [W]www.pensione.com.au. Refurbished and renamed (formerly the Explorers Inn) this well-priced hotel is popular with cost-cutting business types and travellers. Pleasant and well maintained, it offers a variety of modern en-suite singles, doubles and triples, finished in soft, dark tones, plus there's a bar, restaurant and rooftop sundeck. Rooms on the ground floor have retained the Explorers Inn decor for returning customers, and are slightly cheaper, while some triples have three single beds and are ideal for budget travellers. [5]

🏃 **Robinsons in the City** 405 Spencer St, West Melbourne [T]03/9329 2552, [W]www.robinsonsinthecity.com.au. Relatively unknown, tiny boutique hotel with just six luxuriously spacious double rooms. Located in a former bakery built in the 1850s, the service is immaculate, giving it a B&B-type feel. Perfect for those looking for a personal touch in the middle of town. [8]

Hotel Sofitel 25 Collins St [T]03/9653 0000, [W]www.sofitelmelbourne.com.au. An I.M. Pei–designed hotel, set on the top floors of a fifty-storey building, with marvellous views across Melbourne and environs. Gloriously comfortable rooms, which begin on the 36th floor, as well as a good spread of cafés and restaurants, including the airy *Cafe La* located on level 35 (see p.886). [9]

Victoria Hotel 215 Little Collins St [T]03/9669 0000 or 1800 331 147, [W]www.victoriahotel.com.au. Huge refurbished hotel dating back to 1880 in an unbeatable central location, with its own café, bar, a pool and sauna, and a wide range of rooms; the cheapest ones have shared facilities. Under-cover parking available ($15 per day). [5]–[7]

Windsor Hotel 111 Spring St [T]03/9633 6000, [W]www.thewindsor.com.au. A Melbourne landmark built in 1883 opposite Parliament House. This luxurious colonial pile, with 180 spacious, lavishly decorated rooms and suites, has played host to Sir Laurence Olivier, Vivien Leigh and Muhammad Ali. A multi-million-dollar heritage-approved restoration is due to start 2009. [7]

Budget hotels and hostels

All Nations Backpackers 2 Spencer St, at the corner of Flinders St ☎03/9620 1022, ⓦwww .allnations.com.au. Friendly, no-frills hostel that doesn't look like much from the outside and isn't much better inside, though an in-house employment agency, a great bar with free beer on arrival and some of the cheapest beds in the CBD seem to keep the guests happy. There's 24hr reception and good security. Regular events include pool competitions, BBQs and soccer friendlies. Dorms (4–12 beds) $18–36, rooms ④

City Centre Budget Hotel 22 Little Collins St ☎03/9654 5401, ⓦwww.citycentrebudgethotel .com.au. Good option for those on a budget who want their own rooms (shared bathrooms), but the facilities of a hostel. The timber-floored rooms all on the first and second floors (no lift) are nicely designed, and there is a great rooftop garden. Free internet and full tour-booking service is also available. No breakfast. ④

Hotel Discovery 167 Franklin St ☎03/9329 7525, ⓦwww.hoteldiscovery.com.au. A converted former school brightened up with colour-coordinated paintwork, carpets and polished timber floors. Facilities include an employment agency, café, bar and a small cinema with free screenings, plus internet access. All dorms (4–16 beds) have lockers and fans; female dorms available. There are also some spartan singles and doubles, several en suite. Tent accommodation available on the roof terrace with great views. Free airport pick-up if staying three nights or more. Light breakfast included. Dorms $23–32, rooms ④

Exford Hotel 199 Russell St ☎03/9663 2697, ⓦwww.exfordhotel.com.au. Secure, clean and good-value hostel set in an extremely central position in the middle of Chinatown above a refurbished pub, with friendly and helpful staff and the usual amenities, plus a tiny sundeck with BBQ. Accommodation is in four- to ten-bed dorms, which are a little scruffy, though twins and doubles are better looking. Shared facilities only. Dorms $23–26, rooms ③

Greenhouse Backpacker 228 Flinders Lane ☎03/9639 6400, ⓦwww .friendlygroup.com.au. Clean and very friendly

place in a superb sixth-floor location in the heart of the CBD. Sleeping is in spacious dorms (4–6 beds), or in singles and doubles. The big kitchen is well equipped with lots of cookers and plenty of storage space. In addition, there's a lounge, a big TV room, pool table, and a pleasant rooftop garden with BBQ. Staff can help with finding work and there's a travel desk. Rates include breakfast and 30min internet access/day. Dorms $27–30, rooms ④

Melbourne Central YHA 562 Flinders St ☎03/9621 2523, ⓦwww.yha.com.au. Brand-new 208-room hostel occupying a five-storey building in a prime location near to Southern Cross and Flinders St stations. Facilities include a ground-floor bar and café and a roof terrace. Dorms $27–39, doubles ④

Melbourne Connection Travellers Hostel 205 King St ☎03/9642 4464, ⓦwww .melbourneconnection.com. Convenient location close to Southern Cross Station and Queen Victoria Market. A small, clean hostel – the polished wooden floorboards in the corridor are a nice touch – with TV lounge, an internet room and a well-equipped kitchen on the ground floor. Dorms $23–29, rooms ④

Nomads Industry 198 A'Beckett St ☎03/9328 4383, ⓦwww.nomadsindustry .com. One of the new breed of "flashbacker" hostels, this spotless and incredibly social place has an array of decent-sized rooms (some en suite) and very helpful staff. Facilities include kitchen, laundry, rooftop garden and a great bar downstairs – popular with the locals – featuring excellent happy hours, beer garden and a pool table. Free dinner each night is also included in the price. Dorms $21–34, rooms ④

Urban Central 334 City Rd, Southbank ☎03/9693 3700, ⓦwww.urbancentral.com.au. Huge hostel on the city's edge, with modern-looking singles, doubles and four-bed dorms, some en suite. Can be a bit impersonal due to the size but it is clean, well managed, and has a good tour information desk and funky bar downstairs. Price includes free tea and coffee, daily breakfast and rice/pasta for meals. Free airport pick-up if staying for more than three nights. Dorms $25–35, rooms ④

Northern suburbs

The listings below are marked on the **map** on p.856.

Downtowner on Lygon 66 Lygon St, Carlton ☎03/9663 5555 or 1800 800 130, ⓦwww .downtowner.com.au. Chain hotel with 98

attractively refurbished en-suite rooms, some with spas, all with TV, tea- and coffee-making facilities and toaster. There's also a restaurant, bar and free covered parking. Ideally situated on Lygon St and close to the city. ❾

Lygon Lodge 220 Lygon St, Carlton ☏ 03/9663 6633, ⓦ www.lygonlodge.com.au. Good motel in central Carlton with 40 attractive rooms, some with small kitchenette. Undercover car parking. ❺

🏃 **Melbourne Metro YHA** 78 Howard St, off Victoria St, North Melbourne ☏ 03/9329 8599, ⓦ www.yha.com.au. An easy 10min walk from the bus terminal (or tram #57 from Elizabeth St), this huge modern hostel – really more like a smart hotel – has family, double/twin and single rooms, with or without en suite, plus dorms (4–8 beds), and a host of other amenities: kitchen, rooftop garden with barbeque, internet lounge, bicycle hire, car parking, plus a licensed cafeteria and an in-house travel agent. Dorms $26–33.50, rooms ❹

Melbourne Oasis YHA 76 Chapman St, North Melbourne ☏ 03/9328 3595, ⓦ www.yha.com.au; take tram #59 from Elizabeth St. More intimate than

the Melbourne Metro, but further away from the city centre (3km), this hostel has mainly twin-share rooms (no dorms) with a few singles and a four-or five-bed family room. There's also a kitchen, good pancake breakfasts, a leafy garden, free car parking, free DVD hire, swimming passes, bike rental and lockers. Dorms $31.50–35, rooms ❸–❹

The Nunnery 116 Nicholson St, Fitzroy ☏ 03/9419 8637 or 1800 032 635, ⓦ www .nunnery.com.au; take #96 tram from Bourke St. Attractive guesthouse in a former convent with Brunswick St cafés and Melbourne Museum close by. The building retains original stained-glass windows and a grand staircase, and has a range of rooms, all with shared bathroom, from the high-ceilinged rooms of the guesthouse to the budget dorms and doubles, while the newer townhouse offers slightly more sedate boutique-style accommodation. There's also a cosy TV lounge, courtyard, internet facilities and a kitchen. Dorms $26–30, rooms ❸–❺

Eastern suburbs

Amora Hotel Riverwalk 649 Bridge Rd, Richmond ☏ 03/9246 1200, ⓦ www.amorahotels.com.au. Close to the city, but a world away when you are looking at the peaceful rustic setting of the Yarra River from the riverview rooms. Has good-value packages which include full buffet breakfasts. ❼–❾

Central Melbourne Accommodation 21 Bromham Place, Richmond ☏ 03/9427 9826, ⓦ www.centralaccommodation.net. Small place that runs like a shared house with most guests staying long-term. Four- and six-bed dorms (usually single-sex) along with a few single and double rooms, located close to the main drags of Church St and Bridge Rd. Owners have good employment contacts in the area as well as connections within the TV and radio industry so there are usually free tickets for shows and events up for grabs. Excellent weekly rates. Dorms from $21, doubles ❶–❷

Freeman Lodge 153 Hoddle St, Richmond ☏ 03/9421 8038, ⓦ www.freemanlodge.com.au. Renovated, clean budget guesthouse that has a funky sharehouse feel, with well-equipped rooms and single-sex dorms (maximum 4 beds) for a very low price, plus there's a communal kitchen and a pleasant courtyard. It's just around the corner from West Richmond Station, within walking distance of Bridge Rd. Dorms $22, rooms ❷

Knightsbridge Apartments 101 George St, East Melbourne ☏ 03/9419 1333, ⓦ www .knightsbridgeapartments.com.au. See map, p.856. Modern, serviced self-catering studio and

two-bedroom apartments 1km from the centre, on a quiet street running off the east side of Fitzroy Gardens. Laundry and off-street parking. Family suites offer two king beds or four singles. Excellent value. ❸–❽

Magnolia Court Boutique Hotel 101 Powlett St, East Melbourne ☏ 03/9419 4222, ⓦ www .magnolia-court.com.au. See map, p.856. Elegant, family-run hotel in a quiet street, within walking distance of Fitzroy Gardens, the CBD, MCG and Melbourne Park. Some of the en-suite rooms come with a kitchen, sitting room or balcony, in two older, lovingly restored buildings and a newer motel section. Breakfast available (extra for cheaper rooms) in a sunny room overlooking front courtyard garden. Minimum two-night stay at weekends. Website has good deals. ❸

Richmond Hill Hotel 353 Church St (between Bridge Rd and Swan St), Richmond ☏ 03/9428 6501 or 1800 801 618, ⓦ www.richmondhillhotel .com.au. Set in a stately Victorian mansion in a pretty garden, with spacious and cosy dining and sitting rooms. Accommodation consists of economy singles and doubles with balcony and shared bathroom; en-suite singles, doubles and family rooms (3–4 people); apartments (❽); plus a few budget rooms (4–6 beds; ❸) with shared facilities. Prices of all except the budget rooms include continental breakfast ($9 otherwise). ❹–❻

For further accommodation possibilities other than those listed below, check out Gay Share (⊛www.gayshare.com.au), which arranges house shares for gays and lesbians.

169 Drummond Street 169 Drummond St, Carlton ☎03/9663 3081, ⊛www .169drummond.com.au. Discreet B&B in a two-storey refurbished Victorian terrace house. Four rooms with en suite. ❻

Laird Hotel 149 Gipps St, Abbotsford ☎03/9417 2832, ⊛www.lairdhotel.com. One of Melbourne's oldest gay pubs, *The Laird* has large, comfortable rooms upstairs, some en suite, for gay men only. Rates include continental breakfast. The service is especially helpful with tips on nightspots and local eateries. ❹–❺

Opium Den 176 Hoddle St, Collingwood ☎03/9417 2696, ⊛www.opiumden .com.au. Small nightspot that puts on drag shows and cabaret has good-value, pub-style rooms with a touch of velvet opulence. Shared bathrooms. Price includes light breakfast. ❹

Prahran Village Guest House 39 Perth St, Prahran ☎03/9533 6559 ⊛www.guestlink .com.au. Private boutique B&B close to the bars and cafés of Chapel St and Commercial Rd, with four en-suite rooms in tasteful neutral tones. ❻

Southern suburbs

Annies B&B 93 Park St, St Kilda West ☎03/9534 8705, ⊛www.anniesbedandbreakfast.com.au. See St Kilda map on p.883. Small, traditional-style B&B in a renovated Edwardian house with a courtyard garden and BBQ facilities. Guests can use the front lounge with an open fireplace and TV/DVD player. Rooms have en suite or private bathroom. ❻

Base 17 Carlisle St, St Kilda ☎03/8598 6200, ⊛www.stayatbase.com. See St Kilda map on p.883. This funky hostel, rated as one of the best in Australia, is slick and well managed. There are plenty of communal areas including a bar, kitchen and common room, and all rooms have their own bathroom. There's even a girls-only Sanctuary floor (with six- to eight-bed dorms) which provides free champagne of an evening, and even has hair straighteners for hire, all for an extra $6 per night – this is boutique backpacking. Dorms $28–32, rooms ❹

The Beach Accommodation 97 Beaconsfield Parade, Albert Park ☎03/9690 4642, ⊛www .thebeachaccommodation.com.au; tram #1 from Swanston St to South Melbourne Beach. Budget boutique accommodation above a refurbished pub across the road from the beach, and handy for the Tasmanian ferry terminal. Rooms (six-bed dorms and doubles) with shared facilities are clean and basic with pine furniture, lockers and most have sea views. Rates include all-you-can-eat breakfast, tea and coffee, plus there's a TV room and a guest kitchen. Dorms $21, rooms ❶–❷

Boutique Hotel Tolarno 42 Fitzroy St, St Kilda ☎03/9537 0200, ⊛www.hoteltolarno.com.au.

See St Kilda map on p.883. Set right in the thick of things on Fitzroy St in a restored building that once housed the Tolarno Gallery. Stylish and bright en-suite bedrooms with 1950s and 60s retro furnishings, original artwork, polished timber floors and all mod cons. Good value for money. ❻

Chapel Street Backpackers 22 Chapel St, Windsor ☎03/9533 6855, ⊛www.csbackpackers .com.au. This friendly hostel close to Albert Park and St Kilda offers small, clean dorms (4–6 beds; women-only available) and en-suite doubles with free buffet breakfast, tea and coffee. Tight security, internet service and 24hr access. To get there, take the Sandringham-line train from Flinders St Station to Windsor Station; the hostel is across the road. Dorms $28, rooms ❸–❹

College Lawn Hotel 36 Greville St, Windsor ☎03/9510 6057, ⊛www.collegelawnhotel.com.au. Simple, good-value backpacker accommodation above a great pub at the less-noisy end of Greville St. Small kitchen. Dorms $24, rooms ❸

The Como Melbourne 630 Chapel St, South Yarra ☎03/9825 2222 or 1800 033 400, ⊛www .mirvachotels.com. Stylish hotel that often plays host to visiting celebs and businesspeople. All 107 rooms are gratifyingly spacious, with some facing onto Japanese gardens, and feature the usual facilities, plus CD players and gigantic bathtubs that come with a complimentary companion – the hotel's signature rubber duck. The Como's *SOBar* is also a good place for a drink. ❽–❾

Cooee on St Kilda 333 St Kilda Rd, St Kilda ☎03/9537 3777, ⊛www.cooeeonstkilda.com. See St Kilda map on p.883. Friendly hostel with good, clean facilities, and a host of organized activities. The super-large kitchen and courtyard is where travellers tend to swap stories. Has free pancake brekkies (Wed) and sausage-sizzle dinners (Thurs). Free airport pick-up when staying over 3 nights. Dorms (4–10 beds) $26–$34, rooms [6]

Easystay Bayside 63 Fitzroy St, St Kilda ☎ 1300 301 730, [W] www.easystay.com.au. See St Kilda map on p.883. Good, secure budget motel well situated for all the action and within a 10min walk of the beach. If you want quiet, book one of the units facing the car park ($8 per day) out the back (which is locked at night). [4]

The Hatton Hotel 65 Park St, South Yarra ☎ 03/9868 4800, [W] www.hatton.com.au. Modern boutique hotel housed within a grand Italianate house within walking distance of the Botanic Gardens. Each of its twenty stylish rooms is immaculately and individually arranged, including modern bathrooms with deep bathtubs and kitchenettes with real coffee plungers. The hotel's Front Lounge doubles as reception and is a pleasant spot for coffee or a glass of wine. [8]

Olembia Guesthouse 96 Barkly St, St Kilda ☎ 03/9537 1412, [W] www.olembia.com.au. See St Kilda map on p.883. This old Edwardian building provides a peaceful retreat from the bustle of Barkly St. Smallish, rustic-looking rooms with shared facilities are spotlessly clean and simple, as are the three- to four-bed dorms (some women-only). There's also a small kitchen and laundry, plus free tea and coffee, but no breakfast. Its homely drawing room, complete with comfy armchairs, resident cat and open fire, is a treat in winter. Book in advance. Dorms $26–30, rooms [4]

The Prince 2 Acland St, St Kilda ☎ 03/9536 1111, [W] www.theprince.com.au. See St Kilda map on p.883. This 40-room boutique hotel housed within *The Prince* complex is one of Melbourne's most elegant places to lay your head. Minimalist bedrooms include Loewe TVs and DVD players, and Bose radios, while bathrooms are stocked with Aesop products. Other facilities include a day-spa and relaxation centre, the elegant *Circa* restaurant (see p.892), the *Mink Bar* (see p.896) and a club/band room. [9]

Ritz for Backpackers 169B Fitzroy St, St Kilda ☎ 03/9525 3501, [W] www.ritzbackpackers.com. See St Kilda map on p.883. If you like beer and love to party, then this is the place for you. Ideally located in the heart of Fitzroy St (adjacent to a popular pub), the rooms are simple, but most come for the social scene. There are two TV lounges, a pool table, dining room, tiny kitchen and internet and laundry facilities, plus free bike hire. Lots of activities and tours and free pancake breakfast each morning, which can help the hangovers. Dorms from $20, rooms [2]

Camping and caravan parks

There are no campsites anywhere close to the centre; the nearest is the *Melbourne Big 4 Holiday Park*.

Discovery Holiday Park 182 Heidelberg-Warrandyte Rd, East Doncaster ☎ 03/9844 3637, [W] www.discoveryholidayparks.com.au. Modern campsite and holiday park with tennis courts and a pool, 21km northeast of the city centre (20min via the Eastern Freeway). Tents [1], on-site vans and cabins [4]–[5]

Melbourne Big 4 Holiday Park 265 Elizabeth St, Coburg East ☎ 03/9354 3533 or 1800 802 678, [W] www.melbournebig4holidaypark.com.au. Shady park 10km north of the city, with cabins, and powered and unpowered tent sights, plus kitchen and a swimming pool. Take bus #526 to the city (daytime only, no service Sun). Tents [1], cabins [3]–[6]

The City

Melbourne is a city of few sights but plenty of lifestyle, and you'll get to know the city just as well by sitting over a coffee or strolling in the park as by traipsing around museums or attractions. At the heart of the city lies the **Central Business District (CBD)**, bounded by La Trobe, Spring, Flinders and Spencer streets, dotted with fine public buildings and plenty of shops. Sights include the ghoulish **Old Melbourne Gaol**, just north of La Trobe Street, and the **Immigration Museum** in the Old Customs House, dedicated to Victoria's immigration history. The CBD is surrounded by gardens on all sides (save the downtown west): few cities have so much green space so close to the centre. To the north of the CBD a wander through lively, century-old **Queen Victoria Market** will repay both serious shoppers and people-watchers, while the **Melbourne Museum** in tranquil Carlton Gardens draws on the latest technology to give an insight into Australia's flora, fauna and culture. In the east, the CBD rubs up against Eastern Hill, home to **Parliament House** and other government buildings as well as the landscaped **Fitzroy Gardens**, from where it's a short walk to the venerable **Melbourne Cricket Ground (MCG)**, a must for sports fans.

Bordering the south side of the CBD, the muddy and, in former decades, much-maligned **Yarra River** lies at the centre of the massive developments which have transformed the face of the city, with new high-rises still popping up like mushrooms. The shift towards the Yarra River kicked off in the mid-1990s with the waterfront development of **Southgate**, **Crown Casino** and the **Melbourne Exhibition Centre**. These have recently been joined by Southbank's **Eureka Tower** (featuring a stunning observation deck) and the **Docklands** development to the west with its waterside bars and restaurants. **Federation Square** on the north bank of the Yarra River opposite Flinders Street Station is considered the centre of the city; its adjacent park, Birrarung Marr, links Federation Square with the sports arenas further east. Continuing south of the river, the **Victorian Arts Centre** forms a cultural strip on one side of St Kilda Road, while on the other, Government House and the impressive Shrine of Remembrance front the soothing **Royal Botanic Gardens**.

Federation Square and around

The huge, yellow-and-brown **Flinders Street Station**, the city's main suburban railway station, lies sandwiched between the southern edge of the CBD and the Yarra River, and is the gateway to the city for the 1,000,000-plus commuters who pass through it every day. The current building dates back to the early 1900s and "under the clocks" – its entrance with a row of clocks detailing the times of all train departures – is still a traditional Melbourne meeting place.

▲ Federation Square

This famous old city landmark is faced by ultramodern **Federation Square** (or "Fed Square", as it's generally known), which was created in 2002 to provide Melbourne with a single, central unifying focus. Occupying an entire block between Flinders Street and the Yarra River, its bars and cafés are a popular after-work meeting spot, while the Plaza at its core is where crowds gather to check out one of the many events staged throughout the month, including live music, and short art films and major sports events projected from a huge video screen. Rising up from St Kilda Road in a gentle incline, the Plaza narrows into a horseshoe-shape where it is hemmed in by buildings including the Ian Potter Centre: NGV Australia, one of Melbourne's most interesting art museums (see below), and the Australian Centre for the Moving Image. There are also numerous cafés and restaurants. The Melbourne Visitor Centre (see "Information", p.853) is located at the northwestern end of the Plaza, directly across from Flinders Street Station.

On the north side of the Plaza, the **Australian Centre for the Moving Image**, or ACMI (daily 10am–6pm; ☏03/8663 2200, ⒲www.acmi.net.au; some films and exhibitions may attract an entry charge), is devoted to exploring the moving image in all its forms, from film and television to video games and new media. Worth checking out is the screen gallery, an underground exhibition space spanning the entire length of Federation Square, and featuring changing exhibitions of screen-based art; ACMI also presents a wide range of programmes ranging from cinema and educative events to hip-hop festivals. Two state-of-the-art cinemas screen themed programmes and host film festivals and events. The latest development is a free permanent exhibition exploring the last one hundred years of the moving image on the ground floor.

Ian Potter Centre: NGV Australia

Walk from Flinders Street through the **Atrium** – a unique passageway of glass, steel and zinc – or from the Plaza through the similarly narrow **Crossbar** to reach the home of the National Gallery of Victoria's collection of Australian art, the **Ian Potter Centre: NGV Australia** (Tues–Sun 10am–5pm, Thurs till 9pm; free, except special exhibitions; ☏03/8620 2222, ⒲www.ngv.vic.gov.au), named in honour of Sir Ian Potter (1902–94), a local financier, philanthropist and patron of the arts. Occupying three floors, the centre showcases one of the best collections of Australian art in the country, with some seventy thousand works of art, of which about 1800 are usually on display (exhibits are rotated regularly). Traditional and contemporary indigenous art is displayed in four galleries on the ground floor; historic and modern Australian collections are housed on the second floor; while the galleries on the third floor are reserved for special temporary exhibitions. The artworks are complemented by interactive videos, which feature an overview of artists' works, with biographies and interviews.

The building itself is as much a work of art as its exhibits, constructed from two overlapping wings forming a slightly crooked X and offering constantly shifting views, with glimpses of the Yarra and the parklands through the glass walls in the southern part of the building. The best way to get a handle on the collection, as well as the building, is to participate in a **free guided tour** of the main collection (daily at 11am and 2pm).

Galleries 1–4 on the ground floor give an excellent overview of the art produced in Australia's **indigenous communities**, showcasing works in both traditional and contemporary styles. Traditional art is represented by carved and painted figures from Maningrida, masks from Torres Straits Islands, Pukumani poles from the Tiwi Islands north of Darwin, the Wandjina paintings from the north of Western Australia and bark paintings from Yirrkala and other places in Arnhem Land. One of the highlights is undoubtedly *Big Yam Dreaming* (1995), an enormous canvas by Emily Kam Kngwarray (c.1910–96) showing tangled, spidery webs of white against a black background, representing the pencil yam that grows along the creek banks at the artist's birthplace northeast of Alice Springs. In her brief career – she didn't take up painting until she was in her mid-70s – Emily produced a staggering three thousand-plus works, transcending the Western Desert–style dot paintings and developing a uniquely personal style, which, seemingly abstract and vibrantly coloured, is sometimes reminiscent of late Monet or Jackson Pollock.

On the second floor, galleries 5–11 contain paintings, sculptures, drawings, photographs and decorative arts from the mid-nineteenth century to the 1980s displayed in chronological order. One leitmotif is the harsh beauty of the Australian landscape, and (European) peoples' place in it. The early **colonial paintings** – with works by artists such as John Glover, Henry Burn, Frederick McCubbin and Tom Roberts – are particularly interesting, showing European artists struggling to come to terms with an alien land, as well as offering pictorial records of the growth of new cities and the lives of immigrants and pioneers.

Highlights of the twentieth-century collection include paintings by Albert Tucker, Russell Drysdale, John Perceval and, especially, **Sidney Nolan** (1917–92). Dissatisfied with his Eurocentric art training at Prahran Technical College, Nolan strived to express the Australian experience in a fresh style, exploring new ways of seeing and painting the nation's landscapes, as in his *Wimmera* painting of the 1940s. Nolan also showed a unique interest in the histories of convicts, explorers and bushrangers, resulting in pictures such as his well-known *Ned Kelly* series (1946–48). Another highlight is the gallery dedicated to the overwhelming *Pilbara* collection of Fred Williams, painted in 1979 in the Pilbara region of Western Australia.

The CBD

Seen from across the river, Melbourne's CBD (**Central Business District**) presents a spectacular modern skyline; what you notice from close up, however, are the florid nineteenth-century facades, grandiose survivors of the great days of the goldrush and after. The former Royal Mint on William Street near Flagstaff Gardens is one of the finest examples, but the main concentrations are to the south on **Collins Street** and along **Spring Street** to the east. At the centre of the CBD, trams jolt through the busy but somewhat tired-looking **Bourke Street Mall**. A stone's throw from these central thoroughfares, narrow lanes, squares and arcades with quaint, hole-in-the-wall cafés, small restaurants, shops and boutiques add a cosy and intimate feel to the city.

Collins Street

North of Fed Square, **Collins Street** is *the* smart Melbourne address, becoming increasingly exclusive as you climb the hill from the Spencer Street end. At the western end of Collins Street the Stock Exchange squares up to the Rialto Building opposite, an Italianate-Gothic complex built in the 1890s now housing the luxury *Intercontinental Rialto Hotel*. Adjacent to this the massive **Rialto Towers**, built in the 1980s, was Melbourne's tallest structure, until the Eureka Tower opened in 2006 (see p.873). At 235m, the skyscraper is still hairily high; you can take a trip up to the **Observation Deck** on the 55th

floor (daily 10am–10pm; $14.50; ☎03/9629 8222, ⓦwww.melbournedeck
.com.au). There's a licensed café on the deck, and the admission fee includes
the use of binoculars, and a twenty-minute film that highlights the best parts
of Melbourne and Victoria. Nearby, at no. 333, the former **Commercial Bank
of Australia** has a particularly sumptuous interior, with a domed banking
chamber and awesome barrel-vaulted vestibule which you're welcome to
come in and admire during business hours.

Further up Collins Street, beyond the worthwhile diversion down William
Street to the Immigration Museum in the Old Customs House (see below),
shops become the focus of attention. The 1890s **Block Arcade**, at nos.
282–284, is one of Melbourne's grandest shopping centres, its name appropriately taken from the tradition of "doing the block" – promenading around the
city's fashionable shopping lanes. Restored in 1988, the L-shaped arcade sports
a mosaic-tiled floor, ornate columns and mouldings, and a glass-domed roof.
Australia on Collins is a modern alternative next door with an upmarket
food court and adjacent licensed restaurants and bars in its basement. Beyond
this, on the corner of Collins and Swanston streets, the Neoclassical Melbourne
Town Hall stands across the road from City Square, a beleaguered space that
never achieved its intended purpose: to provide Melbourne with a focal point.
There is, however, an unmissable landmark on the south side of the square: the
splendid **St Paul's Cathedral**, built in the 1880s to a Gothic-Revival design
by English architect William Butterfield (who never actually visited Australia).
Across from the cathedral on Swanston Street, the *Young & Jackson's Hotel* is
now protected by the National Trust, not for any intrinsic beauty but as a
showcase for a work of art which has become a Melbourne icon: *Chloe*, a full-
length nude which now reclines upstairs in the comfortable *Chloe's Bar and
Bistro*. Exhibited by the French painter Jules Lefebvre at the Paris Salon of
1875, it was sent to an international exhibition in Melbourne in 1881, where
it caused quite a stir, and has been here ever since.

Back on Collins Street, the pompous **Athenaeum Theatre** next to the Town
Hall houses a cosy library and plays an important role in the rising streetscape
leading up past **Scots' Church**, whose Gothic-Revival design merits a peek,
though it's famous mainly as the place where Dame Nellie Melba first sang in
the choir. Further up, beyond expensive boutiques and souvenir shops, Collins
Place and the towering **Hotel Sofitel** next door dominate the upper part of
Collins Street. The (male) toilet of *Café La* (see p.886) on the 35th floor of the
Sofitel is known as the "loo with a view", but the view from the tables by the
window isn't bad, either. Opposite, overshadowed by the *Sofitel* tower, stands
one of the last bastions of Australian male chauvinism: the very staid, men-only
Melbourne Club.

The Immigration Museum

At the corner of Flinders and William streets, just off the western stretch of
Collins Street, the **Immigration Museum** (daily 10am–5pm; $8; ☎03/9927
2700, ⓦwww.museumvictoria.com.au) is dedicated to one of the central
themes of Australian history. Housed in the beautifully restored Old Customs
House, the museum builds a vivid picture of immigration history through
personal stories, music, moving images, light effects and interactive screens,
evoking the experiences of being a migrant on a square-rigger in the 1840s; a
passenger on a steamship at the beginning of the twentieth century; and a
postwar refugee from Europe. In the **Tribute Garden**, the outdoor centrepiece
of the museum, a film of water flows over polished granite on which are
engraved the names of 7000 migrants to Victoria, symbolizing the passage over

the seas. The names of all the Koorie people living in Victoria prior to white settlement are listed separately at the entrance to the garden.

Bourke Street and Chinatown

Bourke Street Mall extends west from Swanston Street to Elizabeth Street. The mall's western end is dominated by the **General Post Office** (**GPO**), a solid Neoclassical porticoed pile with a distinctive clock tower. So important was this building in its heyday that that all road distances from Melbourne were measured from here. After a fire gutted most of its interior in 2003, it was restored and is now a light and airy shopping complex with high-end designer clothes and upmarket eateries. Running off Bourke Street Mall, the lovely **Royal Arcade** is Melbourne's oldest (1869), paved with black and white marble and lit by huge fanlight windows. A clock on which two two-metre giants, Gog and Magog, strike the hours adds a welcome hint of the grotesque. As you climb the hill east of here, Bourke Street keeps up the interest, with several cafés and bars that put out pavement tables at night – including the eternal and ever-buzzing *Pellegrini's Espresso Bar* (see p.887), Melbourne's first Italian bar, as well as late-opening book and record stores.

North of Bourke Street, and running parallel to it, is Little Bourke Street, with the majestic **Law Courts** by William Street at the western end, and Chinatown in the east between Exhibition and Swanston streets. Australia's oldest continuous Chinese settlement, Melbourne's **Chinatown** began with a few boarding-houses in the 1850s (when the goldrushes attracted Chinese people in droves, many from the Pearl River Delta near Hong Kong) and grew as the gold began to run out and Chinese fortune-seekers headed back to the city. Today the area still has a low-rise, narrow-laned, nineteenth-century character, and it's packed with restaurants and stores. The **Chinese Museum**, in an old warehouse on Cohen Place (daily 10am–5pm; $7.50; ℡03/9662 2888, Ⓦwww.chinesemuseum.com.au), is concerned particularly with the Chinese role in the foundation and development of Melbourne, and is worth a visit for the 92-metre-long Dai Loong dragon alone, paraded each Chinese New Year and during the Moomba Festival (see p.894). The museum organizes the **Chinatown Heritage Walk**, a two-hour guided tour of the building and Chinatown (hours vary depending on bookings; $18 or $34 including lunch). The walk requires a minimum of four people, and should be booked three days in advance.

QV and the State Library of Victoria

North of the Chinese Museum rises the latest bulk development to change the structure and feel of the CBD. **QV** takes in almost the entire block between Russell, Lonsdale, Swanston and La Trobe streets, and is named after the Queen Victoria Women's Hospital which occupied the site from 1896 until the late 1980s. It now houses a shopping complex with a gym, supermarket, restaurants and bars. The building itself is an irregularly formed structure crisscrossed by open-air lanes and passageways with floor-to-ceiling glass walls. The basement houses a busy supermarket, while the levels above offer a diverse range of shops, eateries and bars. The lanes themselves are dedicated to high-end fashion: one of the busiest, **Albert Coates Lane** (named after a World War I stretcher-bearer, who became a leading surgeon at the hospital), runs east from Swanston Street above the intersection with Lonsdale Street and showcases stores from top local and overseas designers including Christensen Copenhagen, Cactus Jam, Guess, Hugo Boss and Wayne Cooper.

To the western edge of QV, along Swanston Street, is the **State Library of Victoria** (Mon–Thurs 10am–9pm, Fri–Sun 10am–6pm; free introductory tours Mon–Fri 2pm; ☏03/8664 7000, ⓦwww.slv.vic.gov.au), which has free internet. The building, dating from 1856, is a splendid example of Victorian architecture, and houses the state's largest public research and reference library. The interior has been painstakingly refurbished and is well worth a visit, in particular the Cowen Gallery with a permanent display of paintings illustrating the changing look of Melbourne and Victoria; the La Trobe Reading Room with its imposing domed roof; and the Dome Gallery dedicated to the history of Victoria. The library houses a trove of paintings and rare and antiquarian books and newspapers, along with the deed of land purchase by John Batman from the Dugitalla Aborigines, Ned Kelly's armour and the famous rage-filled Jerilderie letter which inspired Peter Carey's Booker Prize-winning novel *The True History of the Kelly Gang*, and a leaf of the Gutenberg Bible. Also worth a mention is the **Chess Collection**; with almost 12,000 chess-related items it is reputedly one of the largest public collections in the world. You can play here, too.

Opposite the State Library is the refurbished **Melbourne Central** shopping complex mirroring the QV concept of alleys and passageways lined with cafés, sushi bars and boutiques. On its top levels are several restaurants, a bowling alley and a cinema complex.

Old Melbourne Gaol

The **Old Melbourne Gaol** (daily 9.30am–5pm; $20; ☏03/8663 7228, ⓦwww.oldmelbournegaol.com.au), on Russell Street, a block north of the State Library, is one of the most fascinating sights in the CBD. It's certainly the most popular, largely because Australian folk hero and bushranger **Ned Kelly** (see p.997) was hanged here in 1880 – the site of his execution, the beam from which he was hanged and his death mask are all on display, as is assorted armour worn by the Kelly Gang. The "Hangman's Night Tour" (April–Oct 7.30pm, Nov–March 8.30pm; $30; advance bookings required with Ticketek ☏13 28 49) uses the spooky atmosphere of the prison to full effect.

The bluestone prison was built in stages from 1841 to 1864 – the goldrushes of the 1850s caused such a surge in lawlessness that it kept having to be expanded. A mix of condemned men, remand and short-sentence prisoners, women and "lunatics" (often, in fact, drunks) were housed here; long-term prisoners languished in hulks moored at Williamstown, or at the Pentridge Stockade. Much has been demolished since the jail was closed in 1923, but the entrance and boundary walls survive, and it's worth walking round the building to take a look at the formidable arched brick portal on Franklin Street.

The gruesome collection of **death masks** on show in the tiny cells bears witness to the nineteenth-century obsession with phrenology, a wobbly branch of science which studied how people's characters were related to the size and shape of their skulls. Accompanying the masks are compelling case histories of the murderers and their victims. Most fascinating are the women: Martha Needle, who poisoned her husband and daughters (among others) with arsenic, and young Martha Knorr, the notorious "baby farmer", who advertised herself as a "kind motherly person, willing to adopt a child". After receiving a few dollars per child, she killed and buried them in her backyard. The jail serves up other macabre memorabilia, including a scaffold still in working order, various nooses, and a triangle where malcontents were strapped to receive lashes of the cat-o'-nine-tails. Perhaps the ultimate rite of passage for visitors is the "Art of Hanging", an interpretive display that's part educational tool and part medieval snuff-movie.

Queen Victoria Market

Opened in the 1870s, **Queen Victoria Market** (March–Oct Tues & Thurs 6am–2pm, Fri 6am–5pm, Sat 6am–3pm, Sun 9am–4pm; Nov–Feb same hours plus night market Wed 5.30–10.30pm; Ⓦ www.qvm.com.au) remains one of the best loved of Melbourne's institutions. Its collection of huge, open-sided sheds and high-roofed decorative halls is fronted along Victoria Street by restored shops, with their original wrought-iron canopies. Although undeniably quaint and tourist-friendly, the market is a boisterous, down-to-earth affair where you can buy practically anything from new and secondhand clothes to fresh fish. Stallholders and shoppers seem just as diverse as the goods on offer: Vietnamese, Italian and Greek greengrocers pile their colourful produce high and vie for your attention, while the huge variety of deliciously smelly cheeses effortlessly draws customers to the old-fashioned deli hall. Saturday morning marks a weekly social ritual as Melbourne's foodies turn out for their groceries, while Sunday is for clothing and shoe shopping. The guided **Foodies Tour** (10am Tues, Thurs–Sat; $30 including food sampling, bookings essential) takes in all the culinary delights of the market, while the action-packed Night Market has music stages, bars and over thirty stalls providing on-site cuisine from around the world. The market also runs regular day, evening and weekend cooking classes. For programmes and tour bookings call Ⓣ03/9320 5822; details of the Cooking School programme are shown on the market's website.

Carlton Gardens and Melbourne Museum

At the CBD's northeast corner is **Carlton Gardens**, home to one of Melbourne's most significant historic landmarks – the **Royal Exhibition Building** (Ⓦ www.museumvictoria.com.au/reb). It was built by David Mitchell (father of Dame Nellie Melba) for the International Exhibition of 1880 and visited by 1.5 million people. It is also where Australia's first parliament sat in 1901, and the Victorian State Parliament from 1901–27, as well as being used as a sporting venue for the 1956 Melbourne Olympics. The magnificent Neoclassical edifice, with its soaring dome and huge entrance portal, is the only substantially intact example in the world of a Great Hall from a major exhibition; its scale and grandeur reflect the values and aspirations attached to industrialization, so much so that in 2004 Carlton Gardens and the Royal Exhibition Building were inscribed on the UNESCO World Heritage List. One-hour tours of the building (Mon–Fri 2pm) can be booked via the Melbourne Museum next door on Ⓣ13 11 02.

Melbourne Museum (daily 10am–5pm; $6; Ⓣ13 11 02, Ⓦ www.melbourne .museum.vic.gov.au) is an ultramodern, state-of-the-art museum, which makes a dramatic contrast to its nineteenth-century neighbour, with its geometric forms, vibrant colours, immense blade-like roof and a greenhouse accommodating a lush fern gully flanked by a canopy of tall forest trees. The museum, whose eight galleries include one especially for kids, also houses a 400-seat amphitheatre, a hall for major touring exhibitions, a study centre and a museum shop. Glass-covered display cabinets are few and far between: instead there is an emphasis on interactive exhibits exploring the way science and technology are shaping the future.

Highlights include the **Science and Life Gallery**, which explores the plants and animals inhabiting the southern lands and seas; **Bunjilaka**, the Museum's Aboriginal Centre, showcasing an extraordinary collection of Aboriginal culture from Victoria and further afield (curving for 30m at the entrance is

Wurreka, a wall of zinc panels etched with Aboriginal artefacts, shells, plants and fish); and the **Australia Gallery**, focusing on the history of Melbourne and Victoria, which features the (now stuffed) legendary racehorse Phar Lap (reputedly Australia's most popular museum exhibit). Also of interest are the **Evolution Gallery**, which looks at the earth's history and holds an assortment of dinosaur casts, and the **Children's Museum**, where the exhibition gallery, "Big Box", is built in the shape of a giant, tiled cube painted in brightly coloured squares. One of the most striking exhibits is the **Forest Gallery**, a living, breathing indoor rainforest containing over 8000 plants from more than 120 species, including 25-metre-tall gums, as well as birds, insects, snakes, lizards and fish. Also part of the museum, the **IMAX Melbourne** boasts one of the world's biggest movie screens. Up to eight different IMAX films (daily on the hour 10am–10pm; $17.50; ℡03/9663 5454, ⓦwww.imaxmelbourne.com.au), ranging from natural wonders to artificial marvels and spacewalks, are projected each day; for 3D action liquid crystal glasses are provided.

Parliament House and around

The Eastern Hill area beyond Spring Street has many fine public buildings, centred around **Parliament House** (free 50min tours Mon–Fri 10am, 11am, noon, 2pm, 3pm & 3.45pm on days when parliament is not sitting; ℡03/9651 8568 for dates). Erected in stages between 1856 and 1930, the parliament buildings have a theatrical presence, with a facade of giant Doric columns rising from a high flight of steps, and landscaped gardens either side. Just below, the Old Treasury Building and adjacent State Government office, facing the beautiful Treasury Gardens, are equally imposing. Completed in 1862 to a design by John James Clark, who was just 19 at the time, the building was built to store the city's gold. Today it houses the **City Museum** (Mon–Fri 9am–5pm, Sat & Sun 10am–4pm; $8.50, ℡03/9651 2233, ⓦwww.citymuseummelbourne.org), which has exhibitions on the social and architectural history of Melbourne including *Built on Gold*, an audiovisual presentation, shown in the old gold-vaults deep in the basement, *Making Melbourne* and *Growing up in the Old Treasury*.

East of Parliament House, the broad acres of **Fitzroy Gardens** run a close second to Carlton Gardens as a getaway from the CBD. Originally laid out in the shape of the Union Jack flag, the park's paths still just about conform to the original pattern, though the formal style has been fetchingly abandoned in between. The flowers, statuary and fountains are best appreciated on weekdays, as at the weekend you'll spend most of your time dodging the video cameras of wedding parties. The gardens' much-touted main attraction is really only for kitsch nostalgists: **Captain Cook's Cottage** (daily 9am–5pm; $4.50) was the family home of Captain James Cook, the English navigator who explored the southern hemisphere in three great voyages and first "discovered" the east coast of Australia. Otherwise, there are attractive flower displays at the **Conservatory** (daily 7am–5pm; free).

The MCG and around

East of Birrarung Marr lies **Yarra Park**, containing the hallowed **Melbourne Cricket Ground** (**MCG**) – also easily reached by tram along Wellington Parade or train to Jolimont Station. Hosting state and international cricket matches and some of the top Aussie Rules football games, the 'G', as it is affectionately referred to, is one of sports-mad Melburnians' best-loved icons. Home to the Melbourne Cricket Club since 1853, the complex became the centrepiece of the 1956 Olympic Games after it had been completely reconstructed

▲ Crowds at the Melbourne Cricket Ground

– only the historic members' stand survived. The present-day MCG has a capacity of 100,000 spectators, boosted by the development of the Northern Stand, which was created for the 2006 Commonwealth Games, and houses the National Sport Museum (10am–5pm; $15, or $22 combined with a tour), containing various sports **exhibitions**. One-hour tours of the ground (hourly 10am–3pm; no tours on event days; $15; Ⓦwww.mcg.org.au) offer the chance to visit the players' changing rooms, coaches' boxes and cricket viewing areas and whatever is currently accessible.

From the MCG, three pedestrian bridges over Brunton Avenue lead to **Melbourne Park**, home to a further cluster of sporting venues, including the Rod Laver Arena and Hisense Arena, which host the Australian Open tennis championship in January. The latter can seat up to 10,500 people and has a retractable roof and moveable seating that allows for fully enclosed or open-air events such as cycling, tennis, basketball and concerts. On the other side of Swan Street lies **Olympic Park** where the Melbourne Storm rugby-league team play their matches, and the Lexus Centre, the new training home for Collingwood AFL Club.

Birrarung Marr

Melbourne's newest park, **Birrarung Marr**, forms a green link between the sports precinct of Melbourne Park and Federation Square, giving striking views of the city skyline, the sports arenas, river and parklands. Created from land previously occupied by railway lines, a swimming pool and a road, it now consists of grassy slopes, intersected by a long **footbridge** that crosses the entire park from the southeast to the northwest. The footbridge starts at a small, artificially created wetland area in the southeast by the river called the **Billabong** and leads over Red Gum Gully to the park's centrepiece, the **Federation Bells**, a collection of 39 bells ranging in size from a small handbell to a huge bell weighing a ton, created to commemorate the Centenary of Federation in 2001. The bells are computer-controlled and normally ring every day at 8am, 12.30pm and 5pm.

The Yarra River, Southgate and Eureka Tower

Despite its nondescript appearance, the muddy **Yarra River** was – and still is – an important part of the Melbourne scene. Traditionally home to the city docks, tidal movements of up to 2m meant frequent flooding, a problem only partly solved by artificially straightening the river and building up its banks. This also had the incidental benefit of reserving tracts of low-lying land as recreational space, which are now pleasingly crisscrossed by paths and cycle tracks. Four **bridges** cross the river from the CBD: Spencer Street Bridge at the end of Spencer Street; Kings Bridge on King Street; Queens Bridge, not quite at the end of Queen Street; and Princes Bridge, which carries Swanston Street across. There's also a pedestrian bridge from the bank below Flinders Street Station to the Southgate Centre. The best way to see the Yarra is on a cruise – see the box below.

The riverside's most innovative development is the new 92-storey **Eureka Tower** located on the Southgate site and named after Victoria's goldrush era

River and bay cruises

Most cruises ply the **Yarra River** and the upper reaches of Port Phillip Bay (called Hobsons Bay) between St Kilda and Williamstown at the mouth of the Yarra (see p.884). A cruise on the western suburbs' **Maribyrnong River** reveals a side of Melbourne tourists don't usually get to see, and contrary to local (eastern suburbs) prejudices it is not all factory yards and oil-storage containers either.

The main departure points in the city for cruises along the Yarra River are **Federation Wharf**, at the southern end of Federation Square, **Southgate** and, further west, **Williamstown**. All cruises run weather permitting; in the cooler months (May–Sept) the last scheduled departures of the day may be cancelled.

Melbourne River Cruises (ⓦwww.melbcruises.com.au) depart five to six times daily from berth 5, Southgate and Federation Wharf. Tickets are available at the blue kiosks at Southgate, or call ⓣ03/8610 2600. The River Garden Cruise (1hr 15min; $22) heads upriver past South Yarra and Richmond to Herring Island. The Port and Docklands Cruise (1hr 15min; $22) runs downriver past Crown Casino and Melbourne Exhibition Centre to the Westgate Bridge. Combined up- and downriver cruises cost $29. In addition, cruises to Williamstown and back (approx 1hr; $28) leave daily every half-hour (10.30am–3.30pm, less frequently in the cooler months – enquire at the office).

City River Cruises (ⓣ03/9650 2214, ⓦwww.cityrivercruises.com.au) operate similar Yarra cruises for a marginally cheaper price. Buy tickets at the orange kiosk near the departure point at Northbank Promenade or on board. There are four departures daily between 10am and 2.30pm; additional departure in summer at 4pm.

Williamstown Bay and River Cruises (ⓣ03/9682 9555, ⓦwww.bayandrivercruises.com.au) ply the lower section of the Yarra between Williamstown and Southgate in the west of the city. Departures from Southgate's berth 1 daily every half-hour between 9am and 4.30pm, from Williamstown from 10.30am ($15, or $25 return).

Maribyrnong Cruises (ⓣ03/9689 6431, ⓦwww.blackbirdcruises.com.au). Cruises depart from Wingfield Street and land at Footscray. The Maribyrnong River Cruise passes Flemington Racecourse, Footscray Park and various other parklands to Essendon and shows the tranquil and pretty side of the supposedly drab Western suburbs (2hr; departs Tues, Thurs, Sat & Sun 1pm; $16), while the Port of Melbourne Cruise takes in the industrial aspects of the lower Maribyrnong and Yarra rivers plus the Docklands development (1hr; departs Tues, Thurs, Sat & Sun at 4pm; $8). Take the train to Footscray Station (Watergarden/Werribee line) or take bus #216/#219 from the city to Sunshine, and get off at bus stop 17.

(the top levels are clad in gold). Finished in 2006 and towering 300m, it is the tallest building in Melbourne (having claimed the title from the Rialto Towers) and the highest residential building in the world. Visitors can enjoy amazing views of the city and beyond from the 88th-floor **Skydeck** (10am–10pm; $16.50; ⓦ www.skydeck.com.au), which features the stomach-churning "skywalk" **The Edge** ($12), a three-metre glass cube that juts out over the city below.

At Federation Wharf, on the north side of Princes Bridge, you can **rent bikes** to explore the river banks (see "Listings", p.903); on fine weekends, especially, the Yarra comes to life, with people messing about in boats, cycling and strolling. Southgate, immediately west of Princes Bridge, is an upmarket shopping complex with lots of smart cafés, restaurants, bars and a huge food court with very popular outdoor tables; at lunchtime and weekends it's very hard to find a table, even indoors.

The Crown Casino, Docklands and Etihad Stadium

Providing the Yarra's unavoidable focal point, the **Crown Casino** is Australia's largest gambling and entertainment venue, stretching across 600m of riverfront west of Southgate between Queens Bridge and Spencer Street Bridge. Next door, the **Melbourne Exhibition Centre** (known locally as "Jeff's Shed", a reference to Jeff Kennett, the former state premier behind its construction) is a whimsical example of the city's dynamic new architectural style: facing the river is an immense 450-metre-long glass wall, while the street entrance has an awning resembling a ski jump propped up by wafer-thin pylons. At the time of writing the interesting **Maritime Museum** was closed for extensive renovations. It holds the *Polly Woodside* (enquiries ⓔ polly@nattrust.com.au), a small, barque-rigged sailing ship, built in Belfast in 1885 for the South American coal trade and retired only in 1968, when it was the last deep-water sailing vessel in Australia still afloat.

Opposite the Crown Casino, on the corner of Flinders and King streets, is the **Melbourne Aquarium** (daily 9.30am–6pm, until 9pm Jan 1–26; $31.50; ⓣ 03/9923 5999, ⓦ www.melbourneaquarium.com.au). Resembling a giant fish-and-chip shop, the aquarium harbours thousands of creatures from the Southern Ocean. Part of it is taken up by the Oceanarium tank, which rests 7m below the Yarra, holding over two million litres of water and containing 3200 animals from 150 species (there are over 550 species, or 4000 creatures, in the aquarium in total), as well as a sting-ray-filled beach with a wave machine and a fish bowl turned inside out where you can stand in a glass room surrounded by shark-filled water. The aquarium's latest exhibit, "Antarctica", features two of the larger species of penguin, King and Gentoo. The curved, four-storey building also houses a hands-on learning centre where children get a fish-eye view of life underwater, lecture halls, an amphitheatre, cafés, shop and a restaurant. If you want to come nose-to-nose with a shark, the "Diving With Sharks" experience costs $150 (certified divers with own equipment), $242 (certified divers without own equipment) and $349 for non-divers (includes pre-dive briefing and practical dive). Bookings are essential on ⓣ 039510 9081 or visit ⓦ www.divingheadquarters.com.au.

Further downstream, on what was once the city's old **dock** area, is Melbourne's newest suburb, **Docklands**; a large-scale commercial, residential and leisure development that's slowly rising to the west of Southern Cross Station. Of all the city's new developments this is likely to have the biggest impact on the look and feel of Melbourne: if all goes to plan, when it is completed in 2015 this area is expected to house 20,000 residents, and attract more than 20 million visitors a year. For the time being, the restaurant promenade, NewQuay, on Victoria Harbour, is a bit sterile but is a good place to sit in the warmer months and watch those watching you. Squatting in the middle of it all is another of Melbourne's giant sporting venues, **Etihad Stadium** (formerly the Telstra Dome), a 54,000-seater venue for AFL, cricket, domestic and international soccer and rugby union matches, as well as concerts by big-name artists. A wide pedestrian footbridge crosses the railway tracks at Southern Cross Station, connecting Etihad Stadium and the Docklands with Spencer Street and the older part of the city.

Victorian Arts Centre

The **Victorian Arts Centre** (ⓦwww.theartscentre.com.au), on St Kilda Road, comprises Hamer Hall, the Theatres Building and the Sidney Myer Music Bowl, an open-air venue across St Kilda Road in Kings Domain (see p.876). At the top of the Theatres Building is a 162-metre-tall **spire** whose curved lower sections are meant to evoke the flowing folds of a ballerina's skirt; the mast at its peak turns an iridescent blue at night. A **guided tour** of Hamer Hall and the Theatres Building provides an insight into the history of the buildings and gives an overview of the architecture and design (Mon–Sat 11am; $15), while the **backstage tour** ventures behind the curtains, taking in the dressing rooms and costumes (Sun 12.15pm; $20, ticket from Theatres Building foyer). The centre also houses a Performing Arts Collection research facility covering everything from theatre to rock'n'roll, with exhibits ranging from Dame Edna Everage's spectacles to Kylie's gold hotpants. Viewings are by appointment only, though snapshots of the collection are often displayed in the foyer and gallery spaces, as are splendid temporary exhibitions, normally focusing on the performance schedule. On Sunday between 10am and 5pm the stalls of a good **arts and crafts market** line the pavement outside the Victorian Arts Centre, extending onto the footpath under the Princes Bridge.

The bluestone building next to the Theatres Building is home to the **National Gallery of Victoria** (**NGV**), Australia's oldest public art museum. After extensive refurbishments it was reopened in late 2003 and the gallery now houses a collection of international works under the name **NGV: International** (Wed–Sun 10am–5pm; free; ☎03/8620 2222, ⓦwww.ngv.vic.gov.au), having moved its Australian collection to its new home on Federation Square (see p.864). Features such as the **Waterwall** at the entrance – a water curtain flowing down a glass wall 20m wide and 6m high – and the **Great Hall** on the ground floor, with a beautiful stained-glass ceiling, have been retained, and there's access to the landscaped **Sculpture Garden** via the Great Hall. In addition, individual galleries on the four levels were redesigned, and the overall exhibition space increased. The ground floor contains three large rooms for temporary exhibitions plus galleries dedicated to Oceanic Art, Pre-Columbian, Egyptian and Near Eastern, as well as Greek and Roman Antiquities. Level 1 has rooms displaying European paintings and sculpture from the fourteenth to the seventeenth century. Level 2 comprises paintings, sculpture and decorative arts from the seventeenth to the mid-twentieth centuries: Flemish and Dutch masters, including the Rembrandt Cabinet, are among the highlights here, while the contemporary era is represented using installations and photos on level 3. There's also the pleasant *Garden Restaurant* (daily 10am–5pm) located in the Sculpture Garden. NGV has a regular programme of floor talks, lectures, discussion groups, films and other activities – check out the gallery's *What's On* flyer or its website for details.

Further south, on Sturt Street, next to the Malthouse Theatre, the **Australian Centre for Contemporary Art** (**ACCA**; Tues–Fri 10am–5pm, Sat & Sun

11am–6pm; free; ☎03/9697 9999, ⓦwww.accaonline.org.au) has consistently challenging exhibitions of contemporary international and Australian art.

Kings Domain

Across St Kilda Road from the National Gallery of Victoria, the grassy open parkland of **Kings Domain** encompasses the **Sidney Myer Music Bowl**, which serves as an outdoor music arena for the Victorian Arts Centre. South of the Bowl, and behind imposing iron gates with stone pillars and a British coat of arms, you can glimpse the flag flying over **Government House**, the ivory mansion of the governor of Victoria, set in extensive grounds. The National Trust runs **guided tours** of the house (Mon & Wed; 11am; $15; book in advance on ☎03/663 7260), the highlight being the state ballroom, which occupies the entire south wing and includes a velvet-hung canopied throne, brocade-covered benches, ornate plasterwork and three huge crystal chandeliers.

Further south, on Dallas Brooke Drive, **La Trobe's Cottage** (included in tour) has been re-erected as a memorial to Lieutenant-Governor La Trobe, who lived in this tiny house throughout his term of office (1839–54). The whole thing was sent over from England in prefabricated form. Inside there are interesting displays on La Trobe and the early days of the colony.

The Shrine of Remembrance (daily 10am–5pm; free; ⓦwww.shrine.org .au), in formal grounds in the southwestern corner of the Domain, was built in 1934 to commemorate those who fought in various conflicts. It's a rather Orwellian monument, apparently half-Roman temple, half-Aztec pyramid, given further chill when a mechanical-sounding voice booms out and calls you in to see the symbolic light inside. The shrine is designed so that at 11am on Remembrance Day (Nov 11) a ray of sunlight strikes the memorial stone inside – an effect that's simulated every half-hour.

Royal Botanic Gardens

The **Royal Botanic Gardens** (daily: April, Sept & Oct 7.30am–6pm; May–Aug 7.30am–5.30pm; Nov–March 7.30am–8.30pm; free; ⓦwww.rbg.vic.gov .au) on Dallas Brooke Drive contain twelve thousand different plant species and over fifty thousand individual plants, as well as native wildlife such as cockatoos and kookaburras, in an extensive landscaped setting. Melbourne's much-maligned climate is perfect for horticulture: cool enough for temperate trees and flowers to flourish, warm enough for palms and other subtropical species, and wet enough for anything else. The bright and airy **visitor centre** (Mon–Fri 9am–5pm, Sat & Sun 9.30am–5.30pm) at Observatory Gate on Birdwood Avenue has displays, maps and brochures and is the best place to start your wanderings.

Highlights include the **herb garden**, comprising part of the medicinal garden established in 1880; the **fern gully**, a lovely walk through shady ferns, with cooling mists of water on a hot summer's day; the large ornamental **lake** full of ducks, black swans and eels; and various **hothouses** where exotic cacti and fascinating plants such as the carnivorous Pitcher plant thrive. *The Observatory Gate Café* (daily 7am–5pm) next to the visitor centre has indoor and outdoor seating under sun sails and sells coffee, scrumptious cakes and sandwiches as well as light meals. The *Terrace Tearooms* (daily: April–Sept 9.45am–4pm; Oct–May 9am–5pm) by the lake is licensed and serves meals, or there's a snack bar next door. On summer evenings, plays are often performed in the gardens. Cinema buffs can also swap popcorn for picnic baskets each year from mid-December to mid-March when art-house, cult and classic films are projected onto a big outdoor screen at the **Moonlight Cinema** ($17 or $15 online; recorded info on ☎1300 551 908, or visit ⓦwww.moonlight.com.au). Enter at D Gate on Birdwood Avenue; films start around 8.30pm. Don't forget to take an extra layer of clothing, a rug and, most importantly, insect repellent. Every second Saturday on the month, the **Gardens Market** (9am–2pm; ⓦwww.marketsinthegarden .com.au) is held, where one hundred stallholders sell plants, art, gourmet food and other items.

Guided walks start at the visitor centre: the Gardens Discovery Walk (Tues–Sun 11am & 2pm; free) gives a fine introduction to the history and horticultural diversity of the gardens; and the Aboriginal Heritage Walk (Thurs & one Sunday every month 11am; $18; bookings essential on ☎03/9252 2429) explores the traditional uses of plants for foods, medicine, tools and ceremonies. The painstakingly restored **Observatory Gate**, a group of 19th-century Italianate buildings next door to the visitor centre, can be visited on one of the tours that leaves from the centre: the "Night Sky Experience tour" (Mon 7.30–9pm; during daylight-saving time 9–10.30pm; $18) offers people a chance to gaze up at the stars and planets of the southern hemisphere through large telescopes.

Melbourne suburbs

Far more than in the city centre, it's in Melbourne's **inner suburbs** that you'll really get a feel for what life here is all about. Many have quite distinct characters, whether as ethnic enclaves or self-styled artists' communities. What's more, all can easily be reached by a pleasurable tram ride from the centre. Browsing through markets and shops, cruising across Hobsons Bay, sampling the world's foods and, of course, sipping espresso are the primary attractions. Café society finds its home to the north among the alternative galleries and secondhand shops of **Fitzroy**, while the Italian cafés on Lygon Street in nearby **Carlton** fuelled the Beat Generation with espresso, though these days boutiques far outnumber bookshops. Grungy **Richmond**, to the east, has both Vietnamese and Greek enclaves, is home to a number of good Middle Eastern eateries, and has a diverse music scene in its many pubs. South of the river is the place to shop until you drop, whether at wealthy **South Yarra**, self-consciously groovy **Prahran** or snobby **Toorak**. To the south, **St Kilda** has the advantage of a beachside location to go with its trendy but raucous nightlife. To firm up your itinerary with something more concrete, make for the well-designed **Zoo** in Carlton, or **Scienceworks**, a hugely enjoyable interactive museum in Spotswood. Also of interest is the **Heide Museum of Modern Art** in Bulleen and, a bit further along in the same direction, **Eltham**, with its artists' colony of Montsalvat.

Carlton

Carlton lies just north of the city (tram #1, #3 or #8 from Swanston Street) but, with its university presence and its long-established Italian restaurant scene, it could be a million miles away. **Lygon Street** is the centre of the action, and it was here, in the 1950s, that espresso bars first opened in Melbourne; exotic spots such as the *Caffe Sport*, *La Gina*, *University Caffe* and *Toto's Pizza House* (which claims to have introduced pizza to Australia, see p.889) had an unconventional allure in staid Anglo-Melbourne, and the local intelligentsia soon made the street their second home. Victorian terraced

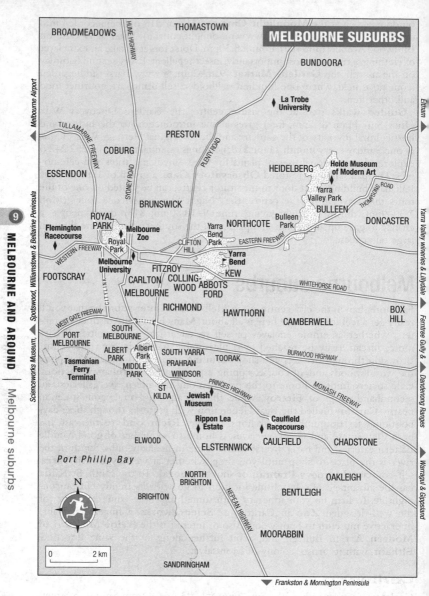

BROADMEADOWS

THOMASTOWN

BUNDOORA

Melbourne Airport ▶

HUME HIGHWAY

TULLAMARINE FREEWAY

La Trobe University ♦

PRESTON

COBURG

PLENTY ROAD

SYDNEY ROAD

ESSENDON

HEIDELBERG

Heide Museum of Modern Art ♦

Flemington Racecourse ♦

ROYAL PARK

Melbourne Zoo ♦

Royal Park

BRUNSWICK

Yarra Valley Park

Bulleen Park

BULLEEN

DONCASTER

THOMPSONS ROAD

NORTHCOTE

Yarra Bend Park

CLIFTON HILL

EASTERN FREEWAY

Yarra Bend

WESTERN FREEWAY

Melbourne University ♦

FITZROY

CARLTON

COLLING-WOOD

ABBOTS FORD

KEW

FOOTSCRAY

MELBOURNE

WHITEHORSE ROAD

RICHMOND

HAWTHORN

CAMBERWELL

BOX HILL

CITYLINK

WEST GATE FREEWAY

PORT MELBOURNE

SOUTH MELBOURNE

Albert Park

SOUTH YARRA

TOORAK

BURWOOD HIGHWAY

Tasmanian Ferry Terminal

ALBERT PARK

MIDDLE PARK

PRAHRAN

WINDSOR

PRINCES HIGHWAY

MONASH FREEWAY

ST KILDA

Jewish Museum ♦

Rippon Lea Estate ♦

Caulfield Racecourse ♦

ELWOOD

ELSTERNWICK

CAULFIELD

CHADSTONE

Port Phillip Bay

NORTH BRIGHTON

OAKLEIGH

BENTLEIGH

N

BRIGHTON

MOORABBIN

0   2 km

SANDRINGHAM

Scienceworks Museum, ◀ Spotswood, Williamstown & Bellarine Peninsula

Eltham ▶

Yarra Valley wineries & Lilydale ▶

Ferntree Gully & ▶

Dandenong Ranges ▶

Warragul & Gippsland ▶

▼ Frankston & Mornington Peninsula

houses provided cheap living, and this became the first of the city's "alternative" suburbs. These days Carlton is no longer bohemian; its residents are older and wealthier, and Lygon Street has gone definitively upmarket, though the smart fashion shops still jostle with bookshops, excellent ethnic restaurants and cafés like *Tiamo 1* (see p.889).

Lygon Street itself is the obvious place to explore, but the elegant architecture also spreads eastwards to Drummond Street, Carlton Gardens, Rathdowne and Nicholson streets. Running along the western side of the university,

Royal Parade gives onto Royal Park, with its memorial to the explorers Burke and Wills (see box, p.526), from where it's a short walk through the park to the zoo.

Melbourne Zoo

When it opened in 1862, **Melbourne Zoo** (daily 9am–5pm; $23.60; ℡03/9285 9300 ⓦ www.zoo.org.au/melbournezoo; tram #55 from William St, or train on Upfield or Gowrie lines from Flinders St Station) was the first in Australia. Some of its original features are still in evidence, including Australian and foreign trees, and landscaped gardens, but the animals have been rehoused in more natural conditions. Popular attractions include an **Orangutan Sanctuary**, featuring a treetop boardwalk, the **Gorilla Rainforest**, home to Riga, a Silverback male, and his family, and the Asian Rainforest, part of the award-winning **Trail of the Elephants**, where you can meet the five resident elephants, learn about the life of a "mahout" or elephant keeper, and eat *nasi goreng* at the Asian food stalls. The Australian area contains a central lake with waterbirds, open enclosures for koalas and other animals, and a bushland setting where you can walk among emus, kangaroos and wallabies. Strolling along the boardwalks of the **Great Flight Aviary** you'll come across areas of rainforest, wetland, and a scrub area with a huge gum tree where many birds nest. The dark **Platypus House** (daily 9.30am–4.30pm) is also worth a look, since the mammals are notoriously difficult to see in the wild – even here there's no guarantee you'll be lucky. **Butterfly House**, a steamy tropical hothouse with hundreds of colourful Australian butterflies flitting about, is also highly enjoyable. In summer, the zoo stays open until 9.30pm on selected nights (usually weekends) for its "Zoo Twilights" music programme, which hosts live bands playing on the central lawn. The zoo also runs the popular **Roar 'n' Snore** sleepover ($185 adults), where you get to sleep in safari tents in the Historic Elephant Enclosure and take an after-dark zoo tour. Dinner, breakfast and snacks are provided, as are tents, but bring your own bedding – for more information call ℡03/9285 9335.

Fitzroy and Collingwood

In the 1970s, **Fitzroy** took over from Carlton as the home of the city's artistic community, and every year at the end of September, the colourful Fringe Parade and a street party on Brunswick Street usher in the **Fringe Festival**, the alternative scene's answer to the highbrow Melbourne International Arts Festival. The **International Comedy Festival** (April) and the **Next Wave Festival** (May, even-numbered years), two other notable arts events, also take place mainly in Fitzroy. The district's focus is **Brunswick Street** (tram #112 from Collins St), especially between Gertrude Street, home to trendy galleries and performance art spaces, and Johnston Street, with its lively Spanish bars. In the shadow of Housing Commission tower-blocks, welfare agencies and charity shops rub shoulders with funky secondhand clothes and junk shops, ethnic supermarkets and restaurants, cafés full of grungy students, artists, writers and musicians, and thriving bookshops that stay open late and are often as crowded as the many bars and music pubs. Most of the rough old hotels have been done up to match the prevailing mood: the *Provincial* is a good example, with its distressed paint-job and café/bar. Some great pubs have remained untouched down the side streets, however, such as the *Napier Hotel* (see p.895) at 210 Napier St opposite Fitzroy Town Hall, and *The Standard* at 293 Fitzroy St which, many say, has Melbourne's best beer-garden.

Fitzroy's fringe art leanings are reflected in wacky street installations such as mosaic chairs, and sculptures like *Mr Poetry*. The eye-catching wrought-iron gate at the entrance to the Fitzroy Nursery at 390 Brunswick St, with its fairy-tale motif, sets the theme for the Artists Garden above the nursery, which exhibits sculptures and other decorative items for garden use. Fitzroy also boasts the unique but overpriced Rose Street **Artists Market** (Oct–May Sat 11am–5pm) at 60 Rose St where fashion designers, painters, photographers, ceramicists, sculptors and other artists sell their work. The **Fitzroy Pool**, in the north of the suburb on the corner of Young and Cecil streets, is a summer meeting place where people occasionally swim between posing sessions.

While not as trendy as Brunswick Street, **Smith Street** (tram #86 from Bourke St), which forms the boundary between Fitzroy and Collingwood to the east, is forever catching up, and still has charity shops, ethnic butchers and cheap supermarkets among its New Age bookshops, quirky little cafés and revamped pubs. North of Johnston Street is a clutch of sportswear factory-seconds outlets. **Collingwood** and the adjacent suburb of Abbotsford have a large **gay** population, with a clutch of gay bars and clubs, particularly on Peel and Glasshouse streets.

East of the CBD, **Richmond**'s Bridge Road (tram #48/#75) is a bargain shopper's paradise, dotted with clothing factory-seconds stores, while running parallel further north, Victoria Street is the bustling heart of Melbourne's Vietnamese community, lined with cheap greengrocers, fishmongers and pho restaurants.

South Yarra, Toorak, Prahran and Windsor

South of the river, the suburbs of **South Yarra**, **Prahran** and, to the east, Toorak, are home to the city's biggest **shopping** area, both grungy and upmarket. **Chapel Street** is the main drag: in South Yarra it extends for a Golden Mile of trendy shopping and *very* chic cafés; heading south beyond Commercial Road through Prahran and Windsor the stereotypically glossy streetscape takes on a refreshingly chequered, ruddier appearance. Crossing Chapel Street at right angles in South Yarra, Toorak Road boasts equally ritzy designer boutiques and, if that's possible, becomes even more exclusive east of Grange Road, as it enters Toorak, a suburb synonymous with wealth.

South Yarra and Toorak

The **South Yarra** stretch of **Chapel Street** is awash with boutiques and speciality shops, bistro bars full of beautiful people and cooler-than-thou nightclubs. Amongst the wall-to-wall chic, it's worth making a beeline for the **Jam Factory** cinema-and-entertainment complex, named after its former incarnation, housing a Virgin Megastore, Borders bookshop and a *TGI Friday*. South Yarra is also home to **Como Historic House and Gardens**, overlooking the river from Lechlade Avenue (entry to house by guided tour only May–Aug Wed, Sat & Sun 10am–5pm; Sept–April daily 10am–4.30pm; $12, gardens $5; for bookings call ☏03/9827 2500, ⓦwww.comohouse.com.au). This elegant white mansion, a mixture of Regency and Italianate architectural styles, is a

---

Trams #5, #6, #8 and #72 leave from Swanston Street and run along St Kilda Road, turning left at some point: #72 turns left into Commercial Road, #8 turns left into Toorak Road, #6 turns left at High Street, #5 turn left into Dandenong Road; get off at the corner of these roads and Chapel Street. Prahran and Windsor can be reached by **train**; take the Sandringham train and get off at Prahran or Windsor Station.

good example of the town houses built by wealthy nineteenth-century landowners. The admission fee includes a one-hour tour of the house; the last tour departs at 4pm. To reach the house, walk east along Toorak Road from Chapel Street, and then north on Williams Road; from the city centre, take tram #8 from Swanston Street.

Toorak has never been short of a bean: when Melbourne was founded, the wealthy built their stately homes here on the high bank of the Yarra, leaving the flood-prone lower ground for the poor; in addition, many European Jews who made good after arriving penniless in Australia celebrated their new wealth by moving to Toorak in the 1950s and 1960s. There's little to see or do in the suburb: the hilly, tree-lined streets are full of huge mansions in extensive private gardens, while so-called Toorak Village is stuffed with wickedly expensive designer boutiques.

Prahran and Windsor

Beyond Commercial Road in **Prahran** proper, Chapel Street still focuses on fashion, but in a more street-smart vein, becoming progressively more downmarket as it heads south. Landmarks include **Prahran Market** (Tues, Thurs & Sat dawn–5pm, Fri dawn–6pm, Sun 10am–3pm), round the corner on Commercial Road, an excellent, though expensive, food emporium (fish, meat, fruit, vegetables and delicatessen) plus cafés and a few clothes shops. **Chapel Street Bazaar**, on the western side of Chapel Street, has good secondhand clothes, Art Deco jewellery, furniture and bric-a-brac. Just opposite, tucked away in Little Chapel Street, a lane off Chapel Street, **Chapel off Chapel** (℡ 03/8290 7000) provides a venue for an eclectic mix of theatre performances, music and art exhibitions. Heading a further 100m south along Chapel Street brings you to **Greville Street**, in the heart of Prahran, which has taken over from Chapel Street as the corridor of cutting-edge cool, with retro and designer boutiques, music outlets, bookshops, and groovy bars and restaurants. Things really hot up over the weekend, and every Sunday the small **Greville Street Market** (noon–5pm) has arts, crafts and secondhand clothes and jewellery on the corner of Gratton Street in Gratton Gardens.

As Chapel Street crosses High Street the suburb changes to **Windsor** and becomes more interestingly ethnic. Discount furniture and household-appliance shops sit cheek by jowl with inexpensive Asian noodle bars, organic produce shops and up-and-coming bars. Busy Dandenong Road marks the boundary of Windsor and **East St Kilda**. Just across Dandenong Road on Chapel Street lies the **Astor Theatre**, a beautifully decorated cinema in an Art Nouveau building.

South Melbourne and Albert Park

Stretching southwest of the Yarra River is **South Melbourne**, whose focus is the excellent **South Melbourne Market** on the corner of Coventry and Cecil streets (Wed 8am–4pm, Fri 8am–6pm, Sat & Sun 8am–4pm; tram #96 from Bourke St), an old-fashioned, value-for-money place where you can browse stalls selling everything from fruit and vegetables to clothes, homeware and continental delicacies. Outside on Cecil Street is the famous *South Melbourne dim sum takeaway* – be prepared to queue. Opposite the market, a number of cafés and upmarket retail stores line **Coventry Street**; across the train line, at no. 399, three portable iron houses, prefabricated residences constructed in England and shipped to Melbourne during the goldrush, have been preserved by the National Trust. At the other end of Coventry Street, **Clarendon Street** is South Melbourne's main shopping precinct, and a fine example of a nineteenth-century streetscape, with original Victorian canopies overhanging numerous cafés, clothing shops and restaurants.

Exclusive **Albert Park** has the feel of a small village, with many lovely old terraced houses and Dundas Place, a shopping centre of mouthwatering delis and bakeries. At the end of Victoria Street there's a beach with a narrow strip of sand that continues west to the up-and-coming suburb of Port Melbourne whose Station Pier (tram #109) is home to the Tasmanian Ferry terminal and a number of good restaurants. In the shadow of St Kilda Road, **Albert Park** itself has a golf course, excellent aquatic centre, with its five pools (see p.904), barbecues, restaurant and a boating lake, and is usually teeming with joggers, cyclists and locals picnicking or playing a game of footy. Every year in March thousands of people descend upon the park for the Australian Grand Prix (see p.58).

St Kilda and around

If it's the bay you're heading for, then **St Kilda** is the obvious destination. The former seaside resort has an air of shabby gentility, which enhances its current schizophrenic reputation as a sophisticated yet seedy suburb, largely residential but blessed with a raging nightlife. Running from St Kilda Road down to the Esplanade, **Fitzroy Street** is Melbourne's red-light district – usually pretty tame, though late at night not a comfortable place for women alone – and epitomizes this split personality, since it's lined with dozens of thoroughly pretentious cafés and bars from which to gawp at the strip's goings-on. On weekend nights these and others throughout St Kilda are filled to overflowing with a style-conscious but fun crowd. During the day there's a very different feel, especially on **Acland Street**, with its wonderful continental cake shops and bakeries.

On Sunday, the **Esplanade Arts and Craft Market** (10am–5pm) lines the waterfront on Upper Esplanade. Going there is part of the ritual that includes taking a look at the beach, feeding your face, ambling into a few shops and listening to a busker.

St Kilda's most famous icon, **Luna Park** (May to mid-Sept Sat & Sun 11am–6pm, or daily during school holidays; mid-Sept to April Fri 7–11pm, Sat 11am–11pm, Sun 11am–6pm, or daily during school holidays; ☏1300 888 272, ⓦ www.lunapark.com.au), is located on the Esplanade, entered through the huge, laughing clown's face of "Mr Moon". Despite a couple of new attractions, there's nothing very high-tech about this 1912 amusement park: the Scenic Railway – the world's oldest operating roller-coaster – runs along wooden trestles and the Ghost Train wouldn't spook a toddler – but then that's half the fun. Wandering around is free, but you pay $8 for individual rides, or $37.95 for a day's unlimited rides. You can sit under the palm trees of **O'Donnell Gardens** next door, or nearby **St Kilda Botanical Gardens**, and eat your Acland Street goodies. The **beachfront** is a popular weekend promenade all year round, with separate cycling and walking paths stretching down to Elwood and Brighton, and a long pier thrusting out into the bay. Near the base of the pier is the botched redevelopment of a historic site, the **St Kilda Sea Baths**, which dates back to 1931, a heroically bad mix of shopping complex and function centre with a Moorish twist.

The quickest and most interesting way to get to St Kilda is on the #96 **tram** from Bourke or Spencer streets, which runs on a light-rail track via South Melbourne and Albert Park. Trams #112 from Collins Street and #16 from Swanston Street run to Fitzroy Street.

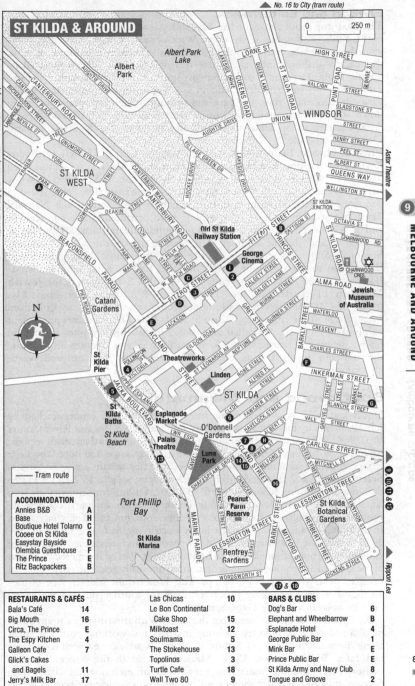

ST KILDA & AROUND

▲ No. 16 to City (tram route)

0 — 250 m

Albert Park Lake

Albert Park

ST KILDA WEST

Old St Kilda Railway Station

George Cinema

WINDSOR

Jewish Museum of Australia

Catani Gardens

St Kilda Pier

Theatreworks

Linden

ST KILDA

St Kilda Baths

St Kilda Beach

Esplanade Market

O'Donnell Gardens

Palais Theatre

Luna Park

Port Phillip Bay

Peanut Farm Reserve

St Kilda Marina

St Kilda Botanical Gardens

Renfrey Gardens

▲ Astor Theatre

▲ Rippon Lea

— Tram route

ACCOMMODATION
Annies B&B	A
Base	H
Boutique Hotel Tolarno	C
Cooee on St Kilda	G
Easystay Bayside	D
Olembia Guesthouse	F
The Prince	E
Ritz Backpackers	B

RESTAURANTS & CAFÉS
Bala's Café	14
Big Mouth	16
Circa, The Prince	E
The Espy Kitchen	4
Galleon Cafe	7
Glick's Cakes and Bagels	11
Jerry's Milk Bar	17
Las Chicas	10
Le Bon Continental Cake Shop	15
Milktoast	12
Soulmama	5
The Stokehouse	13
Topolinos	3
Turtle Cafe	18
Wall Two 80	9

BARS & CLUBS
Dog's Bar	6
Elephant and Wheelbarrow	B
Esplanade Hotel	4
George Public Bar	1
Mink Bar	E
Prince Public Bar	E
St Kilda Army and Navy Club	8
Tongue and Groove	2

Elwood and Elsternwick

The next stop south along the bay, **Elwood**, is a smaller, less colourful version of St Kilda, minus the seedy edge. With scores of high-salaried twenty-somethings moving into the suburb's refurbished apartments in recent years, the slightly shabby, faintly alternative feel of Elwood has been replaced by yuppie bland. Ormond Road, the main street, is now lined with expensive café-restaurants and bars, designed and catering to the tastes of their clientele. Ormond Esplanade runs past parkland through which occasional paths run down to the beach, which is popular with windsurfers. Take tram #96 to Acland Street in St Kilda, then walk south down Barkly Street towards Ormond Esplanade.

East of Elwood, **Elsternwick** (train to Rippon Lea) is a largely Orthodox Jewish area. **Rippon Lea House** at 192 Hotham St (daily 10am–5pm, closed Mon–Wed during winter; $12, garden-only $7; ☎03/9523 6095, ⓦwww .ripponleaestate.com.au) shows how Melbourne's wealthy elite lived a century ago. The 33-room mansion, which is protected by the National Trust, has magnificent gardens, complete with ornamental lake and fernery, and a way-over-the-top interior. The grounds are popular for picnics at weekends, and during summer (Jan–March) when they host "Summer Sessions" (Sun noon–4pm), an afternoon of live music, bocce and wine-tasting. Ten to fifteen minutes' walk away in East St Kilda (also known as Balaclava), at 26 Alma Rd opposite the St Kilda Synagogue, is the **Jewish Museum of Australia** (Tues–Thurs 10am–4pm, Sun 11am–5pm; $10; ☎03/9534 0083, ⓦwww.jewishmuseum.com.au; tram #3 or #67 from Swanston St in the city to stop 32 on St Kilda Rd). The museum's permanent exhibitions focus on Australian and world Jewish history, plus displays on Jewish beliefs and rituals, with a focus on festivals and customs. In addition, the museum regularly puts on special exhibitions that are well worth checking out.

Spotswood and Williamstown

Docks and industry dominate the area west of the city centre, reached by suburban train, by the Williamstown ferry (Williamstown Bay and River Cruises ☎03/9682 9555, ⓦwww.williamstownferries.com.au; for further details see box, p.873), or by heading out on the West Gate Freeway across the huge West Gate Bridge. A good reason for visiting Spotswood, the first suburb across the Yarra, is **Scienceworks**, at 2 Booker St (daily 10am–4.30pm; $6, plus $5 each for Plane-tarium and Lightning Room shows; ☎13 11 02, ⓦhttp://museumvictoria.com .au/scienceworks). Inside a Space Age building, set in appropriately desolate wasteland, the displays and exhibitions are ingenious, fun and highly interactive. In addition, the **Lightning Room** holds electrifying half-hour shows (noon–3pm) explaining the science behind fireworks and featuring high-voltage equipment capable of simulating real lightning bolts. Part of the museum consists of the original Spotswood Pumping Station, an unusually aesthetic early industrial complex with working steam pumps. The Planetarium features state-of-the-art digital technology, taking visitors on a virtual journey through the galaxy (45min shows held hourly 11am–3pm).

On a promontory at the mouth of the Yarra, **Williamstown** is a strange mix of rich and poor: of industry, yachting marinas and working port. The street along the waterfront, named Nelson Place, is nowadays lined with restaurants and cafés. **Williamstown Craft Market** is held in the reserve between Nelson Place and the waterfront (third Sun of each month, 10am–4pm; ⓦwww.williamstowncraftmarket.com.au). The most enjoyable way to get to

Williamstown is by ferry from Southgate in the city with Williamstown Bay and River Cruises; for details, see the box, p.873.

Bulleen and Eltham

Further afield in the northeastern suburbs lie two further attractions: the Heide Museum of Modern Art in **Bulleen** and Montsalvat in **Eltham** – you could make a day of it and visit them en route to the Yarra Valley wineries and the Healesville Sanctuary (see p.218).

The **Heide Museum of Modern Art** (Tues–Fri 10am–5pm, Sat & Sun noon–5pm; $12; ☎03/9850 1500, ⓦwww.heide.com.au) on Templestowe Road in Bulleen was the home of Melbourne art patrons **John Reed** (1901–81) and **Sunday Reed** (1905–81), who in the mid-1930s purchased what was then a derelict dairy farm on the banks of the meandering Yarra River. During the following decades the Reeds fostered and nurtured the talents of young unknown artists and played a central role in the emergence of Australian art movements such as the Angry Penguins, the Antipodeans and the Annandale Realists; the painters Sidney Nolan, John Perceval, Albert Tucker and Arthur Boyd were all members of the artistic circle at Heide at one time or another. The **Heide I Gallery** is set in the farmhouse where the Reeds lived from 1934 until 1967. The gallery exhibits pieces from the museum's extensive collection of paintings and other works purchased by the Reeds over four decades, including works by famous Australian artists of the mid- to late twentieth century, such as Nolan, Perceval and Boyd. Exhibits change every six months. In mid-2006 and at a cost of $3 million, two new galleries, an education centre, an outdoor sculpture area and the restoration of **Heide II** (the later house of John and Sunday built in the mid-1960s) were completed. The most prominent addition is the Albert & Barbara Tucker Gallery (**Heide III**) which features over two hundred artworks from Albert's personal collection. The museum is located 14km from the city centre; take the suburban train to Heidelberg Station (Hurstbridge line) then bus #291 to Templestowe Road (frequent services).

Eltham, a bushy suburb further northeast, about 24km from the city, is known as a centre for **arts and crafts**. Its reputation was established in 1935 when the charismatic painter and architect Justus Jorgensen moved to what was then a separate town and founded **Montsalvat**, a European-style artists' colony. Built with the help of his students and followers, the colony's eclectic design was inspired by medieval European buildings with wonderful quirky results; Jorgensen died before it was completed and it has deliberately been left unfinished. He did, however, live long enough to see his community thrive, and to oversee the completion of the mud-brick Great Hall, whose influence is evident in other mud-brick buildings around Eltham. Today Montsalvat contains a gallery and is still home to a colony of painters and craftspeople (gallery open daily 9am–5pm; $10; ☎03/9439 7712, ⓦwww.montsalvat.com .au). Take a Hurstbridge-line train from Flinders Street Station to Eltham Station, then catch bus #582.

Eating and drinking

Melbourne is Australia's premier city for **eating out**. Sydney may be more style-conscious and Adelaide cheaper, but Melbourne has the best food and the widest choice of cuisines – and almost all of it is exceptionally good value. In the **city centre**, Greek cafés line Lonsdale Street between Swanston and

▲ Melbourne's laneway cafés

Russell streets, while Little Bourke Street is the home of Chinatown. Lygon Street, in inner-city **Carlton**, is just one of many places across the city with a concentration of Italian restaurants. Nearby, Brunswick Street in **Fitzroy** and Smith Street in neighbouring **Collingwood** both have a huge variety of international cuisines as well as trendy bars and cafés. Indeed, Fitzroy and **St Kilda**, another gastronomically mixed bag, are the centres of bar and café society; St Kilda also has great restaurants, bakeries and delis, as does Jewish **Balaclava** (aka East St Kilda). In **Richmond** Vietnamese places dominate Victoria Street, but you'll also find cheap Middle Eastern and Burmese fare. Every year in March, the city celebrates all this culinary diversity with a sixteen-day **Food and Wine Festival** (Ⓦ www.melbournefoodandwine.com.au), with food-themed street parties and events around the city and its environs.

A lot of licensed restaurants still allow you to **bring your own** (BYO) drink, though check first. It is worth noting, however, that most places only allow you to bring in wine, which usually incurs a corkage fee (around $5–10 per bottle. If you're going to be around for a while, *The Age Cheap Eats*, and its more upmarket companion, *The Age Good Food Guide*, are worthwhile investments.

City centre

You can still find the odd old-fashioned **coffee lounge** in the city – the type of place where you can get a milky cappuccino and grilled cheese on toast – but stylish **cafés** with smarter decor and more diverse menus now set the scene. The cheapest places to eat are **food halls** like those in the major department stores and Southgate by the river, while the QV complex on Lonsdale Street also has several good eating places.

The listings below are marked on the **map** on p.856.

Cafés

Café La 35th floor, Hotel Sofitel, corner of Collins and Exhibition sts. Prices at this café are above average but it has the best views in Melbourne, including an incredible one from the toilet. Open daily for breakfast, lunch, dinner, as well as a buffet brunch every Sunday accompanied by live jazz.

Dinkum Pies 29 Block Place. No-frills canteen-style pie shop that does a roaring trade with city workers at lunchtimes. Grab a seat if you can and browse the quirky reading material on the walls in the form of laminated jokes, sayings and email funnies to pass the time. Also does quiche, pastries and cakes. Mon–Thurs 7.30am–4.30pm, Fri 7.30am–5pm.

Hopetoun Tea Rooms Shop2, Block Arcade, 282 Collins St. Traditional tea, scones and delicious cakes have been served in these elegant surroundings for more than one hundred years, but new-fangled delicacies such as focaccia with pesto have now wheedled their way onto the menu. Prices are moderate. Mon–Thurs 9am–5pm, Fri 9am–6pm, Sat 10am–3.30pm.

Koko Black Shop 4 Royal Arcade, 335 Bourke St. A chocoholic's paradise. Watch in awe as the melted chocolate is poured into the moulds before your eyes. The best hot chocolate in town. Branches also at 52 Collins St and 167 Lygon St, Carlton. Mon–Thurs 9am–6pm, Fri 9am–8pm, Sat 10am–6pm, Sun 11am–5.30pm.

Laurent Patisserie 306 Little Collins St (between Collins and Elizabeth sts). Mouthwatering, moderately priced French cakes and pastries, breads, as well as filled baguettes, croissants and soups for lunch. Licensed. Mon–Sat 8am–6pm, Sun 9am–5pm.

Medallion Cafe & Cakes 209 Lonsdale St. Popular Greek café, once shabby, now with an over-the-top, disco-style interior, but still serving authentic, cheap food. Daily 8am until late (3am Fri & Sat).

Pellegrini's Espresso Bar 66 Bourke St. Melbourne's first espresso bar is still an institution, with classic 1950s interior and platefuls of cheap Italian fare (spag bol, risotto, meatballs) presented at the counter at lightning speed. Also good for coffee and home-made cakes. Mon–Sat 8am–11.30pm, Sun noon–8pm.

Restaurants

Bar Lourinha 37 Little Collins St ☎03/9663 7890. It might look like a secluded wine bar, but it's the tapas people come for. Dishes, such as yellow tail

kingfish or house-made chorizo with Nicola potatoes, can be seen being made in the open kitchen (range from $7–18). Mon–Wed noon–11pm, Thurs & Fri noon–1am, Sat 4pm–1am.

Blue Train Café Level 2, Southgate ☎03/0696 0440. One of the many places in the Southgate complex with fine views of the river and the city. Attracts a young, hip crowd and dishes out basic meals like wood-fired pizzas, pasta and salad at reasonable prices. There's also full bar service and plenty of reading material if you're dining solo. Walls display works from local artists. Daily 7am–late.

Chocolate Buddha Federation Square ☎03/9654 5688. A busy space inspired by Japanese canteens serving large portions of inexpensive organic modern Japanese food such as sushi, ramen and donburi on light timber tables. The sake-based cocktails should kick-start your night – but if they don't, you can always look over the sandstone expanse and watch free movies on Fed Square's big screen. Daily noon–1am.

Cookie Level 1, 252 Swanston St ☎03/9663 7660. This place successfully combines cocktail bar, beer hall and Thai restaurant, and serves moderately priced nibbles, salads and full meals, Asian-style, in an upstairs, roomy, modernized former Victorian dining hall. Daily noon–11pm; bar until 3am.

Crossways Food for Life 123 Swanston St ☎03/9650 2939. Dirt-cheap, Indian-style vegetarian food prepared by Hare Krishnas (some practising vows of silence). Nearby is their Gopals at level 1, 139 Swanston St (Mon–Sat 11.30am–8.30pm) which has longer hours. Mon–Sat 11.30am–2.30pm.

ezard 187 Flinders Lane ☎03/9639 6811. This hip, dimly lit place below the Adelphi Hotel is one of Melbourne's coolest eateries, with award-winning chef Teage Ezard's tasty range of East-meets-West favourites. Expensive, with mains from $40 and up. Mon–Fri noon–2.30pm & 6–10.30pm, Sat 6–10.30pm.

Gigi Sushi Bar 237 Swanston St ☎03/9639 2233. Popular with the nearby RMIT students, the sushi

Dining out at Docklands

Melbourne's newest suburb, **Docklands** (see p.874) has a number of glitzy waterside bars and restaurants at the popular district of **NewQuay**, many with fantastic panoramic views of the city and the Bolte Bridge. For high-quality Indian food try Bhoj Docklands (☎03/9600 0884) while for super fresh Mediterranean-style seafood you should head to Livebait (☎03/9642 1500). Mecca Bah (☎03/9642 1300) serves mouthwatering modern Middle Eastern treats and has an outdoor deck, which is perfect for sharing meze platters and watching the boats cruise by.

rolls here are larger than similar outlets around town but just as cheap ($2.30). Get a seat outside on the footpath before others do. Daily 10am–11pm.

Grossi Florentino 80 Bourke St ⓣ03/9662 1811. A Melbourne institution. Downstairs the grill restaurant (moderate) and the adjacent cellar bar (inexpensive), serve home-style pasta dishes, drinks and good coffee, while upstairs is a very pricey and elegant Italian restaurant that's been synonymous with fine dining for many years. Cellar bar Mon–Sat 7.30am–late, restaurant Mon–Fri noon–3pm & 6–11pm, Sat 6–11pm.

MoVida 1 Hosier Lane ⓣ03/9663 3038. Tables are scarce at this popular tapas bar/restaurant but grab a seat at the bar or on the couch and soak up the Spanish flavours. Spanish beers and wine complete the vibe. Tapas $3–7.50. Daily noon–3pm, 5pm–late.

Stalactites 177 Lonsdale St ⓣ03/9663 3316. Operating for over thirty years, the recently spruced-up *Stalactites* serves cheap giros, souvlaki, moussaka and *saganaki* (traditional deep-fried cheese), all dished up in huge portions in a congenial dining area. Most Melburnians have eaten here at least once in their life. Daily 24hr.

Syracuse 23 Bank Place ⓣ03/9670 1777. Situated in a small laneway, *Syracuse's* bright interior is immediately timeless, from its arched ceiling, large wall mirrors, bentwood chairs and wood racks stacked with wine bottles. Come for mouthwatering tapas (served from 3pm), among other dishes, then top it off with fantastic cheese plates, crème caramel and coffee. There's also an extensive wine list and seductive atmosphere.

Mains start at $28. Licensed. Mon–Fri 7.30am–11pm, Sat 6–11pm.

Taxi Dining Room Level 1, Federation Square ⓣ03/9654 8808. Above *Transport* (see p.895), the high ceilings and open windows of this highly designed eatery give a stunning perspective on the city and the Yarra, while the Modern Australian/Japanese food is equally impressive. Alternatively, you can just grab a beer or sake and watch the city lights blur. Daily noon–11pm.

Vue De Monde 430 Little Collins St ⓣ03/9691 3888. Regarded as one of the country's best restaurants, chef Shannon Bennett has blended fine French cuisine with contemporary imagination. It's not cheap (although a 2-course lunch deal is a steal at $55) but you would struggle to find better anywhere. Also excellent value is the lunch box that can be purchased next door at *Café Vue*. Tues–Fri noon–2pm & 6.30–10pm, Sat 6.30–10pm.

Walter's Wine Bar Level 3, Southgate ⓣ03/9690 9211. Long-established restaurant-cum-wine bar, *Walter's* has been preparing excellent contemporary bistro food for over fifteen years. This, combined with knowledgeable staff, good Australian wines by the glass and superb views across the Yarra to the city, makes this a popular choice for breakfast, lunch or post-theatre. Mon–Fri 9am–late, Sat & Sun 8am–late.

William Angliss College 550 Little Lonsdale St ⓣ03/9606 2108. Owned by a catering college, this cheap restaurant aims to dish up fine food and service, and usually succeeds, though occasional hiccups may occur. Two- and three-course lunch $19/26, dinner $25/33. Bookings essential. Open during term time for lunch Mon–Fri and dinner Mon–Thurs.

Chinatown

Yum cha (elsewhere known as dim sum, a series of small delicacies served from trolleys) is available at lunchtime almost everywhere in Chinatown; on Sunday it's a crowded ritual.

The listings below are marked on the **map** on p.856.

Camy Shanghai Dumpling and Noodle Restaurant Tattersalls Lane, between Little Bourke and Lonsdale sts, close to Swanston St ⓣ03/9663 8555. An extremely cheap, partly self-service place, dishing up very simple but delicious dumplings and noodles, with veggie meals available too. Daily 11am–10pm.

China Bar 235 Russell St ⓣ03/9639 1633. Cheap chain with lots of Malaysian-Chinese noodle or rice fast-food classics such as won ton soup, *char kway teow* (fried rice noodles), *nasi lemak* (coconut rice); plus assorted claypot dishes and desserts. BYO.

Other branches at 747 Swanston St, Carlton, and Jam Factory, South Yarra. Mains start at $12. Sun–Thurs 11am–3pm, Fri & Sat 11am–6pm.

Flower Drum 17 Market Lane, between Bourke and Little Bourke sts ⓣ03/9662 3655. This capacious restaurant is quite simply the finest Chinese restaurant in Melbourne, if not Australia. Its sophisticated Cantonese cuisine (Peking duck, dumplings, Hainanese pork, *yi-meen* noodles) and discreet service from an army of waiting staff have garnered it a clutch of top awards. Naturally, this all comes at a price: expect to pay at least $80 per person for three courses. Mon–Sat noon–3pm & 6–10pm, Sun 6–10pm.

Hofbrauhaus 18 Market Lane ☎03/9663 3361. If you're not in the mood for Asian food, head here for large servings of Bavarian fare, including whopping schnitzels and fatty sausages. Help it all down with some German beer on tap, because the other patrons will be. Also provides knee-slapping entertainment Tues–Sun evenings. Lunch Mon–Fri, dinner daily. Mains $22–29.

Kun Ming Restaurant 212 Little Bourke St ☎03/9663 1851. The laminate tables may have gone, to be replaced with smart waiters and table-cloths, but the food is still some of the tastiest you'll find on this busy Chinatown strip, and the prices remain low. Excellent lunch specials for under $10. Daily 11.30am–3pm & 5.30–10pm.

Shark Fin House 131 Little Bourke St ☎03/9663 1555. Award-winning *yum cha* specialists located in a converted three-storey warehouse that is the quintessential Chinese eating experience: preposterously loud, closely packed tables, adrenaline-charged waiters and queues of people waiting to be seated. Mon–Fri 11.30am–3pm & 5.30–11pm, Sat & Sun 11am–3pm & 5.30–11pm.

Supper Inn 15 Celestial Ave ☎03/9663 4759. The decor may be dated but the generous Cantonese food is worth the climb up those stairs. The menu is large, with plenty of unusual options, and the kitchen stays open till very, very late, making it a favourite for those in the hospitality trade. Daily 5.30pm–2.30am.

Northern suburbs

The listings below are marked on the **map** on p.856.

Carlton

Lygon Street, between Grattan and Elgin streets, is mainly wall-to-wall Italian pizza and pasta restaurants spilling out on the footpath, and on most evenings all but the most resolute-looking passers-by are accosted by their touts. *Really* good restaurants are few and far between here, but cheap Asian noodle-bars, catering to the large number of Asian students at Melbourne Uni and the RMIT, are cropping up every month.

Abla's 109 Elgin St ☎03/9347 0006. A homely restaurant serving some of the best Lebanese food in town. The twelve-course banquet (compulsory on Thurs, Fri and Sat nights) for $50 is magnificent. Mon–Wed & Sat 6–11pm Thurs & Fri noon–3pm & 6–11pm.

Big Harvest 151 Elgin St ☎03/9348 0066. Super-small shop with a sole communal table that only seats about 6 people, but this place is all about quality food (they specialize in catering). Great range of specials on the board with a Middle-Eastern slant and coffee that rivals those nearby. Mon–Fri 7.30am–5pm, Sat 8am–3.30pm.

Brunetti 194–204 Faraday St ☎03/9347 2801. What began as a cake shop over twenty years ago is now a café, licensed restaurant, paninoteca, gelateria and pasticceria with an array of display cases filled with a mouthwatering selection of chocolates, pastries, biscuits and cakes, plus coffee. Mon–Thurs & Sun 6.30am–11pm, Fri & Sat 6.30am–midnight.

Jimmy Watson's 333 Lygon St ☎03/9347 3985. Formerly a wine salon, this Lygon St icon has survived the vagaries of Melbourne's food and drinking trends, and still attracts locals, academics, students and anyone who loves a tipple. The strengths are its very good bar meals (modern

Australian cuisine) in convivial, atmospheric surroundings, and a super wine list. Moderate prices. Mon 10.30am–6pm, Tues–Sat 10.30am–late.

Shakahari 201–203 Faraday St ☎03/9347 3848. Excellent and imaginative Asian-influenced vegetarian food such as satays, pasta, curries and laksas at moderate prices. Menu changes according to season. Licensed. Mon–Thurs noon–3pm & 6–9.30pm, Fri & Sat noon–3pm & 6–10pm, Sun 6–9.30pm.

Tiamo 1 303 Lygon St ☎03/9347 5759. One-time beatnik hangout that is still popular with students, with layers of browning 1950s posters and a good-value blackboard menu. The food, including favourites such as lasagne and carbonara, isn't flash but is filling and hearty. Next door is its sibling, which offers a slightly more modern approach to its menu, but is still excellent value. Mon–Sat 7am–11pm, Sun 8am–10pm.

Toto's Pizza House 101 Lygon St ☎03/9347 1630. Melbourne's first pizzeria, dating from the 1950s, serving decent no-frills pizza towards the city end of Lygon St – don't come here looking for an authentic mama's trattoria experience, however. Licensed. Daily noon–11pm.

Fitzroy

Adjacent Fitzroy's focal point, grungy **Brunswick Street**, is packed with great cafés and pubs, while running at right angles across it is **Johnston Street**, known for its Spanish influence and late-night bars. Dissecting Brunswick Street to the south, **Gertrude Street** is fast becoming a chic hub for Melbourne's artistic community and has a couple of cool pubs and cafés.

Arcadia 193 Gertrude St ☎03/9416 1055. Bright, open café with blackboard specials and delicious hearty soups, pasta and focaccia. A popular local hangout; take a seat at the large communal table if you're feeling sociable or nab a seat at the front window for a spot of people-watching. Mon–Fri 8am–5pm, Sat & Sun 9am–5pm.

Babka Bakery Cafe 358 Brunswick St ☎03/9416 0091. A deservedly popular place: the home-made bread and cakes are divine, and dishes from the changing blackboard menu are equally enticing. Try Russian blintzes for breakfast or *borscht* (a tangy, beetroot-based soup) and sourdough bread for lunch. Moderate. Licensed and BYO. Tues–Sun 7am–7pm.

Bimbo Deluxe 376 Brunswick St ☎03/9419 8600. An endless procession of super-cheap and delicious pizzas (only $4 for lunch Mon–Fri and dinner Sun–Thurs) plus a few other favourites keep the diners coming back again and again, so you may need to wait for a table. The large, dimly lit bar out back keeps the drinkers and pool sharks happy. DJs play most nights. Daily noon–3am.

Fitz Curry Cafe 44 Johnston St ☎03/9495 6119. Small, no-frills curry house that dishes up delicious, organic food at low prices. Takeaway available. Licensed and BYO (wine only). Daily 5–10pm.

Ladro 224 Gertrude St ☎03/9415 7575. Sensational yet simple authentic Italian-style pizzas that have won over thousands throughout the city. Booking is essential but takeaway available. Pizzas from $14. Tues–Sun 6pm–late.

Madame Sousou 231 Brunswick St ☎03/9417 0400. Step inside this corner restaurant and you'll feel like you've walked into a Parisian café. From the posters lining the walls and the large chandeliers, the atmosphere is elegantly chic and inviting. The menu naturally has a heavy French influence, but also features risotto and gnocchi. Tues–Sun 9am–late.

Mario's 303 Brunswick St ☎03/9417 3343. If you want to get a true feel of Brunswick St come for brekkie (served until midnight) in this 1950s European-style café with wood counters and tiled floors. While waiting for a seat (it gets very busy at weekends), you can browse the bookstores down the road. Service is always friendly and efficient. Mon–Wed & Sun 7am–midnight, Thurs–Sat 7am–1am.

Thai Thani 293 Brunswick St ☎03/9419 6463. One of Melbourne's best Thai restaurants, on two crowded levels, with moderate prices. Licensed and BYO (wine only). Daily 6–10.30pm.

🏃 **The Vegie Bar** 380 Brunswick St t03/9417 6935. Cheap, popular and hip (rather than hippie) place with simple, fresh vegetarian and vegan food. Licensed and BYO (wine only). Daily 11am–10pm.

Eastern suburbs: Collingwood and Richmond

Swan Street, running from Church Street towards Wattle Park, is home to Greek restaurants, while **Victoria Street**, separating Richmond from Abbotsford, is lined with Vietnamese supermarkets, clothes shops and dozens of cheap, authentic restaurants. Adjacent Collingwood's **Smith Street** also has a burgeoning café scene.

🏃 **Booktalk Café** 91 Swan St, Richmond ☎03/9428 1977. Pop in for great deals on new and secondhand books and discover a fantastic café nestled within. The atmosphere is relaxed and social while the food is wholesome, hearty and cooked daily – choose from dishes such as vegetable frittata, tuna bake, Mediterranean roti, shepherd's pie – plus excellent coffee and cakes. Cheap. Mon–Fri 7.30am–5.30pm, Sat & Sun 8.30am–5.30pm.

Gluttony – It's a Sin 278 Smith St, Collingwood ☎03/9416 0336. Frequented by locals who come here for great breakfasts, lunches and gluten-free cakes, all served in large portions. Licensed and BYO. Mon–Fri 7am–11pm, Sat & Sun 8am–9.30pm.

Ha Long Bay 82 Victoria St, Richmond ☎03/9429 3268. If you're searching for a good Vietnamese restaurant on Victoria St then this is it. Ignore the lurid lime walls – you won't be sitting here long enough for them to take effect – and concentrate on choosing something from the long, long list of dishes. Cheap corkage, plus lunch specials for less than $10. Daily 10am–11pm.

Pacific Seafood BBQ House 240 Victoria St, Richmond ℡03/9427 8225. Despite the name, duck is a particular favourite here, though if that's not your taste go to the tanks and pick which fish to devour. Great ambience and reasonable prices. Licensed and BYO. Mon–Thurs & Sun 10.30am–10.30pm, Fri & Sat 10am–11.30pm.

Soul Food Cafe 273 Smith St, Collingwood ℡03/9419 2949. Large vegetarian café serving a pleasing menu of salads, burgers, curry, *tagines*, *rotis* and risotto, and pumpkin in many variations. Small bar with a few comfy chairs at the back. Mon–Thurs 8am–9pm, Sat & Sun 9am–6pm.

Thy Thy 1 Level 1, 142 Victoria St, Richmond ℡03/9420 1104. Climb the stairs to one of the most popular Vietnamese restaurants in Melbourne. The food, which includes crispy spring rolls, noodles and chicken dishes, is basic but great. Daily 8am–10pm.

Tofu Shop International 78 Bridge Rd, Richmond ℡03/9429 6204. This tiny place has been going for years, serving consistently delicious vegetarian meals to eat in or take away. Treat your body to salads, pasta, stews and tofu (all freshly made on the premises), or try the spring rolls or a "*soyvlaki*" – a massive wrap filled with a choice of salads. Food is ordered according to plate size and prices include dips and ginger. Usually shoulder to shoulder at the counter seats at lunchtimes. Mon–Fri noon–9pm, Sat noon–5pm.

Vlado's 61 Bridge Rd, Richmond ℡03/9428 5833. Vegetarians don't bother. Sausages, hamburger, liver, steak, you name it – if it has four legs it'll end up on long-established *Vlado*'s set-price four-course menu ($80). Heaven for carnivores, the wine list here supports the simple fleshy cuisine. Mon–Fri noon–3pm & 6–11pm, Sat 6–11pm.

Southern suburbs

South Yarra, Prahran and Windsor

Botanical 169 Domain Rd, South Yarra ℡03/9820 7800. Bright, modern restaurant opposite the Botanic Gardens, whose open kitchen offers a sneak peek at chef Paul Wilson's bold signature dishes. If your wallet won't stretch to dinner try the superb breakfasts or the tasty grazing menu with wines by the glass in the adjacent café. There's also a wine shop, and a sleek bar for late-night shenanigans. Mon–Fri 7am–11pm, Sat & Sun 8am–11pm.

Caffe e Cucina 581 Chapel St, South Yarra ℡03/9827 4139. Became the benchmark for Melbourne's restaurant/café style when it opened in 1988, and has spawned a score of imitators with its wood panelling, cute little table lamps and a creative menu written up on a central blackboard. Today it's still one of Melbourne's coolest eating spots, attracting a smart clientele and dishing up fantastic pasta. Licensed. Daily 11.30am–11pm.

Globe Cafe 218 Chapel St, Prahran ℡03/9510 8693. Serves breakfast all day, and has great cakes and bread made on the premises – you're bound to find something on the menu to sate your appetite. Moderate. Licensed. Mon–Fri 8am–late, Sat & Sun 9am–late.

Lucky Coq 179 Chapel St, Windsor ℡03/9525 1288. Renovated pub that has a grungy, bohemian-type feel. Serves excellent gourmet pizzas for just $4 (noon–4pm Sun–Fri) and around $8 at other times. Open noon–3am, making it the prime destination for partygoers.

Jacques Reymond 78 Williams Rd, Prahran ℡03/9525 2178. Jacques Reymond's shrine to fine food brings together eclectic ingredients from Europe, Australia, Asia and the Pacific to startling effect. The space is glamorous and striking, while the menu focuses on small-plate three-, four- or five-course fixed-price menus ($98/$125/$150). There's also a seven-course degustation menu ($150). Tram #64 from Swanston St. Tues, Wed & Sat 6.30–10pm, Thurs & Fri noon–2pm & 6.30–10pm.

Orange 126 Chapel St, Windsor ℡03/9529 1644. Epitomizes the grunge-chic of the Windsor end of Chapel St. Great place to chill out; they serve breakfast all day, light meals for lunch and more substantial fare for dinner, or relax with a cocktail or two until the wee hours. Great garden out the back. Daily 7am–late.

Patersons Cakes & Café 117 Chapel St, Windsor ℡03/9510 8541. This long-established, renowned cake and pastry shop now also runs a good café on the premises. Mon–Fri 9am–5pm, Sat till 3pm.

Sweet Basil 209 Commercial Rd, South Yarra ℡03/9827 3390. Delicious modern Thai cuisine served in simple, relaxed surroundings ensures a loyal following. Choose from an extensive menu featuring contemporary delights such as pumpkin-flavoured steamed dumplings with chicken or crispy stir-fried quail as well as more familiar favourites. Excellent veggie options too. Tues–Sun 6–10pm.

South Melbourne, Albert Park and Port Melbourne

The night-time scene in these suburbs is rather low-key, but there are cafés and delicatessens aplenty dishing up a mouthwatering selection of food during the day.

Andrew's Hamburgers 144 Bridport St, Albert Park ☎03/9690 2126. Much-loved and extremely low-key hamburger shop which serves them big and fatty with all the trimmings. Prices around $7.

Bell's Hotel & Brewery 157 Moray St, South Melbourne ☎03/9690 4511. Typical pub with good chicken parma, burgers and the usual fare, but most people come for their exceptional, award-winning homebrews. Mon–Sat 11am–late, Sun 11am–5pm.

Cafe Sweethearts 263 Coventry St, South Melbourne ☎03/9690 6752. Breakfasts are the order of the day at this sunny corner café, in particular eggs in a variety of ways. Also does lunches that are a cut above your usual café fare. Mon–Fri 7am–3pm, Sat & Sun 8am–3pm.

Dundas & Faussett Corner of Dundas Place and Faussett St, Albert Park ☎03/9645 5155. Large, funky café in the heart of Albert Park village, with an extensive menu that runs the gamut from eggs, pasta, focaccia, noodles and laksa. Great if you fancy something different, and the outside tables occupy the best spot on this busy strip. Mon–Fri 6am–9pm, Sat & Sun 6am–5pm.

Feedings at Readings 253 Bay St, Port Melbourne ☎03/9681 9255. An irresistible bookshop with a licensed café – browse, and read the first pages of your newly acquired book on the café terrace, perched a few steps above Bay St. Daily 9am–6pm.

🏃 **Kamel** 19 Victoria Ave, Albert Park ☎03/9696 1386. Cosy Middle Eastern restaurant with a delectable menu to match. Choose one of the delicious mezes, seafood or grill dishes, and there's also a good vegetarian selection. Mon–Thurs 5.30–10pm, Fri–Sun 8am–3pm, 5.30–10pm.

Misuzu's 7 Victoria Ave, Albert Park ☎03/9699 9022. Pleasant Japanese eatery and very modestly priced given the location. Warm and inviting from the pretty lanterns hanging outside to the dark wood interior, with a menu that ranges from sushi and sashimi to Japanese curries and tasty noodle soups; the extensive sake menu won't disappoint either. Daily noon–10pm.

St Kilda

This suburb's café scene and nightlife revolve around **Acland Street** and **Fitzroy Street**. While the former is good for browsing in shops, for late breakfast and for pigging out on cakes, the latter, especially the block from Grey Street to the waterfront, arguably has the edge on vibrant nightlife.

The listings below are marked on the **map** on p.883.

Bala's Café 1C Shakespeare Grove ☎03/9534 6116. Excellent, cheap Asian takeaway food, including lassis and lots of stir-fried dishes with ultra-fresh ingredients. There are a few tables if you want to eat in, though it gets very busy at lunch and dinner. Daily noon–10pm.

Big Mouth Corner of Acland and Barkly sts ☎03/9534 4611. A great spot for people-watching. The café downstairs is open for breakfast and light meals from 7am till 3am, while the upstairs restaurant (modern Australian cuisine) is open Monday to Friday 5pm–1am, Saturday 10am–late, and Sunday 10.30am–late. Licensed.

Circa, the Prince 2 Acland St ☎03/9536 1122. Part of *The Prince* establishment (see *Mink Bar* and *Prince Public Bar*), this is still one of Melbourne's best spots for fine dining, boasting a magnificently theatrical fit-out and excellent modern food with an award-winning wine list. Mon–Fri & Sun 7–11am, daily noon–3pm & 6.30pm–late.

The Espy Kitchen *Esplanade Hotel*, 11 Upper Esplanade ☎03/9534 0211. Decent pub-style food, especially their burgers ($10 with a pot of beer on Mondays). Mon–Wed 5–11pm, Thurs 5pm–late, Fri noon–late, Sat & Sun 8am–late.

Galleon Cafe 9 Carlisle St ☎03/9534 8934. Breakfast, served until 4pm, is the big attraction in this retro-style café, which is especially popular at weekends. Licensed and BYO. Daily 7am–5pm.

Le Bon Continental Cake Shop 93 Acland St ☎03/9534 2515. Fifty-year-old store, that never fails to tempt the hundreds of passers-by with its array of delicious Mediterranean-influenced cakes and pastries. Daily 8am–11pm.

🏃 **Milktoast** 115 Carlisle St ☎03/9531 3527. The front counter at this café groans with freshly made pastas and salads and pides to die for (try the pumpkin, pea, spinach and feta salad or olive tapenade with salami and sun-dried tomato). From the kitchen there are risottos along with burgers and excellent breakfasts. Mon–Sat 7.30am–5pm.

Soulmama Level 1, St Kilda Sea Baths, 10 Jacka Blvd ☎03/9525 3338. Large, glam vegetarian open-plan café, serving wholesome food in three bowl sizes, including beetroot in tahini and zesty tofu curries. Great beach views from the open beachfront terrace, couch seating and a formidable drinks list make this the perfect place to hole up for the afternoon with a group of friends. Daily noon–late.
The Stokehouse 30 Jacka Blvd ☎03/9525 5555. Right by the beach (it gets packed in warm weather), this restaurant has two sections: a very

affordable downstairs section with lots of unusual pizzas and pastas, fantastic cakes, coffee and wines; and a pricier upstairs section with superb views of the bay and excellent Italian-inspired food, with plenty of seafood. Downstairs open daily noon–late, upstairs daily noon–2.30pm & 6–10pm.
Topolinos 87 Fitzroy St ☎03/9534 1925. A dimly lit and noisy St Kilda institution, which churns out cheap pizzas, generous portions of pasta and good cocktails until very late. Mon–Wed 4pm–1am, Thurs–Sun noon–3am.

Elwood and Balaclava

Elwood's Ormond Street sports wall-to-wall trendy cafés, whereas **Balaclava**, along Carlisle Street, is catching up, but still manages to retain a bit of its old migrant atmosphere.

Las Chicas 203 Carlisle St, Balaclava ☎03/9531 3699. Bright and bustling café that's almost too cool for school but thankfully free of all pretension. On-the-ball staff buzz around its funky brick interior, delivering huge sandwiches, breakfasts, excellent cakes and good coffee to diners who fill every available space. Daily 7am–5pm.
Glick's Cakes and Bagels 330A Carlisle St, Balaclava ☎03/9527 2198. Friendly bakery renowned for bagels and traditional Jewish savouries: try the *kreplach*, *latkes* or *gefilte fish*. Daily 5am–8pm.
Jerry's Milk Bar 345 Barkly St, Elwood ☎03/9531 3078. Cornershop milkbar-cum-café brimming with old-fashioned trappings and locals who come for the cheap delicious soups,

pasta and risotto. Mon–Sat 7am–5pm, Sun 8am–5pm.
Turtle Cafe 34 Glenhuntly Rd, Elwood ☎03/9525 6952. Relaxed, old-corner café that attracts a faithful crowd for breakfast and light meals and snacks including bagels, focaccia, soups and salads, all at moderate prices. Mon–Fri 7am–3pm & 5–11pm, Sat & Sun 7am–6pm.
Wall Two 80 280 Carlisle St (rear), Balaclava ☎03/9539 8280. This former kosher butcher's shop is a simple hole-in-the-wall café that has become the coffee lifeline for those that can find it. Also does simple but delicious food (mostly toasted pides and breakfasts). Inside is a series of small alcoves and a larger space dominated by a wooden communal table, perfect for chitchat. Daily 6.30am–6pm.

Nightlife and entertainment

Melbourne has a rich arts and music scene, and there's always plenty to do in the evening. To find out **what's on**, check out *The Age* on Friday, when the newspaper publishes the small entertainment supplement, "EG". Also check out the great free magazines *Beat* and *Inpress*, which you can pick up at most record shops, cinemas and cafés. For those on a budget looking for the best food and drink specials try the witty ⓦwww.thehappiesthour.com. In 2007 the government introduced a **smoking ban** in all pubs, bars, restaurants and enclosed spaces; as a consequence many establishments responded by adding outside smoking areas, heated with butane lamps in winter.

Annual **festivals** further enliven the scene: the **Melbourne International Arts Festival** (ⓦwww.melbournefestival.com.au) in October presents a selection of visual and performing arts, opera, and features individual performers from Australia and overseas, as well as a host of free events at Federation Square and other places around the city. The more innovative and cutting-edge **Melbourne Fringe Festival** (ⓦwww.melbournefringe.com .au) starts in late September and overlaps a few days with the Melbourne Festival, while the **Melbourne Writers' Festival** (ⓦwww.mwf.com.au)

takes place in late August. The heavily promoted **Moomba Festival** (Ⓦwww .melbournemoombafestival.com.au), held in March, has a more commercial, "fun for the masses" approach, featuring events such as firework displays and dragon-boat races on the banks of the Yarra River in Alexandra Gardens, and Docklands. Three popular outdoor **music festivals** take place in summer: **Summadayze** on January 1 featuring international bands and DJs; the **Big Day Out** on January 26; and **Good Vibrations** in early February. Other events include the **Brunswick Music Festival** in the third week of March, concentrating on folk and world music, and the **St Kilda Festival** which runs for one week early February featuring music, comedy and street perform-ances. The biennial **Next Wave Festival**, held over two weeks in the second half of May (the next one is in 2010), celebrates Victoria's young artists, writers and musicians.

Tickets for most venues can be booked through Ticketmaster (Ⓣ13 61 00, Ⓦwww.ticketmaster.com.au) or Ticketek (Ⓣ13 28 49, Ⓦwww.premier .ticketek.com.au); both take credit-card bookings only. You can buy tickets half-price on the day of performance from Half Tix at Melbourne Town Hall (Mon 10am–2pm, Tues–Thurs 11am–6pm, Fri 11am–6.30pm, Sat 10am–4pm; cash only; Ⓦwww.halftixmelbourne.com).

Bars and pubs

Melbourne's fondness for a drink or three is reflected in its abundance of excellent **bars and pubs** – from places so obscure and cutting-edge you'll only know they exist by word of mouth, to large establishments catering to broader and louder tastes. In general, bars stay **open** to around 1am during the week and 3am at weekends, while some clubs are open until 5am or 7am at the weekend. Some of the more upmarket places have **dress codes** which are often rigidly enforced. A number of drinking places are also listed under "Live music", below. For online guides to the city's drinking spots visit Ⓦwww.melbournepubs.com or Ⓦwww.barfinder.com.au.

City centre

The listings below are marked on the **map** on p.856.

Belgian Beer Café 557 St Kilda Rd. A rare find in St Kilda Rd's sterile office territory: a European-style beer hall in a historic bluestone building set back from the street. Convivial and comfortable in a rustic sort of way but definitely not downmarket. Unusual Belgian beers on tap and a food menu featuring well-prepared, solid European fare. Great beer garden in summer. Only drawback: prices are rather steep.

Elms Family Hotel 269 Spring St. Somebody dropped a country pub in the middle of the CBD. A real bet on the races and have a few cold beers kind of pub, where getting dressed in more than a T-shirt is frowned upon. The food prices are stuck in the 1980s (big steak sandwich for $7.50) and there is a nice little heated beer garden.

Gin Palace 190 Little Collins St (entry via Russell Place). Glamorous subterranean joint with an upmarket drinks-list specializing in cocktails, especially Martinis – not cheap, but delicious and generous. Yummy food and good lounge music, too.

Madame Brussels Level 3, 59 Bourke St. Feels like something out of a David Lynch film, with fake grass and tacky outdoor banana-lounges – and that's inside. Outside, the fantastic beer-garden patio looks through to the city spires. Cocktails come in jugs.

Mai Tai Hawaii Cocktail Bar 234 Russell St. It may feel like a time warp back to the 1980s, but this place, a section of a Thai restaurant, is so completely daggy it just has to be cool. Tasty cocktails complete the picture.

Melbourne Supper Club Level 1, 161 Spring St. Lounge bar with comfy couches that manages to be elegant and laid-back at the same time. Cocktails range from affordable to expensive and there's an extensive wine list; a range of tasty snacks such as veal meatballs or polenta cakes will keep the hunger at bay.

Meyers Place 20 Meyers Place, off Bourke St. This swish, dimly lit hole-in-the-wall bar has proved a massive hit with those in the know and

Melbourne's trendy office-workers who often spill out into the laneway.

Pugg Mahone 106–112 Hardware St. Another Irish theme-pub, with a great party atmosphere of office workers and backpackers, especially on Monday, Friday and Saturday nights when there's live music. Great happy hours as well.

St Jerome's 7 Caledonian Lane. Hard to find but that's the appeal. Dark little entrance leads to a great little outside area in a converted lane. Cheap longneck beers so expect to see fewer business types, more artists and students. Home to the excellent St Jerome's Laneway Festival (ⓦ www.lanewayfestival.com.au) in February.

Tony Starr's Kitten Club 267 Little Collins St. The sleek and stylish Love Lounge is tricked out with slightly oriental furnishings, conducive to lolling on comfy sofas and ottomans while cradling a cocktail and nibbling on Asian-inspired food from the grill, while the Galaxy Space with its retro-style interior hosts cabaret nights.

Transport Federation Square. Enormous pub complex with a staggering range of beers and good local wines. Noisy and fun with DJs and live music most nights, it attracts a mixed crowd of suits, tourists and film-school students. The windows of the airy ground-level pub look out on to St Kilda Rd – a great place for people-watching. Above is the excellent *Taxi Dining Room* (see p.888).

Carlton and Fitzroy

The listings below are marked on the **map** on p.856.

Builders Arms 211 Gertrude St, Fitzroy. Laid-back and unpretentious atmosphere that's more trendy bar than local pub. Guest DJs on weekends and the occasional weekday.

Hotel Lincoln 91 Cardigan St, Carlton. Friendly, revamped corner pub where you can order inexpensive dishes from a blackboard menu in the dining room and wines by the glass from an excellent wine list.

Lambsgo Bar 135 Greeves St, Fitzroy. This unassuming bluestone cottage, tucked off Smith St, is a beer-lover's dream, with over 100 local and imported brews to choose from. Dark and cosy, with quirky amusement machines and art

on the walls, it's a cult favourite of the locals in the know.

Napier Hotel 210 Napier, Fitzroy. Old-school Fitzroy pub that is always busy due to the relaxed surroundings and incredibly enormous meal portions. Try if you dare to finish their Bogan Burger (includes chicken schnitzel, steak, egg, potato cake, beetroot and salad) or just sit in their small, relaxing beer garden.

The Old Bar 74 Johnston St, Fitzroy. Lived-in bar that has an eclectic weekly schedule of live music, DJs, quiz nights, comedy and the odd cult movie; plus $10 jugs. Cover charge may apply some nights.

Collingwood and Richmond

Der Raum 438 Church St, Richmond. German for "the space", this is actually a small, groovy cocktail bar – the Martinis, in particular, are well worth crossing town for.

Great Britain 477 Church St, Richmond. Excellent pub that is hugely popular with the university-student brigade. Has an array of funky couches and chairs, pool tables and a brand-new beer garden for those long, hot nights. Ask for their famous

homebrewed beer on tap called PISS (light beer is called PISS WEAK), which goes down a treat.

The Horn 20 Johnston St, Collingwood ☏ 03/9417 4670. African music lounge that rambles through three rooms out the back of a converted house and plays host to live jazz, African, ska and reggae bands most nights. There's also a kitchen serving cheap Ethiopian food, with a good selection of veggie dishes.

South Yarra and Windsor

Back Bar 67 Green St, off Chapel St, Windsor. Opulent lounge bar reminiscent of a grand manor drawing room, with rich red furnishings, soft cushioned couches, gilt mirrors and a roaring log fire in winter. Upstairs the gold lounge offers much the same but in, you guessed it, gold, with DJs

spinning house and upbeat tunes at weekends till the small hours. Renowned for its relaxed, friendly vibe and excellent cocktail list, you won't want to leave.

Bridie O'Reilly's 462 Chapel St, South Yarra. Irish-themed pub incongruously housed in an old church and saved from terminal tackiness by the pleasant front patio. Has meals and plenty of memorabilia from the Emerald Isle. Can get raucous on

weekends, but fun if you're desperate for a Guinness or British beer.

St Kilda

The listings below are marked on the **map** on p.883.

Dog's Bar 54 Acland St. Chic setting attracting a dedicated clientele. The wine list is terrific and there's great food. The wrought-iron terrace out front is the perfect place for eyeballing passers-by, especially on a sunny afternoon.

Elephant and Wheelbarrow 169 Fitzroy St. Corny English theme-pub that is enormously popular with backpackers looking for love and good times. Has cover bands playing on the weekend and special events during the week such as "Meet the Neighbours" on Mondays, when the cast of the soap play trivia games and generally rub shoulders with the punters.

The Esplanade Hotel 11 Upper Esplanade. Famous for its beachside views, this hotel is the epicentre of St Kilda's drinking scene and shouldn't be missed. Bands play every night and there are inexpensive meals from The Espy Kitchen at the rear, plus pool tables and pinball machines.

The George Public Bar 127 Fitzroy St. Long-established underground bar with an upbeat design. Favoured by locals, it has a large range of beers on tap, a pool table, free live music on Saturday and Sunday, and a trivia night every Monday. The service is friendly and the kitchen is open until late each night, serving a wide range of snacks and good-value meals. Table seats outside.

Mink Bar At *The Prince*, 2B Acland St, St Kilda. Carved out of *The Prince* hotel-bar-restaurant complex, this subterranean vodka-bar has back-lit refrigerated shelves stacked high with an astonishing array of Russian, Polish, Swedish, Finnish, Lithuanian and – gulp – Japanese vodka. A great place for convivial quaffing and mellowing.

The Prince Public Bar 29 Fitzroy St, St Kilda. Defiantly local and no-frills, the downstairs public bar of *The Prince* (see p.863 and *Circa, The Prince*) has an air of stubborn resistance in the face of St Kilda's freewheeling gentrification. Frequented in equal parts by colourful local identities and desperadoes, it's not for the faint-hearted.

St Kilda Army and Navy Club 88 Acland St. In an area where pretentiousness is rife, it doesn't come any more down to earth than this. After signing in at the door, the many locals who spend more time here than their own home, are happy to swap stories and tell you about the good old days. Drink prices are the cheapest in the area, and there is live music every Friday.

Tongue and Groove 16 Grey St. Dedicated backpacker-bar that packs them in due to its late closing time (5am) and ridiculously cheap happy-hours ($2–4 pints).

Live music

Melbourne has a thriving **band** scene, and just about every pub puts on some sort of music – often free – at some time during the week. Grungy Richmond has a big concentration of **music pubs**, as does Fitzroy, while St Kilda is also a worthy area to head to for a range of live music. Note the line between bars, music pubs and clubs is getting increasingly blurred; the pubs listed below are also good places for a drink and always have at least two bars, so you can escape the din if you want to. Most clubs have a **cover charge** of between $5 and $10. Some backpacker hostels give vouchers for reduced or free admission to a rapidly changing array of venues. Free **listings** magazines such as *Beat* and *Inpress* are good sources of information about the local music scene, while local FM stations Triple R (102.7) and PBS (106.7) air alternative music and tell you what's on and where.

City centre and northern suburbs

Bar Open 317 Brunswick St, Fitzroy. The beauty of this place is that you never know what you're going to get. Comedy, acoustic folk, funk, or visual performances are just some of the things

you might encounter. With comfy couches dotted over the two floors, it's a perfect place to see what Fitzroy music is all about. Totally unpretentious.

Bennetts Lane 25 Bennetts Lane, off Little Lonsdale St in the CBD, between Exhibition and Russell sts. One of Melbourne's most interesting jazz venues, now expanded to include a larger back room to complement the original cramped, 1950s-style cellar. Entry from $12.

Ding Dong Lounge Level 1, 18 Market Lane, City. Small and busy place that plays host to jazz musicians, punk and tribute bands, and DJs playing punk, rock and new wave.

Empress Hotel 714 Nicholson St, North Fitzroy. A mecca for Melbourne's emerging bands, featuring anything from electronica to folk and rock most nights, with a friendly, low-key atmosphere, cheap meals and occasional screenings of cult films. Cover charge from $5.

The Hi Fi Bar and Ballroom 125 Swanston St, CBD. Reasonably spacious underground space with two bars on different levels where you can view acts in relative comfort or head for the overheated mosh-pit below. A mainstay venue for high-profile local and international indie rock bands such as The Fratellis and The Kooks.

Pony 68 Little Collins St, CBD. You wouldn't expect to find a gritty rock'n'roll bar deep in the heart of Melbourne's business district, but that's what the *Pony Club* truly is. With a 7am closing time on weekends (5am on weeknights), this is where the people come who don't have to get up next morning, to immerse themselves in all things rock. Also has one of the tiniest men's toilets in the country.

The Rainbow 27 St David St, Fitzroy. Comfy, intimate pub with a mellow atmosphere and interesting crowd, not to mention a good selection of live blues, jazz, funk and roots from local bands four or five nights a week, including Saturday.

The Tote 71 Johnston St, Collingwood. A Melbourne institution for those that like their music loud and raw. Every night of the week you're guaranteed to witness bands plying their trade in the dark and dingy band-room where rock was born to thrive. With a nice beer garden (including BBQ), colourful characters and good happy hours (6–8pm weekdays), it's easy to see why many consider this Melbourne's best place to hear music. Entry $4–14.

Eastern and southern suburbs

Corner Hotel 57 Swan St, Richmond. Big-name, alternative independent bands often play here from overseas. Also has a great beer garden on the roof. Tickets $12–50.

Dizzy's 381 Burnley St, Richmond. *Dizzy's* blasts out contemporary jazz courtesy of local, national and international acts. Comprising a main bar that hosts bands nightly (8pm Tues–Thurs, 9pm Fri & Sat), and breakfast sessions (11am Sunday). Bar snacks and food available, plus Sunday brunch menu. Fri & Sat cover charge $8–16 applies after 8pm.

The Esplanade Hotel 11 Upper Esplanade, St Kilda. The "Espy" is the soul of St Kilda and of Melbourne's eclectic band scene – playing at The Espy is almost a rite of passage – hosting

an interesting nightly line-up of bands in the front bar (free) and Gershwin Room (small admission charge).

The Greyhound 1 Brighton Rd, St Kilda. Old-fashioned pub with cosy band-room playing live music most nights of the week, with an emphasis on stripped-down rock 'n' roll, competing with great drag shows on Saturday nights and karaoke on Sunday night. There's usually a cover charge ($10–12).

The Prince Band Room At *The Prince*, 29 Fitzroy St, St Kilda. Part of the refurbished *Prince* complex, this is another St Kilda icon which has undergone a face-lift to fit in with the smart cafés and restaurants at this end of Fitzroy St. Upstairs late-night venue with good bands. Tickets $25–75.

Clubs

Melbourne's **club culture** is as vibrant as its bar scene. The hot spots are **Chapel Street** in South Yarra and the **CBD**, but clubs take root anywhere they can, from big commercial nights in the suburbs to obscure experimental sessions in inner-city laneways. International DJs visit frequently, and local talent keeps the scene thriving. The bigger the night, the more the **cover charge**, though it rarely tops $15 unless there's an international guest.

Brazen Lounge 169 Exhibition St, City. Spread over two storeys. The programme spans a wide range from indie/alternative, Brit pop, Goth, house, R&B and funk.

The Butterfly Club 204 Bank St, South Melbourne. A dash of artsy cocktail bar mixed with a cabaret salon, the *Butterfly Club* is one of the more camp environments. Nightly cabaret.

Chasers 386 Chapel St, South Yarra. Over two levels, this place remains popular every Friday and Saturday after many years and has a good sound and lighting system.

Club Odeon Crown Casino Entertainment Complex, south of the Yarra. Fresh from a million-dollar face-lift, this highly polished venue with three bars and a dancefloor features rock and pop cover bands every night.

Revolver Upstairs 229 Chapel St, Prahran. Live music in the bandroom most nights, while every night in the lounge room DJs spin electronic beats, reggae and dub sounds.

Viper Room 373 Chapel St, South Yarra. Popular spot at the weekend with Melbourne's dancing crowd.

Gay and lesbian venues and club nights

DT's Hotel 164 Church St, Richmond. Friendly pub that attracts a mixed-gay crowd and hosts

drag shows every Saturday as well as other gay-themed events from BBQs to pool

Gay and lesbian Melbourne

Melbourne's gay and lesbian scene may not be as in-your-face as Sydney's, but it's almost as big, and is also less ghettoized. Fitzroy, Collingwood and Carlton, north of the river, and St Kilda, South Yarra and Prahran, to the south, boast a strong **gay** presence; Fitzroy, Northcote and Clifton Hill are the city's recognized stomping grounds for **lesbians**. *MCV* (*Melbourne Community Voice*), a free gay and lesbian **paper** published weekly, is available at gay and lesbian venues.

Big **events** are mostly organized by the ALSO (Alternative LifeStyle Organisation) Foundation. The scene's annual highlight, however, is the fabulous **Midsumma Festival** (mid-Jan to early Feb; ⓦwww.midsumma.org.au). Already in its 21st year, Midsumma provides an umbrella for a wide range of sporting, artistic and theatrical events, and includes Pride March.

Organizations, support groups, bookshops and radio station

ALSO Foundation Level 8, 225 Bourke St, City ☎03/9660 3900, ⓦwww.also.org.au. Organizes events and publishes the *ALSO Directory*, free from community outlets, which lists everything from gay vets to lesbian psychologists.

Beat Books 157 Commercial Rd, Prahran ☎03/9827 8748. Gay bookshop with a large range of magazines, books, sex toys and leather goods.

Gay and Lesbian Switchboard Victoria ☎03/9663 2939 (Mon, Tues, Thurs 6–10pm, Wed 2–10pm, Fri, Sat & Sun 6–9pm). Counselling, referral and information.

Joy 94.9 FM ⓦwww.joy.org.au. Gay and lesbian radio station, with 24hr music ranging from classical to R&B and world music, plus news and updates about the arts and club scene.

Hares and Hyenas 63 Johnston St, Fitzroy ☎03/9495 6589, ⓦwww.hares-hyenas .com.au. Gay and lesbian bookshop.

Cafés and meeting places

Globe Cafe 218 Chapel St, Prahran ☎03/9510 8693. Good choice for a well-deserved treat after a hard morning's browsing on Chapel St. Mon–Fri 8am–late, Sat & Sun 9am–late.

Ice Café Bar 30 Cato St, Prahran ☎03/9510 8788. Popular gay and lesbian meeting place in a small lane off Commercial Rd, opposite Prahran Market. Breakfasts are served daily until 4pm, with an extensive breakfast menu to choose from, plus light meals (pasta, risotto) and cocktails. Cheap–moderate. Daily 8am–late.

Jackie O 204 Barkly St, St Kilda ☎03/9537 0377. Comfy, atmospheric surroundings complemented by relaxed service and value-for-money food. Daily 7.30am–1am.

See also p.862 for gay- and lesbian-friendly places to stay and above for gay and lesbian club nights.

competitions. Daily happy hour-drinks specials and music. Closed Mon.

Glasshouse Hotel 51 Gipps St, Collingwood. Stylishly revamped hotel with a relaxed and friendly vibe. Good, inexpensive meals, and a regular programme of live music, DJs and cabaret.

Laird Hotel 149 Gipps St, Collingwood. Well-equipped men-only venue with two bars, DJs, a beer garden and games room; popular with the leather crowd. Open daily; cheap drinks until 10pm.

The Market 143 Commercial Rd, South Yarra. Dance club for men only with weekly menu of top-notch drag shows and talent quests. Open Thurs–Sun.

Opium Den 176 Hoddle St, Collingwood. Popular venue hosting drag queens and kings, cabaret and

trans shows. Attracts a mixed crowd most nights, while Saturdays is girls-only featuring girl DJs and shows. Lotus Night every Wednesday is the hotel's longest-running night for Asian men.

The Peel 113 Wellington St (corner of Peel St), Collingwood. Dancefloor, music videos and shows, drawing a large and appreciative crowd, mainly men. Open Thurs–Sun.

Templebar Precinct 98 Smith St, Collingwood. Restaurant/bar that has a super entertaining "spag and drag" night ($12 for beer, spaghetti and drag show on Wednesdays).

Xchange Hotel 119 Commercial Rd, South Yarra. Men-only drinking and dancing spot with chill-out bar and large video screens.

Comedy

Melbourne is the comedy capital of Australia, home of the madcap Doug Anthony All Stars, Wogs Out of Work and comedians from TV shows such as *The Big Gig* and *The Comedy Company*. The highlight of the comedy year is the **Melbourne International Comedy Festival** (Ⓦ www.comedyfestival .com.au) in April, based at the Town Hall in Swanston Street, with performances at over fifty venues around town. As well as local and interstate acts, you're likely to see some of the best stand-up comedians from overseas. For one-off performances and other venues, check out the "EG" supplement to *The Age* on Fridays.

Comedy Club@Athenaeum Theatre 188 Collins St, City ☏ 03/9650 6668. Considered the home of Australia's comedy, this slick, cabaret-style space features largely mainstream comedians, and offers a decent dinner and show deal from $47.

The Comics Lounge 26 Erroll St, North Melbourne ☏ 03/9348 9488. Comedy shows six days a week; all formats from stand-up to cabaret. Tues nights host stand-up comedy newcomers. Pre-show dinner available Wed–Sat.

Theatre

Melbourne's standing as the centre of Australian **theatre** has been recognized since 1871, when visiting English novelist Anthony Trollope remarked on the city's excellent venues and variety of performances. Nowadays, you can see a host of quality productions most nights of the week, from big musicals to experimental drama.

Athenaeum Theatre 188 Collins St, City ☏ 03/9650 1500. Built in 1842, the Athenaeum Theatre stages everything from Shakespearean drama to comedy and fringe performances.

Comedy Theatre 240 Exhibition St, City ☏ 03/9299 9800. Not a comedy venue, but a small theatre. Past shows include *The Rocky Horror Picture Show* and *Avenue Q*.

Her Majesty's Theatre 219 Exhibition St, City ☏ 03/8643 3300. Lavish musicals, from *Billy Elliot* to *Chicago*, in a fabulously ornate old theatre.

La Mama 205 Faraday St, Carlton ☏ 03/9347 6948. A Carlton institution for over forty years,

La Mama hosts low-budget, innovative works by local playwrights.

Malthouse 113 Sturt St, South Melbourne ☏ 03/9685 5111. A renovated malthouse containing three venues – the Beckett Theatre, the larger Merlyn Theatre and the studio Tower Room – hosting guest performances, opera, dance, concerts and readings. The resident company – the Malthouse Theatre – produces contemporary Australian plays.

Playhouse Theatre Victorian Arts Centre, 100 St Kilda Rd ☏ 03/9281 8000. One of the Victorian Arts Centre's Theatre Buildings, the Playhouse offers a wide-ranging choice of programmes, from musical comedy to Shakespeare, as well as plays by the renowned and very popular Melbourne Theatre Company.

Princess Theatre 163 Spring St, City ℡03/9299 9500. Established at the height of the goldrush, this small, exquisitely restored theatre is one of the city's best-loved venues, and stages musicals such as *Guys and Dolls* and other mainstream theatrical productions.

Red Stitch Actors Theatre Rear 2, Chapel St (opposite the Astor Theatre), St Kilda ℡03/9533

8083. Set up by a group of local actors, this theatre specializes in performing cutting-edge works by Melbourne playwrights.

Regent Theatre 191 Collins St, near City Square, City ℡03/9299 9500. This lovingly restored old theatre puts on productions of big-name musicals such as *Wicked* and *Showboat*.

Theatreworks 14 Acland St, St Kilda ℡03/9534 3388. Cutting-edge Australian plays in a reasonably large, wooden-floored space that was formerly a church hall.

Classical music, opera and dance

The **Melbourne Symphony Orchestra** has a season from February to December based at Hamer Hall and the Melbourne Town Hall, while the **State Orchestra of Victoria** performs less regularly at Hamer Hall, often playing works by Australian composers. Ticket prices are around \$40–80 for classical music performances, and \$70–150 for opera.

Chunky Move 111 Sturt St ℡03/9645 5188. Dance company that puts on contemporary dance productions at the adjacent CUB Malthouse, as well as dance classes at the studio.

Hamer Hall Victorian Arts Centre, 100 St Kilda Rd ℡03/9281 8000. Big-name concerts and perform-ances by the Melbourne Symphony Orchestra.

Her Majesty's Theatre 219 Exhibition St, City ℡03/9663 3211. Occasionally hosts some of the great foreign ballet companies.

State Theatre Victorian Arts Centre, 100 St Kilda Rd ℡03/9281 8000. Venue for the Victorian Opera and the Australian Ballet Company.

Film

The Crown Casino, Melbourne Central and the Jam Factory in South Yarra have a number of **cinemas** showing blockbuster movies (cheap tickets available on Tuesdays). In summer, watching a film under the stars at the Moonlight Cinema in the Botanic Gardens (see p.877) can be a real treat (Ⓦwww.moonlight.com.au). The city's independent cinemas screen less obviously commercial US films and foreign-language films; these cinemas tend to offer discounts on Monday. The **Melbourne International Film Festival** in July (Ⓦwww.melbournefilmfestival.com.au) has been going for over fifty years, based at a number of cinemas around the city. The much younger Melbourne Underground Film Festival (Ⓦwww.muff.com.au) held in October continues to grow in popularity at an enormous rate.

ACMI Federation Square ℡03/8663 2583, Ⓦwww.acmi.net.au. Film-buff's cinema; often shows Australian movies.

Astor Theatre Corner of Chapel St and Dandenong Rd, St Kilda ℡03/9510 1414, Ⓦwww.astor-theatre.com.au. Classic and cult movie double bills in a beautiful Art Deco cinema.

Cinema Nova Lygon Court Plaza, 380 Lygon St, Carlton ℡03/9347 5331, Ⓦwww.cinemanova.com.au. A rabbit warren of small but comfortable cinemas specializing in art-house and European films. Also hosts Script Alive, where actors read an unproduced screenplay. Cheap-day Monday.

Como Como Centre, corner of Toorak Rd and Chapel St, South Yarra ℡03/9827 7533, Ⓦwww.palacetheatres.com.au. Boutique, four-cinema complex with a gorgeous plush bar area. Screens international art-house releases and hosts Italian and Greek film festivals.

George 135 Fitzroy St, St Kilda ℡03/9534 6922, Ⓦwww.palacetheatres.com.au. Three screens showing crossover mainstream and alternative releases with an edge. The recently renovated bar and foyer does excellent choc-top ice creams.

IMAX Rathdowne St, Carlton ℡03/9663 5454, Ⓦwww.imaxmelbourne.com.au. Adjacent to the Melbourne Museum (see p.870), with a gigantic screen and film reels so big they require a forklift to move them. Shows both 2-D and 3-D films, mostly documentaries on inaccessible places or anything involving a tyrannosaurus rex, but also the occasional mainstream film specially made in large format.

Kino 45 Collins St, City ☏ 03/9650 2100, ⊛ www .palacccinemas.com.au. Sophisticated and civilized complex beneath the Collins Place atrium showing new – predominantly art-house – releases for the city's cinephiles.

Shopping

Melbourne's big two **department stores**, David Jones and Myer, are located off the Bourke Street Mall. **Shopping hours** are generally 9am to 5.30pm, with late-night shopping till around 9pm on Thursday and Friday evenings; many places are open seven days a week, especially shops in suburban areas such as Carlton, Fitzroy, South Yarra and St Kilda.

Clothes

Bridge Road, Richmond (between Punt Rd and Church St). This is Melbourne's inner-city bargain district: lots of factory outlets, clothes and shoe shops selling seconds, samples and end-of-season stock.

Brunswick St, Fitzroy Interspersed with cafés, bars and "cutting-edge" hairstylists you'll find lots of small, groovy clothes boutiques and accessories shops – great for unusual hats, costume jewellery and "lifestyle" bric-a-brac: unusually shaped wall clocks or whatever is the latest craze in interior decor. It's also the place to pick up vintage clothes.

Chapel St: South Yarra, Prahran and Windsor Many upmarket fashion outlets at the northern (South Yarra) end, getting progressively less expensive, younger and grungier towards Prahran and Windsor in the south.

City Arcades and Lanes Lots of boutiques and small shops, selling designer brands and unusual fashion and shoes, are tucked away in the laneways of the two city blocks bordered by Flinders, Swanston, Bourke and Elizabeth sts.

GPO corner of Bourke and Elizabeth sts, City This grand, magnificently restored Victorian building is now home to high-fashion outlets including Mandarina Duck, Georg Jensen, Ben Sherman, Mimco, Belinda Seper and Karen Millen.

Hardware St and Little Bourke St, City Lots of shops selling travel clothing and equipment. The place to head for if you want to kit yourself out for your skiing, hiking or rafting trip.

Lygon St, Carlton Mainly lined with cafés and restaurants, but there are also a few good shoe shops and fashion retail outlets, most of them at the northern end between Grattan and Elgin sts.

QV, corner of Swanston & Lonsdale Sts, City The latest city development with boutiques clustered

in the "lanes" running from Russell St towards Swanston St, selling high-fashion designer labels.

Smith Street, Collingwood/Fitzroy Has a number of secondhand clothing stores as well as footwear wholesalers and factory discount outlets, especially the section north of Johnston street.

Books

The Avenue Bookstore 127 Dundas Place, Albert Park. The stock in this shop is almost overwhelming – both in subject range and sheer quantity – and the staff really know their stuff. Daily 9am–7pm.

Book Affair 200–202 Elgin St, Carlton. Very good secondhand bookshop, particularly for novels. Daily 10am–8pm.

Books for Cooks 233 Gertrude St, Fitzroy. Australia's largest range of new and secondhand cookbooks and related titles. Mon–Sat 10am–6pm, Sun 11am–5pm.

Brunswick Street Bookstore 305 Brunswick St, Fitzroy. Good independent bookseller, renowned for its huge range of art and design titles, with occasional launches and readings. Daily 10am–11pm.

Chronicles 91 Fitzroy St, St Kilda. Small, well-stocked independent bookseller. Daily 10am–10pm.

Grub Street Bookshop 379 Brunswick St, Fitzroy. Secondhand and antiquarian books. Mon–Wed & Sun 10am–10pm, Thurs–Sat 10am–11pm.

Haunted Bookshop 15 McKillop St, off Bourke St. Decked out with dim lighting and red velour, this is Australia's leading occult, paranormal and mystical bookshop. Mon–Fri 11am–5.30pm.

Kill City Basement, 119 Swanston St. The store for all those with a fixation on hard-boiled characters and true crime. Mon–Thurs 10am–6pm, Fri 10am–7pm, Sat & Sun 11am–6pm.

Map Land 372 Little Bourke St, City. Travel guide and map specialist, plus globes and travel accessories. Mon–Thurs 9am–5.30pm, Fri 9am–6pm, Sat 10am–5pm.

Polyester Books 330 Brunswick St, Fitzroy. Controversial store that's been denounced for its racy and offbeat titles. Among the popular culture, Satanism and conspiracy theory genres, drug titles, adult comics and magazines are works by literary outlaws William Burroughs, Jean Genet, the Marquis de Sade and Adolf Hitler. Mon–Thurs 10am–8pm, Fri & Sat 10am–9pm, Sun 11am–8pm.

Readings 309 Lygon St, Carlton, also at 253 Bay St, Port Melbourne. This independent bookshop is one of Melbourne's best. Both stores have pleasant cafés. Mon–Sat 9am–11pm, Sun 10am–11pm.

Traveller's Bookstore 294 Smith St, Collingwood. Speciality bookstore that has a wide range of travel writing and guides. Mon–Sat 10am–6pm.

Music

Basement Discs 24 Block Place, off Little Collins St, City. Discreet underground space with an exhilarating range of jazz and blues displayed amid inviting sofas and listening stations. Mon–Thurs 10am–6pm, Fri 10am–8pm, Sat 10am–6pm, Sun 11am–5pm.

Blue Moon Records 54 Johnston St, Fitzroy. Specializes in world music, particularly Latin and Spanish. Tues–Fri 11am–7pm, Sat 10am–6pm, Sun noon–6pm.

Discurio 113 Hardware Lane, City. Classical music, jazz, blues and folk. Mon–Thurs 10am–6pm, Fri 10am–7pm, Sat 10am–5pm.

The Last Record Store 304 Smith St, Collingwood. Good range of local artists, Aboriginal music, folk and old-time stringband music. Mon–Fri 10am–6pm, Sat 10am–5pm.

Missing Links 405 Bourke St, City. Melbourne's premier alternative music store and ticket-seller to gigs around town. Mon–Thurs 10am–6pm, Fri 10am–7pm, Sat & Sun 11am–5pm.

Northside Records 236 Gertrude St, Fitzroy. Choice inner-city music store specializing in cool funk, the latest hip-hop, jazz, electronica and Latin music on CD and vinyl. Mon–Wed 10am–6pm, Thurs & Fri 11am–7pm, Sat 11am–5pm, Sun 1–5pm.

Record Collector's Corner 240 Swanston St, City. Mecca for DJs hunting vintage vinyl as well as collectors seeking out rare Japanese import CDs. This is a specialist store with a good range of well-priced old and new CDs and records. Mon–Thurs 10am–7pm, Fri 10am–10pm, Sat & Sun 11am–5pm.

Markets

Abbotsford Convent Farmers' Market 1 St Heliers St, Abbotsford. Good number of stalls selling mostly organic produce in a fantastic setting on the banks of the Yarra River. The Collingwood Children's Farm is next door and is a great intermission. 8am–1pm, 2nd & 4th Saturday of every month; $2.

Camberwell Market Station St, Camberwell. Large flea market with lots of good secondhand clothes stalls, books, records, bric-a-brac, and plenty of food vans and cafés. Sun 6.30am–12.30pm; take the train to Camberwell.

Esplanade Market Upper Esplanade, St Kilda. A Melbourne institution and particularly nice in warm weather: retreat to the beach afterwards or to one of the cafés in Fitzroy or Acland sts. Features works from artists, fresh produce, secondhand clothing and century-old bric-a-brac. Sun 10am–5pm.

Federation Square Book Market New and secondhand books are sold in The Atrium at Federation Square every Saturday 11am–5pm.

Prahran Market Commercial Rd, Prahran. Excellent, upmarket food emporium selling pricey fish, meat, fruit and vegetables. Tues, Thurs & Sat dawn–5pm, Fri dawn–6pm, Sun 10am–3pm.

Queen Victoria Market Corner of Victoria & Elizabeth sts. Probably the best loved of Melbourne's fresh produce markets. A huge range of products is available and the deli section is well worth visiting. Turns into a general clothes market on Sundays, but the fruit and veg section stays open. Tues & Thurs 6am–2pm, Fri 6am–5pm, Sat 6am–3pm, Sun 9am–4pm.

Royal Botanical Gardens Market Limited to 100 stalls; sells a variety of art, food and plants in a great setting. Every 2nd Saturday of the month, 9am–2pm.

South Melbourne Market Corner of Cecil & Coventry sts, South Melbourne. Melbourne's second-oldest market sells a huge range of fresh fruit and vegetables, seafood, meat, delicatessen goods, clothes, furniture and household items. Cecil St has some fantastic eateries serving crepes to tapas – don't leave without trying the famous South Melbourne dimmies, delicious dim sums to take away. Wed 8am–4pm, Fri 8am–6pm, Sat & Sun 8am–4pm.

Suzuki Night Market Held on the premises of the Queen Victoria Market. A lovely market with stalls selling unusual (and good) food, spices, deli items and gifts. Wed 5.30–10pm; end of November until end of February.

Victorian Arts Centre Market Good crafts market on the footpath alongside the Victorian Arts Centre, extending to the underpass towards Southgate. Over 150 stalls selling handmade quality artwork, wood carvings, ceramics, textiles and jewellery. Sun 10am–5pm.

Listings

Airlines (domestic) Jetstar Ⓣ 13 15 18; Pacific Blue Ⓣ 13 16 45; Qantas Ⓣ 13 13 13; Regional Express Ⓣ 13 17 13; Tiger Airways Ⓣ 03/9335 3033; Virgin Blue Ⓣ 13 67 89.

Airlines (international) Aerolineas Argentinas Ⓣ 02/9234 9000; Air Canada Ⓣ 1300 655 767; Air China Ⓣ 02/9232 7277; Air New Zealand Ⓣ 0800 132 476; Air Pacific Ⓣ 1800 230 150; American Airlines Ⓣ 1800 673 486; Austrian Airlines Ⓣ 1800 642 438; British Airways Ⓣ 1300 767 177; Cathay Pacific Ⓣ 13 17 47; Emirates Ⓣ 1300 303 777; Garuda Indonesia Ⓣ 1300 365 330; Japan Airlines Ⓣ 1300 525 287; KLM Ⓣ 1300 392 192; Korean Air Ⓣ 02/9262 6000; Malaysia Airlines Ⓣ 13 26 27; Qantas Ⓣ 13 13 13; Singapore Airlines Ⓣ 13 10 11; South African Airways Ⓣ 1300 435 972; Thai Airways Ⓣ 1300 651 960; United Airlines Ⓣ 13 17 77.

Banks and exchange All major banks can be found on Collins St. Standard banking hours are generally Mon–Fri 9.30am–4pm (Fri until 5pm), although some branches of Westpac/Bank of Melbourne, including the one at the corner of Collins and Swanton sts, are open on Sat (10am–4pm). Branches of Travelex are at 261 Bourke St (Mon–Fri 9am–5pm, Sat 10am–5pm), 233 Collins St (same hours, except Sat 10am–2pm) and 136 Exhibition St (same hours, closed Sat).

Bike rental Hire a Bicycle, riverside at Federation Wharf (daily 10am–5pm, weather permitting; Ⓣ9654 2762, ⓦwww.hireabikc.com) has basic bicycles, mountain bikes and tandems ($15 for first hr then $5 per hr, or $35 per day). The owner also runs a 4hr Real Melbourne Bike Tour ($89 inc. bike hire, coffee and cakes). In St Kilda, try the helpful St Kilda Cycles, 150 Barkly St (Mon–Fri 9am–6pm, Sat 9am–5pm, Sun 10am–4pm; Ⓣ03/9534 3074, ⓦwww .stkildacycles.com.au; $15 per hr, $35 per day).

Consulates Canada, Level 50, 101 Collins St, City Ⓣ03/9653 9674; UK, Level 17, 90 Collins St Ⓣ03/9652 1600; USA, 553 St Kilda Rd Ⓣ03/9526 5900.

Diving Underwater Victoria – Dive Industry Victoria Association (ⓦwww.underwatervictoria.com.au) has a list of members in Greater Melbourne who rent equipment, organize trips and offer dive courses.

Employment Backpackers Resource Centre, at Hotel Discovery (see p.860). Traveller's Xpress (ⓦwww.travellersxpress.com.au) at the Coffee Palace, 24 Grey St, St Kilda (Mon–Fri 10am–6pm; Ⓣ03/8506 0267). In addition the Travellers aid centre (see p.904) has a notice board.

Hospitals and medical centres Alfred Hospital, Commercial Rd, Prahran Ⓣ03/9076 2000; Royal

Children's Hospital, Flemington Rd, Parkville Ⓣ03/9345 5522; Royal Melbourne Hospital, Grattan St, Parkville Ⓣ03/9342 7000; St Vincent's Hospital, Victoria Parade, Fitzroy Ⓣ03/9288 2211. Melbourne Sexual Health Centre, 580 Swanston St, Carlton (Ⓣ03/9347 0244 or 1800 032 017) offers a free service. For vaccinations, anti-malaria tablets and first-aid kits contact the Travellers Medical and Vaccination Centre (TMVC), 2nd Floor, 393 Little Bourke St Ⓣ03/9602 5788, ⓦwww.tmvc.com.au.

Internet There are plenty of internet cafés throughout Melbourne with most charging $3–5 per hr. Most hostels also have internet access. Alternatively, in the City try Global Gossip, 440 Elizabeth St (Mon–Fri 9am–11pm, Sat & Sun 10am–11pm); Elounge, level 1, 9 Elizabeth St (daily 9am–10.30pm); and Traveller's Contact Point, see p.904; in St Kilda: Princy Internet Café, 9 Grey St (daily 9.30am–11pm). Local libraries provide free access, usually limited to one hour per day.

Laundries Almost all of the hostels and hotels have their own laundry. Commercial self-serve coin laundries include City Edge Laundrette, 39 Errol St, North Melbourne (daily 6am–11pm); My Beautiful Laundrette, 153 Brunswick St, Fitzroy (daily 6.30am–9.30pm); The Soap Opera Laundry & Cafe, 128 Bridport St, Albert Park (daily 7.30am–10pm); and Blessington Street Launderette, 22 Blessington St, St Kilda (daily 7.30am–9pm). Machines costs $3–6 per wash and driers $1 for 6–10min.

Left luggage and luggage forwarding Most hotels store luggage. Flinders St Station and Southern Cross Station have self-service lockers ($12–15 per day). Traveller's Contact Point (see p.904) can store luggage, forward it and/or send it home.

Library The Redmond Barry Reading Room at the State Library of Victoria, 328 Swanston St (Mon–Thurs 10am–9pm, Fri–Sun 10am–6pm), has current Australian and overseas magazines; the Newspaper Reading Room has Australian and overseas papers.

Motorbikes The northern end of Elizabeth St in the city centre has a string of motorbike shops. Garner's Motorcycles, 179 Peel St, North Melbourne (Ⓣ03/9326 8676, ⓦwww.garnersmotorcycles .com.au), does rentals and may sell secondhand machines with buy-back deals.

Pharmacies Mulqueeny Midnight Pharmacy, corner of Williams and High sts, Prahran (24hr); Elizabeth Pharmacy, 125 Elizabeth St, City (Mon–Fri 7.30am–6.30pm, Sat 9.30am–5.30pm).

Police Victoria Police station at 637 Flinders St, City (Ⓣ03/9247 6491); emergency Ⓣ000.

Post office The GPO retail shop is located at 250 Elizabeth St (Mon–Fri 8.30am–5.30pm, Sat 9am–5pm, including the poste-restante counter). Other post offices are open Mon–Fri 9am–5pm. For voicemail and mail forwarding, contact Traveller's Contact Point (see below).

Skiing AUSKI Ski Hiring & Information Centre, 9–11 Hardware Lane ☎03/9670 1412, can advise on skiing conditions at Baw Baw, Buffalo, Mount Hotham, Mount Buller, Falls Creek and at Thredbo in New South Wales.

Swimming pools City Baths, 420 Swanston St (Mon–Thurs 6am–10pm, Fri 6am–8.30pm, Sat & Sun 8am–6pm; $5.10 for a swim, $10.95 including the sauna and spa, $18.95 for use of gym, pool, sauna and spa; ☎03/9663 5888), has a 30-metre heated indoor pool for swimming, plus a pool for water-aerobics and a gym. In the state-of-the-art Melbourne Sports & Aquatic Centre, Aughtie Drive, off Albert Park Rd in Albert Park, there are several pools and water slides, as well as a spa (Mon–Fri 5.30am–10pm, Sat & Sun 7am–8pm; admission $6.50 or $9.70 including use of spa, sauna and steam room; ☎03/9926 1555, @www.msac.com .au). Take tram #96 from Bourke St in the city.

Taxis There are taxi ranks on Swanston St outside Flinders St Station and outside Spencer St Station, and plenty to flag down. Call Arrow (☎13 22 11); Embassy Taxis (☎13 17 55); Silver Top Taxis (☎13 10 08); and Yellow Cabs (☎13 CABS).

Telephones There is a plethora of discount phonecards around, which can be used in any payphone for dirt-cheap international calls (as low as 1–3¢ per minute to the UK). They are sold in lots of shops, as well as internet cafés and some hostels. Read the small print before buying – watch out for flagfall billing in units of 3min or more, and a too-short expiry date.

Travel agents For flight bookings: Flight Centre (☎13 31 33), Shop 2, 250 Flinders St, City (☎03/9663 6266), plus many branches throughout the city; STA Travel (☎13 47 82), Shop 5, 240 Flinders St, City, and 144 Acland St, St Kilda, plus other branches throughout the city; Student Flights (☎1800 046 462, @www .studentflights.com.au), many branches, including Shop 4, 250 Flinders St or 357 Little Bourke St.

Travel agent: Backpackers World, Shop 1, 250 Flinders St (Mon–Fri 10.15am–6pm, Sat 10.15am–4pm; ☎03/9654 8477); Peter Pan Adventure Travel, 415 Elizabeth St (☎1800 886 590); Traveller's Contact Point (see below); YHA Travel, 359B Lonsdale St (☎03/9670 9611).

Travellers aid centre Level 3, 225 Bourke St (Mon–Fri 9am–5pm; ☎03/9654 2600, @www .travellersaid.org.au) and Southern Cross Station. As well as information and internet access there's also toilets, lounge rooms, baby-change facilities, lockers, wheelchairs for rent and assistance for disabled and frail people. Traveller's Contact Point, Level 1, 361 Little Bourke St (Mon–Fri 9am–5.30pm, Sat 9am–noon; ☎03/9642 2911, @www.travellers.com.au), sells backpacker discount cards, WWOOF memberships and has an employment notice board.

Travellers with disablties The Travellers Aid Society (@www.travellersaid.org.au) provides information for the disabled; the Southern Cross (under Bourke St Bridge) and Flinders St (between platform 9 & 10, within the ticket area) stations offer assistance and internet facilities. The Melbourne Mobility Centre located on level 1 of Federation Square car park (Mon–Fri 9am–6pm, Sat & Sun 10am–4pm; ☎03/9650 6499) rents mobility equipment and provides information and maps for getting around Melbourne. Other resources include @www.disability.vic.gov.au; @www.accessibility.com.au and @www .paraquad.asn.au. Assistance is available at metropolitan, suburban, country and interstate stations, while relevant information for people with disabilities can be obtained by calling the Met Transport Information Centre on ☎13 16 38. Trams are progressively being replaced with low-floor wheelchair-accessible models, and all trains are wheelchair-accessible from the front carriage. Melbourne City Council produces a free mobility map of the CBD showing accessible routes, transport and toilets, available from the front desk of the Melbourne Town Hall, or download from @www.melbourne.vic.gov.au. Yellow Cabs (☎13 CABS) and Silver Top Taxis (☎13 10 08) have wheelchair-accessible taxis.

Moving on from Melbourne

Three **bus** companies operate from Melbourne:V/Line buses (daily 6am–10pm; ☎13 61 96, @www.vline.com.au), Firefly (reservations daily 6am–9.30pm; ☎1300 730 740, @www.fireflyexpress.com.au), and Greyhound Australia buses (reservation desk daily Mon–Fri 8am–6pm, Sat & Sun 8am–4pm; ☎13 20 30,

@ www.greyhound.com.au), all of which have terminals at Southern Cross Station. For up-to-date **train** information, Southern Cross Station has a staffed information desk with all V/Line train (and bus) timetables. Bikes can be taken on trains free of charge. If you're travelling with a bike on a reserved ticket, you can check it on the train at least thirty minutes prior to travelling. Suburban train information is available from Metlink (see p.854). The **ferry** from Melbourne to Devonport in Tasmania, run by the *Spirit of Tasmania I* and *II*, takes around eleven hours. There's a nightly departure from Station Pier, Port Melbourne, at 9pm, plus additional departures at 9am (daily from mid-Dec to mid-Jan). The cheapest one-way fares range from $132 off-peak to $189 peak. The fare for standard cars and campervans is normally $65; for motorbikes the cost is $45. Reservations with TT Line ☎1800 634 906, @ www.spiritoftasmania.com.au. To get to Station Pier take tram #109 from Collins Street in the City.

Finally, many **car rental** and campervan companies offer one-way rental (see "Basics", p.40). Two used-car companies that offer cheaper rates are Rent-A-Bomb (☎13 15 53) and Ugly Duckling in St Kilda (☎03/9525 4010 or 1800 335 908).

Around Melbourne

There are many possible day-trips out of Melbourne, mainly around the shores of the huge **Port Phillip Bay**, encircled by the arms of the Bellarine and Mornington peninsulas. The **Mornington Peninsula** on the east side has farmland and wineries on gently rolling hills and is home to some of the city's most popular beaches and surfing spots, packed on summer weekends. **Western Port Bay**, beyond the peninsula, encloses two fascinating islands – little-known **French Island**, much of whose wildlife is protected by a national park, and **Phillip Island**, whose nightly "Penguin Parade", when masses of Little penguins waddle ashore each night, is among Australia's biggest tourist attractions. The **Bellarine Peninsula** and the western side of Port Phillip Bay are less exciting, but they do give access to the west coast and the **Great Ocean Road**. A regular ferry service operates from Phillip Island and French Island to the Mornington Peninsula and from here on to the Bellarine Peninsula, making it possible to visit these places in one big loop before continuing along the Great Ocean Road, with no need to backtrack to Melbourne. Even without your own car it is a doable travel option but not one that gets much publicity in Melbourne.

Inland to the east the **Yarra Valley** and the **Dandenong Ranges** offer beautiful countryside, wine-tasting and bushwalking.

The Mornington Peninsula

The **Mornington Peninsula** curves right around Port Phillip Bay, culminating in Point Nepean, well to the southwest of Melbourne. The shoreline facing the bay is beach-bum territory, though the well-heeled denizens of **Sorrento** and **Portsea**, at the tip of the peninsula, might well resent that tag. On the largely

Melbourne can be used as a base for a wide variety of **tours** to the interior of Victoria or along the coast. Popular destinations are the Yarra Valley, the Great Ocean Road, the Grampians and the Penguin Parade at Phillip Island, and a couple of operators also offer walking tours of the gorgeous "Prom" (Wilson's Promontory). Given the distances, **day-trips** to all these destinations (except the Yarra Valley and Phillip Island) would be far too rushed. To get more than the most superficial impression, it is advisable to choose one of the **two- to four-day excursions** offered by various operators. The Great Ocean Road and the Grampians can also be visited on a one-way tour between Melbourne and Adelaide. Some of the smaller outfits do not operate during the winter months.

Adventure Tours Australia ☏1300 654 604, ⓦwww.adventuretours.com.au. A South Australia–based safari-tour operator which has expanded enormously in the last few years. They do runs along the west coast from Perth to Darwin, Darwin to Melbourne and have Tasmania "stitched up". They also do a three-day one-way tour from Melbourne to Adelaide via the Great Ocean Road and the Grampians departing 3 times a week ($407). All the major sights are visited and there is a hop-on, hop-off option with accommodation upgrades possible.

Autopia Tours ☏03/9419 8878 or 1800 000 507, ⓦwww.autopiatours.com.au. Long-established outfit running popular day-trips by minibus along the Great Ocean Road ($105), to Phillip Island ($109) and the Grampians ($99), plus a combined tour to the Great Ocean Road and the Grampians (3 days; $395), including dorm accommodation and most meals. They also offer one-way tours between Melbourne and Sydney via Wilsons Prom, Snowy Mountains and Canberra (3 days; $395); prices include meals and accommodation.

Bunyip Bushwalking Tours ☏03/9650 9680, ⓦwww.bunyiptours.com. Nature-focused tours with – as their name implies – lots of bushwalking, mainly to Wilson's Promontory National Park (1–3 days; $110–195). For the longer trips you need to be reasonably fit and able to carry a pack with your own tent and supplies. The one-and two-day tours can be combined with the Phillip Island Penguin Parade on the way back to Melbourne. A three-day tour of the Great Ocean Road and the Grampians costs $315, and a one-day sunset tour is $105, including lunch. Very small groups.

Echidna Walkabout ☏03/9646 8249, ⓦwww.echidnawalkabout.com.au. Long-running upmarket ecotour operator, with very small groups and enthusiastic, extremely knowledgeable guides, focusing on native wildlife. The Savannah

straight, ocean-facing coast, **Mornington Peninsula National Park** encompasses some fine seascapes, with several walking trails marked out. The western side of the peninsula facing the shallow waters of **Western Port Bay** (and French and Phillip islands) has a much quieter, rural feel. Heading north from the pleasant township of **Flinders** the coastline of rocky cliffs flattens out to sandy beaches, while north of **Stony Point** are mudflats and saltmarshes lined by white mangroves: not particularly visually appealing but an internationally recognized and protected habitat for migratory waterbirds. Further inland, the area around **Arthurs Seat** and **Red Hill** is probably the most scenic: a bucolic landscape of rolling hills, orchards and paddocks. This is also where the bulk of the peninsula's 200 or so **vineyards** are located. They produce superb, if pricey, Pinot Noir and Shiraz wines, as well as good whites. As in the Yarra Valley, good restaurants, especially winery restaurants, have proliferated on the peninsula in recent years, some of them in truly spectacular settings. Two of the best are *Stillwater at Crittenden*, 25 Harrison's Rd, Dromana (☏03/5981 9555,

Walkabout day-tour ($170) goes to Serendip Sanctuary and the You Yangs, southwest of Melbourne, while longer trips head along the Great Ocean Road and to remoter parts of East Gippsland, and include bushwalks; accommodation is in B&Bs or very comfortable camps ($1450).

Eco Platypus Tours ☎1800 819 091, ⓦwww.ecoplatypustours.com. One very long day-trip along the Great Ocean Road, going as far as Loch Ard Gorge and staying at the Twelve Apostles for the sunset. The return trip is along the faster inland route via Colac ($105, but cheaper if more than three people book at the same time).

Go West ☎1300 736 551, ⓦwww.gowest.com.au. This family-run tour company offers day-trips, primarily aimed for the backpacker market, on a 21-seater minibus travelling the Great Ocean Road ($105) and to Phillip Island ($109); tours are very good value, entertaining and informative.

Groovy Grape ☎1800 661 177, ⓦwww.groovygrape.com.au. One-way tour specialist offering regular trips between Melbourne and Adelaide via the Great Ocean Road and the Grampians (3 days; $345). In Adelaide you can join their day-tour to the Barossa Valley ($75) and their one-way tour to Alice Springs (7 days; $865). Maximum 20 people.

Melbourne's Best Tours ☎1300 130 550, ⓦwww.melbournetours.com.au. More conventional half-day and full-day tours in a small (21-seater) luxury coach to various destinations including Mornington Peninsula wineries ($342), Ballarat and Sovereign Hill ($358).

Oz Experience ☎1300 300 028, ⓦwww.ozexperience.com. One-way trips from Melbourne to Adelaide and from Melbourne to Sydney are integral to this (almost) Australia-wide network backpacker bus-company. Primarily attracts a very young, party crowd but a switch in their format to shorter day-long itineraries and more emphasis on hands-on activities such as surfing, hiking, mountain biking, might change this.

Phillip Island Penguin Tours ☎03/9629 5888, ⓦwww.penguinislandtour.com.au. As the name suggests, it focuses solely on day-trips to see penguins ($99) and does it well with good minibuses equipped with DVD players.

Wayward Bus ☎1300 653 510, ⓦwww.waywardbus.com.au. Long-established one-way specialist, their regular tours follow the coast all the way between Melbourne and Adelaide, running via the Great Ocean Road, and the Grampians (3 days; $395 for hostel bed; $460 twin share). In Adelaide, you can join their Kangaroo Island tour ($380) or their trip to all the natural attractions of Wilpena Pound and the Red Centre ($995). Maximum 21 people.

ⓦwww.stillwateratcrittenden.com.au); and *Max's at Red Hill*, 53 Shoreham Rd, Red Hill (☎03/5931 0177, ⓦwww.maxsatredhillestate.com.au), which has superb views over the hills and Western Port Bay; both serve lunch daily and are open for dinner Friday and Saturday. You could also try the equally scenic *Montalto Vineyard and Olive Grove*, 33 Shoreham Rd, Red Hill South (☎03/5989 8412, ⓦwww.montalto.com.au), open for lunches daily and dinner Friday and Saturday (plus Mon–Thurs during summer), with an area of wetlands that's home to over ninety species of birds and other wildlife. For more details, see the *Peninsula Wine Country Annual*, available online at ⓦwww.visitor.com.au or from tourist visitor centres and attractions in the region, or the Mornington Peninsula *Wine Touring Map*, also available at information centres. If you're in the mood for a beer instead, check out the *Red Hill Brewery* at 88 Shoreham Rd, Red Hill South (Thurs–Sun 11am–5pm; ☎03/5989 2959, ⓦwww.redhillbrewery.com.au), which has an excellent range straight from the vat and does hearty food to accompany it.

As well as the beaches, the peninsula's **community markets**, selling local produce and crafts, attract many city dwellers: most are monthly affairs, so there's usually one every weekend. One of the biggest and best is the Red Hill Community Market, held on the first Saturday of every month (Sept–May 8am–1pm), at Red Hill Recreation Reserve, Arthurs Seat Road, 10km east of Dromana; others include Balnarring Racecourse Market at Colaart Road, Balnarring, on the third Saturday of every month (Nov–April 8am–1pm); the Mornington Racecourse Market (year-round every second Sunday 9am–2pm) at Racecourse Road, Mornington; and the Sunday Market at the Dromana Drive-in Cinema (year-round 7am–1pm) on the Bittern–Dromana Road, just off the Mornington Peninsula Freeway.

You can get to the peninsula by **public transport** from Melbourne to Frankston and from there to the main beach resorts and towns along the Nepean Highway on the northern side as well as Flinders and Hastings to the south, but for a sightseeing trip taking in wineries, beaches and Arthurs Seat you'll need your own vehicle. Take a Metlink train from Flinders Street to Frankston (1hr) where you can change onto a train to Stony Point (35min) for Phillip and French islands. From Frankston Station Metlink buses run to various points along the peninsula; #788 to Portsea stops at Mornington, Dromana and Sorrento as well as other points in between, while #782 and #783 head to Flinders and Hastings respectively. For more information call ☏13 16 38 or go to ⓦ www.metlinkmelbourne.com.au. Alternatively, you can head to Dromana and take a Portsea Passenger Service bus #787 to Sorrento Ferry Terminal for ferries to Queenscliff on the Bellarine Peninsula; for timetable information call ☏1800 115 666.

There are **visitor centres** at Frankston, Pier Promenade (☏1300 322 842); Mornington, 320 Main St (☏03/5975 1644); and Dromana, 359B Point Nepean Rd (1800 804 009); all are open daily 9am–5pm.

The western coast

The peninsula starts at suburban **Frankston**, 40km from central Melbourne. From here on down, the western coast, flanked by the Nepean Highway, sports beach after beach, all crowded and traffic-snarled in summer. Fifteen kilometres beyond Frankston, the fishing port of **Mornington** preserves some fine old buildings along Mornington Esplanade; there's a produce and craft market on Main Street every Wednesday. Four kilometres along the Nepean Highway, near Mount Martha, **Briars Park** (9am–5pm; free; ☏03/5974 3686) comprises an 1840s homestead (10am–4pm; entry with tour guide only $5.10; phone for times), complete with a collection of furniture and memorabilia given to the owner, William Balcombe, by Napoleon Bonaparte who reportedly stayed with the family when they lived on the island of St Helena. There is also an enclosed wildlife reserve with woodlands and extensive wetlands. The **visitor centre** near the homestead will put on a short film upon request giving you an overview of the Balcombes' pioneering days in Australia and the history of the homestead, as well as a rundown on the present-day facilities of the park; there's also a wetlands display with turtles and lizards. To the west of the visitor centre are the starting points for two walks through the woodlands, while the adjacent **wetlands**, visited by more than fifty species of waterbirds, can be observed at close distance from two hides accessible via a boardwalk from the visitor centre; pick up a map of these walks from the centre.

Inland from Dromana, where seaside development begins in earnest, the granite outcrop of **Arthurs Seat State Park** rises 305m, providing breathtaking views of Port Phillip Bay. You can drive up to the summit along a winding road dotted with great lookouts. Near the top is the **Enchanted Maze Garden** (daily 10am–6pm; ⓦ www.enchantedmaze.com.au; $15), which combines four landscaped mazes with theme gardens, a sculpture park and a children's animal farm, and offers lots of family-oriented activities and a good restaurant. Alternatively, you can have a drink or a bite to eat at the revamped *Arthurs Hotel*, opposite Arthurs Seat, with live jazz on Fridays.

Sorrento and around

Beyond Arthurs Seat, the peninsula arcs and narrows: the sands around Sorrento and Portsea offer a choice between the rugged surf of the ocean ("back" beaches) or the calmer waters of the bay ("front" beaches). With some of the most expensive real estate outside the Melbourne CBD, **Sorrento** is the traditional haunt of the city's rich during the "season" from Boxing Day to Easter. Well-heeled outsiders also make it their playground in January and on summer weekends, flocking here to swim, surf and dive at the bay and ocean beaches.

Arrival

A reliable **car and passenger ferry** service operated by Peninsula Searoad (ⓣ 03/5258 3244, ⓦ www.searoad.com.au) runs across the mouth of the bay from Sorrento to Queenscliff on the Bellarine Peninsula all year round (hourly 7am–6pm, Boxing Day to end of daylight saving until 7pm; 40min). One-way fares for pedestrians are $10, while standard cars with two passengers costs $63 (depending on the season) for 2 passengers plus $7 for each additional passenger. Motorbikes plus a rider are $31.50. No advance bookings are necessary but cars should be at the terminal thirty to forty-five minutes prior to departure.

Accommodation

Bayplay Adventure Lodge 46 Canterbury Jetty Rd, Blairgowrie ⓣ 03/5984 0888, ⓦ www.bayplay .com.au. Comfortable budget accommodation in a bushland setting near the beach, with a self-catering kitchen, free bicycles, internet access and camping space. The lodge is also a PADI dive resort (see p.910) and offers daily transfers from and to Melbourne in summer. The Frankston–Portsea bus (#788) stops along the Pt Nepean Highway, from where it's a 10min walk. ❹

Carmel of Sorrento 142 Ocean Beach Rd, Sorrento ⓣ 03/5984 3512, ⓦ www.carmelofsorrento.com.au. Charming, sandstone B&B smack in the middle of town. Self-contained units also available. Minimum 2 nights at weekends in summer. ❻–❼

Hotel Sorrento 5 Hotham Rd, Sorrento ⓣ 03/5984 8000, ⓦ www.hotelsorrento.com.au. A charming, 1871 limestone hotel located in a secluded spot on a hill above the jetty. Try to stay in their "Heritage Suites" with sea views. ❽–❾

Sorrento Beach Motel 780 Melbourne Rd, Sorrento ⓣ 03/5984 1356, ⓦ www .sorrentobeachmotel.com.au. Mid-level, well-managed yet quirky motel where the outside of each room looks like an old bathing house. ❼–❽

Sorrento Hostel YHA 3 Miranda St, Sorrento ⓣ 03/5984 4323, ⓦ www.yha.com.au. Cosy place run by friendly staff, with small dorms (some en suite), doubles and twin rooms, and stacks of local information. Dorms $30, rooms ❹

The town and around

Exploring beautiful rock formations and low-tide pools, and swimming with bottlenose dolphins are some of Sorrento's less glitzy attractions, but the smell of money is everywhere – in the wide, tree-lined residential streets, the clifftop mansions boasting million-dollar views, and the town-centre cafés, restaurants, galleries and antique shops, running along Ocean Road down to the beach.

Two kilometres before the town, on Point Nepean Highway, is the **Collins Settlement Historic Site** at Sullivan Bay, where, in 1803, Captain David Collins attempted the first permanent European settlement in what is now

Victoria; the settlers struggled here for eight months before giving up and moving on to Tasmania. One of the convicts in the expedition was the infamous William Buckley who, having escaped, was adopted by the local Aborigines and lived with them for 32 years. When the "wild white man" was seen again by settlers he could scarcely remember how to speak English; his survival against all odds has been immortalized in the phrase "Buckley's chance". You can walk along the cliffs and around the pioneer cemetery; there's a signposted turn-off from the main road.

Swimming with dolphins and seals is one of Port Phillip Bay's prime attractions. Operators include the environmentally conscious Polperro Dolphin Swims (℡03/5988 8437 or ℡0428 174 160, Ⓦwww.polperro.com.au), which takes the smallest groups, and Moonraker (℡03/5984 4211, Ⓦwww .moonrakercharters.com.au). Both run, weather permitting, three- to four-hour trips from Sorrento Pier twice daily during the season (Oct to April/May) for roughly the same prices: $115 for swimmers, including wet suit and snorkelling equipment and $50 for sightseers.

Eating and drinking

As is to be expected in this posh part of the peninsula, most eating places tend to be on the pricey side but some come with great water-views. In winter, a lot of places have restricted opening times or are only open at weekends.

The Baths 3278 Point Nepean Rd ℡03/5984 1500. Best location in Sorrento and with great seafood to match, but high prices. The little fish-and-chip shop (daily noon–late) around the side is a more affordable option. Open Mon–Fri 11.30am–late, Sat & Sun 9am–late.

Continental Hotel 21 Ocean Beach Rd ℡03/5984 2201. Good-looking old-timer with a spacious dining area, a few tables out front and a Mediterranean-influenced menu featuring a range of Mornington Peninsula wines, plus live music and a nightclub at weekends. Daily 9am–late, closed dinner Wed.

Hotel Sorrento 5 Hotham Rd ℡03/5984 8000. Hotel-bar and a restaurant with a Mod-Oz menu featuring seafood dishes and grills that are a cut above your average pub fare, and excellent views across the Bay. Daily 7.30am–10am, noon–2.30pm, 6–9pm.

Shells Café 95 Ocean Beach Rd. This light-filled, breezy café serves good coffee and cakes plus the standard café food, and is a prime spot for people-watching. Popular spot for surfers. 7.30am–4.30pm daily.

Smokehouse Pizza Kitchen 182 Ocean Beach Rd ℡03/5984 1246. Since 1992 this place has been dishing up some of the best pizzas this side of Melbourne. Takeaway available. Daily 6pm–late (winter Thurs–Sun only).

Spargo's 113 Ocean Beach Rd. Big, sometimes chaotic café with nice outdoor seating in which to get stuck into the excellent wine list and seafood specials. Daily 9am–late.

Portsea and Point Nepean

PORTSEA, just beyond Sorrento, is a mecca for divers, with excellent dives of up to 40m off Port Phillip Heads; trips operate from the pier throughout the summer and there are a couple of good dive shops. Portsea Front Beach, on the bay by the pier, is wall-to-wall beautiful people, as is Shelley Beach, which also attracts playful dolphins. On the other shore, Portsea Ocean Beach has excellent surfing, and a hang-gliding pad on a rock formation known as London Bridge. Back on the bay side, the extensive lawns of *Portsea Hotel*, a hugely popular drinking spot which features bands at weekends, overlook the beach. The *Bayplay Adventure Lodge* (see p.909) doubles as a PADI **dive resort** and offers dive courses (all levels) from its shop in Portsea: as well as a wide range of dives for novices and experienced divers, they also run a guided sea-kayaking trip along the coast (daily 3hr; $88). On most days dolphins come to frolic around the boats and often seals and penguins can be sighted. They also provide a free booking service for all kinds of other outdoor activities around the peninsula including horseriding and surfing lessons.

The tip of the peninsula, with its fortifications, tunnels and former army base, is now classified as **Point Nepean National Park**, part of a patchwork of parks sprinkled over the southern end of the peninsula, collectively known as Mornington Peninsula National Park. The visitor centre and a car park are 1km west of Portsea (daily 9am–5pm; free; ☎03/5984 4276). Entrance into the national park costs $7.90. To get to **Point Nepean**, 7km from the visitor centre, you can either rent a bike ($16.50 for 3hr) or board the Transporter "train" – actually a few carriages pulled by a tractor ($13.50 one-way, $16.50 return; these fares include the park admission fee). The Transporter departs from the visitor centre at 10.30am, 11.30am, 12.30pm, 2pm & 3pm; during summer the service runs half-hourly. Alternatively, you can drive to Gunners car park, 2.5km into the park, and walk the rest of the way to Point Nepean.

The Transporter runs to the fortifications at Point Nepean, with four optional drop-offs for walks: the first, the **Walter Pisterman Heritage Walk** (1km), leads through coastal vegetation to the Port Phillip Bay shoreline; the second (1km) leads to the top of Cheviot Hill, where you can look across to Queenscliff, then continues to **Cheviot Beach** where on December 17, 1967, **Harold Holt**, Australia's then prime minister, went for a swim in the rough surf of Bass Strait and disappeared, presumed drowned: his body was never found. The third walk, the **Fort Pearce and Eagle's Nest Heritage Trail** (2km), crosses through defence fortifications. A fourth walk takes you around **Fort Nepean**, right at the tip of the peninsula. Built at the same time as Fort Queenscliff opposite to protect wealthy post-goldrush Melbourne from the imagined threat of Russian invasion, the fort comprises two subterranean levels, whose tunnels lead down to the Engine House at water level.

South and east coast

The rest of Mornington Peninsula National Park spreads along the ocean coast and has a number of sights and activities to keep you occupied. An enjoyable two-day walk (27km) runs from London Bridge along the coast to **Cape Schanck**, site of an 1859 lighthouse (daily 10am–5pm; park entrance $4.40). Here walkways lead down to the sea along a narrow neck of land, providing magnificent coastal views. The three **lighthouse-keepers' cottages** offer the most scenic accommodation on the peninsula (☎03/5988 6184, ⓦwww .austpacinns.com.au; ⑥), each with a cosy lounge and kitchen. There's a small maritime museum ($10) at the lighthouse, which is open daily for tours at half-hour intervals (10am–5pm; $14).

The nearby **Bushrangers Bay Walk** (5km; 2hr) heads from the cape to Main Creek, beginning as a leisurely walk along the clifftop, then leading down to a wild beach facing Elephant Rock. More energetic activities include **horse rides** along Gunnamatta Beach or through bushland, organized by the Gunnamatta Equestrian Centre, Trueman's Road, Rye (from $40 per hr; ☎03/5988 6755, ⓦwww.gunnamatta.com.au), and **surfing** lessons ($50 for 90min, equipment provided), offered by the East Coast Surf School (☎03/5989 2198, ⓦwww.eastcoastsurfschool.net.au) at various spots near Point Leo.

Good-value **accommodation** is available further east in Flinders at the shady *Flinders Caravanpark* (☎03/5989 0458, ⓦwww.flinderscaravanpark.com.au; ④), which has tent sites and cabins, 300m from the beach.

Set in bushland 15km southeast of Frankston, near the northern end of Western Port Bay, **Moonlit Sanctuary Wildlife Conservation Park**, at

550 Tyabb–Tooradin Rd (daily 11am–5pm; $10; ☎03/5978 7935, ⓦwww
.moonlit-sanctuary.com) is home to lots of kangaroos, wallabies, emus and
waterbirds. However, the park's emphasis is on conserving and breeding rare
nocturnal Australian animals, so it's well worth coming late in the day to take
part in their guided **night tour** (1hr 30min; $25; reservations essential). Starting
at dusk, this tour offers the chance to see rare nocturnal Australian creatures
such as eastern quolls, eastern bettongs, pademelons, squirrel gliders and tawny
frogmouths in bushland enclosures. If you really want to get close to the animals,
following this tour is the Feed Out Tour ($44; minimum 3 people; reservations
essential), where you accompany the guide and help feed the animals.

French Island

FRENCH ISLAND, on the eastern side of the Mornington Peninsula, is well
off the beaten track. A former prison farm, about two-thirds of the island is a
national park, with the remaining third used as farmland. The island is renowned
for its rich **wildlife**, especially birds of prey, and a flourishing koala colony.
Make sure you bring mosquito repellent. You need a permit to bring a car onto
the island, but it's a great place to cycle, an activity which is encouraged, with
all walking tracks open to bikes. Contact the French Island National Park office
on ☎03/5980 1294, or Parks Victoria (☎13 19 63, ⓦwww.parkweb.vic.gov.au)
for more information.

Places to stay include *McLeod Eco Farm and Historic Prison* (☎03/5980 1224,
ⓦwww.mcleodecofarm.com; ❸–❹), where you can sleep in former prison cells
converted into twins with bunk beds, or in the slightly more expensive former
officers' quarters with queen-sized beds; all have shared facilities. The farm is
surrounded by national park and has 8km of beach frontage; the very reasonable
rates include organic meals and transfer from the ferry jetty 29km away. The only
camping available is at the small and basic *Fairhaven Campground*, a five-kilometre
walk to the west of the island, which has a pit toilet and tank water, but no
showers or open fires allowed. The island's general store is roughly 2km away.
Camping is free but you must obtain a permit beforehand; phone ☎03/5980
1294 for more information. Near the jetty, the small *Tortoise Head Guesthouse*
(☎03/5980 1234, ⓦwww.tortoisehead.net; ❹–❺) offers B&B accommodation
in guest rooms with shared facilities and four en-suite cabins with water views.
Moderately priced lunches and dinners are also available. *French Island B&B*
(☎03/5980 1209, ⓦwww.frenchislandbandb.com.au; ❺) is a cottage with two
bedrooms, operated by the general store, 2.5km from the jetty; fully catered rates
are also available. The *Bayview Chicory Kiln and Tea Room* (10km from the jetty)
offers scrumptious Devonshire teas and freshly baked scones.

Inter Island Ferries (☎03/9585 5730, ⓦwww.interislandferries.com.au)
connects the Mornington Peninsula with French Island and Phillip Island (see
opposite), departing from **Stony Point**, on the eastern side of the Mornington
Peninsula to **Tankerton jetty** on French Island (daily 8am & 4.15pm, plus
10.15am & noon Tues, Thurs, Sat & Sun; $20 return, bikes $8). To get to Stony
Point from Melbourne, take the Frankston train from Flinders Street Station
and a bus to Stony Point.

For a brief visit to French Island, it's best to book one of the afternoon tours
covering the island's natural attractions and the historic prison. The **French
Island Bus Tour** ($38 including Devonshire tea; ☎03/5980 1241, ⓦwww
.frenchislandtours.com.au) operated by Lois Airs departs on Tuesday, Thursday

and Sunday, and also on Saturday during school holidays. Alternatively, **French Island Eco Tours** ($40; ℡1300 307 054, ⓦwww.frenchislandecotours.com .au) runs tours on Thursday and Sunday and includes light lunch and a tour to the eco farm. For both, take the Inter Island Ferry from Stony Point at noon to Tankerton jetty; the tours meet the ferry and drop off at the jetty at the end of the tour.

Phillip Island

The hugely popular holiday destination of **PHILLIP ISLAND** is famous above all for the nightly roosting of hundreds of Little penguins at Summerland Beach – the so-called **Penguin Parade** – but the island also boasts some dramatic coastline, plenty of surfing, fine swimming beaches, and a couple of well-organized wildlife parks. It is also home to the Australian Motorcycle Grand Prix (ⓦhttp://bikes.grandprix.com.au) held over three days in early October: a History of Motorsport display at the circuit visitor centre (daily 9am–6pm; ℡03/5952 9400, ⓦwww.phillipislandcircuit.com.au; $13.50) features snapshots and memorabilia of the crazy exploits and heroics of Australia's early racers. **Cowes**, on the sheltered bay side, is the main town and a lively and attractive place to stay. Other, smaller, communities worth a visit are **Rhyll**, to the east, and **Ventnor**, just west of Cowes.

A **V/Line bus** to Cowes departs weekdays from Melbourne's Southern Cross Station at 3.50pm (3hr 20min; $10), but there's no public transport on the island itself, so it can be tricky getting around and to the Penguin Parade, over 10km from Cowes. Joining a **tour** solves the transport problem. A few operators specializing in small groups (up to 20 people) run day-tours of the island (taking in a winery, the Nobbies rock formations (see p.914), and a wildlife park) from Melbourne that include the Penguin Parade at dusk; the going rate is $99 including dinner and all entrance fees (see box, p.906 for a list of tour operators).

If you're **driving**, head southeast from Melbourne on the Princes Highway to Dandenong, then follow the South Gippsland Highway to Lang Lang and from there the Bass Highway to Anderson where the road heads directly west to San Remo and the bridge across to the island, a drive of approximately ninety minutes in total. The scenic lookout about 4km before San Remo is worth stopping at, for fantastic views of Western Port Bay and the surrounding countryside. **SAN REMO** itself has lots of motels, a picturesque fishing fleet by its wharf and a cooperative selling fresh fish and crayfish. **NEWHAVEN**, the first settlement you come to after crossing the bridge, has a large tourist information centre (daily 9am–5pm; ℡1300 366 422, ⓦwww.visitphillipisland.com), where you can book accommodation, pick up a free map and buy tickets for the Penguin Parade ($20), Churchill Island ($10), the Koala Conservation Centre ($10), or a combined parks pass for all three ($34), as well as ferry cruises. Tiny **CHURCHILL ISLAND**, accessible by a narrow bridge 1km north of town, is mostly occupied by a working farm and historic homestead in English-style gardens (daily 10am–5pm; adults $10, 4–15-yr-olds $5; ℡03/5956 7214), surrounded by ancient moonah trees which are home to abundant birdlife. The farm puts on a range of daily activities including milking Daisy the cow, sheep-shearing and blacksmith demonstrations, while a leisurely walk leads around the small island (2hr) from the Churchill Island Visitor Centre (free), with views of the unspoilt coastline; the visitor centre has a café.

Phillip Island Reserve and the Penguin Parade

The **Phillip Island Reserve** includes all the public land on the **Summerland Peninsula**, the narrow tip of land at the island's western extremity. The reason for the reserve is the **Little penguin**, the smallest of the penguins, found only in southern Australian waters and whose largest colony breeds at Summerland Beach (around 2000 penguins in the parade area, and 20,000 on the island altogether). The **Penguin Parade** (nightly after dusk; $20; ☏03/5956 8300, ⓦwww.penguins.org.au) is inevitably horribly commercial – and with four thousand visitors a night at the busiest time of the year (around Christmas, January and Easter, when bookings are essential), it can hardly fail to be. Spectators sit in concrete-stepped stadiums looking down onto a floodlit beach, with taped narrations in Japanese, Taiwanese and English. But don't be too hard on it: ecological disaster would ensue if the penguins weren't managed properly, and visitors would still flock here, harming the birds and eroding the sand dunes. As it is, all the money made goes back into research and looking after the penguins, and into facilities such as the excellent **Penguin Parade Visitor Centre** (open from 10am; admission included in the parade ticket): the "Penguin Experience" here is a simulated underwater scene of the hazards of a penguin's life, and there are also interactive displays, videos and even nesting boxes to which penguins have access from the outside, where you can watch the chicks. To escape the majority of the crowds, you can choose the "Penguin Sky Box" option ($50) – an exclusive, elevated viewing-tower with a ranger on hand to answer questions.

The parade itself manages to transcend the setting in any case, as the penguins come pouring onto the beach, waddling comically once they leave the water. They start arriving soon after dark; fifty minutes later the floodlights are switched off and it's all over, at which time (or before) you can move on to the extensive boardwalks over their burrows, with diffused lighting at regular intervals enabling you to watch their antics for hours after the parade finishes – they're active most of the night. If you want to avoid the worst of the crowds, the quietest time to observe them is during the cold and windy winter (you'll need water- or windproof clothing at any time of year). Remember too that you can see Little penguins close to St Kilda Pier in Melbourne and at many other beaches in southern and southeastern Australia, perhaps not in such large numbers, but with far fewer onlookers.

The Nobbies and Seal Rocks

At the tip of the Summerland Peninsula is **Point Grant**, where **The Nobbies**, two huge rock-stacks, are linked to the island at low tide by a wave-cut platform of basalt, affording views across to Cape Schanck on the Mornington Peninsula. From the new Nobbies Centre (daily 10am to 1hr before sunset) car park a boardwalk leads across spongy greenery – vibrant in summer with purple and yellow flowers – along the rounded clifftops to a lookout over a blowhole. This is a wild spot, with views along the rugged southern coastline towards Cape Woolamai, a granite headland at the eastern end of the island. From September to April you may see muttonbirds (shearwaters) here – they arrive in September to breed and head for the same burrows each year, after an incredible flight from the Bering Strait in the Arctic Circle. Two kilometres off Point Grant, **Seal Rocks** are two rocky islets with the largest known colony of Australian fur seals, estimated to number around 5000. It's possible to see seals all year round through the telescopes on the cliff edge ($2), though their numbers peak during the breeding season between late October and December. You can get a better view of the seals from the Nobbies Centre via cameras in the colony; there's also a café and children's play area. **Cruises** to Seal Rocks are available from Cowes (see below).

Phillip Island Wildlife Park, the Koala Conservation Centre and Rhyll Inlet

Two further parks and a mangrove boardwalk complete Phillip Island's rich collection of wildlife attractions. **Phillip Island Wildlife Park**, on Thompson Avenue just 1km south of Cowes (daily 10am–5pm; $11), provides a shady sanctuary for Australian animals: beautiful pure-bred dingoes, Tasmanian devils, fat and dozy wombats, as well as an aviary and a koala reserve. There are also freely ranging emus, Cape Barren geese, wallabies, eastern grey kangaroos and pademelons.

The **Koala Conservation Centre**, on Phillip Island Tourist Road between Newhaven and Cowes (daily 10am–5pm; $10), aims to keep the koala habitat as natural as possible while still giving people a close view. A treetop walk through a part of the bushland park allows visitors to observe the marsupials at close range. At 4pm the rangers provide fresh gum leaves – a very popular photo opportunity. You can learn about koalas in the excellent interpretive centre.

The Conservation Hill Lookout, just off the Cowes–Rhyll Road further north, provides a good view of the **Rhyll Inlet**, a significant roosting and feeding ground for migratory wading birds which come from as far as Siberia. A **boardwalk** starting at the car park takes visitors into the middle of the inlet, a landscape of mangroves, saltmarshes and mudflats. Unlike most other places on the island, the fishing village of **RHYLL** has managed to retain a sleepy charm. There are a couple of cafés on the foreshore with splendid views of the tranquil, shallow waters of Western Port Bay and the South Gippsland coast; occupying the best position is the *Foreshore Bar and Restaurant* (daily noon–2.30pm, 6–9pm; ℡03/5956 9520), a small, homely pub which serves great meals and a good selection of wines.

Cowes and around

Phillip Island's main town, **COWES**, situated at the centre of the north coast, is busy, touristy and even somewhat tacky, though the sandy bays are sheltered enough for good swimming and there are several decent places to eat and stay around **The Esplanade**, a lively strip facing the jetty. Wildlife Coast Cruises (℡1300 763 739, ⓦwww.wildlifecoastcruises.com.au) offers various **cruises** from the jetty, the best being the trip to Seal Rocks (2hr; $60) to see the Australian fur seals close up, as well as ocean rafting trips for the more adventurous.

Inter Island Ferries (see p.912) run transfers between Stony Point and Cowes and French Island (depart Stony Point daily 8am & 5pm, also noon Tues, Thurs, Sat & Sun: $10 one-way, bikes $4), and from Cowes (daily at 8.45am & 5.25pm, also 12.40pm Tues, Thurs, Sat & Sun).

Accommodation

Out of season you shouldn't have any trouble finding somewhere to **stay**, but during the peak Christmas to Easter season accommodation nearly doubles in price and some places require weekly bookings. The Phillip Island tourist information centre in Newhaven handles accommodation bookings for the island.

Amaroo Park 97 Church St, Cowes ☎03/5952 2548, ⓦwww.amaroopark.com. Accommodation comprises a YHA hostel and a caravan park; facilities include a convivial bar, heated swimming pool, cheap meals and bike rental. They also run tours of the island. Dorms $30, rooms ❹

The Castle Villa by the Sea 7–9 Steele St, Cowes ☎03/5952 1228, ⓦwww.thecastle.com.au. Delightful boutique hotel with seven suites in a pleasant and quiet location just around the corner from the Esplanade. Great restaurant as well. ❻–❾

Cliff Top 1 Marlin St, Smiths Beach ☎03/5952 1033, ⓦwww.clifftop.com.au. Stunning secluded views over the water on the south of the island are what make this the island's best accommodation option. The seven rooms are exquisitely decorated and offer everything for a perfect romantic getaway. ❽–❾

Coachman Motel 51 Chapel St, Cowes ☎03/5952 1098, ⓦwww.coachmanmotel.com.au. Spacious motel units, studios and apartments, all with microwave and fridge, some with spa bath big enough for two. Facilities include a heated pool and spa for communal use. ❺

Kaloha Holiday Resort Corner of Chapel and Steele sts, Cowes ☎03/5952 2179, ⓦwww .kaloha.com.au. Motel units with cooking facilities, plus cabins, camping sites and facilities for on-site vans. Located in shady grounds giving onto a quiet swimming beach. ❻–❼

Seahorse Motel 29–31 Chapel St, Cowes ☎03/5952 2003, ⓦwww.seahorsemotel.com.au. An above-average, centrally located motel. ❻

Spice Island 1A Hill St, Sunderland Bay ☎03/5956 7557, ⓦwww.spiceisland.com.au. Three luxurious studio buildings set on rolling hills in a quiet part of the island. With a spa, LCD TV and five-star amenities, it offers excellent value for money. Minimum 2-night stay weekends. ❼

Eating and drinking

Harry's on the Esplanade Level 1, 17 The Esplanade ☎03/5952 6226. Excellent seafood and meat dishes with a European slant – from German sausage and mash to *côte de boeuf* – in a nice setting on the Esplanade. Tues–Sun noon–2.30pm, 5.30pm–late.

Infused 115 Thompson Ave, Cowes ☎03/5952 2655. Busy restaurant and bar, offering excellent modern Australian cuisine using local produce (especially their Phillip Island fillet $30). Lunch 11am–3pm, dinner 5pm–late; closed Tues.

Isola di Capri 2 Thompson Ave, Cowes ☎03/5952 2435. Friendly, moderately priced, Italian restaurant and *gelateria* at the corner of the Esplanade. Daily lunch and dinner.

The Yarra Valley and the Dandenongs

Northeast of Melbourne, the **Yarra Valley** stretches out towards the foothills of the Great Dividing Range, with **Yarra Glen** and **Healesville** the targets for excursions into the wine country and the superb forest scenery beyond. To the east, and still within the suburban limits, the cool **Dandenong Ranges** have been a popular retreat for city folk for over a century, with quaint villages, fine old houses, beautiful flowering gardens and shady forests of eucalypts and tree ferns.

To get to all these destinations and to have a good look round, you really need your own vehicle. From Monday to Saturday it's possible, although not exactly easy, to see the Dandenongs by **public transport**; catch a train from Melbourne to Upper Ferntree Gully Station then take bus #698, which runs via Mount Dandenong Tourist Road to Olinda township and the SkyHigh observatory in the Dandenong Ranges. Alternatively, take a train to Belgrave Station, starting point of the **Puffing Billy** steam train (see p.920), and then bus #694 (Mon–Sat). Bus #688 runs from Olinda via the northern part of Mount Dandenong Tourist Road to Croydon railway station, where you can catch a train back to Melbourne. **Healesville** comes within the orbit of the suburban transport system: take a train from Melbourne to Lilydale and then bus #685 (to visit the Healesville Sanctuary, it's best to go to Lilydale from where there are daily buses). There's a daily bus #684 from Lilydale (departs 1.20pm) to **Eildon** via Healesville and Marysville; the V/Line train service to **Mansfield** passes through Lilydale and Yarra Glen daily (for further information, call V/Line on ☎13 61 96). There are local buses from Belgrave to **Emerald**.

The Yarra Valley

Just half an hour's drive from Melbourne, the **Yarra Valley** is home to around eighty of Victoria's best small **wineries**. The combination of good wine and fine food is really taking off in the valley, and in recent years quite a few winery restaurants have made a name for themselves in culinary circles. Wine country starts in outer suburbia north of the Maroondah Highway just before Lilydale (turn-offs are signposted). North of Lilydale, you can check out wineries (again, all signposted) along or near three routes – the Warburton Highway to the east, the Maroondah Highway to Healesville, and the Melba Highway, heading north past Yarra Glen. The brochure *Wineries of the Yarra Valley* contains a complete list of all local wineries and a map. Even better is the detailed booklet *Wine Regions of Victoria* – both are available at tourist information centres. If you intend to take a few swigs (and can't find a teetotal driver) it's best to join a **winery tour**: Backpacker Tours Australia (☎03/9750 0112, ⓦwww.adventuretravel.com.au) picks up from four locations in central Melbourne, as well as one in St Kilda, visiting four wineries in the Yarra Valley ($98 including transport, tastings, a good restaurant lunch and a cheese platter in the afternoon).

The following are just a few of the wineries and restaurants in the Yarra Valley worth a visit. **Yering Station** (Mon–Fri 10am–5pm, Sat & Sun 10am–6pm; ☎03/9730 0100, ⓦwww.yering.com), 38 Melba Highway, just south of Yarra Glen, is located on the site of the first vineyard planted in the area in 1838 (the cellar door operates from the original brick building) and has a glass-walled

▲ Yering Station Winery

restaurant offering views across the valley, plus a wine bar and a shop selling regional produce. The grounds also host the lively **Yarra Valley Farmers' Market** (every third Sunday of the month 9am–2pm), selling fruit and vegetables, and other valley produce such as smoked trout, honey and jams. On the same property is the **Chateau Yering Historic House Hotel**. For real comfort and luxury, you can wine and dine at the hotel's more casual *Café Sweetwater* or the very posh *Eleonore's Restaurant*, then sink into a four-poster bed in one of the period-style rooms (☎03/9237 3333, ⓦwww.chateauyering .com.au; ⑨). The **Yarra Valley Dairy** (daily 10.30am–5pm; ⓦwww.yvd.com .au) at McMeikans Road, just south of Yering Station, sells gourmet cheeses and serves tasty lunches. **De Bortoli** (daily 10am–5pm; ☎03/5965 2271, ⓦwww .debortoli.com.au) occupies an unbeatable location at 58 Pinnacle Lane, off the Melba Highway at Dixon's Creek north of Yarra Glen, with views over gently rolling hills. This was one of the first places in the valley to offer gourmet food at its restaurant (daily noon–3pm & Sat from 7pm; bookings advisable) along with its wine – both cuisine and decor betray Italian influences.

Domaine Chandon (daily 10.30am–4.30pm; ☎03/9738 9200, ⓦwww .domainechandon.com.au), on the Maroondah Highway near the town of Coldstream, produces fine *méthode champenoise* sparkling wine, which you can sample ($9.50 with cheese) in a modern, bright and airy tastings-room with brilliant views. Free thirty-minute tours depart hourly at 11am, 1pm & 3pm. **Rochford** (☎03/5962 2119, ⓦwww.rochfordwines.com.au) winery and restaurant, further up towards Healesville at the corner of Maroondah Highway and Hill Road, is known for its sparkling Pinot Chardonnay and specializes in locally produced food; it also hosts regular concerts in its gardens.

Heading along the Warburton Highway via Yarra Junction you come to **WARBURTON**, a pretty, old-fashioned town on the Upper Yarra River, whose cool climate and hill-station atmosphere attracts droves of urban dwellers seeking respite from the city. The town is also the final stop on the **Warburton Rail Trail**, a forty-kilometre cycling track that follows the former Warburton Railway from Lilydale. For more information go to ⓦwww.railtrails.org.au.

Wineries apart, **YARRA GLEN** also boasts the splendidly restored *Grand Hotel* (☎03/9730 1230, ⓦwww.yarraglengrand.com.au; ⑥–⑦) with very comfy en-suite rooms and suites, some of them with antique furniture and balconies, as well as a café-bar, a bistro for moderately priced lunches and dinners (both open daily) and a more upmarket restaurant (Thurs–Sat from 6.30pm and Sun 11.30am–2pm). Not far away on the Melba Highway, the National Trust **Gulf Station** (☎03/9656 9800, ⓦwww.gulfstation.com.au; usually Wed–Sun & public holidays 10am–4pm; $9) is a collection of ten 1850s slab farm-buildings set in a large area of farmland stocked with settlers' original breeds such as Clydesdale horse and Berkshire pigs, although at the time of writing it was closed for renovation and the animals had been relocated; it was due to reopen early 2009.

Healesville and beyond

HEALESVILLE is a small, pleasant town nestled in the foothills of the Great Dividing Range; there's a **visitor centre** in the old courthouse building at the southern end of town, just off the Maroondah Highway (daily 9am–5pm; ☎03/5962 2600, ⓦwww.visityarravalley.com.au). The town's main attraction is the renowned **Healesville Sanctuary** (daily 9am–5pm; $23.60; ☎03/5957 2800, ⓦwww.zoo.org.au), a bushland zoo with more than 200 species of

9

▲ Birds of prey display, Healesville Sanctuary

Australian animals and a refuge for injured and orphaned animals, some of which are subsequently returned to the wild; those that stay join the sanctuary's programmes for education and the breeding of endangered species. It's a fascinating place in a beautiful setting, with a stream running through park-like grounds, dense with gum trees and cool ferns, and 3km of walking tracks. Many of the animals are in enclosures, but there are paddocks of emus, wallabies and kangaroos you can stroll through. The informative "meet the keeper" presentations are worth joining, especially the one featuring the birds of prey (noon & 2.30pm, weather permitting).

Sadly, much of the area north of Healesville, including the village of Marysville and the picturesque Steavensons Falls, was completely devastated by the Black Saturday bushfires (see box, p.985). Consequently many of the walks, picnic grounds and parks described below were closed to visitors at the time of writing; these include Maroondah Reservoir Park, Cathedral Range State Park, Kinglake National Park and Yarra Ranges National Park. Sections are slowly being reopened to the public, and many Marysville businesses are up and running, but check the current situation with Parks Victoria (℡13 19 63) or Marysville visitor centre (℡03/5963 4567, ⓦwww.marysvilletourism.com) before setting out.

Despite some fire damage, heading north on the Maroondah Highway over the Black Spur and Dom Dom Saddle towards Alexandra, the scenery becomes progressively more attractive. The Maroondah Reservoir Lookout, just off the highway 3km north of Healesville, is worth a brief stop, with picturesque views across the forest-fringed dam, and popular picnic grounds and gardens in the park on the southwest side of the reservoir. Soon after the reservoir, the highway meanders along bush-clad mountain slopes and enters luxuriant wet eucalypt forest with incredibly tall mountain ash, moss-covered myrtle beech, manna gum, gurgling creeks and waterfalls. The Fernshaw Reserve and Picnic Ground is a good place to stop and view the scenery. After the Dom Dom Saddle, 509m above sea level and 16km past Healesville, the highway descends towards Narbethong, where it enters drier country. Further up, the Maroondah Highway passes the drier Cathedral Range State Park: west of the road here the mighty sandstone cliffs of Cathedral Mountain rise almost vertically behind the paddocks, overlooking the Acheron Valley.

Less than an hour from Healesville is Melbourne's closest alpine resort, **Lake Mountain** (1400m), a very popular place for cross-country skiing and tobogganing (park entry $25–35 per car). Go to Ⓦwww.lakemountainresort.com.au for more details on opening times and rental information.

The Dandenongs

Like the Blue Mountains of New South Wales, the **Dandenong** hills are enveloped in a blue haze rising from forests of gum trees which cover much of the area. Rain ensures the area stays cool and lush, while fine old houses and gardens add to the scenery. Easy bushwalks in the **Dandenong Ranges National Park** start from Upper Ferntree Gully, accessible by train or by car via the Burwood Highway. The most picturesque route is along the winding **Mount Dandenong Tourist Road**, lined with mountain ash trees and quaint little villages, many with small cafés, galleries or craft shops that make for a pleasant pit stop. Atop the ranges there are amazing views of Melbourne and beyond from the newly developed SkyHigh observatory (Mon–Thurs 10am–10pm, Fri 10am–10.30pm, Sat 8am–11pm, Sun 8am–10pm; cars $4; Ⓣ03/9751 0443, Ⓦwww.skyhighmtdandenong.com.au), one of the park's most popular destinations on account of its spectacular views. On a clear day you can see Port Phillip Bay, the Mornington Peninsula and across to You Yangs park (see opposite). The area itself also has a café and bistro, a maze ($6) and gardens. To get there by car, take the Mount Dandenong Tourist Road then turn left at Ridge Road, or take bus #694/#698 from Ferntree Gully or Belgrave stations. A pleasant way to enjoy the forests and fern gullies is to take a ride on the **Puffing Billy** steam train (Ⓣ03/9757 0700, Ⓦwww .puffingbilly.com.au), which runs for 13km from the Puffing Billy station in Belgrave to Lakeside ($38.50 return) on Lake Emerald, stopping at Menzies Creek and Emerald: one train a day continues a further 9km from Lake Emerald to Gembrook ($51 return). The Puffing Billy station is a short, signposted walk from **Belgrave** Station (suburban trains). The train has run more or less continuously since the early 1900s, though its operation now depends on dedicated volunteers; on total-fire-ban days, diesel locomotives are used. Timetables vary seasonally but there are generally several services daily until late afternoon.

Just outside Emerald, man-made **Emerald Lake Park**, adjacent to the station, has over 15km of bush walks, paddleboats for hire ($15 for 30min), a water slide and free swimming pool, as well as picnic and barbecue facilities. Bus #695 runs daily from the Belgrave train station to Emerald.

Australian wildlife

When Australia broke away from the ancestral supercontinent Gondwana about ninety million years ago, its plants and animals took a fork in evolution's road to develop in splendid isolation from the rest of the world. Even though it shares the same latitude as South America and Africa, the country's wildlife is markedly different: most of the few mammal species are marsupials, and there's a huge diversity of birds, reptiles, amphibians and fish.

Marsupials and monotremes

Seventy percent of the world's **marsupials** are found in Australia. The best known are the members of the macropod ("big foot") family: the **kangaroo** (one of the two animals on Australia's coat of arms), and its petite cousins, the **wallaby**, **wallaroo** and **pademelon**. The **red kangaroo**, up to 2m tall, bounds across the savannahs and deserts of the continent, whereas mobs of the smaller **Western** and **Eastern grey kangaroo** frequent eucalypt forests, shrub- and grasslands. Another iconic marsupial is the cuddly, tree-hugging **koala** – found in Eastern and Southern Australia – which is more famous than the tubby **wombat**, which lives a solitary life in burrows in Eastern Australia and Tasmania. However, most marsupials are smaller animals: **possums**, **bettongs**, **numbats** and **gliders**.

Monotremes only occur in Australia and New Guinea. An evolutionary hybrid, they exhibit some characteristics of mammals – they're warm-blooded, have hair and produce milk – but lay soft-shelled eggs and, like reptiles, have the eponymous "single opening" for excretion and reproduction. With any luck, you'll spot shy **platypuses** at dusk or dawn at the edge of temperate rivers and freshwater lakes along the East Coast and in Tasmania. With its duck's bill, webbed feet and otter's body, the animal seemed so implausible that nineteenth-century scientists saw the first stuffed specimen and derided it as a hoax assembled from parts of other animals. The slightly less bizarre spiky **echidna** resembles a big hedgehog and can be found all over Australia.

Koala ▲

Platypus ▼

Dangers down under

Australians take a perverse pleasure in the fact that their country offers more opportunities than most to die by bite or sting. Some of its dangerous animals are large, others small – but all can be lethal. Basking in the former category, the **estuarine crocodile** is not a reptile to be trifled with: sturdy and broad-snouted, a mature male can grow to 6m and weigh up to 100kg. Its common name, the saltwater crocodile, is misleading because "salties" can be found up to 200km inland as well as near the coast – since they are opportunistic hunters whose prey, very occasionally, includes unwary humans, always take local advice on rivers and waterholes in the tropical north.

Australia is home to three-quarters of the world's most venomous **snakes**, among them the inland taipan, the deadliest land snake on the planet. You're more likely to encounter **redback spiders**, which are common in urban and suburban areas countrywide. Just as dangerous are the large, black **funnel-web spiders**, which thrive in eastern Australia, though since the development of antivenoms, no deaths from spider bites have been recorded.

▲ Green tree python

▼ Great white shark

And, of course, there is the **great white shark**, which patrols the temperate coastal waters around southern Australia. It is on the endangered list, and the number of shark attacks per capita has not risen in over a century, despite the increase in people using coastal waters. **Stingrays** became objects of morbid public fascination due to Steve Irwin, the environmentalist and TV personality who died of a barb to the heart in August 2006, but such incidents are extremely rare.

Kookaburra ▲

Zebra finches ▼

Cane toads ▼

Birds

Groups of **emus** roam across all areas of mainland Australia except rainforest and very arid deserts. A flightless, drab bird, the emu can reach speeds of up to 60kph.

A lot of Australian birds can be heard before they are seen: at dusk and dawn, **kookaburras** share private jokes as they guffaw raucously in the bush, and many a camper is awoken by the screeching of **galahs** or **cockatoos**. The gregarious family of parrots to which they belong is abundant in Australia, ranging from impressive birds such as the **yellow-** or **red-tailed black cockatoo** to smaller, equally colourful **lorikeets**, **budgerigars** and **cockatiels**. **Little penguins**, the smallest in the world, are the only penguin species to breed in Australia.

Invasive species

So delicate is the Australian ecosystem that every species introduced to control an indigenous pest – from camels to dingoes – has been spectacularly disastrous. Most insidious of all, however, is the **cane toad**, imported from Latin America in the 1930s in a failed attempt to control cane beetle in the sugar-cane fields of north Queensland. Unfortunately, the toads turned out to be huge pests themselves. With no natural predators to halt their progress, they have waddled down the East Coast to the north coast of New South Wales and across the top of the continent to the floodplains of the Top End, including Kakadu National Park. They are a disaster for native fauna – being highly toxic, the amphibians kill anything that eats them – and in March 2009 the first toad was spotted hopping across the Northern Territory/Western Australia border. Be very afraid.

Geelong and the Bellarine Peninsula

Heading west towards Geelong – for the Bellarine Peninsula and Great Ocean Road – it's just a short detour off the Princes Freeway to **WERRIBEE**, home to the restored **Werribee Park** Mansion (May–Oct Mon–Fri 10am–4pm, Sat & Sun 10am–5pm; Nov–April daily 10am–5pm; $13.50; ℡03/8734 5100, Ⓦwww.werribeepark.com.au), located on K Road, a few kilometres south of town. Built in 1874–77 by Scottish squatters Thomas and Andrew Chirnside, who struck it rich on the back of sheep, the sixty-room mansion is the largest private residence in Victoria. Guides in period costume show you around the ornate homestead and the Victorian-era gardens; alternatively, free audioguides are available at the entrance. The grand sandstone building is surrounded by 25 acres of formal gardens, including the **Victoria State Rose Garden** (daily 10am–5pm; free), which is at its best between November and April when the five thousand rose bushes are in bloom. From March to May the grounds host the **Helen Lempriere National Sculpture Awards**, where visitors can wander through the gardens displaying the finalists' exhibits. Beyond the gardens are the extensive grounds of **Werribee Open Range Zoo** (daily 9am–5pm; $23.60; ℡03/9731 9600, Ⓦwww.zoo.org.au), home to giraffes, cheetahs, lions, rhinoceroses, hippopotamues and monkeys, as well as kangaroos and emus. The magnificent savannah-like conditions are designed to resemble as closely as possible the natural habitats of the animals, which roam freely and can be seen on a 45-minute **safari tour** (10.30am–3.30pm; included in entrance fee), conducted by trained guides. **Werribee Park Shuttle**, a private bus service, provides transport to Werribee Park (mansion and zoo) from Melbourne, departing from the Victorian Arts Centre, St Kilda Road, at 8.30am and 10am ($25 return; advance booking required on ℡03/9748 5094, Ⓦwww.werribeeparkshuttle.com.au). Southeast of here is the **Shadowfax Winery** (Ⓦwww.shadowfax.com.au), an impressive box-like structure that offers cellar-door sales (daily 11am–5pm), glimpses of the wine-making process and tastings (Sat 4pm; $10), along with gourmet food from the deli.

Continuing along the freeway, you can detour west again through Little River to the **You Yangs Regional Park**, small but rugged volcanic peaks which rise sharply out of the surrounding plains. Scramble to the top of the highest, **Flinders Peak** (348m; approx 45min return), and you're rewarded with fine views of Geelong and Port Phillip Bay. The You Yangs, as well as the nearby **Brisbane Ranges**, are excellent places for spotting kangaroos, wallabies, koalas and possums at dusk. Alternatively, you can observe kangaroos, wallabies and emus, as well as numerous waterbirds, in their natural habitat at the little-known **Serendip Sanctuary**, 20km north of Geelong at 100 Windermere Rd, Lara (daily 10am–4.30pm; free; ℡03/5283 8000), which occupies a square kilometre of bush, marsh and wetlands. A refuge for threatened birds of the Western Plains of Victoria, the sanctuary is renowned for its captive breeding programme of brolgas, magpie geese and Australian bustards, which can be viewed on four self-guided walks (pick up a map from the information centre) ranging from 800m to 1400m, along walkways dotted with bird hides and observation areas. There's no public transport to the sanctuary; the nearest train station is Lara from where it's a half-hour walk.

Geelong

Approaching **GEELONG** via its industrial outskirts, you can be forgiven for wanting to zip past the bland melange of fast-food outlets, petrol stations and suburban housing to the beckoning seaside attractions of the Bellarine Peninsula and the Great Ocean Road beyond. However, Geelong has made a big effort to shed its rust-bucket image, mainly by revamping the waterfront it had previously turned its back on, and while still not warranting an extended stay, the city centre is a pleasant enough place to do some exploring, combined with a lunch stop.

Arrival and information

The easiest way to get to Geelong from Melbourne is by **train** (hourly from Southern Cross Station; 1hr; $6.20 one-way); the train station is situated northwest of the centre. To get to the Bellarine Peninsula from Geelong, take a McHarry's Buslines **bus** (☎03/5223 2111, 🌐www.mcharrys.com.au) from the train station for Ocean Grove and Barwon Heads, Point Lonsdale via Queenscliff, St Leonards via Portarlington, and Grovedale via Torquay.

In addition to the **visitor centre** (daily 9am–5pm; ☎031/5222 2900, 🌐www.visitgeelong.org) at the Wool Museum, there's a helpful **tourist information stall** (Mon–Sat 9am–5pm) in the Market Square Shopping Centre at the corner of Moorabool and Malop streets, and a booth on the waterfront (daily 10am–4pm), in front of the carousel. For details of what's going on in the city and southwest pick up a copy of the free *What's On* magazine from visitor centres.

Accommodation

Chifley on the Esplanade Hotel 13 The Esplanade, Geelong ☎03/5224 7700, 🌐www.constellationhotels.com. Upmarket accommodation with water views over Corio Bay, a restaurant, bar and a pool. [5]

Four Points Sheraton 10–14 Eastern Rd ☎03/5223 1377, 🌐www.fourpoints.com/geelong. Some of the best rooms in Geelong can be found at the *Sheraton*'s luxury waterfront tower, and offer grand spa baths and large-screen TVs. Service is impeccable and there's also a decent restaurant and gym. [7]

Irish Murphys 30 Aberdeen St, Geelong West ☎03/5221 4335, 🌐www.irishmurphys.com; bus #35/#36. Backpacker accommodation above a popular traveller's pub that offers basic six-bed dorm accommodation. Entertainment most nights from pub quizzes to live bands (Thurs–Sun). Dorms $20.

The National Hotel 191 Moorabool St, Geelong ☎03/5229 1211, 🌐www.nationalhotel.com.au. Mega-sociable hostel with a relaxed vibe. Rooms are a bit on the small side but guests will be spending most of their time in the excellent pub downstairs anyway; also a popular venue for live bands and its restaurant offers cheap noodle dishes with $7 specials. Dorms $28.

Riverglen Holiday Park 75 Barrabool Rd, Belmont ☎03/5243 5505, 🌐www.riverglenhp.com.au. Good caravan park on the south bank of the Barwon River, with shady tent-sites and timber cottages. Tents $24, cabins [3]

The Sphinx 2 Thompson St, North Geelong ☎03/5278 2911, 🌐www.sphinxhotel.com.au. Bizarre and extremely corny entertainment complex that has really overdone it with the Egyptian motif. Rooms are fine and good for the price though. Look for the huge Sphinx out the front. [5]

The Town

The **National Wool Museum** (Mon–Fri 9.30am–5pm, Sat & Sun 1–5pm; $7.30; ☎031/5227 0701), housed in the Geelong Wool Exchange, a National Trust–listed building at the corner of Brougham and Moorabool streets, is worth a visit. The well-set-up exhibition concentrates on the social history of the wool industry, with reconstructions of typical shearers' quarters and a millworker's 1920s cottage; wool is still auctioned off thirty days a year on the top floor of the exchange. Many of the town's best Victorian buildings are on **Little Malop Street**, including the elegant **Geelong Art Gallery** (Mon–Fri 10am–5pm, Sat & Sun 1–5pm; free, but donation appreciated; 🌐www.geelonggallery.org.au), which has an extensive collection of paintings by nineteenth-century Australian artists such as Tom Roberts and Frederick McCubbin, plus twentieth-century Australian paintings, sculpture and decorative arts. From Little Malop Street and Malop Street, Moorabool Street leads down to **Corio Bay** and the waterfront, with its renovated promenades, rotunda, fountains and a lovely nineteenth-century carousel featuring over thirty sculpted wooden horses. There's a swimming enclosure at Eastern Beach. Nestled among the lawns and trees of Eastern Park around ten minutes' walk from the city centre are Geelong's **Botanic Gardens** (daily 7.30am–5pm; free; free guided walks Wed 10.30am & Sun 2pm). The entrance is through the latest addition to the gardens, the 21st Century Garden, which specializes in resilient native and exotic dry-climate plants. Beyond this are the historic gardens: begun in the late 1850s, they boast lawns, rare trees, a fernery and conservatory, fountains and sculptures, as well as the small *Tea House* (daily 11am–4pm).

On the way to Torquay (see p.933) **Narana Creations** (Mon–Fri 9am–5pm, Sat 10am–4pm; free; ⓦwww.narana.com.au), an Aboriginal arts, crafts and cultural centre at 410 Torquay Rd (Surfcoast Highway) in Grovedale, is worth a brief stop. Paintings and various arts and crafts are sold here, and visitors can sometimes listen to Dreamtime stories or didgeridoo playing.

Eating and drinking

Barwon Club Hotel 509 Moorabool St, South Geelong ℡03/5221 4584. Geelong's most popular band-venue and pub also serves up tasty grub (mains around $20) which you can tuck into on the outdoor tables. Open for lunch & dinner Mon–Fri.

Beach House Restaurant Eastern Beach Reserve ℡03/5221 8322. The café downstairs (open Mon–Sun from 9am; closed evenings) serves breakfast all day as well as other cheap fare, while the upmarket restaurant upstairs (Wed–Sat from 6pm; also lunch Fri–Sun) offers eclectic East-meets-West cuisine. Great views, especially from the restaurant. Mains around $30. Licensed.

The Bended Elbow 69 Yarra St, Geelong ℡03/5229 4477. English-themed pub which has good-portioned lunch specials for $10–13 every day. At night the place fills up with people in search of a pint. Daily 11.30am–late.

Fishermen's Pier Seafood Restaurant Bay end of Yarra St ℡03/5222 4100. Fish and seafood prepared in a range of styles, from African to

Tuscan. Expensive. Licensed. Daily 11.30am–2.30pm & 5.30–9.30pm.

Giuseppe's Café 149 Parkington St, Geelong West ℡03/5223 2187. When the locals crave good Italian cuisine, they head here. Mains around $20. Tues–Sat from 5pm.

Irrewarra Sourdough Store & Café 10 James St ℡03/5221 3909. Outlet of bakery based in Colac in the Otways. Sells their range of outstanding breads, and serves delicious breakfasts and light lunches in the café section. Licensed. Mon–Fri 10am–3pm.

Wharf Shed Cafe 15 Eastern Beach Rd ℡03/5221 6645. Popular café-restaurant in a converted boatshed in Geelong's waterfront precinct that feeds cakes, pizzas and fish and chips to the masses coming here on a sunny weekend. Licensed. Mon–Fri 11am–11pm, Sat & Sun from 9am. Upstairs is the upmarket (and much pricier) *Le Parisien Restaurant* (℡03/5229 3110), open for lunch and dinner daily.

Queenscliff and around

From Geelong, the Bellarine Highway runs 31km southeast to **QUEENSCLIFF** through flat and not particularly scenic grazing country. Queenscliff is essentially a quiet fishing village on Swan Bay – with several quaint cottages on Fishermens Flat – which became a favourite holiday resort for Melbourne's wealthy elite in the nineteenth century, then fell out of favour, but has recently begun to enjoy something of a revival as a popular place for a weekend away or a Sunday drive.

Arrival, information and getting around

Ferries run from Queenscliff across the mouth of Port Phillip Bay to Sorrento (see p.909). The Queenscliff **Visitor Centre** is at 55 Hesse St (daily 9am–5pm;

⊕031/5258 4843, ⓦwww.queenscliff.org). You can rent a bike from *Beacon Resort* ($10–25; see below) and follow the **Bellarine Rail Trail** (map available from the information centre), a fabulous track running 33km from Queenscliff to Geelong through farming and coastal countryside, sharing some of the journey with the Bellarine Railway.

Accommodation

Beacon Resort Holiday Park & Motel 78 Bellarine Highway ⊕03/5258 1133, ⓦwww .beaconresort.com.au. Well-equipped holiday park with a heated pool. Tent sites from $35, cabins ❹–❻, holiday units and motel rooms ❺–❻

Queenscliff Dive Centre Lodge 37 Learmonth St ⊕03/5258 1188, ⓦwww.divequeenscliff.com.au. A good budget option that has good facilities including a sociable lounge with open fireplace. Dorms $32–35, rooms ❹–❺

Queenscliffe Hotel 16 Gellibrand St ⊕03/5258 1066, ⓦwww.queenscliffhotel.com.au. Considered the best Victorian-era hotel in town, the magnificently refined Queenscliff has eighteen period-style rooms and a marvellous dining room. ❽–❾

Queenscliff Inn YHA 59 Hesse St ⊕03/5258 3737, ⓔqueenscliff@yhavic.org.au. Very pleasant hostel set in a Victorian building; its single rooms (❷–❸) are particularly good value. Dorms $27–30, rooms ❹

Vue Grand 46 Hesse St ⊕03/5258 1544, ⓦwww .vuegrand.com. Grand hotel with Spanish-style exterior and a fabulously ornate Victorian interior, plus an award-winning, but expensive, restaurant. ❾

The Town

Queenscliff's position near the narrow entrance to Port Phillip Bay made it strategically important: a **fort** here faces the one at Point Nepean. Planned during the Crimean War, but not completed until 1885, it was built in response to the perceived threat of a Russian invasion, and was used again during World Wars I and II. Its museum can be visited on guided tours (Sat & Sun 1pm & 3pm; $5).

Other than the Bellarine Rail Trail (see above), activities include diving among wrecks and marine life with the **Queenscliff Dive Centre** ($195 for a one-day Scuba Experience; ⊕03/5258 1188, ⓦwww.divequeenscliff.com.au); and a cruise with **Sea All Dolphin Swims** (4hr; $120; twice daily Oct–April; ⊕03/5258 3889, ⓦwww.dolphinswims.com.au) visiting a seal colony, a gannet rookery and the chance to swim with dolphins in Port Phillip Bay.

Among the attractions is the **Queenscliff Maritime Museum**, Weerona Parade (Mon–Fri 10.30am–4.30pm, Sat & Sun 1.30–4.30pm; school holidays daily 10.30am–4.30pm; $5; ⊕03/5258 3440), which concentrates on the many shipwrecks caused by The Rip, a fierce current about 1km wide between Point Lonsdale and Point Nepean. Outside, a tiny fisherman's cottage is set up as it would have been in 1870, and there's a shed where an Italian fisherman painted, in naive style, all the ships he'd seen pass through from 1895 to 1947 (imaginatively including the *Titanic*). Next door, the **Marine Discovery Centre** has a small aquarium stocked with local marine life (Mon–Fri 11am–3pm, 10am–4pm during school holidays; $8; ⊕03/5258 3344); it also organizes a range of activities, mainly during the summer holidays, such as marine-biology cruises, rock-pool rambles and snorkelling tours. Every Sunday, the **Bellarine Peninsula Railway** operates steam trips from the old Queenscliff Railway Station to Drysdale, 20km northwest (11.15am & 2.45pm, plus Tues & Thurs during school holidays; $12 one-way, $20 return; ⊕03/5258 2069, ⓦwww.bpr.org.au). From October to May the railway hosts the Blues Train (6.30–11.30pm $76 return and meal; ⓦwww .thebluestrain.com.au), a round trip with performances by Melbourne's leading blues and jazz musicians.

The **Queenscliff Music Festival** (ⓦ www.qmf.net.au), held annually on the last weekend of November, features an eclectic mix of Australian contemporary music (folk, blues, world music, fusion) and draws ever-growing crowds.

Eating

Some of the town's best **places to eat** can be found along Hesse Street. In addition to the options below are the gorgeous – but pricey – restaurants at the *Vue Grand* (lunch and dinner daily) and the *Queenscliff Hotel* (lunch daily, dinner Thurs–Sat); the latter also has a cheaper courtyard restaurant.

Gusto 25 Hesse St. Serves locally produced wines by the glass and light lunches in a pleasant, Tuscan-style courtyard. Licensed. Daily 9am–5pm, Fri till late.

Harry's 2 Gellibrand St ⓣ03/5258 3750. This renowned old-timer is located on the balcony of the *Esplanade Hotel* with great sea views, and has a good wine list in addition to expensive, but excellent, seafood. Licensed. Daily noon–3pm, 6.30pm–late.

Ripview Bar & Bistro 118 Hesse St. Great-value food can be found at this bistro, situated on the first floor of the Bowling Club, with two-course lunches for $12. Licensed. Daily noon–2pm, 6–8pm.

Point Lonsdale and Portarlington

From Queenscliff it's about 5km to peaceful **Point Lonsdale**, whose most noticeable feature is its magnificent 1902 lighthouse, 120m high and visible for 30km out to sea. Below the lighthouse, on the edge of the bluff, is "Buckley's Cave" where William Buckley is thought to have lived at some stage during his thirty-year sojourn with the Aborigines. Ten kilometres or so west down the highway from Queenscliff, the **Adventure Park** (Oct–April: daily 10am–5pm; closed Tues & Wed Nov, Feb & March; adults $32; ⓣ03/5250 2756, ⓦwww .adventurepark.com.au), 1251 Bellarine Highway, Wallington, boasts Victoria's only water park, and is a big hit with kids and adults alike. Spread over fifty acres of picturesque parkland, it has over twenty rides and provides everything from giant water slides and a raging river to mini-golf, go-karts and paddleboats; to get there by bus phone McHarry's on ⓣ03/5223 2111.

At **PORTARLINGTON**, which sits on Port Phillip Bay about 14km north of Queenscliff, there's a beautifully preserved steam-powered flourmill (Sept–May: Wed, Sat & Sun noon–4pm; closed June to mid-Sept; $2.50; ⓣ03/5259 2804), four storeys of solid stone, owned by the National Trust.

Travel details

Trains

Melbourne to: Adelaide (3 weekly; 10hr); Alice Springs (2 weekly; 36hr); Ballarat (17 daily; 1hr 30min); Bendigo (19 daily; 2hr); Geelong (30 daily; 1hr); Perth (1 weekly; 50hr); Sydney via Albury (1 daily; 11hr 30min); Warrnambool (3 daily; 3hr 15min).

Buses

Melbourne to: Adelaide (3 daily; 10hr); Brisbane via Sydney (3 daily; 29hr); Sydney (5 daily; 13hr); Sydney via Canberra (2 daily; 14hr).

Ferries

Melbourne to: Devonport, Tasmania (1–2 daily; 9–11hr).

Flights

Qantas flies from **Melbourne** to: Adelaide (13 daily; 1hr 20min); Alice Springs (1–5 daily; 2hr 55min direct); Ayers Rock Resort (3–4 daily; 3hr 30min with one stopover); Brisbane (14 daily; 2hr 10min); Cairns (1–6 daily; 3hr 25min direct); Canberra (11 daily; 1hr 5min); Darwin (6 daily; 4hr 10min with one stopover); Hobart (2 daily; 1hr 15min);

Launceston (2 daily; 1hr 20min); Mackay (3 daily; 4hr 35min with one stopover); Perth (7 daily; 4hr 10min); Rockhampton (4 daily; 4hr 30min with one stopover); Sydney (32 daily; 1hr 25min); Townsville (3 daily; 6hr with one stopover).

Jetstar flies from **Melbourne Tullamarine** to: Cairns (1 daily; 3hr 25min); Gold Coast (8 daily; 2hr 5min); Hamilton Island (1 daily; 3hr 5min); Hobart (5 daily; 1hr 15min); Launceston (3 daily; 1hr); Newcastle (3 daily; 1hr 30min); Sunshine Coast (2 daily; 2hr 15min); and from **Melbourne Avalon** (near Geelong) to: Brisbane (3 daily; 2hr 5min); Sydney (7 daily; 1hr 20min).

Tiger Airways flies from **Melbourne** to: Adelaide (1–3 daily; 50min); Canberra (2 daily; 1hr 5min);

Gold Coast (3 daily; 2hr 5min); Hobart (1 daily; 1hr 15min); Launceston (1 daily; 1hr 5min); Mackay (1–2 weekly; 2hr 50min); Perth (2 daily; 4hr); Rockhampton (1–2 weekly; 2hr 35min).

Virgin Blue flies from **Melbourne** to: Adelaide (11 daily; 55min); Brisbane (12 daily; 2hr 10min); Cairns (4 daily; 5hr 10min with one stopover); Canberra (6 daily; 1hr); Darwin (1 daily; 7hr with one stopover); Coffs Harbour (2 daily; 3hr 35min with one stopover); Gold Coast (5 daily; 2hr); Hobart (4 daily; 1hr 15min); Launceston (4 daily; 1hr); Mackay (7 daily; 4hr 20min with one stopover); Perth (4 daily; 4hr 15min); Sydney (27 daily; 1hr 25min); Townsville (7 daily; 5hr 30min with one stopover).

10

Victoria

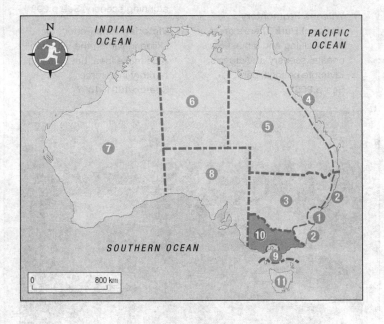

CHAPTER 10 # Highlights

* **Great Ocean Road** Wait until the sun is down and the crowds are gone and watch the fairy penguins come out to play at the Twelve Apostles. See pp.932–950

* **Goldfields** Mining memorabilia and grandiose architecture grace the old gold-towns of Ballarat and Bendigo. See pp.951–968

* **Wilsons Promontory National Park** There's great bushwalking and fantastic coastal scenery at Victoria's favourite national park. See p.986

* **Ned Kelly Country** Follow in the steps of Australia's most famous bush outlaw, in the historic towns that dot the northeast. See p.995

* **Milawa Gourmet Trail** Excellent local produce washed down with great wines from the Brown Brothers winery – all sampled against a backdrop of stunning scenery. See p.998

* **Victorian Alps** Perfect for skiing in winter, the Victorian Alps make ideal bushwalking territory in summer. See pp.1001–1007

▲ The Twelve Apostles

Victoria

A ustralia's second-smallest state, **Victoria** is also the most densely populated and industrialized, and has a wide variety of attractions packed into a small area. Although you're never too far from civilization, there are plenty of opportunities to sample the state's wilder days when it was a centre for **gold prospectors** and **bushrangers**. All routes in the state radiate from **Melbourne**, and no destination is much more than seven hours' drive away. Yet all most visitors see of Victoria apart from its cultured capital is the **Great Ocean Road**, a winding 285-kilometre drive of spectacular coastal scenery. Others may venture to the idyllic **Wilsons Promontory National Park** (the "Prom"), a couple of hours away on the coast of the mainly dairy region of **Gippsland**, or to the **Goldfields**, where the nineteenth-century goldrushes left their mark in the grandiose architecture of old mining towns such as **Ballarat** and **Bendigo**.

There is, however, a great deal more to the state. Marking the end of the Great Dividing Range, the massive sandstone ranges of the **Grampians**, with their Aboriginal rock paintings and dazzling array of springtime flora, rise from the monotonous wheatfields of the **Wimmera** region and the wool country of the western district. To the north of the Grampians is the wide, flat region of the Mallee – scrub, sand dunes and dry lakes heading to the **Murray River**, where Mildura is an irrigated oasis supporting orchards and vineyards. In complete contrast, the **Victorian Alps** in the northeast of the state have several winter **ski slopes**, high country that provides perfect bushwalking and horse-riding territory in summer. In the foothills and plains below, where bushranger **Ned Kelly** once roamed, are some of Victoria's finest wineries (wine buffs should pick up a copy of the excellent hundred-page brochure, *Wine Regions of Victoria*, available from the visitor centre in Melbourne and other towns). Beach culture is alive and well on this **coastline** with some of the best **surfing** in Australia.

The only real drawback is the frequently cursed **climate**. Winter is mild, and the occasional heatwaves in summer are mercifully limited to a few days at most (though they can create bushfires that last for weeks, see p.985), but the problem is that of unpredictability. Cool, rainy "English" weather can descend in any season, and spring and autumn days can be immoderately hot. But even this can be turned to advantage: as the local saying goes, if you don't like the weather, just wait ten minutes and it'll change.

Public transport, by road and rail, is with **V/Line** and subsidiary country bus lines. However, using your own vehicle is definitely a more convenient option, as train and bus services are fairly infrequent and quite a few places can be reached only with difficulty, if at all.

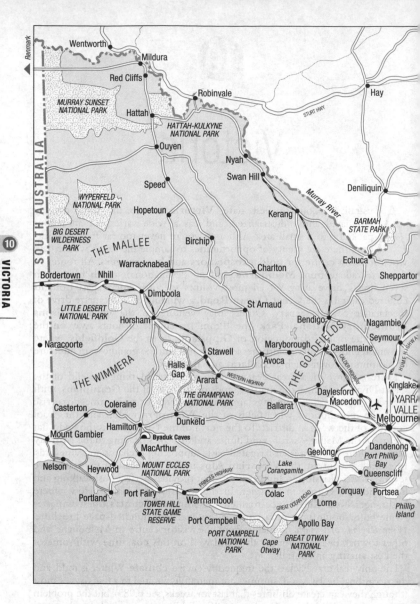

Some history

Semi-nomadic **Koories** have lived in this region for at least forty thousand years, establishing semi-permanent settlements such as those of circular stone houses and fish traps found at Lake Condah in western Victoria. For the colonists, however, Victoria did not get off to an auspicious start: there was an unsuccessful attempt at settlement in the **Port Phillip Bay** area in 1803, but Van Diemen's Land (Tasmania) across the Bass Strait was deemed more suitable. It was in fact from Launceston that Port Phillip Bay was eventually settled, in

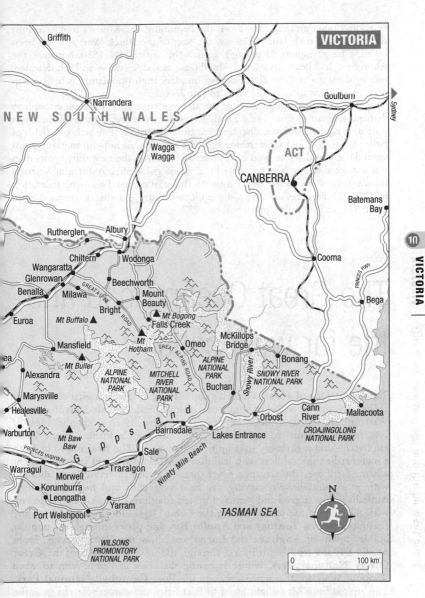

Griffith

Narrandera

NEW SOUTH WALES

Wagga Wagga

ACT

CANBERRA

Goulburn

Sydney

Batemans Bay

Rutherglen

Albury

Cooma

Chiltern

Wodonga

Wangaratta

Beechworth

Glenrowan

Benalla

Milawa

Mount Beauty

Euroa

Bright

Mt Buffalo

Mt Bogong

Falls Creek

Mansfield

Mt Hotham

Omeo

McKillops Bridge

Bonang

Mt Buller

ALPINE NATIONAL PARK

MITCHELL RIVER NATIONAL PARK

ALPINE NATIONAL PARK

SNOWY RIVER NATIONAL PARK

Alexandra

Marysville

Buchan

Healesville

Orbost

Cann River

Mallacoota

Warburton

Mt Baw Baw

Bairnsdale

Lakes Entrance

CROAJINGOLONG NATIONAL PARK

Warragul

Morwell

Sale

Traralgon

Ninety Mile Beach

Korumburra

Leongatha

Yarram

TASMAN SEA

Port Welshpool

WILSONS PROMONTORY NATIONAL PARK

GREAT ALPINE ROAD

GREAT ALPINE ROAD

PRINCES HWY

PRINCES HIGHWAY

Snowy River

Gippsland

N

0   100 km

Bega

1834; other Tasmanians soon followed and **Melbourne** was established. This occupation was in defiance of a British government edict forbidding settlement in the territory, then part of New South Wales, but **squatting** had already begun the previous year when Edward Henty arrived with his stock to establish the first white settlement at **Portland** on the southwest coast. A pattern was created of land-hungry settlers – generally already men of means – responding to Britain's demand for wool, so that during the 1840s and 1850s what was to become Victoria evolved into a prosperous pastoral community with squatters extending huge grazing runs. From the beginning, the Koories fought against the invasion of their land: 1836 saw the start of the **Black War**, as it has been called, a bloody guerrilla struggle against the settlers. By 1850, however, the Aborigines had been decimated – by disease as well as war – and felt defeated, too, by the apparently endless flood of invaders; their population is believed to have declined from around 15,500 to just 2300.

By 1851 the white population of the area was large and confident enough to demand separation from New South Wales, achieved, by a stroke of luck, just nine days before **gold** was discovered in the new colony. The rich goldfields of Ballarat, Bendigo and Castlemaine brought an influx of hopeful migrants from around the world. More gold came from Victoria over the next thirty years than was extracted during the celebrated California goldrush, transforming Victoria from a pastoral backwater into Australia's financial capital. Following federation in 1901, Melbourne was even the political capital – a title it retained until Canberra became fully operational in 1927.

The Great Ocean Road and the far west coast

The **Great Ocean Road**, Victoria's famous southwestern coastal route, starts at Torquay, just over 20km south of Geelong, and extends 285km west to Warrnambool. It was built between 1919 and 1932 with the idea of constructing a scenic road of world repute, equalling California's Pacific Coast Highway – and it certainly lives up to its reputation. The road was to be both a memorial to the soldiers who had died in World War I and an employment scheme for those who returned. Over three thousand ex-servicemen laboured with picks and shovels, carving the road into cliffs and mountains along Australia's most rugged and densely forested coastline; the task was speeded up with the help of the jobless during the Great Depression. The road hugs the coastline between **Torquay** and **Apollo Bay** and passes through the popular holiday towns of **Anglesea** and **Lorne**, set below the Otway Range. From Apollo Bay the road heads inland, through the towering forests of the **Great Otway National Park**, before rejoining the coast at Princetown to wind along the shore for the entire length of the **Port Campbell National Park**. This stretch from Moonlight Head to Port Fairy, sometimes referred to as the "Shipwreck Coast", is the most spectacular – there are two hundred known shipwrecks here, victims of the imprecise navigation tools of the mid-nineteenth century, the rough Southern Ocean and dramatic rock formations such as the **Twelve Apostles**, which sit out to sea beyond the rugged cliffs. Information on all the villages and sights on the Great Ocean Road can be found on the area's website, Ⓦ www.greatoceanroad.org.

From **Warrnambool**, the small regional centre where the Great Ocean Road ends, the Princes Highway continues along the coast, through quaint seaside

Port Fairy and industrial **Portland**, before turning inland for the final stretch to the South Australian border.

Transport

If you don't have your own car, you might want to consider one-way **car rental**, usually available from the big-name companies in Melbourne. There are plenty of parking spots where you can pull over and admire the view, but with narrow roads, steep cliffs and incessant hairpin bends drivers need to keep their eyes glued to the road. In summer the road is filled with **cyclists**, and although the routes are exhilarating they are really only suitable for the experienced and adventurous.

V/Line (⊕13 61 96, ⓦwww.vline.com.au) has a "Great Ocean Road" **bus** service from Geelong to Apollo Bay, calling at Torquay, Anglesea, Lorne and points in between (Mon–Fri three times daily, Sat & Sun twice daily; 2hr 30min; $13.70), and continuing three days a week to Warrnambool (Mon, Wed, Thurs). There is also a **train** service from Melbourne's Southern Cross to Warrnambool (Mon–Sat three daily, Sun twice daily; 3hr 20min; $26) with connecting buses to Port Fairy, Portland and Heywood and on to Mount Gambier in South Australia (1 daily). From Warrnambool you can also return to Melbourne much more quickly on the inland Princes Highway, or go north to Ballarat. See "Travel details" at the end of the chapter for more info.

Tours

One-way tours between Melbourne and Adelaide, via the Great Ocean Road, are a good way to take in the scenery. The backpackers' busline Oz Experience (⊕1300 300 028, ⓦwww.ozexperience.com) covers this route in three days, taking in the Great Ocean Road and the Grampians ($265, transport only). Wayward Bus (⊕1300 653 510, ⓦwww.waywardbus.com.au) offers a similar three-day tour from $395, including hostel accommodation, breakfasts and lunches. The small and friendly Groovy Grape covers the Great Ocean Road–Grampians route in an all-inclusive three-day tour (⊕1800 661 177, ⓦwww .groovygrape.com.au; $355).

A few other reliable tour operators do one- or two-day **round-trips** from Melbourne to the Great Ocean Road, some with an extra Grampians option and/or possible transfer to Adelaide – see the box on pp.906–907.

Hiking

Walking and hiking enthusiasts can choose between two magnificent **walking tracks** along the coast: the **Great Ocean Walk** (ⓦwww.greatoceanwalk.com .au; see also p.941), a 100-kilometre track from Apollo Bay to Glenample (near Princetown); and the long-established **Great Southwest Walk** (ⓦwww .greatsouthwestwalk.com), a superb 250-kilometre circuit starting from just outside Portland. Further sources of information include Parks Victoria (⊕13 19 63, ⓦwww.parkweb.vic.gov.au) and the DSE Information Centre, 8 Nicholson St, East Melbourne (⊕13 61 86, ⓦwww.dse.vic.gov.au).

Torquay

Gateway to the Great Ocean Road, **TORQUAY** is the centre of **surf culture** on Victoria's "surf coast" and two local beaches, **Jan Juc** and **Bells Beach**, are solidly entrenched in Australian surfing mythology. If you're not here for the waves, there's not really a lot happening: in hot weather the place is boisterously alive, but out of season it's somnolent. The big event here is the Rip Curl Pro,

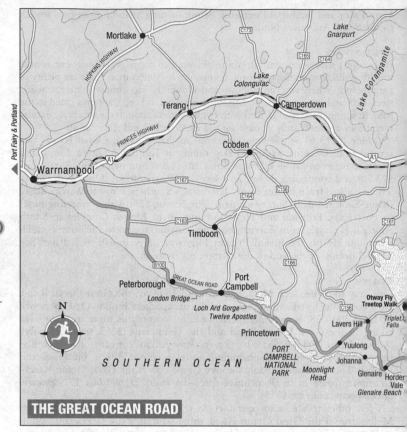

THE GREAT OCEAN ROAD

held at Bells Beach at Easter, which draws national and international contestants and thousands of spectators (call Surfing Victoria on ☎03/5261 2907 or see ⓦwww.ripcurl.com.au for details).

Arrival, information and accommodation

Local **buses** run between Geelong and Torquay via Jan Juc – McHarry's Buslines (☎03/5223 2111, ⓦwww.mcharrys.com.au) has details. **Torquay Visitor Centre** (daily 9am–5pm; ☎1300 614 219), in the Surfworld Museum in the Surf City Plaza, hands out a few leaflets and brochures.

There's a range of **accommodation** to suit all pockets.

Bells Beach Lodge 51–53 Surfcoast Highway ☎03/5261 7070, ⓦwww.bellsbeachbackpackers .com.au. Close to Surf City Plaza and painted with beach-house murals, this place is hard to miss. The small, clean and well-run hostel has dorms and a double, a nice backyard for BBQs and volleyball, plus internet access, bikes, boards and wet suits for hire. Unsurprisingly, it's very popular – book at

least a week in advance, earlier in Jan. Dorms $35, rooms ❹
Grossmans Country Cottages 50 Ashmore Rd ☎03/5261 2656, ⓦwww.grossmans.com.au. Excellent-value, fully equipped cottages positioned on rolling hills, 5min out of town. Has a real country-farm feel to it, making it perfect for those who want a bit of space. Each cottage can sleep

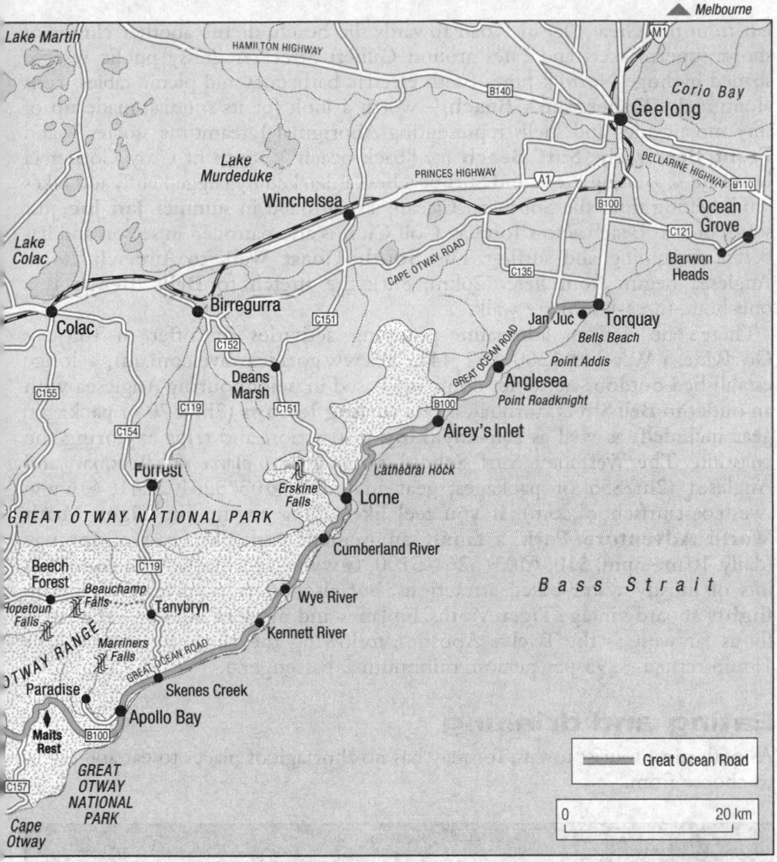

five people, and some have sea views. Owners also run a luxury spa centre on the premises that guests can use. [4]–[5]

Surf City Motel 35 The Esplanade ☎ 03/5261 3492, [W] www.surfcitymotel.com.au. Super location right across from the beach, but rooms are a little dated and prices are on the high side. Does come with a spa bath, heated pool and BBQ area. [4]–[7]

Torquay Hotel 36 Bell St ☎ 03/5261 2001, [W] www.torquayhotel.com.au. Very centrally located option, with good bistro fodder and live bands at the weekend too. The motel-style rooms are okay, but you are really paying for the location. [5]

Torquay Foreshore Caravan Park 35 Bell St ☎ 03/5261 2496, [W] www.gorcc.com.au/torquay-caravan-park. Situated within walking distance of the beach, and close to the shops, this huge park has an array of accommodation options, from powered sites to standard and deluxe cabins. Popular with students in the summer months. [3]–[5]

The Town

As you come into Torquay along the Surfcoast Highway – the main road into Torquay from Geelong – you'll see the **Surf City Plaza** shopping centre on your right, one of the best places in town to rent and buy surf gear. The **Surfworld Museum** at the rear of the plaza (daily 9am–5pm; $9; [W] www.surfworld.org.au) features a wave-making machine, interactive videos that explain how waves are created, and displays about the history of surfing. Turning left from the Great Ocean Road towards the beach, there's another cluster of shops, supermarkets and cafés around Gilbert Street. A grassy public reserve shaded by huge Norfolk pines (with electric barbecues and picnic tables) runs along rocky **Fisherman's Beach** – worth a look for its sundial, made up of tiny mosaic tiles and shells representing Aboriginal Dreamtime stories – and **Front Beach**. The **Surf Beach** (or "back beach"), south of Cosy Corner (a headland separating Front and Surf beaches), is backed by rugged cliffs and takes a full belting from the Southern Ocean; it's patrolled in summer. **Jan Juc**, just south of Surf Beach across Torquay Golf Club, is also patrolled in season and has better swimming and surfing. The **South Coast Walk** to Aireys Inlet via Anglesea begins from here (26km; 8hr); the stretch to **Bells Beach** is a one-hour, three-kilometre walk.

There's no end of adrenaline-pumping activities on offer in Torquay. Go Ride a Wave (T 1300 132 441, W www.gorideawave.com.au), a long-established outdoor-activities company based in neighbouring Anglesea with an outlet in Bell Street, Torquay, offers **surfing lessons** (2hr/$70 or packages; gear included) as well as **sea-kayaking** instruction and trips exploring the coastline. The Westcoast Surf School runs surfing classes in Torquay and Anglesea (2hr/$55 or packages; gear included T 03/5261 2241, W www .westcoastsurfschool.com). If you feel like taking to the air, **Tiger Moth World Adventure Park**, a family amusement park 3km east of Torquay (daily 10am–5pm; $10; T 03/5261 5100, W www.tigermothworld.com), has lots of mostly water-based attractions, but also offers skydives and **scenic flights** aboard vintage Tiger Moths, biplanes and modern aircraft – the latter fly as far west as the Twelve Apostles, following the rugged coastline (1hr 15min return, $295 per person, minimum 2 passengers).

Eating and drinking

As with most tourist towns, Torquay has no shortage of places to eat and drink to choose from.

▲ Surfers in Torquay

Restaurants, cafés and pubs

Bells Beach Hotel 3 Stuart Ave. Popular with beach-goers, this friendly local pub serves up excellent traditional pub food (huge burger $16). Open 9am–late.

Growlers 23 The Esplanade ☏03/5246 1397. Despite the sophisticated cuisine (mains around $20), this place has a laid-back beach vibe due to the Californian bungalow it occupies across from the water. Open Mon–Fri 11am–late, Sat–Sun 9am–late.

Moby 41 The Esplanade. Former run-down beach cottage, which has transformed into a great café serving tasty organic food (around $8–15). A local favourite. Daily 7am–4pm (hours extended in summer).

Sandbah 21 Gilbert St. This large and airy place is one of the nicest cafés on this street; they serve tasty breakfasts, cakes and lunches. Open 7am–6pm.

Scandinavian Ice Cream Company 34 Bell St. Great ice cream option near the beach, where surfers come at the end of the day.

Anglesea to Aireys Inlet

On the way to Anglesea from Torquay, you can make a short but worthwhile detour to **Point Addis**; turn left just beyond Bells Beach. The road goes right out to the headland car park where you look down on the waves crashing onto the point. Steps lead down to an even better vantage point, with surf heaving below you and Bells Beach stretching to the northwest. Just before the headland, there's another car park from where an access track leads to the **Koorie Cultural Walk**. Interpretive signs along this one-kilometre trail point out the use of plants and other aspects of the traditional lifestyle of the Wathaurong clan who inhabited the Geelong region.

ANGLESEA itself is a pleasant place for a holiday, with the Anglesea River running through to the sea, and picnic grounds along its banks; its main claim to fame is a large population of **kangaroos**, which graze on the golf course. Despite tourist development, the beach has managed to retain its sand dunes and untouched aspect. Children can swim safely here, as the surf is fairly gentle, but the waves are high and powerful enough for body-surfers to enjoy. The small *Anglesea Backpackers Hostel* at 40 Noble St (☏03/5263 2664, ⓦwww.angleseabackpackers.com; dorms $30, room ❹), located between the river and the golf course, has two six-bed dorms and an en-suite double. Internet access is also available. A great place to unwind is the friendly *Rivergums B&B* (☏03/5263 3066, ⓦwww.greatoceanroad.org/rivergums; ❼) at 10 Bingley Parade, along the river. There are two self-contained apartments (one with private access to the *Anglesea Hotel*). The local's favourite **café** is *Furios* at 95 Great Ocean Rd, where they serve breakfast, lunch and dinner with an Italian slant seven days a week. Two companies organize surfing and kayaking lessons here; see opposite.

From Anglesea the road goes inland for a few kilometres through scrubby bush. Beyond, the pretty Split Point Lighthouse (tours available Sat & Sun 11am, noon, 1pm, 2pm; $12) with a red cap overlooks the small town of **AIREYS INLET**, where there's a general store, a café and craft shop in what used to be the former lightkeeper's stables (7 Federal St; daily 9am–5pm). The horse-riding outfit Blazing Saddles operates rides through the Angahook-Lorne State Park offering beach rides and pony rides for kids (☏03/5289 7322, ⓦwww.blazingsaddlestrailrides.com). For **accommodation** try *Aireys Inlet Caravan Park* on the Great Ocean Rd (☏03/5289 6230, ⓦwww.aicp.com.au; cabins ❸–❻) or *Split Point Cottages* at 40 Hopkins St (☏03/5289 6566, ⓦwww.splitpointcottages.com.au; ❻–❽), which features accommodation in four mud-brick cottages with two bedrooms.

Lorne and around

Picturesquely set at the foot of the heavily forested **Otway Range**, on the banks of the Erskine River, **LORNE** has long been the premier holiday town of the Great Ocean Road. Only two hours' drive from the city, it's hugely popular with Melbourne weekenders who relish its well-established café society and whiff of 1960s counterculture overlaid on an essentially middle-class 1930s resort. To complete the picture, the **Great Otway National Park**, with its walking tracks, plunging falls and fern gullies, surrounds the town.

Information and accommodation

Lorne's **visitor centre**, at 15 Mountjoy Parade (daily 9am–5pm; ☏1300 891 152, ⊛www.visitsurfcoast.com.au), is very helpful and has a good stock of leaflets packed with local information. Lorne Surf Shop at 132 Mountjoy Parade (daily 9.30am–5pm; ☏03/5289 1673) rents out surf- and boogie-boards and wet suits. Other services, such as banks, a post office and shops, are clustered primarily along Mountjoy Parade and parallel Smith Street.

Most **accommodation** is in the upper price bracket, and in December and January the majority rent by the week, with even B&Bs insisting on a three- or four-night minimum stay. To keep costs down, contact the Lorne Foreshore Committee, Ocean Road by Erskine Bridge (☏03/5289 1382, ⊛www.gorcc .com.au/lorne-caravan-park), which runs four **caravan parks** in the vicinity.

Cumberland Apartments 150 Mountjoy Parade ☏03/5289 4444, ⊛www.cumberland.com.au. Luxurious, fully equipped apartments set right on the beach, many with private balconies overlooking the water. Facilities include gym, tennis and squash courts, indoor swimming pool, and surfboard and mountain-bike hire. ❼–❽

Erskine Falls Cottages Cora-Lynn Court, off Erskine Falls Rd, 4.5km north of town ☏03/5289 2666, ⊛www.lornecottages.com.au. Spacious timber self-contained cottages (1–3 bedrooms) and units in the hills near Erskine Falls, with views of the ocean, big verandas, fireplaces, a pool and a tennis court. ❺–❼

Grand Pacific Hotel 268 Mountjoy Parade, opposite the pier at Point Grey ☏03/5289 1609, ⊛www.grandpacific.com.au. The restored and refurbished Victorian lives up to its name: it has great views over Loutit Bay from the dining room and the bar, and rooms have old-world charm but all the mod cons. It's worth shelling out a bit more for a room with sea views. Hotel rooms ❺, apartments ❼

Great Ocean Road Backpackers YHA 10 Erskine Ave ☏03/5289 1809, ⓔlorne@yhavic.org. This excellent, attractive hostel shares the grounds with *Great Ocean Road Cottages* (see below). The hostel section comprises two large timber cottages with balconies, and there's free use of laundry, bicycles and boogie-boards. Dorm bed $20, rooms ❸

Great Ocean Road Cottages 10 Erskine Ave ☏03/5289 1070, ⊛www.greatoceanroadcottages .com.au. Well-designed, comfortable, self-catering cottages in a lovely forest setting beside the Erskine River, just minutes from the main strip. ❺–❼

Lorne Hotel Mountjoy Parade ☏03/5289 1409, ⊛www.lornehotel.com.au. Super-central pub that has nice enough rooms, but can get noisy on weekends. Some rooms have ocean views with balconies and spa. ❺

The Town

About a thousand people live in Lorne, but from Christmas until the end of January twenty thousand more pour in; if you arrive unannounced, you'll have no hope of finding even a camping spot. The three-day **Falls Festival** (⊛www .fallsfestival.com) held over New Year is celebrated with a big rock concert that attracts droves of teenagers, followed eight days later by the Mountain to Surf Run and one day later by the highlight of the peak season, the **Pier to Pub Swim**. It is said to be the largest blue-water swimming event in the world and attracts as many as four thousand competitors who race the 1200m from Lorne

Pier to the main beach. The atmosphere surrounding these events is a lot of fun, but generally Lorne is more enjoyable when it's less crowded, which means avoiding weekends and the peak summer season.

The town's beachfront is enlivened by the restored *Grand Pacific Hotel* with its 1870s facade, on a headland at the western end, and the modern, pink, terraced *Cumberland Resort*. Between the street and the beach is a foreshore with trampolines and a pool. The **surf beach** itself is one of the safest in Victoria, protected from the Southern Ocean by two headlands, but in summer it gets very crowded.

The Lorne Theatre, 78 Mountjoy Parade (℡03/5289 1272, ⓦwww.greatoceanroadcinemas.com.au), screens films all week during summer and in the school holidays.

Eating and drinking

There are great places to **eat** and **drink** everywhere in town – but they charge Melbourne prices and then some. Most licensed places allow you to bring your own wine but charge a hefty corkage fee.

Andrew's Chicken Joint 134 Mountjoy Parade. Licensed takeaway known for cooking up burgers and souvlakis at affordable prices. Where the surfers come to refuel. Open daily.

Arab 94 Mountjoy Parade ℡ 03/5289 1435. An original beatnik hangout, which opened two weeks before the Olympic Games in 1956 and has been going strong ever since. It now sports minimalist decor and is still good for daytime snacks and fancier meals at night. Licensed and BYO wine. Daily 7am–9.30pm.

Ba Ba Lu Bar and Restaurant 6A Mountjoy Parade. Nice joint at the quieter eastern end of town with a great outdoor area. The restaurant follows a Spanish–Latin American theme with tapas and mains such as *gambas a la plancha* (chargrilled prawns in a sherry sauce). There's also a good range of breakfasts and cheaper lunch items. Licensed and BYO. Daily 9am–1am.

Beach Buns Bakery Shop 2/32 Mountjoy Parade. The place to come to buy straight-out-of-the-oven pies, pastries and snacks for the beach. Also makes gourmet sandwiches for those looking to take a picnic lunch. Open daily.

Kosta's 40 Mountjoy Parade. A popular, Greek-style bar and eating place, serving up good seafood as well as grilled meats. Often has music in the evenings. Licensed or BYO wine. Daily 9am–1am; closed July.

The Lorne Deck 1 William St. The real highlight of this place isn't the modern and reasonably priced menu, but the great sun deck that looks over the town towards the water. A great place to hang out and watch the sunset. Daily 11am–late.

Lorne Hotel 176 Mountjoy Parade. Best pub meals in town ($14–25), plus a dining room and a sensational beer garden overlooking the ocean and live music on Fri and Sat. Daily noon–9pm.

Lorne Pier Seafood Restaurant ℡03/5289 1119. Pricier than the average fish-and-chips shop but this well-known seafood restaurant is worth it for the setting alone. Licensed and BYO. Daily 6–9.30pm, longer in summer.

Qdos Allenvale Rd ℡ 03/5289 1989. Tucked away in the eucalypt-clad hills above Lorne, this art gallery-cum-café serves light lunches, dinners and tasty home-made cakes and coffee in a relaxed atmosphere. Bookings advisable. Mon & Wed–Sun 9am–5.30pm, summer 9am–late.

Around Lorne

Surrounding Lorne are the lush forests of the **Otway Ranges**, which form part of the Great Otway National Park (see p.942). Pockets of temperate rainforest, towering blue-gum forests, cliffs and waterfalls characterize the Lorne section of the park, south of the Erskine River. The **Erskine Falls**, one of the most popular attractions, drop 30m into a fern-fringed pool – you can reach them along a winding eight-kilometre road that ends with a short descent on a very steep but sealed section. From the car park the falls are a few minutes' walk through majestic trees and tall umbrella ferns; another 150m takes you down to the quiet, rocky Erskine River. It's also possible to walk through the bush from

Lorne to the falls (7.5km one-way; 4hr), starting from the *Erskine River Caravan Park* (one of the four caravan parks run by the Lorne Foreshore Committee) next to the bridge over the Erskine River, just off the Great Ocean Road and following the river; after 1km you'll pass the Sanctuary, a natural rock amphitheatre, then Splitter Falls and Straw Falls, before reaching Erskine Falls.

Closer to Lorne, **Teddy's Lookout**, in Queens Park, is either a quick drive from the Great Ocean Road (up Otway St, turn left at the roundabout into George Street), or a three-kilometre walk along the same streets; just follow the signposts. You end up high above the sea, with a view of the St George River below and the Great Ocean Road curving around the cliffs.

Apollo Bay and the Otway Ranges

Between Lorne and Apollo Bay wooded hills fall away steeply into the ocean. If you can, stop for lunch and take advantage of the stunning ocean views at *Wye Beach Hotel* (℡03/5289 0240, ⊛www.wyebeachhotel.com.au) in the sleepy hamlet of **Wye River**. It also has rooms (❺–❻) in case you find it hard to leave. **APOLLO BAY** itself enjoys a picturesque setting between pounding surf and gently rounded green hills.

Information and accommodation

The **Great Ocean Road Visitor Information Centre**, on the foreshore at the eastern end of town (daily 9am–5pm; ℡03/5237 6529), has very helpful staff who can book **accommodation**. There are numerous options in the area, many of them picturesquely located in the hills and valleys surrounding the town – a scenic location is the **Barham River Valley** 8km west of town that has places in a lush rainforest setting. Apollo Bay's main street is lined with **motels**, most of them rather drab 1970s affairs.

There are several **caravan parks**, including the *Apollo Bay Holiday Park* at 27 Cawood St (℡03/5237 7111, ⊛www.apollobayholidaypark.com.au; cabins ❹), *Pisces Caravan Resort*, 2km north of the town centre (℡03/5237 6749, ⊛www.piscespark.com.au; ❶–❹), and the *Marengo Holiday Park* on Marengo Crescent in secluded surroundings on the foreshore (℡03/5237 6162, ⊛www.marengopark.com.au; ❸–❻).

Apollo Bay Backpackers 47 Montrose Ave ℡1800 113 045, ⊛www.apollobaybackpackers .com.au. Small house that has a very chilled "beach bum" vibe. Internet access, BBQ in the backyard and nice tables at the front for socializing. Dorms $20, rooms ❷

Eco Beach YHA 5 Pascoe St ℡03/5237 7899, ⓔapollobay@yhavic.org.au. Easily the state's best budget-accommodation option. This million-dollar property has incredible facilities including a great sun deck looking towards the sea, and state-of-the-art kitchen and lounge rooms. Those not acquainted with such extravagance may want to stay here indefinitely. Dorms $28, rooms ❹

Marriner's Falls Cottages 1090 Barham River Rd, Barham River Valley ℡03/5237 7494, ⊛www.marrinersfalls.com.au. Spacious and cosy cottages, built on a hillside, with spa, open fire, balconies and great views. ❼

A Room with a View 280 Sunnyside Rd, Wongarra ℡03/5237 0218, ⊛www .roomwithaview.com.au. Cozy, aptly named B&B accommodation, 14km east of town, with magnificent views of green rolling hills and the ocean, and gourmet breakfasts to set you up for the day. ❻–❽

Sandpiper Motel 3 Murray St ℡03/5237 6732, ⊛www.sandpiper.net.au. Only 50m from the beach, these stylish apartments (some with ocean views) offer a luxurious setting in the middle of everything. Also has broadband. ❻

Skenes Creek Lodge Motel 61 Great Ocean Rd, Skenes Creek ℡03/5237 6918, ⊛www .skenescreekmotel.com. Good budget motel in a garden setting above the main road, with restaurant and ocean views. ④

Surfside Backpackers Corner of of Great Ocean Rd and Gambier St ☏1800 357 263, ⓔinfo @surfsidebackpacker.com. A friendly place with small dorms and cheap doubles in a scenic location on a hill at the western side of town looking over the water. Facilities include disabled access, pool table, outdoor BBQs and a large vinyl collection. Dorms $22, rooms ❷

The Town

Fishing – commercial and recreational – is the main activity in Apollo Bay. If you're interested in doing a bit yourself, enquire at Apollo Bay Fishing and Adventure Tours (☏03/5237 7888, ⓦwww.apollobayfishing.com.au), which offers fishing trips, seal watching and scenic boat cruises. The town also marks the start of the **Great Ocean Walk**, a 100-kilometre track through forests and some of the state's most stunning coastal scenery. Note that sections of the track become impassable at high tide and in rough weather so make sure you register with the visitor centre (see opposite) which provides updates on its condition. If you're a **cycling** enthusiast enquire about mountain–bike tours run by Otway Expeditions that go from the "rainforest to the beach" (☏0419 007 586; $65, min 6 person). **Flying** is popular here, too: the Wingsports Flight Academy, in Evans Court (☏0419 378 616, ⓦwww.wingsports.com.au), offers courses in hang-gliding and para-gliding and allows those with no prior experience to fly with a fully qualified pilot along the coast in a powered hang-glider. Twelve Apostles Aerial Adventures (☏03/5237 7370, ⓦwww.tigermothworld.com) and Apollo Bay Aviation (☏0407 306 065, ⓦwww.apollobayaviation.com.au), both at the Apollo Bay airfield south of town, do scenic flights to a variety of destinations, including nearby Cape Otway and the Twelve Apostles ($140–200 per person for 45min, depending on size of group), and as far afield as King Island, Tasmania. Otway Eco Tours operates out of the Otway town of Forrest, 37km northwest of Apollo Bay, and runs **canoe trips** in the densely forested hinterland to see platypus and glow-worms (☏03/5236 6345, ⓦwww.platypustours.net.au; 2–6 people; 3.5–4hr; $85). For other sightseeing **tours** (4WD or normal vehicle) enquire at the visitor centre.

Activities aside, the town has an enjoyably alternative feel – a lot of artists and musicians live here and both local pubs often have music at weekends. The weekly **Foreshore Market** (Sat 8.30am–4.30pm) is well worth a browse and showcases locally produced arts and crafts as well as fresh produce. The annual **Apollo Bay Music Festival** (ⓦwww.apollobaymusicfestival.com) takes place over a weekend in mid-March and features jazz, rock, blues and country.

Eating and drinking

In town, the places to eat are strung along the Great Ocean Road. To buy freshly caught seafood, go to the Fishermen's Co-op at the harbour (Mon–Thurs 9.30am–4.30pm, Fri until 5pm, Sat & Sun 10am–3pm).

Apollo Bay Hotel 95 Great Ocean Rd ☏03/5237 6250. Great pub that offers very good bistro meals (lunch around $15) and with an excellent beer garden that looks towards the water.

Bayleaf Café 31 Great Ocean Rd. Good breakfast pit stop where you can fuel up on bacon butties and the like. Daily breakfast and lunch, plus dinner in summer.

Bend Café 3225 Great Ocean Rd ☏03/5237 9102. Halfway to Lavers Hill, this makes the perfect stop to take in the charming rural setting. Food is sourced from local producers. Summer daily for breakfast, lunch and dinner; winter weekends only.

Buffs Bistro 51 Great Ocean Rd. This reliable old-timer serves light snacks, seafood and pasta – leave room for one of the huge desserts from the counter. Daily noon–late.

Chris's Beacon Point Restaurant 2km up Skenes Creek Rd, Skenes Creek ☏03/5237 6411. The renowned restaurant in the hills above Skenes

Creek features Mediterranean cuisine with a Greek accent and specializes in seafood – but it doesn't come cheap (mains $30–36). Daily breakfast, lunch and dinner.

Monsoon 18 Pascoe St ℡03/5237 6766. Very good Thai–Vietnamese cuisine at average prices (mains $11–16). Dinner daily.

Great Otway National Park

From Apollo Bay, the Great Ocean Road soon enters **Great Otway National Park**, a new 53,000-acre park that stretches south along the coast from Anglesea and inland to Lavers Hill and beyond, taking in the lush forests of the Otway Ranges and the former Otway National Park as well as the Carlisle, Melba Gully and Angahook-Lorne state parks. From Maits Rest car park, 15km west of Apollo Bay, you can take an easy stroll through a lovely fern gully, which gives a feel of the dense rainforest that once covered the entire Otway Ranges. A little further down the road, towards Lavers Hill, you'll see a turn-off to the **Cape Otway Lighthouse**, 14km away on a sealed road, where there's a small café (daily 9.30am–4.30pm) and pleasant accommodation in two refurbished lighthouse-keepers' residences, simply but tastefully decorated and fully equipped (℡03/5237 9240, ⓦwww.lightstation.com; ➐–➒). You can visit the lighthouse (daily 9am–5pm; $14.50) or join a guided tour (daily from 9am; 45min; no extra fee). Three kilometres north of Cape Otway, the turn-off to Blanket Bay is a good location for spotting koalas. The only **caravan park** actually within the national park is *Bimbi Park* (℡03/5237 9246, ⓦwww.bimbipark.com.au; cabins ➋–➍), about halfway along the road to the lighthouse. The facilities and some of the cabins are quite basic but the setting is gorgeous – on a small farm with paddocks surrounded by bushland – and the caravan park offers excellent **horse-riding** excursions, including a ride to Station Beach (1hr 30min; $55), a three-kilometre-long stretch of sand with freshwater springs and waterfalls.

Back on the Great Ocean Road, you momentarily return to the ocean at **Castle Cove**, a good lookout point across green, undulating dairy country. As you turn inland again, stepped hills rise sharply from the road as it passes turn-offs to **Johanna**, one of Victoria's best-known surf beaches, and winds up towards **LAVERS HILL**, the highest point in the Otway Ranges. The tiny town has two good cafés: *Gardenside Manor* (9am–5pm daily) and *Blackwood Gully Tea Rooms* (11am–5pm daily); both serve light snacks and Devonshire teas daily. There's motel accommodation at the *Otway Junction Motor Inn* (℡03/5237 3295; ➎) and a small, cosy cottage plus budget rooms at Fauna Australia Wildlife Retreat, a privately run Australian wildlife sanctuary – they also offer guided tours and serve refreshments (℡03/5237 3234, ⓦwww.faunaaustralia.com.au; ➎–➑).

Before continuing west, it's worth taking a detour to the **Otway Fly Treetop Walk**, about fifteen minutes' drive east of Lavers Hill (daily 9am–5pm; $22; ⓦwww.otwayfly.com) – just follow the road signs. A 600-metre steel-trussed walkway here allows you to walk through temperate rainforest at canopy level, 25m above the ground. The Otway Fly Visitor Centre on top of the hill, 300m from the beginning of the walkway, has a good licensed café and a souvenir shop.

The Shipwreck Coast

The 130-kilometre stretch of coast between lonely, windswept Moonlight Head and Port Fairy is known as the **Shipwreck Coast**; it takes in the Twelve Apostles – something of an icon of the Great Ocean Road – and other well-known coastal formations such as Loch Ard Gorge and London Bridge. Most of the coast is protected under the auspices of the Great Otway National Park and **Port Campbell National Park**. Seven hundred ships have come to grief in the coast's treacherous waters – two hundred of which have been found – and the **Historic Shipwreck Trail**, which links the sites of 25 wrecks with informative plaques and signed walking-paths, runs between Moonlight Head and Port Fairy. A brochure about the trail is available at all the visitor centres in the region.

At the tiny hamlet of Princetown, *The 13th Apostle* (℡03/5598 8062, ⓦwww .users.bigpond.com/the13thapostle; dorm beds $19–23, rooms ❸), a modern, purpose-built hostel, provides pleasant and clean budget accommodation. A general store and pub are across the road.

The Twelve Apostles and Loch Ard Gorge

The most awe-inspiring formations on the coast are the **Twelve Apostles** – gigantic limestone pillars, some rising 65m out of the ocean, which retreat in rows as stark reminders of the power of the sea (the cliff faces erode at a rate of about 2cm a year). The (unstaffed) Twelve Apostles Centre at the car park on the northern side of the road provides clean toilet facilities and welcome shelter from the rain and bone-chilling winds blowing off the Southern Ocean. It features wall-length panels of sailcloth with scripted poems about the Shipwreck Coast's awesome, dangerous beauty. Covered walkways lead through a tunnel under the road to the lookout points and a short walk along the clifftop. Sunset here (summer around 9pm, winter around 5.45pm) is a popular time for photographers and, unfortunately, crowds. Wait ten minutes or so after dusk, however, when the tourists have jumped back on their coaches and left, and you'll be treated to another fantastic spectacle, as hordes of fairy penguins waddle onto the shore in droves.

Next stop is underrated **Loch Ard Gorge**, where a small network of clifftop walks and a staircase leading down to a beach give you the chance to view the fantastic rock formations all around. It was here that the *Loch Ard*, an iron-hulled square rig, hit a reef and foundered while transporting immigrants from England to Melbourne in the spring of 1878. Of 53 people on board, only two survived: Eva Carmichael and Tom Pearce, both in their late teens. They were swept into a long gorge that had a narrow entrance, high walls and small beach, and Tom dragged Eva into a cave in the western wall of the gorge before going for help. A walkway leads down to the beach, covered with delicate pink kelp, and you can scramble over craggy rocks to the cave where Eva sheltered, now a nesting site for small birds. The Loch Ard cemetery, where the ship's passengers and crew are buried, is on the clifftop overlooking the gorge. As you drive further, you pass more scenic points, with resonant names such as the Blowhole and the Thundercave, before reaching Port Campbell.

For a bird's-eye view of all this, take a helicopter ride with 12 Apostles Helicopters based on the Great Ocean Road near Loch Ard Gorge, just east of Port Campbell (℡03/5598 8283, ⓦwww.12ah.com).

Port Campbell and around

PORT CAMPBELL is a small settlement on the edge of the Port Campbell National Park, and the main base for those visiting the Twelve Apostles. The **Port Campbell Visitor Centre** on Morris Street (daily 9am–5pm; ℡03/5598 6089, ⓦwww.visit12apostles.com) has displays and information about the area and its national parks, and can also book accommodation. Ask here too about the **Port Campbell Discovery Walk** (90min), which will take you along a clifftop to a viewpoint above Two Mile Bay.

Port Campbell **beach** is a small sandy curve, safe for swimming and patrolled in season – the town climbs the hill behind the beach.

If you're really fascinated by shipwrecks, Port Campbell Boat Charters, at the Mobil Petrol Station at 32 Lord St (☎03/5598 6379), offers **diving** to some wreck sites, fishing trips and can rent out snorkelling or diving gear to those who want to go it alone.

Practicalities

The town itself is a pleasant place to while away an evening, and with two hostels in town, **accommodation** needn't be expensive. In summer and for long weekends, however, it's advisable to book far ahead. The *Port Campbell Hostel* (☎03/5598 6305, ⓦwww.portcambellhostel.com.au; dorms $25, rooms and cabins ❸) on Tregea Street is a pleasant, well-run place with a good kitchen, a spacious common room and TV lounge, internet access, bright dorms, double/twin rooms and two cabins. In comparison, *Ocean House Backpackers* (☎03/5598 6223, ⓦwww.portcampbell.nu/oceanhouse; dorm beds from $30) may have a great location facing the water on Lord Street but the old house is rather dark and somewhat cramped. This hostel is operated by the pleasant Port Campbell National Park Cabin & Camping Park on Morris Street (☎03/5598 6492, ⓦhttp://portcampbellcabincampingpark.street -directory.com.au); small groups are possibly better off booking into one of their beachside cabins (❺). The *Loch Ard Motor Inn* (☎03/5598 6328, ⓦwww .loachardmotorinn.com.au; ❺–❼) is in a prime position opposite the beach, and most of their simple yet comfortable rooms have personal patios facing the water. Rooms also have wireless internet. Moving more upmarket, the *Sea Foam Villas* (☎03/5598 6413, ⓦwww.seafoamvillas.com; ❻) at 14 Lord St are well equipped with private balconies with sea views.

Port Campbell has plenty of places to **eat**, all close to each other on Lord Street. For regular Aussie fare or a late-night drink (they close when the last person leaves), go to the good-quality bistro at the *Port Campbell Hotel* (daily lunch and dinner). The simply titled *Take-Away* opposite the foreshore is a favourite with surfers needing their fish-and-chip fix, while the recently opened *20ate restaurant* (daily dinner), at no. 28, serves well-priced steak, fish and pasta dishes and has a pleasant front terrace with a fountain. Across the road is *Waves* (8am–9.30pm daily; mains from $18.50; booking advised on ☎03/5598 6111), considered the best place in town serving reliably good breakfasts, lunch and dinner.

Port Campbell's expensive **general store** (daily: winter 8am–6pm; summer 7.30am–9pm) also has a bottle shop and an EFTPOS system that takes every type of card; it also functions as the post office and newsagent.

London Bridge, the Grotto and Timboon

Tourists could once walk across the double-arched rock formation known as **London Bridge**, a short distance west of Port Campbell, to the outer end facing the sea. In mid-January 1990, however, the outer span collapsed and fell into the sea, minutes after two very lucky people had crossed it – they were eventually rescued from the far limestone cliff by helicopter. As luck would have it, the couple were conducting an extramarital affair, and fled from the waiting media as soon as the helicopter arrived. Another good place to stop, just before Peterborough, is the **Grotto**, where a path leads from the clifftop to a rock pool beneath an archway.

Moving on, you pass through undulating dairy country on the last stretch of the Great Ocean Road from Peterborough, on Curdies Inlet, to Warrnambool.

Warrnambool and around

Coming into **WARRNAMBOOL** on the Great Ocean Road you see the city's more pleasant aspects: its lovely coastal setting, with **Allansford Cheeseworld** (Mon–Fri 8.30am–5pm, Sat 8.30am–5pm, Sun 10am–4pm; [W] www.cheeseworld.com.au) indicating that this is the centre of rich **dairy country**. As well as selling cheese, it has tastings, a café serving teas and light meals, and a local history museum. However, if you approach Warrnambool from the northeast along the Princes Highway, you'll pass car lots, motels and an ugly factory belching smoke.

Information and accommodation

The well-organized **Warrnambool Visitor Information Centre** (daily 9am–5pm; ☎03/5559 4620, [W] www.warrnamboolinfo.com.au) is part of the Flagstaff Hill complex at 23 Merri St. **Internet** access is available at Southern IT, 168 Timor St (☎03/5561 4087). The visitor centre can help with **accommodation**.

Girt By Sea 52 Banyan St ☎0418 261 969, [W] www.girtbyseabandb.com.au. Tastefully furnished two-bedroom place in a restored historic house (built 1856). Convenient location between the town centre and the beach. 5

Hotel Warrnambool Corner of of Koroit and Kepler sts ☎03/5562 2377, [W] www.hotelwarrnambool.com.au. Upmarket place offering pleasant B&B pub accommodation in the town centre; particularly good value for single travellers. Their British breakfasts are a good start to the day. 5

Lady Bay Apartments 2 Petrobe Rd ☎03/5562 1662, [W] www.ladybayapartments.com.au. Located on the foreshore, these modern self-contained apartments have views towards the sea. There's also an outdoor heated swimming pool and a licensed bistro. 6

Warrnambool Beach Backpackers 17 Stanley St ☎03/5562 4874, [W] www.beachbackpackerscom.au. The best backpacker hostel in town, less than a 5min walk from the beach. It has comfy dorms with lockers (phone ahead for a female dorm) and doubles, some with en suite, and a licensed bar and internet access. Guests are picked up from the bus stop or train station in town on request. Dorms $23, en-suite rooms 3

Warrnambool Surfside Holiday Park Pertobe Rd, opposite Lake Pertobe ☎03/5559 4700, [W] www.surfsidepark.com.au. Self-contained one- to three-bedroom cottages and cabins as well as camping right on the beach. 4–6

The Town

Lady Bay, where Warrnambool is sheltered, was first used by sealers and whalers in the early nineteenth century and was permanently settled from about 1839. **Southern right whales**, hunted almost to extinction, have begun to return in the last decade. Every year between June and September, female whales come to the waters off Logans Beach to calve. Often the whales swim very close to the shore and can be viewed from a specially constructed platform at Logans Beach; follow the signs off the Great Ocean Road for "Whale Nursery". Dive Inn (☎03/5561 6108, [W] www.diveinn.com.au) do whale-watching cruises ($60), scenic tours, **fishing and diving charters** as well as dive courses (SSI open water, 3 days; $599); for **horse rides** along the beach contact Rundell's Mahogany Trail Rides (☎0408 589 546, [W] www.rundellshorseriding.com.au; about $60 per 2hr).

The perils of shipping in the treacherous waters of the Shipwreck Coast are the theme at **Flagstaff Hill** at 23 Merri St (daily 9am–5pm; [W] www.flagstaffhill.com; $15.95). The extensive grounds feature a recreated nineteenth-century coastal village, arranged around the original fort, erected in 1887 when the fear of a Russian invasion was widespread in Australia. Entry is via the building housing the visitor centre, an upmarket restaurant, a souvenir shop plus a theatre and gallery. Flagstaff Hill's *pièce de résistance*, however, is the multi-million-dollar sound and laser show **Shipwrecked** ($25.50; 70min, book at least a day in advance; ☎1800 556 111). Screened nightly after dusk (sometimes a second screening will commence after it if the first show is booked out early), it recounts the story of the Loch Ard disaster (see p.943).

Warrnambool has a bustling downtown, with a major shopping centre on Liebig Street, several galleries and museums, and some fine old churches. Perhaps the best of the sights is the **Warrnambool Art Gallery** on Liebig Street (Mon–Fri 10am–5pm, Sat & Sun noon–5pm; free), a fine provincial gallery with collections of Western District colonial paintings and contemporary Australian prints. The **Botanic Gardens** on Botanic Road, designed in 1877 by William Guilfoyle, then director of the Melbourne Botanic Gardens, are also worth visiting if you have some spare time.

Eating and drinking

There are plenty of good places to **eat** and **drink**, most of them on Liebig Street. Out of town, in a refurbished historic boathouse on the Hopkins River, is *Proudfoots on the River* at 2 Simpson St, with tearooms, a smoke-free bistro and a tavern bar. In terms of **nightlife**, the *Whalers Inn* at the corner of Liebig and Timor streets is popular and has a nightclub next door (*Club 59*) that is open until 3am (Wed, Fri & Sat). Across the road at 62 Liebig St is the *Seanchai Irish Pub*, which fills up on weekends, and, nearby, the *Loft* at no. 58 is the town's best music venue with nightly performances.

Beach Babylon 72 Liebig St. Pleasant place for pizza and pasta or just a glass of wine. Open daily from 6pm, also lunch Fri. Mains around $22.

Fishtales Café 63 Liebig St. Relaxed, funky place with a huge menu that offers a bit of everything, from all-day breakfast, fish meals and focaccia, to Asian, Indian, Italian and over thirty choices of burger. Takeaway available too. Daily 7am–8pm.

Haokai 132 Koroit St. It may be average Chinese food but at least there's lots of it. All-you-can-eat buffet 11.30am–2.30pm ($9.20), 5–9.30pm ($13.90) that attracts backpackers like flies. Open daily.

Mack's Snacks 77 Liebig St. Open since 1948 and still operated by the same family, this US-style

diner (booth seating) is always popular, serving up great burgers ($6), wraps ($8), and an assortment of cakes and biscuits. Mon–Sat breakfast, lunch and dinner.

Pippies by the Bay 91 Merri St ☎03/5561 2188. Located next to the visitor centre at Flagstaff Hill, its main attraction is the views over Flagstaff Hill Maritime Village (see p.945) and Lady Bay. Enquire about dinner and show packages for the *Shipwrecked* programme. Mon–Fri 10am to late, Sat & Sun 9am to late.

Puds Pantry and Deli 60 Kepler St. Excellent home-made bread and pastries, as well as soups, pasta and curries to take away or eat in. Closed Sun.

Port Fairy

PORT FAIRY, the next stop along the coast, was once an early port and whaling centre but is now a quaint crayfishing and tourist town with a busy jetty, a harbour full of yachts, and over fifty National Trust–listed buildings. Heavy southern breakers roll into the surrounding beaches, and on **Griffiths Island**, poised between the ocean and Port Fairy Bay, there's a **muttonbird** rookery with a specially constructed lookout where, between September and April, you can watch the birds roost at dusk.

Information and accommodation

Port Fairy's **visitor centre**, on Bank Street (daily 9am–5pm; ☎03/5568 2682, Ⓦwww.port-fairy.com), has details of all cottages and B&Bs, and of Port Fairy's

⑩

VICTORIA | Port Fairy

946

six caravan parks. With its village-like atmosphere and excellent **accommoda-tion** options, as well as good pubs, tearooms and restaurants, the town makes a good place to break your journey between Melbourne and Adelaide.

Comfort Inn Corner of Cox and Sackville sts ☏ 03/5568 1082, ⓦ www.seacombehouse.com.au. One of many National Trust-listed buildings here, with cheaper hotel rooms including excellent-value singles, gorgeous but pricey modern motel units and historic cottages. ④—⑦

The Douglas on the River 85 Gipps St ☏ 03/5668 1016, ⓦ www.portfairyabed.com. There are a number of B&Bs in town, but those on the Moyne River in quaint colonial cottages are the best, such as this family-run gem with some rooms set right on the river. ⑥—⑦

Moorings Riverside Apartment 69A Gipps St ☏ 03/5561 4690, ⓦ www.mooringsonmoyne.com .au. A beautiful house with deluxe amenities, sleeping up to six people and even with its own fishing and boat jetty. ⑦

Port Fairy YHA 8 Cox St ☏ 03/5568 2468, ⓦ www.portfairyhostel.com.au. A well-run and super-friendly hostel in a lovely old house right in the town centre. They also have wireless and broadband internet access. Dorm beds $25.50, rooms ③

The Town

For a historic small town, Port Fairy is quite a happening place, hosting numerous events. In summer the four-week-long **Moyneyana Festival** focuses on outdoor activities, with events such as a raft race on the Moyne River and its highlight, the Moyneyana New Year's Eve procession. At Easter the annual Queenscliff to Port Fairy yacht race ends here, with a huge party. **Music** is big too, with the Spring Music Festival in mid-October concentrating on classical music, with a bit of opera and jazz thrown in for good measure, and the huge **Port Fairy Folk Festival** over the Labour Day long weekend in March, which takes over the entire town, with Australian and overseas acts playing world, roots and acoustic music. Tickets are sold in early November, and usually sell out in two to three hours. For more information and festival bookings contact the visitor centre. The centre also produces an excellent map of the **Port Fairy Heritage Walk**, which takes you on a route around town to admire the many

▲ Port Fairy

fine buildings. The Port Fairy **Historical Society**, in the old courthouse on Gipps Street by the river (Wed, Sat & Sun 2–5pm, daily during holidays; $3), displays costumes, historic photographs, shipwreck relics and other items relating to the town's pioneer history. Other activities and attractions include the excellent links-style golf course (ⓌWww.portfairygolf.com.au), which has awe-inspiring views over the sea.

Eating and drinking

One of the best places for a **meal** is the *Caledonian Inn* ("The Stump"), on the corner of Bank and James streets, which is open to 1am most nights of the week – it's the oldest continually licensed pub in Victoria (since 1844). In Sackville Street, *Rebecca's* at no. 70 does breakfasts, light lunches, cakes and good coffee, while around the corner are a few more eateries including *Portofino on Bank*, 26 Bank St (Tues–Sat 6pm till late; ℡03/5568 2251), renowned throughout the district for its fusion of Middle Eastern and Mediterranean cuisine. Not to be missed is the ⚘ *Time and Tide Café* (9.30am–5pm; ℡03/5568 2134, closed Tues & Wed) which has stunning views right on the beach, five minutes out of town at 21 Thistle Place. The simple yet delicious delicatessen-style menu complements the setting, and there's an adjacent gallery.

Portland to Nelson

PORTLAND, the last stop on the Victoria coast going west on the Princes Highway, is an important industrial and fishing port, but **Nelson**, a friendly fishing village further west, or **Port Fairy** (see p.946) make for more atmospheric overnight stops on the coast route between Melbourne and Adelaide. The rugged coastal scenery to the southwest around Cape Nelson and Cape Bridgewater, however, is not to be missed.

Portland

Portland likes to describe itself as the "Birthplace of Victoria". Indeed, there are quite a few historic buildings, but unlike Port Fairy they don't add up to form a coherent, captivating townscape. That said, there's plenty here to keep you entertained, and a range of accommodation if you do need to stop over.

Information and accommodation

The excellent, anchor-shaped **visitor centre**, part of the Maritime Discovery Centre (daily 9am–5pm; ℡03/5523 2671 or 1800 035 567), has pamphlets and maps galore, and the staff can advise on local attractions, driving routes and the Great Southwest Walk, which begins and ends in Portland. Absolute Outdoors Australia at 67 Bentinck St (℡03/5521 7646, Ⓦwww.g-adventures.com.au) can kit you out for the Great Southwest Walk and other activities in the region; they sell camping accessories and all sorts of gear, as well as bikes and canoes. **Internet** access is available at 67 Bentinck St (9am–5pm daily; $5 per hr).

There's no shortage of **accommodation** in Portland. At the more affordable end and with a prime location is the *Gordon Hotel* (℡03/5523 1121; ❸), across from the water at 63 Bentinck St. This huge pub has simple rooms with shared facilities and the price includes a light breakfast; ask for a room with sea views. For a bit of history try *Annesley House* (☎03/5521 1434, ⓦwww.annesleyhouse.com .au; min 2-night stay Nov–March; ❺) at 60 Julia St, which blends simple charm with modern amenities. The *Clifftop Accommodation B&B*, 13 Clifton Court (☎03/5523 1126, ⓦwww.portlandaccommodation.au.com; ❻), is within walking distance of the main drag of town and has three spacious, light-filled rooms with en suite and balconies overlooking Portland Bay, one room also has cooking facilities.

The Town

If you want to learn what makes Portland tick, the comprehensive tour of the port and the **aluminium smelter** at Point Danger, 5km from the foreshore, is well worth taking (departs Wed from the visitor centre; 2hr 30min–3hr; free but reservations necessary ☎1800 035 567). Back in town, the small **Maritime Discovery Centre** (daily 9am–5pm; $5.50) extends to the back of the visitor centre on the foreshore down from Bentinck Street. Its centrepiece is a life-sized model of a great white shark, caught 13km west of Cape Bridgewater in 1982. There is also a motley assemblage of boat building tools, memorabilia, photos and marine wildlife information – but strangely, nothing of note on the Koorie people who had lived in the region for a long time prior to white settlement.

A restored and modified vintage **cable tram** (daily 10am–4pm; ⓦwww .portlandcabletrams.com.au; $15) transports sightseers along the foreshore on a round trip of 7.5km, from the depot at Henty Park past the **Powerhouse Motor and Car Museum** (daily 10am–4pm) to **Fawthrop Lagoon** (home to pelicans), then back through the **Botanic Gardens**. Alternatively, you can follow the Historic Buildings Trail (the visitor centre has a brochure) which starts at the former Customs House in Cliff Street (near the southern end of Bentinck Street) and takes in some of the two hundred nineteenth-century buildings in Portland.

Out of town, along the coast to the southwest around craggy **Cape Nelson** and stormy **Cape Bridgewater** (the highest coastal cliffs in Victoria), the scenery is stunning, including caves, blowholes, a petrified forest, and the beach at **Bridgewater Bay**, which extends in a wide, sandy arc from one cape to the other. The best way to explore is along the walking tracks that start from the car park signposted left off the road to Cape Bridgewater. Bring good walking shoes – the volcanic rocks can be very sharp – and food and drink. **Seal Point** at Cape Bridgewater is home to about a thousand **fur seals**. Seals by the Sea run tours (45min) where you can interact with these social creatures (☎03/5526 7247; $30). You can get information about these tours and other activities, and book accommodation, at the *Beach Café* (☎03/5526 7155) in Bridgewater Bay, ten minutes west of town.

Eating

At the southern end of the esplanade (Bentinck Street) is a cluster of **eating** options from where you can look out over the water and across to the busy port. Try the reasonably priced *Kokopelli's* (Sun–Thurs 8.30am–11pm, Fri & Sat 8.30am–1am; winter closes 5pm Sun & Mon), at no. 79, a cool juice-bar and café serving tapas, lunches and dinners. The *Gordon Hotel* serves good pub food (noon–1.30pm & 6–8pm daily) and has bands on the weekends, but for something a bit special try the *Clock by the Bay* restaurant (☎03/5523 4777; dinner Mon–Sat), housed in what was once Portland's post office, built in the 1880s, and now serving Mod Oz cuisine with good views of the harbour.

Lower Glenelg National Park and Nelson

From Portland, the Princes Highway makes its uneventful way, via Heywood, to Mount Gambier in South Australia. After 120km it crosses the **Glenelg River** (which has its source in the Grampians) at Dartmoor, a popular point to begin a four-day canoeing trip down to the river's mouth at Nelson; ask about canoe rental at the Nelson Parks & Visitor Information Centre (see below). For most of the journey, the clear blue river flows through the unspoilt **Lower Glenelg National Park** in a sixty-kilometre gorge cut through limestone. The **Princess Margaret Rose Cave** (daily 45min guided tours at 10am, 11am, noon, then hourly from 1.30pm to 4.30pm, reduced hours during winter; $12; ☏08/8738 4171), a huge chamber of actively growing stalactites and stalagmites, is the main cave in the system and the only one which is open to the public. It lies beside the river as it loops round by the South Australian border. It can be reached by canoe, car (unsealed roads from both sides of the border lead to the caves) or on a cruise from Nelson (see below).

NELSON, at the end of the coastal road and virtually on the Victoria/South Australia border, is well worth an overnight stay. A peaceful, friendly little hamlet, it feels caught in a time warp, and there's little to do but wander along the coast, read on the beach, and **fish** or **canoe** on the Glenelg. Nelson Boat & Canoe Hire on Kellet Street (daily 9am–5pm, closed Thurs; ☏08/8738 4048, ⓦwww.nelsonboatandcanoehire.com.au) rent out canoes and kayaks. They also sell bait; but you'll need a fishing licence, obtained from the visitor centre (see below). Fishing shelters line the river. Glenelg River Cruises on Old Bridge Road operates **cruises** to the Princess Margaret Rose Cave (daily in peak season, other times Sat & Sun and on some weekdays; departs 1pm; 4hr; $25, cave entry not included; ☏08/8738 4191).

The **Nelson Parks & Visitor Centre** (daily 9am–5pm; ☏08/8738 4051) is signposted just off Leake Street; it also covers the Discovery Bay Coastal Park, which protects the shoreline almost all the way from Portland to the border. Here you can get camping permits for this and the Lower Glenelg National Park (book in advance in peak season) and information on walks and activities. They also have internet access ($6 per hr). Nelson Kiosk (daily 8am–5pm; ☏08/8738 4220), on Kellet Street, serves as the local service general store and post office.

If you're **staying overnight**, the best option is the charming *Nelson Cottage B&B* (☏08/8738 4161, ⓦwww.nelsoncottage.bigpondhosting.com; ❹) which has comfortable rooms with shared facilities in an old police station dating from the early 1880s. The *Beach Road B&B* (☏08/8738 4241; ❹), indeed on Beach Road, is very good value, located on the bottom floor of a private house set on the water's edge. The *Pinehaven Motel* on Main Road (☏08/8738 4041; ❹) is a basic motel owned by the petrol station next door. Rooms are small but clean. The *Kywong Caravan Park* on North Nelson Road (☏08/8738 4174, ⓦwww.kywongcp.com) has cheap cabins (❶–❸) 1km north of town. The fantastic *Nelson Hotel* on Kellett Street, is a true country pub, and has excellent fresh **seafood** and huge steaks (daily dinner & lunch Fri & Sat; summer lunch Mon–Fri). The only other places in town are the Kiosk, which sells sandwiches and the usual junk food, and the petrol station on the main road which doubles as a fish-and-chip shop.

Central Victoria: the Goldfields

Central Victoria is classic Victoria: a rich pastoral district, chilly in winter, sweltering in summer, and parched a straw colour after years of drought. Two grand provincial cities, **Ballarat** and **Bendigo**, whose fine buildings were funded by gold, draw large numbers of visitors, while, by contrast, the area's other charming centres such as **Maryborough** and **Castlemaine**, once prosperous gold-towns in their own right, now seem too small for their extravagant architecture.

There's fairly good **transport** from Melbourne with regular V/Line trains and buses to Bendigo, Ballarat and the other major centres in the Goldfields, and a few local buses fill some gaps. However, as elsewhere in the state, your own transport is a big advantage. The easiest way to tour is to follow the **Goldfields Tourist Route**, whose chocolate-brown signs are marked by a distinctive circled capital G. The route links the major cities and towns – Bendigo, Castlemaine, Ballarat, Ararat and Stawell – with many smaller places in between.

The goldrushes

The California goldrushes of the 1840s captured the popular imagination around the world with tales of the huge fortunes to be made gold-prospecting, and it wasn't long before Australia's first goldrush took place – near Bathurst in New South Wales in 1851. Victoria had been a separate colony for only nine days when gold was found at Clunes on July 10, 1851; the **goldrush** began in earnest when rich deposits were found in Ballarat nine months later. The richest goldfields ever known soon opened at Bendigo, and thousands poured into Victoria from around the world. In the golden decade of the 1850s, Victoria's population increased from eighty thousand to half a million, half of whom remained permanently in the state. The British and Irish made up a large proportion of the new population, but over forty thousand Chinese came to make their fortune too, along with experienced American gold-seekers and other nationalities such as Russians, Finns and Filipinos. Ex-convicts and native-born Australians also poured in, leaving other colonies short of workers; even respectable policemen deserted their posts to become "diggers", and doctors, lawyers and prostitutes crowded into the haphazard new towns in their wake.

In the beginning, the fortune-seekers panned the creeks and rivers searching for **alluvial gold**, constantly moving on at the news of another find. But gold was also deep within the earth, where ancient riverbeds had been buried by volcanoes; in Ballarat in 1852 the first **shafts** were dug, and because the work was unsafe and arduous, the men joined in bands of eight or ten, usually grouped by nationality, working a common claim. For deep mining, diggers stayed in one place for months or years, and the major workings rapidly became stable communities with banks, shops, hotels, churches and theatres, evolving more gradually, on the back of income from gold, into grandiose towns.

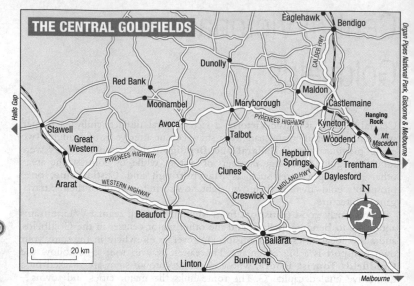

Towards the Goldfields: the Calder Highway

Though you could take the Western Freeway or the train directly to Ballarat, the route along the **CALDER HIGHWAY** towards Bendigo, 150km northwest of Melbourne, is much more interesting. The railway to Bendigo, which continues to Swan Hill, follows the same route, calling at the main towns.

At Diggers Rest, 22km from Melbourne on the highway, a short detour to the east will take you to the tiny **Organ Pipes National Park** (daily 8.30am–4.30pm; summer Sat & Sun & public holidays until 6pm; ☎13 19 63), designated a national park for its outstanding geological interest. The rock formations here form a series of basalt columns, created by lava cooling in an ancient riverbed, and rising up to 20m above Jacksons Creek. The park can be explored along walking tracks and has picnic areas with tables. Back on the highway you'll come to **Gisborne**, 50km from Melbourne, developed as a coaching town for travellers on their way to the Bendigo and Castlemaine goldfields; it's dominated by **Mount Macedon**, an extinct thousand-metre volcano.

Fifteen kilometres or so from Gisborne, **Woodend** is a friendly, bustling place on weekends, with antique shops and cafés lined along the main street, and also the jumping-off point for the **Hanging Rock Reserve**, 6km northeast (daily 9am–5pm; summer 8am–6pm; ⓦ www.hangingrock.info; $10 per car, $4 adult). The rock became famous because of the eerie 1975 film *Picnic at Hanging Rock* (directed by Peter Weir who went on to direct *Dead Poets Society* and *The Truman Show*), about a group of schoolgirls who mysteriously go missing here after a picnic – a story which many people falsely believed to be true. More about that story, as well as scientific information about the geological history of the rock, can be gleaned from the displays in the Hanging Rock Discovery Centre at its base; adjacent to it is a licensed café and a gift shop. You can walk around the base of the rock or climb to the summit with its massive boulders and crags in around an hour; don't forget to take your own picnic – the views are lovely and the place is atmospheric.

KYNETON, 15km further north, features **Piper Street**, a colourful strip lined with a handful of fine, historic bluestone buildings and the **Botanic Gardens**, scenically located above the Campaspe River; but the town lacks Woodend's inviting, friendly charm, however, and only comes alive during the annual food and wine Budburst festival (ⓦwww.budburst.com) in October, when over two dozen local Mount Macedon wineries celebrate the release of a new vintage.

Bendigo

Rich alluvial gold was first discovered in **BENDIGO** in 1851, and, once the initial fields were exhausted, shafts were sunk into a gold-bearing quartz reef. Bendigo became the greatest goldfield of the time, and had the world's deepest mine. Mining continued here until 1954, long after the rest of central Victoria's goldfields were exhausted, so it's a city that has developed over a prosperous century: the nationwide department store Myer began here, as did Australia's first building society in 1858. Although in many ways more magnificent than Ballarat, Bendigo is considerably lower-key. Its most visited sights are legacies of the mining days – the **Chinese Joss House** and the **Central Deborah Mine**.

Arrival, information and transport

Bendigo Airport Service provides a link to Melbourne's Tullamarine Airport (4 Mon–Fri, 3 Sat & Sun; $38 one-way; booking essential on ☏03/5444 3939, ⓦwww.bendigoairportservice.com.au). V/Line trains and buses arrive at the train station on Railway Place, just south of the CBD.

The **visitor centre** on Pall Mall (daily 9am–5pm; ☏1800 813 153, ⓦwww .bendigotourism.com) has a free accommodation-booking service and provides lots of brochures including the free *Bendigo Visitor Guide*, and a range of walking and cycling maps. Wanting to give Bendigo a sophisticated air reminiscent of London, the newly prosperous citizens called its central crossroads **Charing Cross**. Mitchell Street leads south to the **train station**, and High Street (the Calder Highway) is the main exit west out of the city. The other important street is Hargreaves, parallel to Pall Mall one block south, with its impressive town hall and a revamped pedestrianized shopping mall. A good way to get an overall impression of the place is to take the **Vintage Talking Tram Tour** (daily 9.30am–4.30pm; departures on the half-hour, from the Central Deborah Goldmine; 1hr; $15; ☏03/5442 2821). The tram tour ticket includes entrance to the **Bendigo Tram Museum**, located on Tramways Avenue. The route takes in most of Bendigo's main attractions. **Internet** access is available at 70 Pall Mall (Mon–Fri 9.30am–5.30pm; $6 per hr).

Accommodation

In terms of atmosphere and style, the **B&B guesthouses** and **cottages** throughout Bendigo and the whole goldfields area are a much better option than the average, somewhat sterile, motel room.

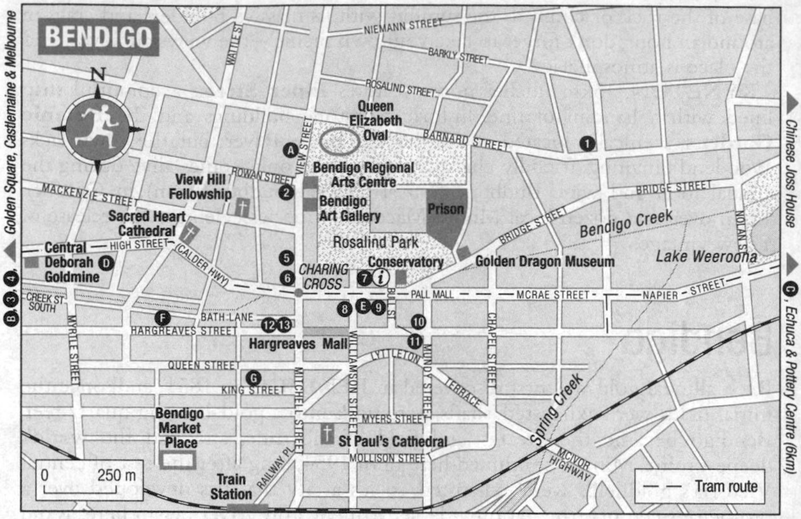

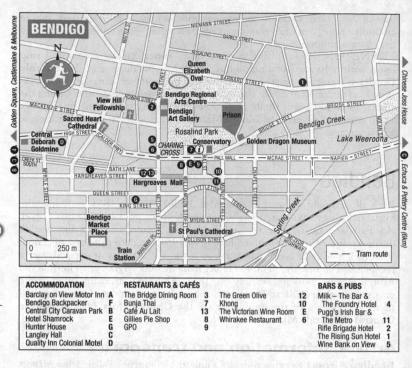

ACCOMMODATION		RESTAURANTS & CAFÉS				BARS & PUBS	
Barclay on View Motor Inn	A	The Bridge Dining Room	3	The Green Olive	12	Milk – The Bar & The Foundry Hotel	4
Bendigo Backpacker	F	Bunja Thai	7	Khong	10	Pugg's Irish Bar & The Metro	11
Central City Caravan Park	B	Café Au Lait	13	The Victorian Wine Room	E	Rifle Brigade Hotel	2
Hotel Shamrock	E	Gillies Pie Shop	8	Whirakee Restaurant	6	The Rising Sun Hotel	1
Hunter House	G	GPO	9			Wine Bank on View	5
Langley Hall	C						
Quality Inn Colonial Motel	D						

Barclay on View Motor Inn 181 View St ☎03/5443 9388, 🌐www.barclayonview.com. The best motel in town, in an excellent location within walking distance of restaurants, bars and shops, across the road from the historic cricket ground. Gym, spa and sauna facilities. [5]–[6]

Bendigo Backpacker 33 Creek St South ☎03/5443 7680, 🌐www.bendigotourism.com.au. Ultra-casual hostel right in the centre of town with dorms ($27), and two twin and two family rooms. Open fire in the lounge, and internet access. Rooms [2]

Central City Caravan Park 362 High St, Golden Square ☎03/5443 6937, 🌐www .centralcitycaravanpark.com.au. Cramped caravan park with modern amenities and a pool. Location is 2.5km southwest of the CBD but there's a bus stop to town just outside. Un/powered sites $23/28, en-suite cabins [4]–[5]

Hotel Shamrock Corner of of Pall Mall and Williamson St ☎03/5443 0333, 🌐www.hotelshamrock.com.au. Centrally located, this fabulous grand Victorian hotel is Bendigo's best with a range of accommodation, from standard rooms to spa suites. [5]–[8]

Hunter House 57 Queen St ☎03/5442 2466, 🌐www.hunterhouse.com.au.A short stroll to the centre, this elegant Victorian mansion has beautifully appointed rooms and a separate bar/lounge and restaurant with open fires. [6]–[7]

Langley Hall 484 Napier St ☎03/5443 3693,🌐www.innhouse.com.au/langleyhall.html. This 1903 Edwardian mansion has delightful heritage rooms, charming common areas and wonderful gardens. [6]

Quality Inn Colonial Motel 483–484 High St ☎03/5447 0122, 🌐www.bendigocolonial.com.au. This comfortable motel has contemporary-designed rooms that belie the old-fashioned "colonial"-inspired exterior. [6]–[7]

The City

At the heart of Bendigo is the vast, leafy **Rosalind Park**, and three important religious buildings constructed with money from gold-mining – All Saints

Church (now View Hill Fellowship), St Paul's Cathedral and **Sacred Heart Cathedral**. Local Catholics imported stonemasons from Italy and England, and their splendid craftsmanship is especially evident in the design and details of Sacred Heart, begun in 1897 in English Gothic style. The interior has beautiful woodcarvings of the Twelve Apostles, and the crypt is the burial place of local bishops (daily 9am–5pm).

Many of Bendigo's finest goldrush buildings are along **Pall Mall**, including the law courts (1896) and the ornate Italianate (1887) edifice which now houses the visitor centre – neither of which would seem out of place in a capital city. The colossal four-storey **Shamrock Hotel** opposite is an extravagant example of Victorian gold-boom architecture. Lively **View Street**, climbing the hill beside Rosalind Park, has a handful of elaborate goldrush buildings now housing charming antique and vintage stores, stylish wine bars and cafés and busy restaurants. The **Bendigo Performing Arts Centre, "The Capital"** (Mon–Fri 9.15am–5.15pm, Sat 10am–1pm; evening performance times vary; ☎03/5434 6100, ⓦwww.thecapital.com.au) at 50 View St is a massive Neoclassical pile, which plays host to classical music, opera and ballet, while **Bendigo Art Gallery**, in another beautifully restored nineteenth century building at no. 42 (daily 10am–5pm; ☎03/5434 6088, ⓦwww.bendigoartgallery.com.au; free), is one of Australia's finest regional galleries, with an extensive collection of Australian painting from Bendigo's goldfield days to the present, as well as nineteenth-century British and European art acquired with all that gold; they also host impressive temporary exhibitions that attract visitors from around the state. The **Queen Elizabeth Oval**, with its historic red-brick grandstand, backs onto Rosalind Park, and you can watch Aussie Rules football here on winter weekends and cricket in summer.

Bridge Street, one of the oldest in Bendigo, was once **Chinatown**, home to the Chinese who came by the thousands in the 1850s and who knew Bendigo as *dai gum san* ("big gold mountain"); when the gold ran out, many turned to market gardening. Until as late as the 1960s old shops sporting faded Chinese signs were still in evidence, but now Chinese customs and ways of life are best seen in the **Golden Dragon Museum and Yi Yuan Classical Chinese Gardens** at 5–11 Bridge St (daily 9.30am–5pm; $8; ⓦwww.goldendragonmuseum.org), where there is an impressive collection of Chinese processional regalia including some of the world's longest and oldest Imperial dragons, Sun Loong and Loong. An exhibition tells the full story of Bendigo's Chinese community since the days of the goldrush, while the adjoining gardens feature a temple to the goddess Kuan Yin. The National Trust–operated **Bendigo Joss House** (Dai Gum San) on Finn Street in North Bendigo (☎03/5443 8255; Wed, Sat & Sun 11am–4pm; $5) was built by the Chinese in the 1860s and is the oldest Chinese temple still in use in Australia. To get to the Joss House, take bus #7, which runs approximately hourly Monday–Friday. The route to the shrine passes man-made Lake Weeroona, whose picnic grounds are the setting for the lovely *Boardwalk Restaurant & Café* (daily 7am till late; ☎03/5443 9855) in an old Chinese teahouse. Virtually dry until recently, due to the long drought, Lake Weeroona is now almost full again – with recycled water – the first urban lake in Australia to undergo such an experiment. Some 6km east of town, on the Midland Highway, is Australia's oldest working pottery centre (daily 9am–5pm), dating back to the 1850s, with a museum, café and shop.

The Central Deborah Goldmine

The **Central Deborah Goldmine**, at the corner of Violet Street and the Calder Highway (daily 9am–5pm; ☎03/5443 8322, ⓦwww.central-deborah.com), was the last mine in the Central Goldfields to close. While exploring the area above ground is free, it's worth taking the 75-minute underground **Mine Experience Tour** (weekdays 5 times daily, weekends 6 times, 9.30am–3.30pm; more during school holidays; $24) if you've never been down in a mine; everybody is issued with a reassuring hard hat, complete with torch and generator. You go down to a depth of 60m in a lift, which takes 85 seconds – it would take thirty minutes to reach the bottom of some of the deepest shafts. The further down you go the hotter it gets, but at 60m it's quite warm and airless, dripping with water and muddy underfoot. If you want to scramble around the mine a bit longer, climb ladders, perhaps operate a drill, you can join a longer **Underground Adventure** which also includes a meal (tours depart 11am & 2pm; $68). For bookings, call ☏03/5443 8255 or see the website.

Eating, drinking and nightlife

Bendigo offers a wonderful choice when it comes to eating and drinking, with lots of brilliant cafés, wine bars, restaurants and pubs on View Street. For after-work drinks, locals love the stylish *Wine Bank on View* at 45 View St, in an atmospheric old building with a superb wine and tapas selection, and the funky *Milk – The Bar* at The Foundry Hotel at 366 High St. For beer-lovers, the *Rifle Brigade Hotel* at 137 View St, a brewery pub with excellent food, has four homebrew beers on tap and a wrought-iron veranda, while *The Rising Sun Hotel* at 85 Barnard St is a stylish contemporary-designed pub with a chic bar and bistro serving beers, cocktails and good bar snacks. There's also a student-influenced nightlife during university terms with several pubs offering **live music** on Friday and Saturday nights, including *Pugg's Irish Bar & The Metro*, on the corner of Bull and Hargreaves streets, which has a beer garden.

Restaurants and cafés

The Bridge Dining Room 49 Bridge St ☏03/5443 7811. In stylish surroundings in a beautifully restored old corner pub, the award-winning Dining Room dishes up good (if not adventurous) Mod Oz cuisine; unfortunately service can be hit and miss. You can get more casual (and cheaper) meals in the adjoining bistro. Dinner from 6pm.

Bunja Thai 32 Pall Mall. Set in a grand 1880s bank building, this Thai restaurant is a local favourite with delicious banquet menus (starting at $40 per person). Tues–Thurs 10am–10.30pm, Fri & Sat 8.30am–10.30pm, Sun 8.30am–3.30pm.

Café au Lait 20 Mitchell St. Bendigo's most beautiful café (with big picture windows and lovely stained glass) is also its most popular café, with delicious breakfasts, scrumptious home-made cakes, and a lovely balcony upstairs. Breakfast and lunch daily.

Gillies Pie Shop Corner of Hargreaves Mall & Williamson St. A Bendigo institution, you can watch through the windows as they make and bake their myriad assortment of pies and pasties. Daily 10am–6pm.

GPO 60–64 Pall Mall ☏03/5443 4343. This sleek contemporary space in a historic nineteenth-century building serves up delicious tapas to a chatty crowd of locals. Daily lunch and dinner.

The Green Olive Bath Lane, Bendigo. Excellent coffee, decadent cakes and light lunches keeps this casual café packed all day with locals. Mon–Fri 7am–5pm, Sat & Sun 8am–3pm.

Khong 200 Hargreaves St. This stylish Asian eatery dishes up delicious great-value Chinese and Thai cuisine. The all-you-can-eat lunches are popular with the office workers. Daily lunch and dinner.

The Victorian Wine Room Shamrock Hotel, Corner of Pall Mall and Williamson St ☏03/5443 0333. Bendigo's most elegant restaurant offers refined contemporary Australian cuisine based on fresh seasonal produce. Extensive wine list. Dinner daily.

Whirakee Restaurant and Wine Bar 17 View Point ☏03/5441 5557. In a splendid heritage building, this local favourite serves quality Mod Oz cuisine and has an excellent wine list. Lunch Wed–Fri, dinner Tues–Sat.

Castlemaine and around

CASTLEMAINE, 39km southwest of Bendigo, is at the centre of the area once known as the Mount Alexander Goldfields. Between 1851 and 1861, when its gullies were among the richest in the world, 105,000kg of gold were found here (modest quantities are still found at Wattle Gully mine at nearby Chewton, the oldest working gold mine in Australia). Castlemaine became the headquarters of the Government Camp for the area in 1852, and its impressive buildings were built during the following ten years. With no deep mines to sustain it, however, the town has developed little since then. Some 19km northwest of Castlemaine lies the quaint, small historic town of **Maldon**.

Information and accommodation

The very helpful **Castlemaine visitor centre** is in the Market Building on Mostyn Street (daily 9am–5pm; ℡03/5471 1795 or 1800 171 888, Ⓦwww .maldoncastlemaine.com) and can arrange **accommodation** in the area. Internet access is available at 155 Barker St (9.30am–5pm daily).

Campbell St Lodge 33 Campbell St ℡03/5472 3477, Ⓦwww.campbellstlodge.com.au. Simple, old-fashioned rooms in a historic National Trust–listed house in the centre of town. ❸–❻

Castlemaine Gardens Caravan Park Doran Ave ℡03/5472 1125, Ⓦwww .castlemainegardenscaravanpark.com. A leafy park just out of the town centre, but next to the open-air swimming pool and Botanic Gardens. Un/powered sites $23/28 & cabins. ❹

Claremont Coach-House Burnett Rd ℡03/5472 2281, Ⓦwww.claremontcoachhouse.com. Fully self-contained double-storey stone cottage built in 1857, 3km north of the CBD near the Botanic Gardens. ❺

Empyre Boutique Hotel 68 Mostyn St ℡03/5472 5166, Ⓦwww.empyre.com.au. Super-stylish luxury accommodation in the heart of town that has embraced the history of the area in its design and has instantly become the town's best accommodation option. ❼–❾

Ken and Chris' B&B 25 Johnstone St ℡03/5472 5292, Ⓦwww.kenandchris.com.au. Quaint self-contained cottage with spa bath, wireless internet and even a BBQ in your own private courtyard. ❺

The Town

The town's finest building is the **Old Castlemaine Market** on Mostyn Street, a wonderfully extravagant piece of Neoclassical architecture. The **Theatre Royal** on Hargreaves Street, one of the oldest theatres in Australia, is also magnificent; it's said that when the famous Lola Montez performed here, miners threw nuggets of gold at her in appreciation. The multi-use theatre (℡03/5472 1196, Ⓦwww.theatreroyal.info) shows art-house and mainstream films, hosts live music and comedy, and has a cabaret-style venue and a licensed bistro downstairs.

Another stunning architectural attraction, a short distance from the centre, is **Buda**, at 42 Hunter St (Wed–Sat noon–5pm, Sun 10am–5pm; $5 for garden, $9 for house and garden; Ⓦwww.budacastlemaine.org), a gracious nineteenth-century home and garden originally built in 1861 by a retired Baptist missionary and extended by its subsequent owner Ernest Leviny, a Hungarian silversmith, in the 1890s. The house and gardens give an insight into the good life enjoyed in the goldrush days, and much work by Leviny and his family is on display, including carved-wood hangings, embroidery, and the family's art and silverware collection. The **Castlemaine Art Gallery and Museum** at 14 Lyttleton St (Mon–Fri 10am–5pm, Sat & Sun noon–5pm; $4, Ⓦwww.castlemainegallery .com) is also worth a visit. It specializes in Australian photographs and paintings, featuring many works by the Heidelberg School, notably Frederick McCubbin and Tom Roberts. Partly because of the big **Castlemaine State Festival**, which takes place over ten days in early April in odd-numbered years, this is quite an arty place, and there are several galleries around town. Throughout the year various gardens in the Castlemaine district open their doors to visitors, especially during the **Festival of Gardens**, which takes place during the Melbourne Cup week in November.

If you're here on a Saturday, trek the 2km out along the Melbourne Road to **Wesley Hill Market**, a giant flea market selling local produce and crafts (7.30am–1pm).

Eating and drinking

Food in Castlemaine is excellent, with a wide variety of places to choose from.

Capones 50 Hargreaves St. A local favourite for those in need of huge if somewhat standard pizzas, in a comfy, cosy setting.

Empyre Hotel 113 Mostyn St ☏ 03/5472 5166. The town's best culinary option is a destination in itself with sophisticated dining and delicious food for breakfast, lunch and dinner.

Railway Hotel 65 Gingell St. Traditional country-style pub, with locals propping up the bar, and happy patrons in the bistro tucking into hearty pub grub, the highlight of which is the enormous succulent steaks. Daily lunch; dinner Wed–Sat.

Saff's 64 Mostyn St. Considered the best café in town, and not just because of the food. Hosts special evening events including recitals and poetry readings. Daily breakfast & lunch; dinner Thurs, Fri and Sat.

Tog's Place 58 Lyttleton St ☏ 03/5470 5090. Good café-style food in a peaceful setting, with sunny courtyard for warmer days. Bookings recommended.

Maldon

MALDON, closely surrounded by low hills, is a tiny, peaceful town that boasts Victoria's most intact historical streetscape. Lined with charming shops and B&Bs, it is an understandably popular weekend getaway. Gold was found here in 1853 and the rich, deep alluvial reefs were mined until 1926. The main shopping street largely preserves its original appearance, with single-storey shopfronts shaded by awnings and decorated with iron-lace work. Apart from enjoying the town's charming shops, cafés and architecture, there aren't many other points of interest, though you can take an underground tour at the stunning candlelit **Carman's Tunnel Goldmine**, off Parkin's Reef Road, 3km south of town (Sat, Sun, school & public holidays; tours depart every 30min from 1.30–4pm; 25min; $8).

During the long weekend before the Melbourne Cup (first weekend of Nov), things get a bit busier than usual as people head to town for the four-day **Maldon Folk Festival** (Ⓦ www.maldonfolkfestival.com; weekend tickets $100, Sunday-only day tickets $40). Since its inception in 1973 the event has steadily grown, and apart from traditional folk, it also features blues, bluegrass and world music as well as some theatre and dance. The main performance space is at the Tarrangower Reserve at the base of Mount Tarrangower, just out of town, but throughout the weekend there are also lots of things happening in town itself where you can listen for free.

Practicalities

Castlemaine Bus Lines run services from Castlemaine to Maldon (timetables and info available at Ⓦ www.castlemainebuslines.com.au). Return buses leave from Maldon post office to connect with trains back to Melbourne. The *Victorian Goldfields Railway*, a tourist **steam train** (or diesel locomotive on days of total fire ban) runs between Maldon and Castlemaine (Sun, also Wed & Sat during school holidays and more frequently during the summer holidays; single trip $22; ⓦwww.vgr.com.au).

For information on the town, check with the **Maldon visitor centre** in the Shire Gardens, High Street (daily 9am–5pm; ⓣ03/5475 2569, ⓦwww .maldoncastlemaine.com).

Places to **stay** include self-contained apartments in the atmospheric *Beehive* (ⓣ03/5475 1154, ⓔhive@bmail.com.au; ❺), a two-storey stone building at 72A Main St. Nearby at no. 58 is the 98-year-old *Maldon Hotel* (ⓣ03/5475 2231; ❸), which has rooms with shared facilities, and includes use of the fantastic balcony overlooking the streetscape. *Heritage Cottages*, 25 Adair St (ⓣ03/5475 1094, ⓦwww.heritagecottages.com.au; ❻–❼), is a selection of historical cottages, most with period furnishings and fireplaces.

Eating options include *Café Maldon* (8am–5pm daily) at 52 Main St and *Berryman's Café* in an old bowling alley at 30 Main St. *McArthur's Coffee & Books*, further up at no. 43, has a very pleasant courtyard and also sells new and second-hand books (Wed–Sun 9am–5pm). The quirky *Gourmet Yabbies Café* at 46 Main St (daily 11am–6pm, closed Tues) specializes in scrumptious yabbie pies (yabbies are like large freshwater shrimps). The *Penny School Gallery Café* (daily 10am–5pm), further out at 11 Church St, is a delightful place for coffee, lunch or afternoon tea, after checking out the latest exhibition at the gallery. A good place for a beer is the 150-year-old *Kangaroo Hotel*, opposite the visitor centre, which has a cosy beer-garden.

Maryborough and around

When Mark Twain visited **MARYBOROUGH**, 47km west of Castlemaine on the Pyrenees Highway, he described it as "a train station with a town attached". Nowadays it's a lovely laid-back country town, interesting mainly for remnants of goldrush architecture which appear far too extravagant for this low-key setting. The grandiose, renovated **Maryborough Railway Station** houses an **Antiques Emporium** and an excellent café (closed Tues, dinner available Fri & Sat). At the heart of town, the Civic Centre is a classic nineteenth-century square with an elegant post office and gracious town hall and courthouse. For more information and accommodation bookings, turn to the **Maryborough visitor centre**, corner of Nolan and Alma streets, just behind High Street (daily 9am–5pm; ⓣ1800 356 511, ⓦwww.visitmaryborough.com.au).

Twenty-one kilometres north of Maryborough is **DUNOLLY**, an attractive town filled with many distinctive old buildings and with kurrajong trees lining the main street. The *Royal Hotel* is a good place to stop for lunch with most bar meals under $20. The goldfields here produced more nuggets than any in Australia, including what's said to be the largest ever found: the 65-kilogram "Welcome Stranger" nugget, found in 1869 by two Cornish miners just 3cm below the surface as they were working around the roots of a tree, and valued at £10,000. Fourteen kilometres south of Maryborough, **TALBOT** is a tiny settlement consisting of little more than a pub and a corner store. It's hard to believe now that at the height of the goldrush the town had 56 hotels and a population of 33,000. Every third Sunday of the month, people congregate here to buy fresh produce at the **Talbot Farmers Market** (10am–2pm).

Daylesford and Hepburn Springs

The attractive, hilly country around Daylesford and Hepburn Springs is known as the "spa centre of Australia", with a hundred **mineral springs** within a fifty-kilometre radius. Daylesford grew from the Jim Crow gold diggings of 1851, but the large Swiss-Italian population here quickly realized the value of the water from the mineral springs, which had been bottled since 1850. People have been taking the waters at Hepburn Springs for almost as long – the spa complex was built in 1895. V/Line has a direct bus service from Melbourne to Daylesford (Mon–Sat 2 daily, Sun 1 daily). Alternatively (Mon–Fri), you can take a train from Melbourne to Ballarat and then transfer to a bus departing Ballarat in the early afternoon. This is the V/Line **bus service** between Geelong and Bendigo via Ballarat, Daylesford and Castlemaine. For enquiries and bookings, phone ☏ 13 61 96 or go to ⓦ www.vline.com.au.

Daylesford

The town of **DAYLESFORD**, a popular weekend retreat for Melburnians, has a New Age, alternative atmosphere, with a large gay community. As a result, the town has several gay-friendly guesthouses, and on the second weekend in March it is the venue for **ChillOut**, Australia's largest rural gay and lesbian festival, featuring a street parade, music and cabaret, dance parties and a carnival at Victoria Park.

Information and accommodation

Daylesford **visitor centre**, servicing the whole area, is at 98 Vincent St in Daylesford (daily 9am–5pm; ☏ 03/5321 6123, ⓦ www.visitdaylesford.com); it has loads of brochures on accommodation and activities in the area, including the many charming places offering bed and breakfast. **Internet** access is also available.

Book well in advance if you want **to stay** in Daylesford at the weekend. Bookings are handled by Escapes Daylesford Accommodation (☏ 03/5348 1448, ⓦ www.escapesdaylesford.com.au) and Daylesford Getaways (☏ 03/5348 4422, ⓦ www.dayget.com.au). As well as the options below, there's also quaint cottage accommodation at Tuki trout farm (see opposite; ⑥–⑧).

35 Hill Street ☏ 03/5348 3878, Ⓔjoanvdf @netconnect.com.au. Early Victorian brick cottage just below the Botanical Gardens, much loved for its casual, friendly attitude. ⑤

Daylesford Caravan Park Ballan Rd ☏ 03/5348 3821. Nice parkland setting close to the lake, 1.7km from town, with un/powered sites and fully contained cabins. ③

Daylesford Hotel 2 Burke Square ☏ 03/5348 2335, ⓦ www.daylesfordhotel.com.au. Simple rooms (popular with backpackers) with shared facilities in a grand old pub; you can't get more central and the price is right. ②

Daylesford Royal Hotel Corner of of Vincent and Albert sts ☏ 03/5348 2205, ⓦ www .daylesfordroyalhotel.com. Refurbished Victorian pub with pleasant, centrally heated rooms with en-suite facilities, some with spa bath. ⑤–⑥

The Lake House King St ☏ 03/5348 3329, ⓦ www.lakehouse.com.au. The town's premier accommodation option and a gastronomic destination, this luxury property continues to add to its collection of awards each year. The beautiful waterfront rooms and suites are a stone's throw from the lake and capture the essence of Daylesford. ⑦–⑧

The Town

Daylesford's well-preserved Victorian and Edwardian streets rise up the side of Wombat Hill, where you'll find the Botanical Gardens, between Hill Street and Central Springs Road, whose lookout tower has panoramic views. Not far away, on the corner of Daly and Hill streets, is the **Convent Gallery** (daily

10am–5pm; ⓦ www.conventgallery.com.au; $5), a rambling former convent that now has three levels of galleries selling high-quality arts, crafts and antiques, and a café and a bar. There's a great Sunday market (8am–2pm) just nearby, on the main road to Castlemaine. The town has "healing centres" aplenty; the spectrum of services ranges from natural therapies to tarot readings – enquire at the visitor centre.

Lake Daylesford, a short distance south from the town centre on Vincent Street, is the location of the Central Springs Reserve, which has several walking tracks and old-fashioned water pumps from which you can drink the mineral springs. The **Lake Daylesford Book Barn** here (open daily 10am–5pm) is a picturesquely situated bookshop, with an extensive range of secondhand books. The charming *Boathouse Café* (9–11am & noon–4pm daily, dinner Sat & Sun; ⓣ 03/5348 1387) has lakeside dining, as well as dinghies, canoes and paddleboats for rent. With your own transport there are some lovely options to explore further afield, including the **Lavandula Swiss Italian Farm** (daily 10.30am–5.30pm; ⓦ www.lavandula.com.au) in nearby Shepherds Flat, 5km north of Hepburn Springs, where you can walk among the historic stone farmhouses, in the extensive gardens and lavender fields, and then have lunch or coffee and cake at *La Trattoria*, the farm's renowned Italian restaurant (ⓣ 03/5476 4393); and **Tuki trout farm** (ⓣ 03/5345 6233, ⓦ www.tuki.com.au; $8, rod hire $5) in Smeaton, 23km west of Daylesford via Creswick, where you can catch your own lunch and have it boned and cooked for you while you wait.

Eating and drinking

In such a sophisticated (and gay-friendly) place you can expect the local bars and eateries to be swish too.

Breakfast and Beer 117 Vincent St. Specializing in great hearty breakfasts, this local institution offers a long list of international beers with pizza and wraps thrown in. Thurs–Sun 8.30am–late.

Cliffy's Emporium 30 Raglan St. In a town of excellent cafés, this delightful deli-café-cum-wine bar rates a special mention for its comfort food and inviting atmosphere. Mon–Thurs 9.30am–4pm, Fridays till late.

D'bar Restaurant Club Lounge 74 Vincent St. Dine on scrumptious Mod Oz food in the first-floor wine bar (Fri–Sun), listen to live jazz on Fri nights, or check out the DJs from 10pm on Sat.

Frangos & Frangos Restaurant/Koukla Café Both at 82 Vincent St ⓣ 03/5348 2363. Specializing in Mediterranean-inspired Modern Australian cuisine, this atmospheric café serves delicious, generously sized breakfasts, and slightly more adventurous and sophisticated lunches and dinners. The wood-fired pizza oven gets a workout at all times of the day and night. Café open Mon &

Tues 8am–4pm, Wed–Sun 8am–late; restaurant Mon & Tues 4pm–late, Fri & Sat 11am–late, Sun 11am–5pm.

Lake House King St near the lake ⓣ 03/5348 3329. Multi-award-winning restaurant that is regarded as one of the state's best. The cuisine is refined Modern Australian with a strong emphasis on using the freshest seasonal local produce. Daily 8–11am, noon–5pm & 7pm–late.

Mercato 32 Raglan St ⓣ 03/5348 4488. Fine Italian-inspired regional cuisine using local ingredients. Main meals start at around $30. Sun noon–3pm, Tues–Fri 6pm–late.

Pastry King Café 60 Vincent St. For the last seventy years or so this place has been baking delicious pies, muffins and other delicacies, perfect for picnic lunches by the lake. Daily 9.30am–4pm.

Sweet Decadence at Locantro 87 Vincent St. Chocolates, coffee and cake served up in an old building full of character. Daily 9.30am–5.30pm, dinner Fri & Sat.

Hepburn Springs

The charming hamlet of **HEPBURN SPRINGS**, set amid lush green hills 4km north of Daylesford, and synonymous with spas and pampering, has become a popular weekend retreat for stressed-out urbanites. From the bus stop, walk through the shady Soldiers Memorial Park to the Mineral Springs

Reserve, where you can taste three kinds of mineral water from old pumps and take advantage of the pool, spa and massage facilities at the sleek **Hepburn Spa & Hepburn Springs Bathhouse** (Sun–Fri 10am–6pm, Sat 9am–7pm, ℡03/5348 8888, Ⓦwww.hepburnspa.com.au). Bookings must be made at least three to six weeks in advance, especially for weekends.

Practicalities

The gracious, grand *Peppers Springs Retreat* at the corner of Main Road and Tenth Street (℡03/5348 2202, Ⓦwww.peppers.com.au; ❽–❾) is located in a famous 1930s Art-Deco hotel that has been tastefully renovated with luxurious en-suite rooms; there's a mineral spa on site too. Tasty meals are available in the bar, and at the more elegant and expensive restaurant on the premises. *Dudley House*, at 101 Main Rd (℡03/5348 3033, Ⓦwww.dudleyhouse.com.au; ❻–❽), is a lovely Federation-style weatherboard house with bed and breakfast. At the budget end of the scale is *Continental House*, 9 Lone Pine Ave (℡03/5348 2005, Ⓦwww.continentalhouse.com.au; ❶–❷), a vegan retreat offering basic accommodation, yoga classes and massages on request. The rambling house is located in a wild garden on a hill above the Mineral Springs Reserve. In addition to small dorms (bed $35) and simple twins/doubles ($80, BYO linen for all) there's a kitchen and several lounge rooms; a café offers vegan banquets on Saturday night ($30). *Wildwood YHA* at 42 Main Rd (℡03/5348 4435, Ⓔdaylesford @yhavic.org.au; dorms $27–32, rooms ❸) is set in a small and lovely renovated guesthouse with a homely kitchen and a deck overlooking a great garden area; booking is essential and pick-ups can be arranged.

A few **eating** places can be found along Main Street. The hippest by far is *The Red Star Café* at 115 Main Rd (daily 8am–5pm, dinner Fri & Sat), which is a likeable laid-back spot with a wide range of pasta and salads. For traditional Thai food try *Jasmine Thai* across the road at no. 114 (dinner daily except Tues; ℡03/5348 1163). *The Palais* at no. 111 (Ⓦwww.thepalais.com.au) is a restaurant and bar (Thurs–Sun night) in a stunning Art Nouveau building with a ballroom used for dance classes and as an entertainment venue – top-notch names from the Melbourne music scene and further afield perform here. Further down the road, *The Old Hepburn Hotel* at no. 236 is good for a drink in the beer garden or for tasty pub grub (dinner Tues–Sun). They also have live bands on Sunday afternoons.

Ballarat

BALLARAT is a grandiose provincial city that makes a memorable first impression, especially if approaching from the west, via the Western Highway, along **Avenue of Honour**. Lined on either side with over 22km of trees and dedicated to soldiers who fought in World War I, it ends at the massive **Arch of Victory**, through which you drive to enter Sturt Street and the city. Over a quarter of all **gold** found in Victoria came from Ballarat's fantastically rich reef mines before they were exhausted in 1918. Nowadays, in addition to the more obvious tourist attractions – especially Sovereign Hill – and fine **architecture**, the town is interesting in its own right, with a fairly large student population that gives the city a somewhat vibrant character and reasonably active nightlife.

Information and transport

The main **Ballarat visitor centre**, located in the Eureka Centre on the corner of Rodier and Eureka streets (daily 9.30am–5pm; ℡1800 446 633,

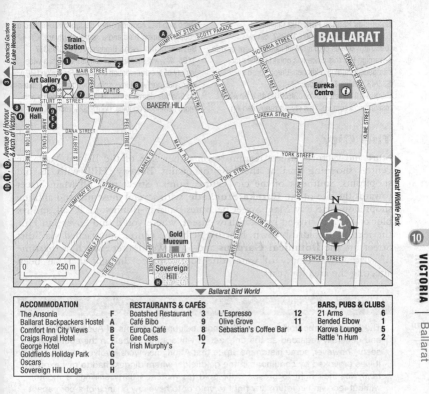

BALLARAT

ACCOMMODATION

The Ansonia	F
Ballarat Backpackers Hostel	A
Comfort Inn City Views	B
Craigs Royal Hotel	C
George Hotel	E
Goldfields Holiday Park	G
Oscars	D
Sovereign Hill Lodge	H

RESTAURANTS & CAFÉS

Boatshed Restaurant	3
Café Bibo	9
Europa Café	8
Gee Cees	10
Irish Murphy's	7
L'Espresso	12
Olive Grove	11
Sebastian's Coffee Bar	4

BARS, PUBS & CLUBS

21 Arms	6
Bended Elbow	1
Karova Lounge	5
Rattle 'n Hum	2

ⓦ www.ballarat.com), has an abundance of free **information**, and town maps, and can book accommodation. There is a more centrally located information office at the Town Hall on Sturt Street (Mon–Fri 9am–5pm), and another at Sovereign Hill. Public **transport** in Ballarat and surrounding areas is handled by Davis Buslines (☎03/5331 7777).

Accommodation

There's plenty of **accommodation** in all price ranges in Ballarat, from hostels to grand hotels, so you shouldn't have a problem finding a room.

The Ansonia 32 Lydiard St ☎03/5332 4678, ⓦwww.ansonia.com.au. This lovely boutique hotel in a heritage building in the historic precinct has elegant rooms and beautiful public spaces. ⑦–⑨
Ballarat Backpackers Hostel 81 Humffray St ☎0427 440 661, ⓦwww.ballarat.com /easternstation. Eclectically decorated with old-fashioned furniture, this popular place has a certain retro charm. There's a range of comfortable rooms, all with shared bathroom, and facilities include kitchen and lounge bar with pool table. ②
Comfort Inn City Views 101 Curtis ☎03/5329 2777, ⓦwww.cityviewsballarat.com.au. Good

value for money with a range of classy rooms, indoor pool and wireless internet in an excellent location. ⑥
Craigs Royal Hotel 10 Lydiard St South ☎03/5331 1377 or 1800 648 051, ⓦwww .craigsroyal.com. The accommodation at this grand Victorian-era hotel is the city's most sumptuous – if you can't afford to stay, at least visit for a drink. ⑧–⑨
George Hotel 27 Lydiard St ☎03/5333 4866, ⓦwww.georgehotelballarat.com.au. Three-storey 1850s hotel with colonial-style decor, an inexpensive bistro and recently renovated rooms. ⑦

Goldfields Holiday Park 108 Clayton St
ⓉΩ03/5332 7888 or 1800 632 237, ⓦwww
.ballaratgoldfields.com.au. Well located, right next to
Sovereign Hill, this place has good facilities for
campers, including a kitchen. Un/powered sites
$33/43, cabins & cottages ❸–❽
Oscars 18 Doveton St ⓉΩ03/5331 1451, ⓦwww
.oscarshotel.com.au. This stylish renovated Art

Deco pub has contemporary-designed rooms and a
couple of smart bars and a sunny courtyard. ❻–❽
Sovereign Hill Lodge Bradshaw St ⓉΩ03/5337
1125, ⓦwww.sovereignhill.com.au. There's a wide
variety of accommodation on site at Sovereign Hill, a
recreated gold rush township, from quality YHA-listed
backpacker dorms to comfortable family rooms and
more upmarket doubles. Dorms $24, rooms ❹–❼

The City

Sturt and Victoria streets terminate on either side of the Bridge Mall, the
central shopping area at the base of quaint **Bakery Hill** with its old
shopfronts. Southeast of the city centre, Eureka Street runs off Main Street
towards the site of the **Eureka Stockade**, with several museums and antique
shops along the way. Main Street becomes Ballarat–Buninyong Road, and six
blocks down is crossed by Bradshaw Street, where you'll find Sovereign Hill,
the recreated goldrush town. Northwest of the centre, approached via Sturt
Street, are the **Botanical Gardens** and Lake Wendouree, which at the time
of writing was empty of water due to the fierce drought that has been
affecting the area for years.

The Eureka Stockade

The **Eureka Rebellion** is one of the most celebrated events of Australian history
and generally regarded as the only act of white armed rebellion the country has
seen – however, some historians argue that Aborigines were involved in it as well.
It was provoked by conditions in the goldfields, where diggers had to pay exorbitantly for their right to prospect for gold (as much as thirty shillings a month),
without receiving in return any right to vote or to have any chance of a permanent
right to the land they worked. The administration at Ballarat was particularly
repressive, and in November 1854 local diggers formed the **Ballarat Reform
League**, demanding full civic rights and the abolition of the licence fee, and
proclaiming that "the people are the only legitimate source of power". At the end
of the month a group of two hundred diggers gathered inside a **stockade** of
logs, hastily flung together, and determined to resist further arrests for non-posses-
sion of a licence. They were attacked at dawn on December 3 by police and
troops; twenty-two died inside, and five members of the government forces also
lost their lives.

The movement was not a failure, however: the diggers had aroused widespread
sympathy, and in 1855 licences were abolished, to be replaced by an annual **Miner's
Right** which carried the right to vote and to enclose land. The leader of the rebellion,
the Irishman Peter Lalor, eventually became a member of parliament.

The **Eureka Flag**, with its white cross and five white stars on a blue background,
has become a symbol of the Left – and indeed of almost any protest movement:
shearers raised it in strikes during the 1890s; wharfies used it before World War II in
their bid to stop pig-iron being sent to Japan; and today the flag is flown by a
growing number of Australians who support the country's transformation to a
republic. On a deeper level, all sorts of claims are made for the Eureka Rebellion's
pivotal role in forming the Australian nation and psyche. The diggers are held up as
a classic example of the Australian (male) ethos of mateship and anti-authoritari-
anism, while the goldrush in general is credited with overthrowing the hierarchical
colonial order, as servants rushed to make their fortune, leaving their masters and
mistresses to fend for themselves.

The city centre

The most complete **nineteenth-century streetscape** is along Lydiard Street, which runs from the centre up past the train station, with historic multi-storey edifices, terraced shopfronts with awnings, and wide verandas with decorative iron-lace work, mostly dating from the mid- to late nineteenth century. The former **Mining Exchange** (1888) has been renovated to its former splendour, and the architecture of Her Majesty's Theatre (1875) also proclaims its goldrush-era heyday. The **Ballarat Art Gallery** at 40 Lydiard St, North Ballarat (daily 9am–5pm; free guided tours Wed–Sun 2pm; free; ☎03/5320 5858, ⓦwww .balgal.com), another superb building, is the oldest provincial art gallery in Australia, established in 1884. The original, frayed **Eureka Flag** (see box opposite) is on display here in a purpose-built space, with subdued lighting to protect the precious relic. The gallery's extensive collection is strong on colonial and Heidelberg School paintings, displayed alongside the watercolours of S.T. Gill, a self-taught artist who painted scenes of goldrush days in Ballarat. In another part of the gallery is a reconstruction of the drawing room of the famous Lindsay family (whose best-known members are the artist Norman and the writer Jack), from nearby Creswick, with several of their paintings. One wing of the gallery, a striking structure with a curved zinc roof and glass-encased staircase, extends out to Camp Street and Alfred Deakin Place, standing cheek by jowl with an 1880s red-brick building, a police station in its previous incarnation and now the *Gallery Café*. Walking from the Art Gallery along Lydiard Street to Sturt Street you'll see more nineteenth-century goldrush architecture: note the imposing Classical-Revival **town hall** on Sturt Street, which dominates the city centre.

There are still over forty old **hotels** in Ballarat – survivors of the hundreds that once watered the thirsty miners. Some of the finest are on Lydiard Street: Craig's *Royal Hotel* at no. 10 and the *George Hotel* at no. 27 are an integral part of Ballarat's architectural heritage, but sadly, during the 1970s, the council forced many old pubs to pull down verandas deemed unsafe, so very few survive in their original form. One that does is attached to the *Golden City Hotel* at 427 Sturt St, which took the council to the Supreme Court to save its magnificent wide veranda with original cast-iron decoration.

The Botanical Gardens

The **Botanical Gardens**, laid out in 1858, cover about half a square kilometre alongside Lake Wendouree, just to the northwest of the city centre (#16 bus from Sturt Street, near the Myer department store). Begonias grow so well in Ballarat that a Begonia Festival runs for ten days in March. The Conservatory at the Botanical Gardens, an impressive glasshouse whose design was inspired by origami, is used to showcase the flowers and other floral displays throughout the year (conservatory daily 9am–5pm; free).

Other highlights are the **Avenue of Big Trees**, with a California redwood among its monsters, and classical statuary donated by rich gold-miners, scattered about the gardens. Pride of place goes to *Benzoni's Flight from Pompeii*, housed in the Statuary Pavilion. Along Prime Minister Avenue there are busts of Australian prime ministers.

Eureka and York streets

As you head east of the centre towards Eureka Street and the Eureka Stockade (bus #8 from outside the ANZ Bank on Sturt St), check out the ornate shop facades on Main Street. The site of the Eureka Stockade is preserved in Eureka Gardens. To commemorate and honour the influential uprising (see box opposite),

▲ Historic buildings in Ballarat

the **Eureka Centre** (daily 9am–4.30pm, last tickets 4pm; $8; ⓦ www
.eurekaballarat.com) was built on the corner of Eureka Street; its exhibits give
a good insight into the historic rebellion. Outside the centre, the big blue-and-
white Eureka sail, shaped like a mining wind sail, is a Ballarat landmark.

Parallel to Eureka Street is York Street, where you'll find the **Ballarat Wildlife
Park**, on the corner of Fussell Street (daily 9am–5.30pm; $20; ⓣ03/5333 5933,
ⓦ www.wildlifepark.com.au); it's home to kangaroos, wombats, koalas and an
array of reptiles. The chance to get up close to the cuddlier animals and have
your photo taken is a highlight and there are daily guided tours. Feeding times
are definitely worth attending (weekends, daily during the school holidays:
between noon & 3pm).

Sovereign Hill and the Gold Museum

The recreated gold-mining township of **Sovereign Hill** (bus #9 from outside the
ANZ Bank on Sturt Street; daily 10am–5pm; $37.50, includes admission to the
Gold Museum and Red Hill Mine; ⓣ03/5331 1944, ⓦ www.sovereignhill.com
.au) is located 1.5km southeast of the city centre, on Bradshaw Street. Planned
around an actual mine-shaft from the 1880s (guided underground tours are
available), the seventy-odd buildings and shops are modelled on those that lined
Ballarat's main street in the 1850s, with a cast of characters in period dress. There
are diggings where you can learn how to pan for gold (and perhaps discover a small
memento), and a mining museum filled with steam-operated machinery. There's a
spectacular outdoor **sound-and-light show**, "Blood on the Southern Cross"
(nightly; 1hr 30min; $42, or joint ticket for show and Sovereign Hill, or for dinner
and show, $75; bookings essential on ⓣ03/5333 5777), which makes use of the
whole panorama of Sovereign Hill to tell the story of the Eureka Stockade.

Opposite Sovereign Hill, the **Gold Museum** (daily 9.30am–5.20pm, in
summer until 6pm; $9 if not going to Sovereign Hill) offers a good overview
of the recreated settlement. It has an outstanding display of real gold, and a
large collection of coins that are arranged in displays exploring the history
and uses of gold. The museum has a small Eureka display which details life

on the goldfields and explains the appalling conditions that provoked the Eureka Stockade. Central to the display is a large painting of the rebellion by George Browning, a mid-nineteenth-century artist: it's interesting to spot the indigenous faces portrayed in the stockade, generally labelled as a white armed uprising.

Ballarat Bird World

The privately run **Ballarat Bird World** (daily 10am–5pm; $10; ☎03/5341 3843, ⓦwww.ballaratbirdworld.com.au) at 408 Eddy Ave, Mount Helen, 7km south of Ballarat, is worth a detour. It has ten acres of landscaped bushland gardens, complete with a small rainforest and a waterfall, and about 150 parrots and cockatoos from Australia, Asia, Africa and South America, some of which were bred here.

Eating

Ballarat has an astonishing number and variety of **eating places**, ranging from atmospheric cafés established by postwar European immigrants to gourmet restaurants, not to mention numerous pubs.

Boatshed Restaurant 27A Wendouree Parade. The lake may have disappeared but that hasn't stopped people coming to relax for a coffee, lunch or dinner while they imagine swans and ducks floating past. Daily 7am–10pm.

Café Bibo 205 Sturt St. The kind of retro diner you might expect to see in the US, with hearty meals hovering around $20. Open daily for breakfast, lunch and dinner.

Europa Café 411 Sturt St. A buzzy café serving good coffee, cakes, snacks and light meals. Mon–Wed & Sun 9am–6pm, Thurs–Sat 9am until late.

Gee Cees 427 Sturt St. The wait may be long on weekend evenings, but it's worth it to try the Mod Oz cuisine at this popular gastropub. Mains around $20 or so. Open daily for lunch and dinner.

Irish Murphy's 36 Sturt St. Big food at small prices, decent beer and frequent live music with minimal Irish kitsch combine to make this bar popular with the backpacking set. Open lunch and dinner daily.

L'Espresso 417 Sturt St. This arty café attracts local uni students, intellectuals and musicians to its good coffee, tasty breakfasts and light meals, good wines by the glass, and CDs for sale. Daily 7am–6pm, also Thurs–Sun 6.30pm until late.

Olive Grove 1303 Sturt St. Excellent delicatessen with a wide range of fresh produce that is a favourite with Ballarat's students. 8.30am–7pm daily.

Sebastian's Coffee Bar 58 Lydiard St North. Café-bar with cool minimalist decor opposite the Regent Multiplex cinemas. Open daily from 11am.

Entertainment and nightlife

Thanks to a burgeoning number of students – over twenty thousand are enrolled at the University of Ballarat, with a high percentage of them studying music, performing arts and fashion – the city has a buzzy live **music** and **club** scene. For up-to-date information about what's on, check *The Courier* on Thursday; most action takes place after 9pm from Thursday to Sunday. *Bended Elbow* at 120 Lydiard St is a boisterous place for a beer, with over twenty varieties on tap; it's popular with students midweek and local football teams at weekends, while *21 Arms* at 21 Armstrong St, Ballarat North, is open until 3am and has four main areas ranging from a lounge bar to the frenetic "*Shed*". *Rattle 'n Hum* at 49 Mair St is another mainstay of the Ballarat club scene. Popular bands from Melbourne and around the country play at the *Karova Lounge* (ⓦwww.karovalounge.com), corner of Field and Camp streets.

The elaborate Victorian-era Her Majesty's Theatre, at 17 Lydiard St (☎03/5333 5800), stages all types of touring **productions**, and the Regent has a three-screen **cinema** on the same street at no. 49 (☎03/5331 1399).

Western Victoria and the Mallee

Several roads run west from the goldfields to the South Australia border through the seemingly endless wheatfields of the **Wimmera**. To the west of the farming centre of **Ararat** is the major attraction of the area, the **Grampians National Park**, the southwestern tail-end of the Great Dividing Range. Stawell and Horsham – the latter regarded as the capital of the Wimmera – are good places to base yourself, but **Halls Gap**, in a valley and surrounded by national park, is even better. North of Horsham is the wide, flat **Mallee** with its twisted mallee scrub, sand dunes and dry lakes. This region, with several state and national parks, extends from **Wyperfeld National Park** in the south, right up to Mildura's irrigated oasis on the Murray River. South of the Grampians is sheep country; following the Hamilton Highway from Geelong you'll end up at **Hamilton**, the major town and wool capital of the western district, also accessible via **Dunkeld** on the southern edge of the Grampians.

V/Line (☎13 61 96, ⊚www.vline.com.au) has a **bus service** from Ballarat to Hamilton via Dunkeld and from Warrnambool to Hamilton. The Grampians Link consists of a **train service** from Melbourne to Ballarat and a connecting bus to Halls Gap, via Ararat and Stawell. The Daylink connection (train from Melbourne to Bendigo, and from there a connecting bus via Horsham and Dimboola to Adelaide) departs Melbourne daily in the morning. Greyhound Australia and Firefly buses to Adelaide travel the Western Highway via Ballarat, Ararat, Stawell, Horsham, Dimboola and Nhill.

Ararat

ARARAT, some 90km west from Ballarat, is still very much a goldfields town, with an overabundance of grandiose Victorian architecture and a main street laid out to show off the best profiles of the nearby mountains: **Mount Ararat** in the west and the **Pyrenees Range** with **Mount Cole** in the east. The town was founded in 1857, when a group of seven hundred hopeful Chinese from Guangdong province in southern China, making the slow trudge from the South Australian ports to the central Victorian goldfields, stumbled across a fabulously rich, shallow alluvial goldfield, the **Canton Lead**.

Information and accommodation

The **visitor centre** is located on High Street near the train station, parallel to the town's main thoroughfare, Barkly Street (daily 9am–5pm; ☎03/5355 0274, ⊚www.visitararat.com.au). It provides information on the Grampians and can book accommodation in the area and has **internet** access. There is cheap **accommodation** at the *Shire Hall Hotel* (☎03/5352 1280, ⊚www.shirehallhotel.com .au; ❶) at 240 Barkly St, which has shared facilities in a building erected in 1860. A more comfortable option is the very good-value *Orchid City Motor Inn* (☎03/5352 1341, ⊚www.orchidcity.com.au; ❺), located at 96 High St, opposite the train station. It has fully renovated, spacious rooms with kitchens and cable TV. Those in need of luxury and serenity should head to the *Links Retreat* (℡ 0419 438 948, ⓦ www.linksretreat.com.au; ❼), a cosy wooden house with full amenities, situated in woodland close to the Chalambar Golf Course at 139 Golf Links Rd.

The Town

The new multi-million-dollar **Gum San Chinese Heritage Centre** (daily 10am–4.30pm; $8; ⓦ www.gumsan.com.au) pays homage to the fact that Ararat is the only town in Australia founded by the Chinese. It was designed by a Melbourne architect of Chinese origin and is a recreation of a two-storey southern Chinese temple set in a traditional Chinese garden. The exhibits recount the tale of the founding of the city and familiarize Western visitors with aspects of Chinese culture.

These days Ararat is the commercial centre for a sheep farming and wine-producing area; local **wineries** include the Montara Winery, 3km south along the Chalambar Road (ⓦ www.montara.com.au; Fri–Sun 11am–4pm), and Mount Langi Ghiran on Vine Road north of Buangor (Mon–Fri 9am–5pm, Sat & Sun 10am–5pm; ⓦ www.langi.com.au), renowned for its superb whites and reds; turn north from the Western Highway towards Warrak.

The **Langi Morgala Museum** (Tues 10am–3pm, Sat & Sun 1–4pm; $5) at 50 Queen St occupies an old brick building banded with bluestone at the base and around the huge arched windows and doors. Along with the usual pioneering displays, there's an important collection of Aboriginal artefacts. A guided tour at **J Ward**, further north across the railway tracks at Girdlestone Street (Mon–Sat at 10am, 11am, 1pm & 2pm; additional tours on Sun and school holidays from 11am to 3pm; $14; ⓦ www.jward.ararat.net.au), gives a chilling insight into one of the darker aspects of the area's social history. The 1859 building started out as a prison, but from the late 1880s it operated as a high-security ward of the Ararat Lunatic Asylum; criminally insane men were incarcerated here, in appalling conditions that were at the time considered acceptable. J Ward itself was closed as late as 1991.

Eating and drinking

For **food**, head for Barkly Street, where you'll find a supermarket, a bakery and a few good cafés. *Vines Café* at no. 74 has good breakfasts, light meals and lots of local wines by the glass and is open daily (except Wed) 9.30am–5.30pm. *Sicilian's Café-Bar-Restaurant* at no. 102 serves good pizza and pasta, open Monday to Wednesday 11am–9pm, Thursday to Saturday till late. For bar meals the slightly upmarket *Hippo Café and Bar* (closed Mon) at no. 157 is popular with locals having a night out, but head to the *Rex Hotel* at 129 Barkly St or the *Blue Duck Hotel* at no. 257 if you want traditional pub grub or a late-night beer. A good-value option is the bistro at the *Ararat RSL Club*, 74 High St, which serves inexpensive meals.

Stawell

STAWELL (pronounced "stall") is most famous for the **Stawell Gift**, a sprint race offering big prize money ($40,000 to the winner) that has been held here every Easter since 1877. It's also the closest major town to the Grampians and the departure point for the bus to Halls Gap. The helpful **Stawell & Grampians**

Visitor Centre is at 52 Western Highway (☎1800 330 080; daily 9am–5pm, ⓦwww.ngshire.vic.gov.au) and has a detailed brochure, *The Cultural Heritage Trail*, listing all the notable buildings and landmarks from the mid- to late 1800s. The **Stawell Gift Hall of Fame** on Main Street (Mon–Fri 9–11am or by appointment; $3; ☎03/5358 1326) charts the history of the race itself. The *Town Hall Hotel* at 62 Main Rd (built in 1873) is a good place to stop for a meal or a beer (lunch noon–2pm, dinner 6–9pm).

The Grampians

Rising from the flat plains of western Victoria's wheat and grazing districts, the sandstone ranges of the **GRAMPIANS**, with their weirdly formed rocky outcrops and stark ridges, seem doubly spectacular. In addition to their scenic splendour, in the **Grampians National Park (Gariwerd)** you'll find a dazzling array of **flora**, with a spring and early summer bonanza of wild flowers; a wealth of **Aboriginal rock art**; an impressive **Aboriginal Cultural Centre**; waterfalls and lakes; and over fifty **bushwalks** along 150km of well-marked tracks. There are also several hundred kilometres of road, from sealed highway to rough track, on which you can make exciting **scenic drives** and **4WD tours**.

The **best times to come** are in autumn, or in spring and early summer when the waterfalls are in full flow and the wild flowers are blooming (although there'll always be something in flower no matter when you come). Between June and August it rains heavily and can get extremely cold; at that time many tracks are closed to avoid erosion. Summers are very hot, with a scarcity of water and the ever-present threat of bushfires. If you're undertaking extended walks in summer, carry a portable radio to get the latest information on the fire risk: on **total fire ban days** no exposed flames – not even that from a portable gas stove – are allowed.

Halls Gap and around

HALLS GAP, 26km from Stawell, on the eastern fringes of the Grampians, is the only settlement actually surrounded by national park. Its setting is gorgeous, in the long flat strip of the Fyans Valley surrounded by the soaring bush and rock of the Wonderland, Mount Difficult and Mount William ranges; koalas are frequently seen in the surrounding trees. Packed with accommodation and other facilities catering to park visitors, this is the obvious place to base yourself, especially if you don't have your own transport.

Information and accommodation

The friendly staff at the **Halls Gap Visitor Centre** (daily 9am–5pm; ☎1800 065 599, ⓦwww.visithallsgap.com.au) on Grampians Road next to the Mobil service station book accommodation, tours and activities as well as having an ATM. Although Halls Gap has lots of **accommodation** of every kind, during school holidays, particularly in January and at Easter, you'll need to book in advance. Note that many places will insist on long stays, and prices rise at weekends.

A permit is required for the **campsites** in the national park, which must be obtained at the National Park Centre at Brambuk (see p.972). After hours you fill in a form and put your money into the box outside the centre. The fee is $13 (for up to 6 people) per site per day. **Bushcamping** is allowed in the park,

Grampians activities

A few companies offer introductory climbing and abseiling; the going rate is about $70 for half a day and $130 for a full day.

Absolute Outdoors Grampians Shop 4, Stoney Creek Stores ☏ 03/5356 4556, ⊛ www .absoluteoutdoors.com.au. In addition to climbing/abseiling tours, they also offer canoeing and kayaking trips, guided nature and night-time spotlight walks as well as mountain-bike tours; they sell outdoor gear and rent mountain bikes too ($40 per hr).

GMAC (Grampians Mountain Adventure Company) ☏ 03/5383 9218 or 0427 747 047, ⊛ www.grampiansadventure.com.au. Trained and accredited by the Australian Mountain Climbers Association; they also operate at Mt Arapiles and can cater for advanced levels.

The Grampians Horse Riding Centre ☏ 03/5383 9255, ⊛ www.grampianshorseriding .com.au. Brimpaen in the Wartook Valley on the northwestern side of the Grampians. Trail rides through the bush twice a day (2hr 30min; $75).

Grampians Scenic Flights ☏ 03/5356 4654 or 0429 954 686. Offers 40-min flights giving the definitive overview of the mountain range; $170 for three-passenger aircraft, $200 for five.

Hangin' Out in the Grampians ☏ 03/5356 4535 or 0407 684 831, ⊛ www.hanginout .com.au. Casual climbing tours start at $65 (4 hours), and rise to $120 for full-day tours that include abseiling.

except in the Wonderland Range and within 20m of a dam, river or creek, or within 50m of a road; but the staff at the National Park Centre will want to be informed about where and when you are going to pitch your tent.

Hostels

Asses Ears Wilderness Lodge 130 Schmidt Rd, Brimpaen ☏ 03/5383 9215, ⊛ www .assesearslodge.com.au. Great backpacker accommodation in timber cabins in a quiet location in the Wartook Valley on the northwestern side of the Grampians. There's a licensed bar, inexpensive restaurant, a swimming pool and a pool table. The owners drop people off for hikes and organize loads of activities. Rates include continental breakfast and linen. Dorms $23–25, cabin ❶

Brambuk Backpackers Grampians Rd ☏ 03/5356 4250, ⊛ www.brambuk.com.au/backpackers.htm. Great lounge area with open fireplace, but the dorm rooms are dated. Ask for a bed in the newer part of the hostel – the older section has been in need of a spruce-up for years. Has broadband and wireless internet. Rates include light breakfast. Dorms $22–25, rooms ❸

Grampians YHA Eco Hostel Grampians Rd ☏ 03/5356 4544, ✉ grampians@yhavic.org .au. Hostel built according to environmentally friendly principles, recycling waste water and using solar electricity and wood-heating stoves. It has excellent facilities, including internet access and spotless same-sex dorms. Office open 8–10am & 3–10pm. Dorms $24, rooms ❸

Neds Beds 2 Heath St, Halls Gap ☏ 03/5356 4516, ⊛ www.grampiansbackpackers.com.au. Old-timer which has expanded over the years to include three camp kitchens and three TV lounges. The central location near the shops, a BBQ area and outdoor veranda are pluses. Free laundry, linen and tea and coffee. Rates include light breakfast. Dorms $23, double ❸

Tim's Place 44 Grampians Rd, Halls Gap ☏ 03/5356 4288, ⊛ www.timsplace.com.au. Friendly small hostel with a lovely, homely feel. There are dorms in the main house, and decent studio apartments out the back. Rates include continental breakfast. Extras include free Internet access and free use of sports equipment and mountain bikes. Dorms $25, rooms ❸

Hotels and apartments

Glengarriff Halls Gap Townhouses 194 Grampians Rd, Halls Gap ☏ 0437 362 458, ⊛ www.hallsgaptownhouses.com.au. Three luxurious two-storey apartments designed to exploit the natural light and scenery. Has BBQ, spa and elegant furnishings. Only 800m from the main shops. ❽

Grand Canyon Motel Less than 1km north of Halls Gap on Grampians Rd ☏ 03/5356 4280,

Ⓦ www.grandcanyonmotel.com.au. Simple and cheap motel accommodation in a good location – good value for the price. ❹

Mountain Grand Hotel Grampians Rd, Halls Gap Ⓣ 03/5356 4232, Ⓦ www.mountaingrand.com.au. This elegant, refurbished 1930s-style guesthouse has comfortable en-suite rooms, some with spa. There's also a good licensed restaurant on the first floor. Dinner, B&B ❽

Caravan parks

Halls Gap Caravan Park Ⓣ 03/5356 4251, Ⓦ www.hallsgapcaravanpark.com.au. Right opposite the shopping centre and so a bit noisy, but it's well equipped, and at the start of many walks. Cabins ❸, on-site vans ❷

Lakeside Caravan Park Ⓣ 03/5356 4281, Ⓦ www.hallsgaplakeside.com.au. Four kilometres out of town on the banks of Lake Bellfield, another good option. Cabins ❹

Brambuk the National Park and Cultural Centre

Just over 2km south of Halls Gap along the Grampians Road (also known as the Dunkeld Road or the Dunkeld–Halls Gap Road) is **Brambuk the National Park and Cultural Centre**, the best place to start your visit. It consists of two separate buildings: the first one (daily 9am–5pm; Ⓣ 03 5361 4000, Ⓦ www.brambuk.com.au) mainly dispenses information on the national park and sells guide books and maps; don't miss the display and videos that trace the development of the Grampians over four hundred million years. There is also a restaurant/café with average food and internet access ($3 per 15min).

Located behind this building is the original **Aboriginal Cultural Centre** (daily 9am–5pm), opened in 1990. With its undulating red-ochre tin roof it blends in wonderfully with the backdrop of bush and rocky ridge; its design incorporates many symbolic features that are important to the five Koorie communities who own and manage the centre. A small exhibition inside features a poignant photographic history of the area's orginal inhabitants, while downstairs the Gariwerd Dreaming Theatre features presentations on the region's creation story and natural history (shows run hourly from 10am–4.30pm; $5).

There are short rock-art tours from the centre, as well as half- and full-day walks to other Aboriginal art sites in the national park. All tours are on demand only, must be booked at least 24 hours in advance, and require a minimum of four people (Mon–Fri 9.30am; 2–3hr; $35).

Bushwalks and scenic drives

The National Park Centre at Brambuk hands out masses of free leaflets, walking guides and more detailed topographic maps; the easy-to-use

---

Rock art in the Grampians

It's estimated that **Koorie** Aborigines lived in the area known to them as **Gariwerd** at least five thousand years ago. The area offered such rich food sources that the Koories didn't have to spend all their time hunting and food-gathering, and could therefore devote themselves to religious and cultural activities. Evidence of this survives in **rock paintings**, which are executed in a linear style, usually in a single colour (either red or white), but sometimes done by handprints or stencils. You can visit some of the rock shelters where Aborigines camped and painted on the sandstone walls, although many more are off-limits. In the northern Grampians one of the best is **Gulgurn Manja** (also known as Flat Rock), 5km south of the Western Highway near the *Hollow Mountain* campsite; from Flat Rock Road it's a signposted fifteen-minute walk. The name means "hands of young people", as many of the handprints here were done by children. In the southern Grampians is **Billimina**, a fifteen-minute walk above the *Buandik* campsite; it's an impressive rock overhang with clearly discernible, quite animated, red stick figures.

Southern Walks, *Northern Walks* and *Wonderland Walks* ($3.30 each) are good all-rounders and handy for short walks. Although most walking tracks are clearly defined and well signposted, it's a good idea to buy *Vicmap*, or the walking maps published by Parks Victoria, and carry a compass if you're planning an overnight trek. Before beginning an extended walk, call into the centre and register. Some **walks** start from the campsite at Halls Gap, while others branch off the Victory and Grampian roads, making them difficult to get to without a car.

You can **drive** on roads through the park to major points and then get out and walk. The most popular section for visitors is the **Wonderland Range**, immediately to the west of Halls Gap. From the Halls Gap campsite you can head directly to **Venus Baths** (1.2km return). **The Pinnacle**, the most popular lookout in the Grampians, is usually accessed from the Wonderland car park (just off Mount Victory Rd; the turn-off is signposted). The 4.2-kilometre return walk is easy, except for the slightly trickier Grand Canyon section where a series of steel ladders must be negotiated – as long as you wear sturdy shoes, are reasonably fit and don't suffer from vertigo, you'll be fine. **Delleys Dell** is another Wonderland walk (5km), through canopies of tree ferns: start at the Delleys Dell car park at the *Rosea Campground* (the turn-off from Mount Victory Rd is signposted). The other major features in the Grampians are the Balconies, Mackenzie Falls and Zumstein, all accessible via the Mount Victory Road northwest of Halls Gap. The walk to the **Balconies** (1.6km return), formerly known as the **Jaws of Death**, begins from the Reed Lookout car park (the turn-off is signposted) and goes for about ten minutes through a stand of lichen-covered tea trees until you have reached the lookout over the Victoria Valley and towards the Balconies. The much photographed, weird rock formation consists of one ledge above another, forming the image of a reptile's elongated, open jaw.

At **Zumstein** (5km east on Mount Victory Rd) there's a picnic area and car park where western grey kangaroos stand passively, waiting for food. They're tame enough to pet, but can be a serious nuisance when you get out your food; don't encourage them by feeding them. A three-kilometre walk runs along the Mackenzie River Gorge from here to the base of **Mackenzie Falls**, which you can also reach more directly from Mount Victory Road. There's parking above the falls, and it's a short but strenuous walk to the base.

If you're reasonably fit, consider tackling the walk to the peak of Mount William (1168m; 3.5km return), the highest point in the park. This starts from the Mount William Road car park, for which you turn off 16km south of Halls Gap. More challenging overnight walks include one to the Major Mitchell Plateau, starting from the same car park but involving a difficult five-hundred-metre climb to the plateau, and the Mount Difficult walk, which starts from Rose Gap and goes across a large, undulating, rocky plateau.

Eating, drinking and entertainment

Halls Gap's main **eating** options are located in the Stoney Creek complex, but around the area are some good country-style pubs worthy of a beer and a feed. For entertainment, there's **live jazz** at the *Mountain Grand* every Saturday from 7pm at their *Balconies Restaurant* upstairs. An alternative **film festival** comes to town at the beginning of November, and there's a jazz festival in mid-February.

Balconies Restaurant ☎03/5356 4232. Situated above the *Mountain Grand Hotel*, it offers elegant dining with reasonably priced good-quality meals and wine. Open for dinner daily.

Black Panther Café and Bar Stoney Creek complex. Good breakfasts and lunch; licensed and BYO. Daily 8am–8pm.

Café Grand *Mountain Grand Hotel*. Licensed café serving light meals, coffee and cake. Daily noon–2pm.

Flying Emu Café Stoney Creek complex. The place to go in between meals for cakes, snacks and something light. Daily 8.30am–4.30pm.

Halls Gap Hotel 1km out of town on Stawell Rd. Serves decent pub meals, but people mostly come here for the views from the balcony looking towards the mountains. Lunch daily except Tues & dinner daily.

Kookaburra Restaurant 125 Grampians Rd ☎03/5356 4222. Dependable bistro-style dishes – including baked duckling, kangaroo filet and home-made ice cream. Lighter pasta and salad dishes are also available. Lunch Sat & Sun, dinner Tues–Sun.

Quarry Restaurant Stoney Creek complex ☎03/5356 4858. Popular spot in a pleasant setting with big windows facing a small reserve. Lunch Sun, dinner daily except Tues..

Hamilton

Three highways converge at **HAMILTON**, a civilized little city where you can see the Grampians from the edge of the main street. Its main claim to fame is as the "Wool Capital of the World" – more accurately, it is responsible for about 15 percent of Australia's wool production. The only reason you're likely to be here is if you're passing through, though there are a few things to distract you and the friendly **Hamilton Visitor Centre** on Lonsdale Street (daily 9am–5pm; ☎1800 807 056, ⓦwww.sthgrampians.vic.gov.au/tourism) can book accommodation if you decide to stay.

The most worthwhile of the town's five museums and galleries is the **Hamilton Art Gallery**, on Brown Street (Mon–Fri 10am–5pm, Sat 10am–noon & 2–5pm, Sun 2–5pm; entry by donation; ⓦwww.hamiltongallery.org), one of the finest provincial art galleries in the state. Its collection of eighteenth-century watercolours of English pastoral scenes by Paul Sandby is the largest outside Britain. Also in the town centre, but of marginal interest, is the **Hamilton History Centre** (2–5pm; closed Sat), located in the Mechanics Institute Building at 43 Gray St. East of town, on the Ballarat Road, is the **Sir Reginald Ansett Transport Museum** (daily 10am–4pm; $4), charting the history of the now-defunct Ansett flight network which began here, while **The Big Woolbales** (Mon–Fri 8am–4.30pm, Sat 8.30am–2.30pm & Sun 9.30am–2.30pm; ⓦwww.bigwoolbales.com.au) on Coleraine Road contains a small exhibition telling you about the wool industry of the Western district and has a restaurant serving cheap meals such as schnitzels, burgers and focaccia, and a Sunday roast for $12 (daily breakfast & lunch).

Practicalities

Hamilton features a wide variety of **accommodation**. Budget travellers can stay at the simple yet central *Commercial Hotel* (☎03/5572 4119; ❶–❷) at 145 Thompson St, which has shared facilities, or the pleasantly located *Lake Hamilton Caravan Park*, 8 Ballarat Rd (☎03/5572 3855, ⓦwww.lakehamilton .com.au; cabins ❹). On the same road at no. 142 is the luxurious *Quality Inn Grange Burn* (☎03/5572 5755, ⓦwww.thegrangeburn.com.au; ❻), which is one of the better places to stay in town.

If you want a bite to **eat**, the *Darriwill Farm Restaurant and Café* at 169 Gray St is a town favourite and has an array of products you can buy and take with you, or you can stay and order a variety of gourmet options (breakfast and lunch Mon–Sat, dinner Thurs, Fri & Sat).

The Wimmera

The Wimmera, dry and hot, relies heavily on irrigation water from the Grampians for its vast wheatfields; before irrigation and the invention of the stump jump plough, the area was little more than mallee scrub, similar to the lands beyond **Warracknabeal**, the northernmost wheat-growing centre.

HORSHAM, capital of the wheatfields, makes a good stop-off point en route to Adelaide; it has an idyllic picnic spot, complete with barbecues by the Wimmera River. There's little else to detain you, though the Grampians National Park (see p.970) is within striking distance to the southeast, and **Mount Arapiles**, 40km west, is one of the most important **rock-climbing** centres in Australia – if you're interested, contact The Climbing Company in Natimuk (☎03/5387 1558, ⓦ www.climbco.com.au), which can also organize **abseiling**. The **Horsham Visitor Centre**, at 20 O'Callaghan Parade (daily 9am–5pm; ☎03/5382 1832 or 1800 633 218, ⓦ www.grampianslittledesert .com.au), books both accommodation and tours. One central, cheap **place to stay** is the *White Hart Hotel*, 55 Firebrace St (☎03/5382 1231; rooms with shared facilities ❷), which is the best of the pub accommodation around town. The best-value meals in town can be found at the *Horsham Sports and Community Club*, 177 Baillie St (noon–2pm daily), while *Bagdad Foods Café* (Mon–Fri 7.30am–5pm) at 50c Darlot St has a changing menu that may include hearty home-made quiche, shepherd's pie or lamb curry. Oasis of Wellbeing, 48 Wilson St, has a very local, slightly arty alternative feel and serves espresso, cakes and ice cream, as well as big portions of soups, lasagne and focaccias (Mon–Wed 9.30am–6pm, Thurs & Fri 9.30am–10pm).

The Mallee

The Mallee, the most sparsely populated area of Victoria, begins north of Warracknabeal, from where the **Henty Highway** heads up to join the Sunraysia Highway and forge its way to Mildura, on the border with New South Wales. You really need your own transport to see anything; the only **public transport** is the small Henty Highway Coach that runs between Horsham and Mildura and mainly carries freight (departs Horsham Atlas Poolside service station Tues & Thurs at 9.15am and Fri at 5.45pm; Mildura train station Mon, Wed & Fri at 7.45am; 6hr; $69; ☎03/5023 5658). Along the way are small dusty towns such as Brim, Bealah and **HOPETOUN** ("Gateway to the Mallee"). Here the *Bon Bon Café* at 74 Austin St is a nice little place with surprisingly good food to break up the journey.

Fifty kilometres west of Hopetoun is **Wyperfeld National Park**, which at 3500 square kilometres is Victoria's third largest. Bushcamping is not allowed in the park but a sealed road leads from Hopetoun via Yampeet to the *Wonga Campground*, where there's shady camping ($13 per site per night, max 6 people; payable by self-registration) and a picnic area with water and toilets.

Beyond Hopetoun, the Henty Highway merges into the Sunraysia Highway. Heading north on the Sunraysia, you pass **SPEED** and **OUYEN**, which don't warrant much time. Heading west on the Mallee Highway, the access track to the picturesque **pink salt lakes** of the **Murray–Sunset (Yanga–Nyawi) National Park** leads north from Linga. Continuing north on the Calder Highway from Ouyen, you pass the **Hattah–Kulkyne National Park**, just east of the highway; the park consists of dry mallee scrub, native woodland, and a lakes system lined with gums. Lake Hattah is reached by turning off the highway at Hattah, 34km north of Ouyen, onto the Hattah–Robinvale Road. From Hattah it's less than 70km to Mildura and the Murray River.

The Murray region

From its source close to Mount Kosciuszko high in the Australian Alps, the **Murray River** forms the border between Victoria and New South Wales until it crosses into South Australia (someone got a ruler out for the rest of the border to the coast), and although the actual watercourse is in New South Wales, the Victoria bank is far more interesting and more populous. After the entire length was navigated in 1836, the river became the route along which cattle were driven from New South Wales to the newly established town of Adelaide, and later in the century there was a thriving paddle-steamer trade on the lower reaches of the river, based at Wentworth on the New South Wales side (see p.363). In 1864, **Echuca** was linked by railway to Melbourne, stimulating the river trade in the upper reaches, and thus became a major inland port, the furthest extent of the navigable river. At the height of the paddle-steamer era, **Mildura** was still a run-down, rabbit-infested cattle station, but in 1887 the Chaffey brothers instituted irrigation projects that now support dairy farms, vineyards, vegetable farms and citrus orchards throughout northwestern Victoria. Between Mildura and Echuca, **Swan Hill** marks the transition to sheep, cattle and wheat country; the **Pioneer Settlement** here explores the extraordinarily hard lives of the early settlers. Above Echuca the Murray loses much of its magic as it flows through the more settled northeast.

Nowadays **paddle steamers** cruise for leisure, and are the best way to enjoy the river and admire magnificent **river red gums** lining its banks, as well as the

Murray River red gums

The magnificent **red gum forests** of the Murray River flood plains are one of the major draws of the Murray River region, with evocative photographs gracing the pages of most tourist brochures. However, while these hardy trees are well adapted to the irregular cycles of drought and flood typical in Australia, human demand for water has created conditions of near-permanent drought they seem unable to cope with. In November 2004, a government report revealed that 75 percent of all red gums along the Murray are stressed, dying or dead. The cause is salinity and a lack of water, exacerbated by long-term natural drought. The infrequently released environmental flows are not sufficient to flush out the saline build-up and supply the trees with the water they need, and though the state and federal governments have agreed to let an additional 500 billion litres flow through the Murray, critics say this is just a third of what the river and the flood plains need in order to be moderately healthy. There is some good news, though; in December 2008 the Victorian Premier John Brumby vowed to create a series of River Red Gum National Parks, with an end to grazing in the forests and a significant reduction in logging. However, his New South Wales counterpart has greeted the decision with the usual silence.

huge array of birds and other wildlife that the Murray sustains. Renting a houseboat is also a relaxing (if expensive) way to travel.

Mildura and around

MILDURA has a mirage-like aura, its vineyards and orange orchards standing out from a hot, dry landscape. To the southwest is the evocatively named **Sunset Country**, with nothing but gnarled mallee scrub, red sand and pink salt lakes (reached via Linga on the Mallee Highway). Mildura makes a good winter getaway, but summer can be stiflingly hot and it's best to avoid the area at this time if you can.

Arrival and information

Mildura is 555km from Melbourne, about as far as you can go in this small state; right on the border of New South Wales, and a little over 100km from South Australia, it's ideally located for **onward transport** to either. Buses on the Sturt Highway, the major route between **Adelaide** and **Sydney**, pass through several times daily. From Melbourne, there's also a V/Line train–bus connection via Bendigo or Swan Hill at least twice daily. **Broken Hill**, north up Silver City Highway, can be reached by bus via Wentworth (departing Mildura train station daily except Fri; 3hr 30min; book at the visitor centre). In terms of **local transport**, Coomealla Buslines runs a service across the river to Wentworth via Buronga (see p.363), while the very regular Sunraysia Buslines (℡03/5023 0274) services the centre from 7th to 15th streets, and to suburban areas further to the east and west, and to the south as far as Red Cliffs. Alternatively, you can **rent a car** from, among others, Budget at 7th Street and Etiwanda Avenue (℡03/5021 4442).

The **Mildura Visitor and Booking Centre** is situated in the state-of-the-art Alfred Deakin Centre at Deakin Avenue and 12th Street (Mon–Fri 9am–5.30pm, Sat & Sun 9am–5pm; ℡03/5018 8380 or 1800 039 043, ⓦwww.visitmildura.com.au), which also houses a pool ($5.05) and gym, a decent café and a library, where you can check your email ($2 per 30min). The visitor centre will book accommodation and supply free town maps: they also have particularly good information on the Murray–Sunset (Yanga–Nyawi) and Hattah–Kulkyne national parks.

Accommodation

Mildura has lots of reasonably priced **accommodation**, and an ever-increasing number of hostels to cater to the hordes of hard-up backpackers who drift here looking for work. If you are staying longer, ask the hostel for their weekly rates – they come much cheaper. There are also a number of houseboats based in Mildura or across the river in Buronga or Wentworth. Call the visitor centre for information and bookings.

Hotels, hostels and caravan parks

Apex Riverbeach Holiday Park Cureton Ave ℡03/5023 6879, ⓦwww.apexriverbeach.com.au. Nestled within the gum trees along the river bank, but still close to the main shops, the fully contained one and two bedroom cabins offer good value in a picturesque setting. ③–④

Mildura City Backpackers 50 Lemon Ave ℡03/5022 7922, ⓦwww.milduracitybackpackers .com.au. Sociable and homely house close to the centre of town, which has a good blend of workers

Cruises, tours and activities

The best **short river cruise** is on the PS *Melbourne* (daily 10.50am & 1.50pm; 2hr 10min; $25; ⓣ03/5023 2200), Mildura's only genuinely steam-driven paddle steamer. Built in 1912, it still has its original boiler and engine. The same company runs *Paddleboat Rothbury*, built in 1881 and in its day the fastest steamboat on the river; it's now been converted to diesel and takes people on cruises to local attractions, such as the Thursday cruise to Trentham Estate Winery (5hr; $60 including lunch and wine tasting).

Away from the river, the most outstanding natural attraction is **Mungo National Park** (see p.364), 110km across the border in New South Wales. It's visited by tour operators from Mildura who charge about $125 for a day tour: Sunraysia Discovery Tours (ⓣ03/5023 5937, ⓦwww.sunraysiadiscoverytours.com.au) and Jumbunna Walkabout Tours (ⓣ0412 581 699). Koorie tour operators belonging to the Barkindji people also lend their perspective on the park with Harry Nanya Tours, based just over the border in Wentworth (day tour $165, $125 from Mungo; ⓣ03/5027 2076, ⓦwww.harrynanyatours.com.au).

Mildura Ballooning (ⓣ03/5024 6848, ⓦwww.milduraballooning.com.au) arranges **hot-air balloon flights** daily, weather permitting, for $285 per person, including breakfast. Rainy days can be passed at the **Deakin Cinema Complex** at 93 Deakin Ave ($10), while a back-to-nature alternative to the swimming pool on Deakin Avenue is available at the sandy **swimming beach** at Chaffey Bend. There are lifeguards in summer, but take local advice and beware of dangerous currents.

and travellers passing through. The couches on the patio are a nightly event. Dorms $22, rooms ❷

Mildura Grand Hotel 7th St, opposite the train station ⓣ03/5023 0511, ⓦwww.milduragrandhotel.com. Restored hotel, complete with ballroom, renowned gourmet restaurant, games room, spa, sauna and outdoor swimming pool. The sparsely decorated rooms range from basic to luxurious, with breakfast included. ❺

Mildura International Backpackers 5 Cedar Ave ⓣ0408 210 132, ⓦwww.mildurabackpackers.com.au. Work-oriented hostel with recreation area, cable TV and laundry. The operators have work contacts, do all the paperwork required and organize transport too. Rooms are twin-, three- and four-bedded. Dorms $25, or $135 per person per week.

Mildura Stopover 29 Lemon Ave ⓣ03/5021 1980, ⓦwww.stopover.com.au. Despite the name, this place mostly houses long-term workers who want a clean place to stay with good facilities, including a sunny courtyard with BBQ. Doesn't have the party atmosphere of the other hostels. Dorms $25, rooms ❷

Riverboat Bungalow 27 Chaffey Ave ⓣ0418 147 363, ⓦwww.workinghostels.com. The 1891 house is a work-and-play-oriented place with work registry, free internet access and cable TV. Dorms $25, rooms ❶–❷

Houseboats

Adventure Houseboats Buronga ⓣ03/5023 4787, ⓦwww.adventurehouseboats.com.au. Large 12-berth self-contained houseboats with all the mod cons; expect to pay from $2500 off-peak for 3 nights.

B&B on a boat ⓣ1800 085 500, ⓦwww.acaciaboats.com.au. Probably no better way to experience the Murray River than to live on it for a few days. Houseboats are air-conditioned, fully equipped and can accommodate up to 6 people. Full breakfast is included (but you have to cook it). ❺–❼ plus $35 per extra adult.

The Town

Deakin Avenue runs northwest through town to the river, with 7th Street and the train station facing the parklands that run along the river. Here, the seventy-year-old **Mildura Weir** system, designed to provide stable pools for irrigation and to enable navigation throughout the year, makes a pleasant place to while away an hour or so. Alternatively, wander down to the **Mildura Arts Centre**, 199 Cureton Ave (daily 10am–5pm; gallery $3.50;

@ www.miduraarts.net.au), which consists of the historic home **Rio Vista**, the Mildura Regional Art Gallery, a theatre and a sculpture park. Rio Vista was built in 1891 for William Chaffey, who lived here with his first and second wives (both called Hattie Schell, the second the niece of the first) until he died in 1926. It's a lovely house, though rather ill-suited to the climate, and inside are various displays about the Chaffeys and the development of Mildura. The art gallery's most important piece is *Woman Combing Her Hair at the Bath*, a pastel by Edgar Degas; it also has some excellent sculpture by Australian artists.

Eating and drinking

Healthy food abounds in Mildura's **cafés** and **restaurants**, most of which are clustered on Langtree Avenue, just south of the mall. If you have your own transport, you can make an enjoyable outing to buy fruit and vegetables from surrounding farms. There are three supermarkets surrounding Langtree Mall.

Mildura's **nightlife** may not be the world's greatest, but there's enough to keep you occupied. The *Mildura Brewery* at 20 Langtree Ave offers incredibly good beer straight from the giant vats visible from the tables, along with well-priced pub grub. *O'Malley's Irish Tavern* at 46 Deakin Ave is a barn-like venue that fills up on weekends and has regular live music. Another good place for a drink and where the locals like to go is the *Sandbar* (nightly till 1am) at 45 Langtree Ave, with an excellent courtyard and live music on weekends.

Restaurants and cafés

Hudak's Bakery Café Corner of 8th St & Langtree Mall, 15th St. Good continental breads, pies, focaccias and cakes, with great seating on the outdoor balcony. Branches also at 15th St & Centro Mildura. Mon–Fri 7am–5.30pm, Sat 7am–4pm, Sun 7am–3pm.

Mildura RSL Corner of Madden Ave & 10th St. Has good-portioned $6.90 lunch specials every day, but the dinner menu is much more expensive.

Quality Hotel Mildura Grand *The Grand*, as it's known, incorporates four eateries. Tucked away in the cellar is its crowning glory, *Stefano's* (dinner Tues–Sat; bookings essential; ☎ 03/5023 0511). There's no menu but the Northern Italian banquets (about $95 for 5 or 6

courses) are excellent. The other options include: *Seasons* (closed Sun), a bistro featuring Australian cuisine sourced locally; the *Spanish Bar & Grill* (closed Mon); and the *Pizza Café* for pasta and wood-fired pizzas.

Restaurant Rendezvous 34 Langtree Ave ☎ 03/5023 1571. Cheap lunches and other meals served in the bistro. There's also an upmarket restaurant, as well as a bar and courtyard seating. Mon–Sat lunch & dinner.

Stefano's Café Bakery 27 Deakin Ave. Owned by celebrity chef Stefano de Pieri, this is just one of his shrines to food that serves delicious breakfasts, lunches, coffee, cakes and bread as well as gourmet grocery items. Mon–Sat 7.30am–3pm, Sun 8am–2pm.

Fruit-picking in Mildura

Mildura has a good reputation as a place to find **fruit-picking work**, though the only guaranteed time is in February, when the grape harvest takes place. Unfortunately, this is also the time when the heat is most intense. If you think you can handle it, come around the end of January, the beginning of the eight-week season. Otherwise, there's a chance of picking up work during the citrus harvest in June and August, and possibly vine pruning. For details, contact MADEC Mildura on ☎ 03/5021 3472, located at 126 Deakin Ave, or call the National Harvest Labour Hotline (☎ 1800 062 332, @ www.jobsearch.gov.au/harvesttrail). Most of the town's backpacker hostels have contacts with a wide range of employers, will find a job for you, assist with the paperwork and provide transport to and from work.

Around Mildura

The easiest excursion from Mildura is to **RED CLIFFS**, some 15km south, with its vineyards and tree-lined streets. The huge **Lindemans Karadoc Winery** (daily 10am–4.30pm; Ⓦ www.lindemans.com.au) is one of the largest **wineries** in Australia, where fifty thousand tonnes of grapes are crushed every year. The range of wines for tasting is extensive, prices are very reasonable and there's a café serving light lunches, coffee and cake (Mon–Fri 10am–3pm).

Across the Murray from Mildura, 15km or so down the Sturt Highway in an idyllic setting overlooking the river, **Trentham Estate Winery** has cellar-door sales (daily 9.30am–5pm); and an upmarket restaurant (lunch Tues–Sun; ☎03/5024 8888, Ⓦ www.trenthamestate.com.au).

Swan Hill and around

As you approach **SWAN HILL**, the landscape changes – this is cattle and sheep country, with wheatfields further north. The Murray here is shallow and tricky to navigate, so there's not much river traffic. Swan Hill is a service centre for the pastoral industry and has a typically solid, conservative atmosphere. Surprisingly, it's quite a multicultural place, having ten percent of Victoria's Aboriginal population, and a large Italian community. The Pioneer Settlement is undoubtedly Swan Hill's main attraction, but while you're here, you could also visit the **Swan Hill Regional Art Gallery** (Tues–Fri 10am–5pm, Sat & Sun 11am–5pm; entry by donation; Ⓦ www.swanhill.vic .gov.au/gallery), which specializes in folk and Aboriginal art and has good touring exhibitions. The town's swimming pool on Monash Drive has several pools and a waterslide (Nov–March daily 11am–7pm; open for morning laps Mon, Wed & Fri 6–8am; $2.80). Next to the train station you can't miss the fake thirteen-metre Murray Cod (built for a film), which doesn't really serve a purpose, but amuses tourists.

Pioneer Settlement

Swan Hill's **Pioneer Settlement**, a reconstruction of a pioneering community at Horseshoe Bend about 1km south of the train station, was the first of its kind in Australia and is still one of the best (daily 9.30am–4pm; $22.60; combination ticket for settlement, sound-and-light show and PS *Pyap* Cruise $45.20; Ⓦ www.pioneersettlement.com.au).

In the settlement's streets many of the **shops** are functional – the baker, the printer, the haberdashery and the porcelain-doll shop – with assistants dressed in vaguely period costume. Generally, though, it's low-key and peaceful: buildings such as the barber's shop and the stock and station agents are open for you to wander around undisturbed, or you can pose for your own "wanted" poster at the print shop. You can go on rides around the settlement in a 1924 Dodge or for free on a horse-drawn carriage. In the evening, the **sound-and-light show** (nightly from dusk; $16.80) is strikingly effective.

The settlement is situated on the banks of the Marraboor River, a branch of the Murray, and a wooden bridge spans the river to Pental Island, which has an assortment of native flora and fauna. Otherwise, an old **paddle steamer**, the *Pyap*, cruises from the settlement upriver past Murray Downs every day at 2.30pm (1hr; $16.80), also 10.30am at weekends and public holidays.

Practicalities

The **Swan Hill Visitor Information Centre**, across the road from the train station, on the corner of McCrae and Curlewis streets (daily 9am–5pm; ℡03/5032 3033 or 1800 625 373, ⓦwww.swanhillonline.com), has a free map of the town giving detailed information on local attractions; it also sells tickets for the Pioneer Settlement, its sound-and-light show and the PS *Pyap* cruises. **Parks Victoria** at 324 Campbell St (Mon–Fri 8.30am–5pm; ℡03/5036 4829) can provide you with information on camping in the nearby Nyah and Vinefera state forests.

There's a strip of **motels**, all with swimming pools, along Campbell Street, where almost all the town's facilities are located. The most luxurious of the lot is the *Sundowner Swan Hill Resort* at no. 405 (℡03/5032 2726, ⓦwww .swanhillresort.bestwestern.com.au; ❻), which has an indoor and outdoor pool and spa, gym and other sports facilities. The *Paddle Steamer Motel* on the Murray Valley Highway, 3km south of the centre, has very good facilities and is much cheaper (℡03/5032 2151, ⓦwww.paddlesteamermotel.com.au; ❹). Also good value and much closer to the centre is *Jacaranda Holiday Units* at 179 Curlewis St (℡03/5032 9077, ⓦwww.jacarandaholidayunits.com.au; ❹). The *Riverside* at 1 Monash Drive (℡03/5032 1494, ⓦwww.swanhillriverside.com.au; cabins ❹) is a good, centrally located **caravan park** right on the riverfront.

Swan Hill **restaurants** still demonstrate an Italian culinary influence. The best restaurant is *Quo Vadis* (open from 5pm daily), an authentic pizzeria at 255 Campbell St that serves mammoth portions of pasta (around $14), yet *Java Spice* at 17 Beveridge St (lunch Thurs–Sun, dinner daily except Mon) is also very good, serving spicy Thai cuisine in a great outdoor setting. A nice place for a cheap meal and a beer with the locals is the *R.S.L. Club* at 138 Curlewis St (daily lunch and dinner).

Echuca and around

ECHUCA, a lively and progressive place, is the most easily accessible river town from Melbourne – it's only three hours or so by bus or car, making it a popular weekend getaway. Echuca became the largest inland port in Australia after the railway line connected it with Melbourne in 1864. The **Port of Echuca**, a

---

River cruises

A wide choice of **cruises with paddle steamers** is on offer, departing from berths just beyond the old wharf, best approached from High Street. One-hour port cruises are available on the PS *Alexander Arbuthnot*, PS *Pevensey* and the PS *Adelaide*; the latter, built in 1866, is the oldest wooden-hulled paddle steamer still operating in the world (about $20 per hr; for all of them call ℡03/5482 4248, ⓦwww.portofechuca.org .au). Other boats offering one-hour cruises are PS *Pride of the Murray*, PS *Canberra* and the PS *Emmylou*, the latter a wood-fired paddle steamer that has a variety of cruises including overnight trips (℡03/5482 5244, ⓦwww.emmylou.com.au), while the MV *Mary Ann* (℡03/5480 2200, ⓦwww.maryann.com.au) does lunch cruises (12.30pm; 1hr 30min; $45) and dinner cruises (7pm; from $75 for two courses). Kingfisher Cruises (℡03/5480 1839, ⓦwww.kingfishercruises.com.au) offers a two-hour eco-cruise (Mon, Wed, Thurs, Sat & Sun, plus other days during busy times; $26.50) through the Barmah wetlands some 30km upstream of the Murray, which contain the world's largest single stand of river red gums.

popular tourist attraction where stores, pubs and businesses have been preserved, gives a good insight into the period. When the **missions** began to close in the 1930s, many Aboriginal families migrated to the Echuca area. Since they weren't made welcome in the towns, the migrants were forced to live on the fringes in badly constructed, flood-prone housing, just close enough to be able to get to work and school. Women commonly worked in the canneries and hospitals, and the men packed fruit, sheared sheep and did other labouring jobs.

Arrival, information and accommodation

The **visitor centre**, 2 Heygarth St (daily 8am–5pm; ☎03/5480 7555 or 1800 804 446, ⓦwww.echucamoama.com), sells tickets to the port complex and for cruises, books accommodation and is an agent for V/Line and Countrylink **bus** tickets. V/Line runs up to six services between Melbourne and Echuca (train–bus); there is also one daily connection with Sydney via Albury, and two to Adelaide (one direct, one via Bendigo). **Internet** access is available at the Tangled Garden Bookshop at 495 High St (Mon–Sat 9am–5pm, Sun 11am–4pm; $2 per 15min).

As well as the **accommodation** options listed below, ask at the visitor centre about the many houseboats available to rent in the area.

The Clocktower 234 Anstruther St ☎03/5482 1932, ⓦwww.clocktowerapartments.com. Luxurious apartments and suites set in a fully renovated post office built in 1879, in the centre of town. Suites ❼, apartments ❾

Echuca Caravan Park Crofton St, Victoria Park ☎03/5482 2157, ⓦwww.echucacaravanpark.com .au. A well-equipped caravan park right on the riverfront. Swimming pool, tennis courts and two kitchens. Cabins ❸–❹

Echuca Gardens YHA 103 Mitchell St ☎03/5480 6522 (8–10am & 5–10pm), ⓔechuca@yhavic.org.au. Budget accommoda- tion in a restored Victorian worker's cottage – cozy atmosphere, but the dorms are cramped and tiny. The location on the edge of the Banyule Forest is very scenic though, and it's a 10min walk through red gums to sandy river beaches where it's safe to swim on the inner bends. Dorms $30, rooms ❷

Nomads Oasis Backpackers 410–424 High St ☎03/5480 7866, ⓔnomads@river.net.au. Centrally located, a/c dorms as well as twins/ doubles at an affordable price. There's a small kitchen and courtyard, and the owner has employ- ment contacts and can provide transport to places of work. Dorms $25, rooms ❷–❸

Shamrock Hotel 579 High St ☎03/5482 1036, ⓦwww.shamrockhotel.com.au. Grand old pub in the old port district offering basic but cheap dorm- style rooms with shared facilities. There's also one double and a triple available. It can get loud on weekends when it turns into a drinking hole. Singles $40 per person, double ❸

🏃 **Steam Packet Inn** Corner of of Leslie St and Murray Esplanade ☎03/5482 3411, ⓦwww .steampacketinn.com.au. A National Trust-listed B&B with super-friendly service, offering traditionally decorated rooms in the heart of the old port area. A good breakfast is included in the price. ❻

The Town

The **Port of Echuca** is where most people head to, with its massive wharves and collection of old buildings. Several cruises ply along the river from here. The town itself, however, is not too touristy, and has retained much of its charm. There are two principal streets: High Street, the former main street, leads to Murray Esplanade and the wharf, and is the centre of tourist activity, with lots of cafés and boutiquey shops, while Hare Street, the present-day main street, is lined with more commercial buildings.

To enter the old wharf area, dubbed the **Historic Wharf** (daily 9am–5pm; ⓦwww.portofechuca.org.au), you'll need to pay a $12 entrance fee. Alternatively, you can combine a tour with a cruise on the *Pevensey* or the *Alexander Arbuthnot* (see box, p.981) for $27.20; boats depart daily at 10.15am, 11.30am, 1.15pm and 2.30pm. The **Star Hotel** was first licensed in 1867 and is a typical pioneer pub, a tiny one-storey building with a tin roof and veranda. As the river trade declined, the *Star* was delicensed (in 1897), along with many of the other 79 hotels in town. Drinking on the premises became illegal, so the loyal clientele dug a tunnel to the street through which they could escape at the first hint of a police raid – you can examine this, along with the cellar and a small museum.

The magnificent red-gum **wharf** was nearly half a kilometre long in its prime and is still fairly extensive. Three landing platforms at different levels allowed unloading, even during times of flooding, and there are wonderful views from the top, high over a bend in the river. At the lowest level, several **old paddle steamers** are moored, including the *Pevensey*, a 1911 cargo boat which you can wander aboard. In the wharf cargo-shed there's a scale model of the working port and a ten-minute audiovisual presentation.

Back outside the wharf complex, along Murray Esplanade opposite Hopwood Gardens, is the **Bridge Hotel**, opened in 1858 but de-licensed in 1916. It was built by the founder of Echuca, Henry Hopwood, an ex-convict who also started a punt service across the Murray. The story goes that if the pub wasn't doing well he'd close the ferry down for a few hours, leaving prospective passengers with little else to do but drink.

Another unique attraction is the **Great Aussie Beer Shed** (9.30am–5pm weekends; ℡03/5480 6904, Ⓦwww.greataussiebeershed.com.au; $9.50) at 377 Mary Ann Rd, which features over 16,000 types of beer can.

Eating, drinking and nightlife

With hungry Melburnians to feed, there's no shortage of decent **restaurants**. The *Star Hotel* is a good place to head for a **drink**, while the *Shamrock Hotel* at 579 High St has the best beer garden in town and plays host to live bands at weekends. If you're looking for somewhere a bit quieter, try the *Harvest Hotel* at 183 Hare St. The OPT Entertainment Complex at 273 Hare St has a restaurant, bar and pool tables (Wed–Sat 5pm–2am, also Sun in summer); the nightclub is open Friday and Saturday nights till 4am. The Paramount Cinemas & Performing Arts Centre at 392 High St has an auditorium and four cinemas with state-of-the-art facilities (℡03/5482 3399, Ⓦwww.echucaparamount .com). If you happen to be around in mid-February, look out for the **Jazz, Food and Wine Weekend**.

Echuca's workers' **clubs** serve very cheap meals and drinks, presumably as an incentive to get you to their gambling machines – non-members can sign in as visitors. There are more clubs across the river in Moama.

Beechworth Bakery 513 High St. A branch of the original, very successful bakery from Beechworth; they sell a variety of breads baked in a wood-fired oven, sandwiches, pastries and other snacks, and there's a sun deck which is a good spot for breakfast or lunch. Daily 6am–6pm.

Bridge Hotel Hopwood Place. Coffee shop, bar and restaurant in the historic port area; good coffee, cakes and desserts, light lunches and mainly traditional Aussie dishes in the restaurant. Open daily for breakfast, lunch and dinner Wed–Sun; the bar is open daily Mon–Fri 9am–late, Sat & Sun 8am–midnight.

Fish in a flash 602 High St. Excellent array of fresh seafood including some of the best battered tiger prawns this side of Melbourne. Open daily.

Leftbank Winebar & Restaurant 551 High St. Housed in an old bank built in 1862, this bar-restaurant offers modern Australian cuisine in a refined setting. Tues–Sat 6pm–late.

Oscar W's Wharfside Murray Esplanade ℡03/5482 5133. This restaurant serves excellent, superbly presented food to match the scenic setting next to the old Echuca Wharf, overlooking the Murray River. The moderately expensive cuisine is Mod Oz with a twist of Asia and the Mediterranean. Service can be poor when the place is full, though. Licensed. Bookings essential. Open daily 11am–late.

Wistaria Tearooms High St, opposite the *Shamrock Hotel*, or enter from the port. Lovely Victorian house where you can get breakfast and light meals, coffee and cakes. Licensed. Daily 8am–4pm.

Around Echuca

Thirty kilometres southeast of Echuca, Kyabram's main attraction is **Kyabram Fauna Park** (daily 9.30am–5.30pm; $14; Ⓦwww.kyabramfaunaparkcom.au.au), a community-owned wildlife park divided into grassland for free-ranging kangaroos, wallabies, emus and other animals, and a huge wetland area. You can wander around the grassland area and through several aviaries; a two-storey observation tower affords views of the more than eighty species of native birdlife. Diamond pythons, tiger snakes, crocodiles and other not-so-pleasant creatures can be viewed from a safe distance at the Reptile House.

BARMAH, some 30km upstream on the Murray, is most easily reached by crossing into New South Wales at Echuca and heading north on the Cobb Highway, then turning east. This small river town is associated with red-gum milling, and with sleeper-cutting in the early railway days. The *Barmah Caravan Park* (Ⓣ03/5869 3225, Ⓦwww.barmahcaravanpark.com.au; ❷–❸) has a great site on the banks of the river among red gums, with a small, sandy beach for swimming, and a few cabins. **Barmah State Park**, 10km out of town, has Australia's largest stands of **river red gum**, some of them 40m tall and five hundred years old. The forest runs along the Murray for over 100km and stands in an extensive flood plain – **canoeing** among the trees at flood time (July–Nov) is a magical experience; you can arrange transport and rent canoes from Echuca Boat and Canoe Hire (canoes from $20 per hr; Ⓣ03/5480 6208, Ⓦwww.echucaboatcanoehire.com). During the wet season more than two hundred species of waterbird come here, and there's plenty of other wildlife; you might even see brumbies (wild horses). When it's dry you can use several well-established walking tracks: the place was of special significance to the local Yorta Yorta Aborigines and you can still see fish traps, middens and scars on trees where the bark was used for canoes.

Yorta Yorta culture and lore are explained in the park's **Dharnya Centre** (daily 10.30am–4pm; Ⓣ03/5869 3302), which also has archeological information and artefacts. A **cruise** in the MV *Kingfisher* – a flat-bottomed boat that glides over Barmah Lake and through stands of red gum – leaves from the bridge near the centre (see box, p.976). Bushcamping is permitted in the park; contact Parks Victoria (Ⓣ13 19 63) for details.

Gippsland

GIPPSLAND stretches southeast of Melbourne from Western Port Bay to the New South Wales border, between the Great Dividing Range and Bass Strait. Green and well watered, it's been the centre of Victoria's dairy industry since the 1880s. South Gippsland has Victoria's most popular national park, **Wilsons Promontory**, or "The Prom", a hook-shaped landmass jutting out into the strait, with some superb scenery and fascinating bushwalks. In the east, around the **Gippsland Lakes** and **Ninety Mile Beach**, the region is beautifully untouched, and just beyond Orbost–Marlo the unspoilt coastline of the **Croajingolong National Park** – with its rocky capes, high sand dunes and endless sandy beaches – stretches to the New South Wales border.

Black Saturday bushfires

February 7, 2009 will be forever etched on most Victorians' minds as the start of Australia's worst bushfires in history. "Black Saturday", as it is known, killed over 170 people and thousands of animals, destroyed over a million acres of bushland, wiped out townships and left 7500 homeless. The state's worst affected areas were northeast of Melbourne in the Kinglake and Yea–Murrindindi regions, encompassing Marysville, Toolangi, Kinglake, Kinglake West, Strathewen, Steels Creek, Narbethong and Flowerdale. In the Gippsland region, southeast of Melbourne, a fire was started deliberately in Churchill and quickly spread to Callignee, Traralgon South, the Otways, Horsham, Coleraine, Dargo, Bendigo and Beechworth. Fires also destroyed thousands of acres of bushland in Wilsons Promontory.

Residents in Victoria's southeast were told to prepare for extreme conditions the day before; temperatures exceeding 47°C and winds of up to 120km/h were predicted, combined with tinder-dry land due to the previous week's heatwave and long-term drought. Many of the places devastated were set in hilly, forested country, including the picturesque village of Marysville. Established in 1863, with a population of just over 500, Marysville had experienced many bushfires during its 146-year history, but none like that in February which killed one in five residents and reduced the town to ashes. To the west, that flames moving at over 100km/h swept through the small hamlet of Kinglake so quickly that people didn't even know they were in danger.

Survivors described how birds began falling from the sky seconds before fireballs sounding like jet engines ripped through their homes. Temperatures within the firestorms were so hot the energy released would have supplied Victoria with electricity for two years. The CFA (Country Fire Association) battled to contain spot fires up to 15km away from the main fire front which were created by embers whipped up by winds. Many fires continued to blaze out of control for over a month afterwards, and National Parks in the area, including Kinglake and Yarra Ranges, were closed to visitors. Sections of the worst affected parks are slowly being opened, but check with Parks Victoria (☎13 19 63, ⊛www.parkweb.vic.gov.au) before setting out. For bushfire safety tips see p.63.

Transport

Having your own **car** is essential for getting off the highway to really experience the region's diverse highlights and to get to the unspoilt bush campsites on the coast. The Princes Highway itself is a very boring drive, particularly the stretch from the Latrobe Valley to Bairnsdale, but after Orbost the highway becomes more scenic as it goes through the tall, dense eucalypt forests of Far East Gippsland. If you don't have a car, you might want to consider travelling with Oz Experience, the **backpacker bus company** that covers the Sydney–Melbourne route in three days, via Wilsons Prom, the Snowy Mountains and Canberra.

V/Line **trains** run from Melbourne to Bairnsdale, basically following the Princes Highway through South Gippsland. From Bairnsdale, **buses** leave for Orbost, stopping at Lakes Entrance. The Sapphire Coast Link is a daily train–bus connection between Melbourne and Narooma on the south coast of New South Wales: take the train to Bairnsdale, then a connecting bus along the Princes Highway via Lakes Entrance, Orbost, Cann River and Genoa. Similarly, the Capital Link train–bus service heads to Canberra via Bairnsdale on Monday, Thursday and Saturday around midday, returning from Canberra Tuesday, Friday and Sunday mornings. Bookings for all the above should be made through V/Line (☎13 61 96, ⊛www.vline.com.au). Premier Motor Service (☎13 34 10, ⊛www.premierms.com.au), an NSW-based coach company, runs a daily service from Melbourne to Sydney along the coast, but it's not very convenient

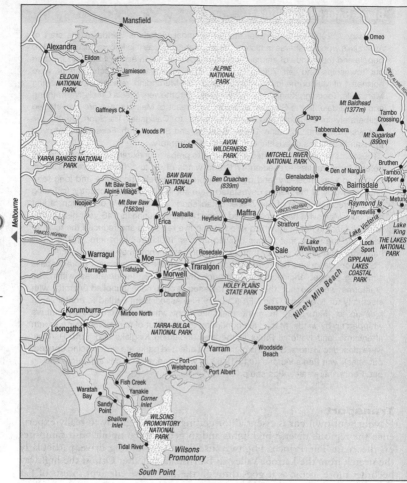

if you want to get off at stops in East Gippsland: the bus leaves Melbourne at 5.45pm Sunday to Friday, and gets to Lakes Entrance and Cann River in the early hours of the morning.

Wilsons Promontory

WILSONS PROMONTORY, or "the Prom", the most southerly part of the Australian mainland, was once joined by a land bridge to Tasmania. Its barbed hook juts out into Bass Strait, with a rocky coastline interspersed with sheltered sandy bays and coves; the coastal scenery is made even more stunning by the backdrop of granite ranges. It's understandably Victoria's most popular **national park**, and though the main campsite gets totally packed in summer, there are

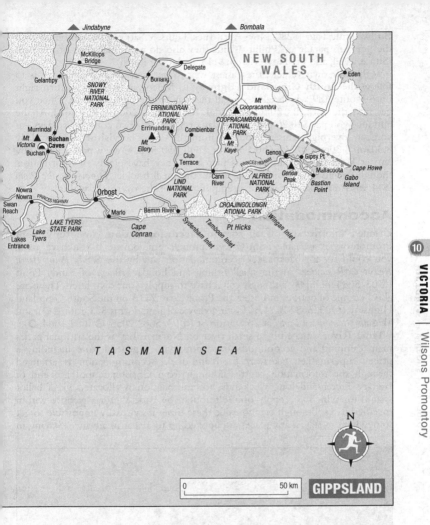

plenty of walking tracks and opportunities for bushcamping, and the park's big enough to allow you to escape the crowds. You can swim at several of the beaches and even **surf**: The Prom Surf School, based at Tidal River, operates courses in summer, for all ages and abilities, with all equipment provided (℡03/5680 8512, ℮peck@pocketmail.com.au).

Arrival and information

There's no public transport to Wilsons Promontory, so if you don't want to hire a car, you can take the evening V/Line bus from Dandenong to Yarram and get off at **FOSTER** on the South Gippsland Highway, from where the Prom Coast YHA (see p.988) can arrange transport to the national park for $15–20 per person.

Melbourne-based ecotour operator Bunyip Tours (℡03/9650 9680, ⓦwww .bunyiptours.com) is a long-established Prom specialist. Their two-day

Bushwalking Tour ($280; Nov–April Tues, Thurs & Sat) can be combined with the penguin parade on Phillip Island; they also do a one-day tour of the park (Sun & Wed, also Fri Nov–March; $115, including lunch).

With your own vehicle, the easiest way to get here from Melbourne is to follow the **South Gippsland Highway** to Meeniyan, where you turn right onto Route 189 which takes you all the way to the park entrance. Once you get into the park, it's 30km to **Tidal River** on a good sealed road. At the entrance you pay $10.20 per car per day, or $16.20 for two consecutive days – if you stay overnight, this is deducted from the cost. The **visitor centre** (daily 8.30am–4.30pm; ☎03/5680 9555 or 1800 350 552, ⓦwww.parkweb.vic.gov.au) at Tidal River is an obvious first stop. They have plenty of information, though not all of it is on display, so ask: the small booklet *Discovering the Prom* ($14.95) is invaluable if you're attempting any of the overnight **walks**.

Accommodation

Detailed information on all sorts of **accommodation** close to Wilsons Promontory is available from ⓦwww.promaccom.com.au. If you have a car, you could try for backpacker accommodation run by the *Sandy Point Beach Resort & Restaurant* in the small fishing and holiday village of Sandy Point (☎03/5684 1448; ❷), although you'd have to supply your own linen. There are also a couple of options in Foster: the Prom Coast YHA on the South Gippsland Highway (☎03/5682 2171, ⓔfoster@yhavic.org.au; dorms $25, rooms ❷), and *Wilsons Promontory Motel* at 26 Station St (☎03/5682 2055, ⓕ5682 1064; ❹).

Tidal River, situated by a small river on Norman Bay, is the national park's main camping and accommodation centre, with a general store including a pricey supermarket, takeaway food and fuel. Accommodation is arranged through the information centre, although from Christmas until the end of January, Easter and long weekends, accommodation is allocated via a ballot system for which you apply online through the Parks Victoria website within specified dates, although even outside these times it's virtually impossible to get somewhere to stay; many places are booked up to a year in advance. Staying in

▲ Wilsons Promontory National Park

the very basic motor huts (use of the campsite's facilities; linen not supplied) works out at around $15 per person if you're in a group of four to six people. The camping area has about 484 non-powered pitches ($22.50 per night for 3 adults and 1 car; additional cars and people extra; max 8 people per site). Facilities include hot showers, a laundry and a summer outdoor cinema. There are also some very comfortable self-contained holiday cabins sleeping up to six people ($150 off peak for two adults, plus $22 each extra adult).

Walks

Many short walks begin from Tidal River, including a track accessible to wheel-chairs. One of the best is the **Squeaky Beach Track** (1hr 30min return), which crosses Tidal River, heads uphill and through a tea-tree canopy, finally ending on a beach of pure quartz sand that is indeed squeaky underfoot. **The Lilly Pilly Gully Nature Walk** (2hr return) is very rewarding, as it affords an excellent overview of the diverse vegetation of "the Prom", from low-growing shrubs to heathland to open eucalypt forest, as well as scenic views. The walk starts at the Lilly Pilly Gully car park near Tidal River, follows a small valley and returns to the car park along the slopes of Mount Bishop. For **overnight camping** ($7.30 per person per night), you need to obtain a **permit** from the information centre at Tidal River (see opposite), as there is a restriction on the number of people allowed on the campsites.

The tracks in the southern section of the park are well defined and not too difficult; the campsites here have pit toilets and fresh water. The most popular walk is the one- to two-day (35.5km) **Sealers Cove–Refuge Cove–Waterloo Bay** route, beginning and ending at the Telegraph Saddle car park. During summer holidays and at long weekends between November and the end of April, the tracks become extremely busy, so book well in advance or show up early. The remote north of the park is only suitable for experienced, properly equipped bushwalkers; there are no facilities (except for pit toilets at Tin Mine Cove) and limited fresh water.

The Gippsland Lakes region

The **Gippsland Lakes**, Australia's largest system of inland waterways, are fed by the waters of the Mitchell, Nicholson and Tambo rivers, and are separated from the sea by Ninety Mile Beach. East of Yarram, the beach stretches long and straight towards **Lakes Entrance**, the tacky focal point of the area and one of Victoria's most popular holiday spots, with the foothills of the high country within easy reach to the north.

Sale

SALE, at the junction of the South Gippsland Highway and the Princes Highway, is a good point from which to head off to explore the coastal park and Ninety Mile Beach. From Seaspray, 35km south, a coastal road hugs the shore for 20km to Golden Beach, from where a scenic drive heads through the Gippsland Lakes Coastal Park to Loch Sport; here you're faced with the enviable dilemma of lakes on one side and ocean beaches with good surfing on the other. An unsealed road then continues on to Sperm Whale Head in the Lakes National Park. Sale's **visitor centre** (daily 9am–5pm; ☎1800 677 520, ⓦwww.tourismwellington.com.au), as you come into town from the west on the Princes Highway, can provide you with all the details. They have internet access ($3 per 15min) and can also give information about the **Bataluk Cultural Trail**, which starts in Sale and links sites of cultural and spiritual significance to the Gunai people, the original inhabitants of the Gippsland coast.

If you'd like to get friendly with the locals, opt for a stay off the beaten track at the small *Cambrai Backpackers* at 117 Johnston St in **Maffra**, a small dairy-farming town, 20km off the Princes Highway in the foothills of the Great Dividing Range. Located in a lovely, refurbished building right in the town centre, the hostel has dorms (6–8 beds) and doubles, a communal kitchen, comfy lounge and licensed bar. The owners pick up from the bus stop (pre-book), arrange walks in the high country and have work contacts (℡1800 101 113, Ⓦwww.maffra.net.au/hostel; dorms $30, rooms ❸).

Bairnsdale and around

BAIRNSDALE is the next major town on the highway east of Sale and serves as another departure point for the lakes to the south. The efficient staff at the **visitor centre** at 240 Main St (daily 9am–5pm; ℡03/5152 3444, Ⓦwww.discovereastgippsland.com.au) will provide all the local information you'll need. A small exhibition at the **Krowathunkooloong Keeping Place**, parallel to the Princes Highway at 37–53 Dalmahoy St, explains the history of the Gunai people (Mon–Fri 9am–noon & 1–5pm; ℡03/5152 1891; $3.50).

For budget **accommodation** in Bairnsdale itself, try the *Grand Terminus Hotel* at 98 McLeod St (℡03/5152 4040, Ⓦwww.grandterminus.com.au; ❷) or the *Bairnsdale Holiday Park* (℡1800 062 885, Ⓦwww.bairnsdaleholidaypark.com; cabins ❸, units ❺) just west of the town at 139 Princes Highway. A gorgeous – if pricey – alternative is the luxurious *Lake Gallery B&B* (℡03/5156 0448, Ⓦwww.lakegallerybedandbreakfast.com; ❼) in **Paynesville**, 16km south of Bairnsdale, which has two designer-decorated guest suites at the water's edge and its own jetty.

A short ferry-ride away across the McMillan Straits from Paynesville is **Raymond Island** which, with its prolific birdlife, kangaroos and koalas, is an idyllic place to stay. The Raymond Island Ferry runs roughly every half-hour throughout the day (Mon–Thurs 7am–11pm, Fri & Sat 7am–midnight, Sun 8am–11pm; cars $8 return, foot passengers free). Accommodation options on the island are *Currawong Cottage* (℡03/5156 7226; ❺), 27 Currawong Close, which sleeps up to four people, or a couple of two-bedroom flats at *Swan Cove Holiday Flats*, 390 Centre Rd (℡03/5156 6716; ❸).

Forty-five kilometres northwest of Bairnsdale is another site on the Bataluk Cultural Trail, the **Den of Nargun** in the **Mitchell River National Park**. According to a Gunai legend, the small cave here was inhabited by a large female creature, a nargun, who would abduct people who wandered off on their own. As the Den of Nargun was a special place for Gunai women and may have been used for initiation ceremonies, the story served the purpose of keeping unauthorized people away. The cave is located in a small, beautiful valley; follow the loop track from the park picnic area via a lookout to the Mitchell River (30min), then take the track along Woolshed Creek to the cave and climb up the steep path back to the starting point (40min).

Lakes Entrance

LAKES ENTRANCE is named after the entrance to the Gippsland Lakes. A sandy barrier between the Gippsland Lakes and the sea formed about six thousand years ago, when first seen by white men in the 1840s; the outlet was a seasonal, intermittent gap, unsuitable for reliable trade. In 1889 the present stable entrance was opened 6km east of the old one: the artificial entrance effectively cuts off the town's access to the length of **Ninety Mile Beach**.

Information and accommodation

Lakes Entrance Visitor Centre (daily 9am–5pm; ☎03/5155 1966), on the Esplanade, provides local advice and tickets for cruises on the lakes. There's **internet** access at 10 Myer St (Mon–Fri 9am–5.30pm, Sat 10am–3pm, Sun 10am–2pm; $7 per hr). The visitor centre can book **accommodation**, a useful service in summer when the place gets very crowded.

Deja Vu Out of town at 17 Clara St ☎03/5155 4330, ⓦwww.dejavu.com.au. A rather special B&B in a pleasant location, with spacious en-suite rooms as well as separate 1- and 2-bedroom cottages overlooking the waterway of North Arm. Minimum 2-night stay at weekends. ❼–❽

Goat and Goose B&B 16 Gay St ☎03/5155 3079, ⓦwww.thegoatandgoose.com. Recommended B&B in a timber house on a hill at the western end of town. There are great ocean views from the balconies, and three of the four suites come with a spa. Breakfast is huge and scrumptious, and, to top it all off, guests get a tour of Lakes Entrance in the owner's Rolls-Royce. ❻–❽

Kalimna Woods Kalimna Jetty Rd ☎03/5155 1957, ⓦwww.kilimnawoods.com.au. Fully self-contained timber cottages in a nice bush setting, some with spas and log fires. ❺

Lakes Waterfront Motel & Cottages 10 Princes Highway ☎03/5155 2841, ⓦwww.lakeswaterfrontmotel.com. The motel rooms are just average, but the self-contained cottages (for 3 people) on the water's edge offer excellent value. Also has pool and cable TV. Rooms ❹, cottages ❻

Riviera Backpackers YHA 669–771 Esplanade ☎03/5155 2444, ⓔlakesentranoo@yhavic.org.au. In the east end of town, this is a friendly place situated close to a beautiful stretch of lake. It has dorms and good en-suite rooms, a large kitchen/common room, internet access, a laundry and a small pool with spa. Dorms $19, rooms ❶

Waters Edge Holiday Park 623 Esplanade ☎03/5155 1914, ⓦwww.watersedgeholidaypark.com.au. Popular option with great amenities such as two pools, games room, playground and modern holiday units. ❸–❹

The Town

As you might expect from the area's popularity, Lakes Entrance is a big, rather tawdry, tourist town, with loads of motels at either end as you enter from the highway. There are all sorts of attractions aimed at keeping holidaying children happy – from Fun Park to minigolf – on the Esplanade, which fronts onto an arm of Lake King. The **Griffiths Sea Shell Museum** at 125 Esplanade (daily 9am–4pm; $6; ☎03/5155 1538), with its rather off-putting 1950s-style facade, has a huge collection of shells and marine life, as well as an aquarium containing an intriguing assortment of fish from the Gippsland Lakes. Lakes Entrance is also a big **fishing port**: the Fishermans Cooperative Wharf has a viewing platform where you can watch the catch being unloaded, as well as a tantalizing fish shop.

Beaches are obviously the big attraction here. Lakes Entrance Surf Beach, a substantial stretch of white sand patrolled in season by surf lifesavers, can be reached via a footbridge across the lake to Hummocks Reserve. A stand on the beach side of the footbridge hires canoes, paddleboats, aquabikes and catamarans. Of the many **lake cruises** on offer, one of the most popular is the trip from the *Club Hotel* jetty at the western end of town, up North Arm to the Wyanga Park Winery (☎03/5155 1508, ⓦwww.wyangapark.com.au) – the most famous local winery – on the fringe of the Colquhoun Forest, in the winery's own boat, the *Corque* (50min; daily lunch cruise $50, Fri & Sat dinner cruise $75; book at Lakes Entrance Visitor Centre, or through the winery). Other waterside activities are three-hour **fishing** trips with Mulloway Fishing Charters (☎0427 943 154; $50), fishing gear and bait supplied.

Eating

Fishing is huge in Lakes Entrance – there's no better place for **fish and chips**.

Ferryman's Seafood Café Situated on the water by Myer St in a 50-year-old ferry, it offers surprisingly well priced seafood in a setting you'd think would be more expensive. Daily lunch noon–3pm, dinner 6pm–late.

Henry's Winery Café Wyanga Park Winery ☎03/5155 1508. 3km from town, it offers excellent cuisine sourced from local producers. Daily 10am–4pm, dinner Fri–Sat.

Lakes Entrance Bowls Club Corner of Rowe and Bulmer St. Perhaps not trendy, but you can't go wrong with the generous portions at good prices. Daily lunch and Fri & Sat dinner.

🏃 **L'Ocean Fish & Chips** 19 Myer St. Fantastic fresh seafood place that, despite its modest exterior, has become an institution. Located just off the Esplanade, they serve gluten-free and wheat-free batter. Daily 11am–8pm.

Tres Amigos Mexican 521 Myer St. A backpacker/surfer favourite since 1977, dishing out cheap Mexican fare. Takeaway available. Wed–Sun dinner.

Metung

If the commercialism of Lakes Entrance turns you off, head for the more refined charms of **METUNG**, a pretty, upmarket boating and holidaying village just 10km west along the shoreline. To get here, take the highway towards Bairnsdale, then turn south on the side road at Swan Reach. There is a visitor office at 50 Metung Rd (daily 9am–5pm; ☎03/5156 2969, 🌐www.metungtourism.com.au) which books accommodation and hires out boats.

A good **accommodation** option is *McMillans of Metung* (☎03/5156 2283, 🌐www.mcmillansofmetung.com.au; ❻–❼), at 155 Metung Rd, which has very comfortable, fully equipped cottages of different sizes in a garden setting, with a solar-heated pool, tennis court and a private jetty. *The Moorings at Metung*, 28 Main Rd (☎03/5156 2750, 🌐www.themoorings.com.au; ❻–❼), are luxury apartments with sun decks and barbecues overlooking Bancroft Bay. Cheaper is the *Metung Hotel* (☎03/5156 2206, 🌐www.metunghotel.com.au; ❹), which also offers food (noon–2pm & 6–8.30pm daily) and a fantastic outdoor table area on the water. *The Seasons* **restaurant** in the *Kings Cove Club* (part of the golf-course development; Wed–Sat dinner, Sun 9am–2pm; ☎03/5156 2927) on Kings Cove Boulevard, serves modern seafood in a chic setting. The bright and pleasant Metung Gallery at 59 Metung Rd serves great breakfasts, lunches and tasty dinners daily at excellent prices.

Buchan and the Snowy River Loop

Nowa Nowa is the inauspiciously named town where you turn north off the Princes Highway for the small town of **BUCHAN**, in the foothills of the Victorian Alps, and take a satisfying loop through the Snowy River National Park. Buchan boasts over six hundred **caves**, the most famous of which – the Royal Cave and the Fairy Cave – can be seen on **guided tours** (Royal Cave daily: April–Sept 11am & 3pm; Oct–March 10am, 1pm, 3.30pm; Fairy Cave daily: April–Sept 1pm; Oct–March 11.15am & 2.15pm; $13.50; ☎03/5162 1900). Both caves are lit and have walkways. In the extensive park surrounding the caves there's an icy, spring-fed swimming pool, a playground, walking tracks and a campsite, plus lots of wildlife.

On the north bank of the Buchan River in the town is *Buchan Lodge* (☎03/5155 9421, 🌐www.buchanlodge.com; ❶), a smallish backpackers' **hostel** with 28 dorm beds (bottom sheet and pillow only supplied), a country-style kitchen, laundry, log fire in winter, barbecue and a nice outdoor garden. The owner will advise about activities in the area, including caving, trail riding and rafting. If you need more than a dorm bed, the *Buchan Valley Log Cabins* (℡03/5155 9494, ⓦwww.buchanlogcabins.com.au; ❹), 16 Gelantipy Rd, consists of a series of spacious two-bedroom cabins with full amenities, plus heating, in a garden setting. For good pub grub head to the *Caves Hotel* (lunch Wed–Sun, dinner Tues–Sun) or the *Buchan Café* (daily 9.30am–4.30pm) on the same road.

The road continues north from Buchan through hilly country, following the Murrindal River and slowly winding its way up to the plateau of the Australian Alps. The sealed road ends at Wulgumerang, just before the turn-off to McKillops Bridge. You can continue straight up to Jindabyne in the Snowy Mountains of New South Wales – a spectacular drive – but about two-thirds of the road is unsealed and can be rough; check conditions before setting out.

Snowy River National Park

Turning right at Wulgumerang, about 55km north of Buchan, enables you to make a scenic, yet at certain times terrifying, arc through part of the **Snowy River National Park**, following the road towards Bonang (check road conditions in advance, as this is an unsealed road that can deteriorate badly in adverse weather conditions). **Little River Falls** are well worth a stop on this stretch: a short walk leads from the car park past snow gums to a lookout with breathtaking views of Little River Gorge and the falls. Equally stunning is the view from the second lookout from the top of the northeastern cliff-face of **Little River Gorge** (about 10min from the car park).

Further on, you descend to the valley of the Snowy River, which you cross at **McKillops Bridge**, set in the landscape that inspired "Banjo" Paterson's famous ballad, *The Man from Snowy River*. The river's sandy banks are a favourite swimming spot, and are also the place to set out on a **rafting** trip through deep gorges, caves, raging rapids and tranquil pools. Snowy River Expeditions offers good-value river expeditions, as well as rafting, abseiling, rock-climbing, horseriding ($35 per hr) and wild caving adventures ($85 per half-day). They also run *Karoonda Park* (℡03/5155 0220, ⓦwww.karoondapark .com; dorms $24, rooms ❸, cabins ❹), a small country **hostel** situated on a beef and sheep farm in Gelantipy offering a variety of accommodation, from dorms to motel-style rooms. Oz Experience buses pass through Gelantipy.

Bonang to Orbost

The road through the Snowy River National Park continues until it meets the Bonang–Orbost road. The general store at **Bonang**, a former goldrush town, sells takeaway food, groceries and fuel, and has some information about the area.

The winding road down from the plateau to the coast, still mostly unsealed, leads past the **Errinundra National Park**, which protects magnificent wetland eucalypt forests containing giant, centuries-old specimens, as well as Victoria's largest surviving stand of **rainforest**. At **Errinundra Saddle**, in the heart of the park, there's a delightful picnic area and a self-guided boardwalk through the forest (about 40min). Take special care while driving, as all the roads in the area are heavily used by logging trucks.

The road from Bonang eventually leads to the old-fashioned town of **ORBOST**, on the Princes Highway where it crosses the Snowy River. The **Orbost Visitor Centre** at 39 Nicholson St (daily 9am–5pm; ℡03/5154 2424) books accommodation and tours. There's a tranquil picnic spot opposite the *Snowy River Orbost Camp Park* (℡03/5154 1097; cabins ❸), on the corner of Lochiel and Nicholson streets, with huge gums lining one bank and cows roaming the paddocks on the other. The *Orbost Club Hotel* (☎03/5154 1003; ➊) at 63 Nicholson St has cheap rooms with shared bathrooms, and offers unusually good Chinese food (daily noon–2pm & 6–8pm). *A lovely little lunch* at 125a Nicholson St is appropriately titled (daily 8.30am–2pm).

Mallacoota and around

MALLACOOTA is an unspoilt village in a gorgeous location surrounded by Croajingolong National Park, on the lake system of the **Mallacoota Inlet**. During the summer and Easter holidays the tranquil place turns into a bustling holiday resort. It's approached via Genoa, 47km east from Cann River along the Princes Highway. About 10km from Genoa, a turn-off to the left leads to **Gipsy Point**, an idyllic spot near the confluence of the Genoa and Wallagaraugh rivers on the upper reaches of the Mallacoota Inlet.

Information and accommodation

The very helpful volunteer-operated Mallacoota Visitor Information Shed is situated on the main wharf (daily 10am–4pm; ☎03/5158 0800) and gives advice on accommodation and attractions around town. Several good **guesthouses** are located in and around Mallacoota; an alternative is **Gipsy Point**, about 20km northwest.

Adobe Flats 17 Karbeethong Ave ☎03/5158 0329, ✆www.adobeholidayflats.com.au. Spacious self-contained mud-brick apartments on a former chicken farm. Popular with couples. ➍–➎

Coopracambra Cottages *Wangarabell* ☎03/5158 8277, ✆www.mallacoota.com /coopracambra. Closer to Genoa than the Gipsy Point options, the *Coopracambra Cottages* offer excellent value, and are a great choice for those wanting a bit of space. ➍

Gipsy Point Lakeside Luxury Apartments Gipsy Point ☎03/5158 8200 or 1800 688 200, ✆www .gipsy.com.au. This boutique resort is set in a garden by the Wallagaraugh River, with attractive apartments, some with spa, all with water frontage on Mallacoota lakes. ➑–➒

Gipsy Point Lodge MacDonald St, Gipsy Point ☎1800 063 556, ✆www.gipsypoint.com. Rooms (dinner, bed and breakfast) and cottages, with free use of canoes and rowing boats; birdwatching and bushwalking excursions can be arranged. Rooms ➏, cottages ➎–➏

Karbeethong Lodge 16 Schnapper Point Drive ☎03/5158 0411, ✆www.karbeethonglodge.com .au. A renovated, old-style weatherboard guesthouse with singles and doubles, most en suite. Has a nice country feel to it. ➍–➎

Mallacoota Foreshore Caravan Park ☎03/5158 0300, ✆www.mallacootaholidaypark .com.au. Great location, just metres from the water. Easily the best place in town to pitch a tent. Their office also offers good advice about where the fish are biting. ➋

Mallacoota Hotel 51 Maurice Ave ☎03/5158 0455, ✆www.mallacootahotel.com.au. Very central on the main shopping strip; offers accommodation in motel rooms and fully self-contained units. Outside there's a swimming pool and BBQ area. ➍–➎

Wave Oasis 36 Vista Drive ☎03/5158 0995, ✆www.thewaveoasis.com.au. One of the best options in town, with extremely comfortable apartments and great views of the surrounding inlet. Breakfast hamper included in price. ➏–➐

Activities

You can go on **bushwalks** and explore the beautiful waterways of the Mallacoota Inlet (Bottom Lake and Top Lake), on your own by renting a boat or canoe from Mallacoota Hire Boats (☎03/5158 0704), located 200m to the left of the information shed (see above), or by taking a cruise with Loch-Ard Cruises ($25 for 2hr; ☎0418 615 282, ✆www.cruisemallacoota.com). The **Parks Victoria office**, on the corner of Allan and Buckland drives (daily 9.30am–3.30pm;

☎03/5161 9500, ⊛www.parkweb.vic.gov.au), has details of secluded camping spots and local bushwalks, and provides fishing licences. It can also provide information on the nearby **Croajingolong National Park**, which begins southeast of the town at Sydenham Inlet and continues for 100km along the coast to the state border. A three-day **bushwalking safari** run by OzStyle Adventures (☎026495 6997, ⊛www.ozstyle.net.au) is a good option without roughing it too much: the tour leaves every Thursday; ($625; includes a tour of Point Hicks Lighthouse and gourmet catering; minimum 6 people or 4 people during NSW and VIC school holidays). Or you can choose to go it alone and stay in the lighthouse-keeper's cottage (entire cottage $295 for 6 people) or a bungalow (sleeps two; ❹) at *Point Hicks* (☎03/5158 4268, ⊛www.pointhicks.com.au). A summer **cinema** operates at the Mallacoota Community Centre, Allan Drive.

Eating and drinking

Choices for **food** are very limited although the standard is high. The *Croajingolong Café* (daily 8.30am–4pm) on Allan Drive serves brunch, light meals and good coffee, while the bakery next door is the pride of the town, selling award-winning pies. For dinner try the *Tide Restaurant & Cocktail Bar* on Maurice Avenue; otherwise, the bistro at the *Mallacoota Hotel* has well-priced meals and cold beer, and there's live music in January.

The northeast

The **Hume Highway**, the direct route between Melbourne and Sydney, cuts straight through Victoria's northeast – an area that has become known as **Ned Kelly Country**. **Benalla** and **Glenrowan** (where he was finally seized after a bloody shoot-out) still bear traces of the masked bushranger's activities, with Glenrowan wholeheartedly cashing in on his fame. Further north, **Wangarrata** is a sizeable town known for its jazz festival and lively nightlife. **Rutherglen**, right up against the state border, is a long-established wine-producing region, while nearby **Chiltern** is a sleepy little town where not much has changed in the last 150 years. Heading east, picturesque **Beechworth** is rich in history, with beautiful streetscapes, haunting attractions and a famous bakery. **Bushwalking** and **mountain biking** in the Alpine region are most easily organized through outdoor tour operators such as the South Australia–based

---

Fruit-picking in the Goulburn Valley

The rich plains of the **Goulburn Valley**, running through Seymour, Nagambie and Shepparton, yield much **fruit**, and it's a popular area for backpackers looking for seasonal work. The small city of **Shepparton** is the operations centre for the SPC and Ardmona canned-fruit companies, with peaches, pears, apples and plums tinned and exported worldwide. The Greater Shepparton Visitor Centre can point you in the right direction regarding **fruit-picking work**. They are located beside Victoria Park Lake in the south of town, at 534 Wyndham St on the Goulburn Valley Highway (daily 9am–5pm; ☎1800 808 839, ⊛www.greatershepparton.com.au).

Ecotrek (☎1300 948 911, ⓦwww.ecotrek.com.au).V/Line runs several **train and bus routes** through the northeast. For bookings and up-to-date timetables call ☎13 61 96 or go to ⓦwww.vline.com.au.

The Hume Highway and Kelly Country

SEYMOUR is the first major stop on the Hume Highway out of Melbourne. An important train interchange, it's an uninspiring place, though the nearby **Tahbilk Winery** (Mon–Fri 9am–5pm, Sat & Sun 10am–5pm; ⓦwww .tahbilk.com.au), 6km southwest, is worth exploring. The oldest continually operating winery and vineyard in Victoria, it opened in 1860, and its Shiraz and Marsanne vines have seen more than 140 harvests. The whitewashed buildings have been well preserved and there are extensive grounds to wander around.

Ninety-two kilometres northeast of Seymour, **BENALLA** is a civilized town on the lake of the same name, formed by the Broken River which runs through town and occasionally floods it. There's a rose festival here every November, which transforms the town's picnic spots and gardens. The helpful **Benalla Visitor Centre**, 14 Mair St (daily 9am–5pm; ☎03/5762 1749), has lots of pamphlets and information on the region, and can also book accommodation. In the same building, the **Costume and Pioneer Museum** (daily 9am–5pm; ⓦwww.benallamuseum.org; $4) displays a collection of women's dresses from the 1920s, ball gowns and male fashion from the late eighteenth century until the early twentieth century, along with a range of Ned Kelly relics, including the green silk cummerbund he was awarded as a child for saving a friend from drowning, and which he proudly wore when captured. The **Benalla Art Gallery** (daily 10am–5pm; free), in a lovely setting across the lake, has a fine collection of early twentieth-century and contemporary Australian art.

If you want to stay you'll find a number of motels along Bridge Street, though more interesting by far is the *Belmont Bed and Breakfast* (☎03/5762 6575, ⓦwww.belmontbnb.com.au; ⑥), 80 Arundel St, a charming 1900s house with elegantly furnished rooms. For something to eat during the day, there's the *Gallery Café* in a serene location at the Art Gallery by the lake (licensed; daily 10am–4pm), or in town, *Hides Bakery* at 111 Bridge St has been preparing excellent pies, salads and sandwiches since 1929. The *Benalla Health Food Shop* (Mon–Fri 9am–5pm) at 67 Nunn St has excellent sandwiches and reasonable breakfasts, and for dinner *Café Raffety's*, 55 Nunn St (Tues–Sat; ☎03/5762 4066), has a blackboard menu featuring daily specials. Further up on the price scale, *Georgina's*, 100 Bridge St (lunch Wed–Fri, dinner Tues–Sat; ☎03/5762 1334), is the best option for excellent contemporary Australian cuisine.

Glenrowan and Kelly's last stand

GLENROWAN, 29km beyond Benalla, was the site of the Kelly Gang's last stand. A gigantic effigy of Ned Kelly, in full iron-armour regalia, greets you as you enter town, and there are lots of other tawdry attractions along the highway, such as the **Last Stand Show** (daily 9.30am–4.30pm; every half-hour; 40min; $22; ☎03/5766 2367, ⓦwww.nedkellyslaststand.com.au), a "computerized animated theatre" using dummies shuffling around on cue to dramatize the story of the siege – your money's better spent elsewhere. The last stand itself took place in Siege Street near the train station. Along the rail lines north of town, a small stone monument marks the spot where Kelly forced railworkers to rip up a section of the track, to try to derail the trainful of troopers he had

The Ned Kelly story

Even before **Ned Kelly** became widely known, folklore and ballads were popularizing the free-ranging bush outlaws as potent symbols of freedom and resistance to authority. Born in 1855, Ned Kelly was the son of an alcoholic rustler and a mother who sold illicit liquor. By the time he was eleven he was already in constant trouble with the police, who considered the whole family troublemakers. Constables in the area were instructed to "endeavour, whenever the Kellys commit any paltry crime, to bring them to justice...the object [is] to take their prestige away from them".

Ned became the accomplice of the established bushranger **Harry Power**, and by his mid-teens had a string of warrants to his name. Ned's brother, Dan, was also wanted by the police, and on one fateful occasion, hearing that he had turned up at his mother's, a policeman set out, drunk and without a warrant, to arrest him. A scuffle ensued and the unsteady constable fell to the floor, hitting his head and allowing Dan to escape. The following day warrants were issued for the arrest of Ned (who was in New South Wales at the time) and Dan for attempted murder, and their mother was sentenced to three years' imprisonment.

From this point on, the **Kelly gang**'s crime spree accelerated and, following the death of three constables in a shoot-out at Stringybark Creek, the biggest manhunt in Australia's history began, with a £1000 reward offered for the gang's apprehension. On December 9, 1878, they robbed the bank at Euroa, taking £2000, before moving on to Jerilderie in New South Wales, where another bank was robbed and Kelly penned the famous **Jerilderie Letter**, describing the "big, ugly, fat-necked, wombat-headed, big-bellied, magpie-legged, narrow-hipped, splay-footed sons of Irish bailiffs or English landlords which is better known as Officers of Justice or Victoria Police" who had forced him onto the wrong side of the law.

After a year on the run, the gang formulated a grand plan: they executed Aaron Sherritt, a police informer, in Sebastopol, thus luring a trainbound posse of armed troopers from nearby Beechworth. This train was intended to be derailed at Glenrowan, with as much bloodshed as possible, before the gang moved on to rob the bank at Benalla and barter hostages for the release of Kelly's mother. In the event, having already sabotaged the tracks, the gang commandeered the Glenrowan Inn and, in a moment of drunken candour, Kelly detailed his ambush to a schoolteacher who escaped, managing to save the special train. As the troopers approached the inn, the gang donned the home-made iron armour that has since become their motif. In the ensuing gunfight Kelly's comrades were either killed or committed suicide as the inn was torched, while Ned himself was taken alive, tried by the same judge who had incarcerated his mother, and sentenced to hang.

Public sympathies lay strongly with Ned Kelly, and a crowd of five thousand gathered outside Melbourne Gaol on November 11, 1880, for his execution, believing that the 25-year-old bushranger would "die game". True to form, his last words are said to have been "Such is life".

lured to the town – though visitors are asked to stay away, as the site is dangerous. Overlooking the town to the west is Mount Glenrowan, which the bushrangers used as a lookout.

More interesting and far better value than the Last Stand Show is **Kate's Cottage Homestead and Museum**, a souvenir and gift shop with a replica of the Kelly home at the back (daily 9am–5.30pm; $5). With its bare earth floor, bark roof and newspaper-lined walls, it speaks volumes of the deprivation that drove the family to crime. An evocative audiotape narrates Ned's story from childhood and is interspersed with folk songs inspired by his life. The original homestead, 9km west along Kelly Gap Road, is now nothing more than rubble and a brick chimney.

Wangaratta

The town of **WANGARATTA**, at the junction of the Ovens and King rivers, 16km from Glenrowan, is a convenient overnight stop between Sydney and Melbourne, but there are few reasons to linger unless you're here for the famous four-day **Wangaratta Festival of Jazz** (ⓦwww.wangaratta-jazz.org.au). Beginning on the Friday prior to the Melbourne Cup (the last weekend in Oct or the first weekend in Nov), this is one of the premier jazz events in the country, attracting national stars and international legends. The highway on either side of "Wang" is lined with motels, and the staff at the new **Wangaratta Tourist Information**, 100 Murphy St (daily 9am–5pm; ⓣ1800 801 065), can book tickets for the festival as well as local tours and accommodation, and give out stacks of leaflets about the area. They also have internet access ($2 per 30min).

There's a vast range of **accommodation** in town. Good choices include the *Pinsent Hotel* (ⓣ03/5721 2183; B&B ❸) at 20 Reid St, a renovated country pub-bistro with reasonable double rooms, and the modern *Parkview Sundowner*, 56 Ryley St (ⓣ03/5721 5655, ⓦwww.parkviewmotorinn.com.au; ❹), which has wireless broadband, cable TV and free DVDs to borrow. For **food**, *Scribbler's Café* (Mon–Sat 8am–4pm, Sun 9am–3pm), at 66 Reid St, serves good cakes and lunchtime fodder, as does the *Yippee Bean Café & Juice Bar* (Mon–Fri 8am–5pm, Sat 10am–3pm) at 76 Ovens St. For dinner, great-value food and drinks can be found at the *Wangarrata RSL* on Victoria Parade (open lunch and dinner daily), while the *Indian Tandoori Restaurant* (Tues–Sun 5.30–11pm) at 54 Ryley St packs them in most nights. For those seeking nightlife, the *Grand Central* at 80 Murphy St and the *Riva Bar* at 40 Faithful St fill up on weekends. Out of town, the *Boorhaman Hotel*, a small country pub with an award-winning **microbrewery**, is worth a detour: they serve hearty country tucker (lunch daily, dinner Fri & Sat), washed down with a lager, dark ale, or wheat beer produced by its Buffalo

---

The Milawa Gourmet Region

The high-country area of Victoria – and in particular the small town of **MILAWA**, 15km southeast of Wangaratta on the Snow Road – is renowned amongst foodies for the excellent quality of its locally produced food and wine, so much so that it has been dubbed the **Milawa Gourmet Region** (ⓦwww.milawagourmet.com). Indeed, Melburnians have been known to make the two-hour trip just to stock up on dinner-party supplies.

If it's a tipple of something special you're after, try a tour of the **Brown Brothers Winery** (daily 9am–5pm; ⓣ03/5720 5500, ⓦwww.brown-brothers.com.au), situated about 2km from Milawa and clearly signposted; there's also a great restaurant here, the *Epicurean Centre* (daily 11am–3pm; bookings essential ⓣ03/5720 5540), which specializes in complementing Brown Brothers wines with seasonal local foods. Back in the town, there's the **Milawa Cheese Factory** (daily 9am–5pm; ⓣ03/5727 3589) on Factory Road, where you'll find award-winning cheeses and another excellent restaurant and bakery. At the crossroads nearby, **Milawa Mustards** (10am–5pm; ⓣ03/5727 3202) offers eighteen home-made seed varieties, while on the Snow Road, **Walkabout Apiaries** (daily 10am–5pm; ⓣ03/5727 3468) sells a variety of meads made from Australian honey, a wide array of sticky, sweet honeys that put commercial brands to shame, candles and other honey products. The **Olive Shop** (Mon–Wed 10am–4pm, Thurs–Sun 10am–5pm; ⓣ03/5727 3887), Snow Road, has locally grown olives and extra virgin olive oil. On the same road, **King River Café** (Mon 10am–3pm, Wed–Sun 10am–late; ⓣ03/5727 3461, ⓦwww.kingrivercafe.com.au) is a popular eatery specializing in local wines and good food – the cakes and coffee are excellent, too.

Brewery. It's on Boorhaman Road, 16km north of Wangaratta towards the Murray Valley Highway – call ☎03/5726 9215 for further directions.

Beechworth

Some 35km east of Wangaratta, off the Ovens Highway (also known as the Great Alpine Road), is **BEECHWORTH**, once the centre of the rich **Ovens gold-mining region**. Sited picturesquely in the foothills of the Victorian Alps, the entire town has been acknowledged by the National Trust as being of historic significance, and the town and surrounding area have been designated a **Historic Park** by the Department of Sustainability and Environment.

Arrival, information and accommodation

V/Line has a **bus service** from Wangaratta to Beechworth and an additional service to Bright via Beechworth. Call V/Line on ☎13 61 96 or consult ⓦwww.vline.com.au for the latest information. The **visitor centre** is located in the fine old Town Hall at 103 Ford St (daily 9am–5pm; ☎1300 366 321, ⓦwww.beechworthonline.com.au), and can book tours as well as provide you with pamphlets on places of interest, including the Gorge Scenic Drive (see p.999). The nearby Beechworth Neighbourhood Centre has **internet** access (Mon–Thurs 9am–4.30pm, Fri 9am–1.30pm). The visitor centre can book **accommodation** for you.

Armour Inn Motel 1 Camp St ☎03/5728 1466, ⓦwww.armour-motor-inn.com.au. Central, comfortable rooms, with pool and cable TV. ❻

Freeman on Ford 97 Ford St ☎03/5728 2371, ⓦwww.freemanonford.com.au. Best option in town for those who can afford it. Four beautifully decorated rooms in traditional Victorian style right in the heart of town. Cooked breakfast included in rates. ❽

Old Priory 8 Priory Lane ☎03/5728 1024, ⓦwww.oldpriory.com.au. Reasonably priced singles ($50–75) are the real drawing card to this historic B&B. If you want peace and quiet, it's best

to come at the weekend, when the school groups have gone. ❹–❺

Rose Cottage 42 Camp St ☎03/5728 1069, ⓦwww.beechworth.com/rosecottage. Central, good-value B&B with equal doses of history and elegance. ❺–❻

Tanswell's Commercial Hotel 50 Ford St ☎03/5728 1480. Beautiful old building on the town's main strip that offers traditional pub accommodation with reasonable double rooms (shared facilities). Has a somewhat haunted feel to it, which some may enjoy. ❸

The Town

As is true of so many other towns in the northeast, Beechworth is rich in **Ned Kelly** history. The **government buildings** on Ford Street house the imposing HM Training Prison, where he and his mother were incarcerated, and the **courthouse** (daily 9am–5pm) where his trial was held. Opposite, underneath the town hall, is the grim cell where he was imprisoned as a teenager (daily 10am–4pm). Other sights of interest in town include the **Burke Museum** on Loch Street (daily 10am–5pm), dedicated to the explorer Robert O'Hara Burke, one-time superintendent of police in Beechworth, who perished with William John Wills on their historic journey from Melbourne to the Gulf of Carpentaria (see box, p.527). To visit these buildings you will need to purchase a Precinct Ticket ($13.50, valid for two days) from the visitor centre, which also includes entry to several other sites, including the Telegraph Station, a Chinese Cultural Centre (closed Tues) and the Powder Magazine (Sat & Sun noon–4pm).

The five-kilometre, one-way route of the **Gorge Scenic Drive** begins at Sydney Road and ends at Bridge Street, along the western edge of the town. It includes the famous Spring and Reid creeks, which supported eight thousand diggers in 1852, and an old storehouse for blasting powder known as the powder magazine, as well as natural features such as Flat Rock, Telegraph Rock and Woolshed Falls.

Eating

For **food**, try the *Beechworth Bakery*, 27 Camp St (daily 6am–7pm). It's famous all over Australia for its delicious pies, bread, cakes and pastries, and on sunny days you can have breakfast on the balcony. Also gaining fame is the *Bridge Road Brewery* situated in an old coach house behind the *Tanswell Commercial Hotel*, which churns out a variety of fantastic ales and pizzas to match (kitchen: Wed–Sun lunch, also dinner Sun). The *Green Gekko* (Tues–Sat 9am–4.30pm, Sun from 7.30am), at 78 Ford St, is a great little café with an excellent garden area out the back, serving big breakfasts and gluten-free Thai-influenced lunches. The stately *The Provenance*, in the Bank of Australia building at 86 Ford St (Wed–Sun from 6pm; Sat & Sun noon–3pm; ☎03/5728 1786), offers à la carte dining with a contemporary Australian menu.

Chiltern

CHILTERN, a sleepy former gold-mining centre with a well-preserved, mid-nineteenth-century streetscape, lies just off the Hume Highway about 40km from Wangaratta. There is a small community-run tourism centre at 30 Main Rd (daily 10am–4pm; ☎03/5726 1611, ⓦ www.chilternvic.com) which stocks the free *Chiltern Visitor's Guide* brochure, explaining the nearby local landmarks and history of the area. For refreshment, the *Telegraph Hotel* (daily lunch and dinner) at 25 Conness St serves up cheap pub grub for around $12, yet most head across the road to the *Mulberry Tree Tearooms*, which also offers pleasant B&B accommodation (☎03/5726 1277; ❹).

Rutherglen

RUTHERGLEN, 18km west of Chiltern and 32km west of Wodonga on the Murray River Highway, is at the heart of Victoria's oldest wine-producing region, renowned for its excellent dessert wines, Rutherglen Muscat and Tokay. Nineteen **wineries** are situated in the area, most of them fourth- or fifth-generation establishments with cellars full of character. The weather partly accounts for the quality of Rutherglen's sweet wines: the long, mild autumns allow the grapes to stay on the vines for longer, producing higher levels of sugar in the fruit. All the wineries are open for free tastings and cellar-door sales (Mon–Sat 10am–5pm; Sun hours differ from place to place). The **Wine Experience Visitor Centre** at 57 Main St (daily 9am–5pm; ☎1800 622 871, ⓦ www.rutherglenvic.com) is local history museum, shop, café and visitor centre all in one – it has informative displays about the goldrush and the agricultural history of the district, including wine making. The shop sells local wines and arts and crafts, and there are stacks of brochures and information on touring the wineries. They also rent mountain bikes ($35 per day, including helmet) and have downloadable cycle route maps on the website above. On the Queen's Birthday weekend in June the town hosts the **Winery Walkabout** – one of Australia's biggest wine-tasting festivals, when the new season's releases are presented to the public. Another festive event, the **Tastes of Rutherglen**, is held over the Victorian Labour Day weekend in mid-March, and sees some of the best local restaurants guest-starring at the wineries.

Practicalities

Around three hours from Melbourne, Rutherglen makes a popular weekend getaway, so **accommodation** can be hard to find at that time; during the week you'll have no problem. Right in the centre of town, you can't miss the 150-year-old *Victoria Hotel* at 90 Main St (☎02/6032 8610, ⓦwww.victoriahotelrutherglen .com.au; ❸—❹) which has standard doubles with shared bathroom, and recently renovated rooms with en suite. Behind the 1860s *Poachers Paradise Motel*, 97 Murray St (☎02/6032 7373, ⓦwww.poachersparadise.com.au; ❹—❺), there are ten modern motel units with air conditioning and the usual mod cons; two of them come with a spa bath. The bar and bistro in front serves breakfast as well as hearty pub grub daily for lunch and dinner. *The Walkabout Motel*, Murray Valley Highway (☎02/6032 9572, ⓦwww.walkaboutmotel.com.au; ❹), offers similar accommodation.

Parker Pies (Mon–Fri 9am–5pm, Sat 8am–5pm, Sun 9am–4pm) at 88 Main St is an award-winning bakery and licensed **café** serving a myriad of excellent pies, while the *Tuileries Restaurant* (☎02/6032 9033; from 6.30pm daily) on Drummond Street has an excellent range of local wines and highly recommended Australian cuisine. For a great beer head to the *Bintara Brewery* (10am–5pm daily) on Drummond Street, where for $10 you can sample their four beers.

The Victorian Alps

The **VICTORIAN ALPS**, the southern extension of the Great Dividing Range, bear little resemblance to their European counterparts; they're too gentle, too rounded, and above all too low to offer really great **skiing**, although they remain a popular winter sports destination. In July and August there is usually plenty of snow and the resorts are packed out. Most people come for the downhill skiing, though the **cross-country skiing**, rapidly growing in popularity, is also excellent: **Lake Mountain** (ⓦwww.lakemountainresort.com.au), 21km from Marysville, is the region's premier cross-country destination. **Snowboarding** was first encouraged at Mount Hotham and is now firmly established everywhere. **Falls Creek**, **Mount Hotham** and **Mount Buller** are the largest and most commercial skiing areas, particularly the last which is within easy reach of Melbourne; smaller resorts such as **Mount Baw Baw** are more suited to beginners.

In summer, when the wild flowers are in bloom, the Alps are ideal **bushwalking** territory with most of the high mountains (and the ski resorts) contained within the vast **Alpine National Park**. The most famous of the walks is the four-hundred-kilometre **Alpine Trail**, which begins in Baw Baw National Park, near Walhalla in Gippsland, and follows the ridges all the way to Mount Kosciuszko in the Snowy Mountains of New South Wales. If you are doing any serious bushwalking, you'll need to be properly equipped. Water can be hard to find, and the weather can change suddenly and unexpectedly: even in summer it can get freezing cold up here, especially at night. After prolonged dry spells, **bushfires** can also pose a very real threat, as was the case in 2009 (see box, p.985), while bushland and resorts were burnt.

Mansfield and **Bright** are good bases for exploration of the Alps, and are great places to unwind. In summer the ski resorts can be ugly and only half the facilities are open, but there are often great bargains to be had on rooms. If you're **driving**, you'll need snow chains in winter (they're compulsory in many parts), and you should heed local advice before venturing off the main roads.

Mansfield

MANSFIELD is located at the junction of the Maroondah and Midland highways, just a few kilometres north of Lake Eildon, 140km east of Seymour and 63km south of Benalla. As the main approach to Mount Buller, it's a lively place with good pubs, restaurants and a cinema. The annual highlight is the **High Country Festival**, which begins the weekend prior to the Melbourne Cup (late Oct/early November); activities include a picnic race known as "Melbourne Cup Day at Mansfield".

V/Line has a year-round bus service from Melbourne to Mansfield. Call V/Line on ☎13 61 96 or consult ⓦwww.vline.com.au for the latest information. The helpful **Mansfield Visitor Centre** at 173 High St (daily 9am–5pm; ☎03/5775 1464 or 1800 060 686 for accommodation bookings, ⓦwww.mansfield-mtbuller .com.au), has complete information on all sights and activities, including skiing and walks in the surrounding country. Out of the snow season, you have a choice of horseriding, hiking, climbing, abseiling, hang-gliding, rafting, canoeing or 4WD tours. Among the many local outfits Stirling Experience (☎03/5777 6441, ⓦwww.stirling.au.com) offer winter and summer activities around Mount Buller (see below) and Mount Stirling.

The *Alzburg Inn Resort*, 39 Malcolm St (☎1300 885 448, ⓦwww.alzburg.com .au; ⑥–⑧), is a resort **hotel** with all mod cons, popular with skiers, while the neat and friendly *Mansfield Traveller's Lodge*, 116 High St (☎03/5775 1800, ⓦwww .mansfieldtravellerslodge.com.au; dorm bed $30, rooms ❹), has motel rooms and a good backpackers' **hostel** in a separate building next door. For a bit of old-world charm, the *Tavistock House* (☎03/5775 1024, ⓦwww.tavistockhouse.com.au; ❾) at the corner of High and Highett streets, is a fully renovated, colonial-style house in the centre of town. Directly across the road is the *Delatite Hotel* (☎03/5775 2004, ⓦwww.hoteldelatite.com.au; ❹), a true country pub with clean rooms and shared facilities that's popular with workers. Rates include continental breakfast.

Merrijig

The small town of **MERRIJIG**, a little under halfway to Mount Buller from Mansfield, is largely responsible for the great number of **riding** outfits in the area. The breathtaking high-country scenery nearby was used as the location for the 1982 kangaroo western, *The Man from Snowy River*, and visitors have been trying to live out their fantasies ever since. If you want to combine horseriding with lodge **accommodation**, try *Merrijig Lodge and Trail Rides*, Mount Buller Road (☎03/5777 5590, ⓦwww.merrijiglodge.com.au; ❹–❺). The *Willawong Bed & Breakfast and Cottage* at Lot 12, Mount Buller Rd, Merrijig (☎03/5777 5750, ⓦwww.willawongbnb.com.au; ❹) offers Bavarian-style accommodation in a gorgeous self-contained wooden cottage in a lovely garden at the foot of the Alps.

Mount Buller

To reach **MOUNT BULLER ALPINE VILLAGE**, 48km from Mansfield, you gradually ascend on the smooth, sealed Summit Road. With 7000 beds, 24 modern ski-lifts and 80km of runs, the village has the greatest capacity of any Australian ski-resort. In winter, Mansfield Mt Buller High Country Reservations dispenses **information** about all things snow-related (☎1800 BULLER, ⓦwww.mtbuller.com.au).

Accommodation

In **winter**, during the ski season, Mansfield Mt Buller High Country Reservations (see above) books **accommodation**. In summer, call the Mansfield Visitor Centre (see above). Most accommodation options also have **restaurants**, otherwise the Village Square has some decent options, though with inflated prices.

Skiing practicalities

The official start of the **ski season** is the Queen's Birthday long weekend in June, though there is often not enough snow cover until August, lasting through to October. Day-trip or weekend **packages** are the best way to go, and are far cheaper than trying to do it yourself. The best value for money are trips organized by the *Alzburg Inn Resort* at Mansfield ([T]1300 885 440, [W]www.alzburg.com.au). The day-tours leave Melbourne at 4.30am and arrive at Mount Buller at about 9am, giving the opportunity for a full day's skiing (from $89, including entrance fees; a 1-day lift/lesson ticket is $140 extra); the 2-day/1-night package includes accommodation at the *Alzburg Inn* (from $260). It's also worth checking out the area around Hardware Street in Melbourne, where such companies as Auski at no. 9 ([T]03/9670 1412) and Mountain Designs at 373 Little Bourke St ([T]03/9670 3354) can advise on skiing conditions at the resorts, and sell or rent equipment.

During the snow season, an entry fee of $30–35 per car applies, depending on the resort. For **weather** and snow conditions go to [W]www.ski.com.au or [W]www.vicsnowreport.com.au.

For accommodation, phone the central reservation hotlines of each mountain resort. The free *Australian Alpine News* is available at the visitor centre in Melbourne as well as in the Alpine region. As a rough guide to **costs**, a lift ticket at Mount Buller is $96 per day, while **lessons** cost $140 for 1-day limited lift and a 3hr lesson. Full equipment rental is about $75 per day.

During the season, Mansfield–Mount Buller Bus Lines, 137 High St, Mansfield ([T]03/5775 2606, [W]www.buslines.com.au/mmbl/), operates a **ski transport service** to Mount Buller eight times a day. In Bright, Adina Ski Hire, 15 Ireland St ([T]03/5755 1177, [W]www.adina.com.au), and Bright Ski Centre, 22 Ireland St ([T]03/5755 1093, [W]www.brightskicentre.com.au), rent out skiing and snowboarding equipment, offer package deals including off-mountain accommodation and transport to Mount Hotham, and have up-to-date snow reports and information on road conditions. There's no transport to Mount Buffalo.

Andre's at Buller Hotel Cobbler Lane [T]03/5777 6966, [W]www.andresatbuller.com. The first B&B built in the area is still the best, mirroring the kind of accommodation you'd more likely see in the French Alps (Andre's home country). Every luxury and stunning views, but it comes at a price. Open all year round. [9]

Arlberg Hotel 53 Summit Rd [T]03/5777 6260, [W]www.arlberg.com.au. Huge property with variety of rooms and six- to eight-bed self-contained apartments. Also has a variety of restaurants for most budgets. [9]

Duck Inn 18 Goal Post Rd [T]03/5777 6326, [W]www.duckinnmtbuller.com. Cosy boutique hotel that has regular rooms as well as lodge-style accommodation with bunk beds. Cooked breakfast included in price. Also has an excellent restaurant on the premises (*Drakes*). Rooms [6], lodge [5]

Monash Alpine Lodge 84 Stirling Rd [T]03/5777 6577, [W]www.sport.monash.edu.au/alpine-lodge.html. Operated by Monash University (but anyone can stay), this two-storey wooden lodge has standard facilities with slightly cramped dorms, kitchen and a good living area. Dorms $37 summer, $88 winter.

YHA Lodge The Avenue [T]03/5777 6181, [E]mountbuller@yhavic.org.au. Unbeatable location right in the centre of the village, with dorm rooms, large living areas and a decent kitchen. Open June–Sept; reception open 8–10am & 5–10pm. Dorms $76.50. Minimum 2-night stay at weekends. Advance booking (available from May 1) is essential. They also organize transport, accommodation and ski/snowboard hire packages.

Bright and around

BRIGHT is at the centre of the picturesque Ovens Valley, between Mount Buffalo and Mount Beauty about 75km southeast of Wangaratta on the Ovens Highway. It began life as a gold-mining town in the 1850s and today still has a faintly elegant air, with tall European trees lining the main street and filling the parks. A clear stream flows through Centennial Park, opposite the visitor centre, and in autumn the glorious colours of the changing leaves make for a very un-Australian scene.

Arrival, information and accommodation

V/Line operates a **bus** service to Bright from Wangaratta. To **get around**, you can rent a mountain bike from Cyclepath, 74 Gavan St (℡03/5750 1442, ⓦwww.cyclepath.com.au; from $28 a day) – which also operates biking tours. Bright Visitor Centre at 76A Gavan St (daily 9am–5pm; ℡1300 551 117, ⓦwww.brightescapes.com.au) has **information** on what's happening around town; there's an **internet** café in the same building. The visitor centre can also book **accommodation**.

Alpine Hotel 7 Anderson St ℡03/5755 1366. Charming century-old place which is the focal point of town, with a rowdy bar, good-value bistro meals and excellent breakfasts; the back bar has bands on Fri night, and outside there's a sunny beer garden. ❸

Bright Hikers Backpackers 4 Ireland St ℡03/5750 1244, ⓦwww.brighthikers.com.au. One of the best budget places to stay, right in the centre of town. Its wide range of facilities includes a games room, bike rental, internet, and a great lounge and balcony where travellers like to socialize. Dorms $25, rooms ❷

The Buckland McCormacks Lane, Buckland Valley ℡03/5756 2383, ⓦwww.thebuckland.com.au. Situated 12km out of town, this eco-oasis has four studio houses and a one-bed chalet all with first-class amenities in a completely relaxing rural setting. Not cheap, but popular with the weekend getaway crowd. ❾

Coach House Inn 100 Gavan St ℡1800 813 992, ⓦwww.coachhousebright.com.au. Medium-priced motel near the visitor centre that has spacious rooms and a bit of character. Great communal BBQ gazebo area. ❺

Elm Lodge Holiday Motel 2 Wood St ℡03/5755 1144, ⓦwww.elmlodge.com.au. Good-value and centrally located motel with a beautiful garden and a pool. Evening meals available. ❹

Eucalypt Mist B&B 152A Delany Ave ℡03/5755 1336. Charming and comfortable house nestled amongst the trees teeming with birdlife, where getting privacy is not a problem. ❺

Riverside Holiday Park 4–10 Toorak Rd ℡03/5755 1118, ⓦwww.riversideholidaypark.com.au. Great riverside location in the heart of town, which offers good-value cabins (4–6 people) and holiday units that sleep up to 5 people. Also has wireless internet throughout. Cabins and units ❹–❺

The Town

As the ski fields of Mount Hotham, Mount Buffalo and Falls Creek are less than an hour's drive away, Bright is popular as a **ski base** in winter. In summer **outdoor activities** are on offer – such as paragliding, hang-gliding, bushwalking, horseriding and cycling. Alpine Paragliding, 6 Ireland St (℡03/5755 1753, ⓦwww.alpineparagliding.com), organizes tandem flights for novices, and introductory and full courses leading to a licence. You could also take to the air in a powered hang-glider from Bright Micro-Lights (℡03/5750 1555; 30min; $155) or with the Eagle School of Micro-Lighting (℡03/5750 1174, ⓦwww.eagleschool.com.au), which also does very enjoyable instructor-accompanied tandem flights.

For a change of pace, visit **Boynton's Winery** (daily 10am–5pm; ℡03/5756 2356, ⓦwww.boynton.com.au), 10km northwest of Bright at Porepunkah, on the northeast slopes of the Ovens River Valley. Enjoy the spectacular views of Mount Buffalo while sampling a house wine – they specialize in cool-climate wines. In the summer months they open a café that serves Mediterranean-inspired cuisine. Alternatively, head south to nearby **Wandiligong**, a beautiful village entirely owned by the National Trust, where you'll find the *Wandiligong Café* and **maze** (Wed–Sun 10am–5pm; closed Aug; ⓦwww.wandimaze.com.au;

$10). The hedge maze itself is a lot of fun, but the café is a truly wonderful find, serving salads, freshly squeezed juices and home-made treats, in a tranquil garden at the end of a six-kilometre bushwalk from Bright.

Eating

Bright has plenty of tempting eating options, with its restaurants making use of the fresh produce available locally.

Bright Brewery 121 Great Alpine Rd (near visitor centre). Popular brewery that attracts the crowds with their multi-award-winning beers, good pizza and relaxed outdoor setting. Live blues Sun 2pm. Daily noon–9pm.

Riverdeck Cafe 119 Gavan St. Great deli sandwiches and hearty breakfast with a good outdoor area looking towards the river. Daily 9am–5pm.

Sasha's of Bright 2D Anderson St ☎03/5750 1711. The Czech owner and chef cooks mainly hearty Central European fare (around $30 for mains), and does it well. This is the place to come for Hungarian goulash, smoked pork neck with sauerkraut or crispy skinned duck. Daily 6pm–late; licensed.

Simone's 98 Gavan St ☎03/5755 2266. One of the top Italian restaurants in Victoria; given the quality of the cooking the prices are very reasonable. Tues–Sat 6.30pm–late.

Sweet Retreat 12A Barnard St. This place sells the best coffee in town, despite primarily being a chocolate shop. Mon–Thurs 9.30am–5.00pm, Fri Sun 9.30am–9.30pm.

Mount Hotham and Dinner Plain

Heading southeast out of Bright on the Great Alpine Road, it is 18km to **HARRIETVILLE**, tucked just below **Mount Hotham** and Mount Feathertop. Originally a gold-mining town, it's now a pretty little village of wide, tree-lined streets, and is also a popular skiing base: there are outlets renting skis and chains, a seasonal shuttle-bus service up to the resorts, and several places to stay and eat. Beyond Harrietville, it's a steep ascent to Mount Hotham in the Alpine National Park, the state's highest ski area and self-proclaimed "powder snow capital of Australia". All this actually means is that the snow here can be marginally less sticky than elsewhere. **Dinner Plain**, a resort village 8km from the summit and about 1500m above sea level, has much more of a cosy, alpine-village feel – complete with architect-designed timber houses that are meant to resemble cattlemen's mountain huts – than the somewhat unsightly Hotham resort. With 15km of groomed cross-country trails around the village and an eleven-kilometre trail leading to Mount Hotham, Dinner Plain is really the domain of cross-country skiers, but a regular shuttle-bus ferries downhill skiers to Mount Hotham. Victorian **snowboarding** started at Hotham so there are lots of special facilities here, equipment rental and lessons. During the ski season, tractor-driven carts ferry you around the village and to the start of cross-country trails and skiing areas (all day until late; free), and helicopter shuttle-flights in winter link Mount Hotham with Falls Creek, only a few minutes away by air ($125 return; ☎03/5759 4470), where you can ski or snowboard on the same lift pass. Following the establishment of a fully fledged airport at Horsehair Plain, 20km south of Mount Hotham, with flights from Melbourne and Sydney, it's now easier than ever to get to Hotham and surrounding areas.

A few centres handle bookings for the mainly lodge-style **accommodation**: Hotham Holidays (☎1800 468 426, ⓦwww.hothamholidays.com.au); Mount Hotham Accommodation Service (☎1800 032 062, ⓦwww.mthothamaccommodation.com.au); and Dinner Plain Central Reservations (☎1800 670 019, ⓦwww.dinnerplain.com). For general information about Dinner Plain, go to ⓦwww.visitdinnerplain.com.

Falls Creek

Some 30km east of Bright, in the Upper Kiewa Valley, the town of **Mount Beauty** lies at the base of the state's highest peak, Mount Bogong (1986m). **FALLS CREEK**, 32km further along, on the edge of the Bogong High Plains, has a much more villagey feel than its sister resort at Mount Hotham. It also has probably Victoria's **best skiing**, with the largest snow-making system in Victoria to supplement any shortage of the real stuff, a wide variety of downhill pistes, and good cross-country trails. **Snowboarding** is really big here, too, and in addition there are rides on snowmobiles and snowbikes and a tube park for snowtubing. In mid-January the entire village of Falls Creek, plus visitors, get together to celebrate "A Taste of Falls Creek", a two-day food and wine festival.

For **accommodation** bookings and information, contact Falls Creek Central Reservations (℡1800 2 FALLS, ⊛www.fallscreek.com.au) or ask at the **Mount Beauty Visitor Centre** (daily 9am–5pm; ℡03/5754 1962, ⊛www .visitalpinevictoria.com.au) at 31 Bogong High Plains Rd. The budget-conscious would do best to stay in Mount Beauty and travel to Falls Creek for their skiing: enquire about packages at the Mount Beauty Visitor Centre. Accommodation options in the valley include *Mountain Creek Motel* in Tawonga (℡03/5754 4247, ⊛www.mountaincreekmotel.com; motel units ❹–❺); the wonderful *Braeview B&B* in Mount Beauty (℡03/5754 4746, ⊛www.braeview .com.au; ❺), which has two luxurious B&B guest rooms, one self-contained studio apartment and a separate cottage, all in an established garden; and the super-fancy *Svarmisk Resort and Spa* (℡03/5754 4544, ⊛www.svarmisk.com .au; ❾), which is pure decadence.

Many of the pubs, **restaurants** and lodges in Falls Creek stay open in summer, notably *The Man Hotel* (daily 5pm–late), a cosy pub with great gourmet pizzas on Telemark Street.

Mount Buffalo National Park

Six kilometres northwest of Bright, back along the Ovens Highway, you can turn off into **Mount Buffalo National Park** ($10.30 per car in summer, $14.40 in winter), which encompasses a huge plateau around Mount Buffalo, and has a number of beautiful walking tracks. In 2007 a bushfire destroyed a number of chalets and lodges in the park, and at the time of writing there was still no "roofed" accommodation or eating places available. The best option is to consult the Bright visitor centre on ℡03/5755 2275 or the Parks Victoria

---

Horseriding

Activities of an **equestrian** nature are available with Bogong Horseback Adventures (℡03/5754 4849, ⊛www.bogonghorse.com.au), a very professional and experienced horse-riding operator based on a farm, specializing in three- to seven-day **packhorse** tours across the high plains which they run from December until the end of April (from $1050 per person). They also run two-hour ($70), three-hour ($80) and day-rides ($190 including lunch) through the Kiewa Valley and the lower levels of the Alpine National Park.

Another horse-riding outfit, Packer's High Country Trail Rides (℡03/5159 7241, ⊛www.horsetreks.com), operates from the small hamlet of **Anglers Rest**, further south towards Omeo. Their rides range from one and a half hours ($80) to longer camping treks (from $1620), and they also offer basic accommodation (outdoor toilets and no electricity) in huts that sleep up to three people (❹) at their farm, *The Willows*.

website Ⓦ www.parkweb.vic.gov.au for latest developments. Meanwhile, you can **camp** at Lake Catani in the summer months (Nov–April; booking essential through Parks Victoria on ☏ 13 19 63).

Mount Baw Baw

The ski village at **MOUNT BAW BAW**, near the edge of the Baw Baw National Park, is considerably south of all the resorts and is, strictly speaking, in Gippsland. It's a quiet little place, commanding magnificent views south over much of Gippsland and consisting mainly of private lodges (reservations on ☏ 1800 629 578). Otherwise, try the *Cascade Apartments* (☏ 1800 229 229, Ⓦ www.cascadeapartments.com.au; ❽–❾), which can sleep up to ten people. The entry fee is $30–35 per vehicle per day during ski season. There are seven ski lifts here, and a lift day-pass costs a reasonable $49–59. As at Mount Buffalo, the ski runs are mainly for beginners and intermediates. In addition to downhill skiing and snowboarding, you can ski cross-country on 10km of groomed trails and have a beginner's lesson ($48). For more on Mount Baw Baw, see Ⓦ www .mountbawbaw.com.au.

Transport to and from the mountain has improved, though it's still far from ideal: Baw Baw Betty shuttle (daily; book 24hr in advance on ☏ 03/5165 1136) provides a bus service from Warragul Station (65km south) to the resort ($60 return). If you drive yourself, access is via Noojee, 48km west of Mount Baw Baw. You get there from Melbourne either on the northeastern route via Lilydale and Yarra Junction, or on the Princes Highway via Dandenong and Pakenham, turning off at Drouin. The road between Noojee and the resort is narrow, steep and winding. To make matters worse, there are lots of logging trucks thundering along, so take care. A better alternative if you want to avoid all the hairpins is to take the **new South Face Road** – continue along the Princes Highway to Moe, turn left and head through Erica and just past the town is the turn off for the South Face Road. It's unsealed but it allows all-weather access and amazing views.

Travel details

V/Line monopolizes transport within Victoria, with a comprehensive combination of train and bus services; Melbourne (see p.851), Ballarat (see p.962) and Geelong (see p.921) are the main interchanges. Following are the main V/Line Victorian services; local buses are detailed in the text. Timetables are subject to frequent change – call V/Line on ☏ 13 61 96 or consult Ⓦ www.vline.com.au for the latest information.

Trains

Melbourne to: Albury (1 daily; 3hr 15min); Ararat (2–3 daily; 2hr 25min); Bairnsdale (3 daily; 3hr 35min); Ballarat (6–19 daily; 1hr 30min); Benalla (1 daily; 1hr 50min); Bendigo (17–23 daily; 2hr–2hr 20min); Castlemaine (12–20 daily; 1hr 35min); Colac (2–3 daily; 1hr 50min–2hr); Echuca (1–2 daily; 3hr 25min); Geelong (19–35 daily; 50min–1hr); Sale (3 daily; 2hr 45min); Shepparton (2–3 daily; 2hr 20min); Swan Hill (1–2 daily; 4hr 25min); Wangaratta (1 daily; 2hr 15min); Warrnambool (2–3 daily; 3hr 20min).

Buses

Apollo Bay to: Geelong (2–4 daily; 2hr 30min); Lorne (2–3 daily; 1hr); Port Campbell (Mon, Wed, Fri only; 2hr 5min); Torquay (2–3 daily; 1hr 55min); Twelve Apostles (Mon, Wed, Fri only; 1hr 10min); Warrnambool (Mon, Wed, Fri only; 3hr 25min). **Bairnsdale** to: Canberra (Capital Link 3 weekly; 6hr 20min) via Lakes Entrance (30min), Orbost

(1hr 15min); Narooma/NSW (Sapphire Coast Link 1 daily; 5hr 35min) via Lakes Entrance (30min) and Orbost (1hr 15min).

Ballarat to: Bendigo (10 weekly; 2hr); Castlemaine (5 weekly; 1hr 30min); Daylesford (6 weekly; 45min); Geelong (2–3 daily; 1hr 40min); Hamilton (1–2 daily; 2hr 20min); Horsham (1–2 daily; 2hr 40min); Mildura (5 weekly; 6hr); Mount Gambier (5 weekly; 3hr 35min); Warrnambool (5 weekly; 3hr 5min).

Beechworth to: Bright (1–2 daily; 1hr); Wangaratta (1–3 daily; 30min).

Bendigo to: Echuca (1–2 daily; 1hr 20min); Geelong (5 weekly; 3hr 35min); Horsham (daily; 3hr 15min); Mildura (1–2 daily; 5hr 45min); Swan Hill (1–3 daily; 3hr 15min).

Bright to: Beechworth (1–2 daily; 1hr); Wangaratta (1–3 daily; 1hr 30min).

Castlemaine to: Ballarat (5 weekly; 1hr 30min); Maryborough (1–5 daily; 50min).

Echuca to: Albury (1 daily; 4hr 10min); Bendigo (1–2 daily; 1hr 20min); Melbourne (1–3 daily; 2hr 45min); Mildura (3 weekly; 5hr 35min); Rutherglen (4 weekly; 3hr 40min–4hr 30min); Shepparton (5 weekly; 1hr 25min); Swan Hill (daily; 2hr 10min).

Foster (closest to Wilsons Promontory NP) to: Melbourne (1–2 daily; 2hr 50min).

Geelong to: Apollo Bay (2–4 daily; 2hr 50min) via Ballarat (2–4 daily; 1hr 25min); Ballarat (2–3 daily 1hr 40min); Bendigo (5 weekly; 3hr 25min); Daylesford (5 weekly; 2hr 15min); Castlemaine (5 weekly; 3hr); Lorne (2–4 daily; 1hr 40min); Maryborough (4 weekly; 3hr 5min); Mildura (6 weekly; 9hr); Torquay (2–4 daily; 40min); Warrnambool (Coastlink via Apollo Bay; Mon, Wed, Fri only; 6hr 40min).

Halls Gap (Grampians) to: Stawell (1 daily; 35min).

Hamilton to: Ballarat (1–2 daily; 2hr 20min); Warrnambool (1–2 daily except Sat; 1hr 35min).

Horsham to: Ararat (3–4 daily; 1hr 35min); Ballarat (1–2 daily; 2hr 40min); Stawell (3–4 daily; 1hr 10min).

Lakes Entrance to: Bairnsdale (1–3 daily; 45min); Canberra (Capital Link 3 weekly; 6hr) via Orbost (45min) and Cann River (1hr 45min); Narooma/NSW (Sapphire Coast Link daily; 5hr 35min) via Orbost and Cann River.

Mansfield to: Melbourne (1–3 daily; 3hr); Mount Buller (snow season only; 1–2 daily; 1hr).

Maryborough to: Ballarat (4 weekly; 1hr); Castlemaine (1–5 daily; 50min).

Mildura to: Bendigo (1–2 daily; 5hr 45min); Ballarat (4 weekly; 6hr); Geelong (6 weekly; 9hr); Swan Hill (1–2 daily; 2hr 45min).

Mount Beauty to: Wangaratta (3 weekly; 2hr 40min).

Mount Buller to: Mansfield (snow season only; 1–2 daily; 1hr).

Portland to: Mount Gambier (1–2 daily; 1hr 35min); Port Fairy (1–3 daily; 1hr); Warrnambool (1–4 daily; 1hr 35min).

Shepparton to: Albury (1–3 daily; 2hr 15min–3hr); Melbourne (1–2 daily; 3hr).

Stawell to: Ballarat (5 weekly; 1hr 40min); Halls Gap (Grampians; 1 daily; 35min); Horsham (3–4 daily; 1hr 10min).

Swan Hill to: Albury (1–2 daily; 5hr 45min–6hr 20min); Bendigo (1–3 daily; 3hr 15min); Echuca (1–2 daily; 2hr 20min); Mildura (1–2 daily; 2hr 45min).

Wangaratta to: Beechworth (1–3 daily; 30min); Bendigo (3 weekly; 3hr); Mount Beauty (2 weekly; 2hr 30min) via Bright (1hr 30min); Rutherglen (8 weekly; 30min).

Warrnambool to: Apollo Bay (Mon, Wed, Fri only; 3hr 25min); Ballarat (5 weekly; 2hr 50min); Geelong (Mon, Wed, Fri only; 8hr 50min); Hamilton (1–2 daily except Sat; 1hr 35min); Mount Gambier (1–2 daily; 3hr 25min); Port Fairy (1–4 daily; 35min); Portland (1–4 daily; 1hr 35min).

Flights

Mildura to: Melbourne (4–8 daily; 1hr 10min).

Portland to: Melbourne (1–3 daily; 40min).

11

Tasmania

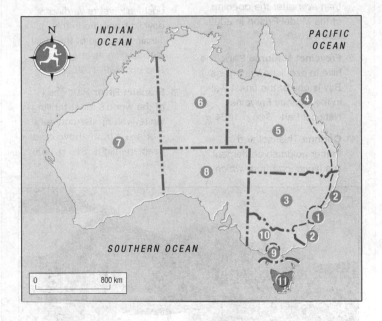

CHAPTER 11 — Highlights

* **Salamanca Market** Lined with old stone warehouses and characterful old pubs, Hobart's Salamanca Place comes alive for its colourful open-air Saturday market. See p.1027

* **Port Arthur** The infamous old penal settlement, the biggest draw on the wild Tasman Peninsula, is more haunting than ever after the opening of the Model Prison in 2008. See p.1049

* **Freycinet National Park** The hike to exquisite Wineglass Bay is one of the finest walks in the glorious Freycinet National Park. See p.1054

* **Corinna** This isolated former goldrush settlement is a launchpad from which to experience the Tarkine, whether by kayak, cruise or foot. See p.1093

* **Gordon River cruise** A cruise up the Gordon River is the easiest way to get a glimpse of the World Heritage-listed rainforest. See p.1099

* **Cradle Mountain–Lake St Clair National Park** Famed for the six-day Overland Track bushwalk, yet rewarding dayhikes abound in this Tassie icon, one of the most glaciated areas in Australia. See pp.1102–1108

* **Franklin River** Raft one of the world's most thrilling white-water roller-coasters – or see it from above on a seaplane flight. See p.1106

▲ Cradle Mountain

Tasmania

There's an otherworldly quality to **TASMANIA**, with its gothic landscape of rain clouds and brooding mountains. This was a prison island whose name, Van Diemen's Land, was so redolent with brutality that when convict transport ended in 1852 it was changed immediately. These days, the island is a far friendlier place. With distances comprehensible to a European traveller – it's roughly the size of Ireland – and resonant echoes of England, Tasmania has a homespun, small-town charm. In winter, when the grass is green, the gentle and cultivated midlands, with their rolling hills, dry-stone walls and old stone villages, are reminiscent of England's West Country. Town names, too, invariably invoke the British Isles – Perth, Swansea, Brighton and Somerset among them. It's a "mainlander's" joke that Tasmania is twenty years behind, and it's true that in some ways it is old-fashioned, a trait that is charming and frustrating by turns. However, things are changing fast. Tasmania now has the fastest-growing tourism sector in Australia, powered by the rise of its cool-climate wine industry, accolades for the superb cuisine of a newly sophisticated café and restaurant scene, booming real estate and immigration, and cheaper and more frequent flights, prompting an increase in luxury accommodation that dares to ditch the chintzy heritage clichés. Recent years have also seen Tasmania re-evaluate its pristine wilderness regions to rebrand itself from heritage island to adventure destination; a sort of New Zealand in the mainland's backyard.

Tasmania is the closest point in Australia to the Antarctic Circle, and the west coast is windswept, wet and savage, bearing the full brunt of the Roaring Forties – and Australia's **whale-stranding** hot spot. The southwest has wild rivers, impassable temperate rainforests, buttongrass plains, and glacially carved mountains and tarns that together form a vast World Heritage Area, crossed only by the Lyell Highway, providing some of the world's best wilderness walking and rafting. With forty percent of the island protected in parks and reserves, it's still one of the cleanest places on Earth: a wilderness walk, breathing the fresh air and drinking freely from tannin-stained streams, is a genuinely exhilarating experience.

When to go

It rarely gets above 25°C in Tasmania, even at the height of summer, and the **weather** is notoriously changeable, particularly in the uplands, where it can sleet and snow at any time of year; the most stable month is February. Winter (June–Aug) is a cold time to visit unless you choose the more temperate east coast; wilderness walks are best left to the most experienced and well equipped at this time of year.

A north–south axis divides the settled areas, with the two major cities, **Hobart**, the capital, in the south, and **Launceston** in the north. The **northwest coast**, facing the mainland across the Bass Strait, is the most densely populated region, the site of Tasmania's two smaller cities, **Devonport** (where the Bass Strait ferries dock) and **Burnie**. Tasmania's **central plateau**, with its thousands of lakes, is sparsely populated, mainly by weekenders in fishing shacks. The sheltered **east coast** is the place to go for sun and watersports; set against a backdrop of bush-clad hills, it has plenty of beautiful deserted beaches and is safe for swimming.

Some history

The Dutch navigator **Abel Tasman** sighted the west coast of the island in 1642. Landing a party on its east coast, he named it **Van Diemen's Land** in honour

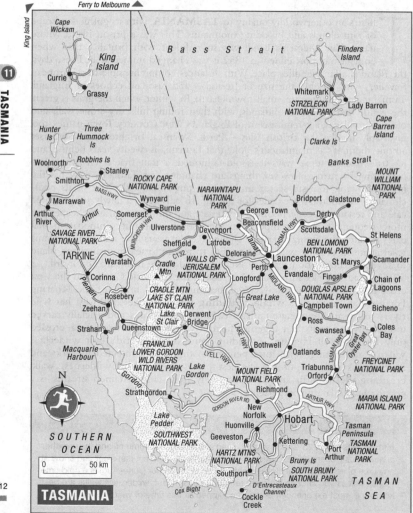

Tasmania's recent history has been shaped not by the postwar industrialization and immigration that transformed the mainland but by a battle over **natural resources**. Forests and water, and the mountainous terrain and fast-flowing rivers meant that forestry and hydroelectricity schemes began early here, under the auspices of the Hydro Electricity Commission (HEC). The flooding of **Lake Pedder** in 1972 led to the formation of the **Wilderness Society**, a conservation organization whose successful **Franklin Blockade** in 1982 saved one of Tasmania's last wild rivers. Bitter controversy over the best balance between conservation and exploitation of natural resources polarizes the state's population between "greenies" and "traditionalists", the former infuriated that both major political parties (Liberal Party and Australian Labour Party) support the clear-felling of old-growth forests (followed by incineration of the remnants). Most wood ends up as woodchips for export to Japanese paper manufacturers; Tasmania is the only state in Australia that woodchips its rainforests. Ongoing conservationist campaigns are aimed at stopping old-growth logging in the **Styx Valley** (p.1046) and nearby Weld and Upper Florentine valleys, and in the **Blue Tier** (p.1059), as well as preventing a pulp mill being built in the bucolic Tamar Valley.

of the governor of the Dutch East Indies. Early maps show it connected to the mainland, and several eighteenth-century French and British navigators, including Bruny d'Entrecasteaux, William Bligh and James Cook – who claimed it for the British – did not prove otherwise. Matthew Flinders' discovery of the **Bass Strait** in 1798 reduced the journey to Sydney by a week. In 1803, after Nicholas Baudin's French expedition had been observed around the island's southern waters, it was decided to establish a second **colony** in Australia and Lieutenant David Bowen was dispatched to Van Diemen's Land, settling with a group of convicts on the banks of the Derwent River at Risdon Cove. In the same year, Lieutenant-Colonel John Collins set out from England with another group to settle the Port Phillip district of what would become Victoria; after a few months they gave up and crossed the Bass Strait to join Bowen's group. **Hobart Town** was founded in 1804 and the first **penal settlement** opened at Macquarie Harbour (Strahan) in 1821, followed by Maria Island and Port Arthur; they were mainly for those who had committed further offences while still prisoners on the mainland. Van Diemen's Land, with its harsh conditions and repressive, violent regime, became part of British folklore as a place of terror, a prison-island hell. Collins was Lieutenant-Governor of Van Diemen's Land until his death in 1810, but it is Lieutenant-Governor **George Arthur** (1824–36) who has the more prominent position in the island's history. His ideas were an influence on the prison settlement at Port Arthur and he was in charge at the time of the **Black Line**, the organized white militia used against the Aboriginal population.

Tasmania practicalities

Although it's small in Australian terms, make sure you give yourself enough time to see Tasmania; if you want to see only its cities, you need no more than a few days, but to get a flavour of the countryside – the great outdoors is the real reason to come here – a couple of weeks or longer is necessary. The Tasmanian Travel and Information Centre in Hobart (℡1800 990 440 or 03/6230 8233, ⓦwww .hobarttravelcentre.com.au) can provide **information** and also book all transport, tours and accommodation; its free information paper, *Tasmanian Travelways*

The attempted genocide of the **Aboriginal peoples of Tasmania** is one of the most tragic episodes of recent history. Ironically, if it were not for American and British sealers and whalers who had operated from the shores of Van Diemen's Land since 1793, abducting Aboriginal women and taking them to the Furneaux Islands in the Bass Strait as their slaves and mistresses, the Tasmanian Aborigines would have disappeared without trace. Until recently, it was stated in schoolbooks that the last Aboriginal Tasmanian was **Truganini**, who died at Oyster Cove, south of Hobart, in 1876. However, a strong Aboriginal movement has grown up in Tasmania in the last thirty years.

The Aboriginal people of Tasmania appear to have been **racially distinct** from those of the mainland, although many of their beliefs and rituals were similar. About twelve thousand years ago, the thawing of the last Ice Age brought rising ocean levels, which separated these people from the mainland and caused their genetic isolation; it's thought that on the mainland new cultures probably entered ten thousand years ago. This isolation was also evident in **cultural development**: they couldn't make fire but kept alight smouldering fire-sticks; their weapons were simpler – they didn't have boomerangs; and although seafood was a main source of food, eating scaly fish was taboo. In **appearance**, the men were startling, wearing their hair in long ringlets smeared with grease and red ochre, while women wore theirs closely shaved. To keep out the cold, they coated their bodies with a mixture of animal fat, ochre and charcoal; women often wore a kangaroo-skin cloak. Men decorated their bodies with linear scar patterns on their abdomens, arms and shoulders. Their **art** consisted of rock carvings of geometric designs, still to be seen in areas on the west and northwest coasts.

When the first **white settlement** was established in the early years of the nineteenth century there were reckoned to be about five thousand Aboriginal people in Tasmania, divided into nine main **tribes**. A tribe consisted of bands of forty to fifty people who lived in adjoining territory, shared the same language and culture, socialized, intermarried and – crucially – fought wars against other tribes. They also traded such items as stone tools, ochre and shell necklaces, and bands moved peaceably across neighbouring tribes' territory along well-defined routes at different times of the year to share resources: the inland Big River tribe, for example, would journey to the coast for sealing. Once they realized the white settlers were not going to "share" their

(ⓦ www.travelways.com.au), is extremely useful, with detailed information on accommodation, attractions, bus timetables, car rental, adventure tours and national parks. It can also be picked up at local tourist offices throughout Tasmania. For general tourist information, check out the government-funded site ⓦ www.discovertasmania.com.au. The **See Tasmania Card** (3-day $165, 7-day $239, 10-day $315; ⓦ www.seetasmaniacard.com), available from visitor centres, provides entry to sixty attractions. Do the sums before you buy – you'll have to travel fast to make it pay its way.

It's easy to find **internet access** in Tasmania, as many towns have a state-government-funded Online Access Centre. The Tasmanian Communities Online website (ⓦ www.tco.asn.au) gives locations of all 66 centres as well as access to town sites.

Getting there

With so many airline companies offering competitive fares from the mainland to Tasmania, and the ferry company now with two ships running between Melbourne and Devonport, it's cheaper and easier to get to Tassie than it's ever been.

resources in this traditional exchange economy but were instead stealing the land, the nomadic people displayed a determination to defend it – by force, if necessary. Confrontation was inevitable, and by the 1820s the white population was in a frenzy of fear – though for every settler who died, twenty Aborigines met a similar fate. In 1828, Governor Arthur declared martial law, expelling all Aboriginal people from the settled districts and giving settlers what was, in practice, a licence to shoot on sight. Alarmed by these events, the British government planned to round up the remaining Aborigines and confine them to **Bruny Island**, south of Hobart Town. In 1830, a mass militia of three thousand settlers formed an armed human barrier, the **Black Line**, which was to sweep across the island, clearing Aborigines before them, in preparation for "resettlement".

The line failed; but unfortunately the final tactic was "divide and rule", in which the Aboriginal people themselves, with their superb tracking skills, were enlisted to help ensnare their tribal enemies. The 135 Aborigines who survived the Black Line were moved in 1834 to a makeshift settlement on Flinders Island. Within four years most of these people died of disease, or as a result of harsh conditions. In 1837, the 47 survivors were transferred to their final settlement at Oyster Cove, near Hobart, where – no longer a threat – they were often dressed up and paraded on official engagements. The skeleton of the last survivor, "Queen" Truganini, originally from Bruny Island, was displayed in the Tasmanian Museum until 1976, when her remains were finally cremated and scattered in the D'Entrecasteaux Channel, according to her final wishes.

The descendants of the original Aboriginal Tasmanians were given a voice with the establishment of the **Tasmanian Aboriginal Centre (TAC)** in the 1970s. The TAC's push for land rights has included the handing over of Wybalenna in Flinders Island and, in 2005, of the whole of Cape Barren Island, to its south. In the 1981 census, 2700 Tasmanians ticked the Aboriginal box; 16,000 did so in 2001. But this huge increase of people proclaiming Aboriginal heritage has ironically not pleased the TAC, whose sympathies lie with the long-documented and distinct Bass Strait communities. Many of those now identifying themselves as Aboriginal are from mainland Tasmania, but of these only descendants of Aborigines such as Fanny Cochrane (see p.1025) and Dolly Dalrymple can produce documents that trace a genealogy back to the time of white settlement.

By ferry

If you've bought a car to travel around Australia, you'll naturally choose to go by ship, and it's also the most romantic way to arrive. From the long-established Port Melbourne departure point, it's a potentially rough, ten-hour trip across the Bass Strait on the TT Line *Spirit of Tasmania* **ferries** to Devonport (daily Port Melbourne and Devonport departing 9pm, arriving 7am; also day sailings daily mid-December to mid-January departing 9am, arriving 7pm; bookings ☏13 20 10, enquiries ☏1800 634 906, ⊛www.spiritoftasmania .com.au). Peak fares operate mid-December to late January; shoulder fares late January to April and September to mid-December, and off-peak fares May to September. On board, there are restaurants, bars and entertainment, and you can choose to sit up on reclining cruise seats (one-way $151–202) or take a private en-suite cabin (pricier with portholes), ranging from basic twins (one-way per person: $231–308) and four-bunk cabins ($193–258) to luxury cabins ($418). Meals are extra.

Book in advance in summer, especially if you want to take a vehicle: cars less than 2m in length cost (one-way) $65, bike/motorbikes cost $6/$45. Cheaper Apex return fares (21-day advance purchase) are available.

By air

Prices are very competitive for **flights** to Tasmania from the mainland with Virgin Blue (☎13 67 89, ⓦwww.virginblue.com.au), with direct services from Melbourne and Sydney to Hobart or Launceston, and from Adelaide to Hobart. Check the website for "Happy Hour" specials (noon–1pm Eastern Standrd Time) and other deals. Qantas' budget arm Jetstar (☎13 15 38, ⓦwww.jetstar.com.au) has direct flights from Melbourne and Sydney to Hobart and Launceston, and from Adelaide to Hobart – a typical advance fare is Melbourne to Launceston one-way at $69, though check the website for specials. Rex Airlines (ⓦwww.rex.com.au) fly from Melbourne to Burnie, as well as from Melbourne to King Island; for other flights to King and Flinders islands, see p.1111.

Qantas itself (☎13 13 13, ⓦwww.qantas.com.au) also has pricier (more comfortable) direct flights from Melbourne and Sydney to Hobart, while QantasLink flies between Devonport and Melbourne. **Fly-drive packages**, which include accommodation, can be particularly good deals; ask at travel agents.

Getting around

With the vagaries of the bus system and the difficulties of using it to get to all those out-of-the-way wilderness places that make Tasmania so attractive a destination, the trend for travellers in the last few years is to hire a car, or for the

---

Bus operators

Bicheno Coach Service ☎03/6257 0293. Runs between Coles Bay and Bicheno, and also offers airport transfers.

Hobart Coaches ☎03/6233 4232, ⓦwww.metrotas.com.au. A regional offshoot of Hobart's city Metro service that heads to Richmond and New Norfolk, and south to Kingston, Snug, Kettering, Woodbridge and Cygnet.

Manion's Coaches ☎03/6383 1221. Launceston to Rosevears, Beaconsfield and Beauty Point.

Maxwell's ☎03/6492 1431 or 0418 584 004. Provides a charter service, based on a minimum of four passengers, from Devonport and Launceston to and around the Cradle Mountain–Lake St Clair area and the Walls of Jerusalem National Park.

Tasmanian Tour Company ☎1300 659 878, ⓦwww.tasmaniantourcompany.com.au. Bushwalking charter service from Devonport to Cradle Mountain, Frenchmans Cap and Walls of Jerusalem.

"Tasmania's Own" Redline Coaches ☎03/6336 1446 or 1300 360 000, ⓦwww.tasredline.com.au. The island's largest operator, referred to in the rest of the text as "Redline", offers frequent scheduled services between Hobart and Launceston via the east coast or direct via the Midland Highway, from Devonport to Hobart via Deloraine and Launceston, and along the northwest coast from Devonport to Burnie and on to Smithton and Stanley.

TassieLink ☎03/6230 8900 or 1300 300 520, ⓦwww.tassielink.com.au. Specializes in scheduled regional transport year-round and bushwalkers' "Wilderness Link" services for the South Coast Track and the Mount Anne Circuit from December to the end of March. Scheduled services run from Hobart to Devonport and Launceston; Hobart to Strahan via Lake St Clair and Queenstown; Hobart to Port Arthur; Hobart south to Dover; Hobart up the east coast to St Helens; Launceston to Bicheno on the east coast via St Marys; and Launceston to Strahan via Devonport, Cradle Mountain and Queenstown. Charters available on request.

Major tour and expedition operators

Another way to get around the island is by taking a **tour**. The excellent **Under Down Under Tours** (☎03/6228 4255 or 1800 064 726, ⊛www.underdownunder.com.au) is a small-group ecotourist outfit aimed at independent-minded travellers. Trips usually depart Launceston or Devonport and include bushwalking and wildlife-spotting, hostel accommodation (which can be upgraded), and some but not all breakfasts and lunches. Their five-day tour ($685) does a loop of the island including Cradle Mountain and the Freycinet Peninsula, while their three-day "Wild West" tour ($440) ticks off Cradle Mountain, Strahan and the Mount Field National Park. Both can be combined into a six- or seven-day trip ($795/825). The "Bloomin Lot" eight-day ($975) or nine-day ($995) versions can be treated as a tour pass with the components done at your leisure.

The operators listed below also offer trips and treks Tasmania-wide:

Bottom Bits Bus ☎03/6234 5093 or 1800 777 103, ⊛www.bottombitsbus.com.au.

Craclair Tours ☎03/6339 4488, ⊛www.craclairtasmania.com.

Island Cycle Tours ☎03/6228 4255 or 1300 880 334, ⊛www.islandcycletours.com.

Rafting Tasmania ☎03/6239 1080, ⊛www.raftingtasmania.com.

Roaring 40s Ocean Kayaking ☎03/6267 5000, ⊛www.roaring40skayaking.com.au.

Tasmanian Expeditions ☎1300 666 856 or 03/6339 3999, ⊛www.tas-ex.com.

Tarkine Trails ☎03/6223 5320, ⊛www.tarkinetrails.com.au.

more intrepid to motorbike or cycle. There are several good-value **tours** aimed at independent travellers that will get you off the beaten track, and any number of **adventure expeditions** will provide transport from the cities as part of the deal (major tour and expedition operators are detailed in the box on above). Alternatively, web-based car-share network CoolPool Tas (⊛www.coolpooltas .com.au) can be a good way to get a cheap ride.

By bus

Several local **bus companies** and charter services (detailed in the box opposite) reach most destinations on the island. You cannot use a mainland bus-pass with any of these, and services are limited, often not running at weekends, especially on the east and west coasts; in winter and spring, services are reduced even further.

Buying a local **bus pass** can be one way of cutting costs, but study timetables carefully before you buy. Redline's **Tassie Pass** comes in 7-, 10-, 14- and 21-day versions ($135/$160/$185/$219) starting from the first day of use. TassieLink's **Explorer Bus Pass** has several formats: a seven-day pass valid for travel over ten days ($208), ten-day over fifteen days ($248), fourteen-day over twenty days ($286), and 21-day over 30 days ($329). A YHA or VIP membership will give you substantial savings on all bus tickets and tours (see p.37).

By car and by bike

Renting a car is a sensible option considering the vagaries of the transport system. Local operators offer reasonable weekly rates including basic insurance (see "Listings" in city accounts); as Tasmania is such a small island, kilometres are usually unlimited, and you don't need a lot of petrol. Though distances seem short compared to the mainland, roads are often winding and mostly two-laned – there are few freeways, except some short stretches on the outskirts of large cities – so **driving** can be slow and tiring. At dusk and night time, you have to be especially careful of animals darting in front of your car, as evidenced by the high number of dead native animals you'll see by the roadside, and huge log trucks are unpleasant and sometimes scary road company. But with relatively few cars, it's easy to relax and enjoy the scenery, also making **cycling** an attractive option, especially in summer, and on the flatter midlands and east-coast routes (otherwise, plenty of gruelling hills will keep you in shape). Several operators in Hobart, Launceston and Devonport rent bikes for touring, or consider the organized cycle tours of Island Cycle Tours (see box, p.1015).

National parks and bushwalking

All **national parks** in Tasmania charge daily (24hr) **entry fees**, often on an honour system, of $11 per pedestrian or cyclist, or $22 per vehicle (including up to eight passengers); if you plan to go bush for longer periods, then a **Parks Pass** will be better value. On offer are an eight-week holiday pass (person, cyclist or motorcyclist $28, vehicle $56) or an annual pass for longer-stayers (car $46 for one park, $90 for all parks); camping fees are not included (though many sites are free anyway). Tasmania's wilderness has always attracted thousands of **bushwalkers**, and many of the churned-up tracks are gradually being boardwalked; keeping to set paths to avoid further erosion is just one of the national park's guidelines, available in a leaflet *Minimal Impact Walking* from the **Tasmania Parks and Wildlife Service**, 134 Macquarie St, Hobart (℡03/6233 2270, ⓦwww.parks.tas.gov.au). This, and all free walking and rafting notes referred to in this chapter, can be downloaded from their website.

Detailed topographic **Tasmaps** (from $9.90) of major walking tracks are available at the Service Tasmania shop at the same address and in all main towns (for locations ℡1300 135 513 or ⓦwww.service.tas.gov.au), as well as in most visitor centres and outdoors shops. It must be emphasized that walking in the wilderness can be dangerous if you're ill prepared: never go by yourself and always register your plans with a park ranger or inform others of your intentions. The brochure *Essential Bushwalking Guide and Trip Planner,* downloadable from ⓦwww.parks.tas.gov.au, gives information about the clothing and equipment needed in these parks, where the weather can change rapidly – even on a warm summer day, hail, sleet or snow can suddenly descend in the highlands, and walkers who have disregarded warnings have died of hypothermia. As a minimum, you'll need wet-weather gear, thermal clothing, walking boots, a sturdy tent, warm sleeping bag, a fuel cooking stove, maps and a compass (which you should know how to use). Gear can be rented from outdoor shops in Hobart, Launceston and Devonport.

Festivals and events

The **Ten Days on the Island** festival is Tasmania's international arts festival, held biennially in March/April in venues around Tasmania (℡03/6233 5700, ⓦwww .tendaysontheisland.org). The big music events are the **Cygnet Folk Festival** (see p.1038, ⓦwww.cygnetfolkfestival.org) and the rock **Falls Festival** (ⓦwww.fallsfestival .com), held over the New Year at Marion Bay (shuttle bus provided from Hobart). On the sports front, the biggest deal is the finale of the **Sydney–Hobart yacht race** (see p.1034), while **Targa Tasmania** is a car rally for GT and sports cars that takes over 2000km of the state's bitumen roads for six days in April or May of each year (ⓦwww.targa.org.au).

Hobart and the east

From Lake St Clair in central Tasmania, the **Derwent River** flows past **Mount Field National Park**, Tasmania's oldest and most popular national park, through well-preserved **New Norfolk**, and towards Hobart, Tasmania's capital. Here, the river estuary widens to form a fine harbour before flowing into the waters of **Storm Bay** and out to the Tasman Sea. **Hobart** is Australia's most southerly city, battered by winter winds and surrounded by a jagged coastline. The hook-shaped **South Arm**, at the entrance to Storm Bay, is echoed by the larger **Tasman Peninsula**, with its infamous convict settlement at **Port Arthur**. To the south, the two tenuously connected halves of **Bruny Island** protect the waters of the **D'Entrecasteaux Channel**. On the mainland opposite Bruny Island is the fertile and cultivated **Huon Valley**, but as you head further south the coastline becomes increasingly wild: there are caves and thermal springs, the **Hartz Mountains National Park** inland, and the **Picton River**, where there's good rafting. The last settlement in this direction is **Cockle Creek**, the starting point for the South Coast Track, which takes you towards the South West National Park (see pp.1108–1111), the great mass of wilderness forming Tasmania's southwest corner.

North of Hobart, the **east coast** of Tasmania is the tamest and most temperate part of the island, providing a popular cycling route past numerous sandy and deserted beaches and some lovely national parks. The **Tasman Highway** follows this coastline from Hobart to Launceston, heading inland through the northeast at **St Helens**, the east coast's largest town. The northeast corner is virtually unpopulated, and the **Mount William National Park** here is a haven for the Forrester kangaroo. Inland are some old tin-mining towns, and superb rainforest remnants and mountain scenery at **Weldborough Pass**, beyond which you pass through rich agricultural and forestry country to Launceston.

Hobart

HOBART is small but beautifully sited, and approaching it from any direction is exhilarating: speeding across the expressway on the Tasman Bridge over the wide expanse of the Derwent River, or swooping down the Southern Outlet with hills, harbour, docks and houses spread out below. The green- and red-tin-roofed timber houses climb up the lower slopes of Mount Wellington, snow-topped for two or three months of the year, and look down on the expansive harbour. It's a city focused on the water: the centre is only a few minutes' walk from the waterfront, where fresh seafood comes straight off the boats in Sullivans Cove, and yachties hang out at old dockside pubs or head for fish and chips served from the punts moored in Constitution Dock. South of Constitution Dock is Salamanca Place, a well-preserved streetscape of waterfront stone warehouses, which is the site of a famous Saturday market, a Hobart highlight. Yacht races and regattas are held throughout the year, while at weekends the water is alive with boats; you can choose any type of craft for a harbour cruise – perfect in the summer when it's dry and not too hot. In winter, though, the wind roars up from the Antarctic and temperatures can drop to 5°C and below.

Australia's second-oldest city, after Sydney, Hobart has managed to escape the worst excesses of developers, and its early architectural heritage is remarkably well preserved – more so than any other antipodean city. There's a wealth of colonial Georgian **architecture**, with more than ninety buildings classified by the National Trust, sixty of which are on Macquarie and Davey streets. **Battery Point**, a village of workers' cottages and grand houses set in narrow, irregular streets, has hardly changed in the last 150 years.

Some history

In 1803, **Lieutenant John Bowen** led a party of 24 convicts from Sydney to settle on the eastern shores of the Derwent River at Risdon Cove. A year later, **Lieutenant-Colonel David Collins** arrived, with about three hundred convicts, a contingent of marines to guard them, and thirty or more free settlers including women and children, and founded Hobart Town on Sullivans Cove, 10km below the original settlement and on the opposite shore. Collins went on to serve as lieutenant-governor of the colony for ten years. For the first two years, food was scarce, and settlers had to hunt local game, creating an early culture based on guns that was later to have terrible effects on the Aboriginal population. The fine deep-water port helped make the town prosperous, and a merchant class became wealthy through whaling, shipbuilding and the transport of crops and wool. The period between the late 1820s and the 1840s was a golden age for building, with the government architect **John Lee Archer** and the convict **James Blackburn** responsible for some of Hobart's finest buildings.

Arrival and information

Hobart **airport** is 17km northeast of the city. Redline's **Airporter Shuttle Bus** ($15 one-way, $25 return; bookings ⓣ 1300 385 511) meets all flights, dropping off at central accommodation, as well as further north in New Town and south in Sandy Bay. A **taxi** into the city centre costs around $40. Redline **coaches** arrive at the **Transit Centre**, 230 Liverpool St (ⓣ 1300 360 000; left luggage $1.50 per item per day; their airport service also drops off and picks up here as well as destinations throughout the city). TassieLink disembarks at the **Hobart Bus Terminal**, 64 Brisbane St (ⓣ 1300 300 520), where there's a free short-term left-luggage service for passengers (or $10 per bag for several days if you're going on a bushwalk). The first stop for general information is the **Tasmanian Travel and Information Centre** at 20 Davey St, corner of Elizabeth St (Mon–Fri 8.30am–5.30pm, Sat & Sun 9am–5pm; ⓣ 1800 990 440 or 03/6230 8233, ⓦ www.hobarttravelcentre.com.au), though it functions mainly as a travel, car-rental and accommodation-booking agency. On a more natural note, the **Tasmanian Environment Centre**, 191 Liverpool St (Mon–Fri 9am–5pm; ⓣ 03/6234 5566, ⓦ www.tasmanianenvironmentcentre.org.au), has lots of books about Tassie's flora and fauna, as well as information on environmental events. For **bushwalking information** and a full range of Tasmaps, head for the Service Tasmania Shop at 134 Macquarie St (Mon–Fri 8.15am–5.30pm; ⓣ 1300 135 513). The Parks and Wildlife Service has an unmanned desk (same hours and number) here with information sheets, or call ⓣ 036233 6191 to talk to a parks officer for advice; other general and bushwalking maps are stocked at the Tasmanian Map Centre, 100 Elizabeth St (ⓣ 03/6231 9043).

City transport

Hobart's public transport system, the **Hobart Metro** (ⓣ 13 22 01, ⓦ www .metrotas.com.au), is useful for getting to more distant accommodation and

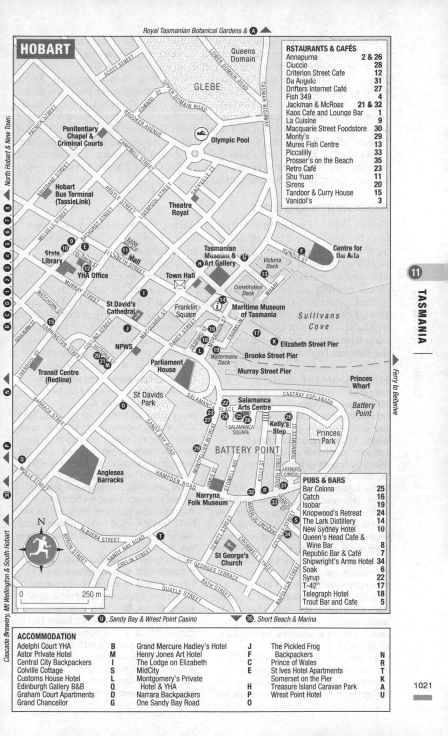

HOBART

Royal Tasmanian Botanical Gardens & **A** ▲

Queens
Domain

GLEBE

RSTAURANTS & CAFÉS

Annapurna	**2 & 26**
Ciuccio	**28**
Criterion Street Cafe	**12**
Da Angelo	**31**
Drifters Internet Café	**27**
Fish 349	**4**
Jackman & McRoss	**21 & 32**
Kaos Cafe and Lounge Bar	**1**
La Cuisine	**9**
Macquarie Street Foodstore	**30**
Monty's	**29**
Mures Fish Centre	**13**
Piccalilly	**33**
Prosser's on the Beach	**35**
Retro Café	**23**
Shu Yuan	**11**
Sirens	**20**
Tandoor & Curry House	**15**
Vanidol's	**3**

Penitentiary
Chapel &
Criminal Courts

Olympic Pool

Hobart
Bus Terminal
(TassieLink)

Theatre
Royal

State
Library

Mall

YHA Office

Town Hall

Tasmanian
Museum &
Art Gallery

Victoria
Dock

Centre for
the Arts

St David's
Cathedral

Franklin
Square

Constitution
Dock

Maritime Museum
of Tasmania

*Sullivans
Cove*

NPWS

Parliament
House

Brooke Street Pier

Elizabeth Street Pier

Murray Street Pier

Watermans
Dock

Transit Centre
(Redline)

St Davids
Park

Salamanca
Arts Centre

SALAMANCA
SQUARE

Kelly's
Step

Princes
Wharf

*Battery
Point*

Princes
Park

BATTERY POINT

Anglesea
Barracks

ARTHURS
CIRCUS

Narryna
Folk Museum

St George's
Church

PUBS & BARS

Bar Celona	**25**
Catch	**16**
Isobar	**19**
Knopwood's Retreat	**24**
The Lark Distillery	**14**
New Sydney Hotel	**10**
Queen's Head Cafe &
Wine Bar	**8**
Republic Bar & Café	**7**
Shipwright's Arms Hotel	**34**
Soak	**6**
Syrup	**22**
T-42°	**17**
Telegraph Hotel	**18**
Trout Bar and Cafe	**5**

0 ____ 250 m

U, Sandy Bay & Wrest Point Casino

35, Short Beach & Marina

North Hobart & New Town:

Cascade Brewery, Mt Wellington & South Hobart

Ferry to Bellerive

ACCOMMODATION

Adelphi Court YHA	**B**	Grand Mercure Hadley's Hotel	**J**	The Pickled Frog	
Astor Private Hotel	**M**	Henry Jones Art Hotel	**F**	Backpackers	**N**
Central City Backpackers	**I**	The Lodge on Elizabeth	**C**	Prince of Wales	**R**
Colville Cottage	**S**	MidCity	**E**	St Ives Hotel Apartments	**T**
Customs House Hotel	**L**	Montgomery's Private		Somerset on the Pier	**K**
Edinburgh Gallery B&B	**Q**	Hotel & YHA	**H**	Treasure Island Caravan Park	**A**
Graham Court Apartments	**D**	Narrara Backpackers	**P**	Wrest Point Hotel	**U**
Grand Chancellor	**G**	One Sandy Bay Road	**O**		

points of interest. The Metroshop, inside the GPO on Elizabeth Street, sells Metro Tens (a pack of ten tickets giving a twenty percent saving) and provides timetables, as do several newsagents; the area outside the GPO – Elizabeth Street, Franklin Square and Macquarie Street – is the **bus** interchange. Single **tickets** cost from $2.20 (valid 1hr 30min); off-peak day-rover passes are $4.40. Captain Fell's Historic Ferries (see p.1025) run a morning and evening commuter **ferry** to Bellerive on the eastern shore (Mon–Fri 7.50am & 5.25pm from Sullivans Cove, 8.15am & 5.40pm from Bellerive; $5; 20min), while the Hobart Yellow Water Cab (☏0407 036 268) has an on-call service (9am–8pm) from only $12. You can hail a **taxi** on the street, or there are taxi stands around the city; central ranks include those outside the *Grand Chancellor* hotel opposite Victoria Dock and on Salamanca Place.

Accommodation

There's plenty of **accommodation** in Hobart, but during the peak season – from Boxing Day and throughout the first week of January, when the yachties hit town – prices shoot up and places can be hard to find. City and dockside **hotels** are the best option for clean, affordable private accommodation, and there are an increasing number of **hostels**, though some are fairly shabby – choose carefully and be aware that bookings are essential in January. In summer, student rooms are available for extended stays at Jane Franklin Hall in South Hobart (☏03/6223 2000). Battery Point is stocked with fairly pricey **B&Bs** as well as several decent holiday **apartments**, with costs comparable to a motel. Most **motels** are situated in Sandy Bay, about 3km south of the centre, or along the Brooker Highway, but B&Bs and guesthouses tend to offer better value.

Hotels and motels

Astor Private Hotel 157 Macquarie St ☏03/6234 6611, ⓦwww.astorprivatehotel.com.au. Old-fashioned character and friendliness in a family-run hotel of 1920s vintage – good value for the central location, too. The cheapest rooms share bathrooms; rates include breakfast. The elegant *Astor Grill* at street level specializes in fine Tasmanian beef and seafood. ❹–❺

Customs House Hotel Corner of Murray and Morrison sts, opposite Watermans Dock ☏03/6234 6645, ⓦwww.customshousehotel.com. Established in 1846, this waterfront pub opposite Parliament House has been stylishly modernized; accommodation is now all en suite, and excellent value for the location. The pub bistro is well regarded and it's a lively drinking spot. ❺

Grand Chancellor 1 Davey St ☏03/6235 4535 or 1800 753 379, ⓦwww.ghihotels.com. Large four-star hotel favoured by older package tourists, with an ugly exterior but a great waterfront location. Facilities include two restaurants, two bars and a health club. ❽

Grand Mercure Hadley's Hotel 34 Murray St ☏03/6223 4355 or 1800 131 689, ⓦwww .hadleyshotel.com.au. National Trust-listed hotel in the heart of the city, an easy walk to the waterfront,

with an old-world feel but all the mod cons of a chain hotel, such as room service and 24hr reception, plus free parking. ❼

Henry Jones Art Hotel 25 Hunter St ☏03/6210 7700, ⓦwww.thehenryjones.com. Combining the ambience of a nineteenth-century waterfront stone warehouse and jam factory with a five-star hotel-cum-contemporary art gallery, this is the place to stay in Hobart. Elegant touches include timber furnishings, sandstone walls, sensuous lighting, huge beds draped in vibrant silks, stunning opaque bathrooms, flat-screen TVs and DVDs. There's dining at the hotel's *Steam Packet Restaurant*, and the adjacent *IXL Bar* is very New York. ❽

MidCity Corner of Elizabeth and Bathurst sts ☏03/6234 6333, ⓦwww.hobartmidcity.com.au. Though rather bland chain fodder, this modern block is central, reasonably priced and rarely full – a handy fallback. ❺

Prince of Wales 55 Hampden Rd, Battery Point ☏03/6223 6355, ⓦwww.princeofwaleshotel.net .au. Ugly modern pub in a great heritage location, whose motel-style rooms have views either of the water or of Mount Wellington. Bathrooms all have tubs. A light breakfast in the bistro is included in the rate. Guest laundry and parking. ❹–❺

Wrest Point Hotel 410 Sandy Bay Rd, Sandy Bay [T] 03/6225 0112, [W] www.wrestpoint.com.au. Attached to the casino at Sandy Bay, this upmarket hotel has riverside rooms, plus a heated indoor pool, sauna and 24hr room service. Luxury tower or cheaper motel section. [5]–[8]

B&Bs and guesthouses

Colville Cottage 32 Mona St, Battery Point [T] 03/6223 6968, [W] www.colvillecottage.com.au. Peaceful, Victorian weatherboard B&B, with lovely en-suite rooms and a pleasant garden. [6]

Edinburgh Gallery B&B 211 Macquarie St [T] 03/6224 9229, [W] www.artaccom.com.au. Funky, retro-styled guesthouse for the post-backpacker market, with a communal kitchen and internet access. Traffic noise is a problem in front rooms. [5]–[6]

The Lodge on Elizabeth 249 Elizabeth St, corner of Warwick St [T] 03/6231 3830, [W] www.thelodge.com.au. Heritage-styled guesthouse in a National Trust-listed mansion; charming or chintzy depending on your taste. Has a guest lounge with fireplace and complimentary port. All rooms en suite, some with spa. Also offers a self-contained cottage with spa (minimum two nights). Light buffet breakfast included. [5]–[6], cottage [6]

Hostels and budget accommodation

Adelphi Court YHA 17 Stoke St, New Town [T] 03/6228 4829, [E] adelphi@yhatas.org.au. Dated motel-like hostel and guesthouse on a quiet suburban street, with the usual facilities. Far from the city (2.5km north), but a 10min walk to North Hobart's restaurant strip, and there's plenty of parking. Bus #15 or #16 from Argyle St, or #25–42, #100 or #105–128 from Elizabeth St. Dorms $20–25, rooms [3]

Central City Backpackers 2nd Floor, 138 Collins St, entrance off Imperial Arcade [T] 03/6224 2404 or 1800 811 507, [W] www.centralbackpackers.com.au. One of Hobart's best hostels, in the spacious quarters of a former hotel. Friendly, efficient management plus clean dorms (three- to twelve-bed, some female-only), singles, twins and doubles. Well-set-up kitchen with dining area, TV and games rooms and internet access. No parking. Dorms $23–27, rooms [3]

Montgomery's Private Hotel & YHA 9 Argyle St [T] 03/6231 2660, [W] www.montgomerys.com.au. Spotless and central small backpackers' a moment's walk from both the action on the water-front and the CBD; its YHA affiliation tends to attract an older clientele. Has a small kitchen and guest lounge. Dorms $28–30, rooms [5]

Narrara Backpackers 88 Goulburn St [T] 03/6231 3191, [W] www.narrarabackpackers.com. Fairly tired hostel in a converted house, whose appeal – such as it is – is its small size and intimate common room; some visitors report that cleanliness is patchy. Dorms, triples, twins and doubles, plus off-street parking. Dorms $23–25, rooms [3]

The Pickled Frog Backpackers 281 Liverpool St [T] 03/6234 7977, [W] www.thepickledfrog.com. Large hostel that's the pick of the backpackers' in the area if only due to its lively vibe, helpful staff and extensive communal area. Other pluses include a bar/café selling cheap beer and meals, sofas, games room with pool table and a wood fire. Functional dorms (four- to eight-bed), plus rooms with sinks; all have free linen. Dorms $23–25, rooms [3]

Caravan parks and self-catering apartments

Graham Court Apartments 15 Pirie St, New Town [T] 03/6278 1333 or 1800 811 915, [W] www.grahamcourt.com.au. Comfortable, well-equipped one- to three-bedroom self-contained apartments set in a pleasant garden, but 2.5km north of the city centre. Disabled access. [4]–[6]

One Sandy Bay Road 1 Sandy Bay Rd [T] 03/6223 3677, [W] www.onesandybayroad.com.au. In a block renovated in 2007, these stylish studio apartments near Salamanca Place all have fully equipped kitchenettes and laundry facilities; some have scenic views. [5]–[6]

Somerset on the Pier Elizabeth St Pier [T] 03/6220 6600 or 1800 766 377, [W] www.somersetonthepier.com. Apartment hotel whose unrivalled location on a pier means water views are guaranteed. Some of the split-level, light-flooded studio and one-bedroom apartments have balconies, all have kitchen and laundry, and there's a gym and sauna. [7]

St Ives Hotel Apartments 67 St Georges Terrace, off Sandy Bay Rd, Battery Point [T] 03/6224 1044, [W] www.stivesmotel.com.au. Recently renovated studios and two-bedroom apartments with full kitchen, TV/dining room, bathrooms with tubs, and neutral decor. All have balconies with water views and free parking. [5]–[6]

Treasure Island Caravan Park 671 Main Rd, Berriedale [T] 03/6249 2379, [E] treasureislandhobart@netspace.net.au. Large park 14km northwest of the city centre, beside the Moorilla wine estate on the banks of the Derwent River; camp kitchen and pool. Camping $25, powered sites $29, vans [2], en-suite cabins [4]

The City

Hobart is small and easy to find your way around, with the streets arranged in a grid pattern running southeast towards **Sullivans Cove**. You can walk anywhere in the city centre, which is mostly flat, although surrounded by some steep hills. The civic centre is **Franklin Square**, bounded by **Macquarie** and **Davey** streets, which between them have a concentration of listed buildings. The main shopping area is **Elizabeth Street Mall**, roughly in the centre of the **CBD** (the Central Business District); Elizabeth Street slopes down from **North Hobart**, known for its many fine restaurants, to the Elizabeth Street Pier on **Franklin Wharf**. Here, at the harbour, fishing boats and yachts are moored, and cruises leave from Brooke Street Pier. **Salamanca Place**, with its row of Georgian warehouses and famous weekly **market**, is on the waterfront on the south side of the cove; a steep climb up Kelly's Steps brings you to **Battery Point**, to the south. Following the Derwent River around from Battery Point, you reach salubrious **Sandy Bay**, with its casino and Royal Yacht Club. To the north of the centre are the parklands of the **Queens Domain**, with the **Royal Botanical Gardens** along the waterfront; from the Domain, the **Tasman Bridge** crosses the river to the residential eastern shore.

There are relatively few sights in Hobart other than the streets themselves, but these are enough to keep you wandering around for hours, stopping at a few museums and parks along the way. While walking through the city, it's worth glancing up occasionally to observe the **street signs**; the streets are often named after important local figures and the signs bear portraits and biographies. Around the docks area, and in Battery Point, interpretive boards point out historic and architectural features. Get self-guided walking maps from the Travel and Information Centre (see p.1020) or go on one of their good historical walking tours.

Franklin Square and around

Set within a fountain in leafy **Franklin Square** is an imposing statue of Sir John Franklin, governor of Van Diemen's Land between 1837 and 1843, and posthumously famous as an Arctic explorer – his ill-fated 1845 expedition discovered the Northwest Passage. From the square, where a giant chess-set gets plenty of use, you can walk south past many of the fine old buildings on Davey Street to **St Davids Park**, at the corner of Murray and Macquarie streets, originally the graveyard of St Davids Cathedral but converted to a park in the early twentieth century. It's a quiet spot containing some important monuments, among them a huge memorial to the first governor, David Collins. Other gravestones have been removed and set into two undulating sandstone walls at the bottom of the park.

Tasmanian Museum and Art Gallery and around

Just north of Franklin Square is the excellent **Tasmanian Museum and Art Gallery** at 40 Macquarie St (daily 10am–5pm; free but charge for some special exhibitions; ⊛ www.tmag.tas.gov.au). The collection is, as the building's name suggests, a mixed bag. Much space is devoted to exploring Tasmania's tragic history, dwelling on penal cruelty, near-genocide and the extinction of animal species.

As you enter, a revamped **Tasmanian Aboriginal room** displays cultural artefacts of the island's indigenous people, including some examples of the kind of exquisite shell necklaces that would have adorned "Queen" Truganini, reputed to be the last Aboriginal Tasmanian. The display gives a comprehensive account of the Aboriginal people, from their tragic near-extermination to

recent events involving land-rights campaigns. Particularly poignant is the
recording of the voice of **Fanny Cochrane** (1834–1905) singing traditional
songs; it is she who was probably the last full-blooded Aboriginal Tasmanian
rather than Truganini, as the myth relates.

Beyond, video-loop footage shows the last known **Tasmanian tiger**
(**thylacine**), which died in captivity in Hobart Zoo in 1936. In 2003, in a
collaborative purchase with Launceston's Queen Victoria Museum and Federal
Hotels in Strahan, the museum acquired a unique, eight-skinned **thylacine rug**
made in the late 1890s, which the three take turns exhibiting. The peculiar,
flesh-eating, dog-like marsupial, which had a rigid tail, stripes and a backwards-
opening pouch, was hunted out of existence by farming families fearful for their
stock and encouraged by the 1888-to-1909 bounty on the creature's head (2184
were paid) – although unconfirmed thylacine sightings still occur. While a
project by Sydney's Australian Museum to resurrect the species using DNA
from pickled specimens was shelved in May 2005, a research team of Pennsyl-
vania University sucessfully sequenced the genetic data in 2008. The feature
introduces a fairly unexciting taxidermy exhibition in the rest of the room;
handy for a heads-up on state fauna, otherwise fairly missable.

There's also is an excellent section on **convicts** – if you can't get to the convict ruins at Port Arthur or Richmond Gaol, this display will convince you of the brutality of the regime – plus an **art gallery** with a display of colonial art featuring several 1830s and 1840s portraits of the well-known "final" Aborigines, including Manalargenna and Truganini, by artists such as **Benjamin Duterrau** and **Thomas Bock**, as well as superb landscape paintings of Tasmania by the nineteenth-century artists **John Glover** and **W.C. Piguenit**. On the same floor an "Islands to Ice" exhibit explores Antarctic ecology and exploration – Tasmania has long been the launchpad for polar expeditions and maintains a scheduled air service to the continent.

Opposite the museum, the modest **Maritime Museum of Tasmania** (daily 9am–5pm; $6; ⓦwww.maritimetas.org), in the red-brick Carnegie Building on the corner of Argyle and Davey streets, houses memorabilia, photographs and exhibits dominated by models of boats – the most impressive is a third-scale model of an open whaling boat. Arranged thematically, it provides an excellent introduction to the history of Hobart as a maritime city.

North of Macquarie Street

There are several worthwhile sights along the straight streets that run north of Macquarie Street (running alongside Franklin Square), particularly Murray and Campbell streets. Three blocks northwest of Macquarie Street, on Murray Street at the corner of Bathurst Street, the **State Library** (Mon–Thurs 9.30am–6pm, Fri 9.30am–8pm, Sat 10am–2pm; ⓦwww.statelibrary.tas.gov.au) holds the **Allport Library and Museum of Fine Arts** (Mon–Fri 9.30am–5pm, Sat 9.30am–2.30pm; free), the Allport family's private collection of eighteenth- and nineteenth-century furnishings, ceramics, silver and glass, paintings, prints and rare books relating to Australia and the Pacific, made as a bequest to the library in 1965. *Zest*, the great little contemporary café at ground level, does good bistro fare and sushi.

The **Theatre Royal**, on Campbell Street at the corner of Sackville Street, is Australia's oldest surviving theatre, built in 1837. It has an intimate interior decorated in Regency style, best seen while attending a performance; otherwise, the staff might let you in for a peek. Further up, at the corner of Brisbane Street, the **Penitentiary Chapel and Criminal Courts** (tours daily except Aug at 10am, 11.30am, 1pm & 2.30pm; 1hr; $8; ⓣ03/6231 0911) comprise a complex of early buildings with two courtrooms, underground tunnels and cells. There's also a rather spooky ghost tour (nightly 8pm or 8.30pm depending on season; $10; 1hr; bookings essential on ⓣ0417 361 392).

The waterfront

The focus of **Sullivans Cove** is busy **Franklin Wharf**, the first commercial centre of Hobart, where merchants erected large warehouses as the colony grew wealthier. In the 1830s, Hobart was one of the world's great whaling centres, and to cater for the growing volume of shipping, the New Wharf – **Princes Wharf** – was built, featuring a row of handsome sandstone warehouses on Salamanca Place. As the new wharf became the focus of port activity, the old wharf developed into an industrial centre of flour mills and factories. Part of the Henry Jones Jam Factory, between Victoria and Macquarie docks on Hunter Street, is now the **Centre for the Arts**, the University of Tasmania's art school. Beyond the original facade in a courtyard there are several large pieces of sculpture and the high-tech face of the art school. Inside, the **Plimsoll Gallery** (daily noon–5pm when there is an exhibition; free; ⓦhttp://fcms.its.utas.edu .au/arts/artschool) has several shows a year featuring the work of contemporary

Tasmanian artists. The rest of the old jam factory has been redeveloped and extended into a complex made up of the luxury *Henry Jones Art Hotel* (see p.1022), with a restaurant, bar, and art galleries featuring Aboriginal art, and wood and furniture design. On the waterfront near the hotel, look out for the several sculptures and a plaque commemorating the links between Hobart and Antarctica, from the first 1840 expedition of the evocatively named *Erebus and Terror* under Captain Ross.

The old docks along Franklin Wharf are thriving: at **Victoria Dock**, lobster boats are moored; at **Constitution Dock**, fish punts sell fresh and cooked seafood and alongside is the Mures Fish Centre, a two-level complex of restaurants and cafés. The stylish development on Elizabeth Street Pier has a slew of hip bars, eateries and luxury hotel-apartments, while Murray Street Pier has been jazzed up with several restaurants. From Brooke Street Pier and Watermans Dock, any number of **cruises** depart (see box, p.1025).

The focus for most visitors, however, is **Salamanca Place**, the old warehouses, shipping offices and storerooms which are now full of arts-and-crafts galleries, speciality shops and cafés, interspersed with atmospheric waterfront pubs. At the end of Salamanca Place, on Castray Esplanade, the old silos have been converted into upmarket apartments. Salamanca Place comes alive for the open-air **Salamanca Market** (Sat 8am–3pm), an event with an alternative feel, wonderful local food – including colourful fruit and vegetable stands – and buskers. Stalls focus on local crafts, particularly woodwork using distinctive Tasmanian timber (often recycled), and there's lots of bric-a-brac and second-hand books and clothes. Several of the narrow lanes and arcades in the area are worth exploring, as is the **Salamanca Arts Centre**, a former jam-canning factory that's now home to a diverse range of arts-based organizations. Downstairs, the Peacock Theatre is the performance venue, and there are several galleries (daily 10am–5pm); upstairs, emerging contemporary artists show at the Long Gallery, with smaller displays in Sidespace.

Through the Arts Centre, Woobies Lane leads to lively **Salamanca Square**, a large public square with a fountain at its centre. The square – nothing special

▲ Salamanca Market

in itself – is ringed with cafés, restaurants and bars with outside seating, and some interesting shops, including the Hobart Bookshop, which has a big Tasmania-related section.

A **guided walk** explores Sullivans Cove and Salamanca Place, starting from outside the Travel and Information Centre (daily 10am; 1hr 30min; $25; bookings ☎03/6230 8233).

Battery Point

Kelly's Steps lead up from Salamanca Place to **Battery Point**, a district with an enduring village atmosphere. With the building of the new wharf in the 1830s, a working-class community grew up behind Salamanca Place; it takes its name from the battery of guns that were once sited on present-day **Princes Park**, protecting the harbour below. The area was first home to waterfront workmen in small cottages and, later, merchants in fine houses. Nowadays, pubs with names such as the *Shipwright's Arms* are the only reminder of the original population. Gentrification has buffed up Battery Point into a prosperous urban village, with streets of immaculately restored historic cottages and the charming flower-filled green of **Arthurs Circus**. The former corner-store shops now host smart cafés and restaurants.

There's a particular concentration of early buildings on De Witt and Cromwell streets. **St George's Church**, on Cromwell, is the joint work of John Lee Archer (responsible for the nave, completed in 1838) and James Blackburn (the tower, added in 1847), the early colony's two best-known architects. **Hampden Road** has more fine nineteenth-century mansions, including one at no. 103 known as "Narryna" (Tues–Fri 10.30am–5pm, Sat & Sun 2–5pm; $6), a house museum furnished with period Georgian antiques.

Queens Domain and Royal Tasmanian Botanical Gardens

The **Queens Domain**, just north of the city centre, is a sparse, bush-covered hill traversed by walking and jogging tracks but positioned between two very busy highways. At the base of the hill on the Derwent, where the trees suddenly become lush and green, are the **Royal Tasmanian Botanical Gardens** (daily 8am–5pm), a formal collection of flower displays and orderly trees. Pick up a leaflet outlining the features of the gardens at any entrance, or from the **Botanical Discovery Centre** at the main entrance on the west side of the park (daily 10am–4.30pm, until 5pm Sept–April; free), where you'll find interactive games and exhibits as well as the **visitor centre**, café and restaurant. It's easy enough to walk to the Domain, following Davey Street or Liverpool Street from the city centre, but the gardens are quite far inside the grounds: from the city centre to the gardens should take you about thirty minutes. Bus #17 or any of the many buses to the Eastern Shore will drop you at Government House, in the centre of the Domain near the gardens, but there's no transport back.

Around the harbour

The estuary of the **Derwent River** is the deepest (and second-busiest) natural port in Australia. Just north of the Queens Domain, at **Cornelian Bay** in **New Town**, you'll find cute fishing shacks and the well-regarded *Cornelian Bay Boat House Restaurant* (☎03/6228 9289), which also has a kiosk for coffees. A bike track runs here from the end of the Queens Domain below the Aquatic Centre (see p.1035). Heading upstream, the scenery becomes increasingly industrial, with a huge zinc-processing plant, but by Berriedale the setting is more unspoilt. Here, the **Moorilla Estate Winery**, off Main Road, has gorgeous river views from its landscaped grounds. Established in 1958, it's one of Tasmania's oldest wineries; you can taste some of its fine cool-climate wines, eat lunch in its wonderful restaurant, *The Source* (T02/6277 9900, Wwww .moorilla.com.au), or stay in five-star chalets ($350), adorned with antiquities from the Moorilla Museum, scheduled to reopen to the public sometime in late 2010; a few exhibits are displayed in the foyer in the meantime. Beyond Berriedale lie Claremont and the riverfront **Cadbury's Factory**, dating from 1921, on Cadburys Road, whose display centre (Mon–Fri Sept–May 8am–4pm, June–Aug 9am–3pm; free) features a video on chocolate production and is an outlet of cut-price goodies. From the city centre, take bus #37, #38 or #39 direct to the factory. Alternatively, you can cruise here (see box, p.1025).

The eastern side of the river is more residential, and looking across you'll see swelling, bush-clad hills with a modest line of homes below. The **Tasman Bridge** connects the eastern shore with the city: it was put out of action for over two years from January 1975, when the 20,000-tonne tanker *Lake Illawarra*, heading for the zinc-smelting works, crashed into it and destroyed two pylons. The ship is still at the bottom of the river, with its cargo of zinc concentrate, as are the bodies of the twelve unfortunate people on board.

The **Kangaroo Bluff Battery** at Bellerive, on the eastern shore – along with its counterparts at Sandy Bay (Alexandra Battery) and Battery Point (Mona Street Battery) – was erected in response to a Russian scare in the late nineteenth century, but it never saw active service. **Bellerive**, which you can reach by ferry from Brooke Street Pier (see p.1024), has a long, sandy beach at the Esplanade; some swim from it, although the water is somewhat polluted. The beach suburb is host to international test cricket at the modern **Bellerive Oval** on Derwent Street (details on T03/6211 4000). There's cleaner water and surf beaches across the promontory from Bellerive at **Opossum Bay** (bus #296 or #300), while **Seven Mile Beach**, on Frederick Henry Bay, offers calmer swimming (bus #292 or #293). Some 10km north of Bellerive is **Risdon Cove**, site of the first European settlement of Van Diemen's Land; interpretive boards explain its early history (bus #267, #269 or #270).

Sandy Bay

Leafy, well-heeled **Sandy Bay**, a suburb just south of Battery Point, is home to a busy shopping centre on Sandy Bay Road. Near the shops, the Royal Yacht Club (where visitors can take a drink) fronts a marina, beside a beach and waterfront park. Further around the bay is the **Wrest Point Casino** on Sandy Bay Road; an incongruous 1970s high-rise, the casino strives to be glamorous, but a rather downmarket tone is set by swarms of tour groups wearing name tags. More glamorous is the annual weekend **Sandy Bay Regatta** in January, when yachts are moored all around Sandy Bay's marinas, the river is filled with boats, and a funfair is held on the waterfront. At weekends throughout the year, too, hundreds of yachts are out on the water. Several buses go to Sandy Bay from the city centre, among them #52–56 and #60, #61 and #94.

Taroona to Kingston

South of the centre, what are defined as Hobart's suburbs terminate at beachside Kingston, reached speedily after 13km on the inland **Southern Outlet** or by a scenic, winding coastal drive via Sandy Bay Road and the **Channel Highway**. En route, at **Taroona**, 10km south of Hobart, the 48-metre-high **Shot Tower** (daily 9am–5pm; $5.50), built in 1870 to make lead shot, gives wonderful views of Hobart and the Derwent Estuary. **Kingston** is a residential suburb with wide, sandy **Kingston Beach**, which is 1km down Beach Road from the large and busy shopping centre. As all sea craft coming into Hobart have to go past the sheltered beach, it's a particularly good place to catch the end of the Sydney–Hobart yacht race. On the Esplanade, there's a cluster of eating options, plus a pub – the *Beachside Hotel* – serving good bistro meals (plus bands Thurs and Fri nights), or the *Citrus Moon* café (daily 9/10am–5pm, Fri till 9pm), diagonally opposite at 23 Beach Rd, is a good choice. Heading south on the Channel Highway, the historical display at Australia's **Antarctic Division Headquarters** (Mon–Fri 9am–5pm; free), on the town's southern edge, can fill you in on Antarctic exploration. To get to Taroona, take bus #60 or #61; bus #61 continues on to Kingston; buses #67, #70 and #80 service Kingston.

Inland to Mount Wellington and Mount Nelson

Heading inland, the route southwest towards Mount Wellington via Davey and Macquarie streets takes you through **South Hobart**, on to Cascade Road and past the pretty **Cascade Gardens** and the nearby **Cascades Female Factory Historic Site** on Degraves Street. The sandstone walls here are all that remain of a prison built in 1827 to house recidivist convict women who were set to work washing and sewing; fascinating interpretive boards tell their story. It's free to visit, though the fudge factory and café beside it (daily 9am–4pm) offer guided tours to fund site conservation (Mon–Fri 9.30am, plus Dec 26–Easter Mon–Fri 2pm; $10; 1hr 15min; bookings ☎03/6233 1559, ⓦwww.femalefactory.com.au). Beyond Cascade Gardens, at 140 Cascade Rd, the magnificent seven-storey **Cascade Brewery** is the oldest in Australia, still using traditional methods and taking advantage of the pure spring water that cascades – of course – down Mount Wellington. **Tours** (daily 9.30am, 10am, 1.30pm & 2pm; 2hr; $20; bookings essential on ☎03/6221 8300; long trousers and covered flat shoes required) are pretty active – there are 220 stairs – but you're rewarded with up to three glasses of draught beer at the end in the brewer's recently renovated original residence. The small **museum** of brewing paraphernalia (Mon–Fri 9.15am–4pm; free) includes a few childhood pictures of the Hollywood actor Errol Flynn, who was brought up in the South Hobart area. If you miss the tour, you can visit the souvenir shop and museum and have a drink at the bar or in the beer garden. To get to the brewery, take bus #43, #44, #46, #47 or #49. Alternatively, you can walk or cycle all the way to Cascades Gardens and past the Female Factory Historic Site along the pathway following the peaceful **Hobart Rivulet** (platypus are often seen here), starting from just behind the Village Cinema on Collins Street near the corner with Molle Street.

In any image of Hobart, **Mount Wellington** (1270m) is always looming in the background, sometimes snow-covered. Access is up winding Huon Road lined with houses as far as **Fern Tree**, from where Pillinger Drive turns into the steep and winding Pinnacle Road to the summit; the nineteen-kilometre drive provides several lookout points. Near the bottom of a walking route that goes right up the mountain (via Fernglade Track, Pinnacle Track and Zig Zag Track; 13km; 2hr 45min one-way; detailed in *Mount Wellington Walks*, $4 from Service Tasmania outlets), the *Fern Tree Tavern* offers teas, meals and views. There are picnic grounds with barbecues, shelters, toilets and information boards at the beginning of the track at Fern Tree, and about halfway up at **The Springs**. Pure, drinkable water cascades from rocks as you climb and the thick bush begins to gradually thin; by the top it's bare and rocky. Here, the stone **Pinnacle Observatory Shelter** (daily 8am–6pm) has details of the magnificent panorama of the city and harbour spread before you, which includes vast tracts of bush and grass plains, and views to Bruny Island to the south and as far as Maria Island to the north; there are toilets but no refreshments available at the top. Metro buses #48 or #49 run to Fern Tree, or the Mount Wellington Shuttle Bus Service can get you to the summit (Mon–Fri 9.30am, noon & 2.30pm, Sat & Sun 9.30am & 1.30pm; $25; 2hr tour includes 30min on top; ℗0408 341 804), leaving from the Travel and Information Centre (see p.1020), or picking up from accommodation. Island Cycle Tours' three-hour Mount Wellington Descent trip includes a visit to the summit, and then a twenty-kilometre downhill mountain-bike ride to Salamanca Place (9.30am & 1.30pm city pick-ups; $75 includes drink and snack; see p.1017). It also offers pedal-and-paddle trips, with kayaking on the harbour.

The views are also terrific from the Old Signal Station on **Mount Nelson** (340m) above Sandy Bay. The station was established in 1811 to announce the appearance of ships in Storm Bay and the D'Entrecasteaux Channel; the signal-man's residence has been converted into a café–restaurant (daily 9.30am–4.30pm), from where you get a panorama of the city below. To get to Mount Nelson, take bus #57 or #58.

Eating and drinking

Hobart may lack the ethnically eclectic range of cuisines of mainland cities, but its dining scene is increasingly sophisticated, boasting a clutch of gourmet **restaurants** that have got the critics salivating. The greatest ethnic diversity of restaurants and cafés is found along the Elizabeth Street strip in North Hobart, including Turkish, Indian, Sudanese and Mexican. In the city centre, inexpensive ethnic places are on Harrington Street between Collins and Liverpool streets, and around the Liverpool Street corner – African, Middle Eastern and the like. **Pubs** are another good source of budget food; menus swing from traditional meat-and-veg stodge to modest Modern Oz dishes. Superlative **seafood** can be had throughout the city, but especially in the restaurants by Victoria Dock and Elizabeth Street Pier, and from the permanently moored punts selling fresh and cooked fish and seafood in Constitution Dock. On Saturdays, the fresh produce and food stalls at **Salamanca Market** (see p.1027) are excellent.

Cafés and takeaways

Ciuccio Shop 9, Salamanca Square. Trendy café-restaurant with big glass windows that offer a grandstand view of the action on the square. Popular with a style-conscious crowd for Italian coffee and food such as gourmet pizza (from $18), salads, pasta and risotto, plus more expensive mains. Mon–Fri from 8.30am, Sat & Sun from 9am.
Criterion Street Cafe 10 Criterion St. The pavement tables outside this relaxed, cosmopolitan café take in appealing Criterion St, with its organic foodstore and retro clothes stores. The Spanish omelette and the gourmet bacon sandwich are both reliable for breakfast, and lunchtime specials include soup, salad, risotto and savoury cheese-cake, with lots of vegetarian options; nothing on main menu over $18. Divine cakes and coffee, too. Mon–Fri 7.30am–5pm, Sat 8.30am–3pm.
Drifters Internet Cafe 33 Salamanca Place, off Montpellier Retreat. Long, cosy nook of a café, its walls covered with paraphernalia of Hobart son

Errol Flynn. Soups, toasted sandwiches and nachos all come under $12. Internet access $1 per 10min, $5 per hour. Daily 10am–6pm.
Jackman & McRoss 57–59 Hampden Rd, Battery Point, and 4 Victoria St. Two stylish eat-in bakeries, both serving excellent pastries and savouries such as gourmet baguettes and pies – the slow-cooked beef is legendary. Battery Point daily 7.30am–6pm (till 5pm Sat & Sun); Victoria St Mon–Fri 7am–4pm.
Kaos Cafe and Lounge Bar 237 Elizabeth St, North Hobart. Trendy, gay-friendly late-night coffee spot, with groovy music and magazines to read. Focaccia, fruit muffins and cakes, plus delicious all-day breakfast.
La Cuisine 85 Bathurst St. Café-patisserie serving excellent French-style pastries and heaps of delicious, healthy salads. Mon–Fri 7am–5pm, Sat 8am–1.30pm.
Macquarie Street Foodstore 356 Macquarie St, South Hobart. Handy stop en route to the Cascade Brewery or Mount Wellington, this colourful, laid-

back café, close to the Hobart Rivulet, is an essential stop for a legendary breakfast – big portions, free-range eggs, and huge and fluffy pancakes – served until 3pm. Mon–Fri 7.30am–6pm, Sat & Sun 8am–5pm. Licensed.

Retro Café 31 Salamanca Place. Relaxed, light and airy place serving one of the best espressos in town, plus wonderful breakfasts. Often full of politicians from the nearby State Parliament and other high-flyers meeting over coffee midweek. Outside tables popular on market day (Sat) and flyers for events cover one wall. Mon–Sat 8am–6pm, Sun 8.30am–6pm.

Shu Yuan Bank Arcade, 64 Liverpool St. This tiny, vibrant place, little more than a takeaway, packs in the customers – many Asian – eager for delicious vegetarian food from a Taiwan-trained chef; delicious, filling and cheap. Also fresh fruit drinks. Mon–Sat 11am–3.30pm.

Restaurants and bistros

Annapurna 305 Elizabeth St, North Hobart ☎03/6236 9500. Popular, casual restaurant serving North and South Indian food. Great masala dosas, plus curry-and-rice lunch specials for under $10. A second, slicker outlet is at 93 Salamanca Place (closed lunch Mon & Tues). Closed lunch Sat & Sun.

Da Angelo 47 Hampden Rd, Battery Point ☎03/6223 7011. A long-standing locals' favourite for an upmarket, tasty Italian meal, including gourmet pizzas; generous portions and good service. Licensed and BYO. Dinner Mon–Sat.

Fish 349 349 Elizabeth St, North Hobart ☎03/6234 7788. A minimalist, modern fish café – order your food at the counter and find a seat. A mite more pricey than other fish-and-chip joints but a considerable cut above the rest ($18–24). Open daily for lunch and dinner. Licensed.

Monty's 37 Montpellier Retreat, Battery Point ☎03/6223 2511. Beloved by locals for a seasonal menu of consistently creative Mod Oz cuisine and a laid-back vibe – fine dining without the fuss. Mains average $26. Booking recommended; dinner only.

Mures Fish Centre Victoria Dock. Set among the yachts and fishing boats, this two-level food centre houses three restaurants, a fishmonger and a café. *Mures Upper Deck* (☎03/6231 1999) is a classy restaurant with lovely harbour views; *Mures Lower Deck* (☎03/6231 2121) has bistro food with cheaper prices; *Orizuru* (☎03/6231 1790; closed Sun) serves Hobart's most authentic sushi – their salmon is delicious.

Piccalilly Corner of Hampden Rd and Francis St, Battery Point ☎03/6224 9900. In an old cottage with village views, this is one of Hobart's best new restaurants; mix-and-match menus are pieced from innovative gourmet taster plates, and Tasmanian wines available by the glass. Expect to pay $75 for a four-plate meal. Bookings recommended; dinner only.

Prosser's on the Beach Long Point Beach Rd, Sandy Bay ☎03/6225 2276. In a relaxing spot in extensive Long Beach Reserve on Little Sandy Bay overlooking the Derwent River, this is Hobart's – and probably Tasmania's – best contemporary seafood restaurant, serving up superb local fresh fish. Asian-influenced dishes vie with simple fish fillets on mash. Prices are very reasonable, with mains around $28–32. Licensed. Lunch Wed–Fri, dinner Mon–Sat from 6pm. Booking essential.

Sirens 6 Victoria St ☎03/6234 2634. Upmarket vegetarian/vegan restaurant serving subtle Mediterranean/North African-inspired food in a lovely plant-filled, high-ceilinged space that's a cross between Gothic and Ottoman Empire styles. Licensed. Mon–Sat from 5.30pm.

Tandoor & Curry House 101 Harrington St ☎03/6234 6905. Good, authentic Indian restaurant serving all the favourites, with mains around $14. Licensed. Closed Sat & Sun lunch.

Vanidol's 353 Elizabeth St, North Hobart ☎03/6234 9307. A popular veteran of the North Hobart scene, this casual, affordable place serves Thai, Indian and Indonesian food. BYO. Dinner Tues–Sun.

Entertainment and nightlife

A lively **nightlife** scene, albeit on a small scale, centres on the waterfront. The focal point is *Knopwood's Retreat* (see p.1033), which attracts a large crowd on Friday and Saturday nights, and has a popular club upstairs. To find out **what's on**, check the gig guide in Thursday's *Mercury*, or pop into *Aroma Records*, 323 Elizabeth St, North Hobart, which has flyers and information, plus a great little café, or in the centre, Ruffcut Records on the mall at 33 Elizabeth St. Online gig guide ⓦwww .thedwarf.com.au is another useful reference.

Tasmania is too small to lure many touring bands, so the ones that play the pubs are mainly local. There's free **live music** in the courtyard at Salamanca

Place on Friday evenings (5.30–7.30pm); also see the *Trout Bar* (p.1034) and *Republic Bar & Cafe* (p.1034). For more interesting gigs, keep an eye on what's happening at the University of Tasmania campus at Sandy Bay (☏03/6220 2861). **Concerts** are staged by the Tasmanian Symphony Orchestra at the Federation Concert Hall and by the Tasmanian Conservatorium of Music at the Conservatorium (5–7 Sandy Bay Rd; ☏03/6226 7306), and in churches around town. Most **tickets** can be booked via Centretainment, at 53 Elizabeth Mall (☏03/6234 5998, ⓦwww.centretainment.com.au).

Pubs, bars, clubs and live music

Bar Celona 24 Salamanca Square. Renovated sandstone warehouse turned into a slick and spacious café (by day) and bar on two levels. The light lunches (from $8.50 to $15) can also be eaten at tables on the square. On Fri and Sat nights DJs play laid-back lounge music on the mezzanine level (9pm–12.30am). Daily 9am–midnight, till 1am Fri & Sat.

Catch 11 Morrison St ☏03/6234 3490. This slick new restaurant and wine bar offers Mod Oz fish dishes (average $28), plus pricey steaks. Mon–Fri & Sun lunch & dinner, Sat dinner only.

Isobar 11 Franklin Wharf. Young and packed, the *Isobar* (Wed 5pm–midnight, Fri 6pm–2am, Sat 7pm–2am) is a weekend favourite, with live music on Fri and Sat; Wed attracts a student crowd. At *The Club* upstairs (Fri & Sat 10pm–5am; Fri $5, Sat $7 or free before 11pm; happy hour 11pm to midnight) DJs play commercial dance on the main floor and there's also an r'n'b room, as well as the quieter *Back Bar*.

Knopwood's Retreat 39 Salamanca Place. A favourite with students, yachties and just about everyone else, this pub has a relaxed, coffee parlour/bar feel, with plenty of magazines and newspapers, plus outside tables. Lunch served Mon–Fri; open until 1am on Fri, when the pavement outside is packed.

The Lark Distillery 14 Davey St. A handy spot to recharge, with pavement tables overlooking Mawson Place. A range of spirits made on the premises can be tasted for free (the single malt whisky has a charge). Also a huge range of whiskies, and an all-Tasmanian wine list. Cheese platters to snack on (and soup in winter). Live folk music on Fri evenings (5.30–8pm; free). A cocktail bar operates nightly except Fri from 6pm to 2am. Mon–Thurs & Sun 10am–2am, Fri 9am–10pm.

New Sydney Hotel 87 Bathurst St ☏03/6234 4516. Hobart's Irish pub, featuring live music nightly except Mon – from traditional Irish to blues and folk. Twelve beers on tap, including Guinness, and decent pub meals (no lunch Sun).

Queen's Head Cafe & Wine Bar 400 Elizabeth St, North Hobart ☏03/6234 4670. Colourful, spacious and casual venue hosting free live music nightly except Sun (Mon–Thurs from 8.30pm, Fri & Sat from 9.30pm), from pub rock to reggae and jazz. Lunch menu ranges from a $5 soup to a $17 chargrilled steak, while dinner includes a $12.50

roast of the day and more meaty mains, including half a kilo of rib-eye steak for $22.

Republic Bar & Café 299 Elizabeth St ☎03/6234 6954. Laid-back lounge atmosphere, funky decor and free music, usually blues and jazz, nightly except Mon; attracts a good crowd, including plenty of students. Excellent meals, too, with lots of seafood on the menu.

Soak 237 Elizabeth St, North Hobart. The funky bar of the *Kaos* café (see above) has plenty of relaxing lounge space, and on Fri and Sat nights there's a club atmosphere, with DJs. Closed Sun.

Shipwright's Arms Hotel Corner of Colville and Trumpeter sts, Battery Point. Old pub with a locals' vibe in posh Battery Point; a great choice for atmosphere after the Sydney–Hobart race. Dishes up a legendary fresh seafood platter.

Syrup 39 Salamanca Place ☎03/6224 8249. Often hosting international guest DJs, this trendy club is on two levels above *Knopwood's*. Different nights and different floors have changing sounds and themes: anything from Sixties theme nights, techno, house, drum'n'bass, and 1980s retro, to live disco and funk. Open from 9pm Thurs, 8pm Fri & Sat (until 6am) and with live bands Sat 3–6pm.

T-42° Elizabeth St Pier ☎03/6224 7742. Stylish lounge bar in a great waterfront location – some tables on the pier – attracting a cross-section of trendies and young professionals. Half the place is an eating area serving well-priced modern Australian meals at lunch and dinner (mains from $20). A good place to try Tasmanian wines, with many available by the glass. Daily 11.30am–1.30am.

Telegraph Hotel 19 Morrison St ☎03/6234 6254. Very popular with the young after-work crowd and university students, possibly due to the lack of cover charge or the cheap beer nights. Occasional DJs and live bands at weekends.

Trout Bar and Cafe Elizabeth St, corner of Federal St, North Hobart ☎03/6236 9777. More an arty café, with a friendly, chatty atmosphere, than a relaxed pub. There's a small menu of pasta, salads, meaty mains and curries, plus music – often jazz or blues, usually free – on Thurs to Sun nights. Lunch Wed–Fri, Sun brunch 11am–3pm, dinner nightly.

Film, theatre and classical music

Centretainment at 53 Elizabeth St Mall (☎03/6234 5998, ⊛www.centretainment.com.au) is a one-stop-shop for all advance theatre and concert tickets.

Federation Concert Hall 1 Davey St ☎1800 001 190, ⊛www.tso.com.au. Home to the Tasmanian Symphony Orchestra, with regular concerts.

The Playhouse Theatre 106 Bathurst St ☎03/6234 1536, ⊛www.playhouse.org.au. The Hobart Repertory Theatre Society, an amateur not-for-profit group established in 1926, puts on at least five plays a year here plus a popular Christmas panto. Premises are also rented out to travelling shows. Advance tickets through Centretainment (see p.1033).

Salamanca Arts Centre 77 Salamanca Place ☎03/6234 8414, ⊛www.salarts.org.au. Base of several performance companies, such as the Terrapin Puppet Theatre, which puts on touring

Festivals and events

Hobart's premier event is the last part of the **Sydney–Hobart yacht race** (see also p.59). The two hundred or so yachts, which leave Sydney on December 26, arrive in Hobart around December 29, making for a lively New Year's Eve waterfront party, complete with fireworks. The race coincides with the fortnight-long **Hobart Summer Festival** (Dec 27 to Jan 9; ⊛www.hobartsummerfestival.com.au), focused on waterfront Sullivans Cove. The major event is **The Taste of Tasmania** (Dec 28–Jan 3: daily 11am–11pm), a gourmet food-fest promoting Tasmanian food, wine and beer, held at Princes Wharf. The main festival features outdoor concerts in St David's Park (the kids' one is free), a circus, symphony concerts, children's theatre in the Botanical Gardens, the 1km Pier-to-Pier River Swim, a Tasmanian film festival, buskers, and night-time gallery openings. The **Australian Wooden Boat Festival** runs over three days in early February in odd-numbered years, marked by a host of boats moored around the docks; activities include theatrical and musical performances and boat-building courses (☎03/6231 6407, ⊛www.australianwoodenboatfestival.com.au). The week-long **Hobart Fringe Festival** in mid-February has visual arts, film and performance components (⊛www.hobartfringe.org; many events free). The whole city shuts down for four days in late October during the **Royal Hobart Show**, an agricultural festival.

shows – including a puppet picnic at the end of Dec in St David's Park. Puppeteers are welcome to come in and look around. Specializing in contemporary works, the Peacock Theatre hosts performances by various local theatre companies. **State Cinema** 375 Elizabeth St, North Hobart ☎03/6234 6318, ⓦwww.statecinema.com.au. Arthouse and foreign films, plus a licensed bar. **Theatre Royal** 29 Campbell St ☎03/6233 2299, ⓦwww.theatreroyal.webcentral.com.au. This

lovely old place (see p.1026) is neither too expensive nor too stuffy, with a broad spectrum of entertainment, from comedy nights to serious drama. Tickets from $17. **Village Cinema Centre** 181 Collins St ☎03/6234 7288, ⓦwww.villagecinemas.com.au. Seven screens showing mainstream new releases; discount day is Tues.

Listings

Airlines Jet Star ☎13 15 38, ⓦwww.jetstar .com.au; King Island Airways ☎03/ 9580 3777, ⓦwww.kingislandair.com.au; Par Avion Wilderness Tours, Cambridge Airport ☎03/6248 5390, ⓦwww.paravion.com.au; Airlines of Tasmania ☎1800 144 460, ⓦwww.airtasmania.com.au; Qantas ☎13 13 13, or their travel centre at 130 Collins St; Tasair, Cambridge Airport ☎03/6427 9777 or 1800 062 900, ⓦwww .tasair.com.au; Virgin Blue ☎13 67 89, ⓦwww .virginblue.com.au.
American Express 74A Liverpool St ☎03/6234 3711.
Banks Branches of all major banks are on Elizabeth St.
Bike rental and tours Ray Appleby at 109 Elizabeth St ($25 for 24hr) is the most central option. Derwent Bike Hire (☎0428 899 169, ⓦwww.derwentbikehire .com; $7 per hr, $20 per day, $90 per week) rents mountain bikes at the beginning of the bike track to Cornelian Bay, by the Cenotaph in the Regatta Grounds.
Bookshops Ellison and Hawker Bookshop, 90 Liverpool St, has an excellent travel section. Fullers Bookshop, 140 Collins St, and The Hobart Bookshop, 22 Salamanca Square, are Hobart's two best literary bookstores. For secondhand books, try Rapid Eye Books, 36–38 Sandy Bay Rd, Battery Point.
Bus companies Redline Coaches, Hobart Transit Centre, 230 Liverpool St ☎1300 360 000; TassieLink, Hobart Bus Terminal, 64 Brisbane St ☎1300 300 520.
Campervan rental Devil Campervans (☎03 6248 4493, ⓦwww.devilcampervans.com.au), Tasmanian Campervan Hire (☎03/6248 9623 or 1800 807 119, ⓦwww.tascamper.com) and Tasmania Campervan Rentals (ⓦwww.tasmaniacampervanrentals.com.au, ☎03 6248 5638), are on Cambridge Rd, near the airport. Prices from $50 per day off-peak to $110 in summer, when minimum rental periods apply.
Camping and outdoor equipment There is a concentration of camping shops on Elizabeth St near Bathurst St, including a big range at Jolly

Swagman Camping World, 107 Elizabeth St; Paddy Pallin, 119 Elizabeth St, has quality outdoor equipment, and provides bushwalking information; Mountain Creek Great Outdoors Centre, 75–77 Bathurst St (☎03/6234 4395), has a big selection and also rents out gear.
Car rental Autorent-Hertz, at the airport and 122 Harrington St (☎03/6237 1111 or 1800 030 222, ⓦwww.autorent.com.au), also has campervans; Avis, at the airport (☎03/6248 5424), offers similar rates; Lo-Cost Auto Rent, at the airport and at 225 Liverpool St (☎03/6231 0550 or 1800 647 060, ⓦwww.locostautorent.com), has older cars and newer models; Rent-A-Bug, 105 Murray St (☎03/6231 0300, ⓦwww.rentabug.com.au), has low-priced VW Beetles.
Diving The Dive Shop, 67A Argyle St (☎03/6234 3428), hires equipment and runs PADI certification courses.
Environment To find out about or to volunteer for environmental conservation programmes, the Wilderness Society's campaign office is at 130 Davey St (☎03/6224 1550, ⓦwww.wilderness .org.au/tas); its shop is at 33 Salamanca Place (beside *Retro Café*).
Hospital Royal Hobart Hospital, 48 Liverpool St ☎03/6222 8308.
Internet There's paid access at the State Library (see p.1026; free for Australian residents, $5.50 per half hr for overseas visitors), but the best rates are at *Drifters Internet Café*, near *Retro Café* at 33 Salamanca Place ($5 per hr; also cheap phone cards for calling overseas).
Laundry 87 Goulbourn St (daily 6.30am–8pm).
Pharmacy Macquarie Pharmacy, 180 Macquarie St (daily 8am–10pm; ☎03/6223 2339); North Hobart Pharmacy, 360–362 Elizabeth St (daily 8am–10pm; ☎03/6234 1136).
Post office GPO, corner of Elizabeth and Macquarie sts (Mon–Fri 8am–6pm). Poste restante: Hobart GPO, TAS 7000.
Swimming pool Hobart Aquatic Centre, corner of Liverpool St and Davies Ave (Mon–Fri 6am–10pm,

Sat & Sun 8am–6pm; $5). Heated swim centre with waterslides and bubblejets. Also gym and fitness centre.

Taxis City Cabs ℡ 13 10 08; Combined Services ℡ 13 22 27.

Travellers with disablities The Commonwealth Carelink Centre (℡ 1800 052 222) and the Aged and Disability Care Information Service, 181 Elizabeth St (℡ 03/6228 5799, ⓦ www.adcis.org .au), are excellent sources of information, providing free mobility maps of Hobart. Hobart City Council produces a free *Hobart CBD Mobility Map*, available from their HQ on the corner of Elizabeth and Davey sts (℡ 03/6238 2711). City Cabs (℡ 13 10 08 or 03/6274 3103) have specially adapted vehicles.

YHA Tasmania Head office, 28 Criterion St ℡ 03/6234 9617, ⓦ www.yha.com.au (Mon–Fri 9am–5pm).

Around Hobart

Picturesque channels, orchards and islands define the landscape south of Hobart. The D'Entrecasteaux Channel region and the Huon Valley form Tasmania's premier **fruit-growing** district, which once exported millions of apples to England; when the UK joined the European Community in the 1970s, however, two-thirds of the apple orchards were abandoned. The region is also heavily forested, and around **Geeveston** magnificent woodlands are still logged. **Hartz Mountains National Park** and the **Picton River** are easily accessible to the west of Geeveston and you can get wonderful views of both, and of old-growth forests, from the **Tahune Forest AirWalk**. As you head down the coast, caves and thermal springs are all accessible en route to **Cockle Creek**, the southern-most point you can drive to in Australia, with foot access along a track into the South West National Park. Offshore, across the D'Entrecasteaux Channel from **Kettering**, **Bruny Island** – Truganini's birthplace – has deserted beaches and coastal bushwalks. To the north, you can head inland to **New Norfolk** and on to **Mount Field National Park**, while to the east lies historic **Richmond** and, on the Tasman Peninsula, the old penal settlement at **Port Arthur**.

South: the D'Entrecasteaux Channel, Huon Valley and beyond

The **Channel Highway** (B68) hugs the coastline south from Hobart and makes a lovely drive around the shores of the **Huon Peninsula**, circling back alongside the Huon River to Huonville. Heading to Huonville directly, it's a much shorter 37km on the **Huon Highway** (A6), which then heads south for 64km, terminating at Southport. An excellent free fold-out guide map, *The Huon Trail*, is available from visitor centres; it outlines the **Huon Discovery Trail**, a series of signs and interpretive boards detailing points of interest off the Channel and Huon highways.

The Channel Highway

On the Channel Highway beyond Taroona and Kingston (see p.1029), **KETTERING**, 34km south of Hobart, is a thriving fishing port, with an attrac-tive marina. It's from Kettering that you catch the ferry for Bruny Island (see p.1042). The unpretentious *Oyster Cove Inn* (℡ 03/6267 4446; ⓦ www .view.com.au/oyster; rooms share bathroom; B&B; ❹) is right on the water, not far from the ferry terminal, and has fantastic views from a restaurant that special-izes in seafood and local produce. More upmarket, *Herons Rise Vineyard* on Saddle Road (℡ 03/6267 4339, ⓦ www.heronsrise.com.au; ❻) has luxury self-contained cabins gazing across the marina. Inside the excellent **visitor centre** at the ferry

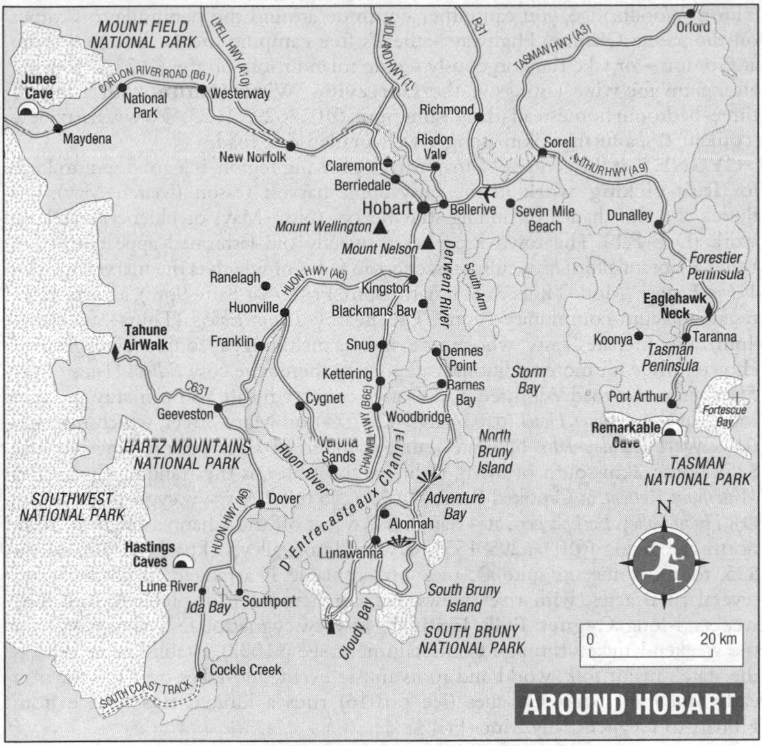

terminal (see opposite), the *Mermaid Café* has good food and coffee (daily 9am–5pm; licensed), plus **internet access**. Roaring 40s Ocean Kayaking, based at the marina (see opposite; ☎03/6267 5000, Ⓦwww.roaring40skayaking.com.au), rents **sea kayaks** (from $20 per hour, $60 per day), and organizes day-trips to Bruny Island ($160), plus longer trips at weekends.

The pretty village of **Woodbridge**, 4km further south, with its quaint general store and wooden meeting hall, had a big makeover when the *Woodbridge Hotel* was demolished in 2003 to make way for the $10-million *Peppermint Bay* (☎03/6267 4088, Ⓦwww.peppermintbay.com.au). An enviable waterfront location offers views across to Bruny in the smart restaurant, or those with tighter budgets can drink in the views from the deck of a bar which serves upmarket pub food. A providore sells local goods, from cheese to smoked salmon, and there's an art gallery featuring Tasmanian art. Another foodie attraction is the **Grandewe Sheep Cheesery** (Sept–June daily 10am–5pm, July & Aug Wed–Sun 10am–4pm; free) 1km south of the centre. You can **stay** in the *Old Woodbridge Rectory* (☎03/6267 4742, Ⓦwww.oldwoodbridgerectory.com.au; [5]), an attractive B&B with disabled access, or there are spectacular self-contained studios 2km uphill at *Peppermint Ridge Retreat* (☎03/6267 4192, Ⓦwww.peppermintridge.com.au; [7]), whose eco-credentials are as impressive as their lofty spaces and Channel views. Woodbridge's **Online Access Centre** is at the West Winds Community Centre. You can get to Kettering and Woodbridge with Hobart Coaches on weekdays (two buses daily).

From Woodbridge, you can either continue around the peninsula to Cygnet on the scenic Channel Highway – there's free camping (no facilities) en route at Gordon – or take the gorgeously scenic inland route on the C627, detouring after 5km for wine tastings at the **Hartzview Wine Centre**, with a luxury three-bedroom homestead (daily 9am–5pm; ℡03/6295 1623, Ⓦ www.hartzview .com.au; Ⓖ), a further 2km along a well-graded dirt road.

CYGNET, at the centre of a major fruit-growing region, is a good spot to look for **fruit-picking work** in the busy apple-harvest season (March–May), but there's also the chance of finding strawberry- (Nov–May) or blueberry-picking work (Dec–Feb). The town itself has a sweetly old-fashioned appearance that belies a vibrant alternative cultural scene, the focus of which is the marvellous *Red Velvet Lounge* (Mon–Thurs & Sun 8am–5pm, Fri & Sat 8am–9pm), an arty café/ restaurant-cum-community centre. The nearby *Lotus Eaters* (Thurs–Sun 9am– 4pm) also prepares tasty wholesome meals, including a couple of vegetarian choices, while for more traditional café society, there's the cosy *School House Coffee Shop* across the road. All three places offer counter meals. You can **stay** in clean rooms at the *Cygnet Hotel* (℡03/6295 1267; Ⓔ) on Mary Street, which manages the *Cygnet Holiday Park* opposite (same number; $10 per person, powered sites $25). Some 2km south of town, right on the water, is the tranquil *Cygnet Bay Waterfront Retreat*, at Crooked Point (℡03/6295 0980, Ⓦ www.cygnetbay.com.au; Ⓖ). *Huon Valley Backpackers*, at 4 Sandhill Rd just off the Channel Highway, 4km north at Cradoc (℡03/6295 1551, Ⓦ www.huonvalleybackpackers.com; dorms $25, rooms, some en suite Ⓒ; pick-ups available if arranged in advance), on several rural acres, with river views, has contacts for fruit-picking work. The weekend-long **Cygnet Folk Festival** (Ⓦ www.cygnetfolkfestival.org; $80 for the weekend; tickets through Centretainment, see p.1033), established in 1982, is the state's major folk, world and roots music event, and takes over the town in early January. Hobart Coaches (see p.1016) runs a limited **bus** service from Hobart to Cygnet (daily Mon–Fri).

The Huon Highway: Huonville and around

The commercial centre of **HUONVILLE** is the focus of the region's apple industry, and another place where the prospect of finding work in the apple-harvest season (March–May) is good; it's also known for its delicious Huon Valley mushrooms. Once a rather redneck place, the town is edging towards a more alternative character suited to its picturesque position on the Huon River. The **Parks and Wildlife Service visitor centre** and shop at 22 Main Rd (Mon–Fri 9am–4.30pm; ℡03/6264 8460) has information on all parks and reserves, and sells park passes, books, maps and basic walking gear. There's also a community-based drop-in **Environment Centre** at 17 Wilmot Rd (daily 9am–5pm; ℡03/6264 1286), northwest of the roundabout near the Parks shop, with a makeshift **café** inside. This, or *Cafe Moto* (daily 8am–6pm) opposite, makes a more appealing option than the outpost of chain bakery *Banjo's* (daily 6am–6pm) on the main street. Another good place to eat is *Huon Manor Bistro* (℡03/6264 1311; Tues–Sat noon–2.30pm & 6–8pm, Sun noon–2.30pm), a reasonably priced restaurant-cum-bar in a Federation-style riverfront homestead, just by the bridge into town.

A jetboat ride ($65) is the most popular of several river excursions with Huon River Cruises (℡03/6264 1838, Ⓦ www.huonjet.com), based at the **Huonville Visitor Centre** (daily 9am–5pm; same phone; internet access $2 per 30min) – it's located on The Esplanade, as the Channel Highway is called coming into town from Cygnet. Huonville's **Online Access Centre** is at 23 Wilmot Rd. TassieLink runs a regular service from Hobart to Huonville on weekdays, and one daily at weekends.

At **GROVE**, 6km back towards Hobart on the Huon Highway (A6), the **Apple Heritage Museum** (daily 9am–5pm; $3) celebrates the local produce. The museum is far more interesting than it sounds, with hundreds of varieties of apples in harvest season (March–May) and assorted apple paraphernalia from what was once a huge export industry.

Some 3km northwest of Huonville via Wilmot Road, the picturesque hamlet of **RANELAGH** is home to the lauded *Matilda's of Ranelagh* at 44 Louisa St ([T]03/6264 3493, [W]www.matildasofranelagh.com.au; [6]), a B&B in an 1850 National Trust-listed mansion within English-style gardens. Arguably more appealing are the luxury tepees and eco-cabins deep within the rainforest provided by *Huon Bush Retreats* ([T]03/6264 2233, [W]www.huonbushretreats.com; camping $15, tepees [5], cabins [7]) – it's signposted 5km south of Ranelagh. Just out of Ranelagh, sleek vineyard-set winery/restaurant *Home Hill*, at 38 Nairn St (wine tasting daily 10am–5pm; lunch Wed–Sun, dinner Fri & Sat, morning and afternoon tea daily; Sun lunch booking essential; [T]03/6264 1200), has a stunning backdrop of the peaks of Sleeping Beauty.

Southwest beyond Huonville, the road follows the west bank of the Huon for 8km to **FRANKLIN**, a bucolic community dating from 1839 with several fine old buildings and weatherboard homes facing the river. The estuarial river brings a hint of the sea to the town, as does Franklin's chief attraction, the **Wooden Boat School**, where you can observe students from around the world on a unique 18-month course learning traditional wooden-boat building and restoration (daily 9.30am–5pm; $6; [W]www.woodenboatschool.com). You can **stay** in the rather heritage-heavy, colonial-era *Franklin Lodge* ([T]03/6266 3506, [W]www.franklinlodge.com.au; [5]) or in self-catering accommodation such as the hilltop cabin *Kay Creek Cottage* ([T]03/6266 3524, [W]www.kaycreekcottage.com; [5] includes breakfast provisions), 1km south of the centre. There's a varied modern menu at the waterfront *Petty Sessions Gourmet Cafe* (daily 10.30am–3.30pm, plus dinner Thurs–Tues; last orders 8pm; licensed). Other options include *Franklin Woodfired Pizza*, around 300m north of *Petty Sessions* (from 5pm Mon–Fri, from 4pm Sat & Sun), and *Aqua Grill*, opposite the fire station, which rustles up tasty fish and chips, delicious Huon Valley mushrooms and Tassie scallops.

Geeveston and around

Two huge upright logs serve as the entrance to sleepy and solid **GEEVESTON**, a traditional logging town in the heart of the Southern Forest whose proximity to the Tahune Forest AirWalk (see p.1040) has brought a touch of tourism gloss. Confrontation between conservationists and the timber industry here led to the so-called "Battle of Farmhouse Creek" in 1986, a dispute won by the conservationists, after which some of the forests were awarded World Heritage listing. The Forestry Commission received millions of dollars in compensation, to be used on special forestry projects, one of which is the **Forest and Heritage Centre** in the town hall on Church Street (daily 9am–5pm; [T]03/6297 1836, [W]www.forestandheritagecentre.com.au; free), which also has a **visitor centre**. Displays explain how the Southern Forests grow, and give a fairly one-sided history of logging in the area, with much talk about sustainable forests. There's also a gallery and outlet of local woodcrafts and a woodturner in residence (lessons are available). The centre serves mostly as a primer for Forestry Tasmania's Tahune Forest AirWalk 26km southwest along the now-sealed Arve Road – it's a good idea to buy tickets here in high summer to avoid queues at the attraction itself. En route to the AirWalk, on the drive along Arve Road, several boardwalks have been constructed through magnificent swamp gum and eucalypt forests, detailed on the free leaflet that's handed out.

Most visitors skip them in their hurry to the **Tahune Forest AirWalk and Visitor Centre** (daily Oct–March 9am–5pm, April–Sept 10am–4pm; $22; ☏03/6297 0068, ⊛www.tasforestrytourism.com.au), a $4.5-million project which has been the major attraction of Tasmania's Far South since it opened in 2001. The 597-metre-long, steel-framed walkway is supported by twelve towers and suspended 25–48m in the air at the level of the tree canopy of the surrounding old-growth forest and, thrillingly, above the confluence of the rivers, with magnificent views across to the Hartz Mountains. For more thrills, there's the **Eagle Glide**, an aerial cable that whizzes you individually across the forest for an extra $33. Below, the riverside Huon Pine boardwalk provides an easy twenty-minute return stroll to huge and ancient Huon pines. The visitor centre has a Forestry Tasmania interpretive display, while the attached licensed café focuses on local gourmet products. If you're picnicking, there are great shelters with roaring fires and gas barbecues for even the wildest day; camping is also allowed here.

Twenty-four kilometres along Arve Road a turn-off heads southwest to the rugged **Hartz Mountains National Park**, with its glacial lakes, rainforests and alpine moorlands; a day-walk map is available from the Forest and Heritage Centre. From Arve Road, a stony, unsealed track winds up for 12km, with several stopping-off points; 2km from the end of the track is a very short walk to Waratah Lookout with great views over the Huon Valley and the Southern Forests. Another walk (4km) heads off to the sometimes-snowcapped Hartz Peak (1255m); most of the trail is boardwalked, but parts are wet and boggy underfoot and there's the potential for fog, icy winds and snow at any time – recommended for well-prepared walkers only.

The **Picton River** skirts the Hartz Mountains from its source deep in the South West National Park; with its frothing rapids, intermittent gentle sections and magnificent wilderness scenery, it's a popular, short (and affordable) **rafting** alternative to the Franklin River. Rafting Tasmania (see p.1017) runs year-round day-trips from Hobart for $115.

One of the few places to **stay** in Geeveston is *Cambridge House*, National Trust-listed home of the Geeves family on the main road 200m beyond the centre (☏03/6297 1596, ⊛www.cambridgehouse.biz; ❺); cheaper, more modern upper rooms share a bathroom. TassieLink has a Hobart–Geeveston service (five daily Mon–Fri, one daily Sat & Sun).

Dover and around

DOVER, 21km from Geeveston, is an attractive fishing village on a large bay, **Port Esperance**, fed by the Esperance River. There are trees everywhere, and lush hills surround the village, backed by the clear, virtually triangular outline of **Adamsons Peak** (1226m), snowcapped in winter. Boats moor off a jetty in the bay, where two tiny tree-covered islets are silhouetted against the sky at dusk.

The hub of Dover is the *Dover Hotel*, on the Huon Highway (☏03/6298 1210, ⊛www.doverhotel.com.au; dorms $20; rooms ❸), beside an apple orchard and rolling fields, with an old-fashioned dining room that overlooks the water. More appealing are the modern waterfront studios of *Driftwood* (☏03/6298 1441, ⊛www.driftwoodcottages.com.au; ❻), while a short way further around the bay, past the jetty, *Dover Beachside Tourist Park* on Kent Beach Road (☏03/6298 1301, ⊛www.dovertouristpark.com.au; camping $20; powered sites $27; cabins ❹) is scenically sited beside a creek. Six kilometres south along the highway at **Strathblane** is the truly marvellous ⚵ *Far South Wilderness Lodge and Backpackers* (☎03/6298 1922, ⓦwww.farsouthwilderness .com.au; dorms $25; TassieLink will drop off outside on request) on an inlet of the Esperance River in eighty acres of unspoilt forest. It rents kayaks when they are not being used by the school groups that occasionally take over the complex – backpackers are housed in a small modern building in the forest away from the main complex. A great place to **eat** in Dover itself is central *Dover Woodfired Pizza* (daily 4–10pm; BYO), whose wall-length windows overlook the water; it's near the **Online Access Centre**. Although you can find fuel and supplies 20km south at **Southport** (the last place to get either), there's more choice and better value in Dover. TassieLink runs a service to Dover (Mon–Fri 1–2 daily, plus extra services Dec–April).

Some 31km from Dover are the Hastings Caves, in the foothills of Adamsons Peak, with the **Thermal Springs State Reserve** en route. The small, shallow and rather tepid springs, ranging from 20–30°C, are no great shakes, but the setting is lush and there are several walks in the grounds, as well as a pleasant café and visitor centre (☎03/6298 3209; ⓦwww.parks.tas.gov.au; $5, or cave ticket includes pool entry). Tickets to visit **Hastings Caves**, a few kilometres further on from the springs, must be bought from here: Newdegate Cave, the best, is open daily for tours (hourly: Sept–April 10am–4pm, May–Aug 11am–3pm; 45min; $24); it's always wet and cold inside, so bring something warm to wear. Southern Wilderness Eco Adventure Tours (☎03/6297 6368 or 0427 976 368) run a Glow Worm Adventure Caving Trip (4hr; $65), though the company's future was uncertain at the time of writing; call for the latest.

Cockle Creek

South of Southport at Ida Bay, the **Ida Bay Railway** (☎03/6298 3110, ⓦwww.idabayrailway.com.au; $25; Oct–April daily 9.30am, 11.30am, 1.30pm & 3.30pm; May–Sept Wed, Sat & Sun 10am, noon & 2pm) is a 1940s bush-train that makes a two-hour return trip to the coast. You can camp by the terminus ($8 per person) or hire a cabin (❸) should you want to stay. Beyond Ida Bay, unsurfaced Cockle Creek Road takes you past picturesque sheltered bays and coastal forests, where wild flowers bloom in summer, to **COCKLE CREEK** on the lovely **Recherche Bay** (pronounced "research" by locals), so named because it was here that the French expedition under **Bruny D'Entrecasteaux**, sent to look for the missing La Pérouse expedition (see "Sydney", p.149), set up for four weeks in 1792 and again in 1793. As well as the important botanical research carried out by naturalist Labillardière, a garden was established and cordial meetings with the Aboriginal people were recorded.

The only provision at the small settlement clustered around the Recherche Bay Community Centre is an emergency phone. Beyond, there are lots of free camping spots along the shore (one-month limit), as well as caravans inhabited semi-permanently mainly by fishing-obsessed retirees after the abundant crayfish, cockles and fish in the bay. Pit toilets and water are the only facilities. The wooden bridge across Cockle Creek leads to the **South West National Park** where an interpretive board outside the intermittently staffed office (to speak to a ranger, contact Huonville NPWS on ☎03/6264 8460; see p.1038) provides a fascinating history from Aboriginal, French, whaling and other perspectives. It's a five-minute walk to a waterfront bronze sculpture of a baby southern right whale, and from here the easy Fishers Point walk takes you around the coast (4km return; up to 2hr), but the most popular walk is the muddy but boardwalked first part of the **South Coast Track** to the beach at South Cape Bay and back (4hr return; moderate difficulty); the entire length of the track is for the very experienced only, but this portion gives you a small taste (see p.1110 for details of the whole walk). TassieLink has a "Wilderness Link" service to Cockle Creek from December to the end of March.

Bruny Island

One of the best places in Tasmania for beautiful, lonely beaches and shorter coastal walks is **Bruny Island**. Almost two distinct islands joined by a narrow isthmus (where you can sometimes see Little penguins from a specially constructed viewing platform), it's roughly 71km from end to end and has a population of only four hundred. The cost of taking a car across on the ferry deters casual visitors, so the island is never very full. The ferry from Kettering goes to substantially rural North Bruny, although most of the settlements, and places to stay and eat, are on South Bruny – the more scenic half, with its state forests and reserves.

Arrival, information and getting around

The **ferry from Kettering** (see p.1036) sails at least nine times daily (Mon–Sat 6.35am–6.30pm, till 7.30pm Fri, Sun 7.45am–6.30pm; 20min; ☎03/6273 6725; $25 return per car or $30 public holidays, motorbikes $11, bikes $3, foot passengers free). The **Bruny D'Entrecasteaux Visitor Centre** at the Kettering ferry terminal on Ferry Road off the Channel Highway (daily 9am–5pm; ☎03/6267 4494, ⓦwww.tasmaniaholiday.com or www.brunyisland.net) books accommodation, much of which is in self-catering cottages (stock up on groceries and petrol in Kingston (see p.1029), as island prices are high and choice limited). The centre can also supply you with **information** on the island, including a good free map. Bruny Island's **Online Access Centre** is near the *Hotel Bruny* on School Road, Alonnah.

As there is no public transport on the island, you'll need your own car or bike to get around unless you come on the excellent small-group **tour** from Hobart with Bruny Island Ventures (☎03/6229 7465, ⓦwww.brunyisland.net.au), or Bruny Island Charters, which will pick you up at the Oyster Cove Marina in

▲ Bruny Island

Kettering (Oct–May daily 9am; $110) for its popular three-hour **wildlife cruise** down the coast and around Fluted Cape, following the spectacular cliff line to a seal colony. If you're lucky you'll see dolphins and maybe even a southern right whale, as well as abundant birdlife (Oct–May daily 11am from the jetty at Adventure Bay; $100; ☎03/6293 1465, ⓦwww.brunycharters.com .au). They also offer the cruise as part of a return trip from Hobart (Hobart pick-up 8am, returning 5.30pm; $165 including lunch).

If you're driving or cycling, be aware that many of the island's roads are unsealed – even the stretch of speedy highway will suddenly become a dusty unsealed road for kilometres at a time. Petrol is only available at Dennes Point, Adventure Bay, Alonnah and Lunawanna. Hobart Coaches operates services from Hobart to Kettering that connect with a couple of the ferries (see p.1036).

Accommodation

Adventure Bay Eco Village Adventure Bay ☎03/6293 1270, ⓦwww.adventurebayholiday village.com.au. In the southern sweep of the bay, a couple of kilometres beyond the *Captain James Cook Caravan Park*, this is a gorgeous setting for cabin accommodation – look out for an endemic colony of white Bennetts wallabies. Motorhome sites $22, cabins ❸–❹, cottages ❺
Bruny Beach House Nebraska Rd, Denees Point ☎0419 315 626, ⓦwww.brunybeachhouse.com. Beach shack chic in a stylish two-bedroom cabin whose deck boasts sweeping views over beach and bay. Minimum two nights. ❺
Captain James Cook Caravan Park Adventure Bay ☎03/6293 1128, ⓦwww.capcookolkid.com .au. You can camp opposite the beach at this caravan park, which is central but less attractive than the *Adventure Bay Eco Village*. Camping $18, powered sites $22, vans ❷, cabins and units ❺
Cloudy Bay Cabin Cloudy Bay ☎03/6293 1171, ⓦwww.cloudybaybrunyisland.com.au. Secluded, self-catering, simple wood cabin located above a sweep of wild beach and powered by solar energy and gas. The getaway par excellence. ❺
Explorers Cottages Lighthouse Rd, 1km south of Lunawanna ☎03/6293 1271, ⓦwww.brunyisland .com. Comfy cottages on Daniels Bay with wood

combustion fires. Facilities include a communal laundry. ❺
Hotel Bruny Alonnah ☎03/6293 1148. Basic motel-style rooms; though it's unattractive, it has uninterrupted water views and meals are available (see p.1044). ❸
Inala Just north of Cloudy Bay ☎03/6293 1217, ⓦwww.inalabruny.com.au. Two comfortable self-contained buildings – one four-star cottage, one five-star spa cottage – owned by a wildlife guide in a pretty area of bush. ❻–❼
Lumeah Quiet Corner ☎03/6293 1265, ⓦwww .lumeah-island.com.au. A good place to stay near Adventure Bay is this three-bedroom, comfortable homestead with an outside spa and attractive garden. ❺
Morella Island Retreats Just north of Adventure Bay ☎03/6293 1131, ⓦwww.morella-island .com.au. Several secluded retreat cabins in 25 acres of gardens, with a café (see p.1044) and great views. ❻–❽
The Tree House 1km north of Alonnah ☎03/5255 5147, ⓦwww.thetreehouse.com.au. Raised wooden house near the beach north of Alonnah that sleeps up to four; open-plan accommodation is stylish but homely, water views are wonderful. ❻

The island

There's no town at **Roberts Point**, where the ferry docks on the north of the island, just a phone box, some public toilets, a post box and, in the summer, a stall selling cherries. The main settlement on **North Bruny** is **DENNES POINT** at the northern extreme of the island, which has a general store (petrol sold) and attached café, and a jetty. This is a popular spot for weekend getaway "shacks" for Hobart citizens fond of fishing. A detour off this route, 3km off the main road along an unsealed road, is the secluded settlement of **Barnes Bay**, where pretty Shelter Cove was the first "Black station" to be established for the forced resettlement of Aboriginal people (see box, p.1088). There's a small jetty which is a peaceful spot to contemplate the boats bobbing in the cove, and a pebbly beach, but no facilities – though you can stay here in the *Bruny Beach House* (see p.1043).

At the northern end of the isthmus connecting the two islands, the **Neck Game Reserve** (free) acts as a sanctuary for Little penguins and muttonbirds which inhabit rookeries in the sand dunes here. A wooden boardwalk (with stairs) descends over the burrows to the beach, and an interpretive board provides information on the birds, best sighted between September and February as they return to their burrows after dusk. Atop the tallest sand dune here, reached by a high wooden stairway, is a small monument to **Truganini** (the "last" Tasmanian Aborigine, who was born here as one of the 70-strong Nuenonne band of the South East tribe), and you can take in superb views of the southern part of the island, where three former reserves have been turned into **South Bruny National Park**. You can see the Fluted Cape State Reserve region to the east of Adventure Bay; here, a steep climb to the top of the Cape (2hr 30min return) offers still better views. The Labillardière State Reserve area occupies the western "hook" of South Bruny Island; a winding, bumpy road leads to the **Cape Bruny Lighthouse** (guided tours by arrangement $8; ℡03/6298 3114), built in 1836 and manned until 1996; beyond this, a seven-hour walking trail explores the peninsula. East of the hook, across **Cloudy Bay**, is the final chunk of the national park, with its great sweep of surf beach. You can do a spot of bushcamping here (pit toilet only, no water), and at Neck Beach about 1.5km from the isthmus viewing point (pit toilet, water, shelter with barbecue). North of Cloudy Bay, *Inala* (see p.1043) doubles as the base for Inala Nature Tours (half-day to extended customized trips) run by a qualified biologist.

ADVENTURE BAY is the main settlement on the east coast of South Bruny, and the principal tourist centre strung along Adventure Bay Road. You can swim from the beautiful sandy sweep of beach, and there's a general store (petrol sold) with an ATM, and several accommodation choices. The **Bligh Museum of Pacific Discovery** (daily 10am–5pm; $4) charts Bruny's links with early explorers and seafarers for whom it provided a safe refuge after the arduous journey across the Southern Ocean, and the museum displays maps, documents, paintings and artefacts relating to landings here. *The Penguin Café* (daily 10am–5pm, plus dinner Sat; ℡03/6293 1352; licensed & BYO) does tasty vegetarian dishes, gourmet burgers and yummy cakes. Just north of town, the *Hothouse Café* at *Morella Island Retreats* (see p.1043; bookings essential for dinner) offers unusual dining in a hothouse surrounded by the veggie patch, and with panoramic views across Neck Beach and all the way to Mount Wellington.

On the west coast, along the D'Entrecasteaux Channel, **ALONNAH** is the main settlement. As well as a general store and post office here (petrol sold) on Bruny Main Road, the *Hotel Bruny* (see p.1043) offers good-value counter meals, and has the island's only bottle shop.

Five kilometres south at **LUNAWANNA**, the Mangana Store (daily 8am–6/7pm) sells petrol, groceries and hamburgers; the bakery next door bakes pizzas (Thurs only). From Lunawanna, it's a scenic drive south to Cloudy Bay.

New Norfolk, Mount Field National Park and Maydena

Heading inland from Hobart through the Derwent Valley towards Mount Field National Park, the A10 hugs the Derwent River for the 50km to agricentre **NEW NORFOLK** – the original settlers were moved here from Norfolk Island (see p.298) between 1806 and 1814. The sizeable town – nothing special despite a few colonial buildings, but a last chance to pick up supplies before a trip to Mount Field National Park – has been at the centre of the hop-growing industry for 150 years, and there are still oast houses in the surrounding hop fields. The broad stretch of the Derwent here is beautiful and swimmable, disturbed only by thrillseekers in jet boats: Devil Jet runs high-speed rides through the rapids (daily 9am–4pm, on the hour; 30min; $60 per person, minimum two people; ☎03/6261 3460, ⓦ www.deviljet.com.au), leaving from the Esplanade. The river-facing *Bush Inn* at 49 Montagu St, the main road, claims to be Australia's oldest continuously licensed **hotel**, which is one excuse for what is now a fairly shabby boozer. On the same street at no. 21, the antique-furnished *Old Colony Inn* in a former hop store lays on the heritage theme fairly thick (☎03/6261 2731; ❹), otherwise *Willow Court Motel* on George Street, on the other side of the main drag, is an excellent modern budget option (☎03/6261 4281, ⓦ www.willowcourt.com.au; dorms $30, rooms ❸). For considerably more comfort, the luxuriously refurbished manor house *Woodbridge on the Derwent* (☎03/6261 5566, ⓦ www.woodbridgenn .com.au; ❽) is located beside the road bridge over the Derwent.

From New Norfolk, you can visit the **Salmon Ponds** (daily Oct–April 9am–5pm, May–Sept 10am–4pm; $7), 18km west on the Glenora Road in Plenty; established in 1864, this is Australia's oldest trout hatchery, set in formal gardens, with six display ponds and a café-restaurant.

Hobart Coaches has eight **buses** on weekdays from Hobart to New Norfolk and three on Saturday; the buses leave from Metro Hobart's Elizabeth Street terminus. TassieLink also runs to New Norfolk (five weekly) on their scheduled year-round service to Queenstown. New Norfolk's **Online Access Centre** is on Charles Street.

Mount Field National Park

It's 37km through pretty rolling countryside full of hop fields from New Norfolk to **Mount Field National Park**, a high alpine area with tarns created by glacial activity where, in winter, there's enough snow to create a small ski field. At the base, the magnificent stands of **swamp gum** (the tallest species of eucalypt and the tallest hardwood in the world), along with the many **waterfalls**, help make this Tasmania's most popular park. Most people come here to see the impressive **Russell Falls**, which cascades in two levels. It's close to the park entrance and can be reached on an easy thirty-minute circuit walk. Longer walks continue on to **Horseshoe Falls** (1hr) and **Lady Barron Falls** (3hr return). The best short walk is the **Tall Trees Track** (1hr 30min), where huge swamp gums dominate; the largest date back to the early nineteenth century.

To get away from the tour-group mob, several shorter walks leave from various spots along the Lake Dobson Road, which leads high up to **Lake Dobson**, 16km into the park in the area of the alpine moorlands and glacial lakes. From the lake car park, you can go on plenty of longer walks, including treks along the tarn shelf that take several days, with huts to stay in along the way. The walk to **Twilight Tarn**, with its historic hut, is one of the most rewarding (4hr return), or you can continue on for the full tarn-shelf circuit (6hr return). A shorter option is the **Pandani Grove Nature Walk** (with an accompanying leaflet available from the ranger station – see below), a forty-minute circuit of the lake, including a section of tall **pandanus** – the striking heath plant which, with its crown of long fronds, looks like a semitropical palm. You'll need your own transport to reach these higher walks, or you could come with the small-group Bottom Bits Bus (see p.1017) from Hobart on a Mount Field day-trip which includes a walk around Lake Dobson ($105).

For information on the walks, to register for overnight hikes and to talk to the ranger, drop in to the **Mount Field Ranger Station** at the entrance to the park (daily 9am–4pm; ℡03/6288 1149), a complex also housing a café, shop and interpretive centre. An excellent range of free pamphlets details the natural environment alongside several of the walks in the park. There's also information here about walks in the South West National Park, several of which can be started from Scotts Peak Road, which runs off the Gordon River Road to the west of Mount Field. If you want to stay in the vicinity, head for the tiny settlement of **NATIONAL PARK** on Maydena Road, a ten-minute walk from the park, where there's basic pub **accommodation** at the *National Park Hotel* (℡03/6288 1103; ❹), with evening **meals** offered from Thursday to Saturday plus Sunday lunch. Just outside the entrance to the park are refurbished 1950s-style chalets at *Russell Falls Holiday Cottages* (℡03/6288 1198; ❺). Within the park there's the well-equipped *Land of the Giants* campsite (℡03/6288 1526; camping $10 per person, powered sites $30) and hikers' cabins (℡03/6288 1149; ❶) at Lake Dobson – an excellent base from which to explore the park's alpine regions. The nearest fuel and basic stores are 7km away at Westerway.

Maydena and around

Nearby **Junee Cave State Reserve** is prime platypus-spotting territory; to get there head 11km southwest to **MAYDENA**, then right onto the narrow, winding Junee Road for 3.5km. A ten-minute walk from the reserve entrance through lush rainforest will bring you to **Junee Cave**, popular with cave divers. As you enter Maydena, *Southwest Adventure Base* (℡03/6288 2210; ⓦwww.southwestadventurebase.com.au; dorms $25, rooms ❸) is a laid-back hostel-style homestay, or at the other end of the village on the Tyenna River there are stylishly renovated cottages at *Giants' Table* (℡03/6288 2293, ⓦwww.giantstable.com.au; ❺–❻); its à la carte **restaurant** serves delicious meals, with plenty of options for vegetarians. A nearby lake has a resident population of platypuses. Maydena's **Online Access Centre** is in the Maydena Kindergarten on Holmes Street.

Out of Maydena, the **Styx Valley** is known as the "**Valley of the Giants**" after its huge swamp gum (*eucalyptus regnans*) – some of which are over 95m tall, 5m wide at the base and over 400 years old – in a large remnant of old-growth forest that's suffered damage from logging activities. There has been a long-running conservationist campaign aimed at protecting 150 square kilometres of this forest as the Styx Valley of the Giants National Park; contact the Wilderness Society (see p.1035) for details and to get hold of a self-guided-drive leaflet.

Richmond

RICHMOND, on the Coal River about 25km north of Hobart and surrounded by undulating countryside scattered with wineries, is one of the oldest and best-preserved towns in Australia. Settlers received land grants in the area not long after the fledgling colony had been set up in 1803, and in 1824 Lieutenant-Governor Sorell founded the town, on the route between Hobart and the east coast. Soon, traffic to the new penal settlement at Port Arthur began to pass through, and Richmond's strategic location made it an important military post and convict station when Richmond Gaol was built in 1825; by the 1830s it was the third-largest town in Tasmania. In 1872, however, the **Sorell Causeway** was opened, bypassing Richmond, which became a rural community with little incentive for change or development. Most of the approximately fifty buildings – plain and functional stone dwellings – date from the 1830s and 1840s, and many are now used as galleries, craft shops, cafés, restaurants and guesthouses; the gorgeous village green is still intact. A free leaflet and map, *Let's Talk About Richmond*, is available at the gaol and details the buildings. Attractions along Bridge Street include the wooden **Richmond Maze** (daily 9am–5pm; $6.50) and the **Old Hobart Town Model Village** (daily 9am–5pm; $12), a large-scale outdoor model of Hobart in the 1820s.

Richmond's most authentic drawing card, however, is the sandstone, slate-roofed **Richmond Gaol** (daily 9am–5pm; $7), Australia's oldest intact example of an early prison. The prison's function was mostly to house prisoners in transit or those awaiting trial, and to accommodate convict road gangs working in the district; the east wing was designed to hold female convicts, who could not be accommodated at Port Arthur. Informative signs explain the features of the gaol, which now seems sombre but incongruously handsome, set around a courtyard. Richmond also has the distinction of having both Australia's oldest Roman Catholic church – that of **St John**, which dates in part from 1837 – and its oldest bridge. The graceful, arched-stone **Richmond Bridge** was constructed in 1823 under harsh conditions using convict labour; legend says that it's haunted by the ghost of the brutal flagellator, George Grover, who was beaten to death by the convicts and thrown into the river during its construction.

Practicalities

Hobart Coaches run four **bus** services a day from Hobart (Mon–Fri; buses leave from Metro Hobart's Elizabeth St terminus), and TassieLink also drops off on their Hobart to Swansea service (1 daily Mon–Fri during term time; Tues, Thurs & Sat only during school holidays). The Richmond Tourist Bus (⊕0408 341 804; $25) departs the tourist centre in Hobart twice daily (9.15am & 12.20pm) and leaves Richmond at 12.50pm & 3.50pm. The **Online Access Centre** is on Torrens Street. Unsurprisingly, heritage properties dominate when it comes to **places to stay**. *Prospect House* (⊕03/6260 2207, ⓦwww .prospect-house.com.au; ➏) is a Georgian country mansion set in landscaped grounds, with a well-regarded licensed restaurant for dinner; it's on your left as you come into town on Cambridge Road. The central *Richmond Arms Hotel*, 42 Bridge St (⊕03/6260 2109; ➍–➎), has decent self-catering accommodation in its converted stone stables, or there's the cheaper *Richmond Cabin and Tourist Park*, on Middle Tea Tree Road behind *Prospect House* (⊕03/6260 2192; camping $10 per person, powered sites $26, cabins ➌–➎), with shady pitches and a small heated pool.

For **food**, the *Richmond Wine Centre* at 27 Bridge St (⊕03/6260 2619; lunch daily, dinner Wed–Sat) is an upmarket café-restaurant in a weatherboard cottage with pretty gardens, outside tables and a focus on Tasmanian produce. The award-winning, Swiss-run *Richmond Bakery* on Edward Street, just off Bridge Street, has an attached café; you can eat in the courtyard or take away to picnic tables on the village green.

The Forestier and Tasman peninsulas

The fastest route from Hobart to the **Tasman Peninsula** heads northeast along the Tasman Highway and then across the **Sorell Causeway** to the small town of **Sorell**, your last chance for shopping and banking; on the huge expanse of Pittwater, windsurfers are out in force on a sunny day. From Sorell, the Arthur Highway heads 34km southeast to **Dunalley** (fuel available), where a bridge crosses the narrow isthmus to the **Forestier Peninsula**. The bridge regularly opens to let boats through, which can cause delays. Once across, it's a further

42km to the infamous **Eaglehawk Neck**, the narrow point connecting the two peninsulas, once guarded by vicious dogs that in effect turned the Tasman Peninsula into a kind of prison island. Of the substantial military station here, only one building survives, the timber **Officers Quarters** dating from 1832. The NPWS has turned it into a fascinating mini-museum, which provides a useful overview of Tasmanian history as well as detailing the site, and there's an entertaining eight-minute sound-and-silhouette diorama which tells the story of the infamous bushranger **Martin Cash**'s swimming escape from Eaglehawk Neck. Entry is free and the museum stays open as long as the nearby Officers Mess General Store, where there's an ATM, café and takeaway.

Eaglehawk Neck Backpackers (☎03/6250 3248; camping $8, dorms $20, rooms ❷), at 94 Old Jetty, 1km west of the Arthur Highway on the Forestier Peninsula side of Eaglehawk Neck, is a fine **place to stay** to explore the area – friendly, non-smoking and green (in both senses of the word). It's also tiny, however, so phone to confirm there's space. For more luxury, the *Lufra Hotel*, near the Officers Quarters, has above-average rear rooms and swish new suites that command awesome views over the bay (☎03/6250 3262 or 1800 639 532 or 03/6250 3262, ⓦwww.lufrahotel.com; ❹–❼). As well as two good-value suites, the *Eaglehawk Café & Guesthouse* (☎03/6250 3331, ⓦwww.theneck.com.au; ❹; café daily: summer 9am–8pm, winter 9am–5pm) prepares a tasty and reasonably priced menu that ranges from filled baguettes to home-made pies (rabbit, venison and seafood). It's located on the main road just past the blowhole turn-off.

Southwest of Eaglehawk Neck at the small settlement of **Koonya**, **Cascades Historic Site** is a well-preserved 1840s Probation Station that has been

Exploring the Tasman Peninsula

While Port Arthur, at the very bottom of the Tasman Peninsula, is the major attraction, the hardly developed peninsula has several good **bushwalks**, and some truly impressive rock formations on the rough ocean side. Some of the finest coastal features are around Eaglehawk Neck: just to the north, there's the **Tessellated Pavement**, onto which you can climb down at low tide; and to the south, off the highway, the fierce **Blowhole**, the huge **Tasman Arch**, and the **Devils Kitchen**, a sheer rock cleft into which the sea surges. Much of this area was proclaimed the **Tasman National Park** (☎03/6250 3497, ⓦwww.parks.tas.gov.au) in 1999; the **Tasman Trail** is an exhilarating 16km coastal walk starting from the Devils Kitchen and ending at **Fortescue Bay**, which has a good camping area (otherwise, the bay is 12km down a dirt road east off the Arthur Highway). You can download walking notes for the Tasman Trail from the NPWS website (see p.1018). South of Port Arthur, several walking tracks begin from **Remarkable Cave**: to Crescent Bay (5hr return), Mount Brown (5hr return) and Maingon Blowhole (3hr return).

The Eaglehawk Dive Centre, 178 Pirates Bay Drive (☎03/6250 3566, ⓦwww.eaglehawkdive.com.au), offers **dive-boat charters** (equipment included) at low rates to caves, shipwrecks, kelp forests and nearby seal colonies, with an underwater visibility of 15–30m. A glorious way to see the towering 190-metre cliffs and surging sea-caves in southern Tasman Peninsula is from the water on an eco-cruise – expect to see and learn about giant kelp, jellyfish, sea eagles, the seals on Tasman Island and, if you're lucky, dolphins and even whales. Sealife Experience (☎03/6253 5325, ⓦwww.sealife.com.au; daily Sept–March 10am, Dec–March also 2pm; 3hr; $99); departing from a car park at Pirates Bay, near the blowhole, operates glass-bottomboat tours, while Tasman Island Cruises (☎03/6250 2200, ⓦwww.tasmancruises.com.au; daily 10am, Dec–May also 2pm; 3hr; $100) jets down the coast from Port Arthur in a high-speed boat. Both cruises hug the coast for over 50km and provide commentaries on geology and fauna.

owned by a farming family for five generations and is now converted into self-catering cottages, most with open fires and one with a spa (*Cascades Colonial Accommodation*; ☎03/6250 3873, ⓦwww.cascadescolonial.com.au; ➏–➐). The peaceful, rural site has a half-hour waterfront walk. The TassieLink Port Arthur service can drop you off at either settlement.

Port Arthur

The most unceasing labour is to be extracted from the convicts...and the most harassing vigilance over them is to be observed.

Governor Arthur

PORT ARTHUR was chosen as the site for a **prison settlement** in September 1830, as a place of secondary punishment for convicts who had committed serious crimes in New South Wales or Van Diemen's Land itself, men who were seen to have no redeeming features and were treated accordingly. The first 150 convicts worked like slaves to establish a timber industry in the wooded surroundings of the "natural penitentiary" of the Tasman Peninsula, with narrow Eaglehawk Neck guarded by dogs. The regime was never a subtle one: **Governor George Arthur**, responsible for all the convicts in Van Diemen's Land, believed that a convict's "whole fate should be ... the very last degree of misery consistent with humanity". Gradually, Port Arthur became a self-supporting industrial centre: the timber industry grew into shipbuilding, there was brickmaking and shoemaking, wheat-growing, and even a flour mill. There was also a separate prison for boys – "the thiefs prison" – at **Point Puer**, where the inmates were taught trades. From the 1840s until transport of convicts ceased in 1853, the penal settlement grew steadily, the early timber constructions later replaced by brick and stone buildings. The lives of the labouring convicts contrasted sharply with those of the prison officers and their families, who had their ornamental gardens, drama club, library and cricket fields. The years after transport ended were in many ways more horrific than those that preceded them, as physical beatings were replaced by psychological punishment. In 1852, the **Model Prison**, based on the spoked-wheel design of Pentonville Prison in London, opened. Here, prisoners could be kept in tiny cells in complete isolation and absolute silence; they were referred to by numbers rather than names, and wore hoods whenever they left their cells. The prison continued to operate until 1877, by now incorporating its own **mental asylum** full of ex-convicts, as well as a geriatric home for ex-convict paupers. The excellent **interpretive centre** in the visitor centre (daily 9am–5pm) provides much more detail on the prison's sad history through artefacts and texts, and there's more fascinating information in the older museum, housed in what was the asylum.

In 1870, Port Arthur was popularized by Marcus Clarke's romantic tragedy, *For the Term of His Natural Life*. The public became fascinated by its buildings and the tragedy behind them, and soon after the prison closed, guided tours were offered by the same men who had been wrecked by the regime. In the 1890s the town around the prison was devastated by bushfires that left most buildings in ruins. A major conservation and restoration project began in the 1970s – ongoing restoration reopened the Model Prison to visitors in 2008 – and today the **Port Arthur Historic Site** covers a huge area (☎03/1800 659 101 or 03/6251 2300, ⓦwww.portarthur.org.au; daily 8.30am–7pm; office 8.30am–11pm; $28 for a 48hr pass – two-year ticket $34 – including 40min guided tour and 30min harbour cruise). There's also a cruise on the MV *Marana* to explore the boys' prison at Point Puer (2hr; $12; daily except Aug) and another to the **Isle of the Dead** (1hr; $12; daily except Aug), Port Arthur's cemetery from

1833 to 1877, where you can view the resting places of 1100 convicts, asylum inmates, paupers and free men. The same company also runs a Tasman Island Wilderness Cruise (subject to demand and weather) from Port Arthur Jetty to see the island's sheer cliffs and its sea birds and fur seals (☎1800 659 101; call for morning times; daily Dec–May; 1hr 30min; $70).

The Port Arthur Historic Site houses more than sixty buildings, some of which – like the poignant **prison chapel** – are furnished and restored. Others, like the ivy-covered **church**, are picturesque ruins set in a landscape of green lawns, shady trees and paths sloping down to the cove. The beautiful setting makes it look more like a serene, old-world university campus than a prison, and indeed, the benign feeling of the place seems to have a capacity to absorb tragedy: another horrific chapter in Port Arthur's history occurred in April 1996, when the massacre of 35 tourists and local people by a lone gunman made international headlines. The café where most of the people were killed has been partially dismantled and a memorial has been built – a garden and reflecting pool laid out around the remaining walls. Visitors are requested to act sensitively and not ask the staff about the tragedy.

If you're staying overnight in Port Arthur, join the nightly lantern-lit **Historic Ghost Tour** (1hr 30min; $20; bookings ☎03/6251 2310), which features lovingly researched and hauntingly retold tales of the settlement's past as you wander through the ruins.

Practicalities

If you don't have your own transport, and want to get to Port Arthur from Hobart on a regular **bus**, you'll usually have to stay overnight. TassieLink has a single afternoon service (Mon–Fri during school terms; Mon, Wed & Fri school holidays), stopping en route at Eaglehawk Neck, Koonya and other places on the Tasman and Forestier peninsulas. However, there are plenty of bus **tours** that sample some of the Tasman Peninsula sights along the way. Among them is small-group tour company Bottom Bits Bus ($110; see box, p.1017), which also takes in peninsula walks and sights and the night-time ghost tour. Navigator Cruises also offers a pricey but spectacular cruise from Hobart (Wed, Fri & Sun, 8am; $229; see box, p.1025) with an optional return coach-trip.

There are various **places to stay** on the outskirts of Port Arthur. The *Comfort Inn Port Arthur* (☎03/6250 2101, 🌐www.portarthur-inn.com.au; [5]–[6]), overlooking the ruined church, is dated and pricey for its small rooms, saved only by the superb location and its on-site bar – albeit open to the public – and reasonable counter meals. Nearby *Port Arthur Villas* (☎03/6250 2239, 🌐www.portarthurvillas.com.au; [5]–[6]) represents better value, with the amenities of a motel and kitchens in the units. Both are just across the road from the site on Safety Cove Road. Otherwise, there are bunkhouse rooms and camping (including an excellent enclosed camp-kitchen) at *Port Arthur Caravan and Cabin Park* 1km north of the site at Garden Point (☎03/6250 2340, 🌐www.portarthurcaravan-cabinpark.com.au; camping $20, dorms $20, en-suite cabins [4]).

At the Port Arthur Historic Site visitor centre, you can **eat** by day at a cafeteria-style café (daily 9am–5pm) or spend more at the good *Felons Restaurant* at night (dinner only); both are licensed. A better bet during the day is *Eucalypt* (Wed–Mon 8am–5pm; licensed) by the site turn-off, which prepares gourmet baguettes and burgers. In **Taranna**, 10km before Port Arthur on the A9, *The Mussel Boys Café* (daily; licensed) serves superb fresh seafood – try the mussels in a dill coconut broth. Though you can sit outside on the veranda and enjoy the water views, the menu offers restaurant food, with dishes priced at $18–28.

The east coast: the Tasman Highway

For much of its length along the sunny **east coast**, the **Tasman Highway** gently rises and falls through grazing land and bush-covered hills. In summer there's something of an unspoilt Mediterranean feel about this stretch, with its long white beaches, blue water stretching to a cloudless sky, a scenic, hilly backdrop, and a thriving local fishing industry. Because the east coast is sheltered from the prevailing westerly winds and is washed by warm offshore currents, it has one of the most temperate climates in Australia. This, and the mainly safe swimming beaches, make it a popular destination for Tasmanians in the school holidays – prices go up and accommodation is scarce from Christmas to the middle of February. Even so, it's still relatively undeveloped and peaceful; there are four national parks, which include a whole island – **Maria Island** – and an entire peninsula – the glorious **Freycinet National Park**. The only blight on the landscape is the huge and controversial export **woodchip mill** at Point Home, one of four in Tasmania, near Triabunna, which can be seen from the ferry to Maria Island.

The east coast is also Tasmania's best **cycling route**: it's relatively flat, and the winter climate is mild enough to tackle it in colder months, too. Distances between towns are reasonable, and there's a string of youth hostels so you don't need to camp. **St Helens** is the largest town on the east coast, with a population of just over a thousand; situated on **Georges Bay**, it makes a good base to explore the northeast corner and **Mount William National Park**. The oldest town, **Swansea**, lies sheltered in **Great Oyster Bay**, facing the Freycinet Peninsula. To the north, the small fishing town of **Bicheno** offers fantastic diving, and it's a convenient place from which to visit both the Freycinet National Park (and its tiny settlement of **Coles Bay**) and the **Douglas Apsley National Park** inland. The highway detours inland at **St Marys**, although there's a more recently built road that allows you to follow the coast and enjoy spectacular views without having to tackle any hills.

Because the east coast is not heavily populated even by Tassie standards, **banking facilities** are minimal outside the few towns. EFTPOS facilities are widely available in shops and service stations as a backup.

A more pressing problem is **transport**. Services offered by Redline and TassieLink don't run to daily schedules, with big gaps at weekends – another good reason to cycle or drive – and a different schedule for the school holidays. You will probably need to change to local bus services at some point to get from one place to another. Unless you enjoy getting stuck somewhere for a couple of days, check timetables carefully. **From Hobart**, TassieLink goes to Orford, Triabunna, Swansea, Bicheno, Scamander and St Helens via the Coles Bay turn-off for Freycinet National Park (1 daily Wed, Fri & Sun). **From Launceston**, Redline has services to the Coles Bay turn-off and Bicheno via towns along the Midlands Highway (1 daily Mon–Fri) and to Scottsdale (2 daily Mon–Fri, 1 daily Sun); TassieLink has a route to Bicheno via St Marys (1 daily Fri & Sun). Three local bus companies fill in the gaps: Stan's (☏03/6356 1662) go between Scottsdale and Bridport; Calows (☏03/6372 5166) between St Helens and Launceston via Derby and Pyengana, and a Sunday-only service from St Helens to Bicheno; and the Bicheno Coach Service (☏03/6257 0293) links to Coles Bay and the Freycinet National Park.

Maria Island National Park

As the Tasman Highway meets the sea at **ORFORD**, a small holiday resort on the estuary of the Prosser River, you get your first views across to **Maria Island**.

The entire island, 15km off the east coast, is a national park, uninhabited save for its ranger. Its wide tracks are ideal for mountain biking, an activity encouraged here – because no other vehicles are allowed, you can ride in perfect safety (bike hire is available at Triabunna). The island's coastal road has no gradient, but inland there are a few hills to climb. **Birdlife** is prolific, with over 130 species; it's the only national park containing all eleven of the state's endemic bird species. The old airstrip is covered with Cape Barren geese, which you'll see if you walk to the **fossil cliffs**, a twenty-minute stroll from Darlington.

The ferry (see below) lands at **DARLINGTON**, where the structures of the former **penal settlement** (dating from 1825 and later a probation station until 1850) still stand, including the commissariat store with its information boards, the convict barn, the cemetery, the mill house and the penitentiary. The latter is now an atmospheric 🕮**bunkhouse** (☎03/6257 1420; dorms $15, rooms ❷); the basic units have wood stoves, table and chairs, and bunks with mattresses, but you'll need to bring your own cooking equipment and bedding. The units are often booked up well in advance, so call before turning up. The **campsite** here ($12, $5 each extra person) is the island's best, with a public phone, toilets, fireplaces, cold-water taps and tank water for drinking. As there is little water elsewhere on the island, free-range camping is best done at **Frenchs Farm** or the more picturesque **Encampment Cove**, two campsites with a rainwater supply and fireplaces. Both are in the south of the island, about four hours' walk from Darlington.

You can take many short **walks** on the island, as well as longer bushwalks (though watch out for cyclists); a range of free pamphlets is in the historic buildings at Darlington, and you can hire bikes at the ranger's office ($15 per day). With a couple of days to spare – or one day on a bike – you can go past the narrow isthmus to the rarely visited **southern end** of the island, which has unspoilt forests and secluded beaches. As there's no water here, be sure to bring supplies with you. The Maria Island Walk (Oct–April; $1950, includes transfers; max 8 people; ☎03/6234 2999, 🌐www.mariaislandwalk.com.au) is a four-day guided walk skirting the coastline and staying in "luxury" wilderness camps and a late nineteenth-century house in Darlington, with gourmet meals each night.

Getting there: Triabunna

The **ferry** to Maria Island (daily mid-Dec to March 9.30am & 4pm, April–Sept Mon, Wed, Fri & Sun 10.30am & 3pm, Oct to mid-Dec Mon, Wed, Fri & Sun 9.30am & 4pm; confirm bookings and departures on ☎0419 746 668, 🌐www .mariaislandferry.com.au; 40min; return $50, bikes $10, kayaks $20) leaves from **TRIABUNNA**, reached by TassieLink from Hobart, Bicheno or St Helens. As well as the ferry fare, standard national park fees apply – if you have a car pass, bring the receipt. You can get a taste of Maria as a day-trip, but given the ferry times, you won't be able to do much more than take in the convict ruins and embark on a three-hour walk.

The **visitor centre** on the Esplanade in Triabunna (☎03/6257 4772) provides details on the island. Triabunna's **Online Access Centre** is on the corner of Vicary and Melbourne streets. **Accommodation** is minimal: apart from the shabby *Spring Bay Hotel* by the jetty (☎03/6257 3115; ❸), the only budget option is the *Triabunna Caravan Park* on Vicary St (☎03/6257 3575; camping $20, powered sites $23, dorms $25). Four-star accommodation is available at the *Tandara Hotel Motel* on the Tasman Highway (☎03/6257 3333; ❺), also your best **eating** option in an otherwise uninspiring small town.

Swansea

On a sunny day, the fifty-kilometre drive north from Triabunna to **SWANSEA** is spectacularly beautiful with brilliant white beaches, the intense aquamarine of Great Oyster Bay and views across to the Freycinet Peninsula, where the pink contours of the Hazards Mountains shimmer in the distance. One of Tasmania's oldest settlements, Swansea is an administrative centre, fishing port and seaside resort, with well-preserved architecture dating from the 1830s to the 1880s. The focus of town has always been **Morris's General Store**, on Franklin Street, run by seven generations of the family since 1868. Swansea's past can be revisited at the volunteer-run **Heritage Centre** (days and times vary; usually 9am–3pm; $3), also on Franklin Street, and at the impressive collection in the restored **Swansea Bark Mill**, 96 Tasman Highway (daily 9am–5pm; $10), once used to produce leather-tanning agents from native blackwattle bark. Swansea's **Online Access Centre** is on Franklin Street.

Accommodation

Meredith House 15 Noyes St ☎03/6257 8119, [W]www.meredith-house.com.au. Gay-friendly B&B in an antiques-filled Georgian manor built by convicts on a hill just off the main street; some rooms have views over the bay. [5]–[6]

Piermont Retreat Tasman Highway, 3km south ☎03/6257 8131, [W]www.piermont.com.au. Glamorous beach-shack chic in self-contained luxury cottages with streamlined Mediterranean styling; the best open directly onto the private beach. [7]–[8]

Swansea Backpackers Lodge Tasman Highway, 600m north of centre ☎03/6257 8650, [W]www.swanseabackpackers.com.au. A spotless, spacious new backpackers' by the Bark Mill run by efficient management – more expensive than your average hostel but also a cut above. Dorms $34 ($28 with own sleeping bag), rooms [3]

Swansea Holiday Park at Jubilee Beach Shaw St, opposite Bark Mill ☎03/6257 8511, [W]www.swansea-holiday.com.au. Campsites and cabins behind the beach north of the centre – a sister site looks over Schouten Beach south of the centre (☎03/6257 8148). Powered sites $30, cabins [4]

Tubby and Padman 20 Franklin St ☎03/6257 8901, [W]www.tubbyandpadman.com.au. Heritage rooms in an upmarket colonial homestead in the centre – look for the huge front veranda – plus contemporary-style self-contained units out back. [6]–[7]

Eating

Recent investment has transformed Swansea's **food** beyond recognition. On either side of Morris's General Store on Franklin Street, you'll find sophisticated Euro-Asian dishes concocted by one of the state's most respected chefs at *The Banc* (☎03/6257 8896; lunch Mon & Sun, dinner Mon & Wed–Sun) and *The Ebb*, a relaxed modern restaurant where the sweeping bay views are almost as magnificent as the seafood (☎03/6257 8088; closed Mon). For cheaper eats, aside from good fish and chips from a takeaway adjoined to the post office, the *Bark Mill Hotel* on the main road beside the bark mill (and backpackers') rustles up bistro meals and above-average pizzas.

The Freycinet Peninsula

Heading for Coles Bay and **Freycinet National Park** (pronounced "fray-zin-ay"), you turn off the Tasman Highway 33km north of Swansea, following the Coles Bay Road. The winding drive from Swansea onwards affords fantastic views of countryside contrasted with dramatic mountain- and seascapes. After about 8km along Coles Bay Road, you can turn left down a side road (3km unsealed) to the **Friendly Beaches**, part of the national park, taking in a length of unspoilt shoreline backed by eucalypt forest. If you're **cycling**, you can cut 40km from your journey by riding along Nine Mile Beach Road, at the end of which an unofficial ferry (book the night before on ☎03/6257 0239; $15;

Oct–April only) crosses the Swan River to **SWANWICK**, about 6km northwest of Coles Bay.

COLES BAY, on the north edge of the Freycinet National Park, is a sheltered inlet with fishing boats moored in the deep-blue water, all set against the striking backdrop of **The Hazards**, three pink-granite peaks – Amos, Dove and Mayson – rising straight from the sea. Since the 1930s, the hamlet of Coles Bay has been the base for the park, and for fishing and recreation; it's also known (in Australia at least) as the first town to ban plastic shopping bags. There are numerous fishing shacks and **holiday houses** available to rent: Freycinet Rentals (☎03/6257 0320) has a wide selection on its books. Just 3.5km west of Coles Bay, *The Edge of the Bay* (☎03/6257 0102, ⓦwww .edgeofthebay.com.au; ❽) has secluded, self-catering two-bedroom cottages set in bushland, or minimalist Japanese-style suites with water views; there are minimum stays and cheaper rates depending on season. There's also a swish restaurant (dinner nightly) and bar open to all. The *Iluka Holiday Centre*, in a great spot behind the Esplanade near Muirs Beach (☎03/6257 0115 or 1800 786 512, ⓦwww.ilukaholidaycentre.com.au; dorms $28, rooms ❷–❸, vans ❸, units ❹–❺), has a wide variety of accommodation, including a **YHA hostel** section. Nearby is a small supermarket which doubles as a visitor centre and a garage with petrol, a pub with bistro meals and the excellent *Freycinet Café & Bakery* (daily 8am–7pm, till 5pm out of season), an eat-in bakery selling bread and pastries, and pizza from 5pm.

At the other end of the township, 1km from Muirs Beach overlooking The Hazards, there's another **general store**, Coles Bay Trading, on Garnet Avenue (daily 8am–6pm, until 7pm Dec 26–Feb; ☎03/6257 0109), with payphones, a post office and a fuel pump. Its coffee shop has great views of The Hazards – when it's open. Next door you can get a wonderful seafood dinner at *Madge Malloy's* (Oct–May dinner Tues–Sat; licensed; ☎03/6257 0399), owned by a fishing family. For more general information, check out the excellent ⓦwww .freycinetcolesbay.com. Redline and TassieLink drop off 31km away from Coles Bay, at the turn-off on the Tasman Highway, connecting with the Bicheno Coach Service to Coles Bay (up to 3 daily; book for off-peak times on ☎03/6257 0293), which can also take you right to the start of the walking tracks.

Freycinet National Park

The **national park office** (daily 9am–5pm; ☎03/6256 7000), just 1km from Coles Bay, sells maps and booklets on day-walks and has an interpretive display on the park. From here, the gravelled, disabled-access Great Oyster Bay path leads down to the beach (10min return). Opposite the centre, the national-park **campsite** ($13, powered sites $16), with water, toilets and showers, is in a sheltered location among bush and dunes behind Richardsons Beach; it's so popular in holiday season that to secure a pitch from mid-December to early February and over Easter you need to apply by ballot by the previous July – entries can be made by email via ⓦwww.parks.tas.gov.au. The park office will advise of any late cancellations – but don't bank on it. At the other end of Richardsons Beach, ⚐ *Freycinet Lodge* (☎03/6257 0101, ⓦwww.freycinetlodge .com.au; ❽) has wooden cabins spread through bushland and offers guided bushwalks among its wealth of activities. There's also a bistro and a smart restaurant with fabulous views overlooking the bay, both open all day and available to non-guests. The only other accommodation in the park itself is the basic *Coles Bay YHA* (no hot water), which must be booked in advance through the Hobart YHA office (see p.1036; dorms $10, rooms ❷). Again, it's absurdly popular during the summer months and Easter.

Tracks into the park begin at the **Walking Track Car Park**, a further 4km from the office. **Water** is scarce, so you must carry all you'll need, although the ranger can advise if there are any streams where the water is safe to drink. The shorter walks are well marked: the strenuous, gravelly walk up to the lookout to exquisite **Wineglass Bay**, with its perfect curve of white beach, is where most walkers head, and many continue on down to the beach itself (2.6km return to the lookout, 1–2hr; 5km return to the beach, 2hr 30min–3hr 30min). The 27-kilometre **peninsula circuit** is a wonderful walk (10hr), best done over two days; it makes a good practice run for the big southwest hikes. There's a **campsite** at **Cooks Beach**, with a pit toilet, water tank, and a rough hut where you can stay.

Schouten Island, off the tip of the peninsula, is part of the national park: it's perfect for really secluded camping, as you're quite likely to have it all to yourself. Freycinet Sea Cruises, in Coles Bay (☎03/6257 0355, ⓦwww.freycinetseacharters.com), will drop you off here for around $85 per person return, as will Freycinet Adventures ($140 return; see below) with its on-demand Aqua Taxi. As well as the Schouten Island trip, Freycinet Sea Cruises also run two cruises to Wineglass Bay from January to March; the Full Wineglass (daily; 4hr; $120) with fine food, or the Beach to Bush tour (daily; 6hr; $180) which returns by guided walk back across The Hazards. You can also charter the boat for a day-trip; options include a nearby seal colony. There are campsites with pit toilet, a hut and two water tanks at **Moreys Bay**, and the creek at **Crocketts Bay** has reliable upstream water. Although there are no proper tracks on the island, walking is easy.

Freycinet Adventures (☎03/6257 0500, ⓦwww.freycinetadventures.com.au) offers three-hour sea-kayaking tours on Coles Bay (8.30am and a sunset trip; $90), which can be extended to include overnight camping in the national park. All4adventure (☎03/6257 0018, ⓦwww.all4adventure.com.au) offers all-terrain-vehicle tours of the park. Both operate from offices by the Esplanade as you enter Coles Bay.

▲ Wineglass Bay

Bicheno

Halfway up the east coast, **BICHENO** (pronounced "bish-eno"), sheltered in **Waubs Bay**, is a busy crayfishing and abalone port. The same conditions that make Bicheno ideal for fishing also make it a perfect spot for diving. Don't let the unattractive inland town centre on the Tasman Highway put you off; it has a beautiful bay setting and there's lots to do.

The 3.5-kilometre, one-way **Bicheno Foreshore Footway** runs from Redbill Point (reached via Gordon St off the Tasman Highway at the western edge of town) and follows several points, bays and beaches, with views of **Governor Island Marine Nature Reserve**, and past the Blowhole. The usually clear waters are rich with a variety of marine life, and the reserve has spectacular large caves and extraordinary vertical rockfaces with swimthroughs and drop-offs. Bicheno Dive Centre, opposite the Sea Life Centre at 2 Scuba Court (℡03/6375 1138), offers dive courses and rents out gear. Among the most popular activities in Bicheno are the evening tours to a local **penguin rookery** with Bicheno Penguin Tours (℡03/6375 1333; nightly; $25; reservations at East Coast Surf in town centre). The French-owned Le Frog Trike Rides (℡0407 511 454) runs a range of fun three-wheeler tours, from $14 for a 10- to 15-minute ride to $195 for a three-hour circuit via Elephant Pass. Bicheno Glass Bottom Boats (℡03/6375 1294) offers fortyminute **glass-bottom-boat tours** of the marine reserve ($15). The **Sea Life Centre** (daily 9am–5pm; $6.50), on the Tasman Highway, has a rather dingy aquarium but a decent seafood restaurant (daily 9am–9pm; dinner bookings ℡03/6375 1121). Bicheno's **Online Access Centre** is at The Oval, Burgess Street.

You have a decent range of **food** options in Bicheno. Apart from the tasty pies at eat-in *Blue Edge Bakery* (daily 8am–4pm) next to the post office, or counter meals at the *Beachfront Tavern*, both on the Tasman Highway, there's classic French cooking in *Cyrano French Restaurant*, at 77 Burgess St (℡03/6375 1137; dinner nightly; mains average $28; BYO), and, nearby, similarly priced modern Australian cooking at the *Gaol House Restaurant* in the gardens of *Bicheno Gaol Cottages* (℡03/6375 1430; dinner Mon–Sat). Locals rate *Seasons*, part of the *Bicheno by the Bay* resort on Foster Street, for cheaper modern European dishes and pizzas (lunch Thurs–Sun summer only, dinner nightly).

The Bicheno Coach Service (℡03/6357 0293) to Freycinet National Park leaves from outside the *Blue Edge Bakery* on the main road.

Accommodation

Bicheno Backpackers 11 Morrison St ℡03/6375 1651, ⓦwww.bichenobackpackers.com. Friendly small backpackers' with wood-pannelled, cabin-like dorms arranged around a kitchen-common room, plus rooms in a separate block, some en suite with sea views. Rental of bikes, kayaks and surfboards for guests. Dorms $23–25, rooms ❸

Bicheno by the Bay The Esplanade ℡03 6375 1171, ⓦwww.bichenobythebay.com.au. Family-friendly resort with twenty cottages, one- to four-bed, spread between the town centre and The Gulch. ❻–❼

Bicheno Gaol Cottages Corner of James and Burgess sts ℡03/6375 1430, ⓦwww .bichenogaolcottages.com. Heritage-style, self-contained two-bed accommodation in the old prison and former school house, plus a studio in the former gaol stables. ❺

Bicheno Hideaway 179 Harveys Farm Rd, signposted 3km south ℡03/6375 1312, ⓦwww.bichenohideaway.com. A unique retreat with a few cylindrical self-contained chalets moments from a private strip of foreshore, all set on six acres of natural bushland teeming with wildlife. ❺–❻

East Coast Holiday Park 4 Champ St ℡03/6375 1999, ⓦwww.bichenoholidaypark.com.au. Small, tidy and well-equipped campsite in central Bicheno. Camping $20, powered sites $30, studios ❹, cabins ❺

The Douglas Apsley National Park to St Marys

Just 4km north of Bicheno on the Tasman Highway there's a turn-off to the **Douglas Apsley National Park**. Demarcated in 1990, it's home to the state's only remaining large dry sclerophyll forest. Because of the temperate weather of the east coast, the park's two-day walk, the **Leeaberra Track** – undertaken north to south – is a good one at any time of the year. Although facilities are being improved, this is a low-maintenance, untouristy park, so be prepared for basic bushcamping; get hold of the *Douglas Apsley Map and Notes* ($10) from outdoors shops in Hobart and Launceston or (in theory) the visitor centre at Bicheno.

Some 30km north of Bicheno, just past Chain of Lagoons, the coastal Tasman Highway continues north to **St Helens**; turn off to the left for a spectacular climb with views of the surrounding coastline on a detour inland to St Marys, 17km away. You can stop at the dramatic **Elephant Pass** for pancakes (plus other dishes), views and atmosphere at the *Mount Elephant Pancake Barn* (daily 8am–6pm).

From Elephant Pass the road heads on to **ST MARYS**, a picturesque little Fingal Valley town surrounded by state forest and waterfalls best viewed from the 832-metre peak of logging-threatened **South Sister**, accessed 6km up unsealed and winding German Town Road. The place has a quiet, old-fashioned feel to it, but an alternative edge focused on the atmospheric *eScApe Tasmanian Wilderness Café Gallery* at 21 Main St (☏03/6372 2444; Mon & Wed–Sun 9.30am–5pm, till 8pm Fri & Sat), with a pool table and regular live music; and the *Purple Possum Wholefoods Café* in the health-food store (closed Sun) by the pub on Storey Street. The best place to stay is the magical ⚑ *Seaview Farm* (☏03/6372 2341 or 0417 382 876, ⓦwww.seaviewfarm.com.au), 8km uphill on German Town Road; the hilltop position gives panoramic views of South Sister and the sea. There's hostel accommodation in a comfortable cottage that has a big kitchen and cosy lounge with a wood stove, and the "dorms" are cottagey rooms with beds not bunks – you rarely have to share a room. Private accommodation is available in en-suite rooms with a veranda that offers fabulous views (dorms $30; rooms ❺). You can arrange a pick-up in advance if you don't have transport.

St Marys' **Online Access Centre** is at 23B Main St. There are **bank services** in the post office at no. 36.

St Helens and the Bay of Fires

ST HELENS is the largest town on the east coast and the last before the Tasman Highway turns inland. It's situated on **Georges Bay**, a long, narrow bay with two encircling arms, and the surrounding coastline holds plenty of interest.

Information and services

Local **information** is available from the **St Helens History Room**, at 55 Cecilia St opposite the post office ($2; ☏03/6376 1744), which details the area's mining history in the nearby Blue Tier (see p.1059) and provides maps and walk information. *St Helens YHA* (see below) hires **bikes** ($25 per day) and kayaks ($60 per day), plus camping gear, should you want to kick back at the Bay of Fires for a while. **Banks** are on Cecilia St, and the **Online Access Centre** is in the library at no. 61. The **Forum Cinema** (☏03/6376 1000, ⓦwww.forumcinema .com.au) at Pendrigh Place shows fairly current releases, plus there's a funky café-bar with couches and art exhibitions.

Accommodation

While Binalong Bay is a far more scenic and relaxing option than St Helens, bear in mind that amenities there are almost nonexistent.

Bay of Fires Character Cottages ☎03/6376 8262. Pleasant holiday cottages stacked on a hillside with to-die-for views of white sands and turquoise sea. ⑥–⑧

Bed in the Treetops 124 Binalong Bay Rd ☎03/6376 1318, ⓦwww.bedinthetreetops.com .au. Two units, two styles – mellow rustic and metropolitan chic – in a luxury retreat 1km from the Bay of Fires beaches. ⑦–⑧

St Helens Backpackers 9 Cecilia St ☎03/6376 2017, ⓦwww.sthelensbackpackers.com.au. Small modern hotel opened in 2006 in the town centre. A "Flashpackers" in a separate building has smaller dorms and family rooms, all en suite and with own TV. Dorms $24–28, rooms ❸

St Helens Caravan Park 2 Penelope St ☎03/6376 1290, ⓦwww.sthelenscp.com.au. Popular family-orientated place a fifteen-minute walk south of the centre. Camping $32, powered/ en-suite sites $35/45, cabins ❺–❻

St Helens YHA 5 Cameron St ☎03/6376 1661. Homely in an old-fashioned way, with a spacious common area, clean rooms and friendly owners. Rarely busy even in peak season; also has a self-contained flat. Dorms $25, rooms ❸, flat ❹

Tidal Waters Resort 1 Quail St ☎03/6376 1999, ⓦwww.tidalwaters.com.au. The most sophisticated place in town, a large, well-patronized four-star resort set on the bay. ⑥–⑦

The town and around

With a large resort hotel, cinema and clutch of cafés, even a vintage clothes store, St Helens is fast changing from a sleepy backwater to a holiday playground as the beauty of the nearby Bay of Fires becomes more widely known and real-estate prices rocket.

The southern arm of Georges Bay is the site of the **St Helens Point Recreation Area**, where there's a large lagoon – Diana's Basin – which the highway skirts as it enters town. On the ocean side the **Peron sand dunes** stretch for several kilometres, and at the point there's good surfing at **Beer Barrel Beach. Binalong Bay**, 10km north of Georges Bay, is another popular surf spot (with a strong current, so beware); there's safer swimming in the large lagoon tucked behind, where people boat and water-ski. Binalong is the southern end of the mesmerizingly beautiful **Bay of Fires** (named for the many fires explorer Tobias Furneaux saw in 1773), where the beach of bright sugary sand stretches for over 30km to Eddystone Point. Binalong Bay is an easy bike ride away from St Helens (hire bikes at the YHA), with only a couple of small climbs. From Binalong Bay, you can walk in around two hours along the beach to **Cosy Corner**; however, unless you want to walk back again you need to arrange to be picked up or go on a tour. There's accommodation, a shop and petrol, and you can **camp** here, as well as further along at Grants Lagoon in the **Bay of Fires Coastal Reserve** which stretches for 13km north alongside the partly sealed coastal drive to the scenic spot known as The Gardens.

To get to the lower half of **Mount William National Park** at the northern end of the Bay of Fires, take the road running inland north for 54km from St Helens to the pink-granite tower of the Eddystone Lighthouse. The northern end of the park is reached via Gladstone, by taking an unsealed track to **Great Musselroe Bay**, where there's a free basic **campsite**. There are no real tracks within the park itself, but plenty of beach and headland walking, and lots of Forrester kangaroos. The ⚞ **Bay of Fires Walk** is a superb four-day guided coastal trek around the bay and through Mount William National Park (☎03/6331 2006, ⓦwww.bayoffires.com.au; $1950–2100 according to season); packs and waterproof jackets are provided and accommodation is in luxury "ecotents" and in a superbly designed ecolodge 40m above the sea with stunning views up and down the coast.

Eating

Food options in St Helens are improving but remain fairly unimpressive, based on noodle bars and snacks rather than full meals, though there are a few exceptions.

Angasi Binalong Bay ⓣ03/6776 8220. Stylish decor, a superb modern Australian menu and bay views that are worth the price alone – reservations are essential for dinner. Breakfast, lunch & dinner daily.

The Captain's Catch On the wharf, St Helens. Some of the best takeaway fish and chips you'll find (daily till 7.30pm), while the attached seafood restaurant *Latris* (ⓣ03/6376 1170) offers elegant sit-down dining.

Deck on the Bay In *Tidal Waters Resort* (see above). This café-bistro is a good bet for fine dining (daily 11am–9.30pm), while the *Ocean View Restaurant* (daily breakfast & dinner) is pricier.

Village Store & More 55 Cecilia St, St Helens. A great menu of fresh bistro fare featuring local organic produce, plus a relaxed café vibe. Mon–Sat 9am–5pm.

St Helens to Scottsdale

From St Helens, the **Tasman Highway (A3)** cuts across the northeast highlands towards Launceston, 170km away. This is mostly dairy country, although there's the odd patch of surviving rainforest and the remnants of a tin-mining industry, based around the **Blue Tier**, a mountain plateau that experienced a mining boom in the 1870s. Many **ghost towns** were left after the mines finally closed in the 1950s.

Some 26km northwest of St Helens on the A3 is the turn-off south for **PYENGANA** (1km) and St Columba Falls (a further 4km). In Pyengana it's worth touring **Healey's Pyengana Cheese Factory** (daily 9am–5pm; free), where you can watch the stuff being made (except Fri & Sat) and buy all the ingredients for a picnic at the falls, or have something to eat at the café. Further along, the *St Columba Falls Hotel* (ⓣ03/6373 6121) – the "Pub in the Paddock" – is a real country local, serving huge steaks and beer for the two resident pigs. You can also **stay** here in cute, tidy rooms with peaceful rural views (❸). At the end of the road (the last bit on dirt) is the **Columba Falls State Reserve**, an area of cool, temperate rainforest. The walk (1km return) to the viewing platform at the base of **St Columba Falls** is easy, passing through a forest of man ferns and under a canopy of sassafras and myrtle. At 90m, the falls are among the highest in Tasmania, pouring with tremendous force over the cliffs – truly thunderous in winter.

Back on the A3 approaching the Blue Tier, **Goshen** is the first of the ghost towns, little more than an old school and the ruins of the *Oxford Arms Inn*. A little further on is the turn-off for **Goulds Country**, with the remaining buildings – all wooden – of what was once a town. Head through Goulds Country and past the site of another abandoned mining town, Lottah, and take the steep, unsealed Poimena Road to the site of Poimena. En route, the "Hands Off The Blue Tier" notices are signs of the fierce environmental campaign against logging of the area (ⓦwww.bluetier.org), one of the few remaining old-growth forests left in the northeast. The boardwalked twenty-minute circuit **Goblin Forest Walk** (wheelchair accessible) provides fascinating interpretive boards that help you to imagine the town once here. There's also a thirty-minute walk to the 810-metre-high Blue Tier Summit, Mount Poimena, for views right across the northeast to the coast, and several other signposted walks taking between two and six hours. Get details on Blue Tier walks at St Helens History Room (see p.1057).

Returning to the Tasman Highway, the Weldborough Pass (595m) is probably the most beautiful part of the drive, with views across the valleys to the sea; it's worth taking the twenty-minute walk through the **Weldborough Pass Scenic Reserve**, predominantly myrtle forest with man ferns and occasional tall black-woods. **WELDBOROUGH** itself, once the centre of a Chinese mining community, now consists of the isolated, characterful *Weldborough Hotel* (☎03/6354 2223; ❸), where you can get a **meal** (Mon–Sat) and a basic shared-bath **room** for the night; there's also a campsite that's free if you buy a meal (otherwise $15).

DERBY, on the Ringarooma River, was made prosperous by the profitable Briseis Tin Mine between 1876 and 1952. The **Tin Centre** (daily Nov–April 9am–5pm, May–Oct 10am–4pm; $16; ☎03/6354 1062), opened in 2008, is one of the only signs of new development in a town that's been closing down since the 1950s; it screens an interesting documentary on the mine's fortune and a flood disaster in 1929 that all but destroyed Derby, and there's a café too. The adjacent volunteer-run Tin Mine Museum (same times and ticket, or $3) fills in the social history, including artefacts belonging to the area's large population of Chinese miners in the late 1800s.

Scottsdale and Bridport

SCOTTSDALE, 99km from St Helens, is a medium-sized town servicing the agricultural and forestry industries of the northeast. The **Scottsdale Forest EcoCentre**, on the outskirts of town at 88 King St (daily 9am–5pm; free), is another Forestry Tasmania public-relations exercise; the unique, energy-smart building looks like a headless Dalek half-sunk into the ground. Inside, an "eco-walk" winds up the circular building, putting the local forest and forestry industry into historical and ecological context, and there's a pleasant café (daily 9am–5pm) and a **visitor centre** (☎03/6352 6520). While far from exciting, Scottsdale has good facilities, including banks, supermarkets, the bustling *Cottage Bakery* at 9 Victoria St, with fresh sandwiches and pies (closed Sun), and an **Online Access Centre** in the library at 51 King St. The Victorian-era B&B *Beulah of Scottsdale*, 9 King St, set among flowery gardens, has attic bedrooms with mountain views, and a guest lounge and dining room (☎03/6352 3723; ❻). There are some beautiful areas to visit nearby, including Ralph Falls in the Mount Victoria Forest Reserve and Evercreech Forest Reserve – get details from the EcoCentre. Alternatively, Pepper Bush Adventures (☎03/6352 2263, ⓦwww .pepperbush.com.au; Launceston pick-ups) can take you off-road to visit some of these places on bespoke high-end wildlife and bush **tours**, including fine food and wine.

Twenty-one kilometres northwest, the fishing town and holiday spot of **BRIDPORT** has several places to **stay** including the modern, purpose-built *Bridport Seaside Lodge YHA Backpackers*, at 47 Main St (☎03/6356 1585, ⓦwww.bridportseasidelodge.com; dorms $22, rooms ❷–❸) right on the river estuary. There's also camping at *Bridport Caravan Park* (☎03/6356 1227; camping $16, powered sites $20), which stretches for about 1km behind the beach at Anderson Bay. The **beaches** in the area are lovely, especially the wide, sandy expanse where the Bird River flows among sand dunes and into the sea.

North and central Tasmania

The **north** of Tasmania is rich and settled agricultural country, and the fertile soil of the **Tamar Valley** in particular made this a prosperous area during the early colonial period. Thirty kilometres inland at the confluence of the Tamar and the North and South Esk rivers, **Launceston** quickly grew as a port and city; gracious early houses and well-preserved villages are still found around the area. Also settled early, due to its fine and open land, was the mostly flat, gently undulating **midlands** area between Launceston and Hobart; the **Midland Highway** more or less follows the old coaching route between the two cities. With its stone walls, hedgerows, haystacks, and small villages and towns, this rural stretch from the Tamar Valley to Hobart is softly appealing but not particularly exciting. In contrast, the area around **Deloraine**, 45km west of Launceston, is spectacular: the early colonial town is surrounded by rich farmland and dramatically located in hilly country below the crest of the **Great Western Tiers** a huge draw for bushwalkers. From Deloraine, the **Lake Highway** heads steeply south up over the Western Tiers and on to the **Central Plateau**, a sparsely populated, lake-filled region dominated by the **Great Lake** and its fishing shacks.

For the **Bass Strait Islands**, off the northern coast, see p.1111.

Launceston and around

LAUNCESTON is dominated by the **Tamar River**, and approaching from the north down the Tamar Highway, zooming through haystack-filled countryside, it's a lovely sight, with grand Victorian houses nestling on hills above the banks. Approaching from the south on the Southern Outlet, however, gives a slightly more accurate picture of Tasmania's "northern capital": the state's second-largest city, with a population of around 98,000, has acquired a sheen of cosmopolitan café society but largely remains an oversized provincial town.

As the third-oldest city in Australia, first settled in 1804, Launceston has hung on to disappointingly little of its colonial Georgian architecture. What the city does have in abundance are many fine examples of colonial **Victorian architecture**: the 1870s and 1880s – years of mineral exploration spurred on by the mainland goldrush – were prosperous times for Launceston, and a number of dignified public buildings date from this boom period.

Launceston's real attractions, though, are its natural assets. It's situated at the confluence of the narrow **North Esk** and **South Esk rivers**, with the breathtaking **Cataract Gorge**, where the South Esk has carved its way through rock to reach the Tamar River, only fifteen minutes' walk from the centre. Yachts and outboard motors ply the 50km of river, and the surrounding countryside of the **Tamar Valley**, with its wineries, strawberry farms and lavender plantations, is idyllic. Beyond the eastern suburbs, bush-covered hills fold back into the distance to **Ben Lomond**, a popular winter skiing destination just an hour's drive away.

Arrival, information and city transport

Launceston Airport is 20km south of the city, near the town of Evandale. The **Airporter Shuttle Bus** (☏03/6343 6677) meets most flights and drops off at accommodation for $14. A **taxi** costs about $45–50, or you could **rent a car** – the main car companies have desks at the airport, or see "Listings", p.1068.

Long-distance **buses** arrive in the city centre at the **Cornwall Square Transit Centre**, on the corner of Cimitiere and St John streets, where both Redline (☎1300 360 000) and TassieLink (☎1300 300 520) have ticket offices; Redline has left-luggage facilities (☎03/6336 1446; $1.50 per bag till closing time) and there's a café and tourist information. If driving, note that most streets operate on a **one-way system**, and that the length of Cameron Street is interrupted by Civic Square, and Brisbane Street by the Mall.

For information, your first stop should be the **Launceston Travel and Information Centre**, on the corner of St John and Cimitiere streets (Mon–Fri 9am–5pm, Sat 9am–3pm, Sun 9am–noon; ☎03/6336 3133 or 1800 651 827, ⓦwww.discoverlaunceston.com), which can also arrange car rental and book accommodation and travel tickets.

Launceston is very compact and most accommodation is within walking distance of the city centre, although **public transport** (the MTT) is useful for a couple of scattered attractions and some outlying accommodation (buses run until 6.15pm Mon–Thurs, until 10pm Fri & Sat; restricted services Sun).

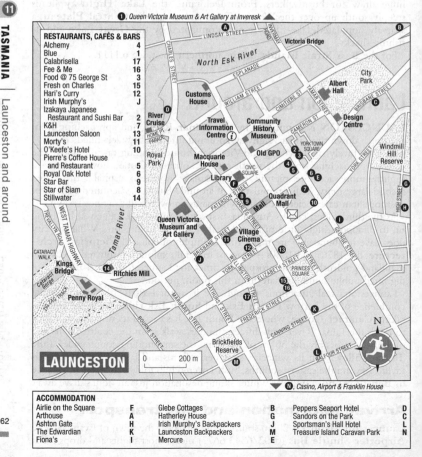

RESTAURANTS, CAFÉS & BARS

Alchemy	4
Blue	1
Calabrisella	17
Fee & Me	16
Food @ 75 George St	3
Fresh on Charles	15
Hari's Curry	12
Irish Murphy's	J
Izakaya Japanese Restaurant and Sushi Bar	2
K&H	7
Launceston Saloon	13
Morty's	11
O'Keefe's Hotel	10
Pierre's Coffee House and Restaurant	5
Royal Oak Hotel	6
Star Bar	9
Star of Siam	8
Stillwater	14

❶, Queen Victoria Museum & Art Gallery at Inveresk ▲

LAUNCESTON

0 ⎯⎯ 200 m

▼ ❶, Casino, Airport & Franklin House

ACCOMMODATION

Airlie on the Square	F	Glebe Cottages	B	Peppers Seaport Hotel	D
Arthouse	A	Hatherley House	G	Sandors on the Park	C
Ashton Gate	H	Irish Murphy's Backpackers	J	Sportsman's Hall Hotel	L
The Edwardian	K	Launceston Backpackers	M	Treasure Island Caravan Park	N
Fiona's	I	Mercure	E		

The **MTT bus interchange** (☎13 22 01, [W]www.metrotas.com.au), where all buses arrive and depart, is on St John Street, on either side of the **Brisbane Street Mall**. While single fares are inexpensive at $2.20, a Day Rover ($2.90) for unlimited off-peak travel is a bargain (buy on board), or you can get a ten-trip ticket (from $17.60; buy at a Metrofare ticket agent, including newsagents in the mall).

Accommodation

Accommodation in Launceston is good value, though rates are hiked up in the busy December-to-February period, when **hostel** beds can be scarce. There's a concentration of **motels** along Brisbane Street and an abundance of **B&Bs** and self-catering accommodation.

Hotels, motels, B&Bs and self-catering

Airlie on the Square 77 Cameron St ☎03/6334 0577, [W]www.airlielodge.com.au. Super-central B&B in an early twentieth-century building tucked away on Civic Square; heritage style but with character and a friendly, well-travelled management. [5]

Ashton Gate 32 High St ☎03/6331 6180, [W]www.ashtongate.com.au. Classified by the National Trust, this weatherboard B&B has been taking guests for over forty years. Antique-style bedrooms are large and light; all are en suite, with TV and hot drinks. [5]–[6]

The Edwardian 229 Charles St ☎03/6334 7771, [W]www.theedwardian.com.au. Lovely, two-storey red-brick Edwardian house near Princes Square, with self-catering suites; breakfast provisions provided. Handy for the supermarket. No children. [5]

Fiona's 141 George St ☎03/6334 5965, [W]www.fionas-bnb.com.au. Quietly luxurious rooms and suites, all individually decorated, in a peaceful residence off George St with free parking. [5]–[6]

Glebe Cottages 14A Cimitiere St ☎03/6334 3688, [W]www.glebecottages.com. Good-value, two- and three-bedroom self-contained cottages, in a convenient location near City Park. Minimum one-week stay. [4]–[5]

Hatherley House 43 High St ☎03/6334 7727, [W]www.hatherleyhouse.com.au. This gorgeous 1830s colonial mansion set in extensive English-style gardens (views stretch off to Ben Lomond) combines original architectural features, tapestries, carvings and sculptures from India, Africa and the Orient with contemporary design and five-star luxury. Scrumptious breakfast served on the veranda, in the library café-bar or out in the garden. [8]

Mercure 3 Earl St ☎1800 030 567 or 03/6333 9999, [W]www.accorhotels.com. Modern business-style rooms – not big on character but good value for its four-star standards and central location. Free parking, too. [6]–[8]

Peppers Seaport Hotel 28 Seaport Boulevard ☎03/6345 3333, [W]www.peppers.com.au. The hotel that gave Launceston a waterfront lifestyle, with its cluster of bars and restaurants. Modern rooms have natural wood furnishings and luxury fabrics, while the spacious suites have kitchenettes. Most rooms have water views; "City view" rooms treat you to a view of a four-lane highway. [7]–[8]

Sandors on the Park 3 Brisbane St ☎03/6331 2055 or 1800 030 140, [W]www.sandorsonthepark.com.au. The best of a bunch of motels on this strip – but not the most expensive – and just a short walk from the centre. Friendly service, laundry and wi-fi. Online booking saves around $30. [5]

Sportsman's Hall Hotel 252 Charles St ☎03/6331 3968. "Sporties" offers functional rooms above an often noisy pub with shared bathrooms. The café-style bistro downstairs serves reasonably priced meals. [3]–[4]

Hostels and caravan parks

Arthouse 20 Lindsay St ☎03/6333 0222 or 1800 041 135, [W]www.arthousehostel.com.au. Impressive new backpackers' on the river's north bank whose renovated Federation-era house offers spacious proportions and historic character. Dorms are four- to eight-bed, some facing onto a front balcony; rooms are singles ($55), twins and doubles. Also has two kitchens and internet access. Friendly young staff can advise on tours and transport. Dorms $23–27, rooms [3]

Irish Murphy's Backpackers 211 Brisbane St ☎03/6331 4440, [W]www.irishmurphys.com.au. Above a lively, centrally located pub, it's cheap but beware noise from traffic and drinkers alike. Facilities include a TV lounge and a fully equipped kitchen, but no laundry. Dorms $17, rooms [2]

Launceston Backpackers 103 Canning St ☎03/6334 2327, [W]www.launcestonbackpackers.com.au. Consistently reliable hostel in a clean, two-storey mansion with an adjoining modern annexe. Well run without being regimental by friendly, well-travelled managers. Internet access available. Dorms in three-, four- and six-bed varieties, single rooms ($48), and some en-suite doubles. Good notice board for onward travel, work and trips. Dorms $20–26, rooms ❸

Treasure Island Caravan Park 94 Glen Dhu St, South Launceston, 2km south of the centre ☎03/6344 2600. A small park, sloping up a hillside and looking right over a noisy freeway yet still crowded in summer. Camp kitchen with TV. Bus #21 or #24 to Wellington St (stop 8). Camping $22, powered sites $26, vans ❷, en-suite cabins ❸–❹

The City

The **Brisbane Street Mall** marks the centre of the city, which is arranged in a typical grid pattern around it. **Brisbane Street**, with the mall as its focus, is the main shopping precinct. The city is small and easy to get around, but if you want some background information, join Launceston Historic Walks (Mon–Fri, call for times; 1hr 15min; $15; bookings ☎03/6331 2213) outside the Travel and Information Centre on the corner of St John and Cimitiere streets.

City Park and the old wharf area

City Park (daily 8am–5pm), with its entrance of impressive wrought-iron gates on Tamar Street, is a real treasure. Established in the 1820s, the impression of a formally organized, very English park is reinforced by the **John Hart Conservatory**, full of flowers and ferns, and by the wrought-iron drinking fountain erected here for Queen Victoria's Diamond Jubilee in 1897. Referred to by the locals as "Monkey Park", it's the closest thing Launceston has to a zoo: its Japanese macaques (over twenty of them) romp around their small, moat-surrounded island.

Within City Park, on the corner of Tamar and Brisbane streets, is the **Design Centre of Tasmania** (daily 9.30am–5.30pm), established in 1976 to support and encourage Tasmanian designers. In a state that's always been perceived by the mainland as lagging behind, it's a source of pride that Tasmanian designers helped furnish the New Parliament House in Canberra. The Design Centre is now the home of the **Tasmanian Wood Design Collection** ($5), which showcases the work of some of these superb local designers, woodworkers and furniture-makers using native Tasmanian woods. Prices are beyond the range of most visitors, but the centre is also one of the best places to buy more portable **craft** items, such as woodwork, leatherwork and jewellery.

The wharves on the North Esk River have disappeared, but the massive Neoclassical **Customs House** is still there on The Esplanade, just east of the Charles Street Bridge. The **old wharf area**, around William Street and the Esplanade, has several interesting industrial buildings, including the 1881, still-operational **J. Boag & Son** brewery. Its popular brewery tours start in the **Boag's Centre For Beer Lovers**, opposite at 39 William St, which includes a **museum** (Mon–Fri 8.45am–4.30pm; free) and gift shop, and finish with a small tasting of four beers (tours Mon–Fri, times vary by season; 1hr $18; 1hr 30min $25; bookings on ☎03/6332 6300 or ⓦwww.boags.com.au).

The North Bank and Heritage Forest

Opposite the Esplanade, reached by Victoria Bridge from Tamar Street, and then a boardwalk along the river, is the **Queen Victoria Museum and Art Gallery** at Inveresk (daily 10am–5pm; free but charges for touring exhibitions; ⓦwww .qvmag.tas.gov.au), part of a multimillion-dollar redevelopment of the complex of old railway yards here. Opened in late 2001, the building's interior – two-thirds of which is home to the University of Tasmania's **Academy of Arts** – has an incredible sense of space. By 2010, a protracted reorganization should have dedicated this wing of the museum to science and history, the latter evident in displays of beautiful shell necklaces created by Tasmanian Aboriginal women, including recent examples from the tradition of Cape Barren Islanders, and a Chinese joss house from Weldborough (see p.1060), constructed in the 1870s by Chinese workers introduced to the east-coast tin mines to provide cheap labour. The revamp should also include displays of state fauna, with sections on the Tasmanian tiger and Tasmanian devil; accounts of the geology of Launceston and the local area, and a **Planetarium** ($5). More appealing, perhaps, are the former **Railway Workshops**, now transformed into a social history museum; the history of railways in Tasmania is hardly compelling stuff (though the Playzone for kids is great), but the walkway through the old Blacksmith Shop, complete with soundtrack of machinery and voices, is eerie, and the exhibition on migration to the state, based on personal stories, gives a different angle on contemporary Tasmania. The sedate licensed café in the Railway Workshops has part of its seating in an old train carriage.

The railway-yards site spans a large expanse of riverfront land dubbed by the council as the **Northbank Experience**. It includes the Tasmanian Conservation Workshops, the Exhibition Centre and the Aurora Stadium (see p.1068), which brings live AFL football to Launceston. The boardwalk to the art gallery continues along the North Esk River to **Heritage Forest**, with walking, bike-riding and horse-riding trails.

Civic Square and the Queen Victoria Museum and Art Gallery

Shady, grassy **Civic Square**, closed to traffic, does convey a tidy spirit of civic-mindedness. Here, **Macquarie House** was built as a warehouse in 1830 for Henry Reed, a wealthy merchant. **Cameron Street** was one of the first streets laid out after the city's settlement in 1806, and the stretch from Civic Square to Wellington Street is an almost perfectly preserved nineteenth-century streetscape, including the imposing Supreme Court building and, opposite, a row of fine Victorian red brick terraced houses adorned with beautiful wrought-iron work.

South of Civic Square is the main shopping thoroughfare, the pedestrianized **Brisbane Street Mall**, a modest precinct taking up one small city block. Just off here is the arc of the **Quadrant Mall**, bounded by Brisbane and St John streets, with several lanes and an arcade leading from it. Gourlay's Sweet Shop here is a Launceston institution – for something really local, try the leatherwood honey drops. East of Quadrant Mall and one block north along George Street, **The Old Umbrella Shop** at no. 60 is a **National Trust visitor centre** (Mon–Fri 9am–5pm, Sat 9am–noon; T03/6331 9248), housed in an 1860s Tasmanian blackwood-lined shop.

West of Cameron Street, the **Queen Victoria Museum and Art Gallery**, on Wellington Street (daily 9am–5pm; free but charges for exhibitions; Wwww .qvmag.tas.gov.au), was opened in 1891 to mark half a century of Queen Victoria's reign. Following renovation (hopefully completed by mid-2010), the historic pile's grand spaces are slated to serve as the city's permanent **gallery**, well worth visiting for its "Aspects of Tasmanian Art" exhibition that contains landscapes by the nineteenth-century painters W.C. Piguenit and John Glover.

Royal Park to Ritchies Mill Arts Centre

Behind the museum, and across Bathurst Street, **Royal Park** has extensive formal parklands running down to the Tamar River; there's even a croquet lawn here, if you were in any doubt about its English lineage. Between Royal Park and Cataract Gorge is a concentrated tourist area. **Ritchies Mill Arts Centre**, at 2 Bridge Rd on the Tamar River, has been converted from a nineteenth-century flour mill and miller's cottage and now contains two galleries and a superb café-restaurant, *Stillwater* (see p.1067).

To the north of the park, the excellent **Tamar River Cruises** (50min–4hr; longer cruises Sept–May only; $22–108; ☎03/6334 9900, ⓦwww .tamarrivercruises.com.au) depart from Home Point, at the end of Home Point Parade, and head along the Tamar and into the mouth of beautiful Cataract Gorge, allowing a close-up view of the Launceston Yacht Club, as well as the wealthy suburb of **Trevallyn**, with classic Victorian mansions strung along the tree-covered hillside. Longer trips, including an evening buffet cruise, continue north up the Tamar as far as the Rosevears vineyards. Nearby, the **Old Launceston Seaport** on Seaport Boulevard provides a clutch of modern waterfront cafés, bars and restaurants around the *Peppers Seaport Hotel*, a pleasant spot with views over the yachts in the marina to the Trevallyn hillside.

Cataract Gorge and beyond

Few cities have such a magnificent natural feature within fifteen minutes' walk of the centre as Launceston. For a beautiful view of **Cataract Gorge**, turn left out of Penny Royal World and walk to the decorative wrought-iron 1863 **Kings Bridge**, which has a span of 60m. From the bridge the cliffs rise almost vertically from the smooth water of the South Esk River as it empties into the Tamar; the natural spectacle is even more dramatic when floodlit after dusk.

The **Zig Zag track** (25min one-way) is the more strenuous of the two walking routes along the gorge: a satisfyingly secluded rock-stepped path shrouded by bush. The track runs steeply along the top of the gorge, from Kings Bridge to the **First Basin**, a large, deep canyon worn away by the river and filled with water. Across the Kings Bridge is the easier but busier **Cataract Walk** (40min one-way), which begins by the small tollhouse; it's suitable for wheelchairs, and offers spectacular views of the gorge. From the trail, you'll see people canoeing, abseiling and even jumping off the cliffs into the water; Tasmania Expeditions offers abseiling trips here (see "Tours", p.1017).

The Cataract Walk leads to the gardens of the **Cliff Grounds**, on the shady northern side of the gorge. These genteel, English-style gardens with parading peacocks are arranged around a lovely 1896 rotunda, and make for a startling contrast with the gorge's wild beauty. *The Basin Café* (☎03/6331 5222) in the grounds has stunning views over the First Basin; less expensive cream teas are served from the kiosk. If you enter the grounds from the First Basin end (where there's a car park, or take bus #51B), you'll find an enormous, unattractive **swimming pool**, built mainly to discourage people from swimming in the basin itself, where some have died.

To get across the First Basin to the Cliff Grounds, the **Launceston Basin Chair Lift** (daily 9am–4.30pm weather permitting; $10, $12 return; ☎03/6331 5915) takes an exhilarating six minutes to cover 457m – it's claimed to have the longest single span (308m) of any chair lift in the world. The views are wonderful, but if you're afraid of heights you might want to cross on foot via the **Basin Walk** directly underneath, although this route is impassable when the river is in flood. The other alternative, the narrow **Alexandra Suspension Bridge**, called the "swinging bridge" by locals, is even shakier when crowded with joggers.

A track starting from the Alexandra Suspension Bridge follows the river through unspoilt bush to the narrower **Second Basin** and the disused **Duck Reach Power Station** (1hr 30min return). From the station you could continue a bit further to the large **Trevallyn State Recreation Area** (daily 8am–dusk; no camping), on the South Esk River, and the **Trevallyn Dam**,

6km west of the city centre. To reach the area by road, go via the suburb of Trevallyn, following Reatta Road. In the recreation area at Aquatic Point, there's a **visitor centre**, summer canoe and windsurf board rental, a playground, toilets and barbecues. The rest of the reserve consists of open eucalypt forest, with marked bushwalks and nature trails shared with horse riders.

Eating

Once a predominantly Anglo-Saxon affair, **eating out** in Launceston has changed beyond recognition in recent years. Indeed, some gourmets reckon its restaurant scene now trumps that in Hobart. If your budget won't stretch to fine dining, **pubs** offer decent cheap meals, or there are a few excellent **cafés**. Old Launceston Seaport around *Peppers Seaport Hotel* (see p.1063) offers a spread of stylish eating and drinking options – from fish and chips to classy Italian cuisine, a relaxed patisserie to funky bars – in one location.

Blue Inveresk Railyards, off Invermay Rd. This café/bar, in a former powerhouse, is a young, lively art-college hangout. It prepares classic café meals as well as more substantial mains up to $26; also has gourmet pizzas and a tapas menu. Outside tables are very popular for the excellent weekend breakfast. Ambient DJs Fri night (from 7pm) and Sun afternoon (2–5pm). Licensed. Mon–Sat from 8.30am, Sun 8am–3pm; dinner Mon–Sat only.

Calabrisella 56 Wellington St ☎03/6331 1958. A crowded, noisy, atmospheric and affordable Italian restaurant. BYO. Dinner nightly except Tues.

Fee & Me 190 Charles St ☎03/6331 3195. Award-winning restaurant serving up international tasting menus featuring regional ingredients. Expensive for Tasmania, but good value compared to mainland Australia. Dinner Mon–Sat.

Food @ 75 George St 75 George St. Relaxed café serving baguettes, pastries, jacket potatoes and cheap pastas, from the usual bolognese to pesto with pumpkin and pine nuts. Takeaway prices are substantially cheaper. Mon–Wed 10.30am–7.30pm, Thurs–Sat 10.30am–8.30pm.

Fresh on Charles 178 Charles St. Delicious modern vegetarian food and smoothies in a café with a funky retro feel. Its notice board and campaign office are a fount of information on the city's alternative and green movements. Mon–Thurs 9am–4pm, Fri & Sat 9am–9pm.

Harl's Curry 152 York St ☎03/6331 6466. Very cheap, well-recommended Indian eatery – average main is $9.50 and there's nothing over $12. BYO. Dinner daily.

Izakaya Japanese Restaurant and Sushi Bar Yorktown Square ☎03/6331 0613. Long-established place with all the favourite Japanese dishes: *ramen*, sushi, tempura and *bento*, though noodles are available lunchtime only. Mains average $15. Licensed (sake) and takeaway. Lunch Wed–Fri, dinner Tues–Sun.

K&H 106 George St. Delicious cakes and pastries accompanied by equally good coffee. A full menu of contemporary meals is served on the upper level with its polished wood floors, and there's a licensed bar with good cocktails, and healthy takeaway sandwiches and wraps too. Mon–Thurs 7.30am–6pm, Fri & Sat 7am–late.

Morty's Corner of Brisbane and Wellington sts. Popular food court near the cinema, with lots of Asian kitchens including Thai and Chinese. Also fish and chips, pancakes, and a juice bar. Licensed. Daily 10am–9.30pm.

O'Keefe's Hotel 124 George St. Tasty pub meals, including a range of international dishes such as curries and seafood, and there are cheap lunch specials.

Pierre's Coffee House and Restaurant 88 George St ☎03/6331 6835. Established in the 1950s by a French immigrant, *Pierre's* is a classic café-bistro despite its makeover into swish metropolitan style. Great coffee, fabulous hot chocolate and cakes, and Tasmanian wines by the glass. Mon–Thurs 10am–9pm, Fri 10am–10pm, Sat 10am–2pm & 6–10pm.

Star of Siam Corner of Charles and Paterson sts ☎03/6331 2786. Launceston's favourite Thai restaurant, worth booking at weekends. Mains average around $18. Licensed and BYO. Lunch Tues–Fri, dinner nightly.

Stillwater Ritchies Mill Arts Centre, Paterson St ☎03/6331 4153. Award-winning and popular riverside café/restaurant and wine bar whose laid-back vibe doesn't stop it oozing class. During the day, it's an alfresco café, with generous breakfasts and gourmet wraps, as well as a few more substantial dishes. At night the menu shifts upscale to offer two- or three-course à la carte dining ($70/85), plus a tasting menu ($105). Daily 10am till late (book for dinner).

Entertainment and nightlife

The *Examiner*, based in Launceston, is the newspaper for the north of Tasmania – Thursday's entertainment section details weekly events. The **Princess Theatre**, 57 Brisbane St (T03/6323 3666, Wwww.theatrenorth.com.au), stages drama, opera, ballet and concerts. Behind the theatre, the **Earl Arts Centre**, 10 Earl St (T03/6334 5579), has fringe theatre productions, while the **Silverdome**, out of town on the Bass Highway at Prospect (T03/6344 9988, Wwww.silverdome.com.au), is the venue for major exhibitions as well as entertainment and sports events. Popular AFL football matches are held in **Aurora Stadium** near the Inveresk development (Wwww.aurorastadiumlaunceston.com.au). The only **cinema**, the four-screen Village 4, at 163 Brisbane St (T03/6331 5066), shows mainstream films. Check the Gay Information Line (see p.1033) for the latest details on the gay scene in Launceston.

Pubs, bars and clubs

Alchemy 90 George St T03/6331 2526. Renovated glass-fronted, light and colourful bar with an emphasis on food (from 8.30am for breakfast). A modern, café-style menu – posh sandwiches and salads, pasta and risotto, plus classic but meaty mains. Occasional gigs at weekends.
Irish Murphy's 211 Brisbane St. Spirited Irish pub with Guinness on tap, live music (Wed–Sun) and pub meals.
Launceston Saloon 191 Charles St T03/6331 7355. Always packed on event nights with a young student crowd. The huge *Saloon Bar* has several plasma screens, local bands (Wed nights) and

occasional interstate and international band events, and DJ nights on Wed, Fri and Sat (9.30pm–5/6am; free) when the mezzanine level becomes a karaoke bar. Big-screen TV and typical pub food in the *Sports Bar* and the *Saloon Bar*.
Royal Oak Hotel 14 Brisbane St T03/6331 5346. Popular, genial boozer with live rock and blues on Thurs to Sat nights. Crowded bistro serves counter meals (mains $14–18).
Star Bar 113 Charles St T03/6331 6111. Popular bar with slick, modern decor and pavement tables. DJs play at weekends and brasserie-style Mediterranean food is available.

Listings

Banks and foreign exchange Branches of major banks are at the bottom of Charles St; Travelex, 98 St John St (Mon–Fri 9am–5.30pm, Sat 10am–1pm).
Bike rental Mountain Designs, 120 Charles St, provides bike hire for $30 per day. It is also the base of Mountain Bike Tasmania (T03/6334 0988, Wwww.mountainbiketasmania.com.au), which runs mountain-bike trips in the Launceston area.
Books Fullers Bookshop, 93 St John St.
Camping equipment A good option for renting or buying gear is Allgoods, with stores at 71–79 York St and 60 Elizabeth St. Paddy Pallin, 110 George St, focuses on the top end of the market and sells a wide range of freeze-dried foods, guidebooks and maps.
Car rental Europcar, airport and 112 George St (T03/6331 8200 or 1800 030 118), also has 4WDs. Autorent-Hertz, airport and 58 Paterson St (T03/6335 1111), also has campervans. For cheaper rates try Economy Car Rentals, 27 William St (T03/6334 3299), or Lo-Cost Auto Rent, 80 Tamar St (T03/6334 6202).

Hospital Launceston General, Charles St T03/6332 7111.
Internet Launceston's Online Access Centre is on the ground floor of the State Library, Civic Square. Cyber King (Mon–Fri 8.30am–7.30pm, Sat & Sun 9.30am–6.30pm) is at 113 George St.
Motorcycle rental Tasmanian Motorcycle Hire, 17 Coachmans Rd, Evandale (T03/6391 9139, Wwww.tasmotorcyclehire.com.au; from $115 per day, helmet included).
Pharmacy Healthwise pharmacy is on Brisbane St, 100m east of the mall (daily 9am–9pm).
Post office 111 St John St, Launceston, TAS 7250 T13 13 18.
Swimming The Launceston Swimming Centre, Windmill Hill Reserve (Nov–March Mon–Fri 6am–7pm, Sat & Sun 9am–7pm, April–Oct daily from 11am; $3.20). Aquarius Roman Baths, 127–133 George St (T03/6331 2255), is an opulent complex of therapeutic warm, hot and cold baths, sauna, steam rooms, gym, massage and solarium (Mon–Fri 9am–6pm, Sat & Sun 9am–6pm; admission to baths and saunas $26, or $44 per couple).

Taxis Taxi ranks are on George St between Brisbane and Paterson sts, on St John St outside Princes Square, and outside the Transit Centre. Taxis Combined ☎ 13 22 27 or 13 10 08.

Tours Tiger Wilderness Tours (☎ 03/6394 3212, ⓦ www.tigerwilderness.com.au) runs small-group half- and full-day tours in the area, focused on wildlife, walks and wine and food. Destinations include Cradle Mountain, the Tamar Valley and Meander Falls near Deloraine. Prices average $120 for a full day. Tasmanian Expeditions (☎ 03/6339 3999 or 1300 666 856, ⓦ www.tas-ex.com) organizes activities, from climbing in Cataract Gorge ($200) to multi-day wilderness hikes.

Around Launceston

Before launching yourself into the beauty of the Tamar Valley, there are several fine Georgian farming estates and mansions around the well-preserved towns of **Evandale** and **Longford**, just twenty-odd kilometres south of Launceston. If you're here in winter, you might consider joining the ski crowd who descend upon **Ben Lomond National Park**, southeast of Launceston; out of season, this is fine bushwalking country.

Evandale and Longford

Though no public transport runs to **EVANDALE**, 20km southeast of Launceston, this National Trust-classified town from the 1830s rewards a visit, particularly for its long-running Sunday market. At the **Evandale Tourism and History Centre** on High Street (daily 9am–4pm; ☎ 03/6391 8128), pick up a $2.20 *Heritage Walk* brochure. Otherwise, the map opposite the popular eat-in *Ingleside Bakery* (licensed), in restored 1867 council chambers, also on High Street, points out notable features – many of the old buildings bear descriptive plaques. The **Clarendon Arms Hotel**, on nearby Russell Street (☎ 03/6391 8181; ❸), was built in 1847 on the site of the former convict station; its mural-covered interior depicts the early history of Tasmania. The **Evandale Market**, held in Falls Park on Logan Road (Sun 8am–2pm), attracts large crowds to its varied hundred-odd stalls, which include local organic produce. Once a year in late February, Evandale hosts the three-day-long **National Penny Farthing Championships** as part of its Village Fair; the races using the old bikes are quite a sight. Eight kilometres south of Evandale via the C416 and the C418 is the National Trust-owned **Clarendon Homestead** on the banks of the South Esk River (daily 10am–5pm, to 4pm June–Aug; $10), a grand white Neoclassical-style country house built in 1838 for a wealthy wool-grower and furnished in Georgian style; it's worth a visit just for the conservatory café at the front.

Australia's oldest continually running **racecourse** was established in 1847 at **LONGFORD**, 20km southwest of Launceston. It's a country classic, with the big event the New Year's Day Longford Cup. On the outskirts of town, along Woolmers Lane (C521), **Brickendon Estate** (Tues–Sun 9.30am–5.30pm; closed July & Aug; $12; ☎ 03/6391 1251, ⓦ www.brickendon.com.au) was set up from land granted to William Archer in 1824; it's still run by sixth-generation Archers as a working sheep property. Earlier members of the family saw fit to preserve the early architecture; walking into the farm compound with its huge Dutch-style wooden barns is like setting foot into a film set for a rural period-piece. Preservation also saw it co-nominated with Woolmers (see below) for World Heritage status in 2007. Its ramshackle appeal is the setting for **accommodation** in charming old estate cottages (❻). William's brother Thomas Archer established his estate **Woolmers** (☎ 03/6391 2230, ⓦ www.woolmers.com.au) in 1819 – just a few kilometres further along the hawthorn-hedgerow-lined Woolmers Lane – which lasted through six generations of Archers until 1994. The original Georgian bungalow with its dark warren of rooms still stands, as does the impressive Italianate villa that was adjoined in 1843. A guided **tour** of the house, with its grand dining room still set up as it was for a royal visit in 1868, is fascinating as much for the interiors as for the family story (daily 10am, 11am, 12.30pm, 2pm & 3.30pm; $18 includes Rose Garden). It's a scenic spot too, perched above the Macquarie River with views across the Great Western Tiers. The **National Rose Garden** (self-guided tour of grounds and garden $12), with over 4000 rose plants, has been set up in former orchards.

Ben Lomond National Park

The plateau of the **Ben Lomond Range**, over 1300m high and 84 square kilometres in area, lies entirely within **Ben Lomond National Park**, 50km southeast of Launceston. A small ski village sits below **Legges Tor** (1572m), the second-highest point in Tasmania, and can be reached in an hour from Launceston; above it the bumpy outline of the range's steep cliffs dominates the horizon. Weather depending, the **ski season** runs from mid-July to September, and **accommodation** is limited to the *Ben Lomond Creek Inn* (☎03/6390 6199; half-board rooms ❼), which is usually booked out at weekends. However, the region's accessibility means there's no real need to stay. **Meals** are available at the inn, or there's fast food from the ski-resort kiosk.

An all-day pass on the **ski lifts** costs around $40 (more details at ⓦwww .ski.com.au/resorts/benlomond). Some ski rental is available on the mountain but there's a better range at Launceston Sports Centre, 88A George St (☎03/6331 4777). The Travel and Information Centre (see p.1062) can advise on ski packages and the **bus service** from Launceston which operates during the season. If you're driving, be warned that the final 20km to the ski village is unsealed and the last leg, **Jacobs Ladder**, is very steep, with hairpin bends, sheer drops and only a wire safety barrier to steady your nerves. You must carry wheel chains, which can be rented from the snow line. Otherwise, you can park just before the Ladder and take the **shuttle bus**. Outside the ski season, all services cease and the businesses close down, but the scenery and the alpine vegetation are magnificent enough to lure **bushwalkers**. There's a 12.5-kilometre track from *Carr Villa*, on the slopes of Ben Lomond, to Legges Tor. Bush **camping** is permitted anywhere in the national park, but *Carr Villa* is an informal camping area with a pit toilet. For more information, contact the ranger (☎03/6230 8233). A thrilling way to experience the mountain in summer is on the Ben Lomond Descent, a downhill cycle from the alpine plateau organized by Mountain Bike Tasmania in Launceston (6–7hr; $150; includes equipment, packed lunch and transfers from Launceston; see "Listings", p.1069).

The Tamar Valley

To the north of Launceston is the beautiful **Tamar Valley**, where, for 64km, the tidal waters meander through orchards, vineyards, strawberry farms, lavender plantations, forested hills and grazing land. Only the Batman Bridge, near Deviot, and the APPM Wood Mill and Bell Bay Power Station, near the river's mouth, mar the idyllic scenery.

West of the Tamar

The West Tamar Highway (A7) follows the line of the Tamar River from Launceston to Beauty Point, and **Brady's Lookout State Reserve** provides magnificent views of the Tamar Valley and Ben Lomond; you can see as far as Low Head, 34km away. Rather than head straight along the highway, it's worth detouring for a stretch through **ROSEVEARS**, on a picturesque sweep of road along the riverbanks that's popular with cyclists. In the village itself you can have a drink in the 1831 *Rosevears Taverne*. A few kilometres west of Rosevears is **Notley Gorge State Reserve**, a beautiful fern gorge with a number of walking tracks, reached by turning west off the highway at Legana. Back on the highway, **EXETER** has the useful **Tamar Visitor Centre** (daily 9am–5pm; ☎1800 637 989, ⓦwww.tamarvalley.com.au), an **Online Access Centre** on Main Road, and the excellent *Exeter Bakery*. Further north, **BEACONS-FIELD** was once at the centre of Tasmania's former gold-mining area, and the mining ruins are still visible; two former mine buildings house the interesting, interactive **Grubb Shaft Gold & Heritage Museum** (daily 9.30am–4.30pm; $11; ☎03/6383 1473, ⓦwww.beaconsfieldheritage.com.au).

The main tourist destination in the area is **Beauty Point**, in part thanks to the **Seahorse World** at Inspection Head Wharf (tours 9.30am–3.30pm, every 30min; $20; 45min–1hr; ⓦwww.seahorseworld.com.au), the world's only commercial seahorse farm. By successfully harvesting the creatures for aquariums and the Chinese market, the farm is helping save those in the oceans from further depletion. The **Australian Maritime College (AMC)**, established in Beauty Point in 1978, has developed the interpretive material at the farm, and there is also an interesting display about the AMC on the top floor, beside a café with wonderful water views. There are more curious critters next door in the **Platypus House** (daily 9am–4pm; ⓦwww.platypushouse.com.au; 1hr tour $18); platypus are elusive in the wild but you are sure to glimpse them here in glass tanks, and also a couple of resident echidnas. A short way south, from the jetty at the marina, where the AMC moors its training craft, the **Shuttlefish Ferry** crosses the Tamar to George Town (2–4 daily except Tues; $10 one-way, $18 return; 20min; $30 cruise to Low Head daily except Tues 11am; 2hr; booking essential on ☎03/6383 4479 or 0412 485 611). Above the marina is the *Beauty Point Waterfront Hotel* (☎03/6383 4363, ⓦwww.beautypointhotel.com.au; ❹–❺), whose faded motel units have fantastic river views. The pub itself is more upmarket, with tables outside over the water and views from the dining room. For somewhere special to stay, *Pomona Spa Cottages* (☎03/6383 4073, ⓦwww.pomonaspacottages.com.au), just across the road on a rise above the river, has B&B accommodation (❺) in a charming Federation-style house with great views from the veranda-cum-breakfast nook, or luxurious, timber self-catering cottages (❻ includes breakfast hamper). As for eating out, the hotel prepares a wide range of seafood. Otherwise, *Carbone's Café* (breakfast & lunch daily, dinner Fri & Sat), on the waterfront a short way north of Seahorse World, rustles up good-value, tasty Mediterranean dishes. The nearest **beach** in the area is Greens Beach, 11km north of Beauty Point.

East of the Tamar: George Town and Low Head

Leaving Launceston and heading north along the East Tamar Highway, it's only a few minutes before you're zooming through scenic countryside, passing through Dilston where cows graze in paddocks at the base of bush-covered hills. After Hillwood and its famous strawberry farm, you're headed for the port of **GEORGE TOWN**, one of the oldest towns in Australia, where Colonel Paterson landed in 1804 to begin settlement of northern Tasmania. The **George Town Visitor Centre** is on Main Road on the way into town (daily: summer 9am–5pm, winter 9am–4pm; ☎03/6382 1700); George Town's **Online Access Centre** is on Macquarie Street.

Despite its history, George Town isn't particularly compelling, with only one colonial building to look at, **The Grove**, an elegant stone Georgian mansion at 25 Cimitiere St, and even here opening days are erratic – ask at the visitor centre or call for times (℡03/6382 1336; $7.50). Unless replica craft in the Bass & Flinders Centre, at 8 Elizabeth St, appeal (daily 10am–4pm; $8) – including one of the brigs that George Bass and Matthew Flinders anchored offshore before they embarked on a circumnavigation of Tasmania in 1798 – you're better off pushing on to **LOW HEAD**, 5km north, with 24 National Trust-listed buildings, whitewashed cottages and rambling houses, all set amid extensive parkland. The convict-built **Pilot Station** now houses a museum (daily 9am–5pm; $5; ⓦwww.lhhp.com.au) of maritime memorabilia. There's also a **Little penguin colony** at Low Head; tours are offered each evening at sunset (1hr; $16; bookings ℡0418 361 860, ⓦwww.penguintours.lowhead .com). Diving options and cruises to a nearby **fur seal colony** on Tenth Island are also available with Seal and Sea Adventure Tours (3hr; $120; bookings ℡0419 357 028, ⓦwww.sealandsea.com).You can catch a ferry to Beauty Point from George Town with the Shuttlefish Ferry (see above). The nearest **beach** is East Beach, reached via a turn just before the Pilot Station.

George Town **accommodation** includes pub rooms in the *George Town Heritage Hotel*, at 77 Macquarie St (℡03/6382 2655; ❸), not nearly as appealing as its nineteenth-century roots should make it, or rooms and apartments by the waterfront at the *Pier Hotel*, at 5 Elizabeth St (℡03/6382 1300, ⓦwww.pierhotel .com.au; rooms ❺, apartments ❻). It also has the best **food** in town.

In Low Head, you can stay in the original but basic cottages of the Pilot Station (see above; ℡03/6382 2826; ❺) or **camp** nearby at *Low Head Tourist Park*, 136 Low Head Rd (℡03/6382 1573, ⓦwww.lowheadtouristpark.com.au; camping $23, powered sites $28.50, en-suite sites $38, cabins ❹).

Around George Town: the Pipers River wine region

Heading east of George Town, a pleasant day can be spent exploring the **vineyards** around the **Pipers River area**, which produce distinctly flavoured, crisp and fresh cool-climate wines. The *Tamar Valley Wine Route* brochure, available from the visitor centres in Launceston (see p.1062) and Exeter (see p.1071), covers 21 vineyards in the Tamar Valley and Pipers Brook area (virtually all open daily 10am–5pm and offering free tastings). One of the best known is **Pipers Brook Vineyard** (now part of Kreglinger), on the sealed C818, 2km off the B82. Established in 1974, the winery is housed in a modern, architect-designed complex, with self-guided tours. It also has a café and vine-covered courtyard. Nearby, also on the C818, lake-fronted **Jansz** makes premium champagne; there's information on the wine-making process in the interpretive centre. The friendly, small-scale **Delamere Vineyard**, on the B82, specializes in Pinot Noir and Chardonnay.Valleybrook and Tiger Wilderness run wine tours from Launceston (see "Tours", p.1069).

The Midland Highway

The **Midland Highway** is a fast three-hour route between Hobart and Launceston, more or less following the old coaching road (look for signs to the "Heritage Highway"), although you'll have to detour if you want to visit some of the towns on the way. Redline has several daily **bus** services between Hobart and Launceston, stopping at the major midland towns.

Campbell Town and Ross

Beyond **CAMPBELL TOWN** – a rather plain community originally settled by Scots but the Midlands' major centre – you drive south through sheep-grazing countryside, eventually turning off the highway to **ROSS**, 2km east. Also settled by Scots, this has a very secluded, rural feel; elm trees line the main Church Street, creating a beautiful avenue, while paddocks with grazing sheep stretch alongside. Old stone buildings along the idyllic street are well preserved, including the characterful sandstone *Man O'Ross Hotel*. From the grounds of St John's Church of England, one of the town's three pretty churches, there are views of the Macquarie River, spanned by the sandstone **Ross Bridge**, designed by John Lee Archer and built by convicts in 1836; the intricate stone carvings on its three arches earned their convict stonemasons a free pardon. A walk in the other direction from the church leads down to the original Ross burial ground and past the site of the **Female Factory**, actually a prison, where women convicts were held before being sent to properties as assigned servants. You can **stay** in several of the old cottages dotted about town: *Colonial Cottages of Ross* (☎03/6381 5354, 🌐www.rossaccommodation.com.au; [5]–[6] including breakfast provisions) has four to choose from. The *Man O'Ross Hotel* (☎03/6381 5445, 🌐www.manoross.com.au; [4] including breakfast) has several intimate rooms in which to **eat or drink**, and shared-bathroom accommodation upstairs. There's **camping** at the pleasant *Ross Caravan Park* on Bridge Street (☎03/6381 5224; camping $17, cabins [3]). A recommended **café** on the main street is the cosy *Old Ross Bakery* (daily 9am–5pm), with delicious pies. The Tasmanian Wool Centre on Church Street (daily 9am–5pm; ☎03/6381 5466; 🌐www.taswoolcentre.com.au) acts as a **visitor centre** (🌐www.visitross.com.au) and also houses a wool exhibition and history museum (entry by donation).

Oatlands

Back on the Midland Highway, it's 88km south from Ross to **OATLANDS**, which has Australia's greatest concentration of colonial **Georgian buildings**. 140 in two square kilometres, most built by convicts. Many are now occupied by antiques and bric-a-brac shops, B&Bs and guesthouses. The most striking edifice is the **Callington Mill** and its outbuildings; the partly restored windmill was built in 1837 and remained in operation until 1892. On the rare chance that it's open, there are fine views of the town. The best way to see the town is to go on one of local historian Peter Fielding's guided **heritage walks** (☎03/6254 1135; $5), which visit several other buildings, including the Old Gaol and courthouse. Contact him to arrange a spooky evening **ghost tour** ($10).

The **Central Tasmania Visitor Centre**, 85 High St (daily 9am–5pm; ☎03/6254 1212), can book **accommodation** in the many colonial-style B&Bs in town; a good choice is the central *Oatlands Lodge* at 92 High St (☎03/6254 1444; [5]). For **food**, *The Stables*, beside the visitor centre, serves breakfast and light lunches daily. Oatlands' **Online Access Centre** is in the library at 68 High St.

The Great Western Tiers and Central Plateau

Deloraine, on the **Meander River**, is nestled in a valley of rich farmland dominated by **Quamby Bluff** (1256m) and the **Great Western Tiers**, where the Central Plateau drops abruptly to the surrounding plains. On the Bass

Highway, it's roughly equidistant from Devonport (51km) and Launceston (48km). From Deloraine the **Lake Highway** begins, rising up over the Western Tiers to the Central Plateau, with its thousands of lakes. To the west of Deloraine are the extensive **cave systems** around **Mole Creek**, while **Walls of Jerusalem National Park** is accessed from **Western Creek**, 32km southwest of Deloraine.

Deloraine and around

Hilly **DELORAINE** is a delightful town, often shrouded in mist, even on summer mornings, and divided into two parts by the bubbling **Meander River**. Although the area was settled by Europeans in the 1830s, Deloraine didn't really begin to develop until after 1846, and today it's National Trust-classified. But don't let that put you off – historic architecture plays second fiddle to a burgeoning arts and crafts scene and an ever-improving café culture.

Arrival, information and tours

The two major **bus** companies both make regular stops in Deloraine: Redline on its daily Launceston–Devonport service, plus its Launceston–Deloraine service continues on to Mole Creek once daily on weekdays; and TassieLink on its Launceston–Queenstown service (Tues/Thurs and Sat); TassieLink is based at *Sullivans Restaurant*, at 17 West Parade. The depot for Redline is the **Great Western Tiers Visitor Centre**, at 98 Emu Bay Rd (Mon–Fri 9am–5pm, Sat & Sun 10am–2pm; ℡03/6362 3471, ⓦwww.greatwesterntiers.org.au). The centre has maps, details on walking times and conditions, and makes free accommodation bookings. The **Online Access Centre** is behind the library at 21 West Parade.

Operators leading **outdoor activities** in the area include Jahadi Indigenous Experiences (℡03/6363 6172, ⓦwww.jahadi.com.au; 4WD tours) and the Tasmanian Fly Fishing School (℡03/6362 3441, ⓦwww.tasmanianflyfishing .com.au).

Accommodation

There are **campsites** at the *Apex Caravan Park* beside the river in Deloraine (℡03/6362 2345; $14) and at Mole Creek (℡03/6363 1150).

Bonney's Farm off Weetah Rd, 4km northwest of Deloraine ℡03/6362 2122. Simple, self-contained two- or three-bed units on a working dairy farm – ideal for kids. ❹

Bonney's Inn 17 West Parade ℡03/6362 2974, ⓦwww.bonneys-inn.com. Pleasant but rather pricey B&B in heritage-styled rooms in the oldest house in town, a Georgian residence beside the *Deloraine Hotel*. Good breakfasts, mind. ❻

Deloraine Highview Lodge YHA 8 Blake St ℡03/6362 2996, ⓔbodach@hotkey.net.au. Set on a hill and enjoying unparalleled views of Quamby Bluff, this YHA of the old school – clean but fairly dated – is about a 10min walk from the visitor centre. Dorms $20, rooms ❷

Deloraine Hotel Corner of Emu Bay Rd and Barrack St ℡03/6362 2022. Functional pub rooms may yet receive the renovation that has taken place below – most share bathroom. ❸

Mole Creek Guest House 100 Pioneer Drive, Mole Creek ℡03/6363 1399, ⓦwww.molecreekgh.com .au. This congenial guesthouse has its own restaurant and tourist information. ❺

Mountain View Country Inn 144 Emu Bay Rd ℡03/6362 2633, ⓦwww.moutainviewcountryinn .com.au. A passable if dated motel on the outskirts of town, some of whose units (nos 11–24) enjoy outstanding views of the Tiers. ❹

Peppers Calstock Lake Highway, 2km south of Deloraine ℡03/6362 2642, ⓦwww.peppers.com.au/calstock. Classic elegance in a refined Georgian country mansion, which features luxurious French style. Also has a superb restaurant for guests. ❽

The town and around

Any history trail, should you fancy it, begins from a roundabout at the bottom of the main street, beside the river. Here, **West Parade** follows the river; at no. 17 Georgian **Bonney's Inn** dates from 1830 and is the town's oldest remaining building (now a B&B; see opposite). At the next block, Westbury Place rises up steeply from West Parade towards the tall spire of **St Mark's Church**, built in 1860, where there's a scenic **lookout** that gives a panoramic view over the town and the Western Tiers to the south. There's a modest history museum at the visitor centre at the top of the main street (see opposite; Mon–Fri 9am–5pm, Sat & Sun 10am–2pm; $7), though it is less appealing than the Yarns exhibition (same ticket) in the same building that showcases three large silk wall-hangings of local scenes. They are one example of Deloraine's alternative arts-and-crafts scene, which supports a smattering of galleries, a strong café culture and plenty of secondhand and antiques shops. It's also in evidence at the **market** on the first Saturday of every month opposite the *Apex Caravan Park* across the river, and at the annual **Tasmanian Craft Fair**, the largest of its type in Australia, which attracts around 40,000 people over four days in early November.

Close to prime **bushwalking** areas in the Western Tiers, Deloraine is an established base for walkers. Popular tracks are the short walk to **Alum Cliffs**, overlooking the Mersey River Gorge (40min return), signposted on the road between Mole Creek and Chudleigh; a difficult walk to **Quamby Bluff**,

▲ A Tasmanian devil

renowned for its myrtle rainforest (6.5km; 6hr; beginning at Brodies Rd, off the Lake Highway); the track to **Liffey Falls** (8km; 3hr; beginning at the picnic ground 5km west of the tiny community of Liffey), and the day-walk to **Meander Falls** through the Meander Forest Reserve, about 25km south of Deloraine, reached via the small settlement of Meander and Meander Falls Road (10km; 6–7hr; beginning from the picnic ground; Tiger Wilderness Tours does an excellent tour from Launceston – see p.1069). There's a walker registration and information booth at the Meander Falls car park. A free leaflet issued by Forestry Tasmania, *Visiting the Great Western Tiers*, has a map of the Meander Forest Reserve and tracks; you can pick it up from the Deloraine visitor centre (see p.1074).

The western end of the Great Western Tiers overlooks **MOLE CREEK**, 24km west of Deloraine. Here, you can get up close to some Tasmanian devils at the **Trowunna Wildlife Park** (daily 9am–5pm; $16; ⓦ www.trowunna.com .au), or buy delicious local honey from **Stephens Leatherwood Honey Factory** (Mon–Fri 8am–5pm). Surrounding the town, the **Mole Creek Karst National Park** has a network of over two hundred underground caves. About 14km west of Mole Creek are two rather spectacular ones: **Marakoopa Cave**, with huge caverns, streams, pools and glow-worms (daily tours roughly hourly 10am–4pm; 50min–1hr 20min; $15); and 6km further west the smaller but more richly decorative **King Solomons Cave**, with stalactites and stalagmites (daily 10.30am, 11.30am, 12.30pm, 2.30pm, 3.30pm & 4.30pm; 40min–1hr; $15). Wild Cave Tours (ⓣ 03/6367 8142, ⓦ www.wildcavetours.com) offers excellent $85 half-day and $170 full-day caving tours of the Mole Creek caves, underground streams and subterranean systems.

Eating

In Deloraine itself, there are plenty of informal **places to eat** on the main street, Emu Bay Road. The pick of the lot is the *Deloraine Deli* at no. 36 (Mon–Fri 9am–5pm, Sat 9am–2.30pm), a combination deli-counter and café with Mediterranean bistro meals under $18. The *Empire Hotel* just downhill serves upmarket meals, including Thai dishes, or try the *Deloraine Hotel* (see p.1074) for pub meals.

Walls of Jerusalem National Park

The **Walls of Jerusalem National Park** is on the western side of the Central Plateau: a series of five mountain peaks that enclose a central basin, an isolated area noted for its lakes, pencil pines and the biblical names of its various features. The best time to visit is November through to April; people have died of exposure here, so make sure you're well prepared. You'll need the *Walls of Jerusalem National Park Map and Notes* ($9.10); the visitor centre at Mole Creek should stock copies, or pick them up at Launceston.

As the Walls of Jerusalem is the only national park in Tasmania that you can't drive into, the walk in begins outside the park boundaries. From King Solomons Cave (see p.1076), head south, following the Mersey River and the unsealed road east of Lake Rowallan; the car park is at Howells Bluff. You walk through wilderness into the park, which is isolated and lacking even basic facilities, without a ranger (although rangers do patrol). However, the track is well kept, with boardwalks laid down over boggy areas, and there's plenty of clean water to drink from the streams and lakes. The few small leaky huts are really for emergencies only. If you just want to walk into the park to the central basin (through **Herods Gate**, with views of Barn Bluff and Cradle Mountain to the northwest), set up camp and then walk back; it's a fourteen-kilometre return hike, which takes seven or eight hours altogether, going at a steady pace over two days. The walk begins with a steep climb then levels out on the plateau. There are numerous routes to the various peaks and lakes – from **Damascus Gate** you get stunning views of Cradle Mountain–Lake St Clair National Park immediately west – and an experienced, well-equipped walker could spend a couple of days here. **Organized walks** are provided by Craclair, and Tasmanian Expeditions run four-day expeditions (both $1040; Oct–April), the latter also offering it as a six-day combined trip walk with Cradle Mountain ($1450); see p.1017 for contact details. Maxwell's (℡03/6492 1431) operates on demand from Devonport (1–4 people $180; 5 or more people $45 per person) and Launceston ($240/$60).

The Central Plateau

At its northern and eastern edges, the **Central Plateau** is rimmed by the long crest of the Great Western Tiers (1440m). At over 1000m above sea level, the plateau is often covered in frost and subject to sleet and snowstorms in winter. The **Great Lake** lies on the plateau about 8km from the escarpment, and only 40km from Deloraine, along the Lake Highway that continues to **BOTHWELL**, the plateau's only town, ending at Melton Mowbray, where it joins the Midland Highway. The major lakes can be reached from roads leading off the Lake Highway. To the west, between Cradle Mountain–Lake St Clair National Park and below the Walls of Jerusalem National Park, is the inaccessible "Land of Three Thousand Lakes".

The Central Plateau has few inhabitants – only around eight hundred live here year-round – but it's full of **fishing shacks**, and on a fine weekend the population sometimes swells to 25,000. It's also the base for the **Hydro Electricity Commission (HEC)**: the countless high-altitude lakes are used as water storage for the generation of electricity. Several temporary HEC villages set up for hydroelectric workers have been transformed into lodge-style accommodation. One is **Tarraleah**, where the workers' Art Deco cottages and former village school have been converted into accommodation in an activity-holiday centre (℡03/6289 0111, Ⓦwww.tarraleah.com; camping $15, studios ❺, cottages ❼). The Art Deco former manager's house is now a luxury country retreat, *The Lodge* (℡03/6289 1199, Ⓦwww.tarraleahlodge.com; ❽). There's also a good café, *Teez* (daily 8am–4pm; licensed) and a pub serving counter meals, the *Highlander Arms*.

TassieLink **buses** calls at Tarraleah off the Lyell Highway on its Hobart–Queenstown service.

The West

The wild **west coast**, densely forested and battered by the rough Southern Ocean and the Roaring Forties, its shores strewn with huge dead trees washed down from the southwest's many rivers, would probably still be uninhabited if it weren't for the **logging** and **mining** industries. The western half of Tasmania is untamed, except for the rich beef, dairy and vegetable-growing land along the northwest coast. This part of the island is very densely populated (by Tasmanian standards), and the **Bass Highway**, which skirts the northwest coast, passes through two unattractive industrial cities, **Devonport** and **Burnie**.

Rocky Cape National Park and the town of Stanley (originally built by the Van Diemen's Land Company – VDL – which still owns the northwest corner of the state) are the most interesting places for visitors.

Just south of Stanley the highway turns inland to Smithton, marking the beginning of a thickly forested region and a logging heartland. The Bass Highway ends at the tiny settlement of Marrawah, on the west coast (popular with surfers), where it meets the Western Explorer road, which runs south to sleepy Arthur River and then through the Arthur Pieman Protected Area to Corinna, where the road heads east via Savage River and Waratah onto the A10 (Murchison Highway). Alternatively, you can continue southwards, taking a barge (the "Fatman") across the Pieman River and then heading on to Zeehan (on the C249) and Strahan (on the B27), on the vast Macquarie Harbour. To reach Strahan on sealed roads, you have to go back to Marrawah and then to Somerset on the northwest coast, from where the Murchison Highway heads south through a copper- and lead-mining backwater. On the way you pass Queenstown; miners' greed which ripped away the surrounding rainforest has scarred the landscape and left only bare moon-like hills.

Strahan sits on the edge of the southwest wilderness, an area of rugged coastlines, wild rivers, open plains, thick rainforest and spectacular peaks – the wettest part of Australia after the tropical lowlands of north Queensland. It's mostly inaccessible, except to experienced and well-prepared bushwalkers, but cruises leave from Strahan to go up the Gordon River, offering a glimpse of its magnificent scenery. Some years ago, a plan to dam the Gordon River below the point where it joins the Franklin River put Strahan at the centre of a struggle between environmentalists and the state government. Eventually the federal government stepped in, and, following a landmark High Court ruling in 1983, the whole of the southwest – including the South West National Park, the Franklin Lower Gordon Wild Rivers National Park and the adjoining heavily glaciated Cradle Mountain–Lake St Clair National Park – became a vast, protected UNESCO World Heritage Area, occupying twenty percent of the state's land area. From Queenstown, en route to Hobart, the Lyell Highway provides limited access to the mainly inaccessible Franklin Lower Gordon Park, and to Lake St Clair at Derwent Bridge.

The northwest coast

A succession of Tasmania's larger towns dots the conservative, agricultural northwest coast, including the cities of Devonport and Burnie, and the smaller community of older Stanley, on a peninsula jutting into the Bass Strait. The Bass Highway, which connects them, becomes spectacularly beautiful beyond Wynyard, passing Table Cape, Boat Harbour Beach and Rocky Cape National Park, though it skirts the very northwest tip (privately owned by the Van Diemen's Land Company). At the end of the highway is Marrawah, from where you can head to Arthur River for a cruise. Redline runs daily services from Devonport to Burnie, and from Burnie to Smithton, stopping at all towns along the Bass Highway; there is no public transport to Marrawah or Arthur River.

Devonport and around

The industrial port of DEVONPORT, which in 1959 replaced Launceston as the terminal of the Bass Strait ferry, the *Spirit of Tasmania*, is not the most inspiring first point of contact with Tasmania. As the ship makes its slow progress up the Mersey River, you might almost think you're arriving at a 1950s

English seaport, but for the tin-roofed weatherboard bungalows, the brittle quality of the light, the bush-covered hills to the east and a *McDonald's* on the waterfront. As a jumping-off point for Cradle Mountain, the Overland Track and the rugged west coast, Devonport has developed a significant tourism infrastructure – car-rental companies, bus companies, camping stores and backpacking information – and though it's hardly a destination in itself, it makes a passable **base** for trips into the surrounding countryside

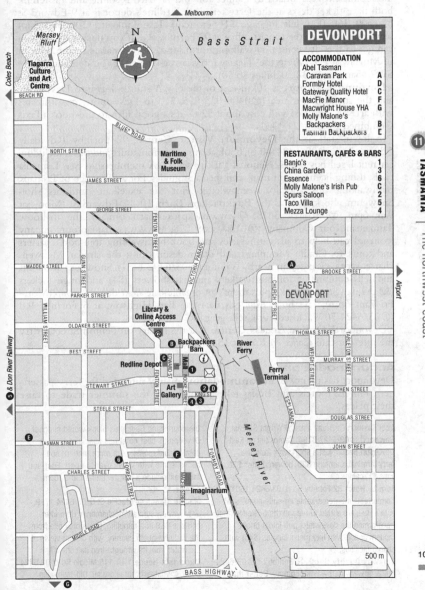

DEVONPORT

ACCOMMODATION

Abel Tasman Caravan Park	A
Formby Hotel	D
Gateway Quality Hotel	C
MacFie Manor	F
Macwright House YHA	G
Molly Malone's Backpackers	B
Tasman Backpackers	E

RESTAURANTS, CAFÉS & BARS

Banjo's	1
China Garden	3
Essence	6
Molly Malone's Irish Pub	C
Spurs Saloon	2
Taco Villa	5
Mezza Lounge	4

The *Spirit of Tasmania* **Bass Strait ferries** (see p.1078) from Melbourne dock at the terminal in East Devonport, just across the Mersey River from the city centre. As the boats have their own tourist information and booking centre, you might have made all your arrangements on board. If not, there are company representatives and car-hire desks in the terminal, and you can buy bus passes and tickets here. Most passengers head immediately for waiting Redline and TassieLink **express buses** to Launceston and Hobart. Redline and TassieLink both have ticket desks at the ferry terminal. Redline's depot is at 9 Edward St (T1300 360 000; left luggage $1 per item); TassieLink (T1300 300 520) services leave from the tourist office at 92 Formby Rd. If you decide to stay, you can get to the city centre by walking north for a short distance to the bottom of Murray Street, where the *Torquay* ferry crosses the river (on demand Mon–Sat 7.45am–6pm; $2.50, bikes $0.50).

Devonport Airport is 10km east of the city. A shuttle bus into Devonport and the surrounding area (T0400 035 995; $10 to Devonport) co-ordinates with arrivals, or a taxi will cost about $20 – it's a good idea to pre-book (Taxis Combined T03/6424 1431).

In town, staff at the **Devonport Visitor Centre**, 92 Formby Rd (daily 7.30am–5pm; T03/6424 4466), book accommodation, tours and travel including car rental, sell bus passes, National Park passes, YHA membership, See Tasmania cards, fishing licences, and maps and specialist guides. For a full range of Tasmaps, bushwalking tips and local knowledge visit the excellent outdoors shop Snowgum, also known as the **Backpackers Barn**, 10–12 Edward St (Mon–Sat 9am–6pm; T03/6424 3628, Wwww.backpackersbarn.com.au); the in-house Tasmanian Tour Company (T01300 659 878, Wwww.tasmaniantourcompany .com.au) can help to plan itineraries and book bushwalking transport charters and tours to Cradle Mountain and other destinations; the similar Maxwells charter service is based in nearby Wilmot (T03/6492 1431). Snowgum also rents and sells equipment for bushwalkers and has showers ($4) and huge lockers ($2 per day, $6 per week), plus there's an organic café next door, *Rosehip* (Mon–Fri 7am–6pm). The huge Allgoods near the Bass Highway, at 6 Formby Rd (T03/6424 7099; closed Sun), sells gear too.

Devonport's **Online Access Centre** is at the library on Fenton Street, or try the internet café *Coffee on King* at 15 King St.

Accommodation

Devonport has plenty of **accommodation**, mainly intended for ferry passengers. Hotels, motels and B&Bs take advantage of the summer trade to raise their prices.

Abel Tasman Caravan Park 6 Wright St, East Devonport T03/6427 8794. Campsites on East Devonport Beach, just a short walk from the ferry terminal. Camping $20, powered sites $26, vans ❸, cabins ❹

Formby Hotel 82 Formby Rd T03/6424 1601. Comfortable if unremarkable en-suite doubles, all with fridge, are slated to receive the makeover that transformed the downstairs pub into a bright modern space. Also has men's singles ($45) with shared facilities. ❸

Gateway Quality Hotel 16 Fenton St T03/6424 4922, Wwww.gatewayinn.com.au. Better than the depressing Seventies block would suggest, Devonport's best hotel has spacious, comfortable rooms, plus more modern spa suites, some with views over the port. Four-star facilities include a bar, restaurant and room service. ❺–❼

MacFie Manor 44 MacFie St T03/6424 1719, Wwww.view.com.au/macfiemanor. Upmarket heritage B&B in a rambling, two-storey pile from the early twentieth century, with distant views of the water from its wrought-iron balcony. ❹

Macwright House YHA 115 Middle Rd T03/6424 5696, Eyhatas@yhatas.org.au. Old-fashioned hostel that's more than half an hour's walk from the city centre – the local Merseylink bus will get you from the city on weekdays. Dorms $18.50, rooms ❷

Molly Malone's Backpackers 34 Best St ☎03/6424 1898, ⓔ mollymalones@vantagegroup .com.au. Convenient backpackers' accommodation, with four-bed dorms and functional rooms – some en suite – well away from the noise of the Irish theme-pub downstairs. Dorms $15, rooms ❷

Tasman Backpackers 114 Tasman St ☎03/6423 2335, ⓦ www.tasmanbackpackers.com.au. Spacious hostel in a former nurses' residence. Mostly well-furnished twins, a couple of en-suite doubles and five- to eight-bed dorms. Affordable tours available to places such as Cradle Mountain, plus harvest work contacts. 20min walk from the river, but free pick-ups on request. Dorms $18, rooms ❷–❸

The City

Central Devonport is bounded by the Mersey to the east; Formby Road runs alongside it, while Stewart Street, at right angles, is dominated by a view of the bulky *Spirit of Tasmania* ferries when they're in port, and sometimes other colourful freighters. The **Devonport Art Gallery** at 45 Stewart St (Mon–Sat 10am–5pm, Sun 2–5pm; free) is a converted church with changing exhibitions and a small permanent collection of Tasmanian ceramics. The city centre caters well to departing tourists in need of last-minute souvenirs, with big-name chain stores on **Rooke Street Mall** and tasteful gift shops on Stewart Street.

The **Devonport Maritime Museum**, north of the city centre at 47 Victoria Parade, near the river's mouth (Tues–Sun 10am–4pm; $4), has an extensive display of model ships ranging from sailing vessels to modern passenger ferries. The **Imaginarium Science Centre**, 19–23 MacFie St, just south of the CBD, is Tasmania's hands-on science discovery centre (Mon–Thurs 10am–4pm, Sat & Sun noon–5pm; $8; ☎03/6423 1466). Considerably more compelling, though, is the **Tiagarra Tasmanian Aboriginal Culture and Art Centre** (☎03/6424 8250; Mon–Sat 9am–5pm; $5), located at the dramatic **Mersey Bluff**, 1.5km northwest of the Maritime and Folk Museum, near the end of Bluff Road. The centre has preserved around 270 Aboriginal rock engravings (eleven of which are on show), and a display centre provides generalized (and rather rushed) taped background information on how the Tasmanian Aborigines lived. Decent beaches lie either side of the bluff, including **Coles Beach**. The **Don River Railway**, which uses steam or diesel locomotives, terminates here on its hourly trips from the Don Recreation Ground, west of town, along the Don River (hourly 10am–4pm; 30min; $15 return; ☎03/6424 6335).

Eating, drinking and nightlife

Banjo's Rooke St Mall. Outpost of the ubiquitous Tasmanian chain of early opening, eat-in bakeries, offering the usual inexpensive fresh-baked goods. Daily 6am–6pm.

China Garden 33 King St ☎03/6424 4148. Popular Cantonese restaurant with $7.50 lunch specials. Licensed.

Essence 28 Forbes St ☎03/6424 6431. This big, old charming house uses the best of Tasmanian produce to create traditional modern European dishes with a contemporary edge. The crisp-skinned confit of duck is always popular. Mains around $26. You can just come in for a drink in the *Lounge Bar*, where several Tasmanian wines are

available by the glass. Lunch Tues–Fri, dinner Tues–Sat, bar from 5.30pm.

Mezza Lounge 12 Rooke St. Contemporary café with comfy sofas and a spread of healthy Mediterranean-style food and fresh juices, plus pastries and yummy cakes. Vegetarian choices include lentil burgers with salad for $14. Licensed. Mon–Sat 9am–4pm.

Molly Malone's Irish Pub 34 Best St. Characterful and sprawling Irish theme-pub that rustles up decent low-priced counter meals. Lots of pub favourites – including a cheap roast of the day – and fish as well as vegetarian choices.

The Tasmanian Trail

The **Tasmanian Trail** is a 480-kilometre multipurpose recreational trail extending from Devonport on the north coast to Dover on the south coast. Created by connecting forestry roads, fire trails and country roads (often going through small towns) and at times traversing private land, it's primarily used for mountain biking and horseriding. For details, consult ⓦ www.tasmaniantrail.com.au; or the *Tasmanian Trail Guidebook* is available from tourist offices and bookshops for $28.

Spurs Saloon 18 King St ⓣ 03/6424 7851. *Warehouse Niteclub* attached. Also a venue for touring bands. Wed–Sun 5pm–late.

Taco Villa Shop 4 Kempling St. Good Mexican food – a local institution for thirty years. Takeaway available. Dinner Wed–Sun.

Listings

Bookshop Angus & Robertson Bookworld, 43 Rooke St ⓣ 03/6424 2022.
Car rental Firms located at the airport and ferry terminal include Autorent-Hertz ⓣ 03/6424 1013, Avis Tasmania ⓣ 03/6427 9797 and Budget ⓣ 03/6427 0650; among cheaper alternatives are Lo-Cost Auto Rent ⓣ 03/6424 9922, ⓦ www.locostautorent.com, and the popular Rent-A-Bug

ⓣ 03/6427 9304, ⓦ www.rentabug.com.au, both on Murray St by the ferry terminal, East Devonport.
Cinema C-Max Cinemas, behind the visitor centre at 5–7 Best St (ⓣ 03/6240 2111), is a four-screen complex.
Post office Corner of Stewart St and Formby Rd, TAS 7310.
Taxi Taxis Combined ⓣ 03/6424 1431.

Around Devonport

East of Devonport are some particularly rewarding spots on the **Rubicon River estuary**, where you'll find the seaside resort of **PORT SORELL**, roughly 19km from Devonport and across the river from the Narawntapu National Park (see below). You can **stay** here in a self-catering three-bedroom solar-heated house at *Heron on Earth Organic Farm* (ⓣ 03/6428 6144, ⓦ www .herononearth.com; ❸), which lends out canoes for you to paddle across to the national park, as well as bikes. More luxurious accommodation is provided 4km northeast at **HAWLEY BEACH**, at the well-regarded, rather grand Victorian-era *Hawley House* (ⓣ 03/6428 6221, ⓦ www.hawleyhousetas.com; ❻–❼), which has a fine restaurant and its own vineyard producing Chardonnay and Pinot Noir. From Hawley Beach there's a 10km-return walk to Point Sorell.

To reach the western edge of the **Narawntapu National Park** (formerly Asbestos Range National Park), on the east side of the Rubicon River estuary, it's a meandering, forty-kilometre drive from Devonport. The remote park is worth the trip – particularly at dusk – for the chance to spot some wildlife: **Forrester kangaroos** come down to feed at **Bakers Beach** at that time, and it's the best place in Tasmania to see **wombats**. The park is renowned for its occasional spectacular storms, accompanied by strong winds roaring along the beach. There's a self-registering **campsite** here, for which you pay a small fee (ranger ⓣ 03/6428 6277), and the beach is good for swimming. You'll need your own transport to get out here.

The quirky town of **LATROBE**, just 5km south of Devonport, has put itself on the map as the self-declared "Platypus Capital of the World", to which end a tacky **Big Platypus** is plonked outside the **Platypus Experience**, a pretty dire adjunct to the Australian Axeman's Hall of Fame (daily 9am–5pm; joint ticket $10) which celebrates the Tasmanian spectator sport of wood-chopping. Spotting the real thing at dusk in the creek outside provides greater thrills or, even better, join a reliable tour to the Warrawee State Reserve 4km south organized by Latrobe Platypus Encounters (dawn and dusk; ☎03/6246 1774; 1hr 30min–2hr; $10); all funds go towards habitat maintenance. You can also book at the **visitor centre** (Mon–Sat 9am–4pm, Sun 9.30am–3pm; ☎03/6421 4599) on the main street beside the *Latrobe Hotel*. Further along, at no. 139, **Reliquaire**, an extraordinary (and fairly kooky) shop selling toys and novelties, is worth a look if you have time to kill.

SHEFFIELD, 30km south of Devonport, is a popular stop en route to Cradle Mountain. The cute, old-fashioned town, set amongst farmland made fertile by red volcanic soils, is situated near the base of Mount Roland (1231m), which provides a scenic backdrop. The town's rural economy was ailing when the community decided to reinvent itself through the medium of visual art; since the mid-1980s over thirty **murals** in various styles have been painted by several local artists, showing the history and folklore of the town, and new works are chosen in an annual competition. You can pick up maps of the locations – and an MP3 audio tour of the murals' history ($5) – from the efficient council-run **Kentish Visitor Centre** (daily 9am–5pm; ☎03/6491 1036); set aside an hour to complete the walking tour. Current entries for the murals competition are displayed in the adjacent park. The centre also books accommodation and offers internet access; the **Online Access Centre** itself is in the high school on Henry Street. The steady stream of tourists has introduced a modest café culture to Sheffield, including *Yvette's* at 43 Main St (usually Mon–Fri 11am–4pm, longer at weekends), which offers fair-trade coffee, inexpensive gourmet sandwiches and salads and light bistro fare, though its opening times can be erratic.

Some 16km southwest of Sheffield at **GOWRIE PARK** at the base of **Mount Roland**, you can **stay** at *Gowrie Park Wilderness Cabins and Backpackers*, with bunk-style quarters and simple en-suite cabins spectacularly sited beneath Mount Roland (☎03/6491 1385; camping $5 per person; dorms $10, cabins ❸). It makes a good base for walks up and around the summit (2hr return), which provide great views of Cradle Mountain. At the other end of the scale, ⚲ *Glencoe* (☎03/6492 3267, ⓦwww.glencoeruralretreat.com; ❻) offers beautiful modern-country style and sensational cooking from its French owners in a renovated home at Barrington, 8km northwest of Sheffield, or for blow-the-budget opulence there's the *Eagles Nest Retreat* (☎03/6491 1511, ⓦwww.eaglesnestretreat.com.au; ❻), whose quirky luxury retreats provide astonishing views of Mount Roland.

You can get to Sheffield and Gowrie Park with TassieLink on their scheduled Launceston–Queenstown service via Cradle Mountain (3 weekly).

Ulverstone and Penguin

Redline buses follow the unremarkable coast from Devonport west to industrial Burnie, stopping at Ulverstone and Penguin. **ULVERSTONE**, 20km west of Devonport where the **Leven River** flows into the sea, is an unremarkable holiday centre which is popular with families due to its unpolluted **beaches**. A population of Little penguins comes to breed on the beach here between September and April, and Penguin Point Twilight Tours takes small groups from the *Ulverstone Waterfront Inn* out at dusk (2–3hr; $15; bookings ☎03/6425 1599). A better reason to stop is to join Todd Walsh on scientific expeditions to map the **giant freshwater crayfish**, a threatened species that can grow up to several kilograms and lives only in the northern flowing rivers of Tasmania (tours by arrangement only; ☎03/6425 5302 or 0439 693 377; payment by donation). The town's **accommodation** includes *Furners Hotel* at 42 Reibey St (☎03/6425 1488; en-suite B&B ❹), a red-brick pile from the early twentieth century complete with carved blackwood staircase and bistro; or you can **camp** at the waterfront *Apex Caravan Park* at Queen St (☎03/6425 2935; camping $11). The best **place to eat** is *Pedro's* jutting above the river on Wharf Road (☎03/6425 6663), the perfect spot for a seafood restaurant and with one of Tassie's most rated fish-and-chips shops beneath. The **Ulverstone Visitor Centre** is at 13–15 Alexander St (daily 9am–5pm; ☎03/6425 2839).

In the picturesque hop-growing countryside just under 25km south of Ulverstone, the **Gunns Plains Caves** (hourly tours daily 10am–4pm; 50min; $10; ☎03/6429 1388), part of the **Gunns Plains State Reserve**, are worth visiting for their remarkable limestone formations which, when lit from behind, glow a succulent red. A permanent stream feeds an underground lake, and platypuses and possums enjoy the cool temperatures.

The best route west from Ulverstone follows the old Bass Highway (Penguin Rd) along the coastline, passing the Three Sisters and Goat Islands bird sanctuaries, Penguin Point where Little penguins roost, and a beautiful array of flowers as you come into **PENGUIN** itself, 12km along the highway. The neat little town has three safe swimming beaches and a strong café culture. Cute blue-and-white penguin-shaped rubbish bins line the beachfront main street, culminating in the two-metre-high **Big Penguin** in the foreshore park. The **Visitor Centre** (summer daily 9am–4pm, otherwise Mon–Fri 9am–4pm, Sat & Sun 9am–12.30pm; ☎03/6437 1421) can provide more details about things to do in the area, including twilight penguin trips (1hr 30min; ☎03/6437 2590; $12). The *Madsen Boutique Hotel* at 64 Main Rd offers stylish bed-and-breakfast **accommodation** (☎03/6437 2588, ⓦwww.themadsen.com; ⑥), while next door, the *Groovy Penguin* (Tues–Sun 10am–4pm) is worth a visit in its own right: it's a fantastically colourful and cluttered **café** with young owners and an alternative feel – the healthy menu includes lentil burgers and lasagne. If it's closed, try the modern Australian cuisine at upmarket café-restaurant *Wild* (lunch & dinner Wed–Sun) a short way along the street. Five kilometres south outside town, there are walking trails in the **Dial Range State Forest**.

Burnie

BURNIE, on Emu Bay 15km west of Penguin, is an industrial and paper-manufacturing centre and container port, and Tasmania's third-largest city with a population of nearly 20,000. The port, with its controversial pile of export woodchips and nearby paper mill, is unattractive, but the city is situated amid rich farmland and beautiful rocky coves, and tourism is now being actively developed. If things go to plan, the focus for visitors will be a beachside development slated for completion in 2010. In theory, this will transfer the **Tasmanian Travel and Information Centre** from its site on Civic Square precinct, off Little Alexander Street (Mon–Fri 9am–5pm, Sat 9am–4pm, Sun 10am–2pm; ☎03/6434 6111), and also take with it the **Pioneer Village Museum**, with its reconstructed early twentieth-century street (Mon–Fri 9am–5pm; $6). The new building was planned principally as a home for the community-based, nonprofit **Creative Paper Mill**, bringing it into the town centre from exile on the Old Surrey Road (C112), 100m off the Bass Highway on the eastern side of Burnie (Oct–April daily 9am–4pm, tours 10am, noon & 2.30pm; May–Sept Mon–Sat 10am–4pm, tours 11am & 2.30pm; $10; ☎03/6430 5831, ⓦwww.creativepapertas.com.au), near the large-scale **Australian Paper Mill**. The paper on show is handmade – you can have a go yourself – and there's a product showroom, as well as an art gallery. Elsewhere in the centre, the **Burnie Regional Art Gallery** (Tues–Fri 10.30am–5pm, Sat & Sun 1.30–4.30pm; free) is on Civic Square.

East of the centre, 3km from the original Creative Paper Mill on Old Surrey Road, Lactos is a prize-winning **cheese factory** (Mon–Fri 9am–5pm, Sat & Sun 10am–4pm; free), where you can sample and buy blends and variations of European cheeses. In the same vein, you can learn about **whisky distillery** and taste the results ($10) in the light-filled visitor centre of nearby Hellyers Road Distillery (daily 10am 4.30pm; ℡03/6433 0439, ⓦwww.hellyersroaddistillery .com.au). Forking off Old Surrey Road, just 1km from the city centre, **Fernglade** is a **platypus reserve** on a peaceful, forested stretch of the Emu River. The platypuses are easy to spot, particularly at dawn and after dusk. Burnie also has a free **penguin interpretive centre**, reached via a one-kilometre boardwalk from the town centre; the long, thin building is open to the Little penguins who, lit by infrared light, can be observed through windows via a periscope-style mirrored tunnel; the best time to view the penguins is after dusk between September and April.

There's plenty of **accommodation**, should you decide to stay in Burnie; the visitor centre does free bookings. The *Burnie Holiday Caravan Park*, 253 Bass Highway, at Cooee on the pleasant, non-industrial side of town towards Wynyard, has something to suit everyone, with an attached *Ocean View Motel*, cabins, a backpackers' section and camping (℡03/6431 1925, ⓦwww .burniebeachaccommodation.com.au; camping $18, powered sites $25, dorms $25, vans ❷, cabins ❹, motel ❹). For more character, *Seabreeze Cottages* (℡0439 353 491, ⓦwww.seabreezecottages.com.au; ❻) maintains three stylish modern houses in the west side of the centre, or *Glen Osborne House*, at 9 Aileen Crescent (℡03/6431 9866, ⓦwww.glenosbornehouse.com.au; ❻), is a large Victorian-era B&B with spacious en-suite rooms and a lovely English-style garden.

Food choices include the veteran Italian, *Rialto*, at 46 Wilmot St (℡03/6431 7718; BYO), and the licensed *Café Europa*, at the corner of Cattley and Wilson streets (Mon–Sat), a cosmopolitan hangout, with some Greek Cypriot offerings on the Mediterranean menu (also good-value toasted Turkish sandwiches, snacks and coffee). The Metro Cinema, at the corner of Marine Terrace and Wilmot Street (℡03/6431 5000, ⓦwww.metrocinemas.com.au), is the entertainment focus. Burnie's **Online Access Centre** is at 2 Spring St. Redline **buses** pick up and drop-off outside the multistorey car park on Wilson Street, while at the time of writing TassieLink operates from the visitor centre on Civic Square.

Wynyard and around

WYNYARD, another 19km along the old Bass Highway from Burnie, snuggles into the lush pasturelands between the **Inglis River** and the sea. The wharf area, with its fishing boats and fresh fish shop, is just off bustling Goldie Street – the main street that parallels the river. There are over 12km of riverside walking tracks, starting from the riverfront park on the corner of Goldie and Hogg streets. It's an easy three-kilometre walk to **Fossil Bluff** where layers of sedimentary rock containing fossilized seashells can easily be examined at low tide, and the beach itself has good views of the 170-metre seaface of **Table Cape**. A drive up to the **lookout** on Table Cape will reward you with magnificent views of the coast and hinterland, particularly pretty when the cape's **tulip fields** are in bloom around October.

Wynyard may well be the first place you see in Tasmania, since "Burnie" **airport** is just a five-minute stroll from the town centre. You can **rent a car** at the airport with Autorent-Hertz (℡03/6431 4242), Avis (℡03/6442 2512) or Budget (℡1800 030 035 or 03/6431 3264). The Burnie Airbus connects the airport with Burnie ($22; ☎0439 322 466). MTT **public transport buses** connect Wynyard with Burnie, departing from 38 Jackson St. Redline stops in the centre on its Burnie–Smithton route, and also the turn-offs to Table Cape, Boat Harbour Beach and Rocky Cape.

Wynyard Visitor Centre, in the large car park behind the intersection of Jackson and Dodgin streets (daily 9am–5pm; ☎03/6443 8330), has the usual flyer confetti on local activities and **accommodation**. There's camping at *Beach Retreat Tourist Park*, at 30B Old Bass Highway on the way out of town to Burnie (☎03/6442 1998, Ⓦwww.beachretreat.touristpark.com.au; rooms ❷, motel units ❸, cabins ❹). However, the best place to stay is *The Waterfront Wynyard*, 1 Goldie St (☎03/6442 2351, Ⓦwww.thewaterfront.net.au; ❹), which overlooks the river right by the wharf. Its recently refurbished motel rooms are equipped with satellite TV and DVD players, and the on-site **café-restaurant** is the best in town, with river views and a diverse menu of modern Australian cooking. The takeaway fish-and-chip shop on the wharf is good too, or try *Buckaneers*, at 4 Inglis St (☎03/6442 4104), which does excellent takeaway fresh fish and has a weekend seafood restaurant. Wynyard's **Online Access Centre** is in the library just across from the visitor centre.

Boat Harbour Beach and Sister Beach

Some 11km west of Wynyard, a turn-off from the Bass Highway winds down to **Boat Harbour Beach**, the prettiest on the northwest coast, with pale-blue water, white sand and very gentle waves. It's good for **diving**, too; rent equipment from the Scuba Centre at 62 Bass Highway in Wynyard (☎03/6442 2247), which also organizes excursions. *Jolly Rogers on the Beach*, a licensed café-restaurant right on the beach with a good modern bistro menu, is tailor-made for lazy days. Attractive Sisters Beach, closer to Rocky Cape, is much less developed (and there are no building works going on); you can stay at *Birdland Holiday Cottages*, 7 Banksia Ave (☎03/6445 1471; ❹), set in forest. Back on the highway, the Boat Harbour Store has petrol and a post office.

Rocky Cape (Tangdimmaa) National Park

Stretching for a mere 12km along the coast, from Sisters Beach to Rocky Cape, are the rugged hills and cliffs of **Rocky Cape (Tangdimmaa) National Park**, Tasmania's smallest national park, created in 1967 for the purpose of preserving some remarkable **Aboriginal archeological finds**. The mainly quartzite hills are pockmarked with caves, of which the two major ones, North Cave and South Cave, contain huge shell middens, bones and stone tools dating back as far as eight thousand years, when the sea was several fathoms below its current level.

Rocky Cape is now managed in consultation with the Tasmanian Aboriginal Land Council, and visitors are no longer allowed to enter the caves, although you can go up to the entrance. To reach North Cave it's a fifteen-minute walk there and back from the road, reached by driving 5km into the park and taking the left fork at the lighthouse – most people prefer just to walk along the various easy tracks. It takes seven hours to traverse the whole length of the park; there's no water, no toilets, and camping is not allowed. Rocky pools, safe swimming beaches and picnic areas are scattered along the route, while in spring and summer there's a profusion of wild flowers on the scrubby heathland, including some unique native orchids. At dusk you may see wallabies, echidnas and various species of bird. Back on the highway, there's **accommodation** at the *Rocky Cape Tavern* (☎03/6443 4110; camping $16, unpowered sites $25, units ❸), and there's a petrol station nearby.

Stanley

It's a 31-kilometre drive from the Rocky Cape turn-off west along the Bass Highway (A2) to the fishing village of **STANLEY**, the original 1826 headquarters of the **Van Diemen's Land Company** and the first settlement in northwest Tasmania; the scenic coastal drive hugging the coast is marred only by the industrial scene at Port Latta. About 5km beyond here, a turn-off leads 27km south on the C225 to the must-see **Dip Falls Big Tree**, a gigantic eucalypt measuring 17m at its base and thought to be over 400 years old.

Back on the highway, long before you arrive at Stanley, 6km off the Bass Highway, you'll see your first view of **The Nut**, described by Matthew Flinders as a "cliffy round lump in form resembling a Christmas cake" that rises directly out of the ocean to a height of nearly 150m. **Circular Head**, as it's officially called (the name also for the surrounding municipality), is thought to be a volcanic plug, with the softer sediments around it having eroded away. The town itself is on a small, foot-shaped peninsula right at the base of The Nut, perched high above Sawyer Bay and Tatlows Beach.

Arrival, information and tours

For visitor information, accommodation bookings and internet access visit the **Stanley Visitor Centre** on the way into Stanley at 45 Main Rd (Mon–Fri 9.30am–5.30pm, Sat & Sun 10am–4pm; ☎03/6458 1330); it also serves as the Redline **bus depot** and sells bus tickets – Stanley is on the route between Burnie and Smithton (Mon–Fri daily either way). The General Store is below the town centre on Wharf Road and has an ATM, while the newsagent towards the end of Church Street also has supplies and is an ANZ **bank** agent; there are more banking facilities a few doors up at the post office.

Stanley-based Wilderness to West Coast Tours (☎03/6458 2038, ⓦwww .wildernesstasmania.com) runs a dusk platypus-viewing tour (2hr; $35) and a penguin tour (1hr; $15; both tours combined $45). Stanley Seal Cruises on Wharf Road will take you to view a colony of rare **Australian fur seals**, weather permitting (daily 10am; also April–June 3pm; $49; ☎0419 550 134).

Accommodation

Stanley is packed with holiday **accommodation**. In keeping with its historic ambience, the town has many "colonial" **B&Bs**, which are actually self-contained cottages with breakfast provisions supplied.

@VDL 16 Wharf Rd ☎03/6458 2032, ⓦwww .atvdlstanley.com.au. The former VDL store has been beautifully renovated to create two glamorous suites, a tasteful union of hip interior design and historic architecture, with custom-designed Tasmanian furniture and art in the shared lounge. ❼

Abbey's Spa Cottage 46 Alexander Terrace ☎1800 222 397, ⓦwww.stanleytasmania.com.au. There are gorgeous Sawyer Bay views from the veranda of this charming, weatherboard self-contained house nestled under The Nut (❺). The same management have several other excellent options, including *Abbey's Cottage*, nearby at no. 34 (❺), and the tiny but tidy two-bed *Pol & Pen Holiday Chalets*, close to Godfrey's Beach on Pearse St – good value (❹).

Beachside Retreat West Inlet Main Rd ☎03/6458 1350, ⓦwww.beachsideretreat.com. 2.5km south of the town centre, some of the stunning designer cabins here have fantastic Nut views framed by huge porthole and picture windows, and there's access to a private beach. ❻–❽

Old Cable Station 435 Greenhills Rd, north of town, beyond Highfield House ☎03/6458 1312, ⓦwww.oldcablestation.com.au. Once linking Tasmania with the mainland via King Island, this is a stylish and peaceful retreat with views stretching across fields to water. Choose from a spacious three-bedroom cottage and two stylish en-suite rooms, all an appealing mix of antique and modern style. Also has a superb restaurant, open to non-guests in peak season. Rooms ❹–❻, cottage ❼

Seaview Inn 1km along Dovecote Rd ⓣ03/6458 1300, ⓦwww.stanleyseaviewinn.com .au. There are some of the best views of The Nut, across green fields, from the *Seaview*'s motel-style units (some self-catering) – fairly dated but comfortable enough and well appointed. Facilities include a bar and a restaurant. ❹–❺

Stanley Cabin and Tourist Park Wharf Rd ⓣ03/6458 1266, ⓦwww.stanleycabinpark.com .au. In a good location behind Tatlows Beach and equidistant between the town centre and fishing wharf, this is the only camping and backpackers' option in town, the latter perennially popular. Also has tidy cabins. Camping $22, powered sites $24, dorms $24, motel-style rooms ❸, cabins ❸–❹

Stanley Hotel Church St ⓣ1800 222 397 or 03/6458 1258. Above-average and pleasant pub rooms above this sprawling, three-storey hotel in the centre. Good single rates ($45). Rooms ❸, en suite ❹

The Town

Stanley's main street, **Church Street**, runs below the foot of The Nut, and its restaurants and crafts shops – check out the contemporary wood designs in Stanley Artworks Studio Gallery near the post office – are high enough above the beach, wharves and the rest of the town to command excellent views. Although it's worth doing the strenuous ten- to twenty-minute walk up the grassy **Nut** itself, you can get to the top more comfortably by means of an exhilarating **chairlift**, reached via the ramp opposite the post office (daily 9.30am–5pm, weather permitting; call ⓣ03/6458 1286 to check; $10 return). The licensed *Nut Rock Café*, next door to the chairlift, has fantastic views and decent coffee. A 2-kilometre circuit walk around the windy **Nut State Reserve** at the top affords views over the town and port, and southeast as far

---

The Van Diemen's Land Company

...how is it that an absentee owner across the world got this magnificent and empty country without having paid one glass bead?

Cassandra Pybus

The Van Diemen's Land Company (VDL) was the brainchild of a group of prominent and well-connected individuals, who in 1824 managed to obtain by Royal Charter 250,000 acres of the mainly thickly forested, unexplored northwest corner of Tasmania. Their plan was to create their own source of fine wool in the colonies, which could be relied upon even if Europe was subject to political upheaval; the *Tranmere* arrived at Circular Head in 1826, with the personnel, livestock, supplies and equipment to create the township of Stanley.

The first flocks were grazed at Woolnorth on Cape Grim, a plateau of tussock grass and trees that might have been made for the purpose but, in fact, was prime Aboriginal hunting land. When hunting parties began to take the precious sheep, whites killed Aborigines in retaliation, and a vindictive cycle of killings began. The most tragic incident (a version of events denied by Woolnorth) was supposed to have occurred around 1826 or 1827: a group of Aboriginal men, seeking revenge for the rape of their women, speared a shepherd and herded one hundred sheep over the cliff edge. These deaths were ruthlessly avenged when a group of thirty unarmed Aborigines, hunting for muttonbirds near the same spot, were killed by shepherds and their bodies thrown over the cliff (now euphemistically called "Suicide Bay"). Ultimately, the Aboriginal people of the northwest were systematically hunted down: the last group, middle-aged parents and their five sons, were captured by sealers near the Arthur River in 1842 after the VDL's chief agent offered a £50 reward.

In the 1840s the company changed its emphasis from wool production to the sale and lease of its land, and it now holds just a fifth of its original land. Still registered on the London Stock Exchange, it is the only remaining company in the world operating under a Royal Charter; its major shareholder, who bought 87.5 percent of the shares in 1993, is a New Zealand-based agribusiness in Dunedin.

as Table Cape. Directly below is the exquisitely deserted **Godfrey's Beach** to the north, with its calm and translucent blue waters. Green Hills Road runs north alongside the beach and winds uphill to the original headquarters of the Van Diemen's Land Company, 2km north of the town, with superb views over Half Moon Bay. Though the rooms themselves of the **Highfield Historic Site** (daily 10am–4pm, closed Sat & Sun June–Aug; $10) are bare of artefacts, the interpretive boards provide a fascinating and honest history of the VDL Company and the Northwest, with lots from the Aboriginal perspective.

Below Church Street and Alexander Terrace, the foreshore area spreads alongside Wharf Road, with the curve of **Tatlows Beach** stretching for kilometres southeast and the busy fishing-port area, the marina full of colourful boats, to the west. By Marine Park, the slate-roofed **Van Diemen's Land Company Store** (now boutique accommodation) was designed in 1844 by John Lee Archer, whose work can be seen notably in Hobart. From the nearby **port area**, at low tide, you can see the remnants of a 1923 **shipwreck**, a victim of the "furies" of the Bass Strait. On Fisherman's Dock, **Stanley Seaquarium** (daily 9.30am–4.30pm; $10) is full of creatures hauled up by fishermen. The hands-on rockpool is fantastic, with sea stars, sea cucumbers and lots of shy hermit crabs in shells.

Eating

The town's **supermarket** is beneath the Stanley Hotel, near the cabin park (see below). Alongside the options listed here, a couple of **cafés** line the main drag, Church Street, though most shut by early evening.

Hurseys Seafoods Next to Marine Park on Wharf Rd. Highly regarded fish-and-chip shop run by a fishing family. Usually Mon–Sat 11am–6pm.

Old Cable Station 435 Greenhills Rd (beyond Highfield House) ☎03/6458 1312. This is dining with wow factor, with modern gourmet cuisine, Mediterranean-influenced and created from fresh local ingredients, and a glamorous dining room. Two-course menus $49. Open summer, dinner only.

Stanley Hotel Corner of Church and Victoria sts ☎03/6458 1258. One of the best bistros in Australia in 2008, according to the Australian Hospitality Association, this local pub is a credit to its breed – fresh seafood and delicious pub fare in a lively lounge bar with terrace dining. Make a reservation or expect to wait in summer. Lunch & dinner daily.

Stanleys on the Bay 15 Wharf Rd ☎03/6458 1404. Well-regarded seafood and steak restaurant in a former seafront VDL bond store. House special is local crayfish. Dinner Mon–Sat; closed July & Aug.

Touchwood Coffee Shop 31 Church St. Everything from octopus salad to crayfish rolls via toasted sandwiches and yummy biscuits in a daytime only café-bistro with expansive views from its terrace. Daily 10am–4pm.

Smithton and around

The only way to see Tasmania's rugged northwest tip, which remains under the control of the Van Diemen's Land Company, is by tour. **Tours** to **Woolnorth**, the original VDL cattle and sheep property, depart from the rather unattractive rural-industrial town of **SMITHTON**, 22km west of Stanley, at the mouth of the Duck River. The tour (☎0428 340 579; half-day $70, full-day $130; includes morning tea and lunch at the board table of the 1970s-built Directors Lodge) takes in **Cape Grim** (see box opposite), where the air carried thousands of kilometres across the Great Southern Ocean by the Roaring Forties is reputed to be the cleanest in the world. It's the site of Australia's baseline air-monitoring station, the most sophisticated in a worldwide network, and Australia's largest **wind farm** takes advantage of these gusting winds (same telephone; tour $17.50). A couple of kilometres east of Cape Grim, you can stand at the point where Bass Strait meets the Southern Ocean and walk along the spectacular, rugged coastline.

What Smithton lacks in aesthetics it makes up for by its usefulness as a service centre, with supermarkets, fuel and banking facilities and an **Online Access Centre** in the library on Nelson Street; Redline **buses** depart from opposite the police station on Smith Street Road. The resort-like *Tall Timbers Hotel Motel* on Scotchtown Road ([T]03/6452 2755, [W]www.talltimbershotel.com.au; [5]–[6]), built from local timbers, has a vast and popular **bistro** and motel or self-catering **accommodation** and offers excellent 4WD tours. South of Smithton, ten **forestry reserves**, ranging from rainforests to blackwood swamps and giant eucalypt forests, are all accessible from a circular route, via Kanunnah Bridge and Taytea Bridge on the C218 (90km return). **Julius River Forest Reserve** and the **Milkshakes Hills Forest Reserve** are the most rewarding. Forestry Tasmania, on West Esplanade on the other side of the river from the town centre ([T]03/6452 4900), provides free maps and route information.

Marrawah

From Smithton, the Bass Highway cuts across the northwest corner to the rich farming settlement of **MARRAWAH** on the west coast. Thirty kilometres along the way, Forestry Tasmania have come up with a startling public-relations exercise: **Tarkine Forest Adventures** (formerly "Dismal Swamp"; daily Nov–March 9am–5pm, April–Oct 10am–4pm; $20; [T]03/6456 7199), whose 110-metre slide (children must be over 8 years old) whizzes you down to the blackwood sinkhole, where a trail through the swamp includes mazes and art installations. There are also a series of graded mountain-bike trails (bike hire: 1hr $15; 3hr $30). There is a smart café attached too.

Marrawah itself has a general store/café with a post office and the last **petrol** until Zeehan on the route south. There's also the *Marrawah Tavern*, the last pub until Corinna, which serves decent counter meals. **Greenpoint Beach**, which has been voted one of the three best **surfing** beaches in Australia, is 2km west from Marrawah and has a small **camping area** as well as the stylish *Ann Bay Cabins* ([T]0428 548 760, [W]www.annbaycabins.com.au; [5]). Excellent, spacious self-contained **accommodation** is available at *Glendonald Cottage* on the Arthur River Road, 3km south of Marrawah ([T]0427 804 101; [4]).

The curve of Ann Bay here is shrouded by the hump of **Mount Cameron West** to the north. Three kilometres north of this bluff, at the end of a long exposed beach, is the most complex Aboriginal art site in Tasmania, now known as **Preminghana Indigenous Protected Area**: rock carvings of geometric or nonfigurative forms cover slabs of rock at the base of a cliff. Access is now restricted to a lookout.

Arthur River and the Arthur Pieman Protected Area

Just over 20km south of Marrawah, the scattering of holiday homes at **ARTHUR RIVER** marks the start of one of the Tasmanian coast's last great wilderness areas, where mighty trees that have been washed down the Frankland and Arthur rivers have crashed against the windswept shoreline. At one time the entire west coast looked like this, but the progressive damming of its rivers has left the **Arthur Pieman Protected Area**, part of the Tarkine, as a unique reminder, complete with a spectacular array of birdlife, such as black cockatoos, Tasmanian rosellas, orange-bellied parrots, black jays, wedge-tail eagles, pied heron and azure kingfishers. Trees on the steep banks of the never-logged river include myrtle, sassafras, celery-top pines and laurels, and there are giant tree ferns. From Gardiners Point – "**The Edge of the World**" – on the south side of the river mouth, the next land west is South America; it's a great vantage point to gaze at the battered coastline. It's obviously dangerous to swim here, due to extremely wild conditions and occasional freak waves – even walking along the beach can be an obstacle course, but it's possible to walk 9km to Sundown Point (arrange a pick-up vehicle or allow a full day to do the return walk.) Another excellent reason to visit Arthur River is Kings Run Wildlife Tours run by Geoff King, a passionate conservationist who is working to regenerate the coastal land and preserve its Aboriginal sites. He guides visitors around the wildlife and flora on his property as a prelude to nocturnal viewings of **Tasmanian devils** in the wild ($100; one hour before sunset until midnight; (T 03/6457 1191, W www.kingsrun.com.au).

As you come into the settlement on the sealed Arthur River Road, get the latest information on conditions (and camping permits) from the Parks and Wildlife office here (daily 9am–5pm; T 03/6457 1225). Opposite, the Arthur River Store (daily 7.30am–8pm; T 03/6457 1207) sells supplies and tickets for the Arthur River Cruise, and books **accommodation**. On the other side of the river, on Gardiner Street, the spacious *Ocean View Holiday Cottage* (T 03/6457 1100; ❸–❹) near the river mouth has stunning views, or there are smaller two-bed apartments at *Sunset Holiday Villas* opposite (T 03/6457 1197; W www.sunsetholidayvillas.com; ❹). **Camping** at Arthur River is a truly pleasurable experience, with facilities that range from the fully serviced *Peppermint Campground* near the base office, to secluded areas among shady trees in the hollows behind the dunes, equipped merely with water taps.

If you want to get out on the river, take a **cruise** (see p.1092) or contact Arthur River Canoe & Boat Hire (T 03/6457 1312), which has canoes and boats available for rent.

The drive to Corinna (see p.1093) south of Arthur River is on the Western Explorer road, the controversial "Road to Nowhere" cut through the Tarkine (see box, p.1092). Allow around three hours for the trip on the unsurfaced road, and bear in mind there is now no fuel until Zeehan – your nearest pump is at Marrawah.

▲ Cruising along the Arthur River

The Tarkine

The Tarkine, covering 377,000 hectares in northwest Tasmania, was named after the Tarkiner band of Aboriginal people who once roved here. It's Tasmania's largest unprotected wilderness area – stretching from the wild west coast to Murchison Highway in the east and from the Arthur River in the north to the Pieman River in the south – though conservationists have been pushing for a Tarkine National Park since the 1960s and the area was recommended for UNESCO's World Heritage list in the 1990s. Of its 593,000 acres of forest, seventy percent constitutes Australia's largest tract of temperate rainforest, second only in global significance to tracts in British Columbia. This "forgotten wilderness" of giant myrtle forests, wild rivers and bare granite mountains is the sort of place where the Tasmanian tiger, long thought extinct, might still be roaming. Tasmania's forests were a key issue in the 2004 Australian federal election, with 180,000 acres (mostly rainforest) of the Tarkine receiving protection from forestry. Dubbed by conservationists as **"The Road to Nowhere"**, the Western Explorer road through the Tarkine, from Arthur River all the way south to Zeehan, was constructed hastily and finished in 1996. A year before, an incredibly vast and ancient Huon pine was found in the area, as big as a city block and thought to date from around 8000 BC. Pick up the *Western Explorer Travel Guide* pamphlet – issued by the Department of Infrastructure, Energy and Resources and available in visitor centres – and remember that the road is rough and Marrawah is the last fuel stop before Zeehan. Alternatively, the Tarkine National Coalition, based in Burnie (℡03/6431 2373, Ⓦwww.tarkine.org), produces guides to three self-drive Tarkine routes that don't involve the Western Explorer; these can be downloaded from their website. Tarkine Trails (see box, p.1017) specializes in area tours; they organize two six-day walking expeditions through giant myrtle forests and next to waterfalls ($1549), five days on the battered west coast via Corinna and the Pieman River Cruise ($1549) or a vehicle-based tour ($2299). Pick-ups for all are available from Hobart, Launceston or Burnie.

The Arthur River Cruise

Perhaps the biggest attraction of the northwest coast is the five-hour **Arthur River Cruise** on the MV *George Robinson* (Sept–May daily 10am; 5hr; enquire about summer evening cruises; $83; bookings ℡03/6457 1158, Ⓦwww .arthurrivercruises.com; they will leave with only one passenger), which sails 14km upriver to the confluence of the Arthur and Frankland rivers at Turks Landing. The slow trip enables you to take in the river and absorb the transition from coastal scrub woodland to the edge of **The Tarkine** – the second-largest tract of temperate rainforest found anywhere in the world; en route you cruise past a white-breasted sea eagles' nest, and see a mating pair being fed. Morning tea on the boat includes rum-spiked hot chocolate. Before a barbecue lunch (with wine) in a clearing, there's an informative half-hour guided bushwalk, where you'll learn about the rainforest species.

The A10 route to the west coast

From Somerset, a suburb of Burnie on the shores of Emu Bay, the A10 (called the Murchison Highway between here and the Zeehan turn-off) heads to **Queenstown**, in the heart of Tasmania's west-coast mining area. This major route to the west coast was only cut in the 1960s; indeed, until the Hobart–Queenstown Lyell Highway was created in 1932, the west coast was only accessible by sea. A few kilometres past the Tewkesbury turn-off, the rural landscape ends and the road rises and winds through temperate rainforest to the **Hellyer Gorge State Reserve**; worth a stop for an easy walk (20min return) through ferns and dense myrtle forest to the Hellyer River.

West to Waratah and the Pieman River

Windswept **WARATAH**, set in mountain heathland 8km off the A10, reached its peak in the early twentieth century after thirty years of tin mining at **Mount Bischoff**, when it was linked to Burnie by the **Emu Bay Railway**, built to facilitate access to the silver fields of Zeehan and Rosebery. Though the mine closed in 1935, Waratah is still a miners' town, with recent mining developments at the Que River. Little more than a scattered collection of scruffy weatherboard cottages, it's a pretty desolate place, worth a visit if you're passing for the **mining museum** in the former courthouse in the centre (daily 9am–5pm; free; keys from the council opposite during the week, or Waratah Roadhouse at weekends) or the old ore stamper in a shed opposite (same hours), and you can get a **meal** at the old pub on the hill and **petrol**. Beyond Waratah, the last fuel stop on the road is the former mining town of **Savage River**, 45km along the B23.

The beautiful, unspoilt **Pieman River**, within the **Pieman River State Reserve**, is reached from the old gold-mining settlement of **CORINNA** on an unsealed road (C247) 26km south of Savage River. It's hard to believe that 2500 people once occupied what is now just a few shacks surrounded by dense rainforest, the last isolated mining village in Tasmania. Corinna even had its own port, despite the difficulties of getting through the narrow **Pieman Heads** from the coastline. Before the goldrush, the reserve was a logging area and still holds one of the largest stands of Huon pine, saved because the water here was too deep to allow a dam to be built. This also means the river can be dangerous for swimming except from the pontoon or from river beaches – seek advice on conditions when you arrive. New owners have renovated the township into a superb eco-resort, *Corinna Wilderness Experience* (☎03/6446 1170, [W]www.corinna.com.au). **Accommodation** options include four original miners' cottages (one- and two-bedroom; [5]), the old pub (with singles and doubles; $35 per person) and new bush-styled one- and two-bedroom cottages ([6]–[7]). You can also **camp** on boardwalk pitches in the rainforest ($15). The marvellous *Tarkine Hotel* pub, rebuilt in 2008, serves beer on a veranda that overlooks the river and the sort of tucker prospectors could only have dreamed of – Sri Lankan tiger prawns, steak and grilled flathead are just some of the options (lunch mains average $16, dinner from $22).

A series of boardwalks allows a number of walks into the forest that last from fifteen minutes to five hours. You can also lose a happy day or two on the river and its tributaries by hiring a sit-on **kayak** (4hr $25), a superb way to experience the solitude and tranquillity of this river, lined by Huon pine, leatherwood and pandanus ferns in the temperate rainforest of the north bank, or brown stringybark eucalypts on the drier southern bank. Alternatively, you can join a **cruise** downriver to the coast on the renovated Huon-pine MV *Arcadia II* (daily 10.30am; 4hr; $79 including morning tea, $12 extra with picnic lunch; bookings advisable on ☎03/6446 1170). This gives you an hour to wander along the wild west coast, or you can link up with Pieman Head Adventure Tours (☎03/6446 1170) for a 4WD excursion to Granville Harbour (6hr; $150, includes BBQ lunch). Ask, too, about evening cruises to the narrower upriver sections in summer. All in all, the antithesis to packaged wilderness resorts such as Strahan, and highly recommended.

The "Fatman" **barge** crosses the Pieman River from Corinna (daily 9am–7pm summer, 9am–5pm winter; $20 car, $10 bike), to continue on the C249 to Zeehan, and then on the B27 to Strahan.

South to Zeehan

Back on the A10, there's no fuel until tiny **TULLAH**, 40km south of Waratah. Fourteen kilometres further on, after crossing forest-covered **Mount Black**, the comparatively large zinc-mining town of **ROSEBERY** is a good place to stock up on supplies, with a couple of banks and an ATM outside the newsagent. In the unlikely event you decide to stop, there's comfortable motel-style **accommodation** at *Mount Black Lodge* on Hospital Road as you enter town from the north (℡03/6473 1039, Ⓦwww.mountblacklodge.com; also licensed restaurant; ❹). It's popular with bushwalkers – the town is hemmed in by looming mounts Black, Read (often recording Tasmania's highest daily rainfall) and Murchison, and there's also a fine walk to the 113-metre **Montezuma Falls** (3hr return), 8km south of the town.

From Rosebery, it's 23km to the turn-off to **ZEEHAN**, 6km southwest off the A10. The town became prosperous from the silver-lead mines that opened in the 1880s, and at its height boasted a population of eight thousand. However, the mines had already begun to fail by 1908, and the town was not to see a revival until the 1970s, when the Renison Bell tin mines were opened. The future of the mine – and by proxy Waratah itself – hung in the balance at the time of writing. Several boom-period buildings are still standing, including the elaborate facade of the **Gaiety Theatre**, once Australia's largest theatre, where Lola Montez trod the boards. The excellent **West Coast Pioneer Memorial Museum** on Main Street (daily 9am–5pm; $10; ℡03/6471 6225, Ⓦwww.westcoastheritage.com.au) has displays on mining and regional history. **Accommodation** is fairly pricey as Zeehan catches Strahan's overspill; options include the *Heemskirk Motor Inn* (℡03/6471 6107, Ⓦwww.heemskirkmotorhotel.com.au; ❺), and pub rooms and refurbished miners' cottages at the *Hotel Cecil* on Main Street (℡03/6471 6221; rooms ❸, cottages ❺), which serves passable counter meals. The *Mount Zeehan Retreat*, at the southern end of town, also provides meals on request (℡03/6471 6424; no en suites; B&B ❺), though was for sale at the time of research. The cheapest option is the friendly *Treasure Island Caravan Park*, north of the centre on Hurst Street (℡03/6471 6633; vans ❷, cabins ❹). The ANZ **bank** has restricted opening hours (Mon & Tues 2–4pm, Wed 9.30am–noon, Thurs 9.30am–4pm & Fri 2–4pm), but there's an ATM at Foodworks supermarket, on the main street by the Strahan turn-off. Incidentally, the supermarket is better stocked than those at Strahan.

From Zeehan it's possible to go direct to Strahan (47km) on the sealed B27, bypassing Queenstown and visiting the Henty Dunes (see p.1100) en route; or you could switch back to the A10 (called the Zeehan Highway until Queenstown) and reach Strahan via Queenstown, another 32km along the highway. You can get to Rosebery and Zeehan on TassieLink's scheduled Launceston–Queenstown service via Cradle Mountain (3 weekly).

Queenstown

QUEENSTOWN is worth a visit, but not for reasons you might expect. One reason is its infamous **"lunar landscape"**, evidence of the devastation that single-minded commercial exploitation can wreak in such a sensitive environment. If you approach the town from Strahan you're confronted by the ugly

copper mine; from Hobart, the road winds down to the town around bare, reddish-brown rock. Almost as celebrated is its defiantly unpolished feel – Tasmanians know it as the redneck capital of the state, and things can get rowdy at weekends.

Queenstown has been a mining centre since 1883, when gold was discovered at Mount Lyell, and it looks like a typical mining town, with its identical, poky tin-roofed weatherboard houses. In 1893 the Mount Lyell Mining and Railway Company was formed and began to mine copper at Mount Lyell. The weird-looking mountains here, chalky-white and, in places, almost totally devoid of vegetation, are the result of a toxic combination of tree-felling, sulphur, fire and rainfall. Since the smelters closed in 1969 there has been some regrowth on the lower slopes, but it's estimated that the damage already done will last some four hundred years. In late 1994 the Mount Lyell mine closed down, but the lease was taken over in 1995 by **Copper Mines of Tasmania**, now part of Indian mining corporation Vedanta. Tailings from the mine are now dumped into a multimillion-dollar dam instead of the town's **Queen River**, where aquatic life is beginning to return. The Queen eventually flows into the **King River**, and its moonscaped banks all the way to the delta near Strahan attest to the lasting and wide-ranging environmental damage of the past century. A good view of the cut slopes is available from the Spion Kopf lookout, reached off Hunter Street, behind the library on the town's through-road. For more mining heritage there's the **Galley Museum** in the old *Imperial Hotel* on Driffield Street, two blocks from the railway station (☎03/6471 1483; Oct–April Mon–Fri 9.30am–6pm, Sat & Sun 12.30–6pm; May–Sept till 5pm; $4), which has extensive photographic displays on west-coast life.

Practicalities

It's no surprise that **accommodation** in Queenstown is noticeably cheaper than Strahan. Options include the *Empire Hotel* at 2 Orr St (☎03/6471 1699, ⓔempirehotel@tassienet.au; ❸), an old-fashioned building noted for its National Trust-listed blackwood staircase; it has a range of typical pub rooms – shabby but reasonably priced – and budget singles ($50), plus good-value meals in the heritage dining room. *Mountain View Holiday Lodge*, at 1 Penghana Rd (☎03/6471 1163; dorms $15, motel units ❸), across the river from the town centre, has been converted from the mine's single-men's lodgings. An upmarket option is *Penghana*, on The Esplanade at no. 32, which provides B&B-style accommodation in the former mine manager's imposing mansion overlooking Queenstown (☎03/6471 2560, ⓦwww.penghana.com.au; ❻).

The Galley Museum (see above) doubles as the **visitor centre**, with information on underground **tours** of the Mount Lyell mine with Douggies Mine Tours, based at the mine office below (daily 1pm; 2hr 30min; $80; ☎0407 049 612 or 03/6471 1472). Mt Lyell Environmental Tours (☎0419 104 138; $55) organizes two-hour, overground trips that focus on the damage. Next door to the mine is the **Parks & Wildlife Service office** (☎03/6471 2511), the base for the Franklin Lower Gordon Wild Rivers National Park and the place to pick up the department's rafting and bushwalking guidelines. Queenstown's **Online Access Centre** is in the library beside the Galley Museum.

Banking facilities in town include a Commonwealth and ANZ bank, and an ATM at the Railway Express General Store on the same street. From Queenstown you can drive to Strahan on the B24 (42km), which starts as a steep, winding road through bare hills, or you continue along the A10 (called the Lyell Highway from Queenstown to Hobart) 88km east to the first fuel at Derwent Bridge, surrounded by the World Heritage Area.

TASMANIA | The A10 route to the west coast

In 2002 the opening of the 35km **West Coast Wilderness Railway** between Queenstown and Strahan fulfilled the $30-million redevelopment of the old **Abt Railway**, which included the restoration or replacement of forty bridges and re-creation of stations and associated buildings. Two of the four surviving locomotives from 1963 were restored and each carriage – replicas of old timber and brass models – was designed using different Tasmanian woods. The original railway was completed in 1896 to connect the Mount Lyell Mining Company in Queenstown with the port of Teepookana for the transport of copper ore, and in 1899 the line was extended to Regatta Point in Strahan. The railway closed in 1963, when it became more economical to transport by road, but years of lobbying finally led to the federal government financing its redevelopment. Reconstruction took three years; the original workers took six months less to hand-cut through the rugged rainforest terrain, struggling in the harsh, wet conditions. In fact, mining heritage is the main thrust of this trip and the informative commentary concentrates on it. The "wilderness" is something of a disappointing misnomer, though – at least for half of the journey the line follows slowly alongside the sadly polluted King River, its banks rusty from mine tailings and lined with tree stumps. Most people take the trip from Strahan: from Dubbil Barril, as the train climbs over 200m up a 1:16 rack gradient using the restored rack-and-pinion track (a system invented by the Swiss engineer Dr Roman Abt), there are stunning gorge views and the train is immersed in up-close rainforest scenery. However, coming into Queenstown, the vision alongside the tracks is a shocking contrast – a shanty town of tin shacks and dilapidated wooden houses.

Trains leave from Queenstown at the reconstructed station on Driffield Street, opposite the *Empire Hotel*, and at Strahan from the original station at Regatta Point (see p.1100). There's a daily service in both directions, both of which provide a one-hour stop at Dubbil Barril (packed lunch included). The train from Queenstown stops at the reconstructed historic settlement of Lynchford for half an hour for morning tea and a try at gold panning; the Lower Landing morning-tea stop from Strahan is on the unscenic polluted King River and includes a tedious mass honey-tasting exercise. Trains are hauled by steam between Queenstown and Dubbil Barril and diesel between here and Strahan. You can choose to go one way from either Strahan or Queenstown with a coach return (with a 30min break in Queenstown or 1hr 30min in Strahan), or return from Dubbil Barril. Either way, try to secure a riverside seat; when facing forward, sit on the right-hand side if coming from Strahan, or left from Queensland. The best return option is from Queenstown, as you avoid the ravaged river, enjoy a thrilling ascent and descent, take the steam train, and there's the morning-tea stop to look forward to; the Strahan return trip is best avoided (departs Queenstown 10am & 3pm, departs Strahan 10.15am & 3.15pm; one-way 4hr, return 5hr; $129 one-way, $195 premier class, includes light lunch; extra $15 for 45min return coach; booking necessary on ℡1800 628 288 or 03/6471 4300, ☏www.puretasmania.com.au).

Strahan and around

STRAHAN is not just the only town and port on the west coast, it is the region's leading resort, and one of the premier tourist destinations in the state. The reason is twofold: its setting on **Macquarie Harbour**, a huge body of water over six times the size of Sydney's harbour; and the surrounding wilderness.

Long before it became a launchpad into the southwestern wilderness, the harbour was home to a brutal, secondary convict settlement on **Sarah Island** between 1822 and 1830 – it can be visited on a Gordon River cruise (see box, p.1099). It was convicts who nicknamed the entrance to Macquarie Harbour, only 80m wide, **Hells Gates**. Abundant **Huon pine**, perfect for shipbuilding, facilitated logging and boatbuilding by convicts' trades, and continued to attract loggers after 1830. Strahan emerged as an export port for the nearby copper and lead fields in 1882 and was Tasmania's third-largest port in 1900. But growing ship sizes – not to mention wild weather – led to its demise by 1970 and the population dwindled to three hundred, most involved in fishing for abalone, crayfish and shark. What changed its fortunes was the **Franklin Blockade** campaign in 1982. When the protest movement based itself here, they put Strahan in the spotlight of the international media for two months. **Cruises** on the **Gordon River** had run before this event, but the declaration of the **World Heritage Area** lured busloads of tourists to see the river for themselves. The West Coast Wilderness Railway (see box, p.1096) was added to the list of attractions in 2003. Federal Resorts owns the railway and Gordon River Cruises, and much of the central accommodation and the pub.

In summer at least, Strahan has ceased to seem "real" in the normal sense – fishing is largely a sideshow to the town's tourism industry. What saves it from tackiness is that it remains an attractive place – the tourism infrastructure is far from the eyesore it could have been – and the surrounding wilderness is as compelling as ever.

Arrival and information

There are scheduled **bus** services from Launceston and Devonport via Cradle Mountain (3 weekly), connecting with a Queenstown–Strahan service (5 weekly), which connects with the service to Hobart via Lake St Clair. The **West Coast Visitor Centre** (daily: Oct–March 10am–7pm; April–Sept 11am–6pm; ☏03/6472 6800, Ⓦ www.westcoast.tas.gov.au), on The Esplanade, handles enquiries and bookings. The Strahan Supermarket (see p.1099) is a Westpac **bank** agent; otherwise, there's an ANZ **ATM** outside *Banjo's* bakery on The Esplanade. At The Esplanade's far end, the old Customs House contains the **post office** (also a Commonwealth Bank agent), and there is a **Parks & Wildlife office** (Mon–Fri 9am–5pm; ☏03/6471 7122), where park passes are available, and an **Online Access Centre**.

Accommodation

Strahan doesn't do cheap. If you have your own transport, you can **camp** at Ocean Beach ($5 per person) and at Henty Dunes (free; see p.1101); there are no facilities, but free hot showers can be had in town in the toilet block opposite the post office. Otherwise, accommodation is expensive and gets booked up in the summer; to be safe, book ahead or bring a tent unless you enjoy backtracking to Zeehan or Queenstown. The Visitor Centre (see above) has a free accommodation-booking service. For something different, you can bunk aboard West Coast Wilderness Yacht Charters' **yacht** *Stormbreaker* for $50 per person (see p.1100); also enquire about their comfortable self-contained apartments *The Crays* (Ⓖ).

Discovery Holiday Parks Corner of Andrew & Innes sts ☏03/6471 7468, Ⓦ www .discoveryholidayparks.com.au. Well positioned near the foreshore, if a fairly bare site for camping and cabins. It also acts as the reception for a backpackers' hostel on Harvey St above. There are dorms and rooms in a main block with a kitchen, as well as timber A-frame cabins, which share the same facilities. The bad news is it's 1km from the centre. Prices drop around $10 out of season. Camping $30, powered sites $45, dorms $40, rooms & huts Ⓙ, cabins Ⓖ

Franklin Manor The Esplanade ☏03/6471 7311, Ⓦ www.franklinmanor.com.au. Boutique B&B in a weatherboard manor on the other side of the bay from the centre. Rooms are elegant, public areas have been attractively done up, and there's a classy restaurant that serves fine modern

Australian cuisine. Four open-plan apartments, each sleeping up to five people, are in the "Stables" in the garden. [6]–[8]

Gordon Gateway Grining St, Regatta Point ☎03/6471 7165, [w]www.gordongateway.com.au. Views of the town and fishing boats are guaranteed from this peaceful spot, on a hill above the bay. Accommodation standards vary from motel-style rooms to swish penthouse suites and spacious A-frame chalets, all with kitchenettes. Gas BBQ for guests in two-acre gardens. [5]–[8]

Risby Cove The Esplanade ☎03/6471 7572, [w]www.risby.com.au. An old sawmill, fully renovated using corrugated iron and Huon pine salvaged from the harbour, now houses bright, upmarket one- and two-bedroom suites with kitchenette area. There's an excellent restaurant-café, gallery, and even a digital film theatre on site too. [6]–[7]

Strahan Colonial Cottages 7 Reid St ☎03/6471 7019, [w]www.strahancolonialcottages.com. Four renovated and well-equipped cottages, one a renovated church, furnished with antique-style pieces. [6]–[7]

Strahan Holiday Park 10 Jones St ☎03/6471 7442, [w]www.islandcabins.com.au. Pleasant spot diagonally opposite *Discovery Holiday Parks* whose appeal is a setting shaded by stands of eucalypt. Has a few tent pitches (more for motorhomes), plus a variety of accommodation options. Powered sites $35, rooms, units, cabins & cottages [5]

Strahan Village The Esplanade ☎03/6471 7160 or 1800 084 620, [w]www.strahanvillage.com.au. Among the various styles of Federal Hotels and Resorts' upmarket accommodation (all en suite) clustered around The Esplanade, best positioned are the spacious "Terrace" rooms above the renovated 1930s *Hamer's Hotel*, with private balcony overlooking the bay ([6]). Of the "Village" units ([6]–[7]) along the Esplanade, some look like cute cottages but are only motel rooms, others have balconies. The most expensive "Hilltop" ([7]–[8]) rooms command great views, with the buffet-style *View 42°* restaurant and bar also taking in the sights. The cheapest "Hilltop Garden View" rooms are tucked behind ([5]).

Wheelhouse Apartments 4 Frazer St ☎03/6471 7777, [w]www.wheelhouseapartments.com.au. These two-bed, two-storey apartments, with abundant use of local timbers and a stylish maritime theme, sit on the edge of a cliff above the harbour. Slanted wall-to-ceiling windows in the downstairs living room give a ship's-prow feel and awesome views. Upstairs, there are less spectacular vistas from the spa in the master bedroom. [8]

The Town

Your first stop should be the wood-and-iron West Coast Visitor Centre (see p.1097), whose exterior design aspires to reflect the area's boatbuilding and timber industries. In the foyer, you can pick up information and use a couple of internet terminals. In an adjoining room a separate **exhibition** ($2) on local history is organized by theme – Aboriginal heritage, convicts, logging, ecology, economy, wilderness and conflict – and arranged around a waterfall. A decade old, it's a mite musty but remains relevant – and there's a good view of the harbour through the glass wall. Outside, the **amphitheatre** is the early-evening venue for an entertaining two-man show, *The Ship That Never Was*, which retells the true story of an 1834 convict escape from Sarah Island (daily 5.30pm, plus 8.30pm in Jan; $17.50). Expect slapstick and much audience participation.

Adjacent to the visitor centre in a corrugated-iron shed, **Strahan Woodworks** (daily 8.30am–5.30pm) sells well-crafted woodwork; you're also free to roam around Morrison's Saw Mill next door, and watch local timbers being processed. The **Forestry Tasmania Office** (Mon–Fri 9am–5pm; ☎03/6472 6000), next to *Hamer's* pub, is also worth a visit for its amazing window display featuring a Huon pine log transforming itself into the bow of a boat; inside you can pick up leaflets describing the trees in the area, as well as other information.

The **Strahan Historic Foreshore Walkway** tracks the shore of the harbour for 1.7km to **Regatta Point** and its train station from where the **West Coast Wilderness Railway** (see p.1096) leaves; self-guided-walk maps are available from the visitor centre. En route you pass the **People's Park**, the starting point for a rainforest walk to **Hogarth Falls** (40min; 2km return).

The **Gordon River** is deep, its waters dark from the tannin leached from buttongrass plains – even the tap water in Strahan is brown (though drinkable). Cruise boats used to travel as far as the landing at Sir John Falls, 30km upriver, but their wakes caused the riverbanks to erode and they now travel only the 14km to **Heritage Landing**, where there's a chance to amble along a boardwalk above the rainforest floor. Trunks and branches of ancient myrtles and **Huon pines** provide homes for mosses, lichens and liverworts on their bark, and ferns and fungi grow from the trunks – even the dead trees support some forms of life, however lowly. The wet and swampy conditions are ideal for Huon pines, a threatened tree species found only in Tasmania: they're the second-oldest living things on Earth after the bristlecone pines of western North America, with some trees found to be more than ten thousand years old. The massive pines, which may reach a height of 40m, can grow from seed but more often regenerate vegetatively, putting down roots where fallen branches touch the soil. The trees are also renowned for their resistance to rot. A tree near the landing, reckoned to be around 2000 years old, split in two during 1997 – one half fell to the ground – but the trunk won't rot for up to one hundred years as the tree's methyl eugenol oil slows fungal growth. The oil content of the wood also explains why Huon pine was so highly sought-after. As one of the few green Tasmanian timbers that floats, pine logs were floated down to the boom camp and there fashioned into huge rafts to be rowed across Macquarie Harbour.

Two operators offer **river cruises**; both visit Sarah Island and make a thirty-minute stop at Heritage Landing. Gordon River Cruises have pre-designated seats, but there are floor-to-ceiling windows and you can move freely on deck; to make the most of the experience on World Heritage Cruises, turn up early to bag a good seat. For both, bring water- and windproof gear, so you can brave the prow of the boat – much the most exhilarating spot when you whizz through Macquarie Heads (**Hells Gates**).

As well as the cruises below, overnight trips are available aboard the ketch of West Coast Yacht Charters (see p.1000).

Gordon River Cruises Federal Resorts operates the high-tech *Jane Franklin II* (departs 8.30am, returns 2pm, Nov–April extra cruise departs 2.45pm, returns 8pm; includes buffet lunch; bow-atrium seat $90, window seats $115, upper-deck seats including lunch, snacks and drinks $195; ☏03/6471 4300 or 1800 420 555, ⓦwww .puretasmania.com.au). Its latest venture fills in time between the morning cruise departure and evening return with a paddle upriver from Heritage Landing by kayak. The full-day Gordon River Paddle costs $345 (includes lunch, dinner and stop at Sarah Island). The booking office for all is the waterfront Strahan Activity Booking Centre, where there's a photographic display of Strahan's history.

World Heritage Cruises Owned and operated by a local family, this is a slightly cheaper cruise, with a one-hour tour of the prison settlement Sarah Island (late Aug– early July daily 9am–3pm; $85 centre, $110 premium and upper deck; includes buffet meal; licensed; ☏03/6471 7174, ⓦwww.worldheritagecruises.com.au). They also offer a similar afternoon cruise in summer (Jan–March 3–8.30pm), and a shorter morning cruise in the warmer months that doesn't stop at Sarah Island (Oct–April; 9am–2pm; $80).

Eating and drinking

Nearly all options are on The Esplanade in the town centre, where *Schowch Seafoods* has takeaway pizza and fish and chips. For a more classy **restaurant** meal, look to the hotels. *Franklin Manor* and *Risby Cove* (for both, see p.1097 & opposite) prepare good modern Australian cuisine; the former is a pricey fine dining place, the latter is more relaxed and cheaper at around $25 a main course. There's a **supermarket** (Mon–Fri 7.30am–7pm, Sat & Sun 8am–6pm) 1km uphill from the centre via Harold St, by *Strahan Central Café*.

⑪

TASMANIA | The A10 route to the west coast

Banjo's The Esplanade. This outlet of the ubiquitous state chain has water-facing tables outside; all the usual coffee, pastries, sandwiches and cooked breakfasts. Daily 6am–8pm.

Hamer's Hotel The Esplanade. Focus of the town's social life with a public bar and attached fine bistro which serves up a varied selection of seafood, pasta, grills and curries (mains around $18).

Regatta Point The Esplanade. On the other side of the bay, beside the terminus of the West Coast

Wilderness Railway, this is the locals' choice for a meal – expect above-average pub grub, including salmon farmed in the cold clear waters of Macquarie Harbour.

Strahan Central Café Harold St. A rather stylish café-restaurant just behind *Hamer's Hotel* with views of the water from the outdoor deck. Excellent coffee and pasta or veggie curry lunches. Daily 11am–8pm.

Around Strahan

Some 6km east of town, **Ocean Beach** is, at 30km, the longest beach in Tasmania but not safe to swim in – no surprise when you consider that the next landmass west is Patagonia. Waves hereabouts have been known to reach 26m high. Come at dusk to observe the marvellous sunsets and to watch – from November to February – the migratory **muttonbirds** roost; in peak season rangers talk visitors through the birds' astounding migration cycles to the Baring Sea. Off the road to Ocean Beach, it's an eleven-kilometre drive on a teeth-jarring gravel road to **Macquarie Heads** (Hells Gates) at the south end of the beach. The extensive thirty-metre **Henty Dunes**, 12km north of town on the Zeehan Road (B27), are also worth seeing; two fun ways to experience them are by quad bike (see below) or by hiring sandboards from The Shack (T03/6471 7396; $30 per 4hr), in a hut beside *Strahan Central Café*. You can **camp** for free at the picnic area or in other clearings. Another destination is the **Teepookana Plateau** to see a stand of ancient Huon pines (some nearly 2000 years old); an elevated walkway leads to a viewing tower offering 360-degree views of forest, mountain and harbour. The tower and the King River railway port ghost town are only accessible by tour (see below).

To get around, you can rent **mountain bikes** from *Strahan Holiday Park* or *Risby Cove* (for both, see p.1098), while The Shack (see above) hires *Easy Rider*-style electric Harleys ($28 per hr).

Tours

You'll run out of cash before you exhaust the tour options. 4 Wheeler Bikes runs popular guided four-wheel **quad bike** tours of Henty Dunes (40min; $40; booking essential on T0419 508 175; full driving licence required) and longer tours to Teepookana. In addition to the Gordon River cruises (see box, p.1099) there's a wide choice of water-based tours. West Coast Yacht Charters, on The Esplanade (T03/6471 7422, W www.tasadventures.com/wcyc), runs evening **crayfish dinner sails** on Macquarie Harbour on an eighteen-metre ketch, *Stormbreaker* (Sept–April daily 6pm; $70 including dinner, $80 with crayfish in season), as well as longer cruises up the Gordon River (leaving 2pm; overnight to Sir John Falls for a morning Franklin rafter pick-up; $250 includes accommodation on boat, breakfast and lunch; overnight Gordon River cruise to Sarah Island and Heritage Landing $320 including all meals). With Wild Rivers Jet, you can blast up the already suffering **King River**, just south of Strahan (50min; $68), but a better option is the combined jet boat-4WD trip to the Teepookana Plateau (11am daily; 1hr 45min; $90); book at The Shack on The Esplanade (see above). Roaring 40s Fishing Tours (T0418 681 098) offers fishing and sightseeing trips.

Strahan Seaplanes & Helicopter, on Strahan Wharf, runs spectacular **flights** over Macquarie Harbour and the wilderness area (daily from 9am; 1hr

20min; $299 for two; ☎03/6471 7718, ⓦwww.adventureflights.com.au), providing the unforgettable image of the smooth dark ribbon of the Franklin River easing through dense forest. The highlight of the trip is the dramatic landing at **Sir John Falls Landing**, further upriver than the cruise boats can reach. You can also charter the plane for longer flights ($680 per hr; maximum four people) – a spectacular way to see the rugged scenery around Frenchmans Cap – or take **helicopter flights** over Hells Gates and Macquarie Harbour (15min; $165 for two people), or the Teepookana Forest, which includes a landing and walk to see the old-growth Huon pine (1hr; $299 for two people). Another high-end trip is Federal Resorts' small-group Piners & Miners tour ($345; includes lunch; ☎03/6471 4300 or 1800 420 555, ⓦwww.puretasmania.com.au). This unique day-trip involves a section of the West Coast Wilderness Railway track by converted 4WD jeep and a rainforest walk to the ghost town of Pillinger, before a cruiser whisks you back across Macquarie Harbour to Strahan.

The World Heritage Area

If we can revise our attitudes towards the land under our feet; if we can accept a role of steward, and depart from the role of conqueror; if we can accept the view that man and nature are inseparable parts of the unified whole – then Tasmania can be a shining beacon in a dull, uniform, and largely artificial world.

Olegas Truchanas, conservationist, 1971

It's the lure of the **wilderness** that attracts a certain type of traveller to Tasmania. The state's vast wilderness areas of the Southwest National Park, Franklin Lower Gordon Wild Rivers National Park and the adjacent Cradle Mountain–Lake St Clair National Park make up the **World Heritage Area**, recognized by UNESCO.

The future of the parks could have been very different had it not been for the bitterly fought battle waged by environmentalists in the 1980s. In 1972 the flooding of the beautiful and unique **Lake Pedder** led to the formation, in 1976, of the **Wilderness Society**, which began a relentless campaign against the next plan for the southwest by the Hydro Electricity Commission (HEC), which was to build a huge dam on the Lower Gordon River that would efface Tasmania's last wild river, the Franklin. Pro-HEC forces included the then Tasmanian Premier Robin Gray. Years of protests and campaigns ensued, but in 1981 the whole southwest area was proposed for the World Heritage List. The **Franklin Blockade**, organized by the Wilderness Society and led by **Dr Bob Brown**, began on December 14, 1982, the day the southwest officially joined the list – a fact the Tasmanian government was choosing to ignore.

For two months, blockaders from all over Australia travelled upriver from a base in Strahan to stand in front of the bulldozers in non-violent protest. The **blockade** attracted international attention, notably when the British botanist David Bellamy joined in the protest and was among the twelve hundred or so arrested for trespassing. During the course of the campaign, Bob Hawke's Labor government was voted in, and in March 1983, following a trailblazing High Court ruling, the federal government forbade further work by the HEC. Though the blockade itself had failed to stop the preparatory work on the dam, it had changed, or at least challenged, the opinion of many Australians.

Cradle Mountain–Lake St Clair National Park

This must be a national park for the people for all time. It is magnificent, and people must know about it and enjoy it.

Gustav Weindorfer, botanist and mountaineer, 1910

Cradle Mountain–Lake St Clair National Park is Tasmania's best-known wilderness region, its northern **Cradle Mountain** end easily accessible from Devonport, Deloraine or Launceston – and with the crowds that go with that in peak season – and its southern **Lake St Clair** end from Derwent Bridge on the Lyell Highway between Queenstown and Hobart. A popular route from Devonport is via Sheffield (see p.1083) on the B14, then the C132 via Wilmot, and for the final stretch to Cradle Valley, the C136. One of the most glaciated areas in Australia, with many lakes and tarns, the park covers some of Tasmania's highest land, with craggy mountain peaks such as **Mount Ossa** (1617m), the state's highest point. At its northern end, **Dove Lake**, backed by the jagged outline of Cradle Mountain, is a breathtaking sight, and at the park's southern end, Lake St Clair is the country's deepest freshwater lake at over 200m, occupying a basin gouged out by two glaciers. Between Cradle Mountain and Lake St Clair, the 65-kilometre **Overland Track** attracts walkers from all over the world, and is the best way to take in the stunning scenery – spread over five or more mud- and often leech-filled days of exhilarating exhaustion. However, you can do just part of the walk, or make several other satisfying day-walks around Cradle Mountain or Lake St Clair.

Getting to the park

TassieLink services both ends of the national park on two year-round **scheduled routes**, and an Overland Track summer service provides additional transport from November until the end of March. A scheduled service from Launceston and Devonport to Queenstown goes via Cradle Mountain (3 weekly; connecting with a Queenstown to Strahan service), while the scheduled Hobart–Strahan service takes the Lyell Highway to Lake St Clair (5 weekly). A daily Launceston–Cradle Mountain summer service runs via Deloraine, Sheffield and Devonport. A Hobart–Lake St Clair summer service via Mount Field National Park runs daily. An alternative is Maxwell's Coaches' charter service (☏03/6492 1431), which connects Devonport and Launceston to Lake St Clair ($70), and Launceston and Devonport to Cradle Mountain ($40).

Cradle Mountain

If you're driving, in high summer you'll probably have to park by the airstrip outside *Cradle Wilderness Cafe*, where there's a secondary visitor centre (daily 8am–5pm) and fuel. It's located 2.5km from the park proper, and linked by a **shuttle bus** which goes to the main visitor centre (see below), then on to Dove Lake (Oct to mid-May daily 8am–7pm; every 20min in summer; Ⓦwww .mcdermotts.com.au); the bus is included in the park entry fee, which can be paid at either visitor centre. Although you can drive to the **Dove Lake car park**, in summer it's often full by 9am and the bus is the best alternative; an electronic reader at the main visitor centre shows space availability. Incidentally, for a more rewarding way to arrive, a boardwalk tracks the road from the main visitor centre to Dove Lake – the total distance is 8km and there are several bus stops on the adjacent road should you tire en route.

Once within the park proper at **Cradle Mountain**, the **Cradle Mountain Visitor Centre** (daily 8am–5pm, later in summer; ☏03/6492 1133) provides information on the many day-walks available in this area of the park, and acts as a registration point for the Overland Track (see box below); it's worth buying *Cradle Mountain Day Walks – Map & Notes* ($4) for more information. You can loosen up here with a gentle ten-minute boardwalk circuit through rainforest and overlooking **Pencil Pine Falls**, ideal for wheelchairs or strollers. There's also the "Enchanted Walk" that follows the creek through rainforest to *Cradle*

The Overland Track

In summer and autumn, around forty people a day depart Cradle Mountain to walk the **Overland Track**, probably Australia's greatest extended bushwalk: 65km, unbroken by roads and passing through buttongrass plains, fields of wild flowers, and forests of deciduous beech, Tasmanian myrtle, pandanus and King Billy pine, with side-walks leading to views of waterfalls and lakes, and starting points for climbs of the various mountain peaks. Most of the track is well-maintained boardwalk but you may still end up ankle-deep in mud. Along the route are six basic coal-stove- or gas-heated huts (not for cooking – bring your own stove), with composting toilets outside. There's no guarantee there'll be space, so you need a good tent; a warm sleeping bag is essential even in the heated huts in summer.

The direct walk generally takes six days – five, if you catch a boat from Narcissus Hut across Lake St Clair; if you want to go on some of the side-walks, allow eight to ten days. On average, most walkers go for six to eight days. You should take enough food and fuel for the duration of your walk, plus extra supplies in case you have an accident or bad weather sets in; there's always plenty of unpolluted fresh water to drink from streams. Around eight thousand people walk the track each year; most come between November and April, but the best time is during February and March when the weather has stabilized, though it's bound to rain at some point, and may even snow. The track is at its most crowded from Christmas to the end of January. To avoid overloading of the track during peak periods, a booking system (Ⓦwww .overlandtrack.com.au) for departure dates applies between November and the end of April, and a fee of $150 per person in addition to the park entry fee will be applicable. At this time you have to walk north to south, a good idea at any rate since it's more downhill than up. The rest of the year you can register at either end in the **national park offices** (see opposite & p.1105), where you receive an obligatory briefing and have your gear checked to make sure it's sufficient. The office also sells camping gear and supplies: fuel stoves, meths, water bottles, trowels, warm hats and gloves. The *Cradle Mountain–Lake St Clair Map and Notes 1:100,000* ($9.90) is an essential purchase, and *The Overland Track – A Walker's Notebook* ($12) is handy too. Once you arrive, mud-encrusted, at Derwent Bridge (see p.1105), you can use the hot showers at the **campsite**, for which there's a small charge.

The logistics of doing a one-way walk are smoothed by a couple of operators: Maxwell's Coaches (Ⓣ03/6289 1141 or 0428 308 813) and the Tasmanian Tour Company (Ⓣ1300 659 878, Ⓦwww.tasmaniantourcompany.com.au) can do **transfers** to get you back to your car, while TassieLink has discounted Overland Track fares that include transfers from Launceston to Cradle Mountain, then back from Lake St Clair to Launceston, Hobart or Devonport or any two combinations ($75–119). They can provide baggage transfer for an extra charge. It's worth knowing that Paddy Pallin (110 George St; Ⓣ03/6331 4240, Ⓦwww.paddypallin.com.au) allow you to hire gear in Launceston and return it in Hobart. **Guided tours** are available, the best offered by Craclair Tours (Ⓣ03/6339 4188; Oct–May; 7 days $2150); you'll still have to camp (except for comfortable cabin accommodation at the start) and carry a ten-kilo pack. The softies' option is to go on a guided walk staying at *Cradle Huts*, **private lodges** with hot showers, beds and delicious meals (Oct–May; 6 days $2550–2750, full board departing and returning Launceston; Ⓣ03/6392 2211, Ⓦwww.cradlehuts.com.au). Several operators combine Cradle Mountain with Walls of Jerusalem (see p.1077).

Mountain Lodge (1km one-way; 20min). Five kilometres into the park from the visitor centre, **Waldheim** ("Forest Home" in German) is the King Billy pine chalet built by the Austrian–Australian **Gustav Weindorfer** in 1912, and now a museum (open 24hr; free) devoted to the man who loved this wilderness area and pushed to have it declared a national park; a fifteen-minute forest walk from the hut shows examples of ancient King Billy pine. Near the hut, there's a day-shelter for a picnic.

Around 2.5km beyond Waldheim, the road concludes at Dove Lake, spectacularly sited beneath the jagged curve of Cradle Mountain itself – an impressive site regardless of the tour groups that swamp the area in high summer. Most day-trippers are content to amble along the Dove Lake circuit (2–3hr), an easy all-weather walk around the shore of the lake – no boots required. For something tougher – and quieter – Marion's Lookout (2–3hr) ascends to a hillside on the west shore for a close-up view of Cradle Mountain, or for a real challenge, embark on the steep day-walk that continues on to the summit of **Cradle Mountain** itself (6hr return; get advice from the ranger first). For spectacular views, try a **scenic helicopter flight** over the area with Cradle Mountain Helicopters (Sept–May weather permitting; $190 per person for 4 people; 50min; landing at Fury Gorge with 20min on the ground; [T]03/6492 1132, [W]www.adventureflights.com.au); it's based by the *Cradle Wilderness Café* (see p.1102). Further on from the café, at *Cradle Mountain Chateau* (see below), the highly recommended nine-room **Wilderness Gallery** (daily 10am–5pm; $5, free for guests) features landscape photography – of Tasmania, Antarctica and the Pacific – from well-known and emerging local and international nature photographers, including the late, great Tasmanian, **Peter Dombrovskis**. Nearby, Devils@Cradle (daily tours 10am–4pm; feeding tours 5.30pm; $25; [T]03/6492 1491, [W]www.devilsatcradle.com) is a conservation and breeding centre for the beleaguered Tasmanian Devil – ask about night-time tours with the rangers.

Accommodation and eating

All hotel **accommodation** is sited between the two visitor centres off Cradle Mountain Road, the main road into the park. None of it is cheap, nor is it widely available in high summer, when reservations are essential. For food, *Cradle Mountain Lodge* has the classy *Highland Restaurant* and the *Tavern Bar* offering fairly reasonably priced counter meals. *Cradle Mountain Chateau* serves up similar fare at its *Grey Gum* and *Quolls* venues respectively. All are open to non-guests; reservations are recommended for the restaurants. *Cradle Mountain Lodge*'s boutique near the main visitor centre also sells snacks, or the *Cradle Wilderness Café* (daily 8am–5pm) at the outer visitor centre has bistro snacks.

Cradle Mountain Chateau 2km from park entrance [T]03/6225 7016 or 1800 420 155, [W]www.puretasmania.com.au. Hotel-style accommodation in ground-floor rooms in two adjoining guest-wings; only Deluxe and King rooms have bush views – Standards look onto the car park. On site are casual and upmarket restaurants, a bar serving snacks, a billiard room, a tour desk, and the Wilderness Gallery photography gallery. Prices are room only. [6]–[8]

Cradle Mountain Highlanders Cottages 1.5km from park entrance [T]03/6492 1116, [W]www.cradlehighlander.com.au. Good-value, characterful cabins, from cosy open-plan studios to two-bedroom spa chalets, most with wood-burning stoves. All are individually decorated in appealing bush style and are fairly private among the eucalypts. [5]–[8]

Cradle Mountain Lodge 100m from park entrance [T]03/6492 1303, [W]www.cradlemountainlodge.com.au. Superbly sited on the edge of the national park, within walking distance of the main visitor centre, are 86 luxurious timber cabins, from contemporary-styled "Pencil

Pine Cabins" to spacious "King Billy Suites", all with log or gas fires and bathrooms (no cooking facilities). At the lodge itself, guest facilities include lounges and the Waldheim Alpine Spa, with outdoor hot tub, cold plunge pool, steam room and sauna, plus massage treatments. All manner of walks, talks and activities are arranged too. ❽

Discovery Holiday Parks (ex Cosy Cabins) ☎03/6492 1395, Ⓦwww.discoveryholidayparks .com.au. 2.5km from park entrance. This is the only backpackers' option, in four-bed dorms or family rooms; rates drop by $10 off-season. If you're desperate, hut shelters have same access to impressive stone-built camp kitchens. Otherwise,

there are well-maintained cabins that sleep up to six, as well as camping, all in a pleasant bush setting. The campsite has a small shop with basic supplies and internet access. Camping $30, powered sites $45; shelters $17 per person; dorms $40; rooms ❹; cabins ❻

Waldheim 5km from visitor centre ☎03/6492 1303. The only beds within the park itself are in basic self-catering hikers' huts for four to eight people. Bunkrooms (linen $7.50 per person), electricity, gas or wood heating, basic gas stoves (cutlery and crockery provided) and a shared amenities block. Managed by NPWS; pick up keys from the visitor centre. ❹

Lake St Clair and Derwent Bridge

The scenery at Lake St Clair, at the south end of the national park, is less dramatic than at Cradle Mountain and correspondingly less busy. Most people treat it as a pause en route to Strahan on the Lyell Highway. Yet there are good walks in the area, and outside peak walking months you can register to walk the Overland Track in the opposite direction at the ranger station at **CYNTHIA BAY** on **Lake St Clair** (daily 8am–5pm; ☎03/6289 1115), which houses an informative interpretive centre and a bistro with views over the lake. **Walks** around Lake St Clair are detailed on a board in the centre. Another option to see the sights is on a **cruise** on the MV *Idaclair*, which will drop you off at Narcissus Hut to begin the Overland Track from the southern end, or you can walk back to the centre (5–6hr); alternatively, get off at Echo Point and return on a three-hour bushwalk (summer: Cynthia Bay 9am, 12.30pm & 3pm; Narcissus Hut 9.30am, 1pm & 3.30pm; 1hr 30min return; to Echo Point $20; to Narcissus Hut $28 one-way, $38 return). Tickets (booking essential) are sold at the restaurant, where you can enquire about renting dinghies with outboard motors, canoes and kayaks.

The restaurant also takes bookings for **accommodation**. *Lakeside St Clair Wilderness Holidays* (☎03/6289 1137, Ⓦwww.lakestclairresort.com.au; ❻) has several expensive lodges, and a backpackers' lodge (dorms $28). The **campsite** ($10 per person, powered sites $25), though in an attractive forest setting, is poorly served – there's no kitchen and even a fee ($1 per 6 min) to use the showers, not that you'll begrudge the price after completing the Overland Track. The site also has laundry facilities. For supplies (and a bottle shop), you have to go to **DERWENT BRIDGE**, 5km away on the Lyell Highway, served by Maxwell's Coaches (☎03/6289 1141 or 0428 308 813), whose $10 shuttle service runs on demand. Here, you can stay at the well-appointed self-catering *Derwent Bridge Chalets* (☎03/6289 1000, Ⓦwww.derwent-bridge .com; B&B ❻–❼), with modern studios and chalets, including a couple of luxurious spa versions, all managed by a friendly, considerate host. The focus of the small community is the *Derwent Bridge Wilderness Hotel* (☎03/6289 1144; ❺), an atmospheric pub with a huge brick fireplace and high-ceilinged, wood-raftered interior. It serves generous bistro meals and offers accommodation in old-fashioned, lodge-style rooms (some en suite) or functional hostel rooms (dorms $30). Derwent Bridge is close to **Lake King William**, equivalent in size to Lake St Clair and popular with anglers. Don't miss the phenomenal **Wall** on Lyell Highway as you enter Derwent Bridge from the south (9am–5pm, till 4pm in winter; $7.50). This work-in-progress by artist Greg Duncan is a frieze carved in Huon pine depicting rural life, each panel some 3m in height. The ten-year project, started in 2005, will eventually be 100m in length.

Franklin Lower Gordon Wild Rivers National Park

The **Franklin Lower Gordon Wild Rivers National Park** was declared in June 1980 and by 1982 had been included with the adjoining parks on the World Heritage List. The park exists for its own sake more than anything, most of it being virtually inaccessible. You can cruise up the Gordon, or fly over it, but the really adventurous can explore by **rafting the Franklin** (see box below) and walking the **Frenchmans Cap Track**, both accessible from the **Lyell Highway**, which extends from Strahan to Hobart and runs through the park between Queenstown and Derwent Bridge. Plenty of short **walks** also lead from the highway to rainforest, rivers and lookouts.

The **Franklin River** is one of the great rivers of Australia, and the only major wild-river system in Tasmania that's not been dammed. It flows for 120km from the Cheyne Range to the majestic **Gordon River**, from an altitude of 1400m down to almost sea level. Swollen by the storms of the Roaring Forties and fed by many other rivers, it can at times become a raging

Rafting on the Franklin

One of the most rugged and inaccessible areas left on Earth, the surrounds of the **Franklin River** can't really be seen on foot – few tracks lead through this twisted, tangled and wet rainforest. **Rafting** is the only way to explore the river and even this is possible only between December and early April. The Franklin is reached by rafting down the Collingwood River from the Lyell Highway, 49km west of Derwent Bridge. The full trip takes eight to fourteen days, ending at the Gordon River, where rafters head finally to Strahan by West Coast Yacht Charter (see p.1100) or take a seaplane with Strahan Seaplanes and Helicopter (see p.1100) from Sir John Falls Camp.

One of the most dangerous Australian rivers to raft, with average **rapids** of grades 3 to 4 – and up to grade 6 in places – the Franklin requires an expedition leader with great skill and experience. Even so, guides have died in the rapids. It's also very remote, and in the event of an accident help can be days away. Despite this, the river's haunting isolation is part of the attraction for most visitors. From **Collingwood River**, it takes about three days to raft to the **Frenchmans Cap Track** on the **Upper Franklin**: alpine country with vegetation adapted to survive snow and icy winds. Watch out for two endemic pines, the Huon pine and celery-top pine. There are lots of intermediate rapids along this stretch and a deep quartzite ravine and large, still pool at Irenabyss. The **Middle Franklin** is a mixture of pools, deep ravines and wild rapids as the river makes a 50km detour around Frenchmans Cap. Dramatic limestone cliffs overhang the **Lower Franklin**, which involves a tranquil paddle through dense myrtle beech forests with flowering leatherwoods overhead. It's a short distance to **Kutikina Caves** and **Deena-reena**; only rafters can gain access to these Aboriginal caves.

It's both unlikely and unwise to attempt the trip **independently** – a rafter died in 2009 attempting the trip with friends – so most visitors go with one of the specialist **tour operators**. You don't have to be experienced to sign up – just fit, with lots of stamina and courage. Prices are high, but this is an experience of a lifetime. Water By Nature (☎0408 242 941 or 1800 111 142, ⊛www.franklinrivertasmania.com) offer a five-day trip ($1740) on the Lower Franklin, a seven-day trip on the Upper Franklin at $2040, or ten days rafting the full navigable length of the river ($2680). The ten-day trip includes a day-walk to Frenchmans Cap (see p.1107). Trips are also offered by Rafting Tasmania and Tasmanian Expeditions (for both, see p.1017) for similar prices.

torrent as it passes through ancient heaths, deep gorges and rainforests. The discovery in 1981 of stone tools in the **Kutikina Cave** on the Lower Franklin proved that during the last Ice Age southwest Tasmania was the most southerly point of human occupation on Earth.

A **seaplane** from Strahan flies over the national park (see p.1100), and from it you can see the confluence of the two rivers – the planned site of the ill-fated dam – surrounded by thick forest, much of it impenetrable and probably never traversed by humans. The Gordon appears wide and slow compared to the narrow, winding Franklin.

Along the Lyell Highway (A10)

Heading east from Queenstown, the Lyell Highway (A10) enters the Franklin Lower Gordon Wild Rivers National Park, reaching Nelson River bridge after 4km, from where **Nelson Falls** is an easy twenty-minute return walk through temperate rainforest. From here, the road begins to wind and rise up to **Collingwood River**, the starting point for raft or canoe trips down the Franklin (see box opposte), with some basic camping facilities.

In fine weather, the white-quartzite dome of Frenchmans Cap, like a dusting of snow, can be seen from the highway. For a more spectacular viewpoint that takes in the Franklin River Valley, **Donaghy's Hill Wilderness Lookout Walk** begins further along the highway on the right. Walk from the parking area along the old road to the top of the hill, where a sign marks the beginning of the forty-minute return track. Further along the highway, the **walking track to Frenchmans Cap** (see p.1107) begins with a fifteen-minute stroll to the suspension bridge over the river. Continuing on the Lyell, you have another opportunity to see the Franklin on a ten-minute **Nature Trail**, at a point where the river is tranquil, as it flows around large boulders; there's also a longer 25-minute circuit. At the start of the trail there's a picnic area and a wooden shelter with an **interpretive board** about the river. Beyond this point, open buttongrass plains take over, huge uninhabited expanses fringed with trees. This is **Wombat Glen**, which looks as though it's been cleared into grazing country until you step out into it and discover its bog-like nature.

At the foot of **Mount Arrowsmith**, the highway begins to ascend, winding around the mountain's southern side above the U-shaped glacial Surprise Valley. The **Surprise Valley Lookout** offers a good view of the valley and, across to the southwest, another excellent aspect of Frenchmans Cap. Continuing down, you come to King William Saddle, another fine lookout point with views of the **King William Range** to the south and **Mount Rufus** to the north.

The Frenchmans Cap Track

The most prominent mountain peak in the Franklin Lower Gordon Wild Rivers National Park is the white-quartzite dome of **Frenchmans Cap** (1446m). Its southeast face has a sheer five-hundred-metre cliff and from its summit there are uninterrupted views of Mount Ossa in the Cradle Mountain–Lake St Clair National Park, Federation Peak, Macquarie Harbour and, on a fine day, the whole of the southwest wilderness. It takes three to five days to do the 54-kilometre return trip to the summit, best done between December and March, though of the seven hundred who walk the track each year, only six hundred do so between these months. Frenchmans Cap is much more demanding than the relatively straightforward Overland Track, as it has some very steep extended climbs and sections of mud, and should be attempted only by skilled bushwalkers – preferably with experience of other Tasmanian walks. The weather is temperamental: it rains frequently, and it can snow even in summer. Beyond Barron Pass, the track is above 900m and at any time of the year is subject to high winds, mist, rain, hail and snowfalls.

The track begins at the Lyell Highway, 55km from Queenstown, served by TassieLink's scheduled Hobart–Queenstown service (5 weekly), or you can charter Maxwell's Coaches (℡03/6492 1431) for $65 from Lake St Clair. A fifteen-minute walk from the road brings you to the suspension bridge across the river for the start of the walk. Record your plans in the registration book here and again in the logbook at the two huts at Lake Vera and Lake Tahune that provide basic **accommodation** (though this is usually full and you must bring tents and stoves with you); Frenchmans Cap is a proclaimed "Fuel Stove Only Area". There are composting toilets at both huts and plenty of camping spots along the way; water along the track is safe to drink. From the Franklin River to Lake Vera the well-defined track crosses plains and foothills, then becomes steep and rough as it climbs to Barron Pass – where there are magnificent views – becoming easier again on the way to Lake Tahune, close to the cliffs of Frenchmans Cap. From here it's a steep one-kilometre walk to the summit, before returning the same way.

For further **information**, see the Parks & Wildlife Service website (𝕎www .parks.tas.gov.au) and pick up the *Frenchmans Cap Map and Notes* ($9.90); or contact the Queenstown Ranger Station (℡03/6471 2511). Craclair Tours (see p.1017) organizes five-day guided treks ($1260), and Tasmanian Expeditions offers a five-day trip (see p.1017; Dec–March; $1260).

The Southwest National Park

Tasmania's **Southwest National Park** is an area of contrast: arrow-sharp, crested ranges of white quartzite cut across buttongrass plains. The isolation, rough terrain and unpredictable weather, even in summer – the southwest has more than two hundred days of rain a year – means that this is an area for experienced bushwalkers only. Being able to use a compass and read a map are important, but so is a tolerance for trudging through deep mud and swampy buttongrass while heavily laden with supplies and plagued by leeches.

The map *South Coast Walks* ($9.90) covers the southern gateways to the World Heritage Area: Cockle Creek through Port Davey to Scotts Peak, as well as Moonlight Ridge and South West Cape, including notes on track conditions, weather and campsites. For the rest of the area you'll need to purchase Tasmap topographic **maps**.

Two airlines operate **flights** into the national park from Cambridge aerodrome, 15km from Hobart. Par Avion (℡03/6248 5390, 𝕎www.paravion .com.au) offers a tour and charter service to Melaleuca, weather permitting (45min; $195 one-way, $370 return); you can register your walk at the airstrip. They also offer a combined scenic flight and boat trip on Melaleuca Inlet (4hr; $200) or Bathurst Harbour (full day; $310), including lunch. Roaring 40s Ocean Kayaking (see p.1017) offers amazing **kayaking expeditions**: you're flown in to Melaleuca and then spend six days camping and kayaking on Port Davey and Bathurst Harbour ($2395; shorter 3-day trip $1650; wilderness weekend $1050). **TasAir** (℡03/6248 5088, 𝕎www.tasair.com.au) flies to Melaleuca or Cox Bight (both $214 one-way, $395 return, minimum 2 passengers), which can cut out the trudge from Melaleuca, and also offers joyrides over the whole of the World Heritage Area from Hobart for $298 (2hr 30min, includes landing and refreshments at Melaleuca). If you're planning an extended walk, you can arrange for either airline to drop food supplies for you ($4.40 per kilo).

Unless you're flying in, or beginning a walk at **Cockle Creek**, south of Hobart, access to the South West National Park is via the **Gordon River Road**, which passes to the south of Mount Field National Park. The ranger for this (northern) end of South West National Park is based at Mount Field (see p.1045) and you should drop in or call to ask about conditions and to check that you're adequately prepared. The good sealed road heads through state forest and the South West Conservation Area, where the amazing craggy landforms of the **Frankland Range** loom above and signposts helpfully point out the names of the features, and past the drowned **Lake Pedder** (see box, p.1109) and the Gordon Dam's power station. The Hydro Tasmania-run Gordon Dam Visitor Centre is at the end of Gordon River Road, above the dam (Nov–April daily 10am–5pm; May–Oct daily 11am–3pm; ☎03/6280 1134). The Gordon Dam lookout here is breathtaking, and if you're after a thrill you can abseil down it with Aardvark Adventures (☎03/6273 7722, ⓦwww.aardvarkadventures.com .au; 4–5hr; $180), who will either meet you at the site or can provide transfers from Hobart on request.

You can **stay** at Lake Pedder at the refurbished *Lake Pedder Chalet* (☎03/6280 1166, ⓦwww.lakepedderchalet.com.au; rooms ❼–❻, chalets ❺), a former staff house for the HEC that has gorgeous lake views from its bar and bistro. Alternatively there are a number of free **campsites** in the area: just down the road on the shore of Lake Pedder, *Ted's Beach* has a shelter shed, electric barbecues, water and toilets; and there are two more campsites at Scotts Peak at the southern end of Lake Pedder, where the Port Davey walk begins (see p.1110). TassieLink runs a "Wilderness Link" service to Scotts Peak and to Condominium Creek (Mount Anne) from Hobart, via Mount Field (Dec–March).

Western Arthurs Traverse and Federation Peak

The most spectacular bushwalk in Tasmania, only 20km in length and 5km in width, **Western Arthurs Traverse** takes in 25 major peaks and 30 lakes. The last glacial period gouged into this range, leaving sharp quartzite ridges, craggy towers and impressive cliffs, and carving cirque valleys that are now filled by dark, tannin-stained lakes, surrounded by contrasting buttongrass plains. Violent storms, mists and continuous rain can plague the route in summer since it's in the direct path of the Roaring Forties. Crossing these ranges makes for a superb but difficult walk, taking between nine and twelve days, and camping areas are limited. Though there's no man-made track, the route, starting at Scotts Peak Road, is not difficult to follow; it involves scrambling over roots and branches

---

The flooding of Lake Pedder

To Senator Bob Brown, Tasmania's foremost Green activist, **Lake Pedder** "was one of the most gently beautiful places on the planet". The glacial lake, in the Frankland Range in Tasmania's southwest, had an area of 9.7 square kilometres until 1972, when it and the surrounding valleys were flooded as part of a huge hydroelectric scheme, creating a reservoir covering a massive 240 square kilometres and reached by the Lake Gordon Road via Maydena. Before then, the lake was so inaccessible that it could only be visited on foot or by light aircraft, which used to land on the perfect sand of the lake beach. In late 1994, a scientist revealed that, beneath the water, the sandy beach remained; in 1995, divers filmed underwater, revealing the still-visible impressions of light-aircraft tyre tracks. Certain scientists and conservationists, backed by the Wilderness Society, believe if Lake Pedder were drained it would revert to its former state, though it might take up to thirty years.

and making short descents and ascents into gullies and cliff lines, and you'll need to use a rope at some point.

The **Eastern Arthur Range** is the location of the major goal for intrepid southwest walkers – **Federation Peak**, often considered the most challenging in Australia, with its steep, almost perfectly triangular outline rising starkly above the surrounding rugged peaks and ridges. It was named by a surveyor in 1901, the year of federation, when most of the major landmarks in the southwest were still unvisited; in fact, the peak was not successfully scaled until 1949, its thick scrub, forests and cliffs having kept walkers at bay. Although the walk is now easier since the terrain has been "broken in", each year many walkers are turned back by the worst weather in Tasmania, and one person has died tackling the route. All the ascents are extremely difficult, and most parties take between seven and ten days to reach the peak and return; minor rock-climbing is required to get to the summit. The walk begins at the same point as the Port Davey Track (see p.1110).

Mount Anne Circuit

The highest peak in the southwest, **Mount Anne** (1423m) is part of a small range capped with red dolerite – a contrast to the surrounding white quartzite. Views from the summit are spectacular in fine weather, but even in summer the route is very exposed and prone to bad weather: it's suitable only for experienced walkers carrying a safety rope. The three- to four-day walk begins 20km along Scotts Peak Road at Condominium Creek (where there are basic camping facilities) and ends 9km south at Red Tape Creek; a car shuttle might be advisable, or you can be picked up and dropped off from Hobart with TassieLink's "Wilderness Link" service (Dec–March).

Port Davey Track

Going straight through the heart of the World Heritage Area, from Scotts Peak Dam south to Melaleuca (where you fly out; see below), is the little-used seventy-kilometre **Port Davey Track**, a wet, muddy four- to five-day trek over buttongrass plains, with views of rugged mountain ranges along the way. It's less interesting than some of the other walks in the area and most groups combine it with the South Coast Track for a ten- to sixteen-day wilderness experience, which requires a drop-off of food supplies. This combined walk is often called the **South West Track**. TassieLink offers a "Wilderness Link" service (Dec–March) to Scotts Peak.

South Coast Track

The **South Coast Track** is known for its magnificent **beaches** and spectacular coastal scenery of Aboriginal **middens**, rainforest and buttongrass ridges. At 85km, it's one of the longest tracks in the South West National Park – a six- to eight-day moderate-to-difficult walk, usually done from Melaleuca east to Cockle Creek. Since the route is mostly along the coast, the climate is milder than in many parts of the World Heritage Area but there is exposure to cold southerly winds and frequent rain; also, while crossing the exposed Ironbound Range (900m) it can sleet or snow, even in summer. Elsewhere, you will need to plough through sections of mud. There are no huts along the way, except at the Melaleuca airstrip. Around a thousand people do the walk each year, 75 percent of them between December and March. The best **approach** is to fly direct to Cox Bight with TasAir, cutting out the dull buttongrass-plains walk from Melaleuca, then head for Cockle Creek where TassieLink provides a "Wilderness Link" (Nov–April) service to Hobart. Alternatively, you can begin at Cockle Creek and fly out at Melaleuca with TasAir or Par Avion, or arrange for extra food supplies to be flown in at Melaleuca and continue along the Port Davey Track across the water, using the rowboats provided.

Tasmanian Expeditions (see p.1017) runs an extended **organized walk** of the South Coast Track (Nov–March; $1990). You need to be very fit for the nine-day trip, as each party member (maximum of ten) carries a share of the food and tents, a weight of 18–20kg. They also offer a 16-day trip ($3200), which combines the South Coast Track with the Port Davey Track, above.

The Bass Strait islands

Located in the rough waters of the Bass Strait, battered by the Roaring Forties, are two groups of islands: the Hunter group, dominated by **King Island** off the northwest tip of Tasmania, and the Furneaux group, the largest of which is **Flinders Island**, lying just beyond the northeast corner of the state. In the nineteenth century, sealers roamed the Bass Strait, but the two main islands now consist of low-key rural communities, while several tall lighthouses, and many shipwrecks offshore, are testimony to the turbulence of the sea at King Island.

Getting to the islands

You can go by **ferry** to Flinders Island from Bridport (see p.1060) on the northeast coast of Tasmania: Southern Shipping Co (Mon or Tues; departure times depend on tides; ☏03/6356 3333, ⓦwww.southernshipping.com.au) operates a car and passenger service. Car costs are prohibitive, but the return passenger fare ($96) is good value if you can put up with a possibly rough, eight-hour trip; book at least four weeks in advance. **Airlines of Tasmania** (☏03/6359 2312 or 1800 144 460, ⓦwww.airtasmania.com.au) flies to Flinders Island from Essendon Airport, just outside of Melbourne ($215 one-way), and from Launceston ($160 one-way). Tasmania's regional airline, Tasair (☏03/6248 5088 or 1800 062 900, ⓦwww.tasair.com.au), flies daily to King Island from Burnie and Devonport ($220 one-way) with connecting Tasair flights from Hobart; Regional Express (REX; ☏13 17 13, ⓦwww.rex.com.au) flies from Melbourne Tullamarine daily ($130 one-way).

King Island

King Island, smaller but more heavily populated than Flinders Island, is chiefly known for its rich dairy produce, with crayfish and kelp and wind farming as secondary industries. Green, low and windswept, it can't offer anything like Flinders Island's dramatic landscape, nor its history, though it has witnessed around sixty **shipwrecks** since 1801 and there are several working lighthouses – **Cape Wickham Lighthouse** in the north is the tallest in the southern hemisphere.

Arrival, information and getting around

King Island Coach Tours, 95 Main St, Currie (☎03/6462 1138 or 1800 647 702), operates pre-booked **airport transfers** to Currie, which is less than 10km away (1–4 passengers $20), and Grassy. They also run various coach, bushwalking and wildlife **tours**; the best is the short evening tour to see the **Little penguin** community at Grassy (Mon & Thurs; $40). Otherwise, to **get around**, Cheapa Island Car Rentals (☎03/6462 1603) and King Island Car Rental (☎03/6462 1282 or 1800 777 282) both do airport drop-offs. The Trend, at 26 Edward St in Currie, provides **tourist information** (Mon–Fri 8.30am–6pm, Sat & Sun 9am–5pm; ☎03/6462 1360), or contact King Island Tourism Inc (☎1800 645 014 or 03/6462 1313, ⓦwww.kingisland.org.au).

Currie has a **bank** with ATM and an **Online Access Centre** at 5 George St.

Accommodation

All options are in or around the main town, Currie. The websites ⓦwww .kingisland.org.au and ⓦwww.kingisland.net.au are good references for sourcing a bed elsewhere on the island.

Bass Caravan Park 100 Main St ☎1800 647 702 or 03/6462 1260. Budget accommodation in vans and cabins right in the town centre – no camping at the time of writing, but phone to check. Vans ❷, cabins ❹

Boomerang By the Sea Golf Club Rd ☎03/6462 1288, ⓦwww.boomerangbythesea.com.au. A five-minute walk south of the centre, this motel's 16 units – pleasant if unremarkable – look over the golf course to Bass Strait beyond. ❺

Devils Gap Retreat Charles St ☎03/6462 1180, ⓔdevilsgap@kingisland.net.au. Two delightful seafront cottages – one with rough stone walls, the other a colourful Fifties bungalow – that are full of artworks by owner and potter Caroline. Both have two bedrooms. ❺

King Island Gem Motel 95 Main St ☎03/6462 1260, ⓔgeraldinedavis2@bigpond.com.au. A quiet motel option in the centre which incorporates three-bed cottages. Airport transfers provided on request. ❹–❺

The island

The island's main town is **CURRIE**, which has a simple museum (daily 2–4pm, closed July & Aug; donation suggested); the bleak village of **GRASSY**, on the eastern side of the island, may experience a revival with the reopening of the tungsten mine that sustained its economy for 73 years from 1917. King Island is renowned for its fresh produce, and one essential stop is the **King Island Dairy** (Mon–Fri & Sun noon–4.30pm, closed Wed May–Sept), 8km north of Currie at Loorna, for free tastings of rich local dairy produce; the brie and thick cream in particular have legendary status around Australia. The island's **kelp factory** is near Currie's golf course; the bull kelp is gathered from the surrounding shores and left to dry outside the factory on racks – you'll see it as you pass by. Once dry, the kelp is milled into granules and shipped to Scotland to be processed into alginates, used as a gelling agent in literally thousands of products ranging from toothpaste to ice cream.

Eating

The best thing about King Island is the food, with free-range lamb and pork and local beef and wallaby, as well as seafood and delicious creamy milk, which you can drink unpasteurized while on the island – a rare treat. For a sit-down meal, the *Boomerang By the Sea* motel (see above) has immediate sea views from its glass-walled **restaurant** and a seafood speciality menu. In the centre, *King Island Bakery* makes delicious pies – including crayfish and King Island beef –

while *Nautilus Coffee Lounge* provides the **café** culture; both are on Main Street. There's also a supermarket (open daily) and a bottle shop in Currie.

Flinders Island

With a population of just 800 (nearly half of whom are absentee landowners), **FLINDERS ISLAND** is nonetheless the largest of 52 named islands that make up the Furneaux group, first mapped by Tobias Furneaux in 1770. Some islanders are descendants of seal hunters who pioneered settlement here a decade or so before the first bases on "mainland" Tasmania and, so legend goes, lured ships to their demise for a spot of piracy. The sea remains a central part of life – the crays brought in by fishermen at Lady Barron are said to be the best in Tasmania – while the dazzling white beaches and granite boulder headlands are similar to those on Tasmania's east coast, but without the people. As locals say, if there's someone on the beach, go to another one. And they're only half joking.

Information, tours and getting around

For **information** on activities such as cruises, scuba diving, fishing, birdwatching and scenic flights, and walking and climbing guides to the island, head for the Area Marketing and Development Office, as you come into Whitemark on Lagoon Road (Mon–Fri 8.15am–5pm; ☏1800 994 477, ⊛www.visitflindersisland.com .au). *Flinders Island Naturally*, a free visitors' guide with map, can be picked up here and at Tasmanian Travel Centres before you arrive on the island. The **Online Access Centre** is just opposite.

Of the island's many **tours**, a good bet is the boat trip to observe muttonbirds return to their nests at dusk with Flinders Island Adventures (Oct–March; 2hr

---

Aboriginal heritage on Flinders Island

More than any other location in the state, Flinders Island is the wellspring of Tasmanian aboriginal culture. Ironically, its survival is down to the piratical European sealers who wreaked devastation on indigenous communites. Their abduction of native women for their seal-hunting skills provided a vital link in the continuing survival of the Tasmanian Aboriginal people. With the demise of sealing, the communities survived by **muttonbird harvesting**, a seasonal industry that continues today for more heritage than economic reasons and whose practice was guaranteed by Aboriginal land-rights claims in 1995 that won the title to several outlying, unoccupied islands. In 2005, Tasmania's Legislative Council approved the largest transfer rights yet, handing over management of Aboriginal-occupied Cape Barren Island (population 75) and Clarke Island (population six) to the Cape Barren Island Aboriginal Association.

The paradox is that Flinders Island itself featured large in the tragedy of the Tasmanian Aboriginal people. Between 1831 and 1834 the remnants of the Tasmanian tribes were persuaded or forced to accept relocation here from territories on "mainland" Tasmania. Settled in a military style camp at windswept **Wybalenna** (literally "Black Man's Houses") on the west coast, without adequate food and shelter, the Aborigines were forcibly Christianized, and as their culture was expunged their numbers dwindled. Of the 135 tribespeople who were sent here, only 47 were still alive when the settlement was abandoned in 1847 and moved to Oyster Cove, near Hobart.

30min–3hr; $35 per person; ℡03/6359 4507, Ⓦwww.flindersisland.com.au). They also offer several other half- or full-day trips, including cruises to the outer islands, fishing and diving trips and 4WD tours.

The post office in Whitemark houses the island's only **bank** – Westpac (Mon–Thurs 10am–2.30pm, Fri 10am–4/5pm) – with EFTPOS, but no ATM. There's no public transport, but you can **rent a car** and arrange to pick it up at the airport on arrival. Prices are reasonable with *Flinders Island Hire and Drive* based near the airport, run by the *Flinders Island Cabin Park* (℡03/6359 2188, Ⓦwww.flindersislandcp.com.au), which also has mountain bikes for hire. Alternatively, Flinders Island Car Rentals (℡03/6359 2168) will meet you off the plane. The Lady Barron Multistore (open daily), tucked away on Henwood Street, is hard to find: head uphill from the pub. It has EFTPOS and a post office, as well as petrol.

Accommodation

The island has plenty of opportunities for **camping**: there's a site with water and showers (℡03/6359 8560) and a shop at topaz-fossicking Killiecrankie Bay in the northwest of the island, or you can camp for free at the coastal reserves, or on any crown land as long as it's 500m from the road. Designated sites are at Allport Beach, Lillies Beach, North East River and Trousers Point Beach; all have toilets and fireplaces, though only the last has water and a gas barbecue.

Flinders Island Cabin Park Bluff Rd ℡03/6359 2188, Ⓦwww.flindersislandcp.com.au. You can camp in comfort a few kilometres out of Whitemark, near the airport, in pleasant sheltered grounds full of spacious and mostly en-suite cabins too. Camping $7 per person, cabins ❸–❹

Furneaux Tavern 11 Franklin Parade, Lady Barron ℡03/6359 3521. Overlooking Adelaide Bay on the dramatic Franklin Sound, with spacious and attractive cabin-style motel units set in native gardens. ❹–❺

Interstate Hotel Patrick St, Whitemark ℡03/6359 2114. Some en-suite rooms and generous meals served in a popular bistro (except Sun). B&B ❹

Partridge Farm A 10min drive from Lady Barron at the end of the road to Badger Corner ℡03/6359 3554. Two four-star cabins in eucalypt forest – a one-bed and a three-bed, both with wood heaters – plus a bungalow, all in a secluded spot with beautiful views. ❺

Vistas on Trousers Point ℡03/6359 4586, Ⓦwww.vistasontrouserpoint.com.au. High-end retreat and spa whose relaxed hosts have a mantra to "relax, heal and rejuvenate" its 14 guests. Located in the idyllic southwest corner of the island, it also serves home-made organic food. ❽

The island

The main town, **Whitemark**, is unlikely to detain you long. The island's principal historic sight is the **chapel at WYBALENNA**, 20km north. Built in 1838 and restored by the National Trust, it is all that remains of the period of enforced Aboriginal settlement here (see box, p.1113) – in the cemetery only the white graves bear headstones. A successful land-rights claim in 1999 allowed the Aboriginal people of Flinders Island to decide how they'll run it – at the time of writing visitors could not enter.

There's a walk to Settlement Point from Wybalenna, where a viewing platform looks over an extensive **muttonbird** rookery – the sight and sound of hundreds of thousands of birds flying to the nesting islands each evening at dusk during the breeding season (Oct to late March) is extraordinary. The only commercial muttonbirding done by Aboriginal people now, however, is on Great Dog Island; in the grounds of the **Furneaux Museum** at **EMITA**, a few kilometres northeast of Wybalenna (Jan daily 1–5pm, otherwise Sat & Sun summer 1–5pm, winter 1–4pm; $2; ℡03/6359 2010), there's a replica of a typical **muttonbirding**

shed, with its floor lined with tussock grass. Inside, shell necklaces made by the Aboriginal people of Cape Barren Island are displayed, and there are exhibits relating to sealing and shipwrecks.

History aside, isolated Flinders Island is a huge draw for **bushwalkers** and **rock-climbers**. Only about half of the island is cultivated, and you can walk its entire length in about six days – arrange with Flinders Island Adventures (see p.1113) to have food and water delivered en route – on the partially signposted north–south **Flinders Trail**, a route designed to provide a sampling of the various terrains. The best-known walk, however, is to the distinctive summit of **Mount Strzelecki**, named after the Polish count, explorer and scientist who climbed it in 1842. The climb to the top starts about 10km south of Whitemark, signposted on Trousers Point Road – look out for a brown national-park sign – the peak is in the **Strzelecki National Park** in the southwest corner (ranger ☏03/6359 2217). Though navigation is easy, it's a strenuous walk – about 5km return (3–5hr). The wind can be fierce at the summit, and mists roll in, so take something wind- and waterproof. **Trousers Point** itself, also in the park, is a good introduction to the delights of the island's deserted beaches. The site, with its fine, white sand and rust coloured rock formations, is particularly spectacular, with Mount Strzelecki rising up behind the granite headland; there's a free camping area here, with a composting toilet, water tank and bins. Nearby, *Retreat Vistas on Trousers Point* (see opposite), with its retreat and day-spa programmes, is a sign of the direction Flinders is heading. The **Flinders Island Ecology Trail** is a circuit designed to be followed in a car, with five stopping points where interpretive material is provided; the *Furneaux Ecological Notebook* ($7), available at the Area Marketing and Development office (see p.1113), is an excellent resource. **Walkers Lookout**, in the Darling Range, is a good starting point, offering the best panorama of Flinders and the surrounding islands, with signs pointing out all the landmarks; the other four points on the route highlight bird habitats. You can see the endemic protected **Cape Barren goose** everywhere, as well as the island's wombats.

Eating

The *Flinders Island Bakery* (closed Sun) in Whitemark has alfresco tables; delicious pies are part of its repertoire. Otherwise, apart from pub grub in the *Interstate Hotel* (see opposite), try the *Flinders Island Sports Club* at the end of the Esplanade for a reasonable meal in pleasant surroundings. In Lady Barron, the *Furneaux Tavern* (see opposite) serves meals in the upmarket *Shearwater Restaurant*, much the island's best place to eat, or there are simple bar meals in the convivial public bar. Whitemark's supermarket (closed Sat afternoon and all Sun) is opposite the pub.

Travel details

Between Tasmania and the mainland states

Ferry

Spirit of Tasmania Bass Strait ferry from Port Melbourne to Devonport (1–2 daily; 10hr).

Flights

Mainly through Sydney's Mascot or Melbourne's Tullamarine airports, with smaller companies operating from Essendon and Moorabbin airports, on the fringes of Melbourne.

Flinders Island to: Launceston (1–5 daily; 40min); Melbourne (Moorabbin 3–4 weekly; 1hr 15min).

King Island to: Burnie (2 daily Mon–Fri, 1 daily Sat & Sun; 45min); Devonport (1 daily Mon–Fri, 2 daily Sat & Sun; 45min); Melbourne (Moorabbin Mon–Fri 4 daily, Sat & Sun 2 daily; 1hr).

Melbourne to: Burnie (4 daily; 1hr 10min); Devonport (4 daily; 1hr 15min); Flinders Island (Essendon 3 weekly; 50min); Hobart (12 daily; 1hr); King Island (Moorabbin Mon–Fri 4 daily, Sat & Sun 1 daily; 45min); Launceston (10 daily; 1hr).

Sydney to: Hobart (4–6 daily; 1hr 50min); Launceston (4 daily; 1hr 35min).

Transport on the island

Buses – scheduled services

Burnie to: Smithton via the northwest coast (1 daily; 1hr 30min).

Deloraine to: Devonport (1–3 daily; 40min); Hobart (2–4 daily; 4hr); Launceston (1–6 daily; 45min).

Devonport to: Burnie (2–5 daily; 50min); Cradle Mountain (Nov–Mar 1 daily, otherwise 3 weekly; 2hr 15min); Deloraine (2–4 daily; 1hr 30min); Hobart (3–4 daily; 4hr 30min); Launceston (3–4 daily; 1hr 30min); Queenstown (3 weekly; 5hr 20min).

Hobart to: Bicheno (3–6 weekly; 4hr); Burnie (3–6 daily; 4hr 45min); Cygnet (3 on Thurs, 1 daily rest of week; 55min); Deloraine (2–4 daily; 4hr); Devonport (2–4 daily; 5hr 30min); Dover (1 daily

Mon–Fri; 55min); Geeveston (4 daily Mon–Fri, 1 daily Sun; 1hr 15min); Kettering (Mon–Fri 4 daily; 40min); Lake St Clair (4 weekly; 3hr); Launceston (3–5 daily; 2hr 30min); New Norfolk (1–8 daily; 30min); Port Arthur (1 daily Mon–Fri; 2hr); Queenstown via New Norfolk, Lake St Clair and Frenchmans Cap with connections to Strahan (5 weekly; 5hr 45min); Richmond (4 daily Mon–Fri; 25min); St Helens (1 daily Fri–Sun; 3hr); Swansea (1–2 daily except Sat; 2hr 30min).

Launceston to: Bicheno (1 daily except Sat; 2hr 40min); Burnie (2–4 daily; 2hr 30min); Cradle Mountain (3 weekly; 3hr); Deloraine (Mon–Fri 5 daily; 45min); Derby (1–5 daily except Sat; 2hr 40min); Devonport (24 daily; 1hr 30min); Hobart (3–5 daily; 2hr 30min); Mole Creek (2 daily Mon–Fri; 1hr 30min); Queenstown (3 weekly; 7hr); St Helens via St Marys (1 daily except Sat; 2hr 45min).

Queenstown to: Strahan (5 weekly; 45min).

Scottsdale to: Bridport (2 daily Mon–Fri; 30min).

Ferries

Beauty Point to: George Town (Nov–April 3 daily Wed–Mon; 30min).

Bridport to: Flinders Island (1 weekly; 8hr).

Kettering to: Bruny Island (10–11 daily Mon–Sat, 8 daily Sun; 20min).

Triabunna to: Maria Island (2 daily summer, 2 daily Mon, Wed, Fri & Sat other seasons; 30min).

Contexts

Contexts

History

The first European settlers saw Australia as *terra nullius* – empty land – on the principle that Aborigines didn't "use" the country in an agricultural sense, a belief that remained uncontested in law until 1992. However, decades of archeological work, the reports of early settlers, and oral tradition, have established that humans have occupied Australia for a minimum of forty thousand years – evidence that Australia's Aboriginal peoples shaped, controlled and used their environment as surely as any farmer. Even so, it's difficult for visitors to form an idea of pre-colonial times, as two centuries of European rule shattered traditional Aboriginal life, and evidence of those earlier times mostly consists of cryptic art sites and legends. If you're lucky enough to get beyond the tourist image, you'll realize that Aboriginal culture, though being redefined, is far from confined to the past. The very simplified outline of Aboriginal history below is intended mainly as background to accounts given in the Guide. Following it is a fuller description of the years since European colonization.

From Gondwana to the Dreamtime

After the break-up of the supercontinent known as **Gondwana** into India, Africa, South America, Australasia and Antarctica, Australia moved away from the South Pole, reaching its current geographical location about fifteen million years ago. Though the mainland was periodically joined to New Guinea and Tasmania, there was never a land link with the rest of Asia, and thus the country developed its unique fauna. Most notably, marsupials, or pouched mammals, became common, but a whole range of giant animals – the **megafauna** (see box, p.1039) – also flourished, along with widespread rainforests, until about fifty thousand years ago. Subsequent Ice Ages dried out the climate; by six thousand years ago the seas had stabilized at their present levels and Australia's environment was much as it is today, an arid centre with a relatively fertile eastern seaboard. **Humans** had been in Australia long before then, of course, most likely taking advantage of low sea levels to cross the Timor Trough into northern Australia, or island-hop from Indonesia via New Guinea onto what is now the Cape York Peninsula. Exactly when this happened, how many times it happened, and what the colonists did next, is debatable. The earliest human remains found in Australia (in New South Wales) are dated to around 40,000 BC, with scientists estimating that humans could have settled here as far back as 70,000 years ago.

The oldest known remains from central Australia are only 22,000 years old, so it's also fairly plausible that initial colonization occurred around the coast, followed by later exploration of the interior – though it's just as likely that corrosive rainforests, which covered the centre until about twenty thousand years ago, obliterated all trace of earlier human habitation. When the European settlers arrived, the **thylacine** (Tasmanian tiger) had disappeared from the Australian mainland but still lived in Tasmania, while the **dingo**, an introduced canine, was prevalent on the mainland but unknown in Tasmania. This indicates that there was a further influx of people and **dogs** more recently than twelve thousand years ago, after rising sea levels separated Tasmania and it had become an island. The earliest inhabitants used crude **stone implements**, gradually replaced by a more refined technology based around lighter tools, **boomerangs**, and the use of core stones to flake "blanks", which were then fashioned into spearheads, knives and scrapers. As only certain types of stone were suitable for the process, tribes living further away from quarries had to trade with those living near them. **Trade networks** for rock, **ochre** (a red clay used for ceremonial purposes) and other products – shells and even wood for canoes – eventually stretched from New Guinea to the heart of the continent, following river systems away from the coast. **Rock art**, preserved in an ancient engraved tradition, and other more recent painted styles, seem to indicate that cultural links also travelled along these trade routes – similar symbols and styles are found in widely separated regions.

It's probable that the disappearance of the megafauna was accelerated by Aboriginal hunting, but the most dramatic change wrought by the original Australians was the controlled use of **fire** to clear forest. Burning promoted new growth and encouraged game, indirectly expanding grassland and favouring certain plants – cycads, grasstrees, banksias and eucalypts – that evolved fire-reliant seeds and growth patterns. But while the Aborigines modified the environment for their own ends, their belief that land, wildlife and people were an interdependent whole engendered sympathy for natural processes, and maintained a balance between the population and natural resources. Tribes were organized and related according to complex kinship systems, reflected in the three hundred different **languages** known to exist at that time. Legends about the mythical **Dreamtime**, when creative forces shaped the landscape, provided verbal maps of tribal territory and linked natural features to the actions of these Dreamtime ancestors, who often had both human and animal forms. This spiritual and practical attachment to tribal areas was expedient in terms of use of resources, but was the weak point in maintaining a culture after white dispossession: separated from the lands they related to, legends lost their meaning, and the people their sense of identity.

The first Europeans

Prior to the sixteenth century, the only regular visitors to Australia were the **Malays**, who established seasonal camps while fishing the northern coasts for trepang, a sea slug, to sell to the Chinese. In Europe, the globe had been carved up between Spain and Portugal in 1494 under the auspices of Pope Alexander VI at the **Treaty of Tordesillas**, and all maritime nations subsequently kept their nautical charts secret, to protect their discoveries. It's possible, therefore, that the inquisitive **Portuguese** knew of **Terra Australis**, the Great Southern Land, soon after founding their colony in East Timor in 1516.

But while the precise date of "discovery" is contentious, it is clear that various nations were making forays into the area: the **Dutch** in 1605 and 1623, who were appalled by the harsh climate and inhabitants of Outback Queensland, and the **Spanish** in 1606, who were looking for both plunder and pagans to convert to Catholicism. The latter, guided by **Luis Vaes de Torres**, blithely navigated the strait between New Guinea and Cape York as if they knew it was there. As Torres hailed from Portugal it is indeed likely that he knew where he was;

there's evidence that the Portuguese had **mapped** a large portion of Australia's northern coastline as early as 1536.

Later in the seventeenth century, the Dutch navigators **Dirk Hartog, Van Diemen** and **Abel Tasman** added to maps of the east and north coasts, but eventually discarded "New Holland" as a barren, worthless country. William Dampier, a buccaneer who wrote popular accounts of his visit to Western Australia, first stirred British interest in 1697. However, it wasn't until the British captured the Spanish port of Manila, in the Philippines, in 1762, that detailed maps of Australia's coast fell into their hands; it took them six more years to assemble an expedition to locate the continent. Sailing in 1768 on the *Endeavour*, **Captain James Cook** headed to Tahiti, then proceeded to map New Zealand's coastline before sailing west in 1770 to search for the Great Southern Land – unsure whether this was New Holland or an as yet undiscovered landmass.

The British sighted the continent in April 1770 and sailed north from Cape Everard to **Botany Bay**, where Cook commented on the Aborigines' initial indifference to seeing the *Endeavour*. When a party of forty sailors attempted to land, however, two Aborigines attacked them with spears; the British drove them off with musket fire. Continuing on up the Queensland coast, the British passed Moreton Bay and Fraser Island before entering the treacherous passages of the Great Barrier Reef where, on June 11, the *Endeavour* ran aground off Cape Tribulation. Cook managed to beach the ship safely at the mouth of the Endeavour River (present-day Cooktown), where the expedition set up camp while the ship was repaired.

Contact between Aborigines and whites during the following six weeks was tinged with a mistrust that never quite erupted into serious confrontation, and Cook took the opportunity to make notes in which he tempered romanticism for the "noble savage" with the sharp observation that European and Aboriginal values were mutually incomprehensible. The expedition was intrigued by some of Australia's wildlife, but otherwise unimpressed with the country, and was glad to sail onwards on August 5. With imposing skill, Cook successfully managed to navigate the rest of the reef, finally claiming possession of the country – which he named **New South Wales** – for King George III on August 21, at Possession Island in the Torres Strait, before sailing off to Timor.

Convicts

The expedition's reports didn't arouse much enthusiasm in London, however, and the disdainful attitude towards the Great Southern Land matched the opinion voiced by the Dutch more than a century before. However, after the loss of its American colonies following the **American War of Independence** in 1783, Britain was deprived of a handy location to offload convicted criminals. They were temporarily housed in prison ships or "hulks", moored around the country, while the government tried to solve the problem. **Sir Joseph Banks**, botanist on the *Endeavour*, advocated Botany Bay as an ideal location for a **penal colony** that could soon become self-sufficient. The government agreed (perhaps also inspired by the political advantages of gaining a foothold in the Pacific), and in 1787 the **First Fleet**, packed with around 730 convicts (570 men and 160 women), set sail for Australia on eleven ships, under the command of **Captain Arthur Phillip**. Reaching Botany Bay in January 1788, Phillip deemed it unsuitable for his purposes and instead founded the settlement at **Sydney Cove**, on Port Jackson's fine natural harbour.

The early years at Sydney were not promising. The colonists suffered erratic weather and starvation, Aboriginal hostility, soil that was too hard to plough, and timber so tough it dented their axes. In 1790, supplies ran so low that a third of the population had to be transferred to a new colony on **Norfolk Island**, 1500km northeast. Even so, in the same year Britain dispatched a second fleet with a thousand more convicts – 267 of whom died en route. To ease the situation, Phillip granted packages of farmland to marines and former convicts before he returned to Britain in 1792. The first **free settlers** arrived the following year, and Britain's preoccupation with the French Revolutionary Wars meant a reduction in the number of convicts being transported to the colony, thus allowing a period of consolidation.

Meanwhile, **John Macarthur** manipulated the temporary governor into allowing his **New South Wales Corps**, which had replaced the marines as the governor's strong arm, to exercise considerable power in the colony. This was temporarily curtailed in 1800 by **Philip King**, who also slowed an illicit rum trade, encouraged new settlements, and speeded production by allowing convicts to work for wages. Macarthur was forced out of the corps into the wool industry, importing Australia's first **sheep** from South Africa. He continued to stir up trouble though, which culminated in the **Rum Rebellion** of 1808, when merchant and pastoral factions, supported by the military, ousted **Governor William Bligh**. Britain finally took notice of the colony's anarchic state and appointed the firm-handed **Colonel Lachlan Macquarie**, backed by the 73rd Regiment, as Bligh's replacement in 1810. Macquarie settled the various disputes – Macarthur had fled to Britain a year earlier – and brought eleven years of disciplined progress to the colony.

Labelled the "Father of Australia", for his vision of a country that could rise above its convict origins, Macquarie implemented enlightened policies towards former convicts or **emancipists**, enrolling them in public offices. He also attempted to educate, rather than exterminate, Aboriginal people and was the driving force behind New South Wales becoming a productive, self-sufficient colony. But he offended the landowner **squatters**, who were concerned that emancipists were being granted too many favours, and also those who regarded the colony solely as a place of punishment. In fact, conditions had improved so much that by 1819 New South Wales had become the major destination for voluntary emigrants from Britain.

In 1821 Macquarie was replaced as governor, and his successor, Sir Thomas Brisbane, was instructed to segregate, not integrate, convicts. To this end, when New South Wales officially graduated from being a penal settlement to a new British colony in 1823, convicts were used to colonize newly explored regions – Western Australia, Tasmania and Queensland – as far away from Sydney's free settlers as possible.

Explorers

Matthew Flinders had already circumnavigated the mainland in 1803 (and suggested the name "**Australia**") in his leaky vessel, the *Investigator*, and with the colony firmly established, expeditions began pushing inland from Sydney. In 1823, John Oxley, the Surveyor General, having previously explored newly discovered pastoral land west of the Blue Mountains, chose the **Brisbane**

River in Queensland as the site of a new penal colony, thus opening up the fertile Darling Downs to future settlement. Meanwhile, townships were being founded elsewhere around the coast, eventually leading to the creation of **separate colonies** to add to that of Van Diemen's Land (Tasmania), settled in 1803 to ward off French exploration. Albany and Fremantle on the west coast were established in 1827 and 1829 respectively, followed by the Yarra River (Melbourne, Victoria) in 1835, and Adelaide (South Australia) in 1836.

But it was the possibilities of the **interior** – which some maintained concealed a vast inland sea – which captured the imagination of the government and squatters. Setting out from Adelaide in 1844, **Charles Sturt** was the first to attempt to cross the centre. Forced to camp for six months at a desert waterhole, where the heat melted the lead in his pencils and unthreaded screws from equipment, he managed to reach the aptly named Sturt's Stony Desert before scurvy forced him back to Adelaide. At the same time, **Ludwig Leichhardt**, a Prussian doctor, had more luck in his crossing between the Darling Downs and Port Essington, near Darwin, which he accomplished in fourteen months. Unlike Sturt, Leichhardt found plenty of potential farmland and returned a hero. He vanished in 1848, however, while again attempting to cross the continent. In the same year, the ill-fated **Kennedy** expedition managed the trek from Tully to Cape York in northern Queensland, but with the loss of most of the party, Kennedy included, as a result of poor planning, starvation and attack by Aborigines. Similarly, **Burke and Wills**' successful 1860 south-to-north traverse between Melbourne and the Gulf of Carpentaria in Queensland was marred by the death of the expedition leaders upon their return south, owing to bad organization and a series of unfortunate errors (see box, p.526 for the full story of their trek). Finally, Australia's centre was located by **John MacDouall Stuart** in 1860, who subsequently managed a safe return journey to Adelaide from the north coast the following year. Hopes of finding an inland sea were quashed, and the harsh reality of a dry, largely infertile interior, began to dawn on developers.

Aboriginal response

British advances had been repulsed from the very first year of the colony's foundation; Governor Phillip reporting that "the natives now attack any straggler they meet unarmed". Forced off their traditional hunting grounds, which were taken by the settlers for agriculture or grazing, the Aborigines began stealing crops and spearing cattle. Response from the British was brutal; the relatively liberal Lieutenant-Governor George Arthur ordered a sweep of Tasmania in 1830, to round up all Aboriginal people and herd them into **reserves**, a symbolic attempt to clear "the uncivilized" from the paths of progress (see box, pp.1014–1015). More direct action, such as the **Myall Creek Massacre** in 1838 (see box, p.340, when 28 Aborigines were roped together and butchered by graziers, created public outcry, but similar "**dispersals**" became commonplace wherever indigenous people resisted white intrusion; more insidious methods – such as poisoning waterholes or lacing gifts of flour with arsenic – were also employed by pastoralists angered over stock losses.

The Aboriginal people were not a single, unified society, and the British exploited existing divisions by creating the notorious **Native Mounted Police**, an Aboriginal force that aided and abetted the extermination of rival groups. By the 1890s, citing a perversion of Darwinian theory which held that

Aboriginal people were less evolved than whites and so doomed to extinction, most states had followed Tasmania's example of "**protectionism**", relocating Aborigines into reserves which were frequently a long way from their traditional lands – in Queensland, for instance, Rockhampton Aborigines were moved to Fraser Island, 500km away.

Gold

The discovery of **gold** in 1851 by Edward Hargraves, fresh from the California fields, had a dramatic bearing on Australia's future. The first major strikes in New South Wales and Victoria brought an immediate rush of hopeful miners from Sydney and Melbourne and, once the news spread overseas, from the USA and Britain. The British government, realizing the absurdity of spending taxes on shipping criminals to a land of gold when there were plenty of people willing to pay for their passage, finally **ended transportation** in 1853. Gold also opened up Australia's interior far more thoroughly than explorers had done; as returns petered out in one area, prospectors moved on into uncharted regions to find more. Western Australia and Queensland (which was saved from bankruptcy by the discovery of gold in 1867) experienced booms up until 1900 and, although mining initially followed in the path of pastoral expansion, the rushes began to attract settlements and markets into previously uncultivated regions.

A new "level society", based on a "mateship" ethic, evolved on the goldfields, where education had little bearing on an ability to endure hard work and Spartan living conditions. Yet the **diggers** were all too aware of their poor social and political rights. At the end of 1854, frustrations over mining licences erupted at **Eureka** (see box, p.964), on the outskirts of Ballarat in Victoria, where miners built a stockade and ended up being charged by mounted police. Twenty-two of the miners were killed and the surviving rebels – put on trial for high treason – were vindicated, and rights, including the vote, were granted to miners. The Victorian goldfields also saw **racial tensions** directed against a new minority, the Chinese, who first arrived there during the 1850s. Disheartened by diminishing returns and infuriated by the Chinese ability to find gold in abandoned claims, diggers stormed a Chinese camp at **Lambing Flat** in 1861. Troops had to be sent in to stop the riots, but the ringleaders were later acquitted by an all-white jury. Throughout the country, goldfields became centres of **nationalism** (despite the irony of the Chinese-run stores and market gardens in mining towns), peaking in Queensland in the 1880s, where the flames were fanned by the importation of **Solomon Islanders** to work on sugar plantations. Ostensibly to prevent slavery, but politically driven by recession and growing white unemployment, the government forced the repatriation of Islanders, taxed the Chinese out of the country, and passed the 1901 Immigration Act – also known as the **White Australia policy** – which greatly restricted non-European immigration.

Federation and war

Central government was first mooted in 1842, but new states were not keen to return to the control of New South Wales, lose interstate customs duties, or share the new-found mineral wealth, which had consolidated separation in the first place. But by the end of the century they began to see advantages to **Federation**, not least as a way to control indentured labour and present a united front against French, German and Russian expansion in the Pacific. A decade of wrangling by the states, to ensure equal representation irrespective of population, saw the formation of a High Court and a two-tier parliamentary system consisting of a House of Representatives and Senate, presided over by a Prime Minister. Each state would have its own premier, and Britain would be represented by a Governor-General. Approved by Queen Victoria shortly before her death, the **Commonwealth of Australia** came into being on January 1, 1901.

It's notable that the Immigration Act (see opposite) was the first piece of legislation to be passed by the new parliament, and reflected the nationalist drive behind federation. Though the intent was to create an Australia largely of European – and preferably British – descent, the policy also sowed the seeds for Australian independence from the "Mother Country". The first pull away came as early as 1912, when the **Commonwealth Bank** opened, evidence that Australia was endeavouring to become less financially reliant on Britain. Centred entirely on white interests, the White Australia policy ensured that Aboriginal people were not included in the national census, nor were they allowed to vote, until 1967. The new government did, however, give white **women** the vote in 1902, and the Australian Labor Party, which had grown out of the economic recession and union battles with the government during the 1890s, established the concept of a **minimum wage** in 1907.

Defence had also been a positive force behind federation. But even though the war between Japan and Russia in 1904 had highlighted the need to build its own defence force, Australia was largely unprepared for the outbreak of hostilities in Europe a decade later, owning little more than a navy made up of secondhand British ships. Promising to support Britain to "the last man and the last shilling", there was a patriotic rush to enlist in the army, and an opportunistic occupation of German New Guinea by Australian forces. Surprisingly, the issue of compulsory conscription, raised by **Prime Minister Billy Hughes**, was twice defeated in referendums during World War I.

From the Australian perspective, the most important stage of the war occurred when Turkey gave its support to Germany in 1915. **Winston Churchill** formulated a plan to defend British shipping in the Dardanelles by occupying the **Gallipoli Peninsula**, and diverted Australian infantry bound for Europe. Between April and December 1915, wave after wave of Australian troops were mown down below Turkish gun emplacements, as they attempted to take control of the peninsula. By the end of the year, it became clear that Gallipoli was not going to fall, and the survivors were evacuated to fight on the Western Front. The long-term effect of the senseless slaughter was the first serious questioning of Anglo-Australian relations: should Australia have committed and sacrificed so much (8,141 soldiers died) to defend a (geographically) distant country's interests? Conversely, Gallipoli, as Australia's debut on the world stage, is still to this day treated as a symbol of national identity and pride.

1918–39

After World War I, the Nationalist Party joined forces with the **Country Party** to assume government under the paternalistic and fiercely anti-socialist guidance of **Earle Page** and **Stanley Bruce**. The Country Party was formed as a result of the widening divisions between the growing urban population and farmers, who felt isolated and politically unrepresented. Under the coalition, pastoral industries were subsidized by overseas borrowing, allowing them to compete internationally, and technology began to close the gap between the city and the Outback. Radio and aviation developments saw the birth of **Qantas** – the Queensland and Northern Territory Aerial Service – and the **Royal Flying Doctor Service** in Queensland's remote west. Development also occurred in the cities: work started on the Sydney Harbour Bridge, and the new Commonwealth capital, **Canberra**, was completed.

On the social front, the USA stopped mass immigration in 1921, deflecting a flood of people from depressed **Southern Europe** to Australia, which the government countered by encouraging British immigrants with assisted passages. While progressive in some areas – a dole was proposed for the unemployed, the sick, pensioners and mothers – the government overreacted to opposition, as exemplified by their response to the **seamen and dockers' strike** of 1928. Citing the arch-villain, "communism", as being behind the dispute, they attempted to stretch the scope of the Immigration Act to allow action to be taken against disturbances that were politically motivated. However, the implication that the law could be altered against anyone who disagreed with the government contributed to the downfall of Bruce and Page the following year. The themes of their rule – differences between rural and urban societies, questions of Australian identity, union disputes, and the effects of heavy borrowing to create artificially high living standards – are issues that are still relevant today.

As the **Great Depression** set in during the early 1930s, Australia faced the collapse of its economic and political systems, with all the parties divided. Pressed for a loan, the Bank of England forced a restructuring of the Australian economy. Adding to national embarrassment, politics and sports became blurred during the 1932 "**body-line**" cricket series: the loan was made virtually conditional on the Australian cricket authorities dropping their allegations that British bowlers were deliberately trying to injure Australian batsmen during the tour.

Meanwhile, worries about communism were succeeded by concern about the rise of fascism, as Mussolini and Hitler took power in Europe and Japanese forces invaded Manchuria – the **Tanaka memorial** in 1927 actually cited Australia as a target for future conquest by Japan. Although displaying ambivalence towards fascism, Australia assisted the immigration of refugees from central Europe, and – after a prolonged union battle – halted iron exports to Japan. When Prime Minister Joseph Lyons died in office, **Robert Menzies**, a firm supporter of everything "British", was elected to the post, in time to side with Britain as hostilities were declared against Hitler in September 1939.

World War II and after

Just as in World War I, Australia cemented its national identity by getting involved on a global scale in World War II, but this time without Britain's involvement. Menzies' United Australia Party barely lasted long enough to form diplomatic ties with the USA – in case Germany overran Europe – before internal divisions saw the government crumble, replaced by **John Curtin** and his Labor Party in 1941.

Curtin, concerned about Australia's vulnerability after the Japanese attack on Pearl Harbor, made the radical decision of shifting the country's commitment in the war from defending Britain and Europe to fighting off an invasion of Australia from Asia. After the **fall of Singapore** in 1942 and the capture of sixteen thousand Australian troops, Curtin succeeded in ordering the immediate recall of Australians fighting in the Middle East, despite opposition from Churchill, who wanted them for the Burma campaign. In February, the Japanese unexpectedly bombed Darwin, launched submarine raids against Sydney and Newcastle, and invaded New Guinea. Feeling abandoned and betrayed by Britain, Curtin appealed to the USA, who quickly adopted Australia as a base for coordinating Pacific operations under **General Douglas MacArthur**. Meanwhile, Australian troops in New Guinea halted Japanese advances along the **Kokoda trail** at Milne Bay, while the Australian and US navies slowed down the Japanese fleet in the **Battle of the Coral Sea** – which, thanks to modern cannons, was notable as the first naval engagement in which the two sides never even saw each other.

Australia came out of World War II realizing that, geographically, the country was closer to Asia than Europe, that it could not count on Britain to help in a crisis (Churchill had been ready to sacrifice Australian territory to protect British interests elsewhere), and that it was able to form political alliances independent of the mother country. From this point on, Australia began to look to the USA and the Pacific, in addition to Britain, for direction. Another consequence of the war was that immigration was speeded up, fuelled by Australia's recent vulnerability. Under the slogan "Populate or Perish", the government reintroduced assisted passages from Britain – the "ten-pound-poms" – and also accepted substantial numbers of European refugees. Even Torres Strait Islanders, previously banned from settling on the mainland, were allowed to move onto Cape York in northern Queensland.

With international right-wing extremism laid low by the war, the old fear of **communism** returned. When North Korea, backed by the Chinese, invaded South Korea in 1950, Australia, led by a revitalized Menzies and his new Liberal Party, was the first country after the USA to commit troops to counter communist forces. Menzies also sent soldiers and pilots to Malaya (as it was known at the time), where communist rebels had been fighting the British colonial administration almost since the end of World War II, under the anti-communist SEATO (Southeast Asia Treaty Organization) banner. At home, he opened up central Australia to British **atomic bomb tests** in the 1950s, because – echoing the beliefs of the first European colonists – "nobody lived there". A number of Aborigines were moved to reserves, but others – along with the British troops involved in the tests – suffered the effects of fallout, and the Aborigines' traditional lands were rendered uninhabitable for the foreseeable future. Wrangles with the British government over compensation, and the clearing of the test sites at **Maralinga** and **Emu Junction**, were finally settled in 1993.

Menzies was still in control when the USA became involved in **Vietnam**, and with conflict in Malaya all but over, Australia volunteered "advisers" to Vietnamese republican forces in 1962. Once fighting became entrenched, the government introduced conscription and – bowing to the wishes of the American president **Lyndon B. Johnson** – sent a battalion of soldiers into the fray in 1965, events that immediately split the country. Menzies quit politics the following year, succeeded by his protégé **Harold Holt**, who, rallying under the catchphrase "All the way with LBJ", willingly increased Australia's participation in the Vietnamese conflict. But as the war dragged on, world opinion shifted to seeing the matter as a civil struggle, rather than as a fight between democratic and communist ideologies, and in 1970 the government began scaling down its involvement. In the meantime, Aboriginal people were finally granted **civil rights** in 1967, and Holt mysteriously disappeared while swimming off the coast of Victoria, leaving the Liberals in turmoil and paving the way for a Labor win under the well-regarded **Gough Whitlam** in 1972.

Whitlam's three years in office had far-reaching effects: he ended national service and participation in Vietnam, granted independence to **Papua New Guinea**, recognized the People's Republic of China, and instituted free health care and higher education systems. The end came in 1975, when a loans scandal involving the government (which was allegedly trying to borrow money illegally) led the conservative majority in the Senate to block supply bills, effectively stopping government expenditure. In an unprecedented move, the **Governor-General John Kerr** (the largely decorative representative of the Crown overseeing Australian affairs) dismissed the government – a move that shocked many into questioning the validity of Britain's hold on Australia – and called an election, which Labor lost. In contrast, the following eight years were uneventful, culminating in the return of Labor in 1983 under the charismatic **Bob Hawke**, a former trade-union leader. Labor's subsequent thirteen years and four terms in office were brought to a close under the leadership of Hawke's successor and former treasurer, **Paul Keating**. While he was unpopular with some for his scornful rhetoric and perceived arrogance and general lack of concern for the country's woes, the Liberal party lost to Keating in the 1993 election. While Keating was always a strong advocate of Australia being part of Asia, news of a secret military agreement with Indonesia created a public backlash, in part resulting in a landslide victory for the **Liberal–National coalition**, led by **John Howard**, in 1996.

Recent history

Previously dismissed by many as an ineffectual character, Howard's performance in the early years of office showed that his critics had underestimated his tenacity and political skills, honed by 22 years in federal politics, notably his ability to grasp any opportunity to rally (potentially flagging) support, thereby detracting from problems and scandals in his own government. This, combined with a superb sense of timing and, arguably, sheer good luck, enabled him to turn many potentially dangerous situations around in his favour.

By 1998, Howard's political position was so secure that the coalition managed to be re-elected on what some considered a suicidal platform of **tax reform** through the implementation of a **GST**, or Goods and Services Tax. When Howard's prospects of winning the next election were slipping away in mid-2001, due to the unfavourable effects of this tax reform, he successfully turned the country's attention to the ongoing issue of **refugees**, playing on the time-honoured Australian fear of being "swamped" by hordes of immigrants. The government's popularity soared, and the tribulations of the GST and shaky economy were all but forgotten. The terrorist attacks on September 11 did nothing to assuage xenophobic fears and, buoyed by his good ratings in the opinion polls, Howard called a federal election for November 10. Predictably, it was a comfortable win for his coalition, and the opposition Labor Party was further diminished.

A year later, Australia's possible involvement in the US- and UK-led war on Iraq dominated the headlines. The carnage of the **car bomb in Kuta, Bali**, on

October 12, 2002 – terrorist action targeted at Westerners but in particular, some argued, Australians – added urgency to the debate.

Defying public opinion, Howard vociferously supported the war in Iraq, and subsequently joined the "coalition of the willing" in the military attack on the country. In contrast to the government's emphatic rhetorical support, Australia's physical contribution to the war was actually quite small – two thousand troops, plus some warships and aircraft.

The domestic arena

When in 2004 it finally transpired that Saddam Hussein's arsenal of weapons of mass destruction, and the immediate threat it posed to international security, was a furphy (see p.1174), it failed to cause a public backlash in Australia. In his speech calling the election for October 9, 2004, Howard deftly sidestepped a debate about his government's sincerity, by saying voters had to decide whom they most trusted to look after Australia and its economic future. By pointing out that in eight and a half years the coalition government had delivered a strong and robust economy, and by warning that interest rates would be higher under a Labor government, Howard played on another typically Australian kind of fear – the "hip-pocket nerve". From then on, foreign affairs, in particular complex and sensitive topics like Iraq and national security, were practically off the radar screen and the election campaign was fought mainly on the theme of economic management, a tactic that paid off handsomely for Howard. At the federal elections in October 2004, the Liberals scored a resounding victory and Howard was elected Prime Minister for the fourth time. By December 2004, he had become **Australia's second-longest serving Prime Minister**, surpassed only by Menzies' eighteen years in office. In addition, from July 2005 the Liberal Party held the absolute majority (39 of 76 seats) in the Senate, enabling it to push through a raft of previously blocked legislation, notably in the area of industrial relations.

By 2007, after eleven years at the helm, John Howard had influenced and shaped Australian culture and society according to his conservative world-view to an extent almost unimaginable back in 1996. Underpinned by an ongoing resources boom, the Australian economy appeared in very good shape, with China's and India's ravenous demands for Australian minerals and metal ore boosting the price of its commodity exports; however, Australia had been running a **trade deficit** for almost five years and the volume of Australian exports had not increased significantly. While high commodity prices had reduced the deficit from $25 billion at the end of 2005 to $12 billion by February 2007, improvements were hampered by increased consumer spending on imports and by the worst drought on record. Hitherto, the Howard government had denounced global warming as scientifically unsound scaremongering; any measures to deal with it, including ratifying the **Kyoto Protocol** and putting a cap on Australia's (abysmally high) emission levels, were rejected on the grounds that they would impact negatively on the Australian economy and jeopardize Australia's living standards. However, the dire warnings contained in the 2007 IPCC reports on climate change could not be so easily dismissed, given the unprecedented length and severity of the drought and, by then, the almost annual occurrence of widespread ferocious bushfires in Australia. In April 2007, the Howard government announced there was a water crisis and proposed the establishment of a **national water management scheme**, while steadfastly denying a link between the increased frequency of bushfires, the drought and climate change. This continuing denial seemed so short-sighted to state premiers that they decided to establish their own **carbon trading system** if the Federal government failed to do so.

As the federal election loomed in late 2007, these topics, as well as whether Howard would see through another complete term, saw cracks appear in the Howard Government. Public support for his "Work Choices" legislation, passed in March 2006, was very low, with many employees feeling that, in terms of remuneration, working conditions and job security, they were worse off than before.

After years of constant leadership struggles, the Australian Labor Party entered into the election year energized and revitalized under the leadership of Queenslander **Kevin Rudd**. A former diplomat, bureaucrat and business consultant, Rudd has a reputation for being very determined, a consummate negotiator, and a sharp and shrewd politician. Next to Howard, Rudd appeared youthful, handled every challenge thrown at him by the Liberal Party with aplomb, and won with a massive swing to Labor. Piling insult on top of injury, Howard lost his electoral seat to a former ABC (Australian Broadcasting Corporation) journalist – an organization that he had been at odds with his whole career. He was only the second sitting Prime Minister to lose his own seat in an election and the first to lose his seat to a woman. After years of adroitly politically outsmarting his opponents, it was a humiliating end to an unexpectedly long political career.

Rudd moved fast, and after being sworn in on December 3, 2007, he first ratified the Kyoto protocol on climate change and then formally apologized to the Australian Aborigines in February 2008, a campaign promise fulfilled in a poignant ceremony. Both were moves strongly opposed by Rudd's predecessor, as was the withdrawal of Australian combat troops from Iraq, which Rudd announced with a stinging rebuke of the former governments' actions in sending troops "without a full and proper assessment".

Rudd's centre-left government had a scandal-free first year in office while Rudd demonstrated his political skills by acting confident and in charge when the global economic crisis hit home in Australia during 2008 and 2009; according to polls, Rudd himself had a personal approval rating of over 70 per cent.

Foreign policy

Looking beyond its shores, for most of the twentieth century Australia faced **Asia** with ambiguity, seeing it partly as a strategic threat, partly as an economic opportunity. The example of Japan is symptomatic: in the 1930s, Japan had become Australia's second-largest trading partner, but during the 1940s Australia had to fight off an impending Japanese invasion. By the 1970s, with the White Australia policy coming to an end, Whitlam initiated a policy shift towards greater engagement with its neighbours, which continued under the Fraser and Hawke–Keating governments in the 1980s and early 1990s, and was intensified under Rudd in 2008–09. This stance was based on the pragmatic recognition of Australia's economic interests, and led to a conciliatory attitude to some Asian countries' more dubious actions against each other, as well as a weak response to regional human-rights abuses. As was the case with many of his political visions, Keating was unable to sell his orientation towards Asia to the general Australian public. The ubiquitous catchphrase of the 1990s, "**Australia is part of Asia**", confused and alienated voters at the time. Howard capitalized on that during his first successful election campaign of 1996, with the recurring reproach that Keating was "obsessed with Asia" and out of touch with what ordinary Australians felt. The "part of Asia" notion did not always wash with other countries in the area either. Australia, with its predominantly white population and strong cultural and political ties to the Anglophone Western world, would not be accepted as "Asian". Australia's most outspoken critic was Malaysia, under the rule of Dr Mahatir Mohamad, who continually vetoed Australia's attempts to join ASEAN, the regional trading bloc. The rough-hewn right-wing outbursts by **Pauline Hanson** and the (short-lived) rise of her **One Nation** party in 1996, which capitalized on xenophobia, did nothing to enhance Australian credibility in the region.

From his first days in office, Howard's statements and actions signalled a backing off, if not complete reversal, from his predecessors' Asia policy. He refused to distance himself emphatically from Pauline Hanson's spiteful, anti-Asian utterances, and in 1996, during his first state visit to Indonesia as prime minister, he stated that Australia did not have to choose between geography and history. While Australia was geographically close to Asia and would eagerly pursue closer economic and security ties in the region, it did not want to be identified as an Asian nation. It would maintain its own culture and traditions, including a security alliance with the US and close ties to Europe.

The Australian-led UN intervention in civil war in East Timor in 1999 put a stop to the massacre and helped the new nation stand on its own feet. Not surprisingly, Australia's relationship with Indonesia deteriorated badly as a result. Subsequent noises about Australia taking a more proactive role in maintaining regional security, and playing the role of America's deputy sheriff, added fuel to the fire and caused a furore across the entire region. Forging closer links with the US was always a high priority of the Howard government. Australia's participation in the war on Iraq, and the signing of the Free Trade Agreement between Australia and the US, are two examples of the importance attributed to the alliance with America.

Engagement with Asia, however – while much more low-key – has never been totally off the agenda. Australia's role in delivering aid to Indonesia's Aceh province, the region worst hit by the **tsunami** on Boxing Day 2004, went a long way towards creating goodwill in the region, and counteracting Australia's "bullyboy" image. With Kevin Rudd as prime minister the pendulum has swung back towards a more substantial engagement with Australia's northern neighbours. Rudd is a fluent Mandarin speaker and spent time in China as a diplomat and business consultant. Now, with Barack Obama as US President, the unease of the relationship Kevin Rudd had with George Bush (who was friends with John Howard) can be relegated to the history books.

Aboriginal rights

During the 1980s there were some advances under Labor in the area of **Aboriginal rights**. An ineffectual inquiry into Aboriginal deaths in custody was overshadowed in June 1992 when the High Court handed down the landmark **Mabo Decision**, legally overturning the concept of *terra nullius*. Eddie Mabo's claim, set around Murray Island (Mer) in the Torres Strait, was granted, and the Merriam were acknowledged as traditional landowners. This decision led to the passing of the Native Title Act of 1993 after extensive discussions with indigenous representatives. Next came the **Wik Decision** in December 1996, which stated that native title and pastoral leases could coexist over the same area. The incoming Howard government initiated an alarmist debate about the implications, triggering something of a public backlash against Aborigines. Support for One Nation increased as the party exploited people's fears, contributing to Australia's racist image overseas, while the government refused to negotiate with indigenous representatives who had sought to bring forward constructive proposals. In 1998, the government introduced amendments to the Wik Decision, winding back indigenous rights under the Native Title Act, whilst enhancing the rights of landholders and developers.

While Mabo and Wik had an effect – such as the handing back of the **Silver Plains** property on Queensland's Cape York to its traditional owners in 2000 – not all similar land claims are likely to succeed. A **Native Title Tribunal** was established to consider each case, but given former resettlement policies, claimants have an uphill struggle to prove constant association with the land in question since white occupation. Nonetheless, a growing acknowledgement that Aboriginal people were in fact the land's original inhabitants, and the perception that they will eventually be re-enfranchised, has seen mining companies, farmers, and notably – and ironically, given its past record – the Queensland government, ignoring political and legal wrangles and making private land-use agreements with, or handovers to, local communities. In this sense, Mabo and Wik have confirmed that Aboriginal people have land rights, despite the best efforts of the Howard government to undermine these.

Australia's indigenous peoples

While white Australians historically grouped the country's indigenous peoples under the term Aborigines, in recent years there has been wider recognition that there are many separate cultures that are as diverse but interrelated as those of Europe.

Today, these cultures include, for example, urbanized **Koorie** communities in Sydney and Melbourne, semi-nomadic groups such as the **Pintupi** living in the western deserts, and the **Yolngu** people of eastern Arnhem Land, an area never colonized by settlers. If there is any thread linking these groups, it is the island continent they inhabit and, particularly in the north, the appalling state of health, education and opportunities they experience, despite the apparent revitalization of and renewed interest in Aboriginal culture.

Colonization

From 1788, the estimated 750,000 indigenous people of Australia were gradually dispossessed of their lands and livelihoods by the British colonists who failed to recognize them as legitimate inhabitants. Australia was annexed to the British Empire on the basis that it was *terra nullius*, or uninhabited wasteland. This legal fiction persisted until the High Court judged in the 1992 **Mabo** case that native title to land still existed in Australia unless it had been extinguished by statute or by some use of the land that was inconsistent with the continuation of native use and ownership. The **Wik Decision** of 1996 went a step further, acknowledging that native title continues to exist on pastoral leases, though with the proviso that "pastoral interest will prevail over native title rights, wherever the two conflict" (for more on the Mabo and Wik decisions, see "History", p.1131).

Upon deciding that the country was unoccupied, successive waves of new settlers hastened to make it so. Violent conflicts between indigenous and recently arrived Australians resulted in the decimation of Aboriginal groups. The most widely known of these conflicts was the **unofficial war** waged against Tasmania's Aboriginal peoples, which resulted in the near-destruction of indigenous Tasmanians (see box, pp.1014–1015). Historians estimate that twenty thousand Aborigines may have died in these mostly unrecorded battles. Measuring the impact of colonization on the indigenous population has been hampered by a lack of information about conditions prior to colonization, as well as the failure of successive governments to record indigenous people as part of the population until the 1960s.

Australia's geographical isolation meant that the introduction of European **diseases** was also a powerful agent in decimating the indigenous populations. Whole populations were wiped out by smallpox and malaria epidemics, and the diaries from the First Fleet record the rapid destruction from smallpox of the Aboriginal camps in the Sydney hinterland within a few years of the establishment of the colony. Those who didn't die fled the area, unwittingly infecting neighbouring groups as they went. When Governor Hunter made the first exploratory expedition to western New South Wales in the 1820s, he recorded evidence of prior smallpox epidemics among Aboriginal groups who had not previously come into contact with European settlers. The lack of immunity to these introduced diseases was exacerbated by the trauma of dispossession, the lack of availability of – or access to – traditional food and water supplies, and the unhygienic consequences of being required to wear European-style clothing.

The **interruption of traditional food and water supplies** became progressively worse through the nineteenth and twentieth centuries as the pastoral industry expanded across rural Australia, and vast areas were stripped of vegetation to provide for grazing land. Grazing animals competed with local animals for food, drained established water sources, and dug up the flora on the soil surface with their hooves, contributing to erosion and salinity, and so creating dust bowls. Other European animals, originally introduced to make the countryside seem more like "home", rapidly multiplied and have now become ubiquitous throughout Australia. Foxes, and especially cats, have been blamed for the near extinction of small mammals and birds throughout arid Australia. Rabbit populations expanded to fill the niche the mammals vacated, and their destructive grazing habits have contributed to the increasing desertification of Australia's rangelands. Aboriginal people in central Australia have witnessed this ecological disaster within the last sixty years, and have lamented the loss of many animal species that once sustained them.

Australia's Aboriginal peoples have also been subjected to various forms of **incarceration**, ranging from prisons to apartheid-style reserves. Much of this systematic imprisonment was instigated between 1890 and 1950 as an official policy of **protection**, in response to the devastating impact of colonization. Missionaries and other well-meaning people believed that Aborigines were a dying race, and that it was a Christian duty to provide for them in their passing. Parliamentary records of the time reveal a harsher mentality. Aborigines were often viewed as a weak and degenerate people who exposed white settlers to physical and moral turpitude. For the wellbeing of Aborigines and settlers alike, state governments enacted legislation to appoint official **Protectors of Aborigines**, established reserves in rural areas, and removed Aboriginal people to them. In some parts of Australia these reserves were established on traditional lands, allowing people to continue to live relatively undisturbed. Elsewhere, notably Queensland, people were forcibly removed from their home areas and relocated in reserves throughout the state. Families were broken up and their ties with the land and spirits shattered. The so-called protectors had autonomy over those in their ward. For example, Aboriginal people required permits to marry or to move from one reserve to another, or were forced into indentured (or simply slave) labour to be paid in flour or tobacco. This treatment persisted in some areas until the late 1960s.

Aboriginal people are still absurdly over-represented in Australia's prison population. In 1991, the situation led to a **Royal Commission into Aboriginal Deaths in Custody**, which reported to the Federal Parliament. It called for wide-ranging changes in police and judicial practice, and substantial changes to social programmes aimed at improving the lot of Aboriginal peoples in the areas of justice, health, education, economics and empowerment. But despite considerable government lip service to the recommendations of the Royal Commission, it has not resulted in any substantial change to incarceration rates.

From the 1920s, Aboriginal children fathered by European Australians but born to black mothers were removed and put into state institutions or with white foster parents as part of a policy of **assimilation**. The practice of "taking the children away" began in Victoria in 1886 and continued until 1969, and still haunts the lives of many Aboriginal Australians, now known as the **Stolen Generation**, who have lost contact with their natal families and their culture. Their plight was poignantly depicted in the 2002 film *Rabbit-Proof Fence* (see p.1150). But despite the policy being the subject of a major government inquiry in 1997, and the subsequent media attention following the release of the report, it was only with the election of the current Rudd Government that there was finally an official **apology**.

Revitalization and setbacks

The **revitalization** of Aboriginal people and their culture effectively began in 1967, when a constitutional referendum overwhelmingly endorsed the rights of indigenous Australians as voting citizens, and gave the federal government the power to legislate for Aboriginal people. Prior to this referendum, Aboriginal people had the status of wards of each of the states. The referendum ushered in a new era of **self-determination** for Aboriginal people, evidenced by the establishment of the first Ministry for Aboriginal Affairs in the Whitlam Labor Government of 1972–75. After more than a hundred years of agitation, **land rights** were accorded to Aboriginal groups in the Northern Territory in 1976 under federal legislation. Since then, other states have legislated to vest title over various pieces of state-owned land to their traditional Aboriginal owners. All the mainland states and territories now have provisions for Aboriginal land rights. Throughout the 1970s and 1980s successive federal governments set up various representative bodies, including the notorious **Aboriginal and Torres Strait Islanders Commission** (**ATSIC**: 1990–2004). This statutory authority gave elected Aboriginal representatives effective control over many of the federal funding programmes directed at Aboriginal organizations and communities. Substantial funds were directed towards training for employment and improved health education. Running at around two billion dollars per annum, this should have seen Aboriginal people thriving right across Australia. The reality was far different: corruption, nepotism and flawed or ill-considered projects conspired to bring about ATSIC's abolition in 2004 and a return to greater federal government control (see "The future", p.1136).

Along with ownership of land and some control over funding came opportunities for economic self-sufficiency and expansion previously unavailable to Aboriginal groups. In many parts of the country, this allowed Aborigines to buy the cattle stations on which they had worked without wages for many years. In central Australia, Aboriginal enterprises include TV and radio stations, transport companies, small airlines, publishing companies, tourist businesses and joint-venture mining operations.

Cooperative agreements with the Australian Nature Conservation Agency led to Aboriginal ownership and joint management of two of Australia's most important conservation reserves, **Uluru–Kata Tjuta** and **Kakadu** national parks in the Northern Territory. These arrangements recognize that Aboriginal owners retain an enormous understanding about the ecology of their traditional lands that are vital in the development of land-management plans.

In 2007, the Howard Government brought in a significant change in policy. A report entitled *Little Children are Sacred* was released, pertaining to the issue of child abuse in Northern Territory indigenous communities. Howard's seven-point plan to combat the problem, labelled "the intervention", included a ban on alcohol in some communities as well as "voluntary" medical checks for sexual abuse for indigenous children younger than 16. Many saw these actions as a gross overreaction, as well as a ploy for re-election, as Howard was sagging in the polls. Indeed many of the recommendations in the report were at odds with the seven-point plan that was ultimately introduced.

Citizenship and its problems

Despite some successes, Australia's indigenous peoples are struggling against considerable disadvantages. Along with citizenship in 1967 came a new-found unemployability (for example, few station owners were willing to pay black workers the same wage as white people), along with the legal right to purchase **alcohol**, a disastrous combination. Institutionalized welfarism compounded feelings of futility, as well as shame towards Aboriginal origins, and substance abuse has been heavily implicated in the destructive spiral sometimes observed in Outback towns (and some inner-city areas). The negative repercussions have been evident in sickness and death, violence and despair, exclusion from education and meaningful employment, as well as families and communities in disarray. The vast over-representation of Aboriginal people in the criminal-justice system is directly attributable to alcohol and substance abuse. **Poor health** continues to reduce substantially the life expectancy of Aborigines. About seventy percent of indigenous Australians die before they turn 65 (compared with just over twenty percent for other Australians), Aboriginal infant mortality is two to three times higher than for white babies, and the death rate from diabetes is eight times higher. As with most areas of social service, health services for Aboriginal peoples have been the province of white professionals until recently; an essential focus of recent strategies has been to empower Aboriginal people by giving resources to them directly.

On the **positive** side, many communities are confronting the problems that alcohol is causing. Many communities choose to be "dry", not allowing alcohol to be brought into the community, and pressure is put on those that break the laws of the community.

The future

The process of **reconciliation** with its "rights"-based approach, as initiated by the Labor government under Keating, was always troubling to Prime Minister John Howard. As Howard claimed he saw it, "symbolic measures" such as an apology or a treaty were an insult to the present generation of non-Aboriginal people who were not responsible for past mistakes, and did nothing to address problems in Aboriginal communities such as alcoholism, appalling health, and lack of access to education. Upon his re-election in 1998, "**practical reconcil-iation**" was the new catchphrase and essentially meant the delivery of welfare services through mainstream programmes. Consistent with this approach, he steadfastly refused to give a formal apology, ignoring the widespread popular movement to that effect in 1999 and 2000. His government promised

$63 million over four years of funding for counselling and "link-up" services for those who had been removed from their families.

In the same year, the Howard government abolished ATSIC and its service delivery arm ATSIS. The new "whole of government" approach meant the responsibility for the delivery of indigenous programmes was to be shared by several government departments. A new, complex bureaucratic structure full of Orwellian acronyms emerged: the **Office of Indigenous Policy Coordination (OIPC)**, which, in addition to coordinating programmes, also provides advice to a Ministerial Task Force on Indigenous Affairs and the **National Indigenous Council (NIC)**. The latter consists of fourteen hand-picked indigenous advisers who meet four times a year and whose function is to advise the government on the future direction of policies and programmes that will impact on every facet of Aboriginal lives. "**Mutual obligation**" and "**shared responsibility**" have been the new buzzwords, a rhetoric that echoed the ideas of Noel Pearson, the Aboriginal lawyer and community leader from the Cape York Peninsula, whose aim is to replace social welfare with social enterprise. On Cape York, he embarked on a community-based social-renewal project which includes having payments of benefits invested in enterprise activity rather than as an individual welfare cheque, with each individual and family making a commitment to contributing as well as receiving.

Aboriginal communities had to enter into **Shared Responsibility Agreements (SRA)** with government departments, committing to "behavioural change" or similar actions in exchange for funding for specified community infrastructure needs. The first SRA released in December 2004 was with Mulan, a remote community in Western Australia. The government agreed to install a petrol bowser, and in return the community agreed to make sure their children showered daily and looked after other health issues. In several places, including Wadeye in the Northern Territory, there was a "no school, no pool" agreement: in return for a swimming pool, kids had to attend school. In most cases, these SRAs were reported to be successful. School attendance rates were up and chronic ear, eye and skin infections that afflict Aboriginal children seemed to be alleviated by the chlorine in the water. At first glance, it seemed a common-sense approach – no more wasting of money by a corrupt organization rife with nepotism, no more "one size fits all" solutions. However, although the inefficient ATSIC had been disbanded, a confusing and costly bureaucratic structure had taken its place, one that distributes funds on a seemingly ad-hoc basis and with few mechanisms in place to check if and how its "mutual obligation" is fulfilled.

In addition, the almost comical machinations of "the intervention" are not promising. Just a few days after calling it "sickening, rotten and worrying", Galarrwuy Yunupingu, the Northern Territory's most powerful Aboriginal leader, changed his mind about "the intervention" following a secret meeting with the government brokered by Noel Pearson in September 2007.

While Galarrwuy Yunupingu might favour the ongoing intervention, many other Aboriginal leaders do not. In early 2009, a group of human rights lawyers lodged a complaint about "the intervention" with the United Nations Committee for the Elimination of Racial Discrimination. The complaint appears likely to succeed because "the intervention" laws are at odds with the Racial Discrimination Act. Bafflingly, despite saying sorry for past mistreatment of the Aboriginals, the Rudd government has failed to significantly alter the thrust of "the intervention" after twelve months in office.

Flora and fauna

D espite forty thousand years of human pressure and manipulation, accelerated in the last two centuries by the effects of introduced species, Australia's ecology and wildlife remain among the most distinctive on Earth. Nonetheless, they are also some of the most endangered: in the last two hundred years, more native mammals have become extinct here than on any other continent, and land clearing – particularly in Queensland – kills an Estimated 7.5 million birds a year, bringing several species to the edge of extinction.

Australians love to tell stories about the **dangers** the bush holds for the inexperienced traveller (see "Health", pp.49–52, for general advice on coping with hazardous wildlife). In reality, fearsome "drop bears" lurking in gums, fallen tree trunks that turn out to be giant snakes, bloodthirsty wild pigs, and other rampaging terrors are mostly confined to hotel bars, the product of suburban paranoia laced with a surprising naivety about the great outdoors. Apart from a couple of avoidable exceptions, there's little to fear from Australia's wildlife, and if you spend any time in the bush, you'll undoubtedly end up far better informed than the yarn-spinners. For more on the dangers down under, see the "Australian Wildlife" colour section.

Marsupials and monotremes

In the years after the demise of the dinosaurs, Australia split away from the rest of the world and the animals here evolved along different lines to anywhere else. As placental mammals gained the ascendancy in South America, Africa, Europe and Asia, it was the marsupials and monotremes that took over in Australia, alongside the megafauna (see box opposite). These orders are not exclusive to Australia (they're also found in New Guinea and South America), but it's here they reached their greatest diversity and numbers.

Marsupials are mammals that give birth to a partially formed embryo, which itself then develops in a **pouch** on the mother; this allows a higher breeding rate in good years. Easiest to find because they actively seek out people, **ringtail** and **brushtail possums** are common in suburbs and campsites, and often hard to avoid if they think there's a chance of getting some food. With a little persistence, you should encounter one of the several species of related **glider possums** on the edges of forests at dusk. **Kangaroos** and **wallabies** are the Australian answer to deer and antelope, and range from tiny, solitary rainforest species to the gregarious two-metre-tall red kangaroo of the central plains – watching these creatures bouncing effortlessly across the landscape is an extraordinary sight. The arboreal, eucalyptus-chewing **koalas** and tubby, ground-dwelling **wombats** are smaller, less active and more sensitive to disturbance; this has made them more elusive, and has placed them on the endangered list as their habitat is cleared. Carnivorous marsupials are mostly shrew-sized today (though a lion equivalent probably survived into Aboriginal times, and fossils of meat-eating kangaroos have been found); two of the largest are spotted native cats or **quolls**, and Tasmania's indigenous **Tasmanian devil**, a terrier-sized scavenger.

Platypuses and echidnas are the only **monotremes**, egg-laying mammals that suckle their young through specialized pores. Once considered a stage in the evolution of placental mammals, they're now recognized as a specialized branch of the family. Neither is particularly rare, but being nocturnal, shy and, in the case of the platypus, aquatic, makes them difficult to find. Ant-eating **echidnas** resemble a long-nosed, thick-spined hedgehog or small porcupine, and are found countrywide. **Platypuses** are confined to the eastern ranges and look like a blend of duck and otter, having a grey, rubbery bill, webbed feet, short fur, and a poison spur on males, a combination that seemed too implausible to nineteenth-century biologists, who initially denounced stuffed specimens as a hoax, assembled from pieces of other animals.

Introduced fauna

Of the **introduced mammals**, dingoes are descended from dogs, introduced to Australia by Aboriginal people in the last twelve thousand years – although there is some merit to the claim that they were introduced from Asia around 3,500 to 4,000 years ago. To keep them away from flocks, graziers built "vermin fences", which were connected by the Australian government to form a 5400-kilometre-long, continuous fence, allegedly the world's longest. The **Dingo Fence** stretches from South Australia into northwest Queensland and down to New South Wales. **Camels** have also become acclimatized to Australia since their introduction in the 1840s; they are doing so well in the central deserts that they are considered a pest. Australia is the only place where dromedaries still occur in the wild, and they are regularly exported to the Middle East. The blight that **hoofed mammals** – horses, cows, sheep and goats – have perpetrated on Australia's fragile fauna is horrendous. Much of the country has been prematurely desertified by their eating habits, abrasive hooves, and demand for water; once extracted from below ground, the water is not replenished, which alters the mineral balance and kills remaining plant life. The damage caused by **rabbits** is equally pervasive, especially in the semi-desert areas where their cyclic population explosions can strip every shred of plant life from fragile dune systems. In an attempt to control the problem, the myxoma virus was introduced in the 1950, and although a large part of the rabbit population was initially wiped out, the rabbits eventually developed a resistance and their numbers increased again in the following decades. Since 1996, another viral disease affecting the European rabbit, the rabbit calicivirus disease (RCD), has been released all over Australia, resulting in a dramatic reduction of rabbit numbers. It remains to be seen, however, whether the unsuccessful story of the myxoma virus will be repeated.

Feral **cats**, which hunt for sport as well as necessity, are currently one of the greatest threats to indigenous fauna, primarily small marsupials and birds. An introduced amphibian, however, has turned out to be the most insidious and rapacious invader of all. The highly poisonous **cane toads**, brought in to combat a plague of greyback beetles marring sugar-cane harvests, have no natural enemies and for thirty years have been on a relentless march from the north Queensland sugar-cane fields southwards along the coast and westwards across northern Australia. In 2004, they invaded the lush Top End floodplains, which have more wildlife per square kilometre than the richest parts of Africa, Asia and the Americas. For more on the cane toad, see the *Australian wildlife* colour section.

Reptiles, birds, bats and marine life

Australian **reptiles** come in all shapes and sizes. In the tropical parts of the country, the pale lizards you see wriggling across the ceiling on Velcro-like pads are **geckos**, and you'll find fatter, sluggish **skinks** – such as the stumpy blue-tongued lizard – everywhere. Other widespread species are **frill-necked lizards**, known for fanning out their necks and running on their hind legs when frightened, and the ubiquitous **goanna** family, which includes the monstrous perentie, third-largest lizard in the world. In central Australia, look out for the extraordinary **thorny devil** or moloch, an animal that seems part rock, part rosebush.

Crocodiles are confined to the tropics and come in two types. The shy, inoffensive **freshwater crocodile** grows to around 3m in length and feeds on fish and frogs. The larger, bulkier, and misleadingly named saltwater or **estuarine crocodile** can grow to 7m, ranges far inland (often in freshwater), and is the only Australian animal that constitutes an active threat to humans. Highly evolved predators, they should be given a very wide berth (see box, p.579 for specific precautions to take while in crocodile country). Despite their bad press, **snakes** are generally timid and pose far less of a problem, even though Australia has everything from constricting pythons through to three-quarters of the world's most venomous species.

With a climate that extends from temperate zones well into the tropics, Australia's **birdlife** is prolific and varied. Small **penguins** and **albatrosses** live along the south coast, while **riflebirds**, related to New Guinea's birds of paradise, and the **cassowary**, a colourful version of the ostrich, live in the tropical rainforests. The drabber **emu** prefers drier plains further west. Among the birds of prey, the countrywide **wedge-tail eagle** and the coastal **white-bellied sea eagle** are most impressive in their size. Both share their environment with the stately grey **brolga**, an Australian crane, and the even larger **jabiru stork**, with its chisel beak and pied plumage. **Parrots**, arguably the country's most spectacular birds, come in over forty varieties, and no matter if they're flocks of green budgerigars, outrageously coloured rainbow lorikeets, or white sulphur-crested cockatoos, they'll deafen you with their noisy song.

Equally raucous are **kookaburras**, giant kingfishers found near permanent water. The quieter **tawny frogmouth**, an incredibly camouflaged cousin of the nightjar, has one of the most disgruntled expressions ever seen on a bird.

Huge colonies of **bats**, of orange, ghost and horseshoe varieties, congregate in caves and fill entire trees all over Australia. The **fruit bat**, or flying fox, is especially common in the tropics, where evenings can be spent watching colonies of the one-metre-winged monsters heading out from their daytime roosts on feeding expeditions.

In addition to what you'll see on the Barrier Reef (covered in the Coastal Queensland chapter), **whales**, **turtles**, **dolphins**, **seals** and **dugongs** (sea cows) are part of the country's marine life, with humpback southern right whales making a welcome return to the coasts in recent decades after being hunted close to extinction.

Flora

Australia's most distinctive and widespread **trees** are those that developed a **dependence on fire**. Some, like the seemingly limitless varieties of **eucalypts** or gum trees, need extreme heat to burst open button-shaped pods and release their seeds, and encourage fires by annually shedding bark and leaves, depositing a thick layer of tinder on the forest floor. Other shrubs with similar habits are **banksias**, **grevillias** and **bottlebrushes**, with their distinctive bushy flowers and spiky seed-pods, while those prehistoric survivors, palm-like **cycads** and **grasstrees**, similarly depend on regular conflagrations to promote new growth. For thousands of years, Aborigines used controlled burn-offs to make the land more suitable for hunting, thereby possibly enhancing these fire-reliant traits.

Despite the country having extensive arid regions, there is no native equivalent to the cactus, although the dry, spiky **spinifex** or porcupine grass, the succulent **samphire** with its curiously jointed stem, and the aptly named **saltbush** come closest in their ability to survive extreme temperatures. After rain, smaller desert plants rush to bloom and seed, covering the ground in a spectacular blanket of colour, a phenomenon for which Australia's Outback regions are well known.

On a larger scale, the Outback is dotted with stands of hardy **mulgas** and **wattles**, which superficially resemble scrawny eucalypts but have different leaf structures, as well as scattered groups of bloated, spindly-branched **bottle trees**, whose sweet, pulpy and moisture-laden cores can be used as emergency stock feed in drought conditions. The similar but far larger **boab**, found in the Kimberley and northern Northern Territory, is thought to be an invader from East Africa. **Mallee scrub** is unique to the southeastern Outback, where clearing of these tangled, bush-sized eucalypts for grazing has endangered both scrub and those animals which rely on it – the mound-building **mallee fowl** being the best known.

Mangrove swamps, found along the tropical and subtropical coasts, are tidal zones of thick grey mud and mangrove trees, whose interlocked aerial roots make an effective barrier to exploration. They've suffered extensive clearing for development, and it wasn't until recently that their importance to the estuarine life-cycle won them limited government protection; Aboriginal people have always found them a rich source of animal and plant products.

Rainforest once covered much of the continent, but today only a small portion of its former abundance survives. Nevertheless, you'll find pockets everywhere, from Tasmania's richly verdant wilderness to the monsoonal examples of northern Queensland and the Top End in the Northern Territory. Trees grow to gigantic heights, as they compete with each other for light, supporting themselves in the poor soil with aerial or buttressed roots. The extraordinary **banyan** and **Moreton Bay fig** trees are fine examples of the two types. They support a huge number of plant species, with tangled **vines** in the lower reaches, and **orchids**, **elkhorns** and other epiphytes using larger plants as roosts. **Palms** and **tree ferns**, with their giant, delicately curled fronds, are found in more open forest, where there's regular water.

Some forest types illustrate the extent of Australia's prehistoric flora. **Antarctic beech** or *Nothafagus*, found south of Brisbane as well as in South America, along with native pines and **kauri** from Queensland, which also occur in New Zealand, are all evidence of the prehistoric supercontinent, Gondwana. Other "living fossils" include primitive marine **stromatolites** – algae corals – still found around Shark Bay, Western Australia, and in fossilized form in the central deserts.

As long as you don't eat them or fall onto the pricklier versions, most Australian plants are harmless – though in rainforests you'd want to avoid entanglement with spiky **lawyer cane** or wait-awhile vine (though it doesn't look like it, this is a climbing palm). Also watch out for the large, pale-green, heart-shaped leaves of the **stinging tree**, a scraggly "regrowth" plant found on the margins of cleared tropical rainforest. Even a casual brush delivers an agonizing and prolonged sting; if you're planning on bushwalking in the tropics, learn to recognize and avoid this plant.

Australian film

A
ustralia has had a connection to film since federation. It is generally agreed (with deference to a 1900 Salvation Army promo, *Stations of the Cross*) that *The Story of the Kelly Gang*, made by Charles Tait in 1906, was the world's first feature-length film. Australians' well-known antagonism towards figures of authority soon led to a hugely popular series of bushranger movies, eventually to be banned in 1912 by the New South Wales police on the grounds that their unsympathetic portrayal in these pictures was corrupting youngsters.

This **early heyday** of Australian film-making predated that of Hollywood and persisted with the production of various World War I morale boosters, despite the creation of a distribution duopoly (known as the "combine") that showed little interest in independent Australian films outside its control. With the ending of the war and its many cinematic testaments to the heroic disaster of Gallipoli, Australian silent cinema reached a creative peak. **Raymond Longford** was Australia's Spielberg of silents at this time, and his 1919 production of *The Sentimental Bloke* and its sequel, *Ginger Mick*, a year later, were popular and notably naturalist dramas about a woman's taming of her larrikin husband's proclivities. Along with the already established contempt for authority, Longford's films featured a distrust of sophistication and formality and, even then, the mythic spell of "the bush" began to make its mark on Australian productions – one that has lasted through to Baz Luhrmann's *Australia* in 2008.

Hollywood domination

The distribution duopoly gradually squeezed the life from Australian cinema, which continued to decline as the powerful Hollywood studios got into their stride and entered the Golden Age of talkies. In 1933 the mildly reformed wild boy from Tasmania, **Errol Flynn**, starred in his first feature film, *In the Wake of the Bounty*, directed by **Charles Chauvel**, a leading figure in Australian film-making until the late 1950s.

During World War II there was a return to newsreels and documentaries, with the legendary cameraman, Damien Parer, earning **Australia's first Oscar** for his documentary account of the fighting in New Guinea (*Kokoda Front Line*, 1942). Following the war, however, Hollywood's global domination of cinema was unassailed, and Australian cinema just about perished. Nevertheless, **Chips Rafferty** turned up as Australia's answer to John Wayne, appearing in an unremarkable series of formulaic films, such as the scenically superb epic of bovine migration, *The Overlanders* (1946).

In the 1950s the British Ealing Studios and the American MGM set up production companies in Australia, turning out the odd Outback drama which was watered down for international consumption. This era produced few notable Australian films other than Cecil Holmes' return to the bushranger format in *Captain Thunderbolt* (1953), and his similarly leftist study of mateship, *Three In One* (1957). Chauvel's remarkable *Jedda, the Uncivilized* (1955, sometimes just known as *Jedda*) was more unusual in that it tackled the tricky issue of an Aboriginal girl's white upbringing, sexual temptation, and subsequent abduction back to tribal life, where a tragic death inevitably awaited her.

Australia was by now nothing more than an exotic, marsupial-speckled location for "**kangaroo westerns**" and other dramas where British and American actors could exercise their skills. In 1959 Stanley Kramer directed *On the Beach*, Nevil Shute's post-nuclear apocalypse drama, with Ava Gardner, Gregory Peck and Fred Astaire tiptoeing through the fallout. A year later Fred Zinnemann directed Deborah Kerr and Robert Mitchum in *The Sundowners*, an affectionate classic about Outback itinerant labour.

The New Wave

The birth of the **New Wave** was a response to the burgeoning counterculture of the late 1960s. Among the many notable reforms of Gough Whitlam's Labor government was support for the long-neglected arts. Film-makers in particular were given a shot in the arm with the introduction of extremely generous grants to more than cover the cost of production. While in its early years this financial support helped produce some of the crassest male-fantasy sex romps ever seen (Tim Burstall's 1973 *Alvin Purple* and Terry Bourke's *Plugg* are matchlessly dire), the opening of the **Australian Film School** in 1973 allowed talents such as Gillian Armstrong, Bruce Beresford and Paul Cox to flourish.

Two years later, the **Australian Film Commission** evolved from previous similar organizations to help produce and market Australian films, and although the grants have been continually reduced ever since, their introduction kick-started the moribund industry.

Peter Weir's unsettlingly eerie *Picnic at Hanging Rock* (1975) remains an early jewel, and the decade ended with further acclaim for his poetic *Gallipoli*, which helped launch the career of one Mel Gibson. Gibson had already starred in the original *Mad Max*, which started with a cult following and ended up becoming a very influential film. The decade also saw Phillip Noyce's outstanding *Newsfront* and Gillian Armstrong's first feature, *My Brilliant Career*, which brought to light the extraordinary talent of NIDA (National Institute of Dramatic Art) graduate Judy Davis.

Australian cinema of the 1980s and 1990s was perhaps most exceptional for establishing a number of **women directors** and **producers** and providing a handful of strong women's roles. Inevitably, only the mainstream hits, such as the uplifting *Strictly Ballroom* and *Death in Brunswick*, achieved wide overseas release, while many equally fine "small" films remained largely unseen. It is these quirky, uniquely Australian films of which the rejuvenated industry can be most proud. The prestige of numerous and consistent awards at the Cannes Film Festival and others proved that Australia's long-established cinematographic heritage, more than any other art form, helped rid the country of its former philistine reputation. Confident and uncompromising films such as *Malcolm, Celia, Sweetie* and *The Year My Voice Broke* were just a few that complemented their better-known siblings. 1994 saw a media-led "renaissance" in Australian film: Stephan Elliott's sartorially outrageous *The Adventures of Priscilla, Queen of the Desert* was the country's biggest box-office success up to that time and won international acclaim, while P.J. Hogan's delightful *Muriel's Wedding* perfectly encapsulated the home-grown film-making idiom and proved that Australia still could make financially viable idiosyncratic films. By 1996, however, Australian film critics (and Australians) had grown weary of quirky, offbeat romances, such as Shirley Barratt's *Love Serenade* and Emma-Kate Croghan's 1996 hit *Love and Other*

Catastrophes; however, the year did produce Scott Hicks' globally acclaimed *Shine*, which won an Academy Award for actor Geoffrey Rush, and a slew of nominations.

Into the new millennium

Towards the start of the new millennium, young writer-directors focused on **crime stories**, often blackly comic, such as Gregor Jordan's first feature, the Sydney-set *Two Hands* (1999), which launched the career of Heath Ledger; Scott Roberts' *The Hard Word* (2002), with Guy Pearce and Rachel Griffiths; and Andrew Dominik's more graphic *Chopper* (2000), based on the autobiography of the celebrity criminal Mark "Chopper" Read and starring Eric Bana. Another trend has been towards telling **Aboriginal stories**: Rolf de Heer's *The Tracker* (2002) and Phillip Noyce's *Rabbit-Proof Fence* (2002) both look critically at the attitudes and atrocities of the 1920s and 1930s (respectively), dealing with the difficult subject matter of massacres (de Heer) and the "Stolen Generation" (Noyce). Two films portray indigenous life in Arnhem Land from very different perspectives: Stephen Johnson's *Yolngu Boy* (2001) confronts contemporary indigenous adolescent experience, including graphic scenes of petrol sniffing, while the dry, humorous storytelling in de Heer's enchanting *Ten Canoes* (2006), exquisitely photographed in the Arafura Swamp, transcends cultural barriers, appealing in equal measure to the local Yolngu audience and Western tastes.

Films such as *Rabbit-Proof Fence*, Ray Lawrence's bleak but brilliant *Lantana*, and Cate Shortland's melancholic *Somersault* show a distinctly Australian sensibility and landscape without exoticism, kitsch suburbia, or cute and quirky characters, and reveal a new level of profundity and maturity in Australian cinema.

As the Liberal government slashed funding to the Australian Film Commission and Film Finance Corporation, Australia's phenomenally successful **actors** now work mostly overseas where the pay, recognition and opportunities are much greater. These actors include Oscar-winners Russell Crowe (*Gladiator* and *Master and Commander*), Nicole Kidman (*Moulin Rouge* and *The Hours*) and Geoffrey Rush (*Shine* and *Quills*), and other major actors such as Judy Davis (*Naked Lunch* and *Celebrity*), Mel Gibson (*Braveheart* and *The Patriot*), Rachel Griffiths (*Blow* and the TV series *Six Feet Under* and *Brothers & Sisters*), Toni Collette (*The Sixth Sense* and *Little Miss Sunshine*), Cate Blanchett (*The Aviator* and *The Lord of the Rings*), Sam Neill (*The Piano* and *Jurassic Park*), Anthony LaPaglia (*29th St* and *Lowdown*), Guy Pearce (*L.A. Confidential* and *Memento*), Hugh Jackman (*Kate & Leopold*, *Swordfish* and *X-Men*), Naomi Watts (*Mulholland Drive* and *2 Grams*), and the late Heath Ledger, who won kudos for his role in *Brokeback Mountain* and a posthumous Academy Award for Best Supporting Actor in 2009 for his role as the Joker in *The Dark Knight*.

While these actors occasionally return home to star in Australian films, these films usually have short runs at home – in 2004, Australian films made up only 1.3 percent of box-office receipts. It usually takes a "blockbuster" Australian film to buck that trend; in 2007, that was the animated penguin film *Happy Feet*, and, in 2008, *Australia* by Baz Luhrmann. Before the release of Luhrmann's epic, Australian films would have comprised around one percent of total box-office receipts, but the film's success in Australia lifted it to 3.8 percent.

Hot spots for film buffs and soap addicts

The majestic scenery of the Northern Territory has featured in many films. **Kakadu National Park** provided the setting for many of the scenes in *Crocodile Dundee*: familiar spots are Anbangbang Billabong (see p.585) and Waterfall Creek (see p.587). *We of the Never Never* was set in the **Mataranka** region, which, predictably, has been rechristened "Never Never" country (see p.600). **Darwin** featured in *Australia*, as did **Kununurra** – where Nicole Kidman claims the waters helped get her pregnant – so be careful, or not.

Desolation and Outback grandeur have a stranglehold on the science fiction and post-apocalyptic genres. Locations for *Mad Max II* include the **Silverton** area of New South Wales (see p.359); as his parting shot, Mel Gibson upscuttled the semi-trailer on the nearby **Mundi Mundi Plains**. In nearby **Broken Hill**, scenes from *The Adventures of Priscilla, Queen of the Desert* were filmed at the kitsch *Mario's Palace Hotel* (see p.354), while the casino scenes were shot in Alice Springs. In South Australia, the pockmarked scenery of **Coober Pedy** (see p.830) has found favour with many film-makers, including Wim Wenders, who made his epic *Until the End of the World* here, while the lunar-like landscape was also an invaluable element in creating the atmosphere of *Mad Max III*. And that Outback pub in *Crocodile Dundee* was none other than the *Walkabout Creek Hotel*, at **McKinlay** in Queensland (see p.538).

More lush surroundings have also caught the imagination: in Victoria, the eponymous **Hanging Rock** (see p.952), which featured in *Picnic at Hanging Rock*, is within striking distance of **Woodend** (though the imposing mansion-school is actually in South Australia, the visitable Martindale Hall in the Clare Valley; see p.876).

The production of big-budget international films at Fox Studios in **Sydney** has provided locals with many location-spotting opportunities: *Mission Impossible II* provided the best haul, including scenes filmed at the **Bare Island** fortifications (see p.150). The soapy teenage angst and surfie bonhomie of *Home and Away* has long revolved around **Palm Beach** in Sydney's northern beaches (see p.149), with the **Barrenjoey Lighthouse** and headland regularly in shot. **Melbourne** is famous for being the filming location of *Home and Away*'s competitor, the veteran soap *Neighbours*; Ramsay Street, Erinsborough, is actually Pin Oak Court in Vermont South, while the hit TV series *The Secret Life of Us* was filmed around St Kilda.

Australians have many skilled technicians – thanks to AFTRS (The Australian Film Television and Radio School) and training at the ABC – and this (along with a weak Australian dollar) has seen Sydney's Fox Studios (see p.129) attract major productions such as *Dark City*, *The Matrix* trilogy, *Mission Impossible II*, *Star Wars Episodes II* and *III*, *Superman Returns*, *Moulin Rouge* and *The Quiet American* to Australia. However, the directors of the New Wave are now the Old Guard and Australia's home-grown cinema is in desperate need of another shot in the arm.

Films to watch out for

While you'd be lucky to catch all the recommendations below on the big screen (although keep an eye on the programmes of art-house, or repertory, cinemas in the major cities), many of the titles can be found in DVD-rental stores.

Humour, black comedy and satire

The Adventures of Priscilla, Queen of the Desert (Stephan Elliott, 1994). A queer romp across the Outback, prying into some musty corners of Australian social life along the way.

Babakiueria (Julian Pringler, 1988). A culture-reversing short-film spoof with Aborigines invading Australia and continuing with an anthropological-style study of white Australia. Well worth the search.

The Castle (Rob Sitch, 1997). A family's struggle to defend their home in the face of a trinity of suburban horrors: toxic-waste dumps, overhead power-lines and airport developers.

Death in Brunswick (John Ruane, 1990). A black comedy about the misfortunes of a hapless dishwasher who becomes embroiled in a gangland killing.

Kenny (Clayton Jacobson, 2006). The eponymous hero is a plumber, owner of a Portaloo business (expect lots of lavatory humour) whose family and ex-wife give him a hard time. A heart-warming "mockumentary" of the quintessential decent Aussie bloke.

Malcolm (Nadia Tass, 1985). A charming, offbeat comedy about a slow-witted tram driver in Melbourne.

Muriel's Wedding (PJ Hogan, 1994). Kleptomaniac frump Muriel wastes away in an Abba-and-confetti dreamworld until ex-schoolchum Rhonda masterminds Muriel's escape from her awful family and ghastly seaside suburb of "Porpoise Spit". Great performances.

Adolescent and misfit romance

Better Than Sex (Jonathan Teplitzky, 2000). In this romantic comedy, Josh has only three days left until he returns to London, so a one-night, after-party fling with Cin shouldn't hold any complications.

Flirting (John Duigan, 1989). This sequel to *The Year My Voice Broke* follows a young boy's adventures in boarding school. Superior coming-of-age film.

Lonely Hearts (Paul Cox, 1981). Following the death of his mother, 50-year-old Peter buys a new toupee and joins a dating agency. A sensitive portrayal of the ensuing, at times awkward, relationship. Other Paul Cox features include *Man of Flowers*, *My First Wife* and *Cactus*.

Looking for Alibrandi (Kate Woods, 2000). Light yet surprisingly layered story of a teenage Sydney girl dealing with suicide, high school, new love and immigrant cultural identity.

Mullet (David Caesar, 2001). A slow-motion plot set in a New South Wales south-coast fishing town where nothing happens until a mysterious prodigal son (Ben Mendelsohn) returns to mixed receptions from his family, former friends and fiancée.

Somersault (Cate Shortland, 2004). Having been caught kissing her mother's no-hoper boyfriend, 16-year-old Heidi (Abbie Cornish) runs away from home winding up in wintery Jindabyne in the snowfields of southern New South Wales. She tries to cobble together a new life there, but her strong sensuality, coupled with emotional fragility, gets her into new trouble. Fine acting and a great debut film.

Strictly Ballroom (Baz Luhrmann, 1991). Mismatched dancers who, together, dare to defy the prescribed routines of a ballroom dancing competition – all its frozen smiles and gaudy gown glory. A feel-good hit and the first feature from the successful director of *Moulin Rouge* (2001).

Urban dysfunctionals

The Boys (Rowan Woods, 1998). This tense and powerful drama follows an ex-prisoner who terrorizes his dysfunctional family and coerces his unemployed brothers into a violent crime.

Careful, He Might Hear You (Carl Shultz, 1982). An absorbing tug-of-love drama set in 1930s Sydney with brilliant images by cinematographer John Seale.

Chopper (Andrew Dominik, 2000). Eric Bana brilliantly plays notorious criminal Mark "Chopper" Read who ruthlessly dominates prison inmates and underworld associates alike. Based on Read's autobiography.

The Devil's Playground (Fred Schepisi, 1975). Burgeoning sexuality creates tension between pupils and their tutors in a Catholic seminary. A fine debut film.

Head On (Ana Kokkinos, 1998). Unemployed Ari (Alex Dimitriades) escapes living with his strict Greek parents by spending a hectic 24 hours nightclubbing, drug taking and graphically exploring his homosexuality.

Lantana (Ray Lawrence, 2001). Set in Sydney, this is a sometimes bleak but thought-provoking tale of trust and secrecy in marriage. Coincidences and consequences bind lives of strangers together in ways that are as twisting, tangled and tough as the Australian plant that provides the film's title. The strong cast includes Geoffrey Rush and Anthony LaPaglia.

The Last Days of Chez Nous (Gillian Armstrong, 1991). A middle-aged woman slowly loses her grip on her marriage and family.

Romper Stomper (Geoffrey Wright, 1991). A bleak account of the violent disintegration of a gang of Melbourne skinheads, notable as Russell Crowe's big-screen debut.

Sweetie (Jane Campion, 1988). Part black comedy, part bleakly disturbing portrait of a bizarre suburban family.

Ockerdom

Australia (Baz Luhrmann, 2008). Hoity-toity Englishwoman Lady Sarah Ashley (Nicole Kidman) comes to Australia to find her pastoralist husband dead. Cue the independent cowboy (Hugh Jackman) and beautifully shot cattle drive. World War II, separation and melodrama follows. Whether you fall for director Baz Luhrmann's epic or not, everyone has fallen under the spell of the Aboriginal character Nullah (newcomer Brandon Walters).

The Adventures of Barry McKenzie (Bruce Beresford, 1972). Ultra-ocker comes to England to teach "pommie sheilas about real men". Ironically, Barry Humphries' satire got beer-spurting ovations from the very people he despised but set Beresford's career back a couple of years.

Crocodile Dundee (Peter Faiman, 1985). The acceptable side of genial, dinky-di ockerdom saw Paul Hogan sell Australian bush mystique to the mainstream and put Kakadu National Park firmly on the tourist agenda. Enjoyable once, but don't bother with the sequels.

Wake in Fright aka Outback (Ted Kotcheff, 1970). A horrifying gem in

its uncut 114min version; a real *Deliverance* down under. A coast-bound teacher blows his fare in Outback Hicksville and his life slowly degenerates into a brutal, beer-sodden nightmare.

Gritty and defiant women

Celia (Ann Turner, 1988). A wonderful allegory that mixes a 1950s rabbit-eradication programme with a communist witch-hunt. Stubborn Celia is determined to keep her bunny.

Dance Me to My Song (Rolf de Heer, 1998). A unique and moving film written by and starring cerebral-palsy-sufferer Heather Rose as she is abused by her carer and falls in love.

The Getting of Wisdom (Bruce Beresford, 1977). Spirited Laura rejects the polite sensibilities and snobbery of an Edwardian boarding school.

My Brilliant Career (Gillian Armstrong, 1978). An early feminist

questions and defies the expectations of 1890s Victoria.

Puberty Blues (Bruce Beresford, 1981). Two teenage beach girls refuse to accept their pushchair-and-shopping-trolley destiny.

Shame (Steve Jodrell, 1988). A woman lawyer on an Outback motorcycle trip breaks down in a small town and becomes embroiled in the town's secrets.

We of the Never Never (Igor Auzins, 1981). A good-looking version of Jeannie Gunn's autobiographical classic of early twentieth-century station life in the Top End.

Men in rugged circumstances

The Dish (Rob Sitch, 2000). Light-hearted take on how Australia saved NASA during the broadcasting of the 1969 Apollo 11 moon landing from New South Wales' Parkes Space Observatory (see p.316), and an aside on how the country's technological skills are often overlooked. Starring Sam Neill.

Gallipoli (Peter Weir, 1980). A deservedly classic buddy movie in which a young Mel Gibson strikingly evokes the ANZACs' cheery idealism and the tragedy of their slaughter.

The Man from Snowy River (George Miller, 1981). Men, horses

and the land from A.B. ("Banjo") Paterson's seminal and dearly loved poem caught the overseas' imagination. A modern kangaroo western.

Plains of Heaven (Ian Pringle, 1982). A spookily atmospheric story of two weathermen in a remote meteorological station slowly losing their minds.

Sunday Too Far Away (Ken Hannam, 1973). A simple tale of macho shearers' rivalries in Outback South Australia, with a charismatic performance by a youthful, bottom-baring, Jack Thompson.

Outback nightmares

Cunnamulla (Dennis O'Rourke, 2000). Controversial and powerful documentary of malaise in Cunnamulla, an isolated Outback town, 800km west of Brisbane, featuring inhabitants' own stories of teen sex and hopelessness, frontier redneckery, racial tension, social dysfunction, and desperate longings for escape to distant cities.

Evil Angels (A Cry in the Dark) (Fred Schepisi, 1987). A dramatic retelling of the Azaria Chamberlain story; Ayers Rock (Uluru) and dingoes will never seem quite the same again. But it's Meryl Streep's atrocious Aussie accent and the line "the dingo's got my baby" that have become classics.

Picnic at Hanging Rock (Peter Weir, 1975). A richly layered tale about the disappearance of a party of schoolgirls and its traumatic aftermath.

Razorback (Russell Mulcahy, 1984). Dark comedy exploiting urban paranoia of the Outback and featuring a remote township, a gigantic, psychotic wild pig, and some bloodthirsty nutters who run the local abattoir.

Walkabout (Nicolas Roeg, 1971). Following their deranged father's suicide during a bush picnic, two children wander through the desert until an Aboriginal boy guides them back to civilization.

Wolf Creek (Greg McLean, 2005). Three backpackers are stuck in the desert at nightfall, hundreds of kilometres from anywhere, when their car won't start. It appears help is at hand in the person of truck-driving Mick Taylor, but his aims are to never let them leave alive. Terrifying, but tasteless considering the inspiration was the real backpacker murders of the 1990s.

About Aboriginal people

The Chant of Jimmie Blacksmith (Fred Schepisi, 1977). Set in the 1800s, a mixed-race boy is forced onto the wrong side of the law. Based on the novel by Thomas Keneally and powerfully directed.

Dead Heart (Brian Brown, 1996). A long-overdue and regrettably overlooked thriller, set on an Aboriginal community near Alice Springs. Bravely gets its teeth into some juicy political and social issues.

The Fringe Dwellers (Bruce Beresford, 1985). An aspiring daughter persuades her family to move from the bush into a suburban white neighbourhood, with expected results.

Jedda, the Uncivilized (Charles Chauvel, 1955). An orphaned

Aboriginal girl brought up by a "civilized" white family cannot resist her "tribal" urges when she is semi-voluntarily abducted by a black outlaw.

Manganinnie (John Honey, 1980). Set during the time of the "black drives" of 1830s Tasmania, a young Aboriginal girl gets separated from her family and meets a white girl in similar straits.

Rabbit-Proof Fence (Phillip Noyce, 2002). A moving film, with beautiful cinematography, set in 1930s Western Australia and based on a true "Stolen Generation" story. Three girls, daughters of absent white fathers and black mothers, are taken from their families according to the policy of the all-powerful Chief Protector of Aborigines to a settlement at Moore River, but manage to escape. The girls – Outback-cast unknowns giving emotive, natural performances – make their way over 2000km home following the fence, pursued by a tracker (David Gulpilil).

Ten Canoes (Rolf de Heer, 2005). A goose-egg-hunting expedition in the Arafura Wetlands in Arnhem Land in tribal times: Dayindi (played by Jamie Gulpilil, son of David Gulpilil) fancies one of the wives of his older brothers – a threat to tribal law. To teach him a lesson, the older brother tells him a parable from the mythical past. The story weaves back and forth between the two timelines, with the Dreamtime events in colour, the goose-egg hunting in black and white. This beautifully photographed and humorously narrated film has a timeless appeal that transcends cultures, the result of close co-operation between de Heer, David Gulpilil and the Arnhem Land community of Ramingining.

The Tracker (Rolf de Heer, 2002). Set in 1922, this is something of a fable in an experimental form: "The Fanatic", a police officer who will stop at nothing, including cold-blooded massacre, leads "The Tracker" (David Gulpilil), "The Follower" (a young, green policeman), and "The Veteran", all in search of "The Accused", an indigenous man wanted for a white woman's murder. Violent massacre scenes are replaced by landscape paintings with a painful soundtrack, while songs (performed by Aboriginal musician Archie Roach) and narration convey the themes, creating a disturbing impression.

Yolngu Boy (Stephen Johnson, 2001). In Yolngu country in Arnhem Land, Lorrpu, Milika and Bortj have always been an inseparable trio. But when adolescence hits, 15-year-old Bortj's petrol-sniffing rampages land him in jail; as Lorrpu and Milika become tribally initiated, Bortj finds himself outside his own culture and unable to become a man, and friendships and loyalties are tested. When the three embark on a (beautifully shot) 500-kilometre overland trek to Darwin, living off the land, distress gives way to joy ... until they hit the city.

Portents of doom

Cane Toads: an Unnatural History (Mark Lewis, 1988). An eccentric, original and amusing documentary about the mixed feelings Queensland's poisonous amphibians arouse and the real threat they may pose to Australia's ecology.

The Last Wave (Peter Weir, 1977). An eerie chiller about a lawyer defending an Aborigine accused of murder – and the powerful, elemental forces his people control.

Mad Max II (George Miller, 1981). The best of the trilogy, set in a near future, where loner Max protects an oil-producing community from fuel-starved crazies. Great machinery and stunts.

Australian music

F or a geographically isolated, sparsely inhabited island with a tiny market for its own recorded music, Australia has, with ever more assurance, shouldered its way in to occupy a distinguished place in the international pop-music hierarchy. In contrast with its fifty-year rock-music heritage, the country's Aboriginal music boasts a creative presence of thousands of years. With a strong influence on contemporary Australian music, its importance in the ongoing reconciliation between black and white Australia can hardly be overstated.

Rock music

The story of Australian contemporary music closely parallels that of Britain and the US – rock'n'roll arrived in the 1950s, and each decade since has offered up its own revolutionary shift in the popular-music landscape. Given the ubiquitous nature of Western popular culture, this is hardly surprising. Less predictable, however, has been the impact of Australian music on the global music scene, beginning in the 1970s with AC/DC, continuing in the 1980s with Midnight Oil and INXS, through to recent years with Silverchair, The Vines, Jet and Wolfmother.

The early years

Australia's very first rock star emerged in 1957 in the form of a lean, throaty, stage-strutting powerhouse named **Johnny O'Keefe**. All snake-hips and sex appeal, "The Wild One", as he became known, was one of the few early rock performers who could very nearly out-Elvis Elvis. Concert footage of his live performances is largely taken up by shots of women screaming, passing out and being carried from concert venues by sweaty police and exhausted security people. O'Keefe discovered early on that all the big players in the industry – performers, managers, promoters and record companies – were expert manipulators, a path he followed: legend has it that he bullied his way into his first recording contract by calling a press conference and announcing that the deal was done, guessing correctly that the publicity would leave the record company no option but to sign him.

Johnny O'Keefe was, to Australians, the embodiment of the defiant new brand of music that was then sweeping the world. He was to become synonymous with 1960s TV programmes that showcased Australian rock'n'roll talent, even as his own recording efforts were gradually swamped by the peace-love-hair movement of the time – a movement he did not warm to. O'Keefe remained a presence on television and radio until his death of a heart attack in 1978, aged just 43. In keeping with the requirements of rock god-dom, his last years were characterized by a series of breakdowns, bouts of depression and problems with alcohol and drugs. His rendition of the classic crowd-anthem *Shout* (1959) remains, to this day, an integral part of early rock'n'roll's global legacy, and his hit *Wild One* (1958) was famously covered by Iggy Pop, renamed *Real Wild Child (Wild One)* in 1986.

Surviving the Sixties

In company with the rest of the world, Australian music rode out the 1960s hanging onto the coattails of the massive British rock invasion. Overwhelmed by the omnipresent Beatles and Rolling Stones, Australia was to produce little ground-breaking rock music beyond the efforts of Billy Thorpe and the Aztecs, The Easybeats, and Russell Morris, each of whom left behind a signature song forever embedded in the Australian psyche, and still played on commercial radio today: *Most People I Know (Think that I'm Crazy)* – Billy Thorpe and the Aztecs (1968); *Friday on My Mind* – The Easybeats (1966); *The Real Thing* – Russell Morris (1969).

The Seekers, however, were operating well clear of the crowded rock-music mainstream, creating their own musical niche by building three-part harmonies around chords strummed on acoustic guitars, the two male voices cushioning the pristine power of lead vocalist Judith Durham. Songs such as *If I Had a Hammer* (1965) might sound like hippie anthems today, but The Seekers' brand of idealism appealed to millions of record-buyers, and several successful comeback tours show that their popularity has barely waned.

It was in 1967, though, that millions of Australians witnessed the decade's most significant music-industry event – and not a single one of them even knew it. A young man named **Johnny Farnham** had appeared on television, performing a too-cute but catchy ditty entitled *Sadie (the Cleaning Lady)* (1967). Good-looking, charming and with a superb voice, Farnham endeared himself immediately to Australian audiences; it was an odd debut, but nobody could have predicted how far he'd go. His name shortened to John (to distance himself from the bubblegum years), from 1982 to 1986 he was a popular frontman for the hugely successful Little River Band (having replaced Glen Shorrock), but it was in 1987 that his career peaked, with the release of his album *Whispering Jack*, which sold millions of copies worldwide, driven, appropriately enough, by the success of the anthemic *You're the Voice* (1987).

Livin' in the Seventies

Having emerged from the shadows of the 1960s, Australian music began to find a voice of its own in the mid-1970s. **Sherbet** and **Skyhooks** pulled off the satin-jumpsuits-and-crazy-make-up combo with singular style, and while they appeared glam, their music was pop-rock with fine songwriters at the helm. The "Mighty Hooks" were at all times the cheekier and sexier of the two. Singer "Shirley" Strachan famously performed in only a pair of tight satin trousers with a large, bright-red hand painted over the crotch; the other band-members were equally indulgent of their penchants for self-expression. There was no sacrifice of substance for style, however, with the band recording several of Australia's catchiest but most enduring pop songs, including such irresistible numbers as *You Just Like Me 'cause I'm Good in Bed* (1974), *Horror Movie* (1974), *Ego (Is Not a Dirty Word)* (1975) and *Women in Uniform* (1978).

Sherbet appeared almost serious by comparison, looking as though they only wore the satin pants, silly shoes and silk scarves because that was what fashion dictated. Highly accomplished musicians, they were led by handsome pop vocalist Daryl Braithwaite and recorded several standout tracks, including *Child's Play* (1976), *Howzat!* (1976), *High Rolling* (1977) and *Summer Love* (1975).

Key songwriters in both bands have gone on to have successful careers. In the case of Sherbet's keyboardist and songwriter, Garth Porter, he is producing many of Australia's top country-music performers. Greg Macainsh, bass player and songwriter for Skyhooks (and one of the first Australian lyricists to reference the suburbs of his city), was an in-demand songwriter for many years after Skyhooks.

But while Australia loved its sometimes-sugary pop, pub-rock was the meat and potatoes of the nation's live scene. Enter a clannish group of young Scottish immigrants playing their own version of Chuck Berry–inspired blues-rock, just three times as loud and with heavily distorted guitars. **AC/DC** not only had the skills, the songs and the "muscle" to back it all up, they also boasted two figures who were destined to become universal icons of rock'n'roll rebellion: guitarist Angus Young's delinquent-schoolboy persona had to share the adulation of wannabe rock rebels with singer Bon Scott, who was possessed not only of a genuine, self-destructive, live-hard-die-young ethos, but also sported the most mischievous grin ever seen in tandem with a microphone. It's unlikely anyone besides Bon could have delivered songs such as *Highway to Hell* (1979), *Whole Lotta Rosie* (1978), and *Dirty Deeds…Done Dirt Cheap* (1976) with the required sass to make them acceptable in a 1970s commercial market.

True to form, Bon died a rock-star's death in London in 1980 in the back of a car, unable to be revived after a hard drinking session. It was, ironically, smack in the middle of a golden age for Australian music, when, during the period 1977–83, bands Men at Work, Midnight Oil, Cold Chisel, INXS, Air Supply and Little River Band were lining up right alongside AC/DC to take the pop-music world by storm.

Oz music grows up

Even as AC/DC managed – in the space of a year following Bon's death – to recruit a new singer (Brian Johnston), settle permanently into life in Britain, and record the most successful heavy-rock album of all time, *Back in Black* (1980), bands back in Australia suddenly found that the world was interested in them, too. **Little River Band**'s sound was so West Coast USA that commercial success in North America had long seemed inevitable; **Air Supply**, meanwhile, had the sort of stranglehold on the American easy-listening love-song market to which Michael Bolton was perhaps, even then, beginning to aspire. More surprising was the impact made by **Men at Work**, a band whose well-crafted songs were invariably, if unfashionably, punctuated by arresting melodies played on a flute, and whose style came to be described as "white reggae". They announced their arrival in 1981 with the ska-ish *Who Can It Be Now?*, followed by *The Land Down Under*, both of which bombarded radio airwaves and shifted by the million.

Top ten great Oz rock albums

1) *Livin' in the Seventies* Skyhooks. Mushroom Records, 1974.
2) *Howzat!* Sherbet. Sherbet Records, 1976.
3) *Goodbye Tiger* Richard Clapton. Infinity Records, 1977.
4) *Back in Black* AC/DC. Albert Records, 1980.
5) *East* Cold Chisel. WEA, 1980.
6) *Business As Usual* Men At Work. CBS, 1981.
7) *Kick* INXS. WEA, 1987.
8) *Diesel and Dust* Midnight Oil. CBS, 1987.
9) *Songs From the South: Paul Kelly's Greatest Hits* Paul Kelly. Mushroom Records, 1997.
10) *Highly Evolved* The Vines. Capitol Records, 2002.

During this period, **Midnight Oil**, **Cold Chisel** and **INXS** stayed closer to home, recognizing perhaps that their styles were less easily translatable from an Australian to a global audience. It is surely no coincidence that among these bands (all highly accomplished, and equally revered at home) the least identifiably "Australian" act – **INXS** – was the first to experience worldwide fame and fortune, when in 1987 their album *Kick* plundered the US charts. Of the other two, most needs to be said about the band that had the biggest impact at home, and the least impact abroad – Cold Chisel. If the period three years either side of 1980 was to be remembered as the grand era of Oz "pub rock", then Chisel was the band that owned it, lock, stock and smoking barrel.

From Chisel to The Church

Formed in Adelaide in 1975, **Cold Chisel** was, like every great band from the Rolling Stones to U2, greater than the sum of its parts. Steve Prestwich (drums) and Phil Small (bass) made a compact and classy rhythm team, variously casting light and shadow about the more illustrious members of the group. Ian Moss's blues-rock guitar virtuosity and awesome soul voice made him a natural star on any stage, in lethal combination with lead singer Jimmy Barnes, Australia's self-styled wild man of rock and working-class hero. A great band must have great songs, and these were duly delivered by the immensely tall and serious man at the piano, **Don Walker**, one of Australia's greatest songwriters.

Among dozens of examples of Don Walker's craftsmanship in capturing the times/places/people/events poignant to Australians, *Khe Sanh* (1978) – a treatise on the Australian experience of surviving the war in Vietnam – remains an Australian classic, while *Star Hotel* (1980) encapsulates, in three verses and a chorus, the mood and events of September 19, 1979, when, in the working-class steel-town of Newcastle, police came to close down the city's main pub-rock venue, *The Star Hotel*, only to find themselves confronted by an angry crowd spoiling for a fight. Police cars were overturned and set alight in the course of a civil disturbance that echoed convict rebellions of two centuries earlier. The hotel was finally closed down, but the punters had made their point – and Chisel weren't going to let the police forget it.

Cold Chisel not only recorded the boozy summer nights, the trips up the coast, the girls, the fights, the pubs, the streets, the cities and towns, they sang it all back to the faithful in sweaty pubs and heaving stadiums night after night. When they called it a day in 1984, Chisel had become Australia's greatest rock band and an iconic symbol of working-class Australia. "Mossy" and "Barnesy" went on to fame and fortune as solo performers: however, their long-awaited return in 1998 with their first studio album in fourteen years, *The Last Wave of Summer*, was anti-climactic, their original audience caring more about mortgages and babies than "Mossy" and "Barnesy".

During this period, **Midnight Oil** by no means played second fiddle to Cold Chisel; rather, they had a different agenda and a different audience, and their commitment and energy in delivering it live were never in question. The twin-guitar attack of Jim Moginie and Martin Rotsey was fierce and central to the sound, the drumming of Rob Hirst was committed, and the energy of the charismatic lead singer, Peter Garrett, was something to behold. While Garrett half-spoke his way through the songs, principal songwriters Rob Hirst and Jim Moginie crafted melodies that belied their intense attack. Always highly political, "the Oils" brought Aboriginal land rights into the forum of pop culture, even as their uncompromising album *Diesel and Dust* (1987) brought them worldwide success. Twenty-five-year veterans with fourteen albums to their credit (and often bracketed by critics with bands like Queen and U2 as the most powerful live act in the world), Midnight Oil's rage against the machine ended in 2002, with Peter Garrett leaving the band in order to resume his political career. Elected a Labor MP in 2004, he became Minister for the Environment, Heritage and the Arts in 2008.

Among the distinguished musicians of the 1970s and 1980s, two songwriters stand (alongside Don Walker) above the rest as chroniclers of their culture and environment: **Richard Clapton** and **Paul Kelly**. Clapton's 1977 album *Goodbye Tiger* is unmatched as a celebration of everyday life in Australia – riding the city tram, searching for the perfect wave, soaking up the streetscapes of Oxford Street and Kings Cross. Paul Kelly is a more contemporary presence, and his songs go unerringly to the heart of the matter: *Have You Ever Seen Sydney from a 727 at Night?* (1985), *From St Kilda to Kings Cross* (1985) and *Adelaide* (1985) capture their respective subjects better than any photograph, while his ode to *Bradman* (1987) – written in homage to Australia's greatest Test cricket batsman Sir Donald Bradman ("The Don"), is the stuff of a true bard.

However, in order to appreciate the depth and diversity of Australian music as it reached **maturity**, one needs to take a stroll out to the fringes. With a well-established canon of "major" Australian bands now in place, others were finding looser creative environments in which to operate. The Triffids, The Birthday Party (with star alumnus Nick Cave), The Church and the Go-Betweens seemed tied to weirder and more eclectic influences (such as The Velvet Underground, David Bowie and Bob Dylan) than their "mainstream" counterparts. Although musically diverse, they held several characteristics in common: their songs seemed more poetic, or just more sensitive to light and shade; and they were also less commercially successful in Australia, yet all made a big impact in Britain and Europe. Nick Cave enjoys a position of enormous respect within the international music industry, thanks to several well-received albums with The Bad Seeds including critical and commercial success in 2008 with *Dig, Lazarus, Dig!!!* as well as success with his side project **Grinderman**, whose self-titled first album was released in 2007. After splitting up in 1989, legendary The Go-Betweens' key songwriters Robert Forster and Grant McLennan reformed their band with new support musicians in 2000 and once again achieved critical acclaim before the premature death of McLennan in 2006. Forster's quirky and angular songs were sometimes at odds with McLennan's softer, more melancholic style, but on their last album, *Oceans Apart* (2005), these two Brisbane songwriters were once again gelling as a team. Oddly enough, it was Brisbane that could also throw up a white-hot punk outfit that pre-dated the Sex Pistols: The Saints. Influenced more by the Ramones, The Stooges and MC5 than anything about to happen in England, their 1976 single, *(I'm) Stranded*, was 3½ minutes of sneering Chris Bailey and the power-chord progressions of Ed Kuepper. While it was raw, there were songsmith smarts already in evidence and both Bailey and Kuepper forged their own paths in their songwriting careers over the ensuing years.

The Nineties to the present day

Strangest perhaps of all the facets of Australia's music industry has been its propensity for throwing up **TV soap stars** who mutated into pop stars. At last count, there were no less than five ex-*Neighbours* cast members at large within the music industry: Kylie Minogue, Danii Minogue, Natalie Imbruglia, Holly Valance and Delta Goodrem. While Goodrem struggles to break the American market (she's hugely successful in Australia), the only one to really make it big internationally is the pop princess **Kylie**. From "singing budgie" to gay icon to mainstream success, Kylie's constant reinvention is the key to her success.

With the industry looking to soap stars to fill the airwaves and the number of venues willing to put on original acts decreasing, a certain listlessness afflicted the music community during the late 1980s and early 1990s. But with the soap stars off overseas to try their luck, bands such as You Am I, The Whitlams, Powderfinger and The Cruel Sea gained popularity with their passion and enigmatic frontmen, if not for their originality. By the mid-1990s, quality Australian bands were once again jostling for position in local and overseas markets, this time led by three scruffy-looking, 15-year-old schoolboys.

In 1994, Newcastle high-school trio Innocent Criminals won a demo tape competition run by the SBS TV show *Nomad*. Renaming themselves **Silverchair**, their demo song *Tomorrow* had the Seattle grunge sound all over it, and an awesome rock vocal performance from 15-year-old singer/guitarist Daniel Johns. *Tomorrow* arrived atop the Australian singles charts where it stayed for several weeks, and their 1995 debut album *frogstomp* took them into league – and onto the stage – with grunge giants such as Pearl Jam and Soundgarden, even as the three "boys" were negotiating their last year of high school. Subsequent Silverchair albums *Freak Show* (1997), *Neon Ballroom* (1999) and *Diorama* (2002) proved Johns was more than just a grunge wannabe, with all albums incurring solid sales and critical approval. Having fought the twin ravages of anorexia and a crippling bout of arthritis, Johns took a break from the band to write and record with prominent Aussie DJ Paul Mac in a band called The Dissociatives. After the hiatus the band quashed rumours of a split in the most empathic way possible, with the hit album *Young Modern* (2007), the most successful of their career.

Tapping into the retro-rock mood that arrived in 2002 with bands such as The Strokes, The White Stripes and The Hives were two local groups of precocious young rockers – The Vines and Jet. **The Vines** exploded onto the world scene with such a rush that they scored both a recording deal and a hit album (*Highly Evolved*, 2002) after having played only a handful of live shows. While touring in support of their second somewhat disappointing album, *Winning Days* (2004), lead singer and songwriter Craig Nicholls was diagnosed with Asperger's Syndrome (a mild form of autism) after his on-stage antics became violent. Nicholls recovered enough to record *Vision Valley* (2006), full of neo-garage pop, and subsequently began touring again. 2008 saw the release of *Melodia*, their forth album, but once again Nicholls' mental condition deteriorated and performances were indefinitely cancelled at the end of 2008.

Jet soared into the hearts and minds of young rock fans, most notably in the UK, with their catchy guitar riffs and their hard-living rock attitude. The album *Get Born* (2003) spent more than a year in the charts, largely on the strength of the single *Are You Gonna Be My Girl?*, a success that has not quite been matched by the band's second album *Shine On* (2006), famously "reviewed" by influential online music website Pitchfork with nothing but a video of a monkey drinking its own urine.

While the music charts in Australia are constantly filled with the sounds of ex-contestants from Australia's version of American Idol, there are some bright spots in Australian talent. Singer-songwriter Sarah Blasko (imagine the love-child of Bjork and Thom Yorke) has released two brilliant albums of ethereal intricate chamber pop, *The Overture & the Underscore* (2004) and *What The Sea Wants, The Sea Will Have* (2006). Another notable female-fronted band is The Audreys who released the acclaimed *When the Flood Comes* in 2008. Rockers to look out for are the evergreen Powderfinger, Jebediah and The Living End. All of these performers are great live and Australia has a fairly active summer music festival season when you can see several of these bands in one hit (see p.57).

Aboriginal music

Aboriginal music is an increasingly powerful and invigorating seam in the fabric of world music. Its instruments and rhythms have a strong influence on contemporary Australian music, and there's probably no better example of the musical crossing of cultural boundaries than in the story of Australia's most recognizable instrument, the didgeridoo. Known also as a *yidaki*, or simply a "didge", this hollowed-out tree branch, when blown into, produces a resonant hum that can be punctuated by imitations of animal and bird noises. Its sound is uniquely evocative of the Australian landscape.

The big surprise for many visitors to Australia is the sheer **diversity** of Aboriginal music. From the big rock sound of the Warumpi Band, and the heartfelt guitar ballads of Archie Roach, to the cruisey island reggae of Saltwater and the echoes of an ancient culture in the work of Nabarlek (who sing mostly in their own language), there is no way of pigeonholing the music. One hot indigenous talent to hit the radio airwaves is Yilila, a band whose music – an energetic mix of pulsing didge, screaming guitar solos and funky bass – is based on the story of *Dhumbala* or Red Flag, which chronicles their ancestors' centuries-old relationship with Indonesian traders. At the other end of the spectrum is Geoffrey Gurrumul Yunupingu, a former member of Yothu Yindi and member of Saltwater whose uplifting debut album, *Gurrumul* (2008), has won rave reviews and a handful of awards. Geoffrey was born blind and sings angelically in his native Yolngu tongue with just acoustic guitar and bass behind him.

It's no problem to see Aboriginal bands playing live, doing everything from metal to hip-hop and performing in all parts of the country, but there's really no better way to immerse yourself than by attending an indigenous music festival.

Festivals

Biggest of the Aboriginal music festivals is the **Barunga Sports & Cultural Festival** (@www.barungafestival.com.au), which showcases up to forty bands, along with team sports, traditional dance, spear-throwing and didge-playing competitions. It's held at Barunga Community, 80km south of Katherine in the NT, over the Queen's Birthday holiday weekend in June (campsites with facilities are available). Also in the Top End, the Milingimbi community's **Gattjirrk Cultural Festival** is purely a music event and, being harder to get to than Barunga, gets fewer white visitors. Dates for this one are hard to nail down, although it's always held sometime mid-year, on Milingimbi Island in the Crocodile archipelago. There are flights from Darwin, otherwise you need permission from the Northern Land Council (Darwin Head Office ℡08/8920 5100, @www.nlc.org.au) to drive across Arnhem Land to Ramingining to catch a barge. Traditional music and dance are featured, along with gospel bands and lots of Arnhem Land rock.

The **Laura Dance Festival** (@www.laurafestival.tv), held every odd-numbered year in far north Queensland, attracts high-profile performers like the Warumpi Band and Christine Anu, plus all the local Murri bands. Held in

June, there are usually quite a few backpackers and hippies about, as well as the local Murri community. It's about three hours' drive (on sealed roads) north from Cairns to Laura, a small town 60km west of Cooktown. The vibrant **Festival of the Dreaming** (⊛www.thedreamingfestival.com) takes place each June near the town of Woodford, northwest of Brisbane. Begun in 2006, this major four-day event features a strong line-up of musical talent alongside other cultural events.

If you're in **Sydney** over summer, there's no better place to be on the Australia Day holiday (January 26) than at **Yabun Survival Day** festival at Victoria Park. This festival began as a highly political event, deliberately juxtaposed with the Australia Day festivities that mark the arrival of the First Fleet of "white invaders". It continues as a celebration of the survival of indigenous people and cultures in the face of white oppression, and draws many of the biggest names in indigenous music.

Artists

Most of the **bands** mentioned above have work available on CD as well as iTunes, while other outstanding artists whose albums are widely available include Yothu Yindi, No Fixed Address, Tiddas, Kev Carmody and Coloured Stone. Compilation albums are also worth looking into, particularly those that cover a wide range of styles: *Meinmuk: Music from the Top End* (1996) and *Culture: Music from Black Australia* (2000) are Triple J compilations that showcase both the quality and diversity of Aboriginal music – from rock, reggae and rap to gospel and metal. CAAMA (Central Australian Aboriginal Media Association) is an excellent source for the latest indigenous CDs and DVDs, all of which are available online at ⊛www.caama.com.au.

Books

Australian writing came into its own in the 1890s, when a strong nation-
alistic movement, leading up to eventual federation in 1901, produced
writers such as Henry Lawson and the balladeer A.B. "Banjo" Paterson,
who romanticized the bush and glorified the mateship ethos, while
outstanding women writers, such as Miles Franklin and Barbara Baynton, gave
a feminine slant to the bush tale and set the trend for strong female authorship.
In the twentieth and twenty-first centuries, Australian novelists came to be
recognized in the international arena: Patrick White was awarded a Nobel
Prize in 1973, Peter Carey won the Booker Prize in 1988 and again in 2001,
and Kate Grenville scored the 2001 Orange Prize for Fiction. Other writers
who have made a name for themselves within Australia, such as David Malouf,
Julia Leigh, Tim Winton (twice nominated for the Booker Prize), Thomas
Keneally, Richard Flanagan, Chloe Hooper and Robyn Davidson, have aroused
curiosity further afield. Literary journals such as *Meanjin*, *Southerly*, *Westerly* and
Heat provide a forum and exposure for short fiction, essays, reviews and new
and established writers. The big prizes in Australian fiction include the Vogel
Prize for the best unpublished novel written by an author under the age of 35,
and the country's most coveted literary prize, the Miles Franklin Award.

Many of the best books by Australian writers or about Australia are not
available overseas, so you may be surprised at the range of local titles available
in Australian **bookshops**. A good website to check is that of Gleebooks
(Ⓦwww.gleebooks.com.au), one of Australia's best literary booksellers, with a
whole host of recent reviews; you can also order books online, to be posted
overseas.

Travel and travel guides

Peter Carey *30 Days in Sydney: a
wildly distorted account*. Part of
Bloomsbury Publishers' "The Writer
and the City" project, where "some
of the finest writers of our time
reveal the secrets of a city they know
best". Now based in New York,
celebrated Australian writer Carey
returns to his old stomping ground
with the perspective only an expat
can have, coupled with the ability of
a great writer to vividly portray it.

Bruce Chatwin *The Songlines*. A
semifictional account of an exploration into Aboriginal nomadism and
mythology that turns out to be one
of the more readable expositions of
this complex subject, though often
pretentious.

Sean Condon *Sean and David's
Long Drive*. Australia's humorous
answer to Kerouac's *On the Road*:

Melbourne-based Condon and his
friend David are fully fledged city
dwellers when they set off on a tour
around their own country, to come
face to face with the dangers of
crocs, tour guides and fellow
travellers.

Robyn Davidson *Tracks*. A compelling account of a young woman's
journey across the Australian desert,
accompanied only by four camels
and a dog. Davidson manages to
break out of the heroic-traveller
mould to write with compassion and
honesty of the people she meets in
the Outback and the doubts, dangers
and loneliness she faces on her way.
A classic of its kind.

Larry Habegger (ed) *Traveller's Tales
Australia*. Excerpts and essays from
some of the world's best travel
writers – Bruce Chatwin, Tim Cahill,

Jan Morris, Tony Horwitz, Pico Iyer and Paul Theroux – as well as new talents.

Tony Horwitz *One for the Road*. Married to an Australian, Pulitzer Prize–winning American author Horwitz comes to live in Sydney, but pines for adventure and sets off to hitchhike through the Outback. Along the way he encounters colourful characters from Aborigines to jackeroos, and hard-drinking men in a multitude of bush pubs. A comical, perceptive account.

Howard Jacobson *In the Land of Oz*. Jacobson focuses his lucidly sarcastic observations on a round-Australia trip in the late 1980s that gets rather close to some home truths for most Australians' tastes.

Mark McCrum *No Worries*. Knowing nothing of the country except the usual clichés, McCrum arrives in 1990s Australia and makes his way around by plane, train, thumb and Greyhound, meeting a surprising cast of characters along the way. As he travels, the stereotypes give way to an insightful picture of modern Australia.

Ruth Park *Ruth Park's Sydney*. Prolific novelist Park's 1973 guide to the city was fully revised and expanded in 1999. A perfect walking companion, full of personal insights, anecdotes and literary quotations.

Nicholas Shakespeare *In Tasmania*. During the seven years writing and researching a biography of Bruce Chatwin, British writer Shakespeare spent time in Australia following in his footsteps. Researching his family history, Shakespeare found living Tasmanian relatives. A brilliantly Chatwinesque book, where historical tales are woven with the writer's own experiences.

Alice Thomson *The Singing Line*. The great-great-granddaughter of Alice Todd, the woman after whom Alice Springs was named, retraces her ancestor's journey to central Australia. Nice change from the usual male-centric view of the early pioneers.

Mark Whittaker and Amy Willesee *The Road to Mount Buggery: a Journey through the Curiously Named Places of Australia*. Australia certainly has some unfortunate, banal and obscure place names, which Mark and Amy seek out on their journey, from Lake Disappointment to Cape Catastrophe. This entertaining, well-informed travelogue gives the fascinating stories behind the names.

Autobiography and biography

Julia Blackburn *Daisy Bates in the Desert*. For almost thirty years from 1913, Daisy Bates was Kabbarli, "the white-skinned grandmother", to the Aboriginal people with whom she lived in the desert. Blackburn's beautifully written biography interweaves fiction with fact to conjure up the life of one of Australia's most eccentric and misunderstood women.

Jill Ker Conway *The Road from Coorain*. Conway's childhood, on a drought-stricken Outback station during the 1940s, is movingly told, as is her battle to establish herself as a young historian in sexist, provincial 1950s Australia.

Robert Drewe *The Shark Net*. Accomplished novelist and journalist, Drewe has written a transfixing memoir of his boyhood and youth in Perth which segues into a literary true-crime story. Against a vividly drawn 1950s middle-class backdrop, Drewe shows how one man's random killing spree struck fear into the 'burbs of sunny, friendly and seemingly innocent Perth.

Albert Facey *A Fortunate Life.* A hugely popular autobiography of a battler, tracing his progress from a bush orphanage to Gallipoli, through the Depression, another war and beyond.

Barry Hill *Broken Song: T.G.H. Strehlow and Aboriginal Possession.* As a child growing up on the Hermannsburg Mission in Central Australia, Strehlow learnt the Aranda (Arrente) language. In 1932, the anthropologist began collecting Aranda songs, myths and tjurunga (sacred objects) for his book *Songs of Central Australia.* Resented by other anthropologists for his unique insight and access, Strehlow's was a fascinating career that ended in disgrace.

Eddie Mabo and Noel Loos *Edward Koiko Mabo: His Life and Struggle for Land Rights.* Mabo spent much of his life fighting for the autonomy of Torres Strait Islanders and in the process overthrew the concept of *terra nullius,* making his name a household word in Australia. Long interviews with the late black hero form the basis of this book and affectionately reveal the man behind the name.

David Malouf *12 Edmondstone Street.* An evocative autobiography-in-snatches of one of Australia's finest literary novelists, describing, in loving detail, the eponymous house in Brisbane where Malouf was born, life in the Tuscan village where he lives for part of each year, and his first visit to India.

Leah Purcell *Black Chicks Talking.* In an effort to overcome Aboriginal stereotypes, indigenous actor and writer Purcell gives insight into the lives of contemporary black women with this collection of lively, lengthy interviews, conducted with nine young females (all under 35).

Hazel Rowley *Christina Stead: a Biography.* Stead (1902–83) has been acclaimed as Australia's greatest novelist. After spending years in Paris, London and New York with her American husband, she returned to Australia in her old age.

Society and culture

Richard Baker *Land is Life: From Bush to Town – the Story of the Yanyuwa People.* The Yanyuwa people inhabited the Gulf of Carpentaria before the Europeans arrived, but most now live in the town of Borroloola, 750km southeast of Darwin. Historian Baker, assigned a "skin" in the Yanyuwa kinship system, gathered the people's oral history and produced this fascinating story told from the Yanyuwa point of view and time.

Geoffrey Blainey *Triumph of the Nomads.* A fascinating account portraying Aboriginal people as masters and not victims of their environment by this controversial conservative historian.

Peter and Gibson Dunbar-Hall *Deadly Sounds Deadly Places.* Comprehensive guide to contemporary Aboriginal music in Australia, from Archie Roach to Yothu Yindi; includes a handy discography.

Monica Furlong *Flight of the Kingfisher: a Journey among Kukatja Aborigines.* Furlong lived among the Aboriginal people of the Great Sandy Desert; this is her account of Kukatja perceptions and spiritual beliefs.

Roslynn Haynes *Seeking the Centre: the Australian Desert in Literature, Art and Film.* The geographical and metaphorical impact of the desert on Australian culture is explored in this illustrated book, as is the connection Aboriginal people have with the desert.

David Headon *North of the Ten Commandments.* An anthology of Northern Territory writings from all perspectives and sources – an excellent literary souvenir for anyone who falls for the charms of Australia's "one percent" territory.

Donald Horne *The Lucky Country.* This seminal analysis of Australian

society, written in 1976, has yet to be matched and is still often quoted.

Peter Singer and Tom Gregg *How Ethical is Australia? An Examination of Australia's Record as a Global Citizen.* Australian Peter Singer, world-renowned philosopher and professor of bioethics at Princeton University, teams up with Tom Gregg to examine Australia's policies on foreign aid, the United Nations, overseas trade, the environment and refugees.

History and politics

Robyn Annear *Nothing But Gold: the Diggers of 1852.* With an eye for interestingly obscure details and managing to convey a sense of irony without becoming cynical, this is a wonderfully readable account of the goldrushes of the nineteenth century, a period in Australia's history which perhaps did more than any other to shape the country's national character.

Len Beadell *Outback Highways.* Extracts from Len Beadell's half-dozen books, cheerfully recounting his life in the central Australian deserts as a surveyor, and his involvement in the construction of Woomera and the atomic bomb test sites.

🏃 **John Birmingham** *Leviathan: the unauthorised biography of Sydney.* Birmingham's tome casts a contemporary eye over the dark side of Sydney's history, from nauseating accounts of Rocks' slum life and the 1900 plague outbreak, through the 1970s traumas of Vietnamese boat people (now Sydney residents) to scandals of police corruption.

Manning Clark *A Short History of Australia.* A condensed version of this leading historian's multi-volume tome, focusing on dreary successions of political administrations over two

centuries, and cynically concluding with the "Age of Ruins".

Inga Clendinnen *Dancing With Strangers.* Empathetic, almost poetically written account imagining the interaction of the British and the Aborigines (whom Clendinnen calls "Australians") in the five years after the arrival of the First Fleet.

Ann Curthoys *Freedom Ride: A Freedom Rider Remembers.* History professor Curthoys was one of the busload of young, idealistic white university students who accompanied Aboriginal activist Charles Perkins (only 29 himself) on his revolutionary trip through northern New South Wales in 1965 to look at Aboriginal living conditions and root out and protest against racial discrimination.

David Day *Claiming a Continent: a New History of Australia.* Award-winning, general and easily readable history, concluding in 2000. The possession, dispossession and ownership of the land – and thus issues of race – are central to Day's narrative. Excellent recommended reading of recent texts at the end of each chapter.

Colin Dyer *The French Explorers and the Aboriginal Australians.* From Bruny d'Entrecasteaux's (1793) to Nicolas

Baudin's (1802) expeditions, the French explorers and on-board scientists kept detailed journals which provide a wealth of information on Aboriginal Australians, particularly those of Tasmania who d'Entrecasteaux noted "seem to offer the most perfect image of pristine society".

Bruce Elder *Blood on the Wattle: Massacres and Maltreatment of Aboriginal Australians Since 1788.* A heart-rending account of the horrors inflicted on the continent's indigenous peoples, covering infamous nineteenth-century massacres as well as more recent mid-twentieth-century scandals of the "Stolen Generation" children.

Tim Flannery (ed) *Watkin Trench 1788.* One of the most vivid accounts of early Sydney written by a twenty-something captain of the marines, Watkin Trench, who arrived with the First Fleet. Trench's humanity and youthful curiosity shine through as he brings alive the characters who peopled the early settlement, such as the Aboriginal Bennelong.

Robert Hughes *The Fatal Shore.* A minutely detailed epic of the origins of transportation and the brutal beginnings of white Australia.

Dianne Johnson *Lighting the Way: Reconciliation Stories.* Twenty-four very personal stories, written in a simple, engaging style, show Aboriginal and non-Aboriginal Australians working with each other, from community artworks to political activism. Positive and inspiring.

Mark McKenna *Looking for Black-fellas Point: an Australian History of Place.* This prize-winning book uncovers the uneasy history of Aboriginals and European settlers on the far south coast of New South Wales and widens its scope to the enduring meaning of land to both Aboriginal and white Australians.

Alan Moorehead *Cooper's Creek.* A historian's dramatic retelling of the ill-fated Burke and Wills expedition that set out in 1860 to make the first south-to-north crossing of the continent. A classic of exploration.

Sarah Murgatroyd *The Dig Tree: the Story of Burke and Wills.* Murgatroyd's recent retelling of the Burke and Wills story is gripping and immaculately researched – she journeyed along the route, and utilized the latest scientific and historical evidence, complemented by maps, photos and paintings.

Rosemary Neill *White Out: How Politics is Killing Black Australia.* Outspoken book which asserts that the rhetoric of self-determination and empowerment excuses the wider society from doing anything to reduce the disparity between black and white Australian populations. Busting taboos about indigenous affairs, Neill criticizes ideologies of both Left and Right.

Cassandra Pybus *Community of Thieves.* Attempting to reconcile past and future, fourth-generation Tasmanian Pybus provides a deeply felt account of the near-annihilation of the island's Aboriginal people.

Henry Reynolds *The Other Side of the Frontier* and *The Law of the Land.* A revisionist historian demonstrates that Aboriginal resistance to colonial invasion was both considerable and organized. *The Whispering in Our Hearts* is a history of those settler Australians who, troubled by the treatment of Aboriginal people, spoke out and took political action. *Why Weren't We Told?* is his most personal, an autobiographical journey showing how he, like many generations of Australians, imbibed a distorted, idealized Australian history, and describing his path to becoming an Aboriginal-history specialist; includes a moving story about his friendship with Eddie Mabo.

Portia Robinson *The Women of Botany Bay.* The result of painstaking research into the records of every female transported from Britain and Ireland between 1787 and 1828, as well as the wives of convicts who settled in Australia, Robinson tells with conviction and passion who these women really were.

Eric Rolls *Sojourners and Citizens* and *Flowers and the Wide Sea.* The first and second volumes of farmer-turned-historian Rolls' fascinatingly detailed history of the Chinese in Australia.

Anne Summers *Damned Whores and God's Police.* Stereotypical images of women in Australian society are explored in this ground-breaking reappraisal of Australian history from a feminist point of view.

Linda Weiss, Elizabeth Thurbon and John Mathews *How to Kill a Country: Australia's Devastating Trade Deal with the United States.* Australia's leading policy analysts examine the recent Free Trade Agreement with the United States, arguing that Australia's interests and identity will be damaged by the quest for a "special relationship".

Ecology and environment

Tim Flannery *The Future Eaters.* Paleontologist and environmental commentator Flannery poses that as the first human beings migrated down to Australasia, the Aborigines, Maoris and other Polynesian peoples changed the region's flora and fauna in startling ways, and began consuming the resources needed for their own future.

Tim Flannery *The Weather Makers: The History and Future Impact of Climate Change.* Written in Flannery's usual easy and engaging style, this book represents scientific journalism at its best – painstakingly tracing the history of climate change and climate science.

Tim Flannery *Chasing Kangaroos: A Continent, a Scientist, and a Search for the World's Most Extraordinary Creature.* Another great piece of scientific journalism, Flannery painstakingly traces the history of Australia's hopping herbivore in an engaging way.

Josephine Flood *The Riches of Ancient Australia.* An indispensable and lavish guide to Australia's most famous landforms and sites. The same author's *Archaeology of the Dreamtime* provides background on the development of Aboriginal society.

Drew Hutton and Libby Connors *A History of the Australian Environmental Movement.* Written by a husband-and-wife team, Queensland academics and prominent in Green politics, this well-balanced book charts the progress of conservation attempts from 1860 to modern protests.

Peter Latz *Bushfires and Bushtucker: Aboriginal Plant Use in Central Australia.* Handbook with photos, published by an Aboriginal-owned press.

Ann Moyal *Platypus: the Extraordinary Story of How a Curious Creature Baffled the World.* When British and French naturalists were first introduced to the platypus, they were flummoxed: Was it bird, reptile or mammal? And did it really lay eggs? Moyal, a science historian, provides a captivating look at the platypus – and Australian nature – through European eyes.

Tim Murray (ed) *Archeology of Australia.* The last thirty-odd years have seen many ground-breaking discoveries in Australian archeology, with three sites in particular of great significance: Kakadu in the Northern Territory, Lake Mungo in New South Wales, and South West Tasmania; a range of specialists contribute essays on the subject.

David Owen *Thylacine: the Tragic Tale of the Tasmanian Tiger*. Hunted to extinction, the last known Tasmanian tiger died in Beaumaris Zoo in Hobart in 1936. But unconfirmed sightings continue: "The longer the thylacine stays dead, the greater the interest it arouses," writes Owen of the marsupial predator's now-mythic status. Packed with fascinating facts and stories.

Mary White *The Greening of Gondwana*. Classic work on the

evolution of Australia's flora and geography.

James Woodford *The Wollemi Pine: the Incredible Discovery of a Living Fossil from the Age of the Dinosaurs*. The award-winning environment writer at the *Sydney Morning Herald* tells the story of the 1994 discovery in Wollemi wilderness near Sydney. *The Secret Life of Wombats* begins as a fascinating account of the "wombat boy", a schoolboy so curious to find out about how wombats lived he crawled into their burrows. In *The Dog Fence: a Journey through the Heart of the Continent* Woodford travels the 5400-kilometre length of the fence built to keep livestock safe from dingoes.

Contemporary fiction

Thea Astley *The Multiple Effects of Rainshadow*. On an Aboriginal island reserve in 1930, a white woman dies in childbirth, and her husband goes on a shotgun-and-dynamite rampage. The novel traces the effects over the years on eight characters who witnessed the violent events, ultimately exploring the brutality and racism in Australian life.

Murray Bail *Eucalyptus*. Beautifully written novel with a fairytale-like plot: New South Wales farmer, Holland, has planted nearly every type of eucalyptus tree on his land. When his extraordinarily beautiful daughter Ellen is old enough to marry, he sets up a challenge for her legion of potential suitors, to name each tree.

John Birmingham *He Died with A Felafel in His Hand*. A collection of squalid and very funny tales emerging from the once-dissolute author's experience of flat-sharing hell in Brisbane.

Anson Cameron *Tin Toys*. The Aboriginal "Stolen Generation" issue explored through the tale of Hunter Carolyn, an unintentional artist who can change skin colour at will.

Peter Carey *Bliss*. Carey's first and perhaps best novel is the story of a Sydney ad executive who drops out to New Age New South Wales. Other novels by Carey to look out for include his two Booker Prize–winners *Oscar and Lucinda* and *The True History of the Kelly Gang*, about the bushranger Ned Kelly. Also worth a read are his bizarre short stories, *The Fat Man in History*, with which he launched his career, and his latest novel *Theft. A Love Story*, an equally bizarre *tour de force* and a take on the international art world.

Steven Carroll *The Time We Have Taken*. The last book of a trilogy about a family living in suburban Melbourne from the 1950s through to the 1970s, is a celebration of the minutiae of suburban life and won the 2008 Miles Franklin Literary Award.

Robert Drewe *The Savage Crows*. A writer whose own life is falling apart in a cockroach-ridden Sydney of the 1970s, sets out to discover the grim truth behind Tasmania's "final solution".

Richard Flanagan *Death of a River Guide*. Narrator, environmentalist Aljaz Cosini, goes over his life and that of his family and forebears as he lies drowning in the Franklin River. Thoughtful writings about Tasmanian landscape, place, migration and the significance of history are the hallmark of Flanagan's novels. His nineteenth-century-set *Gould's Book of Fish: a Novel in Twelve Fish* delves into Tasmania's past as the brutal penal settlement of Van Diemen's Land.

Tom Gilling *Miles McGinty*. Nineteenth-century Sydney comes alive in this riotous, entertaining love story of Miles, who becomes a levitator's assistant and begins to float on air, and Isabel, who wants to fly.

Peter Goldsworthy *Three Dog Night*. It takes three dogs to keep a person warm on a desert night, an allusion to the love triangle which emerges when psychiatrist Martin Blackman returns to Adelaide after a decade in London with his new, much-loved wife, and visits his oldest friend, the difficult Felix, a once-brilliant surgeon dying of terminal cancer. Felix is an initiated man who has lived with Aborigines in the Central Australian desert; when Lucy accompanies him there, Martin must confront his insecurities.

Kate Grenville *The Idea of Perfection*, set in the tiny, fictional New South Wales town of Karakarook, and about two unlikely characters who fall in love, won the 2001 Orange Prize for Fiction. *The Secret River* was shortlisted for the Man Booker Prize in 2006 and won the Commonwealth Writers Prize. This historical novel explores the uneasy terrain of early white contact with Aborigines, telling the story of freed convict William Thornhill taking up land in the Hawkesbury with his family.

Chloe Hooper *A Child's Book of True Crime*. With a claustrophobic Tasmanian setting, this perverse, chilling novel is narrated by a young primary-school teacher having an affair with the married father of her smartest pupil. His writer-wife's true-crime book, about a love triangle that disintegrates into murder, leads the anxious teacher into imagining a child's-classic-Australian-literature-style version, with characters such as Kitty Koala and Wally Wombat.

Douglas Kennedy *The Dead Heart*. A best-selling comic thriller made into a film; an itinerant American journalist gets abducted by man-eating hillbillies in Outback Australia.

Michelle de Kretser *The Lost Dog*. This contemporary Australian love story and intriguing mystery is a layered work with sparkling writing and wonderful observations. It won the 2008 New South Wales Premier's Literary Awards' book of the year and the prize for best fiction.

Julia Leigh *The Hunter*. Intriguing, internationally acclaimed first novel about the rediscovery and subsequent hunt of the Tasmanian tiger; a faceless biotech company after thylacine DNA plays the bad guy.

David Malouf *The Conversations at Curlow Creek*. One of Australia's most important contemporary writers charts the developing relationship between two Irishmen the night before a hanging; one is the officer appointed to supervise the execution and the other the outlaw facing his death. *Remembering Babylon* is the moving story of a British cabin boy in the 1840s who, cast ashore, lives for sixteen years amongst the Aboriginal people of far north Queensland, and finally re-enters the British colonial world.

Andrew McGahan *The White Earth.* A haunting novel set in 1992 in Queensland's Darling Downs wheat-fields as the Mabo land-rights case fills the news. After the death of his father, 8-year-old William and his unstable mother are invited to live on his ageing uncle's Kuran station. In order to prove himself worthy of his uncle's inheritance of the property, William is drawn into his uncle's dark world and association with the racist White League. Questions of Aboriginal dispossession and white belonging reverberate. The polemical tone of *Underground* (2006), a dystopian novel with a somewhat far-fetched plotline, set in a not too distant future in totalitarian Australia, raised the ire of neo-conservative reviewers.

Alex Miller *Journey to the Stone Country.* A betrayed wife leaves her middle-class Melbourne existence and returns to tropical North Queensland, setting out on a journey with a childhood Aboriginal acquaintance into the stone country that is his tribe's remote heartland. However, dark secrets from the lives of their grandparents threaten what future they may have together. *Landscape of Farewell* is his latest (and highly recommended) novel.

Elliot Perlman *Seven Types of Ambiguity.* The chain of events, secrets and lies stretching back a decade that lead to Simon Heywood kidnapping his ex-girlfriend's son are related by seven different narrators. Probing middle-class anxiety in a consumeristic, market-driven society, Perlman's conscience-driven writing can be moralistic at times, but at its best is clever and insightful, providing an intense social portrait of contem-porary Melbourne, from Toorak to St Kilda.

Janette Turner Hospital *Oyster.* Disquieting novel set in the literally off-the-map, opal-mining, one-pub Queensland town of Inner Maroo, whose inhabitants are either rough-as-guts mining people, or religious fundamentalists. Her latest, *Orpheus Lost*, is also wonderful.

Tim Winton *Cloudstreet.* A wonderful, faintly magical saga about the mixed fortunes of two families who end up sharing a house in postwar Perth. His novel *Dirt Music* provides a wonderful evocation of the Western Australian landscape with a compelling narrative and was short-listed for the 2002 Booker Prize. *The Turning*, a collection of seventeen linked short stories set in a fictitious Western Australian coastal town, won the 2005 New South Wales Premier's Literary Award.

Tim Winton *Breath.* Winton's latest novel after a gap of several years is a very good one, with a story based in a small coastal community where two young boys learn to surf from an ageing thrill-seeker and learn plenty of life lessons along the way. Winton captures the spirit of the time (early 1970s) and manages to capture the spirit of surfing and the lure of the ocean – not an easy task.

Danielle Wood *The Alphabet of Light and Dark.* Set evocatively on Bruny Island, in melancholy Tasmanian-Gothic vein. Like the main character Essie, Wood's great-great grandfather was superintendent of the Cape Bruny Lighthouse. Essie returns from Western Australia to the lighthouse after her grandfather's death to write her family history and becomes immersed in her ancestors' tragedies.

Alexis Wright *Carpentaria.* Childhood memories and stories that her Waanyi grandmother told her flowed into Wright's novel about the

Gulf country – in title, subject and scope, reminiscent of Xavier Herbert's classic *Capricornia*, but from an Aboriginal point of view. Short-listed for the Miles Franklin 2007.

Australian classics

Barbara Baynton *Bush Studies*. A collection of nineteenth-century bush stories written from the female perspective.

Rolf Boldrewood *Robbery Under Arms*. The story of Captain Starlight, a notorious bushranger and rustler around the Queensland borders.

Marcus Clarke *For the Term of His Natural Life*. Written in 1870 in somewhat overblown prose, this romantic tragedy is based on actual events in Tasmania's once-notorious prison settlement.

Miles Franklin *My Brilliant Career*. A novel about a spirited young girl in early twentieth-century Victoria who refuses to conform.

May Gibbs *Snugglepot and Cuddlepie*. A timeless children's favourite: the illustrated adventures of two little creatures who live inside gumnuts.

Xavier Herbert *Capricornia*. An indignant and allegorical saga of the brutal and haphazard settlement of the land of Capricornia (tropical Northern Territory thinly disguised).

George Johnston *My Brother Jack*. The first in a disturbing trilogy set in Melbourne suburbia between the wars, which develops into a semi-fictional attempt to dissipate the guilt Johnston felt at being disillusioned with, and finally leaving, his native land.

Thomas Keneally *The Chant of Jimmie Blacksmith*. A prize-winning novel that delves deep into the psyche of an Aboriginal outlaw, tracing his inexorable descent into murder and crime. Sickening, brutal and compelling.

Henry Lawson Ballads, poems and stories from Australia's best-loved chronicler come in a wide array of collections. A few to seek out are: *Henry Lawson Bush Ballads*, *Henry Lawson Favourites* and *While the Billy Boils – Poetry*.

Norman Lindsay *The Magic Pudding*. A whimsical tale of some very strange men and their grumpy, flavour-changing and endless pudding; a children's classic with very adult humour.

Ruth Park *The Harp in the South*. First published in 1948, this first book in a trilogy is a well-loved tale of inner-Sydney slum life in 1940s Surry Hills. The spirited Darcy family's battle against poverty provides memorable characters.

A.B. ("Banjo") Paterson Australia's most famous bush balladeer, author of *Waltzing Matilda* and *The Man from Snowy River*, who helped romanticize the bush's mystique. Some of the many titles published include *Banjo Paterson's Favourites* and *Man from Snowy River and Other Verses*.

Henry Handel Richardson *The Getting of Wisdom*. A gangly country girl's experience of a snobby boarding school in early twentieth-century Melbourne; like Miles Franklin (see above), Richardson was actually a female writer.

Nevil Shute *A Town Like Alice*. A wartime romance that tells of a woman's bravery, endurance and enterprise, both in the Malayan jungle and in the Australian Outback where she strives to create the town of the title.

Christina Stead *For Love Alone.* Set largely around Sydney Harbour, where the late author grew up, this novel follows the obsessive Teresa Hawkins, a poor but artistic girl from a large, unconventional family, who scrounges and saves to head for London and love.

Randolph Stow *The Merry-go-round in the Sea.* An endearing tale of a young boy growing up in rural Western Australia during World War II.

Kylie Tennant *Ride on Stranger.* First published in 1943, this is a humorous portrait of Sydney between the two world wars, seen through the eyes of newcomer Shannon Hicks.

Patrick White Considered dense and symbolic – even visionary (though some claim misogynistic) – White's novels can be heavy going, but try and plough through *Voss, A Fringe of Leaves* or *The Twyborn Affair*, the latter a contemporary exploration of ambiguous sexuality.

Aboriginal writing

Faith Bandler *Welour, My Brother.* A novel by a well-known black activist describing a boy's early life in Queensland, and the tensions of a racially mixed community.

John Muk Muk Burke *Bridge of Triangles.* Powerful, landscape-driven images in this tale of a mixed-race child growing up unable to associate with either side of his heritage, but refusing to accept the downward spiral into despair and alcoholism adopted by those around him.

Evelyn Crawford *Over My Tracks.* Told to Chris Walsh, this oral autobiography is the story of a formidable woman, from her 1930s childhood among the red sandhills of Yantabulla, through her Outback struggles as a mother of fourteen children, to her tireless work, late in life, with Aboriginal students, combating prejudice with education.

Nene Gare *The Fringe Dwellers.* A story of an Aboriginal family on the edge of town and society.

Ruby Langford *Don't Take Your Love to Town.* An autobiography demonstrating a black woman's courage and humour in the face of tragedy and poverty lived out in northern New South Wales and the inner city of Sydney.

Sally Morgan *My Place.* A widely acclaimed and best-selling account of a Western Australian woman's discovery of her black roots.

David Mowaljarlai and Jutta Malnic *Yorro Yorro.* Starry-eyed photographer Malnic's musings while recording sacred Wandjina sites in the west Kimberley and, more interestingly, Mowaljarlai's account of his upbringing and Ngarinyin tribal lore.

Mudrooroo *Wildcat Falling.* The first novel to be published (in 1965) by an Aboriginal writer, under the name Colin Johnson, this is the story of a black teenage delinquent coming of age in the 1950s. *Doctor Wooreddy's Prescription for Enduring the Ending of the World* details the attempted annihilation of the Tasmanian Aborigines. Mudrooroo's three latest novels – *The Kwinkan* (1995), *The Undying* (1998) and *Underground* (1999) – are part of his magic-realist Master of Ghost Dreaming series.

Oodgeroo Noonuccal *My People.* A collection of verse by an established campaigning poet (previously known as Kath Walker).

Paddy Roe *Gularabulu.* Stories from the west Kimberley, both traditional myths and tales of a much more recent origin.

Kim Scott *Benang*. Infuriated at reading the words of A.O. Neville, Protector of Aborigines in Western Australia in the 1930s, who planned to "breed out" Aborigines from Australia, author Scott wrote this powerful tale of Nyoongar history using Neville's own themes to overturn his elitist arguments.

Archie Weller *The Day of the Dog*. Weller's violent first novel, with its searing pace and forceful writing, came out in an angry burst after being released, at 23, from incarceration in Broome jail. The protagonist, in a similar situation, is pressured back into a criminal world by his Aboriginal peers and by police harassment. His second novel, *Land of the Golden Clouds*, is an epic science-fiction fantasy, set 3000 years in the future, which portrays an Australia devastated by a nuclear holocaust and populated by warring tribes.

Specialist and wildlife guides

Jack Absalom *Safe Outback Travel*. The bible for Outback driving and camping, full of sensible precautions and handy tips for preparation and repair.

John Chapman and Monica Chapman *Bushwalking in Australia*. The fourth edition of this bushwalking bible has detailed notes for 25 of the best bushwalks Australia-wide, accompanied by colour topographic maps and photographs. The authors also publish several other excellent walking guides, including the indispensable *South West Tasmania*.

David Clark *Big Things*. From the Big Banana to the Big Lobster, Clark provides a comprehensive guide to Australia's kitsch icons.

Catherine de Courcey and John Johnson *River Tracks: Exploring Australian Rivers*. A practical and up-to-date motoring guide to six river journeys, with lots of insider insight and history.

The Great Barrier Reef A lucid and lavishly illustrated *Reader's Digest* rundown on the Reef. Available both in coffee-table format and in a more portable, edited edition.

James Halliday *Australian Wine Companion*. Released every year, the venerable Halliday provides not only an authoritative guide to the best wines but to the wineries themselves – with profiles of 1661 wineries in the 2009 edition, making it a great companion when visiting any of Australia's wine regions.

David Hampshire *Living and Working in Australia: A Survival Handbook*. Given that so many people come to Australia and don't want to leave, this is a handy book with information from everything from that pesky tax file number to negotiating permits and visa applications.

Tim Low *Bush Tucker: Australia's Wild Food Harvest* and *Wild Food Plants of Australia*. Guides to the bountiful supply of bushtucker that was once the mainstay of the Aboriginal diet; the latter is pocket-sized and contains clear photographs of over 180 plants, describing their uses.

Greg Pritchard *Climbing Australia: the Essential Guide*. Comprehensive guide for rock-climbers, covering everything from the major climbing sites to the best websites, with easy-to-understand route descriptions.

Peter and Pat Slater *Field Guide to Australian Birds*. Pocket-sized, and the easiest to use of the many available guides to Australian birds.

Nick Stock *The Penguin Good Australian Wine Guide*. Released every year in Australia, this is a handy book for a wine buff to buy on the ground, with the best wines and prices detailed to help navigate you around the bottle shop.

Tyrone T. Thomas Regional bushwalking guides by local publisher Michelle Anderson Publishing. A series of ten local guides, from *50 Walks in North Queensland* to *120 Walks in Tasmania*, which make excellent trail companions.

Mark Warren *Atlas of Australian Surfing*. A comprehensive guide to riding the best of Australia's waves by this surfing "hall of fame" recipient. Includes plenty of tips, but omits a few "secret spots".

Australian English

The colourful variant of Australian English, or *strine* (which is how "Australian" is pronounced with a very heavy Australian accent), has its origins in the archaic cockney and Irish of the colony's early convicts as well as the adoption of words from the many Aboriginal languages. For such a vast country, the accent barely varies to the untutored ear (for Australians, however, it's a different story); from Tasmania (sorry, "Tassie") to the northwest you'll find little variation in the national drawl, with a curious, interrogative ending to sentences fairly common – although Queenslanders are noted for their slow delivery. One of the most consistent tendencies of *strine* is to abbreviate words and then stick an "-o" or, more commonly, an "-ie" on the end: as in "bring your cozzie to the barbie this arvo" (bring your swimming costume to the barbecue this afternoon). This informality extends to the frequent use of "bloody", "bugger" and "bastard", all used affectionately. Attempting to abuse someone by calling them a bastard will most likely end up in an offer of a beer. There's also an endearing tendency to genderize inanimate objects as, for example, "she's buggered, mate" (your inanimate object is beyond repair) or "do 'im up nice and tight" (be certain that your inanimate object is well affixed).

The popularity of dire Australian TV soap operas has seen *strine* spread overseas, much as Americanisms have pervaded the English-speaking world. Popular *strinisms* such as "hang a U-ey" (make a U-turn) and the versatile and agreeable "no worries" are now commonly used outside Australia.

The country has its own excellent *Macquarie Dictionary*, the latest edition of which is the ultimate authority on the current state of Australian English. Also worth consulting are *The Dinkum Dictionary: The Origins of Australian Words* by Susan Butler, and *Word Map* by Kel Richards, a dictionary of Australian regionalisms. What follows is our own essential list.

Akubra Wide-brimmed felt hat; a brand name.

ANZAC Australia and New Zealand Army Corps; every town has a memorial to ANZAC casualties from both world wars.

Arvo Afternoon.

Back o'Bourke Outback.

Banana bender Resident of Queensland.

Barbie Barbecue.

Battler Someone who struggles to make a living, as in "little Aussie battler".

Beaut! or **You beauty!** Exclamation of delight.

Beg yours? Excuse me, say again?

Beyond the Black Stump Outback; back of beyond.

Billabong Waterhole in dry riverbed.

Billy Cooking pot.

Bitumen Sealed road as opposed to dirt road.

Blowies Blow flies.

Bludger Someone who does not pull their weight, or a scrounger – as in "dole bludger".

Blue Fight; also a red-haired person.

Blundstones Leather, elastic-sided workmen's boots, now also a fashion item in some circles. Often shortened to "blundies".

Bonzer Good, a good thing.

Bottle shop Off-licence or liquor store.

Brumby Feral horse.

Buckley's No chance; as in "hasn't got a Buckley's".

Bugs Moreton Bay bug – type of crayfish indigenous to southern Queensland.

Bunyip Monster of Aboriginal legend; bogeyman.

Burl Give it a go; as in "give it a burl".

Bush Unsettled country area.

Bushranger Runaway convict; nineteenth-century outlaw.

Bushwhacker Someone lacking in social graces, a hick.

BYO Bring your own. Restaurant which allows you to bring your own alcohol.

Chook Chicken.

Chunder Vomit.

Cocky Small farmer; cow cocky, dairy farmer.

To come the raw prawn To try and deceive or make a fool of someone.

Coo-eee! Aboriginal long-distance greeting, now widely adopted as a kind of "yoo hoo!"

Corroboree Aboriginal ceremony.

Cozzies Bathers, swimmers, togs; swimming costume.

Crim Criminal.

Crook Ill or broken.

Crow eater Resident of South Australia.

Cut lunch Sandwiches.

Dag Nerd.

Daggy Unfashionable. Original meaning: faeces stuck on a sheep's rear end.

Daks or **strides** Trousers/pants.

Dam A man-made body of water or reservoir; not just the dam itself.

Damper Soda bread cooked in a pot on embers.

Dekko To look at; as in "take a dekko at this".

Derro Derelict or destitute person.

Didgeridoo Droning Aboriginal musical instrument made from a termite-hollowed branch.

Digger Old-timer, especially an old soldier.

Dill Idiot.

Dilly bag Aboriginal carry-all made of bark, or woven or rigged twine.

Dinkum True, genuine, honest.

Disposal store Store that sells used army and navy equipment, plus camping gear.

Dob in To tell on someone; as in "she dobbed him in".

Donga Sleeping quarters used often in the mining industry.

Drizabone Voluminous waxed cotton raincoat, originally designed for horseriding; a brand name.

Drongo Fool.

Drover Cowboy or station hand.

Dunny Outside pit toilet.

Esky Portable, insulated box to keep food or beer cold.

Fair dinkum or **dinky di** Honestly, truly.

Fossick To search for gold or gems in abandoned diggings.

Furphy A rumour or false story.

Galah Noisy or garrulous person; after the bird.

Galvo Corrugated iron.

Garbo Garbage or refuse collector.

G'day Hello, hi. Short for "good day".

Gibber Rock or boulder.

Give away To give up or resign; as in "I used to be a garbo but I gave it away".

Grog Alcoholic drink, usually beer.

Gub, gubbah Aboriginal terms for a white person.

Gutless wonder Coward.

Hoon A yob, delinquent. Also someone who drives recklessly.

Humpy Temporary shelter used by Aborigines and early pioneers.

Jackeroo Male station-hand.

Jilleroo Female station-hand.

Joey Baby kangaroo still in the pouch (also, less familiarly, a baby koala).

Koorie Collective name for Aboriginal people from southeastern Australia.

Larrikin Mischievous youth.

Lay by Practice of putting a deposit on goods until they can be fully paid for.

Lollies Sweets or candy.

Manchester Linen goods.

Mate A sworn friend – one you'd do anything for – as essential as beer to the Australian stereotype.

Milk bar Corner shop, and often a small café.

Moleskins Strong cotton trousers worn by bushmen.

Never Never Outback, wilderness.

New Australian Recent immigrants; often a euphemism for Australians of non-British descent.

No worries That's OK; It doesn't matter; Don't mention it.

Ocker Uncultivated Australian male.

Op shop Short for "Opportunity Shop"; a charity shop/thrift store.

Outback Remote, unsettled regions of Australia.

Paddock Field.

Panel van Van with no rear windows and front seating only.

Pashing Kissing or snogging, often in the back of a panel van.

Perve To leer or act as a voyeur (short for pervert); as in "What are you perving at?"

Piss Beer.

Pokies One-armed bandits; gambling machines.

Pommie or **Pom** Person of English descent – not necessarily abusive.

Rapt Very pleased, delighted.

Ratbag An eccentric person; also a term of mild abuse.

Ratshit or **shithouse** How you feel after a night on the piss.

Rego Vehicle registration document.

Ridji didge The real thing or genuine article.

Ripper! Old-fashioned exclamation of enthusiasm.

Rollies Roll-up cigarettes.

Root Vulgar term for sexual congress.

Rooted To be very tired or to be beyond repair; as in "she's rooted, mate" – your [car] is irreparable.

Ropable Furious to the point of requiring restraint.

Rouseabout An unskilled labourer in a shearing shed.

Sandgroper Resident of Western Australia.

She'll be right or **she'll be apples** Everything will work out fine.

Shoot through To pass through or leave hurriedly.

Shout To pay for someone, or to buy a round of drinks; as in "it's your shout, mate".

Sickie To take a day off work due to (sometimes alleged) illness; as in "to pull a sickie".

Singlet Sleeveless cotton vest. The archetypal Australian singlet, in navy, is produced by Bonds.

Skivvy Polo neck.

Slab 24-can carton of beer.

Smoko Tea break.

Snag Sausage.

Speedo Famous Australian brand of swimming costume; speedos (or sluggos) refers to men's swimming briefs.

Spunk Attractive or sexy person of either gender (but generally a young man); as in "what a spunk!" Can also be used as an adjective: spunky.

Squatter Historic term for early settlers who took up public land as their own.

Station Very large pastoral property or ranch.

Sticky beak Nosy person, or to be nosy; as in "let's have a sticky beak".

Stockman Cowboy or station hand.

Stubby Small bottle of beer.

Swag Large bedroll, or one's belongings.

Tall poppy Someone who excels or is eminent. "Cutting down tall poppies" is to bring overachievers back to earth – a national pastime.

Thongs Flip-flops or sandals.

Throw a wobbly Lose your temper.

Tinnie Can of beer, or a small aluminium boat.

Ute Short for "utility" vehicle; pick-up truck.
Wacko! Exclamation of enthusiasm.
Walkabout Temporary migration undertaken by Aborigines; also has the wider meaning of a journey.
Gone walkabout To go missing.
Warm fuzzies Feeling of contentment.
Waxhead Surfer.

Weatherboard Wooden house.
Whinger Someone who complains – allegedly common among Poms.
Wog Derogatory description for those of Mediterranean descent.
Wowser Killjoy.
Yabber To talk or chat.
Yabbie Freshwater crayfish.
Yakka Work, as in "hard yakka".
Yobbo Uncouth person.

Ultimate Aussie adventure!

AUSTRALIA'S GREAT TRAIN JOURNEYS

O FIND OUT MORE VISIT WWW.GSR.COM.AU
R YOUR LICENSED TRAVEL AGENT

THE REAL AUSTRALIA, JUST OUT YOUR WINDOW.

Maui offer a range of motorhomes that sleep 2, 4 or 6 people, plus even a deluxe 4WD. All vehicles feature contemporary design and offer ultimate comfort for your self drive journey around Australia. Maui is the natural choice when you want to travel with an experienced and trusted motorhome operator.

Apartment styled kitchen equipment, freshly laundered linen and bedding plus other useful items are all included with your Maui hire. As an added bonus all our 2 wheel drive vehicles feature automatic transmission.

Maui has branches all over Australia, and a toll free 24 hour Customer Care helpline.

Contact us 24 hours a day, 7 days a week
Worldwide toll free: 00 800 200 80 801

ausinfo@maui-rentals.com

www.maui.com.au

maui™
Spirit of Independence

NOTES

Small print and
Index

A Rough Guide to Rough Guides

Published in 1982, the first Rough Guide – to Greece – was a student scheme that became a publishing phenomenon. Mark Ellingham, a recent graduate in English from Bristol University, had been travelling in Greece the previous summer and couldn't find the right guidebook. With a small group of friends he wrote his own guide, combining a highly contemporary, journalistic style with a thoroughly practical approach to travellers' needs.

The immediate success of the book spawned a series that rapidly covered dozens of destinations. And, in addition to impecunious backpackers, Rough Guides soon acquired a much broader and older readership that relished the guides' wit and inquisitiveness as much as their enthusiastic, critical approach and value-for-money ethos.

These days, Rough Guides include recommendations from shoestring to luxury and cover more than 200 destinations around the globe, including almost every country in the Americas and Europe, more than half of Africa and most of Asia and Australasia. Our ever-growing team of authors and photographers is spread all over the world, particularly in Europe, the US and Australia.

In the early 1990s, Rough Guides branched out of travel, with the publication of Rough Guides to World Music, Classical Music and the Internet. All three have become benchmark titles in their fields, spearheading the publication of a wide range of books under the Rough Guide name.

Including the travel series, Rough Guides now number more than 350 titles, covering: phrasebooks, waterproof maps, music guides from Opera to Heavy Metal, reference works as diverse as Conspiracy Theories and Shakespeare, and popular culture books from iPods to Poker. Rough Guides also produce a series of more than 120 World Music CDs in partnership with World Music Network.

Visit www.roughguides.com to see our latest publications.

Rough Guide travel images are available for commercial licensing at www.roughguidespictures.com

Rough Guide credits

Text editor: Ros Belford, Natasha Foges and Ann-Marie Shaw
Layout: Ajay Verma
Cartography: Maxine Repath, Rajesh Mishra and Alakananda Bhattacharya
Picture editor: Mark Thomas
Production: Rebecca Short
Proofreader: Jan McCann
Cover design: Chloë Roberts
Editorial: Ruth Blackmore, Andy Turner, Keith Drew, Edward Aves, Alice Park, Lucy White, Jo Kirby, James Smart, Róisín Cameron, Emma Traynor, Emma Gibbs, Kathryn Lane, Monica Woods, Mani Ramaswamy, Harry Wilson, Lucy Cowie, Amanda Howard, Lara Kavanagh, Alison Roberts, Joe Staines, Peter Buckley, Matthew Milton, Tracy Hopkins, Ruth Tidball; **Delhi** Madhavi Singh, Karen D'Souza, Lubna Shaheen
Design & Pictures: London Scott Stickland, Dan May, Diana Jarvis, Nicole Newman, Sarah Cummins, Emily Taylor; **Delhi** Umesh Aggarwal, Jessica Subramanian, Ankur Guha, Pradeep Thapliyal, Sachin Tanwar, Anita Singh, Nikhil Agarwal, Sachin Gupta
Production: Vicky Baldwin

Cartography: London Ed Wright, Katie Lloyd-Jones; **Delhi** Rajesh Chhibber, Ashutosh Bharti, Animesh Pathak, Jasbir Sandhu, Karobi Gogoi, Swati Handoo, Deshpal Dabas
Online: London George Atwell, Faye Hellon, Jeanette Angell, Fergus Day, Justine Bright, Clare Bryson, Aine Fearon, Adrian Low, Ezgi Celebi, Amber Bloomfield; **Delhi** Amit Verma, Rahul Kumar, Narender Kumar, Ravi Yadav, Debojit Borah, Rakesh Kumar, Ganesh Sharma, Shisir Basumatari
Marketing & Publicity: London Liz Statham, Niki Hanmer, Louise Maher, Jess Carter, Vanessa Godden, Vivienne Watton, Anna Paynton, Rachel Sprackett, Laura Vipond, Vanessa McDonald; **New York** Katy Ball, Judi Powers, Nancy Lambert; **Delhi** Ragini Govind
Manager India: Punita Singh
Reference Director: Andrew Lockett
Operations Manager: Helen Phillips
PA to Publishing Director: Nicola Henderson
Publishing Director: Martin Dunford
Commercial Manager: Gino Magnotta
Managing Director: John Duhigg

Publishing information

This ninth edition published October 2009 by
Rough Guides Ltd,
80 Strand, London WC2R 0RL
14 Local Shopping Centre, Panchsheel Park, New Delhi 110017, India

Distributed by the Penguin Group
Penguin Books Ltd,
80 Strand, London WC2R 0RL
Penguin Group (USA)
375 Hudson Street, NY 10014, USA
Penguin Group (Australia)
250 Camberwell Road, Camberwell, Victoria 3124, Australia
Penguin Group (Canada)
195 Harry Walker Parkway N, Newmarket, ON, L3Y 7B3 Canada
Penguin Group (NZ)
67 Apollo Drive, Mairangi Bay, Auckland 1310, New Zealand
Cover concept by Peter Dyer.

Typeset in Bembo and Helvetica to an original design by Henry Iles.
Printed in Italy by L.E.G.O. S.p.A, Lavis (TN)
© Margo Daly, Anne Dehne, David Leffman, Chris Scott 2009
Maps © Rough Guides

No part of this book may be reproduced in any form without permission from the publisher except for the quotation of brief passages in reviews.

1208pp includes index
A catalogue record for this book is available from the British Library
ISBN: 978-1-84836-073-0

The publishers and authors have done their best to ensure the accuracy and currency of all the information in **The Rough Guide to Australia**, however, they can accept no responsibility for any loss, injury, or inconvenience sustained by any traveller as a result of information or advice contained in the guide.

1 3 5 7 9 8 6 4 2

Help us update

We've gone to a lot of effort to ensure that the ninth edition of **The Rough Guide to Australia** is accurate and up-to-date. However, things change – places get "discovered", opening hours are notoriously fickle, restaurants and rooms raise prices or lower standards. If you feel we've got it wrong or left something out, we'd like to know, and if you can remember the address, the price, the hours, the phone number, so much the better.

Please send your comments with the subject line "**Rough Guide Australia Update**" to ©mail @roughguides.com. We'll credit all contributions and send a copy of the next edition (or any other Rough Guide if you prefer) for the very best emails.

Have your questions answered and tell others about your trip at
®www.roughguides.com

Acknowledgements

Catherine Le Nevez Cheers to all the locals, tourism professionals, fellow travellers and friends for insight, inspiration and good times throughout my research around northern Inland NSW and Outback Qld. At Rough Guides, major thanks to Natasha Foges for signing me up for the gig and for fantastic support from start to finish, and to editor Ann-Marie Shaw. As ever, thanks above all to my family.

Helen Marsden Thank you to: the Mowanjum Art and Culture Centre in Derby for explaining the finer points of Aboriginal culture to me; all the lovely people of Western Australia who tirelessly answered my neverending questions; and everyone I roped in to help me change the flat tyres. Thank you to Natasha Foges and Annie Shaw at Rough Guides for their excellent project management and editing skills. Most importantly thanks to Matt for chumming me across the scary part, cooking up some sterling feasts on a single burner stove and generally supporting the notion that it was a good idea to quit my job mid

financial crisis in order to drive from Darwin to Perth in an 8ft campervan.

Ian Osborn Thanks to the following for their help: Nick Moon, Ocean Hotels; Anthony O'Rourke, *Airlie Waterfront*; Mercedes Ireland, Cruise Whitsunday; Steve Neals, Fantasea; Pascal Shaeffer, *Airlie Beach Hotel*; Gary Talbot, *Explorers Inn*; Mel, *Sleeping Inn Beachside*.

Paul Whitfield For the kind use of their wonderful house in Paddington I owe a huge debt to Miriam, Martine and Louis. Thanks too to Clive and Terry for dragging me around Sydney's gay bars, Iona McKay for an expert two-up demonstration in Broken Hill, Debbie Elkind for considered restaurant advice, and all the others who suggested favoured activities and haunts from their favourite city – Chris and Sarah in particular. Gratitude is also due to my Sydney co-author, Ben, for sticking with it through difficult times, and most of all to Marion, for great times in Sydney and hanging in there through long absences.

Readers' letters

Thanks to all the readers who took the time to write in with comments and suggestions (and apologies if we've inadvertently omitted or misspelt anyone's name):

Lorraine Ando; Adan Beck; Ben Bernstein; Carol Bowring; Sarah-Jane Brooks; Douglas Dickson; Anna Garde; Stuart Goodall; Clive Paul; Ian Williams; Jill Wookey.

Photo credits

All photos © Rough Guides except the following:

ROUGH GUIDES

SMALL PRINT

Index

Map entries are in colour.

INDEX

I

INDEX

1201

S

Map symbols

maps are listed in the full index using coloured text

▬▬ ▪ ▪	State/territorial boundary		╲	Airfield
▬ ▬ ▬	Chapter division boundary		─Ⓜ─	Metro/monorail
══	Main road		★	Bus/taxi stop
══	Minor road		♦	Point of interest
⋯⋯	Unpaved road		@	Internet access
▬▬	Pedestrianized street (town maps)		ⓘ	Visitor Centre
▥	Steps		⊠	Post office
⇒⇐	Tunnel		⊞	Hospital
⋯⋯	4 wheel drive		🅿	Parking
─ ─ ─	Path/track		⊙	Statue
▬┼▬	Railway		✡	Synagogue
─ ─	Ferry route		♟	Museum
)(	Bridge		ⵣ	Garden
⊠	Gate		✿	Vineyard
﹌	River		⌁	Golf course
▲	Mountain peak		♣	Chinese temple
⌂⌂	Mountain range		⚊	Campsite
﹏	Gorge		◉	Accommodation
⌇⌇	Rocks		▬	Building
﹏	Reef		▭	Market
⚘	Viewpoint		▬┼▬	Church/cathedral
♨	Waterfall		▨	Aboriginal land
◉	Swimming pool		▭	Prohibited area
⌐	Boat/ship		⣿	Beach
⌒	Cave		┼	Cemetery
⌂	Conservation hut		﹏	Marsh
ⵜ	Lighthouse		▨	Park
✈	International airport		▥	Salt lake
✗	Domestic airport			

MAP SYMBOLS